TEACHING THE BIBLE

Creatively

How To Awaken Your Kids To Scripture

Bill McNabb
Steven Mabry

Youth Specialties

Zondervan Publishing House
Grand Rapids, Michigan

Zondervan/Youth Specialties Books

TEACHING THE BIBLE
Creatively

Teaching the Bible Creatively

Copyright © 1990 by Youth Specialties, Inc.

Youth Specialties Books, 1224 Greenfield Drive, El Cajon, California 92021, are published by Zondervan Publishing House, 1415 Lake Drive, S.E., Grand Rapids, Michigan 49506

Library of Congress Cataloging-in-Publication Data

McNabb, Bill.
    Teaching the Bible creatively / Bill McNabb, Steven Mabry.
      p.   cm.
   ISBN 0-310-52921-2
   1. Bible—Study. 2. Youth—Religious life. I. Mabry, Steven, 1950-. II. Title.
   BS603.M33 1990
   268'.433—dc20   90-33626
                                                                CIP

Edited by Tim McLaughlin
Designed by Dan McGowan
Typography by Leah Perry

Printed in the United States of America

90 91 92 93 94 95 96 97 98 99 / CH / 10 9 8 7 6 5 4 3 2 1

About the YOUTHSOURCE™ Publishing Group

YOUTHSOURCE™ books, tapes, videos, and other resources pool the expertise of three of the finest youth-ministry resource providers in the world:

• **Campus Life Books**—publishers of the award-winning *Campus Life* magazine, who for nearly fifty years have helped high schoolers live Christian lives.

• **Youth Specialties**—serving ministers to middle-school, junior-high, and high-school youth for over twenty years through books, magazines, and training events such as the National Youth Workers Convention.

• **Zondervan Publishing House**—one of the oldest, largest, and most respected evangelical Christian publishers in the world.

Campus Life	**Youth Specialties**	**Zondervan**
465 Gundersen Dr.	1224 Greenfield Dr.	1415 Lake Dr. S.E.
Carol Stream, IL 60188	El Cajon, CA 92021	Grand Rapids, MI 49506
708/260-6200	619/440-2333	616/698-6900

To those caught between—

Let not many of you become teachers. (James 3:1)

and

If I say, "I will not remember the Lord or speak any more in his name," then in my heart it becomes like a burning fire, shut up in my bones: and I am weary of holding it in, and I cannot. (Jeremiah 20:9)

and to our parents, Bill and Jackie McNabb and Sam and Bernie Mabry, who taught us to love the Bible, and to our wives Maureen and Marta, who are helping us learn to live it.

Contents

Foreword

I went to Sunday school for one day. When I was eight years old and my brother twelve, my parents decided we needed a religious education and sent us off to a nearby Sunday school in New York City. I remember that day very well. I had to color a picture of Abraham sacrificing Isaac. Perhaps I was a psychiatrist even then, for what I concluded from the experience was that God must be crazy for wanting Abraham to do this; that Abraham must have been crazy for going ahead and doing it; and, above all, that Isaac was crazy for lying in my coloring book with a beatific expression on his face, waiting to be sliced open. When my brother refused to go back, I rode his twelve-year-old coattails out of Sunday school, and that was the extent of my formal religious education.

Yet as the years passed, I was graced with a number of secular-minded mentors who, through their genuine caring for me as an adolescent or young adult, did an enormous amount to prepare me to love Jesus.

When I was thirty-five, I was graced by the opportunity to see *Jesus Christ Superstar* (and later listen to the sound track), which began preparing me to understand Jesus.

When I was forty-one, I was graced by falling into a company of nuns who made no attempt to teach me anything, but welcomed me as an unbaptized person to celebrate the Eucharist with them daily. And thereby I began to incorporate Jesus.

So it was that I came to be baptized at the end of my forty-fourth year.

There is a moral here, one which runs throughout this book: The best way to teach the Bible is not through words, but through actions, through mentoring and entertainment and an accepting community. If we know anything about the creation of a community, it is that it cannot be done from a distance.

I do not regret my journey. But I often wonder what it would have been like if, when I was eight years old on that day in Sunday school, someone had reached out to me. If there had been some mentoring. If there had been some entertainment. If there had been some acceptance. If there had been something beyond showing me to a desk and directing me to color a picture from a distance.

Had it been available fifty years ago, this book could have changed my life. I am delighted that it is now available so that it might change the lives of future generations.

M. Scott Peck

Preface

A woman read somewhere that dogs were healthier if fed a tablespoon of cod liver oil each day. So each day she followed the same routine—she chased her dog until she caught it, wrestled it down, and managed to force the fishy remedy down the dog's throat.

Until one day when, in the middle of this grueling medical effort, the bottle was kicked over. With a sigh, she loosed her grip on the dog so she could wipe up the mess—only to watch the dog trot to the puddle and begin lapping it up. The dog loved cod liver oil. It was just the owner's method of application the dog objected to.

After many years of ministry to young people and adults, we have noticed that almost everyone wants to learn more about God and the Bible—but they are turned off by our method of application. We believe that even the most hardened, apathetic teenager can become interested in the Bible if approached correctly. We've seen it happen. We believe that all people, including teenagers, have a deep spiritual longing and hunger to know more about their Creator.

Yet if that is true, what is the problem? Why aren't kids flocking to our youth groups and Sunday school classes, or holding rallies to demand more time for Bible study? Probably because they do not like our method of application. They have been turned off by boring, predictable, unchallenging, irrelevant, sophomoric attempts to teach them God's Word.

By the time we church-raised kids graduated from high school, we had twelve years of Sunday school and six years of youth group under our belts—and had lost nearly all interest in anything to do with the Bible. After years of enduring discussions characterized by such questions as "Who do you think God would rather us be like—the Apostle Paul or Jack the Ripper?" we still yearned to know God—but weren't sure the Bible had much to say about him. Perhaps

13

Life magazine was on to something in 1957 when it called Sunday school "the most wasted hour of the week."

Fortunately, later we both had experiences in which we encountered gifted Bible teachers who reignited our desire to study and know God's Word.

One of the reasons Christian education is in such bad shape, why apathy is rampant in our Sunday school classes and youth groups, is that we have failed to incorporate tenets of educational psychology into our teaching. During the past half-century researchers have gained incredible insight into how we learn and what motivates us to learn, yet this learning has seldom found its way into the church. It's easy to see why this has happened: because teachers and youth leaders value the Bible and consider it the precious Word of God, they assume that others should naturally feel the same way. This attitude has consequently kept Bible teachers from spending much time on improving their motivation and teaching techniques.

That era is now over. As Bible study has become increasingly difficult to interest kids in, most Christian educators now see the need to dramatically improve their teaching abilities.

Leading a youth group or teaching a Sunday school class is to us one of the most important endeavors in the world. We have between us more than thirty years of experience in youth ministry and Christian education. As a part of Youth Specialties Ministries' Resource Seminar team for the past eight years, we have shared the ideas in this book with thousands of youth workers in cities across the U.S., Canada, and Australia. It is our hope that these educational principles and ideas will help as you seek to teach the Bible to young people.

How to Use the Ideas

Most chapters in this book contain sidebars of Bible teaching ideas that relate to the educational principle discussed in that chapter. Some ideas will immediately strike you as usable with your youth group or class; others will not seem as applicable to your situation. That is natural—not all ideas work with every group.

Over the years, however, we have noticed that some Bible teachers tend to discard ideas too quickly, tossing them aside before they have given them an honest chance. We know the feeling, too, of reading through a book of youth-ministry ideas, all the while noticing why the ideas won't work for our groups. "My group is too small for this . . . too big for that . . . We don't have an adequate facility for this . . . This is too expensive . . . My kids would never do this . . ."

But before you throw out an idea, ask yourself, "How could this idea be changed to make it usable in my situation?" With some fine-tuning, an idea that would not work as written can be customized just right for your group. Ingenuity is the art of taking something that already exists, changing it, and making it better. Loose your ingenuity on these ideas, and put them to work in your situation.

Acknowledgments

We would like to express our thanks to—

• Our colleagues at Youth Specialties—Wayne Rice, Mike Yaconelli, Tic Long, Jim Burns, Rich Van Pelt, Duffy Robbins, Ray Johnston, and Chap Clark—whose creativity is reflected in the pages of this book.

• The many youth workers who contributed their best ideas to the *Ideas* library, in which we found the perfect Bible studies to illustrate the principles in this book.

• Tony Ash, Edward Hobbs, Browne Barr, and Jennings Davis, Stephen Glenn, Doug Adams, Walter Wink, and Karl Irwin, Jr., who modeled what teaching is all about.

• Tim McLaughlin and Noel Becchetti, editors par excellence.

• Dick Wing, who taught us what it means to be a minister of the gospel.

• Scott Peck, Brennan Manning, Rick and Amy Beckett, Larry Thomas, Robert Capon, David and Linda McNabb, Mark Porizky, Jeff Mabry, Larry and Shirly Jeffryes, Randy and Laura Erickson, and Rebecca and Bryan Frank, whose friendship makes life worth living.

• The people of Brentwood Presbyterian Church, The United Church of Los Alamos, First Christian Church of Concord, and Woodland Hills Christian Church, who were a gracious and willing audience to many of these ideas.

1

Basics of Bible Teaching

Bill McNabb

If you look at a window, you see fly-specks, dust, the crack where junior's Frisbee hit it. If you look through a window, you see the world beyond.

Something like this is the difference between those who see the Bible as a Holy Bore and those who see it as the Word of God which speaks out of the depths of an almost unimaginable past into the depths of ourselves.

—Frederick Buechner

$\mathbf{W}$as it always this tough?" I wonder as I struggle to keep the attention of a Bible study class. Did Jesus and Paul have this much trouble when they taught the Scriptures? A teacher friend must have sensed my questions, for he sent me a new slant on the Sermon on the Mount.

Then Jesus took his disciples up onto the mountain and, gathering them around him, he taught them, saying,
"Blessed are the poor in spirit, for theirs is the kingdom of heaven;
Blessed are the meek;
Blessed are they that mourn;
Blessed are the merciful;
Blessed are they that thirst for justice;

Blessed are you when persecuted;
Blessed are you when you suffer;
Be glad and rejoice, for your reward is great in heaven."

Then Simon Peter said, "Are we supposed to know this?"
And Andrew said, "Do we have to write this down?"
And James said, "Will we have a test on this?"
And Philip said, "I don't have any paper."
And Bartholomew said, "Do we have to turn this in?"
And John said, "The other disciples didn't have to learn this."
And Matthew said, "Can I go to the bathroom?"
And Judas said, "What does this have to do with real life?"

And Jesus wept.

When I was in fourth grade, I got my first Bible. It was nothing unusual—the Eastside Church of Christ always gave Bibles to the fourth graders. But I felt so special and unique as the preacher called my name and I walked down the red-carpeted aisle to be presented with The Book. It was a Revised Standard edition in black imitation leather with my name stamped in gold on the front and, inside, Jesus' words in red—so readers would know this was not just anyone talking. Also inside were reproductions of old masters' paintings of the Bible's greatest hits—bearded, fierce Moses receiving the tablets; Daniel calmly praying, surrounded by frustrated lions whose mouths looked like they had been zippered shut; Jesus with kids hanging all over him, with the caption "Let the little children come unto me."

I took it home and treated it with respect, as I had been taught—that is, I never wrote in it or set other books on top of it. Vowing to read it all the way through, I soon began with Genesis, reading a chapter a night. Although I understood little of what was going on, I plugged on until halfway through Numbers I was overcome with numbing boredom, and I gave up. The Bible was extremely overrated, I decided. I could not figure out why everyone made such a big deal about it or how it had become the world's best seller when it only confused and bored me. I put it on my bookshelf where it rested unread and ignored.

For a while the Bible remained for me a locked treasure chest of wisdom and guidance. I continued to go to church and Sunday school, however, and over the years I gradually unlocked the treasure chest. It took the loving guidance of Sunday school teachers, youth leaders, and college and seminary professors. They helped open for me the beauty, wisdom, and truth of the Bible. The Bible now means so much to me that I can think of no greater calling than to be a teacher of the Bible, helping others unlock the treasure chest.

A few years after finishing seminary, I returned to graduate school to obtain a doctorate in educational psychology, which is primarily concerned with how people learn. My main interest was to find ways I could motivate young people to want to learn about the Bible and how to teach in ways that would be remembered and acted upon. But before I could apply the principles to my Bible teaching, I had to take a fresh look at the Bible—what it is and is not.

• **The Bible is a positive book.** Teachers of the Bible must first overcome any tendency to see it as a tool to keep us from having fun—which is all it is to most kids, a book full of rules. We have for far too long treated the Bible as Good Advice rather than as Good News. We need to approach Bible study as if we are about to discover together the greatest news ever heard.

I read of a man who frequently dreamed that God ran after him with a paper in his hand. All his life he ran from God, for he believed that paper contained a warrant for his arrest. After accepting the Christian faith, the man said that now, looking back on his dreams, he realized the paper was not a warrant for his arrest, but a pardon for his sins.

An early duty in teaching the Bible to young people is convincing them that the Bible is a positive book.

• **The Bible is an understandable book.** Granted, much of the Bible is complex and difficult to comprehend. A good commentary or Bible handbook is often necessary to get the fullest understanding from a text. And yet it is important to remember the Bible is for everyone. We need not be seminary graduates to understand the Holy Scriptures. When I was in seminary, I listened to a professor expound a theory on Mark's use of Old Testament symbols, a lecture that left me with the impression that the professor felt he was the first person in two millennia to understand the Gospel of Mark. Such academic elitism has done a great disservice to the Bible.

The sheer size of the Bible or its language (particularly in an older translation such as the King James Version) can intimidate young people. Our job is to present the Bible as an understandable book, a timeless book. It is not mere ancient history or good literature. Even unbelievers would agree that the Bible is worth studying for its historical data and poetical style, but believers see it as a book that has far more than merely literary value. We believe that the values and principles found in the Bible are relevant not only to their original audiences, but to us today.

Often an overlooked "minor" prophet, Amos was the study of a class I recently led. I was amazed at how relevant it was to current American society, despite the book's being written 700 years before Christ. "If God sent a prophet to America today," I asked the class, "what do you think the prophet would say?"

"The same thing Amos said to Israel," students replied. In Amos' description of his society's hedonism and indifference to the poor, the Bible provides a mirror to look at our own society. Sharing this timeless relevance of the Bible with young people is one of the great joys of teaching.

• **The Bible is an open book.** There have been more books written about the Bible than any other book. It is open to a variety of interpretations. We can interact with it and apply it in countless ways. And that very interaction is why Bible study in a group is exciting. Even Jesus' preferred teaching method was to use parables—which require much interpretation and thought from the reader. It is interesting to see how much others can get out of a story. The second-century church father Origen, for example, interpreted the parable of the Good Samaritan allegorically, claiming to find the following symbols:

The man traveling to Jericho: Adam
Jerusalem (from which he was traveling): Paradise
Jericho: The world
Robbers: Hostile influences and enemies of man
Wounds: Disobedience or sins
Priest: Law
Levite: Prophets
Good Samaritan: Christ
Donkey: Body of Christ
Inn: Church
Two denarii: Knowledge of the Father and the Son
Innkeeper: Angels in charge of the church
Return of the Good Samaritan: Second coming of Christ[1]

Whether or not we agree with Origen's interpretation, it is nonetheless interesting to ponder his analogies. A twentieth-century commentator, theologian Robert Capon, claimed the story was not about the Samaritan at all, but about the traveler, beaten, abandoned, left for dead—the Christ figure of the parable.[2]

The point is that there are several levels of truth in the Scriptures. The Bible is a book open to a variety of interpretations, and there is often more than one valid way of looking at a particular passage.

• **The Bible is a challenging book.** Not a book of pat answers and platitudes, it creates tension and forces us to think. When we remember, for example, that Samaritans were not an ancient affiliate of the Red Cross, but hated enemies of the Jews—when we remember this, we see beyond the sweet moralism about being nice to highway casualties. Christ's parable is a stinging indictment of cultural prejudice and the tendency of all societies to exclude certain groups. If Jesus were to tell the story today to American listeners, he would probably describe a PLO terrorist who stopped to help the man after George Bush and Mother Teresa had passed by on the other side.

The Bible challenges our preconceived notions and cherished cultural assumptions. "Jesus is not the answer," noted the great theologian Karl Barth. "He is the question. He is the shattering disturbance that covers our lives and causes us to question that which we had once uncritically accepted."[3] As we help our kids to get inside the Bible, they will discover that it challenges and confronts many of their attitudes and actions.

• **The Bible is a guidebook.** It provides the directions, but not the destination. Its purpose is to lead us to a relationship with God. Technically, in fact, it is not the Word of God. "In the beginning was the Word," says the first chapter of John's Gospel, "and the Word was with God, and the Word was God." In a literal sense, Jesus is the Word of God, and the Bible is the book *about* the Word of God.

Its purpose is to lead us to a knowledge of our savior. "Your word is a lamp to my feet," sang the psalmist, and his words say something about the proper place of the Bible in the Christian life. A lamp does little good at night held either behind your back or up in front of your eyes. Held properly, however, the lamp of the Bible illuminates the paths of our lives.

Like anything, of course, the Bible can become an idol. Some people post it on the coffee table, as if to ward off evil spirits. I was raised to revere the Bible as a holy book; in my circles it was the Holy Bible as Palestine was the Holy Land. As I grew older, I eventually realized that the Bible points us to God, but it is not God. We use it to draw us closer to its author, but we do not worship it.

24

How to Approach Bible Study

Scholars use the terms *exegesis* to describe the process of figuring out what the Bible says, and *hermeneutics* to describe the task of interpreting what it means for our lives. For our purposes, exegesis and hermeneutics can be simplified into four steps:

• **Find the main point of the passage.** We do this by asking what we think the author was trying to convey. Most biblical texts have one main point and several subpoints. If we focus on the subpoints, we risk getting off on side roads, thus missing the main point of the text.

For example, Jesus told a parable about a man who found a treasure hidden in another man's field (Matthew 13:44). The finder did not tell the field's owner about the treasure, but instead he secretly liquidated his assets so he could buy the field and own the treasure. Most scholars agree that this is a parable about the inestimable value of the kingdom of God and the need to sacrifice to obtain it; it is not primarily about how we should respond when we find someone's lost property. If we focus on the ethical propriety of the man's actions, we miss the main point of the parable.

So the first step in Bible study is to consider the intent of the author and determine his main point.

• **Consider the context.** The Bible was not written in a vacuum. Its words were spoken and written to people who lived during a particular century in a particular culture. An understanding of that historical context is vital to discovering the meaning of the text. The story of Zaccheus in Luke 19, for example, makes little sense to those who do not understand how the Jews of Jesus' time felt about tax collectors. Commentaries and Bible dictionaries can assist us in understanding the context.

• **Interpret the part by the whole.** Each individual part of the Bible must be read in light of the whole Scripture. Taking one passage out of the context of the whole can lead to disastrous results. For example, Psalm 137:9 — "Happy is he who seizes your infants and dashes them against the rocks" — must be read in light of Jesus' later admonition to love our enemies. Many of the cults and heresies of history can be traced to failing to heed this principle of interpretation.

What many teenagers need is not merely more Bible knowledge, but a framework that links the bits and pieces they already know. The teenager who wrote the following answer to the question "How would you describe Jesus?" had some details straight, but he needed to see the big picture.

> Jesus is a man who was God's son, and uh, the Virgin Mary got him there and then he started to teach about God and so the Jews didn't believe. So he went to the Gentiles and the Gentiles started to believe and he used to come back and forth to the Jewish city and the chief priest didn't like him and all so they started to want to plan on things so they could kill him. Well, God's plan for Jesus was for him to die for sins. So he died on the cross, the place to die for sins. See, in the Old Testament, they used to have an ark and there was a torn curtain and that means that only one person is supposed to go in there and take a perfect lamb, and Jesus was perfect. Okay. So when Jesus dies for our sins, for all our sins, they are forgiven. So that was just like the lamb but it's for, you don't have to burn a lamb for everything.[4]

This kid needed to see the connections between events and concepts, needed to interpret the parts by the whole. Bits of scriptural knowledge isolated from the whole are useless. Our job as teachers is to help kids see the big picture.

• **Apply the passage to our own lives.** Bible study is worth little if it is based only on intellectual curiosity. The three points mentioned above are only the preparation for the question "What is God saying to me through this passage?" Our job as Bible teachers is more than getting our students to understand what the Bible says about a particular issue; we must help them understand what God is saying to them personally. I like to end each Bible study with the question "How would your life be different if you really took this passage seriously?" This final step of Bible study provides an avenue for the lessons of Scripture to be applied to our everyday lives.

2

The Eureka Principle:

Kids are motivated to learn by learning.

Bill McNabb

The only learning that really sticks is that which is self-discovered.
— *Carl Rogers*

It was Archimedes, the tradition goes, who was stumped in his search for a method of detecting the amount of alloy in the crown of the king of Syracuse. Having pondered a long time in vain for a solution to his dilemma, he was settling one day into a bath, watching the water level rise as it always did—and then the light came on. "Eureka!" he shouted as he leaped from the bath, running through the streets half dressed and dripping wet (some versions of the story have it) back to his experiments. The rest is history—the principle of specific gravity was discovered.

"Eureka!" has persisted in our language to express the joy of sudden discovery, whether the discovery is of the theory of specific gravity or of gold, as in the case of prospectors in California's mother-lode country. In education, too, discovery breeds the desire to keep on discovering. Like everyone, kids are motivated to learn by learning.

Some years ago California's department of education reputedly spent three million dollars discovering that high-school students were motivated to learn when they were learning something. In other words, learning itself creates the desire for more learning; learning is a self-rewarding experience.

This translates into teaching students something easy if we want them to acquire a desire to learn. This is doubly true when the completed learning experience is followed by recognition and praise.

For example, the often-daunting task of Scripture memory can be accomplished with a creative teaching exercise like "Hidden Treasure."

Hidden Treasure

To help motivate your kids to memorize God's Word—while at the same time making them feel capable of doing it—try this. First, distribute pencils and paper to everyone and ask them to write down the following:

1. Their name
2. Their address and phone number
3. Their Social Security number
4. Their school locker combination
5. Their birth date and the birth dates of immediate family members
6. Zip codes of five local towns
7. Phone numbers of five friends
8. Addresses of five friends
9. First verse of a favorite song
10. Five Bible verses

After you have fun sharing answers to the first nine questions, emphasize how Scripture memory can too easily take a back seat to relatively trivial details. Then use the following questions to generate a discussion about Scripture memory.

- How were you able to remember phone numbers, locker combinations, and the rest?
- Have you ever used these same methods to memorize Scripture?
- Why do we need to memorize God's Word? Perhaps these verses will help answer this question:

Psalm 119:9,11
Matthew 4:1-11
Joshua 1:8
2 Timothy 3:16-17
Ephesians 6:11-13,17

Hebrews 4:12
Romans 10:17
Romans 12:2
Philippians 4:8

Remember this: After twenty-four hours we remember five percent of what we hear (Romans 10:17), fifteen percent of what we read (Revelation 1:3), thirty-five percent of what we study (Acts 17:11), and a hundred percent of what we memorize (Psalm 119:11).

Now share some of the following hints for memorizing Scripture — and ask your teens for suggestions and methods of memorizing, too.

- Choose a verse that's special to you. Read and study the verse until you know what it means.
- Meditate on the verse. Think it over again and again until it becomes part of you.
- Write out the verse and reference a number of times.
- Categorize verses. 1 John 5:11-13, for example, would be under the "assurance of salvation" heading.
- When memorizing, quote the topic, the reference, and the verse.
- Break the verse down into smaller phrases and work on memorizing one phrase at a time until you finish the entire verse.
- Start working on a new verse before you go to bed at night. You tend to remember what you are thinking about just before you fall asleep.
- Write out the verses on spiral-bound 3 x 5 index cards so you can carry them with you and work on them wherever you go .
- Use time that's often wasted, such as traveling to and from school, during meals, while exercising or jogging. This is an especially good way to memorize the books of the Bible. Rather than counting push-ups, for instance, recite the Bible books. You just may be able to increase your push-up maximum because you'll have no mental block as you often do when you approach a certain number.
- Accountability! Work with a partner to whom you can be accountable. Check up on each other and quiz each other.
- Set a goal (one or two verses a week, for example), then reward yourself or your partner when either or both of you consistently accomplish your goals over a one- or two-month period.
- Review, review, review. If you don't use them regularly, you will lose them.

A pioneer in applying Adlerian psychology to child rearing, Rudolph Dreikurs pointed out that one of the main goals of people's behavior is to get attention. All of us seek recognition and attention. An expert on motivation, Dr. J. Zink, puts it this way:

> One of the keys to understanding human motivation lies in the power of the emotional response others give to our behavior. Kids who draw powerful emotional responses for being lazy, causing disruptions, fighting with their brothers and sisters, going through your drawers when you're on the phone, taping shut the cat's eyes, etc., have learned how to get our complete and total attention. If you give few other behaviors complete and total attention, they have learned that anger, frustration, and rage are far superior to no attention at all. Most kids get motivated in a positive direction when they experience success at getting the positive emotional attention of others. At the base of the successful experience, like learning to tie one's shoes, learning to sew an even buttonhole, learning to feel the clutch grab as it comes up and the gas pedal goes down, is a common denominator for all human beings. From the success of these activities and others like them we learn how to feel good about being ourselves. And learning to feel good about ourselves and our activities lies at the heart of all motivation.[1]

Have you ever wondered why young boys who would not sit still for even five minutes in Sunday school class will sit for hours on end on cold, hard garage floors tinkering with their bicycles? Or spend weeks hunched and intense before a screen, mastering a video game? Whether the motivators are lights, bells, and whistles or minute gears that fit just so—it feels so good when you master it!

This emotional rush that comes when one discovers or masters or learns something is well known to educators; but it is often overlooked by those who work with under-motivated kids. Good teachers consciously engineer successful experiences for kids in order to generate the honest emotional state in their students of feeling good about themselves.[2]

An appropriate exercise that helps kids feel good about themselves as well as discern their gifts is "What Are My Gifts?"

What Are My Gifts?

For kids to recognize their gifts in this activity, the atmosphere is crucial; the group needs to be relaxed, unhurried, and comfortable with one another.

Read the list of personal gifts below and add any others you like. Keep in mind that this is not a list of skills or talents ("cooks well," "is a good athlete"), but a list of character qualities. Give a copy of the list to everyone.

Get all students in a circle and ask them to read the list and check off the three gifts they feel are their own strongest traits. Then have them place an R beside the three gifts they think best apply to the person sitting on their immediate right, and an L beside the three gifts that best apply to the person on their immediate left.

Now ask those on either side of a student to read their traits for her — that is, the two lists should describe the same person.

Now ask the "described" student to read the list of traits she described herself with so the group can compare the results. Ask her how she felt about the choices of the other two. Have the rest of the group add any other traits that might describe her. Then move on to the next person.

This may take some time, so if you have a large group, you may want to do a few people each meeting for several consecutive meetings.

List of Traits
1. Compassion
2. Listening
3. Trustworthiness
4. Loyalty
5. Sympathy
6. Caring
7. Cheerfulness
8. Ability to cheer up others
9. Helpfulness
10. Ability to make someone who's hurting feel better
11. Ability to mediate between two people or groups
12. Encouragement

13. Teaching
14. Humor
15. Ability to get things done
16. Vision for what the future can be
17. Hospitality — making people feel comfortable
18. Perseverance/tenacity — ability to hang in there
19. Directness — doesn't play games
20. Independence — is not easily influenced by fads or trends
21. Nurturing — ability to help people grow
22. Organization
23. Creativity
24. Acceptance — ability to accept others without judgment
25. Diplomacy — ability to see two sides of an issue
26. Spirituality
27. Humility
28. Hopefulness
29. Optimism
30. Charity — ability to give everything freely
31. Faithfulness
32. Forgiveness
33. Sensitivity
34. Perception — ability to see beyond the superficial level
35. Other _____
36. Other _____

Or give your kids a taste of success at learning this way: Pose a problem and ask for their help in solving it. I once read to my junior-high class a letter I had received from a lady in our church who suffered several illnesses that kept her confined at home. In her letter she wrote about her depression, about how she no longer had reason to keep on living. She wanted to know if there were any Bible passages I could think of that might encourage her.

When I finished the letter, I told the kids I really didn't know what to say to this shut-in; I needed their help in writing my response. I asked them to search their Bibles the following week for any passages that they thought would pertain to the lady's suffering and encourage her.

After years of scant luck getting kids to do their homework, I finally found an approach that worked. The junior highers returned the next week with lots of passages and suggestions, and we had a great time drafting a letter of spiritual encouragement to someone in need. It was rare listening to junior-high kids—who are not known for their scriptural scholarship—arguing with each other about whether Psalm 18 or Psalm 34 offered more spiritual comfort.

The sense of satisfaction they received from creating that letter was amazing. The letter had no sooner been mailed than they asked if I knew of any others who needed the spiritual guidance of the seventh-grade Sunday school class.

These students could very likely have made great use of "Creative Teaching with the Psalms" in their spiritual counseling ministry.

Creative Teaching with the Psalms

Use the Psalms for teaching prayer and petition, praise and thanksgiving—as well as for communicating to a group how individuals and the community of the faithful grapple with grief, despair, sorrow, love, hate, joy, and excitement. Below are two types of psalms which can be used for these purposes.

I. Complaint Psalms
   A. Information
      1. Intention of complaints: to petition God to change or alleviate the situation.
      2. Examples of the two types:
         Individual—Psalms 5, 6, 13, 22, 28, 38, 43, 54, 61.
         Community—Psalms 44, 74, 80, 83, 94.
      3. Historical situations of the complaint: 1 Samuel 1:9-28; 1 Samuel 7; Jeremiah 14:1-9, 17-22.
      4. Situations of the complainers: illness; defeat, persecution; oppression, discouragement, physical needs (children, rain, food, etc), sin.
      5. Constituent parts of all complaints:
         a) invocation.
         b) complaint.
         c) prayer for change.
         In some psalms there are two additional parts:
         d) motivation for God to help.
         e) assurance of God's hearing.

An Example: Psalm 22
I.   Invocation ("My God, my God . . . " — v. 22:1a).
II.   Complaint ("I cry . . . you do not answer . . . " — vv. 1b-2).
III. Motivation ("In you our fathers put their trust . . . " — vv. 3-5).
IV. Complaining (" . . . scorned by men . . . " — vv. 6-8).
V.   Motivation (" . . . you have been my God" — vv. 9-10).
VI. Supplication ("Do not be far from me . . . " — v. 11).
VII. Complaint ("Many bulls surround me . . . " — vv. 12-18).
VIII. Supplication (" . . . be not far off . . . " — vv. 19-21).
IX. Assurance of hearing and praise (" . . . he has not hidden his face . . . " — vv. 22-31).

  B. Group Activity
    1. Lead your group in understanding the parts of a complaint psalm; then ask them to identify the different parts of a particular psalm into its invocation, complaint, and supplication (and motivation and assurance of hearing, if applicable).
    2. Ask them to identify the different emotions and attitudes (despair, anger, sorrow, fear, dread, disgust, etc.) and why the writer had reason to feel this way. Have them examine what the writer wanted God to do about his situation.
    3. As a whole or in small clusters, the group should now share experiences in which they have had similar feelings and attitudes. Ask them how they responded to the situation — e.g., praying, asking for advice from friends, self-pity.
    4. Have the students take ten to fifteen minutes to write psalms of their own, and then share some of them with the whole group. The original psalms can be either a complaint of the community (one that affects the whole group or Christians as a whole) or an individual complaint.

II. Psalms of Praise
  A. Information
    1. Intention of a hymn of praise: To praise God for who he is and what he has done, and to call others to praise him.
    2. Examples:
    Psalms 19:1-6, 29, 30, 33, 47, 48, 65, 66, 92, 93, 95, 96, 97, 98, 100, 101, 103, 111, 113, 145-150.
    3. Situations of the writers: Experiences of deliverance from sickness, distress; thankfulness for God's helping the needy, for the gift of children, for the righteous, for his love, for his justice and mercy; and praise for creation.
  B. Group Activity

1. Ask the group to identify the different moods of one of the psalms (joy, praise, relief, thanks, etc.) and the reasons the writer felt this way.
2. Have the group as a whole or in small groups share times when they have been thankful or wanted to praise God. Ask them to share what they did about it (e.g., shouted, prayed, told a friend).
3. Have all write their own psalms of praise, and then read some of them to the whole group. Remind the group that the criterion of a complaint or praise psalm is not necessarily that it be wonderful poetry, but that it be addressed to God from the heart, not contrived. The results of really putting some thought into this are rewarding, and the group can gain insight about the psalms, themselves, and each other.

The Concept of Chaining

Another way teachers can arrange events to increase motivation is called *chaining*. William James, the father of American psychology, wrote down the idea at the turn of the century:

> Any object not interesting in itself may become interesting through becoming associated with an object in which an interest already exists. The two associated objects grow, as it were, together: the interesting portion sheds its quality over the whole; and thus things not interesting in their own right borrow an interest which becomes as real and as strong as that of any natively interesting thing.[3]

To comply with this common sense principle, we should begin our teaching with something of natural interest to our students and from that point lead them to other areas that will benefit from their original interest. I once began a Bible study series for high schoolers with a lesson I titled "How To Get Someone To Fall in Love With You." This opener definitely lured most teenagers not only to that lesson, but to the following ones, too, which I linked to this first lesson: the nature of love, what attracts people to each other, and eventually an analysis of the qualities we are really looking for. I attached a topic that attracted teen-agers' interest to the study of an important biblical principle.

Or a study of other world religions—the lure—can entice kids to dig deeper into the Christian faith. Adolescents in the West have always been especially fascinated with the religions of the East—Zoroastrianism and Buddhism and Islam. By comparing and contrasting different faiths with Christianity, you are chaining Bible study to already-established interests among your kids.

Or you can chain familiar people with biblical person-alities by using discussion starters like "Who's Who—Then and Now."

Who's Who—Then and Now

This is not only a good discussion starter, but a good crowd breaker as well. You will need to compose and print up two "quizzes," putting one on each side of the same piece of paper. One quiz, entitled "Who's Who—Now," consists of twenty or so questions concerning peo-ple in your church. For example:

1. Who works at Winchell's Donuts?
2. Who is the chairman of our church board?
3. Who teaches our sixth-grade class?
4. Who puts the sermon titles up on the church sign each week?
5. Who is in charge of getting the church bus ready for Sunday?

On the other side of the sheet is a second quiz, "Who's Who—Then," which should contain the same number of questions as the "Now" quiz, except that this one is about people in the Bible. For example:

1. Who built the first temple in Jerusalem?
2. Who led the Exodus from Egypt?
3. Whom did Jesus raise from the dead in the Gospel of John?
4. Who was the first murderer?
5. Who took a ride inside a fish?

All students take both quizzes, and their scores are based on the num-ber of correct answers on each quiz. Each person will have a fraction for a score: The first quiz's score is the numerator, and the second quiz's score is the denominator (a score of 16/19 means sixteen correct for the quiz about people in the church, and nineteen correct on the Bible quiz).

Scores are then compared, and it will surprise everyone to see just how much they vary. Discussion can then center on the relative importance of how much we know about people in the Bible and how much we know about people in the church. Is it good to learn all about people in the Bible and not know each other very well, or vice versa? Is one more important than the other?

Summary

- Learning is a self-motivating experience; it feels good to learn. By successfully teaching someone, we are actually creating more motivation.
- Motivation is increased even more when learning is followed by positive attention.
- We can cultivate an interest in learners about almost any topic by chaining "our" topics to "their" topics.

3

The Conehead Principle:

Kids learn better when they experience.

Bill McNabb

Education, in order to accomplish its ends, both for the learner and for society, must be based on experience—the actual life experience of some individual.
—*John Dewey*

The Conehead Principle is the result of a hard-fought battle between John Dewey and the educational traditionalists during the 1930s and 1940s. Dewey objected to the idea that education was simply the transmission of past knowledge (usually facts and figures) to the present generation. He also objected to *how* knowledge was usually transmitted (through reading or lectures—methods that didn't strike Dewey as particularly effective).

Dewey's pioneering philosophical work was followed by that of the brilliant educational psychologist Edgar Dale, who spent years on a series of experiments in which he measured the effectiveness of various teaching methods. He taught students a certain body of knowledge with a particular method of instruction, then tested his subjects months later in order to determine how much knowledge they retained. He summarized the results of his experiments in the now-famous cone of learning.

Verbal Activities

Visual Symbols

Simulated Experiences

Direct Experiences

The top of the cone represents the least effective teaching methods; the bottom, the most effective. Post-tests revealed that subjects taught by the methods at the top of the cone—lecturing or reading—retained ten percent. On the other hand, subjects who were taught by methods at the bottom of the cone—what he called "direct purposeful experiences"—retained ninety percent of what they were taught. His experiments proved the truth of the maxim, "Tell me, I'll forget; show me, I'll remember; but walk with me, and I will understand."

Researchers since Dale have affirmed the validity of his work. A study addressing the effectiveness of sermons is particularly distressing.

In a large midwestern city undergoing considerable racial tension, the Roman Catholic bishop decreed a program to combat racism. This included, on two successive Sundays, preaching prescribed sermons opposing racial hatred and injustice. To study the effects of the sermons, parishioners from each of twelve parishes were interviewed at home before and after the sermons. Investigators also attended masses in each parish and observed the sermon content. When asked within ten days after the two sermons whether they had heard or read anything about racial prejudice or discrimination since the previous interview, only ten percent of those who had attended at least one of the masses spontaneously recalled the sermon. When the remaining ninety percent were asked directly whether their priest "talked about prejudice or discrimination in the last couple of weeks" more than thirty percent denied hearing such a sermon![1]

So much for the effectiveness of sermons.

Let's take a closer look at the cone of learning.

• **Verbal activities** are, at the top of the cone, the most commonly used teaching methods—lecture, discussion, sermon, listening to a story, reading, and any other type of verbal presentation that depends primarily upon the hearing of learners. Dale's research showed that most people learn poorly by merely *hearing* instruction. In order to be effective, verbal activities must be accompanied by other kinds of experiences. Annotating the genealogy in Matthew chapter one, for example, can increase kids' retention, as outlined in "Matthew One."

Matthew One

It's not easy to make the genealogy of Jesus in Matthew 1 seem exciting to young people, but this idea does exactly that. The following reading is an annotated version of Matthew 1:1-16—that is, it includes brief explanations of who a few of the people were. The annotations

TEACHING THE BIBLE CREATIVELY

reveal to the group what otherwise might be evident only to those who are well educated in the Old Testament. The reading also allows for the group's response to many of the people in Jesus' family tree.

Here's how it works. As the genealogy is read, someone holds up cue cards to the group, who respond as each card indicates. One cue card says "Applause," another says "Boo," another says "Cheer," another says "Hiss," another says "Moan," and another says "Huh?" (The last cue card is used after names of persons in the genealogy who are unknown even to Biblical scholars or who did little or nothing of consequence.) Before the actual reading, it would be a good idea to rehearse the group with the cue cards, just to get everybody in the spirit. When they are ready, then proceed with the reading, pausing as indicated by the parentheses for the appropriate response.

Matthew One

A record of the genealogy of Jesus Christ (*applause, cheer*) the son of David (*applause*), the son of Abraham (*cheers*): Abraham was the father of Isaac (*applause*), the father of Jacob who stole his brother's birthright (*boo*), and Jacob was the father of Judah and his brothers who sold Joseph into slavery (*hiss*). And Judah was the father of Perez and Zerah (*huh?*) by Tamar (*huh?*), and Perez was the father of Hezron, and Hezron the father of Ram, and Ram the father of Amminidab (*huh?*), and Amminidab the father of Nahshon the father of Salmon who was the father of Boaz by Rahab, the prostitute (*boo*), and Boaz was the father of Obed by Ruth (*cheers and applause*); and Obed was the father of Jesse the father of David the King (*cheers*). And David was the father of Solomon by the wife of Uriah whom he had murdered (*hiss*); and Solomon was the father of Rehoboam who was a good king but abandoned God's way for several years (*boo*), and Rehoboam was the father of Abijah who had fourteen wives (*cheers and boos*), and Abijah was the father of Asa, a good king but who did not walk in the way of the Lord at the end of his life and so died of gangrene of the feet (*moans*), and Asa was the father of Jehoshaphat who was a fine king ruling wisely most of the time (*applause*). Jehoshaphat was the father of Joram who was the father of Uzziah whose pride brought his fall (*boo*); but Uzziah was the father of Jotham, a very good king in every way (*cheer*), who was the father of Ahaz, a very bad king in every way (*hiss*). And Ahaz was the father of Hezekiah who cleansed the temple and the kingdom (*cheers and applause*). Hezekiah was the father of Manasseh who ruled for fifty-five years (*applause*), but who was evil for most of that

44

time (*boos*). He was the father of Josiah who did right in the eyes of the Lord (*cheer*); and Josiah was the father of Jeconiah and his brothers at the time of the deportation of Babylon (*huh?*). And after the deportation to Babylon, Jeconiah was the father of Shealtiel who was the father of Zerubbabel, a governor of the people and chosen by God (*applause*). And Jerubbabel was the father of Abiud (*huh?*), and Abiud was the father of Eliakim (*huh?*), who was the father of Azor (*huh?*), who was the father of Zadok (*huh?*) who was the father of Akim (*huh?*), who was the father of Eliud (*huh?*), the father of Eleazar (*huh?*), the father of Matthan (*huh?*), the father of Jacob (*huh?*), the father of Joseph (*applause*), who was husband of Mary (*cheers*), of whom was born Jesus who we call Christ (*applause and cheers*).

A good way to use this (for more than just laughs) is to have the group pay attention to who in fact Jesus' ancestors were. One would think that all of Jesus' ancestors were good people, but that was hardly the case — prostitutes, murderers, and bigamists fill Jesus' family tree. Yet Jesus turned out great. So maybe this means there is hope for us and for our children. Perhaps we ought not blame the way we are on our parents or anyone else, for we are all responsible before God for who we are.

This makes an appropriate reading during Advent or to introduce a Bible study of the Gospel of Matthew.

• **Visual symbols** are another category of teaching activities, which include movies, videos, TV, filmstrips, maps, photos, charts, and virtually any other types of visual presentations. People learn more when what they hear is accompanied with visual stimuli. When visual and verbal symbols are used together, the learning is more effective than when either is used separately.

Objects can be effective visual symbols for teaching, as demonstrated in "Easter Week in Review."

Easter Week in Review

On a table in the center of the room, arrange a number of objects named in the Scriptures that tell of Jesus' last week on earth. Like these:

45

perfume jar (of alabaster) Matt. 26:6-13	whip John 19:1-3	praying hands (ceramic) Matt. 26:36-46
wine bottle Matt. 26:26-30	large nails Matt. 27:32-35	rooster (ceramic) Luke 22:60; Matt. 26:34-35
wine goblet Matt. 26:26-30	dice Matt. 27:32-35	
wash basin (hands and feet) John 13:1-11	palm branch (from florist) Mark 11:1-8	crown of thorns Matt. 27:27-31
sword Matt. 26:47-54	loaf of bread Matt. 26:26-30	cross Matt. 27:32-35
	bag of silver (30) Matt. 26:14-16	linen cloth Matt. 27:57-61

Tell the young people that these objects (others can be used, too) were significant in Jesus' final week on earth. Ask the group to write down the order in which the objects were used — from memory, without consulting their Bibles. Then let them share their thoughts, questions, and their order of objects. Last of all, give them the specific Scriptures and have them look up and read the passages.

This exercise will help give your young people a lasting visual impression of the events of Easter week.

• **Simulated experiences**—activities that require learners to act out feelings or a set of circumstances realistically— move us a step further than verbal and visual activities. Simulated teaching activities include role play, dramatics, simulation games, some field trips, and some creative writing. These types of teaching methods are also especially fun. "Wilderness Wanderings" shows how a simple simulated experience can bring a Bible study to life.

Wilderness Wanderings

Here's a Bible study starter on grumbling and complaining that can be used anywhere.

Give the kids paper and pencil. Announce that you are going to lead them on a journey through the wilderness, like Moses led Israel. Explain that at various stages along the way, you'll ask them to write down their feelings on the sheet of paper. At each such writing stop, they should complete the following statements:

1. Right now I feel —
2. I think this Bible study is —

Now tell them that they must stick together — and take off! Lead them all over the place — down alleys, under buildings, through gullies, across fields, up stairs — and every few minutes call a halt and have the group write as instructed.

Before long they'll start complaining out loud as well as on paper: "I feel shot and want to go back!" "I think this Bible study is stupid!"

But that's just what you want them to do. When you return, you'll have a perfect lead-in for a study of Numbers 11, 13, 14, 20, and 21 — and other passages that deal with the Israelites' grumbling and complaining.

Years ago I put together a simulation based on Jesus' parable of the vineyard laborers (Matthew 20:1-16). You remember the story; the vineyard owner hired one worker in the early morning, another around noon, and a third only an hour before quitting time — and then paid them all the same sum. Few of us like that parable, and most of us have at one time or another attempted to explain it away. It seems unfair, an affront to American values.

I wanted to get my youth group to understand the radical message of grace Jesus illustrated with that parable. So I designed an obstacle course that wound its way through the church property. When kids arrived at our weekly meeting, I told them about the obstacle course — and then wheeled out a cart carrying three giant ice cream sundaes — prizes for the first three people to finish the obstacle course.

When I blew the whistle to start, I got typical responses: some of the kids took off as fast as they could. Others said, "This is so dumb — do we have to do it?" When I assured them that, yes, they did, they flaunted their boredom with my idea of a lesson by slouching through the obstacle course.

When everyone was through the course and back in the youth room, I presented the sundaes to the three winners —

and then our adult sponsors wheeled out carts with identical sundaes for *everyone*.

"Wait a minute," the three winners yelled. "What's going on?" "I decided to give sundaes to everyone," I replied.

"THAT'S NOT FAIR! We won, we really tried, and they weren't even trying—they were just walking."

"I said that the first three to finish would get sundaes," I said, "and you got them." And then I adapted the vineyard owner's piercing line: "Can't I do what I want with my own ice cream, or are you jealous because I am generous?"

With that introductory simulation, we then read together the parable and discussed it with far greater understanding than if we had not used the simulation.

Another effective simulation game is "The Great Button Controversy," a powerful lesson about conformity. The teacher puts a dozen buttons in a box and passes them around the group, with these instructions: all students are to count the buttons when the box is passed to them, and then remember how many buttons they counted. The teacher, however, arranges beforehand that the next-to-the-last person covertly removes one button from the box, so that the last person's count is off by one. You then start at the beginning of the circle of students, asking the kids one at a time how many buttons they counted.

Without fail, the last person in my groups always changed their answers to fit what everyone else said; though they counted eleven buttons, they will inevitably say there were twelve—an obvious springboard to a discussion about denying your personal convictions in the face of group pressure in order to be accepted.

• **Direct experiences**, however—even more than simulated experiences—are what Dale's experiments suggest are the ultimate in teaching methods. Direct experiences are actual, genuine, for-real situations and problems posed for students. Because religious teaching tends to be abstract, instructors often have difficulty designing direct-experience teaching activities—which take more creativity than verbal teaching.

Say for example that you wanted to teach your class or youth group about Jesus' command to love your neighbor as yourself. You could work up a little talk on the subject, you could discuss the concept—but chances are that talks and discussions would render less of an impression than if you selected pictures from magazines to illustrate examples of loving other persons. Better yet, students could dramatize a story or write an ending to several open-ended stories illustrating persons needing love.

Best of all—that is, the teaching method that requires the most student involvement and is therefore the most memorable—you could take your kids to a nursing home or to your congregation's shut-ins, where they could visit with the lonely and unloved and neighborless. The next time the students hear " ... and you shall love your neighbor as yourself," they will have a specific experience as a frame of reference for relating to the concepts of love and neighbor.

A powerful way to give kids a direct experience about life in their community is to arrange a "Nite Life Tour" similar to the one described here.

Nite Life Tour

Here's an intensive, fast-moving twelve-hour (6 p.m. to 6 a.m.) tour of the night life in your town or city. If you take a selected group of senior-high students on a tour like this, they will gain some exposure to the "other side" of life as well as to each other.

Suggested Schedule:

6:00 p.m.	Meet at the church. Orientation. Let the people know where they are going, what to look for, questions to think about.
6:30 p.m.	Dessert and interview at a suicide prevention center.
7:45 p.m.	Movie (secular film at an established theater)
10:30 p.m.	City morgue or emergency room at hospital
11:30 p.m.	Snack
12:30 a.m.	Police department
2:00 a.m.	Control tower at airport
3:00 a.m.	Drug rehabilitation center, or a walk through the red-light district

4:30 a.m.   Breakfast at a pancake house
6:00 a.m.   Home

Additional suggestions: A TV news program (preceded by tour of studios), church-operated coffee houses, telephone company, local newspaper, Salvation Army, Goodwill Industries, store-front churches, a Friday evening or Saturday morning synagogue service, underground church meeting, post office, funeral home (interview with director and tour facilities), bowling, swimming, a play or musical, rap session with students at colleges, fraternities, seminaries, interviews with city officials, etc.

Follow up with a discussion of both the good and the bad of what was seen and heard—though save the discussion for another day, since the group will be pretty tired after the all-nighter.

Early in my pastoral career, my church's Christian education committee took Dale's cone of learning to heart. They realized that the Sunday school format accommodates verbal experiences primarily; it was difficult to have a direct or even simulated experience in forty-five minutes on Sunday morning. So we took the radical step of abolishing the Sunday school and instituting the Concord Christian Club.

The CCC was a monthly twenty-four-hour weekend retreat at the church and open to all first through eighth graders, who arrived at church on Friday evenings—sleeping bags and toothbrushes in hand—and were picked up on Saturday evening. Our Sunday school teachers became CCC sponsors who staffed the events. Parents liked the idea of an occasional child-free weekend; kids not only loved the change, but began bringing friends. Within a few months 150 kids in first through eighth grades were attending—twice the number of kids that had been enrolled in Sunday school. The new format allowed plenty of time for direct experiences—educational field trips, service projects—all sorts of things we could never have done in Sunday school.

Several years ago John Westerhoff suggested that if you could get your kids away for just two weekend retreats a year, they would have more and better Christian education than a year's worth of Sunday school classes.[2]

Such a radical change may not be possible in your situation, but teachers and youth leaders can at least keep the cone of learning in mind when planning their lessons. The cone should be prominently posted wherever you sit when you plan your lessons as a reminder to vary the types of experiences you present to your class.

Matching Your Method with Your Goal

"If you're headed nowhere," the saying goes, "you'll probably get there." Neither will you get anywhere if you do not match the teaching content with an appropriate teaching method. Even experiential-education freaks like John Dewey knew that direct experiences are not always the best way to teach. "Not all experiences are equally educative," he explained. "The central problem of an education based on experience is to select the kind of experiences that live fruitfully and creatively in subsequent experience."[3]

So selecting our methods also means taking a close look at the kind of learning we want to convey to our students. Here, for example, is how educational theorist Benjamin Bloom identifies the various types of thinking that we usually lump together in the general category of "learning."[4]

Type of learning method	Type of teaching method
Acquire information	Lecture, reading
Thinking critically about information	Writing, case study, contrived incident
Clarify and see multiple dimensions	Discussion, role play, films, TV
Apply information to students' world	Simulation games, case studies, discussion
Act on information	Direct experiences (both individual and group)

When planning a series of lessons, teachers would do well to consciously move through each of these types of learning. Say for example you wanted to do a six-week study on what it means to be a disciple of Jesus. You could start by making sure kids acquire the basic information they need through lecture or reading selected biblical passages on the topic. You could then lead them in a contrived incident (of the type found in Youth Specialties' *Tension Getters* series), which poses a difficult situation that requires careful weighing of competing values—which causes students to think critically about what it means to be a disciple.

You could then show them films or videos about people like Dietrich Bonhoeffer or Mother Teresa who have lived out their discipleship in very different ways; such films help them clarify the concept of discipleship and see its multiple dimensions. The next week you could hold a discussion or play a simulation game to help them apply the information about discipleship to their own world. Finally you could plan an evangelistic or service opportunity that would enable them to act upon the knowledge they acquired and clarified in the previous weeks.

This type of thoughtful planning will help you communicate the Christian faith in a way that will continue to live in the minds of your students long after your class sessions are over.

Summary

• Teaching activities at the verbal level—talking and reading—are passive and tend to restrict the participation and learning of many students. Teaching activities involving direct or simulated experiences, on the other hand, tend to involve students and greatly increase the chance that what is taught will be remembered.
• There are various types of learning just as there are various teaching methods. Teachers should choose the teaching method which best fits the type of learning desired.

4

The Sierra Club Principle:

Kids learn better in a comfortable environment.

Steven Mabry

The unseen educators surround us. Not acknowledging their presence, we do their bidding.
— *George Leonard*

Georgia possesses an abundance of granite that found its way into most older buildings, including churches. When I was a kid, my family attended a huge granite church — basement to bell tower, nine stories of stone and stained glass. A grand place for hide-and-seek or for exploring, especially sneaking up the twelve-foot ladder into the bell tower.

The basement, however, was where I spent the formal hours of my early church years, for it housed the children's Sunday school classes. The hall was long, windowless, stone cold, and lined with doors. It *felt* like a basement — cool, poor lighting, hard floors, walls painted a nondescript institutional color, each room equipped with orthopedically designed chairs. Though I never liked the basement, I went to Sunday school to stay out of trouble and get candy.

On Sunday mornings I distinctly remember a lady at the top of the stairs, in the main hall, who let us kids choose our favorite flavors of Life Savers from a big bowl—a cheap but effective way to lure children into the basement where they could be snagged by their teachers.

A few years later my parents changed churches, in the process exchanging our stone edifice for an old house. The living room was the sanctuary, the three Sunday school classes met in bedrooms. I remember adults and kids sitting together on the floor, lots of windows, the one hallway crowded with a mix of men and women and boys and girls and babies. I don't remember much of the lessons I learned there, but I have carried with me to this day many warm feelings for the people in that old house. It was my first taste of Christian community. (No wonder churches build lounges in their CE buildings; designers want to simulate the family living room, where community comes naturally.)

Like the Sierra Club, teachers of the Bible must constantly "lobby" for an environment that gives learners space to learn without distractions, an environment that enhances rather than hinders learning. Classroom settings, unfortunately, are usually overlooked during lesson planning, despite the fact that a warm, friendly atmosphere is crucial for learning. By a warm atmosphere, I mean more than turning up the thermostat on a chilly winter day. Too many of us probably do our share of luring our students, if not with Life Savers, then with promises of socials and retreats—or with guilt—into drab classrooms where we expect our students to learn. Comfortable surroundings that satisfy their physical needs increase attendance and attention—and thus learning.

Buckminster Fuller defined the word *environment* as "everything except me." This chapter focuses not on the students, then, but on everything except them—that is, an effective learning environment, which is characterized by (1) a comfortable physical setting and (2) the creation of an open and receptive attitude.

Physical Comfort

We have many choices when selecting an appropriate physical location for teenage Bible studies. Should we be in a home or at the church? How big a room is required? What kind of seating arrangement is best? How will kids get to and from the study?

Last Wednesday night fifteen-year-old Becky left the Bible study at my house. On her way out the door she said, "I really like being in your home for the Bible study. It's a good place to talk." Translation: "This setting gives me permission to express my feelings and thoughts." The first rule for selecting a location, then, is to consider those who will attend.

The toss-up is usually between a home Bible study and one held at church. Home studies have a decisive advantage—they have kitchens, no small matter to middle-school and high-school meetings. Kitchens, we know, produce Dorito chips, Cokes, hot chocolate, and popcorn with ease. Sofas and carpets create that nice, non-institutional, homey feeling. Opening your home or another adult sponsor's home conveys to your students that you care about them; if you welcome kids into your home, you will likely welcome them—and their problems and friends—into your life, too.

On the other hand, homes often have the distraction of children and pets, inadequate space, the sporadic availability of a sponsor's house if the host travels regularly, regular housecleaning by the host (which is a nagging pressure for some households), a not-as-central location as the church, and the need for everyone in the house—spouses, too—to participate in the study (it feels strange to have non-participants rattling around the house).

Bible studies held at churches boast a central location, adequate meeting space, access to your church library or your office library—generally, a site familiar to both parents and youths alike. Yet this familiar site may work to your

55

disadvantage. A churchy feel to the room or to the seating arrangement—not to mention the mere fact of meeting in a church building—may put off especially unchurched kids.

All things considered, I prefer a private residence. Most of my young people agree.

Ideas for Creating Physical Comfort

Here are some ways to create environments conducive to learning.

• **Temperature.** Rooms too hot or too cold can make students simply incapable of concentrating on anything except the heat or chill. You remember in high school when late spring afternoons turned classrooms into ovens. Ideas don't need *that* kind of incubation.

• **Distractions.** A chattering toddler is a wonderful thing— but not in a Bible study; arrange space with an ear as well an eye to the environment. How about light? You need enough to read by, but warm atmospheres aren't known for lots of it.

• **Seating.** Make it comfortable, and arrange it so that everyone can be easily seen and heard. Even Jesus chose boats and hillsides to teach from; he stood up when reading the Torah in synagogues. If comfort must be compromised, let it be the teacher who endures. Outdoors, for example, if the sun must be in someone's eyes, let it be the teacher's.

• **Room selection.** It should suit the size of the group. Nothing makes a small group feel smaller than meeting in too large a room. And stuffing a big group into a modest living room is great for a Young Life club meeting, but it's probably not the best for study of the Scriptures.

• **Fatigue.** Tired students do not learn well. Nor, at 8:20 p.m., do anxious students who thought the study ended at 8:00. They will tune out, thinking more about tonight's homework and tomorrow's game than about your Sermon on the Mount study.

Finally, here's an idea on how to transform your room emotionally and physically to make it a place kids like to be.

How to Transform a Room

Creativity and tolerance—two words that steer you in the right direction when you create a learning environment for your kids.

Any room can be transformed into a place of their own if kids feel free to say what they need and are then encouraged to plan and do their thing—with adult supervision, of course. When I came to the United Church, the junior highers were meeting in what had been the adult lounge—and it wasn't working. So we brainstormed together and soon received permission to occupy and redecorate another room with typical junior-high flair. After more brainstorming about furnishings, they hustled some old couches and a beat-up stereo, added some lamps, and finally felt the room was theirs. All it took was my encouragement and their released creativity.

Tolerance is allowing kids to keep a room that will never come close to resembling an adult lounge. Tolerance is living with the reality that things will seldom be neat and clean. (Our floor seems perpetually littered with popcorn.) Yet a room of their own—a room that looks and feels like their own—means more to kids than to adults. If your church lacks enough rooms to devote one exclusively to young people, then help the adults learn to tolerate the habits and needs of kids. It is easier for adults to put up with kids than for kids to put up with adults. A little remembering of one's own youth and a lot of patience is all it takes.

The Interpersonal Environment

In preparing the environment for a Bible study, a teacher's attitude is as important as the room's air conditioning. In fact, our interpersonal approach with our kids is the single most important factor in a Bible study's environment.

An open and receptive attitude is hardly a new idea. Consider, for example, Jesus' standard approach to difficult questions. He listened, rejecting neither the question nor the person. Only then did he respond, often with a question of his own. Because he always considered the motivations

57

and thoughts of his questioners and his listeners, he stimulated their thinking and bestowed upon them respect and esteem. He did not argue over different conclusions, but presumed the right of all to choose for themselves.

"Good teacher, what must I do to inherit eternal life?" a rich ruler asked Jesus, who turned another question back to him: "Why do you call me good?" (Luke 18:18-30). Following a brief discussion of the Law, the young man has pointed out to him that although he has obeyed the Law from his youth, he lacks only one thing—his affluence has relegated God to second place. Jesus suggests a remedy that proves too radical for the ruler. Yet Jesus still honored him, granting him the grace to go his own way—even in error.

Honoring your students is essential to the learning environment. The Bible is silent about the eventual outcome of the rich young ruler. The chances for growth and a change of heart, however, are undeniably much greater when students are treated with dignity.

But do not think that treating students with dignity means becoming wimpy teachers who fail to challenge them. In fact, evidence suggests that a degree of anxiety in students actually increases learning; too much anxiety, of course, hinders learning. The trick is not crossing the line.

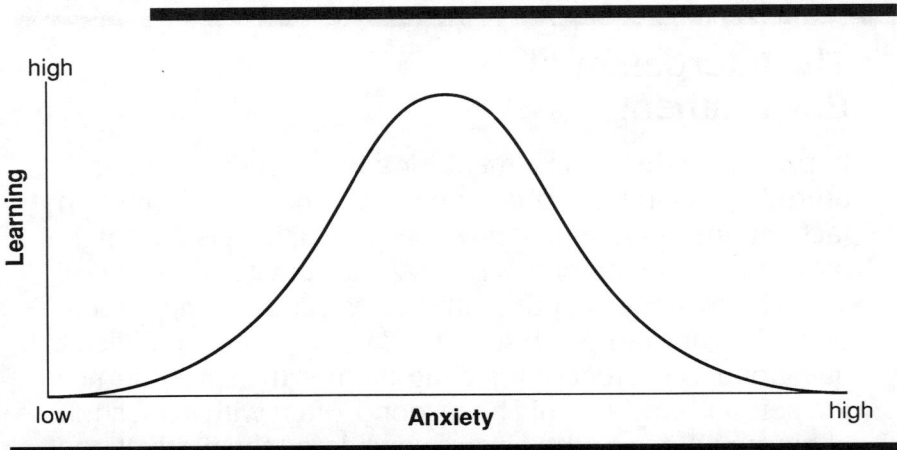

The founder of the youth-resources supplier Serendipity, Lyman Coleman, lists eight assumptions that create environments in which individuals are respected and learning is promoted.[1]

• **Created in God's image.** Each of us is are made in the image of God and blessed by God with great potential. Have faith in the sacredness of each teenager, and hear their thoughts with the ears and eyes of God.

• **Christian community.** The potential of each adolescent can best be realized through the person of Christ, in the company of a supportive Christian community.

• **Commitment.** Christian community is created when we seek to know each other intimately, a task that takes lots of everyone's effort and time.

• **Personal growth.** God wants new life for all your students. Personal growth begins with their response to that desire of God's. This means that the teacher must expect that, somehow, this week's study will make a difference in students' lives.

• **The Holy Spirit.** God has given us the Holy Spirit to minister with us in a supportive community. In response to this gift, we must inspire and lead young people into relationships with one another.

• **The Scripture.** Scripture is the living witness to God's grace and love for people. Youths need to learn the Bible so that it can guide them.

• **Wholeness.** Spiritual growth and wholeness involves our entire being. Through our bodies, minds, and spirits, we learn values and lifestyles, enter (and leave) relationships, and become God's lovers on earth.

• **Acceptance.** When we are set free in Christian community through acceptance and respect, celebration will follow as we reveal the beauty Christ has put within us.

We create environment—both physical and emotional—by meeting physical and emotional needs of our study groups.

Summary

• Environment—"everything but me"—can hinder or enhance learning.
• Two central elements of environment are the physical surroundings and the attitudes of leaders and participants.

5

The Yakety-Yak Principle:

Kids learn better when they discuss what they are learning.

Bill McNabb

Conversation is the laboratory and workshop of the student.
—Ralph Waldo Emerson

As we have seen in chapter three, discussion is not necessarily the best way to teach. But let's face reality: Discussion is by far the most common technique for Christian education, the heart of our Sunday school classes and youth-group meetings. Discussion will always play a major role in Christian education. Our goal is to improve the quality of our discussions in order to increase their effectiveness.

Why Discussion?

The most commonly used alternative to a discussion-format class is the lecture. In most situations, however, discussion is preferable to lecture, for discussion emphasizes learning instead of teaching. Discussion nurtures in students the ability to learn to ask the right questions—which is the beginning of critical thinking.

There are several reasons to choose discussion as a teaching technique.

• **Discussion enhances motivation.** People are naturally curious about what other people think. Although in a lecture you learn only what the lecturer thinks about a subject, a good discussion lets you in on the thinking processes of lots of people. While students listening to a lecture are generally passive, those in a discussion are in the active mode—and that's good. Kids are more motivated to learn if they are active participants in the learning process.

For example, a simple discussion activity like "Human Continuum" can radically increase kids' perceptions of various points of view.

Human Continuum

When discussing subjects that have many points of view, have the kids arrange themselves (prior to the discussion) on a continuum from one extreme viewpoint to the opposite extreme. For example, if you discuss drinking, have those who are "for" drinking line up on one end and those who are "against" it at the other. Undecideds or moderates place themselves somewhere in the middle.

Kids will have to discuss the issue among themselves as they attempt to find the right spot in the line in relationship to each other. After they are settled, further discussion or debate can occur as kids attempt to defend their positions. Anyone may change positions at any time.

• **A good discussion reinforces concepts.** A tenet of social psychology states that group discussion generally strengthens shared convictions. When a teacher presents an idea that is accepted, affirmed, and elaborated upon by the other students, reinforcement occurs. Kids sometimes suspect the thoughts and opinions of adults; but when they hear their peers espouse the same ideas in a discussion, they are more open to accept the new information. An exercise like "Commercial Conformity" is an easy way to put this concept into practice.

Commercial Conformity

When your group discusses the subtle worldliness that tends to creep into Christians' homes and thoughts and behavior (Romans 12:1-2, Matthew 6:19-33, and Colossians 3:1-2), bring with you a video of prime-time commercials that you taped. Replay them as you ponder questions like these:

- What's *really* being sold in this ad?
- What else besides the product itself is being promoted?
- Is there anything unusual or strange in the ad?
- What sells you on the product?
- Does this ad make girls or guys look stupid or used? (Beer commercials usually excel at this.)
- How are you initially affected by the commercial?
- How do certain ads focus on guilt and feelings of inadequacy in us?
- Is your worth to society based on your beauty, youth, or possessions?
- How, if at all, is your value system affected?

- **Discussion nurtures communication skills.** A good discussion educates by its process as well as by its content. The opportunity to share openly one's ideas and opinions challenges kids to become better communicators—a skill that will become of enormous benefit to them.

Several years ago *The Wall Street Journal* reported a study that tried to discover what caused people to rise to the top of their professions. They found that regardless of the profession—law, medicine, business—the people who rose to the top were not the ones who had the most knowledge, but those who had the ability to communicate their knowledge.

For example, "Will the Real Gospel Please Stand Up?" gives kids a chance to practice and improve their communication skills.

Wili the Real Gospel Please Stand Up?

As an intro to the book of Galatians, particularly chapter 1:6-9, this adaptation of the old television game show "What's My Line?" works great. Have six people come to the front of the room, each representing the Christian gospel. They read their "affidavits" (printed below), and then the group discusses the pros and cons of each one. For the best results, the students should know their roles well enough to defend their positions when questioned by group members. Finally, let the group vote on which one (or ones) they feel best represents the gospel.

Add to or change these six "affidavits" as you see fit:

1. I am the gospel of hope. Knowing that mankind is utterly sinful and lost, I claim that Jesus died on the cross and rose from the dead to give all people everywhere forgiveness of sin and eternal life. God does it all, mankind does nothing — therefore, all people everywhere will be saved.

2. My gospel teaches that Jesus died and rose for the forgiveness of all mankind. Those who believe in Jesus will have his forgiveness and eternal life. I also expect you to follow Jesus' command, "Go now and leave your life of sin" (John 8:11).

3. I am the gospel of grace. Jesus suffered and died and rose so that mankind might have forgiveness and life. If you believe, it doesn't matter what you do. You are under a blanket of forgiveness and grace. Enjoy yourself, don't worry how you're doing — Jesus did it all!

4. My gospel teaches that Jesus died and rose for the sins of mankind. This gospel creates a relationship with God in which a person repents and believes in Jesus. This believer's life is one of repentance and faith, expressing itself in love (Galatians 5:6).

5. My gospel is one of action. The same Jesus that suffered and died for the forgiveness of our sins also said, "Let your light shine before men, that they may see your good deeds and praise your Father in heaven." I teach that unless your faith is active, it is no faith at all. Your faith must be visible.

6. I am the gospel of faith. Jesus died and rose for the sins of all who believe. All that God requires of us comes freely through the death and resurrection of his Son. We need only to believe that "since we have been justified through faith, we have peace with God through our Lord Jesus Christ" (Romans 5:1) and this, from John 6:28-29: "Then they asked him, 'What must we do to do the works God requires?' Jesus answered, 'The work of God is this: to believe in the one he has sent.' "

• **Discussion fosters memorizing and understanding better than a lecture.** There are two educational principles at work behind this point. The first is that *improvisation* *increases integration*, which simply means that information learned in a discussion becomes more meaningful to students because they are required to rephrase the information in their own terms. When we read or hear something that prompts a thought of our own, we will often more readily remember the thought than the information which prompted it.

Researchers at the University of Toronto determined that people can more easily recall information they have produced than information they have been told to memorize.[1] Subjects who were given the word *rapid* and who were asked to produce a synonym beginning with the letter *f* later remembered the word *fast* better than did people asked directly to remember *fast*. Not only do we better remember information we produce ourselves, but our attitudes are more likely to be changed by that information.

Social psychologist and Hope College professor David Myers cites others in his field who have

> found that passive exposure to information, through reading or hearing a lecture, has less effect on people's attitudes than when they get the same information through active participation in a group discussion. Other research confirms that when we passively learn about something, our attitudes toward it usually do not change much. When we are stimulated into restating information in our own terms, we are much more likely to remember it and to be persuaded by it.[2]

This concept is readily understood in practice when we use a lively discussion tool like "If You Were to Die."

If You Were to Die

These exercises can be used together in one meeting, or one here and there in order to discuss death and dying.

1. In your opinion, what is the least desirable way to die?

2. If you were to die at eleven o'clock tonight, who would you want most to see before you die? Choose two: parents, brother, a teacher, a neigh-

bor, sister, grandparents, a friend, your pastor, the coach, a child, an enemy.

Discuss your answers and the reasons why you answered the way you did.

3. You are riding in a car down the street. A car coming towards you makes a sudden left turn, smashing into your car and sending it into a light pole. You are rushed by ambulance to the hospital, where you are found to have a fractured skull, broken ribs, a cracked collarbone, and a broken arm and leg. Not only are you in bad shape, but your condition worsens every day. You fear you will soon die; and being as young as you are, you have no will — so you decide to write one.

Write down some of your personal possessions and who you would leave them to. Afterwards, take time to discuss how you felt about writing your will and why you chose to leave certain people certain things.

My Will

I, _____, being of sound mind do hereby bequeath my following possessions to the persons named below.

To _____ I leave my _____
To _____ I leave my _____ [etc.]

As the weeks go by your condition gets worse. Everything is tried — special treatment, surgery by specialists — but to no avail, and finally you die. Next morning your obituary appears in the newspaper. Spend several minutes writing your own obituary; think about what will be said about you after you die. [The leader may want to read an obituary from a newspaper so the students get the idea.]

Take some time to review and talk over feelings about writing your own obituary and what you think will be said about you after your death.

The second educational principle at work is that *context increases internalization*—in other words, a biblical truth may seem meaningless without an exploration of its context and application. I remember leading a Bible study once about idolatry. As we studied the Ten Commandments, we arrived at the verse that forbad worshipping graven images. In the Old Testament context, that almost always had to do with making a statue—such as the golden calf—and worshipping it.

This commandment seemed like a cinch to the kids in my discussion group. "I've never even been tempted to melt down the contents of my piggy bank and make an idol," one said, and most agreed. But then we asked ourselves whether idols had to be statues, or whether they could be other material things. We began to see how we are actually spiritual idolaters when we invest too much of our lives in our material possessions, whether they be cars or CD players or clothes.

After the discussion we realized that maybe the commandment wasn't a cinch after all. A discussion like this— or one triggered by "The Foolish Farmer"—can help us discover the context of a truth and to explore how it applies to our lives.

The Foolish Farmer

Use the parable of the rich fool (Luke 12:13-21) to provoke discussion about materialism by dividing the group into "families" of six to eight people and giving them these instructions:

You are a family and must make a family decision. Everyone in the family must agree; any one person may veto the decision of the others.

You have just received $100,000 from an unexpected source. You must now decide as a family how you will use that money. The only requirements are that you must say very specifically what you will do with the money—and you must decide in the next ten minutes.

Read Luke 12:13-21 before you begin your discussion.

This will obviously result in some heated discussion within each "family." It will be interesting to see how the parable is interpreted and adapted to meet the needs of the group. Some will want to take the parable very literally and radically; others will see it as hyperbole or not applicable to modern-day people.

After each "family" has had sufficient time, have them come back together and share their results, along with the reasoning that went into their decisions.

For an added dimension to this exercise, give the above instructions to all the family groups, but only give half of them the last line that asks them to read the Scripture. There should be a noticeable difference between the groups that use the Bible passage as a basis for their decisions and those who don't. This could lead to a related discussion on the importance of Scripture and how the Bible affects our day-to-day decision making.

The Discussion Leader

Perhaps the most significant factor in the success of any discussion is the teacher's attitude. Some attitudes and roles adopted by teachers are fatal to discussion. You have seen Sunday school teachers who are mere babysitters, mindlessly going through the curriculum, oblivious to their students' apathy. You have been in discussions led by experts whose job apparently was to contradict everyone else's opinion with the "correct" answer.

Or maybe your discussion leader was an entertainer whose perceived duty was to keep everything fun, who would tell any story, however irrelevant, to achieve that end. Or a brainwasher, whose totalitarian teaching style is intended to herd everyone toward the same ideas, who stoops to manipulation and browbeating to achieve the goal.

Such teaching models kill meaningful discussion. To the contrary, the best model I have seen is the teacher as guide. Duke Divinity School's John Westerhoff, a leading Christian education theorist, takes the guide idea a step further; he writes of the need for a teacher to be a shaman. The shamans of some native American tribes led their people on peyote hunts. A tribe's shaman knew where to find water in the desert. He fed his people. He recounted his tribe's history and myths around the campfire. He did a lot of pointing during a day's trek.

A good Bible teacher can learn from a shaman. It is our job, too, to know the way, to lead our people to the water of life, to feed people the Word of God, to tell the stories of our faith, to point the way.

If we see ourselves as co-learners and guides, we are more likely to have discussions filled with active participation and excitement.

The Fine Art of Asking Questions

Good discussion leaders must not only possess the proper attitude, but must be adept at the art of questioning. Possibly the biggest mistake we make in leading discussions—not to mention in our relationships—is asking too many of what psychologist H. Stephen Glenn calls "closed questions." Closed questions can be answered with one word; open questions, on the other hand, elicit a fuller response.

Children are commonly asked closed questions—"How was school today?" "Did you have fun?"—which can be answered with a yes or no, a grunt or a shrug. When we ask closed questions, Glenn points out, we say to them in effect, "I will reduce you to a carefully controlled response by limiting my exposure to your thoughts and ideas." So instead of asking "Did you have a good day?" Glenn proposes asking "What kind of things happened to you today?" That type of question—followed by interested listening, of course—will result in dialogue.[3]

Choosing discussion tools that employ effective questions is a big plus in facilitating successful discussions. Take, for example, the questions posed in "Modern-Day Jesus."

Modern Day Jesus

Curious about how your group perceives Jesus Christ? Want them to grasp some of the implications of being a Christian today? Ask the group to respond to the questions below as if they were each Jesus Christ here and now. Emphasize that there are no right or wrong answers; the main thing is that all respond based on how they think Christ would respond if he were alive today.

1. What kind of clothes do you wear? Do you identify with any particular class of people (poor, middle class, upper class, a minority group, etc.)?
2. Describe your family relationships—with your mother, father, brothers, sisters. Do you have a girlfriend? Will you marry?

3. What kind of people do you hang around with? What do you talk about?
4. What do you look like?
5. Where do you spend most of your time? What is your favorite hangout?
6. Are you a controversial figure? Why or why not?
7. How do you feel about the church today? How do you get along with the religious leaders today?
8. How do you feel about the way things are in this country?
9. What are your goals for the next ten years?
10. How would you get your message out to as many people as possible? (Think this one through carefully, Jesus — are you sure the mass media is the best way to get your message across?)
11. Where do you stand politically? Are you a party member? If so, of which party? What would you consider the important issues — unemployment, inflation, poverty, abortion, equality, environment, capitalism, military spending, nuclear proliferation?

After everyone has answered the questions individually, discuss them with the entire group. To move the discussion from the hypothetical to the actual, ask whether we Christians should respond to those questions in the same manner as our imagined, modern-day Christ. Aren't we to follow Christ and to pattern our lives after his example?

Phrasing good questions is the responsibility of the discussion leader. Here is one educator's classic list of the type of questions there are:

TYPES OF QUESTIONS[4]
Information (listing data, facts, specific content)
Comprehension (asking about the meanings of the content)
Application (asking for places where the content applies)
Analysis (distinguishing meaning in the content)
Synthesis (making connections about the content)
Evaluation (asking for judgments about the content)

Assuming you were to lead a discussion about the parable of the Good Samaritan, for example, the following questions illustrate each of these categories:
• **Information:** Who were the three people that encountered the man lying by the side of the road?

- **Comprehension:** How was it significant that the hero of the story was a Samaritan?
- **Application:** What opportunities do you have to be a neighbor to someone?
- **Analysis:** What was the main point Jesus wanted to make with this story?
- **Synthesis:** How does this parable fit with other teachings in the Bible about our treatment of others?
- **Evaluation:** What is your opinion about Jesus' point?

This order is logical, for it moves from the simple to the complex, each level building on the preceding one. The questions in a typical discussion, however, are seldom scripted and controlled as tightly as the hierarchy of questions suggests. Don't worry about the order of the questions; simply make sure that each type of question is used at least once in each discussion.

In fact, I will let the kids raise their own questions, then lead the group in together searching for the answers. After one of us reads the passage from Scripture, I ask each student to write out as many questions as they can think of concerning the passage. These questions then become the basis of the discussion.

"Questions and Inspirations" is a good example of this technique.

Questions and Inspirations

Here is a simple but effective method of Bible study that works very well with both junior and senior highers. The time allotted for this method can be adjusted to your own time frame, though in general you should allow ten to fifteen minutes of reading time for each chapter or section you study.

Ask the young people to read the assigned passage(s) and write out at least one question and one thing they learned or were inspired by. Then break into small groups of five or so (if your whole group is smaller than ten, just keep everyone together) and spend whatever time it takes sharing each one's questions and inspirations.

The main benefit of this simple system is that in the sharing process, the group teaches itself. The leader takes a very low profile as a facilitator and becomes the speaker/teacher only when the group has no answer for someone's question. Many times one person's inspiration is directly related to someone else's question.

The fact that the Bible study is based on their questions rather than the teacher's usually ensures a higher degree of interest in finding the answers.

Final Tips

• Prepare your basic questions ahead of time; then add other questions as the discussion goes along.
• Don't play "Guess my mind" and call it discussion. Respect others' opinions, even when they differ from yours.
• Try to get all group members to speak during the first few minutes. It is difficult to get a student talking who has been silent early in the discussion.
• If kids are agreeing with each other excessively, play devil's advocate. Stir things up a bit.
• Don't be afraid if a discussion goes off in a direction you don't expect. Trust the process.
• Don't be afraid of silence. Resist the temptation to jump in whenever the conversation lags.

Summary

• The attitude of the teacher is crucial in leading discussions. A good discussion leader is not a propagandist or expert, but a guide.
• A discussion stands or falls on the quality of the questions. Be sure to vary the kinds of questions you pose.
• Allow students to write their own questions about a biblical passage, then use those as the basis for your discussion.

6

The Action-
Attitude Principle:

*Kids believe what they do more
than they do what they believe.*

Bill McNabb

*If we want people to be able to accept or reject the Christian
faith, we have to turn our attention and emphasis from teaching about Christianity to offering within the church experiences which demonstrate our faith.*

—John Westerhoff

During a local political campaign in which my brother
was aggressively involved, he asked if I would post a sign in
my yard that urged voters to elect his candidate. I had heard
neither of the candidate nor of the office he was campaign-
ing for. It strikes me now that, in terms of influence, the
office ranked somewhat beneath municipal dogcatcher.
David was nevertheless persistent, so I agreed to let him
stick the sign in my front yard.

Interesting changes began occurring in me. When I
chanced on small articles in the paper about the candidate
or the race, I found myself reading it instead of skipping
over it. When my neighbors asked me about the sign, I said
to them, "Yeah, he's a good guy, this candidate ... you

oughta vote for him." In short, I began believing in this candidate. On polling day I voted for him with conviction and enthusiasm. When he eventually lost, I was disheartened. I actually cared.

How did I go from apathy to zealous conviction? The attitude-action principle describes how this process happens.

For a long time teachers have generally agreed that if they could persuade kids to believe the right things, the kids would act rightly. We have thought that if we could teach them what the Bible said about honesty, sexuality, you name it, then they would logically, immediately, and cheerfully adopt a biblical lifestyle. Yet in the last thirty years social scientists have discovered much that causes us to question that assumption. In 1964 psychologist Leon Festinger concluded that research had in fact not supported the assumption that changing people's attitudes or beliefs will change their behavior. Festinger and others advanced the radical notion that the attitude-behavior relationship actually works the other way around—that is, people are more likely to behave their way into thinking than think their way into behaving.

In the years since Festinger first circulated his theory, the evidence for it has continued to pile up. A small mountain of research that covers a variety of people, attitudes, and behaviors offered this shocking conclusion: The expressed attitudes of a group of people were almost worthless in predicting how they behaved. People's attitudes about church, for example, had little to do with their church attendance on any given Sunday. Self-described racial attitudes predicted little of the variation in behavior that occurred when people confronted actual interracial situations.

In the course of researching this chapter, I was surprised to read studies that, for instance, compared the tendency of religious and nonreligious college students to do good (e.g., volunteer to help retarded children) and avoid evil (e.g., not cheat when given an easy chance to do so). Smith found that conservative Christian students who were orthodox in their belief about God and Jesus Christ and active in groups such as Campus Crusade for Christ and Navigators were as likely to cheat and as disinclined to volunteer as non-religious and atheist students. Furthermore, these two types of moral behaviors were absolutely unrelated—honest students were no more likely to volunteer than those who cheated; this held true even among the religious students. "As far as moral behavior is concerned," another researcher concluded bluntly, "religion appears to have little effect."[1]

Our beliefs so seldom are translated into action, first of all, because there is a process that a thought must survive before that thought becomes an action. When a teacher attempts to affect a student's behavior with a new thought, that teacher must navigate the following steps:

Does the Learner:

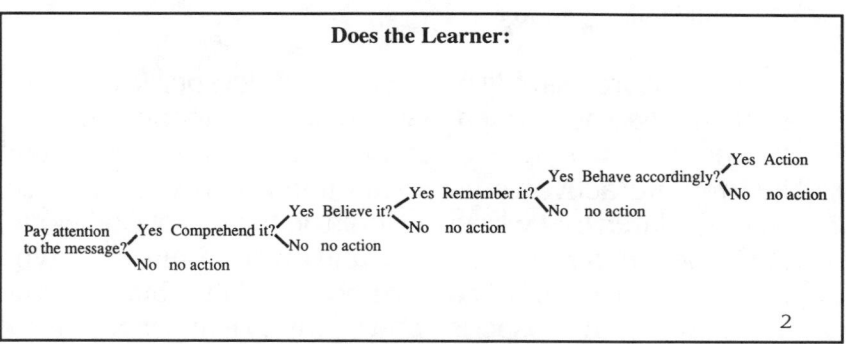

That is a long journey for a teacher's message to travel before it takes root in students' lives. At about the same time that researchers began finding problems with our long-held belief that attitudes determine our actions, social scientists found that actions have a remarkable way of affecting attitudes. Consider the following examples:

- In the laboratory and in everyday situations, evil acts shape the self. People induced to harm an innocent vic-

75

tim typically come to disparage the victim. Those induced to speak or write statements about which they have misgivings will often come to accept their little lies. Saying becomes believing.

- Positive actions—resisting temptation, giving help to someone, behaving amicably in desegregated situations—also shape the self. As social psychologists predicted would happen, changes in racial behavior resulting from desegregation rulings and civil rights legislation have been followed by positive changes in racial attitudes. Evil actions corrupt, but repentant actions renew.

- Many of today's therapy techniques make a constructive use of the self-persuasive effects of behavior. Behavior therapy, assertiveness training, and rational-emotive therapy all coax their clients to rehearse and then practice more productive ways of talking and acting, trusting that by so doing the person's inner disposition will gradually follow along.[3]

This research simply parallels the underappreciated biblical and theological idea that faith follows action. We come to know God by doing his Word. Knowing, loving, and hearing are active verbs, something one does. Likewise, Jesus declared that whoever would do the will of God would know God, that he would come and dwell within those who heed what he said. His call was not to believe, but to follow. The power of the gospel is known only by living it out.[4] Faith therefore grows as we act on the faith we already have. "No truth is taught by words or learned by intellectual means," taught the great Christian educator Horace Bushnell. "Truth must be lived into meaning before it can be truly known."

So what does all this mean for youth workers or teachers who are trying to communicate the Christian faith? It suggests that instead of spending all our time trying to teach kids *about* Christianity, we should involve them in activities that enable them to *live* Christianity.

Action-Attitude at Work— in Mexico

For the last eleven years Steven and I have co-directed an annual workcamp in Tijuana during the Easter vacation break. Over a thousand kids have participated. We do whatever it takes to get them there—including bribing them with visits to Disneyland at the end of the trip. Why? Because we know that one week of building houses for poor families is worth five years of Bible studies on the importance of Christian service. We have taken with us scores of teenagers who did not believe in Jesus' admonition to serve, but who came to believe it by doing it.

Early in our mission-tripping careers, a kid named Bennett came along. He had been in and out of juvenile hall and had been in trouble most of his teenage life. He was a "lowrider"—a Hispanic kid from the poor side of town. As part of his "rehabilitation," his probation officer suggested he get involved with a church. I do not know why, but he picked ours. When the Mexico trip came up, I talked him into going. Bennett was assigned along with fourteen other teenagers and one adult crew chief to build a house for a woman and her three small children who were living in a lean-to made from cardboard refrigerator boxes.

Although back in the States Bennett was the epitome of detached coolness, he threw himself into this challenge with an intensity and enthusiasm that amazed me. Throughout the week I saw him open up spiritually, too. He willingly attended the morning devotional groups and really listened to the campfire talks. Talking with me on the way home, he caught himself.

"I started to say that this had been the best week of my life, but no . . . not the best week. Maybe this has been the only week in my whole life that I have really lived."

Bennett is the rule, not the exception. Nearly all the kids I have taken on a workcamp have returned with profound gratitude for their lives and a taste for the incredible joy and

77

fulfillment that comes from Christian service. It could have taken years to change Bennett's attitude by working on it directly; but one week of the right kind of action caused the attitude itself to change.

It may take a little creativity to get teenagers to act on something before they really believe in it. You can implement a simple yet effective application of the action-attitude principle with simulation games like "The Great Donut Crisis" and "The Great Popcorn Crisis."

The Great Donut Crisis (or The Great Popcorn Crisis)

These two simulation games help your group deal with the problem of world hunger.

Divide your group into three mythical nations, and give them "status papers" describing the situation. The three nations are attending a food-crisis summit. For the purposes of the simulation, each nation's entire food supply is either donuts or popcorn. Each nation represents a different general socioeconomic level—industrialized, agricultural, Third World, etc.

Each group should read its own status paper and then formulate a "position paper" after which the groups meet together to hear each other's positions and intentions. After the three opening statements, the floor is opened for general statements on how the crisis can be averted. Following an adequate period of discussion, a debriefing should follow that discusses the real problem of hunger in the world.

Give all students a copy of the instructions below as well as their specific status paper.

INSTRUCTIONS

You represent one of three nations involved in this serious food shortage. Each group has ten minutes to perform the following tasks:

1. Elect a chairperson for your delegation.
2. Inventory your nation's food supply (see your status paper) and compare it to your needs.
3. After examining your status paper, decide what course of action your country should take and formulate a position paper.

4. Your chairperson should be prepared to present a five-minute statement of your nation's position and intentions at the meeting of the General Assembly, and all members of your delegation should be ready to defend your nation's position paper.

STATUS PAPERS FOR THE
GREAT DONUT CRISIS

- **The United States of Donuts.** You have plenty of food to feed your population and enough left over to export to other countries. Your problem is that your people do not want to give away your food to the needy. Though the donut makers want higher prices, everyone in your country is satisfied because they have all of the donuts that they can eat at prices they can afford. What is your nation's position?

- **The Republic of Bad News.** Your country has a population problem — and on top of that, most of your land area is not suited for agriculture. Furthermore, both your people and your government are very poor and cannot afford modern donut-making equipment that is needed to feed your people. At the conference, you must look to the other two nations for help. What does your nation have to offer in the bargaining? What is your nation's position?

- **The Federation of Big Business.** Your country cannot produce enough food, but you have plenty of industry and money to import all that you need from the U.S. of Donuts. Your economy, however, depends on the sea routes and ports belonging to the Republic of Bad News, with whom you have been good allies for more than a century. You have called this conference in your capital city to try to help in this crisis. What is your nation's position? How will you persuade the United States of Donuts to help your friends in Bad News?

POSITION PAPERS FOR THE
GREAT POPCORN CRISIS

- **The People's Republic of Popcorn.** You are a very wealthy agricultural nation, which produces ninety percent of your continent's main foodstuff, popcorn. Of this popcorn crop, your country needs only fifty percent to feed itself, so that fifty percent is shipped out of the country. Most of those exports go to the United States of Hot Air, which supplies your country with most of its energy in the form of hot air. The present crisis developed when the Kingdom of the Do-Withouts blockaded the Long and Winding River, thus cutting off the main trade route between your country and the U.S. of H.A. Your assignment is to obtain the desperately needed trade route through the Kingdom of the Do-Withouts. Keep in mind that your nation is in critical need of more hot air; you also face the chance of spoilage of this year's huge popcorn crop.

- **The Kingdom of the Do-Withouts.** Your country is very poor and produces only five percent of the popcorn supply. This small amount will just barely supply the needs of only half your population. In the past most of your government's money has gone to buy food to feed the starving people of your country. The popcorn is brought from the People's Republic of Popcorn at very high prices. There is now talk, however, of spending that money on guns and patrol boats in order to completely control the Long and Winding River to force the P.R.P. to lower its prices. The blockade has already begun. It is up to you to try to get more popcorn for your country. It should be noted, however, that each day of the military blockade is costing your country millions of dollars and causes more people to face starvation. You must decide how to act in the best interest of your people.

- **The United States of Hot Air.** Your country is very small and mountainous and produces only five percent of the popcorn supply. This feeds only half your population. Your country, however, has a supply of hot air, which is desperately needed by the People's Republic of Popcorn to run its popcorn factories. Now that the Kingdom of the Do-Withouts has begun its blockade, you have a large supply of hot air, but are running low on food to feed your hot-air factory workers. Find a solution to your country's problem.

Another way to field test this principle with your kids is to find a moral issue which is addressed by the gospel—abortion, the death penalty, etc.—and ask kids to write a letter to the editor of your local paper explaining their views. They are likely to believe more strongly in something they have publicly stood up for.

My Tour in Purgatory

I was once assigned to teaching what the other Sunday school teachers called "the purgatory class"—a group of only seven eighth-grade boys, but the rowdiest, wildest kids I had seen. They attended my Sunday school class only because their parents forced them to attend—and their behavior showed it. I spent most of my teaching energies just trying to maintain class discipline. I spent more time saying, "Listen up, you guys—this stuff is God's Word, and it's important!" than actually explaining the Bible to them.

Two months of this and I was ready to quit—then an idea struck me. I convinced the Sunday school superintendent (who was as desperate as I was) to disband the class and assign the boys in pairs to be "assistant teachers" in the lower Sunday school grades. I spent my time roaming around keeping an eye on them.

The transformation was incredible. The boys became absolutely dedicated to their assigned tasks. After a couple weeks of teaching responsibilities, I walked into classrooms and heard the voice of one of my boys: "Listen up, you guys—this stuff is God's Word, and it's important!" Through being given the job of representing Christianity to those younger than themselves, they came to believe in it more strongly.

The action-attitude principle was at work.

Summary

• Kids are better at finding reasons to believe what they do than doing what they believe.
• When kids publicly act on their beliefs, they come to believe more strongly in their actions.

7

The Agatha Christie Principle:

Kids are motivated to learn when the answer is not obvious.

Bill McNabb

Be patient towards all that is unsolved in your heart and try to love the questions themselves. . . . Live the questions now. Perhaps you will then gradually, without noticing it, live along some distant day into the answer.
——*Rainer Maria Rilke*

I've noticed especially on airplanes that newspaper and magazine readers read casually, almost indifferently. Passengers who are solving crossword puzzles or reading paperback mysteries, on the other hand, are literally engrossed in their pastimes, mentally blocking out all distractions. Considering that the material in newspapers and magazines is generally factual and more pertinent than a fictitious whodunit, I used to wonder why it was that the puzzle and mystery solvers were more captivated by their readings than the newspaper crowd was. The answer is found in the principle I've named after a popular and skillful—maybe the most skillful—writer of mysteries.

Kids learn better when they are challenged to search mentally for an answer they do not possess. Research has consistently shown that learners remember answers to questions they themselves ask. If this is true, one of our most important jobs is to get kids to ask the appropriate questions. Yet what happens in most classes is that teachers ask the questions, try desperately to pry answers out of their students, and usually end up answering their own questions—a process that provides a rich educational experience for the teacher, but not for the students. It takes our patience and wisdom to rein ourselves back from answering questions that have not yet been asked by our students. We must wait for questions to first emerge in our students.

Not to say that we must sit on our hands waiting for kids to ask questions. Teachers can provide information and experiences that can provoke the kinds of questions we want students to grapple with. A great activity that motivates kids to generate their own questions is "Flunk Your Youth Sponsor."

Flunk Your Youth Sponsors

Let your kids see how smart (or not so smart) their youth sponsors are. Students get to play the role of teacher, and the sponsors become the students. It's all done in fun.

Have all the kids in your youth group come up with one question each from any subject they choose. After collecting all the questions, they can then be typed onto one sheet and given to the youth staff. A time limit is set (depending on the number of questions). The results are then announced at the next meeting. Chances are good that most of your sponsors will flunk. But your kids will love it.

You can tie this idea in with your Sunday school curriculum or Bible study, too. Have the kids create questions based on what they've learned during the course of study. The teachers and sponsors, of course, must answer the questions.

Most of you are agonizing your way through final exams this week. Here is your chance to turn the tables, vent your frustration, and

FLUNK YOUR YOUTH SPONSORS!

You are about to write a test that we sponsors will have to take. So make your question as difficult as you possibly can! Here are the instructions:

- Write a test question (one per person) in **true/false**; **matching** (no more than five pairs, please); **multiple choice** (no more than five choices, please); **fill in the blank** (must require a specific answer—no essay questions); or **identification** (can be answered in a sentence or two, and allows for some subjectivity).
- The test question must come out of your knowledge of the various subjects you have been studying this past semester.

Write out your question below, and write the answer on the back of this sheet.

If we can raise questions that create in kids their own questions, then we can set out with them to discover answers—answers that have a far greater chance of being remembered because the students themselves asked the questions.

Prayer Pressure

When a youth worker tried to provoke her students to grapple with the tough theological issues surrounding the subject of prayer, all she heard from the disinterested group were the typical clichés, a regurgitating of the old Sunday school answers they thought she wanted to hear. So she stopped the discussion and instead read two stories to them.

She first read a scriptural passage about God's faithfulness in answering prayer. Then she read a book excerpt about the death of a young girl. The section the youth leader read that night described a hospital visit the father made to his dying daughter. His heart was broken by the sight of his daughter's suffering. Still conscious, the girl asked him to ask God to take away her pain. Not the disease, just the pain. He got down on his knees in the hospital room and prayed harder than he had ever prayed before, every nerve and fiber in his body crying out to the Lord for relief for his daughter. At last finished, he got up from his knees and checked his daughter. There was no change. None. His daughter's pain raged on.

The youth worker closed the book and said to her group, "I'd like you to think this week about how this man's prayer fits into your neat little theories of prayer and how it fits with the Scripture passage we just read. See you next week."

The kids left, stunned and silent. She had started the kids thinking and, more importantly, questioning. Some of the kids told their parents about the question the youth leader had left them with, and asked what they thought about prayer. Others talked to their friends.

When the youth worker opened the next week's meeting with the mention of prayer, there was palpable interest and excitement in the air. They had questions they wanted answers to, and comments they wanted to make. They interrupted each other, waved their hands to be called on, fought for air time. And when they were told about an upcoming Bible study on prayer, the kids showed immediate interest and enthusiasm.

What caused the turnaround in the group? The youth worker had engineered an experience for her kids that caused them to start asking questions. She had provided disturbing information that forced them to abandon their clichés and look beneath the surface for a deeper understanding of prayer.

A master at this kind of teaching, Jesus told stories that had no apparent answer, all in order to tease listeners into reaching for a deeper understanding of God. The Gospel of Luke says that Jesus tried to deliberately shake people up. He taught "so that, though seeing, they may not see; though hearing, they may not understand" (Luke 8:10). He understood that one of the first steps in teaching is to "excavate ignorance."

A big barrier to learning is often the students' perception that they know more about the Bible than they do in fact. This is especially common among Sunday school veterans.

So a first teaching task is to show them exactly how much they don't know—accomplished by some youth leaders by beginning their lesson with a quiz.

When I saw on my schedule that I was due to teach about Noah, I anticipated the teenagers' apathy and prepared a "Noah and the Ark IQ Test."

Noah and the Ark IQ Test

This fun little quiz generates new interest in the familiar story of Noah and the Ark. Most people assume that they know most everything about the facts of the story—but this test may prove otherwise.

1. Why did God decide to destroy all living things with the flood?
   a. Because Israel was disobedient.
   b. Because the Romans were corrupt and needed to be punished.
   c. Because everyone was wicked and evil.
   d. Because he knew it was the only way to get rid of disco dancing and junk food.

2. Why did God pick Noah to survive the Flood?
   a. Noah was the only guy around who knew how to build an ark.
   b. Noah was the only guy around who loved God and would obey him.
   c. Noah won the trip in a sweepstakes.
   d. Noah begged God to save himself and his family.

3. What was Noah's profession?
   a. Animal expert
   b. Boat builder
   c. Farmer
   d. Temple priest

4. How did Noah find out about the coming flood?
   a. He read about it in the Bible.
   b. He had a dream about it.
   c. He was notified by a prophet.
   d. God told him.

5. How long did Noah have to build the ark and get ready for the Flood after he found out about it?
   a. Forty days
   b. One year

c. Three years

d. 120 years

6. What were the names of Noah's three sons?
   a. Ham, Shem, and Japheth
   b. Ham, Sam, and Jeff
   c. Ham, Turkey, on Rye
   d. Huey, Dewey, and Louie

7. How old was Noah when his three sons were born?
   a. In his twenties
   b. In his thirties
   c. About sixty years old
   d. About 500 years old

8. How big was the ark?
   a. 50 cubits high, 30 cubits wide, and 300 cubits long
   b. 300 cubits long, 30 cubits high, and 50 cubits wide
   c. 300 cubits wide, 50 cubits long, and 30 cubits high
   d. About the size of the Queen Mary

9. How long is a cubit?
   a. About three schmuckos
   b. About 2.5 meters
   c. About the length of one's forearm
   d. About a yard (three feet)

10. How many doors did the ark have?
    a. One
    b. Two (one on the side, one on top)
    c. Just the one on the captain's quarters
    d. Who knows?

11. How many floors did the ark have?
    a. One
    b. Three
    c. It was a ranch-style, split-level ark
    d. Who knows?

12. How many people did Noah take on the ark with him?
    a. Three
    b. Seven
    c. Eleven
    d. Thirteen

13. True or False: Noah took only two of each species with him on the ark.

    a. True
    b. False

14. How old was Noah when the flood came?
    a. 35
    b. 50
    c. 120
    d. 600

15. Where did the flood waters come from?
    a. A broken pipe
    b. The sky
    c. Inside the earth
    d. Both b and c

16. How long did the flood last?
    a. A little over a year
    b. Forty days and forty nights
    c. About three months
    d. Who knows?

17. What bird did Noah send out first to see if there was dry land?
    a. Pigeon
    b. Raven
    c. Chicken
    d. Sparrow
    e. None of the above

18. What did the dove return with the first time Noah sent it out?
    a. A pepperoni pizza
    b. Nothing
    c. An olive leaf
    d. An olive branch
    e. An olive pit

19. What did the dove return with the last time Noah sent it out?
    a. Olive Oyl
    b. A message of peace
    c. Nothing
    d. It did not return.

20. Where is the story of Noah in the Bible?
    a. The book of Genesis
    b. The book of Exodus
    c. The book of Noah

d. The book of Moses

21. After the Flood was over, what did Noah do?
    a. He continued his righteous life, never sinning again.
    b. He planted a vineyard.
    c. He got drunk.
    d. He opened a boat store.
    e. Both b and c.

22. God sent a rainbow as a way of saying to Noah —
    a. "There's a pot of god at the end of every rainbow."
    b. "Somewhere over the rainbow . . . "
    c. "Every cloud has a silver lining."
    d. "You don't have to worry about floods anymore, Noah."
    e. "Don't forget what happened, Noah — next time it'll be worse."

23. True or false: Recent scientific expeditions have found remains of the ark on Mt. Sinai.
    a. True
    b. False
    c. Maybe

Answers (all Scripture references from Genesis):

1. c (6:11-13)	13. b (7:2,3)
2. b (6:9; 7:1)	14. d (7:6)
3. c (9:20)	15. d (7:11)
4. d (6:17)	16. a (7:11; 8:14)
5. d (6:3; 7:6)	17. b (8:6-10)
6. a (6:10)	18. b (8:8, 9)
7. d (5:32)	19. d (8:12)
8. b (6:15)	20. a
9. c	21. e (9:20-21)
10. a (6:16)	22. d (9:8-16)
11. b (6:16)	23. b (It was Mt. Ararat,
12. b (7:7)	not Mt. Sinai)

Sure enough, I was met with bored looks when I announced the subject of the lesson.

"We studied that in second grade," they said.

I was prepared. "Great," I replied. "Then you'll ace this test."

No one scored above sixty percent. The test not only illustrated how little they actually understood about the

Deluge, but raised questions in their minds about both the facts and the meaning of the story. They were soon ready to launch into our study with motivation to learn and greater potential for retention—all because we went searching for answers to *their* questions, not mine.

Here are two more "IQ tests" that will get your kids thinking about the holidays in a whole new way.

Christmas IQ Test

Next Christmas give the following quiz to your youths in order to determine how much they really know about the Bible's most popular story. The results will undoubtedly surprise them as well as lead to a better understanding of the events surrounding Christ's birth.

Instructions:

Read and answer each question in the order it appears. When choices are given, read them carefully and select the best one. For all true/false questions, write a T or an F in the blank. Guessing is permitted, cheating is not.

_____ 1. True or false: As long as Christmas has been celebrated, it has been on December 25.

_____ 2. Joseph was from
   a. Bethlehem
   b. Jerusalem
   c. Nazareth
   d. Egypt
   e. Minnesota
   f. None of the above

_____ 3. How did Mary and Joseph travel to Bethlehem?
   a. Camel
   b. Donkey
   c. Walked
   d. Volkswagen
   e. Joseph walked, Mary rode a donkey.
   f. Who knows?

_____ 4. True or false: Mary and Joseph were married when Mary became pregnant.

91

_____ 5. True or false: Mary and Joseph were married when Jesus was born.

_____ 6. True/false: Mary was a virgin when she delivered Jesus.

_____ 7. What did the innkeeper tell Mary and Joseph?
   a. "There is no room in the inn."
   b. "I have a stable you can use."
   c. "Come back after the Christmas rush, and I should have some vacancies then."
   d. Both a and b.
   e. None of the above.

_____ 8. Jesus was delivered in a
   a. Stable
   b. Manger
   c. Cave
   d. Barn
   e. Unknown

_____ 9. A _manger_ is a
   a. Stable for domestic animals
   b. Wooden bin for hay storage
   c. Feeding trough
   d. Barn

_____ 10. Which animals does the Bible say were present at Jesus' birth?
   a. Cows, sheep, goats
   b. Cows, donkeys, sheep
   c. Sheep and goats only
   d. Miscellaneous barnyard animals
   e. Lions, tigers, elephants
   f. None of the above

_____ 11. Who saw "the star in the east"?
   a. Shepherds
   b. Mary and Joseph
   c. Three kings
   d. Both a and c
   e. None of the above

_____ 12. How many angels spoke to the shepherds?
   a. One
   b. Three
   c. A multitude

d. None of the above

_____ 13. What sign did the angels tell the shepherds to look for?
   a. "This way to baby Jesus"
   b. A star over Bethlehem
   c. A baby that doesn't cry
   d. A house with a Christmas tree
   e. A baby in a stable
   f. None of the above

_____ 14. What did the angels sing?
   a. "Joy to the World, the Lord Is Come"
   b. "Alleluia"
   c. "Unto us a child is born, unto us a son is given"
   d. "Glory to God in the highest," etc.
   e. "Glory to the Newborn King"
   f. "My Sweet Lord"

_____ 15. What is a "heavenly host"?
   a. The angel at the gate of heaven.
   b. The angel who invites people to heaven.
   c. The angel who serves drinks in heaven.
   d. An angel choir.
   e. An angel army.
   f. None of the above.

_____ 16. There was snow that first Christmas
   a. Only in Bethlehem
   b. All over Israel
   c. Somewhere in Israel
   d. Mary and Joseph only dreamed of a white Christmas

_____ 17. The baby Jesus cried
   a. When the doctor slapped his behind.
   b. When the little drummer boy started banging on his drum.
   c. Just like other babies cry.
   d. He never cried.

_____ 18. What is frankincense?
   a. A precious metal
   b. A precious fabric
   c. A precious perfume
   d. An Eastern monster story
   e. None of the above

_____ 19. What is myrrh?
   a. An easily shaped metal
   b. A spice used for burying people
   c. A drink
   d. After-shave lotion
   e. None of the above

_____ 20. How many wise men came to see Jesus? (Write in the correct number.)

_____ 21. What does "wise men" refer to?
   a. Men of the educated class
   b. Eastern kings
   c. Astrologers
   d. Men smart enough to follow the star
   e. Sages

_____ 22. The wise men found Jesus in a—
   a. Manger
   b. Stable
   c. House
   d. Holiday Inn
   e. Good mood

_____ 23. The wise men stopped in Jerusalem to
   a. Inform Herod about Jesus.
   b. Find out where Jesus was.
   c. Ask about the star that they saw.
   d. Fill up with gas.
   e. Buy presents for Jesus.

_____ 24. Where do we find the Christmas story in order to check up on all these ridiculous questions?
   a. Matthew
   b. Mark
   c. Luke
   d. John
   e. All of the above
   f. Only a and b
   g. Only a and c
   h. Only a, b, and c
   i. Only x, y, and z
   j. Aesop's Fables

_____ 25. When Joseph and Mary found out that Mary was pregnant with Jesus, what happened?

    a. They got married.
    b. Joseph wanted to break the engagement.
    c. Mary left town for three months.
    d. An angel told them to go to Bethlehem.
    e. Both a and d.
    f. Both b and c.

_____ 26. Who told Mary and Joseph to go to Bethlehem?
    a. The angel
    b. Herod
    c. Caesar Augustus
    d. Alexander the Great
    e. No one told them to

_____ 27. Joseph took the baby Jesus to Egypt
    a. To show him the pyramids.
    b. To teach him the wisdom of the Pharaohs.
    c. To put him in a basket in the reeds by the river.
    d. Because he dreamed about it.
    e. To be taxed.
    f. Joseph did not take Jesus to Egypt.
    g. None of the above.

_____ 28. I think that this test was
    a. Super
    b. Great
    c. Fantastic
    d. All of the above

Answers:
1. False. (Not until the fourth century did it settle on the 25th. Other dates were accepted before then.)
2. a (Luke 2:3,4)
3. f (The Bible doesn't say)
4. False (Matthew 1:18)
5. False (Luke 2:5)
6. True (Matthew 1:25)
7. e (No word about the innkeeper; see Luke 2:7)
8. e (No word about it; see Luke 2:7)
9. c
10. f (The Bible doesn't specify)
11. e (The wise men did—they were not kings; see Matthew 2:2)
12. a (Luke 2:9)
13. f (Luke 2:12)

14. d (Luke 2:14)
15. e (Definition is an *army*; see the Living Bible)
16. d (Mt. Hermon is snow covered)
17. c (We have no reason to believe he wouldn't)
18. c (By definition)
19. b (John 19:30, or a dictionary)
20. No one knows (Matthew 2:1)
21. c (See almost any commentary; they were astrologers or "star gazers")
22. c (Matthew 2:11)
23. b (Matthew 2:1-2)
24. g (Mark begins with John the Baptist, John with "In the beginning was the word . . . ")
25. f (Matthew 1:19, Luke 1:39,56)
26. d (Luke 2:1,4)
27. d (Matthew 2:13)
28. d (of course)

Easter IQ Test

You can use this fun yet educational quiz to usher in Lent and the Easter season.

EASTER IQ TEST
40 Questions for the 40 Days of Lent

Instructions: In the spaces provided on the left, mark the correct answers. Most of the questions are multiple choice; a few are true/false; a couple are fill-in.

_____ 1. As long as Easter has been celebrated, it has been held on the first Sunday after the date of the first full moon that occurs on or after March 21.

_____ 2. Easter was originally a pagan festival.

_____ 3. Ash Wednesday, the beginning of Lent, is always forty days before Easter, not counting
   a. the pastor's day off.
   b. the Sabbath.
   c. Sundays.
   d. Holy Week.

e. Ash Wednesday.

_____ 4. Jesus grew up in
   a. Bethlehem.
   b. Jerusalem.
   c. Nazareth.
   d. Oberammergau.
   e. none of these.

_____ 5. When Jesus came into Jerusalem on Palm Sunday, he entered
   by
   a. walking.
   b. limousine.
   c. riding a white horse.
   d. walking a donkey.
   e. riding a donkey.

_____ 6. With no room in Jerusalem during Holy Week, Jesus had to
   stay in
   a. Bethlehem.
   b. the Garden of Gethsemane.
   c. Bethany.
   d. the YMCA.
   e. a stable.

_____ 7. When Jesus rose from the grave on Easter morning, he
   a. got even with those who crucified him.
   b. saw his shadow and went back inside for forty more days
      of winter.
   c. left the angels in charge of the tomb.
   d. had breakfast with Moses and Elijah on the Mount of
      Transfiguration.
   e. went straight to Galilee and appeared to the disciples.

_____ 8. According to the Gospel of St. Mark, how many women came
   to the tomb Sunday morning?
   a. one
   b. two
   c. three
   d. four
   e. five or more

_____ 9. According to the Gospel of St. John, how many men came to
   the tomb Sunday morning? (Write in the correct number.)

_____ 10. Who was the first person Jesus talked to after he arose?
      a. the gardener
      b. the soldiers on guard
      c. Mary Magdalene
      d. Mary his mother
      e. an Amway distributor
      f. no one

_____ 11. Easter eggs are a part of Easter because
      a. Jesus enjoyed eggs for breakfast.
      b. Jesus was a good egg.
      c. the disciples put all their eggs in one basket.
      d. eggs are a symbol of new life.
      e. rabbits lay eggs.
      f. none of these reasons

_____ 12. Why is the Easter rabbit a part of Easter?
      a. A rabbit's foot is good luck.
      b. Welsh rabbit was a favorite dish of the disciples.
      c. The bunny has nothing to do with anything.
      d. The Easter rabbit is just another commercialization of a religious holiday by Madison Avenue.
      e. It's one of those old German customs.

_____ 13. Jesus was buried on Friday in
      a. a pauper's grave.
      b. a grave he and the family picked out before Holy Week.
      c. a borrowed grave.
      d. a mausoleum.

_____ 14. Jesus was in the tomb for
      a. three days.
      b. an overnight stay.
      c. between 30 and 35 hours.
      d. a much-needed rest.
      e. an unknown period of time.

_____ 15. Jesus was crucified with two others who were
      a. murderers.
      b. thieves.
      c. cutthroats.
      d. blasphemers.
      e. innocent victims like Jesus.
      e. rock musicians.

_____ 16. The Last Supper was held because
  a. Jesus wanted a farewell party.
  b. the Jewish Passover was to be celebrated.
  c. Leonardo da Vinci thought it'd make a great painting.
  d. Judas had to be exposed as a traitor.
  e. none of these reasons.

_____ 17. The word *Easter* appears in which version of the Bible?
  a. RSV
  b. TEV
  c. MTV
  d. KJV
  e. all of these

_____ 18. Lent is
  a. something you find under your bed if you haven't cleaned for awhile.
  b. past tense of *loan*.
  c. a forty-day fast before Easter.
  d. past participle of *lental*.
  e. something I don't know because I'm not Jewish.

_____ 19. How much was Judas paid to betray Jesus?
  a. $100
  b. two loaves and five fish
  c. thirty silver coins
  d. some gold, frankincense, and myrrh
  e. twenty Roman coins

_____ 20. The Joseph who went to Pilate to ask for the body of Jesus was in fact
  a. Jesus' father from Nazareth.
  b. a rich man from Arimathea.
  c. a secret disciple of Jesus.
  d. none of these.
  e. more than one of these.

_____ 21. Who rolled the stone away from the grave Easter morning?
  a. the eleven disciples
  b. two men in white robes
  c. an angel who sat on the stone
  d. Gabriel who blew his horn
  e. St. Peter

_____ 22. How many people did Jesus visit after he rose from the dead?

    a. the eleven disciples
    b. the people of Emmaus
    c. over 500
    d. I don't know.
    e. I wish I did.

_____ 23. How did Jesus look after he arose?
    a. same as always
    b. like Moses
    c. like Elijah
    d. unrecognizable
    e. I give up.

_____ 24. The risen Jesus made breakfast one morning
    a. in the upper room for the disciples.
    b. on the shore of the Sea of Galilee.
    c. at Burger King.
    d. at his friends' home in Bethany.
    e. to start the Easter breakfast tradition.

_____ 25. In the beginning when God created the world, he also created the first computer. How do we know this?
    a. Eve took a byte out of the apple.
    b. Adam and Eve were not compatible.
    c. God monitored their every move.
    d. It's known as a brain.

_____ 26. One disciple was labeled "Doubting Thomas" because he
    a. didn't believe Jesus rose.
    b. missed the reunion party.
    c. didn't believe in the Easter bunny.
    d. was from Missouri.

_____ 27. The date of Easter in the Greek Orthodox tradition is
    a. twelve days later than ours.
    b. the fourteenth of the Jewish month of Nison.
    c. one, four, or five weeks later than ours.
    d. the same as ours.
    e. the same day as Passover.
    f. Who knows?

_____ 28. Where do we find the Easter story in order to check up on all these ridiculous questions?
    a. Matthew
    b. Mark

   c. Luke
   d. John
   e. only a and c
   f. a, b, c, and d
   g. only b and d

_____ 29. The Gospel writers devoted how much of their writings to Holy Week and Easter?
   a. the last chapters of each book
   b. half of their writings
   c. a third of their writings
   d. a quarter of their writings
   e. none of these

_____ 30. Easter is designated a holiday because
   a. it always falls on Sunday.
   b. the Easter bunny lobby was successful in Washington.
   c. college kids needed a break so they could go to Florida.
   d. Easter is the focus of Christian theology.
   e. it comes four months after Christmas.

_____ 31. One of the most famous Easter eggs was
   a. given by a Russian Czar to his wife in 1880.
   b. laid by the original Easter Bunny in 1776.
   c. rolled on the White House lawn in 1952.
   d. a large chocolate egg that took three days to eat in 1967.

_____ 32. The custom of exchanging eggs at Easter comes from
   a. ancient Egypt.
   b. Persia.
   c. medieval Europe.
   d. People's Republic of China.
   e. a and b.
   f. b and d.

_____ 33. Palm Sunday is associated with what other holy days?
   a. Pentecost and Ash Wednesday
   b. Good Friday and Maundy Thursday
   c. Christmas and Epiphany
   d. Advent and Transfiguration

_____ 34. The biblical words "I know that my redeemer lives" were spoken by
   a. Job.
   b. Peter.

      c. Paul.
      d. Matthew.
      e. the Pope.
      f. Billy Graham.

_____ 35. True/false: The cross was the most common instrument of executing criminals in Roman times.

_____ 36. The cross was
      a. always made in the shape of a lower-case *t*.
      b. a stumbling block.
      c. used only by pagans and Gentiles.
      d. made with steel supports.
      e. burned after each use.

_____ 37. Genesis 14:14 has been interpreted as a prediction of Christ's death because
      a. Abraham's kinsmen were taken captive.
      b. Dan was a relative of Jesus.
      c. of the 318 servants.
      d. it was a mistake.
      e. Sorry—I don't know Hebrew.

_____ 38. Jesus was accused by the Jewish leaders before Pilate of
      a. tax evasion.
      b. taking over the temple.
      c. feeding the 5,000.
      d. being a Christian.
      e. selling Amway products.

_____ 39. Easter is
      a. a time for parades.
      b. celebrated every Sunday of the year.
      c. an inspiration for Irving Berlin songs.
      d. the beginning of a new church year.
      e. the time of year to wear your best clothes.

_____ 40. I think this test was
      a. unbelievably simple.
      b. enlightening.
      c. thought-provoking.
      d. unnecessary.
      e. all of these.

Answers to the Easter IQ Test

1. False (The statement is true only since the ninth century for the Western churches. The Council of Nicaea in A.D. 325 had fixed the equinox on March 21, but the Easter date was disputed until the time of Charlemagne.)
2. True (Easter was celebrated as a festival of spring at the vernal equinox in ancient times.)
3. c
4. c
5. e
6. c
7. c
8. c (Mark 16)
9. Two (John 20)
10. c (John 20:11-18)
11. f
12. e (also Egyptian)
13. c
14. c
15. b (Matthew 27:38)
16. b
17. d (Acts 12:4)
18. c
19. c
20. e (Matthew 27:57)
21. c (Matthew 28:2)
22. c (1 Corinthians 15:6)
23. d (John 20:11-18; Luke 24:13-32)
24. b
25. d
26. a
27. c
28. f
29. c
30. d
31. a (A jeweled egg made by the Russian court jeweler Fabergé was given by Czar Alexander to his wife [*World Book Encyclopedia*, Vol. 6, p. 26])
32. e (*World Book Encyclopedia*, Vol. 6, p. 25)
33. b (These are holy days during Holy Week.)
34. a (Job 19:25-26)
35. True

36. b (Galatians 5:11)
37. c (In the apocryphal book of the Epistle of Barnabas, written around A.D. 130-160, it is noted that Abraham had 318 servants. In the Greek alphabet where letters also represented numbers, 318 is expressed as *IHT*. *IH* are the first two letters of Jesus' name, while *T* is a picture of the cross — so there you are, according to Barnabas 9:8.)
38. a (Luke 23:2)
39. b
40. Whatever.

The Educational Power of Suspense

The creative use of suspense can fulfill the Agatha Christie principle as much as entice students to ask their own questions. You heard about the pro who agreed to golf a round with a mere amateur.

"Well, rookie, what's your handicap?" the pro asked his partner for the day. "How many strokes do I give you?"

"No strokes," said the amateur. "Just two gotchas." The pro laughed off what he thought was some sort of a joke, then turned to tee up for his first shot. As he gathered all his concentration, preparing for his drive, the amateur inched up behind him and goosed him with the handle of a club, yelling, "GOTCHA!"

The pro lost the round, waiting for the second gotcha.

Suspense commands attention. Suspense can also arouse interest in a topic that students would otherwise dismiss. A youth leader who wanted to lead his youth group in a study of the book of Hosea, for instance, nevertheless knew the idea would go over like a lead balloon if he presented it at face value. So he put the Agatha Christie principle to work and sent each kid a postcard with this message:

**WHY WOULD GOD WANT YOU
TO MARRY A PROSTITUTE?**
Find out at youth group this Sunday night.

Of course, everybody and his brother (and more than a few parents) showed up to find out what the heck was going on. And this teacher had a captive, interested audience as he explained God's requirement that Hosea remain faithful to his unfaithful wife, as he explained the moving allegory of God's patient husbanding of the whorish Israel. This teacher created motivation and sustained interest through suspense.

Suspense can also inject excitement and attentiveness into a subject kids are already interested in, such as euthanasia. How? Take the issue to court, as described in "Euthanasia on Trial."

Euthanasia on Trial

This mock trial idea not only raises a very timely and difficult issue, but allows the entire youth group to participate in the decision-making process.

The setting is a trial or hearing on the issue of euthanasia (this could also work with any other ethically controversial issue). Part of the youth group is designated the jury, the rest are courtroom observers. Youth sponsors can be used as the lawyers to present the pros and cons sides of the issue to the jury. Youth-group members can be chosen to represent family members in the three cases described. The youth minister or another sponsor plays the part of judge. (It is important that the judge be thoroughly acquainted with the issue, along with portions of Scripture that are applicable.)

The job of the lawyers is to present a convincing case for either the pro or con side of the issue by using whatever sources they can find to prove their argument. They can also call witnesses (youth-group members who represent family members) to bolster their case. Of course, there should be opportunity for cross examination. After both cases have been presented and summary statements made, the jury adjourns for a few minutes to vote on the issues. The jury is not deciding on the pros and cons of euthanasia, but rather on the specific cases. The jury should then vote on each case and give the results to the judge, who will read the results to the "courtroom." (There should be little or no discussion by the jury while deliberating. Save that for the discussion with the whole group later).

The entire group then discusses the decisions. The judge can then wrap up the discussion with some biblical insights without telling the group the conclusions they should have reached. Let the young people go home and struggle with their decision themselves.

Three Cases for the Jury to Consider

A. Robin is a severely retarded nineteen-year-old girl. She has control of her motor (muscular) faculties, but seems to be around the age of one or two mentally. Through nearly eight years of therapy, doctors and aides have finally taught her to button her clothes. The method they used was much like the method a dog trainer would use to teach a dog tricks: stimulus-response. She might be capable of training for an extremely simple factory job, but it would take years to train her and tens of thousands of dollars from both taxpayers and family, in addition to expensive time with a doctor or psychiatrist who could be spending time on more promising patients. Robin's family has asked that they be released from any legal responsibility of her; or, if that is not possible, that she be mercifully put to death. The jury must decide.

B. Alex is a successful forty-seven-year-old businessman who went to the doctor for a routine checkup. The doctor found a large lump in the middle of Alex's back that he didn't like the looks of. X-rays were taken, and it was found to be a form of cancer. A biopsy determined that the cancer was not only malignant, but too far along to take out; so radiation therapy was performed, though unsuccessfully. A month later Alex returned to the hospital in a coma. Doctors believe that he won't live past six months, but he could be given morphine to lessen the pain. He would have to remain in intensive care until his death; that's $120 a day, not to mention thousands of dollars in doctor bills and medication. Alex's family could bear the expense, but they cannot bear to see the pain that Alex is in. So they asked the doctors to either 1) give Alex a lethal dose of morphine, or 2) discontinue all medications and care and let him die naturally and, they hope, quickly. The jury must decide.

C. A baby is born to David and Elizabeth Ritton. They have waited so long for a child, and both eagerly await when they can go on home with their new arrival. The shape of the baby's head bothered a couple of the doctors, so routine tests were conducted to test the baby's brain waves. It was found that during delivery the baby's skull contracted too tightly around the brain and the child suffered severe brain damage to the point that the Ritton baby will be an utter idiot mentally. The baby remained in intensive care while David and Elizabeth went home to think the whole matter over. They are just a young couple and have no finances to put the child in an institution. They decided to go to the doctor and ask if the child could be put out of its misery; the Rittons would try to have another child. It was brought before the courts, and the jury must decide.

Lawyer's Case Against Euthanasia

1. Euthanasia could easily be misconstrued as a mere recommendation of suicide or of wholesale murder of aged or infirmed people.

2. How could a weak and/or unbalanced mind, incapable of properly weighing the conditions that may be held to render death more desirable than life, make this momentous decision?

Case in point: One miraculous cure given a great deal of publicity was that of a clergyman's wife who, in a widely circulated letter, had begged for "scientific kindness" by her physicians to terminate her suffering and give her a painless death. Many laymen supported her arguments, but the physicians ignored them and succeeded in restoring her health. She rejoiced that her pleas were disregarded.

3. What about the obstacles concerning practical applications in our modern society—who will determine who is to die and how?

4. If infants born with idiocy, retardation, or complete body disfigure-ment are put to death under a euthanasia law, this would lead to a degrading of morality, a new form of infanticide—in other words, belated abortion.

5. One alternative to euthanasia is segregation and special training. For example, the feeble minded can actually be made useful, as many of them have considerable physical skill, and they seem to be happy under such conditions.

6. We should hold on to the value of the individual and the value of life at any cost.

7. Wouldn't a pro-euthanasia morality have a hard time dealing with mistakes and/or abuse?

8. What about the danger that the legal machinery initially designed to kill those who are a pain to themselves may someday engulf those who are a pain to others?

Lawyer's Case for Euthanasia

1. What type of life would a baby have who was born with Down's syndrome or a complete vegetable—the issue is *quality* of life, not *quantity*.

2. Special segregation and training involves heavy expense of all sorts, especially emotional and economic.

3. A carefully controlled system of euthanasia would eliminate the most hopeless cases at once.

4. The quality of life of those around the incapacitated individual will be adversely affected if the individual is left to linger in pain.

5. There are those who are afflicted with incurable and painful diseases and want to die quickly. A law that tries to prevent such sufferers from achieving a quick death — a law that thereby forces other people who care for them to watch their pointless pain helplessly — is a cruel law. In such cases the sufferer may be reduced to an obscene image of a human being, a lump of suffering flesh eased only by intervals of drugged stupor.

6. There should be a concern for human dignity, an unwillingness to let animal pain disintegrate a person.

7. Suffering is evil. If it were not, why then do we expend so much energy in trying to relieve it?

8. A society in which euthanasia is accepted "permits an adult person of sound mind, whose life is ending with much suffering, a choice between an easy death and a hard one, and to obtain medical aid in implementing that choice."

With a little creativity all of us can learn how to apply this principle to our own teaching whether it takes place at youth group, in Sunday school, or someplace else.

Summary

- Rarely give kids answers unless they ask the questions. They remember answers to questions that *they* ask.
- When kids assume they already know something, they are not motivated to learn about it. One of your first steps in increasing motivation is to show students they don't know it all.
- Suspense provokes interest. Bible studies that search for unknown, even mysterious answers are more likely to hold students' interest.

8

The Concrete Principle:

Kids learn better when the focus is on the concrete.

Steven Mabry

concrete (kon'-crēt) adj. 1. formed into a solid mass; coalesced. 2. having a material, perceptible existence; of, belonging to, or characterized by things or events that can be perceived by the senses; real; actual. 3. referring to a particular; specific, not general or abstract.
—Webster's New World Dictionary of the American Language

The Bible is about real life. Unfortunately, its message often comes across fuzzy and abstract, irrelevant for today's world. The problem is not so much that the Scriptures speak abstractly, but that in our desire to impart the real meaning of the Scripture, *teachers* often become abstract. Despite the fact that nearly eight million Bibles are sold every year in this country, people largely ignore studying them. Busy people perceive that Scripture is irrelevant and therefore avoid it. Studying it only consumes another slot in an already hurried day.

Helping kids discover that the Bible is a book about real people and a real God is central to effective Bible study.

109

Presenting the words of God with a contemporary image and message for teenagers is a challenge that requires invention; for we must discover methods that employ our imaginations, senses, feelings. By directing students' attention to these tangible handholds, we increase their chances for understanding and retaining Scripture's life-giving lessons. Using specific and concrete examples helps students remember the abstraction and gives them a source of balance and strength wherever they might be. "Power, Authority, and Underwear" illustrates how a passage can be made more tangible, more concrete for the eyes and ears of teenagers—especially by using role playing and the element of surprise.

Power, Authority, and Underwear

"You have heard that it was said, 'Eye for eye, and tooth for tooth.' But I tell you, Do not resist an evil person. If someone strikes you on the right cheek, turn to him the other also. And if someone wants to sue you and take your tunic, let him have your cloak as well. If someone forces you to go one mile, go with him two miles. Give to the one who asks you, and do not turn away from the one who wants to borrow from you." (Matt. 5:38-42)

- Who is Jesus talking *to* (that is, who are the listeners)?
- Who is Jesus talking *about* (that is, who would strike you, take your tunic, or impress you into service to carry their things)?

ROLE PLAY

Have two students enact the striking of one on the right cheek. The striker will immediately realize that there are virtually only two ways to strike the right cheek of another person: hit them with a back hand, or hit them with the left hand

Questions: What does the method of hitting tell you about the victim? About the hitter? Who would strike another with a backhand? If you knew that the left hand was considered unclean and was never used to make contact with another of equal standing, what conclusions would you draw about persons involved? (High schoolers will take only seconds to see that someone of lower social standing or power is being insulted and struck by someone with greater standing or power.)

SCRIPTURE STRIPTEASE

In biblical times the average person wore only two garments, here called the tunic and the cloak. "If someone wants to sue you and take your tunic," Jesus said, "let him have your cloak as well."

Set the scene up for surprise in advance by asking one of your guys to wear a bathing suit under his pants. Then role play the scene — he gets sued and surrenders first his shirt and, next, his pants.

Questions: Who can sue you? How would they feel if you suddenly gave them your cloak (or your pants) as well, leaving yourself publicly naked on their behalf? In these exchanges, who is ultimately humiliated by the end of the scene? What is Jesus saying?

GOING THE EXTRA MILE

A simple discussion suffices for this part of Jesus' story. Explain how in the Roman empire soldiers had the authority to force one to carry their things for a mile.

Questions: What do you suppose happens to a soldier's power when someone voluntarily totes his things for an extra mile? Who is Jesus talking to? Who is he talking about? What does this illustration say about our behavior in contemporary America when peers or employers or even an unreasonable parent leans on us?

Encourage your kids to think of additional questions about the passage. Lead them first in writing a personal story, a contemporary parable that parallels the meaning of this Scripture; then in writing a dialogue between them and Jesus, who explains the meaning of their story.

The concrete method of study provides solid understanding; that it is also entertaining is a bonus. When combined with group participation, stories always turn out to be both fun and meaningful.

Just Give Me the Story

In *The Inflated Self* psychologist David Myers proves the power of personal stories through experiments.[1] When people are presented with thoroughly documented evidence that clearly proves a point, but are then told a specific example or story that contradicts the thoroughly documented evidence, listeners are more likely to believe the one story instead of the documented point.

You know the myth about car buyers who spend a Saturday afternoon in the public library devouring bluebooks and *Consumer Reports* for the latest research about automobile performance, dependability, resale value. Then they make an educated, informed decision. Right?

You know that scenario is mythical. This is usually the way decisions are made:

"Yeah, Larry, I've been doing some reading about the three cars we've narrowed our choice down to. Several trade magazines recommend the '89 Howler GT—you know, the station wagon model. Great gas mileage, and resale value is supposed to stay high for three years, when I'll trade it in."

"Are you kidding, Larry? My sister has a Howler—an '88 or '89, too, I think—and it's always in the shop for one thing or another. The last time it was a $600, six-day drive-shaft repair."

Despite objective research, we cannot discount the experience of a friend—and often put more stock in the experience than in the research. Just the mention of $600 and six days has a tendency to slow a person down. We are simply more likely to accept a specific story than an impersonal report.

Applied to teaching, this knowledge begs us to use methods that make even abstract concepts feel concrete. A good example of this can be seen in the Bible study "Bridge Builders," which takes the term *reconciliation* and gives it a real-life context.

Bridge Builders

Need a program that deals with reconciliation—our being reconciled to God as well as being called to be reconcilers ourselves?

Begin with some fun games, singing, and the like, and then divide the group into bridge-building teams—three to five kids on each team. Give each team lots of popsicle sticks — the more the better. (They aren't expensive, so make sure you get enough.) Provide tape and/or quick drying glue for each team. In the center of the room place a cardboard box. Each team gets an additional smaller box, which they place about four or five feet from the cardboard box in a circle (see diagram). Each team is then instructed to build a bridge from their box to the box in the middle, using the popsicle sticks, tape, and glue only. All the bridges would then be joined together — or, in a word, reconciled.

This activity can produce lots of participation, creativity, and laughs. Encourage "extras" that kids might want to add — toll booths, cars, and so on. Offer a special prize to any group whose bridge supports a toy truck. Follow the whole thing up with a discussion of the unexpected things that happened during the process.

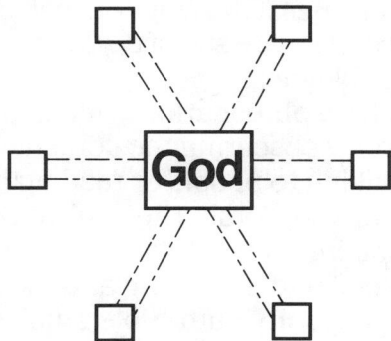

Questions for reflection:
- How many ways are there to reach the same destination?
- How is bridge building similar to reconciliation?
- What do our attempts at bridge building (reconciliation) look like?
- What did God's bridge look like?
- How are the two different? Similar?

Adolescents are bombarded with imaginative images in our society. Trying to combat the almost-tangible MTV, for example, with illusive, abstract notions of a reconciling God is simply ineffective. Thankfully, even Jesus illustrated how to use concrete images — the comparison between the men who built their houses upon the rock and the sand, for instance. Rock and sand are tangible. Anyone who has ever stood barefoot on a beach with waves lapping their feet knows the feel of undertow, of moving sand, of shifting foundations. And that feeling is easy enough to replicate — just stand your kids barefoot in a sandbox and pour water over their feet. They'll immediately sense the instability of the sand they're standing on.

And building our lessons on the bedrock of concrete, realistic imagery is simply good communication.

Making Concrete from Sand

Putting the gospel on a solid footing requires engaging your senses. If you can smell it, taste it, touch it, see it, then you can understand it. Here are specific ways to give teaching a material, perceptible message.

• **Be clear — eschew obfuscation.** That is, avoid bewildering your learners by obscuring the content of your lesson. No one enjoys talking to people or reading books that use difficult-to-understand words. Theological words like *sanctification*, *redemption*, even *salvation*, if they go undefined, will limit teenagers' understanding and the significance of the words. Language in youth Bible studies must simply hold meaning for youths. Talking to kids about the eschatological significance of the return of the Messiah, for example, accomplishes less than asking them how they would feel if Jesus were to physically walk into the room at that moment. Would they be afraid? What questions would they ask him? How would meeting him affect their behavior at school or home?

Paraphrasing historical creeds of the church is a good way to help kids think theologically while using their own vocabulary, as is done in "Youth-Group Creeds."

Youth-Group Creeds

Most churches have definite stands on social and moral issues such as marriage, sex, pollution, war, homosexuality, divorce, alcohol, tobacco, euthanasia, abortion, other religions, materialism, etc. Have your group write up their own creed or statement of belief on one or more of these topics without knowing the "official" position of your church. Then lead them in comparing their stance with your church's. This can lead into a discussion about the difference or similarity of the creeds, as well as about how such creeds are written. They will begin to understand how hard it is for a whole church to agree on something.

A good variation on this activity for a Bible study group is to author a creed based on Romans 12:1-2. Writing a Scripture-based statement is a great way to learn.

The task is not to avoid theological terminology, but to reduce it to believable and understandable forms. Consider, for example, the lyrics to a beloved, old, simple hymn—rendered here, however, in highly technical, clinical, sterile language:

> Unexpected lenience, in the form of a mellifluous phonation,
> That preserved an organism of questionable value commonly associated with the author of this composition.
> Said ego was one time misplaced, but the situation has been altered, and currently there is no doubt as to its location.
> In addition, said ego formerly was incapacitated by a malfunction of the visual sense, but at this moment has recovered the associated ability.

That's one version of "Amazing Grace" that your students probably won't connect with—because it is neither believable nor understandable to most teenagers.

When kids ask you questions, respond in concrete terms and images within their life experiences. I never quite got a handle on just how big an acre of land was until, when I was a teenager, someone told me that an acre was about the same size as a football field. I understood a football field. When a youth asks how far it is between Capernaum and Jerusalem, don't answer like a map maker; give an example. The distance, as the crow flies, is roughly eighty miles—

115

the distance, I told my kids, between Sacramento and San Francisco (or between Charlotte, North Carolina, and Columbia, South Carolina; or Springfield, Massachusetts, and Albany, New York; or Cedar Rapids and Davenport, Iowa). Any kid who had traveled between California's capital and The City immediately had a feel for the distance between Jerusalem and Capernaum. Take your entire youth group out for a mile walk, then tell them to multiply that by eighty—and that's how far Peter and Andrew and John and James commuted. Now you're being concrete.

• **Focus on symbols.** Though it sounds contradictory, looking beyond the literal to the symbolic can actually reinforce concrete images. Take Mark 4:35-41, for example:

> That day when evening came, he said to his disciples, "Let us go over to the other side." Leaving the crowd behind, they took him along, just as he was, in the boat. There were also other boats with him. A furious squall came up, and the waves broke over the boat, so that it was nearly swamped. Jesus was in the stern, sleeping on a cushion. The disciples woke him and said to him, "Teacher, don't you care if we drown?"
>
> He got up, rebuked the wind and said to the waves, "Quiet! Be still!" Then the wind died down and it was completely calm.
>
> He said to his disciples, "Why are you so afraid? Do you still have no faith?"
>
> They were terrified and asked each other, "Who is this? Even the wind and the waves obey him!"

Too often we limit this account of Jesus' mighty power to triumph over the natural elements—wind and water. Says commentator William Barclay,

> We do this story far less than justice if we merely take it in a literalistic sense. If this describes simply a physical miracle in which an actual storm was stilled, it is a very wonder-

ful story, and it is something about which we read and at which we marvel, but nonetheless it is something which happened once and which cannot happen again. In that case it is quite external to us. But if we read it in a symbolic sense it is far more valuable. When the disciples realize the presence of Jesus with them the storm became a calm. Once they knew he was there there was a calm, fearless peace in their hearts no matter what any storm was like. To voyage with Jesus was to voyage in peace even in a storm. Now that is universally true. That is not something which happened once; it is something which still happens and which can happen for us. In the presence of Jesus we can have peace in even the wildest storms of life.[2]

Looking beyond the literal to the symbolic may take on specific forms. In Mark 5, for example, is the story of the demoniac who lived in the tombs. He would break chains that were intended to restrain him. He cut himself with stones, and night and day cried out among the tombs.

A wacko, right? His story has nothing to do with us, right?

Perhaps not, literally. But symbolically, yes. What do the elements of the story represent?

• If tombs can represent our past, how do we live in the past among our own tombs?

• If chains are symbols of being bound up, to what are we captive? What keeps us chained up to old ideas, lifestyles, etc.?

• If injuries inflicted by stones can represent self-abuse, what kinds of self-destructive behaviors do we have?

It is easy to see how using symbols expands the relevance of this story. In this case, symbols make the story more definite and less abstract.

• **Take liberties.** Embellishing a story can bring it alive. For example, the storm passage from Mark can become more sensory and tangible for youth if you add some of your own details to the account of the storm, as in "What Do You Mean, He's Asleep?"

We want to feel the fear, hear the splashing of waves and shouts of the men, taste the lake water, even feel seasick. Try to recover for your students how the disciples felt with the following exercise, which, though it retains virtually all the Scripture, adds just enough detail to jump-start a kid's imagination. (With stories like this, read it through several times before telling it to the group; it's always better to tell a story than to read it.)

"What Do You Mean, He's Asleep?"

On that day—a day of teaching crowds by the sea, of answering an endless stream of questions from never-understanding disciples, a day of telling parable after parable—on that day, when evening had come, he said to his disciples, "Let us go across to the other side." And leaving the crowd, they took him with them in the boat, just as he was. And other boats were with him.

And a great storm of wind arose, and the waves beat into the boat, pouring over every side so that all hands were frantic with bailing. Still the waves beat into the boat, so that the boat was already filling. But he was in the stern, asleep on the cushion; and the gale spun the boat around, and the spray lashed their faces. Clutching the slick gunwales with one hand, they bailed with the other.

Jesus, meanwhile, was in the stern, asleep on the cushion; but they were scared.

Soaked through—and tasting the fishy waters—the disciples heard the wooden dowels groan and the wet sail flap. A line came loose and stood out in the wind as stiff and straight as a laser beam. The boat leaned into the wind, one man was almost overboard.

Jesus was asleep in the stern; they woke him and screamed at him over the wind, "Teacher, do you not care if we perish?" And he awoke and rebuked the wind and the sea, "Peace! Be still!" And the wind ceased, and there was a great calm.

Though you recognized most of the biblical phrases in the account, I've brushed up the story a bit to make it more experiential—and, I hope, more connected to my students. By the same token, allow your students to do this, too. How would the account sound if a teenage boy rewrote it?

118

Another method of embellishing the Scripture is to add background before you read the text, just to set the passage in a real context. An example of this technique is "A God's-Eye View."

A God's-Eye View

Used in conjunction with Psalm 8, the following narrative dramatically illustrates the majesty of God's creation. It is also a good self-image booster as it reminds us of the significance we have in God's eyes.

I want you to use your imagination. Imagine that I have a long sheet of paper that stretches all the way across the front of the room, out the door, outside the building, and continues until you can't see it anymore.

Now imagine that I take a pin and poke a tiny hole in the paper — that is the earth. All the cities, mountains, and oceans of our planet are represented by the speck.

About 5/8 of an inch from the pinhole, make another pinhole — that's the moon.

Now imagine that nineteen feet away, I draw a two-inch circle; that is the sun. Six hundred feet away, the length of two football fields, we come to Neptune.

After leaving the solar system and our pinhole planets, we would have to travel along a thousand miles of paper to come to the nearest star. That's roughly the distance between Chicago and Denver.

Distances in space are so vast they are measured in light-years — that is, the distance that light travels in a year. Light travels at over 186,000 miles per second, so fast that a bullet shot at that speed and circling the earth would hit you seven times before you fell to the ground, even if it took you a full second to fall.

At the speed of light, you could travel from Los Angeles to New York in 1/60 of a second. You could reach the moon in less than a second and a half, the sun in eight minutes, and cover the entire solar system in eleven hours.

But even at those speeds, it would take you forty-three years to reach the nearest star. You would need 400 years to reach the North Star; and crossing just our own galaxy, the Milky Way, would take 120,000 years. And astronomers now estimate that there are over 100 million galaxies.

After reading the narrative aloud to the group, lead your kids in reading Psalm 8 in unison. With this as a background, you can then discuss questions like these:

119

- How does this psalm make you feel about God?
- How does this psalm make you feel about yourself?
- What does this psalm suggest a person's self-image should be? (See also Matthew 10:29-33.)
- What do you think it means when the psalmist says that God crowned human beings with glory and honor?
- Why do you think God needed to create such a large universe?

- **Be inclusive.** Some teachers reduce Bible studies to narrow, constricted "verse studies," with accordingly limiting results. Intense dissection of one or two verses in an hour usually turns kids off. On the other hand, taking whole sections of Scripture—at least when the passages are introduced—will help learners place the passages in context as well as lend depth to the individual stories and verses. Too, readers gain a broader base, which allows the group to focus on areas that may have higher interest.

  For example, if your group is going to study the Beatitudes in Matthew 5, keep them within their proper frame of reference—that is, the Sermon on the Mount. Before you start your Beatitudes study in earnest, read through all three chapters of Matthew's account of the Sermon on the Mount—then go back to the Beatitudes and spend as much time on smaller sections as is needed. Looking at a portion of Scripture as a part of a whole section of the text broadens understanding and enhances the learners' memory. It also gives kids better command of the Bible; kids will know where to find certain passages and will generally be more aware of the context of the Scriptures.

- **Give kids something to find.** Giving the kids something to look for in the passage as they read helps attention and retention. The best way to do this is to do a quick read-through, then ask them to write questions about the passage—questions about theology, personalities, geography, anything they wonder about or want to know. Finally, read the passage a second time, this time searching for answers to their questions. This process does wonders to keep readers' and listeners' attention.

There are lots of ways to turn kids into alert readers: As you read the passage, kids note their favorite verse or the most demanding concept or the most perplexing portion of the passage. Or ask them to note or write down what pops into their minds as you read: their feelings, any of that week's situations at home or school, people, etc. In this way reading becomes active, not passive; it becomes a search for feelings and questions as well as for answers.

Summary

- People are drawn to concrete images.
- Bible studies should present specific and tangible images by encouraging clarity and simplicity; by avoiding meaningless terms; by looking beyond the literal to the symbolic meanings of the passage; by embellishing the stories with details that promote concrete imagine making; by including whole sections of the text and avoiding verse by verse, out of context studies; and by providing kids with things to look for as they read.

9

The Travel Agent Principle:

Kids learn better when they help to choose what they study.

Steven Mabry

I suggest that the Bible is precious to us because it offers us a way of understanding the world in a fresh perspective, a perspective that leads to life, joy, and wholeness.

— Walter Brueggemann

Bill Cosby used to reminisce about his football coach's halftime pep talks during high-school games. After a rousing speech that was heavily seasoned with all the lingo associated with traditional locker room pep talks, after the team gradually got psyched up to fever pitch, the coach climaxed his inspiring talk with a hollered "Let's go!" The fired-up team leaped to their feet and stampeded like frenzied water buffalos to the locker room door—only to find it locked.

Something akin to this happens with youth Bible studies. Leaders get the kids psyched up to come, but then fail to satisfy the students' interests, forget to open the door through which kids can bring their own needs with them to the Bible study. Opening that door for your kids is crucial; your inattention to their needs, on the other hand, will lead them only to crash into the door. Unlock the doors by giving students a choice in topics and methods—then help them choose well.

Perhaps the most important distinction to be made in the process of choice is between need and want. In *All Grown Up and No Place To Go*, David Elkind suggests that American teenagers face potential harm too often because they do not know who they are or what they need. This lack of self-identity and self-image puts them at unnecessary risk. Elkind coined the phrase "the patchwork self" to describe the tendency of adolescents to be one person at church, one person at home, and still another with their school friends. Their need to be accepted by peers and families dictates their personalities and behavior, depending where they are and who they are with.[1]

By focusing on the questions and issues that are significant to young people, we gain their trust and build their self-confidence. They gain the opportunity to learn about their concerns in the context of God's Word, seeking answers from the Scriptures and discovering that God wants to be part of their daily decisions. Providing such a foundation teaches kids to make good decisions, based not on the moment or their company, but on a set of values they have developed and learned to apply to all activities.

To be successful at this task, we must attend to the needs of our students by offering them choices.

Deciding Between Needs and Wants

It was my good luck to be around for much of my nephew's growing up. I remember when Kevin was six, he would burst into the family room with all the energy and thirst of a kid coming in from a hard day at play. He looked his father in the eye and commanded, "I need Coca Cola!"

His dad would grin. "Nobody *needs* Coke," he told his son. "But if you want one, ask, 'Dad, may I please have a Coke?' "

Kevin is in college now and carries a well-tuned set of values. Though raised in an affluent home, he has not become a materialistic kid. I think Kevin knows the difference between needs and wants.

"Okay—so far, Heidi wants us to memorize Lamentations and Lance wants to party until we drop."

Wants and needs are clearly different things. And although adolescents are famous for quickly identifying the former, they usually have an instinctive though unverbalized knowledge of the latter, too. We can help them dig for the answers when they are uncertain. One way to discover the needs of teenagers is to simply and creatively ask them, as "What Do You Need to Know?" demonstrates.

What Do You Need to Know?

Circle the number of the ten topics that most interest you. Then star three of the ten you would most like to learn about.

1. Alcohol
2. Anger
3. Bible studies
4. Competition
5. Careers
6. Colleges
7. Dating
8. Death
9. Drugs
10. Ecology
11. Faith
12. Getting along with brothers and sisters
13. Getting along with parents
14. Getting along with friends
15. Getting along with adults
16. God's will
17. Group pressure
18. World hunger
19. Identity
20. Independence
21. Jealousy
22. Love
23. Marriage
24. Poverty/affluence
25. Race/prejudice
26. Sex
27. School
28. Feminism
29. World religions
30. Values/what's important
31. Inferiority
32. Second Coming/prophecy
33. The Occult/Satan
34. Overcoming laziness
35. Worry
36. Suicide
37. Time management
38. Biblical bodily discipline
39. Humility
40. Handling a big mouth
41. Fasting
42. Depression
43. Patience
44. Persecution
45. Prayer
46. Illness
47. Failure
48. How God can use an introvert
49. Women in the Bible
50. Why believe in the Bible
51. Fear

Unearthing the needs of kids ensures that any effort they make is rewarded with significant and useful information. If we ask sincerely, listen well, and have some patience, young people will tell us what's important to them.

Another way to discover what teenagers need is to hang around with them. In the course of conversation, an observant teacher picks up on the issues where guidance and discussion would be helpful. Or tackle the problem head-on: in a straightforward discussion, just ask students what they feel they need to know more about. This works best when the leader is very patient, permitting time for silence and thought from the students. Facilitate honest, unabridged answers by having students write questions and concerns anonymously.

Become a Travel Agent

There are two basic approaches to learning: passive and participatory. In passive learning students are spoon-fed what the leader thinks they need to learn, having little to do but act as receptacles for the knowledge that the leader pours into their heads. In participatory learning, students make choices. Think of yourself not as a teacher but as a travel agent. Your job is to suggest destinations, assist in the planning, and make sure the people have a rewarding trip. Travel agents would be worthless if they had no suggestions and stifling if they tried to impose destinations on their clients. As guides we help kids choose wisely. Then we teach to their needs.

In his book *How Children Learn*, educational theorist John Holt explains why it is crucial for us to allow young people to have a choice in what they learn.

> In our struggle to make sense out of life, the things we most need to learn are the things we most want to learn. To put this another way, curiosity is hardly ever idle. What we want to know, we want to know for a reason. The reason is that there is a hole, a gap, an empty space in our understanding of things, our mental model of the world. We feel that gap like a hole in a tooth and want to fill it up. It makes us ask, "How, When, Why?"[2]

Carl Rogers sums this principle up nicely when he notes that "the only learning which significantly affects behavior is that learning which is self-appropriated, self-discovered."[3] Since the goal of Bible study is learning that significantly affects behavior and faith, topics must be selected through a process that gives kids an opportunity for self-discovery.

But offering choices to your kids can be threatening. Kids may pick Revelation or another topic you feel inadequate to teach. Just a minute, we protest—they need to learn some basics first. Yet dealing with this dilemma is fairly easy. By providing a framework for their choices, we can include students in the selection process while still retaining some sense of direction for the study. For example, allowing students to pick topics from a curriculum or printed course of study can help the teacher while still involving kids in the selection of topics. This process holds a fringe benefit for us: since we can't be experts on every topic, kids' choices can prod us to involve other adult leaders who may know more about certain topics.

The important thing, of course, is that students participate and that the topics and passages give them maximum opportunity for growth. And whether we like it or not, teenagers and adults are so busy these days that we cannot waste time teaching topics that don't matter. Dog racers, for example, get their hounds out of the gate and across the finish line by using a fake rabbit on the end of a pole. Compelling as this is to the dogs for the duration of a race, not even the dumbest of them will chase a fake rabbit forever.

Neither are kids dumb. In fact, seldom will they chase fake rabbits at all. The genuine quarry for kids is wherever their needs intersect with Scripture, wherever learners are compelled to look carefully at themselves and to decide to act in accordance with God's teachings. The ability to memorize Scripture or recite the books of the Bible or name all the heroes of Hebrews 11 is not the real rabbit. Kids learn that Bible study is relevant to their lives only when we spotlight real-life topics like relationships, love, human sexuality, service to others, parents. Topics such as these create an interest in learning for kids and bring their lives into harmony with the gospel.

Travel Tips

Fake rabbits can be avoided by letting kids determine what the real rabbits will be. Here is what I have found helpful in the selection process:

• **Set the direction.** Deciding the specific purpose of a study makes kids' choosing a topic easier and more meaningful. Before the session begins, ask yourself these questions:

—What are the students' needs? How does this lesson respond to them?

—What is the most important idea that kids can take home with them from this Scripture?

—How will I involve the learners in the lesson?

—What things would need to happen for the study to be successful for me? For the students?

—What is the purpose of my leadership in this study?

• **Know your hopes and fears.** After you have determined your purpose, acknowledge your private hopes and fears for the study.

—What would I be most pleased to have happen?

—How will I adjust to the group if they have a different agenda?

—Am I prepared to jettison or amend personal goals in favor of participants' goals? (For instance, if you plan a discussion, but the conversation takes an unexpected turn, will you quickly turn the group back your way? Discussions will often follow the students' needs, not the teacher's plan. How will you react?)

—What would I least like to have happen?

These and other questions (add your own to the list) are important as you prepare to teach.

• **Select passages with care.** Your reasons for teaching and the purpose of the group play a large part in the selection of the topics and passages to be studied.

—Begin with books or topics that are neither difficult nor lengthy. Initial commitments by kids to study the Bible should not be rewarded with the most difficult passages in the text. It is important that you are acquainted with your kids' level of knowledge and their familiarity with Scripture. Think twice, for example, about beginning with Revelation or Jeremiah—books that tend to be complex and require deeper knowledge of the Bible than most high schoolers have. On the other hand, the Gospels require little previous knowledge and provide something for both experienced and inexperienced readers, making them an ideal beginning point. Some of the shorter letters of the New Testament (especially James) are appropriate as well.

—Select a subject or book of appropriate length. Asking students to read the entire Old Testament in a year may overwhelm them.

—Select Scriptures with good story lines and straightforward theology. Topic and story come together smoothly in the telling of David and Bathsheba (2 Samuel 11), a story of lust, sex, murder, adultery, pregnancy, judgment, and forgiveness. These are contemporary issues of high concern to young people, and there is a definite opinion rendered to us by God through the prophet Nathan.

—When working with very familiar passages, employ new and creative methods that allow insights to get beyond the kids' preconceptions. Spending a lot of time on material that is common knowledge is usually wasted time. Because kids probably are very familiar with the story of the Good Samaritan, they are not likely to take away new insights—unless they study it from a fresh approach, a perspective that surprises them or requires them to identify in new ways to the story's characters. As Christian-education specialist Marlene LeFever says, "Obliterate the familiar and see what emerges."[4]

One way to do this is through identification with a certain character. For instance, how would this story sound to a priest? Take forty-five minutes of a sixty-minute study to learn about the priestly traditions, customs, and governing laws. Then read the story, assuming the role of the priest. Would you even hear the message? Would it make you angry? Could you justify your behavior in the story?

Or what would happen if the parable of the Prodigal Son were updated? Assume that you are the young man—where do you go with all the money? Describe yourself (kind of car, favorite sports, women, where you live, your music). If you died, would you make it into the *New York Times*? What would the obituary say? The secret to creating new insights and discoveries for young minds is creativity, especially when dealing with the familiar. Another example is "Parable."

Parable

Get your kids involved in the parables of Jesus by dividing them into small discussion groups; then give each group a parable from the Scriptures. Ask the groups to work on the following questions about their parable:

- What do you feel was the meaning of the parable in Jesus' time?
- How does it speak to us now?
- What do you find most profound in its message?
- Prepare a short modern skit of how you think this parable would have happened in twentieth-century America.

The groups should be allowed enough time to work through each question and prepare their skits. Then the entire group meets together, and each small group presents its skit and shares its thoughts on the parable. The discussion/preparation period and the presentation of the skits can be done in two different meetings, over two days or even two weeks.

- **Respond to questions.** Display supernatural patience with *all* questions. Be clear with your students that there are no stupid questions (or stupid students) when you all sit down to study the Bible. Treat them all with respect, and do your best to encourage students to seek the answers. Remember, it is okay to say, "I don't know."

131

• **Seek insights as well as answers.** Resist the temptation to say, "Let's find a need that adolescents have and then supply them with answers from the Bible." Questions raised by adolescents will cover the entire range of human existence. Let them find their own answers as active participants in the discussion, as they do in "Scriptures' Common Denominators."

Scriptures' Common Denominators

The next time you want to get your kids into Scripture, give this idea a try. Divide everyone into groups of three, and give each group the following list (without the answers, of course). The object is simple — they are to look up each set of verses and decide on a common theme that links them all together. You can easily add other sets of verses as you like. There are no winners or losers in this exercise; you may want to close by having all or some students share the verse that meant the most to them during the evening.

1. Matthew 9:13, Luke 6:36, 1 Timothy 1:12 ff. (the mercy of God)
2. Acts 10:36, Romans 5:1, Philippians 4:7 (peace between God and man)
3. 1 Corinthians 12:27, Ephesians 1:22, Colossians 1:18 (Christ as head of the church)
4. 2 Corinthians 1:12, 1 Timothy 1:19, 1 John 3:21 (forming a good conscience)
5. Matthew 7:15, Acts 19:9, James 4:4 (friendship)
6. John 7:38, Romans 1:16 or 3:22, Galatians 3:8 (having a visible faith)
7. 1 Corinthians 4:12, 1 Thessalonians 5:15, 1 Peter 3:9 (do not return evil for evil)
8. Matthew 3:15, 1 Corinthians 5:6, James 3:5 (fidelity in little things)
9. Galatians 5:20, Titus 1:7, Matthew 5:22 (anger)
10. Mark 11:25, Luke 7:32, Colossians 3:13 (forgive those who wrong you)
11. 1 Timothy 1:5, 1 Peter 4:8, 1 John 4:17 (charity, or love)
12. John 13:15, 1 Corinthians 15:49, Ephesians 5:17 (we should imitate Christ)
13. Matthew 17:24-27, Romans 14:1, 15, 2 Corinthians 6:3 (don't be a bad example)
14. Matthew 4:22, Mark 7:10, Ephesians 6:1 ff. (children and parents)
15. Philippians 3:13-14, Hebrews 12:28, Jude 1 (serving God)
16 John 16:33, 1 Timothy 6:17, 1 John 3:21 (confidence and trust in God)

17. Luke 15:20, 27, 2 Corinthians 1:3, Ephesians 2:4 (God's goodness and care toward us)
18. Mark 7:6 ff., Acts 5:1 ff, 2 Timothy 3:5 (hypocrisy)
19. 2 Thessalonians 1:4, 7,2 Peter 1:6, James 5:7 (patience)
20. John 13:17, Hebrews 4:2, James 1:2-27 (word of God must be lived)
21. Matthew 5:29 ff., Acts 5:1 ff., Philippians 3:7 (self-denial)
22. 2 Timothy 2:14, 23, Titus 3:1, 2, 9, James 4:1 (avoid discord and arguing)
23. John 15:10 ff., James 2:10, 1 John 5:2 ff. (keeping God's command-ments)
24. 2 Corinthians 6:14, 2 John 6-11, Revelation 18:4 (choose friends well)
25. John 2:7, Acts 4:19, Romans 16:19 (obedience to God)
26. 2 Thessalonians 3:13, 2 John 8, Jude 21 (perseverance)
27. Romans 11:33, Colossians 2:3, James 3:15 (wisdom)

A study on capital punishment provides a context in which your group can look at passages dealing with revenge, justice, judgment, the sacredness of human life, and the eye-for-an-eye laws. Let the kids grapple with forgiveness and revenge. Setting up the Bible as a book full of simplistic solutions to complex questions may not be as helpful as teaching kids a process for asking the right questions, and encouraging them to search for difficult answers.

• **Keep Scripture in context.** One of the ways we assist students in their understanding of Scripture is through helping them see the whole picture. Isolating verses from their surroundings is not helpful. In her book *Using the Bible in Groups*, Roberta Hestenes points out that

because the Bible is a collection of books, the most basic pattern of Bible study is to study one book at a time. Within a book the most convenient unit of study is the chapter. Studying one or two verses is seldom adequate to grasp the thought of the writer and interpret it properly in context. Larger units of study such as the paragraph and the chapter give more with which to interact. Even if thematic or topical study is the method used, the basic building block of study should be more than a single verse or two.[5]

Reading whole stories puts the Scripture in context. Where would the story of David and Bathsheba be without the appearance of Nathan, God's prophet? Let's give our kids complete sections of the text. "The Bible was written in large sections," Roberta Hestenes again writes. "It is best read and studied that way."[6]

Summary

• Choice is essential to the interest and intensity of a student. The things we most need to learn are the things we most want to learn.

• Teachers should be aware of their purpose for teaching and should set goals for their lessons.

• Hints for selecting topics: Begin with simple subjects and build in complexity; welcome *all* questions; use the text as a book of insights, not an answer book; shy away from the overly familiar, unless you can put a new face on it that gives students new insights; and choose a section of Scripture that embraces a complete story or thought.

10

The Emoi Hellēnikē Estin Principle:

Kids learn better when they can translate terms into their own language.

Steven Mabry

There are two basic aspects to the gospel: one expressed through words and ideas, and the other lived as the Good News. . . . The keys to all education are experience and interpretation. Education becomes Christian education when both of these occur to a person within the faith community.

—John H. Westerhoff

E*moi hellēnikē estin*—it's all Greek to me." For centuries the Bible has been translated from one language to another, a necessary process that we take for granted. Yet it is easy to overlook the evolution that has occurred within the language the Bible appears in. A quick comparison between the King James Version and the New International Version, for example, is proof enough that English has changed immensely between the early seventeenth and the late twentieth century. That is why the specific field termed *hermeneutics* has been carved out of theology in general. The Greek word *hermania* means "translate" or "interpret." To reach young people with the biblical message, then, teachers must engage in teaching hermeneutics. That is, we must help students translate and interpret the Scriptures into their language.

The authors of *Helping Youth Interpret the Bible* conducted a study designed to ferret out the perceptions of kids participating in confirmation or catechetical education.

> Young persons, ranging in ages from 12 to 16 years, were asked, "How important is it to read the Bible?" The invariant response was, "Very important." To the question, "Why do you think it is important to read the Bible?" the vast majority responded, "It tells you how to behave" or "It helps you live a good life." At another point in the interview each was asked, "How often do you read the Bible?" The overwhelming majority responded, "Not very often. I can't understand much of it."[1]

A language or comprehension barrier evidently exists between kids and the Bible. Teachers must help students transcend those barriers or the wonders of the Bible may be lost to a generation of young Christians. There was a time in Christian history when the learned priesthood of the church said to lay people, "We will interpret the Bible and tell you what it means; you cannot understand it by yourself." We can avoid historical regression by helping young people read and interpret the meaning of God's words and stories.

An example demonstrating the need to help people put the Bible into comprehensible language is The American Bible Society's publication of *Today's English Version*, subtitled *The Good News Bible*. The TEV was translated for people using English as a second language, for those overwhelmed by the complex vocabulary of other English versions. The goal was to facilitate understanding of the Bible.

The publishers never imagined that their *Good News Bible* would become the all-time best-selling paperback book in history.

I am certain it was with that same good intent that *The Wittenburg Door* facetiously promoted the nonexistent *Valley Bible*.

"Totally Awesome!"
The Valley Bible

So like there was this old dude who had two sons. The youngest one was like y'know a total babe, for sure. The older one was a total zod, like a real space cadet, totally. So this young dude is like freakin' out, like totally bored and stuff. There was nothing to do, like nothing. So he goes to his dad and says, "I'm sure, I'm going to stay here the rest of my life. Like gag me with a spoon. I mean barf me out. This place is totally gross, like grody to the max. I want like my share of your mega-bucks so I can like pig out on junk food and buy clothes, for sure." So his dad like gave him his share of the mega-bucks and like this young babe went totally spaz. For sure. Like scarf and junk food and lowies to the max. And rolfing all night long. Like totally freaked out. I am so sure. Gag me.

Have you ever wondered when somebody was going to put the awkward and formal wording of the Living Bible into a language today's generation can understand? Well, wonder no longer, cuz the Valley Bible is here! That's right. Weekends of extra-credit work by the Inner Vacancy chapter of California's Encino University has produced the definitive translation for the Eighties. The Valley Bible preserves the accuracy of the Living Bible while eliminating ambiguous phrases like, "I don't believe you," or "that makes me upset." Like, we're talking Bible to the max here, so pick up your copy today. For sure!

> *"Yeah; a really tubular Bible."* —F.F. Bruce, Jr.
> *"Like ya know, if you see only one movie a year make sure it's this one for sure."* —Karla Henry, Jr.

Another fine Wycliff product. No. 256 in a series of 700. Collect them all and trade them with your friends.

Though it is dated, Valley talk remains a perfect example of hermeneutics in action. And only God can predict what the language of youth will sound like in another ten years!

The Leader's Role in Translation

The role of the adult leader in translation and interpretation is crucial. Donald Griggs—author, founder of Griggs Educational Service, and noted trainer of teachers—distinguishes between teachers as *transmitters* and teachers as *translators*. "A transmitter sends messages in one direction, from the source to the receiver," says Griggs. "A translator is someone who helps facilitate communication between two persons who are otherwise unable to communicate with each other."[2] Our role is that of translator, not transmitter. Translators assist their students' work of interpretation by giving them background—context, language, history, personality, geography, and other germane data—so that students can interpret the Scriptures into their own language.

Here is how leaders can help kids interpret the Bible and make it meaningful.

• **Build the story into your kids.** We cannot interpret until we are acquainted with the story—that is, how did God act or speak in the given passage? Before we can interpret its message, leaders must internalize the message. For example, I will ask my kids to try an ancient method of memorization—"Getting Acquainted with the Scriptures."

 ## Getting Acquainted with the Scriptures

First choose the passage of Scripture. (Parables work nicely, since they are not lengthy and they normally are complete stories or thoughts.) Instruct students to stand and take their Bibles in hand. While walking around the room, they are to read the passage aloud, with feeling, three times through, attempting to secure it in their minds, word for word. Needless to say, this creates a lot of fun commotion. Next, all students pair off, exchange Bibles with their partners, and then take turns attempting to recite the entire passage by memory to each other while the partners follow along, checking the accuracy of the storytelling and prompting you if you stumble.

This memorization game provides just enough anxiety to increase retention. But because it is not a contest, it will feel like a fun, friendly way to memorize a passage. Once they have experienced the passage written and spoken aloud, their chances for translating it are greatly improved.

Another way to build the understanding of a passage into kids is to have them look at it in the context of everyday situations, as in "What Would You Do?"

What Would You Do?

It's easier to get into Scripture when it can be looked at in light of everyday situations. The following six situations are designed to help kids think through how various passages of Scripture might apply to them personally. One good way to use them would be to divide the entire group into six small groups and type up each of the situations on separate sheets. Then give each group one of the situations, permitting them enough time to work through the discussion questions. When they are finished, each group can then share their conclusions with the other groups.

Jeremiah 17:9-10 (cheating). In an English exam you need an A or B to pass the course for the semester. You studied long and hard. Your friend didn't study at all. While the teacher is busy checking papers, you notice that your friend is copying answers from another student who always does well. You get a C while your friend gets an A.

- How do you feel?
- What would you do as a Christian?
- Does this experience change your relationship with your friend?
- Would you discuss the issue with your friend? Other friends? Your parents? The teacher?
- How would you feel if you were the cheater with an A knowing your friend studied and received only a C when he needed at least a B?

Proverbs 1:29-31 (instant gratification). The group is going to an amusement park and you need $20. Your parents agree to help you earn it by allowing you to keep money from the recycling of aluminum cans and the return deposits on glass soda bottles. Normally the money is put into the family entertainment budget. On the way home with the money, you discover a new album by your favorite rock group and buy it on the spot,

139

thinking that you can get your amusement-trip money from the next recycling batch of returns. When you get home your parents are very upset and tell you that they will not help you earn any more money and, because you broke the agreement, you cannot go on the trip even if you do get the money.

- How do you feel?
- How do you think your parents feel?
- Who was cheated?
- Has an impulsive act such as the above ever cost too high a price?
- If you were the parent, would you have handled this differently? If so, how?

Proverbs 3:1-6 (trust). You are not yet allowed to go on any type of dates. You've agreed to meet your girlfriend (or boyfriend) at the movies. You tell your parents you are going to the movies with your best friend. Your parents discover what you did. Now you can go nowhere unless your parents take you and pick you up. Over the last few weeks you feel they are beginning to trust you again.

- Did you 'fess up or try to fake it?
- Will you sneak another date now that they are beginning to trust you again?
- How do you think your parents felt when you betrayed their trust in you?
- Would a Christian react differently?

Proverbs 16:6 (loyalty). You are at your friend's house. Your friend sneaks a candy bar for you from a little brother's stash. You say nothing, though you think it is not quite right for your friend to just lift it without asking the little brother. On the way home from school you and your friend stop at the store to pick up something for your mom. When you leave the store, your friend gives you another candy bar — which, after you've eaten it, you find out from your friend that he lifted it from the store without paying for it.

- How does the candy taste now?
- How do you feel about your friend?
- Should you tell someone? Who?
- Should you have discussed it earlier when you noticed that the friend was sneaking the candy at home?
- Would you discuss this with your parents? Why or why not?
- If this pattern continues, does your friend deserve your loyalty?
- Can you get into trouble for being loyal? How or why not?
- Does loyalty overlook anything and everything?

Deuteronomy 5:16, 1 Samuel 19:1-3 (obedience). You are not allowed by your parents to call boys on the telephone. Yet you feel times have changed and your parents are old-fashioned. You go to a neighbor's house, you tell your parents, to call a girlfriend. The neighbor, however, discovers you are using the phone to call boys; the neighbor also knows that your parents do not allow it.

- In what position do you place the neighbor?
- Do you know why your parents do not want you to phone boys?
- Do you open discussions with your parents, or just complain to your friends?
- Do you expect parents to know automatically how you feel? Why or why not?
- Will your parents trust you if they find out?
- Did you consider the consequences of being found out?

Matthew 25:34-40 (respect for others). Your youth group goes on a retreat. You find yourself the only person from your group in a discussion group. You are not being included, so you speak up—but the others ignore you. Whenever you ask a question or make a suggestion, they pour cold water on your idea. You attempt to sit closer to the nucleus of the group, only to have someone pull the chair out from under you just as you sit down.

- How do you feel?
- Could you have done anything to improve your situation?
- What should the group have done?
- Did it upset you differently coming from a church group rather than a school group?
- If you had been part of the antagonizing group, what would you or could you have done to improve the situation?
- Have you ever been part of a group that excluded someone? How did you feel? What were your thoughts? Your actions?
- Would a Christian react differently?

- **Identify what is important.** After you build the story into your kids, then direct the students to select the most important points in the passage and translate the Bible's language into contemporary images that *they* choose, images that hold meaning for them. This increases the possibility for interest as well as for understanding. As they select methods and metaphors, they will identify the important parts of the passage, interpreting meaning through their life experiences.

A few years ago three of my junior-high boys created a Christmas rap to illustrate the visit of the Magi. They still know the rap and perform it spontaneously at Christmas parties and youth-group meetings.

The Visit

The visit of the Magi, that is, à la rap music. You'll just have to imagine the chacka-boom-ba accompaniment.

I'm a king
  I'm a king
    I'm a king, too
We do things the way kings do!
Comin' from the East, we seen this star,
Lot's of guys try to come this far.
But we have the know to make this trip
So come on guys, let's be hip!

So we asked
  At the palace
    In the center of town,
We had to know where it was goin' down.
But no one knew as much as we did!
Even Herod didn't know this kid!
So off we went to Beth-le-hem.
And we won't go back to see Herod again.

Now listen
  All ye
    Little kids!
When we got there, this is what we did:
We sang him praises and gave him gifts
(Include that on your Christmas lists!)
So when they ask you what you want on Christmas Day
Tell them, "Jesus — in my heart to stay!!"

Or let creative translation be a metaphor—a ski-boat metaphor for the Psalm 23, for instance.

The Lord Is My Ski Boat

The Lord is my ski boat,
That is just what I have always wanted.
He makes me ski on blue water;
He leads me along quiet seas.
He gives me back my zeal for life,
He guides me behind the wake
For my well-being's sake.
Even though I come to choppy waters,
I show no fear, for someone is watching.
Your life jacket and boots, they comfort me.
You let me jump the wake before my critics and I do not fall.
My skills are mounting.
Certainly exciting and successful times will follow me all the days
    of my life,
And I will dwell in the Skiers Hall of Fame forever.

Okay, so the theology is not always profound. That's not the issue. The bottom line is that kids were engaged on their terms. They participated in the struggle to identify biblical meaning through contemporary expression.

Since kids are often intimidated when they write (thanks to teachers' red pens), you may have to nurture their playfulness. Affirm and inspire them to identify what's important in the text. The adult leader's permission for them to be creative is the key. If you want to bring your kids into this gradually, try "1 Corinthians 13 Fill-in-the-Blank."

1 Corinthians 13 Fill-in-the-Blank

If I have the ability to talk about _____, but have not love, then I am nothing but a big mouth. If I had all the power to _____, but have no love, then my life is a waste of time. If I understand everything about _____, but have no love, then I might as well sit in a gutter. If I give away everything I have, but have no love, then I _____. Love is patient, love is kind, love is _____. Love never _____.

143

It makes it easier for kids just starting out in hermeneutics to get the hang of it. If we affirm and inspire the creativity of young people, they will identify in their own language what the Scriptures mean.

• **Share interpretations.** The discussions really pick up when kids share their interpretations—for example, when you use the "Ski Boat Psalm" in a reflective discussion. Discuss their choices and translations, carefully avoiding any put-downs. Encourage kids to ask questions of their peers. Inquiries that clarify and build on the youths' interpretation are most useful: "What caused you to select a ski boat image for this passage? What made that important to you? How do your critics treat you when you jump the wake in front of them?" As they respond to questions, students learn to analyze their interpretations, defend their faith, and keep an open mind about new insights revealed through discussion.

• **Make general conclusions.** Finally, help the students discern biblical truths that are useful in real-life situations. With the ski-boat metaphor, questions resemble these: "How can you use your translation in the future? Is there anything in your life that you would do differently now that you have translated this passage? What are the choppy waters in your life? How do you deal with them in light of this biblical passage?" Give kids a message for living that they can take with them from the study, for that is when learning begins to be living. For example, notice how "Isaiah's Prophecy" aims its message directly at the student.

Isaiah's Prophecy

Often we fail to appreciate Jesus Christ's death for us. Perhaps we are too familiar with the details of his crucifixion. Maybe the story has become so commonplace that we forget that it was our sins that led Jesus to the cross and to a horribly painful death. In this study and sharing exercise, youth-group members look at the prediction of Jesus' death by Isaiah and recognize that it was their sins that brought the

prophecy's fulfillment. Lead the group in reading Isaiah 53, preferably aloud. Then ask these questions:
• Who do you think Isaiah was talking about?
• What does Isaiah say that reminds you of Jesus?

Next, distribute pen and paper. Instruct students to select verses that are especially meaningful to them. They are to paraphrase these verses, inserting Jesus' name in place of each singular personal pronoun. When finished, let several students read what they have written.

To complete the study, instruct students to read verses 4-6 again. They should paraphrase these verses, writing their own names in place of each plural personal pronoun. When finished, ask these questions:
• Pretend you are the only person who has ever lived. Did Jesus have to die? Why?
• What has Jesus' death done for you?
• What is your response to him right now?

Other Methods for Translating

Writing is only one way for kids to translate a passage into meaning for themselves. Variety increases learning potential—so here are some other methods your students can use to translate. Lead them in the same four steps (build the story into the kids, identify what's important, share interpretations, make general conclusions) regardless of the method you use.

• **Drawing.** Visual images are powerful tools both for memorization and interpretation. Just think for a minute and you will call up mental pictures from cartoons, magazines, even billboards that you habitually passed as a child. Sometimes drawing the narrative of the story—or its meaning—reveals meanings and feelings that other methods miss. Or try the drawing activity "Word Pictures."

Word Pictures

Here's an idea that can help your youths do word studies, examine Bible characters, or delve into theological concepts. Pass out worksheets with a word-picture diagram printed on them. Have your group write the key word (which can be any word or name you suggest) in the center. Then combining the key word with the guide words on the outside, ask them to write in additional descriptive words. It's easiest to write the first thing that comes to mind. When they are through, your group will not only have a better understanding of the key word, but they will be able to see more of the implications in a study of Scripture.

WORD PICTURE

Produce a Word Picture uniquely your own! You will be surprised at the new light you bring to the key word in the center of the picture — and at how creative you really are.

Write the key word in the circle's center. Using the guide words, write a word or a phrase in each outer circle that best fits the mood of the circle. You don't have to put down opposites all the time. The two circles may make you think of two unrelated ideas, or you may see one as positive and the other as negative. However you see fit to fill the circles is okay. It's *your* picture of the key word.

large	hot	God
movement	masculine	touch
cold	outer	baby Jesus
feminine	electric	prayer
inner	word	Transfiguration
soft	spirit	revolutionary
small	judgment	disciples
still	lamb	miracles

- **Music.** The way music creeps into our memories makes it often more available for recall than words. The Christmas rap in this chapter is only one method. Set biblical accounts to modern songs. Try it from scratch—encourage the youths to write music and lyrics that portray the mood and story of a Bible passage. What would the musical score be for the story of David and Bathsheba? How would the mood of the composition change when the prophet Nathan shows up to confront the king? Kids love music and the opportunity to use it creatively. The kids in my group love "Pharaoh Pharaoh," sung to the tune of "Louie Louie."

146

Pharaoh, Pharaoh

Chorus: I said Pharaoh, Pharaoh—oh, baby,
Let my people go—ooh, yeah, yeah, yeah, yeah
(repeat)

Well, a burnin' bush told me just the other day
That I should come over here and stay,
Got to get you people out of Pharaoh's hand
And lead them over to the Promised Land.

So me and my people goin' to the Red Sea,
And Pharaoh's army comin' after me.
I raised my rod, stuck it in the sand,
And all of God's people walked upon dry land.

Well, old Pharaoh's army started comin', too,
So what do you think that I did do?
I raised my rod and I cleared my throat
And all of Pharaoh's army did the dead man's float.

• **Drama.** The parable of the friend at midnight (Luke 11:5) entertains and teaches kids as a skit that they perform—and they always give it different, humorous interpretations each time I see it. Set it up by explaining Israel's ancient tradition of feeding guests in their home. Drama lets us put our whole body into the Scripture; it engages our senses. It is the perfect method to get some kids to relate to a passage in Scripture. Some of the best Bible skits I have seen are impromptu—written in a few minutes and performed by kids who use their imaginations as tools for study. "Family Affair"—about the Prodigal Son—shows how this can be done.

Family Affair

Prior to reading the parable of the Prodigal Son, assign by card a character (father, young son, eldest son) to each person in the group. After your kids hear the story, divide them into three groups—all

147

the fathers in one group, younger sons in another, and eldest sons in another. The three group discussions are intended to clarify the roles in the students' minds and especially talk through the particular feelings of their own character so they can role-play with confidence later in the meeting as they meet their "family."

Each card also bears a number that indicates just what other "brother" and "father" comprise that student's "family." After the discussion groups, each "family" of three meets to role-play what happens the night of the feast, when things have calmed down some and the three of them are alone around the table, finishing up their desserts. Each person responds as his role determines. After the family discussion, meet together with the whole group and discuss what happened.

Summary

- There are many ways to translate—words are only one method. The insights and fun of learning are limited only by our imaginations and ability to grant permission to kids to use their creativity.
- Teachers should serve as translators, not transmitters as they help students put the words of the Bible into their own language. Don't assume that kids view the language of the text as you do. They do have a comprehension barrier that needs to be overcome.
- Four steps that help kids find meaning in the text:
  —Provide creative ways for kids to learn the stories of the Bible.
  —Equip them with methods that encourage translation so that they can identify what is important in the passage.
  —Provide opportunities for their translations to be shared in discussion or presentation.
  —Help them go from the specific truths of the stories to general truths for living.
- Use a variety of creative methods including art, music, and drama as you provide the means for translation.

11

The Show and Tell Principle:

Kids learn better when they are challenged to be creative.

Steven Mabry

Our interest is not in titillating the group with warm fuzzy experiences, or getting people to know one another better, but in finding that subtle intersection between the text and our own life where the sparks fly, the insights are born, the corner is turned—where, in short, we encounter the living God addressing us at the point of our and the world's need.
— *Walter Wink*

In the best-selling *All I Ever Needed to Know I Learned in Kindergarten*, master storyteller Robert Fulghum enthralls readers with his experiences from the Sunday school sand-pile. Fulghum claims that the basic skills for living were right there in kindergarten.

These are the things I learned:
Share everything.
Play fair.
Don't hit people.

149

Put things back where you found them.

Clean up your own mess.

Don't take things that aren't yours.

Say you're sorry when you hurt somebody.

Wash your hands before you eat.

Flush.

Warm cookies and cold milk are good for you.

Live a balanced life—learn some and think some and draw and paint and sing and dance and play and work every day some.

Take a nap every afternoon.

When you go into the world, watch out for traffic, hold hands, and stick together.

Be aware of wonder.

And then remember the Dick and Jane books and the first word you learned—the biggest word of all—LOOK.[1]

A best-selling book about kindergarten? Of course—all of us love to remember familiar experiences and stories in new and different ways. Robert Fulghum attended a kindergarten very much like the one you and I attended. Now an adult, he recounts *our* stories simply by telling his own stories in a fresh way. He invites us to remember and rediscover feelings. He plays with our images of childhood. He calls us once again to look and listen, right out of the Dick and Jane books. He helps us think anew about our learning experience, and—without ever mentioning it—encourages us to compare what we learned with what we now do.

Teachers typically use creative exercises only to spice up a boring Bible study. Their efforts are rewarded because people learn better when they are challenged to use their own creativity and when they are surprised and delighted by the creativity of others. The real purpose for giving students creative license is to enhance their insights. A process that can unearth new learning from too-familiar teachings, stories, and concepts is crucial to the study of the Bible.

"The essence of creativity," says Youth Specialties co-founder Wayne Rice, "is learning how to copy." We learn by emulating our models, by copying their actions. We can go beyond that, however, by helping others to use their God-given imaginations. After all, God is the essence of creativity, and we are created in his image. In fact, the words *imagination* and *image* are from a common root word, as are the words *creator* and *creativity*.

One of many psychologists who have made careers in researching creativity, Guy Lefrancois offers us two choices as we teach: either we are promoting ordinariness, he says, or we are promoting creativity—and we are not always as creative as we think we are, Lefrancois reminds us.

> Creativity is that special quality in students that OTHER teachers in OTHER classrooms stifle. Other teachers are rigid, rule-bound, and authoritarian. . . . They crush the joyful inquisitiveness of young children by not hearing or answering their questions. They are dry, sober, humorless keepers of the culture and their ancestors. . . . But those are OTHER teachers in OTHER classrooms.[2]

Creativity Crushers

Want to promote ordinariness? Here is what stifles creativity in both students *and* teachers.

• **Creativity Crusher 1: The Know It All.** "I'm a teacher. I prepare carefully and know more about the subject than any of my students. There are correct answers, and then there are my students' answers. And of course I grant my students freedom of choice in my classrooms; they can be wrong if they want to—it's their choice."

If you tend to prepare to the point where you always seem to know more than others and have trouble disguising your authoritarian attitude, make that teaching weakness into a strength. Use your gift for study and precision by researching a biblical character. Then appear before your group in costume as that person, as "Guest Speaker from the Early Days" illustrates.

Guest Speaker from the Early Days

This role play is effective for helping youths explore the personalities and feelings of biblical characters who too often seem unrealistic to teenagers. Combined with a Bible study, it can add a great deal of depth to the learning experience.

Someone in the group (perhaps the youth director) first researches that character to be studied and then assumes the identity of that character in a speech to the entire group. For example, he could "become" Peter and try to relate to the group his reactions and feelings during several episodes in his life: when Andrew first introduced him to Jesus; when Jesus stepped into his boat and addressed the crowd; when Peter walked on the water; when he confessed Christ as Lord and then immediately rebuked him for speaking of his death; when he refused (at first) to have his feet washed by Jesus; when the events of Maundy Thursday unfolded; when he denied Christ; when Christ spoke to Peter on the beach after his resurrection, etc.

Following the speech, the group can question "Peter" about the things he said, and "Peter" can respond as he feels the real Peter would have. The group can then be divided into smaller groups for discussion.

• **Creativity Crusher 2: Over-Prepare Your Lesson.** "Just fill in the blanks on your handout." Rigid lesson plans and a teacher's personality that pressure a student to conform to predetermined answers stifle inventive thinking. It isn't necessarily the handouts and blanks, which can be quite helpful. Just leave room for surprise answers. I love it when a youth comes up with an "Aha!" in a group, to which the appropriate response is "Hey, John, I never thought of it that way!" If the student is way off base, share your view (not to *counter* John's answer, but to *supplement* it) and encourage the other youths to share their opinions as well. One example of a fill-in-the-blank format that gets kids into the Scripture with plenty of surprises is "Corinthian Mad Libs."

Corinthian Mad Libs

The next time you discuss the "Love Chapter" of the Bible (1 Corinthians 13), make it come alive by turning it into a "mad lib." Have your group fill in the blanks for the sixteen items below. Then read the chapter aloud as given here (based on Today's English Version), filling in the blanks with their answers. The exercise can help them gain a fresh understanding of Paul's words on love. Take care, however, that the Scripture doesn't become burdened by overly silly responses.

I may be able to speak the language of _____1_____ and even of _____2 _____, but if I have no love, my speech is no more than a noisy _____3_____ or a clanging _____4_____. I may have the gift of _____5_____; I may have all _____6_____ and understand _____7_____; I may have all the faith to move _____8_____ — but if I have no love, I am nothing. I may even give away my _____9_____; but if I have no love, this does me no good.

Love is patient and kind; it is not jealous or conceited or proud; love is not ill-mannered or selfish or irritable; love does not keep a record of wrongs; love is not happy with evil, but is happy with the truth. Love never gives up; and its faith, hope, and patience never fail.

Love is eternal. There are _____10_____, but they are temporary; there are _____11_____, but they will cease; there is _____12_____but it will pass away. These things are only partial; but love is perfect and will go on long after these things are gone.

When I was a child, my _____13_____, _____14_____ and _____15_____, were all those of a child; now that I'm grown up I have no more use of these childish ways. What we see now is like a dim image in a _____16_____; then we shall see face-to-face. What I know is only partial; then it will be complete — as complete as God's knowledge of me.

Meanwhile, these three remain: faith, hope, and love; and the greatest of these is love!

1. Name an animal. _____
2. Name another animal. _____
3. Name a loud musical instrument. _____
4. Name a percussion instrument. _____
5. Name a talent you would like to have that you don't. _____

153

6. Name something that some have lots of. _____
7. Name your hardest subject in school. _____
8. Name something very, very big. _____
9. Name your most cherished possession. _____
10. Name something that lasts a long time. _____
11. Name something else that lasts a long time. _____
12. Name something else that lasts a long time. _____
13. Name something a small child would do. _____
14. Name something else a small child would do. _____
15. Name something else a small child would do. _____
16. Name something shiny. _____

• **Creativity Crusher 3: Encourage by Correcting.** "John, your idea shows insight. But that isn't the way our church tradition interprets this passage. Let me tell you our view . . . " Overemphasis on evaluating students with the classic compliment followed by a *but* is considered nothing less than a put-down, an adult correction of supposedly immature opinions of teenagers.

If you must correct, soften the impact by replacing *but* with *and*, thereby inviting dialogue: "John, your idea shows insight and I bet it would make a good study to lay your interpretation alongside our church traditions. They appear to be different." This response opens the door for discussion and invites the question, "How are they different?"

• **Creativity Crusher 4: Teacher Knows Best.** "Before you decide what that Scripture passage means, it would be best if you checked with me first." Trust students to make their own choices. Even if they goof, what better place than the supportive, nurturing environment of the church in which to make a mistake? Trial and error provides the best learning opportunities. And, as one T-shirt proclaims, "Misteaks R wunderfull opperuniteez 2 lern."[3]

• **Creativity Crusher 5: Great Expectations.** "I appreciate your commitment to being here three hours on Tuesday and Thursdays and for agreeing to read chapters three through nineteen before next Tuesday." Whether in matters of attendance, comprehension, or behavior, unrealistic expectations are a wet blanket on the fires of enthusiasm and originality. Kids will choose what is important to them and make it a priority. By setting realistic expectations and goals, we help students define their participation and encourage commitment. One way to study the Bible and help the group determine expectations for themselves is through a study of Martha and Mary using "Mary and Martha Malpractice." What was expected of them and what is expected of us?

Mary and Martha Malpractice

Here's a good role play that will help your kids better understand two female characters form the New Testament—Mary and Martha.

Introduce the role play this way.

Ever wonder what happened to Mary and Martha after Jesus visited them?

Well, Mary—the one who poured the precious perfume on Jesus' feet—started a convent, where women can pray and worship all the time. Martha—the one who served—opened an inner-city soup kitchen. Mary never does anything to help the poor because she spends all her time praying. Martha hardly ever prays because she's too busy feeding the poor.

Because Martha has become irritated with Mary's lack of concern for the poor, she's suing Mary for malpractice of Christianity.

Now select someone to be Mary and someone to be Martha, each of whom select attorneys (two or three kids) who will represent them. The rest of the group is the jury. After the two sides have had a little time to prepare, conduct a trial, each side presenting its arguments. The jury can ask questions and decide who presents the most convincing argument.

• **Creativity Crusher 6: Get Serious.** "No Humor Allowed" might as well be posted on the wall of many youth rooms. The inability to foster humor and play as we study the Scriptures hampers the ingenuity and insight of students. This becomes increasingly true as we choose methods of Bible study that are person-centered and truly creative.

Most kids possess a healthy sense of humor—so let them shine. The Bible study "Melody in F," for instance, is downright silly, but it requires kids to think about the meaning of the text by asking them to paraphrase the Scriptures. Use "Melody in F" as an example, then have the kids pick a passage of their own and make it new.

Melody in F

The following is a creative paraphrase of the story of the Prodigal Son, which you might want to use next time you discuss the subject.

MELODY IN F

Feeling footloose and frisky, a feather-brained fellow
Forced his fond father to fork over the farthings,
And flew far to foreign fields
And frittered his fortune feasting fabulously with faithless friends.

Fleeced by his fellows in folly, and facing famine,
He found himself a feed flinger in a filthy farmyard.
Fairly famishing, he fain would've filled his frame
With foraged food from fodder fragments.
"Fooey, my father's flunkies fare far finer,"
The frazzled fugitive forlornly fumbled, frankly facing facts.
Frustrated by failure, and filled with foreboding,
He fled forthwith to his family.
Falling at his father's feet, he forlornly fumbled,
"Father, I've flunked,
And fruitlessly forfeited family favor."

The far-sighted father, forestalling further flinching,
Frantically flagged the flunkies to
Fetch a fatling from the flock and fix a feast.

The fugitive's fault-finding brother frowned on
Fickle forgiveness of former folderol.
But the faithful father figured,
"Filial fidelity is fine, but the fugitive is found!

What forbids fervent festivity?
Let flags be unfurled! Let fanfares flare!"

Father's forgiveness formed the foundation
For the former fugitive's future fortitude.

Creativity Emancipators

What teaching traits promote creativity? How will these traits affect my group studies? What will the payoff be for the students? The more you ponder questions like these and then act on some reasonable answers, the more you will see increased participation and creativity in your Bible studies—which spells increased learning.

• **Creativity Emancipator 1: Have It Your Way.** Burger King's old jingle may not exactly be healthy ethics, but it sure points the way to nurturing a creative bunch of students who show and tell their new ideas at the drop of a hat. New ideas require opportunities to make choices. Kids have the right to have their own ideas, to determine their strengths and weaknesses, to test theories and critique them, and to embrace them despite their differences. Learning environments that grant permission and provide resources and room for students to flex their own ideas will be creative places.

We keep a costume box in our senior-high room. During the study of parables, for instance, the kids often turn them into skits or one-act plays. They write the script, choose the costumes, and then perform. These are usually full of surprises and are certainly creative instruments for teaching and learning. Nor do you have to write your own skits. "The Body Life Skit" is one of hundreds already written for your group's performance.

157

The Body Life Skit

Here's a good skit for six characters based on 1 Corinthians 12. All actors who portray parts of the body should wear a sign or T-shirt that identifies the part they play. The reader should have a Bible.

Characters:
  Reader
  Nose (shy, sneezes a lot)
  Foot (wearing big shoes)
  Ear (wearing earphones)
  Eye (wearing big glasses)
  Head (acting conceited)

The skit begins with the body parts in a huddle.

Reader: I'll be reading selections from 1 Corinthians, chapter 12. "The body is a unit, though it is made up of many parts *(the body parts spread apart and begin showing off their individual talents as the Reader continues)*, and though all its parts are many, they form one body. So it is with Christ. For we were all baptized by one Spirit into one body—whether Jews or Greeks, slave or free—and we were all given the one Spirit to drink. Now the body is not made up of one part but of many. If the foot should say—"

Foot: Because I am not a hand, I do not belong to the body!

Reader: " . . . it would not for that reason cease to be part of the body."

Foot: Oh, yes, it would. I mean, I can go places, give the elderly rides to church, and drive for Meals on Wheels. But I can't give a lot of money like a hand could, or cook the best dish at the covered dish supper like a hand could. Maybe I'm just not needed around here!

Reader: "And if the ear should say . . . "

Ear: Because I am not an eye, I do not belong to the body.

Reader: " . . . it would not for that reason cease to be part of the body."

Ear: Oh, yeah? I mean, I can hear and understand a good sermon pretty well, but I can't seem to see places where anyone needs help like an eye could. What good is it to be able to hear and understand if you can't see to do anything? Maybe I'm just not needed around here!

Reader: "If the whole body were an eye, where would the sense of hearing be? If the whole body were an ear, where would the sense of smell be? The eye cannot say to the hand . . . "

158

Eye: I don't need you, hand! I mean, I'm the most important part around here after all. That's pretty obvious. Anyone can see that without me, this body's just stumbling around in the dark. What good are you, hand?

Reader: "Nor can the head say to the feet . . . "

Head: Well, I don't need either of you. I can think and reason and make all the important decisions without any help at all from you guys. I'm the brains of this outfit.

Reader: *(At this point, all the parts of the body begin arguing with each other so that the Reader must plead with them to stop. The nose moves off to the side and begins to cry.)* "On the contrary, those parts of the body that seem to be weaker are indispensable, and the parts that we think are less honorable we treat with special honor. God has combined the members of the body so that there should be no division in the body . . . " *(The arguing gets progressively worse.)* " . . . but that its parts should have equal concern for each other . . . " Oh, I give up! *(Reader walks away exasperated.)*

Ear: Hey wait a minute. Listen! I hear someone crying. *(Everyone finally gets quiet.)*

Eye: Look, it's _____ *(use the name of the person playing the nose)*. Poor guy, I wonder what's wrong.

Head: I've got a idea! We could go over there and find out.

Ear: Hey, I like the sound of that idea!

Head: *(Acting proud)* Of course it's a good idea.

Eye: But how could we get there?

Foot: I could take you, I suppose . . . *(General agreement. Everyone lines up behind the Foot, forms a train, and goes over to the Nose.)*

Ear: *(To nose)* We heard you crying and we're kind of worried about you. Can we help somehow?

Nose: I don't know. I get so lonely sometimes. I wish I had some friends. But who wants to be friends with someone whose greatest talent is sniffing out trouble!

Eye: Well, I don't know about the rest of this crew, but it seems to me that we've got some trouble that needs sniffing out. *(Everyone looks at the Head. Head looks sheepish).*

Head: Well . . . maybe you're right . . .

Foot: You just come with us. We're not perfect yet, but when we all work together, we can do a lot of good after all. *(Body parts form a line with arms around each other's shoulders.)*

Reader: *(Stepping in front to read.)* "If one part suffers, every part suffers with it; if one part is honored, every part rejoices with it. Now you are the body of Christ . . . "

All: And each one of you is a part of it!

• **Creativity Emancipator 2: We Care.** Research repeatedly indicates that people-oriented teachers are more likely than highly organized and businesslike teachers to promote creative behavior in students.[4] In verbal and nonverbal ways, teachers' attitudes communicate acceptance, trust, and respect, permitting freedom and flexibility and feeding students' creativity. One way to help students feel included and important is with "Jigsaw Puzzle."

Jigsaw Puzzle

This crowd breaker can also be an object lesson for a discussion of Christ. Have your kids first assemble a large jigsaw puzzle. The results will include (1) the communication of your students, since they have to work together on a common project; (2) the cultivation of teamwork, with certain people looking for edge pieces, others looking for certain colors, etc.; and (3) a picture of the body of Christ in action. Not only does everyone participate, but the importance of a single puzzle piece is seen, thus demonstrating that all of us are important to the functioning of the body.

• **Creativity Emancipator 3: Aha!** By creating an atmosphere that values a new idea, a fresh concept, or an inventive approach to the Bible, we empower students to explore their faith. As we affirm conclusions and thought processes, we increase their confidence and incentive to discover and grow. They learn more because they become self-initiated learners, prepared and eager to respond to new challenges and solve new problems. Students who are allowed to solve problems in their own way, with an adult as counselor, learn much about themselves and their faith.

I like the Bible study "Commercial Religion" because it begins with something kids see every day—advertisements—and asks them to evaluate their truth. Then it asks kids to compare commercial "truths" to God's truth. It challenges their inventiveness and puts their faith into a medium they understand.

Commercial Religion

Because commercials influence every aspect of our daily lives, they are an effective media technique. Some reasons for their effectiveness, however, are that they tend to—
• Entertain rather than inform.
• Consolidate reality, simplify reality into very black and white categories.
• Exaggerate, manipulate.
• Use symbols.

It is important that a youth group not blindly accept commercials as accurate communication or to feel that by changing a word here or there, the entire meaning will change. For example, the phrase "Coke adds life" changed to "Christ adds life" is catchy—but is it true? In what ways is it true?

But because most people hear commercials all the time, it can be a lot of fun to allow your youth group to make some commercials for God, Christ, or the church by adapting popular commercials or by creating entirely new ones. Divide your group into small groups and give them a few minutes to create their own commercial around whatever theme you give them. Give the kids enough time to practice and gather together whatever props they need.

Then have the groups present their ideas to each other one at a time. You might tell the group something like this: "You have been given sixty seconds (or thirty seconds) on national prime-time television to create and produce a commercial for God, Jesus, or the church. Millions of people will see it. What kind of spot would you create?"

• **Creativity Emancipator 4: Sierra Club.** In Chapter Four we discussed creating the proper environment for learning, for an environment that welcomes students frees them to express themselves. One method for including kids and sparking creativity is through photography. Using the Bible study "Body Life" creates such an environment for expression through the fun of authoring a script and creating slides to go with it. By the way, including everyone in the photos is a perfect way to say "Welcome!"

Body Life

Many youth groups have discovered that producing a slide show can be a unique and captivating way to get into the gospel. Besides being fun to create, the finished product is always a hit at a worship service or youth banquet. To get the most out of a slide show, have the kids create the whole show as a response to a theme you've studied. Have them write the script, design the slides, and do the photography. You'll need a 35mm camera, a photographer who knows how to use it, a slide projector, and enough time to get the slides developed before the presentation.

The following drawings are an example of how you might prepare a script for a slide show. This particular show was created to communicate the unity of the church as seen in 1 Corinthians 12.

(Title)   (Title)   Our Bodies have many parts.   But many parts make up only one body when they are all put together.

So it is with the Body of Christ.   Each of us is a part of the one Body of Christ.   Some of us are Jews.   Some are Gentiles.

Some are slaves.   Some are free.   But the Holy Spirit has fitted us all together into one body.   Yes, the body has many parts.

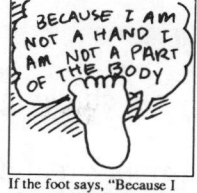

Not just one part.

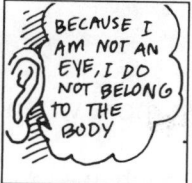

If the foot says, "Because I am not a hand, I am not a part of the body" that doesn't make it any less a part of the body.

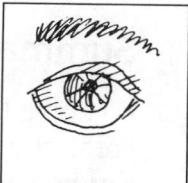

And what would you think if you heard an ear say, "Because I am not an eye, I do not belong to the body"?

Suppose the whole body were an eye?

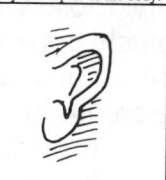

How would you hear?

Or if your whole body were just one big ear . . .

How could you smell anything?

But that isn't the way God made us.

He has made many parts for our bodies.

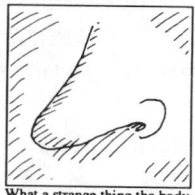

And has put each part just where he wants it.

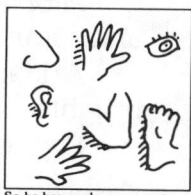

What a strange thing the body would be if it only had one part.

So he has made many parts.

But there is only one body.

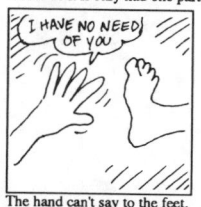

The eye can never say to the hand, "I have no need of you."

The hand can't say to the feet, "I have no need of you."

The head can't say to the hand, "I have no need of you."

God has put us together in such a way that if one suffers,

All parts suffer with it.

And if one part rejoices,

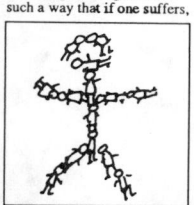

All the parts rejoice.

Now what I'm saying is this: All of you together are the one Body of Christ.

And each of you is a separate and necessary part of it.

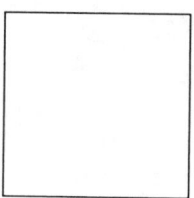

(The End)

163

Summary

- People learn more when they are challenged to use their creativity.
- When we teach we are promoting either creativity or ordinariness.
- These teachers stifle creativity: those who always know more, know best, expect too much, correct their students, and imply that mistakes are abnormal and unacceptable.
- These ingredients encourage creativity in kids:
  —The opportunity to choose topics, locations, and methods.
  —People-oriented teachers who accept their students and communicate that acceptance.
  —A learning atmosphere that values new ideas and insights.
  —Physical environments that are not fixed in location.

12

The Rotation Principle:

Kids learn better in varied settings.

Steven Mabry

I've been surprised by the number of pastors and laypeople I've met who tend to slight wilderness travel, dismissing it as "communing with nature," skeptical that any authentic religious sensibilities could be honored in the open air. . . . More common are laity and clergy who regard wilderness with indifference, as a region useful only for the venting of excess energy by church youth groups. They seem to overlook the scriptural importance of wilderness—as a place of testing for the Hebrews, of solitude for the prophets, and of prayer for Jesus. . . . Wilderness remains not merely a symbol but an actual setting—a spiritual reservoir able to evoke prayer as spontaneously as a house of worship built by human hands.
—David Douglas

When he was four, my nephew went to heaven in an airplane. Or thought he did, or thought he was close. When he awoke at five a.m. on the red-eye from San Francisco to Boston, he turned to his groggy father and blurted out loudly, "Okay, where is God?"

"Shhh," mumbled his quick-thinking dad. "God is still asleep."

Field trips or on-location studies have long been known to stimulate imaginations and wake opportunities for insight that might otherwise remain asleep. Preschool children at 30,000 feet have different questions than they do at home in their kitchens. Wilderness travelers encounter different stimuli than New York City pedestrians. The instinctive curiosity about our surroundings affords teachable moments in youths and adults as well as in young children.

On-location learning rests on two principles: Boredom is deadly to learning. This one is obvious. You know when it is happening. You might as well stop teaching when your students are bored.

About the second principle, however, we need to be reminded: Changing the physical surroundings enhances learning potential. I read a study of factory productivity in which researchers discovered that if they lowered the lights or added music, productivity went up. The strange part is that after some time of dimmed light and soft music, productivity dipped again. So researchers raised the lights and turned off the music. Voilà—productivity went back up. Change itself increases attention and productivity.

Similarly, a change in the location of a Bible study stimulates and reinforces learning. For ten years now Bill and I have taken high-school youth to Mexico for work-study camps. Two things happen with every participant on those trip: First, their motivation to learn something—anything—improves. Some discover Mexico and poverty. Some learn about themselves and others. Many make a first commitment to Christ, and others deepen their faith in God.

Second, these students are rewarded almost instantly through the affirmation of Mexican families and through the support of their peers and their hometown community of faith. Reinforced for what they are doing, they come to understand that learning and growing is fun, that helping others through Christian service makes life meaningful, and that God has given them the ability to make a difference for others. Camp programs impact the lives of participants because they sweep people away from their everyday situations and allow them to be actively involved in the learning process. The new locations stimulate feelings and senses that complement cognitive learning. By thus opening the environment, the minds and hearts of the students are opened as well.

The question, then, is not "Is change beneficial to the health of a Bible study?" but rather "How much change, what kind of switch in setting, and when and where should we alter the environment?"

We don't have to go far from home to stimulate learning through the setting. One example that can easily be done in your town is the Bible study "Jailhouse"—a unique way to get out of your classroom and create excitement.[1] Getting jailed is an experience that kids will remember for years.

Jailhouse

The best presentation of this idea can be found in Rick Bundschuh's collection of out-of-the-classroom meetings, *On Site: 40 On-Location Youth Programs*. Played to the hilt, it puts kids in touch with the feeling of being in prison and is a prime opportunity for publicity and fun. First, create an arrest warrant for your students. (Mail them in advance if you like.) Then persuade an off-duty officer to assist in their "arrests." Transport the whole gang to court and have the judge sentence them to jail. Lock the kids up and go home. Great study, huh? (Just kidding.)

What you do after your kids get locked up is frame yourself as an accomplice and get locked up, too. While you are all in jail, read the first chapter of Philippians together. (Plan ahead so you'll just happen to have a copy of the passage for each kid.) A location like this generates excitement for learning and raises issues that kids seldom conceive of otherwise. Jail gives the kids the boost they need to enhance their memory and understanding of a Bible passage, too. And this on-site program gives you the chance to demonstrate your organizational powers, since you'll need to contact your local police or county sheriff and the court system, not to mention wading through red tape. But it's worth it!

Changing locations can be as simple as swapping rooms at church. I like to take confirmation classes to the sanctuary, where we talk about Communion, the proclamation of the Word, and baptism. The study is more meaningful as kids surround the Communion table, speak from the pulpit, and explore the baptistry.

Or if your church has a basement or underground corridors, use the study "Catacomb Christians" to experience vicariously something of what the early church felt.

Catacomb Christians

Here's an idea that works well during the night at a lock-in or retreat. Blindfold your kids and take them to a mystery location — preferably a dark, musty basement or cave. The only light should be from candles. Once inside, the blindfolds can be removed. Ask the kids to remain quiet. Your adult leaders should dress in early-Christian garb or in grubby clothes to indicate a life of hardship and suffering.

If you cannot locate a place that looks like a cave or catacombs, then find a place that feels like one and keep the blindfolds on the kids throughout the entire experience.

After you've arrived, read or recite from memory the following narration. Adapt it to your situation as you see fit.

The first-century Christians of Rome used to meet in catacombs — underground tunnels where they buried people. Now it may seem a strange place to meet, but there was a good reason for it. At that time it was illegal for people *not* to worship Caesar. And Christians felt they could worship *only* Jesus. If they had been willing to worship Caesar as well, they would have been officially tolerated — but those Christians just couldn't.

So the arrests and persecution began — and the punishment for not worshipping Caesar was death. The Romans had several methods for executing these Christians, these followers of a new Jewish cult called "The Way." At first they pitted them against gladiators, but these fool Christians refused to fight back. So in order to give the crowds more entertainment (Roman spectators paid to watch these spectacles), they released wild, half-starved beasts on them. Often Christians would be tied into the skins of freshly slaughtered cattle or deer in order to attract the fierce attacks of wild dogs — who'd rip them apart. For more entertainment, they'd saturate Christians with oil, coat them with flammable flax, and ignite them as human torches to illuminate nighttime entertainments in the arena. You could hear their screams, but they were soon drowned out by the crowd's screams of delight.

It became common to see roads lined with crucified bodies — some struggling to live, some struggling to die. And the crime posted on their crosses read something like "Seditionist — Christian."

That's why we started hiding in these catacombs — so we could continue worshipping our Jesus, the only true God. We began making secret signs whereby we could identify one another. For example, one of us would draw a straight line in the dirt; when another Christian noticed it, he'd cross it with another straight line, forming a cross. Or one would draw a short curved line, and another — with a similar stroke — would form a simple fish. That really confused the Romans because they didn't know what it meant — at first. You see, the letters in the Greek word *fish* (*ichthus*) were the first letters of the words in the Greek phrase for "Jesus Christ, God's Son, Savior."

But being driven to secrecy made it easier for people to misunderstand us. They said we consumed human flesh and blood — barbarians with a ritual of human sacrifice. But they didn't understand that we were only celebrating our Lord's supper, His last one, with bread and wine and a common meal. The bread represented His body — broken on the cross — and wine represented His blood — shed on the cross, both of which He gave for our sins. They also represented our willingness to die for Jesus.

But rumors spread. Soon they were accusing us of all sorts of crimes. I guess it made it easier for them to do what they did to us in the arena and on the roads. When Rome burned, that madman Nero used us Christians as scapegoats — when he may well have encouraged the arson himself. So much bloodshed for so many evil lies. Since just witnessing would often cost us our lives, we began to be called *martyrs* — Christians who knew that witnessing would mean death.

[Remove blindfolds now; have only candles for light]

As the Apostle Paul said in Romans 10:9, "If you confess with your mouth, 'Jesus is Lord,' and believe in your heart that God raised him from the dead, you will be saved."

To confess Jesus as Lord meant that Caesar wasn't Lord — which was to sign your death warrant. Yet these early followers of the Christ did confess so, because they believed that Jesus would raise them from the dead, just as He is risen. He promises this to all His followers.

And when they would gather together, they'd share and sing of Jesus Christ. And as the Apostle instructed in Colossians 3:16, "Let the word of Christ dwell in you richly as you teach and admonish one another with all wisdom, and as you sing psalms, hymns and spiritual songs with gratitude in your hearts to God."

Let's do some of that now—share Scripture and songs with one another.

After a time of sharing and singing, blindfold the kids again and take them back to church or your original location. Again ask them to be quiet as they leave. After they return, you can discuss the experience with them—how they felt, what they learned, etc.

Part of this environment-altering is just different clothes required by the different settings. Though cool, casual T-shirts and jeans put out the welcome mat for teenagers, dressing out of the ordinary can bring students closer to the passage. And remember when changing locations to be aware of possible dress codes at the destination. Temperature and courtesy to your hosts may affect what you tell the kids to wear or bring. Dressing for jail, you can imagine, presents some restrictions.

So jump into rotating Bible study locations, which require four considerations. The first two are the most laborious, which explains why on-site learning does not happen as often as they should.

Advance Logistics Planning

One reason teachers do not use on-location learning to its full advantage is because of the advance planning it requires. The reality is that staying at home or at the church is easier. But let these steps organize your planning—and start traveling!

• **Carefully decide what to study.** After you have arrived at a topic for your study, brainstorm different locations that could help students grasp the key point of the study. Select the site that gives the most learning for the least hassle. Consider several places—if your Bible study is about the Resurrection, there's the morgue, hospital, mortuary, graveyard. Consider also the time of day for your study. Morgues feel different at two in the afternoon than they do at eleven on a Friday night. (I've always been tempted to hide one of my sponsors in a morgue drawer in order to sit up in the middle of the lesson.)

A less frightening use of the nighttime is "Midnight Picnic."

Midnight Picnic

Here's a Bible study idea that the kids will love. First, have the group look up information about star formations and planets visible from the earth. Then on an evening when there is no or little moon, have a picnic at midnight. Each person should pack a lunch, a lantern, and a blanket. After eating, look at the stars and try to identify the formations. You can even try to count the stars. Tie the evening together with some thoughts on how God created the stars (Genesis 1) and how God's handiwork is expressed through the heavens (Psalms 8 and 19). This could be done anytime after dark, but there's more drama to it for kids if it is done at midnight.

- **Make arrangements in advance.** Since site availability may determine the topic or the time of day for the study, make the arrangements well in advance. Call several of your favorite options to get a feel for who really wants you to come and who thinks you are just another fruitcake. Go where you are welcome.
- **Exchange plans in writing.** Your hosts are less likely to forget details about your visit if they have your plans in writing. So be specific about times, size of your group, duration of the study, etc. Then tour the facility by yourself; become acquainted with your contact person and knowledgeable about the facility. Get the answer to the most frequently asked question ("Where's the bathroom?"). This

firsthand check of the site is a must that smooths out the whole enterprise.

• **Take an appropriate number of people.** Determine how many students can go on this field trip—then arrange transportation. Line up the vehicles and gas them up in advance. Save your drivers the embarrassment of fumbling with gas pumps while the group waits and the study stumbles.

• **Confirm your plan.** A few days before the trip, check with your host as a reminder and make final adjustments.

• **Get signed parental permissions.** The realities of liability mandate this step. My rule of thumb is simple: If students fail to deliver signed permission forms, they stay behind.

Program Planning

• **Be creative.** Now that you have lined up the site and visited it by yourself, unleash your imagination—how can you use this place to reinforce the central theme in your lesson? What feelings might this location spark in the students? Is there any material that you need to bring along—copies of the text, handouts, costumes? What safety considerations need attention?

"Up on the Roof" uses a rooftop and selected Scriptures to reinforce significant growing experiences in your kids' lives.

Up on the Roof

For an effective Bible study, take your group up onto a roof—the roof of the church or of any other building—and present a lesson like this one:

Did you know that in the Bible some significant things happened on roofs? Because roofs were flat back in Bible times, people ate, slept, relaxed—did all sorts of things—on top of their homes. Let's look at some Scriptures about events that took place on rooftops.

First, let's turn to 2 Samuel 11:2 — here David began to lust after Bathsheba from a rooftop. Later on, when David's son Absalom led a rebellion against his father (2 Sam. 16:22), he committed adultery with David's wives on the palace roof. In Jeremiah 32:29 we read that the rooftop was a place of idolatry.

The rooftop was not always a place of sin, however. Rahab hid the Israeli spies on her roof (Josh. 2:6). In Luke 5:18-25 are some men who lowered a diseased friend down through a hole in the roof for healing by Jesus. In 1 Samuel 9:25 Samuel conferred with Saul on a rooftop before he was anointed king of Israel, and in Acts 10:9-17 Peter was on a rooftop when he received a vision that taught him that Gentiles were to be included in God's plan of salvation.

The amazing thing is that God can speak to us anywhere, anytime — even on a rooftop. God is not locked up in the church. He wants to be a part of our lives everywhere, all the time.

Close by asking the kids to name unusual occasions and places where they have had a significant growing experience or encounter with God.

- **Promote with flair.** Got a good program that you are excited about? Sell it with vigor and flash! Occasional on-site learning is a supreme opportunity to promote Bible study as exciting and relevant. Some locations themselves have publicity you can use. Create a WANTED poster the night you do the jail, for instance. Just don't let the opportunity to be inventive pass you by. Plain white paper is great for Sunday morning bulletins, but it seldom captures the imagination of kids.

At the Site

While on site make certain your group knows the behavior expected of them. Are there specific rules of the location? Make sure your kids know them; they need the protocol in order to show the utmost courtesy to the hosting organization. An orientation on site usually makes students more comfortable and better able to learn. Be clear with your host how long you are staying, and honor that plan. Always err on the side of courtesy.

Back at Home

Have the group write a letter of thanks to the host within a week of your visit. This will give your kids an opportunity to express how the experience affected them as they close the event with appreciation for those who made it possible. Good learning as well as good manners ensures future opportunities for the younger kids at your church.

Summary

- On-location learning is based on two principles:
  —Kids learn more when the settings for learning are varied.
  —Boredom is deadly to learning.
- Some tips that will help make a field trip a success:
  —Decide the topic in advance, and choose the most suitable location with care.
  —Allow time for advance planning.
  —Exchange plans and permission with the host facility in writing. Confirm those plans within a few days of the study.
  —Take the number of people appropriate for the location.
  —Get signed permission forms from all your kids.
  —Use your imagination as you plan, and be well prepared.
  —Pull out all the stops for the promotion. Go for it!
  —Give the group a brief orientation of rules, dress, etc.
  —Always send a thank-you after you get home.

13

The Samuel Principle:

Kids learn better under the guidance of a Christian mentor.

Steven Mabry

Faith begins in relationship. Faith implies trust in another, reliance upon another, a counting upon or dependence upon another.

—*James Fowler*

Many years ago when I was a Los Angeles CPA and enrolled in law school, I met Pastor Richard Wing in a little San Fernando Valley church. Dick had something in his life that I couldn't figure out: The man was happy. Thankfully, his zest for life was contagious. At age twenty-three I was among the living freeway-commuter-dead, so I was determined to figure out what Dick had in his life that I didn't. He knew I was searching and began to spend time with me. Starting with tennis, our conversations in a few weeks arrived at loneliness and the lack of joy in my life. We never met in his office. We played tennis, went for coffee, and talked on the way. He never once pressured me to commit to anything or be anything I wasn't. He just kept coming back for conversation and the next round of tennis, which he consistently lost.

Over the months our discussions became the highlight of my week. He asked clarifying questions, and I tried vainly to pry answers from him. During the last six months of our conversations we talked about ministry and service. I raised the issue, he didn't. Though God's claim on my life had long been evident to me, I had never—I mean *never*—actually considered surrendering.

Yet something magical happened when Dick took an interest in me. I felt valued, appreciated, capable. Why Dick paid me this kindness I will never know. I do know that he helped me through a major transition in my life: I traded the keys to my home, company car, and the locker at the racket club for keys to a seminary apartment. Dick is more than a friend—he is my Christian mentor.

The term *mentor* has in the last few years been bandied about and applied to many contexts where it simply doesn't belong. It's become popular in the corporate world, for instance, to assign executives to "mentor" younger, up-and-coming staffers, to cultivate their potential. The significance of the mentor-protégé relationship is blurred, is watered down by reducing it to a mere tutorial internship. The Bible reveals that the Apostle Paul often modeled mentoring. "We loved you so much," he wrote in 1 Thessalonians 2:8, "that we were delighted to share with you not only the gospel of God but our lives as well." But our lives as well. In the Christian sense, mentoring is giving away our lives to assist the spiritual growth and development of others. The buzzword for this in youth work today is "relational ministry." Author Allen Hadidian calls it discipling.

> Discipling [or mentoring] others is the process by which a Christian with a life worth emulating commits himself for an extended period of time to a few individuals who have been won to Christ, the purpose being to aid and guide their growth to maturity and equip them to reproduce themselves in a third spiritual generation.[1]

Call it discipling or mentoring—the relationship can be one of enormous influence and blessing for a young person.

Call for fast service:
(619) 440-2333

BUSINESS REPLY MAIL
FIRST CLASS   PERMIT NO. 16   EL CAJON, CA

POSTAGE WILL BE PAID BY ADDRESSEE

YOUTH SPECIALTIES
1224 Greenfield Dr.
El Cajon, CA 92021-9989

Call for fast service:
(619) 440-2333

BUSINESS REPLY MAIL
FIRST CLASS   PERMIT NO. 16   EL CAJON, CA

POSTAGE WILL BE PAID BY ADDRESSEE

YOUTH SPECIALTIES
1224 Greenfield Dr.
El Cajon, CA 92021-9989

The People Who Brought You This Book...

─────── *Invite you to discover MORE valuable youth ministry resources.* ───────

Youth Specialties offers an assortment of books, publications, tapes and events, all designed to encourage and train youth workers and their kids. Just check what you're interested in below and return this card, and we'll send you FREE information on our products and services.

Please send me FREE information I've checked below:

☐ The Complete Youth Specialties Catalog and information on upcoming Youth Specialties events.

Name _____

Address _____

City _____ State _____ Zip _____

Phone Number ( ) _____

The People Who Brought You This Book...

─────── *Invite you to discover MORE valuable youth ministry resources.* ───────

Youth Specialties offers an assortment of books, publications, tapes and events, all designed to encourage and train youth workers and their kids. Just check what you're interested in below and return this card, and we'll send you FREE information on our products and services.

Please send me FREE information I've checked below:

☐ The Complete Youth Specialties Catalog and information on upcoming Youth Specialties events.

Name _____

Address _____

City _____ State _____ Zip _____

Phone Number ( ) _____

Qualities of a Mentor

It has been said that Christianity is not so much taught as caught. The necessity for providing significant adult models for young people cannot be oversold. Make certain your kids have the chance to be around adult Christians who are making every effort to live out their faith—which does not mean that adults must be perfect Christians to be exemplary models and mentors. It is nice if they lead, as Hadidian suggests, a "life worth emulating," but that may not be the bottom line. God finds ways to use all of us imperfect ones. I know this because I know my mentor, and I am a mentor.

Although I spent my youth attending church regularly, trekking faithfully to camp every summer, serving zealously as a junior deacon, I never committed my life to Christ or to the church. I held myself apart, unwilling to lay aside personal goals. Then Dick stepped into my life.

Yet who was this man Dick? He was hardly perfect. (His imperfection made him easier to be around.) He came to my turf. He knew where I lived and played and was willing to go there with me. He showed empathy in our conversations, having had similar questions when he was younger. (It was nice to know that someone else with my problems had apparently turned out sound.) Dick never asked me to make a commitment; he simply lived his joyful life right in front of me. Fourth, his focus was never on himself even though he was a cool guy leading a fairly together life. He just let me rattle on about how my existence was in disarray. He listened. Finally, after we were on firm ground, he asked significant questions. "What are you going to do about your life?" He listened well and encouraged me to address those parts of my life that were unhappy and unfulfilling.

Because of those five actions of Dick—he came to my turf, empathized with my problems, never required a commitment, listened to me endlessly, and eventually asked significant questions—I was snagged hook, line, and sinker before I knew it. In those five steps you'll find the keys to mentoring students and doing Christian education that will make a difference in the lives of your kids.

Let's turn from one imperfect mentor to another. In the book of 1 Samuel is the account of Eli, the mentor of Samuel. Eli was clearly incompetent in some ways, yet a splendid mentor for Samuel. You remember that Elkanah had two wives, fertile Pininnah and barren Hannah. Hannah prayed to God that she might bear a son, promising in return to give the child to the Lord all the days of his life. God heard Hannah and answered her prayer—she conceived and bore a son, whom she named Samuel. True to her vow, Hannah returned him to the Lord—specifically, to the care of the priest Eli. Now Eli seemed a poor choice to mentor the budding prophet Samuel by at least two counts: He was a priest, not a prophet; and he was apparently dismal at mentoring his own sons, for "Eli's sons were wicked men; they had no regard for the Lord." Yet God nevertheless used Eli to mentor Samuel, who grew in stature and in favor with God and became a very great prophet indeed.

What Counts Is Perception, Not Perfection

Though imperfect, mentors are adults willing to test their Christian faith by living and sharing their experiences and attention with young people. They aid, guide, and love younger generations into Christian maturity. Mentors overlook what people deserve in order to give them what they need. They're willing to give positive regard to younger people whether they earn it or not. It is no psychological mystery that young people thrive if they believe they are held in high esteem. In researching parent-teen relationships, psychologist H. Stephen Glenn discovered that

one of the chief predictors of young people's success— regarding their performance, their motivation, their health, and their productivity—is their perception of their parents' image of them, not necessarily what parents believe about them but rather what they believe their parents believe about them.[2]

Perhaps a Bible study designed to ferret out that information would be helpful for your students? Consider "How to Raise Your Parents."

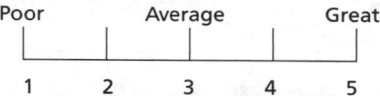

How to Raise Your Parents

Want a lively discussion about parents? For best results, print these up and pass them out to each of your kids. Give the kids time to answer all the questions individually, then discuss them one at a time with the entire group.

1. How would you rate your relationship with your parent(s)?

Poor		Average		Great
1	2	3	4	5

2. What are some of the good points of your relationship with your parent(s)?

3. What are some of the problems in your relationship with your parent(s)?

4. How do your parent(s) feel about you? That is, what do your parent(s) think of you?

5. What do the following teach us about our relationships and responsibilities to our parent(s)? What do they say about the responsibilities of parent(s) to their children?

	Almost never				Almost always
6. Rate yourself in the following areas:					
a. I obey my parents in all things.	1	2	3	4	5
b. I am patient with the weaknesses in my parent(s).	1	2	3	4	5
c. I apologize to my parents when I hurt them.	1	2	3	4	5
d. My parents are patient with my weaknesses.	1	2	3	4	5
e. I try to see life from my parent's point of view.	1	2	3	4	5
f. I ask my parents for their advice.	1	2	3	4	5
g. My parents and I talk about God and Christian faith.	1	2	3	4	5
h. I pray for my parents.	1	2	3	4	5
i. I show my parents I love them.	1	2	3	4	5
j. My parents build me up.	1	2	3	4	5
k. My parents are proud of me.	1	2	3	4	5

7. The areas in which my parents and I most need to improve are (list three) _____

_____

8. My plan for making question 7 happen is _____

_____

As we work with kids in the church, attempting to build their Christian faith and encourage spiritual development, we must help them develop the perception, based in truth, that adults in the church hold them in high esteem, respect them, and believe in them.

What Kids Need From Mentors

Here is a list of their most important needs.

• **Kids in the church need meaningful roles or tasks in which to exercise their developing faith.** "Without a meaningful role," writes Glenn, "it is difficult to develop a sense of meaning, purpose, and significance through being needed, listened to, and taken seriously."[3] Dedicated adults provide that role as we encourage and connect kids to service opportunities. Christian education is effective only when kids see the connection between their activities and their faith. The junior highers in my church raise money every year to build houses for the homeless in Mexico; the high schoolers spend the money on construction material, cross the border, and build the houses. We make certain the younger youth get recognized and affirmed for their very important role in this mission project. We help them interpret their work as normal, mature, Christian behavior.

• **Kids need permission to discover things on their own.** Not that all they need is to dialogue endlessly with their peers. Young minds must relate to adults who are on a higher level of insight if they are to mature and grow in awareness. What I mean is illustrated by the Bible study "Wisdom in Cassette Form."

Wisdom in Cassette Form

Have every kid in your Bible-study group participate in interviews with the wise — that is, with older people from your congregation. After making an appointment, have the kids go out in pairs to record their comments (make certain both the kids and the older folks know this is to be taped) on issues facing young people today. Topics might include friendship, love, marriage, death, grief, the meaning of life, or the virtues of Christian living. Be sensitive to recent life changes of your subjects. Then build a Bible study around each of the topics by combining them with a study of selected Scriptures.

Our task as leaders and mentors goes beyond teaching kids what we have discovered; we must instead enable kids to make discoveries of their own.

• **Kids need adult mentors to walk alongside them and demonstrate living the faith.** My first criteria for youth sponsors in my church program is a genuine interest in kids, a desire to be with them in all kinds of circumstances. Lately some of the adults have become involved in a soup kitchen in Santa Fe, New Mexico. As soon as those adults discovered the program, I heard one of them—a junior-high sponsor, in fact—say, "Hey, let's bring the youth group down once a month to work with us." Demonstrating service to the poor is the most effective lesson plan. It must give God great pleasure to see adults take junior-high students to the local soup kitchen. Said Karl Barth, "Only the doer of the word is its real hearer."

• **Though children must be introduced to the Christian faith, youths need encouragement as they look critically and intellectually at their roots.** Helping kids wrestle with themselves and with God in the tradition of Jacob gives them authority to face and overcome their most difficult doubts and questions. Adult guides provide stability and security through this process. Communities of faith can provide such guidance, as seen in the study "The Family Chapter."

The Family Chapter

This is a study of 1 Thessalonians 2:1-12 that uses the Good News Bible (TEV). It calls attention to the family titles used by Paul in this chapter—"brothers" (vv. 1, 9), "mother" (v. 7), and "father" (v. 11).

Study the chapter together. Other Scriptures that might be helpful include Acts 17 (for information on Paul's ministry in Thessalonica), Jeremiah 31:1, and Ephesians 3:14, 15 (for other references to the family of God). Give the group the following questions to work on, individually or in small groups. Close with sharing insights and commitments with each other.

1. Why is the family of God a good title for the church?
2. What are some characteristics of the love that exists in a family?
3. What are some characteristics of a brother-to-brother reia... nship?
4. Read verses 7-9 again. How does a mother care for her children?
5. Read verses 10-12 again. How does a father act towards his kids?
6. Which of these characteristics of fathers and mothers can you find in God?
7. How are mothers and fathers different in this passage?
8. How does that compare with your parents?

9. What relationships presented in this would be good for the church to embrace? Why?
10. If you could choose an ideal father or mother figure as a guide for your life, how would he or she act towards you?
11. Choose a church "father" or "mother." Who is it? Why did you select them?

Do I Measure Up As a Mentor?

Here are some qualities that are essential to the mentoring task as well as to your own personal cultivation as a mentor. If your students have any of the needs listed above, ask yourself if you have any of these qualities (and perfection is not one of them):

• **Time.** Because choosing only one or two teenagers can be very demanding, different models have been developed to increase the number of adults available to be with young people. One such possibility is "Taking Confirmation Out of the Classroom."

Taking Confirmation Out of the Classroom

Duke University minister William Willimon proposes a new approach to the annual confirmation class, suggesting many ideas that encourage mentor-protégé relationships between adult Christians and young people.[4] His church tried this method because the classroom approach to confirmation did not line up with their vision for Christian education. Though they wanted kids who would, in Willimon's words, "grow up to look like our best Christians," they were instead getting apathetic students whose confirmation was too often their graduation from the church.

In restructuring confirmation, they wanted kids to gain three things from the class:
• The opportunity to become more like the disciples of Jesus.
• To become followers of Christ instead of knowing more about him.
• Life-long learning within a Christian lifestyle.

Working with both students and adults, the congregation carefully selected one adult mentor (later called a guide) for each confirmation student. A learning-activities plan was devised by the committee to be completed at a pace agreeable to the guide and student. It included reading the Gospel of Luke together, sitting with each other in worship, reviewing the church's budget, discussing the policy of the church, attending a church wedding or funeral together, and volunteering with each other in a community or church service project. A special dinner was held the night before the youths were to formally unite with the congregation; and on Sunday morning each student was introduced by his or her guide in worship.

This congregation is obviously dedicated to its confirmation students. First, it fulfilled the students' needs for significant adults; second, it encouraged adults in their responsibility to mentor young Christians. If we could do this consistently in the church, in Bible studies, in Sunday school, and in youth groups, our kids would know that Jesus loves them. His love would be made visible through us.

• **Integrity.** Mentors must follow the ancient decree to "know thyself." Our own awareness of our abilities and limitations, our faith and doubts make us empathetic and helpful to younger persons. Our Christian family needs us to be open and honest, consistent in care for ourselves as well as others. We don't have to be something we are not. We can say no to tasks that threaten to overload us and yes to what is most important. Kids need us to be ourselves with them. If we are Christians, then that includes talking about our faith and forthrightly declaring that we are not ashamed of our love for God.

• **Strength.** This may be spiritual or emotional or physical energy. High schoolers can be hard to keep up with! Mentors had better be prepared to listen attentively for hours, to go where the action is, and, with God's help, keep their own lives together. The amount of energy required is a good reason to limit the number of students we individually try to assist. Having a youth group or Sunday school class split up into small groups for discussions and ease of telephoning is great, but let's be honest—no one can mentor a small group. Select one kid. And be sensitive to "playing favorites," which can often be what parents and other kids perceive in mentoring.

• **Humility and flexibility.** We are not in this to impose Christian discipline or display to the world what great Christian adults we are. We are in it to travel for a time alongside a younger person. We hope to assist kids in their lifelong decisions, not make their decisions for them. We become mentors and models for youth because we must, not because we are necessarily "qualified." In fear and trepidation we accept the responsibility and walk humbly with our God, praying for assistance.

Summary

• Christian mentoring is a process where adults dedicate their experience and energy to nurturing the faith of a younger person, thereby fulfilling the younger person's need for a significant adult model and fulfilling the mentor's need and responsibility to contribute to the coming generation of Christians.

• Mentors are valuable because they—

—Assist in the development of meaningful roles and tasks for younger persons in the church.

—Encourage in-depth discovery of faith and of God.

—Model Christian lifestyles in full view as they talk about their faith and how it affects their living.

—Nurture development of a mature faith that encourages the asking of the most significant and difficult questions.

• For a reasonable chance at success, adult mentors must have time, integrity, spiritual and physical stamina, and humility and flexibility.

14

The Who Cares Principle:

Kids learn better from teachers who care about them.

Steven Mabry

The principal form that the work of love takes is attention. When we love another we give her or him our attention; we attend to that person's growth.
— *M. Scott Peck*

Mrs. Janke taught my ninth-grade Sunday school class. She was an older woman, short, definitely plump, and always wore a dress that flunked the current standards of fashion. She presided in a yellow Sunday school room with concrete block walls, supplied with two tables and a dozen metal folding chairs. A combo blackboard-bulletin board that stated all year long that "God is love" rounded out the furnishings. Armed only with her care for kids and a basic Bible study curriculum, she was the best. Mrs. Janke loved kids. She paid attention to me. I remember even now, twenty-five years later.

The single most important quality of great teachers is their care for each individual student. Thankfully, almost all of us were blessed by a "Mrs. Janke" who embodied that quality—caring for us in a personal way, showing us God's love through the gift of their attention. These teachers enriched our lives and nurtured our self-esteem. If you search your memory, you will find their faces. In response to their care we are simply asked to remember their loving qualities and emulate them. As we do, we begin to understand that teaching is caring. So when kids ask, "Who cares?" our answer should be, "I do."

Love, says psychiatrist M. Scott Peck, "is a committed, thoughtful decision."[1] If we want to be good teachers and models for Christ, we must first decide to be good lovers of kids. There are many methods and techniques for leading studies with youths, and they are important—but secondary. You, the teacher, are the main ingredient. Your method becomes your content. How you teach becomes what you teach. This is what Peck calls the "work of attention."

In *Counseling Teenagers*, psychologist G. Keith Olson suggests that we use reflective exercises to discover the personal characteristics of great counselors. Try a similar exercise to gain insight into the significant qualities of a teacher.

What Makes a Good Teacher?

To start on your road to increased self-discovery, try this reflective exercise (patterned after one mentioned by G. Keith Olson in *Counseling Teenagers*, Group Books, 1984). Make three columns on a sheet of paper. Label the first column "Teachers," the second column "Their Teaching Qualities," and the third column "My Response."

• In the first column: List the names of the teachers who had the greatest impact in your life. Listing the bad ones often reveals as much as listing the good ones.

• In the second column: Record the personal characteristics that caused their influence to be remembered or significant, positive or negative.

• In the third column: Write down your personal response to their presence in your life, including learning as well as behavior.

Take a moment to reflect on your lists. The goal, of course, is to emulate the good behaviors and eliminate the bad from your teaching. No matter how gifted — for some teachers have natural gifts in relationship skills — all teachers can profit from a review of caring skills helpful to Bible study.

Learn Your Students' Names

The ancients believed that knowing another's name gave power. I agree. Here are two ways to use that power in a Bible study. One: Names can be used to show respect and consideration and to build others up. Names welcome students, recognize them in discussions, and encourage relationships with others: "John, you look like you've got an idea. Would you like to share it with us?"

Two: Names can be employed to command and control, to put people on the spot, to embarrass. "Tell us the names of the twelve disciples, Jenny." This is not merely a friendly way to call another by name — it is sheer intimidation. As a student, I learned to appreciate teachers who used my name kindly. As a teacher, I struggle to learn every name and use them with care.

Mrs. Janke called kids by name and recognized us as individuals instead of just the ninth or tenth kid to come through the door on Sunday morning. Knowing the names of your students is a tangible way to show that you are interested in them. Helping them to learn the names of their peers will further their feeling of being accepted. For instance, try "Name Tag Mixer," a get-acquainted game, at the beginning of the first session.

Name Tag Mixer

When the kids come in, hand each a blank name tag (5 x 7 index cards work fine), a straight pin, and a pencil. Have them write on the front of the card 1) their name, and 2) five things they want others to know about them. Collect the name tags and shuffle the deck. Pass them out so that each student gets another's card. Then instruct the students to find the person who belongs to the card they hold. When they find that person, they pin the tag on them. When all have their own name tags pinned to them, students continue to circulate in the room, only now asking each other to autograph their cards.

Stop the mixer before the pace slows, and award a prize to whomever has the most autographs on their name tag.

Learn About Students' Lives

Christians all belong to the family of God. As we form relationships with the youths we lead in Bible study, knowledge on that rather grand scale is of limited use. Don't include them only as attenders at a Bible study, but learn about them in particular. To do that, study the kids as well as the biblical text you teach them each week—what are they like at home, at school, at the mall?

To accomplish this, make time for informal sharing at the beginning of each session. Encourage kids to share by providing a moment for concerns and a prayer at the end of a study. This is particularly helpful as a way of discovering when times are tough for your students and their families. Kids and adults will mention things in a prayer circle that they won't reveal anywhere else—communication problems at home, impending doom with an algebra test, grandparents with cancer, pregnant friends.

Teachers, especially those in a church setting, often have access to parents and siblings, too. Take time to meet them and get acquainted. Eat lunch with kids on campus and attend school games, plays, and concerts. Time spent learning about our students is nothing short of valuable, for it demonstrates our care for their lives, it builds trust, and it encourages learning.

Listen Well

Because many in the church clamor about scriptural ignorance, Bible education is often raised to crusade status. "We must teach our children about the Bible!" becomes the battle cry. Unfortunately, an agenda designed to wipe out the ignorance of others often ignores the perspectives of others, thus producing little or no dialogue between students and teachers. Worse, it generates little dialogue between students and the Bible. Implicit in this understanding is, "I'll teach, you listen."

Transforming Bible study into a war on ignorance places both teacher and students in a dilemma. Crusades leave little room for feelings. "Are you taking me seriously?" kids ask. "Are my opinions valued?" We send kids a resounding yes to these questions when we stop trying to fill them up and instead start listening when they are emptying themselves. If we teach and they listen, their important questions may remain unanswered. Some students come to study the Bible knowing much, others knowing little. All come as individuals of equal value in the eyes of God. We demonstrate our love for the students by listening to each one and by helping others to do the same. Through the work of attention we encourage and foster a rich Christian faith that travels with young people to home and school. Attentive listening supports kids as they search for personal meaning in the Scriptures.

How to Be a
Better Listener

Here are a few specific ways to love your kids by better listening.

• **Prepare.** Take a few minutes in your quiet time before the study to remember what it was like to be a teenager. With all the patience of your own Mrs. Janke, resolve to be empathetic with your students, with their questions, and with their understanding (or lack of understanding) of the Bible. Watch for their participation (or lack of it). Observe their body language as well as their words.

As you prepare, identify their needs and set your sights on resolving them. Select passages and topics with your students (instead of *for* them) to encourage ownership and promote interest. In the first session of the study group, for instance, assume the role of a journalist. Interview the group for an article you are writing: "Significant Issues for Teens in America." When you leave your journalist's role, work with the group to find passages that speak to those issues, and schedule them as your Bible study topics.

This works especially well with new kids who want to know, "Does this book have anything to say to me?" As you prepare the lessons, study your Bible and ponder the meaning. Pray and be open to God's mystery as you decide how to approach that portion of Scripture with teenagers.

• **Withhold judgment.** Be nonjudgmental about your kids' opinions and expressions of faith. All genuine questions about the Bible and its relationship to our lives are good questions. I've actually seen leaders sit and apparently listen to kids express their views, when all the time they were just waiting for the kids to stop talking so they could tell them what the passage *really* means. Disprove the widely held theory of kids that says that asking questions means they are stupid or at least slow. Respect their curiosity. Know that their interpretation of the passage will be the real meaning for them—at least this time around.

• **Accept.** Accept individuals for where they are. Avoid requiring them to change or grow in a particular way before you invest your energy and hours in their nurture.

My congregation has a number of public school teachers who are very familiar with the kids in my youth group. Now and again I've had a teacher remark drily about how much "fun" it must be to have James—who has a reputation for being a rowdy—in my youth group. Actually, it *is* fun to have James around. At our first meeting I knew this kid was high energy—and, frankly, I like that. So I took him to lunch, met him on campus, played a few rounds of Frisbee golf with him, and the next thing I knew he was coming to youth group—where he participates fully in everything, from games to Bible study.

Young people cry out for someone who will accept them and grant them unconditional positive regard.

• **Learn.** Don't assume you or the other leaders know everything. Susan came into my office smoldering over the weekly Fellowship of Christians meeting at her high school. During their morning Bible study, she expressed her interpretation of the passage. The adult leader abruptly told her that she obviously didn't understand the passage. Four days later she still resented the way her views had been dismissed.

Few things are more disrespectful to students than a teacher who knows it all. We are too willing to correct instead of respect the insights of our students. So become a student while you teach. Remember the words of populist philosopher Eric Hoffer: "In times of change, learners inherit the earth, while the learned find themselves beautifully equipped to deal with a world that no longer exists."[2]

If we are to show our students that we care about them, we must become learners with them.

Be There

This is crucial in forming bonds of trust with young people. People who invest themselves in the lives of their students become trusted and reliable sources of knowledge.

"What are you doing here?" kids asked when I first started going to the high-school campus for lunch.

"I came to see you," I replied. When teenagers discover that you're really interested in their lives and that you actually come every Tuesday for lunch, they love it. Committing yourself to teaching the Bible means as much to them as committing to lunch with them. Setting dates for study and keeping them gives the kids a needed continuity. Committed leaders with high availability to teenagers become models of God's love and examples for living.

Know Your Destination

The story is told of an apprentice preacher who was frustrated in his attempts at stirring the congregation with his lackluster sermons. He reported his disappointment to his mentor.

"You don't expect people to be changed *every* time you preach, do you?" the mentor asked his apprentice.

"Of course not."

"That's your problem."[3]

We owe nothing less to our young people than the opportunity for transformation. Bible study is not about learning the names of the twelve tribes of Israel or even of the twelve disciples of Jesus. It is about transforming lives and encouraging people to be able workers for Christ.

I regularly lead work/study camps of high schoolers to Mexico. When we get home, parents commonly ask me, "What did you do to my kid? He cleaned his room and helped with the dishes last night!" or "What happened on this trip? My kid is so grateful for our home now!" They have noticed a positive change in their children's outlook on life and a new appreciation for their blessings.

That is a life transformed. That is the goal of all Christian youth work, including Bible studies. Our job is to call forth the Spirit that God has placed within each person, to help it come alive and make a life new.

The bottom line is that we who teach must show our care for our students. Our action and attitudes are the main conveyers of our faith. Our desire to be with our students influences what they learn. The invitation to go for ice cream after Sunday school, the phone call during the week, a note to a kid who is sick, a birthday card, a cheerful, "Hello, Gene"—these all demonstrate to young people that we care. Most kids will take their first steps at loving Jesus only because they love us—and, most importantly, because we have lived our love for Jesus and for them.

Summary

• Become a Mrs. Janke. Remember that *how* you teach becomes *what* you teach.
• Love kids. Pay attention to them even as you learn from them and about them.
• Be a learner as well as a teacher.
• Be dependable.
• Know where you are going. Always expect the best as you seek transformation in the lives of your students.

15
Putting It All Together:

Kids learn more when their lessons affect their lives.

Steven Mabry

I appeal to you therefore, brethren, by the mercies of God, to present your bodies as a living sacrifice, holy and acceptable to God, which is your spiritual worship. Do not be conformed to this world but be transformed by the renewal of your mind, that you may prove what is the will of God, what is good and acceptable and perfect.   —The Apostle Paul, Romans 12:1-2

Bible studies are life-changing opportunities, not just Christian schooling. Teaching therefore embodies a deliberate and ongoing effort to impart values, behaviors, attitudes, and knowledge. When kids ask, "So what?" it points not to their failure to understand, but to our failure to impart meaning.

Transforming Lives Through Bible Study

Transformation means change, conversion, reformation. It means that students acknowledge God's claim on their lives, that they are not conformed to this world but converted to Christ. It becomes visible in youth when they begin to surrender their lives and lifestyles to God.

Four areas of adolescents' lives must be addressed in Bible study to better nurture Christian transformation: character, community, conversion, and career. Christian psychologist G. Keith Olson sums up these four tasks in what he perceives as vital areas of adolescent need:

• To develop a sense of personal identity that consistently establishes who he or she is as an integrated individual throughout each life role, separate and different from every other person. (character and conversion)

• To begin the process of establishing relationships that are characterized by commitment and intimacy. (community)

• To begin making decisions leading toward training and entry into a particular occupation. (career)[1]

Bible studies that speak to these needs are important to kids. Since adolescents fulfill them on varying time schedules, addressing them in a Bible study is an exercise in flexibility. The Holy Spirit, alive in you and on the pages of God's Word, provides kids with a new identity in Christ. Let's look at each need in greater depth.

• **Character.** Kids ask questions and they need answers. "Who am I? Who tells me who I am? How am I different from others? How am I related?" How does the Bible help students clarify significant issues, deal with problems, and survive the ever-changing atmosphere of American youth culture? Bible studies that respond to these crucial issues bind adolescents and Scripture together. The Bible offers radical opinions and uncompromising challenges to self-understanding. Teenagers welcome that input, for they are searching for their self-image. Teachers serve as a portal to that wisdom. We want to help our kids face tough issues and ask hard questions. The answers, ferreted out in Christian Bible study, have a lasting impact on their character.

One evening we read the entire Sermon on the Mount at a high-school Bible study. We talked about general impressions and the history of the times, taking the whole passage in context. I asked the kids to select a short passage from the section (their choice) and write a dialogue with Jesus about their questions for those few verses (a translation activity). Interestingly enough, every youth focused on a different set of verses (they know their needs better than I do). In the discussion that followed, some shared the conversation they had written and some did not (kids felt permission to pass if they were uncomfortable). An especially interesting interpretation came from Alice, who wrote a dialogue about this passage:

> You have heard that it was said, "Love your neighbor and hate your enemy." But I tell you: Love your enemies and pray for those who persecute you, that you may be sons of your Father in heaven. He causes his sun to rise on the evil and the good, and sends rain on the righteous and the unrighteous. (Matt. 5:43-45)

Alice did not wish to share her written conversation (I respected her comfort level), but she did want to share her problem with the group. "There are these friends I have at school who are always talking about other people, putting them down and making fun of them," she explained. "Some of the people who they make fun of are my friends, too." (Now in a global context of politics and justice and international affairs, this adolescent girl had no problem at all. To Alice, however, her friends were her world, her personal global context—and so this became a significant dilemma.)

There was more, she confessed—she joined in ridiculing some of her own friends, too. "How can I love my enemies when I can't even show love for my friends all of the time?" she asked.

Her peers understood. They suggested that she pray for her friends, by name, and for herself for the next week. One of the group told Alice, "Sometimes when I keep people in my prayers, it improves my attitude towards them."

Another suggested that maybe she should intentionally change the subject when the conversation turned to making fun of others.

Alice was able to make the Bible study meaningful to her. And that is our payoff. When a teenager takes a Scripture and wraps it around her life, there is transformation.

So the Scripture and Alice's problem were not precisely "on point." No matter—she interpreted the Scripture, placed it in a real life context, and allowed it to speak to her daily life. That experience brought her life together with God's Word. It built her character and sense of personal integrity. It built her friendship and trust with the study group, who, empowered by the discussion, affirmed her and increased her confidence and self-esteem.

Adult leaders don't have to sit around and dream up Twenty-Five Ways to Build Personal Integrity or Fifteen Programs to Develop Character. All we need do is take the questions of kids seriously and encourage them to bring their issues to the community of faith. When Bible studies build self-esteem, there is cause for celebration.

• **Community.** Kids need to become part of an ongoing community. In this way their special gifts and talents can be added to the skills and dreams of others. They become—some gradually, others quickly—a functioning part of the body of Christ. Kids need to work through such questions as "Am I my brothers keeper? Who is my neighbor? To whom will I make a commitment? To whom do I belong? To whom will I listen?" Kids are often not truly aware of the influences of their community. How and where and who young people choose to be with makes a significant difference in their development, self-esteem, and direction in life.

The Bible is a guide to community. It speaks of covenants with God and with one another. A Bible study offers kids a place for meaningful community with others, where they can gain needed skills for building relationships.

Our high schoolers recently worked through a four-week session on sexuality. The first evening of the series, we passed out a questionnaire which asked the youths, among other things, to suggest in writing what they needed to learn. Yes, there were questions about physiology and pregnancy and all, but four out of five kids asked questions about *relationships*, about how to be with another person in a caring relationship. Kids hunger for more-than-superficial relationships. When we bring teens together to work through significant issues, they build community as well as character. With adult guidance they find strength in their peers instead of pressure.

Bible studies also enable kids to see themselves as a part of a more intimate community—just them and God. Young people often feel shut out of fellowship with God because they think perfection is required. By accepting kids where they are and encouraging a community of their peers to do likewise, we can nurture in them a receptivity to God's Spirit. The payoff for students and leaders then becomes a strong, nourishing community.

• **Conversion.** Olson says adolescents need a sense of personal identity that consistently tells them who they are—despite the fact that developing this identity has become increasingly difficult in our pluralistic society. Kids often just do not know how to integrate their lives at church with school or work or home. Sure, they often know what the Bible says—but they ignore its teachings because it stands between them and peer acceptance.

Bible studies are a solid footing for identity formation; they are a stable environment built on the rock of God's Word. A Bible study group creates a support network and safe haven in which to choose God's ways. When students start making choices based on what they believe God wants them to do, then there is transformation; then there is conversion. The payoff for teachers is catching the occasional glimpse of students who know that God is in their lives and in their decisions.

• **Career.** Bible studies provide students not only with the gospel message, but with a chance to apply it. In the application process we introduce kids to the needs of others, thereby giving them power and motivation to change their world.

The idea of a vocation dedicated to service and witness is less popular these days than it has been. The average high-school or college student tends to see learning simply as a means to a good job and good money. Active Bible studies that provoke teenagers to live the teachings they glean influence career and vocational choices in positive ways. Though we cannot make lifestyle and career choices for our kids, we can give them a shot at practicing what they are learning. And then, though we may not be around to see what choices they ultimately make, we will still be a part of their foundation—a foundation that, in some kids, will include service to God.

During many years of pastoring, I cannot tell you how many stories I have heard about you—the teacher, the youth leader, the Christian mentor. Adults in my church describe for me the Christian models that led them to choose God and the church. "My Sunday school teacher was a real inspiration in my life," they say, or "My Bible study leader really helped me in my Christian walk" or "My youth sponsor is the reason I'm in church today." Teachers sow the seeds and trust the promise; God provides the growth.

Standing by the Pool

Speaking at the predominantly black Second Baptist Church in Wheaton, Illinois, the Reverend John Perkins enthralled me with a typically moving sermon about healing. Choosing John 5:1-9 as the text, he began preaching and the congregation began participating. He told about the healing pool of Bethesda and a man who had lain invalid for thirty-eight years (congregational gasp). He told of a Jesus who stopped to talk to the lame man, asking him, "Do you want to get well?"

If the invalid hesitated in his answer, the congregation did not. Perkins recounted the man's reply—that he was alone with no one to help him into the pool when the waters were stirred: "While I am trying to get in, someone else goes down ahead of me." The sanctuary moaned with sympathy. When Perkins hit Jesus' words, "Get up! Pick up your mat and walk!" and "At once the man was cured; he picked up his mat and walked," the congregation burst into celebration with amens that raised the roof.

Yet at this climax of the story, Perkins cut through their enthusiasm. "You don't understand what a tragedy this is!" he declared. Sudden silence. Perkins explained that, yes, God wants people to be healed, but then he wants them to stay by the pool in order to help others. The tragedy in the story is that the man left the pool. After thirty-eight years of lying helplessly by the water, wishing others would help him, the invalid is finally healed—but only to leave those who could have used his help.

If you teach young people, you have been touched by the message of the gospel. You have felt in some sense the healing waters of Christ. Others were there to place you into the waters when you were too young to help yourself. The good news is this: you have not gone away. You remained or returned to the pool, helping kids—teaching them creatively and realistically—into the healing waters of the Word of God.

Notes

Chapter 1
Basics of Bible Teaching
The introductory quote by Frederick Buechner is from *Wishful Thinking* (Harper & Row, 1973).
1. Origen, *Commentary on Luke 10:30-35* (Homily XXXIV).
2. Robert Capon, *The Parables of Grace* (Eerdmanns, 1987).
3. Karl Barth, *Evangelical Theology* (Doubleday, 1964).
4. Cited in Roger Goebbel and others, *Helping Youth Interpret the Bible* (John Knox Press, 1984).

Chapter 2
The Eureka Principle
The introductory quote by Carl Rogers is from *Freedom to Learn* (Charles Merrill, 1979).
1. J. Zink, *Champions in the Making: Motivating Kids, Book Two* (J. Zink Inc., 1983).
2. Zink.
3. William James, *Talks to Teachers* (George Ellis Press, 1899).

Chapter 3
The Conehead Principle
The introductory quote by John Dewey is from *Experience and Education* (McGraw Hill, 1938).
1. David Myers, *The Human Puzzle* (Harper & Row, 1978).
2. John Westerhoff, *Values for Tomorrow's Children* (Seabury Press, 1970).
3. John Dewey, *Experience and Education* (McGraw Hill, 1938).
4. For a fuller treatment of this subject, see Bloom's taxonomy of educational objectives.

Chapter 4
The Sierra Club Principle
The introductory quote by George Leonard is from *Education and Ecstasy* (Dell, 1968).
1. Lyman Coleman, *Self-Profile: The Me Nobody Knows* (Abingdon, 1981).

Chapter 5
The Yakety-Yak Principle
The introductory quote by Ralph Waldo Emerson is from *Society and Solitude*.
1. David Myers, "Getting the Message," *Christian Ministry* (January 1981).
2. Myers.
3. H. Stephen Glenn and Jane Nelsen, *Raising Children for Success* (Sunrise Press, 1987).
4. Francis Hunkins, *Questioning Strategies and Techniques* (Allyn & Bacon, 1972).

Chapter 6
The Action-Attitude Principle
The introductory quote by John Westerhoff is from *Will Our Children Have Faith?* (Harper & Row, 1983).
1. David Myers, *The Human Puzzle* (Harper & Row, 1978).
2. Adapted from the writings of Yale University social psychologist William McGuire.
3. Myers.
4. David Myers, "A Social Psychology of Evangelism," *Reformed Review* (Autumn 1987).

Chapter 7
The Agatha Christie Principle
The introductory quote by Rainer Maria Rilke is from *Letters to a Young Poet* (W.W. Norton, 1934).

Chapter 8
The Concrete Principle
1. David Myers, *The Inflated Self* (Seabury Press, 1980)
2. William Barclay, *The Gospel of Mark* (Westminster Press, 1956).

Chapter 9
The Travel Agent Principle
The introductory quote by Walter Brueggemann is from *The Bible Makes Sense* (John Knox Press, 1983).
1. David Elkind, *All Grown Up and No Place To Go* (Addison-Wesley, 1984).
2. John Holt, *How Children Learn* (Dell, 1967).
3. Carl Rogers, *Freedom To Learn* (Charles Merrill, 1979).
4. Marlene LeFever, *Creative Teaching Methods* (David C. Cook, 1985).
5. Roberta Hestenes, *Using the Bible in Groups* (Westminster Press, 1983).
6. Hestenes.

Chapter 10
The Emoi Hellēnikē Estin Principle
The introductory quote by John Westerhoff is from *Values for Tomorrow's Children* (Seabury Press, 1970).
1. Roger Goebbel and others, *Helping Youth Interpret the Bible* (John Knox Press, 1984).
2. Donald Griggs, *Teaching Teachers to Teach* (Abingdon, 1974).

Chapter 11
The Show and Tell Principle
The introductory quote by Walter Wink is from *Transforming Bible Study* (Abingdon, 1980).
1. Robert Fulghum, *All I Ever Needed To Know I Learned in Kindergarten* (Villard Books, 1989).
2. Guy Lefrancois, *Psychology for Teaching, A Bear Always Usually Sometimes Rarely Faces the Front* (Wadsworth Publishing Co., 1982).

3. Available through Sunrise Books, Tapes, and Videos, P.O. Box B, Provo, UT 84603.
4. Fulghum.

Chapter 12
The Rotation Principle

The introductory quote by David Douglas is from *Wilderness Sojourn* (Harper & Row, 1987).

1. This idea and many others are from Rick Bundschuh, *On-Site: 40 On-Location Youth Programs* (Youth Specialties/ Zondervan, 1989).

Chapter 13
The Samuel Principle

The introductory quote is from *Faith Development and Fowler* (Religious Education Press, 1986), edited by Craig Dykstra and Sharon Parks.

1. Allen Hadidian, *Discipleship: Helping Other Christians To Grow* (Moody Press, 1979).
2. H. Stephen Glenn and Jane Nelsen, *Raising Self-Reliant Children in a Self-Indulgent World* (Prima Publishing and Communications, 1988).
3. Glenn and Nelsen.
4. William H. Willimon, "Taking Confirmation Out of the Classroom," *Christian Century* (March 16, 1988).

Chapter 14
The Who Cares Principle

The introductory quote by M. Scott Peck is from *The Road Less Traveled* (Simon & Schuster, 1978).

1. Peck.
2. Eric Hoffer, cited in H. Stephen Glenn with Jane Nelsen, *Raising Children for Success* (Sunrise Press, 1987).
3. Walter Wink, *Transforming Bible Study* (Abingdon, 1980).

Chapter 15
Putting It All Together

1. G. Keith Olson, *Counseling Teenagers* (Group Books, 1984).

Index of Ideas, Games, and Discussion Starters

BaseBall america®
2019 ALMANAC

D0955079

BASEBALL AMERICA INC. · DURHAM, N.C.

BaseBall america

ESTABLISHED 1981

P.O. Box 12877, Durham, NC 27709 • Phone (919) 682-9635

EDITOR AND PUBLISHER B.J. Schecter *@bjschecter*
EXECUTIVE EDITORS J.J. Cooper *@jjcoop36*
Matt Eddy *@MattEddyBA*
CHIEF REVENUE OFFICER Don Hintze
DIRECTOR OF BUSINESS DEVELOPMENT Ben Leigh

EDITORIAL

ASSOCIATE EDITORS Justin Coleman
Kegan Lowe *@KeganLowe*
Josh Norris *@jnorris427*
SENIOR WRITER Ben Badler *@benbadler*
NATIONAL WRITERS Teddy Cahill *@tedcahill*
Carlos Collazo *@CarlosACollazo*
Kyle Glaser *@KyleAGlaser*
WEB EDITOR Mark Chiarelli *@Mark_Chiarelli*
SPECIAL CONTRIBUTOR Tim Newcomb *@tdnewcomb*

PRODUCTION

DESIGN & PRODUCTION DIRECTOR Sara Hiatt McDaniel
MULTIMEDIA MANAGER Linwood Webb
DESIGN ASSISTANT James Alworth

BUSINESS

TECHNOLOGY MANAGER Brent Lewis
ACCOUNT EXECUTIVE Kellen Coleman
MARKETING/OPERATIONS COORDINATOR Angela Lewis
CUSTOMER SERVICE Melissa Sunderman

STATISTICAL SERVICE

MAJOR LEAGUE BASEBALL ADVANCED MEDIA

Alliance
)))) BASEBALL ((((

BASEBALL AMERICA ENTERPRISES

CHAIRMAN & CEO Gary Green
PRESIDENT Larry Botel
GENERAL COUNSEL Matthew Pace
DIRECTOR OF MARKETING Amy Heart
INVESTOR RELATIONS Michele Balfour
DIRECTOR OF OPERATIONS Joan Disalvo
PARTNERS Jon Ashley
Stephen Alepa
Martie Cordaro
Brian Rothschild
Andrew Fox
Maurice Haroche
Dan Waldman
Sonny Kalsi
Glenn Isaacson
Robert Hernreich
Craig Amazeen
Peter Ruprecht
Beryl Snyder
Tom Steiglehner

3 STEP

MANAGING PARTNER David Geaslen
CHIEF CONTENT OFFICER Jonathan Segal
CHIEF FINANCIAL OFFICER Sue Murphy
DIRECTOR OF DIGITAL CONTENT Tom Johnson

BASEBALL AMERICA (ISSN 0745-5372/USPS 591-210) is published bi-weekly with a double issue in August and December, 24 issues per year, by Baseball America Enterprises, LLC, 4319 South Alston Ave, Suite 103, Durham, NC 27713. Subscription rate is $92.95 for one year; Canada $118.95 (U.S. funds); all other foreign $144.95 per year (U.S. funds). Periodicals postage paid at Durham, NC, & additional mailing offices. Occasionally our subscriber list is made available to reputable firms offering goods and services we believe would be of interest to our readers. If you prefer to be excluded, please send your current address label and a note requesting to be excluded from these promotions to Baseball America Enterprises, LLC, 4319 South Alston Ave, Suite 103, Durham, NC 27713, Attn Privacy Coordinator.

©2018 by Baseball America Enterprises, LLC. All Rights Reserved. Printed in Canada

EDITOR'S NOTE: Major league statistics are based on final, unofficial 2018 averages.

» The organization statistics, which begin on page 44, include all players who participated in at least one game during the 2018 season.

» Pitchers' batting statistics are not included, nor are the pitching statistics of field players who pitched in less than two games.

» For players who played with more than one team in the same league, the player's cumulative statistics appear on the line immediately after the player's statistics with each team.

» Innings pitched have been rounded off to the nearest full inning.

BaseBall america
2019 ALMANAC

Editor
Kegan Lowe

Assistant Editors
Ben Badler, Teddy Cahill, Justin Coleman, Carlos Collazo
J.J. Cooper, Matt Eddy, Josh Norris

Database and Application Development
Brent Lewis

Contributing Writers
Jerry Crasnick, Bill Mitchell, Harvey Sahker

Photo Editor
Brendan Nolan

Design & Production
James Alworth, Sara Hiatt McDaniel, Linwood Webb

Programming & Technical Development
Brent Lewis

Cover Photo
Mike Trout of the Los Angeles Angels of Anaheim poses
for a portrait during Angels Photo Day at Tempe Diablo
Stadium on February 21, 2017 in Tempe, Arizona.
Photo by Rob Tringali/Getty Images.

©2018 Baseball America Inc.

No portion of this book may be reprinted or reproduced
without the written consent of the publisher.

For additional copies, visit our Website at
BaseballAmerica.com or call 1-800-845-2726 to order.

US $25.95-$34.95, plus shipping
and handling per order. Expedited shipping available.

Distributed by Simon & Schuster.
ISBN-13: 978-1-932391-81-7

Statistics provided by Major League Baseball Advanced
Media and Compiled by Baseball America.

TABLE OF CONTENTS

Juan Soto

RICH SCHULTZ/GETTY IMAGES

MAJOR
LEAGUES

A Whole New Ballgame

BY JERRY CRASNICK

As the gap between analytics and traditional thinking continues to widen, there are nights when baseball doesn't look or feel much like the sport we've come to know and love through the years. The typical MLB game features a parade of pitchers throwing at velocities previously unseen, to hitters who generate an unprecedented amount of air. It's no longer an oddity to see a shortstop or backup right fielder pitching in the late innings of a 10-3 game, or a third basemen stationed to the right of second base.

The whole production is governed and orchestrated by a terminology that seems utterly foreign. Exit velocity and launch angle were already part of the vernacular. Now starting pitchers have been replaced by "openers" in Tampa Bay and "out-getters" in Milwaukee. And "bullpenning" is increasingly en vogue regardless of venue.

A limitation on mound visits didn't do much to curb those long, painful stretches of inaction in 2018. The 126,294 balls in play were the fewest in 10 seasons, and it was largely a reflection of so much swinging and missing. Before 2018, baseball had never produced a month with more strikeouts than base hits. It happened three times last season—in April, June and September. By season's end, the 30 MLB clubs had produced 189 more whiffs than hits.

Some hitters pointed to increased velocity among pitchers as a major factor. According to FanGraphs, 13 starting pitchers averaged 95 mph or better on the radar gun. Compare that total to 2008, when Colorado's Ubaldo Jimenez led all big-league starters with a 94.9 mph average fastball.

"It's hard now—period," said Matt Carpenter of the St. Louis Cardinals. "Everyone is throwing 95 mph-plus with movement. Every bullpen has guys out there doing that. So just putting the ball in play and not striking out is a challenge in itself."

Defensive shifts have been at the forefront of the game's new dynamic. According to the Baseball Savant website, the 30 clubs employed shifts 17.4 percent of the time—up from 12.1 percent in 2017. The Houston Astros shifted a whopping 2,195 times (and used shifts 59.7 percent of the time) to lead the majors. They were followed by the Rays, who have a reputation for being forward-looking and analytically oriented, and the Minnesota Twins, New York Yankees and Kansas City Royals.

Alex Bregman and the Astros used a defensive shift nearly 60 percent of the time in 2018.

While some hitters grew frustrated making outs every time they hit a ground ball to the right side, others made it their mission to try to hit the ball in the air.

"The reason they shift you in the places they do is because that's what your batted ball data says," said veteran infielder Daniel Murphy. "I heard Joe Maddon say, 'You have three choices: You can try to hit it and beat the shift. That's going to give you a single, but now you're doing something against what you're best at, so the defense wins. You can hit into the shift, and the defense wins. Or you can try not to let the infielders catch the batted ball. No ground balls and no popups. Try to stand on second base.' That's Option C."

In these changing times, the concept of a starting pitcher as a workhorse no longer applies. Just 13 MLB starters surpassed 200 innings, compared to 36 as recently as 2013. Max Scherzer, Corey Kluber and Noah Syndergaard were among a group of eight starters who tied for the MLB lead with two complete games.

And when a game is a blowout, you never know who you might find on the mound in the late innings. The 48 position players who pitched last year were the most in a single season since the start of the expansion era in 1961. In the modern era, black is white, day is night, and moves that were once considered bold or "outside the box" are now standard operating procedure in the big leagues.

New Faces In The Dugout

The concept of manager as policy setter, lineup card-maker and organizational lead dog is now passé. Tony LaRussa, Jim Leyland, Bobby Cox, Joe Torre and Lou Piniella are among the iconic skippers who've retired in recent years. The new wave of managers operates in a different environment. Collaboration is en vogue, and experience is in no way a prerequisite. On the contrary: Teams now regard the manager as less the czar of the clubhouse and the dugout than a cog in the decision-making chain.

"I've likened it to NASA and the space shuttle," said Yankees general manager Brian Cashman. "We'll pick the mission. We're gonna get the trajectory. We're going to hire an astronaut to fly that payload, and they're going to stay in touch with us every single step of the way."

After cutting ties to Joe Girardi, the Yankees concluded an extensive search by hiring Aaron Boone, who had spent the previous eight years as an analyst and color commentator for ESPN. The New York Mets tabbed Mickey Callaway, Terry Francona's pitching coach in Cleveland, as the successor to Terry Collins. The Boston Red Sox replaced John Farrell with Alex Cora, who had worked for ESPN and spent the 2017 season apprenticing as A.J. Hinch's bench coach in Houston. The Philadelphia Phillies hired Gabe Kapler, who was coming off a three-year stint as the Los Angeles Dodgers' farm director. And the Washington Nationals hired Dave Martinez, whose managerial prep consisted of a decade as Joe Maddon's bench coach in Tampa Bay and Chicago.

Cora was the youngest of the new breed at 42, while Martinez was the oldest at 53. The common thread: They all played in the big leagues—and had a scarcity of managerial time on their resumes. Kapler was the only one with any managerial experience, and it consisted of a one-year sabbatical to run the Greenville Drive in the low Class A South Atlantic League in 2007. Kapler managed the team to a 58-81 record before returning to play for three more seasons in Milwaukee and Tampa Bay.

The voyage of discovery was smoother for some of the newcomers than others. Cora led the Red Sox to 108 victories, breaking the franchise record of 105 held by the 1912 Boston squad that featured Tris Speaker, Harry Hooper and Smoky

Joe Wood. In a tough, demanding environment, Cora earned rave reviews for his performance and convinced Dave Dombrowski, Boston's president of baseball operations, that the club had made the right call.

"He's very knowledgeable about the game," Dombrowski said. "He's always been a leader and very well-respected. He's very intelligent and a good communicator, in all directions. He's good with the media. He knows the rules. And we've got a great staff around him. He's got a fire in him. But he just keeps a very calm demeanor about him."

Boone, similarly, fared well as Girardi's replacement in the Bronx. The Yankees won 100 games despite extended injury-related absences by Aaron Judge, Gary Sanchez and Aroldis Chapman. In Philadelphia, Kapler overcame some early stumbles to guide the Phillies to a 63-48 record and a 1.5 game lead over second place Atlanta in the NL East before a late collapse. And just when the Mets' season was declared a disaster, they logged an 18-10 record in September to provide reason to hope that the 2019 season might be better.

But growing pains were inevitable. Callaway was pilloried when the Mets batted out of order in an extra-inning loss to Cincinnati in May. Kapler came under fire for his unconventional bullpen management and numerous other analytically driven moves. The Nationals' disappointing performance produced whispers that Martinez had lost the team and led to one report that the Washington clubhouse was a "mess." Even Boone, who guided the Yankees to their first 100-win season since 2009, became a target for criticism for giving starting pitchers Luis Severino and C.C. Sabathia too long a leash in the American League Division Series loss to Boston.

The Detroit Tigers, the only team to buck the trend toward young, fresh faces in the dugout, put their faith in 60-year-old Ron Gardenhire. The Tigers were 36-37 in mid-June when an 11-game losing streak spelled the end of their .500 aspirations.

Rookie Sensations

It would be an understatement to describe Shohei Ohtani's first appearance at Los Angeles Angels' spring camp as an "event." When Ohtani arrived in Arizona in mid-February, 50 Japanese reporters assembled at the entrance to the player parking lot at Tempe Diablo Stadium. His initial press conference drew a crowd of about 150 media members.

The furor was only natural given the hype. Ohtani, 23, arrived in the U.S. with massive expec-

SCOTT CUNNINGHAM/GETTY IMAGES

Ronald Acuna Jr. set an Atlanta franchise record with eight leadoff home runs in 2018.

tations stemming from his moniker as "Japan's Babe Ruth." He had routinely surpassed 100 mph on the radar gun and launched 22 homers and slugged .588 for the Nippon Ham Fighters at age 21. The Angels emerged from a group of seven finalists to land Ohtani on Dec. 8. He received a signing bonus of $2.135 million and the major-league minimum salary of $545,000 in 2018. If Ohtani had waited two more years, he almost certainly would have commanded a nine-figure contract under the terms of baseball's labor agreement.

It didn't take long for his teammates and American baseball fans to see what the fuss was about. In early June, Ohtani was diagnosed with a sprained ulnar collateral ligament in his right elbow. The injury put a crimp in his pitching workload, but he still managed to post a 4-2 record with a 3.31 ERA and strike out 63 batters in 51.2 innings. Ohtani was even more of a revelation at the plate, hitting 22 homers and posting a .564 slugging percentage in 367 plate appearances. He joined Ruth as the second player in MLB history to record 10 pitching appearances and 20 homers in a season, and became the second Japanese hitter (along with Hideki Matsui) to go deep 20 times in a year.

A late-season test run on the mound put Ohtani over the edge and necessitated Tommy John surgery, prompting the Angels to map out a new course of action for his second season. "It obviously puts him out of pitching in 2019, but he'll be able to hit, and I think he's at peace with that," said Angels manager Mike Scioscia.

About 2,100 miles east of the Cactus League in Orlando, Fla., Atlanta outfielder Ronald Acuna Jr. arrived at spring training to similarly weighty expectations. In March, longtime franchise favorite and spring training guest instructor Ralph Garr watched Acuna launch an array of batting practice bombs and observed that the kid had a touch of Hank Aaron to his game. Acuna began the season with Triple-A Gwinnett and hit .265 in his first month with the big club in Atlanta. But after sitting out most of June with a knee injury, he returned to the lineup and became the talk of baseball.

Acuna's eight homers out of the leadoff spot broke the Atlanta franchise record set by Marquis Grissom in 1996, and he joined Eddie Mathews, Orlando Cepeda, Al Kaline, Tony Conigliaro, Frank Robinson and Mel Ott as one of seven players to record 25 home runs in a season before their 21st birthday. Late in the year, teammate Freddie Freeman observed that Acuna had the ability to become the National League's answer to Mike Trout.

"He hits the ball so hard," Freeman said. "I can only dream of hitting the ball that hard, and he does it with ease. He makes solid contact almost every single time. Obviously, Mike takes a lot more walks, but I think Ronald is going to grow into it. To even compare him to Mike Trout is tough to do, but he has the potential to be that good."

Acuna's feats were joined by a similar output from Nationals outfielder Juan Soto, whose combination of patience, power and bat speed wowed longtime observers, especially considering how little time Soto spent in the minor leagues. "I think we're all amazed every single day," said Nationals pitcher Max Scherzer. "He's got some antics. He's got some flair. He's a great young player."

The Yankees introduced two young infielders with potent bats. Third baseman Miguel Andujar finished the season with 76 extra-base hits—third most by a Yankees rookie behind Joe DiMaggio (88 in 1936) and Aaron Judge (79 in 2017). Gleyber Torres, acquired from the Cubs in the July 2016 trade that sent Aroldis Chapman to Chicago, showed lots of pop and a flair for the big moment. On May 25, Torres became the youngest player in American League history to homer in four straight games.

CONTINUED ON PAGE 11

PLAYER OF THE YEAR

Mike Trout Delivers 'Best Year' Yet

BY KYLE GLASER

I n many ways, 2018 was the best year of Mike Trout's illustrious career.

Trout raised his game yet another notch this season, posting a 1.088 OPS that not only led the majors but also was the second-highest by any player this decade. He finished fifth in MLB in batting average (.312), first in on-base percentage (.460), third in slugging percentage (.628) and tied for fourth in home runs (39). And he did it all without making a single error in the field, something no other center fielder who played at least 120 games can claim.

For his all-around excellence, Trout is the 2018 Baseball America MLB Player of the Year.

"I think just the total package . . . this was my best year," Trout said. "Being up here for seven, eight years now, I'm facing guys over and over again . . . And just knowing my swing, I'm learning how to prevent the long durations without feeling good at the plate."

Trout has now played in 1,065 career games. Through the same amount of games, he has more hits than Cal Ripken Jr., more home runs than Barry Bonds, more runs scored than Ty Cobb and more total bases than Ken Griffey Jr.

And he's getting better. Trout's on-base percentage and OPS this season were the best of his career. His home run total and slugging percentage were second-best. He stole 24 bases in 26 attempts, the best rate of his career.

Then there is his defense. In spring train-

Mike Trout led the majors in on-base percentage (.460) and OPS (1.088) in 2018.

VICTOR DECOLONGON/GETTY IMAGES

ing, Trout declared his goal of winning his first Gold Glove. He sharpened his skills getting jumps off the bat every day in batting practice during camp, and by the time the regular season rolled around, he noticed a distinct difference.

"I've surprised myself a couple times this year with balls I didn't think I could catch and I caught," Trout said. "I wouldn't say it was one particular drill. I think just over time, even in BP when you're not shagging everything, you're getting that first step, getting that reaction time and tell yourself catch everything."

Trout led all AL center fielders with four double plays started and ranked fourth with seven assists. According to Fangraphs, Trout's eight defensive runs saved led all qualified AL center fielders and was tied for third in MLB overall.

"When Mike evaluates himself and if there's maybe a deficiency, he takes it on as a personal challenge," Angels manager Mike Scioscia said. "He's a Gold Glover in center field, there's no doubt in my mind."

That Trout was already considered the best player in baseball and somehow managed to get even better was impressive, but not surprising for those around him on a daily basis.

PREVIOUS POY WINNERS

2008: C.C. Sabathia, LHP, Indians/Brewers
2009: Joe Mauer, C, Twins
2010: Roy Halladay, RHP, Phillies
2011: Matt Kemp, OF, Dodgers
2012: Mike Trout, OF, Angels
2013: Mike Trout, OF, Angels
2014: Clayton Kershaw, LHP, Dodgers
2015: Bryce Harper, OF, Nationals
2016: Mike Trout, OF, Angels
2017: Jose Altuve, 2B, Astros
Full list: BaseballAmerica.com/awards

Several other newcomers made positive first impressions. Dodgers starter Walker Buehler struck out 151 batters in 137.1 innings. Outfielder Harrison Bader showed energy and a terrific glove for the St. Louis Cardinals. The White Sox' Daniel Palka and the Padres' Christian Villanueva each surpassed 20 home runs. Starters Jack Flaherty, Ryan Yarbrough and Dereck Rodriguez, and relievers Lou Trivino, Seranthony Dominguez, Jesse Biddle, Reyes Moronta and Richard Rodriguez were among the rookies who made a positive impression in their first go-rounds.

Vladimir Guerrero Jr. never got the call from the Toronto Blue Jays despite hitting .381 with a 1.073 OPS in four minor league stops. The Jays sent him to the Arizona Fall League to continue to work on his defense and baserunning, and they planned to give him every opportunity to win a big league job in spring training of 2019.

Milestones

Albert Pujols' tenure with the Los Angeles Angels hasn't turned out in a manner that owner Arte Moreno would have hoped or expected when the team signed him to a 10-year, $240 million contract in December 2011. Pujols has been dogged by injuries, and his production had gradually diminished. But for one night in May, it was all about love, appreciation and nostalgia for the artist long known as "The Machine."

In the fifth inning of a 5-0 win over the Mariners at Safeco Field, Pujols flared a single to right field off Mike Leake to join Hank Aaron,

Willie Mays and Alex Rodriguez as the fourth player in history with 3,000 career hits and 600 home runs. Pujols clapped his hands as he passed first base, pointed skyward and embraced first-base coach Alfredo Griffin before accepting congratulations from Mike Trout and other teammates as they streamed from the dugout.

The achievement was doubly gratifying for Pujols because he joined Adrian Beltre as the second Dominican native in the 3,000-hit club.

"There are so many people—if I start thanking them all we might be here to till 2 in the morning," Pujols said. "In the Dominican Republic, there were 10 million-plus people staying up and missing sleep over the last couple days waiting for this moment. To be able to share this with Adrian Beltre, and be the second Dominican to accomplish this is pretty special."

Beltre, like Pujols, has assured himself a spot in Cooperstown with his consistently excellent production over time. The 2018 season was a disappointment for the Rangers, who finished last in the AL West with a 67-95 record, but their 41-year-old third baseman continued to pad his resume. With a second inning double against Oakland on April 5, Beltre passed Panama native Rod Carew to become the career leader in hits by a Latin American player. He also became the 73rd player in history to amass 1,500 doubles.

On a 47-degree night at Target Field—with barely 15,000 people in the stands—Minnesota's Joe Mauer punched a single through a drawn-in infield against Aaron Bummer of the Chicago

CONTINUED ON PAGE 13

AMERICAN LEAGUE STANDINGS

East	W	L	PCT	GB	Manager	General Manager	Attendance	Average	Last Penn.
Boston Red Sox	108	54	.667	—	Alex Cora	Dave Dombrowski	2,895,575	35,748	2018
New York Yankees	100	62	.617	8	Aaron Boone	Brian Cashman	3,482,855	42,998	2009
Tampa Bay Rays	90	72	.556	18	Kevin Cash	Erik Neander	1,154,973	14,259	2008
Toronto Blue Jays	73	89	.451	35	John Gibbons	Ross Atkins	2,325,281	29,066	1993
Baltimore Orioles	47	115	.290	61	Buck Showalter	Dan Duquette	1,564,192	19,800	1983

Central	W	L	PCT	GB	Manager	General Manager	Attendance	Average	Last Penn.
Cleveland Indians	91	71	.562	—	Terry Francona	Mike Chernoff	1,926,701	24,084	2016
Minnesota Twins	78	84	.481	13	Paul Molitor	Thad Levine	1,959,197	24,490	1991
Detroit Tigers	64	98	.395	27	Ron Gardenhire	Al Avila	1,856,970	23,212	2012
Chicago White Sox	62	100	.383	29	Rick Renteria	Rick Hahn	1,608,817	20,110	2005
Kansas City Royals	58	104	.358	33	Ned Yost	Dayton Moore	1,665,107	20,557	2015

West	W	L	PCT	GB	Manager	General Manager	Attendance	Average	Last Penn.
Houston Astros	103	59	.636	—	A.J. Hinch	Jeff Luhnow	2,980,549	36,797	2017
Oakland Athletics	97	65	.599	6	Bob Melvin	David Forst	1,573,616	19,427	1990
Seattle Mariners	89	73	.549	14	Scott Servais	Jerry Dipoto	2,299,489	29,389	Never
Los Angeles Angels	80	82	.494	23	Mike Scioscia	Billy Eppler	3,020,216	37,287	2002
Texas Rangers	67	95	.414	26	J. Bannister/D. Wakamatsu	Jon Daniels	2,107,107	26,014	2011

Wild Card Game: Yankees defeated Athletics. **Division Series:** Red Sox defeated Yankees 3-1 and Astros defeated Indians 3-0 in best-of-five series. **Championship Series:** Red Sox defeated Astros 4-1 in a best-of-seven series.

ROOKIE OF THE YEAR

Shohei Ohtani Does It All In L.A.

BY KYLE GLASER

Shohei Ohtani delivered a nearly unprecedented season as a rookie with the Angels in 2018, simultaneously excelling as both a hitter and pitcher while shattering all notions about what is possible in today's game. Even considering Ohtani was limited to 10 starts and a half-season's worth of plate appearances due to injury, his performance stands out as historic.

Ohtani hit .285 with a .925 OPS and 22 home runs in 367 plate appearances (a 34-homer pace), numbers in line with Paul Goldschmidt's.

He delivered a 3.31 ERA, 11.0 strikeouts per nine innings and a 1.16 WHIP on the mound, numbers in line with Luis Severino's.

Ohtani joined Babe Ruth as the only players in MLB history to hit 15 home runs and pitch 50 innings in a season. He became the first player with 15 homers and 50 strikeouts in a season.

For living starring as both a pitcher and hitter at the highest level of baseball in the world, Ohtani is the 2018 Baseball America Rookie of the Year.

"I didn't really know what to expect here, so I didn't really set any expectations for myself," Ohtani said through a translator. "But once I got here . . . I got the level of competition early, even though there were some struggles."

Ah yes, those struggles. For a moment, it looked like the hype was too good to be true. Ohtani entered spring training with the eyes of the baseball world watching him, and he promptly struck out 10 times in 32 at-bats in while getting pummeled on the mound, even in minor league "B" games. It got so bad evaluators questioned if he'd be best served starting in the minors.

Once the games actually began to count, however, it took Ohtani one week to silence his skeptics. In his first career start, Ohtani beat the Athletics with six strong innings, touching 99.6 mph. He followed by hitting a home run in each of his next three games.

Shohei Ohtani hit 22 home runs at the plate and recorded a 3.31 ERA on the mound.

VICTOR DECOLONGON/GETTY IMAGES

And then he delivered his coup de grace, taking a perfect game into the seventh inning in his first home start and finishing with seven scoreless frames, one hit allowed and 12 strikeouts.

It was a statement. Yes, it was possible to excel as a pitcher and a hitter at the same time. And yes, Ohtani was the man to do it.

There is understandable skepticism Ohtani can hold up long-term with such a dual workload. That sentiment was amplified when Ohtani had Tommy John surgery after the season. Then again, there was skepticism that anyone could excel as both a pitcher and hitter in the today's majors for any extended capacity, and Ohtani did so spectacularly.

With an exhilarating rookie season, Ohtani lived up to the hype. He pitched like an ace and hit like an All-Star, and reset the standard for what is, in fact, achievable in the game today.

PREVIOUS ROY WINNERS

2008: Geovany Soto, C, Cubs
2009: Andrew McCutchen, OF, Pirates
2010: Jason Heyward, OF, Braves
2011: Jeremy Hellickson, RHP, Rays
2012: Mike Trout, OF, Angels
2013: Jose Fernandez, RHP, Marlins
2014: Jose Abreu, 1B, White Sox
2015: Kris Bryant, 3B, Cubs
2016: Corey Seager, SS, Dodgers
2017: Aaron Judge, OF, Yankees
Full list: BaseballAmerica.com/awards

CONTINUED FROM PAGE 11

White Sox to join Kirby Puckett and Carew as the only Twins players to reach 2,000 hits. Mauer, 35, has endured some trying times in the latter stages of his eight-year, $184 million contract with the Twins. But for one night, he enjoyed nothing but love and adulation from an appreciative crowd at Target Field as the "Mauer Meter" flipped from 1,999 to 2,000.

Two other hitting contemporaries added some big, fat numbers to their portfolios. Milwaukee's Ryan Braun notched his 1,000th career RBI with a pinch-hit homer against the Marlins, and Miguel Cabrera became the 30th player to reach 550 doubles with a two-bagger against Baltimore on April 19. Cabrera had season-ending surgery to repair a ruptured left biceps tendon in June, leaving him with 2,676 hits and some work to do in his pursuit of 3,000.

Pitchers joined in the fun, as well. Justin Verlander recorded his 200th career victory and notched his 2,500th strikeout with a whiff of the Angels' Shohei Ohtani. Bartolo Colon, still pumping fastballs at age 45, accompanied Verlander into the 2,500-strikeout fraternity and beat the Kansas City Royals on June 18 for his 244th career win. With the victory, Colon passed Hall of Famer Juan Marichal and became the winningest pitcher ever from the Dominican Republic. Six weeks later, the man known as "Big Sexy" passed Dennis Martinez of Nicaragua and become the all-time leader for wins by a Latin American pitcher.

"It was a long journey, but it finally came and it feels good," said Colon, who beat Felix Hernandez and the Mariners to pass Martinez, aka "El Presidente."

No pitcher enjoyed a more milestone-laden season than Washington's Max Scherzer, who added some traditional and not-so-common flourishes to his portfolio. "Mad Max" joined Randy Johnson as the second pitcher in history to strike out 250 or more batters in six consecutive seasons, while becoming the 17th pitcher since 1900 to record 300 strikeouts in a season.

Two AL West closers went above and beyond the call of duty. Oakland's Blake Treinen became the first pitcher ever to surpass 100 strikeouts and 30 saves with an ERA below 1.00. Seattle's Edwin Diaz, at 24, became the 16th pitcher to record 50 saves and the youngest ever to achieve the feat.

Bryce Harper's Star Turn

Bryce Harper arrived at spring training with plenty of buzz and little to say. Harper entered the 2018 season in the throes of his free agent walk year, and he promptly made it clear that any discussion of future plans or $400 million contracts was off limits. He advised reporters to address any questions to his agent, Scott Boras, and said he was going to be "walking right out the door" if anyone strayed from that directive.

For much of the season, Harper performed like a player who was either pressing, preoccupied with his future or intent on hitting home runs to enhance his value. He arrived at the All-Star Game with 23 homers, a .214 batting average and 102 strikeouts in 327 at-bats. Harper joined Matt Kemp and Nick Markakis in the NL's starting outfield, but his selection was more a tribute to

NATIONAL LEAGUE STANDINGS

East	W	L	PCT	GB	Manager	General Manager	Attendance	Average	Last Penn.
Atlanta Braves	90	72	.556	—	Brian Snitker	Alex Anthopulos	2,555,781	31,553	1999
Washington Nationals	82	80	.506	8	Dave Martinez	Mike Rizzo	2,529,604	31,620	Never
Philadelphia Phillies	80	82	.494	10	Gabe Kapler	Matt Klentak	2,158,124	27,318	2009
New York Mets	77	85	.475	13	Mickey Callaway	Sandy Alderson	2,224,995	28,164	2015
Miami Marlins	63	98	.391	26½	Don Mattingly	Michael Hill	811,104	10,014	2003

Central	W	L	PCT	GB	Manager	General Manager	Attendance	Average	Last Penn.
Milwaukee Brewers	96	67	.589	—	Craig Counsell	David Stearns	2,850,875	35,196	1982 (AL)
Chicago Cubs	95	68	.583	1	Joe Maddon	Jed Hoyer	3,181,089	38,794	2016
St. Louis Cardinals	88	74	.543	7½	M. Matheny/M. Shildt	Mike Girsch	3,403,587	42,020	2013
Pittsburgh Pirates	82	79	.509	13	Clint Hurdle	Neal Huntington	1,465,544	18,786	1979
Cincinnati Reds	67	95	.414	28½	B. Price/J. Riggleman	D. Williams/N. Krall	1,629,356	20,116	1990

West	W	L	PCT	GB	Manager	General Manager	Attendance	Average	Last Penn.
Los Angeles Dodgers	92	71	.564	—	Dave Roberts	Farhan Zaidi	3,857,500	47,043	2018
Colorado Rockies	91	72	.558	1	Bud Black	Jeff Bridich	3,015,880	37,233	2007
Arizona Diamondbacks	82	80	.506	9½	Torey Lovullo	Mike Hazen	2,242,695	27,688	2001
San Francisco Giants	73	89	.451	18½	Bruce Bochy	Bobby Evans	3,156,185	38,965	2014
San Diego Padres	66	96	.407	25½	Andy Green	A.J. Preller	2,168,536	26,772	1998

Wild Card Game: Rockies defeated Cubs. **Division Series:** Brewers defeated Rockies 3-0 and Dodgers defeated Braves 3-1 in best-of-five series. **Championship Series:** Dodgers defeated Brewers 4-3 in a best-of-seven series.

his name recognition and a weak field than his production.

In a bow to sentimentality, Harper acknowledged the support of Washington fans and took part in the Home Run Derby for the first time in his career. Whether it was the excitement of the moment or simply a matter of time, the event brought out the best in him.

Harper chose his father, Ron, as his Derby pitcher, and he came adorned in patriotic garb from head to toe. He wore a bandana styled after the Washington, D.C., flag, a red, white and blue compression sleeve and wrist band and color-coordinated socks. His bat even came in patriotic colors and bore the inscription "We the People" on the barrel.

Harper fed off the crowd of 43,698 and eliminated Freddie Freeman and Max Muncy by identical scores of 13-12 in the first two rounds. When his turn came around in the final round, the event had ascended to full-fledged baseball theatre. A camera caught Harper skipping down the runway and bounding up the steps like Rocky Balboa, and the crowd erupted when he emerged to take aim at Cubs outfielder Kyle Schwarber.

On the verge of an anticlimactic ending, the Harpers began a furious comeback. Down 18-9 to in the final round, Bryce went deep nine times in a span of 10 swings to tie it at the end of regulation. Then he drove Ron's second pitch of bonus time over the fence in center field to win the event. Teammates Sean Doolittle and Max Scherzer came out and handed him the Home Run Derby trophy, and manager Dave Martinez lifted him off the ground in a mammoth bear hug.

"It's unbelievable," Harper said. "We have some of the best fans in baseball, and to be able to do that with my family out there, that's an incredible moment—not only for me, but for the organization and Nationals fans. I'm very blessed and humbled."

Harper's power display provided a fitting lead-in to the main event. On game day, Mike Trout and Aaron Judge got things rolling with early solo shots. The teams combined for an All-Star Game record 10 home runs while striking out 25 times in the American League's 8-6 victory.

All those whiffs and trots were interspersed with some entertaining glimpses of players letting down their hair and engaging with fans on TV. Matt Kemp, Charlie Blackmon, Francisco Lindor, Trout and Harper were among the players miked up for the national TV broadcast. Trout, Judge and Mookie Betts posed for group selfies during an early pitching change. And during one juncture

Bryce Harper won the 2018 Home Run Derby in front of 43,698 fans at Nationals Park.

ROB CARR/GETTY IMAGES

early in the event, Cleveland pitcher Trevor Bauer took to his Twitter account and marveled at the parade of pitchers lighting up the radar gun.

"I love it," Lindor said. "This is a show. We are entertainers. People want to see home runs. People want to see strikeouts. They also want to feel they're in the dugout with us or out at shortstop with me. Having the (microphone) on and being able to interact with guys on the field, that was awesome."

The Great Divide

In recent years, more rebuilding teams have followed the lead of the Astros, Cubs and Nationals. Rather than make incremental changes and muddle along at .500, they've opted to sell off veterans, rebuild through the draft and international signings and hope the fan base would embrace the long-term vision and accept the short-term pain of a 100-loss season.

With multiple teams embracing that approach in 2018, the gap between the haves and have-nots in the American League was startling.

At the top of the food chain, the Boston Red Sox, Houston Astros and New York Yankees became the first trio of teams from the same league to record triple-digit victories. The Indians weren't quite as dominant, but they won the American League Central title by 13 games over the Twins and became the first big-league club to clinch a postseason berth.

The Red Sox were led by versatile right fielder Mookie Betts and outfielder/DH J.D. Martinez,

ALL-ROOKIE TEAM 2018

Pos	Player, Team	Age	AB	AVG	OBP	SLG	2B	HR	RBI	SB	Rundown
C	Jorge Alfaro, Phillies	25	344	.262	.324	.407	16	10	37	3	Ranked eighth among MLB catchers with .262 average
1B	Luke Voit, Cardinals/Yankees	27	143	.322	.398	.671	5	15	36	0	Led MLB hitters (min. 150 PA) with .350 isolated slugging
2B	Joey Wendle, Rays	28	487	.300	.354	.435	33	7	61	16	Led all rookies in average (.300) and triples (six)
3B	Miguel Andujar, Yankees	23	573	.297	.328	.527	47	27	92	2	Led all rookies with 170 hits and 92 RBIs
SS	Gleyber Torres, Yankees	21	431	.271	.340	.480	16	24	77	6	Hit over .300 in his final 40 games of the season
CF	Harrison Bader, Cardinals	24	379	.264	.334	.422	20	12	37	15	His 29.9 ft/sec sprint speed was eighth-fastest in MLB
OF	Ronald Acuna Jr., Braves	20	433	.293	.366	.552	26	26	64	16	Set a franchise record with eight leadoff home runs
OF	Juan Soto, Nationals	19	414	.292	.406	.517	25	22	70	5	Highest OBP (.406) by a teenager in MLB history
DH	Shohei Ohtani, Angels	23	326	.285	.361	.564	21	22	61	10	Also went 4-2, 3.31 with 63 SO in 52 IP as a pitcher

Pos	Pitcher, Team	Age	W	L	SV	ERA	IP	SO	BB	Rundown
SP	Walker Buehler, Dodgers	23	8	5	0	2.62	137	151	37	Led rookie starters in ERA (2.68); allowed 13 ER in final 12 starts
SP	Jack Flaherty, Cardinals	22	8	9	0	3.34	151	182	59	Led rookie starters in SO (182), finished fourth in ERA (3.34)
SP	Brad Keller, Royals	22	9	6	0	3.08	140	96	50	Ranked third among rookie starters in ERA (3.08)
SP	Jaime Barria, Angels	21	10	9	0	3.41	129	98	47	Led Angels starters in both wins (10) and ERA (3.41)
SP	Dereck Rodriguez, Giants	26	6	4	0	2.81	118	89	36	Allowed two earned runs or less in 13 of his 19 starts
RP	Seranthony Dominguez, Phillies	23	2	5	16	2.95	58	74	22	Led the Phillies—and all rookies—with 16 saves

who validated the team's $110 million investment by making a serious run at the Triple Crown. The Red Sox captured the AL East title by eight games over the Yankees, who posted a 100-62 record and launched 267 home runs to break the previous record of 264 held by the 1997 Seattle Mariners. The turning point in the season came in early August, when the Red Sox outscored the Yankees 28-13 in a four-game sweep at Fenway Park.

The Astros survived lengthy, injury-related absences by Jose Altuve, Carlos Correa and George Springer to outlast the Oakland Athletics, who staged a second-half surge to overtake Seattle and make the postseason for the first time since 2014. Justin Verlander and Gerrit Cole were a formidable 1-2 punch at the top of the rotation, and third baseman Alex Bregman emerged as a star on the field and a social media sensation.

Cleveland benefited from a lack of competition in a depleted AL Central division. The Indians' 91-71 record was fueled by an aggregate 49-27 mark against divisional competitors Minnesota, Detroit, Chicago and Kansas City. Nevertheless, the Indians recorded some impressive signature achievements at the plate and on the mound. Corey Kluber, Carlos Carrasco, Trevor Bauer and Mike Clevinger became the first foursome to notch 200-strikeout seasons for the same team, while Francisco Lindor and Jose Ramirez became the first teammates to reach 80 extra-base hits in consecutive seasons since Joe DiMaggio and Lou Gehrig did it for the 1936-37 Yankees.

At the bottom of the food chain, the Baltimore Orioles were the epitome of ineptitude. Before spring training, the O's added free-agent starters Alex Cobb, Andrew Cashner and Chris Tillman in an attempt to make a run at a playoff spot. An 8-20 record in March and April set the tone, and

the Orioles finished the season with a franchise record 114 losses. It was an especially rough season for Chris Davis, whose .168 batting average was the lowest in history by a hitter who qualified for the batting title.

The Kansas City Royals posted a 58-104 record a mere three years after winning the World Series. Eric Hosmer and Lorenzo Cain moved on through free agency, and general manager Dayton Moore sent Mike Moustakas to Milwaukee at the trade deadline. Infielder Whit Merrifield led the majors with 192 hits and 45 stolen bases and was a bright spot for manager Ned Yost's squad.

A Mad Scramble

The only real stretch run drama in baseball played out in the National League, where multiple teams jockeyed for position all the way to the final weekend.

Two division races came down to a one-game tiebreaker. Los Angeles and Colorado posted identical 91-71 records in the NL West, and the Dodgers claimed the title with a 5-2 victory in game 163. In the NL Central, Milwaukee and Chicago finished in a 95-67 regular season deadlock before the Brewers beat the Cubs, 3-1, in a tiebreaker. The Cubs made the playoffs for the fourth straight season before falling 2-1 in 13 innings to the Rockies in the NL Wild Card Game.

The Braves, considered a year away from contention by many observers, bumped up the timetable thanks to an array of contributions from veterans and young players. Shortly after the team's postseason exit against Los Angeles in the NLDS, the Braves signed manager Brian Snitker to a two-year contract extension.

The Mets, who were expected to be in the thick of the race because of their starting pitching, stumbled badly after an 11-1 start and were never a factor. But they received exceptional work from Jacob deGrom, who established himself as the NL Cy Young frontrunner despite just 10 wins. DeGrom set a major league record when he held opponents to three runs or fewer in 29 straight starts. He also became the first pitcher since 1900 to finish with a sub-2.00 ERA, at least 260 strikeouts, 50 or fewer walks and 10 home runs allowed.

In the Central, the Brewers reaped the benefits of a historically active day on Jan. 25, when they signed free agent Lorenzo Cain to a five-year, $80 million contract and acquired Christian Yelich from the Miami Marlins in a five-player trade. The two outfielders provided leadership in the clubhouse and clutch hitting and on-base ability at the top of the order.

The Cubs failed to get much of anything from Yu Darvish, who contributed a mere 40 innings in the first year of a six-year, $126 million contract. Javier Baez played magnificently at multiple positions to inject himself into the MVP debate, but the offense stalled down the stretch and the Cubs' season ended in disappointment. St. Louis put on a second-half surge after replacing manager Mike Matheny with Mike Shildt at the All-Star Game. But the Cardinals followed up a 22-6 August with a 12-15 September to fall short of a postseason berth.

The Arizona Diamondbacks and San Francisco Giants were among baseball's biggest disappointments. The D-backs led the NL West entering the final month, but an 8-19 September ruined their chances of making the postseason. They wasted another strong season by first baseman Paul Goldschmidt, who overcame a dreadful start to hit 33 homers and log a .922 OPS. The Giants brought in Evan Longoria and Andrew McCutchen to supplement their veteran core. But they still finished 14th in the NL in runs, homers and slugging, and they were undermined by a 31-50 record on the road. Worse yet, catcher Buster Posey had hip surgery in late August that necessitated a 6-8 month recovery period.

Among the league's bottom feeders, the Miami Marlins paid the short-term price for trading away Giancarlo Stanton, Christian Yelich, Marcell Ozuna and Dee Gordon in an effort to cut costs under the new Derek Jeter ownership group. The Marlins won 63 games and finished last in the majors with an attendance of 811,104. But the offseason brought reason to hope. In late October, the team signed Cuban outfielder Victor Victor Mesa and his brother, Victor Jr. If management's plan is successful, the Mesa brothers will be the new faces

Jacob deGrom led the majors with a 1.70 ERA in a career-best 2018.

RICH SCHULTZ/GETTY IMAGES

of the franchise for years to come.

Days To Remember

After bottoming out with a .140 batting average in May, St. Louis infielder Matt Carpenter crafted the catchiest comeback narrative of the season. Teammate Adam Wainwright had built him a garden with a variety of fruits and vegetables to cook and can, and Carpenter used many of the ingredients to make his own salsa. With some tomatoes and onions here and a little cilantro and garlic there, he morphed from an automatic out into a home run-hitting, batting glove-free, ERA-decimating machine.

Carpenter's new superpowers were particularly evident the day of July 20, when he took a wrecking ball to the Cubs' pitching staff.

In the signature game of his career, Carpenter homered three times and added two doubles before leaving in the sixth inning of an 18-5 St. Louis victory. Carpenter's 16 total bases tied the franchise record held by Mark Whiten, who hit four homers in a game against Cincinnati in 1993. The carnage could have easily been worse if St. Louis interim manager Mike Shildt hadn't removed Carpenter with St. Louis ahead 15-1 and Cubs infielder Tommy La Stella taking the mound to pitch in the sixth.

Carpenter continued to use the same Marucci maple bat for nine more days until it broke and he sent it to the Hall of Fame in Cooperstown. The Cardinals weren't the only beneficiaries of Carpenter's torrid hitting. T-shirts with the inscription "It's Gotta Be the Salsa" helped raise money for Cardinal Glennon Children's Hospital in St. Louis, and Carpenter was besieged with requests from fellow hitters in search of a salsa pick-me-up.

"I'm getting texts from former teammates and guys on other teams saying, 'Man, you've got to send me some of that stuff,'" he says. "I'm kind of holding all the power to myself right now."

Carpenter injected himself in the NL MVP discussion with his prolonged offensive binge, until a fellow lefty hitter from the NL Central crashed the party. Christian Yelich seized the initiative by hitting .367 with a 1.219 OPS after the all-star break. Yelich's best day came on Aug. 29, when he went 6-for-6 with a cycle in a 13-12 victory over the Reds at Great American Ball Park. He joined Ian Kinsler of the 2009 Rangers, Rondell White of the 1995 Montreal Expos and Bobby Veach of the 1920 Tigers as the fourth player to amass six hits and hit for the cycle in the same game.

"I've never seen a game like that," Brewers manager Craig Counsell said of Yelich's 6-for-6 performance. "It was incredible. He's coming up and you're thinking he can't do it again, and he does it again. He did everything tonight, he really did. He's driving the bus home tonight."

Yelich wasn't done driving the bus. He singled, doubled, tripled and homered against the Reds three weeks later to become the first player to hit for a cycle twice against the same team in one season. He joined Babe Herman of the 1931 Brooklyn Robins and Aaron Hill of the 2012 Arizona Diamondbacks as the third player in the modern era to hit for two cycles in the same year.

"There's been so many great players to play this game," said Yelich. "It just shows how freaky, I guess, that is. A lot of luck goes into that. It's hard enough to get four hits in a Major League Baseball game, yet alone have them all be the right ones and the right sequence."

Every now and then, a pitcher would make a two-way statement. On April 9 against Atlanta, Max Scherzer joined Nolan Ryan as the second pitcher in the live-ball era to throw a shutout, strike out at least 10 batters and steal a base in the same game. Scherzer said he had been lobbying former managers Matt Williams and Dusty Baker for years to let him steal a base. But new Nationals manager Davey Martinez was the first to heed the call.

"I mean, if J-Dub can steal a base, so can I," said Scherzer, in a joking reference to former Nationals

outfielder Jayson Werth.

In a geographical oddity, MLB's three no-hitters in 2018 came in different countries. On April

CONTINUED ON PAGE 19

AMERICAN LEAGUE BEST TOOLS

A Baseball America survey of American League managers, conducted at midseason 2018, ranked players with the best tools.

Best Hitter
1. Mike Trout, Angels
2. Mookie Betts, Red Sox
3. Jose Altuve, Astros

Best Power
1. Aaron Judge, Yankees
2. Giancarlo Stanton, Yankees
3. Mike Trout, Angels

Best Bunter
1. Dee Gordon, Mariners
2. Brett Gardner, Yankees
3. Delino DeShields Jr., Rangers

Best Strike-Zone Judgment
1. Mike Trout, Angels
2. Mookie Betts, Red Sox
3. Jose Ramirez, Indians

Best Hit-And-Run Artist
1. Jose Altuve, Astros
2. Jean Segura, Mariners
3. Andrelton Simmons, Angels

Best Baserunner
1. Dee Gordon, Mariners
2. Mookie Betts, Red Sox
3. Jose Altuve, Astros

Fastest Baserunner
1. Dee Gordon, Mariners
2. Byron Buxton, Twins
3. Delino DeShields Jr., Rangers

Most Exciting Player
1. Mike Trout, Angels
2. Mookie Betts, Red Sox
3. Jose Altuve, Astros

Best Pitcher
1. Chris Sale, White Sox
2. Corey Kluber, Indians
3. Justin Verlander, Astros

Best Fastball
1. Chris Sale, Red Sox
2. Luis Severino, Yankees
3. Aroldis Chapman, Yankees

Best Curveball
1. Corey Kluber, Indians
2. Charlie Morton, Astros
3. Blake Snell, Rays

Best Slider
1. Chris Sale, Red Sox
2. Trevor Bauer, Indians
3. Luis Severino, Yankees

Best Changeup
1. Chris Devenski, Astros
2. Chris Sale, Red Sox
3. Fernando Rodney, Twins

Best Control
1. Corey Kluber, Indians
2. Justin Verlander, Astros
3. Chris Sale, Red Sox

Best Pickoff Move
1. Marco Gonzales, Mariners
2. James Shields, White Sox
3. Dallas Keuchel, Astros

Best Reliever
1. Edwin Diaz, Mariners
2. Craig Kimbrel, Red Sox
3. Aroldis Chapman, Yankees

Best Defensive Catcher
1. Martin Maldonado, Angels
2. Salvador Perez, Royals
3. Mike Zunino, Mariners

Best Defensive 1B
1. Mitch Moreland, Red Sox
2. Matt Olson, Athletics
3. Justin Smoak, Blue Jays

Best Defensive 2B
1. Jose Altuve, Astros
2. Ian Kinsler, Angels
3. Whit Merrifield, Royals

Best Defensive 3B
1. Matt Chapman, Athletics
2. Adrian Beltre, Rangers
3. Kyle Seager, Mariners

Best Defensive SS
1. Andrelton Simmons, Angels
2. Francisco Lindor, Indians
3. Jose Iglesias, Tigers

Best Infield Arm
1. Matt Chapman, Athletics
2. Carlos Correa, Astros
3. Manny Machado, Orioles

Best Defensive OF
1. Jackie Bradley Jr., Red Sox
2. Mookie Betts, Red Sox
3. Mike Trout, Angels

Best Outfield Arm
1. Aaron Judge, Yankees
2. Jackie Bradley Jr., Red Sox
3. Aaron Hicks, Yankees

Best Manager
1. Terry Francona, Indians
2. A.J. Hinch, Astros
3. Alex Cora, Red Sox

ORGANIZATION OF THE YEAR

Brewers' Bold Moves Prove Beneficial

BY TOM HAUDRICOURT

When the Brewers began stripping their roster to embark on a large-scale rebuild in 2015, most people figured it would take four to five years before Milwaukee was competitive again.

As recent examples, the Cubs and Astros endured years of misery before returning to playoff mode. Mindful of those painful years, as well as long rebuilding processes in other cities, David Stearns did not set a timetable for returning to competitiveness when he took over as general manager following the 2015 season, during which the Brewers went 68-94.

"I never even thought about it," Stearns said. "When I got here, we just became so focused on acquiring, developing and retaining as much talent as we possibly could . . ."

Thanks to many astute moves along the way, there would be no protracted, agonizing stretch of losing for the Brewers. They stunned the baseball world in 2018 by wresting the National League Central crown away from the Cubs, sweeping the Rockies in the NL Division Series and battling the Dodgers for seven games before bowing out of the postseason picture in the NL Championship Series.

In becoming so successful in such a short period of time, the Brewers are the Baseball America Organization of the Year in 2018.

"I said at my opening press conference that every situation is unique," said Stearns, who was Houston's assistant GM before joining the Brewers. "I went through (years of losing) in Houston. It's a challenge."

"When I got here in (September) 2015,

David Stearns and the Brewers front office made several bold moves in the offseason.

DYLAN BUELL/GETTY IMAGES

there were a different set of advantages and constraints than some other markets have faced. We tried to focus on the advantages and minimize the constraints."

When the Brewers showed they were ready to go after the Cubs in 2018, Stearns added experienced players such as Mike Moustakas, Jonathan Schoop, Gio Gonzalez and Curtis Granderson.

It hurt to fall one game short of the World Series, but the Brewers had good reason to be satisfied with progress made on the field, which far exceeded the expectations of three years earlier. With a deep, talented core of players, they now appear positioned to succeed for years to come.

"Each year we've taken a step as an organization," Stearns said. "Last year's step certainly informed how we went about the offseason. It informed where we thought our major league team could be and it informed us about the depth we had at the upper levels of our organization, the players who could potentially contribute at the major league level this year."

Yes, you can completely rebuild in three years. As Exhibit A, please see the 2018 Milwaukee Brewers.

PREVIOUS WINNERS

2008: Tampa Bay Rays
2009: Philadelphia Phillies
2010: San Francisco Giants
2011: St. Louis Cardinals
2012: Cincinnati Reds
2013: St. Louis Cardinals
2014: Kansas City Royals
2015: Pittsburgh Pirates
2016: Chicago Cubs
2017: Los Angeles Dodgers
Full list: BaseballAmerica.com/awards

21 at Oakland Coliseum, the Athletics' Sean Manaea struck out 10 batters to vanquish the Boston Red Sox 10-0. Manaea caught a break in the sixth inning when Red Sox outfielder Andrew Benintendi beat out a weak grounder for a hit, but was ruled out after the umpires determined that he had gone outside the base path to a avoid a tag by Oakland first baseman Matt Olson.

On May 4 in Monterrey, Mexico, Dodgers pitchers Walker Buehler, Tony Cingrani, Yimi Garcia and Adam Liberatore threw the 12th combined no-hitter in history in a 4-0 victory over the San Diego Padres. Seattle's James Paxton completed the geographical hat trick four days later in a 5-0 victory over the Blue Jays at Rogers Centre in Toronto. Paxton, a British Columbia native, joined Dick Fowler of the 1945 Phillies as the second Canadian-born pitcher to throw a no-hitter in the big leagues.

The best starting pitcher game score—a 100—was recorded by Houston's Gerrit Cole when he struck out 16 batters in an 8-0 victory over the D-Backs. Chris Owings' fifth-inning double was the only hit off Cole, whose only other blemish was a walk to David Peralta. "I think it would have been the same outcome if any team in the league would have faced him today," said Astros shortstop Carlos Correa. "He was just filthy. Hitting the spots, every pitch was working. There is no plan that could work against him today."

In a season notable for strikeouts, some pitchers generated more than their share of dead air. Milwaukee reliever Josh Hader, who averaged a mind-boggling 15.8 strikeouts per nine innings, whiffed eight Cincinnati Reds in 2.2 innings on April 30. Hader became to first pitcher in history to strike out eight batters in an outing of less than three innings.

Colorado's German Marquez was similarly dominant in a late-season game against the Phillies, tying a major-league record by striking out the first eight batters he faced. Philadelphia starter Nick Pivetta broke the streak with a comebacker to the mound, and Marquez was so caught off guard that he threw wildly to first base—allowing Pivetta to reach on an error.

A Hall Of Fame Class For The Ages

An estimated 53,500 fans packed the field at the Clark Sports Center in Cooperstown, N.Y., for a perennial highlight of the baseball season. It was the second largest induction day crowd in Hall of Fame history—surpassed only by the 2007 cer-

emony featuring Cal Ripken Jr. and Tony Gwynn. The stage was packed, as well. Chipper Jones,

CONTINUED ON PAGE 21

NATIONAL LEAGUE BEST TOOLS

A Baseball America survey of National League managers, conducted at midseason 2017, ranked players with the best tools.

Best Hitter
1. Freddie Freeman, Braves
2. Joey Votto, Reds
3. Paul Goldschmidt, D-backs

Best Power
1. Bryce Harper, Nationals
2. Nolan Arenado, Rockies
3. Jesus Aguilar, Brewers

Best Bunter
1. Cesar Hernandez, Phillies
2. Ender Inciarte, Braves
3. Jose Peraza, Reds

Best Strike-Zone Judgment
1. Joey Votto, Reds
2. Freddie Freeman, Braves
3. Carlos Santana, Phillies

Best Hit-And-Run Artist
1. D.J. LeMahieu, Rockies
2. Jose Peraza, Reds
3. Cesar Hernandez, Phillies

Best Baserunner
1. Trea Turner, Nationals
2. Billy Hamilton, Reds
3. Javier Baez, Cubs

Fastest Baserunner
1. Billy Hamilton, Reds
2. Trea Turner, Nationals
3. Ronald Acuna Jr., Braves

Most Exciting Player
1. Javier Baez, Cubs
2. Ozzie Albies, Braves
3. Nolan Arenado, Rockies

Best Pitcher
1. Max Scherzer, Nationals
2. Jacob deGrom, Mets
3. Clayton Kershaw, Dodgers

Best Fastball
1. Jordan Hicks, Cardinals
2. Noah Syndergaard, Mets
3. Max Scherzer, Nationals

Best Curveball
1. Clayton Kershaw, Dodgers
2. Ross Stripling, Dodgers
3. Stephen Strasburg, Nationals

Best Slider
1. Max Scherzer, Nationals
2. Patrick Corbin, D-backs
3. Jacob deGrom, Mets

Best Changeup
1. Kyle Hendricks, Cubs
2. Stephen Strasburg, Nationals
3. Max Scherzer, Nationals

Best Control
1. Zack Greinke, D-backs
2. Jacob deGrom, Mets
3. Miles Mikolas, Cardinals

Best Pickoff Move
1. Eric Lauer, Padres
2. Julio Teheran, Braves
3. Clayton Richard, Padres

Best Reliever
1. Josh Hader, Brewers
2. Sean Doolittle, Nationals
3. Kenley Jansen, Dodgers

Best Defensive Catcher
1. Buster Posey, Giants
2. Austin Hedges, Padres
3. Yasmani Grandal, Dodgers

Best Defensive 1B
1. Paul Goldschmidt, D-backs
2. Freddie Freeman, Braves
3. Anthony Rizzo, Cubs

Best Defensive 2B
1. D.J. LeMahieu, Rockies
2. Javier Baez, Cubs
3. Ozzie Albies, Braves

Best Defensive 3B
1. Nolan Arenado, Rockies
2. Anthony Rendon, Nationals
3. Johan Camargo, Braves

Best Defensive SS
1. Brandon Crawford, Giants
2. Nick Ahmed, D-backs
3. Trea Turner, Nationals

Best Infield Arm
1. Javier Baez, Cubs
2. Nolan Arenado, Rockies
3. Brandon Crawford, Giants

Best Defensive OF
1. Ender Inciarte, Braves
2. Lorenzo Cain, Brewers
3. Billy Hamilton, Reds

Best Outfield Arm
1. Jason Heyward, Cubs
2. Yasiel Puig, Dodgers
3. Hunter Renfroe, Padres

Best Manager
1. Craig Counsell, Brewers
2. Joe Maddon, Cubs
3. Dave Roberts, Dodgers

DYLAN BUELL/GETTY IMAGES

JIM MCISAAC/GETTY IMAGES

Mookie Betts posted an MLB-best .346 batting average in 2018.

Blake Snell led all MLB pitchers with 21 wins in 2018.

FIRST TEAM

Pos.	Player, Team	AVG	OBP	SLG	AB	R	H	2B	3B	HR	RBI	BB	SO	SB	CS
C	J.T. Realmuto, Marlins	.277	.340	.484	477	74	132	30	3	21	74	38	104	3	2
1B	Freddie Freeman, Braves	.309	.388	.505	618	94	191	44	4	23	98	76	132	10	3
2B	Javier Baez, Cubs	.290	.326	.554	606	101	176	40	9	34	111	29	167	21	9
3B	Jose Ramirez, Indians	.270	.387	.552	578	110	156	38	4	39	105	106	80	34	6
SS	Manny Machado, Orioles/Dodgers	.297	.367	.538	632	84	188	35	3	37	107	70	104	14	2
OF	Christian Yelich, Brewers	.326	.402	.598	574	118	187	34	7	36	110	68	135	22	4
OF	Mike Trout, Angels	.312	.460	.628	471	101	147	24	4	39	79	122	124	24	2
OF	Mookie Betts, Red Sox	.346	.438	.640	520	129	180	47	5	32	80	81	91	30	6
DH	J.D. Martinez, Red Sox	.333	.402	.629	569	111	188	37	2	43	130	69	146	6	1

Pos.	Player, Team	W	L	ERA	G	GS	SV	IP	H	R	ER	HR	BB	SO	WHIP
SP	Jacob deGrom, Mets	10	9	1.70	32	32	0	217	152	48	41	10	46	269	0.91
SP	Max Scherzer, Nationals	18	7	2.53	33	33	0	221	150	66	62	23	51	300	0.91
SP	Justin Verlander, Astros	16	9	2.52	34	34	0	214	152	63	60	28	37	290	0.90
SP	Blake Snell, Rays	21	5	1.89	31	31	0	181	112	41	38	16	64	221	0.97
SP	Aaron Nola, Phillies	17	6	2.39	33	33	0	212	149	57	56	17	58	224	0.97
RP	Blake Treinen, Athletics	9	2	0.78	68	0	38	80	46	12	7	2	21	100	0.83

SECOND TEAM

Pos.	Player, Team	AVG	OBP	SLG	AB	R	H	2B	3B	HR	RBI	BB	SO	SB	CS
C	Wilson Ramos, Rays/Phillies	.306	.358	.487	382	39	117	22	1	15	70	32	80	0	0
1B	Paul Goldschmidt, D-backs	.290	.389	.533	593	95	172	35	5	33	83	90	173	7	4
2B	Whit Merrifield, Royals	.304	.367	.438	632	88	192	43	3	12	60	61	114	45	10
3B	Alex Bregman, Astros	.286	.394	.532	594	105	170	51	1	31	103	96	85	10	4
SS	Francisco Lindor, Indians	.277	.352	.519	661	129	183	42	2	38	92	70	107	25	10
OF	Ronald Acuna Jr., Braves	.293	.366	.552	433	78	127	26	4	26	64	45	123	16	5
OF	Lorenzo Cain, Brewers	.308	.395	.417	539	90	166	25	2	10	38	71	94	30	7
OF	Aaron Judge, Yankees	.278	.392	.528	413	77	115	22	0	27	67	76	152	6	3
DH	Khris Davis, Athletics	.247	.326	.549	576	98	142	28	1	48	123	59	175	0	0

Pos.	Player, Team	W	L	ERA	G	GS	SV	IP	H	R	ER	HR	BB	SO	WHIP
SP	Trevor Bauer, Indians	12	6	2.21	28	27	1	175	134	51	43	9	57	221	1.09
SP	Chris Sale, Red Sox	12	4	2.11	27	27	0	158	102	39	37	11	34	237	0.86
SP	Gerrit Cole, Astros	15	5	2.88	32	32	0	200	143	68	64	19	64	276	1.03
SP	Kyle Freeland, Rockies	17	7	2.85	33	33	0	202	182	64	64	17	70	173	1.25
SP	Mike Foltynewicz, Braves	13	10	2.85	31	31	0	183	130	65	58	17	68	202	1.08
RP	Edwin Diaz, Mariners	0	4	1.96	73	0	57	73	41	17	16	5	17	124	0.79

EXECUTIVE OF THE YEAR

Dave Dombrowski

ADAM GLANZMAN/GETTY IMAGES

When Dave Dombrowski was hired by the Red Sox in 2015, he inherited a team with an excellent young core, but one that had also finished last in their division in three of four years.

Displaying the boldness that has long been his template, Dombrowski showed little reluctance to trade prospects for productive big leaguers. He used the farm system to acquire reliever Craig Kimbrel and Chris Sale. That's what Dombrowski does. And it's worked.

Not only did the Red Sox win the World Series, they also have finished first in the division three straight years under Dombrowski. They had won the pennant three times in the previous 20 seasons before Dombrowski arrived.

PREVIOUS WINNERS

2008: Theo Epstein, Red Sox
2009: Dan O'Dowd, Rockies
2010: Jon Daniels, Rangers
2011: Doug Melvin, Brewers
2012: Billy Beane, Athletics
2013: Dan Duquette, Orioles
2014: Dan Duquette, Orioles
2015: Sandy Alderson, Mets
2016: Chris Antonetti, Indians
2017: Brian Cashman, Yankees

Full list: BaseballAmerica.com/awards

MANAGER OF THE YEAR

Bob Melvin

KELLY GAVIN/GETTY IMAGES

When you lead a band of underdog rebels, you have to be a little different. You must be creative, flexible and adapt quickly to the changes around you.

Bob Melvin is just that way.

The perfect manager for an imperfect team. The A's have an outdated ballpark and a tiny payroll. The Athletics cannot outbid others for top free agents. They must build from within and find a few bargains.

Melvin did all that in 2018. With one of the lowest payrolls in baseball and a rotation in physical collapse, he guided the A's into the postseason. The A's finished 97-65 to earn the second AL wild card despite losing nearly all their Opening Day starting pitchers to injuries.

PREVIOUS WINNERS

2008: Ron Gardenhire, Twins
2009: Mike Scioscia, Angels
2010: Bobby Cox, Braves
2011: Joe Maddon, Rays
2012: Buck Showalter, Orioles
2013: Clint Hurdle, Pirates
2014: Buck Showalter, Orioles
2015: Joe Maddon, Cubs
2016: Terry Francona, Indians
2017: A.J. Hinch, Astros

Full list: BaseballAmerica.com/awards

CONTINUED FROM PAGE 19

Jim Thome, Trevor Hoffman and Vladimir Guerrero matched the monster class of 2015, when Randy Johnson, Pedro Martinez, Craig Biggio and John Smoltz made it to Cooperstown as a quartet. They were joined by former Detroit Tigers teammates Alan Trammell and Jack Morris, who made it in through the Modern Baseball Era Committee.

Jones, an eight-time all-star with the Atlanta Braves and one of the greatest switch-hitters in history, led the way with 97.2 percent of the vote. He received permission to give the first speech of the day because his wife, Taylor, was due to give birth at any moment. Appropriately enough, Chipper and Taylor Jones named the boy "Cooper."

Jones made multiple references in his speech to Mickey Mantle, a longtime hero of his father.

Jones told the story of the first time he met Mantle in 1992 at a card show in Gwinnett, Ga., and was so nervous that he practiced his introduction in front of a mirror.

"I was still so tongue-tied," Jones said, "and eventually I got the courage to carry on a conversation. I asked him, 'Mick, you ever get tired of this [fame]? He said, 'Chipper, I have a recurring dream. I'm standing at the pearly gates, and I must have had a worried look on my face, when God looked at me and said, 'Don't worry, Mick. You'll get in. But, hey, before that, can you please sign these dozen baseballs?'"

Thome, eighth on MLB's career list with 612 home runs, wiped away tears after his daughter, Lila, sang the national anthem to begin the ceremony. He proceeded to give a flawless and eloquent speech that was the product of months of practice. Thome was so intent on getting it right that he traveled to Cooperstown in early July and delivered his speech before a lectern to an empty field.

Hoffman logged 601 career saves, second most in history to the Yankees' Mariano Rivera. He paid tribute to all-time Padres favorites Tony Gwynn and Jerry Coleman in his speech, asked his former teammates in the crowd to stand up and be recognized by the crowd, and shared inspirational quotes from longtime UCLA basketball coach John Wooden.

Guerrero, a nine-time all-star outfielder batted .318 with 449 homers and 1,496 RBIs and is the first player inducted wearing the cap of the Angels. A man of few words during his playing career, Guerrero gave a five-minute speech with Angels broadcaster Jose Mota serving as his interpreter. Several hundred fans waved Dominican flags in tribute.

Trammell played shortstop for 20 seasons—all with Detroit—and earned six All-Star Game selections, four Gold Glove Awards and three Silver Slugger Awards. His .977 fielding percentage ranks sixth among shortstops with at least 2,000 games played.

Trammell formed a stellar double play combination with Lou Whitaker, who was in the audience on a special day for Tigers fans.

"For 19 years Lou Whitaker and I formed the longest-running double play combination in the history of baseball," Trammell said. "Lou, it was an honor and a pleasure to have played alongside you all those years. I hope someday you'll be up here, too."

Morris, known as a ferocious competitor during an 18-year run with the Tigers and three other clubs, showed a softer, more emotional side in his speech.

"I believe in the human heart and human spirit, and no analytics can define them" Morris told the crowd in Cooperstown. "There is no telling what you can accomplish if you have the will and desire to try. God blessed me with a gift, and it was meant to be shared with others. My life in baseball has been an incredible journey, and I am grateful for everything."

Farewells

From the moment Adam Jones arrived in Baltimore via a 2008 trade with the Mariners, he strived to be more than just a name on the lineup card. Jones consistently took the field through injuries and fatigue. He ran out every groundball as if it were his last. And he immersed himself in the community and tried to make a difference

Vladimir Guerrero was one of six players inducted into the Hall of Fame in 2018.

beyond the field. When Jones wasn't serving as the face of the team during periods of racial strife in the city, he was donating tens of thousands of dollars to the local Boys & Girls Clubs.

As Jones' time at Camden Yards grew short, Baltimore baseball fans rose en masse to show their appreciation.

Manager Buck Showalter sent Jones out to right field alone in the top of the ninth inning of a 4-0 victory over Houston in the Orioles' season finale. With 24,916 fans standing and cheering in the stands, Jones acknowledged the love. Joey Rickard came out to replace him, and Jones hugged Rickard and Houston first base coach Alex Cintron before retiring to the dugout and meeting a welcoming committee of teammates.

Jones, in the final year of a five-year, $85 million contract, finished the 2018 season near the top of the leader board in multiple offensive categories for the Orioles. His 263 home runs through 2018 place him fifth on the franchise's career list behind Cal Ripken Jr., Eddie Murray, Boog Powell and Brooks Robinson.

The day before Jones' farewell, David Wright was treated to a similarly heartfelt ceremony at Citi Field. Wright appeared to be on a Hall of Fame track at age 30 before a series of neck, back and shoulder problems limited him to 77 games and a total of 291 at-bats from 2015 through 2018.

In the next-to-last day of the Mets' season, Wright started at third base and went 0-for-1

CONTINUED ON PAGE 24

Bregman, Springer Push AL to 8-6 Win

BY KYLE GLASER

George Springer

ROB CARR/GETTY IMAGES

This is what happens when you hit on your first-round picks. They win games for you. They carry you to the postseason. They represent your franchise glamorously on a national stage.

Alex Bregman and George Springer, again and again, keep doing all of that for the Astros.

Bregman and Springer hit back-to-back home runs in the 10th inning, lifting the American League to an 8-6 victory over the National League in an All-Star slugfest at Nationals Park.

Bregman, the Astros' top pick in 2015, hit the walk-off RBI single to win Game 5 of the World Series last October and was named All-Star Game MVP for hitting the tiebreaking home run on Tuesday. Springer, the Astros first rounder in 2011, won World Series MVP last fall and was responsible for the decisive blast in extras in the All-Star Game.

Again and again, the first-rounders keep delivering on the big stage.

"It never ceases to amaze me with how controlled he is in the big moments, in any game," American League and Astros manager A.J. Hinch said of Bregman. "In any pressure situation . . . He obviously loves the moment. His heartbeat is perfect and so is his execution at the big moments."

Winning MVP in the nation's capital held special meaning for Bregman. His grandfather was general counsel for the Washington Senators. His dad grew up in Washington as a child knowing Ted Williams.

So winning what is officially known as the Ted Williams All-Star Game MVP Award was a particular highlight in the 24-year-old's career, and one he will treasure.

"My dad grew up on Ted Williams' lap, so to see Ted Williams Most Valuable Player on this trophy is pretty special," Bregman said. "He showed me a picture of Ted Williams and him…. I looked at that picture for 10 years growing up and my dad . . . always told me 'You've got to be the next guy to hit .400 in the big leagues' always."

ALL-STAR GAME

2018 ALL-STAR GAME

JULY 17, 2018
AMERICAN LEAGUE 8,
NATIONAL LEAGUE 6

American	AB	R	H	RBI	National	AB	R	H	RBI
Betts, RF	3	0	0	0	Baez, 2B	3	0	1	0
Brantley, LF	2	0	1	1	Albies, 2B	1	0	0	0
Altuve, 2B	3	0	1	0	Gennett, PH-2B	1	1	1	2
Lowrie, 2B	2	0	0	0	Arenado, 3B	2	0	0	0
Trout, CF	2	1	1	1	Suarez, 3B	1	0	0	0
Haniger, RF	2	0	0	0	Goldschmidt, DH	1	0	0	0
Martinez, DH	2	0	1	0	Molina, PH	1	0	0	0
Cruz, PH	0	0	0	0	Aguilar, PH	2	0	0	0
Choo, PH	2	1	1	0	Freeman, 1B	2	0	0	0
Ramirez, 3B	2	0	0	0	Votto, 1B	3	1	1	1
Bregman, PH-3B	3	1	1	1	Kemp, LF	2	0	1	0
Judge, LF	2	1	1	1	Yelich, LF	3	1	1	1
Springer, CF	2	2	2	1	Harper, CF	2	0	0	0
Machado, SS	2	0	0	0	Blackmon, CF	3	0	0	0
Lindor, PH-SS	1	0	0	0	Markakis, RF	1	0	0	0
Segura, PH-SS	2	2	2	3	Cain, RF	3	0	0	0
Abreu, 1B	2	0	0	0	Crawford, SS	2	0	0	0
Moreland, 1B	3	0	2	0	Story, SS	2	1	1	1
Perez, C	2	0	0	0	Contreras, C	2	1	1	1
Gomes, C	3	0	0	0	Realmuto, C	0	1	0	0
Totals	**42**	**8**	**13**	**8**	**Totals**	**37**	**6**	**7**	**6**

2B: Kemp (1, Severino). **HR:** Judge (1, Scherzer, 2nd inn, 0 on, 0 outs); Trout (1, deGrom, 3rd inn, 0 on, 2 outs); Segura (1, Hader, 8th inn, 2 on, 1 out); Bregman (1, Stripling, 10th inn, 0 on, 0 outs); Springer (1, Stripling, 10th inn, 0 on, 0 outs); Contreras (1, Snell, 3rd inn, 0 on, 0 outs); Story (1, Morton, 7th inn, 0 on, 1 out); Yelich (1, Morton, 8th inn, 0 on, 1 out); Gennett (1, Diaz, 9th inn, 1 on, 1 out); Votto (1, Happ, 10th inn, 0 on, 0 outs). **RBI:** Segura 3 (3); Trout (1); Brantley (1); Judge (1); Bregman (1); Springer (1); Gennett 2 (2); Votto (1); Yelich (1); Story (1); Contreras (1). **TB:** Springer 5; Segura 5; Bregman 4; Judge 4; Trout 4; Moreland 2; Martinez; Altuve; Choo; Brantley; Votto 4; Contreras 4; Gennett 4; Yelich 4; Story 4; Kemp 2; Baez.

American	IP	H	R	SO	National	IP	H	R	SO
Sale	1.0	1	0	1	Scherzer	2.0	2	1	4
Severino	1.0	1	0	2	DeGrom	1.0	1	1	1
Snell	1.2	1	1	3	Foltynewicz	1.0	0	0	1
Jimenez	0.1	0	0	1	Nola	1.0	1	0	2
Berrios	1.0	0	0	0	Jeffress	1.0	0	0	0
Treinen	1.0	0	0	0	Vazquez	1.0	1	0	2
Morton	2.0	2	2	2	Hader	0.1	4	3	1
Diaz (W)	1.0	1	2	2	Hand	1.0	0	0	1
Happ (S, 1)	1.0	1	1	1	Stripling (L)	1.2	4	3	1

CONTINUED FROM PAGE 22

with a walk in a 1-0 victory over the Marlins. After Austin Jackson's 13th-inning double drove in the game's only run, the Mets played a video in Wright's honor and he exchanged hugs with longtime teammate Jose Reyes. They received cheers from the crowd in honor of their 878th start together. According to the Elias Sports Bureau, that was the most by any two players in franchise history.

Wright got misty in a postgame address to the crowd. "We've had some pretty good times here and some rough years, but you guys have always had my back and that means the world to me," he said. "I wish I could thank everyone individually but all I can do is say thank you from the bottom of my heart. Thank you for letting me live out my dream here every single night."

With watery eyes, Wright took a bow, blew a kiss to the crowd of 43,928 and came out of the dugout for a curtain call before heading up the runway toward the Mets' clubhouse with several teammates behind him.

Some other franchise staples had said goodbye to their longtime environs earlier in the year. The Pittsburgh Pirates made a long-rumored and emotionally difficult decision when they traded Andrew McCutchen to San Francisco for outfielder Bryan Reynolds and pitcher Kyle Crick in January. When McCutchen returned to PNC Park in May, the Pirates played a video tribute before his first at-bat and fans gave him a 90-second standing ovation and chanted "MVP!" The crowd gave McCutchen a second standing ovation when

he took his position in center field in the bottom of the first inning, and McCutchen waved his cap in response.

Shortly before the All-Star Game, Dodgers second baseman Chase Utley announced his plans to retire at the end of the season. That declaration allowed Utley to say goodbye in a final trip to Philadelphia, where he had become a fan favorite while leading the Phillies to a World Championship in 2008. The Phillies made Utley feel right at home when they played his old walkup song, Led Zeppelin's "Kashmir," before each trip to the plate.

Lorenzo Cain encountered a similarly warm reception in his return to Kansas City in late April. He even received cheers from Royals fans when he hit a home run off Kansas City's Burch Smith. "That's once-in-a-lifetime stuff there," Cain said.

One of the more publicized and least sentimental partings of the season took place in New York, where the Mets finally cut ties with pitcher Matt Harvey. Harvey broke in amid considerable hype in 2012 and was proclaimed the Dark Knight of Gotham. But his performance declined, in large part due to injury, and his relationship with the team's front office grew strained over time. The Mets designated Harvey for assignment on May 4 after he refused a demotion to the minors to work out his problems, and they traded him to the Cincinnati Reds for catcher Devin Mesoraco.

"I think we've tried to find some other solution over a fairly long period of time," said general manager Sandy Alderson. "This was a long time coming. It's something we tried to address, we struggled with, and we wrestled with over two managerial regimes." Alderson left the team a month later due to a recurrence of cancer, and the Mets spent several months seeking a replacement before settling on longtime agent Brodie Van Wagenen in the offseason.

Cincinnati's Bryan Price, St. Louis' Mike Matheny and Texas' Jeff Banister were among the big league managers dismissed during the season. In the final week, Minnesota's Paul Molitor, Baltimore's Buck Showalter and Toronto's John Gibbons were let go, and Angels manager Mike Scioscia announced that he was leaving the team after 19 seasons at the helm in Anaheim.

Among the veteran players to announce their retirement during the 2018 season: Jayson Werth, Brandon McCarthy, Shane Victorino, Ryan Howard, Andre Ethier, Kris Medlen, Brayan Pena and Kyle Lohse.

ACTIVE LEADERS

Career leaders among players who played in a game in 2018. Batters require 3,000 plate appearances and pitchers 1,000 innings to qualify for percentage titles.

BATTERS			PITCHERS		
AVG	Miguel Cabrera	.317	ERA	Clayton Kershaw	2.39
OBP	Joey Votto	.427	SO/9	Chris Sale	10.86
SLG	Mike Trout	.573	BB/9	Corey Kluber	1.91
OPS	Mike Trout	.990	HR/9	Clayton Kershaw	0.62
R	Albert Pujols	1,773	W	Bartolo Colon	247
H	Adrian Beltre	3,166	L	Bartolo Colon	188
2B	Albert Pujols	639	SV	F. Rodriguez	333
3B	Jose Reyes	131	IP	CC Sabathia	3,470
HR	Albert Pujols	633	SO	CC Sabathia	2,986
RBI	Albert Pujols	1,982	BB	CC Sabathia	1,060
BB	Albert Pujols	1,279	AVG	Clayton Kershaw	.207
SO	Mark Reynolds	1,870	G	Fernando Rodney	896
XBH	Albert Pujols	1,288	GS	Bartolo Colon	552
SB	Jose Reyes	517	HR	Bartolo Colon	439

ARIZONA DIAMONDBACKS
Yoshihisa Hirano.................March 29
Joey Krehbiel............. July 2
Yoan Lopez............. Sept. 9

ATLANTA BRAVES
Jesse Biddle..........April 21
Ronald Acuna Jr..............April 25
Mike Soroka.............May 1
Kolby Allard.......... July 31
Adam McCreery ..... Aug. 9
Wes Parsons............ Aug. 9
Chad Sobotka....... Aug. 10
Touki Toussaint.... Aug. 13
Bryse Wilson......... Aug. 20
Kyle Wright .... Sept. 4

BALTIMORE ORIOLES
Pedro Araujo........March31
Engelb Vielma ......April 13
D.J. Snelten..........April 28
David Hess ....May 12
John Andreoli ....May 23
Austin Wynns ....June 5
Yefry Ramirez.......June 13
Steve Wilkerson ...June 20
Paul Fry................June 29
Ryan Meisinger ....June 29
Evan Phillips .... July 3
Cody Carroll .... Aug. 1
Cedric Mullins ...... Aug. 10
Josh Rogers.......... Aug. 28
Luis Ortiz............ Sept. 7
D.J. Stewart .... Sept. 12
John Means .... Sept. 26

BOSTON RED SOX
Bobby Poyner.... March 31
Marcus Walden ......April 1

CHICAGO CUBS
David Bote ....April 21
Justin Hancock .... May 9
Duane Underwood Jr......June 25
James Norwood ... July 11

CHICAGO WHITE SOX
Daniel Palka.........April 25
Alfredo Gonzalez ..May 26
Matt Skole............May 28
Michael Kopech ... Aug. 21
Ryan Burr ....Aug. 23
Ian Hamilton ...... Aug. 31
Caleb Frare.......... Sept. 2
Ryan Cordell .... Sept. 3

CINCINNATI REDS
Alex Blandino.......April 10
Tanner Rainey ......April 10
Brandon Dixon ....May 22
Jesus Reyes .... Aug. 4
Aristides Aquino ..Aug. 19
Blake Trahan .... Sept. 3
Gabriel Guerrero ... Sept. 4

CLEVELAND INDIANS
Adam Cimber .... March 29
Shane Bieber........May 31
Eric Haase............ Sept. 2

COLORADO ROCKIES
Noel Cuevas ....April 22
Harrison Musgrave..............April 23
Sam Howard..........June 10
Yency Almonte.......June 21
Garrett Hampson .. July 21
D.J. Johnson........... Sept. 9

DETROIT TIGERS
Ryan Carpenter ......April 1
Victor Reyes...........April 1
Mike Gerber..........April 20
Grayson Greiner......May 6
Dustin Peterson ....May 28
Ronny Rodriguez ..May 31
Sandy Baez............June 4
Dawel Lugo........... Aug. 30
Christin Stewart.... Sept. 9
Spencer Turnbull. Sept. 14
Matt Hall............. Sept. 15
Harold Castro...... Sept. 23

HOUSTON ASTROS
Kyle Tucker.............. July 7
Cionel Perez .... July 11
Framber Valdez .... Aug. 21
Josh James............ Sept. 1
Dean Deetz .... Sept. 5
Myles Straw........ Sept. 15

KANSAS CITY ROYALS
Tim Hill............... March 29
Brad Keller .... March 29
Rosell Herrera.......April 26
Trevor Oaks ....April 28
Scott Barlow..........April 30
Jason Adam ....May 5
Jerry Vasto...........June 10
Heath Fillmyer.......June 24
Ryan O'Hearn .... July 31
Jake Newberry .....Aug. 20
Meibrys Viloria ...... Sept. 2

LOS ANGELES ANGELS
Shohei Ohtani ... March 29
Jaime Barria ....April 11
Justin Anderson ...April 23
Michael Hermosillo ....May 18
Jose Briceno.........May 26
Jose Fernandez .....June 8
David Fletcher .....June 13
Jake Jewell..........June 16
Francisco Arcia .... July 26
Williams Jerez ...... Aug. 7
Taylor Ward........ Aug. 14
Osmer Morales ... Aug. 16
Ty Buttrey........... Aug. 16
Joe Hudson .... Sept. 8
Sherman Johnson.............Sept. 19

LOS ANGELES DODGERS
Dennis Santana.....June 1
Caleb Ferguson .....June 6

MIAMI MARLINS
Braxton Lee ...... March 30
Trevor Richards.....April 2
Tyler Kinley ....April 7
Merandy Gonzalez...............April 19
Elieser Hernandez...........May 10
Ben Meyer.............June 7
Brett Graves..........June 17
Pablo Lopez..........June 30
Isaac Galloway .... July 31
Austin Dean......... Aug. 15
Jeff Brigham........ Sept. 2

MILWAUKEE BREWERS
Jacob Nottingham.........April 16
Freddy Peralta.......May 13
Corbin Burnes....... July 10

MINNESOTA TWINS
Luke Bard .... March 31
Johnny Field ....April 14
Fernando Romero..................May 2
Jake Cave............May 19
Zack Littell ....June 5
Willians Astudillo.............June 30
Kohl Stewart........ Aug. 12
Stephen Gonsalves...........Aug. 20
Andrew Vasquez ... Sept. 1

NEW YORK METS
Gerson Bautista ...April 17
Corey Oswalt.......April 25
P.J. Conlon ....May 7
Luis Guillorme......May 11
Tim Peterson.........May 30
Drew Smith...........June 23
Kevin Kaczmarski........June 24
Tyler Bashlor.......June 25
Drew Gagnon ...... July 10
Jeff McNeil .... July 24
Daniel Zamora..... Aug. 17
Eric Hanhold .... Sept. 4

NEW YORK YANKEES
Nestor Cortes..... March 31
Gleyber Torres.......April 22
Jonathan Loaisiga.............June 15
Chance Adams....... Aug. 4
Stephen Tarpley ... Sept. 2
Justus Sheffield ... Sept. 19

OAKLAND ATHLETICS
Lou Trivino ....April 17
Nick Martini.........June 6
Jeremy Bleich ...... July 13
Ramon Laureano ... Aug. 3
Beau Taylor .... Sept. 1

PHILADELPHIA PHILLIES
Scott Kingery .... March 30
Jesmuel Valentin .April 29
Seranthony Dominguez...........May 7
Mitch Walding.......May 30
Dylan Cozens ....June 1
Austin Davis..........June 20
Enyel De Los Santos ... July 10
Ranger Suarez....... July 26

PITTSBURGH PIRATES
Clay Holmes...........April 6
Nick Kingham.......April 29
Tanner Anderson ... July 2
Alex McRae........... Aug. 1
Kevin Newman..... Aug. 16
Pablo Reyes .... Sept. 2
Kevin Kramer....... Sept. 5
Nick Burdi.......... Sept. 11

SAN DIEGO PADRES
Joey Lucchesi..... March 30
Kazuhisa Makita............March 30
Colten Brewer.......April 12
Eric Lauer ....April 24
Javy Guerra...........May 4
Franmil Reyes.......May 14
Walker Lockett ......June 1
Jose Castillo ....June 2
Robert Stock........June 24
Nate Orf................ July 2
Trey Wingenter ... Aug. 7
Brett Kennedy ...... Aug. 8
Jacob Nix.............. Aug. 10
Luis Urias............. Aug. 28
Rowan Wick......... Aug. 31
Brad Wieck.......... Sept. 14

SAN FRANCISCO GIANTS
Tyler Beede..........April 10
Andrew Suarez.....April 11
Dereck Rodriguez...........May 29
Ray Black................ July 8
Steven Duggar ...... July 8
Aramis Garcia ..... Aug. 31
Chris Shaw .... Aug. 31
Abiátal Avelino ... Sept. 8

SEATTLE MARINERS
Matt Festa .... July 14

ST. LOUIS CARDINALS
Jordan Hicks ...... March 29
Yairo Munoz........ March 29
Tyler O'Neill ....April 19
Austin Gomber.......June 2
Justin Williams...... July 21
Daniel Poncedeleon...........July 23
Dakota Hudson ... July 28
Adolis Garcia .... Aug. 8
Patrick Wisdom ... Aug. 12
Edmundo Sosa ....Sept. 23

TAMPA BAY RAYS
Ryan Yarbrough March 31
Yonny Chirinos ....April 1
Austin Meadows...May 18
Willy Adames ....May 22
Jaime Schultz........May 29
Diego Castillo ....June 6
Jake Bauers...........June 7
Jalen Beeks............June 7
Michael Perez ...... July 26
Brandon Lowe...... Aug. 5
Andrew Velazquez Sept. 2
Nick Ciuffo........... Sept. 3

TEXAS RANGERS
Carlos Tocci......... March 31
Isiah Kiner-Falefa April 10
Ronald Guzman ...April 13
Brandon Mann .....May 13
Ariel Jurado ....May 19
Jose Trevino ....June 15
Jeffrey Springs .... July 31
Connor Sadzeck... Sept. 1
C.D. Pelham .... Sept. 5

TORONTO BLUE JAYS
Billy McKinney .. March 30
Lourdes Gurriel Jr.April 20
Ryan Borucki ....June 26
Thomas Pannone.. Aug. 10
Danny Jansen ...... Aug. 13
Sean Reid-Foley ... Aug. 13
Justin Shafer....... Aug. 19
Murphy Smith ..... Aug. 27
Jose Fernandez .... Sept. 1
Taylor Guerrieri ... Sept. 1
Jonathan Davis..... Sept. 5
Rowdy Tellez....... Sept. 5
Reese McGuire...... Sept. 6
Jon Berti............. Sept. 26

WASHINGTON NATIONALS
Wander Suero........May 1
Juan Soto ....May 15
Jefry Rodriguez......June 3
Austin Voth .... July 14
Jimmy Cordero ..... Aug. 2
Austen Williams ... Sept. 2
Kyle McGowin ...... Sept. 5

CLUB BATTING

	AVG	G	AB	R	H	2B	3B	HR	RBI	BB	SO	SB	OBP	SLG
Boston	.268	162	5623	876	1509	355	31	208	829	569	1253	125	.339	.453
Cleveland	.259	162	5595	818	1447	297	19	216	786	554	1189	135	.332	.434
Tampa Bay	.258	162	5475	716	1415	274	43	150	664	540	1388	128	.333	.406
Houston	.255	162	5453	797	1390	278	18	205	763	565	1197	71	.329	.425
Seattle	.254	162	5513	677	1402	256	32	176	644	430	1221	79	.314	.408
Oakland	.252	162	5579	813	1407	322	20	227	778	550	1381	35	.325	.439
Minnesota	.250	162	5526	738	1379	317	22	166	704	534	1328	47	.318	.405
New York	.249	162	5515	851	1374	269	23	267	821	625	1421	63	.329	.451
Kansas City	.245	162	5505	638	1350	283	29	155	606	427	1310	117	.305	.392
Toronto	.244	162	5477	709	1336	320	16	217	680	499	1387	47	.312	.427
Los Angeles	.242	162	5472	721	1323	249	23	214	690	514	1300	89	.313	.413
Detroit	.241	162	5494	630	1326	284	35	135	597	428	1341	70	.300	.380
Chicago	.241	162	5523	656	1332	259	40	182	639	425	1594	98	.302	.401
Texas	.240	162	5453	737	1308	266	24	194	696	555	1484	74	.318	.404
Baltimore	.239	162	5507	622	1317	242	15	188	.593	422	1412	81	.298	.391

CLUB PITCHING

	ERA	G	CG	SHO	SV	IP	H	R	ER	HR	BB	SO	AVG
Houston	3.11	162	3	12	46	1455	1164	534	503	152	435	1687	.217
Tampa Bay	3.74	162	0	14	52	1448	1236	646	602	164	501	1421	.230
Boston	3.75	162	2	14	46	1459	1305	647	608	176	512	1558	.237
Cleveland	3.77	162	5	17	41	1457	1349	648	611	200	407	1544	.242
NY Yankees	3.78	162	2	11	49	1456	1311	669	611	177	494	1634	.237
Oakland	3.81	162	2	14	44	1466	1303	674	621	184	474	1237	.236
Seattle	4.13	162	3	12	40	1449	1396	711	664	195	400	1328	.252
LA Angels	4.15	162	1	9	35	1437	1353	722	662	205	546	1386	.248
Minnesota	4.50	162	2	7	37	1443	1425	775	721	198	573	1377	.256
Detroit	4.58	162	0	2	37	1425	1423	796	726	216	491	1215	.258
Chi White Sox	4.83	162	0	8	34	1437	1404	848	771	196	653	1259	.254
Toronto	4.85	162	0	3	39	1434	1476	832	772	208	551	1298	.265
Texas	4.92	162	1	5	42	1431	1516	848	783	222	491	1121	.271
Kansas City	4.94	162	2	8	33	1432	1542	833	786	205	549	1157	.275
Baltimore	5.18	162	2	7	28	1431	1552	892	824	234	589	1203	.276

CLUB FIELDING

	PCT	PO	A	E	DP		PCT	PO	A	E	DP
Baltimore	.982	4293	1537	104	159	Minnesota	.984	4330	1454	97	127
Boston	.987	4376	1366	77	106	New York	.984	4369	1344	94	95
Chicago	.981	4311	1431	114	134	Oakland	.985	4397	1594	89	125
Cleveland	.986	4372	1353	83	123	Seattle	.985	4346	1486	88	153
Detroit	.984	4276	1428	95	126	Tampa Bay	.986	4345	1483	85	136
Houston	.989	4365	1369	63	116	Texas	.980	4293	1558	120	168
Kansas City	.987	4296	1529	77	142	Toronto	.983	4301	1447	101	138
Los Angeles	.987	4312	1502	76	173						

INDIVIDUAL BATTING LEADERS

	AVG	G	AB	R	H	2B	3B	HR	RBI	BB	SO	SB
Mookie Betts, Boston	.346	136	520	129	180	47	5	32	80	81	91	30
J.D. Martinez, Boston	.330	150	569	111	188	37	2	43	130	69	146	6
Jose Altuve, Houston	.316	137	534	84	169	29	2	13	61	55	79	17
Mike Trout, Los Angeles	.312	140	471	101	147	24	4	39	79	122	124	24
Michael Brantley, Cleveland	.309	143	570	89	176	36	2	17	76	48	60	12
Whit Merrifield, Kansas City	.304	158	632	88	192	43	3	12	60	61	114	45
Jean Segura, Seattle	.304	144	586	91	178	29	3	10	63	32	69	20
Joey Wendle, Tampa Bay	.300	139	487	62	146	33	6	7	61	37	96	16
Nick Castellanos, Detroit	.298	157	620	88	185	46	5	23	89	49	151	2
Miguel Andujar, New York	.297	149	573	83	170	47	2	27	92	25	97	2

INDIVIDUAL PITCHING LEADERS

	W	L	ERA	G	GS	CG	SV	IP	H	R	ER	BB	SO
Blake Snell, Tampa Bay	21	5	1.89	31	31	0	0	181	112	41	38	64	221
Trevor Bauer, Cleveland	12	6	2.21	28	27	0	1	175	134	51	43	57	221
Justin Verlander, Houston	16	9	2.52	34	34	1	0	214	156	63	60	37	290
Gerrit Cole, Houston	15	5	2.88	32	32	1	0	200	143	68	64	64	276
Corey Kluber, Cleveland	20	7	2.89	33	33	2	0	215	179	75	69	34	222
Mike Clevinger, Cleveland	13	8	3.02	32	32	1	0	200	164	71	67	67	207
Charlie Morton, Houston	15	3	3.13	30	30	0	0	167	130	63	58	64	201
Carlos Carrasco, Cleveland	17	10	3.38	32	30	2	0	192	173	78	72	43	231
Luis Severino, New York	19	8	3.39	32	32	1	0	191	173	76	72	46	220
Mike Fiers, Oakland	12	8	3.56	31	30	0	0	172	166	71	68	37	139

AWARD WINNERS

Selected by Baseball Writers Association of America

MOST VALUABLE PLAYER

Player	1st	2nd	3rd	Total
Mookie Betts, Red Sox	28	2		410
Mike Trout, Angels	1	24	2	265
Jose Ramirez, Indians		1	10	208
J.D. Martinez, Red Sox	1	2	8	198
Alex Bregman, Astros		1	4	192
Francisco Lindor, Indians			4	169
Matt Chapman, Athletics			2	141
Khris Davis, Athletics				41
Blake Snell, Rays				38
Justin Verlander, Astros				26
Mitch Haniger, Mariners				16
Aaron Judge, Yankees				10
Xander Bogaerts, Red Sox				9
Jose Altuve, Astros				9
Blake Treinen, Athletics				7
Andrelton Simmons, Angels				7
Whit Merrifield, Royals				6
Edwin Diaz, Mariners				5
Giancarlo Stanton, Yankees				4
Didi Gregorius, Yankees				3
Jed Lowrie, Athletics				3
Trevor Bauer, Indians				1
Aaron Hicks, Yankees				1
Chris Sale, Red Sox				1

CY YOUNG AWARD

Player	1st	2nd	3rd	Total
Blake Snell, Rays	17	11	2	169
Justin Verlander, Astros	13	13	3	154
Corey Kluber, Indians		4	12	71
Chris Sale, Red Sox		2	8	59
Gerrit Cole, Astros			3	26
Trevor Bauer, Indians			1	13
Blake Treinen, Athletics			1	13
Edwin Diaz, Mariners				4
Luis Severino, Yankees				1

ROOKIE OF THE YEAR

Player	1st	2nd	3rd	Total
Shohei Ohtani, Angels	25	4		137
Miguel Andujar, Yankees	5	20	4	89
Gleyber Torres, Yankees		3	16	25
Joey Wendle, Rays		3	8	17
Daniel Palka, White Sox			1	1
Ryan Yarbrough, Rays			1	1

MANAGER OF THE YEAR

Player	1st	2nd	3rd	Total
Bob Melvin, Athletics	18	10	1	121
Alex Cora, Red Sox	7	11	11	79
Kevin Cash, Rays	5	6	14	57
A.J. Hinch, Astros		3	2	11
Aaron Boone, Yankees			2	2

GOLD GLOVE WINNERS
Selected by AL Managers

P—Dallas Keuchel, Astros. **C**—Salvador Perez, Royals. **1B**—Matt Olson, Athletics. **2B**—Ian Kinsler, Angels/Red Sox. **3B**—Matt Chapman, Athletics. **SS**—Andrelton Simmons, Angels. **LF**—Alex Gordon, Royals. **CF**—Jackie Bradley Jr., Red Sox. **RF**—Mookie Betts, Red Sox.

DEPARTMENT LEADERS

BATTING

GAMES
Matt Olson, Oakland	162
Marcus Semien, Oakland	159
Giancarlo Stanton, New York	158
Whit Merrifield, Kansas City	158
Francisco Lindor, Cleveland	158

AT-BATS
Francisco Lindor, Cleveland	661
Whit Merrifield, Kansas City	632
Marcus Semien, Oakland	632
Nicholas Castellanos, Detroit	620
Giancarlo Stanton, New York	617

PLATE APPEARANCES
Francisco Lindor, Cleveland	745
Whit Merrifield, Kansas City	707
Alex Bregman, Houston	705
Giancarlo Stanton, New York	705
Marcus Semien, Oakland	703

RUNS
Mookie Betts, Boston	129
Francisco Lindor, Cleveland	129
J.D. Martinez, Boston	111
Jose Ramirez, Cleveland	110
Alex Bregman, Houston	105

HITS
Whit Merrifield, Kansas City	192
J.D. Martinez, Boston	188
Nicholas Castellanos, Detroit	185
Francisco Lindor, Cleveland	183
Mookie Betts, Boston	180

TOTAL BASES
J.D. Martinez, Boston	358
Francisco Lindor, Cleveland	343
Mookie Betts, Boston	333
Jose Ramirez, Cleveland	319
Alex Bregman, Houston	316
Khris Davis, Oakland	316

DOUBLES
Alex Bregman, Houston	51
Miguel Andujar, New York	47
Mookie Betts, Boston	47
Nicholas Castellanos, Detroit	46
Xander Bogaerts, Boston	45

TRIPLES
Yolmer Sanchez, Chicago	10
Mallex Smith, Tampa Bay	10
Kevin Kiermaier, Tampa Bay	9
Dee Gordon, Seattle	8
Teoscar Hernandez, Toronto	7
Brett Gardner, New York	7
Denard Span, Tampa Bay/Seattle	7

EXTRA-BASE HITS
Mookie Betts, Boston	84
Alex Bregman, Houston	83
Francisco Lindor, Cleveland	82
J.D. Martinez, Boston	82
Jose Ramirez, Cleveland	81

HOME RUNS
Khris Davis, Oakland	48
J.D. Martinez, Boston	43
Joey Gallo, Texas	40
Mike Trout, Los Angeles	39
Jose Ramirez, Cleveland	39

RUNS BATTED IN
J.D. Martinez, Boston	130
Khris Davis, Oakland	123

Whit Merrifield

Edwin Encarnacion, Cleveland	107
Jose Ramirez, Cleveland	105
Xander Bogaerts, Boston	103
Alex Bregman, Houston	103

SACRIFICES
Delino DeShields, Texas	12
Dee Gordon, Seattle	9
Alcides Escobar, Kansas City	8
Roberto Perez, Cleveland	7
Guillermo Heredia, Seattle	7
Adam Engel, Chicago	7
Mallex Smith, Tampa Bay	7

SACRIFICE FLIES
Carlos Correa, Houston	11
Giancarlo Stanton, New York	10
Joey Wendle, Tampa Bay	10
Didi Gregorius, New York	9
Adrian Beltre, Texas	8
Evan Gattis, Houston	8

HIT BY PITCHES
Carlos Gomez, Tampa Bay	21
Robinson Chirinos, Texas	19
C.J. Cron, Tampa Bay	17

Khris Davis

Nelson Cruz, Seattle	14
Daniel Robertson, Tampa Bay	13

WALKS
Mike Trout, Los Angeles	122
Jose Ramirez, Cleveland	106
Alex Bregman, Houston	96
Shin-Soo Chin, Texas	92
Aaron Hicks, New York	90

STOLEN BASES
Whit Merrifield, Kansas City	45
Mallex Smith, Tampa Bay	40
Jose Ramirez, Cleveland	34
Adalberto Mondesi, Kansas City	32
Mookie Betts, Boston	30
Dee Gordon, Seattle	30

STOLEN BASE PERCENTAGE
Jackie Bradley Jr., Boston	.944
Mike Trout, Los Angeles	.923
Brett Gardner, New York	.889
Jonathan Villar, Baltimore	.875
Andrew Benintendi, Boston	.875

STRIKEOUTS
Yoan Moncada, Chicago	217

HOME RUNS
Giancarlo Stanton, New York	211
Joey Gallo, Texas	207
Chris Davis, Baltimore	192
Justin Upton, Los Angeles	176

AT-BATS PER STRIKEOUT
Andrelton Simmons, L.A.	12.6
Victor Martinez, Detroit	9.5
Michael Brantley, Cleveland	9.5
Jose Iglesias, Detroit	9.2
Yuli Gurriel, Houston	8.5

DOUBLE PLAYS
Yuli Gurriel, Houston	22
Stephen Piscotty, Oakland	21
Adam Jones, Baltimore	21
Ryon Healy, Seattle	21
Yangervis Solarte, Toronto	21

MULTI-HIT GAMES
J.D. Martinez, Boston	59
Francisco Lindor, Cleveland	58
Nicholas Castellanos, Detroit	56
Mookie Betts, Boston	54
Whit Merrifield, Kansas City	54

ON-BASE PERCENTAGE
Mike Trout, Los Angeles	.460
Mookie Betts, Boston	.438
J.D. Martinez, Boston	.402
Alex Bregman, Houston	.394
Jose Ramirez, Cleveland	.387

ON-BASE PLUS SLUGGING
Mike Trout, Los Angeles	1.088
Mookie Betts, Boston	1.078
J.D. Martinez, Boston	1.031
Jose Ramirez, Cleveland	.939
Alex Bregman, Houston	.926

PITCHING

WINS
Blake Snell, Tampa Bay	21
Corey Kluber, Cleveland	20
Luis Severino, New York	19
Carlos Carrasco, Cleveland	17
J.A. Happ, Toronto/New York	17
Rick Porcello, Boston	17

LOSSES
James Shields, Chicago	16
Dylan Bundy, Baltimore	16
Andrew Cashner, Baltimore	15
Alex Cobb, Baltimore	15
Marco Estrada, Toronto	14
Jason Hammel, Kansas City	14
Felix Hernandez, Seattle	14
Dylan Covey, Chicago	14

GAMES
Ryan Pressly, Minnesota/Houston	77
Jose Alvarez, Los Angeles	76
Yusmeiro Petit, Oakland	74
Joe Kelly, Boston	73
Sergio Romo, Tampa Bay	73
Edwin Diaz, Seattle	73
Tyler Clippard, Toronto	73
Trevor Hildenberger, Minnesota	73

GAMES STARTED
Justin Verlander, Houston	34
Dallas Keuchel, Houston	34
James Shields, Chicago	33
Rick Porcello, Boston	33
Corey Kluber, Cleveland	33

GAMES FINISHED
Edwin Diaz, Seattle	65
Shane Greene, Detroit	58
Blake Treinen, Oakland	58
Craig Kimbrel, Boston	57
Cody Allen, Cleveland	45

COMPLETE GAMES
James Paxton, Seattle	2
Carlos Carrasco, Cleveland	2
Jose Berrios, Minnesota	2
Corey Kluber, Cleveland	2
17 others	1

SHUTOUTS
Sean Manaea, Oakland	1
Daniel Mengden, Oakland	1
James Paxton, Seattle	1
Justin Verlander, Houston	1
7 others	1

SAVES
Edwin Diaz, Seattle	57
Craig Kimbrel, Boston	42
Blake Treinen, Oakland	38
Aroldis Chapman, New York	32
Shane Greene, Detroit	32

INNINGS PITCHED
Corey Kluber, Cleveland	215
Justin Verlander, Houston	214
Dallas Keuchel, Houston	205
James Shields, Chicago	205
Gerrit Cole, Houston	200

HITS ALLOWED
Dallas Keuchel, Houston	211
Mike Leake, Seattle	207
James Shields, Chicago	190
Dylan Bundy, Baltimore	188
Jakob Junis, Kansas City	182

RUNS ALLOWED
Lucas Giolito, Chicago	123
Dylan Bundy, Baltimore	116
James Shields, Chicago	115
Felix Hernandez, Seattle	107
Mike Leake, Seattle	98

HOME RUNS ALLOWED
Dylan Bundy, Baltimore	41
James Shields, Chicago	34
Bartolo Colon, Texas	32

Edwin Diaz

Mike Fiers, Detroit/Oakland	32
Jakob Junis, Kansas City	32

WALKS ALLOWED
Lucas Giolito, Chicago	90
Kyle Gibson, Minnesota	79
James Shields, Chicago	78
Lance Lynn, Minnesota/New York	76
Reynaldo Lopez, Chicago	75

LOWEST WALKS PER NINE
Corey Kluber, Cleveland	1.4
Justin Verlander, Houston	1.6
Mike Leake, Seattle	1.7
Marco Gonzales, Seattle	1.7
Mike Fiers, Detroit/Oakland	1.9

HIT BATTERS
Charlie Morton, Houston	16
Rick Porcello, Boston	16

Lucas Giolito, Chicago	15
Jakob Junis, Kansas City	15
Chris Sale, Boston	14

STRIKEOUTS
Justin Verlander, Houston	290
Gerrit Cole, Houston	276
Chris Sale, Boston	237
Carlos Carrasco, Cleveland	231
Corey Kluber, Cleveland	222

STRIKEOUTS PER NINE
Gerrit Cole, Houston	12.4
Justin Verlander, Houston	12.2
Trevor Bauer, Cleveland	11.3
Blake Snell, Tampa Bay	11.0
Charlie Morton, Houston	10.8

STRIKEOUTS PER NINE
(Relievers)

Aroldis Chapman, New York	16.3
Dellin Betances, New York	15.5
Edwin Diaz, Seattle	15.2
Matt Barnes, Boston	14.0
Craig Kimbrel, Boston	13.9

DOUBLE PLAYS
Mike Leake, Seattle	24
Kyle Gibson, Minnesota	23
Marco Gonzalez, Seattle	23
Yovani Gallardo, Texas	19
Dallas Keuchel, Houston	18
Brad Keller, Kansas City	18

PICKOFFS
Marco Gonzales, Seattle	7
Mike Clevinger, Cleveland	6
Ryan Butcher, Oakland	3
Sonny Gray, New York	3
James Shields, Chicago	3
Masahiro Tanaka, New York	3
Ryan Tepera, Toronto	3

WILD PITCHES
Garrett Richards, Los Angeles	15
Danny Duffy, Kansas City	14
Lance McCullers Jr., Houston	14
Blake Snell, Tampa Bay	13
Lucas Giolito, Chicago	13

WALKS PLUS HITS PER INNING
Justin Verlander, Houston	0.90
Blake Snell, Tampa Bay	0.97
Corey Kluber, Cleveland	0.99
Gerrit Cole, Houston	1.03
Trevor Bauer, Cleveland	1.09

OPPONENT AVERAGE
Blake Snell, Tampa Bay	.178
Gerrit Cole, Houston	.198
Justin Verlander, Houston	.200
Trevor Bauer, Cleveland	.208
Charlie Morton, Houston	.213

WORST ERA
Lucas Giolito, Chicago	6.13
Dylan Bundy, Baltimore	5.45
James Shields, Chicago	4.53
Jake Odorizzi, Minnesota	4.49
Matthew Boyd, Detroit	4.39

FIELDING

PITCHER
PCT	11 players	1.000
PO	Mike Leake, Seattle	20
	Lance McCullers Jr., Houston	20
A	Marcus Stroman, Toronto	28
DP	Carlos Carrasco, Cleveland	5
E	Bartolo Colon, Texas	4
	Dylan Covey, Chicago	4

CATCHER
PCT	Salvador Perez, Kansas City	1.000
PO	Martin Maldonado, L.A./Houston	20
A	Jonathan Lucroy, Oakland	83
DP	Caleb Joseph, Baltimore	11
	Salvador Perez, Kansas City	11
E	Jonathan Lucroy, Oakland	10
CS	Jonathan Lucroy, Oakland	31
PB	Gary Sanchez, New York	18

FIRST BASE
PCT	Justin Smoak, Toronto	.999
PO	Matt Olson, Oakland	1403
A	Matt Olson, Oakland	84
DP	Matt Olson, Oakland	115
E	Yonder Alonso, Cleveland	10

SECOND BASE
PCT	Jed Lowrie, Oakland	.993
PO	Rougned Odor, Texas	218
A	Jed Lowrie, Oakland	336
	Rougned Odor, Texas	336
DP	Rougned Odor, Texas	96
E	Yoan Moncada, Chicago	21

THIRD BASE
PCT	Jeimer Candelario, Detroit	.973
PO	Yolmer Sanchez, Chicago	137
A	Matt Chapman, Oakland	331
DP	Kyle Seager, Seattle	49
E	Rafael Devers, Boston	24

SHORTSTOP
PCT	Didi Gregorius, New York	.987
PO	Andrelton Simmons, Los Angeles	228
A	Marcus Semien, Oakland	458
DP	Andrelton Simmons, Los Angeles	114
E	Marcus Semien, Oakland	20
	Tim Anderson, Chicago	20

OUTFIELD
PCT	4 players	1.000
PO	Adam Engel, Chicago	355
A	Mitch Haniger, Seattle	12
	Andrew Benintendi, Boston	12
DP	Kole Calhoun, Los Angeles	4
	Mike Trout, Los Angeles	4
E	Eddie Rosario, Minnesota	9

CLUB BATTING

	AVG	G	AB	R	H	2B	3B	HR	RBI	BB	SO	SB	OBP	SLG
Chicago	.258	163	5624	761	1453	286	34	167	722	576	1388	66	.333	.410
Atlanta	.257	162	5582	759	1433	314	29	175	717	511	1290	90	.324	.417
Colorado	.256	163	5541	780	1418	280	42	210	748	507	1397	95	.322	.435
Washington	.254	162	5517	771	1402	284	25	191	737	631	1289	119	.335	.419
Cincinnati	.254	162	5532	696	1404	251	25	172	665	559	1376	77	.328	.401
Pittsburgh	.254	161	5447	692	1381	290	38	157	665	474	1229	70	.317	.407
Milwaukee	.252	163	5542	754	1398	252	24	218	711	537	1458	124	.323	.424
Los Angeles	.250	163	5572	804	1394	296	33	235	756	647	1436	75	.333	.442
St. Louis	.249	162	5498	759	1369	248	9	205	725	525	1380	63	.321	.409
San Francisco	.239	162	5541	603	1324	255	30	133	573	448	1467	77	.300	.368
Miami	.237	161	5488	589	1303	222	24	128	554	455	1384	45	.303	.357
Arizona	.235	162	5460	693	1283	259	50	176	658	560	1460	79	.310	.397
San Diego	.235	162	5486	617	1289	250	30	162	583	471	1523	95	.297	.380
New York	.234	162	5468	676	1282	265	34	170	649	566	1404	71	.312	.389
Philadelphia	.234	162	5424	677	1270	241	30	186	653	582	1520	69	.314	.393

CLUB PITCHING

	ERA	G	CG	SHO	SV	IP	H	R	ER	HR	BB	SO	AVG
Los Angeles	3.38	163	0	11	48	1476	1279	610	554	179	422	1565	.230
Chicago	3.65	163	1	18	46	1476	1319	645	598	157	622	1333	.240
Arizona	3.72	162	2	9	39	1463	1313	644	605	174	522	1448	.239
Milwaukee	3.73	163	0	14	49	1461	1259	659	606	173	553	1428	.233
Atlanta	3.75	162	2	11	40	1457	1236	657	607	153	635	1423	.229
St. Louis	3.85	162	1	8	43	1455	1354	691	622	144	593	1337	.246
San Francisco	3.95	162	1	15	36	1461	1387	699	641	156	524	1269	.251
Pittsburgh	4.00	161	3	16	40	1434	1380	693	637	174	497	1336	.251
Washington	4.04	162	2	7	40	1446	1320	682	649	198	487	1417	.242
New York	4.07	162	3	15	41	1446	1364	707	661	185	484	1446	.246
Philadelphia	4.14	162	0	12	44	1446	1366	728	665	171	500	1465	.249
Colorado	4.33	163	0	10	51	1452	1377	745	699	184	525	1409	.250
San Diego	4.40	162	0	5	36	1457	1430	767	713	185	519	1399	.256
Cincinnati	4.63	162	1	6	38	1441	1491	819	741	228	532	1258	.266
Miami	4.76	161	1	12	30	1442	1388	809	762	192	605	1249	.254

CLUB FIELDING

	PCT	PO	A	E	DP		PCT	PO	A	E	DP
Washington	.989	4338	1363	64	115	San Diego	.983	4371	1539	100	127
Arizona	.988	4389	1686	75	152	Chicago	.983	4429	1675	104	155
Colorado	.988	4357	1624	74	162	Los Angeles	.983	4428	1435	100	111
Atlanta	.986	4370	1439	80	134	Pittsburgh	.982	4302	1478	105	129
Miami	.986	4326	1448	83	133	Milwaukee	.982	4383	1453	108	141
New York	.985	4382	1406	88	121	Philadelphia	.979	4337	1478	123	138
Cincinnati	.984	4323	1608	95	144	St. Louis	.978	4366	1540	133	151
San Francisco	.984	4384	1605	97	160						

INDIVIDUAL BATTING LEADERS

	AVG	G	AB	R	H	2B	3B	HR	RBI	BB	SO	SB
Christian Yelich, Milwaukee	.326	147	574	118	187	34	7	36	110	68	135	22
Scotter Gennett, Cincinnati	.310	154	584	86	181	30	3	23	92	42	125	4
Freddie Freeman, Atlanta	.309	162	618	94	191	44	4	23	98	76	132	10
Anthony Rendon, Washington	.308	136	529	88	163	44	2	24	92	55	82	2
Lorenzo Cain, Milwaukee	.308	141	539	90	166	25	2	10	38	71	94	30
Ben Zobrist, Chicago	.305	139	455	67	139	28	3	9	58	55	60	3
Jose Martinez, St. Louis	.305	152	534	64	163	30	0	17	83	49	104	0
Corey Dickerson, Pittsburgh	.300	135	504	65	151	35	7	13	55	21	80	8
Nick Markakis, Atlanta	.297	162	623	78	185	43	2	14	93	72	80	1
Nolan Arenado, Colorado	.297	156	590	104	175	38	2	38	110	73	122	2

INDIVIDUAL PITCHING LEADERS

	W	L	ERA	G	GS	CG	SV	IP	H	R	ER	BB	SO
Jacob deGrom, New York	10	9	1.70	32	32	1	0	217	152	48	41	46	269
Aaron Nola, Philadelphia	17	6	2.37	33	33	0	0	212	149	57	56	58	224
Max Scherzer, Washington	18	7	2.53	33	33	2	0	221	150	66	62	51	300
Miles Mikolas, St. Louis	18	4	2.83	32	32	1	0	201	186	70	63	29	146
Kyle Freeland, Colorado	17	7	2.85	33	33	0	0	202	182	64	64	70	173
Mike Foltynewicz, Atlanta	13	10	2.85	31	31	2	0	183	130	65	58	68	202
Trevor Williams, Pittsburgh	14	10	3.11	31	31	1	0	171	146	64	59	55	126
Patrick Corbin, Arizona	11	7	3.15	33	33	1	0	200	162	70	70	48	246
Jameson Taillon, Pittsburgh	14	10	3.20	32	32	2	0	191	179	69	68	46	179
Zack Greinke, Arizona	15	11	3.21	33	33	0	0	208	181	77	74	43	199

AWARD WINNERS

Selected by Baseball Writers Association of America

MOST VALUABLE PLAYER

Player	1st	2nd	3rd	Total
Christian Yelich, Brewers	29	1		415
Javier Baez, Cubs		19	4	250
Nolan Arenado, Rockies		3	8	203
Freddie Freeman, Braves			8	174
Jacob deGrom, Mets	1	7	1	141
Paul Goldschmidt, D-backs			1	115
Lorenzo Cain, Brewers			1	109
Trevor Story, Rockies			3	108
Matt Carpenter, Cardinals			2	105
Max Scherzer, Nationals			2	59
Anthony Rendon, Nationals				21
Ronald Acuna Jr., Braves				19
Aaron Nola, Phillies				16
Justin Turner, Dodgers				10
Max Muncy, Dodgers				8
Jesus Aguilar, Brewers				7
Anthony Rizzo, Cubs				6
Nick Markakis, Braves				2
Eugenio Suarez, Reds				2

CY YOUNG AWARD

Player	1st	2nd	3rd	Total
Jacob deGrom, Mets	29	1		207
Max Scherzer, Nationals	1	29		123
Aaron Nola, Phillies			27	86
Kyle Freeland, Rockies			2	49
Patrick Corbin, D-backs				23
Miles Mikolas, Cardinals			1	13
Josh Hader, Brewers				4
Mike Foltynewicz, Braves				3
Jon Lester, Cubs				2

ROOKIE OF THE YEAR

Player	1st	2nd	3rd	Total
Ronald Acuna Jr., Braves	27	3		144
Juan Soto, Nationals	2	26	1	89
Walker Buehler, Dodgers	1	1	20	28
Brian Anderson, Marlins			4	4
Jack Flaherty, Cardinals			2	2
Harrison Bader, Cardinals			1	1
Yoshihisa Hirano, D-backs			1	1
Jeff McNeil, Mets			1	1

MANAGER OF THE YEAR

Player	1st	2nd	3rd	Total
Brian Snitker, Braves	17	9	4	116
Craig Counsell, Brewers	11	13	5	99
Bud Black, Rockies	1	6	18	41
Mike Shildt, Cardinals		2	1	7
Joe Maddon, Cubs	1		1	6
Dave Roberts, Dodgers			1	1

GOLD GLOVE WINNERS

Selected by NL Managers

P—Zack Greinke, D-backs. **C**—Yadier Molina, Cardinals. **1B**—Freddie Freeman, Braves; Anthony Rizzo, Cubs. **2B**—D.J. LeMahieu, Rockies. **3B**—Nolan Arenado, Rockies. **SS**—Nick Ahmed, D-backs. **LF**—Corey Dickerson, Pirates. **CF**—Ender Inciarte, Braves. **RF**—Nick Markakis, Braves.

BATTING

GAMES

Nick Markakis, Atlanta	162
Freddy Galvis, San Diego	162
Cody Bellinger, Los Angeles	162
Freddie Freeman, Atlanta	162
Trea Turner, Washington	162

AT-BATS

Trea Turner, Washington	664
Ozzie Albies, Atlanta	639
Jose Peraza, Cincinnati	632
Charlie Blackmon, Colorado	626
Nick Markakis, Atlanta	623

PLATE APPEARANCES

Trea Turner, Washington	740
Cesar Hernandez, Philadelphia	708
Freddie Freeman, Atlanta	707
Nick Markakis, Atlanta	705
Charlie Blackmon, Colorado	696

RUNS

Charlie Blackmon, Colorado	119
Christian Yelich, Milwaukee	118
Matt Carpenter, St. Louis	111
Ozzie Albies, Atlanta	105
Nolan Arenado, Colorado	104

HITS

Freddie Freeman, Atlanta	191
Christian Yelich, Milwaukee	187
Nick Markakis, Atlanta	185
Jose Peraza, Cincinnati	182
Charlie Blackmon, Colorado	182

TOTAL BASES

Christian Yelich, Milwaukee	343
Trevor Story, Colorado	339
Javier Baez, Chicago	336
Nolan Arenado, Colorado	331
Paul Goldschmidt, Arizona	316

DOUBLES

Anthony Rendon, Washington	44
Freddie Freeman, Atlanta	44
Nick Markakis, Atlanta	43
Matt Carpenter, St. Louis	42
Trevor Story, Colorado	42

TRIPLES

Ketel Marte, Arizona	12
Javier Baez, Chicago	9
Billy Hamilton, Cincinnati	9
Chris Taylor, Los Angeles	8
Ian Desmond, Colorado	8
Amed Rosario, New York	8
Brandon Nimmo, New York	8
Margot Manuel, San Diego	8

EXTRA-BASE HITS

Trevor Story, Colorado	85
Javier Baez, Chicago	83
Nolan Arenado, Colorado	78
Matt Carpenter, St. Louis	78
Christian Yelich, Milwaukee	77

HOME RUNS

Nolan Arenado, Colorado	38
Trevor Story, Colorado	37
Christian Yelich, Milwaukee	36
Matt Carpenter, St. Louis	36
Jesus Aguilar, Milwaukee	35
Max Muncy, Los Angeles	35

RUNS BATTED IN

Javier Baez, Chicago	111

Christian Yelich

Christian Yelich, Milwaukee	110
Nolan Arenado, Colorado	110
Jesus Aguilar, Milwaukee	108
Trevor Story, Colorado	108

SACRIFICES

Julio Teheran, Atlanta	12
Jhoulys Chacin, Milwaukee	9
Stephen Strasburg, Washington	8
Kenta Maeda, Los Angeles	8
Zack Godley, Arizona	8
Mike Foltynewicz, Atlanta	8
Jose Peraza, Cincinnati	8

SACRIFICE FLIES

Jesus Aguilar, Milwaukee	10
Bryce Harper, Washington	9
Nick Markakis, Atlanta	9
Anthony Rizzo, Chicago	9
Wilmer Flores, New York	9

HIT BY PITCHES

Brandon Nimmo, New York	22
Derek Dietrich, Miami	21
Anthony Rizzo, Chicago	20
Kris Bryant, Chicago	17
Brian Anderson, Miami	16

WALKS

Bryce Harper, Washington	130
Carlos Santana, Philadelphia	110
Joey Votto, Cincinnati	108
Matt Carpenter, St. Louis	102
Cesar Hernandez, Philadelphia	95

STOLEN BASES

Trea Turner, Washington	43
Billy Hamilton, Cincinnati	34
Starling Marte, Pittsburgh	33
Lorenzo Cain, Milwaukee	30
Ender Inciarte, Atlanta	28

STOLEN BASE PERCENTAGE

Jonathan Villar, Milwaukee	.875
Christian Yelich, Milwaukee	.846
Jarrod Dyson, Arizona	.842
Harrison Bader, St. Louis	.833
Trea Turner, Washington	.827

STRIKEOUTS

Chris Taylor, Los Angeles	178
Paul Goldschmidt, Arizona	173
Bryce Harper, Washington	169
Trevor Story, Colorado	168
Ian Happ, Chicago	167
Javier Baez, Chicago	167

AT-BATS PER STRIKEOUT

Jose Peraza, Cincinnati	8.4
Nick Markakis, Atlanta	7.8
Ben Zobrist, Chicago	7.6
Anthony Rizzo, Chicago	7.1
Miguel Rojas, Miami	7.1

DOUBLE PLAYS

Miguel Rojas, Miami	23
Eugenio Suarez, Cincinnati	20
Jesus Aguilar, Milwaukee	19
Brian Anderson, Miami	18
Nick Markakis, Atlanta	18
Eric Hosmer, San Diego	18
Starlin Castro, Miami	18

MULTI-HIT GAMES

Nolan Arenado, Colorado	57
Nick Markakis, Atlanta	56
Freddie Freeman, Atlanta	53
Scooter Gennett, Cincinnati	53
Javier Baez, Chicago	52
Jose Peraza, Cincinnati	52

ON-BASE PERCENTAGE

Joey Votto, Cincinnati	.417
Brandon Nimmo, New York	.404
Christian Yelich, Milwaukee	.402
Lorenzo Cain, Milwaukee	.395
Bryce Harper, Washington	.393

ON-BASE PLUS SLUGGING

Christian Yelich, Milwaukee	1.000
Nolan Arenado, Colorado	.935
Paul Goldschmidt, Arizona	.922
Trevor Story, Colorado	.914
Anthony Rendon, Washington	.909

PITCHING

WINS

Miles Mikolas, St. Louis	18
Max Scherzer, Washington	18
Jon Lester, Chicago	18
Kyle Freeland, Colorado	17
Aaron Nola, Philadelphia	17

LOSSES

Tanner Roark, Washington	15
Nick Pivetta, Philadelphia	14
Homer Bailey, Cincinnati	14
Andrew Suarez, San Francisco	13
Vince Velasquez, Philadelphia	12
Wei-Yin Chen, Miami	12
Jose Urena, Miami	12
Luis Castillo, Cincinnati	12

GAMES

Brad Ziegler, Miami/Arizona	82
Steve Cishek, Chicago	80
Andrew Chafin, Arizona	77
Archie Bradley, Arizona	76
Yoshihisa Hirano, Arizona	75
Adam Ottavino, Colorado	75

GAMES STARTED

Jhoulys Chacin, Milwaukee	35
Max Scherzer, Washington	33
Zack Greinke, Arizona	33
Kyle Freeland, Colorado	33
German Marquez, Colorado	33
Aaron Nola, Philadelphia	33
Patrick Corbin, Arizona	33
Kyle Hendricks, Chicago	33

Miles Mikolas

DEPARTMENT LEADERS

Max Scherzer

GAMES FINISHED
Wade Davis, Colorado	63
Felipe Vazquez, Pittsburgh	60
Kenley Jansen, Los Angeles	59
Raisel Iglesias, Cincinnati	57
Brad Boxberger, Arizona	45

COMPLETE GAMES
Max Scherzer, Washington	2
Jameson Tallion, Pittsburgh	2
Noah Syndergaard, New York	2
Mike Foltynewicz, Atlanta	2
9 others	1

SHUTOUTS
Max Scherzer, Washington	1
Mike Foltynewicz, Atlanta	1
Chris Stratton, San Francisco	1
Jameson Tallion, Pittsburgh	1
Trevor Williams, Pittsburgh	1
Noah Syndergaard, New York	1
Patrick Corbin, Arizona	1
Miles Mikolas, St. Louis	1

SAVES
Wade Davis, Colorado	43
Kenley Jansen, Los Angeles	38
Felipe Vazquez, Pittsburgh	37
Brad Boxberger, Arizona	32
Raisel Iglesias, Cincinnati	30

INNINGS PITCHED
Max Scherzer, Washington	220
Jacob deGrom, New York	217
Aaron Nola, Philadelphia	212
Zack Greinke, Arizona	208
Kyle Freeland, Colorado	202

HITS ALLOWED
Miles Mikolas, St. Louis	186
Kyle Hendricks, Chicago	184
Kyle Freeland, Colorado	182
Zack Greinke, Arizona	181
Tanner Roark, Washington	181

RUNS ALLOWED
Zack Godley, Arizona	103
Jon Gray, Colorado	102
Clayton Richard, San Diego	98
Tyler Anderson, Colorado	94
Jake Arrieta, Philadelphia	93

HOME RUNS ALLOWED
Tyler Anderson, Colorado	30

Chase Anderson, Milwaukee	30
Zack Greinke, Arizona	28
Luis Castillo, Cincinnati	28
Jon Gray, Colorado	27
Matt Harvey, N.Y./Cincinnati	27

WALKS ALLOWED
Tyler Chatwood, Chicago	95
Julio Teheranm, Atlanta	84
Zack Godley, Arizona	81
Sean Newcomb, Atlanta	81
Gio Gonzalez, Wash./Milwaukee	80

LOWEST WALKS PER NINE
Miles Mikolas, St. Louis	1.3
Zack Greinke, Arizona	1.9
Jacob deGrom, New York	1.9
Kyle Hendricks, Chicago	2.0
Max Scherzer, Washington	2.1

HIT BATTERS
Jose Urena, Miami	12
Zack Godley, Arizona	12
Max Scherzer, Washington	12

Carlos Martinez, St. Louis	11
Jhoulys Chacin, Milwaukee	11
Jack Flaherty, St. Louis	11

STRIKEOUTS
Max Scherzer, Washington	300
Jacob deGrom, New York	269
Patrick Corbin, Arizona	246
German Marquez, Colorado	230
Aaron Nola, Philadelphia	224

STRIKEOUTS PER NINE
Max Scherzer, Washington	12.2
Jacob deGrom, New York	11.2
Patrick Corbin, Arizona	11.1
German Marquez, Colorado	10.6
Nick Pivetta, Philadelphia	10.3

STRIKEOUTS PER NINE
(Relievers)
Josh Hader, Milwaukee	15.8
Corey Knebel, Milwaukee	14.3
Adam Ottavino, Colorado	13.0
Kirby Yates, San Diego	12.9

Will Smith, San Francisco	12.1

DOUBLE PLAYS
Kyle Freeland, Colorado	24
Andrew Suarez, San Francisco	22
Jake Arrieta, Philadelphia	22
Clayton Richard, San Diego	22
Ty Blach, San Francisco	18
Matt Koch, Arizona	18
Kyle Hendricks, Chicago	18
Miles Mikolas, St. Louis	18
Tanner Roark, Washington	18

PICKOFFS
Eric Lauer, San Diego	10
Tyler Anderson, Colorado	6
Julio Teheran, Atlanta	6
Jose Quintana, Chicago	5
Max Fried, Atlanta	4
Kyle Hendricks, Chicago	4
Joey Lucchesi, San Diego	4
Aaron Nola, Philadelphia	4
Noah Syndergaard, New York	4

WILD PITCHES
Zack Godley, Arizona	17
Junior Guerra, Milwaukee	11
Richard Rodriguez, Pittsburgh	11
Jake Arrieta, Philadelphia	11
Clayton Kershaw, Los Angeles	10
Seranthony Dominguez, Philadelphia	10

WALKS PLUS HITS PER INNING
Max Scherzer, Washington	0.91
Jacob deGrom, New York	0.91
Aaron Nola, Philadelphia	0.98
Patrick Corbin, Arziona	1.05
Miles Mikolas, St. Louis	1.07

OPPONENT AVERAGE
Max Scherzer, Washington	.188
Mike Foltynewicz, Atlanta	.195
Julio Teheran, Atlanta	.196
Jacob deGrom, New York	.196
Aaron Nola, Philadelphia	.197

WORST ERA
Jon Gray, Colorado	5.12
Nick Pivetta, Philadelphia	4.77
Zack Godley, Arizona	4.74
Tyler Anderson, Colorado	4.55
Tanner Roark, Washington	4.34

FIELDING

PITCHER
PCT	9 players	1.000
PO	Zack Greinke, Arizona	27
A	Clayton Richard, San Diego	38
DP	Robbie Erlin, San Diego	4
	Brandon McCarthy, Atlanta	4
E	Ivan Nova, Pittsburgh	5

CATCHER
PCT	Yadier Molina, St. Louis	.998
PO	Yasmani Grandal, Los Angeles	1114
A	Willson Contreras, Chicago	71
DP	Willson Contreras, Chicago	9
E	Willson Contreras, Chicago	11
	Austin Hedges, San Diego	11
	Jorge Alfaro, Philadelphia	11
CS	Willson Contreras, Chicago	27
PB	Jorge Alfaro, Philadelphia	10

FIRST BASE
PCT	Cody Bellinger, Los Angeles	.997
	Eric Hosmer, San Diego	.997
PO	Paul Goldschmidt, Arizona	1323
A	Anthony Rizzo, Chicago	147
DP	Paul Goldschmidt, Arizona	131
E	Carlos Santana, Arizona	10

SECOND BASE
PCT	D.J. LeMahieu, Colorado	.993
PO	Scooter Gennett, Cincinnati	280
A	Ozzie Albies, Atlanta	389
DP	Scooter Gennett, Cincinnati	101
E	Cesar Hernandez, Philadelphia	12
	Starlin Castro, Miami	12

THIRD BASE
PCT	Anthony Rendon, Washington	.981
PO	Nolan Arenado, Colorado	104
A	Nolan Arenado, Colorado	312
DP	Nolan Arenado, Colorado	44
E	Eugenio Suarez, Cincinnati	19

SHORTSTOP
PCT	Freddy Galvis, San Diego	.986
PO	Freddy Galvis, San Diego	222
A	Brandon Crawford, San Francisco	435
DP	Brandon Crawford, San Francisco	105
E	Jose Peraza, Cincinnati	22

OUTFIELD
PCT	Charlie Blackmon, Colorado	.997
PO	Ender Inciarte, Atlanta	380
A	Billy Hamilton, Cincinnati	12
DP	Corey Dickerson, Pittsburgh	5
E	Lewis Brinson, Miami	9

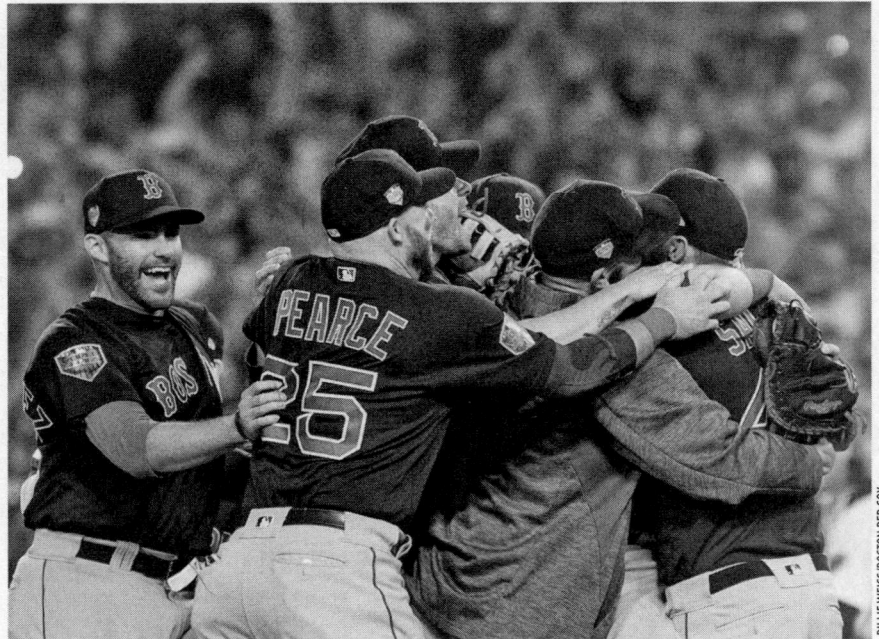

BILLIE WEISS/BOSTON RED SOX

Led by World Series MVP Steve Pearce, the Red Sox won their fourth World Series in the last 15 years.

Red Sox Roll Through Playoffs, Capping Historic Season

BY JERRY CRASNICK

From the first day of spring training, the Red Sox tended to business with supreme focus and a dogged work ethic. The roster was free of divas and big egos—the $206 million payroll notwithstanding—and first-year manager Alex Cora established a workmanlike tone that extended to all corners of the clubhouse.

The Red Sox served notice that they were a force with a 17-2 start coming out of the Grapefruit League. Fittingly enough, when the final pitch was thrown in October, they were the last standing.

The Sox put the finishing touches on one of the most memorable seasons in franchise history three days before Halloween. Chris Sale came out of the bullpen to retire Manny Machado on a swinging strike three to seal a 5-1 victory, and the Sox cel-

ebrated on the Dodger Stadium infield with their fourth World Series title in 15 years.

After setting a franchise record with 108 regular-season victories, the Red Sox rolled to seven wins in nine games against MLB's two other 100-win teams. They eliminated the Yankees in four games in the Division Series and steamrolled MLB's defending champions, the Houston Astros, in five games in the AL Championship Series. The Red Sox finished with a cumulative record of 119-57, and many hailed them as MLB's best team since the 1998 Yankees posted a 114-48 record and then went 11-2 in October on their way to a title.

The Red Sox won despite some underwhelming contributions from pivotal players. Right fielder Mookie Betts, the frontrunner for AL Most Valuable Player, batted .210 (13-for-62) in the postseason, and shortstop Xander Bogaerts hit .136 (3-for-22) in the World Series. Sale, apparently still bothered by the shoulder issues that forced him to take an extended break down the stretch, logged only 15 innings in his three postseason starts. And closer Craig Kimbrel struggled with his command (and some pitch-tipping issues) while posting an uncharacteristic 5.91 ERA in nine October appearances.

The Red Sox benefited from clutch hits by Eduardo Nunez, 21-year-old third baseman Rafael Devers and World Series MVP, Steve Pearce. Joe Kelly, Ryan Brazier and Matt Barnes logged a combined 0.94 ERA and struck out 29 batters in 28.2 October innings, and Nathan Eovaldi made an impact as both a starter and a reliever.

A much-hyped Game 1 World Series matchup between Sale and fellow lefty Clayton Kershaw failed to materialize as expected. The two aces lasted only four innings each—while throwing a combined 180 pitches—and it was left to the bullpens to restore order. Nunez came off the bench to hit a three-run homer off Alex Wood in the seventh to give Boston the cushion it needed in an 8-4 victory. The following night, David Price threw six strong innings and J.D. Martinez's two-run single off Ryan Madson gave Boston a 4-2 victory and a 2-0 series lead heading back to the West Coast.

The most memorable game of the Series took place at Chavez Ravine, where Max Muncy's 18th inning homer off Eovaldi gave the Dodgers a 3-2 victory. The seven-hour, 20-minute game easily set the record for longest game in World Series history. Boston manager Alex Cora exhausted his bullpen in the marathon, but the resilient Red Sox dug deep to clinch the series on the road. The Sox overcame a three-run homer by Yasiel Puig and 4-0 deficit to capture Game 4 by a score of 9-6. In the climactic Game 5, Pearce drove in three runs with a pair of homers and Price threw 89 pitches on short rest to lead Boston to victory and put an exclamation point on a magical season.

The Road To The Fall Classic

The Athletics overcame a slew of starting pitching injuries and won 97 games, but their "bullpenning" strategy went awry when they were clubbed 7-2 by New York in the Wild Card Game at Yankee Stadium. In the National Legaue Wild Card matchup, the Rockies survived an offensive battle of attrition and beat the Cubs 2-1 on catcher Tony Wolters' RBI single in the 13th inning.

Houston eliminated Cleveland in the ALDS behind some dominant pitching from Justin Verlander, Gerrit Cole, Dallas Keuchel and an

David Price went 2-0 with a 1.98 ERA in 13.2 innings during the 2018 World Series.

airtight bullpen. Jose Ramirez's second-half slump continued with an 0-for-11 performance in the three-game sweep, and the Indians scored a total of six runs and batted .144 as a team. Houston third baseman Alex Bregman vented on social media because the defending champion Astros (and the 2016 AL champs, the Indians) were relegated to all day games in the series.

"Does Tiger Woods tee off at 8 a.m. when he's going to win a Masters?' Bregman said. "Does Floyd Mayweather fight the first fight of the night? No, he's the main event, right?"

Boston and New York monopolized the prime-time spotlight during the Division Series, but their matchup lacked much in the way of suspense. After the teams split two games at Fenway Park, the Red Sox demoralized the Yankees with a 16-1 thrashing in Game 3. Brock Holt made history when he became the first player to hit for the cycle in the postseason. Holt completed the cycle with a homer off catcher Austin Romine, who was summoned to pitch in the ninth inning of the blowout.

In the NLDS, Hyun-Jin Ryu and Clayton Kershaw set the tone with 15 innings of shutout ball in the first two games, and the Dodgers eliminated Atlanta in four. Milwaukee overwhelmed Colorado with its deep and versatile bullpen in the other opening-round series, and the Rockies were outscored 13-2 and hit .146 as a team while going down meekly in three games against the Brewers.

The ALCS had all the makings of a classic — until the Red Sox turned it into a walkover. After falling 7-2 to Justin Verlander in Game 1, the Red Sox went to work against Houston's vaunted pitching staff and outscored the Astros 27-14 while winning four straight. Center fielder Jackie Bradley went 3-for-15 in the series, but he drove in nine runs with a grand slam, a two-run homer and a bases-clearing double to capture the MVP award.

Dodgers outfielder/first baseman Cody Bellinger, similarly, made the most of his hits in October. He went a mere 5-for-25 against the Brewers in the NLCS, but contributed a 13th inning walk-off single in Game 4 and a pivotal two-run homer off Jhoulys Chacin in the Dodgers' 5-1 Game 7 victory to earn MVP honors.

"All postseason I felt fairly good," Bellinger said. "I wasn't seeing any results. But luckily for me, I've got a lot of veterans on this team. They said stick with the process and the results will come. That's exactly what I did, and it showed."

Heroes and Goats

The Red Sox had reason to question themselves after losing Game 2 of the Division Series to the Yankees in Boston. But Yankees outfielder Aaron Judge made the mistake of poking the bear when he cranked up the volume to Frank Sinatra's "New York, New York" on his boom box while passing the home clubhouse on his way out of Fenway Park. The Red Sox, properly awakened, pummeled the Yankees 16-1 as the series shifted to New York.

Manager Aaron Boone was forced to defend his pitching moves after New York's disappointing performance against Boston. Boone stuck with starters Luis Severino and C.C. Sabathia for three innings each in Games 3 and 4, and the Yankees dug early holes they could never escape.

Dodgers third baseman Manny Machado was a focal point for all the wrong reasons in October. He hit .227 with 18 strikeouts in 66 at-bats and was guilty of several on-field transgressions. When Machado stepped on Milwaukee first baseman Jesus Aguilar's foot while running out a ground-ball, MLB hit him with a $10,000 fine. Brewers outfielder Christian Yelich responded with an angry post-game diatribe.

"He's a player that has a history of those types of incidents," Yelich told reporters. "One time is an accident. Repeated over and over and over again, you're just a dirty player."

Machado, who was gearing up for a huge free-agent payday at age 26, compounded that misdeed by failing to run hard on multiple occasions. Orioles broadcaster and Hall of Famer Jim Palmer was one of several analysts and onlookers to take aim at Machado for his lack of effort. Machado tried to explain himself in an interview with Ken Rosenthal of Fox Sports 1, but many observers criticized him for being tone deaf and out of touch.

"I'm not the type of player that's going to be 'Johnny Hustle,' and run down the line and slide to first base and … you know, whatever can happen," Machado said. "That's just not my personal-

AMERICAN LEAGUE CHAMPIONS, 1995–2018

American League postseason results in Wild Card Era, 1995-present, where (*) denotes wild card playoff entrant.

YEAR	CHAMPIONSHIP SERIES	ALCS MVP	DIVISION SERIES	DIVISION SERIES
2018	Boston 4, Houston 1	Jackie Bradley Jr., OF, Boston	Boston 3, New York* 1	Houston 3, Cleveland 0
2017	Houston 4, New York 3	Justin Verlander, RHP, Houston	New York* 3, Cleveland 2	Houston 3, Boston 1
2016	Cleveland 4, Toronto 1	Andrew Miller, LHP, Cleveland	Toronto* 3, Texas 0	Cleveland 3, Boston 0
2015	Kansas City 4, Toronto 2	Alcides Escobar, SS, Kansas City	Kansas City 3, Houston* 2	Baltimore 3, Texas 2
2014	Kansas City 4, Baltimore 0	Lorenzo Cain, OF, Kansas City	Kansas City 3, Los Angeles 0	Baltimore 3, Detroit 0
2013	Boston 4, Detroit 2	Koji Uehara, RHP, Boston	Boston 3, Tampa Bay* 1	Detroit, 3, Oakland 2
2012	Detroit 4, New York 0	Delmon Young, OF, Detroit	New York 3, Baltimore* 2	Detroit 3, Oakland 2
2011	Texas 4, Detroit 2	Nelson Cruz, OF, Texas	Detroit 3, New York 2	Texas 3, Tampa Bay* 1
2010	Texas 4, New York 2	Josh Hamilton, OF, Texas	Texas 3, Tampa Bay 2	New York* 3, Minnesota 0
2009	New York 4, Los Angeles 2	C.C. Sabathia, LHP, New York	New York 3, Minnesota 0	Los Angeles 3, Boston* 0
2008	Tampa Bay 4, Boston 3	Matt Garza, RHP, Tampa Bay	Boston* 3, Los Angeles 1	Tampa Bay 3, Chicago 1
2007	Boston 4, Cleveland 3	Josh Beckett, RHP, Boston	Boston 3, Los Angeles 0	Cleveland 3, New York* 1
2006	Detroit 4, Oakland 0	Placido Polanco, 2B, Detroit	Detroit* 3, New York 1	Oakland 3, Minnesota 0
2005	Chicago 4, Los Angeles 1	Paul Konerko, 1B, Chicago	Chicago 3, Boston* 0	Los Angeles 3, New York 2
2004	Boston 4, New York 3	David Ortiz, DH, Boston	Boston* 3, Anaheim 0	New York 3, Minnesota 1
2003	New York 4, Boston 3	Mariano Rivera, RHP, New York	New York 3, Minnesota 1	Boston* 3, Oakland 2
2002	Anaheim 4, Minnesota 1	Adam Kennedy, 2B, Anaheim	Anaheim* 3, New York 1	Minnesota 3, Oakland 2
2001	New York 4, Seattle 1	Andy Pettitte, LHP, New York	Seattle 3, Cleveland 2	New York 3, Oakland* 2
2000	New York 4, Seattle 2	David Justice, OF, New York	New York 3, Oakland 2	Seattle* 3, Chicago 0
1999	New York 4, Boston 1	Orlando Hernandez, RHP, New York	Boston* 3, Cleveland 2	New York 3, Texas 0
1998	New York 4, Cleveland 2	David Wells, LHP, New York	Cleveland 3, Boston* 1	New York 3, Texas 0
1997	Cleveland 4, Baltimore 2	Marquis Grissom, OF, Cleveland	Cleveland 3, New York* 2	Baltimore 3, Seattle 1
1996	New York 4, Baltimore 1	Bernie Williams, OF, New York	Baltimore* 3, Cleveland 1	New York 3, Texas 1
1995	Cleveland 4, Seattle 2	Orel Hershiser, RHP, Cleveland	Cleveland 3, Boston 0	Seattle 3, New York* 2

ity. That's not my cup of tea. That's not who I am."

In the social media age, managers ultimately generated their share of scrutiny in the postseason. In Game 4 of the World Series, Dodgers manager Dave Roberts was pilloried for lifting Rich Hill when the lefty was working on a one-hitter in the seventh inning. Roberts called upon six relievers, and every one allowed at least one run in a 9-6 Red Sox victory. Dodgers closer Kenley Jansen blew two saves in the series, and Ryan Madson allowed all seven of his inherited runners to score.

David Price, who had to lug around a reputation as an October flop thanks to his 2-9, 5.42 record in his first 19 postseason appearances, rehabilitated his image with some gutsy and inspirational pitching against Houston and Los Angeles. Price went 3-0, 2.59 versus the Astros and Dodgers and pitched both as a reliever and a starter on short rest. Within days of the World Series, Price decided to remain with the Red Sox and refrained from exercising an opt-out clause that would have allowed him to test free agency.

Nathan Eovaldi, acquired in a late July trade with Tampa Bay, also had a major impact for the Red Sox in October. Even though Eovaldi allowed the climactic 18th-inning home run to Max Muncy in Boston's 3-2 loss to the Dodgers in Game 3, his teammates appreciated his six-inning, 97-pitch relief outing enough to give him a standing ovation in the clubhouse after the game.

"I felt privileged to be able to watch what Nathan Eovaldi did," said Boston's Rick Porcello.

"That was the most incredible pitching performance I've ever seen. After the game was over I started crying. He literally gave everything he had on every single pitch."

While Chris Sale didn't pitch to expectations in October, he helped his teammates elevate their performance with his oratory. The TV cameras captured Sale screaming at his teammates in the dugout in Game 4 of the World Series, and the Red Sox rallied from a 4-0 deficit to beat the Dodgers 9-6. "We didn't want to see him mad anymore," said Brock Holt. "So we decided to start swinging the bats a little bit."

Steve Pearce, the World Series MVP, came over to Boston from Tampa Bay in a June trade and joined Mark McLemore, Kelly Johnson, Cesar Izturis, Matt Herges and Steve Finley as the sixth player in history to play for all five teams in a division. Pearce went 4-for-12 in the World Series, but his three homers and a double produced eight RBIs and a 1.167 slugging percentage.

While the Red Sox and Dodgers were competing for the World Series, several players received individual honors during the Fall Classic. St. Louis catcher Yadier Molina won the Roberto Clemente Award for his humanitarian work in his native Puerto Rico. Christian Yelich and J.D. Martinez took home the Hank Aaron Award as the top hitters in each league, and Edwin Diaz received the Mariano Rivera Award (American League) and Josh Hader the Trevor Hoffman Award (National League) as MLB's top relievers.

NATIONAL LEAGUE CHAMPIONS, 1995–2018

National League postseason results in Wild Card Era, 1995-present, where (*) denotes wild card playoff entrant.

YEAR	CHAMPIONSHIP SERIES	NLCS MVP	DIVISION SERIES	DIVISION SERIES
2018	Los Angeles 4, Milwaukee 3	Cody Bellinger, 1B/OF, Los Angeles	Los Angeles 3, Atlanta 1	Milwaukee 3, Colorado 0*
2017	Los Angeles 4, Chicago 1	Justin Turner, 3B/Chris Taylor, CF, L.A.	Los Angeles 3, Arizona* 0	Chicago 3, Washington 2
2016	Chicago 4, Los Angeles 2	Javier Baez, 2B/Jon Lester, LHP, Chicago	Chicago 3, San Francisco* 1	Los Angeles 3, Washington 2
2015	New York 4, Chicago 0	Daniel Murphy, 2B, New York	New York 3, Los Angeles 2	Chicago* 3, St. Louis 1
2014	San Francisco 4, St. Louis 1	Madison Bumgarner, LHP, San Francisco	San Francisco 3, Washington 1	St. Louis 3, Los Angeles 1
2013	St. Louis 4, Los Angeles 2	Michael Wacha, RHP, St. Louis	St. Louis 3, Pittsburgh* 2	Los Angeles 3, Atlanta 1
2012	San Francisco 4, St. Louis 3	Marco Scutaro, 2B, San Francisco	St. Louis* 3, Washington 2	San Francisco 3, Cincinnati 2
2011	St. Louis 4, Milwaukee 2	David Freese, 3B, St. Louis	St. Louis* 3, Philadelphia 2	Milwaukee 3, Arizona 2
2010	San Francisco 4, Philadelphia 2	Cody Ross, OF, San Francisco	Philadelphia 3, Cincinnati 0	San Francisco 3, Atlanta* 1
2009	Philadelphia 4, Los Angeles 1	Ryan Howard, 1B, Philadelphia	Los Angeles 3, St. Louis 0	Philadelphia 3, Colorado* 1
2008	Philadelphia 4, Los Angeles 1	Cole Hamels, LHP, Philadelphia	Los Angeles 3, Chicago 0	Philadelphia 3, Milwaukee* 1
2007	Colorado 4, Arizona 0	Matt Holliday, OF, Colorado	Arizona 3, Chicago 0	Colorado* 3, Philadelphia 0
2006	St. Louis 4, New York 3	Jeff Suppan, RHP, St. Louis	New York 3, Los Angeles* 0	St. Louis 3, San Diego 1
2005	Houston 4, St. Louis 2	Roy Oswalt, RHP, Houston	St. Louis 3, San Diego 0	Houston* 3, Atlanta 1
2004	St. Louis 4, Houston 3	Albert Pujols, 1B, St. Louis	St. Louis 3, Los Angeles 1	Houston* 3, Atlanta 2
2003	Florida 4, Chicago 3	Ivan Rodriguez, C, Florida	Florida* 3, San Francisco 1	Chicago 3, Atlanta 2
2002	San Francisco 4, St. Louis 1	Benito Santiago, C, San Francisco	San Francisco* 3, Atlanta 2	St. Louis 3, Arizona 0
2001	Arizona 4, Atlanta 1	Craig Counsell, SS, Arizona	Atlanta 3, Houston 0	Arizona 3, St. Louis* 2
2000	New York 4, St. Louis 1	Mike Hampton, LHP, New York	St. Louis 3, Atlanta 0	New York* 3, San Francisco 1
1999	Atlanta 4, New York 2	Eddie Perez, C, Atlanta	Atlanta 3, Houston 1	New York* 3, Arizona 1
1998	San Diego 4, Atlanta 2	Sterling Hitchcock, LHP, San Diego	Atlanta 3, Chicago* 0	San Diego 3, Houston 1
1997	Florida 4, Atlanta 2	Livan Hernandez, RHP, Florida	Florida* 3, San Francisco 0	Atlanta 3, Houston 0
1996	Atlanta 4, St. Louis 3	Javy Lopez, C, Atlanta	St. Louis 3, San Diego 0	Atlanta 3, Los Angeles* 0
1995	Atlanta 4, Cincinnati 0	Mike Devereaux, OF, Atlanta	Atlanta 3, Colorado* 1	Cincinnati 3, Los Angeles 0

Year	Winner	Loser	Result
1903	Boston (AL)	Pittsburgh (NL)	5-3
1904	NO SERIES		
1905	New York (NL)	Philadelphia (AL)	4-1
1906	Chicago (AL)	Chicago (NL)	4-2
1907	Chicago (NL)	Detroit (AL)	4-0
1908	Chicago (NL)	Detroit (AL)	4-1
1909	Pittsburgh (NL)	Detroit (AL)	4-3
1910	Philadelphia (AL)	Chicago (NL)	4-1
1911	Philadelphia (AL)	New York (NL)	4-2
1912	Boston (AL)	New York (NL)	4-3-1
1913	Philadelphia (AL)	New York (NL)	4-1
1914	Boston (NL)	Philadelphia (AL)	4-0
1915	Boston (AL)	Philadelphia (NL)	4-1
1916	Boston (AL)	Brooklyn (NL)	4-1
1917	Chicago (AL)	New York (NL)	4-2
1918	Boston (AL)	Chicago (NL)	4-2
1919	Cincinnati (NL)	Chicago (AL)	5-3
1920	Cleveland (AL)	Brooklyn (NL)	5-2
1921	New York (NL)	New York (AL)	5-3
1922	New York (NL)	New York (AL)	4-0
1923	New York (AL)	New York (NL)	4-2
1924	Washington (AL)	New York (NL)	4-3
1925	Pittsburgh (NL)	Washington (AL)	4-3
1926	St. Louis (NL)	New York (AL)	4-3
1927	New York (AL)	Pittsburgh (NL)	4-0
1928	New York (AL)	St. Louis (NL)	4-0
1929	Philadelphia (AL)	Chicago (NL)	4-1
1930	Philadelphia (AL)	St. Louis (NL)	4-2
1931	St. Louis (NL)	Philadelphia (AL)	4-3
1932	New York (AL)	Chicago (NL)	4-0
1933	New York (NL)	Washington (AL)	4-1
1934	St. Louis (NL)	Detroit (AL)	4-3
1935	Detroit (AL)	Chicago (NL)	4-2
1936	New York (AL)	New York (NL)	4-2
1937	New York (AL)	New York (NL)	4-1
1938	New York (AL)	Chicago (NL)	4-0
1939	New York (AL)	Cincinnati (NL)	4-0
1940	Cincinnati (NL)	Detroit (AL)	4-3
1941	New York (AL)	Brooklyn (NL)	4-1
1942	St. Louis (NL)	New York (AL)	4-1
1943	New York (AL)	St. Louis (NL)	4-1
1944	St. Louis (NL)	St. Louis (AL)	4-2
1945	Detroit (AL)	Chicago (NL)	4-3
1946	St. Louis (NL)	Boston (AL)	4-3
1947	New York (AL)	Brooklyn (NL)	4-3
1948	Cleveland (AL)	Boston (NL)	4-2
1949	New York (AL)	Brooklyn (NL)	4-1
1950	New York (AL)	Philadelphia (NL)	4-0
1951	New York (AL)	New York (NL)	4-2
1952	New York (AL)	Brooklyn (NL)	4-3
1953	New York (AL)	Brooklyn (NL)	4-2
1954	New York (NL)	Cleveland (AL)	4-0
1955	Brooklyn (NL)	New York (AL)	4-3
1956	New York (AL)	Brooklyn (NL)	4-3
1957	Milwaukee (NL)	New York (AL)	4-3
1958	New York (AL)	Milwaukee (NL)	4-3
1959	Los Angeles (NL)	Chicago (AL)	4-2
1960	Pittsburgh (NL)	New York (AL)	4-3
1961	New York (AL)	Cincinnati (NL)	4-1
1962	New York (AL)	San Francisco (NL)	4-3
1963	Los Angeles (NL)	New York (AL)	4-0
1964	St. Louis (NL)	New York (AL)	4-3
1965	Los Angeles (NL)	Minnesota (AL)	4-3
1966	Baltimore (AL)	Los Angeles (NL)	4-0
1967	St. Louis (NL)	Boston (AL)	4-3
1968	Detroit (AL)	St. Louis (NL)	4-3
1969	New York (NL)	Baltimore (AL)	4-1
1970	Baltimore (AL)	Cincinnati (NL)	4-1

Andrew Benintendi

Year	Winner	Loser	Result
1971	Pittsburgh (NL)	Baltimore (AL)	4-3
1972	Oakland (AL)	Cincinnati (NL)	4-3
1973	Oakland (AL)	New York (NL)	4-3
1974	Oakland (AL)	Los Angeles (NL)	4-1
1975	Cincinnati (NL)	Boston (AL)	4-3
1976	Cincinnati (NL)	New York (AL)	4-0
1977	New York (AL)	Los Angeles (NL)	4-2
1978	New York (AL)	Los Angeles (NL)	4-2
1979	Pittsburgh (NL)	Baltimore (AL)	4-3
1980	Philadelphia (NL)	Kansas City (AL)	4-2
1981	Los Angeles (NL)	New York (AL)	4-2
1982	St. Louis (NL)	Milwaukee (AL)	4-3
1983	Baltimore (AL)	Philadelphia (NL)	4-1
1984	Detroit (AL)	San Diego (NL)	4-1
1985	Kansas City (AL)	St. Louis (NL)	4-3
1986	New York (NL)	Boston (AL)	4-3
1987	Minnesota (AL)	St. Louis (NL)	4-3
1988	Los Angeles (NL)	Oakland (AL)	4-1
1989	Oakland (AL)	San Francisco (NL)	4-0
1990	Cincinnati (NL)	Oakland (AL)	4-0
1991	Minnesota (AL)	Atlanta (NL)	4-3
1992	Toronto (AL)	Atlanta (NL)	4-2
1993	Toronto (AL)	Philadelphia (NL)	4-2
1994	NO SERIES		
1995	Atlanta (NL)	Cleveland (AL)	4-2
1996	New York (AL)	Atlanta (NL)	4-2
1997	Florida (NL)	Cleveland (AL)	4-3
1998	New York (AL)	San Diego (NL)	4-0
1999	New York (AL)	Atlanta (NL)	4-0
2000	New York (AL)	New York (NL)	4-1
2001	Arizona (NL)	New York (AL)	4-3
2002	Anaheim (AL)	San Francisco (NL)	4-3
2003	Florida (NL)	New York (AL)	4-2
2004	Boston (AL)	St. Louis (NL)	4-0
2005	Chicago (AL)	Houston (NL)	4-0
2006	St. Louis (NL)	Detroit (AL)	4-1
2007	Boston (AL)	Colorado (NL)	4-0
2008	Philadelphia (NL)	Tampa Bay (AL)	4-1
2009	New York (AL)	Philadelphia (NL)	4-2
2010	San Francisco (NL)	Texas (AL)	4-1
2011	St. Louis (NL)	Texas (AL)	4-3
2012	San Francisco (NL)	Detroit (AL)	4-0
2013	Boston (AL)	St. Louis (NL)	4-2
2014	San Francisco (NL)	Kansas City (AL)	4-3
2015	Kansas City (AL)	New York (NL)	4-1
2016	Chicago (NL)	Cleveland (AL)	4-3
2017	Houston (AL)	Los Angeles (NL)	4-3
2018	Boston (AL)	Los Angeles (NL)	4-1

WORLD SERIES BOX SCORES

GAME ONE *October 23, 2018*

BOSTON RED SOX 8, LOS ANGELES DODGERS 4

	1	2	3	4	5	6	7	8	9	R	H	E
LA DODGERS	0	1	1	0	1	0	1	0	0	4	8	0
BOSTON	2	0	1	0	2	0	3	0	X	8	11	0

LA DODGERS	AB	R	H	RBI	BB	SO	LOB	AVG
Dozier, B, 2B	2	1	0	0	1	1	0	.000
c-Muncy, PH-1B	2	1	1	0	0	1	0	.500
Turner, 3B	5	1	3	0	0	2	0	.600
Freese, 1B	3	0	2	0	0	1	2	.667
d-Grandal, PH-C	0	0	0	0	1	0	0	.000
Machado, SS	3	0	1	3	0	0	2	.333
Taylor, C, LF	2	0	0	0	0	2	2	.000
a-Bellinger, PH-CF	2	0	0	0	0	0	3	.000
Kemp, M, DH	4	1	1	1	0	1	2	.250
Hernandez, K, CF-LF-2B	4	0	0	0	2	2	0	.000
Puig, RF	3	0	0	0	1	1	0	.000
Barnes, A, C	2	0	0	0	0	1	1	.000
b-Pederson, PH-LF	2	0	0	0	0	0	0	.000
TOTALS	34	4	8	4	3	12	12	

a-Batted for Taylor, C in the 5th. **b-**Grounded out for Barnes, A in the 7th. **c-**Singled for Dozier, B in the 7th. **d-**Batted for Freese in the 7th. **HR:** Kemp, M (1, 2nd inning off Sale, 0 on, 1 out). **TB:** Turner 3; Kemp, M 4; Muncy; Machado; Freese 2. **RBI:** Kemp, M (1); Machado 3 (3). Runners left in scoring position, 2 out: Kemp, M; Bellinger 2. **SF:** Machado. **Team RISP:** 1-for-7. **Team LOB:** 7. **DP:** (Machado-Freese). **Pickoffs:** Kershaw (Martinez, J at 1st base).

BOSTON	AB	R	H	RBI	BB	SO	LOB	AVG
Betts, RF	4	2	1	0	1	2	1	.250
Benintendi, LF	5	3	4	1	0	0	1	.800
Pearce, 1B	2	1	0	0	1	0	2	.000
a-Moreland, PH-1B	1	0	0	0	0	1	1	.000
Martinez, J, DH	3	1	2	1	1	1	3	.667
Bogaerts, SS	3	0	0	1	1	1	4	.000
Devers, 3B	2	0	1	1	1	1	2	.500
b-Nunez, E, PH-3B	1	1	1	3	0	0	0	1.000
Kinsler, 2B	4	0	0	0	0	2	3	.000
Leon, C	4	0	2	0	0	2	0	.500
Bradley Jr., CF	4	0	0	0	0	2	3	.000
TOTALS	33	8	11	8	5	12	20	

a-Struck out for Pearce in the 7th. **b-**Homered for Devers in the 7th. **2B:** Martinez, J 1 (1, Kershaw); Benintendi 1 (1, Urias). **HR:** Nunez, E (1, 7th inning off Wood, A, 2 on, 2 out). **TB:** Benintendi 5; Leon 2; Nunez, E 4; Devers; Martinez, J 3; Betts. **RBI:** Benintendi (1); Martinez, J 2 (2); Bogaerts (1); Devers (1); Nunez, E 3 (3). 2-out RBI: Martinez, J; Devers; Nunez, E 3. Runners left in scoring position, 2 out: Devers; Kinsler. **GIDP:** Bradley Jr. **Team RISP:** 4-for-12. **Team LOB:** 6. **SB:** Betts (1, 2nd base off Kershaw/Barnes, A). **CS:** Martinez, J (1, 2nd base by Kershaw/Barnes, A). **PO:** Martinez, J (1st base by Kershaw).

LA DODGERS	IP	H	R	ER	BB	SO	HR	ERA
Kershaw (L, 0-1)	4.0	7	5	5	3	5	0	11.25
Madson	1.0	1	0	0	1	1	0	0.00
Urias	1.0	1	1	1	0	2	0	9.00
Baez, P	0.2	0	1	1	1	2	0	13.50
Wood, A	1.1	2	1	1	0	2	1	6.75

BOSTON	IP	H	R	ER	BB	SO	HR	ERA
Sale	4.0	5	3	3	2	7	1	6.75
Barnes, M (W, 1-0)	1.0	1	0	0	0	1	0	0.00
Kelly (H, 1)	1.0	0	0	0	0	2	0	0.00
Brasier (H, 1)	0.2	2	1	1	1	0	0	13.50
Rodriguez, E (H, 1)	0.1	0	0	0	0	0	0	0.00
Eovaldi	1.0	0	0	0	0	0	0	0.00
Kimbrel	1.0	0	0	0	0	2	0	0.00

Kershaw pitched to 2 batters in the 5th. Urias pitched to 1 batter in the 7th. Sale pitched to 1 batter in the 5th. **Game Scores:** Kershaw 34; Sale 42. **WP:** Madson; Barnes, M. **IBB:** Bogaerts (by Kershaw); Martinez, J (by Baez, P).

Pitches-strikes: Kershaw 79-52; Madson 14-7; Urias 15-11; Baez, P 10-7; Wood, A 21-14; Sale 91-54; Barnes, M 14-10; Kelly 14-11; Brasier 18-11; Rodriguez, E 3-1; Eovaldi 16-10; Kimbrel 13-10. **Groundouts-flyouts:** Kershaw 3-0; Madson 1-0; Urias 0-0; Baez, P 0-0; Wood, A 1-0; Sale 2-2; Barnes, M 1-1; Kelly 1-0; Brasier 1-1; Rodriguez, E 0-1; Eovaldi 3-0; Kimbrel 1-0. **Batters faced:** Kershaw 20; Madson 5; Urias 4; Baez, P 3; Wood, A 6; Sale 19; Barnes, M 4; Kelly 3; Brasier 5; Rodriguez, E 1; Eovaldi 3; Kimbrel 3. **Inherited runners-scored:** Madson 2-2; Baez, P 1-0; Wood, A 2-2; Barnes, M 1-1; Rodriguez, E 2-0.

GAME TWO *October 24, 2018*

BOSTON RED SOX 4, LOS ANGELES DODGERS 2

	1	2	3	4	5	6	7	8	9	R	H	E
LA DODGERS	0	0	0	2	0	0	0	0	0	2	3	0
BOSTON	0	1	0	0	3	0	0	0	X	4	8	0

LA DODGERS	AB	R	H	RBI	BB	SO	LOB	AVG
Dozier, B, 2B	2	0	0	0	1	0	0	.000
Bellinger, CF	1	0	0	0	0	1	0	.000
Turner, 3B	4	0	0	0	0	1	1	.333
Freese, 1B	2	1	1	0	1	0	0	.600
c-Pederson, PH-LF	1	0	0	0	0	0	0	.000
Machado, SS	4	1	1	0	0	0	1	.286
Taylor, C, LF-2B	3	0	0	0	1	1	0	.000
Kemp, M, DH	3	0	0	1	0	1	0	.143
Hernandez, K, CF-2B	2	0	0	0	1	2	0	.000
a-Muncy, PH-2B-1B	1	0	0	0	0	1	0	.333
Puig, RF	3	0	1	1	0	0	0	.167
Barnes, A, C	2	0	0	0	0	0	2	.000
b-Grandal, PH-C	1	0	0	0	0	1	0	.000
TOTALS	29	2	3	2	3	8	6	

a-Struck out for Hernandez, K in the 7th. **b-**Struck out for Barnes, A in the 7th. **c-**Flied out for Freese in the 8th. **TB:** Puig; Machado; Freese. **RBI:** Kemp, M (2); Puig (1). **2-out RBI:** Puig. Runners left in scoring position, 2 out: Barnes, A. **SF:** Kemp, M. **Team RISP:** 1-for-3. **Team LOB:** 4. **Outfield assists:** Taylor, C (Kinsler at 3rd base).

BOSTON	AB	R	H	RBI	BB	SO	LOB	AVG
Betts, RF	4	1	3	0	0	0	0	.500
Benintendi, LF	3	1	0	0	1	2	2	.500
Pearce, 1B	2	0	0	1	1	0	1	.000
a-Moreland, PH-1B	1	0	0	0	0	1	1	.000
Martinez, J, DH	4	0	1	2	0	0	0	.429
Bogaerts, SS	4	1	1	0	0	2	2	.143
Devers, 3B	4	0	0	0	0	2	1	.167
Kinsler, 2B	3	0	1	1	0	0	0	.143
Bradley Jr., CF	3	0	1	0	0	0	0	.143
Vazquez, C	3	1	1	0	0	1	0	.333
TOTALS	31	4	8	4	2	8	7	

a-Batted for Pearce in the 7th. **2B:** Bogaerts (1, Ryu); Betts (1, Maeda). **TB:** Kinsler; Bradley Jr.; Vazquez; Bogaerts 2; Martinez, J; Betts 4. **RBI:** Kinsler (1); Pearce (1); Martinez, J 2 (4). **2-out RBI:** Kinsler; Pearce; Martinez, J 2. Runners left in scoring position, 2 out: Bogaerts; Moreland. **Team RISP:** 2-for-6. **Team LOB:** 5.

LA DODGERS	IP	H	R	ER	BB	SO	HR	ERA
Ryu (L, 0-1)	4.2	6	4	4	1	2	0	7.71
Madson	0.1	1	0	0	1	1	0	0.00
Urias	1.0	0	0	0	0	0	0	4.50
Maeda	0.2	1	0	0	0	1	0	0.00
Alexander	0.1	0	0	0	0	1	0	0.00
Baez, P	1.0	0	0	0	0	0	0	5.40

BOSTON	IP	H	R	ER	BB	SO	HR	ERA
Price (W, 1-0)	6.0	3	2	2	3	5	0	3.00
Kelly (H, 2)	1.0	0	0	0	0	2	0	0.00
Eovaldi (H, 1)	1.0	0	0	0	0	1	0	0.00
Kimbrel (S, 1)	1.0	0	0	0	0	0	0	0.00

Game Scores: Ryu 47; Price 63. **WP:** Alexander. **Pitches-strikes:** Ryu 69-46; Madson 12-5; Urias 9-8; Maeda 14-8; Alexander 5-3; Baez, P 5-4; Price 88-58; Kelly 11-8; Eovaldi 13-9; Kimbrel 9-7. **Groundouts-flyouts:** Ryu 3-0; Madson 0-0; Urias 0-1; Maeda 1-0; Alexander 0-0; Baez, P 1-2; Price 5-5; Kelly 1-0; Eovaldi 1-1; Kimbrel 2-1. **Batters**

faced: Ryu 20; Madson 3; Urias 3; Maeda 3; Alexander 1; Baez, P 3; Price 24; Kelly 3; Eovaldi 3; Kimbrel 3. **Inherited runners-scored:** Madson 3-3; Alexander 1-0.

GAME 3 *October 26, 2018*

LOS ANGELES DODGERS 3, BOSTON RED SOX 2

	1 2 3 4 5 6 7 8 9 10 11 12 13 14 15 16 17 18	R	H	E
BOSTON	0 0 0 0 0 0 0 1 0 0 0 0 1 0 0 0 0 0	2	7	1
L.A.	0 0 1 0 0 0 0 0 0 0 0 1 0 0 0 0 0 1	3	11	1

None out when winning run scored.

BOSTON	AB	R	H	RBI	BB	SO	LOB	AVG
Betts, RF-CF-RF-CF-RF-CF-RF7	0	0	0	1	3	5	.267
Bogaerts, SS	8	0	0	0	0	2	4	.067
Moreland, 1B	5	0	0	0	0	2	0	.000
Eovaldi, P	2	0	0	0	0	2	0	.000
Martinez, J, LF-RF-LF-RF	3	0	0	0	1	2	0	.300
-Kinsler, PR-2B	3	0	0	0	0	0	1	.100
Holt, 2B-LF-RF-LF	6	1	1	0	1	1	0	.167
Devers, 3B	3	0	0	0	0	2	0	.111
c-Nunez, E, PH-3B	4	0	2	0	0	0	2	.600
Bradley Jr., CF-LF-CF-LF-CF-LF-CF	5	1	2	1	2	1	1	.250
Vazquez, C-1B	7	0	1	0	0	1	4	.200
Porcello, P	0	0	0	0	0	0	0	.000
Rodriguez, E, P	0	0	0	0	0	0	0	.000
a-Swihart, PH	1	0	0	0	0	0	0	.000
Kelly, P	0	0	0	0	0	0	0	.000
Brasier, P	0	0	0	0	0	0	0	.000
Barnes, M, P	0	0	0	0	0	0	0	.000
b-Benintendi, PH	1	0	0	0	0	1	0	.444
Price, P	0	0	0	0	0	0	0	.000
Kimbrel, P	0	0	0	0	0	0	0	.000
d-Pearce, PH	0	0	0	0	1	0	0	.000
Hembree, P	0	0	0	0	0	0	0	.000
Leon, C	2	0	1	0	1	1	2	.500
TOTALS	**57**	**2**	**7**	**1**	**7**	**19**	**18**	

a-Batted for Rodriguez, E in the 6th. **b-**Struck out for Barnes, M in the 9th. **c-**Batted for Devers in the 10th. **d-**Batted for Kimbrel in the 11th. **1-**Ran for Martinez, J in the 10th. **2B:** Leon (1, Floro). **HR:** Bradley Jr. (1, 8th inning off Jansen, 0 on, 2 out). **TB:** Leon 2; Nunez, E 2; Bradley Jr. 5; Vazquez; Holt. **RBI:** Bradley Jr. (1). **2-out RBI:** Bradley Jr. Runners left in scoring position, 2 out: Betts 2; Bogaerts 2. **SAC:** Porcello. **GIDP:** Bogaerts. **Team RISP:** 1-for-7. **Team LOB:** 18. **SB:** Holt (1, 2nd base off Alexander/Barnes, A). **CS:** Bradley Jr. (1, 2nd base by Buehler/Grandal). **E:** Kinsler (1, throw). **Pickoffs:** Price (Bellinger at 1st base).

LA DODGERS	AB	R	H	RBI	BB	SO	LOB	AVG
Pederson, LF	7	1	1	1	0	3	2	.100
Maeda, P	0	0	0	0	0	0	0	.000
Urias, P	0	0	0	0	0	0	0	.000
d-Kershaw, PH	1	0	0	0	0	0	0	.000
Wood, A, P	0	0	0	0	0	0	0	.000
Turner, 3B	8	0	2	0	0	2	1	.294
Muncy, 1B-2B	6	2	2	1	2	1	2	.333
Machado, SS	7	0	1	0	0	1	4	.214
Bellinger, CF	7	0	1	0	0	2	2	.100
Puig, RF	7	0	2	0	0	0	1	.231
Grandal, C	3	0	1	0	1	2	1	.250
1-Barnes, A, PR-C	2	0	0	0	1	0	1	.000
Taylor, C, 2B	4	0	0	0	1	1	3	.000
Madson, P	0	0	0	0	0	0	0	.000
Alexander, P	0	0	0	0	0	0	0	.000
Floro, P	0	0	0	0	0	0	0	.000
c-Freese, PH-1B	2	0	0	0	0	1	0	.429
Buehler, P	2	0	0	0	0	2	1	.000
a-Kemp, M, PH	1	0	0	0	0	0	1	.125
Jansen, P	0	0	0	0	0	0	0	.000
b-Dozier, B, PH	1	0	0	0	0	0	2	.000
Baez, P, P	0	0	0	0	0	0	0	.000
Hernandez, K, 2B-LF	3	0	1	0	0	0	0	.111
TOTALS	**61**	**3**	**11**	**2**	**5**	**15**	**21**	

a-Batted for Buehler in the 7th. **b-**Popped out for Jansen in the 9th. **c-**Grounded out for Floro in the 14th. **d-**Lined out for Urias in the 17th. **1-**Ran for Grandal in the 9th. **2B:** Turner (1, Porcello); Muncy (1, Kimbrel). **HR:** Pederson (1, 3rd inning off Porcello, 0 on, 2 out); Muncy (1, 18th inning off Eovaldi, 0 on, 0 out). **TB:** Puig 2; Turner 3; Pederson 4; Bellinger; Hernandez, K; Muncy 6; Machado; Grandal. **RBI:** Pederson (1); Muncy (1). **2-out RBI:** Pederson. Runners left in scoring position, 2 out: Muncy; Dozier, B; Machado. **Team RISP:** 1-for-4. **Team LOB:** 12. **CS:** Bellinger (1, 2nd base by Price/Vazquez). **PO:** Bellinger (1st base by Price). **E:** Alexander (1, throw). **Outfield assists:** Bellinger (Kinsler at home). **DP:** 2 (Bellinger-Barnes, A; Machado-Muncy-Freese).

	IP	H	R	ER	BB	SO	HR	ERA
Porcello	4.2	3	1	1	1	5	1	1.93
Rodriguez, E	0.1	0	0	0	0	1	0	0.00
Kelly	1.0	1	0	0	0	0	0	0.00
Brasier	1.0	1	0	0	0	1	0	5.40
Barnes, M	1.0	1	0	0	0	2	0	0.00
Price	0.2	1	0	0	0	0	0	2.70
Kimbrel	1.1	1	0	0	1	0	0	0.00
Hembree	1.0	0	0	0	1	1	0	0.00
Eovaldi (L, 0-1)	6.0	3	2	1	1	5	1	1.13

LA DODGERS	IP	H	R	ER	BB	SO	HR	ERA
Buehler	7.0	2	0	0	0	7	0	0.00
Jansen (BS, 1)	2.0	1	1	1	0	2	1	4.50
Baez, P	2.0	1	0	0	2	1	0	2.45
Madson	0.1	0	0	0	0	0	0	0.00
Alexander	1.0	1	1	1	1	1	0	6.75
Floro	1.2	1	0	0	1	3	0	0.00
Maeda	2.0	1	0	0	1	5	0	0.00
Urias	1.0	0	0	0	1	0	0	3.00
Wood, A (W, 1-0)	1.0	0	0	0	1	0	0	3.86

Eovaldi pitched to 1 batter in the 18th. **Game Scores:** Porcello 56; Buehler 85. **IBB:** Betts (by Floro). **Pitches-strikes:** Porcello 61-43; Rodriguez, E 6-5; Kelly 12-9; Brasier 18-15; Barnes, M 23-14; Price 13-7; Kimbrel 28-17; Hembree 25-14; Eovaldi 97-62; Buehler 108-72; Jansen 32-21; Baez, P 26-16; Madson 2-1; Alexander 19-9; Floro 29-19; Maeda 36-24; Urias 11-5; Wood, A 15-6. **Groundouts-flyouts:** Porcello 2-5; Kelly 1-0; Brasier 1-1; Barnes, M 1-0; Price 0-1; Kimbrel 1-0; Hembree 1-1; Eovaldi 2-5; Buehler 7-4; Jansen 1-2; Baez, P 1-2; Madson 1-0; Alexander 1-0; Floro 1-1; Maeda 1-0; Urias 1-1; Wood, A 2-0. **Batters faced:** Porcello 18; Rodriguez, E 1; Kelly 4; Brasier 4; Barnes, M 4; Price 3; Kimbrel 6; Hembree 4; Eovaldi 22; Buehler 22; Jansen 7; Baez, P 8; Madson 1; Alexander 5; Floro 7; Maeda 8; Urias 4; Wood, A 3.

GAME 4 *October 27, 2018*

BOSTON RED SOX 9, LOS ANGELES DODGERS 6

	1	2	3	4	5	6	7	8	9	R	H	E
BOSTON	0	0	0	0	0	0	3	1	5	9	8	1
LA DODGERS	0	0	0	0	4	0	0	2	6	9	0	

BOSTON	AB	R	H	RBI	BB	SO	LOB	AVG
Betts, CF	4	1	0	0	1	1	2	.211
Benintendi, LF	5	1	1	0	0	0	1	.357
Pearce, 1B	4	2	2	4	1	0	1	.250
Martinez, J, RF	4	0	0	0	1	3	1	.214
Bogaerts, SS	4	1	1	1	1	0	0	.105
Nunez, E, 3B	5	0	0	0	0	3	3	.300
Kimbrel, P	0	0	0	0	0	0	0	.000
Holt, 2B	2	2	1	0	2	0	0	.250
Vazquez, C	2	0	1	0	0	0	1	.250
a-Bradley Jr., PH	1	0	0	0	0	0	2	.231
Leon, C	0	0	0	0	0	0	0	.500
c-Devers, PH-3B	1	1	1	1	0	0	0	.200
Rodriguez, E, P	1	0	0	0	0	1	1	.000
Barnes, M, P	0	0	0	0	0	0	0	.000
b-Moreland, PH	1	1	1	3	0	0	0	.125
Kelly, P	0	0	0	0	0	0	0	.000
d-Swihart, PH-C	1	0	0	0	0	0	1	.000
TOTALS	**35**	**9**	**8**	**9**	**6**	**8**	**13**	

a-Popped out for Vazquez in the 7th. **b**-Batted for Barnes, M in the 7th. **c**-Singled for Leon in the 9th. **d**-Batted for Kelly in the 9th. **2B:** Holt (1, Floro); Pearce (1, Maeda). **HR:** Moreland (1, 7th inning off Madson, 2 on, 2 out); Pearce (1, 8th inning off Jansen, 0 on, 1 out). **TB:** Benintendi; Devers; Moreland 4; Vazquez; Bogaerts; Pearce 6; Holt 2. **RBI:** Moreland 3 (3); Pearce 4 (5); Devers (2); Bogaerts (2). **2-out RBI:** Moreland 3; Pearce 3; Bogaerts. Runners left in scoring position, 2 out: Nunez, E. **Team RISP:** 5-for-7. **Team LOB:** 6. **E:** Vazquez (1, throw).

LA DODGERS	AB	R	H	RBI	BB	SO	LOB	AVG
Freese, 1B	2	0	0	0	0	1	0	.333
1-Hernandez, K, PR-2B-LF	2	1	1	2	0	0	0	.182
Muncy, 2B-1B	5	0	1	0	0	1	1	.286
Turner, 3B	4	1	3	0	1	0	1	.381
Machado, SS	4	1	1	0	1	1	3	.222
Bellinger, CF	5	1	0	0	0	2	5	.067
Puig, RF	4	1	1	3	0	0	2	.235
Taylor, C, LF	3	0	2	0	1	1	0	.167
Maeda, P	0	0	0	0	0	0	0	.000
Barnes, A, C	3	0	0	0	0	2	2	.000
b-Grandal, PH-C	1	0	0	0	0	1	2	.200
Hill, R, P	2	0	0	0	0	0	0	.000
Alexander, P	0	0	0	0	0	0	0	.000
Madson, P	0	0	0	0	0	0	0	.000
a-Pederson, PH	1	0	0	0	0	1	0	.091
Jansen, P	0	0	0	0	0	0	0	.000
Floro, P	0	0	0	0	0	0	0	.000
Wood, A, P	0	0	0	0	0	0	0	.000
Dozier, B, 2B	0	1	0	0	1	0	0	.000
TOTALS	36	6	9	5	4	10	16	

a-Struck out for Madson in the 7th. **b**-Batted for Barnes, A in the 8th. **1**-Ran for Freese in the 6th. **2B:** Turner (2, Rodriguez, E). **HR:** Puig (1, 6th inning off Rodriguez, E, 2 on, 2 out); Hernandez, K (1, 9th inning off Kimbrel, 1 on, 0 out). **TB:** Puig 4; Turner 4; Hernandez, K 4; Taylor, C 2; Muncy; Machado. **RBI:** Puig 3 (4); Hernandez, K 2 (2). **2-out RBI:** Puig 3. Runners left in scoring position, 2 out: Grandal; Bellinger. **Team RISP:** 1-for-4. **Team LOB:** 8.

BOSTON	IP	H	R	ER	BB	SO	HR	ERA
Rodriguez, E	5.2	4	4	4	2	6	1	5.68
Barnes, M	0.1	0	0	0	1	1	0	0.00
Kelly (W, 1-0)	2.0	3	0	0	0	3	0	0.00
Kimbrel	1.0	2	2	2	1	0	1	4.15

LA DODGERS	IP	H	R	ER	BB	SO	HR	ERA
Hill, R	6.1	1	1	1	3	7	0	1.42
Alexander	0.0	0	1	1	1	0	0	13.50
Madson (H, 1)	0.2	1	1	1	0	0	1	3.86
Jansen (BS, 2)	1.0	1	1	1	0	1	1	6.00
Floro (L, 0-1)	0.2	2	3	3	1	0	0	11.57
Wood, A	0.0	1	1	1	0	0	0	7.71
Maeda	0.1	2	1	1	1	0	0	3.00

Alexander pitched to 1 batter in the 7th. **Game Scores:** Rodriguez, E 50; Hill, R 74. **IBB:** Betts (by Floro); Martinez, J (by Maeda); Machado (by Rodriguez, E by Hill, R); Freese (by Rodriguez, E). **HBP:** Rodriguez, E (by Hill, R); Freese (by Rodriguez, E). **Pitches-strikes:** Rodriguez, E 93-59; Barnes, M 11-5; Kelly 30-20; Kimbrel 28-15; Hill, R 91-58; Alexander 4-0; Madson 8-5; Jansen 10-8; Floro 10-6; Wood, A 4-4; Maeda 12-9. **Groundouts-flyouts:** Rodriguez, E 5-4; Barnes, M 0-0; Kelly 1-1; Kimbrel 2-1; Hill, R 4-4; Alexander 0-0; Madson 0-0; Jansen 1-1; Floro 1-0; Wood, A 0-0; Maeda 0-1. **Batters faced:** Rodriguez, E 24; Barnes, M 2; Kelly 9; Kimbrel 6; Hill, R 24; Alexander 1; Madson 3; Jansen 4; Floro 5; Wood, A 1; Maeda 4. **Inherited runners-scored:** Alexander 1-0; Madson 2-2; Wood, A 2-0; Maeda 3-3.

GAME 5 *October 28, 2018*

BOSTON RED SOX 5, LOS ANGELES DODGERS 1

	1	2	3	4	5	6	7	8	9	R	H	E
BOSTON	2	0	0	0	1	1	1	0	5	8	0	
LA DODGERS	1	0	0	0	0	0	0	0	0	1	3	0

BOSTON	AB	R	H	RBI	BB	SO	LOB	AVG
Betts, CF-RF	4	1	1	1	0	0	0	.217
Benintendi, LF	4	1	1	0	0	0	0	.333
Pearce, 1B	4	2	2	3	0	0	0	.333
Martinez, J, RF	4	1	2	1	0	1	0	.278
Sale, P	0	0	0	0	0	0	0	.000
Bogaerts, SS	3	0	1	0	1	1	1	.136
Holt, 2B	4	0	0	0	0	0	2	.167
Devers, 3B	4	0	1	0	0	2	0	.214
Vazquez, C	3	0	0	0	0	1	2	.200
Price, P	3	0	0	0	0	1	2	.000
Kelly, P	0	0	0	0	0	0	0	.000
Bradley Jr., CF	0	0	0	0	0	0	0	.231
TOTALS	33	5	8	5	1	6	7	

HR: Pearce 2 (3, 1st inning off Kershaw, 1 on, 1 out; 8th inning off Baez, P, 0 on, 2 out); Betts (1, 6th inning off Kershaw, 0 on, 1 out); Martinez, J (1, 7th inning off Kershaw, 0 on, 0 out). **TB:** Benintendi; Devers; Bogaerts; Martinez, J 5; Pearce 8; Betts 4. **RBI:** Pearce 3 (8); Betts (1); Martinez, J (5). **2-out RBI:** Pearce. Runners left in scoring position, 2 out: Price. **GIDP:** Bogaerts; Holt. **Team RISP:** 0-for-2. **Team LOB:** 2. **DP:** (Devers-Holt-Pearce).

LA DODGERS	AB	R	H	RBI	BB	SO	LOB	AVG
Freese, 1B	3	1	2	1	0	0	0	.417
c-Bellinger, PH	1	0	0	0	0	1	1	.063
Jansen, P	0	0	0	0	0	0	0	.000
Turner, 3B	3	0	0	0	1	0	1	.333
Hernandez, K, CF-2B	4	0	0	0	0	1	2	.133
Machado, SS	4	0	0	0	0	3	0	.182
Muncy, 2B-1B	3	0	0	0	0	1	0	.235
Puig, RF	3	0	1	0	0	0	0	.250
Taylor, C, LF-CF	2	0	0	0	1	1	1	.143
Barnes, A, C	2	0	0	0	0	1	1	.000
a-Kemp, M, PH-LF	1	0	0	0	0	1	1	.111
Kershaw, P	2	0	0	0	0	0	0	.000
Baez, P, P	0	0	0	0	0	0	0	.000
b-Pederson, PH	1	0	0	0	0	1	1	.083
Grandal, C	0	0	0	0	0	0	0	.200
TOTALS	29	1	3	1	2	11	8	

a-Batted for Barnes, A in the 8th. **b**-Struck out for Baez, P in the 8th. **c**-Struck out for Freese in the 8th. **3B:** Freese (1, Price). **HR:** Freese (1, 1st inning off Price, 0 on, 0 out). **TB:** Puig; Freese 7. **RBI:** Freese (1). Runners left in scoring position, 2 out: Hernandez, K. **GIDP:** Hernandez, K. **Team RISP:** 0-for-2. **Team LOB:** 3. **DP:** 2 (Machado-Muncy-Freese; Hernandez, K-Machado-Muncy).

BOSTON	IP	H	R	ER	BB	SO	HR	ERA
Price (W, 2-0)	7.0	3	1	1	2	5	1	1.98
Kelly	1.0	0	0	0	0	3	0	0.00
Sale	1.0	0	0	0	0	3	0	5.40

LA DODGERS	IP	H	R	ER	BB	SO	HR	ERA
Kershaw (L, 0-2)	7.0	7	4	4	0	5	3	7.36
Baez, P	1.0	1	1	1	0	1	1	3.86
Jansen	1.0	0	0	0	1	0	0	4.50

Price pitched to 1 batter in the 8th. **Game Scores:** Price 68; Kershaw 43. **Pitches-strikes:** Price 89-58; Kelly 16-10; Sale 15-11; Kershaw 92-66; Baez, P 15-11; Jansen 9-4. **Groundouts-flyouts:** Price 8-4; Kelly 0-0; Sale 0-0; Kershaw 8-4; Baez, P 0-1; Jansen 2-0. **Batters faced:** Price 25; Kelly 3; Sale 3; Kershaw 27; Baez, P 4; Jansen 3. **Inherited runners-scored:** Kelly 1-0.

AMERICAN LEAGUE WILD CARD GAME

NEW YORK YANKEES 7, OAKLAND ATHLETICS 2

OAKLAND	AB	R	H	RBI	BB	SO	LOB	AVG
Martini, LF	4	0	1	0	0	2	1	.250
a-Canha, PH	1	0	0	0	0	1	1	.000
Chapman, M, 3B	5	0	1	0	0	0	4	.200
Lowrie, 2B	4	1	0	0	0	1	3	.000
Davis, K, DH	4	1	1	2	0	2	2	.250
Olson, 1B	2	0	0	0	2	0	0	.000
Piscotty, RF	3	0	0	0	1	2	3	.000
Laureano, CF	3	0	0	0	0	2	2	.000
Semien, SS	3	0	1	0	1	1	3	.333
Lucroy, C	4	0	1	0	0	2	2	.250
Totals	33	2	5	2	5	13	21	

a-Struck out for Martini in the 9th. **HR:** Davis, K (1, 8th inning off Britton, 1 on, 1 out). **TB:** Lucroy; Martini; Chapman, M; Semien; Davis, K 4. **RBI:** Davis, K 2 (2). Runners left in scoring position, 2 out: Semien 2; Davis, K; Chapman, M. **Team RISP:** 0-for-6. Team LOB: 9. **DP:** (Semien-Lowrie-Olson).

NY YANKEES	AB	R	H	RBI	BB	SO	LOB	AVG
McCutchen, LF	3	1	0	0	1	0	1	.000
Gardner, LF	0	0	0	0	0	0	0	.000
Judge, RF	3	2	2	2	1	1	0	.667
Hicks, A, CF	4	1	1	1	0	1	0	.250
Stanton, DH	3	2	1	1	1	1	0	.333
Voit, 1B	4	1	1	2	0	2	0	.250
Walker, 1B	0	0	0	0	0	0	0	.000
Gregorius, SS	3	0	1	1	0	1	0	.333
Andujar, 3B	1	0	1	0	1	0	1	1.000
Hechavarria, 3B	2	0	0	0	0	0	0	.000
Sanchez, G, C	3	0	0	0	0	3	0	.000
Torres, 2B	3	0	0	0	1	2	0	.000
TOTALS	29	7	7	7	4	6	7	

2B: Judge (1, Rodney); Hicks, A (1, Rodney). **3B:** Voit (1, Treinen). **HR:** Judge (1, 1st inning off Hendriks, 1 on, 0 out); Stanton (1, 8th inning off Treinen, 0 on, 0 out). **TB:** Voit 3; Judge 6; Hicks, A 2; Gregorius; Andujar; Stanton 4. **RBI:** Judge 2 (2); Hicks, A (1); Voit 2 (2); Gregorius (1); Stanton (1). Runners left in scoring position, 2 out: Torres. **SF:** Gregorius. **GIDP:** Sanchez, G. **Team RISP:** 2-for-4. **Team LOB:** 3. **SB:** Stanton (1, 2nd base off Treinen/Lucroy). **E:** Andujar (1, throw).

OAKLAND	IP	H	R	ER	BB	SO	HR	ERA
Hendriks (L, 0-1)	1.0	1	2	2	1	1	1	18.00
Trivino	3.0	1	0	0	1	4	0	0.00
Kelley	1.0	1	0	0	0	0	0	0.00
Rodney	0.0	2	2	2	0	0	0	—
Treinen	2.0	2	3	3	2	0	1	13.50
Familia	1.0	0	0	0	0	1	0	0.00

NY YANKEES	IP	H	R	ER	BB	SO	HR	ERA
Severino	4.0	2	0	0	4	7	0	0.00
Betances (W, 1-0)	2.0	0	0	0	0	3	0	0.00
Robertson, D	1.0	0	0	0	1	0	0	0.00
Britton	1.0	2	2	2	1	0	1	18.00
Chapman, A	1.0	1	0	0	0	2	0	0.00

Rodney pitched to 2 batters in the 6th. Treinen pitched to 1 batter in the 8th. Severino pitched to 2 batters in the 5th. **Game Scores:** Hendriks 31; Severino 59. **WP:** Rodney. **Pitches-strikes:** Hendriks 25-13; Trivino 41-24; Kelley 14-9; Rodney 5-3; Treinen 42-28; Familia 10-6; Severino 87-53; Betances 25-16; Robertson, D 12-7; Britton 13-7; Chapman, A 17-13. **Groundouts-flyouts:** Hendriks 0-1; Trivino 3-0; Kelley 1-0; Rodney 0-0; Treinen 3-0; Familia 1-0; Severino 3-2; Betances 1-1; Robertson, D 0-0; Britton 3-0; Chapman, A 1-0. Batters faced: Hendriks 5; Trivino 10; Kelley 4; Rodney 2; Treinen 10; Familia 3; Severino 19; Betances 6; Robertson, D 3; Britton 6; Chapman, A 4. Inherited runners-scored: Treinen 1-1; Betances 2-0. **Umpires: HP:** Jim Wolf. **1B:** Greg Gibson. **2B:** Gerry Davis. **3B:** Alan Porter. **LF:** Will Little. **RF:** Pat Hoberg. **Weather:** 70 degrees, partly cloudy. **Wind:** 5 mph, Out to CF. **First pitch:** 8:08 PM. **T:** 3:25. **Att:** 49,620. **Venue:** Yankee Stadium.

SCORE BY INNING

											R	H	E
OAKLAND	0	0	0	0	0	0	0	2	0		2	5	0
NY YANKEES	2	0	0	0	0	4	0	1	X		7	7	1

AMERICAN LEAGUE DIVISION SERIES

HOUSTON ASTROS VS CLEVELAND INDIANS

HOUSTON	AVG	G	AB	R	H	2B	3B	HR	RBI	BB	SO	SB
Jose Altuve, 2B	.286	3	14	4	4	1	0	1	2	0	2	0
Alex Bregman, 3B	.556	3	9	5	5	1	0	2	4	4	1	0
Carlos Correa, SS	.100	3	10	1	1	0	0	1	3	3	2	0
Evan Gattis, C	.000	2	2	0	0	0	0	0	0	0	1	0
Marwin Gonzalez, LF	.538	3	13	1	7	2	0	0	5	2	0	0
Yuli Gurriel, 1B	.182	3	11	2	2	1	0	0	0	3	3	0
Tony Kemp, LF	.333	1	3	2	1	0	0	0	0	2	1	0
Martin Maldonado, C	.125	3	8	1	1	0	0	1	1	0	4	0
Jake Marisnick, CF	.000	3	1	0	0	0	0	0	0	0	1	0
Brian McCann, C	.000	1	3	0	0	0	0	0	0	0	2	0
Josh Reddick, RF	.400	3	10	0	4	0	0	0	2	0	1	0
George Springer, CF	.429	3	14	4	6	0	0	3	3	0	2	0
Myles Straw, CF	—	2	0	1	0	0	0	0	0	0	0	1
Tyler White, 1B	.500	3	2	1	1	0	0	0	2	0	0	0
Totals	.327	3	104	21	34	6	0	8	20	14	24	1

HOUSTON	W	L	ERA	G	GS	SV	IP	H	R	ER	BB	SO
Gerrit Cole	1	0	1.29	1	1	0	7	3	1	1	0	12
Wil Harris	0	0	9.00	1	0	0	1	1	1	1	1	0
Dallas Keuchel	0	0	3.60	1	1	0	5	4	2	2	1	2
Lance McCullers Jr.	0	0	0.00	2	0	0	2	2	0	0	0	0
Collin McHugh	1	0	0.00	1	0	0	2	0	0	0	0	4
Roberto Osuna	0	0	0.00	2	0	1	2.1	1	0	0	1	2
Ryan Pressly	0	0	0.00	2	0	0	2.1	0	0	0	1	3
Justin Verlander	1	0	3.38	1	1	0	5.1	2	2	2	2	7
Totals	3	0	2.00	3	3	1	27	13	6	6	6	30

CLEVELAND	AVG	G	AB	R	H	2B	3B	HR	RBI	BB	SO	SB
Greg Allen, CF	.000	1	0	0	0	0	0	0	0	0	0	0
Yonder Alonso, 1B	.000	2	6	0	0	0	0	0	0	0	4	0
Michael Brantley, LF	.200	3	10	0	2	0	0	0	1	1	1	0
Melky Cabrera, RF	.125	3	8	0	1	0	0	0	0	0	0	0
Yandy Diaz, 3B	.333	1	3	0	1	1	0	0	0	0	0	0
Josh Donaldson, 3B	.091	3	11	0	1	0	0	0	1	4	0	0
Edwin Encarnacion, DH	.100	3	10	1	1	0	0	0	0	2	4	0
Yan Gomes, C	.250	3	8	2	2	0	0	0	0	1	4	0
Brandon Guyer, RF	.000	1	2	0	0	0	0	0	0	0	0	0
Jason Kipnis, 2B	.111	3	9	0	1	0	0	0	0	0	6	0
Francisco Lindor, SS	.364	3	11	3	4	0	0	2	2	2	2	0
Jose Ramirez, 3B	.000	3	11	0	0	0	0	0	1	1	3	0
Totals	.144	3	90	6	13	1	0	2	4	6	30	0

CLEVELAND	W	L	ERA	G	GS	SV	IP	H	R	ER	BB	SO
Cody Allen	0	0	54.00	2	0	0	1	4	6	6	2	2
Trevor Bauer	0	1	6.75	3	0	0	4	7	4	3	1	4
Carlos Carrasco	0	1	3.38	1	1	0	5.1	6	2	2	1	3
Adam Cimber	0	0	4.50	2	0	0	2	2	1	1	1	0
Mike Clevinger	0	0	1.80	1	1	0	5	3	1	1	3	9
Brad Hand	0	0	10.80	2	0	0	1.2	3	2	2	1	4
Corey Kluber	0	1	7.71	1	1	0	4.2	6	4	4	2	2
Andrew Miller	0	0	0.00	2	0	0	0.1	1	0	0	3	0
Dan Otero	0	0	9.00	1	0	0	1	2	1	1	0	0
Totals	0	3	7.20	3	3	0	25	34	21	20	14	24

SCORE BY INNING

										R	H	E
HOUSTON	0	0	0	2	3	2	6	7		1	21	
CLEVELAND	0	0	2	0	1	2	0	6				

BOSTON RED SOX VS NEW YORK YANKEES

BOSTON	AVG	G	AB	R	H	2B	3B	HR	RBI	BB	SO	SB
Andrew Benintendi, LF	.286	4	14	5	4	1	0	0	3	3	3	2
Mookie Betts, RF	.188	4	16	3	3	1	0	0	2	3	4	0
Xander Bogaerts, SS	.294	4	17	2	5	0	0	1	2	1	1	0
Jackie Bradley Jr., CF	.167	4	12	2	2	1	0	0	3	3	1	0
Rafael Devers, 3B	.286	2	7	2	2	0	0	0	1	0	1	0
Brock Holt, 2B	.667	1	6	3	4	1	1	1	5	0	0	0

BOSTON	AVG	G	AB	R	H	2B	3B	HR	RBI	BB	SO	SB
Ian Kinsler, 2B	.308	4	13	3	4	2	0	0	2	1	7	1
Sandy Leon, C	.000	2	5	0	0	0	0	0	0	0	0	0
J.D. Martinez, LF	.357	4	14	1	5	0	0	1	6	3	0	0
Mitch Moreland, 1B	.333	2	3	1	1	0	0	0	0	0	1	0
Eduardo Nunez, 2B	.182	3	11	0	2	1	0	0	1	1	2	0
Steve Pearce, 1B	.333	4	12	3	4	0	0	0	2	2	4	0
Blake Swihart, C	.000	1	1	0	0	0	0	0	0	0	1	0
Christian Vazquez, C	.333	3	9	2	3	0	0	1	2	1	2	0
Totals	**.279**	**4**	**140**	**27**	**39**	**7**	**1**	**4**	**26**	**18**	**29**	**5**

BOSTON	W	L	ERA	G	GS	SV	IP	H	R	ER	BB	SO
Matt Barnes	0	0	0.00	2	0	0	2	0	0	0	1	1
Ryan Brasier	0	0	0.00	3	0	0	2.1	1	0	0	2	4
Nathan Eovaldi	1	0	1.29	1	1	0	7	5	1	1	0	5
Heath Hembree	0	0	0.00	2	0	0	3	0	0	0	3	2
Joe Kelly	0	0	0.00	1	0	0	2.1	1	0	0	0	1
Craig Kimbrel	0	0	11.57	2	0	0	2.1	2	3	3	2	4
Rick Porcello	1	0	1.59	2	1	0	5.2	5	1	1	0	1
David Price	0	1	16.20	1	1	0	1.2	3	3	3	2	0
Eduardo Rodriguez	0	0	10.13	2	0	0	2.2	2	3	3	2	2
Chris Sale	1	0	2.84	2	1	0	6.1	5	2	2	2	9
Brandon Workman	0	0	13.50	2	0	0	0.2	4	1	1	1	2
Totals	**3**	**1**	**3.50**	**4**	**4**	**2**	**36**	**28**	**14**	**14**	**15**	**31**

NEW YORK	AVG	G	AB	R	H	2B	3B	HR	RBI	BB	SO	SB
Miguel Andujar, 3B	.111	3	9	0	1	0	0	0	0	0	1	2
Brett Gardner, LF	.000	4	8	1	0	0	0	0	0	1	3	1
Didi Gregorius, SS	.214	4	14	1	3	1	0	0	2	0	3	0
Adeiny Hechavarria, SS	.000	3	1	0	0	0	0	0	0	0	1	0
Aaron Hicks, CF	.200	2	5	0	1	0	0	0	0	0	1	1
Aaron Judge, RF	.375	4	16	4	6	0	0	2	2	2	2	0
Andrew McCutchen, RF	.133	4	15	1	2	0	0	0	1	0	3	0
Gary Sanchez, C	.200	4	15	3	3	1	0	2	5	1	5	0
Giancarlo Stanton, LF	.222	4	18	2	4	0	0	0	0	0	6	0
Gleyber Torres, 2B	.308	4	13	1	4	0	0	0	0	2	2	0
Luke Voit, 1B	.231	4	13	1	3	0	0	0	2	4	4	0
Neil Walker, 1B	.250	3	4	0	1	0	0	0	0	1	2	0
Totals	**.214**	**4**	**131**	**14**	**28**	**2**	**0**	**4**	**14**	**15**	**31**	**0**

NEW YORK	W	L	ERA	G	GS	SV	IP	H	R	ER	BB	SO
Dellin Betances	0	0	2.70	2	0	0	3.1	3	1	1	1	4
Zach Britton	0	0	2.25	3	0	0	4	3	1	1	1	4
Aroldis Chapman	0	0	0.00	2	0	0	2	0	0	0	1	2
Chad Green	0	0	2.45	2	0	0	3.2	4	1	1	3	0
J.A. Happ	0	1	22.50	1	1	0	2	4	5	5	1	2
Jonathan Holder	0	0	4.50	1	0	0	2	2	1	1	1	1
Lance Lynn	0	0	11.57	2	0	0	2.1	3	3	3	2	2
David Robertson	0	0	0.00	2	0	0	2.2	0	0	0	1	6
Austin Romine	0	0	18.00	1	0	0	1	1	2	2	1	0
CC Sabathia	0	1	9.00	1	1	0	3	5	3	3	2	1
Luis Severino	0	1	18.00	1	1	0	3	7	6	6	2	2
Mashiro Tanaka	1	0	1.80	1	1	0	5	3	1	1	1	4
Stephen Tarpley	**0**	**0**	**27.00**	**1**	**0**	**0**	**1**	**4**	**3**	**3**	**1**	
1 Totals	**1**	**3**	**6.94**	**4**	**4**	**0**	**35**	**39**	**27**	**27**	**18**	**29**

SCORE BY INNINGS

BOSTON	3	1	7	9	0	0	2	3	2	27	
NEW YORK	1	2	0	1	1	2	4	0	3	14	

AMERICAN LEAGUE CHAMPIONSHIP SERIES
BOSTON RED SOX VS HOUSTON ASTROS

BOSTON	AVG	G	AB	R	H	2B	3B	HR	RBI	BB	SO	SB
Andrew Benintendi, LF	.208	5	24	4	5	2	0	0	1	0	7	0
Mookie Betts, RF	.217	5	23	5	5	2	0	0	1	1	2	0
Xander Bogaerts, SS	.263	5	19	1	5	1	0	0	3	3	1	0
Jackie Bradley Jr., CF	.200	5	15	3	3	1	0	2	9	4	3	0
Rafael Devers, 3B	.385	4	13	4	5	0	0	1	6	2	5	0
Brock Holt, 2B	.111	4	9	1	1	0	0	0	1	1	3	0
Ian Kinsler, 2B	.182	4	11	1	2	1	0	0	0	0	4	0
Sandy Leon, C	.000	2	5	0	0	0	0	0	0	0	1	0
J.D. Martinez, LF	.278	5	18	3	5	1	0	1	3	4	4	0
Mitch Moreland, 1B	.500	5	6	1	3	1	0	0	2	1	1	0
Eduardo Nunez, 2B	.200	2	5	0	1	0	0	0	0	0	1	0
Steve Pearce, 1B	.214	4	14	4	3	1	0	1	1	3	4	0
Christian Vazquez, C	.154	5	13	1	2	1	0	0	0	0	3	0
Totals	**.233**	**5**	**172**	**29**	**40**	**11**	**0**	**5**	**27**	**20**	**38**	**0**

BOSTON	W	L	ERA	G	GS	SV	IP	H	R	ER	BB	SO
Matt Barnes	1	0	2.08	5	0	0	4.1	1	1	1	4	4
Ryan Brasier	0	0	0.00	4	0	0	4.2	3	0	0	2	2
Nathan Eovaldi	1	0	2.45	2	1	0	7.1	7	2	2	2	5
Heath Hembree	0	0	0.00	1	0	0	0.2	0	0	0	1	0
Joe Kelly	1	1	3.00	3	0	0	3	3	2	1	0	2
Craig Kimbrel	0	0	4.50	3	0	3	4	4	2	2	4	4
Rick Porcello	0	0	7.20	2	1	0	5	7	4	4	1	5
David Price	1	0	3.38	2	2	0	10.2	8	4	4	4	13
Eduardo Rodriguez	0	0	0.00	2	0	0	1	0	0	0	1	2
Chris Sale	0	0	4.50	1	1	0	4	1	2	2	4	5
Brandon Workman	0	0	108.00	1	0	0	0.1	3	4	4	2	1
Totals	**4**	**1**	**4.00**	**5**	**5**	**3**	**45**	**37**	**21**	**20**	**25**	**43**

HOUSTON	AVG	G	AB	R	H	2B	3B	HR	RBI	BB	SO	SB
Jose Altuve, 2B	.250	5	20	4	5	1	0	0	2	3	4	0
Alex Bregman, 3B	.133	5	15	3	2	1	0	0	1	7	3	0
Carlos Correa, SS	.316	5	19	2	6	1	0	0	3	3	7	0
Evan Gattis, C	.000	2	2	0	0	0	0	0	0	0	0	0
Marwin Gonzalez, LF	.200	5	20	2	4	0	0	2	4	1	7	0
Yuli Gurriel, 1B	.250	5	20	3	5	1	0	1	3	2	2	0
Tony Kemp, LF	.273	5	11	1	3	1	0	0	1	3	2	0
Martin Maldonado, C	.091	4	11	2	1	1	0	0	0	0	3	0
Jake Marisnick, CF	.000	2	2	0	0	0	0	0	0	0	0	1
Brian McCann, C	.000	3	5	0	0	0	0	0	0	0	1	0
Josh Reddick, RF	.188	5	16	2	3	1	0	1	2	2	4	0
George Springer, CF	.381	5	21	2	8	3	0	1	5	3	5	1
Tyler White, 1B	.000	5	7	0	0	0	0	0	0	1	3	0
Totals	**.219**	**5**	**169**	**21**	**37**	**10**	**0**	**6**	**21**	**25**	**43**	**2**

HOUSTON	W	L	ERA	G	GS	SV	IP	H	R	ER	BB	SO
Gerrit Cole	0	1	6.00	1	1	0	6	6	5	4	2	5
Josh James	0	1	7.71	2	0	0	4.2	6	4	4	2	7
Dallas Keuchel	0	0	3.60	1	1	0	5	4	2	2	2	0
Lance McCullers Jr.	0	0	3.00	3	0	0	3	2	1	1	2	4
Collin McHugh	0	0	0.00	3	0	0	2	1	0	0	0	1
Charlie Morton	0	0	11.57	1	0	0	2.1	3	3	3	2	2
Roberto Osuna	0	0	12.27	2	0	0	3.2	4	5	5	0	3
Ryan Pressly	0	0	3.38	3	0	0	2.2	1	1	1	2	4
Hector Rondon	0	0	0.00	2	0	0	1	2	0	0	0	0
Tony Sipp	0	0	0.00	3	0	0	1.1	1	0	0	2	2
Joe Smith	0	1	27.00	1	0	0	0.1	1	1	1	0	0
Justin Verlander	1	1	4.50	2	2	0	12	9	6	6	6	10
Totals	**1**	**4**	**5.52**	**5**	**5**	**0**	**44**	**40**	**29**	**27**	**20**	**38**

SCORE BY INNINGS

BOSTON	6	0	5	0	3	6	2	7	0	29	
HOUSTON	1	5	4	1	2	1	1	1	5	21	

NATIONAL LEAGUE WILD CARD GAME

COLORADO ROCKIES 2, CHICAGO CUBS 1

COLORADO	AB	R	H	RBI	BB	SO	LOB	AVG
Blackmon, CF	3	1	1	0	1	0	1	.333
Davis, W, P	0	0	0	0	0	0	0	.000
a-Valaika, PH	1	0	0	0	0	1	1	.000
Oh, P	0	0	0	0	0	0	0	.000
McMahon, 1B	1	0	0	0	0	0	0	.000
LeMahieu, 2B	6	0	1	0	0	1	2	.167
Arenado, 3B	5	0	1	1	0	1	1	.200
Story, SS	6	1	3	0	0	1	2	.500
Holliday, LF	3	0	1	0	0	2	2	.333
Parra, LF	2	0	1	0	1	0	1	.500
Desmond, 1B	5	0	1	0	0	2	4	.200
Rusin, P	0	0	0	0	0	0	0	.000
Wolters, C	1	0	1	1	0	0	0	1.000
Dahl, RF-CF	6	0	0	0	0	1	7	.000
Iannetta, C	3	0	0	0	0	2	0	.000
Ottavino, P	0	0	0	0	0	0	0	.000
Gonzalez, C, RF	2	0	1	0	0	0	0	.500
Freeland, P	2	0	0	0	0	2	0	.000
Butera, C	2	0	0	0	1	0	1	.000
Oberg, P	0	0	0	0	0	0	0	.000
TOTALS	48	2	11	2	3	13	22	

CHI CUBS	AB	R	H	RBI	BB	SO	LOB	AVG
Zobrist, RF-LF-2B	6	0	1	0	0	1	1	.167
Bryant, LF-3B	6	0	1	0	0	3	1	.167
Rizzo, 1B	4	0	1	0	0	0	3	.250
1-Gore, PR-LF	2	1	0	0	0	2	0	.000
Baez, J, SS	5	0	1	1	1	2	1	.200
Almora Jr., CF	5	0	2	0	0	2	1	.400
Murphy, D, 2B-1B	4	0	0	0	1	1	2	.000
Contreras, C	3	0	0	0	2	0	3	.000
Bote, 3B	2	0	0	0	0	2	1	.000
b-La Stella, PH	0	0	0	0	0	0	0	.000
Rosario, R, P	0	0	0	0	0	0	0	.000
Cishek, P	0	0	0	0	0	0	0	.000
Strop, P	0	0	0	0	0	0	0	.000
d-Schwarber, PH	1	0	0	0	0	1	1	.000
Hamels, P	0	0	0	0	0	0	0	.000
e-Caratini, PH	1	0	0	0	0	2	0	.000
Wilson, J, P	0	0	0	0	0	0	0	.000
Hendricks, P	0	0	0	0	0	0	0	.000
De La Rosa, J, P	0	0	0	0	0	0	0	.000
Lester, P	1	0	0	0	0	1	0	.000
a-Happ, I, PH	0	0	0	0	1	0	0	.000
Chavez, P	0	0	0	0	0	0	0	.000
c-Heyward, PH-RF	3	0	0	0	0	1	4	.000
TOTALS	43	1	6	1	5	16	20	

COLORADO	IP	H	R	ER	BB	SO	HR	ERA
Freeland	6.2	4	0	0	1	6	0	0.00
Ottavino (BS, 1)	1.0	2	1	1	1	2	0	9.00
Davis, W	1.1	0	0	0	1	3	0	0.00
Oh	1.2	0	0	0	2	1	0	0.00
Rusin	1.0	0	0	0	0	0	0	0.00
Oberg (W, 1-0)	1.1	0	0	0	0	4	0	0.00

Chi Cubs	IP	H	R	ER	BB	SO	HR	ERA
Lester	6.0	4	1	1	1	9	0	1.50
Chavez	1.0	1	0	0	0	0	0	0.00
Rosario, R	0.1	0	0	0	1	0	0	0.00
Cishek	0.2	0	0	0	0	0	0	0.00
Strop	1.0	1	0	0	0	2	0	0.00
Hamels	2.0	2	0	0	1	1	0	0.00
Wilson, J	0.1	0	0	0	0	0	0	0.00
Hendricks (L, 0-1)	1.1	3	1	1	0	0	0	6.75
De La Rosa, J	0.1	0	0	0	0	1	0	0.00

SCORE BY INNINGS

COLORADO	1	0	0	0	0	0	0	0	0	0	0	0	1	2	11	1
CHI CUBS	0	0	0	0	0	0	0	1	0	0	0	0	0	1	6	0

NATIONAL LEAGUE DIVISION SERIES

MILWAUKEE BREWERS VS COLORADO ROCKIES

MILWAUKEE	AVG	G	AB	R	H	2B	3B	HR	RBI	BB	SO	SB
Jesus Aguilar, 1B	.091	3	11	1	1	0	0	1	1	1	4	0
Orlando Arcia, SS	.250	3	8	2	2	0	0	1	1	0	2	0
Ryan Braun, LF	.385	3	13	1	5	0	0	0	0	0	4	1
Keon Broxton, CF	.500	2	2	1	1	0	0	1	1	0	1	0
Lorenzo Cain, CF	.083	3	12	1	1	0	0	0	0	2	3	0
Jhoulys Chacin, P	.000	1	1	0	0	0	0	0	0	0	0	0
Curtis Granderson, LF	.000	2	2	0	0	0	0	0	0	1	0	0
Jeremy Jeffress, P	.000	3	1	0	0	0	0	0	0	0	0	0
Erik Kratz, C	.625	2	8	1	5	1	0	0	2	1	0	0
Wade Miley, P	.000	1	2	0	0	0	0	0	0	0	2	0
Mike Moustakas, 3B	.364	3	11	2	4	1	0	0	2	2	1	0
Hernan Perez, 2B	.333	3	6	0	2	2	0	0	1	0	2	1
Manny Pina, C	.333	1	3	0	1	0	0	0	0	1	0	0
Domingo Santana, RF	.000	3	2	0	0	0	0	0	0	1	1	0
Jonathan Schoop, 2B	.000	2	2	0	0	0	0	0	0	0	1	0
Traveis Shaw, 3B	.364	3	11	0	4	1	0	0	1	3	2	1
Christian Yelich, LF	.250	3	8	4	2	0	0	1	2	6	0	2
Total	.272	3	103	13	28	5	0	4	11	16	25	5

MILWAUKEE	W	L	ERA	G	GS	SV	IP	H	R	ER	BB	SO
Corbin Burnes	1	0	0.00	2	0	0	4	1	0	0	0	5
Jhoulys Chacin	1	0	0.00	1	1	0	5	3	0	0	3	3
Josh Hader	0	0	0.00	3	0	0	2.1	0	0	0	0	4
Jeremy Jeffress	0	0	5.40	3	0	1	3.1	6	2	2	1	4
Corey Knebel	0	0	0.00	3	0	0	3	0	0	0	1	4
Wade Miley	0	0	0.00	1	1	0	4.2	3	0	0	1	2
Joakim Soria	1	0	0.00	3	0	0	2.2	1	0	0	1	5
Brandon Woodruff	0	0	0.00	1	0	0	3	0	0	0	1	3
Total	3	0	0.64	17	3	1	28	14	2	2	8	30

COLORADO	AVG	G	AB	R	H	2B	3B	HR	RBI	BB	SO	SB
Tyler Anderson, P	.000	1	1	0	0	0	0	0	0	0	1	0
Nolan Arenado, 3B	.182	3	11	0	2	0	0	1	0	5	0	0
Charlie Blackmon, CF	.083	3	12	0	1	0	0	0	1	0	1	0
David Dahl, RF	.000	2	5	0	0	0	0	0	0	0	2	0
Ian Desmond, 1B	.083	3	12	0	1	0	0	0	0	0	3	1
Carlos Gonzalez, RF	.100	3	10	0	1	0	1	0	0	2	5	0
Gerrett Hampson, 2B	.000	2	1	1	0	0	0	0	0	0	0	0
Matt Holliday, LF	.200	3	5	0	1	0	0	0	1	2	0	0
Chris Iannetta, C	.000	3	6	0	0	0	0	0	0	1	1	0
DJ LeMahieu, 2B	.222	3	9	0	2	1	0	0	0	3	2	0
German Marquez, P	.000	1	1	0	0	0	0	0	0	0	1	0
Ryan McMahon, 1B	.000	3	2	0	0	0	0	0	0	1	1	0
Gerardo Parra, LF	.500	2	6	1	3	0	0	0	0	0	1	0
Antonio Senzatela, P	.000	1	1	0	0	0	0	0	0	0	1	0
Trevor Story, SS	.167	3	12	0	2	1	0	0	0	0	6	0
Tony Wolters, C	.500	2	2	0	1	0	0	0	0	0	0	0
Total	.146	3	96	2	14	2	1	0	2	8	30	1

COLORADO	W	L	ERA	G	GS	SV	IP	H	R	ER	BB	SO
Tyler Anderson	0	1	1.50	1	1	0	6	4	1	1	2	5
Wade Davis	0	0	∞	1	0	0	0	2	2	2	2	0
DJ Johnson	0	0	0.00	1	0	0	0.2	1	0	0	0	2
German Marquez	0	1	3.60	1	1	0	5	7	2	2	1	5
Harrison Musgrave	0	0	13.50	2	0	0	0.2	1	1	1	3	2
Scott Oberg	0	0	7.71	3	0	0	2.1	4	2	2	0	6
Seunghwan Oh	0	0	13.50	2	0	0	1.1	3	2	2	2	1
Adam Ottavino	0	1	3.38	2	0	0	2.2	1	1	1	2	1
Chris Rusin	0	0	0.00	3	0	0	3	2	0	0	2	2
Antonio Senzatela	0	0	3.60	1	1	0	5	3	2	2	2	1
Total	0	3	4.39	17	3	0	26.2	28	13	13	16	25

SCORE BY INNINGS

MILWAUKEE	1	0	2	2	0	2	0	3	2	1	13
COLORADO	0	0	0	0	0	0	0	2	0	2	2

LOS ANGELES DODGERS VS ATLANTA BRAVES

LOS ANGELES	AVG	G	AB	R	H	2B	3B	HR	RBI	BB	SO	SB
Cody Bellinger, 1B	.000	4	11	1	0	0	0	0	0	4	4	2
Walker Buehler, P	.000	1	1	0	0	0	0	0	0	0	1	0
Brian Dozier, 2B	.500	1	2	0	1	0	0	0	0	0	1	0
David Freese, 3B	.500	3	2	0	1	0	0	0	3	0	0	0
Yasmani Grandal, C	.077	4	13	2	1	0	0	1	1	3	5	0
Enrique Hernandez, CF	.167	4	12	2	2	0	0	1	1	3	2	2
Rich Hill, P	.000	1	1	0	0	0	0	0	0	0	1	0
Matt Kemp, LF	.250	2	4	0	1	1	0	0	0	0	0	0
Clayton Kershaw, P	.000	1	2	0	0	0	0	0	0	0	1	0
Manny Machado, SS	.176	4	17	2	3	1	0	2	6	1	7	0
Max Muncy, 1B	.182	4	11	4	2	0	0	2	4	6	5	1
Joc Pederson, LF	.286	4	14	3	4	1	0	1	1	0	4	0
Yasiel Puig, RF	.333	4	9	2	3	0	0	0	0	4	3	2
Hyun-Jin Ryu, P	.333	1	3	0	1	0	0	0	0	0	0	0
Chris Taylor, SS	.333	3	3	2	1	0	0	1	2	1	0	0
Justin Turner, 3B	.357	4	14	2	5	1	0	0	1	4	0	1
Totals	.210	4	119	20	25	4	0	8	19	27	35	8

LOS ANGELES	W	L	ERA	G	GS	SV	IP	H	R	ER	BB	SO
Scott Alexander	0	0	0.00	1	0	0	1	0	0	0	0	0
Pedro Baez	0	0	0.00	2	0	0	2.1	0	0	0	1	3
Walker Buehler	0	0	9.00	1	1	0	5	2	5	5	3	7
Caleb Ferguson	0	0	0.00	2	0	0	1.2	0	0	0	0	2
Dylan Floro	0	0	0.00	1	0	0	0.1	0	0	0	0	0
Rich Hill	0	0	4.15	1	1	0	4.1	4	2	2	5	3
Kenley Jansen	0	0	0.00	2	0	1	2	1	0	0	0	1
Clayton Kershaw	1	0	0.00	1	1	0	8	2	0	0	0	3
Ryan Madson	1	0	0.00	2	0	0	1.1	1	0	0	0	1
Kenta Maeda	0	0	0.00	1	0	0	1	2	0	0	0	1
Hyun-Jin Ryu	1	0	0.00	1	1	0	7	4	0	0	0	8
Alex Wood	0	1	9.00	2	0	0	1	3	1	1	0	1
Totals	3	1	2.06	4	4	1	35	19	8	8	9	32

ATLANTA	AVG	G	AB	R	H	2B	3B	HR	RBI	BB	SO	SB
Ronald Acuna Jr., LF	.188	4	16	1	3	1	0	1	4	1	5	0
Lane Adams, CF	.000	2	1	0	0	0	0	0	0	0	1	0
Ozzie Albies, 2B	.200	4	15	1	3	0	0	0	0	0	1	0
Johan Camargo, 3B	.000	4	15	1	0	0	0	0	0	1	5	0
Charlie Culberson, LF	.167	4	12	1	2	0	0	0	0	1	4	0
Lucas Duda, 1B	.000	3	3	0	0	0	0	0	0	0	1	0
Ryan Flaherty, 3B	.000	2	2	0	0	0	0	0	0	0	0	0
Tyler Flowers, C	.143	3	7	1	1	0	0	0	0	1	3	0
Mike Foltynewicz, P	.000	2	2	0	0	0	0	0	0	0	2	0
Freddie Freeman, 1B	.250	4	16	1	4	0	0	1	1	1	3	0
Ender Inciarte, CF	.231	4	13	0	3	0	0	0	0	0	4	0
Nick Markakis, RF	.083	4	12	1	1	0	0	0	0	3	2	0
Anibal Sanchez, P	.000	1	2	0	0	0	0	0	0	0	0	0
Kurt Suzuki, C	.250	4	8	0	2	0	0	0	2	0	1	0
Totals	.154	4	123	7	19	1	0	2	7	8	32	0

ATLANTA	W	L	ERA	G	GS	SV	IP	H	R	ER	BB	SO
Brad Brach	0	0	6.75	2	0	0	1.1	2	1	1	2	2
Anibal Sanchez	0	1	5.79	1	1	0	4.2	5	3	3	1	3
Kevin Gausman	0	0	9.00	1	0	0	2	2	2	2	2	4
Chad Sobotka	0	0	11.57	3	0	0	2.1	2	4	3	4	0
Jonny Venters	0	1	9.00	2	0	0	2	2	2	2	1	1
Mike Foltynewicz	0	1	7.50	2	2	0	6	5	5	5	7	10
Julio Teheran	0	0	0.00	1	0	0	1.2	1	0	0	0	2
Sean Newcomb	0	0	1.93	2	1	0	4.2	2	2	1	3	2
Max Fried	0	0	3.86	4	0	0	2.1	1	1	1	1	1
A.J. Minter	0	0	0.00	2	0	0	2	1	0	0	1	3
Arodys Vizcaino	0	0	0.00	2	0	0	2	1	0	0	1	5
Touki Toussaint	1	0	0.00	2	0	0	3	1	0	0	4	2
Totals	1	3	4.76	4	4	1	34	25	20	18	27	35

SCORE BY INNINGS

LOS ANGELES	4	3	2	0	4	3	3	1	0	20
ATLANTA	0	5	0	2	0	1	0	0	0	8

NATIONAL LEAGUE CHAMPIONSHIP SERIES
MILWAUKEE BREWERS VS LOS ANGELES DODGERS

MILWAUKEE	AVG	G	AB	R	H	2B	3B	HR	RBI	BB	SO	SB
Jesus Aguilar, 1B	.269	7	26	4	7	3	0	1	4	2	11	0
Orlando Arcia, SS	.360	7	25	5	9	0	0	2	3	1	2	0
Ryan Braun, LF	.241	7	29	1	7	2	0	0	4	2	9	1
Lorenzo Cain, CF	.303	7	33	3	10	4	0	0	1	1	9	0
Jhoulys Chacin, P	.200	2	2	0	0	0	0	0	0	0	1	0
Curtis Granderson, LF	.200	5	5	0	1	1	0	0	1	0	2	0
Junior Guerra, P	.000	2	1	0	0	0	0	0	0	0	1	0
Josh Hader, P	.000	4	1	0	0	0	0	0	0	0	1	0
Corey Knebel, P	.000	6	1	0	0	0	0	0	0	0	1	0
Erik Kratz, C	.125	7	16	1	2	1	0	0	1	1	5	0
Wade Miley, P	.500	3	4	1	2	1	0	0	0	0	1	0
Mike Moustakas, 3B	.138	7	29	1	4	1	0	0	1	2	12	0
Freddy Peralta, P	.000	1	0	0	0	0	0	0	0	0	0	0
Hernan Perez, 2B	.125	6	8	0	1	0	0	0	0	1	1	1
Manny Pina, C	.500	4	4	1	2	1	0	0	0	4	1	0
Domingo Santana, RF	.333	7	6	1	2	1	0	0	3	1	4	1
Jonathan Schoop, 2B	.000	2	6	0	0	0	0	0	0	0	2	0
Travis Shaw, 3B	.211	7	19	2	4	1	1	1	1	1	8	0
Brandon Woodruff, P	.500	3	2	1	1	0	0	1	1	1	1	0
Christian Yelich, LF	.179	7	28	3	5	1	0	1	1	5	7	0
Totals	.232	7	246	24	57	17	1	6	22	22	79	3

MILWAUKEE	W	L	ERA	G	GS	SV	IP	H	R	ER	BB	SO
Corbin Burnes	0	0	3.60	4	0	0	5	3	2	2	1	6
Xavier Cedeno	0	0	18.00	4	0	0	1	3	2	2	1	1
Jhoulys Chacin	1	1	2.45	2	2	0	7.1	6	2	2	3	6
Zach Davies	0	0	0.00	1	0	0	1	1	0	0	0	1
Gio Gonzalez	0	0	6.00	2	2	0	3	3	2	2	2	1
Junior Guerra	0	1	1.93	2	0	0	4.2	2	1	1	0	5
Josh Hader	0	0	0.00	4	0	0	7.2	5	0	0	1	12
Jeremy Jeffress	0	1	7.71	5	0	0	4.2	10	4	4	3	7
Corey Knebel	1	0	1.29	6	0	1	7	2	1	1	2	10
Wade Miley	0	0	1.80	3	3	0	10	7	2	2	3	7
Freddy Peralta	0	0	0.00	1	0	0	3	0	0	0	3	6
Joakim Soria	0	0	18.00	4	0	0	2	4	4	4	2	3
Brandon Woodruff	1	1	2.89	3	0	0	9.1	7	3	3	2	17
Totals	3	4	3.15	7	7	1	65.2	53	23	23	23	82

LOS ANGELES	AVG	G	AB	R	H	2B	3B	HR	RBI	BB	SO	SB
Austin Barnes, C	.111	5	18	0	2	0	0	0	2	2	9	0
Cody Bellinger, 1B	.200	7	25	3	5	1	0	1	4	1	6	2
Walker Buehler, P	.000	2	3	0	0	0	0	0	0	0	2	0
Brian Dozier, 2B	.111	6	9	1	1	0	0	0	2	2	2	1
David Freese, 3B	.250	6	8	1	2	1	0	1	2	0	2	0
Yasmani Grandal, C	.182	5	11	0	2	1	0	0	0	0	6	0
Enrique Hernandez, CF	.071	6	14	0	1	0	0	0	0	2	8	0
Rich Hill, P	.000	2	2	0	0	0	0	0	0	0	2	0
Matt Kemp, LF	.200	7	10	0	2	0	0	0	1	1	3	0
Clayton Kershaw, P	.000	3	1	0	0	0	0	0	0	2	0	0
Manny Machado, SS	.296	7	27	5	8	1	0	1	3	2	6	1
Ryan Madson, P	.000	5	1	0	0	0	0	0	0	0	1	0
Max Muncy, 1B	.182	7	22	3	4	0	0	0	1	4	13	0
Joc Pederson, LF	.231	7	13	2	3	0	0	0	0	1	4	0
Yasiel Puig, RF	.333	7	21	1	7	3	0	1	4	1	6	0
Hyun-Jin Ryu, P	.500	2	2	0	1	0	0	0	0	0	0	0
Chris Taylor, SS	.364	7	22	4	8	1	1	0	1	4	7	1
Justin Turner, 3B	.241	7	29	2	7	0	0	0	1	7	1	0
Totals	.223	7	238	23	53	8	1	5	23	23	82	5

LOS ANGELES	W	L	ERA	G	GS	SV	IP	H	R	ER	BB	SO
Pedro Baez	1	0	0.00	4	0	0	4.1	2	0	0	1	7
Walker Buehler	0	1	3.86	2	2	0	11.2	12	5	5	1	15
Caleb Ferguson	0	0	0.00	4	0	0	1.1	0	0	0	1	1
Dylan Floro	0	0	0.00	5	0	0	4.1	3	0	0	2	5
Rich Hill	0	0	1.50	2	1	0	6	4	1	1	4	7
Kenley Jansen	0	0	0.00	4	0	2	4.2	1	0	0	2	7
Clayton Kershaw	1	1	4.09	3	2	0	11	9	6	5	4	13
Ryan Madson	1	0	1.80	5	0	0	5	5	1	1	1	5
Kenta Maeda	0	0	6.75	4	0	0	2.2	3	2	2	1	3
Hyun-Jin Ryu	0	1	8.59	2	2	0	7.1	13	7	7	2	7
Julio Urias	1	0	2.70	4	0	0	3.1	3	1	1	0	3
Alex Wood	0	0	2.70	4	0	0	3.1	2	1	1	3	6
Totals	4	3	3.18	7	7	2	65	57	24	23	22	79

SCORE BY INNINGS

MILWAUKEE	6	1	3	3	2	4	1	1	0	0	0	24
LOS ANGELES	2	3	0	0	2	5	4	5	1	0	0	1	23

ORGANIZATION
STATISTICS

Arizona Diamondbacks

SEASON IN A SENTENCE: On the heels of a playoff appearance in 2017, the D-backs spent 125 days in first place in the National League West—and stood atop the standings on the first day of each month—yet finished in third place at 82-80 after a dismal second half that was punctuated by an 8-19 record in September.

HIGH POINT: At the July 31 trade deadline, the D-backs stood at 60-49 and appeared poised for a postseason run. They held a half-game game lead on the division-rival Dodgers and Rockies and owned the third-best record in the NL.

LOW POINT: The D-backs lost three of four games on the road to the Dodgers in a series ending on Sept. 3, pushing them 1.5 games out of first place and, as it turned out, eliminating them from postseason contention for good. Arizona closed the season winning just eight of its final 27 games.

NOTABLE ROOKIES: With one of the oldest rosters in the NL and with no key prospects knocking on the door at Triple-A, the D-backs had few rookies fill prominent roles in 2018. Reliever Yoshihisa Hirano, a 34-year-old right-hander imported from Japan, appeared in 75 games and pitched well in high-leverage spots all season. He finished with a 2.44 ERA and 8.0 strikeouts per nine innings while showing no platoon split. Righthander Matt Koch picked up 14 starts among his 19 appearances, but the 27-year-old was hammered for 2.0 home runs per nine innings and failed to miss bats.

KEY TRANSACTIONS: The Arizona pitching staff, perhaps aided by the new-in-2018 humidor, was one of the most effective in the NL. Still, the front office made pitching reinforcements a focal point in trades, picking up righthander Matt Andriese and relievers Jake Diekman and Brad Ziegler in July. But as it turned out, signing 34-year-old journeyman Clay Buchholz to a minor league deal in May provided the biggest boost. The D-backs addressed their subpar offense throughout the season, trading for outfielder Steven Souza in February, Jon Jay in June and third baseman Eduardo Escobar in July.

DOWN ON THE FARM: The D-backs' domestic affiliates went 412-350 and compiled a .541 winning percentage that ranked fifth-best in baseball. Double-A Jackson won the Southern League title, thanks to a dynamic pitching staff led by prospects Taylor Widener and Jon Duplantier, and high Class A Visalia lost in the California League finals.

OPENING DAY PAYROLL: $116,038,416 (18th)

PLAYERS OF THE YEAR

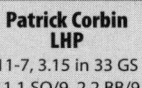

MAJOR LEAGUE	MINOR LEAGUE
Patrick Corbin **LHP**	**Taylor Widener** **RHP**
11-7, 3.15 in 33 GS	(Double-A)
11.1 SO/9, 2.2 BB/9	Ranked second in
and 1.05 WHIP	minors with 176 SO

ORGANIZATION LEADERS

Batting		*Minimum 250 AB
MAJORS		
* AVG	David Peralta	.293
* OPS	Paul Goldschmidt	.922
HR	Paul Goldschmidt	33
RBI	David Peralta	87
MINORS		
* AVG	Juniel Querecuto, Jackson, Reno	.337
* OBP	Ernie De La Trinidad, Kane County, Fort Myers	.403
* SLG	Kevin Cron, Reno	.554
* OPS	Socrates Brito, Reno	.923
R	Socrates Brito, Reno	85
H	Ildemaro Vargas, Reno	167
TB	Ildemaro Vargas, Reno	239
2B	Socrates Brito, Reno	34
2B	Drew Ellis, Visalia	34
3B	Ildemaro Vargas, Reno	10
HR	Jazz Chisholm, Kane County, Visalia	25
RBI	Kevin Cron, Reno	97
BB	Rudy Flores, Jackson	57
BB	Pavin Smith, Visalia	57
SO	Joey Rose, Kane County, Hillsboro	150
SB	Ben DeLuzio, Jackson, Diamondbacks	37

Pitching		#Minimum 75 IP
MAJORS		
W	Zack Greinke	15
W	Zack Godley	15
# ERA	Clay Buchholz	2.01
SO	Patrick Corbin	246
SV	Brad Boxberger	32
MINORS		
W	Taylor Clarke, Reno	13
L	Ryan Atkinson, Jackson	11
# ERA	Taylor Widener, Jackson	2.75
G	Kevin Ginkel, Visalia, Jackson	54
GS	Mack Lemieux, Kane County	27
GS	Taylor Clarke, Reno	27
GS	Connor Grey, Visalia	27
SV	Jimmie Sherfy, Reno	15
IP	Jake Buchanan, Reno	157
BB	Jared Miller, Reno, Jackson	67
SO	Taylor Widener, Jackson	176
# AVG	Taylor Widener, Jackson	.197

2018 PERFORMANCE

General Manager: Mike Hazen. **Farm Director:** Mike Bell. **Scouting Director:** Deric Ladnier.

Class	Team	League	W	L	PCT	Finish	Manager
Majors	Arizona Diamondbacks	National	82	80	.506	t-8th (15)	Torey Luvullo
Triple-A	Reno Aces	Pacific Coast	72	68	.514	t-6th (16)	Greg Gross
Double-A	Jackson Generals	Southern	75	64	.540	3rd (10)	Shelley Duncan
High A	Visalia Rawhide	California	70	70	.500	t-3rd (8)	Joe Mather
Low A	Kane County Cougars	Midwest	72	66	.522	6th (16)	Blake Lalli
Short season	Hillsboro Hops	Northwest	51	25	.671	1st (8)	Shawn Roof
Rookie	Missoula Osprey	Pioneer	39	36	.520	5th (8)	Mike Benjamin
Rookie	AZL D-backs	Arizona	33	21	.611	4th (18)	Darrin Garner
Overall 2018 Minor League Record			412	350	.541	5th (30)	

ORGANIZATION STATISTICS

ARIZONA DIAMONDBACKS
NATIONAL LEAGUE

Batting	B-T	HT	WT	DOB	AVG	vLH	vRH	G	AB	R	H	2B	3B	HR	RBI	BB	HBP	SH	SF	SO	SB	CS	SLG	OBP
Ahmed, Nick	R-R	6-2	195	3-15-90	.235	.256	.223	153	516	61	121	33	5	16	70	40	2	1	5	109	5	4	.411	.290
Avila, Alex	L-R	5-11	210	1-29-87	.165	.207	.158	80	194	13	32	6	0	7	20	37	1	0	2	90	0	0	.304	.299
Brito, Socrates	L-L	6-2	205	9-6-92	.175	.231	.148	24	40	3	7	0	0	1	3	3	0	0	1	9	0	1	.250	.227
Descalso, Daniel	L-R	5-10	190	10-19-86	.238	.286	.227	138	349	54	83	22	4	13	57	64	2	0	7	110	0	1	.436	.353
Dyson, Jarrod	L-R	5-10	165	8-15-84	.189	.250	.173	67	206	29	39	4	2	2	12	27	0	3	1	34	16	3	.257	.282
Escobar, Eduardo	B-R	5-10	185	1-5-89	.268	.319	.240	54	198	30	53	11	0	8	21	18	2	0	5	35	1	1	.444	.327
Goldschmidt, Paul	R-R	6-3	225	9-10-87	.290	.291	.290	158	593	95	172	35	5	33	83	90	6	0	0	173	7	4	.533	.389
Jay, Jon	L-L	5-11	195	3-15-85	.235	.207	.246	84	289	46	68	10	5	2	22	14	15	1	1	56	1	1	.325	.304
Kivlehan, Patrick	R-R	6-2	223	12-22-89	.231	.333	.000	9	13	3	3	0	2	0	0	1	0	0	6	0	0	.539	.286
Lamb, Jake	L-R	6-3	215	10-9-90	.222	.170	.238	56	207	34	46	8	0	6	31	26	1	0	4	65	1	2	.348	.307
Marrero, Deven	R-R	6-1	195	8-25-90	.167	.204	.083	49	78	11	13	1	1	0	7	6	0	0	1	23	3	0	.205	.224
Marte, Ketel	B-R	6-1	165	10-12-93	.260	.321	.224	153	520	68	135	26	12	14	59	54	3	1	2	79	6	1	.437	.332
Mathis, Jeff	R-R	6-0	205	3-31-83	.200	.209	.195	69	195	15	39	9	1	1	20	20	0	1	2	66	0	0	.272	.272
Murphy, John Ryan	R-R	5-11	205	5-13-91	.202	.221	.186	87	208	19	42	9	0	9	24	11	1	2	1	71	0	0	.375	.244
Negron, Kristopher	R-R	6-0	190	2-1-86	.333	.500	.000	2	3	0	1	0	0	0	1	0	0	0	0	0	0	0	.333	.333
Owings, Chris	R-R	5-10	185	8-12-91	.206	.269	.152	106	281	34	58	15	0	4	22	24	2	0	2	75	11	4	.303	.272
Peralta, David	L-L	6-1	210	8-14-87	.293	.237	.318	146	560	75	164	25	5	30	87	48	4	0	2	124	4	0	.516	.352
Pollock, A.J.	R-R	6-1	195	12-5-87	.257	.221	.275	113	413	61	106	21	5	21	65	31	8	1	7	100	13	2	.484	.316
Souza Jr., Steven	R-R	6-4	225	4-24-89	.220	.244	.207	72	241	21	53	15	3	5	29	28	3	0	0	75	6	1	.369	.309
Stewart, Chris	R-R	6-4	215	2-19-82	.000	.000	—	3	1	0	0	0	0	0	0	0	0	0	0	0	0	0	.000	.000
2-team total (5 Atlanta)					.200	.000	.231	8	15	3	3	0	0	0	3	1	0	0	1	1	0	0	.200	.235
Vargas, Ildemaro	B-R	6-0	170	7-16-91	.211	.143	.250	14	19	2	4	0	0	1	4	1	0	0	0	4	1	0	.368	.250
Walker, Christian	R-R	6-0	220	3-28-91	.163	.188	.118	37	49	6	8	2	0	3	6	3	1	0	0	22	1	0	.388	.226

Pitching	B-T	HT	WT	DOB	W	L	ERA	G	GS	CG	SV	IP	H	R	ER	HR	BB	SO	AVG	vLH	vRH	K/9	BB/9
Andriese, Matt	R-R	6-2	225	8-28-89	0	3	9.00	14	1	0	0	19	29	19	19	8	7	19	.354	.395	.308	9.00	3.32
Barrett, Jake	R-R	6-2	240	7-22-91	0	1	5.14	7	0	0	0	7	8	4	4	1	2	6	.286	.400	.222	7.71	2.57
Boxberger, Brad	R-R	6-2	205	5-27-88	3	7	4.39	60	0	0	32	53	44	30	26	9	32	71	.221	.222	.220	11.98	5.40
Bracho, Silvino	R-R	5-10	190	7-17-92	2	0	3.19	31	0	0	0	31	25	12	11	2	12	34	.223	.244	.209	9.87	3.48
Bradley, Archie	R-R	6-4	225	8-10-92	4	5	3.64	76	0	0	3	72	62	30	29	9	20	75	.229	.165	.272	9.42	2.51
Buchholz, Clay	L-R	6-3	190	8-14-84	7	2	2.01	16	16	1	0	98	80	25	22	9	22	81	.220	.191	.249	7.41	2.01
Chafin, Andrew	R-L	6-2	225	6-17-90	1	6	3.10	77	0	0	0	49	41	18	17	0	25	53	.227	.258	.193	9.67	4.56
Corbin, Patrick	L-L	6-3	210	7-19-89	11	7	3.15	33	33	1	0	200	162	70	70	15	48	246	.218	.239	.213	11.07	2.16
De La Rosa, Jorge	L-L	6-1	215	4-5-81	0	2	4.63	42	0	0	0	35	37	19	18	6	19	27	.278	.220	.324	6.94	4.89
2-team total (17 Chicago)					0	2	3.38	59	0	0	1	56	51	25	21	6	27	47	.243	.235	.248	7.55	4.34
Delgado, Randall	R-R	6-4	220	2-9-90	2	0	4.76	10	0	0	0	11	11	6	6	3	6	5	.244	.333	.200	3.97	4.76
Diekman, Jake	L-L	6-4	200	1-21-87	0	1	7.53	24	0	0	0	14	18	15	12	2	8	18	.300	.414	.194	11.30	5.02
Godley, Zack	R-R	6-3	240	4-21-90	15	11	4.74	33	32	0	0	178	177	103	94	16	81	185	.260	.264	.255	9.34	4.09
Greinke, Zack	R-R	6-2	200	10-21-83	15	11	3.21	33	33	0	0	208	181	77	74	28	43	199	.231	.234	.229	8.62	1.86
Hirano, Yoshihisa	R-R	6-1	185	3-8-84	4	3	2.44	75	0	0	3	66	49	22	18	6	23	59	.209	.215	.204	8.01	3.12
Koch, Matt	L-R	6-3	215	11-4-90	5	5	4.15	19	14	0	0	87	88	43	40	19	22	50	.268	.210	.315	5.19	2.28
Krehbiel, Joey	R-R	6-2	185	12-20-92	0	0	0.00	2	0	0	0	3	1	0	0	0	2	0	.100	.000	.111	0.00	6.00
Lopez, Yoan	R-R	6-3	185	1-2-93	0	0	3.00	10	0	0	0	9	7	3	3	2	1	11	.212	.182	.227	11.00	1.00
McFarland, T.J.	L-L	6-3	220	6-8-89	2	2	2.00	47	0	0	1	72	64	18	16	4	22	42	.239	.165	.281	5.25	2.75
Medlen, Kris	B-R	5-10	190	10-7-85	0	1	15.75	1	1	0	0	4	9	7	7	0	4	4	.429	.500	.421	9.00	9.00
Miller, Shelby	R-R	6-3	225	10-10-90	0	4	10.69	5	4	0	0	16	24	21	19	5	8	19	.343	.229	.457	10.69	4.50
Ray, Robbie	L-L	6-2	195	10-1-91	6	2	3.93	24	24	0	0	124	97	55	54	19	70	165	.216	.124	.244	12.01	5.09
Salas, Fernando	R-R	6-2	200	5-30-85	4	4	4.50	41	0	0	0	40	40	20	20	5	13	30	.265	.388	.206	6.75	2.93
Scribner, Troy	L-R	6-3	190	7-2-91	0	1	4.91	1	1	0	0	4	4	2	2	0	6	4	.267	.250	.273	9.82	14.73
Sherfy, Jimmie	R-R	6-0	175	12-27-91	0	0	1.65	15	0	0	0	16	8	3	3	1	10	17	.146	.167	.129	9.37	5.51
Shipley, Braden	R-R	6-1	190	2-22-92	0	0	7.20	3	0	0	0	5	4	4	4	0	2	3	.222	.111	.333	5.40	3.60
Walker, Taijuan	R-R	6-4	235	8-13-92	0	0	3.46	3	3	0	0	13	15	5	5	1	5	9	.294	.385	.200	6.23	3.46
Ziegler, Brad	R-R	6-4	220	10-10-79	1	1	3.74	29	0	0	0	22	22	9	9	1	8	13	.265	.318	.246	5.40	3.32

2-team total (53 Miami)　　2　6　3.91　82　0　0　10　74　71　34　32　8　25　50　.257　.297　.230　6.11　3.05

Fielding

Catcher	PCT	G	PO	A	E	DP	PB
Avila	.998	61	456	39	1	2	3
Mathis	.998	63	516	57	1	1	1
Murphy	.987	68	425	37	6	2	2
Stewart	.800	3	4	0	1	0	0

First Base	PCT	G	PO	A	E	DP
Avila	1.000	3	8	0	0	1
Descalso	.970	11	63	2	2	9
Goldschmidt	.996	155	1323	110	6	131
Walker	1.000	7	38	2	0	3

Second Base	PCT	G	PO	A	E	DP
Descalso	.978	52	58	121	4	25
Marrero	1.000	5	6	4	0	2

Marte	.990	131	190	299	5	83
Mathis	1.000	1	1	0	0	0
Owings	1.000	9	10	19	0	4
Vargas	1.000	2	3	4	0	1

Third Base	PCT	G	PO	A	E	DP
Descalso	.969	37	15	47	2	3
Escobar	.983	54	23	94	2	6
Lamb	.977	52	32	93	3	8
Marrero	.984	33	18	43	1	7
Owings	1.000	5	4	13	0	1
Vargas	.833	3	2	8	2	2

Shortstop	PCT	G	PO	A	E	DP
Ahmed	.985	148	165	432	9	98

Marte	.971	28	21	78	3	15
Vargas	.000	1	0	0	0	0

Outfield	PCT	G	PO	A	E	DP
Brito	1.000	15	20	0	0	0
Descalso	.833	5	5	0	1	0
Dyson	.985	62	130	4	2	2
Jay	1.000	67	119	4	0	1
Kivlehan	1.000	4	2	0	0	0
Negron	1.000	1	1	0	0	0
Owings	.967	60	83	5	3	1
Peralta	.983	140	225	1	4	0
Pollock	.996	109	229	3	1	1
Souza Jr.	.972	65	103	1	3	0
Walker	1.000	1	1	0	0	0

RENO ACES　　　　　　　　　　　　　　　　　　TRIPLE-A
PACIFIC COAST LEAGUE

Batting	B-T	HT	WT	DOB	AVG	vLH	vRH	G	AB	R	H	2B	3B	HR	RBI	BB	HBP	SH	SF	SO	SB	CS	SLG	OBP
Brito, Socrates	L-L	6-2	205	9-6-92	.318	.282	.330	114	428	85	136	34	5	17	69	44	3	0	3	104	15	4	.540	.383
Cron, Kevin	R-R	6-5	245	2-17-93	.309	.402	.271	104	392	57	121	28	1	22	97	36	4	0	6	100	1	0	.554	.368
Decker, Cody	R-R	5-11	218	1-17-87	.268	.318	.248	63	153	23	41	7	2	9	28	22	3	0	4	52	0	0	.516	.363
Dyson, Jarrod	L-R	5-10	165	8-15-84	.200	.333	.000	2	5	0	1	0	0	0	1	0	0	0	0	1	0	0	.200	.333
Flores, Raymel	B-R	5-9	155	9-22-94	.500	—	.500	2	6	0	3	0	0	0	0	1	0	0	0	2	0	0	.500	.571
Fuentes, Rey	L-L	6-0	160	2-12-91	.265	.260	.266	85	302	46	80	11	5	6	39	34	4	0	2	64	10	2	.394	.345
Hazelbaker, Jeremy	L-R	6-3	190	8-14-87	.250	—	.250	1	4	0	1	0	0	0	0	0	0	0	0	1	0	1	.250	.250
Ladendorf, Tyler	R-R	5-11	195	3-7-88	.354	.385	.343	13	48	6	17	3	0	0	5	7	0	0	0	4	0	1	.417	.436
Lara, Luis	B-R	6-0	190	5-6-95	.000	.000	—	1	1	0	0	0	0	0	0	0	0	0	0	1	0	0	.000	.000
Littlewood, Marcus	B-R	6-3	195	3-18-92	.203	.133	.222	22	69	9	14	4	1	2	16	9	1	0	1	25	0	0	.377	.300
Marrero, Deven	R-R	6-1	195	8-25-90	.227	.286	.200	21	66	10	15	4	1	1	7	7	0	2	1	20	0	0	.364	.297
Marzilli, Evan	L-L	6-0	185	3-13-91	.260	.320	.245	43	131	23	34	6	2	2	15	17	0	0	0	44	1	3	.382	.345
Medrano, Kevin	L-R	6-1	155	5-21-90	.333	.000	.409	8	27	5	9	2	0	0	2	2	0	0	0	6	1	0	.407	.379
Negron, Kristopher	R-R	6-0	190	2-1-86	.283	.281	.284	118	371	71	105	17	5	15	45	43	8	1	2	121	10	3	.477	.368
Owings, Chris	R-R	5-10	185	8-12-91	.286	.286	.286	21	91	15	26	4	2	1	11	1	0	0	0	17	1	1	.407	.294
Perez, Michael	L-R	5-11	180	8-7-92	.284	.226	.308	58	218	30	62	9	1	6	29	20	0	0	2	40	0	1	.417	.342
Pollock, A.J.	R-R	6-1	195	12-5-87	.429	1.000	.000	2	7	3	3	1	0	1	3	1	0	0	0	1	0	1	01.000	.500
Prince, Josh	R-R	6-2	180	1-26-88	.000	—	.000	2	3	0	0	0	0	0	0	2	0	0	0	2	0	0	.000	.400
Puello, Cesar	R-R	6-2	220	4-1-91	.317	.293	.325	73	249	43	79	10	3	6	33	35	16	1	5	59	6	3	.454	.426
2-team total (13 Sacramento)					.313	.307	.315	86	294	48	92	11	3	6	37	40	17	1	6	67	6	4	.432	.417
Queliz, Jose	R-R	6-2	224	8-7-92	.400	.222	.546	5	20	2	8	1	0	1	3	0	0	0	0	9	0	0	.600	.400
Querecuto, Juniel	B-R	5-9	155	9-19-92	.315	.448	.275	68	251	33	79	8	2	1	22	18	1	1	3	35	8	3	.375	.359
Recker, Anthony	R-R	6-2	240	8-29-83	.276	.183	.312	74	257	44	71	20	1	15	50	32	2	0	2	73	0	1	.537	.358
Reinheimer, Jack	R-R	6-1	185	7-19-92	.237	.227	.240	50	190	26	45	9	2	3	21	20	3	1	5	45	6	4	.353	.312
2-team total (16 Las Vegas)					.257	.230	.266	66	245	39	63	12	2	5	26	24	4	1	5	55	13	4	.384	.327
Robertson, Daniel	R-R	5-11	200	9-30-85	.253	.214	.261	26	83	12	21	3	0	1	8	15	2	1	2	17	1	1	.325	.373
Rosario, Alberto	R-R	6-0	165	1-10-87	.214	.100	.250	14	42	5	9	1	0	1	4	1	1	2	1	8	0	0	.310	.244
Souza Jr., Steven	R-R	6-4	225	4-24-89	.438	1.000	.400	4	16	5	7	0	2	3	6	2	0	0	0	3	2	0	1.250	.500
Tomas, Yasmany	R-R	6-2	250	11-14-90	.262	.271	.259	106	355	42	93	22	4	14	65	11	0	0	5	101	2	0	.465	.280
Vargas, Ildemaro	B-R	6-0	170	7-16-91	.311	.265	.330	124	537	78	167	31	10	7	54	30	2	0	3	46	10	4	.445	.348
Vinicio, Jose	R-R	5-11	150	7-10-93	.143	.333	.000	4	7	4	1	0	0	0	0	3	0	0	0	1	0	0	.143	.400
Walker, Christian	R-R	6-0	220	3-28-91	.299	.337	.286	84	324	68	97	25	4	18	71	26	4	0	5	86	1	0	.568	.354
Westbrook, Jamie	R-R	5-9	170	6-16-95	.391	.200	.444	7	23	6	9	1	0	1	6	2	0	0	0	2	0	0	.957	.440

Pitching	B-T	HT	WT	DOB	W	L	ERA	G	GS	CG	SV	IP	H	R	ER	HR	BB	SO	AVG	vLH	vRH	K/9	BB/9
Barrett, Jake	R-R	6-2	240	7-22-91	4	0	2.87	42	0	0	8	53	37	19	17	3	29	67	.195	.149	.233	11.31	4.89
Bellow, Kirby	L-L	6-1	220	11-14-91	1	0	0.00	1	0	0	0	2	1	0	0	0	0	2	.200	.000	.500	10.80	0.00
Blazek, Michael	R-R	6-0	205	3-16-89	0	0	81.00	1	0	0	0	0	2	3	3	2	1	0	.667	.500	1.000	0.00	27.00
Bracho, Silvino	R-R	5-10	190	7-17-92	2	2	4.46	27	0	0	8	34	39	19	17	3	8	52	.291	.318	.265	13.63	2.10
Buchanan, Jake	R-R	6-0	235	9-24-89	11	9	5.17	27	26	0	0	157	190	92	90	9	47	86	.304	.281	.324	4.94	2.70
Buchholz, Clay	R-R	6-3	190	8-14-84	0	1	5.40	2	2	0	0	12	12	7	7	0	5	10	.267	.263	.269	7.71	3.86
2-team total (2 Omaha)					1	1	3.52	4	4	0	0	23	21	9	9	2	10	14	.241	.222	.255	5.48	3.91
Clarke, Taylor	R-R	6-4	200	5-13-93	13	8	4.03	27	27	0	0	152	149	76	68	12	44	125	.254	.253	.256	7.40	2.61
Crichton, Stefan	R-R	6-3	200	2-29-92	0	2	10.13	14	0	0	0	16	19	18	18	4	10	17	.292	.267	.314	9.56	5.63
Delgado, Randall	R-R	6-4	220	2-9-90	0	1	2.00	13	1	0	0	18	11	5	4	1	6	14	.169	.129	.206	7.00	3.00
Dimock, Michael	R-R	6-2	195	10-26-89	0	0	4.61	9	0	0	1	14	14	8	7	2	9	16	.269	.200	.333	10.54	5.93
Enright, Barry	R-R	6-3	220	3-30-86	0	0	7.88	4	0	0	0	9	9	7	1	5	4	.344	.278	.429	4.50	5.63
Feliz, Neftali	R-R	6-3	235	5-2-88	6	5	4.81	37	12	0	2	92	85	52	49	9	54	75	.248	.280	.220	7.36	5.30
Gibson, Daniel	R-L	6-3	215	10-16-91	0	0	0.00	1	0	0	0	1	0	0	0	0	1	2	.250	.500	.000	18.00	9.00
Hagens, Bradin	R-R	6-3	210	5-12-89	3	4	7.74	16	8	0	1	55	69	49	47	8	24	43	.308	.207	.379	7.08	3.95
Keele, Tyler	R-R	6-5	195	8-17-93	0	0	22.50	1	0	0	0	2	5	5	5	1	2	2	.455	.667	.000	9.00	4.50
Koch, Matt	L-R	6-3	215	11-2-90	2	4	5.96	11	11	0	0	54	66	41	36	11	12	31	.308	.245	.362	5.13	1.99
Krehbiel, Joey	R-R	6-2	185	12-20-92	3	3	4.24	48	0	0	2	57	49	27	27	9	25	71	.233	.247	.222	11.15	3.92

Pitcher	B-T	HT	WT	DOB	W	L	ERA	G	GS	CG	SV	IP	H	R	ER	HR	BB	SO	AVG	vLH	vRH	K/9	BB/9
Mason, Austin	R-R	6-2	200	12-10-93	0	0	0.00	1	1	0	0	2	2	0	0	0	2	3	.222	.250	.000	13.50	9.00
Medlen, Kris	B-R	5-10	190	10-7-85	0	5	5.03	7	7	0	0	34	39	29	19	6	15	29	.291	.302	.282	7.68	3.97
Miller, Jared	L-L	6-7	240	8-21-93	1	3	7.71	38	0	0	0	42	46	36	36	6	63	52	.286	.327	.268	11.14	13.50
Payamps, Joel	R-R	6-2	170	4-7-94	0	4	7.18	6	5	0	0	26	35	25	21	5	10	26	.313	.267	.365	8.89	3.42
Pill, Tyler	L-R	6-1	199	5-29-90	0	0	15.75	2	0	0	0	4	8	7	7	3	3	2	.421	.250	.546	6.75	6.75
2-team total (19 Oklahoma City)					3	5	5.35	21	13	0	0	74	94	47	44	9	23	53	.314	.320	.310	6.45	2.80
Ray, Robbie	L-L	6-2	195	10-1-91	0	1	2.08	1	1	0	0	4	3	3	1	0	1	9	.200	.500	.154	18.69	2.08
Scribner, Troy	L-R	6-3	190	7-2-91	2	2	5.11	8	8	0	0	44	38	26	25	10	17	44	.236	.241	.232	9.00	3.48
Sherfy, Jimmie	R-R	6-0	175	12-27-91	5	1	1.60	38	0	0	15	45	31	12	8	1	20	58	.190	.263	.126	11.60	4.00
Shipley, Braden	R-R	6-1	190	2-22-92	6	4	5.81	30	6	0	1	74	93	52	48	13	36	58	.311	.321	.302	7.02	4.36
Suarez, Albert	R-R	6-3	235	10-8-89	0	1	4.97	31	4	0	1	63	74	39	35	8	33	51	.298	.330	.272	7.25	4.69
Vasquez, Anthony	L-L	6-0	190	9-19-86	7	4	5.57	18	9	0	1	73	79	46	45	12	31	61	.276	.230	.301	7.56	3.84
Winston, Jake	R-R	6-3	194	9-13-93	1	0	0.00	1	0	0	0	1	1	0	0	0	3	1	.200	.000	.333	6.75	20.25
Young, Alex	L-L	6-2	205	9-9-93	5	4	5.96	20	12	0	0	80	99	56	53	12	23	61	.303	.305	.302	6.86	2.59

Fielding

Catcher	PCT	G	PO	A	E	DP	PB
Littlewood	1.000	2	13	1	0	0	
Perez	.994	57	453	45	3	1	2
Queliz	.956	5	41	2	2	0	0
Recker	.994	66	496	36	3	3	4
Rosario	1.000	13	94	5	0	0	2

First Base	PCT	G	PO	A	E	DP
Cron	.992	46	323	36	3	36
Decker	1.000	26	159	11	0	16
Littlewood	1.000	6	38	4	0	3
Negron	1.000	2	1	0	0	0
Recker	1.000	1	4	1	0	1
Tomas	.983	9	56	3	1	4
Walker	.985	64	497	37	8	60

Second Base	PCT	G	PO	A	E	DP
Flores	1.000	2	3	6	0	1
Ladendorf	.947	6	9	9	1	4
Littlewood	1.000	13	22	32	0	5
Medrano	.933	7	13	15	2	7

	PCT	G	PO	A	E	DP
Negron	.981	43	82	120	4	27
Owings	1.000	10	23	31	0	9
Prince	.750	1	1	2	1	0
Querecuto	.986	34	56	81	2	23
Reinheimer	.952	12	29	31	3	6
Robertson	1.000	2	5	3	0	1
Vargas	.986	17	27	46	1	10

Third Base	PCT	G	PO	A	E	DP
Cron	.954	57	39	86	6	14
Decker	.667	2	1	1	1	0
Ladendorf	1.000	2	0	2	0	1
Marrero	.960	11	10	14	1	1
Negron	1.000	20	17	33	0	2
Owings	1.000	6	4	11	0	3
Querecuto	.986	28	25	45	1	6
Reinheimer	.941	21	8	24	2	1

Shortstop	PCT	G	PO	A	E	DP
Marrero	.900	7	6	21	3	4
Negron	1.000	10	19	30	0	4
Querecuto	1.000	3	4	5	0	1

	PCT	G	PO	A	E	DP
Reinheimer	.955	16	23	41	3	12
Vargas	.977	107	155	274	10	73

Outfield	PCT	G	PO	A	E	DP
Brito	.988	111	231	10	3	4
Decker	.000	1	0	0	0	0
Dyson	1.000	2	5	0	0	0
Fuentes	.971	83	164	6	5	0
Hazelbaker	1.000	1	3	0	0	0
Ladendorf	.941	5	15	1	1	1
Marzilli	.986	41	66	2	1	0
Negron	1.000	41	70	3	0	2
Owings	1.000	4	4	0	0	0
Pollock	.000	2	0	0	0	0
Prince	.000	1	0	0	0	0
Puello	.985	64	124	5	2	2
Robertson	.983	23	57	2	1	1
Souza Jr.	1.000	2	5	0	0	0
Tomas	.956	45	65	0	3	0
Vinicio	1.000	4	9	0	0	0
Walker	1.000	18	21	2	0	0
Westbrook	1.000	6	12	0	0	0

JACKSON GENERALS

SOUTHERN LEAGUE

DOUBLE-A

Batting	B-T	HT	WT	DOB	AVG	vLH	vRH	G	AB	R	H	2B	3B	HR	RBI	BB	HBP	SH	SF	SO	SB	CS	SLG	OBP
Cribbs, Galli	L-R	6-0	170	10-8-92	.211	.118	.241	96	308	45	65	10	8	3	23	31	20	0	0	110	6	5	.325	.323
Decker, Cody	R-R	5-11	218	1-17-87	.125	.000	.143	3	8	0	1	0	0	0	1	0	0	0	1	2	0	0	.250	.111
DeLuzio, Ben	R-R	6-3	190	8-9-94	.262	.310	.245	68	263	43	69	12	3	2	14	25	5	0	2	72	34	9	.354	.336
Flores, Rudy	L-R	6-3	205	12-12-90	.281	.193	.314	126	438	60	123	25	3	17	75	57	16	0	4	124	2	3	.468	.381
Gonzalez, Jay	L-L	5-9	170	12-11-91	.287	.163	.326	55	181	19	52	8	1	0	16	21	0	1	1	49	7	4	.343	.360
Grotjohn, Ryan	L-R	6-2	175	4-25-95	.333	—	.333	1	3	2	1	0	0	0	1	0	0	0	1	0	0	0	.333	.500
Herum, Marty	R-R	6-3	214	12-16-91	.300	.236	.322	76	280	33	84	14	1	5	42	20	1	0	2	46	1	1	.411	.347
Jones, Matt	R-R	6-0	195	4-14-92	.250	.349	.202	41	132	14	33	5	0	3	18	13	1	0	1	51	0	1	.356	.320
Ladendorf, Tyler	R-R	5-11	195	3-7-88	.200	.174	.210	30	85	17	17	4	0	1	8	14	1	0	2	15	0	1	.282	.314
Lara, Luis	B-R	6-0	190	5-6-95	.182	.063	.250	20	44	5	8	1	0	0	2	8	0	0	0	14	0	0	.205	.308
Leyba, Domingo	B-R	5-11	160	9-11-95	.269	.247	.277	83	320	43	86	17	2	5	30	35	2	0	1	46	5	2	.381	.344
Littlewood, Marcus	B-R	6-3	195	3-18-92	.196	.211	.192	54	158	16	31	2	0	4	13	25	0	1	1	36	1	1	.285	.304
Marzilli, Evan	L-L	6-0	185	3-13-91	.133	.083	.167	10	30	6	4	2	0	0	0	8	1	0	0	8	3	0	.200	.333
Medrano, Kevin	L-R	6-1	155	5-21-90	.331	.333	.330	96	369	54	122	30	5	4	48	28	1	5	2	71	9	1	.472	.378
Miroglio, Dominic	R-R	6-0	203	3-10-95	.231	.182	.267	21	78	3	18	4	1	0	10	1	2	0	0	12	0	1	.308	.259
Morozowski, Jason	R-R	6-2	190	6-10-94	.199	.286	.158	85	281	32	56	12	1	6	35	23	2	0	2	85	4	3	.313	.263
Prince, Josh	R-R	6-0	180	1-26-88	.285	.266	.293	102	302	36	86	16	2	6	37	50	1	0	3	81	12	4	.411	.385
Queliz, Jose	R-R	6-2	224	8-7-92	.208	.235	.200	28	72	11	15	4	0	0	11	6	1	0	0	29	0	0	.264	.279
Querecuto, Juniel	B-R	5-9	195	9-19-92	.369	.310	.389	47	168	24	62	15	2	0	23	12	2	1	2	21	10	3	.482	.413
Robertson, Daniel	R-R	5-11	200	9-30-85	.265	.239	.274	73	272	41	72	19	1	8	39	28	12	2	3	44	14	5	.430	.356
Rosario, Alberto	R-R	6-0	165	1-10-87	.266	.240	.273	37	124	11	33	3	0	1	11	7	0	0	2	20	0	2	.315	.303
Sopilka, David	R-R	6-0	180	8-30-93	.333	.000	.429	7	9	1	3	1	0	0	4	6	0	0	1	1	0	0	.444	.563
Vinicio, Jose	R-R	5-11	150	7-10-93	.231	.290	.200	89	268	37	62	12	3	3	24	10	2	5	1	71	10	5	.332	.263
Westbrook, Jamie	R-R	5-9	170	6-18-95	.287	.297	.283	107	408	65	117	20	5	15	68	24	7	0	2	71	4	3	.471	.336

Pitching	B-T	HT	WT	DOB	W	L	ERA	G	GS	CG	SV	IP	H	R	ER	HR	BB	SO	AVG	vLH	vRH	K/9	BB/9
Aguilar, Miguel	L-L	5-11	180	9-26-91	0	0	1.42	11	0	0	0	13	8	2	2	2	5	14	.182	.133	.207	9.95	3.55
Atkinson, Ryan	R-R	6-3	218	5-10-93	5	11	4.79	29	20	1	0	109	98	66	58	14	58	123	.246	.258	.238	10.16	4.79
Bellow, Kirby	L-L	6-1	220	11-14-91	5	3	4.12	47	0	0	1	44	37	26	20	2	29	33	.228	.234	.224	6.80	5.98
Blazek, Michael	R-R	6-0	205	3-16-89	0	0	2.79	9	0	0	1	10	7	3	3	1	4	12	.206	.333	.136	11.17	3.72
Dimock, Michael	R-R	6-2	195	10-26-89	3	0	3.45	14	0	0	0	16	15	7	6	0	4	20	.250	.150	.300	11.49	2.30
Donatella, Justin	R-R	6-6	236	9-16-94	7	8	3.46	27	24	0	0	130	112	53	50	9	47	103	.231	.240	.225	7.13	3.25
Duplantier, Jon	L-R	6-4	225	7-11-94	5	1	2.69	14	14	0	0	67	52	24	20	4	28	68	.217	.227	.210	9.13	3.76

ARIZONA DIAMONDBACKS

Name	B-T	HT	WT	DOB	W	L	ERA	G	GS	CG	SV	IP	H	R	ER	HR	BB	SO	AVG	vLH	vRH	SO/9	BB/9
Ellington, Brian	R-R	6-3	215	8-4-90	2	0	31.50	10	0	0	0	6	6	22	21	1	16	2	.286	.400	.250	3.00	24.00
Enright, Barry	R-R	6-3	220	3-30-86	2	1	4.18	4	4	0	0	24	27	12	11	3	7	17	.297	.300	.294	6.46	2.66
Eveld, Tommy	R-R	6-5	195	12-30-93	1	0	0.00	3	0	0	1	4	1	0	0	0	1	5	.071	.000	.167	10.38	2.08
2-team total (10 Jacksonville)					2	1	0.64	13	0	0	4	14	7	3	1	0	4	19	.146	.100	.179	12.21	2.57
Gibson, Daniel	R-L	6-3	215	10-16-91	2	3	5.40	25	0	0	2	28	32	18	17	2	10	29	.286	.237	.311	9.21	3.18
Ginkel, Kevin	R-R	6-4	210	3-24-94	5	0	1.69	34	0	0	5	43	26	8	8	3	9	60	.176	.177	.174	12.66	1.90
Goldberg, Brad	R-R	6-4	220	2-21-90	2	1	0.64	16	0	0	4	14	4	3	1	1	10	24	.087	.111	.071	15.43	6.43
2-team total (17 Birmingham)					2	1	1.98	33	0	0	4	36	23	13	8	1	25	58	.181	.265	.128	14.37	6.19
Huang, Wei-Chieh	R-R	6-1	170	9-26-93	2	1	2.00	10	2	0	1	27	20	6	6	1	7	32	.208	.243	.186	10.67	2.33
Jeter, Bud	R-R	6-3	205	10-27-91	2	2	2.72	34	0	0	2	46	36	18	14	3	21	47	.213	.206	.217	9.13	4.08
Lewis, Sam	R-R	6-4	195	10-9-91	3	4	5.96	14	6	0	0	45	47	30	30	4	17	40	.269	.339	.227	7.94	3.38
Lopez, Yoan	R-R	6-3	185	1-2-93	2	6	2.92	45	0	0	12	62	38	20	20	4	26	87	.174	.229	.148	12.70	3.79
Mark, Tyler	R-R	6-1	185	10-18-94	2	2	5.40	10	0	0	0	13	17	15	8	0	10	10	.315	.250	.367	6.75	6.75
McCullough, Mason	R-R	6-4	245	1-7-93	0	1	8.53	24	0	0	0	19	17	23	18	1	27	24	.227	.200	.236	11.37	12.79
McKinley, Jayson	R-R	6-4	210	1-18-94	0	0	6.75	2	2	0	0	7	8	6	5	2	9	4	.286	.333	.231	5.40	12.15
Miller, Jared	L-L	6-7	240	8-21-93	0	0	1.50	6	0	0	0	6	3	3	1	0	4	7	.150	.000	.188	10.50	6.00
Miller, Shelby	R-R	6-3	225	10-10-90	0	0	10.57	2	2	0	0	8	13	9	9	1	6	10	.406	.500	.350	11.74	7.04
Nakaushiro, Yuhei	R-R	6-0	160	9-17-89	1	1	5.29	24	0	0	0	34	40	22	20	2	16	36	.296	.340	.271	9.53	4.24
Payamps, Joel	R-R	6-2	170	4-7-94	3	4	2.90	25	10	0	0	90	70	31	29	5	17	96	.217	.257	.183	9.60	1.70
Poche, Colin	L-L	6-3	185	1-17-94	0	0	0.00	9	0	0	1	11	3	0	0	2	2	23	.086	.125	.074	18.82	1.64
2-team total (3 Montgomery)					1	0	0.00	12	0	0	1	16	4	0	0	2	2	32	.080	.143	.056	18.00	1.13
Pujols, Rafael	R-R	6-6	175	8-21-95	0	0	0.00	3	0	0	0	4	1	0	0	0	3	4	.077	.000	.111	9.00	6.75
Speier, Gabe	L-L	6-0	175	4-12-95	1	0	3.03	20	0	0	1	30	28	11	10	1	10	26	.250	.342	.203	7.89	3.03
Takahashi, Bo	R-R	6-0	197	1-23-97	3	3	4.68	14	14	0	0	73	65	38	38	12	20	77	.243	.255	.236	9.49	2.47
Tunnell, West	L-R	6-1	195	11-20-93	0	0	0.00	1	0	0	0	1	0	0	0	0	0	0	.000	.000	.000	0.00	0.00
Vargas, Emilio	R-R	6-3	200	8-12-96	1	3	4.04	6	6	0	0	36	31	16	16	6	8	30	.225	.218	.229	7.57	2.02
Vasquez, Anthony	L-L	6-0	190	9-19-86	0	0	2.08	3	1	0	1	13	16	3	3	0	1	13	.295	.200	.342	9.00	0.69
Widener, Taylor	L-R	6-0	195	10-24-94	5	8	2.75	26	25	1	0	137	99	42	42	12	43	176	.197	.232	.176	11.53	2.82
Young, Alex	L-L	6-2	205	9-9-93	5	1	3.91	9	9	0	0	51	49	24	22	3	16	48	.258	.342	.235	8.53	2.84

Fielding

Catcher	PCT	G	PO	A	E	DP	PB
Jones	.989	26	246	12	3	1	5
Littlewood	.992	49	459	28	4	6	7
Miroglio	.987	18	141	12	2	0	1
Queliz	.982	23	155	12	3	0	2
Rosario	1.000	34	295	35	0	2	3
Sopilka	.000	1	0	0	0	0	0

First Base	PCT	G	PO	A	E	DP
Decker	1.000	3	13	0	0	2
Flores	.990	99	645	70	7	64
Herum	1.000	8	50	4	0	4
Jones	1.000	5	44	1	0	5
Lara	1.000	2	1	0	0	0
Medrano	1.000	10	52	5	0	7
Prince	.977	25	154	19	4	6

Second Base	PCT	G	PO	A	E	DP
Ladendorf	1.000	2	5	1	0	1

Catcher (cont.)	PCT	G	PO	A	E	DP
Leyba	.984	72	111	138	4	37
Medrano	.993	42	67	69	1	17
Prince	.958	16	16	30	2	7
Querecuto	1.000	6	10	13	0	4
Vinicio	.963	11	11	15	1	6

Third Base	PCT	G	PO	A	E	DP
Herum	.973	63	40	104	4	15
Ladendorf	.857	5	2	10	2	0
Lara	.833	4	2	8	2	0
Medrano	.933	22	13	29	3	7
Prince	.862	14	7	18	4	1
Querecuto	.969	37	26	69	3	7
Vinicio	.944	12	12	22	2	3

Shortstop	PCT	G	PO	A	E	DP
Cribbs	.967	73	91	144	8	35
Ladendorf	.923	17	23	37	5	7
Leyba	.967	8	11	18	1	0

Shortstop (cont.)	PCT	G	PO	A	E	DP
Medrano	.964	10	16	11	1	3
Querecuto	.957	6	11	11	1	2
Vinicio	.969	43	47	76	4	15

Outfield	PCT	G	PO	A	E	DP
Cribbs	.983	26	56	2	1	0
DeLuzio	.994	67	166	4	1	0
Flores	.000	2	0	0	0	0
Gonzalez	1.000	50	69	1	0	0
Grotjohn	1.000	1	4	0	0	0
Ladendorf	1.000	6	8	0	0	0
Marzilli	1.000	9	23	1	0	0
Medrano	1.000	13	21	2	0	1
Morozowski	1.000	77	136	6	0	0
Prince	1.000	23	33	3	0	0
Querecuto	.000	1	0	0	0	0
Robertson	.988	71	151	8	2	2
Vinicio	.950	18	16	3	1	1
Westbrook	.970	91	126	5	4	1

VISALIA RAWHIDE   HIGH CLASS A
CALIFORNIA LEAGUE

Batting	B-T	HT	WT	DOB	AVG	vLH	vRH	G	AB	R	H	2B	3B	HR	RBI	BB	HBP	SH	SF	SO	SB	CS	SLG	OBP
Basabe, Luis Alejandro	B-R	5-10	160	8-26-96	.225	.280	.197	63	227	23	51	12	2	2	15	19	1	1	1	50	5	5	.322	.286
Chisholm, Jazz	L-R	5-11	165	2-1-98	.329	.313	.337	36	149	27	49	6	2	10	27	9	1	0	1	52	9	2	.597	.369
Duzenack, Camden	R-R	5-9	170	3-8-95	.225	.253	.216	89	351	49	79	20	3	4	39	30	14	2	2	76	12	8	.333	.310
Ellis, Drew	R-R	6-3	210	12-1-95	.246	.295	.227	120	443	57	109	34	1	15	71	52	5	0	2	98	2	6	.429	.331
Flores, Raymel	B-R	5-9	155	9-22-94	.177	.278	.148	50	158	14	28	8	0	0	9	12	2	6	0	46	6	3	.228	.244
Grier, Anfernee	R-R	6-1	180	10-13-95	.208	.206	.209	34	125	14	26	5	1	3	8	8	3	0	0	46	6	1	.336	.272
Grotjohn, Ryan	L-R	6-2	175	4-25-95	.147	.100	.167	9	34	5	5	0	0	1	4	2	0	0	0	9	3	1	.235	.194
Hernandez, Ramon	R-R	6-4	195	3-2-96	.261	.264	.260	109	425	54	111	28	2	20	77	14	10	0	5	101	3	1	.478	.297
Jefferson, Manny	R-R	6-3	170	3-5-95	.267	.000	.308	5	15	2	4	2	1	0	7	1	0	0	1	6	0	1	.533	.294
Jones, Zachary	R-R	6-0	200	7-4-94	.125	—	.125	3	8	0	1	1	0	0	1	2	0	0	0	4	0	0	.250	.300
Karaviotis, Mark	R-R	6-1	185	10-12-95	.285	.357	.260	91	319	59	91	18	3	4	38	52	8	0	5	84	6	2	.398	.393
Lamb, Jake	L-R	6-3	215	10-9-90	.182	.000	.200	3	11	2	2	2	0	0	0	0	0	0	3	0	0	.364	.182
Lara, Luis	B-R	6-0	190	5-6-95	.625	.750	.500	2	8	2	5	0	0	1	3	1	0	0	0	1	0	0	1.000	.667
Martinez, Renae	R-R	6-1	185	4-15-94	.277	.304	.263	44	170	27	47	11	1	4	19	15	3	0	0	37	2	1	.424	.346
Miroglio, Dominic	R-R	6-0	203	3-10-95	.327	.440	.286	76	278	41	91	23	1	4	42	20	12	0	2	42	5	2	.460	.394
Morozowski, Jason	R-R	6-2	190	6-10-94	.318	.292	.325	30	107	21	34	6	2	3	12	9	0	0	1	28	2	2	.495	.368
Silverio, Luis	R-R	6-3	180	6-27-95	.201	.216	.194	48	159	19	32	11	2	2	13	7	1	0	0	49	2	2	.333	.240
Smith, Pavin	L-L	6-2	210	2-6-96	.255	.250	.257	120	439	63	112	25	1	11	54	57	4	0	6	65	3	2	.392	.343
Smith, Stephen	R-R	6-0	220	11-3-94	.222	.235	.218	77	284	39	63	13	2	8	36	32	6	0	1	99	4	3	.366	.313
Sopilka, David	R-R	6-0	170	8-30-93	.308	—	.308	5	13	2	4	1	0	0	2	2	0	0	0	5	0	0	.385	.400

	B-T	HT	WT	DOB	AVG	vLH	vRH	G	AB	R	H	2B	3B	HR	RBI	BB	HBP	SH	SF	SO	SB	CS	SLG	OBP
Souza Jr., Steven	R-R	6-4	225	4-24-89	.333	.333	.333	2	9	1	3	1	0	0	1	1	0	0	0	4	0	0	.444	.400
Varsho, Daulton	L-R	5-10	190	7-2-96	.286	.367	.252	80	304	44	87	11	3	11	44	30	7	0	1	71	19	3	.451	.363
Vinicio, Jose	R-R	5-11	150	7-10-93	.222	.000	.364	6	18	0	4	0	0	0	2	0	0	1	3	1	0	.222	.211	
Walton, Adam	R-R	6-1	190	9-22-93	.267	.359	.237	80	258	27	69	15	1	5	36	24	3	3	0	68	6	5	.392	.337
Wilson, Marcus	R-R	6-3	175	8-15-96	.235	.299	.209	111	447	60	105	26	2	10	48	44	6	0	5	141	16	6	.369	.309

Pitching	B-T	HT	WT	DOB	W	L	ERA	G	GS	CG	SV	IP	H	R	ER	HR	BB	SO	AVG	vLH	vRH	K/9	BB/9
Aguilar, Miguel	L-L	5-11	180	9-26-91	1	2	3.40	36	0	0	0	45	36	19	17	4	17	51	.222	.222	.222	10.20	3.40
Andriese, Matt	R-R	6-2	225	8-28-89	0	0	0.00	1	1	0	0	4	1	0	0	0	2	5	.083	.125	.000	12.27	4.91
Bain, Jeff	R-R	6-4	200	3-3-96	4	2	4.03	7	7	0	0	38	37	17	17	3	12	33	.255	.273	.241	7.82	2.84
Brill, Matt	R-R	6-2	190	10-25-94	2	3	4.62	20	0	0	5	25	18	16	13	3	18	35	.192	.160	.203	12.43	6.39
Buchholz, Clay	L-R	6-3	190	8-14-84	1	0	3.00	1	1	0	0	6	4	2	2	1	1	6	.191	.200	.188	9.00	1.50
Bustamante, Carlos	R-R	6-0	190	9-25-94	0	0	5.01	22	0	0	1	32	29	18	18	2	14	41	.232	.222	.238	11.41	3.90
Creasy, Jason	R-R	6-4	197	5-13-92	1	1	6.75	6	0	0	0	7	10	8	5	1	3	10	.323	.333	.313	13.50	4.05
Delgado, Randall	R-R	6-4	220	2-9-90	0	0	3.52	7	1	0	0	8	4	3	3	2	3	9	.160	.000	.286	10.57	3.52
Eveld, Tommy	R-R	6-5	195	12-30-93	2	2	1.24	32	0	0	12	36	29	8	5	1	7	42	.216	.200	.228	10.40	1.73
Garcia, Junior	L-L	5-10	220	10-1-95	2	3	1.82	24	0	0	0	35	23	10	7	0	11	44	.186	.146	.205	11.42	2.86
Ginkel, Kevin	R-R	6-4	210	3-24-94	1	1	0.99	20	0	0	4	27	20	6	3	2	3	40	.200	.191	.207	13.17	0.99
Gonzalez, Erbert	R-R	5-10	170	10-21-95	1	1	11.37	12	0	0	0	13	17	16	16	1	10	16	.315	.423	.214	11.37	7.11
Grey, Connor	R-R	6-0	180	5-6-94	10	9	4.54	27	27	0	0	141	154	92	71	21	38	131	.275	.267	.279	8.38	2.43
Huang, Wei-Chieh	R-R	6-1	170	9-26-93	4	1	2.59	19	0	0	0	31	17	9	9	3	16	46	.157	.093	.222	13.21	4.60
Jeter, Bud	R-R	6-3	205	10-27-91	0	0	0.00	1	0	0	0	2	0	0	0	0	0	1	.000	.000	.000	5.40	0.00
Keele, Tyler	R-R	6-3	195	8-17-93	1	2	6.51	9	7	0	1	37	44	29	27	7	16	36	.297	.327	.280	8.68	3.86
Kessay, Sebastian	L-L	6-2	215	6-19-93	0	1	13.50	2	1	0	0	5	9	8	8	0	3	5	.375	.400	.368	8.44	5.06
Long, Keegan	R-R	6-2	190	8-27-93	1	1	6.30	8	0	0	1	10	10	8	7	0	5	6	.263	.400	.214	5.40	4.50
Mark, Tyler	R-R	6-1	195	10-18-94	1	2	1.45	35	0	0	3	50	41	12	8	1	17	66	.222	.270	.197	11.96	3.08
Mason, Austin	R-R	6-2	200	12-10-93	2	5	4.76	29	1	0	1	40	42	25	21	2	19	38	.276	.236	.299	8.62	4.31
McCanna, Kevin	L-R	6-1	185	2-1-94	4	2	3.57	10	9	0	0	53	50	26	21	6	16	51	.242	.266	.213	8.66	2.72
McCullough, Mason	R-R	6-4	245	1-7-93	0	0	16.20	8	0	0	0	7	10	13	12	2	15	12	.323	.286	.353	16.20	20.25
McKinley, Jayson	R-R	6-4	210	1-18-94	0	0	2.25	1	1	0	0	4	3	1	1	0	3	4	.231	.000	.300	9.00	6.75
McWilliams, Sam	R-R	6-7	190	9-4-95	1	1	2.10	5	5	0	0	26	20	7	6	1	6	32	.215	.270	.179	11.22	2.10
Miller, Shelby	R-R	6-3	225	10-10-90	1	0	0.77	2	2	0	0	12	7	1	1	0	0	18	.167	.182	.161	13.89	0.00
Peacock, Matt	R-R	6-1	180	2-27-94	4	3	4.66	11	11	0	0	56	57	32	29	6	17	55	.255	.276	.243	8.84	2.73
Ratliff, Lane	L-L	6-3	185	3-22-95	0	0	9.00	1	1	0	0	4	5	4	4	0	2	4	.313	.200	.364	9.00	4.50
Ray, Robbie	L-L	6-2	195	10-1-91	0	0	7.71	1	1	0	0	2	5	5	2	2	0	3	.385	.429	.333	11.57	0.00
Sexton, Robby	L-L	6-0	225	4-29-94	1	3	4.37	45	0	0	0	56	74	31	27	4	19	57	.326	.208	.381	9.22	3.07
Smith, Riley	R-R	6-1	195	1-15-95	8	6	3.57	26	25	0	0	151	141	64	60	15	48	148	.249	.234	.257	8.80	2.85
Stapler, Cole	R-R	6-4	240	12-22-94	1	7	4.29	10	10	0	0	57	63	34	27	2	10	41	.281	.216	.352	6.51	1.59
Takahashi, Bo	R-R	6-0	197	1-23-97	3	3	3.02	9	9	0	0	48	45	17	16	4	10	53	.250	.315	.206	10.01	1.89
Taylor, Josh	L-L	6-5	225	3-2-93	1	2	2.81	14	0	0	5	16	16	9	5	1	5	20	.262	.125	.311	11.25	2.81
Tunnell, West	L-R	6-1	195	11-20-93	1	0	2.87	11	0	0	0	16	13	6	5	0	7	19	.228	.200	.250	10.91	4.02
Vargas, Emilio	R-R	6-3	200	8-12-96	8	5	2.50	20	19	0	0	108	92	34	30	7	41	140	.230	.184	.262	11.67	3.42
Watson, Jordan	L-L	6-0	185	9-14-93	0	1	6.48	9	0	0	0	8	10	7	6	1	3	10	.313	.333	.304	10.80	3.24
Williams, Breckin	R-R	6-0	200	9-5-93	0	1	2.20	12	0	0	2	16	10	5	4	1	2	22	.170	.182	.154	12.12	1.10
Winston, Jake	R-R	6-3	194	9-13-93	1	0	2.57	9	1	0	0	14	10	4	2		10	17	.200	.111	.250	10.93	6.43

Fielding

Catcher	PCT	G	PO	A	E	DP	PB
Martinez	.993	29	268	25	2	2	3
Miroglio	.983	55	534	42	10	2	4
Sopilka	.947	3	14	4	1	0	1
Varsho	.992	55	558	56	5	3	5

First Base	PCT	G	PO	A	E	DP
Ellis	1.000	2	10	0	0	2
Hernandez	.973	28	200	16	6	22
Karaviotis	.944	2	16	1	1	0
Smith	.993	109	789	79	6	66

Second Base	PCT	G	PO	A	E	DP
Basabe	.960	56	101	113	9	24
Duzenack	.952	6	6	14	1	2
Flores	.955	38	74	97	8	24
Grotjohn	.950	6	7	12	1	2

	PCT	G	PO	A	E	DP
Karaviotis	1.000	3	3	9	0	4
Walton	.949	34	43	69	6	13

Third Base	PCT	G	PO	A	E	DP
Basabe	1.000	1	2	2	0	0
Ellis	.936	108	81	152	16	13
Hernandez	.922	29	16	43	5	2
Jefferson	.000	1	0	0	0	0
Lamb	1.000	2	1	1	0	1
Lara	1.000	1	1	1	0	0
Walton	1.000	4	1	6	0	1

Shortstop	PCT	G	PO	A	E	DP
Chisholm	.961	36	61	87	6	18
Duzenack	.962	83	113	219	13	45
Flores	.952	10	13	27	2	5
Grotjohn	1.000	1	0	2	0	0
Walton	1.000	15	9	35	0	3

Outfield	PCT	G	PO	A	E	DP
Basabe	1.000	1	2	0	0	0
Grier	.971	34	64	4	2	2
Grotjohn	1.000	3	3	0	0	0
Hernandez	1.000	25	34	3	0	1
Jefferson	.917	5	11	0	1	0
Jones	1.000	1	1	0	0	0
Karaviotis	.990	73	89	11	1	0
Morozowski	.982	30	54	2	1	0
Silverio	.946	46	66	4	4	1
Smith	.000	1	0	0	0	0
Smith	.978	76	127	4	3	0
Vinicio	.889	6	8	0	1	0
Walton	1.000	27	34	2	0	2
Wilson	.988	109	250	4	3	1

KANE COUNTY COUGARS
MIDWEST LEAGUE

LOW CLASS A

Batting	B-T	HT	WT	DOB	AVG	vLH	vRH	G	AB	R	H	2B	3B	HR	RBI	BB	HBP	SH	SF	SO	SB	CS	SLG	OBP
Basabe, Luis Alejandro	B-R	5-10	160	8-26-96	.309	.259	.328	27	94	10	29	5	1	0	7	18	0	0	0	23	0	3	.383	.420
Caballero, Jose	R-R	5-10	185	8-30-96	.295	.242	.313	33	129	23	38	7	2	4	16	16	4	1	0	16	5	5	.473	.389
Chisholm, Jazz	L-R	5-11	165	2-1-98	.244	.155	.271	76	307	52	75	17	4	15	43	30	1	0	3	97	6	2	.472	.311
Cintron, Jancarlos	R-R	5-8	170	12-1-94	.298	.315	.294	97	342	51	102	19	2	7	39	18	11	0	6	45	3	4	.427	.348
Connelly, Terence	L-R	6-2	225	3-7-94	.206	.273	.174	11	34	2	7	0	0	0	3	7	0	0	1	12	2	0	.206	.333
De La Trinidad, Ernie	L-L	5-9	165	1-3-96	.311	.290	.317	91	312	52	97	13	2	8	56	45	9	0	9	48	6	7	.442	.403

Batting	B-T	HT	WT	DOB	AVG	vLH	vRH	G	AB	R	H	2B	3B	HR	RBI	BB	HBP	SH	SF	SO	SB	CS	SLG	OBP
Diaz, Eduardo	R-R	6-2	175	7-19-97	.225	.276	.209	33	120	12	27	5	2	2	11	3	3	2	0	40	3	0	.350	.262
Dobson, Ryan	R-R	6-0	165	5-2-95	.192	.348	.145	31	99	15	19	3	1	1	8	14	4	0	1	26	5	1	.273	.314
Gorman, William	L-R	6-4	210	11-8-94	.184	.150	.196	24	76	9	14	2	3	0	6	11	0	0	0	38	1	0	.290	.287
Grotjohn, Ryan	L-R	6-2	175	4-25-95	.303	.254	.315	80	297	51	90	22	6	7	49	25	6	0	7	54	3	5	.488	.361
Herrera, Jose	B-R	5-10	226	2-24-97	.226	.205	.237	32	115	6	26	5	0	1	11	7	0	0	1	21	0	0	.296	.268
Holmes, Tra	R-R			7-10-96	.154	.226	.123	30	104	10	16	5	0	0	7	14	4	2	0	38	9	3	.202	.279
Jefferson, Manny	R-R	6-3	170	3-5-95	.115	.333	.000	8	26	3	3	0	1	0	2	4	0	0	1	7	0	0	.192	.226
Lara, Luis	B-R	6-0	190	5-6-95	.198	.290	.165	36	116	9	23	3	0	0	14	15	1	0	0	26	1	2	.224	.296
Maciel, Gabriel	B-R	5-10	170	1-10-99	.287	.304	.283	68	279	44	80	10	1	0	16	30	3	1	0	50	14	5	.333	.362
2-team total (30 Cedar Rapids)					.280	.267	.283	98	397	60	111	14	2	3	23	35	5	1	1	71	16	10	.348	.345
Martinez, Renae	R-R	6-1	185	4-15-94	.333	.385	.310	44	165	30	55	17	0	5	35	16	5	0	3	36	0	0	.527	.402
Perez, Jorge	L-L	5-8	165	1-18-98	.160	.250	.143	9	25	1	4	0	0	0	3	0	0	0	0	4	0	0	.160	.250
Ramos, Eudy	R-R	6-1	195	2-19-96	.235	.225	.239	99	378	34	89	17	3	11	57	23	3	0	2	121	1	0	.384	.283
Rose, Joey	R-R	6-0	205	1-20-98	.175	.114	.198	50	160	19	28	7	2	3	26	24	3	0	2	71	1	0	.300	.291
Sanchez, Yan	R-R	6-2	170	8-31-96	.275	.336	.252	122	454	55	125	21	2	4	40	37	1	1	4	92	9	9	.344	.329
Silverio, Luis	R-R	6-3	169	6-27-95	.278	.231	.292	43	169	21	47	13	4	3	25	7	1	0	1	54	3	2	.456	.309
Smith, Stephen	R-R	6-1	220	11-3-94	.000	.000	.000	5	13	2	0	0	0	0	1	5	1	0	1	5	0	1	.000	.300
Susnara, Tim	L-R	6-1	185	4-17-96	.258	.148	.258	78	275	32	65	18	0	4	40	37	3	1	2	78	1	2	.346	.331
Tufts, Ryan	R-R	6-2	205	7-27-94	.205	.222	.200	14	44	4	9	3	0	0	2	2	4	0	0	12	0	0	.273	.300
Yanqui, Yoel	L-L	6-1	210	4-25-96	.289	.294	.287	126	495	83	143	22	4	5	60	49	4	1	3	100	13	9	.380	.356

Pitching	B-T	HT	WT	DOB	W	L	ERA	G	GS	CG	SV	IP	H	R	ER	HR	BB	SO	AVG	vLH	vRH	K/9	BB/9
Almonte, Abraham	L-L	5-11	195	12-3-93	0	4	4.07	39	0	0	3	60	59	32	27	10	24	62	.257	.307	.232	9.35	3.62
Bain, Jeff	R-R	6-2	200	3-3-96	7	4	2.52	18	18	0	0	100	85	33	28	2	28	94	.225	.227	.224	8.46	2.52
Bartlett, Cole	R-R	6-2	189	12-22-94	5	4	3.73	26	8	0	0	94	102	43	39	3	17	73	.277	.299	.263	6.99	1.63
Benitez, Anfernee	R-L	6-1	180	7-24-95	0	0	4.15	4	0	0	1	4	2	5	2	0	5	4	.125	.000	.133	8.31	10.38
2-team total (24 Burlington)					3	4	4.87	28	1	0	1	57	53	43	31	1	36	68	.239	.203	.253	10.67	5.65
Brill, Matt	R-R	6-2	190	10-25-94	4	1	2.93	23	0	0	6	28	20	11	9	2	15	30	.202	.212	.197	9.76	4.88
Bustamante, Carlos	R-R	6-0	190	9-25-94	2	1	4.66	19	0	0	4	29	31	16	15	2	12	38	.277	.235	.295	11.79	3.72
Castillo, Luis	R-R	6-3	212	3-10-95	0	2	1.53	12	0	0	3	18	11	3	3	1	6	19	.177	.077	.250	9.68	3.06
Duran, Jhoan	R-R	6-5	175	1-8-98	5	4	4.73	15	15	0	0	65	69	41	34	6	28	71	.269	.257	.276	9.88	3.90
2-team total (6 Cedar Rapids)					7	5	3.75	21	21	0	0	101	88	52	42	8	38	115	.232	.247	.222	10.28	3.40
Gonzalez, Erbert	R-R	5-10	170	10-21-95	3	2	3.40	31	0	0	2	48	41	20	18	3	29	60	.234	.250	.225	11.33	5.48
Hernandez, Carlos	R-R	5-9	171	4-26-94	2	0	4.70	5	0	0	0	8	4	4	4	1	5	5	.154	.100	.188	5.87	5.87
Keele, Tyler	R-R	6-3	195	8-17-93	0	1	3.96	9	2	0	0	25	25	12	11	1	5	14	.260	.359	.193	5.04	1.80
Lemieux, Mack	L-L	6-3	205	9-6-96	4	10	4.20	27	27	0	0	129	149	83	60	12	60	134	.289	.252	.302	9.37	4.20
Long, Keegan	R-R	6-2	190	8-27-93	1	0	0.00	1	0	0	0	2	2	0	0	0	4	.250	—	.250	15.43	0.00	
McCanna, Kevin	L-R	6-1	185	2-1-94	0	3	4.67	4	4	0	0	17	14	13	9	1	8	21	.209	.286	.174	10.90	4.15
McKinley, Jayson	R-R	6-4	210	1-18-94	9	4	3.20	21	13	1	0	90	83	34	32	7	29	83	.248	.219	.270	8.30	2.90
Peacock, Matt	R-R	6-1	180	2-27-94	3	3	3.59	17	5	0	2	43	42	21	17	3	11	35	.253	.258	.250	7.38	2.32
Pujols, Rafael	R-R	6-6	175	8-21-95	1	0	1.61	16	0	0	1	28	19	10	5	1	17	28	.194	.270	.148	9.00	5.46
Ratliff, Lane	L-L	6-3	185	3-22-95	7	2	2.71	14	8	0	0	66	69	21	20	2	19	59	.274	.307	.260	8.01	2.58
Santana, Yeison	R-R	6-0	180	10-25-96	0	0	0.00	1	0	0	0	1	1	0	0	0	1	.333	.500	.000	9.00	0.00	
Shaffer, Brian	R-R	6-5	200	8-12-96	7	5	2.70	19	19	1	0	107	94	37	32	11	21	109	.229	.260	.204	9.20	1.77
Soriano, Franklyn	L-L	6-1	195	7-21-95	2	3	1.82	7	7	0	0	40	30	9	8	3	10	25	.211	.098	.257	5.67	2.27
Stapler, Cole	R-R	6-4	240	12-9-94	1	2	2.95	8	8	0	0	40	38	15	13	2	12	45	.250	.275	.238	10.21	2.72
Stout, Kyler	R-R	6-0	195	10-13-94	2	2	3.00	15	0	0	5	21	17	10	7	0	9	31	.224	.310	.170	13.29	3.86
Torres, Juan	R-R	6-2	180	5-25-95	2	1	5.16	20	0	0	0	30	22	23	17	1	29	30	.198	.214	.188	9.10	8.80
Valdez, Bryan	L-L	6-3	180	11-27-94	0	1	4.73	6	0	0	0	13	17	7	7	0	0	13	.298	.294	.300	8.78	0.00
Watson, Jordan	L-L	6-0	195	9-14-93	2	1	1.20	12	0	0	0	15	11	4	2	0	5	23	.200	.333	.163	13.80	3.00
Williams, Breckin	R-R	6-0	200	9-5-93	3	4	4.04	28	0	0	3	42	37	25	19	4	15	51	.236	.192	.255	10.84	3.19
Winston, Jake	R-R	6-3	194	9-13-93	0	2	5.94	15	4	0	1	33	36	24	22	3	22	26	.277	.341	.244	7.02	5.94

Fielding

C: Herrera 31, Martinez 38, Susnara 70. **1B:** Connelly 4, Ramos 20, Tufts 3, Yanqui 114. **2B:** Basabe 19, Caballero 26, Cintron 64, Grotjohn 9, Jefferson 2, Sanchez 20, Tufts 1. **3B:** Caballero 8, Connelly 1, Grotjohn 8, Lara 12, Ramos 47, Rose 37, Sanchez 29, Tufts 4. **SS:** Chisholm 75, Cintron 31, Dobson 21, Grotjohn 3, Sanchez 10. **OF:** De La Trinidad 90, Diaz 31, Dobson 10, Gorman 17, Grotjohn 60, Holmes 30, Jefferson 6, Maciel 68, Perez 8, Sanchez 57, Silverio 36, Smith 5, Yanqui 3.

HILLSBORO HOPS   SHORT-SEASON
NORTHWEST LEAGUE

Batting	B-T	HT	WT	DOB	AVG	vLH	vRH	G	AB	R	H	2B	3B	HR	RBI	BB	HBP	SH	SF	SO	SB	CS	SLG	OBP
Caballero, Jose	R-R	5-10	185	8-30-96	.290	.371	.262	37	138	24	40	5	2	5	24	14	4	0	2	20	12	3	.464	.367
Connelly, Terence	L-R	6-2	225	3-7-94	.333	.000	.500	1	3	0	1	0	0	0	1	0	0	0	1	0	0	.667	.500	
Dobson, Ryan	R-R	6-0	165	5-2-95	.363	.435	.338	26	91	19	33	6	0	0	9	14	1	3	1	19	14	6	.429	.449
Garza, David	R-R	6-1	200	2-19-95	.300	1.000	.222	3	10	4	3	1	0	1	3	0	0	0	0	1	0	0	.700	.300
Gorman, William	L-R	6-4	210	11-8-94	.257	.381	.226	28	105	17	27	2	3	6	18	1	4	0	0	41	3	4	.505	.291
Herrera, Jose	B-R	5-10	226	2-24-97	.118	.143	.100	6	17	0	2	1	0	0	1	0	0	0	2	0	0	.177	.167	
Hoffpauir, Zach	R-R	6-1	195	9-21-93	.177	.200	.167	13	34	3	6	1	0	0	1	2	0	0	0	16	3	0	.206	.222
Holmes, Tra	R-R	6-0	175	7-10-96	.284	.233	.298	34	134	29	38	8	2	4	13	16	10	9	0	32	19	6	.463	.373
January, Ryan	L-R	6-4	190	5-27-97	.183	.143	.193	43	137	24	25	6	4	0	6	23	5	0	0	61	4	2	.285	.321
Jones, Zachary	R-R	6-0	200	7-4-94	.122	.091	.133	13	41	5	5	0	0	1	2	3	1	0	0	9	1	0	.195	.200
King, Alex	R-R	6-2	200	10-3-95	.143	.250	.111	9	35	2	5	0	0	0	1	1	0	0	0	9	0	0	.143	.189
Lynch, Keshawn	R-R	5-9	190	10-12-96	.214	.178	.224	61	210	45	45	10	2	1	14	22	4	0	3	45	9	4	.295	.297
Martinez, Francis	R-R	6-4	250	6-28-97	.222	.190	.232	66	248	27	55	15	1	8	33	16	3	0	2	88	0	0	.387	.275

Batting	B-T	HT	WT	DOB	AVG	vLH	vRH	G	AB	R	H	2B	3B	HR	RBI	BB	HBP	SH	SF	SO	SB	CS	SLG	OBP
McCarthy, Jake	L-L	6-3	195	7-30-97	.289	.278	.291	55	208	33	60	17	3	3	18	22	9	0	2	40	20	8	.442	.378
Perdomo, Geraldo	B-R	6-2	184	10-22-99	.301	.286	.307	30	103	20	31	3	2	3	14	18	4	1	1	23	9	4	.456	.421
Perez, Jorge	L-L	5-8	165	1-18-98	.272	.194	.285	63	217	30	59	12	2	2	29	25	1	2	1	34	19	11	.373	.348
Rose, Joey	R-R	6-0	205	1-20-98	.236	.186	.251	61	242	23	57	21	2	8	42	14	3	0	6	79	3	2	.438	.279
Swain, Dan	R-R	5-11	200	9-30-94	.209	.207	.210	41	110	12	23	3	0	1	11	13	2	0	2	30	2	1	.264	.299
Tolbert, L.T.	L-R	6-2	200	6-7-96	.290	.250	.299	27	107	10	31	6	1	0	15	10	2	0	1	17	3	3	.365	.358
Tufts, Ryan	R-R	6-2	205	7-27-94	.207	.306	.165	39	121	11	25	7	0	3	15	15	6	1	2	32	0	0	.339	.319
Watson Jr., Kevin	L-R	6-1	190	5-25-99	.200	.000	.250	3	5	1	1	0	1	0	0	0	0	0	4	1	0	.600	.333	
Yerzy, Andy	L-R	6-3	215	7-5-98	.297	.118	.346	63	239	30	71	11	1	8	34	28	6	0	2	67	0	0	.452	.382

Pitching	B-T	HT	WT	DOB	W	L	ERA	G	GS	CG	SV	IP	H	R	ER	HR	BB	SO	AVG	vLH	vRH	K/9	BB/9
Castillo, Luis	R-R	6-3	212	3-10-95	0	0	3.63	10	0	0	0	17	12	7	7	2	3	12	.197	.200	.194	6.23	1.56
Christian, Brian	R-R	6-2	220	6-21-96	2	0	4.26	13	0	0	0	25	23	14	12	3	5	18	.235	.235	.234	6.39	1.78
Del Moral, Adrian	R-R	6-1	190	2-17-99	0	3	4.65	8	8	0	0	31	28	17	16	2	7	30	.239	.278	.222	8.71	2.03
Ellington, Brian	R-R	6-3	215	8-4-90	0	0	0.00	1	0	0	0	1	0	0	0	0	0	0	.000	—	.000	0.00	0.00
Francis, Harrison	R-R		195	10-26-98	3	0	1.53	5	0	0	0	18	15	3	3	0	8	21	.231	.200	.250	10.70	4.08
Frias, Luis	R-R	6-3	180	5-23-98	0	4	3.16	7	7	0	0	26	21	9	9	0	15	27	.221	.154	.268	9.47	5.26
Garcia, Justin	R-R	6-2	175	7-2-95	3	0	3.38	11	0	0	0	16	9	7	6	0	10	25	.177	.120	.231	14.06	5.63
Goddard, Jackson	R-R	6-3	220	12-12-96	1	3	4.18	13	12	0	0	28	19	14	13	1	12	27	.204	.167	.228	8.68	3.86
Green, Josh	R-R	6-3	210	8-31-95	3	1	1.09	25	0	0	11	33	31	9	4	0	9	25	.250	.319	.208	6.82	2.45
Hernandez, Carlos	R-R	5-9	171	4-26-94	0	0	10.80	2	0	0	0	2	2	2	2	0	2	4	.000	.000	.000	10.80	21.60
Hernandez, Kenny	L-L	6-1	197	6-24-98	6	3	4.37	16	5	0	0	68	81	34	33	11	7	59	.296	.227	.322	7.81	0.93
Larrison, Ethan	R-R	6-2	205	8-14-95	6	1	3.10	15	0	0	0	20	16	7	7	1	10	16	.225	.222	.227	7.08	4.43
Lin, Kai-Wei	R-R	5-10	175	3-19-96	4	1	3.44	22	0	0	1	34	26	14	13	3	7	44	.211	.250	.187	11.65	1.85
McCullough, Mason	R-R	6-4	245	1-7-93	0	0	3.00	2	0	0	0	3	1	1	1	1	3	5	.100	.000	.111	15.00	9.00
McKenna, Trevor	L-L	6-0	200	5-17-96	2	1	0.93	20	0	0	3	29	16	7	3	0	14	31	.163	.139	.177	9.62	4.34
McKinley, Jayson	R-R	6-0	210	1-18-94	0	1	10.80	2	1	0	0	5	7	6	6	2	2	3	.318	.125	.429	5.40	3.60
Mercer, Matt	R-R	6-2	180	9-1-96	0	0	3.00	12	12	0	0	27	19	9	9	1	6	37	.192	.200	.188	12.33	2.00
Miller, Ryan	R-R	6-0	180	3-28-96	3	0	3.86	12	0	0	0	12	11	5	5	2	1	10	.244	.133	.300	7.71	0.77
Moths, Travis	R-R	6-1	190	9-22-95	0	1	1.23	4	0	0	0	7	3	1	1	0	1	8	.130	.182	.083	9.82	1.23
Ogando, Cristofer	R-R	6-3	195	10-23-93	0	0	3.86	8	0	0	0	9	9	4	4	2	3	17	.243	.222	.250	16.39	2.89
Owens, Henry	L-L	6-6	220	7-21-92	0	0	10.80	1	0	0	0	2	4	2	2	0	1	2	.444	1.000	.375	10.80	5.40
Pimentel, Chester	R-R	6-5	210	11-12-95	3	0	1.04	15	0	0	7	17	11	3	2	0	4	18	.180	.083	.243	9.35	2.08
Polancic, Jake	R-R	6-3	205	6-8-98	0	0	0.00	2	0	0	0	2	0	0	0	0	0	3	.000	.000	.000	10.80	16.20
Pujols, Rafael	R-R	6-6	175	8-21-95	0	0	0.00	3	0	0	0	3	0	0	0	1	0	3	.000	.000	.000	9.00	3.00
Ratliff, Lane	L-L	6-3	185	3-22-95	0	0	0.00	1	1	0	0	3	2	0	0	0	0	3	.182	—	.182	9.00	0.00
Ricci, Ryan	R-L	6-1	190	2-3-96	0	0	3.52	5	0	0	0	8	11	12	3	2	3	7	.314	.000	.423	8.22	3.52
Rodriguez, Wesley	R-R	5-10	210	12-4-96	2	2	3.48	24	0	0	3	34	28	14	13	0	12	40	.226	.196	.244	10.69	3.21
Santana, Yeison	R-R	6-0	180	10-25-96	2	0	3.71	18	1	0	2	27	24	12	11	2	11	23	.253	.282	.232	7.76	3.71
Scribner, Troy	L-R	6-3	190	7-2-91	0	0	0.00	1	0	0	1	4	1	0	0	0	0	7	.077	.000	.143	15.75	0.00
Soriano, Franklyn	L-L	6-5	195	7-21-95	2	1	4.08	7	3	0	0	29	21	16	13	4	10	29	.202	.188	.208	9.10	3.14
Stapler, Cole	R-R	6-4	240	12-22-94	1	0	0.00	1	0	0	0	3	4	0	0	0		4	.333	.000	.400	12.00	0.00
Stout, Kyler	R-R	6-0	195	10-13-94	0	0	0.79	8	0	0	0	11	5	1	1	1	8	22	.132	.000	.192	17.47	6.35
Tabor, Matt	R-R	6-2	180	7-14-98	2	1	3.26	14	14	0	0	61	59	26	22	4	13	46	.251	.210	.282	6.82	1.93
Toelken, Andy	R-R	6-2	188	1-15-96	1	0	1.80	3	0	0	0	5	4	1	1	0	1	1	.222	.333	.167	1.80	1.80
Tunnell, West	L-R	6-1	195	11-20-93	0	1	2.70	10	0	0	1	17	9	5	5	2	5	19	.170	.000	.273	10.26	2.70
Valdez, Bryan	L-L	6-3	180	11-27-94	2	0	3.38	4	0	0	0	19	21	7	7	3	1	14	.280	.318	.264	6.75	0.48
Weiss, Ryan	R-R	6-4	210	12-10-96	0	1	3.68	12	12	0	0	29	27	13	12	3	3	27	.241	.095	.329	8.28	0.92
Winston, Jake	R-R	6-3	194	9-13-93	0	0	4.50	3	0	0	0	2	3	2	1	0	2	1	.375	.000	.429	4.50	9.00

Fielding

C: Herrera 2, January 23, Jones 12, Yerzy 44. **1B:** Garza 3, King 2, Martinez 53, Tufts 13, Yerzy 8. **2B:** Caballero 7, Lynch 50, Tolbert 18, Tufts 3. **3B:** Caballero 13, Lynch 2, Rose 51, Tufts 10. **SS:** Caballero 15, Dobson 18, King 7, Lynch 1, Perdomo 30, Tolbert 7. **OF:** Dobson 8, Gorman 26, Hoffpauir 10, Holmes 34, January 6, Lynch 4, McCarthy 55, Perez 60, Swain 37, Watson Jr. 3.

MISSOULA OSPREY   ROOKIE
PIONEER LEAGUE

Batting	B-T	HT	WT	DOB	AVG	vLH	vRH	G	AB	R	H	2B	3B	HR	RBI	BB	HBP	SH	SF	SO	SB	CS	SLG	OBP
Alexander, Blaze	R-R	6-0	160	6-11-99	.302	.200	.323	28	116	27	35	9	3	3	17	12	0	0	1	31	3	0	.509	.364
Almond, Zachery	R-R	6-3	210	4-12-96	.345	.209	.376	56	229	43	79	16	1	13	53	13	3	0	2	40	2	0	.594	.385
Barrosa, Jorge	B-L	5-9	165	2-17-01	.167	.000	.188	6	18	3	3	0	1	0	1	1	0	0	1	5	0	0	.278	.200
Cossio, Luis	L-R	6-1	185	12-12-96	.078	.059	.085	23	64	4	5	1	0	0	3	11	1	1	0	25	0	0	.094	.224
Dalesandro, Nick	R-R	6-1	175	10-3-96	.302	.241	.317	45	149	24	45	9	1	0	21	20	0	1	1	22	4	1	.376	.382
Garcia, Cesar	R-R	6-0	190	4-7-98	.245	.180	.267	46	159	28	39	11	3	2	23	20	5	0	1	33	12	4	.390	.346
Gorman, William	L-R	6-4	210	11-8-94	.250	.200	.267	5	20	4	5	1	1	0	2	2	0	0	0	8	1	0	.400	.318
Hernandez, Eddie	B-R	5-9	160	4-18-99	.307	.306	.307	59	251	31	77	14	2	3	27	5	0	0	0	60	5	4	.414	.320
Hoffpauir, Zach	R-R	6-0	195	9-21-93	.182	.000	.200	3	11	0	2	0	1	0	1	0	0	0	0	5	0	0	.182	.250
Jones, Zachary	R-R	6-0	200	7-4-94	.200	.333	.158	7	25	7	5	2	0	0	4	4	0	0	1	10	0	0	.280	.300
Kennedy, Buddy	R-R	6-1	190	10-5-98	.327	.360	.318	57	226	46	74	17	1	4	32	26	1	0	2	34	2	0	.465	.396
King, Alex	R-R	6-2	200	10-3-95	.317	.143	.353	12	41	5	13	2	0	1	8	8	0	0	1	9	0	0	.439	.420
Lanza, Douglas	R-R	6-1	180	3-14-98	.167	1.000	.000	4	12	1	2	1	0	0	1	0	0	0	0	5	0	0	.250	.286
Leyton, Brandon	R-R	5-10	165	12-17-98	.274	.209	.291	56	215	28	59	9	2	6	34	8	4	0	3	28	8	3	.419	.309
Marriaga, Jesus	R-R	6-0	170	12-17-98	.271	.237	.280	43	170	29	46	7	0	0	10	17	4	0	0	48	12	1	.312	.351
Munoz, Jesus	L-L	6-2	160	12-19-98	.230	.255	.221	50	187	22	43	4	1	2	17	8	2	1	1	46	2	0	.294	.268
Perdomo, Geraldo	B-R	6-2	184	10-22-99	.455	.333	.500	6	22	3	10	0	1	0	2	7	0	0	0	4	1	1	.546	.586

	B-T	HT	WT	DOB	AVG	vLH	vRH	G	AB	R	H	2B	3B	HR	RBI	BB	HBP	SH	SF	SO	SB	CS	SLG	OBP
Robbins, Joe	R-R	5-9	195	12-8-93	.319	.333	.314	26	91	19	29	6	1	4	20	15	4	0	0	26	1	0	.539	.436
Robinson, Kristian	R-R	6-3	190	12-11-00	.300	.167	.315	17	60	13	18	1	0	3	10	11	2	0	1	21	5	3	.467	.419
Sanchez, David	R-R	6-1	175	1-6-99	.259	.256	.260	53	197	20	51	14	3	2	30	5	1	0	1	49	2	1	.391	.279
Shannon, Zack	R-R	6-3	230	6-22-96	.355	.279	.377	54	189	45	67	17	1	14	55	28	5	0	6	43	0	0	.677	.439
Thomas, Alek	L-L	5-11	175	4-28-00	.342	.300	.350	28	123	26	42	11	1	2	17	11	0	0	0	19	4	3	.496	.396
Wasinger, Daniel	R-R	5-11	170	11-14-95	.208	.167	.222	8	24	5	5	1	0	0	1	3	1	0	0	7	0	0	.250	.321

Pitching	B-T	HT	WT	DOB	W	L	ERA	G	GS	CG	SV	IP	H	R	ER	HR	BB	SO	AVG	vLH	vRH	K/9	BB/9
Arroyo, Mailon	B-R	6-0	200	1-2-98	0	0	6.20	12	0	0	1	20	23	15	14	3	4	32	.281	.360	.246	14.16	1.77
Autry, Trent	R-R	6-2	215	8-12-97	1	2	7.01	17	0	0	0	26	39	23	20	0	12	23	.361	.419	.338	8.06	4.21
Baldwin, Erin	R-R	6-5	195	4-22-96	4	2	3.40	13	7	0	0	45	42	22	17	3	20	32	.250	.267	.237	6.40	4.00
Castillo, Luis	R-R	6-3	212	3-10-95	1	0	0.00	2	0	0	0	2	0	0	0	0	0	0	.000	.000	.000	0.00	0.00
Cruz, Wilfry	R-R	6-2	160	10-22-97	5	2	5.27	14	14	0	0	68	68	43	40	13	31	60	.257	.214	.291	7.90	4.08
De La Cruz, Ezequiel	L-L	6-2	180	1-21-99	1	0	2.45	2	0	0	0	4	4	1	1	0	0	7	.286	.667	.182	17.18	0.00
Fuenmayor, Liu	L-L	5-11	170	2-2-99	0	0	0.00	1	0	0	0	1	1	0	0	0	0	0	1.000	—	1.000	0.00	0.00
Garcia, Justin	R-R	6-2	175	7-2-95	3	0	0.00	9	0	0	2	12	4	0	0	0	6	16	.098	.222	.000	12.00	4.50
Gelabert, Michel	L-L	6-3	200	1-7-97	0	0	81.00	1	0	0	0	0	4	3	3	0	0	1	.800	.500	1.000	27.00	0.00
Herman, Omar	R-R	5-10	170	3-21-97	1	1	4.76	7	0	0	0	6	7	5	3	1	5	7	.318	.200	.417	11.12	7.94
Hernandez, Carlos	R-R	5-9	171	4-26-94	0	0	0.00	2	0	0	0	3	1	0	0	0	1	2	.100	.000	.125	6.00	3.00
Jandron, Tyler	R-L	6-2	195	5-21-95	1	3	11.68	15	0	0	0	12	16	19	16	3	10	12	.296	.217	.355	8.76	7.30
Ladrech, Matt	R-R	6-1	192	3-11-96	0	1	15.19	4	0	0	0	5	11	10	9	1	2	2	.440	.357	.546	3.38	3.38
Martinez, Edgar	R-R	6-0	175	11-2-97	5	6	5.94	15	15	0	0	67	86	52	44	13	19	32	.308	.310	.307	4.32	2.57
Menendez, Bryan	R-R	5-11	215	1-18-96	2	1	3.09	21	0	0	9	23	20	9	8	2	6	22	.235	.242	.231	8.49	2.31
Ogando, Cristofer	R-R	6-3	195	10-23-93	0	0	9.00	1	0	0	0	1	1	1	1	0	2	2	.250	.500	.000	18.00	0.00
Olivero, Deyni	R-R	6-1	165	1-7-98	4	4	3.94	14	14	0	0	64	62	33	28	5	25	55	.250	.198	.278	7.73	3.52
Ovalles, Melvin	R-R	6-2	180	11-21-96	0	3	10.80	15	0	0	0	22	37	28	26	3	18	13	.374	.226	.441	5.40	7.48
Polancic, Jake	R-R	6-3	205	6-8-98	2	1	5.65	13	0	0	2	14	10	10	9	1	9	11	.196	.067	.250	6.91	5.65
Rosario, Oliver	L-L	6-0	140	6-15-99	0	1	19.29	2	0	0	0	2	5	5	5	0	2	2	.417	.667	.333	7.71	7.71
Sanchez, Geraldo	R-R	6-2	193	8-19-97	0	0	5.56	5	0	0	0	11	9	8	7	2	7	15	.214	.200	.222	11.91	5.56
Santana, Yeison	R-R	6-0	180	10-25-96	1	1	5.40	2	0	0	0	3	2	2	2	0	1	5	.167	.000	.286	13.50	2.70
Stevens, Jacob	B-R	6-3	225	2-11-96	3	0	3.09	16	2	0	1	35	29	17	12	4	22	40	.228	.326	.179	10.29	5.66
Tineo, Marcos	R-R	6-0	165	3-14-97	1	2	3.00	12	12	0	0	57	53	26	19	3	12	40	.249	.230	.262	6.32	1.89
Toelken, Andy	R-R	6-2	188	1-15-96	0	2	3.38	8	4	0	0	21	22	10	8	1	7	15	.272	.314	.239	6.33	2.95
Valdez, Bryan	L-L	6-3	180	11-27-94	0	0	9.45	2	1	0	0	7	13	10	7	4	0	5	.406	.400	.407	6.75	0.00
Whitson, Landon	R-R	6-2	190	9-11-96	0	1	5.23	17	0	0	0	33	50	27	19	3	9	31	.357	.391	.340	8.54	2.48
Workman, Blake	R-R	6-3	195	10-8-97	2	0	2.89	17	0	0	2	28	25	14	9	2	9	18	.233	.229	.233	10.61	2.89
Zorrilla, Pedro	L-L	6-2	168	4-30-96	2	3	3.91	16	6	0	0	46	49	23	20	2	11	38	.263	.273	.261	7.43	2.15

Fielding

C: Almond 35, Dalesandro 30, Jones 5, Lanza 4, Wasinger 4. **1B:** Almond 15, Garcia 3, King 5, Robbins 6, Shannon 48. **2B:** Alexander 4, Garcia 23, Hernandez 30, Leyton 19, Perdomo 1. **3B:** Hernandez 23, Kennedy 50, King 2, Robbins 3. **SS:** Alexander 24, Garcia 10, King 4, Leyton 36, Perdomo 5. **OF:** Barrosa 3, Cossio 21, Garcia 4, Gorman 5, Hoffpauir 3, King 1, Marriaga 43, Munoz 46, Robbins 9, Robinson 17, Sanchez 51, Thomas 28.

AZL D-BACKS
ARIZONA LEAGUE
ROOKIE

Batting	B-T	HT	WT	DOB	AVG	vLH	vRH	G	AB	R	H	2B	3B	HR	RBI	BB	HBP	SH	SF	SO	SB	CS	SLG	OBP
Alexander, Blaze	R-R	6-0	160	6-11-99	.362	.412	.333	27	94	25	34	10	2	2	25	19	3	0	2	21	7	3	.575	.475
Andueza, Axel	R-R	6-0	163	10-27-98	.288	.267	.293	20	73	15	21	4	0	0	11	5	0	0	1	7	1	0	.343	.329
Barrosa, Jorge	B-L	5-9	165	2-17-01	.233	.333	.216	10	43	4	10	0	2	0	1	3	1	0	0	6	2	2	.326	.298
Collie, Dominique	L-L	6-0	160	10-29-99	.127	.100	.137	31	71	10	9	4	0	0	4	13	0	1	0	22	2	2	.183	.262
Connelly, Terence	L-R	6-2	225	3-7-94	.263	.000	.333	7	19	3	5	1	0	0	2	4	1	0	0	3	1	0	.316	.417
Dalesandro, Nick	R-R	6-1	175	10-3-96	.333	.000	.375	2	9	2	3	0	0	0	1	0	0	0	0	1	0	0	.333	.333
DeLuzio, Ben	R-R	6-3	190	8-9-94	.286	.400	.222	4	14	5	4	1	0	0	2	2	0	0	0	5	3	0	.357	.375
Diaz, Dalgeli	L-L	6-3	190	2-3-00	.179	.000	.214	21	67	6	12	1	0	1	5	6	0	0	1	31	2	0	.239	.243
Duzenack, Camden	R-R	5-9	170	3-8-95	.154	.667	.087	7	26	3	4	2	1	0	2	1	0	0	1	7	0	0	.308	.179
Garza, David	R-R	6-1	200	2-19-95	.307	.306	.308	38	127	31	39	11	3	2	26	16	9	0	2	17	4	0	.488	.416
Gillette, Joe	R-R	6-1	190	12-15-95	.203	.162	.215	47	158	18	32	7	3	3	28	26	1	0	0	63	3	0	.342	.319
Gonzalez, Jay	L-L	5-9	170	12-11-91	.350	.222	.455	5	20	5	7	0	0	0	3	2	0	0	0	2	1	0	.350	.409
Gorman, William	L-R	6-4	210	11-8-94	.250	.400	.000	3	8	1	2	0	0	0	1	0	0	0	1	2	1	0	.250	.222
Grier, Anfernee	R-R	6-1	180	10-13-95	.357	.583	.188	9	28	7	10	4	1	0	5	3	1	0	0	6	2	0	.571	.438
Herum, Marty	R-R	6-3	214	12-16-91	.389	.000	.467	5	18	2	7	2	0	0	3	2	0	0	0	6	0	0	.500	.450
Jones, Matt	R-R	6-0	195	4-14-92	.188	.000	.273	5	16	2	3	0	0	1	4	1	0	0	0	4	0	0	.375	.235
King, Alex	R-R	6-2	200	10-3-95	.265	.091	.298	19	68	13	18	6	2	2	8	8	2	1	0	17	6	4	.500	.359
Lanza, Douglas	R-R	6-1	180	3-14-98	.118	.333	.071	9	17	2	2	1	0	0	4	1	1	0	1	6	0	0	.177	.200
Marrero, Deven	R-R	6-1	195	8-25-90	.286	.250	.333	3	7	0	2	0	0	0	2	1	0	0	0	1	0	1	.286	.375
Martinez, Sandy	R-R	6-4	195	5-9-00	.097	.100	.096	24	72	9	7	3	0	0	4	5	0	0	0	33	0	0	.139	.167
Marzilli, Evan	L-L	6-0	185	3-13-91	.429	.333	.500	3	7	2	3	1	0	0	1	1	0	0	2	1	1	0	.571	.556
McArdle, Jordan	L-R	6-0	175	5-2-98	.278	.273	.281	16	54	6	15	1	0	0	8	10	0	0	1	20	0	0	.352	.385
McCarthy, Jake	L-L	6-3	195	7-30-97	.273	.400	.167	3	11	1	3	0	0	0	4	1	0	0	0	1	1	0	.455	.333
Peguero, Liover	R-R	6-1	160	12-31-00	.197	.077	.226	19	66	8	13	0	0	0	5	5	0	0	0	17	3	2	.197	.254
Perdomo, Geraldo	B-R	6-2	184	10-22-99	.314	.273	.340	21	86	20	27	4	2	1	8	14	1	0	0	17	14	1	.442	.416
Reinheimer, Jack	R-R	6-1	185	7-19-92	.250	.167	.333	3	12	2	3	0	0	0	0	0	0	0	0	4	0	0	.250	.250
Robinson, Kristian	R-R	6-3	190	12-11-00	.272	.228	.295	40	162	35	44	11	0	4	31	16	2	0	2	46	7	5	.414	.341
Taylor, Marshawn	L-R	5-10	150	8-27-95	.172	.241	.141	31	93	11	16	1	0	0	7	8	5	0	1	16	5	5	.204	.271
Thomas, Alek	L-L	5-11	175	4-28-00	.325	.378	.302	28	123	24	40	3	5	0	10	13	1	0	0	18	8	2	.431	.394

	B-T	HT	WT	DOB	AVG	vLH	vRH	G	AB	R	H	2B	3B	HR	RBI	BB	HBP	SH	SF	SO	SB	CS	SLG	OBP
Tolbert, L.T.	L-R	6-2	200	6-7-96	.244	.250	.241	12	41	5	10	2	0	0	6	5	0	0	0	3	0	1	.293	.326
Valbuena, Luvin	R-R	5-9	165	5-7-99	.250	.191	.282	17	60	7	15	1	0	0	7	4	0	0	2	12	1	0	.267	.288
Varsho, Daulton	L-R	5-10	190	7-2-96	.500	.200	.714	3	12	4	6	2	1	1	1	0	0	0	0	1	0	0	1.083	.500
Wasinger, Daniel	R-R	5-11	170	11-14-95	.120	.111	.125	8	25	1	3	1	0	0	2	1	1	1	0	6	1	0	.160	.185
Watson Jr., Kevin	L-R	6-1	190	5-25-99	.244	.256	.239	47	156	23	38	7	3	2	25	23	4	1	1	53	7	3	.365	.353

Pitching	B-T	HT	WT	DOB	W	L	ERA	G	GS	CG	SV	IP	H	R	ER	HR	BB	SO	AVG	vLH	vRH	K/9	BB/9
Araujo, Juan	R-R	6-2	195	6-24-98	0	2	12.51	12	0	0	0	14	20	19	19	1	16	11	.345	.273	.389	7.24	10.54
Arroyo, Mailon	B-R	6-0	200	1-2-98	2	0	1.93	7	0	0	3	9	7	3	2	0	3	11	.200	.364	.125	10.61	2.89
Beriguete, Francis	L-L	6-3	165	8-11-99	0	0	1.35	3	3	0	0	13	11	4	2	0	1	11	.216	.000	.275	7.43	0.68
Blazek, Michael	R-R	6-0	205	3-16-89	0	0	0.00	3	0	0	0	3	2	1	0	0	0	6	.154	.250	.111	16.20	0.00
Cardenas, Antonio	R-R	6-2	165	12-24-99	1	2	4.50	12	9	0	0	42	33	23	21	3	23	35	.219	.200	.231	7.50	4.93
Ceballos, Jesus	R-R	5-11	162	1-9-97	0	2	5.56	10	0	0	1	11	14	8	7	3	8	15	.311	.316	.308	11.91	6.35
Custodio, Raibel	R-R	6-3	185	9-8-99	1	2	4.66	16	0	0	5	19	20	13	10	1	12	18	.267	.333	.235	8.38	5.59
De La Cruz, Ezequiel	L-L	6-2	180	1-21-99	6	1	3.10	16	0	0	5	29	25	14	10	2	16	36	.236	.158	.253	11.17	4.97
Duplantier, Jon	L-R	6-4	225	7-11-94	0	0	1.29	2	2	0	0	7	5	1	1	0	2	9	.200	.091	.286	11.57	2.57
Ellington, Brian	R-R	6-3	215	8-4-90	0	0	0.00	4	0	0	0	4	0	0	0	0	1	9	.000	.000	.000	22.85	0.00
Francis, Harrison	R-R	6-2	195	10-26-98	5	0	3.03	9	4	0	0	36	36	13	12	0	11	39	.255	.229	.269	9.84	2.78
Frias, Luis	R-R	6-3	180	5-23-98	1	7	2.48	7	6	0	0	29	17	12	8	1	11	31	.167	.265	.118	9.62	3.41
Fuenmayor, Liu	L-L	5-11	170	2-2-99	4	3	1.95	14	0	0	0	28	19	14	6	0	10	19	.186	.211	.181	6.18	3.25
Gelabert, Michel	L-L	6-3	200	1-7-97	0	0	1.21	5	4	0	1	22	10	4	3	0	12	27	.135	.200	.111	10.88	4.84
Goddard, Jackson	R-R	6-3	220	12-12-96	0	0	0.00	1	1	0	0	1	0	0	0	0	0	0	.000	.000	.000	0.00	0.00
Hagens, Bradin	R-R	6-3	210	5-12-89	1	0	2.84	5	0	0	0	6	2	2	2	1	2	7	.091	.000	.105	9.95	2.84
Herman, Omar	R-R	5-10	170	3-21-97	0	0	2.35	5	0	0	1	8	3	2	2	0	3	9	.120	.143	.111	10.57	3.52
Hernandez, Carlos	R-R	5-9	171	4-26-94	1	0	13.50	2	0	0	0	2	3	3	3	0	0	6	.333	1.000	.250	27.00	0.00
Herrera, Jhoendri	R-R	5-9	170	6-6-94	1	0	4.15	10	0	0	0	9	9	6	4	1	9	7	.265	.286	.250	7.27	9.35
Javier, Joshua	L-L	6-3	195	12-16-98	3	1	2.80	10	4	0	0	35	27	14	11	1	15	33	.209	.100	.242	8.41	3.82
2-team total (2 AZL Rangers)					3	1	2.76	12	6	0	0	42	31	16	13	1	16	45	.201	.094	.230	9.57	3.40
Kelly, Levi	R-R	6-2	205	5-14-99	0	0	0.00	4	4	0	0	6	3	0	0	0	2	6	.143	.111	.167	9.00	3.00
Ladrech, Matt	R-R	6-1	192	3-11-96	0	0	4.05	4	0	0	0	7	6	4	3	1	4	7	.222	.222	.222	9.45	5.40
Lewis, Justin	R-R	6-7	205	8-10-95	0	0	10.13	3	0	0	0	3	3	3	3	1	2	4	.250	.000	.300	13.50	6.75
Lewis, Sam	R-R	6-4	195	10-9-91	2	0	0.00	3	0	0	0	3	4	0	0	0	0	7	.333	.667	.222	23.63	0.00
Mercer, Matt	R-R	6-2	180	9-1-96	0	0	4.50	1	1	0	0	2	2	1	1	1	1	2	.250	.500	.167	4.50	4.50
Moths, Travis	R-R	6-1	190	9-22-95	0	0	4.50	2	1	0	0	2	1	1	1	0	1	2	.143	.000	.250	9.00	4.50
Owens, Henry	L-L	6-6	220	7-21-92	2	0	4.38	4	0	0	0	12	11	8	6	1	14	16	.234	.167	.244	11.68	10.22
Penalver, Carlos	R-R	6-0	170	5-17-94	0	0	4.50	4	0	0	0	4	3	4	2	1	1	4	.188	.222	.143	9.00	2.25
Pimentel, Chester	R-R	6-5	210	11-12-95	0	0	0.00	2	0	0	0	2	0	0	0	0	1	2	.000	.000	.000	9.00	4.50
Polancic, Jake	R-R	6-3	205	6-8-98	0	0	4.26	5	0	0	0	6	5	3	3	0	6	12	.208	.333	.167	17.05	8.53
Ratliff, Lane	L-L	6-3	185	3-22-95	0	0	0.00	1	1	0	0	3	1	0	0	0	1	3	.100	.000	.125	9.00	3.00
Ricci, Ryan	R-L	6-1	190	2-3-96	0	0	1.80	10	0	0	1	10	12	5	2	1	6	11	.286	.182	.323	9.90	5.40
Rosario, Oliver	L-L	6-0	140	6-15-99	1	0	2.08	8	0	0	1	13	10	6	3	3	9	16	.213	.222	.211	11.08	6.23
Sanchez, Geraldo	R-R	6-2	193	8-19-97	0	0	15.00	3	0	0	1	3	5	5	5	0	3	1	.417	.500	.400	3.00	9.00
Scribner, Troy	L-R	6-3	190	7-2-91	0	0	3.26	5	4	0	0	19	18	10	7	1	8	24	.231	.368	.186	11.17	3.72
Valdez, Alex	R-R	6-2	185	12-24-99	1	6	5.79	13	9	0	0	42	43	33	27	0	25	39	.269	.310	.245	8.36	5.36
Valdez, Bryan	L-L	6-3	180	11-27-94	0	0	0.00	1	1	0	0	6	5	1	0	0	0	5	.227	.000	.263	7.50	0.00
Ventura, Carlos	R-R	6-4	185	7-2-97	0	1	13.50	2	0	0	0	2	2	7	3	0	4	5	.222	.000	.286	22.50	18.00
Watson, Jordan	L-L	6-0	185	9-14-93	0	0	0.00	2	0	0	0	2	1	0	0	0	1	4	.143	.000	.167	18.00	4.50
Weiss, Ryan	R-R	6-4	210	12-10-96	0	0	9.00	1	0	0	0	1	2	1	1	0	0	2	.400	1.000	.000	18.00	0.00

Fielding

C: Andueza 3, Dalesandro 2, Jones 5, Lanza 6, Martinez 23, Valbuena 17, Varsho 2, Wasinger 8. **1B:** Andueza 11, Connelly 6, Garza 15, Gillette 9, Herum 1, McArdle 15, Tolbert 1. **2B:** Alexander 11, Duzenack 3, King 7, Perdomo 8, Taylor 30, Tolbert 4. **3B:** Alexander 8, Garza 10, Gillette 33, Herum 4, King 7. **SS:** Alexander 10, Duzenack 2, Garza 1, King 6, Marrero 1, McArdle 1, Peguero 19, Perdomo 14, Reinheimer 3, Tolbert 4. **OF:** Barrosa 10, Collie 25, DeLuzio 4, Diaz 14, Gillette 5, Gonzalez 4, Gorman 2, Grier 4, Marzilli 2, McCarthy 3, Robinson 35, Thomas 26, Watson Jr. 45.

DSL D-BACKS — ROOKIE
DOMINICAN SUMMER LEAGUE

Batting	B-T	HT	WT	DOB	AVG	vLH	vRH	G	AB	R	H	2B	3B	HR	RBI	BB	HBP	SH	SF	SO	SB	CS	SLG	OBP
Amador, Alexander	R-R	6-1	180	12-7-00	.190	.188	.190	28	95	14	18	3	0	0	10	7	3	0	0	33	7	4	.221	.267
Andueza, Axel	R-R	6-0	163	10-27-98	.377	.339	.352	42	162	26	61	13	3	0	25	13	4	0	1	15	5	0	.494	.433
Barrosa, Jorge	B-L	5-9	165	2-17-01	.299	.291	.276	52	204	57	61	8	3	3	21	25	11	0	1	34	37	6	.412	.403
Batista, Juan	R-R	6-1	175	1-9-01	.201	.208	.199	63	224	26	45	9	3	1	14	23	6	6	1	61	10	8	.281	.291
Caraballo, Richard	R-R	6-1	175	4-16-00	.139	.227	.114	32	101	9	14	4	1	0	7	11	5	0	0	35	5	1	.198	.256
Castillo, Neyfy	R-R	6-3	175	3-2-01	.208	.275	.193	60	221	31	46	8	1	2	38	26	6	0	4	64	20	2	.281	.304
Cordero, Andres	L-R	6-0	165	5-18-00	.216	.146	.237	53	176	25	38	5	5	1	20	18	4	0	1	33	4	1	.273	.302
Curpa, Jose	R-R	5-9	160	3-9-00	.267	.340	.241	50	180	34	48	11	0	0	20	26	11	0	1	30	31	4	.328	.390
Garcia, Andy	R-R	6-0	179	5-27-99	.186	.194	.183	32	102	17	19	2	1	0	4	16	6	1	1	38	2	2	.226	.328
Garcia, Manuel	R-R	5-11	170	1-28-00	.240	.250	.238	39	121	10	29	3	0	0	9	14	5	0	0	23	2	5	.265	.343
Goris, Carlos	L-L	5-10	170	12-17-00	.181	.116	.200	57	193	26	35	6	0	0	21	29	5	0	1	50	5	2	.275	.303
Gutierrez, Sergio	B-R	6-1	195	1-18-01	.212	.177	.221	50	179	20	38	7	1	1	22	20	3	0	2	52	7	1	.279	.299
Hernandez, Alexander	R-R	5-11	150	6-20-99	.233	.239	.232	61	223	27	52	7	4	4	21	16	4	0	2	66	2	2	.354	.294
Herrera, Eduardo	B-R	5-9	155	1-5-00	.226	.240	.222	40	106	15	24	4	5	0	11	25	4	2	1	28	9	3	.359	.390
Jaime, Ismael	L-L	6-0	179	11-30-99	.239	.205	.247	58	201	18	48	17	0	4	22	24	1	0	1	63	11	3	.383	.322
Jimenez, Rafael	L-R	6-6	215	8-25-99	.245	.133	.271	61	233	30	57	7	2	7	33	20	1	0	1	78	1	0	.382	.306
Lanza, Douglas	R-R	6-1	180	3-14-98	.182	.429	.091	4	11	0	2	0	0	0	1	1	4	0	0	3	0	0	.182	.438

Name	B-T	HT	WT	DOB	AVG	vLH	vRH	G	AB	R	H	2B	3B	HR	RBI	BB	HBP	SH	SF	SO	SB	CS	OBP	SLG
Malave, Ramses	R-R	5-11	175	9-29-00	.258	.222	.269	39	120	18	31	7	2	1	18	27	2	0	4	37	5	2	.375	.392
Martinez, Sandy	R-R	6-4	195	5-9-00	.253	.314	.142	22	83	10	21	2	0	3	14	2	0	0	3	25	0	0	.386	.261
Montas, Manuel	R-R	6-3	180	3-11-01	.128	.103	.138	45	148	15	19	4	2	1	8	15	7	0	2	61	2	3	.203	.238
Noriega, Kevin	R-R	6-1	175	10-14-99	.201	.114	.227	48	154	20	31	6	1	2	17	19	2	0	2	25	6	5	.292	.294
Padron, Juan	B-R	5-10	160	10-17-00	.114	.071	.125	45	132	15	15	0	1	0	10	16	6	4	2	55	8	1	.129	.237
Patino, Wilderd	R-R	6-1	175	7-18-01	.261	.056	.301	34	111	14	29	6	0	0	9	16	9	0	2	24	6	5	.315	.391
Paulino, Carmelo	L-L	6-0	170	12-29-98	.229	.200	.236	53	175	29	40	8	0	4	31	28	5	0	4	67	12	6	.343	.344
Peguero, Alejandro	B-R	6-0	180	2-28-00	.203	.242	.192	48	153	22	31	3	0	1	11	20	3	3	1	25	9	6	.242	.305
Peguero, Liover	R-R	6-0	160	12-31-00	.309	.094	.304	22	81	14	25	3	3	1	16	6	1	0	2	12	4	1	.457	.356
Reyes, Jose	R-R	5-9	160	10-11-98	.310	.313	.309	58	210	48	65	2	9	5	32	27	2	0	2	20	22	10	.476	.390
Ruiz, Roman	R-R	5-11	175	1-3-01	.245	.200	.256	39	151	12	37	7	2	0	18	11	3	0	1	32	9	1	.318	.307
Sanchez, Pedro	R-R	5-11	185	9-17-00	.103	.238	.070	33	107	15	11	6	0	0	5	11	3	0	0	54	4	0	.159	.207
Santana, Yordeni	R-R	6-5	198	10-8-99	.145	.071	.167	26	62	13	9	0	0	0	3	16	4	0	0	19	1	3	.145	.354
Santilien, Osvaldo	R-R	6-3	195	6-23-99	.205	.222	.202	38	127	18	26	6	0	5	22	21	3	0	1	55	6	3	.370	.329
Vegas, Deivis	R-R	5-11	170	2-9-00	.250	.000	.261	7	24	2	6	1	0	0	1	1	1	0	0	4	1	0	.292	.308

Pitching	B-T	HT	WT	DOB	W	L	ERA	G	GS	CG	SV	IP	H	R	ER	HR	BB	SO	AVG	vLH	vRH	K/9	BB/9
Alcantara, Jose	R-R	6-2	180	8-3-99	1	1	6.55	13	0	0	0	22	29	23	16	0	10	25	.305	.194	.359	10.23	4.09
Almonte, Jonathan	R-R	6-0	175	8-9-00	1	3	1.74	8	3	0	0	21	27	14	4	1	5	22	.310	.310	.310	9.58	2.18
Alvarez, Jhosmer	R-R	6-1	155	6-29-01	2	5	2.72	13	13	0	0	56	41	28	17	0	17	48	.194	.238	.176	7.67	2.72
Avendano, Julio	R-R	6-1	175	12-5-00	0	2	4.88	13	4	0	0	24	25	18	13	0	13	25	.272	.281	.267	9.38	4.88
Beriguete, Francis	L-L	6-2	165	8-11-99	4	2	3.45	10	10	0	0	44	33	23	17	0	21	37	.205	.103	.224	7.51	4.26
Borbolla, Rigoberto	L-L	6-2	170	8-20-01	1	5	4.80	14	11	0	0	54	51	32	29	3	26	59	.243	.186	.258	9.77	4.31
Bravo, Argenis	L-L	5-10	160	1-7-00	6	2	3.35	13	4	0	0	46	42	21	17	2	16	46	.240	.296	.230	9.07	3.15
Carvajal, Roaldo	R-R	6-2	180	12-20-00	0	3	2.35	12	5	0	0	31	19	14	8	0	19	11	.183	.194	.177	3.23	5.58
Caty, Petter	R-R	6-3	195	6-13-00	0	0	5.06	16	0	0	3	27	23	21	15	0	28	27	.221	.314	.174	9.11	9.45
Ceballos, Jesus	R-R	5-11	162	1-9-97	1	1	2.60	8	0	0	2	17	12	6	5	1	13	19	.197	.250	.243	9.87	6.75
De Dios, Fredely	R-R	6-2	165	11-3-00	1	0	12.86	4	0	0	0	7	10	10	10	0	10	6	.333	.400	.300	7.71	12.86
De Jesus, Henler	L-L	6-4	170	6-15-98	3	2	0.40	14	0	0	2	23	10	7	1	0	9	29	.132	.214	.113	11.51	3.57
De Jesus, Lesther	L-L	6-0	165	8-4-00	0	0	6.75	3	0	0	0	4	6	3	3	0	2	3	.353	1.000	.313	6.75	4.50
De La Cruz, Carlos	R-R	6-4	178	5-7-98	1	4	5.73	15	0	0	0	22	20	17	14	0	14	27	.244	.154	.286	11.05	5.73
De La Cruz, Daniel	R-R	6-2	185	4-29-98	1	2	4.62	15	0	0	1	25	25	17	13	1	20	20	.258	.323	.227	7.11	7.11
Dilone, Jander	L-L	6-1	175	3-29-00	2	0	11.00	10	0	0	0	9	6	11	11	0	23	12	.182	.143	.192	12.00	23.00
Gelabert, Michel	L-L	6-3	200	1-7-97	4	1	1.64	9	6	0	0	38	14	9	7	1	16	49	.112	.152	.133	11.50	3.76
Henriquez, Eurys	L-L	6-3	180	10-4-95	2	0	3.18	16	5	0	3	45	33	24	16	0	21	43	.195	.192	.196	8.54	4.17
Hiraldo, Yaramil	R-R	6-1	180	12-31-95	5	1	1.58	16	3	0	2	40	19	11	7	1	14	58	.139	.121	.144	13.05	3.15
Jaquez, Jhonatan	R-R	6-2	175	9-10-96	1	3	2.08	16	1	0	1	26	19	14	6	0	23	39	.194	.152	.215	13.50	7.96
Leal, Jhairon	L-L	6-2	175	8-21-98	3	1	1.96	12	0	0	2	18	9	4	4	0	10	15	.158	.111	.167	7.36	4.91
Martinez, Justin	R-R	6-3	180	7-30-01	0	5	7.57	15	12	0	0	44	51	56	37	3	38	30	.287	.220	.313	6.14	7.77
Martinez, Victor	L-L	6-1	190	8-16-99	1	1	3.10	18	0	0	0	29	18	17	10	1	25	39	.168	.214	.161	12.10	7.76
Mendez, Eric	R-R	6-0	175	12-3-99	4	1	2.42	15	8	0	2	52	30	18	14	2	17	65	.160	.143	.171	11.25	2.94
Meza, Carlos	L-L	6-1	155	2-10-01	1	1	3.80	15	1	0	0	24	17	11	10	0	18	16	.221	.154	.234	6.08	6.85
Mieses, Junior	R-R	6-1	168	10-15-99	0	3	3.64	11	0	0	0	30	16	14	12	0	29	26	.160	.192	.149	8.19	8.80
Ogando, Cristofer	R-R	6-3	195	10-23-93	3	1	0.00	10	0	0	2	23	8	2	0	0	6	26	.110	.188	.146	10.03	2.31
Ogando, Gerald	R-R	6-2	180	7-28-00	1	1	3.29	12	11	0	0	52	45	26	19	3	22	35	.234	.246	.230	6.06	3.81
Pacheco, Cristian	R-R	6-1	165	4-23-01	0	4	4.31	14	13	0	0	56	61	36	27	3	16	45	.281	.329	.259	7.19	2.56
Paulino, Adonis	R-R	6-1	165	3-11-00	1	2	3.32	13	0	0	0	19	13	11	7	1	13	23	.191	.208	.182	10.89	6.16
Pena, Bryam	R-R	6-5	170	2-4-01	3	2	7.58	16	4	0	0	38	39	37	32	2	38	20	.213	.273	.194	4.74	9.00
Perez, Eduardo	L-L	6-1	165	9-27-97	1	2	2.76	12	0	0	3	29	21	12	9	1	22	34	.202	.333	.180	10.43	6.75
Pimentel, Pablo	R-R	6-2	175	11-7-99	1	0	2.89	12	0	0	1	19	12	10	6	0	14	15	.182	.250	.152	7.23	6.75
Rodriguez, Victor	L-L	6-1	165	8-14-01	3	1	1.26	12	8	0	0	43	26	11	6	0	7	34	.169	.214	.164	7.12	1.47
Santamaria, Jose	R-R	6-2	190	11-26-98	1	1	3.24	8	0	0	0	17	13	6	6	1	6	13	.213	.330	.163	7.02	3.24
Santos, Rael	R-R	6-3	165	3-29-01	1	3	3.25	13	10	0	0	44	41	25	16	3	25	45	.250	.250	.250	9.14	5.08
Valdez, Alex	R-R	6-2	185	12-24-99	3	0	1.59	3	3	0	0	17	7	3	3	0	3	17	.123	.270	.210	9.00	1.59
Valdez, Bryan	L-L	6-3	180	11-27-94	2	0	0.50	3	3	0	0	18	10	3	1	0	0	22	.159	.263	.266	11.00	0.00
Valdez, Jhonny	R-R	6-3	187	8-10-98	1	3	3.12	17	0	0	6	40	38	19	14	1	11	31	.247	.296	.220	6.92	2.45
Valencia, Jose	R-R	6-3	204	9-27-00	3	1	3.12	11	0	0	3	17	10	7	6	0	4	13	.170	.125	.200	6.75	2.08
Ventura, Carlos	R-R	6-4	185	7-2-97	1	0	1.64	8	0	0	2	11	8	3	2	0	5	15	.211	.133	.250	12.27	4.09
Vilera, Gabriel	R-R	5-11	175	4-15-00	1	3	9.00	11	0	0	2	16	20	16	16	1	9	22	.308	.294	.313	12.38	5.06

Fielding

C: Andueza 9, Garcia 20, Garcia 27, Gutierrez 46, Lanza 2, Malave 14, Martinez 19, Vegas 2. **1B:** Amador 13, Andueza 13, Cordero 27, Garcia 5, Herrera 2, Jimenez 35, Lanza 1, Malave 17, Peguero 7, Vegas 4. **2B:** Amador 4, Curpa 35, Hernandez 7, Herrera 16, Padron 26, Peguero 13, Reyes 2, Ruiz 7, Sanchez 16. **3B:** Amador 4, Andueza 2, Batista 1, Castillo 59, Cordero 3, Curpa 9, Hernandez 29, Herrera 18, Padron 14, Peguero 1, Sanchez 1. **SS:** Curpa 5, Hernandez 24, Padron 6, Peguero 14, Peguero 21, Reyes 1, Ruiz 31, Sanchez 2. **OF:** Barrosa 52, Batista 61, Caraballo 24, Goris 26, Herrera 1, Jaime 54, Jimenez 10, Montas 21, Noriega 34, Patino 21, Paulino 44, Santana 14, Santilien 23.

Atlanta Braves

SEASON IN A SENTENCE: After a brutal off-season that saw general manager John Coppolella fired and banned from baseball, new GM Alex Anthopoulos and the Braves quickly flipped from rebuilding to contending. Atlanta got off to a fast start, moved into first place in early May and ran away with the NL East in August and September.

HIGH POINT: A four-game sweep of the Phillies in late September wrapped up the Braves' stranglehold on first place in the division and finished off the Phillies' downward spiral as well. The Phillies had led the Braves as late as early August, but after the sweep, Atlanta led the division by 9.5 games.

LOW POINT: The Braves' bullpen was never a strong spot in 2018, but it was even shakier than usual in July, which helped the Braves fall into second place. The bats also cooled for a stretch that resulted in a 5-13 rut that dropped them to 2.5 games behind the Phillies.

NOTABLE ROOKIES: Outfielder Ronald Acuna Jr. proved to be just as good as expected. The 2018 Minor League Player of the Year hit .293/.366/.552 with a team-best 26 home runs despite being held back at Triple-A in April. Lefthander Jesse Biddle made 60 appearances as an effective reliever, fulfilling the promise he'd shown as a Phillies prospect before a series of injuries derailed his career. Bryse Wilson, Touki Toussaint, Mike Soroka, Kolby Allard and Max Fried all made starts as the Braves used 13 rookie pitchers.

KEY TRANSACTIONS: The Braves got excellent value from righthander Anibal Sanchez as the veteran went 7-6, 2.83 after signing a $1 million free agent contract. Needing help for the rotation and the bullpen, Anthopoulos acquired righthanders Kevin Gausman and Brad Brach for international bonus slot money and a quartet of mid-level prospects. Gausman went 5-3, 2.87 in 10 starts with the Braves, showing an effectiveness that he didn't have with the Orioles. Brach had a 1.52 ERA in 27 appearances with the Braves.

DOWN ON THE FARM: Even after graduating Acuna, the system is still one of the deeper ones in baseball, especially on the mound. Third baseman Austin Riley is not far from being big league ready and Wilson, Toussaint, Soroka, Allard, Fried and Kyle Wright could all compete for innings in the Braves' rotation or bullpen in 2019. The lower levels of the farm system are thinner thanks to penalties levied by Major League Baseball that made numerous Braves signees free agents.

OPENING DAY PAYROLL: $83,306,041 (27th)

PLAYERS OF THE YEAR

TONY FIRRIOLO

SCOTT A. MILLER

MAJOR LEAGUE

Freddie Freeman
1B
.309/.388/.505
44 doubles,
23 HR and 98 RBIs

MINOR LEAGUE

Touki Toussaint
RHP
(Double-A/Triple-A)
9-6, 2.38 in 24 GS
163 SO in 136.1 IP

ORGANIZATION LEADERS

Batting		*Minimum 250 AB
MAJORS		
* AVG	Freddie Freeman	.309
* OPS	Ronald Acuna Jr.	.917
HR	Ronald Acuna Jr.	26
RBI	Freddie Freeman	98
MINORS		
* AVG	Michael Reed, Mississippi, Gwinnett	.342
* OBP	Michael Reed, Mississippi, Gwinnett	.453
* SLG	Austin Riley, Mississippi, Gwinnett, Braves	.522
* OPS	Michael Reed, Mississippi, Gwinnett	.972
R	Rio Ruiz, Gwinnett	72
R	Drew Waters, Rome, Florida	72
H	Riley Delgado, Rome, Florida	153
TB	Drew Waters, Rome, Florida	219
2B	Drew Waters, Rome, Florida	39
3B	Drew Waters, Rome, Florida	9
3B	Justin Dean, Danville, Rome	9
HR	Braxton Davidson, Florida	20
RBI	Carlos Franco, Gwinnett	76
BB	Michael Reed, Mississippi, Gwinnett	62
SO	Braxton Davidson, Florida	213
SB	Ray-Patrick Didder, Florida, Mississippi	27

Pitching		#Minimum 75 IP
MAJORS		
W	Mike Foltynewicz	13
# ERA	Anibal Sanchez	2.83
SO	Mike Foltynewicz	202
SV	Arodys Vizcaino	16
MINORS		
W	Kyle Muller, Rome, Florida, Mississippi	11
L	Huascar Ynoa, Rome, Florida	12
# ERA	Touki Toussaint, Mississippi, Gwinnett	2.38
G	Jason Hursh, Mississippi, Gwinnett	53
GS	Jeremy Walker, Florida, Gwinnett	26
SV	Jacob Webb, Mississippi, Gwinnett	18
IP	Jeremy Walker, Florida, Gwinnett	143
BB	Tucker Davidson, Florida	58
BB	Odalvi Javier, Rome	58
SO	Touki Toussaint, Mississippi, Gwinnett	163
# AVG	Ian Anderson, Florida, Mississippi	.199

2018 PERFORMANCE

General Manager: Alex Anthopoulos. **Farm Director:** Dom Chiti. **Scouting Director:** Brian Bridges.

Class	Team	League	W	L	PCT	Finish	Manager
Majors	Atlanta Braves	National	90	72	.556	5th (15)	Brian Snitker
Triple-A	Gwinnett Stripers	International	70	69	.504	7th (14)	Damon Berryhill
Double-A	Mississippi Braves	Southern	67	71	.486	t-5th (10)	Chris Maloney
High A	Florida Fire Frogs	Florida State	51	80	.389	12th (12)	Luis Salazar
Low A	Rome Braves	South Atlantic	71	65	.522	5th (14)	Rocket Wheeler
Rookie	Danville Braves	Appalachian	33	35	.485	t-4th (10)	Barrett Kleinknecht
Rookie	GCL Braves	Gulf Coast	22	32	.407	16th (18)	Nestor Perez
Overall 2018 Minor League Record			314	352	.471	t-22nd (30)	

ORGANIZATION STATISTICS

ATLANTA BRAVES
NATIONAL LEAGUE

Batting	B-T	HT	WT	DOB	AVG	vLH	vRH	G	AB	R	H	2B	3B	HR	RBI	BB	HBP	SH	SF	SO	SB	CS	SLG	OBP
Acuna Jr., Ronald	R-R	6-0	180	12-18-97	.293	.302	.290	111	433	78	127	26	4	26	64	45	6	0	3	123	16	5	.552	.366
Adams, Lane	R-R	6-4	220	11-13-89	.240	.125	.294	26	25	10	6	1	0	2	6	4	0	0	0	8	1	0	.520	.345
Albies, Ozzie	B-R	5-8	165	1-7-97	.261	.335	.231	158	639	105	167	40	5	24	72	36	5	1	3	116	14	3	.452	.305
Bautista, Jose	R-R	6-0	205	10-19-80	.143	.188	.105	12	35	3	5	1	0	2	5	5	0	0	0	12	0	0	.343	.250
3-team total (83 New York, 27 Philadelphia)					.203	.168	.219	122	325	52	66	18	0	13	48	67	6	0	1	111	4	3	.379	.348
Bourjos, Peter	R-R	6-1	175	3-31-87	.205	.182	.227	36	44	5	9	2	1	1	4	2	0	1	0	15	0	0	.364	.239
Camargo, Johan	B-R	6-0	195	12-13-93	.272	.270	.272	134	464	63	126	27	1	19	76	51	6	0	3	108	1	1	.457	.349
Culberson, Charlie	R-R	6-0	200	4-10-89	.270	.262	.275	113	296	47	80	18	2	12	45	21	4	0	1	85	4	2	.466	.326
Duda, Lucas	L-R	6-4	255	2-3-86	.222	—	.222	20	18	1	4	2	0	1	2	4	0	0	0	7	0	0	.500	.364
Duvall, Adam	R-R	6-1	215	9-4-88	.132	.077	.185	33	53	8	7	1	0	0	3	3	1	0	0	17	0	0	.151	.193
2-team total (105 Cincinnati)					.195	.189	.198	138	384	48	75	20	0	15	61	37	5	0	1	117	2	2	.365	.274
Flaherty, Ryan	L-R	6-3	220	7-27-86	.217	.214	.218	81	161	17	35	6	0	2	13	18	1	1	1	41	4	2	.292	.298
Flowers, Tyler	R-R	6-4	260	1-24-86	.227	.349	.184	82	251	34	57	9	0	8	30	35	9	0	1	76	0	0	.359	.341
Freeman, Freddie	L-R	6-5	220	9-12-89	.309	.309	.309	162	618	94	191	44	4	23	98	76	7	0	6	132	10	3	.505	.388
Inciarte, Ender	L-L	5-11	190	10-29-90	.265	.268	.264	156	597	83	158	27	6	10	61	49	6	4	4	86	28	14	.380	.325
Markakis, Nick	L-L	6-1	210	11-17-83	.297	.284	.304	162	623	78	185	43	2	14	93	72	1	0	9	80	1	1	.440	.366
Perez, Carlos	R-R	6-0	210	10-27-90	.143	.000	.158	8	21	0	3	0	0	0	1	0	0	0	0	6	0	0	.143	.182
Peterson, Dustin	R-R	6-2	210	9-10-94	.000	—	.000	2	2	0	0	0	0	0	0	0	0	0	0	1	0	0	.000	.000
Reed, Michael	R-R	6-0	215	11-18-92	.286	.000	.400	7	7	1	2	0	0	0	0	0	0	0	0	3	0	0	.286	.286
Rivera, Rene	R-R	5-10	215	7-31-83	.000	.000	.000	3	4	0	0	0	0	0	0	0	0	0	0	3	0	0	.000	.000
Ruiz, Rio	L-R	6-1	215	5-22-94	.083	—	.083	14	12	1	1	0	0	0	0	2	1	0	0	5	0	0	.083	.267
Santana, Danny	B-R	5-11	185	11-7-90	.179	.250	.150	15	28	4	5	3	0	0	2	3	1	0	0	11	1	1	.286	.281
Stewart, Chris	R-R	6-4	215	2-19-82	.214	.000	.231	5	14	3	3	0	0	0	3	1	0	0	1	1	0	0	.214	.250
2-team total (3 Arizona)					.200	.000	.231	8	15	3	3	0	0	0	3	1	0	0	1	1	0	0	.200	.235
Suzuki, Kurt	R-R	5-11	210	10-4-83	.271	.273	.270	105	347	45	94	24	0	12	50	22	13	0	6	43	0	0	.444	.333
Swanson, Dansby	R-R	6-1	190	2-11-94	.239	.204	.248	136	478	51	114	25	4	14	59	44	2	6	3	122	10	4	.395	.304
Tucker, Preston	L-L	6-0	210	7-6-90	.240	.143	.252	80	129	15	31	10	0	4	22	9	3	0	1	34	0	0	.411	.303
2-team total (17 Cincinnati)					.229	.111	.243	97	166	19	38	11	0	6	27	13	4	0	1	43	0	0	.404	.299

Pitching	B-T	HT	WT	DOB	W	L	ERA	G	GS	CG	SV	IP	H	R	ER	HR	BB	SO	AVG	vLH	vRH	K/9	BB/9
Allard, Kolby	L-L	6-1	190	8-13-97	1	1	12.38	3	1	0	0	8	19	12	11	3	4	3	.463	.571	.407	3.38	4.50
Biddle, Jesse	L-L	6-5	220	10-22-91	6	1	3.11	60	0	0	1	64	50	26	22	6	31	67	.218	.253	.194	9.47	4.38
Brach, Brad	R-R	6-6	215	4-12-86	1	2	1.52	27	0	0	1	24	22	8	4	1	9	22	.237	.303	.200	8.37	3.42
Brothers, Rex	L-L	6-0	215	12-18-87	0	0	—	1	0	0	0	0	0	1	1	0	2	0	—	—	—	—	—
Carle, Shane	R-R	6-4	210	8-30-91	4	1	2.86	53	0	0	1	63	50	22	20	2	27	43	.221	.221	.221	6.14	3.86
Foltynewicz, Mike	R-R	6-4	200	10-7-91	13	10	2.85	31	31	2	0	183	130	65	58	17	68	202	.195	.183	.208	9.93	3.34
Freeman, Sam	R-L	5-11	180	6-24-87	3	5	4.29	63	0	0	0	50	41	26	24	3	32	58	.229	.233	.226	10.37	5.72
Fried, Max	L-L	6-4	190	1-18-94	1	4	2.94	14	5	0	0	34	26	12	11	3	20	44	.226	.224	.224	11.76	5.35
Gausman, Kevin	L-R	6-3	190	1-6-91	5	3	2.87	10	10	0	0	60	50	23	19	5	18	44	.227	.220	.237	6.64	2.72
Gohara, Luiz	L-L	6-3	265	7-31-96	0	1	5.95	9	1	0	1	20	16	13	13	3	8	18	.222	.263	.208	8.24	3.66
Jackson, Luke	R-R	6-2	210	8-24-91	0	1	3.23	35	0	0	1	41	41	22	20	3	21	46	.260	.214	.284	10.18	4.65
McCarthy, Brandon	R-R	6-8	225	7-7-83	6	3	4.92	15	15	0	0	79	94	45	43	15	21	65	.300	.275	.320	7.44	2.40
McCreery, Adam	L-L	6-9	250	12-31-92	0	0	18.00	1	0	0	0	1	4	2	2	0	2	2	.571	.500	.600	18.00	0.00
Minter, A.J.	L-L	6-0	215	9-2-93	4	3	3.23	65	0	0	15	61	57	23	22	3	22	69	.244	.225	.253	10.13	3.23
Moylan, Peter	R-R	6-3	220	12-2-78	0	1	4.45	39	0	0	0	28	32	14	14	4	18	23	.299	.276	.308	7.31	5.72
Newcomb, Sean	L-L	6-5	255	6-12-93	12	9	3.90	31	30	0	0	164	137	74	71	18	81	160	.226	.194	.234	8.78	4.45
Parsons, Wes	R-R	6-5	204	9-6-92	0	1	7.20	1	0	0	0	5	6	4	4	1	3	3	.316	.222	.400	5.40	5.40
Phillips, Evan	R-R	6-2	215	9-11-94	0	0	8.53	4	0	0	0	6	6	6	6	3	4	2	.240	.222	.250	4.26	5.68
Ramirez, Jose	R-R	6-1	210	1-21-90	0	2	17.05	7	0	0	0	6	9	12	12	0	8	7	.321	.333	.313	9.95	11.37
Ravin, Josh	R-R	6-4	215	1-21-88	0	1	6.00	2	0	0	0	3	2	2	2	0	2	1	.200	.250	.167	3.00	6.00
Sanchez, Anibal	R-R	6-0	205	2-27-84	7	6	2.83	25	24	0	0	137	106	48	43	15	42	135	.213	.192	.233	8.89	2.77
Sims, Lucas	R-R	6-2	230	5-10-94	0	0	7.84	6	0	0	0	10	12	9	9	2	8	10	.279	.191	.364	8.71	6.97
2-team total (3 Cincinnati)					0	0	7.47	9	0	0	0	16	15	13	13	3	13	16	.242	.192	.278	9.19	7.47
Sobotka, Chad	R-R	6-7	225	7-10-93	1	0	1.88	14	0	0	0	14	5	3	3	2	9	21	.104	.118	.097	13.19	5.65

Name	B-T	HT	WT	DOB	W	L	ERA	G	GS	CG	SV	IP	H	R	ER	HR	BB	SO	AVG	vLH	vRH	K/9	BB/9
Socolovich, Miguel	R-R	6-1	205	7-24-86	0	1	10.80	4	0	0	0	5	8	6	6	0	2	4	.348	.286	.444	7.20	3.60
Soroka, Mike	R-R	6-5	225	8-4-97	2	1	3.51	5	5	0	0	26	30	14	10	1	7	21	.289	.250	.327	7.36	2.45
Teheran, Julio	R-R	6-2	205	1-27-91	9	9	3.94	31	31	0	0	176	122	80	77	26	84	162	.196	.209	.184	8.30	4.30
Toussaint, Touki	R-R	6-3	185	6-20-96	2	1	4.03	7	5	0	0	29	18	13	13	1	21	32	.182	.143	.211	9.93	6.52
Venters, Jonny	L-L	6-3	200	3-20-85	4	1	3.54	28	0	0	2	20	15	9	8	0	10	16	.206	.111	.297	7.08	4.43
Vizcaino, Arodys	R-R	6-0	245	11-13-90	2	2	2.11	39	0	0	16	38	30	9	9	4	15	40	.213	.227	.200	9.39	3.52
Whitley, Chase	R-R	6-4	220	6-14-89	0	0	18.00	1	0	0	0	1	2	2	2	1	1	1	.400	.250	1.000	9.00	9.00
Wilson, Bryse	R-R	6-1	225	12-20-97	1	0	6.43	3	1	0	0	7	8	5	5	0	6	6	.308	.273	.333	7.71	7.71
Winkler, Dan	R-R	6-3	205	2-2-90	4	0	3.43	69	0	0	2	60	52	27	23	3	20	69	.228	.289	.193	10.29	2.98
Wisler, Matt	R-R	6-3	210	9-12-92	1	1	5.40	7	3	0	0	27	30	16	16	6	5	21	.283	.278	.289	7.09	1.69
2-team total (11 Cincinnati)					1	1	4.28	18	3	0	0	40	41	20	19	8	7	32	.265	.261	.267	7.20	1.58
Wright, Kyle	R-R	6-4	200	10-2-95	0	0	4.50	4	0	0	0	6	4	3	3	2	6	5	.182	.222	.154	7.50	9.00

Fielding

Catcher	PCT	G	PO	A	E	DP	PB
Flowers	.998	76	596	37	1	2	8
Perez	.981	6	47	4	1	0	0
Rivera	1.000	3	10	0	0	0	0
Stewart	1.000	5	28	3	0	0	2
Suzuki	.994	93	744	33	5	5	3

First Base	PCT	G	PO	A	E	DP
Culberson	1.000	2	4	1	0	1
Duda	1.000	2	19	1	0	0
Flaherty	1.000	7	18	0	0	2
Freeman	.995	161	1268	72	7	116

Second Base	PCT	G	PO	A	E	DP
Albies	.985	157	248	389	10	94

	PCT	G	PO	A	E	DP
Camargo	.875	3	1	6	1	1
Culberson	.933	9	9	19	2	5
Flaherty	1.000	1	1	2	0	0

Third Base	PCT	G	PO	A	E	DP
Bautista	.933	8	3	11	1	2
Camargo	.959	114	64	170	10	16
Culberson	.967	20	9	20	1	2
Flaherty	.970	40	16	49	2	6
Ruiz	1.000	1	0	3	0	0

Shortstop	PCT	G	PO	A	E	DP
Camargo	.968	18	25	35	2	13
Culberson	.959	20	21	26	2	4
Swanson	.981	136	165	350	10	77

Outfield	PCT	G	PO	A	E	DP
Acuna Jr.	.974	108	184	3	5	0
Adams	1.000	8	9	0	0	0
Bourjos	1.000	25	17	1	0	0
Culberson	1.000	31	36	2	0	0
Duvall	1.000	14	19	0	0	0
Inciarte	.987	155	380	6	5	3
Markakis	.994	160	313	9	2	0
Reed	.000	1	0	0	0	0
Santana	1.000	9	13	0	0	0
Tucker	1.000	31	47	1	0	0

GWINNETT STRIPERS

TRIPLE-A

INTERNATIONAL LEAGUE

Batting	B-T	HT	WT	DOB	AVG	vLH	vRH	G	AB	R	H	2B	3B	HR	RBI	BB	HBP	SH	SF	SO	SB	CS	SLG	OBP
Acuna Jr., Ronald	R-R	6-0	180	12-18-97	.211	.188	.224	23	90	9	19	2	0	1	3	11	0	0	0	25	5	1	.267	.297
Adams, Lane	R-R	6-4	220	11-13-89	.192	.250	.161	30	94	9	18	5	1	0	6	5	1	0	1	37	3	1	.266	.238
Avery, Xavier	L-L	6-0	190	1-1-90	.261	.286	.253	80	241	36	63	11	1	4	19	36	0	0	1	93	9	2	.365	.356
Bautista, Jose	R-R	6-0	205	10-19-80	.250	.083	.333	10	36	6	9	1	0	1	5	6	2	0	0	8	1	1	.361	.386
Bourjos, Peter	R-R	6-1	175	3-31-87	.277	.353	.260	24	94	16	26	6	5	2	9	10	1	0	0	19	1	0	.511	.352
Brantly, Rob	L-R	6-1	195	7-14-89	.218	.172	.239	57	188	16	41	11	0	1	19	7	3	0	3	37	0	0	.293	.254
2-team total (15 Columbus)					.210	.169	.228	72	229	20	48	11	0	2	21	8	6	0	3	49	0	0	.284	.252
Camargo, Johan	B-R	6-0	195	12-13-93	.303	.286	.308	8	33	6	10	2	0	3	7	3	0	0	0	9	0	0	.636	.361
Carrera, Ezequiel	L-L	5-11	185	6-11-87	.146	.059	.169	26	82	9	12	3	0	1	4	9	0	1	1	20	7	0	.220	.228
Colon, Christian	R-R	5-10	185	5-14-89	.204	.211	.200	16	49	3	10	0	0	0	3	4	1	1	0	8	1	0	.204	.278
Decker, Jaff	L-L	5-9	190	2-23-90	.271	.264	.273	15	48	7	13	6	0	1	4	11	0	0	0	19	1	2	.458	.407
2-team total (24 Syracuse)					.244	.139	.283	39	135	24	33	10	0	3	14	25	2	0	1	49	2	2	.385	.368
Flaherty, Ryan	L-R	6-3	220	7-27-86	.267	.167	.417	8	30	3	8	1	0	0	4	1	1	0	0	9	0	0	.300	.313
Flowers, Tyler	R-R	6-4	260	1-24-86	.000	.000	.000	2	7	0	0	0	0	0	1	0	0	0	0	2	0	0	.000	.000
Franco, Carlos	L-R	6-3	220	12-20-91	.249	.200	.273	119	437	52	109	22	1	16	76	42	0	0	6	153	1	1	.414	.311
Giardina, Sal	B-R	6-4	215	4-30-92	.309	.438	.269	23	68	7	21	4	0	1	6	3	2	0	0	19	0	0	.412	.356
Gosselin, Phil	R-R	6-1	200	10-3-88	.251	.299	.233	81	279	38	70	18	2	5	36	28	1	1	2	59	0	2	.384	.319
2-team total (3 Louisville)					.253	.294	.237	84	292	39	74	19	2	5	40	28	1	1	3	63	0	2	.384	.318
Jackson, Alex	R-R	6-2	215	12-25-95	.204	.129	.234	35	108	15	22	11	2	3	17	12	3	0	2	42	0	0	.426	.296
Kazmar Jr., Sean	R-R	5-9	180	8-5-84	.254	.256	.254	99	338	35	86	15	1	16	26	14	8	1	5	38	3	2	.314	.296
Marte, Luis	R-R	6-1	188	12-15-86	.266	.359	.230	45	188	20	50	8	1	2	15	5	1	1	0	33	5	2	.351	.289
Morales, Jonathan	R-R	5-11	180	1-29-95	.261	.357	.219	16	46	4	12	0	0	0	5	3	1	0	1	8	0	0	.261	.314
Okazaki, Yuta	R-R	5-8	175	7-4-91	.333	.000	.500	3	3	0	1	0	0	0	0	0	0	0	0	2	0	0	.333	.333
Peterson, Dustin	R-R	6-2	210	5-0-94	.269	.279	.264	107	406	46	109	23	0	11	55	30	4	1	1	96	3	0	.406	.324
Reed, Michael	R-R	6-0	215	11-18-92	.363	.409	.339	53	193	36	70	13	0	7	25	32	3	1	0	55	4	0	.539	.459
Riley, Austin	R-R	6-3	220	4-2-97	.282	.303	.274	75	291	41	82	17	0	12	47	26	4	0	3	95	1	0	.464	.346
Ruiz, Rio	L-R	6-1	215	5-22-94	.269	.261	.273	130	498	72	134	25	4	9	72	40	0	0	4	90	2	1	.390	.322
Salazar, Alejandro	R-R	6-0	170	10-5-96	.286	.250	.333	2	7	2	2	0	0	0	0	0	0	0	0	0	0	0	.429	.286
Santana, Danny	B-R	5-11	185	11-7-90	.264	.286	.256	82	322	57	85	21	3	16	40	15	0	2	3	80	12	5	.497	.294
Scivicque, Kade	R-R	6-0	225	3-22-93	.250	.333	.000	1	4	0	1	0	0	0	1	0	0	0	0	1	0	0	.500	.250
2-team total (34 Toledo)					.231	.208	.231	35	117	6	27	8	0	2	8	7	2	1	1	19	0	0	.350	.284
Shumpert, Nicholas	R-R	5-11	180	11-11-96	.167	.000	.200	2	6	0	1	0	0	0	1	0	0	0	0	3	0	0	.167	.167
Smith, Tyler	R-R	6-0	195	7-1-91	.219	.160	.246	52	160	14	35	9	1	4	19	16	2	0	0	46	0	0	.363	.298
Stewart, Chris	R-R	6-3	215	2-19-82	.219	.326	.165	47	137	17	30	6	1	0	10	14	2	2	1	10	0	0	.277	.299
Tucker, Preston	L-L	6-0	210	7-6-90	.250	.077	.298	16	60	7	15	4	1	0	7	3	0	0	0	15	0	0	.350	.274
2-team total (2 Louisville)					.246	.125	.283	18	69	7	17	4	1	0	7	2	0	0	0	7	0	0	.333	.268

Pitching	B-T	HT	WT	DOB	W	L	ERA	G	GS	CG	SV	IP	H	R	ER	HR	BB	SO	AVG	vLH	vRH	K/9	BB/9
Allard, Kolby	L-L	6-1	190	8-13-97	6	4	2.72	19	19	0	0	112	102	37	34	6	34	89	.249	.242	.253	7.13	2.72
Bell, Chad	R-L	6-3	200	2-28-89	2	3	6.22	28	1	0	0	46	49	33	32	5	14	48	.306	.378	.262	9.32	2.72
2-team total (4 Toledo)					2	3	5.88	32	4	0	0	57	68	38	37	8	18	55	.289	.358	.253	8.74	2.86
Biddle, Jesse	L-L	6-5	220	10-22-91	0	0	0.00	4	0	0	1	6	3	0	0	0	1	8	.143	.111	.167	11.37	1.42

Name	B-T	HT	WT	DOB	W	L	ERA	G	GS	CG	SV	IP	H	R	ER	HR	BB	SO	AVG	vLH	vRH	K/9	BB/9
Blair, Aaron	R-R	6-4	220	5-26-92	0	1	0.00	1	1	0	0	3	1	3	0	0	5	3	.100	.000	.200	10.13	16.88
Brothers, Rex	L-L	6-0	215	12-18-87	2	4	7.24	32	0	0	1	27	26	23	22	1	33	37	.257	.286	.237	12.18	10.87
Carle, Shane	R-R	6-4	210	8-30-91	0	0	0.00	2	0	0	0	2	2	0	0	0	0	1	.250	.250	.250	4.50	0.00
Clouse, Corbin	B-L	6-0	230	6-26-95	1	0	2.25	7	3	0	0	16	12	4	4	0	4	18	.207	.111	.250	10.13	2.25
Franco, Enderson	R-R	6-2	180	12-29-92	0	1	1.59	1	1	0	0	6	4	2	1	1	3	1	.182	.400	.118	1.59	4.76
Freeman, Sam	R-L	5-11	180	6-24-87	1	0	0.00	2	0	0	0	2	1	0	0	0	2	3	.143	.333	.000	13.50	9.00
Fried, Max	L-L	6-4	190	1-18-94	2	6	4.61	13	13	0	0	66	66	35	34	4	30	71	.263	.292	.253	9.63	4.07
Gohara, Luiz	L-L	6-3	265	7-31-96	3	4	4.94	12	12	0	0	55	54	33	30	9	15	55	.263	.247	.273	9.05	2.47
Hursh, Jason	R-R	6-2	210	10-2-91	2	5	3.98	39	1	0	1	52	51	29	23	0	31	45	.267	.244	.286	7.79	5.37
Jackson, Luke	R-R	6-2	210	8-24-91	2	1	1.69	10	1	0	0	21	11	5	4	0	10	34	.155	.160	.152	14.34	4.22
Johnstone, Connor	R-R	6-1	195	10-4-94	2	0	4.50	5	4	0	0	22	23	12	11	5	7	15	.261	.279	.244	6.14	2.86
Kennedy, Jon	L-L	6-5	215	9-20-94	0	2	7.59	4	2	0	0	11	14	10	9	0	3	5	.326	.375	.296	4.22	2.53
Leyva, Elian	R-R	6-2	210	3-17-89	1	1	2.70	12	1	0	0	27	23	9	8	1	8	20	.235	.226	.244	6.75	2.70
Mader, Michael	L-L	6-2	205	2-18-94	1	1	3.71	7	4	0	0	27	28	12	11	3	12	22	.277	.355	.243	7.43	4.05
McCarthy, Brandon	R-R	6-8	225	7-7-83	0	1	4.50	3	0	0	0	4	6	2	2	1	0	2	.353	.000	.417	4.50	0.00
McCreery, Adam	L-L	6-9	250	12-31-92	0	0	2.35	8	0	0	0	8	3	2	2	0	4	10	.120	.154	.083	11.74	4.70
Moylan, Peter	R-R	6-3	220	12-2-78	0	0	0.00	3	0	0	0	3	1	0	0	0	1	5	.231	.250	.200	12.00	3.00
Parsons, Wes	R-R	6-5	204	9-6-92	7	4	3.27	16	14	0	1	88	77	33	32	7	25	76	.233	.224	.241	7.77	2.56
Peterson, David	R-R	6-5	205	1-4-90	0	0	6.08	17	0	0	0	24	34	16	16	1	9	10	.347	.405	.304	3.80	3.42
Pfeifer, Philip	L-L	6-0	200	7-15-92	2	3	6.86	29	1	0	0	41	39	38	31	1	29	37	.260	.259	.261	8.19	6.42
Phillips, Evan	R-R	6-2	215	9-11-94	4	4	1.99	31	0	0	8	41	28	12	9	1	14	59	.199	.203	.195	13.06	3.10
2-team total (8 Norfolk)					4	6	2.28	39	0	0	8	51	34	16	13	2	17	72	.190	.183	.196	12.62	2.98
Ramirez, Jose	R-R	6-1	220	1-21-90	0	0	0.00	1	0	0	0	1	0	0	0	0	0	1	.000	.000	—	9.00	0.00
Ravin, Josh	R-R	6-4	215	1-21-88	0	2	0.00	19	0	0	4	19	11	3	0	0	9	30	.157	.152	.162	14.46	4.34
Salas, Fernando	R-R	6-2	200	5-30-85	1	1	12.00	6	0	0	0	6	14	8	8	3	2	9	.438	.375	.500	13.50	3.00
Sanchez, Anibal	R-R	6-0	205	2-27-84	0	1	10.80	2	2	0	0	7	9	8	8	2	4	9	.333	.300	.353	12.15	5.40
Santiago, Andres	R-R	6-1	220	10-26-89	2	4	5.60	17	7	0	0	55	53	39	34	7	32	38	.243	.243	.244	6.26	5.27
Sims, Lucas	R-R	6-2	230	5-10-94	4	3	2.84	15	14	0	0	73	66	29	23	6	34	83	.248	.227	.277	10.23	4.19
2-team total (5 Louisville)					4	5	3.11	20	19	0	0	101	86	43	35	11	39	115	.232	.221	.247	10.21	3.46
Sobotka, Chad	R-R	6-7	225	7-10-93	0	0	1.93	9	0	0	3	9	5	2	2	0	5	12	.152	.250	.059	11.57	8.68
Socolovich, Miguel	R-R	6-1	205	7-24-86	5	4	2.65	30	3	0	0	51	53	18	15	5	12	49	.273	.304	.252	8.65	2.12
Soroka, Mike	R-R	6-5	225	8-4-97	2	1	2.00	5	5	1	0	27	20	6	6	0	6	31	.204	.240	.167	10.33	2.00
Toussaint, Touki	R-R	6-3	185	6-20-96	5	0	1.43	8	8	0	0	50	35	10	8	0	17	56	.193	.180	.214	10.01	3.04
Vasquez, Kelvin	R-R	6-4	195	4-6-93	0	0	0.00	1	0	0	0	1	0	0	0	0	0	1	.000	.000	.000	9.00	0.00
Vizcaino, Arodys	R-R	6-0	245	11-13-90	0	0	0.00	1	0	0	0	1	0	0	0	0	1	0	.000	.000	.000	0.00	9.00
Walker, Jeremy	R-R	6-5	205	6-12-95	0	0	0.00	1	0	0	0	8	3	0	0	0	1	6	.115	.100	.125	6.75	1.13
Webb, Jacob	R-R	6-1	200	8-15-93	2	2	3.13	30	0	0	11	32	20	13	11	3	11	34	.175	.174	.177	9.66	3.13
Whitley, Chase	R-R	6-4	220	6-14-89	0	1	4.18	14	1	0	0	24	26	13	11	1	7	21	.274	.325	.236	7.99	2.66
Wilson, Bryse	R-R	6-1	225	12-20-97	3	0	5.32	5	3	0	0	22	20	13	13	6	3	28	.238	.286	.191	11.45	1.23
Wisler, Matt	R-R	6-3	210	9-12-92	4	4	4.37	13	13	2	0	70	79	35	34	6	14	65	.290	.289	.292	8.36	1.80
2-team total (8 Louisville)					5	5	3.81	21	15	2	0	90	98	40	38	6	17	86	.282	.293	.272	8.63	1.71
Wright, Kyle	R-R	6-4	200	10-2-95	2	1	2.51	7	4	0	0	29	15	9	8	2	8	28	.152	.163	.140	8.79	2.51

Fielding

Catcher	PCT	G	PO	A	E	DP	PB
Brantly	.991	46	390	30	4	3	5
Flowers	1.000	2	8	1	0	0	0
Giardina	.991	13	107	3	1	1	2
Jackson	.977	29	234	18	6	0	4
Morales	1.000	9	60	3	0	0	0
Scivicque	1.000	1	7	0	0	0	0
Stewart	.988	45	364	32	5	0	3

First Base	PCT	G	PO	A	E	DP
Franco	.991	102	724	52	7	104
Gosselin	1.000	5	48	3	0	1
Kazmar Jr.	1.000	2	6	1	0	1
Ruiz	.993	35	259	22	2	19

Second Base	PCT	G	PO	A	E	DP
Camargo	1.000	1	1	1	0	0
Colon	.971	14	30	38	2	12
Flaherty	1.000	3	7	7	0	2
Gosselin	.988	63	108	149	3	42
Kazmar Jr.	.979	32	53	86	3	25
Marte	1.000	2	6	3	0	0
Salazar	1.000	2	1	3	0	1
Santana	.955	14	24	39	3	13
Smith	.959	15	28	19	2	7

Third Base	PCT	G	PO	A	E	DP
Bautista	.933	9	9	19	2	1
Camargo	1.000	3	1	2	0	0
Flaherty	1.000	2	2	3	0	1
Gosselin	1.000	4	1	6	0	0
Riley	.972	71	53	118	5	15
Ruiz	.984	49	36	84	2	16
Smith	1.000	2	1	3	0	2

Shortstop	PCT	G	PO	A	E	DP
Camargo	.909	4	3	7	1	1
Flaherty	.923	2	5	7	1	3
Kazmar Jr.	.977	63	79	175	6	38
Marte	.978	42	42	138	4	22
Smith	.983	31	44	73	2	20

Outfield	PCT	G	PO	A	E	DP
Acuna Jr.	.957	21	22	0	1	0
Adams	.982	25	54	1	1	0
Avery	.966	71	139	5	5	2
Bourjos	1.000	24	48	1	0	1
Carrera	1.000	25	45	0	0	0
Decker	1.000	10	20	1	0	0
Gosselin	.875	4	7	0	1	0
Peterson	.989	98	176	4	2	1
Reed	.976	43	79	4	2	1
Ruiz	.979	31	46	1	1	0
Santana	.992	62	123	7	1	0
Shumpert	1.000	2	8	0	0	0
Tucker	1.000	14	26	0	0	0

MISSISSIPPI BRAVES

DOUBLE-A

SOUTHERN LEAGUE

Batting	B-T	HT	WT	DOB	AVG	vLH	vRH	G	AB	R	H	2B	3B	HR	RBI	BB	HBP	SH	SF	SO	SB	CS	SLG	OBP
Cumberland, Brett	B-R	5-11	205	6-25-95	.111	.000	.118	5	18	1	2	0	0	0	0	1	1	0	0	5	0	0	.111	.200
Demeritte, Travis	R-R	6-0	180	9-30-94	.222	.208	.226	128	428	69	95	22	5	17	63	57	4	1	4	140	6	2	.416	.316
Didder, Ray-Patrick	R-R	6-0	170	10-1-94	.275	.306	.263	46	131	17	36	6	2	1	17	16	5	1	1	37	9	2	.374	.373
Downes, Brandon	R-R	6-3	195	9-29-92	.205	.180	.216	37	127	16	26	1	2	3	14	11	1	1	0	49	2	0	.315	.273
Flowers, Tyler	R-R	6-4	260	1-24-86	.250	.000	.333	1	4	1	1	0	0	0	0	0	0	0	0	1	0	0	.250	.250
Giardina, Sal	B-R	6-4	215	4-30-92	.150	.083	.167	25	60	2	9	0	0	0	4	5	5	2	0	22	1	0	.150	.271
Jackson, Alex	R-R	6-2	215	12-25-95	.200	.220	.196	64	225	27	45	12	1	5	24	20	6	0	1	78	0	0	.329	.282

ATLANTA BRAVES

	B-T	HT	WT	DOB	AVG	vLH	vRH	G	AB	R	H	2B	3B	HR	RBI	BB	HBP	SH	SF	SO	SB	CS	SLG	OBP
Lago, Alay	R-R	6-0	200	7-21-91	.248	.230	.253	80	295	32	73	13	2	2	25	9	1	0	2	34	5	2	.325	.270
Lien, Connor	R-R	6-3	225	3-15-94	.198	.253	.175	99	268	29	53	16	1	7	29	26	9	1	1	113	8	5	.343	.290
Lockhart, Daniel	L-R	5-11	175	11-4-92	.230	.186	.241	119	356	53	82	15	4	6	31	45	1	3	3	100	9	1	.346	.316
Marlette, Tyler	R-R	5-11	195	1-23-93	.244	.300	.226	126	423	58	103	18	1	12	52	49	2	0	0	105	5	2	.376	.325
Marte, Luis	R-R	6-1	188	12-15-93	.313	.321	.311	40	131	14	41	5	1	2	16	7	1	1	0	24	4	0	.412	.353
Martinez, Carlos	R-R	5-11	204	5-2-95	.248	.233	.252	45	137	15	34	7	0	1	19	10	2	0	1	16	0	0	.321	.307
Morales, Jonathan	R-R	5-11	180	1-29-95	.268	.161	.297	46	142	12	38	7	1	1	21	9	4	2	2	21	0	2	.352	.325
Murphy, Taylor	L-R	6-2	200	11-3-92	.107	.333	.046	11	28	1	3	0	0	0	1	3	0	0	0	16	0	0	.107	.194
Neslony, Tyler	L-R	6-1	190	2-13-94	.244	.217	.250	125	451	49	110	24	2	4	48	35	1	0	4	108	5	3	.333	.297
Pache, Cristian	R-R	6-2	185	11-19-98	.260	.407	.208	29	104	10	27	3	1	1	7	5	0	0	0	28	0	2	.337	.294
Reed, Michael	R-R	6-0	215	11-18-92	.314	.400	.296	44	140	33	44	13	0	4	14	30	4	0	1	43	6	3	.493	.446
Riley, Austin	R-R	6-3	220	4-2-97	.333	.188	.361	27	99	17	33	10	3	6	20	8	2	0	0	28	0	0	.677	.395
Rondon, Cleuluis	R-R	6-0	155	4-13-94	.120	.000	.148	29	75	4	9	2	1	0	5	8	0	1	0	24	0	1	.173	.205
Salazar, Alejandro	R-R	6-0	170	10-5-96	.301	.362	.281	54	186	26	56	8	1	0	18	9	0	8	2	33	4	3	.355	.330
Snyder, Michael	R-R	6-4	240	6-17-90	.160	.500	.095	7	25	3	4	0	1	0	1	3	0	0	1	0	0	0	.240	.250
Valenzuela, Luis	L-R	5-10	179	8-25-93	.282	.282	.282	114	369	42	104	22	2	2	42	13	1	1	2	66	5	1	.369	.307

Pitching	B-T	HT	WT	DOB	W	L	ERA	G	GS	CG	SV	IP	H	R	ER	HR	BB	SO	AVG	vLH	vRH	K/9	BB/9
Anderson, Ian	R-R	6-3	170	5-2-98	2	1	2.33	4	4	0	0	19	14	5	5	0	9	24	.203	.207	.200	11.17	4.19
Brothers, Rex	L-L	6-3	215	12-18-87	3	1	4.05	11	0	0	0	13	7	7	6	1	11	19	.149	.188	.129	12.83	7.43
Burrows, Thomas	L-L	6-1	205	9-14-94	0	0	1.42	15	0	0	6	19	10	3	3	0	6	27	.154	.278	.106	12.79	2.84
Clouse, Corbin	B-L	6-0	230	6-26-95	5	2	1.84	38	0	0	4	49	38	11	10	0	21	65	.216	.271	.188	11.94	3.86
Franco, Enderson	R-R	6-2	180	12-29-92	6	9	3.95	28	20	2	1	128	125	65	56	14	42	130	.253	.239	.264	9.16	2.96
Fried, Max	L-L	6-4	190	1-18-94	1	0	0.00	2	2	0	0	11	4	0	0	0	4	16	.108	.000	.138	12.71	3.18
Gohara, Luiz	L-L	6-3	265	7-31-96	0	1	2.70	1	1	0	0	3	5	5	1	0	3	4	.357	.000	.500	10.80	8.10
Graham, Josh	R-R	6-1	215	10-14-93	5	3	6.81	32	0	0	2	40	42	34	30	4	31	41	.276	.328	.239	9.30	7.03
Hursh, Jason	R-R	6-2	210	10-2-91	0	1	2.81	14	0	0	7	16	17	7	5	0	7	13	.270	.273	.268	7.31	3.94
Johnstone, Connor	R-R	6-1	195	10-4-94	0	0	3.12	7	2	0	0	17	18	7	6	0	8	12	.273	.364	.182	6.23	4.15
Kelly, Justin	L-L	6-1	175	4-22-93	1	0	5.06	7	0	0	0	11	10	6	6	0	7	14	.244	.444	.188	11.81	5.91
Leyva, Elian	R-R	6-2	210	3-17-89	3	2	2.69	22	4	0	0	60	61	22	18	2	17	59	.253	.253	.253	8.80	2.54
Lietz, Dan	L-L	6-2	200	6-1-94	0	0	4.60	9	1	0	0	16	16	8	8	1	10	14	.267	.188	.296	8.04	5.74
Mader, Michael	L-L	6-2	205	2-18-94	6	3	3.70	23	12	0	2	75	75	33	31	3	41	63	.263	.271	.260	7.53	4.90
McCreery, Adam	L-L	6-9	225	12-31-92	2	5	3.83	34	0	0	2	47	48	30	20	1	33	61	.258	.222	.276	11.68	6.32
McLaughlin, Sean	L-R	5-11	195	5-16-94	0	2	7.50	11	0	0	0	18	27	16	15	3	5	9	.365	.360	.367	4.50	2.50
Muller, Kyle	R-L	6-6	225	10-7-97	4	1	3.10	5	5	1	0	29	22	10	10	3	6	27	.206	.179	.215	8.38	1.86
Parsons, Wes	R-R	6-5	204	9-6-92	1	2	1.23	8	7	0	0	29	24	11	4	1	10	28	.216	.233	.196	8.59	3.07
Pfeifer, Philip	L-L	6-0	200	7-15-92	0	0	2.51	10	0	0	0	14	9	7	4	1	11	15	.173	.211	.152	9.42	6.91
Pike, Tyler	L-L	6-0	180	1-26-94	0	4	5.87	20	1	0	0	31	21	23	20	1	40	34	.198	.180	.209	9.98	11.74
Sanchez, Ricardo	L-L	5-11	205	4-11-97	2	5	4.06	13	13	1	0	58	65	32	26	3	24	44	.286	.356	.262	6.87	3.75
Santiago, Andres	R-R	6-1	220	10-26-89	4	2	3.55	9	8	1	0	51	54	21	20	6	6	40	.277	.345	.225	7.11	1.07
Sobotka, Chad	R-R	6-7	225	7-10-93	2	3	1.93	22	0	0	0	28	16	9	6	1	13	37	.170	.216	.140	11.89	4.18
Toussaint, Touki	R-R	6-3	185	6-20-96	4	6	2.93	16	16	0	0	86	66	36	28	7	36	107	.208	.205	.210	11.20	3.77
Vasquez, Kelvin	R-R	6-4	195	4-6-93	3	2	5.59	29	1	0	0	48	44	38	30	4	31	40	.240	.284	.206	7.45	5.77
Watts, Devan	R-R	6-0	205	4-21-95	1	0	3.29	10	0	0	0	14	13	5	5	1	5	7	.255	.231	.280	4.61	3.29
Webb, Jacob	R-R	6-1	200	8-15-93	1	2	3.18	21	0	0	7	23	16	12	8	4	12	35	.195	.270	.133	13.90	4.76
Wilson, Bryse	R-R	6-1	225	12-20-97	3	5	3.97	15	15	0	0	77	77	40	34	3	26	89	.258	.237	.275	10.40	3.04
Wright, Kyle	R-R	6-4	200	10-2-95	6	8	3.70	20	20	0	0	109	103	51	45	6	43	105	.249	.237	.259	8.64	3.54
Zimmermann, Bruce	L-L	6-2	215	2-9-95	2	1	3.14	6	6	0	0	29	25	11	10	3	19	26	.243	.147	.290	8.16	5.97

Fielding

Catcher	PCT	G	PO	A	E	DP	PB
Cumberland	.923	3	23	1	2	0	0
Flowers	1.000	1	9	3	0	0	0
Giardina	1.000	8	58	3	0	0	1
Jackson	.990	61	527	56	6	7	8
Marlette	1.000	5	42	4	0	0	1
Martinez	.988	37	303	31	4	1	1
Morales	.992	27	216	24	2	3	3

First Base	PCT	G	PO	A	E	DP
Giardina	1.000	11	66	4	0	4
Lockhart	1.000	8	52	2	0	2
Marlette	.990	106	738	52	8	60
Martinez	1.000	2	7	4	0	1
Morales	1.000	12	82	10	0	9
Snyder	.955	7	42	0	2	7
Valenzuela	1.000	1	1	0	0	0

Second Base	PCT	G	PO	A	E	DP
Lago	.967	68	89	148	8	29
Lockhart	1.000	4	7	5	0	3
Morales	1.000	1	1	0	0	0
Salazar	.979	45	77	113	4	17
Valenzuela	.942	31	49	65	7	12

Third Base	PCT	G	PO	A	E	DP
Demeritte	1.000	1	0	1	0	0
Lockhart	.938	91	67	130	13	12
Morales	1.000	2	2	0	0	0
Riley	.960	27	20	52	3	9
Salazar	1.000	7	2	9	0	0
Valenzuela	.911	26	16	25	4	1

Shortstop	PCT	G	PO	A	E	DP
Didder	.930	46	66	80	11	10
Marte	.981	39	56	98	3	19
Rondon	.910	26	27	64	9	14
Salazar	1.000	1	0	0	0	0
Valenzuela	.962	37	42	85	5	12

Outfield	PCT	G	PO	A	E	DP
Demeritte	.985	120	191	4	3	0
Downes	.984	33	59	3	1	0
Lien	.994	80	164	5	1	1
Lockhart	1.000	3	1	1	0	0
Marlette	1.000	2	3	0	0	0
Murphy	1.000	9	15	2	0	1
Neslony	.990	118	194	7	2	0
Pache	1.000	28	72	2	0	0
Reed	1.000	42	63	1	0	0

FLORIDA FIRE FROGS
FLORIDA STATE LEAGUE

HIGH CLASS A

Batting	B-T	HT	WT	DOB	AVG	vLH	vRH	G	AB	R	H	2B	3B	HR	RBI	BB	HBP	SH	SF	SO	SB	CS	SLG	OBP
Alexander, CJ	L-R	6-5	215	7-17-96	.325	.286	.339	21	80	5	26	5	1	1	7	8	0	0	0	17	3	1	.450	.386
Bautista, Jose	R-R	6-0	205	10-19-80	.286	.500	.200	2	7	1	2	1	0	0	2	0	0	0	0	0	0	0	.429	.444
Camargo, Johan	B-R	6-0	195	12-13-93	.125	.000	.250	2	8	0	1	0	0	0	0	1	0	0	0	3	0	0	.125	.222

	B-T	HT	WT	DOB	AVG	vLH	vRH	G	AB	R	H	2B	3B	HR	RBI	BB	HBP	SH	SF	SO	SB	CS	SLG	OBP
Contreras, William	R-R	6-0	180	12-24-97	.253	.280	.241	23	83	3	21	7	0	0	10	6	0	0	1	16	0	0	.337	.300
Crowley, Alan	R-R	6-2	210	3-4-96	.077	.200	.000	4	13	1	1	0	0	0	1	0	0	0	0	7	1	0	.077	.077
Cumberland, Brett	B-R	5-11	205	6-25-95	.236	.190	.254	82	280	40	66	15	0	11	39	52	7	0	2	85	0	1	.407	.367
Davidson, Braxton	L-L	6-2	230	6-18-96	.171	.167	.172	121	416	49	71	19	1	20	64	58	6	0	1	213	2	2	.365	.281
Delgado, Riley	R-R	5-10	175	2-22-95	.288	.255	.302	44	177	15	51	5	0	0	11	12	2	1	0	18	0	0	.316	.340
Didder, Ray-Patrick	R-R	6-0	170	10-1-94	.209	.203	.212	76	244	37	51	3	5	3	22	28	8	3	2	77	18	3	.299	.309
Ellison, Justin	L-L	6-2	175	2-6-95	.188	.083	.222	15	48	3	9	1	2	1	3	3	0	0	0	14	1	0	.354	.235
Herbert, Lucas	R-R	6-0	200	11-28-96	.202	.206	.200	67	228	20	46	10	0	5	25	16	1	1	2	72	0	1	.311	.255
Hoekstra, Kurt	L-R	6-2	190	6-27-93	.232	.306	.200	67	237	22	55	6	1	2	17	22	0	1	2	66	7	1	.291	.295
James, Jared	L-R	6-1	185	2-22-94	.258	.281	.246	78	279	39	72	15	4	5	30	24	5	0	2	56	6	2	.394	.326
Jenista, Greyson	L-R	6-4	210	12-7-96	.152	.167	.146	19	66	3	10	3	1	0	4	7	0	0	1	15	0	0	.227	.230
Josephina, Kevin	B-R	6-0	170	10-2-96	.227	.207	.232	36	128	11	29	3	0	0	17	8	1	0	3	33	4	3	.250	.271
Michel, Shean	R-R	5-11	170	9-26-97	.232	.294	.200	28	99	10	23	3	0	1	11	6	0	3	0	26	2	2	.293	.276
Mooney, Marcus	R-R	5-7	160	1-20-94	.214	.264	.189	72	215	29	46	6	0	0	13	17	10	7	0	25	1	3	.242	.302
Murphy, Taylor	L-R	6-2	200	11-3-92	.273	.222	.286	14	44	7	12	3	1	1	5	10	0	0	0	15	0	1	.455	.407
Obregon, Omar	R-R	5-10	150	4-18-94	.281	.167	.350	10	32	3	9	1	0	1	5	0	1	0	0	4	0	0	.406	.303
Pache, Cristian	R-R	6-2	185	11-19-98	.285	.330	.265	93	369	46	105	20	5	8	40	15	0	0	2	69	7	6	.431	.311
Rodgers, Jordan	R-R	6-1	185	5-9-95	.219	.209	.225	84	292	27	64	15	4	3	22	10	10	1	1	66	5	0	.329	.268
Salazar, Alejandro	R-R	6-0	170	10-5-96	.271	.307	.257	57	210	12	57	5	1	1	17	10	0	3	1	48	2	4	.319	.303
Schwartz, Garrison	L-L	6-1	205	1-22-96	.237	.217	.246	97	329	28	78	19	2	4	31	36	6	0	3	90	7	4	.384	.321
Seymour, Anfernee	B-R	5-11	165	6-24-95	.195	.214	.186	24	87	7	17	6	1	0	6	6	0	1	2	28	4	2	.287	.242
2-team total (51 Jupiter)					.257	.260	.255	75	288	34	74	17	6	3	30	19	1	4	4	76	20	7	.389	.301
Waters, Drew	B-R	6-2	183	12-30-98	.268	.207	.287	30	123	14	33	7	3	0	3	8	1	0	1	33	3	0	.374	.316
Wilson, Izzy	L-R	6-3	185	3-6-98	.215	.191	.226	40	135	16	29	5	1	2	10	14	0	1	1	43	5	1	.311	.287

Pitching	B-T	HT	WT	DOB	W	L	ERA	G	GS	CG	SV	IP	H	R	ER	HR	BB	SO	AVG	vLH	vRH	K/9	BB/9
Allison, Tanner	L-L	6-1	200	5-23-95	0	1	6.00	1	1	0	0	3	2	3	2	1	4	4	.250	.000	.400	12.00	12.00
Anderson, Ian	R-R	6-3	170	5-2-98	2	6	2.52	20	20	0	0	100	73	31	28	2	40	118	.198	.184	.216	10.62	3.60
Bacon, Troy	R-R	6-0	165	9-26-96	2	1	2.68	20	0	0	1	37	32	12	11	3	15	36	.227	.333	.155	8.76	3.65
Borkovich, Walter	L-R	6-5	217	7-3-95	1	0	0.00	3	3	0	0	17	12	0	0	0	0	12	.203	.179	.226	6.35	0.00
Burrows, Thomas	L-L	6-1	205	9-14-94	6	2	3.28	29	0	0	4	47	38	22	17	0	30	55	.225	.246	.214	10.61	5.79
Cabrera, Mauricio	R-R	6-3	225	9-22-93	0	3	11.03	31	0	0	1	31	43	43	38	4	41	27	.328	.391	.269	7.84	11.90
Camacho, Alex	R-R	6-7	245	7-29-96	0	0	0.00	3	0	0	0	5	1	0	0	0	2	4	.063	.000	.143	7.20	3.60
Cavalieri, Victor	L-L	6-1	180	8-26-95	0	0	16.71	6	0	0	0	7	10	13	13	0	10	5	.370	.357	.385	6.43	12.86
Davidson, Tucker	L-L	6-2	215	3-25-96	7	10	4.18	24	24	1	0	118	120	61	55	5	58	99	.270	.253	.279	7.53	4.41
Graham, Josh	R-R	6-1	215	10-14-93	1	5	3.86	15	0	0	1	23	19	15	10	2	10	33	.216	.237	.200	12.73	3.86
Harrington, Drew	R-L	6-2	225	3-30-95	0	0	10.80	1	0	0	0	2	5	3	2	0	1	0	.500	.250	.667	0.00	5.40
Jerez, Miguel	L-L	5-11	180	10-13-97	0	1	15.00	1	1	0	0	3	6	5	5	0	2	2	.400	.556	.167	6.00	6.00
Johnson-Mullins, Chase	L-L	6-8	270	7-19-94	1	0	3.20	17	0	0	0	20	23	10	7	0	13	19	.299	.368	.231	8.69	5.95
Johnstone, Connor	R-R	6-1	195	10-4-94	1	3	2.81	18	6	0	2	48	38	15	15	2	11	44	.214	.216	.211	8.25	2.06
Kelly, Justin	L-L	6-1	175	4-22-93	3	2	3.05	29	0	0	3	44	31	19	15	1	30	51	.201	.233	.181	10.35	6.09
Kennedy, Jon	L-L	6-5	215	9-20-94	5	5	2.43	25	2	0	1	56	51	18	15	0	13	54	.251	.188	.293	8.73	2.10
Lietz, Dan	L-L	6-2	200	6-1-94	1	2	5.96	12	0	0	2	23	28	16	15	4	11	11	.304	.333	.283	4.37	4.37
Matos, Bladimir	R-R	6-2	190	1-20-94	1	0	5.68	8	0	0	0	13	12	9	8	2	11	11	.261	.313	.233	7.82	7.82
McLaughlin, Sean	L-R	5-11	195	5-16-94	1	5	5.53	29	0	0	2	41	50	32	25	1	17	22	.305	.313	.299	4.87	3.76
Mejia, Dilmer	L-L	5-11	160	7-9-97	0	2	7.82	3	3	0	0	13	20	11	11	2	6	8	.385	.435	.345	5.68	4.26
Muller, Kyle	R-L	6-6	225	10-7-97	4	2	3.24	14	14	0	0	81	80	30	29	2	32	79	.269	.288	.257	8.81	3.57
Rice, Zach	L-L	6-2	205	10-15-95	0	0	8.31	3	0	0	0	4	4	5	4	1	5	6	.222	.333	.200	12.46	10.38
Sanchez, Filyer	L-L	6-1	175	2-8-97	0	1	4.34	4	3	0	0	19	20	9	9	1	6	10	.270	.233	.296	4.82	2.89
Simmons, Connor	L-L	6-2	160	11-7-95	0	0	9.00	1	0	0	0	2	4	2	2	0	0	1	.400	.200	.600	4.50	0.00
Sobotka, Chad	R-R	6-7	225	7-10-93	2	0	2.21	13	1	0	2	20	9	5	5	0	7	28	.132	.120	.140	12.39	3.10
Vasquez, Kelvin	R-R	6-4	195	4-6-93	0	0	0.00	1	0	0	0	3	0	0	0	0	0	0	.000	.000	.000	0.00	0.00
Volquez, Albinson	R-R	6-3	185	8-16-97	0	1	1.50	1	1	0	0	6	3	1	1	0	5	3	.167	.375	.000	4.50	7.50
Walker, Jeremy	R-R	6-5	205	5-14-95	5	11	4.07	25	25	1	0	135	148	71	61	10	46	95	.282	.283	.281	6.33	3.07
Watson, Tyler	L-L	5-11	200	6-9-93	0	2	3.38	5	0	0	0	13	15	6	5	2	0	11	.273	.250	.290	7.43	0.00
Watts, Devan	R-R	6-0	195	4-21-95	0	2	9.49	10	0	0	4	12	17	13	13	3	6	11	.333	.364	.310	8.03	4.38
Wentz, Joey	L-L	6-5	210	10-6-97	3	4	2.28	16	16	0	0	67	49	17	17	3	24	53	.206	.231	.194	7.12	3.22
White, Brandon S.	R-R	6-2	215	12-21-94	1	3	7.77	16	0	0	2	22	30	24	19	3	15	14	.333	.400	.250	5.73	6.14
Whitley, Chase	R-R	6-4	220	6-14-89	0	0	6.75	2	0	0	0	4	4	3	3	0	0	3	.250	.286	.222	6.75	0.00
Wilson, Bryse	R-R	6-1	225	12-20-97	2	0	0.34	5	5	0	0	27	16	4	1	0	7	26	.167	.185	.159	8.78	2.36
Ynoa, Huascar	R-R	6-3	175	5-28-98	1	4	8.03	6	6	0	0	25	33	23	22	1	12	31	.317	.291	.347	11.31	4.38

Fielding

Catcher	PCT	G	PO	A	E	DP	PB
Contreras	.955	20	139	10	7	2	4
Crowley	1.000	4	39	3	0	0	0
Cumberland	.998	57	442	30	1	3	11
Herbert	.984	54	381	54	7	7	8

First Base	PCT	G	PO	A	E	DP
Davidson	.985	94	684	50	11	75
Hoekstra	.992	33	240	15	2	22
Salazar	1.000	9	64	4	0	3
Schwartz	.000	1	0	0	0	0

Second Base	PCT	G	PO	A	E	DP
Josephina	.957	28	44	66	5	11
Mooney	.996	64	121	148	1	32
Obregon	1.000	3	2	4	0	1
Rodgers	.968	16	26	35	2	3
Salazar	.974	25	48	64	3	18

Third Base	PCT	G	PO	A	E	DP
Alexander	.951	17	11	28	2	3
Bautista	1.000	2	0	5	0	1
Camargo	1.000	1	0	2	0	0
Hoekstra	.984	27	14	47	1	5

Josephina	1.000	1	0	1	0	0
Mooney	1.000	1	0	1	0	0
Obregon	1.000	1	0	1	0	0
Rodgers	.927	60	41	111	12	12
Salazar	.941	27	17	47	4	4

Shortstop	PCT	G	PO	A	E	DP
Camargo	1.000	1	3	1	0	0
Delgado	.973	44	68	115	5	24
Didder	.949	76	104	212	17	46
Mooney	.950	7	8	11	1	2
Obregon	.929	4	2	11	1	1

	PCT	G	PO	A	E	DP
Rodgers	.500	1	0	1	1	0
Salazar	1.000	1	0	6	0	1
Outfield						
Ellison	.900	13	16	2	2	1

	PCT	G	PO	A	E	DP
Hoekstra	1.000	1	1	0	0	0
James	.986	51	68	2	1	0
Jenista	1.000	15	33	0	0	0
Michel	1.000	28	56	6	0	0
Murphy	1.000	14	30	0	0	0

	PCT	G	PO	A	E	DP
Pache	.977	93	210	5	5	1
Schwartz	.990	97	198	6	2	2
Seymour	.978	24	43	2	1	1
Waters	1.000	30	68	1	0	0
Wilson	1.000	39	58	3	0	0

ROME BRAVES — LOW CLASS A
SOUTH ATLANTIC LEAGUE

Batting	B-T	HT	WT	DOB	AVG	vLH	vRH	G	AB	R	H	2B	3B	HR	RBI	BB	HBP	SH	SF	SO	SB	CS	SLG	OBP
Almonte, Marcos	R-R	5-10	163	3-28-96	.197	.238	.175	39	122	11	24	5	0	1	14	6	0	1	1	22	2	0	.262	.233
Benson, Griffin	B-R	6-5	210	9-28-97	.200	.250	.177	8	25	3	5	2	0	0	1	3	1	0	0	11	1	0	.280	.310
Bermudez, Jose	B-R	6-2	160	7-9-97	.154	.000	.235	8	26	2	4	0	0	0	3	1	1	1	0	11	2	1	.154	.214
Bush, Austin	L-R	6-6	220	12-27-95	.237	.225	.241	42	152	17	36	8	0	5	19	5	5	0	2	50	0	0	.388	.281
Contreras, William	R-R	6-0	180	12-24-97	.293	.292	.294	82	307	54	90	7	1	11	39	29	4	0	2	73	1	1	.463	.360
Crowley, Alan	R-R	6-2	210	3-4-96	.179	.177	.180	18	56	6	10	4	0	1	3	5	2	0	1	32	0	0	.304	.266
Cruz, Derian	B-R	6-1	180	10-3-98	.222	.246	.211	112	406	41	90	15	4	4	31	12	6	7	1	114	4	9	.308	.254
Dean, Justin	R-R	5-8	180	12-6-96	.257	.225	.274	28	113	20	29	2	5	0	8	11	2	0	0	27	9	3	.363	.333
Delgado, Riley	R-R	5-10	175	2-22-95	.330	.348	.323	78	309	35	102	19	0	2	45	17	11	0	3	30	1	0	.411	.382
Encarnacion, Jean Carlos	R-R	6-3	195	1-17-98	.288	.283	.290	97	361	45	104	23	5	10	57	13	2	0	3	100	5	5	.463	.314
2-team total (26 Delmarva)					.273	.278	.271	123	462	55	126	27	7	12	64	16	2	0	3	134	5	5	.439	.298
Graffanino, AJ	L-R	6-2	170	7-16-97	.301	.235	.337	37	143	19	43	8	0	1	11	8	0	0	2	24	4	3	.378	.333
Harris, Trey	R-R	5-10	219	1-15-96	.286	.231	.310	22	84	10	24	9	0	0	11	7	2	0	1	13	3	0	.393	.351
Hoekstra, Kurt	L-R	6-2	190	6-27-93	.255	.222	.261	32	106	18	27	8	1	2	15	15	0	0	3	21	2	0	.406	.339
Jenista, Greyson	L-R	6-4	210	12-7-96	.333	.263	.367	32	117	20	39	5	3	1	23	10	0	0	3	17	4	1	.453	.377
Josephina, Kevin	B-R	6-0	170	10-2-96	.172	.000	.238	9	29	2	5	2	0	0	1	5	1	1	0	10	0	0	.241	.314
Lugbauer, Drew	L-R	6-3	220	8-23-96	.232	.162	.260	114	409	48	95	22	0	12	46	43	8	0	1	153	3	1	.374	.317
Martinez, Carlos	R-R	5-11	204	5-2-95	.270	.333	.240	21	74	7	20	4	0	0	6	5	0	0	0	5	1	0	.324	.317
Mateja, Michael	R-R	5-11	190	1-25-97	.333	—	.333	1	3	0	1	0	0	0	0	0	0	0	0	0	0	0	.333	.333
Mejia, Luis	B-R	5-10	160	3-8-97	.278	.261	.284	28	97	13	27	5	1	0	6	3	0	2	0	29	1	2	.351	.300
Michel, Shean	R-R	5-11	170	9-26-97	.267	.211	.302	32	101	10	27	6	0	0	5	12	0	1	2	32	1	4	.327	.339
Owenby, Hagen	R-R	6-1	211	7-21-95	.279	.258	.292	45	158	10	44	6	0	1	12	7	2	0	2	24	0	0	.335	.314
Ramos, Jefrey	R-R	6-1	185	2-10-99	.245	.267	.235	122	469	57	115	24	6	16	69	27	4	0	3	89	2	0	.424	.290
Schwartz, Garrison	L-L	6-1	205	1-22-96	.203	.067	.245	20	64	8	13	3	0	0	4	9	2	0	0	22	1	1	.250	.320
Smith, Justin	R-R	6-2	205	2-29-96	.180	.182	.179	33	117	9	21	6	0	3	13	5	4	0	2	42	0	0	.308	.238
Swanson, Dansby	R-R	6-1	190	2-11-94	.500	—	.500	1	2	0	1	0	0	0	0	0	0	0	0	0	0	0	.500	.500
Venter, Brendan	R-R	6-2	205	9-26-96	.175	.163	.180	43	149	17	26	6	0	4	22	10	2	0	6	37	0	0	.295	.228
Waters, Drew	B-R	6-2	183	12-30-98	.303	.250	.325	84	337	58	102	32	6	9	36	21	6	0	1	72	20	5	.513	.353
Wilson, Izzy	L-R	6-3	185	3-6-98	.229	.185	.243	68	223	38	51	10	2	6	25	28	1	4	1	77	11	4	.372	.316

Pitching	B-T	HT	WT	DOB	W	L	ERA	G	GS	CG	SV	IP	H	R	ER	HR	BB	SO	AVG	vLH	vRH	K/9	BB/9
Allison, Tanner	L-L	6-1	200	5-23-95	1	0	13.13	18	0	0	0	24	42	37	35	3	18	19	.400	.425	.385	7.13	6.75
Bacon, Troy	R-R	6-0	165	9-26-96	1	1	2.08	12	0	0	3	17	16	7	4	1	3	19	.232	.192	.256	9.87	1.56
Belinda, Jacob	R-R	6-1	190	9-24-94	2	1	3.48	19	0	0	1	31	29	16	12	4	16	27	.244	.148	.323	7.84	4.65
Borkovich, Walter	L-R	6-5	217	7-3-95	4	1	1.83	31	3	0	2	69	62	18	14	3	15	44	.240	.265	.219	5.77	1.97
Burrows, Thomas	L-L	6-1	205	9-14-94	0	0	0.00	1	0	0	1	2	0	0	0	0	0	4	.000	.000	.000	18.00	0.00
Camacho, Alex	R-R	6-7	245	7-29-96	1	0	9.00	1	0	0	0	2	3	2	2	1	1	1	.333	.250	.400	4.50	4.50
Curtis, John	L-L	6-2	180	10-15-95	1	2	4.06	11	3	0	0	38	38	21	17	2	4	33	.264	.286	.253	7.88	0.96
Daniels, Zach	L-R	5-11	160	4-21-97	1	1	1.08	6	0	0	1	8	5	6	1	1	5	5	.161	.167	.158	5.40	5.40
De La Cruz, Jasseel	R-R	6-1	175	6-26-97	3	4	4.83	15	13	0	0	69	65	40	37	6	34	65	.250	.215	.288	8.48	4.43
Deal, Hayden	L-L	6-4	210	11-4-94	9	1	2.17	27	5	1	2	79	62	23	19	3	17	82	.211	.232	.200	9.38	1.94
Dyals, Cutter	R-R	5-11	205	8-10-95	4	4	3.02	28	0	0	2	48	44	26	16	1	20	43	.242	.221	.260	8.12	3.78
Freeman, Sam	R-L	5-11	180	6-24-87	0	0	13.50	1	0	0	0	1	1	1	1	0	2	1	.333	.000	.500	13.50	27.00
Harrington, Drew	R-L	6-2	225	3-30-95	3	3	7.22	11	6	0	0	34	47	31	27	7	10	25	.343	.311	.359	6.68	2.67
2-team total (14 Kannapolis)					8	8	4.96	25	18	1	1	105	120	63	58	12	26	73	.297	.291	.299	6.24	2.22
Javier, Odalvi	R-R	6-0	180	9-4-96	3	10	4.14	26	25	0	0	126	120	75	58	14	58	133	.252	.218	.282	9.50	4.14
Mejia, Dilmer	L-L	5-11	160	7-9-97	0	1	7.27	3	1	0	1	9	13	8	7	1	3	10	.342	.267	.391	10.38	3.12
Muller, Kyle	R-L	6-6	225	10-7-97	3	0	2.40	6	4	0	0	30	24	10	8	3	8	23	.222	.262	.197	6.90	2.40
Rangel, Alan	R-R	6-2	170	8-21-97	5	7	4.09	25	22	0	0	125	121	62	57	12	31	105	.248	.209	.284	7.54	2.23
Rodriguez, Kelvin	L-L	6-5	195	12-31-93	5	2	2.73	38	0	0	13	59	53	28	18	2	27	66	.240	.218	.252	10.01	4.10
Soroka, Mike	R-R	6-5	225	8-4-97	0	0	0.00	1	1	0	0	4	0	0	0	0	0	3	.000	.000	.000	7.36	0.00
Tarnok, Freddy	R-R	6-3	185	11-24-98	5	5	3.96	27	11	0	0	77	70	56	34	5	41	83	.235	.214	.257	9.66	4.77
Watson, Tyler	L-L	5-11	200	6-9-93	4	4	4.09	13	0	0	0	22	26	11	10	1	2	26	.296	.333	.276	10.64	0.82
Weisenberg, Keith	R-R	6-5	195	12-6-95	2	4	4.91	9	9	0	0	48	50	28	26	3	18	48	.260	.279	.245	9.06	3.40
White, Brandon S.	R-R	6-2	215	12-21-94	2	3	1.23	25	0	0	9	37	22	12	5	0	9	40	.164	.150	.176	9.82	2.21
Wilson, Brooks	L-R	6-2	205	3-15-96	1	1	1.00	7	0	0	0	9	7	2	1	1	3	8	.226	.143	.294	8.00	3.00
Ynoa, Huascar	R-R	6-3	175	5-28-98	7	8	3.63	18	18	0	0	92	69	49	37	7	42	100	.205	.218	.193	9.82	4.12
Zimmermann, Bruce	L-L	6-2	215	2-9-95	7	3	2.76	14	14	0	0	85	74	31	26	5	18	99	.233	.200	.251	10.52	1.91

Fielding
C: Contreras 43, Crowley 15, Lugbauer 65, Martinez 11, Owenby 5. **1B:** Benson 8, Bush 41, Crowley 1, Hoekstra 28, Lugbauer 1, Martinez 7, Owenby 35, Venter 22. **2B:** Almonte 10, Cruz 111, Delgado 2, Josephina 8, Mateja 1, Mejia 8. **3B:** Almonte 17, Encarnacion 92, Hoekstra 2, Mejia 9, Venter 23. **SS:** Almonte 13, Delgado 76, Graffanino 37, Mejia 12, Swanson 1. **OF:** Bermudez 8, Dean 26, Harris 19, Jenista 30, Michel 32, Ramos 105, Schwartz 15, Smith 31, Waters 83, Wilson 67.

DANVILLE BRAVES
APPALACHIAN LEAGUE
ROOKIE

Batting	B-T	HT	WT	DOB	AVG	vLH	vRH	G	AB	R	H	2B	3B	HR	RBI	BB	HBP	SH	SF	SO	SB	CS	SLG	OBP
Alexander, CJ	L-R	6-5	215	7-17-96	.354	.444	.328	22	82	10	29	3	4	0	12	13	1	0	2	21	1	1	.488	.439
Almonte, Marcos	R-R	5-10	163	3-28-96	.500	—	.500	1	4	0	2	0	0	0	1	0	0	1	0	1	0	1	.500	.500
Baerga, Carlos	L-L	5-10	190	9-2-95	.235	.250	.233	45	149	23	35	8	0	1	13	19	0	0	2	27	2	0	.309	.318
Benson, Griffin	B-R	6-5	210	9-8-95	.269	.250	.274	27	104	16	28	6	1	3	15	10	2	0	0	34	1	1	.433	.345
Bermudez, Jose	B-R	6-2	160	7-9-97	.231	.250	.200	5	13	0	3	2	0	0	2	0	1	0	0	4	0	1	.385	.286
Cullen, Greg	L-R	5-10	190	11-13-96	.280	.185	.294	55	207	30	58	12	3	2	33	29	3	0	2	29	0	1	.396	.373
Dean, Justin	R-R	5-8	180	12-6-96	.308	.471	.283	32	130	28	40	8	4	1	15	22	3	0	0	32	7	6	.454	.419
Estrada, Rusber	R-R	6-0	215	6-5-95	.241	.200	.246	25	79	9	19	4	0	0	10	14	1	0	0	23	0	0	.291	.362
Graffanino, AJ	L-R	6-2	170	7-16-97	.407	.250	.435	6	27	2	11	0	0	0	6	1	0	1	2	3	1	0	.407	.400
Jenista, Greyson	R-L	6-4	210	12-7-96	.250	—	.250	10	40	10	10	1	0	3	7	6	0	1	0	9	0	1	.500	.348
Langhorne, Brett	L-R	6-3	210	6-14-96	.281	.276	.282	52	185	23	52	7	2	0	24	28	1	0	2	67	8	2	.341	.375
Mateja, Michael	R-R	5-11	190	1-25-97	.255	.250	.256	20	55	14	14	1	0	0	5	7	5	0	0	13	1	0	.273	.388
Mejia, Luis	B-R	5-10	160	3-8-97	.198	.184	.202	40	157	12	31	6	0	0	15	7	0	0	3	36	0	0	.236	.228
Moritz, Andrew	L-R	5-11	180	12-22-96	.280	.063	.312	31	125	23	35	7	1	1	16	14	1	2	2	24	4	0	.376	.352
Owenby, Hagen	R-R	6-1	211	7-21-95	.500	—	.500	1	2	1	1	0	0	0	0	2	0	0	0	0	0	0	.500	.750
Quintero, Henry	R-R	6-1	193	5-23-96	.262	.250	.265	44	168	14	44	8	3	1	19	3	2	0	1	39	1	1	.363	.282
Rodriguez, Ricardo	R-R	5-10	175	12-20-97	.228	.304	.212	36	136	20	31	6	1	2	16	10	7	0	3	25	0	1	.331	.308
Shumpert, Nicholas	R-R	5-11	180	11-11-96	.248	.200	.262	48	157	28	39	12	3	2	18	10	3	0	2	51	7	3	.401	.302
Smith, Justin	R-R	6-2	205	2-29-96	.246	.194	.264	35	118	16	29	4	1	7	14	14	3	0	0	44	5	0	.475	.341
Soderman, Ray	R-R	6-1	200	5-23-97	.183	.235	.169	26	82	11	15	1	0	0	3	7	5	0	0	31	1	0	.195	.287
Soria, Zack	R-R	5-10	192	10-29-93	.188	.118	.206	27	85	8	16	2	0	1	11	10	2	0	2	34	1	0	.247	.283
Venter, Brendan	R-R	6-2	205	9-26-96	.235	.250	.233	9	34	5	8	2	0	0	5	3	0	1	1	11	1	0	.382	.372
Vizcaino, Nicholas	R-R	6-0	200	3-19-97	.184	.273	.167	37	136	13	25	6	2	0	12	17	2	0	1	40	2	0	.272	.258

Pitching	B-T	HT	WT	DOB	W	L	ERA	G	GS	CG	SV	IP	H	R	ER	HR	BB	SO	AVG	vLH	vRH	K/9	BB/9
Allison, Tanner	L-L	6-1	200	5-23-95	2	0	2.62	13	0	0	1	34	24	10	10	2	12	35	.189	.265	.161	9.17	3.15
Belinda, Jacob	R-R	6-0	190	9-24-94	1	2	6.48	9	0	0	1	17	17	15	12	0	11	19	.250	.348	.200	10.26	5.94
Curtis, John	L-L	6-2	180	10-15-95	0	0	0.00	2	0	0	0	5	3	1	0	0	2	6	.150	.333	.118	10.13	3.38
Daniels, Zach	L-R	5-11	160	4-21-97	2	2	2.65	11	0	0	1	17	19	7	5	1	5	15	.284	.381	.239	7.94	2.65
Gamez, Luis	R-R	6-2	175	6-25-96	0	1	9.00	8	0	0	0	8	10	11	8	2	6	7	.294	.375	.269	7.88	6.75
Guth, Zach	L-L	6-4	210	4-4-97	3	3	4.84	15	0	0	1	22	16	15	12	0	24	27	.203	.263	.183	10.88	9.67
Hartman, Matt	R-R	6-3	220	2-28-96	0	1	2.87	5	5	0	0	16	12	7	5	2	10	8	.214	.227	.206	4.60	5.74
Higginbotham, Jake	L-L	5-10	170	1-11-96	2	1	2.65	13	0	0	1	34	27	12	10	4	12	36	.211	.136	.226	9.53	3.18
Kingham, Nolan	R-R	6-4	200	8-18-96	2	0	4.56	11	3	0	1	24	27	17	12	4	7	18	.297	.278	.309	6.85	2.66
Lawson, Tanner	L-L	6-1	186	10-25-96	0	2	3.68	13	11	0	0	29	28	14	12	1	5	31	.244	.261	.239	9.51	1.53
McReaken, Mason	R-R	6-0	180	2-11-96	0	1	1.50	7	0	0	1	12	5	5	2	0	8	15	.132	.154	.120	11.25	6.00
Mejia, Dilmer	L-L	5-11	160	7-9-97	5	4	2.87	13	13	0	0	69	65	29	22	4	24	53	.249	.229	.254	6.91	3.13
Montilla, Jose	R-R	6-1	170	6-4-94	1	4	4.37	13	13	1	0	70	83	35	34	4	19	53	.299	.339	.270	6.81	2.44
Mora, Luis	R-R	6-4	160	6-17-95	1	1	16.50	6	0	0	0	6	11	11	11	0	7	7	.379	.364	.389	10.50	10.50
Riley, Trey	R-R	6-2	200	4-21-98	0	0	8.00	6	2	0	0	9	10	8	8	1	10	13	.278	.071	.409	13.00	10.00
Rowland, Matt	R-R	6-2	175	2-7-98	1	4	3.83	13	13	0	0	54	47	30	23	5	26	41	.239	.197	.265	6.83	4.33
Sanchez, Ricardo	L-L	5-11	215	4-11-97	1	0	3.09	2	2	0	0	12	11	5	4	1	3	9	.239	.000	.297	6.94	2.31
Seipel, Zach	R-R	6-4	210	10-17-96	3	0	2.63	15	0	0	3	24	19	8	7	0	15	30	.211	.226	.203	11.25	5.63
Shetter, Ryan	R-R	6-3	205	3-5-97	2	3	3.90	11	3	0	0	28	33	19	12	4	3	21	.285	.310	.270	6.83	0.98
Simmons, Connor	L-L	6-2	160	11-7-95	2	2	4.08	17	1	0	2	29	25	14	13	2	14	36	.232	.423	.171	11.30	4.40
Stallings, Mitch	L-L	6-2	180	6-30-95	1	0	3.94	7	0	0	1	16	23	10	7	0	3	18	.333	.333	.333	10.13	1.69
Weisenberg, Keith	R-R	6-5	195	12-6-95	1	1	1.46	3	2	0	0	12	12	5	2	0	5	10	.231	.238	.226	7.30	3.65
Welsh, Bradey	R-R	6-1	190	3-6-97	2	4	4.71	12	0	0	0	21	23	14	11	1	12	16	.284	.192	.327	6.86	5.14
Wilson, Brooks	L-R	6-2	205	3-15-96	2	1	1.45	10	0	0	1	19	13	4	3	2	6	17	.200	.200	.200	8.20	2.89

Fielding

C: Estrada 13, Rodriguez 30, Soderman 16, Soria 13. 1B: Benson 23, Langhorne 13, Venter 1, Vizcaino 32. 2B: Almonte 1, Cullen 55, Mateja 1, Mejia 11, Shumpert 1. 3B: Alexander 20, Langhorne 33, Mateja 6, Mejia 3, Venter 7. SS: Graffanino 6, Langhorne 2, Mejia 27, Shumpert 36. OF: Baerga 43, Bermudez 5, Dean 32, Jenista 9, Mateja 10, Mejia 1, Moritz 31, Quintero 39, Shumpert 9, Smith 33.

GCL BRAVES
GULF COAST LEAGUE
ROOKIE

Batting	B-T	HT	WT	DOB	AVG	vLH	vRH	G	AB	R	H	2B	3B	HR	RBI	BB	HBP	SH	SF	SO	SB	CS	SLG	OBP
Alexander, CJ	L-R	6-5	215	7-17-96	.412	.500	.406	9	34	6	14	0	2	1	8	6	0	0	0	4	0	0	.618	.500
Berne, Mason	R-R	6-3	225	3-11-96	.160	.389	.110	33	100	4	16	7	0	0	7	13	0	0	1	26	1	1	.230	.254
Brown, Logan	L-R	6-1	190	9-14-96	.272	.346	.250	37	114	13	31	5	0	3	16	11	2	0	0	16	0	1	.395	.347
Cerrato, Wiston	B-R	5-10	170	4-9-99	.159	.286	.135	21	44	4	7	1	0	0	4	1	0	0	0	13	0	1	.182	.245
Chapman, Brandon	R-R	6-0	200	5-26-96	.250	.250	.250	19	36	5	9	1	0	0	9	1	0	0	1	9	0	0	.278	.413
De Hoyos, Victor	R-R	5-9	170	2-23-98	.294	.267	.299	29	92	13	27	3	0	4	15	4	5	0	1	22	3	0	.457	.353
Fernandez, Jeremy	R-R	6-1	185	7-11-97	.281	.192	.296	47	185	28	52	9	3	8	29	11	1	0	2	24	5	2	.492	.322
Florentino, Darling	R-R	6-1	190	5-25-01	.217	.292	.202	37	138	16	30	6	1	3	15	5	2	0	1	40	1	2	.341	.253
Harris, Trey	R-R	5-10	219	1-15-96	.314	.333	.310	31	105	24	33	9	2	1	18	21	5	1	0	13	4	3	.467	.450
Hernandez, Ray	R-R	6-3	220	8-19-96	.283	.300	.280	38	138	21	39	11	1	5	25	15	1	0	0	30	1	0	.486	.357
Mateja, Michael	R-R	5-11	190	1-25-97	.364	.385	.355	16	44	17	16	6	0	1	9	13	1	0	9	1	2		.568	.533
Morales, Jonathan	R-R	5-11	180	1-29-95	.259	.000	.318	8	27	1	7	1	0	1	3	2	2	0	0	2	0	0	.407	.355
Morales, Juan	R-R	6-2	165	11-17-98	.202	.167	.210	38	129	15	26	4	0	0	8	9	6	4	2	45	0	1	.233	.281

Batting	B-T	HT	WT	DOB	AVG	vLH	vRH	G	AB	R	H	2B	3B	HR	RBI	BB	HBP	SH	SF	SO	SB	CS	SLG	OBP
Ovando, Luis	R-R	6-1	160	10-29-98	.220	.308	.196	23	59	5	13	0	0	1	7	3	0	0	1	19	3	1	.271	.254
Reyes, Charles	R-R	6-1	165	9-9-99	.252	.208	.264	34	115	10	29	4	1	1	11	3	1	2	1	29	0	1	.330	.275
Reyes, Joel	R-R	6-0	200	10-3-99	.117	.111	.118	31	94	12	11	5	0	1	5	7	0	1	2	36	2	0	.202	.175
Riley, Austin	R-R	6-3	220	4-2-97	.278	.000	.313	6	18	3	5	3	0	1	3	3	1	0	0	6	0	0	.611	.409
Rojas, Luidemid	B-R	5-11	170	5-4-99	.216	.091	.238	25	74	12	16	1	0	0	4	9	0	1	0	27	1	1	.230	.301
Vasquez, Braulio	B-R	6-0	170	4-13-99	.270	.414	.239	45	167	31	45	7	2	4	20	12	1	0	3	40	5	6	.407	.317
Zamora, Christian	R-R	6-4	210	7-4-01	.139	.091	.151	30	108	10	15	3	0	2	8	14	1	0	0	40	0	2	.222	.244

Pitching	B-T	HT	WT	DOB	W	L	ERA	G	GS	CG	SV	IP	H	R	ER	HR	BB	SO	AVG	vLH	vRH	K/9	BB/9
Beck, Tristan	R-R	6-4	165	6-24-96	0	0	0.00	3	1	0	0	5	4	0	0	0	2	7	.235	.200	.250	13.50	3.86
Camacho, Alex	R-R	6-7	245	7-29-96	1	1	4.18	14	0	0	1	24	27	14	11	1	8	25	.287	.219	.323	9.51	3.04
Cavalieri, Victor	L-L	6-1	180	8-26-95	2	2	6.75	10	0	0	1	15	13	11	11	1	12	10	.241	.333	.222	6.14	7.36
Ciriaco, Javier	R-R	6-3	185	1-1-96	1	0	0.96	4	1	0	1	9	6	1	1	0	2	13	.177	.250	.154	12.54	1.93
De Jesus, Luis	R-R	5-11	170	10-8-98	2	2	4.67	11	8	0	0	44	42	27	23	5	25	35	.246	.283	.229	7.11	5.08
Jerez, Miguel	L-L	5-11	180	10-13-97	5	4	3.90	12	10	0	0	58	62	31	25	3	8	50	.266	.226	.278	7.80	1.25
Kurz, Cameron	R-R	6-0	200	5-10-96	1	0	0.00	3	0	0	0	4	2	0	0	0	1	7	.143	.000	.182	14.54	2.08
Lopez, Yoeli	R-R	5-10	167	7-31-97	0	1	8.79	14	0	0	0	14	16	22	14	2	18	18	.281	.250	.289	11.30	11.30
Lourie, Jackson	R-R	6-3	190	10-10-94	0	3	4.76	11	0	0	2	23	19	12	12	2	14	16	.238	.191	.254	6.35	5.56
Pena, Miguel	L-R	6-1	190	11-26-96	1	3	5.32	14	0	0	1	24	33	20	14	3	7	14	.324	.452	.268	5.32	2.66
Polanco, Walner	R-R	6-7	200	12-24-96	1	3	4.80	16	0	0	3	30	33	20	16	2	8	24	.268	.227	.291	7.20	2.40
Rodriguez, Gabriel	L-L	6-1	193	4-9-99	0	0	1.64	11	0	0	0	11	3	4	2	0	22	22	.083	.000	.097	18.00	18.00
Sanchez, Filyer	L-L	6-1	175	2-8-97	4	3	5.22	10	4	0	1	40	39	23	23	7	15	28	.258	.240	.262	6.35	3.40
Sanchez, Ricardo	L-L	5-11	215	4-11-97	0	0	2.08	1	1	0	0	4	3	1	1	0	1	4	.177	.000	.188	8.31	2.08
Santos, Lisandro	L-L	6-0	170	7-24-98	0	3	4.71	11	7	0	0	36	38	24	19	0	23	37	.266	.306	.252	9.17	5.70
Stallings, Mitch	L-L	6-2	180	6-30-95	0	0	4.50	5	2	0	1	12	10	7	6	0	2	15	.222	.167	.215	11.15	1.50
Vodnik, Victor	R-R	6-0	190	10-9-99	1	1	9.64	4	0	0	0	5	8	5	5	1	9	6	.364	.286	.400	17.36	1.93
Volquez, Albinson	R-R	6-3	185	8-16-97	2	3	5.06	12	11	0	0	53	60	33	30	3	21	47	.280	.246	.294	7.93	3.54
Weigel, Patrick	R-R	6-6	240	7-8-94	0	0	0.00	4	3	0	0	4	2	0	0	0	0	6	.167	.000	.200	13.50	0.00
Welsh, Bradey	R-R	6-1	190	3-6-97	1	0	1.93	4	0	0	0	5	6	1	1	0	1	4	.300	.333	.286	7.71	1.93
Whitley, Chase	R-R	6-4	220	6-14-89	0	0	0.00	2	1	0	0	2	1	0	0	0	0	4	.000	.000	.000	18.00	0.00
Woods, William	R-R	6-3	190	12-29-98	0	1	6.10	10	4	0	0	21	22	16	14	0	10	20	.262	.265	.260	8.71	4.35

Fielding

C: Brown 26, Cerrato 14, Chapman 16, De Hoyos 19, Morales 4. **1B:** Berne 27, Hernandez 31. **2B:** Mateja 3, Ovando 18, Rojas 7, Vasquez 31. **3B:** Alexander 5, Florentino 31, Mateja 4, Riley 5, Vasquez 16. **SS:** Morales 38, Rojas 18. **OF:** Fernandez 44, Harris 29, Mateja 5, Reyes 34, Reyes 31, Zamora 30.

DSL BRAVES   ROOKIE
DOMINICAN SUMMER LEAGUE

Batting	B-T	HT	WT	DOB	AVG	vLH	vRH	G	AB	R	H	2B	3B	HR	RBI	BB	HBP	SH	SF	SO	SB	CS	SLG	OBP
Bautista, Asmin	L-L	5-9	198	10-27-00	.165	.065	.186	54	176	16	29	5	1	4	21	28	4	0	3	45	2	1	.273	.289
De La Cruz, Randi	R-R	6-1	180	8-15-01	.178	.177	.179	35	101	7	18	4	0	0	9	11	7	0	0	26	0	2	.218	.303
Encarnacion, Kimberling	R-R	6-0	180	11-22-99	.250	.229	.257	59	196	20	49	11	0	0	19	12	6	0	1	37	0	1	.306	.312
Estrada, Deivi	R-R	5-10	155	1-17-01	.191	.033	.247	45	115	16	22	6	1	0	6	17	3	0	0	29	6	5	.261	.311
Ferreira, Emeli	R-R	6-1	170	4-1-01	.128	.120	.130	39	102	12	13	4	0	0	2	13	3	1	0	48	1	1	.167	.246
Guitian, Enmanuel	R-R	5-11	165	9-14-98	.205	.160	.216	44	127	18	26	2	0	1	5	29	2	0	0	42	2	1	.244	.361
Hernandez, Jose	L-R	6-0	170	10-13-99	.192	.000	.237	24	47	8	9	0	0	0	6	4	0	1	0	15	2	1	.192	.255
Izaguirre, Jonaiker	R-R	5-11	160	9-27-00	.123	.130	.118	26	57	6	7	1	0	0	4	7	3	0	0	24	0	1	.140	.254
Lara, Yandri	R-R	6-0	190	5-31-00	.154	.143	.158	36	104	7	16	4	0	1	8	9	5	0	1	41	1	1	.221	.252
Medina, Yerangel	R-R	6-4	205	3-15-00	.216	.200	.220	46	134	8	29	7	0	0	6	12	4	0	0	47	2	0	.269	.300
Mezquita, Brandol	R-R	6-0	170	7-14-01	.212	.250	.202	52	156	23	33	6	0	4	27	24	9	0	1	52	6	4	.327	.347
Ordonez, Sergio	R-R	6-0	175	4-21-99	.221	.000	.270	26	77	9	17	8	0	0	5	5	0	2	0	20	1	0	.325	.268
Palma, Jose	L-L	6-0	170	6-9-99	.213	.130	.231	46	127	16	27	1	1	0	10	30	1	1	1	24	15	9	.236	.365
Paraguate, Carlos	R-R	5-10	170	2-2-01	.226	.245	.220	62	208	27	47	7	2	0	25	30	6	0	2	56	20	10	.279	.337
Pena, Kelvin	R-R	5-11	210	7-4-00	.196	.154	.209	16	56	3	11	2	0	0	5	0	1	0	0	22	0	1	.232	.211
Quezada, Braian	R-R	6-2	190	9-14-00	.000	.000	.000	6	11	0	0	0	0	0	1	1	2	0	0	7	0	0	.000	.214
Quintero, Henry	R-R	6-1	193	5-23-94	.273	.500	.222	3	11	0	3	0	0	0	2	2	0	0	0	2	1	0	.273	.385
Rodriguez, Jorge	L-L	6-0	160	7-31-01	.125	.286	.080	29	64	10	8	0	0	0	4	16	1	0	0	17	1	2	.125	.309
Sierra, Hector	L-R	5-10	160	12-18-00	.167	.177	.164	32	72	9	12	1	0	0	6	12	1	0	0	21	4	3	.181	.294
Stevens, Eliezel	L-R	6-0	185	10-8-00	.214	.160	.223	52	173	27	37	11	2	2	20	34	3	0	5	65	11	5	.335	.347

Pitching	B-T	HT	WT	DOB	W	L	ERA	G	GS	CG	SV	IP	H	R	ER	HR	BB	SO	AVG	vLH	vRH	K/9	BB/9
Alesandro, Ronaldo	R-R	6-0	170	5-7-98	0	4	2.60	11	0	0	0	35	31	16	10	0	22	47	.244	.250	.242	12.20	5.71
Asencio, Eudi	R-R	6-0	170	2-28-99	5	5	2.63	14	14	0	0	62	44	27	18	1	21	52	.196	.191	.198	7.59	3.06
Bautista, Jorge	R-R	6-0	155	12-10-00	0	0	3.18	8	0	0	1	11	14	4	4	0	8	7	.311	.333	.306	5.56	6.35
Caminero, Carlos	L-L	6-4	185	9-17-97	1	2	1.87	17	0	0	5	34	25	7	7	0	20	40	.205	.095	.228	10.69	5.35
Celedonio, Raulin	R-L	6-6	220	2-8-00	1	1	12.15	18	0	0	0	27	33	45	36	2	40	38	.303	.211	.322	12.83	13.50
Ciriaco, Javier	R-R	6-3	185	1-1-96	3	2	1.76	12	0	0	0	31	18	8	6	0	18	30	.175	.214	.160	8.80	5.28
De La Cruz, Carlos	R-R	6-1	170	9-12-96	1	2	2.28	13	0	0	0	28	19	12	7	0	9	17	.198	.143	.213	5.53	2.93
Diaz, Luis	R-R	6-3	200	9-16-99	0	0	3.58	17	0	0	1	33	33	21	13	2	16	22	.264	.235	.275	6.06	4.41
Jimenez, Edwin	L-L	6-1	170	7-22-00	1	3	6.00	14	4	0	1	24	31	25	16	0	14	17	.304	.556	.250	6.38	5.25
Munoz, Roddery	R-R	6-3	190	4-14-00	1	3	6.88	10	0	0	1	25	28	19	19	1	19	21	.319	.200	.367	9.00	7.41
Nunez, Oscar	R-R	6-0	190	6-16-00	0	1	1.52	7	6	0	0	24	14	5	4	0	12	11	.182	.150	.193	4.18	4.56
Olague, Jose	R-R	6-0	207	12-13-98	3	4	2.43	14	14	0	0	67	75	30	18	1	11	57	.279	.286	.277	7.70	1.49
Rodriguez, Estarlin	R-R	6-0	180	10-24-99	2	6	3.60	13	11	0	0	45	60	28	18	1	30	23	.235	.273	.217	4.60	6.00
Rodriguez, Rainiery	B-R	6-2	200	8-28-00	1	4	3.53	11	7	0	0	36	35	16	14	0	9	22	.240	.290	.226	5.55	2.27

Name																							
Santos, Lisandro	L-L	6-1	170	7-24-98	1	1	2.77	4	1	0	0	13	9	7	4	0	9	12	.184	.000	.237	8.31	6.23
Sepulveda, Jhoniel	R-R	6-2	175	5-15-97	0	1	11.25	7	0	0	0	12	15	16	15	1	11	15	.294	.375	.257	11.25	8.25
Valdez, Nonato	R-R	6-4	210	3-8-97	0	2	10.88	17	0	0	0	22	22	27	27	1	32	21	.256	.375	.210	8.46	12.90
Vallejo, Joselin	R-R	6-2	175	6-5-00	0	0	2.00	6	0	0	0	9	8	4	2	0	7	6	.258	.286	.250	6.00	7.00
Vargas, Leonardo	R-R	6-0	170	1-2-01	1	2	1.50	5	2	0	0	12	10	7	2	0	7	12	.204	.429	.167	9.00	5.25
Vasquez, Willians	R-R	6-1	200	5-7-97	1	5	5.31	17	2	0	1	39	42	42	23	4	21	34	.258	.229	.266	7.85	4.85

Fielding

C: Encarnacion 4, Guitian 35, Ordonez 25, Pena 15. **1B:** Encarnacion 52, Ferreira 1, Guitian 7, Medina 19. **2B:** Estrada 1, Ferreira 19, Sierra 15, Stevens 47. **3B:** Ferreira 22, Lara 35, Medina 28, Sierra 3. **SS:** Ferreira 1, Paraguate 61, Sierra 15. **OF:** Bautista 29, De La Cruz 18, Estrada 40, Hernandez 14, Izaguirre 18, Mezquita 48, Palma 46, Quezada 2, Quintero 2, Rodriguez 25.

Baltimore Orioles

SEASON IN A SENTENCE: In a 115-loss season that was putrid from start to finish, the Orioles traded three of their top four players at midseason, finished with franchise's fewest wins since 1939 and its fewest since moving to Baltimore, then fired manager Buck Showalter and general manager Dan Duquette at season's end.

HIGH POINT: On May 13, the Orioles thrashed the Rays and Cy Young finalist Blake Snell for a season-high 17 runs. Joey Rickard, Danny Valencia and Trey Mancini each went deep off of Snell, representing just less than 20 percent of the home runs Snell allowed in 2018.

LOW POINT: The Orioles finished 61 games behind the Red Sox in the American League East. That figure was the worst since 1935, when the Boston Braves finished 61.5 games behind the Cubs in the National League.

NOTABLE ROOKIES: Righthander David Hess went 3-10, 4.88 in 103.1 innings over 19 starts. The 22 home runs he allowed were the most by any rookie in the AL. He was just one longball behind the Giants' Andrew Suarez and the Padres' Joey Lucchesi, each of whom pitched at least 27 more innings than Hess. D.J. Stewart, Anthony Santander, Austin Wynns and Cedric Mullins each hit their first major league home runs. Of their rookies, Mullins looks the most promising. He has an intriguing combination of power and speed and the ability to play center field.

KEY TRANSACTIONS: The biggest move the Orioles made in 2018 was easily the trade of superstar shortstop Manny Machado to the Dodgers for a package of five prospects. The headliner in that deal, outfielder Yusniel Diaz, stands as the No. 1 prospect in the Orioles' system. The team also dealt lefty reliever Zach Britton to the Yankees, righties Brad Brach and Kevin Gausman to the Braves and second baseman Jonathan Schoop to the Brewers.

DOWN ON THE FARM: Third baseman Ryan Mountcastle continued to show a promising bat but little in the way of defensive chops. Mullins was stellar at Double-A and showed enough at Triple-A to warrant an extended look in the big leagues. Their 2017 first-rounder, lefthander D.L. Hall, excelled in first full pro season, going 2-7, 2.10 at low Class A Delmarva and ranked as the No. 1 prospect in the South Atlantic League. Righthander Hunter Harvey continued to deal with injury issues.

OPENING DAY PAYROLL: $148,160,873 (12th).

PLAYERS OF THE YEAR

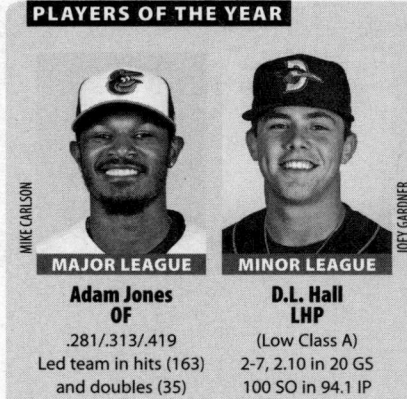

MIKE CARLSON

JOEY GARDNER

MAJOR LEAGUE	**MINOR LEAGUE**
Adam Jones	**D.L. Hall**
OF	LHP
.281/.313/.419	(Low Class A)
Led team in hits (163)	2-7, 2.10 in 20 GS
and doubles (35)	100 SO in 94.1 IP

ORGANIZATION LEADERS

Batting		*Minimum 250 AB
MAJORS		
* AVG	Manny Machado	.315
* OPS	Manny Machado	.963
HR	Manny Machado	24
HR	Trey Mancini	24
RBI	Manny Machado	65
MINORS		
* AVG	Ryan McKenna, Frederick,Bowie	.315
* OBP	Ryan McKenna, Frederick,Bowie	.410
* SLG	Wilson Garcia, Clearwater,Frederick	.521
* OPS	Corban Joseph, Bowie	.878
R	Ryan McKenna, Frederick,Bowie	95
H	Ryan McKenna, Frederick,Bowie	148
TB	Aderlin Rodriguez, Bowie	231
2B	T.J. Nichting, Delmarva,Frederick	36
3B	Mason McCoy, Delmarva	10
HR	Aderlin Rodriguez, Bowie	23
HR	Wilson Garcia, Clearwater,Frederick	23
RBI	Aderlin Rodriguez, Bowie	92
BB	Ryan McKenna, Frederick,Bowie	66
SO	Zach Jarrett, Delmarva	136
SB	Kirvin Moesquit, Delmarva	49

PITCHING		#Minimum 75 IP
MAJORS		
W	Dylan Bundy	8
# ERA	Miguel Castro	3.96
SO	Dylan Bundy	184
SV	Brad Brach	11
MINORS		
W	Keegan Akin, Bowie	14
L	Lucas Long, Bowie,Norfolk	12
# ERA	Zac Lowther, Delmarva,Frederick	2.18
G	Tyler Erwin, Frederick	50
GS	John Means, Bowie,Norfolk	26
GS	Cristian Alvarado, Frederick	26
SV	Tyler Erwin, Frederick	18
IP	John Means, Bowie,Norfolk	157
BB	Michael Kelly, Bowie,Norfolk	77
SO	Zac Lowther, Delmarva,Frederick	151
# AVG	Zac Lowther, Delmarva,Frederick	.195

2018 PERFORMANCE

General Manager: Dan Duquette. **Farm Director:** Brian Graham. **Scouting Director:** Gary Rajsich.

Class	Team	League	W	L	PCT	Finish	Manager
Majors	Baltimore Orioles	American	47	115	.290	15th (15)	Buck Showalter
Triple-A	Norfolk Tides	International	69	71	.493	8th (14)	Ron Johnson
Double-A	Bowie Baysox	Eastern	67	71	.486	6th (12)	Gary Kendall
High A	Frederick Keys	Carolina	65	72	.474	6th (10)	Ryan Minor
Low A	Delmarva Shorebirds	South Atlantic	68	66	.507	t-6th (14)	Buck Britton
Short season	Aberdeen IronBirds	New York-Penn	38	37	.507	t-7th (14)	Kyle Moore
Rookie	GCL Orioles	Gulf Coast	13	42	.236	18th (18)	Carlos Tosca
Overall 2018 Minor League Record			320	359	.471	t-22nd (30)	

ORGANIZATION STATISTICS

BALTIMORE ORIOLES
AMERICAN LEAGUE

Batting	B-T	HT	WT	DOB	AVG	vLH	vRH	G	AB	R	H	2B	3B	HR	RBI	BB	HBP	SH	SF	SO	SB	CS	SLG	OBP
Alvarez, Pedro	L-R	6-3	250	2-6-87	.180	.250	.175	45	111	18	20	3	0	8	18	16	0	0	0	36	0	0	.414	.284
Andreoli, John	R-R	6-1	210	6-9-90	.232	.241	.222	23	56	4	13	2	0	0	4	4	0	0	1	17	2	0	.268	.279
2-team total (3 Seattle)					.230	.226	.233	26	61	4	14	2	0	0	4	5	0	0	1	19	2	0	.262	.284
Beckham, Tim	R-R	6-1	205	1-27-90	.230	.235	.229	96	369	45	85	17	0	12	35	27	3	1	2	100	1	2	.374	.287
Davis, Chris	L-R	6-3	230	3-17-86	.168	.144	.178	128	470	40	79	12	0	16	49	41	7	0	4	192	2	0	.296	.243
Gentry, Craig	R-R	6-2	190	11-29-83	.269	.266	.273	68	156	13	42	5	2	1	11	11	1	1	0	31	12	3	.346	.321
Jones, Adam	R-R	6-2	215	8-1-85	.281	.291	.277	145	580	54	163	35	0	15	63	24	5	0	4	93	7	1	.419	.313
Joseph, Caleb	R-R	6-3	180	6-18-86	.219	.214	.221	82	265	28	58	14	2	3	17	10	3	1	1	48	2	1	.321	.255
Joseph, Corban	L-R	6-0	185	10-28-88	.222	—	.222	14	18	1	4	1	0	0	3	1	0	0	0	5	0	0	.278	.263
Machado, Manny	R-R	6-3	185	7-6-92	.315	.280	.328	96	365	48	115	21	1	24	65	45	0	0	3	51	8	1	.575	.387
Mancini, Trey	R-R	6-4	215	3-18-92	.242	.225	.249	156	582	69	141	23	3	24	58	44	5	0	5	153	0	1	.416	.299
Mullins, Cedric	B-L	5-8	175	10-1-94	.235	.156	.264	45	170	23	40	9	0	4	11	11	2	2	0	37	2	3	.359	.312
Nunez, Renato	R-R	6-1	220	4-4-94	.275	.266	.279	60	200	26	55	13	0	7	20	16	3	0	1	50	0	0	.445	.336
2-team total (13 Texas)					.259	.247	.265	73	236	28	61	14	0	8	22	19	4	0	2	62	0	0	.420	.322
Peterson, Jace	L-R	6-0	215	5-9-90	.195	.097	.213	93	200	21	39	13	2	3	28	30	3	1	1	55	13	2	.325	.308
2-team total (3 New York)					.200	.088	.222	96	210	21	42	13	2	3	28	31	3	1	1	58	13	3	.324	.310
Rasmus, Colby	L-L	6-2	195	8-11-86	.133	.000	.140	18	45	5	6	1	0	1	1	3	1	0	0	19	0	0	.222	.204
Rickard, Joey	R-L	6-1	185	5-21-91	.244	.263	.233	79	213	27	52	10	1	8	23	15	2	0	0	55	4	2	.413	.300
Santander, Anthony	B-R	6-2	190	10-19-94	.198	.200	.197	33	101	8	20	5	1	1	6	6	1	0	0	21	1	0	.297	.250
Sardinas, Luis	B-R	6-1	180	5-16-93	.111	.000	.133	8	18	2	2	0	0	1	1	2	0	0	0	5	0	0	.278	.200
Schoop, Jonathan	R-R	6-1	225	10-16-91	.244	.255	.239	85	349	45	85	18	1	17	40	12	3	1	2	74	0	1	.447	.273
Sisco, Chance	L-R	6-2	195	2-24-95	.181	.143	.185	63	160	13	29	8	0	2	16	13	11	0	0	66	1	0	.269	.288
Stewart, DJ	L-R	6-0	230	11-30-93	.250	.000	.263	17	40	8	10	3	0	3	10	4	2	0	1	12	2	1	.550	.340
Susac, Andrew	R-R	6-1	215	3-22-90	.115	.125	.000	9	26	1	3	1	0	0	0	0	0	0	0	12	0	0	.154	.115
Trumbo, Mark	R-R	6-4	225	1-16-86	.261	.264	.259	90	330	41	86	12	0	17	44	24	2	0	2	87	0	0	.452	.313
Valencia, Danny	R-R	6-2	210	9-19-84	.263	.303	.233	78	255	28	67	8	1	9	28	22	0	0	5	53	1	1	.408	.316
Valera, Breyvic	B-R	5-11	160	1-8-92	.286	.400	.240	12	35	4	10	0	1	0	4	3	0	1	2	9	1	0	.343	.325
Vielma, Engelb	B-R	5-11	155	6-22-94	.143	.250	.000	6	7	1	1	0	0	0	0	1	0	0	0	4	0	0	.143	.250
Villar, Jonathan	B-R	6-1	215	5-2-91	.258	.242	.266	54	209	28	54	4	0	8	24	22	3	1	1	58	21	3	.392	.336
Wilkerson, Steve	B-R	6-1	195	1-11-92	.174	.125	.200	16	46	2	8	3	0	0	3	3	0	0	0	16	1	0	.239	.225
Wynns, Austin	R-R	6-2	205	12-10-90	.255	.196	.297	42	110	16	28	2	0	4	11	5	0	3	0	25	0	0	.382	.287

Pitching	B-T	HT	WT	DOB	W	L	ERA	G	GS	CG	SV	IP	H	R	ER	HR	BB	SO	AVG	vLH	vRH	K/9	BB/9
Araujo, Pedro	R-R	6-3	215	7-2-93	1	3	7.71	20	0	0	0	28	29	24	24	9	18	29	.264	.225	.295	9.32	5.79
Bleier, Richard	L-L	6-3	215	4-16-87	3	0	1.93	31	0	0	0	33	36	7	7	0	4	15	.286	.283	.288	4.13	1.10
Brach, Brad	R-R	6-6	215	4-12-86	1	2	4.85	42	0	0	11	39	50	24	21	4	19	38	.303	.343	.272	8.77	4.38
Britton, Zach	L-L	6-3	195	12-22-87	1	0	3.45	16	0	0	4	16	11	6	6	1	10	13	.212	.250	.188	7.47	5.74
2-team total (25 New York)					2	0	3.10	41	0	0	7	41	29	16	14	3	21	34	.201	.200	.202	7.52	4.65
Bundy, Dylan	B-R	6-1	200	11-15-92	8	16	5.45	31	31	1	0	172	188	116	104	41	54	184	.275	.319	.230	9.65	2.83
Carroll, Cody	R-R	6-5	215	10-15-92	0	2	9.00	15	0	0	0	17	21	17	17	6	13	16	.296	.304	.292	8.47	6.88
Cashner, Andrew	R-R	6-6	235	9-11-86	4	15	5.29	28	28	0	0	153	177	97	90	25	65	99	.291	.278	.304	5.82	3.82
Castro, Miguel	R-R	6-7	205	12-24-94	2	7	3.96	63	1	0	0	86	75	41	38	9	50	57	.236	.244	.230	5.94	5.21
Cobb, Alex	R-R	6-3	205	10-7-87	5	15	4.90	28	28	1	0	152	172	93	83	24	43	102	.284	.276	.292	6.03	2.54
Cortes, Nestor	R-L	5-11	205	12-10-94	0	0	7.71	4	0	0	0	5	10	4	4	2	4	3	.455	.333	.500	5.79	7.71
Fry, Paul	L-L	6-0	190	7-26-92	1	2	3.35	35	0	0	2	38	33	20	14	1	15	36	.236	.264	.218	8.60	3.58
Gausman, Kevin	L-R	6-3	190	1-6-91	5	8	4.43	21	21	0	0	124	139	62	61	21	32	104	.281	.261	.296	7.55	2.32
Gilmartin, Sean	L-L	6-2	205	5-8-90	1	1	3.00	12	0	0	0	27	23	9	9	4	11	15	.230	.146	.288	5.00	3.67
Givens, Mychal	R-R	6-0	210	5-13-90	0	7	3.99	69	0	0	9	77	61	37	34	4	30	79	.218	.245	.201	9.27	3.52
Hart, Donnie	L-L	5-11	180	9-6-90	0	0	5.59	20	0	0	0	19	31	13	12	2	12	13	.361	.333	.390	6.05	5.59
Hess, David	R-R	6-2	180	7-10-93	3	10	4.88	21	19	0	0	103	106	64	56	22	37	74	.262	.254	.271	6.45	3.22
Marinez, Jhan	R-R	6-1	200	8-12-88	0	0	5.63	8	0	0	0	8	9	5	5	1	9	3	.310	.357	.267	3.38	10.13
Means, John	L-L	6-3	230	4-24-93	0	0	13.50	1	0	0	0	3	6	5	5	1	0	4	.375	.429	.333	10.80	0.00
Meisinger, Ryan	R-R	6-4	235	5-4-94	2	1	6.43	18	1	0	0	21	18	15	15	6	10	21	.240	.238	.241	9.00	4.29
O'Day, Darren	R-R	6-4	220	10-22-82	0	2	3.60	20	0	0	2	20	18	9	8	3	4	27	.237	.240	.235	12.15	1.80

	B-T	HT	WT	DOB	W	L	ERA	G	GS	CG	SV	IP	H	R	ER	HR	BB	SO	AVG	vLH	vRH	K/9	BB/9
Ortiz, Luis	R-R	6-3	230	9-22-95	0	1	15.43	2	1	0	0	2	7	6	4	0	3	0	.500	.700	.000	0.00	11.57
Phillips, Evan	R-R	6-2	215	9-11-94	0	1	18.56	5	1	0	0	5	7	13	11	2	6	5	.304	.182	.417	8.44	10.13
Ramirez, Yefry	R-R	6-2	215	11-28-93	1	8	5.92	17	12	0	0	65	64	44	43	11	36	62	.257	.287	.234	8.54	4.96
Rogers, Josh	L-L	6-3	220	7-10-94	1	2	8.49	3	3	0	0	12	17	11	11	2	5	6	.340	.182	.385	4.63	3.86
Scott, Tanner	R-L	6-2	220	7-22-94	3	3	5.40	53	0	0	0	53	55	33	32	6	28	76	.263	.218	.295	12.83	4.73
Tillman, Chris	R-R	6-5	200	4-15-88	1	5	10.46	7	7	0	0	27	42	32	31	6	17	13	.365	.412	.328	4.39	5.74
Wright Jr., Mike	R-R	6-6	215	1-3-90	4	2	5.55	48	2	0	0	84	101	55	52	12	36	74	.299	.284	.310	7.90	3.84
Yacabonis, Jimmy	R-R	6-3	205	3-21-92	0	2	5.40	12	7	0	0	40	40	25	24	8	18	33	.261	.323	.220	7.43	4.05

Fielding

Catcher	PCT	G	PO	A	E	DP	PB
Joseph	.989	81	596	41	7	11	5
Sisco	.997	55	336	26	1	5	1
Susac	1.000	7	48	4	0	0	0
Wynns	.996	41	257	26	1	3	3

First Base	PCT	G	PO	A	E	DP
Alvarez	1.000	1	9	0	0	1
Davis	.995	116	913	67	5	98
Joseph	1.000	2	1	1	0	2
Joseph	1.000	5	18	0	0	0
Mancini	.992	47	331	27	3	34
Trumbo	1.000	3	17	2	0	3
Valencia	1.000	2	9	0	0	0

Second Base	PCT	G	PO	A	E	DP
Beckham	1.000	3	4	7	0	1
Joseph	.000	1	0	0	0	0
Peterson	.982	18	27	29	1	8

Sardinas	.882	8	7	8	2	1
Schoop	.981	85	147	260	8	69
Valera	.925	11	17	20	3	7
Vielma	.875	4	3	4	1	0
Villar	.986	36	51	88	2	17
Wilkerson	1.000	9	12	24	0	4

Third Base	PCT	G	PO	A	E	DP
Alvarez	.941	8	5	11	1	1
Beckham	.938	40	35	71	-7	9
Nunez	.946	59	32	90	7	8
Peterson	.986	35	21	47	1	11
Valencia	.962	39	25	77	4	6
Wilkerson	.846	6	2	9	2	0

Shortstop	PCT	G	PO	A	E	DP
Beckham	.942	49	80	114	12	31
Machado	.980	96	141	247	8	54
Peterson	1.000	3	3	4	0	2

Schoop	1.000	2	1	1	0	1
Valera	1.000	2	1	0	0	0
Vielma	.000	2	0	0	0	0
Villar	.965	18	33	49	3	11
Wilkerson	1.000	1	1	1	0	1

Outfield	PCT	G	PO	A	E	DP
Andreoli	1.000	19	32	0	0	0
Gentry	.979	62	93	2	2	0
Jones	.987	139	309	5	4	2
Mancini	.995	98	185	8	1	1
Mullins	.991	45	108	2	1	0
Peterson	.976	33	39	2	1	0
Rasmus	.947	15	17	1	1	1
Rickard	.992	78	116	8	1	2
Santander	.967	29	57	2	2	0
Stewart	1.000	13	24	2	0	2
Trumbo	1.000	19	26	1	0	0
Valencia	1.000	19	30	1	0	0

NORFOLK TIDES
INTERNATIONAL LEAGUE

TRIPLE-A

Batting	B-T	HT	WT	DOB	AVG	vLH	vRH	G	AB	R	H	2B	3B	HR	RBI	BB	HBP	SH	SF	SO	SB	CS	SLG	OBP
Alvarez, Pedro	L-R	6-3	250	2-6-87	.285	.258	.291	43	165	21	47	6	0	8	32	11	1	0	1	42	0	0	.467	.332
Araiza, Armando	R-R	5-11	205	6-19-93	.139	.143	.138	13	36	1	5	2	0	1	4	3	0	0	1	18	0	0	.278	.200
Beckham, Tim	R-R	6-1	205	1-27-90	.133	.200	.100	4	15	1	2	1	0	0	1	0	0	0	0	5	0	0	.200	.188
Brugman, Jaycob	L-L	6-0	195	1-18-92	.248	.179	.272	66	218	32	54	8	3	5	25	23	1	0	1	59	6	1	.381	.321
Dosch, Drew	L-R	6-2	200	6-24-92	.276	.231	.292	103	355	44	98	24	1	7	40	33	3	0	3	112	1	1	.409	.340
Feliz, Anderson	B-R	6-0	175	5-11-92	.244	.273	.235	12	45	5	11	0	1	0	4	3	0	0	0	19	0	0	.289	.292
Joseph, Caleb	R-R	6-3	180	6-18-86	.273	.273	.273	24	88	10	24	2	0	2	14	8	1	0	0	19	0	0	.364	.340
Levy, Stuart	R-R	6-2	185	8-21-92	.167	.000	.200	3	6	1	1	0	0	1	1	1	0	0	0	2	0	0	.667	.286
Marin, Adrian	R-R	6-0	180	3-8-94	.216	.182	.228	76	255	29	55	9	0	16	14	2	3	2	47	6	0	.251	.260
Mullins, Cedric	B-L	5-8	175	10-1-94	.269	.220	.281	60	242	41	65	17	3	6	19	22	2	2	1	39	12	0	.438	.333
Myers, D'Arby	R-R	6-3	185	12-9-88	.174	.083	.273	11	23	3	4	1	1	0	3	1	1	0	0	4	1	0	.304	.240
Nunez, Renato	R-R	6-1	220	4-4-94	.289	.302	.284	56	201	25	58	14	1	5	25	23	1	0	2	49	1	0	.443	.361
Perez, Audry	R-R	5-10	220	12-23-88	.467	.286	.625	5	15	4	7	0	0	3	6	1	1	0	0	0	0	0	1.067	.529
Presley, Alex	L-L	5-10	195	7-25-85	.275	.250	.288	26	109	19	30	5	1	1	8	11	1	0	0	27	0	0	.367	.347
2-team total (29 Charlotte)					.238	.222	.245	55	210	25	50	8	1	2	20	19	2	0	1	46	0	2	.314	.306
Rickard, Joey	R-L	6-1	185	5-21-91	.275	.277	.274	44	153	25	42	13	1	2	27	26	3	0	3	28	3	0	.412	.384
Rosa, Garabez	R-R	6-2	165	10-12-89	.277	.254	.285	127	481	63	133	22	0	11	56	12	2	0	0	121	2	1	.391	.297
Santander, Anthony	B-R	6-2	190	10-19-94	.182	.100	.206	11	44	3	8	3	0	2	7	2	0	0	1	9	0	0	.386	.213
Sardinas, Luis	B-R	6-1	180	5-16-93	.264	.245	.270	63	231	25	61	15	0	4	21	10	1	5	0	41	2	3	.381	.298
Saunders, Michael	L-R	6-4	225	11-19-86	.161	.087	.188	25	87	11	14	3	1	1	14	16	0	0	0	23	2	0	.253	.291
2-team total (13 Charlotte)					.158	.086	.184	38	133	15	21	4	1	2	18	21	0	0	0	33	2	0	.248	.273
Schoop, Jonathan	R-R	6-1	225	10-16-91	.125	.333	.000	2	8	0	1	0	0	0	0	0	0	0	0	5	0	0	.125	.125
Schoop, Sharlon	R-R	6-2	190	4-15-87	.209	.103	.263	27	86	9	18	5	0	1	16	7	2	1	1	22	0	2	.302	.281
Sisco, Chance	L-R	6-2	195	2-24-95	.242	.167	.260	38	128	22	31	5	0	3	12	16	5	0	2	36	0	0	.352	.344
Stewart, DJ	L-R	6-0	230	11-30-93	.235	.264	.225	116	421	59	99	24	2	12	55	54	8	0	7	103	11	4	.387	.329
Susac, Andrew	R-R	6-1	215	3-22-90	.256	.167	.292	42	125	15	32	7	0	6	26	31	1	0	1	42	0	0	.456	.405
Tejada, Ruben	R-R	5-11	200	10-27-89	.230	.208	.239	101	352	34	81	18	0	2	34	24	8	4	4	69	5	0	.298	.291
Trumbo, Mark	R-R	6-4	225	1-16-86	.286	.250	.333	3	14	2	4	1	0	0	3	0	0	0	0	3	0	0	.357	.286
Valera, Breyvic	B-R	5-11	160	1-8-92	.229	.333	.200	38	140	14	32	6	2	3	14	16	1	2	1	14	3	0	.364	.310
Vielma, Engelb	B-R	5-11	155	6-22-94	.184	.182	.185	12	38	3	7	2	1	0	3	4	0	0	1	9	0	0	.290	.256
Wilkerson, Steve	B-R	6-1	195	11-24-91	.270	.192	.313	20	74	13	20	5	0	4	13	5	3	1	3	15	0	1	.500	.329
Wynns, Austin	R-R	6-2	205	12-10-90	.230	.400	.149	41	139	19	32	4	0	4	16	11	1	0	2	38	0	0	.345	.288
Yastrzemski, Mike	L-L	5-11	180	8-23-90	.265	.284	.260	94	324	48	86	18	6	9	49	44	4	1	1	75	6	4	.441	.359

Pitching	B-T	HT	WT	DOB	W	L	ERA	G	GS	CG	SV	IP	H	R	ER	BB	SO	AVG	vLH	vRH	K/9	BB/9
Aquino, Jayson	L-L	6-1	225	11-22-92	1	2	4.26	4	4	0	0	19	17	11	9	0	12	13	.243	.333	.218	6.16	5.68
Britton, Zach	L-L	6-3	195	12-22-87	0	0	2.70	3	0	0	0	3	3	1	1	0	0	3	.250	.333	.222	8.10	0.00
Carroll, Cody	R-R	6-5	215	10-15-92	1	0	5.79	5	0	0	0	5	4	3	3	0	4	3	.222	.286	.182	5.79	7.71
2-team total (32 Scranton/Wilkes-Barre)					4	0	2.72	37	0	0	9	46	31	16	14	0	22	58	.188	.257	.132	11.27	4.27
Edgin, Josh	L-L	6-1	245	12-17-86	3	0	4.34	12	0	0	0	19	19	10	9	3	5	26	.268	.235	.297	12.05	2.41
2-team total (35 Syracuse)					4	3	3.56	47	0	0	0	43	41	21	17	7	21	64	.253	.183	.325	13.40	4.40
Faulkner, Andrew	R-L	6-3	205	9-12-92	6	2	4.81	46	0	0	2	58	59	37	31	6	29	52	.267	.240	.291	8.07	4.50

Name	T	HT	WT	DOB	W	L	ERA	G	GS	CG	SV	IP	H	R	ER	HR	BB	SO	AVG	vLH	vRH		
Fry, Paul	L-L	6-0	190	7-26-92	0	1	3.47	13	1	0	0	23	22	10	9	2	4	29	.250	.257	.245	11.19	1.54
Gamboa, Eddie	R-R	6-1	215	12-21-84	2	0	2.95	11	0	0	2	21	20	11	7	1	12	17	.238	.279	.195	7.17	5.06
Gilmartin, Sean	L-L	6-2	205	5-8-90	2	0	3.14	7	3	0	0	14	13	5	5	1	2	12	.245	.227	.258	7.53	1.26
Gonzalez, Luis	L-L	6-2	170	1-17-92	0	2	5.04	14	0	0	2	25	31	17	14	1	12	27	.293	.244	.323	9.72	4.32
Grimes, Matthew	R-R	6-5	185	9-4-91	0	0	0.00	1	0	0	0	4	2	0	0	0	0	1	.154	.143	.167	2.45	0.00
Gurka, Jason	L-L	6-0	170	1-10-88	1	2	3.18	16	0	0	0	23	27	9	8	2	6	24	.294	.273	.305	9.53	2.38
Hart, Donnie	L-L	5-11	180	9-6-90	3	2	2.41	32	3	0	6	41	42	14	11	1	10	45	.269	.206	.318	9.88	2.20
Hess, David	R-R	6-2	180	7-10-93	3	2	3.15	9	9	0	0	46	38	16	16	3	19	44	.225	.172	.300	8.67	3.74
Jimenez, Francisco	R-R	6-1	160	10-4-94	0	2	4.64	11	0	0	0	21	21	13	11	1	8	15	.247	.240	.257	6.33	3.38
Kelly, Michael	R-R	6-4	185	9-6-92	0	1	4.91	6	0	0	0	11	13	6	6	0	11	7	.289	.200	.333	5.73	9.00
Lee, Chris	L-L	6-3	180	8-17-92	0	2	10.64	5	3	0	0	11	23	16	13	0	16	8	.426	.421	.429	6.55	8.18
Long, Lucas	R-R	6-0	195	10-7-92	2	3	3.93	12	4	0	0	34	38	17	15	2	7	22	.279	.264	.289	5.77	1.83
Love, Reid	R-L	5-11	195	5-15-92	1	0	2.25	1	0	0	0	4	3	1	1	1	1	1	.214	.000	.375	2.25	2.25
Marinez, Jhan	R-R	6-1	200	8-12-88	2	3	3.21	41	1	0	11	48	52	23	17	6	16	51	.271	.276	.267	9.63	3.02
Means, John	L-L	6-3	230	4-24-93	6	5	3.48	20	19	1	0	111	123	50	43	9	19	89	.277	.206	.307	7.19	1.54
Meisinger, Ryan	R-R	6-4	235	5-4-94	2	0	2.28	21	0	0	1	28	21	7	7	1	10	36	.208	.180	.226	11.71	3.25
Melville, Tim	R-R	6-4	225	10-9-89	9	6	5.33	40	14	0	4	105	115	70	62	15	42	82	.278	.279	.277	7.05	3.61
O'Rourke, Ryan	R-L	6-3	230	4-30-88	0	0	0.00	3	0	0	0	3	1	1	0	0	0	5	.111	.250	.000	16.88	0.00
Ortiz, Luis	R-R	6-3	230	9-22-95	2	1	3.69	6	6	0	0	32	34	13	13	4	8	21	.274	.283	.269	5.97	2.27
Phillips, Evan	R-R	6-2	215	9-11-94	0	2	3.38	8	0	0	0	11	6	4	4	1	3	13	.158	.111	.200	10.97	2.53
2-team total (31 Gwinnett)					4	6	2.28	39	0	0	8	51	34	16	13	2	17	72	.190	.183	.196	12.62	2.98
Ramirez, Yefry	R-R	6-2	215	11-28-93	3	5	3.88	14	14	0	0	72	62	31	31	7	22	72	.227	.271	.178	9.00	2.75
Rodriguez, Joely	L-L	6-1	200	11-14-91	5	3	4.56	33	1	0	2	49	49	28	25	1	18	52	.250	.235	.261	9.49	3.28
Rogers, Josh	L-L	6-3	220	7-10-94	2	1	2.08	5	5	0	0	30	26	9	7	3	7	18	.226	.167	.253	5.34	2.08
2-team total (19 Scranton/Wilkes-Barre)					8	9	3.54	24	24	1	0	140	144	62	55	16	36	101	.263	.201	.290	6.51	2.32
Scott, Tanner	R-L	6-2	220	7-22-94	0	1	0.75	10	0	0	1	12	10	1	1	0	9	13	.250	.231	.259	9.75	6.75
Snelten, D.J.	L-L	6-6	240	5-29-92	2	2	5.52	22	0	0	1	29	40	24	18	2	17	30	.318	.383	.279	9.20	5.22
Tillman, Chris	R-R	6-5	200	4-15-88	0	1	6.60	3	3	0	0	15	25	11	11	2	6	5	.379	.371	.387	3.00	3.60
Wojciechowski, Asher	R-R	6-4	235	12-21-88	5	4	3.51	19	12	0	0	85	68	36	33	14	32	89	.219	.271	.175	9.46	3.40
2-team total (6 Charlotte)					5	9	4.53	25	18	0	0	119	108	63	60	26	37	126	.240	.286	.203	9.50	2.79
Wotherspoon, Matt	R-R	6-2	215	10-6-91	2	8	4.60	39	12	0	0	94	95	52	48	13	38	105	.260	.247	.272	10.05	3.64
Yacabonis, Jimmy	R-R	6-3	205	3-21-92	3	5	4.26	21	21	0	0	76	61	36	36	6	32	62	.219	.227	.209	7.34	3.79
Ysla, Luis	L-L	6-1	185	4-27-92	1	3	6.45	5	5	1	0	22	33	16	16	1	13	18	.347	.333	.354	7.25	5.24

Fielding

Catcher	PCT	G	PO	A	E	DP	PB
Araiza	1.000	13	71	4	0	0	4
Joseph	.993	15	135	8	1	1	2
Levy	1.000	2	14	1	0	0	2
Perez	1.000	4	42	2	0	1	0
Sisco	.989	37	268	9	3	4	3
Susac	.990	36	277	20	3	0	3
Wynns	.994	39	328	15	2	3	4

First Base	PCT	G	PO	A	E	DP
Alvarez	1.000	2	13	0	0	1
Dosch	.994	24	159	13	1	15
Nunez	1.000	6	39	5	0	2
Rosa	.989	114	763	70	9	70
Schoop	.933	2	13	1	1	0
Tejada	1.000	1	7	0	0	0

Second Base	PCT	G	PO	A	E	DP
Dosch	.000	1	0	0	0	0
Feliz	.875	1	2	5	1	2
Marin	.984	18	24	39	1	6
Rosa	1.000	5	6	7	0	1
Sardinas	.941	12	22	26	3	10
Schoop	1.000	2	1	2	0	0
Schoop	1.000	22	34	45	0	6
Tejada	1.000	53	78	115	0	23
Valera	.990	25	38	66	1	13
Wilkerson	1.000	10	9	33	0	5

Third Base	PCT	G	PO	A	E	DP
Beckham	1.000	1	0	1	0	0
Dosch	.912	57	39	75	11	7
Feliz	.905	11	8	11	2	1
Nunez	.936	38	17	56	5	2
Sardinas	1.000	8	5	12	0	3
Schoop	1.000	1	1	0	0	0
Tejada	.973	21	9	27	1	6
Valera	.889	4	4	4	1	2
Wilkerson	1.000	6	3	8	0	3

Shortstop	PCT	G	PO	A	E	DP
Beckham	1.000	2	1	7	0	0
Marin	.986	60	81	128	3	33
Sardinas	.961	39	52	97	6	15
Schoop	1.000	3	3	5	0	1
Tejada	.990	27	40	64	1	13
Valera	1.000	2	2	6	0	0
Vielma	.917	12	10	23	3	3
Wilkerson	1.000	2	4	2	0	2

Outfield	PCT	G	PO	A	E	DP
Brugman	.983	56	113	5	2	1
Mullins	.994	60	155	2	1	1
Myers	1.000	8	12	0	0	0
Presley	1.000	16	34	0	0	0
Rickard	1.000	43	105	5	0	2
Rosa	.958	11	22	1	1	0
Santander	1.000	10	19	1	0	1
Sardinas	1.000	1	2	0	0	0
Saunders	1.000	7	14	0	0	0
Stewart	.972	114	200	8	6	1
Trumbo	1.000	2	2	0	0	0
Valera	.867	7	13	0	2	0
Wilkerson	1.000	4	7	0	0	0
Yastrzemski	.984	91	235	6	4	1

BOWIE BAYSOX · DOUBLE-A
EASTERN LEAGUE

Batting	B-T	HT	WT	DOB	AVG	vLH	vRH	G	AB	R	H	2B	3B	HR	RBI	BB	HBP	SH	SF	SO	SB	CS	SLG	OBP
Araiza, Armando	R-R	5-11	205	6-19-93	.127	.200	.100	22	55	3	7	4	0	0	3	4	1	0	0	18	0	0	.200	.200
Bannon, Rylan	R-R	5-10	180	4-22-96	.204	.091	.218	32	98	16	20	6	0	2	11	22	0	0	2	24	0	0	.327	.344
Beckham, Tim	R-R	6-1	205	1-27-90	.125	.125	—	3	8	1	1	0	0	0	2	0	0	0	0	1	0	.125	.300
Brugman, Jaycob	L-L	6-0	195	1-18-92	.261	.143	.282	12	46	10	12	3	0	3	6	3	0	0	0	15	0	0	.522	.306
Cervenka, Martin	R-R	6-4	225	8-3-92	.258	.250	.261	97	337	41	87	22	0	15	60	30	2	0	6	65	1	0	.457	.317
Clare, Chris	R-R	6-2	175	11-24-94	—	—	—	2	0	0	0	0	0	0	0	0	0	0	0	0	0	0	—	—
Cumberland, Brett	B-R	5-11	205	6-25-95	.191	.250	.184	15	42	6	8	0	0	3	7	4	2	1	0	12	0	0	.405	.292
Diaz, Yusniel	R-R	6-2	195	10-7-96	.239	.316	.226	38	134	23	32	5	1	5	15	18	0	0	0	28	4	5	.403	.329
Feliz, Anderson	B-R	6-0	175	5-11-92	.280	.246	.293	113	393	65	110	19	1	10	48	38	3	1	1	97	20	5	.410	.347
Gentry, Craig	R-R	6-2	190	11-29-83	.600	1.000	.500	3	5	1	3	1	0	0	1	0	0	0	0	2	0	0	.600	.692
Hays, Austin	R-R	6-1	195	7-5-95	.242	.333	.221	66	273	34	66	12	2	12	43	12	0	0	3	59	6	3	.432	.271
Joseph, Corban	L-R	6-0	185	10-28-88	.312	.243	.332	122	459	73	143	30	2	17	68	52	3	6		43	8	2	.497	.381
Juvier, Alejandro	L-R	6-1	180	1-20-96	.000	.000	—	1	3	0	0	0	0	0	0	0	0	0	0	0	0	0	.000	.000

BALTIMORE ORIOLES

Batting	B-T	HT	WT	DOB	AVG	vLH	vRH	G	AB	R	H	2B	3B	HR	RBI	BB	HBP	SH	SF	SO	SB	CS	SLG	OBP
Marin, Adrian	R-R	6-0	180	3-8-94	.247	.412	.206	27	85	10	21	3	0	0	7	13	1	1	0	24	0	1	.282	.354
McKenna, Ryan	R-R	5-11	185	2-14-97	.239	.250	.237	60	213	35	51	8	2	3	16	29	4	4	0	56	4	1	.338	.342
Mountcastle, Ryan	R-R	6-3	195	2-18-97	.297	.315		102	394	63	117	19	4	13	59	26	3	0	5	79	2	0	.465	.341
Mullins, Cedric	B-L	5-8	175	10-1-94	.313	.300	.317	49	201	36	63	12	5	6	28	15	1	0	1	28	9	1	.512	.362
Myers, D'Arby	R-R	6-3	185	12-9-88	.293	.262	.323	44	123	16	36	5	0	0	11	7	0	0	1	20	6	1	.333	.328
Perez, Audry	R-R	5-10	220	12-23-88	.213	.233	.202	38	127	12	27	2	0	8	22	7	0	0	1	20	0	0	.417	.252
Rasmus, Colby	L-L	6-2	195	8-11-86	.214	.200	.222	4	14	2	3	0	0	1	2	3	0	0	0	5	0	0	.429	.353
Rifaela, Ademar	L-L	5-10	180	11-20-94	.265	.299	.255	100	359	36	95	22	2	7	41	30	2	1	4	95	2	3	.396	.322
Rodriguez, Aderlin	R-R	6-3	210	11-18-91	.286	.238	.298	128	483	76	138	20	2	23	92	29	11	0	8	95	1	1	.478	.335
Salcedo, Erick	B-R	5-10	155	6-28-93	.225	.202	.232	127	432	44	97	19	5	0	32	29	3	2	5	54	2	4	.292	.275
Santander, Anthony	B-R	6-2	190	10-19-94	.258	.242	.265	54	209	26	54	9	3	5	22	10	1	0	2	32	4	1	.402	.293
Schoop, Jonathan	R-R	6-1	225	10-16-91	.000	—	.000	1	2	0	0	0	0	0	0	0	0	0	0	1	0	0	.000	.000
Schoop, Sharlon	R-R	6-2	190	4-15-87	.278	.300	.250	8	18	1	5	0	0	1	2	5	1	1	0	7	0	1	.444	.458
Trumbo, Mark	R-R	6-4	225	1-16-86	.100	.000	.200	3	10	0	1	0	0	0	0	0	0	0	0	2	0	0	.100	.250
Wilkerson, Steve	B-R	6-1	195	1-11-92	.158	—	.158	5	19	3	3	1	0	0	0	2	0	0	0	6	0	1	.211	.238
Yastrzemski, Mike	L-L	5-11	180	8-23-90	.202	.174	.210	27	104	13	21	10	0	1	11	10	1	1	1	30	2	1	.327	.276

Pitching	B-T	HT	WT	DOB	W	L	ERA	G	GS	CG	SV	IP	H	R	ER	HR	BB	SO	AVG	vLH	vRH	K/9	BB/9
Akin, Keegan	L-L	6-0	225	4-1-95	14	7	3.27	25	25	0	0	138	114	52	50	16	58	142	.225	.211	.232	9.28	3.79
Aquino, Jayson	L-L	6-2	225	11-22-92	3	4	5.59	8	8	0	0	46	46	26	24	1	14	27	.303	.214	.336	6.28	3.26
Binford, Christian	R-R	6-6	215	12-20-92	1	4	4.95	12	7	1	0	56	77	33	31	9	8	35	.333	.374	.287	5.59	1.28
2-team total (7 Erie)					1	4	4.66	19	9	1	0	77	104	43	40	10	9	57	.324	.347	.298	6.63	1.05
Britton, Zach	L-L	6-3	195	12-22-87	0	0	0.00	1	0	0	0	1	0	0	0	0	0	0	.000	.000	.000	0.00	0.00
Chleborad, Tanner	R-R	6-6	185	11-4-92	6	1	3.61	43	0	0	4	62	69	30	25	2	17	47	.285	.333	.242	6.79	2.45
Flaa, Jay	R-R	6-3	225	6-10-92	3	1	2.77	41	0	0	2	65	35	27	20	7	28	67	.155	.165	.143	9.28	3.88
Fry, Paul	L-L	6-0	190	7-26-92	3	0	2.84	15	0	0	2	19	10	7	6	2	11	28	.154	.111	.184	13.26	5.21
Gamboa, Eddie	R-R	6-1	215	12-21-84	0	0	2.45	1	1	0	0	4	7	1	1	0	1	5	.438	.429	.444	12.27	2.45
Gonzalez, Brian	R-L	6-3	230	10-25-95	8	6	5.69	18	17	0	0	92	110	63	58	15	40	79	.290	.330	.273	7.76	3.93
Gonzalez, Luis	L-L	6-2	170	1-17-92	2	1	2.17	28	0	0	7	46	28	14	11	4	14	58	.167	.221	.130	11.43	2.76
Grimes, Matthew	R-R	6-5	185	9-4-91	0	2	3.94	34	7	0	0	82	84	39	36	8	35	64	.271	.276	.266	7.00	3.83
Harvey, Hunter	R-R	6-3	175	12-9-94	1	2	5.57	9	9	0	0	32	36	20	20	3	9	30	.290	.333	.209	8.35	2.51
Humpal, Lucas	R-R	6-3	180	9-5-93	0	0	13.50	1	1	0	0	3	8	5	5	0	1	1	.471	.539	.250	2.70	2.70
Kelly, Michael	R-R	6-4	185	9-6-92	1	5	9.11	25	8	0	1	56	55	60	57	8	66	55	.258	.244	.281	8.79	10.54
Kipper, Jordan	R-R	6-4	185	10-6-92	1	1	2.41	3	3	1	0	19	17	5	5	2	2	13	.239	.314	.167	6.27	0.96
Kline, Branden	R-R	6-3	210	9-29-91	4	4	1.80	32	0	0	15	45	32	15	9	3	15	48	.199	.129	.276	9.60	3.00
Kremer, Dean	R-R	6-2	180	1-7-96	2	2	2.58	8	8	0	0	45	38	15	13	3	17	53	.228	.169	.286	10.52	3.38
Lee, Chris	L-L	6-3	180	8-17-92	1	1	3.50	10	0	0	0	18	25	9	7	0	7	14	.338	.269	.375	7.00	3.50
Long, Lucas	R-R	6-0	195	10-7-92	2	9	6.60	21	11	0	0	76	102	59	56	11	19	49	.325	.364	.277	5.78	2.24
Love, Reid	R-L	5-11	195	5-15-92	2	5	7.22	17	3	0	0	42	44	29	27	4	10	37	.311	.340	.293	9.89	2.67
Means, John	L-L	6-3	230	4-24-93	1	4	4.30	8	7	0	0	46	43	27	22	6	13	41	.246	.207	.265	8.02	2.54
Meisinger, Ryan	R-R	6-4	235	5-4-94	0	0	4.42	11	0	0	0	18	22	12	9	4	5	19	.293	.250	.333	9.33	2.45
Ming, Cameron	L-L	6-1	177	5-2-96	0	0	6.14	2	0	0	0	7	8	5	5	2	2	7	.276	.267	.286	8.59	2.45
Muckenhirn, Zach	L-L	6-1	185	2-27-95	0	0	5.67	20	0	0	1	27	26	17	17	1	18	27	.252	.290	.231	9.00	6.00
Pop, Zach	R-R	6-4	220	9-20-96	1	1	2.53	14	0	0	1	21	14	7	6	0	6	17	.189	.200	.180	7.17	2.53
Tate, Dillon	R-R	6-2	195	5-1-94	2	3	5.75	7	7	0	0	41	48	27	26	3	9	21	.302	.300	.304	4.65	1.99
2-team total (15 Trenton)					7	5	4.16	22	22	0	0	123	115	60	57	10	34	96	.247	.227	.266	7.01	2.48
Ynoa, Gabriel	R-R	6-2	205	5-26-93	0	0	2.57	2	2	0	0	7	6	3	2	1	0	6	.231	.154	.308	7.71	0.00
Ysla, Luis	L-L	6-1	185	4-27-92	5	5	4.98	28	9	0	0	72	67	46	40	11	45	83	.241	.243	.240	10.33	5.60
Zimmermann, Bruce	L-L	6-2	215	2-9-95	2	3	5.06	5	5	1	0	21	25	17	12	2	7	16	.287	.333	.270	6.75	2.95

Fielding

Catcher	PCT	G	PO	A	E	DP	PB
Araiza	.975	13	72	7	2	1	0
Cervenka	.992	93	762	68	7	6	13
Cumberland	.989	13	83	10	1	1	0
Perez	.989	24	174	13	2	3	2

First Base	PCT	G	PO	A	E	DP
Araiza	1.000	4	17	2	0	4
Joseph	1.000	21	168	9	0	12
Rodriguez	.991	114	834	50	8	80
Trumbo	1.000	1	8	0	0	3
Wilkerson	1.000	1	9	0	0	1

Second Base	PCT	G	PO	A	E	DP
Bannon	.957	30	42	70	5	17
Feliz	.955	26	40	66	5	18
Joseph	.990	52	87	104	2	30
Juvier	1.000	1	2	5	0	1
Marin	.990	25	43	57	1	12

	PCT	G	PO	A	E	DP
Salcedo	1.000	1	2	1	0	1
Schoop	1.000	1	1	2	0	1
Schoop	1.000	6	5	12	0	3
Wilkerson	1.000	1	0	8	0	1

Third Base	PCT	G	PO	A	E	DP
Araiza	1.000	3	0	2	0	0
Bannon	.667	2	0	2	1	0
Beckham	.667	1	1	1	1	0
Feliz	.965	39	21	61	3	8
Joseph	1.000	2	1	0	0	0
Mountcastle	.912	81	49	116	16	12
Rodriguez	.923	11	8	16	2	1
Schoop	1.000	2	0	2	0	0
Wilkerson	1.000	1	1	1	0	0

Shortstop	PCT	G	PO	A	E	DP
Beckham	1.000	1	0	1	0	0
Feliz	.962	13	17	33	2	8

	PCT	G	PO	A	E	DP
Marin	.800	2	1	3	1	0
Salcedo	.957	126	173	300	21	66
Wilkerson	1.000	1	1	4	0	1

Outfield	PCT	G	PO	A	E	DP
Brugman	1.000	10	15	1	0	0
Diaz	.974	35	73	2	2	1
Feliz	.977	36	78	6	2	1
Gentry	1.000	2	7	0	0	0
Hays	.993	61	142	7	1	2
McKenna	.987	60	148	9	2	1
Mullins	.975	46	114	1	3	1
Myers	1.000	31	59	1	0	0
Rasmus	1.000	4	9	0	0	0
Rifaela	.991	69	112	3	1	0
Rodriguez	1.000	2	3	0	0	0
Santander	1.000	49	86	1	0	0
Wilkerson	1.000	1	3	0	0	0
Yastrzemski	.986	25	70	0	1	0

FREDERICK KEYS
CAROLINA LEAGUE

HIGH CLASS A

Batting	B-T	HT	WT	DOB	AVG	vLH	vRH	G	AB	R	H	2B	3B	HR	RBI	BB	HBP	SH	SF	SO	SB	CS	SLG	OBP
Billingsley, Cole	L-L	5-10	165	5-29-94	.208	.200	.211	121	432	53	90	22	3	4	43	53	3	6	3	79	16	4	.301	.297

Batting	B-T	HT	WT	DOB	AVG	vLH	vRH	G	AB	R	H	2B	3B	HR	RBI	BB	HBP	SH	SF	SO	SB	CS	SLG	OBP
Clare, Chris	R-R	6-2	175	11-24-94	.224	.300	.196	120	401	48	90	23	2	5	35	60	9	3	4	76	5	2	.329	.335
Coolbaugh, Tyler	B-R	6-2	190	10-29-93	.000	.000	—	2	1	1	0	0	0	0	0	0	0	0	0	1	0	0	.000	.000
Escarra, J.C.	L-R	6-3	205	4-24-95	.229	.200	.233	12	35	1	8	0	0	1	4	2	0	0	0	6	1	0	.314	.270
Fajardo, Daniel	R-R	6-1	170	11-19-94	.271	.316	.253	63	207	25	56	5	1	4	27	10	0	0	1	24	0	0	.362	.303
Garcia, Wilson	B-R	5-11	160	1-11-94	.295	.263	.308	108	413	60	122	24	0	23	70	21	2	0	6	46	0	0	.521	.334
Gassaway, Randolph	R-R	6-4	210	5-23-95	.272	.340	.249	103	379	45	103	27	1	6	41	43	3	0	3	81	0	0	.396	.348
Gentry, Craig	R-R	6-2	190	11-29-83	.231	—	.231	4	13	1	3	0	0	0	1	0	0	0	1	6	0	0	.231	.214
Hogan, Max	L-R	5-11	195	9-24-93	.000	.000	.000	2	3	0	0	0	0	0	0	0	0	0	0	1	0	0	.000	.000
Juvier, Alejandro	L-R	6-1	180	1-20-96	.219	.175	.229	74	219	26	48	6	0	1	14	15	4	1	0	56	0	2	.260	.282
Levy, Stuart	R-R	6-2	185	8-21-92	.158	.150	.160	48	146	10	23	1	0	3	14	13	7	0	0	46	0	0	.226	.259
McKenna, Ryan	R-R	5-11	185	2-14-97	.377	.459	.352	67	257	60	97	18	2	8	37	37	6	0	0	45	5	6	.556	.467
Murphy, Alex	R-R	5-11	210	10-5-94	.048	.000	.077	6	21	2	1	0	0	0	1	2	1	0	0	3	0	0	.048	.167
Nichting, T.J.	B-R	5-11	188	1-13-95	.253	.255	.252	97	356	41	90	26	0	4	32	13	1	0	3	56	4	7	.360	.279
Palmeiro, Preston	L-R	5-11	180	1-22-95	.251	.279	.240	131	494	62	124	19	2	17	64	39	4	2	4	105	0	1	.401	.309
Quevedo, Yojhan	R-R	6-1	215	11-6-93	.287	.441	.241	38	150	16	43	9	0	4	18	4	2	0	1	17	0	0	.427	.312
Rasmus, Colby	L-L	6-2	195	8-11-86	.297	.000	.333	11	37	8	11	3	1	1	8	2	0	0	1	7	0	0	.514	.325
Reyes, Jomar	R-R	6-3	220	2-20-97	.262	.277	.257	116	431	42	113	27	0	8	48	26	4	0	3	84	0	1	.381	.308
Ring, Jake	L-L	5-11	175	8-11-94	.196	.177	.202	74	224	31	44	11	0	3	21	37	2	3	3	54	5	1	.286	.312
Schoop, Jonathan	R-R	6-1	225	10-16-91	.333	.000	1.000	1	3	0	1	0	0	0	0	2	1	0	0	0	0	0	.333	.500
Torres, Alexis	R-R	6-0	183	12-12-97	.200	.333	.000	2	5	0	1	0	0	0	0	1	0	0	0	0	0	0	.200	.200
Woody, Collin	R-R	6-1	210	8-5-94	.219	.257	.204	79	242	39	53	18	1	10	33	31	8	0	2	72	1	1	.426	.325

Pitching	B-T	HT	WT	DOB	W	L	ERA	G	GS	CG	SV	IP	H	R	ER	HR	BB	SO	AVG	vLH	vRH	K/9	BB/9
Alvarado, Cristian	R-R	6-3	175	9-20-94	12	11	4.18	26	26	0	0	155	173	78	72	19	23	119	.282	.277	.286	6.91	1.34
Araujo, Elvis	L-L	6-7	275	7-15-91	3	0	5.85	15	0	0	1	20	24	13	13	1	5	28	.289	.314	.271	12.60	2.25
Baumann, Michael	R-R	6-4	225	9-10-95	8	5	3.88	17	17	2	0	93	82	42	40	9	40	59	.238	.265	.206	5.73	3.88
Britton, Zach	L-L	6-3	195	12-22-87	1	0	0.00	1	0	0	0	1	1	0	0	0	0	3	.250	.000	1.000	27.00	0.00
Burke, Mike	R-R	6-2	200	8-27-92	0	2	8.39	28	0	0	1	40	62	39	37	7	10	32	.363	.333	.382	7.26	2.27
Dietz, Matthias	R-R	6-5	220	9-20-95	1	6	7.98	11	9	0	0	38	40	41	34	6	39	27	.274	.280	.268	6.34	9.16
Erwin, Tyler	L-L	6-0	185	8-29-94	4	4	1.58	50	0	0	18	68	45	21	12	1	23	84	.183	.191	.178	11.06	3.03
Gonzalez, Brian	R-L	6-3	230	10-25-95	2	2	3.18	7	7	0	0	40	31	17	14	3	18	33	.214	.205	.217	7.49	4.08
Humpal, Lucas	R-R	6-3	180	9-5-93	3	8	4.91	20	13	0	0	81	95	48	44	9	25	59	.297	.292	.301	6.58	2.79
Jimenez, Francisco	R-R	6-1	160	10-4-94	1	2	9.57	14	1	0	0	26	49	35	28	3	9	27	.380	.364	.392	9.23	3.08
Katz, Alex	L-L	5-11	195	10-12-94	0	0	4.50	8	0	0	0	12	14	6	6	1	8	9	.286	.259	.318	6.75	6.00
Klimek, Steven	L-R	6-3	205	4-4-94	3	3	3.43	42	0	0	3	76	75	37	29	7	38	66	.257	.256	.258	7.82	4.50
Kline, Branden	R-R	6-3	210	9-29-91	1	0	1.31	12	0	0	2	21	20	6	3	0	3	23	.253	.290	.220	10.02	1.31
Lowther, Zac	L-L	6-2	235	4-30-96	5	3	2.53	17	16	0	0	93	74	29	26	6	26	100	.220	.207	.227	9.71	2.53
Matson, Zach	L-L	6-3	225	10-24-95	0	0	1.42	4	0	0	0	6	3	1	1	0	5	5	.273	.167	.313	7.11	7.11
Muckenhirn, Zach	L-L	6-1	185	2-27-95	1	1	2.21	12	0	0	4	20	16	5	5	1	4	25	.219	.269	.192	11.07	1.77
O'Day, Darren	R-R	6-4	220	10-22-82	0	0	16.20	2	0	0	0	1.2	2	3	3	0	3	3	.000	.000	.000	16.20	16.20
O'Rourke, Ryan	R-L	6-3	230	4-30-88	0	0	0.00	3	0	0	1	3	1	0	0	0	0	3	.111	.000	.167	9.00	0.00
Peluffo, Jhon	R-R	6-3	140	6-16-97	2	2	6.93	8	4	0	0	25	33	20	19	4	18	17	.320	.279	.350	6.20	6.57
Peralta, Ofelky	R-R	6-5	195	4-20-97	3	6	6.22	12	12	1	0	51	52	43	35	6	38	33	.265	.262	.269	5.86	6.75
Seabrooke, Travis	L-L	6-6	205	9-16-95	0	0	7.09	19	1	0	1	46	58	37	36	5	24	46	.302	.293	.309	9.07	4.73
Sedlock, Cody	R-R	6-3	200	6-19-95	0	2	7.97	6	6	0	0	20	27	19	18	3	12	13	.325	.200	.474	5.75	5.31
Silva, Isaac	L-L	6-2	190	9-12-92	1	1	6.59	7	0	0	0	14	18	12	10	4	6	11	.316	.143	.417	7.24	3.95
Teague, James	R-R	6-0	185	8-29-94	1	3	9.37	13	0	0	0	17	17	17	17	2	13	15	.339	.360	.325	8.27	7.16
Tillman, Chris	R-R	6-5	210	4-15-88	0	1	5.68	1	1	0	0	6	5	6	4	1	3	4	.288	.333	.167	5.68	4.26
Trowbridge, Matt	L-L	5-10	175	3-24-93	5	2	5.75	35	0	0	2	52	57	35	33	5	24	58	.281	.197	.331	10.10	4.18
Wells, Alex	L-L	6-1	190	2-27-97	7	8	3.47	24	24	0	0	135	142	56	52	19	33	101	.271	.270	.271	6.73	2.20

Fielding

Catcher	PCT	G	PO	A	E	DP	PB
Fajardo	.996	59	419	43	2	5	4
Levy	.992	46	362	32	3	3	3
Quevedo	.985	33	248	20	4	0	7

First Base	PCT	G	PO	A	E	DP
Escarra	1.000	7	55	1	0	3
Garcia	.991	59	403	29	4	31
Murphy	1.000	5	30	1	0	4
Palmeiro	.993	20	127	6	1	8
Woody	.992	52	374	20	3	31

Second Base	PCT	G	PO	A	E	DP
Juvier	.974	29	44	69	3	16
Palmeiro	.975	109	165	265	11	48
Schoop	1.000	1	1	3	0	0
Torres	.667	1	1	1	1	0

Third Base	PCT	G	PO	A	E	DP
Juvier	.933	24	7	35	3	5
Reyes	.889	101	71	138	26	12
Woody	.932	19	10	31	3	1

Shortstop	PCT	G	PO	A	E	DP
Clare	.974	120	196	260	12	59
Juvier	.948	21	31	42	4	8

Outfield	PCT	G	PO	A	E	DP
Billingsley	.993	118	270	15	2	5
Gassaway	.973	55	106	1	3	0
Gentry	1.000	3	8	0	0	0
Hogan	1.000	1	2	0	0	0
McKenna	.981	66	149	4	3	0
Nichting	.996	95	213	10	1	3
Rasmus	1.000	7	16	0	0	0
Ring	.985	71	128	2	2	0
Woody	.667	6	4	0	2	0

DELMARVA SHOREBIRDS

LOW CLASS A

SOUTH ATLANTIC LEAGUE

Batting	B-T	HT	WT	DOB	AVG	vLH	vRH	G	AB	R	H	2B	3B	HR	RBI	BB	HBP	SH	SF	SO	SB	CS	SLG	OBP
Becker, Branden	L-R	6-1	175	9-13-96	.273	.254	.277	93	341	40	93	15	0	4	41	24	5	0	2	76	1	1	.352	.328
Breazeale, Ben	L-R	6-0	208	10-21-94	.246	.167	.263	73	240	28	59	10	1	3	25	33	2	0	0	59	0	1	.333	.342
Carrillo, Jean	R-R	6-0	200	6-16-97	.253	.260	.250	67	229	18	58	4	1	3	29	18	6	1	0	52	0	0	.319	.324
Craport, Preston	R-R	5-11	201	8-12-96	.254	.226	.267	122	437	68	112	26	4	11	72	37	13	0	10	77	4	2	.410	.326
Crinella, Frank	R-R	5-11	188	6-9-94	.170	.385	.088	15	47	5	8	0	1	0	4	6	1	0	0	15	1	0	.213	.278
Curran, Seamus	L-R	6-6	245	9-6-97	.221	.220	.222	85	312	43	69	16	0	13	52	34	0	0	1	105	0	3	.397	.297
Encarnacion, Jean Carlos	R-R	6-3	195	1-17-98	.218	.250	.212	26	101	10	22	4	2	2	7	3	0	0	0	34	0	0	.356	.240

	B-T	HT	WT	DOB	AVG	vLH	vRH	G	AB	R	H	2B	3B	HR	RBI	BB	HBP	SH	SF	SO	SB	CS	SLG	OBP
2-team total (97 Rome)					.273	.278	.271	123	462	55	126	27	7	12	64	16	2	0	3	134	5	5	.439	.298
Ferguson, Jaylen	R-R	6-2	180	7-21-97	.171	.267	.146	24	70	9	12	2	0	2	5	3	2	0	0	27	0	0	.286	.227
Grenier, Cadyn	R-R	5-11	188	10-31-96	.216	.205	.220	43	162	23	35	12	2	1	13	17	2	1	1	53	3	2	.333	.297
Hogan, Max	L-R	5-11	195	9-24-93	.215	.180	.229	40	135	15	29	8	0	2	17	11	2	2	0	28	1	2	.319	.284
Jarrett, Zach	R-R	6-4	220	12-8-94	.277	.343	.253	129	501	74	139	26	6	14	72	41	10	0	3	136	4	2	.437	.342
McCoy, Mason	R-R	6-0	175	3-31-95	.266	.230	.278	124	482	66	128	18	10	4	47	45	4	1	3	95	13	2	.369	.332
Moesquit, Kirvin	B-R	5-8	165	3-10-95	.251	.308	.227	112	411	74	103	18	2	4	31	46	4	2	2	93	49	13	.333	.331
Nichting, T.J.	B-R	5-11	188	1-13-95	.326	.255	.361	36	144	21	47	10	1	1	20	7	1	0	1	25	3	1	.431	.360
Ripken, Ryan	L-L	6-6	205	7-26-93	.244	.220	.253	106	398	38	97	12	0	7	44	20	1	0	1	77	0	0	.327	.281
Robertson, Will	R-R	6-2	190	3-2-95	.238	.289	.215	111	386	46	92	27	1	8	37	16	8	0	3	85	0	2	.376	.281
Shaw, Chris	R-R	6-1	215	4-25-94	.185	.259	.132	19	65	6	12	3	0	2	6	3	3	0	1	22	0	0	.323	.250
Tavarez, Davis	R-R	6-2	190	1-7-99	.100	.200	.000	3	10	1	1	1	0	0	0	0	0	0	0	4	0	0	.200	.100
Torres, Alexis	R-R	6-0	183	12-12-97	.250	.667	.154	5	16	2	4	2	0	0	1	1	0	0	0	3	0	0	.375	.294

Pitching

	B-T	HT	WT	DOB	W	L	ERA	G	GS	CG	SV	IP	H	R	ER	HR	BB	SO	AVG	vLH	vRH	K/9	BB/9
Almengo, Diogenes	R-R	6-2	190	6-2-95	1	2	3.77	11	0	0	1	14	11	8	6	0	4	19	.204	.160	.241	11.93	2.51
Baumann, Michael	R-R	6-4	225	9-10-95	5	0	1.42	7	7	0	0	38	23	7	6	0	13	47	.180	.186	.172	11.13	3.08
Bishop, Cameron	L-L	6-4	215	2-14-96	9	7	2.94	22	22	1	0	126	107	47	41	5	20	99	.228	.177	.251	7.09	1.43
Bonilla, Brandon	R-L	6-3	200	10-21-93	0	4	3.18	7	6	0	0	23	15	13	8	2	16	27	.190	.177	.194	10.72	6.35
Burke, Scott	R-R	6-3	200	6-2-94	2	3	5.12	23	4	0	1	58	61	39	33	5	16	47	.275	.291	.257	7.29	2.48
Dietz, Matthias	R-R	6-5	220	9-20-95	6	2	3.56	13	13	0	0	66	56	26	26	2	36	67	.236	.209	.272	9.18	4.93
Fenter, Gray	R-R	6-0	200	1-25-96	3	3	6.75	14	2	0	0	27	31	23	20	3	13	31	.293	.275	.309	10.46	4.39
Gruener, Nick	R-R	6-0	185	5-16-95	1	0	4.56	13	0	0	0	26	25	13	13	1	3	23	.258	.318	.208	8.06	1.05
Hall, DL	L-L	6-2	195	9-19-98	2	7	2.10	22	20	0	0	94	68	31	22	6	42	100	.203	.246	.180	9.54	4.01
Hanifee, Brenan	R-R	6-5	180	5-29-98	8	6	2.86	23	23	1	0	132	120	48	42	8	22	85	.244	.256	.234	5.80	1.50
Hayes, Reed	R-R	6-3	185	3-17-95	0	3	5.50	20	0	0	5	36	30	26	22	3	26	31	.231	.238	.224	7.75	6.50
Katz, Alex	L-L	5-11	195	10-12-94	3	2	4.26	25	0	0	1	44	46	31	21	2	25	47	.277	.250	.296	9.54	5.08
Knutson, Max	L-L	6-2	205	4-1-95	3	0	1.15	19	0	0	1	39	16	7	5	1	18	42	.122	.132	.118	9.69	4.15
Lowther, Zac	L-L	6-2	235	4-30-96	3	1	1.16	6	6	0	0	31	12	4	4	2	9	51	.115	.037	.143	14.81	2.61
Ming, Cameron	L-L	6-1	177	5-2-96	2	2	3.96	22	2	0	1	61	57	30	27	4	15	60	.248	.171	.291	8.80	2.20
Muckenhirn, Zach	L-L	6-1	185	2-27-95	1	0	2.12	12	0	0	3	17	11	5	4	0	6	27	.172	.222	.135	14.29	3.18
Naughton, Timothy	R-R	6-3	195	11-14-95	3	4	4.45	24	0	0	5	32	36	22	16	1	22	33	.275	.318	.219	9.19	6.12
Peluffo, Jhon	R-R	6-3	140	6-16-97	4	6	5.31	16	16	0	0	81	92	55	48	11	19	54	.291	.253	.331	5.98	2.10
Perez, Luis	R-R	6-0	175	5-3-95	5	3	3.34	10	10	0	0	59	45	23	22	7	13	62	.206	.223	.191	9.40	1.97
Seabrooke, Travis	R-L	6-6	205	9-16-95	1	1	3.29	11	0	0	3	27	27	13	10	0	8	19	.260	.237	.273	6.26	2.63
Tillman, Chris	R-R	6-5	200	4-15-88	0	1	5.40	1	1	0	0	3	4	2	2	0	1	3	.308	.300	.333	8.10	2.70
Vespi, Nick	L-L	6-3	215	10-10-95	6	6	2.09	40	0	0	9	65	47	25	15	2	23	68	.198	.209	.192	9.46	3.20
Wilson, Ryan	L-L	6-1	190	11-6-96	0	3	3.50	23	2	0	0	62	52	29	24	4	31	58	.232	.197	.250	8.46	4.52

Fielding

C: Breazeale 59, Carrillo 66, Shaw 12. 1B: Craport 13, Curran 58, Ripken 66. 2B: Becker 39, Hogan 3, McCoy 32, Moesquit 59, Torres 5. 3B: Becker 30, Craport 87, Encarnacion 21. SS: Becker 7, Grenier 39, McCoy 89. OF: Craport 19, Crinella 11, Ferguson 22, Hogan 33, Jarrett 122, Moesquit 52, Nichting 36, Robertson 109, Tavarez 3.

ABERDEEN IRONBIRDS   SHORT-SEASON
NEW YORK-PENN LEAGUE

Batting	B-T	HT	WT	DOB	AVG	vLH	vRH	G	AB	R	H	2B	3B	HR	RBI	BB	HBP	SH	SF	SO	SB	CS	SLG	OBP
Arredondo, Bryndan	R-R	5-10	190	11-8-94	.077	.000	.087	12	26	2	2	0	0	1	4	6	0	0	0	10	0	0	.192	.250
Carmona, Jean	B-R	6-1	183	10-31-99	.226	.200	.229	24	93	9	21	7	0	0	7	6	1	0	0	25	0	1	.301	.280
Coolbaugh, Tyler	B-R	6-2	190	10-29-93	.000	—	.000	3	8	0	0	0	0	0	0	0	0	0	0	0	0	0	.000	.000
Curran, Seamus	L-R	6-6	245	9-6-97	.306	.200	.333	14	49	6	15	4	0	1	5	4	1	0	0	10	0	0	.449	.370
Escarra, J.C.	L-R	6-3	205	4-24-95	.332	.222	.344	51	178	30	59	10	2	6	34	18	9	0	1	22	0	0	.511	.418
Evans, Ian	R-R	5-11	185	7-10-96	.250	.500	.167	3	8	0	2	2	0	0	2	0	0	0	0	0	0	0	.500	.250
Ferguson, Jaylen	R-R	6-2	180	7-21-97	.160	.177	.155	24	75	8	12	3	0	1	8	5	0	0	3	31	1	0	.240	.205
Gassaway, Randolph	R-R	6-4	210	5-23-95	.191	.000	.200	6	21	2	4	0	0	0	2	2	1	0	0	4	0	0	.191	.292
Gonzalez, Alfredo	R-R	6-0	165	12-14-95	.240	.000	.277	27	75	8	18	1	0	0	5	9	0	0	0	16	0	1	.253	.321
Hall, Adam	R-R	6-0	170	5-22-99	.293	.208	.303	62	222	35	65	9	3	1	24	17	11	3	3	58	22	5	.374	.368
Hays, Austin	R-R	6-1	195	7-5-95	.189	.000	.200	9	37	6	7	2	0	0	3	2	0	0	0	7	0	0	.243	.231
Hoiles, Dalton	R-R	6-1	170	4-30-96	.146	.250	.094	19	48	8	7	2	0	0	3	10	1	0	0	11	0	0	.188	.305
Horvath, Nick	R-L	5-10	201	7-13-96	.238	.387	.202	47	160	28	38	11	2	4	22	21	2	1	2	48	3	0	.406	.330
Neustrom, Robert	L-L	6-2	208	11-12-96	.272	.231	.277	61	228	29	62	16	1	4	29	13	1	0	1	45	1	3	.404	.313
Ortega, Irving	R-R	6-2	165	10-30-96	.278	1.000	.188	8	18	4	5	0	1	0	1	2	0	0	1	2	0	1	.389	.333
Ramos, Milton	R-R	5-11	193	10-26-95	.241	.235	.242	35	116	8	28	7	0	1	9	2	1	2	0	22	2	0	.328	.261
Ring, Jake	L-L	5-11	175	8-11-94	.318	.000	.333	6	22	1	7	1	0	0	3	0	0	0	0	6	2	0	.364	.400
Ringhofer, Luke	L-R	6-1	210	2-19-96	.149	.250	.134	30	94	6	14	5	0	2	7	11	0	1	0	27	0	0	.202	.238
Roberts, Cody	R-R	6-1	195	6-16-96	.252	.292	.244	44	155	11	39	9	0	1	14	12	1	0	2	43	0	0	.329	.306
Santander, Anthony	R-R	6-2	190	10-19-94	.286	.500	.250	7	28	6	8	5	0	1	5	2	1	0	0	5	2	0	.571	.355
Thorburn, Robbie	L-R	5-11	175	3-30-95	.253	.360	.237	57	198	33	50	10	0	0	10	18	2	0	0	48	4	8	.303	.321
Torres, Alexis	R-R	6-0	183	12-12-97	.247	.290	.239	54	186	25	46	11	2	2	27	22	2	0	1	66	3	1	.360	.332
Turchin, Doran	R-R	6-2	195	7-7-97	.197	.200	.197	21	71	6	14	7	0	2	6	3	2	0	0	34	0	0	.380	.250
Xu, Guiyuan	L-L	6-0	188	1-29-96	.167	.667	.104	25	54	3	9	3	0	0	5	5	1	0	0	17	0	2	.222	.250
Yahn, Willy	R-R	5-11	185	11-7-95	.275	.394	.256	65	240	33	66	9	1	0	30	7	4	0	3	29	10	3	.321	.303

Pitching	B-T	HT	WT	DOB	W	L	ERA	G	GS	CG	SV	IP	H	R	ER	HR	BB	SO	AVG	vLH	vRH	K/9	BB/9
Almengo, Diogenes	R-R	6-2	190	6-2-95	0	2	3.95	11	0	0	3	14	12	8	6	0	6	17	.226	.130	.300	11.20	3.95

	B-T	HT	WT	DOB	W	L	ERA	G	GS	CG	SV	IP	H	R	ER	HR	BB	SO	AVG	vLH	vRH	K/9	BB/9
Bonilla, Brandon	R-L	6-3	200	10-21-93	1	1	2.19	9	0	0	0	12	7	3	3	0	3	18	.159	.048	.261	13.14	2.19
Conroy, Ryan	R-R	6-3	190	12-31-96	0	1	2.70	14	0	0	6	17	19	6	5	0	3	19	.288	.235	.344	10.26	1.62
Diaz, Jose	R-R	6-3	185	8-1-96	2	0	8.17	16	0	0	1	25	38	25	23	3	8	20	.352	.340	.362	11.71	2.84
Dominguez, Manuel	R-R	6-5	229	1-17-94	0	0	11.25	2	0	0	0	4	5	5	5	1	2	2	.313	.429	.222	4.50	4.50
Echevarria, Juan	R-R	6-3	195	6-25-97	2	2	4.39	17	0	0	1	27	28	18	13	3	11	22	.267	.343	.229	7.43	3.71
Fenter, Gray	R-R	6-0	200	1-25-96	5	3	3.95	13	11	1	0	57	41	25	25	5	25	60	.200	.207	.195	9.47	3.95
Garcia, Ruben	R-R	6-4	220	8-2-96	0	0	5.27	8	0	0	0	14	15	8	8	0	8	8	.294	.444	.212	5.27	5.27
Gruener, Nick	R-R	6-0	185	5-16-95	0	0	3.00	4	0	0	0	9	7	3	3	1	1	10	.219	.267	.177	10.00	1.00
Guance, Hector	R-R	6-6	200	7-12-95	7	6	3.98	15	14	2	0	72	64	41	32	2	30	60	.235	.283	.187	7.47	3.73
Hammonds, Matthew	L-L	6-4	205	5-23-95	4	3	3.74	12	10	0	0	65	53	28	27	4	22	62	.220	.203	.227	8.58	3.05
Joyner, Tyler	R-R	6-4	225	5-10-96	2	0	2.70	9	1	1	0	23	20	7	7	0	3	24	.220	.139	.273	9.26	1.16
Keaton, Josh	R-R	6-1	200	10-20-93	3	1	4.85	16	0	0	1	26	32	15	14	0	11	40	.294	.341	.262	13.85	3.81
Kipper, Jordan	R-R	6-4	185	10-6-92	0	0	0.00	3	3	0	0	4	2	0	0	0	0	4	.154	.400	.000	9.00	0.00
Knight, Blaine	R-R	6-3	165	6-28-96	0	1	2.61	4	4	0	0	10	13	3	3	1	3	8	.302	.208	.421	6.97	2.61
Magee, Kevin	L-L	6-2	210	1-1-96	3	1	1.51	13	3	0	0	36	26	7	6	1	9	32	.206	.150	.233	8.07	2.27
Matson, Zach	L-L	6-3	225	10-24-95	2	1	1.89	16	0	0	2	19	6	4	4	1	12	30	.100	.040	.143	14.21	5.68
Montgomery, J.J.	R-R	6-0	200	6-1-97	1	0	5.11	9	0	0	1	12	12	7	7	0	9	14	.250	.286	.222	10.22	6.57
Murphy, Jimmy	R-R	5-11	195	10-14-94	3	6	3.53	15	11	1	0	71	67	36	28	4	22	50	.246	.276	.217	6.31	2.78
Nolasco, Moises	R-R	6-4	170	2-2-97	0	0	3.00	2	0	0	1	3	2	1	1	0	1	4	.182	.250	.143	12.00	3.00
O'Rourke, Ryan	R-L	6-3	230	4-30-88	0	1	4.50	4	1	0	0	4	4	2	2	1	1	4	.267	.000	.364	9.00	2.25
Perez, Luis	R-R	6-0	175	5-3-95	1	0	0.56	3	3	0	0	16	4	1	1	1	5	14	.077	.042	.107	7.88	2.81
Rios, Willie	B-L	5-11	190	2-6-96	2	4	5.32	12	9	0	0	44	46	30	26	3	27	30	.272	.320	.252	6.14	5.52
Rodriguez, Leonardo	R-R	6-7	215	11-25-97	0	0	0.00	1	1	0	0	3	1	0	0	0	1	1	.111	.167	.000	3.38	3.38
Rodriguez, Yelin	L-L	6-3	200	11-3-98	0	0	9.00	1	0	0	0	1	1	3	1	0	4	0	.250	.000	.333	0.00	36.00
Romero, Victor	R-R	6-3	170	2-17-95	0	2	9.00	2	1	0	0	5	7	6	5	3	0	3	.318	.385	.222	5.40	0.00
Sedlock, Cody	R-R	6-3	190	6-19-95	0	1	2.57	2	2	0	0	7	6	2	2	0	2	5	.250	.308	.182	6.43	2.57
Tillman, Chris	R-R	6-5	200	4-15-88	0	0	13.50	1	1	0	0	2	2	3	3	0	2	1	.250	.500	.167	4.50	9.00
Vichio, Nick	R-R	6-0	190	4-21-95	0	1	2.51	15	0	0	1	29	23	12	8	0	10	27	.219	.250	.197	8.48	3.14

Fielding

C: Arredondo 6, Gonzalez 27, Ringhofer 17, Roberts 32. **1B:** Curran 13, Escarra 49, Evans 2, Ramos 2, Ringhofer 13. **2B:** Carmona 9, Coolbaugh 1, Hall 4, Ramos 17, Torres 45. **3B:** Carmona 4, Coolbaugh 2, Evans 1, Ortega 3, Ramos 7, Yahn 61. **SS:** Carmona 6, Hall 59, Ortega 5, Ramos 7, Torres 1. **OF:** Ferguson 22, Gassaway 1, Hays 5, Hoiles 16, Horvath 47, Neustrom 48, Ring 6, Roberts 2, Santander 5, Thorburn 48, Turchin 21, Xu 14.

GCL ORIOLES — ROOKIE

GULF COAST LEAGUE

Batting	B-T	HT	WT	DOB	AVG	vLH	vRH	G	AB	R	H	2B	3B	HR	RBI	BB	HBP	SH	SF	SO	SB	CS	SLG	OBP
Baez, Carlos	R-R	6-3	175	11-22-97	.204	.265	.185	43	137	9	28	3	0	0	5	4	2	1	0	45	2	2	.226	.238
Beaird, Matt	L-R	6-0	205	5-24-96	.152	.154	.151	23	66	3	10	2	0	1	10	8	3	0	2	25	0	0	.227	.266
Brown, Jacob	R-R	5-9	190	2-16-99	.190	.161	.200	32	116	12	22	2	0	4	14	8	2	1	1	44	0	0	.310	.252
Denning, Jared	L-R	5-11	205	4-30-97	.132	.286	.109	18	53	4	7	1	0	1	3	12	1	0	0	12	0	0	.208	.303
Estrada, Jaime	L-R	5-10	170	12-15-95	.167	.000	.182	3	12	0	2	0	0	0	0	1	0	0	0	4	0	0	.167	.231
Evans, Ian	R-R	5-11	185	7-10-96	.222	.167	.240	46	167	14	37	7	0	0	16	14	6	0	2	25	0	1	.264	.302
Fregia, Andrew	R-R	6-1	170	12-18-96	.222	.143	.250	31	108	10	24	3	2	2	11	8	6	0	0	28	0	1	.343	.312
Gates, Jared	L-R	6-0	205	3-28-96	.289	.353	.274	28	90	9	26	5	0	1	11	4	1	0	1	21	0	1	.378	.323
Ham, John	R-R	5-10	190	8-27-96	.205	.152	.222	38	132	23	27	6	1	1	11	16	3	0	2	32	1	1	.288	.301
Jayne, Andrew	R-R	6-4	195	8-11-99	.212	.200	.214	20	52	4	11	2	0	0	2	6	7	0	0	21	0	0	.250	.369
Jones, Markel	B-R	5-10	175	8-8-94	.250	.150	.278	27	92	16	23	4	1	0	8	17	0	0	0	22	4	3	.315	.367
Lizarraga, Jose	R-R	5-10	190	8-27-97	.270	.214	.286	21	63	4	17	1	0	0	5	5	1	1	0	4	0	0	.286	.333
McLeod, Zachary	R-R	6-1	200	1-19-96	.309	.600	.244	15	55	8	17	3	0	1	7	5	0	0	0	10	0	0	.418	.367
Montanez, Jose	R-R	6-1	200	7-13-98	.250	.300	.233	34	116	12	29	5	0	0	11	12	2	0	1	23	1	0	.293	.328
Montes, Juan	R-R	6-2	185	5-15-95	.301	.389	.280	29	93	12	28	5	0	2	13	7	7	1	1	22	2	1	.419	.389
Ortega, Irving	R-R	6-2	165	10-30-96	.247	.250	.246	23	85	14	21	1	0	0	8	10	1	1	0	11	2	1	.259	.333
Tavarez, Davis	R-R	6-2	190	1-7-99	.187	.188	.187	31	107	6	20	1	1	0	2	4	2	0	0	21	0	1	.215	.230
Truitt, Trey	R-R	6-1	190	6-29-96	.161	.179	.156	40	137	7	22	7	1	1	8	8	3	2	3	53	0	0	.248	.219
Whitley, Trey	R-R	6-2	180	2-9-00	.186	.161	.235	31	81	6	13	3	1	0	6	9	1	2	1	29	0	1	.222	.302
Wilkerson, Steve	B-R	6-1	195	1-11-92	.500	.000	.600	2	6	0	3	1	0	0	2	0	0	0	0	2	1	0	.667	.500

Pitching	B-T	HT	WT	DOB	W	L	ERA	G	GS	CG	SV	IP	H	R	ER	HR	BB	SO	AVG	vLH	vRH	K/9	BB/9
Bautista, Felix	R-R	6-5	190	6-20-95	0	2	4.33	12	1	0	0	27	25	14	13	1	10	30	.253	.208	.294	10.00	3.33
Ciolli, Andrew	R-R	6-5	190	3-28-96	0	2	7.47	18	0	0	1	16	22	18	13	0	14	6	.344	.400	.276	3.45	8.04
Conroy, Ryan	R-R	6-3	190	12-31-96	0	0	6.75	1	1	0	0	4	4	2	2	0	1	2	.364	.429	.250	6.75	3.38
De La Rosa, Matt	L-R	6-2	210	11-15-93	3	0	1.69	17	0	0	2	16	12	10	3	0	11	7	.207	.179	.233	3.94	6.19
Dominguez, Manuel	R-R	6-5	229	1-17-94	0	4	2.87	16	1	0	0	31	33	18	10	1	10	23	.268	.344	.194	6.61	2.87
Hacker, Cody	R-R			6-18-00	0	2	5.02	12	0	0	0	14	19	11	8	0	14	12	.333	.286	.349	7.53	8.79
Hammonds, Matthew	L-L	6-4	205	5-23-95	1	0	5.40	1	1	0	0	5	7	3	3	0	1	4	.350	.429	.308	7.20	1.80
Joyner, Tyler	R-R	6-4	225	5-10-96	1	0	4.09	4	0	0	0	11	17	6	5	0	0	11	.362	.370	.350	9.00	0.00
Lee, Chris	L-L	6-3	180	8-17-92	0	1	12.00	3	3	0	0	3	7	5	4	2	5	4	.438	.500	.429	15.00	6.00
Litscher, Dallas	R-R	6-8	250	1-10-96	0	0	5.00	12	8	0	0	36	34	20	20	3	14	31	.246	.246	.246	7.75	3.50
Lleras, Yeancarlos	R-R	6-0	150	7-22-00	1	2	8.31	10	5	0	0	22	27	22	20	2	15	11	.318	.262	.372	4.57	6.23
Magee, Kevin	L-L	6-2	210	1-1-96	0	0	3.86	2	0	0	0	2	2	1	1	1	1	3	.250	.000	.500	11.57	3.86
Marinez, Jhan	R-R	6-1	190	8-12-88	0	0	0.00	1	1	0	0	1	2	0	0	0	1	2	.400	1.000	.250	18.00	9.00
McFadden, Parker	R-R	6-0	200	6-1-97	0	0	7.36	5	0	0	0	4	4	3	3	0	10	3	.091	.200	.000	7.36	24.55
Meservey, Nick	L-L	6-5	221	9-10-95	0	1	6.23	6	0	0	0	4	4	3	3	0	7	6	.250	.000	.308	12.46	14.54
Montgomery, J.J.	R-R	6-0	200	6-1-97	0	0	0.00	1	0	0	0	1	0	0	0	0	1	0	.000	1.000	.000	0.00	9.00

	B-T	HT	WT	DOB	W	L	ERA	G	GS	CG	SV	IP	H	R	ER	HR	BB	SO	AVG	vLH	vRH	K/9	BB/9
Montville, Jason	L-L	6-2	215	11-16-96	0	3	8.44	15	0	0	0	21	32	23	20	2	13	27	.340	.261	.366	11.39	5.48
Nolasco, Moises	R-R	6-4	170	2-2-97	1	1	3.63	17	1	0	1	40	37	18	16	1	14	37	.248	.276	.219	8.39	3.18
O'Rourke, Ryan	R-L	6-3	230	4-30-88	0	1	0.00	5	0	0	0	5	2	2	0	0	9		.125	.333	.000	17.36	0.00
Rodriguez, Grayson	L-R	6-5	220	11-16-99	0	2	1.40	9	8	0	0	19	17	6	3	0	7	20	.236	.158	.324	9.31	3.26
Rodriguez, Leonardo	R-R	6-7	215	11-25-97	1	7	4.34	12	10	0	0	48	45	31	23	1	23	37	.256	.253	.259	6.99	4.34
Rodriguez, Yelin	L-L	6-3	200	11-3-98	0	0	1.63	13	2	0	0	28	20	8	5	0	10	26	.204	.333	.139	8.46	3.25
Rom, Drew	L-L	6-2	170	12-15-99	0	2	1.76	10	9	0	0	31	20	9	6	1	6	28	.184	.139	.206	8.22	1.76
Sandridge, Jayvien	L-L	6-5	220	2-11-99	3	0	2.00	15	0	0	0	18	10	7	4	1	12	18	.167	.053	.220	9.00	6.00
Sedlock, Cody	R-R	6-3	190	6-19-95	0	0	0.93	5	1	0	0	10	5	1	1	0	4	10	.161	.125	.200	9.31	3.72
Stauffer, Adam	R-R	6-7	240	1-13-99	0	2	5.84	6	0	0	0	12	17	10	8	1	5	6	.333	.310	.364	4.38	3.65
Wernet, Gillian	R-R	6-3	210	10-1-98	0	1	11.12	4	0	0	0	6	8	7	7	0	8	4	.333	.417	.250	6.35	12.71
Zebron, Jake	R-R	6-3	180	2-4-00	1	3	2.97	11	3	0	1	30	30	14	10	0	7	20	.259	.259	.258	5.93	2.08

Fielding

C: Beaird 20, Denning 8, Lizarraga 16, Montanez 16. **1B:** Evans 45, Gates 1, Montanez 1, Montes 11. **2B:** Baez 17, Ham 37, McLeod 5, Wilkerson 1. **3B:** Baez 24, Fregia 1, Gates 25, Ham 1, McLeod 8, Montes 2. **SS:** Baez 5, Fregia 29, McLeod 2, Ortega 22, Wilkerson 1. **OF:** Brown 27, Fregia 1, Jayne 16, Jones 26, Montes 8, Tavarez 29, Truitt 40, Whitley 28.

DSL ORIOLES
ROOKIE
DOMINICAN SUMMER LEAGUE

Batting	B-T	HT	WT	DOB	AVG	vLH	vRH	G	AB	R	H	2B	3B	HR	RBI	BB	HBP	SH	SF	SO	SB	CS	SLG	OBP
Barcenas, Richard	R-R	6-2	182	10-22-97	.276	.222	.288	29	98	12	27	1	2	1	10	4	0	1	0	21	3	2	.357	.304
Bautista, Welbin	R-R	6-0	203	5-7-98	.243	.100	.266	25	74	6	18	6	0	0	10	4	1	0	0	22	0	2	.324	.291
Castro, Ricardo	R-R	6-0	185	12-5-98	.261	.100	.295	60	230	32	60	6	4	0	22	20	4	0	0	59	8	4	.322	.331
Ciriaco, Bryan	R-R	6-1	199	3-29-97	.105	.154	.091	29	57	3	6	0	0	0	5	8	4	0	1	24	1	0	.105	.257
Cruz, Josue	L-L	6-4	175	12-25-00	.140	.065	.157	51	178	15	25	7	0	0	10	13	4	0	1	93	1	1	.180	.214
Estevez, Marcos	R-R	6-0	185	7-12-95	.200	.250	.188	26	80	14	16	8	1	1	13	19	2	0	1	13	4	0	.363	.363
Gonzalez, Frank	L-R	5-11	176	3-5-97	.169	.250	.155	32	83	13	14	3	3	0	11	16	2	0	0	34	0	2	.277	.317
Grullon, Wilkin	R-R	6-0	220	11-28-99	.206	.214	.204	28	68	6	14	2	0	0	7	8	4	0	1	19	2	0	.235	.321
Herrera, Josue	R-R	6-0	165	2-3-97	.245	.159	.267	64	216	30	53	8	1	4	18	34	5	0	0	42	5	5	.347	.361
Jimenez, Hansel	L-L	5-11	181	7-10-96	.151	.071	.170	36	73	8	11	2	1	0	11	25	0	1	2	22	5	0	.206	.360
Leon, Hector	B-R	5-9	171	2-19-01	.207	.212	.206	55	169	17	35	6	0	0	8	25	3	3	3	36	5	11	.243	.315
Mendez, Carlos	R-R	6-4	235	2-15-98	.113	.111	.114	19	53	5	6	0	0	0	2	8	3	0	2	26	0	0	.113	.258
Olivares, Oscar	R-R	6-1	223	9-3-98	.243	.275	.235	56	202	32	49	12	2	0	26	22	3	0	2	55	4	1	.322	.323
Rojas, Edidson	L-R	6-3	193	5-14-99	.259	.238	.264	63	220	34	57	9	1	2	24	39	6	0	1	60	8	7	.336	.384
Santana, Luis	R-R	6-1	160	6-3-99	.207	.000	.250	29	82	10	17	2	0	0	6	5	2	0	1	14	2	4	.232	.267
Tolentino, Frank	R-R	6-1	170	8-5-99	.299	.400	.281	17	67	14	20	2	1	1	8	7	1	0	0	21	2	0	.403	.373
Ventura, Edwin	R-R	6-1	180	8-27-97	.233	.231	.233	60	215	34	50	5	1	0	32	23	4	0	4	43	25	4	.265	.313
Vizcaino, Hector	R-R	6-2	175	3-16-00	.166	.070	.192	54	199	30	33	6	1	1	10	19	7	1	2	68	10	5	.221	.260

Pitching	B-T	HT	WT	DOB	W	L	ERA	G	GS	CG	SV	IP	H	R	ER	HR	BB	SO	AVG	vLH	vRH	K/9	BB/9
Alejandro, Jose	R-R	6-3	200	6-20-95	1	2	2.30	22	0	0	4	31	19	12	8	0	16	45	.167	.140	.183	12.93	4.60
Angomas, Cesar	L-L	6-3	226	4-19-00	2	2	5.15	14	14	0	0	51	48	32	29	0	37	43	.265	.286	.264	7.64	6.57
Arias, Johsson	R-R	6-1	189	4-3-94	4	3	2.81	16	8	0	0	51	46	24	16	1	20	52	.241	.242	.240	9.12	3.51
Brito, Oscar	R-R	6-5	209	12-25-95	2	1	4.78	18	0	0	1	32	31	24	17	1	19	28	.254	.306	.233	7.88	5.34
Constante, Marlon	R-R	5-11	185	7-5-96	3	3	1.67	21	0	0	6	38	30	12	7	0	8	50	.208	.366	.146	11.95	1.91
Daza, Manuel	R-R	6-1	176	9-22-96	4	1	1.03	19	0	0	2	44	24	5	5	0	12	55	.161	.203	.133	11.34	2.47
Dominguez, Manuel	R-R	6-5	229	1-17-94	1	1	1.00	4	4	0	0	18	10	6	2	0	5	12	.156	.000	.182	6.00	2.50
Falconett, Pablo	R-R	6-2	220	10-28-00	1	2	1.88	14	0	0	1	24	14	9	5	0	9	24	.159	.263	.130	9.00	3.38
Gomez, Jose	R-R	6-3	202	9-23-96	4	2	2.35	14	14	0	0	69	52	28	18	1	17	67	.203	.226	.192	8.74	2.22
Herrera, Juan	R-R	6-1	180	1-28-96	5	1	3.02	19	0	0	3	42	34	21	14	1	15	43	.221	.237	.216	9.29	3.24
Lopez, Edinson	L-L	6-0	185	6-5-98	2	5	2.15	15	10	0	0	50	44	18	12	0	21	52	.232	.261	.228	9.30	3.75
Martinez, Jose	R-R	6-1	174	2-2-00	0	1	6.00	16	0	0	0	18	22	21	12	1	30	13	.301	.304	.300	6.50	15.00
Montero, Reynier	R-R	6-2	165	10-29-96	1	1	9.15	14	0	0	0	21	24	28	21	1	17	22	.282	.310	.268	9.58	7.40
Nolasco, Moises	R-R	6-4	170	2-2-97	1	0	1.00	2	2	0	0	9	6	3	1	0	1	14	.216	.333	.194	14.00	1.00
Pujols, Antonio	L-L	6-3	195	1-27-98	1	3	1.92	13	13	0	0	52	40	15	11	0	25	60	.219	.308	.204	10.45	4.35
Rodriguez, Jose A	R-R	6-1	190	12-27-95	1	1	3.91	10	1	0	1	23	27	13	10	0	5	13	.300	.286	.304	5.09	1.96
Tejada, Miguel	R-R	6-2	200	4-12-00	0	0	24.00	4	0	0	0	3	5	8	8	0	3	4	.400	.400		9.00	9.00
Vizcaino, Dember	R-R	6-5	239	5-12-95	3	3	2.92	19	0	0	0	37	37	16	12	1	16	36	.255	.277	.245	8.76	3.89
Wernet, Gillian	R-R	6-3	210	10-1-98	2	2	2.86	6	6	0	0	22	20	11	7	2	9	17	.250	.313	.208	6.95	3.68

Fielding

C: Bautista 20, Grullon 20, Mendez 19, Santana 26. **1B:** Bautista 1, Ciriaco 10, Gonzalez 11, Herrera 54, Santana 2, Ventura 2. **2B:** Ciriaco 1, Gonzalez 13, Herrera 2, Leon 46, Rojas 21. **3B:** Ciriaco 14, Gonzalez 5, Olivares 54, Rojas 11. **SS:** Gonzalez 1, Leon 15, Rojas 10, Vizcaino 53. **OF:** Barcenas 20, Castro 58, Cruz 32, Estevez 25, Jimenez 30, Rojas 1, Tolentino 17, Ventura 56.

Boston Red Sox

SEASON IN A SENTENCE: A potent lineup and strong rotation helped the Red Sox put together one of the greatest seasons in baseball history.

HIGH POINT: After steamrolling their way through the regular season and the first two rounds of the playoffs, the Red Sox manhandled the Dodgers, four games to one, to win their fourth World Series title since 2004. They did so with a mix of superstars young and old, a pair of savvy trade acquisitions and a resurgent David Price. The lefthander sloughed off a series of playoff stinkers in previous seasons to pitch the clinching game at Dodger Stadium. About the only quibble you'll hear from Red Sox fans is that their team didn't clinch a single postseason series at Fenway Park.

LOW POINT: Finding a valley in a season full of peaks is not a particularly easy task, but on June 21 the Red Sox were two games back of the Yankees for the lead in the American League East. They went up by a game on July 2 and never looked back.

NOTABLE ROOKIES: Righty reliever Ryan Brasier was the team's most impactful rookie, racking up a 2-0, 1.60 mark in 34 games. Brasier had gone five seasons since his last major league action (with the Angels) and had spent time in Japan before the Red Sox signed him to a minor league deal in March.

KEY TRANSACTIONS: Their biggest acquisition of the offseason was obviously J.D. Martinez. Boston inked the slugger to a five-year, $110 million deal two weeks into spring training after a disjointed and contentious winter across the sport. His acquisition gave the lineup a huge boost and put the finishing touches on one of the best lineups in history. Dombrowski turned shortstop Santiago Espinal and lefthander Jalen Beeks into slugger Steve Pearce and fireballer Nathan Eovaldi, then watched as his reinforcements thrived.

DOWN ON THE FARM: Third baseman Bobby Dalbec was the clear star of a barren system. The hulking Arizona product led the organization in homers (32) and RBIs (109) and did it with raw power that can match nearly anybody in the minor leagues. Lefthander Jay Groome, the team's top pick in the 2016 draft, had Tommy John surgery in May, wiping away the rest of the 2018 season and probably a good chunk of the 2019 campaign as well. Their first-rounder in 2018, first baseman Triston Casas, broke his thumb early in his pro debut and was limited to just four at-bats.

OPENING DAY PAYROLL: $206,247,686 (2nd).

PLAYERS OF THE YEAR

STEVE MARTINE

MAJOR LEAGUE	MINOR LEAGUE
Mookie Betts	**Bobby Dalbec**
OF	3B
.346/.438/.640	(High Class A/Double-A)
Led MLB in AVG, SLG	.257/.361/.558
and runs (129)	32 HR, 109 RBIs

ORGANIZATION LEADERS

Batting		*Minimum 250 AB
MAJORS		
* AVG	Mookie Betts	.346
* OPS	Mookie Betts	1.078
HR	J.D. Martinez	43
RBI	J.D. Martinez	130
MINORS		
* AVG	Rusney Castillo, Pawtucket	.319
* OBP	Michael Osinski, Greenville, Salem	.370
* SLG	Bobby Dalbec, Salem, Portland	.558
* OPS	Bobby Dalbec, Salem, Portland	.919
R	Bobby Dalbec, Salem, Portland	73
H	Rusney Castillo, Pawtucket	151
TB	Bobby Dalbec, Salem, Portland	254
2B	Bobby Dalbec, Salem, Portland	35
3B	Jarren Duran, Lowell, Greenville	11
HR	Bobby Dalbec, Salem, Portland	32
RBI	Bobby Dalbec, Salem, Portland	109
BB	Josh Ockimey, Portland, Pawtucket	70
SO	Kervin Suarez, Greenville	178
SB	Tyler Hill, Salem	27

Pitching		#Minimum 75 IP
MAJORS		
W	Rick Porcello	17
# ERA	Chris Sale	2.11
SO	Chris Sale	237
SV	Craig Kimbrel	42
MINORS		
W	Denyi Reyes, Greenville, Salem	12
L	Teddy Stankiewicz, Portland, Pawtucket	14
# ERA	Denyi Reyes, Greenville, Salem	1.97
G	Robby Scott, Pawtucket	45
GS	Jhonathan Diaz, Greenville, Salem	27
GS	Kutter Crawford, Greenville, Salem	27
SV	Ryan Brasier, Pawtucket	13
IP	Jhonathan Diaz, Greenville, Salem	157
BB	Darwinzon Hernandez, Salem, Portland	66
BB	Kevin McAvoy, Portland, Salem	66
SO	Kutter Crawford, Greenville, Salem	157
# AVG	Denyi Reyes, Greenville, Salem	.210

2018 PERFORMANCE

General Manager: Dave Dombrowski. **Farm Director:** Ben Crockett. **Scouting Director:** Mike Rikard.

Class	Team	League	W	L	PCT	Finish	Manager
Majors	Boston Red Sox	American	108	54	.667	1st (15)	Alex Cora
Triple-A	Pawtucket Red Sox	International	66	73	.475	9th (14)	Kevin Boles
Double-A	Portland Sea Dogs	Eastern	63	76	.453	10th (12)	Darren Fenster
High A	Salem Red Sox	Carolina	63	75	.457	8th (10)	Joe Oliver
Low A	Greenville Drive	South Atlantic	64	75	.460	12th (14)	Iggy Suarez
Short season	Lowell Spinners	New York-Penn	37	38	.493	9th (14)	Corey Wimberly
Rookie	GCL Red Sox	Gulf Coast	33	22	.600	3rd (18)	Tom Kotchman
Overall 2018 Minor League Record			326	359	.512	20th (30)	

ORGANIZATION STATISTICS

BOSTON RED SOX
AMERICAN LEAGUE

Batting	B-T	HT	WT	DOB	AVG	vLH	vRH	G	AB	R	H	2B	3B	HR	RBI	BB	HBP	SH	SF	SO	SB	CS	SLG	OBP
Benintendi, Andrew	L-L	5-10	170	7-6-94	.290	.247	.305	148	579	103	168	41	6	16	87	71	2	2	7	106	21	3	.465	.366
Betts, Mookie	R-R	5-9	180	10-7-92	.346	.368	.339	136	520	129	180	47	5	32	80	81	8	0	5	91	30	6	.640	.438
Bogaerts, Xander	R-R	6-1	210	10-1-92	.289	.269	.294	136	513	72	148	45	3	23	103	55	6	0	6	102	8	2	.522	.360
Bradley Jr., Jackie	L-R	5-10	200	4-19-90	.234	.185	.251	144	474	76	111	33	4	13	59	46	11	0	4	137	17	1	.403	.314
Butler, Dan	R-R	5-10	210	10-17-86	.167	.000	.200	2	6	0	1	0	0	0	1	0	0	0	1	2	0	0	.167	.143
Devers, Rafael	L-R	6-0	237	10-24-96	.240	.229	.244	121	450	59	108	24	0	21	66	38	0	0	2	121	5	2	.433	.298
Holt, Brock	L-R	5-10	180	6-11-88	.277	.292	.273	109	321	41	89	18	2	7	46	37	7	0	2	73	7	7	.411	.362
Kinsler, Ian	R-R	6-0	200	6-22-82	.242	.167	.271	37	132	17	32	6	0	1	16	10	0	0	1	24	7	3	.311	.294
2-team total (91 Los Angeles)					.240	.191	.259	128	487	66	117	26	0	14	48	40	4	0	3	64	16	7	.380	.302
Leon, Sandy	B-R	5-10	225	3-13-89	.177	.153	.187	89	265	30	47	12	0	5	22	15	4	3	1	75	1	0	.279	.232
Lin, Tzu-Wei	L-R	5-9	155	2-15-94	.246	.063	.306	37	65	15	16	6	1	1	6	8	0	0	0	17	0	1	.415	.329
Martinez, J.D.	R-R	6-3	220	8-21-87	.330	.336	.329	150	569	111	188	37	2	43	130	69	4	0	7	146	6	1	.629	.402
Moreland, Mitch	L-L	6-2	230	9-6-85	.245	.242	.246	124	404	57	99	23	4	15	68	50	0	0	5	102	2	0	.433	.325
Nunez, Eduardo	R-R	6-0	195	6-15-87	.265	.260	.267	127	480	56	127	23	3	10	44	16	2	1	3	69	7	2	.388	.289
Pearce, Steve	R-R	5-11	200	4-13-83	.279	.302	.265	50	136	19	38	8	1	7	26	22	5	0	2	27	0	0	.507	.394
2-team total (26 Toronto)					.284	.304	.266	76	215	35	61	14	1	11	42	29	5	0	2	41	0	0	.512	.379
Pedroia, Dustin	R-R	5-9	175	8-17-83	.091	.000	.125	3	11	1	1	0	0	0	0	2	0	0	0	1	0	0	.091	.231
Phillips, Brandon	R-R	6-0	211	6-28-81	.130	.088	.182	9	23	4	3	0	0	1	2	4	0	0	0	7	0	0	.261	.259
Ramirez, Hanley	R-R	6-2	235	12-23-83	.254	.333	.230	44	177	25	45	7	0	6	29	14	2	0	2	35	4	1	.396	.313
Renda, Tony	R-R	5-8	179	1-24-91	—	—	—	1	0	1	0	0	0	0	0	0	0	0	0	0	0	0	—	—
Swihart, Blake	B-R	6-0	200	4-3-92	.229	.131	.275	82	192	28	44	10	0	3	18	15	0	0	0	57	6	1	.328	.285
Travis, Sam	R-R	6-0	205	8-27-93	.222	.067	.333	19	36	5	8	3	0	1	7	2	0	0	0	10	0	0	.389	.263
Vazquez, Christian	R-R	5-9	195	8-21-90	.207	.231	.199	80	251	24	52	10	0	3	16	13	4	1	0	41	4	1	.283	.258

Pitching	B-T	HT	WT	DOB	W	L	ERA	G	GS	CG	SV	IP	H	R	ER	HR	BB	SO	AVG	vLH	vRH	K/9	BB/9
Barnes, Matt	R-R	6-4	210	6-17-90	6	4	3.65	62	0	0	0	62	47	25	25	5	31	96	.204	.225	.192	14.01	4.52
Beeks, Jalen	L-L	5-11	195	7-10-93	0	1	12.79	2	1	0	0	6	11	9	9	1	4	5	.379	.571	.318	7.11	5.68
2-team total (12 Tampa Bay)					5	1	5.51	14	1	0	0	51	52	31	31	6	24	42	.268	.196	.291	7.46	4.26
Brasier, Ryan	R-R	6-0	225	8-26-87	2	0	1.60	34	0	0	0	34	19	6	6	2	7	29	.171	.232	.109	7.75	1.87
Cuevas, William	B-R	6-2	215	10-14-90	0	2	7.41	9	1	0	0	17	20	14	14	3	11	20	.294	.267	.316	10.59	5.82
Eovaldi, Nathan	R-R	6-2	225	2-13-90	3	3	3.33	12	11	0	0	54	57	28	20	3	12	48	.266	.259	.275	8.00	2.00
2-team total (10 Tampa Bay)					6	7	3.81	22	21	0	0	111	105	55	47	14	20	101	.246	.254	.239	8.19	1.62
Haley, Justin	R-R	6-5	230	6-16-91	0	0	4.70	4	0	0	0	8	10	4	4	2	3	0	.323	.400	.286	0.00	3.52
Hembree, Heath	R-R	6-4	210	1-13-89	4	1	4.20	67	0	0	0	60	53	30	28	10	27	76	.234	.186	.262	11.40	4.05
Johnson, Brian	L-L	6-4	235	12-7-90	4	5	4.17	38	13	0	0	99	104	49	46	16	38	87	.263	.218	.279	7.88	3.44
Kelly, Joe	R-R	6-1	190	6-9-88	4	2	4.39	73	0	0	2	66	57	34	32	4	32	68	.234	.211	.254	9.32	4.39
Kimbrel, Craig	R-R	6-0	210	5-28-88	5	1	2.74	63	0	0	42	62	31	19	19	7	31	96	.146	.153	.139	13.86	4.48
Pomeranz, Drew	R-L	6-6	240	11-22-88	2	6	6.08	26	11	0	0	74	87	53	50	12	44	66	.297	.281	.301	8.03	5.35
Porcello, Rick	R-R	6-5	205	12-27-88	17	7	4.28	33	33	1	0	191	177	97	91	27	48	190	.241	.241	.240	8.94	2.26
Poyner, Bobby	L-L	6-0	205	12-1-92	1	0	3.22	20	0	0	0	22	22	8	8	4	3	24	.256	.143	.292	9.67	1.21
Price, David	L-L	6-5	215	8-26-85	16	7	3.58	30	30	1	0	176	151	75	70	25	50	177	.230	.210	.234	9.05	2.56
Rodriguez, Eduardo	L-L	6-2	220	4-7-93	13	5	3.82	27	23	0	0	130	119	66	55	16	45	146	.238	.234	.238	10.13	3.12
Sale, Chris	L-L	6-6	180	3-30-89	12	4	2.11	27	27	0	0	158	102	39	37	11	34	237	.181	.170	.183	13.50	1.94
Scott, Robby	B-L	6-3	220	8-29-89	0	1	8.10	9	0	0	0	7	10	6	6	2	5	8	.333	.222	.381	10.80	6.75
Smith, Carson	R-R	6-6	215	10-19-89	1	1	3.77	18	0	0	0	14	14	6	6	2	6	18	.241	.100	.316	11.30	3.77
Thornburg, Tyler	R-R	5-11	190	9-29-88	2	0	5.63	25	0	0	0	24	28	15	15	6	10	21	.295	.308	.286	7.88	3.75
Velazquez, Hector	R-R	6-0	180	11-26-88	7	2	3.18	47	8	0	0	85	97	35	30	7	26	53	.290	.276	.301	5.61	2.75
Walden, Marcus	R-R	6-0	195	9-13-88	0	0	3.68	8	0	0	0	15	14	7	6	0	3	14	.255	.227	.273	8.59	1.84
Workman, Brandon	R-R	6-5	235	8-13-88	6	1	3.27	43	0	0	0	41	34	15	15	6	16	37	.230	.204	.245	8.06	3.48
Wright, Steven	R-R	6-2	215	8-30-84	3	1	2.68	20	4	0	1	54	41	17	16	5	26	42	.210	.255	.193	7.04	4.36

Fielding

Catcher	PCT	G	PO	A	E	DP	PB
Butler	1.000	2	7	1	0	0	1
Leon	.999	87	776	37	1	4	13
Swihart	1.000	28	146	9	0	1	0
Vazquez	.996	75	650	27	3	3	11

First Base	PCT	G	PO	A	E	DP
Holt	1.000	7	25	1	0	4
Moreland	.998	116	739	68	2	52
Pearce	.994	31	160	14	1	12
Ramirez	1.000	25	182	8	0	19
Swihart	.980	10	44	4	1	4
Travis	1.000	3	10	0	0	2

Second Base	PCT	G	PO	A	E	DP
Betts	1.000	1	0	2	0	0
Holt	1.000	56	90	91	0	24
Kinsler	.984	37	59	67	2	16
Lin	1.000	4	8	4	0	3
Nunez	.982	74	92	121	4	25

	PCT	G	PO	A	E	DP
Pedroia	1.000	3	7	7	0	1
Phillips	.800	5	2	2	1	0
Swihart	1.000	1	1	1	0	1

Third Base	PCT	G	PO	A	E	DP
Devers	.926	116	57	245	24	14
Holt	1.000	5	4	5	0	0
Lin	1.000	1	0	4	0	0
Nunez	.971	45	30	71	3	3
Phillips	.667	4	2	0	1	0
Swihart	1.000	3	2	1	0	1
Vazquez	.000	2	0	0	0	0

Shortstop	PCT	G	PO	A	E	DP
Bogaerts	.980	136	163	336	10	65

	PCT	G	PO	A	E	DP
Holt	.982	23	18	36	1	3
Lin	.948	23	18	37	3	8

Outfield	PCT	G	PO	A	E	DP
Benintendi	.984	144	241	12	4	2
Betts	.996	131	272	5	1	0
Bradley Jr.	.982	143	326	9	6	3
Holt	1.000	16	15	0	0	0
Lin	.500	6	1	0	1	0
Martinez	1.000	57	116	3	0	1
Pearce	1.000	4	1	0	0	0
Swihart	1.000	21	20	0	0	0
Travis	.909	7	10	0	1	0

PAWTUCKET RED SOX — TRIPLE-A

INTERNATIONAL LEAGUE

Batting	B-T	HT	WT	DOB	AVG	vLH	vRH	G	AB	R	H	2B	3B	HR	RBI	BB	HBP	SH	SF	SO	SB	CS	SLG	OBP
Barfield, Jeremy	R-L	6-5	245	7-12-88	.132	.065	.167	26	91	9	12	3	0	2	6	12	2	0	2	34	0	0	.231	.243
Betts, Jordan	R-R	6-3	220	10-6-91	.265	.296	.247	36	121	13	32	9	0	3	16	12	0	0	1	38	0	0	.413	.328
Bogaerts, Xander	R-R	6-1	210	10-1-92	.667	.500	1.000	1	3	1	2	1	0	1	1	0	0	0	0	0	0	0	2.000	.667
Butler, Dan	R-R	5-10	210	10-17-86	.212	.283	.189	67	212	21	45	9	0	6	26	31	4	1	2	44	0	0	.340	.321
Castillo, Rusney	R-R	5-9	195	7-9-87	.319	.329	.314	117	474	56	151	31	0	5	59	29	4	0	4	80	13	7	.416	.360
Chavis, Michael	R-R	5-10	216	8-11-95	.273	.111	.333	8	33	8	9	3	0	2	7	1	0	0	0	12	0	0	.546	.294
De Jesus Jr., Ivan	R-R	5-11	200	5-1-87	.261	.229	.273	97	349	33	91	16	0	4	31	32	7	1	5	69	2	3	.341	.331
De La Guerra, Chad	L-R	5-11	190	11-24-92	.137	.138	.136	22	73	6	10	2	0	1	4	1	1	0	1	21	2	0	.206	.158
Devers, Rafael	L-R	6-0	237	10-24-96	.333	.250	.353	6	21	3	7	2	0	1	2	1	0	0	0	6	0	0	.571	.364
Flores, Ramon	L-L	5-10	190	3-26-92	.215	.172	.237	56	195	13	42	7	1	3	17	23	1	2	2	42	2	1	.308	.299
Hernandez, Oscar	R-R	6-1	230	7-9-93	.205	.158	.221	47	151	16	31	7	0	1	14	14	3	2	1	37	1	0	.272	.284
Holt, Brock	L-R	5-10	180	6-11-88	.333	.333	—	1	3	0	1	0	0	0	0	0	0	0	0	0	0	0	.333	.333
Lin, Tzu-Wei	L-R	5-9	155	2-15-94	.307	.324	.301	68	277	33	85	20	2	5	25	23	1	1	0	64	3	4	.448	.362
Lind, Adam	L-L	6-2	195	7-17-83	.216	.191	.225	47	171	21	37	7	0	8	32	14	0	0	4	36	0	0	.398	.270
2-team total (16 Scranton/Wilkes-Barre)					.223	.228	.221	63	229	28	51	11	0	10	39	19	0	0	4	49	0	1	.402	.278
Lopez, Deiner	B-R	6-0	165	5-30-94	.250	.500	.200	7	24	2	6	2	0	1	2	1	0	0	0	7	0	0	.458	.280
Miller, Mike	R-R	5-9	170	9-27-89	.284	.314	.274	102	320	42	91	12	0	4	31	30	3	3	5	53	10	5	.359	.346
Ockimey, Josh	L-R	6-1	215	10-18-95	.215	.130	.243	27	93	10	20	2	0	5	15	11	1	0	0	37	1	0	.398	.305
Ohlman, Mike	R-R	6-5	240	12-14-90	.208	.290	.174	69	236	28	49	6	0	10	28	36	1	0	3	91	1	0	.360	.312
Olt, Mike	R-R	6-2	210	8-27-88	.224	.224	.224	71	228	37	51	14	0	11	27	45	3	1	1	86	0	0	.430	.357
Ortega, Jonathan	R-R	5-8	185	9-27-96	.000	—	.000	2	3	1	0	0	0	0	0	0	0	0	0	0	0	0	.000	.000
Pedroia, Dustin	R-R	5-9	175	8-17-83	.071	.000	.111	5	14	1	1	0	0	0	0	3	0	0	0	3	0	0	.071	.235
Phillips, Brandon	R-R	6-0	211	6-28-81	.302	.378	.277	38	149	29	45	14	0	4	19	9	2	0	1	26	1	1	.477	.348
Renda, Tony	R-R	5-8	179	1-24-91	.288	.333	.272	42	170	30	49	8	1	2	11	11	2	0	1	31	6	1	.382	.337
Sturgeon, Cole	L-L	6-0	180	9-17-91	.214	.149	.240	67	238	20	51	6	1	3	20	9	2	3	1	61	8	2	.286	.277
Tavarez, Aneury	L-R	5-9	175	4-14-92	.226	.165	.249	104	394	46	89	18	2	8	34	30	3	1	3	104	9	5	.343	.284
Travis, Sam	R-R	6-0	205	8-27-93	.258	.284	.248	97	361	35	93	13	0	8	43	29	4	0	4	89	1	2	.360	.317
Vazquez, Christian	R-R	5-9	195	8-21-90	.273	.000	.375	3	11	1	3	0	0	0	1	1	0	0	0	1	0	0	.273	.333
Witte, Jantzen	R-R	6-2	195	1-4-90	.252	.167	.288	29	103	13	26	6	2	2	13	7	2	1	0	32	1	0	.408	.313
Wren, Kyle	L-L	5-10	175	4-23-91	.230	.222	.233	37	126	7	29	6	1	1	15	15	0	0	2	34	4	2	.318	.308

Pitching	B-T	HT	WT	DOB	W	L	ERA	G	GS	CG	SV	IP	H	R	ER	HR	BB	SO	AVG	vLH	vRH	K/9	BB/9
Beeks, Jalen	L-L	5-11	195	7-10-93	5	5	2.89	16	16	0	0	87	70	33	28	10	25	117	.215	.220	.213	12.06	2.58
Brasier, Ryan	R-R	6-0	225	8-26-87	2	5	1.34	34	0	0	13	40	29	10	6	1	8	40	.215	.145	.274	8.93	1.79
Buttrey, Ty	L-R	6-6	230	3-31-93	1	1	2.25	32	0	0	1	44	36	16	11	4	14	64	.216	.231	.202	13.09	2.86
Cuevas, William	B-R	6-2	215	10-14-90	10	7	3.39	23	23	0	0	135	120	59	51	17	38	121	.235	.237	.233	8.05	2.53
Elias, Roenis	L-L	6-1	205	8-1-88	1	0	1.23	4	0	0	1	7	2	2	1	1	2	9	.083	.000	.118	11.05	2.45
Gorst, Matthew	R-R	6-1	205	8-24-94	0	2	4.12	11	0	0	0	20	20	13	9	3	3	10	.221	.220	.314	4.58	1.37
Haley, Justin	R-R	6-5	230	6-16-91	6	8	3.80	22	22	0	0	114	124	52	48	10	33	107	.277	.271	.283	8.47	2.61
Jerez, Williams	L-L	6-4	200	5-16-92	1	3	3.63	34	0	0	5	52	48	22	21	6	24	69	.241	.231	.246	11.94	4.15
Jimenez, Dedgar	L-L	6-3	240	3-6-96	1	0	3.00	1	1	0	0	6	5	2	2	0	1	4	.238	.125	.308	6.00	1.50
Kelley, Trevor	R-R	6-2	210	10-20-93	1	1	1.54	13	0	0	1	23	21	6	4	1	9	20	.247	.212	.269	7.71	3.47
Kent, Matthew	L-L	6-0	180	9-13-92	0	0	6.75	1	0	0	0	5	7	4	4	0	1	6	.292	.286	.294	10.13	1.69
Lakins, Travis	R-R	6-1	180	6-29-94	1	0	1.65	10	0	0	2	16	11	6	3	1	5	15	.186	.200	.177	8.27	2.76
Maddox, Austin	R-R	6-2	220	5-13-91	1	0	24.55	1	0	0	0	4	12	10	10	2	8	4	.522	.471	.667	9.82	19.64
Martin, Kyle	R-R	6-7	230	1-18-91	3	2	3.33	30	0	0	1	51	39	24	19	2	28	57	.211	.200	.219	9.99	4.91
Pomeranz, Drew	R-L	6-6	240	11-22-88	0	2	5.49	5	5	0	0	20	16	12	12	7	13	12	.225	.250	.218	5.49	5.95
Poyner, Bobby	L-L	6-0	205	12-1-92	0	0	3.14	33	0	0	6	43	43	17	15	4	11	35	.259	.300	.236	7.33	2.30
Rodriguez Jr., Fernando	R-R	6-3	235	6-18-84	3	4	3.20	30	6	0	2	65	50	28	23	10	26	71	.215	.234	.197	9.88	3.62
Scott, Robby	B-L	6-3	220	8-29-89	3	3	1.86	45	0	0	3	48	35	13	10	1	21	63	.200	.148	.228	11.73	3.91
Shawaryn, Mike	R-R	6-3	205	9-17-94	3	2	3.93	7	6	1	0	37	30	16	16	6	13	34	.221	.192	.254	8.10	2.70
Shepherd, Chandler	R-R	6-3	185	8-25-92	7	10	3.89	25	25	0	0	130	142	66	56	13	34	107	.271	.259	.281	7.43	2.36
Smith, Josh A.	R-R	6-2	220	8-7-87	5	6	4.14	18	10	0	1	74	75	35	34	5	16	76	.258	.248	.269	9.24	1.95
Smith, Josh D.	L-L	6-3	200	10-11-88	9	5	3.01	28	14	0	0	99	85	35	33	4	43	97	.232	.219	.237	8.85	3.92
Stankiewicz, Teddy	R-R	6-4	215	11-25-93	0	1	27.00	1	1	0	0	2	7	6	6	1	3	1	.583	.600	.571	4.50	13.50

	B-T	HT	WT	DOB	W	L	ERA	G	GS	CG	SV	IP	H	R	ER	HR	BB	SO	AVG	vLH	vRH	K/9	BB/9
Taylor, Josh	L-L	6-5	225	3-2-93	0	0	0.00	1	0	0	0	2	1	0	0	0	0	3	.143	.000	.250	13.50	0.00
Thornburg, Tyler	R-R	5-11	190	9-29-88	0	1	4.26	15	1	0	0	13	11	7	6	3	6	11	.216	.238	.200	7.82	4.26
Velazquez, Hector	R-R	6-0	180	11-26-88	0	0	0.00	1	0	0	0	1	0	0	0	0	0	1	.000	.000	.000	9.00	0.00
Walden, Marcus	R-R	6-0	195	9-13-88	0	4	4.96	18	5	0	2	33	44	24	18	2	17	24	.317	.310	.324	6.61	4.68
Weems, Jordan	L-R	6-3	175	11-7-92	0	0	5.40	2	0	0	0	3	3	2	2	1	4	1	.250	.500	.200	2.70	10.80
Workman, Brandon	R-R	6-5	235	8-13-88	2	1	3.90	17	0	0	1	30	21	14	13	3	5	34	.191	.182	.197	10.20	1.50
Wright, Steven	R-R	6-2	215	8-30-84	0	0	3.78	5	3	0	0	17	20	9	7	0	4	9	.294	.308	.276	4.86	2.16

Fielding

Catcher	PCT	G	PO	A	E	DP	PB
Butler	.998	67	596	37	1	7	6
Hernandez	.988	47	368	32	5	7	2
Ohlman	.989	27	247	11	3	0	8
Vazquez	1.000	2	16	0	0	1	0

First Base	PCT	G	PO	A	E	DP
Betts	.989	12	81	8	1	7
Chavis	1.000	1	8	1	0	0
De Jesus Jr.	1.000	1	12	0	0	0
Lind	.989	25	172	15	2	24
Ockimey	.956	20	120	9	6	9
Ohlman	.972	18	133	7	4	11
Olt	.965	16	99	11	4	11
Travis	.994	45	299	22	2	32
Witte	1.000	4	23	4	0	3

Second Base	PCT	G	PO	A	E	DP
De Jesus Jr.	.966	51	83	113	7	26
De La Guerra	.939	9	13	18	2	4

	PCT	G	PO	A	E	DP
Lin	1.000	6	4	7	0	2
Lopez	.962	5	13	12	1	5
Miller	.966	34	56	57	4	13
Olt	1.000	1	0	1	0	0
Pedroia	1.000	4	4	5	0	1
Phillips	.965	19	31	51	3	12
Renda	.967	20	43	44	3	14
Witte	1.000	1	2	0	0	0

Third Base	PCT	G	PO	A	E	DP
Betts	.946	20	11	24	2	3
Chavis	.667	4	3	1	2	0
De Jesus Jr.	.958	29	29	40	3	4
De La Guerra	1.000	6	3	13	0	1
Devers	.917	5	4	7	1	0
Lin	1.000	2	1	1	0	0
Olt	.930	40	30	50	6	6
Phillips	1.000	8	5	11	0	0
Renda	1.000	9	9	16	0	1
Witte	.924	24	20	41	5	5

Shortstop	PCT	G	PO	A	E	DP
Bogaerts	1.000	1	0	1	0	1
De Jesus Jr.	.945	17	20	32	3	4
De La Guerra	.750	5	5	7	4	2
Holt	1.000	1	2	3	0	0
Lin	.961	51	75	123	8	32
Lopez	1.000	2	0	6	0	0
Miller	.987	65	94	128	3	31
Ortega	1.000	1	5	1	0	0

Outfield	PCT	G	PO	A	E	DP
Barfield	1.000	14	30	0	0	0
Castillo	1.000	105	235	4	0	2
Flores	.988	50	83	2	1	1
Lin	1.000	9	26	0	0	0
Renda	.957	12	22	0	1	0
Sturgeon	.980	67	144	3	3	1
Tavarez	.989	94	171	4	2	0
Travis	.983	37	57	2	1	0
Wren	.990	36	91	4	1	1

PORTLAND SEA DOGS
EASTERN LEAGUE
DOUBLE-A

Batting	B-T	HT	WT	DOB	AVG	vLH	vRH	G	AB	R	H	2B	3B	HR	RBI	BB	HBP	SH	SF	SO	SB	CS	SLG	OBP
Betts, Jordan	R-R	6-3	220	10-6-91	.223	.193	.234	58	211	22	47	6	0	8	22	14	4	1	2	61	0	0	.365	.281
Bladel, Johnny	R-R	6-1	190	4-20-91	.170	.200	.158	49	141	21	24	6	0	6	23	2	0	1	41	6	2	.213	.293
Chavis, Michael	R-R	5-10	216	8-11-95	.303	.400	.278	33	122	23	37	7	0	6	17	13	4	0	0	35	3	1	.508	.389
Dalbec, Bobby	R-R	6-4	225	6-29-95	.261	.238	.267	29	111	14	29	8	1	6	24	6	5	0	2	46	0	0	.514	.323
De La Guerra, Chad	L-R	5-11	190	11-24-92	.266	.153	.299	80	316	51	84	13	2	15	54	32	6	0	2	96	4	1	.462	.343
Gregor, Conrad	L-R	6-3	225	2-27-92	.057	.000	.065	12	35	2	2	0	0	1	3	6	1	0	0	12	0	0	.143	.214
Lopez, Deiner	B-R	6-0	165	5-30-94	.226	.071	.282	46	159	15	36	11	3	2	18	7	1	0	1	43	2	4	.371	.262
Lovullo, Nick	R-R	6-0	175	12-1-93	.203	.245	.187	58	187	23	38	8	1	2	14	22	2	3	0	39	1	0	.289	.294
Lucena, Isaias	B-R	5-11	180	11-15-94	.250	.250	.250	8	20	0	5	0	0	0	2	5	0	2	0	5	0	0	.250	.400
Madden, Charlie	R-R	6-3	205	9-1-95	.000	.000	.000	1	4	0	0	0	0	0	0	0	0	0	0	2	0	0	.000	.000
Madera, Chris	R-R	5-10	190	8-23-92	.200	.286	.179	18	70	10	14	2	1	0	5	2	0	1	2	10	2	0	.257	.216
Mars, Danny	B-R	6-0	195	1-22-94	.256	.281	.246	125	411	62	105	21	3	3	32	45	4	6	3	97	19	5	.343	.333
Matheny, Tate	R-R	6-0	185	2-9-94	.254	.291	.241	114	398	50	101	19	5	2	41	41	3	1	3	126	12	10	.342	.326
Nishioka, Tanner	R-R	5-11	180	10-22-94	.300	.250	.333	3	10	2	3	2	0	0	0	0	0	0	0	3	0	0	.500	.300
Nunez, Jhon	B-R	5-9	165	12-5-94	.241	.273	.229	70	232	28	56	7	3	2	21	21	5	1	2	46	4	3	.323	.315
Ockimey, Josh	L-R	6-1	215	10-18-95	.254	.198	.283	90	311	43	79	19	2	15	56	59	1	0	5	112	0	1	.473	.370
Olt, Mike	R-R	6-2	210	8-27-88	.000	.000	.000	3	10	0	0	0	0	0	1	0	1	0	1	4	0	0	.000	.083
Procyshen, Jordan	L-R	5-10	185	3-11-93	.125	.000	.143	2	8	1	1	0	0	0	0	0	0	0	0	5	0	0	.125	.125
Quiroz, Esteban	L-R	5-7	175	2-17-92	.299	.278	.304	24	87	19	26	5	0	7	24	13	4	0	0	19	1	1	.598	.414
Rei, Austin	R-R	6-0	185	10-27-93	.249	.246	.250	83	265	25	66	13	2	7	31	36	9	0	3	72	2	1	.393	.355
Renda, Tony	R-R	5-8	175	1-24-91	.371	.348	.378	26	97	19	36	11	0	3	16	9	2	0	0	13	4	1	.577	.435
Rivera, Jeremy	B-R	5-9	150	1-30-95	.262	.250	.265	120	497	70	130	16	1	5	42	29	2	2	2	86	12	8	.328	.304
Sturgeon, Cole	L-L	6-0	180	9-17-91	.365	.333	.374	31	126	19	46	9	0	6	18	12	1	0	1	20	5	0	.579	.421
Tendler, Luke	L-R	5-11	190	8-25-91	.273	.152	.305	108	374	43	102	18	0	15	62	33	5	0	6	94	1	2	.441	.335
Tobias, Josh	B-R	5-9	195	11-23-92	.228	.158	.239	34	123	12	28	4	0	1	8	7	0	2	2	32	1	0	.285	.265
Vazquez, Christian	R-R	5-9	195	8-21-90	.500	.500	—	1	2	1	1	0	0	0	3	0	0	0	1	0	0	0	.500	.333
Witte, Jantzen	R-R	6-2	195	1-4-90	.277	.299	.269	75	278	43	77	18	1	10	50	31	4	0	2	74	6	3	.457	.356

Pitching	B-T	HT	WT	DOB	W	L	ERA	G	GS	CG	SV	IP	H	R	ER	HR	BB	SO	AVG	vLH	vRH	K/9	BB/9
Ball, Trey	L-L	6-6	185	6-27-94	4	4	7.58	34	1	0	0	65	97	60	55	11	26	56	.340	.255	.385	7.71	3.58
Cooney, Harrison	R-R	6-2	175	3-23-92	0	1	12.27	9	0	0	0	11	15	15	15	2	16	7	.256	.211	.292	5.73	13.09
Cosart, Jake	R-R	6-2	175	2-11-94	2	2	5.94	19	0	0	0	36	39	33	24	6	15	45	.271	.270	.272	11.15	3.72
Gorst, Matthew	R-R	6-1	205	8-24-94	2	0	0.00	9	0	0	1	20	10	1	0	0	7	15	.141	.097	.175	6.64	3.10
Hart, Kyle	L-L	6-5	170	11-23-92	7	9	3.57	24	24	1	0	139	139	68	55	12	49	100	.258	.217	.279	6.49	3.18
Hernandez, Darwinzon	L-L	6-2	245	12-17-96	0	0	3.00	5	0	0	0	6	6	3	2	0	6	10	.250	.250	.250	15.00	9.00
Jimenez, Dedgar	L-L	6-3	240	3-6-96	10	7	4.39	25	24	2	0	137	124	69	67	18	55	116	.242	.200	.260	7.60	3.60
Kelley, Trevor	R-R	6-2	210	10-20-93	1	2	3.82	28	0	0	5	33	31	17	14	1	13	25	.254	.255	.253	6.82	3.55
Kent, Matthew	L-L	6-0	180	9-13-92	11	8	3.58	27	23	0	0	143	143	66	57	13	35	123	.257	.241	.264	7.72	2.20
Lakins, Travis	R-R	6-1	180	6-29-94	2	2	2.61	26	6	0	1	38	27	16	11	3	13	42	.192	.175	.202	9.95	3.08
Lau, Adam	R-R	6-2	210	7-5-94	0	4	4.13	36	0	0	3	57	57	32	26	9	28	59	.265	.231	.290	9.37	4.45
Maddox, Austin	R-R	6-2	220	5-13-91	0	1	9.00	1	0	0	0	2	3	3	2	2	0	1	.375	.500	.250	4.50	0.00

Name	B-T	HT	WT	DOB	W	L	ERA	G	GS	CG	SV	IP	H	R	ER	HR	BB	SO	AVG	vLH	vRH	K/9	BB/9
Martinez, Algenis	R-R	6-1	185	9-12-93	0	0	0.00	1	0	0	1	2	1	0	0	0	0	1	.143	.167	.000	4.50	0.00
McAvoy, Kevin	R-R	6-4	210	7-21-93	0	2	8.64	9	7	0	0	33	36	34	32	4	32	28	.277	.362	.208	7.56	8.64
McGrath, Daniel	R-L	6-3	205	7-7-94	3	3	3.63	33	11	0	1	89	88	40	36	4	37	79	.262	.214	.286	7.96	3.73
O'Linger, Durin	L-R	5-10	185	10-10-93	0	1	23.14	1	1	0	0	2	6	7	6	1	3	1	.429	.556	.200	3.86	11.57
Oliver, Jared	R-R	6-1	185	2-1-93	0	0	21.94	4	0	0	0	5	10	15	13	0	10	8	.400	.400	.400	13.50	16.88
Pimentel, Yankory	R-R	6-2	210	9-29-93	0	1	10.22	7	0	0	0	12	16	17	14	5	13	15	.327	.188	.394	10.95	9.49
Pomeranz, Drew	R-L	6-6	240	11-22-88	1	0	3.38	1	1	0	0	5	4	2	2	1	3	4	.211	.091	.375	6.75	5.06
Poyner, Bobby	L-L	6-0	205	12-1-92	0	0	0.00	1	1	0	0	1	1	0	0	0	0	2	.250	.000	.333	9.00	0.00
Rodriguez, Eduardo	L-L	6-2	220	4-7-93	0	0	0.00	2	2	0	0	8	3	0	0	0	4	14	.111	.000	.158	15.75	4.50
Shawaryn, Mike	R-R	6-2	200	9-17-94	6	8	3.28	19	19	1	0	113	100	45	41	7	27	99	.238	.229	.246	7.91	2.16
Smith, Josh D.	L-L	6-3	200	10-11-89	0	0	5.79	2	0	0	0	5	7	6	3	0	1	6	.318	.000	.467	11.57	1.93
Stankiewicz, Teddy	R-R	6-4	215	11-25-93	8	13	4.67	25	19	1	0	148	156	87	77	23	39	114	.269	.279	.260	6.92	2.37
Taylor, Josh	L-L	6-5	225	3-2-93	2	5	3.79	33	0	0	8	36	42	18	15	1	18	37	.294	.318	.283	9.34	4.54
Thornburg, Tyler	R-R	5-11	190	9-29-88	0	0	7.36	3	0	0	0	4	4	3	3	1	2	4	.286	.667	.000	9.82	4.91
Weems, Jordan	L-R	6-3	175	11-7-92	4	4	4.04	34	0	0	5	42	44	28	19	3	22	45	.275	.250	.296	9.57	4.68

Fielding

Catcher	PCT	G	PO	A	E	DP	PB
Lucena	.969	8	56	7	2	0	0
Nunez	.988	55	396	33	5	0	4
Procyshen	.929	2	11	2	1	0	0
Rei	.983	81	588	42	11	4	10
Vazquez	1.000	1	6	0	0	0	0

Catcher	PCT	G	PO	A	E	DP	PB
Lopez	.964	18	41	40	3	12	
Lovullo	.974	53	94	128	6	36	
Nishioka	.833	2	3	7	2	1	
Quiroz	.989	19	37	49	1	10	
Renda	.950	5	9	10	1	2	
Rivera	1.000	5	6	9	0	2	
Witte	.667	1	1	1	1	0	

Shortstop	PCT	G	PO	A	E	DP
De La Guerra	.974	21	20	54	2	14
Lopez	.941	3	6	10	1	2
Lovullo	1.000	3	4	9	0	2
Rivera	.967	114	124	285	14	48

First Base	PCT	G	PO	A	E	DP
Betts	.987	29	217	17	3	18
Chavis	1.000	11	72	5	0	5
Dalbec	1.000	2	17	0	0	2
Gregor	.947	4	18	0	1	0
Lopez	1.000	1	7	0	0	0
Ockimey	.976	71	537	35	14	54
Olt	1.000	2	15	0	0	0
Renda	1.000	1	4	1	0	0
Witte	.994	25	171	7	1	22

Third Base	PCT	G	PO	A	E	DP
Betts	.929	13	7	19	2	3
Chavis	.913	18	11	31	4	4
Dalbec	.909	18	13	27	4	3
De La Guerra	.943	17	8	25	2	3
Lopez	.895	6	3	14	2	0
Lovullo	1.000	2	3	4	0	1
Olt	1.000	1	2	2	0	0
Renda	.778	6	3	4	2	0
Tobias	.938	28	21	39	4	1
Witte	.968	37	28	64	3	6

Outfield	PCT	G	PO	A	E	DP
Bladel	1.000	48	98	1	0	0
Lopez	.917	18	21	1	2	0
Madera	1.000	18	57	1	0	1
Mars	.996	124	244	8	1	3
Matheny	.978	112	267	4	6	1
Renda	1.000	9	11	0	0	0
Sturgeon	1.000	30	67	1	0	0
Tendler	.983	70	116	3	2	0
Witte	1.000	11	12	2	0	0

Second Base	PCT	G	PO	A	E	DP
De La Guerra	.958	42	77	84	7	28

SALEM RED SOX   HIGH CLASS A
CAROLINA LEAGUE

Batting	B-T	HT	WT	DOB	AVG	vLH	vRH	G	AB	R	H	2B	3B	HR	RBI	BB	HBP	SH	SF	SO	SB	CS	SLG	OBP
Acosta, Victor	R-R	5-11	160	6-2-96	.253	.154	.292	30	91	5	23	9	0	0	12	10	1	2	2	7	0	1	.352	.327
Baldwin, Roldani	R-R	5-11	175	3-16-96	.233	.250	.227	53	202	21	47	7	0	7	27	10	5	0	3	44	2	0	.371	.282
Chatham, C.J.	R-R	6-4	185	12-22-94	.315	.308	.318	95	362	42	114	14	1	3	43	21	4	0	5	72	10	4	.384	.355
Dalbec, Bobby	R-R	6-4	225	6-29-95	.256	.258	.255	100	344	59	88	27	2	26	85	60	8	0	7	130	3	1	.573	.372
Downs, Jerry	L-L	6-2	215	12-22-93	.233	.188	.248	116	407	50	95	15	2	15	52	34	26	1	3	92	3	4	.391	.330
Espinal, Santiago	R-R	5-10	175	11-13-94	.313	.360	.293	65	256	53	80	15	3	7	32	18	4	0	3	35	9	1	.477	.363
Hill, Tyler	R-R	6-0	195	3-4-96	.254	.226	.265	124	426	67	108	20	1	1	38	54	10	4	4	60	27	10	.312	.348
Kemp, Trenton	R-R	6-0	195	9-30-95	.202	.276	.168	59	183	24	37	9	2	9	25	21	1	0	0	68	2	2	.421	.288
Lopez, Deiner	R-R	6-0	165	5-30-94	.280	.308	.250	7	25	5	7	1	1	0	2	4	0	0	0	7	3	1	.400	.379
Lovullo, Nick	R-R	6-0	175	12-1-93	.200	.200	.200	18	50	3	10	0	0	0	2	3	0	0	0	9	0	2	.200	.245
Lucena, Isaias	B-R	5-11	180	11-15-94	.400	.500	.333	2	5	0	2	1	0	0	0	0	0	0	0	2	0	0	.600	.400
Madera, Chris	R-R	5-10	190	8-23-92	.221	.191	.231	102	322	42	71	11	1	2	31	37	4	4	7	46	13	16	.280	.303
Netzer, Brett	L-R	6-0	190	6-4-96	.270	.229	.288	124	481	50	130	31	3	2	50	37	5	2	7	115	3	8	.360	.325
Nunez, Jhon	B-R	5-9	165	12-5-94	.286	.200	.297	13	42	3	12	2	0	0	7	6	0	0	2	10	4	0	.333	.360
Osinski, Michael	R-R	6-2	195	8-4-95	.294	.314	.287	54	187	28	55	8	0	1	22	16	5	1	2	37	7	2	.353	.362
Procyshen, Jordan	R-R	5-10	185	3-11-93	.226	.174	.239	38	115	15	26	4	1	0	15	14	2	0	2	28	0	2	.278	.316
Romanski, Jake	R-R	5-11	200	12-22-90	.224	.130	.273	19	67	9	15	3	1	1	6	2	1	1	1	9	1	0	.343	.254
Rusconi, Jagger	B-R	5-11	165	7-18-96	.218	.214	.220	24	78	7	17	7	0	0	3	6	0	1	0	28	3	1	.308	.274
Sciortino, Nick	R-R	5-9	197	7-21-95	.197	.234	.171	42	117	12	23	5	0	0	5	20	1	3	2	49	1	2	.239	.314
Scott, Ryan	L-R	6-2	195	7-6-93	.194	.239	.177	96	324	38	63	15	4	6	38	35	1	3	2	90	2	4	.321	.274
Tobias, Josh	B-R	5-9	195	11-23-92	.308	.310	.307	28	104	15	32	4	0	4	11	8	2	1	0	21	2	2	.462	.368
Tovar, Carlos	R-R	5-11	170	8-20-95	.222	.179	.239	37	99	11	22	1	1	0	4	6	2	1	0	24	0	0	.253	.280
Washington, Kyri	R-R	5-11	220	7-11-94	.253	.227	.262	25	83	10	21	6	0	4	10	10	4	0	0	35	1	2	.470	.361
Wren, Jordan	L-L	6-0	195	9-23-94	.318	.333	.314	15	44	13	14	0	1	1	3	9	1	0	0	15	2	2	.432	.444

Pitching	B-T	HT	WT	DOB	W	L	ERA	G	GS	CG	SV	IP	H	R	ER	HR	BB	SO	AVG	vLH	vRH	K/9	BB/9
Ahearn, Taylor	R-R	6-1	190	11-25-94	0	1	1.69	5	0	0	0	11	12	5	2	1	1	11	.286	.292	.278	9.28	0.84
Cooney, Harrison	R-R	6-2	175	3-23-92	2	0	3.00	7	0	0	2	12	7	4	4	2	6	20	.156	.174	.136	15.00	4.50
Cosart, Jake	R-R	6-2	175	2-11-94	3	1	3.65	18	0	0	5	25	26	12	10	0	9	32	.263	.317	.224	11.68	3.28
Crawford, Kutter	R-R	6-1	192	4-1-96	2	3	4.31	6	6	0	0	31	28	15	15	0	14	37	.239	.234	.243	10.63	4.02
De Jesus, Enmanuel	L-L	6-3	190	12-10-96	0	2	11.17	3	2	0	0	10	20	12	12	0	3	8	.435	.375	.467	7.45	2.79
Diaz, Jhonathan	R-L	6-0	170	9-13-96	0	1	6.23	11	1	0	0	4	7	3	3	1	2	6	.368	.400	.357	8.31	4.15
Feltman, Durbin	R-R	6-0	205	4-18-97	1	0	2.19	11	0	0	1	12	12	3	3	0	4	15	.261	.238	.280	10.95	2.92

Name	B-T	HT	WT	DOB	W	L	ERA	G	GS	CG	SV	IP	H	R	ER	HR	BB	SO	AVG	vLH	vRH	K/9	BB/9
Glorius, Austin	R-R	6-3	205	5-10-93	1	2	10.24	8	0	0	0	10	12	12	11	1	11	14	.293	.294	.292	13.03	10.24
Gonzalez, Daniel	R-R	6-5	180	2-9-96	8	8	5.01	29	11	0	3	111	135	70	62	13	29	99	.295	.300	.291	8.00	2.34
Gorst, Matthew	R-R	6-1	205	8-24-94	1	2	1.59	20	0	0	8	28	20	7	5	1	7	33	.200	.256	.158	10.48	2.22
Hernandez, Darwinzon	L-L	6-2	245	12-17-96	9	5	3.56	23	23	0	0	101	80	43	40	1	60	124	.220	.214	.223	11.05	5.35
Houck, Tanner	R-R	6-5	210	6-29-96	7	11	4.24	23	23	0	0	119	110	68	56	11	60	111	.245	.274	.219	8.39	4.54
Martinez, Algenis	R-R	6-1	185	9-12-93	4	0	3.94	33	0	0	6	82	85	39	36	11	19	75	.274	.295	.255	8.20	2.08
Martinez, Joan	R-R	6-3	195	8-29-96	2	2	5.19	28	0	0	2	50	47	29	29	6	36	54	.254	.267	.242	9.66	6.44
Mata, Bryan	R-R	6-3	160	5-3-99	6	3	3.50	17	17	0	0	72	58	33	28	1	58	61	.229	.310	.145	7.63	7.25
McAvoy, Kevin	R-R	6-4	210	7-21-93	1	6	5.74	16	8	0	1	58	56	38	37	3	34	56	.262	.290	.240	8.69	5.28
Montgomery, Mark	R-R	6-0	200	8-30-90	0	0	16.20	2	0	0	0	2	2	3	3	0	1	1	.286	.333	.250	5.40	5.40
O'Linger, Durin	L-R	5-10	185	10-10-93	0	1	3.65	6	0	0	0	12	12	8	5	2	8	10	.240	.219	.278	7.30	5.84
Oliver, Jared	R-R	6-1	185	2-1-93	4	3	3.67	32	0	0	1	56	47	26	23	3	52	73	.228	.208	.250	11.66	8.31
Pimentel, Yankory	R-R	6-2	210	9-29-93	1	1	5.36	27	0	0	2	47	63	32	28	5	23	28	.317	.319	.314	5.36	4.40
Raudes, Roniel	R-R	6-1	160	1-16-98	2	5	3.67	11	11	0	0	54	58	24	22	2	19	35	.276	.341	.227	5.83	3.17
Requena, Hildemaro	R-R	6-2	170	7-20-97	0	1	7.90	8	2	0	1	27	36	28	24	2	10	13	.316	.288	.346	4.28	3.29
Reyes, Denyi	R-R	6-4	209	11-2-96	2	2	2.25	6	6	0	0	32	30	13	8	2	6	23	.242	.246	.239	6.47	1.69
Smith, Hunter	R-R	6-3	195	3-18-94	2	2	5.27	34	2	0	0	67	79	44	39	2	22	39	.296	.268	.319	5.27	2.97
Thompson, Jake	R-R	6-1	200	9-22-94	5	13	5.30	26	26	0	0	126	148	91	74	9	47	96	.297	.346	.250	6.88	3.37
Weems, Jordan	L-R	6-3	175	11-7-92	0	0	0.68	7	0	0	0	13	3	1	1	0	8	17	.073	.100	.048	11.48	5.40

Fielding

Catcher	PCT	G	PO	A	E	DP	PB
Baldwin	.984	39	333	41	6	1	10
Lucena	.889	1	8	0	1	0	0
Nunez	.966	13	103	12	4	0	1
Procyshen	.974	31	163	27	5	2	0
Reynoso	1.000	1	4	2	0	0	0
Romanski	.982	19	151	12	3	0	0
Sciortino	.989	41	329	34	4	6	5
Tovar	.000	1	0	0	0	0	0

First Base	PCT	G	PO	A	E	DP
Downs	.994	109	811	57	5	99
Madera	1.000	2	13	1	0	1
Osinski	.994	22	159	5	1	15
Scott	1.000	6	38	5	0	3
Tovar	1.000	4	19	2	0	4

Second Base	PCT	G	PO	A	E	DP
Espinal	1.000	2	3	7	0	2
Lopez	1.000	1	1	4	0	1
Lovullo	1.000	8	7	16	0	5
Netzer	.974	118	213	319	14	76
Tovar	1.000	14	26	33	0	13

Third Base	PCT	G	PO	A	E	DP
Dalbec	.932	91	60	158	16	29
Espinal	1.000	4	2	4	0	0
Lovullo	1.000	1	0	4	0	0
Osinski	.970	15	5	27	1	1
Tobias	.936	21	9	35	3	6
Tovar	.900	8	4	5	1	0

Shortstop	PCT	G	PO	A	E	DP
Chatham	.958	67	97	154	11	39

	PCT	G	PO	A	E	DP
Dalbec	1.000	1	0	1	0	0
Espinal	.956	53	86	130	10	37
Lopez	.929	3	6	7	1	0
Lovullo	1.000	8	10	13	0	4
Tovar	.906	9	12	17	3	6

Outfield	PCT	G	PO	A	E	DP
Acosta	.953	29	38	3	2	1
Hill	.964	115	210	4	8	2
Kemp	.978	56	86	1	2	1
Lopez	1.000	2	5	1	0	0
Madera	.992	100	238	5	2	1
Osinski	1.000	2	2	0	0	0
Rusconi	1.000	24	46	0	0	0
Scott	.986	71	136	8	2	1
Washington	1.000	15	24	1	0	0
Wren	.920	15	21	2	2	0

GREENVILLE DRIVE

SOUTH ATLANTIC LEAGUE

LOW CLASS A

Batting	B-T	HT	WT	DOB	AVG	vLH	vRH	G	AB	R	H	2B	3B	HR	RBI	BB	HBP	SH	SF	SO	SB	CS	SLG	OBP
Acosta, Victor	R-R	5-11	160	6-2-96	.285	.274	.289	75	288	34	82	20	3	8	37	13	5	2	4	36	4	2	.458	.323
Barriento, Juan	R-R	6-2	201	4-28-96	.250	.500	.167	2	8	0	2	0	0	0	2	0	0	0	0	2	0	0	.250	.250
Benge, Garrett	L-R	6-0	205	12-28-95	.327	.357	.322	31	104	19	34	7	0	2	12	27	0	0	0	18	1	1	.452	.466
Berroa, Ramfis	R-R	6-2	190	11-2-95	.158	.231	.120	12	38	1	6	2	0	0	3	3	2	0	2	18	1	1	.211	.244
Brannen, Cole	L-R	6-0	170	8-4-98	.158	.105	.180	32	127	16	20	4	1	0	7	13	2	0	0	43	9	1	.205	.247
Campana, Marino	R-R	6-4	180	11-28-97	.246	.293	.231	111	418	54	103	19	7	16	69	32	7	2	2	120	2	0	.440	.309
Castellanos, Pedro	R-R	6-3	195	12-11-97	.302	.338	.293	88	344	39	104	20	3	1	34	12	6	0	3	50	1	3	.387	.334
Cedrola, Lorenzo	R-R	5-8	152	1-12-98	.318	.269	.333	50	211	40	67	17	3	0	22	5	7	3	3	29	10	8	.427	.350
Chatham, C.J.	R-R	6-4	185	12-22-94	.307	.304	.308	19	75	13	23	6	1	0	9	3	0	1	1	14	1	1	.413	.329
Cottam, Kole	R-R	6-3	220	5-30-97	.000	—	.000	1	3	0	0	0	0	0	0	0	1	0	0	1	0	0	.000	.250
Cubillan, Ricardo	B-R	6-0	155	2-2-96	.214	.250	.196	27	84	10	18	1	1	0	6	12	2	2	0	22	3	5	.250	.327
Duran, Jarren	L-R	6-2	200	9-5-96	.367	.533	.316	30	128	24	47	9	1	1	15	5	1	0	0	22	12	6	.477	.396
Fitzgerald, Ryan	L-R	6-0	185	6-17-94	.274	.339	.258	80	318	44	87	9	3	8	38	29	2	1	1	70	5	3	.396	.337
Lozada, Everlouis	B-R	5-7	150	11-14-98	.239	.219	.244	97	343	33	82	16	1	1	32	24	7	6	1	98	2	3	.300	.301
Lucena, Isaias	R-R	5-11	180	11-15-94	.229	.283	.205	49	170	13	39	6	0	2	14	15	3	3	1	42	0	0	.300	.302
Madden, Charlie	R-R	6-3	205	9-1-95	.252	.375	.215	33	103	15	26	5	0	2	18	15	1	0	2	29	0	0	.359	.347
Marrero, Alan	R-R	5-10	195	2-25-98	.000	—	.000	1	1	0	0	0	0	0	0	0	0	0	0	1	0	0	.000	.000
Miranda, Samuel	R-R	6-1	175	8-21-97	.212	.094	.236	58	193	18	41	9	0	2	22	8	6	3	0	42	0	1	.290	.266
Nishioka, Tanner	R-R	5-11	180	10-22-94	.322	.347	.314	84	301	51	97	20	2	11	52	31	9	1	1	70	4	3	.512	.401
Osinski, Michael	R-R	6-2	195	8-4-95	.298	.240	.324	45	161	20	48	6	1	2	25	18	3	1	0	36	1	1	.385	.379
Rios, Frankie	R-R	5-10	185	5-27-95	.226	.241	.222	79	270	37	61	16	2	1	15	28	9	3	0	93	6	5	.311	.319
Rusconi, Jagger	B-R	5-11	165	7-18-96	.206	.250	.186	35	126	17	26	4	2	3	4	3	2	2	1	40	1	1	.341	.235
Sterry, Zach	L-R	5-11	226	6-4-94	.291	.316	.285	56	203	25	59	8	2	5	30	23	3	0	1	54	0	0	.424	.370
Suarez, Kervin	R-R	6-2	195	12-19-98	.234	.304	.215	119	470	71	110	19	5	7	39	27	5	8	1	178	25	6	.340	.282
Wren, Jordan	L-L	6-1	195	9-23-94	.232	.277	.218	53	194	25	45	8	3	2	31	24	2	1	2	71	2	1	.351	.311

Pitching	B-T	HT	WT	DOB	W	L	ERA	G	GS	CG	SV	IP	H	R	ER	HR	BB	SO	AVG	vLH	vRH	K/9	BB/9
Ahearn, Taylor	R-R	6-1	190	11-25-94	1	0	5.19	3	0	0	0	9	11	6	5	3	1	8	.306	.263	.353	8.31	1.04
Bazardo, Eduard	R-R	6-0	155	9-1-95	1	2	3.21	5	5	0	0	28	28	10	10	2	2	28	.255	.306	.213	9.00	0.64
Crawford, Kutter	R-R	6-1	190	4-1-96	5	4	2.96	21	21	0	0	112	104	45	37	6	34	120	.243	.222	.266	9.61	2.72
De Jesus, Emmanuel	L-L	6-3	190	12-10-96	8	5	3.93	22	17	2	1	112	103	56	49	12	29	117	.239	.272	.227	9.37	2.32
Diaz, Jhonathan	L-L	6-0	170	9-13-96	11	8	3.00	26	26	1	0	153	123	60	51	6	39	147	.223	.201	.233	8.65	2.29

Name	B-T	HT	WT	DOB	W	L	ERA	G	GS	CG	SV	IP	H	R	ER	HR	BB	SO	AVG	vLH	vRH	K/9	BB/9
Duron, Nick	R-R	6-4	190	1-30-96	0	5	7.92	6	6	0	0	25	37	24	22	4	9	23	.339	.228	.462	8.28	3.24
Feltman, Durbin	R-R	6-0	205	4-18-97	0	1	2.57	7	0	0	3	7	6	3	2	0	1	14	.214	.182	.235	18.00	1.29
Fisher, Devon	R-R	6-0	215	5-1-96	4	8	3.57	40	0	0	8	58	47	31	23	7	28	50	.221	.223	.219	7.76	4.34
Florentino, Juan	R-R	5-10	182	9-8-96	5	5	5.63	33	0	0	2	54	60	39	34	10	15	52	.282	.257	.308	8.61	2.48
Franco, Alberto	R-R	5-11	165	8-16-94	0	7	7.15	8	0	0	0	11	11	11	9	1	11	15	.250	.381	.130	11.91	8.74
Glorius, Austin	R-R	6-3	205	5-10-93	0	0	0.00	1	0	0	0	1	0	0	0	0	1	1	.000	.000	.000	9.00	9.00
Gomez, Rio	L-L	6-0	190	10-20-94	0	1	3.24	7	0	0	1	8	10	4	3	2	2	10	.303	.200	.348	10.80	2.16
Haworth, Hunter	R-R	6-4	210	10-2-96	0	4	10.07	5	4	0	0	20	36	32	22	5	9	19	.375	.315	.452	8.69	4.12
Lantigua, Marcos	R-R	6-3	200	12-14-95	0	7	4.28	33	0	0	4	69	84	47	33	8	17	42	.301	.263	.336	5.45	2.21
LoBrutto, Dominic	L-L	6-1	185	5-31-96	3	0	3.73	31	0	0	2	51	50	27	21	3	13	64	.251	.217	.266	11.37	2.31
Nail, Brendan	L-L	6-0	190	10-18-95	0	1	3.52	5	0	0	0	8	6	9	3	0	6	13	.214	.167	.250	15.26	7.04
O'Linger, Durin	L-R	5-10	185	10-10-93	4	1	2.59	14	4	0	0	49	51	16	14	2	15	50	.279	.265	.290	9.25	2.77
Padron, Angel	R-R	5-11	175	9-16-97	6	7	3.99	29	9	0	2	104	99	52	46	10	38	95	.249	.230	.256	8.25	3.30
Requena, Hildemaro	R-R	6-2	170	7-20-97	4	3	5.66	14	14	0	0	70	98	63	44	15	20	48	.323	.336	.313	6.17	2.57
Reyes, Denyi	R-R	6-4	209	11-2-96	10	3	1.89	21	18	2	0	124	92	33	26	11	13	122	.201	.184	.218	8.88	0.95
Schellenger, Zach	R-R	6-5	210	1-8-96	0	0	1.74	9	0	0	0	10	7	5	2	2	0	17	.189	.154	.208	14.81	2.61
Scherff, Alex	B-R	6-3	205	2-5-98	1	5	4.98	15	15	0	0	65	68	38	36	7	23	51	.279	.270	.290	7.06	3.18
Young, Lukas	R-R	6-2	190	7-26-96	1	4	6.12	32	0	0	7	50	55	40	34	6	22	48	.275	.255	.293	8.64	3.96

Fielding

C: Cottam 1, Lucena 49, Madden 32, Marrero 1, Miranda 58. **1B:** Acosta 9, Benge 13, Castellanos 52, Osinski 28, Sterry 40. **2B:** Fitzgerald 1, Lozada 52, Nishioka 9, Rios 27, Rusconi 4, Suarez 46. **3B:** Benge 10, Lozada 28, Nishioka 65, Osinski 10, Rios 28. **SS:** Chatham 4, Cubillan 26, Fitzgerald 79, Lozada 14, Rios 18. **OF:** Acosta 56, Barriento 2, Berroa 11, Brannen 30, Campana 86, Castellanos 16, Cedrola 48, Duran 30, Rios 3, Rusconi 27, Suarez 71, Wren 44.

LOWELL SPINNERS
SHORT-SEASON

NEW YORK-PENN LEAGUE

Batting	B-T	HT	WT	DOB	AVG	vLH	vRH	G	AB	R	H	2B	3B	HR	RBI	BB	HBP	SH	SF	SO	SB	CS	SLG	OBP
Abreu, Juan Carlos	R-R	6-0	175	5-30-97	.174	.000	.191	7	23	1	4	0	0	0	4	3	0	0	0	6	0	0	.174	.269
Batesole, Korby	L-R	6-1	170	2-8-96	.285	.320	.278	46	151	19	43	3	1	0	11	15	1	2	0	40	5	5	.318	.353
Benge, Garrett	L-R	6-0	205	12-28-95	.351	.250	.379	10	37	4	13	3	1	0	7	3	0	0	0	7	0	0	.487	.400
Berroa, Ramfis	R-R	6-2	190	11-2-95	.180	.200	.172	24	78	5	14	3	0	1	7	3	1	0	0	28	2	3	.256	.220
Brannen, Cole	L-R	6-0	170	8-4-98	.181	.208	.175	34	127	16	23	1	1	0	8	17	0	2	1	47	12	1	.205	.276
Chavis, Michael	R-R	5-10	216	8-11-95	.313	.000	.455	5	16	5	5	4	0	1	3	5	0	0	0	5	1	1	.750	.476
Colon, Andre	R-R	6-0	180	2-12-99	.187	.167	.192	29	91	8	17	3	1	0	4	7	3	0	0	23	1	1	.242	.267
Cottam, Kole	R-R	6-3	220	5-30-97	.242	.231	.245	31	120	9	29	8	1	3	24	5	2	0	2	27	2	1	.400	.279
Dearden, Tyler	L-R	6-2	185		.306	.273	.314	47	170	30	52	12	1	4	23	12	4	0	1	60	0	1	.459	.364
Devers, Rafael	L-R	6-0	237	10-24-96	.250	.333	.000	2	4	1	1	0	0	1	0	0	1	0	0	0	0	0	1.000	.250
Duran, Jarren	L-R	6-2	200	9-5-96	.348	.333	.352	37	155	28	54	5	10	2	20	11	1	0	1	26	12	4	.548	.393
Esplin, Tyler	L-R	6-4	225	7-6-99	.217	.175	.229	52	184	18	40	7	4	3	24	23	0	0	1	53	5	2	.348	.303
Ganns, Trey	L-L	6-2	225	10-28-95	.207	.227	.203	40	140	10	29	7	0	1	9	7	0	1	0	37	1	2	.279	.291
Granberg, Devlin	R-R	6-2	224	9-8-95	.300	.326	.294	61	223	40	67	18	0	4	29	25	6	0	2	49	8	1	.435	.383
Hamilton, Nicholas	R-R	5-11	170	12-4-97	.222	.000	.250	6	9	2	2	0	0	0	0	0	0	0	0	4	3	0	.222	.222
Hardy, Dylan	R-R	5-11	175	1-20-97	.167	.226	.146	40	120	14	20	4	2	0	12	12	2	0	2	28	6	3	.233	.250
Howlett, Brandon	R-R	6-1	205	9-12-99	.133	.500	.077	5	15	5	2	1	0	1	2	6	0	0	0	3	1	0	.400	.381
LeGrant, Xavier	R-R	6-0	175	4-19-97	.260	.308	.252	50	169	17	44	13	1	2	20	15	1	0	3	38	3	0	.385	.319
Marrero, Alan	R-R	5-10	195	2-25-98	.125	.000	.154	20	64	6	8	1	0	1	6	2	0	0	0	23	0	0	.188	.222
Marrero, Elih	B-R	5-9	185	6-21-97	.353	.500	.333	4	17	2	6	3	1	0	4	0	0	0	0	5	0	0	.647	.353
Milligan, Lane	L-R	6-2	200	3-22-95	.253	.000	.293	22	87	11	22	5	3	1	11	6	0	0	1	21	2	1	.414	.298
Ortega, Jonathan	R-R	5-8	185	7-27-96	.200	.143	.214	50	145	20	29	5	1	0	13	29	3	3	0	27	19	3	.248	.345
Phillips, Brandon	R-R	6-0	211	6-28-81	.318	.222	.385	6	22	1	7	0	0	1	7	2	0	0	2	3	0	0	.455	.346
Romanski, Jake	R-R	5-11	200	12-22-90	.273	.500	.222	4	11	1	3	2	0	0	1	2	0	0	0	3	0	0	.455	.385
Schmidt, Alberto	R-R	5-9	180	5-29-97	.208	.231	.203	25	77	12	16	2	0	1	4	8	2	0	0	29	0	0	.273	.299
Swihart, Blake	R-L	6-1	200	4-3-92	.000	—	.000	1	3	0	0	0	0	0	0	0	0	0	0	1	0	0	.000	.000
Washington, Kyri	R-R	5-11	220	7-11-94	.000	—	.000	1	1	0	0	0	0	0	0	0	0	0	0	0	0	0	.000	.000
Williams, Grant	L-R	5-10	180	10-3-95	.265	.310	.256	50	166	20	44	8	0	0	17	23	2	5	2	16	9	5	.313	.358

Pitching	B-T	HT	WT	DOB	W	L	ERA	G	GS	CG	SV	IP	H	R	ER	HR	BB	SO	AVG	vLH	vRH	K/9	BB/9
Ahearn, Taylor	R-R	6-0	190	11-25-94	3	5	5.91	12	5	0	0	35	43	34	23	2	22	28	.299	.305	.294	7.20	5.66
Aybar, Yoan	L-L	6-2	165	7-3-97	0	0	4.50	2	0	0	0	2	2	1	1	0	2	2	.250	1.000	.143	9.00	9.00
Bazardo, Eduard	R-R	6-0	155	9-1-95	5	3	2.36	9	9	1	0	50	36	16	13	6	6	56	.195	.205	.186	10.15	1.09
Bethea, Danny	R-R	6-1	210	1-31-90	2	0	4.61	21	0	0	0	27	30	16	14	0	16	20	.294	.432	.190	6.59	5.27
Biondic, Kevin	R-R	6-1	215	1-26-96	1	2	6.26	13	0	0	1	27	35	22	19	3	9	19	.318	.341	.303	6.26	2.96
Brown, Brian	L-L	6-0	183	5-1-96	2	1	1.96	11	10	0	0	37	32	16	8	0	10	32	.237	.277	.216	7.85	2.45
Browning, Logan	L-L	5-8	175	9-3-95	1	1	3.68	6	0	0	0	15	13	6	6	2	4	21	.220	.143	.244	12.89	2.45
Cooney, Harrison	R-R	6-2	175	3-23-92	0	0	2.25	4	0	0	0	4	3	1	1	0	3	4	.214	.222	.200	9.00	6.75
Demchak, Alex	L-L	6-1	175	1-16-95	0	1	6.00	5	0	0	0	6	9	6	4	1	3	6	.346	.200	.381	9.00	4.50
Feltman, Durbin	R-R	6-0	205	4-18-97	0	0	0.00	4	0	0	0	4	0	0	0	0	0	7	.000	.000	.000	15.75	0.00
Franco, Alberto	R-R	5-11	165	8-16-94	1	2	6.39	7	0	0	0	13	8	10	9	2	10	19	.282	.286	.133	13.50	7.11
Garcia, Victor	R-R	6-4	204	6-15-97	3	3	3.55	18	0	0	1	25	20	14	10	2	18	30	.222	.139	.278	10.66	6.39
Glorius, Austin	R-R	6-3	205	5-10-93	0	0	4.50	2	0	0	0	4	4	2	2	0	3	3	.267	.286	.250	6.75	6.75
Gomez, Rio	L-L	6-0	190	10-20-94	2	0	1.65	11	1	0	0	27	19	6	5	1	4	24	.188	.229	.167	7.90	1.32
Gonzalez, Jose	R-R	6-0	175	7-27-98	0	3	5.82	6	4	0	0	22	25	18	14	0	10	19	.247	.189	.289	7.89	4.15
Haworth, Hunter	R-R	6-4	210	10-2-96	5	3	3.28	14	5	0	0	58	45	23	21	3	18	65	.208	.218	.200	10.14	2.81
Jackson, Kris	R-R	5-11	185	3-20-96	2	1	0.47	13	0	0	3	19	11	3	1	0	5	20	.257	.269	.250	9.31	2.33
Lopez-Soto, Francisco	R-R	6-5	220	12-18-96	0	0	6.62	16	0	0	0	18	15	13	13	0	24	21	.246	.250	.242	10.70	12.23

	B-T	HT	WT	DOB	W	L	ERA	G	GS	CG	SV	IP	H	R	ER	HR	BB	SO	AVG	vLH	vRH	K/9	BB/9
Machamer, Chris	R-R	6-1	180	6-4-97	1	2	2.60	10	10	0	0	35	41	15	10	1	10	26	.293	.274	.308	6.75	2.60
Montero, Alexander	R-R	6-3	180	9-21-97	0	1	1.86	4	4	0	0	19	12	5	4	0	4	21	.179	.125	.209	9.78	1.86
Mosqueda, Oddanier	L-L	5-10	155	5-6-99	3	1	2.84	17	0	0	1	32	19	13	10	0	21	40	.171	.133	.185	11.37	5.97
Pantoja, Yorvin	L-L	5-11	175	9-22-97	4	3	3.56	14	13	0	0	68	60	30	27	3	26	47	.238	.250	.233	6.19	3.42
Perez, Juan	R-R	6-1	198	8-30-96	0	1	16.20	2	1	0	0	5	12	11	9	1	3	4	.462	.600	.375	7.20	5.40
Politi, Andrew	R-R	6-0	191	6-4-96	1	1	4.34	21	0	0	7	29	30	15	14	2	10	43	.270	.217	.308	13.34	3.10
Raiburn, Tanner	L-L	5-9	175	12-28-94	2	2	2.45	16	0	0	1	26	15	8	7	1	18	27	.169	.152	.179	9.47	6.31
Santana, Yasel	R-R	6-1	180	12-14-96	0	0	0.00	1	1	0	0	5	1	0	0	0	1	7	.056	.000	.071	12.60	1.80
Shugart, Chase	R-R	5-10	180	10-24-96	0	0	0.00	1	1	0	0	3	0	0	0	0	0	3	.000	.000	.000	9.00	0.00
Walden, Marcus	R-R	6-0	195	9-13-88	0	0	3.38	2	0	0	0	3	2	1	1	0	3	3	.222	.200	.250	10.13	10.13
Ward, Thad	R-R	6-3	182	1-16-97	0	3	3.77	11	11	0	0	31	33	21	13	2	12	27	.275	.288	.259	7.84	3.48

Fielding

C: Cottam 24, Marrero 19, Marrero 4, Milligan 4, Romanski 3, Schmidt 25, Swihart 1. **1B:** Benge 4, Ganns 31, Granberg 39, LeGrant 4. **2B:** Colon 8, Duran 20, LeGrant 14, Ortega 6, Phillips 3, Williams 31. **3B:** Batesole 17, Benge 4, Chavis 4, Colon 1, Devers 1, Howlett 3, LeGrant 21, Northcut 4, Ortega 21, Williams 6. **SS:** Batesole 27, Colon 18, Ortega 23, Williams 11. **OF:** Abreu 7, Berroa 13, Brannen 34, Dearden 42, Duran 15, Esplin 49, Granberg 16, Hamilton 5, Hardy 36, Milligan 17.

GCL RED SOX
GULF COAST LEAGUE
ROOKIE

Batting	B-T	HT	WT	DOB	AVG	vLH	vRH	G	AB	R	H	2B	3B	HR	RBI	BB	HBP	SH	SF	SO	SB	CS	SLG	OBP
Abreu, Juan Carlos	R-R	6-0	175	5-30-97	.351	.293	.369	45	171	38	60	6	8	1	12	21	1	1	1	28	4	5	.497	.423
Arnold, Jecorrah	R-R	6-2	190	1-6-99	.245	.267	.239	42	147	25	36	8	0	1	14	19	8	0	0	35	0	0	.320	.362
Casas, Triston	L-R	6-4	238	1-15-00	.000	—	.000	2	4	0	0	0	0	0	0	1	0	0	0	2	0	0	.000	.200
Colon, Andre	R-R	6-0	180	2-12-99	.125	—	.125	2	8	1	1	0	0	0	1	0	1	0	1	0	0		.250	.222
Cubillan, Ricardo	B-R	6-0	155	2-1-98	.218	.293	.189	46	147	18	32	3	1	0	16	29	3	7	1	25	3	1	.252	.356
Decker, Nick	L-L	6-0	200	10-2-99	.250	—	.250	2	4	1	1	0	0	0	1	0	0	0	0	1	0	0	.500	.400
Diaz, Jonathan	L-R	5-11	170	7-7-99	.261	.154	.279	27	92	6	24	4	3	1	14	8	0	1	0	23	0	0	.402	.317
Flores, Antoni	R-R	6-1	190	10-14-00	.250	.000	.333	2	4	0	1	0	0	0	1	0	0	0	0	1	0	0	.750	.400
Hardy, Chad	R-R	6-2	175	5-20-97	.215	.156	.232	41	144	13	31	10	1	6	27	7	3	0	2	53	1	1	.424	.263
Hernandez, Juan	L-R	5-10	155	4-9-96	.291	.310	.284	37	117	25	34	8	0	1	5	16	5	2	0	38	5	1	.385	.399
Houellemont, Ivan	B-R	6-2	170	9-10-98	.164	.455	.100	22	61	5	10	1	0	0	9	5	5	0	2	22	5	0	.180	.274
Howlett, Brandon	R-R	6-1	205	9-12-99	.307	.393	.284	39	137	24	42	15	0	5	25	22	2	0	2	38	0	1	.526	.405
Marin, Freiberg	B-R	5-11	170	9-5-97	.197	.200	.196	23	66	2	13	1	0	0	5	5	2	0	1	13	1	2	.212	.270
Marrero, Elih	B-R	5-9	185	6-21-97	.289	.222	.321	26	83	14	24	3	1	0	9	14	1	0	2	14	0	0	.349	.390
Milligan, Lane	L-R	6-2	200	3-22-95	.329	.389	.310	20	76	11	25	6	0	1	12	9	2	1	1	16	0	1	.447	.409
Perez, Bramdon	L-R	6-3	180	12-9-99	.220	.111	.250	11	41	2	9	1	0	0	1	2	0	1	0	11	0	1	.244	.256
Petit, Keibert	R-R	6-1	175	8-3-98	.223	.227	.222	34	103	9	23	7	2	1	15	19	1	1	0	40	0	0	.359	.350
Pulido, Carlos	B-R	5-10	170	2-7-98	.213	.063	.254	20	75	6	16	4	0	0	4	1	0	0	0	14	0	0	.267	.263
Qiang, Justin	L-R	6-0	186	1-1-01	.135	.143	.133	17	37	2	5	1	0	0	2	5	1	0	0	9	0	0	.162	.256
Quiroz, Esteban	L-R	5-7	175	2-17-92	.211	.250	.200	8	19	3	4	0	1	0	7	6	1	0	3	3	0	0	.316	.379
Ramsey, Caleb	L-R	5-10	160	10-29-94	.153	.053	.182	29	85	12	13	3	0	0	3	15	1	1	0	26	2	4	.165	.287
Rusconi, Jagger	B-R	5-11	165	7-18-96	.300	.333	.294	6	20	3	6	0	0	0	1	0	0	0	0	6	1	0	.300	.333
Tobias, Josh	B-R	5-9	195	11-23-92	.259	.200	.273	8	27	3	7	1	0	0	3	0	0	0	0	4	1	0	.296	.333

Pitching	B-T	HT	WT	DOB	W	L	ERA	G	GS	CG	SV	IP	H	R	ER	HR	BB	SO	AVG	vLH	vRH	K/9	BB/9
Adams, Rayniel	L-L	6-6	175	9-7-97	3	2	2.51	11	8	0	0	43	40	19	12	2	10	24	.248	.250	.248	5.02	2.09
Aybar, Yoan	L-L	6-2	165	7-3-97	1	1	4.10	15	0	0	0	26	23	13	12	0	12	27	.232	.080	.284	9.23	4.10
Baker, Robbie	R-R	6-1	185	1-31-95	1	0	1.56	11	0	0	1	17	13	4	3	0	7	17	.213	.261	.184	8.83	3.63
Batista, Edilson	L-L	6-3	210	7-7-97	0	2	2.84	9	8	0	0	32	30	12	10	0	7	16	.246	.212	.258	4.55	1.99
Behenna, Kory	L-L	6-2	185	8-2-96	0	1	5.40	4	0	0	0	3	3	3	2	0	3	4	.214	.600	.000	10.80	8.10
2-team total (11 GCL Tigers West)					0	1	6.00	15	0	0	0	15	19	12	10	1	6	24	.250		.302	14.40	3.60
Bello, Brayan	R-R	6-1	170	5-17-99	1	0	0.00	1	0	0	0	3	2	0	0	0	0	6	.182	.250	.143	18.00	0.00
Bens, Jose	R-R	6-3	185	3-4-95	0	2	4.96	13	0	0	1	16	20	14	9	1	14	9	.308	.235	.387	4.96	7.71
Berry, Connor	R-R	6-0	160	12-15-96	1	0	0.00	7	2	0	0	9	7	2	0	0	3	9	.095	.000	.154	11.57	3.86
Browning, Logan	L-L	5-8	175	9-3-95	1	0	1.53	9	0	0	1	18	17	5	3	0	3	19	.250	.273	.246	9.68	1.53
Duron, Nick	R-R	6-4	190	1-30-96	0	1	4.91	4	0	0	0	4	5	3	2	0	1	1	.313	.800	.091	2.45	2.45
Fernandez, Ryan	R-R	6-0	170	6-11-98	1	1	3.46	10	7	0	0	26	28	10	10	3	6	31	.269	.200	.313	10.73	2.08
Franco, Alberto	R-R	5-11	165	8-16-94	0	0	5.28	11	0	0	4	15	16	9	9	1	4	14	.267	.276	.258	8.22	2.35
Glorius, Austin	R-R	6-3	205	5-10-93	1	0	9.82	5	0	0	0	7	8	8	8	0	5	8	.286	.300	.278	9.82	6.14
Gomez, Rafael	R-R	5-11	167	4-17-98	1	3	2.21	14	0	0	1	20	20	8	5	1	4	11	.263	.222	.300	4.87	1.77
Gonzalez, Jose	R-R	6-0	175	7-27-98	1	2	1.22	9	7	0	0	37	28	10	5	0	8	21	.203	.204	.202	5.11	1.95
Jackson, Kris	R-R	5-11	185	3-20-96	0	0	1.29	6	0	0	2	7	6	2	1	0	0	9	.214	.000	.261	11.57	0.00
Jimenez, Andres	R-R	6-1	170	10-23-98	3	1	3.80	12	0	0	1	21	21	10	9	1	3	13	.253	.235	.265	5.48	1.27
Jimenez, Eddie	R-R	6-2	230	8-9-95	1	1	8.53	4	0	0	0	6	7	6	6	0	5	6	.280	.000	.389	8.53	7.11
Maddox, Austin	R-R	6-2	220	5-13-91	0	0	0.00	2	2	0	0	2	4	0	0	0	2	2	.500	.333	.600	9.00	9.00
Montgomery, Mark	R-R	6-0	200	8-30-90	1	0	4.50	2	0	0	0	2	2	1	1	0	1	1	.286	.333	.250	4.50	4.50
Moreno, Rayniel	L-L	6-1	165	9-11-98	0	0	1.59	4	0	0	0	6	4	1	1	0	2	6	.200	.000	.286	7.94	3.18
Morillo, Juan	R-R	6-2	176	9-27-96	2	1	7.94	15	0	0	0	17	19	16	15	1	6	15	.284	.379	.211	2.65	3.18
Padron-Artiles, Yusniel	R-R	6-0	187	11-12-97	3	1	3.74	11	2	0	0	22	23	9	9	1	3	19	.271	.439	.114	7.89	1.25
Reyes, Gregorio	R-R	6-3	170	7-12-98	0	0	4.15	7	5	0	0	13	14	6	6	0	3	6	.264	.364	.238	4.15	2.08
Reynoso, Eddy	R-R	6-0	195	8-7-94	4	1	1.45	15	0	0	2	19	14	5	3	0	7	17	.206	.067	.316	8.20	3.38
Rivero, Luis	R-R	6-3	195	1-23-98	1	0	1.93	12	0	0	4	19	11	6	4	0	5	13	.167	.160	.171	6.27	2.41
Santana, Yasel	R-R	6-1	180	12-14-96	3	1	1.97	10	10	0	0	46	36	12	10	0	8	42	.217	.190	.241	8.28	1.77
Schellenger, Zach	R-R	6-5	210	1-9-96	0	0	1.50	6	1	0	0	6	2	1	1	0	2	8	.105	.167	.077	12.00	1.50

Name	B-T	HT	WT	DOB	W	L	ERA	G	GS	CG	SV	IP	H	R	ER	HR	BB	SO	AVG	vLH	vRH	K/9	BB/9
Scherff, Alex	B-R	6-3	205	2-5-98	0	0	1.80	2	1	0	0	5	5	1	1	0	1	3	.294	.333	.250	5.40	1.80
Shugart, Chase	R-R	5-10	180	10-24-96	0	1	1.80	3	3	0	0	5	4	3	1	0	1	6	.211	.200	.222	10.80	1.80
Suero, Miguel	R-R	6-1	185	1-4-97	0	0	1.69	2	1	0	0	5	3	1	1	0	0	4	.158	.100	.222	6.75	0.00

Fielding

C: Diaz 19, Marrero 24, Milligan 5, Pulido 11, Qiang 6. **1B:** Cubillan 17, Petit 34, Pulido 9. **2B:** Arnold 8, Colon 2, Cubillan 16, Houellemont 12, Marin 13, Quiroz 4, Rusconi 2, Tobias 5. **3B:** Arnold 4, Casas 1, Houellemont 1, Howlett 28, Northcut 23. **SS:** Arnold 29, Cubillan 14, Flores 1, Houellemont 9, Marin 10. **OF:** Abreu 45, Decker 1, Hardy 40, Hernandez 36, Milligan 13, Perez 11, Ramsey 27, Rusconi 2.

DSL RED SOX   ROOKIE
DOMINICAN SUMMER LEAGUE

Batting

Name	B-T	HT	WT	DOB	AVG	vLH	vRH	G	AB	R	H	2B	3B	HR	RBI	BB	HBP	SH	SF	SO	SB	CS	SLG	OBP
Abreu, Nelfy	B-R	5-10	150	3-2-01	.254	—	—	65	248	36	63	15	4	1	31	33	2	3	4	48	13	6	.359	.342
Andrade, Fabian	L-L	5-11	162	4-1-99	.278	.245	.287	66	230	26	64	8	0	0	23	27	5	1	1	25	8	6	.313	.365
Baez, Lewis	L-R	5-9	170	11-7-96	.314	.429	.286	29	105	14	33	7	6	0	19	3	1	1	2	21	6	2	.495	.333
Custodio, Gregori	R-R	6-1	165	3-18-01	.244	—	—	22	78	11	19	2	1	0	10	7	3	1	0	13	3	1	.295	.330
Daza, Denny	R-R	5-11	160	12-27-00	.160	.089	.181	60	200	14	32	2	0	0	12	12	9	2	1	37	1	6	.170	.239
Diaz, Danny	R-R	6-1	160	1-2-01	.238	—	—	26	105	17	25	7	0	6	27	5	2	0	1	27	0	3	.476	.283
Flores, Antoni	R-R	6-1	190	10-14-00	.347	.000	.333	13	49	10	17	3	1	1	14	8	0	0	0	7	0	1	.510	.439
Flores, Erick	L-R	5-9	158	6-10-01	.227	.250	.217	42	132	20	30	8	1	0	14	18	1	0	1	28	1	1	.303	.322
Gari, Andres	L-R	5-11	171	4-27-01	.184	—	—	49	163	18	30	4	2	0	12	18	2	0	0	34	5	1	.233	.273
Gonzalez, Angel	R-R	6-2	180	11-10-98	.286	—	—	25	84	16	24	5	1	0	12	5	9	1	0	16	9	3	.369	.388
Gonzalez, Gamaliel	L-R	6-1	190	7-4-01	.164	.143	.147	19	55	6	9	1	0	0	8	8	1	1	1	11	0	0	.182	.277
Hernandez, Luis	R-R	6-1	165	10-7-98	.218	—	—	62	206	25	45	7	0	0	14	23	5	2	2	39	9	5	.252	.309
Hernandez, Ruben	L-R	5-10	160	10-17-00	.098	.000	.116	25	51	8	5	0	0	0	5	11	3	1	0	12	1	0	.098	.292
Hernandez, Yulis	L-R	5-9	172	1-21-00	.213	—	—	32	108	12	23	5	0	0	11	14	0	1	1	20	4	2	.259	.301
Jimenez, Gilberto	R-R	5-11	160	7-8-00	.319	.204	.350	67	257	42	82	10	8	0	22	19	8	0	0	40	16	14	.420	.384
Jimenez, Leonel	R-R	5-11	160	11-30-99	.325	.320	.327	37	126	21	41	5	2	0	18	19	2	1	1	26	7	3	.397	.419
Licona, Breiner	R-R	6-1	190	8-14-99	.231	.250	.224	29	91	10	21	6	0	1	9	6	4	0	1	27	1	1	.330	.304
Maita, Angel	B-R	5-11	160	5-28-01	.320	—	—	45	181	31	58	8	4	0	15	16	2	1	2	38	9	6	.409	.378
Maita, Jesus	B-R	5-10	160	5-28-01	.220	.171	.233	56	164	22	36	3	2	1	14	22	4	1	2	54	5	7	.281	.323
Martinez, Carlos	R-R	6-5	185	10-5-99	.136	—	—	38	125	8	17	5	0	0	11	9	3	0	1	61	2	3	.176	.210
Mejias, Jose	R-R	6-1	160	3-13-99	.206	.111	.244	22	63	10	13	1	0	1	5	13	0	0	0	12	3	2	.270	.342
Mota, Luis	L-R	5-11	150	2-24-01	.179	.125	.191	30	84	8	15	1	0	0	8	17	1	1	1	27	1	4	.191	.320
Navas, Jose	R-R	5-11	160	7-18-00	.184	.136	.194	41	125	9	23	3	1	0	4	11	2	0	0	44	2	0	.224	.261
Perez, Gabriel	R-R	5-11	145	6-1-01	.225	—	—	44	129	27	29	2	4	1	11	17	2	4	1	47	16	4	.326	.322
Pulgar, Ronaldo	R-R	5-10	158	1-2-97	.264	—	—	64	216	28	57	8	2	2	19	25	4	0	0	41	17	5	.347	.351
Quintero, Gabriel	R-R	6-2	165	12-19-00	.150	—	—	41	120	14	18	7	3	0	8	19	3	0	1	42	2	4	.258	.280
Rafaela, Ceddanne	R-R	5-8	145	9-18-00	.271	.225	.282	54	203	31	55	9	2	3	28	14	4	1	3	39	19	7	.379	.326
Rangel, Oscar	L-R	5-11	175	5-27-98	.247	—	—	45	154	29	38	8	4	1	33	24	2	0	5	22	3	3	.370	.344
Rincones, Brandon	R-R	5-9	145	10-1-00	.238	.257	.232	45	147	25	35	4	1	0	13	21	2	8	0	27	5	2	.279	.341
Rodriguez, Kleiber	B-R	6-2	175	10-8-98	.310	—	—	67	232	33	72	15	1	0	32	33	0	0	5	28	4	0	.397	.389
Rojas, Juan	R-R	6-2	165	4-21-01	.213	—	—	18	47	4	10	1	0	0	7	4	3	0	0	14	2	1	.234	.315
Sanchez, Carlos	R-R	6-4	203	9-7-00	.200	.146	.213	60	215	21	43	7	1	2	20	15	8	0	4	53	12	6	.270	.273
Teran, Nelson	R-R	5-10	160	5-18-01	.111	—	—	6	9	1	1	0	0	0	0	2	1	0	0	3	0	0	.111	.333
Torres, Luis	R-R	5-11	174	9-29-98	.500	—	.500	2	4	0	2	0	0	0	0	0	0	0	0	2	0	1	.500	.500
Vargas, Wilker	L-R	5-9	145	1-8-01	.254	.300	.245	19	59	8	15	2	0	0	3	6	0	1	0	11	2	1	.288	.323

Pitching

Name	B-T	HT	WT	DOB	W	L	ERA	G	GS	CG	SV	IP	H	R	ER	HR	BB	SO	AVG	vLH	vRH	K/9	BB/9
Acosta, Armando	R-R	6-1	174	10-11-98	0	0	2.57	4	0	0	0	7	7	2	2	0	2	4	.304	.000	.389	5.14	2.57
Aquino, Brayan	R-R	6-0	161	11-20-00	0	2	5.40	3	3	0	0	8	7	7	5	0	11	7	.219	.222	.217	7.56	11.88
Batista, Argenis	L-L	6-0	175	8-7-00	0	1	13.09	10	0	0	0	11	9	22	16	0	28	12	.231	—	—	9.82	22.91
Bello, Brayan	R-R	6-1	170	5-17-99	6	2	1.68	13	13	1	0	64	37	16	12	0	10	68	.162	.250	.143	9.51	1.40
Blanco, Royman	R-R	6-1	170	4-17-01	0	0	0.00	2	0	0	0	2	2	0	0	0	0	1	.250	.250	.250	4.50	0.00
Cepeda, Felix	R-R	6-3	170	7-15-00	0	1	1.50	4	4	0	0	6	4	4	1	0	7	10	.174	.200	.167	15.00	10.50
Colmenares, Luis	L-L	6-0	180	4-22-98	4	3	3.69	24	0	0	5	39	21	20	16	1	28	53	.160	.136	.165	12.23	6.46
Cortes, Carlos	R-R	6-1	170	7-26-96	1	3	5.45	18	0	0	2	33	25	25	20	0	36	25	.216	.250	.205	6.82	9.82
Crisostomo, Alejandro	R-R	6-5	184	9-11-00	2	3	7.15	16	0	0	2	23	20	19	18	2	25	23	.247	.000	.077	9.13	9.93
Crisostomo, Juan	R-R	6-5	220	1-11-97	0	1	11.57	3	0	0	0	2	4	3	3	0	7	3	.500	.400	.667	11.57	27.00
De La Rosa, Osvaldo	R-R	6-4	210	10-28-97	1	2	1.63	19	0	0	4	28	20	7	5	0	8	36	.204	.280	.178	11.71	2.60
Gomez, Felix	L-L	6-0	155	9-1-99	0	1	5.28	12	0	0	0	15	8	11	9	0	26	19	.163	.222	.150	11.15	15.26
Guedez, Yoelvis	R-R	5-11	175	9-8-00	5	4	2.39	16	6	0	0	60	45	22	16	1	9	43	.203	.155	.225	6.41	1.34
Gutierrez, Ronald	R-R	6-2	175	4-22-99	0	0	8.03	7	0	0	0	12	12	13	11	0	17	9	.255	.200	.250	6.57	12.41
Jimenez, Richardson	R-R	5-11	173	9-30-99	4	0	2.95	9	0	0	0	18	13	6	6	0	14	23	.206	—	—	11.29	6.87
Larez, Jose	R-R	6-4	195	1-12-97	3	5	4.08	21	0	0	0	35	35	22	16	1	14	21	.273	.444	.207	5.35	3.57
Leal, Alvaro	L-L	6-1	180	4-5-00	1	1	4.76	13	0	0	0	23	19	13	12	1	17	21	.226	.250	.217	8.34	6.75
Lucas, Bryan	R-R	6-2	160	12-13-97	0	2	4.08	7	0	0	0	18	17	10	8	0	9	28	.246	—	—	14.26	4.58
Martinez, Johan	R-R	6-2	180	4-7-99	1	1	4.91	9	0	0	0	18	15	12	10	0	2	17	.224	—	—	9.82	8.35
Medina, Erison	R-R	5-11	190	5-31-97	0	0	11.42	9	0	0	0	9	9	12	11	1	17	10	.290	—	—	10.38	17.65
Montero, Robinson	R-R	5-11	168	11-18-99	3	3	3.02	17	0	0	0	45	43	21	15	1	20	35	.259	—	—	7.05	4.03
Ortiz, Emerson	R-R	6-1	180	2-10-97	4	3	2.61	16	12	1	0	76	72	29	22	2	15	41	.252	.191	.277	4.86	1.78
Ozoria, Isaias	L-L	5-11	180	6-16-98	3	2	1.98	19	0	0	3	36	21	9	8	1	17	44	.165	—	—	10.90	4.21
Parra, Robinson	R-R	6-3	190	9-28-98	1	1	5.12	11	0	0	1	32	18	20	18	0	31	26	.180	—	—	7.39	8.81
Pena, Jeison	R-R	6-2	200	5-15-98	3	1	2.64	14	8	0	1	65	53	24	19	4	12	42	.219	.222	.218	5.85	1.67
Perez, Geraldo	R-R	6-0	200	5-13-96	0	1	22.50	4	0	0	0	4	7	10	10	0	10	2	.467	—	—	4.50	22.50

Ramirez, Aldo	R-R	6-0	180	5-6-01	1	2	0.39	5	5	0	0	23	10	7	1	0	3	17	.127	.000	.161	6.65	1.17
Ramirez, Jose	R-R	6-0	142	3-28-01	1	4	3.16	13	11	0	1	43	30	24	15	1	32	36	.194	—	—	7.59	6.75
Ramirez, Manuel	R-R	5-11	155	2-15-99	1	1	3.74	7	0	0	1	22	18	11	9	4	6	14	.234	.294	.217	5.82	2.49
Rodriguez, Jorge	L-L	5-11	170	8-25-00	3	1	3.41	13	13	1	0	63	66	28	24	1	14	56	.273	—	—	7.96	1.99
Rosillo, Jesus	R-R	6-3	185	1-19-00	0	3	3.89	12	11	0	0	39	35	23	17	0	22	30	.243	.304	.214	6.86	5.03
Sanchez, Kelvin	L-L	6-3	196	5-12-97	5	5	3.03	14	14	0	0	62	48	28	21	2	26	60	.212	.225	.208	8.66	3.75
Segovia, Gregori	R-R	6-1	175	6-27-00	2	3	4.88	18	0	0	3	31	39	17	17	0	9	33	.312	—	—	9.48	2.59
Sosa, Angel	R-R	6-2	175	2-23-01	0	0	28.69	5	0	0	0	5	8	17	17	0	19	5	.381	.667	.333	8.44	32.06
Suero, Miguel	R-R	6-1	185	1-4-97	3	2	1.54	12	9	0	1	47	29	14	8	1	8	45	.179	.091	.191	8.68	1.54
Tineo, Cristofe	R-R	6-2	180	6-17-97	2	2	1.11	13	1	0	0	32	27	11	4	0	15	32	.239	.333	.261	8.91	4.18
Velez, Carlos	L-L	6-2	190	5-4-99	0	2	4.17	14	12	0	0	54	48	32	25	1	32	59	.242	—	—	9.83	5.33
Villarroel, Irvin	R-R	6-4	180	7-26-01	2	6	3.70	14	13	0	0	58	59	33	24	7	22	57	.260	—	—	8.79	3.39
Viola, Hansel	R-R	6-2	190	9-25-99	1	3	3.00	15	0	0	0	30	24	13	10	2	17	19	.224	—	—	5.70	5.10

Fielding

C: Flores 28, Gari 33, Gonzalez 3, Jimenez 2, Licona 9, Navas 40, Rangel 28, Rodriguez 10, Teran 5. **1B:** Andrade 10, Custodio 2, Diaz 1, Flores 1, Gari 4, Licona 18, Mejias 3, Pulgar 1, Rodriguez 51, Rojas 15, Sanchez 43. **2B:** Abreu 9, Custodio 11, Daza 1, Hernandez 4, Hernandez 21, Jimenez 8, Mota 10, Pulgar 29, Rincones 44, Rojas 1, Vargas 12. **3B:** Abreu 1, Custodio 3, Diaz 23, Hernandez 6, Hernandez 3, Jimenez 16, Mota 18, Pulgar 35, Rafaela 44, Rodriguez 1, Rojas 1. **SS:** Daza 59, Flores 13, Hernandez 52, Hernandez 9, Rafaela 11, Rincones 1, Vargas 3. **OF:** Abreu 55, Andrade 56, Baez 24, Gonzalez 23, Hernandez 23, Jimenez 64, Maita 43, Maita 56, Martinez 26, Mejias 10, Perez 39, Quintero 37, Sanchez 4, Torres 2.

Chicago Cubs

SEASON IN A SENTENCE: After spending 75 days in first place in the NL Central, the Cubs ended the season in a tie with the Brewers, then lost Game 163 to cede them the division before falling to the Rockies in the Wild Card Game to bring their season to an abrupt end.

HIGH POINT: Rookie third baseman David Bote lived every child's dream on Aug. 12, when, with his team down 3-0 in the bottom of the ninth, he hit a pinch-hit, walk-off grand slam off Nationals reliever Ryan Madson. It was the Cubs' second walk-off grand slam of the season. Jason Heyward turned the same trick on June 7 against the Dodgers.

LOW POINT: After having as big as a five-game lead in the division as late as Sept. 2, the Cubs fell out of first place and then out of the playoffs in a two-game span, laying waste to what had been a 95-win season.

NOTABLE ROOKIES: Bote's grand slam made the biggest impact of any Cubs rookie in 2018. Overall, Bote showed big exit velocity while hitting six home runs and racking up a .727 OPS over 74 games. He also had a second walk-off home run on his ledger. Catcher Victor Caratini saw sporadic time behind the plate and at the infield corners and managed a .597 OPS. On the mound, lefty Alec Mills was the most-used rookie, with seven games, two starts and 18 innings to his credit.

KEY TRANSACTIONS: The biggest move the Cubs made during the season was the pickup of lefty Cole Hamels from the Rangers for big league reliever Eddie Butler and minor leaguer Rollie Lacy. Hamels was excellent after the trade, pitching to a 4-3, 2.36 mark with 74 strikeouts in 76.1 innings. That helped shore up a rotation that had been weakened by Yu Darvish's disastrous first year as a Cub. The righthander signed a six-year, $126 million deal, then produced just 40 innings, all ineffective, in 2018. His season officially ended in mid-September when he had surgery on his right elbow.

DOWN ON THE FARM: After a series of graduations and trades over the past few years, the Cubs' system is understandably barren. There were few bright spots in the system, led by catcher Miguel Amaya's hot first half and appearance in the Futures Game. First-rounder Nico Hoerner started hot at short-season Eugene but a thumb injury one game after a promotion kept him off the field until the Arizona Fall League.

OPENING DAY PAYROLL: $181,810,002 (3rd).

PLAYERS OF THE YEAR

RON VESELY

JENNIFER STEWART

MAJOR LEAGUE	MINOR LEAGUE
Javier Baez	**David Bote**
2B	**3B**
.290/.326/.554	(Triple-A)
Led Cubs in HR (34),	.268/.342/.494
RBIs (111) and SB (21)	13 HR, 41 RBIs

ORGANIZATION LEADERS

Batting		*Minimum 250 AB
MAJORS		
* AVG	Ben Zobrist	.305
* OPS	Javier Baez	.881
HR	Javier Baez	34
RBI	Javier Baez	111
MINORS		
* AVG	Jared Young, South Bend, Myrtle Beach	.300
* OBP	Mark Zagunis, Jackson, Reno	.395
* SLG	Jared Young, South Bend, Myrtle Beach	.485
* OPS	Jared Young, South Bend, Myrtle Beach	.842
R	Charcer Burks, Tennessee	68
R	Zack Short, Tennessee	68
H	Jared Young, South Bend, Myrtle Beach	134
TB	Jason Vosler, Tennessee, Iowa	220
2B	Jason Vosler, Tennessee, Iowa	29
3B	Jared Young, South Bend, Myrtle Beach	8
HR	Jason Vosler, Tennessee, Iowa	23
RBI	Jason Vosler, Tennessee, Iowa	93
BB	Zack Short, Tennessee	82
SO	Ryan Court, Iowa	149
SO	Jason Vosler, Tennessee, Iowa	149
SB	Zach Davis, South Bend, Myrtle Beach	38

Pitching		#Minimum 75 IP
MAJORS		
W	Jon Lester	18
# ERA	Cole Hamels	2.36
SO	Kyle Hendricks	161
SV	Brandon Morrow	22
MINORS		
W	Michael Rucker, Tennessee	9
W	Keegan Thompson, Myrtle Beach, Tennessee	9
W	Matt Swarmer, Myrtle Beach, Tennessee	9
W	Tyson Miller, Myrtle Beach	9
W	Jeffrey Passantino, South Bend, Eugene	9
L	Jen-Ho Tseng, Iowa	15
# ERA	Cory Abbott, South Bend, Myrtle Beach	2.5
G	Jordan Minch, Myrtle Beach, Tennessee	45
G	Brian Glowicki, South Bend	45
GS	Michael Rucker, Tennessee	26
GS	Jen-Ho Tseng, Iowa	26
GS	Thomas Hatch, Tennessee	26
GS	Duncan Robinson, Tennessee, Iowa	26
SV	Brian Glowicki, South Bend	18
IP	Thomas Hatch, Tennessee	144
BB	Jose Albertos, South Bend, Eugene	65
SO	Matt Swarmer, Myrtle Beach, Tennessee	135
# AVG	Tyson Miller, Myrtle Beach	.220

2018 PERFORMANCE

General Manager: Jed Hoyer. **Farm Director:** Jaron Madison. **Scouting Director:** Matt Dorey.

Class	Team	League	W	L	PCT	Finish	Manager
Majors	Chicago Cubs	National	95	68	.583	2nd (15)	Joe Maddon
Triple-A	Iowa Cubs	Pacific Coast	50	88	.xxx	16th (16)	Marty Pevey
Double-A	Tennessee Smokies	Southern	67	71	.486	t-5th (10)	Mark Johnson
High A	Myrtle Beach Pelicans	Carolina	61	78	.439	9th (10)	Buddy Bailey
Low A	South Bend Cubs	Midwest	64	74	.464	t-11th (16)	Jimmy Gonzalez
Short season	Eugene Emeralds	Northwest	31	45	.408	8th (8)	Steven Lerud
Rookie	AZL Cubs 1	Arizona	38	18	.679	1st (18)	Carmelo Martinez
Rookie	AZL Cubs 2	Arizona	28	25	.528	10th (18)	Jonathan Mota
Overall 2018 Minor League Record			339	399	.459	27th (30)	

ORGANIZATION STATISTICS

CHICAGO CUBS
NATIONAL LEAGUE

Batting	B-T	HT	WT	DOB	AVG	vLH	vRH	G	AB	R	H	2B	3B	HR	RBI	BB	HBP	SH	SF	SO	SB	CS	SLG	OBP
Almora Jr., Albert	R-R	6-2	190	4-16-94	.286	.296	.282	152	444	62	127	24	1	5	41	24	3	2	6	83	1	3	.378	.323
Baez, Javier	R-R	6-0	190	12-1-92	.290	.306	.286	160	606	101	176	40	9	34	111	29	5	1	4	167	21	9	.555	.326
Bote, David	R-R	6-1	210	4-7-93	.239	.275	.226	74	184	23	44	9	2	6	33	19	4	0	3	60	3	4	.408	.319
Bryant, Kris	R-R	6-5	230	1-4-92	.273	.372	.244	102	389	59	106	28	3	13	52	48	17	0	3	107	2	4	.460	.374
Caratini, Victor	B-R	6-1	215	8-17-93	.232	.136	.263	76	181	21	42	7	0	2	21	12	4	2	1	42	0	0	.304	.293
Contreras, Willson	R-R	6-1	210	5-13-92	.249	.250	.249	138	474	50	118	27	5	10	54	53	13	2	2	121	4	1	.390	.340
Davis, Taylor	R-R	5-10	200	11-28-89	.400	—	.400	5	5	0	2	0	0	0	2	0	0	0	1	1	0	0	.400	.333
Freeman, Mike	L-R	6-0	195	8-4-87	—	—	—	1	0	0	0	0	0	0	0	0	0	0	1	0	0	0	—	—
Gimenez, Chris	R-R	6-2	230	12-27-82	.143	—	.143	12	28	1	4	0	0	0	1	3	0	0	1	7	1	0	.143	.219
Gore, Terrance	R-R	5-7	165	6-8-91	.200	.000	.333	14	5	5	1	0	0	0	0	0	0	0	0	1	6	0	.200	.200
Happ, Ian	B-R	6-0	205	8-12-94	.233	.202	.244	142	387	56	90	19	2	15	44	70	3	0	2	167	8	4	.408	.353
Heyward, Jason	L-L	6-5	240	8-9-89	.271	.290	.265	127	440	67	119	23	4	8	57	42	2	2	2	60	1	1	.396	.335
La Stella, Tommy	L-R	5-11	180	1-31-89	.266	.111	.285	123	169	23	45	8	0	1	19	17	2	0	0	27	0	1	.331	.340
Murphy, Daniel	L-R	6-1	221	4-1-85	.297	.219	.321	35	138	23	41	6	0	6	13	7	0	0	1	23	2	0	.471	.329
2-team total (56 Washington)					.299	.238	.319	91	328	40	98	15	0	12	42	20	0	0	3	40	3	0	.454	.336
Navarro, Efren	L-L	6-0	210	5-14-86	.167	—	.167	4	6	0	1	0	0	0	0	0	0	0	0	4	0	0	.167	.167
Rizzo, Anthony	L-L	6-3	240	8-8-89	.283	.248	.295	153	566	74	160	29	1	25	101	70	20	0	9	80	6	4	.470	.376
Russell, Addison	R-R	6-0	200	1-23-94	.250	.273	.242	130	420	52	105	21	1	5	38	40	2	1	2	99	4	0	.341	.317
Schwarber, Kyle	L-R	6-0	235	3-5-93	.238	.224	.242	137	428	64	102	14	3	26	61	78	1	1	2	140	4	3	.467	.356
Zagunis, Mark	R-R	6-0	215	2-5-93	.400	.500	.333	5	5	0	2	1	0	0	1	1	0	0	0	1	0	0	.600	.500
Zobrist, Ben	B-R	6-3	210	5-26-81	.306	.333	.295	139	455	67	139	28	3	9	58	55	2	1	7	60	3	4	.440	.378

Pitching	B-T	HT	WT	DOB	W	L	ERA	G	GS	CG	SV	IP	H	R	ER	HR	BB	SO	AVG	vLH	vRH	K/9	BB/9
Bass, Anthony	R-R	6-2	200	11-1-87	0	0	2.93	16	0	0	0	15	18	6	5	1	3	14	.305	.333	.286	8.22	1.76
Butler, Eddie	R-R	6-2	180	3-13-91	1	1	4.08	4	0	0	0	18	16	10	8	1	7	11	.242	.192	.275	5.60	3.57
Chatwood, Tyler	R-R	6-0	185	12-16-89	4	6	5.30	24	20	0	0	104	92	62	61	9	95	85	.245	.316	.150	7.38	8.25
Chavez, Jesse	R-R	6-2	175	8-21-83	2	1	1.15	32	0	0	4	39	26	5	5	3	5	42	.190	.174	.198	9.69	1.15
Cishek, Steve	R-R	6-6	215	6-18-86	4	3	2.18	80	0	0	4	70	45	19	17	5	28	78	.182	.218	.165	9.98	3.58
Darvish, Yu	R-R	6-5	220	8-16-86	1	3	4.95	8	8	0	0	40	36	24	22	7	21	49	.235	.276	.195	11.03	4.73
De La Rosa, Jorge	L-L	6-1	215	4-5-81	0	0	1.29	17	0	0	1	21	14	6	3	0	8	20	.182	.269	.137	8.57	3.43
2-team total (42 Arizona)					0	2	3.38	59	0	0	1	56	51	25	21	6	27	47	.243	.235	.248	7.55	4.34
Duensing, Brian	L-L	6-0	200	2-22-83	3	0	7.65	48	0	0	1	38	42	33	32	6	29	24	.286	.217	.346	5.73	6.93
Edwards Jr., Carl	R-R	6-3	170	9-3-91	3	2	2.60	58	0	0	0	52	36	17	15	2	32	67	.191	.241	.155	11.60	5.54
Farrell, Luke	R-R	6-6	210	6-7-91	3	4	5.17	20	2	0	0	31	30	22	18	7	16	39	.244	.250	.239	11.20	4.60
Garcia, Jaime	L-L	6-2	215	7-8-86	0	1	4.70	8	1	0	0	8	6	4	4	0	6	4	.222	.182	.250	4.70	7.04
Hamels, Cole	L-L	6-4	205	12-27-83	4	3	2.36	12	12	1	0	76	61	23	20	6	23	74	.226	.197	.234	8.72	2.71
Hancock, Justin	R-R	6-4	185	10-28-90	0	0	1.46	10	0	0	1	12	5	2	2	1	9	15	.125	.167	.091	8.03	6.57
Hendricks, Kyle	R-R	6-3	190	12-7-89	14	11	3.44	33	33	0	0	199	184	82	76	22	44	161	.247	.233	.259	7.28	1.99
Kintzler, Brandon	R-R	6-0	194	8-1-84	2	1	7.00	25	0	0	0	18	27	14	14	3	9	12	.355	.333	.364	6.00	4.50
2-team total (45 Washington)					3	3	4.60	70	0	0	2	61	67	31	31	5	22	49	.286	.264	.299	6.38	3.26
Lester, Jon	L-R	6-4	240	1-7-84	18	6	3.32	32	32	0	0	182	174	75	67	24	64	149	.256	.279	.250	7.38	3.17
Maples, Dillon	R-R	6-2	225	5-9-92	1	0	11.81	9	0	0	0	5	7	7	7	2	5	9	.318	.364	.273	15.19	8.44
Mazzoni, Cory	R-R	6-1	210	6-13-89	1	0	1.04	8	0	0	0	9	5	1	1	0	5	7	.161	.333	.053	7.27	5.19
Mills, Alec	R-R	6-4	190	11-30-91	0	1	4.00	7	2	0	0	18	11	8	8	1	7	23	.172	.185	.162	11.50	3.50
Montgomery, Mike	L-L	6-5	215	7-1-89	5	6	3.99	38	19	0	0	124	131	58	55	10	39	86	.272	.250	.281	6.24	2.83
Morrow, Brandon	R-R	6-3	205	7-26-84	0	0	1.47	35	0	0	22	31	24	5	5	2	9	31	.214	.151	.271	9.10	2.64
Norwood, James	R-R	6-2	215	12-24-93	0	1	4.09	10	0	0	0	11	14	7	5	2	5	10	.298	.353	.267	8.18	4.09
Quintana, Jose	R-L	6-1	220	1-24-89	13	11	4.03	32	32	0	0	174	162	81	78	25	68	158	.246	.248	.246	8.16	3.51
Rosario, Randy	L-L	6-1	200	5-18-94	4	0	3.66	44	0	0	1	47	47	22	19	5	22	30	.264	.174	.321	5.79	4.24
Strop, Pedro	R-R	6-1	220	6-21-85	6	1	2.26	60	0	0	13	60	38	15	15	4	21	57	.179	.217	.155	8.60	3.17
Tseng, Jen-Ho	L-R	6-1	210	10-3-94	0	0	13.50	1	1	0	0	2	4	3	3	1	0	3	.400	1.000	.250	13.50	0.00
Underwood Jr., Duane	R-R	6-2	210	7-20-94	0	1	2.25	1	1	0	0	4	2	1	1	1	3	3	.154	.000	.286	6.75	6.75
Webster, Allen	R-R	6-2	190	2-10-90	1	0	6.00	3	0	0	0	3	2	2	2	1	1	3	.167	.000	.250	9.00	3.00

	B-T	HT	WT	DOB	W	L	ERA	G	GS	CG	SV	IP	H	R	ER	HR	BB	SO	AVG	vLH	vRH	K/9	BB/9
Wilson, Justin	L-L	6-2	205	8-18-87	4	5	3.46	71	0	0	0	55	45	22	21	5	33	69	.223	.190	.244	11.36	5.43
Zastryzny, Rob	R-L	6-3	205	3-26-92	1	0	4.76	6	0	0	0	6	6	3	3	0	4	3	.286	.000	.333	4.76	6.35

Fielding

Catcher	PCT	G	PO	A	E	DP	PB
Caratini	.996	37	267	15	1	2	3
Contreras	.990	133	1013	71	11	9	9
Davis	1.000	3	3	1	0	0	0
Gimenez	.985	10	60	5	1	1	0

First Base	PCT	G	PO	A	E	DP
Baez	1.000	1	1	0	0	0
Bote	1.000	2	0	1	0	0
Bryant	1.000	4	11	2	0	0
Caratini	.990	20	92	6	1	11
Contreras	1.000	1	3	0	0	0
Davis	1.000	1	1	0	0	1
Happ	1.000	2	10	4	0	2
Navarro	1.000	2	8	0	0	1
Rizzo	.995	153	1133	147	7	128
Zobrist	1.000	4	18	2	0	1

Second Base	PCT	G	PO	A	E	DP
Baez	.984	104	163	204	6	60
Bote	.963	13	11	15	1	6
Freeman	1.000	1	2	1	0	1
Happ	.000	2	0	0	0	0
La Stella	.969	15	12	19	1	3
Murphy	.983	33	53	61	2	17
Rizzo	.000	1	0	0	0	0
Zobrist	1.000	63	84	122	0	34

Third Base	PCT	G	PO	A	E	DP
Baez	.940	22	11	36	3	7
Bote	.968	56	27	94	4	11
Bryant	.955	86	53	158	10	12
Caratini	1.000	3	0	1	0	0
Happ	.938	20	9	21	2	1
La Stella	.900	26	3	24	3	4

Shortstop	PCT	G	PO	A	E	DP
Baez	.965	65	67	155	8	29
Bote	1.000	2	2	3	0	1
Russell	.965	129	157	314	17	66

Outfield	PCT	G	PO	A	E	DP
Almora Jr.	.989	138	266	3	3	0
Bote	1.000	1	2	0	0	0
Bryant	.911	27	41	0	4	0
Cishek	.000	1	0	0	0	0
Contreras	.667	5	2	0	1	0
Duensing	.000	1	0	0	0	0
Gore	1.000	7	3	0	0	0
Happ	.988	115	164	6	2	0
Heyward	.988	126	245	7	3	1
Schwarber	.995	120	174	11	1	0
Zagunis	1.000	1	2	0	0	0
Zobrist	.992	84	127	2	1	1

IOWA CUBS
PACIFIC COAST LEAGUE

TRIPLE-A

Batting	B-T	HT	WT	DOB	AVG	vLH	vRH	G	AB	R	H	2B	3B	HR	RBI	BB	HBP	SH	SF	SO	SB	CS	SLG	OBP
Adams, Lane	R-R	6-4	220	11-13-89	.136	.250	.108	32	81	8	11	2	1	0	6	13	2	0	2	32	9	3	.185	.265
Bernard, Wynton	R-R	6-2	195	9-24-90	.204	.050	.262	61	147	17	30	10	3	1	13	6	1	1	0	32	11	2	.333	.240
Bote, David	R-R	6-1	210	4-7-93	.268	.356	.247	61	235	34	63	10	2	13	41	26	1	0	1	63	3	1	.494	.342
Bruno, Stephen	R-R	5-9	175	11-17-90	.240	.321	.219	91	271	27	65	13	0	3	20	18	12	2	2	46	5	6	.321	.314
Bryant, Kris	R-R	6-5	230	1-4-92	.200	.000	.222	4	10	3	2	0	0	0	1	3	0	0	0	4	0	0	.200	.385
Caratini, Victor	B-R	6-1	215	8-17-93	.313	.333	.307	32	115	13	36	7	0	4	22	18	2	0	2	25	0	0	.478	.409
Castillo, Erick	R-R	5-11	178	2-25-93	.143	—	.143	2	7	1	1	0	0	0	0	1	0	0	0	0	0	0	.143	.250
Coghlan, Chris	L-T	6-0	195	6-18-85	.235	.279	.221	53	179	28	42	11	1	4	15	22	4	1	0	34	1	1	.374	.332
Court, Ryan	R-R	6-2	210	5-28-88	.262	.308	.250	114	386	50	101	21	1	11	62	56	6	0	2	149	5	2	.407	.362
Davis, Taylor	R-R	5-10	200	11-28-89	.275	.300	.269	107	356	38	98	18	0	4	41	40	1	8	3	57	0	2	.360	.348
Donahue, Christian	L-R	5-8	180	5-4-95	.000	—	.000	3	6	0	0	0	0	0	0	1	1	0	0	1	0	0	.000	.143
Freeman, Mike	L-R	6-0	195	8-4-87	.274	.261	.278	78	303	51	83	15	2	6	38	25	1	1	1	66	6	6	.396	.330
Gimenez, Chris	R-R	6-2	230	12-27-82	.204	.208	.203	68	201	15	41	12	1	2	18	20	3	0	1	67	1	1	.304	.282
Gore, Terrance	R-R	5-7	165	6-8-91	.118	.000	.133	11	34	6	4	0	0	0	2	1	0	0		13	5	1	.118	.189
2-team total (67 Omah)					.193	.192	.194	78	176	32	34	2	2	0	5	19	3	7	0	49	21	5	.227	.283
Hannemann, Jacob	L-L	6-1	200	4-29-91	.238	.244	.236	116	374	44	89	14	3	6	32	27	5	5	2	84	22	6	.340	.297
Martin, Trey	R-R	6-2	188	12-11-92	.201	.265	.181	46	139	11	28	3	1	0	9	9	1	2	2	54	5	1	.237	.252
Navarro, Efren	L-L	6-0	210	5-14-86	.310	.400	.281	48	184	17	57	10	1	4	29	23	1	0	2	38	0	1	.440	.386
Pearson, Tyler	R-R	6-0	185	4-15-92	.167	.500	.000	2	6	1	1	0	0	0	0	0	0	0	0	3	0	0	.167	.167
Rademacher, Bijan	L-L	6-0	185	6-15-91	.252	.288	.241	114	342	26	86	14	0	2	31	37	2	3	3	67	2	2	.310	.326
Remillard, Will	R-R	6-1	195	9-18-92	.061	.000	.083	15	33	3	2	1	0	0	1	2	0	0	1	17	0	0	.091	.111
Solis, Ali	R-R	6-0	209	9-29-87	.182	.211	.170	27	66	3	12	2	0	1	4	1	0	0	1	24	0	0	.258	.191
Vosler, Jason	L-R	6-2	205	9-6-93	.263	.241	.269	63	236	28	62	11	1	11	47	13	2	0	1	79	0	0	.458	.306
Young, Chesny	R-R	6-0	170	10-6-92	.266	.288	.259	81	271	33	72	8	1	0	20	16	0	1	2	54	4	1	.303	.305
Zagunis, Mark	R-R	6-0	215	2-5-93	.272	.275	.272	115	371	63	101	17	0	7	40	70	7	2	3	101	11	1	.375	.395

Pitching	B-T	HT	WT	DOB	W	L	ERA	G	GS	CG	SV	IP	H	R	ER	HR	BB	SO	AVG	vLH	vRH	K/9	BB/9
Alzolay, Adbert	R-R	6-0	179	3-1-95	2	4	4.76	8	8	0	0	40	43	21	21	4	13	27	.281	.277	.283	6.13	2.95
Baldonado, Alberto	L-L	6-4	250	2-1-93	7	2	4.88	37	1	0	0	59	61	35	32	5	37	66	.275	.258	.282	10.07	5.64
Bass, Anthony	R-R	6-2	200	11-1-87	0	3	3.38	27	0	0	3	32	34	19	12	3	6	25	.266	.364	.214	7.03	1.69
Brooks, Craig	R-R	5-10	180	9-23-92	1	3	4.03	18	0	0	0	22	17	15	10	1	24	22	.210	.206	.213	8.87	9.67
Butler, Eddie	R-R	6-2	180	3-13-91	0	3	8.10	5	5	0	0	13	21	13	12	4	5	9	.368	.417	.356	6.08	3.38
Chatwood, Tyler	R-R	6-0	185	12-16-89	0	1	9.45	2	2	0	0	7	5	7	7	0	10	4	.227	.333	.100	5.40	13.50
Clifton, Trevor	R-R	6-0	170	5-11-95	4	3	3.89	14	12	0	0	69	65	32	30	8	29	56	.258	.245	.267	7.27	3.76
Coleman, Casey	L-R	6-0	185	7-3-87	2	4	6.91	10	5	0	0	29	37	24	22	4	10	23	.314	.400	.269	7.22	3.14
Duensing, Brian	L-L	6-0	200	2-22-83	0	1	6.35	5	0	0	0	6	7	4	4	1	2	2	.318	.143	.400	3.18	3.18
Edwards Jr., Carl	R-R	6-3	170	9-3-91	0	1	9.00	3	0	0	0	2	2	2	2	0	4	3	.333	1.000	.200	13.50	18.00
Farrell, Luke	L-R	6-6	210	6-7-91	1	4	3.64	12	12	0	0	54	40	22	22	4	28	61	.206	.174	.224	10.10	4.64
Hancock, Justin	R-R	6-4	185	10-28-90	2	2	4.57	18	0	0	0	22	25	14	11	2	8	27	.291	.351	.245	11.22	3.32
Hedges, Zach	R-R	6-4	210	10-21-92	0	0	6.20	7	3	0	1	20	26	14	14	3	6	12	.323	.355	.309	4.38	2.92
Hultzen, Danny	L-L	6-3	210	11-28-89	0	0	4.50	2	0	0	0	2	3	1	1	0	1	3	.333	.000	.500	4.50	9.00
Maples, Dillon	R-R	6-2	225	5-9-92	2	3	2.79	41	0	0	10	39	22	14	12	1	39	75	.162	.160	.163	17.46	9.08
Markey, Brad	R-R	5-10	185	3-3-92	3	2	5.12	24	2	0	0	46	51	29	26	11	9	33	.276	.267	.282	6.50	1.77
Mazzoni, Cory	R-R	6-1	210	10-19-89	4	3	4.46	29	0	0	4	38	37	22	19	5	11	34	.248	.236	.255	7.98	2.58
Mekkes, Dakota	R-R	6-7	250	11-6-94	1	0	1.44	25	0	0	3	31	27	6	5	1	16	41	.233	.268	.200	11.78	4.60
Mills, Alec	R-R	6-4	190	11-30-91	5	12	4.84	23	23	0	0	125	121	69	67	10	41	108	.256	.242	.264	7.80	2.96
Morrison, Preston	R-R	6-3	185	7-19-93	0	1	6.23	3	0	0	0	4	7	3	3	1	0	3	.333	.286	.357	6.23	0.00
Norwood, James	R-R	6-2	215	12-24-93	1	1	2.55	15	0	0	0	18	11	5	5	1	12	21	.180	.174	.184	10.70	6.11

Name	B-T	HT	WT	DOB	W	L	ERA	G	GS	CG	SV	IP	H	R	ER	HR	BB	SO	AVG	vLH	vRH	K/9	BB/9
Robinson, Duncan	R-R	6-6	220	12-5-93	1	0	0.82	2	2	0	0	11	9	2	1	0	3	8	.225	.222	.227	6.55	2.45
Rosario, Randy	L-L	6-1	200	5-18-94	0	0	0.79	15	0	0	0	23	13	3	2	1	6	15	.165	.000	.220	5.96	2.38
Roth, Michael	L-L	6-1	210	2-15-90	1	2	3.03	7	5	0	0	30	27	13	10	2	15	23	.265	.150	.293	6.98	4.55
2-team total (14 Round Rock)					6	7	4.35	21	18	0	0	101	122	60	49	12	38	61	.312	.306	.314	5.42	3.38
Ryan, Kyle	L-L	6-5	215	9-25-91	1	2	2.86	22	0	0	0	66	48	21	21	9	18	61	.204	.237	.193	8.32	2.45
Simmons, Shae	R-R	5-11	190	9-3-90	2	2	5.56	24	0	0	2	23	19	15	14	1	21	21	.224	.375	.164	8.34	8.34
Torrez, Daury	R-R	6-3	170	6-11-93	1	2	5.20	8	3	0	0	28	29	16	16	3	10	16	.274	.154	.343	5.20	3.25
Tseng, Jen-Ho	L-R	6-1	210	10-3-94	2	15	6.27	26	26	0	0	136	159	103	95	20	44	115	.290	.289	.291	7.59	2.90
Underwood Jr., Duane	R-R	6-2	210	7-20-94	4	10	4.53	27	20	0	0	119	127	71	60	8	37	105	.275	.289	.266	7.92	2.79
Webster, Allen	R-R	6-2	190	2-10-90	0	0	2.70	4	0	0	0	3	3	1	1	1	0	2	.231	.250	.222	5.40	0.00
Zastryzny, Rob	R-L	6-3	205	3-26-92	3	2	3.86	33	1	0	0	56	47	28	24	5	28	50	.226	.254	.215	8.04	4.50

Fielding

Catcher	PCT	G	PO	A	E	DP	PB
Caratini	.987	18	139	10	2	0	3
Castillo	1.000	2	8	0	1	0	
Davis	.991	67	531	39	5	2	9
Gimenez	.997	38	302	10	1	0	3
Remillard	.980	7	44	4	1	0	1
Solis	.967	10	51	8	2	1	0

First Base	PCT	G	PO	A	E	DP
Caratini	.991	12	107	4	1	4
Coghlan	1.000	25	163	19	0	18
Court	.983	8	56	1	1	7
Davis	1.000	24	167	11	0	23
Gimenez	.984	12	52	9	1	5
Navarro	.995	42	359	20	2	38
Rademacher	1.000	21	121	11	0	11
Remillard	.000	1	0	0	0	0
Solis	.935	5	26	3	2	5
Vosler	1.000	3	15	2	0	1
Young	1.000	1	6	2	0	0

Second Base	PCT	G	PO	A	E	DP
Bote	.972	38	57	80	4	26
Bruno	.988	42	73	93	2	22
Court	.987	17	31	44	1	19
Donahue	1.000	3	3	3	0	2
Freeman	.986	16	34	34	1	8
Vosler	.000	1	0	0	0	0
Young	.980	36	61	86	3	19

Third Base	PCT	G	PO	A	E	DP
Bote	.815	9	6	16	5	2
Bruno	.971	19	7	26	1	1
Bryant	1.000	2	2	0	0	0
Caratini	1.000	1	0	1	0	0
Court	.986	27	13	56	1	3
Davis	.889	12	1	15	2	0
Donahue	.667	1	0	2	1	0
Freeman	1.000	1	0	2	0	1
Gimenez	1.000	5	0	5	0	0
Vosler	.974	60	43	107	4	17
Young	.926	22	12	38	4	4

Shortstop	PCT	G	PO	A	E	DP
Bote	.980	15	9	39	1	13
Court	.950	59	73	135	11	26
Freeman	.987	55	73	154	3	36
Young	.935	14	14	29	3	4

Outfield	PCT	G	PO	A	E	DP
Adams	.953	27	40	1	2	0
Bernard	.951	48	74	3	4	0
Bote	1.000	2	1	0	0	0
Bruno	.967	22	27	2	1	0
Bryant	1.000	1	1	0	0	0
Coghlan	1.000	21	31	0	0	0
Court	1.000	1	1	0	0	0
Freeman	1.000	4	2	0	0	0
Gore	1.000	11	17	0	0	0
Hannemann	.975	107	225	8	6	0
Martin	.990	43	95	1	1	1
Navarro	1.000	3	1	0	0	0
Rademacher	.966	75	110	4	4	1
Young	1.000	6	12	0	0	0
Zagunis	.983	107	172	2	3	2

TENNESSEE SMOKIES
SOUTHERN LEAGUE

DOUBLE-A

Batting

Name	B-T	HT	WT	DOB	AVG	vLH	vRH	G	AB	R	H	2B	3B	HR	RBI	BB	HBP	SH	SF	SO	SB	CS	SLG	OBP
Alamo, Tyler	R-R	6-4	200		.250	.000	.308	5	16	1	4	1	0	0	0	1	0	0	0	4	1	0	.313	.294
Baez, Jeffrey	R-R	6-0	180	10-30-93	.262	.288	.250	88	256	40	67	14	2	7	30	29	5	2	2	81	16	8	.414	.346
Balaguert, Yasiel	R-R	6-2	215	1-9-93	.229	.235	.226	121	450	40	103	24	1	8	57	27	1	0	7	82	1	0	.340	.270
Bernard, Wynton	R-R	6-2	195	9-24-90	.295	.357	.273	37	105	13	31	2	0	2	9	10	1	1	0	20	14	2	.371	.362
Bryant, Kris	R-R	6-5	230	1-4-92	.333	.000	.500	2	6	2	2	0	0	1	3	0	0	0	0	2	0	0	.833	.333
Burks, Charcer	R-R	6-0	170	3-9-95	.229	.248	.221	125	437	68	100	16	4	6	33	60	8	4	4	127	14	5	.325	.330
Castillo, Erick	R-R	5-11	178	2-25-93	.186	.140	.211	42	140	10	26	4	0	2	15	7	2	2	0	22	0	0	.257	.235
Giambrone, Trent	R-R	5-8	175	12-20-93	.251	.214	.266	116	398	56	100	20	2	17	49	46	4	5	3	89	26	9	.440	.333
Higgins, P.J.	R-R	5-10	185	5-10-93	.241	.220	.250	41	145	14	35	5	1	1	15	12	2	0	1	27	1	0	.310	.306
Hodges, Jesse	R-R	6-1	212	3-29-94	.199	.233	.184	100	307	22	61	17	1	3	26	21	1	2	1	96	1	1	.290	.252
Machin, Vimael	L-R	5-10	185	9-25-93	.220	.208	.223	79	250	30	55	10	1	5	28	39	3	2	2	54	2	1	.328	.330
Martin, Trey	R-R	6-2	188	12-11-92	.247	.278	.237	70	227	40	56	16	1	7	30	35	0	2	3	75	12	4	.419	.343
Martinez, Eddy	R-R	6-1	195	1-18-95	.221	.270	.203	119	411	42	91	21	3	12	54	31	1	2	3	91	5	1	.375	.276
Myers, Connor	R-R	5-11	190	2-3-94	.225	.289	.191	39	129	17	29	2	1	1	6	11	1	1	2	43	4	3	.279	.289
Remillard, Will	R-R	6-1	195	9-18-92	.304	.222	.324	14	46	4	14	3	0	1	5	2	0	1	0	15	0	0	.435	.333
Rice, Ian	R-R	6-0	200	8-19-93	.250	.310	.222	88	272	43	68	17	0	8	30	52	9	0	1	85	1	0	.401	.386
Short, Zack	R-R	5-10	195	5-29-95	.227	.254	.217	124	436	68	99	28	2	17	59	82	5	1	0	136	8	3	.417	.356
Spingola, Daniel	L-L	6-1	180	5-5-93	.267	.500	.231	5	15	4	4	1	0	0	1	3	2	0	0	7	1	0	.333	.450
Vosler, Jason	L-R	6-2	205	9-6-93	.238	.134	.280	66	235	33	56	18	1	12	46	37	6	0	4	70	1	0	.477	.351

Pitching

Name	B-T	HT	WT	DOB	W	L	ERA	G	GS	CG	SV	IP	H	R	ER	HR	BB	SO	AVG	vLH	vRH	K/9	BB/9
Brooks, Craig	R-R	5-10	180	9-23-92	2	2	3.00	23	0	0	5	30	19	11	10	2	9	41	.181	.220	.146	12.30	2.70
Buckelew, James	L-L	6-2	155	8-4-91	0	2	4.64	9	1	0	0	21	23	11	11	2	10	15	.284	.222	.315	6.33	4.22
2-team total (2 Jacksonville)					0	2	4.26	11	1	0	0	25	28	12	12	3	11	17	.289	.207	.324	6.04	3.91
Clifton, Trevor	R-R	6-4	170	5-11-95	3	4	2.86	12	12	0	0	57	41	24	18	0	23	45	.200	.221	.185	7.15	3.65
De La Cruz, Oscar	R-R	6-4	200	3-4-95	6	7	5.24	16	16	1	0	77	76	45	45	8	31	73	.259	.230	.276	8.50	3.61
Duensing, Brian	L-L	6-0	200	2-22-83	0	0	0.00	1	0	0	0	1	0	0	0	0	0	0	.000	—	.000	0.00	0.00
Effross, Scott	R-R	6-1	195	12-28-93	2	6	5.97	44	0	0	1	63	83	45	42	7	20	60	.319	.314	.324	8.53	2.84
Hatch, Thomas	R-R	6-1	190	9-29-94	8	6	3.82	26	26	2	0	144	127	62	61	16	61	117	.245	.276	.221	7.33	3.82
Hedges, Zach	R-R	6-4	210	10-21-92	5	2	2.30	29	1	0	1	63	53	17	16	4	10	46	.228	.258	.206	6.61	1.44
Markey, Brad	R-R	5-10	185	3-3-92	0	0	1.64	9	0	0	0	11	9	2	2	1	5	14	.220	.133	.269	11.45	4.09
McNeil, Ryan	R-R	6-3	210	2-1-94	0	0	7.71	9	0	0	0	12	11	10	10	3	14	7	.239	.288	.200	5.40	10.80
Mekkes, Dakota	R-R	6-7	250	11-6-94	3	0	0.81	16	0	0	8	22	9	6	2	1	30	.120	.167	.089	12.09	5.24
Minch, Jordan	L-L	6-3	180	7-16-93	1	4	3.98	27	0	0	0	41	37	22	18	6	26	.247	.212	.274	5.75	4.65
Morrison, Preston	R-R	6-3	185	7-19-93	1	1	4.50	33	1	0	0	58	51	33	29	8	17	51	.232	.323	.165	7.91	2.64

Name	B-T	HT	WT	DOB	W	L	ERA	G	GS	CG	SV	IP	H	R	ER	HR	BB	SO	AVG	vLH	vRH	K/9	BB/9
Nance, Tommy	R-R	6-6	235	3-19-91	1	1	3.48	15	0	0	0	21	14	10	8	1	11	20	.187	.171	.200	8.71	4.79
Norwood, James	R-R	6-2	215	12-24-93	1	2	2.48	25	0	0	2	33	25	10	9	2	12	36	.214	.222	.208	9.92	3.31
Penalver, Carlos	R-R	6-0	170	5-17-94	0	0	9.00	1	0	0	0	1	2	1	1	0	0	0	.400	.333	.500	0.00	0.00
Pugliese, James	R-R	6-3	205	8-12-92	0	2	18.56	6	0	0	0	5	15	11	11	0	6	5	.536	.600	.500	8.44	10.13
Robinson, Duncan	R-R	6-2	220	12-5-93	7	4	3.31	24	24	0	0	131	142	61	48	9	22	111	.275	.297	.255	7.65	1.52
Rucker, Michael	R-R	6-1	185	4-27-94	9	6	3.73	26	26	0	0	133	111	62	55	17	38	118	.223	.242	.208	8.01	2.58
Short, Wyatt	L-L	5-8	180	10-14-94	5	3	3.30	22	0	0	2	30	29	17	11	4	8	28	.259	.238	.271	8.40	2.40
Steele, Justin	L-L	6-2	195	7-11-95	0	1	3.60	2	2	0	0	10	8	4	4	1	3	7	.216	.200	.222	6.30	2.70
Stinnett, Jake	R-R	6-4	205	4-25-92	0	6	4.91	42	0	0	6	51	53	30	28	8	22	57	.259	.352	.184	9.99	3.86
Swarmer, Matt	R-R	6-5	175	9-25-93	4	6	3.84	15	15	0	0	77	70	35	33	8	14	76	.237	.286	.198	8.84	1.63
Thompson, Keegan	R-R	6-0	193	3-13-95	6	3	4.06	13	13	0	0	62	66	29	28	3	21	54	.273	.306	.240	7.84	3.05
Torrez, Daury	R-R	6-3	170	6-11-93	3	2	3.75	25	1	0	1	48	56	21	20	4	12	35	.289	.307	.274	6.56	2.25
Webster, Allen	R-R	6-2	190	2-10-90	0	0	0.00	4	0	0	3	5	3	0	0	0	1	9	.177	.143	.200	17.36	1.93

Fielding

Catcher	PCT	G	PO	A	E	DP	PB
Alamo	1.000	1	10	0	0	0	0
Castillo	.992	42	314	38	3	4	3
Higgins	1.000	21	168	10	0	3	1
Remillard	1.000	13	98	11	0	0	0
Rice	.990	64	467	47	5	2	4

First Base	PCT	G	PO	A	E	DP
Alamo	1.000	3	19	2	0	1
Balaguert	.990	112	898	77	10	90
Higgins	1.000	3	21	0	0	2
Hodges	1.000	3	19	1	0	3
Machin	1.000	12	109	8	0	6
Vosler	1.000	8	62	7	0	2

Second Base	PCT	G	PO	A	E	DP
Giambrone	.976	89	124	247	9	43

Second Base (cont.)	PCT	G	PO	A	E	DP
Machin	.992	36	54	72	1	18
Penalver	.930	17	28	38	5	14
Short	.957	4	8	14	1	5
Vosler	1.000	3	5	6	0	0

Third Base	PCT	G	PO	A	E	DP
Bryant	.750	1	1	2	1	0
Giambrone	.778	6	2	5	2	1
Higgins	1.000	12	9	23	0	2
Hodges	.942	72	43	120	10	13
Machin	1.000	12	7	9	0	1
Vosler	.949	45	30	64	5	1

Shortstop	PCT	G	PO	A	E	DP
Giambrone	.905	13	11	27	4	6
Machin	.875	5	5	9	2	0
Penalver	1.000	5	10	18	0	2

Short						
Short	.964	117	168	308	18	72

Outfield	PCT	G	PO	A	E	DP
Baez	.993	74	134	6	1	0
Balaguert	.000	2	0	0	0	0
Bernard	1.000	30	69	0	0	0
Burks	.980	115	245	4	5	0
Giambrone	1.000	5	9	0	0	0
Machin	.000	1	0	0	0	0
Martin	1.000	66	142	2	0	1
Martinez	.976	99	156	10	4	4
Myers	.989	38	88	4	1	0
Penalver	1.000	2	2	0	0	0
Short	1.000	1	1	0	0	0
Spingola	1.000	5	6	0	0	0

MYRTLE BEACH PELICANS

CAROLINA LEAGUE

HIGH CLASS A

Batting	B-T	HT	WT	DOB	AVG	vLH	vRH	G	AB	R	H	2B	3B	HR	RBI	BB	HBP	SH	SF	SO	SB	CS	SLG	OBP
Ademan, Aramis	L-R	5-11	160	9-13-98	.207	.227	.201	114	396	49	82	11	3	3	38	38	9	8	1	95	9	5	.273	.291
Alamo, Tyler	R-R	6-4	200	5-2-95	.212	.218	.211	71	245	24	52	9	0	8	34	15	4	1	8	66	0	1	.347	.261
Ayala, Luis	L-R	6-0	176	12-21-95	.184	.200	.178	71	207	17	38	4	1	0	12	25	1	1	0	54	7	5	.213	.275
Caro, Roberto	B-R	6-0	185	9-25-93	.263	.158	.303	44	137	13	36	6	0	1	10	25	2	3	0	32	19	4	.329	.384
Cruz, Michael	L-R	5-11	210	1-13-96	.128	.000	.152	12	39	3	5	1	0	1	3	1	1	0	1	9	0	0	.231	.167
Davis, Zach	B-R	5-11	173	6-29-94	.239	.242	.238	38	113	12	27	9	3	0	6	8	0	1		36	7	3	.292	.326
Donahue, Christian	L-R	5-8	180	5-4-95	.282	.444	.233	13	39	7	11	3	0	2	6	6	1	0	0	12	0	0	.513	.391
Galindo, Wladimir	R-R	6-3	210	11-6-96	.216	.222	.214	114	403	40	87	21	0	6	35	31	3	0	1	124	0	2	.313	.276
Gutierrez, Jose	B-R	5-11	185	11-9-98	.239	.177	.276	14	46	5	11	3	2	0	1	5	0	3	0	15	0	1	.391	.314
Higgins, P.J.	R-R	5-10	185	5-10-93	.289	.286	.290	69	232	22	67	17	0	3	37	34	3	4	4	40	3	1	.401	.381
Machin, Vimael	L-R	5-10	185	9-25-93	.209	.235	.204	33	110	20	23	6	0	2	14	28	1	0	2	23	1	0	.318	.369
Mitchell, Kevonte	R-R	6-4	185	8-12-95	.218	.165	.240	80	262	23	57	13	1	4	24	27	3	1	5	78	4	4	.321	.293
Monasterio, Andruw	R-R	6-0	175	5-30-97	.263	.295	.252	109	369	52	97	14	2	3	31	52	5	7	3	64	10	3	.336	.359
2-team total (13 Potomac)					.267	.290	.259	122	408	58	109	14	3	3	36	59	5	7	4	70	12	6	.338	.363
Myers, Connor	R-R	5-11	170	2-3-94	.259	.271	.255	72	247	27	64	14	2	2	24	18	2	2	2	69	14	6	.356	.312
Pearson, Tyler	R-R	6-0	185	4-15-92	.000	.000	.000	9	24	1	0	0	0	0	0	0	0	0	0	11	0	0	.000	.000
Peguero, Yeiler	B-R	5-10	150	9-20-97	.210	.277	.183	60	167	12	35	9	0	0	9	7	2	1		45	1	1	.228	.240
Pereda, Jhonny	R-R	6-1	170	4-18-96	.272	.275	.271	122	441	51	120	12	2	8	57	51	1	1	2	68	4	2	.363	.348
Pieters, Chris	L-L	6-3	185	9-21-94	.226	.316	.203	27	93	9	21	2	2	0	7	7	0	0	2	23	4	0	.290	.275
Spingola, Daniel	L-L	6-1	180	5-5-93	.211	.154	.224	41	133	16	28	8	0	2	10	11	2	2	1	33	1	1	.316	.279
Upshaw, Austin	L-R	6-0	175	7-28-96	.203	.255	.189	72	232	18	47	8	2	2	15	15	1	6	2	44	1	0	.280	.252
Wilson, D.J.	L-L	5-8	177	10-8-96	.226	.195	.236	64	237	27	52	9	2	1	13	32	1	2	0	71	10	6	.287	.315
Young, Jared	L-R	6-2	185	7-9-95	.282	.314	.270	51	188	20	53	6	2	6	23	11	7	0	2	40	6	1	.431	.341

Pitching	B-T	HT	WT	DOB	W	L	ERA	G	GS	CG	SV	IP	H	R	ER	HR	BB	SO	AVG	vLH	vRH	K/9	BB/9
Abbott, Cory	R-R	6-2	210	9-20-95	4	5	2.53	13	13	0	0	68	59	22	19	3	26	74	.234	.264	.212	9.84	3.46
Bloomquist, Casey	R-R	6-3	190	1-25-94	3	4	3.71	30	2	0	1	63	64	29	26	2	23	51	.257	.200	.284	7.29	3.29
Buckelew, James	L-L	6-2	155	8-4-91	0	0	0.00	2	1	0	0	4	2	0	0		2	3	.000	.667	.000	7.36	4.91
Clark, Bailey	R-R	6-4	185	12-3-94	2	2	2.45	12	2	0	0	37	30	14	10	1	14	36	.226	.208	.235	8.84	3.44
Diaz, Elvis	R-R	6-3	185	2-6-93	0	0	9.95	4	0	0	0	6	11	7	7	2	2	3	.407	.429	.400	4.26	2.84
Gomez, Yapson	L-L	5-10	160	10-2-93	1	2	2.45	10	0	0	1	18	17	7	5	1	4	12	.254	.148	.325	5.89	1.96
Hockin, Chad	R-R	6-2	210	10-7-94	0	2	7.94	3	0	0	0	6	8	8	5	0	1	4	.333	.500	.278	6.35	1.59
Hudson, Bryan	L-L	6-8	220	5-8-97	6	11	4.70	23	23	0	0	113	102	72	59	4	58	78	.241	.214	.249	6.21	4.62
Kellogg, Ryan	R-L	6-6	230	2-4-94	3	1	3.58	37	0	0	4	78	81	39	31	4	29	52	.279	.225	.307	6.00	3.35
Kelly, Garrett	R-R	6-1	180	8-2-94	2	1	2.08	5	0	0	0	9	5	4	2		4	9	.161	.182	.150	9.35	4.15
Lacy, Rollie	R-R	6-4	195	7-17-95	1	1	5.79	2	2	0	0	9	11	6	6	2	4	10	.297	.300	.294	9.64	3.86
2-team total (6 Down East)					2	3	4.78	8	8	0	0	38	37	23	20	3	17	37	.262	.257	.268	8.84	4.06
Lange, Alex	R-R	6-3	197	10-2-95	6	8	3.74	23	23	0	0	120	104	52	50	6	38	101	.234	.198	.262	7.55	2.84

Name	B-T	HT	WT	DOB	W	L	ERA	G	GS	CG	SV	IP	H	R	ER	HR	BB	SO	AVG	vLH	vRH	K/9	BB/9
Leal, Erick	R-R	6-3	180	3-17-95	1	1	1.41	21	8	0	1	64	35	12	10	2	17	61	.156	.127	.171	8.62	2.40
Miller, Kyle	R-R	6-3	185	12-2-93	0	0	18.00	2	0	0	0	2	5	4	4	1	3	5	.455	.333	.500	22.50	13.50
Miller, Tyson	R-R	6-5	200	7-29-95	9	9	3.54	23	23	1	0	127	104	53	50	12	35	126	.220	.250	.202	8.93	2.48
Minch, Jordan	L-L	6-3	180	7-16-93	3	1	3.65	18	0	0	1	25	19	15	10	2	13	28	.211	.200	.215	10.22	4.74
Paulino, Jose	L-L	6-2	165	4-9-95	0	7	6.12	29	7	0	3	78	110	80	53	7	21	57	.330	.297	.347	6.58	2.42
Peyton, Tyler	R-R	6-3	200	3-31-94	3	3	3.07	38	0	0	10	67	69	32	23	1	38	52	.265	.341	.229	6.95	5.08
Romero, Jhon	R-R	5-10	195	1-17-95	1	2	3.27	32	0	0	9	44	40	19	16	1	17	57	.237	.276	.216	11.66	3.48
2-team total (4 Potomac)					1	2	2.92	36	0	0	9	49	42	19	16	1	19	64	.225	.246	.213	11.68	3.47
Rondon, Manuel	L-L	6-1	165	3-7-95	2	5	2.10	19	1	0	1	34	25	11	8	2	22	40	.208	.160	.210	10.49	5.77
Short, Wyatt	L-L	5-8	180	10-14-94	1	1	2.27	22	0	0	4	32	19	9	8	1	12	38	.167	.143	.177	10.80	3.41
Steele, Justin	L-L	6-2	195	7-11-95	2	1	2.45	4	4	0	0	18	12	7	5	0	6	19	.185	.273	.140	9.33	2.95
Swarmer, Matt	R-R	6-5	195	9-25-93	5	2	2.28	9	9	0	0	51	43	15	13	2	7	59	.221	.278	.171	10.34	1.23
Thompson, Keegan	R-R	6-0	193	3-13-95	3	3	3.19	12	12	0	0	68	49	27	24	6	13	61	.202	.250	.172	8.11	1.73
Uelmen, Erich	R-R	6-3	185	5-19-96	3	3	4.36	10	9	0	0	33	38	17	16	3	15	24	.292	.339	.246	6.55	4.09

Fielding

Catcher	PCT	G	PO	A	E	DP	PB
Alamo	1.000	3	14	3	0	0	2
Cruz	1.000	9	57	8	0	0	3
Higgins	.981	37	271	41	6	2	5
Pearson	.968	8	58	3	2	0	1
Pereda	.991	83	671	80	7	9	11

First Base	PCT	G	PO	A	E	DP
Alamo	.993	52	391	22	3	35
Cruz	.905	3	19	0	2	2
Higgins	1.000	4	18	0	0	0
Pieters	.000	1	0	0	0	0
Upshaw	.993	50	386	29	3	32
Young	.993	32	271	9	2	30

Second Base	PCT	G	PO	A	E	DP
Donahue	.957	10	23	21	2	8
Machin	.957	17	26	40	3	5
Monasterio	.964	77	135	188	12	47
Peguero	.968	32	64	85	5	18
Upshaw	1.000	8	12	18	0	6

Third Base	PCT	G	PO	A	E	DP
Galindo	.891	105	60	178	29	18
Higgins	.933	5	3	11	1	0
Machin	.931	10	5	22	2	1
Monasterio	.000	1	0	0	1	0
Peguero	.886	22	11	28	5	4
Upshaw	.750	4	3	6	3	1

Shortstop	PCT	G	PO	A	E	DP
Ademan	.948	112	156	265	23	55

	PCT	G	PO	A	E	DP
Monasterio	.957	28	24	65	4	8
Peguero	1.000	2	1	2	0	1

Outfield	PCT	G	PO	A	E	DP
Ayala	.966	69	138	3	5	0
Caro	.986	39	66	3	1	1
Davis	.985	37	61	3	1	1
Gutierrez	.968	14	29	1	1	1
Mitchell	.977	68	122	4	3	1
Myers	.993	70	137	6	1	2
Pieters	.925	26	48	1	4	0
Spingola	.944	39	65	3	4	1
Upshaw	.000	1	0	0	0	0
Wilson	.978	61	132	3	3	1
Young	1.000	8	14	1	0	0

SOUTH BEND CUBS
MIDWEST LEAGUE

LOW CLASS A

Batting	B-T	HT	WT	DOB	AVG	vLH	vRH	G	AB	R	H	2B	3B	HR	RBI	BB	HBP	SH	SF	SO	SB	CS	SLG	OBP
Amaya, Miguel	R-R	6-1	185		.256	.308	.242	116	414	54	106	21	2	12	52	50	11	0	4	91	1	0	.403	.349
Balego, Cam	R-R	5-11	205	6-12-95	.233	.161	.255	38	129	13	30	7	0	0	12	8	4	1	1	25	1	1	.287	.296
Bethencourt, Jhonny	R-R	5-11	160	2-12-97	.274	.242	.284	64	252	33	69	14	5	1	23	17	1	5	4	58	7	3	.381	.318
Caro, Roberto	B-R	6-0	185	9-25-93	.375	.300	.389	38	128	27	48	8	6	1	17	18	3	4	1	30	17	6	.555	.460
Carrier, Chris	R-R	6-2	225	4-18-95	.171	.125	.185	13	35	7	6	1	0	2	11	5	3	0	0	15	1	0	.371	.326
Cruz, Michael	L-R	5-11	210	1-13-96	.246	.217	.252	75	276	34	68	24	0	11	45	25	4	0	3	33	1	0	.453	.315
Daniel, Clayton	R-R	5-7	170	5-10-95	.236	.276	.225	36	127	18	30	8	0	0	9	9	0	0	2	20	1	1	.299	.283
Davis, Zach	B-R	5-11	175	6-29-94	.289	.232	.304	79	273	55	79	5	5	0	25	32	6	4	3	65	31	10	.344	.373
Donahue, Christian	L-R	5-8	180	5-4-95	.287	.300	.285	80	282	41	81	18	1	2	23	29	1	3	3	63	2	3	.379	.352
Filiere, Austin	R-R	6-1	190	9-1-95	.253	.248	.255	120	439	57	111	22	1	8	47	51	5	3	3	129	0	1	.362	.335
Gonzalez, Eric	R-R	5-10	175	9-2-96	.333	.000	.400	4	12	2	4	0	0	0	0	0	0	0	0	1	0	0	.333	.333
Gutierrez, Jose	B-R	5-11	185	11-9-98	.205	.300	.175	21	83	10	17	2	0	2	10	6	1	2	2	26	1	1	.301	.261
Herron, Jimmy	R-L	6-1	195	7-27-96	.246	.265	.237	33	110	12	27	2	0	3	17	12	4	1	3	24	1	3	.346	.333
Hoerner, Nico	R-R	6-1	200	5-13-97	.400	1.000	.308	4	15	1	6	1	0	1	3	2	0	0	0	1	0	0	.667	.471
Hughes, Brandon	B-L	6-2	215	12-1-95	.237	.224	.241	109	375	46	89	14	0	4	35	33	5	3	6	111	22	10	.307	.303
Narea, Rafael	R-R	5-10	160	4-3-98	.237	.205	.248	100	358	43	85	20	0	2	43	29	3	6	6	64	7	3	.310	.296
Payne, Tyler	R-R	5-11	210	10-25-92	.280	.000	.359	13	50	5	14	2	1	0	10	3	0	0	0	10	0	0	.360	.321
Peguero, Yeiler	B-R	5-10	150	9-20-97	.258	.136	.293	28	97	10	25	3	2	1	5	9	0	2	1	26	4	0	.361	.318
Singleton, Chris	R-R	6-0	175	7-5-96	.223	.241	.218	107	368	30	82	26	2	4	28	22	4	9	3	99	12	7	.337	.272
Upshaw, Austin	L-R	6-0	175	7-28-96	.157	.185	.150	39	140	9	22	3	0	4	17	9	0	3	3	32	0	1	.264	.204
Velazquez, Nelson	R-R	6-0	190	12-26-98	.188	.108	.227	31	112	6	21	1	0	0	7	7	1	0	0	43	3	0	.196	.242
Young, Jared	L-R	6-2	185	7-9-95	.313	.317	.312	69	259	41	81	13	6	10	53	20	6	2	6	47	1	0	.525	.368
Zinn, Delvin	R-R	5-10	170	5-29-97	.286	.298	.282	59	217	17	62	3	1	1	21	14	3	3	2	37	3	6	.323	.335

Pitching	B-T	HT	WT	DOB	W	L	ERA	G	GS	CG	SV	IP	H	R	ER	HR	BB	SO	AVG	vLH	vRH	K/9	BB/9
Abbott, Cory	R-R	6-2	210	9-20-95	4	1	2.47	9	9	0	0	47	35	18	13	5	13	57	.207	.246	.185	10.84	2.47
Aguiar, Maikel	R-R	6-1	185	11-20-96	1	1	3.46	6	0	0	0	13	6	5	5	2	6	10	.140	.091	.156	6.92	4.15
Albertos, Jose	R-R	6-1	185	11-7-98	0	5	18.69	9	4	0	0	13	17	28	27	1	32	17	.321	.238	.375	11.77	22.15
Aquino, Luis	R-R	6-1	170	6-30-93	1	2	7.16	10	0	0	0	16	17	20	13	1	10	9	.270	.250	.279	4.96	5.51
Assad, Javier	R-R	6-0	200	7-30-97	5	7	4.40	23	21	0	0	106	124	65	52	6	31	89	.290	.311	.276	7.53	2.62
Camargo, Jesus	R-R	5-11	170	11-23-95	3	2	2.62	11	0	0	0	45	40	15	13	2	10	40	.241	.188	.278	8.06	2.01
Clark, Bailey	R-R	6-4	185	12-3-94	1	0	1.26	5	0	0	0	14	12	5	2	1	3	19	.226	.389	.143	11.93	1.88
Darvish, Yu	R-R	6-5	220	8-16-86	0	0	1.50	2	2	0	0	6	4	1	1	1	1	6	.182	.250	.143	9.00	1.50
De Los Rios, Enrique	R-R	6-1	175	5-2-95	3	4	2.93	31	6	0	4	86	86	36	28	5	16	63	.269	.306	.250	6.59	1.67
Diaz, Elvis	R-R	6-3	185	2-6-93	1	0	1.80	2	0	0	0	5	5	2	1	0	0	4	.250	.000	.417	7.20	0.00
Glowicki, Brian	R-R	5-11	190	10-19-94	5	5	1.20	45	0	0	18	68	52	23	9	4	24	66	.211	.202	.217	8.78	3.19
Gomez, Yapson	L-L	5-10	160	10-2-93	1	1	3.58	28	0	0	1	50	47	25	20	1	17	40	.237	.220	.243	7.15	3.04
Hecht, Ben	R-R	6-2	170	5-31-95	4	1	4.23	34	0	0	6	55	42	29	26	3	29	59	.210	.319	.153	9.60	4.72

Name	B-T	HT	WT	DOB	W	L	ERA	G	GS	CG	SV	IP	H	R	ER	HR	BB	SO	AVG	vLH	vRH	K/9	BB/9
Kelly, Garrett	R-R	6-1	210	8-2-94	1	1	1.34	18	0	0	1	34	19	9	5	1	19	32	.161	.135	.182	8.55	5.08
King, Brendan	R-R	6-1	200	7-8-94	4	7	3.39	35	7	0	3	82	73	35	31	10	24	82	.234	.218	.243	8.96	2.62
Lacy, Rollie	R-R	6-4	195	7-17-95	4	1	2.02	16	10	0	0	71	54	26	16	3	20	84	.203	.207	.201	10.60	2.52
Lawlor, Ryan	R-L	6-1	185	1-8-94	1	2	4.50	4	3	0	0	16	14	8	8	0	5	21	.230	.143	.255	11.81	2.81
Little, Brendon	R-L	6-1	195	8-11-96	5	11	5.15	22	21	0	0	101	106	70	58	8	43	90	.264	.250	.270	7.99	3.82
Marquez, Brailyn	L-L	6-4	185	1-30-99	0	0	2.57	2	2	0	0	7	7	3	2	0	2	7	.259	.400	.227	9.00	2.57
Moreno, Erling	R-R	6-3	200	1-13-97	2	3	3.86	12	11	0	0	68	67	32	29	1	27	41	.265	.307	.237	5.45	3.59
Passantino, Jeffrey	R-R	5-9	225	9-24-95	4	1	3.41	8	4	0	0	34	36	16	13	6	4	37	.267	.224	.299	9.70	1.05
Rodriguez, Manuel	R-R	5-11	205	8-6-96	3	5	7.59	32	0	0	3	40	52	41	34	2	36	64	.308	.345	.288	14.28	8.03
Rondon, Manuel	L-L	6-1	165	3-7-95	1	0	3.78	9	0	0	0	17	12	9	7	2	6	22	.200	.188	.205	11.88	3.24
Smyly, Drew	L-L	6-3	190	6-13-89	0	0	0.00	1	1	0	0	1	0	0	0	0	0	3	.000	—	.000	27.00	0.00
Steffens, Jake	R-R	6-1	215	6-24-94	1	3	3.65	12	0	0	0	25	27	12	10	1	7	12	.270	.231	.295	4.38	2.55
Stophel, Mitch	R-R	6-3	205	11-9-94	0	0	12.54	6	0	0	0	9	20	13	13	3	4	12	.417	.182	.487	11.57	3.86
Thomas, Tyler	R-L	6-1	175	12-22-95	3	5	2.88	15	14	0	1	75	58	31	24	5	14	81	.210	.172	.220	9.72	1.68
Uelmen, Erich	R-R	6-3	185	5-19-96	5	5	3.51	11	11	0	0	56	54	22	22	0	15	58	.251	.222	.269	9.27	2.40
Williams, Ryan	R-R	6-4	220	11-1-91	0	2	4.82	7	6	0	0	37	42	20	20	3	10	29	.290	.284	.295	6.99	2.41

Fielding

C: Amaya 95, Balego 12, Cruz 27, Gonzalez 4, Payne 7. **1B:** Amaya 9, Balego 16, Cruz 6, Filiere 25, Payne 2, Upshaw 34, Young 50. **2B:** Balego 3, Bethencourt 18, Daniel 24, Donahue 49, Narea 12, Peguero 12, Young 2, Zinn 21. **3B:** Balego 9, Bethencourt 13, Daniel 1, Donahue 7, Filiere 86, Narea 2, Peguero 9, Upshaw 1, Zinn 15. **SS:** Bethencourt 31, Daniel 5, Donahue 1, Filiere 1, Hoerner 4, Narea 80, Peguero 6, Zinn 13. **OF:** Caro 31, Carrier 12, Davis 78, Donahue 12, Gutierrez 18, Herron 30, Hughes 100, Singleton 103, Velazquez 26, Young 13.

EUGENE EMERALDS

NORTHWEST LEAGUE

SHORT-SEASON

Batting

Name	B-T	HT	WT	DOB	AVG	vLH	vRH	G	AB	R	H	2B	3B	HR	RBI	BB	HBP	SH	SF	SO	SB	CS	SLG	OBP
Artis, D.J.	L-L	5-9	165	3-20-97	.235	.200	.241	20	68	10	16	2	1	2	9	8	1	0	1	14	6	2	.382	.321
Balego, Cam	R-R	5-11	205	6-12-95	.267	.286	.250	5	15	2	4	2	0	0	2	1	0	0	1	1	2		.400	.389
Daniel, Clayton	R-R	5-7	170	5-10-95	.269	.250	.273	7	26	3	7	1	0	0	2	5	0	1	0	1	1	1	.308	.387
Diaz, Luis	R-R	5-9	160	4-16-99	.212	.132	.239	44	151	16	32	8	1	0	17	14	0	1	1	68	5	3	.278	.277
Durna, Tyler	L-L	6-0	205	11-13-96	.259	.167	.275	24	81	10	21	3	2	1	8	9	0	1	0	17	0	0	.383	.333
Fennell, Grant	R-R	6-1	195	10-12-95	.281	.189	.309	41	160	17	45	11	1	4	21	12	1	0	0	36	3	3	.438	.335
Gonzalez, Eric	R-R	5-10	175	9-2-96	.178	.154	.188	14	45	4	8	3	0	1	4	4	0	0	1	15	0	0	.311	.240
Guerra, Alexander	R-R	5-11	240	4-8-97	.250	.000	.333	1	4	0	1	0	0	0	0	0	0	0	0	1	0	0	.250	.250
Hoerner, Nico	R-R	6-1	200	5-13-97	.318	.429	.267	7	22	6	7	0	1	1	2	5	1	0	0	3	4	1	.546	.464
Jordan, Levi	R-R	5-8	170	9-24-95	.256	.235	.263	39	129	20	33	4	1	1	9	9	1	0	2	30	6	5	.326	.305
Kaleiwahea, Brennon	R-R	6-0	200	5-28-96	.222	.188	.241	18	45	3	10	1	0	1	6	5	2	0	0	18	0	0	.311	.327
Kelli, Fernando	R-R	6-0	180	7-28-98	.236	.278	.218	71	237	29	56	5	0	3	16	19	6	1	1	73	28	13	.295	.308
Knight, Caleb	R-R	5-11	220	1-2-96	.159	.143	.162	16	44	6	7	1	0	1	3	11	4	0	1	9	1	0	.250	.367
Kwon, Kwang-Min	L-L	6-2	210	12-12-97	.191	.154	.200	21	63	8	12	1	0	0	1	7	1	0	0	15	6	1	.206	.282
Mejia, Rafael	R-R	6-1	195	12-12-94	.292	.300	.286	7	24	2	7	2	1	0	2	2	0	0	0	6	0	1	.458	.346
Morel, Christopher	R-R	6-0	140	6-24-99	.165	.214	.143	25	91	7	15	2	0	1	8	0	1	0	1	29	0	1	.220	.172
Perlaza, Yonathan	B-R	5-10	195	11-10-98	.111	.000	.200	2	9	0	1	0	0	0	0	0	0	0	0	2	0	0	.111	.111
Polanco, Gustavo	R-R	6-0	190	6-13-97	.222	.111	.259	41	144	11	32	5	1	3	14	3	1	0	1	31	0	0	.333	.242
Reyes, Ruben	L-L	5-11	170	10-1-95	.000	.000	.000	2	6	0	0	0	0	0	0	0	0	0	0	0	0	0	.000	.000
Reynolds, Luke	L-R	6-1	215	3-20-95	.289	.318	.283	36	121	16	35	11	1	1	16	18	1	0	1	33	0	0	.422	.383
Romano, Ramsey	R-R	6-2	208	5-10-95	.125	.111	.133	7	24	1	3	1	0	0	0	1	0	0	0	5	0	0	.167	.160
Sierra, Jonathan	L-L	6-3	190	10-17-98	.255	.275	.250	68	243	26	62	15	1	3	29	22	1	1	1	60	10	4	.362	.318
Slaughter, Jake	R-R	6-3	200	10-24-96	.233	.262	.221	41	146	7	34	13	1	1	12	7	4	0	0	37	1	1	.356	.287
Soto, Jonathan	L-R	5-9	143	7-9-98	.138	.308	.089	18	58	2	8	3	0	0	5	4	0	0	1	14	1	1	.190	.191
Vazquez, Luis	R-R	6-1	165	10-10-99	.193	.250	.168	59	197	22	38	10	0	3	19	14	3	1	3	48	11	4	.289	.254
Velazquez, Nelson	R-R	6-0	190	12-26-98	.250	.219	.262	72	264	35	66	18	2	11	33	23	5	1	0	81	12	4	.458	.322
Weber, Andy	L-R	6-1	190	7-24-97	.291	.182	.309	23	79	13	23	3	0	0	9	11	1	2	1	19	1	3	.329	.363

Pitching

Name	B-T	HT	WT	DOB	W	L	ERA	G	GS	CG	SV	IP	H	R	ER	HR	BB	SO	AVG	vLH	vRH	K/9	BB/9
Albertos, Jose	R-R	6-1	185	11-7-98	0	4	11.94	11	6	0	0	17	19	27	23	0	33	21	.284	.222	.325	10.90	17.13
Aquino, Luis	R-R	6-1	170	6-30-93	0	0	1.83	12	0	0	2	20	13	6	4	1	7	19	.191	.217	.178	8.69	3.33
Barry, Sean	R-R	6-2	190	5-22-95	2	2	1.77	24	0	0	1	36	23	13	7	3	20	42	.192	.205	.184	10.60	5.05
Carrera, Faustino	L-L	5-10	165	3-29-99	5	2	2.54	13	9	0	0	67	48	20	19	4	19	58	.198	.132	.224	7.75	2.54
Casey, Derek	R-R	6-2	190	2-15-96	0	0	5.87	5	3	0	0	8	6	5	5	1	3	5	.222	.429	.150	5.87	3.52
Cruz, Yovanny	R-R	6-1	190	8-23-99	1	0	0.00	1	1	0	0	5	4	0	0	0	0	5	.222	.154	.400	9.00	0.00
De La Cruz, Yan	R-R	5-11	165	8-5-93	0	2	5.25	19	0	0	1	36	45	27	21	2	15	24	.306	.262	.342	6.00	3.75
Geekie, Dalton	R-R	6-5	200	10-3-94	0	0	0.00	8	0	0	2	12	6	0	0	0	4	16	.150	.000	.250	12.34	3.09
Guerrero, Fauris	R-R	5-11	180	10-5-96	0	1	27.00	1	0	0	0	3	5		1	0	0	1	.500	.500	.500	27.00	0.00
Marquez, Brailyn	L-L	6-4	185	1-30-99	1	4	3.21	10	10	0	0	48	46	22	17	5	14	52	.257	.326	.235	9.82	2.64
McCauley, Riley	R-R	6-1	205	12-5-96	1	0	3.07	14	0	0	0	15	8	5	5	2	10	19	.167	.261	.080	11.66	6.14
Medina, Ivan	R-R	6-3	180	2-26-96	0	0	7.36	3	0	0	1	4	7	3	3	0	1	5	.438	.429	.444	12.27	2.45
Mort, Zach	R-R	6-1	205	5-22-97	0	4	5.79	10	0	0	0	28	36	19	18	5	7	31	.316	.328	.304	9.96	2.25
Palma, Eugenio	L-L	5-11	170	11-26-96	5	1	3.43	24	0	0	2	42	40	20	16	3	20	44	.248	.167	.283	9.43	4.29
Passantino, Jeffrey	R-R	5-9	225	9-24-95	1	0	3.29	8	4	0	0	38	37	14	14	2	9	39	.252	.340	.202	9.16	2.11
Patterson, Jack	L-L	6-0	210	8-3-95	0	0	3.60	1	1	0	0	5	6	2	2	0	2	6	.286	.000	.353	10.80	3.60
Ramos, Eury	R-R	6-3	152	10-10-97	2	5	6.29	12	9	0	0	44	51	35	31	4	21	41	.285	.213	.337	8.32	4.26
Richan, Paul	R-R	6-2	200	3-26-97	0	2	2.12	10	9	0	0	30	19	10	7	2	5	31	.183	.225	.146	9.40	1.52
Ridings, Stephen	R-R	6-8	220	8-14-95	3	3	4.15	22	0	0	0	35	29	19	16	4	15	44	.230	.227	.233	11.42	3.89
Roberts, Ethan	R-R	5-11	170	7-4-97	0	0	5.40	14	0	0	0	15	13	11	9	0	6	13	.232	.381	.143	7.80	3.60

CHICAGO CUBS

Name	B-T	HT	WT	DOB	W	L	ERA	G	GS	CG	SV	IP	H	R	ER	HR	BB	SO	AVG	vLH	vRH	K/9	BB/9
Ryan, Casey	R-R	6-4	230	5-20-94	1	3	5.67	22	0	0	1	33	33	23	21	2	15	28	.260	.254	.265	7.56	4.05
Sanders, Cam	R-R	6-2	175	12-9-96	1	2	4.50	15	0	0	0	16	10	8	8	0	14	22	.182	.238	.147	12.38	7.88
Steffens, Jake	R-R	6-4	215	6-24-94	2	1	1.08	9	0	0	0	17	11	3	2	0	3	19	.186	.208	.171	10.26	1.62
Stophel, Mitch	R-R	6-3	205	11-9-94	1	2	7.67	16	0	0	2	27	25	24	23	4	17	25	.260	.209	.302	8.33	5.67
Sweeney, Nathan	R-R	6-4	185	8-21-97	0	0	9.00	2	0	0	0	3	7	6	3	0	2	2	.389	.600	.308	6.00	6.00
Thompson, Riley	L-R	6-3	205	7-9-96	1	2	2.84	9	8	0	0	25	24	10	8	1	9	25	.253	.250	.255	8.88	3.20
Vega, Carlos	R-R	6-2	220	12-28-95	0	0	3.48	6	0	0	1	10	6	4	4	1	5	13	.162	.111	.179	11.32	4.35
Williams, Ryan	R-R	6-4	220	11-1-91	1	5	5.64	6	6	0	0	30	40	21	19	5	4	15	.313	.283	.329	4.45	1.19

Fielding

C: Gonzalez 14, Guerra 1, Kaleiwahea 14, Knight 15, Polanco 21, Soto 18. **1B:** Balego 4, Durna 23, Fennell 14, Knight 1, Mejia 5, Polanco 11, Reynolds 9, Romano 1, Slaughter 16. **2B:** Daniel 5, Diaz 34, Jordan 20, Perlaza 2, Romano 1, Slaughter 3, Vazquez 4, Weber 9. **3B:** Balego 1, Diaz 7, Fennell 1, Jordan 10, Morel 17, Reynolds 18, Romano 5, Slaughter 19, Vazquez 4, Weber 2. **SS:** Hoerner 5, Jordan 9, Morel 6, Vazquez 50, Weber 10. **OF:** Artis 17, Fennell 15, Jordan 1, Kelli 65, Kwon 17, Reyes 2, Sierra 59, Velazquez 61.

AZL CUBS 1 — ROOKIE

ARIZONA LEAGUE

Batting	B-T	HT	WT	DOB	AVG	vLH	vRH	G	AB	R	H	2B	3B	HR	RBI	BB	HBP	SH	SF	SO	SB	CS	SLG	OBP
Americaan, Edmond	L-L	6-1	170	3-26-97	.295	.200	.322	30	112	22	33	5	2	0	13	1	0	0	30	11	6	.375	.373
Coghlan, Chris	L-R	6-0	195	6-18-85	.345	.250	.381	8	29	7	10	2	1	1	4	7	0	0	0	5	1	0	.586	.472
Cuevas, Yovanny	R-R	6-0	170	7-28-98	.221	.255	.207	48	172	30	38	7	1	0	27	25	4	4	1	40	7	5	.273	.332
Daniel, Clayton	R-R	5-7	175	5-10-95	.370	.400	.355	11	46	7	17	2	1	1	4	4	0	0	0	3	1	2	.522	.420
Filotei, Tolly	L-R	5-6	155	11-28-95	.000	.000	.000	4	8	1	0	0	0	0	0	0	0	0	0	4	0	0	.000	.000
Freeman, Mike	L-R	6-0	195	8-4-87	.308	.500	.143	4	13	1	4	2	0	0	5	0	1	0	0	4	0	0	.462	.357
Galazin, Jamie	R-R	6-4	200	5-20-96	.239	.222	.243	15	46	7	11	4	0	0	3	3	1	0	0	12	2	0	.326	.300
Gonzalez, Eric	R-R	5-10	175	9-2-96	.333	.333	.333	8	27	4	9	1	2	1	11	1	0	0	1	3	0	0	.630	.345
Guerra, Alexander	R-R	5-11	240	4-8-97	.267	.400	.237	46	161	26	43	16	2	3	30	19	4	0	2	39	2	1	.447	.355
Gutierrez, Jose	B-R	5-11	195	11-9-98	.245	.294	.219	17	49	6	12	2	0	0	2	7	0	1	1	12	2	0	.286	.333
Herron, Jimmy	R-L	6-1	195	7-27-96	.310	.300	.316	9	29	6	9	3	0	1	2	8	0	0	0	2	0	0	.517	.460
Hidalgo, Luis	R-R	6-1	190	2-23-96	.182	.250	.118	9	33	6	6	1	0	3	9	4	0	1	0	10	0	0	.485	.270
Hoerner, Nico	R-R	6-1	200	5-13-97	.250	.000	.300	3	12	3	3	1	1	1	2	1	0	0	0	2	0	0	.500	.400
Huma, Josue	R-R	6-1	175	3-17-00	.256	.143	.298	44	156	25	40	8	2	1	17	16	0	0	2	25	7	2	.353	.322
Hurd, Dalton	R-R	5-9	180	12-17-95	.189	.235	.175	25	74	12	14	2	2	0	15	10	0	1	3	20	1	2	.270	.276
Kaleiwahea, Brennon	R-R	6-0	200	5-28-96	.000	—	.000	1	2	0	0	0	0	0	0	0	0	0	0	0	0	0	.000	.000
Knight, Caleb	R-R	5-11	220	1-2-96	.200	.000	.250	5	10	2	2	0	1	0	1	2	1	0	0	2	0	0	.400	.385
Kwon, Kwang-Min	L-L	6-2	210	12-12-97	.253	.381	.207	23	79	5	20	2	2	0	9	11	0	0	0	27	1	6	.329	.344
Mejia, Rafael	R-R	6-1	195	12-12-97	.315	.306	.319	38	127	26	40	7	1	8	29	5	2	1	0	33	5	2	.575	.351
Morel, Christopher	R-R	6-0	140	6-24-99	.257	.345	.226	29	113	20	29	6	0	2	12	11	2	1	1	28	1	4	.363	.331
Moreno, Kevin	R-R	6-3	200	6-19-00	.150	.167	.143	9	20	1	3	1	0	0	3	4	1	0	0	11	1	0	.200	.320
Nunez, Orian	R-R	5-10	160	9-3-98	.261	.316	.250	36	115	14	30	7	1	0	16	5	1	0	0	19	5	3	.339	.346
Pagan, Ezequiel	L-R	6-1	163	7-8-00	.159	.111	.171	13	44	5	7	1	1	0	4	3	0	0	2	15	0	2	.227	.204
2-team total (18 AZL Cubs 2)					.217	.111	.171	31	92	11	20	3	1	0	8	14	0	0	2	27	3	5	.272	.315
Pena, Raymond	R-R	5-10	160	4-7-97	.250	.000	.500	2	4	0	1	0	0	0	0	0	0	0	0	0	0	0	.250	.250
2-team total (20 AZL Cubs 2)					.357	.000	.500	22	56	11	20	3	0	1	9	11	0	0	2	9	2	1	.464	.449
Perez, Herson	R-R	5-11	175	12-19-96	.050	.143	.000	13	20	3	1	0	0	0	3	5	0	1	1	7	1	1	.050	.231
Perlaza, Yonathan	B-S	5-10	195	11-10-98	.317	.372	.300	50	183	34	58	9	2	1	26	15	0	0	2	40	9	3	.404	.365
Reynolds, Luke	L-R	6-1	215	3-20-95	.200	.400	.143	12	45	6	9	4	0	0	4	8	0	0	3	13	1	0	.289	.321
Soto, Jonathan	L-R	5-9	143	7-9-98	.327	.421	.278	16	55	9	18	3	0	1	7	7	0	0	0	17	0	1	.436	.403
Tineo, Franklin	R-R	6-0	176	12-30-94	.156	.091	.177	19	45	6	7	0	1	1	5	7	2	1	0	21	1	0	.267	.296
Ubiera, Luis	R-R	6-2	170	9-17-96	.000	.000	.000	2	5	0	0	0	0	0	0	0	0	0	0	2	0	0	.000	.000
2-team total (3 AZL Cubs 2)					.182	.000	.000	5	11	0	2	0	0	0	2	1	1	0	1	3	0	1	.182	.250
Weber, Andy	L-R	6-1	190	7-24-97	.196	.188	.200	13	51	9	10	2	0	2	3	4	1	0	0	19	1	1	.353	.268
Young, Chesny	R-R	6-0	170	10-6-92	.333	1.000	.273	4	12	2	4	0	0	0	4	0	0	0	0	4	0	0	.333	.500

Pitching	B-T	HT	WT	DOB	W	L	ERA	G	GS	CG	SV	IP	H	R	ER	HR	BB	SO	AVG	vLH	vRH	K/9	BB/9
Aguiar, Maikel	R-R	6-0	185	11-20-96	4	2	2.32	10	0	0	1	31	20	11	8	0	5	48	.170	.083	.207	13.94	1.45
Black, Corey	R-R	5-11	175	8-4-91	2	0	2.45	7	1	0	0	7	4	2	2	1	4	8	.167	.200	.143	9.82	4.91
Bruzual, Jonathan	L-L	6-1	172	2-15-00	0	0	0.00	1	0	0	0	2	1	1	0	0	2	4	.125	.200	.000	18.00	9.00
2-team total (14 AZL Cubs 2)					1	4	9.25	15	1	0	0	24	29	31	25	1	33	23	.296	.000	.000	8.51	12.21
Calderon, Fernando	R-R	6-0	170	10-22-96	0	0	0.00	1	0	0	0	2	1	1	0	0	1	2	.167	.333	.000	9.00	4.50
2-team total (16 AZL Cubs 2)					2	0	5.25	17	0	0	0	36	42	23	21	2	18	30	.288	.333	.000	7.50	4.50
Clark, Bailey	R-R	6-4	185	12-3-94	1	0	0.00	4	3	0	0	6	2	0	0	0	1	8	.100	.000	.154	12.00	1.50
Fernandez, Riger	L-L	6-2	190	1-1-98	4	1	2.94	14	2	0	1	34	26	23	11	1	24	39	.217	.194	.225	10.43	6.42
2-team total (1 AZL Cubs 2)					4	1	2.86	15	2	0	1	35	26	23	11	1	24	39	.211	.194	.225	10.13	6.23
Garcia, Alonso	R-R	6-0	157	5-30-98	2	1	3.43	16	0	0	1	21	14	13	8	1	22	18	.187	.182	.189	7.71	9.43
Geekie, Dalton	R-R	6-2	200	10-3-94	0	0	0.00	2	0	0	1	2	1	1	0	0	1	2	.143	.000	.200	10.80	5.40
Guerrero, Fauris	R-R	5-11	180	10-5-96	4	1	1.62	21	0	0	6	33	25	9	6	1	10	31	.219	.244	.206	8.37	2.70
Hultzen, Danny	L-L	6-3	210	11-28-89	0	0	5.40	8	3	0	0	7	6	4	4	1	2	15	.231	.143	.263	20.25	2.70
Lee, Chi-Feng	R-R	5-11	155	10-14-97	2	1	4.62	13	3	0	1	37	37	21	19	2	10	31	.259	.261	.258	7.54	2.43
Light, Braxton	R-R	5-9	185	10-13-95	1	0	0.00	2	0	0	0	3							.000	.000	.000	13.50	0.00
Miller, Brady	R-R	6-2	190	4-4-96	2	0	4.50	18	0	0	1	24	16	11	12	1	23	11	.187	.194	.182	4.50	9.41
2-team total (1 AZL Cubs 2)					2	0	4.43	20	0	0	1	22	14	16	11	1	23	11	.184	.194	.182	4.43	9.27
Ocampo, Carlos	R-R	6-2	181	9-3-98	1	3	4.88	9	5	0	0	28	20	19	15	0	23	24	.196	.167	.212	7.81	7.48
Orta, Raidel	R-R	5-9	180	3-4-96	1	3	4.11	15	0	0	1	31	40	23	14	2	18	30	.315	.381	.282	8.80	5.28
2-team total (1 AZL Cubs 2)					1	3	4.55	16	0	0	2	32	43	25	16	3	19	30	.326	.381	.282	8.53	5.40

	B-T	HT	WT	DOB	W	L	ERA	G	GS	CG	SV	IP	H	R	ER	HR	BB	SO	AVG	vLH	vRH	K/9	BB/9
Patterson, Jack	L-L	6-0	210	8-3-95	0	0	0.00	3	0	0	0	4	1	0	0	0	1	3	.091	.000	.167	7.36	2.45
2-team total (7 AZL Cubs 2)					2	1	2.70	10	5	0	0	30	29	11	9	3	8	27	.250	.000	.167	8.10	2.40
Perez, Yunior	R-R	6-4	190	12-19-98	2	3	4.63	9	7	0	0	23	22	15	12	1	11	25	.242	.250	.237	9.64	4.24
Remy, Peyton	L-R	6-2	170	8-20-96	6	1	2.58	11	7	0	1	52	40	16	15	3	13	59	.209	.256	.177	10.15	2.24
Steele, Justin	L-L	6-2	195	7-11-95	0	0	1.47	5	5	0	0	18	9	4	3	1	4	27	.143	.333	.123	13.25	1.96
Stone, Niels	L-R	6-1	190	2-10-99	0	0	1.04	7	0	0	0	9	6	3	1	0	7	12	.188	.231	.158	12.46	7.27
Tejada, Jesus	R-R	6-1	168	10-24-96	1	1	2.83	12	12	0	0	57	49	22	18	3	16	49	.230	.304	.187	7.69	2.51
Vargas, Didier	R-L	6-0	175	3-13-99	4	4	3.27	12	8	0	0	52	50	28	19	2	25	43	.260	.245	.266	7.39	4.30
Vega, Carlos	R-R	6-2	220	12-28-95	1	0	6.00	2	0	0	0	3	5	2	2	0	2	6	.357	.286	.429	18.00	6.00
Webb, Ryan	R-R	6-6	245	2-5-86	0	0	1.46	11	0	0	0	12	8	3	2	0	4	17	.186	.278	.120	12.41	2.92

Fielding

C: Gonzalez 8, Guerra 38, Kaleiwahea 1, Knight 3, Pena 2, Soto 9, Tineo 4. **1B:** Hidalgo 9, Mejia 28, Nunez 11, Reynolds 4, Soto 3, Tineo 10. **2B:** Daniel 5, Freeman 2, Huma 6, Nunez 14, Perez 12, Perlaza 24, Weber 6, Young 2. **3B:** Huma 2, Morel 19, Nunez 8, Perlaza 20, Reynolds 7, Young 1. **SS:** Daniel 6, Freeman 2, Hoerner 3, Huma 33, Morel 9, Weber 8. **OF:** Americaan 27, Coghlan 6, Cuevas 44, Filotei 4, Galazin 12, Gutierrez 17, Herron 8, Hurd 21, Kwon 20, Mejia 8, Moreno 5, Pagan 13, Ubiera 2, Young 1.

AZL CUBS 2 *ROOKIE*

ARIZONA LEAGUE

Batting	B-T	HT	WT	DOB	AVG	vLH	vRH	G	AB	R	H	2B	3B	HR	RBI	BB	HBP	SH	SF	SO	SB	CS	SLG	OBP
Alamo, Tyler	R-R	6-4	200	5-2-95	.235	—	—	9	34	1	8	2	0	0	3	0	0	0	1	8	0	0	.294	.229
Artis, D.J.	L-L	5-9	165	3-20-97	.286	—	—	6	14	4	4	0	0	0	0	4	2	0	0	2	3	0	.286	.500
Davis, Brennen	R-R	6-4	175	11-2-99	.298	—	—	18	57	9	17	2	0	0	3	10	4	0	1	12	6	1	.333	.431
Diaz, Luis	R-R	5-9	160	4-16-99	.311	—	—	12	45	7	14	3	1	1	8	6	1	0	1	8	6	1	.489	.396
Durna, Tyler	L-L	6-0	205	11-13-96	.364	—	—	3	11	2	4	1	0	0	7	1	0	0	2	2	0	0	.455	.357
Fennell, Grant	R-R	6-0	195	10-12-00	.355	—	—	20	76	13	27	11	2	1	19	6	2	0	0	15	1	0	.592	.417
Gaitan, Alonso	R-R	6-0	176	2-23-98	.192	—	—	29	73	10	14	2	1	0	8	10	1	0	1	15	2	1	.247	.294
Garcia, Reivaj	R-R	5-11	175	8-12-01	.302	—	—	40	172	28	52	9	0	0	13	15	1	3	0	36	7	3	.355	.362
Gonzalez, Jose Alejandro	R-R	6-1	160	1-12-96	.290	—	—	13	38	8	11	2	0	0	6	2	2	0	0	5	2	2	.342	.357
Jordan, Levi	R-R	5-8	170	9-24-95	.250	—	—	9	32	6	8	2	0	0	7	1	0	0	1	5	2	0	.313	.265
Mejia, Fidel	B-R	5-11	160	8-30-98	.325	—	—	50	188	27	61	9	2	1	24	20	1	0	2	33	3	4	.410	.389
Nunez, Richard	R-R	5-10	170	3-14-95	.192	—	—	14	47	4	9	7	0	0	6	8	0	1	0	12	0	1	.340	.309
Pabon, Miguel	R-R	6-0	165	8-30-00	.148	—	—	23	61	11	9	2	1	0	1	11	2	0	0	32	3	2	.213	.297
Pacheco, Carlos	R-R	5-11	195	4-2-99	.184	—	—	32	114	10	21	4	0	0	12	11	0	0	0	39	4	2	.219	.256
Pagan, Ezequiel	L-R	6-1	163	7-8-00	.271	—	—	18	48	6	13	2	0	0	4	11	0	0	0	12	3	3	.313	.407
2-team total (13 AZL Cubs 1)					.217	.111	.171	31	92	11	20	3	1	0	8	14	0	0	2	27	3	5	.272	.315
Pedra, Henrry	R-R	5-11	175	4-26-94	.333	—	—	19	39	9	13	1	0	0	2	9	2	0	0	7	0	2	.359	.480
Pena, Raymond	R-R	5-10	160	4-7-97	.365	—	—	20	52	11	19	3	0	1	9	11	0	0	2	9	2	1	.481	.462
2-team total (2 AZL Cubs 1)					.357	.000	.500	22	56	11	20	3	0	1	9	11	0	0	2	9	2	1	.464	.449
Perez, Henderson	R-R	5-11	160	6-10-99	.277	—	—	43	159	25	44	6	2	1	24	18	1	0	0	34	1	2	.359	.354
Reyes, Ruben	L-L	5-11	170	10-1-95	1.000	—	—	1	1	1	1	0	0	0	0	0	0	0	0	0	0	0	1.000	1.000
Roederer, Cole	L-L	6-0	175	9-24-99	.275	—	—	36	142	30	39	4	4	5	24	18	0	0	1	37	13	4	.465	.354
Slaughter, Jake	R-R	6-3	200	10-24-96	.200	—	—	3	10	4	2	0	0	0	0	2	2	0	0	3	0	0	.200	.429
Ubiera, Luis	R-R	6-2	170	9-17-96	.333	—	—	3	6	0	2	0	0	0	2	1	0	1	0	1	0	1	.333	.429
2-team total (2 AZL Cubs 1)					.182	.000	.000	5	11	0	2	0	0	0	2	1	0	1	0	3	0	1	.182	.250
Verdugo, Luis	R-R	6-0	172	10-12-00	.193	—	—	47	176	28	34	4	1	4	20	17	1	2	3	45	5	3	.296	.264
Wharton, Drew	R-R	6-0	190	11-28-95	.250	—	—	38	128	18	32	2	0	0	8	13	2	1	1	28	2	4	.266	.326
Zamudio, Kevin	R-R	6-0	200	8-23-97	.215	—	—	25	79	11	17	6	1	0	14	9	1	0	3	25	0	0	.317	.294

Pitching	B-T	HT	WT	DOB	W	L	ERA	G	GS	CG	SV	IP	H	R	ER	HR	BB	SO	AVG	vLH	vRH	K/9	BB/9
Allen, Chris	L-L	6-4	180	6-13-98	0	0	0.63	7	3	0	0	14	15	3	1	0	2	13	.268	—	—	8.16	1.26
Bruzual, Jonathan	L-L	6-1	172	2-15-00	1	4	10.07	14	1	0	0	22	28	30	25	1	31	19	.311	—	—	7.66	12.49
2-team total (1 AZL Cubs 1)					1	4	9.25	15	1	0	0	24	29	31	25	1	33	23	.296	.200	.000	8.51	12.21
Calderon, Fernando	R-R	6-0	170	10-22-96	2	0	5.56	16	0	0	0	34	41	22	21	2	17	28	.293	—	—	7.41	4.50
2-team total (1 AZL Cubs 1)					2	0	5.25	17	0	0	0	36	42	23	21	2	18	30	.288	.333	.000	7.50	4.50
Colorado, Alfredo	R-R	6-1	170	6-22-96	0	1	13.50	1	1	0	0	3	6	4	4	0	1	1	.500	—	—	3.38	3.38
Correa, Danis	R-R	5-11	155	8-26-99	0	0	0.00	2	0	0	0	2	0	0	0	0	1	3	.000	—	—	13.50	4.50
Cruz, Yovanny	R-R	6-1	190	8-23-99	4	2	2.86	10	10	0	0	44	36	18	14	1	13	50	.214	—	—	10.23	2.66
Fernandez, Riger	L-L	6-2	190	1-1-98	0	0	0.00	1	0	0	0	1	0	0	0	0	0	0	.000	—	—	0.00	0.00
2-team total (14 AZL Cubs 1)					4	1	2.86	15	2	0	1	35	26	23	11	1	24	39	.211	.194	.225	10.13	6.23
Ferrebus, Emilio	R-R	6-2	165	11-25-97	0	3	10.03	11	7	0	0	23	34	30	26	3	20	15	.333	—	—	5.79	7.71
Franklin, Kohl	R-R	6-4	190	9-9-99	0	1	6.23	5	3	0	0	9	5	7	6	0	6	8	.161	—	—	8.31	6.23
Herrera, Elias	R-R	6-1	172	9-23-97	5	1	3.86	12	0	0	0	40	38	24	17	1	14	35	.247	—	—	7.94	3.18
McCauley, Riley	R-R	6-1	205	12-5-96	0	0	0.00	2	0	0	0	2	0	0	0	0	0	1	.000	—	—	4.50	0.00
Medina, Ivan	R-R	6-3	180	2-26-96	3	1	1.48	17	0	0	3	30	18	9	5	0	7	27	.164	—	—	8.01	2.08
Miller, Brady	R-R	6-0	190	4-4-96	0	0	0.00	1	0	0	0	0	0	0	0	0	0	0	.000	—	—	0.00	0.00
2-team total (18 AZL Cubs 1)					2	0	4.43	19	0	0	1	22	14	16	11	1	23	11	.184	.194	.182	4.43	9.27
Moreno, Erling	R-R	6-3	200	1-13-97	0	0	0.00	1	1	0	0	5	1	0	0	0	0	5	.063	—	—	9.64	0.00
Nunez, Eduarniel	R-R	6-2	174	6-7-99	1	3	3.19	10	10	0	0	37	28	17	13	0	21	39	.207	—	—	9.57	5.15
Orta, Raidel	R-R	5-9	180	3-4-96	0	0	18.00	1	0	0	1	3	2	2	1	1	0	0	.600	—	—	0.00	9.00
2-team total (15 AZL Cubs 1)					1	3	4.55	10	2	0	1	32	43	25	16	3	19	30	.326	.381	.282	8.53	5.40
Patterson, Jack	L-L	6-0	210	8-3-95	2	1	3.08	7	5	0	0	26	28	11	9	3	7	24	.267	—	—	8.20	2.39
2-team total (3 AZL Cubs 1)					2	1	2.70	10	5	0	0	30	29	11	9	3	8	27	.250	.000	.167	8.10	2.40
Rondon, Andry	R-R	6-2	190	9-16-95	0	0	2.93	11	0	0	2	15	9	5	5	1	12	18	.173	—	—	10.57	7.04
Sanders, Cam	R-R	6-2	175	12-9-96	0	0	0.00	1	0	0	0	3	0	0	0	3	2	.000	—	—	27.00	40.50

	B-T	HT	WT	DOB	W	L	ERA	G	GS	CG	SV	IP	H	R	ER	HR	BB	SO	AVG	vLH	vRH	K/9	BB/9
Silva, Luis	L-L	5-11	165	6-6-97	2	3	4.79	15	1	0	1	36	36	24	19	3	17	33	.265	—	—	8.33	4.29
Sweeney, Nathan	R-R	6-4	185	8-21-97	1	1	8.13	17	0	0	3	28	42	30	25	2	6	25	.347	—	—	8.13	1.95
Valdez, Sucre	R-R	6-2	180	9-1-93	3	1	3.52	15	0	0	1	38	24	15	15	1	9	51	.185	—	—	11.97	2.11
Webster, Allen	R-R	6-2	190	2-10-90	0	0	4.00	9	2	0	0	9	12	7	4	0	2	13	.308	—	—	13.00	2.00
Whitney, Blake	R-R	6-3	185	5-25-96	2	3	2.30	9	9	0	0	31	27	9	8	1	17	37	.237	—	—	10.63	4.88

Fielding

C: Alamo 1, Nunez 7, Pena 17, Perez 33, Zamudio 1. **1B:** Alamo 6, Durna 3, Fennell 6, Mejia 13, Nunez 5, Pedra 8, Perez 3, Zamudio 20. **2B:** Diaz 5, Garcia 38, Pabon 9, Pedra 2. **3B:** Diaz 4, Fennell 1, Jordan 4, Mejia 36, Pedra 3, Slaughter 2, Verdugo 10. **SS:** Diaz 1, Jordan 3, Pabon 14, Pedra 2, Verdugo 40. **OF:** Artis 5, Davis 13, Fennell 9, Gaitan 26, Gonzalez 12, Pacheco 22, Pagan 17, Roederer 33, Ubiera 2, Wharton 36.

DOMINICAN SUMMER LEAGUE

Batting	B-T	HT	WT	DOB	AVG	vLH	vRH	G	AB	R	H	2B	3B	HR	RBI	BB	HBP	SH	SF	SO	SB	CS	SLG	OBP
Acevedo, Augusto	R-R	5-10	165	8-22-00	.100	—	.100	4	10	2	1	0	0	0	0	1	1	0	0	4	0	2	.100	.250
Aliendo, Pablo	R-R	6-0	155	5-29-01	.182	.200	.178	27	55	9	10	3	1	0	7	5	2	0	1	19	5	0	.273	.270
Aular, Efren	R-R	6-1	199	9-28-99	.228	.500	.196	27	57	3	13	2	0	0	8	7	0	0	0	15	2	1	.263	.313
Bautista, Flemin	B-R	5-10	170	3-10-00	.207	.167	.214	29	82	11	17	1	3	2	10	18	1	0	0	24	8	2	.366	.356
Blanco, Santiago	B-R	5-11	165	10-14-99	.238	.077	.269	42	80	13	19	3	1	0	12	14	2	0	3	13	9	4	.300	.354
Brete, Jeinser	R-R	6-0	180	11-26-99	.165	.167	.165	32	97	17	16	3	0	0	4	12	4	0	0	28	4	8	.196	.283
Chacon, Miller	R-R	6-0	189	6-17-98	.247	.083	.277	57	154	21	38	4	3	2	16	13	11	0	1	38	4	2	.351	.346
Cruz, Rochest	L-R	5-11	150	6-24-99	.302	.222	.318	66	225	54	68	9	4	2	25	43	4	4	2	29	56	9	.404	.420
Diaz, Daniel	R-R	5-11	200	4-5-97	.200	.095	.225	47	110	19	22	2	2	2	14	12	5	0	1	23	3	1	.309	.305
Espinal, Christhian	R-R	6-2	180	9-25-00	.220	.261	.210	44	123	21	27	5	0	2	10	20	3	1	0	56	5	2	.309	.343
Fabrizio, Miguel	R-R	5-11	178	9-26-00	.277	.091	.301	39	94	7	26	3	2	1	14	5	4	0	0	17	1	4	.383	.340
Fernandez, Josue	B-R	6-3	180	2-9-01	.142	.118	.146	41	113	14	16	3	1	2	13	27	3	0	1	59	6	6	.239	.319
Heredia, Nestor	R-R	5-11	181	11-25-00	.209	.263	.199	63	249	20	52	11	1	4	33	7	9	1	2	70	8	11	.309	.255
Herrera, Rafael	R-R	5-11	170	9-18-00	.252	.280	.246	50	163	28	41	6	4	3	19	21	6	2	3	32	11	4	.337	.352
Hidalgo, Kelvin	R-R	6-3	190	12-16-00	.228	.250	.225	49	158	36	36	7	0	4	22	17	8	0	5	53	6	4	.348	.325
Hinirio, Albert	B-R	6-2	170	5-15-98	.248	.130	.273	43	133	13	33	5	4	0	12	12	8	0	0	27	10	6	.346	.346
Joaquin, Widimer	R-R	6-2	180	9-8-00	.292	.242	.300	64	233	34	68	12	3	2	30	24	7	2	1	55	10	10	.395	.374
Mancilla, Brayan	R-R	5-10	186	10-28-99	.258	.167	.267	31	66	16	17	5	0	2	12	11	5	0	2	16	2	1	.424	.393
Marchan, Ervis	L-L	5-11	175	8-16-99	.275	.175	.295	69	247	31	68	16	3	1	44	29	3	0	3	22	16	3	.377	.355
Martinez, Pedro	B-R	5-11	165	1-28-01	.310	.310	.310	54	197	36	61	3	5	2	25	26	3	2	0	26	31	9	.406	.398
Miranda, Kevin	L-R	5-11	168	10-2-99	.250	.191	.264	38	112	20	28	3	2	0	7	10	6	0	0	32	6	3	.313	.368
Mora, Juan	R-R	5-9	176	9-30-99	.231	.091	.286	14	39	6	9	4	0	0	3	9	2	0	0	6	2	2	.333	.400
Morfa, Carlos	R-R	6-2	190	12-2-00	.214	.188	.218	31	117	15	25	7	1	5	12	4	3	0	0	41	6	1	.419	.258
Otano, Ignacio	R-R	6-0	175	1-6-97	.269	.286	.268	26	78	14	21	4	1	1	11	4	3	1	1	10	4	2	.385	.326
Ovalles, Alexander	L-L	6-0	180	10-6-00	.316	.300	.318	21	76	13	24	4	0	0	8	16	0	1	1	14	8	5	.368	.430
Pena, Brailin	L-L	5-11	160	5-2-01	.191	.185	.192	61	178	31	34	7	3	0	20	42	3	5	4	40	17	11	.264	.348
Pertuz, Fabian	R-R	6-0	156	9-1-00	.298	.313	.296	62	218	49	65	10	6	2	39	38	9	2	2	32	36	10	.427	.420
Pina, Oswaldo	R-R	5-10	170	8-9-98	.244	.237	.245	67	230	41	56	10	5	2	28	32	0	1	4	67	28	4	.357	.331
Quintero, Malcom	R-R	6-0	165	7-29-00	.243	.333	.231	32	74	5	18	4	1	0	8	11	0	0	0	10	2	2	.324	.341
Rodriguez, Jonathan	R-R	6-0	190	10-9-00	.235	.333	.217	43	153	17	36	3	2	4	26	6	5	1	0	43	9	5	.360	.287
Simon, Ronny	B-R	5-9	150	4-17-00	.185	.200	.180	25	65	12	12	5	0	0	5	10	4	1	2	15	3	5	.262	.321
Valenzuela, Marco	L-R	6-1	170	1-14-00	.220	.095	.237	56	177	29	39	7	4	2	25	23	12	2	1	61	18	5	.339	.347
Vasquez, Juan	R-R	5-11	180	9-7-99	.222	.500	.182	31	63	5	14	2	1	0	6	4	0	0	1	19	0	0	.286	.265
Verenzuela, Ricardo	L-R	6-0	170	1-14-00	.261	.313	.251	65	215	51	56	4	3	0	20	37	6	1	2	44	39	13	.307	.381
Zapata, Orlando	L-R	5-11	160	2-23-99	.239	.125	.258	36	109	12	26	6	1	0	12	5	1	2	0	18	3	2	.312	.278

Pitching	B-T	HT	WT	DOB	W	L	ERA	G	GS	CG	SV	IP	H	R	ER	HR	BB	SO	AVG	vLH	vRH	K/9	BB/9
Acevedo, Anderson	R-R	6-2	220	9-30-93	4	0	6.41	18	0	0	1	27	19	23	19	2	19	31	.198	.208	.186	10.46	6.41
Aguiar, Maikel	R-R	6-0	185	11-20-96	1	1	5.87	5	0	0	0	8	10	6	5	0	3	8	.323	.138	.209	9.39	3.52
Arredondo, Keiber	R-R	6-0	178	10-9-97	2	2	3.38	18	0	0	2	48	40	25	18	1	21	50	.225	.250	.211	9.38	3.94
Auguste, Donato	R-R	6-2	201	1-19-98	0	3	1.14	14	0	0	1	32	23	8	4	0	10	32	.202	.233	.191	9.09	2.84
Cabrera, Willy	R-R	6-3	210	7-10-00	0	8	14.73	13	12	0	0	26	27	44	42	2	50	18	.300	.200	.350	6.23	17.53
Carreno, Kleiber	R-R	6-5	165	10-11-98	0	1	4.81	19	0	0	0	34	32	24	18	1	29	39	.254	.234	.266	10.43	7.75
Devers, Luis	R-R	6-3	178	4-24-00	1	6	2.77	14	13	0	0	55	55	31	17	2	19	48	.258	.227	.275	7.81	3.09
Diaz, Moises	R-R	6-0	195	4-27-01	1	2	3.43	10	0	0	0	21	17	15	8	1	5	14	.215	.256	.175	6.00	2.14
Feliz, Kelvin	R-R	6-1	165	9-30-00	0	5	5.54	13	13	0	0	50	45	37	31	2	32	43	.246	.203	.269	7.69	5.72
Feliz, Wander	R-R	6-2	185	9-7-97	2	3	3.80	20	0	0	3	43	44	29	18	2	11	47	.253	.241	.264	9.91	2.32
Fermin, Francisco	R-R	6-4	175	11-19-98	3	0	6.10	11	0	0	0	21	24	17	14	1	14	17	.293	.250	.315	7.40	6.10
Garcia, Misael	L-L	6-2	194	4-18-01	2	3	3.55	14	14	0	0	46	34	30	18	0	27	46	.205	.167	.211	9.07	5.32
Gomez, Jesus	L-L	6-2	190	4-9-99	5	0	4.61	18	2	0	0	41	32	28	21	1	31	31	.221	.207	.224	6.80	6.80
Gomez, Jose	R-R	6-2	165	3-15-97	2	3	3.00	20	0	0	2	42	28	14	14	2	17	37	.193	.152	.212	7.93	3.64
Gonzalez, Edmar	R-R	5-11	191	8-17-98	3	3	7.16	21	0	0	1	28	26	23	23	3	31	39	.241	.232	.250	12.69	10.08
Gracia, Francisco	R-R	6-0	200	9-4-98	4	2	3.10	21	1	0	3	49	39	30	17	3	13	36	.218	.241	.208	10.03	3.28
Guante, Julio	R-R	6-3	180	5-29-97	1	4	2.63	20	0	0	3	41	35	21	12	1	13	34	.233	.194	.265	7.46	2.85
Heredia, Ferrol	L-L	5-11	200	11-7-98	1	2	2.89	14	3	0	0	44	30	22	14	1	35	40	.195	.178	.202	8.24	7.21
Hernandez, Andy	R-R	6-1	178	11-29-99	3	0	2.80	14	12	0	0	55	48	18	17	2	14	48	.235	.231	.267	7.90	2.30
Herrera, Elias	R-R	6-1	172	9-23-97	2	0	1.53	4	0	0	0	18	13	3	3	0	1	15	.194	.000	.240	7.64	0.51
Jaramillo, Gabriel	R-R	6-1	178	11-3-98	0	0	4.91	4	0	0	0	4	7	2	2	0	1	3	.412	.500	.333	7.36	2.45
Lopez, Johan	L-L	6-6	190	8-31-98	0	6	3.92	11	11	0	0	39	30	30	17	1	29	39	.217	.226	.215	9.00	6.69
Marte, Luis	R-R	6-0	200	2-13-01	3	1	15.43	9	1	0	0	12	15	23	20	0	30	16	.349	.333	.355	9.26	21.60
Parra, Anderson	L-L	6-2	185	4-17-99	1	1	4.40	12	0	0	0	29	23	15	14	1	9	36	.209	.174	.218	11.30	2.83
Paula, Carlos	R-R	6-0	195	1-29-00	2	2	5.04	10	3	0	0	25	27	16	14	1	10	25	.284	.293	.278	9.00	3.60

Perez, Enzo	R-R	5-11	180	6-7-00	1	0	7.40	16	0	0	2	21	27	17	17	1	10	22	.321	.385	.267	9.58	4.35
Ramos, Luis	R-R	6-5	205	12-23-97	3	3	3.86	14	14	0	0	54	38	27	23	0	31	38	.201	.177	.230	6.37	5.20
Remon, Jorge	R-R	6-2	160	2-3-01	2	4	2.86	14	14	0	0	57	40	24	18	2	25	37	.195	.253	.142	5.88	3.97
Rodriguez, Benjamin	R-R	6-1	165	7-27-99	5	5	4.31	15	12	0	0	65	57	39	31	4	25	47	.235	.233	.236	6.54	3.48
Rodriguez, Luis	L-L	6-1	190	9-10-99	5	0	0.73	15	10	0	1	61	38	9	5	2	7	61	.174	.180	.171	8.95	1.03
Tineo, Freddy	R-R	6-0	160	11-22-97	0	1	2.75	8	0	0	0	20	20	11	6	0	6	16	.267	.350	.236	7.32	2.75
Valdez, Sucre	R-R	6-2	180	9-1-93	0	0	5.40	7	0	0	3	12	13	9	7	1	1	13	.283	.273	.292	10.03	0.77
Vasquez, Edward	R-R	6-3	180	7-7-97	3	1	3.21	14	4	0	0	42	35	25	15	1	21	38	.226	.349	.141	8.14	4.50
Vazquez, Saul	L-L	6-1	178	6-25-00	1	1	2.25	4	4	0	0	20	20	9	5	1	6	18	.263	.273	.259	8.10	2.70
Ventura, Omar	R-R	6-2	190	9-10-96	2	0	1.80	15	0	0	2	25	19	6	5	2	20	27	.200	.209	.192	9.72	7.20

Fielding

C: Aliendo 17, Aular 23, Chacon 43, Diaz 45, Fabrizio 20, Mancilla 13, Quintero 32, Vasquez 30. **1B:** Aliendo 1, Brete 27, Chacon 17, Diaz 5, Espinal 27, Mancilla 3, Marchan 66, Otano 1, Ovalles 5, Pena 1, Pina 4, Vasquez 1. **2B:** Acevedo 3, Bautista 8, Cruz 38, Espinal 8, Heredia 10, Joaquin 34, Martinez 4, Mora 13, Otano 7, Pina 9, Simon 7, Zapata 13. **3B:** Brete 3, Cruz 21, Espinal 5, Heredia 3, Joaquin 6, Mancilla 1, Martinez 16, Otano 8, Pertuz 9, Pina 37, Simon 9, Zapata 17. **SS:** Bautista 2, Cruz 5, Heredia 1, Joaquin 13, Martinez 34, Pertuz 51, Pina 15, Simon 6, Zapata 4. **OF:** Fernandez 35, Herrera 49, Hidalgo 32, Hinirio 38, Mancilla 7, Marchan 2, Miranda 36, Morfa 27, Ovalles 15, Pena 60, Rodriguez 39, Simon 4, Valenzuela 6, Verenzuela 63, Zapata 1.

Chicago White Sox

SEASON IN A SENTENCE: The former prospects acquired in the first stages of their 2016 teardown became entrenched in the major leagues, and the results were less than expected.

HIGH POINT: Center fielder Adam Engel dominated highlight shows and social media during August when he robbed three home runs during a homestand. He took longballs from the Yankees' Greg Bird and Kyle Higashioka and the Indians' Yonder Alonso. Those three catches alone were enough to drop the White Sox to 11th place among home runs allowed in 2018. If all three go over the fence, the team finishes in eighth place, just one better than the division champion-Indians.

LOW POINT: When Michael Kopech was called up in the middle of August, excitement was high on the south side of Chicago. Kopech represented the next wave of prospects as part of their rebuild, and he came armed with a triple-digit fastball. That optimism wore off four starts into his career, when a disaster start prompted a doctor's visit that revealed a torn ulnar collateral ligament in his right elbow that required Tommy John surgery.

NOTABLE ROOKIES: Claimed off waivers from the Twins, outfielder Daniel Palka made an impression at the plate all season long. His 27 homers tied with the Yankees' Miguel Andujar for the most among rookies, and he did so in 173 fewer at-bats. Reliever Jace Fry proved to be a particularly effective lefty-killer, holding same-side hitters to a .408 OPS with 34 strikeouts in 92 plate appearances (36.9 percent rate). Kopech made his major league debut in September and was impressive before his elbow blew out.

KEY TRANSACTIONS: The White Sox weren't nearly as busy on the trade front as in the recent past. The biggest trade they made sent reliever Joakim Soria to the Brewers for a pair of pitching prospects. They also dealt reliever Xavier Cedeno to Milwaukee a month later for a pair of low-level prospects. They made another small trade with the Phillies when they exchanged reliever Luis Avilan for righthander Felix Paulino.

DOWN ON THE FARM: Top prospect Eloy Jimenez mashed his way to the cusp of the majors, and Kopech and righthander Dylan Cease dominated on the mound. Cease in particular took big steps forward and now ranks as the system's best arm behind Kopech. First-rounder Nick Madrigal was solid in his professional debut.

OPENING DAY PAYROLL: $86,050,333 (24th)

PLAYERS OF THE YEAR

DAVE DUROCHIK

DAVE DUROCHIK

MAJOR LEAGUE

Jose Abreu
1B
.265/.325/.473
Led team in AVG, OPS
and RBIs (78)

MINOR LEAGUE

Eloy Jimenez
OF
(Double-A/Triple-A)
.337/.384/.577
22 HR, 75 RBIs

ORGANIZATION LEADERS

Batting		*Minimum 250 AB
MAJORS		
* AVG	Omar Narvaez	.275
* OPS	Jose Abreu	.798
HR	Daniel Palka	27
RBI	Jose Abreu	78
MINORS		
* AVG	Eloy Jimenez, Birmingham, Charlotte	.337
* OBP	Jake Elmore, Charlotte	.397
* SLG	Eloy Jimenez, Birmingham, Charlotte	.577
* OPS	Eloy Jimenez, Birmingham, Charlotte	.961
R	Luis Gonzalez, Kannapolis, Winston-Salem	85
H	Luis Gonzalez, Kannapolis, Winston-Salem	148
TB	Eloy Jimenez, Birmingham, Charlotte	240
TB	Luis Gonzalez, Kannapolis, Winston-Salem	240
2B	Luis Gonzalez, Kannapolis, Winston-Salem	40
3B	Blake Rutherford, Winston-Salem	9
HR	Eloy Jimenez, Birmingham, Charlotte	22
RBI	Blake Rutherford, Winston-Salem	78
BB	Zack Collins, Birmingham	101
SO	Zack Collins, Birmingham	158
SB	Joel Booker, Winston-Salem, Birmingham	26

Pitching		#Minimum 75 IP
MAJORS		
W	Lucas Giolito	10
# ERA	Reynaldo Lopez	3.91
SO	James Shields	154
SV	Joakim Soria	16
MINORS		
W	Tanner Banks, Winston-Salem, Birmingham	12
W	John Parke, Kannapolis, Winston-Salem	12
W	Dylan Cease, Winston-Salem, Birmingham	12
L	Spencer Adams, Birmingham, Charlotte	13
# ERA	Dylan Cease, Winston-Salem, Birmingham	2.4
G	Rob Scahill, Charlotte	52
GS	Jordan Stephens, Birmingham, Charlotte	28
GS	Spencer Adams, Birmingham, Charlotte	28
SV	Ian Hamilton, Birmingham, Charlotte	22
IP	Spencer Adams, Birmingham, Charlotte	159
BB	Michael Kopech, Charlotte	60
SO	Michael Kopech, Charlotte	170
# AVG	Dylan Cease, Winston-Salem, Birmingham	.189

General Manager: Rick Hahn. **Farm Director:** Chris Getz. **Scouting Director:** Nick Hostetler.

Class	Team	League	W	L	PCT	Finish	Manager
Majors	Chicago White Sox	American	62	100	.383	13th (15)	Rick Renteria
Triple-A	Charlotte Knights	International	64	75	.460	10th (14)	Mark Grudzielanek
Double-A	Birmingham Barons	Southern	66	72	.478	8th (10)	Ryan Newman
High A	Winston-Salem Dash	Carolina	84	54	.609	1st (10)	Omar Vizquel
Low A	Kannapolis Intimidators	South Atlantic	74	63	.540	3rd (14)	Justin Jirschele
Rookie	Great Falls Voyagers	Pioneer	34	41	.453	7th (8)	Tim Esmay
Rookie	AZL White Sox	Arizona	30	26	.536	t-8th (18)	Tommy Thompson
Overall 2018 Minor League Record			352	331	.515	t-9th (30)	

ORGANIZATION STATISTICS

CHICAGO WHITE SOX
AMERICAN LEAGUE

Batting	B-T	HT	WT	DOB	AVG	vLH	vRH	G	AB	R	H	2B	3B	HR	RBI	BB	HBP	SH	SF	SO	SB	CS	SLG	OBP
Abreu, Jose	R-R	6-3	255	1-29-87	.265	.290	.258	128	499	68	132	36	1	22	78	37	11	0	6	109	2	0	.473	.326
Anderson, Tim	R-R	6-1	185	6-23-93	.240	.282	.224	153	567	77	136	28	3	20	64	30	4	2	3	149	26	8	.406	.282
Castillo, Welington	R-R	5-10	220	4-24-87	.259	.286	.248	49	170	17	44	7	0	6	15	9	2	0	0	46	1	0	.406	.304
Cordell, Ryan	R-R	6-4	195	3-31-92	.108	.167	.080	19	37	3	4	1	0	1	4	0	1	0	2	15	0	0	.216	.125
Davidson, Matt	R-R	6-3	230	3-26-91	.228	.290	.206	123	434	51	99	23	0	20	62	52	7	0	3	165	0	0	.419	.319
Delmonico, Nicky	L-R	6-3	230	7-12-92	.215	.156	.226	88	284	31	61	11	5	8	25	27	6	0	1	80	1	2	.373	.296
Engel, Adam	R-R	6-2	210	12-9-91	.235	.233	.236	143	429	49	101	14	4	6	29	18	8	7	1	129	16	8	.336	.279
Garcia, Avisail	R-R	6-4	240	6-12-91	.236	.279	.222	93	356	47	84	11	2	19	49	20	4	0	5	102	3	1	.438	.281
Garcia, Leury	B-R	5-8	180	3-18-91	.271	.333	.243	82	258	23	70	7	4	4	32	9	3	4	1	69	12	1	.376	.303
Garneau, Dustin	R-R	6-0	200	8-13-87	.500	.500	--	1	2	0	1	0	0	0	1	1	0	0	0	0	0	0	.500	.667
Gonzalez, Alfredo	R-R	6-1	225	7-13-92	.111	.250	.000	3	9	0	1	0	0	0	1	0	0	0	0	4	0	0	.111	.111
LaMarre, Ryan	R-L	6-1	210	11-21-88	.303	.361	.233	33	66	8	20	6	0	2	10	2	1	0	2	20	1	1	.485	.324
2-team total (43 Minnesota)					.279	.333	.240	76	165	15	46	11	0	2	18	10	2	0	3	53	2	2	.382	.322
Moncada, Yoan	B-R	6-2	205	5-27-95	.235	.210	.244	149	578	73	136	32	6	17	61	67	1	2	2	217	12	6	.400	.315
Narvaez, Omar	L-R	5-11	220	2-10-92	.275	.159	.297	97	280	30	77	14	1	9	30	38	2	2	0	65	0	2	.429	.366
Palka, Daniel	L-L	6-2	220	10-28-91	.240	.200	.249	124	417	56	100	15	3	27	67	30	2	0	0	153	2	1	.484	.294
Rondon, Jose	R-R	6-1	195	3-3-94	.230	.196	.259	42	100	15	23	6	0	6	14	.7	0	0	0	30	2	1	.470	.280
Saladino, Tyler	R-R	6-0	200	7-20-89	.250	.250	.250	6	8	2	2	1	0	0	0	0	0	1	0	3	0	0	.375	.250
Sanchez, Yolmer	B-R	5-11	185	6-29-92	.242	.194	.255	155	600	62	145	34	10	8	55	49	8	2	3	138	14	6	.372	.306
Skole, Matt	L-R	6-4	220	7-30-89	.273	.000	.333	4	11	2	3	0	0	1	1	2	0	0	0	3	0	0	.546	.385
Smith, Kevan	R-R	6-4	230	6-28-88	.292	.438	.236	52	171	21	50	6	0	3	21	10	5	0	1	18	1	0	.380	.348
Thompson, Trayce	R-R	6-3	217	3-15-91	.116	.136	.104	48	121	14	14	3	0	3	9	7	0	1	1	46	3	1	.215	.163
2-team total (3 Oakland)					.117	.125	.113	51	128	15	15	3	0	3	9	7	0	1	1	50	3	1	.211	.162
Tilson, Charlie	L-L	6-0	185	12-2-92	.264	.125	.289	41	106	7	28	1	1	0	11	10	1	2	1	20	2	3	.293	.331

Pitching	B-T	HT	WT	DOB	W	L	ERA	G	GS	CG	SV	IP	H	R	ER	HR	BB	SO	AVG	vLH	vRH	K/9	BB/9
Avilan, Luis	L-L	6-2	220	7-19-89	2	1	3.86	58	0	0	2	40	40	20	17	2	14	46	.260	.214	.298	10.44	3.18
Beck, Chris	R-R	6-3	225	9-4-90	0	0	4.18	14	0	0	1	24	24	11	11	5	11	16	.270	.277	.262	6.08	4.18
Bummer, Aaron	L-L	6-3	200	9-21-93	0	1	4.26	37	0	0	0	32	40	19	15	1	10	35	.301	.245	.338	9.95	2.84
Burr, Ryan	R-R	6-4	225	5-28-94	0	0	7.45	8	0	0	0	10	12	8	8	3	6	6	.333	.333	.333	5.59	5.59
Cedeno, Xavier	L-L	5-11	210	8-26-86	2	0	2.84	33	0	0	1	25	19	9	8	1	13	28	.204	.209	.200	9.95	4.62
Covey, Dylan	R-R	6-2	195	8-14-91	5	14	5.18	27	21	0	0	122	129	81	70	13	52	91	.269	.266	.272	6.73	3.85
Danish, Tyler	R-R	6-0	200	9-12-94	1	0	7.11	7	0	0	0	6	8	5	5	2	4	5	.320	.500	.235	7.11	5.68
Farquhar, Danny	R-R	5-9	185	2-17-87	1	1	5.63	8	0	0	0	8	6	5	5	3	0	9	.214	.000	.250	10.13	0.00
Frare, Caleb	L-L	6-1	210	7-8-93	0	1	5.14	11	0	0	0	7	6	4	4	0	4	9	.231	.182	.267	11.57	5.14
Fry, Jace	L-L	6-1	190	7-9-93	2	3	4.38	59	1	0	4	51	37	28	25	4	20	70	.194	.143	.234	12.27	3.51
Fulmer, Carson	R-R	6-0	195	12-13-93	2	4	8.07	9	8	0	0	32	37	32	29	8	24	29	.280	.297	.265	8.07	6.68
Giolito, Lucas	R-R	6-6	245	7-14-94	10	13	6.13	32	32	0	0	173	166	123	118	27	90	125	.250	.271	.227	6.49	4.67
Gomez, Jeanmar	R-R	6-3	215	2-10-88	0	2	4.68	26	0	0	0	25	29	15	13	3	10	27	.293	.343	.266	9.72	3.60
Gonzalez, Miguel	R-R	6-1	185	5-27-84	0	3	12.41	3	3	0	0	12	24	18	17	4	6	5	.400	.348	.432	3.65	4.38
Hamilton, Ian	R-R	6-0	200	6-16-95	1	2	4.50	10	0	0	0	8	6	5	4	2	2	5	.207	.400	.105	5.63	2.25
Infante, Gregory	R-R	6-1	200	7-10-87	1	1	8.00	10	0	0	0	9	12	8	8	0	8	6	.364	.333	.370	6.00	8.00
Jones, Nate	R-R	6-5	220	1-28-86	2	2	3.00	33	0	0	5	30	28	14	10	4	15	32	.239	.235	.242	9.60	4.50
Kopech, Michael	R-R	6-3	205	4-30-96	1	1	5.02	4	4	0	0	14	20	8	8	4	2	15	.328	.258	.400	9.42	1.26
Lopez, Reynaldo	R-R	6-1	200	1-4-94	7	10	3.91	32	32	0	0	189	165	88	82	25	75	151	.234	.220	.249	7.20	3.58
Minaya, Juan	R-R	6-4	210	9-18-90	2	2	3.28	52	0	0	1	47	39	19	17	3	29	58	.220	.164	.255	11.19	5.59
Rodon, Carlos	L-L	6-3	235	12-10-92	6	8	4.18	20	20	0	0	121	97	61	56	15	55	90	.220	.245	.213	6.71	4.10
Rondon, Bruce	R-R	6-3	275	12-9-90	2	3	8.49	35	0	0	1	30	37	30	28	1	27	40	.298	.333	.279	12.13	8.19
Ruiz, Jose	R-R	6-1	190	10-21-94	0	0	4.15	6	0	0	0	4	5	2	2	1	3	6	.278	.200	.308	12.46	6.23
Santiago, Hector	R-L	6-0	215	12-16-87	6	3	4.41	49	7	0	2	102	101	54	50	16	60	103	.258	.276	.252	9.09	5.29
Scahill, Rob	L-R	6-2	220	2-15-87	0	0	5.40	6	0	0	0	5	5	4	3	0	3	3	.250	.429	.154	5.40	5.40
Shields, James	R-R	6-3	210	12-20-81	7	16	4.53	34	33	0	0	205	190	115	103	34	78	154	.245	.214	.278	6.77	3.43
Soria, Joakim	R-R	6-3	200	5-18-84	0	3	2.56	40	0	0	16	39	35	13	11	2	10	49	.230	.264	.200	11.41	2.33
Vieira, Thyago	R-R	6-2	210	7-1-93	1	0	7.13	16	0	0	1	18	21	14	14	4	9	15	.292	.342	.235	7.64	4.58
Volstad, Chris	R-R	6-8	235	9-23-86	1	5	6.27	33	1	0	0	47	65	35	33	9	12	29	.332	.342	.325	5.51	2.28

CHICAGO WHITE SOX

Fielding

Catcher	PCT	G	PO	A	E	DP	PB
Castillo	.997	43	306	22	1	4	5
Garneau	.889	1	7	1	1	0	0
Gonzalez	.957	3	21	1	1	0	1
Narvaez	.989	85	578	40	7	3	12
Smith	.995	47	358	20	2	3	2

First Base	PCT	G	PO	A	E	DP
Abreu	.992	114	903	73	8	81
Davidson	.994	45	335	13	2	23
Delmonico	.980	7	46	2	1	6
Rondon	1.000	1	2	0	0	0
Skole	1.000	1	6	1	0	4

Second Base	PCT	G	PO	A	E	DP
Garcia	1.000	7	15	15	0	3

	PCT	G	PO	A	E	DP
Moncada	.963	149	213	335	21	80
Rondon	.900	4	0	9	1	0
Sanchez	1.000	9	12	17	0	6

Third Base	PCT	G	PO	A	E	DP
Davidson	.949	14	15	22	2	5
Garcia	1.000	1	1	2	0	0
Rondon	.958	8	8	15	1	5
Saladino	1.000	2	3	5	0	0
Sanchez	.968	141	137	254	13	29

Shortstop	PCT	G	PO	A	E	DP
Anderson	.967	151	188	392	20	72
Garcia	1.000	5	2	14	0	2
Rondon	1.000	10	6	17	0	5
Sanchez	.857	4	2	4	1	1

Outfield	PCT	G	PO	A	E	DP
Cordell	1.000	15	23	0	0	0
Delmonico	.969	76	121	5	4	1
Engel	.981	140	355	5	7	1
Garcia	.990	87	189	2	2	0
Garcia	.968	68	117	5	4	2
LaMarre	.952	29	36	4	2	1
Palka	1.000	8	92	3	0	1
Thompson	1.000	46	74	3	0	3
Tilson	.986	35	69	1	1	1

CHARLOTTE KNIGHTS — TRIPLE-A
INTERNATIONAL LEAGUE

Batting	B-T	HT	WT	DOB	AVG	vLH	vRH	G	AB	R	H	2B	3B	HR	RBI	BB	HBP	SH	SF	SO	SB	CS	SLG	OBP
Alvarez, Eddy	B-R	5-9	180	1-30-90	.253	.258	.251	101	308	52	78	26	3	8	37	43	3	7	2	79	5	3	.435	.348
Austin, Brett	B-R	6-1	210	11-24-92	.235	.200	.250	14	34	3	8	2	0	0	2	8	0	1	0	13	0	0	.294	.381
Brett, Ryan	R-R	5-9	180	10-9-91	.071	.000	.111	10	28	1	2	0	0	0	0	1	0	1	0	7	1	0	.071	.103
Castillo, Welington	R-R	5-10	220	4-24-87	.189	.250	.172	10	37	2	7	1	0	0	3	3	0	0	0	11	0	0	.216	.250
Cordell, Ryan	R-R	6-4	195	3-31-92	.239	.234	.240	44	176	15	42	9	2	3	22	11	1	0	4	44	7	2	.364	.281
Cunningham, Todd	R-R	6-0	205	3-20-89	.192	.267	.091	9	26	3	5	1	0	0	2	4	0	1	1	4	2	1	.231	.290
2-team total (9 Indianapolis)					.163	.227	.111	18	49	5	8	2	0	0	3	5	1	3	2	9	2	2	.204	.246
Delmonico, Nicky	L-R	6-3	230	7-12-92	.400	.000	.471	5	20	3	8	4	0	0	2	4	0	0	0	4	0	0	.600	.500
Elmore, Jake	R-R	5-10	180	6-15-87	.289	.351	.257	100	329	47	95	18	1	1	27	55	6	1	3	58	11	2	.359	.397
Flete, Bryant	L-R	5-10	146	1-31-93	.346	.400	.333	8	26	1	9	2	0	0	3	0	2	0	0	7	0	1	.423	.393
Garcia, Avisail	R-R	6-4	240	6-12-91	.360	.400	.333	7	25	5	9	3	0	3	9	3	0	0	0	5	0	0	.840	.429
Garcia, Leury	B-R	5-8	180	3-18-91	.429	.286	.571	4	14	4	6	3	0	0	3	1	0	0	0	3	0	0	.643	.467
Garneau, Dustin	R-R	6-0	200	8-13-87	.252	.229	.264	45	139	19	35	9	0	7	22	16	3	0	1	38	0	2	.468	.340
Giavotella, Johnny	R-R	5-8	185	7-10-87	.225	.150	.300	11	40	4	9	1	0	0	0	0	0	0	0	5	0	0	.250	.225
Gillaspie, Casey	B-L	6-4	240	1-25-93	.220	.159	.249	71	255	20	56	18	0	3	22	24	0	0	2	91	0	0	.326	.285
Gonzalez, Alfredo	R-R	6-1	225	7-13-92	.193	.263	.155	33	109	12	21	2	0	0	5	13	2	1	1	37	0	0	.211	.288
Jimenez, Eloy	R-R	6-4	205	11-27-96	.356	.457	.327	55	211	28	75	13	1	13	33	14	2	0	1	30	0	1	.597	.399
LaMarre, Ryan	R-L	6-1	210	11-21-88	.222	.083	.273	12	45	7	10	2	2	0	2	4	0	0	0	14	2	0	.356	.286
2-team total (13 Rochester)					.269	.185	.303	25	93	12	25	6	3	0	7	9	1	1	0	29	3	0	.398	.340
Leonard, Patrick	R-R	6-4	225	10-20-92	.242	.215	.254	124	430	43	104	29	2	11	50	43	4	1	2	145	3	2	.395	.315
May, Jacob	B-R	5-10	180	1-23-92	.255	.200	.282	81	314	30	80	19	1	2	30	20	2	5	1	73	15	11	.341	.303
Palka, Daniel	L-L	6-2	220	10-28-91	.286	.292	.282	17	63	11	18	3	0	3	7	10	0	0	0	21	1	2	.476	.384
Perez, Juan	L-R	5-11	185	11-1-91	.184	.255	.155	46	163	20	30	6	2	4	11	12	2	1	0	56	9	2	.319	.249
Presley, Alex	L-L	5-10	195	7-25-85	.198	.185	.203	29	101	6	20	3	0	1	12	8	1	0	1	19	0	2	.257	.261
2-team total (26 Norfolk)					.238	.222	.245	55	210	25	50	8	1	2	20	19	2	0	1	46	0	2	.314	.306
Robbins, Mason	L-L	6-0	200	2-1-93	.265	.258	.269	57	215	23	57	10	3	2	24	8	0	0	2	48	3	1	.367	.289
Rondon, Jose	R-R	6-1	195	3-3-94	.249	.263	.245	80	313	41	78	15	4	18	38	16	3	1	3	82	5	6	.495	.290
Saunders, Michael	R-R	6-4	225	11-19-86	.152	.083	.177	13	46	4	7	1	0	1	4	5	0	0	0	10	0	0	.239	.235
2-team total (25 Norfolk)					.158	.086	.184	38	133	15	21	4	1	2	18	21	0	0	0	33	2	0	.248	.273
Skole, Matt	L-R	6-4	220	7-30-89	.237	.220	.243	121	431	50	102	28	1	14	44	61	5	0	3	125	3	1	.404	.336
Smith, Kevan	R-R	6-4	230	6-28-88	.268	.211	.297	30	112	12	30	4	0	4	16	8	3	0	1	18	0	0	.411	.331
Thompson, Trayce	R-R	6-3	217	3-15-91	.213	.296	.181	46	160	22	34	12	0	4	15	15	0	0	1	57	3	1	.363	.278
Tilson, Charlie	L-L	6-0	185	12-2-92	.244	.346	.219	67	270	27	66	12	0	0	25	16	1	4	1	52	10	2	.289	.288
Zavala, Seby	R-R	5-11	215	8-28-93	.243	.300	.227	48	181	18	44	15	0	2	20	6	1	0	3	44	0	2	.359	.267

Pitching	B-T	HT	WT	DOB	W	L	ERA	G	GS	CG	SV	IP	H	R	ER	BB	SO	AVG	vLH	vRH	K/9	BB/9
Adams, Spencer	R-R	6-3	171	4-13-96	4	7	3.19	15	15	0	0	90	82	32	32	10	38	42	.248	.275	.219	4.18	3.79
Beck, Chris	R-R	6-3	225	9-4-90	0	0	2.00	4	2	0	0	9	4	3	2	0	3	13	.129	.222	.000	13.00	3.00
Brennan, Brandon	R-R	6-4	220	7-26-91	1	1	5.40	4	0	0	0	5	3	3	3	0	3	9	.177	.167	.182	16.20	5.40
Bummer, Aaron	L-L	6-0	200	9-21-93	2	3	2.64	31	0	0	0	31	27	11	9	0	11	30	.235	.246	.222	8.80	3.23
Burr, Ryan	R-R	6-4	225	5-28-94	0	1	1.08	7	0	0	0	8	4	2	1	0	2	8	.154	.333	.000	8.64	2.16
Cedeno, Xavier	L-L	5-11	210	8-26-86	0	0	1.25	20	0	0	0	22	12	5	3	1	4	25	.162	.177	.150	10.38	1.66
Covey, Dylan	R-R	6-2	195	8-14-91	3	1	2.33	7	7	0	0	39	32	14	10	3	15	35	.232	.222	.240	8.15	3.49
Danish, Tyler	R-R	6-0	190	9-12-94	2	3	3.01	33	2	0	0	72	63	27	24	6	28	53	.235	.243	.230	6.66	3.52
Frare, Caleb	L-L	6-1	210	7-8-93	1	0	0.71	11	0	0	0	13	5	1	1	0	7	19	.119	.111	.125	13.50	4.97
2-team total (1 Scranton/Wilkes-Barre)					1	0	1.32	12	0	0	0	14	7	2	2	0	7	20	.149	.105	.179	13.17	4.61
Fry, Jace	L-L	6-1	190	7-9-93	0	0	1.35	5	0	0	0	7	3	1	1	1	0	11	.125	.182	.077	14.85	0.00
Fulmer, Carson	R-R	6-0	195	12-13-93	5	6	5.32	25	9	0	0	68	70	41	40	10	41	62	.271	.309	.230	8.25	5.45
Gomez, Jeanmar	R-R	6-3	215	2-10-88	5	0	2.03	30	0	0	2	40	35	11	9	2	13	35	.240	.186	.276	7.88	2.93
Gonzalez, Miguel	R-R	6-1	185	5-27-84	0	0	0.00	1	1	0	0	3	1	0	0	0	1		.091	.000	.143	3.00	3.00
Guerrero, Jordan	L-L	6-3	195	5-31-94	7	2	3.46	12	12	0	0	65	64	28	25	4	28	62	.251	.279	.237	8.58	3.88
Hamilton, Ian	R-R	6-0	200	6-16-95	1	1	1.71	22	0	0	10	26	18	5	5	2	4	28	.198	.167	.233	9.57	1.37
Hasler, Drew	R-R	6-6	245	8-14-93	0	0	6.75	1	0	0	0	3	6	2	2	0	0	3	.462	.200	.625	10.13	0.00

	B-T	HT	WT	DOB	W	L	ERA	G	GS	CG	SV	IP	H	R	ER	HR	BB	SO	AVG	vLH	vRH	K/9	BB/9
House, TJ	R-L	6-1	205	9-29-89	1	6	6.81	9	9	1	0	40	49	40	30	2	18	24	.303	.327	.291	5.45	4.08
Infante, Gregory	R-R	6-1	200	7-10-87	2	4	4.32	44	0	0	9	50	49	26	24	10	10	51	.257	.259	.255	9.18	1.80
Kopech, Michael	R-R	6-3	205	4-30-96	7	7	3.70	24	24	0	0	126	101	58	52	9	60	170	.219	.223	.215	12.11	4.27
Kubat, Kyle	L-L	6-1	195	12-4-92	0	0	13.50	1	0	0	0	2	3	3	3	1	1	3	.333	.400	.250	13.50	4.50
Minaya, Juan	R-R	6-4	210	9-18-90	1	3	4.24	19	0	0	2	23	18	12	11	4	8	27	.217	.188	.235	10.41	3.09
Pinto, Ricardo	R-R	6-0	165	1-20-94	2	2	5.80	27	3	0	0	54	68	35	35	7	22	38	.309	.287	.328	6.29	3.64
Quijada, Jhoan	R-R	6-3	210	12-27-94	0	0	0.00	1	0	0	0	1	0	0	0	0	0	1	.000	.000	.000	9.00	0.00
Roach, Donn	R-R	6-0	195	12-14-89	9	2	2.65	16	15	0	0	95	95	32	28	3	21	61	.262	.239	.281	5.78	1.99
Rodon, Carlos	L-L	6-3	235	12-10-92	1	0	1.42	3	3	0	0	13	10	2	2	0	5	22	.222	.158	.269	15.63	3.55
Rondon, Bruce	R-R	6-3	275	12-9-90	0	0	0.00	1	0	0	0	1	1	0	0	0	0	1	.250	.000	.500	9.00	0.00
Ross Jr., Robbie	L-L	5-11	215	6-24-89	0	2	11.81	11	0	0	0	11	12	16	14	0	17	11	.308	.250	.348	9.28	14.34
Scahill, Rob	L-R	6-2	215	2-15-87	3	4	5.64	52	0	0	5	61	70	41	38	4	25	71	.286	.346	.241	10.53	3.71
Stephens, Jordan	R-R	6-1	190	9-12-92	4	7	4.71	21	21	0	0	107	114	62	56	11	42	99	.271	.296	.242	8.33	3.53
Tomshaw, Matt	R-L	6-2	200	12-17-88	3	1	8.58	6	6	0	0	28	46	27	27	3	8	18	.359	.300	.397	5.72	2.54
Turner, Colton	L-L	6-3	215	1-17-91	0	2	4.76	10	3	0	0	23	19	12	12	5	10	21	.229	.200	.245	8.34	3.97
Vieira, Thyago	R-R	6-2	210	7-1-93	0	4	5.05	36	0	0	6	41	40	25	23	2	24	50	.252	.315	.198	10.98	5.27
Volstad, Chris	R-R	6-8	235	9-23-86	0	1	9.64	1	1	0	0	5	6	5	5	0	2	3	.316	.375	.273	5.79	3.86
Watson, Tyler	L-L	5-11	200	6-9-93	0	0	0.00	1	0	0	0	1	1	0	0	0	0	2	.250	.000	.333	18.00	0.00
Wojciechowski, Asher	R-R	6-4	235	12-21-88	0	5	7.01	6	6	0	0	35	40	27	27	12	5	37	.288	.322	.263	9.61	1.30
2-team total (19 Norfolk Tides)					5	9	4.53	25	18	0	0	119	108	63	60	26	37	126	.240	.286	.203	9.50	2.79

Fielding

Catcher	PCT	G	PO	A	E	DP	PB
Austin	1.000	9	63	3	0	1	1
Castillo	1.000	8	56	6	0	1	1
Garneau	.988	39	309	22	4	2	4
Gonzalez	.993	32	266	14	2	1	1
Smith	.990	22	179	14	2	3	1
Zavala	.996	35	264	19	1	3	4

First Base	PCT	G	PO	A	E	DP
Delmonico	1.000	2	17	0	0	2
Garneau	.900	1	7	2	1	0
Gillaspie	.992	69	600	19	5	50
Leonard	.987	9	70	4	1	5
Skole	.998	63	469	25	1	61

Second Base	PCT	G	PO	A	E	DP
Alvarez	.969	67	107	178	9	44
Brett	.870	3	7	13	3	3
Elmore	.980	33	61	87	3	23
Flete	1.000	4	4	15	0	3
Giavotella	1.000	5	10	16	0	5
Perez	.979	32	42	95	3	19

Third Base	PCT	G	PO	A	E	DP
Alvarez	1.000	1	1	2	0	0
Brett	.000	1	0	0	1	0
Elmore	.957	21	13	32	2	3
Flete	.000	1	0	0	0	0
Leonard	.968	101	58	181	8	20
Rondon	.875	2	3	5	1	0
Skole	1.000	18	12	31	0	3

Shortstop	PCT	G	PO	A	E	DP
Alvarez	.959	31	48	69	5	22
Elmore	.990	25	33	68	1	18
Flete	.867	3	3	10	2	3
Garcia	1.000	1	2	3	0	0
Perez	.941	6	6	26	2	2
Rondon	.976	78	102	220	8	46

Outfield	PCT	G	PO	A	E	DP
Brett	1.000	5	8	0	0	0
Cordell	.989	41	86	3	1	1
Cunningham	.923	9	10	2	1	0
Delmonico	1.000	2	3	0	0	0
Elmore	1.000	14	23	0	0	0
Garcia	1.000	5	7	0	0	0
Garcia	1.000	2	2	0	0	0
Garneau	.000	1	0	0	0	0
Jimenez	.967	46	84	3	3	0
LaMarre	1.000	9	18	1	0	0
May	.994	81	151	8	1	1
Palka	1.000	15	22	1	0	0
Perez	.933	8	13	1	1	0
Presley	.982	29	51	3	1	0
Robbins	1.000	47	79	2	0	0
Saunders	1.000	10	14	2	0	1
Thompson	.970	40	96	1	3	0
Tilson	.985	66	134	1	2	1

BIRMINGHAM BARONS

SOUTHERN LEAGUE

DOUBLE-A

Batting	B-T	HT	WT	DOB	AVG	vLH	vRH	G	AB	R	H	2B	3B	HR	RBI	BB	HBP	SH	SF	SO	SB	CS	SLG	OBP
Barnum, Keon	L-L	6-5	225	1-16-93	.202	.176	.212	79	272	25	55	8	1	15	44	10	2	0	0	96	0	0	.404	.236
Basabe, Luis Alexander	B-R	6-0	160	8-26-96	.251	.327	.227	61	231	41	58	9	3	6	26	30	2	5	2	76	9	4	.394	.340
Basto, Nick	R-R	6-2	210	4-1-94	.165	.161	.167	35	115	15	19	2	1	1	8	16	3	1	0	43	0	1	.226	.284
Booker, Joel	R-R	6-1	190	11-1-93	.266	.364	.241	66	267	43	71	12	2	2	17	22	8	5	2	77	12	8	.348	.338
Brett, Ryan	R-R	5-9	180	10-9-91	.265	.277	.261	47	166	27	44	9	1	3	15	5	2	0	1	43	3	1	.386	.293
Call, Alex	R-R	6-0	180	9-27-94	.242	.192	.254	67	236	28	57	17	1	7	30	25	5	1	2	75	2	1	.411	.325
Collins, Zack	L-R	6-3	220	2-6-95	.234	.212	.242	122	418	58	98	24	1	15	68	101	3	2	7	158	5	0	.404	.382
Cordell, Ryan	R-R	6-4	195	3-31-92	.333	.000	.364	3	12	2	4	0	0	1	3	1	0	0	0	3	0	0	.583	.385
Delmonico, Nicky	L-R	6-3	220	7-12-92	.200	.250	.143	5	15	1	3	0	0	0	1	0	0	0	0	3	0	0	.200	.250
Fisher, Jameson	L-R	6-2	200	12-18-93	.216	.260	.202	97	315	31	68	11	2	6	24	44	6	2	3	113	3	4	.321	.321
Flete, Bryant	R-R	5-10	146	1-31-93	.230	.240	.245	82	258	33	62	10	2	2	25	34	9	1	1	70	4	6	.318	.348
Giavotella, Johnny	R-R	5-8	185	7-10-87	.200	.500	.125	3	10	1	2	0	0	0	3	2	0	0	0	3	0	0	.200	.333
Gonzalez, Alfredo	R-R	6-1	225	7-13-92	.298	.227	.317	31	104	10	31	6	2	1	12	6	1	1	0	26	2	1	.414	.342
Hawkins, Courtney	R-R	6-3	245	11-12-93	.120	.000	.188	9	25	1	3	1	0	0	3	2	0	0	2	10	0	0	.160	.172
Jimenez, Eloy	R-R	6-4	205	11-27-96	.317	.263	.329	53	205	36	65	15	2	10	42	18	1	0	4	39	0	1	.556	.368
Mendick, Danny	R-R	5-10	189	9-28-93	.247	.282	.236	132	453	62	112	25	0	14	59	57	10	2	7	90	20	10	.395	.340
Michalczewski, Trey	B-R	6-3	210	2-27-95	.253	.246	.255	126	451	46	114	26	6	6	65	27	10	3	12	131	4	3	.377	.302
Muno, JJ	L-R	5-11	190	12-21-93	.125	--	.125	1	8	1	1	0	0	0	0	0	0	0	0	0	0	0	.125	.300
Polo, Tito	R-R	5-10	195	8-23-94	.245	.244	.246	46	163	22	40	6	3	1	8	12	4	2	0	34	15	4	.337	.313
Robbins, Mason	L-L	6-0	200	2-1-93	.350	.500	.333	5	20	2	7	0	0	1	3	0	0	0	0	2	0	0	.500	.350
Roman, Mitch	R-R	6-0	161	3-22-95	.232	.214	.235	27	95	11	22	3	0	0	3	3	2	4	1	39	3	0	.263	.267
Rose, Matt	R-R	6-4	195	8-2-94	.183	.167	.188	115	426	42	78	18	0	16	54	35	1	1	4	146	0	0	.338	.245
Schroeder, Casey	B-R	6-2	225	7-12-93	.000	.000	.000	2	7	2	0	0	0	0	0	0	0	2	0	0	3	0	0	.000	.222
Zavala, Seby	R-R	5-11	215	8-28-93	.271	.319	.262	56	199	32	54	7	0	11	31	27	2	0	4	65	0	0	.472	.358

Pitching	B-T	HT	WT	DOB	W	L	ERA	G	GS	CG	SV	IP	H	R	ER	HR	BB	SO	AVG	vLH	vRH	K/9	BB/9
Adams, Spencer	R-R	6-3	171	4-13-96	3	7	4.59	13	13	0	0	69	80	36	35	10	20	53	.290	.328	.258	6.95	2.62
Banks, Tanner	L-L	6-1	195	10-24-91	4	5	2.66	10	10	0	0	61	59	23	18	5	15	44	.258	.214	.267	6.49	2.21
Brennan, Brandon	R-R	6-4	220	7-26-91	4	3	3.10	40	1	0	1	70	54	28	24	4	21	70	.207	.290	.161	9.04	2.71

Name	B-T	HT	WT	DOB	W	L	ERA	G	GS	CG	SV	IP	H	R	ER	HR	BB	SO	AVG	vLH	vRH	K/9	BB/9
Burr, Ryan	R-R	6-4	225	5-28-94	4	2	2.72	30	0	0	2	43	30	15	13	3	23	43	.196	.196	.196	9.00	4.81
Cabrera, Mauricio	R-R	6-3	225	9-22-93	0	0	20.25	2	0	0	0	1	2	3	3	0	4	0	.400	.333	.500	0.00	27.00
Cease, Dylan	R-R	6-2	190	12-28-95	3	0	1.72	10	10	0	0	52	30	11	10	3	22	78	.168	.163	.172	13.41	3.78
Clark, Brian	R-L	6-3	225	4-27-93	2	4	4.76	41	3	0	4	62	62	38	33	5	21	65	.259	.175	.302	9.39	3.03
Clarkin, Ian	L-L	6-2	215	2-14-95	4	5	4.98	18	10	1	0	69	74	43	38	7	31	35	.278	.301	.268	4.59	4.06
Dopico, Danny	R-R	6-2	190	12-18-93	0	0	3.00	1	0	0	0	3	4	1	1	0	1	1	.308	.200	.375	3.00	3.00
Dunning, Dane	R-R	6-4	200	12-20-94	5	2	2.76	11	11	0	0	62	57	24	19	0	23	69	.243	.263	.228	10.02	3.34
Flores, Bernardo	L-L	6-3	170	8-23-95	3	3	2.76	13	13	1	0	78	79	27	24	5	14	47	.271	.206	.290	5.40	1.61
Foster, Matt	R-R	6-0	195	1-27-95	0	4	3.94	24	0	0	1	32	33	19	14	3	13	30	.264	.222	.288	8.44	3.66
Goldberg, Brad	R-R	6-4	220	2-21-90	0	2	2.82	17	0	0	0	22	19	10	7	0	15	34	.235	.355	.160	13.70	6.04
2-team total (16 Jackson)					2	1	1.98	33	0	0	4	36	23	13	8	1	25	58	.181	.265	.128	14.37	6.19
Guerrero, Jordan	L-L	6-3	195	5-31-94	3	6	6.06	14	13	0	0	65	84	48	44	6	19	58	.315	.282	.328	7.99	2.62
Hamilton, Ian	R-R	6-0	200	6-16-95	2	1	1.78	21	0	0	12	25	20	6	5	0	12	34	.211	.237	.193	12.08	4.26
Hansen, Alec	R-R	6-7	235	10-10-94	0	4	6.56	9	9	0	0	36	30	30	26	3	42	35	.238	.157	.293	8.83	10.60
Johansen, Jake	R-R	6-6	235	1-23-91	2	4	4.15	31	0	0	1	48	57	34	22	2	16	35	.291	.306	.282	6.61	3.02
Lambert, Jimmy	R-R	6-2	170	11-18-94	3	1	2.88	5	5	0	0	25	20	8	8	2	6	30	.217	.321	.172	10.80	2.16
Medeiros, Kodi	L-L	6-2	180	5-25-96	0	2	4.98	7	7	0	0	34	31	21	19	4	22	34	.250	.158	.291	8.91	5.77
2-team total (20 Biloxi)					7	7	3.60	27	22	0	0	138	121	66	55	13	67	141	.238	.159	.268	9.22	4.38
Paulino, Felix	R-R	6-1	170	3-24-95	0	2	9.00	2	2	0	0	9	13	13	9	3	7	3	.325	.263	.381	3.00	7.00
Quijada, Jhoan	R-R	6-3	210	12-27-94	0	0	18.00	1	0	0	0	1	3	2	2	0	0	0	.600	.500	.667	0.00	0.00
Rondon, Jorge	R-R	6-1	215	2-16-88	0	1	4.85	9	0	0	0	13	13	7	7	0	8	14	.255	.375	.200	9.69	5.54
Ruiz, Jose	R-R	6-1	190	10-21-94	3	1	3.18	33	0	0	14	45	33	18	16	2	19	55	.204	.185	.213	10.92	3.77
Seitzer, Cameron	L-R	6-5	220	1-11-90	0	0	3.38	5	0	0	0	5	9	2	2	0	1	3	.360	.546	.214	5.06	1.69
Stephens, Jordan	R-R	6-1	190	9-12-92	4	3	2.95	7	7	0	0	40	37	18	13	1	12	40	.259	.307	.222	9.08	2.72
Thompson, Zach	R-R	6-7	230	10-23-93	4	0	1.35	21	0	0	1	40	28	9	6	3	18	40	.194	.180	.202	9.00	4.05
Tomshaw, Matt	R-L	6-2	200	12-17-88	8	5	5.09	21	21	1	0	120	154	75	68	8	21	100	.310	.305	.312	7.48	1.57
Turner, Colton	L-L	6-3	215	1-17-91	7	2	0.86	27	0	0	4	42	25	9	4	0	10	44	.168	.182	.162	9.43	2.14
Walsh, Connor	L-R	6-2	190	10-18-92	0	1	10.67	19	3	0	1	29	46	36	34	6	19	41	.346	.353	.342	12.87	5.97

Fielding

Catcher	PCT	G	PO	A	E	DP	PB
Collins	.987	74	616	56	9	5	13
Gonzalez	.985	31	240	28	4	1	1
Schroeder	.947	2	17	1	1	0	1
Zavala	.996	31	258	20	1	0	8

First Base	PCT	G	PO	A	E	DP
Barnum	.989	65	506	25	6	46
Basto	.989	22	161	11	2	14
Delmonico	1.000	1	4	0	0	0
Rose	.984	58	467	27	8	42

Second Base	PCT	G	PO	A	E	DP
Brett	.905	6	7	12	2	2
Flete	.967	36	54	93	5	20

	PCT	G	PO	A	E	DP
Giavotella	1.000	3	7	10	0	3
Michalczewski	.973	74	121	170	8	43
Roman	.983	23	50	67	2	19

Third Base	PCT	G	PO	A	E	DP
Basto	1.000	2	0	1	0	0
Flete	.934	41	20	79	7	10
Michalczewski	.973	46	23	86	3	10
Rose	.906	54	20	95	12	5

Shortstop	PCT	G	PO	A	E	DP
Flete	.688	3	3	8	5	3
Mendick	.968	131	171	348	17	65
Michalczewski	1.000	1	0	1	0	1
Muno	1.000	1	1	4	0	1
Roman	1.000	2	3	12	0	3

	PCT	G	PO	A	E	DP
Rose	1.000	1	0	1	0	0

Outfield	PCT	G	PO	A	E	DP
Basabe	.993	58	130	4	1	0
Basto	1.000	12	14	0	0	0
Booker	.978	65	124	7	3	2
Brett	1.000	40	83	3	0	0
Call	.982	63	108	4	2	1
Cordell	1.000	2	5	0	0	0
Delmonico	1.000	3	3	0	0	0
Fisher	.946	78	151	7	9	0
Hawkins	.846	8	11	0	2	0
Jimenez	.986	43	66	3	1	0
Muno	1.000	3	5	0	0	0
Polo	.983	45	115	4	2	1
Robbins	1.000	3	3	0	0	0

WINSTON-SALEM DASH
HIGH CLASS A
CAROLINA LEAGUE

Batting	B-T	HT	WT	DOB	AVG	vLH	vRH	G	AB	R	H	2B	3B	HR	RBI	BB	HBP	SH	SF	SO	SB	CS	SLG	OBP
Adolfo, Micker	R-R	6-3	200	9-11-96	.282	.312	.274	79	291	48	82	18	1	11	50	34	8	0	3	92	2	1	.464	.369
Basabe, Luis Alexander	B-R	6-0	160	8-26-96	.266	.327	.245	58	207	36	55	12	5	9	30	34	1	2	1	64	7	8	.502	.370
Booker, Joel	R-R	6-1	190	11-1-93	.297	.283	.302	53	192	39	57	14	2	5	21	22	7	2	0	42	14	9	.469	.389
Brown, Nolan	L-L	5-11	175	1-13-94	.162	.125	.172	14	37	2	6	1	1	0	4	3	1	0	0	12	0	0	.243	.244
Call, Alex	R-R	6-0	188	9-27-94	.256	.302	.243	56	195	35	50	11	3	5	28	35	1	2	3	52	4	6	.421	.368
Duarte, Mikey	R-R	5-11	195	4-8-94	.111	.000	.125	6	9	1	1	0	0	0	0	1	0	1	0	2	1	1	.111	.200
Forbes, Ti'Quan	R-R	6-3	180	8-26-96	.273	.356	.252	119	432	59	118	21	6	6	51	21	5	2	2	74	4	9	.391	.313
Gonzalez, Daniel	R-R	6-1	190	12-6-95	.241	.300	.227	24	54	10	13	0	0	1	5	6	1	1	0	14	1	0	.296	.328
Gonzalez, Luis	L-L	6-1	185	9-10-95	.314	.389	.293	62	252	50	79	24	3	6	45	27	2	0	6	46	3	5	.504	.376
Madrigal, Nick	S-R	5-7	165	3-5-97	.306	.188	.329	26	98	14	30	4	0	0	9	5	3	0	1	5	6	3	.347	.355
Mercedes, Yermin	R-R	5-11	195	2-14-93	.289	.329	.279	103	360	58	104	24	1	14	64	40	4	0	5	67	4	0	.478	.362
Muno, JJ	L-R	5-11	190	12-21-93	.258	.167	.280	20	62	10	16	2	1	1	8	2	2	0	1	17	2	0	.371	.299
Nolan, Nate	R-R	6-1	210	10-11-94	.173	.211	.161	50	162	16	28	7	1	3	20	16	1	0	0	78	0	0	.284	.251
Remillard, Zach	R-R	6-1	200	2-21-94	.250	.244	.252	110	380	58	95	16	5	3	11	52	30	7	1	1	103	8	6	.395	.316
Rivera, Laz	R-R	6-1	185	9-20-94	.280	.366	.261	61	225	38	63	15	2	7	37	7	9	6	2	44	10	7	.458	.325
Robert, Luis	R-R	6-3	185	8-3-97	.244	.400	.214	32	123	21	30	6	1	0	11	8	6	1	2	37	8	2	.309	.317
Roman, Mitch	R-R	6-0	161	3-22-95	.293	.371	.292	99	297	47	87	14	1	3	41	34	2	2	7	70	15	6	.377	.362
Rutherford, Blake	L-R	6-2	195	5-2-97	.293	.284	.295	115	447	67	131	25	9	7	78	34	3	0	3	90	15	8	.436	.345
Sheets, Gavin	L-L	6-4	230	4-23-96	.293	.281	.296	119	437	58	128	28	2	6	61	52	3	0	5	81	1	0	.407	.368
Yrizarri, Yeyson	R-R	6-0	175	2-2-97	.247	.235	.251	101	372	44	92	21	2	6	46	18	9	2	3	75	16	7	.363	.296

Pitching	B-T	HT	WT	DOB	W	L	ERA	G	GS	CG	SV	IP	H	R	ER	HR	BB	SO	AVG	vLH	vRH	K/9	BB/9
Banks, Tanner	L-L	6-1	195	10-24-91	8	2	2.54	13	13	0	0	85	81	33	24	3	17	56	.253	.259	.251	5.93	1.80
Battenfield, Blake	R-R	6-3	220	8-22-94	5	2	4.22	9	9	0	0	53	50	29	25	10	13	46	.248	.299	.200	7.76	2.19

Name	B-T	HT	WT	DOB	W	L	ERA	G	GS	CG	SV	IP	H	R	ER	HR	BB	SO	AVG	vLH	vRH	K/9	BB/9
Cease, Dylan	R-R	6-2	190	12-28-95	9	2	2.89	13	13	0	0	72	52	31	23	5	28	82	.204	.202	.206	10.30	3.52
Clarkin, Ian	L-L	6-2	215	2-14-95	0	0	2.35	4	0	0	0	8	4	2	2	0	3	6	.160	.000	.182	7.04	3.52
Dopico, Danny	R-R	6-2	190	12-18-93	1	4	2.98	32	4	0	5	57	44	24	19	2	26	76	.211	.171	.240	11.93	4.08
Dunning, Dane	R-R	6-4	200	12-20-94	1	1	2.59	4	4	0	0	24	20	7	7	2	3	31	.215	.233	.206	11.47	1.11
Flores, Bernardo	L-L	6-3	170	8-23-95	5	4	2.55	12	12	0	0	78	75	31	22	5	17	58	.253	.277	.246	6.72	1.97
Foster, Matt	R-R	6-0	195	1-27-95	2	1	2.57	21	0	0	7	28	25	10	8	1	7	40	.250	.150	.317	12.86	2.25
Hansen, Alec	R-R	6-7	235	10-10-94	0	1	5.74	5	5	0	0	16	14	10	10	0	17	20	.250	.296	.207	11.49	9.77
Hasler, Drew	R-R	6-6	245	8-14-93	9	2	4.38	29	1	0	1	62	71	32	30	6	11	42	.291	.324	.266	6.13	1.61
Henzman, Lincoln	R-R	6-2	205	7-4-95	0	1	2.60	14	9	0	0	35	34	15	10	1	10	20	.256	.250	.260	5.19	2.60
Hickman, Blake	R-R	6-5	225	10-29-93	3	3	6.82	33	7	0	0	67	76	54	51	11	50	54	.287	.286	.288	7.22	6.68
Johnson, Tyler	R-R	6-3	205	8-21-95	4	0	1.45	21	0	0	7	31	19	7	5	1	6	43	.174	.227	.139	12.48	1.74
Kubat, Kyle	L-L	6-1	195	12-4-92	6	3	3.55	32	9	1	1	91	97	39	36	2	13	77	.279	.256	.285	7.59	1.28
Lambert, Jimmy	R-R	6-2	170	11-18-94	5	7	3.95	13	13	0	0	71	57	38	31	5	21	80	.224	.218	.229	10.19	2.67
Martinez, Luis	R-R	6-0	190	1-29-95	9	7	4.47	26	23	0	0	137	137	76	68	9	59	113	.260	.267	.253	7.42	3.88
Mockbee, Joe	R-L	6-3	205	1-7-95	0	0	4.50	3	0	0	0	4	2	2	2	0	2	1	.143	.286	.000	2.25	4.50
Morrison, Mike	R-R	6-2	195	9-22-93	5	3	3.13	40	0	0	6	60	39	25	21	5	33	55	.184	.167	.197	8.20	4.92
Parke, John	L-L	6-4	205	1-3-95	5	4	4.24	13	13	0	0	76	90	39	36	6	26	52	.301	.292	.304	6.13	3.07
Peralta, Yelmison	R-R	6-2	210	3-3-95	0	0	6.00	6	0	0	1	9	7	6	6	2	6	12	.219	.250	.188	12.00	6.00
Pinto, Ricardo	R-R	6-0	165	1-20-94	1	0	6.75	3	3	0	0	11	13	8	8	2	8	8	.296	.400	.241	6.75	6.75
Ruiz, Jose	R-R	6-1	190	10-21-94	0	0	2.70	10	0	0	2	13	6	4	4	2	5	22	.130	.100	.154	14.85	3.38
Schryver, Hunter	L-L	6-1	198	4-3-95	0	2	1.20	9	0	0	2	15	9	5	2	1	3	21	.170	.177	.167	12.60	1.80
Seitzer, Cameron	L-R	6-5	220	1-11-90	0	1	7.24	9	0	0	0	14	22	11	11	2	5	12	.361	.250	.432	7.90	3.29
Thompson, Zach	R-R	6-7	230	10-23-93	2	1	1.78	22	0	0	1	35	29	12	7	1	11	36	.218	.207	.227	9.17	2.80
Walsh, Connor	L-R	6-2	185	10-18-92	1	1	3.38	18	0	0	2	27	21	11	10	1	20	38	.214	.229	.206	12.83	6.75
Watts, Devan	R-R	6-0	205	4-21-95	1	2	2.75	13	0	0	1	20	17	7	6	2	4	16	.239	.222	.250	7.32	1.83

Fielding

Catcher	PCT	G	PO	A	E	DP	PB
Gonzalez	.986	20	135	6	2	1	1
Mercedes	.990	79	599	73	7	6	11
Nolan	.990	50	372	34	4	4	3

First Base	PCT	G	PO	A	E	DP
Duarte	1.000	5	23	1	0	4
Forbes	1.000	1	1	0	0	0
Gonzalez	1.000	2	4	1	0	0
Mercedes	.988	14	76	3	1	5
Muno	.900	2	8	1	1	0
Remillard	.986	19	137	6	2	13
Sheets	.995	108	805	51	4	83

Second Base	PCT	G	PO	A	E	DP
Forbes	.961	27	42	57	4	17

Madrigal	.991	25	60	54	1	18
Muno	1.000	1	2	3	0	1
Remillard	.973	10	16	20	1	8
Rivera	1.000	1	2	2	0	0
Roman	.972	77	113	198	9	42

Third Base	PCT	G	PO	A	E	DP
Duarte	.000	1	0	0	0	0
Forbes	.898	75	40	110	17	12
Muno	1.000	1	1	0	0	0
Remillard	.925	45	26	72	8	7
Yrizarri	.946	19	6	29	2	3

Shortstop	PCT	G	PO	A	E	DP
Forbes	1.000	8	12	17	0	7
Muno	1.000	1	1	4	0	0
Remillard	.800	2	1	3	1	0

Rivera	.957	56	76	166	11	39
Roman	.946	10	13	22	2	6
Yrizarri	.937	64	66	173	16	33

Outfield	PCT	G	PO	A	E	DP
Basabe	.978	55	128	4	3	1
Booker	.979	50	89	5	2	1
Brown	1.000	11	21	0	0	0
Call	1.000	55	120	4	0	2
Gonzalez	1.000	3	3	0	0	0
Gonzalez	.987	56	147	4	2	0
Muno	.962	15	25	0	1	0
Remillard	.988	35	77	4	1	0
Robert	.967	31	84	4	3	0
Rutherford	.975	102	194	4	5	0
Yrizarri	1.000	17	21	3	0	0

KANNAPOLIS INTIMIDATORS   LOW CLASS A
SOUTH ATLANTIC LEAGUE

Batting	B-T	HT	WT	DOB	AVG	vLH	vRH	G	AB	R	H	2B	3B	HR	RBI	BB	HBP	SH	SF	SO	SB	CS	SLG	OBP
Beltre, Ramon	R-R	5-11	160	10-18-96	.242	.191	.257	28	91	12	22	5	0	1	13	2	0	2	2	26	0	0	.330	.253
Blackman, Tate	R-R	6-0	195	9-7-94	.244	.263	.238	129	450	67	110	18	2	17	65	62	9	1	5	153	6	5	.407	.344
Brown, Nolan	L-L	5-11	175	1-13-94	.285	.289	.284	56	179	34	51	11	1	0	19	19	3	2	3	42	8	2	.358	.358
Cruz, Johan	R-R	6-2	188	10-8-95	.227	.247	.219	91	304	37	69	11	2	1	36	30	2	8	4	64	3	2	.286	.297
Curbelo, Luis	R-R	6-3	185	11-10-97	.237	.231	.239	83	317	35	75	19	2	3	31	18	3	3	2	87	0	0	.338	.282
Dawkins, Ian	R-R	5-11	195	7-6-95	.280	.220	.308	37	132	16	37	6	0	1	8	12	0	1	0	23	6	3	.349	.340
Dedelow, Craig	L-R	6-4	195	11-15-94	.245	.164	.271	129	502	60	123	33	6	12	69	30	5	3	0	128	2	2	.406	.294
Destino, Alex	L-L	6-2	215	10-24-95	.200	.000	.222	3	10	1	2	0	0	0	1	2	0	0	0	2	0	0	.200	.333
Frost, Tyler	L-R	5-10	183	11-21-95	.241	.244	.240	124	407	61	98	21	4	18	65	46	5	4	2	129	7	4	.445	.324
Gonzalez, Luis	L-L	6-1	190	9-10-95	.300	.333	.288	55	230	35	69	16	2	8	26	21	1	1	2	57	7	2	.491	.358
Hickman, Michael	R-R	6-1	215	11-5-96	.241	.210	.254	80	286	29	69	17	1	3	33	19	4	0	0	82	0	3	.339	.298
Madrigal, Nick	R-R	5-7	165	3-5-97	.341	.357	.333	12	44	9	15	3	0	0	6	1	1	0	3	0	2	2	.409	.347
Muno, JJ	L-R	5-11	190	12-21-93	.179	.250	.150	13	28	10	5	0	0	0	1	2	3	0	0	9	5	0	.179	.303
Perez, Carlos	R-R	5-10	160	9-10-96	.290	.226	.318	78	276	33	80	18	1	3	32	4	1	1	4	31	0	1	.395	.298
Rivera, Laz	R-R	5-11	185	9-20-94	.346	.400	.323	63	237	42	82	15	2	6	24	6	14	7	1	48	7	3	.502	.395
Robert, Luis	R-R	6-3	185	8-3-97	.289	.333	.273	13	45	5	13	3	1	0	4	4	1	0	0	12	2	0	.400	.360
Skoug, Evan	L-R	5-11	200	10-21-95	.192	.129	.211	83	271	35	52	10	2	5	31	34	2	0	4	93	4	0	.299	.283
Villa, Anthony	R-R	6-3	220	3-29-94	.261	.263	.259	65	211	25	55	17	0	3	28	28	7	0	3	74	1	0	.384	.361
Walker, Steele	L-L	5-11	190	7-30-96	.186	.156	.198	31	113	13	21	5	0	3	17	8	2	0	3	29	5	1	.310	.246
Yurchak, Justin	L-R	6-1	204	9-17-96	.256	.203	.272	95	313	44	80	17	1	3	36	45	1	1	3	53	0	2	.326	.348
Zangari, Corey	R-R	6-4	240	5-7-97	.000	--	.000	1	1	0	0	0	0	0	0	0	0	0	0	0	0	0	.000	.000

Pitching	B-T	HT	WT	DOB	W	L	ERA	G	GS	CG	SV	IP	H	R	ER	HR	BB	SO	AVG	vLH	vRH	K/9	BB/9
Battenfield, Blake	R-R	6-3	220	8-22-94	5	3	2.00	13	13	0	0	68	52	19	15	6	16	69	.210	.231	.186	9.18	2.13
Elliott, Jake	R-R	6-7	230	3-22-95	1	3	2.99	33	2	0	2	75	57	28	25	6	22	86	.211	.197	.223	10.27	2.63
Escorcia, Kevin	L-L	6-1	170	1-5-95	4	2	2.66	27	0	0	0	44	39	15	13	2	19	62	.238	.262	.223	12.68	3.89
Harrington, Drew	R-L	6-2	225	3-30-95	5	5	3.89	14	12	1	1	72	73	32	31	5	16	48	.273	.277	.272	6.03	2.01

	B-T	HT	WT	DOB	W	L	ERA	G	GS	CG	SV	IP	H	R	ER	HR	BB	SO	AVG	vLH	vRH	K/9	BB/9
2-team total (11 Rome)					8	8	4.96	25	18	1	1	105	120	63	58	12	26	73	.297	.291	.299	6.24	2.22
Henzman, Lincoln	R-R	6-2	205	7-4-95	6	3	2.23	13	13	1	0	73	68	30	18	5	8	60	.241	.243	.239	7.43	0.99
Johnson, Tyler	R-R	6-3	205	8-21-95	5	0	1.33	20	0	0	7	27	16	7	4	1	10	46	.170	.233	.118	15.33	3.33
Kincanon, Will	L-R	6-3	202	10-27-95	3	1	3.63	26	0	0	4	35	29	17	14	2	15	42	.218	.263	.184	10.90	3.89
Ledo, Luis	R-R	6-4	208	5-28-95	7	2	4.95	32	1	0	0	56	56	35	31	6	38	59	.267	.258	.274	9.43	6.07
Lewis, Zach	R-R	6-3	205	5-24-95	6	5	2.60	29	16	1	3	104	69	39	30	6	48	103	.189	.221	.163	8.94	4.17
McClure, Kade	R-R	6-7	230	2-12-96	3	1	3.02	8	8	0	0	42	43	18	14	2	14	42	.265	.274	.258	9.07	3.02
McRee, Aron	R-R	6-0	180	10-29-93	3	3	2.96	18	0	0	3	24	22	11	8	0	13	14	.250	.278	.231	5.18	4.81
Mockbee, Joe	R-L	6-3	205	1-7-95	0	0	2.89	8	0	0	1	9	6	3	3	0	4	10	.182	.133	.222	9.64	3.86
Moran, Spencer	R-R	6-6	180	4-2-96	1	3	5.34	7	7	0	0	32	29	19	19	2	19	24	.246	.245	.246	6.75	5.34
Nin, Jose	R-R	6-3	220	6-20-95	5	5	1.68	37	0	0	10	48	35	15	9	3	13	40	.202	.259	.152	7.45	2.42
Parke, John	L-L	6-4	205	1-3-95	7	4	2.82	14	14	2	0	77	69	32	24	4	13	67	.233	.230	.234	7.87	1.53
Peralta, Yelmison	R-R	6-2	210	3-3-95	1	0	2.51	8	0	0	0	14	14	4	4	1	7	19	.250	.320	.194	11.93	4.40
Perez, Andrew	L-L	6-2	196	7-25-97	0	0	2.88	16	0	0	1	25	21	11	8	0	13	24	.233	.188	.259	8.64	4.68
Portland, Matt	R-L	6-3	225	2-11-94	0	0	6.00	1	1	0	0	6	5	4	4	1	3	4	.238	.000	.313	6.00	4.50
Quijada, Jhoan	R-R	6-3	210	12-27-94	1	4	4.72	17	8	0	1	69	72	41	36	8	18	39	.270	.269	.270	5.11	2.36
Rigler, Parker	L-L	5-11	183	2-16-95	6	9	4.43	27	27	0	0	140	139	77	69	12	53	117	.263	.315	.241	7.50	3.40
Rodon, Carlos	L-L	6-3	235	12-10-92	0	0	1.80	1	1	0	0	5	3	1	1	0	0	6	.177	—	.177	10.80	0.00
Ross Jr., Robbie	L-L	5-11	215	6-24-89	0	0	0.00	1	0	0	1	2	1	0	0	0	1	2	.143	.000	.167	9.00	4.50
Seitzer, Cameron	L-R	6-5	220	1-11-90	0	1	2.89	6	0	0	1	9	10	4	3	1	1	12	.263	.444	.100	11.57	0.96
Solorzano, Yosmer	R-R	6-2	181	2-11-97	3	9	5.55	27	14	0	0	84	74	60	52	6	46	58	.240	.260	.222	6.19	4.91
Sousa, Bennett	L-L	6-3	185	4-6-95	1	0	2.01	11	0	0	1	22	20	7	5	0	7	24	.256	.115	.327	9.67	2.82

Fielding

C: Hickman 28, Perez 53, Skoug 60. **1B:** Hickman 29, Villa 33, Yurchak 80, Zangari 1. **2B:** Beltre 28, Blackman 85, Cruz 6, Madrigal 12, Muno 3, Rivera 3, Villa 1. **3B:** Blackman 38, Cruz 53, Curbelo 20, Muno 2, Rivera 5, Villa 22, Yurchak 1. **SS:** Cruz 28, Curbelo 57, Rivera 54. **OF:** Brown 50, Cruz 2, Dawkins 32, Dedelow 126, Destino 1, Frost 116, Gonzalez 52, Muno 4, Robert 10, Villa 3, Walker 21.

GREAT FALLS VOYAGERS   ROOKIE
PIONEER LEAGUE

Batting	B-T	HT	WT	DOB	AVG	vLH	vRH	G	AB	R	H	2B	3B	HR	RBI	BB	HBP	SH	SF	SO	SB	CS	SLG	OBP
Alfaro, Jhoandro	B-R	6-1	180	11-4-97	.250	.250	.250	28	96	10	24	4	0	3	18	3	4	2	1	18	2	1	.385	.298
Beltre, Ramon	R-R	5-11	160	10-18-96	.290	.267	.297	32	131	22	38	5	3	4	18	6	0	1	1	30	1	0	.466	.319
Bush, Bryce	R-R	6-0	200	12-14-99	.250	.300	.237	24	96	16	24	5	1	2	10	10	1	1	0	21	3	0	.385	.327
Coffey, Micah	L-R	6-1	200	7-22-95	.256	.200	.269	26	82	15	21	5	0	1	10	10	1	0	1	20	0	0	.354	.340
Connell, Bryan	R-R	6-3	195	11-9-98	.050	.000	.059	5	20	1	1	0	0	0	1	0	1	0	0	10	0	0	.050	.095
2-team total (21 Helena)					.183	.235	.171	26	93	12	17	3	0	2	12	6	2	0	0	42	1	1	.280	.248
Dawkins, Ian	R-R	5-11	195	7-6-95	.328	.435	.302	28	119	26	39	7	0	2	13	4	3	0	1	20	8	3	.437	.362
Destino, Alex	L-L	6-2	215	10-24-95	.250	.226	.256	65	260	31	65	18	5	5	35	15	2	0	0	53	0	1	.415	.296
Estes, Jay	R-R	5-10	170	3-3-96	.155	.217	.138	39	110	12	17	7	0	1	5	5	0	1	0	23	0	3	.246	.191
Feliz, Maiker	R-R	6-0	195	8-17-97	.240	.385	.204	37	129	18	31	6	0	2	14	12	1	0	0	35	0	0	.333	.310
Fitzpatrick, Ryan	R-R	6-3	225	3-13-95	.246	.208	.255	41	126	21	31	7	0	6	15	16	14	3	1	32	0	0	.444	.389
Galusky, Jimmy	R-R	6-3	185	4-28-96	.218	.067	.275	20	55	3	12	2	0	0	4	4	1	1	0	13	3	1	.255	.283
Gonzalez, Romy	R-R	6-1	210	9-6-96	.254	.204	.270	54	201	40	51	15	2	10	33	18	3	0	1	65	10	1	.498	.323
McGinnis, Adam	R-R	5-11	225	10-4-94	.235	.188	.244	29	98	17	23	5	0	6	16	9	2	1	1	32	0	0	.469	.309
Moniot, Travis	B-R	6-1	190	6-9-97	.290	.360	.270	38	114	27	33	7	2	1	14	17	2	2	0	29	2	1	.412	.391
Nunez, Amado	R-R	6-2	178	10-10-97	.357	.327	.365	60	241	39	86	21	6	6	52	15	1	0	2	71	3	6	.569	.394
Quintiero, Camilo	R-R	5-11	180	4-11-97	.000	.000	.000	2	3	0	0	0	0	0	1	0	0	0	1	3	0	0	.000	.000
Sosa, Lenyn	R-R	6-0	180	1-25-00	.294	.255	.303	65	276	44	81	13	3	4	35	7	4	1	3	36	2	2	.406	.317
Sowers, Logan	R-R	6-5	230	1-11-96	.296	.359	.270	64	240	42	71	16	1	9	35	32	3	0	0	82	4	0	.483	.386
Troutwine, Gunnar	R-R	6-1	230	3-6-96	.316	.471	.290	35	117	17	37	6	0	2	18	19	0	2	0	20	0	0	.419	.412
Walker, Steele	L-L	5-11	190	7-30-96	.206	.222	.200	9	34	4	7	1	0	2	4	1	2	0	1	7	1	1	.412	.263
Zangari, Corey	R-R	6-2	240	5-7-97	.266	.286	.260	17	64	14	17	1	1	2	9	2	6	1	0	2	16	0	.734	.329

Pitching	B-T	HT	WT	DOB	W	L	ERA	G	GS	CG	SV	IP	H	R	ER	HR	BB	SO	AVG	vLH	vRH	K/9	BB/9
Arobio, Vince	R-R	6-0	185	3-31-95	3	6	5.67	24	0	0	0	33	34	25	21	3	14	44	.260	.233	.273	11.88	3.78
Bilous, Jason	R-R	6-2	185	8-11-97	0	4	7.85	14	14	0	0	37	46	34	32	2	24	31	.324	.250	.362	7.61	5.89
Burns, Wyatt	R-R	5-11	185	11-6-94	4	0	3.92	20	0	0	0	44	56	21	19	4	7	29	.322	.350	.307	5.98	1.44
Comito, Chris	R-R	6-6	240	6-25-96	4	7	6.06	15	8	0	0	71	98	60	48	6	19	67	.323	.371	.291	8.45	2.40
Conway, Austin	R-R	6-1	210	1-16-95	2	2	3.47	16	0	0	1	23	21	10	9	1	9	18	.250	.250	.250	6.94	3.47
Dominguez, Johan	R-R	6-4	190	1-18-96	0	0	0.00	2	0	0	0	2	1	0	0	0	0	4	.143	.000	.167	18.00	0.00
2-team total (2 Helena)					0	0	2.25	4	0	0	0	4	4	2	1	0	1	7	.235	.250	.231	15.75	2.25
Fernandez, Rigo	L-L	6-0	190	11-27-97	0	0	4.15	3	0	0	0	4	6	2	2	0	1	2	.333	.500	.313	4.15	2.08
Folman, Kevin	R-R	6-2	215	10-23-94	0	1	6.75	2	2	0	0	11	19	11	8	1	3	7	.388	.429	.371	5.91	2.53
Heuer, Codi	R-R	6-5	195	7-3-96	0	1	4.74	14	14	0	0	38	49	26	20	4	14	35	.310	.318	.304	8.29	3.32
Johnson, Nick	R-R	6-3	215	7-21-95	0	1	0.90	25	0	0	5	30	25	10	3	0	5	28	.221	.243	.211	8.40	1.50
Love, Carter	R-R	6-6	225	11-27-95	1	0	0.00	2	0	0	0	5	2	0	0	0	0	3	.125	.000	.154	5.40	0.00
Martin, Davis	L-R	6-2	200	1-4-97	0	2	4.50	7	1	0	0	18	18	13	9	1	6	21	.250	.333	.208	10.50	3.00
Maynard, Jack	R-R	5-11	195	7-26-96	4	2	3.00	20	0	0	1	39	40	16	13	2	12	42	.258	.192	.299	9.69	2.77
McCormick, Michael	L-R	6-3	190	12-8-93	4	2	4.42	20	0	0	1	37	38	21	18	1	12	36	.260	.321	.226	8.84	2.95
Minier, Greg	R-L	6-4	235	9-22-95	1	1	8.05	8	0	0	0	19	26	19	17	3	6	16	.325	.222	.355	7.58	2.84
Moran, Spencer	R-R	6-6	180	4-2-96	2	2	3.71	6	4	0	0	34	35	19	14	2	12	32	.265	.244	.276	8.47	3.18
Perez, Andrew	L-L	6-2	196	7-25-97	0	0	1.42	4	0	0	0	6	3	1	1	0	0	7	.136	.167	.125	9.95	0.00
Perez, Devon	R-R	6-5	200	5-15-96	2	1	5.01	14	1	0	0	32	42	23	18	1	2	35	.311	.341	.297	9.74	0.56
Pilkington, Konnor	L-L	6-3	225	9-12-97	0	1	5.25	6	6	0	0	12	14	9	7	1	4	9	.292	.100	.342	6.75	3.00

	B-T	HT	WT	DOB	W	L	ERA	G	GS	CG	SV	IP	H	R	ER	HR	BB	SO	AVG	vLH	vRH	K/9	BB/9
Portland, Matt	R-L	6-3	225	2-11-94	2	3	4.70	11	9	0	0	54	60	32	28	5	21	61	.278	.311	.269	10.23	3.52
Ramsey, Lane	R-R	6-9	245	7-16-96	3	3	5.77	19	1	0	2	48	66	39	31	5	12	38	.316	.296	.328	7.08	2.23
Sousa, Bennett	L-L	6-3	185	4-6-95	1	0	0.00	9	0	0	4	13	4	0	0	0	0	18	.089	.000	.121	12.46	0.00
Stiever, Jonathan	R-R	6-2	205	5-12-97	0	1	4.18	13	13	0	0	28	23	13	13	3	9	39	.223	.250	.203	12.54	2.89
Weston, Drew	L-L	6-2	170	12-13-94	0	1	6.52	7	0	0	0	10	7	8	7	3	3	8	.219	.100	.273	7.45	2.79

Fielding

C: Alfaro 28, Coffey 1, McGinnis 16, Troutwine 34. **1B:** Coffey 16, Feliz 2, Fitzpatrick 41, Nunez 8, Troutwine 1, Zangari 11. **2B:** Beltre 5, Galusky 8, Moniot 13, Nunez 46, Quinteiro 1, Sosa 8. **3B:** Beltre 12, Bush 18, Feliz 29, Moniot 4, Quinteiro 1, Sosa 13. **SS:** Beltre 15, Galusky 8, Moniot 6, Sosa 49. **OF:** Coffey 5, Connell 4, Dawkins 27, Destino 65, Estes 35, Gonzalez 14, Moniot 15, Sowers 62, Walker 8.

AZL WHITE SOX — ROOKIE
ARIZONA LEAGUE

Batting	B-T	HT	WT	DOB	AVG	vLH	vRH	G	AB	R	H	2B	3B	HR	RBI	BB	HBP	SH	SF	SO	SB	CS	SLG	OBP
Abbott, Sam	L-R	6-4	225	4-9-99	.139	.050	.173	28	72	12	10	3	0	3	9	18	5	0	0	33	0	0	.306	.347
Bush, Bryce	R-R	6-0	200	12-14-99	.442	.714	.310	14	43	8	19	4	0	1	8	8	1	0	0	4	1	2	.605	.539
Coffey, Micah	L-R	6-1	200	7-22-95	.275	.200	.306	19	69	12	19	4	0	0	12	11	0	1	0	20	1	1	.333	.375
Colina, Jose	B-R	6-0	180	3-26-98	.170	.177	.167	21	59	5	10	2	0	0	8	8	1	0	2	15	0	0	.203	.271
Comas, Anderson	L-L	6-3	185	2-10-00	.306	.250	.325	41	160	17	49	6	2	1	22	7	2	1	2	26	5	1	.388	.339
Cordell, Ryan	R-R	6-4	195	3-31-92	.267	.200	.300	4	15	1	4	1	0	0	1	0	0	0	0	5	1	0	.333	.267
Coronado, Anthony	R-R	6-1	180	1-21-00	.145	.278	.091	21	62	6	9	1	1	0	4	6	1	0	1	23	3	0	.194	.229
Delgado, Lency	R-R	6-3	215	6-20-99	.233	.297	.208	38	133	20	31	4	1	1	22	9	6	1	1	40	4	0	.301	.309
Galusky, Jimmy	R-R	6-3	185	4-28-96	.388	.400	.385	17	49	13	19	1	1	1	4	7	1	0	1	9	0	2	.510	.466
Greene, Ty	L-R	6-0	185	5-4-97	.313	.220	.356	39	128	19	40	7	0	0	11	17	3	0	1	14	3	3	.367	.403
Guerrero, Josue	R-R	6-2	190	11-23-99	.192	.179	.200	23	73	2	14	5	1	0	8	3	1	0	1	27	0	0	.288	.231
Madrigal, Nick	R-R	5-7	165	3-5-97	.154	.000	.200	5	13	2	2	0	0	0	1	3	0	0	0	1	0	1	.154	.353
Maldonado, Kelvin	R-R	5-11	160	2-21-00	.150	.108	.169	38	120	14	18	0	1	0	4	4	1	3	0	31	0	2	.167	.184
Mendoza, Harvin	L-L	6-2	215	2-18-99	.314	.273	.327	39	137	18	43	9	2	0	23	12	4	0	2	12	3	2	.409	.381
Mieses, Luis	L-L	6-3	180	5-31-00	.226	.286	.206	48	195	19	44	10	2	2	26	4	0	1	4	35	3	0	.328	.237
Nova, Brayant	B-R	6-1	170	8-25-98	.203	.120	.245	24	74	11	15	3	2	0	8	6	0	0	0	28	2	1	.297	.263
Ortiz, Gabriel	L-R	6-0	210	3-15-00	.214	.111	.242	17	42	4	9	1	0	0	5	3	0	0	0	6	0	0	.238	.267
Polo, Tito	R-R	5-10	195	8-23-94	.318	.333	.313	7	22	7	7	0	0	3	7	5	1	0	1	4	5	1	.727	.448
Quinteiro, Camilo	R-R	5-11	180	4-11-97	.286	.297	.282	46	147	28	42	2	0	1	11	36	4	2	1	39	11	2	.320	.436
Robert, Luis	R-R	6-3	185	8-3-97	.389	.143	.546	5	18	5	7	2	1	0	2	0	0	0	0	5	1	0	.611	.389
Sanchez, Kleyder	R-R	5-10	170	12-13-99	.094	.000	.128	22	53	7	5	2	0	0	6	5	2	2	1	8	1	0	.132	.197
Walker, Steele	L-L	5-11	190	7-30-96	.455	1.000	.400	4	11	5	5	0	0	0	1	0	0	0	0	1	0	0	.455	.529
Weaver, Cabera	R-R	6-3	180	12-1-99	.248	.298	.226	50	149	26	37	5	3	1	11	18	10	3	0	52	8	1	.342	.367

Pitching	B-T	HT	WT	DOB	W	L	ERA	G	GS	CG	SV	IP	H	R	ER	HR	BB	SO	AVG	vLH	vRH	K/9	BB/9
Acosta, Hector	L-R	6-4	200	10-24-98	0	2	12.19	6	3	0	0	10	15	14	14	2	6	8	.349	.222	.382	6.97	5.23
Acosta, Nelson	R-R	6-3	195	8-22-97	1	2	4.76	16	0	0	1	23	25	12	12	5	13	19	.272	.400	.193	7.54	5.16
Burdi, Zack	R-R	6-3	205	3-9-95	0	1	2.84	7	1	0	0	6	5	3	2	0	4	7	.217	.250	.200	9.95	5.68
Cabrera, Mauricio	R-R	6-3	230	9-22-93	0	2	11.00	9	2	0	1	9	13	12	11	2	5	13	.310	.500	.214	13.00	5.00
Clarkin, Ian	L-L	6-2	215	2-14-95	0	0	5.19	3	2	0	0	9	9	5	5	1	3	9	.273	.200	.304	9.35	3.12
Conway, Austin	R-R	6-1	210	1-16-95	2	1	2.13	7	0	0	0	13	11	3	3	0	5	14	.239	.300	.192	9.95	3.55
Fernandez, Rigo	L-L	6-0	190	11-27-97	2	0	1.87	15	0	0	8	34	21	12	7	1	14	38	.178	.238	.165	10.16	3.74
Folman, Kevin	R-R	6-2	215	10-23-94	2	2	3.45	6	5	0	0	29	24	11	11	3	5	26	.216	.209	.221	8.16	1.57
Harrington, Drew	R-L	6-2	225	3-30-95	1	0	0.00	1	0	0	0	2	1	0	0	1	0		.500	--	.500	0.00	27.00
Herrera, Brayan	R-R	6-2	185	4-5-98	5	2	2.70	12	11	0	0	57	46	19	17	0	15	43	.216	.286	.177	6.83	2.37
Kiel, Hunter	R-R	6-3	229	7-18-96	0	0	2.65	14	0	0	2	17	4	5	5	0	20	33	.077	.050	.094	17.47	10.59
Lara, Bryan	L-L	6-0	170	11-6-97	3	0	6.66	17	0	0	0	24	33	21	18	2	9	23	.317	.174	.358	8.51	3.33
Love, Carter	R-R	6-6	225	11-27-95	5	1	2.96	13	2	0	0	46	49	24	15	3	5	59	.265	.268	.263	11.63	0.99
Martin, Davis	L-R	6-2	200	1-4-97	0	0	3.00	2	1	0	0	3	3	1	1	0	0	1	.250	.333	.167	3.00	0.00
Perez, Devon	R-R	6-5	200	5-15-96	0	2	0.00	5	0	0	2	9	10	2	0	0	0	18	.278	.273	.280	17.36	0.00
Pilkington, Konnor	L-L	6-3	225	9-12-97	0	0	18.00	2	1	0	0	2	7	4	4	0	1	2	.539	.750	.444	9.00	4.50
Pineda, Ramon	R-R	6-3	200	2-3-98	0	1	12.79	4	0	0	0	6	8	10	9	2	1	6	.296	.667	.111	8.53	1.42
Rosario, Yordi	R-R	6-2	185	1-30-99	1	2	3.42	6	4	0	0	26	28	12	10	3	8	31	.267	.353	.225	10.59	2.73
Soto, Aaron	L-L	5-10	175	9-13-95	3	1	6.85	14	5	0	1	45	58	35	34	9	9	44	.307	.353	.305	8.87	1.81
Thompson, Sean	R-R	6-3	195	9-8-95	3	3	3.68	13	9	0	0	37	42	21	15	4	7	31	.282	.283	.281	7.61	1.72
Varnell, Taylor	L-L	6-1	190	5-5-95	3	1	1.97	10	10	0	0	46	30	20	10	2	10	61	.175	.242	.159	12.02	1.97
Weston, Drew	L-L	6-2	170	12-13-94	1	2	3.77	9	0	0	0	14	18	6	6	0	0	11	.300	.500	.278	6.91	0.00

Fielding

C: Colina 13, Greene 33, Ortiz 6, Sanchez 16. **1B:** Abbott 21, Mendoza 38, Ortiz 1. **2B:** Galusky 2, Madrigal 2, Maldonado 16, Nova 11, Quinteiro 33. **3B:** Bush 12, Coffey 19, Galusky 13, Nova 12, Quinteiro 4. **SS:** Delgado 35, Madrigal 1, Maldonado 18, Quinteiro 6. **OF:** Comas 41, Cordell 2, Coronado 16, Greene 1, Guerrero 19, Mieses 45, Polo 4, Robert 2, Walker 2, Weaver 45.

DSL WHITE SOX — ROOKIE
DOMINICAN SUMMER LEAGUE

Batting	B-T	HT	WT	DOB	AVG	vLH	vRH	G	AB	R	H	2B	3B	HR	RBI	BB	HBP	SH	SF	SO	SB	CS	SLG	OBP
Barreras, Robert	R-R	6-3	205	9-15-98	.214	.167	.227	7	28	3	6	1	0	0	2	0	0	0	0	13	0	0	.250	.214
Betancourt, Jhoneiker	R-R	6-1	174	5-2-00	.213	.188	.221	55	202	21	43	9	2	0	13	13	3	0	0	42	3	0	.277	.271
Diaz, Harold	R-R	5-10	170	1-8-00	.290	.286	.292	18	69	11	20	4	2	0	7	7	4	0	0	6	9	1	.406	.388
Felix, Enrique	R-R	6-3	188	1-7-99	.144	.074	.165	36	118	7	17	5	2	1	6	7	2	0	0	66	1	2	.246	.205

CHICAGO WHITE SOX

Francees, Jerrick	R-R	6-0	188	5-18-00	.174	.000	.217	31	86	3	15	0	0	0	9	7	2	1	0	35	0	4	.174	.253
Garcia, Richard	R-R	6-1	185	9-20-98	.195	.192	.196	41	123	7	24	4	2	1	20	9	2	0	3	26	1	2	.285	.256
Laureano, Johnabiell	R-R	6-0	180	10-11-00	.220	.189	.230	65	214	27	47	9	0	0	13	31	5	0	2	54	4	8	.262	.329
Martinez, Omar	R-R	6-3	192	12-23-98	.198	.213	.192	57	177	20	35	5	0	0	11	5	3	0	2	67	3	7	.226	.230
Martinez, Ulises	R-R	6-1	190	3-2-99	.231	.227	.233	45	147	16	34	7	2	1	12	12	2	0	2	39	2	1	.327	.295
Mendoza, Jefferson	R-R	6-0	170	1-16-01	.207	.162	.226	38	121	8	25	7	0	1	15	12	2	0	0	26	1	3	.289	.289
Peralta, Edwin	R-R	6-3	175	5-10-01	.193	.125	.212	52	145	19	28	3	0	1	18	21	7	1	1	41	5	7	.235	.322
Pimentel, Sidney	B-R	6-1	160	10-27-00	.167	.000	.213	17	60	7	10	2	0	2	7	4	0	0	0	18	2	2	.300	.219
Polanco, Samil	B-R	6-0	160	2-21-00	.274	.237	.290	55	197	25	54	6	5	1	16	10	2	0	1	33	12	4	.371	.314
Rodriguez, Jose	R-R	5-11	175	5-13-01	.291	.200	.316	60	227	31	66	13	3	2	23	9	1	1	2	29	16	4	.401	.318
Rosario, Andres	R-R	6-3	190	3-11-99	.176	.149	.185	59	193	28	34	2	1	3	12	21	2	0	1	85	3	1	.244	.263
Rosas, Jorgen	R-R	5-9	160	1-10-98	.220	.246	.210	66	245	23	54	11	1	0	15	16	6	2	0	54	6	4	.274	.285

Pitching	B-T	HT	WT	DOB	W	L	ERA	G	GS	CG	SV	IP	H	R	ER	HR	BB	SO	AVG	vLH	vRH	K/9	BB/9
Acosta, Hector	L-L	6-4	200	10-24-98	0	1	4.15	4	3	0	0	17	14	13	8	1	5	20	.212	.182	.218	10.38	2.60
Batista, Cristopher	R-R	6-3	180	11-1-98	0	0	9.53	6	0	0	0	11	13	15	12	0	11	11	.277	.231	.294	8.74	8.74
Benitez, Francisco	R-R	6-2	187	9-15-00	0	3	6.10	16	4	0	0	38	26	33	26	1	43	43	.200	.290	.163	10.10	10.10
Caro, Fernando	R-R	6-3	192	2-25-97	1	4	5.18	24	0	0	0	40	41	28	23	0	19	36	.263	.255	.267	8.10	4.28
Castro, Oriel	L-L	6-0	175	5-5-01	1	0	5.23	12	1	0	0	10	5	6	6	0	13	14	.143	.200	.133	12.19	11.32
Ferrer, Jorge	L-L	6-3	180	9-5-00	1	1	0.00	2	0	0	0	4	4	3	0	0	4	5	.286	.000	.308	12.27	9.82
Jimenez, Dionicio	R-R	6-4	190	1-7-01	0	3	6.81	17	6	0	0	40	35	42	30	1	49	46	.235	.244	.231	10.44	11.12
Labourt, Jairo	L-L	6-5	234	3-7-94	0	2	4.76	5	1	0	0	6	1	6	3	0	9	11	.056	.000	.071	17.47	14.29
Lagrange, Daneuris	R-R	6-3	175	6-17-98	2	3	4.86	16	5	0	0	37	44	26	20	1	14	38	.299	.283	.307	9.24	3.41
Lara, Bryan	L-L	6-0	170	11-6-97	0	0	4.00	3	2	0	0	9	12	6	4	2	2	9	.308	.200	.324	9.00	2.00
Melendez, Cristofer	R-R	6-3	170	9-16-97	4	4	1.54	15	11	0	0	70	39	22	12	1	28	93	.158	.111	.189	11.90	3.58
Mola, Carlos	R-R	6-4	190	12-20-00	0	1	9.00	10	1	0	0	10	12	10	10	0	7	9	.300	.375	.250	8.10	6.30
Navarro, Edgar	R-R	6-1	180	2-5-98	3	6	6.36	24	3	0	1	58	70	52	41	0	31	60	.289	.366	.250	9.31	4.81
Nin, Luis	R-R	6-2	185	11-30-96	2	2	3.32	15	0	0	5	19	18	11	7	0	10	21	.250	.231	.261	9.95	4.74
Perez, Erick	R-R	6-1	175	12-9-98	2	3	4.70	28	0	0	3	38	38	23	20	2	37	45	.271	.297	.262	10.57	8.69
Perez, Wilber	R-R	6-2	170	11-3-97	1	2	1.80	6	5	0	0	30	19	7	6	1	8	28	.188	.173	.204	8.40	2.40
2-team total (8 DSL Brewers)					6	3	1.92	14	13	0	0	70	44	18	15	1	21	75	.182	.167	.193	9.60	2.69
Rodriguez, Luis	R-R	6-6	220	4-15-00	0	5	4.68	16	10	0	0	50	44	33	26	4	38	48	.238	.220	.246	8.64	6.84
Rodriguez, Ruddy	R-R	5-11	160	8-6-96	0	0	27.00	4	1	0	0	2	2	5	5	0	7	3	.333	.500	.250	16.20	37.80
Rondon, Jesus	R-R	6-3	178	9-22-99	0	2	5.63	14	1	0	0	24	17	18	15	3	23	27	.200	.172	.214	10.13	8.63
Rosario, Yordi	R-R	6-2	185	1-30-99	0	2	1.82	8	7	0	0	30	23	6	6	1	4	39	.221	.267	.186	11.83	1.21
Silven, Yoelvin	R-R	6-1	176	6-26-99	1	8	3.66	15	10	0	0	64	65	36	26	5	16	71	.262	.265	.261	9.98	2.25
Yanes, Pablo	R-R	6-4	195	10-28-99	0	2	11.05	8	1	0	0	7	10	10	9	1	7	7	.333	.364	.316	8.59	8.59

Fielding

C: Betancourt 17, Garcia 38, Martinez 2, Mendoza 29. **1B:** Barreras 2, Betancourt 23, Martinez 2, Martinez 40, Rosario 1, Rosas 14. **2B:** Diaz 5, Francees 15, Peralta 9, Pimentel 3, Polanco 25, Rodriguez 16, Rosas 10. **3B:** Diaz 4, Peralta 34, Rodriguez 16, Rosario 5, Rosas 25. **SS:** Diaz 9, Peralta 7, Pimentel 10, Polanco 30, Rodriguez 22, Rosas 1. **OF:** Felix 36, Laureano 65, Martinez 56, Rodriguez 1, Rosario 52, Rosas 21.

Cincinnati Reds

SEASON IN A SENTENCE: The rebuilding Reds started the season 3-15—the worst record in baseball at the time—and fired manager Bryan Price, leading to interim manager Jim Riggleman taking over and Cincinnati ultimately finishing 67-95 for its fifth consecutive losing season.

HIGH POINT: The Reds saw much better results after Riggleman took the helm as interim manager. That included a seven-game winning streak from June 17-24 that included a four-game sweep over the Cubs. In fact, the Reds went a combined 28-22 in June and July, a clear bright spot in a season that saw Cincinnati finish 15.5 games back of the Pirates—its closest competitor in the NL Central.

LOW POINT: After winning just three of their first 18 games and having the worst record in baseball for much of April, the Reds fired manager Bryan Price, who went 279-387 in his four-plus seasons in Cincinnati. Then, after an above-average June and July, the Reds once again faded down the stretch, winning just nine of 28 games in the month of August to help secure the No. 7 overall pick in the 2019 draft.

NOTABLE ROOKIES: Despite a season-ending right shoulder injury that ended his rookie campaign in late July, outfielder Jesse Winker slashed .299/.405/.431 with seven home runs and 43 RBIs in 89 games. Winker was especially productive in June and July, when the 24-year-old hit .362/.465/.554 while the Reds were playing their best baseball of the season. Fellow rookie outfielder Phillip Ervin played 78 games in 2018, hitting .252/.324/.404 with seven home runs and six stolen bases.

KEY TRANSACTIONS: As the Reds continue to rebuild, they were able to rake in a slew of young talent at the trade deadline. Cincinnati traded righthanders Dylan Floro and Zach Neal, as well as international slot money, to the Dodgers for minor league pitchers James Marinan and Aneurys Zabala on July 4. Then, toward the end of the month, the Reds sent outfielder Adam Duvall to the Braves and acquired righthanders Lucas Sims and Matt Wisler, as well as outfielder Preston Tucker, in return.

DOWN ON THE FARM: It was a struggle in the minors for Cincinnati, with Rookie-level Billings proving to be the only playoff-bound affiliate. The Mustangs won the Pioneer League's North Division with a 40-36 record before losing in the league's semifinals to Great Falls (White Sox).

OPENING DAY PAYROLL: $101,718,451 (21st)

PLAYERS OF THE YEAR

ALEX TRAUTWIG

MIKE JANES/FOUR SEAM

MAJOR LEAGUE	MINOR LEAGUE
Eugenio Suarez	**Tony Santillan**
3B	**RHP**
.283/.366/.526	(High Class A/Double-A)
Led Reds in HR (34), RBIs	10-7, 3.08 in 26 GS
(104) and OPS (.892)	134 SO, 1.23 WHIP

ORGANIZATION LEADERS

Batting		*Minimum 250 AB
MAJORS		
* AVG	Scooter Gennett	.310
* OPS	Eugenio Suarez	.892
HR	Eugenio Suarez	34
RBI	Eugenio Suarez	104
MINORS		
* AVG	Gabriel Guerrero, Pensacola, Louisville	.293
* OBP	Michael Beltre, Dayton, Daytona	.397
* SLG	Ibandel Isabel, R. Cucamonga, Daytona	.566
* OPS	Ibandel Isabel, R. Cucamonga, Daytona	.900
R	TJ Friedl, Daytona, Pensacola	87
H	Gabriel Guerrero, Pensacola, Louisville	147
TB	Gabriel Guerrero, Pensacola, Louisville	238
2B	Josh VanMeter, Pensacola, Louisville	35
3B	Jose Siri, Daytona, Pensacola	11
HR	Ibandel Isabel, R. Cucamonga, Daytona	35
RBI	Gabriel Guerrero, Pensacola, Louisville	81
BB	Michael Beltre, Dayton, Daytona	69
SO	Taylor Sparks, Pensacola, Louisville	182
SB	Jeter Downs, Dayton	37

Pitching		#Minimum 75 IP
MAJORS		
W	Luis Castillo	10
# ERA	Jared Hughes	1.94
SO	Luis Castillo	165
SV	Raisel Iglesias	30
MINORS		
W	Scott Moss, Daytona	15
L	Jose Lopez, Louisville	13
# ERA	Robert Stephenson, Louisville	2.87
G	Jimmy Herget, Louisville	50
GS	Daniel Wright, Pensacola	28
GS	Packy Naughton, Dayton	28
SV	Kevin Quackenbush, Louisville	25
IP	Packy Naughton, Dayton	154
BB	Robert Stephenson, Louisville	57
SO	Vladimir Gutierrez, Pensacola	145
# AVG	Robert Stephenson, Louisville	.184

2018 PERFORMANCE

General Manager: Dick Williams/Nick Krall. **Farm Director:** Jeff Graupe. **Scouting Director:** Chris Buckley.

Class	Team	League	W	L	PCT	Finish	Manager
Majors	Cincinnati Reds	National	67	95	.414	13th (15)	B. Price/J. Riggleman
Triple-A	Louisville Bats	International	61	76	.445	13th (14)	Pat Kelly
Double-A	Pensacola Blue Wahoos	Southern	69	68	.504	4th (10)	Jody Davis
High A	Daytona Tortugas	Florida State	69	66	.511	t-6th (12)	Ricky Gutierrez
Low A	Dayton Dragons	Midwest	58	80	.420	15th (16)	Luis Bolivar
Rookie	Greeneville Reds	Appalachian	28	40	.412	9th (10)	Travis Dawkins
Rookie	Billings Mustangs	Pioneer	40	36	.526	4th (8)	Ray Martinez
Rookie	AZL Reds	Arizona	13	42	.236	18th (18)	Jose Nieves
Overall 2018 Minor League Record			338	408	.453	29th (30)	

ORGANIZATION STATISTICS

CINCINNATI REDS
NATIONAL LEAGUE

Batting	B-T	HT	WT	DOB	AVG	vLH	vRH	G	AB	R	H	2B	3B	HR	RBI	BB	HBP	SH	SF	SO	SB	CS	SLG	OBP
Aquino, Aristides	R-R	6-4	220	4-22-94	.000	—	.000	1	1	0	0	0	0	0	0	0	0	0	0	1	0	0	.000	.000
Barnhart, Tucker	B-R	5-11	192	1-7-91	.248	.279	.239	138	460	50	114	21	3	10	46	54	2	3	3	96	0	4	.372	.328
Blandino, Alex	R-R	6-0	190	11-6-92	.234	.263	.222	69	128	14	30	4	0	1	8	13	4	2	0	41	0	0	.289	.324
Casali, Curt	R-R	6-3	235	11-9-88	.293	.375	.250	52	140	15	41	10	0	4	16	12	2	1	1	32	0	2	.450	.355
Cruz, Tony	R-R	5-11	215	8-18-86	.154	.214	.083	9	26	2	4	1	0	1	2	0	0	0	0	11	0	0	.308	.154
Dixon, Brandon	R-R	6-2	215	1-29-92	.178	.178	.178	74	118	14	21	6	0	5	10	6	0	0	0	43	0	0	.356	.218
Duvall, Adam	R-R	6-1	215	9-4-88	.205	.224	.199	105	331	40	68	19	0	15	61	34	4	0	1	100	2	2	.399	.287
2-team total (33 Atlanta)					.195	.189	.198	138	384	48	75	20	0	15	61	37	5	0	1	117	2	2	.365	.274
Ervin, Phillip	R-R	5-10	207	7-15-92	.252	.250	.254	78	218	27	55	10	1	7	31	20	5	0	4	60	6	1	.404	.324
Federowicz, Tim	R-R	5-10	215	8-5-87	.333	—	.333	5	6	1	2	1	0	1	2	1	0	0	0	3	0	0	1.000	.429
Gennett, Scooter	L-R	5-10	185	5-1-90	.310	.294	.317	154	584	86	181	30	3	23	92	42	4	3	5	125	4	2	.490	.358
Gosselin, Phil	R-R	6-1	200	10-3-88	.125	.600	.000	20	24	5	3	0	0	1	2	4	0	0	0	8	0	0	.250	.250
Guerrero, Gabriel	R-R	6-3	215	12-11-93	.167	.200	.154	14	18	1	3	0	0	1	1	0	0	0	0	8	0	0	.333	.167
Hamilton, Billy	B-R	6-0	160	9-9-90	.236	.211	.246	153	504	74	119	16	9	4	29	46	1	1	4	132	34	10	.327	.299
Herrera, Dilson	R-R	5-10	210	3-3-94	.184	.211	.163	53	87	11	16	5	0	5	11	8	2	0	0	39	0	0	.414	.268
Herrera, Rosell	B-R	6-3	195	10-16-92	.154	.000	.167	11	13	0	2	0	0	0	0	0	0	0	0	5	0	1	.154	.154
Mesoraco, Devin	R-R	6-1	229	6-19-88	.220	.267	.192	18	41	1	9	2	0	1	3	2	2	0	0	10	0	0	.342	.289
2-team total (66 New York)					.221	.230	.219	84	244	24	54	10	0	11	33	25	4	0	1	52	0	0	.398	.303
Pennington, Cliff	B-R	5-11	195	6-15-84	.138	.333	.115	16	29	1	4	0	0	0	0	5	0	0	0	13	0	0	.138	.265
Peraza, Jose	R-R	6-0	196	4-30-94	.288	.313	.277	157	632	85	182	31	4	14	58	29	9	8	5	75	23	6	.416	.326
Schebler, Scott	L-R	6-0	228	10-6-90	.255	.296	.235	107	380	55	97	19	0	17	49	39	9	0	2	99	4	2	.440	.337
Suarez, Eugenio	R-R	5-11	213	7-18-91	.283	.320	.268	143	527	79	149	22	2	34	104	64	9	0	6	142	1	1	.526	.366
Trahan, Blake	R-R	5-9	180	9-5-93	.214	.000	.273	11	14	2	3	0	0	0	0	0	0	0	0	4	0	0	.214	.214
Tucker, Preston	L-L	6-0	210	7-6-90	.189	.000	.212	17	37	4	7	1	0	2	5	4	1	0	0	9	0	0	.378	.286
2-team total (80 Atlanta)					.229	.111	.243	97	166	19	38	11	0	6	27	13	4	0	1	43	0	0	.404	.299
Votto, Joey	L-R	6-2	220	9-10-83	.284	.260	.298	145	503	67	143	28	2	12	67	108	9	0	3	101	2	0	.420	.417
Williams, Mason	L-R	6-1	195	8-21-91	.293	.211	.308	51	123	10	36	5	1	2	6	7	2	0	2	29	1	2	.398	.331
Winker, Jesse	L-L	6-3	215	8-17-93	.299	.211	.321	89	281	38	84	16	0	7	43	49	2	1	1	46	0	0	.431	.405

Pitching	B-T	HT	WT	DOB	W	L	ERA	G	GS	CG	SV	IP	H	R	ER	HR	BB	SO	AVG	vLH	vRH	K/9	BB/9
Bailey, Homer	R-R	6-4	223	5-3-86	1	14	6.09	20	20	1	0	106	141	82	72	23	33	75	.313	.313	.312	6.35	2.79
Brice, Austin	R-R	6-4	235	6-19-92	2	3	5.79	33	0	0	0	37	39	26	24	9	13	32	.271	.316	.241	7.71	3.13
Castillo, Luis	R-R	6-2	190	12-12-92	10	12	4.30	31	31	0	0	170	158	89	81	28	49	165	.245	.289	.203	8.75	2.60
Crockett, Kyle	L-L	6-2	175	12-15-91	1	0	5.79	15	0	0	0	16	16	8	6	1	2	11	.364	.292	.450	10.61	1.93
DeSclafani, Anthony	R-R	6-1	195	4-18-90	7	8	4.93	21	21	0	0	115	118	68	63	24	30	108	.266	.288	.247	8.45	2.35
Finnegan, Brandon	L-L	5-11	212	4-14-93	0	3	7.40	5	5	0	0	21	27	20	17	5	15	14	.318	.350	.306	6.10	6.53
Floro, Dylan	L-R	6-2	205	12-27-90	3	2	2.72	25	0	0	0	36	39	12	11	2	12	27	.275	.339	.229	6.69	2.97
2-team total (29 Los Angeles)					6	3	2.25	54	0	0	0	64	57	17	16	3	23	58	.237	.292	.204	8.16	3.23
Gallardo, Yovani	R-R	6-2	205	2-27-86	0	0	30.86	3	0	0	0	2	8	8	8	1	4	2	.533	.571	.500	7.71	15.43
Garrett, Amir	R-L	6-5	228	5-3-92	1	2	4.29	66	0	0	0	63	56	30	30	8	25	71	.239	.222	.254	10.14	3.57
Harvey, Matt	R-R	6-4	215	3-27-89	7	7	4.50	24	24	0	0	128	132	66	64	21	28	111	.264	.253	.276	7.80	1.97
2-team total (8 New York)					7	9	4.94	32	28	0	0	155	165	87	85	27	37	131	.271	.264	.279	7.61	2.15
Hernandez, David	R-R	6-3	245	5-13-85	5	2	2.53	57	0	0	0	64	46	20	18	6	17	65	.200	.198	.202	9.14	2.39
Hughes, Jared	R-R	6-7	240	7-4-85	4	3	1.94	72	0	0	7	79	57	17	17	4	23	59	.212	.206	.216	6.75	2.63
Iglesias, Raisel	R-R	6-2	188	1-4-90	2	5	2.38	66	0	0	30	72	52	22	19	12	25	80	.199	.214	.185	10.00	3.13
Lorenzen, Michael	R-R	6-3	217	1-4-92	4	2	3.11	45	3	0	1	81	78	32	28	6	34	54	.258	.282	.242	6.00	3.78
Mahle, Tyler	R-R	6-3	210	9-29-94	7	9	4.98	23	23	0	0	112	125	68	62	22	53	110	.283	.300	.267	8.84	4.26
Mella, Keury	R-R	6-2	200	8-2-93	0	0	8.68	4	0	0	0	9	13	9	9	4	8	8	.351	.364	.333	7.71	7.71
Peralta, Wandy	L-L	6-0	210	7-27-91	2	2	5.36	59	0	0	0	45	58	32	27	2	31	31	.302	.298	.306	6.15	6.15
Quackenbush, Kevin	R-R	6-4	235	11-28-88	0	1	11.00	10	0	0	0	9	13	11	11	3	6	7	.333	.385	.308	7.00	6.00
Rainey, Tanner	R-R	6-2	235	12-25-92	0	0	24.43	8	0	0	0	7	13	19	19	4	12	7	.406	.471	.333	9.00	15.43
Reed, Cody	L-L	6-5	230	4-15-93	1	3	3.98	11	7	0	0	43	45	21	19	5	15	42	.270	.222	.282	8.79	3.14
Reyes, Jesus	R-R	6-2	180	2-21-93	0	0	3.18	5	0	0	0	6	4	4	2	1	2	2	.191	.333	.083	3.18	3.18

CINCINNATI REDS

Pitcher	B-T	HT	WT	DOB	W	L	ERA	G	GS	CG	SV	IP	H	R	ER	HR	BB	SO	AVG	vLH	vRH	K/9	BB/9
Romano, Sal	L-R	6-5	270	10-12-93	8	11	5.31	39	25	0	0	146	155	92	86	23	53	105	.267	.303	.236	6.49	3.27
Shackelford, Kevin	R-R	6-5	210	4-7-89	0	1	7.88	5	0	0	0	8	13	8	7	0	4	7	.382	.368	.400	7.88	4.50
Sims, Lucas	R-R	6-2	230	5-10-94	0	0	6.75	3	0	0	0	5	3	4	4	1	5	6	.158	.200	.143	10.13	8.44
2-team total (6 Atlanta)					0	0	7.47	9	0	0	0	16	15	13	13	3	13	16	.242	.192	.278	9.19	7.47
Stephens, Jackson	R-R	6-2	220	5-11-94	2	3	4.93	29	0	0	0	38	50	30	21	7	15	33	.307	.296	.315	7.75	3.52
Stephenson, Robert	R-R	6-3	215	2-24-93	0	2	9.26	4	3	0	0	12	17	12	12	2	12	11	.340	.333	.346	8.49	9.26
Weiss, Zack	R-R	6-3	210	6-16-92	0	0	—	1	0	0	0	2	4	4	2	2	1	0	1.000	—	1.000	—	—
Wisler, Matt	R-R	6-3	210	9-12-92	0	0	2.03	11	0	0	0	13	11	4	3	2	2	11	.225	.200	.235	7.43	1.35
2-team total (7 Atlanta)					1	1	4.28	18	3	0	0	40	41	20	19	8	7	32	.265	.261	.267	7.20	1.58

Fielding

Catcher	PCT	G	PO	A	E	DP	PB
Barnhart	.998	118	871	53	2	4	4
Casali	.989	38	264	18	3	2	2
Cruz	1.000	6	58	3	0	0	0
Federowicz	1.000	4	9	0	0	0	0
Mesoraco	1.000	10	68	2	0	0	0

First Base	PCT	G	PO	A	E	DP
Barnhart	.984	11	60	3	1	4
Blandino	1.000	1	3	0	0	0
Casali	1.000	6	28	4	0	2
Dixon	1.000	27	89	6	0	12
Duvall	.983	10	49	8	1	8
Gosselin	.750	1	3	0	1	0
Herrera	1.000	1	1	0	0	0
Mesoraco	1.000	1	0	0	0	0
Votto	.996	139	1047	142	5	101

Second Base	PCT	G	PO	A	E	DP
Blandino	.980	21	22	27	1	12
Casali	.000	1	0	0	1	0
Dixon	1.000	8	11	10	0	4
Gennett	.983	142	280	374	11	101
Gosselin	.000	1	0	0	0	0
Herrera	1.000	13	14	17	0	4
Herrera	1.000	1	1	3	0	0
Trahan	.000	3	0	0	0	0

Third Base	PCT	G	PO	A	E	DP
Blandino	.920	15	7	16	2	4
Dixon	1.000	6	1	8	0	1
Duvall	.000	1	0	0	0	0
Gosselin	1.000	8	2	8	0	0
Herrera	1.000	4	1	4	0	0
Pennington	.882	8	1	14	2	1
Suarez	.948	143	94	250	19	23
Trahan	1.000	2	1	1	0	0

Shortstop	PCT	G	PO	A	E	DP
Blandino	.941	11	12	20	2	8
Pennington	1.000	5	1	2	0	1
Peraza	.962	156	161	403	22	85
Suarez	1.000	3	2	3	0	0
Trahan	1.000	5	4	5	0	3

Outfield	PCT	G	PO	A	E	DP
Aquino	.000	1	0	0	0	0
Blandino	.000	1	0	0	0	0
Dixon	1.000	25	9	0	0	0
Duvall	.994	89	160	7	1	2
Ervin	.974	70	111	3	3	0
Gosselin	1.000	1	2	0	0	0
Guerrero	.800	5	4	0	1	0
Hamilton	.994	150	348	12	2	1
Herrera	1.000	11	14	0	0	0
Herrera	.000	2	0	0	0	0
Lorenzen	.000	1	0	0	0	0
Peraza	1.000	1	1	0	0	0
Schebler	.970	101	190	1	6	0
Tucker	1.000	10	12	0	0	0
Williams	1.000	40	51	0	0	0
Winker	.992	76	117	4	1	0

LOUISVILLE BATS
INTERNATIONAL LEAGUE

TRIPLE-A

Batting	B-T	HT	WT	DOB	AVG	vLH	vRH	G	AB	R	H	2B	3B	HR	RBI	BB	HBP	SH	SF	SO	SB	CS	SLG	OBP
Blandino, Alex	R-R	6-0	190	11-6-92	.000	.000	.000	3	8	3	0	0	0	0	0	2	2	0	0	4	1	0	.000	.333
Boulware, Garrett	R-R	6-2	200	9-9-92	.118	—	.118	6	17	3	2	1	1	0	0	0	0	0	0	5	0	0	.294	.118
Cruz, Tony	R-R	5-11	215	8-18-86	.188	.105	.222	18	64	10	12	1	0	3	12	7	0	0	2	19	0	0	.344	.260
Dixon, Brandon	R-R	6-2	215	1-29-92	.346	.373	.336	49	199	28	62	18	2	6	23	12	1	0	1	54	9	3	.570	.389
Elizalde, Sebastian	L-R	6-0	195	11-20-91	.254	.286	.233	21	71	11	18	6	0	2	11	4	2	0	0	14	0	2	.423	.312
Ervin, Phillip	R-R	5-10	207	7-15-92	.289	.234	.310	48	173	25	50	12	4	5	38	20	5	1	3	39	10	7	.491	.373
Federowicz, Tim	R-R	5-10	215	8-5-87	.244	.177	.262	23	78	10	19	6	0	1	9	9	0	0	1	20	0	0	.359	.318
Goeddel, Tyler	R-R	6-4	180	10-20-92	.229	.276	.204	27	83	7	19	5	1	1	10	11	1	1	0	21	1	1	.349	.326
Gosselin, Phil	R-R	6-1	200	10-3-88	.308	.250	.400	3	13	1	4	1	0	0	4	0	0	0	1	4	0	0	.385	.286
2-team total (81 Gwinnett)					.253	.294	.237	84	292	39	74	19	2	5	40	28	1	1	3	63	0	2	.384	.318
Guerrero, Gabriel	R-R	6-3	215	12-11-93	.292	.346	.273	104	404	64	118	15	4	17	65	23	0	0	5	97	1	3	.475	.326
Herrera, Dilson	R-R	5-10	210	3-3-94	.297	.315	.290	50	185	23	55	10	0	7	27	19	2	1	1	50	0	1	.465	.367
Herrera, Rosell	B-R	6-3	195	10-16-92	.267	.308	.250	23	90	11	24	8	2	3	11	6	1	1	0	15	2	1	.500	.320
Hudson, Joe	R-R	6-1	206	5-21-91	.235	.000	.316	16	51	5	12	3	0	0	3	8	0	1	0	15	0	0	.294	.339
Iribarren, Hernan	L-R	6-1	202	6-29-84	.265	.136	.293	82	249	20	66	19	1	0	15	22	0	0	4	48	0	1	.349	.325
Kivlehan, Patrick	R-R	6-2	223	12-22-89	.167	.250	.133	15	42	3	7	0	0	0	4	2	3	0	0	15	1	0	.167	.255
Lofstrom, Morgan	L-R	6-1	185	8-17-95	.300	.333	.250	3	10	0	3	0	0	0	1	0	0	0	1	0	0	0	.300	.300
Longhi, Nick	R-L	6-2	205	8-16-95	.233	.306	.185	32	96	8	21	5	0	0	8	5	1	0	0	27	1	0	.289	.258
Martinez, Valentin	R-R	6-0	175	9-21-96	.136	.286	.067	8	22	1	3	0	0	0	0	0	1	0	0	6	0	0	.136	.136
McElroy, C.J.	R-R	5-10	180	5-29-93	.193	.156	.211	39	140	15	27	2	1	1	6	5	1	1	0	28	10	3	.243	.226
O'Grady, Brian	L-R	6-2	215	5-17-92	.306	.308	.305	42	144	27	44	9	2	8	29	12	2	2	1	39	5	4	.563	.365
Pennington, Cliff	B-R	5-11	195	6-15-84	.267	.222	.286	11	30	4	8	2	0	0	1	6	0	0	1	7	0	1	.333	.378
Peterson, D.J.	R-R	6-1	210	12-31-91	.277	.354	.244	113	422	44	117	28	1	16	52	25	4	0	2	117	2	1	.462	.322
Sanchez, Tony	R-R	5-11	220	5-20-88	.000	.000	.333	2	5	0	1	0	0	0	0	0	0	0	0	3	0	0	.000	.400
Sansone, John	R-R	5-11	200	9-15-93	.143	.000	.167	3	7	0	1	0	0	0	0	3	2	0	1	0	0	0	.143	.500
Schebler, Scott	L-R	6-0	228	10-6-90	.231	.286	.167	8	26	3	6	1	0	1	2	5	0	0	0	6	0	0	.385	.355
Selsky, Steve	R-R	6-0	213	10-24-89	.265	.299	.249	82	268	37	71	15	2	10	35	27	2	0	3	79	1	3	.448	.333
Senzel, Nick	R-R	6-1	205	6-29-95	.310	.288	.321	44	171	23	53	12	2	6	25	19	1	0	2	39	8	2	.509	.378
Sparks, Taylor	R-R	6-4	200	4-3-93	.119	.054	.146	36	126	10	15	4	1	4	9	7	1	0	0	66	1	0	.262	.172
Suarez, Eugenio	R-R	5-11	213	7-18-91	.200	—	.200	2	5	1	1	1	0	0	3	0	0	0	1	0	0	0	.400	.500
Sweet, Daniel	B-L	6-0	190	12-28-94	.000	—	.000	3	0	0	0	0	0	0	0	0	0	0	0	0	0	0	.000	.000
Trahan, Blake	R-R	5-9	180	9-5-93	.246	.222	.256	129	444	55	109	17	1	2	31	49	5	12	0	104	6	3	.302	.327
Tromp, Chadwick	R-R	5-9	205	3-21-95	.264	.281	.256	53	174	20	46	8	1	2	14	15	4	0	2	24	2	3	.356	.333
Tucker, Preston	L-L	6-2	210	7-6-90	.222	.333	.167	2	9	0	2	0	0	1	0	0	0	0	0	2	0	0	.222	.222
2-team total (16 Gwinnett)					.246	.125	.283	18	69	7	17	4	1	0	7	2	0	0	0	7	0	0	.333	.268
Turner, Stuart	R-R	6-2	220	12-27-91	.200	.125	.235	22	75	6	15	1	0	0	9	6	1	0	1	28	0	0	.213	.265
VanMeter, Josh	L-R	5-11	165	3-10-95	.253	.209	.268	98	332	40	84	25	6	11	45	28	0	0	2	73	5	3	.464	.309
Williams, Mason	L-R	6-1	195	8-21-91	.280	.299	.273	87	318	52	89	18	4	6	30	29	1	1	1	57	5	8	.418	.341

Pitching

Pitching	B-T	HT	WT	DOB	W	L	ERA	G	GS	CG	SV	IP	H	R	ER	HR	BB	SO	AVG	vLH	vRH	K/9	BB/9
Astin, Barrett	R-R	6-1	225	10-22-91	0	0	4.70	5	0	0	0	8	10	5	4	1	3	5	.323	.421	.167	5.87	3.52
Bailey, Homer	R-R	6-4	223	5-3-86	2	2	4.78	7	6	0	0	38	41	20	20	4	10	28	.273	.231	.306	6.69	2.39
Bautista, Wendolyn	R-R	6-0	185	3-27-93	0	0	0.00	1	0	0	0	1	0	0	0	0	1	0	.000	.000	.000	0.00	9.00
Brice, Austin	R-R	6-4	235	6-19-92	3	1	2.31	17	0	0	1	23	18	6	6	2	7	24	.225	.278	.182	9.26	2.70
Crockett, Kyle	L-L	6-2	175	12-15-91	2	0	3.00	34	0	0	0	39	37	17	13	3	7	38	.247	.234	.256	8.77	1.62
De Paula, Jose Rafael	R-R	6-2	215	3-24-91	0	0	3.24	5	0	0	0	8	9	3	3	2	5	15	.265	.235	.294	16.20	5.40
DeSclafani, Anthony	R-R	6-1	195	4-18-90	0	2	6.35	2	2	0	0	11	15	8	8	5	2	10	.319	.435	.208	7.94	1.59
Finnegan, Brandon	L-L	5-11	212	4-14-93	2	10	7.05	28	9	0	0	68	90	65	53	10	40	57	.323	.337	.316	7.58	5.32
Floro, Dylan	L-R	6-2	205	12-27-90	0	0	0.00	2	0	0	0	3	4	0	0	0	1	1	.308	.500	.222	3.00	3.00
Herget, Jimmy	R-R	6-3	170	9-9-93	1	3	3.47	50	0	0	9	60	59	28	23	5	21	65	.253	.226	.271	9.80	3.17
Hernandez, David	R-R	6-3	245	5-13-85	0	0	19.29	3	0	0	0	2	6	5	5	0	0	3	.462	.429	.500	11.57	0.00
Lopez, Jose	R-R	6-1	205	9-1-93	5	13	4.47	26	26	0	0	141	142	75	70	19	41	117	.261	.236	.284	7.47	2.62
Mahle, Tyler	R-R	6-3	210	9-29-94	2	1	2.73	5	5	0	0	30	22	9	9	4	11	20	.206	.179	.215	6.07	3.34
Martinez, Juan	L-L	6-2	175	7-15-92	0	1	10.80	2	1	0	0	5	10	7	6	0	1	9	.385	.300	.438	16.20	1.80
Mella, Keury	R-R	6-2	200	8-2-93	2	1	2.74	5	5	0	0	23	20	9	7	1	6	14	.244	.255	.229	5.48	2.35
Mitchell, Evan	R-R	6-2	185	3-18-92	1	1	4.28	19	0	0	0	34	36	17	16	0	20	26	.277	.296	.263	6.95	5.35
Neal, Zach	R-R	6-3	220	11-9-88	2	2	5.90	18	3	0	1	40	52	26	26	10	3	23	.323	.343	.308	5.22	0.68
Nicolino, Justin	L-L	6-3	195	11-22-91	6	6	4.69	25	24	0	0	134	161	76	70	13	35	86	.300	.285	.306	5.76	2.34
Peralta, Wandy	L-L	6-0	220	7-27-91	1	0	3.14	13	0	0	0	14	13	5	5	1	7	10	.255	.177	.294	6.28	4.40
Quackenbush, Kevin	R-R	6-4	235	11-28-88	1	2	2.68	47	0	0	25	47	39	15	14	2	11	56	.225	.267	.194	10.72	2.11
Rainey, Tanner	R-R	6-2	235	12-25-92	7	2	2.65	44	0	0	3	51	25	18	15	2	35	65	.148	.167	.138	11.47	6.18
Reed, Cody	L-L	6-5	230	4-15-93	4	8	3.92	18	17	0	0	106	109	50	46	13	31	105	.267	.231	.281	8.94	2.64
Reyes, Jesus	R-R	6-2	180	2-21-93	1	2	5.27	9	0	0	0	14	15	8	8	3	9	9	.289	.208	.357	5.93	5.93
Rowen, Ben	R-R	6-4	203	11-15-88	0	2	9.28	10	0	0	0	11	19	15	11	3	2	7	.380	.235	.455	5.91	1.69
Shackelford, Kevin	R-R	6-5	210	4-7-89	0	0	3.86	5	0	0	0	5	3	2	2	0	3	6	.188	.000	.333	11.57	5.79
Sims, Lucas	R-R	6-2	230	5-10-94	0	2	3.81	5	5	0	0	28	20	14	12	5	5	32	.192	.200	.185	10.16	1.59
2-team total (15 Gwinnett)					4	5	3.11	20	19	0	0	101	86	43	35	11	39	115	.232	.221	.247	10.21	3.46
Stephens, Jackson	R-R	6-2	220	5-11-94	1	1	5.32	16	7	0	0	44	46	30	26	4	16	35	.266	.314	.233	7.16	3.27
Stephenson, Robert	R-R	6-3	215	2-24-93	11	6	2.87	20	20	1	0	113	74	41	36	12	57	135	.184	.187	.182	10.75	4.54
Tapia, Domingo	R-R	6-3	250	8-4-91	4	5	3.43	47	4	0	1	63	56	29	24	4	26	45	.240	.287	.209	6.43	3.71
Weiss, Zack	R-R	6-3	210	6-16-92	2	2	9.00	11	1	0	1	11	13	14	11	3	15	11	.283	.304	.261	9.00	12.27
Wisler, Matt	R-R	6-3	210	9-12-92	1	1	1.83	8	2	0	0	20	19	5	4	0	3	21	.253	.320	.220	9.61	1.37
2-team total (13 Gwinnett)					5	5	3.81	21	15	2	0	90	98	40	38	6	17	86	.282	.293	.272	8.63	1.71
Wooten, Rob	R-R	6-1	200	7-21-85	0	0	3.00	1	0	0	0	3	3	1	1	0	0	2	.273	.167	.400	6.00	0.00

Fielding

Catcher	PCT	G	PO	A	E	DP	PB
Boulware	1.000	6	46	1	0	0	1
Cruz	.993	15	134	5	1	2	0
Federowicz	1.000	21	165	5	0	1	1
Hudson	.991	15	111	4	1	0	2
Iribarren	1.000	1	1	0	0	0	0
Lofstrom	1.000	3	22	0	0	0	0
Martinez	1.000	8	50	6	0	0	1
Sanchez	1.000	1	5	0	0	0	0
Tromp	.990	51	390	23	4	2	3
Turner	.995	22	176	12	1	0	2

First Base	PCT	G	PO	A	E	DP
Cruz	1.000	2	12	0	0	0
Dixon	1.000	14	98	7	0	11
Iribarren	.981	25	144	11	3	13
Kivlehan	1.000	7	55	6	0	3
Longhi	.975	16	108	11	3	9
O'Grady	.988	12	74	8	1	11
Peterson	.990	37	283	17	3	32
Selsky	.979	36	260	16	6	23

Second Base	PCT	G	PO	A	E	DP
Cruz	.000	1	0	0	0	0
Dixon	.940	14	22	25	3	4
Federowicz	1.000	1	0	1	0	0
Gosselin	1.000	1	1	3	0	0

	PCT	G	PO	A	E	DP
Herrera	.973	35	53	89	4	23
Herrera	1.000	3	3	10	0	2
Iribarren	.952	10	9	11	1	2
Kivlehan	1.000	1	1	0	0	0
Sansone	1.000	3	1	1	0	0
Selsky	1.000	1	1	1	0	0
Senzel	1.000	28	58	79	0	20
Sparks	.500	2	1	0	1	0
Trahan	1.000	2	0	3	0	0
VanMeter	.989	47	77	104	2	27

Third Base	PCT	G	PO	A	E	DP
Blandino	.833	3	0	5	1	1
Dixon	1.000	5	1	5	0	0
Herrera	.952	11	7	33	2	5
Herrera	.833	7	5	5	2	0
Iribarren	.000	1	0	0	0	0
Kivlehan	.714	2	2	3	2	0
Pennington	1.000	7	4	9	0	1
Peterson	.964	51	34	73	4	7
Senzel	.950	14	6	32	2	0
Sparks	.947	34	25	46	4	11
Suarez	1.000	2	1	4	0	0
VanMeter	.964	10	10	17	1	1

Shortstop	PCT	G	PO	A	E	DP
Herrera	1.000	1	1	0	0	0
Iribarren	.000	1	0	0	0	0

	PCT	G	PO	A	E	DP
Pennington	1.000	2	4	3	0	0
Sansone	1.000	2	2	3	0	0
Senzel	1.000	1	1	1	0	0
Sparks	.000	1	0	0	0	0
Trahan	.984	127	150	335	8	66
VanMeter	.960	7	11	13	1	4

Outfield	PCT	G	PO	A	E	DP
Dixon	.955	13	20	1	1	0
Elizalde	1.000	17	44	0	0	0
Ervin	.973	47	108	2	3	0
Goeddel	.956	24	41	2	2	1
Guerrero	.978	102	216	11	5	4
Herget	.000	1	0	0	0	0
Herrera	.962	13	25	0	1	0
Iribarren	1.000	6	6	0	0	0
Kivlehan	1.000	1	1	0	0	0
Longhi	1.000	9	17	0	0	0
Lopez	.000	1	0	0	0	0
McElroy	.989	37	85	1	1	0
O'Grady	1.000	29	54	1	0	0
Schebler	1.000	2	6	0	0	0
Selsky	1.000	24	44	1	0	1
Sweet	1.000	1	2	0	0	0
Tucker	1.000	2	6	0	0	0
VanMeter	1.000	25	40	1	0	0
Williams	.986	85	199	7	3	5

PENSACOLA BLUE WAHOOS
SOUTHERN LEAGUE
DOUBLE-A

Batting	B-T	HT	WT	DOB	AVG	vLH	vRH	G	AB	R	H	2B	3B	HR	RBI	BB	HBP	SH	SF	SO	SB	CS	SLG	OBP
Aquino, Aristides	R-R	6-4	220	4-22-94	.240	.184	.256	114	404	49	97	20	2	20	55	35	4	1	1	112	4	5	.448	.306
Boulware, Garrett	R-R	6-2	200	9-9-92	.200	.429	.130	11	30	2	6	2	0	0	3	0	0	1	0	14	0	0	.267	.265
Brown, Cassidy	R-R	6-3	215	7-21-94	.175	.375	.110	30	97	6	17	3	0	1	5	7	0	0	1	38	0	0	.237	.229
Chavez, Alberti	R-R	5-10	170	7-21-95	.217	.125	.250	28	60	4	13	0	0	1	2	0	1	0	1	11	0	1	.217	.242
Collymore, Malik	R-R	6-0	195	4-29-95	.444	—	.444	7	9	2	4	1	0	0	1	2	0	0	0	3	0	1	.556	.546

	B-T	HT	WT	DOB	AVG	vLH	vRH	G	AB	R	H	2B	3B	HR	RBI	BB	HBP	SH	SF	SO	SB	CS	SLG	OBP
Crook, Narciso	R-R	6-3	220	7-12-95	.286	.286	.286	63	161	18	46	5	2	2	22	18	3	1	3	41	4	4	.379	.362
Featherston, Taylor	R-R	6-1	185	10-8-89	.237	.292	.225	36	135	10	32	2	4	3	15	8	1	0	1	50	2	0	.378	.283
Friedl, TJ	L-L	5-10	170	8-14-95	.276	.283	.274	67	261	47	72	10	3	2	16	28	6	1	0	56	19	5	.360	.359
Gonzalez, Luis	R-R	6-0	175	7-28-94	.243	.205	.253	109	391	46	95	16	1	3	30	17	2	2	1	71	5	4	.312	.277
Guerrero, Gabriel	R-R	6-3	215	12-11-93	.296	.292	.297	26	98	13	29	9	1	2	16	7	0	0	2	26	3	0	.469	.336
LaValley, Gavin	R-R	6-3	235	12-28-94	.209	.214	.207	120	393	43	82	14	0	13	57	44	4	0	5	121	2	1	.344	.292
Long, Shed	L-R	5-8	184	8-22-95	.261	.239	.267	126	452	75	118	22	5	12	56	57	8	4	1	123	19	6	.412	.353
Longhi, Nick	R-L	6-2	205	8-16-95	.250	.244	.252	58	176	20	44	9	0	2	28	13	6	0	3	38	0	0	.335	.318
McElroy, C.J.	R-R	5-10	180	5-29-93	.281	.281	.281	45	128	20	36	7	1	2	11	10	2	3	1	28	9	5	.398	.340
Nay, Mitch	R-R	6-3	200	9-20-93	.262	.275	.259	63	221	34	58	10	0	6	26	31	5	0	2	43	2	0	.389	.363
O'Grady, Brian	L-R	6-2	175	5-17-92	.258	.304	.252	63	178	27	46	12	4	6	30	27	2	1	5	41	4	1	.472	.354
Okey, Chris	R-R	5-11	195	12-29-94	.198	.133	.211	78	263	22	52	13	0	5	26	17	4	1	0	72	2	0	.304	.257
Rodriguez, Alfredo	R-R	6-0	190	6-17-94	.192	.333	.150	9	26	4	5	0	0	0	0	2	1	0	0	7	0	0	.192	.276
Schebler, Scott	L-R	6-0	210	10-6-90	.154	.000	.182	7	26	2	4	1	0	0	1	2	0	0	0	4	0	0	.192	.214
Siri, Jose	R-R	6-2	175	7-22-95	.229	.203	.237	66	253	42	58	8	9	12	34	24	3	0	3	91	14	5	.474	.300
Sparks, Taylor	R-R	6-4	200	4-3-93	.246	.297	.230	90	281	43	69	16	4	10	38	28	6	2	2	116	4	2	.438	.325
Sweet, Daniel	B-L	6-0	190	12-28-94	.161	.053	.189	43	93	10	15	3	1	2	7	14	1	1	0	28	4	2	.280	.278
Tromp, Chadwick	R-R	5-9	205	3-21-95	.247	.250	.246	25	85	9	21	5	0	0	12	0	1	0	0	18	0	1	.306	.340
VanMeter, Josh	L-R	5-11	165	3-10-95	.284	.167	.312	30	95	13	27	10	0	1	14	23	0	2	1	19	5	2	.421	.420

Pitching	B-T	HT	WT	DOB	W	L	ERA	G	GS	CG	SV	IP	H	R	ER	HR	BB	SO	AVG	vLH	vRH	K/9	BB/9
Bender, Joel	L-L	6-4	210	8-3-91	0	1	1.59	19	0	0	0	28	22	8	5	2	6	26	.210	.216	.206	8.26	1.91
Bernardino, Brennan	L-L	6-4	180	1-15-92	1	0	6.30	21	0	0	2	20	22	18	14	2	7	24	.290	.300	.283	10.80	3.15
Canelon, Kevin	L-L	6-0	181	1-16-94	1	0	0.00	2	0	0	0	3	1	0	0	0	0	3	.091	.000	.125	8.10	0.00
Chacin, Alejandro	R-R	6-0	204	6-24-93	1	2	5.50	27	0	0	6	36	38	24	22	7	21	50	.262	.194	.313	12.50	5.25
Davis, Rookie	R-R	6-5	255	4-29-93	2	1	6.14	6	2	0	0	15	17	11	10	3	3	11	.293	.375	.235	6.75	1.84
De Paula, Jose Rafael	R-R	6-2	215	3-24-91	3	4	3.44	37	0	0	3	50	39	24	19	7	25	58	.217	.292	.174	10.51	4.53
DeSclafani, Anthony	R-R	6-1	195	4-18-90	0	1	2.25	2	2	0	0	8	5	3	2	0	1	12	.172	.263	.000	13.50	1.13
Gutierrez, Vladimir	R-R	6-0	190	9-18-95	9	10	4.35	27	27	0	0	147	139	76	71	18	38	145	.246	.203	.275	8.88	2.33
Hernandez, Ariel	R-R	6-4	230	3-2-92	0	0	0.00	3	0	0	2	3	4	0	0	0	3	3	.333	.000	.444	8.10	0.00
Howard, Nick	R-R	6-4	215	4-6-93	2	0	3.00	12	0	0	0	18	16	6	6	1	7	12	.239	.160	.286	6.00	3.50
Kiekhefer, Dean	L-L	6-0	175	6-7-89	0	0	1.13	8	0	0	0	8	7	1	1	0	1	10	.233	.063	.429	11.25	1.13
Leyer, Robinson	R-R	6-2	175	3-13-93	6	3	2.59	42	0	0	2	59	43	19	17	4	28	65	.208	.274	.172	9.92	4.27
Lorenzen, Michael	R-R	6-3	217	1-4-92	0	0	0.00	3	0	0	0	4	1	0	0	0	1	3	.077	.200	.000	6.75	2.25
Martinez, Juan	L-L	6-2	175	7-15-92	1	0	4.62	18	0	0	0	25	25	13	13	3	13	24	.269	.267	.270	8.53	4.62
Mella, Keury	R-R	6-2	200	8-2-93	7	3	3.07	16	16	0	0	85	70	37	29	8	31	87	.222	.230	.216	9.21	3.28
Mitchell, Evan	R-R	6-2	185	3-18-92	1	0	1.80	2	0	0	0	5	5	1	1	0	4	4	.278	.400	.231	7.20	0.00
Navas, Carlos	R-R	6-1	170	8-13-92	4	3	3.19	39	1	0	4	73	68	31	26	6	16	89	.247	.240	.252	10.92	1.96
Payano, Victor	L-L	6-5	185	10-17-92	0	2	4.22	21	3	0	0	32	23	20	15	5	23	45	.202	.182	.210	12.66	6.47
Powers, Alex	R-R	6-4	180	2-26-92	2	2	2.34	39	0	0	18	42	30	12	11	3	11	55	.194	.156	.220	11.69	2.34
Reyes, Jesus	R-R	6-2	180	2-21-93	1	8	3.94	29	6	0	2	64	59	45	28	4	27	53	.242	.269	.225	7.45	3.80
Santillan, Tony	R-R	6-3	240	4-15-97	4	7	3.61	11	11	0	0	62	65	27	25	8	16	61	.264	.276	.257	8.81	2.31
Shackelford, Kevin	R-R	6-5	210	4-7-89	0	0	2.45	3	1	0	0	4	2	1	1	0	3	2	.200	.400	.000	4.91	7.36
Strahan, Wyatt	R-R	6-3	220	4-18-93	7	12	6.38	27	23	0	1	120	144	95	85	15	53	83	.298	.286	.306	6.23	3.98
Tapia, Domingo	R-R	6-3	250	8-4-91	0	0	9.00	1	0	0	0	2	3	2	2	0	3	3	.375	.250	.500	0.00	13.50
Varner, Seth	L-L	6-3	225	1-27-92	9	3	3.39	25	17	0	0	119	104	56	45	19	31	99	.232	.157	.258	7.47	2.34
Weiss, Zack	R-R	6-3	210	6-16-92	1	0	1.17	5	0	0	0	8	5	2	1	0	4	9	.192	.167	.214	10.57	4.70
Wright, Daniel	R-R	6-2	205	4-3-91	7	10	4.16	28	28	1	0	151	148	80	70	25	36	106	.253	.237	.263	6.30	2.14

Fielding

Catcher	PCT	G	PO	A	E	DP	PB
Boulware	.987	10	72	2	1	1	1
Brown	.992	29	234	16	2	0	3
Okey	.991	77	640	42	6	3	2
Tromp	.982	25	201	19	4	0	2

First Base	PCT	G	PO	A	E	DP
LaValley	.992	104	707	50	6	79
Longhi	1.000	15	106	8	0	13
Nay	1.000	24	184	4	0	25
O'Grady	.985	12	62	4	1	6

Second Base	PCT	G	PO	A	E	DP
Chavez	1.000	8	13	19	0	6
Featherston	1.000	4	5	6	0	2
Long	.971	123	212	283	15	90
Nay	.909	3	2	8	1	2

Sparks	.500	1	0	1	1	0
VanMeter	1.000	9	13	13	0	2

Third Base	PCT	G	PO	A	E	DP
Chavez	.889	5	1	7	1	2
Featherston	.947	13	5	31	2	7
LaValley	.625	6	1	4	3	1
Nay	.952	39	24	56	4	3
O'Grady	.000	2	0	0	1	0
Sparks	.945	87	54	136	11	12
VanMeter	1.000	2	1	3	0	0

Shortstop	PCT	G	PO	A	E	DP
Chavez	.889	9	4	12	2	2
Featherston	.948	22	27	65	5	16
Gonzalez	.922	103	112	242	30	66
Rodriguez	1.000	9	8	20	0	5

Sparks	.750	3	3	6	3	3
VanMeter	.889	5	3	5	1	2

Outfield	PCT	G	PO	A	E	DP
Aquino	.972	108	198	12	6	2
Chavez	.000	1	0	0	0	0
Collymore	1.000	3	4	0	0	0
Crook	1.000	43	84	1	0	0
Friedl	.992	62	122	4	1	0
Guerrero	.984	24	58	4	1	1
Longhi	.938	27	30	0	2	0
McElroy	.973	40	72	1	2	0
O'Grady	.981	37	52	1	1	2
Schebler	.900	7	9	0	1	0
Siri	1.000	59	132	3	0	0
Sweet	1.000	23	42	0	0	0
VanMeter	.952	15	20	0	1	0

DAYTONA TORTUGAS   HIGH CLASS A
FLORIDA STATE LEAGUE

Batting	B-T	HT	WT	DOB	AVG	vLH	vRH	G	AB	R	H	2B	3B	HR	RBI	BB	HBP	SH	SF	SO	SB	CS	SLG	OBP
Bell, Brantley	R-R	6-3	185	11-16-94	.251	.228	.261	117	407	50	102	21	3	7	54	31	5	2	3	75	21	5	.369	.309
Beltre, Michael	B-R	6-3	220	7-3-95	.261	.170	.291	58	188	28	49	6	5	1	18	40	0	1	0	48	10	4	.362	.390
Boselli, Robert	R-R	6-4	240	4-17-96	.000	—	.000	1	3	0	0	0	0	0	0	0	0	0	0	3	0	0	.000	.000
Brown, Cassidy	R-R	6-3	215	7-21-94	.136	.125	.143	7	22	2	3	0	1	0	3	3	1	0	0	4	0	0	.227	.269

Name	B-T	HT	WT	DOB	AVG	vLH	vRH	G	AB	R	H	2B	3B	HR	RBI	BB	HBP	SH	SF	SO	SB	CS	OBP	SLG
Chavez, Alberti	R-R	5-10	170	7-21-95	.182	.152	.195	33	110	8	20	1	1	1	6	5	3	1	2	33	0	1	.236	.233
Collymore, Malik	R-R	6-0	195	4-29-95	.243	.325	.194	30	107	18	26	6	1	4	16	9	1	0	0	42	9	1	.430	.308
Crook, Narciso	R-R	6-3	220	7-12-95	.208	.294	.161	15	48	5	10	2	1	1	3	3	3	0	0	11	1	1	.354	.296
Daal, Calten	R-R	6-1	180	8-1-93	.333	.000	.385	4	15	3	5	1	0	0	0	0	0	0	0	3	0	0	.400	.333
Fairchild, Stuart	R-R	6-0	190	3-17-96	.250	.273	.240	63	220	25	55	14	1	2	20	17	2	0	3	63	6	2	.350	.306
Friedl, TJ	L-L	5-10	170	8-14-95	.294	.277	.301	64	228	40	67	10	4	3	35	38	6	0	2	44	11	4	.412	.405
Gonzalez, Luis	R-R	6-0	175	7-12-95	.385	.273	.429	11	39	7	15	1	1	1	5	2	1	0	1	7	1	0	.539	.419
Hawkins, Courtney	R-R	6-3	245	11-12-93	.246	.200	.267	17	65	6	16	1	0	2	4	5	1	0	0	23	3	0	.354	.310
Herrera, Dilson	R-R	5-10	210	3-3-94	.298	.394	.235	21	84	18	25	3	1	2	8	7	1	0	0	19	1	1	.429	.359
Isabel, Ibandel	R-R	6-4	225	6-20-95	.258	.197	.287	104	376	62	97	11	0	35	75	36	7	0	1	152	1	1	.567	.333
Lofstrom, Morgan	L-R	6-1	185	8-17-95	.206	.320	.167	29	97	8	20	2	1	2	8	2	2	0	0	29	0	0	.309	.238
Mardirosian, Shane	L-R	5-10	175	10-13-95	.158	.222	.138	12	38	2	6	0	0	0	1	0	1	0	0	10	0	1	.158	.180
Martinez, Valentin	R-R	6-0	175	9-21-96	—	—	—	1	0	0	0	0	0	0	0	0	1	0	0	0	0	0	—	1.000
Nay, Mitch	R-R	6-3	200	9-20-93	.271	.253	.281	69	251	28	68	18	2	5	44	25	3	0	2	57	1	1	.418	.342
Okey, Chris	R-R	5-11	195	12-29-94	.207	.182	.222	8	29	5	6	0	0	2	3	2	1	0	0	7	0	0	.414	.281
Rivero, Carlos	R-R	6-0	175	4-30-97	.120	.069	.143	28	92	5	11	3	0	0	4	1	2	0	0	38	0	1	.152	.165
Rodriguez, Alfredo	R-R	6-0	190	6-17-94	.207	.281	.177	31	111	12	23	5	1	2	12	8	2	0	1	22	4	0	.324	.271
Sansone, John	R-R	5-11	200	9-15-93	.134	.182	.117	28	82	5	11	3	0	0	3	3	2	0	0	31	0	1	.171	.184
Siri, Jose	R-R	6-2	175	7-22-95	.261	.226	.273	30	119	15	31	9	2	1	9	4	0	1	2	32	9	1	.395	.280
Stephenson, Tyler	R-R	6-4	225	8-16-96	.250	.243	.253	109	388	60	97	20	1	11	59	45	10	0	7	98	1	0	.392	.338
Sweet, Daniel	B-L	6-0	190	12-28-94	.260	.283	.248	47	158	29	41	11	1	4	24	21	2	0	2	34	5	3	.418	.350
Trammell, Taylor	L-L	6-2	195	9-13-97	.277	.310	.262	110	397	71	110	19	4	8	41	58	5	0	1	105	25	10	.406	.375
Vargas, Hector	R-R	6-2	170	1-27-95	.180	.100	.203	28	89	11	16	1	0	0	6	4	2	3	1	13	4	1	.191	.229
Ventura, Randy	B-R	5-9	165	7-11-97	.291	.290	.292	65	254	31	74	7	0	0	17	24	1	1	0	51	10	5	.319	.355
Yari, Bruce	L-L	6-3	224	12-9-94	.272	.234	.284	111	379	40	103	18	0	5	54	61	6	0	3	103	0	3	.359	.379

Pitching

Name	B-T	HT	WT	DOB	W	L	ERA	G	GS	CG	SV	IP	H	R	ER	HR	BB	SO	AVG	vLH	vRH	K/9	BB/9
Adams, Jesse	L-L	6-0	190	8-12-93	2	1	4.40	10	1	0	0	14	17	9	7	0	4	10	.283	.391	.216	6.28	2.51
Antone, Tejay	R-R	6-4	205	12-5-93	6	3	4.03	17	17	0	0	96	95	48	43	6	29	82	.255	.244	.269	7.69	2.72
Bautista, Wendolyn	R-R	6-0	185	3-27-93	0	0	2.25	2	0	0	0	4	4	1	1	0	3	5	.250	.444	.000	11.25	6.75
Bergjans, Tommy	R-R	6-1	190	12-1-92	5	2	3.66	14	14	0	0	79	70	33	32	5	16	51	.236	.239	.233	5.83	1.83
2-team total (2 Clearwater)					5	2	3.68	16	14	0	0	81	73	34	33	6	16	51	.239	.234	.243	5.69	1.79
Boyles, Ty	R-L	6-3	270	9-30-95	5	9	4.90	38	10	0	0	83	95	57	45	7	28	67	.281	.261	.292	7.29	3.05
Byrne, Michael	R-R	6-3	205	4-16-97	1	1	1.25	19	0	0	0	22	19	5	3	0	10	17	.235	.333	.143	7.06	4.15
Canelon, Kevin	L-L	6-0	181	1-16-94	0	2	2.94	37	6	0	0	67	56	23	22	3	12	69	.227	.214	.233	9.22	1.60
Davis, Rookie	R-R	6-5	255	4-29-93	0	1	7.20	1	1	0	0	5	5	5	4	1	1	3	.263	.250	.286	5.40	1.80
Diaz, Carlos	L-L	6-3	190	2-3-92	0	1	3.22	20	0	0	1	22	14	10	8	1	7	37	.184	.250	.136	14.91	2.82
Fossas, Aaron	R-R	6-2	200	9-2-92	5	2	5.40	42	0	0	2	58	58	39	35	3	27	39	.256	.227	.287	6.04	4.17
Hendrix, Ryan	R-R	6-3	185	12-16-94	4	4	1.76	44	0	0	12	51	38	19	10	2	26	79	.205	.218	.191	13.94	4.59
Howard, Nick	R-R	6-4	215	4-6-93	1	4	6.23	26	0	0	2	35	37	29	24	4	27	27	.276	.303	.250	7.01	7.01
Hunter, Brian	R-R	6-3	215	11-22-92	1	1	6.26	18	0	0	1	27	35	21	19	1	17	35	.318	.351	.321	11.52	5.60
Jordan, Andrew	R-R	6-3	180	8-3-97	1	7	8.82	10	10	0	0	34	55	45	33	6	30	28	.360	.380	.338	7.49	8.02
Kivel, Jeremy	R-R	6-1	200	10-16-93	0	0	2.00	10	0	0	0	9	7	3	2	0	7	10	.219	.231	.211	10.00	7.00
Kuhnel, Joel	R-R	6-5	260	2-19-95	1	4	3.04	44	0	0	17	53	54	23	18	2	11	56	.260	.272	.248	9.45	1.86
Martinez, Juan	L-L	6-2	175	7-15-92	0	1	4.38	13	1	0	0	25	28	12	12	1	15	21	.292	.194	.350	7.66	5.47
Moss, Scott	L-L	6-5	215	10-6-94	15	4	3.68	25	25	0	0	132	135	66	54	13	41	112	.262	.271	.257	7.64	2.80
Nutof, Ryan	L-R	6-2	190	11-2-95	0	0	3.86	1	0	0	0	2	6	1	1	0	0	1	.500	.500	.500	3.86	0.00
Ohanian, Sarkis	R-R	5-11	195	8-6-93	0	0	3.38	3	0	0	0	5	4	2	2	0	0	8	.211	.333	.100	13.50	0.00
Olson, Ryan	R-R	6-2	195	11-22-94	4	3	4.64	10	10	0	0	52	58	31	27	5	18	46	.278	.301	.250	7.91	3.10
Quillen, Aaron	R-R	6-0	205	12-19-93	0	0	6.23	5	0	0	0	9	13	6	6	1	2	9	.333	.267	.375	9.35	2.08
Romero, Wennington	L-L	5-11	175	1-29-98	8	10	4.82	24	24	0	0	131	149	78	70	13	37	79	.286	.289	.285	5.44	2.55
Santillan, Tony	R-R	6-3	240	4-15-97	6	4	2.70	15	15	1	0	87	81	31	26	5	22	73	.246	.234	.260	7.58	2.28
Stallings, Jesse	R-R	6-2	198	10-27-94	3	2	2.00	17	0	0	0	18	14	6	4	2	5	12	.212	.200	.222	6.00	2.50
Varner, Seth	L-L	6-3	225	1-27-92	1	0	1.50	1	1	1	0	6	3	1	1	1	0	3	.158	.300	.000	4.50	0.00
Webb, Alex	R-R	6-3	210	7-19-94	0	0	8.20	14	0	0	0	19	29	21	17	3	11	18	.345	.400	.296	8.68	5.30

Fielding

Catcher	PCT	G	PO	A	E	DP	PB
Boselli	1.000	1	4	1	0	0	0
Brown	1.000	6	48	4	0	0	1
Lofstrom	.991	28	196	24	2	0	4
Martinez	1.000	1	1	1	0	0	0
Okey	.971	4	31	3	1	0	0
Stephenson	.996	97	703	61	3	3	5

First Base	PCT	G	PO	A	E	DP
Isabel	.985	37	303	20	5	29
Nay	.964	4	22	5	1	1
Yari	.997	96	730	44	2	65

Second Base	PCT	G	PO	A	E	DP
Bell	.974	41	75	114	5	25
Chavez	.939	7	8	23	2	6
Collymore	1.000	3	2	2	0	1
Daal	1.000	2	3	7	0	2

	PCT	G	PO	A	E	DP
Herrera	.988	19	25	59	1	9
Mardirosian	.975	10	14	25	1	6
Rivero	1.000	2	0	5	0	2
Sansone	1.000	4	1	5	0	0
Vargas	1.000	3	2	10	0	0
Ventura	.947	52	86	130	12	27

Third Base	PCT	G	PO	A	E	DP
Bell	.887	52	35	75	14	8
Nay	.886	63	33	84	15	7
Sansone	.895	24	10	24	4	3
Vargas	.000	1	0	0	0	0

Shortstop	PCT	G	PO	A	E	DP
Bell	.958	21	25	43	3	14
Chavez	.982	26	37	70	2	14
Daal	.800	2	4	4	2	1
Gonzalez	.941	10	13	19	2	4

	PCT	G	PO	A	E	DP
Rivero	.975	26	37	82	3	14
Rodriguez	.958	31	40	74	5	16
Vargas	.935	23	32	55	6	13

Outfield	PCT	G	PO	A	E	DP
Beltre	.958	57	132	6	6	1
Collymore	.949	23	37	0	2	0
Crook	1.000	11	24	1	0	0
Fairchild	1.000	62	127	2	0	0
Friedl	.983	60	115	2	2	1
Hawkins	.941	11	16	0	1	0
Isabel	.882	8	14	1	2	0
Mardirosian	1.000	2	1	0	0	0
Siri	.971	26	68	0	2	0
Sweet	.987	43	74	1	1	0
Trammell	.983	103	233	4	4	0
Ventura	.923	9	11	1	1	0

DAYTON DRAGONS   LOW CLASS A
MIDWEST LEAGUE

Batting	B-T	HT	WT	DOB	AVG	vLH	vRH	G	AB	R	H	2B	3B	HR	RBI	BB	HBP	SH	SF	SO	SB	CS	SLG	OBP
Beltre, Michael	B-R	6-3	220	7-3-95	.297	.282	.302	47	165	27	49	7	3	4	19	29	2	2	2	37	12	1	.449	.404
Cedrola, Lorenzo	R-R	5-8	152	1-12-98	.260	.294	.246	45	169	13	44	4	2	1	11	9	4	4	2	28	13	7	.325	.310
Clementina, Hendrik	R-R	6-0	250	6-17-97	.268	.294	.258	96	340	38	91	22	1	18	59	30	2	0	4	99	1	0	.497	.327
Collymore, Malik	R-R	6-0	195	4-29-95	.290	.412	.254	20	76	10	22	5	1	1	13	3	1	0	0	21	2	1	.421	.325
Crook, Narciso	R-R	6-3	220	7-12-95	.263	.433	.160	25	80	11	21	10	1	3	19	9	1	0	2	27	3	0	.525	.337
Downs, Jeter	R-R	5-11	180	7-27-98	.257	.310	.242	120	455	63	117	23	2	13	47	52	14	2	1	103	37	10	.402	.351
Fairchild, Stuart	R-R	6-0	190	3-17-96	.277	.288	.273	67	235	40	65	12	5	7	37	31	8	0	2	65	17	4	.460	.377
Garcia, Jose	R-R	6-2	175	4-5-98	.245	.246	.244	125	482	61	118	22	4	6	53	19	12	3	1	112	13	9	.344	.290
Gordon, Miles	L-R	6-1	175	12-3-97	.211	.208	.212	57	204	37	43	5	6	2	8	23	1	2	3	46	17	6	.324	.290
India, Jonathan	R-R	6-1	200	12-15-96	.229	.269	.214	27	96	17	22	7	0	3	11	13	3	0	0	28	5	0	.396	.339
Kolozsvary, Mark	R-R	5-8	180	9-4-95	.226	.242	.220	82	275	26	62	16	1	3	27	24	10	0	1	76	3	0	.324	.310
Lofstrom, Morgan	L-R	6-1	185	8-17-95	.250	.000	.318	11	28	3	7	3	0	0	2	3	1	0	0	12	0	0	.357	.344
Lopez, Alejo	R-R	5-10	170	5-5-96	.321	.365	.304	65	234	29	75	16	2	0	17	18	4	1	3	31	7	6	.406	.375
Marshall, Montrell	R-R	6-5	240	4-2-96	.181	.158	.189	65	226	30	41	16	2	3	22	30	4	0	2	89	1	0	.310	.286
Munroe, Reshard	L-L	6-0	170	6-15-96	.192	.120	.216	32	99	16	19	3	2	3	10	14	1	1	1	27	9	2	.354	.296
Piatnik, Mitch	R-R	6-0	170	9-12-94	.174	.053	.209	27	86	8	15	3	0	0	6	5	1	0	0	43	3	2	.209	.228
Sansone, John	R-R	5-11	200	9-15-93	.245	.245	.245	60	216	22	53	10	3	4	27	14	5	1	1	63	5	1	.375	.305
Santana, Leandro	R-R	6-2	200	2-19-97	.217	.188	.227	113	396	39	86	15	1	9	37	37	3	2	4	123	5	1	.328	.286
Scantlin, Nate	L-R	6-1	180	2-17-99	.100	.000	.111	3	10	1	1	0	0	0	0	0	0	0	0	4	0	0	.100	.182
Spooner, Mike	L-R	6-2	204	2-17-97	.091	—	.091	3	11	0	1	0	0	0	0	0	1	0	0	3	0	0	.091	.167
Sugilio, Andy	B-R	6-2	170	10-26-96	.278	.242	.290	91	363	34	101	14	4	5	45	17	1	1	5	61	12	7	.380	.308
Vargas, Hector	R-R	6-2	170	1-27-95	.150	.667	.059	6	20	1	3	0	0	0	1	0	0	0	3	0	0	.150	.150
Ventura, Randy	B-R	5-9	165	7-11-97	.188	.333	.130	7	32	0	6	0	0	0	2	0	0	0	8	5	1	.188	.188
Wallace, Raul	R-R	6-2	215	8-19-95	.254	.200	.266	43	134	18	34	4	1	4	15	5	0	1	2	59	4	3	.388	.277
Williams, J.D.	R-R	5-11	190	3-21-97	.255	.250	.257	46	145	29	37	4	3	0	15	20	4	2	3	36	8	4	.324	.355

Pitching	B-T	HT	WT	DOB	W	L	ERA	G	GS	CG	SV	IP	H	R	ER	HR	BB	SO	AVG	vLH	vRH	K/9	BB/9
Adams, Jesse	L-L	6-0	190	8-12-93	0	0	15.43	2	0	0	0	2	4	4	4	1	2	3	.400	.667	.286	11.57	7.71
Aguilar, Miguel	R-R	6-0	180	7-25-95	4	2	3.49	21	0	0	1	39	33	16	15	3	13	30	.234	.164	.279	6.98	3.03
Alecis, Luis	R-R	6-3	190	6-7-97	0	0	9.72	7	0	0	0	8	8	10	9	0	13	7	.250	.167	.357	7.56	14.04
Bautista, Wendolyn	R-R	6-0	185	3-27-93	5	6	3.75	35	11	0	2	110	122	55	46	10	29	114	.279	.300	.265	9.30	2.37
Bennett, Connor	R-R	5-9	190	4-10-97	1	1	5.27	8	0	0	0	14	16	8	8	2	6	14	.291	.313	.282	9.22	3.95
Buffett, Tyler	R-R	6-1	195	5-22-95	0	0	6.67	17	0	0	0	28	50	25	21	2	8	27	.391	.433	.353	8.58	2.54
Cox, Andy	R-L	6-2	185	10-23-93	1	2	7.43	13	1	0	1	16	16	13	11	2	6	12	.296	.105	.400	8.10	4.05
Ghyzel, John	R-R	6-5	200	5-18-96	3	7	4.40	42	0	0	19	45	42	23	22	3	31	58	.244	.263	.229	11.60	6.20
Greene, Hunter	R-R	6-4	215	8-6-99	3	7	4.48	18	18	0	0	68	66	35	34	6	23	89	.251	.298	.220	11.72	3.03
Hunter, Brian	R-R	6-3	215	11-22-92	1	0	1.98	8	0	0	1	14	16	4	3	0	4	16	.281	.308	.258	10.54	2.63
Jordan, Andrew	R-R	6-2	180	8-3-97	2	3	3.83	10	0	0	0	54	55	28	23	2	17	34	.264	.264	.265	5.67	2.83
McGuff, Patrick	L-R	6-2	200	3-30-94	2	5	4.09	11	10	0	0	51	51	26	23	3	19	35	.266	.282	.254	6.22	3.38
Mondile, Tyler	L-R	6-1	190	11-14-97	2	7	6.51	16	16	1	0	76	112	57	55	15	16	64	.344	.356	.333	7.58	1.89
Moreta, Dauri	R-R	6-2	185	4-15-96	3	2	7.25	28	0	0	1	45	49	40	36	2	18	58	.272	.309	.250	11.69	3.63
Naughton, Packy	R-L	6-2	195	4-16-96	5	10	4.03	28	28	0	0	154	168	73	69	12	34	137	.280	.295	.274	8.01	1.99
Nutof, Ryan	R-R	6-2	190	11-2-95	5	1	2.92	46	0	0	5	71	75	27	23	3	27	76	.277	.255	.290	9.63	3.42
Ohanian, Sarkis	R-R	5-11	195	8-6-93	2	1	9.00	11	0	0	2	12	14	16	12	2	10	15	.280	.462	.216	11.25	7.50
Orewiler, Austin	R-R	6-2	220	5-18-93	5	7	3.72	30	12	0	2	123	129	64	51	12	39	71	.269	.263	.272	5.18	2.85
Quillen, Aaron	R-R	6-6	205	12-19-93	0	0	3.95	7	0	0	0	14	16	6	6	2	3	7	.291	.240	.333	4.61	1.98
Rodriguez, Adrian	R-R	6-1	220	8-8-96	4	5	7.19	15	15	0	0	66	86	54	53	10	25	56	.314	.389	.265	7.60	3.39
Ryan, Connor	R-R	6-1	180	11-20-94	1	0	7.27	8	0	0	0	9	11	7	7	0	8	10	.290	.278	.300	10.38	8.31
Sceroler, Mac	R-R	6-3	200	4-9-95	2	6	6.00	11	11	0	0	54	63	42	36	6	24	47	.294	.263	.319	7.83	4.00
Solomon, Jared	R-R	6-2	180	6-10-97	0	1	5.40	6	6	0	0	25	32	19	15	1	18	13	.305	.320	.291	4.68	6.48
Thompson, Cory	R-R	5-11	180	9-23-94	6	6	3.25	46	0	0	5	72	76	31	26	6	13	67	.272	.318	.244	8.38	1.63
Wotell, Max	R-L	6-3	190	9-13-96	0	0	16.88	5	0	0	0	3	2	5	5	1	9	3	.200	.333	.143	10.13	30.38
Zabala, Aneurys	R-R	6-2	259	12-21-96	0	3	3.31	16	0	0	3	16	14	8	6	1	9	13	.222	.273	.195	7.16	4.96
2-team total (24 Great Lakes)					2	5	4.39	40	0	0	4	53	45	28	26	3	34	43	.228	.219	.234	7.26	5.74

Fielding

C: Clementina 64, Kolozsvary 74, Lofstrom 3. **1B:** Clementina 1, Lofstrom 6, Marshall 61, Munroe 9, Sansone 13, Santana 54. **2B:** Downs 73, Garcia 29, Lopez 19, Piatnik 1, Sansone 17, Vargas 2, Williams 7. **3B:** India 21, Lopez 46, Sansone 26, Santana 53, Vargas 1. **SS:** Downs 43, Garcia 93, India 4, Lopez 1. **OF:** Beltre 41, Cedrola 44, Collymore 13, Crook 19, Fairchild 61, Gordon 55, Munroe 22, Piatnik 24, Sansone 1, Scantlin 3, Spooner 3, Sugilio 82, Ventura 7, Wallace 41, Williams 9.

BILLINGS MUSTANGS   ROOKIE
PIONEER LEAGUE

Batting	B-T	HT	WT	DOB	AVG	vLH	vRH	G	AB	R	H	2B	3B	HR	RBI	BB	HBP	SH	SF	SO	SB	CS	SLG	OBP
Azcona, Francis	B-R	5-10	165	11-20-95	.162	.143	.167	15	37	5	6	2	0	0	2	7	0	3	0	11	0	1	.216	.296
Bautista, Mariel	R-R	6-3	170	10-15-97	.330	.250	.352	56	209	43	69	12	4	8	37	16	5	0	3	29	16	3	.541	.386
Boselli, Robert	R-R	6-4	240	4-17-96	.167	.000	.400	5	12	2	2	0	0	0	2	0	0	0	3	0	0	.167	.286
Case, Cash	L-R	6-1	190	5-12-99	.221	.313	.203	25	95	12	21	2	2	0	5	9	4	1	0	22	0	1	.284	.315
Conde, Mauro	R-R	6-0	205	6-1-97	.333	.000	.500	5	9	2	3	1	0	0	1	0	0	0	5	0	0	.444	.333
Harris, Dylan	R-R	5-11	195	1-27-95	.314	.255	.331	61	223	38	70	20	2	1	43	12	6	3	3	29	7	5	.435	.361
Hernandez, Miguel	R-R	6-0	170	4-13-99	.083	.000	.091	7	24	4	2	0	0	0	2	3	0	0	0	2	0	0	.083	.185

Batting	B-T	HT	WT	DOB	AVG	vLH	vRH	G	AB	R	H	2B	3B	HR	RBI	BB	HBP	SH	SF	SO	SB	CS	SLG	OBP
India, Jonathan	R-R	6-1	200	12-15-96	.250	1.000	.143	3	8	1	2	0	0	0	0	0	2	0	0	4	0	1	.250	.400
Juaquin, Urwin	R-R	6-0	170	12-29-97	.207	.200	.210	49	87	10	18	1	1	0	10	3	1	1	1	22	2	0	.241	.239
Ljatifi, Nadir	R-R	5-10	175	2-21-98	.183	.294	.140	21	60	12	11	4	0	0	6	7	1	0	0	9	1	1	.250	.279
Manzanero, Pabel	R-R	6-3	240	1-30-96	.291	.316	.284	66	251	31	73	13	0	9	44	8	1	0	3	55	0	0	.450	.312
Martinez, Juan	R-R	6-0	179	11-8-98	.274	.256	.280	47	164	22	45	6	1	8	33	12	1	1	3	39	0	1	.470	.322
Martinez, Valentin	R-R	6-0	175	9-21-96	.308	.455	.200	12	26	3	8	0	0	1	4	1	3	1	0	5	0	0	.423	.400
McElroy, Satchel	R-R	5-10	170	8-13-96	.222	.154	.240	21	63	12	14	0	0	0	3	3	0	1	0	19	2	1	.222	.258
Mount, Drew	L-R	5-11	205	3-24-96	.310	.321	.307	65	242	42	75	19	0	8	58	18	3	0	2	40	7	2	.488	.362
Munroe, Reshard	L-L	6-0	170	6-15-96	.313	.182	.351	28	99	13	31	5	0	3	12	6	0	0	0	26	6	7	.455	.387
Ozuna, Reniel	R-R	6-2	180	7-29-98	.158	.000	.177	7	19	3	3	0	0	0	3	0	4	0	1	6	1	0	.158	.292
Rivero, Carlos	L-R	6-0	175	4-30-97	.255	.188	.267	64	204	23	52	5	2	0	21	8	1	3	3	53	7	3	.299	.282
Ruiz, Victor	R-R	6-1	190	10-20-99	.278	.000	.333	8	18	2	5	0	0	0	3	1	0	0	0	5	0	0	.278	.316
Schuyler, Jay	R-R	6-2	190	4-11-97	.272	.243	.279	58	191	38	52	6	0	1	23	28	4	1	6	31	5	4	.319	.367
Seminati, Leonardo	R-R	6-2	210	1-2-99	.279	.333	.270	15	43	3	12	1	1	1	8	1	0	0	1	9	0	0	.419	.289
Spillane, Bren	R-R	6-4	210	9-21-96	.237	.097	.274	48	148	28	35	9	3	5	22	30	4	0	2	76	2	2	.439	.375
Spooner, Mike	L-R	6-3	204	2-17-97	.083	.091	.081	17	48	5	4	2	0	0	3	4	0	0	0	13	0	0	.125	.154
Stallings, Brandt	R-R	6-4	215	9-5-96	.211	.143	.226	12	38	3	8	2	0	0	1	0	1	0	0	9	1	0	.263	.231
Turnbull, Jake	L-R	6-1	190	2-16-98	.242	.214	.250	19	62	11	15	6	0	1	20	6	0	1	0	20	0	1	.387	.329
Wallace, Raul	R-R	6-2	215	8-19-95	.250	—	.250	1	4	1	1	0	0	0	0	0	0	0	0	2	0	0	.250	.250
White, Zeek	R-R	6-0	170	1-7-97	.236	.265	.228	45	157	32	37	10	3	3	17	17	5	1	1	57	10	2	.395	.328
Willems, Jonathan	R-R	5-11	180	11-7-98	.211	.750	.067	6	19	3	4	0	0	0	0	1	0	0	0	3	0	1	.211	.250

Pitching	B-T	HT	WT	DOB	W	L	ERA	G	GS	CG	SV	IP	H	R	ER	HR	BB	SO	AVG	vLH	vRH	K/9	BB/9
Alecis, Luis	R-R	6-3	190	6-7-97	3	4	4.42	14	14	0	0	59	49	35	29	2	31	67	.227	.235	.221	10.22	4.73
Bennett, Connor	R-R	5-9	190	4-10-97	0	0	0.00	1	0	0	0	2	0	0	0	2	3	.000	.000	.000	13.50	9.00
Campbell, Ryan	R-R	6-3	220	1-11-96	3	3	3.65	23	1	0	1	37	28	16	15	3	10	34	.203	.205	.202	8.27	2.43
Castillo, Jose	R-R	6-4	190	6-10-96	0	0	6.14	4	0	0	0	7	10	9	5	2	3	8	.303	.364	.273	9.82	3.68
Cox, Andy	R-L	6-2	185	10-23-93	0	1	1.35	6	0	0	0	7	5	3	1	0	5	8	.200	.000	.263	10.80	6.75
Curlis, Connor	L-L	6-0	180	11-29-96	3	0	4.56	16	1	0	0	26	23	16	13	1	10	33	.223	.323	.181	11.57	3.51
Demurias, Eddy	R-R	6-0	184	8-1-97	1	5	4.97	20	0	0	3	29	33	22	16	2	10	25	.306	.290	.312	7.76	3.10
Dunne, Ryan	L-R	6-3	220	3-17-95	2	0	2.66	16	0	0	5	24	14	8	7	0	9	26	.175	.208	.161	9.89	3.42
Escoboza, Edward	R-R	6-5	185	12-5-95	3	0	5.55	21	0	0	1	36	43	26	22	6	8	35	.289	.348	.262	8.83	2.02
Kivel, Jeremy	R-R	6-1	200	10-16-93	1	1	1.74	10	0	0	0	10	8	2	2	0	3	15	.216	.214	.217	13.06	2.61
Machorro, Carlos	R-R	6-2	175	9-20-96	1	0	2.45	3	0	0	0	4	7	1	1	4	6	.389	.500	.357	14.73	9.82
Marinan, James	R-R	6-5	220	10-10-98	3	2	3.98	11	11	0	0	43	49	23	19	1	19	39	.287	.370	.256	8.16	3.98
McDonald, Andrew	R-R	6-6	225	12-24-94	3	2	4.46	22	0	0	2	38	34	24	19	2	18	43	.235	.255	.223	10.10	4.23
McGregor, Justin	R-R	6-1	185	12-13-95	1	0	4.50	4	1	0	0	8	7	4	4	1	3	10	.226	.200	.235	11.25	3.38
Moreta, Dauri	R-R	6-2	185	4-15-96	1	1	4.91	11	0	0	3	11	10	6	6	1	9	21	.222	.200	.233	17.18	7.36
Nova, Moises	R-R	6-3	190	8-2-95	0	1	6.55	9	0	0	0	11	14	8	8	1	9	13	.318	.333	.310	10.64	7.36
Pidich, Matt	R-R	6-2	220	12-25-94	1	2	5.28	19	1	0	0	31	30	22	18	3	9	34	.244	.192	.276	9.98	2.64
Rodriguez, Adrian	R-R	6-1	200	8-8-96	1	2	3.66	6	0	0	0	32	35	19	13	4	5	27	.273	.296	.257	7.59	1.41
Ryan, Connor	R-R	6-1	180	11-20-94	0	0	4.45	20	0	0	0	28	25	16	14	1	14	20	.234	.259	.225	6.35	4.45
Salinas, Ricky	R-R	6-2	220	3-26-96	2	2	4.53	14	14	0	0	56	64	32	28	9	15	59	.281	.282	.280	9.54	2.43
Sceroler, Mac	R-R	6-3	200	4-9-95	2	2	3.07	7	7	0	0	29	31	19	10	4	6	34	.256	.273	.247	10.43	1.84
Smith, Ricardo	R-R	6-2	175	2-16-96	3	5	5.64	15	11	0	0	59	79	46	37	3	14	49	.316	.321	.314	7.47	2.14
Solomon, Jared	R-R	6-2	180	6-10-97	4	2	2.27	9	0	0	0	48	32	13	12	4	14	54	.187	.177	.194	10.20	2.64
Stallings, Jesse	R-R	6-2	198	10-21-94	1	0	0.00	3	0	0	2	4	2	0	0	0	3	.143	.200	.111	6.75	2.25
Wyrick, Jake	L-L	6-0	195	11-14-95	1	1	6.20	14	0	0	0	25	25	19	17	3	10	29	.260	.406	.180	10.58	3.65

Fielding

C: Boselli 5, Manzanero 29, Martinez 5, Ruiz 5, Schuyler 39. **1B:** Case 1, Harris 6, Manzanero 27, Martinez 2, Martinez 3, Schuyler 10, Seminati 14, Spillane 15, Spooner 1, Turnbull 10. **2B:** Azcona 10, Case 17, Harris 35, Hernandez 5, Juaquin 22, Ljatifi 5, Rivero 2. **3B:** Azcona 3, Harris 1, Juaquin 7, Ljatifi 16, Manzanero 1, Martinez 45, Turnbull 8, Willems 6. **SS:** Azcona 1, Hernandez 4, India 3, Juaquin 20, Rivero 62. **OF:** Bautista 46, Conde 5, Harris 1, McElroy 20, Mount 59, Munroe 22, Ozuna 7, Schuyler 4, Spillane 25, Spooner 12, Stallings 9, Wallace 1, White 36.

GREENEVILLE REDS

APPALACHIAN LEAGUE

ROOKIE

Batting	B-T	HT	WT	DOB	AVG	vLH	vRH	G	AB	R	H	2B	3B	HR	RBI	BB	HBP	SH	SF	SO	SB	CS	SLG	OBP
Bellinger, Justin	L-L	6-6	245	8-18-95	.209	.000	.231	35	115	11	24	8	0	3	18	11	1	0	0	42	0	0	.357	.284
Boselli, Robert	R-R	6-4	240	4-17-96	.225	.333	.196	24	71	10	16	3	0	2	9	12	2	0	0	27	0	0	.352	.353
Case, Cash	L-R	6-1	190	5-12-99	.314	.600	.283	12	51	8	16	2	2	1	12	3	1	0	0	13	0	0	.490	.364
Conde, Mauro	R-R	6-0	205	6-1-97	.000	—	.000	1	1	0	0	0	0	0	0	0	0	0	0	1	0	0	.000	.000
Finol, Claudio	R-R	5-11	150	4-13-00	.294	.206	.315	49	177	26	52	7	0	0	16	9	2	1	3	32	1	1	.333	.330
Hernandez, Miguel	R-R	6-0	170	4-13-98	.301	.474	.265	60	219	29	66	11	3	2	29	13	0	1	2	37	2	1	.406	.338
India, Jonathan	R-R	6-1	200	12-15-96	.261	.357	.219	14	46	11	12	2	1	3	12	15	1	0	0	12	1	0	.544	.452
Juarez, Raul	R-R	6-1	165	5-21-98	.208	.177	.214	32	101	12	21	4	0	2	13	5	3	2	1	26	0	0	.307	.264
Liberatore, Ernesto	R-R	6-0	180	3-26-96	.333	—	.333	2	6	2	2	0	0	1	2	0	0	1	0	1	0	0	.833	.286
Martinez, Juan	R-R	6-0	179	11-8-98	.240	1.000	.200	9	25	9	6	4	0	0	1	8	1	1	0	5	0	0	.400	.441
Martinez, Valentin	R-R	6-0	175	9-21-96	.000	.000	.000	1	2	0	0	0	0	0	0	0	0	0	0	1	0	0	.000	.000
McElroy, Satchel	R-R	5-10	170	8-13-96	.071	.000	.095	14	28	5	2	1	0	0	0	6	0	0	0	11	0	0	.107	.235
Oliver, Hunter	R-R	6-1	190	11-20-97	.256	.138	.292	38	125	27	32	5	0	6	20	7	3	2	0	39	0	2	.440	.307
Ozuna, Reniel	R-R	6-2	180	7-29-98	.252	.270	.249	60	218	27	55	7	1	2	27	31	0	0	2	63	2	5	.321	.343
Rey, Brian	R-R	5-11	170	2-22-98	.269	.200	.287	49	171	27	46	7	0	2	21	12	9	0	1	14	3	1	.345	.347
Ruiz, Victor	R-R	6-1	190	10-20-99	.174	.333	.150	6	23	0	4	0	0	0	4	0	0	0	1	8	0	0	.174	.167
Scantlin, Nate	L-R	6-1	180	2-17-99	.241	.125	.248	48	137	25	33	6	2	0	14	23	1	0	1	35	3	2	.314	.352

Player	B-T	HT	WT	DOB	AVG	vLH	vRH	G	AB	R	H	2B	3B	HR	RBI	BB	HBP	SH	SF	SO	SB	CS	SLG	OBP
Siani, Mike	L-L	6-1	180	7-16-99	.288	.214	.301	46	184	24	53	6	3	2	13	16	3	0	2	35	6	4	.386	.351
Stallings, Brandt	R-R	6-4	215	9-5-96	.160	.154	.162	20	50	12	8	0	0	2	6	2	0	0	1	24	1	0	.280	.189
Tello, Jose	R-R	6-0	170	5-21-98	.245	.375	.220	20	49	3	12	1	0	0	6	4	2	1	1	15	1	1	.265	.321
Thomas, Rylan	R-R	5-11	235	6-25-97	.257	.171	.278	55	179	34	46	12	0	10	33	41	3	0	2	49	0	2	.492	.400
White, Zeek	R-R	6-0	170	1-7-97	.438	.333	.462	9	32	10	14	0	0	2	5	4	1	1	0	6	3	0	.625	.514
Willems, Jonathan	R-R	5-11	180	11-7-98	.263	.286	.258	55	217	30	57	13	4	8	39	7	5	1	1	54	0	2	.470	.300
Yon, Edwin	R-R	6-5	180	7-24-98	.263	.308	.250	18	57	8	15	2	1	4	11	5	1	0	0	21	1	0	.544	.333

Pitching	B-T	HT	WT	DOB	W	L	ERA	G	GS	CG	SV	IP	H	R	ER	HR	BB	SO	AVG	vLH	vRH	K/9	BB/9
Bennett, Connor	R-R	5-9	190	4-10-97	3	0	0.86	15	0	0	6	21	10	3	2	0	6	28	.139	.286	.078	12.00	2.57
Bono, Michael	R-R	6-1	177	11-3-96	0	0	16.62	6	0	0	0	4	2	9	8	0	13	3	.143	.000	.200	6.23	27.00
Cachutt, Manuel	R-R	6-0	185	6-7-97	2	1	4.15	16	0	0	1	30	39	19	14	1	15	15	.305	.319	.296	4.45	4.45
D'Andrea, Jerry	L-L	6-2	192	5-23-96	2	3	3.20	16	0	0	2	20	11	12	7	0	14	27	.159	.130	.174	12.36	6.41
De La Fuente, Daniel	R-R	6-2	210	7-18-97	0	1	4.32	4	2	0	0	17	14	15	8	0	8	12	.222	.182	.244	6.48	4.32
Diaz, Alexis	R-R	6-2	170	9-26-96	3	3	3.02	11	9	0	0	54	51	22	18	6	18	67	.244	.256	.236	11.24	3.02
German, Uarlim	R-R	6-5	215	8-2-96	0	0	15.19	4	0	0	0	5	10	9	9	3	7	3	.417	.500	.333	5.06	11.81
Gray, Josiah	R-R	6-1	190	12-21-97	2	2	2.58	12	12	0	0	52	29	17	15	1	17	59	.155	.134	.171	10.15	2.92
Heatherly, Jacob	L-L	6-2	208	5-20-98	1	5	5.82	11	11	0	0	39	34	25	25	3	40	49	.241	.372	.184	11.41	9.31
Heitler, Cory	R-R	6-2	210	8-27-97	2	0	2.50	14	0	0	1	18	18	7	5	1	3	19	.257	.207	.293	9.50	1.50
Jones, Francis	R-R	6-3	200	12-6-96	2	2	6.92	13	0	0	0	39	43	32	30	5	15	43	.272	.239	.297	9.92	3.46
Karcher, Ricky	L-R	6-4	195	9-18-97	0	3	8.33	10	0	0	0	31	46	35	29	3	27	22	.349	.178	.430	6.32	7.76
Keller, Stephen	B-R	6-2	210	11-19-97	1	1	9.42	9	0	0	1	14	23	16	15	0	13	11	.371	.304	.410	6.91	8.16
Knowles, Perez	R-L	6-0	205	7-6-95	0	0	5.73	6	0	0	0	11	10	10	7	0	11	14	.222	.154	.250	11.45	9.00
Koch, Ian	R-R	6-4	220	8-18-97	0	0	1.17	6	0	0	0	8	6	2	1	0	4	8	.214	.111	.263	9.39	4.70
McGregor, Justin	R-R	6-1	185	12-13-95	1	1	8.62	9	0	0	0	16	22	18	15	3	9	15	.328	.387	.278	8.62	5.17
Medrano, Miguel	R-R	6-0	165	1-4-98	2	4	5.50	12	12	0	0	54	75	40	33	8	17	55	.328	.330	.326	9.17	2.83
Moore, A.J.	R-R	6-3	205	1-4-96	2	1	5.72	12	1	0	0	28	31	22	18	2	13	26	.272	.364	.214	8.26	4.13
Norman, Doug	R-R	6-3	208	10-20-95	0	1	9.53	6	0	0	0	6	7	7	6	2	5	4	.292	.600	.211	6.35	7.94
Nova, Moises	R-R	6-3	190	8-2-95	1	1	5.59	9	0	0	0	10	9	7	6	1	5	10	.237	.385	.160	9.31	4.66
Olson, Ryan	R-R	6-2	195	11-22-94	0	0	11.57	2	0	0	0	2	6	4	3	0	0	4	.500	.750	.000	15.43	0.00
Quillen, Aaron	R-R	6-6	205	12-19-93	0	2	3.52	5	0	0	0	8	8	3	3	1	1	12	.267	.125	.318	14.09	1.17
Rich, Josh	R-R	6-1	205	2-26-96	0	1	9.95	14	0	0	0	19	24	25	21	0	23	10	.304	.290	.313	4.74	10.89
Richardson, Lyon	B-R	6-2	175	1-18-00	0	5	7.14	11	11	0	0	29	37	27	23	3	16	24	.308	.354	.278	7.45	4.97
Salazar, Eduardo	R-R	6-2	165	5-9-95	2	0	6.57	4	0	0	0	12	10	9	9	2	6	11	.217	.059	.310	8.03	4.38
Schneider, Johnnie	R-R	6-5	180	6-30-97	2	4	5.61	15	0	0	1	26	31	19	16	3	13	15	.293	.283	.300	5.26	4.56
Wotell, Max	R-L	6-3	190	9-13-96	0	0	8.22	4	0	0	0	8	13	9	7	1	8	8	.382	.300	.417	9.39	9.39

Fielding

C: Boselli 21, Liberatore 2, Martinez 1, Oliver 33, Ruiz 6, Tello 15. 1B: Bellinger 16, Juarez 13, Thomas 44. 2B: Case 6, Finol 17, Rey 2, Willems 47. 3B: Finol 22, India 12, Juarez 14, Martinez 7, Thomas 10, Willems 5. SS: Finol 10, Hernandez 58, India 2, Juarez 1, Willems 1. OF: Conde 1, McElroy 11, Ozuna 51, Rey 42, Scantlin 31, Siani 45, Stallings 13, White 9, Yon 11.

AZL REDS
ARIZONA LEAGUE
ROOKIE

Batting	B-T	HT	WT	DOB	AVG	vLH	vRH	G	AB	R	H	2B	3B	HR	RBI	BB	HBP	SH	SF	SO	SB	CS	SLG	OBP
Amador, Ranser	R-R	6-2	165	3-15-99	.224	.067	.257	28	85	8	19	2	1	0	9	5	1	0	0	29	7	2	.271	.275
Castro, Fidel	L-R	6-3	175	12-26-98	.315	.100	.364	17	54	9	17	4	2	1	5	8	1	0	0	23	2	1	.519	.413
Franco, Rafael	R-R	6-0	155	6-20-01	.256	.417	.229	33	82	10	21	5	0	0	3	8	4	0	0	25	6	1	.317	.351
Gomez, Elvis	R-R	6-0	170	5-27-99	.179	.231	.163	21	56	5	10	1	0	0	3	1	2	1	0	8	0	1	.196	.220
Guzman, Edward	R-R	6-1	195	9-30-99	.184	.333	.138	15	38	5	7	1	1	0	3	7	2	0	2	21	2	0	.263	.327
Lantigua, Danny	B-R	6-1	175	3-7-99	.223	.189	.236	52	197	26	44	12	6	8	37	13	2	0	3	75	5	4	.467	.274
Lopez, Luis	R-R	5-11	165	11-30-99	.226	.364	.177	29	84	14	19	2	0	1	7	2	2	1	2	24	4	0	.286	.305
McElroy, C.J.	R-R	5-10	180	5-29-93	.167	.000	.333	2	6	0	1	1	0	0	1	0	0	0	0	0	0	0	.333	.167
Olivo, Cristian	L-L	6-2	190	9-30-99	.157	.094	.176	38	140	14	22	3	3	2	11	4	1	0	0	61	4	0	.264	.186
Plaz, Peterson	L-L	5-10	155	3-6-99	.320	.250	.342	34	103	12	33	3	0	0	4	9	2	1	0	3	3		.350	.386
Reina, Carlos	B-R	6-0	175	12-11-98	.220	.375	.182	26	82	14	18	4	2	1	11	10	3	0	1	18	3	0	.390	.323
Remy, Danielito	B-R	6-1	170	5-5-98	.295	.256	.308	40	156	19	46	11	0	1	14	6	2	0	0	38	11	1	.385	.329
Reyes, Reyny	R-R	6-2	185	3-20-99	.223	.325	.282	43	157	21	46	5	0	2	14	8	1	1	0	37	5	2	.363	.331
Rodriguez, Alfredo	R-R	6-0	170	6-17-94	.250	.000	.278	6	20	3	5	3	0	0	3	1	0	0	0	3	0	0	.400	.286
Ruiz, Victor	R-R	6-1	190	10-20-99	.303	.546	.262	22	76	12	23	4	0	1	4	1	0	0	0	15	0	0	.434	.346
Santana, Debby	R-R	6-2	185	8-24-98	.250	.289	.238	50	188	23	47	7	4	6	25	10	2	0	0	44	0	0	.426	.295
Seminati, Leonardo	R-R	6-2	210	1-2-99	.240	.238	.240	27	96	12	23	1	0	3	10	6	2	0	0	29	0	0	.344	.298
Silverio, Isaias	R-R	6-2	185	2-18-00	.165	.160	.167	27	79	5	13	7	0	1	11	3	2	0	2	34	1	0	.291	.209
Taylor, Logan	R-R	5-9	175	6-21-94	.143	—	.143	3	7	3	1	0	0	0	0	3	0	0	0	3	1	0	.143	.400
Tello, Jose	R-R	6-0	170	5-21-98	.296	.143	.350	7	27	5	8	4	0	1	4	0	0	1	0	6	0	0	.556	.296
Turner, Stuart	R-R	6-2	220	12-27-91	.269	.143	.316	18	26	7	7	2	0	0	5	6	0	0	1	2	0	0	.346	.394
Yon, Edwin	R-R	6-5	180	7-24-98	.227	.192	.242	25	88	12	20	6	2	0	9	11	0	0	0	36	2	1	.341	.313

Pitching	B-T	HT	WT	DOB	W	L	ERA	G	GS	CG	SV	IP	H	R	ER	HR	BB	SO	AVG	vLH	vRH	K/9	BB/9
Abril, Juan Manuel	R-R	6-0	160	3-11-98	2	2	3.94	14	0	0	1	30	23	18	13	1	11	41	.213	.235	.203	12.44	3.34
Aranguren, Frainger	R-R	6-2	190	3-17-97	4	1	4.01	16	0	0	1	34	31	18	15	2	9	29	.250	.170	.299	7.75	2.41
Carreno, Carlos	R-R	6-2	174	9-4-98	2	6	6.75	10	10	0	0	32	38	28	24	2	16	30	.292	.359	.247	8.44	4.50
Conoropo, Omar	B-L	5-10	165	5-29-01	1	3	4.91	17	4	0	0	40	46	26	22	4	9	40	.284	.296	.280	8.93	2.01
Davis, Rookie	R-R	6-5	255	4-29-93	0	0	6.75	2	2	0	0	6	9	7	5	1	2	10	.321	.750	.150	13.50	2.70
De La Fuente, Daniel	R-R	6-2	210	7-18-97	0	5	3.00	10	5	0	0	39	28	21	13	0	21	32	.200	.205	.198	7.38	4.85

Name	B-T	HT	WT	DOB	W	L	ERA	G	GS	CG	SV	IP	H	R	ER	HR	BB	SO	AVG	vLH	vRH	K/9	BB/9
German, Uarlim	R-R	6-5	215	8-2-96	0	2	5.02	11	0	0	1	14	17	10	8	0	13	11	.293	.269	.313	6.91	8.16
Gonzalez, Alberto	R-R	6-1	180	7-26-99	1	2	4.76	15	0	0	1	23	23	13	12	0	15	24	.264	.241	.276	9.53	5.96
Hanson, Nick	R-R	6-5	205	6-10-98	0	1	4.50	3	3	0	0	4	3	2	2	0	1	2	.214	.333	.125	4.50	2.25
Machorro, Carlos	R-R	6-2	175	9-20-96	0	0	0.00	3	1	0	0	4	1	0	0	0	0	6	.077	.000	.167	13.50	0.00
Mallen, Jorge	R-R	6-0	160	4-5-98	1	0	17.36	4	0	0	0	5	8	9	9	0	6	4	.381	.500	.273	7.71	11.57
Mateo, Marvin	R-R	6-3	170	1-8-98	0	2	1.96	17	0	0	2	18	13	8	4	1	7	14	.186	.172	.195	6.87	3.44
Maysonet, Yomil	R-R	6-1	180	1-9-00	0	1	15.19	4	2	0	0	5	14	11	9	0	4	5	.452	.462	.444	8.44	6.75
Mojica, Ariel	R-R	6-2	185	9-20-98	0	1	4.67	10	0	0	1	17	21	12	9	0	7	15	.300	.385	.250	7.79	3.63
Mota, Reinaldo	R-R	6-2	165	11-14-98	0	0	8.72	14	0	0	0	22	33	23	21	1	14	12	.363	.357	.367	4.98	5.82
Nino, Jeffry	R-R	6-4	170	9-26-96	1	2	5.19	16	0	0	0	26	31	17	15	0	12	20	.301	.267	.328	6.92	4.15
Noriega, Orlando	R-R	6-0	175	5-15-99	0	5	5.09	14	12	0	0	53	59	43	30	4	24	48	.278	.330	.242	8.15	4.08
Peguero, Francis	R-R	6-1	185	8-11-97	0	1	6.04	13	0	0	1	22	33	19	15	1	6	13	.337	.350	.328	5.24	2.42
Rijo, Oliver	R-R	6-2	180	1-11-98	0	2	12.71	6	2	0	0	6	12	16	8	0	10	7	.375	.500	.333	11.12	6.58
Salazar, Eduardo	R-R	6-2	165	5-5-98	0	1	5.29	7	6	0	0	17	17	12	10	3	6	15	.243	.143	.286	7.94	3.18
Severino, Moises	R-R	5-11	185	9-20-97	0	0	9.00	5	0	0	0	5	6	6	5	0	9	4	.300	.375	.250	7.20	16.20
Sparles, Luis	R-R	6-3	170	5-1-97	0	0	4.50	10	0	0	0	14	13	10	7	1	11	14	.236	.304	.188	9.00	7.07
Stallings, Jesse	R-R	6-2	198	10-27-94	0	0	9.00	2	2	0	0	2	3	2	2	1	2	1	.375	.500	.000	4.50	9.00
Valenzuela, Jose	R-R	6-1	190	5-5-98	1	1	8.18	7	2	0	0	11	14	11	10	1	4	9	.311	.316	.308	7.36	3.27
Weiss, Zack	R-R	6-3	210	6-16-92	0	1	4.26	5	1	0	0	6	6	4	3	0	1	6	.240	.385	.083	8.53	1.42
Wooten, Rob	R-R	6-1	200	7-21-85	0	3	8.16	7	3	0	0	14	24	16	13	1	1	15	.343	.522	.255	9.42	0.63

Fielding

C: Gomez 15, Guzman 11, Reina 19, Ruiz 12, Tello 1, Turner 4. **1B:** Gomez 5, Reyes 5, Santana 3, Seminati 25, Silverio 15, Tello 6. **2B:** Amador 1, Lopez 8, Remy 37, Reyes 12. **3B:** Reyes 11, Santana 43, Seminati 2. **SS:** Amador 27, Lopez 18, Reyes 12, Rodriguez 3. **OF:** Castro 17, Franco 29, Lantigua 47, McElroy 1, Olivo 27, Plaz 30, Silverio 3, Taylor 1, Yon 22.

DSL REDS
ROOKIE
DOMINICAN SUMMER LEAGUE

Batting	B-T	HT	WT	DOB	AVG	vLH	vRH	G	AB	R	H	2B	3B	HR	RBI	BB	HBP	SH	SF	SO	SB	CS	SLG	OBP
Acosta, Jose	B-R	5-10	170	3-20-00	.199	.111	.211	39	141	20	28	3	3	1	15	24	2	0	1	29	12	3	.284	.321
Aleixo, Axel	L-L	6-1	172	9-11-99	.292	.375	.284	42	171	27	50	6	0	2	21	14	0	1		21	11	9	.363	.344
Almonte, Sebastian	R-R	6-0	185	10-22-99	.201	.304	.186	47	179	21	36	9	2	1	8	10	3	0	0	58	8	2	.291	.255
Amador, Ranser	R-R	6-2	165	3-15-99	.259	.286	.254	19	81	10	21	1	0	1	4	2	1	0	1	20	10	3	.309	.282
Castro, Fidel	L-R	6-3	175	12-26-98	.262	.177	.276	35	122	21	32	10	6	3	22	25	4	0	0	42	2	2	.516	.404
Cerda, Allan	R-R	6-3	170	11-24-99	.272	.333	.265	51	173	35	47	11	0	6	34	25	14	0	2	45	3	2	.439	.402
Colmenarez, Samuel	B-R	5-10	160	7-23-99	.213	.083	.226	42	127	15	27	2	1	1	7	16	2	0	1	40	7	4	.268	.308
Garcia, Emilio	R-R	6-2	200	6-15-99	.205	.250	.196	47	171	18	35	7	1	0	11	20	6	0	0	60	1	1	.257	.310
Guzman, Darlin	L-L	6-1	165	9-27-00	.252	.167	.261	49	171	22	43	8	7	4	28	20	0	0	2	52	4	6	.450	.326
Jimenez, Fraudys	L-R	5-11	175	5-24-99	.289	.250	.295	37	121	19	35	2	3	0	12	6	2	1	0	16	10	4	.355	.381
Lozano, Deybert	L-R	6-1	165	11-15-99	.179	.235	.169	36	106	14	19	2	1	1	5	3	1	1	3	31	3	1	.245	.235
Melo, Junior	R-R	6-2	175	5-10-97	.237	.263	.232	36	114	15	27	5	1	1	11	6	2	0	2	16	3	0	.325	.282
Palacios, Aiverson	B-R	6-0	150	4-13-00	.174	.077	.188	35	98	16	17	0	2	0	5	18	4	4	1	50	10	2	.214	.322
Sencion, Jorge	R-R	6-4	194	10-3-98	.200	.167	.204	32	115	19	23	7	2	1	11	2	6	0	0	58	1	2	.348	.252
Sequera, Jorge	R-R	6-0	175	3-20-99	.219	.500	.196	34	105	16	23	5	0	0	11	23	2	0	1	12	7	4	.267	.366
Soto, Ronard	R-R	6-2	185	5-18-99	.167	.000	.191	22	72	11	12	2	0	1	4	8	5	0	0	17	2	2	.236	.294
Tejada, Luis	R-R	6-0	160	9-3-99	.282	.333	.276	41	149	29	42	3	1	2	16	16	10	0	0	41	6	2	.389	.389
Vellojin, Daniel	B-R	5-11	160	3-15-00	.199	.136	.211	38	131	20	26	4	2	2	21	26	2	0	1	30	3	2	.305	.338

Pitching	B-T	HT	WT	DOB	W	L	ERA	G	GS	CG	SV	IP	H	R	ER	HR	BB	SO	AVG	vLH	vRH	K/9	BB/9
Beltre, Allan	R-R	6-4	195	9-12-99	3	3	4.17	15	13	0	0	50	57	35	23	0	14	35	.282	.265	.288	6.34	2.54
Capellan, Jairo	R-R	6-8	190	8-17-99	2	3	6.25	18	0	0	0	32	26	26	22	2	26	39	.228	.267	.214	11.08	7.39
Castillo, Zamil	L-L	5-10	160	10-17-99	3	1	5.93	16	0	0	1	27	20	24	18	1	28	38	.194	.091	.207	12.51	9.22
Cuevas, Andry	R-R	6-0	185	8-4-98	2	2	5.00	19	0	0	3	27	16	18	15	0	26	31	.182	.208	.172	10.33	8.67
Diaz, Yoel	R-R	6-1	190	1-9-99	3	1	2.76	17	0	0	4	29	20	12	9	1	9	35	.194	.149		10.74	2.76
Falcon, Andres	R-R	6-3	165	10-22-97	3	2	3.03	15	3	0	1	36	38	21	12	0	19	41	.259	.225	.271	10.35	4.79
Hernandez, Raul	R-R	6-3	190	2-2-99	2	4	2.29	14	13	0	0	51	36	23	13	1	22	77	.196	.209	.192	13.59	3.88
Lantigua, Israel	R-R	6-3	190	2-9-99	0	1	4.45	18	0	0	3	28	19	19	14	2	20	26	.192	.233	.174	8.26	6.35
Lar, Miguel	R-R	6-1	170	10-3-99	3	2	3.04	18	0	0	1	44	44	23	16	1	22	43	.254	.204	.277	8.18	4.18
Manuel, Maiker	R-R	6-2	175	7-29-98	1	6	4.32	14	7	0	0	50	43	28	24	3	24	48	.226	.216	.230	8.64	4.32
Moreno, Pedro	R-R	6-5	200	3-8-98	6	4	4.85	14	13	0	0	56	60	42	30	2	24	53	.273	.231	.290	8.57	3.88
Ortega, Jose	R-R	6-3	190	11-8-99	1	1	2.77	8	4	0	0	13	11	8	4	1	8	8	.244	.000	.333	5.54	5.54
Peguero, Francis	R-R	6-1	185	8-11-97	0	0	7.11	3	0	0	0	6	11	7	5	0	4	5	.379	1.000	.280	7.11	5.68
Peralta, Jose	R-R	6-1	170	10-2-99	4	2	2.12	16	6	0	0	47	42	20	11	3	12	31	.231	.192	.244	5.98	2.31
Salvador, Jose	L-L	6-1	170	9-21-99	3	0	1.18	14	12	0	0	53	28	8	7	0	20	72	.155	.150	.155	12.15	3.38
Santos, Carlos	R-R	6-1	180	7-12-98	1	1	5.40	12	0	0	1	20	18	14	12	0	22	17	.257	.333	.231	7.65	9.90
Tavarez, Dannysmel	R-R	6-3	190	3-10-98	2	2	7.71	14	0	0	0	23	28	25	20	1	27	19	.308	.240	.333	7.33	10.41
Zorrilla, Jose	L-R	6-1	180	10-2-98	1	1	2.08	14	1	0	2	22	16	9	5	1	7	32	.203	.240	.185	13.29	2.91

Fielding

C: Melo 22, Sequera 18, Vellojin 36. **1B:** Acosta 1, Melo 12, Sencion 27, Sequera 14, Soto 21. **2B:** Acosta 18, Almonte 2, Colmenarez 8, Jimenez 28, Palacios 15, Tejada 7. **3B:** Almonte 38, Colmenarez 2, Jimenez 4, Soto 1, Tejada 30. **SS:** Almonte 5, Amador 18, Colmenarez 30, Jimenez 2, Palacios 18, Tejada 2. **OF:** Aleixo 36, Castro 35, Cerda 49, Garcia 33, Guzman 38, Lozano 32, Sencion 3.

Cleveland Indians

SEASON IN A SENTENCE: After an excellent season fueled by two of the game's best infielders, one of its preeminent aces and a universally respected manager, the Indians rolled to another AL Central crown but were roughed up by the Astros in the first round of the playoffs.

HIGH POINT: With a core that included finalists for the AL Cy Young (Corey Kluber) and AL MVP (Jose Ramirez) awards, as well as superstar shortstop Francisco Lindor and burgeoning ace Trevor Bauer, the Indians won their third straight division title.

LOW POINT: After spending the regular season coasting to the AL Central title, the Indians were summarily swept out of the playoffs by the Astros and managed just six runs in three games. Because of the way the 2017 Division Series unfolded against the Yankees, the Indians ran their postseason losing streak to six consecutive games.

NOTABLE ROOKIES: Control artist Shane Bieber got his chance in the rotation and held his own, working to an 11-5, 4.55 mark over 19 starts. He racked up 9.3 strikeouts per nine innings against just 1.8 walks but was hamstrung by more than 10 hits per nine innings. His 118 strikeouts were second to Tampa Bay's Ryan Yarbrough among AL rookies. Outfielder Greg Allen and utility infielder Erik Gonzalez also saw significant time and made modest contributions.

KEY TRANSACTIONS: The Indians struck early on the trade market to strengthen their bullpen by adding Padres relievers Brad Hand and Adam Cimber in exchange for top catching prospect Francisco Mejia. They made another big move toward the end of August when they pried former AL MVP Josh Donaldson from the Blue Jays in exchange for a player to be named later.

DOWN ON THE FARM: After a bit of forearm tightness that kept him out for a portion of the early season, righthander Triston McKenzie made his upper-level debut and established himself as the organization's clear No. 1 prospect. Shortstop Tyler Freeman, the team's supplemental second-round selection in 2017, led the New York-Penn League in average (.352), slugging (.511), runs (49), hits (95) and doubles (29). Another shortstop, 17-year-old Brayan Rocchio, turned heads in the Rookie-level Arizona League and was named as the league's top prospect. The Indians also landed the No. 2 prospect in the AZL with their acquisition of Jhon Torres from the Cardinals.

OPENING DAY PAYROLL: $136,652,167 (15th).

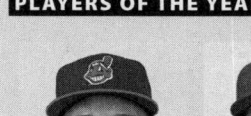

PLAYERS OF THE YEAR

ALEX TRAUTWIG

MAJOR LEAGUE	MINOR LEAGUE
Jose Ramirez	**Tyler Freeman**
3B	SS
.270/.387/.552	(Short-season)
Led Indians in HR (39)	.352/.405/.511
OPS (.939) and SB (34)	95 H, 29 2B in 72 G

ORGANIZATION LEADERS

Batting		*Minimum 250 AB
MAJORS		
* AVG	Michael Brantley	.309
* OPS	Jose Ramirez	.939
HR	Jose Ramirez	39
RBI	Edwin Encarnacion	107
MINORS		
* AVG	Tyler Freeman, Mahoning Valley	.352
* OBP	Yandy Diaz, Columbus	.409
* SLG	Tyler Freeman, Mahoning Valley	.511
* OPS	Tyler Freeman, Mahoning Valley	.916
R	Andrew Calica, Akron	78
H	Brandon Barnes, Columbus	136
TB	Bobby Bradley, Akron, Columbus	225
2B	Brandon Barnes, Columbus	39
3B	Bobby Bradley, Akron, Columbus	5
3B	Sam Haggerty, Akron, Columbus	5
3B	Connor Marabell, Akron, Columbus	5
3B	Mitch Longo, Lynchburg	5
HR	Bobby Bradley, Akron, Columbus	27
RBI	Bobby Bradley, Akron, Columbus	83
BB	Nolan Jones, Lake County, Lynchburg	89
SO	Brandon Barnes, Columbus	152
SO	Will Benson, Lake County	152
SB	Todd Isaacs, Lake County	30

Pitching		#Minimum 75 IP
MAJORS		
W	Corey Kluber	20
# ERA	Trevor Bauer	2.21
SO	Carlos Carrasco	231
SV	Cody Allen	27
MINORS		
W	Zach Plesac, Lynchburg, Akron	11
L	Juan Hillman, Lake County	12
# ERA	Zack Draper, Lake County, Mahoning Valley	3.1
G	Henry Martinez, Lynchburg, Akron, Columbus	48
GS	Sean Brady, Akron, Columbus	28
SV	Henry Martinez, Lynchburg, Akron, Columbus	15
SV	Dalbert Siri, Lynchburg	15
IP	Adam Wilk, Columbus	165
BB	Adam Wilk, Columbus	58
SO	Kirk McCarty, Lake County, Lynchburg	161
# AVG	Eli Morgan, Lake County, Lynchburg	.231

2018 PERFORMANCE

General Manager: Mike Chernoff. **Farm Director:** James Harris. **Scouting Director:** Scott Barnsby.

Class	Team	League	W	L	PCT	Finish	Manager
Majors	Cleveland Indians	American	91	71	.562	5th (15)	Terry Francona
Triple-A	Columbus Clippers	International	73	67	.521	5th (14)	Chris Tremie
Double-A	Akron Rubberducks	Eastern	78	62	.557	3rd (12)	Tony Mansolino
High A	Lynchburg Hillcats	Carolina	71	66	.518	4th (10)	Rouglas Odor
Low A	Lake County Captains	Midwest	60	79	.432	14th (16)	Luke Carlin
Short season	M. Valley Scrappers	New York-Penn	42	33	.560	2nd (14)	Jim Pankovits
Rookie	AZL Indians 1	Arizona	36	18	.667	3rd (18)	Larry Day
Rookie	AZL Indians 2	Arizona	32	24	.571	5th (18)	Jerry Owens
Overall 2018 Minor League Record			392	349	.529	7th (30)	

ORGANIZATION STATISTICS

CLEVELAND INDIANS
AMERICAN LEAGUE

Batting	B-T	HT	WT	DOB	AVG	vLH	vRH	G	AB	R	H	2B	3B	HR	RBI	BB	HBP	SH	SF	SO	SB	CS	SLG	OBP
Allen, Greg	B-R	6-0	175	3-15-93	.257	.208	.267	91	265	36	68	11	3	2	20	14	7	4	1	58	21	4	.343	.310
Alonso, Yonder	L-R	6-1	230	4-8-87	.250	.227	.258	145	516	64	129	19	0	23	83	51	2	0	5	123	0	0	.421	.317
Barnes, Brandon	R-R	6-2	210	5-15-86	.263	.143	.333	19	19	2	5	0	0	1	2	2	0	0	0	5	0	0	.421	.333
Brantley, Michael	L-L	6-2	200	5-15-87	.309	.277	.321	143	570	89	176	36	2	17	76	48	5	1	6	60	12	3	.468	.364
Cabrera, Melky	B-L	5-10	210	8-11-84	.280	.309	.269	78	250	28	70	17	0	6	39	20	3	0	5	38	1	1	.420	.335
Chisenhall, Lonnie	L-R	6-2	190	10-4-88	.321	.286	.325	29	84	11	27	6	1	1	9	2	1	0	1	12	1	0	.452	.394
Davis, Rajai	R-R	5-10	195	10-19-80	.225	.221	.228	101	196	33	44	6	1	1	6	11	4	4	1	48	21	7	.281	.278
Diaz, Yandy	R-R	6-2	185	8-8-91	.312	.289	.328	39	109	15	34	5	2	1	15	11	0	0	0	19	0	0	.422	.375
Donaldson, Josh	R-R	6-1	210	12-8-85	.280	.267	.286	16	50	8	14	3	0	3	7	10	0	0	0	10	0	0	.520	.400
2-team total (36 Toronto)					.246	.276	.233	52	187	30	46	14	0	8	23	31	0	0	1	54	2	0	.449	.352
Encarnacion, Edwin	R-R	6-1	230	1-7-83	.246	.217	.255	137	500	74	123	16	1	32	107	63	8	0	7	132	3	0	.474	.336
Gomes, Yan	R-R	6-2	215	7-19-87	.266	.288	.257	112	403	52	107	26	0	16	48	21	8	0	3	119	0	0	.449	.313
Gonzalez, Erik	R-R	6-3	195	8-31-91	.265	.211	.304	81	136	17	36	10	1	1	16	5	2	0	0	34	3	0	.375	.301
Guyer, Brandon	R-R	6-2	200	1-28-86	.206	.233	.176	103	194	25	40	11	0	7	27	15	11	1	0	48	1	1	.371	.300
Haase, Eric	R-R	5-10	180	12-18-92	.125	.143	.111	9	16	0	2	0	0	0	1	0	0	0	0	6	0	0	.125	.177
Kipnis, Jason	L-R	5-11	195	4-3-87	.230	.222	.233	147	530	65	122	28	1	18	75	60	7	1	3	112	7	1	.389	.315
Lindor, Francisco	B-R	5-11	190	11-14-93	.277	.343	.253	158	661	129	183	42	2	38	92	70	8	3	3	107	25	10	.519	.352
Martin, Leonys	L-R	6-2	200	3-6-88	.333	—	.333	6	15	3	5	0	0	2	4	1	0	0	1	2	0	1	.733	.353
2-team total (78 Detroit)					.255	.176	.279	84	318	48	81	15	3	11	33	30	3	0	2	77	7	4	.425	.323
Mejia, Francisco	B-R	5-10	180	10-27-95	.000	.000	—	1	2	0	0	0	0	0	0	2	0	0	0	0	0	0	.000	.500
Naquin, Tyler	L-R	6-2	195	4-24-91	.264	.250	.266	61	174	22	46	7	0	3	23	6	2	0	1	42	1	1	.356	.295
Perez, Roberto	R-R	5-11	220	12-23-88	.168	.250	.150	62	179	16	30	9	1	2	19	21	1	7	2	70	1	0	.263	.256
Ramirez, Jose	B-R	5-9	165	9-17-92	.270	.267	.271	157	578	110	156	38	4	39	105	106	8	0	6	80	34	6	.552	.387
Rosales, Adam	R-R	6-0	200	5-20-83	.211	.000	.235	13	19	4	4	1	0	1	2	1	0	1	0	5	0	0	.421	.250
Zimmer, Bradley	L-R	6-5	220	11-27-92	.226	.233	.224	34	106	14	24	5	0	2	9	7	1	0	0	44	4	1	.330	.281

Pitching	B-T	HT	WT	DOB	W	L	ERA	G	GS	CG	SV	IP	H	R	ER	HR	BB	SO	AVG	vLH	vRH	K/9	BB/9
Allen, Cody	R-R	6-1	210	11-20-88	4	6	4.70	70	0	0	27	67	58	35	35	11	33	80	.231	.252	.212	10.75	4.43
Bauer, Trevor	R-R	6-1	190	1-17-91	12	6	2.21	28	27	0	1	175	134	51	43	9	57	221	.208	.203	.213	11.34	2.93
Belisle, Matt	R-R	6-3	230	6-6-80	0	0	5.06	8	0	0	0	11	9	6	6	1	4	8	.220	.111	.304	3.38	0.84
2-team total (25 Minnesota)					1	1	7.86	33	0	0	0	34	49	32	30	6	11	25	.336	.343	.329	6.55	2.88
Beliveau, Jeff	L-L	6-1	190	1-17-87	0	0	11.57	9	0	0	1	5	7	6	6	2	5	2	.350	.250	.500	3.86	9.64
Bieber, Shane	R-R	6-3	195	5-31-95	11	5	4.55	20	19	0	0	115	130	60	58	13	23	118	.285	.316	.252	9.26	1.81
Carrasco, Carlos	R-R	6-3	212	3-21-87	17	10	3.38	32	30	2	0	192	173	78	72	21	43	231	.238	.248	.229	10.83	2.02
Cimber, Adam	R-R	6-4	180	8-15-90	1	3	4.05	28	0	0	0	20	26	9	9	3	7	7	.325	.467	.292	3.15	3.15
Clevinger, Mike	R-R	6-4	210	12-21-90	13	8	3.02	32	32	1	0	200	164	71	67	21	67	207	.223	.234	.211	9.32	3.02
Drake, Oliver	R-R	6-4	215	1-13-87	0	0	12.46	4	0	0	0	4	7	6	6	1	4	4	.350	.400	.333	8.31	2.08
4-team total (8 Los Angeles, 19 Minnesota, 2 Toronto)					0		14.89	33	0	0	0	35	38	20	19	4	9	36	.270	.328	.221	9.26	2.31
Edwards, Jon	R-R	6-5	235	1-8-88	0	0	3.12	9	0	0	0	9	6	4	3	2	4	10	.182	.214	.158	10.38	4.15
Goody, Nick	R-R	5-11	195	7-6-91	0	2	6.94	12	0	0	0	12	15	9	9	4	5	12	.289	.263	.303	9.26	3.86
Hand, Brad	L-L	6-3	228	3-20-90	0	1	2.28	28	0	0	8	28	19	7	7	3	13	41	.192	.163	.220	13.34	4.23
Kluber, Corey	R-R	6-4	215	4-10-86	20	7	2.89	33	33	2	0	215	179	75	69	25	34	222	.224	.227	.220	9.29	1.42
Kontos, George	R-R	6-3	225	6-12-85	0	0	3.38	6	0	0	0	5	3	2	2	1	2	4	.158	.167	.154	6.75	3.38
2-team total (1 New York)					0	0	2.57	7	0	0	0	7	4	2	2	1	2	6	.160	.286	.111	7.71	2.57
Marshall, Evan	R-R	6-2	225	4-18-90	0	0	7.71	10	0	0	0	7	12	6	6	0	4	9	.375	.308	.421	11.57	5.14
McAllister, Zach	R-R	6-6	240	12-8-87	1	2	4.97	41	0	0	0	42	47	25	23	7	10	34	.285	.329	.253	7.34	2.16
2-team total (3 Detroit)					1	2	6.20	44	0	0	0	45	57	33	31	8	10	39	.310	.363	.269	7.80	2.00
Miller, Andrew	L-L	6-7	205	5-21-85	2	4	4.24	37	0	0	2	34	31	16	16	3	16	45	.233	.227	.236	11.91	4.24
Ogando, Alexi	R-R	6-4	200	10-5-83	0	1	18.00	1	0	0	0	1	2	2	2	0	3	1	.400	.000	.667	9.00	27.00
Olson, Tyler	R-L	6-3	195	10-2-89	2	1	4.94	43	0	0	0	27	26	16	15	4	12	40	.245	.182	.314	13.17	3.95
Otero, Dan	R-R	6-3	205	2-19-85	2	1	5.22	61	0	0	1	59	69	36	34	12	5	43	.289	.337	.259	6.60	0.77
Perez, Oliver	L-L	6-3	225	8-15-81	1	1	1.39	51	0	0	0	32	17	6	5	1	7	43	.155	.194	.104	11.97	1.95
Plutko, Adam	R-R	6-3	200	10-3-91	4	5	5.28	17	12	0	1	77	78	45	45	21	23	60	.261	.319	.209	7.04	2.70

	B-T	HT	WT	DOB	W	L	ERA	G	GS	CG	SV	IP	H	R	ER	HR	BB	SO	AVG	vLH	vRH	K/9	BB/9
Ramirez, Neil	R-R	6-4	215	5-25-89	0	3	4.54	47	0	0	0	42	36	21	21	9	18	51	.228	.218	.233	11.02	3.89
Rzepczynski, Marc	L-L	6-2	220	8-29-85	0	0	0.00	5	0	0	0	3	3	0	0	0	1	1	.333	.500	.200	3.38	3.38
2-team total (18 Seattle)					0	1	6.97	23	0	0	0	10	16	11	8	2	10	11	.340	.258	.500	9.58	8.71
Taylor, Ben	R-R	6-3	225	11-12-92	0	0	6.00	6	0	0	0	6	6	4	4	2	1	8	.250	.364	.154	12.00	1.50
Tomlin, Josh	R-R	6-1	190	10-19-84	2	5	6.14	32	9	0	0	70	92	52	48	25	12	46	.304	.353	.264	5.89	1.54

Fielding

Catcher	PCT	G	PO	A	E	DP	PB
Gomes	.991	111	994	49	9	6	6
Haase	.967	7	29	0	1	0	0
Perez	.991	58	538	26	5	3	3

First Base	PCT	G	PO	A	E	DP
Alonso	.990	138	980	54	10	89
Diaz	1.000	9	51	7	0	1
Encarnacion	.994	23	147	14	1	16
Gonzalez	1.000	9	28	6	0	4
Rosales	1.000	5	12	0	0	0

Second Base	PCT	G	PO	A	E	DP
Barnes	.000	1	0	0	0	0

	PCT	G	PO	A	E	DP
Gonzalez	.901	30	19	45	7	6
Kipnis	.982	131	175	308	9	68
Ramirez	.950	16	24	33	3	5
Rosales	1.000	4	4	5	0	0

Third Base	PCT	G	PO	A	E	DP
Diaz	.909	9	0	10	1	1
Donaldson	.882	12	3	12	2	0
Gonzalez	.963	20	6	20	1	2
Ramirez	.965	137	94	205	11	21
Rosales	1.000	3	1	4	0	0

Shortstop	PCT	G	PO	A	E	DP
Gonzalez	1.000	16	8	20	0	4
Lindor	.976	157	189	383	14	82

Rosales	1.000	2	1	0	0	0

Outfield	PCT	G	PO	A	E	DP
Allen	.995	87	184	2	1	1
Barnes	1.000	19	14	0	0	0
Brantley	.996	134	221	6	1	2
Cabrera	1.000	71	99	4	0	1
Chisenhall	.976	28	38	2	1	1
Davis	1.000	75	112	3	0	1
Guyer	.971	96	97	2	3	0
Kipnis	1.000	14	16	0	0	0
Martin	1.000	6	10	0	0	0
Naquin	1.000	60	123	2	0	0
Zimmer	1.000	34	82	4	0	1

COLUMBUS CLIPPERS   TRIPLE-A
INTERNATIONAL LEAGUE

Batting	B-T	HT	WT	DOB	AVG	vLH	vRH	G	AB	R	H	2B	3B	HR	RBI	BB	HBP	SH	SF	SO	SB	CS	SLG	OBP
Allen, Greg	B-R	6-0	175	3-15-93	.298	.362	.274	47	171	31	51	13	0	2	14	19	9	5	1	44	12	6	.409	.395
Barnes, Brandon	R-R	6-2	210	5-15-86	.273	.310	.261	132	498	75	136	39	2	14	81	47	12	2	5	152	19	5	.444	.347
Berti, Jon	R-R	5-10	195	1-22-90	.217	.316	.171	25	60	10	13	1	0	0	3	9	2	1	1	8	1		.233	.333
2-team total (4 Buffalo)					.221	.300	.188	29	68	11	15	1	0	0	4	9	2	1	1	16	8	1	.235	.325
Bradley, Bobby	L-R	6-1	225	5-29-96	.254	.263	.250	32	114	11	29	7	2	3	19	11	1	1	1	43	0	0	.430	.323
Brantly, Rob	L-R	6-1	195	7-14-89	.171	.154	.179	15	41	4	7	0	0	1	2	1	3	0	0	12	0	0	.244	.244
2-team total (57 Gwinnett)					.210	.169	.228	72	229	20	48	11	0	2	21	8	6	0	3	49	0	0	.284	.252
Cabrera, Melky	B-L	6-1	210	8-11-84	.321	.304	.327	19	78	7	25	6	1	0	8	2	0	0	0	10	2	0	.423	.338
Chang, Yu	R-R	6-1	175	8-18-95	.256	.264	.254	127	457	56	117	28	2	13	62	44	9	3	5	144	4	3	.411	.330
Chisenhall, Lonnie	L-R	6-1	190	10-4-88	.263	.667	.188	6	19	5	5	2	0	1	2	4	0	0	0	5	0	0	.526	.391
Chu, Li-Jen	R-R	5-11	200	3-13-94	.250	.333	.000	2	4	1	1	1	0	0	0	0	0	0	0	1	0	0	.500	.250
Diaz, Yandy	R-R	6-2	185	8-8-91	.293	.311	.288	98	348	53	102	24	0	3	40	70	2	1	5	70	3	3	.388	.409
Donaldson, Josh	R-R	6-1	210	12-8-85	.500	—	.500	1	2	1	1	0	0	1		4	1	0	0	0	0		2.000	.667
Field, Johnny	R-R	5-10	180	2-20-92	.333	.500	.273	5	15	7	5	2	0	1	4	5	0	0	0	3	0	0	.667	.500
3-team total (10 Durham, 10 Rochester)					.258	.320	.234	25	89	14	23	6	0	1	9	9	2	0	0	18	2	1	.360	.340
Gantt, Tre	L-L	5-10	180	5-10-96	.000	—	.000	1	1	0	0	0	0	0	0	0	0	0	0	1	0	0	.000	.000
Guyer, Brandon	R-R	6-2	200	1-28-86	.125	.300	.046	9	32	6	4	0	0	2	2	1	4	0	0	4	0	0	.313	.243
Haase, Eric	R-R	5-10	180	12-18-92	.236	.221	.241	120	433	54	102	24	3	20	71	31	4	2	7	143	3	1	.443	.288
Haggerty, Sam	B-R	5-11	175	5-26-94	.177	.000	.190	7	17	3	3	0	0	0	2	2	1	1	0	6	2	0	.177	.300
Hankins, Todd	R-R	5-9	180	11-18-90	.273	.208	.301	64	161	21	44	8	1	1	9	13	1	4	1	51	11	6	.354	.330
Maggi, Drew	R-R	6-0	192	5-16-89	.272	.276	.270	64	232	37	63	12	1	1	14	21	1	5	1	57	11	5	.345	.333
Marabell, Connor	L-R	6-1	195	3-28-94	.214	.258	.198	31	117	12	25	8	1	2	9	3	0	0	0	16	1	0	.350	.233
Mejia, Francisco	B-R	5-10	180	10-27-95	.279	.321	.264	79	305	32	85	22	1	7	45	18	6	4	3	58	0	0	.426	.328
Mercado, Oscar	R-R	6-2	175	12-16-94	.252	.206	.275	32	103	12	26	5	1	0	5	13	1	2	0	23	6	4	.320	.342
Napoli, Mike	R-R	6-1	225	10-31-81	.042	.000	.056	8	24	3	1	0	0	1	4	7	0	0	0	11	0	0	.167	.258
Naquin, Tyler	L-R	6-2	195	4-24-91	.125	.100	.125	5	16	1	2	1	0	0	0	0	0	0	0	5	0	0	.188	.125
Papi, Mike	L-R	6-3	215	9-19-92	.247	.191	.259	83	243	38	60	17	1	7	26	47	2	4	0	78	1	1	.412	.373
Paulino, Dorssys	R-R	6-0	175	11-21-94	.182	.333	.125	4	11	2	2	1	0	0	0	4	0	0	0	5	0	0	.273	.400
Rodriguez, Nellie	R-R	6-2	225	6-12-94	.204	.260	.190	76	240	24	49	11	0	10	39	23	2	1	2	95	0	0	.375	.277
Rosales, Adam	R-R	6-2	200	5-20-83	.240	.235	.241	114	380	52	91	22	1	18	61	38	5	0	5	94	3	3	.445	.313
Salters, Daniel	L-R	6-3	210	2-5-93	.200	1.000	.000	2	5	1	1	0	0	0	0	1	0	0	0	1	0	0	.200	.333
Sever, Joe	R-R	6-0	205	8-10-92	.219	.200	.227	19	64	5	14	5	0	0	3	3	2	0	0	15	0	1	.297	.275
Shaffer, Richie	R-R	6-3	230	3-15-91	.164	.192	.156	32	116	9	19	5	0	4	13	8	0	0	1	43	0	0	.310	.216
Stamets, Eric	R-R	6-0	190	9-25-91	.202	.167	.214	78	238	22	48	10	2	5	16	18	5	8	0	63	5	2	.324	.272
Urshela, Gio	R-R	6-0	215	10-11-91	.324	.455	.269	11	37	6	12	4	0	0	7	5	0	0	0	9	0	0	.432	.405
3-team total (24 Buffalo, 27 Scranton/W-B)					.286	.300	.282	62	224	27	64	14	2	2	24	13	1	1	1	31	0	0	.393	.326
Zimmer, Bradley	L-R	6-5	220	11-27-92	.148	.000	.222	6	27	1	4	0	0	1	1	1	0	0	0	11	1	0	.259	.179

Pitching	B-T	HT	WT	DOB	W	L	ERA	G	GS	CG	SV	IP	H	R	ER	HR	BB	SO	AVG	vLH	vRH	K/9	BB/9
Belisle, Matt	R-R	6-3	230	6-6-80	0	0	4.22	9	0	0	1	11	10	5	5	1	1	11	.263	.231	.280	9.28	0.84
Beliveau, Jeff	L-L	6-1	190	1-17-87	0	1	6.92	26	0	0	2	26	23	20	20	2	16	31	.232	.200	.259	10.73	5.54
Bieber, Shane	R-R	6-3	195	5-31-95	3	1	1.66	8	8	1	0	49	30	10	9	3	6	47	.178	.167	.187	8.69	1.11
Brady, Sean	L-L	6-0	175	6-9-94	1	0	3.60	1	1	0	0	5	5	2	2	1	2	5	.263	.400	.214	9.00	3.60
Chiang, Shao-Ching	R-R	6-0	175	11-10-93	4	5	5.01	13	11	0	0	66	69	38	36	7	11	39	.271	.290	.255	5.43	1.53
Claiborne, Preston	R-R	6-2	225	1-21-88	0	0	27.00	1	0	0	0	2	5	5	5	0	1	0	.500	.500	.500	5.40	16.20
DeMasi, Dominic	R-R	6-3	190	5-18-93	1	2	5.21	5	4	0	0	19	23	12	11	3	7	14	.319	.342	.294	6.63	3.32
Edwards, Jon	R-R	6-5	235	1-8-88	2	1	3.60	25	0	0	4	30	23	12	12	2	9	42	.204	.220	.194	12.60	2.70
Eubank, Luke	R-R	6-0	180	2-24-94	3	2	4.54	32	0	0	2	40	40	25	20	4	16	31	.267	.313	.229	7.03	3.63
Fife, Stephen	R-R	6-2	225	10-4-86	5	7	6.80	20	17	0	0	86	124	69	65	8	20	56	.341	.301	.374	5.86	2.09
Head, Louis	R-R	6-1	180	4-23-90	1	1	12.64	15	0	0	0	16	24	22	22	3	10	20	.389	.423	.370	11.49	5.74

Name	T	HT	WT	DOB	W	L	ERA	G	GS	CG	SV	IP	H	R	ER	HR	BB	SO	AVG	vLH	vRH	H9	BB9
Hill, Cam	R-R	6-1	185	5-24-94	0	0	6.59	16	0	0	3	14	15	11	10	5	8	13	.278	.100	.382	8.56	5.27
Hoyt, James	R-R	6-6	230	9-30-86	0	1	10.13	3	0	0	0	3	5	3	3	1	2	2	.385	.500	.286	6.75	6.75
Jaye, Myles	R-R	6-0	170	12-28-91	2	5	9.62	9	5	0	0	29	44	35	31	9	10	16	.352	.397	.307	4.97	3.10
2-team total (8 Rochester)					5	8	6.43	17	13	0	0	71	89	56	51	14	25	35	.308	.329	.289	4.42	3.15
Kontos, George	R-R	6-3	225	6-12-85	2	0	1.13	14	0	0	3	16	15	2	2	0	0	12	.259	.056	.350	6.75	0.00
2-team total (8 Scranton/Wilkes-Barre)					3	2	1.85	22	0	0	3	24	25	5	5	1	1	16	.278	.167	.352	5.92	0.37
Leathersich, Jack	R-L	5-11	205	7-14-90	2	2	3.98	35	0	0	0	32	19	15	14	2	26	34	.173	.157	.186	9.66	7.39
Lovegrove, Kieran	R-R	6-4	185	7-28-94	0	0	0.00	1	0	0	0	3	1	0	0	0	0	3	.111	.167	.000	9.00	0.00
Marshall, Evan	R-R	6-2	225	4-18-90	1	1	1.13	20	0	0	4	24	18	5	3	1	3	21	.205	.138	.237	7.88	1.13
Martin, Josh	R-R	6-5	230	12-30-89	4	0	2.91	19	0	0	1	22	19	13	7	1	8	24	.232	.250	.217	9.97	3.32
Martinez, Henry	R-R	6-1	180	4-27-94	1	0	10.64	10	0	0	0	11	18	13	13	0	4	14	.367	.409	.333	11.45	3.27
Merritt, Ryan	L-L	6-0	180	2-21-92	3	3	3.79	15	13	0	0	71	82	30	30	10	2	52	.292	.303	.288	6.56	0.25
Milbrath, Jordan	R-R	6-6	215	8-1-91	1	2	5.93	9	0	0	0	14	21	10	9	0	8	12	.356	.433	.276	7.90	5.27
Miller, Andrew	L-L	6-7	205	5-21-85	0	0	1.93	5	0	0	0	5	2	1	1	0	0	6	.125	.125	.125	11.57	0.00
Morimando, Shawn	L-L	6-0	200	11-20-92	1	3	7.03	5	5	0	0	24	44	22	19	1	10	11	.396	.269	.435	4.07	3.70
2-team total (4 Buffalo)					2	6	5.89	9	9	0	0	44	65	33	29	6	12	22	.339	.250	.362	4.47	2.44
Ogando, Alexi	R-R	6-4	200	10-5-83	2	0	3.89	14	6	0	0	35	38	17	15	4	10	25	.284	.340	.250	6.49	2.60
Olson, Tyler	R-L	6-3	195	10-2-89	2	1	3.65	17	0	0	1	12	8	7	5	0	3	18	.186	.227	.143	13.14	2.19
Orlan, R.C.	R-L	6-0	185	9-28-90	0	0	0.00	2	0	0	0	2	2	0	0	0	2	3	.286	.250	.316	16.20	10.80
Pasquale, Nick	R-R	6-0	190	10-27-90	0	0	27.00	1	0	0	0	1	4	2	2	0	0	1	.667	.500	.750	13.50	0.00
Peoples, Michael	R-R	6-5	190	9-5-91	0	2	16.50	4	4	0	0	12	29	23	22	3	7	15	.453	.500	.412	11.25	5.25
Plutko, Adam	R-R	6-3	200	10-3-91	7	3	1.70	14	14	1	0	85	47	16	16	5	16	81	.158	.160	.157	8.61	1.70
Ramirez, Neil	R-R	6-4	215	5-25-89	2	1	3.38	14	0	0	3	19	16	7	7	4	3	32	.229	.320	.178	15.43	1.45
Rzepczynski, Marc	L-L	6-2	220	8-29-85	0	0	3.38	6	0	0	0	3	4	1	1	0	3	1	.364	.333	.500	3.38	10.13
Sulser, Cole	R-R	6-0	190	3-12-90	5	4	4.53	41	0	0	1	52	52	31	26	4	16	78	.265	.164	.325	13.59	2.79
Talbot, Mitch	R-R	6-1	180	10-17-83	4	5	2.52	18	17	0	0	104	98	31	29	9	22	66	.256	.235	.275	5.56	1.91
Taylor, Ben	R-R	6-3	225	11-12-92	7	2	2.51	46	0	0	11	57	42	17	16	5	9	70	.204	.141	.242	10.99	1.41
Tomlin, Josh	R-R	6-1	190	10-19-84	0	1	6.75	3	3	0	0	9	19	7	7	3	0	8	.422	.286	.542	7.71	0.00
Whitehouse, Matt	L-L	6-1	175	4-13-91	0	1	8.69	6	5	0	0	20	31	19	19	3	12	19	.365	.150	.431	8.69	5.49
Wilk, Adam	L-L	6-2	180	12-9-87	6	9	3.66	27	27	1	0	165	170	76	67	23	58	107	.269	.290	.261	5.85	3.17
Zarate, Robert	L-L	6-3	200	2-1-87	3	1	3.30	29	0	0	1	30	27	15	11	4	17	40	.229	.245	.215	12.00	5.10

Fielding

Catcher	PCT	G	PO	A	E	DP	PB
Brantly	1.000	15	96	9	0	1	0
Chu	1.000	1	11	0	0	0	0
Haase	.992	90	654	48	6	4	10
Mejia	1.000	41	323	27	0	2	5
Salters	1.000	2	12	0	0	0	1

First Base	PCT	G	PO	A	E	DP
Bradley	.992	29	248	10	2	28
Diaz	.989	12	84	4	1	7
Napoli	.973	5	36	0	1	2
Papi	1.000	6	14	1	0	3
Rodriguez	.991	73	491	34	5	55
Rosales	.995	32	174	13	1	14
Sever	1.000	2	8	0	0	1
Shaffer	1.000	4	29	3	0	5
Urshela	1.000	2	17	1	0	2

Second Base	PCT	G	PO	A	E	DP
Berti	1.000	6	7	16	0	3
Chang	1.000	9	20	19	0	4
Haggerty	.857	3	2	4	1	1
Hankins	.964	12	10	17	1	8
Maggi	.968	46	76	133	7	36
Rosales	.992	36	47	80	1	19
Sever	1.000	1	0	1	0	0
Stamets	.977	40	72	100	4	21
Urshela	1.000	4	4	5	0	2

Third Base	PCT	G	PO	A	E	DP
Berti	1.000	4	2	6	0	0
Chang	.944	23	15	36	3	3
Chu	.000	1	0	0	0	0
Diaz	.961	73	40	109	6	7
Donaldson	.000	1	0	0	0	0
Maggi	1.000	4	2	11	0	1
Rosales	1.000	28	17	48	0	5
Sever	1.000	14	10	17	0	4
Shaffer	1.000	3	2	3	0	0
Urshela	1.000	4	2	6	0	3

Shortstop	PCT	G	PO	A	E	DP
Chang	.975	94	126	229	9	63
Maggi	1.000	3	2	7	0	0
Rosales	.971	9	6	28	1	6
Stamets	.975	38	47	109	4	25
Urshela	.800	2	3	1	1	0

Outfield	PCT	G	PO	A	E	DP
Allen	.982	47	105	7	2	1
Barnes	.975	117	260	12	7	1
Berti	1.000	14	15	0	0	0
Cabrera	1.000	14	22	4	0	2
Chisenhall	1.000	5	11	1	0	1
Field	1.000	5	10	1	0	0
Gantt	.000	1	0	0	0	0
Guyer	1.000	9	13	1	0	0
Haggerty	1.000	6	2	0	0	0
Hankins	.974	51	76	0	2	0
Maggi	1.000	9	13	0	0	0
Marabell	1.000	30	70	7	0	1
Mejia	1.000	28	36	0	0	0
Mercado	.972	32	70	0	2	0
Naquin	1.000	5	12	0	0	0
Papi	.992	66	126	4	1	0
Paulino	1.000	4	4	0	0	0
Sever	.000	1	0	0	0	0
Shaffer	.929	17	39	0	3	0
Zimmer	1.000	5	11	0	0	0

AKRON RUBBERDUCKS   DOUBLE-A
EASTERN LEAGUE

Batting	B-T	HT	WT	DOB	AVG	vLH	vRH	G	AB	R	H	2B	3B	HR	RBI	BB	HBP	SH	SF	SO	SB	CS	SLG	OBP
Bradley, Bobby	L-R	6-1	225	5-29-96	.214	.184	.225	97	369	49	79	19	3	24	64	45	4	0	3	105	1	0	.477	.304
Calica, Andrew	L-R	6-1	190	3-5-94	.278	.286	.275	115	421	78	117	21	1	6	49	55	22	2	1	104	27	5	.375	.389
Carter, Jodd	R-R	5-10	170	7-20-96	.290	.381	.250	19	69	6	20	0	1	1	4	3	2	1	0	12	0	0	.362	.338
Castro, Willi	R-B	6-1	165	4-24-97	.245	.232	.250	97	371	55	91	20	2	5	39	28	3	7	1	84	13	4	.350	.303
2-team total (26 Erie)					.263	.260	.264	123	476	67	125	29	4	9	52	34	4	9	1	109	17	5	.397	.317
Chisenhall, Lonnie	L-R	6-2	190	10-4-88	.333	1.000	.250	3	9	1	3	1	0	1	4	2	0	0	0	0	0	0	.778	.455
Chu, Li-Jen	R-R	5-11	200	3-13-94	.241	.400	.180	16	54	4	13	1	0	2	6	3	0	0	0	13	0	0	.370	.281
Clement, Ernie	R-R	6-0	170	3-22-96	.246	.100	.311	15	65	9	16	5	1	0	5	3	0	0	0	7	2	1	.354	.279
Davis, Rajai	R-R	5-10	195	10-19-80	.000	.000	—	2	6	0	0	0	0	0	0	0	0	0	0	2	0	0	.000	.000
Gonzalez, Gianpaul	R-R	6-0	185	1-11-96	.091	.000	.200	3	11	0	1	0	0	0	1	0	0	0	0	5	0	0	.091	.091
Guyer, Brandon	R-R	6-0	200	1-28-86	.000	.000	.000	3	12	2	0	0	0	0	0	0	0	0	0	3	0	0	.000	.000
Haggerty, Sam	B-R	5-11	175	5-26-94	.243	.205	.257	87	280	44	68	21	5	4	37	57	4	5	5	77	24	7	.396	.373
Hankins, Todd	R-R	5-9	180	11-18-90	.271	.222	.282	12	48	8	13	4	0	1	5	2	0	0	4	12	0	0	.417	.364
Ice, Logan	B-R	5-10	180	5-27-95	.250	.143	.268	17	48	6	12	3	2	0	8	5	0	1	1	18	0	0	.396	.315
Krieger, Tyler	B-R	6-2	170	1-16-94	.276	.276	.276	123	468	69	129	22	4	5	55	38	4	3	5	88	10	0	.372	.332

Player	B-T	HT	WT	DOB	AVG	vLH	vRH	G	AB	R	H	2B	3B	HR	RBI	BB	HBP	SH	SF	SO	SB	CS	SLG	OBP
Laureano, Jonathan	R-R	6-1	200	12-21-95	.000	.000	.000	2	7	0	0	0	0	0	0	1	0	0	0	2	0	0	.000	.125
Loopstok, Sicnarf	R-R	5-11	195	4-26-93	.225	.286	.203	58	182	29	41	4	2	9	35	36	5	1	4	57	1	2	.418	.361
Marabell, Connor	L-R	6-1	195	3-28-94	.296	.282	.300	89	345	52	102	23	4	11	64	23	3	2	4	58	4	3	.481	.341
Mathias, Mark	R-R	6-0	200	8-2-94	.232	.275	.215	117	397	65	92	25	3	8	45	59	9	3	8	94	11	2	.370	.338
Murphy, Taylor	L-R	6-2	200	11-3-92	.222	—	.222	3	9	1	2	1	0	0	1	1	0	1	0	3	0	0	.333	.300
Naquin, Tyler	L-R	6-2	195	4-24-91	.000	.000	.000	1	2	0	0	0	0	0	0	1	0	0	0	1	0	0	.000	.333
Pantoja, Alexis	L-R	5-11	150	1-18-96	.190	.167	.200	24	79	8	15	2	0	0	5	3	0	0	0	23	0	0	.215	.220
Paulino, Dorssys	R-R	6-0	175	11-21-94	.196	.189	.198	44	133	15	26	4	1	4	17	18	0	1	1	29	0	1	.331	.290
Perez, Elvis	R-R	6-0	165	1-10-96	.273	.000	.333	3	11	1	3	1	0	0	0	1	0	0	0	6	0	0	.364	.333
Rodriguez, Jorma	R-R	5-10	150	3-25-96	.333	.571	.235	7	24	4	8	3	0	0	3	2	0	0	0	4	0	1	.458	.385
Rodriguez, Nellie	R-R	6-2	225	6-12-94	.283	.094	.365	31	106	15	30	7	1	5	23	16	1	0	3	47	0	0	.509	.373
Salters, Daniel	L-R	6-3	210	2-5-93	.240	.174	.266	74	246	20	59	10	0	5	30	17	9	0	2	68	1	1	.342	.310
Sever, Joe	R-R	6-0	205	8-12-94	.262	.297	.247	107	424	60	111	27	0	7	57	36	4	1	8	72	10	2	.375	.320
Tom, Ka'ai	L-R	5-9	185	5-29-94	.245	.207	.260	121	421	60	103	21	4	12	64	46	10	1	6	102	13	10	.399	.329
Zimmer, Bradley	L-R	6-5	220	11-27-92	.333	—	.333	2	3	2	1	0	0	0	0	2	2	0	0	2	0		.333	.714

Pitching	B-T	HT	WT	DOB	W	L	ERA	G	GS	CG	SV	IP	H	R	ER	HR	BB	SO	AVG	vLH	vRH	K/9	BB/9
Anderson, Cody	R-R	6-4	240	9-14-90	0	0	0.00	1	1	0	0	1	0	0	0	0	0	1	.000	.000		0.00	9.00
Angulo, Argenis	R-R			2-26-94	2	5	5.23	47	0	0	8	52	59	36	30	4	29	64	.286	.247	.319	11.15	5.05
Bieber, Shane	R-R	6-3	195	5-31-95	3	0	1.16	5	5	0	0	31	26	6	4	1	1	30	.215	.276	.159	8.71	0.29
Brady, Sean	L-L	6-0	175	6-9-94	7	7	4.53	27	27	0	0	143	148	85	72	17	53	95	.272	.259	.276	5.98	3.34
Brown, Mitch	R-R	6-1	195	4-13-94	1	5	1.99	37	0	0	4	45	26	13	10	1	36	52	.166	.110	.214	10.32	7.15
Carrasco, Carlos	R-R	6-3	212	3-21-87	0	0	0.00	1	1	0	0	4	1	0	0	0	1	4	.091	.200	.000	9.00	2.25
Chiang, Shao-Ching	R-R	6-0	175	11-10-93	5	2	2.90	12	12	0	0	71	65	25	23	6	13	54	.243	.235	.250	6.81	1.64
Civale, Aaron	R-R	6-2	215	6-12-95	5	7	3.89	21	21	0	0	106	115	56	46	12	21	78	.276	.302	.252	6.60	1.78
Claiborne, Preston	R-R	6-2	225	1-21-88	0	1	15.00	3	0	0	0	3	6	5	5	2	3	1	.400	.400	.400	3.00	9.00
DeMasi, Dominic	R-R	6-3	190	5-18-93	8	2	7.24	28	7	0	1	68	85	64	55	9	19	48	.300	.274	.319	6.32	2.50
Dowdy, Kyle	R-R	6-1	195	2-3-93	1	4	6.52	6	6	0	0	29	30	21	21	4	18	28	.273	.261	.293	8.69	5.59
2-team total (13 Erie)					4	8	5.68	19	11	0	2	70	73	44	44	10	29	76	.274	.271	.278	9.82	3.75
Edwards, Jon	R-R	6-5	235	1-8-88	0	1	3.72	9	0	0	0	10	6	4	4	1	6	14	.177	.200	.167	13.03	5.59
Eubank, Luke	R-R	6-0	180	2-24-94	0	0	0.56	13	0	0	3	16	12	1	1	0	7	26	.203	.136	.243	14.63	3.94
Kaminsky, Rob	R-L	5-11	190	9-2-94	1	1	3.08	23	0	0	4	26	22	12	9	2	18	22	.229	.188	.271	7.52	6.15
Karinchak, James	R-R	6-3	230	9-22-95	0	1	2.61	10	0	0	0	10	7	3	3	1	12	16	.189	.125	.308	13.94	10.45
Krauth, Ben	L-L	6-0	180	3-10-94	0	0	0.00	1	0	0	0	2	3	1	0	0	1	0	.333	.500	.286	0.00	4.50
Linares, Leandro	R-R	6-3	205	1-27-94	2	2	6.05	14	0	0	1	19	21	13	13	1	14	13	.288	.200	.349	6.05	6.52
Lovegrove, Kieran	R-R	6-4	185	7-28-94	1	0	3.46	30	0	0	1	39	28	21	15	2	27	38	.197	.140	.235	8.77	6.23
Martinez, Henry	R-R	6-1	180	4-27-94	2	1	2.76	32	0	0	11	33	30	12	10	1	9	32	.248	.236	.258	8.82	2.48
McKenzie, Triston	R-R	6-5	165	8-2-97	7	4	2.68	16	16	0	0	91	63	31	27	8	28	87	.192	.193	.191	8.64	2.78
Milbrath, Jordan	R-R	6-6	215	8-1-91	2	4	3.42	34	0	0	1	50	42	23	19	1	21	49	.227	.229	.226	8.82	3.78
Miller, Andrew	L-L	6-7	205	5-21-85	0	0	108.00	1	0	0	0	0	2	4	4	0	1	0	1.000	—	1.000	0.00	27.00
Mingo, Cameron	R-R	6-5	185	9-10-93	0	0	3.65	3	3	0	0	12	13	6	5	1	4		.271	.333	.133	2.92	0.73
Orlan, R.C.	R-L	6-0	185	9-28-90	1	0	0.00	10	0	0	2	16	8	1	0	0	2	14	.140	.130	.147	8.04	1.15
Pasquale, Nick	R-R	6-0	190	10-7-90	3	3	3.21	22	0	0	0	34	24	16	12	2	17	24	.197	.246	.154	6.42	4.54
Paulson, Jake	R-R	6-7	220	2-17-92	8	5	3.04	20	19	1	0	115	104	42	39	10	32	91	.241	.276	.210	7.10	2.50
Peoples, Michael	R-R	6-5	190	9-5-91	1	2	1.11	6	6	0	0	32	17	5	4	1	6	26	.152	.133	.164	7.24	1.67
Plesac, Zach	R-R	6-3	200	1-21-95	3	1	2.45	4	4	0	0	22	19	6	6	1	4	21	.235	.283	.143	8.59	1.64
Ramirez, Neil	R-R	6-4	215	5-25-89	0	0	0.00	1	0	0	0	1	0	0	0	0		1	.000	.000	.000	9.00	9.00
Robinson, Jared	R-R	6-0	190	11-20-94	1	0	4.50	1	0	0	0	2	3	1	1	0	0	1	.333	.500	.000	4.50	0.00
Sandlin, Nick	R-R	5-11	175	1-10-97	1	0	10.38	5	0	0	0	4	8	5	5	1	7	4	.400	.231	.714	14.54	2.08
Speer, David	L-L	6-1	185	8-14-92	4	3	3.48	46	1	0	1	62	64	32	24	1	13	49	.275	.286	.268	7.11	1.89
Sulser, Cole	R-R	6-0	190	3-12-90	3	0	0.00	6	0	0	1	9	3	0	0	0		17	.103	.091	.111	17.00	1.00
Tomlin, Josh	R-R	6-1	190	10-19-84	0	0	0.00	1	1	0	0	3	1	0	0	0	0	3	.100	.000	.200	9.00	0.00
Whitehouse, Matt	L-L	6-0	175	4-13-91	4	1	2.63	29	10	0	0	65	52	25	19	4	34	58	.219	.193	.234	8.03	4.71

Fielding

Catcher	PCT	G	PO	A	E	DP	PB
Chu	.987	10	69	8	1	1	1
Gonzalez	.938	1	13	2	1	0	0
Ice	1.000	17	128	11	0	2	0
Laureano	1.000	1	8	1	0	0	0
Loopstok	.993	55	407	37	3	1	13
Salters	.989	63	431	37	5	4	6

First Base	PCT	G	PO	A	E	DP
Bradley	.990	97	871	77	10	75
Mathias	1.000	1	5	1	0	1
Rodriguez	.992	31	221	16	2	19
Sever	.991	14	104	8	1	7

Second Base	PCT	G	PO	A	E	DP
Haggerty	1.000	8	14	18	0	5
Hankins	1.000	2	4	3	0	1
Krieger	.960	17	35	37	3	8
Mathias	.987	105	164	304	6	65
Pantoja	1.000	5	15	14	0	4
Perez	.000	1	0	0	0	0
Rodriguez	1.000	7	8	20	0	4

Third Base	PCT	G	PO	A	E	DP
Haggerty	.896	41	26	60	10	3
Hankins	.944	8	6	11	1	2
Pantoja	1.000	10	6	22	0	2
Perez	.000	1	0	0	0	0
Sever	.933	83	50	174	16	17

Shortstop	PCT	G	PO	A	E	DP
Castro	.966	96	96	279	13	50
Clement	.985	15	27	39	1	8
Haggerty	.972	19	17	52	2	12
Hankins	.800	2	2	2	1	1
Pantoja	.952	9	15	25	2	6
Perez	1.000	1	1	3	0	1

Outfield	PCT	G	PO	A	E	DP
Calica	.984	93	180	2	3	1
Carter	1.000	18	23	0	0	0
Chisenhall	1.000	3	3	0	0	0
Davis	1.000	1	2	0	0	0
Guyer	1.000	3	3	0	0	0
Haggerty	1.000	12	23	0	0	0
Hankins	1.000	2	5	0	0	0
Krieger	.994	87	175	1	1	0
Marabell	1.000	75	148	8	0	3
Murphy	1.000	2	1	0	0	0
Paulino	.948	27	54	1	3	0
Tom	.970	108	247	9	8	5
Zimmer	1.000	1	2	0	0	0

CLEVELAND INDIANS

Batting	B-T	HT	WT	DOB	AVG	vLH	vRH	G	AB	R	H	2B	3B	HR	RBI	BB	HBP	SH	SF	SO	SB	CS	SLG	OBP
Brooks, Trenton	L-L	6-0	180	7-3-95	.281	.182	.315	107	388	47	109	28	3	5	52	45	7	1	5	66	2	1	.407	.362
Capel, Conner	L-L	6-1	185	5-19-97	.261	.167	.285	89	322	47	84	17	3	6	44	49	2	3	7	72	15	10	.388	.355
Carter, Jodd	R-R	5-10	170	7-20-96	.244	.256	.240	103	365	54	89	20	3	10	52	47	4	4	3	96	11	6	.397	.334
Cerda, Erlin	R-R	5-9	170	5-5-94	.222	.333	.202	32	99	12	22	8	0	0	5	8	0	3	0	27	1	1	.303	.280
Chu, Li-Jen	R-R	5-11	200	3-13-94	.278	.265	.282	81	295	33	82	20	1	8	45	32	4	0	5	68	1	0	.434	.351
Clement, Ernie	R-R	6-0	180	3-22-96	.346	.382	.333	33	133	29	46	7	0	1	13	15	4	3	1	7	5	3	.421	.425
Collins, Gavin	R-R	5-11	190	7-17-95	.233	.217	.236	62	228	28	53	20	1	5	36	14	6	3	1	46	1	2	.395	.293
Friis, Tyler	B-R	5-9	180	2-12-96	.153	.125	.163	20	59	8	9	3	0	0	6	8	0	2	0	9	0	0	.203	.254
Gantt, Tre	L-L	5-10	180	5-10-96	.200	.333	.000	6	15	1	3	1	1	0	0	4	0	0	0	7	0	0	.400	.368
Gonzalez, Gianpaul	R-R	6-0	185	1-11-96	.217	.000	.263	6	23	3	5	2	0	0	1	2	1	0	0	9	0	0	.304	.308
Ice, Logan	B-R	6-0	180	5-27-95	.194	.286	.157	43	144	15	28	5	1	1	21	18	2	0	2	46	0	0	.264	.289
Jones, Nolan	L-R	6-4	185	5-7-98	.298	.191	.325	30	104	23	31	9	1	0	17	26	0	0	0	34	0	0	.471	.439
Longo, Mitch	L-R	6-0	185	1-12-95	.276	.250	.282	119	461	73	127	28	5	8	52	41	4	2	4	97	18	8	.410	.337
Lopez Alvarez, Angel	R-R	5-10	194	3-14-97	.278	.333	.222	6	18	4	5	1	0	1	4	4	0	0	0	5	0	0	.500	.409
Medina, Jose	L-L	6-1	185	2-14-95	.250	.250	.250	30	100	9	25	5	1	2	7	13	0	0	0	21	0	1	.380	.336
Miller, Anthony	L-R	6-4	240	10-4-94	.264	.148	.302	74	250	38	66	16	1	8	30	32	8	1	2	101	0	1	.432	.363
Pantoja, Alexis	L-R	5-11	150	1-18-96	.205	.196	.207	76	259	24	53	8	1	0	21	13	1	5	3	46	7	3	.243	.243
Persinger, Dillon	R-R	5-11	180	1-31-96	.254	.218	.267	99	342	44	87	19	1	5	33	35	11	4	4	100	2	6	.360	.339
Rodriguez, Jorma	R-R	5-10	150	3-25-98	.232	.177	.254	71	237	26	55	7	2	0	15	12	5	7	1	46	7	1	.279	.282
Rolette, Josh	L-R	5-11	195	5-21-96	.250	—	.250	2	4	2	1	0	0	0	0	2	0	1	0	2	0	0	.250	.500
Tapia, Emmanuel	L-L	6-3	215	2-26-96	.186	.143	.198	89	301	29	56	10	1	9	44	37	5	0	2	112	0	0	.316	.284
Wade, Austen	L-L	6-1	185	2-17-96	.212	.100	.238	30	104	4	22	4	0	1	6	13	0	2	0	36	0	1	.279	.299
Wakamatsu, Luke	B-R	6-3	185	10-10-96	.197	.245	.179	55	193	30	38	9	1	1	16	29	1	1	1	65	1	3	.269	.304

Pitching	B-T	HT	WT	DOB	W	L	ERA	G	GS	CG	SV	IP	H	R	ER	HR	BB	SO	AVG	vLH	vRH	K/9	BB/9
Echols, Riley	R-R	6-4	205	4-12-95	0	0	11.57	1	0	0	0	2	5	3	3	1	0	1	.556	.500	.571	3.86	0.00
Esparza, Matt	R-R	6-2	195	8-22-94	0	0	4.50	1	0	0	0	2	2	1	1	0	4	0	.333	1.000	.200	0.00	18.00
Garcia, Justin	R-R	6-1	180	9-16-92	0	1	7.07	8	0	0	1	14	13	11	11	1	9	12	.245	.286	.219	7.71	5.79
Garza, Justin	R-R	5-10	170	3-20-94	5	6	3.71	16	16	0	0	68	56	31	28	5	22	69	.227	.225	.228	9.13	2.91
Hentges, Sam	L-L	6-6	245	7-18-96	6	6	3.27	23	23	0	0	118	114	51	43	4	53	122	.260	.265	.258	9.28	4.03
Jimenez, Luis	R-R	6-4	170	1-2-95	3	3	5.74	23	0	0	0	31	36	26	20	4	20	25	.295	.362	.253	7.18	5.74
Kaminsky, Rob	R-L	5-11	190	9-2-94	0	0	0.00	2	0	0	0	2	1	0	0	0	1	1	.143	.500	.000	4.50	4.50
Karinchak, James	R-R	6-3	230	9-22-95	1	1	1.00	25	0	0	13	27	14	6	3	1	17	45	.161	.195	.130	15.00	5.67
Krauth, Ben	L-L	6-0	180	3-10-94	4	2	1.99	38	0	0	2	68	47	18	15	2	25	100	.191	.184	.194	13.24	3.31
Linares, Leandro	R-R	6-3	205	1-27-94	4	1	5.20	18	1	0	0	28	29	17	16	2	32	34	.274	.250	.288	11.06	10.41
Lovegrove, Kieran	R-R	6-4	185	7-28-94	3	0	1.56	10	0	0	2	17	12	4	3	0	4	25	.188	.192	.184	12.98	2.08
Martinez, Henry	R-R	6-1	180	4-27-94	0	0	1.29	6	0	0	4	7	3	1	1	1	3	10	.125	.200	.071	12.86	3.86
McCarty, Kirk	L-L	5-10	185	10-12-95	1	2	3.19	5	5	0	0	31	26	12	11	2	4	29	.234	.361	.173	8.42	1.16
Mejia, Jean Carlos	R-R	6-4	205	8-26-96	0	1	6.00	1	1	0	0	6	5	4	4	0	1	3	.227	.231	.222	4.50	1.50
Miniard, Micah	R-R	6-7	195	4-12-94	3	5	5.00	30	7	0	1	76	72	45	42	1	46	52	.253	.304	.204	6.19	5.47
Morgan, Eli	R-R	5-10	190	5-13-96	7	7	3.91	19	19	1	0	99	93	50	43	11	26	100	.247	.242	.251	9.09	2.36
Nelson, Kyle	L-L	6-1	175	7-8-96	3	0	4.35	10	0	0	0	10	9	6	5	0	7	16	.243	.250	.238	13.94	6.10
Orlan, R.C.	R-L	6-0	185	9-28-90	0	0	1.59	5	0	0	0	6	5	1	1	0	2	8	.227	.222	.231	12.71	3.18
Pasquale, Nick	R-R	6-0	190	10-27-90	1	0	3.31	9	0	0	0	16	12	7	6	0	8	24	.207	.167	.225	13.22	4.41
Paulson, Jake	R-R	6-7	220	2-17-92	2	2	4.71	4	4	0	0	21	20	12	11	1	6	10	.253	.289	.206	4.29	2.57
Plesac, Zach	R-R	6-3	200	1-21-95	8	5	4.04	22	22	1	0	123	124	63	55	8	33	111	.264	.236	.287	8.14	2.42
Polanco, Anderson	L-L	6-3	190	9-6-92	2	2	3.72	29	7	0	0	65	56	31	27	8	56	78	.231	.157	.269	10.74	7.71
Robinson, Jared	R-R	6-0	190	11-20-94	5	3	2.65	29	0	0	0	51	40	17	15	3	21	56	.220	.239	.207	9.88	3.71
Sandlin, Nick	R-R	5-11	175	1-10-97	1	0	1.42	7	0	0	4	6	2	1	1	0	2	10	.091	.000	.125	14.21	2.84
Scott, Adam	L-L	6-4	220	10-10-95	0	0	0.00	2	0	0	0	4	3	0	0	0	4	4	.214	.200	.222	9.00	9.00
Siri, Dalbert	R-R	6-2	190	7-19-95	1	5	2.45	42	0	0	15	48	31	21	13	4	29	71	.182	.219	.160	13.41	5.48
Strode, Billy	L-L	6-0	180	8-10-92	3	1	4.05	26	0	0	0	47	53	29	21	0	16	44	.279	.265	.287	8.49	3.09
Tati, Felix	R-R	6-2	190	4-1-97	2	2	4.66	6	6	0	0	29	28	17	15	2	15	21	.252	.222	.267	6.52	4.66
Tully, Tanner	L-L	6-0	200	11-30-94	6	11	4.47	26	26	2	0	147	176	87	73	17	20	109	.297	.272	.308	6.67	1.22

Fielding

Catcher	PCT	G	PO	A	E	DP	PB
Chu	.981	57	536	45	11	1	9
Collins	.979	30	257	22	6	0	11
Gonzalez	.982	6	49	5	1	0	0
Ice	.997	38	286	29	1	1	3
Lopez Alvarez	1.000	6	36	4	0	1	2
Rolette	1.000	2	18	1	0	1	0

First Base	PCT	G	PO	A	E	DP
Miller	.994	66	501	38	3	50
Tapia	.976	72	532	32	14	53

Second Base	PCT	G	PO	A	E	DP
Cerda	.949	12	16	21	2	7
Friis	1.000	1	2	5	0	0
Pantoja	.984	15	29	33	1	6
Persinger	.978	90	154	202	8	59
Rodriguez	.988	23	32	50	1	12

Third Base	PCT	G	PO	A	E	DP
Cerda	.898	19	14	30	5	1
Collins	.923	26	19	41	5	1
Jones	.886	28	23	47	9	4
Pantoja	.923	39	35	49	7	4
Rodriguez	.902	29	10	36	5	2

Shortstop	PCT	G	PO	A	E	DP
Clement	.982	30	36	73	2	16
Friis	1.000	16	17	48	0	6
Pantoja	.990	23	34	63	1	15
Persinger	.818	2	4	5	2	0
Rodriguez	.963	14	19	33	2	5
Wakamatsu	.938	55	75	152	15	34

Outfield	PCT	G	PO	A	E	DP
Brooks	.975	71	112	4	3	0
Capel	.954	83	156	9	8	1
Carter	.989	99	166	14	2	3
Gantt	1.000	6	14	0	0	0
Longo	.974	103	182	4	5	0
Medina	.981	24	49	4	1	1
Rodriguez	1.000	3	3	0	0	0
Wade	1.000	28	46	0	0	0

LAKE COUNTY CAPTAINS   LOW CLASS A
MIDWEST LEAGUE

Batting	B-T	HT	WT	DOB	AVG	vLH	vRH	G	AB	R	H	2B	3B	HR	RBI	BB	HBP	SH	SF	SO	SB	CS	SLG	OBP
Benson, Will	L-L	6-5	225	6-16-98	.180	.277	.152	123	416	54	75	11	1	22	58	82	7	0	1	152	12	6	.370	.324
Berardi, Jesse	L-R	5-10	185	1-13-96	.234	.280	.223	69	261	30	61	13	2	3	25	19	3	0	3	54	11	2	.333	.290
Cantu, Ulysses	R-R	5-11	220	5-1-98	.173	.179	.171	69	237	27	41	12	0	8	20	24	5	1	0	78	0	0	.325	.263
Cerda, Erlin	R-R	5-9	170	5-5-94	.179	.111	.211	9	28	4	5	0	0	0	1	0	1	1	0	9	2	0	.179	.207
Clement, Ernie	R-R	6-0	170	3-22-96	.267	.327	.247	54	221	34	59	14	1	1	15	23	1	1	1	21	11	6	.353	.337
Eladio, Miguel	R-R	6-1	160	5-10-96	.230	.180	.248	52	183	14	42	6	3	3	28	9	0	3	0	45	2	0	.344	.266
Friis, Tyler	B-R	5-9	180	2-12-96	.266	.324	.254	59	214	32	57	12	2	3	27	31	1	0	2	26	8	5	.383	.359
Gantt, Tre	L-L	5-10	180	5-10-96	.167	.250	.150	9	24	2	4	1	0	0	0	7	0	1	0	10	1	1	.208	.355
Gonzalez, Gianpaul	R-R	6-0	185	1-11-96	.233	.333	.222	8	30	3	7	2	0	1	4	2	0	0	0	11	0	0	.400	.281
Gonzalez, Oscar	R-R	6-2	180	1-10-98	.292	.294	.292	114	462	52	135	25	1	13	52	12	2	0	4	107	5	6	.435	.310
Hutcheon, Dane	L-R	5-9	177	7-14-94	.289	.375	.270	13	45	6	13	1	0	0	3	4	0	0	0	9	1	1	.311	.347
Isaacs, Todd	R-R	5-11	175	5-22-96	.232	.217	.237	106	388	47	90	20	3	4	31	17	8	2	0	115	30	6	.330	.279
Jones, Nolan	L-R	6-4	185	5-7-98	.279	.184	.308	90	323	46	90	12	0	16	49	63	0	0	3	97	2	1	.464	.393
Laureano, Jonathan	R-R	6-1	200	12-21-95	.245	.260	.241	89	326	40	80	18	0	9	38	21	6	2	2	86	1	3	.383	.301
Medina, Jose	L-L	6-1	185	2-14-95	.278	.283	.276	48	169	22	47	11	1	4	16	15	0	1	2	29	1	1	.426	.335
Mejia, Gabriel	B-R	5-11	160	7-30-95	.226	.214	.230	32	115	10	26	4	1	0	8	12	1	1	2	20	4	4	.278	.300
Palacios, Richard	L-R	5-11	180	5-16-97	.300	.353	.286	20	80	10	24	2	1	2	7	2	0	0	0	13	3	0	.425	.317
Perez, Elvis	B-R	6-0	165	1-10-96	.229	.292	.205	48	175	17	40	10	1	4	22	11	0	2	2	41	1	2	.366	.271
Persinger, Dillon	R-R	5-11	180	1-31-96	.095	.000	.125	7	21	1	2	0	0	0	1	0	0	0	0	7	0	1	.095	.136
Reeves, Mitch	R-R	6-2	210	11-18-94	.286	.444	.242	12	42	6	12	1	1	1	6	6	2	0	0	6	0	0	.429	.400
Rivera, Mike	R-R	5-10	200	12-12-95	.195	.273	.167	14	41	10	8	3	0	0	3	15	0	1	0	10	0	0	.268	.411
Rodriguez, Eric	R-R	6-1	188	7-28-98	.286	—	.286	2	7	0	2	0	0	0	1	0	0	0	0	0	0	0	.286	.286
Rodriguez, Jhan	R-R	6-0	165	7-2-98	.167	.000	.200	2	6	1	1	0	0	0	0	2	0	0	0	2	0	0	.167	.375
Rodriguez, Jorma	R-R	5-10	150	3-25-96	.345	.294	.361	35	142	18	49	6	2	1	20	4	1	0	1	30	6	2	.437	.365
Rolette, Josh	L-R	5-11	180	5-21-96	.253	.119	.297	56	170	15	43	11	0	4	21	28	2	0	3	57	1	0	.388	.360
Schneemann, Daniel	L-R	6-1	180	1-23-97	.000	—	.000	2	7	1	0	0	0	0	0	0	0	0	0	4	0	0	.000	.000
Smith, Connor	R-R	5-10	180	4-22-97	.000	.000	.000	4	14	0	0	0	0	0	0	1	0	0	0	8	0	1	.000	.067
Vicente, Jose	R-R	5-11	175	11-13-95	.260	.284	.253	101	385	47	100	22	2	17	52	19	0	0	2	81	0	2	.460	.293
Wade, Austen	L-L	6-1	185	2-17-96	.260	.206	.277	41	146	19	38	10	1	2	16	27	2	0	0	42	8	4	.384	.383

Pitching	B-T	HT	WT	DOB	W	L	ERA	G	GS	CG	SV	IP	H	R	ER	HR	BB	SO	AVG	vLH	vRH	K/9	BB/9
Alvarez, Manuel	R-R	6-3	200	9-17-95	1	2	10.97	12	0	0	0	11	14	15	13	1	7	10	.333	.357	.321	8.44	5.91
Arias, Skylar	L-L	6-3	190	6-30-97	0	1	4.63	15	0	0	1	23	24	14	12	1	15	33	.267	.115	.328	12.73	5.79
Broom, Robert	R-R	6-1	195	1-19-96	2	1	1.17	17	0	0	2	23	11	3	3	0	10	30	.141	.160	.132	11.74	3.91
Clemmer, Dakody	R-R	6-2	185	1-19-96	1	2	3.49	15	0	0	0	28	38	13	11	1	12	21	.325	.391	.282	6.67	3.81
DeJuneas, Tommy	R-R	6-1	175	10-24-95	2	2	3.38	20	0	0	1	29	27	17	11	2	8	39	.248	.281	.234	11.97	2.45
Draper, Zack	L-L	6-3	200	10-18-94	0	1	3.38	3	2	0	0	13	12	5	5	1	3	9	.250	.500	.200	6.08	2.03
Echols, Riley	R-R	6-4	205	4-12-95	1	5	4.10	27	0	0	2	37	34	21	17	6	22	31	.248	.311	.217	7.47	5.30
Gallagher, Nick	R-R	6-3	200	9-9-95	2	2	4.00	18	6	0	1	54	55	33	24	6	14	54	.256	.278	.240	9.00	2.33
Hillman, Juan	L-L	6-2	185	5-15-97	6	12	5.18	26	26	0	0	129	140	95	74	7	52	110	.273	.267	.275	7.69	3.64
Hockin, Grant	R-R	6-4	200	3-5-96	1	3	6.27	4	4	0	0	19	22	15	13	1	4	16	.293	.387	.227	7.71	1.93
Jimenez, Domingo	R-R	6-3	175	8-29-93	3	0	4.63	6	0	0	0	12	5	8	6	1	10	18	.128	.250	.074	13.89	7.71
Jimenez, Luis	R-R	6-4	170	1-2-95	0	1	3.20	15	0	0	1	25	24	11	9	2	14	18	.250	.229	.262	6.39	4.97
Karinchak, James	R-R	6-3	230	9-22-95	3	0	0.79	7	0	0	1	11	8	1	1	0	7	20	.200	.200	.200	15.88	5.56
Kery, Adoni	R-R	6-0	170	2-18-96	0	0	0.00	1	0	0	0	1	2	0	0	0	1	0	.667	—	.667	0.00	13.50
Kime, Dace	R-R	6-4	200	3-6-92	2	1	4.50	7	0	0	0	8	3	4	4	2	5	7	.107	.200	.056	7.88	5.63
Manzanillo, Maiker	R-R	6-2	190	10-14-96	0	1	6.26	17	0	0	0	27	36	21	19	3	9	18	.330	.415	.279	5.93	2.96
McCarty, Kirk	L-L	5-10	185	10-12-95	4	9	4.29	22	22	0	0	115	120	60	55	14	34	132	.270	.281	.266	10.30	2.65
Mejia, Jean Carlos	R-R	6-4	205	8-26-96	4	8	3.13	17	15	0	0	92	84	41	32	3	20	97	.241	.304	.199	9.49	1.96
Miller, Andrew	L-L	6-7	205	5-21-85	0	0	27.00	1	0	0	0	1	3	4	2	0	0	1	.500	.000	.600	13.50	0.00
Mingo, Cameron	R-R	6-4	185	9-10-93	2	1	3.48	6	1	0	2	21	24	9	8	2	6	18	.282	.219	.321	7.84	2.61
Morgan, Eli	R-R	5-10	190	5-13-96	2	0	1.83	8	8	0	0	44	31	10	9	2	8	56	.194	.190	.196	11.37	1.62
Nelson, Kyle	L-L	6-1	175	7-8-96	3	1	0.76	25	0	0	6	35	28	6	3	0	2	51	.211	.152	.230	12.99	0.51
Oviedo, Luis	R-R	6-4	170	5-15-99	1	0	3.00	2	2	0	0	9	5	3	3	0	7	6	.179	.000	.263	6.00	7.00
Perez, Francisco	L-L	6-2	195	7-20-97	8	10	4.07	26	25	0	0	139	125	69	63	8	54	111	.240	.196	.251	7.17	3.49
Ponticelli, Thomas	R-R	6-1	195	4-15-97	1	0	0.00	1	0	0	0	4	2	0	0	0	1	4	.143	.200	.111	9.00	2.25
Sandlin, Nick	R-R	5-11	175	1-10-97	0	0	1.74	10	0	0	1	10	9	2	2	0	0	15	.237	.200	.261	13.06	0.00
Scheftz, Jordan	R-R	6-3	190	8-31-95	1	0	4.26	5	0	0	0	6	4	4	3	0	9	5	.191	.444	.000	7.11	12.79
Scott, Adam	L-L	6-4	220	10-10-95	0	1	2.45	5	0	0	0	11	10	3	3	1	1	15	.244	.250	.242	12.27	0.82
Tati, Felix	R-R	6-2	190	4-1-97	1	5	4.94	20	5	0	2	75	89	52	41	9	24	67	.292	.278	.300	8.08	2.89
Teaney, Jonathan	R-R	6-2	195	1-28-96	3	3	5.94	43	0	0	8	53	46	44	35	4	42	76	.223	.227	.221	12.91	7.13
Vasquez, Gregori	R-R	6-1	185	9-8-97	6	7	4.07	28	23	0	1	148	144	76	67	17	40	94	.255	.264	.251	5.72	2.43

Fielding

C: Cerda 1, Gonzalez 8, Laureano 58, Rivera 12, Rodriguez 2, Rolette 52, Vicente 15. **1B:** Cantu 64, Laureano 10, Medina 23, Reeves 2, Vicente 47. **2B:** Berardi 42, Cerda 2, Eladio 18, Friis 23, Hutcheon 1, Laureano 1, Palacios 18, Persinger 3, Rodriguez 2, Rodriguez 30, Smith 4. **3B:** Cerda 5, Friis 23, Hutcheon 10, Jones 77, Laureano 7, Perez 17, Persinger 4. **SS:** Berardi 14, Clement 52, Eladio 34, Friis 13, Perez 26, Schneemann 1. **OF:** Benson 117, Berardi 1, Gantt 9, Gonzalez 104, Isaacs 8, Laureano 1, Medina 23, Mejia 28, Reeves 6, Wade 38.

MAHONING VALLEY SCRAPPERS   SHORT-SEASON
NEW YORK-PENN LEAGUE

Batting	B-T	HT	WT	DOB	AVG	vLH	vRH	G	AB	R	H	2B	3B	HR	RBI	BB	HBP	SH	SF	SO	SB	CS	SLG	OBP
Cardenas, Ruben	R-R	6-2	185	10-10-97	.385	.000	.455	5	13	5	5	2	0	0	4	5	0	0	0	1	0	1	.539	.556

CLEVELAND INDIANS

	B-T	HT	WT	DOB	AVG	vLH	vRH	G	AB	R	H	2B	3B	HR	RBI	BB	HBP	SH	SF	SO	SB	CS	SLG	OBP
Cooper, Michael	L-R	6-5	180	7-27-99	.222	.000	.316	9	27	0	6	2	0	0	2	2	0	0	0	6	1	0	.296	.276
Dominguez, Ronny	R-R	6-0	175	6-5-97	.227	.267	.207	32	88	11	20	5	1	0	4	7	0	2	0	26	3	5	.307	.284
Eladio, Miguel	R-R	6-1	160	5-10-96	.125	.000	.250	4	8	2	1	1	0	0	0	2	0	1	0	3	0	0	.250	.300
Engelmann, Jonathan	R-R	6-4	210	9-18-96	.400	1.000	.333	3	10	2	4	0	1	1	3	1	0	0	0	4	0	0	.900	.455
Fermin, Jose	R-R	5-11	160	3-29-99	.279	.127	.321	71	251	47	70	12	4	2	26	39	9	5	3	26	17	4	.383	.391
Freeman, Tyler	R-R	6-0	170	5-21-99	.352	.417	.328	72	270	49	95	29	4	2	38	8	19	0	4	22	14	3	.511	.405
Gantt, Tre	L-L	5-10	180	5-10-96	.188	.206	.181	40	128	18	24	3	1	1	10	9	1	1	2	31	4	1	.250	.243
Gonzalez, Gianpaul	R-R	6-0	185	1-11-96	.243	.083	.320	13	37	2	9	0	0	0	2	6	0	1	0	15	2	1	.243	.349
Kwan, Steven	L-L	5-9	175	9-5-97	.333	.000	.444	4	12	1	4	1	0	0	1	2	0	0	0	2	1	0	.417	.429
Lopez Alvarez, Angel	R-R	5-10	194	3-14-97	.197	.200	.196	37	122	10	24	9	0	1	7	13	2	5	0	25	0	0	.295	.285
Lucas, Simeon	L-R	6-2	195	2-7-96	.260	.194	.281	39	127	15	33	11	0	3	17	17	0	0	0	51	1	1	.417	.347
Mejia, Gabriel	B-R	5-11	160	7-30-95	.283	.417	.244	15	53	9	15	2	1	0	7	5	0	0	2	8	5	1	.359	.333
Nelson, Hosea	L-L	6-0	210	11-22-96	.233	.246	.229	63	232	27	54	11	1	8	36	12	6	0	1	80	2	3	.392	.287
Palacios, Richard	L-R	5-11	180	5-16-97	.411	.571	.373	20	73	12	30	5	1	2	17	11	0	0	2	12	2	1	.589	.477
Perez, Elvis	B-R	6-0	165	1-10-96	.366	.313	.400	12	41	9	15	0	1	2	10	4	1	0	0	6	0	3	.561	.435
Pujols, Henry	R-R	6-3	195	12-10-98	.229	.217	.232	57	201	19	46	10	1	7	26	8	5	2	0	84	0	0	.393	.276
Reeves, Mitch	R-R	6-2	210	11-18-94	.274	.283	.270	60	219	29	60	12	0	4	36	22	5	0	3	42	4	1	.384	.349
Rodriguez, Jason	R-R	5-11	180	1-11-95	.167	.069	.200	35	114	12	19	4	0	1	12	13	2	1	2	18	0	0	.228	.260
Rodriguez, Jhan	R-R	6-0	165	7-2-98	.077	.000	.125	12	26	4	2	1	0	0	1	2	1	2	0	16	0	1	.115	.172
Scolamiero, Clark	L-L	6-0	175	1-24-96	.240	.196	.251	61	221	27	53	10	1	2	24	23	2	0	3	72	5	1	.321	.313
Smith, Connor	R-R	5-10	180	4-22-97	.212	.211	.213	19	66	8	14	2	0	2	10	4	1	0	0	14	0	0	.333	.268
Tinsley, Michael	L-R	6-0	195	5-10-95	.147	.107	.161	34	109	16	16	3	0	0	7	3	1	3	1	25	2	1	.174	.207
Wilson, Billy	L-R	5-11	185	5-28-96	.200	.000	.222	3	10	1	2	0	0	0	1	0	1	0	0	3	0	0	.200	.273

Pitching	B-T	HT	WT	DOB	W	L	ERA	G	GS	CG	SV	IP	H	R	ER	HR	BB	SO	AVG	vLH	vRH	K/9	BB/9
Algarin, Erick	R-R	6-1	195	3-31-95	2	2	3.04	21	0	0	7	24	14	13	8	2	8	34	.177	.182	.174	12.93	3.04
Alvarez, Manuel	R-R	6-3	200	9-17-95	1	0	2.28	22	0	0	5	28	14	10	7	1	18	26	.151	.200	.113	8.46	5.86
Anderson, Cody	R-R	6-4	240	9-14-90	0	0	0.00	1	1	0	0	1	0	1	0	0	0	2	.000	.000	.000	18.00	0.00
Araujo, Luis	R-R	6-1	155	8-1-96	2	1	5.60	21	1	0	2	35	35	22	22	2	14	34	.261	.220	.286	8.66	3.57
Arias, Skylar	L-L	6-3	190	6-30-97	0	0	1.64	7	0	0	0	11	10	2	2	0	2	18	.238	.250	.233	14.73	1.64
Burgos, Raymond	L-L	6-3	170	11-29-98	0	0	0.00	1	1	0	0	6	5	0	0	0	0	9	.227	.286	.240	14.29	0.00
Clemmer, Dakody	R-R	6-2	185	1-19-96	2	0	1.77	13	0	0	3	20	13	7	4	0	2	22	.171	.182	.163	9.74	0.89
Draper, Zack	L-L	6-3	200	10-18-94	7	4	3.04	14	13	1	0	68	69	30	23	4	14	65	.261	.339	.238	8.60	1.85
Garza, Justin	R-R	5-10	170	3-20-94	0	0	0.00	2	2	0	0	7	2	0	0	0	0	7	.091	.000	.143	9.00	0.00
Kery, Adoni	R-R	6-0	170	2-18-96	1	2	5.29	15	3	0	0	34	29	21	20	2	23	36	.232	.205	.247	9.53	6.09
Lantrip, Andrew	R-R	6-2	180	5-11-95	0	0	6.75	3	0	0	0	3	4	2	2	0	0	3	.333	.250	.375	10.13	0.00
Lingos, Eli	L-L	6-0	192	5-21-96	1	0	4.76	5	0	0	0	11	12	6	6	0	2	13	.267	.077	.344	10.32	1.59
Lopez, Francisco	R-R	5-11	170	2-13-94	0	0	3.65	10	0	0	0	12	10	6	5	1	7	16	.217	.357	.156	11.68	5.11
McCarthy, Shane	R-R	6-2	190	7-29-96	1	1	0.43	6	4	0	0	21	13	2	1	0	2	16	.178	.231	.149	6.86	0.86
Mingo, Cameron	R-R	6-4	185	9-10-93	2	5	5.03	15	14	0	0	63	82	44	35	4	18	37	.329	.333	.327	5.31	2.59
Mota, Juan	R-R	6-4	190	5-4-96	4	6	5.53	15	15	0	0	68	76	48	42	2	18	63	.283	.293	.276	8.30	2.37
Oviedo, Luis	R-R	6-4	170	5-15-99	4	2	1.88	9	9	0	0	48	34	14	10	3	10	61	.192	.188	.196	11.44	1.88
Royalty, Alex	R-R	6-4	190	3-19-97	0	0	2.40	5	5	0	0	15	17	6	4	0	3	16	.283	.273	.290	9.60	1.80
Santos, Luis	R-R	6-4	180	12-18-94	5	2	3.15	23	0	0	3	34	31	13	12	4	15	34	.246	.333	.187	8.91	3.93
Scheftz, Jordan	R-R	6-3	190	8-31-95	1	1	4.39	18	0	0	0	27	32	17	13	2	21	27	.305	.243	.338	9.11	7.09
Scott, Adam	L-L	6-4	220	10-10-95	2	0	3.09	5	0	0	0	12	11	5	4	1	2	14	.244	.313	.207	10.80	1.54
Valdez, Luis	R-R	6-3	170	10-14-96	2	4	5.77	17	1	0	1	34	34	28	22	3	20	33	.254	.214	.282	8.65	5.24
Valladares, Randy	L-L	5-11	155	7-6-94	0	2	2.29	19	0	0	0	39	31	14	10	2	11	44	.212	.192	.222	10.07	2.52
Yannuzzi, Yeffersson	L-L	6-2	175	10-4-96	0	3	3.38	6	6	0	0	27	22	13	10	2	14	25	.220	.200	.225	8.44	4.73

Fielding

C: Gonzalez 11, Lopez Alvarez 35, Rodriguez 31. **1B:** Cooper 7, Lucas 24, Pujols 1, Reeves 46. **2B:** Eladio 3, Fermin 37, Freeman 10, Palacios 15, Rodriguez 4, Smith 10. **3B:** Eladio 1, Fermin 4, Perez 9, Pujols 52, Rodriguez 6, Smith 6. **SS:** Fermin 22, Freeman 52, Palacios 1. **OF:** Cardenas 3, Dominguez 24, Gantt 40, Kwan 4, Mejia 14, Nelson 58, Scolamiero 57, Tinsley 30, Wilson 2.

AZL INDIANS 1   *ROOKIE*
ARIZONA LEAGUE

Batting	B-T	HT	WT	DOB	AVG	vLH	vRH	G	AB	R	H	2B	3B	HR	RBI	BB	HBP	SH	SF	SO	SB	CS	SLG	OBP
Alfonseca, Pedro	R-R	6-0	178	9-4-97	.216	.273	.202	31	111	28	24	3	3	2	14	7	6	0	0	35	7	1	.351	.298
Benavente, Brandon	B-R	5-10	200	9-3-97	.000	—	.000	1	4	0	0	0	0	0	1	0	0	0	0	1	0	0	.000	.000
Cardenas, Ruben	R-R	6-2	185	10-10-97	.300	.250	.319	37	130	20	39	13	3	0	26	18	3	1	0	19	3	0	.446	.397
Cespedes, Cristopher	R-R	6-3	200	5-18-98	.163	.167	.161	13	43	1	7	3	0	0	2	0	0	0	1	10	0	0	.233	.159
2-team total (28 Indians 2)					.223	.167	.164	41	130	15	29	8	1	1	12	11	2	0	2	34	2	1	.323	.290
Cooper, Michael	L-R	6-5	180	7-27-99	.279	.238	.293	39	158	23	44	7	0	3	22	10	1	0	4	36	2	0	.380	.318
Dominguez, Ronny	R-R	6-0	175	6-5-97	.276	.333	.261	10	29	8	8	1	2	0	7	1	0	0		9	2	1	.448	.432
Farhat, Cody	R-R	6-1	185	9-26-96	.271	.563	.185	20	70	10	19	5	1	1	10	7	3	0	0	11	3	1	.414	.363
Fernandez, Felix	R-R	6-0	185	12-9-96	.179	.000	.217	8	28	1	5	1	1	0	3	1	0	1	0	6	0	1	.286	.207
2-team total (21 Indians 2)					.235	.000	.217	29	85	10	20	6	1	1	14	6	1	0	2	17	0	1	.365	.287
Gonzalez, Marcos	R-R	5-11	165	10-12-99	.305	.286	.313	35	131	22	40	7	2	3	20	14	6	2	0	28	4	4	.458	.397
Holmes, Quentin	R-R	6-3	175	7-7-99	.000	—	.000	1	2	0	0	0	0	0	0	0	0	0	0	1	0	0	.000	.000
2-team total (6 Indians 2)					.143	—	.000	7	21	5	3	1	0	0	1	4	0	0	0	8	2	1	.191	.280
Jerez, Miguel	R-R	6-1	178	10-24-97	.274	.200	.284	48	175	30	48	11	0	14	37	21	3	0	1	56	2	0	.577	.360
Kwan, Steven	L-L	5-9	175	9-5-97	.350	.333	.355	13	40	8	14	2	1	0	4	9	1	0		3	2	0	.450	.480
Lavastida, Bryan	R-R	6-0	200	11-27-98	.292	.393	.261	33	120	23	35	4	1	0	20	22	4	2	1	23	5	5	.367	.415
Lopez, Jonathan	B-R	6-2	175	8-13-99	.203	.095	.241	24	79	8	16	3	0	0	4	13	1	1	0	22	0	1	.241	.323

	B-T	HT	WT	DOB	AVG	vLH	vRH	G	AB	R	H	2B	3B	HR	RBI	BB	HBP	SH	SF	SO	SB	CS	SLG	OBP
2-team total (14 Indians 2)					.233	.095	.241	38	129	19	30	3	2	0	11	22	2	1	0	35	3	3	.287	.353
Palacios, Richard	L-R	5-11	180	5-16-97	.438	.143	.667	5	16	4	7	1	0	2	6	6	0	0	0	2	2	0	.875	.591
Rodriguez, Eric	R-R	6-1	188	7-28-98	.200	.296	.151	23	80	9	16	2	0	2	8	9	1	1	0	18	0	0	.300	.289
Rodriguez, Jhan	R-R	6-0	165	7-2-98	.246	.167	.275	17	69	9	17	2	0	1	6	5	2	1	0	24	3	2	.319	.316
Rodriguez, Johnathan	B-R	6-3	180	11-4-99	.294	.333	.284	47	187	36	55	10	4	1	22	22	1	0	1	44	8	3	.406	.370
Santiago, Wilbis	R-R	6-0	180	1-20-96	.311	.367	.294	35	132	20	41	2	4	1	24	5	1	0	5	9	1	3	.409	.329
2-team total (7 Indians 2)					.315	.367	.294	42	159	27	50	3	4	1	26	7	1	0	5	12	2	3	.403	.337
Schneemann, Daniel	L-R	6-1	180	1-23-97	.206	.278	.180	41	136	29	28	8	1	3	14	22	0	1	2	37	2	0	.346	.313
Smith, Connor	R-R	5-10	180	4-22-97	.292	.375	.274	27	89	14	26	5	1	1	17	11	3	0	2	18	3	0	.405	.381
Wade, Austen	L-L	6-1	185	2-17-96	.286	.000	.296	8	28	5	8	3	0	0	2	2	0	0	1	3	0	0	.393	.323

Pitching	B-T	HT	WT	DOB	W	L	ERA	G	GS	CG	SV	IP	H	R	ER	HR	BB	SO	AVG	vLH	vRH	K/9	BB/9
Burgos, Raymond	L-L	6-5	170	11-29-98	3	2	3.78	12	8	0	0	52	55	26	22	2	17	58	.275	.370	.247	9.97	2.92
Esparza, Matt	R-R	6-2	195	8-22-94	0	1	6.75	3	3	0	0	7	8	5	5	0	2	9	.320	.500	.200	12.15	2.70
Feliz, Ignacio	L-L	6-1	180	10-23-99	1	1	5.73	3	3	0	0	11	11	9	7	0	4	18	.250	.191	.304	14.73	3.27
2-team total (7 Indians 2)					5	3	3.00	10	10	0	0	45	34	22	15	0	14	54	.207	.191	.304	10.80	2.80
Figueroa, Hector	R-R	6-3	190	11-30-94	1	0	2.78	14	0	0	2	23	22	7	7	0	10	22	.247	.256	.240	8.74	3.97
Gutierrez, Jhonneyver	R-R	6-5	200	12-24-98	2	5	4.14	12	10	0	0	59	64	40	27	3	18	42	.281	.316	.254	6.44	2.76
Herrin, Tim	L-L	6-5	225	10-8-96	0	1	6.16	13	0	0	3	19	29	17	13	1	8	22	.354	.231	.377	10.42	3.79
Jenkins, Liam	R-R	6-8	225	4-9-97	4	0	4.91	14	0	0	0	22	18	13	12	0	16	37	.228	.167	.265	15.14	6.55
Lantrip, Andrew	R-R	6-2	180	5-11-95	1	0	2.45	8	3	0	0	7	6	3	2	0	3	8	.222	.222	.222	9.82	3.68
Lingos, Eli	L-L	6-0	192	5-21-96	2	0	2.61	12	0	0	3	21	19	7	6	1	2	34	.232	.286	.221	14.81	0.87
Martin, Josh	R-R	6-5	230	12-30-89	0	0	7.36	3	1	0	0	4	3	3	3	1	0	6	.214	.000	.273	14.73	0.00
2-team total (1 Indians 2)					0	0	5.79	4	1	0	0	5	3	3	3	1	0	8	.177	.000	.273	15.43	0.00
McCarthy, Shane	R-R	6-2	190	7-29-96	2	0	1.35	9	0	0	1	20	18	3	3	0	2	20	.240	.179	.277	9.00	0.90
Mendoza, Dante	R-R	6-5	186	12-16-98	2	2	4.58	10	3	0	0	37	33	22	19	5	20	37	.232	.259	.216	8.92	4.82
Miednik, Jake	L-L	5-10	185	5-1-96	0	1	1.93	13	1	0	1	19	15	7	4	0	2	25	.214	.211	.216	12.05	0.96
Orlan, R.C.	R-R	6-0	185	9-28-90	0	0	0.00	1	0	0	1	2	0	0	0	0	4	.333	.000	.400	27.00	0.00	
2-team total (5 Indians 2)					0	0	1.35	6	1	0	1	7	5	1	1	0	1	14	.208	.000	.400	18.90	1.35
Pinto, Aaron	L-R	6-0	200	7-3-96	3	1	1.00	11	0	0	2	18	10	4	2	0	4	20	.164	.150	.171	10.00	2.00
2-team total (7 Indians 2)					3	2	1.95	18	0	0	2	28	20	10	6	0	5	30	.198	.150	.171	9.76	1.63
Ponticelli, Thomas	R-R	6-1	195	4-15-97	3	1	2.96	11	3	0	0	24	30	9	8	1	3	31	.303	.282	.317	11.47	1.11
Rholl, Kellen	L-L	6-3	200	5-13-96	1	0	1.31	16	0	0	0	21	17	4	3	0	13	24	.233	.077	.267	10.45	5.66
Royalty, Alex	R-R	6-4	190	3-19-97	1	0	0.00	4	1	0	0	8	4	0	0	0	2	13	.167	.143	.177	15.26	2.35
Sandlin, Nick	R-R	5-11	175	1-10-97	0	0	0.00	3	0	0	0	3	2	0	0	0	0	4	.200	.000	.333	12.00	0.00
Santana, Christophers	R-R	6-2	195	2-26-98	0	0	10.80	1	0	0	0	2	3	5	2	0	2	1	.333	.000	.375	5.40	10.80
2-team total (15 Indians 2)					1	1	4.97	16	0	0	0	25	21	21	14	1	14	18	.226	.000	.375	6.39	4.97
Scott, Adam	L-L	6-4	220	10-10-95	1	0	0.00	4	0	0	0	7	4	0	0	0	1	14	.148	.250	.130	17.18	1.23
Thomas, Tahnaj	R-R	6-4	190	6-16-99	0	0	4.58	6	0	0	0	20	13	12	10	2	10	27	.188	.217	.174	12.36	4.58
Turner, Matt	L-L	6-4	180	8-4-99	3	3	3.75	11	0	0	0	36	35	18	15	1	8	36	.250	.296	.239	9.00	2.00
Varela, Jahir	L-L	5-10	175	2-7-98	1	0	0.00	1	0	0	0	2	2	0	0	0	0	3	.250	—	.250	11.57	0.00
2-team total (15 Indians 2)					2	3	5.47	16	0	0	0	26	23	20	16	2	22	23	.245	—		7.86	7.52
Wyatt, Jonas	R-R	6-1	185	9-16-97	0	0	9.82	5	3	0	0	4	8	4	4	0	4	5	.471	.625	.333	12.27	9.82
Yannuzzi, Yeffersson	L-L	6-2	175	10-4-96	3	0	2.21	8	6	0	0	37	31	11	9	3	15	42	.225	.250	.219	10.31	3.68

Fielding

C: Benavente 1, Fernandez 5, Lavastida 26, Rodriguez 22. **1B:** Cooper 35, Fernandez 2, Jerez 13, Lopez 2, Santiago 3. **2B:** Palacios 5, Santiago 31, Schneemann 22, Smith 4. **3B:** Lopez 22, Rodriguez 15, Schneemann 15, Smith 6. **SS:** Gonzalez 35, Schneemann 6, Smith 20. **OF:** Alfonseca 31, Cardenas 31, Cespedes 13, Dominguez 9, Farhat 19, Holmes 1, Jerez 14, Kwan 12, Rodriguez 41, Schneemann 1, Wade 7.

AZL INDIANS 2   ROOKIE
ARIZONA LEAGUE

Batting	B-T	HT	WT	DOB	AVG	vLH	vRH	G	AB	R	H	2B	3B	HR	RBI	BB	HBP	SH	SF	SO	SB	CS	SLG	OBP
Cerda, Erlin	R-R	5-9	170	5-5-94	.333	—	—	1	3	1	1	0	0	0	0	0	0	0	0	1	0	0	.333	.333
Cespedes, Cristopher	R-R	6-3	200	5-18-98	.253	—	—	28	87	14	22	5	1	1	10	11	2	0	1	24	2	1	.368	.347
2-team total (13 Indians 1)					.223	.167	.161	41	130	15	29	8	1	1	12	11	2	0	2	34	2	1	.323	.290
Collins, Gavin	R-R	5-11	190	7-17-95	.177	—	—	5	17	0	3	1	0	0	0	0	0	0	0	3	0	0	.235	.177
De Oleo, Henderson	R-R	6-4	210	2-11-98	.220	—	—	47	173	24	38	8	1	3	19	19	4	0	2	62	2	2	.330	.308
Delgado, Raynel	B-R	6-2	185	4-4-00	.306	—	—	46	173	34	53	10	0	1	21	30	0	1	0	44	10	2	.382	.409
Diaz, Yainer	R-R	6-0	195	9-21-98	.355	—	—	41	155	27	55	9	4	2	28	7	1	1	0	18	1	0	.503	.387
Engelmann, Jonathan	R-R	6-4	210	9-18-96	.315	—	—	35	108	23	34	6	2	4	24	11	6	0	0	25	8	3	.519	.408
Fernandez, Felix	R-R	6-0	185	12-9-96	.263	—	—	21	57	9	15	5	0	1	11	5	1	0	2	11	0	0	.404	.323
2-team total (8 Indians 1)					.235	.000	.217	29	85	10	20	6	1	1	14	6	1	0	2	17	0	1	.365	.287
Holland, Korey	R-R	5-11	170	1-1-00	.245	—	—	31	94	20	23	3	1	0	12	23	2	0	1	30	7	1	.298	.400
Holmes, Quentin	R-R	6-3	175	7-7-99	.158	—	—	6	19	5	3	1	0	0	1	4	0	0	0	8	2	1	.211	.304
2-team total (1 Indians 1)					.143	—	.000	7	21	5	3	1	0	0	1	4	0	0	0	8	2	1	.191	.280
Jimenez, Pablo	R-R	6-2	175	2-6-99	.208	—	—	34	106	19	22	6	1	5	23	8	1	0	1	50	0	0	.425	.267
Kelkboom, Makesiondon	R-R	5-11	152	7-12-00	.127	—	—	26	71	9	9	1	1	1	3	15	2	1	1	27	5	5	.211	.292
Lopez, Jonathan	B-R	6-2	175	8-13-99	.280	—	—	14	50	11	14	0	2	0	7	9	1	0	0	13	3	2	.360	.400
2-team total (24 Indians 1)					.233	.095	.241	38	129	19	30	2	2	0	11	22	2	1	0	35	3	3	.287	.353
Naylor, Bo	L-R	6-0	195	2-21-00	.274	—	—	33	117	17	32	3	3	2	17	21	0	0	1	28	5	1	.402	.381
Ramirez, Micael	R-R	5-11	170	6-8-99	.338	—	—	24	77	10	26	2	1	1	9	6	1	0	0	11	1	1	.429	.393
Rocchio, Brayan	B-R	5-10	150	1-13-01	.343	—	—	35	143	21	49	10	1	1	16	10	2	1	2	17	14	8	.448	.389
Santiago, Wilbis	L-R	6-0	180	1-20-96	.333	—	—	7	27	7	9	1	0	0	2	2	0	0	0	3	1	0	.370	.379
2-team total (35 Indians 1)					.315	.367	.294	42	159	27	50	3	4	1	26	7	1	0	5	12	2	3	.403	.337

	B-T	HT	WT	DOB	AVG	vLH	vRH	G	AB	R	H	2B	3B	HR	RBI	BB	HBP	SH	SF	SO	SB	CS	SLG	OBP
Torres, Jhon	R-R	6-4	199	3-29-00	.273	—	—	27	99	16	27	3	0	4	16	11	1	0	0	24	3	0	.424	.351
Turner, Gionti	R-R	6-2	178	8-17-00	.296	—	—	46	169	25	50	10	2	1	22	12	2	3	1	42	9	6	.396	.348
Valera, George	L-L	5-10	160	11-13-00	.333	—	—	6	18	4	6	1	0	1	6	3	0	0	1	3	1	1	.556	.409
Wilson, Billy	L-R	5-11	185	5-28-96	.219	—	—	48	169	40	37	7	3	10	24	22	10	3	1	62	14	4	.473	.342

Pitching	B-T	HT	WT	DOB	W	L	ERA	G	GS	CG	SV	IP	H	R	ER	HR	BB	SO	AVG	vLH	vRH	K/9	BB/9
Anderson, Cody	R-R	6-4	240	9-14-90	0	0	0.00	1	1	0	0	1	1	0	0	0	1	2	.250	—	—	18.00	9.00
Broom, Robert	R-R	6-1	190	9-17-96	0	0	1.69	5	0	0	2	5	5	2	1	0	0	9	.250	—	—	15.19	0.00
Claiborne, Preston	R-R	6-2	225	1-21-88	0	0	0.00	5	1	0	0	5	3	0	0	0	0	8	.158	—	—	14.40	0.00
Feliz, Daritzon	L-L	6-2	175	8-19-99	1	3	7.64	10	8	0	0	33	46	32	28	1	22	36	.338	—	—	9.82	6.00
Feliz, Ignacio	R-R	6-1	180	10-23-99	4	2	2.12	7	7	0	0	34	23	13	8	0	10	36	.192	—	—	9.53	2.65
2-team total (3 Indians 1)					5	3	3.00	10	10	0	0	45	34	22	15	0	14	54	.207	.191	.304	10.80	2.80
Garcia, Luis D.	R-R	6-2	180	6-23-00	4	1	4.31	10	7	0	0	48	57	27	23	4	11	39	.300	—	—	7.31	2.06
Garcia, Mike	R-R	6-4	183	8-11-00	4	0	3.12	7	1	0	0	26	25	9	9	2	9	41	.243	—	—	14.19	3.12
Hankins, Ethan	R-R	6-6	200	5-23-00	0	0	6.00	2	2	0	0	3	4	2	2	0	0	6	.308	—	—	18.00	0.00
Lopez, Francisco	R-R	5-11	170	2-13-94	0	1	5.63	9	0	0	1	8	7	5	5	0	5	13	.233	—	—	14.63	5.63
Manzanillo, Maiker	R-R	6-2	190	10-14-96	1	0	0.00	4	0	0	0	5	2	0	0	0	0	11	.118	—	—	19.80	0.00
Marshall, Evan	R-R	6-2	225	4-18-90	0	0	0.00	1	1	0	0	1	0	0	0	0	0	2	.000	—	—	18.00	0.00
Martin, Josh	R-R	6-5	230	12-30-89	0	0	0.00	1	0	0	0	1	0	0	0	0	0	2	.000	—	—	18.00	0.00
2-team total (3 Indians 1)					0	0	5.79	4	1	0	0	5	3	3	3	1	0	8	.177	.000	.273	15.43	0.00
Mejia, Wilmer	R-R	6-2	170	1-15-99	4	2	4.30	10	8	0	0	46	49	26	22	1	15	40	.271	—	—	7.83	2.93
Meyer, Brendan	L-R	6-5	200	10-8-94	1	2	5.31	13	0	0	1	20	26	15	12	0	7	16	.292	—	—	7.08	3.10
Meza, Wuilson	R-R	5-11	170	10-5-98	0	1	7.20	19	0	0	1	30	34	25	24	0	17	29	.276	—	—	8.70	5.10
Morillo, Sergio	R-R	6-3	190	9-13-99	1	1	0.84	4	3	0	0	16	3	2	0	0	6	12	.208	—	—	5.06	2.53
Oca, Jose	R-R	6-0	150	2-28-99	1	0	3.63	9	1	0	1	22	18	9	9	1	3	26	.214	—	—	10.48	1.21
Orlan, R.C.	R-L	6-0	185	9-28-90	0	0	1.69	5	1	0	0	5	3	1	1	0	1	10	.167	—	—	16.88	1.69
2-team total (1 Indians 1)					0	0	1.35	6	1	0	1	7	5	1	1	0	1	14	.208	.000	.400	18.90	1.35
Paredes, Juan	R-R	6-3	200	9-25-98	1	1	4.33	19	0	0	5	27	32	20	13	1	10	34	.296	—	—	11.33	3.33
Pinto, Aaron	L-R	6-0	200	7-3-96	0	1	3.72	7	0	0	0	10	10	6	4	0	1	10	.250	—	—	9.31	0.93
2-team total (11 Indians 1)					3	2	1.95	18	0	0	2	28	20	10	6	0	5	30	.198	.150	.171	9.76	1.63
Ramirez, Jerson	R-R	6-1	185	11-24-98	4	2	2.01	14	0	0	4	22	15	10	5	0	13	30	.183	—	—	12.09	5.24
Sanchez, Wilton	R-R	6-4	175	9-8-98	3	1	8.54	15	1	0	0	26	24	26	25	1	21	23	.250	—	—	7.86	7.18
Santana, Christophers	R-R	6-2	195	2-26-98	1	1	4.56	15	0	0	0	24	18	16	12	1	12	17	.214	—	—	6.46	4.56
2-team total (1 Indians 1)					1	1	4.97	16	0	0	0	25	21	21	14	1	14	18	.226	.000	.375	6.39	4.97
Torres, Lenny	R-R	6-1	190	10-15-00	0	0	1.76	6	5	0	0	15	14	4	3	0	2	22	.246	—	—	12.91	2.35
Varela, Jahir	L-L	5-10	175	2-7-98	1	3	6.00	15	1	0	0	24	21	20	16	2	22	20	.244	—	—	7.50	8.25
2-team total (1 Indians 1)					2	3	5.47	16	0	0	0	26	23	20	16	2	22	23	.245	—	.250	7.86	7.52
Vargas, Carlos	R-R	6-3	180	10-13-99	1	2	3.93	10	9	0	0	34	33	18	15	2	24	41	.256	—	—	10.75	6.29

Fielding

C: Collins 1, Diaz 26, Fernandez 10, Naylor 19, Ramirez 10. **1B:** De Oleo 39, Engelmann 2, Fernandez 8, Ramirez 7, Santiago 2, Wilson 2. **2B:** Delgado 13, Kelkboom 7, Lopez 3, Ramirez 2, Rocchio 1, Santiago 5, Turner 1, Wilson 1. **3B:** Cerda 1, Collins 3, De Oleo 6, Delgado 12, Kelkboom 15, Lopez 12, Naylor 5, Ramirez 1, Rocchio 8. **SS:** Delgado 18, Kelkboom 3, Rocchio 26, Turner 15. **OF:** Cespedes 23, Engelmann 30, Holland 31, Holmes 5, Jimenez 25, Torres 25, Turner 6, Valera 5, Wilson 43.

DSL INDIANS   ROOKIE

DOMINICAN SUMMER LEAGUE

Batting	B-T	HT	WT	DOB	AVG	vLH	vRH	G	AB	R	H	2B	3B	HR	RBI	BB	HBP	SH	SF	SO	SB	CS	SLG	OBP
Aguilar, Daniel	L-L	5-8	175	9-16-00	.284	.233	.299	42	127	27	36	6	3	0	12	28	1	3	2	36	8	7	.378	.411
Contreras, Jeikol	L-R	6-0	175	4-14-00	.190	.308	.156	18	58	6	11	4	0	0	10	11	0	0	1	20	1	2	.259	.314
2-team total (38 DSL Indians/Brewers)					.194	.139	.208	56	180	15	35	11	1	3	32	34	1	0	5	59	3	8	.317	.318
De La Cruz, Moises	B-R	5-8	155	8-9-01	.069	.143	.046	7	29	0	2	1	0	0	2	1	0	0	0	9	1	0	.103	.100
2-team total (42 DSL Indians/Brewers)					.193	.206	.191	49	181	22	35	5	2	0	15	16	1	0	0	52	10	3	.243	.263
Flores, Jothson	B-R	5-11	160	10-6-98	.190	.357	.149	46	142	18	27	4	1	0	17	20	4	1	1	38	4	2	.232	.305
Idrogo, Cesar	B-R	5-11	170	3-26-01	.309	.306	.310	45	165	18	51	8	2	3	28	13	2	0	3	16	7	0	.436	.361
Marmol, Roger	R-R	5-11	190	10-5-99	.190	.156	.198	49	158	24	30	7	0	3	18	13	10	0	0	57	0	0	.291	.293
Montero, Jean	R-R	5-11	175	2-26-99	.220	.241	.214	50	141	30	31	2	1	1	14	25	2	5	1	40	12	3	.270	.343
Noel, Jhonkensy	R-R	6-1	180	7-15-01	.243	.283	.233	64	218	34	53	11	0	10	34	25	14	2	1	58	6	4	.431	.357
Palacio, Gaspar	B-R	5-8	155	3-2-00	.211	.242	.204	58	175	23	37	5	3	0	15	17	1	1	3	47	6	5	.274	.281
Paz, Richard	L-R	5-7	150	6-12-01	.236	.143	.255	39	123	17	29	1	0	1	13	20	3	1	2	11	0	2	.268	.351
Peralta, Wilfri	R-R	6-0	155	12-10-00	.244	.208	.253	33	119	17	29	5	2	0	12	17	5	0	1	23	5	8	.319	.359
2-team total (23 DSL Indians/Brewers)					.239	.205	.247	56	209	31	50	8	3	0	19	26	6	0	1	46	8	11	.306	.339
Perez, Derian	L-L	6-3	175	6-8-00	.244	.158	.260	46	123	15	30	4	0	0	13	15	3	2	2	25	5	6	.276	.336
Planez, Alexfri	R-R	6-2	180	8-17-01	.279	.383	.255	61	251	39	70	18	3	9	40	9	7	1	3	55	5	7	.482	.319
Rocchio, Brayan	B-R	5-10	150	1-13-01	.323	.235	.342	25	99	19	32	2	3	1	12	5	6	1	0	14	8	5	.434	.391
Rodriguez, Skeiling	L-R	6-0	175	2-26-01	.217	.180	.226	56	194	32	42	3	6	0	17	32	3	4	2	72	5	5	.294	.333
Tena, Jose	L-R	5-9	159	3-20-01	.313	.279	.322	51	195	28	61	8	4	1	23	15	4	0	4	29	10	7	.410	.367

Pitching	B-T	HT	WT	DOB	W	L	ERA	G	GS	CG	SV	IP	H	R	ER	HR	BB	SO	AVG	vLH	vRH	K/9	BB/9
Bautista, Adenys	R-R	6-3	170	8-6-98	1	0	4.78	13	1	0	0	26	24	22	14	2	16	22	.242	.260	.225	7.52	5.47
Cruz, Robert	R-R	6-3	170	4-11-00	0	1	6.14	2	2	0	0	7	14	9	5	2	7	5	.412	.375	.500	6.14	8.59
2-team total (10 DSL Indians/Brewers)					0	4	8.16	12	10	0	2	43	69	44	39	2	22	22	.369	.340	.402	4.60	4.60
Figueroa, Abraham	L-L	6-1	170	2-27-01	0	0	14.29	4	0	0	0	6	8	9	9	1	8	3	.348	.333	.353	7.94	12.71
2-team total (13 DSL Indians/Brewers)					2	2	10.45	17	0	0	1	21	26	27	24	2	29	16	.325	.238	.356	6.97	12.63
Figueroa, Daniel	R-R	6-0	172	9-25-00	0	0	3.91	12	0	0	0	23	18	10	10	0	21	19	.231	.180	.282	7.43	8.22
Flores, David	L-L	5-10	180	11-2-00	0	1	7.94	7	0	0	0	11	11	14	10	0	9	8	.239	.077	.303	6.35	7.15

Player	B-T	HT	WT	DOB	W	L	ERA	G	GS	CG	SV	IP	H	R	ER	HR	BB	SO	AVG	vLH	vRH	K/9	BB/9
Franco, Logan	R-R	6-3	170	10-11-99	1	0	8.20	13	0	0	0	26	29	28	24	2	24	16	.284	.261	.304	5.47	8.20
2-team total (1 DSL Indians/Brewers)					1	0	7.71	14	0	0	0	28	30	28	24	2	26	18	.278	.255	.298	5.79	8.36
Garcia, Frederic	R-R	6-4	195	12-17-00	0	0	27.00	1	0	0	0	1	0	2	2	0	3	0	.000	.000	.000	0.00	50.00
2-team total (12 DSL Indians/Brewers)					0	1	7.29	13	0	0	0	21	15	24	17	3	33	15	.217	.143	.294	6.43	14.14
Garcia, Luis C.	R-R	6-3	180	4-26-97	2	1	2.70	17	1	0	5	37	25	15	11	1	13	43	.187	.179	.194	10.55	3.19
Garcia, Mike	R-R	6-4	183	8-11-00	1	2	2.05	5	5	0	0	22	12	6	5	1	8	11	.169	.154	.188	4.50	3.27
Garcia, Yonaiker	R-R	5-11	165	12-15-00	0	0	10.80	2	0	0	0	2	0	2	2	0	2	1	.000	.000	.000	5.40	10.80
Gervacio, Yeury	L-L	6-1	168	7-1-99	2	1	5.93	9	4	0	0	27	34	22	18	2	14	26	.321	.250	.346	8.56	4.61
Heredia, Erick	R-R	6-4	175	3-17-97	2	5	3.68	16	0	0	3	29	25	19	12	3	14	27	.227	.246	.208	8.28	4.30
Hernandez, Roberto	R-R	6-2	180	12-2-00	2	2	2.36	13	11	0	0	46	41	23	12	0	14	49	.227	.205	.247	9.66	2.76
Jimenez, Diarlin	R-R	6-5	180	3-18-00	1	5	3.18	15	15	0	0	65	68	44	23	2	23	46	.260	.273	.244	6.37	3.18
Lopez, Euclides	R-R	5-10	170	10-13-00	0	0	3.38	2	0	0	1	3	2	2	1	0	2	2	.222	.000	.400	6.75	6.75
2-team total (14 DSL Indians/Brewers)					0	3	10.13	16	0	0	2	21	29	26	24	1	26	17	.341	.349	.333	7.17	10.97
Morillo, Sergio	R-R	6-3	190	9-13-99	1	2	3.38	6	4	0	0	16	12	7	6	0	8	13	.218	.222	.214	7.31	4.50
2-team total (2 DSL Indians/Brewers)					1	2	2.45	8	6	0	0	22	15	8	6	0	12	22	.200	.189	.211	9.00	4.91
Munoz, Brauny	R-R	6-1	170	8-20-00	5	2	2.84	14	14	0	0	63	52	28	20	1	21	51	.226	.238	.212	7.25	2.98
Noboa, Darlin	R-R	6-1	175	2-19-00	2	0	2.48	13	2	0	1	29	29	13	8	1	15	18	.276	.296	.255	5.59	4.66
Oca, Jose	R-R	6-0	150	2-28-99	3	1	2.54	10	1	0	0	28	20	11	8	0	6	24	.192	.234	.158	7.62	1.91
Parra, Ronald	L-L	6-1	160	11-5-98	1	2	4.19	12	0	0	2	19	12	12	9	0	18	19	.188	.250	.159	8.84	8.38
Peguero, Luis	R-R	6-1	165	11-15-99	5	2	5.18	19	0	0	3	42	41	26	24	4	20	32	.270	.342	.192	6.91	4.32
Perez, Steven	L-L	6-0	155	4-21-01	0	1	2.04	8	4	0	0	18	17	5	4	1	11	18	.250	.167	.296	9.17	5.60
Ramirez, Jerson	R-R	6-1	185	11-24-98	1	1	2.08	6	0	0	3	9	8	5	2	0	3	11	.242	.333	.167	11.42	3.12
Sanchez, Luis	R-R	6-1	190	3-9-95	1	0	2.25	3	0	0	0	4	3	1	1	0	2	6	.231	.000	.300	13.50	4.50
Santana, Christophers	R-R	6-2	195	2-26-98	1	0	7.94	3	0	0	0	6	4	5	5	0	6	5	.182	.222	.154	7.94	9.53
Vasquez, Wardquelin	R-R	6-3	194	7-25-01	0	2	3.29	4	4	0	0	14	16	17	5	0	9	11	.291	.333	.250	7.24	5.93
Vicente, Adauri	R-R	6-2	188	12-18-00	1	0	9.00	7	0	0	0	8	13	10	8	0	7	4	.333	.368	.300	4.50	7.88
Vinicio, Miguel	R-R	6-3	170	9-1-99	0	4	3.86	10	4	0	1	30	27	18	13	1	15	26	.237	.138	.339	7.71	4.45
Zapata, Juan	R-R	6-1	198	11-19-98	0	0	0.00	3	0	0	0	3	8	0	0	0	1	2	.500	.500	.500	5.40	2.70
2-team total (14 DSL Indians/Brewers)					1	4	5.50	17	2	0	1	34	42	26	21	3	12	29	.296	.297	.295	7.60	3.15

Fielding

C: Idrogo 12, Marmol 44, Paz 24. **1B:** Contreras 9, Flores 8, Idrogo 16, Marmol 3, Noel 43. **2B:** Contreras 1, De La Cruz 1, Flores 12, Palacio 31, Peralta 9, Rocchio 8, Tena 14. **3B:** Contreras 7, De La Cruz 1, Flores 26, Noel 19, Palacio 21, Rocchio 1. **SS:** De La Cruz 5, Palacio 1, Peralta 21, Rocchio 15, Tena 35. **OF:** Aguilar 37, Montero 50, Perez 40, Planez 52, Rodriguez 48.

DSL INDIANS/BREWERS   ROOKIE
DOMINICAN SUMMER LEAGUE

Batting	B-T	HT	WT	DOB	AVG	vLH	vRH	G	AB	R	H	2B	3B	HR	RBI	BB	HBP	SH	SF	SO	SB	CS	SLG	OBP
Celesten, Nehemias	R-R	6-1	195	2-3-00	.163	.000	.180	13	43	2	7	2	1	0	6	8	0	0	1	12	0	1	.256	.289
Contreras, Jeikol	L-R	6-0	175	4-14-00	.197	.044	.232	38	122	9	24	7	1	3	22	23	1	0	4	39	2	6	.344	.320
2-team total (18 DSL Indians)					.194	.139	.208	56	180	15	35	11	1	3	32	34	1	0	5	59	3	8	.317	.318
De La Cruz, Moises	B-R	5-8	155	8-9-01	.217	.222	.216	42	152	22	33	4	2	0	13	15	1	0	0	43	9	3	.270	.292
2-team total (7 DSL Indians)					.193	.206	.191	49	181	22	35	4	2	0	15	16	1	0	0	52	10	3	.243	.263
Made, Marlin	L-L	5-10	165	4-16-01	.263	.208	.271	53	194	26	51	12	2	1	24	23	0	0	2	37	2	4	.361	.338
Maestre, Jesus	R-R	5-10	155	2-4-00	.329	.429	.319	25	76	14	25	4	2	1	16	15	6	0	1	19	7	0	.474	.469
Paulino, Joseph	R-R	5-11	165	8-5-01	.164	.179	.161	49	165	24	27	8	1	1	10	20	4	0	2	52	2	3	.242	.267
Peralta, Wilfri	L-R	6-0	155	12-10-00	.233	.200	.240	23	90	14	21	3	1	0	7	9	1	0	0	23	3	3	.289	.310
2-team total (33 DSL Indians)					.239	.205	.247	56	209	31	50	8	3	0	19	26	6	0	1	46	8	11	.306	.339
Planchart, Victor	B-R	5-8	165	5-17-01	.301	.385	.282	43	143	15	43	13	1	0	18	26	2	0	2	25	2	0	.406	.410

Pitching	B-T	HT	WT	DOB	W	L	ERA	G	GS	CG	SV	IP	H	R	ER	HR	BB	SO	AVG	vLH	vRH	K/9	BB/9
Cruz, Robert	R-R	6-3	170	4-11-00	0	2	8.58	10	2	0	2	36	55	35	34	0	15	17	.360	.329	.390	4.29	3.79
2-team total (2 DSL Indians)					0	4	8.16	12	10	0	2	43	69	44	39	0	22	22	.369	.340	.402	4.60	4.60
Figueroa, Abraham	L-L	6-1	170	2-27-01	2	2	9.00	13	0	0	1	15	18	18	15	1	21	11	.316	.200	.357	6.60	12.60
2-team total (4 DSL Indians)					2	2	10.45	12	0	0	1	21	26	27	24	2	29	16	.325	.238	.356	6.97	12.63
Franco, Logan	R-R	6-3	170	10-11-99	0	0	0.00	1	0	0	0	2	1	0	0	0	2	2	.167	.200	.000	10.80	10.80
2-team total (13 DSL Indians)					1	0	7.71	14	0	0	0	28	30	28	24	2	26	18	.278	.255	.298	5.79	8.36
Garcia, Frederic	R-R	6-4	195	12-17-00	0	1	6.64	12	0	0	0	20	15	22	15	3	30	15	.224	.147	.303	6.64	13.28
2-team total (1 DSL Indians)					0	1	7.29	13	0	0	0	21	15	24	17	3	33	15	.217	.143	.294	6.43	14.14
Lopez, Euclides	R-R	5-10	170	10-13-00	0	3	11.09	14	0	0	1	19	27	24	23	1	24	15	.355	.385	.324	7.23	11.57
2-team total (2 DSL Indians)					0	3	10.13	16	0	0	2	21	29	26	24	1	26	17	.341	.349	.333	7.17	10.97
Martinez, Daniel	R-R	6-4	150	9-25-99	1	4	5.96	19	0	0	2	26	24	23	17	0	15	25	.245	.255	.234	8.77	5.26
Perez, Eric	R-R	6-6	190	7-27-97	0	0	9.82	3	0	0	0	4	2	4	4	0	5	3	.154	.250	.000	7.36	12.27
Reyes, Tomas	L-L	5-11	150	9-23-99	0	0	3.27	8	0	0	1	11	8	4	4	2	4	15	.186	.154	.200	12.27	3.27
Rubio, Andy	R-R	6-4	175	2-5-01	1	1	9.00	14	0	0	0	13	15	14	13	1	18	16	.353	.391	.308	7.58	8.53
Taveras, Heylin	R-R	5-11	163	8-3-99	1	1	7.88	19	1	0	1	32	37	31	28	2	19	19	.301	.309	.291	5.34	5.34
Varela, Jahir	L-L	5-10	175	2-7-98	2	0	9.82	3	0	0	0	7	8	11	8	0	9	5	.267	.182	.316	6.14	11.05
Vasquez, Samuel	R-R	6-3	170	9-20-99	2	4	5.88	12	12	0	0	41	51	34	27	1	21	34	.298	.357	.241	7.40	4.57
Vergara, Jhon	R-R	6-3	170	4-4-00	3	5	4.09	12	11	0	0	55	56	35	25	0	17	26	.262	.296	.214	4.25	2.78
Zapata, Juan	R-R	6-1	198	11-19-98	1	4	6.10	14	2	0	1	31	34	26	21	3	11	27	.270	.283	.258	7.84	3.19
2-team total (3 DSL Indians)					1	4	5.50	17	2	0	1	34	42	26	21	3	12	29	.296	.297	.295	7.60	3.15

Fielding

C: Planchart 35. **1B:** Celesten 8, Contreras 9, Paulino 10. **2B:** Contreras 1, De La Cruz 14, Maestre 12, Paulino 5, Peralta 7, **3B:** Celesten 3, Contreras 7, De La Cruz 5, Maestre 6, Paulino 22, Peralta 1, **SS:** De La Cruz 19, Maestre 2, Paulino 6, Peralta 11, **OF:** Made 50.

Colorado Rockies

SEASON IN A SENTENCE: Behind breakout seasons from starters Kyle Freeland and German Marquez, as well as continued high-level production from Nolan Arendado, the Rockies made it to the postseason for the second consecutive year, beating the Cubs in the NL Wild Card Game before being swept by the Brewers in the NLDS.

HIGH POINT: Known as a light-hitting backup catcher, Tony Wolters forever etched his name into Rockies lore with his game-winning RBI single in the 13th inning of the NL Wild Card Game at Wrigley Field on Oct. 2. Righthander Scott Oberg made sure Wolters' heroics stood tall, as the veteran reliever struck out all four hitters he faced to secure the Rockies' first playoff win since 2009.

LOW POINT: Blown out by the Mets on June 18, the Rockies dropped to 34-38 and had won just four of their last 17 games. The struggles didn't last long, as the Rockies went 57-34 the rest of the way and had a 3.83 team ERA in the second half.

NOTABLE ROOKIES: The Rockies' No. 2 prospect, Ryan McMahon filled a variety of backup roles on the infield while hitting .232/.307/.376 in 181 at-bats. Middle infielder Garrett Hampson made his major league debut after starting the season in Double-A, slashing .275/.396/.400 in 40 at-bats, while lefthander Harrison Musgrave went 2-3, 4.63 in 44.2 innings over 35 appearances.

KEY TRANSACTIONS: The Rockies spent $106 million on relievers Wade Davis, Jake McGee and Bryan Shaw in the offseason, yet the trio went a combined 9-16, 5.41 with 179 strikeouts in 171.1 innings. Davis did set a single-season franchise record with 43 saves, however. The Rockies continued adding at the trade deadline, acquiring righthander Seung-Hwan Oh from the Blue Jays. Oh appeared in 25 games for the Rockies, posting a 2.53 ERA and 24 strikeouts in 21.1 innings.

DOWN ON THE FARM: None of the Rockies' full-season affiliates finished above .500, though some of the system's top-end talent is pushing toward Colorado. Brendan Rodgers, the Rockies' No. 1 prospect, ended the season in Triple-A, as did top righthander Peter Lambert. Third baseman Colton Welker led the California League in hitting, while first baseman Roberto Ramos hit 32 home runs between stops at high Class A and Double-A. Righthander Riley Pint, the Rockies' 2016 first-round pick, struggled with injuries all season and completed just 8.1 innings while dealing with shoulder stiffness and an oblique strain.

OPENING DAY PAYROLL: $139,328,498 (14th).

PLAYERS OF THE YEAR

ANDY KUNO

ANDY KUNO

MAJOR LEAGUE

Nolan Arenado
3B
.297/.374/.561
Led NL with 38 HR;
won sixth Gold Glove

MINOR LEAGUE

Garrett Hampson
2B/SS
(Double-A/Triple-A)
.311/.382/.462
10 HR, 36 SB

ORGANIZATION LEADERS

Batting		*Minimum 250 AB
MAJORS		
* AVG	Nolan Arenado	.297
* OPS	Nolan Arenado	.935
HR	Nolan Arenado	38
RBI	Nolan Arenado	110
MINORS		
* AVG	Coco Montes, Grand Junction	.333
* AVG	Colton Welker, Lancaster	.333
* OBP	Niko Decolati, Grand Junction	.414
* SLG	Chad Spanberger, Asheville, Lansing, Dunedin	.579
* OPS	Mike Tauchman, Albuquerque	.978
R	Bret Boswell, Asheville, Lancaster	97
H	Josh Fuentes, Albuquerque	180
TB	Josh Fuentes, Albuquerque	285
2B	Josh Fuentes, Albuquerque	39
3B	Josh Fuentes, Albuquerque	12
HR	Casey Golden, Asheville	34
RBI	Josh Fuentes, Albuquerque	95
RBI	Casey Golden, Asheville	95
BB	Vince Fernandez, Lancaster	65
SO	Casey Golden, Asheville	180
SB	Garrett Hampson, Hartford, Albuquerque	36

Pitching		#Minimum 75 IP
MAJORS		
W	Kyle Freeland	17
# ERA	Adam Ottavino	2.43
SO	German Marquez	230
SV	Wade Davis	43
MINORS		
W	Rico Garcia, Lancaster, Hartford	13
L	Nick Kennedy, Asheville	13
L	Antonio Santos, Asheville, Lancaster	13
L	Matt Dennis, Lancaster	13
# ERA	Rico Garcia, Lancaster, Hartford	2.96
G	Matt Pierpont, Hartford	55
G	Justin Lawrence, Lancaster	55
GS	Matt Dennis, Lancaster	28
SV	Matt Pierpont, Hartford	32
IP	Rico Garcia, Lancaster, Hartford	167
BB	Ryan Castellani, Hartford	70
SO	Rico Garcia, Lancaster, Hartford	162
# AVG	Rico Garcia, Lancaster, Hartford	.243

2018 PERFORMANCE

General Manager: Jeff Bridich. **Farm Director:** Zach Wilson. **Scouting Director:** Bill Schmidt.

Class	Team	League	W	L	PCT	Finish	Manager
Majors	Colorado Rockies	National	91	72	.558	4th (15)	Bud Black
Triple-A	Albuquerque Isotopes	Pacific Coast	63	77	.450	14th (16)	Glenallen Hill
Double-A	Hartford Yard Goats	Eastern	65	72	.474	7th (12)	Warren Schaeffer
High A	Lancaster JetHawks	California	70	70	.500	t-3rd (8)	Fred Ocasio
Low A	Asheville Tourists	South Atlantic	64	73	.467	10th (14)	Robinson Cancel
Short season	Boise Hawks	Northwest	35	41	.461	t-6th (8)	Scott Little
Rookie	Grand Junction Rockies	Pioneer	43	33	.566	t-2nd (8)	Jake Opitz
Overall 2018 Minor League Record			340	366	.482	18th (30)	

ORGANIZATION STATISTICS

COLORADO ROCKIES
NATIONAL LEAGUE

Batting	B-T	HT	WT	DOB	AVG	vLH	vRH	G	AB	R	H	2B	3B	HR	RBI	BB	HBP	SH	SF	SO	SB	CS	SLG	OBP
Arenado, Nolan	R-R	6-2	205	4-16-91	.297	.368	.267	156	590	104	175	38	2	38	110	73	3	1	6	122	2	2	.561	.374
Blackmon, Charlie	L-L	6-3	210	7-1-86	.291	.293	.289	156	626	119	182	31	7	29	70	59	8	1	2	134	12	4	.502	.358
Butera, Drew	R-R	6-1	205	8-9-83	.214	.250	.000	10	14	2	3	0	0	1	3	2	0	0	0	6	0	0	.429	.313
Castro, Daniel	R-R	5-11	190	11-14-92	.174	.500	.083	18	46	2	8	1	0	1	6	1	0	0	0	7	0	0	.261	.192
Cuevas, Noel	R-R	6-2	210	10-2-91	.233	.231	.236	75	146	16	34	4	1	2	10	6	1	0	0	24	1	0	.315	.268
Dahl, David	L-R	6-2	195	4-1-94	.273	.234	.287	77	249	31	68	11	3	16	48	19	1	0	2	68	5	3	.534	.325
Desmond, Ian	R-R	6-3	215	9-20-85	.236	.280	.216	160	555	82	131	21	8	22	88	53	6	1	4	146	20	6	.422	.307
Gonzalez, Carlos	L-L	6-1	220	10-17-85	.277	.259	.284	132	463	71	128	32	4	16	64	37	1	0	3	113	5	2	.467	.329
Hampson, Garrett	R-R	5-11	185	10-10-94	.275	.429	.242	24	40	3	11	3	1	0	4	7	1	0	0	12	2	0	.400	.396
Holliday, Matt	R-R	6-4	240	1-15-80	.283	.313	.238	25	53	3	15	2	0	2	3	12	0	0	0	18	0	0	.434	.415
Iannetta, Chris	R-R	6-0	230	4-8-83	.224	.232	.219	110	299	36	67	13	1	11	36	50	7	1	3	87	0	0	.385	.345
LeMahieu, DJ	R-R	6-4	215	7-13-88	.276	.330	.249	128	533	90	147	32	2	15	62	37	2	2	7	82	6	5	.428	.321
McMahon, Ryan	L-R	6-2	185	12-14-94	.232	.313	.215	91	181	17	42	9	1	5	19	18	2	0	1	64	1	0	.376	.307
Murphy, Tom	R-R	6-1	220	4-3-91	.226	.226	.226	37	93	5	21	7	1	2	11	3	0	0	0	44	0	1	.387	.250
Parra, Gerardo	L-L	5-11	210	5-6-87	.284	.202	.309	142	401	52	114	17	0	6	53	32	5	2	3	75	11	4	.372	.342
Story, Trevor	R-R	6-1	210	11-15-92	.291	.326	.277	157	598	88	174	42	6	37	108	47	7	0	4	168	27	6	.567	.348
Tapia, Raimel	L-L	6-2	180	2-4-94	.200	.143	.222	25	25	6	5	2	1	1	6	2	0	0	0	7	0	0	.480	.259
Tauchman, Mike	L-L	6-2	200	12-3-90	.094	.083	.100	21	32	5	3	1	0	0	4	0	1	0	1	15	1	0	.125	.194
Valaika, Pat	R-R	5-11	200	9-9-92	.156	.167	.143	68	122	8	19	5	0	2	5	9	0	2	0	30	0	0	.246	.214
Wolters, Tony	L-R	5-10	200	6-9-92	.170	.194	.164	74	182	19	31	4	4	3	27	26	6	0	2	33	2	0	.286	.292

Pitching	B-T	HT	WT	DOB	W	L	ERA	G	GS	CG	SV	IP	H	R	ER	HR	BB	SO	AVG	vLH	vRH	K/9	BB/9
Almonte, Yency	B-R	6-3	205	6-4-94	0	0	1.84	14	0	0	0	15	15	5	3	1	4	14	.273	.250	.286	8.59	2.45
Anderson, Tyler	L-L	6-4	210	12-30-89	7	9	4.55	32	32	0	0	176	165	94	89	30	59	164	.248	.283	.239	8.39	3.02
Bettis, Chad	R-R	6-1	200	4-26-89	5	2	5.01	27	20	0	0	120	121	72	67	18	47	80	.265	.232	.290	5.98	3.52
Davis, Wade	R-R	6-5	225	9-7-85	3	6	4.13	69	0	0	43	65	43	31	30	8	26	78	.185	.140	.227	10.74	3.58
Dunn, Mike	L-L	6-0	215	5-23-85	0	0	9.00	25	0	0	0	17	22	17	17	1	18	12	.344	.308	.368	6.35	9.53
Freeland, Kyle	L-L	6-3	170	5-14-93	17	7	2.85	33	33	0	0	202	182	64	64	17	70	173	.240	.185	.255	7.70	3.11
Gray, Jon	R-R	6-4	235	11-5-91	12	9	5.12	31	31	0	0	172	180	102	98	27	52	183	.266	.270	.262	9.56	2.72
Hoffman, Jeff	R-R	6-5	225	1-8-93	0	0	9.35	6	1	0	0	9	15	9	9	0	7	5	.405	.526	.278	5.19	7.27
Howard, Sam	R-L	6-3	170	3-5-93	0	0	2.25	4	0	0	0	4	5	1	1	0	3	1	.313	.000	.385	2.25	6.75
Johnson, DJ	L-R	6-4	235	8-30-89	1	0	4.26	7	0	0	0	6	6	3	3	0	2	9	.240	.333	.154	12.79	2.84
Marquez, German	R-R	6-1	185	2-22-95	14	11	3.77	33	33	0	0	196	179	90	82	24	57	230	.241	.290	.188	10.56	2.62
McGee, Jake	L-L	6-3	230	8-6-86	2	4	6.49	61	0	0	1	51	59	39	37	10	16	47	.285	.307	.273	8.24	2.81
Musgrave, Harrison	L-L	6-1	205	3-3-92	2	3	4.63	35	0	0	0	45	36	23	23	7	22	32	.224	.217	.228	6.45	4.43
Oberg, Scott	R-R	6-2	205	3-13-90	8	1	2.45	56	0	0	1	59	45	17	16	4	12	57	.213	.250	.185	8.74	1.84
Oh, Seunghwan	R-R	5-10	205	7-15-82	2	0	2.53	25	0	0	1	21	15	7	6	3	7	24	.197	.250	.159	10.13	2.95
Ottavino, Adam	B-R	6-5	220	11-22-85	6	4	2.43	75	0	0	6	78	41	25	21	5	36	112	.158	.179	.142	12.98	4.17
Pounders, Brooks	R-R	6-5	265	9-26-90	0	1	7.63	14	0	0	0	15	25	13	13	3	2	17	.368	.281	.444	9.98	1.17
Rusin, Chris	L-L	6-2	195	10-22-86	2	3	6.09	41	0	0	0	55	56	42	37	7	26	47	.268	.225	.300	7.74	4.28
Senzatela, Antonio	R-R	6-1	220	1-21-95	6	6	4.38	23	13	0	0	90	94	45	44	10	30	69	.266	.265	.267	6.87	2.99
Shaw, Bryan	R-R	6-1	220	11-8-87	4	6	5.93	61	0	0	0	55	70	43	36	9	28	54	.313	.272	.341	8.89	4.61
Vasto, Jerry	L-L	6-2	195	2-12-92	0	0	40.50	1	0	0	0	1	3	3	3	0	1	1	.600	.000	.750	13.50	13.50

Fielding

Catcher	PCT	G	PO	A	E	DP	PB
Butera	1.000	6	45	4	0	1	0
Iannetta	.994	99	692	29	4	2	4
Murphy	.974	22	183	8	5	0	1
Wolters	.993	64	488	43	4	5	6

First Base	PCT	G	PO	A	E	DP
Butera	1.000	4	6	1	0	1
Desmond	.995	138	1111	84	6	113

	PCT	G	PO	A	E	DP
Holliday	1.000	1	2	0	0	0
McMahon	.995	31	179	9	1	17
Valaika	.986	15	63	9	1	12

Second Base	PCT	G	PO	A	E	DP
Castro	1.000	16	18	32	0	7
Hampson	.926	7	9	16	2	3
LeMahieu	.993	128	209	378	4	90
McMahon	1.000	10	14	27	0	6

	PCT	G	PO	A	E	DP
Valaika	1.000	17	30	31	0	11
Wolters	1.000	2	1	2	0	1

Third Base	PCT	G	PO	A	E	DP
Arenado	.967	152	104	312	14	44
McMahon	1.000	17	7	18	0	4
Valaika	1.000	8	1	8	0	2
Wolters	.000	1	0	0	0	0

Shortstop	PCT	G	PO	A	E	DP
Castro	.000	1	0	0	0	0
Desmond	1.000	3	0	1	0	0
Hampson	.938	8	1	14	1	1
Story	.979	156	197	416	13	92
Valaika	1.000	7	3	9	0	4

Outfield	PCT	G	PO	A	E	DP
Blackmon	.997	151	293	3	1	1
Cuevas	1.000	45	48	1	0	1
Dahl	1.000	62	109	2	0	1
Desmond	1.000	20	29	1	0	0
Gonzalez	.991	117	213	6	2	1

	PCT	G	PO	A	E	DP
Hampson	.000	1	0	0	0	0
Holliday	.846	13	10	1	2	1
Parra	.981	119	194	9	4	3
Tapia	1.000	5	5	0	0	0
Tauchman	1.000	9	9	0	0	0
Wolters	1.000	2	1	0	0	0

ALBUQUERQUE ISOTOPES   TRIPLE-A
PACIFIC COAST LEAGUE

Batting	B-T	HT	WT	DOB	AVG	vLH	vRH	G	AB	R	H	2B	3B	HR	RBI	BB	HBP	SH	SF	SO	SB	CS	SLG	OBP
Bemboom, Anthony	L-R	6-2	195	1-18-90	.232	.167	.246	70	211	25	49	10	0	5	29	32	3	1	2	49	0	0	.351	.339
Cardullo, Stephen	R-R	6-0	215	8-31-87	.286	.267	.290	73	199	34	57	13	4	3	30	17	1	6	42	3	0	.437	.336
Castro, Daniel	R-R	5-11	190	11-14-92	.307	.314	.305	69	251	35	77	16	1	3	30	13	2	1	3	24	2	0	.414	.342
Cuevas, Noel	R-R	6-2	210	10-2-91	.331	.280	.341	44	160	17	53	10	4	5	29	16	0	0	1	23	3	5	.538	.390
Dahl, David	L-R	6-2	195	4-1-94	.286	.154	.313	19	77	7	22	7	0	2	9	1	0	0	0	19	1	0	.455	.295
Fuentes, Josh	R-R	6-2	215	2-19-93	.327	.323	.327	135	551	93	180	39	12	14	95	21	6	1	7	103	3	5	.517	.354
Gibson, Derrik	R-R	6-1	195	12-5-89	.275	.217	.289	34	120	25	33	5	6	4	16	15	0	0	2	27	2	3	.517	.350
Hampson, Garrett	R-R	5-11	185	10-10-94	.314	.264	.325	72	296	53	93	17	4	6	25	30	1	3	2	58	17	4	.460	.377
Hatch, LJ	R-R	5-11	175	5-18-94	.000	—	.000	1	1	0	0	0	0	0	0	0	0	0	0	1	0	0	.000	.000
Holliday, Matt	R-R	6-4	240	1-15-80	.346	.600	.319	15	52	12	18	4	0	3	14	9	1	0	0	9	0	0	.596	.452
McMahon, Ryan	L-R	6-2	185	12-14-94	.290	.217	.317	55	224	40	65	15	3	11	48	15	2	0	1	61	3	2	.531	.339
Metzler, Ryan	R-R	6-3	190	3-20-93	.381	1.000	.350	8	21	1	8	1	0	0	4	1	0	1	0	6	0	0	.429	.409
Moberg, Jeff	R-R	5-9	170	7-18-94	.125	—	.125	4	8	0	1	0	0	0	2	0	0	0	0	2	0	0	.125	.125
Murphy, Tom	R-R	6-1	220	4-3-91	.259	.286	.254	64	236	40	61	16	3	17	49	22	5	0	1	76	4	2	.568	.333
O'Malley, Shawn	B-R	5-11	175	12-28-87	.279	.143	.302	55	147	19	41	6	2	1	16	9	1	10	2	29	3	3	.367	.321
Patterson, Jordan	L-L	6-4	215	2-12-92	.271	.253	.276	118	413	77	112	23	2	26	76	42	22	0	3	128	6	2	.525	.367
Phillips, Anthony	R-R	5-9	160	4-11-90	.318	.625	.250	14	44	9	14	6	0	2	5	5	1	0	0	9	1	0	.591	.434
Rodgers, Brendan	R-R	6-0	180	8-9-96	.232	.222	.233	19	69	5	16	4	0	0	5	1	2	0	0	16	0	0	.290	.264
Soto, Elliot	R-R	5-9	160	8-21-89	.286	.342	.274	81	238	33	68	10	5	1	28	24	0	3	3	41	2	1	.382	.347
Tapia, Raimel	L-L	6-2	180	2-4-94	.302	.303	.301	105	434	81	131	33	9	11	62	32	2	3	1	85	21	3	.495	.352
Tauchman, Mike	L-L	6-2	200	12-3-90	.323	.378	.307	112	403	84	130	26	7	20	81	60	2	0	6	70	12	10	.571	.408
Valaika, Pat	R-R	5-11	200	9-9-92	.216	.261	.207	37	139	13	30	4	1	8	20	7	0	0	1	30	1	1	.432	.252
Vazquez, Jan	B-R	5-10	165	4-29-91	.230	.206	.237	55	148	20	34	7	0	4	18	21	6	1	2	42	0	1	.358	.345
Weeks, Drew	R-R	6-2	200	6-9-93	.267	.222	.275	49	180	27	48	8	4	8	28	15	5	1	1	43	3	4	.489	.348

Pitching	B-T	HT	WT	DOB	W	L	ERA	G	GS	CG	SV	IP	H	R	ER	HR	BB	SO	AVG	vLH	vRH	K/9	BB/9
Almonte, Yency	R-R	6-3	205	6-4-94	3	5	5.56	18	10	0	1	44	44	27	27	8	14	34	.268	.321	.221	7.01	2.89
Bettis, Chad	R-R	6-2	200	4-26-89	0	0	5.14	3	3	0	0	14	16	8	8	2	3	10	.281	.412	.225	6.43	1.93
Broyles, Shane	R-R	6-1	180	8-19-91	3	2	5.63	42	0	0	0	54	62	35	34	6	27	63	.295	.377	.240	10.44	4.47
Casilla, Santiago	R-R	6-0	210	7-25-80	0	2	8.03	12	0	0	0	12	16	14	11	2	9	12	.308	.391	.241	8.76	6.57
Diaz, Jairo	R-R	6-0	200	5-27-91	0	0	9.82	4	0	0	0	4	3	5	4	0	4	5	.214	.000	.375	12.27	9.82
Dunn, Mike	L-L	6-0	215	5-23-85	0	1	5.79	5	0	0	0	5	5	3	3	0	3	4	.278	.333	.250	7.71	5.79
Estevez, Carlos	R-R	6-4	210	12-28-92	0	1	6.35	28	0	0	1	28	37	21	20	6	11	35	.314	.460	.206	11.12	3.49
Flemer, Matt	R-R	6-2	210	11-22-90	1	1	10.29	5	4	0	0	21	36	24	24	12	6	17	.395	.359	.429	7.29	2.57
Gonzalez, Nelson	R-R	6-1	170	2-15-90	3	2	5.36	20	5	0	0	47	52	30	28	10	16	45	.278	.269	.284	8.62	3.06
Gray, Jon	R-R	6-4	235	11-5-91	1	0	3.38	2	2	0	0	11	7	5	4	1	4	13	.175	.238	.105	10.97	3.38
Hessler, Keith	L-L	6-4	244	3-15-89	3	2	5.47	42	0	0	0	53	63	44	32	9	34	57	.293	.256	.314	9.74	5.81
Hoffman, Jeff	R-R	6-5	225	1-8-93	6	8	4.94	21	21	0	0	106	105	60	58	9	47	102	.267	.289	.248	8.69	4.00
Holman, David	R-R	6-6	220	5-31-90	5	5	5.25	20	8	0	0	72	81	48	42	12	26	36	.292	.361	.239	4.50	3.25
Holmberg, David	R-L	6-3	245	7-19-91	7	8	5.21	22	18	0	0	107	136	73	62	17	30	65	.313	.302	.318	5.47	2.52
House, Austin	R-R	6-4	200	1-24-91	1	2	8.48	34	0	0	1	40	49	40	38	8	23	28	.297	.352	.255	6.25	5.13
Howard, Sam	R-L	6-3	170	3-5-93	3	8	5.06	21	21	0	0	96	106	55	54	13	34	80	.285	.319	.270	7.50	3.19
Jensen, Chris	R-R	6-4	200	9-30-90	0	0	7.13	5	2	0	0	18	24	14	14	3	10	15	.329	.389	.270	7.64	5.09
2-team total (15 Round Rock)					1	2	5.54	20	7	0	0	65	80	43	40	8	33	43	.309	.339	.284	5.95	4.57
Johnson, DJ	L-R	6-4	235	8-30-89	3	5	3.90	50	0	0	18	55	56	27	24	5	15	84	.262	.239	.279	13.66	2.44
Lambert, Peter	R-R	6-2	185	4-18-97	2	5	5.04	11	11	0	0	55	72	41	31	5	15	30	.320	.288	.351	5.04	2.44
McGough, Scott	R-R	5-11	190	10-31-89	7	3	5.55	43	1	0	1	71	87	47	44	13	22	81	.300	.290	.307	10.22	2.78
Melotakis, Mason	R-L	6-2	220	6-28-91	0	0	12.60	16	0	0	0	15	27	21	21	4	11	6	.391	.217	.478	3.60	6.60
Musgrave, Harrison	L-L	6-1	205	3-3-92	0	1	5.40	8	3	0	0	23	23	12	10	2	6	16	.324	.292	.340	9.72	3.24
Oberg, Scott	R-R	6-2	205	3-13-90	1	0	1.76	13	0	0	3	15	14	3	3	1	2	14	.264	.238	.281	8.22	1.17
Oberholtzer, Brett	L-L	6-1	225	7-1-89	7	10	5.77	24	23	0	0	133	167	91	85	25	43	91	.313	.311	.315	6.17	2.92
Pounders, Brooks	R-R	6-5	265	9-26-90	2	3	3.48	26	0	0	0	31	28	12	12	3	10	36	.235	.229	.239	10.45	2.90
Rosscup, Zac	R-L	6-2	220	6-9-88	0	0	1.08	10	0	0	0	8	4	2	1	0	3	9	.133	.067	.200	9.72	3.24
2-team total (1 Oklahoma City)					0	0	1.00	11	0	0	0	9	4	2	1	0	4	10	.125	.063	.188	10.00	4.00
Rusin, Chris	L-L	6-2	195	10-22-86	0	0	5.40	3	0	0	0	3	5	2	2	0	2	3	.231	.250	.222	2.70	5.40
Schlitter, Craig	R-R	6-0	195	5-16-92	0	1	3.60	3	0	0	0	5	3	2	2	1	2	2	.300	.222	.364	3.60	3.60
Senzatela, Antonio	R-R	6-1	180	1-21-95	3	1	2.15	8	8	0	0	38	29	10	9	1	12	42	.215	.269	.162	10.04	2.87
Shaw, Bryan	B-R	6-2	220	11-8-87	0	0	9.00	2	0	0	0	2	3	2	2	1	2	1	.333	.250	.400	4.50	9.00
Vasto, Jerry	L-L	6-2	195	2-12-92	2	1	3.16	37	0	0	3	37	32	18	13	3	18	44	.232	.269	.209	10.70	4.38
2-team total (1 Omaha)					3	1	3.08	38	0	0	3	38	34	19	13	3	18	45	.236	.259	.222	10.66	4.26

Fielding

Catcher	PCT	G	PO	A	E	DP	PB
Bemboom	.996	52	407	36	2	4	3

	PCT	G	PO	A	E	DP	PB
Murphy	.981	52	426	35	9	3	6
Vazquez	.993	37	264	21	2	3	5

First Base	PCT	G	PO	A	E	DP
Bemboom	1.000	1	2	0	0	0

COLORADO ROCKIES

	PCT	G	PO	A	E	DP
Fuentes	1.000	21	158	12	0	25
Holliday	1.000	2	17	0	0	1
McMahon	.976	43	339	25	9	41
Patterson	.994	71	585	43	4	68
Valaika	1.000	8	80	4	0	9

Second Base	PCT	G	PO	A	E	DP
Cardullo	1.000	1	2	5	0	1
Castro	.959	23	47	71	5	25
Fuentes	1.000	1	3	3	0	1
Gibson	.989	25	37	56	1	13
Hampson	.980	44	76	119	4	36
Hatch	.000	1	0	0	0	0
McMahon	.976	10	22	19	1	7
Metzler	.941	4	8	8	1	4
Moberg	1.000	2	2	5	0	1
O'Malley	.966	19	33	51	3	18
Rodgers	1.000	3	6	6	0	0

Soto	.962	8	9	16	1	5
Valaika	1.000	9	18	26	0	8

Third Base	PCT	G	PO	A	E	DP
Castro	1.000	1	0	4	0	0
Fuentes	.966	110	67	216	10	25
Gibson	.938	8	5	10	1	3
McMahon	1.000	2	1	3	0	0
Metzler	1.000	3	0	2	0	0
Moberg	.000	1	0	0	0	0
Phillips	1.000	5	3	9	0	1
Rodgers	1.000	4	4	6	0	1
Soto	.750	4	3	3	2	1
Valaika	.957	8	6	16	1	2

Shortstop	PCT	G	PO	A	E	DP
Castro	.988	41	51	118	2	27
Hampson	.942	23	22	59	5	16

Metzler	.000	1	0	0	0	0
O'Malley	1.000	4	1	7	0	1
Phillips	1.000	7	12	19	0	7
Rodgers	.962	11	9	16	1	5
Soto	.959	56	70	139	9	43
Valaika	1.000	9	12	26	0	8

Outfield	PCT	G	PO	A	E	DP
Cardullo	.975	51	72	5	2	0
Cuevas	.967	41	58	1	2	0
Dahl	.976	17	39	2	1	0
Hampson	1.000	6	16	1	0	0
Holliday	1.000	6	8	0	0	0
O'Malley	.958	16	22	1	1	0
Patterson	.974	44	72	3	2	0
Tapia	.981	104	203	3	4	0
Tauchman	.988	106	233	12	3	2
Weeks	.965	46	52	3	2	0

HARTFORD YARD GOATS

DOUBLE-A

EASTERN LEAGUE

Batting	B-T	HT	WT	DOB	AVG	vLH	vRH	G	AB	R	H	2B	3B	HR	RBI	BB	HBP	SH	SF	SO	SB	CS	SLG	OBP
Bednar, Brandon	R-R	6-4	195	3-21-92	.283	.233	.300	55	173	20	49	5	1	5	15	14	3	0	1	35	2	1	.410	.346
2-team total (31 Reading)					.279	.225	.299	86	272	28	76	15	2	7	29	16	3	0	2	54	2	2	.427	.324
Bugner, Tyler	L-R	6-2	195	10-29-94	.333	.500	.000	3	3	1	1	0	0	0	0	1	0	0	0	0	0	0	.333	.500
Burcham, Scott	R-R	5-11	185	6-17-93	.263	.342	.241	53	175	22	46	9	0	2	15	17	1	1	2	51	6	5	.349	.328
Carrizales, Omar	L-L	6-0	175	1-30-95	.229	.191	.242	90	279	34	64	16	2	7	31	22	2	5	1	76	11	2	.376	.290
Daza, Yonathan	R-R	6-2	200	2-28-94	.306	.296	.309	54	219	27	67	18	2	4	29	7	1	1	0	24	4	5	.461	.330
Hampson, Garrett	R-R	5-11	185	10-10-94	.304	.300	.305	38	148	28	45	8	2	4	15	21	0	3	0	17	19	1	.466	.391
Hilliard, Sam	L-L	6-5	225	2-21-94	.262	.211	.279	121	435	58	114	22	9	35	101	40	2	4	2	151	23	14	.509	.327
Jones, Mylz	R-R	6-1	185	4-13-94	.250	.250	.250	117	404	49	101	19	3	10	35	14	2	4	5	94	10	5	.386	.275
Metzler, Ryan	R-R	6-3	190	3-20-93	.230	.243	.225	98	292	34	67	16	0	8	37	31	3	4	4	86	14	4	.366	.306
Molina, Nelson	L-R	6-3	175	4-30-95	.204	.094	.236	49	142	17	29	9	0	2	12	6	0	1	0	34	0	1	.310	.237
Mundell, Brian	R-R	6-3	230	2-28-94	.263	.250	.267	128	441	49	116	25	1	7	41	53	5	2	5	77	1	3	.372	.345
Nunez, Dom	L-R	6-0	175	1-17-95	.222	.231	.220	92	324	34	72	12	0	9	42	46	2	2	3	73	8	6	.343	.320
Perkins, Robbie	R-R	6-0	175	5-29-94	.214	.250	.200	5	14	1	3	0	0	0	0	2	1	1	0	5	0	1	.214	.353
Phillips, Anthony	R-R	5-9	160	4-11-92	.250	.000	.385	6	20	9	5	0	0	3	9	3	0	0	0	5	1	0	.700	.348
Rabago, Chris	R-R	5-11	185	4-22-93	.213	.200	.217	66	202	22	43	14	2	4	23	22	1	2	1	52	9	1	.361	.292
2-team total (7 Trenton)					.196	.158	.208	73	230	23	45	14	2	5	23	24	1	2	1	62	9	1	.326	.273
Ramos, Roberto	L-R	6-5	220	12-28-94	.231	.164	.257	61	199	26	46	9	0	15	34	26	1	0	2	75	2	1	.503	.320
Rodgers, Brendan	R-R	6-0	180	8-9-96	.275	.269	.277	95	357	49	98	23	2	17	62	30	9	1	5	76	12	3	.493	.342
Rogers, Wes	R-R	6-3	180	3-7-94	.200	.048	.248	54	175	17	35	4	1	2	15	15	2	4	1	44	14	4	.269	.269
Tidaback, Sam	R-R	6-0	210	10-6-93	.263	.000	.286	12	38	4	10	2	0	0	4	3	0	0	0	10	1	0	.316	.317
Wall, Forrest	L-R	6-0	176	11-20-95	.206	.217	.202	46	170	27	35	6	1	2	12	17	3	0	0	42	8	3	.359	.290
2-team total (35 New Hampshire)					.234	.242	.231	81	299	46	70	13	3	7	25	30	7	0	1	88	18	6	.368	.318
Weeks, Drew	R-R	6-2	200	6-9-93	.239	.241	.238	31	109	13	26	3	1	3	11	8	0	1	0	32	2	0	.367	.288
Wernes, Bobby	R-R	6-0		7-4-94	.242	.333	.222	12	33	4	8	2	1	0	6	1	0	1	2	11	0	0	.364	.290

Pitching	B-T	HT	WT	DOB	W	L	ERA	G	GS	CG	SV	IP	H	R	ER	HR	BB	SO	AVG	vLH	vRH	K/9	BB/9
Castellani, Ryan	R-R	6-4	220	4-1-96	7	9	5.49	26	26	0	0	134	135	86	82	15	70	91	.265	.268	.261	6.10	4.69
Cozart, Logan	R-R	6-2	215	1-27-93	8	5	2.23	54	0	0	2	69	54	20	17	6	16	62	.213	.231	.196	8.13	2.10
Duncan, Frank	R-R	6-4	215	1-30-92	3	4	4.84	16	10	0	0	61	63	35	33	7	21	24	.273	.268	.277	3.52	3.08
French, Parker	L-R	6-2	215	3-19-93	1	4	7.95	27	8	0	0	60	79	55	53	7	42	28	.336	.406	.252	4.20	6.30
Garcia, Jason	R-R	6-0	185	11-21-92	2	1	9.64	15	0	0	0	19	27	23	20	3	15	17	.365	.410	.314	8.20	7.23
Garcia, Rico	R-R	5-11	190	1-10-94	6	2	2.28	11	11	0	0	67	54	19	17	8	20	61	.223	.233	.212	8.19	2.69
Gonzalez, Rayan	R-R	6-3	175	10-18-90	0	1	5.19	19	0	0	0	17	19	11	10	4	8	17	.271	.207	.317	8.83	4.15
Griggs, Scott	R-R	6-4	215	5-13-91	4	0	3.47	49	0	0	4	57	52	25	22	6	22	63	.240	.232	.246	9.95	3.47
Grills, Evan	L-L	6-4	210	4-5-92	4	5	3.90	16	16	0	0	85	89	38	37	8	16	81	.271	.269	.271	8.54	1.69
Holder, Heath	R-R	6-6	211	8-23-92	0	1	13.50	1	0	0	0	3	2	2	1	0	2	0	.429	.600	.000	0.00	6.00
Horacek, Mitch	L-L	6-5	185	12-3-91	3	3	2.20	51	0	0	2	61	50	17	15	3	27	75	.222	.204	.235	11.01	3.96
Humphreys, Reid	R-R	6-1	205	11-21-94	0	1	3.18	7	0	0	4	6	3	3	2	0	7	7	.167	.083	.333	11.12	11.12
Jensen, Chris	R-R	6-4	200	9-30-90	1	2	10.13	7	3	0	0	19	36	23	21	5	10	16	.405	.420	.385	5.79	4.82
Lambert, Peter	R-R	6-2	185	4-18-97	8	2	2.23	15	15	1	0	93	80	25	23	6	12	75	.236	.241	.231	7.28	1.17
Magliaro, Marc	R-R	5-11	175	2-17-90	3	4	4.44	36	0	0	0	49	49	32	24	6	15	51	.257	.318	.208	9.43	2.77
Moran, Brian	L-L	6-3	210	9-30-88	0	1	2.42	19	0	0	0	22	15	7	6	1	7	32	.188	.143	.217	12.90	2.82
Nolin, Sean	L-L	6-3	235	12-26-89	2	4	4.24	29	3	0	0	40	42	20	19	6	11	45	.266	.293	.250	10.04	3.35
Pierpont, Matt	R-R	6-2	215	1-25-91	1	5	1.95	55	0	0	32	60	44	19	13	3	21	77	.209	.228	.186	11.55	3.15
Schlitter, Craig	R-R	6-0	195	5-16-92	0	1	5.01	22	3	0	1	47	47	26	26	10	19	40	.266	.309	.229	7.71	3.66
Schuh, Max	L-L	6-4	210	3-13-92	0	0	7.50	9	0	0	0	6	5	5	5	0	9	4	.227	.200	.235	6.00	13.50
Tinoco, Jesus	R-R	6-4	190	4-30-95	9	12	4.79	26	26	1	0	141	149	77	75	23	38	132	.269	.215	.328	8.43	2.43
Wynkoop, Jack	L-L	6-5	200	11-2-93	3	7	6.58	16	16	0	0	81	124	63	59	11	16	40	.357	.378	.347	4.13	1.79

Fielding

Catcher	PCT	G	PO	A	E	DP	PB
Nunez	.995	70	520	33	3	2	3
Perkins	.975	5	36	3	1	0	1
Rabago	.992	61	459	60	4	11	5
Tidaback	1.000	3	17	1	0	0	0

First Base

First Base	PCT	G	PO	A	E	DP
Metzler	1.000	3	23	3	0	5
Mundell	.991	92	662	72	7	66
Ramos	.994	42	295	17	2	34
Wernes	1.000	5	35	3	0	7

Second Base

Second Base	PCT	G	PO	A	E	DP
Bednar	.981	38	65	86	3	20
Burcham	.968	7	14	16	1	4
Hampson	.986	17	24	46	1	13
Metzler	.963	47	76	105	7	26
Molina	.970	16	31	34	2	4
Phillips	1.000	3	6	6	0	1
Rodgers	1.000	21	40	44	0	14

Third Base

Third Base	PCT	G	PO	A	E	DP
Bednar	.769	13	1	9	3	1
Burcham	1.000	16	7	20	0	2
Jones	.967	73	43	102	5	12
Metzler	.931	13	10	17	2	3
Molina	.983	20	17	40	1	6
Rodgers	.944	17	12	22	2	3
Wernes	.857	5	2	4	1	1

Shortstop

Shortstop	PCT	G	PO	A	E	DP
Bednar	.000	1	0	0	0	0
Burcham	.981	31	41	62	2	13
Hampson	.972	18	25	45	2	14
Metzler	.942	31	52	78	8	23
Phillips	1.000	3	7	14	0	2
Rodgers	.986	58	93	126	3	34

Outfield

Outfield	PCT	G	PO	A	E	DP
Bugner	.000	2	0	0	0	0
Burcham	.000	1	0	0	0	0
Carrizales	.994	78	173	4	1	1
Daza	.975	50	111	8	3	1
Hampson	1.000	3	6	0	0	0
Hilliard	.982	110	218	6	4	2
Jones	.973	46	68	3	2	1
Molina	.909	4	9	1	1	0
Mundell	.977	24	40	2	1	2
Rogers	.978	44	87	3	2	0
Wall	.967	44	112	4	4	1
Weeks	.986	30	68	0	1	0

LANCASTER JETHAWKS HIGH CLASS A
CALIFORNIA LEAGUE

Batting

Batting	B-T	HT	WT	DOB	AVG	vLH	vRH	G	AB	R	H	2B	3B	HR	RBI	BB	HBP	SH	SF	SO	SB	CS	SLG	OBP
Abreu, Willie	L-L	6-4	225	3-21-95	.266	.297	.261	65	252	41	67	12	2	7	27	20	1	4	0	62	19	9	.413	.322
Bosiokovic, Jacob	R-R	6-5	240	12-21-93	.159	.177	.150	42	151	12	24	1	0	4	17	12	6	1	1	66	6	3	.245	.247
Boswell, Bret	L-R	6-1	180	10-4-94	.322	.235	.357	30	118	28	38	5	1	10	28	13	1	1	2	41	2	0	.636	.388
Castro, Luis	R-R	6-1	187	9-19-95	.354	.546	.297	27	96	18	34	10	0	3	13	5	8	0	0	24	0	1	.552	.431
Diaz, Joel	R-R	6-1	195	9-18-95	.268	.354	.242	57	209	19	56	10	0	3	30	19	4	2	3	45	1	0	.359	.336
Fernandez, Vince	L-R	6-3	210	7-25-95	.265	.175	.291	117	423	82	112	25	8	24	75	65	7	2	2	172	10	5	.532	.370
George, Max	R-R	5-9	180	4-7-96	.209	.219	.205	98	297	61	62	15	3	14	42	44	19	7	3	87	27	6	.421	.344
Herrera, Carlos	L-R	6-0	145	9-23-96	.278	.215	.294	106	399	63	111	21	8	6	50	25	3	16	5	103	15	11	.416	.322
Linkous, Steven	R-R	6-0	171	9-28-94	.260	.250	.264	44	150	21	39	7	1	0	19	15	2	3	2	49	13	3	.320	.331
Melendez, Manuel	L-L	5-11	165	1-10-97	.291	.290	.291	119	499	76	145	18	11	5	66	25	5	4	8	81	17	16	.401	.328
Nevin, Tyler	R-R	6-4	200	5-29-97	.328	.354	.319	100	378	59	124	25	1	13	62	34	3	0	2	77	4	3	.503	.386
Ramos, Roberto	L-R	6-5	220	12-28-94	.304	.263	.313	60	214	44	65	15	3	17	43	32	7	2	0	65	3	1	.640	.411
Rogers, Wes	R-R	6-3	180	3-7-94	.287	.354	.263	52	185	30	53	8	0	6	34	17	1	0	3	48	10	3	.427	.345
Serven, Brian	R-R	6-0	195	5-5-95	.268	.286	.263	83	291	53	78	22	3	12	46	23	6	9	8	68	1	1	.488	.326
Stephens, Brett	L-R	6-0	190	3-18-95	.148	.200	.136	8	27	2	4	1	2	0	2	1	0	1	0	6	0	0	.333	.179
Trejo, Alan	R-R	6-2	185	5-30-96	.278	.262	.284	114	449	65	125	28	4	10	67	31	6	5	6	113	3	6	.425	.329
Wall, Forrest	L-R	6-0	176	11-20-95	.305	.382	.290	47	203	43	62	11	5	3	19	23	2	2	0	47	20	8	.453	.382
Welker, Colton	R-R	6-2	195	10-9-97	.333	.356	.326	114	454	74	151	32	0	13	82	42	2	0	11	103	5	1	.489	.383

Pitching

Pitching	B-T	HT	WT	DOB	W	L	ERA	G	GS	CG	SV	IP	H	R	ER	HR	BB	SO	AVG	vLH	vRH	K/9	BB/9
Baker, Bryan	R-R	6-6	220	12-2-94	4	2	3.80	43	0	0	1	45	47	36	19	7	34	58	.264	.279	.255	11.60	6.80
Bowden, Ben	L-L	6-4	235	10-21-94	4	2	4.17	34	0	0	0	37	35	21	17	6	15	53	.245	.226	.256	13.01	3.68
Culbreth, Ty	L-L	5-11	175	4-9-94	6	8	5.87	21	21	0	0	123	162	87	80	23	25	98	.316	.307	.320	7.19	1.83
Dennis, Matt	R-R	6-1	210	1-3-95	8	13	5.59	28	28	0	0	153	195	105	95	24	48	128	.310	.292	.320	7.53	2.82
Diaz, Jairo	R-R	6-0	200	5-27-91	0	0	5.79	5	0	0	0	5	3	3	3	0	4	3	.133	.500	.000	5.79	7.71
Dunn, Mike	L-L	6-0	215	5-23-85	0	0	0.00	1	0	0	0	1	0	0	0	0	1	2	.000	—	.000	18.00	9.00
Garcia, Rico	R-R	5-11	190	1-10-94	7	7	3.42	16	15	0	0	99	100	42	38	12	22	100	.255	.299	.255	9.09	1.98
Gold, Brandon	R-R	6-3	203	9-16-94	9	9	5.44	27	27	0	0	154	204	101	93	20	32	121	.319	.345	.307	7.07	1.87
Gonzalez, Rayan	R-R	6-3	175	10-18-90	0	0	6.75	3	0	0	0	3	3	2	2	0	0	2	.273	.667	.125	6.75	0.00
Guillen, Alexander	R-R	6-2	175	11-23-95	3	3	4.15	51	0	0	1	65	58	32	30	7	27	81	.239	.228	.244	11.22	3.74
Hill, David	R-R	6-2	195	5-27-94	2	4	4.58	7	7	0	0	35	35	18	18	5	11	33	.257	.217	.278	8.41	2.80
Hoffman, Jeff	R-R	6-5	225	1-8-93	0	0	6.00	1	1	0	0	3	5	2	2	0	2	2	.385	.600	.250	6.00	6.00
Holder, Heath	R-R	6-2	215	8-23-92	9	1	3.42	45	3	0	0	84	60	37	32	6	30	117	.199	.165	.218	12.49	3.20
Humphreys, Reid	R-R	6-1	205	11-21-94	2	2	1.83	35	0	0	22	34	22	10	7	1	13	51	.179	.152	.189	13.37	3.41
Justo, Salvador	R-R	6-5	210	10-14-94	4	1	5.93	43	0	0	0	58	61	40	38	6	24	47	.276	.276	.276	7.34	3.75
Killian, Trey	R-R	6-3	190	3-24-94	0	2	9.75	6	6	0	0	24	36	26	26	2	29	20	.360	.356	.364	5.63	10.50
Lawrence, Justin	R-R	6-2	210	11-25-94	0	2	2.65	55	0	0	11	54	36	16	16	2	27	62	.188	.209	.176	10.27	4.47
Longwith, Logan	R-R	6-3	170	3-30-94	4	5	6.52	19	19	0	0	90	105	70	65	17	40	62	.289	.346	.256	6.22	4.01
Oakley, Kenny	R-R	6-3	195	8-30-93	0	5	7.17	30	0	0	1	48	64	46	38	7	26	42	.323	.319	.325	7.93	4.91
Oberg, Scott	R-R	6-2	205	3-13-90	0	0	0.00	1	0	0	0	1	0	0	0	0	1	2	.000	.000	.000	18.00	9.00
Pena, Juan	R-R	6-2	175	8-25-95	4	1	6.48	37	1	0	0	42	68	33	30	6	14	39	.366	.265	.424	8.42	3.02
Santos, Antonio	R-R	6-3	180	10-6-96	4	3	5.21	12	12	0	0	66	74	44	38	15	21	56	.278	.253	.288	7.68	2.88
Tyler, Robert	R-R	6-4	226	6-18-95	0	1	9.64	12	0	0	0	9	17	11	10	2	5	5	.425	.273	.483	4.82	4.82

Fielding

Catcher	PCT	G	PO	A	E	DP	PB
Diaz	.996	57	432	48	2	3	3
Serven	.990	83	741	59	8	5	14

First Base	PCT	G	PO	A	E	DP
Bosiokovic	.991	14	101	9	1	13
Castro	.993	18	129	12	1	13
Nevin	.989	67	484	37	6	49
Ramos	.992	42	332	27	3	34
Welker	1.000	6	31	1	0	5

Second Base	PCT	G	PO	A	E	DP
Boswell	.969	19	31	32	2	12
George	.983	87	148	193	6	44
Herrera	.981	35	67	91	3	26
Trejo	1.000	2	6	4	0	1

Third Base	PCT	G	PO	A	E	DP
Boswell	.938	8	3	12	1	1
Nevin	.900	17	8	28	4	3
Trejo	.929	28	27	52	6	4
Welker	.968	92	40	142	6	13

Shortstop	PCT	G	PO	A	E	DP
Herrera	.969	63	71	149	7	35
Trejo	.964	80	112	239	13	52

Outfield	PCT	G	PO	A	E	DP
Abreu	.962	56	99	3	4	0
Bosiokovic	.981	24	51	1	1	0
Fernandez	.980	108	238	12	5	3
Herrera	1.000	3	2	0	0	0
Linkous	.919	30	57	0	5	0
Melendez	.971	115	259	8	8	1

Nevin	.000	1	0	0	0	0		Stephens	1.000	3	7	0	0	0
Rogers	1.000	45	70	2	0	0		Wall	.987	40	73	1	1	0

ASHEVILLE TOURISTS
SOUTH ATLANTIC LEAGUE
LOW CLASS A

Batting	B-T	HT	WT	DOB	AVG	vLH	vRH	G	AB	R	H	2B	3B	HR	RBI	BB	HBP	SH	SF	SO	SB	CS	SLG	OBP
Bernard, Austin	B-R	5-10	195	3-14-96	.185	.200	.179	58	184	28	34	7	1	5	13	21	5	4	0	58	1	2	.315	.286
Boswell, Bret	L-R	6-1	180	10-4-94	.288	.234	.314	97	379	69	109	20	4	17	50	21	5	5	3	103	7	5	.496	.331
Bouchard, Sean	R-R	6-3	215	5-16-96	.257	.291	.242	125	463	77	119	34	2	14	75	41	7	0	4	128	22	9	.430	.324
Bugner, Tyler	L-R	6-2	195	10-29-94	.211	.267	.190	54	166	17	35	2	1	0	9	14	1	4	0	29	8	4	.235	.276
Cunningham, Kyle	R-R	6-0	205	10-5-94	.000	—	.000	1	2	0	0	0	0	0	0	0	2	0	0	0	0	0	.000	.500
Czinege, Todd	R-R	6-2	204	7-28-94	.320	.362	.301	49	181	34	58	15	2	13	39	11	4	0	2	50	4	2	.641	.369
Golden, Casey	R-R	6-2	185	9-1-94	.278	.288	.273	124	461	92	128	23	3	34	95	38	22	1	2	180	24	8	.562	.360
Gonzalez, Hidekel	R-R	6-0	189	10-7-96	.129	.087	.154	19	62	5	8	1	0	0	2	4	3	1	1	18	0	0	.145	.214
Hearn, Matt	L-R	5-9	165	2-29-96	.271	.281	.268	31	129	18	35	3	1	0	10	12	0	2	0	23	6	5	.310	.333
Linkous, Steven	L-R	6-0	171	9-28-94	.296	.280	.304	24	81	12	24	4	1	0	4	9	3	0	0	22	9	5	.370	.387
Marcelino, Ramon	L-R	6-1	175	12-23-96	.221	.215	.224	113	429	46	95	16	4	22	68	4	2	1	116	4	3	.431	.249
McLaughlin, Matt	R-R	6-1	185	2-2-96	.263	.270	.259	98	350	35	92	23	2	4	48	31	10	6	2	65	8	13	.374	.338
Mendoza, Shael	L-R	6-0	165	10-15-96	.251	.300	.230	60	235	30	59	6	2	2	13	7	0	5	1	64	12	7	.319	.272
Moberg, Jeff	R-R	5-9	170	7-18-94	.205	.177	.213	23	78	13	16	8	1	2	11	4	1	0	5	30	1	0	.410	.239
Motley, Nic	R-R	6-3	210	8-1-96	.239	.229	.244	36	117	16	28	5	0	6	13	7	5	2	2	40	1	1	.436	.305
Perkins, Robbie	R-R	6-0	175	5-29-94	.234	.191	.247	27	94	6	22	2	0	2	6	3	0	1	0	23	1	0	.319	.258
Snyder, Taylor	R-R	6-2	165	9-28-94	.264	.272	.260	84	284	33	75	22	3	8	39	24	4	3	6	87	8	6	.447	.324
Spanberger, Chad	L-R	6-3	235	11-1-95	.315	.283	.331	92	349	65	110	23	3	22	75	20	8	0	3	82	16	4	.579	.363
Stephens, Brett	L-R	6-0	190	3-18-95	.205	.250	.194	13	39	7	8	0	1	5	1	4	1	1	6	1	0	.256	.273
Vilade, Ryan	R-R	6-2	194	2-18-99	.274	.298	.264	124	457	77	125	20	4	5	44	49	9	13	4	96	17	13	.368	.353

Pitching	B-T	HT	WT	DOB	W	L	ERA	G	GS	CG	SV	IP	H	R	ER	HR	BB	SO	AVG	vLH	vRH	K/9	BB/9
Agis, Michael	R-R	5-11	190	9-6-94	0	0	0.00	1	0	0	0	1	0	0	0	0	0	0	.000	.000	.000	0.00	0.00
Bowden, Ben	L-L	6-4	235	10-21-94	3	0	3.52	15	0	0	0	15	17	6	6	2	5	25	.274	.360	2.16	14.67	2.93
Bunal, Mike	R-R	6-2	205	11-18-93	0	1	5.73	10	0	0	1	11	16	7	7	1	5	4	.372	.381	.364	3.27	4.09
Ceja, Moises	R-R	6-0	175	8-17-95	2	2	4.05	17	0	0	0	27	31	15	12	1	7	26	.310	.418	.178	8.78	2.36
Doyle, Tommy	R-R	6-6	235	5-1-96	7	6	2.31	52	0	0	18	58	52	29	15	2	12	66	.233	.227	.239	10.18	1.85
Eusebio, Breiling	L-L	6-1	175	10-21-96	0	1	4.82	3	3	0	0	9	12	5	5	1	3	11	.316	.364	.296	10.61	2.89
Gilbreath, Lucas	L-L	6-1	185	3-5-96	7	8	5.04	26	21	1	2	116	133	72	65	9	24	119	.285	.250	.301	9.23	1.86
Harris, Nate	R-R	6-0	190	9-7-94	2	1	3.86	40	2	0	2	70	76	31	30	7	7	81	.269	.284	.250	10.41	0.90
Hathcock, Colton	R-R	6-2	185	11-2-95	0	1	40.50	3	0	0	0	2	10	10	9	4	4	2	.588	.667	.500	9.00	18.00
Julio, Erick	R-R	6-1	175	9-22-96	4	4	3.99	34	10	0	1	97	90	48	43	10	25	103	.246	.246	.246	9.56	2.32
Kennedy, Nick	R-L	5-11	205	6-20-96	4	13	7.09	27	23	0	0	124	180	108	98	30	37	116	.343	.274	.372	8.40	2.68
Lorenzini, Braxton	R-R	6-4	172	4-5-95	4	0	2.57	23	0	0	1	28	24	12	8	1	16	37	.231	.208	.255	11.89	5.14
Moore, Austin	R-R	6-2	230	6-21-94	1	3	4.40	36	0	0	0	45	55	30	22	2	12	41	.296	.271	.322	8.20	2.40
Oakley, Kenny	R-R	6-3	195	8-30-93	0	1	12.00	2	0	0	0	3	5	4	4	0	0	2	.385	.400	.375	6.00	0.00
Parra, Frederis	R-R	6-3	162	10-22-94	4	4	4.73	11	11	0	0	65	91	37	34	3	12	42	.329	.360	.291	5.85	1.67
Pint, Riley	R-R	6-4	195	11-6-97	0	1	81.00	1	1	0	0	0	2	5	3	0	2	0	.500	.333	1.000	54.00	54.00
Roberts, Hayden	R-R	6-0	187	8-22-95	4	0	1.38	21	0	0	0	26	18	8	4	0	8	20	.188	.156	.216	6.92	2.77
Santos, Antonio	R-R	6-3	180	10-6-96	1	10	4.48	15	15	0	0	86	100	56	43	8	12	86	.287	.259	.312	8.97	1.25
Schilling, Garrett	R-R	6-2	185	10-25-95	8	5	3.87	26	25	0	0	144	156	74	62	16	45	135	.279	.262	.297	8.42	2.81
Tyler, Robert	R-R	6-4	226	6-18-95	4	2	3.99	34	0	0	8	38	37	24	17	5	7	52	.243	.217	.275	12.21	1.64
Valdespina, Justin	R-R	6-0	200	3-20-95	2	3	7.19	18	3	0	0	41	53	35	33	4	25	33	.325	.279	.369	7.19	5.44
Watson, Derrik	R-R	6-2	175	8-21-94	1	1	4.93	28	0	0	0	35	38	19	19	5	21	36	.282	.286	.278	9.35	5.45
Williams, Hunter	L-L	6-1	220	2-7-96	0	0	1.93	12	0	0	1	14	16	9	3	3	2	12	.281	.368	.237	7.71	1.29

Fielding

C: Bernard 58, Cunningham 1, Gonzalez 18, Motley 36, Perkins 27. **1B:** Bouchard 45, Czinege 23, Gonzalez 1, Spanberger 70. **2B:** Boswell 36, McLaughlin 43, Moberg 15, Snyder 45. **3B:** Boswell 56, Bouchard 10, Czinege 13, McLaughlin 45, Moberg 8, Snyder 10. **SS:** Boswell 1, McLaughlin 5, Snyder 15, Vilade 116. **OF:** Bouchard 42, Bugner 45, Czinege 5, Golden 108, Hearn 30, Linkous 22, Marcelino 100, Mendoza 56, Snyder 1, Stephens 13.

BOISE HAWKS
NORTHWEST LEAGUE
SHORT-SEASON

Batting	B-T	HT	WT	DOB	AVG	vLH	vRH	G	AB	R	H	2B	3B	HR	RBI	BB	HBP	SH	SF	SO	SB	CS	SLG	OBP
Abreu, Willie	L-L	6-4	225	3-21-95	.162	.200	.148	10	37	3	6	2	0	0	3	3	0	1	0	9	2	0	.216	.225
Anderson, Cole	R-R	5-11	190	2-7-97	.193	.211	.187	40	145	20	28	5	1	5	13	9	1	0	1	70	1	2	.345	.244
Bohling, Jeff	B-R	5-10	190	5-4-94	.205	.281	.177	33	117	8	24	4	0	4	12	5	1	0	0	46	2	6	.342	.244
Boyd, LeeMarcus	R-R	5-10	170	10-6-95	.221	.091	.246	19	68	11	15	3	2	0	8	4	3	1	0	13	6	0	.324	.290
Castro, Luis	R-R	6-1	187	9-19-95	.349	.364	.345	30	106	16	37	7	2	5	23	15	4	0	2	24	8	1	.594	.441
Datres, Kyle	R-R	6-0	180	1-5-96	.239	.286	.219	11	46	6	11	3	1	2	6	1	0	0	1	2	4	1	.478	.250
Edgeworth, Danny	L-R	6-3	210	7-26-95	.255	.293	.240	54	216	34	55	15	2	1	34	11	3	1	2	49	5	3	.357	.297
Gonzalez, Hidekel	L-R	6-0	189	10-7-96	.165	.235	.144	42	152	13	25	7	1	0	13	10	0	0	0	39	1	0	.224	.216
Harris, Cade	L-R	6-2	195	5-27-97	.249	.375	.218	59	205	40	51	6	1	8	25	43	4	1	2	69	13	8	.405	.386
Hatch, LJ	R-R	5-11	195	5-18-94	.258	.364	.230	42	159	26	41	6	3	2	20	11	3	1	1	36	4	2	.371	.316
Hearn, Matt	L-R	5-9	165	2-29-96	.378	.367	.380	36	151	24	57	4	4	0	17	9	2	2	0	29	12	6	.457	.420
Jacobs, Trey	L-R	6-2	195	5-13-97	.245	.250	.244	12	49	5	12	1	0	0	7	0	0	0	0	13	3	0	.265	.245
Jipping, Daniel	R-R	6-2	232	4-10-96	.285	.239	.298	59	207	37	59	10	2	10	33	29	3	0	1	62	15	1	.498	.379
Jones, Greg	L-R	6-2	220	10-17-94	.161	.286	.143	17	56	5	9	1	0	0	3	5	1	3	0	23	0	1	.179	.242

	B-T	HT	WT	DOB	AVG	vLH	vRH	G	AB	R	H	2B	3B	HR	RBI	BB	HBP	SH	SF	SO	SB	CS	SLG	OBP
MacIver, Willie	R-R	6-2	205	10-28-96	.284	.239	.297	54	194	25	55	10	3	5	30	18	5	0	1	44	4	6	.443	.358
McCarty, Aubrey	B-B	6-3	205	1-24-95	.205	.100	.227	34	117	9	24	5	0	1	10	9	1	0	1	44	0	3	.274	.266
McDowell, Kennard	R-R	6-2	195	9-15-93	.179	.129	.194	37	134	18	24	7	1	1	11	10	0	1	1	42	0	2	.269	.235
Morgan, Luke	R-R	6-2	195	5-13-96	.312	.312	.312	67	260	46	81	17	7	4	39	24	3	1	2	60	16	3	.477	.374
Vavra, Terrin	L-R	6-1	185	5-12-97	.302	.412	.274	44	169	22	51	8	4	4	26	26	1	2	1	40	9	1	.468	.396

Pitching	B-T	HT	WT	DOB	W	L	ERA	G	GS	CG	SV	IP	H	R	ER	HR	BB	SO	AVG	vLH	vRH	K/9	BB/9
Ausua, Miguel	L-L	6-0	180	7-15-96	0	3	6.02	16	8	0	0	40	54	37	27	4	12	26	.320	.275	.333	5.80	2.68
Biechler, Reagan	L-L	6-1	195	11-9-94	0	0	0.00	4	0	0	0	4	4	0	0	0	1	3	.222	.200	.231	6.23	2.08
Bunal, Mike	R-R	6-2	205	11-18-93	3	0	3.04	14	0	0	0	27	27	10	9	2	7	26	.262	.368	.200	8.78	2.36
Bush, Nick	L-L	5-11	173	8-23-96	2	3	4.34	9	9	0	0	37	48	18	18	2	10	28	.316	.378	.296	6.75	2.41
Byrd, Alec	L-L	6-3	175	3-31-95	3	3	3.00	16	10	0	0	60	50	23	20	7	23	53	.226	.073	.261	7.95	3.45
Condreay, Joel	L-R	6-3	185	7-5-96	0	0	4.50	14	0	0	0	14	17	7	7	0	11	8	.315	.368	.286	5.14	7.07
Diaz, Jairo	R-R	6-0	200	5-27-91	1	0	2.25	4	0	0	0	4	3	1	1	0	1	3	.200	.167	.222	6.75	2.25
Gray, Peyton	R-R	6-3	200	6-2-95	4	0	2.11	16	0	0	0	21	12	6	5	3	3	36	.158	.063	.227	15.19	1.27
Hepple, Eric	R-R	6-0	218	3-28-96	1	0	2.48	22	0	0	0	29	29	10	8	2	7	27	.257	.239	.269	8.38	2.17
Johnson, Boby	R-R	6-1	185	4-8-97	2	0	2.53	13	0	0	0	21	23	10	6	0	1	19	.271	.235	.294	8.02	0.42
Lackey, Shelby	R-R	6-3	190	7-8-97	1	3	1.60	21	0	0	1	34	23	10	6	1	10	32	.195	.205	.190	8.55	2.67
Lepore, Jesse	R-R	6-4	210	6-15-96	0	0	2.70	8	0	0	0	10	9	3	3	0	6	11	.257	.100	.320	9.90	5.40
McMahan, Pearson	L-R	6-2	190	7-1-96	3	5	6.03	15	14	0	0	69	92	54	46	7	33	62	.322	.324	.320	8.13	4.33
Medina, Javier	R-R	6-2	200	8-9-96	0	3	7.17	6	4	0	0	21	29	18	17	3	6	7	.333	.270	.380	2.95	2.53
Nikorak, Mike	R-R	6-5	205	9-16-96	0	0	4.32	9	2	0	0	8	7	4	4	0	11	10	.233	.167	.278	10.80	11.88
Ocando, Jeffri	R-R	6-1	180	5-15-99	1	5	6.23	13	13	0	0	56	84	47	39	11	14	41	.350	.310	.379	6.55	2.24
Olivares, Keinter	L-L	6-0	170	12-1-97	2	4	6.09	19	0	0	0	34	44	28	23	6	13	26	.308	.279	.320	6.88	3.44
Parra, Frederis	R-R	6-3	162	10-22-94	1	1	4.41	3	3	0	0	16	22	8	8	1	2	10	.324	.571	.213	5.51	1.10
Pate, Colton	R-R	6-1	195	1-29-96	1	1	7.36	5	1	0	0	7	9	9	6	2	5	7	.290	.250	.304	8.59	6.14
Pint, Riley	R-R	6-4	195	11-6-97	0	2	1.13	3	3	0	0	8	4	2	1	0	9	8	.167	.100	.214	9.00	10.13
Polanco, Carlos	R-R	6-2	175	2-18-94	0	0	27.00	5	0	0	0	2	3	7	7	0	8	3	.300	.500	.000	11.57	30.86
Poulin, PJ	R-L	6-1	185	7-25-96	1	3	1.96	24	0	0	7	23	15	10	5	0	10	33	.177	.231	.153	12.91	3.91
Roberts, Hayden	R-R	6-0	187	8-22-95	0	0	1.29	7	0	0	4	7	3	1	1	0	1	9	.125	.125	.125	11.57	1.29
Schmidt, Colten	L-L	6-1	175	11-25-95	0	1	10.80	9	0	0	0	10	17	12	12	2	5	10	.395	.500	.345	9.00	4.50
Schreiber, Brad	R-R	6-3	225	2-13-91	0	0	8.44	7	0	0	0	5	5	5	5	0	5	8	.167	.273	.000	13.50	8.44
Todd, Reagan	L-L	6-3	218	8-30-95	0	1	7.20	5	0	0	0	5	7	4	4	0	2	6	.350	.000	.438	10.80	3.60
Valdespina, Justin	R-R	6-0	200	3-20-95	4	2	3.00	10	9	0	0	45	47	21	15	4	15	25	.270	.250	.284	5.00	3.00
Valdez, Jefry	R-R	6-1	165	8-20-95	3	1	5.82	27	0	0	4	34	48	27	22	2	9	45	.331	.240	.379	11.91	2.38
Williams, Hunter	L-L	6-1	220	2-7-96	2	0	1.35	14	0	0	1	20	17	4	3	0	3	22	.230	.222	.234	9.90	1.35

Fielding

C: Gonzalez 35, Jones 11, MacIver 31. **1B:** Bohling 1, Castro 16, Edgeworth 11, Gonzalez 6, Jipping 45. **2B:** Bohling 16, Datres 10, Hatch 23, McDowell 15, Vavra 16. **3B:** Bohling 16, Datres 1, Edgeworth 43, Hatch 7, Jacobs 11. **SS:** Boyd 19, Hatch 7, McDowell 24, Vavra 28. **OF:** Abreu 8, Anderson 40, Harris 56, Hatch 5, Hearn 36, McCarty 22, Morgan 66.

GRAND JUNCTION ROCKIES ROOKIE
PIONEER LEAGUE

Batting	B-T	HT	WT	DOB	AVG	vLH	vRH	G	AB	R	H	2B	3B	HR	RBI	BB	HBP	SH	SF	SO	SB	CS	SLG	OBP
Barnwell, Jacob	R-R	5-10	170	8-8-97	.143	.000	.194	12	42	2	6	1	0	0	1	4	1	0	0	9	1	0	.167	.234
Bartosic, Joey	R-R	6-0	190	7-29-94	.306	.400	.269	11	36	11	11	0	1	0	6	8	1	1	1	2	5	2	.361	.435
Berberet, Reese	R-R	6-3	225	11-1-97	.228	.257	.221	51	180	29	41	7	3	11	34	14	4	0	2	70	3	1	.483	.295
Cresto, John	R-R	6-3	225	12-15-96	.257	.250	.260	29	101	20	26	9	0	7	22	3	3	0	3	38	1	1	.555	.291
Czinege, Todd	R-R	6-2	204	7-28-94	.359	.313	.378	14	53	14	19	6	1	3	10	5	1	0	3	13	0	0	.679	.403
Decolati, Niko	R-R	6-1	215	8-12-97	.327	.275	.340	69	263	55	86	15	3	11	56	34	6	0	1	56	17	5	.532	.415
Garcia, Franklin	R-R	6-0	170	3-3-98	.225	.227	.224	27	98	12	22	8	1	1	15	2	2	0	0	25	2	1	.357	.255
Golsan, Will	R-R	6-1	185	3-6-96	.321	.300	.327	63	265	58	85	13	2	3	26	30	2	0	2	42	16	10	.419	.391
Guevara, Javier	R-R	5-11	165	9-25-97	.279	.194	.299	49	183	19	51	11	2	4	32	9	2	1	2	31	2	1	.426	.316
Hall, Zach	L-L	6-0	195	6-26-96	.192	.138	.205	49	156	21	30	5	4	8	17	12	3	0	2	58	0	0	.430	.260
Hatch, LJ	R-R	5-11	175	5-18-94	.118	.375	.039	11	34	2	4	0	0	0	2	4	1	0	0	10	0	0	.118	.231
Holliday, Matt	R-R	6-4	240	1-15-80	.333	1.000	.000	1	3	0	1	1	0	0	1	0	0	0	0	0	0	0	.667	.500
Lavigne, Grant	R-R	6-4	220	8-27-99	.350	.323	.354	59	206	45	72	13	2	6	38	45	6	0	1	40	12	7	.519	.477
Moberg, Jeff	R-R	5-9	170	7-18-94	.261	.400	.222	7	23	3	6	1	0	0	1	1	0	0	0	9	1	0	.304	.292
Montano, Daniel	L-R	6-1	170	3-31-99	.279	.200	.303	62	240	32	67	15	5	4	29	21	1	1	1	57	9	5	.433	.338
Montes, Coco	R-R	6-1	175	10-7-96	.333	.310	.340	69	267	55	89	18	3	8	42	35	4	0	4	69	7	6	.513	.413
Navarro, Cristopher	R-R	6-0	152	6-14-99	.217	.442	.156	65	244	30	53	11	1	1	23	18	2	2	0	28	7	5	.283	.277
Stephens, Brett	L-R	6-0	190	3-18-95	.000	.000	.000	2	5	1	0	0	0	0	0	1	0	0	0	2	0	0	.000	.167
Stovall, Hunter	R-R	5-8	170	9-5-96	.297	.333	.288	49	199	38	59	16	6	10	41	8	2	1	6	29	3	7	.588	.321
Weeks, Drew	R-R	6-2	200	6-9-93	.154	.091	.200	7	26	4	4	1	0	0	2	1	0	0	0	6	1	0	.192	.241

Pitching	B-T	HT	WT	DOB	W	L	ERA	G	GS	CG	SV	IP	H	R	ER	HR	BB	SO	AVG	vLH	vRH	K/9	BB/9
Agis, Michael	R-R	5-11	190	9-6-94	6	5	3.18	25	0	0	2	40	46	21	14	1	12	39	.293	.273	.308	8.85	2.72
Biechler, Reagan	L-L	6-1	195	11-9-94	2	0	2.70	18	0	0	1	27	16	10	8	2	7	25	.168	.035	.227	8.44	2.36
Bird, Jacob	R-R	6-3	200	12-4-95	4	1	3.38	17	0	0	0	31	27	10	12	2	10	32	.202	.194	.206	10.13	4.05
Cabrera, Wander	L-L	6-1	185	11-7-97	2	2	9.87	11	7	0	0	31	40	35	34	6	23	22	.348	.146	.382	6.39	6.68
Ceja, Moises	R-R	6-0	175	8-17-95	1	0	1.64	13	0	0	0	22	20	4	4	0	5	19	.247	.194	.289	7.77	2.05
Duarte, Aneudy	R-R	6-3	190	10-20-97	1	1	2.91	26	0	0	3	34	29	12	11	3	13	35	.232	.275	.203	9.26	3.44
Feltner, Ryan	R-R	6-4	190	9-2-96	0	0	0.88	9	9	0	0	31	16	3	3	1	4	39	.157	.163	.151	11.45	1.17
Fennell, Trent	R-R	6-5	205	11-26-95	1	2	4.24	13	7	0	0	34	34	19	16	2	15	32	.260	.179	.320	8.47	3.97

Name	B-T	HT	WT	DOB	W	L	ERA	G	GS	CG	SV	IP	H	R	ER	HR	BB	SO	AVG	vLH	vRH	K/9	BB/9
Filpo, Eris	R-R	6-3	170	5-3-98	6	4	5.64	14	14	0	0	67	84	49	42	10	25	38	.308	.312	.305	5.10	3.36
Garcia, Alfredo	L-L	6-1	175	7-22-99	2	5	4.99	11	10	0	0	49	58	35	27	8	21	27	.302	.345	.284	4.99	3.88
Harlow, Colton	L-L	5-10	170	9-21-95	1	0	4.57	19	0	0	0	22	21	11	11	1	12	22	.250	.167	.296	9.14	4.98
Hatcher, Cayden	R-R	6-5	200	9-9-95	2	0	5.54	11	4	0	0	26	24	20	16	3	11	23	.245	.194	.274	7.96	3.81
Lepore, Jesse	R-R	6-4	210	6-15-96	2	1	11.57	14	0	0	0	16	29	28	21	7	11	15	.377	.486	.286	8.27	6.06
Martinez, Alexander	R-R	6-1	165	12-28-96	0	0	3.07	28	0	0	19	29	26	13	10	1	9	39	.232	.308	.167	11.97	2.76
Mejia, Alejandro	L-L	6-1	168	7-2-98	3	5	7.83	13	12	0	0	56	86	65	49	8	38	30	.360	.301	.391	4.79	6.07
Rolison, Ryan	R-L	6-2	195	7-11-97	0	1	1.86	9	9	0	0	29	15	8	6	2	8	34	.149	.095	.163	10.55	2.48
Skolnicki, Jared	B-L	6-2	195	7-22-94	4	1	2.78	21	0	0	1	32	29	14	10	2	3	26	.236	.209	.250	7.24	0.84
Smith, Shameko	R-R	6-1	190	6-4-97	0	0	4.50	3	0	0	0	4	5	4	2	1	5	3	.313	.222	.429	6.75	11.25
Stinnett, Jesse	R-R	6-4	225	7-12-95	1	1	4.15	6	1	0	0	13	15	8	6	2	4	14	.306	.227	.370	9.69	2.77
Supple, Rayne	B-R	6-3	185	8-18-97	0	1	4.97	21	0	0	0	29	27	18	16	1	22	21	.239	.270	.224	6.52	6.83
Todd, Reagan	L-L	6-3	218	8-30-95	1	1	7.20	12	3	0	0	20	32	19	16	5	9	18	.364	.379	.356	8.10	4.05
Tribucher, Will	L-L	6-3	210	9-23-96	4	2	2.32	20	0	0	0	31	18	12	8	2	10	40	.164	.189	.151	11.61	2.90

Fielding

C: Barnwell 11, Garcia 26, Guevara 43. **1B:** Berberet 13, Czinege 9, Guevara 1, Lavigne 53. **2B:** Cresto 3, Hatch 6, Moberg 6, Montes 28, Navarro 2, Stovall 33. **3B:** Berberet 29, Cresto 15, Czinege 1, Hatch 4, Montes 24, Stovall 9. **SS:** Montes 13, Navarro 63, Stovall 1. **OF:** Bartosic 8, Decolati 60, Golsan 59, Hall 38, Montano 59, Stephens 2, Stovall 5, Weeks 5.

DSL ROCKIES   ROOKIE

DOMINICAN SUMMER LEAGUE

Batting	B-T	HT	WT	DOB	AVG	vLH	vRH	G	AB	R	H	2B	3B	HR	RBI	BB	HBP	SH	SF	SO	SB	CS	SLG	OBP
Baptista, Jesus	L-R	6-0	160	1-12-99	.287	.317	.279	53	181	26	52	6	1	0	21	22	3	4	0	25	16	4	.332	.374
Carreras, Julio	R-R	6-1	166	1-12-00	.252	.136	.274	41	135	32	34	5	3	3	14	23	8	2	0	28	8	6	.400	.392
Chal, Welington	L-R	6-1	170	11-18-97	.178	.111	.200	23	73	9	13	4	0	0	13	10	6	0	0	14	0	1	.233	.326
Colon, Jose	R-R	5-11	135	9-17-00	.194	.229	.186	52	175	23	34	9	0	1	19	32	2	5	1	53	8	4	.263	.324
Concepcion, Branfiel	L-R	6-0	170	9-28-99	.231	.120	.257	40	134	17	31	4	6	1	17	15	1	0	3	32	8	2	.373	.307
Cordova, Jose	R-R	6-0	200	1-11-00	.309	.240	.327	32	123	16	38	7	1	1	19	6	2	2	2	16	0	2	.407	.346
Cruz, Fadriel	L-R	5-10	170	11-12-00	.269	.200	.282	45	149	32	40	3	1	1	8	31	0	2	0	38	31	6	.322	.394
Gil, Gabriel	R-R	5-10	173	3-9-01	.182	.161	.191	33	99	11	18	4	1	0	14	3	1	0	42	1	0	.242	.302
Guerrero, Junior	R-R	6-1	170	9-11-00	.180	.171	.183	43	150	13	27	5	2	0	10	8	2	1	0	38	2	6	.240	.231
Liberato, Johan	L-L	5-11	184	11-12-00	.216	.200	.221	33	102	12	22	4	0	1	17	13	2	0	4	17	3	2	.284	.306
Mezquita, Jonatan	R-R	6-0	180	1-11-99	.163	.250	.135	16	49	2	8	1	0	2	5	2	0	0	18	1	0	.306	.226
Oferman, Justin	B-R	5-10	145	1-12-01	.169	.219	.156	48	154	22	26	5	0	0	12	30	1	2	1	52	7	5	.201	.307
Palma, Francisco	L-L	5-11	165	7-4-01	.304	.333	.296	55	184	21	56	12	3	2	13	15	1	3	0	31	6	4	.435	.360
Palma, Ronaiker	R-R	5-9	161	1-2-00	.350	.389	.343	33	123	15	43	5	1	1	19	6	2	0	2	9	5	7	.431	.384
Ramos, Gerard	R-R	6-3	175	1-19-01	.214	.143	.234	62	220	27	47	14	0	0	21	21	4	2	3	81	2	3	.277	.290
Restituyo, Bladimir	R-R	5-10	151	7-2-01	.291	.256	.301	46	182	27	53	9	5	0	21	7	6	2	1	38	12	8	.396	.337
Vasquez, Johendry	R-R	6-1	170	11-30-00	.235	.238	.233	23	81	10	19	2	0	1	9	4	2	0	1	24	2	4	.296	.296

Pitching	B-T	HT	WT	DOB	W	L	ERA	G	GS	CG	SV	IP	H	R	ER	HR	BB	SO	AVG	vLH	vRH	K/9	BB/9
Amarista, Anderson	R-R	6-1	185	9-15-98	4	5	3.64	10	8	0	0	54	56	35	22	2	12	52	.269	.163	.336	8.61	1.99
Azor, Victor	R-R	6-2	180	11-11-00	1	3	7.58	13	5	0	0	30	39	29	25	2	23	23	.310	.308	.311	6.98	6.98
Cabrera, Jerald	R-R	6-1	185	8-26-01	0	0	6.75	6	0	0	0	13	15	11	10	0	8	13	.283	.500	.205	8.78	5.40
Cabrera, Wander	L-L	6-1	185	11-7-97	1	0	2.70	2	2	0	0	10	7	4	3	1	3	12	.189	.000	.200	10.80	2.70
Castillo, Brayan	R-R	6-0	145	9-11-00	1	3	4.87	13	10	0	0	44	47	26	24	1	21	38	.280	.233	.306	7.71	4.26
Cespedes, Richard	R-R	6-0	185	8-29-97	2	4	5.49	21	0	0	2	39	59	31	24	4	9	37	.362	.510	.295	8.47	2.06
Chalas, Gregoris	R-R	5-10	143	8-12-00	1	1	6.35	5	0	0	0	11	12	8	8	0	6	16	.267	.368	.192	10.32	4.76
Franco, Junior	R-R	6-3	178	2-17-99	0	0	7.15	8	0	0	1	11	11	11	9	1	9	10	.250	.412	.148	7.94	7.15
Garcia, Kevin	L-L	6-0	170	11-25-99	1	4	3.46	13	13	0	0	55	53	35	21	1	27	58	.255	.343	.237	9.55	4.45
Hernandez, Robinson	R-R	6-0	186	6-11-99	0	1	6.14	3	1	0	0	7	12	5	5	0	3	10	.364	.400	.333	12.27	3.68
Lopez, Raul	R-R	6-4	172	6-3-01	0	3	11.49	15	0	0	0	16	24	22	20	5	9	12	.353	.292	.386	6.89	5.17
Mejia, Juan	R-R	6-1	181	7-4-00	2	4	4.67	9	9	1	0	44	51	32	23	3	15	48	.291	.290	.293	9.74	3.05
Mendez, Victor	L-L	6-4	177	1-24-00	0	3	5.40	18	0	0	0	37	37	31	22	3	20	39	.259	.200	.271	9.57	4.91
Moya, Ever	L-L	6-4	150	5-25-99	2	7	5.18	18	2	0	1	42	50	30	24	2	11	43	.289	.185	.308	9.29	2.38
Noguera, Luis	L-L	6-2	160	3-20-00	0	2	7.71	15	1	0	0	21	20	28	18	1	26	8	.253	.294	.242	3.43	11.14
Olivarez, Helcris	L-L	6-2	192	8-8-00	4	1	2.78	9	9	0	0	36	25	17	11	1	22	36	.205	.333	.183	9.00	5.55
Ozoria, Luis	L-L	6-0	145	8-30-01	0	1	14.63	7	0	0	0	8	13	16	13	3	8	7	.351	.200	.375	7.88	9.00
Perdomo, Alan	R-R	6-4	150	8-24-01	0	1	6.99	12	4	0	0	28	39	27	22	4	13	17	.333	.290	.349	5.40	4.13
Pilar, Anderson	R-R	6-2	175	3-2-98	2	3	2.08	20	0	0	4	22	19	10	5	0	7	18	.235	.219	.245	7.48	2.91
Pio, Enmanuel	R-R	5-11	145	4-11-00	0	0	8.64	7	0	0	0	8	16	16	8	2	11	8	.372	.533	.286	8.64	11.88
Ramires, Felix	L-L	6-1	199	9-26-99	1	0	3.54	17	3	0	2	41	36	21	16	2	25	35	.235	.250	.231	7.75	5.53
Sanchez, Stalyn	R-R	6-1	161	7-10-00	0	3	9.82	5	0	0	0	15	22	17	16	1	9	12	.333	.333	.333	7.36	5.52
Tovar, Manual	L-L	6-6	166	4-29-00	0	2	7.71	10	1	0	1	16	25	15	14	0	6	13	.347	.267	.368	7.16	3.31

Fielding

C: Baptista 7, Cordova 13, Gil 31, Palma 25. **1B:** Baptista 36, Cordova 11, Liberato 1, Mezquita 6, Ramos 20. **2B:** Baptista 1, Carreras 2, Colon 19, Cruz 34, Oferman 16, Restituyo 7. **3B:** Baptista 7, Carreras 23, Colon 17, Mezquita 6, Oferman 1, Restituyo 5, Vasquez 16. **SS:** Carreras 15, Colon 4, Oferman 28, Restituyo 21, Vasquez 6. **OF:** Baptista 1, Chal 7, Concepcion 40, Cruz 7, Guerrero 42, Liberato 26, Palma 51, Ramos 41, Restituyo 12.

Detroit Tigers

SEASON IN A SENTENCE: The Tigers are in the midst of a transitional phase and it showed on the field, because they posted a 26-55 road record and finished 64-98—an identical mark to their 2017 record—while missing the playoffs for a fourth consecutive season.

HIGH POINT: A 15-14 record in May clinched the Tigers their only winning month of the season and included a series win against the eventual AL Central-winning Indians. The Tigers then selected Auburn righthander Casey Mize with the No. 1 overall pick in the 2018 draft, giving the organization a new No. 1 prospect and helping expedite the franchise's ongoing rebuild.

LOW POINT: The Tigers started the season by losing their first three games and never spent a single day in first place in the AL Central. August was the team's worst month, when Detroit won just eight of its 27 games—bad enough for a season-worst .296 winning percentage.

NOTABLE ROOKIES: A Twins second-round pick in 2010, second baseman Niko Goodrum had a decent season for the Tigers after signing a minor league free agent deal. Goodrum hit 16 home runs to go along with 53 RBIs in 131 games, slashing .245/.315/.432 at the major league level. In addition, powerful outfield prospect Christin Stewart made his big league debut in September, driving in 10 runs across 17 games while hitting .267/.375/.417.

KEY TRANSACTIONS: Just before the July 31 trade deadline, the Tigers traded major league outfielder Leonys Martin and minor league righthander Kyle Dowdy to Cleveland for shortstop Willi Castro. Then in August Detroit flipped major league righthander Mike Fiers to the Athletics and acquired minor league righthanders Nolan Blackwood and Logan Shore as the Tigers' front office continues their organizational rebuild with a focus on minor league talent.

DOWN ON THE FARM: Triple-A Toledo won the International League West Division championship with a 73-66 record. Though the Mud Hens could not follow through with the IL championship in the playoffs, the Rookie-level Gulf Coast League Tigers West team delivered a minor league title for the organization. GCL Tigers West won 37 games during the regular season and beat the GCL Cardinals in a three-game championship series, punctuated by an 11-hit, nine-run outburst in the series finale.

OPENING DAY PAYROLL: $111,286,000 (20th).

PLAYERS OF THE YEAR

TONY FIRRIOLO

MAJOR LEAGUE

Nick Castellanos
OF
.298/.354/.500. Led
Tigers in HR (23), 2B
(46) and OPS (.854)

MINOR LEAGUE

Christin Stewart
OF
(Triple-A)
.264/.364/.480
23 HR, 77 RBIs

ORGANIZATION LEADERS

Batting		*Minimum 250 AB
MAJORS		
* AVG	Nicholas Castellanos	.298
* OPS	Nicholas Castellanos	.854
HR	Nicholas Castellanos	23
RBI	Nicholas Castellanos	89
MINORS		
* AVG	Daniel Woodrow, Lakeland, Erie	.317
* OBP	Troy Montgomery, Erie, Lakeland	.386
* SLG	Christin Stewart, Toledo, Tigers East, Tigers West	.488
* OPS	Christin Stewart, Toledo, Tigers East, Tigers West	.851
R	Jacob Robson, Erie, Toledo	82
H	Jacob Robson, Erie, Toledo	142
TB	Christin Stewart, Toledo, Tigers East, Tigers West	221
2B	Jacob Robson, Erie, Toledo	29
3B	Jose Azocar, Lakeland, West Michigan	9
3B	Daz Cameron, Lakeland, Erie, Toledo	9
HR	Christin Stewart, Toledo, Tigers East, Tigers West	25
RBI	Christin Stewart, Toledo, Tigers East, Tigers West	80
BB	Christin Stewart, Toledo, Tigers East, Tigers West	68
SO	Jacob Robson, Erie, Toledo	140
SB	Derek Hill, Lakeland	35

Pitching		#Minimum 75 IP
MAJORS		
W	Matthew Boyd	9
# ERA	Mike Fiers	3.48
SO	Matthew Boyd	159
SV	Shane Greene	32
MINORS		
W	A.J. Ladwig, Toledo, Erie	10
W	Spenser Watkins, Lakeland, Toledo, Erie	10
W	Beau Burrows, Erie	10
L	Alex Faedo, Lakeland, Erie	10
# ERA	Matt Hall, Erie, Toledo	2.13
G	John Schreiber, Erie	49
GS	Beau Burrows, Erie	26
SV	John Schreiber, Erie	18
IP	Tyler Alexander, Erie, Toledo	140
BB	Gregory Soto, Lakeland	70
SO	Matt Manning, West Michigan, Lakeland, Erie	154
# AVG	Matt Hall, Erie, Toledo	.193

2018 PERFORMANCE

General Manager: Al Avila. **Farm Director:** Dave Owen. **Scouting Director:** Scott Pleis.

Class	Team	League	W	L	PCT	Finish	Manager
Majors	Detroit Tigers	American	64	98	.395	12th (15)	Ron Gardenhire
Triple-A	Toledo Mud Hens	International	73	66	.525	4th (14)	Doug Mientkiewicz
Double-A	Erie Seawolves	Eastern	63	77	.450	11th (12)	Andrew Graham
High A	Lakeland Flying Tigers	Florida State	72	61	.541	4th (12)	Mike Rabelo
Low A	West Michigan Whitecaps	Midwest	69	70	.496	9th (16)	Lance Parrish
Short season	Connecticut Tigers	New York-Penn	29	44	.397	14th (14)	Gerald Laird
Rookie	GCL Tigers East	Gulf Coast	26	28	.481	10th (18)	Luis Lopez
Rookie	GCL Tigers West	Gulf Coast	37	16	.698	2nd (18)	Gary Cathcart
Overall 2018 Minor League Record			369	362	.505	12th (30)	

ORGANIZATION STATISTICS

DETROIT TIGERS
AMERICAN LEAGUE

Batting	B-T	HT	WT	DOB	AVG	vLH	vRH	G	AB	R	H	2B	3B	HR	RBI	BB	HBP	SH	SF	SO	SB	CS	SLG	OBP
Adduci, Jim	L-L	6-2	210	5-15-85	.267	.100	.289	59	176	19	47	8	2	3	21	6	0	2	1	45	1	0	.386	.290
Cabrera, Miguel	R-R	6-4	249	4-18-83	.299	.267	.308	38	134	17	40	11	0	3	22	22	0	0	1	27	0	0	.448	.395
Candelario, Jeimer	B-R	6-1	221	11-24-93	.225	.291	.200	144	539	78	121	28	3	19	54	66	9	0	5	160	3	2	.393	.317
Castellanos, Nicholas	R-R	6-4	203	3-4-92	.298	.381	.273	157	620	88	185	46	5	23	89	49	6	0	3	151	2	1	.500	.354
Castro, Harold	L-R	6-0	165	11-30-93	.300	—	.300	6	10	2	3	0	0	0	0	0	0	0	0	2	1	0	.300	.300
Gerber, Mike	L-R	6-0	190	7-8-92	.095	.000	.108	18	42	2	4	1	0	0	2	4	0	0	1	21	0	0	.119	.170
Goodrum, Niko	B-R	6-3	198	2-28-92	.246	.303	.225	131	444	55	109	29	3	16	53	42	4	0	2	132	12	4	.432	.315
Greiner, Grayson	R-R	6-6	239	10-11-92	.219	.412	.177	30	96	9	21	6	0	0	12	17	0	0	3	32	0	1	.281	.328
Hicks, John	R-R	6-2	230	8-31-89	.260	.291	.249	81	288	35	75	12	1	9	32	22	0	1	1	84	0	1	.403	.312
Iglesias, Jose	R-R	5-11	194	1-5-90	.269	.318	.256	125	432	43	116	31	3	5	48	19	8	3	2	47	15	6	.389	.310
Jones, JaCoby	R-R	6-2	201	5-10-92	.208	.194	.212	129	429	54	89	22	6	11	34	24	11	1	2	142	13	5	.364	.266
Kozma, Pete	R-R	6-0	190	4-11-88	.217	.158	.240	27	69	7	15	4	1	1	8	2	0	1	1	15	0	1	.348	.236
Lugo, Dawel	R-R	6-0	190	12-31-94	.213	.250	.205	27	94	10	20	4	1	1	8	7	0	0	0	20	0	0	.309	.267
Machado, Dixon	R-R	6-1	190	2-22-92	.206	.279	.187	67	214	20	44	13	1	1	21	14	3	1	1	41	1	1	.290	.263
Mahtook, Mikie	R-R	6-1	216	11-30-89	.202	.164	.216	67	223	24	45	4	2	9	29	21	3	0	3	66	4	1	.359	.276
Martin, Leonys	L-R	6-2	190	3-6-88	.251	.176	.275	78	303	45	76	15	3	9	29	29	3	0	1	75	7	3	.409	.321
2-team total (6 Cleveland)					.255	.176	.279	84	318	48	81	15	3	11	33	30	3	0	2	77	7	4	.425	.323
Martinez, Victor	B-R	6-2	235	12-23-78	.251	.256	.249	133	467	32	117	21	0	9	54	32	2	0	7	49	0	0	.353	.297
McCann, James	R-R	6-3	225	6-13-90	.220	.177	.234	118	427	31	94	16	0	8	39	26	2	0	2	116	0	3	.314	.267
Reyes, Victor	B-R	6-5	194	10-5-94	.222	.216	.223	100	212	35	47	5	3	1	12	5	0	1	1	46	9	1	.288	.239
Rodriguez, Ronny	R-R	6-0	170	4-17-92	.220	.278	.197	62	191	17	42	7	0	5	20	10	0	3	2	42	2	0	.335	.256
Saltalamacchia, Jarrod	B-R	6-4	235	5-2-85	.000	.000	.000	5	7	0	0	0	0	0	0	0	0	0	0	4	0	0	.000	.125
Stewart, Christin	L-R	6-0	205	12-10-93	.267	.200	.280	17	60	7	16	1	1	2	10	10	1	0	1	13	0	0	.417	.375

Pitching	B-T	HT	WT	DOB	W	L	ERA	G	GS	CG	SV	IP	H	R	ER	HR	BB	SO	AVG	vLH	vRH	K/9	BB/9
Alcantara, Victor	R-R	6-2	190	4-3-93	1	1	2.40	27	0	0	0	30	25	8	8	5	6	21	.223	.234	.215	6.30	1.80
Baez, Sandy	R-R	6-2	180	11-25-93	0	0	5.02	9	0	0	0	14	12	12	8	2	9	10	.222	.214	.225	6.28	5.65
Barbato, Johnny	R-R	6-1	231	7-11-92	0	0	12.15	7	0	0	0	7	11	9	9	3	5	2	.379	.467	.286	2.70	6.75
Bell, Chad	R-L	6-3	200	2-28-89	0	1	8.59	3	0	0	0	7	14	7	7	1	2	7	.424	.563	.294	8.59	2.45
Boyd, Matthew	L-L	6-3	234	2-2-91	9	13	4.39	31	31	0	0	170	146	87	83	27	51	159	.229	.215	.232	8.40	2.69
Carpenter, Ryan	L-L	6-5	210	8-22-90	1	2	7.25	6	5	0	0	22	34	19	18	8	4	15	.347	.292	.365	6.04	1.61
Coleman, Louis	R-R	6-4	205	4-4-86	4	1	3.51	51	0	0	0	51	43	21	20	5	24	41	.235	.222	.243	7.19	4.21
Farmer, Buck	R-R	6-4	232	2-20-91	3	4	4.15	66	1	0	0	69	67	34	32	6	41	57	.255	.168	.320	7.40	5.32
Fiers, Mike	R-R	6-2	202	6-15-85	7	6	3.48	21	21	0	0	119	121	49	46	20	26	87	.258	.255	.261	6.58	1.97
2-team total (10 Oakland)					12	8	3.56	31	30	0	0	172	166	71	68	32	37	139	.249	.231	.268	7.27	1.94
Fulmer, Michael	R-R	6-3	246	3-15-93	3	12	4.69	24	24	0	0	132	128	75	69	19	46	110	.254	.241	.270	7.48	3.13
Greene, Shane	R-R	6-4	197	11-17-88	4	6	5.12	66	0	0	32	63	68	39	36	11	19	65	.268	.246	.292	9.24	2.70
Hall, Matt	L-L	6-0	200	7-23-93	0	0	14.63	5	0	0	0	8	19	16	13	1	3	5	.452	.556	.424	5.63	3.38
Hardy, Blaine	L-L	6-2	218	3-14-87	4	5	3.56	30	13	0	1	86	79	37	34	10	22	66	.245	.232	.250	6.91	2.30
Jimenez, Joe	R-R	6-3	272	1-17-95	5	4	4.31	68	0	0	3	63	53	34	30	5	22	78	.222	.211	.231	11.20	3.16
Lewicki, Artie	R-R	6-3	195	4-8-92	0	2	4.89	13	3	0	0	39	48	24	21	4	14	30	.320	.350	.286	6.98	3.26
Liriano, Francisco	L-L	6-3	218	10-26-83	5	12	4.58	27	26	0	0	134	127	84	68	19	73	110	.253	.171	.270	7.41	4.92
McAllister, Zach	R-R	6-6	240	12-8-87	0	0	21.60	3	0	0	0	3	10	8	8	1	0	5	.526	.600	.444	13.50	10.80
2-team total (41 Cleveland)					0	2	6.20	44	0	0	0	45	57	33	31	8	10	39	.310	.363	.269	7.80	2.00
Norris, Daniel	L-L	6-2	185	4-25-93	0	5	5.68	11	8	0	0	44	46	28	28	8	19	51	.261	.325	.243	10.35	3.86
Reininger, Zac	B-R	6-3	185	1-28-93	1	0	7.59	18	0	0	0	21	28	18	18	5	9	18	.311	.326	.298	7.59	3.80
Saupold, Warwick	R-R	6-2	223	1-16-90	4	1	4.46	31	0	0	1	34	41	17	17	6	13	16	.293	.349	.247	4.19	3.41
Smoker, Josh	L-L	6-2	255	11-26-88	0	0	0.00	1	0	0	0	2	0	0	0	0	2	2	.000	.000	.000	10.80	10.80
Stumpf, Daniel	L-L	6-2	208	1-4-91	1	5	4.93	56	0	0	0	38	44	23	21	5	16	37	.286	.247	.325	8.69	3.76
Turnbull, Spencer	R-R	6-3	215	9-18-92	0	2	6.06	4	3	0	0	16	17	11	11	1	4	15	.262	.278	.243	8.27	2.20
Turner, Jacob	R-R	6-5	215	5-21-91	0	1	45.00	1	1	0	0	1	6	7	5	1	1	1	.600	.600	.600	9.00	9.00
VerHagen, Drew	R-R	6-6	230	10-22-90	3	3	4.63	41	1	0	0	56	46	29	29	6	19	53	.222	.250	.205	8.47	3.04
Wilson, Alex	R-R	6-0	227	11-3-86	2	4	3.36	59	0	0	0	62	50	24	23	8	15	43	.223	.269	.191	6.28	2.19

Zimmermann, Jordan R-R 6-2 225 5-23-86 7 8 4.52 25 25 0 0 131 140 76 66 28 26 111 .269 .261 .277 7.61 1.78

Fielding

Catcher	PCT	G	PO	A	E	DP	PB
Greiner	.996	30	238	12	1	1	3
Hicks	.987	21	142	13	2	3	0
McCann	.994	114	847	50	5	10	5
Saltalamacchia	.000	1	0	0	0	0	

First Base	PCT	G	PO	A	E	DP
Adduci	.981	48	351	14	7	22
Cabrera	.996	32	248	13	1	22
Goodrum	.984	37	169	16	3	15
Hicks	.986	59	402	33	6	48
Martinez	1.000	1	1	0	0	0
Rodriguez	.967	10	53	5	2	3
Saltalamacchia	.917	1	11	0	1	0

Second Base	PCT	G	PO	A	E	DP
Castro	1.000	2	4	3	0	1

Goodrum	.967	64	85	147	8	23
Kozma	1.000	4	8	7	0	6
Lugo	.964	27	37	44	3	6
Machado	.982	64	119	157	5	45
Rodriguez	.984	17	20	40	1	9

Third Base	PCT	G	PO	A	E	DP
Candelario	.973	140	116	241	10	26
Goodrum	.920	10	9	14	2	2
Kozma	1.000	6	4	12	0	0
Rodriguez	.895	12	5	12	2	0

Shortstop	PCT	G	PO	A	E	DP
Castro	1.000	4	3	5	0	1
Goodrum	.926	12	9	16	2	4
Iglesias	.983	122	148	316	8	63
Kozma	1.000	15	18	35	0	7

Rodriguez	.921	24	25	45	6	5

Outfield	PCT	G	PO	A	E	DP
Castellanos	.990	142	287	10	3	0
Gerber	1.000	12	25	1	0	0
Goodrum	.971	19	33	0	1	0
Jones	.997	120	284	8	1	2
Mahtook	.976	61	120	3	3	2
Martin	.992	74	228	9	2	1
Reyes	1.000	63	111	4	0	1
Rodriguez	.000	1	0	0	0	0
Stewart	.953	15	41	0	2	0

TOLEDO MUD HENS
INTERNATIONAL LEAGUE
TRIPLE-A

Batting	B-T	HT	WT	DOB	AVG	vLH	vRH	G	AB	R	H	2B	3B	HR	RBI	BB	HBP	SH	SF	SO	SB	CS	SLG	OBP
Adduci, Jim	L-L	6-2	210	5-15-85	.309	.247	.333	70	272	39	84	22	1	7	44	22	0	0	2	60	8	1	.474	.358
Cameron, Daz	R-R	6-2	195	1-15-97	.211	.143	.233	15	57	8	12	4	1	0	6	2	1	1	1	15	2	2	.316	.246
Candelario, Jeimer	B-R	6-1	221	11-24-93	.250	.333	.000	2	8	3	2	0	0	0	1	1	0	0	0	1	0	0	.250	.333
Castro, Harold	L-R	6-0	165	11-30-93	.257	.225	.266	74	241	24	62	8	0	2	19	5	0	3	2	47	3	3	.315	.270
Castro, Willi	B-R	6-1	165	4-24-97	.286	.200	.313	5	21	0	6	0	0	0	2	0	0	0	5	1	0	.286	.286
Eaves, Kody	L-R	6-0	175	7-8-93	.160	.115	.184	22	75	7	12	4	1	0	4	6	1	0	0	21	0	0	.240	.232
Espinal, Edwin	R-R	6-2	250	1-27-94	.242	.298	.213	100	335	38	81	8	0	6	24	40	5	1	2	65	0	0	.319	.330
Gerber, Mike	L-R	6-0	190	7-8-92	.213	.241	.202	74	287	35	61	14	2	13	34	22	4	2	1	103	2	2	.411	.277
Greiner, Grayson	R-R	6-6	239	10-11-92	.266	.289	.257	46	158	12	42	8	1	4	23	21	0	1	1	42	0	0	.405	.350
Huffman, Chad	R-R	6-1	215	4-29-85	.268	.245	.279	85	291	40	78	17	1	12	40	33	9	0	1	78	0	1	.457	.359
Jones, JaCoby	R-R	6-2	201	5-10-92	.083	.000	.111	3	12	1	1	0	0	0	0	0	0	0	0	3	0	0	.083	.083
Kozma, Pete	R-R	6-0	190	4-11-88	.203	.241	.185	83	271	23	55	18	2	1	17	19	3	0	3	52	6	1	.295	.260
Krizan, Jason	L-R	6-0	185	6-28-89	.250	.216	.261	106	368	49	92	19	2	8	55	46	0	0	1	67	4	0	.378	.333
Lugo, Dawel	R-R	6-0	190	12-31-94	.269	.231	.283	123	509	56	137	26	3	3	59	9	2	0	6	66	12	4	.350	.283
Machado, Dixon	R-R	6-1	190	2-22-92	.225	.298	.190	43	147	19	33	5	0	1	8	18	3	3	0	28	4	2	.279	.321
Mahtook, Mikie	R-R	6-1	216	11-30-89	.251	.320	.226	72	283	40	71	12	6	11	35	25	5	0	2	82	6	4	.452	.321
Martin, Leonys	L-R	6-2	200	3-6-88	.300	.333	.250	3	10	2	3	2	0	0	1	1	0	0	0	3	0	0	.500	.417
Quintana, Gabriel	R-R	6-3	215	9-7-92	.133	.250	.091	4	15	1	2	0	0	0	2	0	1	0	0	5	0	0	.267	.188
Robson, Jacob	L-R	5-10	175	11-20-94	.305	.245	.323	57	220	36	67	13	1	4	15	23	0	1	1	62	7	6	.427	.369
Rodriguez, Herlis	L-L	6-0	170	6-10-94	.182	.333	.158	6	22	0	4	0	1	0	1	0	0	0	0	5	1	0	.273	.182
Rodriguez, Ronny	R-R	6-0	170	4-17-92	.339	.400	.316	63	260	42	88	20	5	9	40	10	1	2	2	47	10	8	.558	.365
Saltalamacchia, Jarrod	B-R	6-4	235	5-2-85	.174	.143	.182	67	218	21	38	7	1	5	28	33	1	0	1	81	1	1	.284	.285
Scivicque, Kade	R-R	6-0	225	3-22-93	.230	.262	.211	34	113	6	26	7	0	2	8	7	2	1	1	18	0	0	.345	.285
2-team total (1 Gwinnett)					.231	.267	.208	35	117	6	27	8	0	2	8	7	2	1	1	19	0	0	.350	.284
Stewart, Christin	L-R	6-0	205	12-10-93	.264	.274	.259	122	444	69	117	21	3	23	77	67	6	0	5	108	0	0	.480	.364
Wilson, Kenny	R-R	6-0	205	1-30-90	.177	.278	.063	10	34	5	6	0	0	2	3	1	0	0	1	11	0	0	.353	.263

Pitching	B-T	HT	WT	DOB	W	L	ERA	G	GS	CG	SV	IP	H	R	ER	HR	BB	SO	AVG	vLH	vRH	K/9	BB/9
Alcantara, Victor	R-R	6-2	190	4-3-93	5	2	2.81	29	1	0	3	51	52	20	16	3	7	47	.263	.318	.237	8.24	1.23
Alexander, Tyler	R-L	6-2	200	7-14-94	3	6	4.79	17	15	0	0	92	120	58	49	9	13	60	.319	.299	.326	5.87	1.27
Aumont, Phillippe	L-R	6-7	240	1-7-89	4	6	6.58	29	4	0	3	53	57	39	39	9	25	62	.277	.253	.291	10.46	4.22
Barbato, Johnny	R-R	6-1	231	7-11-92	0	3	1.45	33	2	0	12	37	25	10	6	1	10	37	.191	.208	.181	8.92	2.41
Bell, Chad	R-L	6-3	200	2-28-89	0	0	4.35	4	3	0	0	10	8	5	5	3	4	7	.205	.143	.219	6.10	3.48
2-team total (28 Gwinnett)					2	3	5.88	32	4	0	0	57	68	38	37	8	18	55	.289	.358	.253	8.74	2.86
Carpenter, Ryan	L-L	6-5	210	8-22-90	2	8	5.07	14	14	0	0	76	96	46	43	8	21	73	.309	.247	.329	8.61	2.48
Cervenka, Hunter	L-L	6-1	245	1-3-90	3	2	2.36	24	0	0	0	27	21	10	7	2	8	31	.219	.177	.242	10.46	2.70
Chapman, Kevin	L-L	6-3	230	2-19-88	0	0	3.45	14	0	0	2	16	12	7	6	2	10	13	.231	.353	.171	7.47	5.74
Coleman, Louis	R-R	6-4	205	4-4-86	0	0	2.40	13	0	0	8	15	8	4	4	1	5	15	.157	.250	.114	9.00	3.00
Comer, Kevin	R-R	6-3	205	8-1-92	3	1	3.86	48	1	0	4	56	56	24	24	5	20	57	.261	.200	.296	9.16	3.21
Dowdy, Kyle	R-R	6-1	195	2-3-93	5	4	4.47	11	9	0	0	54	61	27	27	2	21	44	.291	.218	.333	7.29	3.48
Funkhouser, Kyle	R-R	6-2	220	3-16-94	0	2	6.23	2	2	0	0	9	8	6	6	0	10	7	.258	.333	.188	7.27	10.38
Gutierrez, Alfred	R-R	6-1	200	6-12-95	0	0	72.00	1	0	0	0	1	7	8	8	0	1	0	.636	.714	.500	0.00	0.00
Hall, Matt	L-L	6-0	200	7-23-93	4	0	2.67	10	10	0	0	57	46	18	17	1	20	59	.219	.206	.225	9.26	3.14
Hardy, Blaine	L-L	6-2	218	3-14-87	0	1	1.03	9	4	0	0	26	14	3	3	0	4	34	.156	.185	.143	11.62	1.37
Houston, Zac	R-R	6-5	250	11-30-94	0	1	1.18	33	0	0	10	38	20	5	5	1	16	55	.156	.149	.161	13.03	3.79
Ladwig, A.J.	R-R	6-5	180	12-24-92	6	4	6.19	16	14	0	0	80	104	57	55	16	13	50	.319	.336	.307	5.63	1.46
Lewicki, Artie	R-R	6-3	195	4-8-92	5	6	4.67	12	12	0	0	62	64	32	32	5	16	55	.270	.239	.290	8.03	2.34
Liriano, Francisco	L-L	6-2	180	10-26-83	0	1	18.00	1	1	0	0	4	11	8	8	2	0	7	.500	.000	.550	15.75	0.00
Montgomery, Mark	R-R	6-0	200	8-30-90	1	0	1.98	12	0	0	0	14	17	6	3	0	8	17	.293	.200	.342	11.20	5.27
Norris, Daniel	L-L	6-2	185	4-25-93	0	0	2.25	1	1	0	0	4	3	1	1	0	1	4	.214	.000	.273	9.00	2.25

Name	B-T	HT	WT	DOB	W	L	ERA	G	GS	CG	SV	IP	H	R	ER	HR	BB	SO	AVG	vLH	vRH	K/9	BB/9
Reininger, Zac	B-R	6-3	185	1-28-93	5	1	2.63	37	0	0	6	51	46	18	15	3	16	53	.236	.254	.227	9.29	2.81
Russell, James	L-L	6-4	205	1-8-86	0	1	15.00	2	0	0	0	3	5	5	5	1	1	2	.385	.500	.364	6.00	3.00
Saupold, Warwick	R-R	6-2	223	1-16-90	3	2	4.89	15	8	0	0	53	59	30	29	6	17	43	.278	.297	.265	7.26	2.87
Smoker, Josh	L-L	6-2	255	11-26-88	0	1	5.23	10	0	0	0	10	13	6	6	0	4	11	.302	.400	.273	9.58	3.48
2-team total (32 Indianapolis)					3	2	3.38	42	0	0	0	45	45	19	17	4	16	50	.250	.258	.246	9.93	3.18
Spomer, Kurt	B-R	6-2	215	7-10-89	1	0	1.00	4	0	0	0	9	5	1	1	0	3	5	.172	.273	.111	5.00	3.00
Stumpf, Daniel	L-L	6-2	208	1-4-91	1	0	3.48	9	0	0	0	10	12	4	4	1	0	13	.293	.333	.276	11.32	0.00
Tazawa, Junichi	R-R	5-11	200	6-6-86	0	1	9.39	7	0	0	0	8	11	9	8	1	5	10	.344	.444	.304	11.74	5.87
Thielbar, Caleb	R-L	6-0	205	1-31-87	4	1	3.32	12	0	0	0	19	20	9	7	2	2	11	.270	.304	.255	5.21	0.95
Turley, Josh	L-L	6-0	185	8-26-90	5	3	4.90	12	9	0	0	61	53	35	33	1	46	50	.241	.246	.239	7.42	6.82
Turnbull, Spencer	R-R	6-3	215	9-18-92	1	1	2.03	2	2	0	0	13	8	3	3	0	3	19	.178	.167	.182	12.83	2.03
Turner, Jacob	R-R	6-5	215	5-21-91	3	4	3.50	15	15	0	0	82	74	33	32	6	29	58	.247	.246	.247	6.34	3.17
VerHagen, Drew	R-R	6-6	230	10-22-90	2	1	1.65	10	6	0	0	33	18	7	6	0	10	51	.155	.171	.147	14.05	2.76
Voelker, Paul	R-R	5-10	185	8-19-92	6	3	3.18	43	1	0	0	68	56	27	24	7	24	58	.219	.198	.230	7.68	3.18
Watkins, Spenser	R-R	6-2	220	8-27-92	1	1	4.66	2	2	0	0	10	8	5	5	2	5	6	.222	.208	.250	5.59	4.66
Wilson, Alex	R-R	6-0	227	11-3-86	0	0	0.00	1	1	0	0	1	0	0	0	0	1	2	.000	—	.000	13.50	6.75
Zimmermann, Jordan	R-R	6-2	225	5-23-86	0	1	14.40	2	2	0	0	5	10	8	8	1	4	6	.417	.222	.533	10.80	7.20

Fielding

Catcher	PCT	G	PO	A	E	DP	PB
Greiner	.998	44	365	35	1	2	5
Saltalamacchia	.993	63	500	34	4	3	7
Scivicque	.990	34	269	24	3	4	7

First Base	PCT	G	PO	A	E	DP
Adduci	.974	10	72	2	2	7
Espinal	.995	97	714	72	4	84
Huffman	1.000	10	78	4	0	9
Krizan	.981	25	198	8	4	23
Quintana	1.000	1	6	0	0	1

Second Base	PCT	G	PO	A	E	DP
Castro	.951	12	17	22	2	6
Kozma	1.000	8	12	18	0	4
Krizan	.990	29	42	61	1	18
Lugo	.987	80	124	169	4	53
Machado	1.000	16	31	48	0	8
Rodriguez	1.000	1	2	2	0	0

Third Base	PCT	G	PO	A	E	DP
Candelario	1.000	2	1	3	0	0
Castro	.885	30	19	58	10	4
Eaves	.958	19	11	35	2	4
Espinal	1.000	2	1	7	0	0
Kozma	1.000	10	4	16	0	2
Krizan	.875	3	3	4	1	1
Lugo	.941	43	26	70	6	8
Rodriguez	.958	34	22	70	4	9

Shortstop	PCT	G	PO	A	E	DP
Castro	.928	22	27	50	6	13
Castro	1.000	5	4	10	0	2
Kozma	.987	64	75	156	3	38
Lugo	.000	1	0	0	0	0
Machado	.980	25	38	61	2	21
Rodriguez	.968	26	28	63	3	16

Outfield	PCT	G	PO	A	E	DP
Adduci	.980	48	97	1	2	1
Cameron	1.000	15	40	0	0	0
Castro	1.000	7	3	2	0	0
Gerber	1.000	67	149	1	0	0
Huffman	1.000	5	6	1	0	0
Jones	1.000	2	7	1	0	1
Kozma	.000	1	0	0	0	0
Krizan	1.000	27	59	2	0	0
Mahtook	.994	66	151	3	1	0
Martin	1.000	2	2	0	0	0
Robson	.992	55	119	1	1	1
Rodriguez	1.000	4	7	0	0	0
Rodriguez	1.000	4	8	0	0	0
Stewart	.987	108	223	5	3	0
Wilson	1.000	10	33	2	0	0

DETROIT TIGERS

ERIE SEAWOLVES

DOUBLE-A

EASTERN LEAGUE

Batting	B-T	HT	WT	DOB	AVG	vLH	vRH	G	AB	R	H	2B	3B	HR	RBI	BB	HBP	SH	SF	SO	SB	CS	SLG	OBP
Alcantara, Sergio	B-R	5-9	168	7-10-96	.272	.236	.291	120	442	53	120	18	3	1	37	42	1	7	2	95	8	5	.333	.335
Cameron, Daz	R-R	6-2	195	1-15-97	.285	.310	.275	53	200	32	57	12	5	5	35	25	1	0	0	53	12	5	.470	.367
Castro, Harold	L-R	6-0	165	11-30-93	.282	.265	.290	29	110	10	31	5	0	0	10	4	1	0	1	21	2	1	.327	.310
Castro, Willi	B-R	6-1	165	4-24-97	.324	.314	.333	26	105	12	34	9	2	4	13	6	1	2	0	25	4	1	.562	.366
2-team total (97 Akron)					.263	.260	.264	123	476	67	125	29	4	9	52	34	4	9	1	109	17	5	.397	.317
Eaves, Kody	R-R	6-0	175	7-8-93	.209	.155	.230	71	254	35	53	13	1	4	21	34	0	2	5	67	4	3	.315	.297
Ficociello, Dominic	B-R	6-4	200	4-10-92	.268	.291	.257	97	366	50	98	15	1	8	56	43	4	0	4	117	8	7	.380	.348
Gibson, Cam	L-R	6-1	215	2-12-94	.250	.234	.257	48	152	26	38	7	2	4	28	19	1	3	4	43	6	2	.401	.330
Lester, Josh	L-R	6-3	216	7-17-94	.259	.230	.272	127	464	71	120	22	3	21	75	61	5	0	8	118	1	0	.455	.346
Maddox, Will	L-R	5-10	180	6-11-92	.300	.291	.304	102	397	59	119	17	5	4	41	24	4	4	5	67	7	7	.398	.342
Montgomery, Troy	L-L	5-10	185	8-13-94	.249	.250	.248	64	209	30	52	7	3	1	14	34	1	1	1	61	9	3	.325	.355
Paredes, Isaac	R-R	5-11	225	2-18-99	.321	.297	.330	39	131	20	42	9	0	3	22	19	2	0	3	22	1	0	.458	.407
Perez, Arvicent	R-R	5-10	180	1-14-94	.256	.500	.212	11	39	1	10	1	0	0	3	0	0	2	0	8	0	1	.282	.256
Quintana, Gabriel	R-R	6-3	215	9-7-92	.183	.220	.167	35	137	17	25	2	0	4	12	8	3	0	0	54	0	0	.285	.243
Robson, Jacob	L-R	5-10	175	11-20-94	.286	.247	.306	67	262	46	75	16	3	7	32	39	2	7	1	78	11	4	.450	.382
Rodriguez, Herlis	L-L	6-0	170	6-10-94	.194	.235	.182	24	72	7	14	5	0	0	7	4	1	3	2	12	4	3	.264	.241
Rogers, Jake	R-R	6-1	190	4-18-95	.219	.200	.227	99	352	57	77	15	1	17	56	41	6	2	7	112	7	1	.412	.305
Salter, Blaise	R-R	6-5	245	6-25-93	.192	.000	.243	12	47	2	9	1	0	1	9	0	0	0	1	15	0	0	.277	.188
Scivicque, Kade	R-R	6-0	225	3-22-93	.244	.273	.304	10	34	2	10	1	0	0	6	3	0	0	2	7	0	0	.324	.333
Sedio, Chad	L-R	6-3	200	3-30-94	.255	.279	.240	48	165	21	42	8	1	2	23	13	6	0	3	46	1	0	.352	.326
Simcox, A.J.	R-R	6-3	185	6-22-94	.205	.278	.170	51	166	22	34	4	2	0	20	12	1	3	1	45	3	2	.289	.261
Thole, Josh	L-R	6-1	205	10-28-86	.238	.167	.267	21	63	11	15	1	0	1	10	8	1	1	3	14	1	0	.302	.320
Wilson, Kenny	R-R	6-0	205	1-30-90	.278	.300	.269	31	108	15	30	4	3	0	14	18	1	0	3	36	10	4	.370	.377
Woodrow, Daniel	L-R	5-10	160	1-26-95	.313	.340	.301	92	342	48	107	13	3	3	37	31	3	5	6	71	19	13	.395	.369

Pitching	B-T	HT	WT	DOB	W	L	ERA	G	GS	CG	SV	IP	H	R	ER	HR	BB	SO	AVG	vLH	vRH	K/9	BB/9
Alexander, Tyler	R-L	6-2	200	7-14-94	3	2	3.75	9	9	0	0	48	64	22	20	7	9	35	.325	.288	.344	6.56	1.69
Aumont, Phillippe	L-R	6-7	240	1-7-89	0	0	0.00	2	0	0	0	3	1	0	0	1	0	2	.111	.250	.000	6.00	3.00
Baez, Sandy	R-R	6-2	180	11-25-93	1	9	5.64	33	15	0	1	104	114	71	65	19	46	86	.284	.259	.311	7.47	3.99
Binford, Christian	R-R	6-5	215	12-20-92	0	0	3.86	7	2	0	0	21	27	10	9	1	1	22	.300	.277	.326	9.43	0.43
2-team total (12 Bowie)					1	4	4.66	19	9	1	0	77	104	43	40	10	9	57	.324	.347	.298	6.63	1.05
Blackwood, Nolan	R-R	6-5	185	3-16-95	0	1	4.50	6	0	0	0	8	7	4	4	2	3	7	.241	.294	.167	7.88	3.38
Breto, Liarvis	L-L	5-11	175	4-10-93	2	3	3.82	9	5	0	0	31	34	15	13	2	6	31	.276	.231	.289	9.10	1.76

DETROIT TIGERS

Name	B-T	HT	WT	DOB	W	L	ERA	G	GS	CG	SV	IP	H	R	ER	HR	BB	SO	AVG	vLH	vRH	SO/9	BB/9
Burrows, Beau	R-R	6-2	200	9-18-96	10	9	4.10	26	26	0	0	134	126	66	61	12	56	127	.252	.265	.238	8.53	3.76
Carlton, Drew	R-R	6-1	210	9-8-95	0	0	1.64	5	0	0	0	11	11	3	2	0	1	11	.275	.364	.167	9.00	0.82
Castro, Anthony	R-R	6-2	180	4-13-95	0	0	8.10	3	3	0	0	10	8	10	9	1	12	4	.229	.182	.308	3.60	10.80
Cervenka, Hunter	L-L	6-1	245	1-3-90	0	0	0.00	3	0	0	0	6	2	0	0	2	4		.111	.000	.154	6.35	3.18
Dowdy, Kyle	R-R	6-1	195	2-3-93	3	4	5.09	13	5	0	2	41	43	23	23	6	11	48	.276	.281	.272	10.62	2.43
2-team total (6 Akron)					4	8	5.68	19	11	0	2	70	73	44	44	10	29	76	.274	.271	.278	9.82	3.75
Ecker, Mark	R-R	6-0	180	5-27-95	4	6	3.66	44	0	0	1	59	44	30	24	7	31	51	.212	.188	.232	7.78	4.73
Faedo, Alex	R-R	6-5	230	11-12-95	3	6	4.95	12	12	0	0	60	54	37	33	15	22	59	.239	.198	.264	8.85	3.30
Funkhouser, Kyle	R-R	6-2	220	3-16-94	4	5	3.74	17	17	0	0	89	88	42	37	10	39	89	.266	.240	.288	9.00	3.94
Gutierrez, Alfred	R-R	6-1	200	6-12-95	2	3	6.09	7	7	0	0	34	48	24	23	3	15	32	.329	.377	.294	8.47	3.97
Hall, Matt	L-L	6-0	200	7-23-93	5	2	1.58	27	4	0	0	57	33	16	10	1	25	76	.165	.253	.112	12.00	3.95
Houston, Zac	R-R	6-5	250	11-30-94	1	1	2.60	13	0	0	0	17	8	5	5	1	9	25	.136	.039	.212	12.98	4.67
Ladwig, A.J.	R-R	6-5	180	12-24-92	4	2	2.68	9	9	0	0	54	51	19	16	2	12	48	.255	.275	.242	8.05	2.01
Manning, Matt	R-R	6-6	190	1-28-98	0	1	4.22	2	2	0	0	11	1	6	5	0	4	13	.282	.350	.211	10.97	3.38
Moreno, Gerson	R-R	6-0	175	9-10-95	0	1	5.29	14	0	0	1	17	11	10	10	2	14	21	.266	.237	.308	11.12	7.41
Navilhon, Joe	R-R	6-0	200	7-13-93	2	3	3.89	24	1	0	0	37	39	23	16	6	9	46	.265	.246	.279	11.19	2.19
Perez, Fernando	R-R	6-3	181	12-17-93	0	0	10.03	8	0	0	0	12	18	14	13	3	10	6	.360	.320	.400	4.63	7.71
Ravenelle, Adam	R-R	6-3	185	10-5-92	0	0	4.05	13	0	0	0	20	19	10	9	3	11	15	.253	.313	.209	6.75	4.95
Schreiber, John	R-R	6-3	215	3-5-94	7	2	2.48	49	0	0	18	58	47	25	16	2	19	59	.224	.245	.205	9.16	2.95
Schwaab, Andrew	R-L	6-1	205	2-8-93	0	0	5.87	7	0	0	0	8	13	5	5	1	3	6	.371	.438	.316	7.04	3.52
2-team total (13 Trenton)					2	3	4.85	20	0	0	1	26	26	16	14	1	14	25	.271	.255	.289	8.65	4.85
Spomer, Kurt	B-R	6-2	215	7-10-89	3	0	4.18	28	0	0	1	32	39	20	15	1	10	18	.302	.283	.316	5.01	2.78
Szkutnik, Trent	R-L	6-1	195	8-21-93	4	2	3.43	34	0	0	1	45	44	22	17	4	18	51	.251	.233	.265	10.28	3.63
Tepesch, Nick	R-R	6-4	240	10-12-88	0	0	8.22	4	0	0	0	12	7	7	7	0	4	4	.353	.375	.333	4.70	4.70
2-team total (10 New Hampshire)					1	2	5.63	14	8	0	1	56	67	38	35	6	20	34	.298	.307	.290	5.46	3.21
Thielbar, Caleb	R-L	6-0	205	1-31-87	3	0	1.42	27	0	0	0	38	28	7	6	1	3	40	.201	.214	.196	9.47	0.71
Thompson, Jeff	R-R	6-6	245	9-23-91	0	1	5.29	14	0	0	0	17	24	13	10	3	13	17	.329	.317	.344	9.00	6.88
Turley, Josh	L-L	6-0	185	8-26-90	1	0	6.14	2	1	0	0	7	7	6	5	1	3	6	.241	.000	.280	7.36	3.68
Turnbull, Spencer	R-R	6-3	215	9-18-92	4	7	4.47	19	19	1	0	99	92	50	49	4	40	105	.248	.231	.265	9.58	3.65
Watkins, Spencer	R-R	6-2	220	8-27-92	1	2	5.40	3	3	0	0	15	16	9	9	1	7	18	.262	.290	.233	10.80	4.20

Fielding

Catcher	PCT	G	PO	A	E	DP	PB
Perez	.990	11	86	9	1	1	2
Rogers	.995	98	857	102	5	7	11
Scivicque	.988	10	74	10	1	1	3
Thole	.994	21	165	10	1	2	1

First Base	PCT	G	PO	A	E	DP
Ficociello	.988	56	388	27	5	31
Lester	.990	66	435	37	5	53
Maddox	1.000	1	4	0	0	0
Quintana	.974	6	35	2	1	4
Rodriguez	.977	9	39	4	1	6
Rogers	1.000	1	6	1	0	0
Salter	.986	8	68	5	1	8
Sedio	1.000	1	6	1	0	1

Second Base	PCT	G	PO	A	E	DP
Alcantara	.965	20	36	47	3	14

	PCT	G	PO	A	E	DP
Castro	1.000	14	21	23	0	5
Castro	1.000	9	15	18	0	1
Eaves	.778	4	3	4	2	1
Maddox	.960	84	140	195	14	55
Paredes	1.000	1	1	5	0	1
Simcox	.985	13	27	37	1	8

Third Base	PCT	G	PO	A	E	DP
Castro	1.000	8	4	15	0	1
Eaves	.906	40	21	56	8	9
Ficociello	1.000	2	1	3	0	0
Lester	.929	60	34	83	9	5
Paredes	.909	18	5	25	3	3
Quintana	1.000	1	0	5	0	0
Sedio	.000	1	0	0	0	0
Simcox	.893	15	5	20	3	2

Shortstop	PCT	G	PO	A	E	DP
Alcantara	.960	93	142	215	15	53
Castro	1.000	1	4	2	0	0
Castro	.958	10	20	26	2	2
Paredes	.918	15	22	34	5	10
Simcox	.950	22	28	48	4	11

Outfield	PCT	G	PO	A	E	DP
Cameron	.990	49	92	5	1	1
Castro	.889	5	8	0	1	0
Ficociello	1.000	28	42	1	0	0
Gibson	.975	47	112	4	3	0
Montgomery	.985	64	124	7	2	1
Robson	.993	66	133	5	1	2
Rodriguez	1.000	13	25	2	0	1
Sedio	.986	36	70	1	1	0
Wilson	.967	29	56	3	2	1
Woodrow	.991	89	220	2	2	2

LAKELAND FLYING TIGERS

FLORIDA STATE LEAGUE

HIGH CLASS A

Batting	B-T	HT	WT	DOB	AVG	vLH	vRH	G	AB	R	H	2B	3B	HR	RBI	BB	HBP	SH	SF	SO	SB	CS	SLG	OBP
Athmann, Austin	R-R	6-2	210	4-27-95	.243	.271	.233	76	276	23	67	11	1	0	29	17	5	0	1	63	1	0	.290	.298
Azocar, Jose	R-R	5-11	185	5-11-96	.290	.268	.297	82	300	34	87	14	3	1	34	9	2	0	7	64	5	2	.367	.308
Bauml, Cole	L-R	6-3	205	11-2-92	.186	.125	.200	12	43	4	8	2	0	0	3	1	0	0	0	8	0	1	.233	.205
Brinkman, Clark	R-R	6-2	195	3-6-96	.136	.250	.111	6	22	3	3	0	1	2	5	1	1	1	0	8	0	0	.500	.208
Burch, Luke	L-L	6-2	185	4-18-94	.300	.280	.304	67	257	31	77	10	0	0	27	14	1	5	1	75	12	5	.339	.337
Burdeaux, Dylan	R-R	6-2	215	2-21-94	.245	.288	.234	102	364	49	89	16	2	6	43	26	5	0	3	95	4	2	.349	.302
Cameron, Daz	R-R	6-2	195	1-15-97	.259	.328	.234	58	216	35	56	9	3	3	20	25	4	0	1	69	10	4	.370	.346
Clemens, Kody	L-R	6-1	170	5-15-96	.238	.143	.286	11	42	6	10	2	0	1	3	2	1	0	1	12	1	0	.357	.283
Deatherage, Brock	L-L	6-1	175	9-12-95	.333	.333	.333	12	45	12	15	1	1	1	5	6	0	0	1	13	4	0	.467	.404
Escobar, Elys	R-R	6-0	190	9-21-96	.143	.500	.000	3	7	0	1	0	0	0	0	1	1	0	0	5	0	0	.143	.333
Gibson, Cam	L-R	6-1	215	2-12-94	.240	.265	.233	66	229	32	55	7	3	4	24	36	5	3	1	61	16	6	.349	.354
Hill, Derek	R-R	6-2	190	12-30-95	.239	.230	.242	106	343	45	82	9	3	4	33	33	1	5	1	109	35	12	.318	.307
Montgomery, Troy	L-L	5-10	185	8-13-94	.336	.367	.327	39	131	16	44	9	0	1	19	25	0	1	3	27	5	5	.428	.434
Paredes, Isaac	R-R	5-11	225	2-18-99	.259	.318	.244	84	301	50	78	19	2	12	48	32	7	1	6	54	1	0	.455	.338
Pereira, Anthony	R-R	6-0	195	11-28-96	.201	.222	.195	58	194	19	39	7	3	3	17	10	1	1	1	60	0	1	.314	.264
Peterson, Cole	L-R	5-11	160	8-2-95	.220	.269	.209	38	141	14	31	6	0	0	12	6	1	3	2	7	0	0	.262	.253
Pinero, Daniel	R-R	6-5	235	5-2-94	.263	.281	.258	119	414	66	109	26	1	9	59	54	7	0	8	81	5	0	.396	.352
Rodriguez, Herlis	L-L	6-0	170	6-10-94	.250	.125	.313	7	24	5	6	0	1	0	3	3	0	0	0	6	0	0	.333	.333
Salter, Blaise	R-R	6-5	245	6-25-93	.294	.296	.293	28	109	7	32	6	2	3	20	7	2	0	0	14	0	0	.468	.322
Scivicque, Kade	R-R	6-0	225	3-22-93	.277	.214	.290	23	83	12	23	5	0	2	11	10	0	0	1	15	0	0	.410	.351

Name	B-T	HT	WT	DOB	AVG	vLH	vRH	G	AB	R	H	2B	3B	HR	RBI	BB	HBP	SH	SF	SO	SB	CS	SLG	OBP
Sedio, Chad	L-R	6-3	200	3-30-94	.287	.258	.300	55	216	31	62	9	2	2	32	11	11	0	4	36	1	1	.375	.347
Shepherd, Zac	R-R	6-3	185	9-14-95	.190	.081	.216	62	190	27	36	13	2	5	25	28	5	0	2	90	0	0	.358	.307
Simcox, A.J.	R-R	6-3	185	6-22-94	.235	.194	.248	39	136	17	32	1	4	2	22	15	0	1	3	34	3	0	.346	.305
Sthormes, Andres	R-R	5-10	195	8-7-96	.177	.208	.171	48	153	18	27	3	1	0	11	6	4	2	0	39	1	0	.209	.227
Valente, John	B-R	5-11	190	6-23-95	.571	1.000	.500	2	7	0	4	0	0	0	0	0	0	0	0	0	1	0	0	.571	.571
Verdon, Jordan	L-R	6-3	190	1-7-97	.143	.000	.200	2	7	0	1	0	0	0	1	0	0	0	1	0	0	0	.143	.250
Wilson, Kenny	R-R	6-0	205	1-30-90	.273	.429	.273	6	18	4	6	4	0	1	3	4	1	0	0	5	2	0	.722	.478
Woodrow, Daniel	L-R	5-10	160	1-26-95	.381	.667	.267	5	21	5	8	1	0	0	1	0	0	0	0	5	4	1	.429	.409

Pitching

Name	B-T	HT	WT	DOB	W	L	ERA	G	GS	CG	SV	IP	H	R	ER	HR	BB	SO	AVG	vLH	vRH	K/9	BB/9
Barbato, Johnny	R-R	6-1	231	7-11-92	0	0	40.50	1	1	0	0	1	1	3	3	0	2	1	.333	.000	1.000	13.50	27.00
Belisario, Johan	R-R	5-11	165	8-13-93	0	0	0.00	1	0	0	0	3	1	0	0	0	0	3	.100	.000	.250	9.00	0.00
Breto, Liarvis	L-L	5-11	175	4-10-93	3	2	2.61	10	3	0	0	31	24	11	9	1	12	42	.214	.205	.221	12.19	3.48
Briceno, Endrys	R-R	6-5	175	2-7-92	0	1	6.75	1	1	0	0	4	7	7	3	0	3	2	.350	.455	.222	4.50	6.75
Carlton, Drew	R-R	6-1	210	9-8-95	4	2	2.38	34	0	0	9	57	46	19	15	0	11	57	.217	.198	.238	9.05	1.75
Carpenter, Ryan	L-L	6-5	210	8-22-90	0	0	3.00	1	1	0	0	3	4	2	1	1	1	3	.333	—	.333	3.00	3.00
Castro, Anthony	R-R	6-2	180	4-13-95	9	4	2.93	22	20	2	0	117	112	42	38	8	43	101	.253	.267	.232	7.79	3.32
Cervenka, Hunter	L-L	6-1	245	1-3-90	0	0	0.00	2	0	0	0	1	0	0	0	0	0	5	.091	.200	.000	13.50	0.00
Crosby, Drew	R-L	6-0	196	11-16-95	0	0	13.50	1	0	0	0	2	6	3	3	1	9	1	.546	.600	.500	9.00	0.00
de Blok, Tom	R-R	6-4	240	5-8-96	4	4	5.98	11	11	0	0	56	65	38	37	7	20	41	.293	.285	.303	6.63	3.23
DeCaster, Ethan	R-R	6-3	190	10-27-94	0	0	0.00	1	0	0	0	2	1	0	0	0	2	4	.125	.000	.500	15.43	7.71
Faedo, Alex	R-R	6-5	230	11-12-95	2	4	3.10	12	12	0	0	61	49	25	21	3	13	51	.217	.244	.187	7.52	1.92
Fulmer, Michael	R-R	6-3	246	3-15-93	0	0	0.00	2	2	0	0	6	1	0	0	0	0	6	.053	.083	.000	16.50	0.00
Gutierrez, Alfred	R-R	6-1	200	6-12-95	2	4	2.42	23	11	0	3	74	50	23	20	3	27	78	.189	.221	.146	9.44	3.27
Guzman, Carlos	R-R	6-1	170	5-16-98	0	0	0.00	1	0	0	0	1	0	0	0	0	0	2	.000	.000	.000	18.00	0.00
Hill, Evan	L-L	6-5	190	8-18-93	0	2	4.60	13	0	0	1	16	18	10	8	3	5	16	.290	.333	.257	9.19	2.87
Idrogo, Eudis	L-L	6-1	198	6-6-95	4	3	4.50	21	5	0	2	68	72	45	34	7	15	42	.274	.322	.249	5.56	1.99
Jimenez, Eduardo	R-R	6-2	225	4-4-95	3	3	3.42	40	0	0	15	50	62	23	19	3	20	51	.301	.347	.257	9.18	3.60
Manning, Matt	R-R	6-6	190	1-28-98	4	4	2.98	9	9	0	0	51	32	17	17	4	19	65	.176	.167	.186	11.40	3.33
Mize, Casey	R-R	6-3	220	5-1-97	0	1	4.63	4	4	0	0	12	13	6	6	2	2	10	.296	.292	.300	7.71	1.54
Navilhon, Joe	R-R	6-0	200	7-13-93	1	3	1.72	12	0	0	2	16	13	6	3	0	2	21	.224	.147	.332	12.06	1.15
Norris, Daniel	L-L	6-2	185	4-25-93	0	0	3.00	1	1	0	0	3	2	1	1	0	2	4	.182	.000	.250	12.00	6.00
Perez, Fernando	R-R	6-3	181	12-17-93	5	1	2.95	29	1	0	1	55	49	20	18	0	21	63	.239	.220	.260	10.31	3.44
Perez, Franklin	R-R	6-3	197	12-6-97	0	1	7.94	4	4	0	0	11	15	10	10	2	8	9	.341	.435	.238	7.15	6.35
Pinto, Wladimir	R-R	5-11	170	2-12-98	3	2	6.75	25	0	0	0	33	26	25	25	5	21	47	.213	.222	.203	12.69	5.67
Schmidt, Clate	R-R	6-1	190	12-10-93	0	0	2.45	2	0	0	0	4	4	1	1	0	0	3	.267	.222	.333	7.36	0.00
Sittinger, Brandyn	R-R	6-1	200	6-6-94	0	0	1.80	10	0	0	1	15	12	3	3	0	12	21	.211	.242	.167	12.60	7.20
Sodders, Austin	L-L	6-4	205	4-29-95	3	2	4.05	8	8	0	0	47	36	22	21	4	8	41	.213	.245	.198	7.91	1.54
Soto, Gregory	L-L	6-1	240	2-11-95	8	8	4.45	25	23	0	0	113	101	67	56	4	70	115	.235	.227	.238	9.13	5.56
Szkutnik, Trent	R-L	6-1	195	8-21-93	2	2	0.53	10	0	0	0	17	13	3	1	0	1	10	.228	.136	.286	5.29	0.53
Teakell, Trey	R-R	6-5	210	2-17-92	1	2	6.43	7	0	0	1	14	16	11	10	3	3	5	.291	.393	.185	3.21	1.93
Thompson, Jeff	R-R	6-6	245	9-23-91	1	0	7.24	11	0	0	0	14	21	13	11	0	13	7	.368	.345	.393	4.61	8.56
Turnbull, Spencer	R-R	6-3	215	9-18-92	0	0	0.00	1	1	0	0	5	2	0	0	0	0	6	.125	.200	.000	11.57	0.00
Vest, Will	R-R	6-0	180	6-6-95	1	0	6.08	10	0	0	0	13	16	9	9	1	2	12	.286	.333	.217	8.10	1.35
Warner, Burris	R-R	6-0	185	10-15-94	4	1	2.18	20	2	0	0	41	41	13	10	0	13	38	.260	.250	.270	8.27	2.83
Watkins, Spenser	R-R	6-2	220	8-27-92	8	4	2.24	22	13	2	1	112	91	31	28	5	33	89	.225	.213	.237	7.13	2.64

Fielding

Catcher	PCT	G	PO	A	E	DP	PB
Athmann	.990	72	562	42	6	2	12
Escobar	.933	3	14	0	1	0	0
Scivicque	.989	17	166	14	2	2	4
Sthormes	.979	44	341	31	8	2	10

First Base	PCT	G	PO	A	E	DP
Burdeaux	.994	82	632	41	4	60
Pinero	.994	19	162	4	1	16
Rodriguez	1.000	1	0	0	0	2
Salter	.981	20	152	5	3	12
Sedio	1.000	1	12	1	0	0
Shepherd	.987	10	72	4	1	9
Verdon	1.000	1	4	1	0	1

Second Base	PCT	G	PO	A	E	DP
Clemens	1.000	11	14	26	0	3
Paredes	1.000	22	38	59	0	17
Pereira	.954	41	63	124	9	20

Third Base	PCT	G	PO	A	E	DP
Paredes	1.000	3	2	4	0	0
Pereira	1.000	8	3	20	0	3
Peterson	1.000	5	3	7	0	0
Pinero	.965	65	47	89	5	10
Sedio	.947	21	12	42	3	5
Shepherd	.922	28	19	40	5	5
Simcox	1.000	5	3	9	0	0

Shortstop	PCT	G	PO	A	E	DP
Paredes	.964	59	63	154	8	27
Pereira	.941	9	13	19	2	8
Peterson	.987	20	30	44	1	15

(2B/SS)	PCT	G	PO	A	E	DP
Pinero	.974	30	36	78	3	15
Simcox	.968	17	21	39	2	4

Outfield	PCT	G	PO	A	E	DP
Azocar	.986	70	135	4	2	0
Bauml	1.000	3	2	0	0	0
Brinkman	1.000	6	6	0	0	0
Burch	.957	51	86	4	4	1
Cameron	.978	56	134	2	3	1
Deatherage	1.000	11	15	0	0	0
Gibson	.989	49	88	2	1	1
Hill	.985	101	194	7	3	0
Montgomery	.986	35	68	5	1	2
Pinero	1.000	2	4	0	0	0
Rodriguez						
Sedio	1.000	8	16	1	0	0
Wilson	1.000	4	9	0	0	0
Woodrow	1.000	5	7	0	0	0

WEST MICHIGAN WHITECAPS LOW CLASS A
MIDWEST LEAGUE

Batting	B-T	HT	WT	DOB	AVG	vLH	vRH	G	AB	R	H	2B	3B	HR	RBI	BB	HBP	SH	SF	SO	SB	CS	SLG	OBP
Alvarado, Darwin	L-R	6-0	170	11-10-98	.175	.111	.194	13	40	3	7	0	0	0	4	2	1	0	2	10	1	0	.175	.222
Azocar, Jose	R-R	5-11	185	5-11-96	.317	.482	.260	27	104	19	33	3	6	1	16	5	1	0	0	21	6	2	.490	.355
Bauml, Cole	L-R	6-3	205	11-2-92	.167	.400	.000	3	12	1	2	0	0	0	0	1	0	0	3	0	0	.167	.231
Bojarski, Ulrich	R-R	6-3	190	9-15-98	.222	.000	.276	10	36	6	8	3	1	1	5	0	0	0	1	15	0	0	.444	.216

DETROIT TIGERS

	B-T	HT	WT	DOB	AVG	vLH	vRH	G	AB	R	H	2B	3B	HR	RBI	BB	HBP	SH	SF	SO	SB	CS	SLG	OBP
Bortles, Colby	R-R	6-5	225	5-28-95	.246	.286	.231	115	407	42	100	27	0	5	53	43	6	0	5	121	5	5	.349	.323
Burch, Luke	L-L	6-2	185	4-18-94	.313	.333	.305	37	134	22	42	6	2	0	22	12	0	6	1	36	10	3	.388	.367
Clemens, Kody	L-R	6-1	170	5-15-96	.302	.250	.319	41	149	18	45	10	2	4	17	21	1	1	2	27	3	1	.477	.387
De La Rosa, Eric	R-R	6-4	175	6-3-97	.174	.158	.185	14	46	6	8	2	0	0	4	1	3	1	0	17	4	2	.217	.240
Deatherage, Brock	L-L	6-1	175	9-12-95	.313	.341	.303	46	176	25	55	7	5	2	18	14	3	0	2	50	15	3	.443	.369
Garcia, Alexis	B-R	6-2	170	7-1-97	.213	.271	.191	64	211	28	45	8	2	1	17	8	5	0	1	66	9	6	.284	.258
Gonzalez, Cesar	R-R	6-2	175	5-31-95	.105	.000	.182	11	38	1	4	1	0	0	2	0	1	1	0	15	1	0	.132	.128
Hampton, Reece	B-R	5-10	170	7-19-96	.218	.308	.191	16	55	2	12	3	0	0	2	8	0	0	0	10	0	1	.273	.318
McCain, Garrett	R-L	6-0	180	2-28-96	.245	.192	.267	85	269	39	66	11	1	0	23	38	12	0	0	73	6	9	.294	.364
Morgan, Joey	R-R	6-0	185	8-26-96	.217	.220	.216	87	290	25	63	12	1	4	21	32	6	6	2	76	1	1	.307	.306
Pearce, Jordan	L-R	6-2	200	6-14-96	.220	.149	.241	123	413	50	91	19	0	6	49	65	1	3	8	94	2	0	.310	.322
Pereira, Anthony	R-R	6-0	195	11-28-96	.197	.177	.204	46	147	13	29	10	0	1	11	16	0	2	3	32	2	2	.286	.271
Perez, Wenceel	B-R	5-11	170	10-30-99	.309	.154	.346	16	68	8	21	3	3	0	9	2	0	0	1	8	4	1	.441	.324
Peterson, Cole	L-R	5-11	160	8-2-95	.277	.369	.246	66	260	40	72	8	5	0	21	18	2	2	2	37	13	7	.346	.326
Policelli, Brady	R-R	5-11	195	6-24-95	.248	.192	.268	98	359	43	89	19	6	7	28	33	5	2	1	78	19	8	.393	.319
Proctor, Christopher	L-R	6-1	180	3-8-97	.111	.154	.104	31	90	6	10	1	1	0	6	8	0	3	1	22	3	0	.144	.182
Quero, Jose	L-L	6-0	190	9-5-98	.030	.000	.035	10	33	4	1	0	0	0	2	5	1	0	0	9	0	0	.030	.180
Rivera, Reynaldo	R-R	6-6	250	6-14-97	.237	.198	.251	115	410	41	97	28	4	9	62	36	1	0	7	119	3	2	.390	.295
Rosa, Dylan	R-R	6-2	200	6-27-96	.229	.211	.235	107	376	53	86	15	6	11	53	42	3	0	0	129	5	6	.388	.311
Shepherd, Zac	R-R	6-3	185	9-14-95	.254	.154	.278	22	67	12	17	3	0	0	6	19	1	0	0	20	1	1	.299	.425
Sherley, Luke	R-R	6-1	190	5-7-96	.171	.200	.161	24	76	2	13	0	1	0	7	9	0	0	2	19	4	1	.197	.253
Valdez, Ignacio	R-R	6-3	195	7-16-95	.192	.167	.200	29	104	7	20	5	1	1	15	5	0	0	1	38	0	0	.289	.227
Valente, John	B-R	5-11	190	6-23-95	.333	.467	.282	13	54	7	18	5	0	0	1	1	0	0	·	9	0	3	.426	.357
Warner, Cam	R-R	6-2	188	3-4-94	.150	.111	.161	11	40	2	6	3	0	0	3	0	1	1	0	13	0	0	.225	.205

Pitching	B-T	HT	WT	DOB	W	L	ERA	G	GS	CG	SV	IP	H	R	ER	HR	BB	SO	AVG	vLH	vRH	K/9	BB/9
Bass, Brad	R-R	6-6	250	2-15-96	7	7	4.05	21	21	0	0	118	116	57	53	9	43	91	.259	.301	.236	6.96	3.29
Belisario, Johan	R-R	5-11	165	8-13-93	3	2	1.48	21	0	0	3	49	36	15	8	2	10	58	.206	.265	.168	10.73	1.85
Briceno, Endrys	R-R	6-5	175	2-7-92	4	2	4.50	17	2	0	1	42	47	26	21	3	22	37	.285	.344	.248	7.93	4.71
Castillo, Oswaldo	R-R	6-0	193	8-18-96	3	2	4.19	22	0	0	0	39	34	18	18	3	22	41	.245	.305	.200	9.54	5.12
Crosby, Drew	R-L	6-0	196	11-16-95	0	1	3.29	6	0	0	0	14	11	6	5	0	3	8	.220	.333	.195	5.27	1.98
de Blok, Tom	R-R	6-4	240	5-8-96	1	2	3.15	8	8	0	0	46	44	17	16	4	16	30	.253	.222	.275	5.91	3.15
DeCaster, Ethan	R-R	6-3	190	10-27-94	0	0	0.71	7	0	0	1	13	7	1	1	0	1	13	.167	.214	.143	9.24	0.71
Fernandez, Aaron	R-R	6-2	190	9-25-94	0	0	18.00	1	0	0	0	4	4	8	8	2	4	6	.250	.000	.333	13.50	9.00
Green, Max	L-L	6-1	175	5-28-96	2	3	4.11	17	0	0	1	35	40	23	16	3	19	34	.286	.342	.265	8.74	4.89
Hayes, John	R-R	6-6	225	1-7-93	1	2	1.54	7	0	0	2	12	15	10	2	0	7	11	.333	.350	.320	8.49	5.40
Hernandez, Wilkel	R-R	6-3	160	4-13-99	2	5	4.71	10	10	0	0	42	40	22	22	4	16	34	.250	.206	.278	7.29	3.43
Idrogo, Eudis	L-L	6-1	198	6-6-95	2	2	0.49	6	2	0	0	37	24	3	2	0	8	34	.188	.167	.196	8.27	1.95
King, Garett	R-R	6-4	189	6-12-96	0	1	4.45	6	0	0	0	28	28	17	14	6	8	30	.250	.333	.180	9.53	2.54
Kirby, Chance	R-R	5-11	165	7-19-95	0	2	4.87	4	0	0	0	19	11	11	10	2	4	20	.247	.417	.170	8.85	1.77
Lance, Carson	R-R	6-5	245	5-3-95	0	3	5.30	4	0	0	0	19	24	15	11	1	14	15	.308	.379	.265	7.23	6.75
Lescher, Billy	R-R	6-4	215	9-17-95	3	1	0.92	19	0	0	8	29	20	4	3	1	8	33	.192	.237	.167	10.13	2.45
Manning, Matt	R-R	6-6	190	1-28-98	3	3	3.40	11	11	0	0	56	47	22	21	3	28	76	.229	.230	.229	12.29	4.53
Myers, Dane	R-R	6-2	205	3-8-96	3	3	3.33	14	14	0	0	73	67	28	27	5	24	61	.245	.248	.242	7.52	2.96
Pinto, Wladimir	R-R	5-11	170	2-12-98	1	0	0.00	11	0	0	7	17	4	0	0	0	13	30	.077	.080	.074	16.20	6.48
Rodriguez, Elvin	R-R	6-3	160	3-31-98	8	7	3.34	21	21	0	0	113	108	49	42	9	32	109	.255	.253	.256	8.66	2.54
Rodriguez, Jesus	R-R	6-3	170	2-16-98	5	7	4.35	22	22	0	0	124	133	72	60	9	37	90	.270	.271	.269	6.53	2.69
Schmidt, Clate	R-R	6-1	190	12-10-93	9	2	2.59	33	1	0	4	76	75	26	22	4	20	73	.264	.318	.232	8.61	2.36
Sittinger, Brandyn	R-R	6-1	200	6-6-94	2	1	4.67	15	0	0	1	35	32	21	18	2	20	46	.241	.333	.193	11.94	5.19
Skubal, Tarik	L-L	6-3	215	11-20-96	2	0	0.00	3	0	0	1	7	5	0	0	0	1	11	.200	.143	.222	13.50	1.23
Stalsberg, Mitchell	L-L	6-0	215	1-12-96	0	0	0.00	3	0	0	0	8	4	1	0	0	5	7	.143	.143	.143	7.88	5.63
Stock, Dylan	R-R	6-4	195	7-21-96	1	0	3.38	5	1	0	0	13	13	9	5	0	3	14	.245	.143	.313	9.45	2.03
Vasquez, Jose	R-R	6-0	175	3-19-96	1	3	9.00	4	0	0	0	15	25	18	15	2	11	6	.385	.357	.405	3.60	6.60
Vest, Will	R-R	6-0	180	6-6-95	3	4	4.84	20	0	0	5	35	43	28	19	0	12	44	.297	.309	.289	11.21	3.06
Viloria, Felix	L-L	6-1	165	12-2-96	2	2	3.64	16	0	0	1	30	32	18	12	3	10	23	.283	.212	.313	6.98	3.03
Warner, Burris	R-R	6-0	190	10-15-94	1	3	1.14	14	3	0	1	39	37	15	5	0	8	49	.237	.242	.234	11.21	1.83
Zimmermann, Jordan	R-R	6-2	225	5-23-86	0	0	1.69	1	1	0	0	5	7	1	1	0	0	6	.350	.364	.333	10.13	0.00

Fielding

C: Morgan 79, Policelli 34, Proctor 31. **1B:** Pearce 73, Pereira 1, Quero 4, Rivera 60, Shepherd 4. **2B:** Clemens 39, Garcia 63, Pereira 8, Policelli 12, Shepherd 5, Sherley 1, Valente 11, Warner 3. **3B:** Bortles 99, Pearce 26, Pereira 2, Shepherd 4, Sherley 3, Valente 1, Warner 6. **SS:** Bortles 3, Pereira 32, Perez 14, Peterson 65, Shepherd 5, Sherley 18, Warner 3. **OF:** Alvarado 12, Azocar 26, Bauml 1, Bojarski 8, Burch 33, De La Rosa 11, Deatherage 44, Gonzalez 10, Hampton 16, McCain 74, Policelli 41, Quero 2, Rivera 26, Rosa 92, Valdez 25.

CONNECTICUT TIGERS — SHORT-SEASON
NEW YORK-PENN LEAGUE

Batting	B-T	HT	WT	DOB	AVG	vLH	vRH	G	AB	R	H	2B	3B	HR	RBI	BB	HBP	SH	SF	SO	SB	CS	SLG	OBP
Alvarado, Darwin	L-R	6-1	170	11-10-98	.174	.126	.161	48	155	12	27	5	2	0	18	20	2	0	3	49	2	2	.232	.272
Ames, Nick	L-R	6-3	240	11-25-96	.198	.200	.198	36	126	12	25	5	0	4	9	13	1	0	1	45	0	0	.333	.277
Aristigueta, Keyder	R-R	5-11	165	2-2-96	.000	.000	.000	3	9	0	0	0	0	0	0	2	1	0	0	2	1	0	.000	.250
Bojarski, Ulrich	R-R	6-3	190	9-15-98	.162	.143	.167	21	74	10	12	3	0	1	7	5	3	0	1	33	3	0	.243	.241
Brinkman, Clark	R-R	6-2	195	3-6-96	.208	.238	.196	23	72	11	15	1	0	0	5	8	1	0	0	22	3	1	.222	.296
Burks, Jeremiah	R-R	6-1	175	1-8-97	.200	.118	.222	24	80	12	16	2	1	1	6	11	2	1	2	23	1	1	.288	.305
Cooper, Shane	R-R	5-11	185	12-19-94	.180	.200	.177	24	61	7	11	1	0	0	10	2	0	0	3	23	1	1	.197	.315
De La Cruz, Isrrael	B-R	6-0	150	6-15-97	.195	.031	.238	46	154	24	30	4	2	1	9	18	2	0	1	52	11	2	.266	.286

Batting	B-T	HT	WT	DOB	AVG	vLH	vRH	G	AB	R	H	2B	3B	HR	RBI	BB	HBP	SH	SF	SO	SB	CS	SLG	OBP
De La Rosa, Eric	R-R	6-4	175	6-3-97	.229	.250	.226	36	131	12	30	7	0	0	12	13	2	0	0	48	9	0	.282	.308
Dugas, Dayton	R-R	6-3	230	6-9-97	.230	.200	.237	36	122	12	28	5	1	3	12	6	2	0	1	47	2	1	.361	.275
Garcia, Alexis	B-R	6-2	170	7-1-97	.232	.318	.211	33	112	10	26	3	3	1	11	12	3	0	1	39	0	4	.339	.320
Gonzalez, Cesar	R-R	6-2	175	5-31-95	.250	.167	.300	5	16	4	4	1	0	0	0	2	1	0	0	7	1	0	.313	.368
Hampton, Reece	B-R	5-10	170	7-19-96	.185	.000	.240	22	65	10	12	2	1	1	6	15	1	0	1	14	4	2	.292	.342
Hoffman, Teddy	R-R	6-0	195	8-3-96	.194	.333	.136	9	31	3	6	3	0	0	4	1	0	0	0	16	2	1	.290	.219
Karstetter, Ryan	R-R	6-0	200	1-30-97	.220	.200	.224	25	82	11	18	5	0	0	6	5	0	0	0	26	1	0	.281	.264
King, Jose	L-R	6-0	160	1-16-99	.212	.143	.234	25	85	5	18	7	1	0	16	5	0	1	0	29	2	0	.318	.256
Liniak, Kingston	R-R	6-2	170	11-11-99	.250	.333	.222	3	12	1	3	0	0	1	2	1	0	0	0	5	1	1	.500	.308
Martinez, Hector	R-R	5-11	175	11-1-96	.083	.143	.069	11	36	2	3	1	0	1	2	2	2	0	0	13	0	0	.194	.175
Martinez, Julio	R-R	6-2	195	12-15-97	.219	.125	.250	9	32	1	7	0	1	0	0	2	0	0	0	13	0	0	.281	.265
McMillan, Sam	R-R	6-1	195	12-1-98	.158	.235	.137	50	165	16	26	6	1	0	8	25	12	1	0	47	7	2	.206	.312
Meadows, Parker	L-R	6-5	185	11-2-99	.316	.143	.417	6	19	4	6	1	0	0	2	2	0	0	0	6	0	0	.368	.381
Nunez, Moises	R-R	6-2	190	2-7-97	.275	.273	.275	16	51	7	14	3	0	1	6	7	0	1	0	15	0	0	.392	.362
Perez, Wenceel	B-R	5-11	170	10-30-99	.244	.333	.219	21	82	8	20	2	0	1	8	5	0	0	0	12	7	3	.305	.287
Quero, Jose	L-L	6-0	190	9-5-98	.138	.200	.125	9	29	0	4	1	0	0	3	3	0	0	1	11	0	0	.172	.212
Reyes, Daniel	R-R	6-1	200	9-7-96	.320	.600	.250	6	25	4	8	2	0	0	6	1	0	0	0	5	0	0	.400	.346
Sherley, Luke	R-R	6-1	190	5-7-96	.246	.333	.229	17	57	6	14	2	0	1	6	8	0	0	0	14	4	0	.333	.339
Silverio, Gresuan	B-R	6-0	175	1-5-99	.232	.208	.237	40	138	11	32	10	0	0	17	11	2	1	4	35	0	0	.304	.290
Valentin, Yomar	B-R	5-8	145	12-26-97	.143	.200	.130	12	28	4	4	0	0	0	1	3	1	0	0	5	5	1	.143	.250
Verdon, Jordan	L-R	6-3	190	1-7-97	.206	.250	.198	29	107	7	22	4	0	0	9	2	0	0	0	19	0	1	.243	.280
Warner, Cam	R-R	6-2	188	3-4-94	.197	.240	.186	37	127	15	25	7	1	1	16	14	2	1	2	35	2	0	.291	.283

Pitching	B-T	HT	WT	DOB	W	L	ERA	G	GS	CG	SV	IP	H	R	ER	HR	BB	SO	AVG	vLH	vRH	K/9	BB/9
Aguilera, Juan	R-R	6-1	183	9-24-96	1	1	1.13	6	0	0	0	16	10	4	2	0	9	13	.167	.292	.083	7.31	5.06
Arriera, Gio	R-R	6-2	220	6-7-98	2	5	4.38	12	12	0	0	64	58	33	31	5	29	57	.248	.187	.315	8.06	4.10
Castillo, Oswaldo	R-R	6-0	193	8-18-96	0	0	0.00	2	0	0	0	4	2	0	0	0	2	2	.143	.000	.222	4.50	4.50
Chentouf, Yaya	R-S	5-9	170	6-18-97	0	0	2.23	23	0	0	9	32	22	9	8	0	8	22	.193	.250	.152	6.12	2.23
Crosby, Drew	R-L	6-0	196	11-16-95	4	0	1.78	16	0	0	1	25	21	6	5	0	7	27	.223	.220	.226	9.59	2.49
DeCaster, Ethan	R-R	6-3	190	10-27-94	1	0	0.61	8	0	0	1	15	9	3	1	0	3	19	.177	.158	.188	11.66	1.84
Fernander, Chavez	R-R	6-3	205	7-7-97	0	0	9.00	1	0	0	0	1	2	1	1	0	1	2	.400	.500	.333	18.00	9.00
Fernandez, Aaron	R-R	6-2	190	9-25-94	0	1	10.80	3	0	0	0	3	7	5	4	0	1	3	.438	.625	.250	8.10	2.70
Gizzi, Michael	R-R	6-4	195	5-15-95	0	0	0.00	1	0	0	0	1	0	0	0	0	1	0	.000	—	.000	0.00	9.00
Gonzalez, Daniel	R-R	6-3	200	8-15-95	0	1	13.50	6	0	0	0	5	9	9	8	0	3	7	.346	.385	.308	11.81	5.06
Guzman, Carlos	R-R	6-1	170	5-16-98	3	4	3.86	12	12	0	0	51	45	24	22	5	14	52	.232	.216	.245	9.12	2.45
Hernandez, Wilkel	R-R	6-3	160	4-13-99	0	2	7.94	2	2	0	0	6	6	7	5	2	4	11	.250	.273	.231	17.47	6.35
Javier, Xavier	R-R	6-4	170	2-9-98	0	1	1.80	1	0	0	0	5	4	2	1	0	2	4	.235	.333	.125	7.20	3.60
Kirby, Chance	R-R	5-11	165	7-19-95	2	3	4.68	5	5	0	0	25	25	18	13	2	5	25	.253	.323	.211	9.00	1.80
Lance, Carson	R-R	6-5	245	5-3-95	1	3	4.53	9	9	0	0	48	46	27	24	1	26	28	.258	.322	.193	5.29	4.91
Ledesma, Stevie	R-R	6-5	195	11-22-95	1	2	7.80	4	3	0	0	15	21	14	13	1	6	15	.333	.423	.270	9.00	3.60
Lescher, Billy	R-R	6-4	215	9-17-95	0	0	0.00	3	0	0	1	7	2	1	0	0	2	6	.095	.111	.083	7.71	2.57
Mateo, Jhonny	R-R	6-3	170	8-19-94	1	1	6.14	4	0	0	0	7	7	5	5	0	7	10	.241	.412	.000	12.27	8.59
Mueses, Victor	R-R	6-1	175	10-13-95	1	3	5.17	17	0	0	0	31	33	29	18	3	23	24	.264	.321	.217	6.89	6.61
Murphy, Kacey	L-L	6-0	190	1-21-97	2	0	9.00	5	3	0	0	11	16	11	11	2	4	7	.348	.471	.276	5.73	3.27
Noble, Wes	R-R	5-11	195	5-27-96	1	0	6.48	2	0	0	0	8	5	6	6	1	6	6	.161	.286	.059	6.48	6.48
O'Loughlin, Jack	L-L	6-5	210	3-14-00	0	1	4.35	7	1	0	1	21	15	12	10	1	12	25	.211	.222	.205	10.89	5.23
Reyes, Angel	R-R	6-2	200	10-17-97	0	0	0.00	1	0	0	0	2	2	0	0	0	1	3	.250	.333	.200	13.50	4.50
Silva, Alfredo	L-L	6-0	180	7-27-98	0	2	9.35	5	2	0	0	9	7	11	9	0	13	7	.233	.385	.118	7.27	13.50
Skubal, Tarik	L-L	6-3	215	11-20-96	0	0	0.75	4	0	0	1	12	8	1	1	0	2	17	.195	.111	.219	12.75	1.50
Stalsberg, Mitchell	L-L	6-0	215	1-12-96	1	0	1.95	14	0	0	0	28	18	10	6	0	15	34	.186	.205	.172	11.06	4.88
Stock, Dylan	R-R	6-4	195	7-21-96	2	3	3.94	22	0	0	0	30	31	23	13	2	18	30	.265	.304	.230	9.10	5.46
Vancena, Jayce	R-R	6-5	225	4-25-96	0	2	0.00	3	1	0	0	8	5	2	0	0	1	7	.179	.100	.222	8.22	1.17
Vasquez, Jose	R-R	6-0	175	3-19-96	5	4	3.45	13	13	1	0	60	61	36	23	1	23	42	.260	.262	.257	6.30	3.45
Viloria, Felix	L-L	6-1	165	12-2-96	2	0	7.52	9	0	0	0	20	23	17	17	1	14	12	.291	.276	.300	5.31	6.20
Welhaf, Robbie	R-R	6-1	190	5-19-95	0	0	4.76	5	0	0	0	6	7	3	3	0	2	6	.292	.200	.375	7.94	3.18
Wolf, Adam	L-L	6-6	225	12-26-96	1	1	2.67	10	10	0	0	30	25	9	9	0	8	27	.225	.222	.227	8.01	2.37

Fielding

C: McMillan 34, Nunez 13, Silverio 26. **1B:** Ames 28, Karstetter 21, Nunez 1, Quero 9, Verdon 18. **2B:** Burks 22, Cooper 7, De La Cruz 19, Garcia 19, Martinez 6, Cooper 2. **SS:** De La Cruz 13, King 25, Martinez 6, Valentin 2. **3B:** Aristigueta 3, Cooper 14, Garcia 14, Karstetter 1, Martinez 1, Sherley 3, Valentin 6, Warner 35. **SS:** De La Cruz 13, King 25, Perez 21, Sherley 12, Valentin 3. **OF:** Alvarado 45, Bojarski 20, Brinkman 22, De La Cruz 10, De La Rosa 36, Dugas 32, Gonzalez 5, Hampton 22, Hoffman 8, Liniak 3, Martinez 8, Meadows 6, Reyes 6.

GCL TIGERS EAST   ROOKIE
GULF COAST LEAGUE

Batting	B-T	HT	WT	DOB	AVG	vLH	vRH	G	AB	R	H	2B	3B	HR	RBI	BB	HBP	SH	SF	SO	SB	CS	SLG	OBP
Arias, Kevynn	R-R	6-0	215	2-11-97	.150	.500	.111	20	40	4	6	0	0	0	3	5	0	0	0	11	0	0	.150	.244
Aristigueta, Keyder	R-R	5-11	165	2-2-96	.196	.067	.250	18	51	6	10	2	0	1	2	15	3	1	0	9	2	1	.294	.406
2-team total (4 GCL Tigers West)					.183	.111	.214	22	60	7	11	2	0	1	2	17	3	1	0	13	3	1	.267	.388
Azuaje, Jheyser	R-R	5-9	165	2-12-97	.118	.154	.105	15	51	1	6	0	0	0	1	2	0	0	1	6	0	0	.118	.148
2-team total (11 GCL Tigers West)					.154	.125	.161	26	78	3	12	1	0	0	2	2	1	1	1	13	1	0	.167	.183
Bello, Moises	R-S	5-10	160	6-13-97	.200	.129	.216	45	165	19	33	6	0	0	21	11	5	1	2	33	9	1	.236	.268
2-team total (2 GCL Tigers West)					.214	.152	.229	47	173	20	37	6	1	0	23	11	5	1	2	34	9	1	.260	.278
Bojarski, Ulrich	R-R	6-3	190	9-15-98	.225	.154	.235	29	98	12	22	6	1	4	14	12	4	0	1	31	3	2	.429	.330
Brinkman, Clark	R-R	6-2	195	3-6-96	.271	.353	.238	17	59	11	16	4	1	0	11	16	2	0	0	5	7	2	.373	.442

Player	B-T	HT	WT	DOB	AVG	vLH	vRH	G	AB	R	H	2B	3B	HR	RBI	BB	HBP	SH	SF	SO	SB	CS	SLG	OBP
Childers, Justin	R-R	6-2	210	10-27-95	.255	.250	.256	14	51	14	13	2	0	3	11	8	1	0	2	19	1	0	.471	.355
2-team total (26 GCL Tigers West)					.200	.241	.188	40	125	25	25	7	0	3	14	25	3	0	2	41	2	0	.328	.342
Escobar, Elys	R-R	6-0	190	9-21-96	.300	.500	.269	12	30	0	9	1	0	0	5	2	0	0	0	9	0	0	.333	.344
2-team total (8 GCL Tigers West)					.273	.429	.243	20	44	1	12	1	0	1	8	6	0	0	0	14	0	1	.364	.360
Esposito, Vinny	R-R	5-11	200	3-10-96	.235	.250	.231	5	17	3	4	2	0	0	2	3	0	0	0	9	0	0	.353	.350
2-team total (40 GCL Tigers West)					.312	.310	.313	45	141	34	44	14	0	4	26	25	4	0	2	42	10	2	.497	.424
Figueroa, Gustavo	R-R	6-0	170	9-22-98	.241	.286	.227	15	29	2	7	0	0	0	8	1	0	0	2				.241	.250
2-team total (13 GCL Tigers West)					.271	.333	.260	28	59	6	16	2	0	0	8	5	0	0	2	11	0	0	.305	.318
Gonzalez, Gerardo	R-R	5-9	170	12-21-98	.143	.500	.083	3	14	3	2	0	0	1	2	1	0	0	0	7	1	0	.357	.200
Hoffman, Teddy	R-R	6-0	195	8-3-96	.278	.250	.286	21	72	15	20	0	3	6	15	11	5	0	2	29	4	1	.611	.400
2-team total (7 GCL Tigers West)					.267	.208	.288	28	90	22	24	1	3	6	17	14	8	0	2	36	5	1	.544	.404
Jarecki, Matthew	R-R	6-2	205	5-12-96	.241	.207	.250	37	133	23	32	12	2	3	17	14	8	0	1	31	5	5	.429	.346
2-team total (5 GCL Tigers West)					.245	.242	.246	42	151	28	37	13	2	4	20	15	9	1	1	34	10	6	.437	.347
Laurencio, Luis	R-R	6-2	215	10-6-98	.238	.244	.236	48	181	27	43	7	2	4	21	22	1	0	0	89	7	1	.365	.324
Liniak, Kingston	R-R	6-2	170	11-11-99	.224	.167	.235	37	156	14	35	7	0	0	9	7	1	0	2	51	5	4	.269	.259
2-team total (8 GCL Tigers West)					.234	.179	.244	45	188	19	44	8	0	0	13	7	3	0	2	58	7	4	.277	.270
Malis, Zach	L-R	6-4	190	11-7-96	.273	.500	.250	6	22	2	6	1	1	0	3	2	0	0	0	5	1	0	.409	.333
2-team total (25 GCL Tigers West)					.202	.250	.192	31	89	15	18	2	1	0	7	14	0	0	1	22	1	1	.247	.308
Martinez, Julio	R-R	6-2	195	12-15-97	.333	.000	.500	1	3	0	1	1	0	0	2	1	0	0	0	0	0	0	.667	.500
2-team total (31 GCL Tigers West)					.245	.227	.250	32	98	15	24	4	0	0	16	8	2	0	1	31	3	1	.286	.312
Noworyta, David	R-R	6-4	180	5-24-96	.270	.444	.200	29	63	3	17	1	0	0	8	11	1	0	0	12	0	0	.286	.387
Reyes, Daniel	R-R	6-1	200	9-7-96	.286	.256	.295	47	161	29	46	15	1	7	27	22	2	0	3	33	12	5	.522	.372
Rosoff, Jon	L-R	5-9	175	11-14-94	.000	.000	.000	3	4	2	0	0	0	0	0	1	0	0	0	3	0	0	.000	.200
2-team total (21 GCL Tigers West)					.260	.500	.214	24	50	11	3	2	1	0	6	10	1	1	0	7	3	2	.340	.393
Smith, Kelvin	R-R	6-1	185	10-30-99	.202	.292	.180	34	124	17	25	4	1	2	9	8	3	0	1	51	9	2	.298	.265
Stewart, Christin	L-R	6-0	205	12-10-93	.200	—	.200	2	5	1	1	0	0	1	0	1	1	0	0	0	0	0	.800	.333
2-team total (1 GCL Tigers West)					.222	—	.222	3	9	2	2	0	0	2	0	3	1	0	0	0	0	0	.889	.300
Torres, Mike	R-R	5-10	140	2-10-98	.246	.350	.222	38	110	18	27	5	0	0	4	11	1	0	1	34	6	3	.291	.317
Tuck, Avery	L-R	6-4	195	12-28-97	.214	.667	.091	4	14	4	3	0	0	1	1	5	1	0	0	5	0	0	.429	.450
2-team total (33 GCL Tigers West)					.165	.263	.144	30	109	11	18	6	0	3	12	19	5	0	2	55	5	1	.303	.311
Ynirio, Jorge	R-R	5-11	170	10-19-97	.250	.250	.250	37	124	14	31	7	0	2	7	7	2	0	0	27	6	1	.355	.301

Pitching	B-T	HT	WT	DOB	W	L	ERA	G	GS	CG	SV	IP	H	R	ER	HR	BB	SO	AVG	vLH	vRH	K/9	BB/9
Aguilera, Juan	R-R	6-1	183	9-24-96	3	0	0.43	10	0	0	2	21	5	1	1	0	10	26	.077	.067	.080	11.14	4.29
Anderson, Austin	R-R	5-11	197	11-20-95	2	1	2.84	10	1	0	1	19	15	7	6	0	10	14	.227	.273	.205	6.63	4.74
Appleton, Jose	R-R	6-3	170	7-2-97	1	0	9.31	5	4	0	0	19	23	20	20	3	10	15	.319	.278	.333	6.98	4.66
Barbato, Johnny	R-R	6-1	231	7-11-92	0	0	9.00	1	1	0	0	1	1	1	1	0	0	2	.250	.000	.500	18.00	0.00
Bargfeldt, Jeb	L-L	6-0	175	10-13-95	2	0	4.56	14	0	0	2	26	32	15	13	2	12	22	.308	.304	.309	7.71	4.21
De Jesus, Angel	R-R	6-3	185	2-13-97	4	3	3.12	11	11	0	0	43	32	19	15	4	17	54	.199	.149	.219	11.22	3.53
Domnarski, Doug	R-L	5-11	190	7-8-94	0	0	9.53	5	0	0	0	6	5	6	6	0	6	6	.263	.500	.200	9.53	9.53
Escalona, Edgar	R-R	6-4	193	3-30-98	1	3	5.66	11	7	0	0	41	55	32	26	2	10	24	.327	.295	.346	5.23	2.18
Farish, Chris	R-R	6-3	205	8-5-94	0	0	0.00	4	0	0	3	4	1	0	0	0	3	15	.083	.000	.125	6.75	0.00
Fernander, Chavez	R-R	6-3	205	7-7-97	1	0	0.75	4	0	0	0	12	7	1	1	0	4	15	.171	.267	.115	11.25	3.00
2-team total (10 GCL Tigers West)					4	1	1.40	14	5	0	0	39	26	7	6	0	8	39	.193	.222	.178	9.08	1.86
Ledesma, Stevie	R-R	6-5	195	11-22-95	1	0	1.23	5	0	0	0	7	3	1	1	0	4	5	.143	.250	.070	6.14	4.91
2-team total (4 GCL Tigers West)					1	2	2.70	7	4	0	0	23	23	7	7	1	7	24	.264	.280	.258	9.26	2.70
Lopez, Ronaldo	R-R	6-2	165	1-7-98	1	0	4.91	14	0	0	0	18	18	10	10	1	17	19	.261	.273	.255	9.33	8.35
Mateo, Jhonny	R-R	6-3	170	8-19-94	2	1	3.38	10	0	0	0	16	18	13	6	1	11	9	.281	.308	.263	5.06	6.19
Murphy, Kacey	L-L	6-0	190	1-21-97	1	0	0.00	4	2	0	0	8	5	0	0	0	1	7	.179	.200	.174	7.88	1.13
Noble, Wes	R-R	5-11	195	5-27-96	1	1	1.84	9	3	0	1	29	20	7	6	0	12	26	.202	.172	.214	7.98	3.68
2-team total (4 GCL Tigers West)					2	1	2.52	13	3	0	1	36	25	11	10	0	17	32	.205	.184	.214	8.07	4.29
Norris, Daniel	L-L	6-2	185	4-25-93	0	0	0.00	1	1	0	0	2	1	0	0	0	1	2	.167	.000	.200	9.00	4.50
2-team total (1 GCL Tigers West)					0	0	1.93	2	1	0	0	5	4	2	1	0	2	9	.235	.000	.267	17.36	3.86
Perez, Franklin	R-R	6-3	197	12-6-97	0	1	4.50	3	3	0	0	8	3	4	4	0	0	5	.120	.154	.083	5.63	0.00
Rodriguez, Hector	R-R	6-4	210	12-4-96	1	2	6.95	12	0	0	0	22	25	18	17	0	10	17	.287	.219	.327	6.95	4.09
Santana, Kilber	R-R	6-1	160	10-15-98	3	1	4.88	13	0	0	1	31	33	18	17	3	7	31	.266	.222	.286	8.90	2.01
Tobey, Jared	R-L	6-4	225	3-11-96	1	4	4.17	11	10	0	0	37	36	19	17	3	20	29	.265	.160	.288	7.12	4.91
Tortosa, Cristhian	L-L	6-4	170	10-30-98	0	1	13.89	12	0	0	0	12	16	18	18	2	17	12	.327	.375	.317	9.26	13.11
Vancena, Jayce	R-R	6-5	225	4-25-96	1	2	5.49	11	0	0	0	41	50	32	25	4	10	33	.308	.246	.347	7.24	2.20
Villanueva, Eric	R-R	6-0	179	3-19-98	0	2	1.50	4	0	0	0	6	8	4	1	0	6	2	.296	.000	.421	3.00	9.00
Welhaf, Robbie	R-R	6-1	190	5-19-95	1	1	3.77	14	1	0	3	31	31	14	13	2	8	27	.261	.262	.260	7.84	2.32

Fielding

C: Arias 19, Azuaje 14, Escobar 8, Figueroa 15, Noworyta 27, Rosoff 3. **1B:** Aristigueta 3, Childers 5, Escobar 1, Laurencio 45, Malis 2. **2B:** Aristigueta 1, Bello 17, Torres 36, Ynirio 6. **3B:** Aristigueta 10, Bello 10, Escobar 3, Gonzalez 3, Malis 5, Smith 1, Ynirio 30. **SS:** Bello 24, Smith 33, Ynirio 1. **OF:** Aristigueta 4, Bello 1, Bojarski 27, Brinkman 16, Esposito 4, Hoffman 17, Jarecki 33, Liniak 37, Martinez 1, Reyes 21, Stewart 1, Tuck 4.

GCL TIGERS WEST ROOKIE
GULF COAST LEAGUE

Batting	B-T	HT	WT	DOB	AVG	vLH	vRH	G	AB	R	H	2B	3B	HR	RBI	BB	HBP	SH	SF	SO	SB	CS	SLG	OBP
Alfonzo, Eliezer	B-R	5-10	155	9-23-99	.217	.177	.231	22	69	7	15	1	0	1	12	9	0	0	2	9	3	1	.275	.300
Ames, Nick	L-R	6-3	240	11-25-96	.304	.429	.282	12	46	9	14	6	0	5	19	5	0	1	1	11	0	0	.761	.365
Aristigueta, Keyder	R-R	5-11	165	2-2-96	.111	.333	.000	4	9	1	1	0	0	0	2	0	0	0	4	1	0		.111	.273
2-team total (18 GCL Tigers East)					.183	.111	.214	22	60	7	11	2	0	1	2	17	3	1	0	13	3	1	.267	.388
Azuaje, Jheyser	R-R	5-9	165	2-12-97	.222	.000	.250	11	27	2	6	1	0	0	1	0	1	1	0	7	1	0	.259	.250

Batting	B-T	HT	WT	DOB	AVG	vLH	vRH	G	AB	R	H	2B	3B	HR	RBI	BB	HBP	SH	SF	SO	SB	CS	OBP	SLG
2-team total (15 GCL Tigers East)					.154	.125	.161	26	78	3	12	1	0	0	2	2	1	1	1	13	1	0	.167	.183
Bello, Moises	R-R	5-10	160	6-13-97	.500	.500	.500	2	8	1	4	0	1	0	2	0	0	0	0	1	0	0	.750	.500
2-team total (45 GCL Tigers East)					.214	.152	.229	47	173	20	37	6	1	0	23	11	5	1	2	34	9	1	.260	.278
Burks, Jeremiah	R-R	6-1	175	1-8-97	.260	.200	.275	13	50	10	13	5	1	1	8	7	1	0	0	11	1	0	.460	.362
Childers, Justin	R-R	6-2	210	10-27-95	.162	.235	.140	26	74	11	12	5	0	0	3	17	2	0	0	22	1	0	.230	.333
2-team total (14 GCL Tigers East)					.200	.241	.188	40	125	25	25	7	0	3	14	25	3	0	2	41	2	0	.328	.342
De La Rosa, Eric	R-R	6-4	175	6-3-97	.462	.000	.500	3	13	4	6	1	0	1	3	1	0	0	0	4	0	0	.769	.500
Deatherage, Brock	L-L	6-1	175	9-12-95	.556	.000	.625	2	9	6	5	0	0	4	7	1	0	0	0	1	0	0	1.889	.600
Dugas, Dayton	R-R	6-3	230	6-9-97	.333	—	.333	4	15	3	5	0	0	1	6	1	0	0	2	4	0	0	.533	.333
Escalona, Ildemaro	R-R	6-0	170	2-12-99	.294	.238	.313	23	85	8	25	7	0	0	7	3	3	0	1	19	0	1	.377	.337
Escobar, Elys	R-R	6-0	190	9-21-96	.214	.333	.182	8	14	1	3	0	0	1	3	4	0	0	0	5	0	1	.429	.389
2-team total (12 GCL Tigers East)					.273	.429	.243	20	44	1	12	1	0	1	8	6	0	0	0	14	0	1	.364	.360
Esposito, Vinny	R-R	5-11	200	3-10-96	.323	.320	.323	40	124	31	40	12	0	4	24	22	4	0	2	33	10	2	.516	.434
2-team total (5 GCL Tigers East)					.312	.310	.313	45	141	34	44	14	0	4	26	25	4	0	2	42	10	2	.497	.424
Figueroa, Gustavo	R-R	6-0	170	9-22-98	.300	.500	.286	13	30	4	9	2	0	0	4	0	0	0	0	6	0	0	.367	.382
2-team total (15 GCL Tigers East)					.271	.333	.260	28	59	6	16	2	0	0	8	5	0	0	2	11	0	0	.305	.318
Hampton, Reece	B-R	5-10	170	7-19-96	.378	.000	.424	10	37	10	14	2	2	0	2	5	0	0	0	5	4	1	.541	.452
Hoffman, Teddy	R-R	6-0	195	8-3-96	.222	.125	.300	7	18	7	4	1	0	0	2	3	0	0	0	7	1	0	.278	.417
2-team total (21 GCL Tigers East)					.267	.208	.288	28	90	22	24	1	3	6	17	14	8	0	2	36	5	1	.544	.404
Hurtado, Pedro	B-R	5-11	160	3-1-99	.228	.177	.250	23	57	7	13	3	0	1	9	7	0	0	0	12	0	0	.333	.313
Jarecki, Matthew	R-R	6-2	205	5-12-96	.278	.500	.214	5	18	5	5	0	1	0	3	1	1	1	0	3	5	1	.500	.350
2-team total (37 GCL Tigers East)					.245	.242	.246	42	151	28	37	13	2	4	20	15	9	1	1	34	10	6	.437	.347
King, Jose	L-R	6-0	160	1-16-99	.314	.273	.320	24	86	20	27	2	3	2	12	4	4	1	0	21	5	4	.477	.372
Liniak, Kingston	R-R	6-2	170	11-11-99	.281	.250	.286	8	32	5	9	1	0	0	4	0	2	0	0	7	2	0	.313	.324
2-team total (37 GCL Tigers East)					.234	.179	.244	45	188	19	44	8	0	0	13	7	3	0	2	58	7	4	.277	.309
Malis, Zach	L-R	6-4	190	11-7-96	.179	.214	.170	25	67	13	12	1	0	0	4	12	0	0	1	17	0	1	.194	.300
2-team total (6 GCL Tigers East)					.202	.250	.192	31	89	15	18	2	1	0	7	14	0	0	1	22	1	1	.247	.308
Martinez, Hector	R-R	5-11	175	11-1-96	.366	.350	.370	29	101	22	37	11	3	3	20	2	1	0	0	27	5	1	.624	.385
Martinez, Julio	R-R	6-2	195	12-15-97	.242	.238	.243	31	95	15	23	3	0	0	14	7	2	0	1	31	3	1	.274	.305
2-team total (1 GCL Tigers East)					.245	.227	.250	32	98	15	24	4	0	0	16	8	2	0	1	31	3	1	.286	.312
Meadows, Parker	L-R	6-5	185	11-2-99	.284	.667	.231	22	74	16	21	2	1	4	8	8	3	0	0	25	3	1	.500	.377
Perez, Wenceel	B-R	5-11	170	10-30-99	.383	.533	.349	20	81	20	31	7	0	2	14	12	0	0	0	14	2	1	.543	.462
Proctor, Christopher	R-R	6-1	180	3-8-97	.167	.000	.200	2	6	1	1	0	1	0	0	1	0	0	0	2	0	1	.500	.286
Quero, Jose	L-L	6-0	190	9-5-98	.150	.000	.214	6	20	6	3	1	0	0	2	4	0	0	0	2	0	0	.200	.292
Rosoff, Jon	L-R	5-9	175	11-14-94	.283	.571	.231	21	46	9	13	2	1	0	6	9	1	1	0	4	3	2	.370	.411
2-team total (3 GCL Tigers East)					.260	.500	.214	24	50	11	13	2	1	0	6	10	1	1	0	7	3	2	.340	.393
Salas, Jose	R-R	6-0	160	4-17-97	.179	.100	.203	25	84	9	15	3	0	3	11	5	0	0	2	14	0	3	.321	.220
Sherley, Luke	R-R	6-1	190	5-7-96	.167	—	.167	2	6	2	1	1	0	0	1	4	0	0	0	0	1	0	.333	.500
Stewart, Christin	L-R	6-0	205	12-10-93	.250	—	.250	1	4	1	1	0	0	1	2	0	0	0	0	0	0	0	1.000	.250
2-team total (2 GCL Tigers East)					.222	—	.222	3	9	2	2	0	0	2	3	1	0	0	0	0	0	0	.889	.300
Tuck, Avery	L-R	6-4	195	12-28-97	.158	.188	.152	33	95	7	15	6	0	2	11	14	4	0	2	50	5	1	.284	.287
2-team total (4 GCL Tigers East)					.165	.263	.144	37	109	11	18	6	0	3	12	19	5	0	2	55	5	1	.303	.311
Valente, John	B-R	5-11	190	6-23-95	.344	.423	.324	33	128	19	44	8	1	2	21	5	0	0	1	7	10	4	.469	.366
Verdon, Jordan	L-R	6-3	190	1-7-97	.381	.500	.344	12	42	10	16	5	2	1	16	8	1	0	3	4	0	0	.667	.463

Pitching	B-T	HT	WT	DOB	W	L	ERA	G	GS	CG	SV	IP	H	R	ER	HR	BB	SO	AVG	vLH	vRH	K/9	BB/9
Baez, Jorge	R-R	6-2	185	5-9-95	0	1	10.38	5	0	0	0	4	4	6	5	0	1	3	.235	.200	.250	6.23	2.08
Baker, Jake	R-L	6-2	200	6-12-98	2	1	5.73	14	2	0	1	22	21	18	14	2	20	35	.244	.316	.224	14.32	8.18
Behenna, Kory	L-L	6-2	185	8-2-96	0	0	6.17	11	0	0	0	12	16	9	8	1	3	20	.314	.000	.364	15.43	2.31
2-team total (4 GCL Red Sox)					0	1	6.00	15	0	0	0	15	19	12	10	1	6	24	.292	.250	.302	14.40	3.60
Beyer, Drew	R-R	6-3	200	5-16-96	2	0	4.15	7	1	0	0	13	18	8	6	1	1	6	.305	.278	.317	4.15	0.69
Carpenter, Ryan	L-L	6-2	210	8-22-90	0	0	0.00	1	0	0	0	3	1	0	0	0	0	4	.100	.500	.000	12.00	3.00
Chentouf, Yaya	R-R	5-9	170	6-18-97	0	0	0.00	1	0	0	0	4	3	0	0	0	0	7	.231	.333	.000	17.18	0.00
Conger, Maddux	R-R	6-3	200	6-28-96	2	1	1.93	8	5	0	0	28	20	6	6	1	8	39	.200	.321	.153	12.54	2.57
De La Cruz, Sandel	R-R	6-2	185	3-6-96	1	0	3.86	17	0	0	4	26	25	11	11	3	18	40	.258	.231	.276	14.03	6.31
De La Rosa, Bairon	R-R	6-0	195	7-17-96	2	2	7.59	15	1	0	0	21	24	22	18	1	25	26	.282	.238	.297	10.97	10.55
DeCaster, Ethan	R-R	6-3	190	10-27-94	0	0	3.86	2	0	0	0	2	1	1	1	0	2	3	.222	.000	.286	11.57	0.00
Fernander, Chavez	R-R	6-2	205	7-7-97	3	1	1.69	10	5	0	0	27	19	6	5	0	4	24	.202	.200	.203	8.10	1.35
2-team total (4 GCL Tigers East)					4	1	1.40	14	5	0	0	39	26	7	6	0	8	39	.193	.222	.178	9.08	1.86
Gizzi, Michael	R-R	6-4	195	5-15-95	4	1	1.84	13	0	0	6	15	11	8	3	0	3	23	.193	.200	.192	14.11	1.84
Gonzalez, Daniel	R-R	6-3	200	8-15-95	3	0	1.17	10	4	0	0	31	17	4	4	1	11	36	.165	.188	.161	10.57	3.23
Hardman, Ian	R-R	6-5	240	9-16-95	0	0	5.40	3	0	0	1	3	3	2	2	0	3	5	.250	—	.250	13.50	8.10
Hill, Garrett	R-R	6-0	175	1-16-96	3	3	3.11	9	6	0	0	38	43	20	13	2	10	46	.281	.318	.266	10.99	2.39
Javier, Xavier	R-R	6-4	170	2-9-98	3	2	2.79	10	10	0	0	52	46	18	16	3	27	38	.240	.250	.236	6.62	4.70
Kirby, Chance	R-R	5-11	165	7-19-95	0	0	0.71	3	1	0	0	13	9	1	1	0	3	15	.200	.333	.152	10.66	2.13
Ledesma, Stevie	R-R	6-5	195	11-22-95	0	2	3.38	4	4	0	0	16	20	6	6	1	3	19	.303	.294	.306	10.69	1.69
2-team total (3 GCL Tigers East)					1	2	2.70	7	4	0	0	23	23	7	7	1	7	24	.264	.280	.258	9.26	2.70
Mize, Casey	R-R	6-3	220	5-1-97	0	0	0.00	1	1	0	0	2	0	0	0	0	0	4	.000	—	.000	18.00	4.50
Noble, Wes	R-R	5-11	195	5-27-96	1	0	5.68	4	0	0	0	6	5	4	4	0	5	6	.217	.222	.214	8.53	7.11
2-team total (9 GCL Tigers East)					2	1	2.52	13	3	0	1	36	25	11	10	0	17	32	.205	.184	.214	8.07	4.29
Norris, Daniel	L-L	6-2	185	4-25-93	0	0	3.38	1	1	0	0	3	3	1	1	0	1	7	.273	.000	.300	23.63	3.38
2-team total (1 GCL Tigers East)					0	0	1.93	2	1	0	0	5	4	2	1	0	2	9	.235	.000	.267	17.36	3.86
Paulino, Miguel	R-R	6-1	185	8-21-98	1	1	3.15	15	0	0	1	20	20	10	7	0	13	20	.256	.360	.208	9.00	5.85
Reyes, Angel	R-R	6-2	200	10-17-97	5	0	3.09	15	0	0	1	23	21	12	8	1	16	25	.241	.263	.235	9.64	6.17
Silva, Alfredo	L-L	6-3	180	7-27-98	4	1	2.25	8	7	0	0	40	28	10	10	3	18	38	.200	.235	.195	8.55	4.05

DETROIT TIGERS

	B-T	HT	WT	DOB	W	L	ERA	G	GS	CG	SV	IP	H	R	ER	HR	BB	SO	AVG	vLH	vRH	K/9	BB/9
Skubal, Tarik	L-L	6-3	215	11-20-96	1	0	0.00	2	1	0	0	3	2	2	0	0	1	5	.167	—	.167	15.00	3.00
Turnbull, Spencer	R-R	6-3	215	9-18-92	0	0	0.00	1	1	0	0	3	1	0	0	0	3	3	.111	.000	.167	10.13	10.13
Wolf, Adam	L-L	6-6	225	12-26-96	0	0	0.00	2	2	0	0	7	5	0	0	0	4	5	.217	.000	.250	6.75	5.40

Fielding

C: Alfonzo 14, Azuaje 11, Escobar 8, Figueroa 10, Hurtado 18, Proctor 2, Rosoff 15. **1B:** Alfonzo 3, Ames 8, Bello 1, Childers 26, Malis 6, Quero 5, Verdon 6. **2B:** Burks 10, Escalona 10, Martinez 18, Salas 12, Valente 6. **3B:** Aristigueta 2, Bello 1, Malis 14, Martinez 6, Salas 8, Valente 25. **SS:** Bello 1, Escalona 9, King 24, Perez 19, Sherley 2. **OF:** De La Rosa 3, Deatherage 2, Dugas 4, Esposito 40, Hampton 10, Hoffman 6, Jarecki 4, Liniak 7, Malis 1, Martinez 31, Meadows 20, Quero 1, Salas 4, Tuck 32, Verdon 3.

DSL TIGERS — ROOKIE

DOMINICAN SUMMER LEAGUE

Batting	B-T	HT	WT	DOB	AVG	vLH	vRH	G	AB	R	H	2B	3B	HR	RBI	BB	HBP	SH	SF	SO	SB	CS	SLG	OBP
Acevedo, Yoneiry	B-R	5-10	150	12-4-00	.212	—	—	61	198	18	42	5	2	0	15	22	2	6	5	38	8	5	.258	.291
Adames, Ernesto	L-L	6-0	180	12-29-99	.175	.136	.182	47	154	15	27	8	0	1	8	12	2	1	0	59	0	4	.247	.244
Alfonzo, Eliezer	B-R	5-10	155	9-23-99	.391	.177	.231	33	110	22	43	10	1	0	21	20	3	0	3	8	3	1	.500	.485
Batista, Enrique	R-R	5-9	170	2-10-00	.219	—	—	47	146	19	32	5	4	1	18	14	0	0	0	45	7	6	.329	.288
Chacon, Esney	R-R	6-1	160	3-17-00	.263	.286	.257	72	270	49	71	5	6	1	20	36	1	2	3	33	48	15	.337	.348
De La Cruz, Danuerys	R-R	5-11	160	4-27-01	.165	.000	.083	33	97	12	16	4	1	1	11	19	2	0	0	32	1	5	.258	.314
Dominguez, Antonio	R-R	5-9	150	4-25-01	.276	.214	.293	41	127	12	35	10	0	1	12	11	8	3	0	12	2	2	.378	.370
Figuereo, Adonis	L-L	6-2	170	5-5-01	.167	.200	.159	33	102	12	17	3	2	1	9	15	1	5	0	23	4	4	.265	.280
Garcia, Pedro	R-R	6-1	170	5-22-01	.253	.125	.286	47	158	20	40	6	2	1	14	16	1	1	1	38	9	4	.335	.324
Gonzalez, Alvaro	R-R	6-0	165	9-16-00	.245	.324	.225	46	163	19	40	4	6	1	17	23	5	1	2	36	8	9	.362	.352
Irigoyen, Carlos	R-R	6-2	165	3-21-01	.265	—	—	33	121	18	32	2	1	0	4	13	0	2	0	25	4	7	.298	.336
Jimenez, Jeremy	R-R	6-2	180	3-3-01	.226	.300	.206	28	93	7	21	2	0	0	7	10	1	0	0	27	1	2	.247	.308
Leonardo, Iverson	L-L	6-0	173	8-21-01	.236	—	—	62	195	31	46	8	7	1	17	31	11	1	2	59	7	8	.364	.368
Marte, Kendry	B-R	6-0	160	5-10-00	.224	—	—	52	143	26	32	5	0	1	17	33	1	2	1	45	17	9	.280	.371
Martinez Jr., Pedro	R-R	6-0	185	8-30-00	.225	—	—	47	147	20	33	7	1	1	23	19	12	0	5	25	2	2	.306	.350
Medrano, Carlos	L-R	5-11	170	11-11-99	.159	—	—	45	132	10	21	2	3	1	12	11	5	1	1	52	4	3	.242	.248
Mojica, Jimmy	R-R	6-0	175	5-4-00	.312	—	—	60	218	52	68	7	6	3	32	19	1	1	3	38	10	5	.440	.381
Montes, Sergio	R-R	5-11	165	5-10-00	.157	.056	.192	27	70	6	11	0	0	0	6	11	4	2	0	32	4	0	.157	.306
Moreno, Jhenry	L-R	5-11	160	3-28-00	.184	—	—	35	87	13	16	4	1	0	9	17	3	0	0	38	5	3	.253	.336
Nivar, Kevin	R-R	5-10	170	9-28-00	.261	.234	.269	65	222	34	58	12	1	1	18	33	4	0	0	42	10	5	.338	.367
Olivas, Martin	R-R	6-0	170	7-25-01	.198	.150	.210	61	197	21	39	6	6	2	15	8	6	3	3	53	2	2	.320	.248
Oviedo, Luis	L-L	5-10	170	10-16-00	.156	.125	.171	37	109	12	17	4	0	0	13	1	1	0	40	2	3	.193	.252
Perez, Yerjeni	R-R	165		2-6-00	.262	.333	.244	59	168	27	44	7	2	0	18	21	0	8	1	45	4	6	.327	.342
Reina, Jose	R-R	6-2	160	2-28-01	.231	.294	.214	67	243	28	56	10	6	0	30	23	6	4	5	49	26	13	.321	.307
Rodriguez, Jose	R-R	6-1	170	3-19-01	.225	—	—	57	169	19	38	10	0	2	23	23	3	2	4	65	3	10	.320	.322
Sandoval, Jhon	R-R	6-2	172	11-14-99	.181	—	—	32	105	11	19	5	1	0	9	16	2	0	1	51	3	2	.248	.298
Valencia, Eduardo	R-R	6-2	180	1-25-00	.313	.250	.331	57	198	30	62	13	1	0	26	21	4	3	5	35	6	5	.389	.382
Veliz, Frank	R-R	5-11	160	9-10-99	.282	—	—	57	206	40	58	7	1	1	17	18	8	1	3	40	16	7	.340	.357

Pitching	B-T	HT	WT	DOB	W	L	ERA	G	GS	CG	SV	IP	H	R	ER	HR	BB	SO	AVG	vLH	vRH	K/9	BB/9
Acosta, Victor	R-R	6-3	190	6-24-98	2	0	1.85	19	0	0	7	34	28	7	7	0	5	35	.239	—	—	9.26	1.32
Bauza, Adolfo	R-R	6-2	160	9-27-00	0	4	7.36	11	10	0	0	26	22	24	21	1	34	19	.234	.286	.203	6.66	11.92
Burgos, Ronald	R-R	6-3	190	12-22-99	2	2	4.09	14	9	0	0	55	61	39	25	1	13	54	.279	—	—	8.84	2.13
Chavez, Alejandro	R-R	6-2	170	7-14-99	2	5	4.12	17	0	0	0	55	39	23	18	0	18	40	.271	.304	.255	9.15	4.12
Cortes, Maximo	R-R	6-1	170	11-18-99	1	5	5.69	12	10	0	0	55	63	41	35	3	14	42	.286	—	—	6.83	2.28
Dacosta, Francarlos	R-R	6-1	175	2-27-00	1	1	4.35	12	4	0	1	21	20	12	10	1	9	9	.244	—	—	3.92	3.92
De Jesus, Angel	R-R	6-4	185	2-13-97	1	0	1.69	3	1	0	0	11	8	2	2	1	3	14	.211	.149	.219	11.81	2.53
De La Cruz, Sandel	R-R	6-2	185	8-6-96	1	0	0.00	3	0	0	0	7	8	0	0	0	1	7	.296	.231	.276	9.45	1.35
De Los Reyes, Raul	R-R	6-4	220	8-24-97	2	1	2.96	12	0	0	3	24	23	11	8	2	7	21	.250	.325	.192	7.77	2.59
Diaz, Jose	R-R	6-5	200	5-12-00	3	1	5.40	18	0	0	0	28	20	21	17	1	27	25	.198	—	—	7.94	8.58
Escalona, Edgar	R-R	6-4	193	3-30-98	1	0	7.11	2	0	0	0	6	8	5	5	1	4	4	.308	.296	.342	5.68	5.68
Fajardo, Rodolfo	L-L	6-3	165	2-17-00	3	0	1.07	14	13	0	0	59	39	14	7	2	10	67	.183	.121	.194	10.22	1.53
Fenelon, Wilmer	R-R	6-3	170	10-18-00	0	0	3.65	10	0	0	0	12	6	5	5	0	4	9	.255	.167	.310	6.57	2.92
Francisco, Roberto	R-R	6-3	190	3-1-99	4	1	4.60	21	0	0	4	31	44	23	16	2	14	27	.339	—	—	7.76	4.02
Galea, Maiker	R-R	6-0	190	8-30-98	1	0	7.30	10	0	0	1	12	14	13	10	0	12	16	.264	—	—	11.68	8.76
Gardea, Dario	R-R	6-2	210	1-29-99	5	1	2.05	12	9	1	1	48	32	15	11	2	13	51	.189	.185	.191	9.50	2.42
Guerrero, Yonson	R-R	6-1	175	5-12-00	2	2	4.99	16	3	0	2	38	23	19	17	1	18	25	.204	—	—	7.34	5.28
Hernandez, Jhoan	R-R	6-0	145	4-21-99	3	2	4.88	18	0	0	0	24	27	13	13	0	13	21	.276	—	—	7.88	4.88
Herrera, Martin	L-R	6-1	170	9-22-00	1	3	3.73	12	11	0	0	31	41	19	13	1	6	28	.318	—	—	8.04	1.72
Jimenez, Francisco	R-R	6-2	194	3-23-99	2	1	2.66	8	5	0	0	24	16	10	7	0	15	24	.195	—	—	9.13	5.70
Jimenez, Marco	R-R	165		12-6-99	1	1	3.18	4	0	0	0	3	2	4	1	0	2	4	.200	—	—	6.35	3.18
Lopez, Johan	R-R	6-4	190	4-5-99	1	2	4.67	17	0	0	9	35	21	18	2	29	28	.271	.300	.258	7.27	7.53
Montero, Keider	R-R	6-1	145	7-6-00	2	2	2.14	15	7	0	5	46	45	12	11	1	16	40	.249	.242	.252	7.77	3.11
Moreno, Williander	R-R	6-0	160	3-13-99	3	4	3.61	19	9	0	5	57	55	27	23	4	14	47	.261	.250	.266	7.38	2.20
Nunez, Hendry	R-R	6-4	180	7-22-99	0	2	4.50	13	2	0	2	28	24	19	14	1	21	29	.226	.238	.219	9.32	6.75
Ozuna, Angel	R-R	5-10	180	9-25-98	3	2	5.06	20	0	0	0	37	37	26	21	2	22	26	.264	—	—	6.32	5.30
Perdomo, Carlos	L-L	6-1	167	4-25-98	1	1	1.59	10	0	0	0	11	5	3	2	0	14	15	.128	—	—	11.91	11.12
Perez, Cleiverth	L-L	5-11	167	2-5-00	1	3	3.64	14	13	0	0	54	49	25	22	2	21	52	.245	—	—	8.61	3.48
Pina, Jose	R-R	6-3	170	5-24-01	1	2	0.64	6	5	0	0	14	8	1	1	0	6	12	.226	.321	.147	7.71	3.86
Pinales, Erick	R-R	6-2	185	1-27-99	1	3	3.48	11	6	0	0	21	9	11	8	0	18	24	.132	—	—	10.45	7.84
Quinones, Emmanuel	R-R	6-1	185	4-15-99	2	3	2.26	13	9	0	0	60	53	27	15	0	13	37	.238	—	—	5.58	1.96
Ramirez, Jose	R-R	6-1	170	8-18-97	0	1	6.62	13	0	0	0	18	12	13	13	0	21	19	.203	.067	.250	9.68	10.70

DETROIT TIGERS

Player	B-T	Ht	Wt	DOB	W	L	ERA	G	GS	CG	SV	IP	H	R	ER	HR	BB	SO	AVG	vLH	vRH		
Reyes, Marcos	R-R	6-0	170	4-4-98	3	0	7.43	15	0	0	0	23	34	27	19	2	20	15	.330	.276	.351	5.87	7.83
Salazar, Joseph	R-R	6-1	175	9-24-99	3	5	3.90	14	13	0	0	58	57	37	25	2	24	43	.259	.286	.248	6.71	3.75
Santana, Andy	R-R	6-3	190	10-27-99	2	1	3.27	7	0	0	1	11	10	5	4	2	7	11	.238	.091	.290	9.00	5.73
Santana, Kilber	R-R	6-1	160	10-15-98	1	1	4.22	3	0	0	0	11	11	6	5	1	0	11	.268	.235	.281	9.28	0.00
Severino, Oscar	R-R	6-1	175	2-26-98	0	0	2.45	10	0	0	3	15	10	4	4	1	6	18	.196	.316	.125	11.05	3.68
Silva, Ricardo	L-L	6-1	165	4-14-00	2	5	3.51	14	6	0	1	56	61	30	22	0	3	57	.275	.244	.282	9.11	0.48
Tejeda, Briant	R-R	6-2	185	2-19-00	1	0	4.76	13	0	0	0	17	14	12	9	0	20	17	.233	.211	.244	9.00	10.59
Torres, Oswal	R-R	6-3	185	5-5-00	1	3	7.66	16	1	0	1	25	23	22	21	1	27	17	.267	.167	.368	6.20	9.85
Valdez, Albert	L-L	6-2	165	7-5-99	0	2	7.71	10	0	0	0	12	15	13	10	2	6	9	.313	—	—	6.94	4.63
Vazquez, Juan	L-L	6-2	165	7-2-99	0	3	2.49	16	0	0	4	25	28	12	7	0	9	21	.272	—	—	7.46	3.20
Yeguez, Enrique	R-R	6-0	165	12-4-00	1	2	7.15	7	0	0	0	11	15	13	9	1	7	14	.313	.375	.281	11.12	5.56

Fielding

C: Alfonzo 18, De La Cruz 4, Garcia 27, Jimenez 20, Medrano 21, Rea 27, Valencia 24. **1B:** Adames 11, Alfonzo 12, Batista 15, De La Cruz 14, Dominguez 17, Garcia 14, Jimenez 1, Marte 13, Medrano 14, Perez 8, Rea 15, Valencia 33, Veliz 1. **2B:** Acevedo 20, Batista 1, Marte 14, Montes 10, Nivar 59, Olivas 1, Perez 7, Veliz 44. **3B:** Batista 6, Dominguez 22, Garcia 1, Marte 26, Martinez Jr. 42, Montes 5, Olivas 45, Perez 15, Veliz 6. **SS:** Acevedo 42, Gonzalez 36, Irigoyen 31, Olivas 8, Perez 33, Veliz 4. **OF:** Adames 29, Batista 14, Chacon 71, Figuereo 32, Leonardo 51, Marte 1, Medrano 1, Mojica 59, Moreno 27, Oviedo 28, Reina 66, Rodriguez 55, Sandoval 22.

Houston Astros

SEASON IN A SENTENCE: It was always going to be hard to repeat as World Series champs, and the Astros push for back-to-back titles ended against the Red Sox in the AL Championship Series, ending an excellent 103-win season.

HIGH POINT: The Astros were dominant from day one until the final day of the season. They managed to survive and weather a variety of injuries. Carlos Correa missed more than a month with a back injury, and Jose Altuve played through a knee injury that required offseason surgery. The high point was a 12-game winning streak in June, capped off by a walk-off 5-4 win over the Rays.

LOW POINT: The first time the Astros truly struggled was in the playoffs, when they were eliminated in five games by the Red Sox after sweeping the Indians. The Astros' excellent pitching staff, which had been one of the team's strengths, let the team down in the ALCS. Gerrit Cole, Charlie Morton and even Justin Verlander struggled to handle a deep Red Sox lineup.

NOTABLE ROOKIES: Righthander Josh James proved to be a useful swingman in a late-season callup. He went 2-0, 2.35 with 29 strikeouts in 23 innings. Outfielder Kyle Tucker was given a chance to win the left field job in the second half of the season, but when he struggled right away (.141/.236/.206) the Astros moved on because they were in the midst of a pennant race.

KEY TRANSACTIONS: Righthander Ryan Pressly, acquired for outfielder Gilberto Celestino and righthander Jorge Alcala in a midseason trade with the Twins, had a 0.77 ERA in 23 innings with the Astros. Catcher Martin Maldonado, acquired from the Angels for lefthander Patrick Sandoval, became the club's primary catcher. Righthander Roberto Osuna was acquired in a trade that sent Ken Giles, David Paulino and Hector Perez to the Blue Jays. On the field Osuna was excellent, but the trade brought the Astros widespread scorn because of his domestic violence suspension.

DOWN ON THE FARM: The Astros don't have as much prospect depth as they had a few years ago, but the system still has prospects with star potential. Righthander Forrest Whitley is one of the best pitching prospects in baseball while outfielders Kyle Tucker and Yordan Alvarez are both nearly ready sluggers. The Astros pitching development and ability to develop their arms is exemplified by the fact that the Astros' top five farm teams led their respective leagues in pitcher strikeouts.

OPENING DAY PAYROLL: $172,038,900 (7th).

PLAYERS OF THE YEAR

MAJOR LEAGUE	MINOR LEAGUE
Alex Bregman 3B	**Kyle Tucker** OF
.286/.394/.532	(Triple-A)
Led the Astros in 2B	.332/.400/.590
(51) and HR (31)	24 HR, 20 SB

ORGANIZATION LEADERS

Batting		*Minimum 250 AB
MAJORS		
* AVG	Jose Altuve	.316
* OPS	Alex Bregman	.926
HR	Alex Bregman	31
RBI	Alex Bregman	103
MINORS		
* AVG	J.D. Davis, Fresno	.342
* OBP	J.D. Davis, Fresno	.406
* SLG	Kyle Tucker, Fresno	.590
* OPS	Kyle Tucker, Fresno	.989
R	Myles Straw, Corpus Christi, Fresno	95
H	Myles Straw, Corpus Christi, Fresno	150
TB	Kyle Tucker, Fresno	240
2B	Abraham Toro-Hernandez, Buies Creek, Corpus Christi	35
3B	Osvaldo Duarte, Buies Creek	9
3B	Jonathan Arauz, Quad Cities, Buies Creek	9
HR	AJ Reed, Fresno	28
RBI	AJ Reed, Fresno	108
BB	Myles Straw, Corpus Christi, Fresno	73
SO	Miguelangel Sierra, Quad Cities	143
SB	Myles Straw, Corpus Christi, Fresno	70

Pitching		#Minimum 75 IP
MAJORS		
W	Justin Verlander	16
# ERA	Justin Verlander	2.52
SO	Justin Verlander	290
SV	Hector Rondon	15
MINORS		
W	Ryan Hartman, Corpus Christi	11
L	Brandon Bielak, Buies Creek, Corpus Christi	8
L	Trent Thornton, Fresno	8
L	Brandon Bailey, Buies Creek, Corpus Christi	8
L	Yohan Ramirez, Quad Cities, Buies Creek	8
# ERA	Brandon Bielak, Buies Creek, Corpus Christi	2.23
G	Brendan McCurry, Fresno	46
GS	Trent Thornton, Fresno	22
SV	Brendan McCurry, Fresno	14
IP	Cy Sneed, Fresno	127
IP	Brock Dykxhoorn, Corpus Christi, Fresno	127
BB	Cesar Rosado, Quad Cities	63
SO	Josh James, Corpus Christi, Fresno	171
# AVG	Cristian Javier, Quad Cities, Buies Creek	.185

2018 PERFORMANCE

General Manager: Jeff Luhnow. **Farm Director:** Pete Putila. **Scouting Director:** Mike Elias.

Class	Team	League	W	L	PCT	Finish	Manager
Majors	Houston Astros	American	103	59	.636	2nd (15)	A.J. Hinch
Triple-A	Fresno Grizzlies	Pacific Coast	82	57	.590	3rd (16)	Rodney Linares
Double-A	Corpus Christi Hooks	Texas	82	56	.594	1st (8)	Omar Lopez
High A	Buies Creek Astros	Carolina	80	57	.584	2nd (10)	Morgan Ensberg
Low A	Quad Cities River Bandits	Midwest	81	59	.579	2nd (16)	Mickey Storey
Short season	Tri-City Valleycats	New York-Penn	42	33	.560	3rd (14)	Jason Bell
Rookie	GCL Astros	Gulf Coast	27	28	.491	9th (18)	Wladimir Sutil
Overall 2018 Minor League Record			394	290	.576	2nd (30)	

ORGANIZATION STATISTICS

HOUSTON ASTROS
AMERICAN LEAGUE

Batting	B-T	HT	WT	DOB	AVG	vLH	vRH	G	AB	R	H	2B	3B	HR	RBI	BB	HBP	SH	SF	SO	SB	CS	SLG	OBP
Altuve, Jose	R-R	5-6	165	5-6-90	.317	.282	.329	137	534	84	169	29	2	13	61	55	6	3	1	79	17	4	.451	.386
Bregman, Alex	R-R	6-0	180	3-30-94	.286	.315	.274	157	594	105	170	51	1	31	103	96	12	0	3	85	10	4	.532	.394
Correa, Carlos	R-R	6-4	215	9-22-94	.239	.286	.224	110	402	60	96	20	1	15	65	53	2	0	1	111	3	0	.406	.323
Davis, J.D.	R-R	6-3	225	4-27-93	.175	.231	.141	42	103	9	18	2	0	1	5	10	0	0	0	29	0	0	.223	.248
Federowicz, Tim	R-R	5-10	215	8-5-87	.206	.231	.191	10	34	4	7	3	0	0	2	1	0	0	0	13	0	0	.294	.229
Fisher, Derek	L-R	6-3	205	8-21-93	.165	.286	.139	42	79	13	13	2	2	4	11	5	0	0	2	42	2	0	.392	.209
Gattis, Evan	R-R	6-4	270	8-18-86	.226	.241	.218	128	407	49	92	17	0	25	78	33	3	0	8	101	1	0	.452	.284
Gonzalez, Marwin	B-R	6-1	205	3-14-89	.247	.273	.235	145	489	61	121	25	3	16	68	53	3	5	2	126	2	3	.409	.324
Gurriel, Yuli	R-R	6-0	190	6-9-84	.291	.331	.273	136	537	70	156	33	1	13	85	23	6	0	7	63	5	1	.428	.323
Kemp, Tony	L-R	5-6	165	10-31-91	.263	.268	.261	97	255	37	67	15	0	6	30	32	3	3	1	44	9	3	.392	.351
Maldonado, Martin	R-R	6-0	230	8-16-86	.232	.293	.194	41	108	15	25	4	1	4	12	3	1	1	1	25	0	0	.398	.257
2-team total (78 Los Angeles)					.225	.233	.222	119	373	39	84	18	1	9	44	16	11	2	2	98	0	1	.351	.276
Marisnick, Jake	R-R	6-4	220	3-30-91	.211	.231	.193	103	213	34	45	8	1	10	28	15	4	1	1	84	6	2	.399	.275
McCann, Brian	L-R	6-3	225	2-20-84	.212	.200	.215	63	189	22	40	3	0	7	23	19	6	0	2	40	0	1	.339	.301
Reddick, Josh	L-R	6-2	195	2-19-87	.243	.269	.231	134	433	63	105	13	2	17	47	49	0	1	2	77	7	2	.400	.318
Reed, AJ	L-L	6-4	275	5-10-93	.000	—	.000	1	3	0	0	0	0	0	0	0	0	0	0	1	0	0	.000	.000
Springer, George	R-R	6-3	215	9-19-89	.265	.285	.257	140	544	102	144	26	0	22	71	64	5	0	3	122	6	4	.434	.346
Stassi, Max	R-R	5-10	200	3-15-91	.226	.228	.225	88	221	28	50	13	0	8	27	23	6	0	0	74	0	0	.394	.316
Straw, Myles	R-R	5-10	180	10-17-94	.333	—	.333	9	9	4	3	0	0	1	1	1	0	0	0	2	0	0	.667	.400
Tucker, Kyle	L-R	6-4	190	1-17-97	.141	.364	.094	28	64	10	9	2	1	0	4	6	2	0	0	13	1	1	.203	.236
White, Tyler	R-R	5-11	225	10-29-90	.276	.305	.265	66	210	27	58	12	3	12	42	24	2	0	1	49	0	1	.533	.354

Pitching	B-T	HT	WT	DOB	W	L	ERA	G	GS	CG	SV	IP	H	R	ER	HR	BB	SO	AVG	vLH	vRH	K/9	BB/9
Cole, Gerrit	R-R	6-4	225	9-8-90	15	5	2.88	32	32	1	0	200	143	68	64	19	64	276	.198	.162	.231	12.40	2.88
Deetz, Dean	R-R	6-1	195	11-29-93	0	0	5.40	4	0	0	0	3	4	2	2	1	1	3	.308	.167	.429	8.10	2.70
Devenski, Chris	R-R	6-3	210	11-13-90	2	3	4.18	50	1	0	2	47	42	23	22	9	13	51	.236	.220	.256	9.70	2.47
Giles, Ken	R-R	6-2	205	9-20-90	0	2	4.99	34	0	0	12	31	36	17	17	2	3	31	.286	.273	.296	9.10	0.88
2-team total (21 Toronto)					0	3	4.65	55	0	0	26	50	54	28	26	6	7	53	.266	.225	.305	9.48	1.25
Guduan, Reymin	L-L	6-4	205	3-16-92	0	0	2.70	3	0	0	0	3	1	1	1	1	0	4	.091	.000	.125	10.80	0.00
Harris, Will	R-R	6-4	250	8-28-84	5	3	3.49	61	0	0	0	57	48	22	22	3	14	64	.226	.267	.187	10.16	2.22
Hoyt, James	R-R	6-6	230	9-30-86	0	0	0.00	1	0	0	0	1	0	0	0	0	1	0	.500	1.000	.000	0.00	27.00
James, Josh	R-R	6-3	206	3-8-93	2	0	2.35	6	3	0	0	23	15	6	6	3	7	29	.183	.195	.171	11.35	2.74
Keuchel, Dallas	L-L	6-3	205	1-1-88	12	11	3.74	34	34	1	0	205	211	92	85	18	58	153	.263	.281	.259	6.73	2.55
McCullers Jr., Lance	L-R	6-2	205	10-2-93	10	6	3.86	25	22	0	0	128	100	60	55	12	50	142	.215	.177	.251	9.96	3.51
McHugh, Collin	R-R	6-2	190	6-19-87	6	2	1.99	58	0	0	0	72	45	18	16	6	21	94	.177	.228	.135	11.70	2.61
Morton, Charlie	R-R	6-5	235	11-12-83	15	3	3.13	30	30	0	0	167	130	63	58	18	64	201	.214	.207	.219	10.83	3.45
Osuna, Roberto	R-R	6-2	215	2-7-95	2	2	1.99	23	0	0	12	23	17	5	5	1	3	19	.210	.300	.122	7.54	1.19
2-team total (15 Toronto)					2	2	2.37	38	0	0	21	38	33	10	10	1	4	32	.234	.280	.182	7.58	0.95
Peacock, Brad	R-R	6-1	210	2-2-88	3	5	3.46	61	1	0	3	65	56	26	25	11	20	96	.226	.264	.204	13.29	2.77
Perez, Cionel	L-L	5-11	170	4-21-96	0	0	3.97	8	0	0	0	11	6	5	5	3	7	12	.158	.083	.192	9.53	5.56
Pressly, Ryan	R-R	6-3	210	12-15-88	1	0	0.77	26	0	0	2	23	11	2	2	1	3	32	.138	.103	.171	12.34	1.16
2-team total (51 Minnesota)					2	1	2.54	77	0	0	2	71	57	21	20	6	22	101	.216	.172	.242	12.80	2.79
Rondon, Hector	R-R	6-3	230	2-26-88	2	5	3.20	63	0	0	15	59	58	22	21	4	20	67	.252	.246	.258	10.22	3.05
Sipp, Tony	L-L	6-0	190	7-12-83	3	1	1.86	54	0	0	0	39	27	8	8	1	13	42	.200	.191	.209	9.78	3.03
Smith, Joe	R-R	6-2	205	3-22-84	5	1	3.74	56	0	0	0	46	34	20	19	7	12	46	.207	.192	.214	9.07	2.36
Valdez, Framber	L-L	5-11	170	11-19-93	4	1	2.19	8	5	0	0	37	22	10	9	3	24	34	.175	.125	.192	8.27	5.84
Verlander, Justin	R-R	6-5	225	2-20-83	16	9	2.52	34	34	1	0	214	156	63	60	28	37	290	.200	.177	.219	12.20	1.56

Fielding

Catcher	PCT	G	PO	A	E	DP	PB
Federowicz	.990	10	87	8	1	0	1
Gattis	1.000	2	2	0	0	0	0
Maldonado	1.000	40	347	21	0	1	3
McCann	.995	62	569	27	3	1	3
Stassi	.997	82	668	32	2	4	8

First Base	PCT	G	PO	A	E	DP
Davis	1.000	13	73	8	0	3
Gonzalez	1.000	24	128	11	0	14
Gurriel	.995	109	770	48	4	61

Reed	1.000	1	6	0	0	1
White	1.000	42	258	15	0	29

Second Base	PCT	G	PO	A	E	DP
Altuve	.984	130	159	262	7	63
Bregman	1.000	2	1	2	0	1
Gonzalez	.987	32	33	45	1	9
Gurriel	.969	15	11	20	1	6
Kemp	1.000	7	2	6	0	2

Third Base	PCT	G	PO	A	E	DP

Bregman	.962	136	84	245	13	23
Davis	.927	23	7	31	3	4
Gonzalez	.833	3	2	3	1	1
Gurriel	1.000	21	8	29	0	5

Shortstop	PCT	G	PO	A	E	DP
Bregman	.964	28	22	58	3	10
Correa	.984	109	106	268	6	43
Gonzalez	.939	39	27	65	6	14
Gurriel	1.000	2	1	3	0	1

Outfield	PCT	G	PO	A	E	DP
Bregman	.000	1	0	0	0	0
Davis	1.000	5	5	1	0	0
Fisher	1.000	37	43	0	0	0
Gonzalez	.991	73	102	4	1	1
Kemp	1.000	85	138	1	0	1
Marisnick	.993	98	141	1	1	1
Reddick	1.000	128	209	9	0	2
Springer	.996	128	252	8	1	2
Straw	1.000	9	9	0	0	0
Tucker	.917	23	20	2	2	0

HOUSTON ASTROS

FRESNO GRIZZLIES

PACIFIC COAST LEAGUE

TRIPLE-A

Batting	B-T	HT	WT	DOB	AVG	vLH	vRH	G	AB	R	H	2B	3B	HR	RBI	BB	HBP	SH	SF	SO	SB	CS	SLG	OBP
Altuve, Jose	R-R	5-6	165	5-6-90	.333	—	.333	1	3	0	1	0	0	0	0	1	0	0	1	0	0	.333	.500
Alvarez, Yordan	L-R	6-5	225	6-27-97	.259	.302	.239	45	166	24	43	8	0	8	28	23	0	0	1	47	1	0	.452	.349
Angarita, Alfredo	B-R	5-10	155	11-16-96	.000	.000	—	1	2	0	0	0	0	0	0	1	0	0	0	1	0	0	.000	.000
Bohanek, Cody	R-R	6-1	195	7-2-95	.195	.143	.206	11	41	2	8	0	0	0	1	0	0	1	0	17	1	0	.195	.209
Davis, J.D.	R-R	6-3	225	4-27-93	.342	.408	.323	85	333	56	114	25	2	17	81	36	3	0	5	69	3	0	.583	.406
De Goti, Alex	R-R	5-10	165	8-19-94	.287	.261	.296	27	94	14	27	8	0	1	12	10	1	1	2	15	3	1	.404	.355
de Oleo, Eduardo	R-R	5-10	180	1-25-93	.267	.429	.237	12	45	6	12	3	0	0	2	2	0	0	0	14	0	0	.333	.298
Federowicz, Tim	R-R	5-10	215	8-5-87	.328	.389	.319	38	134	24	44	13	0	6	22	16	1	0	0	27	0	0	.560	.404
Ferguson, Drew	R-R	5-11	180	8-3-92	.305	.271	.314	65	233	43	71	11	3	4	29	46	10	1	2	61	6	4	.429	.436
Fisher, Derek	L-R	6-3	205	8-21-93	.251	.264	.246	67	239	44	60	12	1	10	34	39	3	0	0	85	11	1	.435	.363
Garcia, Alejandro	R-R	5-10	182	6-21-91	.225	.136	.243	36	129	14	29	2	1	1	19	6	1	0	2	12	0	2	.279	.261
Jones, Taylor	R-R	6-7	225	12-6-93	.210	.243	.198	39	143	16	30	7	1	5	17	16	2	0	2	46	0	0	.378	.295
Kemmer, Jon	L-L	6-2	230	11-17-90	.253	.146	.274	77	285	40	72	16	4	13	44	31	5	2	0	88	3	2	.474	.334
Kemp, Tony	L-R	5-6	165	10-31-91	.335	.444	.322	38	161	33	54	6	5	0	19	19	1	1	1	15	13	2	.435	.407
Marisnick, Jake	R-R	6-4	220	3-30-91	.343	.375	.333	19	73	18	25	8	2	4	13	6	2	0	1	17	3	1	.671	.402
Mayfield, Jack	R-R	5-11	190	9-30-90	.270	.282	.267	113	433	66	117	31	1	16	66	33	5	1	7	92	5	4	.457	.324
McCann, Brian	L-R	6-3	225	2-20-84	.143	.333	.000	2	7	1	1	0	0	0	0	0	0	0	2	0	0	.143	.250
Nunez, Antonio	R-R	5-9	165	1-10-93	.190	.308	.164	69	216	24	41	8	2	1	20	18	2	3	3	77	9	6	.259	.255
Reed, AJ	L-L	6-4	275	5-10-93	.255	.205	.273	123	462	72	118	24	4	28	108	64	4	0	10	128	0	0	.507	.344
Ritchie, Jamie	R-R	6-2	205	4-9-93	.321	.263	.339	25	81	16	26	7	0	3	9	14	2	0	0	16	2	0	.519	.433
Straw, Myles	R-R	5-10	180	10-17-94	.257	.281	.249	66	265	48	68	10	3	0	14	38	0	0	1	60	35	3	.317	.349
Stubbs, Garrett	L-R	5-10	175	5-26-93	.310	.275	.323	84	297	60	92	19	6	4	38	35	2	2	4	53	6	0	.455	.382
Tanielu, Nick	R-R	5-11	215	9-4-92	.289	.300	.284	76	277	40	80	17	1	5	37	19	2	1	2	38	2	2	.412	.337
Tucker, Kyle	L-R	6-4	190	1-17-97	.332	.307	.337	100	407	86	135	27	3	24	93	48	2	1	6	84	20	4	.590	.400
White, Tyler	R-R	5-11	225	10-29-90	.333	.327	.335	70	255	55	85	18	0	14	53	46	8	0	4	39	1	1	.569	.444

Pitching	B-T	HT	WT	DOB	W	L	ERA	G	GS	CG	SV	IP	H	R	ER	HR	BB	SO	AVG	vLH	vRH	K/9	BB/9
Armenteros, Rogelio	R-R	6-1	215	6-30-94	8	1	3.74	22	21	1	1	118	106	51	49	15	48	134	.237	.260	.214	10.22	3.66
Boshers, Buddy	L-L	6-3	205	5-9-88	2	1	3.18	41	0	0	4	51	48	23	18	5	15	55	.249	.300	.204	9.71	2.65
Bostick, Akeem	R-R	6-6	215	5-4-95	0	0	7.20	1	1	0	0	5	5	4	4	1	2	8	.263	.250	.286	14.40	3.60
Deetz, Dean	R-R	6-1	195	11-29-93	2	0	0.79	21	0	0	0	34	22	3	3	1	18	50	.186	.151	.215	13.24	4.76
Devenski, Chris	R-R	6-3	210	11-13-90	0	0	0.00	2	0	0	0	2	4	0	0	0	0	6	.444	.500	.333	21.60	0.00
Dorris, Jacob	R-R	6-2	165	3-24-93	0	2	7.71	12	0	0	0	16	18	17	14	3	10	13	.286	.222	.333	7.16	5.51
Dykxhoorn, Brock	R-R	6-8	250	7-2-94	6	3	4.60	14	12	0	0	74	69	39	38	8	16	79	.246	.278	.218	9.57	1.94
Emanuel, Kent	L-L	6-4	212	6-4-92	5	4	5.59	31	10	0	1	84	107	57	52	10	26	86	.308	.299	.315	9.25	2.80
Feldmann, Brendan	R-R	6-4	205	4-7-94	1	0	13.50	1	0	0	0	2	4	3	3	0	2	2	.400	.500	.250	9.00	0.00
Ferrell, Riley	R-R	6-2	200	10-18-93	2	1	6.75	22	0	0	2	28	34	21	21	4	16	34	.296	.308	.286	10.93	5.14
Garza, Ralph	R-R	6-2	195	4-6-94	1	2	3.71	18	0	0	0	34	29	16	14	3	23	40	.227	.175	.277	10.59	6.09
Giles, Ken	R-R	6-2	205	9-20-90	0	0	8.44	6	0	0	0	5	9	5	5	0	2	8	.360	.273	.429	13.50	3.38
Guduan, Reymin	L-L	6-4	205	3-16-92	3	3	3.74	43	0	0	2	55	46	24	23	5	32	83	.217	.128	.288	13.50	5.20
Hauschild, Mike	R-R	6-3	210	1-22-90	7	6	4.88	19	19	0	0	98	113	61	53	7	38	93	.293	.264	.323	8.57	3.50
Hoyt, James	R-R	6-6	230	9-30-86	0	3	2.25	25	0	0	5	28	19	11	7	2	8	33	.192	.195	.190	10.61	2.57
James, Josh	R-R	6-3	206	3-8-93	6	4	3.40	17	17	0	0	93	62	39	35	8	39	133	.187	.178	.195	12.92	3.79
Martes, Francis	R-R	6-1	225	11-24-95	0	1	6.75	4	4	0	0	19	25	14	14	3	8	16	.329	.387	.289	7.71	8.20
McCurry, Brendan	R-R	5-10	170	1-7-92	6	7	3.69	46	0	0	14	63	64	32	26	5	17	73	.262	.278	.250	10.37	2.42
Nunn, Chris	L-L	6-5	200	10-5-90	0	0	13.50	7	0	0	0	7	9	13	11	3	6	9	.290	.500	.158	11.05	7.36
Paulino, David	R-R	6-7	222	2-6-94	0	0	5.50	4	0	0	0	18	16	12	11	3	5	23	.232	.250	.220	11.50	2.50
Perez, Cionel	L-L	5-11	170	4-21-96	1	0	3.38	4	0	0	0	5	5	2	2	0	6	6	.250	.300	.000	10.13	10.13
Ramsey, Matt	R-R	5-11	205	9-24-89	2	2	2.30	33	0	0	0	47	37	13	12	5	16	54	.216	.206	.222	10.34	3.06
Rodgers, Brady	R-R	6-2	210	9-17-90	3	3	5.49	8	8	0	0	41	48	25	25	4	10	30	.289	.300	.276	6.59	2.20
Sneed, Cy	R-R	6-4	215	10-1-92	10	6	3.83	26	20	1	0	127	120	56	54	6	53	114	.253	.291	.221	8.08	3.76
Thome, Andrew	R-R	6-3	216	1-13-93	4	2	4.91	25	0	0	0	37	38	22	20	5	15	18	.262	.268	.258	4.42	3.68
Thornton, Trent	R-R	6-0	175	9-30-93	9	8	4.42	24	22	0	0	124	118	67	61	13	31	122	.248	.283	.217	8.83	2.24
Valdez, Framber	L-L	5-11	170	11-19-93	2	0	4.15	2	1	0	0	9	8	4	4	0	3	9	.250	.273	.238	9.35	3.12

Fielding

Catcher	PCT	G	PO	A	E	DP	PB
de Oleo	.963	11	99	6	4	1	3
Federowicz	.988	33	299	20	4	2	5
McCann	1.000	1	6	0	0	0	0
Ritchie	1.000	24	258	9	0	2	1
Stubbs	.993	75	694	41	5	4	5

First Base	PCT	G	PO	A	E	DP
Davis	1.000	10	62	12	0	10
Federowicz	1.000	3	11	2	0	0

Fielding

	PCT	G	PO	A	E	DP
Jones	.983	29	210	15	4	14
Reed	.984	90	623	72	11	61
Stubbs	1.000	1	2	0	0	0
White	.988	10	74	6	1	3

Second Base	PCT	G	PO	A	E	DP
Altuve	1.000	1	1	3	0	1
Angarita	1.000	1	2	2	0	2
Bohanek	1.000	11	15	32	0	6
Federowicz	1.000	1	0	1	0	0
Kemp	1.000	25	38	52	0	10
Mayfield	.986	62	85	128	3	24
Nunez	1.000	6	2	8	0	0
Tanielu	.919	14	9	25	3	7
White	.974	26	46	67	3	14

Third Base	PCT	G	PO	A	E	DP
Davis	.972	51	29	77	3	6
De Goti	1.000	1	1	3	0	1
Mayfield	.900	4	1	8	1	0
Tanielu	.930	63	42	104	11	14
White	.952	23	16	43	3	2

Shortstop	PCT	G	PO	A	E	DP
Bohanek	.000	1	0	0	0	0
De Goti	.989	26	34	53	1	15
Mayfield	.962	48	63	87	6	25
Nunez	.966	61	83	146	8	23
Straw	1.000	1	1	0	0	0
White	1.000	8	9	17	0	3

Outfield	PCT	G	PO	A	E	DP
Alvarez	1.000	34	45	2	0	0
Davis	.968	20	28	2	1	0
de Oleo	.000	1	0	0	0	0
Ferguson	.979	64	138	4	3	0
Fisher	.982	56	106	2	2	0
Garcia	.981	36	47	4	1	0
Jones	1.000	1	1	0	0	0
Kemmer	1.000	32	52	0	0	0
Kemp	.964	14	27	0	1	0
Marisnick	1.000	18	28	2	0	0
Nunez	1.000	1	2	0	0	0
Straw	.976	66	156	7	4	1
Stubbs	.000	2	0	0	0	0
White	1.000	2	3	0	0	0

CORPUS CHRISTI HOOKS   DOUBLE-A
TEXAS LEAGUE

Batting	B-T	HT	WT	DOB	AVG	vLH	vRH	G	AB	R	H	2B	3B	HR	RBI	BB	HBP	SH	SF	SO	SB	CS	SLG	OBP
Alvarez, Yordan	L-R	6-5	225	6-27-97	.325	.396	.293	43	169	39	55	13	0	12	46	19	0	0	2	45	5	2	.615	.390
Benedetti, Carmen	L-L	6-2	215	10-29-94	.277	.218	.304	80	271	45	75	17	2	8	49	39	1	0	4	82	11	5	.443	.365
Birk, Ryne	L-R	5-10	185	11-11-94	.216	.208	.219	116	412	44	89	11	7	1	36	42	7	1	7	89	13	7	.284	.295
Celestino, Gilberto	R-L	6-0	170	2-13-99	.000	.000	.000	3	8	0	0	0	0	0	0	0	0	0	1	0	5	0	0	.000	.000
Cesar, Randy	R-R	6-1	180	1-11-95	.296	.398	.265	116	446	59	132	25	2	10	62	36	1	0	2	112	3	4	.428	.349
Correa, Carlos	R-R	6-4	215	9-22-94	.188	.500	.083	5	16	1	3	1	0	1	2	2	0	0	0	5	0	0	.438	.278
Dawson, Ronnie	L-R	6-2	225	5-19-95	.290	.259	.299	29	114	18	33	6	1	6	14	6	3	0	0	34	6	3	.518	.342
De Goti, Alex	R-R	5-10	165	8-19-94	.282	.321	.271	98	358	43	101	21	3	11	50	18	8	1	2	65	5	6	.450	.329
de Oleo, Eduardo	R-R	5-10	180	1-25-93	.250	.263	.247	27	92	12	23	2	0	3	10	3	0	0	0	26	0	0	.370	.274
Encarnacion, Luis	R-R	6-2	185	8-9-97	.000	.000	.000	2	6	0	0	0	0	0	0	0	1	0	0	3	0	0	.000	.143
Gurriel, Yuli	R-R	6-0	190	6-9-84	.429	.500	.400	5	21	3	9	4	0	0	3	0	0	0	4	0	0	.619	.429
Jones, Taylor	R-R	6-5	225	12-6-93	.314	.315	.314	84	309	45	97	25	1	13	63	45	8	0	5	78	2	0	.528	.409
Marisnick, Jake	R-R	6-4	220	3-30-91	.167	—	.167	2	6	1	1	0	0	0	0	0	0	0	1	1	0	.167	.250
McCann, Brian	L-R	6-3	225	2-20-84	.200	—	.200	5	15	1	3	0	0	1	3	2	0	0	0	3	0	0	.400	.294
McCormick, Chas	R-L	6-0	190	4-19-95	.280	.340	.264	69	250	33	70	10	1	2	28	24	3	0	5	32	12	4	.352	.344
Michelena, Arturo	R-R	5-11	165	10-15-94	.119	.133	.111	12	42	5	5	0	1	0	4	1	0	0	0	8	0	0	.167	.213
Pineda, Andy	L-R	6-1	165	11-11-96	.339	.500	.286	16	65	9	22	2	1	2	6	4	2	0	0	16	3	3	.492	.394
Quintana, Lorenzo	R-R	5-10	198	3-1-89	.254	.291	.243	70	244	38	62	19	2	11	42	15	7	0	0	47	7	4	.484	.316
Reddick, Josh	L-R	6-2	195	2-19-87	.500	1.000	.429	2	4	1	4	1	0	0	0	0	0	0	0	1	0	0	.625	.500
Ritchie, Jamie	R-R	6-2	205	4-9-93	.280	.244	.293	45	161	15	45	9	1	0	22	17	6	0	1	41	1	1	.348	.368
Rojas, Josh	L-R	6-1	185	6-30-94	.251	.231	.258	106	390	64	98	23	4	7	45	53	1	1	6	76	26	14	.385	.338
Sierra, Anibal	R-R	6-1	190	2-15-94	.204	.255	.188	68	221	28	45	11	1	2	17	14	3	0	1	69	3	5	.290	.259
Straw, Myles	R-R	5-10	180	10-17-94	.327	.371	.309	65	251	47	82	7	3	1	17	35	4	2	2	42	35	6	.390	.414
Tanielu, Nick	R-R	5-11	215	9-4-92	.287	.314	.275	29	115	16	33	5	0	4	22	9	0	0	1	12	1	0	.435	.336
Toro, Abraham	B-R	6-1	190	12-20-96	.230	.314	.207	50	178	16	41	15	2	2	22	17	6	0	1	46	3	3	.371	.317
Wrenn, Stephen	R-R	6-2	185	10-7-94	.248	.200	.264	121	472	79	117	23	4	9	55	44	7	5	4	138	44	10	.371	.319

Pitching	B-T	HT	WT	DOB	W	L	ERA	G	GS	CG	SV	IP	H	R	ER	HR	BB	SO	AVG	vLH	vRH	K/9	BB/9
Adcock, Brett	L-L	6-1	225	8-28-95	4	2	3.49	9	5	0	0	39	34	16	15	2	22	28	.238	.143	.269	6.52	5.12
Alcala, Jorge	R-R	6-3	180	7-28-95	2	3	3.54	9	5	0	1	41	36	17	16	1	17	37	.243	.250	.238	8.19	3.76
Bailey, Brandon	R-R	5-10	175	10-19-94	1	0	4.01	5	1	0	1	25	21	13	11	5	9	23	.221	.283	.163	8.39	3.28
Bielak, Brandon	L-R	6-1	210	4-2-96	2	5	2.35	11	10	0	0	61	52	18	16	4	22	57	.235	.198	.270	8.36	3.23
Blanco, Ronel	R-R	6-0	180	8-31-93	2	0	7.08	13	0	0	1	20	23	17	16	3	11	30	.277	.342	.222	13.28	4.87
Bostick, Akeem	R-R	6-6	215	5-4-95	2	5	3.48	21	15	0	3	93	85	39	36	7	35	97	.245	.237	.251	9.39	3.39
Bukauskas, J.B.	R-R	6-0	196	10-11-96	0	0	0.00	1	1	0	0	6	1	0	0	0	2	8	.056	.091	.000	12.00	3.00
Deetz, Dean	R-R	6-1	195	11-29-93	0	0	0.00	3	0	0	0	4	2	0	0	0		6	.154	.200	.125	14.73	0.00
Devenski, Chris	R-R	6-3	210	11-13-90	0	1	12.00	3	2	0	0	3	7	4	4	2	1	6	.467	.500	.429	18.00	3.00
Dykxhoorn, Brock	R-R	6-8	250	7-2-94	3	1	3.08	11	9	0	0	53	40	20	18	6	23	46	.211	.253	.183	7.86	3.93
Feldmann, Brendan	R-R	6-4	205	4-7-94	1	0	4.26	5	0	0	1	6	10	4	3	0	5	6	.357	.700	.167	8.53	5.68
Ferrell, Justin	R-R	6-7	205	4-21-94	6	3	3.38	27	1	0	2	48	39	22	18	4	21	58	.219	.213	.223	10.88	3.94
Ferrell, Riley	R-R	6-2	200	10-18-93	2	2	1.90	21	0	0	7	24	14	8	5	1	18	33	.171	.250	.138	12.55	6.85
Garza, Ralph	R-R	6-2	195	4-6-94	6	0	3.31	17	0	0	0	33	27	15	12	0	9	34	.227	.245	.212	9.37	2.48
Hartman, Ryan	L-L	6-3	205	4-21-94	11	4	2.69	25	18	0	0	121	104	41	36	11	26	143	.235	.255	.229	10.67	1.94
Hill, Kevin	R-R	6-0	230	8-12-92	1	1	1.96	10	0	0	1	18	16	5	4	1	10	14	.239	.238	.239	6.87	4.91
Hiraldo, Carlos	L-L	5-10	175	7-15-96	0	0	3.38	2	0	0	0	3	2	3	1	1	2	3	.182	.000	.250	10.13	6.75
James, Josh	R-R	6-3	206	3-8-93	0	0	2.49	6	4	0	1	22	17	6	6	1	10	38	.205	.179	.218	15.78	4.15
Martin, Corbin	R-R	6-2	200	12-28-95	7	2	2.97	21	18	0	0	103	84	38	34	7	28	96	.221	.214	.225	8.39	2.45
Nunn, Chris	L-L	6-5	200	10-5-90	3	0	1.80	8	0	0	0	20	19	6	4	1	8	23	.264	.278	.259	10.35	3.60
Osuna, Roberto	R-R	6-2	215	2-7-95	0	0	0.00	1	0	0	0	1	0	0	0	0	0	1	.250	.000	.333	9.00	0.00
Perez, Cionel	L-L	5-11	170	4-21-96	6	1	1.98	16	11	0	1	68	54	18	15	3	22	83	.213	.227	.211	10.93	2.90
Perez, Hector	R-R	6-3	190	6-6-96	0	1	3.24	4	2	0	0	17	12	6	6		8	18	.197	.250	.138	9.72	4.32
Pinales, Erasmo	R-R	5-11	180	11-25-94	3	4	5.17	38	0	0	7	56	50	36	32	5	31	72	.240	.154	.292	11.64	5.01
Quiala, Yoanys	R-R	6-3	235	1-15-94	6	5	5.97	13	9	0	1	57	64	39	38	5	22	44	.283	.309	.269	6.91	3.45
Scheetz, Kit	L-L	5-10	185	5-18-94	2	1	2.75	25	0	0	4	39	39	14	12	0	8	43	.262	.265	.260	9.84	1.83
Sierra, Carlos	R-R	6-3	195	10-18-94	0	1	6.00	16	0	0	2	21	17	15	14	6	11	19	.218	.294	.159	8.14	4.71

	B-T	HT	WT	DOB	W	L	ERA	G	GS	CG	SV	IP	H	R	ER	HR	BB	SO	AVG	vLH	vRH	K/9	BB/9
Smith, Joe	R-R	6-2	205	3-22-84	0	0	0.00	2	0	0	0	2	4	0	0	0	0	1	.400	.200	.600	4.50	0.00
Stutzman, Sean	L-L	5-9	175	7-8-93	2	4	5.84	15	0	0	0	25	25	18	16	6	24	17	.275	.346	.246	6.20	8.76
Valdez, Framber	L-L	5-11	170	11-19-93	4	5	4.10	20	13	0	1	94	92	47	43	7	29	120	.256	.214	.276	11.45	2.77
Whitley, Forrest	R-R	6-7	195	9-15-97	0	2	3.76	8	8	0	0	26	15	11	11	2	11	34	.160	.195	.132	11.62	3.76
Winkelman, Alex	L-L	6-2	180	2-8-94	5	3	3.13	32	6	0	4	78	64	39	27	3	58	81	.229	.132	.266	9.39	6.72

Fielding

Catcher	PCT	G	PO	A	E	DP	PB
de Oleo	.983	26	219	19	4	7	5
McCann	1.000	3	26	2	0	0	0
Quintana	.993	69	646	43	5	5	8
Ritchie	.989	44	421	30	5	2	9

First Base	PCT	G	PO	A	E	DP
Alvarez	1.000	5	34	0	0	5
Cesar	.994	42	334	10	2	34
Encarnacion	1.000	2	16	0	0	1
Gurriel	.947	3	18	0	1	3
Jones	.998	70	488	52	1	57
Rojas	.991	13	96	10	1	10
Tanielu	.984	9	55	5	1	6

Second Base	PCT	G	PO	A	E	DP
Birk	.987	106	167	210	5	67

	PCT	G	PO	A	E	DP
De Goti	.957	17	32	34	3	12
Michelena	1.000	3	1	6	0	1
Rojas	.962	12	25	26	2	8
Tanielu	1.000	2	4	6	0	1

Third Base	PCT	G	PO	A	E	DP
Cesar	.922	50	29	89	10	11
De Goti	1.000	16	11	31	0	3
Gurriel	1.000	1	1	0	0	0
Michelena	.889	3	1	7	1	2
Rojas	.942	16	15	34	3	3
Sierra	.000	1	0	0	0	0
Tanielu	.923	11	7	17	2	1
Toro	.952	43	30	70	5	13

Shortstop	PCT	G	PO	A	E	DP
Correa	1.000	4	3	7	0	0
De Goti	.977	66	94	164	6	45

	PCT	G	PO	A	E	DP
Michelena	1.000	5	10	12	0	5
Rojas	1.000	9	11	15	0	6
Sierra	.956	60	53	142	9	26

Outfield	PCT	G	PO	A	E	DP
Alvarez	.965	31	51	4	2	1
Benedetti	.974	52	72	4	2	0
Celestino	1.000	3	4	0	0	0
Dawson	.984	29	61	0	1	0
Jones	1.000	7	6	0	0	0
Marisnick	1.000	2	2	1	0	0
McCormick	1.000	68	120	5	0	1
Pineda	1.000	15	25	0	0	0
Reddick	1.000	1	2	0	0	0
Rojas	.987	46	69	6	1	2
Straw	.975	63	145	10	4	4
Wrenn	.991	105	210	4	2	1

BUIES CREEK ASTROS

CAROLINA LEAGUE

HIGH CLASS A

Batting

	B-T	HT	WT	DOB	AVG	vLH	vRH	G	AB	R	H	2B	3B	HR	RBI	BB	HBP	SH	SF	SO	SB	CS	SLG	OBP
Adams, Jake	R-R	6-2	250	12-23-95	.222	.194	.234	63	216	28	48	12	0	7	23	22	3	0	2	60	8	5	.375	.300
Angarita, Alfredo	B-R	5-10	155	11-16-96	.232	.108	.293	32	112	18	26	4	0	0	10	9	0	0	0	31	6	1	.268	.289
Arauz, Jonathan	B-R	6-0	150	8-3-98	.167	.197	.157	71	233	25	39	10	3	4	18	16	1	2	1	36	1	2	.288	.223
Beer, Seth	L-R	6-3	195	9-18-96	.262	.172	.295	27	107	15	28	4	0	5	19	4	3	0	0	2	0	1	.439	.307
Bohanek, Cody	R-R	6-1	195	7-2-95	.212	.313	.169	65	212	28	45	7	0	2	20	27	8	0	1	56	6	4	.274	.323
Canelon, Carlos	R-R	5-11	168	12-14-94	.208	.225	.200	72	226	23	47	7	0	3	23	28	3	2	5	62	1	2	.279	.298
Dawson, Ronnie	L-R	6-2	225	5-19-95	.247	.237	.251	90	332	51	82	18	1	10	49	39	3	1	1	96	29	11	.398	.331
De La Cruz, Bryan	R-R	6-2	175	12-16-96	.297	.357	.270	54	182	26	54	11	1	0	30	27	2	0	2	41	7	2	.368	.390
Duarte, Osvaldo	R-R	5-9	160	1-18-96	.276	.275	.276	132	486	64	134	22	9	7	52	44	2	0	3	120	21	19	.401	.336
Julks, Corey	R-R	6-1	185	2-27-96	.282	.333	.258	61	227	39	64	18	2	6	31	28	2	0	3	58	16	5	.458	.362
Marquez, Orlando	R-R	5-10	180	3-12-96	.111	.000	.174	10	36	2	4	1	0	1	4	2	0	0	1	10	2	0	.222	.154
Mathis, Patrick	L-L	6-1	195		.100	1.000	.000	3	10	2	1	0	0	0	1	0	0	0	0	9	1	1	.100	.250
Matijevic, J.J.	L-R	6-0	206	11-14-95	.266	.187	.295	88	335	58	89	20	3	19	57	36	1	0	4	103	10	13	.513	.335
McCormick, Chas	R-L	6-0	190	4-19-95	.264	.289	.254	51	182	26	48	13	3	2	27	19	2	1	5	34	7	0	.401	.332
Meyers, Jacob	R-L	6-0	200	6-18-96	.250	.353	.214	60	196	28	49	13	0	3	24	28	2	1	6	40	3	7	.362	.341
Payano, Luis	R-R	6-1	175	5-12-96	.269	.286	.262	46	145	16	39	4	0	2	13	15	3	1	0	43	3	4	.338	.350
Robinson, Chuckie	R-R	5-11	225	12-14-94	.239	.319	.207	75	260	27	62	10	1	7	30	21	1	0	2	58	3	4	.365	.296
Rojas, Josh	L-R	6-1	185	6-30-94	.311	.364	.294	24	90	20	28	11	2	1	10	15	0	0	1	13	12	0	.511	.410
Shaver, Colton	R-R	6-1	210	9-18-95	.216	.375	.172	12	37	3	8	1	0	1	5	6	2	0	0	7	0	0	.324	.356
Sieber, Troy	L-R	5-11	215	6-22-95	.228	.257	.219	46	149	14	34	11	0	2	19	20	2	1	1	43	1	3	.342	.326
Sierra, Anibal	R-R	6-1	190	2-15-94	.245	.290	.227	35	106	17	26	7	0	4	15	13	3	0	0	38	2	5	.425	.355
Toro, Abraham	B-R	6-1	190	12-20-96	.257	.289	.244	83	296	54	76	20	1	14	56	45	5	0	3	62	5	1	.473	.361
Trompiz, Kristian	R-R	6-1	184	12-2-95	.184	.200	.178	55	179	17	33	4	1	0	16	17	1	0	0	33	11	5	.218	.259

Pitching

	B-T	HT	WT	DOB	W	L	ERA	G	GS	CG	SV	IP	H	R	ER	HR	BB	SO	AVG	vLH	vRH	K/9	BB/9
Adcock, Brett	L-L	6-1	225	8-28-95	5	3	2.54	16	9	0	1	67	32	23	19	1	36	67	.140	.041	.168	8.96	4.81
Alcala, Jorge	R-R	6-3	180	7-28-95	1	4	3.00	10	7	0	2	39	25	15	13	2	18	45	.183	.264	.131	10.47	4.19
Bailey, Brandon	R-R	5-10	175	10-19-94	5	8	2.49	20	16	0	0	98	69	30	27	6	43	113	.199	.176	.215	10.41	3.96
Balaguer, Jesus	R-R	6-4	195	8-12-93	3	4	5.13	23	0	0	1	33	20	20	19	4	32	43	.174	.163	.181	11.61	8.64
Bielak, Brandon	L-R	6-1	210	4-2-96	5	3	2.10	14	7	0	2	56	44	15	13	2	17	74	.217	.133	.266	11.96	2.75
Blanco, Ronel	R-R	6-0	180	8-31-93	5	1	1.73	19	0	0	4	36	18	10	7	1	18	41	.146	.136	.152	10.16	4.46
Bleday, Adam	L-L	5-11	175	11-2-94	0	0	7.27	7	0	0	0	9	4	8	7	2	12	9	.133	.111	.143	9.35	12.46
Bukauskas, J.B.	R-R	6-0	196	10-11-96	3	0	1.61	5	5	0	0	28	13	5	5	1	13	31	.138	.212	.098	9.96	4.18
Corniel, Robert	R-R	6-3	190	6-23-95	0	0	6.75	6	0	0	0	7	5	5	5	2	6	6	.217	.250	.200	8.10	8.10
DeJuneas, Tommy	R-R	6-1	175	10-24-95	1	2	2.20	12	0	0	3	16	12	7	4	1	13	16	.214	.143	.257	8.82	7.16
Duncan, Tanner	R-R	6-2	205	8-12-94	0	0	5.40	5	0	0	0	8	8	5	5	0	9		.242	.111	.292	9.72	6.48
Feldmann, Brendan	R-R	6-4	205	4-7-94	0	1	5.40	4	0	0	0	5	4	3	3	1	5	5	.222	.333	.167	9.00	9.00
Ferrell, Justin	R-R	6-7	205	4-21-94	1	0	1.62	7	0	0	2	17	6	3	3	2	4	24	.109	.087	.125	12.96	2.16
Hernandez, Jose	R-R	6-0	180	5-1-95	2	2	2.35	9	7	1	0	46	40	16	12	2	8	38	.234	.147	.302	7.43	1.57
Ivey, Tyler	R-R	6-4	195	5-12-96	3	3	2.69	15	12	1	1	70	50	26	21	5	21	82	.196	.247	.167	10.49	2.69
Javier, Cristian	R-R	6-1	170	3-26-97	5	4	3.41	14	11	0	0	61	44	26	23	6	27	66	.201	.258	.162	9.79	4.01
LaRue, Carson	R-R	6-1	175	3-6-96	8	7	4.18	25	17	0	0	116	109	56	54	13	40	99	.248	.219	.267	7.66	3.09
Martin, Corbin	R-R	6-2	200	12-28-95	2	0	0.00	4	3	0	1	19	4	1	0	0	7	26	.065	.074	.057	12.32	3.32
McKee, Colin	R-R	6-3	225	6-21-94	3	2	4.17	25	0	0	7	37	35	20	17	5	32	56	.238	.192	.260	13.25	5.40
Paredes, Enoli	R-R	5-11	165	9-28-95	4	1	1.35	8	0	0	0	13	6	3	2	1	3	19	.133	.130	.136	12.83	2.03
Perez, Hector	R-R	6-3	190	6-6-96	3	3	3.84	17	11	1	2	73	50	31	31	5	40	83	.196	.149	.220	10.28	4.95

	B-T	HT	WT	DOB	W	L	ERA	G	GS	CG	SV	IP	H	R	ER	HR	BB	SO	AVG	vLH	vRH	K/9	BB/9
Ramirez, Yohan	R-R	6-4	190	5-6-95	1	1	3.15	14	0	0	2	20	16	9	7	0	14	20	.222	.290	.171	9.00	6.30
Rodgers, Brady	R-R	6-2	210	9-17-90	0	0	1.50	4	4	0	0	12	12	2	2	0	0	7	.261	.200	.290	5.25	0.00
Saldana, Abdiel	R-R	5-11	195	3-13-96	8	2	3.25	26	14	0	0	108	106	42	39	1	26	100	.260	.243	.274	8.33	2.17
Sanabria, Carlos	R-R	6-0	165	1-24-97	1	0	4.50	11	0	0	2	18	16	9	9	1	12	18	.246	.231	.256	9.00	6.00
Sandoval, Patrick	L-L	6-3	190	10-18-96	2	0	2.74	5	3	0	1	23	12	8	7	1	4	26	.156	.167	.153	10.17	1.57
Scheetz, Kit	L-L	5-10	185	5-18-94	0	0	1.55	13	0	0	3	29	24	7	5	1	9	44	.220	.212	.224	13.66	2.79
Sierra, Carlos	R-R	6-3	195	10-18-94	1	1	3.32	10	0	0	2	22	13	9	8	1	10	21	.173	.179	.170	8.72	4.15
Solomon, Peter	R-R	6-4	201	8-16-96	1	0	1.96	5	3	0	0	23	16	5	5	0	4	26	.195	.196	.194	10.17	1.57
Valdez, Gabriel	R-R	6-2	185	10-25-95	7	5	3.86	23	8	0	0	75	63	38	32	7	28	60	.224	.224	.224	7.23	3.38

Fielding

Catcher	PCT	G	PO	A	E	DP	PB
Canelon	.995	66	586	66	3	5	8
Marquez	1.000	1	10	1	0	0	1
Robinson	.994	70	630	74	4	2	9

First Base	PCT	G	PO	A	E	DP
Adams	.988	63	464	36	6	33
Beer	.983	6	51	6	1	6
De La Cruz	1.000	11	84	2	0	5
Robinson	1.000	2	18	1	0	1
Rojas	.980	7	45	5	1	6
Sieber	1.000	33	219	9	0	20
Trompiz	.993	18	127	7	1	11

Second Base	PCT	G	PO	A	E	DP
Angarita	.988	24	44	38	1	6
Arauz	.667	1	1	1	1	0

	PCT	G	PO	A	E	DP
Bohanek	.994	40	55	103	1	17
Canelon	1.000	1	1	3	0	0
Duarte	.979	40	63	77	3	17
Rojas	.976	10	19	22	1	9
Trompiz	.974	23	27	47	2	12

Third Base	PCT	G	PO	A	E	DP
Bohanek	1.000	22	11	42	0	2
Duarte	.932	23	14	27	3	4
Rojas	.750	1	1	2	1	0
Shaver	1.000	12	7	12	0	1
Toro	.959	81	58	128	8	13
Trompiz	1.000	1	0	1	0	0

Shortstop	PCT	G	PO	A	E	DP
Angarita	1.000	2	4	5	0	0
Arauz	.991	70	77	142	2	25
Duarte	.908	27	36	53	9	12

	PCT	G	PO	A	E	DP
Rojas	1.000	1	2	3	0	0
Sierra	.970	32	28	68	3	17
Trompiz	.864	8	6	13	3	2

Outfield	PCT	G	PO	A	E	DP
Adams	.000	1	0	0	0	0
Beer	.950	13	19	0	1	0
Dawson	.995	88	198	4	1	1
De La Cruz	.961	37	70	3	3	0
Duarte	.986	43	68	1	1	0
Julks	.963	54	76	2	3	0
Mathis	1.000	3	8	0	0	0
Matijevic	.958	49	91	0	4	0
McCormick	.991	51	106	1	1	0
Meyers	.976	56	117	3	3	1
Payano	.929	25	39	0	3	0
Rojas	1.000	3	3	0	0	0

QUAD CITIES RIVER BANDITS
MIDWEST LEAGUE

LOW CLASS A

Batting	B-T	HT	WT	DOB	AVG	vLH	vRH	G	AB	R	H	2B	3B	HR	RBI	BB	HBP	SH	SF	SO	SB	CS	SLG	OBP
Adams, Jake	R-R	6-2	250	12-23-95	.277	.371	.254	48	177	29	49	11	2	8	31	19	1	0	1	53	1	1	.497	.349
Almonte, Marcos	R-R	5-10	163	3-28-96	.221	.150	.246	23	77	5	17	5	0	0	13	7	0	0	3	27	1	4	.286	.276
Angarita, Alfredo	B-R	5-10	155	11-16-96	.247	.200	.260	63	235	23	58	9	3	1	24	28	3	3	2	44	5	8	.323	.332
Arauz, Jonathan	B-R	6-0	150	8-3-98	.299	.315	.293	54	204	31	61	11	6	4	29	30	2	0	1	38	7	6	.441	.392
Beer, Seth	L-R	6-3	195	9-18-96	.348	.300	.359	29	112	15	39	7	0	3	16	15	4	0	0	17	1	0	.491	.443
Bohanek, Cody	R-R	6-1	195	7-2-95	.223	.171	.240	44	139	22	31	2	2	4	17	21	8	0	1	29	7	1	.353	.355
Bracamonte, Gabriel	R-R	5-9	165	5-15-95	.200	.250	.188	12	40	4	8	0	0	0	5	0	0	0	6	2	0	.200	.289
Castro, Ruben	L-R	5-10	182	7-10-96	.299	.229	.323	38	134	19	40	7	2	0	10	9	3	0	1	27	1	4	.381	.395
Costes, Marty	R-R	5-9	205	12-18-95	.243	.306	.228	49	181	32	44	11	3	3	13	18	15	0	0	29	8	2	.387	.360
Dawson, Trey	R-R	6-0	177	10-2-96	.162	.111	.179	12	37	7	6	0	0	0	2	8	1	0	0	14	0	1	.162	.326
De La Cruz, Bryan	R-R	6-2	175	12-16-96	.283	.264	.288	65	237	34	67	11	3	2	32	24	1	0	2	56	3	5	.380	.349
Garcia, Roman	R-R	6-1	210	11-22-95	.179	.000	.218	30	106	5	19	6	0	0	5	4	0	0		27	1	0	.236	.209
Hensley, David	R-R	6-6	190	3-28-96	.209	.225	.205	63	234	24	49	11	2	4	20	31	0	1	2	79	2	6	.325	.300
Julks, Corey	R-R	6-1	185	2-27-96	.259	.274	.253	64	232	40	60	12	2	4	31	27	2	0	0	50	14	6	.379	.341
Lacroix, Jonathan	L-R	6-1	195	2-8-97	.256	.245	.258	76	266	30	68	11	6	5	28	22	5	0	1	78	2	2	.399	.323
Matijevic, J.J.	L-R	6-0	206	11-14-95	.354	.167	.381	13	48	8	17	6	1	3	5	8	0	0	0	13	3	0	.708	.446
Mattix, Logan	R-R	6-0	185	5-16-96	.203	.167	.208	44	149	13	30	6	0	1	14	9	1	0	4	47	3	4	.262	.245
McKenna, Alex	R-R	6-2	200	9-6-97	.271	.214	.294	12	48	5	13	1	1	2	7	3	0	0		16	0	0	.458	.314
Meyers, Jacob	R-L	6-0	200	6-18-96	.302	.327	.295	61	225	35	68	18	3	5	23	7	1	1	43	13	7	.476	.383
Papierski, Michael	B-R	6-4	225	2-26-96	.185	.203	.180	93	297	44	55	12	0	5	27	64	8	0	0	69	4	1	.276	.344
Salazar, Cesar	L-R	5-9	185	3-15-96	.182	.250	.175	14	44	5	8	0	0	3	7	4	2	0	0	13	0	0	.386	.280
Schreiber, Scott	R-R	6-3	230	10-13-95	.219	.250	.210	60	219	20	48	10	1	6	15	4	0	0	87	5	2	.356	.282
Shaver, Colton	R-R	6-1	210	9-18-95	.223	.262	.214	95	327	44	73	18	1	15	50	34	9	0	8	84	2	2	.422	.307
Sierra, Miguelangel	R-R	5-11	165	12-2-97	.230	.301	.211	100	391	36	90	16	3	11	48	26	0	1	1	143	3	4	.371	.278
Taylor, Chandler	L-L	6-1	215	2-7-96	.214	.130	.237	63	215	26	46	9	2	9	27	46	0	0	1	92	3	8	.400	.351
Tovalin, Adrian	R-R	6-2	222	2-11-96	.215	.161	.227	46	163	21	35	8	2	3	21	16	6	0	0	59	0	1	.344	.308

Pitching	B-T	HT	WT	DOB	W	L	ERA	G	GS	CG	SV	IP	H	R	ER	HR	BB	SO	AVG	vLH	vRH	K/9	BB/9
Abreu, Bryan	R-R	6-1	175	4-22-97	4	1	1.64	10	5	0	3	38	22	8	7	2	17	68	.165	.213	.125	15.97	3.99
Aquino, Dariel	R-R	6-1	190	1-30-96	1	0	11.25	13	0	0	1	12	19	18	15	4	15	18	.359	.368	.353	13.50	11.25
Bleday, Adam	L-L	5-11	175	11-2-94	2	2	1.96	11	0	0	1	23	11	6	5	0	14	37	.141	.161	.128	14.48	5.48
Bukauskas, J.B.	R-R	6-0	196	10-11-96	1	2	4.20	4	4	0	0	15	15	7	7	0	7	21	.259	.286	.233	12.60	4.20
Castellanos, Humberto	R-R	5-11	170	4-3-98	3	2	2.09	21	0	0	4	43	40	18	10	5	11	48	.234	.271	.214	10.05	2.30
Collado, Willy	R-R	6-2	165	3-30-98	1	0	2.23	23	0	0	6	40	28	16	10	1	10	55	.192	.250	.156	12.27	2.23
Corniel, Robert	R-R	6-3	190	6-23-95	0	1	5.84	9	0	0	0	12	13	9	8	0	8	22	.265	.250	.280	16.05	5.84
Deetz, Dean	R-R	6-1	195	11-29-93	0	0	3.00	3	1	0	0	3	3	1	1	0	5	5	.300	.500	.167	21.00	15.00
Donato, Chad	R-R	6-0	180	6-3-95	6	0	2.04	12	10	0	2	62	38	15	14	2	19	77	.176	.172	.179	11.24	2.77
Duncan, Tanner	R-R	6-2	205	8-12-94	4	3	2.35	26	0	0	5	46	19	15	12	4	24	58	.121	.129	.115	11.35	4.70
Feldman, Brendan	R-R	6-4	205	4-7-94	0	0	1.64	23	0	0	7	33	24	9	6	1	11	44	.202	.149	.236	12.00	3.00
France, J.P.	R-R	6-0	216	4-4-95	1	0	0.90	4	1	0	0	10	6	1	1	0	4	14	.177	.133	.211	12.60	3.60
Garcia, Luis	R-R	6-1	216	12-13-96	7	2	2.48	19	10	0	1	69	58	23	19	4	33	70	.230	.265	.207	9.13	4.30
Hardy, Tim	L-L	6-7	250	3-1-96	0	0	2.84	6	0	0	0	13	12	4	4	1	6	23	.245	.143	.286	16.34	4.26

Name	B-T	HT	WT	DOB	W	L	ERA	G	GS	CG	SV	IP	H	R	ER	HR	BB	SO	AVG	vLH	vRH	K/9	BB/9
Hiraldo, Carlos	L-L	5-10	175	7-15-96	1	0	0.84	5	0	0	0	11	7	8	1	0	11	10	.163	.143	.172	8.44	9.28
Ivey, Tyler	R-R	6-4	195	5-12-96	1	3	3.46	9	6	0	2	42	36	20	16	2	8	53	.221	.222	.220	11.45	1.73
Javier, Cristian	R-R	6-1	170	3-26-97	2	2	1.82	11	7	0	1	49	28	11	10	3	23	80	.165	.194	.146	14.59	4.20
McKee, Colin	R-R	6-3	225	6-21-94	3	1	3.24	7	0	0	0	8	4	3	3	0	7	14	.148	.222	.111	15.12	7.56
Mushinski, Parker	L-L	6-0	225	11-22-95	4	2	2.33	27	12	0	2	89	62	27	23	4	45	114	.190	.187	.191	11.53	4.55
Paredes, Enoli	R-R	5-11	165	9-28-95	2	3	1.46	16	5	0	2	56	28	14	9	0	26	71	.143	.171	.127	11.48	4.20
Paulino, Hansel	R-R	6-2	170	1-3-96	2	1	3.57	9	0	0	1	18	16	8	7	2	5	19	.229	.214	.238	9.68	2.55
Ramirez, Yohan	R-R	6-4	190		5	7	2.95	15	10	0	1	58	40	26	19	6	28	62	.192	.199		9.62	4.34
Robles, Juan	R-R	6-0	185	11-6-97	2	0	4.05	3	0	0	0	11	3	3	0	2	6		.393	.444	.368	8.10	2.70
Rodriguez, Leovanny	R-R	6-0	160	6-13-96	4	7	4.11	19	16	0	0	92	92	47	42	9	23	102	.261	.272	.255	9.98	2.25
Rosado, Cesar	R-R	6-1	172	6-22-96	5	4	4.15	27	18	0	2	108	96	54	50	5	63	102	.242	.256	.233	8.47	5.23
Sanabria, Carlos	R-R	6-0	165	1-24-97	2	1	3.86	25	0	0	8	37	30	19	16	5	11	55	.217	.182	.234	13.26	2.65
Sandoval, Edgardo	R-R	6-0	170	7-9-96	1	3	3.82	7	5	0	1	31	31	15	13	2	10	43	.261	.170	.333	12.62	2.93
Sandoval, Patrick	L-L	6-3	190	10-18-96	7	1	2.49	14	10	0	1	65	58	22	18	4	11	71	.231	.182	.249	9.83	1.52
Solis, Jairo	R-R	6-2	160	12-22-99	2	3	3.55	13	11	0	0	51	49	23	20	1	32	51	.259	.253	.263	9.06	5.68
Solomon, Peter	R-R	6-4	201	8-16-96	8	1	2.43	19	10	0	0	78	62	26	21	2	28	88	.218	.226	.212	10.20	3.24
Watts, Cole	R-L	6-4	205	11-2-95	0	0	7.88	9	0	0	0	8	18	13	7	1	10	11	.419	.417	.419	12.38	11.25

Fielding

C: Bracamonte 11, Castro 30, Papierski 89, Salazar 10. **1B:** Adams 37, Beer 7, Bracamonte 1, Garcia 19, Papierski 2, Schreiber 44, Shaver 32, Tovalin 1. **2B:** Almonte 11, Angarita 39, Arauz 17, Bohanek 19, Castro 2, Dawson 5, Hensley 10, Shaver 3, Sierra 34. **3B:** Almonte 3, Angarita 14, Arauz 3, Bohanek 9, Dawson 1, Garcia 1, Hensley 25, Shaver 46, Sierra 1, Tovalin 38. **SS:** Almonte 1, Angarita 1, Arauz 33, Bohanek 14, Dawson 4, Hensley 22, Sierra 65. **OF:** Almonte 6, Angarita 6, Beer 19, Costes 41, De La Cruz 57, Julks 53, Lacroix 64, Matijevic 12, Mattix 41, McKenna 8, Meyers 60, Schreiber 7, Shaver 1, Taylor 52.

TRI-CITY VALLEYCATS   SHORT-SEASON
NEW YORK-PENN LEAGUE

Batting	B-T	HT	WT	DOB	AVG	vLH	vRH	G	AB	R	H	2B	3B	HR	RBI	BB	HBP	SH	SF	SO	SB	CS	SLG	OBP
Beer, Seth	L-R	6-3	195	9-18-96	.293	.000	.324	11	41	9	12	3	0	4	7	6	4	0	0	10	0	0	.659	.431
Campos, Oscar	R-R	5-10	170	12-8-96	.233	.241	.231	43	150	15	35	10	0	3	22	7	3	1	1	20	2	0	.360	.280
Carrasco, Deury	L-R	5-9	165	9-20-99	.250	.200	.263	7	24	3	6	2	0	0	2	1	0	0	0	10	0	1	.333	.280
Carrillo, Jose	R-R	6-0	178	1-24-98	.250	.333	.214	6	20	2	5	1	0	1	2	1	1	0	0	9	1	0	.450	.318
Celestino, Gilberto	R-L	6-0	170	2-13-99	.323	.167	.371	34	127	18	41	8	0	4	21	10	4	0	1	25	14	0	.480	.387
Costes, Marty	R-R	5-9	205	12-18-95	.071	.000	.100	4	14	2	1	0	1	0	2	1	0	0	0	1	0	0	.214	.133
Davis, Kyle	R-R	6-0	195	12-30-95	.500	—	.500	1	2	1	1	0	0	1	2	2	0	0	0	0	0	0	2.000	.750
Dawson, Trey	R-B	6-0	177	10-2-96	.232	.265	.222	43	142	19	33	9	0	1	13	31	0	0	2	40	9	1	.317	.366
Dennis, Austin	R-R	5-11	170	6-6-97	.242	.140	.273	53	186	28	45	11	0	1	13	19	1	0	2	30	16	4	.317	.313
Encarnacion, Luis	R-B	6-2	185	8-9-97	.213	.194	.219	44	150	18	32	6	0	10	33	22	0	0	2	62	1	2	.453	.310
Ferguson, Drew	R-R	5-11	180	8-3-92	.300	.429	.231	6	20	2	6	3	0	1	4	3	0	0	1	7	0	2	.600	.375
Goetzman, Granden	R-R	6-4	200	11-14-92	.125	.000	.167	2	8	2	1	0	0	0	0	1	0	0	0	2	0	0	.125	.222
Holderbach, Alex	R-R	6-0	205	12-9-96	.201	.180	.210	42	144	15	29	8	2	3	23	12	2	0	2	39	2	0	.347	.269
Machado, Carlos	R-R	6-2	170	6-5-98	.304	.326	.298	52	194	25	59	10	1	3	28	14	0	0	3	26	5	2	.412	.346
Marquez, Orlando	R-R	5-10	180	3-12-96	.182	1.000	.100	4	11	1	2	0	0	1	3	1	0	0	0	4	0	0	.455	.250
Mattix, Logan	R-R	6-1	195	5-16-96	.254	.214	.267	15	59	9	15	4	0	2	6	0	0	0	0	15	4	0	.424	.254
McKenna, Alex	R-R	6-2	200	9-6-97	.328	.357	.318	32	116	14	38	7	1	5	21	11	9	0	1	24	6	5	.535	.423
Pena, Jeremy	R-R	6-0	179	9-22-97	.250	.321	.232	36	136	22	34	5	0	1	10	18	1	0	1	19	3	0	.309	.340
Perry, Nathan	L-R	6-2	195	7-7-99	.172	.231	.157	18	64	5	11	2	1	2	7	4	0	0	1	13	0	0	.328	.217
Pineda, Andy	L-R	6-1	165	11-11-96	.253	.353	.230	30	91	15	23	4	2	1	4	10	2	0	0	27	9	3	.374	.340
Pineda, Juan	R-R	5-10	145	1-31-98	.198	.250	.183	30	91	8	18	2	0	0	9	9	2	0	2	30	2	1	.220	.279
Rodriguez, Ramiro	L-L	5-10	145	2-2-98	.216	.171	.231	55	171	26	37	11	2	2	13	28	7	0	0	47	8	4	.339	.350
Salazar, Cesar	L-R	5-9	185	3-15-96	.206	.046	.275	22	73	5	15	6	0	0	10	4	4	0	0	15	1	1	.288	.284
Santana, Andres	R-R	6-1	180	11-5-98	.400	.000	.500	2	5	0	2	1	0	0	0	0	1	0	0	2	0	0	.600	.500
Valdez, Enmanuel	L-R	5-9	171	12-28-98	.244	.213	.254	63	238	40	58	16	1	8	22	22	2	0	2	53	11	6	.420	.311
Wielansky, Michael	R-B	6-2	175	3-18-97	.204	.231	.198	43	137	24	28	7	1	2	13	18	2	0	2	36	4	1	.314	.302

Pitching	B-T	HT	WT	DOB	W	L	ERA	G	GS	CG	SV	IP	H	R	ER	HR	BB	SO	AVG	vLH	vRH	K/9	BB/9
Abreu, Bryan	R-R	6-1	175	4-22-97	2	0	1.13	4	2	0	0	16	11	3	2	2	6	22	.196	.233	.154	12.38	3.38
Billingsley, Jacob	R-R	5-11	185	7-27-94	0	1	5.63	9	0	0	1	16	20	10	10	1	4	15	.294	.344	.250	8.44	2.25
Bravo, Jose	R-R	6-3	185	6-10-97	0	0	9.00	3	1	0	0	7	10	7	7	3	2	8	.345	.294	.417	10.29	2.57
Bukauskas, J.B.	R-R	6-0	196	10-11-96	0	0	0.00	3	3	0	0	8	8	0	0	0	2	9	.258	.214	.294	9.72	2.16
Cabral, Riley	R-R	5-11	200	1-25-97	1	0	3.57	16	0	0	0	18	21	11	7	0	11	17	.284	.306	.263	8.66	5.60
Castellanos, Humberto	R-R	5-11	170	4-3-98	0	0	0.00	2	0	0	1	2	1	0	0	0	0	2	.143	.000	.250	9.00	0.00
Conine, Brett	R-R	6-3	210	10-16-96	1	1	1.99	11	0	0	0	32	23	9	7	0	11	37	.198	.250	.156	10.52	3.13
Conn, Devin	R-R	6-0	170	4-3-97	0	2	2.65	12	2	0	0	17	15	5	5	0	9	13	.140	.167	.111	6.88	4.76
Daniels, Brett	R-R	6-0	170	2-29-96	3	0	1.62	11	2	0	0	33	21	11	6	5	7	36	.175	.175	.172	9.72	1.89
De Paula, Luis	R-R	6-0	160	11-15-96	1	5	7.52	18	0	0	3	20	22	20	17	2	20	25	.275	.297	.256	11.07	8.85
Deason, Cody	R-R	6-4	205	12-26-96	1	0	4.00	9	4	0	0	18	20	9	8	0	10	14	.303	.310	.297	7.00	5.00
Donato, Chad	R-R	6-3	195	8-6-95	3	0	0.00	3	2	0	0	16	8	2	0	0	3	21	.143	.053	.189	11.81	1.69
Dubin, Shawn	R-R	6-1	160	9-6-95	2	1	4.60	14	5	0	0	29	23	15	15	4	11	31	.215	.267	.177	9.51	3.38
France, J.P.	R-R	6-2	216	4-4-95	1	0	0.00	6	0	0	2	8	4	0	0	0	2	14	.148	.250	.067	15.75	2.25
Freure, R.J.	R-R	6-2	210	7-6-97	3	0	0.98	11	3	0	0	28	17	4	3	2	13	29	.172	.188	.157	9.43	4.23
Garcia, Luis	R-R	6-2	216	12-13-96	0	0	0.00	5	3	0	0	16	7	3	0	0	8	28	.121	.087	.143	15.43	4.41
Gonzalez, Joey	R-R	5-11	175	1-10-97	0	0	0.00	2	0	0	0	4	0	0	0	0	3		.000	.000	.000	6.75	0.00
Hansen, Austin	R-R	6-0	195	8-25-96	2	3	1.76	14	2	0	2	31	14	7	6	2	13	45	.130	.163	.102	13.21	3.82
Hardman, Ian	R-R	6-5	240	9-16-95	0	1	8.10	5	0	0	0	3	4	3	3	0	8	5	.308	.600	.125	13.50	21.60

Name	B-T	HT	WT	DOB	W	L	ERA	G	GS	CG	SV	IP	H	R	ER	HR	BB	SO	AVG	vLH	vRH	K/9	BB/9
Hardy, Tim	L-L	6-7	250	3-1-96	2	2	1.50	12	1	0	4	18	13	6	3	0	9	26	.203	.200	.205	13.00	4.50
Henderson, Layne	R-R	6-4	200	6-8-96	0	0	5.14	4	0	0	1	7	5	4	4	0	4	9	.208	.125	.375	11.57	5.14
Hernandez, Jose	R-R	6-0	180	5-1-95	0	0	2.38	4	4	0	0	11	15	3	3	0	2	10	.313	.217	.400	7.94	1.59
Hiraldo, Carlos	L-L	5-10	175	7-15-96	4	0	3.32	13	4	0	0	43	45	22	16	1	21	41	.268	.271	.266	8.52	4.36
House, Alex	R-R	6-3	194	8-24-96	0	2	1.80	3	3	0	0	5	5	2	1	1	1	7	.263	.375	.182	12.60	1.80
Jaquez, Ernesto	R-R	6-2	190	6-11-99	1	1	19.64	2	1	0	0	4	6	9	8	2	3	4	.333	.400	.250	9.82	7.36
Lopez, Juan Pablo	R-R	6-4	170	2-17-99	4	1	3.70	16	3	0	2	41	46	27	17	3	13	30	.275	.264	.281	6.53	2.83
Moclair, Mark	R-R	6-2	205	3-13-97	2	4	4.61	14	5	0	0	27	20	16	14	0	30	48	.213	.111	.276	15.80	9.88
Paulino, Hansel	R-R	6-2	170	1-3-96	0	1	3.57	9	1	0	1	23	15	9	9	3	6	26	.192	.273	.133	10.32	2.38
Ramirez, Manny	R-R	5-11	170	11-21-99	0	0	0.00	2	1	0	0	5	1	0	0	0	4	9	.063	.000	.167	15.19	6.75
Rivera, Jose Alberto	R-R	6-3	160	2-14-97	1	2	4.50	10	1	0	0	10	9	6	5	2	8	14	.237	.227	.250	12.60	7.20
Robles, Juan	R-R	6-0	185	11-6-97	0	1	8.22	2	2	0	0	8	8	7	7	1	4	9	.267	.364	.211	10.57	4.70
Rodgers, Brady	R-R	6-2	210	9-17-90	0	0	18.00	1	1	0	0	2	3	4	4	1	1	3	.333	.667	.167	13.50	4.50
Rodriguez, Nivaldo	R-R	6-1	170	4-16-97	4	1	2.91	14	7	0	1	56	45	18	18	3	13	50	.218	.257	.181	8.08	2.10
Ruppenthal, Matt	R-R	6-4	225	10-21-95	0	0	6.35	6	1	0	0	6	7	5	4	0	3	5	.304	.364	.250	7.94	4.76
Sandoval, Edgardo	R-R	6-0	170	7-9-96	0	1	4.50	2	1	0	0	6	4	3	3	0	3	10	.182	.375	.071	15.00	4.50
Tejada, Felipe	R-R	6-1	190	2-27-98	4	5	4.50	15	7	0	2	54	51	29	27	4	16	66	.243	.277	.216	11.00	2.67

Fielding

C: Campos 29, Holderbach 22, Marquez 1, Perry 10, Salazar 15. **1B:** Beer 4, Campos 9, Carrillo 2, Encarnacion 37, Holderbach 13, Perry 4, Pineda 9, Wielansky 1. **2B:** Dawson 9, Dennis 21, Pena 4, Pineda 3, Valdez 21, Wielansky 18. **3B:** Davis 1, Dawson 7, Dennis 2, Pineda 12, Valdez 39, Wielansky 15. **SS:** Carrasco 7, Dawson 26, Pena 32, Pineda 5, Wielansky 6. **OF:** Beer 7, Campos 1, Celestino 31, Costes 3, Dennis 22, Ferguson 5, Goetzman 1, Machado 43, Mattix 15, McKenna 30, Pineda 26, Rodriguez 49, Santana 2.

GCL ASTROS   ROOKIE
GULF COAST LEAGUE

Batting	B-T	HT	WT	DOB	AVG	vLH	vRH	G	AB	R	H	2B	3B	HR	RBI	BB	HBP	SH	SF	SO	SB	CS	SLG	OBP
Abreu, Wilyer	L-L	6-0	180	6-24-99	.223	.370	.188	41	139	22	31	11	0	0	16	18	0	2	1	32	8	4	.302	.310
Carrasco, Deury	L-R	5-9	165	9-20-99	.242	.107	.283	38	120	17	29	3	5	1	8	16	1	1	0	34	17	6	.375	.336
Castillo, Gerry	R-R	5-10	170	10-3-97	.160	.000	.250	19	25	3	4	1	0	0	1	3	0	0	0	7	0	0	.200	.250
Ceuta, Yorbin	B-R	6-0	165	1-14-00	.206	.235	.200	34	107	10	22	2	2	0	8	15	0	1	1	13	1	1	.262	.301
Cortez, Cesar	R-R	6-0	165	4-1-99	.133	.000	.222	5	15	1	2	0	0	0	0	1	1	0	0	6	0	0	.133	.235
Diaz, Carlos	L-L	6-2	175	7-15-99	.202	.286	.189	29	104	14	21	2	0	0	7	11	0	0	0	36	6	1	.221	.278
Martinez, Hector	R-R	6-1	185	7-6-98	.207	.250	.198	40	121	25	25	7	0	2	14	19	3	0	1	52	5	2	.334	.326
Mathis, Patrick	L-L	6-1	190	3-23-96	.191	.000	.333	6	21	5	4	2	0	1	3	2	0	0	0	8	0	0	.429	.261
Mendoza, Sean	B-R	5-8	150	6-2-00	.270	.174	.294	34	115	14	31	6	1	0	10	18	0	1	0	17	6	1	.339	.368
Nova, Freudis	R-R	6-1	180	1-12-00	.308	.208	.328	41	146	21	45	3	1	6	28	6	1	0	4	21	9	5	.466	.331
Paulino, Juan	L-R	5-11	192	12-10-97	.130	.200	.122	24	54	6	7	2	1	1	5	13	3	0	1	23	1	2	.259	.324
Perez, Joe	R-R	6-2	215	8-12-99	.364	.000	.571	4	11	1	4	0	0	0	0	3	0	0	0	1	0	0	.364	.500
Perry, Nathan	L-R	6-2	195	7-7-99	.244	.167	.256	33	90	5	22	6	2	0	13	12	1	0	1	20	1	1	.356	.337
Ramirez, Juan	L-L	5-9	160	4-9-99	.248	.222	.255	38	133	13	33	8	3	0	16	12	1	1	1	21	3	5	.353	.313
Ramirez, Yeuris	R-R	6-0	170	11-28-98	.172	.192	.167	39	128	13	22	4	3	3	18	13	6	1	2	42	4	2	.320	.275
Rodriguez, Nerio	R-R	6-2	205	9-21-99	.189	.150	.198	40	106	13	20	8	0	0	8	14	0	0	0	38	0	0	.264	.283
Sanchez, Rhandall	R-R	6-1	180	11-29-98	.171	.125	.183	26	76	6	13	2	0	0	3	6	0	0	0	20	0	1	.197	.232
Santana, Andres	R-R	6-1	180	11-5-98	.175	.154	.182	35	114	7	20	9	0	1	9	7	2	0	1	28	1	0	.281	.234
Urdaneta, Ronaldo	B-R	5-10	155	11-18-98	.274	.300	.266	37	124	19	34	9	1	2	16	14	1	0	0	31	15	2	.411	.353

Pitching	B-T	HT	WT	DOB	W	L	ERA	G	GS	CG	SV	IP	H	R	ER	HR	BB	SO	AVG	vLH	vRH	K/9	BB/9
Bello, Daniel	L-L	6-2	197	1-8-97	1	1	6.23	12	0	0	0	17	20	14	12	1	14	21	.278	.353	.255	10.90	7.27
Bermudez, Jonathan	L-L	6-2	170	10-16-95	1	1	3.29	10	0	0	0	14	13	8	5	1	5	10	.265	.222	.275	6.59	3.29
Bravo, Jose	R-R	6-3	185	6-10-97	2	4	3.06	10	6	0	0	35	34	14	12	0	1	26	.256	.192	.296	6.62	0.25
Bukauskas, J.B.	R-R	6-0	196	10-11-96	0	0	10.80	1	1	0	0	2	5	2	2	0	0	2	.500	.000	.556	10.80	0.00
Chavez, Jervic	L-L	6-0	175	2-8-97	1	1	3.18	15	0	0	6	17	12	6	6	0	7	14	.218	.250	.213	7.41	3.71
Figueroa, Miguel	R-R	6-2	203	3-22-97	2	1	2.53	10	2	0	0	21	13	8	6	0	14	21	.173	.167	.177	8.86	5.91
Garcia, Freylin	R-R	6-3	170	12-6-97	0	0	2.89	7	0	0	1	9	8	6	3	0	8	7	.242	.333	.333	6.75	7.71
Gonzalez, Joey	R-R	5-11	175	1-10-97	4	2	1.72	13	0	0	3	16	13	9	3	0	4	22	.210	.091	.275	12.64	2.30
Guerrero, Fredis	R-R	6-3	175	2-16-96	0	0	3.86	2	0	0	0	2	3	1	1	0	0	0	.300	.750	.000	0.00	0.00
Henderson, Layne	R-R	6-4	200	6-8-96	3	0	3.93	7	0	0	0	18	15	9	8	0	10	17	.231	.217	.238	8.35	4.91
Jaquez, Ernesto	R-R	6-2	190	6-11-99	0	0	1.06	5	1	0	0	17	9	3	2	1	5	21	.150	.158	.146	11.12	2.65
Jimenez, Alfredi	R-R	6-1	175	10-19-99	1	3	3.00	3	1	0	0	12	8	4	4	2	3	12	.191	.231	.172	9.00	2.25
Macuare, Angel	R-R	6-2	188	3-3-00	4	3	3.43	12	4	0	1	39	44	19	15	2	17	40	.282	.239	.300	9.15	3.89
Martes, Francis	R-R	6-1	225	11-24-95	0	0	0.00	1	1	0	0	1	1	0	0	0	0	1	.500	.500	.000	9.00	0.00
Medina, Fredy	R-R	5-10	160	9-26-97	1	1	2.25	9	3	0	0	28	17	7	7	1	14	34	.179	.205	.161	10.93	4.50
Mejias, Christian	R-R	6-0	160	5-19-99	1	1	5.27	12	0	0	0	27	32	16	16	0	17	30	.281	.267	.286	9.92	5.60
Navas, Javier	L-L	5-11	165		0	0	9.00	1	0	0	0	1	1	1	1	0	1	1	.500	1.000	.000	9.00	9.00
Paulino, David	R-R	6-7	222	2-6-94	0	0	3.00	3	3	0	0	9	7	5	3	0	1	10	.226	.200	.250	10.00	1.00
Ramirez, Manny	R-R	5-11	170	11-21-99	1	1	4.76	10	5	0	0	34	29	22	18	0	15	46	.232	.200	.240	12.18	3.97
Ramsey, Matt	R-R	5-11	205	9-24-89	1	0	0.00	5	2	0	0	6	5	1	0	0	1	9	.250	.250	.250	13.50	0.00
Rivera, Jose Alberto	R-R	6-3	160	2-14-97	1	2	3.23	10	4	0	0	39	30	16	14	4	6	39	.206	.222	.202	9.00	1.38
Robaina, Julio	L-L	5-11	170	3-23-01	0	4	6.84	11	4	0	2	25	22	20	19	1	17	27	.225	.261	.213	9.72	6.12
Rodriguez, Elian	R-R	6-2	205	3-10-97	1	4	5.09	10	4	0	0	23	16	17	13	1	26	19	.205	.160	.226	7.43	10.17
Ruppenthal, Matt	R-R	6-4	225	10-21-95	0	0	3.86	2	2	0	0	7	3	3	3	0	3	6	.222	.500	.143	19.29	3.86
Sandoval, Edgardo	R-R	6-0	170	7-9-96	1	0	2.00	4	4	0	0	9	11	2	2	0	1	6	.314	.308	.318	6.00	1.00
Schroeder, Jayson	R-R	6-2	195	11-14-99	0	0	1.50	7	5	0	0	18	13	3	3	0	9	18	.220	.261	.194	9.00	4.50
Serrano, Kyle	R-R	6-1	190	7-6-95	1	0	2.70	4	0	0	0	3	2	3	1	0	2	5	.154	.000	.182	13.50	5.40

	B-T	HT	WT	DOB		W	L	ERA	G	GS	CG	SV	IP	H	R	ER	HR	BB	SO	AVG	vLH	vRH	K/9	BB/9
Sierra, Carlos	R-R	6-3	195	10-18-94		0	0	0.00	2	0	0	0	3	1	0	0	0	1	2	.111	.000	.167	6.00	3.00
Solano, Bryan	R-R	6-4	190	1-25-98		2	1	3.38	13	0	0	2	24	22	9	9	0	6	22	.256	.320	.230	8.25	2.25

Fielding

C: Castillo 19, Paulino 9, Perry 22, Rodriguez 30, Sanchez 10. **1B:** Mendoza 1, Paulino 9, Ramirez 15, Sanchez 15, Urdaneta 16. **2B:** Carrasco 12, Ceuta 14, Mendoza 13, Nova 9, Urdaneta 10. **3B:** Ceuta 8, Mendoza 16, Perez 4, Ramirez 22, Urdaneta 9. **SS:** Carrasco 18, Ceuta 13, Mendoza 3, Nova 24. **OF:** Abreu 37, Cortez 3, Diaz 26, Martinez 31, Mathis 4, Ramirez 36, Ramirez 1, Santana 34, Urdaneta 2.

DSL ASTROS   ROOKIE
DOMINICAN SUMMER LEAGUE

Batting	B-T	HT	WT	DOB	AVG	vLH	vRH	G	AB	R	H	2B	3B	HR	RBI	BB	HBP	SH	SF	SO	SB	CS	SLG	OBP
Alvarez, Jose	R-R	6-1	180	6-4-00	.359	.370	.356	44	131	23	47	8	0	0	15	17	2	0	2	27	5	2	.420	.434
Barajas, Luis	R-R	6-1	190	7-13-98	.333	.000	.500	1	3	0	1	0	0	0	1	0	0	0	0	0	0	1	.333	.333
Bermudez, Javier	B-R	5-11	155	1-2-99	.184	.250	.170	54	163	21	30	5	1	1	12	20	6	0	3	39	9	8	.245	.292
Carrillo, Yefri	R-R	6-2	170	1-13-01	.221	.370	.180	59	213	33	47	9	3	1	11	28	7	0	0	66	18	7	.305	.331
Castillo, Abraham	R-R	6-0	180	12-5-00	.232	.281	.220	51	155	20	36	5	1	0	14	24	3	0	1	38	6	2	.277	.344
Castillo, Jeury	L-R	5-10	170	1-14-00	.240	.267	.233	45	150	12	36	6	0	0	11	15	1	3	1	36	5	3	.280	.311
Cortabarria, Yimmi	R-R	6-2	175	1-10-01	.156	.036	.182	52	160	18	25	5	0	2	14	21	3	1	2	73	3	2	.225	.263
Espinosa, Rolando	R-R	6-0	177	1-5-01	.170	.135	.179	59	188	14	32	5	2	1	10	18	1	1	1	54	10	6	.234	.245
Grullon, Sebastian	R-R	6-1	170	7-19-01	.204	.250	.195	30	103	6	21	1	0	0	9	4	0	1	0	23	7	5	.214	.234
Hurtado, Carlos	R-R	6-0	170	5-18-01	.200	.240	.190	39	120	9	24	12	0	1	14	9	1	0	3	18	5	3	.325	.256
Lopez, Jonarkys	R-R	5-11	160	8-13-01	.154	.000	.177	24	39	5	6	2	0	0	4	8	1	0	1	14	2	0	.205	.306
Marte, Junior	L-R	6-2	165	4-14-00	.172	.192	.167	42	128	12	22	6	0	0	6	17	0	1	0	37	8	5	.219	.269
Mascai, Victor	L-R	6-2	188	2-10-01	.259	.273	.255	56	201	24	52	9	1	5	29	23	2	0	3	47	8	2	.388	.336
Mendoza, Jose	R-R	5-11	165	6-19-01	.273	.348	.253	33	110	13	30	2	0	0	8	14	0	0	2	16	8	3	.291	.349
Morillo, Enmanuel	R-R	6-0	175	12-6-00	.239	.240	.239	43	142	15	34	6	0	1	17	12	8	1	0	24	4	2	.303	.333
Pinto, Franklin	R-R	6-1	160	4-26-01	.241	.278	.235	34	116	13	28	1	1	0	6	11	4	0	2	16	14	3	.267	.323
Toro, Ricardo	R-R	6-1	170	2-24-01	.161	.105	.172	41	112	10	18	4	0	0	9	11	11	0	1	24	3	2	.196	.296
Van Der Wijst, Marco	R-R	5-10	180	2-23-98	.231	.125	.278	10	26	5	6	2	1	0	3	3	1	1	1	8	0	1	.385	.323

Pitching	B-T	HT	WT	DOB	W	L	ERA	G	GS	CG	SV	IP	H	R	ER	HR	BB	SO	AVG	vLH	vRH	K/9	BB/9
Bellozo, Valente	R-R	5-10	170	1-4-00	2	1	1.74	14	8	0	1	52	29	11	10	0	16	42	.164	.167	.163	7.32	2.79
Betances, Jose	R-R	6-0	170	10-17-99	0	0	6.75	10	0	0	0	11	13	10	8	0	6		.325	.333	.321	5.06	7.59
Blanco, Alex	R-R	6-1	180	10-3-97	1	1	7.45	9	0	0	0	10	10	8	0	11	11		.286	.250	.296	10.24	10.24
Cobos, Franny	R-R	5-9	170	2-1-01	1	2	0.60	14	5	0	1	45	29	4	3	0	7	39	.192	.159	.206	7.80	1.40
Garcia, Ronny	R-R	6-3	170	12-2-99	0	2	2.92	17	0	0	2	12	16	12	4	0	9	14	.308	.308	.308	10.22	6.57
Gonzalez, Flaer	R-R	5-10	160	9-27-96	1	1	4.05	15	0	0	3	20	29	16	9	1	8	17	.345	.267	.389	7.65	3.60
Hernandez, Jose Antonio	R-R	6-0	161	6-18-99	4	4	1.90	15	7	0	0	47	41	17	10	0	18	41	.236	.277	.221	7.80	3.42
Jaquez, Ernesto	R-R	6-2	190	6-11-99	4	0	0.25	9	4	0	0	36	10	2	1	0	9	49	.086	.083	.088	12.25	2.25
Jimenez, Alfredi	R-R	6-1	175	10-19-99	1	2	1.25	11	4	1	2	43	27	9	6	0	10	51	.177	.163	.183	10.59	2.08
Leon, Ricardo	L-L	6-4	165	3-26-01	2	1	4.91	8	1	0	0	11	7	12	6	0	29	11	.212	.250	.207	9.00	23.73
Lopez, Jairo	R-R	5-11	150	11-21-00	1	3	3.32	14	0	0	0	43	37	24	16	1	15	41	.222	.163	.246	8.52	3.12
Mejias, Christian	R-R	6-0	160	5-19-99	0	0	0.00	3	1	0	1	9	3	1	0	0	3	11	.097	.111	.091	11.00	3.00
Mezquita, Cristofer	L-L	6-0	175	6-6-00	2	1	2.92	12	0	0	1	12	10	9	4	0	9	9	.217	.000	.270	6.57	6.57
Molero, Jeremy	R-R	6-2	170	11-8-99	0	4	2.70	13	0	0	0	13	7	11	4	0	17	17	.143	.211	.100	11.48	11.48
Oberto, Wender	R-R	6-0	170	12-9-99	4	3	1.91	15	6	0	1	57	45	12	12	1	18	39	.226	.224	.227	6.19	2.86
Pereira, Jherson	R-R	6-2	175	1-27-97	0	3	4.26	13	3	0	1	32	44	29	15	1	14	25	.324	.209	.376	7.11	3.98
Placencia, Antonio	R-R	6-0	170	8-17-99	1	0	1.80	2	0	0	0	5	3	1	1	0	1	3	.167	.000	.250	5.40	1.80
Reina, Fabricio	R-R	6-3	175	2-26-00	4	7	9.66	14	6	0	0	32	38	42	34	1	40	27	.317	.189	.374	7.67	11.37
Solano, Bryan	R-R	6-4	190	1-25-98	0	0	0.00	2	0	0	0	2	2	1	0	0	3	3	.200	.333	.143	11.57	11.57
Taveras, Diosmerky	R-R	6-3	180	9-23-99	2	3	4.14	15	4	0	3	37	28	19	17	0	27	35	.211	.233	.200	8.51	6.57
Tokar, Heitor	R-R	6-6	256	10-25-00	0	1	1.66	13	0	0	0	43	27	11	8	0	6	35	.181	.270	.152	7.27	1.25
Torres, Jojanse	R-R	6-2	175	8-4-95	1	2	2.20	13	8	0	1	41	36	11	10	1	8	48	.232	.230	.223	10.54	1.76

Fielding

C: Alvarez 32, Hurtado 34, Lopez 12, Toro 21. **1B:** Alvarez 9, Barajas 1, Castillo 2, Espinosa 1, Hurtado 1, Mascai 35, Morillo 17, Toro 14. **2B:** Bermudez 6, Castillo 21, Espinosa 3, Grullon 17, Marte 12, Mendoza 7, Morillo 14, Van Der Wijst 2. **3B:** Bermudez 8, Castillo 16, Espinosa 24, Grullon 2, Marte 16, Mendoza 6, Morillo 5, Van Der Wijst 2. **SS:** Bermudez 26, Espinosa 19, Grullon 1, Marte 11, Mendoza 20. **OF:** Bermudez 8, Carrillo 58, Castillo 51, Castillo 3, Cortabarria 50, Espinosa 15, Mascai 10, Pinto 32, Van Der Wijst 2.

Kansas City Royals

SEASON IN A SENTENCE: Just three years after winning the World Series, the Royals couldn't keep the band together, with much of the 2015 core departing for free agency and launching the organization into a major rebuilding phase.

HIGH POINT: Fitting for a 104-loss team, the Royals' must successful moment didn't come on the field, but rather in the draft room. On June 4, the Royals, armed with five picks in the first two rounds, jump-started the remaking of their farm system by selecting a full rotation of advanced college pitchers, including first-rounders Brady Singer, Jackson Kowar and Daniel Lynch, who all rank among the organization's top prospects.

LOW POINT: By the end of April, the Royals had already suffered a nine-game losing streak and were 14 games below .500, a telling sign of what was to come. In all, the Royals' 58-104 record was the organization's worst mark since losing 106 games in 2005, and it was only the third time since the franchise's inaugural season in 1969 that the franchise lost more than 100 games.

NOTABLE ROOKIES: The Royals drafted Brad Keller in the Rule 5 draft in December, and his acquisition turned out to be a steal. The former D-backs righthander moved into the Royals' rotation in June and turned out to be one of the better pitchers on the staff. He finished with a 9-6 record and led all qualified Royals pitchers with a 3.08 ERA. First baseman Ryan O'Hearn got the call to Kansas City on July 31 and showed more over-the-fence power than he did in the minors, blasting 12 home runs in 149 at-bats.

KEY TRANSACTIONS: The Royals' rebuild moved forward when they traded Jon Jay to the D-backs and Kelvin Herrera to the Nationals in June. Just before the July 31 deadline, they dealt Mike Moustakas to the Brewers, but perhaps the most beneficial moves came from the decisions not to re-sign Eric Hosmer and Lorenzo Cain after 2017, which netted them two additional first-round picks in 2018.

DOWN ON THE FARM: The best story on the farm came from low Class A Lexington, which put up a 76-60 regular season record and went on to win the South Atlantic League title for the first time since 2001. Outfielder Seuly Matias hit 31 home runs, catcher M.J. Melendez led the team in RBIs with 73 in his first full pro season and outfielder Brewer Hicklen led the team in hitting (.307), OPS (.930) and stolen bases (29).

OPENING DAY PAYROLL: $115,483,116 (19th).

PLAYERS OF THE YEAR

CHRIS BERMACCHI

CHRIS BERMACCHI

MAJOR LEAGUE	MINOR LEAGUE
Whit Merrifield	**Nicky Lopez**
2B	SS
.304/.367/.438	(Double-A/Triple-A)
Led the majors in hits	.308/.382/.417
(192) and SB (45)	155 hits, 15 SB

ORGANIZATION LEADERS

Batting		*Minimum 250 AB
MAJORS		
* AVG	Whit Merrifield	.304
* OPS	Whit Merrifield	.806
HR	Salvador Perez	27
RBI	Salvador Perez	80
MINORS		
* AVG	Nathan Eaton, Idaho Falls	.354
* OBP	Nathan Eaton, Idaho Falls	.427
* SLG	Nathan Eaton, Idaho Falls	.581
* OPS	Nathan Eaton, Idaho Falls	1.008
R	Erick Mejia, NW Arkansas	79
R	Nick Pratto, Lexington	79
H	Nicky Lopez, NW Arkansas, Omaha	155
TB	Frank Schwindel, Omaha	258
2B	Frank Schwindel, Omaha	38
3B	MJ Melendez, Lexington	9
HR	Seuly Matias, Lexington	31
RBI	Frank Schwindel, Omaha	93
BB	Nicky Lopez, NW Arkansas, Omaha	60
SO	Chase Vallot, Wilmington, Idaho Falls	151
SB	Nick Heath, Wilmington, NW Arkansas	39

Pitching		#Minimum 75 IP
MAJORS		
W	Jakob Junis	9
W	Brad Keller	9
# ERA	Brad Keller	3.08
SO	Jakob Junis	164
SV	Kelvin Herrera	14
SV	Wily Peralta	14
MINORS		
W	Arnaldo Hernandez, Wilmington, Omaha, NW Arkansas	12
W	J.C. Cloney, Idaho Falls, Lexington	12
L	Foster Griffin, NW Arkansas	12
# ERA	Gerson Garabito, Wilmington	3.16
G	Richard Lovelady, Omaha	46
GS	Gerson Garabito, Wilmington	26
GS	Foster Griffin, NW Arkansas	26
GS	Emilio Ogando, NW Arkansas	26
GS	Daniel Tillo, Lexington, Wilmington	26
SV	Tyler Zuber, Lexington, Wilmington	18
IP	Foster Griffin, NW Arkansas	153
BB	Gerson Garabito, Wilmington	73
SO	Jake Kalish, NW Arkansas, Omaha	124
# AVG	Gerson Garabito, Wilmington	.226

2018 PERFORMANCE

General Manager: Dayton Moore. **Farm Director:** Alec Zumwalt. **Scouting Director:** Lonnie Goldberg.

Class	Team	League	W	L	PCT	Finish	Manager
Majors	Kansas City Royals	American	58	104	.358	14th (15)	Ned Yost
Triple-A	Omaha Storm Chasers	Pacific Coast	66	74	.471	12th (16)	Brian Poldberg
Double-A	NW Arkansas Naturals	Texas	70	70	.500	5th (8)	Mike Rojas
High A	Wilmington Blue Rocks	Carolina	68	72	.486	5th (10)	Darryl Kennedy
Low A	Lexington Legends	South Atlantic	76	60	.559	2nd (14)	Scott Thorman
Rookie	Idaho Falls	Pioneer	43	33	.566	3rd (8)	Omar Ramirez
Rookie	Burlington	Appalachian	25	43	.368	10th (10)	Brooks Conrad
Rookie	AZL Royals	Arizona	22	43	.423	14th (18)	Tony Pena Jr.
Overall 2018 Minor League Record			370	382	.492	17th (30)	

ORGANIZATION STATISTICS

KANSAS CITY ROYALS
AMERICAN LEAGUE

Batting	B-T	HT	WT	DOB	AVG	vLH	vRH	G	AB	R	H	2B	3B	HR	RBI	BB	HBP	SH	SF	SO	SB	CS	SLG	OBP
Almonte, Abraham	B-R	5-9	210	6-27-89	.179	.100	.213	50	134	15	24	1	2	3	9	15	0	1	1	36	2	2	.284	.260
Bonifacio, Jorge	R-R	6-1	225	6-4-93	.225	.230	.223	69	236	31	53	16	2	4	23	29	2	1	2	71	0	1	.360	.312
Butera, Drew	R-R	6-1	205	8-9-83	.188	.167	.196	51	149	11	28	9	0	2	18	13	2	0	2	37	0	0	.289	.259
Cuthbert, Cheslor	R-R	6-1	210	11-16-92	.194	.256	.156	30	103	11	20	2	0	3	7	11	2	0	1	23	0	1	.301	.282
Dozier, Hunter	R-R	6-4	220	8-22-91	.229	.207	.239	102	362	36	83	19	4	11	34	24	1	0	1	109	2	3	.395	.278
Duda, Lucas	L-R	6-4	255	2-3-86	.242	.180	.267	87	310	34	75	12	1	13	48	24	8	0	3	95	1	0	.413	.310
Escobar, Alcides	R-R	6-1	205	12-16-86	.231	.239	.228	140	485	54	112	22	3	4	34	29	5	8	4	74	8	2	.313	.279
Gallagher, Cam	R-R	6-3	230	12-6-92	.206	.105	.250	22	63	5	13	3	0	1	7	3	1	1	1	15	0	0	.302	.250
Goins, Ryan	L-R	5-10	180	2-13-88	.226	.200	.232	41	115	10	26	8	1	0	6	4	0	1	0	29	0	0	.313	.252
Goodwin, Brian	L-R	6-0	200	11-2-90	.266	.188	.282	27	94	11	25	5	0	3	13	6	1	0	0	31	1	1	.415	.317
Gordon, Alex	L-R	6-1	225	2-10-84	.245	.211	.259	141	506	56	124	24	0	13	54	50	10	0	2	124	12	2	.370	.324
Herrera, Rosell	B-R	6-3	190	10-16-92	.238	.189	.263	75	265	25	63	14	3	1	20	19	2	1	2	52	3	4	.325	.292
Jay, Jon	L-L	5-11	195	3-15-85	.307	.286	.314	59	238	28	73	9	2	1	18	19	3	4	2	39	3	2	.374	.363
Merrifield, Whit	R-R	6-0	195	1-24-89	.304	.357	.282	158	632	88	192	43	3	12	60	61	6	2	6	114	45	10	.438	.367
Mondesi, Adalberto	B-R	6-1	190	7-27-95	.276	.289	.270	75	275	47	76	13	4	14	37	11	1	3	1	77	32	7	.498	.306
Moustakas, Mike	L-R	6-0	225	9-11-88	.249	.256	.245	98	378	46	94	21	1	20	62	30	5	0	4	63	3	0	.468	.309
O'Hearn, Ryan	L-L	6-3	200	7-26-93	.262	.108	.313	44	149	23	39	10	2	12	30	20	1	0	0	45	0	0	.597	.353
Orlando, Paulo	R-R	6-2	215	11-1-85	.167	.189	.151	25	90	6	15	3	0	0	5	3	0	0	0	25	0	0	.200	.194
Perez, Salvador	R-R	6-4	240	5-10-90	.235	.241	.233	129	510	52	120	23	0	27	80	17	12	0	5	108	1	1	.439	.274
Phillips, Brett	L-R	6-0	185	5-30-94	.188	.156	.200	36	112	13	21	4	2	2	7	9	1	0	1	50	1	1	.313	.252
Soler, Jorge	R-R	6-4	230	2-25-92	.265	.315	.249	61	223	27	59	18	0	9	28	28	4	0	2	69	3	1	.466	.354
Torres, Ramon	B-R	5-11	190	1-22-93	.179	.250	.125	9	28	4	5	1	0	0	1	1	0	0	0	3	0	0	.214	.207
Viloria, Meibrys	L-R	5-11	220	2-15-97	.259	.000	.292	10	27	4	7	2	0	0	4	1	0	1	0	9	0	0	.333	.286

Pitching	B-T	HT	WT	DOB	W	L	ERA	G	GS	CG	SV	IP	H	R	ER	HR	BB	SO	AVG	vLH	vRH	K/9	BB/9
Adam, Jason	R-R	6-4	225	8-4-91	0	3	6.12	31	0	0	0	32	30	22	22	9	15	37	.246	.234	.253	10.30	4.18
Barlow, Scott	R-R	6-3	215	12-18-92	1	1	3.60	6	0	0	0	15	16	7	6	2	3	15	.258	.250	.263	9.00	1.80
Boyer, Blaine	R-R	6-3	235	7-11-81	2	1	12.05	21	0	0	1	22	32	33	29	7	13	9	.344	.233	.397	3.74	5.40
Duffy, Danny	L-L	6-3	205	12-21-88	8	12	4.88	28	28	0	0	155	161	86	84	23	70	141	.264	.268	.263	8.19	4.06
Fillmyer, Heath	R-R	6-1	195	5-16-94	4	2	4.26	17	13	0	0	82	78	41	39	11	32	57	.255	.229	.286	6.23	3.50
Flynn, Brian	L-L	6-7	255	4-19-90	3	5	4.04	48	0	0	1	76	87	37	34	5	35	47	.295	.284	.300	5.59	4.16
Grimm, Justin	R-R	6-3	210	8-16-88	1	3	13.50	16	0	0	0	13	17	19	19	2	14	8	.347	.400	.310	5.68	9.95
2-team total (5 Seattle)					1	3	10.38	21	0	0	0	17	19	20	20	3	14	11	.297	.333	.275	5.71	7.27
Hammel, Jason	R-R	6-6	225	9-2-82	4	14	6.02	39	18	0	0	127	168	91	85	18	39	92	.315	.257	.366	6.52	2.76
Herrera, Kelvin	R-R	5-10	200	12-31-89	1	1	1.05	27	0	0	14	26	19	3	3	2	2	22	.207	.167	.232	7.71	0.70
Hill, Tim	R-L	6-2	200	2-10-90	1	4	4.53	70	0	0	2	46	46	28	23	4	14	42	.257	.230	.276	8.28	2.76
Junis, Jakob	R-R	6-2	225	9-16-92	9	12	4.37	30	30	1	0	177	182	94	86	32	43	164	.265	.278	.251	8.34	2.19
Keller, Brad	R-R	6-5	230	7-27-95	9	6	3.08	41	20	1	0	140	133	50	48	7	50	96	.252	.268	.239	6.16	3.21
Kennedy, Ian	R-R	6-0	205	12-19-84	3	9	4.66	22	22	0	0	120	125	66	62	20	40	105	.265	.257	.274	7.90	3.01
Lively, Ben	R-R	6-4	190	3-5-92	0	1	1.35	5	0	0	0	7	7	1	1	0	5	5	.280	.273	.286	6.75	6.75
Lopez, Jorge	R-R	6-3	195	2-10-93	2	4	6.35	7	7	0	0	34	41	24	24	5	9	23	.297	.276	.333	6.09	2.38
Maurer, Brandon	R-R	6-5	225	7-3-90	0	4	7.76	37	0	0	1	31	42	29	27	7	25	31	.323	.348	.295	8.90	7.18
McCarthy, Kevin	R-R	6-3	215	2-22-92	5	4	3.25	65	0	0	0	72	70	28	26	7	20	46	.259	.263	.257	5.75	2.50
Newberry, Jake	R-R	6-2	195	11-20-94	2	0	4.73	14	0	0	0	13	13	8	7	3	9	11	.255	.261	.250	7.43	6.08
Oaks, Trevor	R-R	6-3	225	3-26-93	0	2	7.24	4	2	0	0	14	21	11	11	1	6	10	.375	.467	.269	6.59	3.95
Peralta, Wily	R-R	6-1	255	5-8-89	1	0	3.67	37	0	0	14	34	28	14	14	4	23	35	.230	.191	.277	9.17	6.03
Romero, Enny	R-L	6-3	232	1-24-91	0	0	20.25	4	0	0	0	4	11	9	9	3	2	3	.524	.429	.571	6.75	4.50
Skoglund, Eric	L-L	6-7	210	10-26-92	1	6	5.14	14	13	0	0	70	66	41	40	12	19	49	.246	.196	.257	6.30	2.44
Smith, Burch	R-R	6-4	225	4-12-90	1	6	6.92	38	6	0	0	78	90	60	60	15	40	77	.292	.327	.261	8.88	4.62
Sparkman, Glenn	B-R	6-2	210	5-11-92	0	3	4.46	15	3	0	0	38	47	20	19	5	11	27	.303	.294	.310	6.34	3.52
Stout, Eric	L-L	6-3	205	3-27-93	0	0	23.14	3	0	0	0	2	7	7	6	2	2	2	.500	.400	.556	7.71	7.71
Vasto, Jerry	L-L	6-2	195	2-12-92	0	1	2.45	5	0	0	0	4	3	2	1	1	1	3	.214	.143	.286	7.36	2.45

Fielding

Catcher	PCT	G	PO	A	E	DP	PB
Butera	.994	48	309	10	2	0	5
Gallagher	.992	20	118	3	1	0	0
Perez	1.000	96	690	69	0	11	4
Viloria	1.000	10	60	7	0	0	1

First Base	PCT	G	PO	A	E	DP
Butera	1.000	2	14	3	0	2
Cuthbert	.986	10	68	0	1	8
Dozier	.991	51	406	20	4	45
Duda	.994	61	496	36	3	41
Merrifield	1.000	5	38	1	0	4
Moustakas	1.000	4	31	3	0	4
O'Hearn	.983	31	279	13	5	18
Perez	1.000	3	25	1	0	2

Second Base	PCT	G	PO	A	E	DP
Escobar	1.000	3	5	6	0	0

	PCT	G	PO	A	E	DP
Goins	.990	28	42	62	1	15
Herrera	.987	17	26	49	1	10
Merrifield	.987	108	175	287	6	71
Mondesi	1.000	12	19	30	0	8
Torres	.867	3	6	7	2	2

Third Base	PCT	G	PO	A	E	DP
Cuthbert	.935	12	4	25	2	2
Dozier	.958	37	16	53	3	6
Escobar	.963	29	25	53	3	7
Goins	1.000	5	3	7	0	1
Herrera	1.000	5	1	13	0	0
Moustakas	.969	76	51	171	7	21
Torres	1.000	6	5	9	0	2

Shortstop	PCT	G	PO	A	E	DP
Escobar	.976	104	129	243	9	49
Goins	1.000	4	0	1	0	0

Mondesi	.975	61	100	169	7	36

Outfield	PCT	G	PO	A	E	DP
Almonte	1.000	39	83	2	0	2
Bonifacio	.982	60	105	3	2	1
Dozier	1.000	2	3	0	0	0
Escobar	.923	6	12	0	1	0
Goodwin	.984	26	61	1	1	0
Gordon	.993	136	281	9	2	1
Herrera	1.000	40	79	2	0	0
Jay	1.000	51	129	2	0	0
Merrifield	.990	39	98	1	1	0
O'Hearn	1.000	1	1	0	0	0
Orlando	.960	21	47	1	2	0
Phillips	1.000	33	83	3	0	1
Soler	.975	52	117	2	3	0

OMAHA STORM CHASERS TRIPLE-A
PACIFIC COAST LEAGUE

Batting	B-T	HT	WT	DOB	AVG	vLH	vRH	G	AB	R	H	2B	3B	HR	RBI	BB	HBP	SH	SF	SO	SB	CS	SLG	OBP
Arteaga, Humberto	R-R	6-1	160	1-23-94	.292	.340	.276	118	414	42	121	19	1	6	49	21	0	4	6	73	2	3	.387	.322
Bonifacio, Jorge	R-R	6-1	225	6-4-93	.392	.429	.378	13	51	11	20	5	1	0	9	7	0	0	0	12	0	0	.529	.466
Burns, Billy	B-R	5-9	170	8-30-89	.255	.297	.242	102	376	51	96	9	1	4	36	30	4	11	4	54	10	8	.317	.314
Collins, Tyler	L-L	5-11	215	6-6-90	.132	.250	.111	18	53	3	7	0	0	0	2	7	1	0	1	14	0	1	.132	.242
Cuthbert, Cheslor	R-R	6-1	210	11-16-92	.235	.500	.200	6	17	2	4	1	0	1	4	1	0	0	1	5	0	0	.471	.263
Dewees, Donnie	L-L	5-11	204	9-29-93	.266	.308	.253	64	222	31	59	11	3	6	29	15	1	3	0	45	8	2	.423	.315
Dini, Nick	R-R	5-8	180	7-27-93	.333	.200	.379	14	39	4	13	4	0	3	6	1	0	0	0	5	0	0	.667	.350
Dozier, Hunter	R-R	6-4	220	8-22-91	.254	.217	.263	35	118	18	30	7	0	1	11	24	1	0	0	43	2	1	.339	.385
Duda, Lucas	L-R	6-4	255	2-3-86	.313	.200	.364	4	16	5	5	1	0	2	7	2	0	0	0	5	0	0	.750	.389
Gallagher, Cam	R-R	6-3	230	12-6-92	.265	.328	.245	77	268	28	71	13	0	4	42	26	3	4	2	38	1	0	.358	.334
Goodwin, Brian	R-R	6-0	200	11-2-90	.225	.133	.280	10	40	6	9	2	0	2	9	4	0	0	0	11	0	0	.475	.296
Gordon, Alex	L-R	6-1	225	2-10-84	.222	.000	.250	3	9	2	2	1	0	0	2	2	0	0	0	2	0	0	.333	.364
Gore, Terrance	R-R	5-7	165	6-8-91	.211	.209	.212	67	142	26	30	2	2	0	5	17	2	7	0	36	16	4	.254	.304
2-team total (11 Iowa)					.193	.192	.194	78	176	32	34	2	2	0	5	19	3	7	0	49	21	5	.227	.283
Hernandez, Elier	R-R	6-3	197	11-21-94	.279	.455	.243	40	129	13	36	8	1	0	15	14	1	1	2	37	0	1	.357	.349
Herrera, Rosell	B-R	6-3	195	10-16-92	.278	.091	.360	10	36	8	10	3	2	1	5	5	0	0	0	7	4	1	.556	.366
Lopez, Jack	R-R	5-9	165	12-16-92	.251	.178	.278	113	395	53	99	10	3	8	34	14	3	8	4	106	14	6	.352	.279
Lopez, Nicky	L-R	5-11	175	3-13-95	.278	.294	.273	57	223	33	62	6	2	7	26	27	3	3	0	29	6	2	.417	.364
Mondesi, Adalberto	B-R	6-1	190	7-27-95	.250	.220	.266	29	120	19	30	8	3	5	21	8	0	4	1	30	10	0	.492	.295
Moon, Logan	R-R	6-2	195	2-15-92	.193	.200	.189	34	114	10	22	2	0	0	12	7	0	0	1	34	2	1	.211	.238
Morin, Parker	L-R	5-11	195	7-2-91	.265	.364	.237	52	151	16	40	10	0	1	9	11	2	2	1	34	1	0	.351	.321
O'Hearn, Ryan	L-L	6-3	200	7-26-93	.232	.271	.220	100	353	47	82	21	1	11	52	45	3	2	3	97	2	0	.391	.322
Olloque, Manny	R-R	6-2	165	5-11-96	.207	.000	.273	9	29	3	6	3	0	0	2	1	0	0	0	8	0	0	.310	.233
Orlando, Paulo	R-R	6-2	215	11-1-85	.270	.284	.264	75	289	46	78	17	2	12	41	17	4	1	0	58	2	0	.467	.319
Perez, Salvador	R-R	6-4	240	5-10-90	.400	.500	.385	4	15	3	6	2	0	1	3	0	0	0	0	6	0	0	.733	.400
Schwindel, Frank	R-R	6-1	205	6-29-92	.286	.353	.266	134	510	65	146	38	1	24	93	34	7	0	5	71	2	2	.506	.336
Soler, Jorge	R-R	6-4	230	2-25-92	.250	—	.250	2	8	0	2	0	0	0	1	2	0	0	0	6	0	0	.250	.400
Starling, Bubba	R-R	6-4	215	8-3-92	.257	.286	.250	11	35	5	9	2	0	0	2	5	0	1	0	14	0	1	.314	.350
Torres, Ramon	B-R	5-11	190	1-22-93	.230	.200	.238	97	370	44	85	20	2	6	27	25	1	7	2	59	6	3	.343	.279
Toups, Corey	R-R	5-10	170	2-12-93	.184	.238	.143	15	49	10	9	3	0	1	4	6	2	0	1	19	1	0	.306	.298
Villegas, Luis	R-R	5-10	170	12-2-92	.241	.263	.231	18	58	7	14	2	0	2	5	5	0	0	0	12	0	0	.379	.302

Pitching	B-T	HT	WT	DOB	W	L	ERA	G	GS	CG	SV	IP	H	R	ER	HR	BB	SO	AVG	vLH	vRH	K/9	BB/9
Adam, Jason	R-R	6-4	225	8-4-91	2	0	1.42	11	0	0	4	13	6	4	2	0	7	15	.140	.125	.148	10.66	4.97
Barlow, Scott	R-R	6-3	215	12-18-92	1	4	6.11	13	10	0	1	46	54	33	31	9	21	50	.294	.338	.260	9.85	4.14
Boyer, Blaine	R-R	6-3	235	7-11-81	1	0	1.59	5	0	0	0	6	7	1	1	1	2	5	.304	.273	.333	7.94	3.18
Broadway, Mike	R-R	6-5	215	3-30-87	4	1	7.91	20	0	0	1	19	25	17	17	5	12	23	.313	.333	.300	10.71	5.59
Buchholz, Clay	L-R	6-3	190	8-14-84	1	0	1.59	2	2	0	0	11	9	2	2	2	5	4	.214	.177	.240	3.18	3.97
2-team total (2 Reno)					1	1	3.52	4	4	0	0	23	21	9	9	2	10	14	.241	.222	.255	5.48	3.91
Camp, Justin	R-R	5-11	230	5-17-93	0	0	0.00	1	0	0	0	1	0	0	0	0	1	2	.333	.500	.000	21.60	10.80
Dziedzic, Jonathan	R-L	6-1	190	2-4-91	8	9	3.94	25	24	0	1	139	141	68	61	11	43	96	.262	.289	.253	6.20	2.78
Fernandez, Pedro	R-R	6-0	175	5-25-94	1	0	7.00	6	0	0	0	9	12	7	7	1	7	6	.324	.333	.320	6.00	7.00
Fillmyer, Heath	R-R	6-1	195	5-16-94	4	5	5.73	13	13	0	0	67	82	46	43	5	28	47	.303	.270	.325	6.28	3.74
Grimm, Justin	R-R	6-3	210	8-16-88	1	1	8.68	9	0	0	0	9	15	9	9	0	6	13	.366	.286	.407	12.54	5.79
2-team total (10 Tacoma)					2	1	4.87	19	0	0	0	20	23	11	11	0	8	30	.291	.172	.360	13.28	3.54
Hahn, Jesse	R-R	6-4	215	7-30-89	0	0	0.00	1	0	0	0	1	0	0	0	0	0	2	.333	.500	.000	0.00	0.00
Hernandez, Arnaldo	R-R	6-0	175	2-9-96	5	1	3.55	10	9	2	0	58	45	26	23	8	19	36	.210	.190	.227	5.55	2.93
Kalish, Jake	B-L	6-2	210	7-9-91	6	6	3.34	17	14	1	0	89	94	35	33	3	13	85	.273	.298	.264	8.60	1.31
Kennedy, Ian	R-R	6-0	205	12-19-84	0	1	7.36	1	1	0	0	4	3	3	3	0	1	2	.286	.500	.250	4.91	2.45
Lenik, Kevin	R-R	6-5	225	8-1-91	0	2	4.93	34	0	0	4	49	45	30	27	4	25	51	.243	.234	.248	9.30	4.56
Lohse, Kyle	R-R	6-2	215	10-4-78	0	1	12.46	2	2	0	0	9	17	12	12	5	5	5	.405	.333	.458	5.19	5.19

Name	B-T	HT	WT	DOB	W	L	ERA	G	GS	CG	SV	IP	H	R	ER	BB	SO	AVG	vLH	vRH	K/9	BB/9
Lopez, Jorge	R-R	6-3	195	2-10-93	1	0	4.00	2	2	0	0	9	8	4	4	2	1	11	.235	.250	.214	11.00	1.00
2-team total (24 Colorado Springs)					4	3	5.26	26	2	0	5	38	41	27	22	5	11	34	.277	.310	.256	8.12	2.63
Lovelady, Richard	L-L	6-0	175	7-7-95	3	3	2.47	46	0	0	9	73	53	24	20	3	21	71	.204	.157	.228	8.75	2.59
Lovvorn, Zach	R-R	6-0	185	5-26-94	2	6	5.71	12	9	0	1	63	70	41	40	5	23	30	.286	.301	.279	4.29	3.29
Machado, Andres	R-R	6-0	220	4-22-93	0	4	9.72	7	6	0	0	25	41	33	27	4	16	25	.360	.417	.318	9.00	5.76
Maness, Seth	R-R	6-0	190	10-14-88	0	1	4.63	5	1	0	0	12	17	9	6	2	1	8	.347	.368	.333	6.17	0.77
Mariot, Michael	R-R	6-0	190	10-20-88	1	2	3.81	18	2	0	2	28	23	12	12	3	7	31	.219	.265	.197	9.85	2.22
2-team total (10 El Paso)					1	3	6.48	28	3	0	3	42	46	30	30	8	14	45	.277	.338	.235	9.32	3.02
Maurer, Brandon	R-R	6-5	225	7-3-90	1	3	5.48	19	0	0	5	23	23	17	14	1	13	24	.256	.286	.236	9.39	5.09
McCarthy, Kevin	R-R	6-3	215	2-22-92	0	1	5.40	3	0	0	0	3	5	2	2	0	1	3	.333	.500	.273	8.10	2.70
Newberry, Jake	R-R	6-2	195	11-20-94	3	0	0.90	16	0	0	3	20	13	3	2	1	6	16	.191	.238	.170	7.20	2.70
Oaks, Trevor	R-R	6-3	225	3-26-93	8	8	3.23	22	22	1	0	128	130	50	46	5	44	70	.266	.323	.230	4.91	3.09
Peralta, Wily	R-R	6-1	255	5-8-89	0	1	4.37	18	2	0	1	35	36	18	17	3	21	39	.267	.304	.241	10.03	5.40
Selman, Sam	R-L	6-3	190	11-14-90	0	2	4.13	23	0	0	0	28	22	14	13	0	19	37	.212	.125	.250	11.75	6.04
Skoglund, Eric	L-L	6-7	210	10-26-92	0	1	4.32	2	2	0	0	8	8	4	4	2	0	6	.250	.273	.238	6.48	0.00
Sparkman, Glenn	B-R	6-2	210	5-11-92	5	1	4.01	12	12	0	0	67	76	32	30	10	11	48	.288	.311	.265	6.42	1.47
Staumont, Josh	R-R	6-3	200	12-21-93	2	5	3.51	41	5	0	1	74	59	31	29	4	52	103	.217	.222	.213	12.47	6.30
Stout, Eric	L-L	6-3	205	3-27-93	3	4	4.75	38	2	0	4	55	70	30	29	5	13	44	.308	.275	.327	7.20	2.13
Vasquez, Luis	R-R	6-4	200	4-3-86	2	2	9.00	12	0	0	0	20	33	22	20	3	14	24	.355	.366	.346	10.80	6.30
Vasto, Jerry	L-L	6-2	195	2-12-92	1	0	0.00	1	0	0	0	1	2	1	0	0	0	1	.333	.000	.500	9.00	0.00
2-team total (37 Albuquerque)					3	1	3.08	38	0	0	3	38	34	19	13	3	18	45	.236	.259	.222	10.66	4.26

Fielding

Catcher	PCT	G	PO	A	E	DP	PB
Dini	.973	11	69	3	2	0	2
Gallagher	.995	72	525	29	3	3	7
Morin	.986	51	328	25	5	3	7
Perez	1.000	2	13	0	0	2	0
Villegas	1.000	16	118	5	0	1	1

First Base	PCT	G	PO	A	E	DP
Arteaga	1.000	9	63	4	0	3
Dozier	1.000	4	17	2	0	1
O'Hearn	.989	69	539	22	6	63
Olloque	1.000	1	4	0	0	0
Schwindel	1.000	63	488	26	0	52

Second Base	PCT	G	PO	A	E	DP
Arteaga	.985	28	48	81	2	27
Lopez	.986	50	86	130	3	31
Lopez	1.000	18	33	53	0	18

	PCT	G	PO	A	E	DP
Mondesi	.966	6	8	20	1	2
Torres	.960	38	67	100	7	24
Toups	1.000	2	0	6	0	0

Third Base	PCT	G	PO	A	E	DP
Arteaga	.937	51	23	96	8	8
Cuthbert	1.000	6	2	6	0	0
Dozier	.961	19	15	34	2	7
Lopez	.979	19	11	36	1	6
Olloque	.882	8	5	10	2	1
Torres	.949	30	21	53	4	4
Toups	1.000	13	6	23	0	1

Shortstop	PCT	G	PO	A	E	DP
Arteaga	.981	31	31	75	2	15
Lopez	.959	29	39	77	5	27
Lopez	.972	36	43	96	4	19
Mondesi	.984	18	16	45	1	7

	PCT	G	PO	A	E	DP
Torres	.967	27	28	61	3	13

Outfield	PCT	G	PO	A	E	DP
Bonifacio	.966	13	27	1	1	0
Burns	.991	101	220	4	2	0
Collins	.926	18	25	0	2	0
Dewees	1.000	61	185	3	0	1
Dozier	.970	13	29	3	1	0
Goodwin	.818	7	8	1	2	0
Gordon	1.000	3	1	0	0	0
Gore	.973	59	106	3	3	0
Hernandez	.986	37	70	0	1	0
Herrera	.967	9	29	0	1	0
Lopez	.917	13	11	0	1	0
Moon	.965	30	54	1	2	0
O'Hearn	1.000	13	19	0	0	0
Orlando	.985	57	128	2	2	0
Starling	.963	11	26	0	1	0

NORTHWEST ARKANSAS NATURALS   DOUBLE-A
TEXAS LEAGUE

Batting	B-T	HT	WT	DOB	AVG	vLH	vRH	G	AB	R	H	2B	3B	HR	RBI	BB	HBP	SH	SF	SO	SB	CS	SLG	OBP
Brontsema, John	R-R	6-2	187	12-13-94	.229	.154	.253	37	109	17	25	5	1	2	10	8	5	0	1	31	5	1	.349	.309
Dewees, Donnie	L-L	5-11	204	9-29-93	.253	.246	.255	70	285	35	72	12	5	2	25	20	2	2	1	48	8	4	.351	.305
Dini, Nick	R-R	5-8	180	7-27-93	.239	.206	.251	80	280	40	67	10	0	8	37	12	8	1	3	64	7	1	.361	.287
Downes, Brandon	R-R	6-3	195	9-29-92	.146	.267	.077	16	41	4	6	3	0	1	5	7	1	2	0	20	2	2	.293	.286
Duenez, Samir	L-R	6-0	211	6-11-96	.282	.256	.294	80	287	44	81	18	2	10	60	35	1	0	5	68	5	0	.463	.357
Escalera, Alfredo	R-R	6-1	186	2-17-95	.240	.326	.198	39	129	22	31	5	0	4	12	10	3	0	2	40	4	2	.372	.306
Esposito, Nathan	R-R	5-11	180	6-25-93	.156	.125	.162	18	45	5	7	2	0	0	1	2	1	0	0	15	1	0	.200	.208
Fernandez, Xavier	R-R	5-11	197	7-15-95	.328	.546	.244	36	119	21	39	8	2	3	14	10	1	0	1	17	2	2	.504	.382
Flores, Jecksson	R-R	5-11	145	10-28-93	.314	.305	.317	122	459	74	144	31	3	7	52	30	7	10	2	72	27	7	.440	.364
Gutierrez, Kelvin	R-R	6-3	215	8-28-94	.277	.254	.286	65	242	29	67	8	3	6	40	20	2	0	0	46	10	3	.409	.337
Heath, Nick	L-L	6-1	187	11-27-93	.257	.250	.259	36	105	22	27	3	3	0	7	13	0	6	1	33	10	0	.343	.336
Hernandez, Elier	R-R	6-3	197	11-21-94	.287	.308	.280	91	355	45	102	22	1	3	50	14	6	2	4	71	10	8	.380	.322
Lee, Khalil	L-L	5-10	170	6-26-98	.245	.161	.282	29	102	15	25	5	0	2	10	11	2	3	0	28	2	2	.353	.330
Liddi, Alex	R-R	6-4	225	8-14-88	.247	.327	.217	107	393	54	97	18	3	23	72	25	2	1	1	126	4	3	.484	.295
Lopez, Nicky	L-R	5-11	175	3-13-95	.331	.370	.317	73	281	42	93	8	5	2	27	33	0	8	3	23	9	4	.416	.398
Martin, Rudy	L-L	5-7	155	1-31-96	.000	—	.000	1	1	0	0	0	0	0	0	0	0	0	0	0	0	0	.000	.000
Mejia, Erick	B-R	5-11	155	11-9-94	.263	.278	.257	136	540	79	142	27	7	5	59	43	2	14	3	98	34	17	.367	.318
Miller, Anderson	L-L	6-3	208	5-6-94	.255	.279	.247	120	432	50	110	22	4	13	46	33	1	2	2	83	10	8	.414	.308
Perez, Salvador	R-R	6-4	240	5-10-90	.333	.000	.375	3	9	1	3	0	0	1	3	0	0	1	0	2	0	0	.667	.364
Peterson, Kort	L-R	6-1	195	4-29-94	.229	.238	.226	50	166	24	38	8	3	7	27	12	5	0	0	61	6	3	.440	.301
Porter, Logan	R-R	6-0	200	7-12-95	.000	—	.000	1	1	0	0	0	0	0	0	0	0	0	0	0	0	0	.000	.000
Toups, Corey	R-R	5-10	170	2-12-93	.249	.313	.215	61	185	24	46	6	1	4	21	24	1	2	1	67	10	3	.357	.337
Villegas, Luis	R-R	5-10	170	12-2-92	.236	.438	.168	38	127	13	30	3	1	3	16	11	0	0	2	30	1	1	.347	.293

Pitching	B-T	HT	WT	DOB	W	L	ERA	G	GS	CG	SV	IP	H	R	ER	BB	SO	AVG	vLH	vRH	K/9	BB/9
Adam, Jason	R-R	6-4	225	8-4-91	1	0	1.59	6	0	0	0	11	5	2	2	0	4	17	.132	.222	.103	13.50	3.18
Barlow, Scott	R-R	6-3	215	12-18-92	0	0	2.25	1	1	0	0	4	3	1	1	0	0	4	.214	.333	.125	9.00	0.00
Beeler, Dallas	R-R	6-5	225	6-12-89	0	0	13.50	4	2	0	0	11	26	17	17	4	5	8	.448	.588	.390	6.35	3.97
Blewett, Scott	R-R	6-6	210	4-10-96	8	6	4.79	26	25	1	0	148	164	84	79	12	49	100	.282	.281	.283	6.07	2.97
Bodner, Jacob	R-R	5-10	185	1-31-93	0	0	17.05	6	0	0	0	6	15	13	12	6	1	8	.441	.571	.407	11.37	1.42

Name																							
Boyer, Blaine	R-R	6-3	235	7-11-81	0	0	0.00	3	1	0	0	3	2	0	0	0	1	3	.200	.000	.250	10.13	3.38
Brickhouse, Bryan	R-R	6-0	195	6-6-92	0	5	11.81	11	0	0	0	11	18	18	14	5	12	11	.353	.333	.364	9.28	10.13
Buchholz, Clay	L-R	6-3	190	8-14-84	0	0	0.00	1	1	0	0	5	1	0	0	0	2	5	.067	.000	.125	9.64	3.86
Castillo, Cristian	L-L	6-0	190	9-25-94	2	2	5.40	11	0	0	0	22	20	13	13	3	4	22	.233	.200	.250	9.14	1.66
Fernandez, Pedro	R-R	6-0	175	5-25-94	4	2	2.81	26	3	0	2	58	54	18	18	2	19	43	.250	.237	.255	6.71	2.97
Gavin, Grant	R-R	6-2	185	7-10-95	0	1	3.19	21	0	0	1	31	27	11	11	4	17	30	.237	.200	.253	8.71	4.94
Griffin, Foster	R-L	6-3	200	7-27-95	10	12	5.13	28	26	0	0	153	197	94	87	20	40	117	.315	.330	.311	6.90	2.36
Hahn, Jesse	R-R	6-4	215	7-30-89	0	0	0.00	3	2	0	0	3	2	0	0	0	2	0	.200	.500	.125	6.00	5.40
Hernandez, Arnaldo	R-R	6-0	175	2-9-96	1	0	4.41	3	3	0	0	16	20	9	8	1	6	16	.323	.261	.359	8.82	3.31
Kalish, Jake	B-L	6-2	210	7-9-91	2	2	5.12	16	4	0	0	39	46	28	22	6	8	39	.279	.258	.284	9.08	1.86
Kennedy, Ian	R-R	6-0	205	12-19-84	0	1	13.50	1	1	0	0	4	7	6	6	0	2	5	.389	.364	.429	11.25	4.50
Lovvorn, Zach	R-R	6-0	185	5-26-94	4	3	4.80	15	15	0	0	81	90	45	43	9	26	52	.290	.218	.325	5.80	2.90
Lugo, Luis	L-L	6-5	200	3-5-94	1	2	4.18	8	4	0	0	24	25	11	11	3	11	21	.263	.071	.296	7.99	4.18
Machado, Andres	R-R	6-0	220	4-22-93	2	3	3.72	30	6	0	9	58	60	31	24	5	22	47	.269	.302	.256	7.29	3.41
Mariot, Michael	R-R	6-0	190	10-20-88	1	0	0.96	7	0	0	1	9	4	1	1	0	0	11	.125	.000	.167	10.61	0.00
Marte, Yunior	R-R	6-2	180	2-2-95	4	4	2.91	43	0	0	2	80	69	33	26	7	29	80	.226	.186	.241	8.96	3.25
Newberry, Jake	R-R	6-2	195	11-20-94	2	0	2.12	25	0	0	12	30	29	7	7	2	8	37	.254	.310	.235	11.22	2.43
Ogando, Emilio	L-L	6-2	180	8-13-93	11	7	4.79	26	26	0	0	118	127	71	63	22	72	94	.279	.329	.267	7.15	5.48
Perrin, Jon	R-R	6-5	220	5-23-93	1	2	3.38	5	5	0	0	21	19	11	8	1	11	20	.241	.200	.273	8.44	4.64
Ray, Corey	R-R	6-3	175	12-15-92	0	1	10.80	8	0	0	0	8	13	11	10	2	11	8	.342	.143	.387	8.64	11.88
Ruxer, Jared	R-R	6-3	200	7-29-92	0	0	67.50	1	0	0	0	1	3	5	5	0	2	0	.750	1.000	.667	0.00	27.00
Selman, Sam	R-L	6-3	190	11-14-90	1	2	6.57	12	0	0	0	12	12	9	9	0	11	21	.250	.200	.263	15.32	8.03
Sheller, Walker	R-R	6-3	195	5-21-95	3	2	3.53	35	0	0	1	51	49	23	20	5	14	27	.263	.213	.281	4.76	2.47
Skoglund, Eric	L-L	6-7	210	10-26-92	0	0	4.00	2	2	0	0	9	12	5	4	1	2	4	.324	.143	.367	4.00	2.00
Sparkman, Glenn	B-R	6-2	215	5-11-92	3	2	2.94	6	6	0	0	34	35	13	11	0	1	26	.263	.275	.258	6.95	0.27
Speier, Gabe	L-L	6-0	175	4-12-95	0	0	3.73	26	0	0	0	31	46	19	13	2	10	22	.326	.231	.363	6.32	2.87
Terrero, Franco	R-R	6-0	180	5-20-95	3	6	5.37	44	0	0	4	64	74	49	38	11	39	62	.288	.250	.301	8.76	5.51
Vasquez, Luis	R-R	6-4	200	4-3-86	2	0	0.00	7	0	0	3	7	4	0	0	0	4	15	.160	.125	.177	19.29	5.14
Vines, Jace	R-R	6-3	215	9-4-94	4	3	6.48	9	7	0	0	42	52	31	30	5	15	28	.325	.381	.289	6.05	3.24

Fielding

Catcher	PCT	G	PO	A	E	DP	PB
Dini	.994	71	468	44	3	1	9
Esposito	1.000	17	100	12	0	1	1
Fernandez	.992	34	229	12	2	2	3
Perez	1.000	2	13	0	0	0	0
Villegas	1.000	27	205	16	0	1	2

First Base	PCT	G	PO	A	E	DP
Brontsema	1.000	15	100	7	0	9
Dini	1.000	1	2	0	0	0
Duenez	.989	76	529	27	6	62
Liddi	.991	56	416	36	4	37
Porter	1.000	1	2	0	0	0

Second Base	PCT	G	PO	A	E	DP
Flores	.996	44	101	143	1	27
Lopez	1.000	14	28	35	0	7
Mejia	.967	63	150	145	10	42
Toups	.972	21	46	58	3	15

Third Base	PCT	G	PO	A	E	DP
Brontsema	.833	6	2	8	2	2
Flores	.933	40	23	88	8	7
Gutierrez	.936	62	36	95	9	8
Liddi	.923	8	3	21	2	1
Toups	.836	28	11	40	10	3

Shortstop	PCT	G	PO	A	E	DP
Flores	.949	22	30	64	5	21
Gutierrez	.875	2	3	4	1	0
Lopez	.996	58	69	161	1	29
Mejia	.952	59	86	170	13	31

Outfield	PCT	G	PO	A	E	DP
Brontsema	1.000	1	1	0	0	0
Dewees	.990	69	189	10	2	1
Downes	1.000	10	17	4	0	1
Escalera	.971	36	67	1	2	0
Flores	.950	14	17	2	1	0
Heath	.975	33	76	3	2	2
Hernandez	.974	82	176	8	5	1
Lee	.961	26	43	6	2	0
Liddi	.938	9	14	1	1	0
Martin	.000	1	0	0	0	0
Mejia	.980	14	49	1	1	0
Miller	.995	99	179	9	1	3
Peterson	.954	36	81	2	4	1
Toups	.000	1	0	0	0	0

WILMINGTON BLUE ROCKS   HIGH CLASS A
CAROLINA LEAGUE

Batting	B-T	HT	WT	DOB	AVG	vLH	vRH	G	AB	R	H	2B	3B	HR	RBI	BB	HBP	SH	SF	SO	SB	CS	SLG	OBP
Brontsema, John	R-R	6-2	187	12-13-94	.250	.000	.333	4	12	2	3	0	0	0	0	4	0	0	0	4	0	1	.250	.438
Burt, D.J.	R-R	5-9	160	10-13-95	.281	.322	.263	111	410	72	115	14	7	3	46	59	0	12	5	98	32	10	.371	.367
Cancel, Gabriel	R-R	6-1	185	12-8-96	.259	.220	.276	120	455	54	118	31	1	8	73	35	7	1	9	91	7	4	.385	.316
Castellano, Angelo	R-R	6-0	170	1-13-95	.221	.227	.219	120	375	39	83	16	2	2	36	35	4		6	81	12	9	.291	.291
DeVito, Chris	L-R	6-2	220	12-1-94	.181	.208	.168	65	221	22	40	7	0	1	23	29	2	1	2	67	0	0	.226	.280
Downes, Brandon	R-R	6-3	195	9-29-92	.235	.333	.167	13	51	5	12	4	0	2	11	3	1	0	1	16	2	0	.431	.286
Esposito, Nathan	R-R	5-11	180	6-25-93	.175	.063	.220	21	57	4	10	0	0	0	6	8	3	2	1	12	1	0	.175	.304
Fernandez, Xavier	R-R	5-11	197	7-15-95	.252	.250	.253	36	135	12	34	13	0	2	10	7	1	0	1	19	1	1	.393	.292
Heath, Nick	L-L	6-1	187	11-27-93	.284	.172	.331	54	194	37	55	8	1	2	20	35	2	5	1	65	29	9	.366	.397
Hicklen, Brewer	R-R	6-2	208	2-9-96	.211	.208	.213	22	71	11	15	4	0	1	3	4	1	2	0	26	6	0	.310	.263
Jones, Travis	R-R	6-4	210	9-29-95	.298	.211	.343	67	205	31	61	4	1	2	18	29	22	2	0	54	17	5	.356	.438
Lee, Khalil	L-L	5-10	170	6-26-98	.281	.282	.265	71	244	42	66	13	4	4	41	48	7	0	2	75	14	3	.406	.402
Lueck, Jackson	B-R	6-1	170	2-19-97	.172	.222	.150	9	29	3	5	4	0	0	2	6	1	0	0	12	1	0	.310	.200
Martin, Rudy	L-L	5-7	155	1-31-96	.232	.177	.259	75	259	42	60	13	4	4	37	39	6	10	0	93	29	6	.359	.345
Nunez, Oliver	B-R	5-10	170	2-21-95	.200	.250	.159	45	125	15	25	3	0	2	14	11	2	2	1	30	4	4	.272	.273
Perkins, Blake	B-R	6-1	165	9-10-96	.240	.230	.247	64	233	48	56	11	1	2	18	46	5	0	5	67	17	4	.322	.381
2-team total (65 Potomac)					.237	.245	.233	129	485	87	115	22	1	3	39	92	6	5		134	29	9	.305	.362
Peterson, Kort	L-R	6-1	195	4-29-94	.292	.297	.290	62	219	34	64	17	2	8	33	17	8	2	0	59	5	1	.498	.365
Rivera, Emmanuel	R-R	6-2	195	6-29-96	.280	.307	.268	99	375	45	105	25	6	6	61	29	3	0	4	59	3	2	.427	.333
Vallot, Chase	R-R	6-0	215	8-21-96	.108	.152	.088	47	148	19	16	4	0	7	24	31	5	0	1	80	0	0	.277	.281
Viloria, Meibrys	L-R	5-11	220	2-15-97	.260	.272	.255	100	358	34	93	16	1	6	44	40	5	3	1	75	2	1	.360	.342
Vizcaino, Vance	L-R	6-3	215	8-1-94	.241	.222	.247	73	241	31	58	9	2	1	28	17	2	3	2	62	2	2	.307	.294

Pitching

Pitching	B-T	HT	WT	DOB	W	L	ERA	G	GS	CG	SV	IP	H	R	ER	HR	BB	SO	AVG	vLH	vRH	K/9	BB/9
Becker, Nolan	R-L	6-6	225	6-13-91	1	0	2.70	8	0	0	0	13	14	6	4	2	2	13	.292	.500	.188	8.78	1.35
Beckwith, Andrew	R-R	6-0	180	3-22-95	1	0	1.42	11	0	0	0	13	15	3	2	0	1	11	.306	.280	.333	7.82	0.71
Bender, Anthony	R-R	6-4	205	2-3-95	6	3	3.57	30	9	0	1	93	91	41	37	7	38	54	.260	.288	.235	5.21	3.66
Brickhouse, Bryan	R-R	6-0	195	6-6-92	1	0	1.99	27	0	0	14	32	11	7	7	0	19	39	.106	.076	.137	11.08	5.40
Camp, Justin	R-R	5-11	230	5-17-93	3	2	3.47	37	0	0	0	57	56	28	22	3	26	43	.262	.250	.270	6.79	4.11
Castillo, Cristian	L-L	6-0	190	9-25-94	4	5	5.16	17	9	0	0	59	66	35	34	10	13	49	.281	.284	.280	7.43	1.97
Condra-Bogan, Jacob	R-R	6-3	220	8-30-94	0	0	27.00	1	0	0	0	1	3	3	3	0	1	1	.600	.500	.667	9.00	9.00
2-team total (11 Potomac)					1	2	3.94	12	0	0	2	16	11	8	7	0	4	14	.196	.318	.118	7.88	2.25
Dye, Josh	L-L	6-5	180	9-14-96	1	0	1.80	1	1	0	0	5	3	1	1	0	1	6	.158	.182	.125	10.80	1.80
Garabito, Gerson	R-R	6-0	160	8-19-95	8	6	3.16	26	26	1	0	142	117	59	50	12	73	116	.226	.191	.256	7.33	4.62
Gavin, Grant	R-R	6-2	185	7-10-95	1	0	3.18	13	0	0	0	23	13	8	8	3	9	31	.167	.276	.102	12.31	3.57
Gomez, Ofreidy	R-R	6-0	190	7-6-95	6	10	3.40	27	22	0	1	135	134	65	51	13	61	104	.260	.261	.259	6.93	4.07
Hernandez, Arnaldo	R-R	6-0	175	2-9-96	4	4	4.22	14	12	1	0	64	77	31	30	3	19	53	.301	.325	.277	7.45	2.67
Hinton, Kyle	R-R	6-0	200	2-12-97	0	0	0.00	1	0	0	0	2	2	0	0	0	2	0	.250	.286	.000	0.00	9.00
Hope, Carter	L-R	6-3	195	2-5-95	6	3	4.93	27	4	0	3	73	92	47	40	6	18	47	.309	.291	.325	5.79	2.22
Mitchell, Josh	R-L	6-2	220	9-8-94	2	1	8.39	21	0	0	0	25	28	24	23	2	12	22	.283	.308	.267	8.03	4.38
Pinto, Julio	R-R	6-3	185	11-18-95	1	4	6.11	26	0	0	10	28	34	21	19	2	19	28	.321	.420	.232	9.00	6.11
Ray, Corey	R-R	6-4	175	12-15-92	2	1	4.78	17	0	0	0	32	30	17	17	4	25	28	.256	.204	.294	7.88	7.03
Ruxer, Jared	R-R	6-3	200	7-29-92	1	2	4.19	10	0	0	0	19	18	9	9	3	6	14	.257	.250	.265	6.52	2.79
Sheller, Walker	R-R	6-3	195	5-21-95	1	1	1.42	5	0	0	1	6	5	1	1	0	2	6	.227	.300	.167	8.53	2.84
Sotillet, Andres	R-R	6-1	175	3-2-97	2	6	5.40	10	1	0	1	52	70	32	31	5	21	25	.337	.340	.333	4.35	3.66
Tatum, Vance	L-L	6-4	215	5-2-95	3	2	3.33	19	0	0	0	27	28	14	10	2	17	19	.277	.175	.344	6.33	5.67
Tillo, Daniel	L-L	6-5	215	6-13-96	3	5	4.94	19	19	0	0	93	99	54	51	3	51	69	.279	.272	.282	6.68	4.94
Vines, Jace	R-R	6-3	215	9-4-94	2	8	5.04	18	17	1	1	95	122	62	53	5	28	59	.310	.328	.297	5.61	2.66
Watson, Nolan	R-R	6-2	195	1-25-97	6	4	4.60	11	11	1	0	59	65	33	30	5	26	30	.292	.331	.248	4.60	3.99
Wynne, Matthew	R-R	6-4	235	7-5-93	0	1	3.06	14	0	0	3	18	20	7	6	1	10	14	.282	.214	.326	7.13	5.09
Zuber, Tyler	R-R	5-11	175	6-16-95	1	4	4.91	20	0	0	9	22	22	17	12	1	9	22	.265	.293	.238	9.00	3.68

Fielding

Catcher	PCT	G	PO	A	E	DP	PB
Esposito	1.000	21	110	16	0	2	5
Fernandez	.975	21	147	11	4	1	0
Vallot	.988	11	82	3	1	0	3
Viloria	.993	88	585	86	5	9	9

First Base	PCT	G	PO	A	E	DP
DeVito	.988	65	465	46	6	44
Fernandez	.982	6	49	5	1	3
Jones	.986	61	444	45	7	61
Vallot	.944	6	50	1	3	6
Vizcaino	.971	4	33	1	1	3

Second Base	PCT	G	PO	A	E	DP
Brontsema	.923	4	7	5	1	2

	PCT	G	PO	A	E	DP
Burt	.988	35	73	95	2	28
Cancel	.975	87	154	237	10	56
Nunez	.988	18	34	45	1	7

Third Base	PCT	G	PO	A	E	DP
Burt	.973	38	24	48	2	3
Cancel	.765	8	7	6	4	2
Jones	.857	4	2	10	2	1
Nunez	.833	4	0	5	1	0
Rivera	.963	89	76	133	8	16

Shortstop	PCT	G	PO	A	E	DP
Burt	.872	13	17	24	6	3
Cancel	.964	12	21	32	2	8
Castellano	.960	120	194	312	21	83

	PCT	G	PO	A	E
Nunez	.750	1	3	3	2	1

Outfield	PCT	G	PO	A	E	DP
Burt	.952	12	20	0	1	0
Downes	1.000	11	20	0	0	0
Heath	.992	53	112	8	1	0
Hicklen	1.000	21	39	3	0	2
Jones	1.000	1	0	0	0	0
Lee	.972	66	165	6	5	1
Lueck	.933	9	13	1	1	0
Martin	.993	75	136	8	1	0
Perkins	.989	62	170	9	2	2
Peterson	.977	60	117	11	3	1
Vizcaino	.977	55	124	5	3	2

LEXINGTON LEGENDS
SOUTH ATLANTIC LEAGUE

LOW CLASS A

Batting

Batting	B-T	HT	WT	DOB	AVG	vLH	vRH	G	AB	R	H	2B	3B	HR	RBI	BB	HBP	SH	SF	SO	SB	CS	SLG	OBP
Aracena, Ricky	B-R	5-8	160	10-2-97	.261	.270	.257	95	303	46	79	10	0	3	40	21	4	11	4	61	17	6	.323	.313
Carrasco, Dennicher	R-R	5-11	195	10-12-95	.250	.206	.268	62	232	34	58	9	1	10	30	11	4	0	1	58	2	3	.427	.294
Diaz, Carlos	R-R	5-8	145	11-15-92	.291	.333	.279	22	79	15	23	4	0	1	4	4	1	3	0	8	1	0	.380	.333
Gasparini, Marten	B-R	6-0	195	5-24-97	.222	.238	.214	103	343	38	76	16	2	4	34	23	2	8	2	119	18	9	.315	.273
Gigliotti, Michael	L-L	6-1	180	2-14-96	.235	.250	.231	6	17	3	4	1	0	1	2	6	0	1	0	5	1	0	.471	.435
Gonzalez, Julio	L-R	5-10	185	6-14-95	.235	.333	.182	6	17	4	4	1	0	0	3	4	0	0	0	5	0	1	.294	.381
Guzman, Jeison	L-R	6-2	180	10-8-98	.239	.197	.259	60	209	27	50	11	3	2	21	18	4	5	0	58	12	4	.349	.312
Hancock, William	L-R	6-2	200	10-31-96	.200	.000	.222	6	20	1	4	1	0	0	1	0	0	1	0	9	0	0	.250	.227
Hicklen, Brewer	R-R	6-2	208	2-9-96	.307	.345	.292	82	306	59	94	18	3	17	65	24	13	0	4	98	29	6	.552	.378
Isbel, Kyle	L-R	5-11	183	3-3-97	.289	.382	.240	39	159	30	46	12	1	3	14	12	2	0	1	43	12	3	.434	.345
Jones, Cal	R-R	6-0	175	9-16-97	.253	.301	.235	89	304	49	77	14	3	8	41	24	3	1	4	95	5	6	.398	.310
Jones, Travis	R-R	6-4	210	9-29-95	.285	.257	.298	62	228	41	65	13	1	5	32	17	14	0	2	56	14	7	.417	.368
Matias, Seuly	R-R	6-3	200	9-4-98	.231	.227	.232	94	338	62	78	13	1	31	63	24	12	0	2	131	6	0	.550	.303
Melendez, MJ	L-R	6-1	185	11-29-98	.251	.254	.249	111	419	52	105	26	9	19	73	43	4	0	6	143	4	6	.492	.322
Morales, Matt	R-R	5-11	170	11-26-96	.198	.160	.209	38	111	16	22	2	0	1	9	16	0	1	1	42	5	1	.243	.297
Nunez, Oliver	B-R	5-10	170	2-21-95	.219	.353	.170	19	64	9	14	2	1	0	3	4	0	1	1	16	2	0	.281	.261
Olloque, Manny	R-R	6-2	165	5-11-96	.254	.271	.248	48	177	21	45	12	2	7	29	7	2	0	2	67	3	2	.463	.287
Perez, Cristian	R-R	5-10	170	10-26-98	.278	.354	.252	87	320	48	89	14	0	3	37	11	3	8	3	43	10	7	.350	.306
Pratto, Nick	L-L	6-1	195	10-6-98	.280	.289	.277	127	485	79	136	33	2	14	62	45	3	0	4	150	22	5	.443	.343
Rivero, Sebastian	R-R	6-1	180	11-16-98	.258	.256	.259	77	279	41	72	16	0	7	34	17	2	4	4	59	0	1	.391	.301
Vizcaino, Vance	R-R	6-1	185	10-1-95	.192	.154	.205	16	52	7	10	2	1	0	5	8	0	1	0	13	4	3	.327	.312

Pitching

Pitching	B-T	HT	WT	DOB	W	L	ERA	G	GS	CG	SV	IP	H	R	ER	HR	BB	SO	AVG	vLH	vRH	K/9	BB/9
Beckwith, Andrew	R-R	6-0	180	3-22-95	3	1	1.84	25	0	0	2	49	33	17	10	3	13	43	.192	.141	.241	7.90	2.39
Biasi, Sal	R-R	6-0	190	9-30-95	3	3	5.06	27	0	0	3	48	42	27	24	9	17	46	.259	.222	.289	9.70	3.59
Capps, Holden	R-L	6-2	180	3-24-97	1	1	2.98	24	4	0	2	63	68	28	21	5	10	69	.265	.269	.263	9.81	1.42

	B-T	HT	WT	DOB	W	L	ERA	G	GS	CG	SV	IP	H	R	ER	HR	BB	SO	AVG	vLH	vRH	K/9	BB/9
Cloney, J.C.	L-L	6-1	226	8-3-94	3	1	2.73	5	5	0	0	30	32	11	9	2	9	18	.288	.279	.294	5.46	2.73
Condra-Bogan, Jacob	R-R	6-3	220	8-30-94	1	1	2.08	16	0	0	5	26	18	9	6	2	2	39	.190	.186	.192	13.50	0.69
Davila, Garrett	L-L	6-2	180	1-17-97	7	7	4.21	25	18	0	0	107	94	58	50	22	49	84	.235	.248	.229	7.07	4.12
Del Rosario, Yefri	R-R	6-2	180	9-23-99	6	5	3.19	15	15	0	0	79	69	36	28	10	29	72	.227	.200	.252	8.20	3.30
Drabble, Dillon	R-R	6-2	190	7-12-96	0	1	45.00	2	0	0	0	1	2	5	5	1	2	2	.333	.250	.500	18.00	18.00
Duarte, Daniel	R-R	6-0	170	12-4-96	1	0	2.31	6	0	0	0	12	8	3	3	1	5	11	.195	.273	.105	8.49	3.86
Garcia, Robert	R-L	6-4	225	6-14-96	0	2	2.25	13	0	0	1	24	21	13	6	0	11	31	.244	.188	.278	11.63	4.13
Hensley, Bryce	L-L	6-4	215	10-3-95	0	0	0.00	1	0	0	0	1	1	0	0	0	0	2	.200	.000	.500	13.50	0.00
Hernandez, Carlos	R-R	6-4	175	3-11-97	6	5	3.29	15	15	0	0	79	71	36	29	7	23	82	.236	.242	.229	9.30	2.61
Hope, Carter	L-R	6-3	195	2-5-95	4	0	1.32	6	0	0	1	14	6	3	2	1	1	16	.128	.100	.177	10.54	0.66
Hrbek, Danny	L-R	5-11	195	12-27-94	4	2	4.50	24	0	0	0	36	24	21	18	5	16	35	.202	.245	.167	8.75	4.00
Kowar, Jackson	R-R	6-5	180	10-4-96	0	1	3.42	9	9	0	0	26	19	10	10	2	12	22	.200	.177	.227	7.52	4.10
Lara, Janser	R-R	6-0	170	8-10-96	3	4	3.41	23	8	0	1	66	54	34	25	5	28	75	.214	.222	.206	10.23	3.82
Lynch, Daniel	L-L	6-6	190	11-17-96	5	1	1.58	9	9	0	0	40	35	9	7	1	6	47	.243	.135	.280	10.58	1.35
Martinez, Marcelo	L-L	6-2	190	8-10-96	1	0	4.50	1	1	0	0	6	4	3	3	1	1	9	.182	.273	.091	13.50	1.50
Mitchell, Josh	R-L	6-2	220	8-9-94	1	0	0.90	7	0	0	0	10	8	4	1	1	1	11	.205	.250	.185	9.90	0.90
Neuweiler, Charlie	R-R	6-1	205	2-8-99	2	3	5.58	11	11	0	0	50	50	39	31	8	23	46	.258	.259	.257	8.28	4.14
Pinto, Julio	R-R	6-3	185	11-18-95	2	0	4.86	10	0	0	0	17	12	9	9	4	7	21	.200	.235	.154	11.34	3.78
Ratliff, Tad	R-R	6-2	240	4-3-96	2	0	1.68	27	0	0	10	48	45	12	9	3	9	47	.289	.209	.209	8.87	1.86
Snider, Collin	R-R	6-4	200	10-10-95	5	7	5.57	29	9	0	1	76	111	62	47	13	16	50	.330	.337	.323	5.92	1.89
Sotillet, Andres	R-R	6-1	175	3-2-97	6	5	3.93	16	13	1	0	89	107	46	39	6	13	84	.296	.314	.273	8.46	1.31
Suchey, Garrett	R-R	6-2	215	11-25-94	2	2	1.36	21	0	0	1	33	27	8	5	2	4	30	.221	.193	.246	8.18	1.09
Tatum, Vance	L-L	6-4	215	5-2-95	0	0	0.00	3	0	0	0	5	1	0	0	0	2	7	.063	.000	.100	11.81	3.38
Tillo, Daniel	L-L	6-5	215	6-13-96	1	1	4.35	7	7	0	0	41	37	22	20	3	14	31	.233	.306	.200	6.75	3.05
Watson, Nolan	R-R	6-2	195	1-25-97	4	6	5.81	13	13	1	0	67	94	55	43	9	21	63	.331	.341	.322	8.51	2.84
Zuber, Tyler	R-R	5-11	175	6-16-95	2	2	3.10	23	0	0	0	29	26	11	10	4	4	48	.241	.211	.275	14.90	1.24

Fielding

C: Hancock 6, Melendez 73, Rivero 60. **1B:** Jones 7, Olloque 6, Pratto 125. **2B:** Aracena 94, Diaz 7, Gonzalez 6, Morales 20, Nunez 13. **3B:** Carrasco 57, Diaz 15, Guzman 7, Jones 23, Morales 4, Nunez 3, Olloque 15, Perez 14. **SS:** Guzman 51, Morales 15, Nunez 3, Perez 69. **OF:** Gasparini 100, Gigliotti 6, Hicklen 71, Isbel 37, Jones 84, Jones 23, Matias 75, Olloque 10, Vizcaino 12.

BURLINGTON ROYALS   ROOKIE
APPALACHIAN LEAGUE

Batting	B-T	HT	WT	DOB	AVG	vLH	vRH	G	AB	R	H	2B	3B	HR	RBI	BB	HBP	SH	SF	SO	SB	CS	SLG	OBP
Aplin, Rhett	L-L	6-2	220	10-10-95	.288	.333	.275	39	132	17	38	4	2	0	9	20	2	0	2	28	3	1	.349	.385
Bewley, Bhret	R-R	5-11	182	1-30-97	.285	.345	.271	46	151	25	43	12	1	1	11	27	2	1	1	34	7	1	.397	.398
Bradshaw, Montae	R-R	5-10	170	4-29-96	.160	.160	.160	38	125	10	20	5	0	0	13	5	9	1	0	27	2	2	.200	.245
Cole, Eric	B-R	5-11	170	1-17-97	.281	.111	.314	42	167	19	47	11	2	1	25	17	2	0	1	40	6	0	.389	.353
Emodi, Michael	R-R	6-4	225	4-18-96	.206	.130	.230	27	97	16	20	6	0	3	13	8	7	0	0	40	0	0	.361	.313
Fermin, Freddy	R-R	5-10	185	5-16-95	.246	.296	.236	47	167	28	41	9	1	2	18	25	2	1	1	15	2	1	.347	.349
Griffin, Dalton	L-L	6-3	200	9-2-97	.150	.000	.162	14	40	5	6	2	1	0	4	13	0	0	0	19	0	0	.250	.359
Guzman, Jeison	L-R	6-2	180	10-8-98	.283	.077	.312	25	106	17	30	1	1	2	8	12	0	1	0	16	14	1	.368	.356
Henry, Isaiah	R-R	6-3	185	3-22-99	.214	.250	.212	17	56	12	12	2	1	0	5	9	0	1	0	30	2	1	.286	.323
Hudgins, Chris	R-R	6-1	190	3-2-96	.238	.219	.243	37	143	19	34	11	2	5	26	9	2	0	2	39	0	0	.448	.289
Lueck, Jackson	B-R	6-1	170	2-19-97	.245	.233	.248	43	163	24	40	9	1	5	19	19	5	0	2	52	4	3	.405	.339
Marquez, Jose	B-R	6-0	175	10-7-97	.301	.300	.302	59	229	47	69	14	5	7	35	16	4	2	2	49	9	4	.498	.355
Medina, Angel	R-R	6-1	180	11-2-98	.179	.000	.189	14	56	8	10	1	2	1	8	3	0	0	0	22	0	1	.321	.220
Morales, Matt	R-R	5-11	170	11-26-96	.212	.276	.191	29	113	15	24	5	1	1	10	16	0	1	1	44	5	2	.301	.308
Negret, Juan Carlos	R-R	6-0	190	6-19-99	.224	.227	.223	54	201	30	45	11		9	32	13	5	0	3	60	3	2	.423	.284
Romero, Rafael	R-R	5-10	155	11-14-98	.233	.191	.242	36	120	12	28	4	0	0	14	12	0	1	0	28	1	2	.267	.303
Schultz, Colby	L-R	6-0	180	12-13-94	.244	.235	.246	39	127	13	31	3	2	0	14	16	3	3	1	29	3	2	.299	.340
Strong, Hunter	L-L	6-2	200	3-25-97	.143	.111	.149	16	56	5	8	2	0	0	3	4	0	0	0	13	2	0	.179	.200

Pitching	B-T	HT	WT	DOB	W	L	ERA	G	GS	CG	SV	IP	H	R	ER	HR	BB	SO	AVG	vLH	vRH	K/9	BB/9
Acevedo, Randy	R-R	6-1	155	3-14-97	0	2	6.67	5	4	0	0	27	40	24	20	0	8	13	.336	.367	.305	4.33	2.67
Alcantara, Luis	R-R	6-0	150	11-1-97	0	0	10.61	3	0	0	0	9	17	11	11	1	4	8	.378	.438	.345	7.71	3.86
Cillis, Ted	L-L	6-2	225	8-12-94	1	1	2.25	8	0	0	0	16	7	4	4	0	6	18	.132	.067	.158	10.13	3.38
Cox, Austin	L-L	6-4	185	3-28-97	1	1	3.78	9	9	0	0	33	29	19	14	1	15	51	.228	.320	.206	13.77	4.05
De Leon, Jose	R-R	5-11	175	4-19-95	0	1	5.57	17	0	0	0	21	20	15	13	2	15	26	.253	.160	.296	11.14	6.43
Dye, Josh	R-R	6-5	180	9-14-96	1	3	4.54	11	7	0	0	36	45	32	18	4	5	34	.304	.282	.312	8.58	1.26
Estevez, Emmanuel	R-R	6-3	210	8-22-96	1	1	8.80	10	0	0	0	15	21	16	15	2	10	14	.318	.250	.357	8.22	5.87
Garcia, Yerelmy	R-R	6-2	180	11-5-95	5	2	4.58	11	8	1	0	55	55	31	28	2	14	35	.254	.268	.244	5.73	2.29
Gonzalez, Kelvin	R-R	6-0	170	12-24-97	0	2	4.19	11	0	0	1	19	20	13	9	2	7	17	.256	.280	.245	7.91	3.26
Greenlees, Stephen	L-L	6-4	215	5-7-96	0	0	5.40	3	0	0	0	7	5	4	4	0	5	10	.222	.500	.143	13.50	6.75
Hinton, Kyle	R-R	6-0	200	2-12-97	1	2	3.52	19	0	0	6	31	21	14	12	2	18	46	.189	.209	.177	13.50	5.28
Johnson, Bryar	R-R	6-3	200	8-17-99	2	5	7.54	11	2	0	1	37	49	35	31	6	30	40	.316	.400	.256	9.73	7.30
Lambright, Austin	R-R	6-3	205	8-26-94	0	3	4.84	16	0	0	1	22	21	16	12	0	27	31	.233	.207	.246	12.49	10.88
Lara, Janser	R-R	6-0	170	8-10-96	0	0	10.38	2	2	0	0	4	9	6	5	0	3	5	.474	.364	.625	10.38	5.19
Luciano, Elvis	R-R	6-2	184	2-15-00	3	5	4.66	11	11	0	0	56	55	30	29	4	20	56	.255	.235	.272	9.00	3.21
Lynch, Daniel	L-L	6-6	190	11-17-96	0	0	1.59	3	3	0	0	11	9	3	2	0	4	11	.209	.000	.265	11.12	1.59
Maldonado, Ismael	R-R	6-0	170	9-28-95	2	1	6.32	15	0	0	1	31	34	29	22	4	24	35	.264	.256	.267	10.05	6.89
Martinez, Marcelo	L-L	6-2	190	8-10-96	5	3	2.68	10	10	1	0	57	46	18	17	3	11	71	.216	.217	.216	11.21	1.74
Neuweiler, Charlie	R-R	6-1	205	2-8-99	0	1	6.30	2	2	0	0	13	7	7	2	2	10	13	.310	.375	.269	9.00	1.80
Nunez, Andres	R-R	6-4	240	9-20-95	0	0	2.45	4	0	0	0	7	6	2	1	2	4	7	.222	.333	.167	8.59	4.91

	B-T	HT	WT	DOB	W	L	ERA	G	GS	CG	SV	IP	H	R	ER	HR	BB	SO	AVG	vLH	vRH	K/9	BB/9
Van Buren, Malcolm	R-R	6-4	185	7-5-98	0	5	8.91	10	7	0	0	33	39	34	33	7	31	37	.291	.267	.303	9.99	8.37
Willis, Marlin	L-L	6-4	190	6-5-98	3	5	8.38	11	3	0	0	39	49	40	36	5	34	32	.310	.292	.313	7.45	7.91

Fielding

C: Emodi 14, Fermin 37, Hudgins 17. **1B:** Aplin 36, Bewley 6, Griffin 14, Hudgins 15, Schultz 1. **2B:** Marquez 49, Romero 8, Schultz 13. **3B:** Bewley 39, Medina 10, Romero 19, Schultz 1. **SS:** Guzman 23, Morales 29, Romero 7, Schultz 10. **OF:** Bradshaw 37, Cole 41, Henry 16, Lueck 36, Negret 51, Schultz 10, Strong 16.

IDAHO FALLS CHUKARS   ROOKIE
PIONEER LEAGUE

Batting	B-T	HT	WT	DOB	AVG	vLH	vRH	G	AB	R	H	2B	3B	HR	RBI	BB	HBP	SH	SF	SO	SB	CS	SLG	OBP
Atencio, Jesus	R-R	5-10	165	8-22-96	.309	.296	.313	35	139	25	43	7	0	1	22	12	4	0	1	22	0	0	.381	.378
Caraballo, Jose	R-R	6-1	180	1-7-97	.293	.333	.282	66	280	44	82	23	3	5	48	15	1	0	1	76	2	4	.450	.330
Collado, Offerman	L-R	5-10	140	6-10-96	.273	.205	.290	56	227	38	62	6	3	2	33	25	0	4	3	36	9	3	.352	.341
Cox, Brady	R-R	6-0	205	10-24-94	.221	.136	.250	27	86	14	19	8	1	2	14	16	2	0	1	23	0	0	.407	.352
Diaz, Carlos	R-R	5-8	145	11-15-92	.435	.000	.526	5	23	4	10	2	0	0	3	0	0	0	0	2	0	0	.522	.435
Eaton, Nathan	R-R	5-11	185	12-22-96	.354	.412	.333	66	260	59	92	20	12	5	53	33	4	1	5	60	19	5	.581	.427
Fermin, Freddy	R-R	5-10	185	5-16-95	.300	.333	.286	3	10	3	3	1	0	0	1	0	0	0	0	2	0	0	.400	.300
Gonzalez, Julio	L-R	5-10	185	6-14-95	.218	.250	.210	34	124	25	27	4	3	0	19	16	1	2	1	17	3	2	.298	.310
Hutchins, Nick	R-R	6-1	200	11-17-95	.292	.282	.295	48	178	35	52	19	0	7	40	20	6	0	3	40	0	0	.517	.377
Isbel, Kyle	L-R	5-11	185	3-3-97	.381	.292	.407	25	105	27	40	10	1	4	18	14	0	0	0	17	12	3	.610	.454
James, Tyler	L-R	5-10	162	9-14-96	.312	.383	.281	47	199	55	62	8	2	2	20	29	4	4	0	54	38	8	.402	.410
Jaquez, Rubendy	B-R	5-11	174	2-13-99	.387	.600	.346	9	31	5	12	2	0	0	5	6	0	1	1	6	2	2	.452	.474
Kasser, Kyle	L-R	5-10	180	10-12-95	.357	.429	.333	42	171	25	61	6	0	1	29	13	0	1	1	17	1	0	.409	.400
Lopez, Raymond	B-R	6-1	155	12-4-98	.250	.000	.333	1	4	1	1	0	0	0	0	1	0	0	0	0	0	0	.250	.400
Marquez, Jose	B-R	6-0	175	10-7-97	.333	.000	.429	2	9	1	3	0	0	0	2	0	0	0	0	1	0	1	.333	.333
Martin, Andres	R-R	6-0	190	2-14-97	.288	.368	.265	45	153	23	44	2	5	1	21	16	1	1	1	34	10	1	.386	.357
Martin, Rudy	L-L	5-7	155	1-31-96	.265	.182	.304	9	34	9	9	2	1	2	9	6	0	2	2	11	0	0	.559	.357
Medina, Angel	R-R	5-10	180	11-2-98	.218	.217	.218	31	124	22	27	5	1	2	14	7	0	0	1	32	3	1	.323	.258
Olloque, Manny	R-R	6-2	165	5-11-96	.474	.750	.400	5	19	7	9	2	1	2	9	4	0	0	1	5	0	1	1.000	.542
Rohlman, Reed	L-L	6-1	190	1-5-95	.286	.203	.310	67	262	59	75	23	3	6	56	38	4	0	1	57	3	1	.466	.384
Romero, Rafael	R-R	5-10	155	11-14-98	.750	1.000	.667	2	4	3	3	1	0	0	1	0	0	0	0	0	0	0	1.000	.750
Starling, Bubba	R-R	6-4	215	8-3-92	.500	—	.500	5	8	5	4	3	0	1	4	5	0	0	0	2	0	1	1.250	.692
Strong, Hunter	L-L	6-1	200	3-25-97	.336	.231	.349	32	119	26	40	10	2	2	21	16	1	0	1	18	3	0	.504	.416
Vallot, Chase	R-R	6-0	215	8-21-96	.262	.235	.270	37	145	23	38	15	0	7	28	14	9	0	0	71	0	0	.510	.363

Pitching	B-T	HT	WT	DOB	W	L	ERA	G	GS	CG	SV	IP	H	R	ER	HR	BB	SO	AVG	vLH	vRH	K/9	BB/9
Bowlan, Jonathan	R-R	6-6	262	12-1-96	1	4	6.94	9	9	0	0	35	51	30	27	6	9	23	.329	.300	.343	5.91	2.31
Bubic, Kris	L-L	6-3	220	8-19-97	2	3	4.03	10	10	0	0	38	38	25	17	2	19	53	.253	.256	.252	12.55	4.50
Cillis, Ted	L-L	6-2	225	8-12-94	1	1	7.36	4	0	0	1	7	9	6	6	0	5		.281	.200	.318	6.14	6.14
Cloney, J.C.	L-L	6-1	226	8-3-94	9	0	1.93	9	9	0	0	56	49	13	12	2	10	50	.234	.214	.240	8.04	1.61
Duarte, Daniel	R-R	6-0	170	12-4-96	0	1	0.00	7	0	0	1	14	12	1	0	0	3	14	.235	.191	.267	9.00	1.93
Edwards, Andrew	R-R	6-6	265	10-7-91	1	0	3.86	2	0	0	0	2	1	1	1	0	1	3	.125	.000	.200	11.57	3.86
Eldred, C.J.	R-R	6-2	225	5-6-95	6	2	6.00	13	13	0	0	72	86	59	48	6	12	39	.292	.265	.306	4.88	1.50
Floyd, Jordan	L-L	6-3	240	2-23-95	3	2	5.40	16	0	0	0	27	28	19	16	1	10	23	.272	.258	.278	7.76	3.38
Garcia, Robert	R-L	6-4	225	6-14-96	0	0	1.61	10	0	0	3	22	18	5	4	1	8	18	.222	.261	.207	7.25	3.22
Gray, Tyler	R-R	6-2	180	3-12-97	3	2	4.56	12	2	0	2	47	48	31	24	4	20	57	.253	.191	.287	10.84	3.80
Greenlees, Stephen	L-L	6-4	215	5-7-96	0	2	7.56	11	0	0	0	17	16	16	14	0	15	18	.254	.188	.277	9.72	8.10
Haake, Zach	R-R	6-4	186	10-8-96	0	0	1.59	2	2	0	0	6	2	1	1	0	2	4	.111	.200	.077	6.35	3.18
Heasley, Jon	R-R	6-3	215	1-27-97	1	3	5.15	12	11	0	0	51	55	38	29	4	16	35	.264	.310	.241	6.22	2.84
Hellinger, Jaret	R-L	6-4	170	11-18-96	2	1	4.60	17	0	0	4	29	35	20	15	3	6	25	.294	.233	.315	7.67	1.84
James, Daniel	R-R	6-4	215	1-19-96	0	0	1.59	6	0	0	3	6	3	2	1	0	3	5	.158	.200	.143	7.94	4.76
Kaufman, Rylan	L-L	6-4	190	6-23-99	0	0	1.80	2	2	0	0	5	2	2	1	0	1	7	.111	.000	.182	12.60	1.80
Klein, Jackson	R-R	6-2	185	7-13-94	0	1	12.71	14	0	0	1	11	16	17	16	0	23	15	.327	.304	.346	11.91	18.26
Luciano, Elvis	R-R	6-2	184	2-15-00	2	0	0.00	2	1	0	0	11	6	1	0	0	3	14	.162	.250	.059	11.45	2.45
Lugo, Rito	L-L	5-10	185	11-3-95	2	0	2.01	4	0	0	2	22	19	5	5	2	2	30	.226	.214	.229	12.09	0.81
Maldonado, Ismael	R-R	6-4	170	9-28-95	0	0	4.50	1	1	0	0	2	3	1	1	0	0	3	.333	.000	.429	13.50	0.00
Markus, Joey	R-L	6-7	220	5-29-96	0	0	3.00	2	0	0	0	3	2	1	1	0	5	3	.200	.500	.125	9.00	15.00
Marte, Christopher	R-R	6-1	190	7-9-96	0	0	14.85	6	0	0	0	7	15	12	11	0	3	2	.455	.455	.455	2.70	4.05
Martinez, Marcelo	L-L	6-2	190	8-10-96	0	1	1.50	2	0	0	0	6	4	1	1	1	2	10	.191	.222	.167	15.00	3.00
Mayes, Connor	R-R	6-2	205	5-23-96	5	2	5.52	13	11	0	0	62	81	40	38	7	25	52	.309	.340	.289	7.55	3.63
Messier, Michael	R-L	6-6	205	5-12-95	1	0	7.20	3	0	0	0	5	5	4	4	1	3	6	.263	.333	.250	10.80	5.40
Pena, Domingo	R-R	6-2	171	4-7-98	3	4	7.27	12	0	0	0	43	59	37	35	7	15	36	.321	.246	.354	7.48	3.12
Ramirez, Jose	R-R	6-2	225	1-10-98	0	2	6.75	14	0	0	3	21	29	20	16	3	11	14	.322	.318	.324	5.91	4.64
Webb, Nathan	R-R	6-2	215	8-20-97	1	2	10.42	11	1	0	0	38	54	44	44	10	29	36	.333	.383	.304	8.53	6.87

Fielding

C: Atencio 29, Cox 19, Fermin 2, Hutchins 9, Vallot 19. **1B:** Cox 4, Hutchins 17, Rohlman 58. **2B:** Diaz 3, Eaton 20, Gonzalez 14, James 7, Kasser 31, Marquez 2. **3B:** Eaton 20, Gonzalez 15, Jaquez 9, Medina 31, Olloque 3, Romero 1. **SS:** Collado 56, Diaz 2, Gonzalez 6, Kasser 11, Romero 1. **OF:** Caraballo 62, Eaton 21, Isbel 22, James 41, Lopez 1, Martin 43, Martin 8, Starling 4, Strong 32.

AZL ROYALS
ARIZONA LEAGUE
ROOKIE

Batting	B-T	HT	WT	DOB	AVG	vLH	vRH	G	AB	R	H	2B	3B	HR	RBI	BB	HBP	SH	SF	SO	SB	CS	SLG	OBP
Aplin, Rhett	L-L	6-2	220	10-10-95	.348	.333	.355	12	46	6	16	2	0	0	9	3	2	0	0	10	1	0	.391	.412
Bewley, Brhet	R-R	5-11	182	1-30-97	.357	.000	.455	8	14	4	5	0	0	1	1	6	0	2	0	5	0	1	.357	.550
Diaz, Carlos	R-R	5-8	145	11-15-92	.500	1.000	.429	3	8	2	4	0	0	1	3	0	0	0	0	2	0	0	.500	.636
Duenez, Samir	L-R	6-1	230	6-11-96	.238	.250	.231	7	21	1	5	2	0	1	4	2	0	0	1	7	1	0	.476	.292
El-Abour, Tarik	R-R	5-11	180	6-20-92	.000	.000	.000	4	6	0	0	0	0	0	0	0	0	0	0	3	0	0	.000	.000
Emodi, Michael	R-R	6-4	225	4-18-96	.100	.000	.167	4	10	3	1	1	0	0	1	5	0	0	1	4	0	0	.200	.375
Escalera, Alfredo	R-R	6-1	186	2-17-95	.250	.300	.227	10	32	6	8	1	0	1	6	5	0	0	1	5	5	0	.375	.342
Garcia, Maikel	R-R	6-0	145	3-3-00	.228	.229	.228	40	149	15	34	2	1	0	9	15	0	6	0	38	13	6	.255	.299
Hancock, William	L-R	6-2	200	10-31-96	.224	.182	.241	24	76	6	17	5	1	1	7	8	4	0	2	25	0	1	.355	.322
Henry, Isaiah	R-R	6-3	185	3-22-99	.275	.267	.278	24	69	9	19	2	3	0	6	7	0	1	1	30	2	1	.391	.338
Hollie, David	R-R	6-0	190	10-25-99	.225	.206	.232	38	129	11	29	6	2	2	19	12	0	0	1	42	4	2	.349	.289
Hughes, Gage	B-R	6-1	170	8-15-99	.208	.316	.182	26	96	11	20	6	2	0	6	2	1	3	1	25	5	2	.313	.274
Jackson, Kevon	R-R	5-9	180	6-14-00	.178	.233	.155	38	101	14	18	1	3	0	7	20	2	0	0	47	7	3	.248	.325
Jaquez, Rubendy	B-R	5-11	174	2-13-99	.303	.364	.273	46	165	27	50	6	3	4	27	22	2	1	1	34	16	5	.449	.390
Lopez, Raymond	R-R	6-1	155	12-4-98	.164	.143	.173	42	146	14	24	5	1	0	10	8	1	5	0	55	7	3	.212	.213
Lueck, Jackson	B-R	6-1	170	2-19-97	.625	.800	.333	2	8	5	5	2	1	0	2	0	0	0	1	0	0	1	1.125	.700
Mondesi, Paul	R-R	6-0	235	7-7-98	.250	.412	.200	25	72	4	18	2	0	0	5	2	1	2	0	21	1	0	.278	.280
Nacero, Kember	R-R	5-11	155	3-5-00	.209	.254	.186	46	172	25	36	7	1	0	11	17	2	1	0	64	5	2	.262	.288
Pineda, Hector	R-R	5-10	160	8-22-98	.246	.231	.250	20	57	8	14	1	0	0	4	5	1	1	2	15	0	0	.263	.308
Porter, Logan	R-R	6-0	200	7-12-95	.317	.364	.294	34	101	14	32	11	1	1	16	19	5	1	0	22	0	0	.475	.448
Rivera, Emmanuel	R-R	6-2	195	6-29-96	.192	.167	.200	7	26	4	5	0	1	0	2	1	0	0	0	6	0	0	.269	.222
Rodriguez, Ismaldo	R-R	6-0	175	7-3-98	.234	.364	.120	13	47	12	11	2	0	4	9	4	0	0	1	16	2	0	.532	.289
Schultz, Colby	L-R	6-0	180	12-13-94	.333	1.000	.000	1	3	0	1	0	0	0	2	0	0	1	0	0	1	0	.333	.333
Smith, Isaiah	R-R	6-3	190	6-19-99	.160	.167	.154	9	25	4	4	0	1	1	3	3	0	0	0	5	2	1	.360	.250
Soto, Edickson	R-R	5-11	165	2-28-00	.158	.167	.155	24	76	6	12	1	0	0	2	6	1	1	0	20	2	1	.171	.229
Starling, Bubba	R-R	6-4	215	8-3-92	.273	.500	.222	4	11	3	3	0	0	3	5	0	1	0	0	6	0	1	1.091	.333
Strong, Hunter	L-L	6-1	200	3-25-97	.125	.000	.167	3	8	2	1	0	0	0	0	2	2	0	0	1	0	0	.125	.417
Vidal, Stephan	R-R	6-1	215	4-4-96	.286	.214	.321	13	42	5	12	1	0	0	2	4	2	0	0	12	0	1	.310	.375

Pitching	B-T	HT	WT	DOB	W	L	ERA	G	GS	CG	SV	IP	H	R	ER	HR	BB	SO	AVG	vLH	vRH	K/9	BB/9
Alcantara, Adrian	R-R	6-1	178	8-29-99	1	1	6.04	12	7	0	0	45	49	32	30	4	30	33	.290	.379	.233	6.65	6.04
Barlow, Scott	R-R	6-3	215	12-18-92	0	0	0.00	2	2	0	0	4	2	0	0	0	3	6	.154	.000	.250	13.50	6.75
Bryant, Noah	R-R	6-3	200	10-15-98	1	1	4.80	13	0	0	0	15	14	8	8	1	18	11	.255	.300	.200	6.60	10.80
Capellan, Delvin	R-R	6-1	167	12-6-98	1	5	5.24	13	8	0	0	55	68	36	32	8	11	61	.293	.274	.307	9.98	1.80
Castillo, Adriam	R-R	6-5	230	11-19-98	5	2	3.27	12	0	0	0	22	20	12	8	1	15	18	.241	.262	.220	7.36	6.14
Cillis, Ted	L-L	6-2	225	8-12-94	0	1	2.16	4	0	0	1	8	7	4	2	0	5	9	.226	.000	.304	9.72	5.40
Cosby, Christian	R-R	6-5	215	12-21-96	2	0	3.43	13	0	0	2	39	37	17	15	0	14	42	.243	.246	.242	9.61	3.20
Edwards, Andrew	R-R	6-6	265	10-7-91	0	2	9.53	5	2	0	0	6	9	8	6	0	3	2	.360	.455	.286	14.29	3.18
Feliz, Darwin	R-R	6-1	175	9-19-96	0	1	19.64	4	3	0	0	4	4	8	8	0	7	2	.286	.500	.200	4.91	17.18
Frias, Adan	L-L	6-0	200	5-18-99	2	4	4.85	12	7	0	0	43	44	26	23	4	29	41	.262	.250	.266	8.65	6.12
Haake, Zach	R-R	6-4	186	10-8-96	0	0	1.86	5	4	0	0	10	7	2	2	1	2	10	.200	.417	.087	9.31	1.86
Hahn, Jesse	R-R	6-4	215	7-30-89	0	0	0.00	2	1	0	0	2	1	0	0	0	0	2	.167	.000	.200	9.00	0.00
Hensley, Bryce	L-L	6-4	215	10-3-95	2	0	1.42	11	0	0	2	19	15	5	3	0	5	21	.208	.238	.196	9.95	2.37
James, Daniel	R-R	6-4	215	1-19-96	2	0	0.73	10	0	0	4	12	12	1	1	0	4	17	.267	.278	.259	12.41	2.92
Kaufman, Rylan	L-L	6-4	190	6-23-99	0	1	9.00	2	2	0	0	2	4	3	2	0	1	1	.400	.333	.429	4.50	4.50
Lara, Janser	R-R	6-0	170	8-10-96	0	1	9.00	1	1	0	0	1	2	1	1	0	0	1	.400	.667	.000	9.00	0.00
Lugo, Rito	L-L	5-10	185	11-3-95	0	0	2.00	2	0	0	0	9	8	2	2	0	3	15	.235	.375	.192	15.00	3.00
Morel, Yohanse	R-R	6-0	170	8-23-00	1	2	3.71	12	7	0	0	44	40	18	18	1	16	47	.240	.295	.208	9.69	3.30
Nunez, Andres	R-R	6-4	240	9-20-95	1	0	3.12	11	0	0	1	17	13	6	6	0	3	20	.200	.143	.243	10.38	1.56
Rosillo, Eduard	R-R	6-4	210	12-22-93	0	1	14.73	4	0	0	0	4	2	6	6	0	8	6	.154	.333	.000	14.73	19.64
Skoglund, Eric	L-L	6-7	210	10-26-92	0	0	0.00	1	1	0	0	3	2	0	0	0	1	2	.200	.400	.000	6.00	3.00
Wang, Chih-Ting	L-L	6-1	230	1-24-99	1	2	4.95	13	0	0	2	40	45	23	22	1	22	40	.285	.270	.289	9.00	4.95
Zerpa, Angel	L-L	6-0	175	9-27-99	3	6	3.88	11	7	0	0	49	52	30	21	5	12	34	.277	.256	.283	6.29	2.22

Fielding

C: Emodi 3, Hancock 20, Mondesi 23, Porter 2, Vidal 10. **1B:** Aplin 12, Duenez 6, Hollie 4, Mondesi 2, Pineda 8, Porter 27. **2B:** Bewley 2, Diaz 2, Hughes 7, Jaquez 8, Nacero 37. **3B:** Bewley 6, Diaz 1, Jaquez 33, Pineda 10, Rivera 5, Schultz 1. **SS:** Garcia 40, Hughes 9, Jaquez 2, Nacero 7. **OF:** El-Abour 2, Escalera 7, Henry 23, Hollie 23, Jackson 32, Lopez 40, Lueck 2, Rodriguez 10, Smith 9, Soto 20, Starling 3, Strong 3.

DSL ROYALS1
DOMINICAN SUMMER LEAGUE
ROOKIE

Batting	B-T	HT	WT	DOB	AVG	vLH	vRH	G	AB	R	H	2B	3B	HR	RBI	BB	HBP	SH	SF	SO	SB	CS	SLG	OBP
Almanzar, Luis	B-R	6-1	170	5-11-99	.200	.071	.227	34	80	10	16	2	1	0	4	11	1	0	0	27	8	1	.250	.304
Asencio, Bryan	R-R	6-1	183	2-27-01	.232	.200	.232	45	155	18	36	9	0	2	13	11	3	0	2	48	4	1	.329	.292
Biegel, Daytan	R-R	6-0	175	2-4-00	.225	.100	.194	49	151	14	34	9	0	2	16	11	11	0	1	44	0	3	.325	.322
Camarillo, Gary	R-R	6-1	157	7-5-01	.265	.200	.279	55	189	22	50	6	2	1	16	11	3	0	1	43	8	7	.333	.314
Carvajal, Jean	R-R	5-10	153	12-8-00	.160	.059	.169	50	131	17	21	3	1	0	5	19	5	0	2	54	8	10	.199	.287
De Leon, Ruben	R-R	5-9	175	2-12-01	.158	.200	.143	19	38	4	6	2	0	0	1	4	2	0	0	4	0	5	.211	.347
Familia, Felix	R-R	6-2	205	10-13-98	.207	.222	.204	54	121	14	25	1	0	0	9	27	9	4	4	16	4	0	.215	.379
Febres, Nicolas	R-R	5-11	178	10-11-98	.270	—	—	63	211	24	57	13	2	0	39	29	5	2	1	23	6	2	.351	.370
Fernandez, Guillermo	R-R	6-2	165	7-15-01	.141	.200	.172	43	99	9	14	2	0	0	1	14	2	1	0	21	5	3	.162	.261

Name	B-T	HT	WT	DOB	AVG	vLH	vRH	G	AB	R	H	2B	3B	HR	RBI	BB	HBP	SH	SF	SO	SB	CS	OBP	SLG
Florian, Jose	L-L	6-0	170	9-27-00	.186	.240	.176	51	156	17	29	6	0	2	11	16	3	1	0	58	1	2	.263	.274
Garcia, Maikel	R-R	6-0	145	3-3-00	.194	.232	.217	12	36	8	7	3	0	0	2	8	1	2	0	7	7	0	.278	.356
Garcia, Xionel	R-R	6-2	180	12-15-00	.206	—	—	59	219	26	45	14	1	0	15	17	2	1	3	73	7	6	.279	.266
Gonzalez, Herard	B-R	5-11	167	5-16-01	.216	.414	.174	55	167	28	36	4	0	1	15	24	2	5	0	42	22	6	.258	.321
Grullon, Francis	B-R	5-10	170	10-13-00	.205	—	—	47	151	22	31	8	1	0	19	19	3	2	1	29	7	4	.272	.305
Hernandez, Diego	L-L	6-0	150	11-21-00	.325	.546	.241	10	40	7	13	0	1	0	3	4	1	0	1	4	5	3	.375	.391
Herrera, Frank	B-R	6-1	170	3-20-01	.212	.276	.197	48	156	9	33	6	0	0	15	9	2	1	0	32	3	3	.250	.264
Maican, Diego	R-R	6-3	180	10-24-00	.267	.375	.241	51	165	14	44	7	1	0	21	20	6	0	2	33	6	6	.321	.363
Marinez, Neyfi	L-R	6-1	175	9-7-00	.269	—	—	59	212	29	57	14	6	1	23	14	2	1	2	44	2	4	.406	.317
Martinez, Edgar	R-R	5-10	150	2-14-01	.246	—	.083	55	191	29	47	9	2	0	14	24	5	4	1	49	15	13	.314	.344
Medina, Yesi	R-R	5-10	185	4-18-00	.238	1.000	.000	24	63	6	15	4	0	0	8	13	0	1	0	9	0	1	.302	.368
Moreno, Olivber	R-R	6-1	187	6-28-01	.225	.222	.226	53	173	17	39	3	2	1	10	18	3	2	0	39	13	3	.283	.309
Pire, Enmanuel	R-R	5-10	165	5-18-01	.224	—	—	34	116	13	26	3	0	0	8	7	2	0	1	21	2	0	.250	.278
Quintana, Guillermo	R-R	6-0	180	3-16-01	.276	.343	.257	57	181	15	50	2	0	0	19	19	3	0	3	36	5	3	.287	.350
Ramirez, Jean	L-L	5-10	180	10-25-00	.267	.222	.278	17	45	5	12	1	0	0	3	7	1	0	0	8	7	2	.289	.377
Reyes, Jesus	R-R	5-10	160	9-14-00	.212	.000	.100	49	137	15	29	5	0	0	13	17	1	1	3	41	7	7	.248	.298
Reynoso, Reynin	L-L	5-11	162	11-25-99	.250	.417	.224	47	148	20	37	8	2	1	12	13	1	2	0	25	4	4	.351	.315
Rodriguez, Omar	R-R	6-1	190	4-9-00	.227	.455	.140	34	88	7	20	6	0	0	10	6	4	0	0	25	2	0	.296	.306
Rodriguez, Rodrigo	B-R	6-0	170	9-25-00	.168	—	—	31	95	7	16	5	0	0	6	8	4	0	0	27	0	1	.221	.262
Sanchez, Javier	R-R	5-11	160	10-27-99	.234	—	—	56	184	20	43	10	0	0	16	22	2	3	1	39	3	4	.288	.321
Valdez, Enrique	L-R	6-0	158	5-15-01	.287	.167	.279	53	192	24	55	5	2	0	15	14	2	2	1	46	14	9	.333	.340
Vargas, Randor	L-L	5-10	160	12-9-99	.167	.000	.222	26	78	4	13	2	0	1	9	6	2	0	0	41	5	3	.231	.244
Vicente, Warling	R-R	5-10	165	6-8-99	.284	.000	.056	64	229	46	65	8	4	0	19	25	8	2	2	63	19	10	.354	.371

Pitching	B-T	HT	WT	DOB	W	L	ERA	G	GS	CG	SV	IP	H	R	ER	HR	BB	SO	AVG	vLH	vRH	K/9	BB/9
Abreu, Brian	R-R	6-2	194	6-3-99	0	3	3.92	12	0	0	0	41	38	22	18	0	17	34	.253	—	—	7.40	3.70
Almonte, Junior	R-R	6-1	175	4-10-00	2	3	2.00	12	7	0	0	36	16	14	8	0	20	34	.137	.118	.137	8.50	5.00
Avila, Luinder	R-R	6-3	170	8-21-01	1	2	3.18	9	2	0	1	23	15	16	8	0	11	20	.188	.227	.172	7.94	4.37
Ballista, Jose	R-R	5-10	168	9-4-00	2	3	3.07	14	0	0	3	29	27	11	10	0	10	24	.250	—	—	7.36	3.07
Barroso, Luis	R-R	6-3	165	9-7-98	2	2	2.08	12	11	0	0	43	49	13	10	0	9	35	.288	.234	.309	7.27	1.87
Benua, Carlos	R-R	6-2	180	4-24-00	0	1	9.42	12	0	0	0	14	15	17	15	1	26	12	.273	—	.000	7.53	16.33
Breton, Fraicy	L-L	6-3	196	6-10-01	0	2	5.63	8	5	0	0	24	25	18	15	2	11	18	.258	—	—	6.75	4.13
Cabrera, Daury	R-R	6-4	190	10-23-00	5	2	1.16	13	9	0	0	54	37	13	7	0	10	36	.197	.000	.208	5.96	1.66
Cabrera, Rovaldis	L-L	5-10	176	11-22-99	2	2	2.19	13	9	0	2	53	43	16	13	1	9	52	.215	.364	.213	8.78	1.52
Camargo, Cesar	R-R	6-1	195	7-21-99	0	1	6.75	13	0	0	0	17	18	13	13	1	19	13	.254	.211	.269	6.75	9.87
Castillo, Adriam	R-R	6-5	230	11-19-98	1	2	2.84	3	3	0	0	13	6	5	4	0	6	14	.133	.262	.220	9.95	4.26
Cepeda, Luis	L-L	6-1	160	10-12-00	1	0	1.98	10	6	0	0	27	25	6	6	1	9	31	.248	.200	.263	10.21	2.96
Correa, Jean	R-R	6-1	145	2-16-98	2	0	4.50	4	0	0	0	6	6	3	3	0	3	6	.273	—	—	9.00	4.50
De Los Santos, Kelvin	R-R	6-4	215	2-13-98	1	2	2.77	14	0	0	4	26	26	13	8	0	10	19	.265	—	—	6.58	3.46
Diaz, Andres	R-R	6-1	155	7-6-01	1	2	3.38	12	0	0	0	21	14	8	8	1	4	22	.187	.182	.189	9.28	1.69
Fana, Jeisson	R-R	5-11	155	1-29-99	0	1	7.15	6	0	0	0	11	11	12	9	0	16	7	.250	.000	.000	5.56	12.71
Garcia, Heribert	R-R	6-0	190	10-2-99	4	2	0.94	11	10	0	0	48	19	7	5	1	7	44	.119	.107	.125	8.31	1.32
Guaba, Yordy	R-R	6-3	175	9-8-00	1	1	1.74	10	2	0	0	21	13	5	4	0	17	21	.188	1.000	.333	9.15	7.40
Jimenez, Axsel	R-R	6-1	180	9-8-00	0	0	1.96	10	0	0	0	18	13	6	4	1	10	19	.197	—	—	9.33	4.91
Jimenez, Wilmer	L-L	5-11	162	6-1-98	3	0	0.89	12	1	0	3	30	22	4	3	1	10	48	.193	.154	.205	14.24	2.97
Lugo, Rito	L-L	5-10	185	11-3-95	0	2	1.15	4	2	0	0	16	11	5	2	0	4	27	.204	.258	.213	15.51	2.30
Marquez, Emilio	L-L	5-8	170	4-28-98	2	0	0.61	9	0	0	3	15	9	3	1	0	3	20	.180	.200	.175	12.27	1.84
Matos, Yonathan	R-R	6-3	194	7-6-98	0	2	4.62	15	0	0	2	25	18	14	13	1	10	26	.198	.100	.161	9.24	3.55
Medina, Victor	R-R	5-10	170	2-9-00	0	2	3.12	15	4	0	1	40	34	21	14	0	13	26	.233	—	—	5.80	2.90
Mendez, Leandro	R-R	5-11	181	4-21-00	0	7	5.58	13	12	0	0	50	62	38	31	2	9	34	.302	—	—	6.12	1.62
Morales, Austin	R-R	6-2	185	1-23-98	2	1	3.51	14	0	0	1	26	22	11	10	0	7	24	.232	.364	.192	8.42	2.45
Noriega, Cruz	R-R	6-1	175	10-1-97	2	4	4.18	14	3	0	3	32	33	19	15	0	8	30	.262	.200	.277	8.35	2.23
Nunez, Braulio	L-L	6-1	178	12-21-99	0	2	2.62	16	1	0	2	34	22	13	10	2	18	22	.179	—	—	5.77	4.72
Ovalle, Luilly	R-R	6-3	170	10-13-00	2	3	6.43	12	1	0	0	21	22	18	15	0	13	25	.275	—	—	10.71	5.57
Paulino, Anderson	R-R	6-2	200	9-12-98	1	3	7.47	8	2	0	0	16	18	15	13	0	10	11	.286	.333	.267	6.32	5.74
Peralta, Dario	R-R	6-1	170	10-12-00	1	1	12.00	6	0	0	0	12	23	19	16	1	7	8	.404	—	—	6.00	5.25
Pinales, Gerson	R-R	6-2	166	9-2-99	3	3	5.45	14	5	0	0	35	28	28	21	3	29	23	.217	—	—	5.97	7.53
Polanco, Gustavo	L-L	6-2	170	5-9-00	5	0	5.96	14	0	0	0	23	19	20	15	1	19	22	.238	.500	.000	8.74	7.54
Rodriguez, Diogenes	R-R	6-1	178	2-17-99	0	4	4.78	14	6	0	0	26	25	28	14	3	21	26	.236	—	—	8.89	7.18
Roman, Jesus	L-L	6-4	185	5-25-00	0	1	8.38	5	1	0	0	10	13	10	9	0	4	10	.325	.333	.318	9.31	3.72
Sanchez, Carlos	R-R	6-0	175	6-20-99	1	2	6.11	12	2	0	0	28	33	23	19	1	20	17	.317	—	—	5.46	6.43
Solano, Adrian	R-R	6-1	165	10-17-99	0	3	3.91	12	1	0	0	23	24	14	10	1	15	22	.270	.360	.234	8.61	5.87
Valenzuela, Oscar	R-R	5-11	171	3-2-01	3	0	2.95	11	0	0	2	21	14	10	7	0	7	8	.182	.174	.185	3.38	2.95
Vasquez, Javier	R-R	6-2	180	1-6-00	2	2	4.45	14	0	0	0	28	25	21	14	1	20	30	.234	.231	.222	9.53	6.35
Vasquez, Richi	R-R	6-1	155	9-18-00	0	3	8.78	12	5	0	0	27	32	28	26	2	25	23	.317	—	—	7.76	8.44
Villar, Luis	L-L	5-10	160	11-8-00	4	1	1.49	12	6	0	0	36	35	14	6	0	6	35	.252	.323	.232	8.67	1.49
Vitriago, Daniel	L-L	5-10	155	12-5-00	2	2	2.81	12	4	0	1	26	19	9	8	0	14	25	.214	.111	.258	8.77	4.91

Fielding

C: Familia 51, Febres 5, Florian 2, Herrera 2, Medina 1, Medina 2, Pire 32, Quintana 1, Rodriguez 18, Rodriguez 15. **1B:** Familia 4, Febres 57, Florian 37, Herrera 12, Medina 2, Quintana 31, Sanchez 18. **2B:** Carvajal 6, De Leon 9, Gonzalez 54, Grullon 45, Martinez 16, Reyes 2. **3B:** Almanzar 14, Carvajal 4, De Leon 6, Fernandez 19, Grullon 1, Herrera 39, Martinez 4, Sanchez 40. **SS:** Almanzar 16, Carvajal 2, Febres 1, Garcia 12, Martinez 12, Reyes 2, Valdez 26. **OF:** Asencio 13, Biegel 9, Camarillo 47, De Leon 1, Garcia 52, Hernandez 10, Maican 34, Marinez 49, Moreno 46, Ramirez 14, Reynoso 21, Vargas 8, Vicente 56.

Los Angeles Angels

SEASON IN A SENTENCE: Despite a career year from Mike Trout and a brilliant rookie debut from Japanese two-way star Shohei Ohtani, pitching injuries and a lack of depth once again sabotaged the Angels as they limped to an 80-82 record in Mike Scioscia's final season as manager.

HIGH POINT: Ohtani became the talk of baseball with his two-way heroics in the season's first full week. He won his first career start, homered in his next three games and capped his first week by taking a perfect game into the seventh inning against Oakland. Buoyed by their rookie sensation, the Angels won 13 of 16 games to open the season.

LOW POINT: With J.C. Ramirez (Tommy John surgery) and Matt Shoemaker (forearm surgery) already down, the Angels lost their two aces in the span of a week in June. Ohtani left his June 6 start with elbow soreness, and Garrett Richards left his June 13 start with a hamstring strain. With their rotation eviscerated, the Angels spiraled into a 4-13 stretch, falling from 3.5 games back in the American League West to 13.5 games back. Shortly after, Richards had Tommy John surgery and Ohtani eventually followed.

NOTABLE ROOKIES: Ohtani hit 22 home runs as the Angels' DH while going 4-2, 3.31 with 63 strikeouts in 51.2 innings on the mound. He became the first player since Babe Ruth in 1919 to hit 20 home runs and strike out 50 batters in the same season. Righthander Jaime Barria joined the rotation in April and led the team in wins (10) and ERA (3.41). Reliever Justin Anderson and second baseman David Fletcher made their major league debuts and became constants in the Angels' bullpen and infield. Third baseman Taylor Ward, the club's 2015 first-round pick as a catcher, came up in August and ended the season with a walk-off home run in the Angels' final game.

KEY TRANSACTIONS: The Angels won the fevered recruiting pitch for Ohtani in December and signed him for $2.315 million. They also signed Zack Cozart and traded for Ian Kinsler, but Cozart had season-ending labrum surgery in June and Kinsler was traded to the Red Sox in July.

DOWN ON THE FARM: Outfielder Jo Adell shot from low Class A all the way to Double-A in his first full season, batting .290 with 20 home runs, 77 RBIs, 15 stolen bases and an .897 OPS. Righthander Griffin Canning (4-3, 3.65) and lefthander Jose Suarez (3-6, 3.92) vaulted from high Class A to Triple-A.

OPENING DAY PAYROLL: $171,248,332 (7th).

PLAYERS OF THE YEAR

ROBERT BINDER

BILL MITCHELL

MAJOR LEAGUE	MINOR LEAGUE
Mike Trout **OF**	**Jo Adell,** **OF**
.312/.460/.628	(Low Class A/High
39 HR, 24 SB	Class A/Double-A)
1.088 OPS led majors	.897 OPS, 20 HR

ORGANIZATION LEADERS

Batting		*Minimum 250 AB
MAJORS		
* AVG	Mike Trout	.312
* OPS	Mike Trout	1.088
HR	Mike Trout	39
RBI	Justin Upton	85
MINORS		
* AVG	Taylor Ward, Mobile, Salt Lake	.349
* OBP	Taylor Ward, Mobile, Salt Lake	.446
* SLG	Jo Adell, Burlington, Inland Empire, Mobile	.543
* OPS	Taylor Ward, Mobile, Salt Lake	.977
R	Luis Rengifo, Inland Empire, Mobile, Salt Lake	109
H	Luis Rengifo, Inland Empire, Mobile, Salt Lake	150
TB	Jared Walsh, Inland Empire, Mobile, Salt Lake	255
2B	Matt Thaiss, Mobile, Salt Lake	34
2B	Jared Walsh, Inland Empire, Mobile, Salt Lake	34
3B	Luis Rengifo, Inland Empire, Mobile, Salt Lake	13
HR	Jabari Blash, Salt Lake	29
HR	Jared Walsh, Inland Empire, Mobile, Salt Lake	29
RBI	Jared Walsh, Inland Empire, Mobile, Salt Lake	99
BB	David MacKinnon, Burlington, Inland Empire	95
SO	Brandon Marsh, Burlington, Inland Empire	158
SB	Luis Rengifo, Inland Empire, Mobile, Salt Lake	41

Pitching		#Minimum 75 IP
MAJORS		
W	Jaime Barria	10
# ERA	Jaime Barria	3.41
SO	Andrew Heaney	180
SV	Blake Parker	14
MINORS		
W	Alex Klonowski, Salt Lake, Inland Empire, Mobile	12
L	Erik Manoah, Inland Empire	12
# ERA	Jeremy Beasley, Burlington, Inland Empire, Mobile	2.66
G	Jeremy Rhoades, Mobile, Salt Lake	54
GS	Jose Suarez, Inland Empire, Mobile, Salt Lake	26
SV	Matt Custred, Inland Empire, Mobile, Salt Lake	10
SV	Ryan Clark, Inland Empire, Mobile, Salt Lake	10
IP	Alex Klonowski, Salt Lake, Inland Empire, Mobile	136
BB	Nate Bertness, Inland Empire	66
SO	Jose Suarez, Inland Empire, Mobile, Salt Lake	142
# AVG	Jeremy Beasley, Burlington, Inland Empire, Mobile	.236
# AVG	Griffin Canning, Inland Empire, Mobile, Salt Lake	.236

General Manager: Billy Eppler. **Farm Director:** Mike LaCassa. **Scouting Director:** Matt Swanson.

Class	Team	League	W	L	PCT	Finish	Manager
Majors	Los Angeles Angels	American	80	82	.494	8th (15)	Mike Scioscia
Triple-A	Salt Lake Bees	Pacific Coast	71	68	.511	8th (16)	Keith Johnson
Double-A	Mobile BayBears	Southern	66	70	.485	7th (10)	Lou Marson
High A	Inland Empire 66ers	California	67	73	.479	6th (8)	Ryan Barba
Low A	Burlington Bees	Midwest	50	84	.373	16th (16)	Jack Howell
Rookie	Orem Owlz	Pioneer	22	54	.289	8th (8)	David Stapleton
Rookie	AZL Angels	Arizona	16	38	.296	16th (18)	Jack Santora
Overall 2018 Minor League Record			292	387	.430	30th (30)	

ORGANIZATION STATISTICS

LOS ANGELES ANGELS
AMERICAN LEAGUE

Batting	B-T	HT	WT	DOB	AVG	vLH	vRH	G	AB	R	H	2B	3B	HR	RBI	BB	HBP	SH	SF	SO	SB	CS	SLG	OBP
Arcia, Francisco	L-R	5-11	195	9-14-89	.204	.300	.194	40	103	10	21	5	0	6	23	1	2	0	0	27	1	0	.427	.226
Blash, Jabari	R-R	6-5	235	7-4-89	.103	.059	.136	24	39	4	4	1	0	0	1	5	0	0	1	24	2	1	.128	.200
Briceno, Jose	R-R	6-1	210	9-19-92	.239	.289	.200	46	117	12	28	2	0	5	10	8	2	1	0	35	0	1	.385	.299
Calhoun, Kole	L-L	5-10	200	10-14-87	.208	.207	.208	137	491	71	102	18	2	19	57	53	1	0	6	133	6	2	.369	.283
Cowart, Kaleb	B-R	6-3	225	6-2-92	.134	.115	.140	47	112	7	15	7	1	1	10	10	1	0	1	44	1	0	.241	.210
Cozart, Zack	R-R	6-0	205	8-12-85	.219	.173	.233	58	224	29	49	13	2	5	18	19	7	0	3	42	0	0	.362	.296
Fernandez, Jose	L-R	5-10	185	4-27-88	.267	.263	.268	36	116	9	31	8	0	2	11	6	1	0	0	15	1	0	.388	.309
Fletcher, David	R-R	5-10	175	5-31-94	.275	.262	.283	80	284	35	78	18	2	1	25	15	3	3	2	34	3	0	.363	.316
Fontana, Nolan	L-R	5-11	195	6-6-91	.091	.000	.143	8	11	1	1	0	0	1	1	1	0	0	0	6	0	0	.364	.167
Graterol, Juan	R-R	6-1	205	2-14-89	1.000	—	1.000	1	1	0	1	0	0	0	0	0	0	0	0	0	0	0	1.000	1.000
2-team total (3 Minnesota)					.250	.333	.200	4	8	2	2	0	0	0	0	1	0	0	0	0	0	0	.250	.333
Hermosillo, Michael	R-R	5-11	190	1-17-95	.211	.261	.177	31	57	7	12	4	0	1	1	3	2	0	0	17	0	1	.333	.274
Hudson, Joe	R-R	6-1	206	5-21-91	.167	.500	.000	8	12	0	2	1	0	0	1	0	0	0	0	4	0	0	.250	.167
Johnson, Sherman	L-R	5-10	190	7-15-90	.000	.000	.000	10	10	0	0	0	0	0	0	0	1	0	0	4	0	0	.000	.091
Kinsler, Ian	R-R	6-0	200	6-22-82	.239	.200	.255	91	355	49	85	20	0	13	32	30	4	0	2	40	9	4	.406	.304
2-team total (37 Boston Red Sox)					.240	.191	.259	128	487	66	117	26	0	14	48	40	4	0	3	64	16	7	.380	.302
Maldonado, Martin	R-R	6-0	230	8-16-86	.223	.200	.232	78	265	24	59	14	0	5	32	13	10	1	1	73	0	1	.332	.284
2-team total (41 Houston)					.225	.233	.222	119	373	39	84	18	1	9	44	16	11	2	2	98	0	1	.351	.276
Marte, Jefry	R-R	6-1	220	6-21-91	.217	.217	.216	90	194	28	42	7	1	7	22	13	2	0	0	41	1	1	.371	.273
Pujols, Albert	R-R	6-3	240	1-16-80	.245	.200	.259	117	465	50	114	20	0	19	64	28	2	0	3	65	1	0	.411	.289
Rivera, Rene	R-R	5-11	215	7-31-83	.244	.188	.280	30	82	8	20	4	0	4	11	4	1	0	0	32	0	0	.439	.287
Schimpf, Ryan	L-R	5-9	180	4-11-88	.200	1.000	.000	5	5	2	1	0	0	1	2	2	0	0	0	3	0	0	.800	.429
Simmons, Andrelton	R-R	6-2	200	9-4-89	.292	.277	.299	146	554	68	162	26	5	11	75	35	5	1	5	44	10	2	.417	.337
Trout, Mike	R-R	6-2	235	8-7-91	.312	.292	.318	140	471	101	147	24	4	39	79	122	10	0	4	124	24	2	.629	.460
Upton, Justin	R-R	6-2	205	8-25-87	.257	.195	.277	145	533	80	137	18	1	30	85	64	10	0	6	176	8	2	.463	.344
Valbuena, Luis	L-R	5-10	215	11-30-85	.199	.222	.196	96	266	23	53	9	0	9	33	19	1	0	2	100	3	0	.335	.254
Ward, Taylor	R-R	6-1	200	12-14-93	.178	.244	.144	40	135	14	24	3	0	6	15	9	3	0	0	45	2	0	.333	.245
Young Jr., Eric	B-R	5-10	195	5-25-85	.202	.237	.183	41	109	12	22	4	2	1	8	6	1	0	1	28	5	1	.303	.248
Young, Chris	R-R	6-2	200	9-5-83	.168	.192	.152	56	113	17	19	2	1	6	13	11	2	1	1	37	2	0	.363	.252

Pitching	B-T	HT	WT	DOB	W	L	ERA	G	GS	CG	SV	IP	H	R	ER	HR	BB	SO	AVG	vLH	vRH	K/9	BB/9
Almonte, Miguel	R-R	6-2	210	4-4-93	0	0	10.29	8	0	0	0	7	9	8	8	1	3	7	.300	.273	.316	9.00	3.86
Alvarez, Jose	L-L	5-11	180	5-6-89	6	4	2.71	76	0	0	1	63	51	20	19	3	22	59	.217	.206	.232	8.43	3.14
Anderson, Justin	L-R	6-3	220	9-28-92	3	3	4.07	57	0	0	4	55	42	25	25	3	40	67	.214	.215	.214	10.90	6.51
Bard, Luke	R-R	6-3	202	11-13-90	0	0	5.40	8	0	0	0	12	10	7	7	4	5	13	.222	.231	.211	10.03	3.86
Barria, Jaime	R-R	6-1	210	7-18-96	10	9	3.41	26	26	0	0	129	117	50	49	17	47	98	.242	.216	.269	6.82	3.27
Bedrosian, Cam	R-R	6-0	230	10-2-91	5	4	3.80	71	0	0	1	64	63	30	27	7	26	57	.263	.280	.252	8.02	3.66
Bridwell, Parker	R-R	6-4	185	8-2-91	1	0	17.55	5	1	0	0	7	14	13	13	5	2	3	.438	.417	.450	4.05	2.70
Buttrey, Ty	L-R	6-6	230	3-31-93	0	1	3.31	16	0	0	4	16	15	7	6	0	5	20	.238	.300	.182	11.02	2.76
Cole, Taylor	R-R	6-4	215	8-20-89	4	2	2.75	18	2	0	0	36	20	11	11	3	12	39	.170	.164	.175	9.75	3.00
Despaigne, Odrisamer	R-R	6-0	200	4-4-87	0	3	8.20	8	4	0	0	19	30	18	17	3	11	17	.361	.357	.366	8.20	5.30
Drake, Oliver	R-R	6-4	215	1-13-87	0	1	5.19	8	0	0	0	9	15	5	5	2	1	8	.385	.500	.263	8.31	1.04
4-team total (4 Cleveland, 19 Minnesota, 2 Toronto)					0	1	4.89	33	0	0	0	35	38	20	19	4	9	36	.270	.328	.221	9.26	2.31
Heaney, Andrew	L-L	6-2	185	6-5-91	9	10	4.15	30	30	1	0	180	171	91	83	27	45	180	.248	.230	.253	9.00	2.25
Jerez, Williams	L-L	6-4	200	5-16-92	0	0	6.00	17	0	0	0	15	17	14	10	3	8	15	.270	.304	.250	9.00	4.80
Jewell, Jake	R-R	6-3	200	5-16-93	0	1	9.00	3	0	0	0	2	2	2	2	0	1	2	.250	.333	.000	4.50	4.50
Johnson, Jim	R-R	6-6	250	6-27-83	5	3	3.84	62	1	0	2	63	64	38	27	9	22	45	.268	.301	.243	6.39	3.13
Krol, Ian	L-L	6-1	210	5-9-91	0	0	0.00	1	0	0	0	2	1	0	0	0	1	2	.143	.333	.000	9.00	4.50
Lamb, John	L-L	6-4	205	7-10-90	0	1	7.20	3	3	0	0	10	15	10	8	4	4	11	.326	.375	.316	9.90	3.60
McGuire, Deck	R-R	6-6	220	6-23-89	0	2	6.07	17	4	0	0	30	29	22	20	7	21	26	.266	.245	.286	7.89	6.37
2-team total (4 Toronto)					0	2	6.16	21	4	0	0	38	38	28	26	9	26	33	.266	.214	.315	7.82	6.16
Middleton, Keynan	R-R	6-2	215	9-12-93	0	0	2.04	16	0	0	6	18	14	4	4	1	9	16	.233	.273	.185	8.15	4.58
Morales, Osmer	R-R	6-3	196	10-30-92	0	0	0.00	1	0	0	0	1	0	0	0	0	0	1	.000	.500	1.000	0.00	0.00
Morris, Akeel	R-R	6-1	205	11-14-92	0	0	5.79	9	0	0	0	14	18	9	9	3	8	7	.316	.323	.308	4.50	5.14
Ohtani, Shohei	L-R	6-4	200	7-5-94	4	2	3.31	10	10	0	0	52	38	19	19	6	22	63	.203	.192	.211	10.97	3.83

Name	B-T	HT	WT	DOB	W	L	ERA	G	GS	CG	SV	IP	H	R	ER	HR	BB	SO	AVG	vLH	vRH	K/9	BB/9
Paredes, Eduardo	R-R	6-1	230	3-6-95	0	0	6.87	14	0	0	0	18	25	14	14	5	7	15	.325	.290	.348	7.36	3.44
Parker, Blake	R-R	6-3	225	6-19-85	2	1	3.26	67	0	0	14	66	63	24	24	12	19	70	.249	.269	.231	9.50	2.58
Pena, Felix	R-R	6-2	185	2-25-90	3	5	4.18	19	17	0	0	93	87	45	43	12	28	85	.247	.274	.220	8.26	2.72
Ramirez, JC	R-R	6-4	250	8-16-88	0	2	9.45	2	2	0	0	7	7	8	7	3	7	4	.269	.222	.375	5.40	9.45
Ramirez, Noe	R-R	6-3	195	12-22-89	7	5	4.54	69	1	0	1	83	75	43	42	15	30	95	.237	.248	.230	10.26	3.24
Richards, Garrett	R-R	6-3	210	5-27-88	5	4	3.66	16	16	0	0	76	64	43	31	11	34	87	.222	.207	.239	10.26	4.01
Robles, Hansel	R-R	5-11	185	8-13-90	0	1	2.97	37	0	0	2	36	32	15	12	2	15	36	.237	.200	.263	8.92	3.72
Shoemaker, Matt	R-R	6-2	225	9-27-86	2	2	4.94	7	7	0	0	31	29	17	17	3	10	33	.244	.192	.284	9.58	2.90
Skaggs, Tyler	L-L	6-4	200	7-13-91	8	10	4.02	24	24	0	0	125	127	60	56	14	40	129	.262	.231	.273	9.26	2.87
Tazawa, Junichi	R-R	5-11	200	6-6-86	0	0	2.25	9	0	0	0	8	7	3	2	1	3	4	.226	.125	.261	4.50	3.38
Tropeano, Nick	R-R	6-4	200	8-27-90	5	6	4.74	14	14	0	0	76	68	41	40	16	31	64	.242	.269	.213	7.58	3.67
Wood, Blake	R-R	6-5	233	8-8-85	1	0	2.31	13	0	0	0	12	8	3	3	1	7	10	.211	.250	.192	7.71	5.40

Fielding

Catcher	PCT	G	PO	A	E	DP	PB
Arcia	.990	34	190	15	2	1	1
Briceno	.993	41	269	32	2	2	4
Graterol	1.000	1	0	3	0	0	0
Hudson	1.000	8	39	2	0	0	0
Maldonado	.994	77	674	33	4	4	10
Rivera	.996	26	216	15	1	3	3

First Base	PCT	G	PO	A	E	DP
Arcia	1.000	1	6	1	0	3
Briceno	1.000	2	1	0	0	0
Cowart	1.000	5	20	1	0	5
Fernandez	1.000	28	170	6	0	29
Johnson	1.000	2	6	0	0	0
Marte	.992	71	335	33	3	35
Pujols	.993	70	529	53	4	60
Rivera	1.000	2	1	0	0	0
Valbuena	.983	39	161	10	3	24

Second Base	PCT	G	PO	A	E	DP
Cowart	1.000	14	24	28	0	9
Cozart	1.000	16	24	34	0	9
Fernandez	1.000	1	1	3	0	0
Fletcher	.994	43	65	103	1	33
Fontana	1.000	3	1	3	0	0
Johnson	1.000	7	5	6	0	3
Kinsler	.983	91	154	243	7	73
Schimpf	.000	1	0	0	0	0
Valbuena	.000	1	0	0	0	0

Third Base	PCT	G	PO	A	E	DP
Cowart	1.000	24	6	31	0	3
Cozart	.957	35	18	49	3	5
Fernandez	1.000	2	1	1	0	1
Fletcher	.986	33	10	63	1	3
Fontana	1.000	2	1	1	0	0
Marte	.929	10	5	8	1	1
Schimpf	1.000	1	0	2	0	1
Valbuena	.953	57	21	80	5	11

	PCT	G	PO	A	E	DP
Ward	.939	40	15	62	5	3

Shortstop	PCT	G	PO	A	E	DP
Cowart	1.000	5	4	7	0	2
Cozart	.979	15	17	30	1	8
Fletcher	1.000	7	2	8	0	2
Fontana	.857	2	3	3	1	2
Simmons	.984	145	228	372	10	114

Outfield	PCT	G	PO	A	E	DP
Blash	.955	20	21	0	1	0
Calhoun	.984	136	231	8	4	4
Cowart	1.000	4	4	1	0	0
Fletcher	1.000	4	1	0	0	0
Hermosillo	.983	27	57	0	1	0
Marte	1.000	2	1	0	0	0
Schimpf	.000	2	0	0	0	0
Trout	1.000	125	271	7	0	4
Upton	.987	140	294	7	4	1
Young Jr.	.986	37	69	4	1	2
Young	.983	48	56	2	1	0

SALT LAKE BEES

TRIPLE-A

PACIFIC COAST LEAGUE

Batting	B-T	HT	WT	DOB	AVG	vLH	vRH	G	AB	R	H	2B	3B	HR	RBI	BB	HBP	SH	SF	SO	SB	CS	SLG	OBP
Ackley, Dustin	L-R	6-1	205	2-26-88	.286	.240	.298	72	241	32	69	13	1	4	39	37	1	1	4	32	1	0	.398	.378
Arcia, Francisco	L-R	5-11	195	9-14-89	.283	.308	.274	42	145	18	41	3	2	3	26	11	5	6	1	25	2	1	.393	.352
Barash, Michael	R-R	6-1	200	10-12-94	.250	.333	.222	3	12	0	3	0	0	0	2	0	0	0	0	1	0	0	.250	.250
Blash, Jabari	R-R	6-5	235	7-4-89	.317	.349	.308	83	287	73	91	21	1	29	68	49	9	0	1	102	5	7	.700	.431
Briceno, Jose	R-R	6-1	210	9-19-92	.277	.364	.256	29	112	22	31	5	0	8	25	4	0	0	2	22	3	0	.536	.297
Calhoun, Kole	L-L	5-10	200	10-14-87	.316	.200	.357	5	19	3	6	1	1	1	2	1	0	0	0	0	0	0	.632	.350
Carter, Chris	R-R	6-4	245	12-18-86	.255	.320	.242	38	145	29	37	9	1	13	43	16	3	0	4	49	2	0	.600	.333
Cowart, Kaleb	B-R	6-3	225	6-2-92	.287	.308	.282	64	258	36	74	20	3	6	45	18	1	0	2	52	8	1	.457	.333
Fernandez, Jose	L-R	5-10	185	4-27-88	.333	.317	.338	91	357	66	119	19	1	17	59	33	4	0	0	34	2	2	.535	.396
Fletcher, David	R-R	5-10	175	5-31-94	.350	.351	.350	58	254	55	89	25	5	6	37	16	3	1	1	21	7	2	.559	.394
Fontana, Nolan	L-R	5-11	195	6-6-91	.235	.267	.226	45	145	27	34	11	3	3	24	40	1	2	3	38	4	1	.414	.397
Graterol, Juan	R-R	6-1	205	2-14-89	.322	.231	.338	24	90	11	29	5	0	0	13	3	1	1	1	10	0	0	.378	.347
Hermosillo, Michael	R-R	5-11	190	1-17-95	.267	.311	.259	68	273	43	73	14	4	12	46	30	11	4	5	87	10	5	.480	.357
Houchins, Zach	R-R	6-2	210	9-16-92	.309	.222	.329	27	94	14	29	6	0	3	16	3	2	0	1	15	1	2	.468	.340
Hudson, Joe	R-R	6-1	206	5-21-91	.311	.308	.313	26	90	13	28	6	0	3	14	10	0	1	0	18	0	0	.478	.380
Johnson, Sherman	L-R	5-10	190	7-15-90	.277	.222	.301	46	148	32	41	7	4	4	14	20	0	1	2	47	2	0	.460	.359
Leon, Julian	R-R	5-11	200	1-24-96	.182	.333	.125	4	11	3	2	1	0	0	1	4	1	0	0	5	0	1	.273	.438
Liriano, Rymer	R-R	6-0	230	6-20-91	.268	.220	.278	65	239	42	64	7	3	16	48	25	3	1	1	84	6	5	.523	.343
2-team total (37 Colorado Springs)					.253	.185	.268	102	352	62	89	11	3	20	59	45	4	1	2	125	11	9	.472	.342
McGee, Stephen	R-R	6-3	215	2-7-91	.233	.444	.177	14	43	9	10	4	0	0	7	11	0	0	0	16	0	0	.326	.389
2-team total (18 El Paso)					.184	.286	.152	32	87	14	16	6	0	1	11	16	0	0	0	39	0	0	.287	.311
Rengifo, Luis	B-R	5-10	165	2-26-97	.274	.296	.267	46	190	36	52	9	5	3	27	25	1	1	2	31	6	6	.421	.358
Revere, Ben	L-R	5-9	175	5-3-88	.277	.316	.265	40	155	27	43	7	2	3	18	10	0	0	1	11	2	0	.407	.319
Rojas, Jose	L-R	6-0	200	2-24-93	.217	.200	.225	19	69	10	15	3	0	0	6	2	0	0	2	13	1	0	.261	.233
Schimpf, Ryan	L-R	5-9	180	4-11-88	.178	.136	.188	30	107	14	19	6	2	3	13	16	1	0	1	49	1	1	.355	.288
Thaiss, Matt	L-R	6-0	195	5-6-95	.277	.315	.265	85	368	54	102	24	6	10	51	28	1	0	3	68	6	3	.457	.328
Triunfel, Alberto	R-R	5-11	160	2-1-94	.274	.250	.281	35	117	14	32	6	2	4	17	7	1	4	2	30	1	5	.462	.315
Unroe, Riley	B-R	5-10	180	8-3-95	.263	.000	.333	6	19	1	5	2	0	0	1	0	0	0	0	5	1	0	.368	.300
Walsh, Jared	L-L	6-1	210	7-30-93	.270	.314	.259	47	178	32	48	13	0	8	37	16	2	2	2	56	0	0	.478	.333
Ward, Taylor	R-R	6-1	200	12-14-93	.352	.365	.349	60	227	42	80	18	0	8	35	36	2	0	2	61	10	2	.537	.442
Wass, Wade	R-R	6-0	215	9-23-91	.222	.000	.250	3	9	1	2	0	0	1	1	0	0	0	0	5	0	0	.556	.222
Way, Bo	L-L	6-0	180	11-17-91	.342	.303	.356	33	123	19	42	8	0	0	14	5	1	3	0	18	5	1	.407	.372
Young Jr., Eric	B-R	5-10	195	5-25-85	.300	.333	.289	84	307	46	92	18	7	5	34	35	0	2	4	66	10	6	.453	.367

Pitching	B-T	HT	WT	DOB	W	L	ERA	G	GS	CG	SV	IP	H	R	ER	HR	BB	SO	AVG	vLH	vRH	K/9	BB/9
Alexander, Jason	R-R	6-3	200	3-1-93	0	1	6.75	2	1	0	0	7	11	6	5	2	4	7	.393	.250	.500	9.45	5.40
Almonte, Miguel	R-R	6-2	210	4-4-93	1	1	10.18	25	0	0	0	20	34	23	23	4	15	22	.366	.270	.429	9.74	6.64

LOS ANGELES ANGELS

Name	B-T	HT	WT	DOB	W	L	ERA	G	GS	CG	SV	IP	H	R	ER	HR	BB	SO	AVG	vLH	vRH	K/9	BB/9
Anderson, Justin	L-R	6-3	220	9-28-92	0	0	0.00	3	0	0	0	5	0	0	0	0	1	6	.000	.000	.000	10.80	1.80
Barria, Jaime	R-R	6-1	210	7-18-96	0	0	3.50	5	5	0	0	18	20	7	7	2	5	19	.282	.286	.278	9.50	2.50
Belton, Greg	R-R	5-10	190	12-31-92	0	2	9.49	6	1	0	0	12	17	13	13	1	7	14	.309	.296	.321	10.22	5.11
Bridwell, Parker	R-R	6-4	185	8-2-91	1	1	8.68	6	6	0	0	28	50	27	27	4	9	19	.391	.347	.418	6.11	2.89
Buttrey, Ty	L-R	6-6	230	3-31-93	0	1	2.25	4	0	0	0	4	2	1	1	0	1	7	.143	.500	.000	15.75	2.25
Campos, Vicente	R-R	6-3	230	7-27-92	1	2	12.60	4	0	0	0	5	8	7	7	1	6	5	.381	.500	.273	9.00	10.80
Canning, Griffin	R-R	6-1	170	5-11-96	3	3	5.49	13	13	0	0	59	68	36	36	6	22	64	.294	.320	.273	9.76	3.36
Cash, Ralston	R-R	6-3	215	8-20-91	5	2	7.11	29	0	0	0	44	46	37	35	8	27	48	.264	.214	.298	9.74	5.48
Clark, Ryan	R-R	6-5	220	12-9-93	1	2	8.82	26	0	0	5	34	45	35	33	9	19	33	.324	.355	.299	8.82	5.08
Cole, Taylor	R-R	6-1	200	8-20-89	3	0	5.37	34	0	0	6	55	55	34	33	6	27	65	.261	.277	.248	10.57	4.39
Custred, Matt	R-R	6-6	240	9-8-93	0	0	14.40	4	0	0	0	5	8	8	8	0	9	4	.381	.400	.364	7.20	16.20
Drake, Oliver	R-R	6-4	215	1-13-87	0	0	1.17	8	0	0	0	8	3	1	1	0	1	8	.120	.000	.231	9.39	1.17
Hofacket, Adam	R-R	6-1	195	2-18-94	5	1	8.17	18	0	0	0	25	35	23	23	3	11	14	.347	.333	.356	4.97	3.91
Isaac, Sean	R-R	6-4	225	12-17-92	1	1	6.67	11	2	0	2	27	26	20	20	3	13	28	.250	.385	.169	9.33	4.33
Jankowski, Jordan	R-R	6-1	225	5-17-89	2	0	8.20	15	0	0	1	19	23	18	17	2	15	23	.299	.206	.372	11.09	7.23
Jerez, Williams	L-L	6-4	200	5-16-92	0	1	17.18	4	0	0	1	4	8	7	7	0	2	5	.421	.143	.583	12.27	4.91
Jewell, Jake	R-R	6-3	200	5-16-93	2	4	3.60	19	0	0	3	25	23	11	10	2	17	24	.240	.353	.177	8.64	6.12
Johnson, Jim	R-R	6-6	250	6-27-83	0	0	0.00	2	1	0	0	2	2	0	0	0	0	2	.250	.333	.200	9.00	0.00
Klonowski, Alex	R-R	6-4	195	4-1-92	1	2	11.25	3	2	0	0	12	24	16	15	3	6	8	.429	.316	.487	6.00	4.50
Krol, Ian	L-L	6-1	210	5-9-91	1	0	1.71	18	0	0	4	21	16	6	4	0	9	20	.208	.194	.220	8.57	3.86
2-team total (25 Las Vegas 51s)					3	0	2.72	43	0	0	4	56	63	21	17	4	26	59	.280	.296	.268	9.43	4.15
Lamb, John	L-L	6-4	205	7-10-90	1	0	3.44	13	13	0	0	50	49	21	19	7	15	54	.255	.234	.269	9.79	2.72
Lillis-White, Conor	L-L	6-4	220	7-22-92	2	2	3.86	26	0	0	0	37	36	18	16	5	16	52	.243	.179	.283	12.54	3.86
Mahle, Greg	L-L	6-2	230	4-17-93	3	3	8.88	17	0	0	0	25	33	25	25	4	13	21	.314	.255	.362	7.46	4.62
Malmin, Jon	R-L	6-1	170	9-2-94	0	0	19.29	1	0	0	0	2	6	5	5	1	2	1	.546	.000	.600	3.86	7.71
Mathews, Simon	R-R	6-2	180	9-24-95	1	0	1.23	2	1	0	0	7	7	1	1	0	3	6	.259	.400	.177	7.36	3.68
McGuire, Deck	R-R	6-6	220	6-23-89	1	1	4.91	6	3	0	0	11	9	6	6	2	5	10	.225	.083	.286	8.18	4.09
2-team total (1 Round Rock)					1	1	7.82	7	3	0	0	13	14	11	11	3	9	10	.286	.188	.333	7.11	6.39
Middleton, Keynan	R-R	6-2	215	9-12-93	0	0	0.00	1	1	0	0	1	0	0	0	0	0	2	.000	.000	.000	18.00	18.00
Morales, Osmer	R-R	6-3	196	10-30-92	4	5	6.44	24	22	0	0	102	125	80	73	16	57	93	.304	.332	.281	8.21	5.03
Morris, Akeel	R-R	6-1	205	11-14-92	4	3	7.04	40	0	0	5	46	48	42	36	4	28	45	.271	.225	.309	8.80	5.48
Paredes, Eduardo	R-R	6-1	230	3-6-95	2	1	4.68	38	0	0	5	42	44	22	22	5	19	35	.279	.266	.287	7.44	4.04
Pena, Felix	R-R	6-2	185	2-25-90	1	2	3.51	10	9	0	0	33	30	14	13	2	16	38	.250	.232	.266	10.26	4.32
Pena, Luis	R-R	5-11	190	8-24-95	4	3	5.59	11	11	0	0	47	47	30	29	8	32	38	.260	.238	.278	7.33	6.17
Pineyro, Ivan	R-R	6-1	200	9-29-91	5	7	6.81	24	18	0	0	112	145	88	85	16	31	96	.317	.314	.319	7.69	2.48
Rhoades, Jeremy	R-R	6-4	225	2-12-93	6	4	2.87	40	0	0	4	53	57	25	17	4	15	51	.278	.403	.203	8.61	2.53
Smith, Blake	R-R	6-5	240	8-12-92	0	1	13.50	4	0	0	0	4	6	7	6	0	3	2	.400	.250	.571	4.50	6.75
Stevens, Tyler	R-R	6-0	215	4-4-96	2	1	10.93	20	0	0	0	28	58	35	34	4	14	36	.430	.446	.418	11.57	4.50
Suarez, Jose	L-L	5-10	170	1-3-98	1	4	4.48	17	17	0	0	78	81	43	39	5	35	73	.268	.221	.282	8.39	4.02
Tazawa, Junichi	R-R	5-11	200	6-6-86	0	1	7.11	7	0	0	2	6	10	6	5	1	2	5	.357	.214	.500	7.11	2.84
Tropeano, Nick	R-R	6-4	200	8-27-90	0	0	0.00	1	1	0	0	4	3	0	0	0	3	7	.231	.143	.333	17.18	7.36
Unsworth, Dylan	R-R	6-1	175	9-23-92	6	1	5.53	19	12	0	1	86	107	54	53	14	20	62	.305	.241	.360	6.46	2.08

Fielding

Catcher	PCT	G	PO	A	E	DP	PB
Arcia	.992	41	335	30	3	6	6
Barash	1.000	3	17	1	0	0	0
Briceno	.986	29	256	23	4	1	3
Graterol	.977	24	195	17	5	2	1
Hudson	1.000	25	216	21	0	2	5
Leon	1.000	3	25	2	0	1	0
McGee	1.000	13	129	4	0	1	1
Wass	1.000	2	18	0	0	0	0

First Base	PCT	G	PO	A	E	DP
Ackley	.990	14	97	4	1	12
Carter	1.000	25	181	5	0	10
Cowart	1.000	1	7	0	0	0
Fernandez	.992	17	104	14	1	10
Houchins	1.000	2	19	1	0	1
Rojas	1.000	2	10	0	0	1
Thaiss	.987	77	589	40	8	65
Walsh	1.000	6	41	2	0	5

Second Base	PCT	G	PO	A	E	DP
Ackley	1.000	16	27	38	0	11
Cowart	.964	7	13	14	1	3

	PCT	G	PO	A	E	DP
Fernandez	.983	33	38	76	2	21
Fletcher	.988	18	41	39	1	10
Fontana	1.000	7	12	13	0	4
Johnson	.985	16	23	41	1	9
Rengifo	.992	31	51	68	1	19
Rojas	.000	1	0	0	0	0
Schimpf	.971	18	28	39	2	7
Triunfel	1.000	3	2	3	0	1
Unroe	.000	1	0	0	0	0
Young Jr.	1.000	1	0	1	0	0

Third Base	PCT	G	PO	A	E	DP
Cowart	.923	10	7	17	2	3
Fernandez	1.000	16	8	27	0	0
Fletcher	.962	8	5	20	1	1
Houchins	.978	21	15	30	1	1
Johnson	1.000	10	9	12	0	2
Rojas	.862	12	6	19	4	1
Schimpf	.889	9	7	17	3	0
Triunfel	1.000	4	2	15	0	1
Unroe	.000	1	0	0	0	0
Ward	.944	53	27	75	6	4

Shortstop	PCT	G	PO	A	E	DP
Cowart	.980	28	42	55	2	23
Fletcher	.982	31	27	85	2	18
Fontana	.970	34	47	82	4	13
Houchins	1.000	1	0	2	0	1
Johnson	.931	7	6	21	2	4
Rengifo	.957	16	22	44	3	14
Triunfel	.962	26	46	56	4	19

Outfield	PCT	G	PO	A	E	DP
Ackley	1.000	21	42	0	0	0
Blash	.972	71	130	11	4	2
Calhoun	1.000	2	4	0	0	0
Cowart	1.000	12	15	1	0	0
Hermosillo	.974	63	143	9	4	0
Johnson	1.000	15	26	0	0	0
Liriano	.975	58	109	7	3	3
Revere	.989	34	83	3	1	1
Rojas	1.000	2	4	0	0	0
Schimpf	1.000	4	13	0	0	0
Triunfel	1.000	1	5	0	0	0
Unroe	1.000	3	9	0	0	0
Walsh	.940	41	62	1	4	0
Way	1.000	33	73	0	0	0
Young Jr.	1.000	78	154	1	0	0

MOBILE BAYBEARS
SOUTHERN LEAGUE

DOUBLE-A

Batting	B-T	HT	WT	DOB	AVG	vLH	vRH	G	AB	R	H	2B	3B	HR	RBI	BB	HBP	SH	SF	SO	SB	CS	SLG	OBP
Adell, Jo	R-R	6-3	208	4-8-99	.238	.308	.220	17	63	14	15	6	0	2	6	6	2	0	0	22	2	0	.429	.324
Arcia, Francisco	L-R	5-11	195	9-14-89	.200	.200	.200	4	15	3	3	0	0	0	0	0	0	0	0	2	0	0	.200	.200
Baldoquin, Roberto	R-R	5-11	199	5-14-94	.269	.382	.225	51	193	16	52	7	2	1	27	13	3	0	3	46	3	3	.342	.321

	B-T	HT	WT	DOB	AVG	vLH	vRH	G	AB	R	H	2B	3B	HR	RBI	BB	HBP	SH	SF	SO	SB	CS	SLG	OBP
Barash, Michael	R-R	6-1	200	10-12-94	.224	.414	.182	49	161	21	36	9	0	5	19	33	2	2	1	43	2	1	.373	.360
Ghelfi, Mitch	B-R	5-11	185	9-24-92	.272	.250	.281	24	81	11	22	4	1	3	17	6	0	0	2	19	3	0	.457	.315
2-team total (14 Biloxi)					.252	.300	.238	38	131	12	33	5	1	3	18	9	2	0	2	25	4	0	.374	.306
Gibbons, Zach	R-R	5-8	186	10-14-93	.261	.267	.259	108	395	61	103	21	4	4	45	42	0	0	3	59	6	5	.365	.330
Houchins, Zach	R-R	6-2	210	9-16-92	.235	.300	.222	50	183	25	43	7	1	11	35	13	0	0	2	52	1	1	.465	.283
Hudson, Joe	R-R	6-2	206	5-21-91	.346	.500	.278	7	26	2	9	1	1	1	5	1	1	0	0	7	0	0	.577	.393
Johnson, Sherman	L-R	5-10	190	7-15-90	.194	.240	.167	20	67	8	13	5	1	0	6	11	1	0	0	17	1	2	.299	.317
Jones, Jahmai	R-R	6-0	215	8-4-97	.245	.274	.230	48	184	33	45	10	4	2	20	24	2	0	2	51	11	1	.375	.335
Justus, Connor	R-R	6-0	190	11-2-94	.170	.129	.184	77	247	30	42	9	1	0	18	40	7	2	1	82	1	4	.215	.302
Kruger, Jack	R-R	6-1	185	10-26-94	.305	.382	.269	41	174	25	53	10	1	4	24	4	2	0	0	31	2	2	.443	.328
Leon, Julian	R-R	5-11	200	1-24-96	.200	.000	.250	2	5	1	1	0	0	0	0	1	2	0	0	3	0	0	.200	.429
Lund, Brennon	L-R	5-10	185	11-27-94	.264	.168	.299	100	401	63	106	20	6	8	59	43	6	1	2	102	21	5	.404	.343
Moyer, Hutton	B-R	6-1	185	4-30-93	.200	.184	.206	35	135	20	27	4	1	6	19	8	1	0	2	52	7	4	.378	.247
Olmeda, Alexis	R-R	6-0	225	4-5-94	.143	.250	.100	5	14	1	2	1	0	0	2	1	0	0	1	8	0	0	.214	.188
Rengifo, Luis	B-R	5-10	165	2-26-97	.305	.290	.308	40	151	37	46	10	5	2	21	23	7	0	0	22	13	2	.477	.420
Rojas, Jose	R-R	6-0	200	2-24-93	.305	.333	.294	84	312	57	95	21	3	17	65	36	3	0	1	75	9	4	.555	.381
Sandoval, Brandon	R-R	6-1	180	6-24-95	.271	.217	.292	72	247	33	67	9	0	2	18	25	0	0	1	65	15	5	.332	.337
Sanger, Brendon	L-R	6-0	195	9-11-93	.234	.273	.220	93	304	37	71	12	0	7	41	50	1	0	3	72	4	4	.342	.341
Spires, Mitch	R-R	6-1	195	3-11-96	.246	.214	.255	19	61	5	15	1	0	0	3	2	0	0	1	12	2	0	.262	.266
Thaiss, Matt	L-R	6-0	195	5-6-95	.287	.184	.319	40	157	24	45	10	2	6	25	16	1	0	2	35	2	1	.490	.352
Unroe, Riley	B-R	5-10	180	8-3-95	.226	.200	.238	106	345	45	78	9	2	4	42	52	2	1	2	96	10	9	.299	.329
Walsh, Jared	L-L	6-1	210	7-30-93	.289	.167	.319	41	149	26	43	13	0	8	26	21	2	0	1	48	1	0	.537	.382
Ward, Taylor	R-R	6-1	200	12-14-93	.345	.382	.333	42	148	26	51	8	0	6	25	29	1	0	1	33	8	1	.520	.453
Wass, Wade	R-R	6-0	215	9-23-91	.159	.118	.174	19	63	6	10	3	0	2	6	8	3	0	0	27	1	0	.302	.284
Way, Bo	L-L	6-0	180	11-17-91	.279	.042	.345	35	111	12	31	5	1	0	12	17	4	1	0	19	2	5	.342	.394
Yacinich, Jake	L-R	6-2	195	3-2-93	.182	.000	.222	4	11	1	2	0	0	1	1	1	0	0	2	0	0	.364	.308

Pitching

	B-T	HT	WT	DOB	W	L	ERA	G	GS	CG	SV	IP	H	R	ER	HR	BB	SO	AVG	vLH	vRH	K/9	BB/9
Alexander, Jason	R-R	6-3	200	3-1-93	2	5	4.09	13	11	0	0	62	63	30	28	5	15	40	.267	.303	.250	5.84	2.19
Almeida, Adrian	L-L	6-0	160	2-25-95	2	4	4.25	33	0	0	0	49	30	26	23	3	51	54	.179	.113	.209	9.99	9.43
Anderson, Justin	L-R	6-3	220	9-28-92	0	0	0.00	3	0	0	0	4	2	0	0	0	1	8	.167	.000	.222	19.64	2.45
Ball, Matt	R-R	6-5	200	1-23-95	1	3	5.79	4	4	0	0	19	22	13	12	0	7	13	.301	.323	.286	6.27	3.38
Bates, Nathan	R-R	6-8	205	3-1-94	0	0	9.00	1	0	0	0	1	1	1	1	0	0	1	.250	.500	.000	9.00	0.00
Beasley, Jeremy	R-R	6-3	215	11-20-95	3	3	2.44	10	7	0	0	44	32	13	12	3	14	37	.207	.233	.190	7.51	2.84
Beltre, Dario	R-R	6-3	170	11-19-92	1	2	5.14	21	0	0	1	28	20	18	16	2	17	33	.196	.167	.212	10.61	5.46
Campos, Vicente	R-R	6-3	230	7-27-92	0	1	5.50	8	1	0	0	18	25	12	11	2	7	15	.333	.333	.333	7.50	3.50
Canning, Griffin	R-R	6-2	170	5-11-96	1	0	1.97	10	10	0	0	46	27	11	10	2	19	49	.170	.200	.149	9.66	3.74
Cash, Ralston	R-R	6-3	215	8-20-91	2	2	4.03	18	0	0	0	22	23	12	10	2	13	29	.258	.211	.294	11.69	5.24
Castillo, Jesus	R-R	6-2	165	8-27-95	9	5	4.94	21	20	0	0	98	97	56	54	7	31	60	.264	.277	.254	5.49	2.84
Clark, Ryan	R-R	6-5	220	12-9-93	2	3	2.19	18	0	0	5	25	17	7	6	0	12	33	.198	.321	.138	12.04	4.38
Cox, Cortland	R-R	6-1	185	11-3-94	0	0	9.00	1	0	0	0	1	2	1	1	0	1	1	.500	.000	.667	9.00	9.00
Custred, Matt	R-R	6-6	240	9-8-93	3	5	3.26	34	0	0	8	50	36	24	18	2	29	53	.201	.111	.250	9.60	5.26
De Los Santos, Samil	R-R	6-4	175	1-94	1	1	7.15	25	0	0	1	34	37	32	27	5	35	32	.282	.321	.256	8.47	9.26
Gatto, Joe	R-R	6-3	220	6-14-95	3	4	5.75	16	16	0	0	77	85	54	49	8	36	49	.283	.333	.254	5.75	4.23
Herrmann, Max	L-L	6-3	210	7-17-93	0	0	0.00	1	0	0	0	1	1	0	0	0	2	0	.250	—	.250	0.00	18.00
Hofacket, Adam	R-R	6-1	195	2-18-94	0	0	9.00	8	0	0	0	11	20	15	11	1	6	6	.377	.368	.382	4.91	4.91
Isaac, Sean	R-R	6-4	225	12-17-92	0	1	6.43	7	1	0	0	14	11	13	10	2	14	22	.208	.304	.133	14.14	9.00
Jewell, Jake	R-R	6-3	200	5-16-93	1	0	2.08	7	0	0	2	13	15	3	3	1	2	11	.313	.263	.345	7.62	1.38
Klonowski, Alex	R-R	6-4	195	4-1-92	10	3	3.97	18	13	0	0	95	96	43	42	7	26	83	.258	.242	.266	7.84	2.45
Lillis-White, Conor	L-L	6-4	220	7-22-92	2	0	3.12	20	0	0	3	35	26	13	12	1	16	46	.205	.257	.185	11.94	4.15
Mahle, Greg	L-L	6-2	230	4-17-93	3	1	1.73	26	0	0	3	36	22	10	7	2	11	36	.180	.077	.229	8.92	2.72
Pena, Luis	R-R	5-11	190	8-24-95	2	4	4.27	12	12	0	0	59	46	29	28	7	25	63	.201	.255	.176	9.61	3.81
Pineyro, Ivan	R-R	6-1	200	9-29-91	0	1	5.23	2	2	0	0	10	9	7	6	0	1	14	.231	.278	.191	12.19	0.87
Procopio, Daniel	R-R	6-0	190	9-18-95	1	3	7.11	26	0	0	0	38	42	33	30	5	27	44	.280	.315	.260	10.42	6.39
Rhoades, Jeremy	R-R	6-4	225	2-12-93	4	0	1.82	14	0	0	0	25	14	6	5	2	5	16	.161	.182	.148	6.93	1.46
Rodriguez, Jose	R-R	6-2	175	8-29-95	7	10	6.12	23	23	0	0	115	144	86	78	10	41	105	.304	.316	.296	8.24	3.22
Ryan, Zac	R-R	6-1	201	5-28-94	1	4	5.68	20	0	0	2	32	35	22	20	1	21	31	.287	.395	.228	8.81	5.97
Sandoval, Patrick	L-L	6-3	190	10-18-96	1	0	1.37	4	4	0	0	20	12	3	3	0	8	27	.174	.227	.149	12.36	3.66
Stevens, Tyler	R-R	6-0	215	4-4-96	2	1	3.17	13	0	0	4	20	9	7	3	2	6	30	.130	.111	.143	13.73	2.75
Suarez, Jose	L-L	5-10	170	1-3-98	2	1	3.03	7	7	0	0	30	34	11	10	0	8	51	.286	.265	.294	15.47	2.43
Unsworth, Dylan	R-R	6-1	175	9-23-92	0	3	6.88	5	3	0	0	17	23	14	13	3	4	11	.307	.171	.425	5.82	2.12
Wesely, Jonah	L-L	6-1	215	12-8-94	0	1	12.46	3	0	0	0	4	8	9	6	0	9	2	.400	.000	.500	4.15	18.69

Fielding

Catcher	PCT	G	PO	A	E	DP	PB
Arcia	.981	4	51	2	1	0	0
Barash	.996	48	433	27	2	2	4
Ghelfi	.995	22	162	19	1	1	5
Hudson	.971	4	34	0	1	0	0
Kruger	.990	36	268	21	3	1	2
Leon	1.000	2	14	2	0	0	1
Olmeda	1.000	3	11	0	0	0	0
Wass	.985	17	124	9	2	2	2

First Base	PCT	G	PO	A	E	DP
Ghelfi	1.000	1	4	0	0	1

	PCT	G	PO	A	E	DP
Houchins	.993	20	129	6	1	18
Hudson	1.000	2	17	1	0	5
Johnson	1.000	3	31	1	0	3
Olmeda	1.000	2	17	0	0	3
Rojas	.997	36	270	17	1	26
Spires	.889	1	8	0	1	1
Thaiss	.997	36	275	25	1	26
Unroe	1.000	2	10	0	0	4
Walsh	.993	37	254	27	2	27

Second Base	PCT	G	PO	A	E	DP
Baldoquin	1.000	2	2	4	0	1

	PCT	G	PO	A	E	DP
Jones	.940	45	90	112	13	29
Justus	.963	24	41	63	4	16
Moyer	.968	6	12	18	1	4
Rengifo	1.000	9	21	17	0	4
Rojas	1.000	3	3	3	0	0
Unroe	.964	47	99	116	8	38
Yacinich	1.000	1	1	0	0	0

Third Base	PCT	G	PO	A	E	DP
Baldoquin	1.000	14	10	14	0	3
Houchins	.937	24	20	39	4	9
Johnson	1.000	11	4	15	0	0

	PCT	G	PO	A	E	DP
Moyer	1.000	11	7	25	0	2
Rojas	.886	12	7	24	4	3
Spires	1.000	1	0	1	0	0
Unroe	.914	33	14	60	7	4
Ward	.910	33	22	39	6	6

Shortstop	PCT	G	PO	A	E	DP
Baldoquin	.931	34	32	102	10	16
Justus	.947	51	63	133	11	39

	PCT	G	PO	A	E	DP
Moyer	1.000	6	7	15	0	2
Rengifo	.938	30	25	50	5	15
Unroe	.919	16	22	35	5	8

Outfield	PCT	G	PO	A	E	DP
Adell	.973	17	34	2	1	0
Gibbons	.994	95	157	7	1	1
Houchins	1.000	4	5	0	0	0
Johnson	.833	2	5	0	1	0

	PCT	G	PO	A	E	DP
Lund	.986	100	201	4	3	1
Rojas	1.000	2	6	0	0	0
Sandoval	.987	69	150	6	2	2
Sanger	.975	82	146	7	4	3
Unroe	1.000	1	3	0	0	0
Way	.974	35	71	5	2	1
Yacinich	1.000	3	6	2	0	1

INLAND EMPIRE 66ERS

CALIFORNIA LEAGUE

HIGH CLASS A

Batting	B-T	HT	WT	DOB	AVG	vLH	vRH	G	AB	R	H	2B	3B	HR	RBI	BB	HBP	SH	SF	SO	SB	CS	SLG	OBP
Adell, Jo	R-R	6-3	208	4-8-99	.290	.306	.286	57	238	46	69	19	3	12	42	15	6	0	2	63	9	2	.546	.345
Baldoquin, Roberto	R-R	5-11	199	5-14-94	.293	.333	.284	31	116	10	34	2	6	1	13	10	2	2	1	28	3	2	.440	.357
Camargo, Bernabe	R-R	6-1	180	1-22-96	.290	.524	.200	24	76	8	22	0	2	0	5	10	2	0	2	23	1	1	.342	.378
Fecteau, Richie	L-R	5-10	190	3-17-94	.244	.204	.252	84	299	37	73	13	8	4	37	20	2	2	1	97	2	2	.381	.295
Fuchs, Michael	R-R	6-0	190	9-1-95	.000		.000	1	2	1	0	0	0	0	0	0	1	0	0	1	0	0	.000	.333
Gurwitz, Zane	R-R	5-8	185	12-1-94	.227	.250	.220	29	110	8	25	8	2	2	12	7	1	0	0	28	1	1	.391	.280
Hunter Jr., Torii	R-R	6-2	180	6-7-95	.327	.385	.310	13	55	4	18	1	1	0	1	2	2	1	0	18	5	0	.382	.373
Jenkins, DJ	R-R	5-8	155	2-11-94	.219	.211	.222	77	260	33	57	6	2	1	21	22	2	1	1	63	7	5	.269	.284
Jones, Jahmai	R-R	6-0	215	8-4-97	.235	.277	.227	75	298	47	70	10	5	8	35	43	4	0	1	63	13	3	.383	.338
Justus, Connor	R-R	6-0	190	11-2-94	.290	.320	.278	47	176	30	51	8	1	6	29	24	7	0	3	37	6	5	.449	.391
Kruger, Jack	R-R	6-1	185	10-26-94	.294	.387	.279	56	221	25	65	12	0	3	16	27	3	0	4	66	11	3	.389	.379
Leon, Julian	R-R	5-11	200	1-24-96	.219	.233	.215	64	201	30	44	8	0	11	41	40	9	0	5	70	0	1	.423	.365
MacKinnon, David	R-R	6-2	200	12-15-94	.285	.273	.290	90	305	51	87	22	0	5	47	60	7	0	5	73	0	0	.407	.409
Marsh, Brandon	L-R	6-4	210	12-18-97	.256	.235	.263	93	371	59	95	15	6	7	46	52	1	0	1	118	10	4	.385	.348
Marte, Jefry	R-R	6-1	220	6-21-91	.143	1.000	.077	4	14	1	2	0	0	0	1	2	0	0	0	6	0	0	.143	.250
Navarro, Franklin	B-R	5-10	181	10-17-94	.237	.069	.282	38	139	13	33	8	0	2	17	3	0	0	2	50	0	0	.338	.250
Rengifo, Luis	B-R	5-10	165	2-26-97	.323	.263	.331	41	161	36	52	11	3	2	16	27	2	0	0	22	22	8	.466	.426
Rivera, Rene	R-R	5-10	215	7-31-83	.286	.500	.154	6	21	4	6	0	0	2	3	3	1	0	0	5	0	0	.571	.400
Rosario, Rayneldy	L-L	5-8	139	4-30-98	.130	.250	.105	7	23	1	3	0	1	0	1	1	1	0	0	10	1	0	.217	.200
Sandoval, Brandon	R-R	6-1	180	6-24-95	.352	.167	.372	33	125	19	44	5	2	0	15	11	1	1	2	20	9	5	.424	.403
Sanger, Brendon	L-R	6-0	195	9-11-93	.319	.429	.273	13	47	12	15	3	1	2	4	9	1	0	0	13	0	0	.553	.439
Sanjur, Mario	R-S	5-7	174	12-23-95	.222	.000	.250	4	9	1	2	0	0	0	2	2	0	0	0	3	0	0	.222	.364
Taylor, Cole	R-R	6-0	200	6-11-96	.152	.091	.171	13	46	4	7	2	0	0	2	4	1	1	0	22	0	0	.196	.235
Todd, Jonah	L-L	6-0	185	9-18-95	.204	.200	.205	113	417	35	85	13	7	0	36	58	0	0	3	130	4	3	.269	.299
Torres, Franklin	R-R	6-0	175	10-27-96	.216	.308	.184	12	51	8	11	1	1	3	8	4	0	0	1	12	0	0	.451	.268
Triunfel, Alberto	R-R	5-11	160	2-1-94	.216	.225	.214	68	232	26	50	18	0	2	28	20	2	4	1	63	4	1	.319	.282
Vega, Ryan	R-R	6-2	180	9-17-96	.750	.000	1.000	1	4	0	3	0	0	0	1	0	0	0	0	0	0	0	.750	.750
Walsh, Jared	L-L	6-1	210	7-30-93	.275	.133	.291	40	149	28	41	8	1	13	36	24	0	0	5	50	0	1	.604	.365
Williams, Kevin	R-R	6-0	190	6-17-96	.188	.158	.195	27	96	11	18	3	1	2	9	9	2	0	0	41	1	2	.302	.271
Yacinich, Jake	L-R	6-2	195	3-2-93	.148	.000	.160	7	27	1	4	0	0	0	1	2	0	0	0	12	0	0	.148	.233
Zimmerman, Jordan	R-R	6-1	195	11-21-94	.231	.282	.219	111	446	53	103	27	5	11	60	22	3	1	6	123	3	1	.388	.268

Pitching	B-T	HT	WT	DOB	W	L	ERA	G	GS	CG	SV	IP	H	R	ER	HR	BB	SO	AVG	vLH	vRH	K/9	BB/9
Alexander, Jason	R-R	6-3	200	3-1-93	2	4	4.50	9	9	0	0	48	41	32	24	7	13	48	.222	.256	.194	9.00	2.44
Almeida, Adrian	L-L	6-0	160	2-25-95	0	0	0.75	7	0	0	1	12	4	1	1	0	4	19	.146	.091	.167	14.25	3.00
Ball, Matt	R-R	6-5	200	1-23-95	4	1	3.81	14	13	0	0	54	44	24	23	5	12	55	.223	.269	.200	9.11	1.99
Beasley, Jeremy	R-R	6-3	215	11-20-95	3	2	3.05	9	6	0	1	44	48	20	15	4	11	48	.281	.302	.269	9.74	2.23
Belton, Greg	R-R	5-10	190	12-31-92	1	1	3.38	6	0	0	2	8	9	4	3	1	5	6	.290	.455	.200	6.75	5.63
Beltre, Dario	R-R	6-3	170	11-19-92	0	0	1.46	6	0	0	1	12	10	3	2	1	5	18	.217	.353	.138	13.14	3.65
Bertness, Nate	L-L	6-6	205	8-4-95	3	7	5.33	27	17	0	1	110	116	74	65	11	66	93	.273	.281	.270	7.63	5.42
Bower, Matt	R-L	6-5	190	6-16-94	0	1	3.52	8	0	0	0	15	13	6	6	1	10	17	.220	.222	.219	9.98	5.87
Brakeman, Marc	L-R	6-2	185	6-15-94	3	0	5.24	24	0	0	0	45	41	30	26	4	24	48	.238	.256	.223	9.67	4.84
Canning, Griffin	R-R	6-1	170	5-11-96	0	0	0.00	2	2	0	0	9	4	0	0		3	12	.133	.333	.048	12.46	3.12
Clark, Ryan	R-R	6-2	220	12-9-93	2	0	0.00	5	0	0	0	7	5	1	0	0	1	10	.185	.091		12.86	1.29
Cordy, Max	R-R	6-4	220	6-9-93	2	2	2.92	7	0	0	0	12	12	7	4	0	9	7	.267	.167	.333	5.11	6.57
Cox, Aaron	R-R	6-3	205	8-5-94	0	1	4.11	11	0	0	2	15	14	9	7	0	7	21	.246	.143	.306	12.33	4.11
Custred, Matt	R-R	6-6	240	9-8-93	0	0	5.40	4	0	0	2	5	3	3	3	0	2	6	.158	.143	.167	16.20	3.60
De Horta, Adrian	R-R	6-3	185	3-13-95	0	2	5.60	9	9	0	0	34	42	25	22	6	16	39	.284	.267	.291	9.93	4.08
De La Cruz, Kida	R-R	6-5	240	8-10-94	1	3	9.55	15	0	0	0	22	19	26	23	0	21	27	.226	.189	.255	11.22	8.72
Diaz, Dayan	R-R	5-10	195	2-10-89	1	0	4.02	11	0	0	0	16	17	7	7	2	6	25	.274	.211	.302	14.94	3.45
Gatto, Joe	R-R	6-3	220	6-14-95	5	2	4.15	9	9	0	0	43	43	21	20	2	18	51	.256	.197	.304	10.59	3.74
Halbohn, Kyle	R-R	6-8	230	1-19-93	1	1	4.00	6	0	0	1	9	7	5	4	0	2	9	.226	.154	.278	9.00	2.00
Hanewich, Brett	B-R	6-3	200	12-15-94	3	0	1.90	26	0	0	0	43	26	11	9	2	31	51	.179	.160	.190	10.76	6.54
Heaney, Andrew	L-L	6-2	185	6-5-91	1	0	1.42	1	1	0	0	6	2	1	1	0	1	6	.095		.095	8.53	1.42
Herrin, Travis	R-R	6-2	220	4-29-95	3	1	3.00	5	0	0	0	6	4	2	2	2	0	6	.191	.167	.200	9.00	0.00
Herrmann, Max	L-L	6-3	210	7-17-93	0	1	3.00	4	0	0	0	3	2	1	1	0	1	3	.200	.000	.222	0.00	0.00
Hunt, Dustin	R-R	6-5	195	8-2-94	0	0	3.00	2	0	0	0	3	2	1	1	0	1	3	.182	.400	.000	9.00	3.00
Isaac, Sean	R-R	6-4	225	12-17-92	2	0	3.04	9	0	0	0	27	15	9	9	0	17	39	.166	.257	.111	13.16	5.74
Johnson, Jim	R-R	6-6	250	6-27-83	0	0	18.00	1	0	0	0	1	1	2	2	0	1	1	.500	.250	1.000	9.00	9.00
Kaelin, Mike	R-R	5-9	185	3-30-94	1	3	5.94	20	0	0	2	36	41	26	24	4	16	36	.275	.291	.266	8.92	3.96
Kelly, Zack	R-R	6-3	205	3-3-95	1	0	5.40	4	0	0	1	7	4	4	4	0	4	7	.310	.500	.261	9.45	2.70
Klonowski, Alex	R-R	6-4	195	4-1-92	5	4	5.34	15	4	0	0	29	35	17	17	3	8	17	.307	.395	.263	5.34	2.51
Madero, Luis	R-R	6-3	175	4-15-97	1	2	2.44	9	9	0	0	44	41	14	12	3	12	46	.246	.320	.214	9.34	2.44

Name	B-T	HT	WT	DOB	W	L	ERA	G	GS	CG	SV	IP	H	R	ER	HR	BB	SO	AVG	vLH	vRH	K/9	BB/9
Manoah, Erik	R-R	6-2	190	12-22-95	2	12	7.29	25	25	0	0	104	119	87	84	19	64	99	.292	.353	.254	8.59	5.56
Mathews, Simon	R-R	6-2	180	9-24-95	4	7	5.14	16	13	0	1	68	75	53	39	7	31	64	.276	.267	.281	8.43	4.08
Mattson, Isaac	R-R	6-3	205	7-14-95	2	1	3.62	11	0	0	2	37	30	17	15	2	12	39	.216	.192	.230	9.40	2.89
Procopio, Daniel	R-R	6-0	190	9-18-95	0	0	2.25	12	0	0	1	20	11	5	5	0	12	33	.157	.400	.060	14.85	5.40
Richards, Garrett	R-R	6-3	210	5-27-88	0	1	13.50	1	1	0	0	3	7	5	5	2	0	4	.412	.222	.625	10.80	0.00
Riley, Connor	R-R	6-0	185	5-7-95	0	1	17.18	2	2	0	0	4	6	8	7	1	5	3	.353	.600	.250	7.36	12.27
Rivera, Eduardo	R-R	6-5	190	9-24-92	2	5	7.36	30	0	0	2	44	39	38	36	7	48	67	.239	.263	.226	13.70	9.82
Ryan, Zac	R-R	6-1	201	5-28-94	3	1	3.66	22	0	0	1	39	32	17	16	2	19	44	.227	.309	.174	10.07	4.35
Salazar, Carlos	R-R	6-0	200	11-23-94	0	3	6.46	12	0	0	0	15	13	17	11	3	13	15	.245	.286	.219	8.80	7.63
Sandoval, Patrick	L-L	6-3	190	10-18-96	1	0	0.00	3	3	0	0	15	6	0	0	0	6	21	.118	.111	.119	12.89	3.68
Santos, Michael	R-R	6-4	205	5-29-95	0	1	7.23	4	3	0	1	19	24	17	15	4	3	13	.320	.130	.404	6.27	1.45
Shoemaker, Matt	R-R	6-2	225	9-27-86	0	0	0.00	1	1	0	0	4	0	1	0	0	2	6	.000	.000	.000	13.50	4.50
Smith, Blake	R-R	6-5	240	8-12-92	2	0	5.18	12	0	0	1	24	21	15	14	3	9	20	.231	.250	.220	7.40	3.33
Stevens, Tyler	R-R	6-0	215	4-4-96	3	2	2.28	16	0	0	2	24	20	8	6	3	4	28	.217	.220	.216	10.65	1.52
Suarez, Jose	L-L	5-10	170	1-3-98	0	1	2.00	2	2	0	0	9	6	4	2	0	1	18	.182	.500	.138	18.00	1.00
Tavarez, Jorge	R-R	5-10	150	8-4-95	5	1	1.87	19	0	0	1	34	28	7	7	2	17	35	.228	.233	.225	9.36	4.54
Tropeano, Nick	R-R	6-4	200	8-27-90	1	1	2.00	2	2	0	0	9	9	3	2	1	1	9	.257	.250	.267	9.00	1.00
Wesely, Jonah	L-L	6-1	215	12-8-94	2	1	6.75	16	0	0	0	24	30	20	18	2	16	28	.306	.206	.359	10.50	6.00
Wood, Blake	R-R	6-5	233	8-8-85	0	0	7.71	3	3	0	0	2	4	2	2	0	0	2	.333	.143	.600	7.71	0.00

Fielding

Catcher	PCT	G	PO	A	E	DP	PB
Kruger	.992	47	443	35	4	2	4
Leon	.991	52	482	48	5	5	9
Navarro	.994	38	342	16	2	3	2
Rivera	1.000	4	34	3	0	0	0
Sanjur	.963	4	23	3	1	0	1

First Base	PCT	G	PO	A	E	DP
Camargo	1.000	1	2	0	0	1
Fecteau	.941	6	29	3	2	1
MacKinnon	.994	83	623	45	4	44
Marte	1.000	2	8	0	0	0
Walsh	1.000	26	191	19	0	12
Zimmerman	.990	25	191	12	2	17

Second Base	PCT	G	PO	A	E	DP
Baldoquin	1.000	5	4	7	0	0
Camargo	1.000	4	4	8	0	2
Gurwitz	.976	21	33	48	2	14
Jones	.951	70	110	144	13	31
Justus	1.000	7	11	27	0	3
Rengifo	1.000	2	2	2	0	0
Taylor	.889	6	7	9	2	0
Torres	.957	11	21	24	2	5
Triunfel	1.000	8	25	22	0	5
Yacinich	.800	4	2	6	2	1
Zimmerman	1.000	2	4	3	0	0

Third Base	PCT	G	PO	A	E	DP
Baldoquin	.933	6	3	11	1	0
Camargo	1.000	1	1	2	0	2
Fecteau	.891	47	31	83	14	7
Justus	1.000	5	4	10	0	0
Marte	1.000	1	0	3	0	0
Taylor	1.000	2	1	2	0	0
Triunfel	.953	20	19	42	3	4
Yacinich	.000	1	0	0	0	0
Zimmerman	.928	58	43	98	11	9

Shortstop	PCT	G	PO	A	E	DP
Baldoquin	.986	19	21	50	1	6
Camargo	.967	17	23	36	2	8
Fuchs	1.000	1	0	3	0	0
Justus	.945	33	32	88	7	10
Rengifo	.953	36	43	98	7	14
Taylor	.882	5	4	11	2	2
Triunfel	.992	29	45	74	1	9
Yacinich	.000	1	0	0	0	0

Outfield	PCT	G	PO	A	E	DP
Adell	.968	51	91	1	3	1
Gurwitz	1.000	5	7	2	0	0
Hunter Jr.	.962	12	25	0	1	0
Jenkins	.971	71	127	7	4	3
Marsh	.975	89	189	9	5	1
Rosario	.933	7	13	1	1	0
Sandoval	.970	32	64	1	2	1
Sanger	1.000	10	23	1	0	0
Todd	.989	113	183	5	2	0
Triunfel	.750	4	3	0	1	0
Vega	1.000	1	1	0	0	0
Walsh	1.000	5	10	1	0	0
Williams	1.000	25	43	2	0	0
Yacinich	1.000	1	4	0	0	0
Zimmerman	.000	1	0	0	0	0

BURLINGTON BEES
LOW CLASS A

MIDWEST LEAGUE

Batting	B-T	HT	WT	DOB	AVG	vLH	vRH	G	AB	R	H	2B	3B	HR	RBI	BB	HBP	SH	SF	SO	SB	CS	SLG	OBP
Adell, Jo	R-R	6-3	208	4-8-99	.326	.276	.349	25	95	23	31	7	1	6	29	11	1	0	1	26	4	1	.611	.398
Barnes, Jimmy	R-R	6-4	190	6-16-97	.118	.150	.107	27	76	6	9	1	0	2	13	12	2	0	3	41	1	1	.211	.247
Fitzsimons, Connor	R-R	5-10	190	8-29-94	.271	.214	.285	42	144	22	39	8	1	4	16	10	1	0	1	54	1	1	.424	.321
Garcia, Julio	B-R	6-0	175	7-31-97	.233	.155	.255	122	456	27	106	19	3	5	53	17	4	7	2	132	3	6	.320	.265
Griffin, Spencer	R-R	6-1	170	10-24-96	.221	.284	.199	108	394	56	87	8	7	2	40	50	2	1	3	150	11	7	.292	.310
Gurwitz, Zane	R-R	5-8	185	12-1-94	.177	.077	.204	37	124	12	22	4	2	0	8	11	0	0	0	29	0	0	.242	.244
Hunter Jr., Torii	R-R	6-2	180	6-7-95	.255	.232	.262	97	381	59	97	14	8	2	44	44	0		4	106	24	6	.349	.335
MacKinnon, David	R-R	6-2	200	12-15-94	.261	.407	.214	35	111	21	29	7	0	3	35	13	0	0	0	30	0	0	.351	.438
Marsh, Brandon	L-R	6-4	210	12-18-97	.296	.296	.295	34	132	26	39	12	1	3	24	21	0	0	1	40	4	0	.470	.390
Martinez, Orlando	L-L	6-0	185	2-17-98	.289	.362	.263	53	218	27	63	12	1	3	25	17	1	0	2	56	6	5	.395	.340
Menendez, Kiki	R-R	6-2	205	2-7-95	.235	.321	.203	27	102	11	24	1	1	4	6	0	0	0		36	0	0	.304	.278
Millard, Tim	R-R	6-2	200	5-29-95	.243	.281	.227	30	107	9	26	4	0	2	12	12	2	0	1	30	1	0	.336	.328
Olmeda, Alexis	R-R	6-0	225	4-5-94	.362	.222	.395	13	47	10	17	5	0	4	13	4	0	0	0	14	0	1	.723	.412
Pina, Keinner	R-R	5-10	165	2-12-94	.256	.290	.245	82	313	26	80	8	2	0	36	20	4	2	3	72	3	0	.294	.306
Pineda, Gleyvin	L-R	5-11	160	8-19-96	.248	.225	.257	46	149	21	37	3	0	2	16	21	1	0	1	38	2	1	.309	.343
Rivas, Leonardo	B-R	5-10	150	10-10-97	.234	.336	.196	119	454	62	106	16	7	4	34	84	3	4	2	138	16	10	.326	.355
Rubalcaba, Alvaro	R-R	5-8	165	4-4-97	.221	.241	.212	29	95	10	21	6	1	1	12	4	0		1	24	0	0	.337	.330
Sanchez, Jeyson	R-R	5-10	174	7-4-94	.183	.206	.175	43	131	19	24	6	0	3	14	16	8	0	0	35	0	1	.298	.310
Torres, Franklin	R-R	6-0	175	10-27-96	.285	.301	.279	82	288	36	82	12	4	4	39	44	2	1	2	60	12	1	.382	.381
Wenson, Harrison	R-R	6-3	235	4-21-95	.114	.163	.099	58	185	21	21	4	0	6	17	27	5	3	0	101	4	0	.232	.244
Williams, Cam	R-R	5-11	185	1-16-97	.177	.000	.243	16	51	6	9	1	1	0	3	4	1	1	0	20	0	1	.235	.250
Williams, Kevin	R-R	6-0	190	6-17-96	.245	.258	.240	91	347	27	85	18	3	4	35	28	2	3	1	111	3	4	.349	.304

Pitching	B-T	HT	WT	DOB	W	L	ERA	G	GS	CG	SV	IP	H	R	ER	HR	BB	SO	AVG	vLH	vRH	K/9	BB/9
Beasley, Jeremy	R-R	6-3	215	11-20-95	0	2	2.35	6	5	0	0	23	16	6	6	0	7	19	.198	.222	.178	7.43	2.74
Belton, Greg	R-R	5-10	190	12-31-92	0	1	3.18	4	0	0	0	6	6	3	2	2	1	8	.223	.222	.308	12.71	1.59
Benitez, Anfernee	R-L	6-1	180	7-24-95	3	4	4.92	24	1	0	0	53	51	38	29	1	31	64	.248	.206	.266	10.87	5.26
2-team total (4 Kane County)					3	4	4.87	28	1	0	1	57	53	43	31	1	36	68	.239	.203	.253	10.67	5.65
Brady, Denny	R-R	6-1	200	1-18-97	0	5	4.72	13	13	0	0	48	51	29	25	1	15	47	.274	.319	.248	8.87	2.83

Name	B-T	HT	WT	DOB	W	L	ERA	G	GS	CG	SV	IP	H	R	ER	HR	BB	SO	AVG	vLH	vRH	K/9	BB/9
Brakeman, Marc	L-R	6-2	185	6-15-94	1	0	0.00	1	0	0	0	3	1	0	0	0	0	3	.091	.000	.143	8.10	0.00
De La Cruz, Kida	R-R	6-5	240	8-10-94	2	2	3.94	18	0	0	1	32	25	18	14	2	26	43	.212	.178	.233	12.09	7.31
Del Rosario, Eduardo	R-R	6-0	145	5-19-95	3	5	3.38	33	0	0	2	64	58	30	24	4	35	74	.241	.248	.236	10.41	4.92
Eagle, Matt	R-R	6-3	230	11-25-95	0	0	5.40	4	0	0	0	7	8	4	4	3	2	9	.308	.400	.286	12.15	2.70
Halbohn, Kyle	R-R	6-8	230	1-19-93	1	0	5.25	5	1	0	0	12	11	7	7	1	6	9	.250	.200	.276	6.75	4.50
Hanewich, Brett	B-R	6-3	200	12-15-94	0	2	3.76	16	0	0	2	26	25	12	11	0	15	23	.275	.394	.207	7.86	5.13
Herrmann, Max	L-L	6-3	210	7-17-93	2	9	5.78	29	12	0	0	81	113	58	52	7	34	68	.332	.356	.324	7.56	3.78
Isaac, Sean	R-R	6-4	225	12-17-92	1	1	3.38	3	0	0	1	5	4	2	2	0	2	8	.211	.000	.286	13.50	3.38
Jobst, Nick	R-R	6-2	260	4-20-94	0	0	9.45	5	0	0	1	7	7	8	7	0	6	7	.280	.167	.316	9.45	8.10
Kelly, Zack	R-R	6-3	205	3-3-95	3	3	2.86	12	0	0	0	28	26	10	9	3	12	25	.260	.216	.286	7.94	3.81
Krzeminski, Austin	R-R	6-2	210	9-30-96	5	6	2.23	39	5	0	4	93	91	31	23	5	34	72	.267	.254	.275	6.99	3.30
Madero, Luis	R-R	6-3	175	4-15-97	2	7	4.26	14	14	0	0	61	69	33	29	5	15	49	.283	.306	.265	7.19	2.20
Malmin, Jon	R-L	6-1	170	9-2-94	0	1	7.04	8	1	0	0	15	14	16	12	3	18	13	.233	.333	.191	7.63	10.57
Mathews, Simon	R-R	6-1	180	9-24-95	0	2	4.22	10	8	0	0	43	44	23	20	4	10	46	.267	.317	.238	9.70	2.11
Mattson, Isaac	R-R	6-3	205	7-14-95	5	3	3.95	14	0	0	0	57	59	25	25	1	19	46	.272	.269	.274	7.26	3.00
Ortega, Oliver	R-R	6-0	185	10-2-96	4	5	3.51	19	18	0	0	82	64	36	32	6	41	86	.216	.258	.186	9.44	4.50
Pastrone, Sam	R-R	6-0	185	6-28-97	2	2	5.23	7	3	0	0	21	19	18	12	1	26	17	.247	.229	.262	7.40	11.32
Perez, Mayky	R-R	6-5	235	9-26-96	1	0	2.58	25	0	0	3	38	16	14	11	1	22	57	.125	.111	.133	13.38	5.17
Rogalla, Keith	R-R	6-3	205	9-15-95	0	0	1.93	.2	2	0	0	5	4	1	1	0	4	7	.222	.286	.182	13.50	7.71
Salazar, Carlos	R-R	6-0	200	11-23-94	0	0	0.00	1	0	0	0	2	1	0	0	0	1	1	.143	.000	.333	4.50	4.50
Santos, Michael	R-R	6-4	205	5-29-95	3	1	2.89	15	5	0	0	47	34	16	15	2	18	50	.205	.264	.160	9.64	3.47
Soriano, Jose	R-R	6-3	168	10-20-98	1	6	4.47	14	14	0	0	46	34	24	23	1	35	42	.217	.231	.207	8.16	6.80
Tavarez, Jorge	R-R	5-10	150	8-4-95	2	4	2.86	21	1	0	0	44	39	19	14	0	19	55	.239	.215	.255	11.25	3.89
Traver, Mitchell	R-R	6-7	255	5-3-94	5	7	4.08	20	20	0	0	82	83	46	37	9	32	69	.264	.275	.256	7.60	3.53
Wantz, Andrew	R-R	6-4	235	10-13-95	1	2	3.71	14	0	0	0	17	11	8	7	2	12	35	.180	.261	.132	18.53	6.35
Warren, Austin	R-R	6-0	170	5-5-96	0	2	3.00	15	0	0	3	21	17	9	7	3	5	27	.224	.200	.239	11.57	2.14
Ziemba, James	R-L	6-10	230	8-10-94	3	2	4.48	39	0	0	6	78	90	54	39	7	40	59	.280	.308	.266	6.78	4.60

Fielding

C: Fitzsimons 5, Olmeda 3, Pina 76, Wenson 51. **1B:** Fitzsimons 36, MacKinnon 32, Menendez 26, Millard 3, Olmeda 5, Sanchez 7, Torres 25. **2B:** Garcia 53, Gurwitz 4, Pineda 1, Rivas 26, Rubalcaba 12, Torres 40. **3B:** Garcia 30, Gurwitz 26, Millard 23, Pineda 26, Rubalcaba 14, Sanchez 2, Torres 16. **SS:** Garcia 38, Pineda 2, Rivas 92, Rubalcaba 2. **OF:** Adell 20, Barnes 24, Griffin 93, Gurwitz 1, Hunter Jr. 82, Marsh 33, Martinez 51, Pineda 13, Sanchez 1, Williams 15, Williams 73.

OREM OWLZ   ROOKIE
PIONEER LEAGUE

Batting	B-T	HT	WT	DOB	AVG	vLH	vRH	G	AB	R	H	2B	3B	HR	RBI	BB	HBP	SH	SF	SO	SB	CS	SLG	OBP
Adams, Jordyn	R-R	6-2	180	10-18-99	.314	.167	.345	9	35	5	11	4	1	0	8	4	0	0	1	7	0	1	.486	.375
Barnes, Griffin	R-R	5-10	180	10-18-95	.157	.192	.146	34	115	12	18	2	0	1	10	12	2	0	2	37	1	1	.200	.244
Bond, Brett	B-R	6-1	216	10-15-95	.000	—	.000	1	1	0	0	0	0	0	0	0	0	0	0	1	0	0	.000	.000
Clawson, David	L-R	6-1	180	5-20-97	.177	.111	.212	14	51	3	9	2	0	0	3	0	0	0	0	14	0	0	.216	.177
Del Valle, Francisco	L-L	6-1	187	8-18-98	.250	.206	.270	65	240	27	60	11	3	5	33	33	5	0	2	77	5	1	.383	.350
Fitzsimons, Connor	R-R	5-10	190	8-29-94	.211	.174	.221	31	109	13	23	2	0	2	17	12	6	0	0	33	2	0	.284	.323
Jackson, Jeremiah	R-R	6-0	165	3-26-00	.198	.000	.231	22	91	13	18	6	3	2	9	8	0	0	1	34	4	1	.396	.260
Jones, Justin	R-R	5-11	185	5-20-96	.211	.071	.246	24	71	10	15	5	0	2	5	11	0	0	0	12	2	1	.366	.317
Knowles, D'Shawn	B-R	6-0	165	1-16-01	.321	.318	.322	28	109	27	35	9	2	4	15	13	1	0	0	38	2	3	.551	.398
Maitan, Kevin	B-R	6-0	190	2-12-00	.248	.200	.267	63	262	42	65	13	1	8	26	19	3	0	6	66	1	2	.397	.306
Martinez, Orlando	L-L	6-0	185	2-17-98	.375	.375	.375	12	48	11	18	5	0	2	10	4	0	0	1	9	3	2	.604	.415
Menendez, Kiki	R-R	6-2	205	2-7-95	.294	.217	.319	24	92	19	27	7	0	7	21	11	1	0	0	17	0	1	.598	.375
Millard, Tim	R-R	6-0	200	5-29-95	.299	.347	.276	41	154	30	46	10	0	7	29	21	3	0	1	27	1	2	.500	.391
Olmeda, Alexis	R-R	6-0	225	4-5-94	.000	.000	.000	2	8	0	0	0	0	0	0	0	0	0	0	7	0	0	.000	.000
Ozoria, Daniel	L-R	5-9	135	8-24-00	.333	—	.333	2	3	1	1	0	0	0	0	1	0	0	0	1	0	0	.333	.500
Roper, Erven	L-R	6-0	205	2-28-95	.268	.290	.260	41	142	14	38	5	0	5	23	13	4	0	1	40	2	1	.409	.344
Rosario, Rayneldy	L-L	5-8	139	4-30-98	.252	.233	.258	45	163	23	41	4	1	13	33	9	0	0	0	14	5	5	.307	.265
Rubalcaba, Alvaro	R-R	5-8	165	4-24-95	.000	.000	.000	5	16	0	0	0	0	0	0	1	1	0	0	4	1	0	.000	.056
Sala, Johan	R-R	6-1	175	12-17-97	.260	.357	.238	42	150	13	39	8	2	1	15	7	2	1	0	38	3	1	.360	.302
Sanjur, Mario	R-R	5-7	174	12-23-95	.244	.222	.250	28	90	10	22	5	0	1	18	10	3	1	0	25	1	2	.333	.340
Soto, Livan	R-R	6-0	160	6-22-00	.291	.233	.310	44	172	31	50	10	0	1	11	24	3	0	1	24	9	3	.349	.385
Spires, Mitch	R-R	6-1	195	3-11-96	.259	.342	.228	36	139	18	36	5	1	3	19	12	1	0	3	31	6	0	.374	.316
Stefanic, Michael	R-R	5-10	180	2-24-96	.222	—	.222	5	9	1	2	0	0	0	1	0	1	0	0	3	0	1	.222	.300
Taylor, Cole	R-R	6-0	200	6-11-96	.164	.200	.150	18	55	10	9	4	1	1	2	12	3	0	0	21	1	2	.327	.343
Verrier, Jose	R-R	6-0	180	12-2-97	.000	—	.000	1	2	0	0	0	0	0	0	0	0	0	0	1	0	0	1.000	.333
Williams, Cam	R-R	5-11	185	1-16-97	.261	.263	.260	28	92	13	24	3	0	3	9	9	2	0	0	27	2	2	.391	.340
Williams, Nonie	R-R	6-2	180	5-22-98	.193	.267	.164	40	161	27	31	8	5	2	24	14	4	0	2	50	3	1	.342	.271

Pitching	B-T	HT	WT	DOB	W	L	ERA	G	GS	CG	SV	IP	H	R	ER	HR	BB	SO	AVG	vLH	vRH	K/9	BB/9
Alvarado, Luis	R-R	6-4	210	1-5-97	0	1	6.00	14	0	0	0	18	17	12	12	3	8	23	.246	.174	.283	11.50	4.00
Aragon, Christian	L-L	6-2	183	7-18-96	0	0	8.53	7	0	0	0	13	15	16	12	1	9	12	.289	.529	.171	8.53	6.39
Benitez, Anfernee	R-L	6-1	180	7-24-95	0	0	3.00	4	0	0	0	6	3	3	0	6	10		.188	.091	.238	10.00	6.00
Chock, Tanner	B-R	6-1	190	8-8-96	0	1	4.31	11	3	0	0	31	29	15	15	3	17	30	.250	.300	.224	8.62	4.88
Cole, Dazon	R-R	5-11	180	5-3-96	1	1	4.71	16	0	0	0	21	20	17	11	3	7	21	.233	.217	.238	9.00	3.00
De Horta, Adrian	R-R	6-3	185	3-13-95	0	0	0.00	1	0	0	0	4	4	0	0	0	3	2	.267	.286	.250	6.75	0.00
Duensing, Cole	L-R	6-4	175	6-16-98	0	10	10.32	15	13	0	0	52	86	64	60	11	33	39	.381	.375	.383	6.71	5.68
Eagle, Matt	R-R	6-3	230	11-25-95	3	0	7.06	11	0	0	0	22	36	20	17	2	6	30	.360	.429	.333	12.46	2.49
Eckerson, Cody	L-L	5-8	175	2-22-95	1	2	14.29	5	2	0	0	11	33	24	18	1	4	9	.508	.500	.511	7.15	3.18
Franco, Sadrac	R-R	6-0	155	6-4-00	1	1	14.54	4	0	0	0	4	7	7	0	2	4		.389	.500	.333	8.31	4.15

	B-T	HT	WT	DOB	W	L	ERA	G	GS	CG	SV	IP	H	R	ER	HR	BB	SO	AVG	vLH	vRH	K/9	BB/9
Guzman, Emilker	R-R	5-10	160	2-10-99	0	1	4.70	2	1	0	0	8	6	4	4	0	4	5	.231	.364	.133	5.87	4.70
Higgins, Connor	R-L	6-5	240	7-21-96	0	0	0.00	2	0	0	0	1	0	0	0	0	1	0	.000	—	.000	0.00	9.00
Jobst, Nick	R-R	6-2	260	4-20-94	0	0	9.35	15	0	0	0	26	37	30	27	7	11	27	.325	.316	.329	9.35	3.81
Kelly, Zack	R-R	6-3	205	3-3-95	1	0	1.13	2	0	0	0	8	5	2	1	0	2	9	.192	.429	.105	10.13	2.25
Lee, Jake	R-R	6-4	215	6-30-95	0	1	2.66	17	0	0	5	24	21	12	7	1	4	30	.223	.086	.305	11.41	1.52
Leon, Matt	R-R	5-11	185	9-25-95	2	5	6.20	13	8	0	0	45	56	34	31	4	15	34	.298	.310	.291	6.80	3.00
Malmin, Jon	R-L	6-1	170	9-2-94	0	1	10.24	5	0	0	0	10	15	16	11	2	6	9	.333	.375	.324	8.38	5.59
Molina, Cristopher	R-R	6-3	170	6-10-97	4	4	5.23	16	12	0	0	65	52	44	38	8	35	70	.209	.235	.191	9.64	4.82
Morell, Johnny	R-R	6-2	200	10-30-97	0	5	15.34	14	10	0	0	29	49	61	50	7	34	31	.363	.408	.337	9.51	10.43
Morrison, Ben	L-R	5-11	185	1-20-95	1	1	5.26	20	0	0	1	26	30	19	15	4	6	26	.280	.270	.286	9.12	2.10
Murrah, Rion	R-R	6-0	180	12-21-94	1	1	6.75	17	0	0	0	43	62	42	32	6	11	32	.330	.344	.323	6.75	2.32
Natera, Jose	R-R	6-1	180	11-30-99	0	1	9.00	2	2	0	0	7	11	7	7	0	5	5	.367	.500	.333	6.43	6.43
Pena, Adalberto	R-R	6-2	173	3-11-95	1	1	4.85	8	0	1	0	13	11	8	7	2	10	9	.229	.208	.250	6.23	6.92
2-team total (3 Ogden)					2	2	5.66	11	1	0	1	21	21	16	13	2	13	17	.263	.268	.256	7.40	5.66
Pina, Robinson	R-R	6-4	180	11-26-98	1	1	3.21	5	0	0	0	14	13	6	5	1	8	18	.245	.250	.244	11.57	5.14
Rivera, Jerryell	L-L	6-3	180	4-19-99	0	5	14.00	5	4	0	0	9	16	22	14	4	18	3	.410	.250	.452	3.00	18.00
Smith, Tyler	R-R	6-0	230	11-20-95	2	1	3.95	17	0	0	1	27	27	14	12	3	14	32	.252	.184	.290	10.54	4.61
Swanda, John	R-R	6-2	185	3-18-99	0	4	4.50	10	10	0	0	30	37	20	15	4	7	26	.291	.250	.317	7.80	2.10
Tyler, Kyle	R-R	6-0	185	12-27-96	1	1	5.11	15	0	0	2	25	26	14	14	5	6	22	.277	.333	.241	8.03	2.19
Voss, Jacob	R-R	6-9	255	4-20-97	2	1	6.20	16	0	0	1	20	21	17	14	0	15	28	.259	.233	.275	12.39	6.64
Wantz, Andrew	R-R	6-4	235	10-13-95	0	0	0.00	4	0	0	0	6	3	3	0	0	3	12	.130	.333	.059	18.00	4.50
Warren, Austin	R-R	6-0	170	5-5-96	0	0	7.11	4	0	0	0	6	11	5	5	1	4	11	.355	.615	.167	15.63	5.68
Yan, Hector	L-L	5-11	180	4-26-99	0	0	4.55	10	0	0	0	30	29	17	15	3	20	29	.274	.185	.304	8.80	6.07

Fielding

C: Barnes 29, Clawson 12, Roper 13, Sanjur 26. **1B:** Clawson 1, Del Valle 7, Fitzsimons 31, Menendez 24, Millard 12, Spires 3. **2B:** Jackson 1, Jones 22, Rubalcaba 3, Soto 18, Spires 19, Stefanic 2, Taylor 16. **3B:** Maitan 40, Millard 27, Spires 9. **SS:** Jackson 21, Jones 1, Maitan 21, Ozoria 1, Rubalcaba 2, Soto 28, Spires 5. **OF:** Adams 8, Del Valle 36, Jones 2, Knowles 27, Martinez 10, Rosario 43, Sala 40, Williams 27, Williams 39.

AZL ANGELS   ROOKIE
ARIZONA LEAGUE

Batting	B-R	HT	WT	DOB	AVG	vLH	vRH	G	AB	R	H	2B	3B	HR	RBI	BB	HBP	SH	SF	SO	SB	CS	SLG	OBP
Adams, Jordyn	R-R	6-2	180	10-18-99	.243	.091	.313	20	70	8	17	2	0	0	5	10	2	0	0	23	5	2	.329	.354
Barnes, Griffin	R-R	5-10	180	10-18-95	.125	.000	.167	3	8	0	1	0	0	0	1	1	0	0	0	4	0	0	.125	.222
Bond, Brett	B-R	6-1	216	10-15-95	.292	.233	.322	30	89	11	26	5	0	0	9	9	0	0	0	18	0	0	.348	.357
Bray, Datren	R-R	5-9	189	4-28-99	.130	.235	.096	23	69	8	9	1	1	0	4	10	5	0	1	34	3	0	.174	.282
Camargo, Bernabe	R-R	6-1	180	1-22-96	.227	.231	.225	21	66	13	15	1	0	0	7	8	3	0	2	19	1	0	.242	.329
Clawson, David	L-R	6-1	180	5-20-97	.297	.261	.317	24	64	10	19	6	2	0	13	9	0	0	3	14	1	0	.453	.368
De La Cruz, Julio	R-R	5-11	182	8-3-00	.189	.125	.216	14	53	4	10	4	1	1	6	3	1	0	1	20	0	2	.359	.241
Deveaux, Trent	R-R	6-0	160	5-4-00	.199	.267	.174	44	166	20	33	5	0	1	11	24	3	0	1	68	7	4	.247	.309
Flores, Jeans	R-R	5-11	165	3-20-98	.173	.000	.213	23	75	4	13	2	0	0	3	6	1	1	1	14	0	0	.200	.241
Gomez, Cristian	L-R	6-2	205	10-29-96	.500	.000	.600	2	6	2	3	3	0	0	3	0	0	0	0	2	0	0	1.000	.667
Jackson, Jeremiah	R-R	6-0	165	3-26-00	.317	.143	.377	21	82	13	26	4	2	5	14	7	1	0	1	25	6	1	.598	.374
Jones, Justin	R-R	5-11	185	5-20-96	.246	.177	.269	24	69	13	17	2	0	0	9	11	4	0	0	11	5	1	.275	.381
Knowles, D'Shawn	B-R	6-0	165	1-16-01	.301	.317	.292	30	113	19	34	4	1	1	14	15	1	0	1	27	7	4	.381	.385
Marcano, Marlon	R-R	5-11	211	9-14-99	.250	.125	.313	7	24	1	6	0	0	0	2	0	0	0	1	6	0	0	.250	.240
Mendoza, Willian	R-R	5-11	185	12-1-97	.114	.200	.080	11	35	2	4	0	0	0	2	2	0	0	0	17	0	1	.114	.162
Menendez, Kiki	R-R	6-2	205	2-7-95	.177	.000	.300	6	17	3	3	1	0	1	1	2	0	0	0	3	0	0	.412	.263
Ozoria, Daniel	L-R	5-9	135	8-24-00	.193	.193	.193	49	197	14	38	3	1	0	12	11	2	2	0	56	6	6	.218	.243
Rivas, Leonardo	B-R	5-10	150	10-10-97	.250	.000	.286	2	8	2	2	1	0	1	3	0	0	0	0	2	0	0	.750	.250
Rivera, William	R-R	6-3	184	4-21-00	.152	.261	.116	27	92	5	14	1	0	0	8	2	0	0	0	36	1	0	.163	.235
Sala, Johan	R-R	6-1	175	12-17-97	.375	.444	.348	13	32	7	12	2	3	0	6	6	2	0	1	9	1	2	.625	.488
Stefanic, Michael	R-R	5-10	180	2-24-96	.393	.500	.364	9	28	2	11	0	1	0	4	4	0	1	0	2	0	0	.464	.469
Taylor, Cole	R-R	6-0	200	6-15-96	.300	.333	.286	3	10	1	3	2	0	0	0	0	1	0	0	2	0	0	.700	.364
Verrier, Jose	R-R	6-1	180	12-2-97	.219	.245	.208	50	178	15	39	8	1	2	22	16	6	0	1	69	8	6	.309	.304
Wenson, Harrison	R-R	6-3	235	4-21-95	.417	.500	.400	3	12	1	5	0	2	0	2	0	0	0	0	4	0	0	.750	.417
Williams, Cam	R-R	5-11	185	1-16-97	.333	.500	.286	4	9	0	3	1	0	0	3	2	0	0	0	1	0	0	.444	.455
Williams-Nelson, Drevian	R-R	5-7	175	1-00-00	.217	.393	.141	30	92	11	20	3	0	0	9	11	0	0	0	31	6	2	.250	.301

Pitching	B-T	HT	WT	DOB	W	L	ERA	G	GS	CG	SV	IP	H	R	ER	HR	BB	SO	AVG	vLH	vRH	K/9	BB/9
Adkins, Chase	R-R	5-11	180	5-14-95	0	4	2.22	14	0	0	3	24	16	13	6	2	7	27	.172	.061	.233	9.99	2.59
Agramonte, Galvi	R-R	5-11	190	5-19-98	1	0	2.03	5	0	0	0	13	8	6	3	0	5	15	.160	.133	.171	10.13	3.38
Almonte, Miguel	R-R	6-2	210	4-4-93	0	0	0.00	1	1	0	0	1	1	0	0	0	2	2	.250	.000	.500	18.00	0.00
Alvarado, Luis	R-R	6-4	210	1-5-97	0	1	4.50	2	0	0	0	4	2	2	2	0	4	7	.133	.250	.091	15.75	9.00
Aragon, Christian	L-L	6-2	183	7-18-96	0	2	3.07	9	0	0	0	15	14	7	5	0	5	19	.255	.313	.231	11.66	3.07
Arvelaez, Kiber	R-R	6-2	170	5-9-98	0	1	13.11	11	0	0	0	12	21	17	17	1	13	8	.412	.474	.375	6.17	10.03
Belton, Greg	R-R	5-10	190	12-31-92	0	0	7.11	5	0	0	0	6	4	5	5	0	5	10	.182	.182	.182	14.21	7.11
Buttrey, Ty	L-R	6-6	230	3-31-93	0	0	0.00	1	1	0	0	1	0	0	0	0	0	3	.000	.000	.000	27.00	0.00
Chatham, Clayton	R-R	6-6	200	6-29-95	0	0	5.40	12	0	0	0	22	18	15	13	1	14	26	.225	.161	.265	10.80	5.82
Chock, Tanner	B-R	6-1	190	8-8-96	0	1	4.70	5	0	0	0	8	7	5	4	1	3	9	.226	.222	.227	10.57	3.52
Cole, Dazon	R-R	5-11	180	5-3-96	0	0	5.40	2	0	0	0	5	5	4	3	1	1	9	.227	.375	.143	16.20	1.80
De Horta, Adrian	R-R	6-3	185	3-3-96	0	0	5.40	2	2	0	0	5	6	3	3	1	1	6	.300	.333	.286	10.80	1.80
De Leon, Yoel	L-L	6-2	200	11-23-97	2	3	4.30	11	4	0	0	38	41	26	18	1	14	32	.263	.243	.269	7.65	3.35
Eckerson, Cody	L-L	5-8	175	2-22-95	1	2	4.86	8	0	0	0	17	16	11	9	1	11	18	.242	.091	.273	9.72	5.94
Eregua, Greyfer	R-R	5-11	160	10-15-93	0	0	0.00	4	2	0	0	6	2	1	0	0	1	4	.095	.000	.143	6.00	1.50
Franco, Sadrac	R-R	6-0	155	6-4-00	1	1	4.94	12	0	0	0	31	30	20	17	1	19	32	.250	.293	.228	9.29	5.52

	B-T	HT	WT	DOB	W	L	ERA	G	GS	CG	SV	IP	H	R	ER	HR	BB	SO	AVG	vLH	vRH	K/9	BB/9
Guzman, Emilker	R-R	5-10	160	2-10-99	1	2	3.38	11	9	0	0	37	36	16	14	2	7	31	.250	.283	.231	7.47	1.69
Herrin, Travis	R-R	6-2	220	4-29-95	0	0	0.00	4	2	0	0	6	2	0	0	0	0	4	.100	.167	.071	6.00	0.00
Higgins, Connor	R-L	6-5	240	7-21-96	2	1	3.86	14	0	0	1	21	16	11	9	0	17	24	.198	.250	.180	10.29	7.29
Hofacket, Adam	R-R	6-1	195	2-18-94	0	0	3.86	8	0	0	0	12	10	6	5	0	2	14	.217	.125	.267	10.80	1.54
Leon, Matt	R-R	5-11	185	9-25-95	0	0	0.00	3	0	0	0	6	3	0	0	0	1	10	.150	.167	.143	15.88	1.59
Natera, Jose	R-R	6-1	180	11-30-99	0	4	4.17	11	9	0	0	37	50	29	17	2	11	38	.319	.222	.369	9.33	2.70
Pastrone, Sam	R-R	6-0	185	6-28-97	0	0	0.00	2	0	0	0	2	3	0	0	3	3	.375	1.000	.286	16.20	16.20
Pina, Robinson	R-R	6-4	180	11-26-98	1	1	3.14	6	1	0	0	14	12	9	5	0	5	17	.218	.250	.205	10.67	3.14
Reyes, Cristian	R-R	6-5	220	9-19-94	0	1	12.00	9	0	0	0	12	15	16	16	0	10	17	.319	.636	.222	12.75	7.50
Rivera, Jerryell	L-L	6-3	180	4-19-99	0	3	6.85	7	6	0	0	22	29	20	17	0	11	19	.312	.333	.303	7.66	4.43
Robinson, Parker Joe	R-R	6-5	230	8-16-95	2	0	0.44	11	0	0	1	20	13	3	1	0	1	22	.186	.261	.149	9.74	0.44
Rodriguez, Jose M.	R-R	6-3	195	9-8-00	0	3	17.25	9	5	0	0	12	12	24	23	0	34	13	.279	.333	.259	9.75	25.50
Salazar, Carlos	R-R	6-0	200	11-23-94	1	0	3.86	6	0	0	0	7	5	3	3	0	6	11	.200	.200	.200	14.14	7.71
Santa Maria, Tulio	R-R	6-4	170	6-6-00	1	3	5.23	9	6	0	0	21	20	16	12	0	15	15	.263	.185	.306	6.53	6.53
Tucker, Bo	L-L	6-4	210	5-23-95	0	2	18.69	4	3	0	0	4	8	9	9	0	6	3	.444	.333	.500	6.23	12.46
Voss, Jacob	R-R	6-9	255	4-20-97	1	0	0.00	2	0	0	1	3	2	0	0	0	6	.200	.333	.143	18.00	0.00
Williams, Darrien	R-R	6-3	205	6-24-96	2	2	4.01	15	0	0	1	25	17	14	11	0	16	21	.191	.250	.158	7.66	5.84

Fielding

C: Barnes 3, Bond 9, Clawson 10, Flores 23, Marcano 7, Mendoza 9, Wenson 1. **1B:** Bond 21, Camargo 14, Clawson 9, Gomez 2, Jones 3, Mendoza 2, Menendez 1, Stefanic 5. **2B:** De La Cruz 11, Jones 2, Ozoria 13, Stefanic 1, Taylor 1, Verrier 29. **3B:** Camargo 7, De La Cruz 2, Jones 17, Ozoria 3, Rivera 1, Stefanic 2, Taylor 2, Verrier 19. **SS:** Camargo 1, Jackson 21, Jones 1, Ozoria 32, Rivas 1. **OF:** Adams 15, Bray 20, De La Cruz 1, Deveaux 43, Knowles 28, Menendez 1, Rivera 22, Sala 12, Williams 3, Williams-Nelson 25.

DSL ANGELS   ROOKIE
DOMINICAN SUMMER LEAGUE

Batting	B-T	HT	WT	DOB	AVG	vLH	vRH	G	AB	R	H	2B	3B	HR	RBI	BB	HBP	SH	SF	SO	SB	CS	SLG	OBP
Apolinar, Samy	L-R	5-11	217	12-1-97	.174	.171	.175	55	172	20	30	6	2	1	9	35	0	0	1	53	6	3	.250	.313
De La Cruz, Julio	R-R	5-11	182	8-3-00	.194	.188	.196	50	180	22	35	10	0	5	29	24	2	0	0	65	4	3	.333	.296
Diaz, Luis	L-R	5-11	185	1-13-00	.207	.130	.222	49	140	22	29	7	0	1	17	41	6	0	1	50	2	3	.279	.404
Gonzalez, Andres	R-R	5-10	170	9-8-00	.200	.188	.203	34	95	7	19	2	0	0	10	13	0	0	1	21	1	0	.221	.294
Gutierrez, Nishell	B-R	5-10	165	5-4-00	.177	.154	.184	25	62	6	11	0	1	0	6	20	3	0	0	16	0	0	.210	.400
Guzman, Jose	R-R	5-11	162	9-15-00	.282	.478	.241	44	131	20	37	4	5	1	7	21	2	0	0	32	6	3	.412	.390
Marcano, Marlon	R-R	5-11	211	9-14-99	.265	.357	.241	27	68	10	18	3	0	1	11	11	4	0	1	11	0	1	.353	.393
Moya, Kendy	B-R	5-10	150	12-14-98	.242	.344	.217	53	161	27	39	8	5	0	23	46	6	1	2	39	9	6	.354	.423
Nunez, Geison	R-R	6-1	203	7-30-00	.205	.400	.179	38	127	20	26	5	1	2	16	11	3	0	1	44	1	3	.307	.282
Pineda, Maikel	R-R	6-1	175	10-19-96	.198	.300	.178	37	121	14	24	8	0	2	11	7	2	0	0	27	1	2	.314	.254
Quezada, Jose	R-R	5-9	159	7-26-98	.258	.325	.245	63	248	39	64	4	5	2	35	31	3	0	3	52	26	13	.339	.344
Reyes, Jose	L-R	6-2	180	9-22-00	.225	.152	.237	63	227	36	51	12	8	2	27	37	4	0	2	74	9	6	.374	.341
Rijo, Jeison	R-R	6-0	165	10-14-99	.146	.000	.162	13	41	3	6	0	0	0	2	6	3	0	0	11	0	1	.146	.300
Rivas, Rainier	L-L	6-3	220	6-29-01	.242	.188	.253	27	99	15	24	2	1	1	7	14	0	0	0	31	6	1	.313	.336
Santana, Adderlin	B-R	5-8	160	5-31-00	.167	.079	.184	66	234	29	39	8	6	0	33	33	2	1	3	84	10	3	.252	.272
Uceta, Raider	L-L	6-0	215	1-29-01	.263	.281	.258	42	160	18	42	11	1	2	25	5	3	0	3	40	1	3	.381	.292

Pitching	B-T	HT	WT	DOB	W	L	ERA	G	GS	CG	SV	IP	H	R	ER	HR	BB	SO	AVG	vLH	vRH	K/9	BB/9
Agramonte, Galvi	R-R	5-11	190	5-19-98	0	5	9.25	9	6	0	0	24	35	34	25	1	17	24	.333	.275	.369	8.88	6.29
Antigua, Faustino	R-R	6-5	202	5-23-99	0	5	13.92	22	0	0	0	21	21	37	33	0	42	18	.256	.189	.311	7.59	17.72
Aquino, Ewdy	R-R	5-9	170	2-24-00	1	1	4.70	14	0	0	0	23	24	14	12	0	9	17	.276	.310	.259	6.65	3.52
Bonilla, Christopher	R-R	6-0	199	1-13-99	2	2	4.09	23	0	0	1	44	42	29	20	2	19	32	.258	.296	.239	6.55	3.89
Caceres, Kelvin	R-R	6-1	180	1-26-00	2	7	4.98	14	10	0	0	47	39	29	26	5	18	32	.216	.190	.228	6.13	3.45
Duran, Emmanuel	R-R	6-1	182	10-9-00	0	5	6.57	14	9	0	0	38	35	37	28	3	33	42	.283	.133	.333	9.86	7.75
Espinal, Andersson	L-L	6-0	184	9-1-99	1	0	3.22	13	0	0	0	22	14	14	8	0	28	27	.180	.154	.185	10.88	11.28
Gomez, Victor	R-R	5-11	184	10-19-00	1	2	7.34	22	0	0	1	31	37	35	25	2	27	28	.289	.180	.337	8.22	7.92
Gomez, Wilson	L-L	6-0	177	4-20-01	0	1	14.82	18	0	0	1	17	16	33	28	0	30	21	.242	.167	.259	11.12	15.88
Gonzalez, Jenrry	L-L	5-10	185	6-7-01	1	4	3.56	13	11	0	0	43	39	25	17	1	15	38	.236	.265	.229	7.95	3.14
Leon, Jesus	L-L	5-10	162	2-6-01	1	5	5.18	21	1	0	0	38	28	31	19	1	38	32	.230	.130	.253	9.00	10.36
Lopez, Nehemias	R-R	5-10	152	5-9-00	2	1	5.85	13	3	0	0	32	31	25	21	2	15	25	.256	.220	.275	6.96	5.85
Lucas, Jean Carlos	R-R	6-3	185	12-2-00	2	3	2.98	15	12	0	0	51	52	20	17	3	15	39	.267	.264	.268	6.84	2.63
Moncion, Kelvin	L-L	6-1	201	12-23-98	1	4	3.04	14	13	0	0	50	46	24	17	1	19	61	.253	.333	.210	10.91	3.40
Pena, Andres	R-R	6-1	183	10-22-99	1	3	15.26	4	1	0	0	8	13	13	1	15	6	.296	.167	.333		17.61
Pena, Elian	R-R	6-4	171	3-12-00	2	1	10.02	23	0	0	0	32	34	44	36	2	39	22	.272	.348	.228	6.12	10.86
Perez, Samuel	L-L	5-11	175	11-29-99	2	0	1.44	13	0	0	2	31	28	9	5	0	3	32	.228	.333	.206	9.19	0.86
Pina, Robinson	R-R	6-4	180	11-26-98	0	2	4.02	8	0	0	1	12	10	7	6	0	6	26	.214	.182	.235	14.94	3.45
Portorreal, Samir	R-R	6-0	200	5-29-99	0	1	15.00	4	0	0	0	3	11	9	5	1	3	5	.524	.600	.500	15.00	9.00
Rodriguez, Jose M.	R-R	6-3	195	9-8-00	0	0	0.00	2	2	0	0	6	2	1	0	0	3	7	.105	.167	.077	10.50	4.50
Velez, Yeyson	R-R	6-0	165	8-15-98	0	1	2.82	8	4	0	0	22	18	8	7	0	15	16	.217	.185	.232	6.45	6.04

Fielding

C: Gonzalez 27, Gutierrez 5, Marcano 24, Nunez 30. **1B:** Apolinar 50, Diaz 2, Marcano 1, Nunez 1, Pineda 23. **2B:** De La Cruz 30, Gutierrez 6, Guzman 25, Moya 1, Quezada 10, Santana 4. **3B:** Apolinar 5, De La Cruz 14, Gutierrez 11, Guzman 5, Moya 31, Rijo 12. **SS:** Guzman 3, Moya 13, Santana 60. **OF:** Diaz 39, Moya 12, Pineda 4, Quezada 49, Reyes 62, Rivas 25, Santana 1, Uceta 31.

Los Angeles Dodgers

SEASON IN A SENTENCE: The Dodgers over-came a 16-26 start and myriad of injuries to return to the World Series for the second straight year, but the Red Sox dispatched them in five games to squash Los Angeles' title dreams.

HIGH POINT: At the end of a trying season that saw the Dodgers need to win their final three games just to force a one-game tiebreaker, rookie Walker Buehler took the mound in Game 163 with the National League West title on the line. The righthander brilliantly pitched 6.2 scoreless, one-hit innings against the Rockies, leading the way in a 5-2 win that gave the Dodgers their sixth straight division crown.

LOW POINT: After the Dodgers won an 18-inning marathon in Game 3 of the World Series on Max Muncy's walk-off home run, they held a 4-0 lead in the seventh inning of Game 4 and were nine outs away from tying the series at two games apiece. Instead, manager Dave Roberts pulled Rich Hill in the midst of a one-hitter and the Dodgers' bullpen imploded, surrendering nine runs in the final three innings to lose the game and turn the series permanently in Boston's favor.

NOTABLE ROOKIES: Buehler graduated from top prospect to ace of the future, leading all rookies with a 2.63 ERA and .193 opponent average while blowing 96-99 mph fastballs and dirty upper-80s sliders by hitters. He started six innings of a com-bined no-hitter in May, pitched the Dodgers to victory in the NL West tiebreaker and tossed seven scoreless innings with just two hits allowed in his lone World Series start. Lefthander Caleb Ferguson emerged as one of the Dodgers' few reliable reliev-ers, going 7-2, 3.49 out of the bullpen.

KEY TRANSACTIONS: The Dodgers reacquired Matt Kemp before the season, and he hit .290 with 21 home runs in a rebound season. With Corey Seager out for the year after Tommy John surgery, the Dodgers acquired Manny Machado from the Orioles at the all-star break. Machado hit .273 with 13 homers for the Dodgers, but hit just .227 in the playoffs. Brian Dozier and David Freese also came over in midseason trades.

DOWN ON THE FARM: Double-A Tulsa, high Class A Rancho Cucamonga and the Rookie-level Arizona League Dodgers all won league champion-ships. The organization posted the third-best win-ning percentage (.552) in baseball. Catcher Keibert Ruiz, shortstop Gavin Lux and righthander Dustin May headlined the system's banner year.

OPENING DAY PAYROLL: $157,496,785 (11th).

PLAYERS OF THE YEAR

ALEX TRAUTWIG

ZACHARY LUCY/FOUR SEAM

MAJOR LEAGUE	MINOR LEAGUE
Max Muncy	**Gavin Lux**
1B/3B	**SS**
.263/.391/.582	(High Class A/Double-A)
35 HR, 79 RBIs	.324/.399/.514
Led MLB in AB/HR	15 HR, 13 SB

ORGANIZATION LEADERS

Batting		*Minimum 250 AB
MAJORS		
* AVG	Justin Turner	.312
* OPS	Max Muncy	.973
HR	Max Muncy	35
RBI	Matt Kemp	85
MINORS		
* AVG	Alex Verdugo, Oklahoma City	.329
* OBP	Connor Joe, Tulsa, Oklahoma City	.408
* SLG	Rylan Bannon, R. Cucamonga, Bowie	.559
* OPS	Rylan Bannon, R. Cucamonga, Bowie	.961
R	Omar Estevez, R. Cucamonga	87
H	Cristian Santana, R. Cucamonga	150
H	Gavin Lux, R. Cucamonga, Tulsa	150
TB	Cody Thomas, R. Cucamonga	248
2B	Omar Estevez, R. Cucamonga	43
3B	Jared Walker, Great Lakes, R. Cucamonga	8
3B	Gavin Lux, R. Cucamonga, Tulsa	8
HR	DJ Peters, Tulsa	29
RBI	Cristian Santana, R. Cucamonga	109
BB	Connor Joe, Tulsa, Oklahoma City	60
SO	DJ Peters, Tulsa	192
SB	Brayan Morales, Great Lakes	46

Pitching		#Minimum 75 IP
MAJORS		
W	Rich Hill	11
# ERA	Hyun-Jin Ryu	1.97
SO	Clayton Kershaw	155
SV	Kenley Jansen	38
MINORS		
W	Isaac Anderson, R. Cucamonga, Tulsa	10
W	Tony Gonsolin, R. Cucamonga, Tulsa	10
L	Logan Bawcom, Tulsa, Oklahoma City	10
# ERA	Tony Gonsolin, R. Cucamonga, Tulsa	2.6
G	Brian Schlitter, Oklahoma City	58
GS	Tony Gonsolin, R. Cucamonga, Tulsa	26
SV	Brian Schlitter, Oklahoma City	21
IP	Justin DeFratus, Tulsa, Oklahoma City	133
BB	Riley Ottesen, Great Lakes, Dodgers	52
SO	Tony Gonsolin, R. Cucamonga, Tulsa	155
# AVG	Tony Gonsolin, R. Cucamonga, Tulsa	.219

2018 PERFORMANCE

General Manager: Farhan Zaidi. **Farm Director:** Brandon Gomes. **Scouting Director:** Billy Gasparino.

Class	Team	League	W	L	PCT	Finish	Manager
Majors	Los Angeles Dodgers	National	92	71	.564	3rd (15)	Dave Roberts
Triple-A	Oklahoma City Dodgers	Pacific Coast	75	65	.536	4th (16)	Bill Haselman
Double-A	Tulsa Drillers	Texas	74	65	.532	2nd (8)	Scott Hennessey
High A	R. Cucamonga Quakes	California	87	53	.621	1st (8)	Drew Saylor
Low A	Great Lakes Loons	Midwest	60	77	.438	12th (16)	John Shoemaker
Rookie	Ogden Raptors	Pioneer	46	30	.605	1st (8)	Jeremy Rodriguez
Rookie	AZL Dodgers	Arizona	37	18	.673	2nd (18)	Mark Kertenian
Overall 2018 Minor League Record			379	308	.552	3rd (30)	

ORGANIZATION STATISTICS

LOS ANGELES DODGERS
NATIONAL LEAGUE

Batting	B-T	HT	WT	DOB	AVG	vLH	vRH	G	AB	R	H	2B	3B	HR	RBI	BB	HBP	SH	SF	SO	SB	CS	SLG	OBP
Barnes, Austin	R-R	5-10	190	12-28-89	.205	.246	.151	100	200	32	41	5	0	4	14	31	6	1	0	67	4	3	.290	.329
Bellinger, Cody	L-L	6-4	210	7-13-95	.260	.226	.278	162	557	84	145	28	7	25	76	69	3	0	3	151	14	1	.470	.343
Dozier, Brian	R-R	5-11	200	5-15-87	.182	.152	.208	47	143	16	26	9	0	5	20	24	1	0	2	33	4	0	.350	.300
Farmer, Kyle	R-R	6-0	214	8-17-90	.235	.256	.207	39	68	1	16	4	1	0	9	5	3	0	1	15	0	0	.324	.312
Forsythe, Logan	R-R	6-1	205	1-14-87	.207	.177	.232	70	193	18	40	10	0	2	13	17	0	0	1	43	2	0	.290	.270
Freese, David	R-R	6-2	220	4-28-83	.385	.464	.182	19	39	9	15	2	1	2	9	6	2	0	0	16	0	0	.641	.489
2-team total (94 Pittsburgh)					.296	.321	.273	113	280	38	83	12	2	11	51	24	5	0	3	72	0	0	.471	.359
Gale, Rocky	R-R	6-1	185	2-22-88	.000	.000	.000	3	2	0	0	0	0	0	0	0	0	0	0	1	0	0	.000	.000
Grandal, Yasmani	B-R	6-1	235	11-8-88	.241	.206	.252	140	440	65	106	23	2	24	68	72	3	0	3	124	2	1	.466	.349
Hernandez, Enrique	R-R	5-11	200	8-24-91	.256	.260	.253	145	402	67	103	17	3	21	52	50	1	4	5	78	3	0	.470	.336
Kemp, Matt	R-R	6-4	210	9-23-84	.290	.273	.301	146	462	62	134	25	0	21	85	36	1	0	7	115	0	0	.481	.338
Locastro, Tim	R-R	6-1	200	7-14-92	.182	.222	.000	18	11	6	2	1	0	0	2	1	0	1	0	5	4	0	.273	.357
Machado, Manny	R-R	6-3	185	7-6-92	.273	.318	.253	66	267	44	73	14	2	13	42	25	2	0	2	53	6	1	.487	.338
Muncy, Max	L-R	6-0	210	8-25-90	.263	.255	.266	137	395	75	104	17	2	35	79	79	5	0	2	131	3	0	.582	.391
Pederson, Joc	L-L	6-1	220	4-21-92	.248	.170	.260	148	395	65	98	27	3	25	56	40	4	1	3	85	1	5	.522	.321
Puig, Yasiel	R-R	6-2	240	12-7-90	.267	.209	.297	125	405	60	108	21	1	23	63	36	1	0	2	87	15	5	.494	.327
Seager, Corey	L-R	6-4	220	4-27-94	.267	.231	.290	26	101	13	27	5	1	2	13	11	2	0	1	17	0	0	.396	.348
Taylor, Chris	R-R	6-1	195	8-29-90	.254	.232	.265	155	536	85	136	35	8	17	63	55	9	0	4	178	9	6	.444	.331
Toles, Andrew	L-R	5-9	192	5-24-92	.233	.167	.250	17	30	5	7	2	0	0	4	2	0	0	0	8	1	0	.300	.281
Turner, Justin	R-R	5-11	205	11-23-84	.312	.336	.301	103	365	62	114	31	1	14	52	47	12	0	2	54	2	1	.518	.406
Utley, Chase	L-R	6-1	195	12-17-78	.213	.143	.220	87	164	18	35	10	1	1	14	17	5	0	1	34	3	1	.305	.305
Valera, Breyvic	B-R	5-11	160	1-8-92	.172	.250	.160	20	29	4	5	0	0	0	4	4	0	1	0	4	0	0	.172	.273
Verdugo, Alex	L-L	6-0	205	5-15-96	.260	.222	.271	37	77	11	20	6	0	1	4	8	0	1	0	14	0	0	.377	.329

Pitching	B-T	HT	WT	DOB	W	L	ERA	G	GS	CG	SV	IP	H	R	ER	HR	BB	SO	AVG	vLH	vRH	K/9	BB/9
Alexander, Scott	L-L	6-2	190	7-10-89	2	1	3.68	73	1	0	3	66	57	28	27	4	27	56	.240	.172	.288	7.64	3.68
Axford, John	R-R	6-5	220	4-1-83	0	0	17.18	5	0	0	0	4	8	8	7	0	2	4	.444	.200	.539	9.82	4.91
Baez, Pedro	R-R	6-0	230	3-11-88	4	3	2.88	55	0	0	0	56	46	19	18	4	23	62	.220	.164	.247	9.91	3.67
Buehler, Walker	R-R	6-2	175	7-28-94	8	5	2.62	24	23	0	0	137	95	43	40	12	37	151	.193	.195	.191	9.90	2.42
Chargois, JT	B-R	6-3	200	12-3-90	2	4	3.34	39	0	0	0	32	26	13	12	4	15	40	.222	.276	.205	11.13	4.18
Cingrani, Tony	L-L	6-4	214	7-5-89	1	2	4.76	30	0	0	0	23	19	12	12	2	6	36	.221	.200	.235	14.29	2.38
Corcino, Daniel	R-R	5-11	210	8-26-90	0	0	2.25	2	0	0	1	4	2	2	1	0	3	1	.143	.250	.000	2.25	6.75
Ferguson, Caleb	R-L	6-3	215	7-2-96	7	2	3.49	29	3	0	2	49	43	21	19	8	12	59	.230	.217	.237	10.84	2.20
Fields, Josh	R-R	6-0	195	8-19-85	2	2	2.20	45	0	0	2	41	28	10	10	4	11	33	.196	.179	.207	7.24	2.41
Floro, Dylan	L-R	6-2	205	12-27-90	3	1	1.63	29	0	0	0	28	18	5	5	1	11	31	.182	.200	.174	10.08	3.58
2-team total (25 Cincinnati)					6	3	2.25	54	0	0	0	64	57	17	16	3	23	58	.237	.292	.204	8.16	3.23
Font, Wilmer	R-R	6-4	265	5-24-90	0	2	11.32	6	0	0	0	10	18	13	13	5	1	7	.383	.526	.286	6.10	0.87
Garcia, Yimi	R-R	6-1	220	8-18-90	1	2	5.64	25	0	0	0	22	29	18	14	7	6	19	.305	.290	.316	7.66	1.61
Goeddel, Erik	R-R	6-3	191	12-20-88	1	0	3.38	26	0	0	0	29	22	11	11	4	15	35	.202	.177	.224	10.74	4.60
Hill, Rich	L-L	6-5	220	3-11-80	11	5	3.66	25	24	0	0	133	108	57	54	20	41	150	.219	.206	.223	10.18	2.78
Hudson, Daniel	R-R	6-3	225	3-9-87	3	2	4.11	40	1	0	0	46	38	25	21	6	18	44	.217	.194	.232	8.61	3.52
Jansen, Kenley	B-R	6-5	275	9-30-87	1	5	3.01	69	0	0	38	72	54	28	24	13	17	82	.201	.194	.207	10.30	2.13
Kershaw, Clayton	L-L	6-4	228	3-19-88	9	5	2.73	26	26	0	0	161	139	55	49	17	29	155	.227	.243	.223	8.65	1.62
Liberatore, Adam	L-L	6-3	243	5-12-87	2	1	2.77	17	0	0	0	13	10	4	4	1	8	12	.227	.200	.241	8.31	5.54
Madson, Ryan	L-R	6-6	234	8-28-80	0	0	6.48	9	0	0	0	8	10	6	6	1	1	13	.294	.429	.200	14.04	1.08
2-team total (49 Washington)					2	5	5.47	58	0	0	4	53	58	34	32	7	16	54	.282	.289	.276	9.23	2.73
Maeda, Kenta	R-R	6-1	175	4-11-88	8	10	3.81	39	20	0	2	125	115	58	53	13	43	153	.240	.276	.209	10.99	3.09
Neal, Zach	R-R	6-3	220	11-9-88	0	0	9.00	1	0	0	0	2	1	1	1	0	0	0	.400	.333	.500	0.00	0.00
Paredes, Edward	L-L	6-0	180	9-30-86	2	0	5.87	15	0	0	0	8	7	5	5	2	2	8	.233	.177	.308	9.39	2.35
Rosscup, Zac	R-L	6-2	220	6-9-88	0	1	4.76	17	0	0	0	11	9	6	6	3	4	20	.209	.143	.273	15.88	3.18
Ryu, Hyun-Jin	R-L	6-3	250	3-25-87	7	3	1.97	15	15	0	0	82	68	23	18	9	15	89	.222	.250	.213	9.73	1.64
Santana, Dennis	R-R	6-2	160	4-12-96	1	0	12.27	1	0	0	0	4	6	5	5	0	1	6	.375	.333	.400	9.82	2.45
Stewart, Brock	L-R	6-3	210	10-3-91	0	1	6.11	9	2	0	0	18	23	15	12	4	9	14	.303	.355	.267	7.13	4.58

	B-T	HT	WT	DOB	W	L	ERA	G	GS	CG	SV	IP	H	R	ER	HR	BB	SO	AVG	vLH	vRH	K/9	BB/9
Stripling, Ross	R-R	6-3	210	11-23-89	8	6	3.02	33	21	0	0	122	123	42	41	18	22	136	.257	.241	.274	10.03	1.62
Urias, Julio	L-L	6-0	215	8-12-96	0	0	0.00	3	0	0	0	4	1	0	0	0	0	7	.077	.000	.100	15.75	0.00
Venditte, Pat	L-B	6-1	185	6-30-85	0	0	2.57	15	0	0	0	14	11	4	4	1	3	9	.212	.194	.238	5.79	1.93
Wood, Alex	R-L	6-4	215	1-12-91	9	7	3.68	33	27	0	0	152	143	70	62	14	40	135	.247	.264	.240	8.01	2.37

Fielding

Catcher	PCT	G	PO	A	E	DP	PB
Barnes	.998	61	478	15	1	3	1
Farmer	1.000	1	0	1	0	0	0
Gale	1.000	2	4	0	0	0	0
Grandal	.994	135	1114	47	7	6	9

First Base	PCT	G	PO	A	E	DP
Bellinger	.997	110	717	19	2	58
Farmer	1.000	1	2	0	0	0
Forsythe	.000	1	0	0	0	0
Freese	.977	14	80	4	2	3
Grandal	.909	2	9	1	1	1
Hernandez	1.000	8	38	2	0	2
Muncy	.990	84	458	24	5	31
Utley	1.000	2	9	0	0	1

Second Base	PCT	G	PO	A	E	DP
Barnes	.966	19	11	17	1	4
Dozier	.974	45	68	82	4	19
Forsythe	.979	51	73	115	4	25
Hernandez	.989	41	40	49	1	12
Muncy	.980	13	25	24	1	8
Taylor	1.000	12	13	10	0	3
Utley	.975	50	51	64	3	9
Valera	1.000	5	11	7	0	3

Third Base	PCT	G	PO	A	E	DP
Farmer	.976	22	6	35	1	4
Forsythe	.889	12	7	25	4	2
Freese	1.000	3	0	1	0	0
Hernandez	.800	9	4	4	2	0
Machado	.981	16	13	40	1	2
Muncy	.908	38	9	60	7	3
Turner	.962	96	57	199	10	12
Valera	1.000	3	2	0	0	0

Shortstop	PCT	G	PO	A	E	DP
Hernandez	.983	22	26	33	1	11
Machado	.976	51	53	110	4	19
Seager	.968	25	26	64	3	11
Taylor	.967	81	95	197	10	28

Outfield	PCT	G	PO	A	E	DP
Bellinger	.986	81	135	1	2	0
Hernandez	.992	87	118	1	1	1
Kemp	.988	120	154	5	2	1
Locastro	1.000	5	7	0	0	0
Muncy	1.000	6	2	0	0	0
Pederson	.994	132	163	6	1	1
Puig	.958	118	171	10	8	4
Taylor	.981	63	100	2	2	1
Toles	1.000	10	12	0	0	0
Valera	1.000	1	2	0	0	0
Verdugo	.972	28	34	1	1	0

OKLAHOMA CITY DODGERS

TRIPLE-A

PACIFIC COAST LEAGUE

Batting	B-T	HT	WT	DOB	AVG	vLH	vRH	G	AB	R	H	2B	3B	HR	RBI	BB	HBP	SH	SF	SO	SB	CS	SLG	OBP
Ahmed, Mike	R-R	6-2	195	1-20-92	.231	.250	.226	14	39	8	9	3	0	0	1	3	1	0	0	6	0	0	.308	.302
Beaty, Matt	L-R	6-0	210	4-28-93	.277	.192	.307	31	101	13	28	10	0	1	12	12	5	1	1	17	0	0	.406	.378
Brockmeyer, Cael	R-R	6-5	235	10-8-91	.415	.444	.406	14	41	7	17	5	0	0	2	3	0	0	0	10	0	0	.537	.455
Burg, Alex	R-R	6-0	190	8-9-87	.234	.188	.258	24	47	6	11	3	0	1	4	0	1	0	0	10	0	0	.362	.250
Darvill, Wes	L-R	6-2	190	9-10-91	.100	—	.100	5	10	2	1	0	0	0	0	1	0	0	0	2	0	1	.100	.100
Espinosa, Danny	B-R	6-0	205	4-25-87	.150	.333	.104	19	60	4	9	1	0	2	6	2	2	1	0	24	0	1	.267	.203
Farmer, Kyle	R-R	6-2	214	8-17-90	.288	.282	.291	79	288	37	83	24	1	7	36	17	4	0	3	50	1	1	.451	.333
Gale, Rocky	R-R	6-1	185	2-22-88	.281	.299	.275	85	295	24	83	14	2	4	34	12	0	7	4	50	1	2	.383	.306
Garlick, Kyle	R-R	6-1	210	1-26-92	.253	.256	.252	97	324	49	82	18	2	17	46	14	2	0	1	105	2	0	.478	.287
Goeddel, Tyler	R-R	6-4	180	10-20-92	.250	.000	.286	4	8	2	2	0	0	0	0	0	0	0	0	0	0	0	.250	.250
Joe, Connor	R-R	6-2	205	8-16-92	.294	.303	.287	49	160	34	47	10	2	6	25	22	3	1	2	31	2	0	.494	.385
Landon, Logan	R-R	6-2	180	2-17-93	.250	.500	.167	4	8	2	2	0	0	0	1	0	0	1	0	1	0	0	.250	.250
Locastro, Tim	R-R	6-0	200	7-14-92	.279	.311	.265	83	301	61	84	23	2	4	25	28	26	1	0	52	18	2	.409	.389
Mora, Angelo	B-R	5-11	150	2-25-93	.275	.263	.280	68	200	24	55	6	2	5	37	17	0	1	4	42	5	3	.400	.326
Muncy, Max	L-R	6-0	210	8-25-90	.313	.000	.345	9	32	7	10	2	0	2	4	6	0	0	0	5	0	0	.563	.421
Peter, Jake	L-R	6-1	185	4-5-93	.243	.161	.260	107	329	44	80	10	4	7	34	29	5	0	2	95	4	4	.362	.312
Puig, Yasiel	R-R	6-2	240	12-7-90	.222	.000	.250	3	9	2	2	0	0	0	1	1	0	0	1	1	0	1	.222	.273
Ramos, Henry	B-R	6-2	220	4-15-92	.297	.304	.294	106	357	45	106	22	4	10	58	31	0	4	1	69	8	4	.465	.352
Rios, Edwin	L-R	6-3	220	4-21-94	.304	.291	.309	88	309	45	94	25	0	10	55	23	4	0	5	110	0	1	.482	.355
Scavuzzo, Jacob	R-R	6-4	185	1-15-94	.200	.000	.263	16	50	7	10	1	0	2	6	4	0	0	0	20	0	0	.340	.259
Segedin, Rob	R-R	6-2	220	11-10-88	.211	.364	.174	35	114	13	24	4	0	3	15	15	1	0	4	24	0	0	.325	.299
Smith, Will	R-R	6-0	192	3-28-95	.138	.375	.085	25	87	9	12	4	0	1	7	11	1	2	1	37	1	0	.218	.206
Solano, Donovan	R-R	5-10	205	12-17-87	.319	.322	.317	81	314	38	100	21	1	4	43	16	4	0	6	40	4	1	.430	.353
Taijeron, Travis	R-R	6-2	224	1-20-89	.271	.218	.292	87	280	40	76	18	2	11	44	33	3	0	2	110	1	3	.468	.352
Toles, Andrew	L-R	5-9	185	5-24-92	.306	.227	.333	71	258	43	79	17	1	7	39	13	3	0	1	56	3	2	.461	.346
Valera, Breyvic	B-R	5-11	160	1-8-92	.284	.319	.264	56	201	36	57	8	2	6	25	21	0	0	1	20	4	6	.433	.350
Verdugo, Alex	L-L	6-0	205	5-15-96	.329	.396	.304	91	343	44	113	19	0	10	44	34	1	0	1	47	8	2	.472	.391

Pitching	B-T	HT	WT	DOB	W	L	ERA	G	GS	CG	SV	IP	H	R	ER	HR	BB	SO	AVG	vLH	vRH	K/9	BB/9
Alexander, Scott	L-L	6-2	190	7-10-89	1	0	0.00	4	0	0	0	4	4	0	0	0	1	5	.250	.000	.286	11.25	2.25
Allie, Stetson	R-R	6-2	230	3-13-91	3	0	6.30	13	0	0	0	10	6	8	7	2	8	8	.177	.250	.154	7.20	7.20
Asher, Alec	R-R	6-4	240	10-4-91	0	0	3.00	1	1	0	0	3	3	2	1	0	0	1	.273	.200	.333	3.00	0.00
2-team total (21 Colorado Springs)					6	4	5.96	22	17	0	0	100	121	71	66	12	36	50	.300	.291	.306	4.52	3.25
Baez, Pedro	R-R	6-0	230	3-11-88	0	0	0.00	2	0	0	0	2	1	0	0	0	0	3	.143	.333	.000	13.50	0.00
Banuelos, Manny	R-L	5-10	215	3-13-91	9	7	3.73	31	18	0	0	109	109	47	45	10	42	127	.261	.239	.270	10.52	3.48
Bawcom, Logan	R-R	6-2	220	11-2-88	2	4	6.52	8	0	0	0	39	44	29	28	4	21	31	.288	.339	.250	7.22	4.89
Broussard, Joe	R-R	6-1	220	1-28-91	5	4	3.52	57	0	0	10	66	62	28	23	4	22	71	.250	.305	.223	9.63	2.98
Buehler, Walker	R-R	6-2	175	7-28-94	1	0	2.08	3	3	0	0	13	10	4	3	0	4	16	.204	.200	.207	11.08	2.77
Chargois, JT	B-R	6-3	200	12-3-90	1	0	1.80	11	0	0	0	15	13	3	3	0	7	9	.241	.320	.172	5.40	4.20
Copping, Corey	R-R	6-1	195	11-4-94	1	0	2.45	5	0	0	1	7	9	2	2	1	2	3	.321	.286	.357	4.91	2.45
Corcino, Daniel	R-R	5-11	210	8-26-90	4	3	3.40	24	19	0	0	103	83	44	39	9	41	102	.217	.273	.185	8.88	3.57
Crawford, Leo	L-L	6-0	180	2-2-97	0	1	81.00	1	0	0	0	0	4	3	1	2	0	0	.500	—	.500	0.00	54.00
De Leon, Emmanuel	R-R	6-1	175	12-25-90	0	1	6.23	6	1	0	0	9	6	6	6	2	11	6	.154		.235	6.23	11.42
DeFratus, Justin	B-R	6-4	225	10-21-87	3	4	5.27	12	12	1	0	68	82	41	40	8	17	44	.304	.320	.295	5.80	2.24
Ferguson, Caleb	R-L	6-3	215	7-2-96	0	2	2.25	2	2	0	0	8	6	3	2	0	7	12	.194	.000	.222	13.50	7.88
Fields, Josh	R-R	6-0	195	8-19-85	0	0	6.75	5	0	0	0	4	7	3	3	2	0	2	.368	.600	.286	4.50	0.00

LOS ANGELES DODGERS

Name	B-T	HT	WT	DOB	W	L	ERA	G	GS	CG	SV	IP	H	R	ER	HR	BB	SO	AVG	vLH	vRH	K/9	BB/9
Floro, Dylan	L-R	6-2	205	12-27-90	0	1	9.00	1	0	0	0	1	1	1	1	1	0	1	.250	.000	1.000	9.00	-0.00
Garcia, Yimi	R-R	6-1	220	8-18-90	1	0	4.30	14	0	0	1	15	16	7	7	2	0	14	.281	.333	.256	8.59	0.00
Girodo, Chad	L-L	6-1	190	2-6-91	0	1	4.50	6	3	0	0	8	10	6	4	0	3	11	.286	.133	.400	12.38	3.38
Hernandez, Ariel	R-R	6-4	230	3-2-92	3	2	3.20	21	0	0	1	25	22	10	9	1	20	21	.234	.273	.200	7.46	7.11
2-team total (5 Colorado Springs)					4	2	3.82	26	0	0	1	31	24	14	13	1	31	26	.216	.231	.203	7.63	9.10
Hudson, Daniel	R-R	6-3	225	3-9-87	1	0	0.00	5	0	0	0	5	0	0	0	0	4	5	.000	.000	.000	9.64	7.71
Hutchison, Drew	L-R	6-3	205	8-22-90	4	1	2.14	9	7	0	0	42	38	10	10	1	13	40	.241	.286	.189	8.57	2.79
Istler, Andrew	R-R	5-11	175	9-18-92	0	0	0.00	2	0	0	0	6	2	0	0	0	2	7	.105	.167	.077	11.12	3.18
Johnson, Michael	L-L	6-1	185	1-3-91	0	1	3.15	14	0	0	0	20	22	8	7	1	7	8	.293	.294	.293	3.60	3.15
Kowalczyk, Karch	R-R	6-1	215	3-31-91	0	0	18.00	1	0	0	0	1	3	3	2	0	0	1	.500	.333	.667	9.00	0.00
Lee, C.C.	R-R	5-11	190	10-21-86	2	2	3.91	22	0	0	0	25	17	13	11	3	9	41	.233	.217	.171	14.57	3.20
Liberatore, Adam	L-L	6-3	243	5-12-87	2	2	5.19	18	0	0	0	17	29	16	10	3	6	17	.372	.600	.293	8.83	3.12
Lobstein, Kyle	L-L	6-3	220	5-12-87	1	1	5.14	7	0	0	0	35	36	24	20	1	15	31	.261	.263	.261	7.97	3.86
McAllister, Zach	R-R	6-6	240	12-8-87	1	1	9.00	5	0	0	0	6	6	6	6	2	6	6	.261	.250	.263	13.50	3.00
Moran, Brian	L-L	6-3	210	9-30-88	1	1	6.17	9	0	0	0	12	16	9	8	0	5	10	.333	.364	.324	7.71	3.86
Moscoso, Guillermo	R-R	6-1	200	11-14-83	3	4	4.90	16	13	0	0	72	80	43	39	13	25	65	.279	.273	.285	8.16	3.14
Neal, Zach	R-R	6-2	200	11-9-88	3	2	3.82	14	11	0	0	61	66	30	26	5	12	45	.272	.248	.289	6.60	1.76
Ondrusek, Logan	R-R	6-8	230	2-13-85	0	1	5.30	13	0	0	0	19	23	12	11	5	6	23	.303	.342	.257	11.09	2.89
Paredes, Edward	L-L	6-0	180	9-30-86	3	2	3.79	36	0	0	2	36	37	17	15	3	19	41	.268	.228	.296	10.35	4.79
Pill, Tyler	L-R	6-1	199	5-29-90	3	5	4.76	19	13	0	0	70	86	40	37	6	20	50	.307	.325	.295	6.43	2.57
2-team total (2 Reno)					3	5	5.35	21	13	0	0	74	94	47	44	9	23	53	.314	.320	.310	6.45	2.80
Richman, Jason	L-L	6-4	210	10-15-93	1	0	6.00	2	0	0	0	3	6	2	2	1	2	3	.462	.333	.571	9.00	6.00
Rosscup, Zac	R-L	6-2	220	6-9-88	0	0	0.00	1	0	0	0	1	0	0	0	0	1	1	.000	.000	.000	13.50	13.50
2-team total (10 Albuquerque)					0	0	1.00	11	0	0	0	9	4	2	1	0	4	10	.125	.063	.188	10.00	4.00
Ryu, Hyun-Jin	R-L	6-3	250	3-25-87	0	1	1.80	1	1	0	0	5	5	1	1	0	0	3	.250	.500	.222	5.40	0.00
Santana, Dennis	R-R	6-2	160	4-12-96	1	1	2.45	2	2	0	0	11	10	3	3	0	2	14	.238	.231	.241	11.45	1.64
Sborz, Josh	R-R	6-3	225	12-17-93	1	1	4.38	33	0	0	0	37	38	19	18	0	15	47	.266	.279	.256	11.43	3.65
Schlitter, Brian	R-R	6-5	235	12-21-85	7	2	3.36	58	0	0	21	67	66	31	25	2	26	46	.256	.303	.226	6.18	3.49
Schueller, Sven	R-R	6-3	205	1-17-96	0	0	6.75	1	0	0	0	3	4	2	2	0	0	3	.364	.500	.200	10.13	0.00
Spitzbarth, Shea	R-R	6-1	195	10-4-94	0	0	9.00	2	0	0	0	3	5	3	3	1	3	2	.385	.375	.400	6.00	9.00
Stewart, Brock	L-R	6-3	210	10-3-91	3	3	2.99	19	19	0	0	96	83	34	32	7	29	80	.233	.184	.262	7.47	2.71
Urias, Julio	L-L	6-0	215	8-12-96	0	0	18.00	1	0	0	0	1	2	2	2	0	3	0	.400	—	.400	0.00	27.00
Venditte, Pat	L-B	6-1	185	6-30-85	4	2	1.75	45	0	0	4	51	30	13	10	1	14	62	.168	.197	.150	10.87	2.45
Younginer, Madison	R-R	6-3	209	11-3-90	0	0	48.60	3	0	0	0	2	3	9	9	0	8	2	.375	.000	.600	10.80	43.20
2-team total (18 Sacramento)					1	1	11.00	21	1	0	0	27	43	36	33	1	30	26	.347	.281	.417	8.67	10.00

Fielding

Catcher	PCT	G	PO	A	E	DP	PB
Brockmeyer	1.000	12	98	4	0	1	1
Burg	1.000	2	7	1	0	0	0
Farmer	.992	29	236	16	2	4	2
Gale	.995	84	706	55	4	7	3
Smith	1.000	16	118	7	0	1	3

First Base	PCT	G	PO	A	E	DP
Ahmed	1.000	1	1	0	0	0
Beaty	1.000	16	91	8	0	9
Burg	.982	8	50	4	1	4
Darvill	1.000	1	3	1	0	1
Farmer	1.000	5	34	3	0	4
Joe	.994	41	292	17	2	21
Locastro	.987	11	76	1	1	4
Muncy	.974	7	35	2	1	2
Peter	1.000	7	58	3	0	2
Rios	.986	28	197	11	3	25
Scavuzzo	1.000	1	2	0	0	1
Segedin	.992	19	124	6	1	15
Taijeron	.986	22	131	6	2	13

Second Base	PCT	G	PO	A	E	DP
Beaty	1.000	4	2	6	0	1
Espinosa	1.000	1	1	2	0	1
Farmer	1.000	2	2	2	0	0
Gale	.000	1	0	0	1	0
Locastro	.962	30	47	55	4	13
Mora	.985	19	27	38	1	7
Peter	.984	86	118	193	5	46
Solano	.980	10	19	29	1	6
Valera	.966	16	28		2	10

Third Base	PCT	G	PO	A	E	DP
Ahmed	1.000	6	2	8	0	1
Beaty	.846	4	5	6	2	1
Darvill	1.000	2	1	6	0	2
Farmer	.988	31	18	64	1	10
Joe	.900	4	3	6	1	0
Mora	.930	21	12	28	3	0
Muncy	.900	3	1	8	1	0
Peter	.969	12	5	26	1	1
Rios	.925	38	23	51	6	7
Segedin	.971	13	7	27	1	5
Smith	.963	10	9	17	1	2
Solano	.933	4	3	11	1	2
Valera	.950	15	10	28	2	1

Shortstop	PCT	G	PO	A	E	DP
Ahmed	.842	6	7	9	3	4
Espinosa	.986	17	21	49	1	6
Farmer	1.000	8	8	14	0	4
Mora	.967	26	33	56	3	12
Segedin	.923	3	3	9	1	1
Solano	.963	65	76	157	9	25
Valera	.956	25	26	61	4	9

Outfield	PCT	G	PO	A	E	DP
Ahmed	1.000	1	1	0	0	0
Beaty	1.000	5	13	0	0	0
Garlick	.993	82	133	5	1	1
Goeddel	.000	4	0	0	0	0
Landon	1.000	4	6	0	0	0
Locastro	.988	54	81	3	1	1
Peter	1.000	3	6	0	0	0
Puig	1.000	3	5	0	0	0
Ramos	.982	86	157	5	3	1
Rios	.938	17	30	0	2	0
Scavuzzo	1.000	12	18	1	0	0
Taijeron	.980	55	97	1	2	0
Toles	.990	56	99	3	1	1
Valera	1.000	4	4	0	0	0
Verdugo	.978	82	165	9	4	3

TULSA DRILLERS

TEXAS LEAGUE

DOUBLE-A

Batting	B-T	HT	WT	DOB	AVG	vLH	vRH	G	AB	R	H	2B	3B	HR	RBI	BB	HBP	SH	SF	SO	SB	CS	SLG	OBP
Ahmed, Mike	R-R	6-2	195	1-20-92	.251	.208	.268	65	195	24	49	9	2	5	22	20	3	0	4	63	1	1	.395	.324
Brockmeyer, Cael	R-R	6-5	235	10-8-91	.279	.286	.276	59	183	25	51	8	0	4	31	17	8	0	2	55	3	0	.388	.362
Colvin, Chad	L-L	6-3	210	9-5-85	.286	.250	.300	15	42	7	12	2	0	1	5	4	0	0	1	12	0	0	.405	.340
Darvill, Wes	L-R	6-2	190	9-10-91	.203	.200	.203	48	148	18	30	5	0	2	13	12	0	1	1	38	0	2	.277	.261
Diaz, Yusniel	R-R	6-1	195	10-7-96	.314	.300	.319	59	220	36	69	10	4	6	30	41	3	0	0	39	8	8	.477	.428
Garlick, Kyle	R-R	6-1	210	1-26-92	.282	.267	.286	19	78	11	22	4	0	5	14	6	0	0	1	33	0	0	.526	.329
Goeddel, Tyler	R-R	6-4	180	10-20-92	.212	.289	.178	51	146	25	31	3	2	3	17	12	3	1	1	33	3	1	.322	.284
Jackson, Drew	R-R	6-2	200	7-28-93	.252	.224	.261	103	342	57	86	20	1	15	46	45	13	6	4	93	22	7	.447	.356

Batting	B-T	HT	WT	DOB	AVG	vLH	vRH	G	AB	R	H	2B	3B	HR	RBI	BB	HBP	SH	SF	SO	SB	CS	SLG	OBP
Joe, Connor	R-R	6-0	205	8-16-92	.304	.327	.295	57	204	35	62	16	1	11	30	38	5	0	0	57	1	2	.554	.425
Landon, Logan	R-R	6-2	180	2-17-93	.172	.286	.158	24	64	7	11	3	0	1	2	1	1	0	0	26	1	0	.266	.197
Lux, Gavin	L-R	6-2	190	11-23-97	.324	.217	.354	28	105	21	34	1	4	9	14	1	0	0		20	2	2	.495	.408
Marte, Hamlet	R-R	5-10	180	2-3-94	.143	.000	.200	2	7	1	1	0	0	0	0	0	0	1	0	4	0	0	.143	.143
McKinstry, Zach	L-R	6-0	180	4-29-95	.193	.182	.194	25	83	7	16	2	1	2	8	4	0	0		21	0	0	.313	.230
Mora, Angelo	B-R	5-11	150	2-25-93	.263	.281	.256	30	114	12	30	10	2	3	11	6	0	0		22	0	0	.465	.300
O'Brien, Peter	R-R	6-4	235	7-15-90	.150	.208	.132	31	100	12	15	3	0	7	22	10	2	0		44	0	0	.390	.241
Peters, DJ	R-R	6-6	225	12-12-95	.236	.264	.227	132	491	79	116	23	3	29	60	45	18	0	5	192	1	2	.473	.320
Peterson, Eric	R-R	5-11	190	9-22-93	.471	.500	.462	7	17	3	8	3	0	1	1	1	0	0		4	0	0	.824	.500
Raley, Luke	L-R	6-3	220	9-19-94	.275	.333	.255	93	386	65	106	17	5	17	53	24	20	0	5	105	3	0	.477	.345
Reks, Zach	L-R	6-2	190	11-12-93	.289	.333	.277	78	260	37	75	14	1	3	33	34	0	0	2	73	5	3	.385	.368
Robinson, Errol	R-R	6-0	180	10-1-94	.247	.202	.264	117	433	53	107	14	1	10	50	37	3	0	2	104	18	9	.353	.310
Ruiz, Keibert	B-R	6-0	200	7-20-98	.268	.238	.277	101	377	44	101	14	0	12	47	26	9	0	3	33	0	1	.401	.328
Scavuzzo, Jacob	R-R	6-4	185	1-15-94	.266	.278	.262	95	342	56	91	25	0	24	79	22	6	0	5	88	12	1	.550	.317
Smith, Will	R-R	6-0	192	3-28-95	.264	.258	.266	73	265	48	70	14	0	19	53	36	4	0	2	75	4	0	.532	.358

Pitching	B-T	HT	WT	DOB	W	L	ERA	G	GS	CG	SV	IP	H	R	ER	HR	BB	SO	AVG	vLH	vRH	K/9	BB/9
Allie, Stetson	R-R	6-2	230	3-13-91	1	0	2.84	11	0	0	3	12.2	13	6	5	1	8	18	.180	.214	.107	12.79	5.68
Alvarez, Yadier	R-R	6-3	175	3-7-96	1	7	4.66	17	8	0	1	48	37	31	25	2	43	52	.211	.178	.235	9.68	8.01
Anderson, Isaac	R-R	6-0	185	9-4-93	0	1	16.20	1	1	0	0	3.1	7	6	6	1	2	1	.412	.286	.500	2.70	5.40
Baez, Pedro	R-R	6-0	230	3-11-88	0	0	6.75	1	0	0	0	1.1	1	1	1	0	0	1	.200	—	.200	6.75	0.00
Baker, Dylan	R-R	6-2	205	4-6-92	3	6	6.08	34	0	0	8	37	43	29	25	6	17	22	.293	.302	.289	5.35	4.14
Bawcom, Logan	R-R	6-2	220	11-2-88	4	6	4.43	12	12	0	0	61	63	38	30	11	19	42	.258	.289	.242	6.20	2.80
Boyle, Michael	R-L	6-3	200	4-12-94	1	0	5.54	10	0	0	0	13	10	9	8	4	9	7	.208	.154	.229	4.85	6.23
Copping, Corey	R-R	6-1	175	1-11-94	3	0	2.53	30	0	0	2	46	35	16	13	1	24	55	.208	.254	.181	10.68	4.66
Corcino, Daniel	R-R	5-11	210	8-26-90	1	1	3.52	4	0	0	0	8	7	5	3	1	1	9	.226	.231	.222	10.57	1.17
Curry, Parker	R-R	6-0	185	11-21-93	1	3	6.75	5	5	0	0	21	29	21	16	7	9	12	.305	.219	.349	5.06	3.80
De Leon, Emmanuel	R-R	6-1	175	12-25-90	0	1	14.54	3	1	0	0	4.1	8	7	7	0	3	2	.391	.286	.438	4.15	6.23
DeFratus, Justin	B-R	6-4	225	10-21-87	1	4	5.18	11	11	0	0	65	74	41	30	10	14	49	.280	.304	.262	6.82	1.95
Duncan, Frank	R-R	6-4	215	1-30-92	1	3	5.79	7	4	0	0	28	37	21	18	4	4	14	.314	.286	.333	4.50	1.29
Ferguson, Caleb	R-L	6-3	215	12-2-96	3	0	1.38	8	8	0	0	39	31	11	6	2	10	40	.205	.221	.209	9.23	2.31
Girodo, Chad	L-L	6-1	190	2-6-91	0	0	5.40	7	0	0	0	12	10	7	7	2	3	8	.227	.214	.233	6.17	2.31
Gonsolin, Tony	R-R	6-2	180	5-14-94	6	0	2.44	9	9	0	0	44	32	14	12	3	16	49	.203	.254	.161	9.95	3.25
Hamilton, Austin	L-L	6-0	185	8-11-93	1	0	0.00	1	0	0	0	2	0	0	0	0	0	2	.167	—	.167	9.00	0.00
Hernandez, Ariel	R-R	6-2	230	3-2-92	0	0	2.11	13	0	0	4	21	13	5	5	0	9	25	.183	.154	.200	10.55	3.80
Holmes, Ben	L-L	6-1	195	9-12-91	2	2	2.82	6	6	0	0	38	25	12	12	3	12	30	.189	.278	.156	7.04	2.82
Hoyt, Justin	L-L	6-0	210	4-30-95	0	0	0.00	1	0	0	0	0	0	0	0	0	0	0	.000	.000	.000	0.00	0.00
Istler, Andrew	R-R	5-11	175	9-18-92	4	4	2.53	29	1	0	1	57	42	21	16	1	13	46	.212	.159	.240	7.26	2.05
Johnson, Michael	L-L	6-1	185	1-3-91	1	2	5.70	29	2	0	0	47	51	30	30	9	20	40	.276	.286	.271	7.61	3.80
Kasowski, Marshall	L-R	6-2	215	3-10-95	1	2	2.77	10	0	0	1	13	7	4	4	2	9	18	.159	.250	.125	12.46	6.23
Kowalczyk, Karch	R-R	6-1	215	3-31-91	1	1	6.16	22	0	0	1	31	39	24	21	0	17	31	.350	.281	.510	9.10	4.99
Kremer, Dean	R-R	6-3	180	1-7-96	0	0	0.00	1	1	0	0	7	3	0	0	0	3	11	.130	.091	.167	14.14	3.86
Lobstein, Kyle	L-L	6-3	220	8-12-89	3	2	2.56	7	7	0	0	39	35	15	11	3	9	35	.238	.297	.218	8.15	2.09
Long, Nolan	R-R	6-10	255	1-19-94	3	0	5.05	24	0	0	0	36	26	21	20	2	17	40	.180	.213	.109	10.09	4.29
May, Dustin	R-R	6-6	180	9-6-97	2	3	3.67	6	6	0	0	34	27	14	14	0	12	28	.209	.267	.179	7.34	3.15
Moran, Brian	L-L	6-3	210	9-30-88	1	1	3.71	22	0	0	3	27	30	13	11	3	10	34	.294	.313	.286	11.48	3.38
Ondrusek, Logan	R-R	6-8	230	2-13-85	1	0	0.00	3	0	0	0	3	3	0	0	0	2	1	.250	.200	.286	2.70	5.40
Pill, Tyler	L-R	6-1	199	5-29-90	0	1	5.40	2	1	0	0	8	11	7	5	2	3	4	.297	.111	.357	4.32	3.24
Richman, Jason	L-L	6-4	210	10-15-93	1	1	6.75	5	0	0	0	11	14	11	8	1	8	9	.326	.400	.286	7.59	6.75
Santana, Dennis	R-R	6-2	160	4-12-96	0	2	2.56	8	8	0	0	39	26	17	11	3	14	51	.183	.146	.202	11.87	3.26
Santarsiero, Vinny	R-R	6-7	185	12-10-93	0	0	4.76	4	0	0	0	6	4	3	3	1	4	4	.200	.250	.125	6.35	6.35
Sborz, Josh	R-R	6-3	225	12-17-93	3	1	2.76	13	0	0	6	16	11	6	5	1	5	24	.193	.208	.182	13.22	2.76
Scrubb, Andre	R-R	6-4	265	1-13-95	0	0	1.93	5	0	0	0	9	6	2	2	0	5	10	.177	.294	.059	9.64	4.82
Smeltzer, Devin	R-L	6-3	195	9-7-95	5	5	4.73	23	14	0	0	84	94	48	44	9	19	67	.281	.289	.278	7.21	2.04
Somsen, Layne	R-R	6-0	190	6-5-89	1	0	0.73	11	0	0	2	12	10	1	1	0	2	18	.227	.286	.200	13.14	1.46
Sopko, Andrew	R-R	6-2	205	8-7-94	3	1	3.88	14	10	0	0	53	66	26	23	9	13	48	.310	.329	.301	8.10	2.19
Spitzbarth, Shea	R-R	6-1	195	10-4-94	3	4	4.10	38	0	0	3	64	61	31	29	10	23	84	.229		.206	11.87	3.25
White, Mitchell	R-R	6-4	207	12-28-94	6	7	4.53	22	22	0	0	105	114	63	53	12	34	88	.273	.298	.258	7.52	2.91
Younginer, Madison	R-R	6-3	209	11-3-90	0	0	10.80	1	0	0	0	2	2	2	2	0	2	2	.333	—	.333	10.80	10.80

Fielding

Catcher	PCT	G	PO	A	E	DP	PB
Brockmeyer	1.000	28	160	10	0	1	0
Marte	1.000	2	11	5	0	0	0
Ruiz	.995	86	717	62	4	3	11
Smith	.993	33	244	25	2	2	5

First Base	PCT	G	PO	A	E	DP
Ahmed	1.000	10	76	3	0	7
Brockmeyer	.985	25	187	11	3	28
Colvin	1.000	7	55	6	0	8
Darvill	1.000	3	8	1	0	0
Joe	.988	21	149	10	2	13
O'Brien	.990	26	189	5	2	6
Peterson	1.000	1	8	0	0	1

Outfield	PCT	G	PO	A	E	DP
Raley	.997	44	363	23	1	31
Reks	.977	6	41	1	1	8

Second Base	PCT	G	PO	A	E	DP
Ahmed	.957	12	15	30	2	4
Darvill	.972	10	13	22	1	8
Jackson	.959	64	118	160	12	35
Joe	1.000	2	2	2	0	1
McKinstry	1.000	9	22	24	0	9
Mora	.973	19	37	35	2	6
Peterson	1.000	1	5	5	0	2
Robinson	.970	29	52	79	4	23

Third Base	PCT	G	PO	A	E	DP
Ahmed	.867	26	10	42	8	8
Darvill	.932	22	13	42	4	6
Joe	.886	34	18	60	10	3
McKinstry	1.000	14	6	21	0	1
Mora	.852	9	4	19	4	1
Peterson	.000	1	0	0	0	0
Robinson	.900	12	8	19	3	2
Smith	.880	33	16	50	9	7

Shortstop	PCT	G	PO	A	E	DP
Ahmed	.867	9	19	4	1	
Jackson	.949	30	42	89	7	18
Lux	.945	26	42	62	6	20

McKinstry	.833	2	2	3	1	1		Darvill	1.000	10	15	2	0	1
Robinson	.951	76	97	176	14	28		Diaz	.950	59	133	1	7	0

Garlick	1.000	16	35	1	0	0

Outfield	PCT	G	PO	A	E	DP		Goeddel	.986	41	71	2	1	0
Ahmed	1.000	2	4	0	0	0		Jackson	.957	7	21	1	1	0
Colvin	1.000	5	3	1	0	1								

Landon	1.000	21	20	1	0	0
Peters	.984	127	294	6	5	1
Raley	.981	48	99	3	2	0
Reks	.981	32	50	1	1	0
Scavuzzo	.992	70	116	1	1	0

RANCHO CUCAMONGA QUAKES HIGH CLASS A
CALIFORNIA LEAGUE

Batting	B-T	HT	WT	DOB	AVG	vLH	vRH	G	AB	R	H	2B	3B	HR	RBI	BB	HBP	SH	SF	SO	SB	CS	SLG	OBP
Bannon, Rylan	R-R	5-10	180	4-22-96	.296	.304	.295	89	338	58	100	17	6	20	61	59	3	0	3	103	4	4	.559	.402
Berman, Steve	6-2	225	11-28-94	.302	.500	.268	33	96	24	29	5	1	4	19	19	5	0	0	15	0	0	.500	.442
Casey, Donovan	R-R	6-2	190	2-23-96	.253	.286	.246	62	241	43	61	8	2	6	30	23	1	0	4	72	2	1	.378	.316
Estevez, Omar	R-R	5-10	168	2-25-98	.278	.293	.275	128	515	87	143	43	2	15	84	45	5	2	10	138	3	1	.456	.336
Forsythe, Logan	R-R	6-1	205	1-14-87	.100	1.000	.000	3	10	0	1	0	0	0	0	0	0	0	0	0	0	0	.200	.100
Isabel, Ibandel	R-R	6-4	225	6-20-95	.238	.000	.294	6	21	1	5	2	0	1	3	2	0	0	0	9	0	0	.476	.304
Jenco, Saige	L-L	5-10	185	8-7-94	.247	.231	.250	59	170	25	42	8	1	0	11	34	0	1	1	49	7	5	.306	.371
Kendall, Jeren	L-R	6-0	190	2-4-96	.215	.173	.224	114	438	68	94	20	3	12	42	52	2	1	1	158	30	14	.356	.300
Landon, Logan	R-R	6-2	180	2-17-93	.268	.217	.277	85	317	56	85	16	2	12	41	33	3	1	3	76	22	5	.445	.340
Lux, Gavin	L-R	6-2	190	11-23-97	.324	.230	.343	88	358	64	116	23	7	11	48	43	1	0	2	68	11	7	.520	.396
Marte, Hamlet	R-R	5-10	180	2-3-94	.272	.300	.267	77	257	40	70	15	2	12	47	29	2	0	3	67	1	0	.486	.347
McKinstry, Zach	L-R	6-0	180	4-29-95	.308	.238	.329	33	91	20	28	7	1	2	8	17	6	0	0	22	0	0	.473	.447
Montgomery, Brandon	R-R	6-0	180	2-12-96	.318	.250	.344	23	85	15	27	5	3	4	21	5	2	0	2	23	1	0	.588	.362
Puig, Yasiel	R-R	6-2	240	12-7-90	.000	—	.000	1	4	0	0	0	0	0	0	0	0	0	0	1	0	0	.000	.000
Reks, Zach	L-R	6-2	190	11-12-93	.405	.286	.433	10	37	8	15	3	1	2	7	1	0	0	0	5	1	0	.703	.421
Rincon, Carlos	R-R	6-3	190	10-14-97	.327	.412	.312	29	110	36	36	9	0	15	35	16	4	0	1	31	0	1	.818	.428
Santana, Cristian	R-R	6-2	175	2-24-97	.274	.211	.286	131	548	75	150	23	0	24	109	20	5	0	7	143	2	2	.447	.302
Thomas, Cody	L-R	6-4	211	10-8-94	.285	.299	.282	127	499	82	142	35	7	19	87	48	8	0	3	163	5	2	.497	.355
Turner, Justin	R-R	5-11	205	11-23-84	.000	—	.000	2	6	0	0	0	0	0	0	1	0	0	0	0	0	0	.000	.143
Walker, Jared	L-R	6-2	195	2-4-96	.260	.194	.274	56	204	48	53	11	4	17	45	25	14	0	1	73	2	0	.603	.377
Wong, Connor	R-R	6-1	181	5-19-96	.269	.324	.257	102	383	64	103	20	2	19	60	38	10	0	0	138	6	2	.480	.350
Yarnall, Nick	L-L	6-0	200	10-17-94	.241	.100	.265	42	141	27	34	10	0	7	18	18	0	0	0	48	3	1	.461	.327

Pitching	B-T	HT	WT	DOB	W	L	ERA	G	GS	CG	SV	IP	H	R	ER	HR	BB	SO	AVG	vLH	vRH	K/9	BB/9
Abdullah, Imani	R-R	6-4	205	4-20-97	1	1	12.38	6	2	0	0	8	8	11	11	1	13	7	.229	.143	.357	7.88	14.63
Allie, Stetson	R-R	6-2	230	3-13-91	3	1	6.98	22	0	0	0	23	23	17	15	6	15	31	.288	.345	.255	14.43	6.98
Anderson, Isaac	R-R	6-2	185	9-4-93	10	6	3.67	31	16	0	1	118	121	55	48	8	32	120	.264	.204	.292	9.18	2.45
Boyle, Michael	R-L	6-3	200	4-12-94	1	2	1.47	23	0	0	6	31	24	13	5	2	11	37	.212	.191	.217	10.86	3.23
Buehler, Walker	R-R	6-2	175	7-28-94	0	0	3.00	1	1	0	0	3	2	1	1	0	1	5	.182	.250	.143	15.00	3.00
Carter, James	R-R	6-1	185	3-10-94	0	0	20.25	1	0	0	0	1	3	3	3	1	1	3	.429	.250	.667	20.25	6.75
Cespedes, Yeison	R-R	6-1	178	3-5-98	0	1	2.00	5	0	0	0	9	7	4	2	0	5	6	.206	.333	.136	6.00	5.00
Crawford, Leo	L-L	6-0	180	2-2-97	8	0	2.77	13	11	0	0	68	59	22	21	3	19	61	.228	.263	.218	8.03	2.50
Curry, Parker	R-R	6-0	185	11-21-93	7	3	3.41	34	6	0	1	74	71	32	28	6	24	95	.245	.247	.244	11.55	2.92
Gamboa, Max	R-R	6-5	190	11-22-95	4	2	6.56	9	9	0	0	48	57	37	35	6	13	53	.297	.377	.266	9.94	2.44
Gonsolin, Tony	R-R	6-2	180	5-14-94	4	2	2.69	17	17	0	0	84	72	31	25	5	26	106	.227	.215	.235	11.40	2.80
Hamilton, Austin	L-L	6-0	185	8-11-93	1	3	5.23	8	3	0	0	21	25	16	12	3	6	13	.291	.231	.317	5.66	2.61
Hill, Rich	L-L	6-5	220	3-11-80	0	1	0.00	1	1	0	0	5	4	2	0	0	0	10	.211	—	.211	19.29	0.00
Holmes, Ben	L-L	6-1	195	9-12-91	1	0	1.06	6	3	0	0	17	9	2	2	1	5	25	.150	.167	.146	13.24	2.65
Hoyt, Justin	L-L	6-0	210	4-30-95	0	0	36.00	1	0	0	0	1	5	4	4	1	0	2	.625	.800	.333	27.00	0.00
Istler, Andrew	R-R	5-11	175	9-18-92	0	0	2.65	10	0	0	0	17	8	7	5	1	4	20	.136	.185	.094	10.59	2.12
Jagiello, Dan	R-R	6-3	200	5-23-95	0	1	5.14	10	0	0	0	14	7	8	8	3	8	22	.143	.188	.121	14.14	5.14
Kasowski, Marshall	L-R	6-3	215	3-10-95	2	0	1.14	16	0	0	4	24	10	3	3	1	11	44	.128	.167	.117	16.73	4.18
Kremer, Dean	R-R	6-3	180	1-7-96	5	3	3.30	16	16	0	0	79	67	33	29	7	26	114	.230	.215	.241	12.99	2.96
Long, Nolan	R-R	6-10	255	1-19-94	5	0	1.03	19	0	0	3	35	18	4	4	1	12	52	.151	.122	.171	13.37	3.09
Mathewson, Chris	L-R	6-1	200	5-26-95	1	1	5.75	7	3	0	0	30	33	16	13	2	7	15	.208	.194	.220	4.64	3.10
May, Dustin	R-R	6-6	180	9-6-97	7	3	3.29	17	17	0	0	98	91	42	36	9	17	94	.241	.237	.242	8.60	1.56
Montgomerie, Wills	R-R	6-3	225	6-2-95	1	1	4.67	6	0	0	0	17	21	12	9	3	14	19	.292	.250	.308	9.87	7.27
Moseley, Ryan	R-R	6-1	190	10-6-94	3	4	4.32	47	3	0	2	73	74	46	35	3	49	83	.259	.347	.213	10.23	6.04
Muhammad, Jeremiah	R-R	6-2	195	11-14-94	0	1	18.00	2	0	0	0	4	8	8	8	1	6	4	.400	.375	.429	9.00	12.00
Navarro, Orlandy	R-R	6-2	175	6-3-99	0	0	18.00	1	0	0	0	2	3	4	4	2	1	2	.333	.000	.600	9.00	4.50
Pop, Zach	R-R	6-4	220	9-20-96	1	0	0.33	19	0	0	7	27	13	1	1	0	6	23	.149	.167	.140	7.67	2.00
Richman, Jason	L-L	6-4	210	10-15-93	2	5	3.97	37	0	0	5	59	69	35	26	5	18	53	.288	.226	.309	8.08	2.75
Rosscup, Zac	R-L	6-2	220	6-9-88	0	0	0.00	1	0	0	0	1	0	0	0	0	0	1	.000	—	.000	9.00	0.00
Ruibal, Evy	R-R	6-4	230	9-29-95	0	0	0.00	3	0	0	0	2	0	0	0	0	6	4	.000	.000	.000	18.00	7.71
Ryu, Hyun-Jin	R-L	6-3	250	3-25-87	0	0	0.00	1	1	0	0	4	2	0	0	0	0	4	.154	—	.154	9.00	0.00
Salow, Logan	L-L	6-1	185	9-27-94	4	2	2.82	34	0	0	3	45	41	14	14	2	12	56	.238	.279	.225	11.28	2.42
Schueller, Sven	R-R	6-2	205	1-17-96	0	2	6.16	21	0	0	1	31	46	35	21	2	14	17	.343	.364	.333	4.99	4.11
Scrubb, Andre	R-R	6-3	215	3-31-95	4	0	0.38	14	0	0	3	24	8	3	1	0	11	28	.098	.056	.109	10.65	4.18
Serrano, Elio	R-R	5-11	160	8-2-98	0	1	13.50	1	0	0	0	1	2	1	1	0	0	3	.500	.000	.667	27.00	0.00
Sheffield, Jordan	R-R	5-10	190	6-1-95	1	3	6.88	14	7	0	0	34	39	28	26	8	20	40	.283	.245	.306	10.59	5.29
Sopko, Andrew	R-R	6-2	205	8-7-94	3	4	3.22	12	12	0	0	64	59	25	23	4	14	70	.272	.268	.225	10.31	1.96
Strain, Connor	R-R	6-1	180	8-4-94	3	2	6.46	17	0	0	0	24	32	18	17	2	11	73	.323	.484	.250	10.27	4.18
Uceta, Edwin	R-R	6-0	155	1-9-98	0	0	6.97	5	5	0	0	21	17	16	16	7	12	28	.224	.227	.222	12.19	5.23
Urias, Julio	L-L	6-0	215	8-12-96	0	0	4.91	4	4	0	0	7	6	4	4	3	4	13	.231	.250	.222	15.95	4.91

Fielding

Catcher	PCT	G	PO	A	E	DP	PB
Berman	.988	32	315	14	4	0	1
Marte	.987	44	433	26	6	0	4
Wong	.986	71	646	49	10	4	12

First Base	PCT	G	PO	A	E	DP
Isabel	.977	6	40	3	1	2
Marte	.991	15	112	1	1	0
Reks	1.000	4	20	3	0	3
Santana	.976	42	297	23	8	26
Walker	1.000	37	276	12	0	28
Yarnall	.989	39	264	16	3	28

Second Base	PCT	G	PO	A	E	DP
Bannon	.974	22	35	41	2	11
Estevez	.970	47	83	113	6	30

	PCT	G	PO	A	E	DP
Forsythe	1.000	2	1	3	0	1
Lux	.953	17	34	47	4	12
McKinstry	.971	17	28	38	2	5
Montgomery	1.000	16	28	35	0	11
Walker	1.000	17	32	35	0	7
Wong	1.000	11	22	27	0	5

Third Base	PCT	G	PO	A	E	DP
Bannon	.901	54	39	97	15	7
McKinstry	.941	5	4	12	1	3
Montgomery	1.000	5	4	8	0	2
Santana	.888	76	38	137	22	14
Turner	1.000	1	1	1	0	0
Wong	1.000	1	0	3	0	1

Shortstop	PCT	G	PO	A	E	DP
Estevez	.955	74	91	184	13	38

	PCT	G	PO	A	E	DP
Lux	.921	66	75	170	21	34
McKinstry	1.000	5	5	8	0	2
Montgomery	1.000	2	1	4	0	1

Outfield	PCT	G	PO	A	E	DP
Casey	.965	55	82	0	3	0
Jenco	.973	54	71	2	2	0
Kendall	.969	107	211	11	7	2
Landon	.986	78	138	1	2	1
McKinstry	1.000	5	14	0	0	0
Puig	1.000	1	2	0	0	0
Reks	1.000	1	2	0	0	0
Rincon	.943	18	32	1	2	0
Thomas	.975	107	190	4	5	0
Yarnall	1.000	1	1	0	0	0

GREAT LAKES LOONS
MIDWEST LEAGUE

LOW CLASS A

Batting	B-T	HT	WT	DOB	AVG	vLH	vRH	G	AB	R	H	2B	3B	HR	RBI	BB	HBP	SH	SF	SO	SB	CS	SLG	OBP
Amaya, Jacob	R-R	6-0	180	9-3-98	.265	.353	.247	27	98	13	26	1	0	1	5	20	0	1	0	18	3	3	.306	.390
Avans, Drew	L-L	5-10	195	6-13-96	.228	.185	.240	36	123	17	28	5	2	2	21	17	3	1	4	29	12	2	.350	.327
Carpenter, Brock	R-R	6-3	200	6-5-95	.244	.366	.207	50	176	19	43	11	4	4	17	19	1	0	0	61	2	1	.421	.321
Chiu, Marcus	R-R	6-2	208	1-13-97	.221	.244	.214	54	181	33	40	8	1	9	22	18	18	0	1	55	9	2	.425	.349
Cogen, Matt	L-R	6-0	195	8-19-95	.200	.000	.250	2	5	1	1	1	0	0	3	0	0	0	0	2	0	0	.400	.200
Cuadrado, Romer	R-R	6-4	185	9-12-97	.210	.270	.191	123	472	43	99	19	4	5	44	40	2	0	2	159	7	5	.299	.273
Feduccia, Hunter	L-R	6-2	183	6-5-97	.290	.240	.307	31	100	6	29	6	0	0	9	15	1	1	2	31	1	0	.350	.381
Hansen, Mitchell	L-L	6-4	210	5-1-96	.232	.200	.247	32	108	10	25	3	1	2	13	7	0	0	2	32	3	2	.333	.274
Heredia, Starling	R-R	6-2	200	2-6-99	.182	.167	.187	53	203	18	37	9	1	6	26	16	1	0	0	81	3	0	.325	.246
Heyer, Luke	R-R	6-0	200	9-26-96	.262	.177	.289	58	210	23	55	9	0	1	12	18	6	0	1	57	3	4	.319	.336
Hope, Garrett	R-R	6-3	235	12-27-93	.105	.091	.109	19	57	6	6	2	0	2	6	13	2	0	1	24	0	1	.246	.288
Liput, Deacon	L-R	5-10	185	6-27-96	.280	.273	.282	42	168	31	47	7	3	5	21	13	1	0	2	48	5	2	.446	.332
Mann, Devin	R-R	6-3	180	2-11-97	.241	.267	.232	63	224	26	54	13	1	2	30	34	4	0	2	50	7	4	.335	.349
McKinstry, Zach	L-R	6-0	180	4-29-95	.377	.368	.382	18	53	12	20	2	2	3	8	16	3	0	0	16	2	1	.660	.542
McLain, Josh	R-R	6-1	170	9-23-96	.303	.392	.271	52	195	26	59	11	1	1	18	7	4	1	3	39	7	7	.385	.335
Miller, Darrell	R-R	6-2	220	9-29-93	.310	.214	.341	15	58	6	18	3	1	2	8	4	1	0	0	9	0	0	.500	.365
Montgomery, Brandon	R-R	6-0	180	2-12-96	.251	.290	.236	92	347	44	87	11	4	9	40	17	1	1	4	87	11	4	.383	.285
Morales, Brayan	R-L	6-1	170	12-8-95	.273	.241	.285	86	326	47	89	15	6	3	23	22	11	6	2	105	46	15	.383	.338
Perez, Moises	R-R	6-0	160	7-18-97	.227	.268	.215	73	251	24	57	12	3	1	21	12	4	1	4	62	8	3	.311	.269
Peterson, Eric	R-R	5-11	190	9-22-93	.255	.231	.262	52	165	18	42	7	1	3	20	13	6	0	2	39	10	2	.364	.328
Pitre, Gersel	R-R	6-0	203	7-23-96	.282	.378	.252	56	188	20	53	10	0	0	16	4	1	0	1	37	4	0	.335	.299
Rincon, Carlos	R-R	6-3	190	10-14-97	.226	.233	.222	81	288	28	65	13	2	7	33	41	6	0	3	91	5	1	.358	.331
Rodriguez, Ramon	R-R	5-11	194	10-30-98	.209	.222	.205	33	110	7	23	4	0	1	13	8	1	1	0	17	0	0	.273	.269
Roller, Chris	R-R	6-0	190	10-8-96	.233	.167	.250	28	86	6	20	4	0	1	7	10	2	2	1	31	6	1	.314	.323
Vargas, Miguel	R-R	6-3	198	11-17-99	.213	.278	.193	23	75	4	16	1	1	0	6	10	1	1	2	20	0	0	.253	.307
Walker, Jared	L-R	6-2	195	2-4-97	.250	.218	.262	54	200	33	50	15	4	8	30	28	5	0	2	59	4	0	.485	.353
Yarnall, Nick	L-L	6-0	200	10-17-94	.268	.207	.294	25	97	13	26	2	0	6	16	11	0	0	0	25	1	0	.474	.343

Pitching	B-T	HT	WT	DOB	W	L	ERA	G	GS	CG	SV	IP	H	R	ER	HR	BB	SO	AVG	vLH	vRH	K/9	BB/9
Alvino, Jasiel	R-R	6-1	180	1-11-97	2	0	4.56	17	0	0	0	26	20	15	13	3	11	23	.215	.256	.185	8.06	3.86
Carrillo, Gerardo	R-R	6-0	154	9-13-98	2	1	1.65	9	9	0	0	49	35	10	9	3	15	37	.200	.191	.209	6.80	2.76
Carter, James	R-R	6-3	185	3-10-94	2	1	5.06	12	0	0	0	21	21	13	12	1	7	18	.259	.300	.220	7.59	2.95
Castro, Jeronimo	R-R	6-4	200	9-3-96	1	2	6.63	6	6	0	0	19	23	14	14	2	10	26	.291	.267	.306	12.32	4.74
Cespedes, Yeison	R-R	6-1	178	3-5-98	0	1	12.60	5	0	0	0	5	5	11	7	1	6	3	.263	.300	.222	5.40	10.80
Chacin, Jose	R-R	6-4	168	3-25-97	0	3	4.36	7	6	0	0	33	41	22	16	3	10	28	.297	.327	.279	7.64	2.73
Crawford, Leo	L-L	6-0	180	2-2-97	0	5	4.02	14	9	0	0	47	52	26	21	2	6	33	.286	.313	.276	6.32	1.15
Drury, Austin	L-L	5-11	180	8-13-97	3	1	0.51	10	0	0	0	18	8	1	1	0	5	18	.136	.000	.182	9.17	2.55
Gamboa, Max	R-R	6-5	190	11-22-95	3	4	4.22	17	11	0	0	53	53	37	25	2	25	51	.249	.242	.252	8.61	4.22
Gonzalez, Victor	L-L	6-0	180	11-16-95	0	3	5.61	6	6	0	0	26	33	17	16	3	5	18	.314	.138	.382	6.31	1.75
Hagenman, Justin	R-R	6-3	205	10-7-96	1	0	6.75	4	0	0	0	8	13	6	6	2	2	6	.361	.385	.348	6.75	2.25
Hamilton, Austin	L-L	6-0	185	8-11-93	2	0	3.60	10	0	0	0	20	22	10	8	2	4	22	.272	.227	.288	9.90	1.80
Hemmerich, Devin	R-L	6-1	195	7-11-96	5	5	2.73	31	0	0	2	56	46	25	17	3	27	34	.228	.192	.240	5.46	4.34
Hernandez, Ricardo	R-R	6-1	205	2-4-98	0	1	4.50	1	0	0	0	2	2	2	1	0	2	3	.286	.000	.333	13.50	9.00
Hoyt, Justin	L-L	6-0	210	4-30-95	1	1	5.48	11	0	0	0	21	21	13	13	1	11	16	.269	.364	.232	6.75	4.64
Inoa, Joel	R-R	6-2	210	2-21-96	1	2	5.34	7	5	0	0	30	30	19	18	5	4	16	.261	.184	.318	6.23	4.15
Jackson, Andre	R-R	6-3	187	5-1-96	1	5	4.35	14	14	0	0	50	48	29	24	3	41	45	.257	.237	.270	8.15	7.43
Jagiello, Dan	R-R	6-3	200	5-23-95	2	2	2.60	32	0	0	3	52	32	17	15	0	32	60	.182	.179	.184	10.38	5.54
Jimenez, Melvin	R-R	6-0	170	7-23-99	3	7	4.22	24	9	0	0	60	41	30	28	4	29	59	.198	.218	.183	8.90	4.37
Kasowski, Marshall	L-R	6-3	215	3-10-95	0	1	2.57	15	1	0	0	28	13	11	8	1	18	49	.133	.156	.113	15.75	5.79
Kolek, Stephen	R-R	6-3	220	4-18-97	2	0	0.66	14	0	0	2	27	16	2	2	0	6	27	.168	.171	.167	8.89	1.98
Montgomerie, Wills	R-R	6-3	225	6-2-95	0	1	1.45	7	4	0	0	31	16	9	5	1	21	36	.154	.135	.164	10.45	6.10
Navarro, Orlandy	R-R	6-2	175	6-3-99	0	0	0.00	1	0	0	0	3	0	0	0	0	1	1	.000	.000	.000	3.38	3.38

	B-T	HT	WT	DOB	W	L	ERA	G	GS	CG	SV	IP	H	R	ER	HR	BB	SO	AVG	vLH	vRH	K/9	BB/9
Nunez, Darien	L-L	6-2	205	3-19-93	1	2	2.67	17	0	0	2	30	28	9	9	2	12	46	.246	.281	.232	13.65	3.56
Ottesen, Riley	R-R	6-1	185	10-30-94	1	4	11.39	12	4	0	0	28	22	35	35	0	38	25	.227	.250	.213	8.13	12.36
Pasen, Luis	R-R	6-0	175	1-14-95	1	0	8.68	6	0	0	0	9	12	9	9	1	10	11	.324	.182	.385	10.61	9.64
Pop, Zach	R-R	6-4	220	9-20-96	0	2	2.20	11	0	0	0	16	12	8	4	1	7	24	.194	.214	.177	13.22	3.86
Rooney, John	L-L	6-5	235	1-28-97	0	0	2.40	6	0	0	0	15	12	4	4	0	7	14	.240	.400	.200	8.40	4.20
Salow, Logan	L-L	6-1	185	9-27-94	1	0	5.06	3	0	0	0	5	5	3	3	1	2	8	.227	.000	.294	13.50	3.38
2-team total (4 Beloit)					3	0	3.27	7	0	0	0	11	6	5	4	1	4	16	.158	.000	.207	13.09	3.27
Santarsiero, Vinny	R-R	6-7	185	12-10-93	0	0	0.00	1	0	0	0	2	1	0	0	0	0	3	.143	.200	.000	13.50	0.00
Schueller, Sven	R-R	6-3	205	1-17-96	1	2	4.84	14	0	0	0	22	25	15	12	1	5	23	.269	.349	.200	9.27	2.01
Scrubb, Andre	R-R	6-4	265	1-13-95	3	2	5.10	19	0	0	2	30	33	21	17	3	16	34	.277	.250	.296	10.20	4.80
Sequera, Gregorio	R-R	6-1	165	12-9-97	0	0	4.91	2	0	0	0	4	3	2	2	0	5	4	.214	.000	.333	9.82	12.27
Strain, Connor	R-R	6-1	180	8-4-94	2	0	1.40	16	0	0	0	26	20	5	4	1	12	21	.217	.161	.246	7.36	4.21
Tavarez, Alfredo	R-R	6-5	190	11-27-97	3	6	3.30	20	18	0	0	95	80	40	35	4	47	67	.231	.232	.230	6.33	4.44
Uceta, Edwin	R-R	6-0	155	1-9-98	5	5	3.25	20	20	0	0	100	91	40	36	9	27	103	.241	.196	.273	9.30	2.44
Vargas, Jesus	R-R	6-2	175	8-18-98	4	3	3.28	8	8	0	0	36	30	14	13	4	9	28	.229	.192	.253	7.07	2.27
Warzek, Bryan	L-L	6-0	205	1-17-97	1	1	2.75	8	3	0	0	20	21	6	6	1	3	33	.280	.111	.333	15.10	1.37
Washington, Mark	R-R	6-2	205	3-22-96	1	1	2.95	8	0	0	0	18	16	6	6	1	9	13	.242	.273	.227	6.38	4.42
Willeman, Zach	R-R	6-2	175	3-27-96	2	0	2.16	3	1	0	0	8	10	3	2	0	1	10	.333	.400	.300	10.80	1.08
Zabala, Aneurys	R-R	6-3	259	12-21-96	2	2	4.86	24	0	0	1	37	31	20	20	2	25	30	.231	.196	.253	7.30	6.08
2-team total (16 Dayton)					2	5	4.39	40	0	0	4	53	47	28	26	3	34	43	.228	.219	.234	7.26	5.74

Fielding

C: Feduccia 31, Hope 18, Miller 14, Pitre 45, Rodriguez 33. **1B:** Carpenter 35, Chiu 1, Hansen 16, Heyer 13, Mann 11, Peterson 17, Pitre 1, Walker 28, Yarnall 23. **2B:** Amaya 5, Chiu 38, Heyer 1, Liput 12, Mann 46, McKinstry 5, Montgomery 28, Perez 6, Peterson 4, Pitre 1, Walker 1. **3B:** Carpenter 2, Chiu 10, Heyer 39, Mann 1, Montgomery 21, Perez 1, Peterson 21, Pitre 4, Vargas 19, Walker 24. **SS:** Amaya 21, Liput 22, McKinstry 11, Montgomery 22, Perez 63. **OF:** Avans 32, Cogen 2, Cuadrado 110, Hansen 12, Heredia 39, McKinstry 1, McLain 48, Montgomery 16, Morales 82, Peterson 4, Pitre 1, Rincon 54, Roller 27.

OGDEN RAPTORS   *ROOKIE*
PIONEER LEAGUE

Batting	B-T	HT	WT	DOB	AVG	vLH	vRH	G	AB	R	H	2B	3B	HR	RBI	BB	HBP	SH	SF	SO	SB	CS	SLG	OBP
Amaya, Jacob	R-R	6-0	180	9-3-98	.347	.310	.365	32	127	41	44	9	3	3	24	27	1	0	0	29	11	4	.535	.465
Amon, Pascal	L-R	6-1	183	12-26-97	.267	.429	.125	4	15	1	4	2	0	0	2	2	0	0	0	5	0	1	.400	.353
Aponte, Kevin	R-R	6-1	175	10-26-97	.233	.300	.200	8	30	6	7	0	1	0	1	2	2	0	0	14	1	0	.300	.324
Arocho, Jeremy	B-R	5-10	165	6-6-98	.313	.255	.331	59	208	44	65	10	2	0	21	29	3	1	2	31	12	7	.380	.401
Avans, Drew	L-L	5-10	195	6-13-96	.350	.546	.306	16	60	23	21	0	2	5	20	16	0	0	1	10	5	3	.667	.481
Betancourt, Kenneth	R-R	5-8	160	2-5-00	.279	.313	.271	22	86	17	24	3	1	0	8	3	1	0	1	18	5	2	.337	.308
Brito, Ronny	R-R	6-0	165	3-22-99	.288	.250	.301	53	219	37	63	11	0	11	52	21	2	0	2	74	1	6	.489	.353
Camargo, Jair	R-R	5-10	150	7-1-99	.273	.238	.289	18	66	9	18	2	1	3	18	3	1	0	1	22	1	0	.470	.310
Chiu, Marcus	R-R	6-2	200	1-13-97	.271	.200	.303	13	48	8	13	1	2	2	13	2	5	0	0	11	3	0	.500	.364
Cogen, Matt	L-R	6-0	195	8-19-95	.316	.296	.321	54	206	51	65	10	6	9	50	29	3	0	0	37	3	0	.553	.408
De Jongh, Aldrich	R-R	5-9	160	9-1-98	.333	.000	.500	2	3	0	1	0	0	0	0	0	0	0	0	2	0	0	.333	.333
Feduccia, Hunter	L-R	6-2	183	6-5-97	.250	.000	.400	3	8	2	2	0	0	0	1	3	1	0	0	1	0	0	.250	.500
Grand Pre, Preston	R-R	6-4	175	7-15-95	.268	.267	.269	12	41	2	11	3	2	1	6	1	0	0	0	15	0	1	.512	.286
Heady, Connor	R-R	5-11	158	7-3-94	—	—	—	1	0	0	0	0	0	0	0	0	0	0	0	0	0	0	—	—
Hernandez, Marco	R-R	6-2	170	6-22-98	.325	.250	.357	13	40	8	13	3	0	1	7	5	1	0	0	6	0	0	.475	.413
Heyer, Luke	R-R	6-0	205	9-26-96	.286	.167	.375	5	14	1	4	1	0	1	4	0	0	0	0	2	1	0	.571	.286
Hulsizer, Niko	R-R	6-2	200	2-1-97	.281	.432	.224	48	160	47	45	13	0	9	32	30	11	0	1	52	12	2	.531	.426
Littell, Jon	R-R	6-3	218	8-16-95	.244	.125	.274	21	78	11	19	7	0	2	16	5	1	0	1	24	1	1	.410	.294
Osorio, Felix	R-R	6-4	195	11-13-96	.313	.333	.286	4	16	1	5	1	0	0	3	1	0	0	0	2	0	1	.375	.353
Outman, James	L-R	6-2	195	5-14-97	.264	.232	.276	55	208	50	55	8	3	11	33	24	4	0	1	56	12	2	.490	.350
Paulson, Dillon	L-L	6-3	200	6-10-97	.272	.286	.267	58	224	54	61	20	3	10	61	42	3	0	6	51	1	0	.522	.386
Perez, Moises	R-R	6-0	160	7-18-97	.313	.750	.167	5	16	2	5	1	0	0	2	0	0	0	1	3	0	0	.375	.294
Peterson, Eric	R-R	5-11	190	9-22-93	.231	.500	.182	13	39	13	9	2	1	2	7	4	2	0	3	6	3	0	.487	.313
Pitre, Gersel	R-R	6-0	203	7-23-96	.500	.500	.500	3	12	2	6	1	0	1	5	0	0	0	0	0	0	0	.833	.500
Robinson, Daniel	L-L	6-2	215	10-30-96	.332	.365	.320	57	205	50	68	13	4	2	36	32	2	0	2	24	11	4	.463	.423
Rodriguez, Ramon	R-R	5-11	194	10-30-98	.250	.250	.250	37	116	15	29	5	0	0	13	14	0	0	2	13	0	1	.293	.326
Roller, Chris	R-R	6-0	190	10-8-96	.312	.256	.352	26	93	28	29	9	1	5	17	15	4	0	1	28	6	3	.591	.425
Rubi, Alvaro	R-R	6-2	185	2-16-97	.242	.200	.261	11	33	3	8	3	0	0	3	6	0	0	0	5	1	1	.333	.359
Souffront, Jefrey	R-R	6-1	180	5-23-97	.302	.256	.318	48	149	28	45	7	2	1	24	19	0	0	4	44	2	1	.396	.372
Todd, Tre	L-R	6-1	205	9-29-96	.227	.333	.196	22	66	11	15	4	1	1	13	18	1	0	0	19	1	0	.364	.400
Valera, Leonel	R-R	6-1	165	7-9-99	.111	.000	.250	3	9	0	1	1	0	0	1	0	0	0	0	6	0	0	.222	.111
Vargas, Miguel	R-R	6-1	198	11-17-99	.394	.462	.368	32	94	25	37	11	1	2	22	8	1	0	0	13	6	1	.596	.442
Vison, Jeremiah	R-R	5-4	145	8-27-97	.000	.000	.000	1	3	0	0	0	0	0	0	0	0	0	0	0	0	0	.000	.000

Pitching	B-T	HT	WT	DOB	W	L	ERA	G	GS	CG	SV	IP	H	R	ER	HR	BB	SO	AVG	vLH	vRH	K/9	BB/9
Aleaziz, Reza	R-R	6-4	225	7-11-95	1	1	5.32	17	0	0	2	24	27	16	14	0	8	22	.290	.314	.276	8.37	3.04
Alvino, Jasiel	R-R	6-1	180	1-11-97	1	0	4.91	7	0	0	1	7	5	4	4	1	4	10	.179	.111	.211	12.27	4.91
Bruihl, Justin	L-L	6-2	215	6-26-97	1	2	8.24	21	0	0	1	32	33	32	29	1	24	44	.246	.209	.264	12.51	6.82
Cespedes, Yeison	R-R	6-1	178	3-5-98	0	1	9.42	11	0	0	0	14	22	17	15	2	10	18	.355	.231	.444	11.30	6.28
Chacin, Jose	R-R	6-4	168	3-25-97	6	2	2.85	12	12	0	0	66	77	31	21	2	14	51	.293	.326	.276	6.92	1.90
de Geus, Brett	R-R	6-1	190	11-4-97	4	5	7.26	15	14	0	0	62	78	56	50	10	27	58	.305	.374	.267	8.42	3.92
Drury, Austin	L-L	5-11	180	8-13-97	1	0	2.25	7	0	0	1	12	10	3	3	0	1	10	.233	.100	.273	7.50	0.75
Gonzalez, Victor	L-L	6-0	180	11-16-95	1	2	13.50	4	2	0	0	8	18	14	12	1	4	7	.429	.267	.519	7.88	4.50
Hagenman, Justin	R-R	6-3	205	10-7-96	3	0	4.09	10	0	0	0	22	19	10	10	2	6	23	.232	.148	.273	9.41	2.45

Name	B-T	HT	WT	DOB	W	L	ERA	G	GS	CG	SV	IP	H	R	ER	HR	BB	SO	AVG	vLH	vRH	K/9	BB/9
Hamilton, Austin	L-L	6-0	185	8-11-93	2	0	1.00	4	0	0	0	9	9	3	1	0	0	6	.265	.546	.130	6.00	0.00
Helsabeck, Wes	L-L	6-0	195	7-7-92	0	0	8.56	10	1	0	0	14	19	13	13	3	5	15	.328	.294	.342	9.88	3.29
Hemmerich, Devin	R-L	6-1	195	7-11-95	0	1	1.23	5	0	0	2	7	3	1	1	0	0	7	.125	.000	.200	8.59	0.00
Hernandez, Ricardo	R-R	6-1	205	2-4-98	0	0	23.63	3	0	0	0	3	9	7	7	1	1	1	.600	.000	.900	3.38	3.38
Hoyt, Justin	L-L	6-0	210	4-30-95	0	0	0.00	1	0	0	0	1	2	0	0	0	1	1	.500	1.000	.333	13.50	13.50
Inoa, Joel	R-R	6-2	180	2-21-96	4	2	4.91	11	11	0	0	51	65	41	28	4	16	43	.297	.369	.252	7.54	2.81
Kolek, Stephen	R-R	6-3	220	4-18-97	0	0	6.23	3	0	0	1	4	6	3	3	1	1	3	.316	.375	.273	6.23	2.08
Lewis, Justin	B-L	6-2	210	10-12-96	1	1	5.40	17	4	0	0	27	32	19	16	1	15	28	.314	.357	.297	9.45	5.06
Malisheski, Kevin	R-R	6-3	200	9-7-97	3	2	5.88	16	16	0	0	64	89	61	42	7	31	51	.333	.333	.333	7.13	4.34
Martinez, Jose	R-R	6-0	175	4-23-99	0	0	2.25	1	0	0	0	4	4	2	1	0	0	3	.235	.111	.375	6.75	0.00
Mitchell, Connor	L-L	6-4	180	9-11-95	4	0	6.67	17	0	0	0	30	49	30	22	3	6	20	.358	.333	.367	6.07	1.82
Muhammad, Jeremiah	R-R	6-2	195	11-14-94	0	0	2.35	4	0	0	0	8	3	2	2	1	1	9	.125	.125	.125	10.57	1.17
Navarro, Orlandy	R-R	6-2	175	6-3-99	1	1	2.35	11	3	0	0	23	12	7	6	1	8	24	.156	.226	.109	9.39	3.13
Nealy, Colby	R-R	6-5	185	3-18-96	0	0	7.20	4	0	0	0	5	10	6	4	1	2	3	.400	.444	.375	5.40	3.60
Nunez, Darien	L-L	6-2	205	3-19-93	0	0	0.00	1	0	0	0	1	0	0	0	0	0	3	.000	—	.000	27.00	0.00
Pasen, Luis	R-R	6-0	175	1-14-95	1	1	4.57	14	0	0	3	22	20	16	11	2	11	19	.247	.278	.222	7.89	4.57
Pena, Adalberto	R-R	6-2	173	3-11-95	1	1	7.04	3	1	0	0	8	10	8	6	0	3	8	.313	.353	.267	9.39	3.52
2-team total (8 Orem)					2	2	5.66	11	1	0	1	21	21	16	13	2	13	17	.263	.268	.256	7.40	5.66
Richert, Riley	R-R	6-3	200	1-28-97	0	0	20.25	2	0	0	0	1	1	3	3	1	6	2	.250	—	.250	13.50	40.50
Ruibal, Evy	R-R	6-4	232	9-29-95	2	1	3.66	17	0	0	1	20	26	9	8	0	8	13	.342	.261	.377	5.95	3.66
Sampen, Caleb	R-R	6-2	185	7-23-96	0	2	5.04	13	11	0	0	30	31	21	17	2	9	43	.250	.290	.233	12.76	2.67
Santarsiero, Vinny	R-R	6-7	185	12-10-93	0	1	9.64	4	0	0	0	5	9	10	5	1	6	4	.375	.539	.182	7.71	11.57
Sequera, Gregorio	R-R	6-1	165	12-9-97	1	2	4.22	17	0	0	1	21	16	15	10	2	9	14	.205	.154	.231	5.91	3.80
Serrano, Elio	R-R	5-11	160	8-2-98	0	0	4.20	9	0	0	0	15	13	7	7	2	3	10	.241	.111	.306	6.00	1.80
Speer, Hunter	R-R	6-0	180	5-18-95	2	2	4.33	18	0	0	3	27	32	13	13	2	8	18	.302	.316	.294	6.00	2.67
Vargas, Jesus	R-R	6-2	175	8-18-98	0	0		1	1	0	0	0	1	1	1	0	0	0	1.000	—	1.000	—	—
Washington, Mark	R-R	6-2	205	3-22-96	2	0	3.32	10	0	0	0	22	25	16	8	2	9	19	.278	.258	.288	7.89	3.74

Fielding

C: Camargo 16, Feduccia 2, Hernandez 13, Rodriguez 37, Rubi 1, Todd 20. **1B:** Hernandez 1, Paulson 55, Pitre 2, Rubi 7, Souffront 10, Vargas 6. **2B:** Amaya 8, Arocho 55, Betancourt 9, Brito 5, Chiu 2, Perez 1, Peterson 1, Pitre 1, Souffront 2, Valera 1, Vargas 2. **3B:** Betancourt 8, Brito 4, Camargo 2, Chiu 6, Grand Pre 11, Heyer 5, Perez 1, Peterson 8, Souffront 31, Vargas 13. **SS:** Amaya 27, Arocho 7, Betancourt 5, Brito 38, Grand Pre 4, Perez 3, Valera 2. **OF:** Amon 4, Aponte 7, Avans 12, Cogen 39, De Jongh 1, Hulsizer 39, Littell 17, Osorio 4, Outman 39, Peterson 1, Robinson 42, Roller 26, Shaps 5, Souffront 7, Vison 1.

AZL DODGERS
ARIZONA LEAGUE
ROOKIE

Batting	B-T	HT	WT	DOB	AVG	vLH	vRH	G	AB	R	H	2B	3B	HR	RBI	BB	HBP	SH	SF	SO	SB	CS	SLG	OBP
Ackerman, Aaron	B-R	6-3	210	5-1-97	.253	.360	.204	26	79	11	20	0	1	1	8	13	1	0	0	33	1	0	.317	.366
Alcantara, Ismael	R-R	6-1	165	9-25-98	.168	.243	.125	36	101	18	17	4	1	3	12	13	3	2	0	33	5	2	.317	.282
Aponte, Kevin	R-R	6-2	175	10-26-97	.149	.125	.163	24	67	11	10	1	0	0	6	16	2	0	2	30	8	1	.164	.322
Avans, Drew	L-L	5-10	195	6-13-96	.393	.286	.429	8	28	6	11	1	1	3	10	2	0	0	0	4	3	0	.821	.433
Beaty, Matt	L-R	6-0	210	4-28-93	.375	.333	.400	3	8	0	3	0	0	0	2	0	0	0	0	0	0	0	.375	.375
Betancourt, Kenneth	R-R	5-8	160	2-5-00	.313	.550	.213	22	67	14	21	2	4	0	10	5	0	1	0	11	4	1	.463	.361
Camargo, Jair	R-R	5-10	150	7-1-99	.234	.235	.233	15	47	4	11	5	0	1	7	0	0	0	1	12	2	0	.404	.229
Casey, Donovan	R-R	6-2	190	2-23-96	.316	.200	.357	7	19	4	6	3	1	1	6	1	0	0	1	6	0	0	.737	.333
Chiu, Marcus	R-R	6-2	208	1-13-97	.200	—	.200	2	5	0	1	1	0	0	2	0	0	0	0	0	0	0	.400	.200
Darvill, Wes	L-R	6-2	190	9-10-91	.100	.000	.250	4	10	1	1	0	1	0	2	1	0	0	0	5	0	0	.300	.182
De Jongh, Aldrich	L-R	5-9	160	9-1-98	.221	.154	.233	23	86	11	19	4	1	1	12	6	0	1	1	16	2	1	.326	.269
Espinoza, Aldo	R-R	6-0	148	9-11-98	.333	.500	.282	18	51	10	17	5	0	0	10	1	0	0	1	3	0	0	.431	.340
Heredia, Starling	R-R	6-2	200	2-6-99	.269	.429	.211	8	26	6	7	0	0	1	2	4	0	0	0	11	1	0	.385	.367
Hernandez, Marco	R-R	6-2	195	6-22-98	.256	.143	.310	14	43	6	11	2	0	0	3	9	1	0	2	4	3	1	.302	.382
Landry, Meaux	R-R	6-4	230	1-18-98	.210	.154	.225	19	62	9	13	7	1	2	10	10	2	0	0	25	1	0	.452	.338
Lao, Sauryn	R-R	6-2	182	8-14-99	.262	.125	.309	40	126	18	33	11	2	4	22	18	1	0	0	41	4	1	.476	.359
Lebron, Rolando	R-R	5-9	170	5-10-98	.286	.375	.254	34	91	16	26	6	3	2	11	10	1	1	1	24	9	4	.484	.359
Littell, Jon	R-R	6-3	218	8-16-95	.327	.316	.333	14	49	10	16	3	3	1	7	6	0	0	0	14	2	1	.571	.400
Locastro, Tim	R-R	6-1	200	7-14-92	.412	.500	.385	6	17	3	7	0	1	0	4	3	2	0	1	0	1	1	.529	.522
Mann, Devin	R-R	6-3	180	2-11-97	.200	.000	.250	2	5	0	1	0	0	0	0	1	0	0	0	3	0	1	.200	.333
McLain, Josh	R-R	6-1	170	9-23-96	.333	1.000	.200	2	6	1	2	1	0	0	0	0	0	0	0	1	0	0	.500	.333
McWilliams, Sam	R-R	6-2	190	4-30-96	.276	.375	.250	25	76	14	21	6	1	1	18	11	2	0	1	19	9	1	.421	.378
Mendoza, Cesar	R-R	5-11	175	2-28-97	.105	.000	.167	6	19	3	2	0	0	0	1	0	0	0	0	9	0	0	.105	.227
Pages, Andy	R-R	6-1	180	12-8-00	.192	.167	.200	10	26	5	5	1	0	1	3	6	2	0	0	4	1	1	.346	.382
Perez, Moises	R-R	6-0	160	7-18-97	.333	.500	.250	3	6	1	2	0	0	0	0	1	0	0	1	3	0		.333	.429
Rodriguez, Luis	B-R	6-0	150	3-2-99	.190	.217	.179	28	79	8	15	3	1	0	11	9	2	1	5	29	3	1	.253	.270
Sanchez, Frank	R-R	6-3	170	8-25-98	.233	.250	.226	28	90	13	21	3	2	0	9	8	0	0	1	29	3	0	.311	.293
Solano, Donovan	R-R	5-10	205	12-17-87	.440	.500	.421	8	25	3	11	5	0	0	3	0	1	0	1	1	0	0	.480	.444
Suarez, Albert	L-R	5-11	150	11-30-99	.231	.208	.242	40	143	18	33	6	1	0	17	12	0	2	2	31	11	2	.287	.287
Taylor, Zach	R-R	6-1	220	10-29-95	.000	.000	.000	2	3	1	0	0	0	0	0	4	0	0	0	2	1	0	.000	.571
Valera, Leonel	R-R	6-1	165	7-9-99	.293	.325	.280	42	147	23	43	4	2	1	13	16	1	0	1	45	13	1	.367	.364
Vargas, Miguel	R-R	6-3	198	11-17-99	.419	.500	.353	8	31	6	13	3	1	0	2	5	1	0	0	3	1	0	.581	.514
Vison, Jeremiah	R-R	5-4	145	8-27-97	.253	.385	.184	28	75	15	19	0	2	0	2	8	1	0	0	9	7	2	.307	.313
Zabala, Juan	R-R	5-10	170	7-3-99	.139	.100	.154	24	72	7	10	2	0	0	5	9	1	0	2	18	0	2	.167	.238

Pitching	B-T	HT	WT	DOB	W	L	ERA	G	GS	CG	SV	IP	H	R	ER	HR	BB	SO	AVG	vLH	vRH	K/9	BB/9
Acosta, Aldry	R-R	6-4	200	9-7-99	2	2	4.39	12	7	0	1	41	38	20	20	2	15	36	.245	.328	.192	7.90	3.29
Alvarez, Yadier	R-R	6-3	175	3-7-96	0	0	1.29	2	2	0	0	7	5	1	1	0	1	10	.208	.286	.177	12.86	1.29

	B-T	HT	WT	DOB	W	L	ERA	G	GS	CG	SV	IP	H	R	ER	HR	BB	SO	AVG	vLH	vRH	K/9	BB/9
Carrillo, Gerardo	R-R	6-0	154	9-13-98	2	0	0.82	4	1	0	1	11	6	1	1	0	2	13	.154	.067	.208	10.64	1.64
Castro, Jeronimo	R-R	6-4	200	9-3-96	2	0	0.87	3	0	0	0	10	4	1	1	0	0	19	.114	.136	.077	16.55	0.00
Contreras, Nelfri	L-L	6-0	177	12-25-98	0	1	4.50	17	0	0	3	22	24	16	11	1	14	15	.279	.286	.277	6.14	5.73
Cuello, Edward	R-R	6-0	170	10-20-98	1	1	3.57	15	0	0	3	18	19	12	7	3	5	19	.264	.250	.275	9.68	2.55
Fields, Josh	R-R	6-0	195	8-19-85	0	0	6.00	3	3	0	0	3	3	2	2	1	1	4	.300	.200	.400	12.00	3.00
Fisher, Braydon	R-R	6-4	180	7-26-00	1	2	2.05	11	9	0	0	22	21	8	5	2	9	19	.259	.268	.250	7.77	3.68
Garcia, Yimi	R-R	6-1	220	8-18-90	0	0	0.00	3	2	0	0	3	2	1	0	0	0	4	.182	.333	.125	12.00	0.00
Gilliland, Jacob	R-R	6-2	180	1-16-00	3	1	4.19	13	1	0	0	19	17	11	9	2	15	12	.246	.250	.244	5.59	6.98
Helsabeck, Wes	L-L	6-0	195	7-7-92	0	0	0.00	2	0	0	0	1	0	0	0	0	3	2	.000	.000	.000	13.50	20.25
Hernandez, Antonio	L-L	5-8	187	9-27-99	3	0	1.09	12	0	0	0	25	19	9	3	1	8	26	.198	.263	.182	9.49	2.92
Hernandez, Jose	L-L	6-3	170	12-31-97	2	1	2.96	15	0	0	0	27	18	12	9	2	14	38	.180	.000	.240	12.51	4.61
Hernandez, Ricardo	R-R	6-1	205	2-4-98	2	0	1.83	13	0	0	0	20	17	4	4	1	8	17	.221	.219	.222	7.78	3.66
Jackson, Andre	R-R	6-3	187	5-1-96	2	0	3.44	4	3	0	0	18	18	7	7	0	4	31	.254	.217	.271	15.22	1.96
Jimenez, Melvin	B-R	6-0	170	7-23-99	2	0	0.00	4	0	0	0	4	2	0	0	0	2	6	.133	.143	.125	13.50	4.50
Marinan, James	R-R	6-5	220	10-10-98	0	0	0.84	3	3	0	0	11	11	4	1	0	4	11	.290	.304	.267	9.28	3.38
Martinez, Jose	R-R	6-0	175	4-23-99	3	2	3.06	10	2	0	1	32	27	11	11	1	7	41	.229	.238	.224	11.41	1.95
Montgomerie, Wills	R-R	6-3	225	6-2-95	1	1	6.35	3	2	0	0	6	5	5	4	0	4	11	.217	.417	.000	17.47	6.35
Morillo, Juan	R-R	6-1	150	3-19-99	0	0	3.22	6	3	0	1	22	12	9	8	1	13	28	.160	.161	.159	11.28	5.24
Mortillaro, Joe	R-R	6-2	205	9-14-93	0	0	54.00	1	0	0	0	0	2	2	0	0	3	0	.000	—	.000	0.00	81.00
Navarro, Orlandy	R-R	6-1	175	6-3-99	1	0	0.00	5	0	0	1	8	2	0	0	0	2	12	.083	.154	.000	14.09	2.35
Nunez, Darien	L-L	6-2	205	3-19-93	0	0	0.00	2	0	0	0	3	1	0	0	0	0	5	.100	.000	.125	15.00	0.00
Nunez, Mateo	R-R	6-5	220	6-11-97	0	0	0.00	1	0	0	0	1	1	0	0	0	1	1	.200	.333	.000	6.75	6.75
Ortiz, Robinson	L-L	6-0	180	1-4-00	2	2	4.18	11	9	0	0	32	27	16	15	2	12	42	.231	.381	.198	11.69	3.34
Ottesen, Riley	R-R	6-1	185	10-30-94	2	0	7.20	12	0	0	0	10	7	8	8	0	14	13	.189	.273	.154	11.72	12.60
Rooney, John	L-L	6-5	235	1-28-97	0	0	0.00	2	2	0	0	5	2	0	0	0	1	7	.143	.000	.167	12.60	1.80
Serrano, Elio	R-R	5-11	160	8-2-98	0	0	1.29	7	0	0	2	14	7	3	2	0	2	23	.143	.105	.167	14.79	1.29
Sheffield, Jordan	R-R	5-10	190	6-1-95	0	0	0.00	3	1	0	0	3	1	0	0	0	0	4	.100	.000	.200	12.00	6.00
Urias, Julio	L-L	6-0	215	8-12-96	0	0	2.70	2	2	0	0	3	2	1	1	0	0	6	.167	.000	.182	16.20	0.00
Vargas, Jesus	R-R	6-2	175	8-18-98	0	1	5.40	4	1	0	0	12	13	9	7	3	3	14	.260	.375	.206	10.80	2.31
Warzek, Bryan	L-L	6-0	205	1-17-97	1	1	3.38	2	0	0	0	3	0	1	1	0	2	5	.000	.000	.000	16.88	6.75
Willeman, Zach	R-R	6-2	175	3-27-96	1	0	0.84	5	0	0	0	11	2	1	1	0	7	14	.065	.071	.059	11.81	5.91
Witt, Nathan	R-R	6-4	210	4-19-96	2	0	3.46	14	0	0	0	13	12	6	5	2	6	24	.240	.208	.269	9.69	4.15
Younginer, Madison	R-R	6-3	209	11-3-90	0	0	0.00	3	0	0	0	2	0	0	0	0	0	4	.000	.000	.000	12.00	6.00
Zuniga, Guillermo	R-R	6-3	195	10-10-98	3	1	3.86	12	2	0	2	37	41	17	16	0	13	41	.289	.308	.278	9.88	3.13

Fielding

C: Ackerman 15, Camargo 10, Hernandez 8, Mendoza 5, Taylor 2, Zabala 22. 1B: Ackerman 7, Beaty 1, Betancourt 2, Espinoza 8, Hernandez 6, Landry 17, Lao 20, Rodriguez 1, Vargas 5. 2B: Betancourt 9, Chiu 2, Darvill 1, Espinoza 8, Locastro 1, Mann 1, McWilliams 15, Rodriguez 9, Solano 1, Suarez 18, Valera 4. 3B: Beaty 1, Betancourt 11, Camargo 1, Darvill 2, Lao 20, Rodriguez 12, Suarez 1, Valera 11, Vargas 4. SS: Betancourt 1, Perez 3, Rodriguez 6, Solano 5, Suarez 21, Valera 26. OF: Alcantara 35, Aponte 20, Avans 7, Casey 5, De Jongh 21, Lebron 31, Littell 8, Locastro 3, McLain 1, McWilliams 2, Pages 9, Sanchez 20, Shaps 5, Vison 23.

DSL DODGERS   ROOKIE
DOMINICAN SUMMER LEAGUE

Batting	B-T	HT	WT	DOB	AVG	vLH	vRH	G	AB	R	H	2B	3B	HR	RBI	BB	HBP	SH	SF	SO	SB	CS	SLG	OBP
Alvarez, Oscar	R-R	5-9	145	6-20-00	.143	.200	.134	30	77	9	11	0	0	1	6	7	2	0	0	22	2	0	.182	.233
Bastardo, Kiumel	R-R	6-0	180	1-12-00	.318	.667	.263	6	22	5	7	0	0	0	5	1	0	0	0	7	1	2	.318	.348
Bentura, Railison	R-R	5-10	155	1-16-00	.000	.000	.000	7	17	3	0	0	0	0	0	6	1	0	0	3	0	0	.000	.292
Brito, Ronny	R-R	6-0	165	3-22-99	.400	.267	.305	8	15	3	6	3	0	0	3	2	0	0	1	4	0	0	.600	.444
Cathalina, Mayron	R-R	6-0	145	2-12-01	.132	.000	.143	12	38	3	5	1	0	1	4	5	0	0	1	20	1	2	.237	.227
Chalo, Wladimir	R-R	5-8	170	4-21-00	.270	.214	.280	28	89	7	24	6	0	0	18	14	4	0	0	22	1	1	.337	.393
Chirinos, Yhostin	R-R	5-10	165	9-29-00	.266	.308	.254	52	177	24	47	18	2	1	20	26	8	1	1	30	12	1	.407	.382
Diaz, Luis Carlos	R-R	6-1	155	12-19-99	.233	.359	.200	58	189	32	44	11	0	1	20	48	5	0	4	32	5	4	.307	.394
Diaz, Luis Yanel	R-R	5-11	170	9-9-99	.206	.194	.208	56	204	30	42	4	1	5	28	20	0	0	1	64	15	2	.309	.276
Dominguez, Jesus	L-R	5-9	189	4-6-01	.197	.000	.228	23	66	6	13	1	1	1	8	10	1	0	0	17	1	0	.288	.312
Enrique, Julio	R-R	6-1	184	2-21-00	.206	.148	.217	52	165	30	34	5	1	3	14	25	5	0	1	59	13	8	.303	.327
Feliz, Jimmie	B-R	5-11	180	8-1-00	.158	.125	.167	16	38	11	6	2	1	1	3	13	1	0	0	19	3	1	.342	.385
Fernandez, Alejandro	R-R	5-10	155	3-7-01	.119	.095	.125	30	101	4	12	2	0	0	8	12	2	1	1	19	0	0	.139	.224
Garcia, Jeans	L-R	6-1	185	6-21-01	.073	.083	.070	19	55	8	4	2	0	0	6	6	0	0	0	27	0	0	.109	.164
Garcia, Yunior	R-R	6-0	198	7-29-01	.226	.258	.219	45	168	32	38	8	4	5	24	19	4	0	0	41	8	2	.411	.319
Heredia, Gorge	R-R	6-3	200	12-1-00	.167	.333	.111	18	48	3	8	2	0	0	3	7	1	0	0	21	1	0	.208	.286
Hernandez, Jorge	R-R	5-10	145	1-12-01	.174	.250	.158	9	23	1	4	0	0	0	2	3	0	0	0	8	0	3	.174	.269
Jardines, Jenderson	B-R	5-11	160	1-31-01	.171	.238	.157	40	123	23	21	3	1	3	10	22	2	0	0	27	5	2	.285	.306
Leonard, Eddys	R-R	6-0	160	11-10-00	.248	.148	.271	45	149	36	37	10	0	4	16	28	5	0	0	33	13	6	.396	.385
Loaisiga, Mike	B-R	5-11	167	8-29-99	.113	.000	.130	21	53	8	6	0	0	0	1	14	1	0	0	9	1	0	.113	.309
Luis, Deivi	L-L	6-0	164	10-11-99	.202	.077	.224	33	89	16	18	5	0	0	16	20	3	0	1	27	2	2	.258	.363
Machin, Eynar	R-R	5-10	155	10-3-00	.272	.286	.269	41	125	12	34	7	0	2	20	7	7	0	4	28	3	5	.376	.336
Martinez, Hector	R-R		135	8-22-00	.190	.143	.198	43	142	25	27	2	0	1	19	21	6	1	4	27	7	5	.225	.312
Mateo, Edwin	L-L		160	11-18-98	.257	.243	.261	61	202	38	52	3	5	2	17	34	4	1	1	35	19	5	.352	.373
Nava, Jose	L-R	6-2	190	1-15-99	.230	.400	.200	35	100	11	23	5	1	2	23	19	4	0	3	21	0	0	.360	.365
Noriega, Andres	R-R	6-1	190	1-3-01	.237	.167	.254	47	152	14	36	8	0	2	19	16	8	1	1	40	1	2	.329	.339
Pages, Andy	R-R	6-1	180	12-8-00	.236	.243	.225	42	140	34	33	8	0	9	33	23	14	0	1	31	9	6	.486	.393
Perez, Jaime	R-R	6-1	178	4-5-00	.275	.345	.260	48	160	35	44	9	3	6	26	19	7	0	0	49	14	3	.481	.376
Perez, Vladimir	R-R	5-9	138	1-3-01	.195	.250	.185	44	128	23	25	5	1	2	19	29	5	0	1	55	6	6	.297	.362

Restituyo, Harold	R-R	6-2	185	9-1-00	.269	.000	.304	11	26	6	7	2	0	1	2	3	2	0	0	6	0	1	.462 .387
Rodriguez, Brayan	R-R	6-4	190	11-23-00	.235	.000	.250	16	34	4	8	0	0	0	4	6	0	1	0	14	0	0	.235 .350
Rodriguez, Randy	B-R	5-10	175	9-4-95	.241	.455	.200	43	137	18	33	3	5	1	19	12	1	3	3	27	10	4	.358 .301
Santiago, Carlos	B-R	5-11	145	7-24-01	.138	.294	.119	45	152	21	21	3	1	2	12	21	1	1	1	38	4	2	.211 .246
Sequera, Yohandry	R-R	5-10	150	1-25-00	.150	.167	.147	16	40	5	6	0	0	0	2	7	2	0	0	8	0	0	.150 .306
Tomsjansen, Rushenten	R-R	6-0	150	5-14-01	.222	.333	.200	41	126	15	28	3	0	0	7	3	3	3	1	30	4	5	.246 .256
Valdez, Amin	L-R	6-0	155	11-18-00	.184	.200	.181	38	125	17	23	3	4	0	14	22	3	0	0	42	5	1	.272 .320
Valdez, Jesus	R-R	6-0	175	12-29-97	.230	.400	.201	60	204	44	47	11	4	6	27	28	8	0	2	46	16	7	.412 .343
Vargas, Imanol	L-R	6-3	185	6-29-98	.264	.212	.274	62	201	28	53	9	3	4	39	52	2	0	2	50	10	7	.398 .416
Vivas, Jorbit	L-R	5-10	145	3-9-01	.222	.278	.207	51	176	33	39	11	1	0	11	26	11	0	4	35	16	4	.296 .350
Yan, Luis	B-R	6-3	180	1-1-99	.225	.167	.235	36	120	14	27	5	4	0	17	17	0	0	0	36	4	3	.333 .321

Pitching	B-T	HT	WT	DOB	W	L	ERA	G	GS	CG	SV	IP	H	R	ER	HR	BB	SO	AVG	vLH	vRH	K/9	BB/9
Abreu, Jeffry	R-R	6-4	200	1-28-00	0	2	4.01	11	6	0	0	25	30	18	11	0	8	18	.300	.226	.383	6.57	2.92
Acevedo, Axel	R-R	6-2	170	9-23-00	1	1	5.14	20	0	0	2	28	32	20	16	2	14	18	.288	.229	.316	5.79	4.50
Alejo, Carlos	R-R	6-1	165	8-23-99	3	3	3.86	13	8	0	0	44	41	32	19	0	25	34	.237	.287	.186	6.90	5.08
Baez, Wilkin	R-R	6-1	175	11-12-99	1	1	2.19	16	0	0	5	25	17	9	6	0	21	32	.198	.233	.179	11.68	7.66
Beltran, Hugo	R-R	6-1	190	6-13-00	3	3	5.40	22	0	0	3	40	43	29	24	3	12	28	.267	.253	.284	6.30	2.70
Berroa, Israily	R-R	5-11	165	11-17-00	0	3	3.14	12	11	0	0	49	44	25	17	3	20	54	.237	.221	.253	9.99	3.70
Budier, Andrew	L-L	6-0	165	10-20-99	3	3	3.66	18	0	0	0	32	23	18	13	0	27	23	.209	.097	.253	6.47	7.59
Cabrera, Jeisson	R-R	6-2	170	9-5-98	1	3	2.19	14	14	0	0	53	41	17	13	2	22	62	.219	.204	.226	10.46	3.71
Camilo, Darlin	R-R	6-1	190	11-17-99	1	3	6.20	22	0	0	2	25	28	25	17	5	15	27	.283	.300	.275	9.85	5.47
Castillo, Yamil	R-R	6-1	200	8-18-99	1	1	1.13	4	0	0	1	8	4	4	1	1	3	10	.138	.214	.067	11.25	3.38
Castro, Jeronimo	R-R	6-4	200	9-3-96	2	0	4.50	2	0	0	0	4	5	2	2	1	0	6	.294	.211	.270	13.50	0.00
Cruz, Daniel	R-R	6-3	185	10-5-97	2	4	2.55	14	8	0	0	42	33	24	12	0	23	45	.213	.203	.221	9.57	4.89
De Avila, Carlos	R-R	5-11	170	2-11-00	4	2	2.10	22	0	0	1	34	34	15	8	1	9	22	.250	.220	.263	5.77	2.36
De La Paz, Franklin	L-L	6-2	190	3-29-99	5	2	3.28	17	4	0	0	47	43	29	17	0	23	48	.244	.154	.270	9.26	4.44
De Los Santos, Carlos	R-R	6-2	170	11-18-00	2	0	6.85	23	0	0	0	24	21	18	18	0	20	20	.236	.207	.250	7.61	7.61
De Paula, Reinaldo	R-R	5-11	177	10-20-98	6	1	4.28	24	0	0	3	40	30	26	19	1	16	51	.199	.296	.113	11.48	3.60
Duran, Carlos	R-R	6-7	230	7-30-01	0	2	1.50	12	12	0	0	42	29	9	7	1	3	30	.196	.152	.216	6.43	0.64
Galindo, Harold	R-R	6-2	175	1-22-01	0	0	1.93	13	3	0	0	28	18	7	6	0	15	21	.196	.231	.150	6.75	4.82
Gomez, Duany	R-R	6-5	186	9-30-00	1	1	5.53	19	0	0	1	28	29	23	17	4	14	18	.266	.355	.149	5.86	4.55
Gonzalez, Juan	R-R	6-0	165	6-24-00	3	3	2.68	15	11	0	0	57	43	19	17	1	6	38	.211	.246	.196	6.00	0.95
Gutierrez, Stiven	R-L	6-1	180	6-21-01	1	1	6.75	14	0	0	0	15	11	11	11	0	12	12	.208	.200	.209	7.36	6.75
Lara, Breidy	R-R	6-4	180	3-16-99	2	0	2.67	14	3	0	0	27	17	14	8	3	13	27	.179	.094	.222	9.00	4.33
Marcano, Enmanuel	R-R	6-1	185	12-4-98	3	5	2.36	25	0	0	5	34	30	14	9	3	4	33	.227	.225	.230	8.65	1.05
Martinez, Michael	R-R	6-1	185	7-11-99	1	1	2.14	18	0	0	3	21	16	11	5	1	18	18	.211	.333	.172	7.71	7.71
Montilla, Carlos	R-R	5-11	165	7-24-99	4	1	1.87	12	12	0	0	53	40	21	11	2	5	42	.200	.229	.165	7.13	0.85
Moya, Abel	R-R	6-1	172	6-6-01	2	0	3.31	12	0	0	1	16	16	9	6	1	12	10	.246	.250	.245	5.51	6.61
Nunez, Darien	L-L	6-2	205	3-19-93	0	0	0.00	1	0	0	0	2	1	0	0	0	1	3	.143	.270	.206	13.50	4.50
Perez, Luisenyer	L-L	5-11	180	11-9-01	1	1	3.95	14	2	0	0	27	27	15	12	0	24	28	.214	.222	.211	9.22	7.90
Rabsatt, Maykel	R-R	6-3	180	11-14-98	2	2	10.19	15	0	0	1	18	27	24	20	0	12	15	.346	.500	.239	7.64	6.11
Ramirez, Adolfo	R-R	6-0	165	6-1-99	4	2	2.15	18	7	1	3	50	37	14	12	1	10	46	.201	.210	.197	8.23	1.79
Robles, Benony	L-L	6-4	185	10-1-00	2	5	5.30	12	6	0	0	37	31	26	22	1	29	33	.233	.290	.216	7.96	6.99
Rodriguez, Carlos	R-R	6-2	194	4-2-99	0	0	6.75	4	0	0	0	7	8	5	5	0	5	8	.286	.188	.417	10.80	6.75
Rodulfo, Jose	R-R	6-0	165	8-20-00	5	3	1.61	14	13	0	0	62	41	16	11	1	12	57	.186	.128	.218	8.32	1.75
Romero, Jonny	R-R	6-2	170	3-5-99	0	3	6.97	17	0	0	0	21	26	18	16	2	15	21	.310	.390	.233	9.15	6.53
Santana, Martin	R-R	6-1	165	1-30-01	1	1	5.23	19	5	0	0	31	31	20	18	0	35	32	.274	.233	.321	9.29	10.16
Turizo, Jesus	R-R	6-2	192	5-9-01	2	0	6.00	11	0	0	0	15	17	13	10	0	9	7	.298	.235	.325	4.20	5.40
Valdez, Joan	R-R	6-4	175	3-10-99	2	3	2.93	14	14	0	0	58	46	21	19	3	15	59	.214	.223	.204	9.10	2.31
Vasquez, Jonathan	R-R	6-0	170	1-25-00	1	0	5.25	11	0	0	0	12	6	7	7	1	10	12	.146	.071	.185	9.00	7.50
Villicana, Fernando	L-L	5-11	186	8-2-01	1	0	12.19	11	0	0	0	10	16	14	14	1	13	6	.356	.231	.406	5.23	11.32

Fielding

C: Alvarez 16, Chalo 26, Dominguez 12, Fernandez 25, Jardines 12, Noriega 46, Restituyo 1. **1B:** Alvarez 8, Bastardo 6, Bentura 7, Chalo 2, Diaz 15, Garcia 10, Hernandez 4, Jardines 13, Loaisiga 21, Nava 34, Valdez 9, Vargas 30. **2B:** Chirinos 5, Hernandez 4, Leonard 4, Machin 21, Martinez 35, Perez 8, Rodriguez 9, Santiago 2, Sequera 9, Valdez 10, Valdez 22, Vivas 29. **3B:** Chirinos 11, Diaz 35, Leonard 1, Machin 22, Martinez 2, Perez 30, Rodriguez 3, Santiago 8, Sequera 1, Valdez 20, Vivas 16. **SS:** Brito 4, Chirinos 33, Leonard 40, Machin 1, Martinez 3, Perez 5, Rodriguez 2, Santiago 33, Sequera 7, Valdez 23, Valdez 3. **OF:** Catalina 10, Diaz 51, Dominguez 1, Enrique 48, Feliz 9, Garcia 31, Heredia 10, Loaisiga 1, Luis 31, Mateo 57, Pages 34, Perez 41, Restituyo 9, Rodriguez 13, Rodriguez 23, Tomsjansen 37, Vargas 25, Yan 23.

Miami Marlins

SEASON IN A SENTENCE: After trading away outfielders Giancarlo Stanton, Christian Yelich and Marcell Ozuna, as well as second baseman Dee Gordon, in the offseason, the Marlins entered Year One of the Bruce Sherman/Derek Jeter-led rebuild and finished with an NL-worst 63-98 record.

HIGH POINT: The Marlins never managed to break above .500 in 2018, though they did have a season-high four-game winning streak from April 28-May 1. They won two games apiece against the Rockies and Phillies by a combined score of 17-6.

LOW POINT: Hosting the Cubs on Opening Day, Marlins righthander Jose Urena surrendered a home run to Cubs outfielder Ian Happ on the first pitch of the 2018 season, perhaps a sign of things to come. The Marlins suffered three different six-game losing streaks—May 29-June 3, July 30-August 5, August 12-17—and finished last among major league teams in total attendance (811,104) and average attendance (10,013).

NOTABLE ROOKIES: Twenty-six rookies saw action for the Marlins, but none performed better than Brian Anderson, who led the team in on-base percentage (.357), runs (87) and doubles (34) while playing above-average defense at both third base and in right field. Righthander Trevor Richards tied for the team lead in strikeouts (130) while posting a 4.42 ERA in 126.1 innings. Lewis Brinson entered the year as the Marlins' No. 1 prospect, leadoff hitter and everyday center fielder, but he hit just .199/.240/.338 with 11 home runs and 120 strikeouts in 109 games.

KEY TRANSACTIONS: The Marlins' major moves came prior to the season, with the trades of Stanton (Yankees), Yelich (Brewers), Ozuna (Cardinals) and Gordon (Mariners). The trades lowered payroll and helped rebuild a farm system that had become one of the worst in baseball. The Marlins also traded reliever Brad Ziegler (D-backs) and outfielder Cameron Maybin (Mariners) before the July 31 trade deadline.

DOWN ON THE FARM: Triple-A New Orleans, Double-A Jacksonville and low Class A Greensboro all finished below .500 in 2018, while high Class A Jupiter won a system-best 70 games. After the season, it was announced that the Marlins' low Class A affiliate would no longer be in Greensboro, where it had been located for the past 16 seasons. Instead the organization signed a two-year Player Development Contract with the Clinton LumberKings of the Midwest League.

OPENING DAY PAYROLL: $85,843,000 (25th).

PLAYERS OF THE YEAR

ELIOT J. SCHECHTER

MAJOR LEAGUE	MINOR LEAGUE
J.T. Realmuto C	**Nick Neidert** RHP,
.277/.340/.484	(Double-A)
24 HR, 74 RBIs	3.24 ERA, 1.13 WHIP
first-time all-star	154 SO in 153 IP

ORGANIZATION LEADERS

Batting		*Minimum 250 AB
MAJORS		
* AVG	Starlin Castro	.278
* OPS	J.T. Realmuto	.825
HR	J.T. Realmuto	21
RBI	J.T. Realmuto	74
MINORS		
,* AVG	Austin Dean, Jacksonville, New Orleans	.345
* OBP	Eric Campbell, New Orleans	.420
* SLG	Austin Dean, Jacksonville, New Orleans	.511
* OPS	Austin Dean, Jacksonville, New Orleans	.922
R	Monte Harrison, Jacksonville	85
H	Brian Miller, Jupiter, Jacksonville	153
TB	Monte Harrison, Jacksonville	208
2B	Brian Schales, Jacksonville	27
3B	Rafael Ortega, New Orleans	10
HR	Peter O'Brien, Tulsa, Jacksonville, New Orleans	23
RBI	Joe Dunand, Jupiter, Jacksonville	70
BB	Isan Diaz, Jacksonville, New Orleans	68
SO	Monte Harrison, Jacksonville	215
SB	Brian Miller, Jupiter, Jacksonville	40

Pitching		#Minimum 75 IP
MAJORS		
W	Jose Urena	9
# ERA	Jose Urena	3.98
SO	Trevor Richards	130
SV	Kyle Barraclough	10
SV	Brad Ziegler	10
MINORS		
W	Nick Neidert, Jacksonville	12
L	Cody Poteet, Jacksonville, Jupiter	15
# ERA	Dustin Beggs, Greensboro, Jupiter, Jacksonville	2.12
G	Jose Quijada, Jacksonville, New Orleans	44
G	Kyle Keller, Jupiter, Jacksonville, New Orleans	44
G	Dylan Lee, Jupiter, Jacksonville, New Orleans	44
GS	Nick Neidert, Jacksonville	26
SV	Jumbo Diaz, New Orleans, Marlins	12
SV	Chad Smith, Jupiter	12
IP	Nick Neidert, Jacksonville	153
BB	Jorge Guzman, Jupiter	64
SO	Nick Neidert, Jacksonville	154
# AVG	Dustin Beggs, Greensboro, Jupiter, Jacksonville	.216

2018 PERFORMANCE

General Manager: Michael Hill. **Farm Director:** Gary Denbo. **Scouting Director:** Stan Meek/D.J. Svihlik.

Class	Team	League	W	L	PCT	Finish	Manager
Majors	Miami Marlins	National	63	98	.391	15th (15)	Don Mattingly
Triple-A	New Orleans Baby Cakes	Pacific Coast	69	70	.496	10th (16)	Arnie Beyeler
Double-A	Jacksonville Jumbo Shrimp	Southern	55	82	.401	10th (10)	Randy Ready
High A	Jupiter Hammerheads	Florida State	70	64	.522	5th (12)	Kevin Randel
Low A	Greensboro Grasshoppers	South Atlantic	60	76	.441	13th (14)	Todd Pratt
Short season	Batavia Muckdogs	New York-Penn	36	40	.474	t-10th (14)	Mike Jacobs
Rookie	GCL Marlins	Gulf Coast	25	31	.446	12th (18)	John Pachot
Overall 2018 Minor League Record			**315**	**363**	**.465**	**26th (30)**	

ORGANIZATION STATISTICS

MIAMI MARLINS
NATIONAL LEAGUE

Batting	B-T	HT	WT	DOB	AVG	vLH	vRH	G	AB	R	H	2B	3B	HR	RBI	BB	HBP	SH	SF	SO	SB	CS	SLG	OBP
Anderson, Brian	R-R	6-3	185	5-19-93	.273	.252	.280	156	590	87	161	34	4	11	65	62	16	0	2	129	2	4	.400	.357
Bostick, Christopher	R-R	5-10	200	3-24-93	.214	.143	.286	13	14	0	3	1	0	0	2	2	0	0	0	6	0	0	.286	.313
2-team total (2 Pittsburgh)					.188	.143	.222	15	16	0	3	1	0	0	2	2	0	0	0	7	0	0	.250	.278
Bour, Justin	L-R	6-3	265	5-28-88	.227	.197	.241	112	374	43	85	10	1	19	54	69	1	0	3	111	1	0	.412	.347
2-team total (29 Philadelphia)					.227	.192	.242	141	423	49	96	13	1	20	59	73	2	0	3	124	2	0	.404	.341
Brinson, Lewis	R-R	6-3	195	5-8-94	.199	.214	.194	109	382	31	76	10	5	11	42	17	4	0	2	120	2	1	.338	.240
Castro, Starlin	R-R	6-2	230	3-24-90	.278	.293	.274	154	593	76	165	32	2	12	54	48	0	6		124	6	4	.400	.329
Cooper, Garrett	R-R	6-6	230	12-25-90	.212	.429	.154	14	33	2	7	1	0	0	2	4	1	0	0	12	0	0	.242	.316
Dean, Austin	R-R	6-1	190	10-14-93	.221	.130	.244	34	113	16	25	4	0	4	14	7	2	0	0	22	1	0	.363	.279
Dietrich, Derek	L-R	6-0	205	7-18-89	.265	.227	.274	149	499	72	132	26	2	16	45	29	21	0	2	140	2	0	.421	.330
Galloway, Isaac	R-R	6-2	205	10-10-89	.203	.269	.158	43	64	7	13	3	0	3	7	9	0	1	0	21	1	1	.391	.301
Holaday, Bryan	R-R	6-0	205	11-19-87	.205	.156	.226	61	151	7	31	5	0	1	16	10	2	1	2	29	0	0	.258	.261
Lee, Braxton	L-R	5-10	185	8-23-93	.177	.000	.188	8	17	0	3	0	0	0	2	1	0	0	0	8	0	0	.177	.222
Maybin, Cameron	R-R	6-3	215	4-4-87	.251	.262	.243	99	251	20	63	12	1	3	20	32	2	0	2	55	8	5	.343	.338
O'Brien, Peter	R-R	6-4	235	7-15-90	.273	.333	.259	22	66	8	18	5	0	4	10	7	0	0	1	22	0	0	.530	.338
Ortega, Rafael	L-R	5-11	160	5-15-91	.233	.304	.218	41	133	10	31	3	1	0	7	10	0	0	0	23	5	2	.271	.287
Prado, Martin	R-R	6-0	215	10-27-83	.244	.211	.252	54	197	16	48	9	0	1	18	11	1	0	0	35	1	1	.305	.287
Realmuto, J.T.	R-R	6-1	210	3-18-91	.277	.204	.298	125	477	74	132	30	3	21	74	38	10	0	4	104	3	2	.484	.340
Riddle, JT	L-R	6-1	180	10-12-91	.231	.171	.248	102	308	28	71	10	4	9	36	20	0	3	1	67	0	3	.377	.277
Rivera, Yadiel	R-R	6-3	185	5-2-92	.173	.213	.152	111	139	13	24	3	0	1	9	9	0	2		51	2	1	.216	.269
Rojas, Miguel	R-R	5-11	195	2-24-89	.252	.235	.258	153	488	44	123	13	0	11	53	24	9	2	4	69	6	3	.346	.297
Shuck, JB	L-L	5-11	195	6-18-87	.192	.227	.185	70	130	10	25	3	1	0	4	10	1	1	0	22	2	2	.231	.255
Sierra, Magneuris	L-L	5-11	160	4-7-96	.191	.333	.167	54	147	10	28	3	0	0	7	6	0	3	0	39	3	2	.211	.222
Telis, Tomas	B-R	5-8	220	6-18-91	.207	.000	.261	23	29	2	6	1	0	0	1	2	0	0	0	8	0	0	.241	.258
Wallach, Chad	R-R	6-3	230	11-4-91	.178	.182	.177	15	45	4	8	1	0	1	5	4	2	1	0	23	0	0	.267	.275

Pitching	B-T	HT	WT	DOB	W	L	ERA	G	GS	CG	SV	IP	H	R	ER	HR	BB	SO	AVG	vLH	vRH	K/9	BB/9
Alcantara, Sandy	R-R	6-4	170	9-7-95	2	3	3.44	6	6	0	0	34	25	13	13	3	23	30	.214	.191	.241	7.94	6.09
Barraclough, Kyle	R-R	6-3	225	5-23-90	1	6	4.20	61	0	0	10	56	40	27	26	8	34	60	.197	.175	.217	9.70	5.50
Brigham, Jeff	R-R	6-0	200	2-16-92	0	4	6.06	4	4	0	0	16	16	11	11	2	13	12	.271	.250	.296	6.61	7.16
Chen, Wei-Yin	R-L	6-0	200	7-21-85	6	12	4.79	26	26	0	0	133	131	75	71	19	47	111	.256	.198	.272	7.49	3.17
Cloyd, Tyler	R-R	6-3	210	5-16-87	0	0	8.66	7	0	0	0	18	25	17	17	3	10	13	.329	.391	.302	6.62	5.09
Conley, Adam	L-L	6-3	205	5-24-90	3	4	4.09	52	0	0	3	51	37	25	23	5	18	50	.207	.180	.228	8.88	3.20
Despaigne, Odrisamer	R-R	6-0	200	4-4-87	2	0	5.31	11	1	0	0	20	22	16	12	1	8	18	.279	.313	.255	7.97	3.54
Garcia, Jarlin	L-L	6-3	215	1-18-93	3	3	4.91	29	7	0	0	66	59	37	36	16	28	40	.239	.250	.234	5.45	3.82
Gonzalez, Merandy	R-R	6-0	216	10-9-95	2	1	5.73	8	1	0	0	22	31	14	14	4	8	19	.326	.385	.286	7.77	3.27
Graves, Brett	R-R	6-1	170	1-30-93	1	1	5.40	21	0	0	1	33	41	22	20	3	12	21	.311	.350	.278	5.67	3.24
Guerra, Javy	R-R	6-1	225	10-31-85	1	1	5.55	32	0	0	1	36	42	27	22	4	12	30	.292	.275	.307	7.57	3.03
Guerrero, Tayron	R-R	6-8	210	1-9-91	1	3	5.43	60	0	0	0	58	64	40	35	8	30	68	.275	.307	.250	10.55	4.66
Hernandez, Elieser	R-R	6-0	210	5-3-95	2	7	5.21	32	6	0	0	66	68	38	38	11	27	45	.272	.286	.258	6.17	3.70
Kinley, Tyler	R-R	6-4	205	1-31-91	0	0	7.04	9	0	0	0	8	6	6	6	0	4	9	.207	.067	.357	10.57	4.70
Lopez, Pablo	L-R	6-3	200	3-7-96	2	4	4.14	10	10	0	0	59	56	28	27	8	18	46	.252	.246	.259	7.06	2.76
Meyer, Ben	R-R	6-5	180	1-30-93	0	0	10.42	13	0	0	0	19	26	23	22	2	14	9	.338	.385	.290	4.26	6.63
O'Grady, Chris	R-L	6-4	225	4-17-90	0	1	6.43	8	0	0	0	7	7	5	5	2	4	8	.250	.333	.211	10.29	5.14
Peters, Dillon	L-L	5-9	195	8-31-92	2	2	7.16	7	5	0	0	28	34	22	22	4	15	17	.306	.300	.309	5.53	4.88
Richards, Trevor	R-R	6-2	190	5-15-93	4	9	4.42	25	25	0	0	126	121	65	62	15	54	130	.253	.230	.272	9.26	3.85
Rucinski, Drew	R-R	6-2	190	12-30-88	4	2	4.33	32	0	0	0	35	34	21	17	2	13	27	.254	.255	.253	6.88	3.31
Smith, Caleb	R-L	6-2	205	7-28-91	5	6	4.19	16	16	0	0	77	63	36	36	10	33	88	.220	.287	.191	10.24	3.84
Steckenrider, Drew	R-R	6-5	215	1-10-91	4	4	3.90	71	0	0	5	65	55	29	28	7	27	74	.227	.241	.216	10.30	3.76
Straily, Dan	R-R	6-2	220	12-1-88	5	6	4.12	23	23	0	0	122	107	62	56	20	52	99	.237	.264	.207	7.28	3.83
Tazawa, Junichi	R-R	5-11	200	6-6-86	1	1	9.00	22	0	0	0	20	28	21	20	6	14	20	.329	.278	.367	10.80	5.85
Turner, Jacob	R-R	6-5	215	5-21-91	0	0	15.88	4	0	0	0	6	13	10	10	1	5	2	.448	.385	.500	3.18	7.94
Urena, Jose	R-R	6-2	200	9-12-91	9	12	3.98	31	31	1	0	174	155	78	77	19	51	130	.242	.255	.227	6.72	2.64
Wittgren, Nick	R-R	6-2	210	5-29-91	2	1	2.94	32	0	0	0	34	29	13	11	1	15	31	.223	.221	.226	8.29	4.01

				W	L	ERA	G	GS	CG	SV	IP	H	R	ER	HR	BB	SO	AVG	OBP	SLG	K/9	BB/9
Ziegler, Brad	R-R	6-4	220 10-10-79	1	5	3.98	53	0	0	10	52	49	25	23	7	17	37	.254	.292	.221	6.40	2.94
2-team total (29 Arizona)				2	6	3.91	82	0	0	10	74	71	34	32	8	25	50	.257	.297	.230	6.11	3.05

Fielding

Catcher	PCT	G	PO	A	E	DP	PB
Holaday	1.000	50	325	23	0	1	1
Realmuto	.992	112	826	46	7	6	8
Telis	1.000	4	13	1	0	1	0
Wallach	.984	14	112	8	2	1	1

First Base	PCT	G	PO	A	E	DP
Bour	.996	103	707	54	3	75
Cooper	1.000	4	26	3	0	1
Dietrich	.987	33	209	11	3	16
O'Brien	.991	17	105	8	1	11
Prado	1.000	1	8	1	0	0
Realmuto	1.000	13	77	5	0	8
Rivera	1.000	5	4	0	0	1
Rojas	.990	49	89	9	1	14
Telis	1.000	2	7	0	0	1

Second Base	PCT	G	PO	A	E	DP
Bostick	1.000	2	2	1	0	1
Castro	.981	150	271	349	12	77
Dietrich	1.000	4	2	3	0	0
Rivera	1.000	11	6	11	0	4
Rojas	1.000	11	15	27	0	7

Third Base	PCT	G	PO	A	E	DP
Anderson	.942	71	42	87	8	7
Dietrich	.000	2	0	0	0	0
Prado	.981	48	30	71	2	11
Rivera	1.000	29	11	39	0	4
Rojas	.989	39	28	58	1	6

Shortstop	PCT	G	PO	A	E	DP
Riddle	.983	95	115	227	6	47
Rivera	.925	28	16	33	4	8
Rojas	.994	83	123	195	2	31

Outfield	PCT	G	PO	A	E	DP
Anderson	.994	91	167	8	1	1
Bostick	1.000	1	3	0	0	0
Brinson	.968	106	270	2	9	0
Cooper	1.000	9	12	1	0	0
Dean	.983	31	57	1	1	0
Dietrich	.993	97	138	5	1	1
Galloway	1.000	38	45	1	0	0
Lee	1.000	6	7	0	0	0
Maybin	.987	82	154	1	2	1
O'Brien	1.000	2	3	0	1	0
Ortega	.961	34	70	3	3	1
Rivera	1.000	9	9	0	0	0
Shuck	.980	42	48	2	1	0
Sierra	.962	51	98	4	4	0

NEW ORLEANS BABY CAKES
PACIFIC COAST LEAGUE
TRIPLE-A

Batting	B-T	HT	WT	DOB	AVG	vLH	vRH	G	AB	R	H	2B	3B	HR	RBI	BB	HBP	SH	SF	SO	SB	CS	SLG	OBP
Adames, Cristhian	R-B	6-0	185	7-26-91	.270	.361	.244	122	449	58	121	18	3	7	57	38	1	4	6	67	6	3	.370	.324
Bostick, Christopher	R-R	5-10	200	3-24-93	.281	.250	.300	16	64	6	18	1	0	0	6	5	1	0	1	19	1	1	.297	.338
Brinson, Lewis	R-R	6-3	195	5-8-94	.222	.750	.130	6	27	0	6	1	1	0	3	0	0	0	0	6	0	0	.333	.222
Campbell, Eric	R-R	6-3	215	4-9-87	.313	.333	.309	95	326	54	102	21	2	6	68	58	9	0	9	61	8	4	.445	.420
Cooper, Garrett	R-R	6-6	230	12-25-90	.300	.000	.310	9	30	2	9	1	0	1	5	3	1	0	0	5	0	0	.433	.382
Culver, Cito	R-R	6-0	205	8-26-92	.219	.182	.228	67	215	21	47	5	1	4	24	20	0	4	1	78	0	1	.307	.284
Dean, Austin	R-R	6-1	190	10-14-93	.326	.403	.305	87	316	58	103	12	4	9	54	33	6	0	3	49	2	2	.475	.397
Diaz, Chris	R-R	5-10	190	11-9-90	.188	.105	.222	25	64	2	12	0	0	0	7	7	0	3	0	18	1	0	.188	.268
Diaz, Isan	L-R	5-10	185	5-27-96	.204	.217	.198	36	137	19	28	4	4	3	14	15	0	2	1	45	4	0	.358	.281
Galloway, Isaac	R-R	6-2	205	10-10-89	.262	.227	.273	92	324	64	85	21	3	9	30	21	5	4	2	75	20	7	.429	.315
Giavotella, Johnny	R-R	5-8	185	7-10-87	.214	.200	.217	10	28	2	6	2	0	0	3	8	0	0	0	6	1	0	.250	.389
Lee, Braxton	L-R	5-10	185	8-23-93	.235	.264	.222	47	179	24	42	6	2	0	9	19	0	2	1	37	4	6	.291	.307
Millan, J.C.	R-R	6-0	185	1-18-96	.250	.000	.333	3	4	0	1	0	0	0	0	0	0	0	0	1	0	0	.250	.250
Mooney, Peter	L-R	5-6	155	8-19-90	.297	.226	.322	75	239	26	71	8	2	6	35	27	4	3	3	32	3	3	.423	.374
Nola, Austin	R-R	6-0	195	12-28-89	.279	.367	.254	69	226	26	63	16	0	2	32	27	7	0	2	43	2	0	.376	.370
O'Brien, Peter	R-R	6-4	235	7-15-90	.277	.314	.260	36	112	22	31	6	0	8	33	20	1	0	2	40	1	0	.598	.385
Ortega, Rafael	L-R	5-11	160	5-15-91	.275	.274	.275	92	280	51	77	10	10	2	28	44	1	3	0	31	12	1	.404	.375
Othman, Sharif	L-R	5-11	190	3-23-89	.185	.000	.227	8	27	0	5	2	0	0	3	3	0	1	0	5	0	1	.259	.267
Riddle, JT	L-R	6-1	180	10-12-91	.346	.294	.359	21	81	17	28	4	1	3	19	8	0	1	1	15	2	0	.531	.400
Rodriguez, Jonathan	R-R	6-2	250	8-21-89	.248	.230	.253	97	286	50	71	14	0	14	45	50	3	1	4	94	2	0	.444	.362
Shuck, JB	L-L	5-11	195	6-18-87	.327	.265	.353	51	165	28	54	13	0	3	16	23	0	0	2	23	11	1	.461	.405
Sierra, Magneuris	L-L	5-11	160	4-7-96	.260	.270	.258	86	346	48	90	12	5	2	17	13	1	5	2	73	14	5	.341	.287
Telis, Tomas	B-R	5-8	220	6-18-91	.309	.349	.296	76	282	36	87	7	3	4	47	20	2	1	1	30	3	2	.397	.357
Van Slyke, Scott	R-R	6-4	215	7-24-86	.248	.258	.245	45	137	19	34	6	0	8	28	21	2	0	1	43	1	1	.467	.354
Wallach, Chad	R-R	6-3	230	11-4-91	.225	.233	.222	44	147	20	33	7	0	3	16	20	3	1	3	47	0	1	.333	.324

Pitching	B-T	HT	WT	DOB	W	L	ERA	G	GS	CG	SV	IP	H	R	ER	BB	SO	AVG	vLH	vRH	K/9	BB/9
Alcantara, Sandy	R-R	6-4	170	9-7-95	6	3	3.89	19	19	0	0	116	107	51	50	38	88	.246	.258	.237	6.85	2.96
Brigham, Jeff	R-R	6-0	200	2-16-92	5	2	3.44	9	9	0	0	52	53	20	20	13	48	.266	.260	.271	8.25	2.24
Buckelew, James	L-L	6-2	155	8-4-91	1	1	3.38	6	0	0	0	13	15	10	5	6	9	.289	.294	.286	6.08	4.05
Burnett, Sean	L-L	5-11	185	9-17-82	1	2	5.49	17	0	0	0	20	30	13	12	5	23	.361	.364	.361	10.53	2.29
Cloyd, Tyler	R-R	6-3	210	5-16-87	6	5	5.17	17	15	0	0	85	96	52	49	18	68	.282	.276	.286	7.17	1.90
Conley, Adam	L-L	6-3	200	5-24-90	2	4	5.18	8	8	0	0	40	45	24	23	14	25	.280	.267	.282	5.63	3.15
Despaigne, Odrisamer	R-R	6-0	200	4-4-87	2	3	4.36	13	4	0	2	43	52	22	21	12	40	.296	.273	.313	8.31	2.49
Diaz, Jumbo	R-R	6-4	315	2-27-84	6	2	2.34	36	0	0	12	42	35	15	11	19	48	.227	.212	.235	10.20	4.04
Gallen, Zac	R-R	6-2	191	8-3-95	8	9	3.65	25	25	0	0	133	148	60	54	48	136	.281	.312	.262	9.18	3.24
Garcia, Jarlin	L-L	6-3	215	1-18-93	2	2	4.81	9	0	0	0	49	57	31	26	14	33	.291	.269	.299	6.10	2.59
Gonzalez, Severino	R-R	6-2	205	9-28-92	2	2	5.61	21	0	0	3	34	39	22	21	9	23	.298	.321	.285	6.15	2.41
Guerra, Javy	R-R	6-1	225	10-31-85	3	0	0.00	12	0	0	5	17	9	1	0	3	24	.161	.214	.107	12.96	1.62
Gunkel, Joe	R-R	6-5	225	12-30-91	1	1	3.03	22	6	0	1	65	63	23	22	7	49	.260	.250	.266	6.75	0.96
Hernandez, Elieser	R-R	6-0	210	5-3-95	0	0	6.75	1	1	0	0	3	5	3	2	1	2	.417	.333	.500	6.75	3.38
Keller, Kyle	R-R	6-4	200	4-28-93	0	0	1.35	5	0	0	1	7	4	1	1	2	10	.174	.250	.133	13.50	2.70
Kickham, Mike	L-L	6-4	220	12-12-88	1	1	4.06	17	2	0	1	38	36	19	17	7	33	.250	.132	.293	7.88	1.67
Kinley, Jeff	L-L	6-1	195	2-15-92	1	1	3.32	11	0	0	0	19	16	13	7	12	12	.213	.125	.237	5.82	5.82
Kinley, Tyler	R-R	6-4	205	1-31-91	2	2	2.93	40	0	0	8	40	32	18	13	22	56	.213	.230	.202	12.60	4.95
Lee, Dylan	L-L	6-4	210	8-1-94	1	1	3.38	10	0	0	1	16	14	6	6	9	19	.237	.177	.262	10.69	5.06
Lopez, Pablo	L-R	6-3	200	3-7-96	1	1	3.38	4	4	0	0	19	16	9	7	4	15	.222	.286	.127	7.23	1.93
Mahoney, Kolton	R-R	6-1	195	5-20-92	0	1	10.80	1	1	0	0	5	8	6	6	4	5	.381	.385	.375	9.00	7.20
Mazza, Chris	R-R	6-4	180	10-17-89	1	1	3.94	7	0	0	0	16	14	7	7	8	14	.277	.241	.306	7.88	4.50
Meyer, Ben	R-R	6-5	180	1-30-93	4	4	4.24	15	11	0	0	64	67	36	30	19	49	.271	.233	.292	6.93	2.69

Name	B-T	HT	WT	DOB	W	L	ERA	G	GS	CG	SV	IP	H	R	ER	HR	BB	SO	AVG	vLH	vRH	K/9	BB/9
Murray, Colton	R-R	6-0	195	4-22-90	0	0	17.36	4	0	0	0	5	11	11	9	2	2	2	.440	.333	.539	3.86	3.86
Pena, Jose	R-R	6-0	190	3-22-91	0	0	1.08	5	0	0	0	8	3	2	1	0	5	4	.107	.091	.118	4.32	5.40
Peters, Dillon	L-L	5-9	195	8-31-92	6	7	5.61	19	19	0	0	103	129	69	64	15	29	85	.312	.299	.317	7.45	2.54
Quijada, Jose	L-L	6-0	175	11-9-95	2	4	3.32	27	0	0	3	41	24	17	15	2	22	52	.171	.148	.186	11.51	4.87
Richards, Trevor	R-R	6-2	190	5-15-93	3	2	2.06	6	6	0	0	39	31	10	9	4	4	37	.215	.125	.260	8.47	0.92
Rucinski, Drew	R-R	6-2	190	12-30-88	0	0	2.52	14	0	0	0	25	27	10	7	0	6	21	.287	.270	.298	7.56	2.16
Squier, Scott	R-L	6-5	185	9-17-92	0	0	0.00	1	0	0	0	2	0	0	0	0	3	1	.000	.000	.000	3.86	11.57
Turner, Jacob	R-R	6-5	215	5-21-91	1	0	5.82	11	0	0	1	22	31	16	14	4	8	17	.333	.343	.328	7.06	3.32
Wimmers, Alex	L-R	6-2	215	11-1-88	0	0	9.82	4	0	0	0	4	5	4	4	1	3	0	.357	.429	.286	0.00	7.36
Wittgren, Nick	R-R	6-2	210	5-29-91	0	5	5.22	25	0	0	2	29	34	21	17	4	8	34	.283	.300	.271	10.43	2.45

Fielding

Catcher	PCT	G	PO	A	E	DP	PB
Nola	.988	68	529	43	7	1	5
Othman	.967	8	57	2	2	0	1
Telis	.980	29	224	18	5	0	0
Wallach	1.000	40	290	19	0	4	6
Culver	1.000	10	21	24	0	6	
Diaz	1.000	6	4	7	0	1	
Diaz	.969	35	76	80	5	21	
Giavotella	.970	8	13	19	1	3	
Millan	1.000	3	1	3	0	0	
Mooney	1.000	8	19	24	0	8	
Diaz	.971	9	9	24	1	6	
Mooney	.971	66	92	143	7	27	
Riddle	1.000	21	32	65	0	9	

First Base	PCT	G	PO	A	E	DP
Campbell	1.000	8	40	2	0	3
Cooper	1.000	5	26	2	0	4
Culver	1.000	1	3	0	0	0
O'Brien	.992	14	112	7	1	11
Rodriguez	.988	66	465	20	6	38
Telis	.992	29	229	12	2	27
Van Slyke	.987	27	202	19	3	23

Second Base	PCT	G	PO	A	E	DP
Adames	.988	17	30	51	1	12
Bostick	1.000	3	6	8	0	1
Campbell	.984	58	102	145	4	30

Third Base	PCT	G	PO	A	E	DP
Adames	.962	98	60	170	9	12
Bostick	1.000	2	0	3	0	0
Campbell	.963	24	13	39	2	1
Culver	.867	12	3	10	2	1
Diaz	.917	6	5	6	1	2
Rodriguez	.870	7	7	13	3	0

Shortstop	PCT	G	PO	A	E	DP
Adames	1.000	5	3	15	0	2
Campbell	1.000	2	2	8	0	2
Culver	.974	47	66	122	5	35

Outfield	PCT	G	PO	A	E	DP
Bostick	1.000	12	17	1	0	0
Brinson	.889	5	7	1	1	0
Campbell	.500	3	1	0	1	0
Cooper	1.000	4	11	0	0	0
Dean	.977	77	121	4	3	2
Diaz	1.000	2	5	0	0	0
Galloway	.977	86	166	3	4	0
Lee	.980	46	94	4	2	2
O'Brien	1.000	17	40	2	0	0
Ortega	.979	65	92	2	2	0
Shuck	1.000	45	87	3	0	1
Sierra	.981	82	197	12	4	3
Van Slyke	1.000	7	10	1	0	0

JACKSONVILLE JUMBO SHRIMP · DOUBLE-A
SOUTHERN LEAGUE

Batting	B-T	HT	WT	DOB	AVG	vLH	vRH	G	AB	R	H	2B	3B	HR	RBI	BB	HBP	SH	SF	SO	SB	CS	SLG	OBP
Barrett, Kyle	L-R	5-11	185	8-4-93	.228	.143	.250	36	101	12	23	5	4	0	12	9	1	2	2	33	6	1	.356	.292
Brigman, Bryson	R-R	5-11	180	6-19-95	.310	.263	.348	12	42	1	13	2	0	1	6	2	1	0	1	6	2	0	.429	.348
Brinson, Lewis	R-R	6-3	195	5-8-94	.130	.154	.100	8	23	1	3	0	0	1	3	0	0	0	5	1	0	.261	.231
Culver, Cito	R-R	6-0	205	8-26-92	.600	1.000	.500	2	5	1	3	0	0	0	3	3	0	0	0	1	0	1	.600	.750
Davis, Mason	B-R	5-9	175	1-11-93	.193	.174	.198	37	119	14	23	6	3	0	8	7	0	2	1	24	4	2	.294	.236
Dean, Austin	R-R	6-1	190	10-14-93	.420	.526	.387	22	81	13	34	8	1	3	14	6	1	0	0	7	0	0	.654	.466
Diaz, Chris	R-R	5-10	190	11-9-90	.214	.152	.241	57	154	17	33	1	0	0	9	27	2	6	2	44	2	2	.221	.335
Diaz, Isan	L-R	5-10	185	5-27-96	.245	.254	.242	83	294	44	72	19	1	10	42	53	4	3	2	95	10	3	.418	.365
Dunand, Joe	R-R	6-2	205	9-20-95	.212	.206	.215	61	217	25	46	13	0	7	28	16	4	0	2	71	0	1	.369	.276
Ewing, Skyler	R-R	6-1	225	8-22-92	.159	.105	.200	24	44	4	7	2	0	2	3	2	0	0	0	20	0	0	.341	.245
Gotta, Cade	R-R	6-4	205	8-1-91	.254	.177	.278	44	142	27	36	8	3	1	10	19	1	2	1	31	18	3	.373	.344
Harrison, Monte	R-R	6-3	220	8-10-95	.240	.207	.252	136	521	85	125	20	3	19	48	44	14	3	1	215	28	9	.399	.316
Hoo, Chris	R-R	5-9	190	2-19-92	.316	.500	.231	5	19	1	6	0	0	1	1	0	0	0	0	9	0	0	.474	.316
Jagielo, Eric	L-R	6-3	210	5-17-92	.198	.153	.210	121	399	37	79	20	0	11	64	33	5	0	5	138	1	0	.331	.265
Lee, Braxton	L-R	5-10	185	8-23-93	.218	.240	.212	29	110	16	24	6	0	1	7	16	0	0	1	19	3	1	.300	.315
Lusignan, Colby	L-R	6-4	230	11-15-92	.200	.125	.227	10	30	1	6	2	0	0	7	3	0	0	0	16	0	0	.267	.273
Millan, J.C.	R-R	6-0	185	1-18-96	.200	.111	.273	11	20	1	4	4	0	0	2	3	0	0	1	3	1	0	.200	.292
Miller, Brian	L-R	6-1	186	8-20-95	.267	.271	.266	66	262	29	70	8	2	0	14	18	2	5	0	39	21	7	.313	.319
Mooney, Peter	L-R	5-6	155	8-19-90	.000	.000	.000	4	1	0	0	0	0	0	0	0	0	1	0	4	0	0	.000	.000
Norwood, John	R-R	6-1	225	9-24-92	.242	.275	.230	123	396	41	96	18	2	7	32	41	0	0	1	120	14	9	.351	.313
O'Brien, Peter	R-R	6-4	235	7-15-90	.215	.152	.234	43	144	22	31	4	0	13	31	28	1	0	1	49	0	0	.514	.345
Othman, Sharif	L-R	5-11	190	3-23-89	.191	.167	.197	51	162	11	31	5	0	3	17	16	3	1	0	66	0	0	.278	.276
Pintor, Luis	R-R	5-9	170	6-6-95	.050	.059	.044	21	40	0	2	1	0	0	1	4	0	2	0	14	0	0	.075	.136
Riddle, JT	L-R	6-1	180	10-12-91	.286	—	.286	2	7	0	2	0	0	0	0	0	0	0	0	1	0	0	.286	.286
Schales, Brian	R-R	6-1	170	2-13-96	.258	.220	.273	127	422	52	109	27	2	10	49	57	7	1	3	108	4	2	.403	.354
Seymour, Anfernee	B-R	5-11	165	6-24-95	.255	.217	.286	25	51	6	13	4	0	1	5	6	1	0	0	9	4	1	.392	.345
Silviano, John	L-R	5-11	190	7-11-94	.167	.158	.171	20	54	8	9	0	1	3	7	7	3	0	0	24	0	0	.370	.297
Twine, Justin	R-R	5-11	205	10-7-95	.402	.360	.414	28	112	18	45	5	1	4	23	5	2	1	1	23	5	2	.571	.433
Vigil, Rodrigo	R-R	6-0	165		.245	.211	.260	83	286	26	70	13	0	5	22	10	9	5	3	37	1	1	.343	.289

Pitching	B-T	HT	WT	DOB	W	L	ERA	G	GS	CG	SV	IP	H	R	ER	HR	BB	SO	AVG	vLH	vRH	K/9	BB/9
Barker, Brandon	R-R	6-3	210	8-20-92	0	0	10.45	6	1	0	0	10	19	12	12	2	11	11	.396	.529	.323	9.58	9.58
Beggs, Dustin	R-R	6-3	180	6-14-93	1	2	1.44	4	4	1	0	25	17	6	4	1	8	23	.193	.281	.143	8.28	2.88
Brigham, Jeff	R-R	6-0	200	2-16-92	4	1	1.18	7	7	0	0	38	27	5	5	1	9	41	.211	.242	.177	9.71	2.13
Buckelew, James	L-L	6-2	155	8-4-91	0	0	2.25	2	0	0	0	4	5	1	1	1	2		.313	.000	.357	4.50	2.25
2-team total (9 Tennessee)					0	2	4.26	11	1	0	0	23	22	12	11	3	11	17	.289	.207	.324	6.04	3.91
Cavanerio, Jorgan	R-R	6-1	155	8-18-94	0	1	4.97	13	0	0	0	25	32	14	14	3	8	26	.320	.324	.318	9.24	2.84
Crescentini, Marcus	R-R	6-4	240	12-26-92	1	0	3.91	23	0	0	5	35	23	14	11	5	9	34	.250	.419	.164	8.53	6.75
De La Rosa, Esmerling	R-R	6-2	199	5-15-91	0	1	5.14	8	0	0	1	14	17	11	8	1	6	13	.293	.444	.225	8.36	3.86
Del Pozo, Miguel	L-L	6-1	180	10-14-92	5	0	3.97	28	0	0	1	34	37	16	15	3	15	34	.274	.294	.262	9.00	3.97

MIAMI MARLINS

MIAMI MARLINS

Name	B-T	HT	WT	DOB	W	L	ERA	G	GS	CG	SV	IP	H	R	ER	HR	BB	SO	AVG	vLH	vRH		
Dugger, Robert	R-R	6-2	180	7-3-95	7	6	3.79	18	18	3	0	109	100	54	46	13	36	107	.245	.244	.246	8.81	2.96
Duval, Max	R-R	6-5	235	4-15-91	2	11	7.16	24	16	0	0	88	112	80	70	23	30	76	.306	.296	.313	7.77	3.07
Eveld, Tommy	R-R	6-5	195	12-30-93	1	1	0.93	10	0	0	3	10	6	3	1	0	3	14	.177	.167	.182	13.03	2.79
2-team total (3 Jackson)					2	1	0.64	13	0	0	4	14	7	3	1	0	4	19	.146	.100	.179	12.21	2.57
Gonzalez, Merandy	R-R	6-0	216	10-9-95	3	6	4.32	14	14	0	0	73	68	37	35	7	33	47	.256	.320	.201	5.79	4.07
Graves, Brett	R-R	6-1	170	1-30-93	1	1	5.11	5	1	0	0	12	13	7	7	2	6	10	.265	.188	.303	7.30	4.38
Guerrero, Tayron	R-R	6-8	210	1-9-91	0	0	0.00	3	0	0	0	3	1	0	0	0	1	2	.111	.000	.200	6.00	3.00
Hernandez, Elieser	R-R	6-0	210	5-3-95	0	0	4.00	2	2	0	0	9	7	4	4	3	4	10	.219	.125	.250	10.00	4.00
Holmes, Ben	L-L	6-1	195	9-12-91	0	0	4.70	5	0	0	0	8	11	4	4	1	1	5	.324	.364	.304	5.87	1.17
Hovis, Reilly	R-R	6-3	195	10-27-93	0	2	6.14	12	0	0	0	22	25	15	15	3	16	21	.291	.294	.289	8.59	6.55
Keller, Kyle	R-R	6-4	200	4-28-93	1	3	4.34	24	0	0	4	29	22	15	14	2	18	46	.210	.214	.206	14.28	5.59
Kickham, Mike	L-L	6-4	220	12-12-88	0	0	0.00	2	0	0	0	-3	0	0	0	0	0	3	.000	.000	.000	8.10	0.00
Kinley, Jeff	L-L	6-1	195	2-15-92	2	3	3.08	30	0	0	2	38	23	20	13	1	12	39	.166	.154	.172	9.24	2.84
Lee, Dylan	L-L	6-4	210	8-1-94	1	0	0.00	12	0	0	3	15	5	0	0	0	1	19	.100	.091	.107	11.40	0.60
Lemond, Zech	R-R	6-1	170	10-9-92	1	0	4.50	13	0	0	0	20	17	10	10	3	8	19	.230	.259	.213	8.55	3.60
Lopez, Pablo	L-R	6-3	200	3-7-96	1	2	0.62	8	8	0	0	44	30	6	3	3	8	51	.184	.219	.162	10.51	1.65
Mahoney, Kolton	R-R	6-1	195	5-20-92	3	9	4.23	29	11	0	2	89	106	50	42	8	23	67	.295	.343	.266	6.75	2.32
Mazza, Chris	R-R	6-4	180	10-17-89	0	0	4.26	2	0	0	0	6	8	3	3	2	2	2	.320	.333	.313	2.84	2.84
Mills, McKenzie	R-R	6-4	205	11-19-95	0	3	8.10	4	4	0	0	17	22	16	15	3	4	8	.339	.250	.359	4.32	2.16
Neidert, Nick	R-R	6-1	180	11-20-96	12	7	3.24	26	26	0	0	153	142	63	55	17	31	154	.250	.207	.279	9.08	1.83
Newell, Ryan	R-R	6-2	215	6-18-91	0	0	1.93	12	0	0	1	14	17	4	3	1	3	12	.298	.407	.200	7.71	1.93
Pena, Jose	R-R	6-0	190	3-22-91	2	3	5.54	30	0	0	0	37	32	28	23	5	27	41	.230	.300	.191	9.88	6.51
Poteet, Cody	R-R	6-1	190	7-30-94	3	12	5.26	22	21	1	0	120	133	77	70	15	44	99	.287	.283	.289	7.45	3.31
Quijada, Jose	L-L	6-0	175	11-9-95	0	2	2.42	17	0	0	4	22	13	6	6	1	7	29	.171	.103	.213	11.69	2.82
Reed, Chris	L-L	6-3	225	5-20-90	0	1	0.00	1	0	0	0	2	2	1	0	0	0	1	.250	.200	.333	4.50	0.00
Schiraldi, Lukas	R-R	6-6	210	7-25-93	0	1	8.66	14	0	0	0	18	18	18	17	2	24	18	.261	.286	.244	9.17	12.23
Squier, Scott	R-L	6-5	185	9-17-92	1	0	7.62	11	0	0	0	13	17	11	11	1	6	7	.333	.211	.406	4.85	4.15
Straily, Dan	R-R	6-2	220	12-1-88	1	0	5.06	1	1	0	0	5	6	4	3	2	1	6	.261	.667	.200	10.13	1.69
Wittgren, Nick	R-R	6-2	210	5-29-91	0	1	13.50	2	0	0	0	1	4	2	2	2	0	1	.571	.667	.500	6.75	0.00
Yamamoto, Jordan	R-R	6-0	185	5-11-96	1	0	2.12	3	3	0	0	17	12	6	4	1	4	23	.191	.148	.222	12.18	2.12

Fielding

Catcher	PCT	G	PO	A	E	DP	PB
Ewing	.929	2	13	0	1	0	0
Hoo	1.000	5	42	6	0	0	1
Othman	.993	51	411	17	3	2	3
Vigil	.994	83	658	64	4	9	11

First Base	PCT	G	PO	A	E	DP
Diaz	1.000	1	6	0	0	1
Ewing	1.000	5	30	2	0	2
Jagielo	.990	96	660	42	7	76
Lusignan	1.000	5	36	3	0	3
O'Brien	.979	23	130	7	3	14
Silviano	.989	15	88	5	1	10

Second Base	PCT	G	PO	A	E	DP
Brigman	1.000	10	14	21	0	9
Davis	.957	9	21	23	2	6
Diaz	1.000	4	7	7	0	3
Diaz	.975	82	153	200	9	45

	PCT	G	PO	A	E	DP
Millan	1.000	1	1	1	0	1
Pintor	1.000	6	6	9	0	2
Schales	1.000	2	1	1	0	0
Twine	.976	28	50	73	3	20

Third Base	PCT	G	PO	A	E	DP
Davis	1.000	5	1	5	0	0
Diaz	1.000	3	2	4	0	0
Jagielo	.857	9	2	10	2	1
Millan	1.000	5	3	0	0	0
Pintor	.000	1	0	0	0	0
Schales	.924	127	97	171	22	29

Shortstop	PCT	G	PO	A	E	DP
Brigman	1.000	2	1	3	0	0
Culver	1.000	2	3	3	0	0
Davis	.922	20	17	30	4	3
Diaz	.942	45	52	95	9	25
Dunand	.979	60	89	140	5	36

	PCT	G	PO	A	E	DP
Mooney	.952	4	8	12	1	3
Pintor	.960	8	8	16	1	2
Riddle	1.000	2	1	2	0	0

Outfield	PCT	G	PO	A	E	DP
Barrett	1.000	19	37	0	0	0
Brinson	.875	8	14	0	2	0
Davis	.000	1	0	0	0	0
Dean	1.000	21	37	2	0	0
Diaz	1.000	3	4	0	0	0
Gotta	.988	39	78	6	1	1
Harrison	.994	131	310	8	2	0
Lee	.930	25	49	4	4	1
Miller	.992	63	124	2	1	0
Norwood	.974	96	173	12	5	6
O'Brien	1.000	10	17	0	0	0
Pintor	.000	1	0	0	0	0
Seymour	1.000	13	22	2	0	0
Silviano	.000	1	0	0	0	0

JUPITER HAMMERHEADS HIGH CLASS A
FLORIDA STATE LEAGUE

Batting	B-T	HT	WT	DOB	AVG	vLH	vRH	G	AB	R	H	2B	3B	HR	RBI	BB	HBP	SH	SF	SO	SB	CS	SLG	OBP
Allen, Will	R-R	6-3	220	3-25-92	.195	.308	.143	21	82	9	16	5	0	0	4	4	2	0	1	22	1	0	.256	.247
Alonso, Lazaro	L-R	6-3	220	12-17-94	.194	.179	.202	48	160	14	31	4	1	3	19	23	2	0	1	62	2	1	.288	.301
Arcaya, Luis	R-R	6-1	170	2-26-99	—	—	—	1	0	0	0	0	0	0	0	0	0	0	0	0	0	0	—	—
Ayarza, Rodrigo	L-R	5-8	145	2-20-95	.205	.209	.203	43	117	12	24	5	1	0	13	17	2	0	4	12	3	2	.265	.307
Baranek, Cameron	L-L	5-10	195	2-20-95	.208	.127	.246	54	197	22	41	7	1	2	24	13	1	0	1	60	7	6	.284	.259
Bird, Corey	L-L	6-1	185	8-11-95	.215	.222	.212	34	121	21	26	3	0	0	8	20	1	2	1	28	5	2	.240	.329
Brigman, Bryson	R-R	5-11	180	6-19-95	.338	.259	.386	17	71	9	24	4	0	0	5	3	1	1	1	13	4	0	.394	.368
Brown, Micah	R-R	6-2	200	5-9-96	.236	.333	.178	22	72	10	17	1	3	0	3	4	0	0	1	25	0	2	.333	.273
Cespedes, Ricardo	L-L	6-1	195	8-24-97	.500	—	.500	1	2	0	1	0	0	0	0	0	0	0	0	1	0	0	.500	.500
Cooper, Garrett	R-R	6-6	230	12-25-90	.167	.000	.214	7	18	0	3	0	0	0	2	0	0	0	2	0	0		.167	.250
Davis, Mason	B-R	5-9	175	1-11-93	.167	.000	.200	3	12	0	2	0	0	0	1	0	0	0	1	0	1		.167	.154
Devers, Jose	L-R	6-0	155	12-7-99	.250	.000	.400	2	8	1	2	0	0	0	0	0	0	0	0	0	0		.250	.333
Dinicola, Harrison	L-R	6-0	195	4-28-97	.290	.250	.304	9	31	3	9	1	1	1	3	2	0	0	0	8	0	0	.484	.333
Donadio, Michael	L-R	6-0	195	4-23-95	—	—	—	1	0	1	0	0	0	0	0	0	0	0	0	0	0	0	—	—
Dunand, Joe	R-R	6-2	205	9-20-95	.263	.291	.250	66	243	39	64	8	1	7	42	20	5	0	5	54	2	0	.391	.326
Ewing, Skyler	R-R	6-1	225	8-22-92	.091	.111	.077	7	22	2	2	1	0	0	2	6	0	0	0	6	0	0	.273	.286
Garrett, Stone	R-R	6-2	195	11-22-95	.243	.210	.259	64	251	30	61	9	4	5	30	10	3	0	0	85	14	5	.371	.280
Gotta, Cade	R-R	6-4	205	8-1-91	.455	.667	.375	3	11	2	5	0	0	1	2	0	0	0	0	2	0		.727	.455
Gutierrez, Eric	R-L	5-10	205	12-28-93	.293	.333	.266	32	106	17	31	8	1	1	7	8	6	0	0	12	0	1	.415	.375

Name	B-T	HT	WT	DOB	AVG	vLH	vRH	G	AB	R	H	2B	3B	HR	RBI	BB	HBP	SH	SF	SO	SB	CS	SLG	OBP
Hernandez, Michael	R-R	5-10	195	5-24-95	.192	.364	.139	14	47	5	9	1	0	1	4	0	3	0	0	26	0	0	.277	.240
Hollins, Bubba	R-R	6-1	200	12-6-95	.167	.160	.171	21	66	2	11	1	0	1	5	5	2	1	1	15	0	1	.227	.243
Hoo, Chris	R-R	5-9	190	2-19-92	.167	.182	.156	18	54	4	9	5	0	0	5	4	3	0	1	17	0	0	.259	.258
Knapp, Aaron	L-R	5-10	175	11-4-94	.230	.197	.247	74	217	26	50	6	3	0	18	44	2	5	1	52	18	4	.286	.364
Lee, Braxton	L-R	5-10	185	8-23-93	.292	.400	.214	8	24	6	7	0	0	0	3	3	1	1	0	3	0	1	.292	.393
Lopez, B.J.	R-R	5-9	185	9-29-94	.171	.194	.160	36	111	9	19	0	0	0	2	12	1	2	0	32	0	0	.171	.258
Mahan, Riley	L-R	6-3	185	12-31-95	.250	.282	.233	110	424	38	106	23	3	3	40	24	7	3	4	127	7	2	.340	.299
Millan, J.C.	R-R	6-0	185	1-18-96	.292	.222	.333	7	24	3	7	3	0	1	2	1	1	1	0	3	0	0	.542	.346
Miller, Brian	L-R	6-1	186	8-20-95	.324	.337	.317	62	256	28	83	13	3	0	29	14	1	2	3	27	19	6	.398	.358
Morales, Roy	R-R	6-2	195	6-25-95	.255	.267	.247	46	145	23	37	4	1	0	13	14	4	3	3	21	4	0	.297	.331
Nelson, James	R-R	6-2	180	10-18-97	.211	.206	.213	62	232	27	49	10	0	2	28	13	4	1	3	66	1	0	.280	.262
Pintor, Luis	R-R	5-9	170	6-6-95	.179	.286	.136	40	123	17	22	5	0	0	10	13	6	2	1	27	0	0	.220	.287
Pompey, Tristan	B-R	6-4	200	3-23-97	.291	.391	.254	24	86	13	25	5	0	1	13	13	2	0	0	21	4	1	.384	.396
Prado, Martin	R-R	6-0	215	10-27-83	.250	.357	.143	10	28	3	7	1	0	0	2	3	0	0	0	2	0	0	.286	.323
Realmuto, J.T.	R-R	6-1	210	3-18-91	1.000	1.000	1.000	1	3	3	3	1	0	1	1	0	0	0	0	0	0	0	2.333	1.000
Riddle, JT	L-R	6-1	180	10-12-91	.167	.000	1.000	2	6	1	1	1	0	0	1	0	0	0	0	2	0	0	.333	.286
Rindfleisch, Jarett	R-R	6-1	225	9-4-95	.290	.375	.261	13	31	6	9	1	0	0	5	11	7	0	1	14	0	0	.323	.540
Santos, Jhonny	R-R	6-0	160	10-2-96	.196	.200	.194	28	102	11	20	4	0	1	9	6	1	0	1	21	4	1	.265	.246
Schubert, Gunnar	R-R	5-11	205	5-19-96	.424	.375	.440	10	33	3	14	3	0	0	2	4	0	0	0	8	0	0	.515	.487
Seymour, Anfernee	B-R	6-2	165	6-24-95	.284	.278	.287	51	201	27	57	11	5	3	24	13	1	3	2	48	16	5	.433	.327
2-team total (24 Florida)					.257	.260	.255	75	288	34	74	17	6	3	30	19	1	4	4	76	20	7	.389	.301
Silviano, John	L-R	5-11	190	7-11-94	.281	.230	.305	65	228	31	64	8	2	12	39	30	0	0	1	61	1	5	.491	.363
Smith, Milton	L-L	5-10	165	9-25-97	.455	.500	.444	5	11	3	5	0	1	0	0	0	0	0	0	1	0	0	.636	.455
Sullivan, Zach	R-R	6-3	180	11-26-95	.125	.208	.075	22	64	8	8	2	1	0	1	1	0	0	0	27	1	0	.188	.139
Twine, Justin	R-R	5-11	205	10-7-95	.235	.179	.268	70	226	22	53	8	5	3	31	10	4	1	3	54	8	4	.354	.276
Vazquez, Boo	L-R	6-4	220	4-4-93	.224	.200	.238	20	67	8	15	6	2	1	6	9	1	0	0	20	0	0	.418	.325

Pitching

Name	B-T	HT	WT	DOB	W	L	ERA	G	GS	CG	SV	IP	H	R	ER	HR	BB	SO	AVG	vLH	vRH	K/9	BB/9
Aiello, Vincenzo	R-R	6-3	220	8-6-94	4	1	4.76	24	0	1	0	28	20	15	15	3	7	26	.200	.200	.200	8.26	2.22
Alcantara, Sandy	R-R	6-4	170	9-7-95	3	0	3.97	3	3	0	0	11	10	5	5	0	5	8	.238	.267	.167	6.35	3.97
Beggs, Dustin	R-R	6-3	180	6-14-93	2	2	2.01	7	7	1	0	45	33	16	10	3	6	35	.203	.230	.171	7.05	1.21
Bugg, Parker	R-R	6-6	210	10-26-94	2	1	3.07	37	1	0	1	67	49	27	23	9	13	81	.203	.259	.157	10.83	1.74
Burnett, Sean	L-L	5-11	185	9-17-82	0	0	0.00	1	0	0	0	1	1	0	0	0	0	1	.250	.000	.500	9.00	0.00
Castano, Daniel	L-L	6-4	230	9-17-94	5	8	4.74	14	14	0	0	76	95	48	40	3	24	56	.306	.260	.329	6.63	2.84
Cavanerio, Jorgan	R-R	6-1	155	8-18-94	6	2	2.54	28	0	0	3	46	48	22	13	2	5	42	.260	.259	.260	8.22	0.98
Chen, Wei-Yin	R-L	6-0	200	7-21-85	1	0	1.17	2	2	1	0	8	5	1	1	0	1	11	.172	.182	.167	12.91	1.17
Clark, Ethan	R-R	6-5	235	10-26-94	1	5	4.01	10	8	0	0	43	46	26	19	4	22	40	.281	.296	.263	8.44	4.64
Crescentini, Marcus	R-R	6-4	240	12-26-92	0	0	4.50	2	0	0	1	2	1	1	1	1	2	1	.143	.250	.000	9.00	4.50
De La Rosa, Esmerling	R-R	6-2	199	5-15-91	0	3	4.70	25	5	0	1	52	59	28	27	6	15	39	.291	.298	.283	6.79	2.61
Despaigne, Odrisamer	R-R	6-0	200	4-4-87	0	0	9.00	1	1	0	0	1	1	1	1	1	1	1	.250	.333	.000	9.00	9.00
Dugger, Robert	R-R	6-2	180	7-3-95	3	1	2.40	7	7	0	0	41	40	14	11	2	7	34	.252	.246	.258	7.40	1.52
Farnworth, Steven	R-R	6-2	175	9-6-93	0	0	67.50	2	0	0	0	1	5	5	5	0	3	1	.714	.500	1.000	9.00	40.50
Graves, Brett	R-R	6-1	170	1-30-93	0	1	6.43	2	2	0	0	7	8	5	5	1	1	7	.308	.286	.333	9.00	1.29
Guenther, Sean	L-L	5-11	194	12-29-95	0	1	4.83	7	7	0	0	32	48	22	17	5	3	13	.358	.375	.355	3.69	0.85
Guzman, Jorge	R-R	6-2	182	1-28-96	0	9	4.03	21	21	0	0	96	84	49	43	7	64	101	.239	.273	.204	9.47	6.00
Hernandez, Elieser	R-R	6-0	210	5-3-95	0	1	6.00	2	2	0	0	6	9	6	4	2	4	5	.333	.125	.421	7.50	6.00
Holmes, Ben	L-L	6-0	195	9-12-91	0	0	7.36	3	0	0	0	4	7	3	3	1	4	4	.438	.500	.400	9.82	9.82
Hovis, Reilly	R-R	6-3	195	10-27-93	2	1	3.58	22	0	0	0	28	24	12	11	1	11	34	.233	.326	.167	11.06	3.58
Keller, Kyle	R-R	6-4	200	4-28-93	1	1	1.59	15	0	0	4	17	11	5	3	1	1	22	.177	.174	.180	11.65	0.53
Lee, Dylan	L-L	6-4	210	8-1-94	6	2	1.45	22	0	0	0	31	19	6	5	1	12	25	.174	.200	.159	7.26	3.48
Lemond, Zech	R-R	6-1	170	10-9-92	3	0	0.64	20	0	0	2	28	16	7	2	1	8	25	.172	.130	.213	8.04	2.57
Lillie, Ryan	R-R	6-2	210	5-1-96	0	4	4.93	7	7	0	0	35	32	20	19	4	11	27	.246	.282	.203	7.01	2.86
Mateo, Alejandro	R-R	6-2	200	1-18-94	2	1	3.31	35	0	0	0	71	59	32	26	6	25	72	.224	.274	.187	9.17	3.18
McGrane, Jameson	R-R	6-4	190	6-3-96	1	0	0.00	2	0	0	0	2	2	0	0	0	1	3	.286	.500	.000	16.20	5.40
McKay, Ryan	R-R	6-4	195	9-20-96	0	0	1.29	3	0	0	0	7	6	1	1	0	2	10	.240	.333	.211	12.86	2.57
Mertz, Michael	R-R	6-2	220	9-24-93	2	0	6.75	9	0	0	0	11	13	13	8	1	10	5	.310	.294	.320	4.22	8.44
Neubeck, Travis	L-R	6-2	180	3-13-95	0	1	3.09	10	0	0	0	12	11	8	4	1	3	13	.239	.269	.200	10.03	2.31
Perez, Sam	R-R	6-2	210	8-19-94	2	2	4.14	9	8	0	0	41	34	19	19	2	23	26	.235	.288	.198	5.66	5.01
Poteet, Cody	R-R	6-1	190	7-30-94	1	3	3.60	4	4	0	0	25	21	12	10	2	5	29	.228	.250	.205	10.44	1.80
Puckett, Brady	R-R	6-8	220	7-31-95	7	1	2.33	12	11	0	1	70	69	18	18	0	13	42	.264	.270	.258	5.43	1.68
Roeder, Josh	R-R	6-2	175	12-2-94	6	6	3.63	16	15	0	0	92	90	45	37	9	20	60	.254	.275	.228	5.89	1.96
Rucinski, Drew	R-R	6-2	190	12-30-88	0	0	0.00	2	0	0	0	3	1	0	0	0	0	2	.100	.000	.250	6.00	0.00
Schiraldi, Lukas	R-R	6-6	210	7-25-93	2	2	1.69	22	0	0	0	27	17	9	5	1	11	30	.181	.136	.220	10.13	3.71
Smith, Chad	R-R	6-4	200	6-8-95	5	3	3.57	30	0	0	12	35	22	14	2	22	45	.200	.266	.131	11.46	5.60
Squier, Scott	R-L	6-5	185	9-17-92	1	0	0.00	7	0	0	1	9	6	0	0	0	1	9	.188	.077	.263	9.00	1.00
Straily, Dan	R-R	6-2	220	12-1-88	1	1	8.22	2	2	0	0	8	11	8	7	2	3	6	.314	.182	.375	7.04	3.52
Villalobos, Eli	R-R	6-4	195	6-26-97	0	0	18.00	1	0	0	0	1	2	2	2	0	1	0	.500	.333	1.000	0.00	9.00
Yamamoto, Jordan	R-R	6-0	185	5-11-96	4	1	1.55	7	7	0	0	41	26	8	7	0	8	47	.182	.250	.143	10.40	1.77

Fielding

Catcher	PCT	G	PO	A	E	DP	PB
Allen	.961	8	69	5	3	1	2
Arcaya	.000	1	0	0	0	0	0
Ewing	1.000	4	35	0	0	2	0
Hernandez	.983	14	100	13	2	0	2
Hoo	1.000	18	122	17	0	0	2
Lopez	.991	36	291	28	3	3	1
Morales	.986	45	321	27	5	2	2
Realmuto	1.000	1	2	1	0	0	0
Rindfleisch	.990	13	85	13	1	0	1

First Base	PCT	G	PO	A	E	DP
Allen	1.000	6	57	5	0	4
Alonso	.966	31	243	16	9	20
Brown	.965	11	82	1	3	7
Cooper	1.000	4	22	2	0	1

	PCT	G	PO	A	E	DP
Dinicola	1.000	9	72	8	0	3
Ewing	1.000	2	17	0	0	1
Gutierrez	.994	23	162	12	1	14
Hollins	.990	12	87	11	1	7
Millan	1.000	1	7	0	0	0
Silviano	.991	40	326	19	3	32

Second Base	PCT	G	PO	A	E	DP
Ayarza	1.000	21	29	54	0	15
Brown	.933	3	4	10	1	1
Davis	1.000	1	3	1	0	0
Mahan	.970	92	160	267	13	49
Millan	1.000	1	1	1	0	0
Pintor	.909	2	7	3	1	0
Twine	.965	17	19	36	2	5

Third Base	PCT	G	PO	A	E	DP
Ayarza	.917	19	10	34	4	3

	PCT	G	PO	A	E	DP
Brown	.938	7	3	12	1	1
Davis	1.000	2	2	2	0	0
Hollins	1.000	9	4	11	0	1
Millan	1.000	3	2	1	0	0
Nelson	.948	48	28	63	5	4
Pintor	.889	8	3	13	2	1
Prado	.923	10	6	18	2	2
Twine	.925	40	23	75	8	7

Shortstop	PCT	G	PO	A	E	DP
Brigman	1.000	16	25	44	0	11
Brown	1.000	2	3	6	0	2
Devers	1.000	2	1	3	0	0
Dunand	.962	62	85	165	10	29
Pintor	.912	30	50	64	11	15
Riddle	1.000	2	3	4	0	1
Schubert	.953	10	14	27	2	2
Twine	.892	13	12	21	4	5

Outfield	PCT	G	PO	A	E	DP
Baranek	.975	49	111	5	3	1
Bird	1.000	32	58	4	0	2
Cespedes	1.000	1	2	0	0	0
Cooper	1.000	3	3	0	0	0
Garrett	.979	61	130	7	3	0
Gotta	1.000	3	7	0	0	0
Knapp	.975	71	148	6	4	0
Lee	1.000	7	9	0	0	0
Miller	.992	59	119	3	1	0
Pompey	.964	16	27	0	1	0
Santos	.984	26	58	2	1	0
Seymour	.953	45	76	5	4	0
Smith	1.000	4	8	0	0	0
Sullivan	1.000	20	36	1	0	1
Twine	.000	2	0	0	0	0
Vazquez	1.000	13	22	0	0	0

GREENSBORO GRASSHOPPERS

LOW CLASS A

SOUTH ATLANTIC LEAGUE

Batting	B-T	HT	WT	DOB	AVG	vLH	vRH	G	AB	R	H	2B	3B	HR	RBI	BB	HBP	SH	SF	SO	SB	CS	SLG	OBP
Allen, Will	R-R	6-3	220	3-25-92	.267	.147	.302	43	150	25	40	9	1	9	29	10	2	2	1	34	1	0	.520	.319
Alonso, Lazaro	L-R	6-3	220	12-17-94	.336	.311	.346	43	149	20	50	15	0	4	25	23	1	0	0	51	2	0	.517	.428
Ayarza, Rodrigo	L-R	5-8	145	2-20-95	.231	.143	.250	14	39	5	9	2	0	2	5	3	0	0	0	6	0	0	.436	.286
Banfield, Will	R-R	6-0	200	11-18-99	.208	.235	.194	15	48	5	10	0	0	3	4	4	0	0	0	15	0	0	.396	.269
Baranek, Cameron	L-L	5-10	195	2-20-95	.319	.200	.342	28	94	22	30	3	0	4	15	13	1	0	2	19	4	2	.479	.400
Brown, Micah	R-R	6-2	200	5-9-96	.221	.194	.232	74	249	29	55	11	1	6	26	20	4	3	2	82	11	1	.345	.287
Castro, Samuel	B-R	5-10	160	10-16-97	.262	.179	.295	61	195	24	51	12	2	1	23	11	9	1	0	52	6	2	.359	.330
Cespedes, Ricardo	L-L	6-1	205	8-24-97	.215	.238	.209	33	107	9	23	4	1	1	6	6	1	2	1	26	5	0	.299	.261
Devers, Jose	L-R	6-0	155	12-7-99	.273	.275	.272	85	337	46	92	12	4	0	24	15	5	4	1	49	13	6	.332	.313
Dinicola, Harrison	L-R	6-0	195	4-28-97	.206	.200	.206	23	73	3	15	3	0	0	6	11	0	0	1	21	0	1	.247	.306
Encarnacion, Jerar	R-R	6-4	219	10-22-97	.074	.118	.054	16	54	3	4	0	0	0	2	5	0	0	0	23	0	0	.074	.153
Fortes, Nick	R-R	6-0	210	11-11-96	.118	—	.118	5	17	1	2	0	0	0	1	3	0	0	1	1	0	0	.118	.250
Gutierrez, Eric	R-L	5-10	205	12-28-93	.264	.105	.321	19	72	5	19	4	0	2	11	4	1	0	1	15	1	0	.403	.308
Hernandez, Michael	R-R	5-10	195	5-24-95	.176	.228	.157	62	210	21	37	10	0	4	23	15	2	2	2	88	0	1	.281	.236
Hollins, Bubba	R-R	6-1	200	12-6-95	.065	.125	.044	11	31	0	2	0	0	0	1	3	0	0	4	0	0	0	.065	.216
Johnson, Osiris	R-R	6-0	181	10-18-00	.188	.120	.271	23	85	4	16	3	0	2	6	1	1	0	1	34	0	2	.294	.205
Jones, Thomas	R-R	6-4	195	12-9-97	.222	.232	.219	103	396	55	88	17	2	9	33	25	7	4	5	140	20	8	.343	.277
Karas, Denis	R-R	5-11	180	11-27-95	.200	.333	.177	6	20	2	4	1	0	0	1	2	0	0	0	6	0	0	.250	.273
Knapp, Aaron	L-R	5-10	175	11-4-94	.303	.222	.316	21	66	10	20	2	1	1	9	10	3	1	16	4	2	.409	.454
Lara, Garvis	L-R	6-0	170	5-19-96	.217	.200	.221	82	258	35	56	17	2	4	29	18	4	5	1	74	10	7	.345	.278
Lopez, B.J.	R-R	5-9	185	9-29-94	.205	.095	.246	24	78	11	16	4	0	0	6	7	2	1	1	21	0	0	.256	.284
Millan, J.C.	R-R	6-0	185	1-18-96	.224	.304	.194	25	85	13	19	3	0	2	6	12	0	1	0	11	2	0	.329	.320
Osborne, J.D.	R-R	6-1	215	7-13-95	.245	.214	.257	16	49	3	12	2	2	1	4	1	0	0	0	8	0	0	.429	.260
Pompey, Tristan	B-R	6-4	200	3-23-97	.314	.267	.324	24	86	12	27	4	0	2	9	16	0	1	0	22	5	3	.430	.422
Rivera, Marcos	R-R	6-1	160	5-31-97	.232	.195	.247	110	392	41	91	14	1	12	43	25	1	3	5	142	4	2	.365	.277
Santos, Jhonny	R-R	6-0	160	10-2-96	.268	.286	.262	79	265	32	71	17	2	7	35	28	4	5	4	64	15	7	.426	.342
Schubert, Gunnar	R-R	5-11	205	5-19-96	.162	.500	.069	12	37	4	6	0	0	0	2	3	0	0	0	15	1	0	.162	.225
Scott, Connor	L-L	6-4	180	10-8-99	.211	.250	.196	23	76	4	16	2	0	1	5	10	0	1	2	27	1	3	.276	.296
Soto, Isael	L-L	6-0	190	11-6-96	.230	.197	.238	96	339	47	78	20	3	15	69	32	4	0	5	97	2	3	.440	.300
Sullivan, Zach	R-R	6-3	180	11-26-95	.226	.167	.260	34	115	14	26	10	0	2	14	5	1	5	0	32	3	1	.365	.265
Torres, Christopher	B-R	5-11	170	2-6-98	.250	.130	.292	30	88	20	22	0	1	1	6	21	0	1	0	30	3	1	.307	.395

Pitching	B-T	HT	WT	DOB	W	L	ERA	G	GS	CG	SV	IP	H	R	ER	HR	BB	SO	AVG	vLH	vRH	K/9	BB/9
Aiello, Vincenzo	R-R	6-3	220	8-6-94	1	0	0.50	3	0	0	7	18	11	2	1	0	2	22	.172	.250	.111	11.00	2.00
Bautista, Nestor	L-L	6-3	200	5-13-92	1	2	2.64	37	1	0	2	75	64	23	22	10	13	89	.225	.211	.234	10.68	1.56
Beggs, Dustin	R-R	6-3	180	6-14-93	3	1	2.66	14	4	0	1	41	38	20	12	4	6	53	.242	.299	.188	11.73	1.33
Braley, Taylor	R-R	5-11	140	1-13-96	5	9	4.79	18	18	0	0	103	119	60	55	13	24	83	.285	.303	.266	7.23	2.09
Cabrera, Edward	R-R	6-4	175	4-13-98	4	8	4.22	22	22	1	0	100	105	57	47	11	42	93	.270	.299	.239	8.34	3.77
Castano, Daniel	L-L	6-4	230	9-17-94	4	3	2.70	8	8	1	0	50	48	18	15	10	4	52	.247	.116	.285	9.36	0.72
Castellanos, Gabriel	L-L	6-1	165	12-28-93	1	2	7.71	20	0	0	0	26	33	28	22	0	15	27	.317	.290	.333	9.47	5.26
Clark, Ethan	R-R	6-5	235	10-26-94	1	2	4.45	6	4	0	0	30	34	17	15	2	12	38	.276	.213	.316	11.27	3.56
Farnworth, Steven	R-R	6-2	175	9-6-93	0	0	2.89	9	0	0	1	10	9	4	3	1	2	10	.256	.313	.217	9.64	1.93
Frohwirth, Tyler	R-R	6-1	165	9-13-93	0	0	6.14	8	0	0	2	7	10	7	5	2	0	4	.313	.316	.308	4.91	0.00
Guenther, Sean	L-L	5-11	194	12-29-95	4	3	4.45	13	8	1	0	55	65	37	27	5	9	40	.294	.227	.323	6.59	0.82
Hock, Colton	R-R	6-4	220	3-15-96	9	8	4.45	30	10	0	1	91	97	50	45	12	21	77	.275	.343	.214	7.62	2.08
Hovis, Reilly	R-R	6-3	195	10-27-93	1	0	3.60	3	0	0	0	5	4	2	2	0	1	9	.222	.364	.000	16.20	1.80
Howe, Bryce	R-R	6-2	250	11-27-95	1	2	3.86	14	0	0	2	21	32	15	9	2	8	19	.364	.381	.343	8.14	3.43
Lillie, Ryan	R-R	6-0	210	5-1-96	6	2	2.58	14	14	2	0	80	68	32	23	8	10	77	.227	.204	.254	8.63	1.12
McGrane, Jameson	R-R	6-4	190	6-25-92	0	0	27.00	1	0	0	0	3	3	3	3	0	3	1	.500	.000	.600	9.00	27.00
McKay, Ryan	R-R	6-4	195	9-20-96	1	1	9.53	9	0	0	1	11	17	12	12	1	5	9	.333	.278	.364	7.15	3.97
Mertz, Michael	R-R	6-2	220	9-24-93	2	6	5.36	33	0	0	5	47	44	33	28	6	23	55	.266	.242	.235	10.53	4.40
Miller, Brandon	R-R	6-4	210	6-16-95	3	9	5.21	28	17	0	1	123	138	77	71	23	30	101	.282	.270	.293	7.41	2.20

MIAMI MARLINS

	B-T	HT	WT	DOB	W	L	ERA	G	GS	CG	SV	IP	H	R	ER	HR	BB	SO	AVG	vLH	vRH	K/9	BB/9
Neubeck, Travis	L-R	6-2	180	3-13-95	2	1	1.71	18	0	0	2	21	18	6	4	0	5	26	.234	.231	.237	11.14	2.14
Ovalle, Jeremy	R-R	6-3	185	1-17-97	0	3	5.82	16	0	0	3	22	28	16	14	4	20	28	.311	.447	.212	11.63	8.31
Peace, RJ	R-R	6-2	175	6-24-97	2	0	9.42	11	0	0	1	14	16	15	15	3	6	17	.286	.211	.444	10.67	3.77
Puckett, Brady	R-R	6-8	220	7-31-95	1	3	1.99	8	8	0	0	50	51	18	11	2	4	48	.266	.262	.270	8.70	0.72
Reed, Chris	L-L	6-3	225	5-20-90	1	0	1.80	3	0	0	0	5	7	1	1	0	1	3	.333	.167	.400	5.40	1.80
Reed, Remey	R-R	6-5	230	5-5-95	1	0	1.80	2	0	0	0	5	2	1	1	1	2	7	.133	.167	.111	12.60	3.60
Rodriguez, Manuel	L-L	6-2	160	12-23-96	1	1	4.32	17	0	0	3	25	27	17	12	6	13	23	.262	.265	.261	8.28	4.68
Rogers, Trevor	L-L	6-5	185	11-13-97	2	7	5.82	17	17	0	0	73	86	48	47	4	27	85	.295	.303	.290	10.53	3.34
Sebald, Scott	L-L	6-5	230	6-16-94	2	3	5.79	10	5	0	0	28	31	20	18	6	11	24	.267	.296	.250	7.71	3.54
Wolf, Zach	R-R	5-8	175	11-15-97	1	0	0.00	6	0	0	0	7	3	0	0	0	4	10	.125	.100	.143	13.50	5.40

Fielding

C: Allen 23, Banfield 14, Fortes 5, Hernandez 62, Lopez 24, Osborne 10. **1B:** Allen 20, Alonso 31, Brown 25, Dinicola 18, Encarnacion 1, Gutierrez 17, Hollins 4, Lara 13, Millan 5, Osborne 3. **2B:** Ayarza 13, Brown 6, Castro 37, Devers 15, Lara 43, Schubert 7, Torres 21. **3B:** Brown 24, Castro 11, Hollins 6, Karas 6, Lara 11, Millan 14, Rivera 67. **SS:** Brown 1, Devers 59, Johnson 23, Lara 11, Rivera 35, Schubert 5, Torres 6. **OF:** Baranek 21, Brown 11, Cespedes 26, Encarnacion 12, Jones 92, Knapp 20, Pompey 20, Santos 77, Scott 22, Soto 75, Sullivan 34.

BATAVIA MUCKDOGS

NEW YORK-PENN LEAGUE

SHORT-SEASON

Batting	B-T	HT	WT	DOB	AVG	vLH	vRH	G	AB	R	H	2B	3B	HR	RBI	BB	HBP	SH	SF	SO	SB	CS	SLG	OBP
Baez, Igor	R-R	6-1	214	6-6-95	.207	.152	.227	39	121	12	25	5	0	1	11	13	2	0	3	26	0	0	.273	.288
Bird, Corey	L-L	6-1	185	8-11-95	.188	.250	.167	5	16	2	3	1	0	0	1	6	0	0	0	1	2	2	.250	.409
Bradshaw, Davis	L-R	6-3	175	4-25-98	.324	.235	.352	19	71	7	23	2	0	0	6	3	2	0	1	14	5	4	.352	.368
Brooks, Matt	R-R	6-0	185	3-21-96	.212	.261	.200	35	113	10	24	2	0	1	6	10	1	2	0	29	3	0	.257	.282
Cespedes, Ricardo	L-L	6-1	205	8-24-97	.241	.211	.250	23	83	13	20	3	2	0	13	5	1	1	1	12	4	1	.325	.289
Donadio, Michael	L-R	6-0	195	4-23-95	.274	.258	.277	56	197	26	54	12	1	5	26	19	5	2	3	63	8	2	.421	.348
Encarnacion, Jerar	R-R	6-4	219	10-22-97	.284	.359	.254	43	183	30	52	14	2	4	24	4	2	0	1	57	1	1	.448	.305
Fish, Keegan	B-R	5-11	190	9-11-99	.333	.000	.500	1	3	0	1	0	0	0	1	1	0	0	0	2	1	0	.333	.500
Fortes, Nick	R-R	6-0	210	11-11-96	.500	.250	.667	3	10	3	5	0	0	0	3	2	1	0	0	0	0	0	.500	.615
Garcia, Pablo	R-R	5-10	170	9-26-96	.278	.364	.256	19	54	3	15	2	0	0	5	5	0	0	0	9	0	0	.315	.339
Guaimaro, Albert	R-R	6-0	180	1-17-99	.257	.226	.270	57	210	28	54	8	3	1	17	17	3	1	2	37	5	5	.338	.319
Hernandez, Brayan	R-R	6-2	175	9-11-97	.215	.303	.177	55	219	28	47	13	3	3	18	20	1	5	1	58	10	2	.343	.282
Hollins, Bubba	R-R	6-1	200	12-6-95	.222	.375	.158	25	81	11	18	5	0	1	11	14	1	0	0	16	1	2	.321	.344
Jarvis, Luke	R-R	5-10	191	12-7-94	.217	.233	.212	48	161	12	35	9	1	2	12	11	2	1	1	39	6	3	.323	.274
Karas, Denis	R-R	5-11	180	11-27-95	.223	.236	.217	55	193	19	43	10	1	2	30	19	2	0	4	72	1	0	.316	.294
Nunez, Gerardo	R-R	6-1	180	2-6-98	.135	.179	.118	33	96	8	13	0	0	1	4	3	0	5	0	30	4	3	.167	.162
Osborne, J.D.	R-R	6-1	215	7-13-95	.340	.424	.301	30	106	15	36	7	1	3	20	13	3	0	3	14	1	1	.509	.416
Reynolds, Sean	L-R	6-7	237	4-19-98	.193	.178	.198	76	270	49	52	12	2	17	52	42	3	0	2	133	13	1	.441	.306
Reynoso, Ronal	L-R	6-1	165	5-23-98	.125	.000	.143	6	8	1	1	0	0	0	0	1	0	1	0	1	0	0	.125	.222
Schubert, Gunnar	L-R	5-11	205	5-19-96	.293	.222	.306	17	58	5	17	6	1	0	4	4	0	0	0	16	0	1	.431	.339
Sims, Demetrius	R-R	6-2	200	7-14-95	.227	.210	.235	57	194	30	44	8	1	1	16	18	5	6	2	53	9	4	.294	.306
Torres, Christopher	B-R	5-11	170	2-6-98	.348	.143	.438	7	23	6	8	1	1	1	4	4	0	0	1	5	0	1	.609	.429
Turner, Andrew	R-R	6-2	190	9-26-95	.286	.333	.000	3	7	0	2	1	0	0	0	1	0	0	0	4	0	1	.429	.375
White, Harrison	L-R	5-11	175	11-18-94	.000	.000	.000	5	11	2	0	0	0	0	1	0	0	0	0	5	0	0	.000	.267

Pitching	B-T	HT	WT	DOB	W	L	ERA	G	GS	CG	SV	IP	H	R	ER	HR	BB	SO	AVG	vLH	vRH	K/9	BB/9
Alcala, Elkin	R-R	5-11	175	8-2-97	4	2	3.30	21	0	0	5	30	33	16	11	2	5	22	.277	.178	.338	6.60	1.50
Anderson, Martin	R-L	6-1	175	1-13-93	1	1	8.16	7	2	0	0	14	20	22	13	4	18	11	.333	.333	.333	6.91	11.30
Andrews, Tanner	R-R	6-3	220	11-15-95	2	0	3.72	12	2	0	0	29	29	14	12	3	5	25	.254	.239	.265	7.76	1.55
Bennett, Dakota	B-L	6-2	160	7-12-99	0	2	8.68	3	3	0	0	9	21	21	9	2	4	9	.438	.429	.444	8.68	3.86
Boyd, Logan	L-L	6-2	205	11-26-93	0	2	2.81	3	3	0	0	16	15	7	5	0	4	9	.254	.333	.200	5.06	2.25
Carter, C.J.	R-R	6-0	165	5-29-97	3	2	3.95	18	0	0	4	27	18	14	12	2	17	35	.184	.219	.167	11.52	5.60
Craigie, Karl	L-L	6-1	215	1-22-95	0	1	5.40	6	0	0	0	7	9	6	4	0	4	8	.310	.200	.368	10.80	5.40
Culbertson, Peyton	R-R	6-1	220	4-18-97	1	3	2.08	9	7	0	0	30	32	8	7	0	7	29	.271	.390	.208	8.60	2.08
Cyphert, Dylan	L-L	6-0	186	9-10-96	1	1	5.46	18	0	0	0	28	34	20	17	1	25	33	.293	.250	.313	10.61	8.04
Domnarski, Doug	R-L	5-11	190	7-8-94	0	0	0.00	2	0	0	1	2	2	0	0	0	1	4	.222	.333	.000	15.43	3.86
Estes, Evan	R-R	6-2	185	11-29-96	0	2	5.74	18	0	0	0	27	34	18	17	0	18	20	.321	.361	.300	6.75	6.08
Guerrero, Alberto	R-R	6-3	192	12-13-97	3	6	3.49	15	14	0	0	70	61	31	27	6	22	63	.233	.230	.235	8.14	2.84
Holloway, Jordan	R-R	6-4	190	6-13-96	0	0	0.00	2	2	0	0	5	0	0	0	0	4	4	.000	.000	.000	7.20	0.00
Howe, Bryce	R-R	6-2	250	11-27-95	2	2	2.19	15	10	0	0	53	55	18	13	1	20	52	.268	.263	.272	8.78	3.38
Kolek, Tyler	R-R	6-5	260	12-15-95	1	2	4.50	8	0	0	0	14	12	9	7	0	7	12	.222	.261	.194	7.71	4.50
Martin, Chad	R-R	6-4	215	1-2-94	0	0	10.80	4	0	0	0	3	5	6	4	0	5	5	.333	.333	.286	13.50	13.50
McGrane, Jameson	R-R	6-4	190	6-25-92	3	0	1.52	13	0	0	3	24	14	4	4	0	20	33	.180	.094	.239	12.55	7.61
McKay, Ryan	R-R	6-4	195	9-20-96	1	0	5.17	11	0	0	0	16	17	10	9	1	4	18	.262	.296	.237	10.34	2.30
Mejia, Humberto	R-R	6-3	175	3-3-97	1	6	3.30	15	12	0	0	63	55	27	23	8	14	59	.232	.321	.160	8.47	2.01
Mitzel, Tyler	R-R	6-4	210	5-10-96	2	1	4.35	16	0	0	1	21	22	14	10	3	9	27	.268	.167	.327	11.76	3.92
Mojica, Luis	R-R	6-1	190	2-18-98	0	0	0.00	3	0	0	0	4	0	0	0	0	3	8	.308	.400	.250	8.10	0.00
Ovalle, Jeremy	R-R	6-3	185	1-17-97	1	0	3.60	3	0	0	0	5	6	2	2	0	6	9	.316	.000	.500	16.20	0.00
Peace, RJ	R-R	6-2	175	6-24-97	2	0	4.12	4	0	0	0	20	18	10	9	1	5	22	.240	.214	.273	10.07	2.29
Roberson, Josh	R-R	6-5	175	5-12-96	1	1	3.00	2	2	0	0	6	7	5	2	0	3	6	.269	.000	.313	4.50	0.00
Rodriguez, Manuel	L-L	6-2	160	12-23-96	3	2	1.06	13	0	0	0	51	43	12	6	1	9	42	.228	.206	.238	7.41	1.59
Vallimont, Chris	R-R	6-5	220	3-18-97	0	2	6.21	12	11	0	0	29	23	20	20	3	23	20	.215	.175	.239	6.21	7.14
Vesia, Alex	L-L	6-2	195	4-11-96	3	0	1.82	10	0	0	0	25	27	7	5	1	4	31	.276	.344	.242	11.31	1.46
Villalobos, Eli	R-R	6-4	195	6-26-97	1	1	5.79	14	0	0	0	19	16	12	12	0	9	17	.273	.259	.280	8.20	4.34
Wolf, Zach	R-R	5-8	175	11-15-97	1	1	3.00	13	0	0	5	15	10	7	5	0	5	21	.182	.222	.162	12.60	3.00

MIAMI MARLINS

Fielding

C: Baez 38, Fish 1, Fortes 3, Garcia 19, Osborne 19. **1B:** Osborne 1, Reynolds 75. **2B:** Jarvis 37, Karas 6, Nunez 31, Schubert 5, Sims 2. **3B:** Hollins 24, Karas 49, Osborne 1, Reynoso 2, Schubert 1, Turner 1. **SS:** Jarvis 11, Reynoso 2, Schubert 9, Sims 54, Torres 6. **OF:** Bird 4, Bradshaw 17, Brooks 15, Cespedes 22, Donadio 28, Encarnacion 37, Guaimaro 52, Hernandez 55, White 3.

GCL MARLINS
GULF COAST LEAGUE
ROOKIE

Batting	B-T	HT	WT	DOB	AVG	vLH	vRH	G	AB	R	H	2B	3B	HR	RBI	BB	HBP	SH	SF	SO	SB	CS	SLG	OBP
Arcaya, Luis	R-R	6-1	170	2-26-99	.231	.400	.206	19	39	5	9	2	0	0	5	3	1	0	0	8	0	1	.282	.302
Banfield, Will	R-R	6-0	200	11-18-99	.256	.250	.257	24	82	7	21	8	1	0	14	7	3	0	2	28	0	1	.378	.330
Barnes, Jared	R-R	6-0	185	11-21-95	.105	.000	.118	5	19	2	2	0	0	0	1	2	1	0	0	7	0	0	.105	.227
Bird, Corey	L-L	6-1	185	8-11-95	.091	.000	.100	3	11	0	1	0	0	0	0	0	0	0	0	2	0	0	.091	.091
Bradshaw, Davis	L-R	5-9	175	4-25-98	.376	.467	.359	27	93	18	35	4	3	0	13	10	3	0	0	13	15	1	.484	.453
Caballero, Jorge	R-R	6-1	170	1-10-00	.300	.154	.328	45	160	19	48	8	1	0	21	29	1	3	1	49	2	2	.363	.408
Castro, Samuel	B-R	5-10	160	10-16-97	.000	.000	.000	2	9	0	0	0	0	0	0	0	0	0	0	1	0	0	.000	.000
Dinicola, Harrison	L-R	6-0	195	4-30-97	.263	.429	.240	16	57	10	15	5	0	0	5	5	2	0	0	14	5	1	.351	.432
Espinal, Walner	R-R	6-0	170	12-21-99	.252	.320	.238	45	151	17	38	8	1	3	26	11	3	2	4	46	0	2	.378	.308
Fish, Keegan	B-R	5-11	190	9-19-99	.184	.000	.200	16	38	3	7	2	0	0	3	9	1	0	1	15	0	0	.237	.347
Fortes, Nick	R-R	6-0	210	11-11-96	.200	.333	.172	11	35	8	7	2	0	0	7	6	1	0	3	4	0	0	.257	.311
Garrett, Stone	R-R	6-2	195	11-22-95	.333	.667	.250	4	15	2	5	1	2	1	5	0	1	0	1	3	0	0	.867	.353
Grant, Connor	R-R	6-0	195	11-15-96	.246	.313	.235	35	114	23	28	6	0	1	8	12	1	1	1	23	16	3	.325	.320
Johnson, Osiris	R-R	6-0	181	10-18-00	.301	.375	.287	25	103	12	31	8	2	1	13	4	2	0	2	19	7	2	.447	.333
Lebron, Omar	L-L	6-0	175	4-11-99	.225	.111	.241	42	151	23	34	9	0	6	17	14	6	2	2	38	5	4	.404	.312
Marinez, Ynmanol	R-R	6-0	170	4-12-01	.170	.500	.111	11	53	3	9	0	0	0	6	1	0	0	0	9	2	2	.170	.185
Paulino, Daniel	R-R	6-1	155	11-23-98	.260	.400	.238	25	73	14	19	4	1	0	7	7	1	1	1	16	5	1	.343	.329
Pena, Miguel	R-R	6-0	175	1-14-97	.333	1.000	.294	6	18	3	6	1	1	0	1	2	0	0	0	3	0	0	.500	.400
Pompey, Tristan	B-R	6-4	200	3-23-97	.250	—	.250	4	12	1	3	0	0	0	1	3	0	0	0	4	1	1	.250	.400
Reynoso, Ronal	L-R	6-1	165	5-23-98	.283	.368	.266	36	113	15	32	3	2	1	13	11	3	3	2	30	4	3	.372	.357
Rodriguez, Christopher	R-R	6-1	190	12-22-99	.186	.231	.175	39	129	12	24	6	1	3	21	14	4	1	3	37	1	0	.318	.280
Schubert, Gunnar	R-R	5-11	205	5-19-96	.269	.500	.227	8	26	4	7	2	1	0	3	3	1	0	0	9	1	1	.423	.367
Scott, Connor	L-L	6-4	180	10-8-99	.223	.143	.236	27	103	15	23	1	4	0	8	14	1	0	1	29	8	5	.311	.319
Silviano, John	L-R	5-11	190	7-11-94	.125	.000	.133	5	16	2	2	0	0	1	2	2	1	0	0	4	1	0	.313	.263
Smith, Milton	L-L	5-10	165	9-25-97	.352	.235	.375	31	105	23	37	6	0	2	14	12	2	0	2	21	7	3	.410	.433
Torres, Christopher	B-R	5-11	170	2-6-98	.000	.000	.000	2	6	1	0	0	0	0	0	1	0	0	0	1	0	0	.000	.143
Turner, Andrew	R-R	6-2	190	9-26-95	.171	.154	.174	33	105	17	18	6	0	1	7	14	6	1	0	22	1	2	.257	.304
Wallach, Chad	R-R	6-3	230	11-4-91	.357	.500	.333	4	14	2	5	1	0	1	0	5	2	0	0	4	0	0	.429	.438

Pitching	B-T	HT	WT	DOB	W	L	ERA	G	GS	CG	SV	IP	H	R	ER	HR	BB	SO	AVG	vLH	vRH	K/9	BB/9
Alexander, Nathan	R-R	6-4	185	6-7-96	0	2	2.45	12	0	0	0	18	19	12	5	0	5	22	.247	.208	.264	10.80	2.45
Anderson, Martin	R-L	6-1	175	1-13-93	0	0	7.20	3	0	0	0	5	6	5	4	0	3	8	.316	.375	.273	14.40	5.40
Andrews, Tanner	R-R	6-3	220	11-15-95	0	0	0.00	1	0	0	1	2	1	0	0	0	0	0	.400	.500	.333	0.00	0.00
Baird, Cam	R-R	6-2	195	5-15-96	1	1	4.00	13	0	0	1	18	16	10	8	0	11	22	.232	.227	.234	11.00	5.50
Bennett, Dakota	B-L	6-2	160	7-12-99	2	1	1.46	9	7	0	0	37	30	7	6	0	9	37	.217	.200	.221	9.00	2.19
Braley, Taylor	R-R	5-11	140	1-13-96	0	0	0.00	2	0	0	0	6	6	0	0	0	0	4	.250	.222	.267	6.00	0.00
Brigham, Jeff	R-R	6-0	200	2-16-92	1	0	0.00	1	1	0	0	5	2	0	0	0	0	5	.118	.250	.077	9.00	0.00
Carter, C.J.	R-R	6-2	165	5-27-97	1	0	0.00	3	0	0	0	2	1	0	0	0	0	3	.125	.000	.167	11.57	0.00
Castano, Daniel	L-L	6-4	230	9-17-94	0	1	4.00	2	1	0	0	9	10	5	4	0	0	8	.286	.273	.292	8.00	0.00
Craigie, Karl	L-L	6-1	215	1-22-95	2	1	1.88	9	1	0	0	14	10	4	3	0	2	16	.189	.158	.206	10.05	1.26
Crescentini, Jared	L-R	6-4	240	8-29-94	1	0	45.00	2	0	0	0	1	3	5	5	0	3	0	.600	1.000	.500	0.00	27.00
Culbertson, Peyton	R-R	6-1	220	4-18-97	0	0	4.15	2	1	0	0	4	3	2	2	0	5	2	.214	.000	.250	4.15	10.38
Diaz, Jumbo	R-R	6-4	315	2-27-84	0	0	0.00	2	2	0	0	3	2	0	0	0	0	4	.200	.167	.250	12.00	0.00
Farnworth, Steven	R-R	6-2	175	9-6-93	0	0	8.68	9	2	0	1	9	17	10	9	1	1	13	.370	.438	.333	12.54	0.96
Frias, Julio	L-L	6-2	160	6-1-98	1	4	4.68	8	5	0	0	33	34	18	17	1	18	23	.281	.235	.289	6.34	4.96
Guenther, Sean	L-L	5-11	194	12-9-95	0	0	0.00	1	0	0	0	2	0	0	0	0	0	2	.000	.000	.000	9.00	0.00
Gunkel, Joe	R-R	6-5	225	12-30-91	1	1	3.60	3	2	0	0	5	6	2	2	0	0	5	.286	.143	.357	9.00	0.00
Holloway, Jordan	R-R	6-4	190	6-13-96	0	0	0.00	3	3	0	0	3	4	2	0	0	0	5	.286	.250	.300	16.88	0.00
Hoover, Chevis	R-R	6-3	240	10-18-93	0	0	2.89	8	0	0	0	9	5	3	3	0	3	12	.152	.000	.238	11.57	2.89
Jones, Tyler	R-R	6-3	200	12-7-95	1	1	2.00	12	0	0	0	18	10	6	4	0	3	25	.159	.000	.217	12.50	1.50
Kickham, Mike	L-L	6-4	220	12-12-88	0	0	0.00	1	0	0	0	1	0	0	0	0	0	2	.000	.000	.000	18.00	0.00
Kolek, Tyler	R-R	6-5	260	12-15-95	0	0	21.60	2	2	0	0	2	5	4	4	0	2	2	.500	.500	.500	10.80	10.80
Leban, Zack	R-R	6-3	245	5-30-96	0	2	7.24	12	0	0	0	14	24	13	11	1	7	11	.407	.438	.395	7.24	4.61
Lemond, Zech	R-R	6-1	170	10-9-92	0	0	3.00	2	0	0	0	3	4	1	1	0	0	3	.333	.250	.500	9.00	0.00
Lilek, Brett	L-L	6-4	220	8-10-93	2	0	1.80	5	1	0	0	5	5	1	1	0	1	2	.263	.200	.294	3.60	1.80
Lillie, Ryan	R-R	6-0	180	5-1-96	0	1	10.13	1	1	0	0	3	6	3	3	0	3	6	.400	.500	.385	20.25	10.13
Lopez, Giovanni	R-R	6-1	204	9-16-96	1	0	6.55	10	0	0	0	11	10	8	8	1	13	11	.250	.214	.269	9.00	10.64
Martinez, Edgar	R-R	6-1	170	7-13-97	0	4	8.18	12	8	0	0	44	63	43	40	1	18	39	.342	.396	.324	7.98	3.68
McGrane, Jameson	R-R	6-0	190	6-25-92	0	0	0.00	1	0	0	0	1	0	0	0	0	0	2	.000	.000	.000	18.00	0.00
Miller, Andrew	L-L	6-3	195	12-15-96	0	0	4.50	2	0	0	0	2	1	1	1	0	0	3	.250	.400	.000	13.50	0.00
Mitzel, Tyler	R-R	6-4	210	5-10-96	0	0	0.00	1	0	0	1	1	0	0	0	0	0	1	.000	.000	.000	6.75	0.00
Neubeck, Travis	L-R	6-2	180	3-13-95	0	0	0.00	1	0	0	0	1	1	0	0	0	1	2	.250	.333	.000	0.00	0.00
Norton, Jake	R-R	6-4	190	8-28-96	0	1	0.00	4	0	0	0	5	2	0	0	0	5	2	.182	.000	.250	5.40	13.50
Puckett, Brady	R-R	6-8	220	7-31-95	0	1	8.59	2	2	0	0	7	12	8	7	0	1	8	.375	.444	.286	9.82	1.23
Roberson, Josh	R-R	6-3	175	5-12-96	5	3	1.06	11	8	0	0	42	28	8	5	0	12	31	.184	.137	.208	6.59	2.55
Rose, Jackson	R-R	6-2	185	4-25-96	0	0	4.91	10	0	0	0	11	9	6	6	1	7	13	.225	.167	.250	10.64	5.73

Pitching	B-T	HT	WT	DOB	W	L	ERA	G	GS	CG	SV	IP	H	R	ER	HR	BB	SO	AVG	vLH	vRH	K/9	BB/9
Sebald, Scott	L-L	6-5	230	6-16-94	0	1	2.08	1	0	0	0	4	2	1	1	0	0	5	.133	.400	.000	10.38	0.00
Sherrod, Cason	R-R	6-4	215	6-25-96	2	3	5.68	15	0	0	3	19	12	15	12	1	8	23	.177	.130	.200	10.89	3.79
Soriano, George	R-R	6-2	170	3-24-99	2	1	1.91	11	3	0	1	42	28	13	9	0	9	36	.183	.200	.175	7.65	1.91
Strzelecki, Joe	R-R	6-4	220	3-16-96	1	2	6.60	11	0	0	0	15	15	14	11	2	8	12	.259	.267	.256	7.20	4.80
Suriel, Edison	L-L	5-10	160	10-24-98	0	0	6.75	13	0	0	1	15	16	11	11	2	12	18	.276	.200	.292	11.05	7.36
Vesia, Alex	L-L	6-2	195	4-11-96	1	0	0.00	4	0	0	0	9	4	1	0	0	3	7	.133	.000	.191	7.27	3.12
Villalobos, Eli	R-R	6-4	195	6-26-97	0	0	0.00	1	0	0	0	1	0	0	0	0	0	2	.000	—	.000	18.00	0.00
Villalobos, Jonaiker	L-L	6-0	160	7-11-99	0	0	11.40	13	0	0	1	15	29	23	19	2	7	18	.397	.364	.403	10.80	4.20
Yamamoto, Jordan	R-R	6-0	185	5-11-96	1	0	2.45	3	3	0	0	11	5	3	3	1	2	15	.135	.091	.200	12.27	1.64

Fielding

C: Arcaya 16, Banfield 22, Barnes 3, Fish 15, Fortes 7, Pena 6, Wallach 3. **1B:** Arcaya 1, Dinicola 11, Lebron 22, Reynoso 1, Rodriguez 18, Silviano 4, Turner 1. **2B:** Castro 2, Espinal 43, Grant 1, Turner 12. **3B:** Dinicola 1, Espinal 1, Reynoso 19, Rodriguez 20, Turner 19. **SS:** Johnson 23, Marinez 11, Reynoso 17, Schubert 8, Torres 1. **OF:** Bird 2, Bradshaw 19, Caballero 39, Garrett 3, Grant 34, Lebron 8, Paulino 20, Pompey 3, Scott 22, Smith 30.

DSL MARLINS

ROOKIE

DOMINICAN SUMMER LEAGUE

Batting	B-T	HT	WT	DOB	AVG	vLH	vRH	G	AB	R	H	2B	3B	HR	RBI	BB	HBP	SH	SF	SO	SB	CS	SLG	OBP
Campos, Brhayan	R-R	6-1	185	9-17-98	.262	.222	.273	15	42	8	11	4	0	0	1	7	3	1	1	8	1	1	.357	.396
Chinchilla, Jonathan	R-R	5-11	160	11-18-00	.175	.333	.155	28	80	5	14	2	0	0	7	7	3	0	1	15	1	2	.200	.264
Cumana, Arquimedes	R-R	6-3	175	4-28-00	.071	.000	.083	5	14	1	1	0	0	0	0	0	2	0	0	7	1	0	.143	.188
Felipe, Anthony	R-R	5-11	170	9-16-00	.214	.000	.250	7	14	2	3	0	0	0	0	6	0	0	0	5	2	1	.214	.450
Gilma, Joseph	B-R	5-9	145	3-18-99	.281	.200	.296	17	32	3	9	0	0	0	2	7	1	0	0	4	0	0	.281	.425
Giron, Adonis	R-R	5-10	190	2-22-01	.255	.212	.262	67	243	29	62	11	3	3	30	21	8	0	3	56	12	8	.362	.331
Machado, Julio	R-R	6-0	185	9-12-00	.231	.133	.246	67	225	26	52	6	0	0	20	30	8	5	4	24	14	7	.258	.337
Marinez, Ynmanol	R-R	6-0	170	4-12-01	.267	.294	.261	54	210	27	56	10	1	0	28	14	0	2	0	35	7	3	.324	.313
Mercado, Jan	R-R	6-1	185	8-28-99	.189	.115	.208	43	127	17	24	4	0	0	8	13	4	2	1	38	6	5	.221	.283
Montero, Alvaro	L-R	5-11	155	6-27-00	.312	.400	.300	64	215	51	67	6	2	0	24	38	9	1	3	42	30	18	.358	.430
Osorio, Jhonaiker	L-R	6-0	160	9-2-00	.212	.077	.229	40	118	11	25	0	1	0	14	9	0	3	0	20	2	2	.229	.268
Ozoria, Elvin	R-R	6-0	180	7-16-01	.227	.500	.194	28	75	15	17	3	0	1	7	17	1	0	0	23	5	3	.307	.376
Paulino, Jandel	R-R	6-1	175	11-3-00	.205	.318	.188	53	166	25	34	5	0	1	17	22	10	3	1	46	6	7	.253	.332
Pena, Miguel	R-R	6-0	175	1-14-98	.228	.333	.212	35	114	12	26	0	0	0	15	10	3	0	3	24	2	3	.228	.300
Pineda, Bryan	R-R	6-3	165	2-28-00	.234	.167	.246	27	77	13	18	2	0	0	7	5	1	0	0	24	3	1	.260	.289
Romero, Carlos	R-R	6-1	175	7-31-01	.192	.177	.194	39	125	13	24	5	0	0	7	17	0	1	1	37	5	3	.232	.287
Rosario, Dalvy	R-R	6-0	160	7-22-00	.257	.171	.271	67	249	42	64	13	2	4	42	22	1	3	4	63	26	3	.374	.315
Sosa, Maicol	R-R	6-2	185	2-9-99	.279	.375	.266	58	197	29	55	9	0	5	22	23	6	1	1	49	15	11	.401	.370

Pitching	B-T	HT	WT	DOB	W	L	ERA	G	GS	CG	SV	IP	H	R	ER	HR	BB	SO	AVG	vLH	vRH	K/9	BB/9
Alegre, Delvis	R-R	6-2	180	2-2-01	1	2	3.06	14	5	0	2	47	50	26	16	3	15	36	.269	.203	.299	6.89	2.87
Borges, Juan	R-R	6-1	180	1-6-98	1	1	1.86	19	0	0	1	29	26	9	6	1	9	26	.239	.219	.247	8.07	2.79
Brito, Raul	R-R	6-1	180	5-23-97	2	2	2.35	13	0	0	1	23	23	12	6	0	15	21	.250	.306	.214	8.22	5.87
De Paula, Brayan	L-L	6-3	175	6-25-99	1	1	2.23	15	4	0	1	44	45	15	11	2	12	45	.266	.243	.273	9.14	2.44
Eysseric, Rafael	R-R	6-0	170	6-27-00	2	1	3.60	11	0	0	1	20	13	9	8	1	16	16	.191	.182	.196	7.20	7.20
Galindez, Geremy	R-R	6-1	170	4-29-98	4	3	2.86	21	0	0	10	28	24	17	9	0	7	32	.207	.182	.222	10.16	2.22
Jimenez, Yeuris	R-R	6-3	185	3-23-01	2	0	9.64	11	0	0	0	14	15	16	15	0	11	9	.294	.250	.314	5.79	7.07
Lara, Yeremin	R-R	6-0	160	11-6-98	2	3	2.50	14	9	0	1	58	43	18	16	0	17	58	.202	.197	.204	9.05	2.65
Martinez, Leudy	R-R	6-2	180	6-9-00	6	1	2.44	14	5	0	1	52	36	20	14	1	19	55	.197	.194	.198	9.58	3.31
Mendez, Josan	R-R	6-2	180	7-10-00	3	4	3.93	14	9	0	0	55	56	31	24	1	6	42	.259	.271	.253	6.87	0.98
Palacios, Luis	L-L	6-2	160	7-1-00	8	0	0.85	15	4	0	0	64	34	9	6	4	6	62	.155	.158	.154	8.76	0.57
Puentes, Zaquiel	R-R	6-1	160	12-30-00	0	2	5.87	5	5	0	0	8	8	10	5	0	5	4	.235	.000	.333	4.70	5.87
Quinonez, Yoilan	R-R	6-4	200	8-11-99	1	2	4.91	12	7	0	0	33	36	25	18	1	12	27	.277	.302	.264	7.36	3.27
Reyes, Juan	R-L	6-4	170	7-24-00	0	1	—	1	1	0	0	0	1	3	2	0	3	0	1.000	1.000	—	—	—
Rodriguez, Eliezer	L-L	6-0	160	2-17-99	0	1	3.48	10	0	0	0	31	26	13	12	0	19	25	.245	.333	.224	7.26	5.52
Rosario, Jesus	R-R	6-1	180	10-25-99	0	0	5.40	2	0	0	0	2	5	5	1	1	2	1	.500	.333	.571	5.40	10.80
Sanchez, Jesus	R-R	5-11	150	4-8-99	2	1	1.47	17	0	0	2	31	18	6	5	2	12	28	.175	.143	.187	8.22	3.52
Valencio, Henry	R-R	6-1	170	5-11-99	4	3	2.79	13	10	0	0	52	49	23	16	1	14	38	.251	.193	.275	6.62	2.44
Valera, Frank	R-R	6-3	210	10-2-99	3	2	4.35	12	4	1	1	39	33	21	19	2	17	35	.231	.314	.185	8.01	3.89

Fielding

C: Campos 8, Chinchilla 19, Cumana 1, Mercado 28, Osorio 24, Pena 24. **1B:** Campos 6, Chinchilla 9, Cumana 3, Gilma 5, Mercado 19, Montero 13, Osorio 19, Ozoria 10, Pena 18, Sosa 3. **2B:** Gilma 3, Machado 15, Montero 41, Ozoria 7, Romero 11, Rosario 9. **3B:** Chinchilla 1, Gilma 7, Machado 42, Marinez 6, Montero 3, Ozoria 2, Romero 8, Rosario 18. **SS:** Machado 8, Marinez 40, Romero 21, Rosario 7. **OF:** Felipe 5, Gilma 2, Giron 60, Paulino 51, Pineda 26, Rosario 39, Sosa 50.

MIAMI MARLINS

Milwaukee Brewers

SEASON IN A SENTENCE: The Brewers tied a franchise record with 96 wins and finished first in the NL Central for the first time since 2011. As they had in 2011, the 2018 Brew Crew also ended their season with a loss in the NLCS, this time in a seven-game series with the Dodgers.

HIGH POINT: Milwaukee broke off a seven-game winning streak from Sept. 23-30, going from 2.5 games out of the division lead to a first-place tie with the Cubs. The Brewers then beat their division rival, 3-1, in Game 163 to secure the NL Central and avoid the Wild Card Game, which the Cubs went on to lose to the Rockies.

LOW POINT: It was a generally positive season for the Brewers, with a seven-game losing streak in mid-July being one of the few low points to speak of. Even then, Milwaukee fell just three games out of the division lead. Thus losing Game 7 of the NLCS to narrowly miss out on the organization's second World Series appearance might be the better example here.

NOTABLE ROOKIES: Righthander Freddy Peralta started 14 games and logged 78.1 innings, posting a 4.25 ERA with an 11.0 strikeouts per nine innings. Lefthander Brandon Woodruff improved his numbers after a brief major league stint in 2017, posting a 3.61 ERA, mostly out of the bullpen. Righthander Corbin Burnes made his major league debut and posted a 2.61 ERA across 38 innings out of the bullpen.

KEY TRANSACTIONS: The biggest move the Brewers made came prior to the season, when the team included three of its top prospects—outfielders Luis Brinson and Monte Harrison plus second baseman Isan Diaz—in a trade with the Marlins for outfielder Christian Yelich. The gamble paid off in a big way. Yelich went on to have a career year, leading the National League in hitting (.326), slugging (.598), OPS (1.000), adjusted-OPS+ (164) and total bases (343) while playing all three outfield positions.

DOWN ON THE FARM: Keston Hiura, the club's 2017 first-round pick, started the year hot with the bat, hitting .320/.382/.529 through 50 games with high Class-A Carolina. He faded down the stretch once he was promoted to Double-A and started playing second base more regularly. Hiura hit just .272/.339/.416 with Biloxi. Corey Ray had his best pro season with 27 home runs and 37 stolen bases in Double-A after re-working his swing, but he needs to cut down his strikeouts.

OPENING DAY PAYROLL: $90,827,856 (23rd).

PLAYERS OF THE YEAR

DAVE DUROCHIK

ROBERT BINDER

MAJOR LEAGUE	MINOR LEAGUE
Christian Yelich	**Corey Ray**
OF	OF
.326/.402/.598	(Double-A)
Led NL in AVG, SLG	.239/.323/.477
and OPS (1.000)	27 HR, 37 SB

ORGANIZATION LEADERS

Batting		*Minimum 250 AB
MAJORS		
* AVG	Christian Yelich	.326
* OPS	Christian Yelich	1.000
HR	Christian Yelich	36
RBI	Christian Yelich	110
MINORS		
* AVG	Dylan Moore, Biloxi, Colorado Springs	.299
* OBP	Nate Orf, Colorado Springs	.397
* OBP	Cooper Hummel, Carolina	.397
* SLG	Dylan Moore, Biloxi, Colorado Springs	.522
* OPS	Dylan Moore, Biloxi, Colorado Springs	.885
R	Corey Ray, Biloxi	86
H	Keston Hiura, Carolina, Biloxi	142
TB	Corey Ray, Biloxi	254
2B	Keston Hiura, Carolina, Biloxi	34
3B	Tyrone Taylor, Colorado Springs	9
3B	Dylan Moore, Biloxi, Colorado Springs	9
3B	Ryan Aguilar, Carolina	9
HR	Corey Ray, Biloxi	27
RBI	Tyrone Taylor, Colorado Springs	80
BB	Troy Stokes Jr., Biloxi	65
BB	Dallas Carroll, Carolina	65
SO	Corey Ray, Biloxi	176
SB	Corey Ray, Biloxi	37
Pitching		#Minimum 75 IP
MAJORS		
W	Jhoulys Chacin	15
# ERA	Jeremy Jeffress	1.29
SO	Jhoulys Chacin	156
SV	Corey Knebel	16
MINORS		
W	Nick Ramirez, Biloxi, Colorado Springs	11
L	Nelson Hernandez, Wisconsin	10
L	Dylan File, Wisconsin	10
L	Bowden Francis, Wisconsin, Carolina	10
L	Alec Bettinger, Wisconsin, Carolina	10
# ERA	Zack Brown, Biloxi, Brewers	2.40
G	Tristan Archer, Biloxi, Colorado Springs	52
GS	Nelson Hernandez, Wisconsin	28
SV	Nate Griep, Biloxi	34
IP	Christian Taugner, Wisconsin, Carolina	149
BB	Marcos Diplan, Carolina, Biloxi	74
SO	Braden Webb, Carolina, Biloxi	128
# AVG	Zack Brown, Biloxi, Brewers	.210

General Manager: David Stearns. **Farm Director:** Tom Flanagan. **Scouting Director:** Tod Johnson.

Class	Team	League	W	L	PCT	Finish	Manager
Majors	Milwaukee Brewers	National	96	67	.589	1st (15)	Craig Counsell
Triple-A	Colorado Springs Sky Sox	Pacific Coast	73	66	.525	5th (16)	Rick Sweet
Double-A	Biloxi Shuckers	Southern	81	59	.579	1st (10)	Mike Guerrero
High A	Carolina Mudcats	Carolina	65	73	.471	7th (10)	Joe Ayrault
Low A	Wisconsin Timber Rattlers	Midwest	68	71	.489	10th (16)	Matt Erickson
Rookie	Helena Brewers	Pioneer	36	40	.474	6th (8)	Nestor Corredor
Rookie	AZL Brewers	Arizona	22	33	.400	15th (18)	Rafael Neda
Overall 2018 Minor League Record			345	342	.502	t-13th (30)	

ORGANIZATION STATISTICS

MILWAUKEE BREWERS
NATIONAL LEAGUE

Batting	B-T	HT	WT	DOB	AVG	vLH	vRH	G	AB	R	H	2B	3B	HR	RBI	BB	HBP	SH	SF	SO	SB	CS	SLG	OBP
Aguilar, Jesus	R-R	6-3	250	6-30-90	.274	.282	.272	149	492	80	135	25	0	35	108	58	6	0	10	143	0	0	.539	.352
Arcia, Orlando	R-R	6-0	165	8-4-94	.236	.244	.233	119	348	32	82	16	0	3	30	15	1	1	1	87	7	4	.308	.269
Bandy, Jett	R-R	6-4	235	3-26-90	.188	.182	.189	24	64	5	12	2	0	1	1	3	4	0	0	23	0	0	.266	.268
Braun, Ryan	R-R	6-2	205	11-17-83	.254	.246	.258	125	405	59	103	25	1	20	64	34	2	0	3	85	11	5	.469	.313
Broxton, Keon	R-R	6-3	195	5-7-90	.180	.115	.212	51	78	15	14	2	2	4	11	11	0	0	0	28	5	1	.410	.281
Cain, Lorenzo	R-R	6-2	205	4-13-86	.308	.373	.285	141	539	90	166	25	2	10	38	71	8	0	2	94	30	7	.417	.395
Choi, Ji-Man	L-R	6-1	230	5-19-91	.233	.250	.231	12	30	4	7	2	0	2	5	2	0	0	0	14	0	0	.500	.281
Franklin, Nick	B-R	6-1	190	3-2-91	.000	—	.000	1	2	0	0	0	0	0	0	0	0	0	0	0	0	0	.000	.000
Granderson, Curtis	L-R	6-1	200	3-16-81	.220	.500	.205	19	41	12	9	1	1	2	3	12	1	0	0	10	0	0	.439	.407
Kratz, Erik	R-R	6-4	250	6-15-80	.237	.196	.252	67	203	18	48	6	0	6	23	6	7	1	2	40	1	0	.355	.280
Miller, Brad	L-R	6-2	215	10-18-89	.230	.200	.234	27	74	5	17	3	1	2	8	6	0	0	0	31	0	0	.378	.288
Moustakas, Mike	L-R	6-0	225	9-11-88	.256	.267	.252	54	195	20	50	12	0	8	33	19	2	0	2	40	1	1	.441	.326
Nottingham, Jacob	R-R	6-2	230	4-3-95	.000	.000	.222	9	20	2	4	1	0	0	4	0	0	0	0	8	0	0	.250	.333
Orf, Nate	R-R	5-9	180	2-1-90	.095	.111	.083	15	21	4	2	0	0	1	1	3	1	0	0	8	1	0	.238	.240
Perez, Hernan	R-R	6-1	215	3-26-91	.253	.277	.239	132	316	36	80	11	2	9	29	17	0	0	1	71	11	3	.386	.290
Phillips, Brett	L-R	6-0	185	5-30-94	.182	.000	.235	15	22	2	4	0	1	0	4	2	0	0	0	11	0	0	.273	.250
Pina, Manny	R-R	6-0	215	6-5-87	.252	.217	.262	98	306	39	77	13	2	9	28	21	5	1	4	62	2	0	.395	.307
Saladino, Tyler	R-R	6-0	200	7-20-89	.246	.180	.279	52	118	11	29	3	0	5	16	9	1	1	1	38	2	2	.398	.302
Santana, Domingo	R-R	6-5	220	8-5-92	.265	.172	.301	85	211	21	56	14	1	5	20	20	1	0	3	77	1	1	.412	.328
Schoop, Jonathan	R-R	6-1	225	10-16-91	.202	.204	.200	46	124	16	25	4	0	4	21	7	1	0	2	41	1	0	.331	.246
Shaw, Travis	L-R	6-4	230	4-16-90	.241	.209	.251	152	498	73	120	3	0	32	86	78	4	1	6	108	5	2	.480	.345
Sogard, Eric	L-R	5-9	180	5-22-86	.134	.167	.129	55	97	7	13	3	0	0	2	12	2	1	1	23	3	0	.165	.241
Thames, Eric	L-R	6-0	210	11-10-86	.219	.185	.223	96	247	41	54	10	3	16	37	29	2	0	0	97	7	0	.478	.306
Villar, Jonathan	B-R	6-1	215	5-2-91	.261	.300	.251	87	257	26	67	13	0	6	22	19	2	0	1	80	14	2	.377	.315
Yelich, Christian	L-R	6-3	195	12-5-91	.326	.337	.321	147	574	118	187	34	7	36	110	68	7	0	2	135	22	4	.598	.403

Pitching	B-T	HT	WT	DOB	W	L	ERA	G	GS	CG	SV	IP	H	R	ER	HR	BB	SO	AVG	vLH	vRH	K/9	BB/9
Albers, Matt	L-R	6-1	225	1-20-83	3	3	7.34	34	0	0	1	34	45	29	28	10	12	32	.321	.321	.321	8.39	3.15
Anderson, Chase	R-R	6-1	200	11-30-87	9	8	3.93	30	30	0	0	158	131	71	69	30	57	128	.228	.217	.239	7.29	3.25
Asher, Alec	R-R	6-4	240	10-4-91	0	0	0.00	2	0	0	0	3	2	0	0	0	1	2	.167	.200	.143	6.00	3.00
Barnes, Jacob	R-R	6-2	220	4-14-90	0	1	3.33	49	0	0	2	49	51	24	18	4	23	47	.266	.298	.241	8.69	4.25
Burnes, Corbin	R-R	6-3	205	10-22-94	7	0	2.61	30	0	0	1	38	27	11	11	4	11	35	.199	.170	.214	8.29	2.61
Cedeno, Xavier	L-L	5-11	210	8-26-86	0	0	1.13	15	0	0	0	8	7	1	1	0	3	6	.226	.200	.250	6.75	3.38
Chacin, Jhoulys	R-R	6-3	215	1-7-88	15	8	3.50	35	35	0	0	193	153	83	75	18	71	156	.220	.261	.178	7.29	3.32
Davies, Zach	R-R	6-0	155	2-7-93	2	7	4.77	13	13	0	0	66	67	36	35	8	21	49	.269	.263	.274	6.68	2.86
Drake, Oliver	R-R	6-4	215	1-13-87	1	0	6.39	11	0	0	0	13	14	9	9	0	8	15	.286	.348	.231	10.66	5.68
Gonzalez, Gio	R-L	6-0	203	9-19-85	3	0	2.13	5	5	0	0	25	14	7	6	2	10	22	.157	.077	.171	7.82	3.55
2-team total (27 Washington)					10	11	4.21	32	32	0	0	171	167	84	80	17	80	148	.256	.219	.265	7.79	4.21
Guerra, Junior	R-R	6-0	205	1-16-85	6	9	4.09	31	26	0	0	141	143	74	64	19	55	136	.264	.267	.260	8.68	3.51
Hader, Josh	L-L	6-3	185	4-7-94	6	1	2.43	55	0	0	12	81	36	23	22	9	30	143	.132	.090	.153	15.82	3.32
Hoover, J.J.	R-R	6-3	240	8-13-87	0	1	20.25	2	0	0	0	1	4	3	3	1	2	0	.500	.500	.500	0.00	13.50
Houser, Adrian	R-R	6-4	235	2-2-93	0	0	3.29	7	0	0	0	14	13	5	5	0	7	8	.255	.136	.345	5.27	4.61
Jeffress, Jeremy	R-R	6-0	205	9-21-87	8	1	1.29	73	0	0	15	77	49	12	11	5	27	89	.182	.183	.182	10.45	3.17
Jennings, Dan	L-L	6-3	210	4-17-87	4	5	3.22	72	1	0	1	64	66	27	23	6	23	45	.275	.226	.320	6.30	3.22
Knebel, Corey	R-R	6-4	220	11-26-91	4	3	3.58	57	0	0	16	55	38	23	22	7	22	88	.194	.177	.213	14.31	3.58
Logan, Boone	R-L	6-5	215	8-13-84	1	0	5.91	16	0	0	0	11	15	7	7	3	10	14	.326	.409	.250	11.81	8.44
Lopez, Jorge	R-R	6-3	195	2-10-93	0	1	2.75	10	0	0	0	20	16	6	6	1	13	15	.225	.162	.294	6.86	5.95
Lyles, Jordan	R-R	6-4	230	10-19-90	1	0	3.31	11	0	0	0	16	12	7	6	0	9	22	.203	.160	.235	12.12	4.96
2-team total (24 San Diego)					3	4	4.11	35	8	0	0	88	83	42	40	12	28	84	.249	.185	.300	8.62	2.87
Miley, Wade	L-L	6-0	220	11-13-86	5	2	2.57	16	16	0	0	81	71	28	23	3	27	50	.237	.225	.240	5.58	3.01
Peralta, Freddy	R-R	5-11	175	6-4-96	6	4	4.25	16	14	0	0	78	49	37	37	8	40	96	.178	.252	.111	11.03	4.60
Soria, Joakim	R-R	6-3	200	5-18-84	3	1	4.09	26	0	0	0	22	18	11	10	2	6	26	.214	.250	.182	10.64	2.45
Suter, Brent	L-L	6-5	195	8-29-89	8	7	4.44	20	18	0	0	101	102	55	50	18	19	84	.258	.222	.269	7.46	1.69
Wilkerson, Aaron	R-R	6-3	190	5-24-89	0	1	10.00	3	1	0	0	9	12	10	10	4	3	10	.308	.400	.211	10.00	3.00

Name	B-T	HT	WT	DOB	W	L	ERA	G	GS	CG	SV	IP	H	R	ER	HR	BB	SO	AVG	vLH	vRH	K/9	BB/9
Williams, Taylor	B-R	5-11	195	7-21-91	1	3	4.25	56	0	0	0	53	53	28	25	6	25	57	.260	.347	.209	9.68	4.25
Woodruff, Brandon	L-R	6-4	215	2-10-93	3	0	3.61	19	4	0	1	42	36	18	17	4	14	47	.226	.221	.232	9.99	2.98
Zagurski, Mike	L-L	6-0	240	1-27-83	0	1	63.00	2	0	0	0	1	5	7	7	0	2	2	.625	.800	.333	18.00	18.00

Fielding

Catcher	PCT	G	PO	A	E	DP	PB
Bandy	.994	22	167	7	1	1	4
Kratz	.994	61	508	23	3	3	4
Nottingham	.967	8	54	5	2	0	0
Pina	.995	92	720	45	4	6	2

First Base	PCT	G	PO	A	E	DP
Aguilar	.996	132	894	86	4	92
Braun	.979	18	85	8	2	8
Choi	1.000	2	10	2	0	5
Kratz	.000	1	0	0	0	0
Miller	1.000	1	4	0	0	0
Perez	1.000	6	7	1	0	1
Pina	.000	1	0	0	0	0
Shaw	1.000	17	39	2	0	4
Thames	.986	29	194	15	3	15

Second Base	PCT	G	PO	A	E	DP
Franklin	1.000	1	0	1	0	0
Miller	.983	15	26	31	1	9

	PCT	G	PO	A	E	DP
Orf	1.000	3	1	5	0	1
Perez	.981	51	38	63	2	17
Saladino	.857	6	2	4	1	0
Schoop	.934	31	38	61	7	17
Shaw	.992	39	59	69	1	11
Sogard	.971	22	18	16	1	4
Villar	.974	74	100	129	6	29

Third Base	PCT	G	PO	A	E	DP
Aguilar	1.000	5	1	3	0	0
Moustakas	.961	52	32	90	5	11
Orf	1.000	1	1	2	0	0
Perez	1.000	22	8	26	0	2
Saladino	1.000	1	1	2	0	0
Shaw	.959	107	66	168	10	19

Shortstop	PCT	G	PO	A	E	DP
Arcia	.964	116	154	243	15	57
Miller	.769	6	6	4	3	1
Orf	1.000	2	2	2	0	1

	PCT	G	PO	A	E	DP
Perez	.962	20	18	33	2	11
Saladino	.938	28	38	68	7	13
Schoop	.974	15	13	24	1	4
Sogard	.981	24	13	39	1	8

Outfield	PCT	G	PO	A	E	DP
Braun	.993	93	138	1	1	0
Broxton	1.000	43	57	2	0	0
Cain	.981	138	304	11	6	3
Choi	.000	1	0	0	0	0
Granderson	1.000	15	14	0	0	0
Orf	.000	1	0	0	0	0
Perez	1.000	44	35	2	0	0
Phillips	1.000	12	11	0	0	0
Santana	.988	55	82	1	1	0
Sogard	.000	1	0	0	0	0
Thames	.967	37	57	2	2	1
Yelich	.989	145	266	4	3	1

COLORADO SPRINGS SKY SOX

PACIFIC COAST LEAGUE   **TRIPLE-A**

Batting	B-T	HT	WT	DOB	AVG	vLH	vRH	G	AB	R	H	2B	3B	HR	RBI	BB	HBP	SH	SF	SO	SB	CS	SLG	OBP
Arcia, Orlando	R-R	6-0	165	8-4-94	.341	.240	.383	22	85	16	29	5	1	2	8	10	1	0	0	15	2	1	.494	.417
Bandy, Jett	R-R	6-4	235	3-26-90	.292	.307	.285	59	192	23	56	15	0	9	35	10	10	0	3	32	3	0	.510	.354
Berry, Quintin	L-L	6-1	195	11-21-84	.214	.286	.200	42	84	14	18	3	0	2	11	8	1	0	0	31	10	1	.321	.290
Bethancourt, Christian	R-R	6-2	213	9-2-91	.297	.274	.304	104	391	59	116	22	0	20	71	20	1	0	6	76	6	1	.506	.328
Blanco, Andres	B-R	5-10	192	4-11-84	.271	.226	.288	96	306	51	83	17	3	9	47	35	11	0	4	47	6	3	.435	.362
Bonifacio, Emilio	R-R	5-10	210	4-23-85	.231	.400	.125	5	13	2	3	2	0	0	2	0	0	0	0	6	0	0	.385	.231
Broxton, Keon	R-R	6-3	195	5-7-90	.254	.281	.247	82	299	47	76	16	2	10	37	30	2	0	3	119	27	4	.421	.323
Choi, Ji-Man	L-R	6-1	230	5-19-91	.302	.208	.324	40	129	17	39	9	0	5	23	32	0	0	2	31	1	0	.488	.436
Coulter, Clint	R-R	6-3	225	7-30-93	.268	.143	.294	13	41	5	11	3	0	1	2	3	1	0	0	11	0	0	.415	.333
Davis, Johnny	B-R	5-10	180	4-26-90	.118	.200	.083	9	17	2	2	0	0	0	1	1	0	0	0	8	2	0	.118	.167
Dubon, Mauricio	R-R	6-0	160	7-19-94	.343	.440	.313	24	108	16	37	9	2	4	18	2	0	2	2	19	6	3	.574	.348
Hager, Jake	R-R	6-1	170	3-4-93	.267	.278	.263	33	116	18	31	8	1	1	11	5	1	0	1	17	2	3	.379	.301
Heineman, Tyler	B-R	5-11	205	6-19-91	.211	.200	.214	6	19	1	4	0	0	0	1	4	0	0	0	4	1	0	.211	.348
Houle, Dustin	R-R	6-1	205	11-9-93	.444	.500	.400	8	9	3	4	1	0	1	2	3	0	0	1	2	1	0	.889	.539
Liriano, Rymer	R-R	6-0	230	6-20-91	.221	.125	.247	37	113	20	25	4	0	4	11	20	1	0	1	41	5	4	.363	.341
2-team total (65 Salt Lake)					.253	.185	.268	102	352	62	89	11	3	20	59	45	4	1	2	125	11	9	.472	.342
Meyer, Charlie	R-R	5-10	180	1-10-93	1.000	1.000	—	1	1	0	1	0	0	0	0	0	0	0	0	0	0	0	1.000	1.000
Miller, Brad	L-R	6-2	215	10-18-89	.185	.200	.182	8	27	4	5	3	0	0	1	2	3	0	0	9	1	0	.296	.258
Moore, Dylan	R-R	6-0	200	8-2-92	.280	.330	.261	97	325	58	91	24	6	11	40	28	6	1	2	52	17	6	.492	.346
Noriega, Gabriel	R-R	6-0	180	9-13-90	.279	.273	.281	37	86	11	24	4	0	1	13	6	1	1	1	24	0	1	.361	.330
Nottingham, Jacob	R-R	6-0	230	4-3-95	.281	.227	.299	50	178	33	50	10	2	10	36	14	4	0	0	59	2	1	.528	.347
Opitz, Shane	L-R	6-1	180	1-10-92	.252	.120	.299	61	147	22	37	6	3	2	16	20	1	1	1	33	5	1	.374	.343
Orf, Nate	R-R	5-9	180	2-1-90	.298	.316	.292	108	399	67	119	27	3	6	55	50	20	2	7	72	22	4	.426	.397
Phillips, Brett	L-R	6-0	185	5-30-94	.240	.210	.250	71	258	42	62	12	7	6	25	36	1	0	4	94	11	0	.411	.331
Rojas, Robie	R-R	5-7	185	12-3-94	.083	.000	.125	4	12	1	1	0	0	0	1	1	0	0	0	6	0	0	.083	.154
Saladino, Tyler	R-R	6-0	200	7-20-89	.262	.200	.280	36	130	23	34	4	3	3	19	21	2	0	1	28	10	0	.408	.370
Santana, Domingo	R-R	6-5	220	8-5-92	.283	.309	.273	55	187	30	53	10	2	8	35	36	2	0	2	75	2	0	.487	.401
Shaffer, Richie	R-R	6-3	230	3-15-91	.167	.000	.235	19	48	9	8	3	0	2	6	10	0	0	0	26	0	0	.354	.310
Sogard, Eric	L-R	5-9	180	5-22-86	.225	.063	.260	27	89	10	20	4	0	0	11	10	0	0	2	16	0	1	.270	.297
Taylor, Tyrone	R-R	6-0	185	1-22-94	.278	.273	.280	119	446	73	124	23	9	20	80	27	3	1	4	74	13	4	.505	.321
Thames, Eric	L-R	6-0	210	11-10-86	.429	.429	.429	4	14	3	6	0	0	1	3	0	0	0	0	0	0	0	.643	.467
Villar, Jonathan	B-R	6-1	215	5-2-91	.600	.500	.667	3	10	4	6	0	0	1	1	1	0	0	0	1	1	0	.900	.636
Wren, Kyle	L-L	5-10	175	4-23-91	.294	.177	.311	47	136	23	40	7	1	2	28	16	0	1	5	33	6	3	.404	.357

Pitching	B-T	HT	WT	DOB	W	L	ERA	G	GS	CG	SV	IP	H	R	ER	HR	BB	SO	AVG	vLH	vRH	K/9	BB/9
Albers, Matt	L-R	6-1	225	1-20-83	0	0	0.00	1	0	0	0	2	1	0	0	0	0	3	.200	.000	.333	16.20	0.00
Ames, Jeff	R-R	6-4	220	1-31-91	0	0	54.00	1	0	0	0	1	3	4	4	0	5	1	.600	.000	.750	13.50	67.50
Archer, Tristan	R-R	6-2	200	10-18-90	4	4	4.52	50	1	0	3	74	72	47	37	7	25	66	.255	.260	.253	8.06	3.05
Asher, Alec	R-R	6-4	240	10-4-91	6	4	6.05	21	16	0	0	97	118	69	65	12	36	49	.300	.293	.305	4.56	3.35
2-team total (1 Oklahoma City)					6	4	5.96	22	17	0	0	100	121	71	66	12	36	50	.300	.291	.306	4.52	3.25
Barnes, Jacob	R-R	6-2	220	4-14-90	1	0	1.54	11	0	0	2	12	5	3	2	0	8	10	.128	.167	.111	7.71	6.17
Brady, Michael	R-R	6-0	195	3-21-87	1	4	6.91	33	3	0	1	55	89	43	42	5	9	46	.372	.370	.374	7.57	1.48
Brooks, Aaron	R-R	6-4	225	4-27-90	9	4	3.35	26	15	1	0	99	100	40	37	8	28	74	.263	.284	.246	6.70	2.54
Burnes, Corbin	R-R	6-3	205	10-22-94	3	3	5.15	19	13	0	0	79	83	48	45	7	31	81	.275	.286	.267	9.27	3.55
Davies, Zach	R-R	6-0	155	2-7-93	0	3	6.35	5	5	0	0	17	18	12	12	0	12	13	.277	.242	.313	6.88	6.35

Name	B-T	HT	WT	DOB	W	L	ERA	G	GS	CG	SV	IP	H	R	ER	HR	BB	SO	AVG	vLH	vRH	K/9	BB/9
Davis, Erik	R-R	6-3	205	10-8-86	4	6	3.99	49	0	0	2	65	67	38	29	4	25	56	.269	.323	.233	7.71	3.44
Derby, Bubba	L-R	5-11	185	2-24-94	6	5	4.49	31	16	1	0	118	127	65	59	9	50	96	.279	.271	.284	7.30	3.80
Dillard, Tim	R-R	6-4	220	7-19-83	2	4	9.70	25	1	0	1	34	54	46	37	7	17	24	.360	.420	.330	6.29	4.46
Espino, Paolo	R-R	5-10	215	1-10-87	4	5	4.83	19	10	0	0	54	62	31	29	7	22	52	.293	.338	.270	8.67	3.67
2-team total (3 Round Rock)					4	5	5.85	22	10	0	0	60	72	42	39	9	26	58	.301	.370	.266	8.70	3.90
Guerra, Junior	R-R	6-0	205	1-16-85	1	0	1.59	1	1	0	0	6	2	1	1	1	1	6	.100	.000	.182	9.53	1.59
Hernandez, Ariel	R-R	6-4	230	3-2-92	1	0	6.75	5	0	0	0	5	2	4	4	0	11	5	.118	.000	.222	8.44	18.56
2-team total (21 Oklahoma City)					4	2	3.82	26	0	0	1	31	24	14	13	1	31	26	.216	.231	.203	7.63	9.10
Hoover, J.J.	R-R	6-3	240	8-13-87	0	0	0.00	1	0	0	0	1	1	0	0	0	0	0	.333	1.000	.000	0.00	0.00
Houser, Adrian	R-R	6-4	235	2-2-93	2	3	5.19	13	13	0	0	52	66	30	30	6	18	37	.314	.410	.252	6.40	3.12
Jankins, Thomas	R-R	6-3	200	7-2-95	0	0	0.00	1	0	0	0	5	2	0	0	0	2	4	.118	.000	.250	7.20	3.60
Knebel, Corey	R-R	6-4	220	11-26-91	0	0	0.00	1	0	0	0	1	1	0	0	0	1	1	.250	.000	.333	9.00	9.00
Liz, Radhames	R-R	6-2	200	10-6-83	4	3	6.75	18	0	0	1	23	26	19	17	3	17	28	.277	.188	.323	11.12	6.75
Logan, Boone	R-L	6-5	215	8-13-84	0	0	0.00	1	0	0	0	1	0	0	0	0	1	3	.000	.000	.000	27.00	9.00
Lopez, Jorge	R-R	6-3	195	2-10-93	3	3	5.65	24	0	0	5	29	33	23	18	3	10	23	.290	.342	.263	7.22	3.14
2-team total (2 Omaha)					4	3	5.26	26	2	0	5	38	41	27	22	5	11	34	.277	.310	.256	8.12	2.63
Peralta, Freddy	R-R	5-11	175	6-4-96	6	2	3.10	13	13	0	0	61	49	23	21	1	28	87	.218	.267	.175	12.84	4.13
Perrin, Jon	R-R	6-5	220	5-23-93	2	0	2.59	18	0	0	0	24	16	8	7	2	12	18	.186	.206	.173	6.66	4.44
Ramirez, Nick	L-L	6-3	225	8-1-89	3	3	5.73	20	2	0	0	38	44	26	24	3	21	18	.297	.304	.294	4.30	5.02
Reynolds, Danny	R-R	6-0	190	5-2-91	0	0	13.50	2	0	0	0	2	5	3	3	1	2	1	.556	.800	.250	4.50	9.00
Roegner, Cameron	L-L	6-6	205	6-19-93	0	1	7.11	2	1	0	0	6	10	8	5	0	5	6	.385	.250	.444	8.53	7.11
Sanchez, Miguel	R-R	6-3	190	12-31-93	0	0	0.00	1	0	0	0	2	1	0	0	0	2	3	.143	.000	.200	13.50	9.00
Thompson, Jake	R-R	6-4	225	1-31-94	0	0	1.69	5	0	0	1	5	6	1	1	0	3	6	.286	.250	.333	10.13	5.06
Torres-Costa, Quintin	L-L	5-11	190	9-11-94	2	0	1.50	22	0	0	2	24	10	5	4	0	12	21	.132	.150	.111	7.88	4.50
Ventura, Angel	R-R	6-2	185	4-7-93	1	0	10.13	3	0	0	0	5	7	6	6	2	3	5	.318	.200	.353	8.44	5.06
Wilkerson, Aaron	R-R	6-3	190	5-24-89	4	5	2.49	15	12	0	0	72	64	27	20	3	25	61	.236	.216	.250	7.59	3.11
Williams, Taylor	B-R	5-11	195	7-21-91	0	0	4.50	2	0	0	1	2	2	1	1	0	1	2	.250	.500	.000	9.00	4.50
Woodruff, Brandon	L-R	6-4	215	2-10-93	3	2	4.04	17	17	0	0	71	67	35	32	8	32	68	.246	.198	.277	8.58	4.04
Zagurski, Mike	L-L	6-0	240	1-27-83	1	1	3.20	49	0	0	4	45	39	21	16	5	17	66	.227	.210	.242	13.20	3.40

Fielding

Catcher	PCT	G	PO	A	E	DP	PB
Bandy	.986	29	206	12	3	2	1
Bethancourt	.991	74	541	35	5	1	7
Heineman	.980	5	48	2	1	1	0
Houle	1.000	7	20	1	0	0	0
Nottingham	.984	32	226	16	4	1	1
Rojas	.950	3	18	1	1	0	1

First Base	PCT	G	PO	A	E	DP
Bandy	.995	21	179	8	1	14
Bethancourt	1.000	8	51	5	0	3
Blanco	.997	44	322	25	1	43
Choi	.989	38	268	14	3	28
Coulter	1.000	1	1	0	0	0
Heineman	1.000	1	9	1	0	1
Moore	.981	9	52	1	1	4
Nottingham	.985	9	59	6	1	6
Opitz	1.000	10	67	3	0	9
Ramirez	1.000	3	6	0	0	1
Shaffer	.976	12	74	6	2	12
Thames	1.000	2	17	0	0	2

Second Base	PCT	G	PO	A	E	DP
Blanco	.979	14	14	32	1	9
Dubon	.955	4	9	12	1	3

	PCT	G	PO	A	E	DP
Hager	.970	16	31	33	2	9
Miller	1.000	1	2	2	0	1
Moore	.973	25	52	56	3	16
Noriega	1.000	8	10	12	0	3
Opitz	1.000	10	6	17	0	4
Orf	.991	48	92	136	2	37
Saladino	.969	9	10	21	1	4
Sogard	.988	18	32	52	1	10
Villar	1.000	3	0	11	0	0

Third Base	PCT	G	PO	A	E	DP
Bandy	.000	1	0	0	0	0
Blanco	.945	32	19	50	4	6
Bonifacio	1.000	3	1	3	0	0
Moore	.930	54	26	107	10	9
Noriega	1.000	22	14	24	0	1
Opitz	.943	30	13	37	3	3
Orf	.966	14	6	22	1	2
Saladino	.750	2	3	0	1	0

Shortstop	PCT	G	PO	A	E	DP
Arcia	.991	22	35	77	1	15
Blanco	1.000	5	4	11	0	3
Dubon	.944	23	38	63	6	19
Hager	.983	16	9	48	1	10

	PCT	G	PO	A	E	DP
Miller	.900	6	7	20	3	6
Moore	1.000	7	11	26	0	5
Noriega	1.000	1	0	1	0	0
Orf	.964	39	42	93	5	22
Saladino	1.000	25	36	63	0	19
Sogard	1.000	5	4	14	0	1

Outfield	PCT	G	PO	A	E	DP
Berry	.978	27	45	0	1	0
Bonifacio	1.000	2	1	0	0	0
Broxton	.982	74	163	5	3	1
Choi	1.000	1	3	0	0	0
Coulter	1.000	11	23	0	0	0
Davis	1.000	6	6	0	0	0
Liriano	.986	34	64	5	1	1
Moore	.889	7	8	0	1	0
Orf	.952	10	19	1	1	0
Phillips	.985	67	133	2	2	0
Santana	.935	50	70	2	5	0
Shaffer	.000	3	0	0	0	0
Taylor	.996	115	215	18	1	4
Thames	1.000	2	2	0	0	0
Wren	.966	39	55	2	2	1

BILOXI SHUCKERS

DOUBLE-A

SOUTHERN LEAGUE

Batting	B-T	HT	WT	DOB	AVG	vLH	vRH	G	AB	R	H	2B	3B	HR	RBI	BB	HBP	SH	SF	SO	SB	CS	SLG	OBP
Allemand, Blake	B-R	5-10	175	7-1-92	.259	.241	.266	106	305	36	79	12	1	6	19	30	6	0	3	62	2	2	.364	.334
Aviles Jr., Luis	R-R	6-1	170	3-16-95	.251	.266	.245	64	207	24	52	14	0	4	23	23	1	1		52	14	3	.377	.328
Berry, Quintin	L-L	6-1	195	11-21-84	.250	.500	.000	1	4	2	1	0	0	0	1	0	0	0		1	0	0	.250	.400
Coulter, Clint	R-R	6-3	225	7-30-93	.256	.269	.252	78	223	36	57	11	3	11	35	17	5	0	3	70	2	2	.480	.319
Erceg, Lucas	L-R	6-3	210	5-1-95	.248	.255	.247	123	463	52	115	21	1	13	51	37	3	1	4	82	3	1	.382	.306
Franklin, Nick	B-R	6-1	190	3-2-91	.288	.188	.326	20	59	10	17	3	0	2	8	11	0	0	1	7	4	1	.441	.394
Gatewood, Jake	R-R	6-5	190	9-25-95	.244	.326	.218	94	352	45	86	19	1	19	59	28	3	0	5	114	2	0	.466	.302
Ghelfi, Mitch	B-R	5-11	185	9-24-92	.220	.500	.182	14	50	1	11	1	0	0	3	2	0	0		6	1	0	.240	.291
2-team total (24 Mobile)					.252	.300	.238	38	131	12	33	5	1	3	18	9	2	0	2	25	4	0	.374	.306
Grisham, Trent	L-L	6-0	205	11-1-96	.233	.250	.227	107	335	45	78	10	2	7	31	63	2	3	2	87	11	3	.337	.356
Hager, Jake	R-R	6-1	170	3-4-93	.292	.263	.303	64	219	28	64	18	1	10	40	28	1	1	6	44	6	0	.521	.371
Heineman, Tyler	B-R	5-11	205	6-19-91	.255	.321	.234	72	224	29	57	11	0	4	23	36	4	4	5	32	3	1	.357	.361
Hiura, Keston	R-R	5-11	190	8-2-96	.272	.269	.274	73	279	36	76	18	2	6	20	22	6	0	0	56	11	5	.416	.339
Houle, Dustin	R-R	6-1	205	11-9-93	.197	.318	.128	24	61	6	12	2	0	1	9	4	0	0	1	15	0	0	.230	.306

	B-T	HT	WT	DOB	AVG	vLH	vRH	G	AB	R	H	2B	3B	HR	RBI	BB	HBP	SH	SF	SO	SB	CS	SLG	OBP
McDowell, Max	R-R	6-1	208	1-12-94	.226	.276	.206	37	102	13	23	4	0	1	13	15	5	0	3	18	3	0	.294	.344
Mojica, Johan	R-R	6-1	220	10-15-95	.000	.000	—	3	2	0	0	0	0	0	0	0	0	0	0	2	0	0	.000	.000
Moore, Dylan	R-R	6-0	200	8-2-92	.374	.367	.377	24	83	12	31	7	3	3	18	7	1	0	0	16	6	1	.639	.429
Noriega, Gabriel	R-R	6-2	180	9-13-90	.214	.243	.200	44	117	7	25	1	0	1	16	6	0	0	4	30	1	1	.248	.244
Ray, Corey	L-L	6-0	195	9-22-94	.239	.243	.237	135	532	86	127	32	7	27	74	60	7	0	1	176	37	7	.477	.323
Rijo, Wendell	R-R	5-11	170	9-4-95	.200	.179	.212	32	80	14	16	2	0	4	14	12	0	1	0	20	1	3	.375	.304
Seferina, Darren	L-R	5-9	175	1-24-94	.111	.000	.120	14	27	3	3	0	0	0	0	1	0	0	9	2	0	.111	.143
Shaffer, Richie	R-R	6-3	230	3-15-91	.218	.333	.204	15	55	5	12	3	1	4	7	3	1	0	0	23	0	0	.527	.271
Stokes Jr., Troy	R-R	5-8	182	2-2-96	.233	.246	.229	129	467	74	109	23	6	19	58	65	15	0	4	147	19	2	.430	.343
Vogt, Stephen	L-R	6-0	225	11-1-84	.286	.000	.333	3	7	1	2	0	0	1	1	2	0	0	0	0	0	0	.714	.444
Wilson, Weston	R-R	6-3	195	9-11-94	.239	.269	.200	12	46	5	11	1	0	1	3	3	0	1	3	4	3	0	.286	.286

Pitching

	B-T	HT	WT	DOB	W	L	ERA	G	GS	CG	SV	IP	H	R	ER	HR	BB	SO	AVG	vLH	vRH	K/9	BB/9
Albers, Matt	L-R	6-1	225	1-20-83	1	0	0.00	3	0	0	0	4	2	0	0	0	0	6	.143	—	.143	13.50	0.00
Ames, Jeff	R-R	6-4	220	1-31-91	2	0	0.66	10	0	0	1	14	8	1	1	1	7	14	.163	.059	.219	9.22	4.61
Archer, Tristan	R-R	6-2	200	10-18-90	0	0	0.00	2	0	0	0	3	1	0	0	0	1	3	.091	.000	.333	3.00	0.00
Brown, Zack	R-R	6-1	180	12-15-94	9	1	2.44	22	21	1	0	126	95	44	34	8	36	116	.207	.220	.199	8.31	2.58
Davies, Zach	R-R	6-0	155	2-7-93	1	1	4.09	2	2	0	0	11	7	5	5	1	4	12	.189	.222	.179	9.82	3.27
Diplan, Marcos	R-R	6-0	170	9-16-96	2	6	4.58	12	11	0	0	57	58	35	29	6	36	57	.266	.277	.261	9.00	5.68
Diplan, Nattino	R-R	6-3	180	12-30-93	0	0	3.95	8	0	0	0	14	10	6	6	1	9	13	.208	.133	.242	8.56	5.93
Griep, Nate	R-R	6-2	190	10-11-93	2	1	3.34	51	0	0	34	57	48	22	21	4	35	53	.225	.260	.207	8.42	5.56
Harber, Conor	R-R	6-2	205	12-18-93	1	1	3.98	4	4	0	0	20	21	9	9	2	6	18	.276	.250	.286	7.97	2.66
Houser, Adrian	R-R	6-4	235	2-2-93	0	1	4.73	8	8	0	0	27	30	16	14	3	7	30	.286	.280	.291	10.13	2.36
Jankins, Thomas	R-R	6-3	200	7-2-95	10	9	4.42	23	21	0	0	130	130	69	64	13	36	95	.268	.260	.272	6.56	2.49
Knebel, Corey	R-R	6-4	220	11-26-91	0	0	0.00	3	0	0	0	3	1	0	0	0	1	4	.111	.250	.000	13.50	3.38
Kuntz, Brad	L-L	6-0	180	5-14-92	4	2	3.52	36	2	0	0	54	56	26	21	5	26	61	.272	.281	.266	10.23	4.36
Logan, Boone	R-L	6-5	215	8-13-84	0	0	9.00	5	0	0	0	3	3	3	3	0	4	3	.273	.250	.286	9.00	12.00
Medeiros, Kodi	L-L	6-2	180	5-25-96	7	5	3.14	20	15	0	0	103	90	45	36	9	45	107	.234	.160	.261	9.32	3.92
2-team total (7 Birmingham)					7	7	3.60	27	22	0	0	138	121	66	55	13	67	141	.238	.159	.268	9.22	4.38
Miley, Wade	L-L	6-0	220	11-13-86	1	2	3.55	7	7	0	0	25	27	12	10	3	4	28	.294	.324	.276	9.95	1.42
Olczak, Jon	R-R	6-0	180	11-14-93	10	3	1.44	42	0	0	4	56	36	17	9	1	18	60	.184	.175	.188	9.59	2.88
Ortiz, Luis	R-R	6-3	230	9-22-95	3	4	3.71	16	11	0	2	68	63	31	28	7	18	65	.240	.262	.224	8.60	2.38
Perrin, Jon	R-R	6-5	220	5-23-93	0	2	5.09	10	1	0	1	23	23	13	13	2	8	26	.296	.238	.238	10.17	3.13
Ponce, Cody	R-R	6-6	240	4-25-94	7	6	4.36	29	11	0	0	95	88	54	46	10	34	88	.244	.230	.255	8.34	3.22
Ramirez, Nick	L-L	6-3	225	8-1-89	8	0	1.76	19	0	0	1	31	17	9	6	2	13	33	.159	.266	.094	9.68	3.82
Reynolds, Danny	R-R	6-0	190	5-2-91	2	1	3.56	21	0	0	2	30	28	14	12	3	13	24	.237	.286	.222	7.12	3.86
Rodriguez, Wuilder	R-R	6-2	180	1-21-93	2	1	4.19	11	1	0	0	19	22	10	9	1	8	14	.293	.382	.220	6.52	3.72
Roegner, Cameron	L-L	6-6	205	6-19-93	0	1	5.74	5	5	0	0	16	21	10	10	5	6	11	.333	.333	.333	6.32	3.45
Sanchez, Miguel	R-R	6-3	190	12-31-93	1	1	2.63	23	0	0	1	41	32	13	12	3	14	62	.213	.227	.208	13.61	3.07
Supak, Trey	R-R	6-5	235	5-31-96	6	6	2.91	16	16	0	0	87	74	36	28	4	28	75	.232	.172	.266	7.79	2.91
Torres-Costa, Quintin	L-L	5-11	190	9-11-94	1	2	1.16	21	0	0	2	31	17	5	4	0	13	44	.160	.182	.145	12.77	3.77
Uhen, Josh	R-R	6-3	215	4-7-92	0	2	6.85	24	0	0	0	26	16	20	18	2	30	22	.188	.267	.171	8.37	11.41
Ventura, Angel	R-R	6-2	185	4-7-93	0	1	6.17	8	1	0	0	23	29	16	16	5	13	28	.296	.269	.326	10.80	5.01
Webb, Braden	R-R	6-2	195	4-25-95	1	0	1.80	4	3	0	0	20	13	4	4	0	10	24	.186	.100	.220	10.80	4.50

Fielding

Catcher	PCT	G	PO	A	E	DP	PB
Franklin	1.000	3	14	4	0	0	1
Ghelfi	.991	11	96	10	1	2	4
Heineman	.991	71	638	60	6	7	4
Houle	.977	24	150	22	4	2	2
McDowell	.983	36	264	29	5	0	4
Mojica	1.000	2	7	0	0	0	0
Vogt	.952	3	17	3	1	1	0

First Base	PCT	G	PO	A	E	DP
Coulter	.970	8	57	7	2	6
Franklin	1.000	1	8	0	0	0
Gatewood	.993	87	693	53	5	68
Ghelfi	1.000	1	7	0	0	1
Moore	1.000	7	50	1	0	7
Noriega	.988	23	151	17	2	17
Ramirez	1.000	3	15	1	0	1
Shaffer	.990	12	93	4	1	10
Wilson	1.000	4	33	2	0	4

Second Base	PCT	G	PO	A	E	DP
Allemand	.988	46	66	103	2	27
Franklin	1.000	4	5	7	0	1
Hiura	.964	64	110	129	9	38
Moore	.969	9	10	21	1	4
Noriega	1.000	1	1	3	0	0
Rijo	.962	21	32	43	3	12
Seferina	1.000	2	5	5	0	2

Third Base	PCT	G	PO	A	E	DP
Allemand	1.000	3	1	4	0	1
Erceg	.924	117	77	204	23	27
Franklin	1.000	4	0	5	0	0
Gatewood	1.000	1	0	2	0	0
Moore	1.000	2	2	5	0	2
Noriega	1.000	7	3	10	0	0
Rijo	.800	1	0	4	1	1
Wilson	1.000	8	13	13	0	6

Shortstop	PCT	G	PO	A	E	DP
Allemand	1.000	6	6	8	0	3
Aviles Jr.	.951	64	91	161	13	34
Franklin	.714	1	0	5	2	0
Hager	.971	64	63	168	7	34
Moore	.900	3	3	6	1	1
Noriega	1.000	5	5	14	0	2
Rijo	1.000	1	1	0	0	0
Seferina	1.000	3	6	5	0	3

Outfield	PCT	G	PO	A	E	DP
Allemand	1.000	4	4	0	0	0
Berry	1.000	1	2	0	0	0
Coulter	.962	55	68	7	3	1
Franklin	1.000	6	7	2	0	0
Gatewood	.000	3	0	0	0	0
Ghelfi	1.000	1	1	0	0	0
Grisham	.972	104	165	11	5	5
Moore	1.000	2	1	0	0	0
Ray	.976	135	314	8	8	0
Shaffer	1.000	3	1	0	0	0
Stokes Jr.	.995	123	217	2	1	0

CAROLINA MUDCATS   HIGH CLASS A
CAROLINA LEAGUE

Batting	B-T	HT	WT	DOB	AVG	vLH	vRH	G	AB	R	H	2B	3B	HR	RBI	BB	HBP	SH	SF	SO	SB	CS	SLG	OBP
Aguilar, Ryan	L-L	6-2	168	9-11-94	.223	.239	.217	126	430	51	96	21	9	8	56	64	2	6	4	138	5	1	.370	.324
Aviles Jr., Luis	R-R	6-1	170	3-16-95	.256	.242	.262	67	238	30	61	11	2	2	15	14	2	2	2	71	16	4	.345	.301
Belonis, Carlos	R-R	6-3	175	8-19-94	.165	.118	.188	35	103	9	17	1	1	2	10	14	2	0	0	43	3	0	.252	.277

	B-T	HT	WT	DOB	AVG	vLH	vRH	G	AB	R	H	2B	3B	HR	RBI	BB	HBP	SH	SF	SO	SB	CS	SLG	OBP
Carroll, Dallas	R-R	6-0	205	5-18-94	.224	.230	.222	134	508	54	114	24	1	7	53	65	4	4	6	113	9	4	.317	.314
Coulter, Clint	R-R	6-3	225	7-30-93	.241	.211	.256	15	58	8	14	7	1	1	2	5	1	0	0	21	0	0	.448	.313
Feliciano, Mario	R-R	6-1	195	11-20-98	.206	.260	.177	42	146	20	30	7	1	3	12	13	3	1	1	59	2	0	.329	.282
Franklin, Nick	B-R	6-1	190	3-2-91	.636	.000	.700	3	11	3	7	2	1	1	4	3	0	0	0	2	0	0	1.273	.714
Ghelfi, Mitch	B-R	5-11	185	9-24-92	.143	.182	.100	7	21	2	3	0	0	0	1	1	0	0	0	7	1	0	.143	.182
Gideon, Ronnie	R-R	6-2	225	9-20-94	.221	.258	.204	58	213	23	47	12	0	7	26	20	3	0	2	86	1	2	.376	.294
Hairston, Devin	R-R	5-8	175	4-7-96	.195	.197	.195	13	41	2	8	1	1	0	10	17	0	2	0	80	0	2	.256	.254
Henry, Rob	R-R	6-1	195	5-19-95	.202	.242	.187	48	124	15	25	6	1	2	15	31	3	2	1	40	6	1	.315	.371
Hiura, Keston	R-R	5-11	190	8-2-96	.320	.442	.279	50	206	38	66	16	3	7	23	14	7	0	1	47	4	6	.529	.382
Houle, Dustin	R-R	6-1	205	11-9-93	.296	.263	.314	17	54	5	16	4	0	0	7	4	2	2	2	16	0	0	.370	.355
Hummel, Cooper	B-R	5-10	190	11-28-94	.260	.265	.258	102	327	51	85	25	0	8	50	63	12	1	1	93	3	1	.410	.397
McDowell, Max	R-R	6-1	208	1-12-94	.222	.255	.208	47	153	16	34	6	1	2	12	14	5	3	1	36	2	1	.314	.306
McInerney, Pat	R-R	6-5	245	9-14-94	.112	.147	.094	33	98	6	11	4	0	0	5	17	0	1	1	38	0	0	.153	.241
Morrison, Trever	L-R	6-0	175	4-21-95	.194	.083	.220	19	62	4	12	2	0	2	6	10	0	0	1	23	1	0	.323	.301
Neuhaus, Tucker	L-R	6-3	190	6-18-95	.232	.184	.248	79	306	35	71	18	5	8	39	26	3	0	3	106	5	0	.402	.296
Orimoloye, Demi	R-R	6-4	225	1-6-97	.237	.232	.239	65	253	30	60	11	1	7	32	19	6	0	2	76	7	5	.372	.304
Rodriguez, Nathan	R-R	5-10	210	9-30-95	.202	.273	.183	35	104	11	21	3	0	2	9	16	2	0	0	17	1	0	.289	.320
Rojas, Robie	R-R	5-7	185	12-3-94	.351	.143	.400	13	37	7	13	2	0	0	5	6	1	0	0	15	0	0	.405	.455
Roscetti, Nick	R-R	6-3	190	11-6-93	.243	.260	.233	47	140	9	34	4	1	0	10	19	2	2	2	32	2	1	.286	.337
Segovia, Joantgel	R-R	6-1	175	11-8-96	.233	.177	.253	62	228	20	53	5	2	1	10	24	2	5	2	42	2	1	.285	.309
Thomas, Dillon	L-L	6-1	225	12-10-92	.293	.375	.273	13	41	7	12	2	0	0	5	11	3	0	1	17	1	1	.342	.464
Wilson, Weston	R-R	6-3	195	9-11-94	.274	.259	.280	105	383	60	105	23	2	13	62	31	4	0	6	93	7	4	.447	.330

Pitching

	B-T	HT	WT	DOB	W	L	ERA	G	GS	CG	SV	IP	H	R	ER	HR	BB	SO	AVG	vLH	vRH	K/9	BB/9
Barker, Luke	R-R	6-3	230	3-11-92	6	4	2.21	46	0	0	20	61	47	23	15	3	16	63	.213	.196	.225	9.30	2.36
Beckman, Cody	R-L	6-2	190	11-1-94	1	0	4.98	15	0	0	0	22	15	16	12	3	19	24	.190	.133	.225	9.97	7.89
Benoit, Rodrigo	R-R	6-2	170	2-23-94	0	1	2.38	7	0	0	0	11	12	3	3	0	0	18	.267	.292	.238	14.29	0.00
Bettinger, Alec	R-R	6-2	185	7-13-95	1	6	6.91	13	12	1	0	55	70	43	42	10	17	56	.315	.336	.294	9.22	2.80
Bickford, Phil	R-R	6-4	200	7-10-95	0	0	4.67	21	0	0	0	35	37	21	18	3	18	41	.276	.250	.300	10.64	4.67
Brown, Daniel	L-L	5-10	185	3-22-95	7	4	4.20	39	0	0	2	64	57	34	30	3	34	61	.235	.202	.255	8.53	4.76
Crawford, Alec	R-R	6-2	205	1-10-92	1	1	2.77	10	0	0	2	13	14	6	4	4	3	15	.275	.188	.314	10.38	2.08
Diaz, Victor	R-R	6-1	178	10-6-93	6	8	4.42	27	13	2	0	126	133	69	62	12	51	99	.275	.294	.263	7.05	3.63
Diplan, Marcos	R-R	6-0	170	9-18-96	3	2	3.52	13	13	0	0	61	58	26	24	3	38	60	.261	.196	.308	8.80	5.58
Diplan, Nattino	R-R	6-3	180	12-30-93	5	3	3.91	34	0	0	3	46	43	26	20	2	31	40	.246	.271	.229	7.83	6.07
Francis, Bowden	R-R	6-5	240	4-22-96	2	2	4.88	4	4	0	0	24	19	13	13	3	9	11	.216	.239	.191	4.13	3.38
Harber, Conor	R-R	6-2	205	12-18-93	4	5	2.26	25	11	0	0	96	73	25	24	4	45	78	.214	.205	.220	7.34	4.23
Kenilvort, Alec	R-R	6-6	230	1-7-93	4	3	4.24	40	0	0	1	68	61	38	32	6	26	66	.236	.204	.256	8.74	3.44
Kirby, Nathan	L-L	6-2	200	11-23-93	3	5	4.82	27	11	0	0	71	70	39	38	7	46	75	.256	.180	.294	9.51	5.83
Olczak, Jon	R-R	6-0	180	11-14-93	0	0	0.00	2	0	0	2	2	0	0	0	1	3	.250	.500	.167	13.50	4.50
Ortega, Jorge	R-R	6-1	165	6-20-93	0	5	8.88	8	6	0	0	24	40	30	24	4	4	7	.364	.390	.348	2.59	1.48
Ortiz, Braulio	R-R	6-7	253	12-20-91	0	0	8.10	10	0	0	0	6	9	9	9	1	9	12	.177	.143	.200	10.80	8.10
Rodriguez, Wuilder	R-R	6-2	180	1-21-93	0	0	5.28	16	0	0	0	31	38	22	18	5	14	18	.302	.255	.338	5.28	4.11
Roegner, Cameron	L-L	6-6	205	6-19-93	9	5	2.16	19	19	0	0	108	97	28	26	4	28	71	.246	.262	.240	5.90	2.33
Sanchez, Miguel	R-R	6-3	190	12-31-93	1	0	2.53	10	0	0	0	21	14	6	6	4	6	30	.182	.217	.167	12.66	2.53
Supak, Trey	R-R	6-5	235	5-31-96	2	1	1.76	9	9	0	0	51	37	10	10	2	16	48	.208	.239	.189	8.47	2.82
Taugner, Christian	R-R	6-3	215	5-14-95	3	1	4.91	5	5	1	0	26	27	15	14	4	7	19	.267	.245	.289	6.66	2.45
Webb, Braden	R-R	6-2	195	4-25-95	5	8	4.20	21	21	0	0	101	89	50	47	9	56	104	.239	.207	.266	9.30	5.01
Williams, Chase	R-R	6-6	210	11-23-92	2	3	6.86	18	0	0	3	21	20	17	16	2	21	19	.267	.200	.311	8.14	9.00
Williams, Devin	R-R	6-2	165	9-21-94	0	3	5.82	14	14	0	0	34	40	26	22	2	22	35	.301	.273	.328	9.26	5.82

Fielding

Catcher	PCT	G	PO	A	E	DP	PB
Feliciano	.986	25	201	15	3	1	0
Ghelfi	.980	6	44	4	1	0	0
Houle	.992	17	111	11	1	1	1
Hummel	.953	8	56	5	3	0	0
McDowell	.989	47	379	61	5	7	5
Rodriguez	.981	35	237	19	5	2	1
Rojas	.968	8	55	6	2	1	0

First Base	PCT	G	PO	A	E	DP
Aguilar	.995	28	200	13	1	10
Gideon	.991	52	391	28	4	39
McInerney	1.000	25	176	23	0	10
Neuhaus	1.000	1	5	0	0	1
Roscetti	.000	1	0	0	0	0
Wilson	1.000	38	280	22	0	28

Second Base	PCT	G	PO	A	E	DP
Carroll	.976	9	18	22	1	3
Franklin	1.000	2	3	0	0	0
Hairston	.987	22	27	47	1	5
Hiura	1.000	15	22	37	0	9
Neuhaus	.970	43	62	97	5	22
Roscetti	.988	39	70	91	2	16
Wilson	.977	13	18	24	1	9

Third Base	PCT	G	PO	A	E	DP
Carroll	.929	113	66	194	20	17
Morrison	.000	1	0	0	0	0
Neuhaus	.600	3	1	2	2	0
Roscetti	1.000	4	2	7	0	0
Wilson	.927	18	16	35	4	1

Shortstop	PCT	G	PO	A	E	DP
Aviles Jr.	.976	67	111	170	7	41

	PCT	G	PO	A	E	DP
Hairston	1.000	36	49	89	0	13
Morrison	.976	18	34	49	2	7
Neuhaus	.957	17	26	40	3	7
Roscetti	.714	2	2	3	2	1
Wilson	1.000	2	2	5	0	1

Outfield	PCT	G	PO	A	E	DP
Aguilar	.991	100	219	11	2	2
Belonis	.946	33	52	1	3	0
Coulter	1.000	15	29	2	0	1
Henry	1.000	47	68	6	0	0
Hummel	.978	51	83	5	2	2
Neuhaus	1.000	12	13	1	0	0
Orimoloye	.994	62	163	3	1	0
Segovia	.974	61	108	6	3	2
Thomas	1.000	13	25	3	0	1
Wilson	1.000	34	68	3	0	0

WISCONSIN TIMBER RATTLERS
MIDWEST LEAGUE

LOW CLASS A

Batting	B-T	HT	WT	DOB	AVG	vLH	vRH	G	AB	R	H	2B	3B	HR	RBI	BB	HBP	SH	SF	SO	SB	CS	SLG	OBP
Broxton, Keon	R-R	6-3	195	5-7-90	.167	.400	.000	3	12	1	2	0	0	0	0	2	0	0	0	7	2	0	.167	.286
Clark, Zach	R-R	6-2	200	12-5-95	.246	.250	.245	108	382	50	94	15	8	8	35	36	4	4	1	166	19	12	.390	.317

Batting	B-T	HT	WT	DOB	AVG	vLH	vRH	G	AB	R	H	2B	3B	HR	RBI	BB	HBP	SH	SF	SO	SB	CS	SLG	OBP
Corey, Kenny	L-R	6-1	185	2-15-95	.253	.308	.242	45	150	15	38	8	0	0	13	12	2	2	4	37	3	1	.307	.310
Diaz, Brent	R-R	6-1	205	3-22-96	.194	.188	.196	26	72	9	14	2	0	3	13	12	1	0	2	22	0	0	.347	.310
Feliciano, Jay	R-R	6-2	215	9-28-95	.187	.207	.180	69	230	26	43	12	0	4	29	20	5	0	0	62	0	1	.291	.267
Fry, David	R-R	6-0	195	11-20-95	.222	.333	.000	2	9	0	2	0	0	0	0	0	0	0	0	3	0	0	.222	.222
Garcia, Gabriel	R-R	6-3	185	12-16-97	.197	.250	.180	106	325	41	64	16	2	5	35	43	7	3	3	115	5	4	.305	.302
Hairston, Devin	R-R	5-8	175	4-7-96	.218	.333	.176	39	124	18	27	2	2	0	12	24	1	0	0	41	2	0	.266	.349
Harrison, KJ	R-R	6-0	208	8-11-96	.228	.281	.213	115	417	45	95	29	0	12	51	39	5	0	5	147	2	2	.384	.298
Henry, Payton	R-R	6-2	215	6-24-97	.234	.203	.244	98	337	44	79	15	2	10	41	38	10	1	3	124	1	3	.380	.327
Henry, Rob	R-R	6-1	195	5-19-95	.253	.333	.227	26	87	12	22	3	2	0	10	11	2	0	0	19	8	2	.333	.350
Lara, Gilbert	R-R	6-4	198	10-30-97	.249	.315	.231	115	430	45	107	26	2	5	46	18	2	0	2	94	1	3	.354	.281
Lutz, Tristen	R-R	6-3	210	8-22-98	.246	.260	.241	119	444	63	109	33	3	13	63	46	6	1	6	139	9	3	.421	.321
Mallen, Franly	R-R	6-1	160	5-27-97	.177	.250	.167	11	34	5	6	2	1	0	1	3	0	1	0	11	0	0	.294	.243
McClanahan, Chad	L-R	6-5	200	12-22-97	.171	.200	.164	21	76	8	13	2	0	1	8	6	4	0	2	33	0	0	.237	.261
McInerney, Pat	R-R	6-0	245	9-14-94	.230	.162	.247	56	187	32	43	8	1	10	25	37	3	1	2	68	5	3	.444	.362
Morrison, Trever	L-R	6-0	175	4-21-95	.253	.174	.263	54	198	22	50	8	0	0	23	18	3	3	3	58	8	2	.293	.320
Orimoloye, Demi	R-R	6-4	225	11-4-97	.261	.347	.235	61	215	27	56	9	5	5	23	22	6	0	2	52	15	5	.419	.343
Pierre, Nic	R-R	6-3	170	11-13-96	.174	.174	.174	30	92	11	16	4	0	0	4	3	0	1	1	28	2	1	.217	.198
Pina, Manny	R-R	6-0	215	6-5-87	.333	—	.333	1	3	0	1	0	0	0	1	0	0	0	0	0	0	0	.333	.500
Roscetti, Nick	R-R	6-3	190	11-6-93	.326	.345	.321	39	141	19	46	6	1	0	19	5	0	0	1	25	5	3	.383	.347
Saladino, Tyler	R-R	6-0	200	7-20-89	.000	.000	.000	3	8	0	0	0	0	0	0	3	0	0	0	2	0	0	.000	.273
Seferina, Darren	L-R	5-9	175	1-24-94	.242	.220	.247	63	240	37	58	10	3	3	16	40	0	1	1	52	13	8	.346	.349
Segovia, Joantgel	R-R	6-1	175	11-8-96	.347	.415	.329	50	202	25	70	11	1	2	24	13	4	4	0	29	12	5	.441	.397
Silva, Eddie	R-R	6-0	218	4-12-96	.321	.371	.302	33	131	16	42	8	1	5	20	7	2	0	2	23	3	3	.512	.359

Pitching	B-T	HT	WT	DOB	W	L	ERA	G	GS	CG	SV	IP	H	R	ER	HR	BB	SO	AVG	vLH	vRH	K/9	BB/9
Albers, Matt	L-R	6-1	225	1-20-83	0	0	0.00	1	0	0	0	1	0	0	0	0	0	0	.000	.000	.000	0.00	0.00
Andrews, Clayton	L-L	5-6	160	1-4-97	6	1	1.33	14	0	0	0	27	14	6	4	3	5	42	.156	.143	.161	14.00	1.67
Ashby, Aaron	R-L	6-1	170	5-24-98	1	1	2.17	7	7	0	0	37	40	9	9	1	9	47	.274	.321	.263	11.33	2.17
Beckman, Cody	R-L	6-2	190	11-1-94	1	1	2.84	25	0	0	1	38	26	18	12	1	16	36	.194	.155	.224	8.53	3.79
Benoit, Rodrigo	R-R	6-2	170	2-23-94	0	3	3.56	31	0	0	10	43	46	21	17	3	18	56	.233	.220	.239	11.72	3.77
Bettinger, Alec	R-R	6-2	185	7-13-95	5	4	3.73	12	11	0	0	63	59	28	26	6	17	50	.250	.269	.235	7.18	2.44
Biasi, Sal	R-R	6-0	190	9-30-95	0	0	2.03	6	0	0	0	13	10	3	3	1	8	11	.208	.177	.226	7.43	5.40
Davies, Zach	R-R	6-0	155	2-7-93	1	0	2.84	4	4	1	0	19	19	6	6	2	0	19	.271	.324	.222	9.00	0.00
De La Cruz, Joaquin	R-R	6-2	195	10-13-95	0	2	7.00	4	1	0	0	9	16	8	7	1	9	9	.421	.389	.450	3.00	9.00
File, Dylan	R-R	6-1	180	6-4-96	8	10	3.96	25	25	0	0	136	152	68	60	15	28	114	.284	.249	.312	7.53	1.85
Francis, Bowden	R-R	6-5	240	4-22-96	5	8	4.41	22	19	0	0	104	120	63	51	9	29	95	.288	.292	.284	8.22	2.51
Friese, Gabe	L-R	6-3	180	5-5-95	3	5	4.70	35	0	0	6	61	66	32	32	6	17	37	.274	.299	.257	5.43	2.49
Hardy, Matt	R-R	6-0	160	7-15-95	5	1	5.72	36	0	0	0	50	49	33	32	5	17	45	.257	.207	.294	8.05	3.04
Hernandez, Nelson	R-R	6-2	170	3-13-97	10	10	4.95	28	28	0	0	135	158	80	74	8	47	83	.293	.341	.259	5.55	3.14
Herrera, Carlos	R-R	6-2	150	10-26-97	3	6	5.46	28	11	0	1	86	95	54	52	5	48	60	.292	.281	.301	6.30	5.04
Hintzen, J.T.	R-R	6-0	185	6-1-96	3	1	3.22	15	1	0	1	36	32	16	13	2	10	41	.230	.286	.193	10.16	2.48
Hitt, Robbie	R-R	6-2	185	6-21-96	2	4	4.04	39	0	0	9	62	69	30	28	0	23	58	.286	.279	.292	8.37	3.32
Meister, Christian	R-R	6-3	210	10-29-93	1	1	4.50	7	0	0	1	8	4	4	4	0	9	10	.148	.250	.105	11.25	10.13
Montas, Jenri	R-R	6-3	200	8-10-96	0	0	8.22	5	0	0	0	8	10	7	7	0	9	5	.303	.231	.350	5.87	10.57
Ortiz, Braulio	R-R	6-7	253	12-20-91	0	0	3.38	10	0	0	0	13	10	7	5	0	17	22	.196	.191	.200	14.85	11.48
Pennington, Josh	R-R	6-0	190	7-6-95	0	0	0.00	2	0	0	0	2	0	0	0	0	3	2	.000	.000	.000	9.00	13.50
Peralta, Freddy	R-R	5-11	175	6-4-96	0	0	4.50	1	1	0	0	2	1	1	1	0	0	5	.143	.000	.167	22.50	0.00
Petersen, Michael	R-R	6-7	195	5-16-94	2	1	3.46	32	0	0	4	68	61	28	26	5	25	62	.247	.248	.247	8.25	3.33
Salaman, Wilfred	L-L	5-11	210	10-5-97	0	2	6.43	9	6	0	0	28	34	21	20	0	17	29	.296	.286	.300	9.32	5.46
Sunitsch, Scott	L-L	6-1	205	6-16-96	3	0	1.71	4	4	0	0	21	25	4	4	0	6	14	.298	.200	.319	6.00	2.57
Taugner, Christian	R-R	6-3	215	5-14-95	7	7	3.49	22	22	0	0	124	136	52	48	11	19	90	.278	.304	.260	6.55	1.38

Fielding

C: Diaz 26, Harrison 26, Henry 93. **1B:** Corey 1, Garcia 33, Harrison 54, McClanahan 8, McInerney 47. **2B:** Corey 20, Hairston 15, Mallen 11, Morrison 7, Roscetti 36, Seferina 39, Silva 14. **3B:** Garcia 65, Lara 66, Roscetti 1, Silva 14. **SS:** Hairston 24, Lara 50, Morrison 48, Roscetti 1, Saladino 3, Seferina 17. **OF:** Broxton 3, Clark 105, Feliciano 46, Garcia 7, Henry 6, Lutz 109, McClanahan 13, Orimoloye 46, Pierre 28, Segovia 46.

HELENA BREWERS
PIONEER LEAGUE

ROOKIE

Batting	B-T	HT	WT	DOB	AVG	vLH	vRH	G	AB	R	H	2B	3B	HR	RBI	BB	HBP	SH	SF	SO	SB	CS	SLG	OBP
Abreu, Pablo	R-R	6-0	170	10-19-99	.250	.303	.240	61	208	33	52	14	0	7	33	28	0	2	3	61	9	1	.418	.335
Alescio, Mike	R-R	6-1	200	6-4-96	.180	.214	.170	21	61	8	11	2	0	1	6	4	1	1	2	21	0	1	.262	.235
Avila, Luis	R-R	5-11	150	3-5-99	.300	.182	.338	26	90	12	27	4	1	0	8	2	0	0	1	20	2	1	.367	.312
Carmona, Jean	B-R	6-1	183	10-31-99	.239	.194	.250	39	155	28	37	8	3	4	24	13	1	1	2	45	5	3	.407	.298
Castillo, Leugim	R-R	6-2	215	7-18-99	.285	.314	.278	65	260	28	74	5	5	5	39	8	1	1	1	61	5	7	.400	.307
Coca, Yeison	B-R	5-10	155	5-22-99	.281	.373	.261	68	281	49	79	14	7	3	21	13	1	9	0	66	16	9	.413	.315
Connell, Bryan	R-R	6-3	195	11-9-98	.219	.286	.203	21	73	11	16	3	0	2	11	6	1	0	0	32	1	1	.343	.288
2-team total (5 Great Falls)					.183	.235	.171	26	93	12	17	3	0	2	12	6	2	0	0	42	1	1	.280	.248
Egnatuk, Nick	R-R	6-2	185	12-21-98	.220	.258	.207	30	118	14	26	3	1	4	16	4	2	1	0	39	2	2	.364	.258
Fry, David	R-R	6-0	195	11-20-95	.315	.317	.315	61	222	44	70	15	2	12	57	29	7	0	3	42	2	1	.563	.406
Lujano, Jesus	L-L	5-10	160	2-18-99	.297	.299	.299	60	196	34	55	9	3	1	22	16	1	6	0	32	8	6	.372	.338
McClanahan, Chad	L-R	6-5	200	12-22-97	.301	.211	.324	49	183	30	55	14	3	8	35	24	2	0	3	55	3	4	.541	.382
McVey, Connor	R-R	5-11	190	4-10-95	.250	.125	.273	16	52	8	13	2	0	1	2	10	2	0	0	13	2	1	.346	.391
Pinero, Antonio	B-R	6-1	155	3-15-99	.238	.143	.286	5	21	3	5	1	0	0	5	0	0	1	0	4	0	0	.286	.238
Rojas, Robie	R-R	5-7	185	12-3-94	.429	—	.429	3	7	4	3	0	0	1	4	2	0	0	0	1	0	0	.857	.556

	B-T	HT	WT	DOB	AVG	vLH	vRH	G	AB	R	H	2B	3B	HR	RBI	BB	HBP	SH	SF	SO	SB	CS	SLG	OBP
Sibrian, Jose	R-R	5-11	175	10-24-98	.197	.231	.188	37	127	11	25	5	0	1	8	7	6	0	0	28	0	0	.260	.271
Silva, Eddie	R-R	6-0	218	4-12-96	.361	.455	.344	20	72	14	26	11	0	1	17	2	4	1	0	12	2	2	.556	.410
Torres, Bryan	L-R	5-11	165	7-2-97	.278	.211	.290	37	126	12	35	6	1	1	16	6	0	3	0	16	4	5	.365	.311
Turang, Brice	L-R	6-1	165	11-21-99	.268	.261	.270	29	112	26	30	4	1	1	11	22	0	0	1	28	6	1	.348	.385
Ward, Je'Von	L-R	6-5	190	10-25-99	.307	.375	.290	64	238	40	73	13	2	2	21	32	1	0	0	57	13	5	.403	.391

Pitching	B-T	HT	WT	DOB	W	L	ERA	G	GS	CG	SV	IP	H	R	ER	HR	BB	SO	AVG	vLH	vRH	K/9	BB/9
Andrews, Clayton	L-L	5-6	160	1-4-97	0	0	6.00	5	0	0	0	6	9	4	4	0	2	12	.346	.200	.381	18.00	3.00
Ashby, Aaron	R-L	6-1	170	5-24-98	1	2	6.20	6	3	0	1	20	18	15	14	3	8	19	.234	.273	.218	8.41	3.54
Budnick, Tate	R-R	6-0	205	4-25-96	0	2	5.92	13	0	0	0	24	28	19	16	3	5	25	.292	.286	.295	9.25	1.85
Bullock, Justin	R-R	6-2	195	5-12-99	2	5	5.68	13	13	0	0	59	68	39	37	9	23	66	.294	.316	.287	10.13	3.53
Castaneda, Victor	R-R	6-1	185	8-27-98	2	6	5.13	14	8	0	0	47	59	40	27	10	15	40	.298	.313	.291	7.61	2.85
Delgado, Roberto	R-R	6-5	240	7-27-96	2	1	2.73	17	0	0	1	26	35	15	8	2	10	18	.318	.241	.346	6.15	3.42
Dominguez, Johan	R-R	6-4	190	1-18-96	0	0	4.50	2	0	0	0	2	3	2	1	0	1	3	.300	.333	.286	13.50	4.50
2-team total (2 Great Falls)					0	0	2.25	4	0	0	0	4	4	2	1	0	1	7	.235	.250	.231	15.75	2.25
Gillaspie, Logan	R-R	6-2	195	4-17-97	0	0	3.94	10	0	0	2	16	15	8	7	0	2	15	.238	.200	.256	8.44	1.13
Hall, Chris	R-R	6-2	212	1-27-94	0	0	2.70	4	0	0	0	3	4	1	1	0	3	5	.308	.333	.300	13.50	8.10
Hernandez, Franklin	R-R	6-0	175	10-29-95	0	0	6.75	2	0	0	0	3	3	2	2	0	1	0	.300	.000	.375	0.00	3.38
Hintzen, J.T.	R-R	6-0	185	6-1-96	0	0	0.00	2	0	0	0	1	0	0	0	0	0	2	.100	.000	.125	18.90	2.70
Lazar, Max	R-R	6-3	165	6-3-99	3	3	4.37	14	14	0	0	68	74	37	33	7	15	55	.269	.310	.250	7.28	1.99
Lemons, Caden	R-R	6-6	175	12-2-98	1	2	6.27	5	5	0	0	19	26	17	13	2	9	17	.321	.394	.271	8.20	4.34
Lillis, Blake	L-L	6-3	180	3-10-98	2	5	5.24	12	10	0	0	46	52	36	27	5	20	27	.280	.220	.297	5.24	3.88
Matulovich, Joey	R-R	6-3	195	7-6-97	3	3	2.75	12	2	0	0	36	27	14	11	1	14	49	.209	.222	.202	12.25	3.50
Mediavilla, Michael	L-L	6-5	225	8-14-95	3	1	0.00	14	0	0	4	20	7	3	0	0	3	22	.117	.077	.128	10.07	1.37
Montas, Jenri	R-R	6-3	200	8-10-96	2	2	6.92	16	0	0	0	26	39	24	20	4	10	13	.345	.471	.291	4.50	3.46
Pinto, Joel	R-R	6-3	180	9-25-96	1	2	8.56	5	4	0	0	14	23	16	13	0	6	5	.371	.320	.405	3.29	3.95
Presley, Brandon	R-L	6-7	205	11-21-96	0	2	9.16	18	0	0	0	19	27	22	19	3	10	18	.342	.290	.375	8.68	4.82
Rock, Kody	R-R	6-4	220	5-17-94	1	0	9.95	4	0	0	0	5	9	7	0	2	2	2	.469	.600	.444	2.84	2.84
Rubick, Austin	R-R	6-3	210	8-11-97	1	0	14.09	8	0	0	0	8	5	12	12	0	15	6	.208	.200	.211	7.04	17.61
Salaman, Wilfred	L-L	5-11	210	10-5-97	4	1	2.66	8	8	0	0	44	35	14	13	2	20	31	.219	.268	.202	6.34	4.09
Schanuel, Brady	R-R	6-3	180	2-21-97	0	0	16.39	8	0	0	0	9	19	18	17	0	10	13	.413	.357	.438	12.54	9.64
Strzelecki, Peter	R-R	6-1	195	10-24-94	2	2	5.60	21	0	0	3	27	26	20	17	2	11	38	.248	.324	.211	12.51	3.62
Sunitsch, Scott	L-L	6-1	205	6-16-96	2	0	4.75	8	5	0	0	30	28	16	16	1	12	23	.237	.200	.250	6.82	3.56
Tungate, Tyler	R-R	6-3	195	2-2-96	1	0	3.51	15	0	0	0	26	26	13	10	3	6	22	.268	.162	.333	7.71	2.10
Vassalotti, Michele	R-R	6-2	180	8-2-00	0	1	7.29	6	4	0	0	21	34	19	17	4	8	12	.374	.345	.387	5.14	3.43
Whitmer, Chad	R-R	6-3	190	5-11-95	3	3	2.66	22	0	0	7	24	24	11	7	0	7	24	.267	.458	.197	9.13	2.66
Zhao, Lun	R-R	5-10	180	8-29-01	0	0	2.25	3	0	0	0	4	4	1	1	1	2		.267	.333	.222	4.50	0.00

Fielding

C: Alescio 20, Fry 23, Rojas 1, Sibrian 34, Torres 3. **1B:** Connell 5, Egnatuk 3, Fry 11, McClanahan 37, McVey 2, Torres 22. **2B:** Avila 17, Carmona 4, Coca 45, McVey 1, Silva 5, Torres 1, Turang 5. **3B:** Avila 7, Carmona 7, Egnatuk 26, Fry 8, McClanahan 10, McVey 13, Silva 7. **SS:** Avila 1, Carmona 27, Coca 22, Pinero 4, Turang 23. **OF:** Abreu 60, Castillo 56, Connell 7, Lujano 53, Ward 57.

AZL BREWERS   ROOKIE
ARIZONA LEAGUE

Batting	B-T	HT	WT	DOB	AVG	vLH	vRH	G	AB	R	H	2B	3B	HR	RBI	BB	HBP	SH	SF	SO	SB	CS	SLG	OBP
Alescio, Mike	R-R	6-1	200	6-4-96	.364	—	.364	4	11	1	4	0	1	0	3	0	0	0	0	3	0	0	.546	.364
Avalo, Luis	R-R	5-11	190	11-24-98	.213	.130	.235	28	108	10	23	10	0	1	16	4	3	0	3	39	0	0	.333	.254
Avila, Luis	R-R	5-11	150	3-5-99	.320	.000	.348	7	25	5	8	1	2	0	3	0	0	0	3	2	1		.520	.320
Bello, Micah	R-R	5-11	165	7-21-00	.240	.195	.257	39	154	25	37	4	3	1	15	18	1	1	0	41	10	1	.325	.324
Cipion, Arbert	R-R	6-2	186	5-9-00	.118	.111	.121	26	93	9	11	1	2	0	2	10	0	0	0	45	2	1	.172	.204
Ernesto, Larry	B-R	6-2	175	9-12-00	.350	.500	.250	5	20	4	7	2	0	0	2	1	0	0	1	6	0	1	.450	.364
Familia, Aaron	R-R	6-2	170	3-16-99	.206	.222	.200	32	102	19	21	5	0	0	4	17	3	0	0	37	2	0	.255	.336
Feliciano, Mario	R-R	6-1	195	11-20-98	.286	.250	.300	4	14	0	4	1	0	0	2	2	0	0	0	3	0	1	.357	.375
Florentino, Francis	R-R	6-1	180	10-13-99	.253	.250	.254	29	95	14	24	3	0	0	9	8	2	0	1	28	9	4	.284	.321
Franklin, Nick	B-R	6-1	190	3-2-91	.500	.333	.600	3	8	1	4	0	0	1	1	0	0	0	0	1	0	0	.875	.500
Garabitos, Pablo	L-L	6-1	170	7-30-00	.230	.231	.230	25	74	11	17	4	0	0	6	11	0	1	0	23	3	1	.284	.329
Gray, Joe	R-R	6-1	195	11-24-00	.182	.167	.186	24	77	14	14	5	0	2	9	18	2	0	1	25	6	0	.325	.347
Hall, Alex	B-R	5-8	161	6-8-00	.244	.111	.279	27	86	9	21	6	1	2	15	7	1	0	1	20	1	0	.407	.305
Howell, Korry	R-R	6-2	175	9-1-98	.311	.423	.273	28	103	15	32	4	0	0	6	14	1	1	0	24	12	4	.350	.398
Marquez, Caleb	R-R	6-3	240	12-22-99	.164	.133	.174	19	61	6	10	4	0	1	7	6	2	0	0	39	0	0	.279	.261
Martinez, Ernesto	L-L	6-4	225	6-20-99	.224	.087	.255	35	125	15	28	5	1	0	10	16	5	0	0	48	5	3	.280	.336
McVey, Connor	R-R	5-11	190	4-10-95	.267	.333	.250	11	30	4	8	1	0	1	4	6	0	1	0	9	2	2	.400	.389
Melendez, Anderson	R-R	6-2	165	5-31-00	.135	.143	.131	23	89	7	12	1	1	1	8	1	3	1	1	37	0	0	.202	.170
Melendez, Andres	R-R	5-10	150	5-21-01	.182	.167	.200	3	11	1	2	0	0	0	1	0	0	0	0	1	0	0	.182	.182
Perez, Moises	R-R	6-1	190	8-17-98	.077	.250	.000	5	13	1	1	0	0	0	2	0	1	1	0	8	0	0	.077	.143
Pierre, Nic	R-R	6-3	170	11-13-96	.333	.333	.333	4	18	1	6	3	0	0	3	5	1	0	0	3	0	0	.611	.368
Rios, Kekai	R-R	5-11	200	6-6-97	.333	.375	.324	19	42	10	14	5	0	0	6	16	2	0	0	7	1	1	.452	.533
Rodriguez, Carlos	L-L	5-10	150	12-7-00	.350	.333	.353	5	20	4	7	0	0	0	1	2	0	0	0	1	2	1	.350	.409
Saint, Orveo	R-R	6-2	190	11-10-99	.126	.148	.117	28	87	9	11	3	2	0	10	22	0	0	0	60	3	4	.207	.303
Sano, Edwin	B-R	5-9	160	12-12-98	.281	.211	.294	37	128	22	36	5	3	1	18	10	2	3	1	18	11	2	.391	.340
Sogard, Eric	L-R	5-9	185	5-22-86	.429	.333	.500	2	7	0	3	1	0	0	0	0	0	0	1	0	0	0	.571	.429
Torres, Bryan	L-R	5-11	165	7-2-97	.500	1.000	.333	2	4	3	2	0	0	0	2	2	0	0	0	1	0	1	.500	.667
Turang, Brice	L-R	6-1	165	11-21-99	.319	.333	.314	13	47	11	15	2	0	0	7	9	0	0	1	6	8	1	.362	.421
Williams, Jess	L-R	5-11	183	5-31-99	.270	.207	.286	39	141	13	38	5	3	0	21	7	2	0	2	36	4	2	.348	.309

MILWAUKEE BREWERS

MILWAUKEE BREWERS

Pitching	B-T	HT	WT	DOB	W	L	ERA	G	GS	CG	SV	IP	H	R	ER	HR	BB	SO	AVG	vLH	vRH	K/9	BB/9
Adames, Freisis	R-R	6-3	175	11-18-96	2	1	3.89	10	5	0	0	37	35	21	16	3	11	31	.241	.259	.231	7.54	2.68
Beasley, Wade	R-R	6-3	210	12-14-99	0	1	10.38	5	2	0	0	9	16	11	10	1	4	3	.364	.300	.417	3.12	4.15
Brea, Jesus	R-R	6-3	194	12-25-95	1	1	1.80	19	0	0	3	20	17	6	4	1	4	20	.227	.250	.216	9.00	1.80
Brown, Zack	R-R	6-1	180	12-15-94	0	0	0.00	1	1	0	0	2	3	0	0	0	1	3	.333	.333	.333	13.50	4.50
Budnick, Tate	R-R	6-0	205	4-25-96	0	1	3.24	5	0	0	0	8	9	5	3	0	2	5	.265	.222	.280	5.40	2.16
Dominguez, Johan	R-R	6-4	190	1-18-96	2	0	0.00	15	0	0	2	19	5	0	0	0	7	21	.085	.125	.070	9.78	3.26
Gillaspie, Logan	R-R	6-2	195	4-17-97	0	0	0.00	2	0	0	0	3	0	0	0	0	2	1	.000	.000	.000	5.40	
Gonzalez, Luis	R-R	6-3	175	5-6-99	1	2	6.35	7	2	0	0	11	15	14	8	2	13	6	.319	.444	.241	4.76	10.32
Hernandez, Franklin	R-R	6-0	175	10-29-95	0	0	2.53	5	2	0	0	11	12	4	3	0	5	12	.293	.177	.375	10.13	4.22
Jarvis, Justin	R-R	6-2	168	2-2-00	1	2	6.63	10	3	0	0	19	24	14	14	2	4	18	.329	.281	.366	8.53	1.89
Lemons, Caden	R-R	6-6	175	12-2-98	0	0	1.38	5	4	0	0	13	7	4	2	0	5	11	.149	.200	.125	7.62	3.46
Luna, Carlos	R-R	6-3	175	9-25-96	2	2	3.38	11	4	0	0	29	21	13	11	2	7	22	.196	.200	.194	6.75	2.15
McIntyre, Mitchell	R-R	6-3	195	10-22-94	1	0	2.41	18	0	0	0	19	16	12	5	0	9	23	.219	.217	.220	11.09	4.34
Mediavilla, Michael	L-L	6-5	225	8-14-95	0	0	1.69	8	0	0	1	11	7	2	2	0	2	9	.171	.167	.171	7.59	1.69
Meister, Christian	R-R	6-3	210	10-29-93	0	0	1.50	6	0	0	1	6	3	2	1	0	5	12	.136	.333	.000	18.00	7.50
Morales, Karlos	L-L	6-3	170	8-10-99	1	3	8.28	10	2	0	0	29	43	33	27	1	20	25	.331	.324	.333	7.67	6.14
Olson, Reese	R-R	6-1	160	7-31-99	0	2	5.23	4	2	0	0	10	11	8	6	0	4	6	.290	.333	.261	5.23	3.48
Ortega, Jorge	R-R	6-1	165	6-20-93	0	3	4.50	6	6	0	0	18	18	9	9	1	1	14	.257	.241	.268	7.00	0.50
Parra, Jose	R-R	6-3	180	3-18-97	0	3	7.97	12	2	0	0	20	34	26	18	3	5	19	.370	.378	.364	8.41	2.21
Pinto, Joel	R-R	6-3	180	9-25-96	1	2	4.07	7	3	0	1	24	25	12	11	0	6	21	.255	.256	.254	7.77	2.22
Robinson, Cam	R-R	5-11	187	9-6-99	1	4	5.50	11	7	0	0	36	43	30	22	0	25	37	.291	.368	.242	9.25	6.25
Rose, Jayson	R-R	6-0	180	2-20-96	0	0	0.00	2	2	0	0	3	2	0	0	1	1	1	.182	.000	.250	3.00	3.00
Salaya, Brayan	R-R	6-1	178	2-13-00	3	3	3.93	11	5	0	0	37	34	23	16	1	26	21	.252	.327	.205	5.15	6.38
Schanuel, Brady	R-R	6-3	180	2-21-97	0	0	4.22	9	0	0	2	11	6	5	5	0	7	19	.162	.143	.174	16.03	5.91
Strzelecki, Peter	R-R	6-2	195	10-24-94	0	0	4.50	2	0	0	0	2	3	2	1	0	0	3	.333	1.000	.000	13.50	0.00
Tolentino, Renny	R-R	6-0	190	7-11-96	1	2	6.08	15	0	0	0	24	27	21	16	2	9	31	.273	.243	.290	11.79	3.42
Tungate, Tyler	R-R	6-3	195	2-2-96	0	0	5.87	5	0	0	0	8	11	5	5	0	2	7	.324	.250	.364	8.22	2.35
Vassalotti, Michele	R-R	6-2	180	8-2-00	5	1	3.21	7	3	0	0	28	23	10	10	2	8	19	.226	.300	.177	6.11	2.57
Zhao, Lun	R-R	5-10	180	8-29-01	0	0	0.00	3	0	0	0	4	2	0	0	0	2	4	.133	.143	.125	8.31	4.15

Fielding

C: Alescio 2, Avalo 21, Feliciano 3, Hall 19, Marquez 8, Melendez 2, Perez 3, Rios 11, Torres 1. **1B:** Avalo 5, Familia 18, Martinez 32, Perez 1, Torres 1. **2B:** Avila 2, Franklin 3, McVey 3, Saint 12, Sano 29, Sogard 1, Williams 10. **3B:** Familia 14, Howell 7, McVey 6, Sano 4, Williams 27. **SS:** Avila 5, Howell 20, Saint 16, Sano 3, Turang 12. **OF:** Bello 38, Cipion 25, Ernesto 5, Florentino 27, Garabitos 24, Gray 22, Melendez 20, Pierre 4, Rodriguez 4.

DSL BREWERS   ROOKIE
DOMINICAN SUMMER LEAGUE

Batting	B-T	HT	WT	DOB	AVG	vLH	vRH	G	AB	R	H	2B	3B	HR	RBI	BB	HBP	SH	SF	SO	SB	CS	SLG	OBP
Casado, Francis	R-R	5-11	170	10-30-00	.111	.000	.143	12	36	3	4	2	0	0	2	3	0	0		12	1	0	.167	.180
Castillo, Daniel	B-R	5-11	150	1-25-01	.212	.211	.212	57	170	20	36	3	1	0	15	25	5	3	1	38	9	8	.241	.328
Chirinos, Jesus	R-R	6-0	165	7-27-01	.254	.225	.263	58	173	20	44	17	0	2	26	39	3	0	3	52	0	0	.387	.395
Cristian, Jeicor	L-L	6-3	155	5-31-01	.195	.231	.188	28	82	7	16	3	0	0	5	11	4	1	0	34	3	5	.232	.320
Cruz, Jean	R-R	6-0	155	10-27-99	.143	.333	.091	6	14	3	2	1	0	0	2	3	1	0	0	6	0	0	.214	.333
David, Jhonny	R-R	6-3	195	7-5-01	.314	.000	.379	12	35	6	11	4	0	0	6	2	1	0	0	17	2	1	.429	.368
Ernesto, Larry	B-R	6-2	175	9-12-00	.237	.096	.285	53	203	38	48	13	2	5	20	14	3	0	1	68	9	4	.394	.294
Ferrer, Alberis	R-R	6-0	150	12-17-00	.226	.211	.233	42	124	21	28	4	5	1	17	17	3	1	3	42	11	2	.363	.327
Frias, Juan	R-R	6-0	175	11-7-00	.221	.208	.225	32	104	11	23	2	0	1	15	12	1	0	1	21	9	1	.269	.305
Gonzalez, Francisco	B-R	5-11	174	3-9-00	.146	.130	.152	30	89	8	13	3	1	0	10	3	2	0	0	19	3	0	.202	.192
Leones, Oswel	L-R	6-0	165	10-6-00	.289	.277	.293	56	187	40	54	7	0	3	16	28	4	4	2	25	12	6	.374	.389
Manon, Farlyn	R-R	5-9	178	10-22-96	.211	.129	.250	33	95	11	20	3	1	1	15	11	4	1	0	13	4	0	.295	.318
Maria, Victor	R-R	6-2	160	9-22-99	.224	.256	.214	59	179	37	40	5	0	1	13	25	5	2	2	40	25	5	.268	.332
Melendez, Andres	R-R	5-10	150	5-21-01	.290	.167	.324	41	138	21	40	6	3	2	18	17	4	1	4	17	4	2	.399	.374
Rodriguez, Carlos	L-L	5-10	150	12-7-00	.323	.269	.339	56	217	38	70	13	1	2	32	7	5	1	0	19	12	8	.419	.358
Silva, Luis	R-R	6-0	178	7-6-01	.238	.261	.232	59	210	23	50	5	1	0	30	13	3	0	4	26	5	5	.271	.287
Valdez, Alwinson	R-R	6-3	195	4-1-01	.258	.225	.268	55	178	39	46	10	0	7	22	30	1	1	1	60	14	4	.433	.367
Valdez, Luis	R-R	6-3	195	9-12-99	.200	.000	.250	3	5	1	1	0	0	0	1	0	0	0	0	4	0	0	.200	.333
Vargas, Victor	R-R	5-7	160	8-15-00	.302	.059	.354	44	96	25	29	7	3	0	14	17	2	2	1	28	16	7	.438	.414

Pitching	B-T	HT	WT	DOB	W	L	ERA	G	GS	CG	SV	IP	H	R	ER	HR	BB	SO	AVG	vLH	vRH	K/9	BB/9
Alberro, Jose	L-L	6-1	168	2-2-98	4	2	1.80	18	0	0	2	45	28	16	9	2	11	56	.176	.148	.182	11.20	2.20
Arias, Deybi	R-R	6-1	155	5-27-01	0	1	22.50	4	0	0	0	2	3	8	5	1	6	3	.333		.333	13.50	27.00
Atagua, Alis	R-R	6-1	160	3-14-01	0	1	20.25	5	0	0	0	4	9	9	9	0	3	4	.438	.500	.417	6.75	20.25
Colina, Leoner	R-R	5-11	165	11-1-00	4	2	2.31	13	13	1	0	70	67	29	18	1	17	50	.253	.270	.242	6.43	2.19
Cruz, Jhoan	R-R	5-9	147	5-31-00	2	2	3.51	18	1	0	2	33	28	14	13	3	4	28	.233	.279	.208	7.56	1.08
De Jesus, Wilmy	R-R	6-0	170	2-26-00	1	3	4.81	10	7	0	0	34	21	19	18	2	21	20	.181	.120	.198	5.35	5.61
Diaz, Wilber	R-R	6-0	170	8-7-00	1	1	1.35	10	2	0	4	27	12	6	4	0	9	25	.133	.214	.097	8.44	3.04
Dominguez, Johan	R-R	6-4	190	1-18-96	1	0	1.54	6	0	0	0	12	7	3	2	0	5	12	.175	.188	.167	9.36	3.86
Elizondo, Santiago	R-R	5-9	142	10-25-99	5	3	4.42	14	7	0	1	53	49	28	26	2	13	44	.248	.225	.263	7.47	2.21
Espiritu, Jose	R-R	6-4	172	11-20-98	0	0	2.35	4	0	0	0	8	2	4	2	0	11	4	.083	.000	.125	4.70	12.91
Gonzalez, Davison	L-L	6-0	165	8-10-97	0	0	3.00	2	0	0	0	3	3	1	1	0	1	2	.250	.000	.273	6.00	3.00
Javier, Starling	R-L	6-2	172	12-17-00	0	0	27.00	1	0	0	0	1	1	2	2	0	1	1	.333	.500	.000	13.50	13.50
2-team total (8 DSL Indians/Brewers)					2	0	6.23	9	0	0	0	9	6	11	6	0	19	7	.200	.250	.182	7.27	19.73
Medina, Henry	R-R	6-0	175	9-5-97	4	2	1.41	13	13	1	0	76	71	23	12	1	10	33	.247	.255	.243	3.89	1.18
Mota, Claudio	R-R	6-3	194	7-19-97	0	0	9.00	2	0	0	0	5	7	6	5	1	4	4	.318	.250	.357	7.20	7.20

Name	B-T	HT	WT	DOB	W	L	ERA	G	GS	CG	SV	IP	H	R	ER	HR	BB	SO	AVG	vLH	vRH	K/9	BB/9
2-team total (18 DSL Indians/Brewers)					0	2	4.97	20	0	0	0	38	37	26	21	1	24	19	.250	.261	.241	4.50	5.68
Nunez, Wellington	R-R	6-2	171	10-17-99	0	0	18.69	10	0	0	1	9	16	19	18	1	12	4	.421	.500	.406	4.15	12.46
2-team total (1 DSL Indians/Brewers)					0	0	16.76	11	0	0	2	10	16	19	18	1	12	4	.381	.429	.371	3.72	11.17
Ortiz, Robert	R-R	6-3	185	7-23-01	1	0	3.60	7	0	0	0	10	10	6	4	0	9	1	.294	.333	.280	0.90	8.10
Perez, Wilber	R-R	6-2	170	11-3-97	5	1	2.01	8	0	0	0	40	25	11	9	0	13	47	.177	.160	.187	10.49	2.90
2-team total (6 DSL White Sox)					6	3	1.92	14	13	0	0	70	44	18	15	1	21	75	.182	.167	.193	9.60	2.69
Ramirez, Alexis	R-R	6-2	170	7-20-99	1	1	4.71	4	4	0	0	21	16	12	11	1	6	20	.211	.348	.151	8.57	2.57
2-team total (8 DSL Indians/Brewers)					1	3	4.72	12	11	0	0	55	50	31	29	4	21	52	.240	.280	.209	8.46	3.42
Ramirez, Dantel	R-R	6-1	170	1-7-99	4	1	2.94	19	0	0	5	34	32	16	11	2	6	35	.246	.214	.261	9.36	1.60
Romero, Jose	R-R	6-1	170	11-1-97	2	4	2.83	12	11	0	0	54	52	22	17	3	25	49	.257	.200	.288	8.17	4.17
Rosario, Leony	R-R	6-2	198	10-21-00	1	5	6.42	15	6	0	0	41	57	34	29	2	23	33	.341	.333	.344	7.30	5.09
Tolentino, Joandris	L-L	6-1	201	11-21-99	2	3	6.75	10	0	0	0	16	23	15	12	1	10	14	.333	.308	.339	7.88	5.63
2-team total (4 DSL Brewers)					2	5	5.18	14	4	0	0	33	47	23	19	1	13	27	.348	.241	.377	7.36	3.55
Uribe, Abner	R-R	6-2	200	6-20-00	2	0	3.32	12	0	0	0	19	10	8	7	0	10	21	.164	.200	.146	9.95	4.74
Vasquez, Victor	R-R	6-4	205	3-16-97	0	0	21.60	2	0	0	0	2	1	4	4	0	3	2	.167	1.000	.000	10.80	16.20
Vega, Ariel	R-R	6-2	190	4-4-01	0	0	0.00	2	0	0	0	3	0	0	0	0	1	1	.000	.000	.000	3.00	3.00

Fielding

C: Chirinos 20, Manon 31, Melendez 32, Silva 1. **1B:** Chirinos 34, Cruz 4, Frias 8, Gonzalez 17, Manon 3, Maria 12, Silva 12, Valdez 1, Vargas 1. **2B:** Castillo 2, Cruz 1, Gonzalez 11, Maria 17, Silva 18, Valdez 1, Vargas 31. **3B:** Cruz 1, Ferrer 24, Gonzalez 2, Maria 22, Silva 31. **SS:** Castillo 55, Ferrer 14, Maria 8, Silva 1. **OF:** Casado 4, Cristian 13, David 9, Ernesto 50, Frias 17, Leones 40, Rodriguez 51, Valdez 42, Valdez 1.

DSL INDIANS/BREWERS   ROOKIE
DOMINICAN SUMMER LEAGUE

Batting	B-T	HT	WT	DOB	AVG	vLH	vRH	G	AB	R	H	2B	3B	HR	RBI	BB	HBP	SH	SF	SO	SB	CS	SLG	OBP
Arteaga, Jose	B-R	5-8	155	1-25-01	.137	.133	.138	33	95	8	13	0	2	0	1	5	0	1	0	22	3	2	.179	.180
Avila, Luis	R-R	5-11	150	3-5-99	.243	.242		9	37	7	9	0	0	0	5	2	0	0	0	6	5	1	.243	.282
Brito, Rafael	R-R	6-2	180	10-25-98	.191	.120	.205	45	157	13	30	6	1	3	20	8	1	0	4	19	5	2	.299	.229
Connell, Bryan	R-R	6-3	195	11-9-98	.256	.267	.254	27	82	19	21	4	1	5	13	17	4	0	0	24	0	0	.512	.408
Dimas, Bryan	B-R	6-1	165	2-4-00	.137	.133	.138	51	139	20	19	3	2	1	11	29	4	0	3	90	5	6	.209	.297
Gonzalez, Elian	R-R	6-2	175	4-15-00	.212	.211	.212	44	151	20	32	7	3	2	9	17	3	0	0	34	7	7	.338	.304
Lugo, Eduin	R-R	5-11	170	7-14-01	.333	.500	.294	8	21	1	7	1	0	0	4	2	0	0	0	4	0	0	.381	.391
Marte, Alejandro	R-R	6-2	180	5-23-00	.228	.250	.223	37	114	11	26	4	2	4	12	15	2	0	4	31	3	1	.404	.319
Mercado, Reidy	B-R	5-11	153	1-6-01	.194	.300	.167	50	196	25	38	2	0	0	5	18	2	0	0	52	18	7	.204	.269
Molina, Roberto	R-R	5-9	160	12-7-99	.197	.200	.196	41	122	19	24	5	0	0	11	22	10	0	1	31	3	2	.238	.361
Munoz, Joel	R-R	5-10	155	12-26-96	.200	.500	.125	3	10	2	2	2	0	0	3	1	0	0	1	2	0	0	.400	.250
Valderrama, Luis	R-R	5-10	150	10-11-00	.180	.200	.177	14	39	3	7	1	0	0	3	4	1	0	0	7	0	1	.205	.273
Watanabe, Vitor	L-R	5-7	155	4-21-01	.154	.000	.179	29	78	7	12	1	2	0	5	10	4	1	0	25	1	1	.218	.283

Pitching	B-T	HT	WT	DOB	W	L	ERA	G	GS	CG	SV	IP	H	R	ER	HR	BB	SO	AVG	vLH	vRH	K/9	BB/9
Acosta, Daniel	R-R	6-1	185	2-27-97	1	4	6.46	20	0	0	0	31	28	28	22	1	39	29	.248	.275	.226	8.51	11.45
Bordones, Kleiber	R-R	6-3	175	12-10-00	1	6	5.71	13	11	0	0	52	49	36	33	6	37	35	.248	.265	.230	6.06	6.40
Javier, Starling	R-L	6-2	172	12-17-00	2	0	4.50	8	0	0	0	8	5	9	4	0	18	6	.185	.167	.191	6.75	20.25
2-team total (1 DSL Brewers)					2	0	6.23	9	0	0	0	9	6	11	6	0	19	7	.200	.250	.182	7.27	19.73
Morillo, Sergio	R-R	6-3	190	9-13-99	0	0	0.00	2	2	0	0	6	3	1	0	0	4	9	.158	.100	.200	13.50	6.00
2-team total (6 DSL Indians)					1	2	2.45	8	6	0	0	22	15	8	6	0	12	22	.200	.189	.211	9.00	4.91
Mota, Claudio	R-R	6-3	194	7-19-97	0	2	4.36	18	0	0	0	33	30	20	16	0	20	15	.238	.262	.215	4.09	5.45
2-team total (2 DSL Brewers)					0	2	4.97	20	0	0	0	38	37	26	21	1	24	19	.250	.261	.241	4.50	5.68
Nunez, Wellington	R-R	6-2	171	10-17-99	0	0	0.00	1	0	0	1	0	0	0	0	0	0	0	.000	.000	.000	0.00	0.00
2-team total (10 DSL Brewers)					0	0	16.76	11	0	0	2	10	16	19	18	1	12	4	.381	.429	.371	3.72	11.17
Ramirez, Alexis	R-R	6-2	170	7-20-99	0	2	4.72	8	7	0	0	34	34	19	18	3	15	32	.258	.257	.258	8.39	3.93
2-team total (4 DSL Brewers)					1	3	4.72	12	11	0	0	55	50	31	29	4	21	52	.240	.280	.209	8.46	3.42
Ruiz, Moises	R-R	6-2	170	10-3-98	2	5	4.01	14	12	0	0	52	48	28	23	1	29	33	.241	.237	.247	5.75	5.05
Tolentino, Joandris	L-L	6-1	201	11-21-99	0	2	3.71	4	4	0	0	17	24	8	7	0	3	13	.364	.188	.420	6.88	1.59
2-team total (10 DSL Brewers)					2	5	5.18	14	4	0	0	33	47	23	19	1	13	27	.348	.241	.377	7.36	3.55
Velasquez, Ricardo	R-R	6-2	175	8-9-99	2	0	2.83	19	0	0	1	41	32	18	13	2	27	32	.221	.333	.127	6.97	5.88

Fielding

C: Lugo 1, Molina 28, Valderrama 10. **1B:** Brito 18, Connell 9, Contreras 21, Gonzalez 2, Lugo 2, Molina 4, Valderrama 3. **2B:** Arteaga 22, Avila 1, Brito 4, Gonzalez 7. **3B:** Arteaga 4, Avila 1, Brito 17, Gonzalez 6. **SS:** Arteaga 5, Avila 5, Gonzalez 25. **OF:** Arteaga 1, Brito 3, Connell 14, Dimas 51, Marte 30, Mercado 50, Watanabe 26.

MILWAUKEE BREWERS

Minnesota Twins

SEASON IN A SENTENCE: The Twins finished second in the AL Central, but that's not saying much considering the historical weakness of the division as a whole and the fact that Minnesota finished the season below .500 (78-84) and 13 games behind the division-winning Indians.

HIGH POINT: The Twins entered a late May series with the Indians with a 22-29 record and beat the Tribe 3-1 before taking another series against their division rival, 2-1, a few weeks later. The team showed signs of life and the potential to follow up 2017 with back-to-back playoff appearances.

LOW POINT: After winning a Gold Glove and finishing top 20 in MVP voting in 2017, out-fielder Byron Buxton played just 28 games in the majors and didn't look like the same player when he was on the field. Third baseman Miguel Sano dealt with injuries and poor performance as well, managing just a .199/.281/.398 line while striking out 38.5 percent and being sent to the minors to try to figure things out. Additionally, the Twins were victims of 15 walk-off losses during the season—the most in the AL.

NOTABLE ROOKIES: Outfielder Jake Cave made his major league debut and hit .269/.316/.481 with 13 home runs and 17 doubles across 91 games, while catcher Mitch Garver logged 102 games and hit 268/.335/.414. Catcher Willians Astudillo got a brief callup in July but solidified his place with the team at the end of the season, when he hit .378/.397/.554 in 22 games. His unique build, high-contact approach and ability to play five positions made him eminently watchable.

KEY TRANSACTIONS: The Twins made a number of moves to bring in talented prospects at the trade deadline, most notably acquiring righthander Jorge Alcala and outfielder Gilberto Celestino from the Astros for reliever Ryan Pressley. Righthanders Jhoan Duran (D-backs) and Luis Rijo (Yankees) are other intriguing pitching prospects the Twins acquired in trades.

DOWN ON THE FARM: The system's No. 1 prospect is shortstop Royce Lewis, who continued to live up to the expectations that come with being the No. 1 overall pick in 2017. He hit .292/.352/.451 in the Midwest and Florida State leagues. Lewis' teammate, outfielder Alex Kirilloff, had a terrific year with the bat, hitting .348/.392/.578 with 20 home runs, 44 doubles and 101 RBIs.

OPENING DAY PAYROLL: $129,560,000 (16th).

PLAYERS OF THE YEAR

MICHAEL WINS

BRACE HEMMELGARN

MAJOR LEAGUE	MINOR LEAGUE
Jose Berrios	**Alex Kirilloff**
RHP	OF
12-11, 3.84 in 32 GS	(Low Class A/High Class A)
202 SO in 192.1 IP	.348/.392/.578
1.14 WHIP	20 HR, 101 RBIs

ORGANIZATION LEADERS

Batting		*Minimum 250 AB
MAJORS		
* AVG	Jorge Polanco	.288
* AVG	Eddie Rosario	.288
* OPS	Eduardo Escobar	.852
HR	Eddie Rosario	24
RBI	Eddie Rosario	77
MINORS		
* AVG	Alex Kirilloff, Cedar Rapids, Fort Myers	.348
* OBP	Alex Kirilloff, Cedar Rapids, Fort Myers	.392
* SLG	Alex Kirilloff, Cedar Rapids, Fort Myers	.578
* OPS	Alex Kirilloff, Cedar Rapids, Fort Myers	.970
R	Akil Baddoo, Cedar Rapids	83
R	Royce Lewis, Cedar Rapids, Fort Myers	83
H	Alex Kirilloff, Cedar Rapids, Fort Myers	178
TB	Alex Kirilloff, Cedar Rapids, Fort Myers	296
2B	Alex Kirilloff, Cedar Rapids, Fort Myers	44
3B	Jean Carlos Arias, Cedar Rapids, Elizabethton	12
HR	Brent Rooker, Chattanooga	22
RBI	Alex Kirilloff, Cedar Rapids, Fort Myers	101
BB	Akil Baddoo, Cedar Rapids	74
SO	Brent Rooker, Chattanooga	150
SB	Royce Lewis, Cedar Rapids, Fort Myers	28

Pitching		#Minimum 75 IP
MAJORS		
W	Jose Berrios	12
# ERA	Kyle Gibson	3.62
SO	Jose Berrios	202
SV	Fernando Rodney	25
MINORS		
W	Stephen Gonsalves, Chattanooga, Rochester	12
L	Dietrich Enns, Rochester, Chattanooga	12
# ERA	Tyler Wells, Fort Myers, Chattanooga	2.49
G	Andrew Vasquez, Fort Myers, Chattanooga, Rochester	40
GS	Lewis Thorpe, Chattanooga, Rochester	25
SV	John Curtiss, Rochester	10
IP	Omar Bencomo, Chattanooga, Rochester	133
BB	Stephen Gonsalves, Chattanooga, Rochester	65
SO	Lewis Thorpe, Chattanooga, Rochester	157
# AVG	Stephen Gonsalves, Chattanooga, Rochester	.184

2018 PERFORMANCE

General Manager: Thad Levine. **Farm Director:** Jeremy Zoll. **Scouting Director:** Sean Johnson.

Class	Team	League	W	L	PCT	Finish	Manager
Majors	Minnesota Twins	American	78	84	.481	9th (15)	Paul Molitor
Triple-A	Rochester Red Wings	International	64	76	.457	t10th (14)	Joel Skinner
Double-A	Chattanooga Lookouts	Southern	65	72	.474	9th (10)	Tommy Watkins
High A	Fort Myers Miracle	Florida State	68	69	.496	9th (12)	Ramon Borrego
Low A	Cedar Rapids Kernels	Midwest	77	62	.554	4th (16)	Toby Gardenhire
Rookie	Elizabethton Twins	Appalachian	39	27	.591	3rd (10)	Ray Smith
Rookie	GCL Twins	Gulf Coast	32	24	.571	5th (xx)	Dan Ramsay
Overall 2018 Minor League Record			345	330	.511	11th (30)	

ORGANIZATION STATISTICS

MINNESOTA TWINS

AMERICAN LEAGUE

Batting	B-T	HT	WT	DOB	AVG	vLH	vRH	G	AB	R	H	2B	3B	HR	RBI	BB	HBP	SH	SF	SO	SB	CS	SLG	OBP
Adrianza, Ehire	B-R	6-1	170	8-21-89	.251	.264	.246	114	335	42	84	23	1	6	39	24	1	4	2	82	5	1	.379	.301
Astudillo, Willians	R-R	5-9	225	10-14-91	.355	.357	.354	29	93	9	33	4	1	3	21	2	1	0	1	3	0	0	.516	.371
Austin, Tyler	R-R	6-2	220	9-6-91	.236	.222	.241	35	123	18	29	4	0	9	24	11	0	0	2	42	0	1	.488	.294
2-team total (34 New York)					.230	.236	.226	69	244	34	56	10	0	17	47	19	2	0	3	95	1	2	.480	.287
Buxton, Byron	R-R	6-2	190	12-18-93	.156	.111	.167	28	90	8	14	4	0	0	4	3	0	1	0	28	5	0	.200	.183
Castro, Jason	L-R	6-3	215	6-18-87	.143	.000	.155	19	63	4	9	3	0	1	3	9	1	0	1	26	0	0	.238	.257
Cave, Jake	L-L	6-0	200	12-4-92	.265	.194	.287	91	283	54	75	16	2	13	45	18	3	2	3	102	2	1	.474	.313
Dozier, Brian	R-R	5-11	200	5-15-87	.227	.247	.220	104	410	65	93	21	2	16	52	46	3	0	3	96	8	3	.405	.307
Escobar, Eduardo	B-R	5-10	185	1-5-89	.275	.257	.282	97	368	45	101	37	3	15	63	34	3	0	3	91	1	3	.514	.338
Field, Johnny	R-R	5-10	180	2-20-92	.250	.179	.333	21	52	8	13	4	0	3	7	0	1	0	1	14	0	0	.500	.259
2-team total (62 Tampa Bay)					.222	.239	.211	83	221	28	49	13	0	9	21	7	3	1	1	72	4	0	.403	.254
Forsythe, Logan	R-R	6-1	205	1-14-87	.258	.246	.265	50	178	19	46	6	0	0	14	24	3	0	0	40	1	0	.292	.356
Garver, Mitch	R-R	6-1	220	1-15-91	.268	.227	.288	102	302	38	81	19	2	7	45	29	2	1	1	72	0	0	.414	.335
Gimenez, Chris	R-R	6-2	230	12-27-82	.276	.125	.333	13	29	6	8	1	0	2	6	3	1	0	1	9	0	0	.517	.353
Graterol, Juan	R-R	6-1	205	2-14-89	.143	.333	.000	3	7	2	1	0	0	0	1	0	0	0	0	0	0	0	.143	.250
2-team total (1 Los Angeles)					.250	.333	.200	4	8	2	2	0	0	0	1	0	0	0	0	0	0	0	.250	.333
Grossman, Robbie	B-L	6-0	215	9-16-89	.273	.325	.248	129	396	50	108	27	1	5	48	60	2	2	5	83	0	1	.384	.367
Kepler, Max	L-L	6-4	205	2-10-93	.224	.245	.216	156	532	80	119	30	4	20	58	71	5	0	3	96	4	5	.408	.319
LaMarre, Ryan	R-L	6-1	210	11-21-88	.263	.303	.242	43	99	7	26	5	0	0	8	8	1	0	1	33	1	1	.313	.321
2-team total (33 Chicago)					.279	.333	.240	76	165	15	46	11	0	2	18	10	2	0	3	53	2	2	.382	.322
Mauer, Joe	L-R	6-5	225	4-19-83	.282	.300	.275	127	486	64	137	27	1	6	48	51	2	1	3	86	0	1	.379	.351
Morrison, Logan	L-L	6-3	245	8-25-87	.186	.218	.175	95	318	41	59	13	0	15	39	34	6	0	1	80	1	0	.368	.276
Motter, Taylor	R-R	6-1	195	9-18-89	.053	.111	.000	9	19	0	1	0	0	0	1	2	0	0	0	3	1	0	.053	.143
2-team total (7 Seattle)					.147	.191	.077	16	34	2	5	0	0	1	2	4	0	0	0	8	1	0	.235	.237
Petit, Gregorio	R-R	5-10	200	12-10-84	.246	.182	.260	26	61	7	15	2	0	0	3	6	0	0	0	14	3	1	.279	.313
Polanco, Jorge	B-R	5-11	200	7-5-93	.288	.233	.317	77	302	38	87	18	3	6	42	25	2	3	1	62	7	7	.427	.346
Rosario, Eddie	L-R	6-1	180	9-28-91	.288	.284	.290	138	559	87	161	31	2	24	77	30	0	1	2	104	8	2	.479	.323
Sano, Miguel	R-R	6-4	260	5-11-93	.199	.186	.204	71	266	32	53	14	0	13	41	31	0	0	2	115	0	0	.399	.281
Wilson, Bobby	R-R	6-0	230	4-8-83	.178	.156	.185	47	135	12	24	8	0	2	16	12	0	2	2	37	0	0	.282	.242

Pitching	B-T	HT	WT	DOB	W	L	ERA	G	GS	CG	SV	IP	H	R	ER	HR	BB	SO	AVG	vLH	vRH	K/9	BB/9
Belisle, Matt	R-R	6-3	230	6-6-80	1	1	9.13	25	0	0	0	24	40	26	24	5	10	21	.381	.423	.340	7.99	3.80
2-team total (8 Cleveland)					1	1	7.86	33	0	0	0	34	49	32	30	6	11	25	.336	.343	.329	6.55	2.88
Berrios, Jose	R-R	6-0	185	5-27-94	12	11	3.84	32	32	2	0	192	159	83	82	25	61	202	.222	.213	.231	9.45	2.85
Busenitz, Alan	R-R	6-1	180	8-22-90	4	1	7.82	23	0	0	0	25	37	25	22	8	14	26	.339	.263	.380	9.24	4.97
Curtiss, John	R-R	6-4	200	4-5-93	0	1	5.68	8	0	0	0	6	8	4	4	0	4	7	.308	.167	.350	9.95	5.68
De Jong, Chase	L-R	6-4	205	12-29-93	1	1	3.57	4	4	0	0	18	18	9	7	3	6	13	.265	.200	.316	6.62	3.06
Drake, Oliver	R-R	6-4	215	1-13-87	0	0	2.21	19	0	0	0	20	12	6	5	2	7	22	.164	.212	.125	9.74	3.10
4-team total (4 Cleveland, 8 Los Angeles, 2 Toronto)					0	1	4.89	33	0	0	0	35	38	20	19	4	9	36	.270	.328	.221	9.26	2.31
Duffey, Tyler	R-R	6-3	220	12-27-90	2	2	7.20	19	1	0	0	25	26	22	20	6	4	19	.260	.314	.204	6.84	1.44
Duke, Zach	L-L	6-2	210	4-19-83	3	4	3.62	45	0	0	0	37	44	19	15	0	15	39	.282	.237	.309	9.40	3.62
2-team total (27 Seattle)					5	5	4.15	72	0	0	0	52	57	28	24	1	21	51	.271	.220	.311	8.83	3.63
Gibson, Kyle	R-R	6-6	215	10-23-87	10	13	3.62	32	32	0	0	197	177	88	79	23	79	179	.242	.270	.215	8.19	3.62
Gonsalves, Stephen	L-L	6-5	213	7-8-94	2	2	6.57	7	4	0	0	25	28	22	18	2	22	16	.283	.300	.279	5.84	8.03
Hale, David	R-R	6-2	210	9-27-87	0	0	12.00	1	0	0	0	3	4	4	4	1	4	2	.333	.143	.600	6.00	12.00
2-team total (3 New York)					0	0	4.61	4	0	0	0	14	16	7	7	3	5	8	.286	.385	.200	5.27	3.29
Hildenberger, Trevor	R-R	6-2	211	12-15-90	4	6	5.42	73	0	0	7	73	75	46	44	12	26	70	.263	.255	.269	8.63	3.21
Hughes, Phil	R-R	6-5	240	6-24-86	0	0	6.75	7	2	0	0	12	14	9	9	4	5	8	.292	.158	.379	6.00	3.75
Kinley, Tyler	R-R	6-4	205	1-31-91	0	0	24.30	4	0	0	0	3	9	9	9	2	4	4	.474	.400	.556	10.80	10.80
Littell, Zack	R-R	6-4	220	10-5-95	0	2	6.20	8	2	0	0	20	25	17	14	3	11	14	.298	.350	.250	6.20	4.87
Lynn, Lance	B-R	6-5	280	5-12-87	7	8	5.10	20	20	0	0	102	105	61	58	12	62	100	.263	.288	.247	8.79	5.45
2-team total (11 New York)					10	10	4.77	31	29	0	0	157	163	87	83	14	76	161	.265	.299	.239	9.25	4.37
Magill, Matt	R-R	6-3	210	11-10-89	3	3	3.81	40	0	0	0	57	58	24	24	11	23	56	.262	.258	.266	8.89	3.65

May, Trevor	R-R	6-5	240	9-23-89	4	1	3.20	24	1	0	3	25	21	9	9	4	5	36	.221	.195	.241	12.79	1.78
Mejia, Adalberto	R-L	6-3	195	6-20-93	2	0	2.01	5	4	0	0	22	17	5	5	1	9	13	.215	.118	.242	5.24	3.63
Moya, Gabriel	L-L	6-0	175	1-9-95	3	1	4.71	35	6	0	0	36	35	19	19	6	13	31	.245	.250	.242	7.68	3.22
Odorizzi, Jake	R-R	6-2	190	3-27-90	7	10	4.49	32	32	0	0	164	151	89	82	20	70	162	.242	.237	.246	8.87	3.83
Pressly, Ryan	R-R	6-3	210	12-15-88	1	1	3.40	51	0	0	0	48	46	19	18	5	19	69	.250	.217	.266	13.03	3.59
2-team total (26 Houston)					2	1	2.54	77	0	0	2	71	57	21	20	6	22	101	.216	.172	.242	12.80	2.79
Reed, Addison	R-R	6-4	230	12-27-88	1	6	4.50	55	0	0	0	56	65	30	28	11	15	44	.298	.337	.273	7.07	2.41
Rodney, Fernando	R-R	5-11	230	3-18-77	3	2	3.09	46	0	0	25	44	42	18	15	5	19	50	.249	.208	.283	10.31	3.92
2-team total (22 Oakland)					4	3	3.36	68	0	0	25	64	62	27	24	7	32	70	.250	.185	.310	9.79	4.48
Rogers, Taylor	L-L	6-3	170	12-17-90	1	2	2.63	72	0	0	2	68	49	20	20	3	16	75	.206	.180	.225	9.88	2.11
Romero, Fernando	R-R	6-0	215	12-24-94	3	3	4.69	11	11	0	0	56	60	31	29	6	19	45	.279	.274	.283	7.28	3.07
Santana, Ervin	R-R	6-2	175	12-12-82	0	1	8.03	5	5	0	0	25	31	22	22	9	9	16	.310	.267	.375	5.84	3.28
Slegers, Aaron	R-R	6-10	245	9-4-92	1	1	5.27	4	2	0	0	14	17	8	8	3	2	6	.298	.217	.353	3.95	1.32
Stewart, Kohl	R-R	6-3	195	10-7-94	2	1	3.68	8	4	0	0	37	34	16	15	1	18	24	.246	.246	.246	5.89	4.42
Vasquez, Andrew	L-L	6-6	228	9-14-93	1	0	5.40	9	0	0	0	5	5	4	3	0	2	7	.238	.364	.100	12.60	3.60

Fielding

Catcher	PCT	G	PO	A	E	DP	PB
Astudillo	.992	16	114	7	1	0	0
Castro	1.000	19	187	17	0	5	1
Garver	.994	86	617	34	4	2	9
Gimenez	.983	8	55	2	1	0	0
Graterol	1.000	3	20	2	0	0	0
Mauer	.000	1	0	0	0	0	0
Wilson	.998	47	399	21	1	2	2

First Base	PCT	G	PO	A	E	DP
Adrianza	1.000	10	35	4	0	7
Austin	1.000	15	101	7	0	14
Garver	1.000	5	7	1	0	1
Gimenez	.944	3	16	1	1	2
Kepler	.000	1	0	0	0	0
Mauer	.996	90	633	61	3	56
Morrison	.993	50	380	24	3	31
Petit	1.000	1	2	0	0	0
Sano	.977	11	78	8	2	5

Second Base	PCT	G	PO	A	E	DP
Adrianza	1.000	5	6	10	0	1
Astudillo	1.000	2	0	2	0	0
Dozier	.981	103	150	260	8	60
Escobar	1.000	1	4	3	0	0
Forsythe	.984	48	74	105	3	28
Motter	1.000	2	1	0	0	0
Petit	1.000	10	17	28	0	9

Third Base	PCT	G	PO	A	E	DP
Adrianza	.972	28	21	48	2	5
Astudillo	.846	6	3	8	2	0
Escobar	.983	77	47	130	3	13
Gimenez	1.000	1	0	1	0	0
Motter	1.000	2	1	3	0	0
Petit	.941	6	4	12	1	2
Rosario	1.000	1	0	2	0	0
Sano	.946	56	41	100	8	5

Shortstop	PCT	G	PO	A	E	DP
Adrianza	.966	64	61	138	7	30
Escobar	.986	21	26	43	1	10
Motter	1.000	1	1	4	0	0
Petit	.923	9	11	13	2	4
Polanco	.953	76	90	172	13	42

Outfield	PCT	G	PO	A	E	DP
Adrianza	1.000	5	3	0	0	0
Astudillo	1.000	1	2	0	0	0
Buxton	1.000	27	69	1	0	0
Cave	.976	85	157	5	4	1
Field	1.000	20	25	0	0	0
Forsythe	.000	1	0	0	0	0
Grossman	.979	84	138	3	3	0
Kepler	.997	150	327	7	1	2
LaMarre	1.000	38	63	0	0	0
Mauer	.000	1	0	0	0	0
Morrison	.000	2	0	0	0	0
Motter	1.000	5	7	0	0	0
Rosario	.964	127	234	9	9	0

ROCHESTER RED WINGS
INTERNATIONAL LEAGUE

TRIPLE-A

Batting	B-T	HT	WT	DOB	AVG	vLH	vRH	G	AB	R	H	2B	3B	HR	RBI	BB	HBP	SH	SF	SO	SB	CS	SLG	OBP
Astudillo, Willians	R-R	5-9	225	10-14-91	.276	.319	.262	78	286	30	79	17	1	12	38	10	7	1	3	14	7	4	.469	.314
Austin, Tyler	R-R	6-2	220	9-6-91	.263	.091	.333	9	38	6	10	2	1	3	8	1	1	0	0	10	0	0	.605	.300
2-team total (26 Scranton/Wilkes-Barre)					.256	.214	.274	35	137	20	35	11	1	9	22	9	2	0	0	42	0	0	.547	.311
Buss, Nick	L-R	6-2	190	12-15-86	.239	.280	.231	47	159	14	38	8	1	2	11	14	3	0	2	36	4	1	.340	.309
Buxton, Byron	R-R	6-2	190	12-18-93	.272	.268	.274	35	136	22	37	11	1	4	14	9	3	0	0	42	4	1	.456	.331
Carter, Chris	R-R	6-4	245	12-18-86	.187	.241	.170	36	123	18	23	8	0	7	15	19	1	0	1	43	0	0	.423	.299
Cave, Jake	L-L	6-0	200	12-4-92	.269	.296	.259	59	216	26	58	9	1	6	28	26	4	0	4	55	4	2	.403	.352
Corcino, Edgar	B-R	6-1	210	6-7-92	.261	.419	.175	29	88	8	23	4	1	2	6	4	0	0	1	21	0	0	.398	.290
Curtis, Jermaine	R-R	5-11	190	7-10-87	.200	.147	.219	42	130	14	26	4	0	1	10	24	8	0	3	33	3	0	.254	.352
Featherston, Taylor	R-R	6-1	185	10-8-89	.167	.056	.194	55	180	17	30	4	2	4	21	20	7	2	4	70	7	1	.278	.270
Field, Johnny	R-R	5-10	180	2-20-92	.135	.000	.167	10	37	1	5	1	0	0	1	2	1	0	0	8	1	0	.162	.200
3-team total (5 Columbus, 10 Durham)					.258	.320	.234	25	89	14	23	6	0	1	9	2	0	0	0	18	2	1	.360	.340
Gordon, Nick	L-R	6-0	160	10-24-95	.212	.243	.200	99	382	40	81	13	4	2	29	23	3	1	1	82	13	3	.283	.262
Granite, Zack	L-L	6-1	175	9-17-92	.211	.167	.222	68	237	28	50	8	0	0	4	22	2	1	1	28	9	4	.245	.282
Graterol, Juan	R-R	6-1	205	2-24-89	.285	.235	.305	34	116	12	33	6	0	0	10	2	4	0	1	3	0	0	.336	.317
Grossman, Robbie	B-L	6-0	215	9-16-89	.455	.500	.400	3	11	1	5	1	0	0	3	1	0	0	1	1	0	0	.546	.462
Hazelbaker, Jeremy	L-R	6-3	190	8-14-87	.188	.160	.197	35	96	14	18	4	2	3	9	16	1	0	0	38	5	0	.365	.310
2-team total (62 Durham)					.203	.177	.212	97	310	46	63	20	2	11	36	38	4	0	0	121	14	0	.387	.298
Kemmer, Jon	L-L	6-2	230	11-17-90	.224	.286	.206	39	125	17	28	8	1	4	18	11	4	0	0	37	2	0	.400	.307
Kerrigan, Jimmy	R-R	6-1	215	3-16-94	.300	.333	.286	4	10	2	3	0	0	1	2	1	0	0	2	0	0		.600	.462
LaMarre, Ryan	R-R	6-1	210	11-21-88	.313	.267	.333	13	48	5	15	4	1	0	5	5	1	0	0	15	1	0	.438	.389
2-team total (12 Charlotte)					.269	.185	.303	25	93	12	25	6	3	0	7	9	1	1	0	29	3	0	.398	.340
Mauer, Joe	L-R	6-5	225	4-19-83	.000	.000	.000	3	10	0	0	0	0	0	0	0	0	0	0	2	0	0	.000	.000
Miller, Sean	R-R	5-11	175	10-10-94	.091	.143	.077	10	33	0	3	0	0	0	1	1	0	0	0	8	0	0	.091	.118
Motter, Taylor	R-R	6-1	195	9-18-89	.182	.200	.175	47	159	23	29	10	1	5	14	22	1	0	1	37	3	4	.352	.284
Pacheco, Jordan	R-R	6-1	200	1-30-86	.163	.040	.209	30	92	10	15	3	0	0	2	7	3	0	0	15	0	0	.196	.245
Perez, Alex	L-R	5-10	180	10-24-92	.244	.222	.250	14	45	7	11	2	0	0	3	4	0	0	0	10	0	0	.289	.300
Petit, Gregorio	R-R	5-10	180	12-10-84	.268	.282	.263	79	284	31	76	12	1	7	29	17	3	5	3	47	4	1	.328	.313
Polanco, Jorge	B-R	5-11	200	7-5-93	.462	.167	.714	4	13	0	6	1	0	0	2	0	0	0	0	2	0	0	.615	.533
Ramsey, James	L-R	6-0	200	12-19-89	.240	.105	.286	22	75	10	18	2	0	0	6	6	1	0	0	30	1	1	.267	.305
Reginatto, Leonardo	R-R	6-2	180	4-10-90	.207	.192	.212	61	203	18	42	8	1	2	21	12	2	2	3	51	3	2	.286	.255
Rupp, Cameron	R-R	6-2	260	9-28-88	.141	.214	.120	21	64	5	9	0	0	3	6	11	0	0	1	32	0	0	.281	.263

	B-T	HT	WT	DOB	AVG	vLH	vRH	G	AB	R	H	2B	3B	HR	RBI	BB	HBP	SH	SF	SO	SB	CS	SLG	OBP
Sano, Miguel	R-R	6-4	260	5-11-93	.267	.667	.222	9	30	2	8	1	0	2	5	6	0	0	0	8	0	0	.500	.389
Sawyer, Wynston	R-R	6-3	205	11-14-91	.318	.250	.340	23	66	13	21	2	0	1	11	11	5	0	1	16	0	0	.394	.446
Stassi, Brock	L-L	6-2	190	8-7-89	.211	.150	.223	32	114	14	24	6	0	2	13	15	3	0	1	28	0	1	.316	.316
Tademo, Victor	R-R	6-1	170	7-9-99	.250	.333	.000	1	4	0	1	0	0	0	0	0	0	0	0	1	0	0	.250	.250
Vargas, Kennys	B-R	6-5	290	8-1-90	.240	.265	.231	130	463	41	111	23	0	21	73	58	5	0	7	133	0	0	.426	.327
Wade, LaMonte	L-L	6-1	189	1-1-94	.229	.187	.247	74	253	24	58	9	3	4	21	38	3	0	0	54	5	1	.336	.337
Wiel, Zander	R-R	6-3	232	1-11-93	.196	.273	.175	15	51	5	10	0	1	3	7	3	2	0	2	13	1	0	.412	.259
Wilkins, Andy	L-R	6-1	225	9-13-88	.162	.059	.193	22	74	5	12	2	0	2	8	6	0	0	0	23	1	0	.270	.225
Wilson, Bobby	R-R	6-0	230	4-8-83	.125	.000	.156	11	40	2	5	1	0	0	3	3	1	0	1	13	0	0	.150	.182

Pitching	B-T	HT	WT	DOB	W	L	ERA	G	GS	CG	SV	IP	H	R	ER	HR	BB	SO	AVG	vLH	vRH	K/9	BB/9
Anderson, Brady	L-R	6-0	185	11-10-92	0	0	4.50	1	0	0	0	4	3	2	2	0	1	1	.214	.250	.167	2.25	2.25
Anderson, Nick	R-R	6-1	195	7-5-90	8	2	3.30	39	0	0	4	60	49	26	22	8	19	88	.221	.204	.233	13.20	2.85
Bard, Luke	R-R	6-3	202	11-13-90	3	3	4.66	32	0	0	1	48	54	29	25	6	18	52	.286	.321	.261	9.68	3.35
Baxendale, D.J.	R-R	6-2	190	12-8-90	0	3	3.74	32	10	0	1	67	81	31	28	5	19	61	.299	.269	.329	8.15	2.54
Bencomo, Omar	R-R	6-1	170	2-10-89	1	0	3.46	2	2	0	0	13	6	5	5	1	2	10	.136	.125	.150	6.92	1.38
Busenitz, Alan	R-R	6-1	180	8-22-90	2	3	2.48	27	1	0	7	40	32	14	11	3	8	45	.219	.222	.217	10.13	1.80
Crosby, Casey	R-L	6-5	225	9-17-88	0	0	1.69	5	0	0	1	5	6	1	1	0	3	5	.300	.250	.333	8.44	5.06
Curtiss, John	R-R	6-4	200	4-5-93	2	4	2.77	38	1	0	10	55	41	21	17	3	31	61	.214	.219	.219	9.92	5.04
De Jong, Chase	L-R	6-4	205	12-29-93	2	3	3.20	7	5	0	0	39	37	14	14	2	12	34	.247	.206	.281	7.78	2.75
Duffey, Tyler	R-R	6-3	220	12-27-90	4	4	2.90	31	0	0	3	59	48	24	19	5	20	63	.220	.154	.281	9.61	3.05
Eades, Ryan	R-R	6-2	200	12-15-91	0	0	0.59	7	3	0	0	15	13	2	1	0	4	20	.224	.217	.229	11.74	2.35
Enns, Dietrich	L-L	6-1	210	5-16-91	5	7	5.14	14	13	1	0	68	76	40	39	8	30	45	.285	.253	.299	5.93	3.95
Gonsalves, Stephen	L-L	6-5	213	7-8-94	9	3	2.96	19	18	0	0	100	65	33	33	6	55	95	.187	.244	.160	8.52	4.93
Harper, Ryne	R-R	6-3	215	3-27-89	0	3	5.19	14	0	0	0	26	26	16	15	2	5	35	.252	.163	.333	12.12	1.73
Jaye, Myles	B-R	6-3	170	12-28-91	3	3	4.25	8	8	0	0	42	45	21	20	5	15	19	.274	.273	.276	4.04	3.19
2-team total (9 Columbus)					5	8	6.43	17	13	0	0	71	89	56	51	14	25	35	.308	.329	.289	4.42	3.15
Littell, Zack	R-R	6-3	220	10-5-95	6	6	3.57	19	15	0	0	106	100	47	42	5	40	98	.248	.288	.200	8.32	3.40
Magill, Matt	R-R	6-3	210	11-10-89	0	0	0.00	5	0	0	2	9	5	0	0	0	2	13	.161	.118	.214	13.50	2.08
May, Trevor	R-R	6-5	240	9-23-89	0	4	4.00	13	4	0	2	27	24	14	12	2	16	25	.238	.177	.300	8.33	5.33
Mejia, Adalberto	R-L	6-3	195	6-20-93	5	3	3.27	15	12	0	0	63	55	25	23	3	20	62	.224	.240	.224	8.81	2.84
Melotakis, Mason	R-L	6-2	220	6-28-91	2	1	3.07	8	0	0	0	15	15	7	5	2	5	14	.268	.056	.368	8.59	3.07
Moya, Gabriel	L-L	6-0	175	1-9-95	1	1	1.90	26	4	0	4	43	38	11	9	2	12	50	.242	.217	.258	10.55	2.53
Pineda, Michael	R-R	6-7	260	1-18-89	1	0	2.25	1	0	0	0	4	2	1	1	1	2	2	.167	.667	.000	4.50	4.50
Reed, Addison	L-R	6-4	230	12-27-88	0	0	4.50	2	0	0	1	2	2	1	1	0	2	1	.250	.333	.200	4.50	9.00
Reed, Jake	R-R	6-2	190	9-29-92	0	3	1.89	30	1	0	2	48	34	13	10	1	21	50	.204	.192	.214	9.44	3.97
Romero, Fernando	R-R	6-0	215	12-24-94	5	6	3.50	16	13	0	0	91	85	40	36	5	32	69	.247	.244	.250	6.85	3.18
Santana, Ervin	R-R	6-2	175	12-12-82	0	1	3.09	2	2	0	0	12	6	4	4	3	4	8	.150	.143	.158	6.17	3.09
Slegers, Aaron	R-R	6-10	245	9-4-92	5	7	3.80	15	15	1	0	85	85	41	36	12	19	57	.263	.203	.314	6.01	2.00
Stewart, Kohl	R-R	6-3	195	10-7-94	0	3	3.98	7	5	0	0	41	45	19	18	4	12	30	.300	.277	.328	6.64	2.66
Thorpe, Lewis	R-L	6-1	160	11-23-95	0	3	3.32	4	4	0	0	22	20	11	8	3	6	26	.244	.286	.230	10.80	2.49
Vasquez, Andrew	L-L	6-6	228	9-14-93	0	0	1.59	4	0	0	1	6	5	1	1	0	4	12	.217	.000	.333	19.06	6.35

Fielding

Catcher	PCT	G	PO	A	E	DP	PB
Astudillo	.995	39	343	19	2	4	1
Graterol	.983	34	273	13	5	5	2
Pacheco	.989	19	175	6	2	0	1
Rupp	.976	20	150	12	4	1	2
Sawyer	.994	22	153	13	1	1	3
Wilson	1.000	11	84	4	0	0	1

First Base	PCT	G	PO	A	E	DP
Astudillo	1.000	2	1	1	0	0
Austin	.983	7	55	2	1	4
Carter	1.000	10	71	4	0	12
Curtis	1.000	3	12	1	0	3
Mauer	1.000	1	2	0	0	1
Motter	.000	1	0	0	0	0
Sano	1.000	1	6	1	0	0
Sawyer	1.000	2	11	3	0	1
Stassi	.988	20	151	12	2	18
Vargas	.995	73	523	48	3	51
Wiel	1.000	14	111	5	0	8
Wilkins	.987	11	71	5	1	7

Second Base	PCT	G	PO	A	E	DP
Featherston	.972	47	79	131	6	34
Gordon	.992	30	46	76	1	14
Miller	1.000	4	8	11	0	4
Motter	1.000	9	14	19	0	5
Perez	.971	10	19	15	1	6
Petit	.966	28	41	73	4	14
Reginatto	.983	14	27	30	1	8
Tademo	.833	1	2	3	1	2

Third Base	PCT	G	PO	A	E	DP
Astudillo	.939	28	25	37	4	4
Curtis	.960	30	14	34	2	5
Featherston	.824	8	3	11	3	2
Miller	1.000	3	0	2	0	0
Motter	.980	20	13	36	1	5
Pacheco	.933	10	2	12	1	0
Perez	1.000	4	1	3	0	1
Petit	.935	16	6	23	2	1
Reginatto	.964	26	19	34	2	6
Sano	.900	4	4	5	1	0
Wilkins	1.000	1	1	1	0	0

Shortstop	PCT	G	PO	A	E	DP
Gordon	.977	69	92	162	6	36
Miller	1.000	3	1	10	0	1
Motter	.963	10	11	15	1	4
Petit	.985	36	43	90	2	24
Polanco	1.000	3	2	3	0	0
Reginatto	.988	21	29	52	1	11

Outfield	PCT	G	PO	A	E	DP
Astudillo	1.000	6	10	0	0	0
Buss	.980	46	90	6	2	1
Buxton	.988	28	81	3	1	1
Cave	.992	58	116	8	1	3
Corcino	.981	23	50	1	1	0
Curtis	1.000	9	13	0	0	0
Field	.929	10	11	2	1	0
Granite	.976	68	161	2	4	2
Grossman	1.000	1	1	0	0	0
Hazelbaker	1.000	34	74	0	0	0
Kemmer	.984	36	61	0	1	0
Kerrigan	1.000	4	8	0	0	0
LaMarre	.960	12	23	1	1	0
Motter	1.000	8	15	1	0	1
Ramsey	1.000	21	37	0	0	0
Stassi	1.000	1	3	0	0	0
Wade	.979	72	133	7	3	0
Wilkins	1.000	2	2	0	0	0

CHATTANOOGA LOOKOUTS
SOUTHERN LEAGUE
DOUBLE-A

Batting	B-T	HT	WT	DOB	AVG	vLH	vRH	G	AB	R	H	2B	3B	HR	RBI	BB	HBP	SH	SF	SO	SB	CS	SLG	OBP
Arraez, Luis	L-R	5-10	155	4-9-97	.298	.267	.308	48	178	25	53	6	0	2	16	13	1	1	2	16	2	0	.365	.345
Corcino, Edgar	B-R	6-1	210	6-7-92	.264	.277	.261	56	208	32	55	14	3	5	32	22	3	0	4	37	3	1	.433	.338
Cronin, Joe	R-R	5-10	185	5-15-94	.115	.000	.130	9	26	3	3	0	0	0	0	4	2	0	0	11	0	0	.115	.281

Name	B-T	HT	WT	DOB	AVG	vLH	vRH	G	AB	R	H	2B	3B	HR	RBI	BB	HBP	SH	SF	SO	SB	CS	OBP	SLG
Davis, Jaylin	R-R	6-1	190	7-1-94	.275	.352	.253	63	240	30	66	14	2	6	34	21	4	0	2	69	5	2	.425	.341
English, Tanner	R-R	5-10	160	3-11-93	.221	.220	.221	97	299	42	66	17	6	4	28	21	3	5	3	97	13	8	.358	.276
Gordon, Nick	L-R	6-0	160	10-24-95	.333	.273	.356	42	162	22	54	10	3	5	20	11	4	0	4	27	7	2	.525	.381
Gore, Jordan	B-R	6-0	180	8-3-94	.250	.257	.248	41	136	24	34	7	3	1	18	15	0	0	2	29	1	0	.368	.320
Kerrigan, Jimmy	R-R	6-1	215	3-16-94	.226	.239	.222	55	195	21	44	7	0	6	21	10	2	0	2	67	0	3	.354	.268
Kranson, Mitchell	L-R	5-9	210	1-11-94	.262	.118	.294	56	187	15	49	9	1	3	20	26	1	0	4	36	0	1	.369	.349
Miller, Sean	R-R	5-11	175	10-10-94	.220	.243	.212	46	150	20	33	5	0	1	8	10	2	2	0	36	1	0	.273	.278
Motter, Taylor	R-R	6-1	195	9-18-89	.133	.000	.143	4	15	2	2	1	0	0	0	1	0	0	0	6	0	0	.200	.188
Navarreto, Brian	R-R	6-4	220	12-29-94	.247	.250	.245	97	357	37	88	19	0	4	28	14	6	2	1	57	0	1	.333	.286
Olson, Brian	R-R	6-0	171	1-21-93	.207	.000	.255	17	58	8	12	1	0	0	3	8	0	1	0	19	0	0	.224	.303
Paul, Chris	R-R	6-2	200	10-12-92	.254	.233	.262	92	338	48	86	22	1	6	48	21	4	0	3	75	2	0	.379	.303
Perez, Alex	L-R	5-10	180	10-24-92	.249	.222	.258	69	241	28	60	8	2	0	28	35	2	0	2	55	2	0	.299	.346
Raley, Luke	L-R	6-3	220	9-19-94	.276	.333	.257	27	98	15	27	2	3	3	16	12	4	0	2	32	1	0	.449	.371
Ramsey, James	L-R	6-0	200	12-19-89	.250	.120	.299	26	92	17	23	1	0	4	10	16	1	0	0	24	2	1	.391	.367
Robles, Alex	R-R	6-0	200	7-7-95	.143	.333	.091	5	14	0	2	0	0	0	1	2	0	0	0	2	0	0	.143	.250
Rooker, Brent	R-R	6-3	211	11-9-94	.255	.225	.264	130	503	72	128	32	4	22	79	56	5	0	4	150	6	1	.465	.333
Sawyer, Wynston	R-R	6-3	205	11-14-91	.143	.000	.156	13	35	4	5	1	0	1	2	5	1	0	0	5	0	0	.257	.268
Wade, LaMonte	L-L	6-1	189	1-1-94	.298	.194	.326	46	171	30	51	2	1	7	27	26	2	0	2	20	5	2	.444	.393
Walker, Ryan	L-R	6-1	157	3-26-92	.227	.122	.257	55	181	20	41	3	0	4	21	22	2	0	0	34	4	2	.309	.317
White, T.J.	R-R	5-10	200	1-24-92	.187	.250	.170	39	134	12	25	4	0	4	14	8	4	0	0	38	1	2	.306	.253
Wiel, Zander	R-R	6-3	232	1-11-93	.311	.333	.303	101	386	53	120	27	2	7	58	40	6	0	3	82	8	4	.446	.382
Wilkins, Andy	L-R	6-1	225	9-13-88	.221	.259	.211	40	136	21	30	5	1	12	28	21	2	0	0	40	1	0	.537	.333

Pitching	B-T	HT	WT	DOB	W	L	ERA	G	GS	CG	SV	IP	H	R	ER	HR	BB	SO	AVG	vLH	vRH	K/9	BB/9
Adams, Austin	R-R	5-11	200	8-19-86	1	0	1.00	5	3	0	0	9	8	1	1	1	4	10	.235	.250	.214	10.00	4.00
Alcala, Jorge	R-R	6-3	180	7-28-95	0	4	5.85	5	4	0	0	20	23	16	13	4	14	22	.281	.356	.189	9.90	6.30
Beeker, Clark	R-R	6-3	205	11-22-92	0	0	0.00	1	1	0	0	4	2	0	0	0	0	2	.143	.167	.000	4.50	0.00
Bencomo, Omar	R-R	6-1	170	2-10-89	8	6	3.45	26	17	0	2	120	128	56	46	16	17	102	.278	.276	.280	7.65	1.28
Clay, Sam	L-L	6-2	190	6-21-93	2	6	5.88	34	1	0	1	52	54	43	34	1	36	61	.266	.154	.319	10.56	6.23
Crosby, Casey	R-L	6-5	225	9-17-88	1	0	4.91	6	1	0	0	7	6	4	4	0	14	9	.231	.222	.235	11.05	17.18
Eades, Ryan	R-R	6-2	200	12-15-91	4	3	4.28	29	3	0	0	61	66	34	29	5	18	68	.276	.275	.277	10.03	2.66
Enns, Dietrich	L-L	6-1	210	5-16-91	1	5	4.01	11	9	0	0	61	60	28	27	4	13	61	.259	.239	.267	9.05	1.93
Gonsalves, Stephen	L-L	6-5	213	7-8-94	3	0	1.77	4	4	0	0	20	11	4	4	2	10	25	.167	.188	.160	11.07	4.43
Harper, Ryne	R-R	6-3	215	3-27-89	1	2	2.54	24	0	0	6	39	35	18	11	0	5	51	.241	.196	.270	11.77	1.15
Jay, Tyler	L-L	6-1	185	4-19-94	5	4	4.22	38	2	0	2	60	74	38	28	7	20	49	.310	.276	.329	7.39	3.02
Jones, Zack	R-R	6-1	195	12-4-90	1	1	2.49	17	0	0	1	25	10	10	7	2	25	39	.119	.175	.068	13.86	8.88
LeBlanc, Randy	R-R	6-4	185	3-7-92	6	1	2.17	9	9	0	0	50	50	13	12	2	13	40	.270	.230	.297	7.25	2.36
Littell, Zack	R-R	6-4	220	10-5-95	0	3	5.87	5	5	0	0	23	28	15	15	3	7	32	.308	.207	.355	12.52	2.74
Marzi, Anthony	L-L	6-1	205	11-27-92	0	8	5.49	22	12	0	0	82	97	55	50	8	30	65	.286	.383	.241	7.13	3.29
McIver, Anthony	L-L	6-5	210	4-8-92	0	0	2.70	8	0	0	0	13	19	5	4	0	5	15	.328	.546	.277	10.13	3.38
Poppen, Sean	R-R	6-3	205	3-15-94	5	7	3.83	18	14	2	0	94	88	45	40	11	28	79	.254	.265	.243	7.56	2.68
Ramirez, Williams	R-R	6-1	200	8-8-92	2	6	5.67	39	1	0	7	54	55	38	34	4	34	76	.264	.278	.254	12.67	5.67
Rodriguez, Paco	L-L	6-3	220	4-16-91	3	1	4.26	19	3	0	0	25	20	13	12	0	16	19	.220	.237	.208	6.75	5.68
Sammons, Bryan	L-L	6-4	235	4-27-95	0	1	11.25	1	1	0	0	4	5	6	5	0	3	6	.278	.000	.357	13.50	6.75
Santana, Ervin	R-R	6-2	175	12-12-82	0	1	5.14	2	2	0	0	7	6	4	4	2	0	7	.231	.214	.250	9.00	0.00
Smeltzer, Devin	R-L	6-3	195	9-7-95	0	0	3.00	10	0	0	4	12	14	6	4	0	2	16	.280	.294	.273	12.00	1.50
Stashak, Cody	R-R	6-2	169	6-4-94	1	1	2.75	35	2	0	4	56	47	18	17	4	13	69	.230	.231	.230	11.16	2.10
Stewart, Kohl	R-R	6-3	195	10-7-94	3	4	4.76	14	14	0	0	68	84	41	36	3	21	71	.301	.336	.268	9.40	2.78
Thorpe, Lewis	R-L	6-1	160	11-23-95	8	4	3.58	22	21	0	0	108	105	57	43	13	30	131	.251	.230	.259	10.92	2.50
Van Steensel, Todd	R-R	6-1	215	1-14-91	5	1	3.07	25	2	0	4	44	26	15	15	1	23	49	.169	.179	.161	10.02	4.70
Vasquez, Andrew	L-L	6-6	228	9-14-93	1	0	1.16	17	1	0	0	31	21	9	4	1	4	59	.196	.200	.195	17.13	1.16
Wells, Tyler	R-R	6-8	265	8-26-94	2	2	1.65	6	5	0	1	33	23	6	6	1	14	39	.205	.204	.207	10.74	3.86

Fielding

Catcher

Catcher	PCT	G	PO	A	E	DP	PB
Kranson	.988	18	139	22	2	2	1
Navarreto	.990	96	885	88	10	5	8
Olson	1.000	16	139	11	0	0	1
Sawyer	1.000	10	88	8	0	1	2
Perez	.979	55	96	136	5	36	
Robles	1.000	2	2	3	0	0	
Walker	.976	35	59	64	3	17	
White	1.000	5	8	11	0	4	
Miller	.954	36	40	84	6	22	
Motter	.000	1	0	0	1	0	
Perez	.982	15	20	34	1	7	
Walker	.750	3	2	4	2	2	

First Base

First Base	PCT	G	PO	A	E	DP
Kranson	1.000	8	50	2	0	5
Paul	1.000	7	51	4	0	5
Raley	1.000	7	50	7	0	2
Rooker	.986	47	332	14	5	36
Sawyer	1.000	3	18	3	0	2
Wiel	.992	50	350	26	3	44
Wilkins	1.000	18	105	10	0	15

Second Base

Second Base	PCT	G	PO	A	E	DP
Arraez	1.000	27	49	54	0	17
Cronin	.917	5	5	6	1	4
Gordon	1.000	6	15	11	0	2
Kranson	1.000	1	1	0	0	0
Miller	.974	10	16	22	1	8

Third Base

Third Base	PCT	G	PO	A	E	DP
Arraez	1.000	10	8	17	0	4
Gore	1.000	1	0	4	0	0
Kranson	.957	22	16	28	2	1
Paul	.948	69	51	112	9	9
Perez	.750	2	1	2	1	0
Robles	1.000	2	1	1	0	0
Walker	.895	15	11	23	4	5
White	.953	22	12	29	2	2
Wilkins	1.000	3	2	4	0	0

Shortstop

Shortstop	PCT	G	PO	A	E	DP
Arraez	.944	9	15	19	2	8
Cronin	1.000	4	4	13	0	1
Gordon	.958	34	48	88	6	24
Gore	.964	39	40	93	5	25

Outfield

Outfield	PCT	G	PO	A	E	DP
Arraez	.500	1	2	0	2	0
Corcino	.967	55	81	6	3	2
Davis	.971	51	96	6	3	1
English	.987	93	229	3	3	0
Kerrigan	.991	51	113	3	1	0
Motter	1.000	2	4	0	0	0
Paul	1.000	15	15	2	0	0
Raley	1.000	15	29	1	0	0
Ramsey	1.000	24	45	2	0	
O Rooker	.949	44	53	3	3	0
Wade	1.000	40	65	4	0	1
Walker	1.000	6	7	0	0	0
Wiel	1.000	28	37	3	0	0

FORT MYERS MIRACLE
FLORIDA STATE LEAGUE

HIGH CLASS A

Batting	B-T	HT	WT	DOB	AVG	vLH	vRH	G	AB	R	H	2B	3B	HR	RBI	BB	HBP	SH	SF	SO	SB	CS	SLG	OBP
Arraez, Luis	L-R	5-10	155	4-9-97	.320	.286	.338	60	228	27	73	14	3	1	20	19	2	6	3	28	2	3	.421	.373
Blankenhorn, Travis	L-R	6-2	208	8-3-96	.231	.202	.241	124	442	52	102	24	6	11	57	34	10	5	2	127	6	4	.387	.299
Buxton, Byron	R-R	6-2	190	12-18-93	.000	—	.000	1	4	0	0	0	0	0	0	0	0	0	0	0	0	0	.000	.000
Carrier, Shane	R-R	6-2	215	6-3-96	.138	.184	.107	27	94	9	13	0	0	4	13	5	1	0	2	33	2	2	.266	.186
Contreras, Mark	L-R	6-0	185	1-24-95	.212	.215	.211	97	335	60	71	15	4	9	39	35	9	2	2	92	12	9	.361	.302
Costello, Ryan	L-R	6-2	200	6-13-96	.229	.250	.221	27	96	15	22	1	0	4	9	14	0	0	0	19	0	0	.365	.327
Crites, Carson	R-R	6-0	195	1-18-95	.167	.333	.000	3	6	1	1	0	0	0	0	1	0	1	0	2	0	0	.167	.167
Cronin, Joe	R-R	5-10	185	5-15-94	.228	.324	.181	68	206	37	47	8	1	5	23	32	6	1	2	66	4	2	.350	.346
Davis, Jaylin	R-R	6-1	190	7-1-94	.271	.267	.273	57	199	23	54	10	0	5	19	23	3	1	1	57	3	2	.397	.354
De La Trinidad, Ernie	L-L	5-9	165	1-15-94	.303	.130	.364	27	89	13	27	2	0	1	12	9	1	3	1	17	1	4	.360	.363
Diaz, Lewin	L-L	6-3	180	11-19-96	.225	.274	.205	79	294	21	66	11	3	6	35	10	3	0	3	56	1	0	.344	.255
Foster, Jared	R-R	6-1	200	11-2-92	.167	.121	.187	32	108	9	18	1	0	1	7	5	0	2	1	25	2	1	.204	.202
Grzelakowski, Taylor	L-R	5-11	245	12-20-93	.298	.182	.340	95	332	46	99	23	3	8	40	37	2	1	2	98	1	2	.458	.370
Hamilton, Caleb	R-R	6-0	185	2-5-95	.205	.239	.191	91	297	38	61	19	4	2	42	36	1	0	6	72	5	2	.323	.288
Kerrigan, Jimmy	R-R	6-1	215	3-16-94	.281	.286	.278	53	196	26	55	15	2	6	24	14	6	0	3	59	3	4	.469	.343
Kirilloff, Alex	L-L	6-2	195	11-9-97	.362	.356	.364	65	260	39	94	24	2	7	45	14	2	0	4	39	3	2	.550	.393
Kranson, Mitchell	L-R	5-9	210	1-11-94	.240	.273	.226	21	75	7	18	5	0	0	14	5	0	1	0	6	0	0	.307	.288
Lewis, Royce	R-R	6-2	188	6-5-99	.255	.239	.261	46	188	33	48	6	3	5	21	19	1	0	0	35	6	4	.399	.327
Lopez, Brandon	R-R	6-1	190	9-9-93	.221	.228	.218	68	199	24	44	8	0	0	15	30	1	9	2	54	1	4	.261	.323
Miranda, Jose	R-R	6-2	180	6-29-98	.216	.250	.200	27	102	9	22	5	0	3	10	5	6	0	0	11	2	0	.353	.292
Molina, Nelson	L-R	6-3	175	4-30-95	.234	.222	.237	25	77	5	18	3	0	0	7	6	2	3	0	14	1	5	.273	.306
Molina, Robert	B-R	5-11	175	11-9-94	.071	.000	.091	4	14	0	1	0	0	0	0	0	0	0	0	2	0	0	.071	.071
Perez, Alex	L-R	5-10	180	10-24-92	.208	.167	.220	17	53	4	11	1	0	0	3	2	0	0	0	12	0	1	.226	.236
Polanco, Jorge	B-R	5-11	200	7-5-93	.333	.000	1.000	2	6	1	2	0	0	1	1	2	0	0	0	2	0	0	.833	.500
Rinn, Robby	L-L	6-1	205	10-17-92	.254	.316	.225	18	59	2	15	5	0	0	5	7	0	0	1	19	0	0	.339	.328
Robles, Alex	R-R	6-0	200	7-7-95	.160	.091	.214	7	25	1	4	0	0	0	1	1	0	0	0	3	0	0	.160	.192
Rodriguez, Ben	R-R	6-6	235	11-9-94	.172	.111	.200	7	29	3	5	0	0	1	3	1	0	0	0	9	0	0	.276	.200
Rortvedt, Ben	L-R	5-10	190	9-25-97	.250	.184	.269	51	172	20	43	7	1	4	27	21	2	0	1	29	0	0	.372	.337
Sano, Miguel	R-R	6-4	260	5-11-93	.328	.286	.340	19	64	11	21	2	0	2	12	13	0	0	0	21	0	0	.453	.442
Tademo, Victor	R-R	6-1	170	7-9-99	.000	.000	.000	2	5	1	0	0	0	0	0	1	0	0	0	4	0	0	.000	.167
Whitefield, Aaron	R-R	6-4	200	9-2-96	.211	.226	.206	65	213	33	45	7	0	2	10	17	2	2	3	56	20	7	.272	.272

Pitching	B-T	HT	WT	DOB	W	L	ERA	G	GS	CG	SV	IP	H	R	ER	HR	BB	SO	AVG	vLH	vRH	K/9	BB/9
Anderson, Brady	L-R	6-0	185	11-10-92	1	4	6.00	12	7	0	0	42	53	30	28	5	12	28	.301	.272	.333	6.00	2.57
Barnes, Charlie	L-L	6-2	180	10-1-95	8	6	2.81	23	23	0	0	118	115	39	37	6	44	84	.260	.258	.260	6.39	3.35
Beeker, Clark	R-R	6-3	205	11-22-92	5	7	4.59	20	17	0	0	100	122	57	51	9	23	64	.307	.327	.287	5.76	2.07
Bray, Adam	R-R	6-3	200	4-13-94	2	0	1.88	19	0	0	2	38	35	8	8	3	7	40	.241	.303	.190	9.39	1.64
Colina, Edwar	R-R	5-11	182	5-3-97	0	1	3.97	2	0	0	0	11	13	5	5	1	3	11	.289	.286	.292	8.74	2.38
Cordy, Max	R-R	6-4	220	6-9-93	0	1	7.15	6	0	0	0	11	16	11	9	1	4	12	.348	.400	.250	9.53	3.18
Cutura, Andro	R-R	6-0	195	8-22-93	4	6	3.65	20	17	1	1	101	100	46	41	3	28	83	.260	.231	.294	7.40	2.50
Davis, Colton	R-R	6-1	190	1-5-94	1	3	4.14	24	0	0	4	41	33	21	19	0	27	47	.214	.236	.195	10.23	5.88
Faucher, Calvin	R-R	6-1	175	9-22-95	0	0	7.30	6	0	0	0	12	19	10	10	0	3	7	.359	.394	.300	5.11	2.19
Graterol, Brusdar	R-R	6-1	180	8-26-98	5	2	3.12	11	11	0	0	61	59	22	21	0	19	56	.261	.207	.313	8.31	2.82
Hackimer, Tom	R-R	5-11	190	6-28-94	2	4	6.20	16	0	0	3	25	26	18	17	0	16	21	.289	.316	.269	7.66	5.84
Hughes, Phil	R-R	6-5	240	6-24-86	2	0	2.70	2	2	0	0	10	11	3	3	0	1	9	.275	.276	.273	8.10	0.90
Jax, Griffin	R-R	6-2	195	11-22-94	3	4	3.70	15	14	0	0	88	93	44	36	3	15	66	.274	.294	.262	6.78	1.54
Lombana, Logan	R-R	6-3	220	7-17-94	2	1	4.94	17	0	0	0	31	35	20	17	4	7	27	.285	.286	.283	7.84	2.03
Lujan, Hector	R-R	6-3	230	8-23-94	5	5	2.64	38	0	0	4	72	68	27	21	3	22	68	.248	.240	.255	8.54	2.76
Marnon, Kevin	R-L	6-7	245	3-16-94	1	4	4.76	18	2	0	3	28	36	24	15	5	13	21	.305	.310	.303	6.67	4.13
Marzi, Anthony	L-L	6-1	205	11-29-92	1	1	2.00	6	4	0	0	27	23	8	6	1	5	26	.230	.206	.242	8.67	1.67
Mason, Ryan	R-R	6-6	215	10-4-94	9	3	2.84	36	0	0	5	70	70	23	22	5	12	62	.271	.278	.264	8.01	1.55
May, Trevor	R-R	6-5	240	9-23-89	0	0	0.00	1	1	0	0	3	1	0	0	0	3	5	.100	.143	.000	15.00	9.00
Moran, Jovani	L-L	6-1	167	4-24-97	6	1	2.56	15	0	0	4	32	20	10	9	1	8	37	.179	.242	.152	10.52	2.27
Phillips, Alex	R-R	6-4	230	12-16-94	1	0	0.00	2	0	0	0	3	0	0	0	0	3	.000	.000	.000	8.10	0.00
Pineda, Michael	R-R	6-7	260	1-18-89	0	0	1.50	2	2	0	0	6	7	1	1	0	0	4	.304	.294	.333	6.00	0.00
Poppen, Sean	R-R	6-3	205	3-15-94	1	2	2.41	8	6	0	0	34	30	12	9	3	11	44	.236	.329	.111	11.76	2.94
Robinson, Alex	L-L	6-3	217	8-11-94	1	3	4.98	25	0	0	3	34	27	22	19	3	23	45	.208	.231	.190	11.88	6.03
Rodriguez, Paco	L-L	6-3	220	4-16-91	0	0	0.00	3	1	0	0	6	6	2	0	0	3	7	.250	.200	.286	11.12	4.76
Sammons, Bryan	L-L	6-4	235	4-27-95	1	2	8.49	4	4	0	0	23	32	24	22	3	14	20	.323	.314	.328	7.71	5.40
Santana, Ervin	R-R	6-2	175	12-12-82	0	3	3.48	3	3	0	0	10	7	4	4	1	1	7	.184	.217	.133	6.10	0.87
Stashak, Cody	R-R	6-2	169	6-4-94	1	0	4.50	2	0	0	0	4	2	2	2	1	2	5	.143	.143	.143	11.25	4.50
Stowell, Dylan	R-R	6-2	189	1-13-95	0	0	3.38	1	0	0	0	3	4	1	1	1	1	2	.364	.375	.333	6.75	3.38
Suniaga, Carlos	R-R	6-2	187	5-26-91	0	0	3.00	2	0	0	1	3	1	1	1	0	1	2	.111	.167	.000	6.00	3.00
Vasquez, Andrew	L-L	6-6	228	9-14-93	0	2	1.38	19	0	0	5	33	24	8	5	1	13	37	.202	.189	.212	10.19	3.58
Watson, Tyler	R-L	6-5	200	5-22-97	0	1	5.40	4	4	0	0	20	23	15	12	1	4	14	.281	.400	.254	6.30	1.80
Wells, Tyler	R-R	6-8	265	8-26-94	8	4	2.80	16	16	1	0	87	60	28	27	6	17	82	.191	.211	.164	8.52	1.77

Fielding

Catcher	PCT	G	PO	A	E	DP	PB
Grzelakowski	.983	22	152	20	3	1	4
Hamilton	.993	67	485	49	4	7	16

	PCT	G	PO	A	E	DP	PB
Kranson	.980	6	45	3	1	0	0
Molina	1.000	3	17	6	0	1	0
Rortvedt	.981	45	329	35	7	3	1

First Base	PCT	G	PO	A	E	DP
Costello	1.000	26	194	13	0	18
Cronin	1.000	6	22	1	0	1

MINNESOTA TWINS

Diaz	.989	74	573	50	7	57
Grzelakowski	1.000	13	108	9	0	12
Hamilton	.941	2	12	4	1	1
Kranson	1.000	7	65	5	0	7
Molina	1.000	1	5	1	0	0
Rinn	1.000	6	58	2	0	6
Robles	1.000	2	16	1	0	0
Rodriguez	1.000	7	48	4	0	5

Second Base	PCT	G	PO	A	E	DP
Arraez	.990	40	74	116	2	19
Blankenhorn	.966	58	89	111	7	28
Crites	1.000	1	4	2	0	1
Cronin	.974	18	27	49	2	12
Lopez	.714	2	1	4	2	1
Miranda	1.000	6	12	20	0	3
Molina	.895	4	2	15	2	1
Perez	1.000	11	12	23	0	3
Tademo	.000	1	0	0	0	0

Third Base	PCT	G	PO	A	E	DP
Arraez	1.000	6	9	9	0	2
Blankenhorn	.946	41	28	78	6	7
Costello	.667	1	2	0	1	0
Crites	1.000	1	1	1	0	0
Cronin	.912	14	7	24	3	1
Hamilton	.882	22	12	33	6	3
Lopez	1.000	15	8	29	0	1
Miranda	.914	19	10	22	3	5
Molina	.950	12	14	24	2	1
Molina	1.000	1	1	0	0	0
Sano	.957	10	6	16	1	2
Tademo	.667	1	1	1	1	0

Shortstop	PCT	G	PO	A	E	DP
Arraez	1.000	5	6	20	0	4
Cronin	.948	28	33	58	5	12
Lewis	.977	45	70	101	4	22
Lopez	.960	51	70	121	8	37

Miranda	1.000	2	2	3	0	0
Molina	1.000	6	8	14	0	3
Perez	.857	5	4	8	2	1
Polanco	1.000	1	3	4	0	1

Outfield	PCT	G	PO	A	E	DP
Blankenhorn	1.000	4	11	0	0	0
Carrier	.975	20	35	4	1	2
Contreras	.986	87	201	11	3	1
Cronin	1.000	4	3	2	0	0
Davis	1.000	52	69	5	0	1
De La Trinidad	1.000	25	27	0	0	0
Foster	.983	27	56	2	1	1
Grzelakowski	1.000	29	52	4	0	2
Kerrigan	.992	51	120	5	1	1
Kirilloff	.982	54	102	6	2	1
Perez	1.000	1	1	0	0	0
Robles	1.000	3	5	0	0	0
Whitefield	.994	63	166	3	1	1

CEDAR RAPIDS KERNELS

LOW CLASS A

MIDWEST LEAGUE

Batting	B-T	HT	WT	DOB	AVG	vLH	vRH	G	AB	R	H	2B	3B	HR	RBI	BB	HBP	SH	SF	SO	SB	CS	SLG	OBP
Akins, Jared	L-R	6-3	220	12-12-96	.209	.333	.182	18	67	7	14	2	1	0	8	2	0	0	0	24	0	1	.269	.232
Arias, Jean Carlos	L-L	5-11	170	1-14-98	.246	.216	.255	79	305	35	75	11	9	5	29	12	1	2	1	70	6	6	.390	.276
Baddoo, Akil	L-L	5-11	195	8-16-98	.243	.220	.250	113	437	83	106	22	11	11	40	74	1	2	3	124	24	5	.419	.352
Banuelos, David	R-R	6-0	205	10-1-96	.220	.232	.216	73	259	28	57	14	0	2	22	10	1	2	5	77	1	3	.297	.247
Bechtold, Andrew	R-R	6-1	185	4-18-96	.216	.272	.197	106	366	43	79	17	0	2	34	51	2	1	1	115	8	0	.279	.314
Cabbage, Trey	L-R	6-3	204	5-3-97	.244	.258	.241	99	340	34	83	22	4	8	45	28	4	0	3	119	3	0	.403	.307
Carrier, Shane	R-R	6-2	215	6-3-96	.231	.310	.193	37	130	12	30	5	1	5	22	10	1	0	3	36	2	0	.400	.285
Contreras, Mark	L-R	6-0	185	1-24-95	.440	.500	.435	7	25	4	11	3	0	0	5	2	0	1	0	7	1	0	.560	.482
Davis, Michael	L-R	6-0	200	1-22-96	.294	.273	.303	42	143	25	42	9	1	9	28	6	1	0	0	47	1	0	.559	.327
Gore, Jordan	B-R	6-0	180	8-3-94	.307	.357	.293	63	199	31	61	6	1	2	22	27	2	4	1	44	5	3	.377	.393
Helman, Michael	R-R	6-1	190	5-23-96	.355	.393	.342	27	107	20	38	6	1	2	15	6	3	0	2	14	4	5	.486	.398
Jeffers, Ryan	R-R	6-4	228	6-3-97	.288	.281	.290	36	139	19	40	10	0	4	17	14	2	0	0	30	0	0	.446	.361
Kirilloff, Alex	L-L	6-2	195	11-9-97	.333	.367	.323	65	252	36	84	20	5	13	56	24	2	0	3	47	1	1	.607	.392
Larnach, Trevor	L-R	6-4	210	2-26-97	.297	.353	.284	24	91	17	27	8	1	3	10	11	0	0	0	17	1	0	.506	.373
Lewis, Royce	R-R	6-2	188	6-5-99	.315	.237	.335	75	295	50	93	23	0	9	53	44	3	1	4	49	22	4	.485	.368
Maciel, Gabriel	B-R	5-10	170	1-10-99	.263	.200	.284	30	118	16	31	4	2	2	7	5	2	0	1	21	2	5	.381	.302
2-team total (68 Kane County)					.280	.267	.283	98	397	60	111	14	2	3	23	35	5	1	1	71	16	10	.348	.345
Miranda, Jose	R-R	6-2	180	6-29-98	.277	.304	.268	104	401	52	111	22	1	13	72	26	6	0	5	51	0	1	.434	.326
Molina, Robert	R-R	5-11	170	9-16-96	.133	.000	.154	5	15	2	2	0	0	0	0	0	0	1	0	5	0	0	.133	.125
Montesino, Ariel	R-R	5-10	188	9-21-95	.184	.294	.125	31	98	12	18	5	1	1	4	7	1	2	0	24	3	0	.286	.245
Pearson, Jacob	L-R	6-1	185	6-1-98	.237	.233	.237	78	279	51	66	12	3	7	36	29	2	1	1	69	6	5	.376	.312
Rinn, Robby	L-L	6-1	205	10-17-92	.305	.262	.317	48	187	26	57	12	1	3	21	15	3	0	1	28	0	0	.428	.364
Rodriguez, Ben	R-R	6-6	235	11-9-94	.258	.262	.256	83	279	46	72	21	1	10	44	33	2	0	6	96	2	2	.448	.334
Rortvedt, Ben	L-R	5-10	190	9-25-97	.276	.276	.276	39	145	14	40	9	2	1	16	10	1	0	1	35	1	0	.386	.325
Tademo, Victor	R-R	6-1	170	7-9-99	.500	.000	.556	3	10	2	5	1	0	1	2	1	0	0	1	1	0	0	.900	.546

Pitching	B-T	HT	WT	DOB	W	L	ERA	G	GS	CG	SV	IP	H	R	ER	HR	BB	SO	AVG	vLH	vRH	K/9	BB/9
Acosta, Melvi	R-R	6-1	188	6-2-95	2	4	2.95	21	6	0	3	55	64	23	18	3	15	41	.298	.310	.290	6.71	2.45
Balazovic, Jordan	R-R	6-4	175	9-17-98	7	3	3.94	12	11	0	0	62	54	27	27	5	18	78	.233	.293	.188	11.38	2.63
Brown, Nick	R-R	6-1	190	11-20-94	1	2	8.42	9	2	0	1	26	34	25	24	5	10	23	.321	.326	.317	8.06	3.51
Colina, Edwar	R-R	5-11	182	5-3-97	7	4	2.48	19	18	0	0	98	71	31	27	4	50	95	.200	.192	.204	8.72	4.59
Dobnak, Randy	R-R	6-1	210	1-17-95	10	5	3.14	24	20	1	0	129	138	51	45	6	25	84	.274	.276	.273	5.86	1.74
Duran, Jhoan	R-R	6-5	175	1-8-98	2	1	2.00	6	6	0	0	36	19	11	8	2	10	44	.155	.222	.115	11.00	2.50
2-team total (15 Kane County)					7	5	3.75	21	21	0	0	101	88	52	42	8	38	115	.232	.247	.220	10.28	3.40
Enlow, Blayne	R-R	6-3	170	3-21-99	3	5	3.26	20	17	0	1	94	94	40	34	4	35	71	.263	.216	.298	6.80	3.35
Faucher, Calvin	R-R	6-1	175	9-22-95	4	4	3.35	30	0	0	3	54	49	25	20	5	33	55	.248	.284	.222	9.22	5.53
Finkel, Jared	R-R	6-3	205	4-27-96	5	3	3.39	33	0	0	3	64	65	32	24	3	22	43	.268	.276	.263	6.08	3.11
Gomez, Moises	R-R	6-1	215	2-8-97	0	1	3.77	15	0	0	2	29	26	15	12	2	9	24	.271	.371	.213	7.53	2.83
Graterol, Brusdar	R-R	6-1	180	8-26-98	3	2	2.18	8	8	0	0	41	30	12	10	3	9	51	.195	.290	.130	11.10	1.96
Kiest, Tanner	R-R	6-3	200	9-16-94	0	1	7.98	7	2	0	1	15	17	14	13	0	14	14	.288	.417	.255	8.59	8.59
Marnon, Kevin	R-L	6-7	245	3-16-94	2	0	1.90	11	0	0	3	24	16	6	5	1	6	29	.191	.280	.153	11.03	2.28
Martinez, Jose	R-R	6-2	192	10-29-96	1	4	4.52	34	0	0	7	68	56	36	34	7	25	67	.224	.161	.254	8.91	3.33
Mason, Ryan	R-R	6-6	215	10-4-94	1	0	1.80	3	0	0	2	5	3	1	1	0	2	5	.188	.111	.286	9.00	0.00
Molina, Derek	R-R	6-3	206	7-27-97	3	0	2.83	16	0	0	2	35	25	13	11	0	16	47	.194	.109	.241	12.09	4.11
Moran, Jovani	L-L	6-1	167	4-24-97	3	2	2.03	22	1	0	4	44	25	11	10	1	27	70	.169	.171	.168	14.21	5.48
Neff, Zach	L-L	6-1	195	3-14-96	1	0	0.00	2	0	0	0	5	1	0	0	0	0	4	.067	.333	.000	7.71	0.00
Ober, Bailey	R-R	6-8	215	7-12-95	7	1	3.84	14	14	0	0	75	71	32	32	7	9	88	.249	.269	.231	10.56	1.08
Quezada, Johan	R-R	6-6	200	8-25-94	1	1	0.93	4	0	0	2	10	7	3	1	0	2	10	.200	.111	.231	9.31	1.86
Ramirez, Rickey	R-R	6-0	168	10-20-96	0	3	5.75	14	0	0	2	20	23	13	13	1	9	18	.291	.500	.189	7.97	3.98
Sammons, Bryan	L-L	6-4	225	4-27-95	5	5	2.32	15	15	0	0	66	49	21	17	4	22	75	.225	.194	.233	7.91	2.32
Suniaga, Carlos	R-R	6-2	187	5-26-97	4	4	3.50	19	2	0	2	46	38	22	18	5	16	40	.229	.207	.241	7.77	3.11
Watson, Tyler	R-L	6-5	200	5-22-97	5	7	4.76	18	17	1	0	87	91	56	46	7	44	85	.275	.254	.280	8.79	4.55

MINNESOTA TWINS

Fieldng

C: Banuelos 68, Jeffers 22, Molina 4, Rodriguez 21, Rortvedt 29. 1B: Bechtold 2, Cabbage 37, Rinn 43, Rodriguez 61. 2B: Bechtold 23, Gore 33, Helman 26, Miranda 53, Montesino 7. 3B: Bechtold 79, Cabbage 2, Gore 6, Miranda 41, Montesino 13, Tademo 3. SS: Davis 41, Gore 24, Lewis 67, Miranda 1, Montesino 11. OF: Akins 16, Arias 70, Baddoo 99, Cabbage 47, Carrier 25, Contreras 6, Kirilloff 53, Larnach 17, Maciel 28, Pearson 65.

ELIZABETHTON TWINS ROOKIE
APPALACHIAN LEAGUE

Batting	B-T	HT	WT	DOB	AVG	vLH	vRH	G	AB	R	H	2B	3B	HR	RBI	BB	HBP	SH	SF	SO	SB	CS	SLG	OBP
Akins, Jared	L-R	6-3	220	12-12-96	.269	.000	.309	22	78	21	21	4	1	1	8	8	3	0	2	22	3	2	.385	.352
Arias, Jean Carlos	L-L	5-11	170	1-14-98	.220	.571	.173	17	59	6	13	1	3	0	6	4	1	0	1	12	3	1	.339	.277
Burns, Colton	L-R	6-2	201	10-19-95	.247	.077	.275	30	93	20	23	6	0	6	14	17	2	0	0	33	1	0	.505	.375
Casanova, Trevor	L-R	6-0	200	6-22-96	.331	.219	.363	38	145	24	48	14	0	3	17	13	2	0	2	38	2	1	.490	.389
Celestino, Gilberto	R-L	6-0	170	2-13-99	.266	.500	.252	27	109	13	29	4	1	1	13	6	1	0	1	16	8	2	.349	.308
Cosgrove, Andrew	R-R	6-0	200	7-31-96	.262	.143	.294	19	65	11	17	3	0	1	12	10	1	0	0	17	0	0	.354	.368
Davis, Michael	L-R	6-0	200	1-22-96	.429	.250	.500	3	14	4	6	0	0	1	4	2	0	0	0	0	0	0	.643	.500
De La Torre, Ricky	B-R	6-2	204	7-21-99	.254	.276	.250	49	169	25	43	10	1	4	18	15	4	0	1	52	1	0	.396	.328
Encarnacion, Yeltsin	L-R	5-11	170	6-28-98	.291	.273	.294	24	79	15	23	6	0	0	11	6	0	1	0	17	2	4	.367	.341
Helman, Michael	R-R	6-1	190	5-23-96	.375	.429	.364	12	40	8	15	0	1	2	7	3	2	0	1	4	6	1	.575	.435
Jeffers, Ryan	R-R	6-4	228	6-3-97	.422	.333	.449	28	102	29	43	7	0	3	16	20	7	0	0	16	0	1	.725	.543
Keirsey, DaShawn	L-L	6-2	195	5-13-97	.301	.250	.317	26	103	20	31	7	3	0	13	12	0	0	1	20	4	1	.427	.371
Larnach, Trevor	L-R	6-4	210	2-26-97	.312	.143	.333	18	61	10	19	5	0	2	16	10	2	0	2	11	2	0	.492	.413
Lee, Hunter	L-R	5-9	180	1-17-96	.250	.000	.304	10	28	4	7	0	0	1	5	6	0	1	0	8	0	0	.357	.382
Marrero, Lean	L-R	5-10	189	9-19-97	.283	.286	.282	51	184	32	52	7	1	2	17	15	4	3	0	36	8	5	.364	.350
Molina, Robert	B-R	5-11	175	9-16-96	.231	.375	.211	18	65	4	15	1	0	2	17	4	0	0	0	9	0	0	.339	.275
Montesino, Ariel	R-R	5-10	188	9-01-95	.333	.500	.280	9	33	8	11	3	0	0	5	1	1	0	0	5	3	1	.424	.371
Robles, Alex	R-R	6-0	200	7-7-95	.297	.293	.298	59	222	26	66	12	0	2	35	19	2	0	1	32	2	2	.378	.357
Severino, Yunior	B-R	6-1	189	10-3-99	.263	.212	.273	49	198	32	52	8	0	8	28	17	1	0	2	52	0	1	.424	.321
Webb, Tyler	R-R	6-0	175	4-15-96	.268	.250	.273	10	41	8	11	0	0	0	5	2	0	0	0	12	3	0	.268	.302
Weiss, Albee	R-R	6-1	225	9-20-95	.200	.167	.211	36	120	16	24	6	0	4	11	9	1	0	1	38	0	0	.350	.260
Williams, Chris	R-R	6-1	225	11-23-96	.252	.400	.218	62	214	39	54	6	1	15	51	40	3	0	4	52	2	1	.500	.372

Pitching	B-T	HT	WT	DOB	W	L	ERA	G	GS	CG	SV	IP	H	R	ER	HR	BB	SO	AVG	vLH	vRH	K/9	BB/9
Berroa, Prelander	R-R	5-11	170	4-18-00	0	0	11.57	1	0	0	0	2	2	3	3	0	3	3	.250	.667	.000	11.57	11.57
Blank, Jacob	R-R	6-4	215	2-16-96	1	0	3.97	7	0	0	1	11	10	5	5	0	3	13	.244	.250	.242	10.32	2.38
Broussard, Christian	R-R	6-2	265	10-21-96	0	1	12.66	5	0	0	0	11	20	15	15	0	4	13	.377	.464	.280	10.97	3.38
Cabezas, Andrew	R-R	5-10	175	12-5-96	1	3	2.74	11	9	0	0	46	30	16	14	4	14	44	.180	.197	.170	8.61	2.74
Cha, Erik	L-L	6-2	190	6-19-97	0	0	0.00	2	0	0	1	4	2	1	0	0	3	8	.143	.200	.111	19.64	7.36
Funderburk, Kody	L-L	6-4	230	11-27-96	2	1	4.93	10	9	0	0	35	45	20	19	2	15	32	.324	.333	.321	8.31	3.89
Gamez, Juan	R-R	5-11	247	3-7-94	1	1	6.00	14	0	0	0	24	30	21	16	1	18	27	.294	.211	.344	10.13	6.75
Garcia, Pedro	R-R	6-2	240	7-21-95	4	3	5.40	12	5	0	1	33	25	25	20	2	31	29	.207	.200	.211	7.83	8.37
Gomez, Moises	R-R	6-1	215	2-8-97	2	0	3.48	9	0	0	0	21	17	16	8	4	10	26	.215	.222	.212	11.32	4.35
Howell, Tanner	R-R	6-5	210	3-29-95	1	2	6.20	10	0	0	0	20	23	16	14	3	8	18	.291	.440	.222	7.97	3.54
Lakso, Blair	R-R	6-2	235	8-23-94	6	2	3.66	15	0	0	0	32	27	16	13	2	22	35	.233	.146	.280	9.84	6.19
Molina, Derek	L-R	6-3	206	7-27-97	0	0	2.70	8	0	0	3	13	8	5	4	0	8	21	.163	.053	.231	14.18	5.40
Neff, Zach	L-L	6-1	195	3-14-96	3	2	4.87	14	0	0	5	20	21	14	11	3	6	22	.263	.227	.276	9.74	2.66
Palm, Tyler	R-R	6-2	226	12-10-94	2	4	4.06	11	11	0	0	51	60	23	23	1	11	45	.306	.280	.322	7.94	1.94
Perez, J.T.	L-L	6-4	215	10-26-95	0	1	7.20	5	0	0	0	11	9	9	8	1	4	18	.268	.222	.281	12.60	7.20
Pinkerton, Seth	R-R	6-3	225	7-26-96	1	1	6.57	15	0	0	2	25	23	24	18	3	22	28	.256	.294	.232	10.22	8.03
Quezada, Johan	R-R	6-6	200	8-25-94	2	2	2.35	12	0	0	2	23	18	8	6	0	12	21	.207	.306	.137	8.22	4.70
Ramirez, Rickey	R-R	6-0	168	10-20-96	2	0	0.00	5	0	0	1	7	0	0	0	0	2	9	.000	.000	.000	11.57	2.57
Rapp, Brian	R-R	6-0	197	8-10-95	1	3	3.52	10	6	0	0	38	46	19	15	2	10	37	.291	.269	.308	8.69	2.35
Rijo, Luis	R-R	6-1	200	9-6-98	2	0	1.27	5	5	0	0	21	15	8	3	1	4	17	.195	.261	.167	7.17	1.69
2-team total (5 Pulaski)					5	1	2.05	10	8	0	0	48	43	19	11	1	5	43	.231	.224	.235	8.01	0.93
Schulfer, Austin	R-R	6-2	175	12-22-95	8	0	1.58	11	7	0	0	40	33	13	7	1	15	34	.231	.268	.207	7.65	3.38
Stowell, Dylan	R-R	6-2	189	1-13-95	0	1	16.20	2	0	0	0	3	8	6	6	0	2	8	.444	.500	.400	21.60	5.40
Suniaga, Carlos	R-R	6-2	187	5-26-97	2	1	3.82	9	5	0	0	33	38	19	14	1	9	28	.277	.289	.271	7.64	2.45
Winder, Josh	R-R	6-5	210	10-11-96	3	1	3.72	9	9	0	0	39	37	17	16	1	6	42	.248	.270	.233	9.78	1.40

Fielding

C: Casanova 25, Cosgrove 19, Jeffers 10, Molina 13. 1B: Casanova 1, Molina 4, Weiss 3, Williams 59. 2B: Encarnacion 14, Helman 7, Lee 8, Montesino 1, Severino 38. 3B: De La Torre 6, Lee 1, Montesino 3, Robles 57. SS: Davis 2, De La Torre 43, Encarnacion 9, Helman 1, Montesino 3, Severino 10. OF: Akins 20, Arias 14, Burns 21, Celestino 23, Helman 1, Keirsey 22, Larnach 14, Marrero 50, Montesino 1, Webb 10, Weiss 27.

GCL TWINS ROOKIE
GULF COAST LEAGUE

Batting	B-T	HT	WT	DOB	AVG	vLH	vRH	G	AB	R	H	2B	3B	HR	RBI	BB	HBP	SH	SF	SO	SB	CS	SLG	OBP
Carrier, Shane	R-R	6-2	215	6-3-96	.387	.500	.348	9	31	6	12	3	0	1	7	2	2	0	0	6	1	1	.581	.457
Cavaness, Christian	L-L	6-2	190	3-16-94	.160	.125	.177	8	25	5	4	0	0	1	2	3	0	0	0	11	0	0	.280	.250
De La Cruz, Yeremi	R-R	5-11	185	7-15-97	.750	.333	1.000	2	8	3	6	3	0	1	9	0	0	0	0	0	0	0	1.500	.750
Encarnacion, Yeltsin	L-R	5-11	170	6-28-98	.307	.333	.297	21	88	22	27	2	1	1	11	7	0	1	0	12	4	0	.386	.358
Garry Jr., Willie Joe	L-L	6-1	170	5-29-00	.161	.235	.141	33	81	13	13	4	0	0	5	8	4	1	1	28	5	2	.210	.266
Hale, Austin	R-R	6-0	190	10-16-95	.232	.278	.211	26	56	7	13	4	0	1	5	4	1	2	1	13	0	0	.357	.290
Herrera, Edgar	L-L	6-0	170	4-19-97	.220	.154	.243	17	50	5	11	2	0	0	5	4	0	1	1	10	1	0	.260	.273
Lee, Hunter	L-R	5-9	180	1-17-96	.270	.278	.267	23	63	9	17	3	0	1	7	9	3	0	0	15	0	4	.365	.387

Name	B-T	HT	WT	DOB	AVG	vLH	vRH	G	AB	R	H	2B	3B	HR	RBI	BB	HBP	SH	SF	SO	SB	CS	SLG	OBP
Mack, Charles	L-R	6-0	190	11-12-99	.216	.192	.224	30	102	13	22	4	1	0	3	13	2	0	1	23	1	1	.275	.314
Marte, Agustin	B-R	6-0	180	12-9-98	.243	.241	.244	33	111	17	27	4	0	2	9	8	0	2	1	25	4	1	.333	.292
Nunez, Alberoni	R-R	6-1	180	2-17-99	.189	.237	.175	46	164	17	31	6	1	1	19	9	0	2	1	53	2	2	.256	.230
Pacheco, Jordan	R-R	6-1	200	1-30-86	.333	.500	.200	4	9	3	3	0	0	0	2	2	0	1	2	0	0	0	.333	.500
Perez, Yeison	R-R	5-11	200	4-9-96	.273	.214	.300	35	88	6	24	8	0	1	16	7	1	0	0	15	0	0	.398	.333
Rivera, Erick	L-L	6-0	183	11-11-00	.246	.429	.167	23	69	6	17	4	0	0	7	11	1	1	0	22	1	2	.304	.358
Salva, Kidany	R-R	5-11	185	3-24-98	.240	.292	.225	36	104	16	25	5	0	0	9	8	4	0	1	17	2	0	.289	.316
Smith, LaRon	R-R	6-2	200	9-16-00	.205	.300	.172	13	39	3	8	2	0	0	2	7	0	0	0	9	1	0	.256	.326
Snyder, Gabe	L-L	6-5	235	3-4-95	.265	.184	.294	48	147	17	39	7	0	3	25	20	4	0	5	36	3	3	.374	.358
Tademo, Victor	R-R	6-1	170	7-9-99	.255	.250	.256	44	157	11	40	5	0	0	15	10	1	1	2	32	2	2	.287	.304
Urena, Estamy	R-R	6-0	175	5-27-99	.293	.302	.289	41	147	18	43	6	2	0	21	11	1	0	3	13	5	1	.361	.340
Vasquez, Samuel	L-L	5-10	155	1-15-97	.240	.296	.219	36	100	23	24	6	0	0	9	14	1	2	1	21	3	1	.300	.336
Villalobos, Janigson	R-R	5-9	195	5-10-97	.310	.316	.308	31	84	8	26	3	2	0	15	7	0	0	0	11	1	1	.393	.363
Webb, Tyler	R-R	6-0	175	4-15-96	.294	.250	.318	31	102	22	30	4	0	1	11	12	7	0	2	15	8	2	.363	.398
Whitefield, Aaron	R-R	6-4	200	9-2-96	.250	.375	.125	5	16	2	4	1	0	0	2	4	0	0	0	4	0	0	.313	.400

Pitching	B-T	HT	WT	DOB	W	L	ERA	G	GS	CG	SV	IP	H	R	ER	HR	BB	SO	AVG	vLH	vRH	K/9	BB/9
Balan, Petru	L-L	6-0	185	2-22-96	1	3	2.35	16	0	0	1	23	21	9	6	0	18	22	.247	.177	.265	8.61	7.04
Benninghoff, Tyler	R-R	6-4	180	9-17-97	2	2	3.89	10	7	0	0	39	27	19	17	1	26	28	.194	.197	.192	6.41	5.95
Bentley, Denny	L-L	6-2	195	5-28-98	1	1	2.60	13	0	0	1	17	16	6	5	2	6	21	.242	.158	.277	10.90	3.12
Berroa, Prelander	R-R	5-11	170	4-18-00	2	0	2.29	9	8	0	0	39	31	17	10	0	15	38	.217	.250	.190	8.69	3.43
Breek, Donny	R-R	6-2	205	11-8-99	2	1	2.89	10	8	0	0	37	26	14	12	0	17	41	.197	.189	.203	9.88	4.10
Cha, Erik	L-L	6-2	190	6-19-97	2	0	1.59	13	0	0	2	23	21	12	4	1	4	21	.247	.158	.273	8.34	1.59
Crosby, Casey	R-L	6-5	225	9-17-88	0	2	2.08	6	3	0	0	9	2	4	2	0	6	11	.074	.167	.048	11.42	6.23
Cruz, Amilcar	R-R	6-2	190	3-28-96	2	0	6.00	3	0	0	0	6	6	4	4	0	3	4	.273	.222	.308	6.00	4.50
Cruz, Steven	R-R	6-2	185	6-15-99	1	3	3.12	13	2	0	2	26	14	12	9	0	24	33	.156	.178	.133	11.42	8.31
Featherstone, Zach	L-L	6-2	215	12-18-95	0	0	9.00	3	1	0	0	3	4	3	3	0	4	3	.308	.000	.333	9.00	12.00
German, Osiris	R-R	6-1	170	11-2-98	2	2	2.57	17	0	0	2	21	21	8	6	3	4	23	.273	.310	.250	9.86	1.71
Grace, Regi	L-R	6-1	215	12-10-99	2	1	5.06	6	1	0	0	11	13	9	6	1	6	8	.310	.357	.286	6.75	3.38
Howell, Tanner	R-R	6-5	210	3-29-95	0	0	0.75	7	0	0	3	12	8	1	1	0	2	14	.191	.191	.191	10.50	1.50
Jorge, Felix	R-R	6-2	170	1-2-94	1	0	0.00	2	1	0	0	3	2	1	0	0	0	2	.167	.000	.222	6.00	0.00
Leach, Landon	R-R	6-4	220	7-12-99	0	1	2.18	7	6	0	0	21	16	9	5	1	10	16	.216	.216	.216	6.97	4.35
Marin, Andriu	R-R	6-2	205	7-6-98	3	2	5.54	9	7	0	0	37	45	25	23	1	9	37	.298	.333	.273	8.92	2.17
Montero, Michael	R-R	6-3	190	1-6-00	4	1	2.41	12	1	0	1	34	26	12	9	1	10	21	.210	.250	.177	5.61	2.67
Navas, Junior	R-R	6-4	185	9-8-99	0	0	1.38	8	0	0	1	13	13	2	2	0	2	10	.283	.389	.214	6.92	1.38
Perez, J.T.	L-L	6-4	215	10-26-95	1	0	2.31	10	0	0	0	12	14	6	3	0	5	14	.298	.308	.294	10.80	3.86
Pineda, Michael	R-R	6-7	260	1-18-89	0	0	0.00	1	1	0	0	2	1	0	0	1	3	.143	.333	.000	13.50	4.50
Rimmel, Niklas	R-R	6-3	200	7-5-99	0	1	3.86	8	0	0	1	14	21	8	6	0	3	6	.356	.414	.300	3.86	1.93
Stowell, Dylan	R-R	6-2	189	1-13-95	1	0	2.74	12	1	0	2	23	21	9	7	1	7	21	.236	.152	.286	8.22	2.74
Teng, Kai-Wei	R-R	6-4	260	12-1-98	3	3	3.59	10	9	0	0	43	36	17	17	0	15	47	.226	.154	.277	9.91	3.16
Torres, Frandy	R-R	5-10	160	8-4-95	2	1	3.38	15	0	0	0	19	16	7	7	1	11	24	.229	.214	.238	11.57	5.30

Fielding

C: De La Cruz 1, Hale 25, Pacheco 2, Perez 22, Salva 24, Villalobos 20. 1B: Herrera 1, Pacheco 1, Perez 4, Salva 8, Smith 3, Snyder 47, Urena 2. 2B: Lee 20, Marte 18, Urena 24. 3B: Mack 27, Smith 1, Tademo 23, Urena 11. SS: Encarnacion 21, Marte 13, Tademo 20, Urena 4. OF: Carrier 8, Cavaness 6, Garry Jr. 24, Herrera 14, Nunez 45, Rivera 23, Smith 1, Vasquez 32, Webb 28, Whitefield 4.

DSL TWINS   ROOKIE
DOMINICAN SUMMER LEAGUE

Batting	B-T	HT	WT	DOB	AVG	vLH	vRH	G	AB	R	H	2B	3B	HR	RBI	BB	HBP	SH	SF	SO	SB	CS	SLG	OBP
Aguiar, Carlos	L-L	6-2	175	8-28-01	.228	.120	.263	33	101	19	23	5	4	2	24	14	2	2	2	30	6	5	.416	.328
Baez, Luis	R-R	5-11	170	11-23-00	.188	.300	.141	50	101	23	19	2	1	1	12	14	6	1	1	22	14	3	.257	.320
Caceres, Jim	B-R	5-11	165	10-13-00	.265	.180	.288	55	185	38	49	5	7	3	23	27	6	0	2	29	15	5	.416	.373
Carrillo, Brahiap	L-L	6-0	170	4-26-99	.299	.286	.303	44	137	28	41	5	6	1	23	20	0	0	2	35	9	4	.445	.384
Castro, Wilfri	R-R	5-11	165	3-21-01	.160	.111	.175	22	75	11	12	2	0	0	2	8	5	2	0	16	3	2	.187	.284
Feliz, Jesus	R-R	6-0	185	6-7-00	.289	.323	.279	38	142	18	41	11	4	3	21	3	5	1	2	25	9	6	.486	.322
Gomez, Luis	L-R	5-11	160	10-22-00	.326	.286	.340	43	138	34	45	7	3	0	22	31	2	1	1	32	15	6	.420	.454
Heredia, Victor	R-R	6-2	230	6-1-00	.331	.357	.322	60	233	47	77	16	4	8	56	14	5	0	8	40	1	4	.537	.369
Martinez, Francisco	B-R	6-5	220	4-25-99	.278	.200	.308	36	126	19	35	3	8	2	24	13	1	0	2	48	2	2	.476	.345
Milla, Luis	L-R	6-0	175	9-5-98	.301	.378	.273	51	173	31	52	9	4	3	26	26	1	4	2	39	11	9	.451	.391
Morales, Jeferson	R-R	5-8	175	5-13-99	.303	.239	.326	53	178	44	54	15	6	1	22	41	13	0	9	29	17	11	.472	.466
Pena, Yelinson	R-R	5-11	175	9-16-00	.239	.174	.262	27	88	10	21	3	0	0	9	17	1	1	0	17	3	3	.273	.368
Reyes, Felix	L-L	6-0	180	3-1-99	.143	.077	.167	19	49	3	7	1	0	0	4	2	0	0	21	2	1	.163	.236
Roberto, Nelson	R-R	6-2	200	10-7-00	.156	.188	.148	24	77	8	12	1	3	0	7	4	2	0	2	44	2	1	.247	.212
Santana, Ruben	R-R	5-9	160	11-30-97	.324	.300	.331	51	173	44	56	15	6	0	30	23	3	1	2	19	15	6	.480	.408
Toribio, Sergio	B-R	5-11	170	8-16-98	.203	.364	.172	23	69	8	14	2	2	0	11	7	0	1	1	19	1	0	.290	.273
Urdaneta, Nomar	B-R	6-0	175	11-18-00	.261	.348	.240	38	119	27	31	1	3	0	13	16	5	2	2	26	2	6	.319	.366
Valdez, Wander	R-R	6-0	200	11-22-99	.278	.255	.278	51	177	32	46	7	5	3	24	15	4	3	4	40	7	4	.407	.354

Pitching	B-T	HT	WT	DOB	W	L	ERA	G	GS	CG	SV	IP	H	R	ER	HR	BB	SO	AVG	vLH	vRH	K/9	BB/9
Banks, Alex	R-R	6-2	160	10-7-00	1	1	8.59	10	2	0	0	15	20	15	14	1	9	13	.318	.346	.297	7.98	5.52
Bermudez, Jose	R-R	6-4	190	1-8-98	4	4	4.01	16	14	0	0	67	64	34	30	2	15	67	.245	.203	.264	8.96	2.00
Castro, Cristian	R-R	6-1	165	4-21-98	3	6	4.73	17	9	0	0	53	46	41	28	4	30	60	.231	.187	.258	10.13	5.06
Causado, Moises	R-R	6-1	170	1-7-01	0	0	0.00	5	0	0	0	6	3	0	0	0	3	6	.150	.125	.167	6.35	4.76
Cruz, Amilcar	R-R	6-2	190	3-28-96	1	0	3.75	4	0	0	0	12	13	7	5	0	5	12	.255	.118	.324	9.00	3.75

De La Cruz, Luciano	L-L	5-11	200	2-4-99	7	0	3.93	20	4	0	2	55	53	29	24	4	21	56	.241	.250	.238	9.16	3.44
Escobar, Anthony	R-R	5-11	170	8-25-00	5	1	1.10	14	10	0	0	57	29	14	7	1	14	53	.144	.194	.121	8.32	2.20
Feliz, Rafael	R-R	6-0	160	11-20-00	2	1	8.00	12	0	0	0	18	23	20	16	1	7	15	.295	.222	.333	7.50	3.50
Garcia, Yeremi	R-R	6-2	185	11-16-99	4	0	2.33	15	0	0	1	27	28	9	7	0	16	24	.267	.290	.254	8.00	5.33
German, Giovahniey	R-R	6-2	165	10-8-00	2	0	10.26	14	0	0	0	17	22	19	19	2	17	11	.344	.310	.371	5.94	9.18
German, Osiris	R-R	6-1	170	11-2-98	0	1	2.53	3	2	0	0	11	9	5	3	0	5	16	.225	.177	.261	13.50	4.22
Guevara, Jose	R-R	6-3	180	10-2-98	2	2	2.48	17	0	0	6	29	29	14	8	1	15	35	.252	.186	.292	10.86	4.66
Guzman, Yolby	R-R	6-2	175	11-11-00	1	0	7.59	20	0	0	3	32	34	36	27	1	26	35	.256	.351	.219	9.84	7.31
Mateo, Yordin	R-R	6-1	165	12-10-00	3	1	3.26	12	8	0	1	39	33	18	14	2	14	28	.231	.200	.250	6.52	3.26
Moreno, Danny	R-R	6-1	180	10-10-99	0	0	1.14	18	1	0	7	24	13	4	3	0	4	21	.157	.111	.179	7.99	1.52
Perez, Bryant	R-R	6-0	160	6-25-00	3	0	1.06	10	5	0	0	34	22	8	4	1	10	40	.182	.227	.156	10.59	2.65
Rodriguez, Miguel	R-R	6-2	180	2-25-99	3	1	4.99	13	5	0	0	31	28	19	17	0	12	35	.235	.167	.282	10.27	3.52
Sanchez, Fernando	R-R	5-9	155	2-20-00	6	2	3.12	20	0	0	2	40	27	18	14	1	16	28	.192	.122	.228	6.25	3.57
Toledo, Jesus	L-L	5-11	180	8-25-99	2	2	3.21	14	12	0	0	53	44	25	19	1	21	67	.217	.159	.233	11.31	3.54

Fielding

C: Castro 20, Heredia 2, Morales 34, Toribio 20. **1B:** Feliz 1, Heredia 55, Santana 4, Toribio 1, Valdez 20. **2B:** Caceres 20, Feliz 7, Gomez 5, Santana 19, Urdaneta 25. **3B:** Caceres 5, Feliz 10, Gomez 7, Pena 20, Santana 5, Valdez 33. **SS:** Caceres 21, Feliz 20, Gomez 27, Santana 1, Urdaneta 6. **OF:** Aguiar 33, Baez 43, Carrillo 42, Gomez 2, Martinez 19, Milla 51, Morales 1, Reyes 17, Roberto 23, Santana 20.

New York Mets

SEASON IN A SENTENCE: While the Mets' final standing is unremarkable—fourth in the National League East at 77-85—the same is not true for their path to that record; New York went 15-39 (.278) in May and June but 62-46 (.574) in the other 108 games.

HIGH POINT: First-year manager Mickey Callaway could do no wrong when the Mets opened the year 16-9. That run included a nine-game winning streak, with five wins coming against the division-rival Phillies and Nationals.

LOW POINT: The Mets crashed to earth in May by opening the month with six straight losses to the Braves and Rockies, both eventual NL playoff teams. New York then lost eight in a row from May 31-June 9, which included two defeats at the hands of the 115-loss Orioles.

NOTABLE ROOKIES: Jeff McNeil opened the season as a nondescript 26-year-old but finished the year entrenched as the Mets' second baseman. He hit .342/.411/.617 with 19 home runs in the minors to force his July 24 callup. He continued to mash in the majors by batting .329 with a 140 OPS+. Righthander Corey Oswalt picked up 12 starts and tossed 65 innings as he recorded a 5.85 ERA. A host of relievers made at least 15 appearances, including righthanders Jacob Rhame (30), Drew Smith (27), Tyler Bashlor (24) and Tim Peterson (22) and lefty Daniel Zamora (16). Rhame, Smith and Zamora were the products of trades the Mets made to improve the velocity and dominance of their relief corps.

KEY TRANSACTIONS: The Mets opted to hang on to their biggest potential trade chips—right-handers Jacob deGrom, Noah Syndergaard and Zack Wheeler—but did make two notable dead-line deals. They shipped Jeurys Familia to the Athletics for a return headlined by $1 million in international bonus pool money, and they traded Asdrubal Cabrera to the Phillies for 23-year-old Double-A righthander Franklyn Kilome.

DOWN ON THE FARM: Mets farm clubs finished 21st in the game with a .472 winning percentage, and only Rookie-level Kingsport qualified for the playoffs. However, many of the organization's top prospects turned in productive seasons, headlined by shortstop Andres Gimenez and first baseman Peter Alonso, who both participated in the Futures Game. Recent first-round college pitchers Justin Dunn, Anthony Kay and David Peterson all stayed healthy and progressed towards Queens.

OPENING DAY PAYROLL: $172,761,459 (5th)

PLAYERS OF THE YEAR

ELIOT J. SCHECHTER

MAJOR LEAGUE	MINOR LEAGUE
Jacob deGrom RHP	**Peter Alonso** 1B
10-9, 1.70 in 32 GS	(Double-A/Triple-A)
11.2 SO/9, 1.9 BB/9	.285/.395/.579
Led majors in ERA	36 HR, 119 RBIs

ORGANIZATION LEADERS

Batting		*Minimum 250 AB
MAJORS		
* AVG	Asdrubal Cabrera	.277
* OPS	Brandon Nimmo	.886
HR	Michael Conforto	28
RBI	Michael Conforto	82
MINORS		
* AVG	Jeff McNeil, Binghamton, Las Vegas	.342
* OBP	Jeff McNeil, Binghamton, Las Vegas	.411
* SLG	Jeff McNeil, Binghamton, Las Vegas	.617
* OPS	Jeff McNeil, Binghamton, Las Vegas	1.028
R	Zach Borenstein, Las Vegas	92
R	Peter Alonso, Binghamton, Las Vegas	92
H	Peter Alonso, Binghamton, Las Vegas	136
TB	Peter Alonso, Binghamton, Las Vegas	277
2B	Zach Borenstein, Las Vegas	32
3B	Ross Adolph, Brooklyn	12
HR	Peter Alonso, Binghamton, Las Vegas	36
RBI	Peter Alonso, Binghamton, Las Vegas	119
BB	Zach Borenstein, Las Vegas	81
SO	Zach Borenstein, Las Vegas	182
SB	Andres Gimenez, St. Lucie, Binghamton	38

Pitching		#Minimum 75 IP
MAJORS		
W	Noah Syndergaard	13
# ERA	Jacob deGrom	1.70
SO	Jacob deGrom	269
SV	Jeurys Familia	17
MINORS		
W	Nabil Crismatt, Binghamton, Las Vegas	11
L	Harol Gonzalez, St. Lucie, Las Vegas, Binghamton	16
# ERA	Christian James, Binghamton, St. Lucie, Brooklyn	1.90
G	Kyle Regnault, Las Vegas	48
GS	Drew Gagnon, Binghamton, Las Vegas	28
SV	Trey Cobb, Columbia, St. Lucie	12
IP	Drew Gagnon, Binghamton, Las Vegas	164
BB	Nabil Crismatt, Binghamton, Las Vegas	56
SO	Drew Gagnon, Binghamton, Las Vegas	172
# AVG	Christian James, Binghamton, St. Lucie, Brooklyn	.220

2018 PERFORMANCE

General Manager: Sandy Alderson. **Farm Director:** Ian Levin. **Scouting Director:** Marc Tramuta.

Class	Team	League	W	L	PCT	Finish	Manager
Majors	New York Mets	National	77	85	.475	11th (15)	Mickey Callaway
Triple-A	Las Vegas 51s	Pacific Coast	71	69	.507	9th (16)	Chad Kreuter
Double-A	Binghamton Rumble Ponies	Eastern	64	76	.457	9th (12)	Luis Rojas
High A	St. Lucie Mets	Florida State	54	76	.415	11th (12)	Tony DeFrancesco
Low A	Columbia Fireflies	South Atlantic	64	70	.478	9th (14)	Pedro Lopez
Short season	Brooklyn Cyclones	New York-Penn	40	35	.533	5th (14)	Edgardo Alfonzo
Rookie	Kingsport Mets	Appalachian	33	35	.485	5th (10)	Sean Ratliff
Rookie	GCL Mets	Gulf Coast	24	31	.436	14th (18)	David Davalillo
Overall 2018 Minor League Record			350	392	.472	21st (30)	

ORGANIZATION STATISTICS

NEW YORK METS
NATIONAL LEAGUE

Batting	B-T	HT	WT	DOB	AVG	vLH	vRH	G	AB	R	H	2B	3B	HR	RBI	BB	HBP	SH	SF	SO	SB	CS	SLG	OBP
Bautista, Jose	R-R	6-0	205	10-19-80	.204	.169	.217	83	245	37	50	13	0	9	37	51	5	0	1	84	2	2	.367	.351
3-team total (12 Atlanta, 27 Philadelphia)					.203	.168	.219	122	325	52	66	18	0	13	48	67	6	0	1	111	4	3	.379	.348
Bruce, Jay	L-L	6-3	225	4-3-87	.223	.230	.219	94	319	31	71	18	1	9	37	41	0	0	1	75	2	3	.370	.310
Cabrera, Asdrubal	B-R	6-0	205	11-13-85	.277	.261	.285	98	375	48	104	23	1	18	58	29	1	0	2	81	0	0	.488	.329
2-team total (49 Philadelphia)					.262	.250	.267	147	546	68	143	36	1	23	75	41	3	0	2	119	0	0	.458	.316
Cespedes, Yoenis	R-R	5-10	220	10-18-85	.262	.167	.288	38	141	20	37	6	0	9	29	13	1	0	2	50	3	0	.497	.325
Conforto, Michael	L-R	6-1	215	3-1-93	.243	.249	.241	153	543	78	132	25	1	28	82	84	7	0	4	159	3	4	.448	.350
d'Arnaud, Travis	R-R	6-2	210	12-10-89	.200	.250	.182	4	15	1	3	0	0	1	3	1	0	0	0	5	0	0	.400	.250
den Dekker, Matthew	L-L	6-2	210	8-10-87	.000	.000	.000	8	18	0	0	0	0	0	0	1	2	0	0	1	9	0	0	.000	.095
Evans, Phillip	R-R	5-10	223	9-10-92	.143	.143	.143	15	21	1	3	0	0	0	1	2	0	0	0	8	1	0	.143	.217
Flores, Wilmer	R-R	6-3	205	8-6-91	.267	.237	.283	126	386	43	103	25	0	11	51	29	5	0	9	42	0	0	.417	.319
Frazier, Todd	R-R	6-3	220	2-12-86	.213	.162	.232	115	408	54	87	18	0	18	59	48	8	0	8	112	9	4	.390	.303
Gonzalez, Adrian	L-L	6-2	215	5-8-82	.237	.227	.238	54	169	15	40	5	0	6	26	15	1	0	2	34	0	0	.373	.300
Guillorme, Luis	L-R	5-10	195	9-27-94	.209	.227	.200	35	67	4	14	2	0	0	5	7	0	0	0	3	1	0	.239	.284
Jackson, Austin	R-R	6-1	198	2-1-87	.248	.200	.266	57	198	17	49	9	1	3	19	12	0	0	0	74	1	2	.349	.291
2-team total (59 San Francisco)					.245	.252	.241	116	347	29	85	17	1	3	32	26	1	0	1	133	3	3	.326	.299
Kaczmarski, Kevin	L-R	6-0	192	12-31-91	.000	.000	.000	4	4	0	0	0	0	0	0	1	0	0	0	1	0	1	.000	.200
Kelly, Ty	B-R	6-0	180	7-20-88	.091	.500	.000	9	11	1	1	0	0	0	1	0	0	0	0	2	0	0	.091	.167
Lagares, Juan	R-R	6-1	215	3-17-89	.339	.300	.379	30	59	9	20	1	1	0	6	3	1	0	1	9	3	1	.390	.375
Lobaton, Jose	B-R	6-0	205	10-21-84	.143	.118	.156	22	49	3	7	2	1	0	4	7	0	0	1	15	0	0	.225	.246
McNeil, Jeff	L-R	6-1	195	4-8-92	.329	.281	.345	63	225	35	74	11	6	3	19	14	5	4	0	24	7	1	.471	.381
Mesoraco, Devin	R-R	6-1	229	6-19-88	.222	.217	.223	66	203	23	45	8	0	10	30	23	2	0	1	42	0	0	.409	.306
2-team total (18 Cincinnati)					.221	.230	.219	84	244	24	54	10	0	11	33	25	4	0	1	52	0	0	.398	.303
Nido, Tomas	R-R	6-0	210	4-12-94	.167	.267	.145	34	84	10	14	3	0	1	9	4	0	0	2	27	0	0	.238	.200
Nimmo, Brandon	L-R	6-3	207	3-27-93	.263	.234	.275	140	433	77	114	28	8	17	47	80	22	0	0	140	9	6	.483	.404
Plawecki, Kevin	R-R	6-2	210	2-26-91	.210	.235	.203	79	238	33	50	13	2	7	30	28	9	1	1	65	0	1	.370	.315
Reinheimer, Jack	R-R	6-1	185	7-19-92	.167	.250	.154	21	30	4	5	0	0	0	5	0	0	0	9	1	1	.167	.286
Reyes, Jose	B-R	6-0	195	6-11-83	.189	.197	.186	110	228	30	43	12	3	4	16	22	0	1	0	39	5	2	.320	.260
Rosario, Amed	R-R	6-2	189	11-20-95	.256	.284	.247	154	554	76	142	26	8	9	51	29	3	3	3	119	24	11	.381	.295
Smith, Dominic	L-L	6-0	239	6-15-95	.224	.167	.232	56	143	14	32	11	1	5	11	4	2	0	0	47	0	0	.420	.255
Wright, David	R-R	6-0	205	12-20-82	.000	—	.000	2	2	0	0	0	0	0	0	1	0	0	0	0	0	0	.000	.333

Pitching	B-T	HT	WT	DOB	W	L	ERA	G	GS	CG	SV	IP	H	R	ER	HR	BB	SO	AVG	vLH	vRH	K/9	BB/9
Bashlor, Tyler	R-R	6-0	195	4-16-93	0	3	4.22	24	0	0	0	32	26	16	15	6	12	25	.219	.193	.242	7.03	3.38
Baumann, Buddy	L-L	5-11	198	12-9-87	0	1	24.00	3	0	0	0	3	7	8	8	1	5	4	.438	.400	.455	12.00	15.00
2-team total (1 San Diego)					0	2	27.00	4	0	0	0	3	9	13	10	1	7	4	.474	.571	.417	10.80	18.90
Bautista, Gerson	R-R	6-3	195	5-31-95	0	1	12.46	5	0	0	0	4	8	6	6	2	5	3	.444	.600	.385	6.23	10.38
Beck, Chris	R-R	6-3	225	9-4-90	0	0	5.23	6	0	0	0	10	10	6	6	3	9	5	.270	.308	.250	4.35	7.84
Blevins, Jerry	L-L	6-6	190	9-6-83	3	2	4.85	64	1	0	1	43	36	24	23	6	22	41	.225	.264	.193	8.65	4.64
Conlon, P.J.	L-L	5-11	192	11-11-93	0	0	8.22	3	2	0	0	8	15	7	7	2	2	5	.417	.385	.435	5.87	2.35
Copeland, Scott	R-R	6-3	220	12-15-87	0	0	0.00	1	0	0	0	1	1	0	0	0	0	2	.200	.333	.000	13.50	0.00
deGrom, Jacob	L-R	6-4	180	6-19-88	10	9	1.70	32	32	1	0	217	152	48	41	10	46	269	.196	.219	.172	11.16	1.91
Familia, Jeurys	R-R	6-3	240	10-10-89	4	4	2.88	40	0	0	17	41	36	13	13	1	14	43	.234	.288	.185	9.52	3.10
Flexen, Chris	R-R	6-3	250	7-1-94	0	2	12.79	4	1	0	0	6	14	13	9	2	6	3	.424	.444	.417	4.26	8.53
Gagnon, Drew	R-R	6-4	215	6-26-90	2	1	5.25	5	1	0	0	12	15	7	7	2	5	8	.319	.350	.296	6.00	3.75
Gsellman, Robert	R-R	6-4	205	7-18-93	6	3	4.28	68	0	0	13	80	76	44	38	8	28	70	.250	.216	.279	7.88	3.15
Hanhold, Eric	R-R	6-5	220	11-1-93	0	0	7.71	3	0	0	0	2	4	2	2	0	1	2	.364	.500	.200	7.71	3.86
Harvey, Matt	R-R	6-4	215	3-27-89	0	2	7.00	8	4	0	0	27	33	21	21	6	9	20	.303	.315	.291	6.67	3.00
2-team total (24 Cincinnati)					7	9	4.94	32	28	0	0	155	165	87	85	27	37	131	.271	.264	.279	7.61	2.15
Lugo, Seth	R-R	6-4	225	11-17-89	3	4	2.66	54	5	0	3	101	81	36	30	9	28	103	.217	.184	.245	9.15	2.49
Matz, Steven	R-L	6-2	200	5-29-91	5	11	3.97	30	30	0	0	154	134	77	68	25	58	152	.232	.236	.231	8.88	3.39
Oswalt, Corey	R-R	6-5	250	9-3-93	3	3	5.85	17	12	0	0	65	69	43	42	14	20	45	.269	.232	.295	6.26	2.78
Peterson, Tim	R-R	6-1	215	2-22-91	2	2	6.18	22	0	0	0	28	29	19	19	8	5	25	.261	.304	.231	8.13	1.63
Ramos, AJ	R-R	5-10	200	9-20-86	2	2	6.41	28	0	0	0	20	17	14	14	3	15	22	.236	.300	.191	10.07	6.86

Name	B-T	HT	WT	DOB	W	L	ERA	G	GS	CG	SV	IP	H	R	ER	HR	BB	SO	AVG	vLH	vRH	K/9	BB/9
Rhame, Jacob	R-R	6-1	215	3-16-93	1	2	5.85	30	0	0	1	32	38	21	21	8	8	28	.295	.316	.278	7.79	2.23
Robles, Hansel	R-R	5-11	185	8-13-90	2	2	5.03	16	0	0	0	20	21	11	11	7	10	23	.280	.323	.250	10.53	4.58
Sewald, Paul	R-R	6-3	207	5-26-90	0	7	6.07	46	0	0	2	56	62	39	38	8	23	58	.277	.271	.281	9.27	3.67
Smith, Drew	R-R	6-2	190	9-24-93	1	1	3.54	27	0	0	0	28	34	11	11	2	6	18	.309	.268	.333	5.79	1.93
Swarzak, Anthony	R-R	6-4	215	9-10-85	0	2	6.15	29	0	0	4	26	28	18	18	6	14	31	.280	.268	.288	10.59	4.78
Syndergaard, Noah	L-R	6-6	240	8-29-92	13	4	3.03	25	25	2	0	154	148	55	52	9	39	155	.250	.258	.241	9.04	2.27
Vargas, Jason	L-L	6-0	215	2-2-83	7	9	5.77	20	20	0	0	92	100	60	59	18	30	84	.276	.250	.284	8.22	2.93
Wahl, Bobby	R-R	6-2	210	3-21-92	0	1	10.13	7	0	0	0	5	9	6	6	2	4	7	.360	.500	.231	11.81	6.75
Wheeler, Zack	L-R	6-4	195	5-30-90	12	7	3.31	29	29	0	0	182	150	69	67	14	55	179	.225	.238	.213	8.84	2.71
Zamora, Daniel	L-L	6-3	195	4-15-93	1	0	3.00	16	0	0	0	9	6	3	3	1	3	16	.194	.222	.154	16.00	3.00

Fielding

Catcher	PCT	G	PO	A	E	DP	PB
d'Arnaud	.978	4	43	1	1	0	0
Lobaton	.993	18	133	8	1	0	0
Mesoraco	.998	57	484	22	1	6	8
Nido	.983	30	218	8	4	1	1
Plawecki	.994	71	597	31	4	1	0

First Base	PCT	G	PO	A	E	DP
Bautista	1.000	2	14	3	0	2
Bruce	.994	21	150	10	1	14
Evans	1.000	1	3	0	0	0
Flores	.995	83	576	32	3	49
Gonzalez	.997	48	333	34	1	31
Plawecki	1.000	3	12	0	0	0
Smith	.982	28	153	13	3	15

Second Base	PCT	G	PO	A	E	DP
Bautista	.000	1	0	0	0	0
Cabrera	.986	90	153	198	5	56

	PCT	G	PO	A	E	DP
Evans	1.000	2	2	0	0	0
Flores	1.000	13	11	18	0	3
Guillorme	1.000	8	5	14	0	0
Kelly	.000	2	0	0	0	0
McNeil	.991	54	96	123	2	29
Reinheimer	1.000	1	1	3	0	0
Reyes	.909	13	9	21	3	3

Third Base	PCT	G	PO	A	E	DP
Bautista	1.000	11	3	16	0	2
Evans	1.000	3	4	4	0	0
Flores	.864	10	6	13	3	2
Frazier	.959	109	80	203	12	28
Guillorme	.938	14	6	9	1	1
Kelly	1.000	1	1	0	0	1
McNeil	.875	4	2	5	1	2
Reinheimer	1.000	4	3	3	0	0
Reyes	.953	28	12	29	2	3
Wright	1.000	1	0	1	0	0

Shortstop	PCT	G	PO	A	E	DP
Reinheimer	1.000	3	1	6	0	1
Reyes	.955	25	15	48	3	6
Rosario	.969	146	160	332	16	58

Outfield	PCT	G	PO	A	E	DP
Bautista	.975	58	110	5	3	2
Bruce	.984	64	117	3	2	0
Cespedes	1.000	35	63	4	0	0
Conforto	.990	144	293	5	3	0
den Dekker	1.000	7	19	0	0	0
Evans	1.000	1	1	0	0	0
Jackson	.992	53	123	1	1	0
Kaczmarski	1.000	1	2	0	0	0
Kelly	1.000	1	1	0	0	0
Lagares	1.000	20	34	0	0	0
Nimmo	.996	126	249	4	1	2
Reinheimer	1.000	6	3	0	0	0
Smith	.929	13	13	0	1	0

LAS VEGAS 51S

PACIFIC COAST LEAGUE

TRIPLE-A

Batting	B-T	HT	WT	DOB	AVG	vLH	vRH	G	AB	R	H	2B	3B	HR	RBI	BB	HBP	SH	SF	SO	SB	CS	SLG	OBP
Alonso, Peter	R-R	6-3	245	12-7-94	.260	.261	.259	67	258	50	67	19	1	21	67	33	7	0	3	78	0	1	.585	.356
Asche, Cody	L-R	6-1	205	6-30-90	.231	.186	.246	89	269	46	62	17	4	10	38	31	2	0	0	71	0	4	.435	.315
Biondi, Patrick	L-R	5-8	171	1-9-91	.219	.241	.211	60	119	17	26	4	0	0	6	12	0	0	0	31	12	3	.252	.296
Borenstein, Zach	L-R	6-0	225	7-23-90	.248	.250	.247	133	484	92	120	32	2	25	90	81	3	0	4	182	3	4	.477	.357
Brentz, Bryce	R-R	6-0	215	12-30-88	.264	.333	.241	55	193	39	51	16	0	15	47	19	1	0	1	67	1	0	.580	.332
Burdick, Dale	R-R	6-0	175	10-12-95	.000	.000	.000	4	4	1	0	0	0	0	0	3	0	1	0	3	0	0	.000	.429
Carrera, Ezequiel	L-L	5-11	185	6-11-87	.254	.357	.225	17	63	8	16	4	0	0	4	1	0	1	0	10	4	1	.318	.266
Cecchini, Gavin	R-R	6-2	200	12-22-93	.294	.333	.279	30	109	14	32	11	1	2	9	7	1	2	0	15	1	1	.468	.342
Colon, Christian	R-R	5-10	185	5-14-89	.304	.309	.302	82	270	44	82	22	1	6	38	36	6	0	1	30	11	5	.459	.396
den Dekker, Matthew	L-L	6-2	210	8-10-87	.278	.227	.294	87	313	52	87	19	5	14	44	21	0	1	3	85	8	3	.505	.321
Evans, Phillip	R-R	5-10	223	9-10-92	.256	.362	.217	62	219	34	56	8	1	14	39	21	3	0	2	42	4	3	.493	.327
Frazier, Todd	R-R	6-3	220	2-12-86	.444	.500	.333	3	9	2	4	0	0	3	0	0	0	0	0	0	0	0	.444	.546
Glenn, Jeff	R-R	6-3	221	9-22-91	.000	.000	.000	6	6	0	0	0	0	0	0	0	1	0	0	2	0	0	.000	.143
Guillorme, Luis	L-R	5-10	195	9-27-94	.304	.316	.300	69	247	41	75	15	2	3	33	30	1	2	1	39	2	1	.417	.380
Kaczmarski, Kevin	L-R	6-0	192	12-31-91	.300	.310	.297	60	160	23	48	6	2	0	19	17	3	1	3	44	3	5	.375	.372
Kelly, Ty	R-R	6-0	180	7-20-88	.260	.194	.286	108	370	60	96	24	5	8	52	48	2	4	0	92	2	1	.416	.348
Kivlehan, Patrick	R-R	6-2	223	12-22-89	.314	.315	.313	98	354	59	111	29	4	20	67	30	4	0	2	84	4	3	.588	.372
Lobaton, Jose	B-R	6-1	205	3-21-85	.349	.241	.379	39	132	22	46	9	0	8	27	18	1	0	0	31	1	0	.599	.431
Mazzilli, L.J.	R-R	6-1	190	9-6-90	.333	1.000	.200	4	6	1	2	0	0	0	1	0	1	0	0	1	0	0	.500	.429
McNeil, Jeff	L-R	6-1	195	4-8-92	.368	.286	.392	31	125	23	46	10	2	5	28	14	1	0	3	19	3	0	.600	.427
Michael, Levi	R-R	5-10	180	2-9-91	.333	.333	.333	3	9	1	3	0	0	0	0	1	0	0	0	3	0	0	.333	.400
Monell, Johnny	R-R	6-1	210	3-27-86	.263	.170	.304	65	194	31	51	17	1	3	34	20	1	0	3	52	0	0	.407	.330
Nido, Tomas	R-R	6-0	210	4-12-94	.235	.333	.182	6	17	3	4	2	0	0	1	2	0	0	0	2	0	0	.353	.316
Nimmo, Brandon	L-R	6-3	207	3-27-93	.500	.000	1.000	1	4	2	2	0	0	0	1	1	0	0	0	0	0	0	.500	.600
Oberste, Matt	R-R	6-2	240	8-9-91	.000	—	.000	2	2	0	0	0	0	0	0	0	0	0	0	1	0	0	.000	.000
Plaia, Colton	R-R	6-2	219	9-25-90	.255	.234	.265	66	196	33	50	14	1	9	29	23	0	2	1	62	0	0	.475	.332
Plawecki, Kevin	R-R	6-2	210	2-26-91	.231	—	.231	4	13	2	3	0	0	1	3	0	0	0	0	5	0	0	.462	.333
Reinheimer, Jack	R-R	6-1	185	7-19-92	.327	.230	.333	16	55	13	18	3	0	2	5	4	1	0	0	10	7	0	.491	.383
2-team total (50 Reno)					.257	.230	.266	66	245	39	63	12	2	5	26	24	4	1	5	55	13	4	.384	.327
Rivera, T.J.	R-R	6-1	203	10-27-88	.000	—	.000	1	3	0	0	0	0	0	0	0	0	0	0	1	0	0	.000	.000
Sergakis, Nick	R-R	5-8	178	4-6-93	.000	—	.000	2	2	0	0	0	0	0	0	0	0	0	0	0	0	0	.000	.000
Smith, Dominic	L-L	6-0	239	6-15-95	.258	.264	.256	84	337	52	87	21	1	6	41	34	2	0	2	76	3	0	.380	.328
Thompson, David	R-R	6-2	210	8-28-93	.258	.177	.286	22	66	10	17	5	0	1	5	4	3	0	0	20	2	2	.379	.329
Wong, Joey	L-R	5-10	180	4-12-88	.000	.000	.000	6	8	1	0	0	0	0	0	1	0	0	0	3	0	1	.000	.273
Wright, David	R-R	6-0	205	12-20-82	.111	.333	.000	2	9	1	1	0	0	0	0	1	0	0	0	3	0	0	.111	.111

Pitching	B-T	HT	WT	DOB	W	L	ERA	G	GS	CG	SV	IP	H	R	ER	HR	BB	SO	AVG	vLH	vRH	K/9	BB/9
Baumann, Buddy	L-L	5-11	198	12-9-87	1	0	6.04	26	0	0	0	25	27	20	17	5	12	26	.262	.269	.260	9.24	4.26
2-team total (8 El Paso)					1	0	4.78	34	0	0	1	32	29	20	17	5	17	35	.234	.211	.244	9.84	4.78
Bautista, Gerson	R-R	6-3	195	5-31-95	3	1	5.22	31	0	0	3	40	54	30	23	3	18	54	.314	.333	.298	12.25	4.08

Name	B-T	HT	WT	DOB	W	L	ERA	G	GS	CG	SV	IP	H	R	ER	HR	BB	SO	AVG	vLH	vRH	K/9	BB/9
Beck, Chris	R-R	6-3	225	9-4-90	1	1	8.15	17	0	0	3	18	24	16	16	0	11	16	.338	.273	.395	8.15	5.60
Callahan, Jamie	R-R	6-2	230	8-24-94	0	1	9.72	7	0	0	1	8	14	10	9	0	4	9	.378	.412	.350	9.72	4.32
Church, Andrew	R-R	6-2	200	10-7-94	1	1	6.00	2	1	0	0	9	12	6	6	1	3	7	.316	.200	.444	7.00	3.00
Conlon, P.J.	L-L	5-11	192	11-11-93	4	9	6.55	23	21	0	0	114	147	88	83	20	39	82	.311	.244	.334	6.47	3.08
Copeland, Scott	R-R	6-3	220	12-15-87	3	3	3.09	8	8	0	0	47	48	22	16	1	15	33	.261	.303	.212	6.36	2.89
Crismatt, Nabil	R-R	6-1	215	12-25-94	3	4	8.84	9	9	0	0	39	61	40	38	8	19	35	.365	.395	.341	8.15	4.42
Flexen, Chris	R-R	6-3	250	7-1-94	6	7	4.40	18	17	1	0	92	109	53	45	11	31	78	.300	.258	.333	7.63	3.03
Gage, Matt	R-L	6-4	240	2-11-93	1	1	6.30	2	2	0	0	10	13	7	7	0	4	16	.317	.250	.345	14.40	3.60
2-team total (11 Sacramento)					5	8	6.43	13	12	0	0	63	96	52	45	4	19	48	.350	.393	.330	6.86	2.71
Gagnon, Drew	R-R	6-4	215	6-26-90	6	6	4.57	27	27	2	0	158	151	82	80	23	43	167	.257	.283	.236	9.53	2.45
Gonzalez, Harol	R-R	6-0	160	3-2-95	0	1	3.00	1	1	1	0	6	4	2	2	0	2	1	.182	.125	.214	1.50	3.00
Griffin, A.J.	R-R	6-5	230	1-28-88	0	2	48.00	2	2	0	0	3	13	16	16	3	6	1	.619	.600	.625	3.00	18.00
Hanhold, Eric	R-R	6-5	220	11-1-93	2	2	7.11	14	0	0	0	19	25	15	15	1	7	20	.333	.346	.327	9.47	3.32
Jannis, Mickey	R-R	5-9	195	12-16-87	0	2	14.63	2	2	0	0	8	17	13	13	1	4	4	.415	.522	.278	4.50	4.50
Krol, Ian	L-L	6-1	210	5-9-91	2	0	3.31	25	0	0	0	35	47	15	13	4	17	39	.318	.355	.291	9.93	4.33
2-team total (18 Salt Lake)					3	0	2.72	43	0	0	4	56	63	21	17	4	26	59	.280	.296	.268	9.43	4.15
Laffey, Aaron	L-L	5-11	190	4-15-85	0	3	18.00	3	3	0	0	13	28	29	26	9	4	8	.424	.263	.489	5.54	2.77
Martin, Cody	R-R	6-3	230	9-4-89	3	4	7.03	17	17	0	0	81	97	69	63	18	39	70	.297	.299	.294	7.81	4.35
McGowan, Kevin	R-R	6-5	233	10-18-91	6	2	4.07	28	3	0	0	60	65	29	27	6	26	52	.278	.250	.302	7.84	3.92
Molina, Marcos	R-R	6-3	225	3-8-95	0	1	9.35	2	2	0	0	9	11	9	9	1	5	7	.324	.313	.333	7.27	5.19
Oswalt, Corey	R-R	6-5	250	9-3-93	4	4	6.02	11	11	0	0	52	58	37	35	9	20	52	.280	.271	.287	8.94	3.44
Peterson, Tim	R-R	6-1	215	2-22-91	0	1	3.49	32	0	0	8	39	29	15	15	4	10	55	.199	.180	.212	12.80	2.33
Pobereyko, Matt	R-R	6-3	220	12-24-91	0	0	12.00	1	0	0	0	3	6	6	6	0	2	0	.375	.500	.333	0.00	6.00
Prevost, Josh	R-R	6-7	223	1-15-92	1	1	4.91	2	2	0	0	11	12	7	6	2	4	4	.267	.375	.143	3.27	3.27
Purke, Matt	L-L	6-4	215	7-17-90	2	2	7.14	38	0	0	1	47	54	38	37	2	37	42	.290	.228	.336	8.10	7.14
Regnault, Kyle	L-L	6-2	228	12-13-88	4	1	4.77	48	0	0	3	60	62	38	32	8	25	82	.267	.271	.265	12.23	3.73
Rhame, Jacob	R-R	6-1	215	3-16-93	1	2	3.06	25	0	0	11	32	22	14	11	4	8	41	.190	.200	.180	11.41	2.23
Robles, Hansel	R-R	5-11	185	8-13-90	0	3	3.52	6	0	0	2	8	7	3	3	1	5	2	.241	.429	.182	8.22	5.87
Roseboom, David	R-R	6-3	215	5-17-92	0	0	17.18	3	0	0	0	4	6	7	7	4	5	5	.400	.571	.250	12.27	12.27
Secrest, Kelly	L-L	6-0	225	9-13-91	0	0	11.12	4	0	0	0	6	8	10	7	3	5	5	.308	.091	.467	7.94	7.94
Sewald, Paul	R-R	6-3	207	5-26-90	3	0	1.13	7	0	0	1	8	7	1	1	0	1	7	.241	.211	.300	7.88	1.13
Smith, Drew	R-R	6-2	190	9-24-93	5	1	2.76	23	1	0	2	33	26	12	10	3	12	30	.260	.260	.200	8.27	3.31
Swarzak, Anthony	R-R	6-4	215	9-10-85	2	0	10.13	3	0	0	0	3	4	3	3	0	2	3	.333	.286	.400	10.13	6.75
Taylor, Blake	L-L	6-2	220	8-17-95	2	0	4.09	2	2	0	0	11	11	7	5	0	9	11	.282	.200	.310	9.00	7.36
Taylor, Corey	R-R	6-2	240	1-8-93	2	1	4.26	16	0	0	0	25	28	12	12	1	8	22	.289	.333	.259	7.82	2.84
Taylor, Logan	R-R	6-5	248	12-13-91	1	1	6.47	19	3	0	0	32	35	23	23	4	19	29	.280	.315	.254	8.16	5.34
Torres, Joshua	R-R	6-0	170	4-26-94	0	0	12.96	5	0	0	0	8	17	13	12	4	7	10	.415	.462	.393	10.80	7.56
Vargas, Jason	L-L	6-0	215	2-2-83	0	1	6.75	1	1	0	0	4	3	3	3	0	2	4	.231	.400	.125	9.00	4.50
Wahl, Bobby	R-R	6-2	210	3-21-92	1	0	1.69	4	0	0	1	5	3	1	1	0	2	8	.188	.250	.167	13.50	3.38
2-team total (34 Nashville)					4	2	2.20	38	1	0	12	45	20	17	11	2	19	73	.136	.184	.112	14.60	3.80
Wheeler, Zack	L-R	6-4	195	5-30-90	1	0	1.80	1	1	0	0	5	3	1	1	1	1	6	.177	.222	.125	10.80	1.80
Worley, Vance	R-R	6-2	240	9-25-87	0	3	13.50	4	4	0	0	17	29	27	25	6	12	5	.382	.425	.333	2.70	6.48
Zanghi, Joe	R-R	6-3	240	12-1-94	0	0	9.00	2	0	0	1	5	6	5	5	1	3	4	.300	.333	.273	7.20	5.40

Fielding

Catcher	PCT	G	PO	A	E	DP	PB
Evans	.000	1	0	0	0	0	0
Lobaton	.994	37	305	15	2	0	1
Monell	.985	44	311	27	5	1	10
Nido	.979	6	44	3	1	0	0
Plaia	.992	60	490	35	4	8	9
Plawecki	.941	3	15	1	1	0	1

First Base	PCT	G	PO	A	E	DP
Alonso	.994	59	454	48	3	50
Asche	1.000	2	15	1	0	1
Evans	1.000	7	35	5	0	7
Kivlehan	.988	21	156	10	2	22
Monell	1.000	3	19	1	0	2
Smith	.995	53	398	44	2	34

Second Base	PCT	G	PO	A	E	DP
Biondi	1.000	2	1	2	0	0
Burdick	1.000	2	3	3	0	2
Cecchini	.954	18	25	37	3	6
Colon	.973	43	79	103	5	31
Evans	.946	18	26	27	3	12
Guillorme	1.000	9	15	15	0	6
Kelly	.968	45	59	93	5	19
McNeil	.970	24	47	49	3	14
Reinheimer	1.000	1	1	5	0	0
Wong	.875	2	3	4	1	2

Third Base	PCT	G	PO	A	E	DP
Asche	.959	66	48	92	6	9
Cecchini	.000	1	0	0	0	0
Colon	.947	25	11	43	3	3
Evans	.956	22	16	27	2	0
Frazier	.800	3	3	1	1	1
Guillorme	1.000	5	2	10	0	0
Kelly	1.000	1	0	2	0	0
Kivlehan	.941	19	6	26	2	3
McNeil	1.000	3	4	5	0	1
Rivera	1.000	1	0	2	0	0
Thompson	.930	21	10	30	3	3
Wright	1.000	2	0	4	0	0

Shortstop	PCT	G	PO	A	E	DP
Asche	.000	2	0	0	0	0
Cecchini	1.000	11	9	29	0	5
Colon	.920	7	12	11	2	3
Evans	.987	19	29	45	1	13
Guillorme	.958	54	62	145	9	38
Kelly	.987	42	57	97	2	23
Michael	1.000	2	1	8	0	1
Reinheimer	.980	15	14	36	1	7
Wong	1.000	1	1	2	0	0

Outfield	PCT	G	PO	A	E	DP
Asche	1.000	6	8	0	0	0
Biondi	.988	40	77	2	1	0
Borenstein	.995	126	186	9	1	0
Brentz	.984	43	60	1	1	0
Carrera	.949	16	36	1	2	0
Colon	1.000	10	22	0	0	0
den Dekker	.993	72	142	5	1	1
Evans	.500	2	1	1	2	1
Kaczmarski	.962	46	75	0	3	0
Kelly	1.000	23	34	3	0	1
Kivlehan	.990	53	97	7	1	1
Mazzilli	1.000	1	2	0	0	0
McGowan	.000	1	0	0	0	0
McNeil	1.000	1	5	0	0	0
Nimmo	1.000	1	2	0	0	0
Smith	.940	26	46	1	3	0

BINGHAMTON RUMBLE PONIES   DOUBLE-A
EASTERN LEAGUE

Batting	B-T	HT	WT	DOB	AVG	vLH	vRH	G	AB	R	H	2B	3B	HR	RBI	BB	HBP	SH	SF	SO	SB	CS	SLG	OBP
Allen, Josh	R-R	5-10	185	3-26-91	.248	.250	.247	42	153	15	38	12	0	2	20	18	1	0	6	47	5	2	.366	.320
Alonso, Peter	R-R	6-3	245	12-7-94	.314	.310	.315	65	220	42	69	12	0	15	52	43	8	0	2	50	0	2	.573	.440

Name	B-T	HT	WT	DOB	AVG	vLH	vRH	G	AB	R	H	2B	3B	HR	RBI	BB	HBP	SH	SF	SO	SB	CS	SLG	OBP
Biondi, Patrick	L-R	5-8	171	1-9-91	.225	.280	.206	32	98	13	22	2	0	0	7	21	1	0	0	26	7	5	.245	.367
Carpio, Luis	R-R	5-11	190	7-11-97	.250	.250	—	1	4	1	1	0	0	0	0	1	0	0	0	1	1	0	.250	.400
Cespedes, Yoenis	R-R	5-10	220	10-18-85	.500	—	.500	2	4	0	2	2	0	0	0	0	0	0	0	0	0	0	1.000	.500
Cone, Gene	L-L	6-0	175	9-21-94	.125	.250	.063	7	24	1	3	0	0	0	2	1	0	0	0	6	1	0	.125	.160
Ely, Andrew	L-R	5-11	180	1-23-93	.162	.167	.160	60	179	24	29	5	2	1	13	34	5	2	2	49	0	1	.229	.309
Franco, J.J.	R-R	5-9	180	2-2-92	.120	.059	.152	22	50	5	6	2	0	0	2	11	0	1	0	17	0	1	.160	.279
Garcia, Jose	L-R	6-0	228	11-3-94	.333	.600	.231	8	18	0	6	0	0	0	0	3	0	0	5	0	0	.333	.429
Gimenez, Andres	L-R	5-11	161	9-4-98	.277	.194	.307	37	137	19	38	9	1	0	16	9	5	2	0	22	10	3	.358	.344
Mazeika, Patrick	L-R	6-3	208	10-14-93	.231	.203	.240	87	295	32	68	12	0	9	39	39	5	0	2	35	0	0	.363	.328
McNeil, Jeff	L-R	6-1	195	4-8-92	.327	.214	.367	57	214	49	70	16	3	14	43	22	5	0	0	23	3	0	.626	.403
Michael, Levi	R-R	5-10	180	2-9-91	.305	.315	.300	103	387	72	118	30	2	10	36	35	20	4	1	93	13	6	.470	.391
Moore, Tyler	L-R	6-0	209	8-8-93	.118	.000	.162	16	51	7	6	2	0	0	5	4	0	0	0	20	0	0	.157	.182
Mora, John	L-L	5-11	195	5-31-93	.234	.188	.248	105	351	44	82	16	7	5	30	37	4	1	3	88	4	8	.362	.311
Nido, Tomas	R-R	6-0	210	4-12-94	.274	.364	.225	58	215	23	59	18	1	5	30	7	2	0	4	36	0	0	.437	.298
Oberste, Matt	R-R	6-2	240	8-9-91	.185	.159	.197	61	216	24	40	3	1	6	20	12	3	0	2	53	0	1	.292	.236
Pascual, Oliver	R-R	5-9	178	11-16-96	.280	.167	.385	7	25	1	7	1	0	0	3	0	0	1	0	9	0	0	.320	.280
Sergakis, Nick	R-R	5-8	178	4-6-93	.170	.091	.216	23	59	5	10	3	0	2	10	3	1	0	1	18	0	0	.322	.219
Strom, Ian	R-L	6-2	205	12-12-94	.083	.182	.000	7	24	3	2	0	0	0	1	4	1	0	0	7	0	1	.083	.241
Stuart, Champ	R-R	6-0	181	10-11-92	.136	.133	.139	55	110	19	15	2	0	4	7	22	0	2	0	47	11	2	.264	.280
Taylor, Kevin	L-R	6-0	197	7-13-91	.263	.301	.244	126	437	46	115	18	2	3	42	31	3	0	5	55	3	1	.332	.313
Tebow, Tim	L-L	6-3	245	8-14-87	.273	.281	.269	84	271	32	74	14	1	6	36	22	4	0	1	103	1	0	.399	.336
Terdoslavich, Joey	B-R	6-2	200	9-9-88	.308	.296	.314	74	286	36	88	9	1	12	41	28	1	0	3	42	0	0	.472	.368
Toffey, Will	L-R	6-2	205	12-21-94	.254	.238	.261	41	134	23	34	10	2	1	19	30	1	0	0	36	2	0	.433	.394
Urena, Jhoan	B-R	6-1	225	9-1-94	.261	.266	.259	123	421	47	110	20	2	14	63	39	2	0	4	112	2	4	.418	.324
Wong, Joey	L-R	5-10	185	4-12-88	.213	.150	.230	36	94	12	20	5	0	3	9	16	2	1	0	26	0	0	.362	.339

Pitching

Name	B-T	HT	WT	DOB	W	L	ERA	G	GS	CG	SV	IP	H	R	ER	HR	BB	SO	AVG	vLH	vRH	K/9	BB/9
Atkins, Adam	R-R	6-3	210	9-8-93	0	0	4.15	2	0	0	0	4	6	3	2	0	2	4	.316	.286	.333	8.31	4.15
Bashlor, Tyler	R-R	6-0	195	4-16-93	0	3	2.63	20	0	0	7	24	14	8	7	2	12	30	.177	.139	.209	11.25	4.50
Bautista, Gerson	R-R	6-3	195	5-31-95	1	0	4.82	6	0	0	0	9	12	5	5	0	0	15	.316	.250	.429	14.46	0.00
Blackham, Matt	R-R	5-10	150	1-7-93	1	2	3.42	22	0	0	0	26	18	12	10	2	17	36	.190	.087	.286	12.30	5.81
Cavallaro, Joe	R-R	6-4	190	7-19-95	0	0	9.00	1	1	0	0	5	9	5	5	2	1	5	.375	.389	.333	9.00	1.80
Church, Andrew	R-R	6-2	200	10-7-94	1	5	6.44	7	7	0	0	36	49	30	26	5	7	31	.329	.318	.344	7.68	1.73
Copeland, Scott	R-R	6-3	220	12-15-87	6	4	3.63	14	14	0	0	79	83	34	32	5	29	67	.273	.312	.239	7.63	3.29
Crismatt, Nabil	R-R	6-1	215	12-25-94	8	8	3.59	18	18	1	0	105	99	51	42	8	37	105	.243	.216	.269	8.97	3.16
Dunn, Justin	R-R	6-2	185	9-22-95	6	5	4.22	15	15	0	0	90	85	49	42	7	37	105	.258	.290	.234	10.54	3.71
Gage, Matt	R-L	6-4	240	2-11-93	2	1	3.12	3	3	0	0	17	24	7	6	0	4	17	.338	.167	.354	8.83	2.08
2-team total (4 Richmond)					2	3	3.15	7	7	0	0	40	48	19	14	3	7	32	.300	.222	.316	7.20	1.58
Gagnon, Drew	R-R	6-4	215	6-26-90	1	0	0.00	1	1	0	0	6	2	0	0	0	1	5	.095	.071	.143	7.50	1.50
Gibbons, Michael	R-R	6-4	205	4-24-93	1	1	0.00	2	0	0	0	8	10	2	0	0	2	7	.294	.417	.000	7.56	2.16
Gonzalez, Harol	R-R	6-0	160	3-2-95	9	9	7.79	9	9	0	0	52	79	48	45	10	17	30	.359	.357	.361	5.19	2.94
Hanhold, Eric	R-R	6-5	220	11-1-93	3	1	2.84	17	0	0	8	25	21	8	8	1	9	32	.223	.227	.220	11.37	3.20
James, Christian	R-R	6-3	210	5-24-98	0	1	2.25	1	1	0	0	4	3	1	1	0	1	4	.200	.375	.000	9.00	2.25
Jannis, Mickey	R-R	5-9	195	12-16-87	10	6	3.60	24	23	1	0	142	157	65	57	12	36	114	.280	.288	.272	7.21	2.28
Kilome, Franklyn	R-R	6-6	175	6-25-95	0	3	4.03	7	7	0	0	38	31	19	17	3	16	42	.223	.293	.173	9.95	2.37
2-team total (19 Reading)					4	9	4.18	26	26	0	0	140	127	80	65	10	61	125	.248	.275	.223	8.04	3.92
Knapp, Ricky	R-R	6-0	217	5-20-92	0	1	5.40	3	3	0	0	10	14	8	6	0	4	2	.350	.414	.182	1.80	3.60
Magliozzi, Johnny	R-R	5-10	193	7-21-91	0	1	10.29	5	1	0	0	7	16	10	8	0	8	6	.471	.462	.476	7.71	10.29
McGeorge, Austin	R-R	6-2	215	11-27-94	1	1	7.96	22	0	0	0	26	44	25	23	5	8	27	.386	.326	.427	9.35	2.77
McGowan, Kevin	R-R	6-5	233	10-18-91	0	3	6.26	5	4	0	0	23	24	17	16	6	8	25	.267	.263	.269	9.78	3.13
Molina, Marcos	R-R	6-3	225	3-8-95	7	9	6.66	14	14	0	0	73	102	59	54	14	29	57	.329	.288	.363	7.03	3.58
Nogosek, Stephen	R-R	6-2	205	1-11-95	0	0	8.10	16	0	0	0	20	16	20	18	3	21	21	.211	.263	.158	9.45	9.45
Pobereyko, Matt	R-R	6-3	220	12-24-91	1	0	0.00	5	0	0	0	6	2	0	0	1	6	.111	.200	.077	9.53	1.59
Prevost, Josh	R-R	6-7	223	1-15-92	0	0	7.94	1	1	0	0	9	5	5	0	3	4	.375	.167	.444	6.35	4.76
Roseboom, David	L-L	6-3	215	5-17-92	3	3	2.72	40	0	0	1	50	40	20	15	3	19	61	.213	.225	.204	11.05	3.44
Ryan, Ryder	R-R	6-2	205	5-11-95	3	3	4.13	26	0	0	3	33	27	17	15	5	10	36	.223	.259	.191	9.92	2.76
Shaw, Joseph	R-R	6-5	225	12-20-93	1	4	6.47	12	12	0	0	65	77	50	47	9	29	49	.298	.297	.300	6.75	3.99
Smith, Drew	R-R	6-2	190	9-24-93	0	0	2.08	2	0	0	1	4	1	1	1	0	1	6	.143	.222	.000	12.46	2.08
Taylor, Corey	R-R	6-1	240	1-8-93	2	1	2.41	29	3	0	6	41	50	12	11	1	9	34	.313	.343	.287	7.46	1.98
Torres, Joshua	R-R	6-0	170	4-26-94	9	0	1.19	35	0	0	6	45	36	8	6	1	14	58	.220	.136	.267	11.51	2.78
Uceta, Adonis	R-R	6-1	225	5-10-94	0	1	4.26	16	0	0	1	25	27	13	12	2	12	28	.258	.222	.302	9.95	4.26
Villines, Stephen	R-R	6-2	175	7-15-95	1	3	3.18	7	0	0	0	11	6	4	4	1	2	17	.154	.188	.130	13.50	1.59
Zamora, Daniel	L-L	6-3	195	4-15-93	1	1	3.48	40	1	0	2	52	37	20	20	3	16	69	.197	.244	.157	12.02	2.79
Zanghi, Joe	R-R	6-3	240	12-1-94	1	1	5.11	17	0	0	0	25	25	16	14	1	8	22	.258	.255	.261	8.03	2.92

Fielding

Catcher	PCT	G	PO	A	E	DP	PB
Garcia	.982	8	53	3	1	0	0
Mazeika	.994	75	616	45	4	6	10
Moore	.991	14	103	7	1	1	1
Nido	.993	48	414	35	3	4	6

	PCT	G	PO	A	E	DP
Oberste	.973	12	67	4	2	9
Taylor	.982	16	105	7	2	9
Terdoslavich	.985	65	502	25	8	47

	PCT	G	PO	A	E	DP
McNeil	.966	47	68	128	7	25
Michael	1.000	19	35	52	0	13
Moore	.000	1	0	0	0	0
Pascual	.966	5	12	16	1	3
Sergakis	1.000	8	9	19	0	5

First Base	PCT	G	PO	A	E	DP
Alonso	.986	51	396	33	6	35
Mazeika	1.000	2	9	0	0	3

Second Base	PCT	G	PO	A	E	DP
Allen	.980	38	71	123	4	27
Ely	.981	15	23	29	1	9
Franco	.976	14	10	30	1	2
Gimenez	.875	1	3	4	1	1

Third Base	PCT	G	PO	A	E	DP
Ely	.923	8	2	10	1	2
Franco	1.000	2	1	5	0	0

McNeil	.842	9	3	13	3	2
Michael	.903	34	18	38	6	2
Oberste	.920	41	20	60	7	8
Sergakis	.800	7	4	8	3	0
Toffey	.964	37	26	55	3	3
Urena	.846	6	2	9	2	0
Wong	.900	4	2	7	1	1

Shortstop	PCT	G	PO	A	E	DP
Carpio	1.000	1	1	2	0	0
Ely	.964	38	60	101	6	29

Gimenez	.974	36	38	74	3	14
McNeil	1.000	3	4	3	0	0
Michael	.986	44	58	88	2	29
Pascual	1.000	1	2	2	0	1
Wong	.975	29	39	76	3	18

Outfield	PCT	G	PO	A	E	DP
Allen	1.000	2	5	0	0	0
Biondi	1.000	32	68	2	0	0
Cespedes	.000	1	0	0	0	0
Cone	1.000	6	17	0	0	0

Franco	.000	1	0	0	0	0
Michael	1.000	12	17	0	0	0
Mora	.983	97	176	2	3	0
Strom	.929	7	12	1	1	0
Stuart	.990	44	94	5	1	4
Taylor	.977	87	123	7	3	1
Tebow	.988	59	79	3	1	0
Terdoslavich	1.000	2	6	1	0	0
Urena	.967	101	164	12	6	3

ST. LUCIE METS — HIGH CLASS A
FLORIDA STATE LEAGUE

Batting	B-T	HT	WT	DOB	AVG	vLH	vRH	G	AB	R	H	2B	3B	HR	RBI	BB	HBP	SH	SF	SO	SB	CS	SLG	OBP
Becerra, Wuilmer	R-R	6-3	243	10-1-94	.256	.205	.278	40	129	9	33	6	1	0	11	11	3	2	3	27	5	0	.318	.322
Brodey, Quinn	L-L	6-1	200	12-1-95	.245	.250	.244	31	102	11	25	3	1	3	17	10	0	0	0	31	4	0	.382	.313
Brosher, Brandon	R-R	6-3	225	2-17-95	.124	.129	.121	28	89	4	11	1	0	2	8	4	2	0	1	42	3	0	.202	.177
Bruce, Jay	L-L	6-3	225	4-3-87	.360	.300	.400	7	25	3	9	1	0	1	2	0	0	0	0	6	0	0	.520	.407
Burdick, Dale	R-R	6-0	175	10-12-95	.171	.125	.192	60	176	16	30	7	5	1	10	27	1	1	0	63	7	1	.284	.284
Carpio, Luis	R-R	5-11	190	7-11-97	.219	.272	.190	112	389	38	85	21	0	12	40	40	1	0	6	80	8	9	.365	.289
Cecchini, Gavin	R-R	6-2	200	12-22-93	.500	—	.500	1	4	1	2	0	0	0	0	0	0	0	0	0	0	0	.500	.500
Cone, Gene	L-L	6-0	175	9-21-94	.234	.235	.234	110	380	34	89	15	0	0	31	30	3	2	4	80	11	2	.274	.293
Dimino, Anthony	L-R	5-11	180	8-5-93	.265	.318	.247	75	253	29	67	13	1	3	23	21	1	1	1	38	12	2	.360	.323
Flores, Wilmer	R-R	6-3	205	8-6-91	.546	.500	.571	3	11	1	6	2	0	1	4	0	0	0	0	0	0	0	1.000	.546
Franco, J.J.	R-R	5-9	180	2-2-92	.296	.361	.244	33	81	9	24	3	0	0	5	10	1	1	2	17	1	2	.333	.372
Frazier, Todd	R-R	6-3	220	2-12-86	.250	1.000	.000	2	4	0	1	1	0	0	2	1	0	0	0	0	0	0	.500	.400
Garcia, Jose	L-R	6-0	228	11-3-94	.071	.000	.083	4	14	1	0	0	0	0	1	1	0	0	0	7	1	0	.071	.133
Gimenez, Andres	L-R	5-11	161	9-4-98	.283	.298	.275	85	308	43	87	20	4	6	30	22	11	6	4	70	28	11	.432	.348
Gladu, Raphael	L-R	6-2	195	6-23-95	.206	.200	.208	18	68	6	14	4	0	2	12	4	0	0	1	10	2	1	.353	.247
Kaczmarski, Kevin	L-R	6-0	192	12-31-91	.296	.273	.313	9	27	3	8	0	0	0	3	6	0	0	0	3	1	1	.296	.424
Lindsay, Desmond	R-R	6-0	200	1-15-97	.218	.273	.190	84	294	27	64	11	5	3	30	37	3	0	1	89	7	3	.320	.310
Nimmo, Brandon	L-R	6-3	205	3-27-93	.333	.000	.500	2	6	1	2	0	0	0	2	0	0	0	0	1	0	0	.333	.500
Paez, Michael	R-R	5-8	175	12-8-94	.270	.297	.256	121	408	54	110	20	1	11	48	41	7	3	9	79	4	8	.404	.340
Reyes, Wilmer	R-R	6-0	161	12-22-97	.231	.000	.333	5	13	2	3	0	0	1	1	0	0	0	0	4	0	0	.462	.231
Rivera, T.J.	R-R	6-1	203	10-27-88	.211	.250	.143	5	19	1	4	1	0	0	1	0	0	0	0	3	0	0	.263	.211
Rizzie, Dan	R-R	6-2	200	11-26-93	.248	.266	.237	67	214	20	53	9	0	2	20	20	0	0	6	33	0	2	.318	.304
Sanchez, Ali	R-R	6-1	196	1-20-97	.274	.283	.270	38	135	11	37	9	0	2	16	5	0	0	2	15	1	1	.385	.296
Strom, Ian	R-L	6-2	175	12-12-94	.224	.233	.218	67	210	30	47	7	1	2	11	18	4	3	2	44	12	5	.295	.295
Tiberi, Blake	L-R	6-0	205	2-16-95	.168	.125	.183	31	95	12	16	5	1	1	5	5	0	0	2	23	1	0	.274	.210
Vasquez, Jeremy	L-L	6-1	205	7-17-96	.264	.256	.267	45	163	25	43	7	1	4	14	19	1	0	1	26	0	1	.393	.342
Winningham, Dash	L-L	6-2	225	10-11-95	.236	.273	.217	66	220	18	52	11	0	3	24	21	4	0	2	53	2	2	.327	.312
Wright, David	R-R	6-0	205	12-20-82	.188	.000	.273	10	32	3	6	1	0	0	2	2	0	0	0	6	0	0	.219	.235
Zanon, Jacob	R-R	6-1	180	6-25-95	.206	.220	.199	63	233	22	48	11	1	0	11	20	1	1	2	49	14	7	.262	.270

Pitching	B-T	HT	WT	DOB	W	L	ERA	G	GS	CG	SV	IP	H	R	ER	HR	BB	SO	AVG	vLH	vRH	K/9	BB/9
Atkins, Adam	R-R	6-2	210	9-8-93	3	3	2.17	36	0	0	5	58	41	20	14	2	18	64	.196	.216	.218	9.93	2.79
Blackham, Matt	R-R	5-10	150	1-7-93	4	1	1.90	17	0	0	2	24	11	5	5	1	13	29	.145	.129	.156	11.03	4.94
Campusano, Brian	R-R	6-2	174	3-26-96	0	1	2.25	1	1	0	0	4	2	1	1	0	3	4	.167	.111	.333	9.00	6.75
Cavallaro, Joe	R-R	6-4	190	7-19-95	2	4	4.84	9	8	0	0	45	48	25	24	1	18	41	.271	.304	.227	8.26	3.63
Cobb, Trey	R-R	6-2	190	6-24-94	0	1	4.50	15	0	0	2	22	19	11	11	3	6	19	.229	.300	.121	7.77	2.45
Cornish, Gary	R-R	6-3	225	1-21-94	2	8	6.63	12	10	0	0	58	70	47	43	7	32	41	.306	.299	.312	6.33	4.94
Davis, Seth	L-L	5-9	189	5-01-94	1	0	3.51	17	0	0	2	26	18	13	10	3	15	29	.194	.220	.173	10.17	5.26
Debora, Nicolas	R-R	6-4	189	12-6-93	1	0	2.70	1	0	0	0	3	3	1	1	0	0	2	.231	.200	.250	5.40	0.00
Dunn, Justin	R-R	6-2	185	9-22-95	2	3	2.36	9	9	0	0	46	43	17	12	2	15	51	.243	.222	.264	10.05	2.96
Gibbons, Michael	R-R	6-4	205	4-24-93	5	7	3.51	18	17	0	0	90	83	40	35	6	35	69	.249	.285	.189	6.93	3.51
Gonzalez, Harol	R-R	6-0	160	3-2-95	1	6	2.82	13	12	2	0	73	62	27	23	6	19	59	.223	.250	.199	7.24	2.33
Hernandez, Carlos	R-R	5-11	172	11-3-94	0	0	1.59	3	0	0	0	6	3	1	1	0	3	4	.150	.154	.143	6.35	4.76
James, Christian	R-R	6-3	210	5-24-98	0	0	0.00	1	0	0	0	5	1	0	0	0	1	5	.056	.125	.000	9.00	0.00
Kay, Anthony	L-L	6-0	218	3-21-95	3	7	3.88	10	10	0	0	53	51	28	23	1	27	45	.262	.299	.242	7.59	4.56
Llanes, Gabriel	R-R	6-3	190	1-15-96	7	9	4.27	23	22	1	0	124	150	66	59	8	34	66	.305	.327	.278	4.78	2.46
Magliozzi, Johnny	R-R	5-10	193	7-21-91	0	0	4.50	1	0	0	0	2	2	1	1	0	1	3	.250	.400	.000	13.50	4.50
McGeorge, Austin	R-R	6-2	215	11-27-94	1	1	2.73	21	0	0	1	30	24	10	9	4	9	29	.220	.278	.164	8.80	2.73
McIlraith, Thomas	R-R	6-4	200	2-17-94	1	3	4.38	28	0	0	0	51	65	30	25	6	21	43	.311	.354	.260	7.54	3.68
Mena, Malky	R-R	6-0	164	10-3-96	0	0	0.00	1	0	0	0	2	2	1	0	0	2	2	.222	.400	.000	0.00	0.00
Nogosek, Stephen	R-R	6-2	205	1-11-95	1	3	3.06	23	0	0	1	32	22	12	11	4	18	37	.190	.179	.200	10.30	5.01
Oxford, Billy	R-R	6-1	215	10-22-95	0	0	0.00	2	0	0	0	3	4	4	0	1	0	1	.267	.125	.429	2.70	2.70
Palsha, Alex	R-R	6-1	190	5-10-92	0	1	5.19	11	0	0	2	17	21	10	10	0	8	14	.300	.313	.290	7.27	4.15
Peterson, David	L-L	6-6	240	9-3-95	6	6	4.33	13	13	0	0	69	74	39	33	1	19	58	.273	.250	.288	7.60	2.49
Pobereyko, Matt	R-R	6-3	220	12-24-91	2	3	3.19	36	0	0	10	48	30	20	17	3	24	55	.175	.177	.174	10.31	4.50
Prevost, Josh	R-R	6-7	223	1-15-92	5	2	3.77	11	11	1	0	60	66	32	25	2	13	50	.276	.314	.237	7.54	1.96
Ryan, Ryder	R-R	6-2	205	5-11-95	0	1	1.77	16	0	0	2	20	14	4	4	0	5	23	.200	.207	.195	10.18	2.21
Selmer, Ryan	R-R	6-8	220	5-20-94	0	1	13.50	2	0	0	0	2	4	5	3	1	4	3	.400	.800	.000	4.50	4.50
Taylor, Blake	L-L	6-2	220	8-17-95	1	8	5.59	17	16	0	0	76	72	49	47	4	45	72	.250	.244	.253	8.56	5.35
Villines, Stephen	R-R	6-2	175	7-15-95	2	0	0.41	16	0	0	4	22	7	1	1	0	6	25	.100	.071	.119	10.23	2.45

	B-T	HT	WT	DOB	W	L	ERA	G	GS	CG	SV	IP	H	R	ER	HR	BB	SO	AVG	vLH	vRH	K/9	BB/9
Zabaleta, Ezequiel	R-R	6-0	175	8-20-95	1	0	1.59	3	0	0	1	6	3	2	1	1	1	3	.167	.286	.091	4.76	1.59
Zanghi, Joe	R-R	6-3	240	12-1-94	2	0	1.15	18	0	0	1	31	24	4	4	1	5	23	.214	.204	.222	6.61	1.44

Fielding

Catcher	PCT	G	PO	A	E	DP	PB
Brosher	1.000	14	101	10	0	1	6
Dimino	.995	25	175	15	1	0	13
Garcia	1.000	4	31	6	0	0	1
Rizzie	.990	65	470	50	5	7	8
Sanchez	.990	27	192	14	2	1	3

First Base	PCT	G	PO	A	E	DP
Brosher	1.000	4	28	3	0	4
Bruce	1.000	3	23	5	0	3
Burdick	.991	14	103	11	1	7
Dimino	1.000	1	4	0	0	0
Flores	1.000	2	15	2	0	2
Franco	1.000	1	4	2	0	0
Vasquez	.989	45	333	37	4	26
Winningham	.986	65	471	33	7	42

Second Base	PCT	G	PO	A	E	DP
Burdick	1.000	9	11	15	0	1
Carpio	.972	80	109	206	9	42
Cecchini	1.000	1	0	1	0	1
Franco	.917	9	8	14	2	3
Gimenez	1.000	2	2	4	0	0
Paez	.974	11	17	21	1	2
Reyes	1.000	2	2	7	0	1
Rivera	1.000	3	5	1	0	0
Tiberi	.929	25	33	58	7	13

Third Base	PCT	G	PO	A	E	DP
Burdick	.857	17	13	17	5	3
Flores	1.000	1	0	1	0	0
Franco	1.000	6	5	11	0	1
Frazier	1.000	2	2	3	0	1
Paez	.917	106	73	148	20	12
Reyes	.000	1	0	0	0	0
Tiberi	.000	2	0	0	0	0
Wright	.933	10	8	6	1	0

Shortstop	PCT	G	PO	A	E	DP
Burdick	1.000	16	21	34	0	5
Carpio	.960	32	39	82	5	14
Gimenez	.970	83	127	224	11	42
Paez	.875	2	2	5	1	1

Outfield	PCT	G	PO	A	E	DP
Becerra	.985	38	64	0	1	0
Brodey	1.000	28	47	3	0	0
Bruce	1.000	3	3	0	0	0
Burdick	.909	5	10	0	1	0
Cone	1.000	103	182	5	0	1
Dimino	.900	5	8	1	1	1
Gladu	.974	17	36	2	1	0
Kaczmarski	1.000	8	16	0	0	0
Lindsay	.984	75	178	7	3	3
Nimmo	1.000	2	7	0	0	0
Reyes	1.000	1	2	0	0	0
Strom	.933	65	123	2	9	1
Zanon	.987	56	143	4	2	0

COLUMBIA FIREFLIES

SOUTH ATLANTIC LEAGUE — **LOW CLASS A**

Batting	B-T	HT	WT	DOB	AVG	vLH	vRH	G	AB	R	H	2B	3B	HR	RBI	BB	HBP	SH	SF	SO	SB	CS	SLG	OBP
Alfonzo, Giovanny	R-R	5-11	185	12-19-92	.215	.247	.202	75	251	26	54	12	1	2	26	19	2	3	2	47	1	5	.295	.274
Becerra, Wuilmer	R-R	6-3	243	10-1-94	.265	.188	.289	19	68	5	18	2	0	0	4	3	1	0	0	21	2	1	.294	.306
Brizuela, Jose	L-R	6-0	180	8-31-92	.224	.300	.300	33	116	14	26	3	0	3	11	8	0	1	0	25	0	0	.328	.272
Brodey, Quinn	L-L	6-1	200	12-1-95	.217	.190	.228	84	314	36	68	14	5	10	46	26	6	0	2	93	7	2	.389	.287
Fermin, Edgardo	R-R	6-0	171	5-28-98	.210	.220	.206	109	429	56	90	19	7	8	39	28	4	3	7	108	9	8	.343	.261
Gladu, Raphael	L-R	6-2	195	6-23-95	.275	.256	.283	71	262	31	72	13	4	1	25	16	3	1	1	41	12	5	.366	.323
Jabs, Jay	L-R	6-0	195	9-30-94	.167	.143	.174	36	114	12	19	6	2	2	9	9	3	0	1	36	0	0	.307	.244
Manea, Scott	R-R	5-11	216	12-21-95	.261	.238	.271	100	345	48	90	23	0	12	53	35	24	0	1	66	0	0	.432	.368
Mena, Jose	R-R	6-0	208	12-22-96	.000	.000	.000	2	6	0	0	0	0	0	0	0	0	0	0	0	0	0	.000	.000
Miranda, David	L-L	6-0	210	3-23-95	.250	.263	.246	21	76	9	19	3	0	0	6	6	2	0	0	17	0	1	.290	.321
Moreno, Hansel	B-R	6-4	180	11-3-96	.248	.256	.245	89	319	44	79	16	4	8	33	24	4	5	2	101	21	11	.398	.307
Pascual, Oliver	B-R	5-9	178	11-16-96	.091	.000	.156	17	55	2	5	1	0	0	1	2	0	1	0	16	0	1	.109	.123
Paulino, Dionis	L-L	6-1	223	6-20-94	.259	.182	.285	49	174	19	45	6	0	6	18	10	0	0	0	47	5	1	.397	.299
Rasquin, Walter	R-R	5-9	200	3-21-96	.298	.308	.294	13	47	10	14	3	1	1	9	3	1	1	0	11	3	0	.468	.353
Rheams, Zach	L-L	6-0	230	7-5-96	.226	.278	.210	45	155	19	35	8	0	8	25	15	5	0	1	48	0	0	.432	.313
Rizzie, Dan	R-R	6-2	200	11-26-93	.318	.143	.400	6	22	3	7	0	0	0	2	1	1	0	0	3	0	0	.318	.375
Sanchez, Ali	R-R	6-1	196	1-20-97	.259	.200	.283	50	193	26	50	11	1	4	22	10	0	0	2	23	1	1	.389	.293
Sanchez, Carlos	R-R	6-0	203	6-6-96	.178	.167	.185	32	107	6	19	2	0	0	5	3	0	0	1	23	0	1	.196	.198
Terrazas, Rigoberto	B-R	6-2	180	4-14-96	.176	.129	.198	85	295	21	52	7	1	0	20	30	0	1	1	58	0	0	.207	.252
Tiberi, Blake	L-R	6-0	205	2-16-95	.265	.279	.259	83	298	53	79	13	1	4	27	53	4	0	4	61	5	1	.356	.379
Vasquez, Jeremy	L-L	6-1	205	7-17-96	.289	.250	.305	80	284	33	82	18	3	6	44	43	3	0	4	65	0	0	.437	.383
Winaker, Matt	L-L	6-1	195	11-29-95	.254	.248	.257	121	425	65	108	23	7	13	61	62	21	0	8	88	4	3	.433	.370

Pitching	B-T	HT	WT	DOB	W	L	ERA	G	GS	CG	SV	IP	H	R	ER	HR	BB	SO	AVG	vLH	vRH	K/9	BB/9
Campos, Yeizo	R-R	5-9	172	4-29-96	3	4	3.88	17	7	0	1	67	65	33	29	4	16	64	.255	.239	.268	8.55	2.41
Campusano, Briam	R-R	6-2	174	3-26-96	1	1	3.55	3	2	0	0	13	15	6	5	0	3	15	.290	.375	.222	10.66	2.13
Cavallaro, Joe	R-R	6-4	190	7-19-95	8	2	2.09	13	12	0	0	77	54	24	18	5	26	83	.199	.207	.192	9.66	3.03
Chadwick, Cannon	R-R	6-0	195	12-2-94	0	0	12.60	4	0	0	0	5	7	7	7	1	6	7	.368	.333	.400	12.60	10.80
Cobb, Trey	R-R	6-1	190	6-24-94	3	1	2.22	27	0	0	10	28	34	12	7	4	4	33	.298	.333	.267	10.48	1.27
Debora, Nicolas	R-R	6-4	189	12-6-93	3	5	3.65	21	7	0	0	74	72	37	30	4	27	64	.252	.228	.273	7.78	3.28
Dibrell, Tony	R-R	6-3	190	11-8-95	7	6	3.50	23	23	1	0	131	112	60	51	10	54	147	.228	.214	.243	10.10	3.71
Diehl, Jeff	R-R	6-5	235	9-30-93	0	0	8.10	4	0	0	0	3	4	3	3	2	4	3	.231	.143	.333	10.80	10.80
Ford, Aaron	L-L	5-11	190	9-9-94	2	2	2.03	19	0	0	1	27	27	8	6	0	2	32	.260	.229	.275	10.80	0.68
Grotz, Zac	R-R	6-2	195	2-17-93	3	7	4.61	13	13	0	0	80	91	51	41	4	12	83	.284	.289	.280	9.34	1.35
Henry, Taylor	L-L	6-2	200	7-6-93	1	2	4.33	25	0	0	0	35	36	20	17	0	11	24	.261	.279	.247	6.11	2.80
Hernandez, Carlos	R-R	5-11	172	11-3-94	1	3	3.59	28	0	0	4	43	31	21	17	4	19	51	.205	.212	.200	10.76	4.01
Johnson, Trent	R-R	6-5	205	8-12-96	0	0	5.00	6	0	0	0	9	13	8	5	2	6	4	.342	.263	.421	4.00	6.00
Kay, Anthony	L-L	6-0	218	3-21-95	4	4	4.54	13	13	0	0	69	73	41	35	6	22	78	.276	.301	.264	10.13	2.86
O'Neil, Conner	R-R	6-2	195	9-25-94	6	0	2.86	27	0	0	4	44	38	17	14	1	16	56	.230	.284	.187	11.45	3.27
Payne, Joshua	R-R	6-6	260	10-3-94	4	3	4.39	28	0	0	1	41	44	25	20	4	10	43	.279	.250	.300	9.44	2.20
Peterson, David	L-L	6-6	240	9-3-95	1	4	1.82	9	9	0	0	59	46	16	12	1	11	57	.214	.123	.247	8.65	1.67
Ramos, Darwin	R-R	6-2	192	11-23-95	4	3	4.74	37	0	0	2	74	83	39	39	2	26	73	.283	.305	.267	8.88	3.16
Rennie, Luc	R-R	6-2	200	4-26-94	3	4	4.07	10	9	1	0	55	61	26	25	4	11	60	.277	.278	.277	9.76	1.79
Renteria, Marcel	R-R	5-11	185	9-27-94	5	3	4.23	15	15	0	0	77	77	43	36	6	23	72	.269	.284	.257	8.45	2.70
Sanchez, Ronald	R-R	6-5	195	9-20-93	0	0	5.19	6	0	0	0	9	6	5	5	1	5	8	.273	.263	.286	8.31	5.19
Selmer, Ryan	R-R	6-8	220	5-20-94	0	0	0.00	2	0	0	0	3	1	0	0	0	0	1	.091	.333	.000	3.00	0.00

Player	B-T	HT	WT	DOB	W	L	ERA	G	GS	CG	SV	IP	H	R	ER	HR	BB	SO	AVG	vLH	vRH	K/9	BB/9
Simon, Jake	L-L	6-2	189	1-21-97	0	5	4.04	11	9	0	0	42	50	24	19	4	14	34	.294	.333	.277	7.23	2.98
Viall, Chris	R-R	6-9	253	9-28-95	3	7	4.75	15	15	0	0	66	61	42	35	8	41	94	.244	.269	.221	12.75	5.56
Villines, Stephen	R-R	6-2	175	7-15-95	2	4	4.86	24	0	0	6	33	33	21	18	2	5	54	.256	.207	.296	14.58	1.35

Fielding

C: Jabs 2, Manea 65, Mena 2, Rizzie 6, Sanchez 36, Sanchez 28. 1B: Alfonzo 13, Brizuela 12, Jabs 1, Paulino 31, Sanchez 3, Terrazas 1, Vasquez 75. 2B: Alfonzo 31, Brizuela 3, Moreno 15, Pascual 7, Rasquin 4, Tiberi 77. 3B: Alfonzo 16, Brizuela 19, Moreno 22, Pascual 3, Terrazas 77. SS: Alfonzo 6, Fermin 83, Moreno 42, Pascual 7. OF: Alfonzo 4, Becerra 18, Brodey 82, Fermin 27, Gladu 68, Jabs 26, Miranda 21, Moreno 13, Paulino 14, Rasquin 6, Rheams 28, Winaker 98.

BROOKLYN CYCLONES
NEW YORK-PENN LEAGUE

SHORT-SEASON

Batting	B-T	HT	WT	DOB	AVG	vLH	vRH	G	AB	R	H	2B	3B	HR	RBI	BB	HBP	SH	SF	SO	SB	CS	SLG	OBP
Adolph, Ross	L-R	6-1	203	12-17-96	.276	.300	.269	61	232	47	64	9	12	7	35	21	7	0	4	52	14	3	.509	.349
Avant, Chandler	R-R	5-11	170	7-11-95	.246	.275	.234	43	134	18	33	4	0	1	12	10	4	1	0	16	5	4	.299	.318
Brizuela, Jose	L-R	6-0	180	8-31-92	.235	.227	.238	28	102	15	24	4	2	2	10	14	1	0	1	22	1	1	.373	.331
Chambers, Chase	L-L	6-1	250	8-22-95	.281	.217	.298	59	217	34	61	13	1	3	30	21	3	0	2	43	2	0	.350	.350
Coleman, Kendall	L-L	6-4	190	5-22-95	.156	.182	.143	9	32	4	5	0	0	1	6	4	2	0	0	14	1	0	.250	.290
Cortes, Carlos	L-B	5-7	197	6-30-97	.264	.270	.262	47	178	26	47	5	2	4	24	17	4	1	2	34	1	0	.382	.338
Dirocie, Anthony	R-R	5-11	175	4-24-97	.230	.258	.222	44	148	19	34	9	1	2	22	22	2	1	1	47	5	1	.345	.335
Foley, Matthew	R-R	6-4	230	4-15-94	.000	.000	.000	2	6	1	0	0	0	0	0	0	0	0	0	3	0	0	.000	.000
Frazier, Todd	R-R	6-3	220	2-12-86	.250	1.000	.143	2	8	1	2	0	0	1	1	0	0	0	0	2	0	0	.625	.250
Hall, Kevin	R-R	6-2	210	11-13-93	.220	.000	.265	16	41	3	9	5	0	0	2	4	0	0	0	22	0	0	.342	.289
Lagrange, Wagner	R-R	5-11	187	9-6-95	.282	.152	.315	62	227	31	64	13	2	0	32	22	6	0	3	43	9	3	.357	.357
Manzanarez, Angel	R-R	5-10	160	5-19-97	.274	.222	.281	27	73	8	20	4	0	0	9	7	1	3	1	8	3	2	.329	.342
Medina, Jose Miguel	R-R	6-3	180	10-21-96	.271	.143	.304	54	210	33	57	16	1	5	32	22	1	2	1	41	12	8	.429	.342
Meyer, Nick	R-R	6-1	200	2-18-97	.226	.265	.214	43	137	15	31	4	1	0	9	9	1	0	2	19	2	1	.270	.275
Miranda, David	L-L	6-0	210	3-23-95	.200	.250	.182	20	45	9	9	2	0	0	4	11	1	0	2	12	4	1	.244	.356
Pascual, Oliver	R-R	5-9	178	11-16-96	.290	.231	.320	10	38	3	11	2	0	0	5	0	0	0	0	9	0	1	.342	.290
Paulino, Dionis	L-L	6-1	223	6-20-94	.265	.200	.276	9	34	4	9	1	0	0	2	2	0	0	0	15	1	0	.294	.306
Rasquin, Walter	R-R	5-9	200	3-21-96	.299	.242	.315	40	144	23	43	9	0	1	16	16	2	0	2	28	8	2	.382	.372
Rodriguez, Manny	R-R	5-10	166	7-4-96	.236	.300	.216	51	174	19	41	8	2	2	18	14	2	1	1	58	5	2	.339	.298
Sanchez, Carlos	R-R	6-0	203		.308	.286	.316	9	26	5	8	1	0	0	3	4	0	0	0	3	1	1	.346	.400
Senger, Hayden	R-R	6-1	210	4-3-97	.250	.250	.250	22	68	9	17	3	1	0	12	9	5	0	1	23	0	1	.324	.374
Sharp, Brian	L-R	6-2	205	2-18-97	.250	.192	.261	50	168	20	42	4	2	5	22	25	1	1	2	72	8	2	.387	.347
Thompson, David	R-R	6-2	210	8-28-93	.167	—	.167	3	12	1	2	1	0	0	1	0	0	0	0	2	0	0	.250	.231
Tice, Dylan	B-R	5-8	190	12-15-92	.296	.500	.250	14	44	10	13	1	0	0	5	9	2	1	0	12	1	1	.318	.436
Uriarte, Juan	R-R	6-0	182	9-17-97	.000	—	.000	1	1	0	0	0	0	0	0	0	0	0	0	1	0	0	.000	.000
Woodard, L.A.	R-R	5-11	165	6-3-97	.500	.500	.500	3	4	2	2	1	0	0	1	0	0	0	0	1	0	0	.500	.600

Pitching	B-T	HT	WT	DOB	W	L	ERA	G	GS	CG	SV	IP	H	R	ER	HR	BB	SO	AVG	vLH	vRH	K/9	BB/9
Butto, Jose	R-R	6-1	152	3-19-98	1	2	6.11	6	5	0	0	28	31	20	19	6	11	24	.279	.294	.267	7.71	3.54
Campos, Yeizo	R-R	5-9	172	4-29-96	0	0	4.05	1	1	0	0	7	8	3	3	1	0	4	.296	.308	.286	5.40	0.00
Campusano, Briam	R-R	6-2	174	3-26-96	3	6	5.26	13	13	0	0	53	58	37	31	3	22	53	.279	.263	.294	9.00	3.74
Colon, Yeudy	R-R	6-1	230	6-9-95	4	4	1.95	25	0	0	3	32	21	14	7	1	23	31	.183	.196	.170	8.63	6.40
Davis, Seth	L-L	5-9	189	5-8-93	0	0	3.60	4	0	0	0	5	4	2	2	0	1	7	.211	.143	.250	12.60	1.80
Debora, Nicolas	R-R	6-4	189	12-6-93	0	0	4.91	3	0	0	0	15	16	8	8	1	7	15	.291	.364	.242	9.00	4.30
Gilliam, Ryley	R-R	5-10	170	8-11-96	0	1	2.08	17	0	0	5	17	11	4	4	1	13	31	.180	.250	.135	16.10	6.75
Hanhold, Eric	R-R	6-5	220	11-1-93	0	0	0.00	1	0	0	0	4	1	0	0	0	0	2	.077	.111	.000	4.50	0.00
Hill, Adam	R-R	6-6	185	3-24-97	1	1	2.35	9	0	0	0	15	16	7	4	1	7	26	.262	.296	.235	15.26	4.11
Huertas, Joel	B-L	6-3	236	2-14-96	0	1	20.25	3	0	0	0	4	9	9	9	1	4	4	.368	.571	.250	9.00	9.00
James, Christian	R-R	6-3	210	5-24-98	4	2	2.01	13	13	0	0	72	61	22	16	4	20	45	.232	.182	.275	5.65	2.51
Johnson, Trent	R-R	6-5	205	8-12-96	1	1	5.40	12	0	0	0	18	24	11	11	1	5	15	.320	.448	.239	7.36	2.45
Lozer, Mac	R-R	6-1	200	7-18-95	0	2	3.07	11	0	0	2	15	12	6	5	2	2	20	.250	.200		12.17	1.23
McAuliffe, Ryan	R-R	6-4	195	6-19-95	0	0	2.89	6	1	0	0	9	4	3	2	0	2	10	.273	.191	.417	9.64	1.93
Megill, Tylor	R-R	6-7	230	7-28-95	1	2	3.21	10	2	0	0	28	18	17	10	2	14	36	.180	.105	.226	11.57	4.50
Mitchell, Andrew	L-L	6-0	180	10-23-94	1	1	1.64	8	0	0	0	11	5	2	2	1	3	16	.244	.125	.320	13.09	2.45
Oxford, Billy	R-R	6-1	215	10-22-96	8	1	1.34	26	0	0	0	40	36	8	6	1	14	26	.237	.262	.218	5.80	3.12
Sanchez, Ronald	R-R	5-9	195	9-20-93	0	2	8.31	11	0	0	1	13	14	13	12	1	11	12	.269	.296	.240	8.31	7.62
Selmer, Ryan	R-R	6-8	220	5-20-94	1	0	5.65	22	0	0	1	29	33	19	18	1	14	15	.287	.277	.294	4.71	4.40
Smith, Kevin	R-R	6-5	200	5-13-97	4	1	0.76	12	3	0	0	24	12	3	2	1	6	28	.156	.083	.189	10.65	2.28
Swarzak, Anthony	R-R	6-4	215	9-10-85	0	0	0.00	1	0	0	0	1	0	0	0	0	0	2	.000	.000	.000	18.00	0.00
Syndergaard, Noah	L-R	6-6	240	8-29-92	0	0	1.80	1	1	0	0	5	2	1	1	0	1	7	.111	.167	.083	12.60	1.80
Vargas, Jason	L-L	6-0	215	2-2-83	0	0	1.50	2	2	0	0	12	7	2	2	0	0	19	.143	.143	.143	14.25	0.00
Vilera, Jaison	R-R	6-0	188	5-13-97	0	3	1.83	13	0	0	0	74	50	20	15	1	22	78	.191	.136	.236	9.53	2.69
Walker, Joshua	L-L	6-6	225	12-1-94	0	0	4.18	10	0	0	0	32	33	17	15	4	15	40	.271	.313	.256	11.13	4.18
Wilson, Kyle	R-R	6-1	185	9-27-96	4	4	3.86	11	11	0	0	54	49	27	23	3	14	59	.241	.262	.220	9.89	2.35
Wilson, Tommy	R-R	6-0	220	5-26-96	1	0	1.33	11	0	0	0	13	9	3	3	0	3	16	.211	.091	.213	11.05	2.84
Zabaleta, Ezequiel	R-R	6-0	175	8-20-95	0	1	1.47	13	0	0	2	18	15	5	3	0	3	16	.211	.171	.171	7.85	1.47

Fielding

C: Foley 1, Hall 12, Meyer 42, Sanchez 9, Senger 22, Uriarte 1. **1B:** Brizuela 1, Chambers 52, Paulino 6, Sharp 22. **2B:** Avant 13, Brizuela 3, Cortes 45, Manzanarez 5, Pascual 5, Tice 4, Woodard 2. **3B:** Avant 23, Brizuela 20, Frazier 2, Sharp 29, Thompson 2, Tice 3. **SS:** Avant 1, Manzanarez 22, Pascual 4, Rodriguez 51, Tice 1. **OF:** Adolph 57, Coleman 4, Dirocie 44, Lagrange 55, Medina 53, Miranda 17, Rasquin 1, Tice 6.

NEW YORK METS

KINGSPORT METS · ROOKIE
APPALACHIAN LEAGUE

Batting	B-T	HT	WT	DOB	AVG	vLH	vRH	G	AB	R	H	2B	3B	HR	RBI	BB	HBP	SH	SF	SO	SB	CS	SLG	OBP
Adon, Ranfy	R-R	6-3	177	8-2-97	.295	.344	.281	40	146	29	43	6	6	5	26	7	3	3	1	52	10	5	.521	.338
Beracierta, Raul	R-R	6-0	211	5-24-99	.270	.207	.285	46	159	35	43	8	3	3	29	26	5	0	0	36	7	2	.415	.390
Capra, Phil	B-R	5-10	205	10-1-96	.146	.059	.163	32	103	19	15	1	0	1	11	17	1	0	3	32	0	0	.185	.266
Dirocie, Anthony	R-R	5-11	175	4-24-97	.408	.500	.390	14	49	11	20	4	2	3	14	6	3	0	1	8	1	3	.755	.492
Garay, Gavin	R-R	6-2	205	6-18-97	.329	.111	.404	18	70	15	23	3	0	5	20	4	1	0	2	17	0	0	.586	.364
Granadillo, Guillermo	R-R	5-11	197	2-12-97	.303	.250	.315	51	198	44	60	3	0	1	23	26	5	2	0	38	21	8	.333	.397
Hernandez, Kenny	L-R	6-0	194	8-13-98	.176	.143	.184	56	193	30	34	6	1	1	15	34	2	0	3	59	2	1	.233	.302
Kelenic, Jarred	L-L	6-1	196	7-16-99	.253	.357	.233	44	174	33	44	8	4	5	33	22	4	0	0	39	11	1	.431	.350
Kidwell, Robby	L-R	6-3	200	10-21-97	.150	.000	.171	12	40	5	6	2	0	1	5	4	0	0	1	20	0	0	.275	.222
Martinez, Domingo	R-R	5-10	214	4-2-95	.245	.333	.213	41	147	24	36	10	0	2	13	15	5	0	0	38	1	0	.354	.335
Mauricio, Ronny	B-R	6-3	166	4-4-01	.233	.111	.286	8	30	6	7	3	0	0	4	3	0	0	2	9	1	0	.333	.286
Newton, Shervyen	B-R	6-4	180	4-24-99	.280	.302	.274	56	207	50	58	16	2	5	41	46	4	1	8	84	4	0	.449	.408
Reyes, Wilmer	R-R	6-0	161	12-22-97	.000	.000	.000	2	8	0	0	0	0	0	0	0	0	0	0	0	0	0	.000	.000
Rheams, Zach	L-L	6-0	230	7-5-96	.208	.000	.217	6	24	3	5	0	0	0	1	1	1	0	0	8	0	0	.208	.269
Romero, Yoel	R-R	6-0	180	4-10-98	.265	.226	.278	53	204	42	54	10	0	4	38	33	2	1	3	41	12	7	.373	.368
Santana, Luis	R-R	5-8	175	7-20-99	.348	.350	.348	53	204	34	71	13	0	4	35	27	10	0	1	23	8	3	.471	.446
Senger, Hayden	R-R	6-1	210	4-3-97	.400	.333	.414	10	35	12	14	4	0	1	6	4	2	0	0	8	0	0	.600	.488
Vientos, Mark	R-R	6-4	185	12-11-99	.287	.381	.265	60	223	32	64	17	4	11	52	37	1	0	1	43	1	0	.489	.389
Woodard, L.A.	R-R	5-11	165	6-3-97	.239	.231	.241	24	71	14	17	4	0	0	11	16	2	0	1	14	8	0	.296	.389

Pitching	B-T	HT	WT	DOB	W	L	ERA	G	GS	CG	SV	IP	H	R	ER	HR	BB	SO	AVG	vLH	vRH	K/9	BB/9
Acosta, Daison	R-R	6-2	160	8-24-98	2	5	4.46	10	9	0	0	42	38	28	21	8	18	46	.236	.188	.268	9.78	3.83
Bryant, Garrison	L-R	6-3	189	12-3-98	1	3	5.24	11	8	0	0	46	52	34	27	7	19	54	.272	.290	.264	10.49	3.69
Butto, Jose	R-R	6-1	152	3-19-98	3	0	1.93	6	6	1	0	33	27	7	7	3	11	31	.227	.153	.300	8.54	3.03
Cleveland, Matt	R-R	6-3	187	3-18-98	1	4	4.97	10	10	0	0	42	41	39	23	0	40	26	.255	.339	.202	5.62	8.64
Hickey, Mitch	R-R	6-0	184	11-16-95	1	0	3.71	13	0	0	2	17	15	8	7	3	12	18	.242	.250	.237	9.53	6.35
Huertas, Joel	B-L	6-3	236	2-14-96	0	0	19.29	5	0	0	0	5	5	10	10	0	12	8	.313	.167	.400	15.43	23.14
Jean, Ivan	L-L	6-1	211	9-14-93	2	1	3.00	7	0	0	0	9	4	4	3	0	12	8	.138	.111	.150	8.00	12.00
Leon, Nelson	R-R	6-1	154	3-1-95	2	2	7.01	21	0	0	0	26	37	22	20	3	8	22	.349	.342	.353	7.71	2.81
McCall, Liam	R-R	6-4	180	2-19-99	0	2	9.00	12	1	0	0	22	28	30	22	1	34	18	.318	.333	.308	7.36	13.91
Metoyer, Brian	R-R	6-4	160	11-13-96	0	1	5.56	11	0	0	1	11	11	12	7	2	9	11	.239	.214	.250	8.74	7.15
Mitchell, Andrew	L-L	6-0	180	10-23-94	1	2	0.75	10	0	0	2	12	11	6	1	1	3	16	.239	.154	.273	12.00	2.25
Montijo, Marbin	R-R	6-3	181	7-4-96	1	4	8.34	17	0	0	0	23	24	23	21	4	24	19	.273	.371	.208	7.54	9.53
Moreno, Jose	R-R	6-4	165	7-31-96	3	0	4.12	8	2	0	0	24	11	9	9	1	8	26	.164	.194	.139	11.90	3.66
Nunez, Dedniel	R-R	5-11	210	6-5-96	4	1	3.79	11	7	0	1	40	38	18	17	2	16	36	.255	.258	.253	8.03	3.57
Nunez, Noah	R-R	6-4	210	12-28-98	1	2	6.43	8	4	0	0	21	29	19	15	6	7	20	.326	.355	.310	8.57	3.00
Peden, Nate	R-R	6-4	170	10-16-98	2	5	6.48	11	10	0	0	50	67	42	36	5	17	35	.319	.250	.362	6.30	3.06
Rivera, Dariel	R-R	6-1	186	10-1-97	0	0	13.50	1	0	0	0	1	1	1	1	1	1	1	.333	—	.333	13.50	13.50
Rojas, Oscar	R-R	5-11	200	5-5-99	2	0	6.75	2	2	0	0	8	11	7	6	2	3	2	.333	.250	.381	2.25	3.38
Ryan, Andrew	R-R	6-2	215	9-14-96	0	0	6.06	11	0	0	0	16	18	14	11	2	14	17	.261	.261	.261	9.37	7.71
Silva, Luis	R-R	6-0	200	11-17-96	0	0	4.76	19	0	0	0	28	28	17	15	0	26	25	.267	.306	.246	7.94	8.26
Taveras, Willy	R-R	5-11	158	1-20-98	5	0	2.93	7	7	0	0	43	37	17	14	3	6	32	.231	.276	.206	6.70	1.26
Tripp, Christian	R-R	6-7	220	3-13-97	2	0	4.05	15	0	0	1	20	18	11	9	0	8	14	.247	.304	.220	6.30	3.60
Villanueva, Eric	R-R	6-0	179	3-19-98	1	0	5.14	13	0	0	2	14	10	12	8	1	13	10	.204	.177	.219	6.43	8.36
Walker, Joshua	L-L	6-6	225	12-1-94	1	0	0.00	3	0	0	0	9	9	1	0	0	0	12	.265	.182	.304	12.00	0.00
Winans, Allan	R-R	6-2	165	8-10-95	0	1	4.66	11	0	0	0	19	19	14	10	1	7	15	.257	.192	.292	6.98	3.26
Woods Richardson, Simeon	R-R	6-3	210	9-27-00	0	0	4.50	2	2	0	0	6	6	3	3	1	0	11	.250	.125	.313	16.50	0.00

Fielding

C: Capra 30, Kidwell 10, Martinez 24, Senger 8. **1B:** Garay 8, Hernandez 52, Kidwell 1, Martinez 10. **2B:** Newton 3, Reyes 1, Romero 16, Santana 51. **3B:** Hernandez 6, Newton 2, Romero 9, Santana 1, Vientos 54. **SS:** Mauricio 8, Newton 49, Romero 4, Woodard 9. **OF:** Adon 34, Beracierta 46, Dirocie 14, Granadillo 47, Kelenic 43, Rheams 4, Romero 19.

GCL METS · ROOKIE
GULF COAST LEAGUE

Batting	B-T	HT	WT	DOB	AVG	vLH	vRH	G	AB	R	H	2B	3B	HR	RBI	BB	HBP	SH	SF	SO	SB	CS	SLG	OBP
Astudillo, Wilfred	B-R	5-11	209	3-14-00	.260	.286	.256	14	50	7	13	4	0	0	5	3	1	0	0	5	2	0	.340	.315
Bohorquez, Anderson	R-R	5-11	180	10-3-97	.250	.150	.272	37	112	14	28	4	4	0	12	10	3	1	1	35	9	4	.357	.325
Brentz, Bryce	R-R	6-0	215	12-30-88	.200	—	.200	2	5	1	1	0	0	1	2	0	0	0	0	2	0	0	.800	.200
Cespedes, Yoenis	R-R	5-10	220	10-18-85	.250	.000	.286	2	8	1	2	0	0	1	3	0	0	0	0	1	0	0	.625	.250
Consuegra, Stanley	R-R	6-2	167	9-24-00	.217	.189	.224	51	189	23	41	12	3	2	26	17	5	0	1	41	4	4	.344	.297
Ely, Andrew	L-R	5-11	180	1-23-93	.316	.333	.308	7	19	6	6	0	2	0	5	6	1	0	0	1	0	1	.526	.500
Espino, Sebastian	R-R	6-2	176	5-29-00	.267	.323	.252	46	150	20	40	13	1	0	18	15	0	2	2	39	4	3	.367	.329
Kelenic, Jarred	L-L	6-1	196	7-16-99	.413	.500	.367	12	46	9	19	2	2	1	9	4	0	0	1	11	4	0	.609	.451
Kidwell, Robby	R-R	6-3	200	10-21-97	.077	.125	.056	8	26	1	2	0	0	0	2	2	1	0	1	15	0	0	.077	.167
Lebron, Luis	R-R	5-10	197	1-6-97	.310	.200	.333	10	29	5	9	0	0	3	6	2	1	0	0	8	2	1	.621	.375
Lindsay, Desmond	R-R	6-0	200	1-15-97	.300	1.000	.263	6	20	4	6	2	0	0	3	3	1	0	1	7	2	0	.400	.400
Lozano, David	R-R	5-11	177	5-11-98	.235	.143	.254	30	85	21	20	3	0	0	7	9	0	3	1	10	7	3	.271	.305
Mauricio, Ronny	B-R	6-3	166	4-4-01	.279	.371	.259	49	197	26	55	13	3	3	31	10	0	0	5	31	1	6	.421	.307
Mena, Jose	R-R	6-0	208	12-22-96	.295	.222	.304	23	78	8	23	4	0	0	2	6	1	0	0	14	1	0	.346	.353
Mompierre, Nelson	L-R	6-0	195	9-26-95	.171	.000	.203	23	70	9	12	3	1	2	7	14	2	0	1	28	3	1	.329	.322

Name	B-T	HT	WT	DOB	AVG	vLH	vRH	G	AB	R	H	2B	3B	HR	RBI	BB	HBP	SH	SF	SO	SB	CS	SLG	OBP
Palmer, Jaylen	R-R	6-3	195	7-31-00	.310	.250	.320	25	87	13	27	4	1	1	11	8	4	1	0	27	5	2	.414	.394
Peroza, Jose	R-R	6-1	214	6-15-00	.184	.364	.158	24	87	4	16	3	1	0	7	8	0	0	0	25	2	2	.241	.253
Pujols, Cristopher	R-R	6-2	180	8-19-97	.219	.250	.212	42	146	23	32	8	1	1	13	17	0	0	5	35	6	3	.308	.292
Rasquin, Walter	R-R	5-9	200	3-21-96	.524	.750	.471	6	21	3	11	1	1	1	8	4	1	0	0	4	5	1	.810	.615
Reyes, Wilmer	R-R	6-0	161	12-22-97	.269	.296	.261	32	119	18	32	5	2	3	10	3	2	0	0	17	2	5	.420	.298
Saez, Jhoander	B-R	6-0	165	3-24-98	.230	.323	.204	41	139	20	32	5	1	0	11	11	0	0	0	54	11	2	.281	.287
Strom, Ian	R-L	6-2	205	12-12-94	.238	.333	.222	6	21	2	5	0	0	0	2	0	0	0	0	7	0	0	.238	.238
Valdez, Edinson	R-R	6-2	212	1-22-99	.272	.400	.253	32	114	13	31	4	1	1	11	3	2	0	0	17	1	4	.351	.303
Zanon, Jacob	R-R	6-1	180	6-25-95	.250	.000	.267	5	16	2	4	1	1	0	3	2	1	0	0	4	0	1	.438	.368

Pitching	B-T	HT	WT	DOB	W	L	ERA	G	GS	CG	SV	IP	H	R	ER	HR	BB	SO	AVG	vLH	vRH	K/9	BB/9
Cespedes, Jorge	L-R	6-0	215	6-26-96	2	1	4.03	11	2	0	0	38	34	19	17	3	8	28	.235	.226	.239	6.63	1.89
Correa, Marcos	R-R	6-3	195	1-31-00	0	0	5.87	6	0	0	2	15	20	12	10	0	9	10	.313	.200	.364	5.87	5.28
De Jesus, Jender	R-R	6-2	165	1-3-98	1	3	7.03	11	2	0	1	24	27	26	19	3	13	23	.276	.257	.286	8.51	4.81
Dominguez, Christofer	L-L	6-2	222	1-3-00	1	0	6.35	3	0	0	0	6	6	5	4	0	4	6	.286	.600	.188	9.53	6.35
Flores, Yadiel	R-R	6-2	165	7-31-99	0	0	6.39	16	0	0	0	13	22	9	9	2	3	9	.400	.389	.405	6.39	2.13
Gonzalez, Saul	R-R	6-7	235	12-28-99	0	0	11.57	3	0	0	0	2	5	3	3	1	2	1	.455	1.000	.400	3.86	7.71
Guzman, Ramon	R-R	6-4	154	10-16-96	5	2	2.05	11	5	0	0	48	42	18	11	1	18	36	.236	.203	.257	6.70	3.35
Hammer, Zachary	R-R	6-2	165	7-4-00	0	1	19.29	3	0	0	0	2	4	5	5	0	3	3	.364	.000	.500	11.57	11.57
Hanhold, Eric	R-R	6-5	220	11-1-93	0	0	0.00	1	0	0	0	1	0	0	0	0	0	3	.000	.000	.000	27.00	0.00
Hardy, Brendan	R-R	6-4	170	12-15-99	1	1	3.31	9	0	0	0	16	11	9	6	1	14	19	.186	.115	.242	10.47	7.71
Hutchinson, Bryce	R-R	6-6	245	10-21-98	1	2	2.25	9	5	0	0	20	18	12	5	1	7	13	.237	.250	.229	5.85	3.15
Jimenez, Jurgen	R-R	6-2	197	1-14-96	3	2	5.19	6	4	0	0	26	26	15	15	2	13	20	.265	.222	.290	6.92	4.50
Knapp, Ricky	R-R	6-0	217	5-20-92	0	0	0.00	3	0	0	0	7	6	2	0	0	1	9	.231	.000	.240	11.57	1.29
Kuhns, Max	R-R	6-2	209	8-11-94	0	2	3.00	5	5	0	0	6	7	3	2	1	1	3	.292	.000	.368	4.50	1.50
Loaiza, Cesar	L-L	6-3	165	7-10-98	0	2	3.24	5	1	0	0	8	6	5	3	0	7	8	.200	.222	.191	8.64	7.56
Mena, Malky	R-R	6-0	164	10-3-96	2	1	3.48	14	2	0	1	21	16	9	8	1	6	19	.213	.238	.204	8.27	2.61
Metoyer, Brian	R-R	6-4	160	11-13-96	0	0	0.00	1	0	0	0	1	0	0	0	0	1	0	.333	—	.333	0.00	9.00
Otanez, Michel	R-R	6-2	215	7-3-97	1	6	7.64	11	7	0	0	35	42	39	30	2	24	33	.284	.327	.263	8.41	6.11
Parra, Franklin	L-L	6-1	185	9-13-99	1	0	0.90	6	0	0	0	10	5	1	1	0	11	10	.147	.100	.167	9.00	9.90
Planck, Cameron	R-R	6-4	218	3-5-98	0	0	27.00	2	1	0	0	1	1	2	2	0	1	1	.250	.000	.333	13.50	13.50
Ramirez, Miguel	R-R	6-1	140	3-10-97	0	1	2.60	17	0	0	0	17	13	7	5	1	14	15	.213	.182	.231	7.79	7.27
Rodriguez, Hector	L-L	6-2	166	12-27-97	0	0	4.33	11	2	0	0	27	20	14	13	1	18	27	.206	.103	.250	9.00	6.00
Rojas, Oscar	R-R	5-11	200	5-5-99	3	3	3.83	8	7	0	0	42	34	19	18	1	12	40	.224	.310	.191	8.50	2.55
Sanchez, Boris	L-R	6-2	180	6-20-97	0	2	3.86	15	0	0	2	21	19	14	9	2	9	17	.244	.192	.269	7.29	3.86
Santos, Junior	R-R	6-8	218	8-16-01	0	0	0.00	3	0	0	0	5	4	0	0	0	0	3	.222	.167	.250	5.40	0.00
Sierra, Julian	L-L	6-3	190	2-22-96	0	0	13.50	1	0	0	0	1	1	1	1	0	2	0	.333	.000	.500	0.00	27.00
Taveras, Willy	R-R	5-11	158	1-20-98	2	1	1.23	4	1	0	0	22	15	6	3	1	8	25	.185	.174	.190	10.23	3.27
Taylor Jr., Ronnie	R-R	6-3	220	10-6-98	0	1	3.68	11	1	0	0	22	20	13	9	2	19	19	.233	.273	.219	7.77	7.77
Taylor, Logan	R-R	6-5	248	12-13-91	0	0	0.00	3	3	0	0	4	2	2	0	0	1	4	.133	.000	.250	9.00	2.25
Uceta, Adonis	R-R	6-1	225	5-10-94	0	0	0.00	2	0	0	0	1	2	0	0	0	2	1	.500	1.000	.333	13.50	27.00
Woods Richardson, Simeon	R-R	6-3	210	9-27-00	1	0	0.00	5	2	0	1	11	9	2	0	0	4	15	.209	.200	.214	11.91	3.18

Fielding

C: Astudillo 7, Kidwell 5, Lebron 4, Mena 22, Mompierre 20. 1B: Astudillo 7, Bohorquez 23, Cespedes 1, Lebron 5, Lozano 14, Pujols 3, Rasquin 2, Reyes 7. 2B: Ely 1, Espino 43, Lozano 15, Reyes 3. 3B: Ely 3, Lozano 3, Palmer 9, Peroza 15, Pujols 28. SS: Ely 1, Espino 4, Mauricio 45, Palmer 6. OF: Bohorquez 14, Brentz 2, Cespedes 1, Consuegra 50, Kelenic 9, Lindsay 5, Lozano 1, Pujols 4, Rasquin 3, Reyes 22, Saez 41, Strom 5, Valdez 25, Zanon 3.

DSL METS1   ROOKIE
DOMINICAN SUMMER LEAGUE

Batting	B-T	HT	WT	DOB	AVG	vLH	vRH	G	AB	R	H	2B	3B	HR	RBI	BB	HBP	SH	SF	SO	SB	CS	SLG	OBP
Almario, Fidel	B-R	6-0	165	11-17-99	.266	.282	.262	53	169	23	45	3	0	0	13	15	6	1	1	36	3	5	.284	.346
Arias, Eliam	B-R	5-11	165	3-6-01	.176	.046	.202	39	131	12	23	6	0	0	16	18	4	2	1	40	6	2	.221	.292
Astudillo, Wilfred	B-R	5-11	209	3-14-00	.256	.235	.261	25	82	11	21	5	0	1	7	12	3	0	0	8	2	1	.354	.371
Cabrera, Jan	R-R	6-1	170	9-10-01	.156	.080	.170	53	160	22	25	6	1	3	21	36	8	0	0	56	7	4	.263	.338
Consuegra, Stanley	R-R	6-2	167	9-24-00	.192	.178	.219	13	52	9	10	1	1	2	13	9	1	0	1	5	5	0	.365	.318
De La Rosa, Juan	R-R	6-3	207	6-22-98	.255	.259	.253	60	224	27	57	6	8	3	34	15	4	0	0	71	9	8	.393	.313
Diaz, Patricio	L-R	5-10	171	3-13-01	.207	.219	.204	43	135	22	28	4	2	0	13	30	6	0	3	48	4	3	.267	.368
Gonzalez, Moises	R-R	6-1	163	6-10-00	.199	.259	.186	47	151	25	30	4	2	1	14	24	5	1	1	31	13	9	.272	.326
Hernandez, Adrian	R-R	5-9	210	2-8-01	.261	.250	.264	63	249	50	65	12	2	5	34	17	18	0	1	52	9	5	.386	.351
Loyo, Juan	R-R	5-11	180	3-16-99	.292	.323	.283	48	144	19	42	4	0	1	14	22	16	2	2	27	7	4	.340	.435
Lozano, David	R-R	5-11	177	5-11-98	.256	.148	.268	11	39	8	10	0	1	0	3	6	2	0	1	3	3	3	.308	.375
Marquez, Alexis	R-R	6-0	181	6-1-99	.172	.188	.169	31	93	11	16	3	0	0	5	4	1	1	0	16	3	0	.204	.243
Martinez, Jorge	R-L	5-10	192	3-23-96	.242	.333	.226	53	157	24	38	8	2	0	18	27	3	0	1	22	7	2	.319	.362
Medina, Alejandro	R-R	6-1	183	4-7-00	.188	.125	.208	33	101	13	19	7	1	0	15	14	2	0	0	29	0	1	.297	.299
Monegro, Ruben	R-R	6-2	180	12-2-97	.165	.212	.151	54	152	25	25	9	1	1	15	42	2	1	2	52	7	0	.257	.349
Nunez, Malvin	B-R	5-11	152	1-20-99	.202	.195	.204	61	198	32	40	7	2	0	13	38	6	2	1	43	14	6	.258	.346
Parra, Andres	B-R	6-0	150	9-9-99	.206	.191	.209	63	214	24	44	9	3	0	16	23	1	2	2	56	8	5	.276	.283
Pena, Ezequiel	R-R	6-0	190	5-25-99	.141	.111	.153	38	99	10	14	4	0	1	8	15	9	1	0	47	1	3	.212	.309
Pereira, Walter	R-R	5-10	165	11-2-99	.212	.200	.217	9	33	7	7	2	0	1	6	2	0	2	0	9	2	0	.364	.257
Polanco, Federico	L-R	5-10	155	3-20-01	.201	.154	.210	64	249	28	50	6	3	0	18	19	2	0	0	53	11	3	.249	.263
Regnault, Andres	R-R	6-0	251	12-21-98	.333	.389	.321	53	192	33	64	17	1	9	45	22	8	0	2	33	5	3	.573	.420
Rene, Julio	R-R	6-2	182	11-6-97	.194	.240	.184	44	134	14	26	5	1	0	15	6	5	0	3	45	6	4	.246	.250
Rodriguez, Endy	B-R	6-0	170	5-26-00	.261	.188	.273	35	115	22	30	6	2	2	23	20	2	0	4	26	2	2	.400	.369
Rodriguez, Jeison	R-R	6-2	204	1-27-98	.201	.208	.200	49	144	17	29	10	2	4	11	29	0	0	1	49	6	3	.382	.333

Player	B-T	HT	WT	DOB	AVG	vLH	vRH	G	AB	R	H	2B	3B	HR	RBI	BB	HBP	SH	SF	SO	SB	CS	OBP	SLG
Salazar, Eduardo	R-R	6-3	167	12-15-00	.288	.400	.257	42	139	21	40	3	1	0	12	17	0	1	3	37	2	2	.324	.359
Sanchez, Eulises	R-R	6-1	172	3-7-97	.186	.185	.186	53	156	27	29	6	6	1	29	36	5	1	1	51	10	5	.321	.354
Soto, Jean Carlos	L-L	6-0	165	4-3-00	.213	.241	.207	50	174	21	37	7	2	2	17	15	0	1	0	38	6	4	.310	.275
Torres, Kevin	R-R	6-0	169	5-4-99	.226	.177	.239	49	164	24	37	7	1	1	20	31	3	0	2	30	4	4	.299	.355
Valdez, Wilmy	R-R	6-6	206	7-3-97	.219	.225	.217	50	169	20	37	10	0	0	26	9	3	1	1	37	8	6	.278	.269
Valerio, Felix	R-R	5-7	165	12-26-00	.319	.467	.289	67	263	54	84	17	2	3	22	34	6	0	0	21	16	6	.434	.409
Velasquez, Wilker	R-R	6-0	155	1-18-01	.217	.125	.237	23	92	6	20	3	0	0	4	5	0	1	0	18	4	4	.250	.258

Pitching	B-T	HT	WT	DOB	W	L	ERA	G	GS	CG	SV	IP	H	R	ER	HR	BB	SO	AVG	vLH	vRH	K/9	BB/9
Almonte, Enmanuel	R-R	6-5	197	11-9-97	1	3	7.62	16	1	0	0	28	28	25	24	0	17	35	.267	.242	.278	11.12	5.40
Angela, Nelmerson Xavier	L-L	6-1	170	2-20-98	3	1	2.37	16	0	0	1	30	18	10	8	1	6	33	.164	.200	.150	9.79	1.78
Armado, Johan	L-L	6-1	175	5-4-01	2	1	9.11	15	0	0	1	28	38	31	28	2	17	23	.322	.227	.344	7.48	5.53
Aybar, Adrian	R-R	6-4	180	3-8-98	1	4	2.57	12	10	0	0	42	37	19	12	3	21	38	.239	.263	.225	8.14	4.50
Baez, Darling	R-R	6-1	198	6-26-97	1	3	4.54	19	0	0	5	34	33	20	17	3	12	26	.266	.293	.242	6.95	3.21
Castellanos, Carlos	L-L	6-3	170	1-27-01	0	0	—	2	0	0	0	0	1	2	1	0	4	0	1.000	1.000	—	—	—
Cespedes, Jorge	L-R	6-0	215	6-26-96	0	1	7.71	2	2	0	0	7	10	6	6	2	4	7	.345	.213	.274	9.00	5.14
Colina, Robert	R-R	5-11	175	4-24-01	3	2	2.94	13	9	0	0	49	42	19	16	3	12	49	.240	.276	.222	9.00	2.20
Colon, Jeffrey	R-R	6-1	170	11-9-99	4	2	4.24	15	3	0	2	34	30	17	16	0	16	33	.236	.155	.304	8.74	4.24
Cornielly, Joshua	R-R	6-2	175	1-15-01	4	0	3.25	14	0	0	2	38	35	16	10	0	8	27	.302	.279	.315	8.78	2.60
Correa, Marcos	R-R	6-3	195	1-31-00	0	0	2.79	3	3	0	0	10	6	5	3	0	4	6	.177	.200	.302	5.59	3.72
De Jesus, Jender	R-R	6-2	165	1-3-98	0	1	6.30	3	3	0	0	10	9	12	7	0	4	11	.225	.235	.276	9.90	3.60
Diaz, Edinson	R-R	6-0	170	12-25-99	3	2	3.68	8	4	0	1	22	19	9	9	0	9	22	.250	.300	.217	9.00	3.68
Dominguez, Christofer	L-L	6-2	222	1-3-00	6	1	1.36	10	10	0	0	53	34	9	8	2	17	46	.189	.238	.189	7.81	2.89
Escalona, Jhonfran	R-R	5-10	159	4-8-99	4	0	1.88	16	1	0	4	48	32	13	10	1	6	31	.186	.162	.202	5.81	1.13
Escorcha, Jefferson	L-L	5-11	178	10-4-99	5	3	1.57	20	3	0	5	57	33	15	10	3	12	63	.165	.135	.172	9.89	1.88
Garcia, Benito	R-R	6-0	165	3-10-00	2	3	3.93	14	10	0	1	50	51	27	22	1	11	58	.260	.280	.248	10.37	1.97
German, Andres	R-R	6-1	150	5-16-97	5	2	1.97	15	12	2	0	73	57	25	16	1	15	58	.210	.135	.258	7.15	1.85
Gonzalez, Brailin	L-L	6-2	180	9-23-99	4	4	3.71	14	11	0	0	51	50	25	21	1	23	53	.272	.361	.250	9.35	4.06
Guzman, Daniel	L-L	6-1	194	2-16-98	1	3	1.17	21	0	0	4	46	29	10	6	1	15	26	.188	.250	.170	5.05	2.91
Guzman, Ramon	R-R	6-4	154	10-16-96	0	0	7.45	3	3	0	0	10	13	8	8	1	4	9	.310	.233	.261	8.38	3.72
Hernandez, Kevin	L-L	6-0	170	4-23-01	0	2	6.50	6	5	0	0	18	21	18	13	2	9	14	.284	.250	.290	7.00	4.50
Huizi, Eiker	R-R	6-0	155	10-8-00	0	0	1.59	5	0	0	0	6	5	4	1	0	3	5	.273	.200	.294	7.94	4.76
Isturiz, Victor	R-R	6-2	208	3-8-97	0	4	4.17	15	4	0	1	41	42	29	19	2	20	48	.258	.208	.278	10.54	4.39
Jimenez, Jurgen	R-R	6-2	197	1-14-96	0	1	2.25	3	3	0	0	12	9	3	3	1	5	7	.209	.232	.259	5.25	3.75
Loaiza, Cesar	L-L	6-2	176	10-5-99	4	0	1.16	9	6	0	0	39	21	6	5	0	15	49	.162	.231	.149	11.41	3.49
Madera, Christopher	R-R	6-2	188	10-1-96	0	0	2.70	3	0	0	0	3	4	1	1	0	0	2	.308	.286	.333	5.40	0.00
Marcano, David	R-R	6-2	180	8-28-01	3	3	6.18	14	11	0	0	39	35	31	27	1	31	32	.250	.296	.229	7.32	7.09
Martinez, Juan	R-R	6-1	187	2-14-96	1	2	4.22	20	0	0	4	32	21	18	15	1	24	36	.186	.229	.167	10.13	6.75
Mata, Miguel	R-R	6-6	191	5-5-97	2	1	6.42	21	0	0	2	34	44	30	24	3	13	27	.326	.298	.341	7.22	3.48
Mejia, Jenrry	R-R	6-0	205	10-11-89	0	0	0.00	2	2	0	0	7	2	0	0	0	1	10	.087	.111	.071	12.86	1.29
Ogando, Haniel	R-R	6-2	180	7-15-99	1	1	3.21	9	0	0	0	14	15	8	5	1	8	9	.268	.273	.265	5.79	5.14
Paniagua, Jaison	R-R	6-2	190	2-25-98	0	0	9.64	5	0	0	0	5	6	5	5	1	5	5	.316	.375	.273	3.86	9.64
Pena, Jasson	R-R	6-3	171	6-9-98	0	2	9.00	2	0	0	0	3	3	4	3	1	1	5	.231	.286	.167	15.00	3.00
Rodriguez, Hector	L-L	6-2	166	12-27-97	0	0	1.50	3	3	0	0	12	6	3	2	0	5	9	.146	.075	.235	6.75	3.75
Rodriguez, Martin	R-R	6-1	195	1-13-00	2	0	2.77	13	0	0	3	26	20	9	8	0	7	16	.208	.180	.239	5.54	2.42
Rodriguez, Ragui	L-L	5-11	165	4-27-99	1	1	3.67	14	0	0	1	27	24	11	11	0	12	36	.245	.200	.265	12.00	4.00
Santos, Junior	R-R	6-8	218	8-16-01	1	1	2.80	11	10	0	0	45	35	15	14	1	6	36	.219	.188	.239	7.20	1.20
Santos, Reyson	R-R	6-2	190	1-22-99	2	0	5.66	9	0	0	1	19	13	13	12	6	13	15	.136	.286	.067	9.15	6.97
Silva, Nixon	L-L	5-10	165	8-20-99	6	0	1.24	11	2	0	1	36	28	7	5	1	4	33	.224	.179	.237	8.17	0.99
Sosa, Felix	R-R	6-0	169	3-13-98	3	0	2.60	8	0	0	0	28	17	9	8	1	14	23	.179	.146	.204	7.48	4.55
Suarez, Joander	R-R	6-3	181	2-27-00	0	1	4.35	8	4	0	0	21	16	10	10	0	5	19	.208	.286	.163	8.27	2.18
Vargas, Rolfy	R-R	6-3	160	8-25-00	0	2	8.25	7	0	0	0	12	14	13	11	1	5	9	.280	.167	.344	6.75	3.75
Ventura, Jordany	R-R	6-0	162	7-6-00	0	1	0.00	3	1	0	0	7	7	4	0	0	7	3	.292	.167	.333	4.05	9.45
Villalba, Antonio	R-R	6-3	175	7-10-99	3	2	1.77	22	0	0	6	41	21	16	8	0	27	30	.150	.191	.133	6.64	5.98
Villegas, Marco	R-R	6-0	168	4-17-01	0	0	7.20	4	1	0	0	5	2	4	4	1	10	6	.118	.111	.125	10.80	18.00

Fielding

C: Astudillo 6, Loyo 28, Marquez 16, Martinez 2, Medina 3, Regnault 34, Rodriguez 6, Torres 44. **1B:** Astudillo 14, Gonzalez 1, Loyo 18, Marquez 9, Martinez 24, Medina 6, Rodriguez 3, Sanchez 1, Valdez 27. **2B:** Almario 5, Arias 1, Lozano 5, Monegro 1, Nunez 36, Polanco 16, Valerio 40, Velasquez 4. **3B:** Almario 41, Arias 21, Lozano 6, Medina 8, Monegro 26, Nunez 15, Parra 9, Pereira 17, Polanco 30, Velasquez 2. **SS:** Arias 16, Lozano 2, Monegro 28, Nunez 9, Parra 52, Pereira 8, Polanco 30, Velasquez 2. **OF:** Cabrera 51, Consuegra 12, De La Rosa 57, Diaz 22, Gonzalez 42, Hernandez 61, Pena 27, Rene 16, Rodriguez 37, Salazar 17, Sanchez 28, Soto 43.

New York Yankees

SEASON IN A SENTENCE: After falling a win short of the World Series in 2017, the Yankees dealt with injuries and ineffectiveness to some of their key pieces in 2018 and fell to the Red Sox in the ALDS despite a 100-win season.

HIGH POINT: On June 20, after the Yankees had clawed their way back to the top of the division and erased what had been a 7.5-game deficit, Giancarlo Stanton hit a walk-off home run against the Mariners to extend the Yankees' brief division lead to two games over the Red Sox. They kept their lead until July 1, when they relinquished the top of the division to Boston for the final time.

LOW POINT: Five days before the July 31 trade deadline, Aaron Judge broke his wrist after being hit by a pitch from Royals righthander Jake Junis. Judge didn't return until Sept. 14, and the Yankees weren't able to patch the hole left by his absence until they acquired Andrew McCutchen from the Giants at the end of August. They lost five games in the standings before he returned.

NOTABLE ROOKIES: Two of the best rookies in the American League played on the Yankees' infield. Third baseman Miguel Andujar and second baseman Gleyber Torres each went through periods of adjustment, but their contributions were predominantly positive. The pair contributed 51 home runs—19 percent of the team's total output—and drove in a combined 169 runs. Andujar also etched a spot in the team record books with 47 doubles, eclipsing Joe DiMaggio's record for the most two-baggers by a Yankees rookie.

KEY TRANSACTIONS: The Yankees' biggest transaction of 2018 occurred in December 2017, when New York dealt Starlin Castro and two prospects to the Marlins for reigning NL MVP Stanton, who swatted 38 homers and drove in 100 runs in his first season in pinstripes. To prepare for a playoff run, the team dipped into its prospect depth to acquire reliever Zach Britton, starters Lance Lynn and J.A. Happ, shortstop Adeiny Hechavarria and outfielder McCutchen.

DOWN ON THE FARM: After Torres and Andujar graduated from prospect eligibility, the farm had an up-and-down year. Top prospect Justus Sheffield had an acceptable, if not standout, season. The lefthander moved to the bullpen in September and made his major league debut late in the month. Outfielder Estevan Florial missed significant time with a broken hamate bone in his left wrist and never really got going at high Class A Tampa.

OPENING DAY PAYROLL: $161,305,917 (10th).

PLAYERS OF THE YEAR

MIKE CARLSON

MAJOR LEAGUE	MINOR LEAGUE
Aaron Judge	**Michael King**
OF	**RHP**
.278/.392/.528	(High Class A/
One of four Yankees	Double-A/Triple-A)
to hit 27 home runs	11-5, 1.79 in 24 GS

ORGANIZATION LEADERS

Batting		*Minimum 250 AB
MAJORS		
* AVG	Miguel Andujar	.297
* OPS	Aaron Judge	.919
HR	Giancarlo Stanton	38
RBI	Giancarlo Stanton	100
MINORS		
* AVG	Ryan McBroom, Scranton/W-B, Trenton	.302
* OBP	Hoy Jun Park, Tampa	.387
* SLG	Dom Thompson-Williams, Charleston, SC, Tampa	.546
* OPS	Dom Thompson-Williams, Charleston, SC, Tampa	.909
R	Brandon Wagner, Tampa, Trenton	68
H	Ryan McBroom, Scranton/W-B, Trenton	139
TB	Ryan McBroom, Scranton/W-B, Trenton	211
2B	Bruce Caldwell, Trenton, Scranton/W-B	30
3B	Evan Alexander, Charleston, SC, Pulaski	9
HR	Dom Thompson-Williams, Charleston, SC, Tampa	22
RBI	Dom Thompson-Williams, Charleston, SC, Tampa	74
RBI	Trey Amburgey, Trenton	74
BB	Brandon Wagner, Tampa, Trenton	70
SO	Isiah Gilliam, Tampa	151
SB	Ben Ruta, Trenton, Tampa	37

Pitching		#Minimum 75 IP
MAJORS		
W	Luis Severino	19
# ERA	Chad Green	2.50
SO	Luis Severino	220
SV	Aroldis Chapman	32
MINORS		
W	Adonis Rosa, Tampa, Trenton, Scranton/W-B	14
L	Brian Keller, Trenton	9
L	Trevor Stephan, Tampa, Trenton	9
L	Rony Garcia, Charleston, SC, Tampa	9
# ERA	Michael King, Tampa, Trenton, Scranton/W-B	1.79
G	Matt Wivinis, Charleston, SC, Tampa, Trenton	45
GS	Nick Nelson, Charleston, SC, Tampa, Trenton	25
SV	Matt Wivinis, Charleston, SC, Tampa, Trenton	19
IP	Michael King, Tampa, Trenton, Scranton/W-B	161
BB	Nick Green, Tampa, Trenton	64
SO	Michael King, Tampa, Trenton, Scranton/W-B	152
# AVG	Justus Sheffield, Trenton, Scranton/W-B	.195

2018 PERFORMANCE

General Manager: Brian Cashman. **Farm Director:** Kevin Reese. **Scouting Director:** Damon Oppenheimer.

Class	Team	League	W	L	PCT	Finish	Manager
Majors	New York Yankees	American	100	62	.617	3rd (15)	Aaron Boone
Triple-A	Scranton/W-B RailRiders	International	73	65	.529	3rd (14)	Bobby Mitchell
Double-A	Trenton Thunder	Eastern	79	61	.564	2nd (12)	Jay Bell
High A	Tampa Tarpons	Florida State	70	67	.511	7th (12)	Pat Osborn
Low A	Charleston RiverDogs	South Atlantic	64	72	.471	10th (14)	Julio Mosquera
Short-season	Staten Island Yankees	New York-Penn	37	36	.507	7th (14)	Lino Diaz
Rookie	Pulaski Yankees	Appalachian	32	36	.471	6th (10)	Nick Ortiz
Rookie	GCL Yankees East	Gulf Coast	19	35	.352	17th (18)	Edgar Gonzalez
Rookie	GCL Yankees West	Gulf Coast	25	27	.481	11th (18)	David Adams
Overall 2018 Minor League Record			399	399	.500	15th (30)	

ORGANIZATION STATISTICS

NEW YORK YANKEES
AMERICAN LEAGUE

Batting	B-T	HT	WT	DOB	AVG	vLH	vRH	G	AB	R	H	2B	3B	HR	RBI	BB	HBP	SH	SF	SO	SB	CS	SLG	OBP
Andujar, Miguel	R-R	6-0	215	3-2-95	.297	.264	.309	149	573	83	170	47	2	27	92	25	4	0	4	97	2	1	.527	.328
Austin, Tyler	R-R	6-2	220	9-6-91	.223	.245	.206	34	121	16	27	6	0	8	23	8	2	0	1	53	1	1	.471	.280
2-team total (35 Minnesota)					.230	.236	.226	69	244	34	56	10	0	17	47	19	2	0	3	95	1	2	.480	.287
Bird, Greg	L-R	6-4	220	11-9-92	.199	.224	.192	82	272	23	54	16	1	11	38	30	5	0	4	78	0	0	.386	.286
Drury, Brandon	R-R	6-2	210	8-21-92	.177	.177	.177	18	51	2	9	2	0	1	7	5	1	0	0	12	0	0	.275	.263
2-team total (8 Toronto)					.169	.167	.170	26	77	5	13	4	0	1	10	7	2	0	0	20	0	0	.260	.256
Frazier, Clint	R-R	6-1	190	9-6-94	.265	.455	.174	15	34	9	9	3	0	0	1	5	2	0	0	13	0	0	.353	.390
Gardner, Brett	L-L	5-11	195	8-24-83	.236	.239	.235	140	530	95	125	20	7	12	45	65	5	4	5	107	16	2	.368	.322
Gregorius, Didi	L-R	6-3	205	2-18-90	.268	.278	.264	134	504	89	135	23	5	27	86	48	7	1	9	69	10	6	.494	.335
Hechavarria, Adeiny	R-R	6-0	195	4-15-89	.194	.111	.222	18	36	3	7	0	0	2	2	1	0	0	0	10	1	0	.361	.216
2-team total (61 Tampa Bay)					.249	.300	.230	79	253	32	63	7	0	5	28	13	0	2	6	47	2	0	.336	.279
Hicks, Aaron	B-R	6-1	202	10-2-89	.248	.224	.258	137	480	90	119	18	3	27	79	90	3	2	6	111	11	2	.467	.366
Higashioka, Kyle	R-R	6-1	205	4-20-90	.167	.160	.170	29	72	6	12	2	0	3	6	6	1	0	0	16	0	0	.319	.241
Judge, Aaron	R-R	6-7	282	4-26-92	.279	.261	.285	112	413	77	115	22	0	27	67	76	4	0	5	152	6	3	.528	.392
McCutchen, Andrew	R-R	5-11	195	10-10-86	.253	.208	.270	25	87	18	22	2	1	5	10	22	4	0	1	22	1	3	.471	.421
McKinney, Billy	L-L	6-1	205	8-23-94	.250	—	.250	2	4	1	0	0	0	0	0	0	0	0	0	1	0	0	.250	.250
2-team total (36 Toronto)					.252	.143	.276	38	119	14	30	7	0	6	13	11	1	0	1	33	1	0	.462	.318
Peterson, Jace	L-R	6-0	215	5-9-90	.300	.000	.429	3	10	0	3	0	0	0	0	1	0	0	0	3	0	1	.300	.364
2-team total (93 Baltimore)					.200	.088	.222	96	210	21	42	13	2	3	28	31	3	1	1	58	13	3	.324	.310
Robinson, Shane	R-R	5-9	170	10-30-84	.143	.000	.226	25	49	8	7	1	0	1	2	4	0	1	0	6	1	0	.225	.208
Romine, Austin	R-R	6-1	220	11-22-88	.244	.262	.237	77	242	30	59	12	0	10	42	17	2	1	3	67	1	0	.417	.296
Sanchez, Gary	R-R	6-2	230	12-2-92	.186	.229	.171	89	323	51	60	17	0	18	53	46	3	0	2	94	1	0	.406	.291
Stanton, Giancarlo	R-R	6-6	245	11-8-89	.266	.316	.250	158	617	102	164	34	1	38	100	70	8	0	10	211	5	0	.509	.343
Torres, Gleyber	R-R	6-1	200	12-13-96	.272	.254	.278	123	431	54	117	16	1	24	77	42	5	1	5	122	6	2	.480	.340
Torreyes, Ronald	R-R	5-8	151	9-2-92	.280	.259	.288	41	100	9	28	7	1	0	7	2	0	0	0	16	0	0	.370	.294
Voit, Luke	R-R	6-3	225	2-13-91	.333	.349	.326	39	132	28	44	5	0	14	33	15	1	0	0	39	0	0	.689	.405
Wade, Tyler	L-R	6-1	185	11-23-94	.167	.083	.185	36	66	8	11	4	0	1	5	4	0	0	0	23	1	0	.273	.214
Walker, Neil	B-R	6-3	210	9-10-85	.219	.164	.234	113	347	48	76	12	1	11	46	42	5	0	4	87	0	0	.355	.309

Pitching	B-T	HT	WT	DOB	W	L	ERA	G	GS	CG	SV	IP	H	R	ER	HR	BB	SO	AVG	vLH	vRH	K/9	BB/9
Adams, Chance	R-R	6-1	220	8-10-94	0	1	7.04	3	1	0	0	8	8	7	6	3	4	4	.267	.235	.308	4.70	4.70
Betances, Dellin	R-R	6-8	265	3-23-88	4	6	2.70	66	0	0	4	67	44	22	20	7	26	115	.186	.200	.175	15.53	3.51
Britton, Zach	L-L	6-3	195	12-22-87	1	0	2.88	25	0	0	3	25	18	10	8	2	11	21	.196	.160	.209	7.56	3.96
2-team total (16 Baltimore)					2	0	3.10	41	0	0	7	41	29	16	14	3	21	34	.201	.200	.202	7.52	4.65
Cessa, Luis	R-R	6-0	210	4-25-92	1	4	5.24	16	5	0	2	45	51	27	26	5	13	39	.282	.266	.294	7.86	2.62
Chapman, Aroldis	L-L	6-4	212	2-28-88	3	0	2.45	55	0	0	32	51	24	15	14	2	30	93	.136	.136	.135	16.31	5.26
Cole, A.J.	R-R	6-5	238	1-5-92	3	1	4.26	28	0	0	0	38	39	23	18	9	16	49	.258	.373	.200	11.61	3.79
Gallegos, Giovanny	R-R	6-2	210	8-14-91	0	0	4.50	4	0	0	1	10	10	5	5	2	1	10	.278	.375	.200	9.00	2.70
German, Domingo	R-R	6-2	175	8-4-92	2	6	5.57	21	14	0	0	86	81	55	53	15	33	102	.242	.256	.228	10.72	3.47
Gray, Sonny	R-R	5-10	190	11-7-89	11	9	4.90	30	23	0	0	130	138	73	71	14	57	123	.270	.255	.284	8.49	3.94
Green, Chad	L-R	6-3	210	5-24-91	8	3	2.50	63	0	0	0	76	64	22	21	9	15	94	.229	.234	.225	11.18	1.78
Hale, David	R-R	6-2	210	9-27-87	0	0	2.53	3	0	0	0	11	12	3	3	2	1	6	.273	.474	.120	5.06	0.84
2-team total (1 Minnesota)					0	0	4.61	4	0	0	0	14	16	7	7	3	5	8	.286	.385	.200	5.27	3.29
Happ, J.A.	L-L	6-5	205	10-19-82	7	0	2.69	11	11	0	0	64	51	20	19	10	16	63	.217	.136	.236	8.91	2.26
2-team total (20 Toronto)					17	6	3.65	31	31	0	0	178	150	81	72	27	51	193	.225	.171	.238	9.78	2.58
Holder, Jonathan	R-R	6-2	235	6-9-93	1	3	3.14	60	1	0	0	66	53	27	23	4	19	60	.214	.212	.215	8.18	2.59
Kahnle, Tommy	R-R	6-1	235	8-7-89	2	0	6.56	24	0	0	1	23	23	22	17	3	15	30	.256	.222	.289	11.57	5.79
Kontos, George	R-R	6-3	225	6-12-85	0	0	0.00	1	0	0	0	2	1	0	0	0	0	2	.167	1.000	.000	10.80	0.00
2-team total (6 Cleveland)					0	0	2.57	7	0	0	0	7	4	2	2	1	2	6	.160	.286	.111	7.71	2.57
Loaisiga, Jonathan	R-R	5-11	165	11-2-94	2	0	5.11	9	4	0	0	25	26	17	14	3	12	33	.271	.273	.269	12.04	4.38
Lynn, Lance	B-R	6-5	280	5-12-87	3	2	4.14	11	9	0	0	54	58	26	25	2	14	61	.267	.317	.221	10.10	2.32
2-team total (20 Minnesota)					10	10	4.77	31	29	0	0	157	163	87	83	14	76	161	.265	.299	.239	9.25	4.37

Name	B-T	HT	WT	DOB	W	L	ERA	G	GS	CG	SV	IP	H	R	ER	HR	BB	SO	AVG	vLH	vRH	W9	H9
Montgomery, Jordan	L-L	6-6	225	12-27-92	2	0	3.62	6	6	0	0	27	25	11	11	3	12	23	.240	.000	.269	7.57	3.95
Robertson, David	R-R	5-11	195	4-9-85	8	3	3.23	69	0	0	5	70	46	30	25	7	26	91	.183	.177	.188	11.76	3.36
Sabathia, CC	L-L	6-6	300	7-21-80	9	7	3.65	29	29	0	0	153	150	72	62	19	51	140	.250	.180	.264	8.24	3.00
Severino, Luis	R-R	6-2	215	2-20-94	19	8	3.39	32	32	1	0	191	173	76	72	19	46	220	.238	.252	.227	10.35	2.16
Sheffield, Justus	L-L	6-0	200	5-13-96	0	0	10.13	3	0	0	0	3	4	3	3	1	3	0	.364	.200	.500	0.00	10.13
Shreve, Chasen	L-L	6-4	195	7-12-90	2	2	4.26	40	0	0	1	38	39	23	18	8	18	46	.262	.245	.270	10.89	4.26
Tanaka, Masahiro	R-R	6-3	215	11-1-88	12	6	3.75	27	27	1	0	156	141	68	65	25	35	159	.240	.236	.243	9.17	2.02
Tarpley, Stephen	R-L	6-1	235	2-17-93	0	0	3.00	10	0	0	0	9	6	3	3	0	6	13	.177	.067	.263	13.00	6.00
Warren, Adam	R-R	6-1	224	8-25-87	0	1	2.70	24	0	0	0	30	26	9	9	3	12	37	.228	.291	.170	11.10	3.60
2-team total (23 Seattle)					3	2	3.14	47	0	0	0	52	48	18	18	6	20	52	.240	.274	.216	9.06	3.48

Fielding

Catcher	PCT	G	PO	A	E	DP	PB
Higashioka	.996	27	225	14	1	1	2
Romine	.994	76	668	48	4	3	5
Sanchez	.992	76	731	35	6	5	18

First Base	PCT	G	PO	A	E	DP
Austin	.995	27	193	9	1	14
Bird	.996	74	503	37	2	37
Drury	1.000	2	8	1	0	0
Voit	.991	32	219	11	2	16
Walker	.997	42	271	19	1	17

Second Base	PCT	G	PO	A	E	DP
Drury	1.000	5	4	7	0	1
Torres	.970	109	163	230	12	40
Torreyes	1.000	20	19	35	0	4

	PCT	G	PO	A	E	DP
Wade	.980	26	21	28	1	8
Walker	.981	32	36	65	2	13

Third Base	PCT	G	PO	A	E	DP
Andujar	.948	136	93	178	15	6
Drury	.842	9	5	11	3	2
Hechavarria	1.000	4	0	3	0	0
Torreyes	.882	11	2	13	2	0
Wade	.000	1	0	0	0	0
Walker	.976	25	10	31	1	2

Shortstop	PCT	G	PO	A	E	DP
Gregorius	.987	132	160	309	6	54
Hechavarria	.975	16	16	23	1	5
Torres	.928	21	22	42	5	8
Torreyes	1.000	9	3	22	0	5

	PCT	G	PO	A	E	DP
Wade	1.000	2	0	3	0	0

Outfield	PCT	G	PO	A	E	DP
Frazier	1.000	10	15	0	0	0
Gardner	.989	136	265	6	3	2
Hicks	.993	131	268	2	2	0
Judge	.984	91	171	9	3	2
McCutchen	1.000	24	34	0	0	0
McKinney	1.000	2	2	0	0	0
Peterson	1.000	3	6	0	0	0
Robinson	.976	24	36	4	1	1
Stanton	.992	72	111	6	1	0
Voit	.000	1	0	0	0	0
Wade	1.000	7	4	0	0	0
Walker	.952	16	18	2	1	0

SCRANTON/WILKES-BARRE RAILRIDERS

TRIPLE-A

INTERNATIONAL LEAGUE

Batting	B-T	HT	WT	DOB	AVG	vLH	vRH	G	AB	R	H	2B	3B	HR	RBI	BB	HBP	SH	SF	SO	SB	CS	SLG	OBP
Asche, Cody	L-R	6-1	205	6-30-90	.170	.214	.156	16	59	4	10	1	0	1	1	6	1	0	0	21	0	0	.237	.258
Austin, Tyler	R-R	6-2	220	9-6-91	.253	.258	.250	26	99	14	25	9	0	6	14	8	1	0	0	32	0	0	.525	.315
2-team total (9 Rochester)					.256	.214	.274	35	137	20	35	11	1	9	22	9	2	0	0	42	0	0	.547	.311
Avelino, Abiatal	R-R	5-11	195	2-14-95	.252	.264	.246	74	274	33	69	6	6	5	38	14	1	1	0	61	10	2	.372	.291
Barrios, Daniel	R-R	5-11	183	4-18-95	.000	—	.000	3	1	0	0	0	0	0	0	0	0	0	0	0	0	0	.000	.000
Berry, Quintin	L-L	6-1	195	11-21-84	.154	.000	.182	7	13	1	2	1	0	0	0	0	0	0	0	3	0	0	.231	.154
Bird, Greg	L-R	6-4	220	11-9-92	.250	.333	.200	4	16	3	4	0	0	2	5	2	0	0	0	7	0	0	.625	.333
Bolasky, Devyn	L-L	5-11	185	1-24-93	.214	.300	.188	30	89	9	19	1	1	0	8	7	2	0	0	7	1	0	.247	.286
Caldwell, Bruce	L-R	5-11	175	11-27-91	.231	.238	.229	48	160	21	37	6	0	6	22	16	2	0	2	49	0	0	.381	.306
Castillo, Wilkin	B-R	6-0	215	6-1-84	.250	.286	.234	41	136	11	34	6	1	2	13	5	0	3	0	19	0	0	.353	.277
Conde, Vicente	R-R	6-0	195	10-13-93	.000	.000	.000	4	9	0	0	0	0	0	1	2	0	0	0	5	0	0	.000	.182
Crawford, Rashad	L-R	6-3	225	10-15-93	.333	.400	.308	16	18	5	6	1	1	0	3	1	1	1	0	2	0	0	.500	.400
Diaz, Cesar	B-R	5-10	165	4-12-93	.333	.000	1.000	2	3	1	1	0	0	0	0	1	0	0	1	0	0	0	.333	.500
Diaz, Francisco	B-R	5-11	185	3-21-90	.268	.296	.257	34	97	12	26	2	1	0	9	15	0	4	0	24	0	0	.309	.366
Drury, Brandon	R-R	6-2	210	8-21-92	.292	.327	.278	56	199	30	58	13	1	5	30	32	4	0	0	58	3	1	.442	.400
Estrada, Thairo	R-R	5-10	185	2-22-96	.152	.250	.120	8	33	1	5	1	0	0	3	0	1	0	0	8	0	0	.182	.177
Fleming, Billy	R-R	6-1	210	9-20-92	.275	.345	.242	27	91	12	25	7	0	0	6	2	1	1	0	19	0	0	.352	.330
Ford, Mike	L-R	6-0	225	7-4-92	.253	.220	.267	102	367	48	93	21	0	15	52	37	4	0	2	70	1	0	.433	.327
Frazier, Clint	R-R	6-1	190	9-6-94	.311	.348	.299	48	190	38	59	14	3	10	21	23	2	0	1	52	4	2	.574	.389
Hicks, Aaron	B-R	6-1	202	10-2-89	.333	.000	.400	2	6	0	2	1	0	0	0	1	0	0	0	0	0	0	.500	.429
Higashioka, Kyle	R-R	6-1	205	4-20-90	.202	.203	.202	53	188	16	38	10	1	5	22	17	3	0	2	44	2	0	.346	.276
Kratz, Erik	R-R	6-4	250	6-15-80	.269	.313	.250	17	52	10	14	2	0	4	6	7	0	1	0	10	0	0	.539	.356
Lind, Adam	L-L	6-2	195	7-17-83	.241	.333	.209	16	58	7	14	4	0	2	7	5	0	0	0	13	0	1	.414	.302
2-team total (47 Pawtucket)					.223	.228	.221	63	229	28	51	11	0	10	39	19	0	0	4	49	0	1	.402	.278
Mazzilli, L.J.	R-R	6-1	190	9-6-90	.244	.250	.241	79	230	28	56	15	0	7	25	22	3	1	2	44	1	2	.400	.315
McBroom, Ryan	R-L	6-3	235	4-9-92	.295	.273	.305	96	359	49	106	18	1	11	46	25	2	0	6	106	1	4	.443	.339
McKinney, Billy	L-L	6-1	205	8-23-94	.226	.225	.227	56	212	27	48	8	5	13	32	21	1	0	0	56	0	0	.495	.299
2-team total (20 Buffalo)					.221	.206	.229	76	276	37	61	11	7	16	40	29	1	0	0	72	0	0	.486	.297
Navarro, Rey	R-R	5-10	185	12-22-89	.242	.321	.214	62	215	20	52	6	0	10	28	13	0	1	0	28	1	1	.409	.285
Payton, Mark	L-L	5-8	190	12-7-91	.259	.213	.273	62	197	29	51	6	2	6	25	34	1	3	2	49	2	6	.401	.368
Peterson, Jace	L-R	6-0	215	5-9-90	.250	—	.250	1	4	1	1	0	0	0	0	0	0	0	0	1	0	0	.250	.250
Robinson, Shane	R-R	5-9	170	10-30-84	.261	.193	.290	50	188	25	49	7	3	0	14	8	2	3	1	29	9	0	.330	.297
Sanchez, Gary	R-R	6-2	230	12-2-92	.179	.000	.192	7	28	4	5	0	0	4	4	0	0	0	0	10	0	0	.607	.179
Surum, Ricky	R-R	5-10	170	12-7-94	.240	.375	.177	10	25	4	6	1	0	0	3	2	0	0	0	6	1	1	.280	.296
Torres, Gleyber	R-R	6-1	200	12-13-96	.347	.250	.394	14	49	6	17	3	1	1	11	5	0	0	2	10	1	1	.510	.393
Torreyes, Ronald	R-R	5-8	151	9-2-92	.247	.233	.254	26	97	9	24	3	0	0	8	7	1	0	1	11	0	0	.278	.302
Urshela, Gio	R-R	6-0	215	10-11-91	.307	.364	.291	27	101	14	31	7	2	2	12	4	1	1	0	13	0	0	.475	.340
3-team total (24 Buffalo, 11 Columbus)					.286	.300	.282	62	224	27	64	14	2	2	24	13	1	1	1	31	0	0	.393	.326
Voit, Luke	R-R	6-3	225	2-13-91	.310	.167	.348	9	29	2	9	2	0	1	3	3	0	0	0	7	0	0	.483	.375
Wade, Tyler	L-R	6-1	185	11-23-94	.256	.234	.265	91	364	46	93	18	4	4	27	37	3	2	2	82	11	8	.360	.328
Zehner, Zack	R-R	6-4	220	8-8-92	.262	.319	.237	87	302	39	79	19	3	10	42	23	4	1	2	94	1	1	.444	.320

Pitching

Pitching	B-T	HT	WT	DOB	W	L	ERA	G	GS	CG	SV	IP	H	R	ER	HR	BB	SO	AVG	vLH	vRH	K/9	BB/9
Adams, Chance	R-R	6-1	220	8-10-94	4	5	4.78	27	23	2	0	113	101	65	60	16	58	113	.236	.249	.221	9.00	4.62
Bollinger, Ryan	L-L	6-5	230	2-4-91	0	1	3.00	3	3	0	0	15	12	6	5	1	5	10	.235	.133	.278	6.00	3.00
Camarena, Daniel	L-L	6-0	210	11-9-92	2	3	5.08	8	8	0	0	39	44	23	22	3	20	34	.288	.256	.298	7.85	4.62
Carroll, Cody	R-R	6-5	215	10-15-92	3	0	2.38	32	0	0	9	42	27	13	11	0	18	55	.184	.254	.125	11.88	3.89
2-team total (5 Norfolk)					4	0	2.72	37	0	0	9	46	31	16	14	0	22	58	.188	.257	.132	11.27	4.27
Cessa, Luis	R-R	6-0	210	4-25-92	3	0	2.73	6	5	0	0	26	19	9	8	1	4	25	.196	.235	.152	8.54	1.37
Cole, A.J.	R-R	6-5	238	1-5-92	0	1	27.00	2	1	0	0	2	6	5	5	1	3	1	.546	.333	.625	5.40	16.20
Cortes, Nestor	R-L	5-11	205	12-10-94	6	6	3.71	23	18	1	0	112	95	50	46	13	37	96	.228	.172	.257	7.74	2.98
Coshow, Cale	R-R	6-5	270	7-16-92	1	4	4.95	38	0	0	5	56	54	35	31	9	28	66	.249	.224	.273	10.54	4.47
Espinal, Raynel	R-R	6-3	199	10-6-91	7	2	3.09	41	3	0	2	67	55	27	23	4	26	95	.222	.233	.211	12.76	3.49
Feyereisen, J.P.	R-R	6-2	215	2-7-93	6	6	3.45	37	0	0	1	60	56	24	23	5	25	59	.253	.231	.274	8.85	3.75
Frare, Caleb	L-L	6-1	210	7-8-93	0	0	9.00	1	0	0	0	1	2	1	1	0	0	1	.400	.000	.500	9.00	0.00
2-team total (11 Charlotte)					1	0	1.32	12	0	0	0	14	7	2	2	0	7	20	.149	.105	.179	13.17	4.61
Gallegos, Giovanny	R-R	6-2	210	8-14-91	2	1	3.90	17	0	0	2	28	24	13	12	1	7	41	.231	.205	.250	13.34	2.28
German, Domingo	R-R	6-2	175	8-4-92	0	0	18.00	1	1	0	0	1	2	2	2	1	0	0	.400	.000	.500	0.00	0.00
Gomez, Anyelo	R-R	6-1	185	3-1-93	0	1	2.45	7	0	0	1	7	7	3	2	1	3	8	.250	.294	.182	9.82	3.68
Hale, David	R-R	6-2	210	9-27-87	3	2	4.20	11	11	0	0	56	58	27	26	5	17	44	.261	.215	.317	7.11	2.75
Harvey, Joe	R-R	6-2	235	1-9-92	3	2	1.66	38	0	0	8	54	33	11	10	1	21	61	.174	.165	.182	10.10	3.48
Holder, Jonathan	R-R	6-2	235	6-9-93	1	0	3.00	4	1	0	0	6	5	2	2	1	1	8	.217	.267	.125	12.00	1.50
Kahnle, Tommy	R-R	6-1	235	8-7-89	2	2	4.01	25	0	0	1	25	23	14	11	2	11	37	.245	.182	.300	13.50	4.01
King, Michael	R-R	6-3	210	5-25-95	4	0	1.15	6	6	1	0	39	20	5	5	3	6	31	.147	.187	.098	7.15	1.38
Koerner, Brody	R-R	6-2	220	10-17-93	1	3	5.65	9	5	0	0	37	40	24	23	2	9	20	.276	.243	.310	4.91	2.21
Kontos, George	R-R	6-3	225	6-12-85	1	2	3.24	8	0	0	0	8	10	3	3	1	1	4	.313	.278	.357	4.32	1.08
2-team total (14 Columbus)					3	2	1.85	22	0	0	3	24	25	5	5	1	1	16	.278	.167	.352	5.92	0.37
Lail, Brady	R-R	6-2	205	8-9-93	4	6	5.36	27	0	0	0	44	43	28	26	6	28	46	.259	.284	.242	9.48	5.77
Perez, Oliver	L-L	6-3	225	8-15-81	1	0	2.57	16	0	0	0	14	17	5	4	1	3	15	.327	.357	.292	9.64	1.93
Reeves, James	R-L	6-3	215	6-7-93	0	0	5.40	1	0	0	0	2	1	1	1	0	3	1	.200	.000	.500	5.40	16.20
Rogers, Josh	L-L	6-3	220	7-10-94	6	8	3.95	19	19	1	0	109	118	53	48	13	29	83	.273	.211	.299	6.83	2.39
2-team total (5 Norfolk)					8	9	3.54	24	24	1	0	140	144	62	55	16	36	101	.263	.201	.290	6.51	2.32
Rosa, Adonis	R-R	6-1	160	11-17-94	2	1	3.92	4	4	0	0	21	23	13	9	3	7	14	.267	.171	.356	6.10	3.05
Sheffield, Justus	L-L	6-0	200	5-13-96	6	4	2.56	20	15	0	0	88	66	28	25	3	36	84	.204	.176	.216	8.59	3.68
Sosebee, David	R-R	6-2	220	8-25-93	0	0	1.59	4	0	0	0	6	5	2	1	1	3	6	.227	.100	.333	9.53	4.76
Swanson, Erik	R-R	6-3	235	9-4-93	3	2	3.86	14	13	1	0	72	63	32	31	10	14	78	.230	.199	.261	9.71	1.74
Tanaka, Masahiro	R-R	6-3	215	11-1-88	0	0	3.60	1	1	0	0	5	3	2	2	1	0	4	.167	.200	.125	7.20	0.00
Tarpley, Stephen	R-L	6-1	235	2-17-93	2	2	2.65	17	0	0	0	34	23	10	10	3	11	38	.192	.151	.224	10.06	2.91
Warren, Adam	R-R	6-1	224	8-25-87	0	1	54.00	1	1	0	0	1	4	4	0	2	1	.333	.000	.500	13.50	27.00

Fielding

Catcher

Catcher	PCT	G	PO	A	E	DP	PB
Castillo	.992	39	344	10	3	0	5
Diaz	1.000	33	265	12	0	2	4
Higashioka	.986	49	410	26	6	4	2
Kratz	.987	17	141	10	2	0	2
Sanchez	1.000	5	33	4	0	1	0

First Base

First Base	PCT	G	PO	A	E	DP
Austin	.976	17	118	3	3	8
Bird	.958	3	21	2	1	1
Castillo	1.000	1	7	1	0	2
Drury	1.000	5	27	3	0	3
Ford	.998	57	378	31	1	33
Lind	1.000	5	32	2	0	5
McBroom	1.000	45	351	30	0	22
McKinney	.950	2	18	1	1	0
Navarro	1.000	2	3	1	0	2
Voit	.913	3	20	1	2	1

Second Base

Second Base	PCT	G	PO	A	E	DP
Avelino	.938	16	21	39	4	5
Barrios	.000	1	0	0	0	0
Caldwell	.978	12	16	28	1	9
Conde	1.000	1	3	3	0	1
Drury	1.000	2	2	2	0	0
Estrada	.950	3	6	13	1	3

Third Base

Third Base	PCT	G	PO	A	E	DP
Fleming	.975	12	11	28	1	5
Mazzilli	.940	44	59	97	10	13
Navarro	.957	26	29	37	3	10
Surum	1.000	8	11	13	0	1
Torres	.917	3	3	8	1	2
Torreyes	1.000	11	12	17	0	2
Urshela	1.000	1	1	5	0	0
Wade	.954	10	22	40	3	10

Shortstop

Third Base	PCT	G	PO	A	E	DP
Asche	1.000	6	8	2	0	0
Avelino	1.000	3	1	1	0	0
Caldwell	.978	31	30	61	2	5
Castillo	.000	1	0	0	0	0
Conde	1.000	3	2	4	0	0
Drury	.954	45	24	80	5	11
Fleming	.944	9	7	10	1	0
Mazzilli	.000	1	0	0	1	0
Navarro	1.000	12	4	16	0	2
Surum	.000	1	0	0	0	0
Torres	1.000	8	3	11	0	0
Torreyes	1.000	6	7	6	0	0
Urshela	1.000	20	8	26	0	3
Wade	1.000	3	5	5	0	3

Shortstop	PCT	G	PO	A	E	DP
Avelino	.989	52	65	117	2	22

Outfield

	PCT	G	PO	A	E	DP
Estrada	1.000	5	9	12	0	2
Navarro	.938	21	22	39	4	6
Torres	.938	3	6	9	1	3
Torreyes	1.000	6	4	13	0	2
Urshela	.950	8	10	9	1	3
Wade	.967	51	62	112	6	18

Outfield	PCT	G	PO	A	E	DP
Asche	1.000	6	7	0	0	0
Austin	1.000	3	7	0	0	0
Avelino	1.000	1	4	0	0	0
Berry	1.000	6	15	0	0	0
Bolasky	.982	29	54	1	1	0
Crawford	1.000	6	8	0	0	0
Diaz	.000	2	0	0	0	0
Frazier	.989	46	89	3	1	0
Hicks	1.000	2	2	0	0	0
Mazzilli	1.000	23	38	2	0	0
McBroom	.989	43	84	2	1	0
McKinney	.990	48	101	2	1	0
Payton	.982	55	108	2	2	0
Peterson	1.000	1	2	0	0	0
Robinson	.993	50	131	3	1	2
Torreyes	1.000	2	0	0	0	0
Wade	.946	30	67	3	4	0
Zehner	.958	78	156	4	7	0

TRENTON THUNDER   DOUBLE-A
EASTERN LEAGUE

Batting	B-T	HT	WT	DOB	AVG	vLH	vRH	G	AB	R	H	2B	3B	HR	RBI	BB	HBP	SH	SF	SO	SB	CS	SLG	OBP
Aguilar, Angel	R-R	6-0	170	6-13-95	.083	.500	.000	4	12	2	1	0	0	1	1	2	0	0	0	5	0	0	.333	.214
Alvarez, Mandy	R-R	6-1	195	7-14-94	.262	.286	.253	99	359	54	94	25	3	11	54	25	3	0	2	48	2	1	.440	.314
Amburgey, Trey	R-R	6-2	210	10-24-94	.258	.302	.241	125	481	65	124	25	2	16	74	22	9	0	5	108	12	2	.418	.300
Avelino, Abiatal	R-R	5-11	195	2-14-95	.337	.311	.345	49	190	32	64	7	2	10	28	18	0	2	1	37	15	4	.553	.392

Name	B-T	HT	WT	DOB	AVG	vLH	vRH	G	AB	R	H	2B	3B	HR	RBI	BB	HBP	SH	SF	SO	SB	CS	OBP	SLG
Bird, Greg	L-R	6-4	220	11-9-92	.133	.333	.000	5	15	5	2	0	0	1	1	5	0	0	0	2	0	0	.333	.350
Bolasky, Devyn	L-L	5-11	185	1-24-93	.365	.268	.402	38	148	19	54	6	2	0	11	12	2	0	1	16	0	1	.432	.417
Caldwell, Bruce	L-R	5-11	175	11-27-91	.274	.265	.279	74	266	32	73	24	1	4	35	38	0	1	2	72	1	1	.417	.363
Conde, Vicente	R-R	6-0	195	10-13-93	.119	.046	.156	25	67	7	8	2	0	1	6	10	0	2	1	14	0	0	.194	.231
Crawford, Rashad	L-R	6-3	225	10-15-93	.223	.200	.233	52	184	14	41	7	1	2	21	17	3	1	1	52	8	4	.304	.298
Deglan, Kellin	L-R	6-2	205	5-3-92	.100	.000	.167	3	10	0	1	0	0	0	0	0	0	0	0	3	0	0	.100	.100
Diaz, Andy	L-L	5-11	190	11-21-95	.000	.000	.000	1	3	0	0	0	0	0	0	0	0	0	0	2	0	0	.000	.000
Diaz, Cesar	B-R	5-10	165	4-12-93	.276	.222	.300	10	29	5	8	1	0	1	10	5	0	1	1	6	2	0	.414	.371
Diaz, Francisco	B-R	5-11	185	3-21-90	.344	.444	.327	19	64	12	22	4	0	1	12	8	0	1	0	12	0	0	.453	.417
Drury, Brandon	R-R	6-2	210	8-21-92	.263	.167	.308	6	19	4	5	0	0	1	2	5	0	0	1	10	0	0	.421	.400
Fleming, Billy	R-R	6-1	210	9-20-92	.298	.333	.288	44	168	22	50	12	1	6	23	16	1	0	3	35	2	1	.488	.356
Gittens, Chris	R-R	6-4	250	2-4-94	.197	.095	.227	53	183	21	36	8	0	6	26	27	1	0	2	65	0	1	.339	.301
Hendrix, Jeff	L-R	6-0	195	7-16-93	.195	.128	.217	91	308	34	60	7	1	1	21	46	9	5	2	114	8	5	.234	.315
Holder, Kyle	L-R	6-1	185	5-25-94	.248	.200	.273	32	117	10	29	4	1	1	10	8	1	4	2	15	0	1	.325	.297
Jackson, Jhalan	R-R	6-4	240	2-12-93	.205	.277	.179	102	346	52	71	16	2	17	44	38	8	1	2	148	7	2	.410	.297
Katoh, Gosuke	L-R	6-2	200	10-8-94	.229	.142	.259	118	433	55	99	27	2	5	35	62	3	2	3	123	11	6	.335	.327
Lidge, Ryan	B-R	6-2	216	10-27-94	.206	.138	.233	30	102	9	21	1	0	1	7	7	0	1	0	17	1	2	.245	.319
McBroom, Ryan	R-L	6-3	235	4-9-92	.324	.367	.306	25	102	13	33	5	1	4	14	7	2	0	0	27	0	3	.510	.378
McKinney, Billy	L-L	6-1	205	8-23-94	.222	.429	.091	5	18	2	4	1	0	0	3	0	0	0	4	1	1	.278	.333
Navarro, Rey	B-R	5-10	185	12-22-89	.188	.077	.263	10	32	3	6	2	0	1	2	0	1	0	1	6	0	0	.344	.206
Numata, Chace	B-R	6-0	175	8-14-92	.180	.250	.156	38	128	6	23	6	1	0	8	7	0	0	0	25	1	1	.242	.222
Perez, Danienger	R-R	5-10	155	11-6-96	.222	.273	.188	9	27	4	6	0	0	1	3	4	0	1	0	7	0	0	.333	.323
Rabago, Chris	R-R	5-11	185	4-22-93	.071	.000	.125	7	28	1	2	0	0	0	0	2	0	0	0	10	0	0	.071	.133
2-team total (66 Hartford)					.196	.158	.208	73	230	23	45	14	2	4	23	24	1	2	1	62	9	1	.326	.273
Rijo, Wendell	R-R	5-11	170	9-4-95	.217	.276	.188	49	175	19	38	10	1	0	12	20	0	2	0	29	2	2	.286	.297
Ruta, Ben	L-R	6-3	195	6-8-94	.314	.514	.233	36	121	17	38	8	1	0	13	11	0	0	2	25	12	3	.397	.366
Saez, Jorge	R-R	5-10	200	8-28-90	.237	.243	.235	47	152	20	36	4	0	5	19	10	1	0	1	42	2	2	.362	.324
Snyder, Matt	L-R	6-5	230	6-17-90	.267	.250	.273	4	15	2	4	1	0	0	1	0	0	0	0	4	0	1	.333	.267
Surum, Ricky	L-R	5-10	170	12-7-94	.000	.000	.214	5	15	3	3	0	1	0	1	1	0	0	1	4	0	0	.333	.235
Wagner, Brandon	L-R	6-0	210	8-24-95	.262	.233	.276	37	130	16	34	8	0	1	10	27	1	0	1	38	1	0	.346	.390
Zehner, Zack	R-R	6-4	220	8-8-92	.293	.286	.296	32	116	15	34	6	3	4	21	17	1	0	1	33	2	2	.500	.385

Pitching	B-T	HT	WT	DOB	W	L	ERA	G	GS	CG	SV	IP	H	R	ER	HR	BB	SO	AVG	vLH	vRH	K/9	BB/9
Abreu, Albert	R-R	6-2	175	9-26-95	0	0	0.00	1	1	0	0	5	0	0	0	0	1	4	.000	.000	.000	7.20	1.80
Acevedo, Domingo	R-R	6-7	250	3-6-94	3	3	2.92	14	10	0	0	65	51	24	21	3	20	52	.217	.188	.239	7.24	2.78
Bollinger, Ryan	L-L	6-2	230	2-4-91	8	5	4.00	17	17	0	0	97	90	45	43	6	28	87	.246	.217	.256	8.10	2.61
Carter, Will	L-R	6-3	195	1-18-93	0	2	6.07	7	0	0	0	30	33	24	20	1	23	20	.285	.298	.271	6.07	6.98
Cessa, Luis	R-R	6-0	210	4-25-92	0	1	2.70	2	2	0	0	10	6	3	3	1	1	12	.167	.192	.100	10.80	0.90
Cortes, Nestor	R-L	5-11	205	12-10-94	0	0	2.70	1	0	0	0	3	3	1	1	0	1	3	.250	.167	.333	8.10	2.70
Diehl, Phillip	L-L	6-2	180	7-16-94	0	1	1.35	14	0	0	1	27	18	4	4	2	11	29	.196	.235	.172	9.79	3.71
Foley, Jordan	R-R	6-4	225	7-12-93	4	4	2.98	37	2	0	10	66	65	27	22	6	35	67	.265	.281	.252	9.09	4.75
Frare, Caleb	L-L	6-1	210	7-8-93	4	1	0.62	31	0	0	5	44	25	5	3	1	15	57	.167	.167	.167	11.75	3.09
Frawley, Matt	R-R	6-1	195	8-8-95	1	1	5.56	15	0	0	0	23	23	14	14	4	11	17	.267	.273	.264	6.75	4.37
Garcia, Deivi	R-R	5-10	163	5-19-99	1	0	0.00	1	1	0	0	5	0	0	0	0	2	7	.000	.000	.000	12.60	3.60
Green, Nick	R-R	6-1	175	3-25-95	1	2	3.63	3	0	0	0	17	12	9	7	2	7	9	.200	.200	.200	4.67	3.63
Harris, Hobie	R-R	6-3	200	6-23-93	1	1	4.70	5	0	0	0	8	8	7	4	3	8	7	.258	.313	.200	8.22	9.39
Harvey, Joe	R-R	6-2	235	1-9-92	0	0	1.80	5	0	0	3	5	1	1	1	1	4	7	.063	.000	.111	12.60	7.20
Hodson, Chase	L-R	6-1	205	7-10-92	1	1	4.60	11	0	0	0	16	16	8	8	1	10	14	.271	.231	.303	8.04	5.74
Kamplain, Justin	R-L	6-0	175	2-13-93	1	1	7.20	2	0	0	0	5	2	5	4	0	3	5	.118	.400	.000	9.00	5.40
Keller, Brian	R-R	6-3	210	6-21-94	10	9	3.74	22	21	0	0	125	120	55	52	13	37	114	.253	.253	.253	8.21	2.66
King, Michael	R-R	6-3	210	5-25-95	6	2	2.09	12	11	1	0	82	65	23	19	4	13	76	.220	.218	.221	8.34	1.43
Koerner, Brody	R-R	6-2	220	10-17-93	1	1	3.33	12	2	0	0	27	26	15	10	1	9	21	.255	.292	.222	7.00	3.00
Lail, Brady	R-R	6-2	205	8-9-93	1	0	5.59	10	0	0	0	19	22	12	12	2	8	20	.297	.257	.333	9.31	3.72
Lane, Trevor	L-L	5-11	185	4-26-94	1	1	3.98	11	0	0	0	20	26	13	9	1	6	21	.299	.259	.317	9.30	2.66
Loaisiga, Jonathan	R-R	5-11	165	11-2-94	3	1	3.93	9	9	0	0	34	37	15	15	6	6	40	.278	.324	.226	10.49	1.57
Mesa Jr., Jose	R-R	6-4	215	8-13-93	2	1	5.19	9	0	0	0	17	14	11	10	4	12	21	.212	.226	.190	10.90	6.23
Nelson, Nick	R-R	6-1	195	12-5-95	0	0	5.19	3	3	0	0	9	10	6	5	1	9	10	.278	.318	.214	10.38	9.35
Ort, Kaleb	R-R	6-4	240	2-5-92	1	1	2.18	22	0	0	3	33	23	10	8	0	22	42	.193	.170	.217	11.45	6.00
Reeves, James	R-L	6-3	215	6-7-93	2	2	2.80	32	0	0	2	55	32	19	17	4	31	71	.166	.161	.168	11.69	5.10
Rosa, Adonis	R-R	6-1	160	11-17-94	0	2	4.63	2	2	0	0	12	12	7	6	1	0	5	.255	.261	.250	3.86	0.00
Sanmartin, Reiver	L-L	6-2	160	4-15-96	0	1	1.80	1	1	0	0	5	4	2	1	0	0	4	.222	.000	.286	7.20	0.00
Schwaab, Andrew	R-R	6-1	205	2-8-93	1	1	4.42	13	0	0	1	18	11	9	9	0	11	19	.213	.171	.269	9.33	5.40
2-team total (7 Erie)					2	3	4.85	20	0	0	1	26	26	16	14	1	14	25	.271	.255	.289	8.65	4.85
Sheffield, Justus	L-L	6-0	200	5-13-96	1	2	2.25	5	5	0	0	28	16	9	7	1	14	39	.163	.094	.197	12.54	4.50
Sosebee, David	R-R	6-2	220	8-25-93	4	2	3.66	20	0	0	1	32	35	19	13	4	13	39	.282	.322	.246	10.97	3.66
Stephan, Trevor	R-R	6-5	225	11-25-95	3	8	4.54	17	17	0	0	83	80	43	42	5	29	91	.253	.273	.235	9.83	3.13
Swanson, Erik	R-R	6-3	235	9-4-93	5	0	0.42	8	7	0	0	43	22	3	2	0	15	55	.155	.143	.160	11.60	3.15
Tarpley, Stephen	R-L	6-1	235	2-17-93	5	0	1.26	19	0	0	2	36	18	7	5	0	13	33	.145	.143	.146	8.33	3.79
Tate, Dillon	R-R	6-2	195	5-1-94	5	2	3.38	15	15	0	0	83	67	33	31	7	25	75	.218	.186	.247	8.17	2.72
2-team total (7 Bowie)					7	5	4.16	22	22	0	0	123	115	60	57	10	34	96	.247	.227	.266	7.01	2.48
Vargas, Alexander	R-R	6-4	203	7-24-97	0	0	2.25	2	2	0	0	8	6	2	2	0	4	7	.222	.231	.214	7.88	4.50
Warren, Adam	R-R	6-1	224	8-25-87	0	0	0.00	1	1	0	0	1	0	0	0	0	0	3	.100	.000	.167	9.00	0.00
Whitlock, Garrett	R-R	6-5	190	6-11-96	1	0	0.84	2	1	0	0	11	7	1	1	0	7	4	.263	.182	.296	3.38	5.91
Wivinis, Matt	R-R	6-0	170	7-24-93	1	1	4.86	12	0	0	0	17	13	11	9	2	6	19	.220	.316	.175	10.26	3.24
Young, Paul	R-R	6-2	205	3-15-93	0	0	40.50	1	0	0	0	1	5	6	6	0	1	2	.625	.500	1.000	13.50	6.75

NEW YORK YANKEES

Fielding

Catcher	PCT	G	PO	A	E	DP	PB
Deglan	1.000	3	25	1	0	1	0
Diaz	1.000	19	177	14	0	2	1
Lidge	.993	33	266	27	2	2	3
Numata	.994	38	307	22	2	3	11
Rabago	.986	7	66	7	1	1	0
Saez	.988	43	379	29	5	3	3

First Base	PCT	G	PO	A	E	DP
Alvarez	.857	1	6	0	1	0
Bird	.938	4	29	1	2	2
Caldwell	1.000	3	17	1	0	1
Fleming	1.000	18	131	3	0	13
Gittens	.986	41	269	18	4	32
Katoh	1.000	36	221	19	0	24
McBroom	.988	20	142	20	2	15
Snyder	1.000	1	5	0	0	0
Wagner	1.000	22	171	12	0	21

Second Base	PCT	G	PO	A	E	DP
Aguilar	1.000	1	0	3	0	0
Alvarez	1.000	1	4	5	0	0
Avelino	1.000	2	0	7	0	0
Caldwell	.975	57	104	126	6	44
Conde	1.000	2	1	5	0	1
Fleming	.962	13	19	31	2	6
Katoh	1.000	33	58	80	0	20
Navarro	.875	3	2	5	1	0
Perez	.833	1	3	2	1	1
Rijo	1.000	20	36	50	0	14
Surum	1.000	1	2	4	0	2
Wagner	.971	9	21	13	1	3

Third Base	PCT	G	PO	A	E	DP
Aguilar	1.000	2	3	6	0	1
Alvarez	.954	87	67	140	10	17
Caldwell	.000	2	0	0	1	0
Drury	1.000	4	4	5	0	0
Fleming	1.000	9	8	14	0	4
Katoh	.981	24	13	40	1	2
Navarro	1.000	3	1	2	0	0
Perez	.800	5	4	4	2	1
Rijo	.750	2	0	3	1	0
Wagner	.500	4	2	1	3	0

Shortstop	PCT	G	PO	A	E	DP
Aguilar	1.000	1	1	0	0	0
Avelino	.944	44	56	112	10	25
Conde	.899	22	24	38	7	5
Holder	1.000	28	29	68	0	17
Katoh	.929	19	24	41	5	9
Navarro	1.000	4	4	4	0	2
Perez	1.000	1	1	5	0	1
Rijo	.957	20	34	54	4	12
Surum	1.000	4	6	13	0	4

Outfield	PCT	G	PO	A	E	DP
Amburgey	.996	103	214	8	1	1
Bolasky	.960	31	47	1	2	0
Crawford	.983	50	117	2	2	1
Diaz	1.000	1	3	0	0	0
Diaz	1.000	9	14	1	0	0
Hendrix	.995	83	194	9	1	4
Jackson	.993	82	146	2	1	1
Katoh	1.000	7	9	0	0	0
McBroom	1.000	2	5	0	0	0
McKinney	1.000	5	14	0	0	0
Ruta	.982	31	53	1	1	0
Zehner	.981	23	53	0	1	0

TAMPA TARPONS

HIGH CLASS A

FLORIDA STATE LEAGUE

Batting	B-T	HT	WT	DOB	AVG	vLH	vRH	G	AB	R	H	2B	3B	HR	RBI	BB	HBP	SH	SF	SO	SB	CS	SLG	OBP
Aguilar, Angel	R-R	6-0	170	6-13-95	.232	.215	.241	114	413	45	96	19	7	10	51	15	5	2	4	103	12	6	.385	.265
Alvarez, Mandy	R-R	6-1	195	7-14-94	.185	.000	.227	9	27	5	5	0	0	2	2	5	0	0	0	6	0	0	.407	.313
Barrios, Daniel	R-R	5-11	183	4-18-95	.182	.120	.212	26	77	7	14	1	0	1	7	11	0	0	0	34	0	1	.234	.284
Bird, Greg	L-R	6-4	220	11-9-92	.250	.400	.000	3	8	1	2	0	0	0	2	3	0	0	0	2	0	0	.250	.455
Cabrera, Leobaldo	R-R	6-0	170	1-21-98	.429	.500	.400	2	7	2	3	0	0	0	0	2	0	0	0	2	0	0	.429	.556
Castillo, Diego	R-R	6-0	170	10-28-97	.260	.277	.253	120	469	58	122	20	2	2	51	30	3	9	3	47	11	4	.324	.307
Conde, Vicente	R-R	6-0	195	10-13-93	.000	.000	.000	1	3	0	0	0	0	0	0	0	0	0	0	2	0	0	.000	.000
Coronado, Nathaniel	R-R	6-3	205	6-5-92	.206	.333	.063	10	34	3	7	0	0	0	3	3	0	0	0	10	0	0	.206	.270
Crawford, Rashad	L-R	6-3	225	10-15-93	.238	.200	.250	23	80	9	19	5	1	0	9	8	0	2	0	25	0	2	.325	.307
Deglan, Kellin	R-L	6-2	205	5-3-92	.184	.150	.192	32	98	8	18	6	0	2	14	9	3	1	0	32	0	0	.306	.273
Diaz, Cesar	B-R	5-10	165	4-12-93	.333	.500	.316	5	21	2	7	0	1	0	1	0	0	1	0	4	0	0	.429	.364
Diaz, Francisco	B-R	5-11	185	3-21-90	.213	.188	.222	21	61	9	13	2	0	0	7	13	2	1	0	13	0	0	.246	.368
Estrada, Thairo	R-R	5-10	185	2-20-96	.222	.188	.241	10	45	4	10	2	0	0	2	0	0	5	0	9	0	0	.267	.234
Florial, Estevan	L-R	6-1	185	11-25-97	.255	.278	.245	75	294	45	75	16	3	3	27	44	1	0	0	87	11	10	.361	.354
Frazier, Clint	R-R	6-1	190	9-6-94	.250	.000	.294	6	20	6	5	1	0	1	3	4	1	0	1	3	2	0	.450	.385
Gilliam, Isiah	B-R	6-3	220	7-23-96	.260	.244	.268	125	474	59	123	22	2	13	71	36	4	0	6	151	4	5	.397	.314
Holder, Kyle	L-R	6-1	185	5-25-94	.267	.177	.321	11	45	7	12	1	0	2	12	6	1	0	0	5	1	1	.422	.365
Lidge, Ryan	B-R	6-2	216	10-27-94	.333	.300	.350	9	30	7	10	0	0	2	6	3	0	0	1	4	0	0	.533	.382
Lind, Adam	L-L	6-2	195	7-17-83	.429	.333	.500	8	28	5	12	2	0	1	7	3	0	0	0	4	0	0	.607	.484
Lopez, Jason	R-R	5-10	160	3-16-98	.196	.294	.138	13	46	6	9	3	1	0	5	2	0	0	2	11	0	0	.304	.220
Lynch, Tim	L-R	6-2	220	6-3-93	.197	.130	.226	23	76	5	15	3	0	1	9	5	2	0	1	15	0	0	.276	.262
McGarry, Matt	R-R	5-10	175	3-24-96	.286	.333	.000	2	7	1	2	1	0	0	1	0	0	0	0	1	0	0	.429	.286
McKinney, Billy	L-L	6-1	205	8-23-94	.250	.250	.250	3	8	1	2	1	0	0	3	4	0	0	0	2	0	0	.375	.500
Metzgar, David	R-R	5-8	170	12-10-94	.200	.333	.152	15	45	7	9	1	0	0	4	6	1	1	1	10	1	0	.267	.302
Mora, Gabriel	R-R	5-11	155	6-1-00	.111	.000	.167	4	9	1	1	0	0	0	1	0	0	0	0	3	0	0	.111	.200
Numata, Chace	B-R	6-0	170	1-26-96	.286	.167	.318	9	28	7	8	2	1	1	3	3	1	0	0	4	0	0	.536	.375
Olivares, Pablo	R-R	6-0	160	1-27-98	.244	.308	.214	14	41	7	10	0	0	2	4	4	1	4	0	11	0	0	.390	.326
Palma, Alexander	R-R	6-0	201	10-18-95	.299	.420	.232	52	194	27	58	8	1	7	26	11	4	0	1	28	3	1	.459	.348
Park, Hoy Jun	L-R	6-1	175	4-7-96	.258	.296	.243	103	341	46	88	9	2	6	34	68	5	5	2	69	18	5	.349	.387
Pita, Matt	R-R	5-10	175	4-21-97	.000	.000	.000	3	7	0	0	0	0	0	0	0	0	0	0	4	0	0	.000	.125
Rijo, Wendell	R-R	5-11	170	9-4-95	.125	.000	.200	3	8	1	1	0	0	0	1	1	2	0	1	3	0	0	.250	.333
Robinson, Timmy	R-R	6-1	225	6-17-94	.216	.280	.184	28	74	10	16	6	0	2	10	15	2	0	1	31	1	0	.378	.359
Ruta, Ben	L-R	6-3	195	6-8-94	.295	.283	.300	83	326	44	96	17	6	8	40	24	1	2	1	53	25	13	.457	.344
Sands, Donny	R-R	6-2	190	5-16-96	.267	.095	.323	25	86	10	23	5	0	0	7	5	2	0	1	22	0	0	.326	.319
Seitz, Jerry	R-R	5-10	180	9-27-94	.091	.000	.200	3	11	1	1	0	0	0	0	0	0	0	0	6	0	0	.091	.091
Sensley, Steven	L-L	6-1	220	9-6-95	.203	.226	.189	43	143	19	29	3	0	7	16	17	1	0	0	47	0	0	.371	.292
Skinner, Keith	L-R	6-1	200	4-14-94	.221	.229	.216	27	86	8	19	3	1	0	4	9	1	0	0	19	2	1	.279	.302
Surum, Ricky	R-R	5-10	170	12-7-94	.205	.250	.188	13	44	3	9	1	0	0	2	1	0	1	0	12	2	2	.227	.222
Thompson-Williams, Dom	L-L	6-0	191	4-21-95	.290	.313	.281	90	331	56	96	16	4	17	65	31	5	0	4	95	17	7	.517	.356
Torrealba, Eduardo	R-R	5-8	140	3-26-99	.125	.000	.143	3	8	1	1	0	0	0	1	0	1	0	0	1	0	0	.125	.222
Torres, Gleyber	R-R	6-1	200	12-13-96	.333	.000	.375	3	9	3	3	1	0	0	2	0	0	0	0	1	0	0	.444	.455
Torres, Miguel	R-R	6-0	170	3-3-00	.111	.000	.125	3	9	1	1	0	0	0	0	0	1	0	0	4	0	0	.111	.200
Torreyes, Ronald	R-R	5-8	151	9-2-92	.286	.000	.333	4	14	2	4	0	0	0	1	0	0	0	0	0	0	0	.286	.267
Wagner, Brandon	L-R	6-0	210	8-24-95	.270	.224	.285	87	304	52	82	13	0	20	57	43	10	0	2	97	1	1	.510	.376

Pitching

Pitching	B-T	HT	WT	DOB	W	L	ERA	G	GS	CG	SV	IP	H	R	ER	HR	BB	SO	AVG	vLH	vRH	K/9	BB/9
Abreu, Albert	R-R	6-2	175	9-26-95	4	3	4.16	13	13	0	0	63	54	34	29	9	29	65	.229	.233	.224	9.34	4.16
Bristo, Braden	R-R	6-0	180	11-1-94	0	0	2.45	7	0	0	0	11	13	6	3	1	10	6	.296	.235	.333	4.91	8.18
Carter, Will	L-R	6-3	195	1-18-93	0	1	5.06	5	4	0	0	21	21	13	12	2	16	14	.253	.292	.200	5.91	6.75
Cessa, Luis	R-R	6-0	210	4-25-92	0	1	10.80	1	1	0	0	2	3	2	2	0	4	1	.375	.667	.200	5.40	21.60
Diehl, Phillip	L-L	6-2	180	7-16-94	2	3	3.14	25	0	0	3	49	37	20	17	2	12	79	.209	.206	.212	14.61	2.22
Frawley, Matt	R-R	6-1	195	8-8-95	1	5	4.26	27	1	0	3	44	43	22	21	4	18	57	.252	.209	.294	11.57	3.65
Garcia, Deivi	R-R	5-10	163	5-19-99	2	0	1.27	5	5	0	0	28	19	6	4	0	8	35	.192	.222	.167	11.12	2.54
Garcia, Rony	R-R	6-3	200	12-19-97	1	5	4.50	9	9	0	0	48	47	30	24	2	15	45	.257	.248	.268	8.44	2.81
German, Domingo	R-R	6-2	175	8-4-92	0	0	0.00	2	2	0	0	6	3	1	0	0	2	8	.150	.250	.083	12.00	3.00
Green, Nick	R-R	6-1	175	3-25-95	7	5	3.28	20	20	1	0	115	104	57	42	5	57	93	.240	.209	.269	7.26	4.45
Harris, Hobie	R-R	6-3	200	6-23-93	0	1	2.15	21	0	0	2	38	30	9	9	4	7	46	.217	.215	.219	10.99	1.67
Hodson, Chase	R-R	6-1	205	7-10-92	0	0	1.35	5	0	0	0	7	3	1	1	0	5	8	.158	.000	.273	10.80	6.75
Kamplain, Justin	R-L	6-0	175	2-13-93	2	1	4.38	30	0	0	1	62	62	35	30	1	25	68	.261	.281	.248	9.92	3.65
King, Michael	R-R	6-3	210	5-25-95	1	3	1.79	7	7	0	0	40	33	15	8	1	10	45	.219	.224	.214	10.04	2.23
Lane, Trevor	L-L	5-11	185	4-26-94	1	3	3.97	29	0	0	3	48	49	25	21	6	14	61	.265	.284	.252	11.52	2.64
Lehnen, Dalton	L-L	6-3	222	5-16-96	1	3	5.09	10	9	0	0	46	49	29	26	3	29	30	.269	.309	.252	5.87	5.67
Loaisiga, Jonathan	R-R	5-11	165	11-2-94	3	0	1.35	4	4	0	0	20	19	3	3	0	1	26	.244	.238	.250	11.70	0.45
Morris, Christian	R-R	6-4	195	1-23-94	1	1	5.92	14	1	0	0	24	27	17	16	6	11	17	.270	.259	.283	6.29	4.07
Nelson, Nick	R-R	6-1	195	12-5-95	7	5	3.36	18	17	0	0	88	69	37	33	1	47	99	.214	.222	.206	10.09	4.79
Ort, Kaleb	R-R	6-4	240	2-5-92	1	1	6.04	13	0	0	0	22	22	18	15	1	20	27	.250	.205	.286	10.88	8.06
Perez, Freicer	R-R	6-8	240	3-14-96	0	4	7.20	6	6	0	0	25	28	21	20	3	19	20	.283	.308	.267	7.20	6.84
Rijo, Luis	R-R	6-1	200	9-6-98	1	0	3.00	1	1	0	0	6	6	2	2	0	0	3	.261	.267	.250	4.50	0.00
Rosa, Adonis	R-R	6-1	160	11-17-94	12	3	3.84	20	15	0	1	96	100	48	41	7	29	89	.268	.276	.260	8.34	2.72
Sanmartin, Reiver	L-L	6-2	160	4-15-96	2	0	0.00	2	1	0	0	12	8	1	0	0	0	10	.191	.263	.130	7.50	0.00
Schwaab, Andrew	R-R	6-1	205	2-8-93	1	4	5.88	21	0	0	1	26	27	20	17	0	17	28	.278	.308	.259	9.69	5.88
Semple, Shawn	R-R	6-1	220	10-9-95	0	1	6.75	1	1	0	0	4	5	3	3	0	1	2	.313	.200	.364	4.50	2.25
Severino, Anderson	L-L	5-10	165	9-17-94	0	0	4.91	2	0	0	0	4	3	2	2	0	3	4	.214	.500	.100	9.82	7.36
Sosebee, David	R-R	6-2	220	8-25-93	4	2	0.72	18	0	0	5	25	11	6	2	0	8	30	.133	.167	.106	10.80	2.88
Stephan, Trevor	R-R	6-5	225	11-25-95	3	1	1.98	7	7	1	0	41	23	9	9	5	9	49	.160	.141	.178	10.76	1.98
Trieglaff, Brian	R-R	6-1	190	6-13-94	1	0	1.62	9	0	0	0	17	13	3	3	1	4	15	.217	.182	.259	8.10	2.16
Vargas, Alexander	R-R	6-4	203	7-24-97	1	0	9.00	1	0	0	0	1	1	1	1	0	1	0	.333	.000	.500	0.00	9.00
Weissert, Greg	R-R	6-2	215	2-4-95	2	2	3.76	19	0	0	4	26	20	17	11	0	16	36	.211	.222	.200	12.30	5.47
Whitlock, Garrett	R-R	6-5	190	6-11-96	5	3	2.44	14	13	1	0	70	60	23	19	2	27	74	.231	.222	.240	9.51	3.47
Wivinis, Matt	R-R	6-0	180	7-24-93	1	2	1.76	24	0	0	8	31	21	9	6	3	9	44	.184	.143	.235	12.91	2.64
Young, Paul	R-R	6-2	205	3-15-93	0	1	7.11	5	0	0	0	6	6	5	5	1	8	8	.250	.200	.286	11.37	11.37
Zurak, Kyle	R-R	6-1	192	11-28-94	3	2	4.32	10	0	0	1	17	21	9	8	1	9	15	.313	.429	.231	8.10	4.86

Fielding

Catcher	PCT	G	PO	A	E	DP	PB
Deglan	.993	30	247	20	2	1	2
Diaz	.987	21	211	15	3	1	1
Lidge	.988	9	71	9	1	0	1
Lopez	.992	13	101	16	1	1	3
Mora	1.000	3	31	1	0	0	0
Numata	1.000	8	75	7	0	2	2
Sands	.996	24	208	18	1	1	7
Seitz	1.000	3	25	1	0	0	0
Skinner	.985	27	244	19	4	2	5
Torres	.958	3	22	1	1	0	2

First Base	PCT	G	PO	A	E	DP
Alvarez	1.000	4	25	2	0	4
Barrios	.977	6	39	4	1	4
Bird	1.000	2	14	0	0	1
Coronado	.966	7	52	5	2	5
Deglan	1.000	2	13	1	0	1
Lind	1.000	4	25	0	0	0
Lynch	1.000	11	77	2	0	5
Ruta	.985	8	61	4	1	4
Sensley	.984	34	226	22	4	27
Wagner	.993	67	496	42	4	46

Second Base	PCT	G	PO	A	E	DP
Aguilar	.962	20	31	44	3	13
Castillo	.969	51	88	128	7	27
Conde	1.000	1	2	2	0	1
Holder	1.000	3	4	8	0	2
Metzgar	.750	1	2	1	1	0
Park	.954	45	69	98	8	20
Pita	1.000	2	1	5	0	2
Rijo	1.000	2	2	6	0	0
Ruta	1.000	1	0	1	0	0
Surum	1.000	11	22	21	0	9
Torrealba	.929	3	8	5	1	1
Torres	.882	2	8	7	2	3
Torreyes	1.000	1	3	1	0	0

Third Base	PCT	G	PO	A	E	DP
Aguilar	.954	92	68	138	10	9
Alvarez	.923	3	5	7	1	3
Barrios	.897	14	8	18	3	4
Coronado	.667	3	1	1	1	0
Holder	1.000	2	4	0	0	1
Metzgar	.951	13	8	31	2	5
Wagner	.950	15	10	28	2	0

Shortstop	PCT	G	PO	A	E	DP
Aguilar	1.000	1	0	2	0	1
Castillo	.941	68	73	167	15	32
Estrada	1.000	8	10	20	0	7
Holder	1.000	6	7	14	0	2
Park	.956	53	66	129	9	22
Surum	1.000	2	2	4	0	2
Torreyes	.917	3	2	9	1	3

Outfield	PCT	G	PO	A	E	DP
Cabrera	1.000	2	1	0	0	0
Crawford	.976	19	39	2	1	0
Diaz	1.000	5	13	1	0	0
Florial	.980	68	145	3	3	1
Frazier	1.000	3	7	0	0	0
Gilliam	.967	104	167	7	6	0
McKinney	1.000	2	1	0	0	0
Metzgar	.000	1	0	0	0	0
Olivares	1.000	14	24	0	0	0
Palma	1.000	41	66	2	0	1
Robinson	1.000	21	18	0	0	0
Ruta	1.000	57	93	2	0	0
Sensley	1.000	5	9	0	0	0
Thompson-Williams	.967	77	144	3	5	1
Wagner	1.000	1	1	0	0	0

CHARLESTON RIVERDOGS   LOW CLASS A
SOUTH ATLANTIC LEAGUE

Batting	B-T	HT	WT	DOB	AVG	vLH	vRH	G	AB	R	H	2B	3B	HR	RBI	BB	HBP	SH	SF	SO	SB	CS	SLG	OBP
Alexander, Evan	L-L	6-2	175	2-26-98	.100	.111	.091	6	20	1	2	0	0	0	2	2	2	0	0	6	1	1	.100	.250
Barrios, Daniel	R-R	5-11	183	4-18-95	.143	.200	.000	2	7	0	1	0	0	0	1	0	0	0	0	3	0	0	.143	.143
Blaser, Dalton	L-L	6-1	200	1-31-94	.202	.208	.197	40	124	15	25	4	0	2	12	14	4	0	3	21	2	1	.282	.297
Cabrera, Oswaldo	B-R	5-10	145	3-1-99	.229	.207	.239	126	485	48	111	24	1	6	48	28	3	5	5	66	4	9	.320	.273
Cuevas, Frederick	L-L	5-11	185	10-27-97	.219	.204	.224	55	183	14	40	7	2	1	14	13	2	3	1	53	3	0	.295	.276
Deglan, Kellin	L-R	6-2	205	5-3-92	.250	—	.250	1	4	0	1	0	0	0	0	0	0	0	0	2	0	0	.250	.250

Name	B-T	HT	WT	DOB	AVG	vLH	vRH	G	AB	R	H	2B	3B	HR	RBI	BB	HBP	SH	SF	SO	SB	CS	SLG	OBP
Ferreira, Ricardo	B-R	5-11	175	2-3-95	.196	.177	.205	18	56	6	11	1	2	0	6	4	0	0	2	25	3	4	.286	.242
Flames, Miguel	R-R	6-2	210	9-14-97	.333	.375	.308	6	21	5	7	2	0	0	3	1	0	0	0	4	0	0	.429	.364
Garcia, Dermis	R-R	6-3	200	1-7-98	.241	.275	.230	88	324	37	78	17	2	15	50	36	2	0	1	111	3	2	.444	.320
Garcia, Wilkerman	R-R	6-0	176	4-1-98	.218	.200	.226	121	478	57	104	20	2	6	34	35	3	2	2	105	16	7	.305	.274
Gasper, Mickey	B-R	5-10	205	10-11-95	.000	—	.000	1	1	0	0	0	0	0	0	0	0	0	0	0	0	0	.000	.000
Hansen, Mitchell	L-L	6-4	210	5-1-96	.190	.139	.212	40	121	12	23	5	5	0	7	12	2	3	0	37	3	1	.314	.274
Hess, Chris	R-R	6-2	195	12-3-94	.233	.259	.224	115	407	41	95	21	4	9	46	31	20	0	5	116	2	3	.371	.315
Holder, Kyle	L-R	6-1	185	5-25-94	.286	.250	.294	5	21	1	6	1	0	0	0	1	0	0	0	1	0	1	.333	.318
Lidge, Ryan	B-R	6-2	216	10-27-94	.103	.143	.091	9	29	1	3	0	0	0	1	2	0	0	0	7	0	0	.103	.161
Lopez, Jason	R-R	5-10	160	3-16-98	.285	.290	.283	72	256	35	73	19	0	8	30	15	2	1	0	57	7	3	.453	.330
Mateo, Welfrin	R-R	5-10	170	9-8-95	.233	.250	.228	60	210	26	49	10	0	3	19	17	1	4	4	52	6	2	.324	.289
McPhearson, Matt	L-L	5-8	175	4-18-95	.266	.333	.237	33	109	14	29	6	2	0	12	17	0	0	0	31	10	2	.358	.365
Metzgar, David	R-R	5-8	170	12-10-94	.281	.222	.309	40	139	14	39	4	1	1	9	8	3	0	3	27	1	3	.345	.327
Molina, Leonardo	R-R	6-2	180	7-31-97	.251	.208	.269	119	418	48	105	21	7	2	39	23	3	5	4	105	4	7	.349	.292
Navas, Eduardo	B-R	5-10	180	4-5-96	.180	.196	.174	54	172	19	31	4	0	2	14	12	6	4	1	51	0	0	.238	.257
Olivares, Pablo	R-R	6-0	160	1-27-98	.338	.350	.333	56	201	30	68	11	0	4	26	16	7	1	1	35	10	4	.453	.404
Seitz, Jerry	R-R	5-10	180	9-27-94	.093	.167	.065	14	43	3	4	0	0	0	2	2	1	0	1	16	0	0	.093	.149
Sensley, Steven	L-L	6-1	220	9-6-95	.277	.278	.277	67	231	32	64	15	3	10	22	21	7	0	1	66	2	4	.498	.354
Surum, Ricky	R-R	5-10	170	12-7-94	.226	.500	.130	11	31	0	7	1	0	0	2	2	0	2	0	6	1	0	.258	.273
Thompson-Williams, Dom	L-L	6-0	190	4-21-95	.378	.444	.357	10	37	7	14	1	0	5	9	2	1	0	0	7	3	2	.811	.425
Vidal, Carlos	L-L	5-11	160	11-29-95	.244	.250	.242	79	270	35	66	16	6	3	27	35	2	1	4	56	5	4	.382	.331

Pitching	B-T	HT	WT	DOB	W	L	ERA	G	GS	CG	SV	IP	H	R	ER	HR	BB	SO	AVG	vLH	vRH	K/9	BB/9
Alvarez, Daniel	R-R	6-3	228	6-28-96	2	2	0.87	14	0	0	2	21	12	4	2	0	5	25	.169	.152	.184	10.89	2.18
Bristo, Braden	R-R	6-0	180	11-1-94	0	4	2.06	28	0	0	7	44	34	12	10	2	15	57	.213	.238	.184	11.75	3.09
Cedeno, Luis	R-R	5-11	154	7-14-94	0	1	0.68	11	0	0	2	13	10	5	1	0	4	11	.208	.286	.100	7.43	2.70
2-team total (16 Lakewood)					5	3	2.91	27	0	0	2	43	33	25	14	2	24	49	.208	.244	.164	10.18	4.98
Contreras, Roansy	R-R	6-0	175	11-7-99	3	3	3.38	7	7	0	0	35	29	14	13	4	12	28	.225	.254	.194	7.27	3.12
DeCarr, Austin	R-R	6-3	218	3-14-95	1	1	3.50	20	0	0	0	36	28	16	14	3	25	39	.211	.210	.211	9.75	6.25
Espinal, Carlos	R-R	5-11	175	10-21-96	1	2	2.51	10	0	0	4	14	16	6	4	0	4	13	.286	.320	.258	8.16	2.51
Garcia, Deivi	R-R	5-10	163	5-19-99	2	4	3.76	8	8	0	0	41	31	19	17	5	10	63	.205	.224	.184	13.94	2.21
Garcia, Rony	R-R	6-3	200	12-19-97	3	4	4.18	14	14	0	0	71	73	44	33	5	13	62	.259	.291	.224	7.86	1.65
Higgins, Dalton	R-R	6-1	185	8-8-95	5	5	2.65	24	0	0	1	58	44	22	17	3	16	44	.208	.245	.173	6.87	2.50
Junk, Janson	R-R	6-1	177	1-15-96	7	5	3.77	17	15	1	0	88	82	39	37	9	31	71	.245	.246	.243	7.23	3.16
Kahnle, Tommy	R-R	6-1	235	8-7-89	0	1	4.50	1	1	0	0	2	3	1	1	1	0	2	.375	.250	.500	9.00	0.00
Kriske, Brooks	R-R	6-3	190	2-3-94	0	0	4.50	2	0	0	0	4	4	2	2	0	1	6	.267	.286	.250	13.50	2.25
Lehnen, Dalton	L-L	6-3	222	5-16-96	6	3	2.67	13	11	0	0	71	59	23	21	3	24	73	.222	.175	.242	9.30	3.06
Martin, Chad	R-R	6-4	215	1-2-94	2	1	0.84	11	0	0	1	21	7	6	2	1	2	21	.106	.118	.094	8.86	5.06
Martinez, Nolan	R-R	6-2	165	6-30-98	0	0	6.48	5	5	0	0	25	24	18	18	2	14	15	.264	.195	.320	5.40	5.04
Mauricio, Alex	R-R	6-0	180	9-24-96	1	1	4.82	7	0	0	0	37	40	22	20	0	12	28	.278	.286	.273	6.75	2.89
Nelson, Nick	R-R	6-1	195	12-5-95	1	1	3.65	5	5	0	0	25	18	10	10	1	7	35	.198	.244	.152	12.77	2.55
Orozco, Jio	R-R	6-1	210	8-15-97	1	3	4.50	10	9	0	1	46	43	24	23	3	13	36	.252	.209	.294	7.04	2.54
Otto, Glenn	R-R	6-5	240	3-11-96	1	1	3.48	2	2	0	0	10	8	5	4	1	7	8	.216	.211	.222	6.97	6.10
Ramos, Daniel	R-R	5-10	169	3-6-95	8	2	3.57	24	5	0	1	71	73	33	28	7	27	69	.268	.238	.295	8.79	3.44
Sanmartin, Reiver	L-L	6-2	160	4-15-96	2	6	4.19	8	8	0	0	43	48	26	20	2	4	31	.282	.156	.328	6.49	0.84
Sears, JP	R-L	5-11	180	2-19-96	1	5	2.67	11	10	0	0	54	38	19	16	7	11	54	.191	.216	.171	9.00	1.83
Semple, Shawn	R-R	6-1	220	10-9-95	2	0	1.50	2	2	0	0	12	7	2	2	0	1	17	.167	.167	.167	12.75	0.75
Severino, Anderson	L-L	5-10	165	9-17-94	2	3	3.64	8	0	0	1	42	52	24	17	0	14	35	.306	.286	.316	7.50	3.00
Trieglaff, Brian	R-R	6-1	190	6-13-94	2	1	1.42	8	0	0	0	19	17	4	3	0	0	18	.236	.209	.276	8.53	0.00
Vargas, Alexander	R-R	6-4	203	7-24-97	4	1	4.14	19	5	0	4	74	83	39	34	7	11	43	.283	.287	.280	5.23	1.34
Vizcaino, Alexander	R-R	6-2	165	5-22-97	0	1	13.50	1	1	0	0	4	8	6	6	2	2	2	.421	.539	.167	4.50	4.50
Weissert, Greg	R-R	6-2	215	2-4-95	2	2	2.62	17	0	0	0	34	28	17	10	4	12	50	.211	.180	.236	13.11	3.15
Whitlock, Garrett	R-R	6-5	190	6-11-96	2	2	1.13	7	7	0	0	40	23	5	5	1	7	44	.168	.194	.143	9.90	1.58
Wivinis, Matt	R-R	6-0	170	7-24-93	0	0	0.00	9	0	0	6	9	3	1	0	0	0	14	.107	.077	.133	14.54	0.00
Yajure, Miguel	R-R	6-1	175	5-1-98	4	3	3.90	14	14	0	0	65	64	38	28	3	15	56	.258	.259	.257	7.79	2.09
Zurak, Kyle	R-R	6-1	192	11-28-94	2	1	2.51	25	0	0	10	43	31	13	12	1	10	46	.200	.211	.185	9.63	2.09

Fielding

C: Deglan 1, Gasper 1, Lidge 9, Lopez 65, Navas 52, Seitz 13. 1B: Blaser 33, Flames 5, Garcia 44, Hess 54, Sensley 2. 2B: Barrios 2, Cabrera 52, Garcia 43, Hess 4, Mateo 17, Metzgar 18, Surum 1. 3B: Cabrera 15, Garcia 20, Hess 44, Mateo 32, Metzgar 19, Surum 7. SS: Cabrera 55, Garcia 76, Holder 4, Surum 1. OF: Alexander 4, Blaser 1, Cuevas 47, Ferreira 13, Hansen 33, Lopez 1, Mateo 5, McPhearson 26, Molina 112, Navas 1, Olivares 45, Sensley 49, Thompson-Williams 9, Vidal 70.

STATEN ISLAND YANKEES   SHORT-SEASON

NEW YORK-PENN LEAGUE

Batting	B-T	HT	WT	DOB	AVG	vLH	vRH	G	AB	R	H	2B	3B	HR	RBI	BB	HBP	SH	SF	SO	SB	CS	SLG	OBP
Barrios, Daniel	R-R	5-11	183	4-18-95	.000	—	.000	1	2	0	0	0	0	0	0	0	0	0	0	1	0	0	.000	.000
Bastidas, Jesus	R-R	5-10	145	9-14-98	.246	.256	.243	56	191	24	47	5	1	1	16	14	5	3	1	48	3	3	.298	.313
Breaux, Josh	R-R	6-1	200	10-7-97	.280	.111	.317	27	100	6	28	9	0	0	13	3	0	0	2	20	0	0	.370	.295
Chaparro, Andres	R-R	6-1	200	5-4-99	.191	.191	.191	60	204	21	39	11	0	7	20	12	4	1	1	56	0	3	.348	.249
Cuevas, Frederick	L-L	5-11	185	10-27-97	.286	.250	.289	18	56	11	16	4	0	2	5	11	1	1	1	20	4	1	.464	.406
Diaz, Andy	L-L	5-11	190	11-21-95	.122	.000	.130	23	49	6	6	2	2	0	2	3	0	1	0	20	0	0	.245	.173
Ferreira, Ricardo	B-R	5-11	175	2-3-95	.180	.208	.169	37	89	22	16	3	1	1	10	17	0	3	0	30	13	3	.270	.311
Flames, Miguel	R-R	6-2	210	9-14-97	.254	.250	.255	24	71	7	18	3	0	1	10	2	0	1	0	24	0	0	.338	.274
Ford, Mike	L-R	6-0	225	7-4-92	.211	.375	.091	6	19	2	4	1	0	1	2	2	1	0	0	3	0	0	.421	.318

	B-T	HT	WT	DOB	AVG	vLH	vRH	G	AB	R	H	2B	3B	HR	RBI	BB	HBP	SH	SF	SO	SB	CS	SLG	OBP
Gittens, Chris	R-R	6-4	250	2-4-94	.143	—	.143	4	14	0	2	1	0	0	1	1	0	0	0	5	0	0	.214	.200
Gray, Kyle	L-R	5-10	175	3-25-97	.170	.136	.176	48	153	21	26	6	0	7	21	22	2	1	1	47	2	2	.346	.281
Jackson, Jhalan	R-R	6-4	240	2-12-93	.333	.000	.500	1	3	1	1	1	0	0	0	0	0	0	0	2	0	0	.667	.333
Junior, Alex	L-L	5-10	188	5-28-96	.208	.152	.220	57	192	29	40	10	4	0	15	33	7	2	2	75	10	4	.302	.342
Lidge, Ryan	B-R	6-2	216	10-27-94	.306	.500	.294	10	36	3	11	4	0	1	6	2	0	0	1	4	0	0	.500	.333
Lockridge, Brandon	R-R	6-1	185	3-14-97	.216	.125	.233	16	51	6	11	3	1	1	6	8	1	0	1	15	0	2	.373	.328
Metzgar, David	R-R	5-8	170	12-10-94	.125	.000	.143	3	8	2	1	0	0	0	0	3	0	0	0	1	0	0	.125	.364
Mora, Gabriel	R-R	5-11	155	6-1-00	.500	—	.500	1	2	0	1	1	0	0	0	0	0	1	0	1	0	0	1.000	.500
Narvaez, Carlos	R-R	6-0	190	11-26-98	.000	.000	.000	3	9	0	0	0	0	0	0	0	0	0	0	2	0	0	.000	.000
Perez, Danienger	R-R	5-10	155	11-6-96	.105	.071	.125	14	38	1	4	1	0	0	5	1	0	0	2	9	0	1	.132	.122
Rodriguez, Meure	R-R	6-2	200	5-20-99	.000	—	.000	1	1	0	0	0	0	0	0	0	0	0	0	1	0	0	.000	.000
Seitz, Jerry	R-R	5-10	180	9-27-94	.274	.400	.234	22	62	5	17	2	0	3	3	3	0	1		25	0	1	.307	.333
Skinner, Keith	L-R	6-1	200	4-14-94	.167	.500	.000	2	6	1	1	0	0	0	0	0	0	0	0	3	0	0	.167	.167
Smith, Canaan	L-R	6-0	215	4-30-99	.191	.091	.208	45	152	13	29	8	1	3	16	19	0	0	0	52	0	0	.316	.281
Soto, Junior	R-R	6-3	175	1-21-97	.224	.196	.231	61	219	20	49	12	0	5	27	10	0	0	0	69	4	3	.347	.258
Surum, Ricky	R-R	5-10	170	12-7-94	.000	—	.000	3	8	0	0	0	0	0	0	1	0	0	0	4	0	0	.000	.111
Thoreson, Jackson	R-R	6-1	200	6-25-95	.218	.231	.215	28	78	10	17	4	0	2	8	10	0	1	1	25	0	1	.346	.303
Torrealba, Eduardo	R-R	5-8	140	3-26-99	.240	.182	.252	59	200	21	48	11	1	0	20	11	6	9	1	45	1	1	.305	.298
Vazquez, Charles	R-R	6-1	200	9-24-93	.286	.250	.300	5	14	2	4	1	0	0	1	0	0	1	0	1	0	0	.357	.313
Wagaman, Eric	R-R	6-4	210	8-14-97	.194	.227	.185	64	222	19	43	14	1	5	18	14	2	0	4	73	0	0	.333	.244

Pitching	B-T	HT	WT	DOB	W	L	ERA	G	GS	CG	SV	IP	H	R	ER	HR	BB	SO	AVG	vLH	vRH	K/9	BB/9
Acevedo, Domingo	R-R	6-7	250	3-6-94	0	0	3.86	2	2	0	0	5	5	2	2	0	1	3	.294	.333	.250	5.79	1.93
Alvarez, Daniel	R-R	6-3	228	6-28-96	1	0	1.93	2	0	0	0	14	12	4	3	1	3	28	.226	.111	.346	18.00	1.93
Bies, Daniel	R-R	6-8	245	4-9-96	1	0	0.00	1	0	0	0	4	2	0	0	0	0	3	.154	.250	.000	6.75	0.00
Contreras, Roansy	R-R	6-0	175	11-7-99	0	0	1.26	5	5	0	0	29	15	5	4	1	9	32	.158	.158	.158	10.05	2.83
Cortijo, Harold	R-R	6-2	180	9-29-98	4	1	2.63	10	9	0	0	51	44	20	15	5	12	60	.233	.243	.221	10.52	2.10
Curtis, Keegan	R-R	6-0	175	9-30-95	0	1	20.25	3	0	0	0	3	5	6	6	2	4	4	.417	.667	.167	13.50	13.50
De Paula, Juan	R-R	6-3	165	9-22-97	2	2	1.71	10	9	0	0	47	35	11	9	1	26	46	.207	.195	.217	8.75	4.94
Duarte, Abel	R-R	6-1	190	5-20-94	4	1	1.14	14	0	0	0	24	20	13	3	1	15	26	.225	.243	.212	9.89	5.70
Finley, Drew	R-R	6-3	200	7-10-96	2	4	7.24	16	1	0	0	27	27	25	22	4	20	33	.252	.350	.194	10.87	6.59
Gardner, Austin	R-R	6-2	215	12-22-97	0	0	0.00	2	0	0	1	6	2	0	0	0	1	8	.100	.167	.071	12.00	1.50
German, Frank	R-R	6-2	195	9-22-97	1	3	2.22	10	4	0	1	28	22	9	7	0	6	38	.206	.239	.180	12.07	1.91
Gil, Luis	R-R	6-3	176	6-3-98	0	2	5.40	2	2	0	0	7	11	7	4	1	6	10	.344	.429	.278	13.50	8.10
Hodson, Chase	R-R	6-1	205	7-10-92	1	1	2.93	11	0	0	0	15	15	6	5	0	1	23	.263	.136	.343	13.50	0.59
Hutchison, Rodney	R-R	6-5	225	8-9-96	2	1	1.97	9	6	0	1	32	26	9	7	2	6	31	.220	.250	.197	8.72	1.69
Johnson, Kyle	R-R	6-4	220	9-19-93	0	0	1.80	5	0	0	0	10	9	2	2	0	2	9	.231	.177	.273	8.10	1.80
Kriske, Brooks	R-R	6-3	190	2-3-94	2	2	1.09	14	0	0	3	25	21	4	3	0	8	33	.244	.286	.205	12.04	2.92
Maciejewski, Josh	R-L	6-3	175	8-14-95	0	0	5.68	3	0	0	0	6	8	4	4	0	6	8	.296	.250	.316	11.37	5.68
Marinaccio, Ron	R-R	6-2	205	7-1-95	0	0	9.22	7	0	0	0	14	21	14	14	0	3	21	.356	.320	.382	13.83	1.98
Martinez, Nolan	R-R	6-2	165	6-30-98	4	0	1.23	8	5	0	0	37	21	7	5	1	11	26	.172	.161	.182	6.38	2.70
Mauricio, Alex	R-R	6-0	180	9-24-96	2	2	2.14	4	4	0	0	21	16	9	5	0	6	21	.211	.242	.186	9.00	2.57
McGarity, Aaron	R-R	6-3	185	1-31-95	2	0	0.35	13	0	0	3	26	19	5	1	0	3	32	.207	.188	.227	11.22	1.05
Morris, Christian	R-R	6-4	195	1-23-94	2	0	0.92	12	0	0	0	20	11	4	2	1	6	27	.157	.188	.132	12.36	2.75
Mundell, Garrett	R-R	6-6	245	2-16-93	4	3	1.87	18	0	0	4	34	24	12	7	0	10	33	.195	.250	.149	8.82	2.67
Myatt, Tanner	R-R	6-7	220	5-21-98	0	0	0.00	1	1	0	0	2	1	0	0	0	2	2	.167	.000	.250	9.00	9.00
Rijo, Luis	R-R	6-1	200	9-6-98	0	0	3.00	1	1	0	0	6	8	2	2	0	2	3	.348	.400	.333	4.50	3.00
Sanmartin, Reiver	L-L	6-2	160	4-15-96	1	0	0.00	2	0	0	1	7	5	0	0	0	0	13	.185	.000	.294	15.95	0.00
Sauer, Matt	R-R	6-4	195	1-21-99	3	6	3.90	13	13	0	0	67	60	31	29	3	18	45	.236	.188	.277	6.04	2.42
Schmidt, Clarke	R-R	6-1	200	2-20-96	0	1	1.08	2	2	0	0	8	4	1	1	0	2	10	.143	.222	.105	10.80	2.16
Semple, Shawn	R-R	6-1	220	10-9-95	3	4	3.00	10	7	0	0	45	40	20	15	1	12	43	.263	.216	.299	8.60	2.40
Swanson, Erik	R-R	6-3	235	9-4-93	0	0	4.05	2	2	0	0	7	8	3	3	0	2	7	.308	.286	.333	8.10	0.00
Young, Paul	R-R	6-2	205	3-15-93	0	0	7.36	2	0	0	0	4	4	3	3	0	2	7	.286	.000	.400	17.18	4.91

Fielding

C: Breaux 21, Lidge 9, Mora 1, Narvaez 3, Seitz 22, Skinner 2, Thoreson 21, Vazquez 2. **1B:** Flames 14, Ford 4, Gittens 2, Vazquez 1, Wagaman 57. **2B:** Bastidas 30, Gray 31, Perez 5, Torrealba 7. **3B:** Barrios 1, Chaparro 57, Gray 7, Metzgar 3, Perez 6, Surum 1. **SS:** Bastidas 23, Surum 1, Torrealba 49. **OF:** Cuevas 31, Diaz 10, Ferreira 31, Jackson 1, Junior 57, Lockridge 15, Smith 38, Soto 60.

PULASKI YANKEES   ROOKIE
APPALACHIAN LEAGUE

Batting	B-T	HT	WT	DOB	AVG	vLH	vRH	G	AB	R	H	2B	3B	HR	RBI	BB	HBP	SH	SF	SO	SB	CS	SLG	OBP
Alexander, Evan	L-L	6-2	175	2-26-98	.278	.344	.261	47	151	28	42	1	9	5	23	26	5	0	1	57	10	3	.503	.399
Barrios, Daniel	R-R	5-11	183	4-18-95	.167	.000	.222	9	12	4	2	1	0	0	1	5	0	0	0	3	1	1	.250	.412
Brown, Cody	L-R	5-11	190	4-1-94	.385	.333	.400	4	13	3	5	0	0	1	4	4	0	0	0	2	0	0	.615	.529
Burt, Max	R-R	6-3	185	8-28-96	.274	.302	.266	56	186	27	51	11	3	0	21	18	5	0	4	31	5	2	.366	.347
De Leon, Juan	R-R	6-2	185	9-13-97	.243	.256	.238	43	144	24	35	9	2	5	23	15	6	0	0	57	6	0	.438	.339
Duran, Ezequiel	R-R	5-11	185	5-22-99	.201	.222	.194	53	219	34	44	8	2	4	20	9	6	0	1	65	7	0	.311	.251
Gallardo, Carlos	R-R	5-10	160	1-26-97	.167	—	.167	2	6	0	1	0	0	0	1	1	0	0	0	3	0	0	.333	.375
Garabito, Griffin	R-R	5-11	180	8-2-97	.208	.333	.182	22	53	6	11	3	0	0	7	7	1	0	1	10	0	1	.264	.307
Garcia, Anthony	B-R	6-5	204	9-5-00	.095	.000	.118	5	21	4	2	1	0	0	2	0	0	0	0	7	0	0	.143	.174
Gasper, Mickey	B-R	5-10	205	10-11-95	.259	.188	.280	42	139	25	36	6	0	9	30	30	2	0	1	21	0	0	.496	.395
Gomez, Nelson	R-R	6-1	200	10-8-97	.213	.193	.220	58	221	36	47	14	0	11	30	17	7	0	1	93	0	0	.425	.289
Javier, Robert	R-R	5-8	173	2-1-99	.268	.219	.282	39	142	12	38	7	1	0	19	10	4	0	3	42	4	4	.331	.327
Metzgar, David	R-R	5-8	170	12-10-94	.333	.000	.391	12	27	2	9	1	1	1	6	3	0	0	0	6	2	0	.556	.400

Name	B-T	HT	WT	DOB	AVG	vLH	vRH	G	AB	R	H	2B	3B	HR	RBI	BB	HBP	SH	SF	SO	SB	CS	SLG	OBP
Narvaez, Carlos	R-R	6-0	190	11-26-98	.280	.217	.298	32	107	18	30	3	0	1	9	24	1	0	0	26	0	1	.336	.417
Peraza, Oswald	R-R	6-0	176	6-15-00	.250	.129	.284	36	140	25	35	3	2	1	11	14	4	0	1	41	8	1	.321	.333
Pereira, Everson	R-R	6-0	191	4-10-01	.264	.260	.265	41	167	21	44	8	2	3	26	15	0	0	1	60	3	2	.389	.322
Robertson, Terrance	L-L	6-0	175	11-18-96	.080	.100	.100	12	25	1	2	0	0	0	3	9	0	0	0	13	1	0	.080	.324
Rosario, Hemmanuel	R-R	6-2	200	8-21-00	.200	.000	.333	3	10	1	2	0	0	0	0	0	0	0	0	3	0	0	.200	.200
Scott, Jordan	B-R	6-0	210	5-23-97	.175	.138	.184	45	143	21	25	6	1	4	16	29	3	1	1	65	4	1	.315	.324
Seigler, Anthony	B-B	6-0	200	6-20-99	.209	.500	.097	12	43	4	9	1	0	0	5	8	1	0	1	5	0	0	.233	.340
Tatis, Carlos	R-R	6-5	211	12-19-96	.220	.222	.220	48	186	17	41	6	0	1	16	15	3	0	1	43	1	2	.269	.288
Thoreson, Jackson	L-R	6-1	200	6-25-95	.250	—	.250	1	4	1	1	0	0	0	0	0	0	0	0	2	0	0	.250	.250
Torres, Miguel	R-R	6-0	170	3-3-00	.069	.000	.087	13	29	2	2	0	0	0	2	7	1	0	0	18	0	0	.069	.270
Torres, Saul	R-R	6-2	190	2-19-99	.170	.059	.233	13	47	4	8	2	0	1	3	0	0	0	0	23	0	0	.277	.220
Vazquez, Charles	R-R	6-1	200	9-24-93	.286	.000	.333	3	7	0	2	0	0	0	2	1	1	0	0	3	0	0	.286	.444

Pitching	B-T	HT	WT	DOB	W	L	ERA	G	GS	CG	SV	IP	H	R	ER	HR	BB	SO	AVG	vLH	vRH	K/9	BB/9
Barrios, Pedro	R-R	6-1	199	3-27-99	2	2	5.12	7	6	0	1	32	33	20	18	5	10	32	.268	.192	.316	9.09	2.84
Bies, Daniel	R-R	6-8	245	4-9-96	1	2	4.13	10	3	0	0	24	25	13	11	3	6	37	.258	.239	.275	13.88	2.25
Blanton, Bryan	R-R	6-0	190	12-19-95	0	3	7.77	16	0	0	0	22	33	21	19	1	10	25	.359	.390	.333	10.23	4.09
Caceres, Wellington	R-R	5-11	185	1-29-96	1	4	5.45	10	7	0	0	36	50	28	22	5	16	31	.319	.388	.267	7.68	3.96
Correa, Nelvin	R-R	6-1	170	1-25-97	1	0	3.18	1	1	0	0	6	5	2	2	0	3	3	.250	.200	.267	4.76	4.76
Diaz, Wellington	R-R	6-4	190	4-25-97	3	2	4.61	11	1	0	1	41	40	25	21	4	19	40	.253	.246	.258	8.78	4.17
Espinal, Carlos	R-R	5-11	175	10-21-96	3	0	0.43	8	0	0	1	21	8	1	1	1	4	26	.114	.107	.119	11.14	1.71
Espinola, Pedro	R-R	6-4	207	2-1-96	1	2	3.77	11	11	0	0	45	35	25	19	5	32	58	.211	.205	.216	11.51	6.35
Evey, Marcus	R-R	5-10	175	8-4-97	2	1	3.60	13	0	0	1	25	26	11	10	0	7	37	.268	.267	.269	13.32	2.52
Gardner, Austin	R-R	6-2	215	12-2-94	1	0	1.53	16	0	0	3	29	20	6	5	0	7	40	.185	.213	.164	12.27	2.15
Gil, Luis	R-R	6-3	176	6-3-98	2	1	1.37	10	10	0	0	39	21	10	6	1	25	58	.154	.167	.143	13.27	5.72
Marinaccio, Ron	R-R	6-2	205	7-1-95	0	2	1.77	10	0	0	2	20	15	7	4	1	3	33	.197	.129	.244	14.61	1.33
Marquina, Yoiber	R-R	5-10	190	2-3-96	0	1	3.00	8	0	0	0	9	5	4	3	0	5	14	.143	.250	.087	14.00	5.00
Medina, Luis	R-R	6-1	175	5-3-99	1	3	6.25	12	10	0	0	36	32	35	25	3	46	47	.239	.230	.250	11.75	11.50
Mejias, Alex	R-R	5-11	185	11-26-96	1	0	2.25	5	0	0	1	8	4	2	2	0	4	6	.148	.231	.071	6.75	4.50
Montas, Kenlly	R-R	6-0	187	5-31-96	0	1	8.22	2	1	0	0	8	12	8	7	0	3	6	.355	.364	.400	7.04	3.52
Morales, Brett	R-R	6-1	200	1-10-95	2	4	3.82	17	0	0	2	31	31	16	13	2	10	33	.263	.271	.254	9.68	2.93
Munoz, Jhonatan	R-R	5-10	200	8-10-99	2	2	3.90	8	1	0	1	28	28	13	12	2	4	25	.257	.218	.296	8.13	1.30
Ojeda, Luis	R-R	5-11	180	1-10-97	0	1	10.80	3	0	0	0	5	11	6	6	2	2	6	.440	.500	.385	10.80	3.60
Rijo, Luis	R-R	6-1	200	9-6-98	3	1	2.67	5	3	0	0	27	28	11	8	0	1	26	.257	.205	.292	8.67	0.33
2-team total (5 Elizabethton)					5	1	2.05	10	8	0	0	48	43	19	11	1	5	43	.231	.224	.235	8.01	0.93
Troya, Gilmael	R-R	6-0	196	4-4-97	2	0	1.63	15	0	0	2	39	25	8	7	1	18	55	.180	.207	.161	12.80	4.19
Vizcaino, Alexander	R-R	6-2	160	5-22-97	3	3	4.50	11	11	0	0	54	49	29	27	7	21	55	.239	.217	.257	9.17	3.50
Wilson, Justin	R-R	6-0	180	9-9-96	1	1	7.71	5	1	0	0	12	14	10	10	0	11	5	.298	.222	.345	3.86	8.49

Fielding

C: Gallardo 2, Narvaez 31, Rosario 2, Seigler 11, Thoreson 1, Torres 13, Torres 12, Vazquez 3. **1B:** Barrios 4, Burt 11, Gasper 19, Gomez 4, Tatis 41. **2B:** Barrios 1, Brown 1, Burt 4, Duran 51, Garabito 10, Metzgar 4. **3B:** Barrios 1, Brown 3, Burt 8, Garabito 7, Gomez 51, Metzgar 6. **SS:** Barrios 4, Burt 35, Duran 1, Metzgar 2, Peraza 32. **OF:** Alexander 37, De Leon 35, Garabito 2, Garcia 5, Javier 35, Pasteur 9, Pereira 36, Robertson 12, Scott 42.

GCL YANKEES EAST *ROOKIE*
GULF COAST LEAGUE

Batting	B-T	HT	WT	DOB	AVG	vLH	vRH	G	AB	R	H	2B	3B	HR	RBI	BB	HBP	SH	SF	SO	SB	CS	SLG	OBP
Alvarez, Asdrubal	R-R	6-0	160	10-10-99	.263	.200	.276	42	118	11	31	6	0	0	13	15	0	1	1	35	5	3	.314	.343
Andrade, Christian	L-R	6-0	215	4-14-99	.191	.059	.215	36	110	13	21	3	0	4	11	12	2	0	0	51	3	2	.327	.282
Breaux, Josh	R-R	6-1	220	10-7-97	.125	.333	.000	3	8	0	1	0	0	0	1	0	0	0	0	1	0	0	.125	.222
Campero, Gustavo	B-R	5-6	182	9-20-97	.200	.000	.250	2	5	0	1	0	0	0	1	0	0	0	0	1	0	0	.200	.200
Carrera, Jose	B-R	5-2	155	10-22-94	.000	.000	.000	4	5	0	0	0	0	0	0	1	1	0	0	2	0	0	.000	.286
Diaz, Pedro	R-R	6-2	202	11-6-97	.226	.313	.196	24	62	5	14	4	0	1	8	9	0	0	2	28	1	0	.339	.315
Florial, Estevan	L-R	6-1	185	11-25-97	.647	.500	.667	5	17	5	11	3	1	2	5	2	0	0	0	2	3	0	1.294	.684
2-team total (4 GCL Yankees West)					.548	.500	.552	9	31	10	17	3	1	3	8	4	0	0	0	5	5	0	1.000	.600
Garabito, Griffin	R-R	5-11	180	8-2-97	.235	.500	.200	5	17	4	4	0	2	1	4	0	1	0	0	3	0	0	.647	.278
2-team total (3 GCL Yankees West)					.333	.333	.333	8	27	8	9	2	2	1	4	0	1	0	0	6	0	0	.667	.357
Green, Ryder	R-R	6-0	200		.203	.053	.250	26	79	11	16	2	2	3	10	11	3	0	2	35	3	2	.392	.316
Guerrero, Alex	L-R	6-0	185	3-10-00	.164	.083	.184	23	61	1	10	0	0	0	2	6	0	0	0	16	2	1	.164	.239
Jimenez, Brayan	R-R	6-0	140	5-31-99	.260	.280	.254	32	96	12	25	2	0	0	8	6	0	1	1	14	3	4	.281	.301
Martinez, Luis	R-R	5-11	170	11-24-98	.000	.000	.000	4	9	1	0	0	0	0	1	0	0	0	0	5	1	0	.000	.100
McGarry, Matt	R-R	5-10	175	3-24-96	.268	.320	.250	33	97	15	26	4	1	0	8	8	0	0	1	15	2	1	.330	.423
Mendez, Borinquen	B-R	5-11	165	2-1-98	.226	.346	.196	45	133	15	30	5	3	0	12	16	1	1	1	17	19	4	.308	.311
Mora, Gabriel	R-R	5-11	155	6-1-00	.286	.500	.250	6	14	1	4	0	0	0	1	2	0	0	0	5	0	0	.286	.444
2-team total (4 GCL Yankees West)					.227	.667	.158	10	22	2	5	0	0	0	1	3	2	0	0	6	0	0	.227	.370
Moreno, Raymundo	R-R	6-1	185	3-9-98	.221	.300	.197	32	86	11	19	3	2	1	8	11	5	0	1	21	6	1	.337	.340
Mota, Sandy	R-R	6-0	170	9-25-96	.210	.250	.200	39	124	14	26	4	2	0	13	14	3	1	2	29	9	7	.274	.301
Numata, Chace	R-R	6-0	175	8-14-92	.231	—	.231	5	13	1	3	2	0	0	3	2	1	0	2	0	0	0	.385	.333
2-team total (2 GCL Yankees West)					.211	.000	.235	7	19	2	4	3	0	0	4	3	1	0	2	1	0	0	.368	.292
Paulino, Starlin	R-R	6-1	170	2-24-00	.175	.143	.183	38	114	16	20	6	0	1	8	12	6	0	0	27	1	0	.254	.288
Rodriguez, Andres	R-R			5-20-99	.000	—	.000	1	0	0	0	0	0	0	0	0	0	0	0	0	0	0	.000	.500
2-team total (18 GCL Yankees West)					.238	.286	.229	19	42	4	10	3	0	1	5	7	0	0	0	16	0	0	.310	.347
Rosario, Hemmanuel	R-R	6-2	200	8-21-00	.000	.000	.000	1	3	1	0	0	0	0	0	0	0	0	0	2	0	0	.000	.000
2-team total (28 GCL Yankees West)					.149	.111	.159	29	87	4	13	3	0	1	5	7	2	0	0	33	0	0	.207	.229
Sanchez, Gary	R-R	6-2	230	12-2-92	.000	.000	.000	1	3	1	0	0	0	0	0	1	0	0	0	0	0	0	.000	.250

Batting	B-T	HT	WT	DOB	AVG	vLH	vRH	G	AB	R	H	2B	3B	HR	RBI	BB	HBP	SH	SF	SO	SB	CS	SLG	OBP
Sands, Donny	R-R	6-2	190	5-16-96	.250	—	.250	2	4	0	1	0	0	0	0	1	0	0	0	0	0	0	.250	.400
2-team total (1 GCL Yankees West)					.333	—	.333	3	6	1	2	0	0	0	0	2	0	0	0	0	0	0	.333	.500
Santana, Alexander	R-R	6-0	175	7-7-00	.196	.200	.195	40	133	13	26	9	1	0	8	10	4	0	0	54	0	2	.278	.272
Severino, Jesus	R-R	6-0	186	6-7-00	.248	.320	.232	45	137	24	34	5	3	3	18	14	12	0	0	54	18	5	.394	.368
Skinner, Keith	L-R	6-1	200	4-14-94	.000	—	.000	1	2	0	0	0	0	0	0	0	0	0	0	1	0	0	.000	.000
2-team total (3 GCL Yankees West)					.222	.000	.250	4	9	0	2	0	0	0	2	2	0	0	1	2	0	0	.222	.333
Torres, Miguel	R-R	6-0	170	3-3-00	.053	.000	.067	11	19	1	1	0	0	0	1	1	0	0	0	8	0	0	.053	.100
Torres, Saul	R-R	6-2	190	2-19-99	.073	.250	.054	13	41	3	3	1	0	0	0	2	0	0	0	15	0	0	.098	.116
Villa, Jose	R-R	6-1	170	11-16-98	.371	.417	.365	33	116	12	43	8	3	2	21	1	4	0	0	27	5	3	.543	.397

Pitching	B-T	HT	WT	DOB	W	L	ERA	G	GS	CG	SV	IP	H	R	ER	HR	BB	SO	AVG	vLH	vRH	K/9	BB/9
Abreu, Albert	R-R	6-2	175	9-26-95	0	1	18.00	1	1	0	0	2	4	4	4	0	0	2	.400	.667	.286	9.00	0.00
2-team total (2 GCL Yankees West)					0	3	23.40	3	3	0	0	5	14	14	13	0	2	5	.452	.750	.348	9.00	3.60
Bies, Daniel	R-R	6-8	245	4-9-96	0	0	0.00	1	0	0	0	2	0	0	0	0	1	3	.000	—	.000	13.50	4.50
Brown, Blakely	R-R	6-0	165	8-20-96	0	1	3.18	6	0	0	0	6	7	6	2	0	2	4	.259	.231	.286	6.35	3.18
Craft, Derek	R-R	6-8	220	7-11-96	1	1	8.02	15	0	0	0	21	29	20	19	0	10	33	.322	.333	.316	13.92	4.22
Curtis, Keegan	R-R	6-0	175	9-30-95	0	0	3.68	11	0	0	1	15	12	7	6	2	5	15	.207	.256	.196	9.00	3.07
Garcia, Jairo	R-R	5-11	182	1-25-95	1	0	4.63	13	0	0	0	23	23	15	12	1	21	21	.277	.400	.238	8.10	8.10
German, Domingo	R-R	6-2	175	8-4-92	0	1	33.75	1	0	0	0	1	3	5	5	1	2	2	.429	.500	.333	13.50	13.50
Gomez, Yoendrys	R-R	6-3	175	10-15-99	3	1	2.33	10	9	0	0	39	27	10	10	1	15	43	.194	.177	.200	10.01	3.49
Harris, Hobie	R-R	6-3	200	6-23-93	0	0	4.50	1	0	0	0	2	3	2	1	0	0	2	.429	—	.429	9.00	0.00
Hebert, Chaz	L-L	6-2	180	9-4-92	0	0	0.00	2	2	0	0	4	1	0	0	0	2	3	.091	.000	.143	7.36	4.91
2-team total (3 GCL Yankees West)					0	0	1.08	5	5	0	0	8	5	1	1	0	4	7	.192	.182	.200	7.56	4.32
Hernandez, Tony	L-L	6-2	215	8-8-96	0	1	11.25	3	1	0	0	8	13	11	10	0	7	2	.371	.250	.387	2.25	7.88
Johnson, Kyle	R-R	6-4	220	9-19-93	0	0	10.80	1	0	0	0	2	7	3	2	0	0	0	.539	.333	.600	0.00	0.00
2-team total (6 GCL Yankees West)					2	0	2.92	7	0	0	1	12	12	5	4	0	5	11	.250	.067	.333	8.03	3.65
Johnson, Tyler	R-R	6-0	195	7-12-96	1	0	0.96	13	0	0	1	19	8	2	2	0	4	14	.123	.154	.115	6.75	1.93
Jones, Connor	R-L	6-2	195	11-17-94	0	1	63.00	2	0	0	0	1	7	7	7	0	2	1	.875	.000	1.000	9.00	18.00
2-team total (3 GCL Yankees West)					0	3	12.86	5	3	0	0	7	14	10	10	0	3	9	.412	.200	.448	11.57	3.86
Loseke, Barrett	R-R	6-0	170	11-12-96	1	1	3.60	10	0	0	0	10	10	6	4	0	4	10	.250	.000	.357	9.00	3.60
Luna, Anyelo	R-R	6-3	184	12-16-97	1	3	6.45	7	2	0	0	22	33	17	16	4	7	17	.351	.478	.310	6.85	2.82
Maciejewski, Josh	R-L	6-3	175	8-14-95	2	2	3.81	15	0	0	2	26	26	17	11	3	7	35	.255	.250	.256	12.12	2.42
Marquina, Yoiber	R-R	5-10	190	2-3-96	0	1	3.60	3	0	0	0	5	5	4	2	0	4	3	.250	.333	.235	5.40	7.20
2-team total (2 GCL Yankees West)					1	1	2.00	5	1	0	0	9	6	4	2	0	4	6	.188	.125	.208	6.00	4.00
Marten, Daniel	R-R	6-0	179	5-7-97	0	1	21.60	2	0	0	0	2	4	4	4	1	2	1	.286	.000	.333	5.40	10.80
Mejias, Alex	R-R	5-11	185	11-26-96	4	2	1.66	13	0	0	1	22	13	11	4	2	5	16	.173	.200	.160	6.65	2.08
Munoz, Anderson	R-R	5-8	158	8-4-98	1	5	5.20	11	9	0	0	36	38	28	21	4	26	38	.262	.220	.279	9.41	6.44
Myatt, Tanner	R-R	6-7	220	5-21-98	0	1	6.06	9	5	0	0	16	12	11	11	3	7	20	.211	.150	.243	11.02	3.86
Ojeda, Luis	R-R	5-11	180	1-10-97	0	0	4.82	3	0	0	0	9	7	5	5	0	2	6	.226	.333	.158	5.79	1.93
2-team total (6 GCL Yankees West)					0	0	3.65	9	0	0	0	25	20	10	10	1	8	16	.222	.313	.172	5.84	2.92
Oronel, Nestor	L-L	6-1	175	12-13-96	0	2	5.19	8	3	0	0	11	9	5	1	0	6	8	.290	.000	.324	8.31	6.23
2-team total (4 GCL Yankees West)					0	2	4.60	12	3	0	0	16	19	12	8	2	7	17	.284	.111	.310	9.77	4.02
Peguero, Elvis	R-R	6-5	208	3-20-97	0	3	6.25	9	6	0	0	32	43	29	22	7	17	23	.314	.339	.295	6.54	4.83
Peguero, Jose	R-R	6-1	177	8-8-98	1	1	8.31	10	0	0	0	13	17	12	12	5	5	17	.315	.308	.317	11.77	3.46
Ruegger, Charlie	R-R	6-6	218	7-14-97	0	1	2.79	9	1	0	2	10	11	4	3	0	2	7	.306	.308	.304	6.52	1.86
Schmidt, Clarke	R-R	6-1	200	2-20-96	0	2	7.04	3	2	0	0	8	8	7	6	1	2	12	.267	.077	.412	14.09	2.35
2-team total (3 GCL Yankees West)					0	2	4.20	6	5	0	0	15	12	8	7	1	4	20	.222	.167	.267	12.00	2.40
Then, Juan	R-R	6-1	155	2-7-00	0	3	2.70	11	11	0	0	50	38	21	15	2	11	42	.210	.192	.217	7.56	1.98
Villaman, Abismael	L-L	6-2	195	9-27-95	3	1	3.19	8	2	0	0	31	29	16	11	2	13	23	.248	.261	.245	6.68	3.77

Fielding

C: Breaux 2, Campero 2, Diaz 22, Guerrero 22, Mora 2, Numata 4, Rodriguez 1, Rosario 1, Sands 1, Skinner 1, Torres 9, Torres 10. 1B: Alvarez 1, Andrade 6, Garabito 1, Jimenez 12, Mora 4, Mota 11, Paulino 17, Torres 1, Villa 13. 2B: Alvarez 19, Carrera 1, Jimenez 10, McGarry 29, Mendez 2, Mota 1. 3B: Alvarez 16, Carrera 2, Garabito 2, Jimenez 4, McGarry 2, Mota 9, Paulino 16, Villa 13. SS: Alvarez 5, Jimenez 8, Mendez 41, Mota 8. OF: Andrade 23, Florial 3, Green 23, Martinez 3, Moreno 25, Mota 10, Pasteur 17, Santana 35, Severino 42, Villa 4.

GCL YANKEES WEST — ROOKIE
GULF COAST LEAGUE

Batting	B-T	HT	WT	DOB	AVG	vLH	vRH	G	AB	R	H	2B	3B	HR	RBI	BB	HBP	SH	SF	SO	SB	CS	SLG	OBP
Alvarez, Nelson	L-L	6-3	210	3-10-96	.103	.050	.119	33	87	13	9	1	0	1	6	22	0	1	1	20	1	0	.149	.282
Arias, Antonio	R-R	6-2	180	6-12-98	.157	.227	.134	36	89	4	14	2	0	0	11	7	0	0	4	23	1	1	.180	.210
Cabello, Antonio	R-R	5-10	160	11-24-00	.321	.371	.304	40	137	21	44	9	4	5	20	21	4	0	0	34	5	5	.555	.426
Chirinos, Roberto	R-R	5-11	172	9-8-00	.219	.077	.248	41	155	18	34	6	0	2	14	9	3	1	1	40	5	2	.297	.274
Florial, Estevan	L-R	6-1	185	11-25-97	.429	—	.429	4	14	5	6	0	0	1	3	2	0	0	0	3	2	0	.643	.500
2-team total (5 GCL Yankees East)					.548	.500	.552	9	31	10	17	3	1	3	8	4	0	0	0	5	5	0	1.000	.600
Garabito, Griffin	R-R	5-11	180	8-2-97	.500	.000	.556	9	14	5	2	0	0	0	0	0	0	0	0	3	0	0	.700	.500
2-team total (5 GCL Yankees East)					.333	.333	.333	8	27	8	9	2	2	1	4	0	1	0	0	6	0	0	.667	.357
Garcia, Anthony	B-R	6-5	204	9-5-00	.244	.194	.258	44	156	18	38	6	3	10	20	18	0	0	1	73	3	0	.513	.320
Graterol, Jesus	R-R	5-11	175	4-11-97	.256	.273	.250	32	90	8	23	3	1	1	9	3	3	1	2	27	2	3	.344	.340
Lockridge, Brandon	R-R	6-1	185	3-14-97	.367	.333	.375	10	30	8	11	2	2	0	2	4	0	0	0	9	0	3	.567	.460
Luaces, Edel	R-R	6-5	205	5-14-94	.000	—	.000	2	2	0	0	0	0	0	0	0	0	0	0	2	0	0	.000	.000
Martinez, Jose	R-R	6-0	198		.198	.227	.191	33	106	15	21	4	1	5	16	1	0	2	23	2	1		.396	.315
Mora, Gabriel	R-R	5-11	155	6-1-00	.125	1.000	.000	4	8	1	1	0	0	0	1	0	0	0	0	1	0	0	.125	.222
2-team total (6 GCL Yankees East)					.227	.667	.158	10	22	2	5	0	0	0	1	3	2	0	0	6	0	0	.227	.370
Numata, Chace	B-R	6-0	175	8-14-92	.167	.000	.250	2	6	1	1	1	0	0	1	0	0	0	0	1	0	0	.333	.167

NEW YORK YANKEES

Batting	B-T	HT	WT	DOB	AVG	vLH	vRH	G	AB	R	H	2B	3B	HR	RBI	BB	HBP	SH	SF	SO	SB	CS	SLG	OBP
2-team total (5 GCL Yankees East)					.211	.000	.235	7	19	2	4	3	0	0	4	2	1	0	2	1	0	0	.368	.292
Pita, Matt	R-R	5-10	175	4-21-97	.212	.150	.231	27	85	9	18	3	2	0	5	7	2	0	0	20	3	1	.294	.287
Polonia, Jose	R-R	5-11	175	12-11-95	.133	.000	.154	7	15	1	2	0	0	0	1	2	0	0	0	1	0	1	.133	.235
Robinson, Mitchell	R-R	6-3	200	3-17-96	.271	.409	.230	31	96	6	26	7	0	1	12	10	3	0	2	23	0	0	.375	.351
Rodriguez, Meure	R-R	6-2	200	5-20-99	.244	.286	.235	18	41	4	10	3	0	0	5	6	0	0	0	15	0	0	.317	.340
2-team total (1 GCL Yankees East)					.238	.286	.229	19	42	4	10	3	0	0	5	7	0	0	0	16	0	0	.310	.347
Rosario, Hemmanuel	R-R	6-2	200	8-21-00	.155	.118	.164	28	84	3	13	2	0	1	5	6	2	0	0	31	0	0	.214	.228
2-team total (1 GCL Yankees East)					.149	.111	.159	29	87	4	13	2	0	1	5	7	2	0	0	33	0	0	.207	.229
Rosario, Stanley	L-R	6-2	195	12-1-00	.208	.206	.209	50	168	23	35	10	1	4	19	19	3	0	1	45	2	2	.351	.298
Salinas, Raimfer	R-R	6-0	175	12-31-00	.125	.000	.133	5	16	0	2	0	0	0	0	2	2	0	0	5	0	1	.125	.300
Sands, Donny	R-R	6-2	190	5-16-96	.500	—	.500	1	2	1	1	0	0	0	0	1	0	0	0	0	0	0	.500	.667
2-team total (2 GCL Yankees East)					.333		.333	3	6	1	2	0	0	0	0	2	0	0	0	2	0	0	.333	.500
Santos, Luis	R-R	5-8	160	1-4-00	.209	.219	.205	40	115	17	24	3	3	0	8	15	3	1	0	19	12	1	.287	.316
Seigler, Anthony	B-B	6-0	200	6-20-99	.333	.273	.360	12	36	7	12	2	0	1	4	6	0	0	0	7	0	0	.472	.429
Skinner, Keith	L-R	6-2	200	4-14-94	.286	.000	.333	3	7	0	2	0	0	0	2	0	0	1	0	0	0	0	.286	.400
2-team total (1 GCL Yankees East)					.222	.000	.250	4	9	0	2	0	0	0	2	0	0	1	2	0	0	.222	.333
Smith, Sincere	R-R	5-11	170	3-13-00	.161	.100	.191	12	31	1	5	0	1	0	1	3	0	0	0	5	2	1	.226	.235

Pitching	B-T	HT	WT	DOB	W	L	ERA	G	GS	CG	SV	IP	H	R	ER	HR	BB	SO	AVG	vLH	vRH	K/9	BB/9
Abreu, Albert	R-R	6-2	175	9-26-95	0	2	27.00	2	2	0	0	3	10	10	9	0	2	3	.476	.800	.375	9.00	6.00
2-team total (1 GCL Yankees East)					0	3	23.40	3	3	0	0	5	14	14	13	0	2	5	.452	.750	.348	9.00	3.60
Barrios, Pedro	R-R	6-1	199	3-27-99	1	0	0.70	5	4	0	0	26	22	7	2	0	3	20	.222	.222	.227	7.01	1.05
Barrios, Wilser	R-R	6-2	160	3-21-98	3	0	3.55	7	0	0	0	13	8	5	5	1	6	9	.186	.000	.250	6.39	4.26
Bertsch, Jackson	L-R	6-3	225	2-14-95	1	1	4.15	13	0	0	7	17	22	9	8	2	2	15	.306	.407	.244	7.79	1.04
Boyle, Sean	R-R	6-1	205	10-29-96	1	0	3.60	10	0	0	1	15	15	7	6	2	4	20	.254	.174	.306	12.00	2.40
Burgos, Havid	R-R	6-0	186	8-6-94	0	1	5.30	11	0	0	0	19	25	11	11	1	9	15	.309	.263	.323	7.23	4.34
Calderon, Daniel	L-L	6-1	170	10-13-97	0	0	10.13	4	0	0	0	5	5	9	6	1	8	8	.227	.000	.238	13.50	13.50
Cordero, Diego	R-R	6-0	160	10-21-99	1	0	1.50	3	0	0	0	6	8	1	1	0	0	6	.308	.500	.250	9.00	0.00
Correa, Nelvin	R-R	6-1	170	1-25-97	2	3	3.82	7	4	0	0	31	35	18	13	0	5	35	.278	.143	.330	10.27	1.47
Diaz, Deivi	L-L	5-10	197	6-9-99	1	2	4.32	10	5	0	0	33	37	20	16	2	12	38	.287	.143	.304	10.26	3.24
Evey, Marcus	R-R	5-10	175	8-4-97	0	0	0.00	2	0	0	0	4	1	0	0	0	2	8	.083	.000	.111	19.64	4.91
German, Frank	R-R	6-2	195	9-22-97	0	0	0.00	1	1	0	0	2	0	0	0	0	0	3	.000	.000	.000	13.50	0.00
Hebert, Chaz	L-L	6-2	180	9-4-92	0	1	1.93	3	3	0	0	5	4	1	1	0	2	4	.267	.286	.250	7.71	3.86
2-team total (2 GCL Yankees East)					0	1	1.08	5	5	0	0	8	5	1	1	0	4	7	.192	.182	.200	7.56	4.32
Herrera, Argelis	L-L	6-5	165	10-17-98	0	1	16.43	10	0	0	0	8	9	19	14	0	17	7	.300	.167	.333	8.22	19.96
Johnson, Kyle	R-R	6-4	220	9-19-93	2	0	1.69	6	0	0	1	11	5	2	2	0	5	11	.143	.000	.217	9.28	4.22
2-team total (1 GCL Yankees East)					2	0	2.92	7	0	0	1	12	12	5	4	0	5	11	.250	.067	.333	8.03	3.65
Jones, Connor	R-L	6-2	195	11-17-94	0	2	4.50	3	3	0	0	6	7	3	3	0	1	6	.269	.250	.273	12.00	1.50
2-team total (1 GCL Yankees East)					0	3	12.86	5	3	0	0	7	14	10	10	0	3	9	.412	.200	.448	11.57	3.86
Loaisiga, Jonathan	R-R	5-11	165	11-2-94	0	0	0.00	1	1	0	0	2	1	0	0	0	0	1	.167	.500	.000	5.40	5.40
Marquina, Yoiber	R-R	5-10	190	2-3-96	1	0	0.00	2	1	0	0	4	1	0	0	0	0	3	.083	.000	.143	6.75	0.00
2-team total (3 GCL Yankees East)					1	1	2.00	5	1	0	0	9	6	4	2	0	4	6	.188	.125	.208	6.00	4.00
Mendez, Bringnel	R-R	6-0	239	1-31-94	1	1	4.85	10	0	0	3	13	14	9	7	0	5	9	.255	.412	.184	6.23	3.46
Montas, Kenlly	R-R	6-0	187	5-31-96	2	6	4.50	9	8	0	0	42	53	30	21	3	16	27	.314	.341	.304	5.79	3.43
Ojeda, Luis	R-R	5-11	180	1-10-97	0	0	2.93	6	0	0	0	15	13	5	5	1	6	10	.220	.300	.180	5.87	3.52
2-team total (3 GCL Yankees East)					0	0	3.65	9	0	0	0	25	20	10	10	1	8	16	.222	.313	.172	5.84	2.92
Oronel, Nestor	L-L	6-1	175	12-13-96	0	0	3.86	4	0	0	0	7	8	3	3	1	1	9	.276	.200	.292	11.57	1.29
2-team total (8 GCL Yankees East)					0	2	4.60	12	3	0	0	16	19	12	8	2	7	17	.284	.111	.310	9.77	4.02
Paredes, Edward	R-R	5-11	170	1-7-99	1	0	2.86	12	0	0	0	22	16	7	7	2	7	18	.198	.200	.197	7.36	2.86
Pestana, Leonardo	R-R	6-4	198	7-30-98	1	3	8.44	7	6	0	0	21	30	22	20	1	11	31	.330	.438	.271	13.08	4.64
Reynoso, Anderson	R-R	6-2	180	11-25-97	3	1	3.18	7	3	0	0	28	26	12	10	0	4	19	.243	.250	.241	6.04	1.27
Rodriguez, Carlos D.	R-R	5-10	155	12-13-98	4	3	2.44	10	5	0	0	44	34	17	12	3	12	44	.210	.255	.189	8.93	2.44
Schmidt, Clarke	R-R	6-1	200	2-20-96	0	0	1.23	3	3	0	0	7	4	1	1	0	2	8	.167	.273	.077	9.82	2.45
2-team total (3 GCL Yankees East)					0	2	4.20	6	3	0	0	15	12	8	7	1	4	20	.222	.167	.267	12.00	2.40
Van Hoose, Connor	R-R	6-1	195	2-1-96	0	0	6.00	3	0	0	0	3	4	2	2	0	2	2	.200	.000	.250	6.00	12.00
Vasquez, Randy	R-R	6-0	165	11-3-98	0	1	3.09	3	3	0	0	12	10	4	4	1	6	6	.233	.231	.233	4.63	4.63

Fielding

C: Graterol 1, Mora 4, Numata 2, Rodriguez 18, Rosario 27, Sands 1, Seigler 10, Skinner 2. **1B:** Alvarez 30, Graterol 18, Polonia 3, Robinson 5. **2B:** Chirinos 7, Garabito 1, Graterol 10, Pita 20, Polonia 1, Santos 19. **3B:** Garabito 1, Graterol 4, Martinez 24, Polonia 1, Robinson 23, Santos 4. **SS:** Chirinos 28, Polonia 1, Santos 17, Smith 10. **OF:** Arias 35, Cabello 33, Florial 3, Garcia 37, Lockridge 10, Luaces 2, Pita 1, Polonia 1, Rosario 45, Salinas 3.

DSL YANKEES   ROOKIE
DOMINICAN SUMMER LEAGUE

Batting	B-T	HT	WT	DOB	AVG	vLH	vRH	G	AB	R	H	2B	3B	HR	RBI	BB	HBP	SH	SF	SO	SB	CS	SLG	OBP
Arrieche, Bryant	R-R	6-1	180	6-29-01	.182	.000	.222	29	99	16	18	1	0	0	10	5	0	0	0	26	3	2	.192	.290
Ascanio, Enyerberth	R-R	5-10	170	12-3-00	.245	.063	.279	34	102	20	25	7	0	0	19	25	11	0	3	29	0	2	.314	.433
Cabello, Antonio	R-R	5-10	160	11-1-00	.227	.143	.267	6	22	5	5	0	1	0	1	6	2	0	0	6	5	1	.318	.433
Chirinos, Roberto	R-R	5-11	172	9-8-00	.346	.286	.368	6	26	5	9	4	0	0	4	2	0	0	1	4	2	0	.577	.379
Crisp, Juan	R-R	6-1	170	5-23-00	.256	.263	.254	41	160	27	41	6	1	2	23	11	4	0	0	35	0	4	.344	.320
Favelo, Wilfre	R-R	6-0	170	4-1-01	.190	.071	.227	17	58	2	11	0	0	0	4	5	1	0	1	17	2	1	.190	.262
Garcia, Anthony	B-R	6-5	204	9-5-00	.125	.250	.083	4	16	3	2	1	1	0	4	3	0	0	0	8	0	0	.313	.263
Marte, Miguel	R-R	5-11	165	5-26-01	.246	.222	.252	49	195	26	48	13	7	1	25	11	5	0	3	44	10	6	.400	.299
Martinez, Omar	L-R	5-11	192	7-5-01	.000	.000	—	1	2	0	0	0	0	0	0	0	0	0	0	0	0	0	.000	.000
Medina, Nelson	R-R	6-2	175	9-14-00	.204	.268	.188	57	201	36	41	10	5	1	17	38	6	0	0	89	12	9	.318	.347

Name	B-T	HT	WT	DOB	AVG	vLH	vRH	G	AB	R	H	2B	3B	HR	RBI	BB	HBP	SH	SF	SO	SB	CS	SLG	OBP
Mejia, Alan	R-R	6-0	165	7-20-01	.329	.308	.340	20	76	19	25	5	2	5	16	7	1	0	1	25	3	2	.645	.388
Moreno, Carlos	R-R	6-0	176	1-31-99	.230	.250	.223	38	122	13	28	3	4	0	11	9	3	0	1	39	4	1	.320	.296
Morillo, Mario	R-R	5-11	155	4-17-99	.154	.182	.146	15	52	14	8	1	1	1	6	11	1	0	1	11	1	0	.269	.308
Mota, Sandy	R-R	6-0	170	9-25-96	.389	.250	.500	5	18	2	7	2	0	0	5	3	0	0	0	1	1	2	.500	.476
Munoz, Deivi	B-R	5-8	153	11-30-99	.344	.370	.337	41	131	26	45	10	9	0	19	9	1	0	1	16	12	4	.557	.387
Naranjo, Marco	R-R	5-11	155	3-26-01	.150	.000	.171	12	40	5	6	1	1	0	5	3	1	0	1	12	2	1	.225	.222
Rodriguez, Carlos A.	R-R	6-0	170	3-12-99	.152	.000	.192	11	33	6	5	2	1	0	3	2	4	0	0	13	0	0	.273	.282
Rodriguez, Jhoiner	R-R	5-11	180	20-9-99	.185	.211	.180	33	108	13	20	6	0	0	8	10	4	1	0	34	4	0	.241	.279
Rojas, Angel	R-R	6-0	160	11-26-00	.285	.283	.286	55	214	41	61	10	9	5	30	30	2	0	1	60	15	11	.486	.377
Rojas, Ronny	B-R	6-1	180	8-23-01	.169	.178	.167	53	183	31	31	8	5	5	21	45	3	0	0	93	4	2	.350	.342
Salinas, Raimfer	R-R	6-0	175	12-31-00	.095	.333	.000	6	21	4	2	1	0	0	2	5	2	0	0	5	4	2	.143	.321
Sanabria, Oscar	R-R	5-10	160	5-24-01	.170	.300	.135	16	47	6	8	1	0	0	4	7	1	0	1	11	0	2	.192	.286
Santos, Madison	R-R	5-10	165	9-6-99	.315	.342	.306	43	159	28	50	10	9	3	28	25	1	0	1	32	11	7	.547	.409
Valenzuela, Anthony	R-R	5-11	180	6-16-01	.220	.185	.226	46	164	21	36	11	1	5	27	11	4	0	1	80	4	1	.390	.283
Vallejo, Dionys	R-R	6-1	153	5-25-00	.275	.348	.258	34	120	17	33	7	1	3	16	10	2	0	3	18	5	4	.425	.333
Villa, Jose	R-R	6-1	170	11-16-98	.500	—	.500	6	16	4	8	0	3	0	5	1	1	0	0	0	0	0	.875	.556

Pitching

Name	B-T	HT	WT	DOB	W	L	ERA	G	GS	CG	SV	IP	H	R	ER	HR	BB	SO	AVG	vLH	vRH	K/9	BB/9
Abreu, Joensy	R-R	6-1	190	12-29-97	0	0	4.61	9	0	0	0	14	13	8	7	0	8	15	.245	.294	.222	9.88	5.27
Alonzo, Felix	R-R	6-2	185	6-3-99	2	2	4.14	13	1	0	2	50	61	30	23	2	18	47	.292	.281	.299	8.46	3.24
Arguello, Marcos	L-L	6-2	180	11-10-97	1	0	2.45	10	0	0	0	18	15	8	5	0	8	16	.217	.316	.180	7.85	3.93
Barrios, Wilser	R-R	6-2	160	3-21-98	0	1	2.79	7	0	0	2	10	5	3	3	1	3	18	.147	.071	.200	16.76	2.79
Carderon, Juan	R-R	6-0	172	8-1-98	0	1	4.60	9	0	0	1	16	19	10	8	0	7	20	.307	.269	.333	11.49	4.02
Carrizo, Albert	R-R	6-4	165	11-11-99	0	1	3.97	9	0	0	0	11	12	7	5	0	5	9	.267	.353	.214	7.15	3.97
Castano, Blas	R-R	5-11	150	9-8-98	1	5	5.40	11	7	0	0	40	44	30	24	2	20	30	.270	.183	.337	6.75	4.50
Castro, Yon	R-R	5-11	201	5-23-99	4	4	3.81	14	5	0	0	52	60	40	22	3	21	44	.272	.263	.278	7.62	3.63
Cordero, Diego	R-R	6-0	160	10-21-99	3	3	3.00	17	0	0	1	24	25	12	8	0	8	29	.255	.244	.264	10.88	3.00
Diaz, Deivi	L-L	5-10	197	6-9-99	1	0	0.00	2	1	0	0	6	3	0	0	0	4	14	.143	.000	.188	19.89	5.68
Diaz, Wellington	R-R	6-4	190	4-25-97	0	0	4.15	1	1	0	0	4	4	2	2	0	1	8	.235	.200	.286	16.62	2.08
Espana, Carfred	R-R	5-11	195	1-3-00	0	0	9.00	4	0	0	0	3	4	3	3	0	4	1	.308	.200	.375	3.00	12.00
Espinal, Carlos	R-R	5-11	175	10-21-96	0	0	2.45	1	0	0	0	4	2	1	1	1	0	4	.143	.143	.143	9.82	0.00
Estevez, Abel	R-R	6-1	170	1-17-00	0	2	8.27	12	0	0	1	21	29	22	19	2	6	20	.322	.333	.315	8.71	2.61
Gomez, Carlos	R-R	6-1	175	6-14-98	1	3	4.40	12	12	0	0	43	42	24	21	1	18	47	.252	.233	.262	9.84	3.77
Gomez, Ismael	R-R	5-10	170	12-9-99	0	0	4.61	10	0	0	3	14	16	11	7	0	4	18	.291	.191	.353	11.85	2.63
Gomez, Yoendrys	R-R	6-3	175	10-15-99	1	0	1.00	2	2	0	0	9	2	1	1	0	7	7	.080	.125	.059	7.00	7.00
Hernandez, Franyer	R-R	6-0	171	2-1-01	1	0	6.17	7	0	0	0	12	13	8	8	0	7	10	.302	.308	.300	7.71	5.40
Marten, Daniel	R-R	6-0	179	5-7-97	1	0	0.00	1	0	0	0	2	0	0	0	0	3	.000	.000	.000	13.50	0.00	
Martinez, Thowar	R-R	6-1	160	3-29-98	2	1	4.68	13	0	0	0	33	29	19	17	0	22	42	.242	.216	.261	11.57	6.06
Munoz, Jhonatan	R-R	5-10	200	8-10-99	0	0	0.00	1	1	0	0	5	2	0	0	0	2	.118	.250	.077	3.60	0.00	
Obando, Angel	R-R	5-11	178	1-19-99	2	4	3.40	13	8	0	1	48	32	20	18	1	21	43	.192	.155	.219	8.12	3.97
Peguero, Jose	R-R	6-1	177	8-8-98	0	0	0.00	2	0	0	0	3	2	0	0	0	4	4	.200	.250	.167	13.50	13.50
Pestana, Leonardo	R-R	6-4	198	7-30-98	0	1	5.27	4	2	0	1	14	11	11	8	0	9	22	.204	.191	.212	14.49	5.93
Reynoso, Anderson	R-R	6-2	180	11-25-97	0	0	8.53	2	1	0	0	6	8	6	6	2	3	10	.296	.111	.389	14.21	4.26
Rodriguez, Carlos D.	R-R	5-10	155	12-13-98	0	1	8.44	1	1	0	0	5	9	6	5	0	0	7	.360	.286	.455	11.81	0.00
Santana, Carlos	R-R	6-7	195	1-4-99	1	1	8.31	8	2	0	0	17	23	19	16	2	13	9	.343	.292	.372	4.67	6.75
Serrano, Elvin	R-R	6-1	180	2-15-99	0	0	24.92	7	0	0	0	4	10	13	12	1	11	4	.435	.200	.615	8.31	22.85
Sumoza, Cristian	R-R	5-10	164	11-18-00	2	5	5.31	12	10	0	0	42	49	36	25	0	16	32	.285	.352	.238	6.80	3.40
Vasquez, Randy	R-R	6-0	165	11-3-98	1	0	0.96	6	4	0	0	19	6	4	2	0	6	22	.102	.111	.098	10.61	2.89
Vega, Alfred	R-R	6-1	169	1-19-01	3	7	3.99	14	12	0	0	59	65	38	26	5	15	42	.284	.268	.296	6.44	2.30
Villaman, Abismael	L-L	6-2	195	9-27-95	2	0	0.53	4	2	0	0	17	11	5	1	0	7	15	.193	.167	.200	7.94	3.71

Fielding

C: Ascanio 25, Crisp 27, Martinez 1, Morillo 11, Rodriguez 6, Rodriguez 8. **1B:** Moreno 24, Mota 5, Munoz 10, Rodriguez 4, Rodriguez 22, Sanabria 10. **2B:** Marte 19, Moreno 1, Munoz 10, Rojas 27, Rojas 13, Sanabria 3, Vallejo 2. **3B:** Moreno 9, Munoz 17, Rojas 25, Sanabria 3, Vallejo 19, Villa 5. **SS:** Chirinos 5, Marte 25, Moreno 2, Rojas 23, Rojas 11, Vallejo 8. **OF:** Arrieche 26, Cabello 5, Favelo 17, Garcia 4, Medina 54, Mejia 17, Moreno 1, Munoz, Naranjo 12, Salinas 5, Santos 42, Valenzuela 41, Villa 1.

Oakland Athletics

SEASON IN A SENTENCE: The Athletics entered the season with the lowest payroll in the majors, but thanks to a potent offense and dominating bullpen they finished with 97 wins and a date with the Yankees in the AL Wild Card Game.

HIGH POINT: Oakland won the first two games of a mid-August series against the Astros and entered the third game tied with Houston for first place in the AL West. The A's had won 40 out of 53 games to erase an 11.5-game deficit.

LOW POINT: The A's placed lefthander Sean Manea, their most dependable starter, on the disabled list on Aug. 26 and lost him for the season. He later had surgery to repair a left shoulder impingement, which will cost him all of 2019.

NOTABLE ROOKIES: Lou Trivino, a nondescript 26-year-old righthander, established himself as a high-leverage bullpen option by recording a 2.92 ERA in 69 appearances with 10.0 strikeouts per nine innings. His fastball averaged nearly 98 mph. Ramon Laureano served as the club's regular center fielder following his Aug. 3 callup. He hit .288/.358/.474 (128 OPS+) in 48 games. Minor league free agent pickup Nick Martini earned a share of the left field job in July and served as leadoff hitter when he started. The 28-year-old put up a .399 on-base percentage against righthanders.

KEY TRANSACTIONS: The A's helped compensate for an injury-decimated rotation by making a series of summer trades for pitchers. Oakland nabbed journeyman righthander Mike Fiers from the Tigers on Aug. 6 and watched him go 5-2, 3.74 in 53 innings in green and gold. They also traded for high-leverage relievers Jeurys Familia, Shawn Kelley and Fernando Rodney. Oakland completed the deals without having to sacrifice significant future assets. Their most notable losses were Double-A starter Logan Shore, high Class A third baseman Will Toffey and international bonus pool money that the club couldn't spend because it was under penalty for this year's signing class.

DOWN ON THE FARM: Two A's affiliates qualified for the playoffs—low Class A Beloit in the Midwest League and high Class A Stockton in the California League—but neither advanced past the first round. The organization's domestic affiliates compiled a .515 winning percentage that ranked ninth in baseball. If lefthanders Jesus Luzardo and A.J. Puk—who missed the year with Tommy John surgery—and catcher Sean Murphy develop, they could form the battery of the future in Oakland.

OPENING DAY PAYROLL: $62,652,500 (30th)

PLAYERS OF THE YEAR

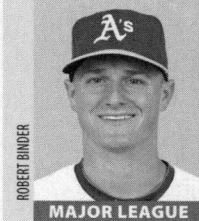

ROBERT BINDER

MAJOR LEAGUE	MINOR LEAGUE
Matt Chapman	**Jesus Luzardo**
3B	LHP
.278/.356/.508	(High Class A/
Gold Glover hit	Double-A/Triple-A)
24 HR and 42 2B	10-5, 2.88 in 23 GS

ORGANIZATION LEADERS

Batting		*Minimum 250 AB
MAJORS		
* AVG	Matt Chapman	.278
* OPS	Khris Davis	.874
HR	Khris Davis	48
RBI	Khris Davis	123
MINORS		
* AVG	Eli White, Midland	.306
* OBP	Eli White, Midland	.388
* SLG	Anthony Garcia, Nashville	.479
* OPS	Eli White, Midland	.838
R	Eli White, Midland	81
H	Eli White, Midland	154
TB	Anthony Garcia, Nashville	230
2B	Seth Brown, Midland	38
3B	Jorge Mateo, Nashville	16
HR	Anthony Garcia, Nashville	25
RBI	Anthony Garcia, Nashville	91
BB	Anthony Garcia, Nashville	65
SO	Sheldon Neuse, Nashville	172
SB	Richie Martin, Midland	25
SB	Jorge Mateo, Nashville	25

Pitching		#Minimum 75 IP
MAJORS		
W	Sean Manaea	12
# ERA	Blake Treinen	0.78
SO	Sean Manaea	108
SV	Blake Treinen	38
MINORS		
W	Parker Dunshee, Stockton, Midland	13
L	Jean Ruiz, Beloit	12
# ERA	Parker Dunshee, Stockton, Midland	2.33
G	Angel Duno, Stockton	48
GS	James Naile, Nashville, Midland	26
SV	Angel Duno, Stockton	15
SV	Seth Martinez, Beloit	15
IP	Matt Milburn, Stockton, Nashville	152
BB	Wyatt Marks, Beloit, Stockton	51
SO	Parker Dunshee, Stockton, Midland	163
# AVG	Parker Dunshee, Stockton, Midland	.221

2018 PERFORMANCE

General Manager: David Forst. **Farm Director:** Billy Owen. **Scouting Director:** Eric Kubota.

Class	Team	League	W	L	PCT	Finish	Manager
Majors	Oakland Athletics	American	97	65	.599	4th (15)	Bob Melvin
Triple-A	Nashville Sounds	Pacific Coast	72	68	.514	6th (16)	Fran Riordan
Double-A	Midland Rockhounds	Texas	68	71	.489	6th (8)	Scott Steinmann
High A	Stockton Ports	California	77	63	.550	2nd (8)	Rick Magnante
Low A	Beloit Snappers	Midwest	69	69	.500	7th (16)	Webster Garrison
Short season	Vermont Lake Monsters	New York-Penn	39	37	.513	6th (14)	Aaron Nieckula
Rookie	AZL Athletics	Arizona	29	25	.537	7th (18)	Eddie Menchaca
Overall 2018 Minor League Record			354	333	.515	t9th (30)	

ORGANIZATION STATISTICS

OAKLAND ATHLETICS
AMERICAN LEAGUE

Batting	B-T	HT	WT	DOB	AVG	vLH	vRH	G	AB	R	H	2B	3B	HR	RBI	BB	HBP	SH	SF	SO	SB	CS	SLG	OBP
Barreto, Franklin	R-R	5-10	190	2-27-96	.233	.192	.255	32	73	10	17	4	0	5	16	1	1	0	0	29	0	0	.493	.253
Canha, Mark	R-R	6-2	210	2-15-89	.249	.282	.227	122	365	60	91	22	0	17	52	34	10	0	2	88	1	2	.449	.329
Chapman, Matt	R-R	6-0	210	4-28-93	.278	.288	.274	145	547	100	152	42	6	24	68	58	9	0	2	146	1	2	.508	.356
Davis, Khris	R-R	5-10	195	12-21-87	.247	.219	.257	151	576	98	142	28	1	48	123	59	12	0	7	175	0	0	.549	.326
Fowler, Dustin	L-L	6-0	195	12-29-94	.224	.154	.229	69	192	19	43	3	2	6	23	8	1	0	2	47	6	4	.354	.256
Joyce, Matt	L-R	6-2	205	8-3-84	.208	.158	.213	83	207	34	43	9	0	7	15	35	1	1	2	53	0	2	.353	.322
Laureano, Ramon	R-R	5-11	185	7-15-94	.289	.267	.297	48	156	27	45	12	1	5	19	16	2	0	2	50	7	1	.474	.358
Lowrie, Jed	B-R	6-0	180	4-17-84	.267	.254	.273	157	596	78	159	37	1	23	99	78	3	0	3	128	0	0	.448	.353
Lucroy, Jonathan	R-R	6-0	200	6-13-86	.241	.236	.243	126	415	41	100	21	1	4	51	29	3	1	6	65	0	0	.325	.291
Martini, Nick	L-L	5-11	205	6-27-90	.296	.125	.306	55	152	26	45	9	3	1	19	21	5	0	1	36	0	0	.415	.397
Maxwell, Bruce	L-R	6-1	250	12-20-90	.182	.067	.225	18	55	5	10	4	0	1	6	2	0	0	1	13	0	0	.309	.207
Olson, Matt	L-R	6-5	230	3-29-94	.247	.251	.244	162	580	85	143	33	0	29	84	70	8	0	2	163	2	1	.453	.335
Phegley, Josh	R-R	5-10	230	2-12-88	.204	.161	.226	39	93	13	19	7	0	2	15	6	1	0	2	27	0	0	.344	.255
Pinder, Chad	R-R	6-2	195	3-29-92	.258	.289	.233	110	298	43	77	12	1	13	27	7	6	2	0	88	0	2	.436	.332
Piscotty, Stephen	R-R	6-3	210	1-14-91	.267	.241	.279	151	546	78	146	41	0	27	88	42	12	0	5	114	2	0	.491	.331
Powell, Boog	L-L	5-10	185	1-14-93	.167	.000	.174	7	24	3	4	1	0	0	1	0	0	0	0	6	1	1	.292	.200
Semien, Marcus	R-R	6-0	195	9-17-90	.255	.250	.257	159	632	89	161	35	2	15	70	61	1	2	7	131	14	6	.388	.318
Smolinski, Jake	R-R	5-11	205	2-9-89	.128	.125	.133	19	39	2	5	1	1	0	2	1	1	0	0	10	1	0	.205	.171
Taylor, Beau	L-R	6-0	205	2-13-90	.200	.000	.333	7	5	0	1	1	0	0	0	1	0	0	0	2	0	0	.400	.333
Thompson, Trayce	R-R	6-3	217	3-15-91	.143	.000	.333	3	7	1	1	0	0	0	0	0	0	0	0	4	0	0	.143	.143
2-team total (48 Chicago)					.117	.125	.113	51	128	15	15	3	0	3	9	7	0	1	1	50	3	1	.211	.162

Pitching	B-T	HT	WT	DOB	W	L	ERA	G	GS	CG	SV	IP	H	R	ER	HR	BB	SO	AVG	vLH	vRH	K/9	BB/9
Anderson, Brett	L-L	6-3	230	2-1-88	4	5	4.48	17	17	0	0	80	90	42	40	10	13	47	.285	.257	.293	5.27	1.46
Bassitt, Chris	R-R	6-5	220	2-22-89	2	3	3.02	11	7	0	0	48	40	21	16	4	19	41	.221	.218	.223	7.74	3.59
Blackburn, Paul	R-R	6-1	195	12-4-93	2	3	7.16	6	6	0	0	28	33	23	22	2	6	19	.303	.318	.283	6.18	1.95
Bleich, Jeremy	L-L	6-2	215	6-18-87	0	0	54.00	2	0	0	0	0	2	2	2	0	1	0	.667	.500	1.000	27.00	0.00
Brooks, Aaron	R-R	6-4	225	4-27-90	0	0	0.00	3	0	0	0	3	1	0	0	0	2	1	.125	.000	1.000	3.38	6.75
Buchter, Ryan	L-L	6-4	258	2-13-87	6	0	2.75	54	0	0	0	39	32	17	12	4	15	41	.219	.169	.286	9.38	3.43
Cahill, Trevor	R-R	6-4	240	3-1-88	7	4	3.76	21	20	0	0	110	90	52	46	8	41	100	.227	.243	.212	8.18	3.35
Casilla, Santiago	R-R	6-0	210	7-25-80	0	0	3.16	26	0	0	1	31	18	11	11	0	20	22	.170	.167	.173	6.32	5.74
Coulombe, Danny	L-L	5-10	190	10-26-89	1	1	4.56	27	0	0	0	24	24	13	12	5	11	26	.279	.317	.244	9.89	4.18
Dull, Ryan	R-R	5-9	175	10-2-89	0	0	4.26	28	0	0	0	25	22	12	12	3	7	21	.242	.219	.254	7.46	2.49
Familia, Jeurys	R-R	6-3	240	10-10-89	4	2	3.45	30	0	0	1	31	24	13	12	2	14	40	.205	.208	.203	11.49	4.02
Fiers, Mike	R-R	6-2	202	6-15-85	5	2	3.74	10	9	0	0	53	45	22	22	12	11	52	.228	.178	.289	8.83	1.87
2-team total (21 Detroit)					12	8	3.56	31	30	0	0	172	166	71	68	32	37	139	.249	.231	.268	7.27	1.94
Font, Wilmer	R-R	6-4	265	5-24-90	0	0	14.85	4	0	0	0	7	13	11	11	5	4	9	.394	.273	.455	12.15	5.40
2-team total (9 Tampa Bay)					2	1	4.28	13	5	0	0	34	28	16	16	7	15	29	.219	.175	.254	7.75	4.01
Gearrin, Cory	R-R	6-1	205	4-14-86	0	0	6.00	6	0	0	0	6	10	4	4	0	2	2	.385	.308	.462	3.00	3.00
2-team total (21 Texas)					1	0	3.29	27	0	0	0	27	23	10	10	2	8	22	.230	.128	.295	7.24	2.63
Gossett, Daniel	R-R	6-2	185	11-13-92	0	3	5.18	5	5	0	0	24	25	14	14	5	8	12	.269	.267	.270	4.44	2.96
Graveman, Kendall	R-R	6-2	200	12-21-90	1	5	7.60	7	7	0	0	34	44	32	29	9	13	27	.306	.314	.297	7.08	3.41
Hatcher, Chris	R-R	6-1	200	1-12-85	3	3	4.95	34	0	0	0	36	43	23	20	7	17	30	.289	.385	.214	7.43	4.21
Hendriks, Liam	R-R	6-0	200	2-10-89	0	1	4.13	25	8	0	0	24	25	11	11	3	10	22	.272	.184	.333	8.25	3.75
Jackson, Edwin	R-R	6-2	215	9-9-83	6	3	3.33	17	17	0	0	92	75	37	34	12	37	68	.221	.216	.227	6.65	3.62
Kelley, Shawn	R-R	6-2	237	4-26-84	1	0	2.16	19	0	0	0	17	7	4	4	0	6	18	.127	.211	.083	9.72	3.24
Kiekhefer, Dean	L-L	6-0	175	6-7-89	0	0	18.00	4	0	0	0	2	7	4	4	1	1	1	.583	.667	.333	4.50	4.50
Lucas, Josh	R-R	6-6	185	11-5-90	0	0	6.28	8	0	0	0	14	16	11	10	1	9	14	.286	.259	.310	8.79	5.65
Manaea, Sean	R-L	6-5	245	2-1-92	12	9	3.59	27	27	1	0	161	141	67	64	21	32	108	.232	.236	.231	6.05	1.79
Mengden, Daniel	R-R	6-2	190	2-19-93	7	6	4.05	22	17	1	0	116	103	58	52	18	26	72	.234	.221	.244	5.60	2.02
Montas, Frankie	R-R	6-2	255	3-21-93	5	4	3.88	13	11	0	0	65	74	34	28	5	21	43	.290	.305	.276	5.95	2.91
Pagan, Emilio	L-R	6-3	210	5-7-91	3	1	4.35	55	0	0	0	62	55	30	30	13	19	63	.230	.296	.196	9.15	2.76
Petit, Yusmeiro	R-R	6-1	255	11-22-84	7	3	3.00	74	0	0	0	93	76	32	31	13	18	76	.221	.183	.251	7.35	1.74

	B-T	HT	WT	DOB	W	L	ERA	G	GS	CG	SV	IP	H	R	ER	HR	BB	SO	AVG	vLH	vRH	K/9	BB/9
Ramirez, Carlos	R-R	6-5	205	4-24-91	0	0	3.00	3	0	0	0	6	2	2	2	0	4	2	.111	.000	.143	3.00	6.00
2-team total (2 Toronto)					0	0	3.24	5	0	0	0	8	3	3	3	0	9	5	.115	.100	.125	5.40	9.72
Rodney, Fernando	R-R	5-11	230	3-18-77	1	1	3.92	22	0	0	0	21	20	9	9	2	13	20	.253	.143	.378	8.71	5.66
2-team total (46 Minnesota)					4	3	3.36	68	0	0	25	64	62	27	24	7	32	70	.250	.185	.310	9.79	4.48
Treinen, Blake	R-R	6-5	225	6-30-88	9	2	0.78	68	0	0	38	80	46	12	7	2	21	100	.158	.192	.124	11.20	2.35
Triggs, Andrew	R-R	6-4	220	3-16-89	3	1	5.23	9	9	0	0	41	37	24	24	7	18	43	.231	.231	.232	9.36	3.92
Trivino, Lou	R-R	6-5	225	10-1-91	8	3	2.92	69	1	0	4	74	53	24	24	8	31	82	.201	.223	.182	9.97	3.77
Wendelken, J.B.	R-R	6-0	220	3-24-93	0	0	0.54	13	0	0	0	17	8	1	1	1	5	14	.140	.080	.188	7.56	2.70

Fielding

Catcher	PCT	G	PO	A	E	DP	PB
Lucroy	.989	125	857	83	10	3	10
Maxwell	1.000	16	126	12	0	0	1
Phegley	.996	39	210	18	1	2	6
Taylor	1.000	6	10	1	0	0	0

First Base	PCT	G	PO	A	E	DP
Canha	1.000	15	59	2	0	2
Olson	.995	162	1403	84	7	115
Pinder	1.000	1	3	0	0	0

Second Base	PCT	G	PO	A	E	DP
Barreto	.973	26	35	36	2	6

	PCT	G	PO	A	E	DP
Lowrie	.993	136	194	336	4	73
Pinder	1.000	21	21	26	0	2

Third Base	PCT	G	PO	A	E	DP
Chapman	.959	145	133	331	20	37
Lowrie	1.000	14	10	22	0	1
Pinder	.935	16	11	18	2	2

Shortstop	PCT	G	PO	A	E	DP
Barreto	1.000	2	3	3	0	0
Pinder	.857	3	3	9	2	1
Semien	.970	159	198	458	20	79

Outfield	PCT	G	PO	A	E	DP
Canha	1.000	108	201	1	0	0
Davis	1.000	11	17	0	0	0
Fowler	.991	62	110	1	1	0
Joyce	.989	57	86	1	1	0
Laureano	.991	47	103	9	1	1
Martini	.977	50	83	1	2	0
Pinder	.984	73	123	4	2	0
Piscotty	.989	151	273	5	3	1
Powell	.941	7	16	0	1	0
Smolinski	1.000	16	30	0	0	0
Thompson	1.000	2	4	0	0	0

NASHVILLE SOUNDS

PACIFIC COAST LEAGUE

TRIPLE-A

Batting

	B-T	HT	WT	DOB	AVG	vLH	vRH	G	AB	R	H	2B	3B	HR	RBI	BB	HBP	SH	SF	SO	SB	CS	SLG	OBP
Barreto, Franklin	R-R	5-10	190	2-27-96	.259	.188	.280	77	282	54	73	16	1	18	46	39	7	0	5	106	5	2	.514	.357
Boyd, BJ	L-R	5-11	230	7-16-93	.271	.260	.275	105	391	36	106	15	3	3	49	26	4	4	2	71	6	3	.348	.322
Canha, Mark	R-R	6-2	210	2-15-89	.250	.500	.167	2	8	1	2	1	0	1	1	1	0	0	0	1	0	0	.750	.333
Fowler, Dustin	L-L	6-0	195	12-29-94	.341	.344	.339	55	229	37	78	17	6	4	27	9	0	0	1	41	13	2	.520	.364
Garcia, Anthony	R-R	6-0	180	1-4-92	.254	.293	.242	131	480	78	122	31	1	25	91	65	15	0	6	107	1	3	.479	.357
Garneau, Dustin	R-R	6-0	200	8-13-87	.208	.381	.137	22	72	8	15	3	0	2	9	5	1	0	2	10	0	0	.333	.263
Goldby, Cooper	R-R	5-10	190	1-18-95	.500	—	.500	1	2	1	1	1	1	0	0	2	0	0	0	0	0	0	1.000	.500
Goldstein, Jason	R-R	5-11	195	3-9-94	—	—	—	1	0	1	0	0	0	0	0	1	0	0	0	0	0	0	—	1.000
Heathcott, Slade	L-L	6-1	205	9-28-90	.266	.263	.267	30	109	15	29	9	0	1	9	10	1	0	0	37	4	0	.376	.333
Joyce, Matt	L-R	6-2	205	8-3-84	.281	.263	.308	9	32	4	9	3	0	0	3	3	0	0	0	5	0	0	.375	.343
Laureano, Ramon	R-R	5-11	185	7-15-94	.297	.297	.297	64	246	44	73	12	1	14	35	31	4	0	3	70	11	2	.524	.380
Lombardozzi, Steve	B-R	6-0	195	9-20-88	.243	.215	.253	120	412	67	100	15	3	1	42	51	2	6	9	64	4	7	.301	.323
Martini, Nick	L-L	5-11	205	6-27-90	.297	.258	.316	76	276	44	82	12	2	6	40	51	1	0	2	68	5	1	.420	.406
Mateo, Jorge	R-R	6-0	190	6-23-95	.230	.246	.224	131	470	50	108	17	16	3	45	29	5	2	4	139	25	10	.353	.280
Maxwell, Bruce	L-R	6-1	220	12-20-90	.219	.203	.227	51	178	9	39	8	0	1	17	21	0	0	1	61	0	0	.281	.300
Mercedes, Melvin	B-R	5-8	170	1-13-92	.232	.118	.269	51	142	18	33	3	0	3	15	20	3	1	1	31	1	3	.296	.337
Murphy, Sean	R-R	6-3	215	10-10-94	.250	.500	.167	3	8	2	2	0	0	0	3	1	0	0	2	0	0	0	.250	.500
Neuse, Sheldon	R-R	6-0	195	12-10-94	.263	.312	.247	135	499	48	131	26	3	5	55	32	0	1	5	172	4	1	.357	.304
Nunez, Renato	R-R	6-1	220	4-4-94	.357	.400	.348	7	28	3	10	0	0	4	2	0	0	0	6	0	0	.357	.400
Phegley, Josh	R-R	5-10	230	2-12-88	.235	.394	.174	36	119	12	28	6	3	3	18	15	3	0	2	31	0	0	.412	.331
Powell, Boog	L-L	5-10	185	1-14-93	.225	.182	.250	38	147	18	33	2	0	0	8	23	1	3	0	36	5	6	.238	.333
Smolinski, Jake	R-R	5-11	205	2-9-89	.278	.297	.270	36	126	25	35	4	0	10	19	18	1	0	0	42	1	0	.548	.372
Sportman, J.P.	R-R	5-9	190	1-26-92	.235	.231	.238	10	34	5	8	4	0	1	6	1	0	0	1	9	0	0	.441	.250
Taylor, Beau	L-R	6-0	205	2-13-90	.248	.193	.261	90	302	39	75	15	3	3	39	50	3	0	1	89	2	0	.348	.360
Vertigan, Brett	L-L	5-9	175	8-21-90	.274	.177	.299	33	84	10	23	7	2	0	7	9	0	2	0	21	1	0	.405	.344
Ward, Nick	L-R	5-10	180	10-19-95	.000	.000	.000	2	3	0	0	0	0	0	0	0	0	0	0	1	0	0	.000	.000

Pitching

	B-T	HT	WT	DOB	W	L	ERA	G	GS	CG	SV	IP	H	R	ER	HR	BB	SO	AVG	vLH	vRH	K/9	BB/9
Alcantara, Raul	R-R	6-4	220	12-4-92	5	7	5.29	32	10	0	5	83	100	54	49	10	14	53	.292	.282	.298	5.72	1.51
Anderson, Brett	L-L	6-3	230	2-1-88	2	1	2.78	7	7	0	0	32	32	17	10	0	6	36	.248	.314	.223	10.02	1.67
Aquino, Ismael	R-R	6-2	170	9-2-98	0	0	18.00	1	0	0	0	1	1	2	2	0	4	2	.250	.000	.333	18.00	36.00
Bassitt, Chris	R-R	6-5	220	2-22-89	5	5	4.30	18	14	0	0	82	86	42	39	6	25	83	.271	.215	.313	9.15	2.76
Bleich, Jeremy	L-L	6-2	215	6-18-87	1	2	2.63	38	0	0	1	51	47	18	15	5	13	48	.247	.211	.269	8.42	2.28
Bracewell, Ben	R-R	6-0	195	9-19-90	2	3	4.12	8	8	0	0	39	41	21	18	4	13	29	.272	.250	.293	6.64	2.97
Bragg, Sam	R-R	6-2	190	3-23-93	0	0	9.00	1	1	0	0	4	4	4	4	2	0	4	.333	.000	.429	9.00	0.00
Buchter, Ryan	L-L	6-4	258	2-13-87	1	0	0.00	4	0	0	0	3	1	0	0	0	1	3	.100	.000	.143	8.10	2.70
Cahill, Trevor	R-R	6-4	240	3-1-88	0	1	2.63	3	3	0	0	14	7	5	4	0	8	17	.146	.177	.129	11.20	5.27
Camacho, Joseph	R-R	5-9	175	6-23-94	0	0	45.00	1	0	0	0	1	5	5	5	2	1	0	.714	.500	.800	0.00	9.00
Castro, Simon	R-R	6-5	230	4-9-88	1	1	7.56	6	0	0	0	8	11	8	7	1	6	12	.314	.091	.417	12.96	6.48
Coker, Calvin	R-R	6-3	174	3-6-96	0	0	7.71	2	0	0	1	2	2	2	2	0	1	0	.250	.500	.167	0.00	3.86
Coulombe, Danny	L-L	5-10	190	10-26-89	2	1	2.54	23	1	0	0	28	30	11	8	3	6	28	.280	.326	.246	8.89	1.91
Dull, Ryan	R-R	5-9	175	10-2-89	3	2	3.54	23	0	0	0	28	27	12	11	5	8	36	.273	.308	.250	11.57	2.57
Finnegan, Kyle	R-R	6-2	170	9-4-91	0	2	7.13	13	0	0	0	18	22	16	14	2	7	17	.297	.280	.306	8.66	3.57
Friedrichs, Kyle	R-R	6-1	195	11-23-90	0	1	3.18	1	1	0	0	6	4	2	2	0	1	1	.200	.286	.154	1.59	1.59
Gossett, Daniel	R-R	6-2	185	11-13-92	4	0	1.63	7	5	0	0	39	26	10	7	1	16	42	.190	.146	.208	9.78	3.72
Graveman, Kendall	R-R	6-2	200	12-21-90	2	1	4.50	4	4	0	0	24	35	14	12	3	7	16	.365	.258	.415	6.00	2.63
Hatcher, Chris	R-R	6-1	200	1-12-85	0	1	2.08	5	0	0	0	9	10	4	2	0	7	7	.286	.429	.250	7.27	4.15
Hendriks, Liam	R-R	6-0	200	2-10-89	4	1	2.84	23	1	0	6	25	21	9	8	1	4	43	.217	.205	.224	15.28	1.42

Name	B-T	HT	WT	DOB	W	L	ERA	G	GS	CG	SV	IP	H	R	ER	HR	BB	SO	AVG	vLH	vRH	K/9	BB/9
Jackson, Edwin	R-R	6-2	215	9-9-83	0	1	4.02	3	3	0	0	16	12	7	7	1	8	16	.207	.222	.194	9.19	4.60
Jokisch, Eric	R-L	6-2	205	7-29-89	5	11	4.06	26	23	0	1	149	165	84	67	12	46	121	.278	.272	.280	7.33	2.78
Kiekhefer, Dean	L-L	6-0	175	6-7-89	8	1	3.83	32	1	0	0	45	50	24	19	4	6	36	.278	.203	.330	7.25	1.21
Lucas, Josh	R-R	6-6	185	11-5-90	0	2	2.56	31	0	0	5	39	28	12	11	2	15	32	.207	.180	.224	7.45	3.49
Luzardo, Jesus	L-L	6-1	205	9-30-97	1	1	7.31	4	4	0	0	16	25	13	13	2	7	18	.362	.667	.317	10.13	3.94
Martin, Jarret	L-L	6-3	230	8-14-89	0	0	4.91	3	0	0	0	4	3	2	2	0	8	5	.214	.200	.222	12.27	19.64
Martinez, Daniel	L-R	5-11	190	7-28-98	0	0	3.00	1	0	0	0	3	2	1	1	1	0	1	.182	.000	.222	3.00	0.00
McIntyre, Aiden	R-R	6-5	220	8-27-95	1	0	0.00	1	0	0	0	4	2	0	0	0	1	3	.143	.000	.182	6.75	2.25
Mengden, Daniel	R-R	6-2	190	2-19-93	4	1	2.98	9	8	0	0	45	39	17	15	2	7	34	.231	.279	.204	6.75	1.39
Milburn, Matt	R-R	6-3	210	7-29-93	1	0	2.61	2	2	0	0	10	9	3	3	0	1	7	.231	.143	.333	6.10	0.87
Montas, Frankie	R-R	6-2	255	3-21-93	4	5	4.65	15	15	1	0	72	69	40	37	7	26	61	.255	.190	.290	7.66	3.27
Morban, Richard	R-R	6-2	162	12-24-97	1	0	2.25	1	0	0	0	4	3	1	1	0	1	0	.200	.200	.200	0.00	2.25
Naile, James	R-R	6-4	185	2-8-93	7	10	4.71	24	24	1	0	136	156	80	71	12	40	77	.293	.289	.296	5.11	2.65
Pagan, Emilio	L-R	6-3	210	5-7-91	1	0	3.00	5	0	0	0	6	5	3	2	2	0	11	.208	.000	.278	16.50	0.00
Ramirez, Carlos	R-R	6-5	205	4-24-91	2	2	3.10	26	1	0	1	41	28	18	14	3	17	39	.193	.183	.200	8.63	3.76
Ruiz, Norge	R-R	6-0	185	3-15-94	1	1	6.75	3	2	0	0	13	15	11	10	3	4	10	.273	.200	.360	6.75	2.70
Sanchez, Jake	R-R	6-1	205	8-19-89	0	1	4.15	30	0	0	0	39	45	18	18	4	9	37	.285	.303	.272	8.54	2.08
Trivino, Lou	R-R	6-5	225	10-1-91	0	0	1.69	4	0	0	1	5	2	1	1	0	1	10	.111	.111	.111	16.88	1.69
Wahl, Bobby	R-R	6-2	210	3-21-92	3	2	2.27	34	1	0	11	40	17	16	10	2	17	65	.130	.178	.105	14.75	3.86
2-team total (4 Las Vegas)					4	2	2.20	38	1	0	12	45	20	17	11	2	19	73	.136	.184	.112	14.60	3.80
Wendelken, J.B.	R-R	6-0	220	3-24-93	1	1	2.80	22	1	0	3	35	29	11	11	2	10	52	.223	.189	.247	13.25	2.55

Fielding

Catcher	PCT	G	PO	A	E	DP	PB
Garneau	.993	18	136	11	1	1	2
Maxwell	.997	38	289	12	1	0	8
Murphy	1.000	3	18	3	0	0	0
Phegley	1.000	19	147	14	0	3	5
Taylor	.991	69	534	25	5	5	3

First Base	PCT	G	PO	A	E	DP
Canha	1.000	1	9	1	0	0
Garcia	1.000	1	9	1	0	1
Heathcott	.985	29	247	16	4	25
Lombardozzi	.995	70	542	23	3	63
Martini	.989	41	331	25	4	33
Nunez	1.000	1	14	1	0	1
Vertigan	1.000	2	24	1	0	1

Second Base	PCT	G	PO	A	E	DP
Barreto	.981	60	107	152	5	45
Lombardozzi	1.000	39	61	111	0	22
Mateo	1.000	4	8	10	0	8
Mercedes	.962	34	44	83	5	17
Neuse	1.000	1	1	2	0	0
Sportman	1.000	8	9	23	0	5
Ward	1.000	1	3	1	0	0

Third Base	PCT	G	PO	A	E	DP
Lombardozzi	.882	7	1	14	2	1
Mercedes	.875	5	3	4	1	0
Neuse	.935	130	97	249	24	25
Nunez	.750	2	1	2	1	0

Shortstop	PCT	G	PO	A	E	DP
Barreto	.959	11	12	35	2	7
Lombardozzi	1.000	1	2	0	0	1
Mateo	.955	123	146	340	23	72
Mercedes	.958	7	11	12	1	1
Neuse	.889	1	3	5	1	1

Outfield	PCT	G	PO	A	E	DP
Boyd	.984	101	183	3	3	1
Canha	1.000	1	2	0	0	0
Fowler	.947	53	85	4	5	0
Garcia	.970	67	125	3	4	1
Heathcott	1.000	1	1	1	0	0
Joyce	1.000	6	10	0	0	0
Laureano	.978	64	123	13	3	2
Lombardozzi	1.000	5	4	0	0	0
Martini	1.000	34	63	2	0	0
Mercedes	1.000	3	3	0	0	0
Nunez	.000	2	0	0	1	0
Powell	.978	38	81	6	2	1
Smolinski	1.000	34	66	0	0	0
Sportman	1.000	2	2	0	0	0
Vertigan	1.000	27	48	0	0	0

MIDLAND ROCKHOUNDS
TEXAS LEAGUE

DOUBLE-A

Batting	B-T	HT	WT	DOB	AVG	vLH	vRH	G	AB	R	H	2B	3B	HR	RBI	BB	HBP	SH	SF	SO	SB	CS	SLG	OBP
Barrera, Luis	L-L	6-0	180	11-15-95	.328	.314	.333	36	131	24	43	8	4	0	18	9	2	1	1	18	13	3	.450	.378
Bolt, Skye	B-R	6-3	190	1-15-94	.256	.228	.267	78	285	41	73	18	3	5	37	27	2	1	0	75	10	1	.446	.325
Brown, Seth	L-L	6-3	220	7-13-92	.283	.261	.294	131	502	66	142	38	3	14	90	47	1	0	5	142	5	0	.454	.342
Chavez, Santiago	R-R	5-11	175	8-5-95	.209	.250	.194	28	91	13	19	9	0	0	4	3	1	3	0	17	0	0	.308	.242
Diaz, Edwin	R-R	6-2	223	8-25-95	.155	.194	.139	31	103	6	16	4	0	2	13	8	0	1	0	32	1	0	.252	.209
Goldstein, Jason	R-R	5-11	195	3-9-94	.164	.200	.143	16	55	5	9	2	0	1	2	1	1	0	0	19	0	0	.255	.220
Heim, Jonah	B-R	6-4	225	6-27-95	.183	.085	.233	39	137	16	25	4	0	1	11	10	1	3	3	22	0	0	.234	.238
Marincov, Tyler	R-R	6-2	205	10-20-91	.225	.270	.204	92	325	39	73	11	1	14	46	35	1	2	4	112	11	6	.394	.299
Marinez, Eric	B-R	6-1	160	9-12-95	.143	.000	.286	5	14	1	2	0	0	0	0	0	0	0	0	6	0	0	.143	.143
Martin, Richie	R-R	5-11	190	12-22-94	.300	.294	.303	118	453	68	136	29	8	6	42	44	6	3	3	86	25	10	.439	.368
Mercedes, Melvin	B-R	5-8	190	1-13-92	.455	.000	.500	3	11	3	5	0	0	0	2	1	0	0	0	1	2	0	.455	.500
Mondou, Nate	L-R	5-10	205	3-24-95	.255	.151	.304	48	165	15	42	7	0	0	14	19	6	2	4	26	2	1	.297	.345
Murphy, Sean	R-R	6-3	215	10-10-94	.288	.337	.261	68	257	51	74	26	2	8	43	23	6	1	2	47	3	0	.498	.358
Ramirez, Tyler	L-L	5-9	185	2-21-95	.287	.293	.285	134	512	73	147	35	4	10	79	62	10	2	8	148	5	4	.430	.370
Siddall, Brett	L-L	6-1	210	10-3-94	.206	.209	.204	74	253	22	52	10	2	2	28	23	4	1	4	64	2	1	.285	.278
Sportman, J.P.	R-R	5-9	190	1-26-92	.277	.287	.272	103	401	55	111	25	2	13	56	22	2	0	3	83	18	13	.446	.315
Vertigan, Brett	L-L	5-9	175	8-21-90	.243	.291	.215	78	280	43	68	12	1	0	19	39	1	3	4	57	9	5	.293	.333
White, Eli	R-R	6-2	175	10-24-94	.306	.289	.313	130	504	81	154	30	8	9	55	62	8	0	4	116	18	9	.450	.388
White, Mikey	R-R	6-1	200	9-3-93	.218	.165	.247	64	225	21	49	6	0	6	29	25	4	0	1	81	0	1	.324	.306

Pitching	B-T	HT	WT	DOB	W	L	ERA	G	GS	CG	SV	IP	H	R	ER	HR	BB	SO	AVG	vLH	vRH	K/9	BB/9
Blackwood, Nolan	R-R	6-5	185	3-16-95	6	3	4.08	39	0	0	9	53	60	31	24	3	16	48	.280	.231	.309	8.15	2.72
Bowers, Heath	R-R	6-4	190	7-25-93	0	0	1.50	2	1	0	0	6	5	1	1	1	0	4	.227	.357	.000	6.00	0.00
Bracewell, Ben	R-R	6-0	195	9-19-90	5	7	3.03	17	17	2	0	110	101	44	37	9	16	98	.242	.303	.198	8.02	1.31
Bragg, Sam	R-R	6-2	190	3-23-93	4	5	3.62	33	5	0	0	70	78	34	28	3	26	44	.281	.287	.277	5.68	3.36
Camacho, Joseph	R-R	5-9	175	6-23-94	0	0	10.80	3	0	0	0	3	5	4	4	0	4	0	.357	.400	.333	0.00	10.80
Cochran-Gill, Trey	R-R	5-10	190	12-10-92	1	1	5.09	22	0	0	1	35	41	20	20	2	12	23	.293	.388	.242	5.86	3.06
Dunshee, Parker	R-R	6-1	205	2-12-95	7	4	2.01	12	12	0	0	81	59	21	18	5	14	81	.205	.186	.220	9.04	1.56

Name	B-T	HT	WT	DOB	W	L	ERA	G	GS	CG	SV	IP	H	R	ER	HR	BB	SO	AVG	vLH	vRH	K/9	BB/9
Finnegan, Kyle	R-R	6-2	170	9-4-91	1	1	2.16	21	0	0	13	25	18	11	6	0	11	28	.207	.184	.225	10.08	3.96
Friedrichs, Kyle	R-R	6-1	195	1-22-92	6	5	5.66	15	14	0	0	76	90	54	48	13	23	60	.291	.238	.326	7.07	2.71
Gorman, John	R-R	6-1	230	2-19-92	3	3	2.78	42	0	0	2	65	55	25	20	7	15	47	.226	.241	.219	6.54	2.09
Healy, Tucker	L-R	6-1	210	6-15-90	1	0	3.86	5	0	0	0	7	6	3	3	1	3	1	9	.231	.200	.250	11.57	1.29
Howard, Brian	R-R	6-9	185	4-25-95	4	4	3.48	12	12	0	0	67	65	36	26	7	23	63	.249	.252	.247	8.42	3.07
Kiekhefer, Dean	L-L	6-0	175	6-7-89	0	0	3.18	5	0	0	3	6	8	2	2	0	1	5	.348	.250	.400	7.94	1.59
Krall, Pat	L-L	6-6	220	8-27-94	0	0	7.20	3	0	0	0	5	8	4	4	0	2	3	.364	.429	.333	5.40	3.60
Luzardo, Jesus	L-L	6-0	205	9-30-97	7	3	2.29	16	16	0	0	79	58	22	20	5	18	86	.204	.203	.204	9.84	2.06
Martin, Jarret	L-L	6-3	230	8-14-89	1	4	3.91	37	0	0	0	46	41	25	20	2	27	53	.241	.174	.266	10.37	5.28
Naile, James	R-R	6-4	185	2-8-93	1	0	3.00	2	2	0	0	15	17	5	5	1	2	7	.288	.276	.300	4.20	1.20
Romero, Miguel	R-R	6-2	180	4-22-94	1	1	6.00	22	0	0	1	30	35	25	20	4	12	33	.297	.286	.303	9.90	3.60
Ruiz, Norge	R-R	6-0	185	3-15-94	5	9	4.69	21	21	1	0	121	142	66	63	12	34	76	.303	.335	.281	5.65	2.53
Sanchez, Jake	R-R	6-1	205	8-19-89	0	0	2.25	4	0	0	4	4	3	1	1	0	3	3	.200	.200	.200	6.75	6.75
Seddon, Joel	L-R	6-1	165	7-13-92	9	7	4.81	28	17	0	0	118	131	67	63	19	38	80	.281	.345	.244	6.10	2.90
Shore, Logan	R-R	6-2	215	12-28-94	1	6	5.50	13	13	0	0	69	85	44	42	7	19	49	.306	.283	.320	6.42	2.49
Stull, Cody	L-L	6-2	160	3-23-92	1	1	5.23	28	0	0	0	43	56	28	25	1	17	40	.306	.254	.331	8.37	3.56
Walter, Corey	R-R	6-3	215	8-11-92	4	6	6.21	26	9	0	0	75	93	55	52	6	27	39	.297	.342	.270	4.66	3.23
Wendelken, J.B.	R-R	6-0	220	3-24-93	0	1	3.38	11	0	0	3	13	11	6	5	3	10	23	.220	.222	.219	15.53	6.75

Fielding

Catcher	PCT	G	PO	A	E	DP	PB
Chavez	.985	26	177	26	3	6	3
Goldstein	.977	12	78	8	2	0	1
Heim	.990	38	286	13	3	4	3
Murphy	.994	65	498	39	3	5	4
Mercedes	1.000	2	3	7	0	1	
Mondou	1.000	5	10	14	0	6	
Sportman	.966	33	53	87	5	26	
Vertigan	.000	1	0	0	0	0	
White	.967	66	127	166	10	36	
White	.963	16	38	41	3	14	

First Base	PCT	G	PO	A	E	DP
Brown	.988	115	907	72	12	85
Diaz	1.000	6	33	3	0	3
Goldstein	1.000	1	1	0	0	0
Vertigan	1.000	13	122	8	0	9
White	.987	9	69	5	1	7

Second Base	PCT	G	PO	A	E	DP
Diaz	1.000	1	1	2	0	0
Martin	.951	21	43	54	5	12

Third Base	PCT	G	PO	A	E	DP
Chavez	.000	1	0	0	0	0
Diaz	.953	25	15	66	4	2
Marinez	1.000	4	2	3	0	0
Mondou	.981	41	34	71	2	9
Sportman	.867	14	7	19	4	2
White	.872	19	11	30	6	1
White	.938	40	29	77	7	8

Shortstop	PCT	G	PO	A	E	DP
Martin	.963	96	139	282	16	50
Mercedes	1.000	1	2	7	0	2
Sportman	1.000	1	2	2	0	2
White	.951	42	52	122	9	18

Outfield	PCT	G	PO	A	E	DP
Barrera	.988	31	79	2	1	1
Bolt	.969	69	152	6	5	2
Brown	1.000	12	23	3	0	1
Marincov	.966	80	136	7	5	1
Ramirez	.983	111	218	9	4	0
Siddall	1.000	19	20	0	0	0
Sportman	.984	55	115	5	2	2
Vertigan	1.000	45	107	2	0	0
White	1.000	3	5	0	0	0

STOCKTON PORTS   HIGH CLASS A
CALIFORNIA LEAGUE

Batting	B-T	HT	WT	DOB	AVG	vLH	vRH	G	AB	R	H	2B	3B	HR	RBI	BB	HBP	SH	SF	SO	SB	CS	SLG	OBP
Barrera, Luis	L-L	6-0	180	11-15-95	.284	.284	.285	88	313	51	89	18	7	3	46	32	3	1	2	63	10	4	.415	.354
Blanco, Dairon	R-R	6-0	170	4-26-93	.291	.313	.285	82	313	39	91	13	10	1	37	25	2	0	5	66	22	2	.406	.342
Bolt, Skye	B-R	6-3	190	1-15-94	.266	.286	.262	46	169	28	45	8	4	9	32	31	3	1	4	47	9	3	.521	.382
Calabuig, Chase	L-L	5-11	185	12-10-95	.239	.366	.206	51	201	32	48	12	0	0	16	21	3	2	0	40	3	1	.299	.320
Chapman, Matt	R-R	6-0	210	4-28-93	.250	—	.250	1	4	0	1	0	0	0	0	0	0	0	0	0	1	0	0	.250	.250
Chavez, Santiago	R-R	5-11	175	8-5-95	.268	.409	.233	34	112	13	30	2	0	3	12	11	1	2	1	38	2	1	.366	.336
Deichmann, Greg	L-R	6-2	190	5-31-95	.199	.152	.211	47	166	18	33	14	0	6	21	17	1	0	1	63	0	1	.392	.276
Diaz, Edwin	R-R	6-2	223	8-25-95	.237	.286	.227	84	296	44	70	19	0	13	37	39	3	3	3	98	3	0	.432	.328
Goldstein, Jason	R-R	5-11	195	3-9-94	.300	.231	.324	14	50	5	15	5	0	1	5	9	3	0	0	10	0	0	.460	.340
Heim, Jonah	B-R	6-4	225	6-27-95	.292	.369	.271	80	312	41	91	21	1	7	49	29	3	0	4	60	3	1	.433	.353
Lage, Jesus	R-R	6-1	155	12-1-97	.132	.286	.100	16	53	3	7	1	0	1	2	1	0	0	0	23	1	1	.208	.148
Loehr, Trace	L-R	5-10	175	5-23-95	.259	.441	.220	49	193	18	50	12	1	0	11	10	1	1	1	47	1	1	.332	.298
Marinez, Eric	B-R	6-1	160	9-12-95	.226	.241	.221	36	124	13	28	6	3	0	6	10	1	0	0	40	1	1	.323	.289
Mercedes, Melvin	B-R	5-8	170	1-13-92	.232	.100	.250	25	82	11	19	4	1	1	14	20	0	0	1	21	2	3	.342	.379
Merrell, Kevin	R-R	6-1	180	12-14-95	.267	.364	.242	62	270	38	72	10	3	0	24	15	1	4	0	66	5	4	.326	.308
Mondou, Nate	L-R	5-10	205	3-24-95	.291	.207	.308	88	344	64	100	20	5	8	61	33	7	3	4	58	8	5	.448	.361
Perez, Brallan	R-R	5-10	160	1-27-96	.265	.292	.257	87	313	47	83	9	4	0	13	31	9	3	1	56	2	4	.320	.348
Persico, Luke	R-R	6-3	180	10-4-95	.287	.250	.297	112	429	58	123	32	5	5	60	44	2	1	6	78	5	5	.420	.351
Phegley, Josh	R-R	5-10	230	2-12-88	.143	—	.143	2	7	0	1	0	0	0	0	0	0	0	0	3	0	0	.143	.143
Pimentel, Sandber	L-L	6-3	220	9-12-94	.219	.122	.238	68	247	36	54	11	1	15	47	33	1	0	0	93	0	1	.453	.313
Pinder, Chad	R-R	6-2	195	3-29-92	.286	—	.286	2	7	1	2	1	0	1	1	1	0	0	0	1	0	0	.857	.444
Powell, Boog	L-L	5-10	185	1-14-93	.200	.500	.125	4	10	4	2	1	0	0	1	5	0	0	0	1	1	1	.300	.467
Rosa, Viosergy	L-L	6-3	185	6-16-90	.309	.278	.317	25	97	15	30	9	0	5	22	10	4	0	1	23	0	0	.557	.393
Siddall, Brett	L-L	6-1	195	10-3-94	.212	.208	.212	44	156	14	33	5	1	6	22	14	3	0	2	50	0	0	.372	.286
Theroux, Collin	R-R	6-2	220	3-10-94	.181	.238	.168	73	227	34	41	6	2	12	32	43	3	2	2	101	3	1	.383	.316
Toffey, Will	L-R	6-2	205	12-31-94	.244	.256	.240	48	164	17	40	8	0	5	32	29	1	1	2	49	0	0	.384	.357
Vance, Cobie	R-R	5-8	185	8-24-97	.229	.250	.224	27	96	9	22	1	0	0	4	3	2	0	0	16	1	1	.240	.267

Pitching	B-T	HT	WT	DOB	W	L	ERA	G	GS	CG	SV	IP	H	R	ER	HR	BB	SO	AVG	vLH	vRH	K/9	BB/9
Altamirano, Xavier	R-R	6-3	195	7-20-94	5	6	6.62	13	13	0	0	71	96	54	52	11	17	62	.308	.304	.348	7.90	2.17
Bayer, Peter	R-R	6-4	195	3-6-94	0	0	40.50	3	1	0	0	1	3	6	6	2	6	2	.500	.500	.500	13.50	40.50
Biegalski, Boomer	R-R	6-2	177	7-13-94	3	0	2.91	14	0	0	1	22	17	10	7	2	5	36	.210	.259	.185	14.95	2.08
Blackburn, Paul	R-R	6-1	195	12-4-93	0	0	7.36	1	1	0	0	4	3	3	0	1	1	.444	.400	.500	2.45	2.45
Bray, Jake	R-R	6-0	190	12-8-92	1	3	5.01	15	8	0	0	47	48	28	26	8	20	41	.265	.327	.240	7.91	3.86

Name	B-T	HT	WT	DOB	W	L	ERA	G	GS	CG	SV	IP	H	R	ER	HR	BB	SO	AVG	vLH	vRH	K/9	BB/9
Buchter, Ryan	L-L	6-4	258	2-13-87	0	0	0.00	2	1	0	0	2	2	0	0	0	1	2	.286	—	.286	9.00	4.50
Butler, Brendan	L-R	6-3	217	5-2-93	2	2	5.71	36	1	0	0	69	76	56	44	8	28	60	.271	.250	.282	7.79	3.63
Casilla, Santiago	R-R	6-0	210	7-25-80	0	0	0.00	1	1	0	0	1	1	0	0	0	0	1	.250	.000	.500	9.00	0.00
Cochran-Gill, Trey	R-R	5-10	190	12-10-92	1	2	2.89	18	0	0	2	28	31	10	9	3	10	29	.279	.306	.267	9.32	3.21
Damron, Ty	L-L	6-2	200	7-28-94	1	0	3.24	13	0	0	0	17	15	6	6	3	10	24	.238	.167	.267	12.96	5.40
Duno, Angel	R-R	6-0	180	1-10-94	5	4	2.62	48	0	0	15	65	63	21	19	4	17	66	.250	.226	.264	9.09	2.34
Dunshee, Parker	R-R	6-1	205	2-12-95	6	2	2.70	12	10	0	0	70	61	23	21	7	17	82	.238	.260	.224	10.54	2.19
Erwin, Zack	L-L	6-5	195	1-24-94	8	11	5.44	25	25	0	0	136	172	84	82	15	36	108	.308	.302	.310	7.16	2.39
Friedrichs, Kyle	R-R	6-1	195	1-22-92	2	2	3.27	9	9	0	0	52	49	20	19	6	17	48	.245	.235	.252	8.25	2.92
Gilbert, Will	L-L	5-11	170	2-9-94	4	4	2.71	38	0	0	1	63	51	24	19	2	20	62	.223	.200	.231	8.86	2.86
Holmes, Grant	L-R	6-1	215	3-22-96	0	0	4.50	2	2	0	0	6	4	4	3	1	2	8	.174	.333	.118	12.00	3.00
Howard, Brian	R-R	6-9	185	4-25-95	7	3	2.38	12	11	0	0	72	53	21	19	9	14	77	.201	.230	.186	9.63	1.75
Hurlbutt, Dustin	R-R	6-1	195	11-5-92	3	4	3.86	9	9	0	0	44	37	21	19	7	18	39	.228	.208	.244	7.92	3.65
Krall, Pat	L-L	6-6	220	8-27-94	4	1	1.06	23	0	0	0	42	30	9	5	1	8	29	.208	.106	.258	6.17	1.70
Luzardo, Jesus	L-L	6-1	205	9-30-97	2	1	1.23	3	3	0	0	15	6	2	2	0	5	25	.120	.167	.105	15.34	3.07
Manarino, Evan	L-L	6-1	195	12-28-92	4	6	5.40	17	14	0	1	85	101	56	51	11	28	68	.295	.250	.314	7.20	2.96
Marks, Wyatt	R-R	6-0	205	6-28-95	2	0	3.58	5	5	0	0	28	23	11	11	4	16	32	.226	.303	.188	10.41	5.20
Marsonek, Brandon	L-L	5-11	185	6-12-94	0	1	11.88	6	0	0	0	8	11	12	11	3	8	6	.324	.000	.367	6.48	8.64
Milburn, Matt	R-R	6-3	210	7-29-93	9	5	3.49	23	22	2	0	142	161	63	55	13	16	111	.287	.256	.305	7.04	1.01
Romero, Miguel	R-R	6-2	180	4-23-94	1	2	1.84	22	0	0	13	29	21	9	6	3	5	33	.202	.344	.139	10.13	1.53
Sheehan, Sam	R-R	6-2	195	8-8-93	3	2	4.32	44	0	0	1	50	35	25	24	1	32	78	.199	.246	.174	14.04	5.76
Shore, Logan	R-R	6-2	215	12-28-94	2	0	1.21	4	4	0	0	22	18	3	3	0	2	25	.220	.292	.190	10.07	0.81
Tomasovich, Andrew	L-L	6-4	215	9-24-93	2	2	3.14	41	0	0	3	52	42	21	18	4	30	61	.222	.184	.236	10.63	5.23

Fielding

Catcher	PCT	G	PO	A	E	DP	PB
Chavez	1.000	28	213	21	0	5	2
Goldstein	1.000	4	39	2	0	0	2
Heim	.996	55	495	40	2	4	10
Theroux	.994	56	491	34	3	2	7

First Base	PCT	G	PO	A	E	DP
Barrera	1.000	1	5	0	0	1
Deichmann	1.000	5	27	3	0	1
Diaz	.990	26	195	11	2	15
Persico	.991	38	314	16	3	32
Pimentel	.992	54	445	22	4	40
Rosa	.987	19	132	15	2	11

Second Base	PCT	G	PO	A	E	DP
Loehr	.982	41	61	106	3	28
Mondou	.990	72	119	171	3	36
Perez	.959	21	31	40	3	7
Pinder	1.000	1	2	4	0	1
Vance	.950	8	16	22	2	5

Third Base	PCT	G	PO	A	E	DP
Chapman	.750	1	0	3	1	1
Diaz	.944	26	16	52	4	5
Marinez	1.000	1	0	2	0	0
Mercedes	.911	19	13	38	5	3
Mondou	.929	4	2	11	1	0
Perez	.928	27	21	43	5	3
Persico	1.000	7	6	12	0	0
Toffey	.903	43	26	95	13	8
Vance	.957	19	13	31	2	2

Shortstop	PCT	G	PO	A	E	DP
Diaz	.957	33	55	77	6	22
Lage	.875	12	11	24	5	3
Loehr	1.000	1	3	2	0	1
Marinez	.951	17	23	54	4	7
Mercedes	1.000	2	0	8	0	1
Merrell	.951	59	74	139	11	30
Perez	.951	21	34	63	5	11

Outfield	PCT	G	PO	A	E	DP
Barrera	.985	86	184	11	3	3
Blanco	.993	80	146	4	1	1
Bolt	1.000	46	83	1	0	0
Calabuig	1.000	51	113	1	0	0
Deichmann	.944	39	63	4	4	0
Goldstein	1.000	1	1	0	0	0
Lage	1.000	3	2	1	0	0
Loehr	1.000	1	2	0	0	0
Marinez	1.000	11	21	0	0	0
Mercedes	.667	3	2	0	1	0
Mondou	1.000	4	9	0	0	0
Perez	1.000	2	1	0	0	0
Persico	.984	65	115	6	2	1
Pinder	1.000	1	1	0	0	0
Powell	1.000	4	6	0	0	0
Siddall	1.000	36	59	5	0	1

BELOIT SNAPPERS
MIDWEST LEAGUE
LOW CLASS A

Batting

Name	B-T	HT	WT	DOB	AVG	vLH	vRH	G	AB	R	H	2B	3B	HR	RBI	BB	HBP	SH	SF	SO	SB	CS	SLG	OBP
Allen, Nick	R-R	5-9	155	10-8-98	.239	.227	.242	121	460	51	110	17	6	0	34	34	9	3	6	85	24	8	.302	.301
Armenteros, Lazaro	R-R	6-0	182	5-22-99	.277	.250	.283	79	292	43	81	8	2	8	39	36	10	0	2	115	8	6	.401	.374
Beck, Austin	R-R	6-1	200	11-21-98	.296	.303	.294	123	493	58	146	29	4	2	60	30	3	0	8	117	8	6	.383	.335
Churlin, Anthony	R-R	6-1	205	5-27-97	.186	.304	.111	19	59	5	11	2	2	0	6	7	2	0	1	18	0	1	.288	.290
Devencenzi, Jordan	R-R	5-11	190	6-26-93	.266	.250	.271	81	282	32	75	13	1	1	25	21	6	4	5	40	0	2	.330	.325
Farrar, Logan	L-R	5-10	180	4-16-95	.235	.222	.229	117	421	50	99	14	5	12	57	45	7	0	5	102	2	1	.378	.316
Gridley, Ryan	R-R	5-8	180	5-4-95	.269	.250	.274	68	227	25	61	10	1	3	24	28	4	1	1	46	3	5	.361	.358
Hargrove, Hunter	R-R	6-0	215	9-9-94	.290	.307	.285	126	469	59	136	28	0	9	68	37	11	2	6	61	1	0	.407	.352
Lage, Jesus	R-R	6-1	155	12-1-97	.191	.267	.176	29	89	11	17	2	0	2	14	13	1	3	1	31	1	0	.281	.298
Loehr, Trace	L-R	5-10	175	5-23-95	.286	.244	.291	69	252	38	72	14	2	3	22	27	2	6	3	47	15	6	.393	.356
Lopez, Jesus	R-R	5-11	170	10-5-96	.239	.276	.231	84	301	33	72	15	2	10	41	18	5	2	0	56	2	2	.402	.293
Lumley, Jake	R-R	6-1	178	2-13-95	.232	.231	.233	15	56	7	13	0	1	0	6	2	0	0	0	13	0	0	.268	.259
McDonald, Mickey	B-R	6-4	180	6-2-95	.284	.244	.296	110	391	59	111	15	3	2	25	41	3	7	0	76	22	0	.353	.356
Meggs, Jack	L-L	6-1	175	4-18-95	.261	.235	.265	97	345	40	90	22	3	6	35	31	0	0	3	69	2	1	.394	.319
Mercedes, Miguel	R-R	6-4	255	9-12-95	.191	.286	.169	41	152	14	29	7	1	5	24	5	3	0	1	52	0	0	.349	.230
Mullen, Robert	R-R	5-11	225	5-23-96	.222	.000	.267	6	18	2	4	2	0	0	1	1	0	0	0	4	0	0	.333	.263
Shelby, JaVon	R-R	6-1	190	5-6-95	.118	.261	.071	27	93	12	11	1	2	3	10	6	1	0	0	48	5	0	.269	.180
Weber, Skyler	L-R	5-10	176	6-6-95	.227	.037	.258	63	194	23	44	10	1	0	15	28	0	0	2	51	6	1	.289	.321

Pitching

Name	B-T	HT	WT	DOB	W	L	ERA	G	GS	CG	SV	IP	H	R	ER	HR	BB	SO	AVG	vLH	vRH	K/9	BB/9
Altamirano, Xavier	R-R	6-3	195	7-20-94	4	2	3.09	12	12	0	0	70	58	25	24	5	16	63	.221	.158	.246	8.10	2.06
Andueza, Ivan	L-L	5-11	180	2-7-95	4	10	5.35	22	16	0	1	104	110	69	62	5	46	74	.273	.244	.286	6.38	3.97
Bowers, Heath	R-R	6-4	190	7-25-93	6	2	5.40	37	0	0	1	52	55	34	31	6	34	50	.275	.342	.234	8.71	5.92
Camacho, Joseph	R-R	5-9	175	6-23-94	0	1	7.65	16	0	0	2	20	17	17	17	3	12	23	.236	.167	.286	10.35	5.40
Chalmers, Dakota	R-R	6-3	175	10-8-96	0	0	0.00	2	1	0	0	5	3	1	0	0	8	10	.150	.100	.200	18.00	14.40

Name	B-T	HT	WT	DOB	W	L	ERA	G	GS	CG	SV	IP	H	R	ER	HR	BB	SO	AVG	vLH	vRH	K/9	BB/9
Charles, Wandisson	R-R	6-6	220	9-7-96	0	0	4.09	11	0	0	0	11	6	6	5	1	17	19	.158	.200	.130	15.55	13.91
Conley, Bryce	R-R	6-3	200	8-22-94	3	7	4.46	20	16	0	1	85	66	44	42	8	37	98	.213	.226	.203	10.42	3.93
Damron, Ty	L-L	6-2	200	7-28-94	4	2	2.97	24	0	0	0	33	33	16	11	2	17	49	.254	.231	.264	13.23	4.59
Danielak, Michael	R-R	6-4	215	3-16-94	0	2	9.35	3	2	0	0	9	18	17	9	3	3	7	.400	.333	.444	7.27	3.12
Feigl, Brady	R-R	6-5	230	11-27-95	0	1	3.00	3	3	0	0	6	5	2	2	1	1	7	.217	.182	.250	10.50	1.50
Highberger, Nick	R-R	5-10	190	11-4-93	6	3	3.35	34	0	0	6	48	42	27	18	4	25	41	.236	.318	.188	7.63	4.66
Hurtado, Jhenderson	L-L	5-11	205	3-28-96	0	2	6.10	5	3	0	0	21	18	17	14	4	13	20	.234	.227	.236	8.71	5.66
Jordan, Mitchell	R-R	6-2	205	4-10-95	8	4	2.67	25	19	1	0	125	110	40	37	9	34	105	.239	.228	.246	7.58	2.45
Lebron, Jaimito	R-R	6-2	195	10-20-96	0	0	6.55	10	0	0	1	11	12	8	8	2	14	7	.286	.412	.200	5.73	11.45
Lee, Slater	R-R	5-11	230	3-5-95	0	0	0.00	4	0	0	0	6	6	0	0	0	0	2	.300	.444	.182	3.00	0.00
Marks, Wyatt	R-R	6-3	205	6-28-95	5	6	3.23	20	18	0	0	106	90	44	38	8	35	127	.227	.233	.223	10.78	2.97
Martinez, Seth	R-R	6-2	200	8-29-94	3	5	3.28	42	0	0	15	71	68	32	26	5	18	58	.260	.313	.229	7.32	2.27
Poche', Jared	R-L	6-1	215	11-21-94	8	6	4.41	25	22	0	0	131	127	69	64	9	34	105	.259	.244	.264	7.23	2.34
Reagan, Josh	B-L	6-1	185	10-2-94	3	3	5.52	30	1	0	4	46	50	32	28	4	19	33	.286	.342	.269	6.50	3.74
Reuss, Adam	R-R	6-4	220	3-14-95	0	0	4.91	3	0	0	0	7	8	4	4	0	2	7	.267	.182	.316	8.59	2.45
Ruiz, Jean	R-R	6-1	165	9-6-96	5	12	4.66	27	20	0	0	120	123	71	62	14	41	77	.261	.274	.252	5.79	3.08
Salow, Logan	R-R	6-1	185	9-27-94	2	0	1.59	4	0	0	0	6	1	2	1	0	2	8	.063	.000	.083	12.71	3.18
2-team total (3 Great Lakes)					3	0	3.27	7	0	0	0	11	6	5	4	1	4	16	.158	.000	.207	13.09	3.27
Varland, Gus	L-R	6-1	205	11-6-96	0	0	0.93	5	5	0	0	19	8	2	2	1	3	28	.123	.179	.081	13.03	1.40
Withers, Brandon	R-R	6-0	200	7-4-94	0	0	7.20	4	0	0	0	5	10	4	4	1	1	6	.400	.400	.400	10.80	1.80
Zambrano, Jesus	R-R	5-11	170	8-23-96	8	1	3.64	39	0	0	6	77	83	39	31	8	24	81	.269	.298	.250	9.51	2.82

Fielding

C: Devencenzi 77, Mullen 6, Weber 60. 1B: Devencenzi 2, Hargrove 118, Lumley 2, Meggs 12, Mercedes 11. 2B: Gridley 52, Lage 14, Loehr 69, Lopez 6, Lumley 1, McDonald 1. 3B: Gridley 8, Lage 13, Lopez 69, Lumley 14, McDonald 18, Mercedes 24. SS: Allen 121, Gridley 8, Lage 4, Lopez 8. OF: Armenteros 69, Beck 113, Churlin 13, Farrar 60, McDonald 78, Meggs 69, Shelby 23.

VERMONT LAKE MONSTERS
SHORT-SEASON
NEW YORK-PENN LEAGUE

Batting	B-T	HT	WT	DOB	AVG	vLH	vRH	G	AB	R	H	2B	3B	HR	RBI	BB	HBP	SH	SF	SO	SB	CS	SLG	OBP
Akau, Lana	R-R	5-11	205	8-31-95	.146	.000	.200	14	41	4	6	2	0	0	4	8	0	2	0	14	0	0	.195	.286
Arruda, Aaron	R-R	6-3	230	6-21-95	.199	.214	.193	45	156	18	31	4	0	4	17	21	2	0	2	68	2	2	.301	.298
Bride, Jonah	R-R	5-10	208	12-27-95	.287	.347	.267	54	195	29	56	17	0	3	34	24	6	0	4	35	3	2	.421	.376
Brito, Marcos	B-R	6-0	165	3-6-00	.241	.228	.245	54	212	29	51	5	1	1	20	27	0	1	1	50	7	6	.288	.325
Churlin, Anthony	R-R	6-1	205	5-27-97	.202	.194	.204	37	129	20	26	8	0	4	13	11	3	0	2	41	1	0	.357	.276
Eierman, Jeremy	R-R	6-1	205	9-10-96	.235	.281	.219	62	247	36	58	8	2	8	26	13	4	2	1	70	10	4	.381	.283
Foyle, Devin	B-L	6-3	190	11-18-96	.169	.107	.184	49	142	21	24	5	1	0	12	21	2	2	3	44	11	1	.218	.280
Godard, Javier	R-R	6-0	170	12-13-95	.133	.111	.143	8	30	5	4	2	0	1	3	2	0	1	0	8	0	0	.300	.182
Goldby, Cooper	R-R	5-10	190	1-18-95	.000	—	.000	1	1	0	0	0	0	0	0	0	0	0	0	0	0	0	.000	.000
Hannah, Jameson	L-L	5-9	185	8-10-97	.279	.211	.302	23	86	14	24	4	1	1	10	9	0	0	0	24	6	0	.384	.347
Lage, Jesus	R-R	6-1	155	12-1-97	.222	.000	.286	7	18	4	4	1	0	0	1	3	1	0	0	4	0	0	.278	.364
McCray, Jeramiah	R-L	5-10	160	3-3-98	.167	.500	.000	5	12	2	2	1	0	0	0	0	0	0	0	3	0	0	.250	.167
Merrell, Kevin	L-R	6-1	180	12-14-95	.500	—	.500	5	16	4	8	0	0	0	1	0	0	0	0	3	0	0	.625	.579
Mullen, Robert	R-R	5-11	225	5-23-96	.183	.182	.184	19	60	5	11	5	0	1	11	5	4	2	0	12	0	0	.317	.290
Osborne, Nick	R-R	6-2	205	2-20-97	.235	.333	.209	31	115	13	27	7	0	2	14	12	1	0	1	35	1	0	.348	.310
Pantoja, Enrry	R-R	5-11	215	9-27-96	.222	.200	.231	6	18	0	4	0	0	0	0	1	1	0	0	4	0	0	.222	.300
Pena, Joseph	B-R	5-9	175	10-27-95	.218	.103	.246	44	147	27	32	4	4	0	16	26	5	1	3	32	9	1	.299	.348
Piscotty, Austin	R-R	6-2	190	4-16-96	.143	.167	.125	5	14	1	2	0	0	0	1	1	0	0	0	8	0	0	.143	.200
Rivas, Alfonso	L-L	6-0	180	9-13-96	.285	.327	.272	61	214	33	61	16	1	1	28	36	5	0	2	44	7	4	.383	.397
Rivas, Jose	R-R	5-11	220	8-5-98	.215	.282	.191	45	144	16	31	4	0	2	16	11	4	2	1	25	0	0	.285	.288
Rodriguez, J.C.	R-R	5-11	175	1-12-96	.125	.000	.333	2	8	0	1	0	0	0	0	1	0	0	0	1	0	0	.125	.222
Schuemann, Max	R-R	6-1	186	6-11-97	.195	.046	.228	45	123	19	24	1	0	0	6	13	9	0	2	31	11	1	.203	.313
Schwarz, JJ	R-R	6-2	215	3-28-96	.230	.625	.170	18	61	7	14	2	1	0	6	10	1	0	1	17	0	0	.295	.343
Spitz, Adrian	R-R	5-11	185	10-21-93	.000	—	.000	2	1	1	0	0	0	0	0	0	0	0	0	1	0	0	.000	.000
Squier, Payton	L-R	6-0	220	10-29-95	.323	.184	.367	43	158	25	51	8	2	2	29	22	1	0	4	14	5	2	.437	.400
Terrell, James	R-R	5-11	165	1-10-97	.286	.500	.000	2	7	2	2	0	0	0	0	0	0	0	0	4	0	0	.286	.286
Vaughan, Noah	R-R	5-11	200	6-6-97	.194	.179	.197	50	160	15	31	7	3	2	21	7	5	2	1	71	6	3	.313	.249

Pitching	B-T	HT	WT	DOB	W	L	ERA	G	GS	CG	SV	IP	H	R	ER	HR	BB	SO	AVG	vLH	vRH	K/9	BB/9
Birlingmair, Reid	L-R	5-10	210	11-13-96	1	0	2.25	5	3	0	0	16	10	5	4	1	10	8	.172	.136	.194	4.50	5.63
Cerny, Charlie	R-R	6-5	230	9-23-96	1	1	4.32	16	1	0	3	25	26	17	12	0	12	15	.271	.229	.295	5.40	4.32
Charles, Wandisson	R-R	6-6	220	9-7-96	0	0	—	1	1	0	0	0	0	1	1	0	1	0	—	—	—	—	—
Cohen, Chase	R-R	6-1	183	4-26-97	1	2	4.13	12	9	0	0	33	30	17	15	2	14	42	.234	.231	.237	11.57	3.86
Coker, Calvin	R-R	6-3	174	3-6-96	0	0	0.00	1	0	0	0	2	1	0	0	0	0	4	.125	.000	.200	15.43	0.00
Cota, Clark	R-R	6-2	230	10-6-96	3	1	6.11	14	0	0	1	18	18	16	12	1	17	14	.281	.310	.257	7.13	8.66
Evans, Caleb	R-R	6-8	220	3-4-95	1	1	8.64	5	1	0	0	8	13	8	8	1	9	9	.361	.600	.191	9.72	9.72
Feigl, Brady	R-R	6-5	230	11-27-95	1	1	1.35	8	5	0	0	20	6	3	3	0	7	27	.091	.065	.114	12.15	3.15
Hurtado, Jhenderson	L-L	5-11	205	3-28-96	2	2	2.86	9	7	0	0	44	34	14	14	2	13	45	.218	.235	.210	9.20	2.66
Kelly, Rafael	R-R	6-2	190	6-9-97	5	6	4.59	14	10	0	0	69	65	40	35	7	27	59	.247	.171	.298	7.73	3.54
Kohler, Chris	L-L	6-2	210	5-4-95	3	2	4.21	15	10	0	0	36	33	26	17	3	16	28	.241	.268	.222	6.94	3.96
Lebron, Jaimito	R-R	6-2	195	10-20-96	1	0	2.50	10	0	0	2	18	8	5	5	0	9	21	.136	.148	.125	10.50	4.50
Lee, Slater	R-R	5-11	230	3-5-95	1	3	1.95	14	0	0	6	28	21	11	6	0	6	27	.204	.244	.172	8.78	1.95
Marsonek, Brandon	L-L	5-11	185	6-12-94	1	0	4.41	14	1	0	0	33	24	22	16	2	28	27	.211	.125	.257	7.44	7.71
Mejia, Jeferson	R-R	6-7	255	8-2-94	2	1	4.03	15	0	0	0	29	15	18	13	4	19	42	.143	.125	.154	13.03	5.90
Mendoza, Abdiel	R-R	5-10	160	9-19-98	2	3	3.32	13	10	0	0	57	46	25	21	3	22	41	.220	.264	.186	6.47	3.47

OAKLAND ATHLETICS

Name	B-T	HT	WT	DOB	W	L	ERA	G	GS	CG	SV	IP	H	R	ER	HR	BB	SO	AVG	vLH	vRH	K/9	BB/9
Mora, Jose	R-R	6-3	200	10-1-97	1	5	4.67	14	9	0	0	54	48	42	28	4	39	64	.226	.247	.211	10.67	6.50
Morban, Richard	R-R	6-2	162	12-24-97	0	1	22.50	1	1	0	0	2	3	6	5	1	3	4	.300	.200	.400	18.00	13.50
Nightengale, Bryce	R-R	6-5	215	8-16-96	0	2	5.09	14	1	0	2	23	25	14	13	2	17	23	.281	.256	.300	9.00	6.65
Reagan, Josh	B-L	6-1	185	10-2-94	1	1	3.46	6	0	0	0	13	12	6	5	2	2	12	.231	.333	.161	8.31	1.38
Reuss, Adam	R-R	6-4	220	3-14-95	5	2	3.88	14	12	0	0	65	63	32	28	4	22	54	.258	.243	.271	7.48	3.05
Tovar, Oscar	R-R	6-1	200	3-19-98	4	1	2.03	16	0	0	1	27	23	13	6	0	13	29	.235	.225	.241	9.79	4.39
Varland, Gus	L-R	6-1	205	11-6-96	0	1	1.02	7	5	0	0	18	14	5	2	0	4	22	.215	.333	.114	11.21	2.04
Withers, Brandon	R-R	6-0	200	7-4-94	1	1	0.88	15	0	0	5	31	17	4	3	1	10	27	.165	.158	.169	7.92	2.93

Fielding

C: Akau 14, Goldby 1, Mullen 13, Rivas 40, Schwarz 14. **1B:** Arruda 34, Mullen 7, Rivas 40. **2B:** Brito 52, Eierman 2, Godard 1, Lage 1, Pena 20, Rodriguez 1, Schuemann 4. **3B:** Bride 48, Godard 7, Lage 2, Pena 1, Piscotty 4, Rodriguez 1, Schuemann 19. **SS:** Brito 1, Eierman 56, Lage 4, Merrell 5, Rodriguez 1, Schuemann 13. **OF:** Churlin 18, Foyle 49, Godard 1, Hannah 18, McCray 4, Osborne 31, Pantoja 6, Pena 20, Rivas 4, Schuemann 6, Spitz 1, Squier 35, Terrell 2, Vaughan 47.

AZL ATHLETICS   ROOKIE
ARIZONA LEAGUE

Batting	B-T	HT	WT	DOB	AVG	vLH	vRH	G	AB	R	H	2B	3B	HR	RBI	BB	HBP	SH	SF	SO	SB	CS	SLG	OBP
Astorri, Cesarre	R-R	6-0	188	6-26-98	.289	.294	.286	16	45	6	13	2	0	0	5	5	0	0	0	7	0	0	.333	.360
Bautista, Danny	R-R	6-2	185	9-20-00	.200	.250	.183	43	110	19	22	7	3	0	11	14	4	0	1	41	3	1	.318	.310
Bell, George	R-R	6-2	170	1-3-00	.214	.409	.149	41	89	11	19	1	1	0	5	8	2	0	0	32	2	1	.247	.293
Bride, Jonah	R-R	5-10	208	12-27-95	.000	.000	.000	2	5	0	0	0	0	0	0	0	0	0	0	1	0	0	.000	.000
Butler, Lawrence	L-R	6-4	185	7-10-00	.226	.120	.259	46	106	20	24	4	2	1	15	18	0	0	0	43	3	1	.330	.339
Calabuig, Chase	L-L	5-11	185	12-10-95	.406	.556	.348	16	32	7	13	3	1	0	5	5	1	0	1	5	0	0	.563	.487
Campos, Alexander	R-R	6-0	178	2-20-00	.127	.158	.115	28	71	11	9	2	1	0	4	11	1	0	1	28	4	1	.183	.250
Cross, Matt	R-R	6-1	205	7-28-98	.217	.200	.222	13	23	2	5	0	0	0	3	3	0	0	1	5	0	0	.217	.296
Deichmann, Greg	L-R	6-2	190	5-31-95	.290	.250	.308	11	38	9	11	2	2	1	7	5	0	0	0	8	0	0	.526	.372
Diaz, Jordan	R-R	5-10	175	8-13-00	.277	.317	.263	48	159	23	44	11	2	1	25	19	6	0	2	22	0	2	.390	.371
Dingcong, Gio	R-R	6-3	245	5-23-95	.216	.235	.207	38	116	17	25	8	1	5	18	11	5	0	0	42	4	0	.431	.311
Gonzalez, Yhoelnys	R-R	6-0	170	10-30-96	.242	.313	.227	41	91	15	22	1	0	0	8	12	0	2	0	27	9	0	.253	.330
Gordon, Jorge	R-R	5-10	175	10-28-97	.186	.182	.188	24	59	7	11	1	1	0	4	9	0	0	2	14	0	1	.237	.286
Jones, Alonzo	R-R	5-9	197	2-24-97	.267	.250	.273	6	15	2	4	0	0	0	1	0	0	0	0	4	1	0	.267	.313
Jones, John	R-R	5-10	190	10-9-94	.333	.385	.321	31	69	13	23	6	0	0	14	24	1	1	3	11	3	0	.420	.495
Medina, Alonzo	R-R	6-2	190	2-2-99	.225	.154	.237	30	89	13	20	3	0	1	14	13	2	0	0	34	2	1	.292	.337
Mercedes, Miguel	R-R	6-4	255	9-12-95	.250	.222	.267	8	24	3	6	2	0	1	4	3	0	0	0	5	0	0	.458	.333
Merrell, Kevin	L-R	6-0	180	12-14-95	.600	1.000	.556	4	10	3	6	0	2	0	1	1	0	0	0	1	2	1	1.000	.636
Murphy, Sean	R-R	6-3	215	10-10-94	.200	—	.200	2	5	1	1	0	0	0	0	1	0	0	0	1	0	0	.400	.200
Pena, Joseph	B-R	5-9	175	10-27-95	.143	.000	.200	4	7	3	1	0	0	0	1	4	0	1	0	3	1	1	.143	.455
Piscotty, Austin	R-R	6-2	190	4-16-96	.111	.200	.000	4	9	1	1	0	0	0	1	1	0	0	0	2	0	0	.111	.273
Quintin, Christopher	R-R	6-2	135	6-7-99	.217	.281	.198	43	138	17	30	5	0	2	13	11	0	0	0	47	5	2	.297	.275
Richards, Kevin	R-R	6-2	160	1-8-00	.248	.229	.256	42	121	21	30	6	2	0	8	8	1	2	1	32	7	0	.331	.298
Rincones, Rafael	R-R	6-0	159	7-1-99	.209	.227	.203	36	86	13	18	0	3	1	18	10	3	0	2	36	2	1	.349	.307
Sanchez, Santis	L-R	6-1	199	8-21-98	.056	.000	.091	7	18	1	1	0	0	0	1	4	0	0	0	9	0	0	.056	.227
Schwarz, JJ	R-R	6-2	215	3-28-96	.389	.333	.417	7	18	5	7	3	0	0	4	6	1	0	0	1	0	0	.556	.560
Vance, Cobie	R-R	5-8	185	8-24-97	.304	.250	.318	24	56	8	17	2	2	1	10	5	0	0	0	5	1	0	.464	.361
Vargas, Yerdel	R-R	6-0	170	2-17-00	.180	.143	.185	19	61	15	11	1	2	0	4	14	0	1	0	20	3	4	.262	.333
Ward, Nick	L-R	5-10	180	10-19-95	.273	.327	.248	48	154	33	42	4	7	2	27	30	4	0	2	37	8	4	.429	.400

Pitching	B-T	HT	WT	DOB	W	L	ERA	G	GS	CG	SV	IP	H	R	ER	HR	BB	SO	AVG	vLH	vRH	K/9	BB/9
Aquino, Ismael	R-R	6-2	170	9-2-98	2	2	4.54	14	11	0	0	34	29	20	17	0	22	37	.230	.216	.240	9.89	5.88
Berrios, Osvaldo	R-R	6-2	200	11-29-99	3	4	3.71	13	10	0	0	51	57	27	21	1	13	43	.284	.249	.252	7.59	2.29
Birlingmair, Reid	L-R	5-10	210	11-13-96	2	0	1.45	8	2	0	0	19	15	5	3	0	6	25	.214	.167	.239	12.05	2.89
Bray, Jake	R-R	6-0	190	12-8-92	0	0	0.00	2	2	0	0	4	2	0	0	0	1	5	.143	.167	.125	11.25	2.25
Briggs, Austin	R-L	6-1	205	10-10-95	0	1	3.12	16	1	0	3	26	24	15	9	0	14	28	.245	.292	.230	9.69	4.85
Cohen, Chase	L-R	6-1	183	4-26-97	0	0	0.00	1	0	0	0	1	0	0	0	0	0	0	.000	.000	.000	0.00	0.00
Coker, Calvin	R-R	6-3	174	3-6-96	0	0	4.00	13	1	0	2	18	20	11	8	1	9	23	.270	.400	.204	11.50	4.50
Cota, Clark	R-R	6-2	230	10-6-96	0	0	0.00	2	0	0	0	2	0	0	0	0	2	5	.000	.000	.000	22.50	9.00
Evans, Caleb	R-R	6-8	220	3-4-95	1	0	1.56	11	1	0	2	17	15	4	3	0	7	22	.234	.391	.146	11.42	3.63
Finnegan, Kyle	R-R	6-2	170	9-4-91	0	0	18.00	2	2	0	0	2	4	4	4	0	1	3	.400	.400	.400	13.50	4.50
Infante, Angello	R-R	6-1	180	4-16-99	4	3	3.12	9	5	0	0	43	40	15	15	0	9	37	.244	.328	.194	7.68	1.87
Jefferies, Daulton	L-R	6-0	180	8-2-95	0	0	0.00	1	1	0	0	1	1	0	0	0	0	5	.143	.000	.200	22.50	0.00
Jones, Malik	R-R	6-1	185	3-14-96	1	0	4.44	16	0	0	0	24	22	14	12	0	17	26	.256	.188	.296	9.62	6.29
Martinez, Daniel	L-R	5-11	190	7-28-98	1	1	3.13	15	1	0	4	23	17	14	8	0	12	28	.210	.211	.209	10.96	4.70
Martinez, Jorge	L-L	5-11	170	1-5-96	3	2	6.51	15	1	0	0	28	30	23	20	3	13	28	.286	.279	.291	9.00	4.23
McIntyre, Aiden	R-R	6-5	180	8-27-95	1	2	3.38	14	5	0	0	29	19	11	11	0	13	43	.181	.171	.188	13.19	3.99
Monserratt, Jesus	R-R	6-0	180	1-3-97	2	2	5.11	15	2	0	2	25	27	18	14	1	12	23	.278	.359	.224	8.39	4.38
Morban, Richard	R-R	6-2	162	12-24-97	6	3	1.92	13	7	0	0	61	45	24	13	3	23	64	.195	.263	.161	9.44	3.39
Nightengale, Bryce	R-R	6-5	215	8-16-96	0	0	27.00	1	0	0	0	0	2	2	1	0	1	1	.500	.000	.667	27.00	27.00
Pantuso, Alexander	L-R	6-6	235	10-14-95	0	0	3.33	15	0	0	0	24	15	10	9	0	13	35	.177	.237	.128	12.95	4.81
Pineda, Leudeny	R-R	6-1	205	1-29-96	1	3	7.32	13	1	0	0	20	20	18	16	1	14	14	.267	.296	.250	6.41	6.41
Varland, Gus	L-R	6-1	205	11-6-96	0	0	0.00	1	1	0	0	1	0	0	0	0	0	1	.000	—	.333	9.00	9.00
Walter, Corey	R-R	6-3	215	8-11-92	0	0	4.50	3	0	0	0	4	4	2	2	0	4	4	.250	.333	.143	9.00	9.00
Woolfolk, Dallas	R-R	6-2	225	10-30-96	2	1	7.31	11	0	0	2	16	14	16	13	3	16	20	.222	.250	.205	11.25	9.00

Fielding

C: Astorri 16, Cross 12, Gordon 20, Jones 18, Murphy 2, Sanchez 5, Schwarz 4. **1B:** Diaz 1, Dingcong 29, Gordon 3, Jones 1, Medina 28, Mercedes 3, Quintin 8, Schwarz 1. **2B:** Campos 10, Diaz 1, Gordon 1, Quintin 25, Vance 10, Ward 28. **3B:** Bride 2, Diaz 44, Medina 1, Mercedes 4, Piscotty 2, Quintin 5, Vance 10. **SS:** Campos 18, Merrell 3, Pena 3, Quintin 6, Vance 4, Vargas 16, Ward 19. **OF:** Bautista 39, Bell 35, Butler 40, Calabuig 16, Deichmann 11, Gonzalez 38, Jones 3, Quintin 1, Richards 41, Rincones 23, Vance 1.

DSL ATHLETICS   ROOKIE
DOMINICAN SUMMER LEAGUE

Batting	B-T	HT	WT	DOB	AVG	vLH	vRH	G	AB	R	H	2B	3B	HR	RBI	BB	HBP	SH	SF	SO	SB	CS	SLG	OBP
Alvarez, Wilson	R-R	5-10	155	5-19-98	.259	.207	.271	47	147	15	38	4	1	0	8	14	2	3	1	15	11	2	.299	.329
Avila, Albert	L-L	6-2	160	9-26-00	.180	.214	.176	47	139	10	25	5	1	0	15	16	1	2	4	42	6	5	.230	.263
Basilia, Givaine	R-R	6-1	160	6-22-00	.216	.240	.211	47	139	24	30	5	1	0	11	16	2	1	0	43	26	6	.266	.306
Bautista, Danny	R-R	6-2	185	9-20-00	.261	.333	.250	12	46	8	12	1	0	1	7	9	0	1	1	10	6	4	.348	.375
Betancourt, Marcos	R-R	6-0	165	1-17-01	.204	.222	.200	17	54	6	11	2	0	0	6	1	3	0	1	18	1	0	.241	.254
Bonilla, Jose	R-R	6-3	180	2-20-01	.206	.317	.176	59	189	21	39	7	0	3	22	25	6	0	1	78	4	4	.291	.317
Cantillo, Marshall	R-R	6-1	183	3-28-01	.167	.000	.193	34	66	9	11	0	1	0	2	12	4	1	0	24	5	5	.197	.329
Davila, Geykler	R-R	5-11	180	10-19-00	.188	.278	.157	28	69	5	13	2	0	0	12	6	0	1	1	10	1	2	.217	.250
Garcia, Kelvin	R-R	6-3	194	10-14-00	.088	.111	.080	32	68	5	6	1	0	0	3	11	1	0	0	38	0	0	.103	.225
Lopez, Hansen	R-R	5-9	170	7-3-00	.146	.250	.130	33	89	12	13	3	1	0	2	8	4	1	1	33	1	1	.202	.245
Mackey, Davonn	R-R	6-2	170	10-10-00	.111	.125	.107	58	135	18	15	2	1	1	10	25	3	3	0	68	9	4	.163	.264
Mujica, Jose	R-R	6-0	164	3-28-01	.164	.000	.189	24	61	3	10	1	0	0	5	5	2	1	0	10	0	0	.180	.250
Pastrano, Jose	B-R	5-11	150	11-25-00	.143	.056	.170	30	77	10	11	0	1	0	5	22	0	1	0	22	12	7	.169	.333
Paulino, Jhoan	R-R	6-1	176	6-11-01	.242	.242	.242	55	186	15	45	9	0	0	21	16	2	3	1	42	11	2	.290	.307
Salom, Dereck	R-R	5-10	135	2-22-01	.250	.286	.241	46	140	27	35	2	0	0	12	20	2	2	3	20	9	6	.264	.346
Sanchez, Saul	B-R	5-11	160	1-5-01	.109	.000	.140	24	55	5	6	0	0	0	5	2	0	0	0	18	3	0	.109	.140
Santana, Juan	L-L	6-2	180	7-17-01	.171	.130	.186	33	82	9	14	0	1	0	4	20	4	0	0	23	5	2	.195	.359
Serrano, Iraj	L-L	5-11	165	2-19-99	.236	.182	.250	67	216	29	51	5	1	0	24	53	8	4	1	30	11	4	.269	.403
Wright, Joshwan	R-R	5-8	170	11-9-00	.221	.177	.233	53	163	17	36	7	1	0	16	20	4	1	0	20	4	4	.276	.321

Pitching	B-T	HT	WT	DOB	W	L	ERA	G	GS	CG	SV	IP	H	R	ER	HR	BB	SO	AVG	vLH	vRH	K/9	BB/9
Benjamin-Garnett, Mario	R-R	6-4	200	11-22-99	0	0	12.27	3	0	0	0	4	5	5	5	1	3	5	.294	.600	.167	12.27	7.36
Cedano, Alexis	L-R	6-0	180	11-12-97	2	1	3.48	15	1	0	0	21	21	11	8	0	15	24	.256	.261	.254	10.45	6.53
De Leon, Yonatan	R-R	6-3	184	9-4-98	1	2	13.00	6	2	0	0	9	11	13	13	0	12	11	.324	.333	.320	11.00	12.00
Delgado, Gabriel	R-R	6-0	175	11-1-00	2	1	4.78	18	0	0	1	26	30	20	14	1	11	22	.286	.323	.270	7.52	3.76
Diaz, Cesar	R-R	5-11	180	1-8-97	2	0	5.91	17	0	0	2	21	20	20	14	1	24	25	.235	.250	.230	10.55	10.13
Guasch, Richard	R-R	6-4	205	4-10-98	1	0	1.16	7	5	0	0	23	17	5	3	1	4	27	.205	.214	.200	10.41	1.54
Hernandez, Marcelo	R-R	6-1	170	1-23-99	1	3	4.94	20	0	0	0	31	33	22	17	1	11	29	.262	.143	.321	8.42	3.19
Juan, Jorge	R-R	6-8	200	3-6-99	0	5	2.51	15	6	0	0	43	32	18	12	0	24	48	.204	.109	.243	10.05	5.02
Leandro, Carlos	L-L	6-1	170	1-1-01	1	7	9.43	13	6	0	0	28	28	40	29	1	37	22	.259	.336	.247	7.16	12.04
Manzanillo, Manuel	R-R	5-11	185	3-21-98	1	0	3.12	19	0	0	4	26	19	15	9	1	19	34	.198	.167	.212	11.77	6.58
Minaya, Yeudy	R-R	6-4	206	5-11-96	0	3	4.38	8	2	0	0	25	31	18	12	0	12	19	.298	.267	.311	6.93	4.38
Montilla, Stiven	R-R	6-2	197	11-29-98	0	2	3.77	11	7	0	0	31	21	16	13	2	21	23	.196	.172	.205	6.68	6.10
Munoz, Keiro	R-R	6-3	195	9-23-98	1	2	6.41	6	3	0	0	20	31	18	14	2	2	12	.352	.323	.368	5.49	0.92
Noa, Yorlenis	L-L	6-3	185	4-12-96	0	1	1.04	14	7	0	1	52	29	10	6	0	13	48	.166	.222	.155	8.31	2.25
Ortega, Teodoro	R-R	6-0	145	3-12-00	3	1	2.11	14	6	0	0	43	27	14	10	0	11	48	.174	.192	.165	10.13	2.32
Ramos, Wilkin	R-R	6-5	165	10-31-00	3	3	3.15	14	8	0	0	40	39	18	14	0	17	38	.260	.356	.219	8.55	3.83
Rojas, Edwin	R-R	6-1	160	11-1-00	3	3	1.20	13	4	0	0	45	29	18	6	0	17	33	.181	.098	.220	6.60	3.40
Sanchez, Carlos	R-R	5-11	150	12-26-97	2	0	2.35	9	0	0	4	15	12	5	4	0	4	19	.211	.235	.200	11.15	2.35
Sanchez, Livan	L-L	6-0	165	10-21-97	6	2	1.61	14	8	0	0	62	37	16	11	2	12	57	.171	.167	.172	8.32	1.75
Vazquez, Robin	R-R	6-2	187	4-15-98	1	3	2.33	8	4	0	1	27	21	12	7	0	14	16	.214	.167	.242	5.33	4.67

Fielding

C: Betancourt 15, Davila 18, Lopez 33, Mujica 23. **1B:** Alvarez 1, Bonilla 4, Serrano 65. **2B:** Alvarez 11, Basilia 40, Pastrano 13, Paulino 1, Salom 10, Sanchez 4, Wright 2. **3B:** Alvarez 27, Salom 1, Sanchez 6, Wright 42. **SS:** Paulino 43, Salom 29, Sanchez 5. **OF:** Alvarez 4, Avila 38, Bautista 12, Bonilla 55, Cantillo 30, Garcia 17, Mackey 54, Santana 29.

Philadelphia Phillies

SEASON IN A SENTENCE: The Phillies flirted with postseason contention, leading the National League East at one point in August, but a meltdown in September dropped their record to 80-82, resulting in a third-place finish and the franchise's sixth straight losing season.

HIGH POINT: After beating Arizona on Aug. 7, the Phillies improved to 64-49, giving them a 1.5 game lead over the Braves in the NL East. It was the Phillies' sixth win in their last seven games, and the apex of the team's division lead in August.

LOW POINT: Things crumbled in a big way for the Phillies in September. A late August slip caused them to drop to two games behind the Braves in the NL East standings by the end of the month, and an 8-20 September—including nine straight losses, five of which were against Atlanta—sank their season.

NOTABLE ROOKIES: The Phillies were counting on shortstop J.P. Crawford and second baseman Scott Kingery to contribute in 2018, though neither player was effective in their rookie seasons. The team's top rookie turned out to be righthander Seranthony Dominguez, who overpowered hitters with his high-octane fastball and notched 16 saves out of the bullpen. Catcher Jorge Alfaro showed outstanding arm strength and raw power in a solid rookie campaign.

KEY TRANSACTIONS: The Phillies tried to clear a path for Crawford before the season by trading shortstop Freddy Galvis to the Padres in December 2017 for righthander Enyel de los Santos. They also kept Kingery on the Opening Day roster by locking him up to a six-year contract with team options for 2024, 2025 and 2026. In July, the Phillies dipped into their pipeline of young Latin American pitchers, dealing righthander Franklyn Kilome to the Mets for infielder Asdrubal Cabrera.

DOWN ON THE FARM: The Phillies' farm system tilts heavily towards pitching prospects, though the organization's best arm, righthander Sixto Sanchez, threw just 46.2 innings in 2018 because of right elbow inflammation. The upper levels of the system are thin on position players, but Philadelphia addressed that to some extent by adding Wichita State third baseman Alec Bohm with the No. 3 overall pick in the 2018 draft. They also have an exciting Dominican shortstop, Luis Garcia, who played great defense and won the batting title in the Rookie-level Gulf Coast League at just 17 years old.

OPENING DAY PAYROLL: $93,188,166 (22nd).

PLAYERS OF THE YEAR

ROBBIE ROGERS

MAJOR LEAGUE

Aaron Nola
RHP
17-6, 2.37
224 SO, 0.97 WHIP
First-time all-star

MINOR LEAGUE

Enyel de los Santos, RHP
(Triple-A)
10-5, 2.63 ERA
110 SO, 1.16 WHIP

ORGANIZATION LEADERS

Batting		*Minimum 250 AB
MAJORS		
* AVG	Maikel Franco	.270
* OPS	Rhys Hoskins	.850
HR	Rhys Hoskins	34
RBI	Rhys Hoskins	96
MINORS		
* AVG	Austin Listi, Clearwater, Reading	.312
* OBP	Austin Listi, Clearwater, Reading	.412
* SLG	Zach Green, Reading, Lehigh Valley	.532
* OPS	Austin Listi, Clearwater, Reading	.915
R	Adam Haseley, Clearwater, Reading	77
H	Joey Meneses, Lehigh Valley	153
TB	Joey Meneses, Lehigh Valley	251
2B	Zach Green, Reading, Lehigh Valley	35
3B	Malquin Canelo, Reading	6
HR	Darick Hall, Clearwater, Reading	26
RBI	Darick Hall, Clearwater, Reading	87
BB	Mitch Walding, Lehigh Valley	73
SO	Jose Pujols, Clearwater, Reading	162
SB	Malquin Canelo, Reading	24

Pitching		#Minimum 75 IP
MAJORS		
W	Aaron Nola	17
# ERA	Aaron Nola	2.37
SO	Aaron Nola	224
SV	Seranthony Dominguez	16
MINORS		
W	Cole Irvin, Lehigh Valley	14
L	Tom Eshelman, Lehigh Valley	13
# ERA	David Parkinson, Lakewood, Clearwater	1.45
G	Pedro Beato, Lehigh Valley	63
GS	Harold Arauz, Reading, Lehigh Valley	26
GS	Tom Eshelman, Lehigh Valley	26
SV	Pedro Beato, Lehigh Valley	35
IP	Cole Irvin, Lehigh Valley	161
BB	Franklyn Kilome, Reading, Binghamton	51
SO	Spencer Howard, Lakewood	147
# AVG	David Parkinson, Lakewood, Clearwater	.202

General Manager: Matt Klentak. **Farm Director:** Joe Jordan. **Scouting Director:** Johnny Almaraz.

Class	Team	League	W	L	PCT	Finish	Manager
Majors	Philadelphia Phillies	National	80	82	.494	10th (15)	Gabe Kapler
Triple-A	Lehigh Valley IronPigs	International	84	56	.600	1st (14)	Gary Jones
Double-A	Reading Fightin Phils	Eastern	64	73	.467	8th (12)	Greg Legg
High A	Clearwater Threshers	Florida State	77	60	.562	2nd (12)	Shawn Williams
Low A	Lakewood BlueClaws	South Atlantic	87	51	.630	1st (14)	Marty Malloy
Short season	Williamsport Crosscutters	New York-Penn	32	44	.421	t-12th (14)	Pat Borders
Rookie	GCL Phillies East	Gulf Coast	30	24	.556	t-6th (18)	Roly de Armas
Rookie	GCL Phillies West	Gulf Coast	30	24	.556	t-6th (18)	Nelson Prada
Overall 2018 Minor League Record			404	332	.549	4th (30)	

ORGANIZATION STATISTICS

PHILADELPHIA PHILLIES
NATIONAL LEAGUE

Batting	B-T	HT	WT	DOB	AVG	vLH	vRH	G	AB	R	H	2B	3B	HR	RBI	BB	HBP	SH	SF	SO	SB	CS	SLG	OBP
Alfaro, Jorge	R-R	6-2	225	6-11-93	.262	.256	.264	108	344	35	90	16	2	10	37	18	14	0	1	138	3	0	.407	.324
Altherr, Aaron	R-R	6-5	215	1-14-91	.181	.190	.177	105	243	28	44	11	1	8	38	36	4	0	2	91	3	2	.333	.295
Bautista, Jose	R-R	6-0	205	10-19-80	.244	.150	.320	27	45	12	11	4	0	2	6	11	1	0	0	15	2	1	.467	.404
3-team total (12 Atlanta, 83 New York)					.203	.168	.219	122	325	52	66	18	0	13	48	67	6	0	1	111	4	3	.379	.348
Bour, Justin	L-R	6-3	265	5-28-88	.225	.125	.244	29	49	6	11	3	0	1	5	4	1	0	0	13	1	0	.347	.296
2-team total (112 Miami)					.227	.192	.242	141	423	49	96	13	1	20	59	73	2	0	3	124	2	0	.404	.341
Cabrera, Asdrubal	B-R	6-0	205	11-13-85	.228	.220	.231	49	171	20	39	13	0	5	17	12	2	0	0	38	0	0	.392	.287
2-team total (98 New York)					.262	.250	.267	147	546	68	143	36	1	23	75	41	3	0	2	119	0	0	.458	.316
Cozens, Dylan	L-L	6-6	235	5-31-94	.158	.167	.156	26	38	2	6	2	0	1	2	6	0	0	0	24	1	0	.290	.273
Crawford, J.P.	L-R	6-2	180	1-11-95	.214	.118	.230	49	117	17	25	6	3	3	12	13	5	2	0	37	2	0	.393	.319
Florimon, Pedro	B-R	6-2	185	12-10-86	.225	.308	.207	50	71	13	16	6	1	2	5	5	0	0	0	30	1	2	.423	.276
Franco, Maikel	R-R	6-1	215	8-26-92	.270	.222	.286	131	433	48	117	17	1	22	68	29	0	0	3	62	1	0	.467	.314
Hernandez, Cesar	B-R	5-10	160	5-23-90	.253	.272	.247	161	605	91	153	15	3	15	60	.95	4	1	3	155	19	6	.362	.356
Herrera, Odubel	L-R	5-11	205	12-29-91	.255	.288	.244	148	550	64	140	19	3	22	71	38	7	1	1	122	5	2	.420	.310
Hoskins, Rhys	R-R	6-4	225	3-17-93	.246	.192	.260	153	558	89	137	38	0	34	96	87	9	0	5	150	5	3	.496	.354
Kingery, Scott	R-R	5-10	180	4-29-94	.226	.220	.228	147	452	55	102	23	2	8	35	24	3	0	5	126	10	3	.339	.267
Knapp, Andrew	B-R	6-1	195	11-9-91	.198	.167	.204	84	187	19	37	6	2	4	15	24	2	1	1	75	1	0	.316	.294
Plouffe, Trevor	R-R	6-2	215	6-15-86	.250	.286	.200	7	12	1	3	0	0	1	3	0	0	0	6	0	0	.500	.250
Quinn, Roman	B-R	5-10	170	5-14-93	.260	.302	.239	50	131	13	34	6	4	2	12	10	1	1	0	35	10	4	.412	.317
Ramos, Wilson	R-R	6-1	245	8-10-87	.337	.300	.348	33	89	9	30	8	1	1	17	10	0	0	2	19	0	0	.483	.396
Santana, Carlos	B-R	5-11	210	4-8-86	.229	.255	.219	161	560	82	128	28	2	24	86	110	1	0	8	93	2	1	.414	.352
Valentin, Jesmuel	B-R	5-9	180	5-12-94	.177	.222	.164	46	79	8	14	5	1	1	6	8	1	0	1	24	0	0	.304	.258
Walding, Mitch	L-R	6-3	190	9-10-92	.059	.000	.067	13	17	1	1	0	0	1	2	2	0	0	0	12	0	0	.235	.158
Williams, Nick	L-L	6-3	195	9-8-93	.256	.232	.262	140	407	53	104	12	3	17	50	32	9	0	0	111	3	2	.425	.324

Pitching	B-T	HT	WT	DOB	W	L	ERA	G	GS	CG	SV	IP	H	R	ER	HR	BB	SO	AVG	vLH	vRH	K/9	BB/9
Anderson, Drew	R-R	6-3	185	3-22-94	0	1	4.97	5	1	0	0	13	17	7	7	0	2	11	.309	.296	.321	7.82	1.42
Arano, Victor	R-R	6-2	200	2-7-95	1	2	2.73	60	0	0	3	59	54	19	18	6	17	60	.239	.286	.207	9.10	2.58
Arrieta, Jake	R-R	6-4	225	3-6-86	10	11	3.96	31	31	0	0	173	165	93	76	21	57	138	.254	.281	.234	7.19	2.97
Avilan, Luis	L-L	6-2	220	7-19-89	0	0	3.18	12	0	0	0	6	4	2	2	1	4	5	.191	.250	.111	7.94	6.35
Curtis, Zac	L-L	5-9	190	7-4-92	0	0	1.86	7	0	0	0	10	6	2	2	0	10	10	.188	.125	.208	9.31	9.31
Davis, Austin	L-L	6-4	245	12-3-93	1	2	4.15	32	0	0	0	35	35	20	16	4	12	38	.265	.293	.243	9.87	3.12
De Los Santos, Enyel	R-R	6-3	170	12-25-95	1	0	4.74	7	2	0	0	19	19	10	10	2	8	15	.271	.182	.351	7.11	3.79
Dominguez, SeranthonyR-R	6-1	185	11-25-94	2	5	2.95	53	0	0	16	58	32	19	19	4	22	74	.157	.188	.126	11.48	3.41
Eflin, Zach	R-R	6-6	215	4-8-94	11	8	4.36	24	24	0	0	128	130	69	62	16	37	123	.261	.286	.240	8.65	2.60
Eickhoff, Jerad	R-R	6-4	245	7-2-90	0	1	6.75	3	1	0	0	5	4	4	4	1	0	11	.385	.471	.222	18.56	0.00
Garcia, Luis	R-R	6-3	230	1-30-87	3	1	6.07	59	0	0	1	46	49	31	31	4	18	51	.271	.280	.264	9.98	3.52
Hunter, Tommy	R-R	6-2	250	7-3-86	5	4	3.80	65	0	0	4	64	65	28	27	6	15	51	.260	.236	.284	7.17	2.11
Hutchison, Drew	L-R	6-3	205	8-22-90	1	1	4.64	11	0	0	0	21	21	11	11	4	13	19	.273	.333	.220	8.02	5.48
Leiter Jr., Mark	R-R	6-0	195	3-13-91	0	1	5.40	12	0	0	0	17	22	17	10	5	8	13	.297	.258	.326	7.02	4.32
Lively, Ben	R-R	6-4	190	3-5-92	0	2	6.85	5	5	0	0	24	34	18	18	4	10	22	.337	.364	.304	8.37	3.80
Loup, Aaron	L-L	5-11	210	12-19-87	0	0	4.50	9	0	0	0	4	4	2	2	0	1	2	.267	.250	.333	4.50	2.25
Milner, Hoby	L-L	6-2	165	1-13-91	0	0	7.71	10	0	0	0	5	6	4	4	1	3	4	.286	.267	.333	7.71	5.79
Morgan, Adam	L-L	6-1	200	2-27-90	0	2	3.83	67	0	0	1	49	49	25	21	5	22	50	.259	.267	.250	9.12	4.01
Neris, Hector	R-R	6-2	215	6-14-89	1	3	5.10	53	0	0	11	48	46	27	27	11	16	76	.250	.267	.234	14.35	3.02
Neshek, Pat	B-R	6-3	220	9-4-80	3	2	2.59	30	0	0	5	24	23	9	7	2	5	15	.245	.300	.219	5.55	1.85
Nola, Aaron	R-R	6-2	195	6-4-93	17	6	2.37	33	33	0	0	212	149	57	56	17	58	224	.197	.187	.207	9.49	2.46
Pivetta, Nick	R-R	6-5	220	2-14-93	7	14	4.77	33	32	0	0	164	163	91	87	24	51	188	.261	.276	.250	10.32	2.80
Ramos, Edubray	R-R	6-0	160	12-19-92	3	1	2.32	52	0	0	1	43	34	14	11	4	15	42	.218	.208	.223	8.86	3.16
Rios, Yacksel	R-R	6-3	185	6-27-93	3	2	6.75	36	0	0	0	36	43	28	27	6	15	36	.293	.328	.270	9.00	3.75
Suarez, Ranger	L-L	6-1	180	8-26-95	1	1	5.40	4	3	0	0	15	21	14	9	3	6	11	.339	.250	.381	6.60	3.60
Thompson, Jake	R-R	6-4	225	1-31-94	1	0	4.96	9	0	0	2	16	14	10	9	1	11	14	.230	.290	.167	7.71	6.06
Velasquez, Vince	R-R	6-3	205	6-7-92	9	12	4.85	31	30	0	0	147	138	83	79	16	59	161	.250	.288	.212	9.88	3.62

Fielding

Catcher	PCT	G	PO	A	E	DP	PB
Alfaro	.989	104	888	59	11	6	10
Knapp	.982	53	404	21	8	2	6
Ramos	.995	23	190	13	1	0	2

First Base	PCT	G	PO	A	E	DP
Bour	.984	10	57	3	1	6
Hoskins	1.000	17	105	11	0	9
Knapp	1.000	1	2	0	0	0
Santana	.992	149	1167	76	10	114

Second Base	PCT	G	PO	A	E	DP
Cabrera	1.000	2	2	5	0	1
Florimon	1.000	4	2	6	0	1
Hernandez	.981	154	243	378	12	92
Kingery	.900	4	4	5	1	1
Plouffe	1.000	1	1	0	0	0

	PCT	G	PO	A	E	DP
Valentin	.875	9	4	10	2	3

Third Base	PCT	G	PO	A	E	DP
Alfaro	.000	1	0	0	0	0
Bautista	1.000	2	0	1	0	0
Cabrera	1.000	22	12	22	0	1
Crawford	.933	13	1	13	1	1
Florimon	.000	1	0	0	0	0
Franco	.949	117	85	196	15	20
Kingery	.870	10	7	13	3	3
Plouffe	1.000	2	0	2	0	0
Santana	.974	19	9	29	1	3
Valentin	1.000	11	7	11	0	2
Walding	1.000	7	3	3	0	0

Shortstop	PCT	G	PO	A	E	DP
Cabrera	.988	31	20	59	1	18
Crawford	.931	30	36	72	8	18

	PCT	G	PO	A	E	DP
Florimon	.964	21	18	36	2	11
Kingery	.975	119	98	251	9	45
Quinn	.000	1	0	0	0	0
Valentin	1.000	4	0	4	0	0

Outfield	PCT	G	PO	A	E	DP
Altherr	.990	79	95	2	1	0
Bautista	1.000	19	15	2	0	1
Cozens	1.000	14	16	0	0	0
Florimon	1.000	5	1	0	0	0
Herrera	.990	145	305	2	3	1
Hoskins	.976	135	235	5	6	0
Kingery	1.000	7	8	1	0	0
Plouffe	1.000	1	1	0	0	0
Quinn	.975	37	77	2	2	2
Valentin	1.000	5	4	0	0	0
Williams	.980	106	143	5	3	0

LEHIGH VALLEY IRONPIGS — TRIPLE-A
INTERNATIONAL LEAGUE

Batting	B-T	HT	WT	DOB	AVG	vLH	vRH	G	AB	R	H	2B	3B	HR	RBI	BB	HBP	SH	SF	SO	SB	CS	SLG	OBP
Altherr, Aaron	R-R	6-5	215	1-14-91	.244	.292	.232	34	119	15	29	5	0	2	12	14	0	0	1	37	4	0	.336	.321
Amarista, Alexi	L-R	5-6	160	4-6-89	.238	.207	.244	51	160	18	38	3	1	1	14	11	0	1	1	25	2	2	.288	.285
Anna, Dean	L-R	5-11	180	11-24-86	.271	.291	.263	122	446	73	121	20	4	1	34	51	18	12	3	56	9	5	.341	.367
Chambers, Adron	L-L	5-10	200	10-8-86	.278	.368	.262	39	126	20	35	13	2	1	15	10	0	1	1	35	3	1	.437	.329
Cowgill, Collin	R-L	5-9	190	5-22-86	.230	.263	.211	93	304	54	70	16	1	12	43	32	4	1	3	74	3	2	.408	.309
Cozens, Dylan	L-L	6-6	235	5-31-94	.246	.146	.289	88	297	49	73	17	2	21	58	46	1	0	4	124	9	6	.529	.345
Crawford, J.P.	L-R	6-2	180	1-11-95	.259	.313	.238	16	58	6	15	2	1	1	7	5	4	1	0	17	1	0	.379	.358
Espinosa, Danny	B-R	6-0	205	4-25-87	.200	.115	.228	31	105	11	21	4	0	4	14	5	2	0	3	30	3	0	.352	.244
2-team total (13 Buffalo)					.211	.154	.230	44	161	16	34	7	0	4	16	8	2	1	3	45	3	0	.329	.253
Florimon, Pedro	R-R	6-2	185	12-10-86	.214	.667	.091	3	14	1	3	0	0	0	3	0	0	0	0	4	0	0	.214	.214
Goins, Ryan	L-R	5-10	180	2-13-88	.221	.296	.200	42	127	20	28	6	0	2	8	13	0	2	1	32	4	1	.315	.291
Green, Zach	R-R	6-3	210	3-7-94	.248	.328	.221	37	125	16	31	12	1	3	22	10	2	0	1	49	0	2	.432	.312
Knapp, Andrew	B-R	6-1	195	11-9-91	.250	.000	.357	6	20	2	5	1	0	0	1	5	0	0	0	6	0	0	.300	.400
McBride, Matt	R-R	6-2	185	5-23-85	.242	.222	.252	60	190	30	46	13	1	0	26	26	1	4	2	42	0	1	.479	.333
Meneses, Heiker	R-R	5-9	200	7-1-91	.170	.115	.238	16	47	1	8	0	0	0	1	5	0	3	0	10	0	0	.170	.250
Meneses, Joey	R-R	6-3	220	5-6-92	.311	.374	.286	130	492	75	153	27	1	23	82	40	0	0	4	110	0	1	.510	.360
Moore, Logan	L-R	6-3	200	8-22-90	.188	.250	.176	75	229	21	43	8	0	3	14	29	4	1	1	62	0	0	.262	.289
Ortiz, Danny	L-L	5-11	190	1-9-90	.230	.210	.240	118	392	43	91	20	0	15	61	19	3	0	4	101	0	1	.398	.270
Plouffe, Trevor	R-R	6-2	215	6-15-86	.230	.257	.218	73	226	31	52	16	0	12	37	41	2	0	5	68	2	0	.460	.347
Pullin, Andrew	L-R	6-0	190	9-25-93	.171	.071	.202	36	117	10	20	6	1	2	8	8	0	0	0	41	1	0	.291	.224
Quinn, Roman	B-R	5-10	170	5-14-93	.296	.243	.328	25	98	14	29	2	3	2	11	8	0	1	0	19	13	1	.439	.349
Rickles, Nick	R-R	6-2	220	2-2-90	.245	.217	.267	57	188	14	46	7	0	7	26	7	1	0	3	43	0	0	.394	.271
Tomscha, Damek	R-R	6-2	200	8-27-91	.181	.200	.172	26	83	6	15	4	0	2	8	7	2	1	0	16	0	0	.301	.261
Tromp, Jiandido	R-R	5-11	175	9-27-93	.200	.200	.200	6	15	1	3	1	0	0	1	1	0	0	0	4	0	0	.267	.250
Valentin, Jesmuel	B-R	5-9	180	5-12-94	.240	.225	.247	37	129	17	31	5	1	2	13	19	3	1	2	27	3	0	.341	.346
Walding, Mitch	L-R	6-3	190	9-10-92	.266	.218	.284	119	388	70	103	20	2	19	69	73	8	0	3	148	2	0	.474	.390

Pitching	B-T	HT	WT	DOB	W	L	ERA	G	GS	CG	SV	IP	H	R	ER	HR	BB	SO	AVG	vLH	vRH	K/9	BB/9
Anderson, Drew	R-R	6-3	185	3-22-94	9	4	3.87	19	19	0	0	105	92	47	45	14	29	84	.231	.221	.241	7.22	2.49
Arano, Victor	R-R	6-2	200	2-7-95	0	0	9.00	1	0	0	0	1	1	1	1	0	1	1	.250	.000	.333	9.00	9.00
Arauz, Harold	R-R	6-2	185	5-29-95	0	0	6.23	2	2	0	0	9	13	6	6	2	2	12	.351	.333	.360	12.46	2.08
Beato, Pedro	R-R	6-6	230	10-27-86	8	4	3.04	63	0	0	35	68	57	28	23	7	20	67	.229	.205	.248	8.87	2.65
Casimiro, Ranfi	R-R	6-8	200	7-16-92	4	1	3.67	15	2	0	0	27	28	19	11	2	14	22	.264	.327	.211	7.33	4.67
Curtis, Zac	L-L	5-9	190	7-4-92	3	2	3.00	33	0	0	0	42	39	18	14	4	22	48	.201	.154	.228	10.29	4.71
Davis, Austin	L-L	6-4	245	2-3-93	0	1	2.59	24	0	0	0	31	23	9	9	2	8	40	.202	.293	.151	11.49	2.30
De Los Santos, Enyel	R-R	6-3	170	12-25-95	10	5	2.63	22	22	1	0	127	104	41	37	12	43	110	.226	.222	.229	7.82	3.06
DeNato, Joey	L-L	5-10	175	3-3-91	0	0	0.00	1	0	0	1	1	0	0	0	0	2	1	.000	.000	.250	6.75	13.50
Dominguez, Seranthony	R-R	6-1	185	11-25-94	1	0	0.00	4	0	0	0	4	0	0	0	0		3	.000	.000	.000	7.36	2.45
Eflin, Zach	R-R	6-6	215	4-8-94	2	2	4.05	4	4	0	0	20	20	10	9		5	15	.256	.242	.267	6.75	2.25
Eickhoff, Jerad	R-R	6-4	245	7-2-90	0	0	2.44	4	4	0	0	19	17	6	5	1	5	13	.239	.147	.324	4.82	3.86
Eshelman, Tom	R-R	6-3	210	6-20-94	2	13	5.84	27	26	1	0	140	189	105	91	21	45	104	.321	.365	.281	6.67	2.89
Garcia, Edgar	R-R	6-1	180	10-4-96	0	1	7.71	5	0	0	0	5	5	4	4	2	2	4	.235	.250	.222	7.71	3.86
Garcia, Luis	R-R	6-3	230	1-30-87	0	0	10.80	2	0	0	0	2	3	2	2	1	1	0	.375	.250	.500	16.20	0.00
Gilbert, Tyler	L-L	6-3	190	12-22-93	3	1	3.63	25	0	0	3	35	27	14	14	4	6	28	.214	.132	.250	7.27	1.56
Hibbs, Will	R-R	6-7	245	10-27-93	0	1	54.00	1	0	0	0	1	5	9	8	1	2	1	.625	.667	.600	6.75	13.50
Irvin, Cole	L-L	6-4	180	1-31-94	14	4	2.57	26	25	1	0	161	135	51	46	11	35	131	.227	.217	.230	7.31	1.95
Leibrandt, Brandon	L-L	6-4	190	12-13-92	4	1	1.42	20	6	0	0	51	34	8	8	1	10	32	.192	.123	.225	5.68	1.78
Leiter Jr., Mark	R-R	6-0	195	3-13-91	3	1	3.81	20	4	0	0	28	28	15	12	3	13	30	.257	.341	.200	9.53	4.13
Lively, Ben	R-R	6-4	190	3-5-92	3	2	2.42	11	8	0	0	52	37	15	14	3	15	47	.199	.202	.195	8.13	2.60
Milner, Hoby	L-L	6-2	165	1-13-91	0	0	2.39	25	0	0	0	26	21	7	7	2	14	28	.219	.225	.214	9.57	4.78
2-team total (15 Durham)					1	0	2.88	40	1	0	2	41	35	16	13		15	49	.233	.210	.250	10.84	3.76

Name	B-T	HT	WT	DOB	W	L	ERA	G	GS	CG	SV	IP	H	R	ER	HR	BB	SO	AVG	vLH	vRH	K/9	BB/9
Neris, Hector	R-R	6-2	215	6-14-89	2	0	1.45	19	0	0	1	19	9	3	3	0	7	31	.139	.161	.118	14.95	3.38
Ramos, Edubray	R-R	6-0	160	12-19-92	0	0	9.00	6	0	0	0	6	8	6	6	1	1	5	.333	.273	.385	7.50	1.50
Rios, Yacksel	R-R	6-3	185	6-27-93	0	0	3.97	22	0	0	1	23	18	12	10	2	17	26	.220	.212	.225	10.32	6.75
Rivero, Alexis	R-R	6-0	180	10-18-94	0	0	0.00	1	0	0	0	1	0	0	0	0	0	0	.000	.000	.000	0.00	0.00
Singer, Jeff	L-L	6-0	200	9-13-93	0	1	19.64	4	1	0	0	4	5	8	8	1	4	0	.313	.000	.357	0.00	9.82
Suarez, Ranger	L-L	6-1	180	8-26-95	2	0	2.74	9	9	0	0	49	48	17	15	2	15	31	.257	.164	.296	5.66	2.74
Thompson, Jake	R-R	6-4	225	1-31-94	1	2	4.60	28	4	0	2	47	41	25	24	5	26	49	.244	.236	.250	9.38	4.98
Viza, Tyler	R-R	6-3	170	10-21-94	1	1	5.40	5	0	0	0	8	9	5	5	0	6	9	.273	.133	.389	9.72	6.48
Waguespack, Jacob	R-R	6-6	225	11-5-93	3	5	5.06	14	8	0	1	53	54	34	30	4	20	48	.263	.302	.235	8.10	3.38
2-team total (7 Buffalo)					5	9	5.05	21	14	1	1	93	101	60	52	7	30	81	.277	.282	.272	7.87	2.91
Windle, Tom	L-L	6-4	215	3-10-92	9	4	4.17	50	0	0	3	54	48	30	25	6	28	52	.233	.246	.227	8.67	4.67

Fielding

Catcher	PCT	G	PO	A	E	DP	PB
Knapp	1.000	4	28	3	0	0	1
McBride	.984	23	168	15	3	1	2
Moore	.995	75	527	40	3	5	7
Rickles	.997	48	352	16	1	1	1

First Base	PCT	G	PO	A	E	DP
Green	.993	17	141	8	1	13
McBride	.994	21	152	20	1	17
Meneses	.997	96	680	60	2	61
Plouffe	1.000	15	126	5	0	15
Tomscha	1.000	2	14	2	0	1
Walding	1.000	4	27	1	0	3

Second Base	PCT	G	PO	A	E	DP
Amarista	.982	38	71	96	3	26
Anna	.978	38	71	107	4	27
Espinosa	1.000	5	5	9	0	2
Florimon	1.000	1	4	5	0	2
Goins	1.000	7	10	18	0	4

Meneses	.981	10	19	34	1	8	
Plouffe	1.000	22	27	48	0	10	
Valentin	.980	26	43	54	2	11	

Third Base	PCT	G	PO	A	E	DP
Goins	1.000	6	2	5	0	0
Green	.933	12	8	20	2	1
Knapp	.500	1	1	0	1	0
Meneses	.833	2	1	4	1	1
Plouffe	1.000	9	6	13	0	0
Tomscha	.960	10	5	19	1	2
Valentin	.778	3	1	6	2	0
Walding	.941	108	65	220	18	21

Shortstop	PCT	G	PO	A	E	DP
Amarista	1.000	4	4	7	0	2
Anna	.979	77	87	198	6	44
Crawford	.964	16	16	38	2	6
Espinosa	.973	26	39	69	3	22
Florimon	1.000	1	1	4	0	0
Goins	.976	11	12	29	1	7

Meneses	1.000	5	4	6	0	0
Valentin	1.000	6	5	8	0	1

Outfield	PCT	G	PO	A	E	DP
Altherr	1.000	31	67	4	0	0
Amarista	1.000	6	9	0	0	0
Chambers	1.000	33	63	3	0	0
Cowgill	.989	81	180	5	2	2
Cozens	.993	84	148	4	1	1
Florimon	1.000	1	3	0	0	0
Goins	1.000	14	22	0	0	0
Knapp	1.000	1	1	0	0	0
McBride	1.000	2	1	0	0	0
Meneses	.983	30	58	1	1	0
Ortiz	.995	96	189	5	1	1
Pullin	.977	27	42	1	1	1
Quinn	.950	24	55	2	3	0
Tomscha	1.000	10	15	1	0	1
Tromp	1.000	6	6	1	0	0
Valentin	1.000	2	7	0	0	0

READING FIGHTIN PHILS

EASTERN LEAGUE

DOUBLE-A

Batting	B-T	HT	WT	DOB	AVG	vLH	vRH	G	AB	R	H	2B	3B	HR	RBI	BB	HBP	SH	SF	SO	SB	CS	SLG	OBP
Antequera, Jose	R-R	5-10	160	8-1-95	.333	—	.333	1	3	0	1	0	0	0	0	0	0	0	0	0	0	0	.333	.333
Bednar, Brandon	R-R	6-4	195	3-21-92	.273	.214	.296	31	99	8	27	10	1	2	14	2	0	0	1	19	0	1	.455	.284
2-team total (55 Hartford)					.279	.225	.299	86	272	28	76	15	2	7	29	16	0	3	2	54	2	2	.427	.324
Bossart, Austin	R-R	6-2	210	7-4-93	.273	.340	.244	54	176	17	48	6	1	7	29	11	2	0	0	38	0	0	.438	.323
Canelo, Malquin	R-R	5-10	156	9-5-94	.251	.219	.262	128	470	63	118	15	6	9	32	37	2	3	5	110	24	5	.366	.305
Coppola, Zach	L-R	5-10	180	4-7-94	.194	.200	.192	38	129	19	25	1	0	0	7	26	1	4	3	30	10	8	.202	.327
Florimon, Pedro	B-R	6-2	185	12-10-86	.222	.300	.125	4	18	2	4	0	0	1	1	2	0	0	0	5	0	0	.389	.300
Green, Zach	R-R	6-3	210	3-7-94	.296	.333	.284	77	277	50	82	23	2	17	53	28	7	0	0	80	1	0	.578	.375
Grullon, Deivi	R-R	6-1	180	2-17-96	.273	.313	.260	90	326	36	89	14	1	21	59	18	2	1	6	81	0	0	.515	.310
Hall, Darick	L-R	6-4	236	7-25-95	.224	.253	.212	80	295	40	66	10	1	15	52	18	14	0	4	79	1	0	.417	.296
Haseley, Adam	L-L	6-1	195	4-12-96	.316	.238	.351	39	136	23	43	4	0	6	17	16	5	0	2	19	0	1	.478	.403
Hernandez, Jan	R-R	6-1	195	1-3-95	.263	.270	.260	103	350	59	92	15	1	14	53	30	4	1	3	120	7	2	.431	.326
Listi, Austin	R-R	6-0	218	11-5-93	.281	.253	.297	65	217	26	61	9	0	9	39	28	5	0	3	52	0	0	.447	.372
Marrero, Emmanuel	B-R	5-11	169	5-16-93	.189	.138	.202	53	143	8	27	5	0	2	11	15	1	3	1	47	3	0	.266	.269
Martin, Kyle	L-R	6-2	240	11-13-92	.196	.161	.205	48	143	23	28	11	0	4	19	22	2	0	4	37	0	0	.357	
.304 Meneses, Heiker	R-R	5-9	200	7-1-91	.187	.200	.180	51	150	15	28	4	0	1	9	13	4	0	1	39	2	3	.233	.268
Pujols, Jose	R-R	6-3	175	9-29-95	.270	.174	.303	26	89	11	24	2	0	4	18	14	0	0	1	35	2	2	.427	.365
Quinn, Roman	B-R	5-10	170	5-14-93	.333	—	.333	1	3	2	1	1	0	0	0	0	0	0	0	1	0	0	.667	.500
Randolph, Cornelius	L-R	5-11	205	6-2-97	.242	.258	.236	118	410	52	99	18	0	5	40	48	3	2	2	92	3	3	.322	.324
Sandberg, Cord	L-L	6-3	215	1-2-95	.231	.179	.242	54	156	23	36	4	0	3	11	9	0	0	1	35	2	2	.314	.271
Stankiewicz, Drew	L-R	5-9	160	6-18-93	.199	.128	.222	54	156	25	31	10	0	2	14	19	1	2	1	46	1	1	.301	.288
Tomscha, Damek	R-R	6-2	200	8-27-91	.294	.250	.312	93	344	53	101	12	1	15	54	26	8	1	6	58	1	1	.465	.352
Tromp, Jiandido	R-R	5-11	175	9-27-93	.225	.238	.218	89	289	40	65	12	3	4	23	33	4	1	1	83	4	4	.329	.312

Pitching	B-T	HT	WT	DOB	W	L	ERA	G	GS	CG	SV	IP	H	R	ER	HR	BB	SO	AVG	vLH	vRH	K/9	BB/9
Arano, Victor	R-R	6-2	200	2-7-95	0	0	9.00	1	0	0	1	2	1	2	2	0	0	2	.400	.000	.667	18.00	0.00
Arauz, Harold	R-R	6-2	185	5-29-95	9	7	4.59	24	24	0	0	131	144	74	67	17	42	113	.278	.284	.271	7.74	2.88
Bergjans, Tommy	R-R	6-1	190	12-1-92	0	0	1.80	3	0	0	0	5	4	1	1	0	3	0	.222	.200	.250	0.00	5.40
Berry, Tim	L-L	6-3	180	3-18-91	0	0	10.38	4	0	0	0	4	7	5	5	2	2	7	.333	.333	.333	14.54	4.15
Bettencourt, Trevor	R-R	6-0	195	7-21-94	1	0	3.18	11	0	0	2	17	14	6	6	2	9	18	.226	.222	.229	9.53	4.76
Brown, Aaron	L-L	6-2	220	6-20-92	1	2	4.88	18	0	0	1	24	16	15	13	1	23	17	.203	.167	.225	6.38	8.63
Casimiro, Ranfi	R-R	6-8	200	7-16-92	5	4	3.62	18	7	0	0	60	54	30	24	8	26	52	.243	.272	.206	7.84	3.92
Cleavinger, Garrett	R-L	6-1	210	4-23-94	0	1	5.40	7	0	0	0	8	8	5	5	0	10	14	.229	.250	.217	15.12	10.80
Davis, Austin	L-L	6-4	245	2-3-93	1	1	3.86	4	0	0	0	7	7	7	3	1	2	10	.241	.125	.286	12.86	2.57
DeNato, Joey	L-L	5-10	175	3-17-92	0	0	0.00	4	0	0	0	5	4	0	0	0	1	6	.222	.500	.200	11.57	1.93
Dohy, Kyle	L-L	6-2	188	9-17-96	2	5	5.56	18	0	0	1	21	13	15	14	3	22	30	.169	.214	.143	11.91	8.74
Dominguez, Seranthony	R-R	6-1	185	11-25-94	1	2	2.08	8	0	0	0	13	8	6	3	0	2	18	.178	.231	.105	12.46	1.38

Name	B-T	HT	WT	DOB	W	L	ERA	G	GS	CG	SV	IP	H	R	ER	HR	BB	SO	AVG	vLH	vRH	K/9	BB/9
Eickhoff, Jerad	R-R	6-4	245	7-2-90	0	0	5.40	1	1	0	0	3	5	3	2	1	1	3	.385	.333	.429	8.10	2.70
Garcia, Edgar	R-R	6-1	180	10-4-96	7	2	3.32	47	0	0	8	60	45	24	22	6	25	68	.204	.204	.203	10.26	3.77
Garcia, Elniery	L-L	6-0	155	12-24-94	0	6	6.38	10	9	1	0	42	60	41	30	7	21	29	.319	.429	.288	6.17	4.46
Garcia, Luis	R-R	6-3	230	1-30-87	0	1	27.00	1	0	0	0	1	3	2	2	2	0	1	.600	1.000	.333	13.50	0.00
Gilbert, Tyler	L-L	6-3	190	12-22-93	4	1	2.86	23	0	0	2	35	27	14	11	3	9	41	.208	.196	.215	10.64	2.34
Hibbs, Will	R-R	6-7	245	10-27-93	0	0	54.00	1	0	0	0	0	2	6	2	1	3	0	.500	.333	1.000	0.00	81.00
Hunter, Tommy	R-R	6-3	250	7-3-86	0	0	0.00	1	0	0	0	1	0	0	0	0	0	2	.000	—	.000	18.00	0.00
Kilome, Franklyn	R-R	6-6	175	6-25-95	4	6	4.24	19	19	0	0	102	96	61	48	7	51	83	.257	.270	.245	7.32	4.50
2-team total (7 Binghamton)					4	9	4.18	26	26	0	0	140	127	80	65	10	61	125	.248	.275	.223	8.04	3.92
Leftwich, Luke	L-R	6-3	205	6-9-94	3	4	3.73	44	1	0	3	63	55	29	26	3	25	72	.234	.271	.197	10.34	3.59
McGarry, Seth	R-R	6-0	180	1-5-94	2	4	3.99	45	0	0	4	68	58	37	30	6	41	65	.238	.248	.228	8.65	5.45
Neshek, Pat	B-R	6-3	220	9-4-80	0	0	9.00	2	0	0	0	2	4	2	2	0	0	4	.400	.429	.333	18.00	0.00
Paulino, Felix	R-R	6-1	170	3-24-95	3	1	5.46	6	6	0	0	30	32	19	18	2	13	20	.274	.225	.309	6.07	3.94
Quinn, Blake	R-R	6-4	222	4-29-94	0	2	10.80	3	3	0	0	7	6	8	8	1	12	4	.286	.143	.571	5.40	16.20
Ramos, Edubray	R-R	6-0	160	12-19-92	0	0	0.00	1	0	0	0	1	1	0	0	0	1	0	.333	.000	1.000	0.00	13.50
Rivero, Alexis	R-R	6-0	180	10-18-94	3	1	3.45	25	4	0	0	47	40	20	18	6	24	36	.230	.247	.214	6.89	4.60
Romero, JoJo	L-L	6-0	190	9-9-96	7	6	3.80	18	18	0	0	107	97	49	45	13	41	100	.241	.213	.253	8.44	3.46
Seabold, Connor	R-R	6-3	190	1-24-96	1	4	4.91	11	11	0	0	59	55	32	32	10	19	64	.241	.273	.212	9.82	2.91
Singer, Jeff	L-L	6-0	200	9-13-93	1	2	2.70	27	0	0	12	33	20	11	10	1	19	38	.195	.206	.163	10.26	5.13
Suarez, Ranger	L-L	6-1	180	8-26-95	4	3	2.76	12	12	1	0	75	64	23	23	2	20	54	.235	.224	.239	6.48	2.40
Taveras, Jose	L-R	6-4	210	11-6-93	0	1	5.95	6	3	0	0	20	24	14	13	4	10	17	.282	.356	.200	7.78	4.58
Tols, Josh	L-L	5-7	185	10-6-89	1	1	3.27	23	1	0	1	33	13	12	12	3	18	42	.122	.111	.132	11.45	4.91
Viza, Tyler	R-R	6-3	170	10-21-94	3	5	2.75	19	11	1	0	75	70	29	23	5	20	68	.249	.231	.263	8.12	2.39
Waguespack, Jacob	R-R	6-6	225	11-5-93	1	1	3.99	7	7	0	0	29	31	14	13	0	16	31	.261	.222	.304	9.51	4.91

Fielding

Catcher	PCT	G	PO	A	E	DP	PB
Bossart	.996	51	447	45	2	1	7
Grullon	.984	87	682	58	12	8	10

First Base	PCT	G	PO	A	E	DP
Green	.982	25	203	12	4	18
Hall	.992	73	551	52	5	39
Listi	.977	12	76	10	2	5
Martin	.996	31	248	22	1	17

Second Base	PCT	G	PO	A	E	DP
Bednar	.964	23	33	48	3	10
Canelo	.984	14	25	35	1	3
Florimon	1.000	1	1	1	0	0
Marrero	.987	36	59	97	2	16
Meneses	.992	29	53	64	1	14

	PCT	G	PO	A	E	DP
Stankiewicz	.970	45	62	97	5	21

Third Base	PCT	G	PO	A	E	DP
Bednar	.800	4	0	4	1	0
Florimon	1.000	1	0	2	0	0
Green	.937	40	18	56	5	1
Listi	1.000	3	2	2	0	0
Marrero	.000	2	0	0	0	0
Meneses	.800	4	1	3	1	0
Stankiewicz	1.000	2	1	1	0	0
Tomscha	.950	88	54	135	10	10

Shortstop	PCT	G	PO	A	E	DP
Antequera	1.000	1	3	4	0	0
Canelo	.959	115	165	307	20	60
Florimon	.800	1	2	2	1	1

	PCT	G	PO	A	E	DP
Marrero	.933	7	3	11	1	1
Meneses	.968	19	21	40	2	7

Outfield	PCT	G	PO	A	E	DP
Coppola	.957	37	85	4	4	0
Haseley	.986	36	70	2	1	0
Hernandez	.969	95	183	7	6	2
Listi	1.000	24	39	4	0	2
Martin	1.000	3	3	0	0	0
Pujols	.951	24	38	1	2	0
Quinn	1.000	1	5	0	0	0
Randolph	.976	103	155	8	4	1
Sandberg	1.000	38	82	4	0	1
Tomscha	.667	1	2	0	1	0
Tromp	.970	70	126	5	4	1

CLEARWATER THRESHERS

HIGH CLASS A

FLORIDA STATE LEAGUE

Batting	B-T	HT	WT	DOB	AVG	vLH	vRH	G	AB	R	H	2B	3B	HR	RBI	BB	HBP	SH	SF	SO	SB	CS	SLG	OBP
Antequera, Jose	R-R	5-10	160	8-1-95	.333	.500	.250	11	30	3	10	1	0	0	5	2	0	2	0	4	0	0	.367	.375
Brito, Daniel	L-R	6-1	170	1-23-98	.250	.125	.276	27	92	8	23	5	2	0	7	6	1	0	1	19	1	1	.348	.300
Cabral, Edgar	R-R	5-11	210	9-12-95	.252	.252	.251	81	294	41	74	10	2	6	39	28	4	0	3	64	1	1	.361	.322
Crawford, J.P.	L-R	6-2	180	1-11-95	.143	.000	.188	12	42	8	6	1	0	1	4	7	0	0	0	14	0	0	.238	.265
Cumana, Grenny	R-R	5-5	145	11-10-95	.282	.281	.282	59	206	18	58	8	1	2	16	5	4	0	0	15	2	6	.359	.312
Florimon, Pedro	B-R	6-0	185	12-10-86	.222	.000	.364	6	18	4	4	1	1	0	1	3	2	0	0	8	0	0	.389	.391
Gamboa, Arquimedes	B-R	6-0	175	9-23-97	.214	.203	.220	114	434	49	93	14	4	2	37	53	4	3	3	111	6	4	.279	.304
Garcia, Wilson	B-R	5-11	160	1-11-94	.250	.143	.286	7	28	2	7	3	0	0	6	0	0	0	1	0	0	0	.357	.250
Gomez, Jose	R-R	5-11	175	12-10-96	.224	.229	.221	103	357	33	80	7	2	1	24	15	2	11	0	65	7	2	.263	.259
Hall, Darick	L-R	6-4	236	7-25-95	.278	.233	.301	48	173	28	48	12	0	11	35	18	7	0	1	39	1	0	.538	.367
Haseley, Adam	L-L	6-1	195	4-12-96	.300	.322	.288	79	330	54	99	13	5	5	38	19	3	1	1	54	7	3	.415	.343
Lartigue, Henri	B-R	6-0	205	2-24-95	.251	.236	.259	100	374	44	94	14	2	7	45	33	6	0	0	88	1	1	.356	.322
Lino, Gabriel	B-R	6-3	200	5-17-93	.214	.214	.150	20	56	3	12	1	0	2	4	4	1	0	0	17	0	0	.339	.279
Listi, Austin	R-R	6-0	218	11-5-93	.345	.333	.352	58	209	37	72	16	1	9	45	34	9	0	2	42	0	0	.560	.453
Markham, Kevin	L-R	6-0	195	4-14-94	.254	.333	.226	45	138	25	35	5	2	0	14	13	2	0	2	25	5	1	.319	.323
Martin, Kyle	L-L	6-2	240	11-13-92	.199	.164	.217	62	216	17	43	14	0	6	26	20	1	0	2	64	2	0	.347	.268
Mayer, Danny	R-R	6-5	245	6-25-95	.385	1.000	.333	4	13	2	5	1	0	0	0	1	0	0	0	4	0	0	.462	.429
Mims, Brian	R-R	5-11	185	3-14-96	.318	.333	.310	15	44	9	14	4	0	0	4	8	0	1	0	11	1	0	.409	.423
Moniak, Mickey	L-R	6-2	185	5-13-98	.270	.294	.259	114	433	50	117	28	3	5	55	22	2	1	7	100	6	3	.383	.304
Nieporte, Quincy	R-R	6-1	225	7-29-94	.250	.000	.333	1	4	0	1	0	0	0	0	0	0	0	0	1	0	0	.250	.250
Pujols, Jose	R-R	6-3	175	9-29-95	.301	.286	.311	95	352	56	106	16	4	18	58	33	2	0	0	127	1	1	.523	.364
Quinn, Roman	B-R	5-10	170	5-14-93	.400	.400	—	2	5	2	2	0	0	0	2	0	0	0	0	1	0	0	.400	.500
Ramos, Wilson	R-R	6-1	245	8-10-87	.444	.000	.571	3	9	2	4	3	0	0	0	0	0	0	0	2	0	0	.778	.444
Rivas, Raul	B-R	5-10	160	10-27-96	.242	.155	.283	104	343	46	83	10	4	3	35	22	3	3	2	69	10	6	.321	.292
Williams, Luke	R-R	6-1	180	8-9-96	.245	.264	.233	110	388	51	95	13	1	9	43	35	9	1	4	76	14	7	.353	.319

Pitching	B-T	HT	WT	DOB	W	L	ERA	G	GS	CG	SV	IP	H	R	ER	HR	BB	SO	AVG	vLH	vRH	K/9	BB/9
Bergjans, Tommy	R-R	6-1	190	12-1-92	0	0	4.50	2	0	0	0	2	3	1	1	1	0	0	.333	.000	.500	0.00	0.00
2-team total (14 Daytona)					5	2	3.68	16	14	0	0	81	73	34	33	6	16	51	.239	.234	.243	5.69	1.79

PHILADELPHIA PHILLIES

Name	B-T	HT	WT	DOB	W	L	ERA	G	GS	CG	SV	IP	H	R	ER	HR	BB	SO	AVG	vLH	vRH	K/9	BB/9
Bettencourt, Trevor	R-R	6-0	195	7-21-94	1	1	0.53	10	0	0	0	17	13	5	1	0	2	21	.213	.143	.273	11.12	1.06
Brown, Aaron	L-L	6-2	220	6-20-92	2	4	4.91	28	0	0	4	37	46	23	20	4	17	41	.307	.439	.226	10.06	4.17
Brown, Andrew	R-R	6-1	180	10-24-97	0	0	2.25	1	1	0	0	4	4	1	1	0	1	2	.286	.400	.222	4.50	2.25
Cabrera, Ismael	R-R	6-1	185	6-19-94	0	1	7.16	11	0	0	2	16	17	14	13	3	8	14	.258	.353	.156	7.71	4.41
Casimiro, Ranfi	R-R	6-8	200	7-16-92	0	0	4.50	1	1	0	0	4	4	2	2	0	2	5	.286	.222	.400	11.25	4.50
Cedeno, Luis	R-R	5-11	154	7-14-94	0	0	—	1	0	0	0	0	3	3	3	0	1	0	1.000	1.000	1.000	—	—
Cleavinger, Garrett	R-L	6-1	210	4-23-94	1	0	10.80	5	0	0	0	5	5	7	6	0	2	4	.278	.143	.364	7.20	3.60
Dohy, Kyle	L-L	6-2	188	9-17-96	2	1	1.64	7	0	0	2	11	5	3	2	1	3	18	.135	.133	.136	14.73	2.45
Dyer, Grant	R-R	6-1	195	7-31-95	1	1	4.78	23	0	0	0	32	39	17	17	6	7	25	.310	.328	.290	7.03	1.97
Eickhoff, Jerad	R-R	6-4	245	7-2-90	0	1	3.00	3	3	0	0	9	3	3	3	2	4	10	.107	.083	.125	10.00	4.00
Falter, Bailey	R-L	6-4	175	4-24-97	8	4	2.69	17	17	0	0	94	87	35	28	6	15	83	.247	.250	.245	7.98	1.44
Fanti, Nick	L-L	6-2	185	12-30-96	3	3	7.22	6	6	0	0	29	31	23	23	6	9	18	.287	.368	.243	5.65	2.83
Hammer, JD	R-R	6-3	215	7-12-94	1	2	2.79	9	0	0	0	10	8	6	3	0	4	12	.216	.167	.263	11.17	3.72
Hennigan, Jonathan	L-L	6-4	193	8-27-94	0	0	1.53	15	0	0	0	18	17	6	3	1	6	14	.250	.212	.286	7.13	3.06
Hernandez, Jakob	L-L	6-4	260	5-19-96	3	3	2.80	43	0	0	5	71	61	26	22	2	31	92	.242	.236	.247	11.72	3.95
Hibbs, Will	R-R	6-2	245	10-27-93	3	0	6.75	17	0	0	2	21	19	17	16	1	12	24	.226	.189	.255	10.13	5.06
Hunter, Tommy	R-R	6-3	250	7-3-86	0	0	0.00	1	0	0	0	1	1	0	0	0	1	1	.200	.333	.000	6.75	6.75
Leiter Jr., Mark	R-R	6-0	195	3-13-91	0	0	0.00	3	0	0	0	5	1	0	0	0	1	9	.063	.125	.000	16.20	1.80
Llovera, Mauricio	R-R	5-11	200	4-17-96	8	7	3.72	23	22	1	0	121	100	59	50	14	34	137	.221	.213	.231	10.19	2.53
Medina, Adonis	R-R	6-1	185	12-18-96	10	4	4.12	22	21	1	0	111	103	59	51	11	36	123	.245	.256	.234	9.94	2.91
Mills, McKenzie	L-L	6-4	205	11-19-95	2	5	3.51	20	16	0	0	90	88	43	35	7	33	85	.256	.239	.264	8.53	3.31
Neshek, Pat	B-R	6-3	220	9-4-80	0	0	0.00	1	0	0	0	1	0	0	0	0	0	2	.000	.000	—	18.00	0.00
Parkinson, David	R-L	6-2	210	12-14-95	3	0	1.24	5	4	0	0	29	17	4	4	1	9	26	.175	.081	.233	8.07	2.79
Paulino, Felix	R-R	6-1	170	3-24-95	1	3	3.18	25	3	0	1	62	67	24	22	6	21	54	.276	.323	.221	7.80	3.03
Quinn, Blake	R-R	6-4	222	4-29-94	3	6	6.33	34	0	0	0	48	51	35	34	4	28	50	.268	.284	.253	9.31	5.21
Requena, Alejandro	R-R	6-2	200	11-29-96	4	4	3.60	12	12	0	0	65	55	26	26	3	23	60	.235	.246	.220	8.31	3.18
Rivero, Alexis	R-R	6-0	180	10-18-94	0	0	6.91	9	0	0	1	14	16	11	11	1	5	8	.286	.276	.296	5.02	3.14
Rosso, Ramon	R-R	6-4	215	6-9-96	6	2	2.91	11	10	0	0	56	49	21	18	1	20	58	.238	.290	.182	9.38	3.23
Russ, Addison	R-R	6-1	190	10-29-94	4	0	1.69	29	0	0	14	32	25	6	6	1	11	42	.205	.188	.224	11.81	3.09
Sanchez, Sixto	R-R	6-0	185	7-29-98	4	3	2.51	8	8	1	0	47	39	14	13	1	11	45	.224	.217	.231	8.68	2.12
Seabold, Connor	R-R	6-3	190	1-24-96	4	4	3.77	12	12	1	0	72	57	31	30	6	14	68	.214	.209	.218	8.54	1.76
Singer, Jeff	L-L	6-0	200	9-13-93	0	3	3.86	13	0	0	3	16	16	11	7	2	4	17	.262	.348	.211	9.37	2.20
Tirado, Alberto	R-R	6-0	180	12-10-94	3	1	2.18	23	0	0	1	33	20	9	8	0	21	31	.170	.102	.237	8.45	5.73
Tols, Josh	L-L	5-7	185	10-6-89	1	0	0.93	4	1	0	0	10	2	1	0	4	13		.069	.000	.118	12.10	3.72

Fielding

Catcher	PCT	G	PO	A	E	DP	PB
Cabral	.994	60	509	32	3	3	6
Garcia	.960	3	21	3	1	0	0
Lartigue	.994	72	632	62	4	1	6
Lino	1.000	2	11	3	0	0	0
Ramos	1.000	2	17	2	0	0	0

First Base	PCT	G	PO	A	E	DP
Hall	.995	42	337	27	2	19
Listi	.994	22	162	12	1	9
Martin	.994	61	462	34	3	37
Mayer	1.000	1	1	0	0	0
Nieporte	1.000	1	6	0	0	0
Williams	1.000	14	91	13	0	10

Second Base	PCT	G	PO	A	E	DP
Antequera	1.000	10	14	31	0	3
Brito	.980	24	34	65	2	14
Florimon	1.000	1	1	0	0	0
Gomez	.977	31	41	84	3	14
Mims	1.000	10	14	27	0	7
Rivas	.976	63	97	143	6	22
Williams	.857	1	3	3	1	0

Third Base	PCT	G	PO	A	E	DP
Crawford	1.000	3	6	4	0	1
Florimon	1.000	2	1	0	0	0
Gomez	.951	48	25	72	5	4
Mims	1.000	3	2	3	0	0
Rivas	.955	31	17	47	3	3
Williams	.975	58	35	80	3	7

Shortstop	PCT	G	PO	A	E	DP
Crawford	.950	8	8	11	1	3
Florimon	1.000	1	2	1	0	0
Gamboa	.971	109	153	243	12	46
Gomez	.989	25	32	59	1	7

Outfield	PCT	G	PO	A	E	DP
Cumana	.987	43	69	9	1	0
Haseley	.975	79	149	4	4	2
Listi	1.000	7	10	0	0	0
Markham	.977	43	79	6	2	2
Mayer	1.000	1	4	0	0	0
Moniak	.996	110	227	6	1	1
Pujols	.949	88	156	11	9	1
Quinn	1.000	2	2	0	0	0
Rivas	1.000	5	6	0	0	0
Williams	.961	40	73	1	3	0

LAKEWOOD BLUECLAWS
SOUTH ATLANTIC LEAGUE
LOW CLASS A

Batting	B-T	HT	WT	DOB	AVG	vLH	vRH	G	AB	R	H	2B	3B	HR	RBI	BB	HBP	SH	SF	SO	SB	CS	SLG	OBP
Alastre, Jesus	R-R	6-1	155	11-25-96	.231	.231	.231	17	52	3	12	1	0	0	3	4	2	1	0	10	2	1	.250	.310
Antequera, Jose	R-R	5-10	160	8-1-95	.263	.296	.245	54	156	20	41	8	0	2	15	18	2	5	5	33	2	6	.353	.337
Brito, Daniel	L-R	6-1	170	1-23-98	.252	.250	.253	92	329	33	83	13	2	4	31	27	2	5	5	64	15	6	.340	.309
Duran, Rodolfo	R-R	5-9	181	2-19-98	.261	.174	.301	88	311	44	81	17	1	18	46	20	1	1	3	75	1	1	.495	.305
Fitch, Colby	L-R	5-11	215	7-27-95	.236	.224	.243	77	254	39	60	14	3	5	28	40	6	1	2	86	0	2	.374	.351
Gurrola, Yahir	R-R	6-0	190	3-19-96	.127	.103	.150	25	79	11	10	1	0	1	1	4	0	0	0	30	1	1	.177	.169
Guthrie, Dalton	R-R	5-11	160	12-23-95	.241	.191	.267	91	307	42	74	16	0	5	30	21	6	6	7	56	3	6	.342	.296
Markham, Kevin	L-R	6-0	195	4-14-94	.282	.271	.287	53	170	22	48	8	1	2	15	15	4	0	1	31	12	7	.377	.353
Martinez, Nerluis	L-R	6-2	175	4-10-96	.000		.000	1	2	0	0	0	0	0	0	0	0	0	0	0	0	0	.000	.000
Maton, Nick	L-R	6-1	165	2-18-97	.236	.234	.264	114	406	52	104	26	5	8	51	43	5	5	7	103	5	3	.404	.330
Matos, Malvin	R-R	6-3	170	8-19-96	.250	.500	.167	3	8	1	2	1	1	0	1	1	1	0	0	4	0	0	.625	.400
Mayer, Danny	R-R	6-5	245	6-25-95	.148	.143	.152	16	54	5	8	1	0	2	2	2	0	1	0	22	0	0	.278	.179
Muzziotti, Simon	L-L	6-1	175	12-27-98	.263	.330	.228	68	278	33	73	12	2	1	20	14	5	1	6	40	18	4	.331	.299
Nieporte, Quincy	R-R	6-1	225	7-29-94	.258	.287	.244	89	306	33	79	18	1	6	35	21	6	0	4	43	0	0	.382	.315
Ortiz, Jhailyn	R-R	6-3	215	11-18-98	.225	.205	.233	110	405	51	91	18	2	13	47	35	9	0	5	148	2	2	.375	.297
Rivero, Gregori	B-R	6-0	202	5-27-96	.217	.182	.231	48	161	18	35	6	2	3	21	5	1	0	2	42	0	2	.335	.243
Rodriguez, Edwin	L-L	6-1	170	6-8-97	.200	.000	.357	7	25	2	5	1	0	0	1	0	0	0	0	4	0	0	.240	.200

Name	B-T	HT	WT	DOB	AVG	vLH	vRH	G	AB	R	H	2B	3B	HR	RBI	BB	HBP	SH	SF	SO	SB	CS	SLG	OBP
Scheiner, Jake	R-R	6-1	200	8-13-95	.296	.338	.275	122	453	65	134	30	5	13	67	49	8	3	4	81	10	6	.470	.372
Stephen, Josh	L-L	6-0	185	9-22-97	.242	.254	.239	99	314	28	76	17	2	4	35	19	2	0	2	71	4	1	.347	.288
Stobbe, Cole	R-R	6-2	194	8-30-97	.209	.316	.125	12	43	5	9	3	0	1	7	3	0	0	0	15	0	0	.349	.261
Stokes, Madison	R-R	6-2	200	4-25-96	.260	.286	.250	27	100	12	26	4	1	1	11	4	1	0	1	23	0	0	.350	.293
Vierling, Matt	R-R	6-3	205	9-16-96	.294	.386	.252	50	184	24	54	15	0	6	25	10	5	2	3	38	5	5	.473	.342

Pitching	B-T	HT	WT	DOB	W	L	ERA	G	GS	CG	SV	IP	H	R	ER	HR	BB	SO	AVG	vLH	vRH	K/9	BB/9
Alcantara, Randy	R-R	5-11	173	11-9-96	0	1	7.02	10	0	0	1	17	27	15	13	5	6	10	.365	.415	.303	5.40	3.24
Armas, Gustavo	R-R	6-1	195	1-15-96	3	1	2.32	8	8	1	0	50	35	14	13	4	9	47	.193	.227	.161	8.40	1.61
Brogdon, Connor	R-R	6-6	192	1-29-95	5	3	2.47	31	7	0	5	69	59	21	19	3	16	79	.228	.234	.221	10.25	2.08
Brown, Andrew	R-R	6-1	180	10-24-97	6	3	2.10	14	10	1	0	69	49	19	16	2	16	58	.199	.200	.198	7.60	2.10
Cabrera, Ismael	R-R	6-1	185	6-19-94	0	2	6.23	12	0	0	0	22	29	19	15	4	13	24	.322	.450	.220	9.40	5.40
Carrasco, Luis	R-R	6-3	181	9-11-94	5	2	3.11	30	1	0	4	67	64	25	23	2	27	59	.262	.235	.287	7.97	3.65
Cedeno, Luis	R-R	5-11	154	7-14-94	5	2	3.90	16	0	0	0	30	23	20	13	2	20	38	.207	.224	.189	11.40	6.00
2-team total (11 Charleston)					5	3	2.91	27	0	0	2	43	33	25	14	2	24	49	.208	.244	.164	10.18	4.98
Dohy, Kyle	L-L	6-2	188	9-17-96	3	3	0.80	24	0	0	7	34	16	5	3	1	17	63	.144	.086	.171	16.84	4.54
Fallwell, Tyler	R-R	6-5	210	11-8-95	1	1	6.75	12	0	0	0	21	31	20	16	1	6	21	.344	.415	.286	8.86	2.53
Garcia, Julian	L-R	6-3	206	5-13-95	7	3	2.54	28	8	0	1	78	63	24	22	3	26	94	.223	.256	.193	10.85	3.00
Hennigan, Jonathan	L-L	6-4	193	8-27-94	1	1	2.83	22	0	0	2	35	30	13	11	1	14	32	.238	.172	.294	8.23	3.60
Howard, Spencer	R-R	6-3	205	7-28-96	9	8	3.78	23	23	1	0	112	101	52	47	6	40	147	.241	.211	.271	11.81	3.21
Jones, Damon	L-L	6-5	225	9-30-94	10	7	3.41	23	22	0	0	113	105	53	43	7	50	123	.247	.295	.228	9.77	3.97
Killgore, Keylan	L-L	6-3	185	9-30-96	0	0	0.00	1	0	0	0	1	0	0	0	0	0	0	.000	.000	.000	0.00	0.00
McArthur, James	R-R	6-7	230	12-11-96	0	0	0.00	1	1	0	0	4	0	0	0	1	2	.000	.000	.000	4.50	2.25
Parkinson, David	R-L	6-2	210	12-14-95	8	1	1.51	17	17	1	0	95	74	27	16	4	26	115	.210	.301	.161	10.86	2.45
Ramirez, Luis	R-R	5-11	175	9-14-97	0	4	4.41	22	0	0	1	33	40	21	16	3	13	40	.299	.343	.254	11.02	3.58
Rosso, Ramon	R-R	6-4	215	6-9-96	5	1	1.33	12	12	0	0	68	45	13	10	3	20	81	.192	.156	.245	10.77	2.66
Russ, Addison	R-R	6-1	190	10-29-94	5	2	1.67	25	0	0	13	32	19	8	6	3	4	37	.171	.186	.154	10.30	1.11
Stewart, Will	L-L	6-2	175	7-14-97	8	1	2.06	20	20	2	0	114	90	29	26	5	21	90	.218	.235	.208	7.13	1.66
Warren, Zach	L-L	6-5	200	6-9-96	3	2	1.91	39	0	0	15	57	33	15	12	2	28	100	.172	.115	.211	15.88	4.45
Young, Kyle	L-L	6-10	205	12-2-97	3	3	3.10	9	9	1	0	52	46	20	18	2	7	44	.240	.230	.246	7.57	1.20

Fielding

C: Duran 81, Fitch 27, Rivero 31. **1B:** Nieporte 71, Rivero 12, Rodriguez 7, Scheiner 30, Stokes 23. **2B:** Antequera 11, Brito 92, Guthrie 34, Maton 3. **3B:** Antequera 36, Guthrie 35, Scheiner 59, Stobbe 9, Stokes 4. **SS:** Antequera 8, Guthrie 22, Maton 110. **OF:** Alastre 11, Gurrola 23, Markham 51, Matos 3, Mayer 10, Muzziotti 67, Ortiz 96, Scheiner 26, Stephen 96, Vierling 38.

WILLIAMSPORT CROSSCUTTERS — *SHORT-SEASON*
NEW YORK-PENN LEAGUE

Batting	B-T	HT	WT	DOB	AVG	vLH	vRH	G	AB	R	H	2B	3B	HR	RBI	BB	HBP	SH	SF	SO	SB	CS	SLG	OBP
Aklinski, Ben	R-R	5-11	210	6-3-96	.255	.263	.252	53	204	28	52	8	3	7	25	16	4	1	0	54	4	0	.427	.321
Azuaje, Jesus		5-9	165	8-11-97	.222	.333	.167	3	9	1	2	0	0	0	1	0	0	0	0	2	0	0	.222	.222
Bocio, Keudy	R-R	5-10	161	11-15-98	.205	.220	.200	56	190	19	39	4	0	0	15	13	1	4	1	43	6	1	.226	.259
Bohm, Alec	R-R	6-5	225	8-3-96	.224	.258	.211	29	107	9	24	5	1	0	12	10	4	0	0	19	1	0	.290	.314
Francisco, Julio	L-L	6-1	140	3-19-98	.125	.000	.200	2	8	1	1	0	0	1	2	0	0	0	0	1	0	0	.500	.125
Gonzalez, Brayan	B-R	5-11	172	1-14-00	.198	.236	.183	56	197	21	39	10	1	1	24	14	2	1	2	87	3	1	.274	.256
Guzman, Jonathan	R-R	6-0	156	8-17-99	.210	.279	.187	62	243	28	51	7	1	2	14	10	1	2	3	61	3	4	.272	.241
Henriquez, Jesus	B-R	6-0	168	4-7-98	.221	.286	.204	45	136	15	30	5	2	0	15	13	0	3	2	30	4	2	.287	.285
Holmes, Jake	R-R	6-3	185	7-2-98	.252	.406	.183	29	103	11	26	2	0	0	9	10	2	1	0	23	3	2	.272	.330
Kroon, Matt	R-R	6-1	195	12-5-96	.250	.235	.256	38	120	22	30	3	1	2	9	24	1	0	1	38	2	3	.342	.377
Lancaster, Seth	L-R	6-2	208	6-21-96	.196	.185	.198	41	133	13	26	9	3	1	14	23	0	0	0	49	5	0	.331	.314
Marchan, Rafael	B-R	5-9	170	2-25-99	.301	.377	.273	51	196	28	59	8	2	0	12	11	2	0	1	18	9	6	.362	.343
Martinez, Nerluis	L-R	6-2	175	4-10-96	.130	.400	.056	7	23	2	3	0	0	0	1	3	0	0	0	8	2	0	.130	.231
Mayer, Danny	R-R	6-5	245	6-25-95	.250	.244	.252	43	164	18	41	11	2	5	19	9	3	0	1	46	0	1	.433	.299
O'Brien, Stoney	R-R	6-3	200	5-18-94	.167	.000	.286	3	12	1	2	0	0	0	1	1	0	0	0	3	1	0	.167	.231
Pelletier, Ben	R-R	6-1	170	6-8-97	.250	.218	.303	69	256	29	71	17	4	9	45	16	8	1	5	63	1	1	.481	.333
Rodriguez, Edwin	L-L	6-1	170	6-8-97	.250	.304	.237	34	120	12	30	9	1	3	24	4	2	0	0	29	1	1	.417	.286
Rodriguez, Lenin	R-R	5-9	165	3-26-98	.213	.389	.140	21	61	6	13	5	0	0	8	4	0	0	13	1	0	.295	.343
Stokes, Madison	R-R	6-2	200	4-25-96	.338	.400	.316	22	77	16	26	8	1	1	11	15	1	0	0	16	1	1	.507	.452
Vierling, Matt	R-R	6-3	205	9-16-96	.420	.438	.412	12	50	8	21	3	1	6	3	0	0	0	2	2	1	.580	.453
Wilkening, Jesse	R-R	5-11	200	8-29-96	.270	.353	.239	20	63	5	17	5	0	0	7	6	1	0	0	15	0	0	.349	.343

Pitching	B-T	HT	WT	DOB	W	L	ERA	G	GS	CG	SV	IP	H	R	ER	HR	BB	SO	AVG	vLH	vRH	K/9	BB/9
Alcantara, Randy	R-R	5-11	173	11-9-96	4	1	2.15	20	0	0	4	46	32	12	11	3	12	29	.194	.185	.200	5.67	2.35
Aris, Abdallah	R-L	5-11	155	10-8-96	2	5	4.28	16	0	0	0	27	30	18	13	0	15	20	.283	.255	.305	6.59	4.94
Armas, Gustavo	R-R	6-1	195	1-15-96	1	3	4.70	4	4	0	0	23	23	12	12	3	1	20	.253	.277	.227	7.83	0.39
Brown, Ben	R-R	6-6	210	9-9-99	0	2	7.04	2	2	0	0	8	9	7	6	1	5	3	.281	.235	.333	3.52	5.87
Carr, Tyler	R-R	5-10	175	5-16-96	3	2	2.42	13	1	0	0	26	31	13	7	1	4	23	.295	.273	.312	7.96	1.38
Carvajal, Rafael	R-R	6-0	170	11-13-96	2	2	1.59	16	0	0	1	34	31	12	6	1	11	32	.242	.280	.218	8.47	2.91
Eastman, Colton	R-R	6-3	185	8-22-96	0	2	3.00	4	4	0	0	18	18	6	6	1	7	23	.269	.290	.250	11.50	3.50
Escorcia, Juan	R-R	6-1	161	5-30-96	1	4	3.29	11	6	0	1	41	31	22	15	1	25	49	.204	.129	.256	10.76	5.49
Evanko, Ethan	L-L	6-4	185	6-7-95	0	0	1.29	3	0	0	0	7	5	1	1	0	2	2	.217	.250	.182	2.57	2.57
Jimenez, Jose	L-L	5-11	175	9-25-97	2	1	3.71	17	0	0	0	27	32	13	11	1	9	33	.288	.200	.338	11.14	3.04
Killgore, Keylan	L-L	6-3	185	9-30-96	0	0	0.81	14	0	0	10	22	11	2	2	0	5	29	.145	.185	.112	11.69	2.01
Kuznetsov, Anton	R-L	6-1	185	5-26-98	1	1	11.25	3	0	0	0	4	6	5	5	1	2	4	.375	.714	.111	9.00	4.50
Lindow, Ethan	R-L	6-3	180	10-15-98	3	2	2.19	13	13	1	0	70	58	20	17	2	19	63	.228	.181	.250	8.10	2.44

Name	B-T	HT	WT	DOB	W	L	ERA	G	GS	CG	SV	IP	H	R	ER	HR	BB	SO	AVG	vLH	vRH	K/9	BB/9
Marcelino, Oscar	R-R	6-3	166	6-8-97	1	0	12.94	14	0	0	0	16	24	26	23	0	17	18	.348	.207	.450	10.13	9.56
Martinez, Denny	B-L	6-0	157	11-1-96	0	0	3.00	2	0	0	0	3	3	1	1	0	0	5	.250	.286	.200	15.00	0.00
Martinez, Robinson	R-R	6-0	190	3-20-98	1	2	4.67	10	0	0	1	17	21	13	9	1	6	24	.284	.344	.238	12.46	3.12
McArthur, James	R-R	6-7	230	12-11-96	2	0	0.64	8	5	0	0	28	15	2	2	0	10	31	.158	.211	.123	9.85	3.18
Melendez, Orestes	L-L	5-11	180	6-8-95	0	0	6.75	2	0	0	0	4	4	3	3	0	2	4	.267	.167	.333	9.00	4.50
Mezquita, Jhordany	L-L	6-1	185	1-30-98	1	0	3.60	9	9	0	0	35	28	14	14	1	17	41	.219	.293	.184	10.54	4.37
Morales, Francisco	R-R	6-4	185	10-27-99	4	5	5.27	13	13	0	0	56	54	37	33	6	33	68	.244	.242	.246	10.86	5.27
Perkins, Jack	R-R	6-4	200	8-6-97	1	1	4.50	8	2	0	0	18	17	9	9	1	4	18	.262	.172	.333	9.00	2.00
Ramirez, Luis	R-R	5-11	175	9-14-97	0	4	6.08	12	0	0	3	13	17	12	9	2	6	14	.304	.286	.314	9.45	4.05
Ross, Austin	R-R	6-1	185	8-16-94	1	1	3.34	16	0	0	1	32	24	16	12	1	20	52	.209	.227	.197	14.47	5.57
Silva, Manuel	L-L	6-2	145	12-18-98	2	5	2.60	13	12	0	0	62	54	22	18	4	27	60	.236	.270	.214	8.66	3.90
White, Eric	R-R	6-3	208	3-25-96	0	0	13.50	1	0	0	0	1	1	2	2	1	1	2	.200	.000	.250	13.50	6.75
Young, Kyle	L-L	6-10	205	12-2-97	0	0	0.00	1	1	0	0	3	0	0	0	0	0	2	.000	.000	.000	6.00	0.00

Fielding

C: Marchan 47, Martinez 5, Rodriguez 11, Wilkening 18. **1B:** Henriquez 7, Kroon 25, Martinez 2, Mayer 1, O'Brien 2, Rodriguez 24, Stokes 15. **2B:** Azuaje 3, Gonzalez 51, Henriquez 7, Kroon 1, Lancaster 15. **3B:** Bohm 20, Henriquez 14, Holmes 22, Kroon 8, Lancaster 12, Stokes 3. **SS:** Guzman 61, Lancaster 15. **OF:** Aklinski 52, Bocio 55, Francisco 2, Henriquez 15, Mayer 24, Pelletier 69, Vierling 12.

GCL PHILLIES EAST · ROOKIE
GULF COAST LEAGUE

Batting	B-T	HT	WT	DOB	AVG	vLH	vRH	G	AB	R	H	2B	3B	HR	RBI	BB	HBP	SH	SF	SO	SB	CS	SLG	OBP
Aklinski, Ben	R-R	5-11	210	6-3-96	.267	.286	.261	10	30	4	8	1	0	0	4	8	0	0	1	3	0	1	.300	.410
Aparicio, Juan	R-R	5-11	175	5-26-00	.339	.250	.359	39	112	24	38	9	1	3	15	4	3	0	0	26	0	1	.518	.378
Bohm, Alec	R-R	6-5	225	8-3-96	.222	.000	.286	4	9	0	2	0	0	0	2	0	0	1	0	4	0	0	.222	.200
2-team total (7 GCL Phillies West)					.344	.000	.286	11	32	8	11	1	1	0	5	2	2	0	1	4	2	0	.438	.405
Conley, Jack	R-R	6-1	190	1-16-97	.329	.222	.362	33	76	18	25	4	0	2	11	14	3	0	1	17	0	0	.461	.447
Crawford, J.P.	L-R	6-2	180	1-11-95	.000	—	.000	1	1	2	0	0	0	0	3	4	0	0	0	1	0	0	.000	.800
De La Cruz, Carlos	R-R	6-8	210	10-6-99	.284	.265	.290	43	148	20	42	8	0	6	21	11	4	0	2	56	2	1	.460	.346
Edwards, Mitchell	B-R	5-11	200	8-1-99	.250	.333	.242	16	36	5	9	3	0	1	3	3	0	0	0	11	0	1	.417	.308
Florimon, Pedro	R-R	6-2	185	12-10-86	.000	.000	—	1	1	0	0	0	0	0	1	0	0	0	0	0	0	0	.000	.500
2-team total (1 GCL Phillies West)					.200	.000	—	2	5	1	1	0	0	0	1	0	0	1	0	0			.200	.333
Francisco, Julio	L-L	6-1	170	3-19-98	.293	.267	.299	44	167	28	49	9	4	0	11	12	3	0	0	18	14	4	.395	.352
Guthrie, Dalton	R-R	5-11	160	12-23-95	.182	.000	.250	3	11	1	2	1	0	0	0	0	0	0	0	1	0	0	.273	.182
2-team total (1 GCL Phillies West)					.231	.000	.250	4	13	1	3	1	0	0	0	0	0	0	0	1	0	0	.308	.214
Holmes, Jake	R-R	6-3	185	7-2-98	.353	.375	.345	31	116	18	41	5	2	4	29	10	0	3	1	9	4	1	.535	.395
Made, Edgar	R-R	5-10	145	12-15-99	.253	.091	.278	29	83	13	21	3	1	2	15	4	2	0	1	18	2	3	.386	.300
Mercado, Jose	R-R	6-1	170	1-4-00	.165	.316	.121	26	85	8	14	2	0	2	5	3	1	0	0	26	1	1	.259	.202
Miller, Luke	R-R	6-2	192	7-17-96	.284	.313	.280	32	109	17	31	5	0	2	21	17	0	0	0	18	1	0	.385	.381
Muzziotti, Simon	L-L	6-1	175	12-27-98	.091	.000	.118	6	22	2	2	0	0	0	2	2	0	0	1	0	0	0	.091	.167
Oropeza, Carlos	R-R	6-0	170	12-22-98	.281	.385	.263	34	89	11	25	5	0	0	8	8	1	1	0	20	2	2	.337	.347
Pickett, Greg	L-R	6-4	215	10-30-96	.071	.000	.143	4	14	1	1	0	0	0	3	1	0	0	0	6	0	0	.286	.133
2-team total (7 GCL Phillies West)					.059	.000	.143	11	34	2	2	1	0	0	6	6	0	0	0	15	0	0	.177	.200
Rivera, Jose	R-R	5-10	165	5-26-99	.277	.050	.333	35	101	13	28	5	1	0	19	12	2	0	4	19	0	0	.347	.353
Simmons, Logan	R-R	6-2	180	4-11-00	.232	.294	.218	32	95	21	22	7	0	3	11	9	8	0	1	30	2	4	.400	.345
Smith, James	R-R	6-1	210	8-27-95	.280	.304	.275	44	132	27	37	8	2	3	22	13	2	1	1	23	1	0	.439	.351
Stokes, Madison	R-R	6-2	200	4-25-96	.375	.833	.100	5	16	4	6	2	1	0	3	1	0	0	0	2	0	0	.625	.412
2-team total (1 GCL Phillies West)					.353	.833	.100	6	17	5	6	2	1	0	3	1	1	0	0	2	0	0	.588	.421
Torres, Nicolas	R-R	5-10	155	9-23-99	.302	.394	.274	39	139	19	42	8	1	1	19	8	0	4	0	27	7	1	.396	.340
Wilkening, Jesse	R-R	5-11	200	8-29-96	.250	.333	.000	3	4	0	1	0	0	0	0	0	1	0	0	0	0	0	.250	.400
Zoellner, Jack	L-R	6-2	205	10-29-94	.236	.324	.213	47	161	31	38	5	2	7	26	32	1	0	1	42	1	0	.422	.364

Pitching	B-T	HT	WT	DOB	W	L	ERA	G	GS	CG	SV	IP	H	R	ER	HR	BB	SO	AVG	vLH	vRH	K/9	BB/9
Alcala, Bryan	R-R	6-5	215	8-14-97	0	0	4.50	2	1	0	0	4	5	2	2	0	3	4	.313	.125	.500	9.00	6.75
Antonac, Yoan	R-R	6-9	183	7-27-00	0	0	7.71	2	0	0	0	2	2	2	2	0	0	3	.222	.333	.167	11.57	0.00
Arjona, Kyle	R-R	5-10	195	1-17-97	0	0	2.25	5	0	0	0	8	8	2	2	1	1	5	.267	.364	.211	5.63	1.13
Auerbach, Brian	R-R	6-4	195	8-30-96	2	0	1.59	13	0	0	3	23	22	6	4	1	4	19	.237	.200	.250	7.54	1.59
Bettencourt, Trevor	R-R	6-5	195	7-21-94	0	0	4.91	3	0	0	0	4	2	2	2	0	1	4	.154	.200	.125	9.82	2.45
Carr, Tyler	R-R	5-10	175	5-1-96	0	0	0.00	2	0	0	0	4	4	1	0	0	0	1	.267	.250	.273	2.25	0.00
Cotto, Gabriel	L-L	6-5	175	5-15-00	0	2	9.39	8	7	0	0	15	16	19	16	0	16	15	.258	.200	.269	8.80	9.39
Cox, Adam	R-R	6-3	187	8-31-95	0	1	0.00	3	0	0	0	3	2	1	0	0	0	4	.200	.500	.125	13.50	0.00
2-team total (12 GCL Phillies West)					0	2	2.70	15	0	0	1	20	18	9	6	2	9	21	.231	.500	.125	9.45	4.05
Cummings, Bailey	R-R	6-3	200	12-20-97	2	2	1.88	17	0	0	2	24	17	7	5	1	6	31	.187	.240	.167	11.63	2.25
De La Cruz, Jonas	R-R	6-3	175	1-1-98	5	2	4.46	10	6	0	0	34	31	22	17	3	19	31	.244	.389	.187	8.13	4.98
Falter, Bailey	R-L	6-4	195	4-24-97	0	0	0.00	1	1	0	0	2	0	0	0	0	0	6	.154	.000	.167	14.73	0.00
2-team total (1 GCL Phillies West)					0	1	3.38	2	2	0	0	8	9	4	3	1	0	13	.265	.000	.167	14.63	0.00
Francisco, Carlos	R-R	6-2	179	3-28-98	4	8	6.51	11	8	0	0	37	45	29	27	1	18	41	.302	.283	.311	9.88	4.34
Hammer, JD	R-R	6-3	215	7-12-94	0	0	0.00	2	0	0	0	3	1	0	0	0	0	5	.100	.000	.125	15.00	0.00
2-team total (1 GCL Phillies West)					0	0	2.25	3	1	0	1	4	3	1	1	0	0	5	.200	.000	.125	11.25	0.00
Hibbs, Will	R-R	6-7	245	10-27-93	0	0	0.00	3	0	0	0	4	1	0	0	0	0	4	.167	.250	.125	10.80	0.00
Kinney, Jake	R-R	6-2		1-14-97	1	0	0.00	2	0	0	0	2	1	0	0	0	2	3	.143	.250	.000	13.50	9.00
2-team total (5 GCL Phillies West)					1	0	3.00	7	0	0	0	9	6	3	3	1	5	11	.177	.250	.000	11.00	5.00
Lehman, Taylor	L-L	6-8	240	12-30-95	0	1	7.02	13	0	0	0	17	20	13	13	1	7	17	.286	.286	.286	9.18	3.78
Lin, Hsin-Chieh	R-R	6-2	198	3-18-99	0	0	0.00	3	0	0	0	3	0	0	0	0	1	1	.000	.000	.000	3.00	12.00
Lively, Ben	R-R	6-4	190	3-5-92	0	0	0.00	1	1	0	0	3	1	0	0	0	1	4	.111	.000	.143	12.00	3.00

BaseballAmerica.com

	B-T	HT	WT	DOB	W	L	ERA	G	GS	CG	SV	IP	H	R	ER	HR	BB	SO	AVG	vLH	vRH	K/9	BB/9
2-team total (1 GCL Phillies West)					0	0	0.00	3	1	0	0	4	1	0	0	0	1	6	.083	.000	.143	13.50	2.25
Made, Alejandro	R-R	6-4	190	12-29-97	4	2	2.66	14	0	0	0	24	20	19	7	0	9	25	.215	.290	.177	9.51	3.42
Martinez, Robinson	R-R	6-0	190	3-20-98	0	0	3.00	2	0	0	0	3	1	1	1	0	1	7	.100	.000	.125	21.00	3.00
2-team total (3 GCL Phillies West)					0	0	2.70	5	0	0	0	7	5	2	2	0	2	8	.192	.000	.125	10.80	2.70
McKay, Tyler	R-R	6-6	180	8-18-97	1	0	2.45	4	1	0	0	7	7	2	2	0	2	2	.250	.125	.300	2.45	2.45
Miller, Justin	R-R	6-4	183	5-17-98	1	5	4.50	10	4	0	0	28	36	27	14	2	19	27	.303	.286	.308	8.68	6.11
Pipkin, Dominic	R-R	6-4	160	11-5-99	1	2	3.64	10	8	0	0	30	27	12	12	3	8	18	.252	.194	.276	5.46	2.43
Potter, Mark	R-R	6-6	284	11-12-97	1	0	1.96	11	0	0	0	23	18	8	5	1	4	13	.212	.192	.220	5.09	1.57
Sanchez, Mario	R-R	6-1	166	10-31-94	0	1	5.40	4	3	0	0	5	4	3	3	0	0	4	.222	.167	.250	7.20	0.00
2-team total (3 GCL Phillies West)					0	1	8.00	7	4	0	0	9	12	8	8	1	0	8	.316	.167	.250	8.00	0.00
Santos, Victor	R-R	6-1	191	7-12-00	6	1	3.03	11	11	0	0	59	63	21	20	4	4	65	.268	.311	.241	9.86	0.61
Sobil, Victor	R-R	6-2	215	7-17-96	0	0	18.69	5	0	0	0	4	10	14	9	0	3	5	.435	.400	.444	10.38	6.23
Taveras, Jose	L-R	6-4	210	11-6-93	0	0	0.00	3	0	0	0	3	0	0	0	0	0	3	.000	.000	.000	0.00	0.00
Tejada, Junior	L-L	6-1	170	5-23-97	2	0	5.06	9	0	0	0	11	21	15	6	1	10	8	.389	.539	.342	6.75	8.44
2-team total (5 GCL Phillies West)					3	0	3.00	13	0	0	0	21	24	17	7	2	14	16	.273	.539	.342	6.86	6.00
Vilchez, Daniel	R-R	6-1	155	10-4-00	1	1	7.27	8	0	0	0	9	14	10	7	2	3	8	.350	.231	.407	8.31	3.12
Viza, Tyler	R-R	6-3	170	10-21-94	0	0	0.00	2	1	0	0	2	1	0	0	0	2	.125	.333	.000	9.00	0.00
2-team total (1 GCL Phillies West)					0	1	0.00	3	0	0	0	4	3	2	0	0	5	.177	.333	.000	11.25	0.00
White, Eric	R-R	6-3	208	3-25-96	1	0	0.82	6	0	0	0	11	8	1	1	0	1	7	.200	.300	.167	5.73	0.82
Yanez, Gabriel	L-L	6-3	168	7-22-99	0	0	6.43	15	3	0	2	35	53	26	25	4	3	33	.344	.400	.333	8.49	0.77

Fielding

C: Aparicio 24, Conley 27, Edwards 12, Oropeza 25, Wilkening 2. **1B:** Miller 3, Oropeza 6, Pickett 2, Stokes 5, Zoellner 41. **2B:** Guthrie 3, Made 2, Made 17, Miller 1, Rivera 6, Torres 36. **3B:** Bohm 4, Holmes 27, Made 7, Miller 15, Rivera 7. **SS:** Crawford 1, Florimon 1, Mercado 25, Simmons 32. **OF:** Aklinski 10, De La Cruz 40, Francisco 43, Made 4, Miller 9, Muzziotti 5, Rivera 19, Smith 43.

GCL PHILLIES WEST   ROOKIE
GULF COAST LEAGUE

Batting	B-T	HT	WT	DOB	AVG	vLH	vRH	G	AB	R	H	2B	3B	HR	RBI	BB	HBP	SH	SF	SO	SB	CS	SLG	OBP
Azuaje, Jesus	R-R	5-9	165	8-11-97	.169	—	—	28	65	14	11	2	0	0	4	6	4	1	0	8	7	0	.200	.280
Bohm, Alec	R-R	6-5	225	8-3-96	.391	—	—	7	23	8	9	1	1	0	3	2	2	0	0	2	0	0	.522	.482
2-team total (4 GCL Phillies East)					.344	.000	.286	11	32	8	11	1	1	0	5	2	2	0	1	4	2	0	.438	.405
Bowles, Trent	R-R	6-3	205	5-21-95	.256	—	—	39	133	22	34	8	1	1	16	11	1	2	4	33	9	3	.353	.309
Florimon, Pedro	B-R	6-2	185	12-10-86	.250	—	—	1	4	1	1	0	0	0	0	0	0	0	0	1	0	0	.250	.250
2-team total (1 GCL Phillies East)					.200	.000	—	2	5	1	1	0	0	0	0	1	0	0	0	1	0	0	.200	.333
Garcia, Luis	B-R	5-11	170	10-1-00	.369	—	—	43	168	33	62	11	3	1	32	15	4	0	0	21	12	8	.488	.433
Guthrie, Dalton	R-R	5-11	160	12-23-95	.500	—	—	1	2	0	1	0	0	0	2	0	0	0	1	0	0	0	.500	.333
2-team total (3 GCL Phillies East)					.231	.000	.250	4	13	1	3	1	0	0	2	0	0	0	1	1	0	0	.308	.214
Gutierrez, Abrahan	R-R	6-2	214	10-31-99	.315	—	—	41	162	24	51	10	1	1	30	10	3	0	2	16	2	2	.407	.362
Kroon, Matt	R-R	6-1	195	12-5-96	.563	—	—	4	16	2	9	1	0	0	1	3	0	0	0	4	4	1	.625	.632
Litton, Connor	R-R	6-3	220	1-14-97	.188	—	—	6	16	1	3	1	0	0	3	2	0	0	1	5	0	0	.250	.263
Matera, Nick	R-R	6-2	215	8-29-96	.224	—	—	25	76	13	17	6	0	0	5	13	2	0	1	17	0	1	.303	.348
Matos, Luis	B-R	6-0	175	12-17-99	.270	—	—	36	111	13	30	2	0	0	11	5	1	3	2	29	8	5	.288	.303
Mead, Curtis	R-R	6-2	171	10-26-00	.167	—	—	2	6	1	1	0	0	0	0	0	0	0	0	0	0	0	.167	.167
O'Brien, Stoney	R-R	6-3	200	5-18-94	.325	—	—	37	123	27	40	8	1	3	26	15	4	0	3	33	2	2	.480	.407
O'Hoppe, Logan	R-R	6-2	185	2-2-00	.367	—	—	34	109	19	40	10	1	2	21	10	1	0	4	28	2	1	.532	.411
Pickett, Greg	L-R	6-4	215	10-30-96	.050	—	—	7	20	1	1	0	0	0	3	5	0	0	0	8	0	0	.100	.240
2-team total (4 GCL Phillies East)					.059	.000	.143	11	34	2	2	1	0	1	6	6	0	0	0	15	0	0	.177	.200
Rojas, Luis	R-R	5-9	150	4-19-00	.227	—	—	33	110	19	25	1	0	0	7	8	0	2	2	10	3	3	.236	.275
Stewart, D.J.	R-R	6-2	205	2-2-99	.281	—	—	36	114	18	32	8	0	0	16	11	2	1	1	31	1	1	.351	.352
Stokes, Madison	R-R	6-2	200	4-25-96	.000	—	—	1	1	0	0	0	0	0	0	1	0	0	0	0	0	0	.000	.500
2-team total (5 GCL Phillies East)					.353	.833	.100	16	17	5	6	2	1	0	3	1	1	0	0	2	0	0	.588	.421
Taylor-Wingrove, Rixon	L-R	6-5	230	5-23-00	.241	—	—	23	79	12	19	5	0	1	8	8	0	0	0	22	1	1	.342	.310
Trejo, Yerwin	R-R	6-0	170	1-3-97	.301	—	—	52	196	40	59	6	1	0	20	23	6	3	1	31	23	9	.342	.389
Valerio, Christian	R-R	6-1	155	2-24-00	.270	—	—	38	126	15	34	10	0	1	18	13	1	3	1	22	6	2	.373	.340
Williams, Corbin	R-R	6-2	170	1-19-98	.289	—	—	29	83	17	24	1	1	0	9	7	1	3	1	27	12	4	.325	.348

Pitching	B-T	HT	WT	DOB	W	L	ERA	G	GS	CG	SV	IP	H	R	ER	HR	BB	SO	AVG	vLH	vRH	K/9	BB/9
Aponte, Leonel	R-R	6-4	144	7-2-99	3	2	4.40	12	1	0	1	31	30	17	15	3	7	30	.242	—	—	8.80	2.05
Avendano, Eudiver	R-R	6-3	200	2-1-99	1	0	3.00	2	2	0	0	9	5	3	3	0	5	8	.152	—	—	8.00	5.00
Brown, Ben	R-R	6-6	210	9-9-99	4	2	3.12	10	8	1	0	49	43	21	17	2	15	62	.230	—	—	11.39	2.76
Canizales, Antonio	R-R	6-1	160	1-24-98	1	4	7.43	6	0	0	0	23	35	28	19	4	7	16	.343	—	—	6.26	2.74
Conopoima, Jose	R-R	6-0	157	3-1-00	1	2	3.53	14	5	0	1	43	42	21	17	1	8	29	.252	—	—	6.02	1.66
Cox, Adam	R-R	6-3	187	8-31-95	0	1	3.12	12	0	0	1	17	16	8	6	2	9	17	.235	.000	.125	8.83	4.67
2-team total (3 GCL Phillies East)					0	2	2.70	15	0	0	1	20	18	9	6	2	9	21	.231	.500	.125	9.45	4.05
Evanko, Ethan	L-L	6-4	185	6-7-95	2	2	3.38	11	0	0	1	21	24	8	8	0	10	19	.289	—	—	8.02	4.22
Falter, Bailey	R-L	6-4	175	4-24-97	0	1	6.23	1	1	0	0	4	7	4	3	1	0	7	.333	—	—	14.54	0.00
2-team total (1 GCL Phillies East)					0	1	3.38	2	2	0	0	8	9	4	3	1	0	13	.265	.000	.167	14.63	0.00
Garcia, Alex	R-R	6-3	190	6-16-96	1	0	9.00	10	0	0	0	11	13	15	11	1	23	11	.283	—	—	9.00	18.82
Glogoski, Kyle	R-R	6-2	183	1-6-99	4	0	2.31	10	8	0	0	39	30	10	10	2	11	47	.204	—	—	10.85	2.54
Gomez, Michael	R-R	6-3	210	8-15-96	1	0	3.52	6	0	0	0	8	8	5	3	0	5	5	.276	—	—	5.87	5.87
Gonell, Rafi	R-R	6-2	190	2-26-97	5	1	4.65	10	8	0	0	41	37	24	21	1	20	41	.243	—	—	9.07	4.43
Hammer, JD	R-R	6-3	215	7-12-94	0	0	9.00	1	0	0	0	1	1	0	0	0	1	0	.400	—	—	0.00	0.00
2-team total (2 GCL Phillies East)					0	0	2.25	3	1	0	1	4	3	1	1	0	2	5	.200	.000	.125	11.25	0.00
Kinney, Jake	R-R	6-7	225	1-14-97	0	0	3.86	5	0	0	0	7	5	3	3	1	3	8	.185	—	—	10.29	3.86

	B-T	HT	WT	DOB	W	L	ERA	G	GS	CG	SV	IP	H	R	ER	HR	BB	SO	AVG	vLH	vRH	K/9	BB/9
2-team total (2 GCL Phillies East)					1	0	3.00	7	0	0	0	9	6	3	3	1	5	11	.177	.250	.000	11.00	5.00
Lively, Ben	R-R	6-4	190	3-5-92	0	0	0.00	1	1	0	0	1	0	0	0	0	0	2	.000	—	—	18.00	0.00
2-team total (2 GCL Phillies East)					0	0	0.00	3	1	0	0	4	1	0	0	0	1	6	.083	.000	.143	13.50	2.25
Martinez, Denny	B-L	6-0	157	11-1-96	0	0	0.00	1	0	0	0	1	1	0	0	0	0	1	.250	—	—	9.00	0.00
Martinez, Robinson	R-R	6-0	190	3-20-98	0	0	2.45	3	0	0	0	4	4	1	1	0	1	1	.250	—	—	2.45	2.45
2-team total (2 GCL Phillies East)					0	0	2.70	5	0	0	0	7	5	2	2	0	2	8	.192	.000	.125	10.80	2.70
McArthur, James	R-R	6-7	230	12-11-96	0	0	0.00	1	0	0	0	1	0	0	0	0	0	2	.250	—	—	18.00	0.00
Perkins, Jack	R-R	6-4	200	8-6-97	0	0	0.00	1	0	0	0	2	1	0	0	0	1	2	.167	—	—	9.00	4.50
Ramey, Brandon	R-R	6-3	170	8-31-00	1	0	6.00	4	0	0	1	9	7	6	6	1	4	7	.206	—	—	7.00	4.00
Requena, Alejandro	R-R	6-2	200	11-29-96	0	0	0.00	1	1	0	0	3	0	0	0	0	1	5	.000	—	—	15.00	3.00
Ross, Austin	R-R	6-1	185	8-16-94	0	0	0.00	2	0	0	0	3	2	1	0	0	1	3	.154	—	—	9.00	3.00
Sanchez, Mario	R-R	6-1	166	10-31-94	0	0	11.25	3	1	0	0	4	8	5	5	1	0	4	.400	—	—	9.00	0.00
2-team total (4 GCL Phillies East)					0	1	8.00	7	4	0	0	9	12	8	8	1	0	8	.316	.167	.250	8.00	0.00
Santa Cruz, Sati	R-R	6-3	230	9-3-96	1	2	10.38	14	0	0	0	17	22	20	20	0	23	11	.319	—	—	5.71	11.94
Smith, Jayle	L-L	5-11	170	11-5-99	0	1	7.11	11	0	0	0	13	17	10	10	0	12	7	.309	—	—	4.97	8.53
Sutera, Tom	R-R	6-5	190	5-29-97	0	0	1.35	5	0	0	1	7	6	3	1	0	1	8	.222	—	—	10.80	1.35
Tejada, Junior	L-L	6-1	170	5-23-97	1	0	0.87	5	0	0	0	10	3	2	1	1	4	8	.088	—	—	6.97	3.48
2-team total (8 GCL Phillies East)					3	0	3.00	13	0	0	0	21	24	17	7	2	14	16	.273	.539	.342	6.86	6.00
Vargas, Victor	R-R	6-1	175	9-3-00	1	4	6.00	10	9	0	0	45	62	37	30	8	11	34	.332	—	—	6.80	2.20
Viza, Tyler	R-R	6-3	170	10-21-94	0	1	0.00	1	0	0	0	2	2	2	0	0	0	3	.222	—	—	13.50	0.00
2-team total (2 GCL Phillies East)					0	1	0.00	3	0	0	0	4	3	2	0	0	0	5	.177	.333	.000	11.25	0.00
Young, Kyle	L-L	6-10	205	12-2-97	0	0	0.00	3	3	0	0	4	2	1	0	0	2	4	.143	—	—	9.00	4.50

Fielding

C: Gutierrez 28, Matera 11, O'Hoppe 20. **1B:** Litton 1, O'Brien 33, Pickett 5, Stokes 1, Taylor-Wingrove 18. **2B:** Azuaje 15, Guthrie 1, Kroon 3, Mead 2, Rojas 5, Valerio 31. **3B:** Azuaje 10, Bohm 5, Litton 5, Rojas 7, Stewart 34, Valerio 1. **SS:** Azuaje 3, Garcia 43, Kroon 1, Rojas 4, Valerio 5. **OF:** Bowles 39, Florimon 1, Matos 36, O'Brien 1, Rojas 15, Trejo 50, Williams 27.

DSL PHILLIES   ROOKIE

DOMINICAN SUMMER LEAGUE

Batting	B-T	HT	WT	DOB	AVG	vLH	vRH	G	AB	R	H	2B	3B	HR	RBI	BB	HBP	SH	SF	SO	SB	CS	SLG	OBP
Alfonso, Victor	B-R	5-11	140	8-27-99	.210	.234	.203	57	210	18	44	13	1	0	29	20	3	1	4	37	4	2	.281	.283
Asencio, Ryan	R-R	5-11	195	3-1-99	.162	.000	.186	20	68	8	11	1	1	2	7	8	0	0	1	7	2	0	.294	.247
Barboza, Edward	R-R	5-11	175	4-2-01	.226	.091	.255	20	62	7	14	2	1	0	5	6	1	0	0	15	3	1	.290	.304
Barreto, Freddy	R-R	6-0	155	9-27-99	.206	.154	.220	40	126	15	26	2	0	1	10	6	2	0	1	25	1	1	.246	.252
Boekhoudt, Mani	R-L	6-5	165	9-20-99	.255	.361	.231	55	192	26	49	4	3	0	22	17	3	1	3	45	9	2	.307	.321
Cedeno, Jose	L-L	6-2	168	3-19-01	.195	.000	.235	13	41	10	8	0	1	0	6	6	1	0	0	10	9	0	.244	.313
De Freitas, Arturo	R-R	6-0	170	5-28-01	.266	.250	.270	59	173	30	46	16	1	3	28	28	10	0	2	39	3	1	.422	.394
De La Rosa, Maximo	R-R	6-2	205	9-15-99	.111	.000	.143	4	9	0	1	0	0	0	2	0	0	0	0	2	0	2	.111	.273
Dipre, Guarner	R-R	6-0	160	10-26-00	.222	.225	.221	67	248	24	55	12	2	2	26	18	7	1	2	68	11	7	.311	.291
Duran, Christopher	R-R	5-10	165	11-2-00	.252	.192	.271	43	111	23	28	6	2	2	17	14	1	1	2	28	10	4	.396	.336
Encarnacion, Jefferson	L-L	6-1	185	8-28-01	.245	.222	.249	68	229	28	56	3	3	0	17	26	4	0	2	57	5	10	.284	.330
Flores, Wilfredo	R-R	5-10	170	5-14-00	.320	.267	.333	62	228	35	73	12	0	2	21	24	5	2	1	48	18	11	.390	.395
Francisco, Freddy	R-R	5-11	180	2-7-01	.287	.294	.286	46	167	24	48	11	3	0	18	16	1	0	1	26	10	1	.389	.351
Garcia, Wilbert	R-R	5-11	179	1-20-00	.239	.182	.253	36	113	15	27	5	1	2	8	9	3	1	1	34	10	8	.354	.310
Gonzalez, Oscar	R-R	6-0	184	11-21-00	.216	.111	.245	70	250	29	54	8	2	1	32	24	5	1	2	37	2	3	.276	.295
Gonzalez, Ronaldo	R-R	5-11	178	10-14-98	.000	—	.000	4	6	2	0	0	0	0	0	0	2	0	0	1	0	1	.000	.250
Hernandez, Carlos	L-R	5-10	168	5-1-01	.209	.118	.232	33	86	14	18	3	0	0	7	14	0	1	1	15	2	0	.244	.317
Hernandez, Jevi	R-R	6-0	140	3-2-99	.275	.333	.260	53	200	43	55	7	5	2	20	27	1	0	1	31	32	9	.390	.362
Herrera, Juan	R-R	6-3	165	12-14-99	.278	.216	.298	45	151	24	42	9	3	1	17	10	2	0	0	38	5	2	.397	.331
Jerez, Albert	R-R	6-2	165	5-18-01	.178	.100	.195	35	107	7	19	0	0	0	8	10	0	2	3	25	3	2	.178	.242
Mendoza, Carlos	L-L	5-9	164	2-18-01	.261	.192	.279	72	249	42	65	10	3	0	29	39	3	3	6	32	16	9	.325	.360
Mora, Raymond	R-R	6-0	155	7-29-00	.191	.143	.203	53	173	18	33	6	1	0	12	15	6	4	2	39	4	7	.237	.276
Mujica, Luiggi	B-R	5-10	155	11-25-99	.250	.261	.246	27	92	20	23	0	2	0	9	13	5	1	1	24	3	4	.294	.369
Peguero, Giuseppe	R-R	6-0	175	6-30-00	.186	.238	.173	60	204	35	38	5	6	3	20	34	7	1	1	74	7	3	.314	.321
Rodriguez, Cesar	B-R	5-10	160	12-26-00	.241	.196	.254	67	224	24	54	10	0	1	30	28	4	0	4	33	4	7	.299	.331
Rojas, Johan	R-R	6-1	165	8-14-00	.321	.306	.324	68	259	42	83	12	4	2	31	18	8	2	5	37	19	8	.421	.376
Rondon, Ellian	L-R	5-11	166	6-24-00	.201	.163	.211	72	209	30	42	5	2	0	23	37	7	5	2	48	9	5	.244	.337
Smith, Juan Carlos	R-R	6-1	188	8-22-97	.259	.234	.265	65	232	43	60	7	4	4	42	21	10	0	2	48	24	10	.444	.343
Valdez, Wilson	R-R	6-2	168	10-25-99	.269	.275	.268	62	208	31	56	8	3	0	20	12	2	2	2	16	8	5	.337	.313

Pitching	B-T	HT	WT	DOB	W	L	ERA	G	GS	CG	SV	IP	H	R	ER	HR	BB	SO	AVG	vLH	vRH	K/9	BB/9
Aleman, Edinso	L-L	5-11	178	10-6-00	0	1	6.86	14	2	0	0	20	24	21	15	2	13	14	.282	.105	.333	6.41	5.95
Aponte, Ruben	R-R	6-0	180	5-18-97	0	3	6.49	16	1	0	0	26	23	24	19	2	23	31	.235	.267	.221	10.59	7.86
Araujo, Alexis	R-R	6-5	200	1-7-99	1	1	2.43	20	0	0	2	41	41	22	11	2	20	32	.277	.258	.293	7.08	4.43
Arauz, Osvaldo	R-R	6-1	150	1-8-00	0	0	6.46	13	0	0	0	15	19	17	11	0	12	9	.292	.368	.261	5.28	7.04
Betancourt, Carlos	R-R	6-1	160	3-27-01	0	2	4.50	4	4	0	0	14	16	9	7	0	10	8	.302	.462	.250	5.14	6.43
Bido, Nathanael	L-L	6-2	190	6-22-97	1	1	3.75	17	0	0	0	24	25	13	10	1	16	22	.275	.286	.273	8.25	6.00
Candelo, Luis	R-R	5-11	190	6-27-97	3	3	3.07	21	0	0	8	29	20	16	10	1	10	16	.196	.277	.127	4.91	3.07
Cruz, Cristofer	R-R	6-0	155	4-5-99	1	2	9.39	14	0	0	0	23	30	24	24	1	18	25	.326	.357	.313	9.78	7.04
Estevez, Engel	R-R	6-1	180	2-8-00	3	3	3.44	10	6	0	0	37	27	20	14	1	14	27	.205	.163	.225	6.63	3.44
Garrido, Maikel	L-L	6-4	175	1-24-00	0	2	5.14	5	0	0	1	7	5	4	4	0	5	4	.200	.000	.227	5.14	6.43
Geraldo, Juan	R-R	6-0	175	8-6-01	3	4	4.43	15	12	0	1	61	60	32	30	3	20	52	.258	.325	.224	7.67	2.95
Gomez, Luis	R-R	6-0	174	5-14-01	2	0	2.25	9	3	0	0	24	13	8	6	0	9	16	.151	.069	.193	6.00	3.38
Guzman, Michael	L-L	6-0	175	7-31-00	1	0	4.82	7	0	0	0	9	11	5	5	1	3	9	.297	.333	.290	8.68	2.89

Name	B-T	Ht	Wt	DOB	W	L	ERA	G	GS	CG	SV	IP	H	R	ER	HR	BB	SO	AVG	vLH	vRH		
Hernandez, Cristian	R-R	6-3	180	9-23-00	2	3	2.57	13	13	0	0	63	62	28	18	2	10	49	.250	.263	.242	7.00	1.43
Hernandez, Joan	R-R	6-0	180	7-7-99	0	0	45.00	1	0	0	0	1	4	5	5	0	2	0	.571	.333	.750	0.00	18.00
Herrera, Alexis	R-R	6-3	180	5-6-99	3	1	1.93	14	0	0	3	28	18	10	6	0	15	37	.190	.050	.227	11.89	4.82
Liendo, Wilberson	R-R	6-3	160	9-13-99	1	3	3.18	16	0	0	1	34	26	13	12	4	17	31	.213	.118	.282	8.21	4.50
Lima, Cristian	R-R	6-2	190	7-5-00	2	0	6.93	17	0	0	0	25	28	25	19	1	24	20	.275	.206	.309	7.30	8.76
Liriano, Elias	R-R	6-5	192	3-19-99	1	0	2.66	12	1	0	0	20	17	8	6	0	10	23	.227	.130	.269	10.18	4.43
Marcano, Rafael	L-L	6-1	170	4-20-00	1	0	1.35	9	1	0	0	13	10	3	2	0	6	11	.208	.167	.214	7.43	4.05
Martinez, Alejandro	R-R	6-6	190	5-8-98	1	0	3.60	4	0	0	0	5	3	2	2	1	2	4	.167	.000	.250	7.20	3.60
Martinez, Jordi	L-L	6-2	185	7-18-00	1	4	5.44	14	10	0	0	41	45	27	25	0	14	37	.276	.267	.280	8.06	3.05
Mejia, Hernando	R-R	6-3	230	6-8-00	1	1	3.54	12	3	0	0	20	23	11	8	0	12	16	.284	.303	.271	7.08	5.31
Miranda, Juan	L-L	5-11	165	2-27-99	0	2	0.99	15	5	0	7	46	25	6	5	0	8	48	.159	.103	.172	9.46	1.58
Morales, Efrain	R-R	6-0	191	6-26-01	3	3	3.50	13	5	0	0	36	29	25	14	1	22	34	.218	.291	.167	8.50	5.50
Moreno, Noelis	R-R	6-2	207	1-23-99	1	0	1.08	13	0	0	0	17	11	4	2	0	8	13	.190	.191	.189	7.02	4.32
Naranjo, Yosmel	L-L	6-4	205	3-8-00	2	4	4.50	22	0	0	1	36	31	24	18	2	15	37	.235	.216	.242	9.25	3.75
Pacheco, Luis	R-R	6-2	185	4-22-99	5	3	2.00	16	11	0	0	63	44	25	14	1	33	61	.191	.197	.188	8.71	4.71
Palacio, Jose	B-L	6-0	165	2-7-00	3	2	3.27	15	9	0	0	55	59	27	20	2	22	40	.282	.222	.303	6.55	3.60
Parraga, Roger	R-R	6-2	170	2-15-01	0	0	3.60	3	0	0	0	5	6	2	2	0	2	5	.316	.222	.400	9.00	3.60
Perez, Daivin	L-L	6-1	177	10-19-98	1	3	8.00	7	4	0	0	18	26	22	16	1	12	14	.329	.267	.344	7.00	6.00
Perez, Jose	R-R	6-3	170	8-16-98	1	0	2.57	4	4	0	0	14	13	10	4	0	7	13	.228	.300	.189	8.36	4.50
Pina, Nicoly	R-R	6-3	203	10-8-99	1	3	4.00	17	11	0	1	54	41	26	24	0	35	53	.220	.171	.255	8.83	5.83
Puello, Israel	R-R	6-3	200	10-10-00	4	6	4.52	14	14	0	0	66	43	37	33	3	37	60	.182	.132	.214	8.22	5.07
Reyes, Andy	R-R	6-0	160	3-11-00	1	1	3.44	17	1	0	2	34	31	21	13	1	20	22	.250	.146	.301	5.82	5.29
Rivas, Aldemar	R-R	6-1	170	1-21-99	5	1	5.01	17	0	0	0	32	29	22	18	1	15	44	.232	.291	.186	12.25	4.18
Rosario, Dalvin	R-R	6-1	167	6-15-00	4	4	4.47	13	13	0	0	50	48	32	25	2	33	47	.258	.273	.252	8.40	5.90
Sanchez, Sergio	L-L	6-1	160	12-16-00	4	0	2.74	13	0	0	0	23	20	8	7	1	17	25	.233	.269	.217	9.78	6.65
Sanchez, Yeison	R-R	6-0	170	11-13-97	3	1	2.35	15	0	0	4	23	10	9	6	0	13	29	.132	.156	.114	11.35	5.09
Segovia, Eduar	R-R	6-0	180	1-10-01	1	2	0.59	10	0	0	5	15	6	3	1	0	10	18	.118	.000	.188	10.57	5.87
Suarez, Luis	L-L	6-1	155	11-1-99	0	0	9.00	2	0	0	1	1	1	1	1	0	2	0	.250	—	.250	0.00	18.00
Torres, Alberto	L-L	6-0	155	4-28-01	1	0	2.45	2	0	0	0	4	2	1	1	0	3	4	.167	.500	.100	9.82	7.36
Urias, Manuel	R-R	6-6	200	3-8-01	2	4	1.95	12	11	0	0	60	56	19	13	0	11	44	.242	.269	.221	6.60	1.65

Fielding

C: Asencio 3, Barboza 13, Barreto 7, De Freitas 18, Francisco 25, Gonzalez 21, Gonzalez 4, Hernandez 32, Rodriguez 37. **1B:** Asencio 19, Barboza 3, Barreto 2, De Freitas 21, De La Rosa 2, Francisco 9, Gonzalez 45, Hernandez 1, Herrera 2, Jerez 1, Mendoza 1, Rodriguez 11, Smith 25, Valdez 4. **2B:** Alfonso 20, Boekhoudt 1, Dipre 2, Duran 3, Flores 50, Hernandez 5, Jerez 5, Mujica 26, Rondon 29. **3B:** Alfonso 9, De Freitas 1, Duran 14, Flores 1, Gonzalez 1, Hernandez 1, Hernandez 32, Herrera 43, Valdez 56. **SS:** Alfonso 19, Dipre 54, Jerez 28, Mujica 1, Rondon 44, Valdez 1. **OF:** Boekhoudt 53, Cedeno 8, Duran 2, Encarnacion 61, Flores 1, Garcia 29, Gonzalez 5, Hernandez 19, Herrera 1, Jerez 1, Mendoza 69, Mora 45, Peguero 57, Rojas 68, Smith 32, Valdez 1.

Pittsburgh Pirates

SEASON IN A SENTENCE: Entering the season without much in the way of expectations, the Pirates hovered around .500 and eventually acquired Rays ace Chris Archer prior to the July 31 trade deadline, only to see their playoff hopes fizzle with an August slump that led to a third consecutive season without a postseason appearance.

HIGH POINTS: The Pirates moved into first place in the NL Central by winning eight of their first 10 games. In all, the Pirates spent 26 days leading the division, the last of which was on May 17, following a 5-4 victory against the Padres. The win improved the Pirates' record to 26-17. The club also won 11 games in a row from July 11-24, giving the city and its franchise renewed playoff hopes as the trade deadline neared.

LOW POINT: After trading for Archer, the Pirates went just 4-10 against their division rivals in August. This led to a 10-17 overall record for the month, which eventually pushed Pittsburgh to make additional September callups and stymied their playoff push.

NOTABLE ROOKIES: After signing as a minor league free agent in the offseason, righthander Richard Rodriguez fit well in the Pirates' bullpen, tossing 69.1 innings after appearing in five games for the Orioles in 2017. The 28-year-old posted an impressive 2.47 ERA while striking out 88 hitters and walking just 19. Third baseman Colin Moran performed well after coming to Pittsburgh from the Astros via the Gerrit Cole trade. The University of North Carolina product started 107 games and hit .277/.340/.407 with 11 home runs and 58 RBIs.

KEY TRANSACTIONS: Pirates general manager Neal Huntington decided to be aggressive at the trade deadline. He acquired Archer from Tampa Bay in a trade that cost the Pirates righthander Tyler Glasnow and outfielder Austin Meadows as well as a player to be named, which turned out to be 2017 first-round righthander Shane Baz. In addition, Pittsburgh beefed up the bullpen by adding Rangers closer Keone Kela for two prospects.

DOWN ON THE FARM: With the exception of Double-A Altoona, no other Pirates farm team qualified for the playoffs. Third baseman Ke'Bryan Hayes and first baseman Will Craig provided offensive fire power for Altoona, helping the club win 78 games. Their playoff run fell short when they were eliminated by Akron (Indians) in the semifinals of the Eastern League playoffs.

OPENING DAY PAYROLL: $84,585,833 (26th).

PLAYERS OF THE YEAR

ROBBIE ROGERS

CLIFF WELCH/GETTY IMAGES

MAJOR LEAGUE	MINOR LEAGUE
Gregory Polanco OF	**Ke'Bryan Hayes** 3B
.254/.340/.499. Led	(Double-A)
Pirates in HR (23), RBIs	.293/.375/.444
(81) and OPS (.839)	45 XBH, 12 SB

ORGANIZATION LEADERS

Batting		*Minimum 250 AB
MAJORS		
* AVG	Corey Dickerson	.300
* OPS	Gregory Polanco	.839
HR	Gregory Polanco	23
RBI	Gregory Polanco	81
MINORS		
* AVG	Kevin Kramer, Indianapolis	.311
* OBP	Alfredo Reyes, Bradenton, Altoona, Indianapolis	.386
* SLG	Kevin Kramer, Indianapolis	.492
* OPS	Kevin Kramer, Indianapolis	.856
R	Cole Tucker, Altoona	77
H	Kevin Kramer, Indianapolis	148
TB	Kevin Kramer, Indianapolis	234
2B	Kevin Kramer, Indianapolis	35
3B	Jason Martin, Altoona, Indianapolis	8
3B	Patrick Dorrian, Pirates, Bristol	8
HR	Will Craig, Altoona	20
RBI	Will Craig, Altoona	102
BB	Mason Martin, West Virginia, Bristol	60
SO	Mason Martin, West Virginia, Bristol	149
SB	Alfredo Reyes, Bradenton, Altoona, Indianapolis	35
SB	Cole Tucker, Altoona	35

Pitching		#Minimum 75 IP
MAJORS		
W	Jameson Taillon	14
W	Trevor Williams	14
# ERA	Trevor Williams	3.44
SO	Jameson Taillon	179
SV	Felipe Vazquez	37
MINORS		
W	Tyler Eppler, Indianapolis	13
W	Cam Vieaux, Bradenton, Altoona	13
L	Mike Wallace, Bradenton	11
# ERA	J.T. Brubaker, Altoona, Indianapolis	2.81
G	Geoff Hartlieb, Altoona	47
GS	J.T. Brubaker, Altoona, Indianapolis	28
SV	Matt Eckelman, Bradenton, Altoona	17
IP	James Marvel, Bradenton, Altoona	167
BB	Luis Escobar, Bradenton, Altoona	59
SO	Mitch Keller, Altoona, Indianapolis, Bradenton	135
# AVG	Luis Escobar, Bradenton, Altoona	.225

General Manager: Neal Huntington. **Farm Director:** Larry Broadway. **Scouting Director:** Joe Delli Carri.

Class	Team	League	W	L	PCT	Finish	Manager
Majors	Pittsburgh Pirates	National	82	79	.509	7th (15)	Clint Hurdle
Triple-A	Indianapolis Indians	International	73	67	.521	t-5th (14)	Brian Esposito
Double-A	Altoona Curve	Eastern	78	60	.565	1st (12)	Mike Ryan
High A	Bradenton Marauders	Florida State	56	74	.431	2nd (12)	Gera Alvarez
Low A	West Virginia Power	South Atlantic	71	62	.534	4th (14)	Wyatt Toregas
Short season	West Virginia Black Bears	New York-Penn	32	44	.421	t-12th (14)	Kieran Mattison
Rookie	Bristol Pirates	Appalachian	31	37	.456	7th (10)	Miguel Perez
Rookie	GCL Pirates	Gulf Coast	27	25	.519	8th (18)	Dave Turegon
Overall 2018 Minor League Record			368	369	.499	16th (30)	

ORGANIZATION STATISTICS

PITTSBURGH PIRATES
NATIONAL LEAGUE

Batting	B-T	HT	WT	DOB	AVG	vLH	vRH	G	AB	R	H	2B	3B	HR	RBI	BB	HBP	SH	SF	SO	SB	CS	SLG	OBP
Bell, Josh	B-R	6-4	235	8-14-92	.262	.254	.265	148	501	74	131	31	4	12	62	77	0	0	5	104	2	5	.411	.357
Bostick, Christopher	R-R	5-10	200	3-24-93	.000	—	.000	2	2	0	0	0	0	0	0	0	0	0	0	1	0	0	.000	.000
2-team total (13 Miami)					.188	.143	.222	15	16	0	3	1	0	0	2	2	0	0	0	7	0	0	.250	.278
Cervelli, Francisco	R-R	6-1	210	3-6-86	.259	.244	.264	104	332	39	86	15	3	12	57	51	15	2	4	84	2	3	.431	.378
Diaz, Elias	R-R	6-1	215	11-17-90	.286	.346	.257	82	252	33	72	12	0	10	34	21	1	0	3	40	0	1	.452	.339
Dickerson, Corey	L-R	6-1	200	5-22-89	.300	.293	.302	135	504	65	151	35	7	13	55	21	1	4	0	4	80	8	3	.474	.330
Frazier, Adam	L-R	5-10	180	12-14-91	.277	.224	.291	113	318	52	88	23	2	10	35	29	3	1	1	53	1	3	.456	.342
Freese, David	R-R	6-2	220	4-28-83	.282	.284	.280	94	241	29	68	10	1	9	42	18	3	0	3	56	0	0	.444	.336
2-team total (19 Los Angeles)					.296	.321	.273	113	280	38	83	12	2	11	51	24	5	0	3	72	0	0	.471	.359
Harrison, Josh	R-R	5-8	185	7-8-87	.250	.219	.262	97	344	41	86	13	1	8	37	18	5	2	5	68	3	0	.363	.293
Hechavarria, Adeiny	R-R	6-0	195	4-15-89	.233	.455	.156	15	43	2	10	4	0	1	3	3	0	0	1	11	0	0	.395	.277
Kang, Jung Ho	R-R	6-0	210	4-5-87	.333	—	.333	3	6	0	2	0	0	0	0	0	0	0	0	1	0	0	.333	.333
Kramer, Kevin	L-R	6-0	200	10-3-93	.135	.000	.139	21	37	5	5	0	0	0	4	2	0	0	1	20	0	0	.135	.175
Lavarnway, Ryan	R-R	6-4	240	8-7-87	.667	.000	.800	6	6	1	4	1	0	0	1	0	0	0	0	1	0	0	.833	.667
Luplow, Jordan	R-R	6-1	195	9-26-93	.185	.211	.167	37	92	16	17	1	3	3	7	10	1	0	0	18	2	2	.359	.272
Marte, Starling	R-R	6-1	190	10-9-88	.277	.237	.291	145	559	81	155	32	5	20	72	35	8	1	3	109	33	14	.460	.327
Meadows, Austin	L-L	6-3	210	5-3-95	.292	.302	.287	49	154	16	45	8	2	5	13	8	1	0	2	35	4	1	.468	.327
Mercer, Jordy	R-R	6-3	210	8-27-86	.251	.286	.239	117	394	43	99	29	2	6	39	32	6	1	3	87	2	0	.381	.315
Moran, Colin	L-R	6-4	205	10-1-92	.277	.177	.295	144	415	49	115	19	1	11	58	39	4	0	7	82	0	2	.407	.340
Moroff, Max	B-R	5-10	185	5-13-93	.186	.240	.147	26	59	7	11	1	0	3	9	7	1	0	0	24	0	0	.356	.284
Newman, Kevin	R-R	6-1	180	8-4-93	.209	.357	.182	31	91	7	19	2	0	0	6	4	1	0	1	23	0	1	.231	.247
Osuna, Jose	R-R	6-3	240	12-12-92	.226	.255	.196	51	106	14	24	9	0	3	11	3	1	0	1	22	0	0	.396	.252
Polanco, Gregory	L-L	6-5	235	9-14-91	.254	.248	.256	130	461	75	117	32	6	23	81	61	3	0	7	117	12	2	.499	.340
Reyes, Pablo	R-R	5-8	170	5-5-93	.293	.364	.250	18	58	9	17	2	0	3	7	5	0	0	0	11	0	1	.483	.349
Rodriguez, Sean	R-R	6-0	200	4-26-85	.167	.227	.142	66	150	21	25	5	1	5	19	22	1	0	0	60	1	0	.313	.278
Stallings, Jacob	R-R	6-5	220	12-22-89	.216	.100	.259	14	37	2	8	0	0	0	5	3	0	0	1	9	0	0	.216	.268

Pitching	B-T	HT	WT	DOB	W	L	ERA	G	GS	CG	SV	IP	H	R	ER	HR	BB	SO	AVG	vLH	vRH	K/9	BB/9
Anderson, Tanner	R-R	6-2	195	5-27-93	1	0	6.35	6	0	0	0	11	15	10	8	1	8	6	.333	.353	.321	4.76	6.35
Archer, Chris	R-R	6-2	195	9-26-88	3	3	4.30	10	10	0	0	52	53	27	25	8	18	60	.262	.239	.282	10.32	3.10
Brault, Steven	L-L	6-0	200	4-29-92	6	3	4.61	45	5	0	0	92	84	51	47	10	57	82	.244	.213	.259	8.05	5.60
Burdi, Nick	R-R	6-5	220	1-19-93	0	0	20.25	2	0	0	0	1	3	4	3	1	2	2	.375	1.000	.167	13.50	13.50
Crick, Kyle	L-R	6-4	220	11-30-92	3	2	2.39	64	0	0	2	60	45	18	16	3	23	65	.202	.255	.154	9.70	3.43
Feliz, Michael	R-R	6-4	230	6-28-93	1	2	5.66	47	0	0	0	48	49	33	30	6	23	55	.261	.259	.262	10.38	4.34
Glasnow, Tyler	L-R	6-8	220	8-23-93	1	2	4.34	34	0	0	0	56	47	28	27	5	34	72	.226	.247	.209	11.57	5.46
Holmes, Clay	R-R	6-5	230	3-27-93	1	3	6.84	11	4	0	0	26	30	21	20	2	23	21	.291	.271	.309	7.18	7.86
Kela, Keone	R-R	6-1	215	4-16-93	0	1	2.93	16	0	0	0	15	10	5	5	2	5	22	.182	.154	.207	12.91	2.93
Kingham, Nick	R-R	6-5	225	11-8-91	5	7	5.21	18	15	0	0	76	79	50	44	18	26	69	.259	.293	.228	8.17	3.08
Kontos, George	R-R	6-3	225	6-16-85	2	3	5.03	21	0	0	1	20	23	12	11	4	5	9	.295	.286	.306	4.12	2.29
Kuhl, Chad	R-R	6-3	216	9-10-92	5	5	4.55	16	16	0	0	85	89	47	43	14	33	81	.275	.265	.284	8.58	3.49
McRae, Alex	R-R	6-2	220	4-6-93	0	1	5.68	2	0	0	0	6	8	4	4	0	5	5	.308	.154	.462	7.11	7.11
Musgrove, Joe	R-R	6-5	260	12-4-92	6	9	4.06	19	19	0	0	115	113	56	52	12	23	100	.253	.277	.233	7.80	1.79
Neverauskas, Dovydas	R-R	6-3	225	1-14-93	0	0	8.00	25	0	0	0	27	30	25	24	9	10	27	.280	.356	.226	9.00	3.33
Nova, Ivan	R-R	6-5	250	1-12-87	9	9	4.19	29	29	0	0	161	171	82	75	26	35	114	.268	.288	.250	6.37	1.96
Rodriguez, Richard	R-R	6-4	205	3-4-90	4	3	2.47	63	0	0	0	69	55	19	19	5	19	88	.217	.155	.270	11.42	2.47
Romero, Enny	R-L	6-3	232	1-24-91	0	0	4.50	2	0	0	0	4	7	5	2	0	3	5	.350	.167	.429	11.25	6.75
2-team total (2 Washington)					0	0	7.50	4	0	0	0	6	12	8	5	1	4	7	.387	.308	.444	10.50	6.00
Sadler, Casey	R-R	6-3	220	7-13-90	0	0	8.31	2	0	0	0	4	9	7	4	0	3	3	.409	.539	.222	6.23	6.23
Santana, Edgar	R-R	6-2	195	10-16-91	3	4	3.26	69	0	0	0	66	61	25	24	7	12	54	.240	.214	.266	7.33	1.63
Smoker, Josh	L-L	6-2	255	11-26-88	0	0	11.12	7	0	0	0	6	11	7	7	2	5	2	.423	.250	.500	3.18	7.94
Taillon, Jameson	R-R	6-5	230	11-18-91	14	10	3.20	32	32	2	0	191	179	69	68	20	46	179	.246	.266	.225	8.43	2.17
Vazquez, Felipe	L-L	6-2	210	7-5-91	4	2	2.70	70	0	0	37	70	63	24	21	4	24	89	.233	.175	.250	11.44	3.09
Williams, Trevor	R-R	6-3	230	4-25-92	14	10	3.11	31	31	1	0	171	146	64	59	15	55	126	.231	.228	.234	6.64	2.90

PITTSBURGH PIRATES

Fielding

Catcher	PCT	G	PO	A	E	DP	PB
Cervelli	.996	94	750	62	3	8	8
Diaz	.984	70	501	41	9	6	0
Stallings	1.000	13	96	9	0	1	0

First Base	PCT	G	PO	A	E	DP
Bell	.995	137	1021	83	6	90
Cervelli	.975	5	38	1	1	3
Freese	.990	15	95	9	1	8
Osuna	.989	12	83	9	1	9
Rodriguez	1.000	2	6	0	0	0

Second Base	PCT	G	PO	A	E	DP
Frazier	.975	55	72	121	5	30
Harrison	.982	87	126	209	6	47
Kramer	.933	4	7	7	1	3
Moroff	.975	17	18	21	1	6

Newman	.952	8	11	9	1	3
Reyes	1.000	1	0	1	0	0
Rodriguez	.968	26	25	36	2	9

Third Base	PCT	G	PO	A	E	DP
Freese	.965	55	27	84	4	10
Harrison	.000	2	0	0	0	0
Kang	1.000	1	1	1	0	0
Kramer	1.000	7	4	8	0	1
Moran	.962	116	64	188	10	15
Osuna	1.000	7	0	6	0	1
Reyes	.875	3	2	5	1	0
Rodriguez	.000	1	0	0	1	0

Shortstop	PCT	G	PO	A	E	DP
Hechavarria	.974	15	16	21	1	7

Mercer	.977	117	151	273	10	50
Moroff	1.000	6	4	10	0	3
Newman	.956	24	25	40	3	9
Rodriguez	.944	16	15	36	3	9

Outfield	PCT	G	PO	A	E	DP
Bostick	.000	1	0	0	0	0
Dickerson	.996	124	255	7	1	5
Frazier	.959	35	45	2	2	0
Luplow	.982	29	51	4	1	0
Marte	.991	139	338	11	3	3
Meadows	.974	39	75	0	2	0
Osuna	1.000	7	11	0	0	0
Polanco	.992	124	229	8	2	1
Reyes	.960	12	22	2	1	1
Rodriguez	1.000	18	25	0	0	0

INDIANAPOLIS INDIANS
INTERNATIONAL LEAGUE

TRIPLE-A

Batting	B-T	HT	WT	DOB	AVG	vLH	vRH	G	AB	R	H	2B	3B	HR	RBI	BB	HBP	SH	SF	SO	SB	CS	SLG	OBP
Bostick, Christopher	R-R	5-10	200	3-24-93	.295	.292	.297	78	298	32	88	24	3	4	32	24	2	1	66	6	3	.436	.351
Cunningham, Todd	B-R	6-0	205	3-20-89	.130	.143	.125	9	23	2	3	1	0	0	1	1	1	2	1	5	0	1	.174	.192
2-team total (9 Charlotte)					.163	.227	.111	18	49	5	8	2	0	0	3	5	1	3	2	9	2	2	.204	.246
Frazier, Adam	L-R	5-10	180	12-14-91	.223	.211	.229	32	121	10	27	5	2	0	18	11	1	2	20	1	3	.298	.289
Kang, Jung Ho	R-R	6-0	210	4-5-87	.235	.375	.192	9	34	4	8	1	0	0	5	3	1	0	1	5	0	1	.265	.308
Kramer, Kevin	L-R	6-0	200	10-3-93	.311	.312	.311	129	476	73	148	35	3	15	59	38	5	3	5	127	13	5	.492	.365
Lavarnway, Ryan	R-R	6-4	240	8-7-87	.288	.241	.308	77	264	29	76	23	1	9	33	29	8	2	0	57	0	0	.485	.375
Luplow, Jordan	R-R	6-1	195	9-26-93	.287	.273	.292	88	314	41	90	25	3	8	49	39	2	0	2	64	7	2	.462	.367
Martin, Jason	L-R	5-10	185	9-5-95	.211	.250	.192	59	213	20	45	5	3	4	21	17	0	4	0	52	5	4	.319	.270
Mathisen, Wyatt	R-R	6-0	227	12-30-93	.248	.264	.238	78	242	34	60	13	0	9	45	23	9	3	5	59	2	2	.413	.330
Meadows, Austin	L-L	6-3	210	5-3-95	.279	.328	.250	42	165	27	46	13	0	2	21	9	1	3	1	24	11	1	.394	.318
2-team total (27 Durham)					.303	.322	.293	69	261	46	79	24	0	12	43	17	2	3	2	37	12	2	.533	.348
Moroff, Max	B-R	5-10	185	5-13-93	.223	.256	.207	74	247	38	55	14	2	8	38	43	0	4	3	68	5	0	.393	.335
Newman, Kevin	R-R	6-1	180	8-4-93	.302	.336	.286	109	437	74	132	30	2	4	35	31	2	5	1	50	28	11	.407	.350
Osuna, Jose	R-R	6-3	240	12-12-92	.321	.319	.322	82	302	45	97	26	0	9	59	31	1	1	7	51	5	3	.497	.378
Pabst, Arden	R-R	6-1	202	3-14-95	.667	—	.667	1	3	1	2	0	0	0	0	0	0	0	0	0	0	0	.667	.667
Ratledge, Logan	R-R	5-11	190	7-20-92	.000	—	.000	1	3	0	0	0	0	0	0	1	0	0	0	1	0	0	.000	.250
Reyes, Alfredo	R-R	6-2	160	10-6-95	.200	.000	.250	6	10	1	2	0	0	0	1	0	1	0	1	5	1	0	.200	.273
Reyes, Pablo	R-R	5-8	170	9-5-93	.289	.254	.306	110	356	52	103	20	4	8	36	28	2	8	4	71	13	7	.435	.341
Rodriguez, Sean	R-R	6-0	200	4-26-85	.250	.000	.300	10	36	5	9	1	0	2	7	5	1	0	0	10	1	1	.444	.357
Stallings, Jacob	R-R	6-5	225	12-22-89	.285	.395	.234	68	256	37	73	22	1	3	40	15	5	0	2	51	1	2	.414	.335
Suiter, Jerrick	R-R	6-4	230	3-4-93	.204	.197	.208	67	191	21	39	13	1	2	27	21	2	0	5	72	6	0	.314	.283
Weiss, Erich	L-R	6-2	200	9-11-91	.234	.225	.237	76	218	26	51	11	4	5	21	15	3	0	0	54	1	0	.390	.292
Williams, Jackson	R-R	5-10	200	5-14-86	.222	.250	.206	16	54	4	12	2	0	1	5	5	0	0	1	15	0	0	.315	.283
Wood, Eric	R-R	6-1	210	11-22-92	.269	.294	.258	86	283	44	76	25	1	11	39	20	5	0	0	68	3	0	.481	.328

Pitching	B-T	HT	WT	DOB	W	L	ERA	G	GS	CG	SV	IP	H	R	ER	HR	BB	SO	AVG	vLH	vRH	K/9	BB/9
Anderson, Tanner	R-R	6-2	195	5-27-93	3	2	2.64	39	0	0	6	61	65	25	18	2	15	49	.277	.344	.230	7.19	2.20
Boshers, Buddy	L-L	6-3	205	5-9-88	0	1	4.50	7	0	0	1	6	6	3	3	0	3	7	.273	.333	.231	10.50	4.50
Brault, Steven	L-L	6-0	200	4-29-92	0	1	3.38	5	0	0	0	5	6	2	2	0	4	7	.273	.091	.455	11.81	6.75
Brubaker, J.T.	R-R	6-4	175	11-17-93	8	4	3.10	22	22	0	0	119	121	47	41	7	36	96	.268	.322	.225	7.26	2.72
Burdi, Nick	R-R	6-5	220	1-19-93	0	0	5.40	5	0	0	0	5	9	4	3	0	4	5	.375	.444	.333	9.00	7.20
Coley, Austin	R-R	6-2	203	7-14-92	1	3	9.64	9	7	0	0	28	46	31	30	5	13	15	.368	.333	.388	4.82	4.18
Crick, Kyle	L-R	6-4	220	11-30-92	1	0	2.25	3	0	0	1	4	1	1	1	0	0	5	.353	.500	.273	11.25	0.00
DuRapau, Montana	R-R	5-11	175	3-27-92	1	0	6.33	11	0	0	0	21	21	15	15	5	10	25	.250	.286	.225	10.55	4.22
Eppler, Tyler	R-R	6-5	230	1-5-93	13	6	3.59	24	23	0	0	153	160	63	61	13	39	118	.272	.250	.287	6.94	2.29
Feliz, Michael	R-R	6-4	230	6-28-93	2	1	7.20	9	0	0	2	10	13	8	8	2	1	12	.317	.313	.320	10.80	0.90
Hellweg, Johnny	R-R	6-7	235	10-29-88	1	1	1.33	24	0	0	11	27	18	6	4	0	13	25	.192	.100	.259	8.33	4.33
Holmes, Clay	R-R	6-5	230	3-27-93	8	3	3.40	22	16	1	0	95	94	40	36	4	40	100	.260	.246	.274	9.44	3.78
Jones, Tyler	R-R	6-4	240	9-5-89	2	1	5.40	12	0	0	0	20	14	10	3	7	10	.222	.367	.220	9.18	3.78
Keller, Mitch	R-R	6-3	195	4-4-96	3	2	4.82	10	10	0	0	52	59	34	28	3	22	57	.280	.293	.271	9.80	3.78
Kingham, Nick	R-R	6-5	225	11-8-91	4	2	3.61	12	12	1	0	62	57	26	25	5	16	58	.246	.239	.252	8.37	2.31
Liranzo, Jesus	R-R	6-3	225	3-7-95	2	3	5.00	32	0	0	3	45	31	27	25	7	31	47	.195	.192	.198	9.40	6.20
Magnifico, Damien	R-R	6-1	205	5-24-91	3	4	3.57	42	4	0	0	71	60	31	28	1	44	64	.236	.278	.210	8.15	5.60
McKinney, Brett	R-R	6-0	225	11-19-90	0	0	9.53	5	0	0	0	6	7	6	6	1	7	5	.304	.143	.375	7.94	11.12
McRae, Alex	R-R	6-2	220	4-6-93	3	10	4.77	26	19	0	1	117	134	67	62	9	50	104	.295	.283	.307	8.00	3.85
Musgrove, Joe	R-R	6-5	260	12-4-92	1	1	5.06	2	2	0	0	11	10	6	6	2	2	10	.244	.450	.048	9.28	1.69
Neverauskas, Dovydas	R-R	6-3	225	1-14-93	2	3	2.53	34	0	0	4	46	31	15	13	2	30	58	.195	.153	.220	11.27	5.83
Rodriguez, Richard	R-R	6-4	205	3-4-90	0	0	0.00	2	0	0	0	5	1	0	0	0	2	9	.063	.000	.100	16.20	3.60
Romero, Enny	R-L	6-3	232	1-24-91	1	1	6.23	5	0	0	0	4	3	4	3	1	5	5	.071	.000	.083	10.38	10.38
Sadler, Casey	R-R	6-3	220	7-13-90	6	5	3.39	27	8	1	1	77	79	38	29	7	26	61	.264	.262	.267	7.13	3.04
Schugel, A.J.	R-R	6-0	195	6-27-89	1	0	6.23	12	0	0	0	13	18	9	9	4	4	12	.340	.435	.267	8.31	2.77

	B-T HT WT DOB	W	L	ERA	G	GS	CG	SV	IP	H	R	ER	HR	BB	SO	AVG	vLH	vRH	K/9	BB/9
Schultz, Bo	R-R 6-3 220 9-25-85	0	1	2.00	24	0	0	3	27	29	9	6	0	10	22	.271	.244	.290	7.33	3.33
Smoker, Josh	L-L 6-2 255 11-26-88	3	1	2.83	32	0	0	0	35	32	13	11	4	12	39	.234	.231	.235	10.03	3.09
2-team total (10 Toledo)		3	2	3.38	42	0	0	0	45	45	19	17	4	16	50	.250	.258	.246	9.93	3.18
Waddell, Brandon	L-L 6-3 180 6-3-94	5	8	4.19	19	15	0	0	82	91	42	38	3	36	60	.285	.284	.286	6.61	3.97

Fielding

Catcher	PCT	G	PO	A	E	DP	PB
Lavarnway	.992	60	471	26	4	7	1
Pabst	.917	1	11	0	1	0	0
Stallings	.993	63	516	41	4	5	4
Williams	1.000	16	128	16	0	1	4
Reyes	.950	9	19	19	2	4	
Rodriguez	1.000	2	7	9	0	3	
Weiss	1.000	1	3	2	0	1	
Reyes	.946	9	16	19	2	6	
Rodriguez	.833	2	2	3	1	1	

First Base	PCT	G	PO	A	E	DP
Mathisen	.994	57	448	23	3	47
Osuna	.995	24	201	14	1	27
Suiter	.981	6	49	3	1	12
Weiss	.991	44	319	28	3	35
Wood	.993	17	140	6	1	16

Second Base	PCT	G	PO	A	E	DP
Frazier	1.000	17	24	47	0	16
Kramer	.976	82	153	216	9	70
Mathisen	1.000	1	1	0	0	0
Moroff	.979	10	15	31	1	5
Newman	.972	21	40	66	3	21
Reyes	1.000	1	0	1	0	0

Third Base	PCT	G	PO	A	E	DP
Kang	1.000	5	4	14	0	0
Kramer	.978	19	7	38	1	7
Mathisen	.962	15	3	22	1	0
Moroff	.957	19	9	36	2	2
Osuna	.976	47	25	98	3	11
Reyes	1.000	27	16	48	0	8
Rodriguez	1.000	2	1	6	0	0
Weiss	.000	1	0	0	0	0
Wood	.957	11	6	16	1	1

Shortstop	PCT	G	PO	A	E	DP
Kang	1.000	4	1	10	0	1
Kramer	.985	15	22	42	1	19
Moroff	.914	29	29	67	9	10
Newman	.982	83	103	221	6	51

Outfield	PCT	G	PO	A	E	DP
Bostick	.993	73	133	0	1	0
Cunningham	1.000	8	17	0	0	0
Frazier	1.000	13	25	0	0	0
Luplow	.977	78	117	9	3	4
Martin	1.000	59	117	1	0	0
Meadows	1.000	39	72	0	0	0
Moroff	1.000	8	10	0	0	0
Osuna	1.000	9	17	2	0	1
Ratledge	1.000	1	2	0	0	0
Reyes	1.000	1	1	0	0	0
Reyes	.990	58	96	4	1	1
Rodriguez	1.000	1	0	1	0	0
Suiter	.989	45	78	8	1	2
Weiss	.000	1	0	0	1	0
Wood	.944	44	82	2	5	0

PITTSBURGH PIRATES

ALTOONA CURVE   DOUBLE-A
EASTERN LEAGUE

Batting	B-T	HT	WT	DOB	AVG	vLH	vRH	G	AB	R	H	2B	3B	HR	RBI	BB	HBP	SH	SF	SO	SB	CS	SLG	OBP
Alemais, Stephen	R-R	6-0	190	4-12-95	.279	.316	.267	120	402	56	112	16	4	1	34	44	2	5	8	69	16	9	.346	.347
Bormann, John	R-R	6-0	205	4-4-93	.000	—	.000	2	3	0	0	0	0	0	0	3	0	0	0	1	0	0	.000	.500
Cervelli, Francisco	R-R	6-1	210	3-6-86	.200	—	.200	2	5	0	1	0	0	0	0	1	0	0	3	0	0	.200	.556
Craig, Will	R-R	6-3	212	11-16-94	.248	.241	.250	132	480	73	119	30	3	20	102	42	15	0	12	128	6	3	.448	.321
Gaffney, Tyler	R-R	6-1	225	4-20-91	.194	.257	.169	51	124	20	24	4	0	3	15	12	10	0	1	27	4	0	.298	.313
George, Jordan	R-R	6-0	200	7-16-92	.263	.203	.278	110	342	46	90	12	0	5	43	41	8	1	0	47	0	1	.342	.356
Harrison, Josh	R-R	5-8	185	7-8-87	.167	.000	.182	3	12	2	2	0	0	0	1	0	0	0	3	0	0	.167	.231
Hayes, Ke'Bryan	R-R	6-1	210	1-28-97	.293	.255	.304	117	437	64	128	31	7	7	47	57	4	4	6	84	12	5	.444	.375
Hill, Logan	R-R	6-3	230	5-26-93	.228	.270	.215	117	391	48	89	14	2	17	72	41	8	0	4	132	1	5	.404	.311
Jackson, Bralin	R-L	6-2	183	12-2-93	.214	.269	.195	64	206	19	44	7	1	3	14	11	1	0	1	63	5	3	.301	.256
Jhang, Jin-De	L-R	5-9	225	5-17-93	.320	.375	.306	35	122	13	39	8	0	1	23	11	0	1	1	14	0	0	.410	.373
Kelley, Christian	R-R	5-10	190	9-23-93	.235	.231	.236	90	311	36	73	13	2	8	38	25	9	0	2	64	0	0	.367	.308
Krause, Kevin	R-R	6-2	200	11-23-92	.000	—	.000	2	3	0	0	0	0	0	0	1	0	0	1	0	0	.000	.250
Martin, Jason	L-R	5-10	185	9-5-95	.326	.320	.327	68	255	49	83	13	5	9	34	28	1	3	2	61	7	8	.522	.392
Mathisen, Wyatt	R-R	6-0	227	12-30-93	.385	.286	.421	12	26	9	10	3	1	1	3	11	3	0	1	7	1	1	.692	.585
Pabst, Arden	R-R	6-1	202	3-14-95	.193	.375	.122	19	57	6	11	2	0	2	7	5	0	1	0	15	0	1	.333	.258
Ratledge, Logan	R-R	5-11	190	7-20-92	.182	.063	.231	28	55	5	10	3	0	2	8	5	2	0	2	13	1	0	.346	.266
Reyes, Alfredo	R-R	6-2	160	10-4-93	.250	.368	.225	34	108	16	27	4	0	1	11	10	1	2	0	37	11	1	.315	.319
Reyes, Pablo	R-R	5-8	170	9-5-93	.244	.143	.263	12	45	3	11	3	0	0	5	4	0	0	0	5	3	0	.311	.306
Reynolds, Bryan	R-B	6-3	205	1-27-95	.302	.233	.322	88	331	56	100	18	7	7	46	43	3	0	6	73	4	4	.438	.381
Tucker, Cole	B-R	6-3	200	7-3-96	.259	.311	.246	133	517	77	134	21	7	5	44	55	6	3	8	104	35	12	.356	.333
Williams, Jackson	R-R	5-10	200	5-14-86	.219	.286	.200	10	32	1	7	0	0	1	5	2	0	0	4	0	0	.313	.265

Pitching	B-T	HT	WT	DOB	W	L	ERA	G	GS	CG	SV	IP	H	R	ER	HR	BB	SO	AVG	vLH	vRH	K/9	BB/9
Agrazal, Dario	R-R	6-2	225	12-28-94	5	6	3.99	15	14	0	0	86	91	41	38	9	13	52	.301	.241	.346	5.46	1.37
Brentz, Jake	L-L	6-2	195	9-14-94	0	1	13.50	12	0	0	0	11	12	19	17	1	21	15	.267	.333	.233	11.91	16.68
Brubaker, J.T.	R-R	6-4	175	11-17-93	2	2	1.80	6	6	0	0	35	29	9	7	1	8	35	.218	.279	.130	9.00	2.06
Burdi, Nick	R-R	6-5	220	1-19-93	0	0	6.75	3	0	0	0	4	6	3	3	0	2	3	.375	.546	.000	6.75	4.50
Coley, Austin	R-R	6-2	203	7-14-92	2	0	3.57	5	5	0	0	23	24	9	9	1	8	14	.270	.346	.162	5.56	3.18
DuRapau, Montana	R-R	5-11	175	3-27-92	0	1	2.89	8	0	0	2	9	7	3	3	1	0	13	.206	.167	.250	12.54	0.00
Eckelman, Matt	R-R	6-4	240	10-6-93	1	1	1.82	23	0	0	11	25	18	7	5	1	15	17	.207	.216	.194	6.20	5.47
Escobar, Elvis	L-L	5-8	181	9-16-94	1	0	12.46	3	0	0	0	4	7	6	6	1	5	8	.333	.286	.357	16.62	10.38
Escobar, Luis	R-R	6-2	210	5-30-96	4	0	4.54	7	7	0	0	36	30	18	18	4	21	25	.227	.200	.286	6.31	5.30
Garcia, Yeudy	R-R	6-2	200	10-6-92	3	5	5.23	37	0	0	3	53	53	35	31	3	32	68	.257	.273	.235	11.48	5.40
Hartlieb, Geoff	R-R	6-6	210	12-9-93	8	2	3.24	47	0	0	10	58	56	29	21	3	24	56	.253	.238	.273	8.64	3.70
Hearn, Taylor	L-L	6-5	210	8-30-94	3	6	3.12	19	19	2	0	104	75	41	36	6	38	107	.198	.200	.197	9.26	3.29
Helton, Bret	R-R	6-3	215	7-25-93	6	6	6.12	35	1	0	0	60	62	46	41	8	38	45	.276	.313	.227	6.71	5.67
Hightower, Scooter	R-R	6-6	215	10-15-93	2	1	2.41	11	7	0	0	37	30	13	10	1	9	31	.217	.250	.182	7.47	2.17
Keller, Mitch	R-R	6-3	195	4-4-96	9	2	2.72	14	14	0	0	86	64	29	26	7	32	76	.208	.229	.175	7.95	3.35
Keselica, Sean	L-L	6-2	210	6-14-93	2	3	4.94	40	1	0	0	58	39	34	32	4	43	49	.195	.180	.205	7.56	6.63
Kingham, Nick	R-R	6-5	225	11-8-91	0	1	7.20	1	1	0	0	5	7	4	4	0	1	4	.318	.600	.235	7.20	1.80
Liranzo, Jeison	R-R	6-3	225	3-7-95	0	0	0.00	9	0	0	4	12	7	0	0	0	6	3	.167	.211	.130	13.50	2.25
Marvel, James	R-R	6-4	197	9-17-93	3	1	3.00	5	5	1	0	33	29	11	11	1	9	22	.236	.214	.254	6.00	2.45
Musgrove, Joe	R-R	6-5	260	12-4-92	0	1	2.25	1	1	0	0	4	2	1	1	1	0	4	.143	.200	.000	9.00	0.00
Romero, Enny	R-L	6-3	232	1-24-91	0	0	0.00	2	0	0	0	2	1	0	0	1	0	1	.167	.000	.200	4.50	4.50

Name	B-T	HT	WT	DOB	W	L	ERA	G	GS	CG	SV	IP	H	R	ER	HR	BB	SO	AVG	vLH	vRH	K/9	BB/9
Scioneaux, Tate	R-R	6-1	200	12-14-92	2	3	4.87	43	2	0	7	61	71	39	33	10	19	69	.283	.274	.295	10.18	2.80
Sendelbach, Logan	R-R	6-3	185	5-5-94	4	3	4.24	35	3	0	0	70	68	34	33	6	41	47	.258	.258	.258	6.04	5.27
Street, Sam	R-R	6-3	215	3-18-92	0	0	0.00	3	0	0	1	3	2	1	0	0	0	3	.182	.143	.250	9.00	0.00
Vasquez, Pedro	R-R	6-4	190	9-23-95	2	6	5.12	13	12	0	0	63	70	40	36	9	18	46	.287	.268	.314	6.54	2.56
Vera, Eduardo	R-R	6-2	185	7-3-94	8	3	3.62	17	17	0	0	97	83	41	39	11	23	68	.231	.242	.217	6.31	2.13
Vieaux, Cam	L-L	6-4	200	12-5-93	9	5	3.59	15	15	0	0	88	79	35	35	10	17	72	.242	.242	.241	7.39	1.75
Waddell, Brandon	L-L	6-3	180	6-3-94	2	1	2.68	9	8	0	0	54	39	18	16	4	19	43	.206	.104	.241	7.21	3.19
Weiman, Blake	R-L	6-4	208	11-5-95	1	0	0.00	3	0	0	0	7	4	0	0	0	1	5	.182	.300	.083	6.75	1.35

Fielding

Catcher	PCT	G	PO	A	E	DP	PB
Bormann	1.000	2	13	1	0	0	1
Jhang	.994	22	163	11	1	1	4
Kelley	.993	90	637	64	5	3	5
Pabst	.992	17	119	11	1	0	1
Williams	.988	10	69	10	1	0	0

First Base	PCT	G	PO	A	E	DP
Craig	.993	122	1021	87	8	110
George	1.000	14	102	10	0	8
Mathisen	1.000	5	37	3	0	2

Second Base	PCT	G	PO	A	E	DP
Alemais	.977	114	166	334	12	71

	PCT	G	PO	A	E	DP
Harrison	.875	2	2	5	1	0
Mathisen	1.000	5	13	7	0	3
Ratledge	1.000	16	16	29	0	6
Reyes	.973	9	15	21	1	5
Reyes	1.000	3	8	8	0	1

Third Base	PCT	G	PO	A	E	DP
George	.833	11	2	8	2	1
Hayes	.978	116	72	200	6	29
Mathisen	1.000	1	0	3	0	1
Ratledge	1.000	5	2	5	0	1
Reyes	1.000	10	6	6	0	0

Shortstop	PCT	G	PO	A	E	DP
Alemais	1.000	7	9	26	0	5

	PCT	G	PO	A	E	DP
Reyes	1.000	2	1	3	0	0
Tucker	.973	131	182	315	14	77

Outfield	PCT	G	PO	A	E	DP
Escobar	1.000	30	47	0	0	0
Gaffney	.988	42	83	2	1	0
George	.962	35	50	0	2	0
Hill	.982	92	162	3	3	1
Jackson	.977	55	123	5	3	2
Krause	.000	1	0	0	0	0
Martin	.988	68	162	0	2	0
Ratledge	.000	1	0	0	0	0
Reyes	.969	14	30	1	1	0
Reyes	.938	7	15	0	1	0
Reynolds	.984	88	181	6	3	0

BRADENTON MARAUDERS — HIGH CLASS A
FLORIDA STATE LEAGUE

Batting	B-T	HT	WT	DOB	AVG	vLH	vRH	G	AB	R	H	2B	3B	HR	RBI	BB	HBP	SH	SF	SO	SB	CS	SLG	OBP
Arbet, Trae	R-R	6-0	185	7-1-94	.143	.115	.155	26	84	6	12	4	0	0	4	4	2	0	0	28	3	2	.191	.200
Baur, Albert	L-R	6-4	215	3-22-92	.266	.277	.262	117	436	55	116	22	1	13	57	37	5	3	5	73	1	2	.411	.327
Bormann, John	R-R	6-0	205	4-4-93	.218	.214	.220	18	55	6	12	2	0	0	6	2	2	0	0	11	1	0	.255	.318
Brown, Garrett	L-R	6-0	185	3-23-93	.257	.478	.198	36	109	13	28	0	1	0	12	6	1	1	1	22	6	7	.275	.299
Delay, Jason	R-R	5-11	185	3-7-95	.247	.333	.209	67	219	23	54	4	1	2	21	21	5	4	1	51	2	0	.301	.325
Gaffney, Tyler	R-R	6-1	225	4-20-91	.291	.310	.283	38	134	27	39	9	3	3	21	9	13	1	0	27	10	5	.470	.391
Harrer, Justin	R-R	6-2	195	3-2-97	.200	.500	.000	2	5	0	1	0	0	0	0	1	0	2	0	0	.200	.200
Haug, Ryan	R-R	6-2	165	12-29-94	.000	—	.000	1	3	0	0	0	0	0	0	0	0	0	0	0	0	0	.000	.000
Hughston, Casey	L-R	6-2	200	6-9-94	.201	.149	.220	105	339	42	68	12	5	3	21	39	3	6	2	130	6	4	.292	.287
Kang, Jung Ho	R-R	6-0	210	4-5-87	.417	.400	.421	7	24	5	10	2	0	3	11	6	1	0	1	3	1	0	.875	.531
Madris, Bligh	R-R	6-2	200	9-8-95	.239	.294	.215	103	369	40	88	12	5	9	53	28	3	3	7	88	3	4	.371	.292
Medrano, Jesse	R-R	5-11	200	3-27-95	.000	.000	.000	5	8	0	0	0	0	0	0	0	0	1	0	4	0	0	.000	.111
Oliva, Jared	R-R	6-3	187	11-27-95	.275	.302	.262	108	396	75	109	24	4	9	47	40	11	2	5	91	33	8	.424	.354
Owen, Hunter	R-R	6-0	195	9-22-93	.262	.244	.270	111	401	53	105	21	3	18	60	19	14	5	1	114	4	1	.464	.317
Pabst, Arden	R-R	6-1	202	3-14-95	.281	.235	.300	46	171	19	48	12	2	8	29	10	0	1	2	27	2	0	.515	.317
Peurifoy, Ryan	R-R	6-2	206	3-26-95	.000	.000	.000	3	7	0	0	0	0	0	-1	0	0	0	3	0	0	.000	.125
Pope, Brett	L-R	6-0	180	5-25-94	.243	.275	.232	48	152	17	37	6	0	0	12	22	2	2	1	27	2	7	.283	.345
Reyes, Alfredo	R-R	6-2	160	10-4-93	.310	.307	.311	61	197	34	61	6	0	3	19	39	1	5	1	60	23	3	.386	.424
Rodriguez, Sean	R-R	6-0	200	4-26-85	.125	.000	.143	2	8	2	1	0	0	0	1	0	0	0	1	0	0	.125	.222
Siri, Raul	R-R	5-9	175	10-21-94	.333	.222	.378	19	63	5	21	4	0	1	10	3	2	0	0	21	1	0	.444	.382
Tancas, Lucas	R-R	6-2	220	11-12-93	.213	.188	.225	92	310	29	66	20	4	6	46	23	7	1	0	88	6	2	.316	.282
Tolman, Mitchell	L-R	5-11	195	6-8-94	.250	.286	.233	68	240	28	60	16	1	2	37	51	1	7	7	77	7	3	.350	.359
Valerio, Adrian	R-R	5-11	150	3-13-97	.243	.261	.235	117	466	51	113	26	1	6	49	15	1	16	2	101	11	4	.341	.267

Pitching	B-T	HT	WT	DOB	W	L	ERA	G	GS	CG	SV	IP	H	R	ER	HR	BB	SO	AVG	vLH	vRH	K/9	BB/9
Agrazal, Dario	R-R	6-3	225	12-28-94	0	0	0.00	2	2	0	0	8	3	0	0	0	0	4	.120	.177	.000	4.50	0.00
Agustin, Ronny	L-L	6-2	185	9-18-94	1	5	3.33	32	0	0	5	46	33	23	17	1	35	39	.199	.200	.198	7.63	6.85
Amedee, Jess	R-R	6-2	205	9-5-93	1	1	6.75	14	0	0	1	19	22	16	14	1	16	22	.290	.297	.282	10.61	7.71
Brentz, Jake	L-L	6-2	195	9-14-94	0	0	8.02	19	0	0	0	21	25	20	19	1	18	30	.281	.313	.263	12.66	7.59
Burdi, Nick	R-R	6-5	220	1-19-93	0	0	4.50	2	2	0	0	2	1	1	1	1	0	6	.143	.200	.000	27.00	0.00
Cederlind, Blake	R-R	6-3	190	1-4-96	1	2	7.59	17	0	0	3	21	26	20	18	2	19	18	.302	.256	.340	7.59	8.02
Eckelman, Matt	R-R	6-4	240	10-6-93	4	0	2.28	17	0	0	6	24	19	6	6	2	8	27	.218	.206	.226	10.27	3.04
Escobar, Luis	R-R	6-2	210	5-30-96	7	6	3.98	17	16	0	0	93	76	43	41	9	38	85	.224	.224	.223	8.26	3.69
German, Angel	R-R	6-4	185	5-25-96	1	3	6.92	35	0	0	3	40	41	34	31	5	28	47	.263	.228	.299	10.49	6.25
Hightower, Scooter	R-R	6-6	215	10-15-93	5	0	1.47	18	0	0	3	31	23	6	5	2	4	35	.211	.258	.149	10.27	1.17
Holmes, Clay	R-R	6-5	230	3-27-93	0	0	1.50	1	1	0	0	6	4	1	1	0	0	8	.191	.000	.250	12.00	0.00
Jess, Jordan	L-L	6-2	245	1-29-93	4	5	4.71	33	0	0	3	50	51	29	26	5	11	54	.264	.228	.290	9.79	1.99
Keller, Mitch	R-R	6-3	195	4-4-96	0	0	2.25	1	1	0	0	4	7	2	1	0	1	2	.389	.600	.308	4.50	2.25
Marvel, James	R-R	6-2	197	9-17-93	9	6	3.68	22	21	2	0	134	132	64	55	10	31	100	.261	.268	.253	6.70	2.08
Mendez, Deivy	R-R	6-2	190	10-27-95	0	2	8.31	11	0	0	0	13	12	12	12	1	10	13	.245	.250	.238	9.69	6.23
2-team total (11 Charlotte)					0	4	8.53	22	0	0	0	25	23	24	24	1	21	31	.240	.239	.240	11.01	7.46
Musgrove, Joe	R-R	6-5	260	12-4-92	0	0	6.00	1	1	0	0	3	5	2	2	0	0	2	.385	.333	.429	6.00	0.00
Nunez, Oddy	L-L	6-8	230	12-20-96	4	9	4.70	19	17	1	0	100	102	60	52	9	44	61	.270	.292	.258	5.51	3.97
Oller, Adam	R-R	6-4	225	10-17-94	2	4	6.75	24	5	0	0	59	70	48	44	14	21	53	.299	.350	.248	8.13	3.22
Piechota, Evan	R-R	6-1	225	10-19-93	0	5	5.28	14	7	0	1	58	72	35	34	10	15	33	.310	.326	.289	5.12	2.33
Robles, Domingo	L-L	6-2	170	4-29-98	0	3	4.76	5	5	0	0	28	32	15	15	1	10	19	.294	.370	.238	6.04	3.18

	B-T	HT	WT	DOB	W	L	ERA	G	GS	CG	SV	IP	H	R	ER	HR	BB	SO	AVG	vLH	vRH	K/9	BB/9
Romero, Enny	R-L	6-3	232	1-24-91	0	1	13.50	1	1	0	0	1	3	1	1	1	0	1	.600	.500	.667	13.50	0.00
Schugel, A.J.	R-R	6-0	195	6-27-89	0	0	7.71	5	2	0	0	5	8	5	4	0	1	8	.381	.375	.385	15.43	1.93
Schultz, Bo	R-R	6-3	220	9-25-85	0	0	0.00	8	0	0	0	11	2	0	0	0	4	10	.061	.000	.087	8.44	3.38
Vasquez, Pedro	R-R	6-4	190	9-23-95	0	3	4.21	6	6	0	0	26	26	14	12	2	12	19	.268	.298	.225	6.66	4.21
Vera, Eduardo	R-R	6-2	185	7-3-94	3	2	2.95	9	9	0	0	58	48	19	19	6	10	30	.230	.183	.276	4.66	1.55
Vieaux, Cam	L-L	6-4	200	12-5-93	4	1	3.81	10	10	0	0	57	54	26	24	9	18	52	.251	.209	.270	8.26	2.86
Wallace, Gavin	R-R	6-5	210	11-14-95	3	4	6.32	10	10	0	0	57	82	41	40	10	15	40	.340	.333	.348	6.32	2.37
Wallace, Mike	R-R	6-5	180	5-21-94	5	11	5.56	27	14	1	1	110	155	76	68	18	20	71	.341	.339	.345	5.81	1.64
Weiman, Blake	R-L	6-4	208	11-5-95	2	1	3.90	22	0	0	2	32	33	15	14	3	6	37	.260	.226	.284	10.30	1.67

Fielding

Catcher	PCT	G	PO	A	E	DP	PB
Bormann	1.000	17	118	9	0	2	5
Delay	.992	66	452	42	4	3	7
Haug	.909	1	7	3	1	1	0
Owen	1.000	3	19	5	0	0	3
Pabst	.995	44	332	36	2	2	2

First Base	PCT	G	PO	A	E	DP
Baur	.995	76	603	45	3	69
Pope	1.000	1	2	0	0	0
Reyes	1.000	1	1	0	0	0
Tancas	.990	56	456	25	5	50

Second Base	PCT	G	PO	A	E	DP
Arbet	.981	24	45	61	2	19
Medrano	1.000	3	5	2	0	2

	PCT	G	PO	A	E	DP
Pope	.984	13	21	42	1	11
Reyes	.981	32	63	93	3	25
Siri	1.000	4	8	12	0	2
Tolman	.972	54	90	149	7	36
Valerio	.909	2	5	5	1	1

Third Base	PCT	G	PO	A	E	DP
Kang	1.000	2	2	3	0	0
Medrano	1.000	1	1	5	0	0
Owen	.938	76	52	143	13	18
Pope	.982	24	18	37	1	2
Reyes	.964	21	23	31	2	5
Siri	.667	1	2	0	1	1
Tolman	.938	7	4	11	1	2

Shortstop	PCT	G	PO	A	E	DP
Kang	1.000	4	11	8	0	5

	PCT	G	PO	A	E	DP
Pope	1.000	6	4	13	0	1
Reyes	.939	9	14	17	2	6
Rodriguez	1.000	1	1	6	0	0
Tolman	.833	1	3	2	1	2
Valerio	.966	113	164	294	16	76

Outfield	PCT	G	PO	A	E	DP
Brown	1.000	34	64	1	0	0
Gaffney	.981	30	50	1	1	1
Harrer	1.000	2	7	0	0	0
Hughston	.991	105	204	8	2	4
Madris	.989	92	164	8	2	1
Oliva	.996	101	218	4	1	1
Peurifoy	1.000	3	4	1	0	1
Siri	1.000	11	14	1	0	0
Tancas	.960	22	46	2	2	1

WEST VIRGINIA POWER

LOW CLASS A

SOUTH ATLANTIC LEAGUE

Batting	B-T	HT	WT	DOB	AVG	vLH	vRH	G	AB	R	H	2B	3B	HR	RBI	BB	HBP	SH	SF	SO	SB	CS	SLG	OBP
Bengtson, Ben	R-R	6-0	205	7-28-95	.220	.173	.232	74	246	31	54	13	1	4	27	14	3	2	4	71	4	1	.329	.266
Bormann, John	R-R	6-0	205	4-4-93	.265	.500	.233	11	34	6	9	3	0	0	5	3	2	0	0	5	0	0	.353	.359
Busby, Dylan	R-R	6-2	196	11-28-95	.244	.346	.214	33	115	19	28	8	1	5	20	13	4	2	0	37	3	1	.461	.341
Castro, Rodolfo	B-R	6-0	200	5-21-99	.231	.180	.244	105	385	47	89	19	4	12	50	26	1	8	6	100	6	3	.395	.278
Cruz, Oneil	L-R	6-6	175	10-4-98	.286	.375	.261	103	402	66	115	25	7	14	59	34	3	0	4	100	11	5	.488	.343
Glendinning, Robbie	R-R	6-2	196	10-6-95	.282	.296	.277	34	110	16	31	4	1	2	18	13	0	2	0	28	1	3	.391	.358
Gonzalez, Yoel	R-R	6-1	180	8-1-96	.000	—	.000	2	4	0	0	0	0	0	0	0	0	0	0	2	0	0	.000	.000
Hernandez, Raul	R-R	6-0	182	12-20-95	.325	.368	.312	47	160	20	52	12	0	1	22	11	2	1	1	33	2	1	.419	.374
Herrera, Jhoan	L-R	6-1	185	6-14-95	.125	—	.125	2	8	0	1	0	0	0	1	0	0	0	0	1	0	0	.250	.125
Kaiser, Connor	R-R	6-4	195	11-20-96	.302	.250	.314	16	63	7	19	2	0	1	8	4	0	1	1	15	0	1	.381	.338
Lorenzo, Rafelin	R-R	6-2	200	1-15-97	.307	.200	.329	24	88	15	27	4	0	3	13	1	1	0	2	14	0	1	.455	.315
Macias, Fabricio	R-R	6-0	188	3-11-98	.222	.394	.161	40	126	22	28	6	2	1	19	14	4	2	2	42	5	1	.325	.315
Mangieri, Luke	L-R	6-3	215	10-15-96	.147	.143	.148	11	34	4	5	2	0	0	4	3	2	0	0	8	0	1	.206	.256
Martin, Mason	R-R	6-0	200	6-16-99	.200	.281	.178	45	150	16	30	8	0	4	18	18	4	1	0	62	1	1	.333	.302
Medrano, Jesse	R-R	5-11	200	3-27-95	.229	.308	.203	48	157	21	36	9	0	2	22	12	2	3	2	36	8	2	.325	.289
Mitchell, Calvin	L-L	6-0	209	3-8-99	.280	.357	.258	119	443	55	124	29	3	10	65	41	5	1	5	109	4	5	.427	.344
Peurifoy, Ryan	R-R	6-2	200	3-26-95	.197	.167	.207	77	239	31	47	16	3	3	24	29	4	3	0	66	4	4	.326	.294
Pope, Brett	L-R	6-0	180	5-28-96	.274	.235	.282	29	95	12	26	7	0	3	17	13	3	2	1	24	4	2	.442	.375
Sanchez, Lolo	R-R	5-11	168	4-23-99	.243	.220	.250	114	378	57	92	18	1	4	34	41	5	12	5	72	30	13	.328	.322
Sharpe, Chris	R-R	6-1	195	6-6-96	.263	.245	.266	85	278	50	73	11	2	4	28	39	6	7	3	98	11	4	.360	.362
Siri, Raul	R-R	5-9	175	10-21-94	.120	.167	.105	8	25	5	3	2	0	0	3	3	1	0	0	8	0	2	.200	.241
Stafford, Deon	R-R	5-11	211	3-17-96	.253	.275	.246	94	344	60	87	19	5	11	49	28	5	1	3	99	0	3	.433	.316
Swaggerty, Travis	L-L	5-11	180	8-19-97	.129	.100	.135	16	62	6	8	1	1	1	5	7	1	0	1	18	0	0	.226	.225
Watson, Kyle	R-R	6-3	195	1-14-96	.188	.167	.193	96	293	45	55	12	2	4	33	39	2	4	3	120	10	1	.283	.285

Pitching	B-T	HT	WT	DOB	W	L	ERA	G	GS	CG	SV	IP	H	R	ER	HR	BB	SO	AVG	vLH	vRH	K/9	BB/9
Alldred, Cam	L-L	6-3	205	7-25-96	0	1	3.86	2	0	0	0	2	2	1	1	0	2	2	.364	.500	.286	7.71	3.86
Bolton, Cody	R-R	6-3	185	6-19-98	3	3	3.65	9	9	0	0	44	43	19	18	6	7	45	.253	.272	.236	9.14	1.42
Cederlind, Blake	R-R	6-3	190	1-4-96	3	2	2.86	19	1	0	1	28	21	9	9	1	9	36	.208	.208	.208	11.44	2.86
Cesar, Joel	R-R	5-11	191	1-26-96	2	1	3.15	29	0	0	3	54	44	30	19	4	23	50	.222	.195	.243	8.28	3.81
Cubilete, Sergio	R-R	6-4	185	3-19-95	5	5	5.17	23	13	0	0	87	98	68	50	8	42	79	.284	.286	.283	8.17	4.34
Economos, Nicholas	R-R	6-6	215	6-27-95	0	0	3.00	1	0	0	1	3	2	1	1	0	0	3	.182	.200	.167	9.00	0.00
Escobar, Elvis	L-L	5-8	181	9-6-94	3	2	2.08	15	0	0	1	26	17	7	6	2	12	28	.187	.261	.162	9.69	4.15
Fischer, Drew	R-R	6-3	205	6-3-96	2	2	3.83	28	0	0	0	45	41	23	19	1	20	50	.238	.270	.214	10.07	4.03
Kranick, Max	R-R	6-3	175	7-21-97	4	5	3.81	17	16	0	1	78	72	35	33	7	18	77	.242	.237	.244	8.88	2.08
MacGregor, Travis	R-R	6-3	180	10-15-97	1	4	3.25	15	15	0	0	64	53	35	23	7	21	74	.239	.252	.226	10.46	2.97
Nunez, Oddy	L-L	6-4	230	12-20-96	1	1	2.17	7	5	0	1	37	31	11	9	2	8	24	.226	.256	.214	5.79	1.93
Ogle, Braeden	L-L	6-2	170	7-30-97	2	0	2.65	4	4	0	0	17	16	5	5	1	10	21	.262	.320	.222	11.12	5.29
Oller, Adam	R-R	6-4	225	10-17-94	1	1	4.40	5	0	0	1	14	10	8	7	1	3	15	.200	.241	.115	9.42	1.88
Piechota, Evan	R-R	6-1	225	10-19-93	2	2	3.38	12	3	0	2	45	47	17	17	5	6	49	.267	.218	.306	9.73	1.19
Pomeroy, John	L-R	6-5	210	10-9-94	0	1	2.45	8	0	0	2	7	2	3	2	0	6	12	.074	.143	.050	14.73	7.36
Prohoroff, Dylan	R-R	6-3	215	11-29-94	1	0	3.60	3	0	0	0	5	6	2	2	0	0	6	.286	.333	.250	10.80	0.00
Reyes, Samuel	R-R	5-11	180	3-13-96	4	3	2.72	18	2	0	3	43	41	15	13	1	13	36	.243	.235	.248	7.53	2.72

	B-T	HT	WT	DOB	W	L	ERA	G	GS	CG	SV	IP	H	R	ER	HR	BB	SO	AVG	vLH	vRH	K/9	BB/9
Robles, Domingo	L-L	6-2	170	4-29-98	9	6	2.97	21	21	0	0	115	118	60	38	8	26	88	.259	.231	.269	6.89	2.03
Schlabach, Ike	R-L	6-5	185	12-27-96	8	4	3.55	29	10	0	0	89	98	46	35	7	32	68	.282	.248	.296	6.90	3.25
Seelinger, Matt	R-R	6-0	205	4-19-95	1	3	3.03	28	0	0	7	33	30	14	11	6	11	52	.236	.206	.271	14.33	3.03
Stoelke, Logan	R-R	6-3	185	8-26-95	0	0	0.00	3	0	0	1	2	0	0	0	0	1	4	.000	.000	.000	15.43	3.86
Stratton, Hunter	R-R	6-4	225	11-17-96	6	5	4.16	22	20	1	0	102	93	56	47	8	52	82	.246	.211	.272	7.26	4.60
Sulser, Beau	R-R	6-2	195	5-5-94	5	8	2.35	36	0	0	8	57	43	22	15	4	4	63	.205	.182	.225	9.89	0.63
Taylor, Jacob	R-R	6-3	205	7-5-95	0	1	4.05	7	0	0	2	13	10	7	6	3	7	12	.213	.167	.261	8.10	4.73
Valdes, Ryan	R-R	5-11	185	8-22-93	0	0	0.87	3	0	0	1	10	4	1	1	1	2	10	.121	.059	.188	8.71	1.74
Wallace, Gavin	R-R	6-5	210	11-14-95	6	2	3.69	14	14	0	0	76	65	34	31	11	13	43	.230	.254	.211	5.11	1.55
Weiman, Blake	R-L	6-4	208	11-5-95	1	0	1.29	14	0	0	3	28	21	5	4	2	2	35	.212	.167	.246	11.25	0.64

Fielding

C: Bormann 7, Gonzalez 2, Hernandez 26, Lorenzo 20, Medrano 5, Stafford 81. **1B:** Bengtson 15, Hernandez 8, Herrera 1, Mangieri 11, Martin 43, Watson 65. **2B:** Castro 89, Glendinning 17, Medrano 11, Pope 11, Siri 5, Watson 6. **3B:** Bengtson 45, Busby 28, Glendinning 12, Medrano 29, Pope 16, Siri 1, Watson 8. **SS:** Castro 12, Cruz 102, Glendinning 5, Kaiser 16. **OF:** Bengtson 1, Macias 36, Mitchell 110, Peurifoy 54, Sanchez 108, Sharpe 81, Swaggerty 16.

WEST VIRGINIA BLACK BEARS
NEW YORK-PENN LEAGUE

SHORT-SEASON

Batting	B-T	HT	WT	DOB	AVG	vLH	vRH	G	AB	R	H	2B	3B	HR	RBI	BB	HBP	SH	SF	SO	SB	CS	SLG	OBP
Amaral, Daniel	R-R	5-11	180	3-7-97	.244	.318	.212	58	217	32	53	5	5	5	24	23	5	1	1	46	25	6	.383	.329
Bejerano, Manny	R-R	6-3	185	5-14-97	.294	.286	.300	6	17	1	5	0	0	0	1	0	2	0	4	0	0		.294	.333
Bengtson, Ben	R-R	6-0	205	7-28-95	.207	.250	.191	15	58	4	12	2	1	0	3	2	0	1		19	1	1	.276	.254
Brands, Paul	R-R	6-1	185	5-13-97	.234	.211	.241	25	77	4	18	2	0	0	3	7	0	2	0	29	3	3	.260	.298
De La Cruz, Michael	L-L	6-1	165	7-10-96	.207	.292	.172	26	82	9	17	2	0	1	6	11	0	5	1	26	8	3	.268	.298
Glendinning, Robbie	R-R	6-2	196	10-6-95	.250	.320	.220	25	84	14	21	8	1	0	11	13	2	1	0	28	1	1	.369	.364
Gretler, Mike	R-R	6-2	180	1-1-96	.274	.250	.289	45	164	22	45	10	2	2	30	20	6	1	1	38	3	1	.396	.372
Herrera, Jhoan	R-R	6-1	185	6-14-96	.215	.189	.225	37	135	11	29	11	0	4	18	6	0	1	1	36	1	0	.385	.247
Jhang, Jin-De	L-R	5-9	225	5-17-93	.182	.143	.200	6	22	2	4	0	0	0	1	1	0	0	1	6	0	0	.182	.208
Jimenez, Melvin	B-R	5-10	170	9-9-95	.200	.119	.239	40	130	11	26	1	0	0	9	16	3	4	1	17	0	1	.223	.300
Kaiser, Connor	R-R	6-4	195	11-20-96	.212	.276	.187	31	104	14	22	2	0	1	9	13	2	2	3	31	7	1	.260	.303
Kinneman, Brett	L-L	6-1	195	8-28-96	.253	.286	.237	60	225	33	57	16	4	4	44	30	3	0	4	74	3	3	.413	.344
Koch, Grant	R-R	6-0	190	2-5-97	.188	.191	.187	40	133	10	25	2	1	2	11	12	1	0	2	35	1	0	.263	.304
Kone, Zack	R-R	6-3	202	11-5-96	.250	.313	.224	44	164	29	41	10	1	1	11	20	0	1	0	43	7	3	.342	.332
Lantigua, Edison	L-L	6-0	175	1-9-97	.277	.281	.274	53	188	24	52	9	5	3	22	19	1	1	1	57	5	3	.426	.345
Macias, Fabricio	R-R	6-0	188	3-11-98	.325	.263	.345	19	77	9	25	4	2	0	5	6	0	0	0	12	2	3	.429	.374
Mangieri, Luke	L-R	6-3	215	10-15-96	.247	.149	.287	44	162	23	40	8	1	2	16	18	4	1	0	35	9	1	.346	.337
Siri, Raul	R-R	5-9	175	10-21-94	.268	.313	.255	21	71	10	19	5	1	2	8	11	3	1	1	19	2	4	.451	.384
Susi, Zac	L-R	6-1	200	10-30-96	.206	.222	.200	22	63	4	13	3	0	0	6	11	0	2	0	17	1	0	.254	.324
Swaggerty, Travis	L-L	5-11	185	8-11-97	.288	.342	.265	36	139	22	40	9	1	4	15	15	5	2	0	40	9	3	.453	.365
Valaika, Nick	R-R	5-11	185	12-7-95	.213	.222	.208	26	80	12	17	3	0	2	7	2	3	0	0	34	1	0	.325	.259
Vinicio, Felix	L-L	5-10	175	10-28-94	.118	.000	.143	5	17	3	2	0	0	1	5	2	0	0	1	4	0	1	.294	.200
Watson, Kyle	R-R	6-3	195	1-14-96	.205	.188	.214	14	44	4	9	1	0	0	6	10	0	0	0	17	8	1	.227	.352
Weiss, Erich	L-R	6-2	190	9-11-91	.231	.000	.250	3	13	2	3	2	0	0	0	0	0	0	0	5	1	0	.385	.231
Wood, Eric	R-R	6-1	210	11-22-92	.333	.000	.400	2	6	2	2	1	0	1	2	1	0	0	0	0	0	1	1.000	.429

Pitching	B-T	HT	WT	DOB	W	L	ERA	G	GS	CG	SV	IP	H	R	ER	HR	BB	SO	AVG	vLH	vRH	K/9	BB/9
Alldred, Cam	L-L	6-3	205	7-25-96	0	1	1.63	18	0	0	1	28	16	5	5	0	9	30	.180	.154	.191	9.76	2.93
Bido, Osvaldo	R-R	6-3	175	10-18-95	4	6	4.18	14	14	0	0	75	74	37	35	2	19	58	.263	.220	.298	6.93	2.27
Case, Brad	R-R	6-6	220	9-13-96	1	0	1.80	1	1	0	0	5	3	2	1	0	2		.177	.000	.300	3.60	1.80
Del Orbe, Francis	R-R	6-4	173	10-9-98	5	2	3.59	17	3	0	0	48	37	26	19	1	19	46	.213	.229	.202	8.69	3.59
Economos, Nicholas	R-R	6-6	215	6-27-95	3	2	2.52	15	5	0	1	54	46	17	15	4	18	58	.237	.231	.243	9.73	3.02
Flynn, Michael	R-R	6-4	185	8-7-96	0	3	5.94	5	5	0	0	17	16	11	11	1	4	17	.269	.280	.262	9.18	2.16
Gardner, Will	R-R	6-2	200	5-8-96	0	2	2.45	11	0	0	0	15	12	6	4	0	9	15	.245	.389	.161	9.20	5.52
Henriquez, Juan	R-R	6-3	185	10-22-96	1	0	4.70	10	0	0	0	15	14	8	8	2	7	14	.250	.174	.303	8.22	4.11
Hernandez, Miguel	R-R	6-5	175	11-3-95	2	1	5.26	19	1	0	1	38	52	25	22	2	16	25	.329	.294	.356	5.97	3.82
Jacques, Joe	L-L	6-4	210	3-11-95	0	0	9.00	1	0	0	0	3	5	3	3	0	1	1	.417	.000	.625	3.00	3.00
Loeprich, Conner	R-R	6-3	215	9-13-97	1	4	2.83	22	0	0	7	29	18	13	9	1	14	31	.178	.116	.224	9.73	4.40
LoPresti, Mike	R-R	6-4	220	10-22-96	2	4	5.33	13	12	0	0	49	57	37	29	4	16	22	.301	.322	.355	4.04	2.94
Manasa, Alex	L-R	6-4	195	1-6-98	4	7	4.48	15	15	0	0	80	84	45	40	4	26	46	.274	.215	.316	5.15	2.91
Mears, Nick	R-R	6-4	185	10-7-96	0	0	0.00	3	0	0	0	4	1	0	0	0	1	8	.077	.000	.111	18.00	2.25
Montgomery, Allen	R-R	6-3	190	8-15-96	1	0	0.00	2	0	0	0	3	1	0	0	0	3		.000	.000	.000	8.10	0.00
Murray, Shea	R-R	6-6	215	11-5-93	0	0	7.36	10	0	0	0	7	3	8	6	0	16	7	.130	.000	.214	8.59	19.64
Pomeroy, John	L-R	6-5	210	10-9-94	0	2	4.70	15	0	0	0	15	14	10	8	0	16	17	.237	.136	.297	9.98	9.39
Rennard, Alec	R-R	6-3	210	5-6-95	1	0	3.00	6	0	0	0	9	10	3	3	0	3	6	.303	.231	.350	6.00	3.00
Romano, Argenis	R-R	6-1	190	6-16-95	2	0	3.65	5	0	0	0	12	12	5	5	0	8	18	.245	.389	.161	13.14	5.84
Shortridge, Aaron	R-R	6-3	196	5-29-97	1	1	2.67	8	8	0	0	30	27	10	9	1	7	38	.231	.208	.250	11.27	2.08
Smith, Cody	R-R	6-0	202	9-12-95	2	2	3.90	17	0	0	1	28	27	13	12	0	7	30	.252	.273	.238	9.76	2.28
Spears, Zach	L-L	6-7	237	6-3-97	1	6	6.07	12	12	0	0	43	55	32	29	4	19	30	.322	.250	.350	6.28	3.98
Stoelke, Logan	R-R	6-3	185	8-26-95	0	1	1.77	17	0	0	6	20	8	4	4	1	8	31	.116	.179	.073	13.72	3.54
Valdes, Ryan	R-R	5-11	185	8-22-93	1	1	4.75	16	0	0	1	30	31	23	16	0	18	29	.254	.214	.275	8.60	5.34

Fielding

C: Bejerano 6, Brands 10, Gretler 2, Jhang 5, Koch 36, Susi 21. **1B:** Bengtson 7, Brands 1, Herrera 10, Mangieri 37, Valaika 11, Watson 9, Weiss 2, Wood 2. **2B:** Brands 8, Glendinning 11, Gretler 2, Jimenez 23, Kone 12, Siri 14, Valaika 4, Watson 5. **3B:** Bengtson 8, Brands 1, Glendinning 1, Gretler 38, Jimenez 16, Kaiser 4, Siri 5, Valaika 7. **SS:** Glendinning 13, Gretler 2, Jimenez 2, Kaiser 28, Kone 32. **OF:** Amaral 58, Brands 5, De La Cruz 26, Kinneman 55, Lantigua 32, Macias 18, Mangieri 1, Swaggerty 36, Vinicio 3.

PITTSBURGH PIRATES

BRISTOL PIRATES

APPALACHIAN LEAGUE

Batting	B-T	HT	WT	DOB	AVG	vLH	vRH	G	AB	R	H	2B	3B	HR	RBI	BB	HBP	SH	SF	SO	SB	CS	SLG	OBP
Apostel, Sherten	R-R	6-4	200	3-11-99	.259	.353	.246	41	139	28	36	7	0	7	26	32	3	0	1	42	3	1	.460	.406
Bejerano, Manny	R-R	6-3	185	5-14-97	.145	.125	.148	20	62	7	9	2	0	0	3	8	3	0	0	18	0	0	.177	.274
Brito, Gabriel	R-R	5-9	170	11-3-97	.239	.368	.213	36	113	12	27	3	0	0	16	22	1	1	4	27	0	1	.266	.357
Busby, Dylan	R-R	6-2	196	11-28-95	.250	.250	.250	4	16	1	4	0	0	1	5	2	0	0	2	6	0	0	.438	.300
Citta, Brendt	R-R	6-2	180	7-12-96	.250	.276	.244	44	156	19	39	12	1	2	27	22	10	0	4	33	1	4	.378	.370
Contreras, Yondry	R-R	5-11	180	9-11-97	.193	.200	.191	36	109	18	21	4	0	3	13	11	5	0	1	30	3	2	.312	.294
Davis, Jonah	L-R	5-10	181	7-2-97	.306	.233	.318	51	206	46	63	15	6	12	34	27	6	0	2	59	6	5	.612	.398
De Jesus, Johan	R-R	6-0	165	8-1-96	.107	.333	.080	9	28	2	3	0	0	1	2	2	0	0	0	12	0	0	.214	.167
Dorrian, Patrick	L-R	6-2	188	6-26-96	.367	.000	.458	9	30	6	11	2	2	1	5	4	1	0	0	8	0	0	.667	.457
Granberry, Mikell	R-R	6-1	190	8-19-95	.305	.214	.325	43	151	31	46	11	1	5	24	28	2	0	2	35	5	3	.490	.415
Lambert, Chase	R-R	5-11	175	6-28-96	.348	.429	.337	32	112	19	39	4	1	2	20	16	3	0	3	12	6	0	.455	.433
Lockery, Dean	L-R	5-11	185	5-28-96	.274	.344	.250	39	124	25	34	5	1	2	20	25	1	0	2	18	4	1	.379	.395
Martin, Mason	L-R	6-0	201	6-2-99	.233	.237	.232	59	223	42	52	10	1	10	40	42	2	0	2	87	2	2	.422	.357
Mepris, Francisco	B-R	5-11	165	10-10-97	.248	.286	.238	31	105	16	26	3	1	0	16	0	0	0	0	22	15	4	.295	.347
Navarro, Christian	R-R	6-0	190	12-18-95	.250	.273	.246	22	72	13	18	3	3	0	6	10	0	0	0	14	5	2	.375	.342
Ngoepe, Victor	R-R	5-8	150	2-9-98	.223	.311	.199	56	211	36	47	7	2	0	11	20	3	6	0	54	10	6	.275	.299
Portorreal, Jeremias	L-L	6-3	195	8-7-97	.172	.188	.169	27	87	8	15	1	0	2	11	14	2	0	1	36	1	0	.253	.298
Susi, Zac	L-R	6-1	200	10-30-96	.273	.300	.265	14	44	7	12	0	0	3	6	3	6	1	2	10	1	1	.273	.373
Uselton, Conner	R-R	6-3	185	5-20-98	.225	.111	.248	43	160	15	36	2	1	0	14	12	1	0	2	31	0	2	.250	.280
Vizcaino, Eddy	L-L	5-11	165	7-19-96	.240	.177	.259	24	75	13	18	5	0	0	9	9	0	1	0	14	6	0	.307	.321

Pitching	B-T	HT	WT	DOB	W	L	ERA	G	GS	CG	SV	IP	H	R	ER	HR	BB	SO	AVG	vLH	vRH	K/9	BB/9
Baz, Shane	R-R	6-3	190	6-17-99	4	3	3.97	10	10	0	0	45	45	23	20	2	23	54	.250	.250	.250	10.72	4.57
2-team total (2 Princeton)					4	5	4.47	12	12	0	0	52	56	30	26	3	29	59	.267	.247	.280	10.15	4.99
Case, Brad	R-R	6-6	220	9-13-96	1	1	3.72	2	2	0	0	10	10	5	4	0	4	5	.263	.357	.208	4.66	3.72
De Los Santos, Yerry	R-R	6-2	160	12-12-97	0	0	3.00	3	0	0	0	6	5	3	2	0	3	10	.217	.250	.200	15.00	4.50
Deyzel, Vince	R-R	6-2	180	2-9-98	4	2	6.23	19	0	0	1	26	24	24	18	2	23	25	.245	.235	.250	8.65	7.96
Diaz, Luis	L-L	6-2	190	6-25-97	0	0	6.00	5	0	0	1	6	9	7	4	1	3	4	.321	.400	.278	6.00	4.50
Dicent, Lizardy	R-R	6-3	178	2-11-97	0	0	2.45	2	0	0	0	4	4	3	1	0	3	3	.267	.333	.222	7.36	7.36
Garcia, Oliver	R-R	6-3	213	1-8-98	2	4	7.28	10	10	0	0	38	45	35	31	5	23	28	.298	.238	.341	6.57	5.40
Gardner, Will	R-R	6-2	200	5-8-96	0	0	0.82	8	0	0	3	11	5	6	1	1	8	15	.128	.133	.125	12.27	6.55
Jacques, Joe	L-L	6-4	210	3-11-95	0	2	6.33	17	0	0	1	21	19	19	15	1	19	19	.232	.227	.233	8.02	8.02
Jennings, Steven	R-R	6-2	175	11-13-98	3	4	4.82	13	13	0	0	65	68	44	35	5	27	53	.260	.278	.247	7.30	3.72
Kobos, Will	R-R	6-2	180	8-3-97	2	2	7.11	14	3	0	0	32	30	28	25	4	19	42	.238	.256	.229	11.94	5.40
Manzanillo, Yeudry	R-R	6-3	175	12-7-98	2	3	6.08	12	3	0	1	40	49	29	27	4	15	31	.293	.306	.284	6.98	3.38
Montgomery, Allen	R-R	6-3	190	8-15-96	0	1	4.82	12	0	0	0	19	23	12	10	2	10	19	.307	.083	.412	9.16	4.82
Nova, Luis	R-R	6-1	191	6-10-98	0	2	11.25	6	0	0	0	8	8	12	10	3	9	9	.250	.308	.211	11.25	10.13
O'Reilly, John	R-R	6-5	195	10-4-95	2	1	5.33	12	0	0	1	25	12	15	15	2	21	21	.242	.184	.283	7.46	4.26
Pichardo, Adonis	R-R	6-3	195	4-9-96	0	0	12.42	7	0	0	0	17	32	27	23	2	13	8	.395	.444	.370	4.32	7.02
Pina, Leandro	R-R	6-3	174	9-23-98	1	1	3.86	5	0	0	1	12	8	7	5	2	3	13	.195	.167	.217	10.03	2.31
Rennard, Alec	R-R	6-3	210	5-6-95	1	0	2.31	9	0	0	2	12	12	5	3	0	7	9	.267	.400	.200	6.94	5.40
Roman, Denny	L-L	5-9	180	9-30-98	1	0	6.75	4	4	0	0	15	17	11	11	2	6	17	.293	.583	.217	10.43	3.68
Romano, Argenis	R-R	6-1	190	6-16-95	2	0	3.03	10	0	0	1	33	25	11	11	4	12	30	.219	.227	.214	8.27	3.31
Santana, Roger	L-L	6-1	168	9-26-97	5	6	5.83	12	12	0	0	59	64	39	38	5	21	47	.278	.255	.284	7.21	3.22
Selby, Colin	R-R	6-1	218	10-24-97	1	3	4.15	11	11	0	0	48	43	27	22	4	16	41	.240	.182	.274	7.74	3.02
Shields, Austin	L-R	6-5	220	11-23-97	0	2	13.08	17	0	0	0	21	37	38	31	3	27	29	.349	.282	.388	12.23	11.39
Webb, Jacob	R-R	6-4	200	6-5-99	0	0	7.56	7	0	0	0	8	8	7	0	3	7	.235	.250	.227	7.56	3.24

Fielding

C: Bejerano 20, Brito 36, Granberry 1, Susi 14. **1B:** De Jesus 2, Granberry 15, Martin 52. **2B:** Lambert 29, Lockery 18, Mepris 22. **3B:** Apostel 35, Busby 4, De Jesus 7, Dorrian 9, Lockery 9, Mepris 7. **SS:** Lambert 3, Lockery 10, Ngoepe 56. **OF:** Citta 34, Contreras 33, Davis 51, Navarro 21, Portorreal 11, Uselton 41, Vizcaino 22.

GCL PIRATES

GULF COAST LEAGUE

Batting	B-T	HT	WT	DOB	AVG	vLH	vRH	G	AB	R	H	2B	3B	HR	RBI	BB	HBP	SH	SF	SO	SB	CS	SLG	OBP
Acuna, Francisco	R-R	5-7	150	1-12-00	.230	.345	.191	36	113	22	26	6	0	0	9	10	4	1	2	23	1	0	.283	.310
Alcime, Larry	R-R	6-2	207	10-15-98	.167	.200	.143	4	12	0	2	0	0	0	1	1	0	0	0	3	0	0	.167	.231
Babilonia, Yair	R-R	6-2	215	8-25-97	.000	.000	.000	5	8	1	0	0	0	0	1	0	1	0	2	0	0	.000	.111
Bae, Ji-Hwan	L-R	6-0	170	7-26-99	.271	.359	.233	35	129	24	35	6	2	0	13	15	5	0	3	16	10	4	.349	.362
Bostick, Christopher	R-R	5-10	200	3-24-93	.375	.667	.200	3	8	3	3	1	0	0	2	0	0	0	0	0	0	.500	.546
Busby, Dylan	R-R	6-2	196	11-28-95	.091	.143	.067	8	22	1	2	1	0	1	3	0	1	0	0	11	0	0	.273	.130
Calderon, Williams	R-R	6-0	182	12-22-97	.300	.400	.200	4	10	0	3	1	0	0	2	1	0	0	0	1	0	0	.400	.364
Dorrian, Patrick	L-R	6-2	188	6-26-96	.329	.387	.311	40	137	28	45	10	6	1	34	24	1	0	2	24	2	1	.511	.427
Dotel, Mariano	B-R	5-10	155	1-4-00	.083	.333	.000	5	12	0	1	0	0	0	0	1	0	0	2	0	0	.167	.154
Eusebio, Jean	L-R	6-1	170	8-22-00	.236	.091	.274	31	106	15	25	5	2	1	15	6	1	2	1	27	4	4	.349	.281
Fishback, Mason	R-R	6-1	190	9-19-94	.375	.333	.400	7	8	2	3	0	0	0	1	3	4	0	0	4	2	0	.375	.667
Garcia, Carlos	L-L	5-10	180	4-7-99	.222	.333	.167	3	9	0	2	0	0	0	0	1	0	0	0	5	0	0	.222	.300
Harrer, Justin	R-R	6-2	195	3-2-97	.183	.136	.195	33	104	19	19	3	2	5	18	16	7	1	0	39	2	1	.394	.331
Haug, Ryan	R-R	6-0	165	12-29-94	.324	.500	.303	17	37	5	12	2	0	1	4	1	10	0	1	4	1	2	.460	.469
Herman, Jack	R-R	6-0	190	9-30-99	.340	.457	.302	37	141	28	48	9	3	2	22	24	2	2	2	24	2	2	.489	.435

PITTSBURGH PIRATES

	B-T	HT	WT	DOB	AVG	vLH	vRH	G	AB	R	H	2B	3B	HR	RBI	BB	HBP	SH	SF	SO	SB	CS	SLG	OBP
Hernandez, Raul	R-R	6-0	182	12-20-95	.333	.000	.375	2	9	1	3	0	0	0	1	0	0	0	0	3	0	0	.333	.333
Inoa, Samuel	R-R	5-10	211	10-6-98	.289	.450	.247	28	97	18	28	2	5	3	17	4	2	3	2	17	2	1	.505	.324
Kraft, Steven	R-R	6-5	185	7-7-96	.321	.387	.295	31	109	18	35	9	1	2	29	13	3	0	1	11	3	2	.477	.405
Lantigua, John	L-R	6-1	170	8-26-97	.232	.280	.211	30	82	9	19	2	1	0	8	4	3	3	1	22	2	3	.281	.289
Lorenzo, Rafelin	R-R	6-2	200	1-15-97	.308	.167	.350	9	26	3	8	3	0	1	3	1	0	0	0	6	0	0	.539	.333
Medina, Joseivin	L-L	6-2	222	2-2-00	.164	.250	.146	18	67	8	11	1	1	0	7	0	1	0	0	17	3	0	.209	.177
Morris, Justin	L-R	6-2	215	3-26-96	.222	.250	.214	9	18	4	4	1	0	0	5	2	0	0	0	3	0	1	.278	.300
Morrow, Matt	L-R	5-10	180	1-9-96	.286	.267	.289	33	98	20	28	4	0	0	8	15	0	2	0	11	5	1	.327	.381
Mottice, Kyle	L-R	6-0	183	1-18-96	.283	.120	.333	35	106	26	30	3	1	0	9	24	14	4	0	12	16	0	.330	.472
Patten, Nick	R-R	6-4	205	9-12-96	.195	.120	.215	37	118	19	23	5	2	3	16	15	7	3	1	30	0	0	.348	.319
Perez, Cristopher	R-R	6-1	170	8-7-97	.000	.000	.000	2	5	0	0	0	0	0	0	1	0	0	0	0	0	0	.000	.167
Ramos, Robinson	R-R	5-11	185	5-24-98	.157	.100	.171	20	51	3	8	1	0	0	1	3	2	0	0	3	0	0	.177	.232
Simmons, Kyle	R-R	5-11	181	12-12-96	.000	.000	.000	4	9	1	0	0	0	0	0	0	1	0	0	4	0	0	.000	.100
Villegas, Fernando	R-R	5-10	176	6-28-98	.296	.240	.318	25	88	16	26	7	3	0	16	12	7	0	3	15	4	3	.443	.409

Pitching	B-T	HT	WT	DOB	W	L	ERA	G	GS	CG	SV	IP	H	R	ER	HR	BB	SO	AVG	vLH	vRH	K/9	BB/9
Arrieta, Andres	R-R	6-0	185	1-10-98	1	1	9.82	11	0	0	0	11	17	15	12	1	8	7	.347	.182	.395	5.73	6.55
Arrieta, Luis	R-R	6-2	180	6-21-99	1	4	6.75	11	8	0	0	36	36	31	27	7	29	30	.269	.242	.277	7.50	7.25
Ashcraft, Braxton	L-R	6-5	195	10-5-99	0	1	4.58	5	5	0	0	18	16	9	9	2	5	12	.242	.125	.280	6.11	2.55
Burrows, Michael	R-R	6-2	183	11-8-99	0	0	0.00	4	3	0	0	14	6	1	0	0	4	9	.133	.100	.143	5.79	2.57
Case, Brad	R-R	6-6	220	9-13-96	3	0	3.38	8	6	0	0	40	42	16	15	3	4	33	.271	.286	.267	7.43	0.90
Contreras, Wilmer	R-R	6-4	213	2-5-98	3	0	4.22	14	0	0	0	32	31	16	15	2	11	22	.261	.269	.258	6.19	3.09
De La Cruz, Saul	R-R	6-4	174	10-26-97	2	2	5.24	14	0	0	2	22	19	16	13	1	14	32	.232	.409	.167	12.90	5.64
De Los Santos, Yerry	R-R	6-2	160	12-12-97	0	0	0.00	2	0	0	0	3	1	0	0	0	1	1	.100	.000	.143	3.00	3.00
Dicent, Lizardy	R-R	6-3	178	2-11-97	1	0	4.22	12	0	0	0	21	18	14	10	1	10	25	.217	.318	.180	10.55	4.22
Florez, Santiago	R-R	6-5	222	5-9-00	5	2	4.15	10	10	0	0	43	37	23	20	0	23	35	.230	.205	.238	7.27	4.78
Gong, Hai-Cheng	R-R	6-2	168	12-28-98	1	0	5.40	11	0	0	1	17	18	12	10	0	4	14	.269	.273	.267	7.56	2.16
Henriquez, Juan	R-R	6-3	185	10-22-98	2	0	1.65	7	0	0	1	16	13	5	3	0	4	15	.213	.214	.213	8.27	2.20
Jimenez, Randy	L-L	6-2	200	6-21-98	1	5	6.49	12	5	0	2	35	34	27	25	1	21	35	.260	.350	.243	9.09	5.45
MacGregor, Travis	R-R	6-3	180	10-15-97	2	2	2.57	2	2	0	0	7	6	2	2	1	1	6	.222	.143	.250	7.71	1.29
Machado, Kleiner	R-R	5-10	169	3-8-99	3	3	3.52	12	0	0	0	23	27	18	9	1	15	15	.284	.208	.310	5.87	5.87
Marcano, Jose	L-L	6-1	204	3-10-99	0	0	0.00	3	0	0	0	4	4	0	0	0	1	4	.267	.000	.333	9.82	2.45
Martinez, Angel	L-L	6-3	198	11-14-96	0	0	0.00	1	0	0	0	0	0	0	0	0	1	0	.000	—	.000	0.00	27.00
Mielock, Jake	R-R	6-3	220	1-9-95	1	0	12.19	9	0	0	1	10	15	16	14	3	12	9	.341	.385	.323	7.84	10.45
Nova, Luis	R-R	6-1	191	6-10-98	0	1	3.00	9	0	0	1	27	30	12	9	0	4	23	.289	.150	.321	7.67	1.33
O'Reilly, John	R-R	6-5	195	10-4-95	0	1	13.50	2	0	0	0	5	3	3	0	0	0	5	.625	.333	.800	0.00	0.00
Reed, Will	R-R	6-2	190	11-3-95	0	1	4.91	4	0	0	0	4	2	3	2	0	3	4	.154	.000	.167	9.82	7.36
Rosario, Braham	L-L	6-1	198	2-18-00	0	1	4.50	1	1	0	0	4	5	3	2	2	0	3	.294	.000	.385	6.75	0.00
Santana, Pablo	R-R	6-1	186	2-28-99	0	0	22.50	2	0	0	0	2	5	5	5	1	3	1	.500	.500	.500	4.50	13.50
Toribio, Noe	R-R	6-2	194	8-25-99	3	2	5.68	12	12	0	0	51	55	38	32	3	22	43	.267	.219	.289	7.64	3.91
Webb, Jacob	R-R	6-4	200	6-5-99	0	1	3.86	4	0	0	0	5	6	2	2	1	5	4	.333	.250	.357	7.71	9.64

Fielding

C: Babilonia 4, Fishback 7, Haug 17, Hernandez 2, Inoa 8, Lorenzo 9, Morris 7, Ramos 20. **1B:** Calderon 1, Inoa 5, Mottice 13, Patten 37, Perez 1. **2B:** Acuna 21, Bae 2, Dorrian 1, Dotel 2, Kraft 2, Morrow 26, Mottice 11, Simmons 2. **3B:** Acuna 10, Busby 8, Calderon 1, Dorrian 34, Kraft 1, Mottice 1, Perez 2, Simmons 2. **SS:** Acuna 8, Bae 34, Dorrian 3, Dotel 3, Morrow 4, Mottice 7. **OF:** Alcime 3, Bostick 3, Eusebio 29, Garcia 3, Harrer 32, Herman 37, Kraft 8, Lantigua 23, Medina 9, Villegas 24.

DSL PIRATES   *ROOKIE*
DOMINICAN SUMMER LEAGUE

Batting	B-T	HT	WT	DOB	AVG	vLH	vRH	G	AB	R	H	2B	3B	HR	RBI	BB	HBP	SH	SF	SO	SB	CS	SLG	OBP
Angulo, Daniel	L-R	5-10	164	8-10-98	.245	.000	.269	37	102	22	25	1	2	0	4	16	2	1	1	14	5	2	.294	.355
Apostel, Shendrik	R-R	6-5	245	4-24-00	.250	.546	.193	41	136	15	34	12	0	6	29	17	5	0	0	46	0	0	.471	.354
Arroyo, Carlos	R-R	5-9	170	7-11-01	.294	.188	.318	58	180	35	53	2	0	1	20	33	8	4	5	27	15	4	.322	.416
Baez, Darwin	R-R	6-0	186	11-6-00	.205	.222	.262	49	166	17	34	7	1	1	11	11	0	1	0	36	2	1	.277	.254
Barrios, Edgar	R-R	5-9	145	7-20-00	.232	—	—	63	211	34	49	4	0	0	16	32	7	2	3	31	15	9	.251	.348
Basabe, Angel	L-L	6-0	153	12-12-00	.260	—	—	50	181	34	47	9	5	3	18	21	2	3	1	46	8	5	.414	.342
Castillo, Pedro	L-L	6-2	170	4-23-00	.255	—	—	50	165	28	42	6	0	2	17	22	2	1	1	32	10	1	.327	.347
Ceballo, Yeison	R-R	5-11	175	2-20-01	.239	.286	.219	34	113	11	27	3	3	0	13	8	1	0	1	24	1	2	.319	.293
Dotel, Mariano	B-R	5-10	155	1-4-00	.257	.333	.000	43	152	24	39	4	4	0	9	7	4	2	0	32	13	5	.336	.307
Fajardo, Yoyner	L-R	6-0	179	4-6-99	.311	.319	.326	62	222	44	69	13	8	1	34	29	5	0	0	28	17	3	.455	.402
Gonzalez, Ruben	R-R	5-11	205	9-13-97	.202	.333	.192	34	84	5	17	2	0	0	6	4	0	0	1	21	0	1	.226	.236
Hernandez, Jommer	R-R	5-11	181	10-20-00	.247	.345	.223	45	150	20	37	5	1	0	19	17	4	0	5	37	2	0	.293	.330
Jerez, Mario	R-R	6-3	185	9-4-00	.206	—	—	48	136	13	28	3	2	1	12	15	2	3	1	42	4	4	.279	.292
Lopez, Germin	R-R	6-0	170	2-13-99	.238	.333	.212	50	172	30	41	2	5	2	22	18	3	4	1	39	15	3	.343	.320
Marcos, Norkis	R-R	6-0	170	5-26-01	.230	.222	.231	57	209	47	48	3	0	0	16	45	4	5	2	50	14	1	.263	.373
Mateo, Bryan	L-L	6-2	180	10-20-98	.265	—	—	53	170	17	45	6	1	0	22	16	10	0	1	33	2	0	.312	.360
Matos, Omar	B-R	6-0	170	5-27-00	.168	—	—	45	131	16	22	7	1	0	7	16	3	1	0	28	13	4	.237	.273
Medina, Joseivin	L-L	6-4	222	2-2-00	.343	.222	.226	10	35	3	12	4	0	0	2	3	1	0	0	10	1	2	.457	.410
Melfor, Tilsaimy	R-R	6-0	183	2-14-01	.212	—	—	33	118	12	25	1	1	2	12	7	3	2	2	40	6	1	.288	.269
Mena, Juan	R-R	5-11	180	8-3-00	.211	—	—	34	95	12	20	4	1	0	8	16	2	2	0	29	0	0	.274	.336
Mercedes, Matthew	R-R	6-1	195	8-26-98	.257	—	—	39	109	15	28	5	0	1	18	13	5	0	1	10	1	1	.440	.359
Nova, Fleury	R-R	5-11	160	1-17-01	.204	—	—	45	137	19	28	4	0	0	10	19	2	1	2	31	14	2	.234	.306
Paulino, Ronaldo	R-R	6-3	232	9-30-98	.240	.200	.180	45	129	23	31	9	1	6	25	27	2	1	2	60	0	1	.465	.375
Pie, Juan	L-L	6-2	170	4-1-01	.258	.258	.258	58	209	35	54	12	8	2	21	36	7	1	2	47	7	9	.421	.382

Name	B-T	HT	WT	DOB	AVG	vLH	vRH	G	AB	R	H	2B	3B	HR	RBI	BB	HBP	SH	SF	SO	SB	CS	OBP	SLG
Polanco, Jhan	B-R	5-11	175	11-4-00	.200	—	—	15	35	3	7	1	0	0	2	3	2	2	0	4	0	0	.229	.300
Ramirez, Eduar	R-R	5-11	200	6-4-01	.301	—	—	39	123	15	37	7	2	1	27	18	3	0	2	24	0	1	.415	.397
Ramos, Robinson	R-R	5-11	185	5-24-98	.000	.100	.171	1	1	0	0	0	0	0	0	0	0	0	0	0	0	0	.000	.000
Rivero, Daniel	R-R	6-1	191	1-22-01	.317	.200	.339	61	230	38	73	10	1	0	31	20	5	0	3	17	11	6	.370	.380
Rodriguez, Rayvi	L-L	5-11	142	4-16-98	.283	.310	.278	59	173	32	49	5	4	0	23	12	5	3	1	23	6	5	.358	.346
Romero, Randy	R-R	5-11	155	8-10-99	.253	.273	.250	53	174	28	44	7	2	1	24	17	2	4	0	23	12	4	.333	.326
Rosado, Emilson	R-R	6-3	229	2-11-01	.287	.273	.289	51	171	21	49	11	0	1	36	22	6	0	5	51	0	2	.368	.378
Rosario, Ivan	R-R	6-2	155	11-9-98	.204	—	—	38	103	9	21	0	0	6	7	0	3	1		25	8	4	.204	.252
Susana, Bladimir	B-R	5-9	154	5-20-00	.180	.273	.164	23	78	5	14	0	0	0	4	8	1	0	0	23	2	2	.180	.264
Valerio, Stiwatt	R-R	6-2	186	9-9-00	.128	—	—	34	94	6	12	0	0	0	9	5	1	4		27	1	2	.128	.232

Pitching	B-T	HT	WT	DOB	W	L	ERA	G	GS	CG	SV	IP	H	R	ER	HR	BB	SO	AVG	vLH	vRH	K/9	BB/9
Amaya, Jose	L-L	6-1	169	2-28-00	0	1	4.56	14	0	0	2	24	24	17	12	2	11	22	.255	.077	.324	8.37	4.18
Arrieta, Andres	R-R	6-0	185	1-10-98	1	0	2.57	3	0	0	0	7	3	3	2	0	3	8	.120	.091	.346	10.29	3.86
Basil, Willy	R-R	6-4	189	4-27-97	2	3	3.40	11	9	0	1	42	42	23	16	2	18	46	.255	—		9.78	3.83
Camacho, Wilger	R-R	6-4	185	10-16-97	1	3	3.18	18	0	0	2	23	17	15	8	1	19	26	.200	.250	.156	10.32	7.54
Campos, Carlos	R-R	6-1	169	5-10-01	2	1	6.81	22	0	0	3	36	44	35	27	3	27	43	.303	.500	.400	10.85	6.81
Charle, Christian	R-R	6-1	208	6-2-00	0	2	6.04	14	3	0	0	28	33	24	19	0	23	20	.280	—		6.35	7.31
Concepcion, Xavier	R-R	6-2	175	1-22-98	2	2	4.94	9	3	0	0	24	22	23	13	2	22	27	.237	—		10.27	8.37
De Dios, Arlinthon	R-R	6-2	183	1-24-00	0	5	5.28	15	11	0	0	46	52	37	27	1	29	40	.281	.321	.250	7.83	5.67
De Los Santos, Enmanuel	R-R	6-4	163	10-14-00	0	4	4.08	6	6	0	0	18	14	10	8	1	16	22	.237	—		11.81	8.15
De Los Santos, Yerry	R-R	6-2	160	12-12-97	0	0	2.89	7	0	0	0	9	7	5	3	0	4	13	.200	.192	.191	12.54	3.86
Del Rosario, Joelvis	R-R	5-11	170	4-16-01	0	1	1.64	7	0	0	1	11	5	2	2	0	6	4	.147	.188	.111	3.27	4.91
Diaz, Miguel	R-R	6-0	160	8-19-01	0	1	4.64	16	1	0	2	21	14	12	11	0	22	19	.197	.172	.258	8.02	9.28
Dicent, Lizardy	R-R	6-3	178	2-11-97	0	0	10.38	4	0	0	0	4	7	6	5	0	4	5	.350	.342	.200	10.38	8.31
Echarry, Oscar	R-R	6-3	175	1-6-99	5	6	7.16	20	1	0	0	33	45	31	26	4	26	21	.349	.271	.368	5.79	7.16
Garcia, Mario	R-R	6-1	183	12-27-98	3	2	1.94	13	6	0	0	46	43	19	10	0	12	39	.258	—		7.58	2.33
Gonzalez, Domingo	R-R	6-0	185	9-27-99	2	3	5.84	16	0	0	3	25	28	20	16	0	15	18	.292	.275	.311	6.57	5.47
Hodge, Francisco	L-L	6-3	209	5-23-00	1	2	2.76	10	10	0	0	42	33	21	13	0	18	41	.214	—		8.72	3.83
Linarez, Valentin	R-R	6-5	226	2-14-00	2	3	3.86	18	7	0	1	40	38	20	17	1	22	29	.245	.276	.215	6.58	4.99
Maldonado, Jose	R-R	6-2	198	1-17-99	0	0	3.29	6	2	0	0	14	11	5	5	1	7	17	.216	.296	.125	11.20	4.61
Marcano, Jose	L-L	6-1	204	3-10-99	1	0	1.35	4	0	0	1	7	8	3	1	0	2	10	.286	.091	.350	13.50	2.70
Mateo, Oliver	R-R	6-2	170	11-7-97	2	2	10.13	22	0	0	0	29	19	35	33	0	42	49	.190	—		15.03	12.89
Nova, Luis	R-R	6-1	191	6-10-98	1	0	1.69	3	0	0	0	11	7	3	2	0	13	17	.175	.177	.288	10.97	1.69
Ortega, Jordy	R-R	6-2	184	10-17-99	1	1	12.15	10	0	0	0	13	17	20	18	1	10	8	.309	.379	.231	5.40	6.75
Ortiz, Estalin	L-L	6-4	213	11-20-98	1	7	4.53	15	14	0	0	56	59	37	28	1	33	51	.280	—		8.25	5.34
Peralta, Luis	L-L	5-11	170	1-6-01	3	4	5.63	19	4	0	1	48	48	30	30	2	26	62	.257	—		11.63	4.88
Peralta, Miguel	R-R	6-2	212	4-20-99	0	4	8.31	16	8	0	0	39	48	43	36	1	19	28	.302	.298	.307	6.46	4.38
Polonia, Eddison	R-R	6-5	198	10-10-98	0	1	4.26	8	0	0	1	13	10	11	6	0	13	15	.222	—		10.66	9.24
Reyes, Yoelvis	L-L	6-2	192	12-10-99	5	2	4.14	14	10	0	0	54	43	29	25	3	29	50	.216	.193	.225	8.28	4.80
Reynoso, Starlyn	L-L	6-0	168	7-29-97	1	4	4.04	16	6	0	0	33	31	26	16	0	26	25	.235	.185	.248	7.07	6.56
Roman, Denny	L-L	5-9	180	9-30-98	0	1	2.28	10	2	0	3	24	17	8	6	1	3	44	.189	.583	.217	16.73	1.14
Romero, Wander	R-R	6-3	184	7-25-99	1	0	6.61	13	0	0	1	16	18	14	12	0	9	17	.286	.000	1.000	9.37	4.96
Rosario, Braham	L-L	6-1	198	2-18-00	1	2	1.84	14	4	0	0	44	33	13	9	2	18	37	.205	.000	.385	7.57	3.68
Rosario, Julio	R-R	6-2	200	6-5-99	3	4	3.09	20	0	0	3	35	27	18	12	0	12	41	.211	.185	.238	10.54	3.09
Santana, Enrique	R-R	5-11	190	9-23-97	1	2	10.32	15	1	0	1	23	27	27	26	2	23	29	.294	.318	.313	11.51	9.13
Santos, Yeison	L-L	6-2	170	4-6-01	5	0	2.06	17	0	0	1	44	43	13	10	1	12	33	.258	—		6.80	2.47
Suero, Angel	R-R	6-4	202	8-27-99	0	4	5.75	11	11	0	0	36	36	27	23	0	22	39	.252	—		9.75	5.50
Torres, Bryan	R-R	6-2	211	4-12-01	4	3	2.61	13	8	0	0	52	42	19	15	2	14	33	.230	.242	.214	5.75	2.44
Valles, Jesus	R-R	6-3	178	12-15-97	3	0	3.86	13	8	0	0	51	49	26	22	2	8	40	.248	.239	.258	7.01	1.40
Vargas, Eddy	L-L	6-0	170	10-12-97	4	2	6.75	21	0	0	0	31	25	30	23	1	25	24	.225	—		7.04	7.34
Vega, Yandy	R-R	6-0	160	12-2-98	1	1	4.42	15	9	0	0	55	56	32	27	2	16	39	.256	.231	.286	6.38	2.62
Velette, Raydel	R-R	6-6	196	6-20-01	0	2	4.87	11	0	0	1	20	17	13	11	0	13	18	.227	.167	.000	7.97	5.75

Fielding

C: Angulo 3, Baez 20, Ceballo 19, Gonzalez 24, Hernandez 33, Mena 23, Polanco 13. **1B:** Angulo 3, Apostel 34, Baez 7, Gonzalez 9, Mateo 42, Mena 2, Mercedes 12, Paulino 27, Ramirez 14, Romero 7. **2B:** Arroyo 45, Barrios 14, Dotel 1, Fajardo 18, Marcos 4, Matos 31, Mena 6, Rosario 36, Susana 12. **3B:** Arroyo 11, Barrios 22, Fajardo 22, Matos 7, Melfor 27, Mena 1, Mercedes 3, Paulino 1, Ramirez 14, Rosado 41, Rosario 1, Susana 1. **SS:** Barrios 31, Dotel 43, Fajardo 11, Marcos 52, Matos 11, Susana 10. **OF:** Arroyo 1, Basabe 45, Castillo 45, Fajardo 8, Jerez 43, Lopez 21, Mateo 7, Medina 9, Nova 45, Pie 42, Rivero 50, Rodriguez 52, Romero 48, Rosario 1, Valerio 24.

St. Louis Cardinals

SEASON IN A SENTENCE: A tumultuous season marked by the firing of manager Mike Matheny ended with Cardinals missing the playoffs for the third straight year, but interim manager Mike Shildt guided a second-half turnaround to salvage an 88-74 record and provide hope for the future.

HIGH POINT: With Shildt and an influx of midseason callups delivering a much-needed injection of energy, the Cardinals went 22-6 in August to catapult from fourth place in the NL Central to first place in the NL wild card race by Sept. 1.

LOW POINT: After back-to-back 9-1 and 8-2 losses to the lowly Reds dropped the Cardinals to 47-46 on July 14, the club fired Matheny along with hitting coaches John Mabry and Bill Mueller.

NOTABLE ROOKIES: Righthanded reliever Jordan Hicks jumped from high Class A straight to the majors and became the hardest-throwing pitcher in the majors, touching 105 mph twice to tie Aroldis Chapman's record for fastest pitch. Righthander Jack Flaherty joined the rotation in April and logged a 3.34 ERA while emerging as a Rookie of the Year contender. Outfielder Harrison Bader established himself as one of the top defensive outfielders in the game while seizing the starting center field job. Lefthander Austin Gomber and righthanders Dakota Hudson and Daniel Poncedeleon helped stabilize the pitching staff during an on-the-fly midseason bullpen rebuild. Shortstop Yairo Munoz and outfielder Tyler O'Neill debuted while showing flashes of being keepers.

KEY TRANSACTIONS: The Cardinals signed Miles Mikolas from Japan before the season, and he emerged as their top starter, going 18-4, 2.83 and making the All-Star Game. They also remade their outfield in the offseason, acquiring Marcell Ozuna from the Marlins in a December blockbuster and trading away Stephen Piscotty and Randal Grichuk. They continued tweaking during the year, trading outfielder Tommy Pham to the Rays and first baseman Luke Voit to the Yankees in July.

DOWN ON THE FARM: Triple-A Memphis won its second straight Pacific Coast League championship largely on the backs of players who earned in-season callups to St. Louis, such as Hudson, O'Neill, Gomber and catcher Carson Kelly. Nolan Gorman, Elehuris Montero and Cuban signee Malcom Nunez emerged as promising sluggers at the lower levels, and overall four of the Cardinals' six affiliates qualified for the playoffs.

OPENING DAY PAYROLL: $146,916,999 (13th)

PLAYERS OF THE YEAR

MAJOR LEAGUE	MINOR LEAGUE
Matt Carpenter	**Dakota Hudson**
1B	**RHP**
.257/.374/.523	(Triple-A)
3rd in NL with 36 HR,	13-3, 2.50
4th with 42 2B	1 HR in 111.2 IP

ORGANIZATION LEADERS

Batting		*Minimum 250 AB
MAJORS		
* AVG	Jose Martinez	.305
* OPS	Matt Carpenter	.897
HR	Matt Carpenter	36
RBI	Marcell Ozuna	88
MINORS		
* AVG	Elehuris Montero, Peoria, Palm Beach	.315
* OBP	John Nogowski, Springfield, MO, Cardinals	.394
* SLG	Elehuris Montero, Peoria, Palm Beach	.504
* OPS	Rangel Ravelo, Memphis	.879
R	Lane Thomas, Springfield, MO, Memphis	84
R	Tommy Edman, Springfield, MO, Memphis	84
H	Tommy Edman, Springfield, MO, Memphis	156
TB	Lane Thomas, Springfield, MO, Memphis	252
2B	Elehuris Montero, Peoria, Palm Beach	37
3B	Lane Thomas, Springfield, MO, Memphis	6
HR	Lane Thomas, Springfield, MO, Memphis	27
RBI	Lane Thomas, Springfield, MO, Memphis	88
BB	Nick Plummer, Peoria	67
SO	Victor Roache, Springfield, MO, Memphis	143
SB	Oscar Mercado, Memphis, Columbus	31

Pitching		#Minimum 75 IP
MAJORS		
W	Miles Mikolas	18
# ERA	Miles Mikolas	2.83
SO	Jack Flaherty	182
SV	Bud Norris	28
MINORS		
W	Dakota Hudson, Memphis	13
L	Jake Woodford, Springfield, MO, Memphis	13
# ERA	Alex Fagalde, Peoria, Palm Beach	2.16
G	Jacob Patterson, Palm Beach	51
GS	Jake Woodford, Springfield, MO, Memphis	28
SV	Edward Mujica, Memphis	13
IP	Anthony Shew, Palm Beach, Springfield, MO	157
BB	Johan Oviedo, Peoria	79
SO	Anthony Shew, Palm Beach, Springfield, MO	130
# AVG	Alex Fagalde, Peoria, Palm Beach	.212

2018 PERFORMANCE

General Manager: Mike Girsch. **Farm Director:** Gary LaRocque. **Scouting Director:** Randy Flores.

Class	Team	League	W	L	PCT	Finish	Manager
Majors	St. Louis Cardinals	National	88	74	.543	6th (15)	M. Matheny/M. Shildt
Triple-A	Memphis Redbirds	Pacific Coast	83	57	.593	1st (16)	Stubby Clapp
Double-A	Springfield Cardinals	Texas	60	79	.432	7th (8)	Johnny Rodriguez
High A	Palm Beach Cardinals	Florida State	75	58	.564	1st (12)	Dann Bilardello
Low A	Peoria Chiefs	Midwest	76	63	.547	5th (16)	Chris Swauger
Short season	State College Spikes	New York-Penn	36	40	.474	t-10th (14)	Joe Kruzel
Rookie	Johnson City Cardinals	Appalachian	31	37	.456	t-7th (10)	Roberto Espinoza
Rookie	GCL Cardinals	Gulf Coast	40	16	.714	1st (18)	Erick Almonte
Overall 2018 Minor League Record			401	350	.534	6th (30)	

ORGANIZATION STATISTICS

ST. LOUIS CARDINALS
NATIONAL LEAGUE

Batting	B-T	HT	WT	DOB	AVG	vLH	vRH	G	AB	R	H	2B	3B	HR	RBI	BB	HBP	SH	SF	SO	SB	CS	SLG	OBP
Adams, Matt	L-R	6-3	245	8-31-88	.158	.250	.151	27	57	5	9	1	0	3	9	3	0	0	0	18	0	0	.333	.200
2-team total (94 Washington)					.239	.220	.242	121	306	42	73	10	0	21	57	27	4	0	0	73	0	0	.477	.309
Bader, Harrison	R-R	6-0	195	6-3-94	.264	.292	.251	138	379	61	100	20	2	12	37	31	11	2	4	125	15	3	.422	.334
Baron, Steven	R-R	6-0	205	12-7-90	.200	—	.200	2	5	0	1	0	0	0	0	0	0	0	0	2	0	0	.200	.200
Carpenter, Matt	L-R	6-3	205	11-26-85	.257	.232	.268	156	564	111	145	42	0	36	81	102	6	0	4	158	4	1	.523	.374
DeJong, Paul	R-R	6-1	195	8-2-93	.241	.198	.255	115	436	68	105	25	1	19	68	36	12	0	5	123	1	1	.434	.313
Fowler, Dexter	B-R	6-5	195	3-22-86	.180	.161	.185	90	289	40	52	10	0	8	31	38	3	0	4	75	5	2	.298	.278
Garcia, Adolis	R-R	6-1	180	3-2-93	.118	.000	.182	21	17	3	2	1	0	0	1	0	0	0	0	7	0	0	.177	.118
Garcia, Greg	L-R	6-0	190	8-8-89	.221	.167	.229	114	181	15	40	6	0	3	15	20	4	1	2	37	3	1	.304	.309
Gyorko, Jedd	R-R	5-10	215	9-23-88	.262	.309	.244	125	351	49	92	19	1	11	47	44	3	0	4	77	2	0	.416	.346
Kelly, Carson	R-R	6-2	220	7-14-94	.114	.091	.125	19	35	1	4	0	0	0	3	3	1	3	0	7	0	0	.114	.205
Martinez, Jose	R-R	6-6	215	7-25-88	.305	.279	.313	152	534	64	163	30	0	17	83	49	2	2	3	104	0	3	.457	.364
Molina, Yadier	R-R	5-11	205	7-13-82	.261	.268	.259	123	459	55	120	20	0	20	74	29	9	0	6	66	4	3	.436	.314
Munoz, Yairo	R-R	6-1	201	1-23-95	.277	.267	.280	108	293	39	81	16	0	8	42	30	4	0	2	71	5	4	.413	.350
O'Neill, Tyler	R-R	5-11	210	6-22-95	.254	.267	.250	61	130	29	33	5	0	9	23	7	3	0	2	57	2	0	.500	.303
Ozuna, Marcell	R-R	6-1	225	11-12-90	.280	.314	.270	148	582	69	163	16	2	23	88	38	5	0	4	110	3	0	.433	.325
Pena, Francisco	R-R	6-2	230	10-12-89	.203	.114	.235	58	133	10	27	3	0	2	8	6	1	0	2	43	1	0	.271	.239
Pham, Tommy	R-R	6-1	210	3-8-88	.248	.266	.243	98	351	67	87	11	0	14	41	42	2	0	1	97	10	6	.399	.331
Sosa, Edmundo	R-R	5-11	190	3-6-96	.000	.000	.000	3	2	1	0	0	0	0	0	0	0	0	0	1	0	0	.000	.333
Voit, Luke	R-R	6-3	225	2-13-91	.182	.286	.000	8	11	2	2	0	0	1	3	2	0	0	0	4	0	0	.455	.308
Wisdom, Patrick	R-R	6-2	220	8-27-91	.260	.333	.207	32	50	11	13	1	0	4	10	6	2	0	0	19	2	1	.520	.362
Wong, Kolten	L-R	5-9	185	10-10-90	.249	.241	.252	127	353	41	88	18	2	9	38	31	14	6	3	60	6	5	.388	.332

Pitching	B-T	HT	WT	DOB	W	L	ERA	G	GS	CG	SV	IP	H	R	ER	HR	BB	SO	AVG	vLH	vRH	K/9	BB/9
Bowman, Matt	R-R	6-0	175	5-31-91	0	2	6.26	22	0	0	0	23	29	16	16	4	11	26	.309	.296	.320	10.17	4.30
Brebbia, John	L-R	6-1	185	5-30-90	3	3	3.20	45	0	0	2	51	43	18	18	5	16	60	.226	.250	.206	10.66	2.84
Cecil, Brett	R-L	6-3	235	7-2-86	1	1	6.89	40	0	0	0	33	39	27	25	5	25	19	.302	.310	.296	5.23	6.89
Flaherty, Jack	R-R	6-4	205	10-15-95	8	9	3.34	28	28	0	0	151	108	59	56	20	59	182	.199	.194	.204	10.85	3.52
Gallegos, Giovanny	R-R	6-2	210	8-14-91	0	0	0.00	2	0	0	0	1	1	0	0	0	0	2	.200	.333	.000	13.50	0.00
Gant, John	R-R	6-3	200	8-6-92	7	6	3.47	26	19	0	0	114	91	54	44	9	57	95	.216	.208	.224	7.50	4.50
Gomber, Austin	L-L	6-5	230	11-23-93	6	2	4.44	29	11	0	0	75	81	40	37	7	32	67	.277	.289	.272	8.04	3.84
Gregerson, Luke	L-R	6-3	205	5-14-84	0	0	7.11	17	0	0	0	13	14	10	10	2	6	12	.275	.191	.333	8.53	4.26
Guilmet, Preston	R-R	6-2	200	7-27-87	0	1	22.50	2	0	0	0	2	7	5	5	2	0	3	.583	.500	.625	13.50	0.00
Hicks, Jordan	R-R	6-2	185	9-6-96	3	4	3.59	73	0	0	6	78	59	33	31	2	45	70	.208	.264	.150	8.11	5.21
Holland, Greg	R-R	5-10	205	11-20-85	0	2	7.92	32	0	0	0	25	34	28	22	1	22	22	.312	.269	.351	7.92	7.92
2-team total (24 Washington)					2	2	4.66	56	0	0	3	46	43	30	24	2	32	47	.242	.205	.270	9.13	6.22
Hudson, Dakota	R-R	6-5	215	9-15-94	4	1	2.63	26	0	0	0	27	19	9	8	0	18	19	.196	.275	.140	6.26	5.93
Leone, Dominic	R-R	5-11	210	10-26-91	1	2	4.50	29	0	0	0	24	27	12	12	3	8	26	.287	.319	.255	9.75	3.00
Lyons, Tyler	L-L	6-4	210	2-21-88	1	0	8.64	27	0	0	0	17	24	16	16	3	8	19	.343	.333	.357	10.26	4.32
Martinez, Carlos	R-R	6-0	190	9-21-91	8	6	3.11	33	18	0	5	119	100	48	41	5	60	117	.228	.237	.216	8.87	4.55
Mayers, Mike	R-R	6-3	200	12-6-91	2	1	4.70	50	0	0	1	52	59	28	27	7	15	49	.289	.247	.324	8.54	2.61
Mikolas, Miles	R-R	6-5	220	8-23-88	18	4	2.83	32	32	1	0	201	186	70	63	16	29	146	.245	.283	.195	6.55	1.30
Norris, Bud	R-R	6-0	215	3-2-85	3	6	3.59	64	0	0	28	58	51	27	23	8	21	67	.237	.184	.297	10.46	3.28
Poncedeleon, Daniel	R-R	6-4	185	1-16-92	0	2	2.73	11	4	0	1	33	24	10	10	2	13	31	.205	.140	.267	8.45	3.55
Reyes, Alex	R-R	6-3	175	8-29-94	0	0	0.00	1	1	0	0	4	3	0	0	0	2	2	.250	.200	.286	4.50	4.50
Ross, Tyson	R-R	6-6	245	4-22-87	2	0	2.73	9	1	0	0	26	20	9	8	1	10	15	.222	.290	.173	5.13	3.42
2-team total (22 San Diego)					8	9	4.15	31	23	0	0	150	132	73	69	17	62	122	.237	.294	.176	7.34	3.73
Sherriff, Ryan	L-L	6-1	185	5-25-90	0	0	6.35	5	0	0	0	6	8	4	4	1	2	3	.333	.200	.429	4.76	3.18
Shreve, Chasen	L-L	6-4	195	7-12-90	1	2	3.07	20	0	0	0	15	14	5	5	3	9	16	.259	.323	.174	9.82	5.52
Tuivailala, Sam	R-R	6-3	225	10-19-92	3	3	3.69	31	0	0	0	32	35	14	13	3	11	26	.273	.333	.230	7.39	3.13
Wacha, Michael	R-R	6-6	215	7-1-91	8	2	3.20	15	15	0	0	84	68	36	30	9	36	71	.221	.217	.225	7.58	3.84
Wainwright, Adam	R-R	6-7	235	8-30-81	2	4	4.46	8	8	0	0	40	41	21	20	5	18	40	.263	.256	.269	8.93	4.02
Weaver, Luke	R-R	6-2	170	8-21-93	7	11	4.95	30	25	0	0	136	150	83	75	19	54	121	.277	.291	.261	7.99	3.56
Webb, Tyler	L-L	6-5	230	7-20-90	0	0	1.76	18	0	0	0	15	16	3	3	1	6	11	.276	.194	.370	6.46	3.52

2-team total (4 San Diego)		0	1	4.43	22	0	0	0	20	22	15	10	3	9	15	.279	.238	.324	6.64 3.98

Fielding

Catcher	PCT	G	PO	A	E	DP	PB
Baron	1.000	2	12	2	0	0	1
Kelly	1.000	16	85	6	0	0	0
Molina	.998	121	966	42	2	8	4
Pena	.997	56	296	11	1	0	2

First Base	PCT	G	PO	A	E	DP
Adams	.981	15	92	10	2	12
Carpenter	.987	95	552	46	8	62
Gyorko	1.000	5	12	1	0	0
Martinez	.989	84	608	31	7	57
Molina	.917	5	9	2	1	3
Pena	1.000	2	1	0	0	0
Voit	1.000	3	15	4	0	1
Wisdom	.920	4	23	0	2	5

Second Base	PCT	G	PO	A	E	DP
Carpenter	1.000	11	22	23	0	5
Garcia	.988	31	29	56	1	14
Gyorko	.926	17	16	34	4	7
Munoz	.953	26	41	61	5	18
Sosa	1.000	1	0	1	0	1
Wong	.981	119	165	306	9	73

Third Base	PCT	G	PO	A	E	DP
Carpenter	.958	76	54	128	8	12
Garcia	.882	15	5	10	2	1
Gyorko	.943	96	46	119	10	19
Munoz	.900	24	5	22	3	2
Wisdom	.941	13	13	11	1	1

Shortstop	PCT	G	PO	A	E	DP
DeJong	.974	114	153	289	12	64
Garcia	.962	17	16	34	2	12
Gyorko	.818	5	5	4	2	0
Munoz	.938	40	49	73	8	24

Outfield	PCT	G	PO	A	E	DP
Bader	.989	113	257	8	3	1
Fowler	.969	75	124	2	4	0
Garcia	.800	11	4	0	1	0
Martinez	1.000	46	61	3	0	1
Munoz	.895	22	17	0	2	0
O'Neill	.968	42	60	1	2	0
Ozuna	.985	147	264	6	4	4
Pham	.976	91	203	2	5	0

MEMPHIS REDBIRDS   TRIPLE-A
PACIFIC COAST LEAGUE

Batting	B-T	HT	WT	DOB	AVG	vLH	vRH	G	AB	R	H	2B	3B	HR	RBI	BB	HBP	SH	SF	SO	SB	CS	SLG	OBP
Arozarena, Randy	R-R	5-11	170	2-28-95	.232	.283	.220	89	267	42	62	16	0	5	28	28	11	3	2	59	17	5	.348	.328
Baron, Steven	R-R	6-0	205	12-7-90	.213	.316	.197	41	136	8	29	5	0	0	7	8	1	0	0	33	0	1	.250	.262
DeJong, Paul	R-R	6-1	195	8-2-93	.308	1.000	.250	4	13	3	4	2	0	1	3	1	0	0	1	4	0	0	.692	.333
Edman, Tommy	R-R	5-10	180	5-9-95	.318	.154	.359	17	66	13	21	0	1	1	5	8	0	0	2	11	3	0	.394	.382
Garcia, Adolis	R-R	6-1	180	3-2-93	.256	.333	.238	112	406	62	104	25	4	22	71	14	2	1	5	99	10	3	.500	.281
Kelly, Carson	R-R	6-2	220	7-14-94	.269	.349	.246	83	294	38	79	14	1	7	41	48	5	0	2	48	0	0	.395	.378
Knizner, Andrew	R-R	6-1	200	2-3-95	.315	.250	.326	17	54	3	17	5	0	0	4	4	2	1	0	8	0	0	.407	.383
Martinez, Jeremy	R-R	5-11	195	12-29-94	.235	.000	.333	6	17	3	4	2	0	0	1	0	0	1	0	0	0	0	.353	.278
Mejia, Alex	R-R	6-1	200	1-18-91	.273	.257	.278	108	322	39	88	4	1	4	35	19	3	1	4	54	6	3	.329	.316
Mercado, Oscar	R-R	6-2	175	12-16-94	.285	.313	.278	100	382	73	109	21	1	8	42	36	4	2	3	64	31	8	.408	.351
Munoz, Yairo	R-R	6-1	201	1-23-95	.287	.263	.293	26	94	11	27	3	1	3	13	5	1	0	0	18	1	0	.436	.330
O'Neill, Tyler	R-R	5-11	210	6-22-95	.311	.397	.283	64	238	61	74	9	2	26	63	29	2	0	4	68	3	1	.693	.385
Ravelo, Rangel	R-R	6-1	225	4-24-92	.308	.267	.320	100	347	57	107	19	2	13	67	42	7	0	2	49	0	1	.487	.392
Roache, Victor	R-R	6-1	225	9-17-91	.143	.333	.000	5	7	0	1	0	0	0	1	0	0	0	0	1	0	0	.143	.143
Schrock, Max	L-R	5-8	180	10-12-94	.249	.247	.250	114	417	41	104	22	0	4	42	24	7	1	8	36	10	5	.331	.296
Sosa, Edmundo	R-R	5-11	170	3-6-96	.262	.245	.268	56	191	31	50	13	0	5	27	13	4	0	1	42	5	2	.408	.321
Thomas, Lane	R-R	6-1	210	8-23-95	.275	.161	.310	32	131	21	36	7	2	6	21	7	2	0	0	33	4	1	.496	.321
Tovar, Wilfredo	R-R	5-10	180	8-11-91	.297	.271	.306	108	360	41	107	15	1	5	47	24	2	0	3	42	11	5	.386	.342
Urias, Ramon	R-R	5-10	150	6-3-94	.261	.476	.223	46	142	20	37	9	0	5	14	6	0	1	0	29	0	0	.430	.291
Voit, Luke	R-R	6-3	225	2-13-91	.299	.231	.319	67	234	35	70	16	2	9	36	31	5	0	1	49	0	1	.500	.391
Williams, Justin	L-R	6-2	215	8-20-95	.217	.143	.236	21	69	8	15	3	0	1	5	1	0	1	0	17	0	1	.391	.276
Wisdom, Patrick	R-R	6-2	220	8-27-91	.288	.321	.280	107	371	65	107	24	1	15	61	43	3	0	4	112	11	2	.480	.363

Pitching	B-T	HT	WT	DOB	W	L	ERA	G	GS	CG	SV	IP	H	R	ER	HR	BB	SO	AVG	vLH	vRH	K/9	BB/9
Beck, Landon	R-R	6-3	215	12-9-92	0	0	2.96	18	0	0	0	27	26	10	9	2	7	21	.252	.319	.196	6.91	2.30
Bowman, Matt	R-R	6-0	175	5-31-91	0	1	4.30	18	0	0	1	23	23	13	11	2	8	30	.256	.290	.222	11.74	3.13
Brebbia, John	L-R	6-1	185	5-30-90	2	0	4.61	11	0	0	2	14	16	7	7	3	4	24	.281	.167	.333	15.80	2.63
Cabrera, Genesis	L-L	6-1	170	10-10-96	0	0	0.00	1	0	0	0	2	0	0	0	0	1	3	.000	.000	.000	13.50	4.50
Cecil, Brett	R-L	6-3	235	7-2-86	0	0	0.00	5	0	0	0	5	3	0	0	0	1	2	.177	.000	.273	3.60	1.80
Ellis, Chris	L-R	6-5	205	9-22-92	4	3	3.76	16	14	0	0	79	72	36	33	7	21	68	.244	.224	.259	7.75	2.39
Flaherty, Jack	R-R	6-4	205	10-15-95	4	1	2.27	5	5	1	0	32	22	10	8	2	7	41	.190	.216	.177	11.65	1.99
Gallegos, Giovanny	R-R	6-2	210	8-14-91	0	0	0.54	13	0	0	1	17	7	1	1	0	3	16	.130	.040	.207	8.64	1.62
Gant, John	R-R	6-3	200	8-6-92	5	1	1.65	8	8	0	0	49	45	13	9	5	16	42	.243	.203	.267	7.71	2.94
Garcia, Elniery	L-L	6-0	155	12-24-94	0	1	18.00	1	0	0	0	2	3	4	4	1	1	3	.333	.333	.333	13.50	4.50
Gilmartin, Sean	L-L	6-3	205	5-14-90	4	2	4.66	24	6	0	0	46	48	26	24	6	16	33	.276	.192	.307	6.41	3.11
Gomber, Austin	L-L	6-5	230	11-23-93	7	3	3.42	12	11	0	0	68	65	26	26	9	20	76	.247	.276	.239	10.01	2.63
Gonzalez, Derian	R-R	6-3	190	1-31-95	0	0	5.91	8	0	0	1	11	13	7	7	0	4	12	.296	.200	.345	10.13	3.38
Greene, Conner	R-R	6-3	185	4-4-95	0	2	3.66	29	0	0	0	39	33	21	16	2	31	26	.243	.177	.297	5.95	7.09
Gregerson, Luke	L-R	6-3	205	5-14-84	0	0	0.00	2	0	0	0	2	2	1	0	0	3	.286	.500	.000	13.50	0.00
Guilmet, Preston	R-R	6-2	200	7-27-87	0	0	0.93	21	0	0	11	29	9	4	3	3	5	35	.098	.103	.094	10.86	1.55
Helsley, Ryan	R-R	6-1	195	7-18-94	2	1	3.71	5	5	0	0	27	18	14	11	2	9	36	.188	.108	.237	11.48	3.04
Herget, Kevin	L-R	5-10	185	4-3-91	9	11	4.61	28	22	1	0	139	153	76	71	21	34	121	.284	.288	.280	7.85	2.21
Holland, Greg	R-R	5-10	205	11-20-85	0	1	9.00	3	0	0	0	3	3	3	3	1	4	2	.250	.500	.125	6.00	12.00
Hudson, Dakota	R-R	6-5	215	9-15-94	13	3	2.50	19	19	0	0	112	107	34	31	0	38	87	.254	.276	.238	7.01	3.06
Jones, Connor	R-R	6-3	200	10-10-94	1	0	6.46	4	4	0	0	15	20	14	11	1	14	16	.318	.306	.333	9.39	8.22
Layne, Tommy	L-L	6-2	195	11-2-84	2	1	1.35	27	0	0	3	27	21	9	4	0	4	34	.206	.250	.152	11.48	1.35
Leone, Dominic	R-R	5-11	210	10-26-91	1	1	7.20	10	0	0	0	10	14	8	8	2	6	7	.333	.412	.280	6.30	5.40
Lyons, Tyler	L-L	6-4	210	2-21-88	1	1	2.49	7	3	0	1	22	11	6	6	2	6	21	.149	.033	.227	8.72	2.49
Mayers, Mike	R-R	6-3	200	12-6-91	0	0	0.00	5	0	0	3	8	5	0	0	0	4	8	.185	.222	.167	9.39	4.70
Mendoza, Hector	R-R	6-2	176	3-5-94	1	2	7.25	10	0	0	0	22	25	20	18	5	14	14	.278	.242	.298	5.64	5.64
Morales, Andrew	R-R	6-0	185	11-9-92	0	1	3.88	46	0	0	6	60	58	26	26	6	25	69	.261	.178	.250	10.29	3.73
Mujica, Edward	R-R	6-3	220	5-10-84	3	2	3.68	48	0	0	13	51	58	32	21	7	6	35	.282	.224	.315	6.14	1.05
O'Reilly, Mike	R-R	5-11	180	9-3-94	0	1	5.84	6	0	0	0	12	14	10	8	3	3	5	.292	.286	.294	3.65	2.19
Ponceledeon, Daniel	R-R	6-4	185	1-16-92	9	4	2.24	19	18	1	0	96	69	37	24	4	50	110	.197	.224	.177	10.28	4.67

Name	B-T	HT	WT	DOB	W	L	ERA	G	GS	CG	SV	IP	H	R	ER	HR	BB	SO	AVG	vLH	vRH	K/9	BB/9
Reyes, Alex	R-R	6-3	175	8-29-94	1	0	0.00	1	1	0	0	7	1	0	0	0	1	13	.048	.000	.083	16.71	1.29
Reyes, Arturo	R-R	5-11	185	4-6-92	2	2	6.68	23	0	0	0	34	47	26	25	5	17	35	.331	.261	.365	9.36	4.54
Sherriff, Ryan	L-L	6-1	185	5-25-90	0	1	6.75	5	0	0	0	4	6	3	3	1	1	4	.375	.500	.357	9.00	2.25
Tuivailala, Sam	R-R	6-3	225	10-19-92	0	0	2.25	3	1	0	1	4	3	1	1	0	1	3	.231	.250	.222	6.75	2.25
Wainwright, Adam	R-R	6-7	235	8-30-81	1	0	0.00	2	2	0	0	9	8	0	0	0	4	11	.250	.235	.267	11.00	4.00
Warner, Austin	L-L	5-11	185	6-27-94	1	2	4.33	7	7	0	0	35	56	20	17	7	11	23	.371	.381	.367	5.86	2.80
Weaver, Luke	R-R	6-2	170	8-21-93	0	0	4.50	1	1	0	0	4	3	2	2	1	0	7	.200	.125	.286	15.75	0.00
Webb, Tyler	L-L	6-5	230	7-20-90	0	0	2.29	11	1	0	0	20	9	5	5	1	2	21	.143	.273	.073	9.61	1.83
2-team total (19 El Paso)					1	1	2.16	30	1	0	0	42	29	11	10	2	12	49	.200	.298	.136	10.58	2.59
Woodford, Jake	R-R	6-4	210	10-28-96	5	5	4.50	12	12	0	0	64	64	37	32	5	27	45	.261	.284	.245	6.33	3.80

Fielding

Catcher

Catcher	PCT	G	PO	A	E	DP	PB
Baron	.995	40	343	23	2	1	3
Kelly	.993	83	670	42	5	5	5
Knizner	.993	16	128	9	1	0	3
Martinez	1.000	6	40	8	0	0	0

First Base

First Base	PCT	G	PO	A	E	DP
Kelly	1.000	1	3	0	0	0
Mejia	.995	29	202	11	1	16
Ravelo	.998	54	388	33	1	37
Urias	1.000	6	45	0	0	4
Voit	.988	56	378	37	5	40
Wisdom	.980	7	46	3	1	8

Second Base

Second Base	PCT	G	PO	A	E	DP
Edman	.986	14	29	44	1	14
Mejia	.970	12	12	20	1	3
Munoz	.857	1	4	2	1	1
Schrock	.969	80	107	177	9	51
Sosa	.981	12	18	34	1	6
Tovar	1.000	13	18	24	0	4
Urias	.987	18	30	45	1	10

Third Base

Third Base	PCT	G	PO	A	E	DP
Mejia	.947	22	11	25	2	1
Munoz	.818	4	3	6	2	0
Schrock	.967	14	9	20	1	5
Sosa	1.000	10	11	14	0	1
Urias	.929	7	7	6	1	0
Wisdom	.945	93	53	135	11	10

Shortstop

Shortstop	PCT	G	PO	A	E	DP
DeJong	1.000	4	9	14	0	3
Edman	1.000	3	6	7	0	2
Mejia	.968	19	24	36	2	11
Munoz	.981	13	15	37	1	8
Sosa	.966	28	39	74	4	15
Tovar	.969	81	119	198	10	49
Urias	.000	1	0	0	0	0

Outfield

Outfield	PCT	G	PO	A	E	DP
Arozarena	.984	76	116	4	2	0
Garcia	.962	104	216	14	9	0
Mejia	1.000	4	9	1	0	0
Mercado	.978	97	216	4	5	0
Munoz	1.000	5	8	0	0	0
O'Neill	.973	58	101	6	3	2
Ravelo	1.000	37	53	0	0	0
Roache	1.000	2	1	0	0	0
Schrock	1.000	4	6	1	0	0
Thomas	.988	32	78	2	1	1
Tovar	1.000	4	10	0	0	0
Voit	1.000	1	1	0	0	0
Williams	.980	17	44	4	1	0

SPRINGFIELD CARDINALS

TEXAS LEAGUE

DOUBLE-A

Batting	B-T	HT	WT	DOB	AVG	vLH	vRH	G	AB	R	H	2B	3B	HR	RBI	BB	HBP	SH	SF	SO	SB	CS	SLG	OBP
Arozarena, Randy	R-R	5-11	170	2-28-95	.396	.414	.387	24	91	22	36	5	0	7	21	6	4	1	0	25	9	3	.681	.455
Billings, Shane	R-L	5-11	190	12-14-94	.154	.000	.267	11	26	3	4	0	0	1	1	1	0	0	5	0	0		.269	.214
Chinea, Chris	R-R	5-11	220	5-3-94	.231	.247	.224	89	299	39	69	12	0	14	39	15	1	0	1	72	0	0	.411	.269
Drake, Blake	R-R	6-1	175	7-11-93	.235	.230	.237	93	289	31	68	19	0	6	34	21	1	1	2	76	5	3	.363	.288
Dykstra, Luke	R-R	6-1	195	11-7-95	.225	.257	.216	49	151	17	34	5	0	0	8	7	2	0	1	25	0	0	.258	.267
Edman, Tommy	B-R	5-10	180	5-9-95	.299	.350	.281	109	452	71	135	23	3	6	36	35	3	4	4	76	27	5	.403	.350
Godoy, Jose	L-R	5-11	180	10-13-94	.226	.167	.263	9	31	3	7	1	0	0	2	2	0	0	0	3	0	0	.258	.273
Goetzman, Granden	R-R	6-4	200	11-14-92	.244	.318	.219	48	172	19	42	12	4	3	20	7	0	1	1	39	3	1	.413	.272
Herrera, Ivan	R-R	6-0	180	6-1-00	.000	.000	.000	2	4	0	0	0	0	0	0	1	0	0	2	0	0	.000	.200
Knizner, Andrew	R-R	6-1	200	2-3-95	.313	.299	.318	77	281	39	88	13	0	7	41	23	3	1	5	40	0	1	.434	.365
Martinez, Jeremy	R-R	5-11	195	12-29-94	.237	.180	.260	58	173	19	41	6	1	1	26	30	3	0	3	28	0	0	.358	.315
Martinez, Jose	B-R	5-10	180	8-15-96	.200	.154	.213	24	60	4	12	3	0	0	6	7	0	2	1	20	1	0	.250	.279
Mendoza, Evan	R-R	6-2	200	6-28-96	.254	.220	.266	98	366	36	93	12	2	5	26	30	2	1	7	77	1	1	.339	.315
Mieses, Johan	R-R	6-2	185	7-13-95	.206	.259	.186	57	219	26	45	8	1	9	31	11	2	1	0	62	0	0	.374	.250
Molina, Yadier	R-R	5-11	205	7-13-82	.000	—	.000	2	5	0	0	0	0	0	0	1	0	1	1	0	0	.000	.143
Munoz, Yairo	R-R	6-1	201	1-23-95	.200	.000	.250	2	5	1	1	0	0	0	0	0	0	0	0	1	0	.400	.200
Nogowski, John	R-L	6-2	210	1-5-93	.309	.349	.293	83	298	41	92	10	0	12	61	41	3	0	5	21	0	2	.463	.392
Pinder, Chase	R-R	6-1	190	3-16-96	.267	.600	.200	11	30	2	8	0	0	0	1	4	0	0	0	7	0	0	.267	.353
Roache, Victor	R-R	6-1	225	9-17-91	.218	.218	.218	121	426	50	93	11	2	18	58	44	3	0	2	142	4	1	.380	.295
Seferina, Darren	L-R	5-9	175	1-24-94	.159	.273	.138	20	69	8	11	2	0	3	4	3	0	1	3	20	2	1	.319	.197
Sosa, Edmundo	R-R	5-11	180	3-6-96	.276	.233	.293	67	261	34	72	11	7	3	32	9	4	2	2	52	1	2	.429	.308
Spitz, Thomas	R-R	6-1	180	4-16-92	.260	.226	.274	36	104	19	27	4	3	3	13	12	1	1	2	38	1	2	.442	.336
Thomas, Lane	R-R	6-1	210	8-23-95	.260	.256	.262	100	384	63	100	16	4	21	67	43	3	2	3	101	13	9	.487	.337
Trosclair, Stefan	R-R	6-2	195	7-23-94	.267	.320	.250	29	101	18	27	3	0	4	13	6	1	0	1	34	1	1	.416	.312
Urias, Ramon	R-R	5-10	180	6-3-94	.333	.341	.331	44	168	28	56	19	0	8	27	18	4	2	2	29	1	2	.589	.406
Voit, Luke	R-R	6-3	225	2-13-91	.333	—	.333	2	6	1	2	0	0	1	1	1	0	0	0	0	0	.833	.429
Young, Andy	R-R	6-0	195	5-10-94	.319	.302	.326	35	135	18	43	3	1	9	24	7	10	0	0	26	2	0	.556	.395

Pitching	B-T	HT	WT	DOB	W	L	ERA	G	GS	CG	SV	IP	H	R	ER	HR	BB	SO	AVG	vLH	vRH	K/9	BB/9
Arias, Estarlin	R-R	6-1	175	5-22-94	1	1	4.50	21	0	0	0	34	41	17	17	5	15	31	.306	.367	.271	8.21	3.97
Beck, Landon	R-R	6-3	215	12-9-92	2	4	5.05	25	0	0	1	36	39	24	20	5	16	36	.281	.235	.307	9.08	4.04
Bowen, Brady	R-L	6-1	160	7-24-92	0	0	5.40	4	0	0	0	5	4	3	3	1	2	4	.200	.143	.231	7.20	3.60
Bray, Tyler	R-R	6-5	200	10-3-91	0	0	4.32	5	0	0	0	8	7	4	4	1	2	7	.219	.294	.133	7.56	2.16
Cabrera, Genesis	L-L	6-1	175	10-10-96	1	3	4.74	5	0	0	0	25	24	15	13	3	13	21	.255	.189	.298	7.66	4.74
Carter, Eric	R-R	5-11	202	7-21-92	0	0	4.35	8	0	0	0	10	10	5	5	2	3	13	.256	.333	.191	11.32	2.61
Cecil, Brett	R-L	6-3	235	7-2-86	0	0	0.00	1	0	0	0	1	0	0	0	0	0	1	.333	—	.333	9.00	0.00
Elledge, Seth	R-R	6-3	210	5-20-96	3	1	4.32	13	0	0	4	17	13	10	8	3	6	20	.220	.250	.194	10.80	3.24
Ellis, Chris	L-R	6-5	205	9-22-92	4	4	4.19	13	0	0	2	54	46	27	25	6	16	56	.228	.236	.221	9.39	2.68
Evans, Jacob	L-L	6-2	215	11-27-93	1	5	5.06	29	2	0	1	48	44	31	27	3	16	38	.253	.271	.246	7.13	3.00
Fernandez, Junior	R-R	6-1	180	3-2-97	0	0	5.14	16	0	0	0	21	19	12	12	1	16	17	.253	.316	.189	7.29	6.86
Garcia, Elniery	L-L	6-0	155	12-24-94	1	1	4.26	13	1	0	0	25	19	15	12	0	9	14	.333	.273	.381	6.63	4.26
Gonzalez, Derian	R-R	6-3	190	1-31-95	4	0	2.76	13	0	0	1	16	13	6	5	0	7	10	.224	.348	.143	5.51	3.86

Pitching	B-T	HT	WT	DOB	W	L	ERA	G	GS	CG	SV	IP	H	R	ER	HR	BB	SO	AVG	vLH	vRH	K/9	BB/9
Greene, Conner	R-R	6-3	185	4-4-95	4	3	4.44	11	10	0	0	49	43	29	24	1	32	43	.242	.112	.371	7.95	5.92
Gregerson, Luke	L-R	6-3	205	5-14-84	1	0	0.00	3	0	0	0	3	1	0	0	0	0	2	.111	.000	.200	6.00	0.00
Helsley, Ryan	R-R	6-1	195	7-18-94	3	2	4.39	7	7	1	0	41	30	22	20	5	20	44	.203	.246	.172	9.66	4.39
Holland, Greg	R-R	5-10	205	11-20-85	0	1	4.50	2	0	0	0	2	2	1	1	1	1	2	.250	.250	.250	9.00	4.50
Jones, Connor	R-R	6-3	200	10-10-94	5	5	3.80	22	17	0	0	95	96	48	40	4	51	66	.264	.281	.249	6.27	4.85
Kruczynski, Evan	L-L	6-5	215	3-31-95	2	3	2.50	6	6	0	0	40	27	11	11	1	10	33	.200	.238	.183	7.49	2.27
Latcham, Will	R-R	6-2	200	1-26-96	1	1	5.11	10	0	0	3	12	13	8	7	1	5	8	.289	.333	.238	5.84	3.65
Layne, Tommy	L-L	6-2	195	11-2-84	0	0	0.00	2	0	0	0	2	1	0	0	0	0	2	.125	.000	.200	7.71	0.00
Lyons, Tyler	L-L	6-4	210	2-21-88	0	0	6.75	3	0	0	1	3	3	2	2	1	1	1	.273	.250	.286	3.38	3.38
Martinez, Carlos	R-R	6-0	190	9-21-91	0	0	3.86	3	1	0	0	7	6	3	3	3	0	6	.222	.100	.294	7.71	0.00
McKinney, Ian	L-L	5-11	185	11-18-94	3	2	5.17	18	0	0	1	31	31	19	18	5	23	24	.254	.303	.236	6.89	6.61
Medina, Yeison	R-R	6-2	210	10-2-92	0	3	5.88	23	0	0	4	26	36	19	17	2	13	19	.340	.357	.328	6.58	4.50
Meisner, Casey	R-R	6-7	190	5-22-95	2	2	3.60	7	6	0	0	40	31	17	16	3	14	33	.208	.174	.238	7.43	3.15
Mendoza, Hector	R-R	6-2	176	3-5-94	3	2	3.82	32	0	0	4	38	27	17	16	4	14	32	.200	.196	.203	7.65	3.35
Morales, Andrew	R-R	6-0	185	1-16-93	0	0	10.80	3	0	0	0	3	5	4	4	1	4	5	.357	.333	.375	13.50	10.80
O'Reilly, Mike	R-R	5-11	180	9-3-94	3	6	5.32	13	13	0	0	66	70	45	39	10	25	43	.269	.227	.300	5.86	3.41
Pearce, Matt	R-R	6-3	205	2-24-94	0	7	5.40	10	10	0	0	53	66	33	32	8	11	46	.301	.340	.271	7.76	1.86
Ramirez, Roel	R-R	6-1	210	5-26-95	0	0	5.06	10	0	0	0	11	8	6	6	1	5	10	.211	.250	.182	8.44	4.22
Reyes, Alex	R-R	6-3	175	8-29-94	1	0	0.00	1	1	0	0	8	1	0	0	0	3	13	.046	.000	.077	15.26	3.52
Santos, Ramon	R-R	6-2	160	9-20-94	0	2	5.49	34	1	0	7	57	67	39	35	6	26	46	.289	.405	.217	7.22	4.08
Sexton, Austin	R-R	6-2	185	7-17-94	2	0	5.32	14	0	0	0	22	24	13	13	1	9	22	.273	.290	.260	9.00	3.68
Shew, Anthony	R-R	6-2	191	11-3-93	6	8	4.50	19	19	0	0	114	128	57	57	13	32	96	.288	.276	.297	7.58	2.53
Tewes, Sam	R-R	6-5	200	2-6-95	0	2	4.78	7	7	0	0	32	38	19	17	5	13	18	.304	.255	.343	5.06	3.66
Thomson, Colton	L-L	6-0	190	7-22-92	0	2	4.41	15	0	0	2	16	19	9	8	1	9	10	.297	.455	.214	5.51	4.96
Wacha, Michael	R-R	6-6	215	7-1-91	0	1	11.57	1	1	0	0	2	6	5	3	1	1	3	.429	.556	.200	11.57	3.86
Wainwright, Adam	R-R	6-7	235	8-30-81	1	0	0.00	3	3	0	0	10	5	0	0	0	0	9	.143	.133	.150	8.10	0.00
Warner, Austin	L-L	5-11	185	6-27-94	2	3	5.34	6	6	0	0	32	28	19	19	3	19	25	.231	.200	.247	7.03	5.34
Williams, Ronnie	R-R	6-0	170	1-6-96	1	1	13.50	2	0	0	0	3	4	5	5	2	2	2	.286	.143	.429	5.40	5.40
Woodford, Jake	R-R	6-4	210	10-28-96	3	8	5.22	16	16	0	0	81	94	52	47	13	35	56	.290	.240	.322	6.22	3.89
Zgardowski, Jason	R-R	6-5	190	9-27-93	0	0	6.00	6	0	0	0	9	10	6	6	2	6	4	.323	.300	.333	4.00	6.00

Fielding

Catcher	PCT	G	PO	A	E	DP	PB
China	1.000	13	78	10	0	2	0
Godoy	.987	9	69	7	1	2	0
Herrera	1.000	1	12	0	0	0	0
Knizner	.993	74	523	34	4	3	7
Martinez	.994	50	310	23	2	3	2
Molina	1.000	2	10	2	0	0	0

First Base	PCT	G	PO	A	E	DP
China	1.000	48	357	30	0	42
Dykstra	1.000	3	21	1	0	3
Nogowski	.994	78	571	81	4	56
Roache	.000	1	0	0	0	0
Troslair	.980	12	81	17	2	14
Urias	1.000	1	8	0	0	0
Voit	1.000	2	8	2	0	0

Second Base	PCT	G	PO	A	E	DP
Dykstra	.981	26	37	69	2	15
Edman	.977	22	53	73	3	18
Munoz	1.000	1	1	2	0	1
Seferina	.982	14	15	41	1	8
Sosa	.974	10	16	21	1	8
Troslair	.960	11	21	27	2	6
Urias	.985	30	62	70	2	14
Young	.992	30	63	62	1	11

Third Base	PCT	G	PO	A	E	DP
China	1.000	2	1	4	0	0
Dykstra	1.000	2	1	6	0	1
Edman	.950	22	17	40	3	5
Martinez	1.000	2	0	1	0	0
Mendoza	.967	88	76	159	8	22
Munoz	.000	1	0	0	0	0
Seferina	.625	4	0	5	3	0
Sosa	.967	11	8	21	1	1
Urias	1.000	7	1	5	0	2
Young	1.000	7	4	5	0	0

Shortstop	PCT	G	PO	A	E	DP
Edman	.962	65	86	164	10	33
Martinez	.966	17	26	31	2	7
Mendoza	.938	9	16	14	2	5
Munoz	1.000	1	0	4	0	0
Sosa	.951	43	75	98	9	25
Urias	.895	7	7	27	4	4

Outfield	PCT	G	PO	A	E	DP
Arozarena	.976	23	37	4	1	1
Billings	.900	6	8	1	1	1
Drake	.989	80	179	8	2	1
Goetzman	.966	32	54	3	2	0
Meisner	.000	1	0	0	0	0
Mieses	.972	49	98	7	3	1
Munoz	.000	1	0	0	0	0
Nogowski	1.000	2	3	0	0	0
Pinder	1.000	10	22	1	0	1
Roache	.985	102	188	6	3	1
Spitz	.982	30	54	1	1	0
Thomas	1.000	93	238	8	0	3

PALM BEACH CARDINALS

FLORIDA STATE LEAGUE   HIGH CLASS A

Batting	B-T	HT	WT	DOB	AVG	vLH	vRH	G	AB	R	H	2B	3B	HR	RBI	BB	HBP	SH	SF	SO	SB	CS	SLG	OBP
Billings, Shane	R-L	5-11	190	12-14-94	.273	.266	.277	101	388	39	106	14	1	4	37	14	1	6	0	68	11	5	.345	.300
Bryant, Taylor	R-R	6-1	180	12-16-94	.180	.138	.200	29	89	4	16	5	1	1	14	10	1	0	1	34	0	1	.292	.267
Capel, Conner	L-L	6-1	185	5-19-97	.248	.214	.258	29	117	11	29	6	1	1	19	7	1	1	0	30	0	1	.342	.296
Carlson, Dylan	B-L	6-3	195	10-23-98	.247	.302	.223	99	376	63	93	19	3	9	53	52	7	1	5	78	6	3	.386	.346
Denton, Bryce	R-R	6-0	190	8-1-97	.182	—	.182	3	11	1	2	0	0	0	1	0	0	0	0	4	1	0	.182	.182
Fiedler, Matt	R-R	5-10	195	3-22-95	.267	.167	.333	6	15	3	4	0	0	1	2	0	1	0	0	4	0	0	.467	.313
Godoy, Jose	L-R	5-11	180	10-13-94	.289	.235	.299	68	211	25	61	10	1	2	18	25	7	5	1	37	2	0	.374	.381
Hudzina, Danny	R-R	5-11	185	2-27-94	.168	.091	.200	44	149	14	25	6	0	4	16	7	3	1	2	44	0	0	.289	.217
Hurst, Scott	L-R	5-10	175	3-25-96	.354	.462	.314	14	48	10	17	6	0	1	9	8	0	0	1	10	1	0	.542	.439
Jackson, Zach	L-R	6-3	215	5-24-98	.500	—	.500	2	6	1	3	0	0	0	0	0	0	0	0	2	0	0	.500	.500
Lopez, Irving	L-R	5-10	170	6-30-95	.298	.414	.259	33	114	14	34	6	0	2	22	13	1	3	1	13	0	0	.404	.372
Martinez, Jose	B-R	5-10	150	8-15-96	.182	.235	.163	19	66	6	12	2	0	0	7	4	1	0	2	17	0	1	.212	.233
McCarvel, Ryan	R-R	6-2	200	12-23-94	.226	.255	.210	79	261	29	59	5	0	5	32	27	5	1	2	85	1	2	.303	.309
Mendoza, Evan	R-R	6-2	200	6-28-96	.349	.400	.330	37	149	22	52	7	0	3	16	9	2	2	0	27	1	0	.456	.394
Mieses, Johan	R-R	6-2	185	7-13-95	.251	.325	.217	65	243	33	61	8	2	10	40	19	4	0	4	53	3	0	.424	.311
Montero, Elehuris	R-R	6-3	195	8-17-98	.286	.321	.271	24	98	13	28	9	0	1	13	5	2	0	1	22	1	0	.408	.330
Myers, Wood	L-R	5-10	180	10-11-94	.000	.000	.000	2	5	0	0	0	0	0	0	1	0	0	0	2	0	0	.000	.167
O'Keefe, Brian	R-R	6-0	210	7-15-93	.243	.242	.243	73	243	37	59	23	0	6	44	40	4	0	1	49	0	0	.412	.358
Ozuna, Raffy	B-R	6-3	196	9-6-98	.273	.250	.286	3	11	1	3	0	0	0	0	1	0	0	0	4	0	0	.273	.333

Name	B-T	HT	WT	DOB	AVG	vLH	vRH	G	AB	R	H	2B	3B	HR	RBI	BB	HBP	SH	SF	SO	SB	CS	SLG	OBP
Pinder, Chase	R-R	6-1	190	3-16-96	.252	.294	.231	78	278	37	70	13	2	4	30	44	3	2	2	62	3	5	.356	.358
Robertson, Kramer	R-R	5-10	166	9-20-94	.252	.299	.233	121	460	74	116	24	3	2	37	49	18	10	1	52	15	10	.330	.347
Shaw, Josh	R-R	6-1	195	11-30-96	.200	.000	.250	3	10	0	2	0	0	0	0	0	0	0	0	3	0	0	.200	.200
Toerner, Justin	L-L	5-10	165	8-11-96	.300	.267	.320	10	40	8	12	5	0	0	3	5	1	0	0	9	0	0	.425	.391
Troslair, Stefan	R-R	6-2	195	7-23-94	.242	.286	.223	84	297	44	72	14	4	8	45	27	14	2	4	78	3	2	.397	.330
Woodman, J.B.	L-R	6-2	195	12-13-94	.246	.220	.251	68	228	30	56	9	1	6	29	23	2	2	2	106	1	3	.373	.318
Yepez, Juan	R-R	6-1	200	2-19-98	.208	.171	.229	67	226	30	47	12	0	2	22	12	3	1	0	52	2	1	.288	.257
Young, Andy	R-R	6-0	195	5-10-94	.276	.247	.290	84	297	43	82	10	2	12	34	31	17	2	4	59	4	0	.444	.373

Pitching	B-T	HT	WT	DOB	W	L	ERA	G	GS	CG	SV	IP	H	R	ER	HR	BB	SO	AVG	vLH	vRH	K/9	BB/9
Arias, Estarlin	R-R	6-1	175	5-22-94	1	1	4.70	6	0	0	0	8	8	4	4	0	6	10	.276	.250	.294	11.74	7.04
Balestrieri, Paul	R-R	6-0	210	9-4-94	0	1	9.82	5	0	0	0	4	5	5	4	0	5	1	.357	.600	.222	2.45	12.27
Calvano, Robert	R-R	6-2	225	2-27-93	0	0	9.00	2	0	0	0	1	1	1	1	0	2	0	.250	.000	.333	0.00	18.00
Carter, Eric	R-R	5-11	202	7-21-92	2	3	2.20	18	0	0	3	29	18	9	7	2	6	27	.182	.178	.185	8.48	1.88
Cordero, Diego	L-L	6-2	171	9-8-97	0	1	1.46	2	2	0	0	12	7	3	2	1	3	3	.159	.158	.160	2.19	2.19
Cruz, Jesus	R-R	6-1	225	4-15-95	6	0	3.54	25	11	0	1	69	49	27	27	5	33	85	.198	.215	.178	11.14	4.33
Dobzanski, Bryan	R-R	6-4	220	8-31-95	3	1	1.13	13	0	0	4	16	12	3	2	0	6	15	.207	.185	.226	8.44	3.38
Fagalde, Alex	R-R	6-3	225	4-29-94	4	2	3.20	7	7	0	0	39	34	14	14	3	9	39	.238	.263	.206	8.92	2.06
Fernandez, Junior	R-R	6-1	180	3-2-97	1	0	0.00	8	0	0	3	10	9	2	0	0	2	7	.265	.177	.353	6.52	1.86
Gordon, Robbie	R-R	6-2	205	6-8-93	3	1	3.00	16	0	0	0	21	17	8	7	1	7	24	.215	.182	.257	10.29	3.00
Gregerson, Luke	L-R	6-3	205	5-14-84	0	0	0.00	4	0	0	0	4	0	0	0	0	0	6	.286	.143	.429	13.50	0.00
Guillory, Evan	R-R	6-3	210	1-6-96	1	3	6.12	13	10	0	0	60	84	45	41	7	20	39	.331	.339	.323	5.82	2.98
Holland, Greg	R-R	5-10	205	11-20-85	0	0	4.50	2	1	0	0	2	2	1	1	0	0	2	.250	.400	.000	9.00	0.00
Kilichowski, John	L-L	6-5	217	5-17-94	1	2	7.75	28	2	0	0	38	41	35	33	3	28	42	.277	.304	.253	9.86	6.57
Kruczynski, Evan	L-L	6-5	215	3-31-95	5	3	4.03	15	15	0	0	76	74	37	34	6	21	74	.249	.238	.255	8.76	2.49
Latcham, Will	R-R	6-2	200	1-26-96	4	3	3.00	34	0	0	9	42	29	16	14	2	18	52	.190	.183	.195	11.14	3.86
McKinney, Ian	L-L	5-11	185	11-18-94	2	1	3.68	5	1	0	0	7	3	3	3	0	3	14	.115	.083	.143	17.18	3.68
Medina, Yeison	R-R	6-2	210	10-2-92	3	4	3.78	25	0	0	0	33	30	17	14	0	17	26	.233	.262	.206	7.02	4.59
Meisner, Casey	R-R	6-7	190	5-22-95	5	3	3.64	15	15	0	0	82	72	39	33	10	34	60	.233	.221	.245	6.61	3.75
O'Reilly, Mike	R-R	5-11	180	9-3-94	2	1	3.21	13	2	0	0	34	27	16	12	7	8	36	.214	.161	.266	9.22	2.14
Osnowitz, Mitchell	R-R	6-5	245	7-2-91	0	0	0.00	2	0	0	0	3	3	1	0	0	3	1	.273	.333	.250	3.38	10.13
Oxnevad, Ian	R-L	6-4	205	10-3-96	7	6	4.79	22	18	0	0	115	137	66	61	10	34	63	.302	.341	.277	4.94	2.67
Patterson, Jacob	R-L	6-2	200	10-30-95	4	3	3.64	51	0	0	4	64	51	29	26	2	23	72	.219	.244	.195	10.07	3.22
Reyes, Alex	R-R	6-3	175	8-29-94	0	0	0.00	1	1	0	0	3	4	0	0	1	1	6	.286	.286	.286	16.20	2.70
Roberts, Griffin	R-R	6-3	205	6-13-96	0	0	0.00	1	0	0	0	1	0	0	0	0	0	2	.000	.000	.000	18.00	0.00
Santos, Ramon	R-R	6-2	160	9-20-94	0	1	4.50	4	0	0	0	4	2	2	2	0	6	1	.167	.250	.000	2.25	13.50
Sexton, Austin	R-R	6-2	185	7-17-94	2	4	4.50	23	1	0	4	32	27	19	16	1	20	30	.241	.271	.219	8.44	5.63
Shew, Anthony	R-R	6-2	191	11-3-93	4	1	2.11	8	8	1	0	43	40	14	10	2	7	34	.248	.276	.224	7.17	1.48
St. Clair, Thomas	R-R	6-1	186	5-16-94	0	1	4.61	14	0	0	0	14	16	7	7	0	15	14	.296	.478	.161	9.22	9.88
Tewes, Sam	R-R	6-5	200	2-6-95	2	3	4.91	6	6	0	0	29	40	18	16	2	6	21	.336	.322	.350	6.44	1.84
Thomson, Colton	L-L	6-0	190	7-22-92	1	1	1.36	22	0	0	0	33	23	5	5	0	8	38	.198	.212	.188	10.36	2.18
Wacha, Michael	R-R	6-6	215	7-1-91	0	0	6.23	2	2	0	0	4	2	3	3	0	2	5	.133	.200	.118	8.08	4.15
Wainwright, Adam	R-R	6-7	235	8-30-81	0	0	0.00	2	2	0	0	3	1	0	0	0	0	5	.111	.143	.000	15.00	0.00
Walsh, Jake	R-R	6-1	192	7-20-95	7	4	2.24	17	16	1	0	96	81	32	24	7	21	69	.227	.243	.205	6.45	1.96
Warner, Austin	L-L	5-11	185	6-27-94	3	3	3.41	12	12	1	0	74	78	30	28	1	13	77	.274	.266	.279	9.36	1.58
Williams, Ronnie	R-R	6-0	170	1-6-96	0	0	0.73	6	1	0	0	12	6	1	1	0	6	13	.143	.238	.048	9.49	4.38
Zgardowski, Jason	R-R	6-5	190	9-27-93	2	1	3.35	31	0	0	2	43	45	22	16	2	18	45	.271	.314	.240	9.42	3.77

Fielding

Catcher	PCT	G	PO	A	E	DP	PB
Godoy	.998	62	474	46	1	5	6
Jackson	1.000	2	13	1	0	0	0
McCarvel	1.000	15	111	10	0	1	3
O'Keefe	.994	64	475	37	3	3	4

First Base	PCT	G	PO	A	E	DP
Bryant	1.000	3	18	2	0	2
McCarvel	.989	37	259	19	3	33
Troslair	.993	54	358	49	3	27
Yepez	.997	50	352	31	1	32

Second Base	PCT	G	PO	A	E	DP
Bryant	1.000	5	6	9	0	1
Lopez	.978	28	54	82	3	19
Martinez	.897	8	10	16	3	3
Myers	1.000	2	4	2	0	1
Ozuna	1.000	2	0	4	0	0

	PCT	G	PO	A	E	DP
Robertson	1.000	1	2	1	0	1
Shaw	1.000	2	4	7	0	4
Troslair	.970	17	20	45	2	13
Young	.983	73	127	162	5	29

Third Base	PCT	G	PO	A	E	DP
Bryant	.968	14	6	24	1	1
Hudzina	.913	44	24	70	9	7
Lopez	1.000	4	1	2	0	0
Martinez	1.000	5	7	8	0	0
Mendoza	.946	37	32	55	5	10
Montero	.830	20	10	29	8	7
Yepez	1.000	7	3	10	0	3
Young	.941	7	10	6	1	0

Shortstop	PCT	G	PO	A	E	DP
Bryant	1.000	6	6	13	0	4
Lopez	.875	2	3	4	1	1

	PCT	G	PO	A	E	DP
Martinez	.939	7	12	19	2	4
Ozuna	.667	1	1	1	1	0
Robertson	.961	119	170	270	18	50
Shaw	1.000	1	0	1	0	0
Young	1.000	1	4	3	0	2

Outfield	PCT	G	PO	A	E	DP
Billings	.986	94	203	6	3	1
Capel	1.000	28	56	3	0	0
Carlson	.978	86	167	9	4	4
Denton	1.000	1	2	1	0	0
Fiedler	1.000	4	11	0	0	0
Hurst	1.000	13	20	3	0	1
Mieses	.992	51	119	8	1	0
Pinder	.994	64	162	1	1	0
Toerner	1.000	10	28	0	0	0
Troslair	.941	12	16	0	1	0
Woodman	.957	42	60	6	3	0

PEORIA CHIEFS

MIDWEST LEAGUE

LOW CLASS A

Batting	B-T	HT	WT	DOB	AVG	vLH	vRH	G	AB	R	H	2B	3B	HR	RBI	BB	HBP	SH	SF	SO	SB	CS	SLG	OBP
Ascanio, Rayder	B-R	5-11	155	3-17-96	.246	.304	.228	66	236	27	58	6	0	4	18	19	3	0	1	36	3	5	.322	.309
Baker, Luken	R-R	6-4	265	3-10-97	.288	.200	.312	37	139	16	40	9	0	3	15	16	0	0	1	31	0	0	.417	.359
Benson, Brandon	R-R	6-1	195	6-13-96	.188	.192	.186	33	112	7	21	4	0	2	9	9	0	0	0	41	3	0	.277	.248
Bryant, Taylor	R-R	6-1	180	12-16-94	.242	.200	.253	28	99	17	24	5	0	1	10	15	4	2	0	30	0	1	.323	.364
Carlson, Dylan	B-L	6-3	195	10-23-98	.234	.091	.278	13	47	5	11	3	0	2	9	10	0	0	0	10	2	0	.426	.368

Name	B-T	HT	WT	DOB	AVG	vLH	vRH	G	AB	R	H	2B	3B	HR	RBI	BB	HBP	SH	SF	SO	SB	CS	SLG	OBP
Davis, J.R.	R-R	5-10	190	8-10-94	.278	.301	.269	76	270	32	75	14	2	4	27	11	4	1	0	40	5	3	.389	.316
Denton, Bryce	R-R	6-0	190	8-1-97	.258	.237	.265	91	329	38	85	14	1	8	34	23	2	1	1	82	4	0	.380	.310
Dunn, Nick	L-R	5-10	175	1-29-97	.167	.143	.177	14	48	3	8	0	0	0	3	1	3	0	0	9	0	1	.167	.231
Fiedler, Matt	L-R	6-1	195	3-22-95	.258	.308	.237	38	132	14	34	5	2	4	20	11	2	0	1	25	5	0	.417	.322
Figuera, Edwin	R-R	5-10	160	9-2-97	.304	.308	.304	20	69	11	21	0	0	1	5	3	3	1	0	14	4	2	.348	.360
Gonzalez, Yariel	B-R	6-1	190	6-1-94	.311	.238	.331	107	395	51	123	23	1	11	64	31	1	0	7	58	3	1	.458	.357
Gorman, Nolan	L-R	6-1	210	5-10-00	.202	.200	.203	25	94	8	19	3	0	6	16	10	1	0	2	39	0	2	.426	.280
Hurst, Scott	L-R	5-10	175	3-25-96	.295	.233	.313	49	190	28	56	11	1	3	25	19	3	0	4	41	7	4	.411	.361
Kirtley, Zach	R-R	6-1	190	10-1-96	.262	.279	.257	74	271	34	71	16	1	1	20	29	7	0	0	60	0	1	.340	.349
Lopez, Irving	L-R	5-10	170	6-30-95	.273	.220	.287	77	289	46	79	20	1	4	26	31	13	1	3	54	2	2	.391	.366
Luna, Andres	R-R	5-10	175	7-17-97	.250	.316	.220	17	60	7	15	2	0	0	4	2	1	0	0	15	3	4	.283	.286
Machado, Jonatan	L-L	5-9	155	1-21-99	.185	.231	.177	23	92	8	17	4	0	0	8	3	0	0	1	15	3	2	.228	.208
Martinez, Jose	B-L	5-10	150	8-15-96	.241	.191	.258	54	166	18	40	10	0	1	13	24	1	2	4	33	2	0	.319	.333
Montero, Elehuris	R-R	6-3	195	8-17-98	.322	.222	.349	103	382	68	123	28	3	15	69	33	6	0	4	81	2	0	.529	.381
Moreno, Angel	R-R	6-2	200	7-31-96	.222	.182	.240	10	36	3	8	1	0	1	5	3	1	0	0	13	0	1	.333	.300
Myers, Wood	L-R	5-10	180	10-11-94	.314	.167	.355	35	140	16	44	10	0	1	11	5	1	0	0	24	4	2	.407	.343
Ortega, Dennis	R-R	6-2	180	6-11-97	.257	.193	.277	65	245	37	63	13	0	6	27	21	0	2	2	51	7	3	.384	.313
Plummer, Nick	L-L	5-10	200	7-31-96	.205	.155	.219	104	336	54	69	15	3	8	30	67	7	1	0	131	10	7	.339	.349
Riley, Brandon	L-R	6-0	170	12-13-96	.192	.143	.211	9	26	2	5	1	0	0	1	6	0	0	0	6	0	1	.231	.344
Rodriguez, Julio	R-R	6-0	197	6-11-97	.258	.242	.262	76	291	26	75	15	2	8	47	13	0	0	2	60	0	0	.406	.288
Toerner, Justin	L-L	5-10	165	8-11-96	.500	.400	.533	7	20	4	10	0	1	0	4	5	0	0	0	2	0	1	.600	.600
Wilson, Alexis	R-R	5-10	168	8-13-96	.130	.000	.177	8	23	1	3	0	0	0	3	0	0	0	0	9	0	0	.130	.231
Wong, Kolten	L-R	5-9	185	10-10-90	.000	.000	.000	1	3	0	0	0	0	0	0	1	0	0	0	0	0	0	.000	.250
Yepez, Juan	R-R	6-1	200	2-19-98	.415	.250	.449	25	94	20	39	10	2	1	20	10	0	0	2	14	4	1	.596	.462

Pitching	B-T	HT	WT	DOB	W	L	ERA	G	GS	CG	SV	IP	H	R	ER	HR	BB	SO	AVG	vLH	vRH	K/9	BB/9
Balestrieri, Paul	R-R	6-0	210	9-4-94	7	5	4.99	18	16	1	0	88	101	57	49	6	33	64	.295	.351	.266	6.52	3.36
Blanco, Fabian	L-L	6-0	165	12-22-97	2	1	4.33	44	0	0	8	54	50	29	26	1	26	54	.250	.262	.247	9.00	4.33
Calvano, Robert	R-R	6-2	225	2-27-93	0	0	7.36	2	0	0	0	4	3	3	3	1	3	5	.250	.333	.222	12.27	7.36
Casadilla, Franyel	R-R	6-3	175	4-5-97	0	2	12.00	3	3	0	0	12	29	17	16	3	4	9	.468	.556	.400	6.75	3.00
Cruz, Jesus	R-R	6-1	225	4-15-95	1	1	2.16	5	5	0	0	17	17	6	4	0	8	19	.266	.300	.235	10.26	4.32
Dahlberg, Jake	L-L	6-0	205	12-1-93	4	3	2.87	7	7	1	0	47	48	16	15	1	9	33	.270	.250	.277	6.32	1.72
Dayton, Patrick	L-L	6-0	170	7-20-95	0	0	0.78	20	0	0	2	35	27	6	3	0	11	51	.202	.177	.210	13.24	2.86
Dobzanski, Bryan	R-R	6-4	220	8-31-95	5	3	2.89	29	0	0	4	44	39	19	14	3	12	46	.241	.180	.268	9.48	2.47
Fagalde, Alex	R-R	6-3	225	4-29-94	6	3	1.63	13	12	0	0	77	56	17	14	6	17	77	.199	.200	.199	8.96	1.98
Gonzalez, Noel	R-R	5-11	190	2-27-94	1	0	6.23	4	0	0	0	4	5	3	3	0	6	3	.294	.167	.364	6.23	12.46
Gordon, Robbie	R-R	6-2	205	6-8-93	2	1	0.36	15	0	0	0	25	11	2	1	1	7	32	.131	.094	.154	11.37	2.49
Guillory, Evan	R-R	6-3	210	1-6-96	6	5	4.01	13	13	0	0	76	88	39	34	8	21	62	.289	.304	.279	7.31	2.48
Hamann, Kevin	R-R	6-4	180	11-24-93	0	2	10.61	6	0	0	0	9	15	12	11	1	11	9	.385	.500	.333	8.68	10.61
Kilichowski, John	L-L	6-5	217	5-17-94	0	0	0.00	1	0	0	0	3	1	0	0	0	1	5	.100	.000	.125	15.00	3.00
Malcom, Cory	R-R	6-0	190	1-31-95	0	1	4.66	8	0	0	1	10	10	6	5	1	6	20	.250	.200	.257	18.62	5.59
MaVorhis, Levi	R-R	6-2	215	7-30-95	3	0	6.57	19	1	0	1	37	46	30	27	4	11	25	.309	.291	.319	6.08	2.68
Nicacio, Winston	R-R	6-2	180	12-29-96	1	1	7.00	6	5	0	0	27	28	23	21	6	15	18	.269	.395	.197	6.00	5.00
Oviedo, Johan	R-R	6-6	210	3-2-98	10	10	4.22	25	23	0	1	122	108	63	57	6	79	118	.238	.275	.214	8.73	5.84
Prendergast, Zach	R-R	6-2	175	5-6-95	7	4	3.08	27	10	0	1	79	78	33	27	7	15	80	.253	.232	.265	9.11	1.71
Reyes, Alex	R-R	6-3	175	8-29-94	1	0	0.00	1	1	0	0	5	1	0	0	0	2	12	.063	.000	.091	21.60	3.60
Rondon, Angel	R-R	6-2	185	12-1-97	3	2	2.90	10	10	0	0	59	49	29	19	7	17	57	.220	.263	.188	8.69	2.59
Saylor, C.J.	R-R	5-11	195	10-14-93	0	2	4.29	35	0	0	3	50	47	26	24	6	29	76	.245	.253	.239	13.59	5.19
Seijas, Alvaro	R-R	6-1	175	10-10-98	5	8	4.52	25	22	1	0	129	149	72	65	14	61	84	.301	.322	.289	5.85	4.24
St. Clair, Thomas	R-R	6-1	186	5-16-94	2	5	3.72	30	1	0	5	46	29	25	19	2	27	54	.185	.300	.113	10.57	5.28
Summerville, Andrew	L-L	6-3	195	9-4-95	2	0	0.68	8	0	0	0	13	4	1	1	0	15	20	.095	.000	.108	13.50	10.13
Walsh, Jake	R-R	6-1	192	7-20-95	2	1	3.12	8	8	0	0	43	30	15	15	4	15	47	.192	.210	.181	9.76	3.12
Whitley, Kodi	R-R	6-4	220	2-21-95	4	2	2.51	41	2	0	9	72	67	25	20	2	26	68	.248	.270	.235	8.54	3.27
Yokley, Ben	R-R	6-1	190	9-1-92	2	1	3.86	15	0	0	0	21	11	9	9	1	13	20	.157	.192	.136	8.57	5.57

Fielding

C: Ortega 62, Rodriguez 72, Wilson 8. **1B:** Baker 20, Bryant 1, Gonzalez 56, Kirtley 48, Rodriguez 3, Yepez 16. **2B:** Bryant 9, Davis 7, Dunn 14, Gonzalez 11, Lopez 71, Martinez 7, Myers 24, Wong 1. **3B:** Bryant 6, Gonzalez 22, Gorman 25, Lopez 3, Martinez 11, Montero 77, Myers 1. **SS:** Ascanio 66, Bryant 14, Figuera 20, Gonzalez 4, Martinez 36, Myers 2. **OF:** Benson 33, Carlson 13, Davis 51, Denton 83, Fiedler 27, Gonzalez 12, Hurst 49, Lopez 1, Luna 17, Machado 22, Moreno 10, Myers 6, Plummer 95, Riley 9, Toerner 6.

STATE COLLEGE SPIKES　　SHORT-SEASON
NEW YORK-PENN LEAGUE

Batting	B-T	HT	WT	DOB	AVG	vLH	vRH	G	AB	R	H	2B	3B	HR	RBI	BB	HBP	SH	SF	SO	SB	CS	SLG	OBP
Benson, Brandon	R-R	6-1	195	6-13-96	.233	.333	.194	13	43	6	10	2	1	0	4	4	0	0	0	8	3	1	.326	.298
Diaz, Imeldo	R-R	6-0	175	11-24-97	.174	.104	.211	41	138	9	24	4	0	1	3	2	2	2	0	14	0	0	.225	.197
Donovan, Brendan	L-R	6-1	195	1-16-97	.188	.400	.091	4	16	2	3	1	1	0	2	1	0	0	1	7	0	0	.375	.222
Duce, Matt	L-R	5-11	190	11-22-95	.143	.050	.175	28	77	8	11	5	0	0	2	13	1	3	0	20	0	0	.208	.275
Dunn, Nick	L-R	5-10	175	1-29-97	.274	.286	.269	51	201	34	55	14	2	3	32	22	3	1	2	21	3	3	.408	.351
Espinal, Stanley	R-R	6-2	190	11-15-96	.286	.232	.303	64	241	34	69	9	4	8	41	19	6	0	3	47	1	1	.456	.349
Figuera, Edwin	R-R	5-10	160	9-2-97	.285	.227	.306	62	246	33	70	8	4	0	18	8	20	4	1	52	15	3	.350	.356
Gomez, Joe	R-R	6-0	190	12-3-94	.258	.444	.182	13	31	4	8	1	0	0	5	5	3	1	2	17	0	0	.290	.390
Knight, Cameron	R-R	6-0	205	11-15-94	.212	.158	.234	22	66	6	14	1	0	0	3	8	4	2	0	20	0	0	.227	.333
Luna, Andres	R-R	5-10	175	7-17-97	.300	.214	.346	16	40	9	12	2	0	1	5	2	2	0	0	13	2	0	.425	.364
Machado, Jonatan	L-L	5-9	155	1-21-99	.048	.100	.031	10	42	2	2	0	0	0	2	3	0	0	1	15	0	0	.048	.109
Myers, Wood	L-R	5-10	180	10-11-94	.348	.474	.259	12	46	7	16	4	0	0	4	0	0	4	0	0	7	2	0	.435	.400

Name	B-T	HT	WT	DOB	AVG	vLH	vRH	G	AB	R	H	2B	3B	HR	RBI	BB	HBP	SH	SF	SO	SB	CS	SLG	OBP
Nootbaar, Lars	L-R	6-3	210	9-8-97	.227	.340	.189	56	198	14	45	5	0	2	26	22	2	0	1	43	2	2	.283	.309
Perez, Delvin	R-R	6-3	175	11-24-98	.213	.313	.177	64	239	22	51	5	3	1	21	28	2	0	0	54	8	6	.272	.301
Robbins, Walker	L-L	6-3	215	11-18-97	.153	.200	.140	36	118	7	18	4	0	0	1	9	0	0	0	38	0	0	.186	.213
Toerner, Justin	L-L	5-10	165	8-11-96	.292	.275	.300	50	171	26	50	5	1	1	10	24	4	2	1	34	11	2	.351	.390
Whalen, Brady	B-R	6-4	180	1-15-98	.209	.312	.170	65	220	26	46	13	1	6	37	38	7	1	2	56	1	0	.359	.341
Wilson, Alexis	R-R	5-10	168	8-13-96	.220	.154	.250	27	82	9	18	6	1	0	5	18	1	0	0	17	0	0	.317	.366
Woodall, Kevin	R-R	6-6	240	3-20-96	.164	.238	.130	18	67	3	11	7	0	0	8	9	1	0	0	19	1	1	.269	.273
Ynfante, Wadye	R-R	6-0	160	8-15-97	.213	.225	.209	70	253	34	54	15	1	4	25	21	11	0	1	101	10	5	.328	.301

Pitching	B-T	HT	WT	DOB	W	L	ERA	G	GS	CG	SV	IP	H	R	ER	HR	BB	SO	AVG	vLH	vRH	K/9	BB/9
Baird, Michael	R-R	6-5	210	7-9-95	2	2	1.61	12	4	0	1	45	28	9	8	4	5	44	.180	.153	.196	8.87	1.01
Casadilla, Franyel	R-R	6-3	175	4-5-97	4	3	3.84	12	9	0	1	61	46	29	26	8	17	43	.203	.178	.219	6.34	2.51
Changarotty, Will	R-R	6-0	165	10-19-95	1	1	3.38	20	0	0	0	27	20	13	10	1	7	21	.206	.229	.194	7.09	2.36
Cordero, Diego	L-L	6-2	171	9-8-97	2	5	4.70	10	10	0	0	61	73	33	32	3	12	33	.299	.365	.276	4.84	1.76
Dahlberg, Jake	L-L	6-0	205	12-1-93	1	2	2.15	9	8	0	0	50	45	13	12	1	10	44	.245	.200	.257	7.87	1.79
Dayton, Patrick	L-L	6-0	170	7-20-95	0	0	13.50	2	0	0	0	3	6	4	4	0	1	3	.429	.250	.500	10.13	3.38
Gentner, Gabe	R-R	6-1	235	9-6-95	2	2	6.00	16	0	1	0	21	23	15	14	1	17	27	.281	.321	.259	11.57	7.29
Gonzalez, Edgar	R-R	6-1	200	12-26-97	1	1	4.99	20	1	0	2	31	40	17	17	0	10	31	.313	.277	.333	9.10	2.93
Hamann, Kevin	R-R	6-4	180	11-24-93	1	1	1.95	25	0	0	10	32	25	10	7	0	19	21	.221	.257	.205	5.85	5.29
Holba, Chris	R-R	6-3	190	8-31-96	3	3	5.05	12	10	0	0	46	52	33	26	3	11	39	.272	.342	.223	7.58	2.14
Kraus, Eli	L-L	6-1	190	2-3-96	3	2	3.15	13	6	0	1	40	34	14	14	2	9	34	.231	.180	.250	7.65	2.03
Malcom, Cory	R-R	6-0	190	1-31-95	3	0	4.91	19	0	0	5	22	20	13	12	1	10	25	.230	.207	.241	10.23	4.09
Montemayor, Troy	R-R	6-1	160	6-6-96	3	1	5.46	20	0	1	0	28	39	22	17	0	9	22	.325	.222	.387	7.07	2.89
Nicacio, Winston	R-R	6-2	180	12-29-96	3	2	3.24	16	5	0	1	42	32	19	15	1	22	20	.207	.183	.221	9.07	4.75
Rondon, Angel	R-R	6-2	185	12-1-97	0	4	3.72	5	5	0	0	29	29	12	12	3	7	23	.264	.250	.274	7.14	2.17
Schlesener, Jacob	L-L	6-3	175	10-8-96	2	6	4.47	17	10	0	0	52	49	28	26	1	28	69	.249	.208	.262	11.87	4.82
Seeburger, Brett	L-L	6-2	205	1-19-95	0	0	10.80	2	0	0	0	2	3	3	2	0	2	1	.333	.500	.286	5.40	10.80
Villalobos, Hector	L-L	5-11	182	8-19-96	2	2	3.16	14	0	0	1	26	27	14	9	1	8	26	.267	.294	.254	9.12	2.81
Voyles, Jim	R-R	6-7	205	3-20-95	3	3	2.70	12	8	0	0	50	40	17	15	5	11	35	.222	.242	.211	6.30	1.98

Fielding

C: Duce 25, Gomez 11, Knight 20, Wilson 24. **1B:** Espinal 17, Whalen 56, Woodall 3. **2B:** Diaz 19, Dunn 47, Figuera 8, Myers 5. **3B:** Diaz 6, Donovan 4, Espinal 20, Figuera 50. **SS:** Diaz 13, Figuera 2, Perez 64. **OF:** Benson 9, Luna 13, Machado 9, Nootbaar 49, Robbins 30, Toerner 44, Woodall 13, Ynfante 66. Johnson City CardinalsRookie

JOHNSON CITIY CARDINALS   *ROOKIE*
APPALACHIAN LEAGUE

Batting	B-T	HT	WT	DOB	AVG	vLH	vRH	G	AB	R	H	2B	3B	HR	RBI	BB	HBP	SH	SF	SO	SB	CS	SLG	OBP
Castillo, Moises	R-R	6-1	170	7-14-99	.253	.222	.259	49	170	25	43	5	0	4	13	18	2	1	2	38	3	1	.353	.328
Cedeno, Leandro	R-R	6-2	195	8-22-98	.336	.297	.344	59	223	47	75	13	1	14	47	22	11	0	2	69	2	1	.592	.419
Flores, Luis	B-R	6-0	190	10-22-96	.252	.227	.256	45	143	23	36	10	1	1	11	11	0	1	2	34	4	4	.357	.301
Gomez, Dariel	L-R	6-4	190	7-15-96	.270	.211	.278	49	152	26	41	8	1	6	36	28	3	0	2	43	1	0	.454	.389
Gorman, Nolan	L-R	6-1	210	5-10-00	.350	.318	.355	38	143	41	50	10	1	11	28	24	0	0	0	37	1	3	.664	.443
Jackson, Zach	R-R	6-3	215	5-24-98	.239	.292	.229	44	155	15	37	13	0	3	24	26	1	0	2	63	1	1	.381	.348
Machado, Jonatan	L-L	5-9	155	1-21-99	.292	.265	.298	49	192	30	56	10	0	2	21	17	3	0	2	41	9	5	.375	.355
Perri, Michael	R-R	6-3	195	9-5-95	.267	.371	.246	57	202	35	54	14	3	4	19	11	5	1	0	21	7	0	.426	.321
Purcell, Brandon	R-R	6-1	205	7-2-94	.300	1.000	.222	3	10	1	3	0	0	0	1	3	0	0	0	1	0	0	.300	.462
Riley, Brandon	L-R	6-0	170	12-13-96	.294	.105	.327	37	126	22	37	4	0	2	12	35	0	1	2	21	1	5	.373	.442
Rosendo, Sanel	R-R	6-2	205	5-7-97	.257	.333	.241	25	70	8	18	3	1	1	9	15	4	0	1	13	1	0	.371	.411
Sabino, Liam	R-R	6-0	205	5-1-96	.339	.200	.383	19	62	11	21	6	1	3	11	9	1	0	0	15	1	2	.613	.431
Sanchez, Brian	L-R	6-0	180	4-18-96	.173	.286	.157	24	81	10	14	2	1	2	11	4	0	0	2	25	1	1	.296	.207
Santiago, Benito	L-R	6-0	190	3-31-95	.182	.286	.170	20	66	7	12	3	0	3	11	4	1	0	0	28	2	0	.364	.239
Soto, Carlos	L-R	6-2	220	4-27-99	.276	.111	.313	29	98	14	27	7	0	2	23	16	2	0	4	26	0	1	.408	.375
Warner, Andrew	R-R	6-2	225	12-4-95	.214	.250	.210	21	70	17	15	1	0	3	11	15	4	0	0	21	1	0	.357	.382
Williams, Donivan	R-R	6-0	190	7-25-99	.246	.154	.269	55	199	36	49	8	1	5	30	25	4	0	2	71	7	3	.372	.339
Woodall, Kevin	R-R	6-6	240	3-20-96	.286	.000	.327	30	112	23	32	9	0	9	25	15	2	0	1	31	0	0	.607	.377

Pitching	B-T	HT	WT	DOB	W	L	ERA	G	GS	CG	SV	IP	H	R	ER	HR	BB	SO	AVG	vLH	vRH	K/9	BB/9
Aker, Cole	R-R	6-2	205	9-18-96	3	2	4.36	7	6	0	0	33	30	22	16	0	16	33	.242		.247	9.00	4.36
Alvarez, Juan	R-R	6-4	180	12-28-96	3	2	8.46	17	0	0	0	28	41	29	26	7	11	21	.339	.375	.326	6.83	3.54
Brettell, Michael	R-R	6-3	195	7-13-97	1	3	8.78	17	4	0	1	28	44	28	27	4	9	29	.364	.404	.338	9.43	2.93
De Jesus, Noel	R-R	6-3	181	1-18-97	2	1	8.10	6	6	1	0	27	37	29	24	2	12	16	.336	.344	.333	5.40	4.05
Diaz, Oneiver	R-R	6-2	160	8-28-96	0	1	9.12	9	4	0	0	25	46	31	25	7	12	20	.397	.500	.361	7.30	4.38
Gonzalez, Junior	R-R	6-3	175	11-7-96	0	3	10.25	16	1	0	0	26	49	32	30	5	11	18	.402	.447	.381	6.15	3.76
Hunt, Chris	R-R	6-3	210	1-16-95	0	1	7.45	2	2	0	0	10	15	9	8	1	1	8	.333	.412	.286	7.45	0.93
Kelly, Parker	R-R	6-1	235	4-1-97	4	3	3.81	20	0	0	3	28	27	13	12	1	7	20	.255	.212	.274	6.35	2.22
Leahy, Kyle	B-R	6-5	200	6-4-97	4	3	5.52	13	10	0	2	59	88	48	36	7	11	45	.345	.383	.314	6.90	1.69
Oca, David	L-L	5-10	165	7-4-95	2	6	4.58	18	2	0	0	39	51	29	20	2	13	51	.309	.184	.362	11.67	2.97
Parsons, Tommy	R-R	6-4	185	9-1-95	5	1	3.00	13	9	1	1	57	59	23	19	7	10	43	.268	.293	.248	6.79	1.58
Perez, Enrique	L-R	6-2	180	8-10-97	0	2	4.67	19	0	0	0	27	24	18	14	2	14	29	.238	.083	.286	9.67	4.67
Ramirez, Edwar	R-R	6-3	190	3-15-98	1	1	10.91	6	2	0	0	16	28	20	19	2	9	10	.418	.417	.419	5.74	5.17
Schmid, Colin	L-L	6-1	195	8-13-97	2	2	5.64	13	8	0	1	48	49	33	29	4	16	36	.265	.310	.256	6.75	3.00
Sisk, Evan	L-L	6-2	209	4-23-97	0	0	1.76	20	1	0	5	31	23	6	6	1	12	35	.211	.067	.266	10.27	3.52
Sylvester, Jacob	R-R	6-7	235	9-26-95	2	2	6.20	17	0	0	0	25	33	19	17	3	9	24	.306	.342	.286	8.76	3.28
Villalobos, Hector	L-L	5-11	182	8-19-96	0	1	7.88	3	2	0	0	8	13	8	7	1	2	7	.351	.000	.382	7.88	2.97
Zamora, Dionis	R-R	6-2	193	8-2-96	2	3	3.86	12	11	0	0	61	64	33	26	12	20	57	.268	.284	.260	8.46	2.97

Fielding

C: Jackson 33, Purcell 3, Santiago 19, Soto 14. **1B:** Cedeno 23, Gomez 39, Sabino 4, Soto 2, Woodall 10. **2B:** Castillo 9, Flores 7, Perri 1, Williams 54. **3B:** Castillo 16, Flores 10, Gorman 33, Perri 2, Sabino 14. **SS:** Castillo 26, Perri 47. **OF:** Cedeno 33, Flores 26, Gomez 2, Machado 48, Riley 36, Rosendo 22, Sanchez 19, Warner 14, Woodall 17.

GCL CARDINALS — ROOKIE
GULF COAST LEAGUE

Batting	B-T	HT	WT	DOB	AVG	vLH	vRH	G	AB	R	H	2B	3B	HR	RBI	BB	HBP	SH	SF	SO	SB	CS	SLG	OBP
Baker, Luken	R-R	6-4	265	3-10-97	.500	.667	.444	8	24	10	12	2	0	1	7	3	0	0	1	4	0	0	.708	.536
Benson, Brandon	R-R	6-1	195	6-13-96	.250	.250	.250	11	28	8	7	1	0	2	5	4	1	0	0	7	0	2	.500	.364
Del Rio, Diomedes	L-L	5-10	160	9-15-97	.256	.177	.268	37	129	27	33	7	5	1	17	10	1	3	2	32	5	4	.411	.310
Freiday, Joe	R-R	6-3	240	1-17-96	.212	.333	.200	13	33	5	7	0	0	0	4	8	1	0	2	12	0	0	.212	.364
Fuller, Terry	L-R	6-4	210	12-5-98	.243	.333	.235	11	37	11	9	1	0	3	5	9	3	0	0	14	2	0	.514	.429
Gahagan, Zack	R-R	6-1	195	8-3-95	.278	.278	.278	35	108	16	30	4	1	1	14	18	4	0	1	21	5	2	.361	.397
Garcia, Victor	R-R	6-3	235	9-16-99	.304	.227	.320	33	125	25	38	4	2	1	19	7	7	0	0	24	0	0	.392	.374
Gil, Mateo	R-R	6-1	180	7-24-00	.252	.214	.259	45	171	27	43	6	1	1	20	20	3	0	0	51	2	2	.316	.340
Herrera, Ivan	R-R	6-0	180	6-1-00	.348	.438	.333	28	112	23	39	6	4	1	25	11	5	0	2	20	1	1	.500	.423
Hurst, Scott	L-R	5-10	175	3-25-96	.400	.333	.417	5	15	5	6	3	0	0	2	5	0	0	0	2	2	0	.600	.550
Jimenez, William	R-R	5-10	171	1-23-96	.329	.375	.319	41	143	27	47	6	4	2	25	17	1	1	1	33	3	2	.469	.401
Knight, Cameron	R-R	6-0	205	11-15-94	.667	—	.667	1	3	2	2	0	0	0	1	0	0	0	0	0	0	0	.667	.750
Kreuter, Cole	R-R	6-0	190	11-29-95	.153	.143	.155	34	98	12	15	5	0	0	15	11	10	0	2	39	2	1	.204	.298
Moreno, Angel	R-R	6-2	200	7-31-96	.233	.125	.273	8	30	4	7	2	1	1	3	3	0	1	0	5	0	1	.467	.303
Nogowski, John	R-L	6-2	210	1-5-93	.345	.500	.304	8	29	5	10	0	0	3	3	1	0	1	4	1	0	.345	.412
Ozuna, Raffy	B-R	6-3	196	9-6-98	.181	.214	.171	35	133	24	24	4	4	0	14	17	2	0	0	70	2	0	.271	.283
Purcell, Brandon	R-R	6-1	205	7-2-94	.262	.294	.250	21	61	8	16	5	0	3	20	7	0	0	0	13	1	0	.459	.338
Sabino, Liam	R-R	6-0	205	5-1-96	.192	.250	.175	23	73	10	14	7	0	0	7	10	0	1	2	31	2	0	.288	.272
Shaw, Josh	R-R	6-1	195	11-30-96	.266	.214	.275	46	177	31	47	7	2	2	30	14	2	1	3	14	6	2	.362	.321
Soler, Carlos	L-R	6-2	163	10-29-96	.246	.333	.222	15	57	8	14	4	3	0	9	2	2	0	0	17	1	1	.421	.295
Soto, Carlos	L-R	6-2	220	4-27-99	.200	.000	.235	11	40	7	8	2	0	3	10	5	1	0	0	9	0	0	.475	.304
Torres, Jhon	R-R	6-4	199	3-29-00	.397	.500	.362	17	63	11	25	6	0	4	14	8	4	0	0	13	1	1	.683	.493
Vargas, Kevin	R-R	6-1	175	2-14-00	.218	.267	.208	31	87	17	19	4	0	0	7	11	5	1	0	32	1	3	.264	.340
Warner, Andrew	R-R	6-2	225	12-4-95	.342	.167	.375	31	114	24	39	16	1	4	27	13	8	0	1	26	3	1	.605	.441

Pitching	B-T	HT	WT	DOB	W	L	ERA	G	GS	CG	SV	IP	H	R	ER	HR	BB	SO	AVG	vLH	vRH	K/9	BB/9
Aker, Cole	R-R	6-2	205	9-18-96	3	0	4.15	6	1	0	0	17	18	10	8	0	8	14	.273	.350	.239	7.27	4.15
Avelino, Rodard	R-R	6-1	170	6-3-99	1	0	5.87	8	0	0	0	8	6	9	5	0	12	7	.194	.250	.174	8.22	14.09
Cohen, Ty	R-R	6-1	195	2-23-96	3	1	2.64	18	0	0	1	31	31	12	9	1	12	23	.272	.222	.317	6.75	3.52
Cordero, Diego	L-L	6-2	171	9-8-97	2	0	2.25	2	2	0	0	12	8	3	3	1	4	9	.191	.267	.148	6.75	3.00
Coward, Connor	R-R	6-0	200	5-31-96	4	0	0.88	10	6	0	0	41	23	4	4	0	7	38	.170	.164	.175	8.34	1.54
DellaValle, Perry	R-R	6-0	185	1-23-96	0	2	1.97	11	7	0	1	46	43	13	10	0	7	67	.247	.256	.240	13.20	1.38
Escobar, Edgar	R-R	6-1	220	1-20-97	2	2	1.21	19	0	0	0	22	13	4	3	0	3	33	.169	.200	.154	13.30	1.21
Gallegos, Alex	R-R	6-3	175	5-14-98	0	0	4.50	13	0	0	0	14	17	12	7	0	7	4	.304	.316	.297	2.57	4.50
Geronimo, Jose	R-R	6-3	239	10-26-97	1	1	6.65	15	0	0	0	21	21	19	16	1	12	12	.241	.313	.200	4.98	4.98
Gonzalez, Derian	R-R	6-3	190	1-31-95	0	1	1.42	6	6	0	0	6	4	2	1	0	4	10	.182	.250	.100	14.21	5.68
Helsley, Ryan	R-R	6-1	195	7-18-94	0	0	0.00	1	1	0	0	3	1	0	0	0	3	4	.111	.000	.125	13.50	10.13
Hunt, Chris	R-R	6-3	210	1-16-95	4	0	1.82	10	3	0	0	30	25	6	6	1	6	20	.225	.250	.211	6.07	1.82
Justo, Francisco	R-R	6-4	205	12-20-98	0	1	5.46	13	4	0	2	28	29	20	17	6	10	25	.266	.283	.254	8.04	3.21
Pacheco, Freddy	R-R	5-11	203	4-17-98	1	2	0.55	9	1	0	1	16	9	9	1	0	10	21	.164	.071	.195	11.57	5.51
Pereira, Wilfredo	R-R	5-11	197	4-26-99	3	4	5.53	11	7	0	0	42	53	33	26	4	17	27	.303	.277	.318	5.74	3.61
Pirela, Brian	R-R	6-2	221	1-19-98	10	0	2.71	12	11	1	0	70	65	25	21	2	20	44	.252	.271	.238	5.68	2.58
Ramirez, Edwar	R-R	6-3	190	3-15-98	0	1	6.14	2	2	0	0	7	13	7	5	0	6	3	.419	.286	.458	3.68	7.36
Rivera, Chris	R-R	5-9	175	1-15-97	3	1	4.50	16	0	0	2	30	36	18	15	0	3	23	.298	.391	.240	6.90	0.90
Rivera, Wilberto	R-R	6-3	207	4-26-99	0	0	8.22	9	0	0	0	8	9	7	7	1	11	2	.310	.308	.313	2.35	12.91
Roberts, Griffin	R-R	6-3	205	6-13-96	0	1	6.23	7	2	0	1	9	6	7	6	0	4	11	.194	.333	.063	11.42	4.15
Solano, Enmanuel	R-R	6-1	160	9-23-98	2	0	4.26	3	3	0	0	19	17	9	9	0	3	8	.239	.240	.239	3.79	1.42
Yokley, Ben	R-R	6-1	190	9-1-92	0	0	2.25	3	0	0	1	4	5	3	1	0	1	7	.278	.444	.111	15.75	2.25
Zamora, Dionis	R-R	6-2	193	8-2-96	1	0	2.25	1	0	0	0	4	4	1	1	0	0	3	.267	.143	.375	6.75	0.00

Fielding

C: Freiday 12, Herrera 20, Knight 1, Purcell 20, Soto 9. **1B:** Baker 5, Gahagan 28, Kreuter 7, Nogowski 7, Sabino 9, Shaw 1, Soto 1, Warner 7. **2B:** Kreuter 15, Sabino 2, Shaw 25, Vargas 18. **3B:** Gahagan 6, Kreuter 5, Ozuna 25, Sabino 7, Shaw 17, Vargas 2. **SS:** Gil 41, Ozuna 8, Shaw 2, Vargas 10. **OF:** Benson 2, Del Rio 37, Fuller 2, Gahagan 3, Garcia 28, Hurst 3, Jimenez 39, Kreuter 4, Moreno 5, Sabino 4, Soler 15, Torres 15, Vargas 2, Warner 20.

DSL CARDINALS BLUE — ROOKIE
DOMINICAN SUMMER LEAGUE

Batting	B-T	HT	WT	DOB	AVG	vLH	vRH	G	AB	R	H	2B	3B	HR	RBI	BB	HBP	SH	SF	SO	SB	CS	SLG	OBP
Andujar, Luis	R-R	6-1	165	1-19-00	.248	—	—	43	133	19	33	6	1	1	20	12	2	0	0	35	6	0	.331	.320
Burgos, Diowill	L-R	6-0	190	1-29-01	.210	.167	.227	56	210	29	44	8	4	6	31	30	1	0	1	72	3	4	.371	.310
Cruz, Adanson	R-R	6-2	175	10-6-00	.300	.227	.316	67	240	50	72	15	6	2	39	38	7	0	3	64	11	2	.438	.406
De Jesus, Elvin	B-R	5-11	160	8-29-01	.260	.300	.292	40	100	22	26	5	2	0	9	20	0	0	0	31	2	4	.350	.383
De Jesus, Freddy	R-R	6-1	200	10-15-99	.263	.146	.301	67	228	39	60	26	0	3	44	49	14	0	4	72	0	2	.417	.417
De Los Santos, Joerlin	R-R	5-11	175	9-16-00	.359			64	234	66	84	18	6	1	28	41	3	3	1	36	30	9	.500	.459
Del Rio, Diomedes	L-L	5-10	160	9-15-97	.339	.242	.291	20	62	23	21	4	8	2	17	21	0	0	2	14	4	1	.758	.494
Del Villar, Darlyn	R-R	6-0	176	11-8-00	.282	.222	.311	34	135	21	38	9	1	1	22	17	2	0	3	33	5	1	.385	.363
Garcia, Joyser	R-R	5-10	165	10-14-99	.233	—	—	31	103	11	24	6	0	0	14	4	3	0	1	20	0	0	.291	.279

ST. LOUIS CARDINALS

Name	B-T	HT	WT	DOB	AVG	vLH	vRH	G	AB	R	H	2B	3B	HR	RBI	BB	HBP	SH	SF	SO	SB	CS	SLG	OBP
Gomez, Pablo	R-R	5-11	170	9-4-99	.234	.161	.260	56	214	40	50	15	3	3	34	16	1	4	2	44	7	4	.374	.288
Hernandez, Francisco	R-R	5-11	190	10-8-99	.293	—	—	64	222	48	65	14	2	3	37	33	8	2	4	56	3	7	.414	.397
Longa, Cristhian	R-R	5-11	180	4-28-00	.263	—	—	64	236	50	62	14	3	4	49	20	15	1	6	57	2	3	.398	.350
Mendoza, Ramon	R-R	5-11	174	8-31-00	.311	.154	.366	41	151	29	47	9	5	3	33	22	6	0	0	29	0	1	.497	.419
Montano, Luis	L-R	6-2	170	4-10-00	.272	—	—	66	235	47	64	20	5	3	44	42	6	2	4	85	2	5	.438	.390
Moquete, Darlin	R-R	5-11	175	9-19-99	.275	.315	.260	56	204	53	56	8	3	1	19	19	3	2	1	38	21	5	.358	.344
Mora, Sander	R-R	5-9	155	2-23-01	.234	.184	.141	54	188	43	44	11	1	0	17	35	7	1	1	46	12	7	.303	.372
Nunez, Malcom	R-R	5-11	205	3-9-01	.415	.383	.427	44	164	44	68	16	2	13	59	26	5	0	4	29	3	0	.774	.498
Orecchia, Jesus	R-R	6-1	175	4-22-01	.172	—	—	42	134	14	23	7	0	0	13	13	1	0	1	37	0	0	.224	.248
Pena, Erik	B-R	5-8	140	1-6-00	.290	.000	.100	41	124	23	36	2	3	1	21	9	7	1	3	22	4	3	.379	.364
Pena, Leudy	L-R	6-3	197	11-17-00	.246	.367	.200	29	110	13	27	6	1	3	13	10	2	0	0	31	0	0	.400	.320
Ramirez, Claudio	R-R	6-1	185	11-3-00	.211	—	—	60	199	39	42	16	2	2	26	39	6	0	2	64	2	1	.342	.354
Rodriguez, Luis	R-R	6-0	175	2-26-00	.188	.220	.174	37	133	13	25	4	0	1	12	12	3	0	3	36	2	1	.241	.265
Rosario, Yowelfy	R-R	6-5		6-9-00	.255	.200	.282	57	196	49	50	15	8	3	36	33	5	1	2	61	7	2	.459	.373
Samuel, Alexander	R-R	6-3	190	3-24-00	.191	.273	.133	39	136	19	26	7	2	2	26	20	2	0	3	52	4	1	.316	.298
Selmo, Jean	R-R	6-2	190	4-25-00	.301	.188	.338	54	193	47	58	16	5	2	38	34	2	0	1	45	7	3	.466	.409
Soler, Carlos	L-R	6-2	163	10-29-99	.372	.315	.345	35	145	38	54	10	5	1	31	16	4	0	3	32	6	6	.531	.441
Soto, Franklin	R-R	5-11	168	9-23-99	.305	—	—	61	233	49	71	11	8	0	37	38	2	0	3	31	23	12	.421	.402
Zapata, Jose	R-R	5-11	195	2-14-01	.192	.250	.171	35	120	18	23	6	0	0	20	17	5	0	3	42	1	0	.242	.310

Pitching	B-T	HT	WT	DOB	W	L	ERA	G	GS	CG	SV	IP	H	R	ER	HR	BB	SO	AVG	vLH	vRH	K/9	BB/9
Avelino, Rodard	R-R	6-1	170	6-3-99	0	1	11.74	17	0	0	0	15	12	21	20	0	34	23	.218	.250	.174	13.50	19.96
Benitez, Allinson	R-R	6-4	200	11-4-99	2	2	4.54	11	10	0	0	38	39	21	19	2	21	32	.283	—	—	7.65	5.02
Calderon, Augusto	R-R	6-0	190	10-6-00	1	0	10.66	11	0	0	0	13	14	20	15	2	14	5	.280	—	—	3.55	9.95
Contreras, Gabriel	R-R	6-2	175	8-16-00	0	0	24.23	16	0	0	0	13	28	35	35	1	32	11	.475	—	—	7.62	22.15
Cordova, Martin	R-R	6-0	175	6-28-99	7	2	3.09	10	9	0	0	47	53	24	16	0	9	28	.287	—	—	5.40	1.74
Cuenca, Angel	R-R	6-1	160	7-10-01	2	1	4.15	12	5	0	1	35	38	22	16	1	13	33	.277	.344	.234	8.57	3.38
De Los Santos, Hector	R-R	6-0	170	9-18-98	2	0	5.23	17	0	0	1	33	32	20	19	0	32	31	.269	—	—	8.54	8.82
Diaz, Derek	R-R	5-11	185	1-29-01	2	0	11.05	13	0	0	0	15	16	19	18	1	14	12	.286	.316	.270	7.36	8.59
Fernandez, Ramon	R-R	6-2	180	10-26-98	1	0	7.27	10	0	0	0	9	5	8	7	0	13	8	.156	.200	.136	8.31	13.50
Garcia, Roy	R-R	6-0	190	8-28-00	1	2	8.37	19	0	0	1	33	30	37	31	1	43	38	.238	—	—	10.26	11.61
Geronimo, Jose	R-R	6-3	239	10-26-97	0	3	5.79	5	0	0	0	5	2	8	3	0	7	3	.118	.313	.200	5.79	13.50
Jimenez, Ludwin	R-R	6-2	165	8-9-01	4	4	3.55	14	12	1	1	63	57	40	25	4	18	69	.241	—	—	9.81	2.56
Madera, Wilman	R-R	6-2	200	3-10-99	2	2	3.52	19	3	0	3	46	52	21	18	2	15	47	.291	—	—	9.20	2.93
Maiz, Miguel	R-R	6-1	170	6-27-01	2	1	3.55	14	4	0	1	33	28	16	13	1	13	38	.228	—	—	10.36	3.55
Moreno, Jose	R-R	6-1	170	8-20-00	3	5	4.30	14	14	0	0	67	68	42	32	4	27	59	.266	—	—	7.93	3.63
Ortega, Angel	R-R	6-1	180	11-18-99	2	0	1.38	13	0	0	2	26	19	5	4	0	11	28	.214	.108	.289	9.69	3.81
Ortiz, Luis	R-R	6-3	170	7-23-00	2	4	5.81	14	11	0	1	53	66	46	34	1	18	44	.311	—	—	7.52	3.08
Pacheco, Freddy	R-R	5-11	203	4-17-98	3	0	1.50	11	0	0	4	18	7	4	3	0	8	35	.117	.128	.145	17.50	4.00
Paniagua, Inohan	R-R	6-1	148	2-6-00	3	3	3.77	14	14	0	0	57	53	29	24	3	16	51	.245	.298	.212	8.01	2.51
Pereira, Wilfredo	R-R	5-11	197	4-26-99	0	0	1.64	2	2	0	0	11	10	5	2	0	1	11	.244	.277	.318	9.00	0.82
Prada, Nelson	L-L	6-2	170	5-6-00	4	1	3.49	19	0	0	2	28	25	15	11	1	11	32	.240	—	—	10.16	3.49
Puello, Julio	R-R	6-4	185	1-7-99	7	0	2.05	15	13	0	0	75	57	21	17	0	23	82	.210	.232	.195	9.88	2.77
Ramirez, Josue	R-R	6-1	185	6-1-00	2	0	7.52	16	0	0	0	20	23	19	17	0	25	16	.299	.344	.267	7.08	11.07
Rodriguez, Dionys	L-R	6-0	188	9-3-00	4	0	7.40	19	0	0	2	24	21	24	20	1	32	26	.228	.000	.400	9.62	11.84
Rodriguez, Gustavo J.	R-R	6-3	160	1-8-01	0	1	2.25	8	1	0	0	12	12	6	3	0	8	4	.267	—	—	3.00	6.00
Santana, Saniel	R-R	6-1	213	8-12-99	0	2	5.16	20	0	0	2	23	21	17	13	2	20	21	.253	.242	.260	8.34	7.94
Solano, Enmanuel	R-R	6-1	160	9-23-98	7	1	3.27	10	10	0	0	55	63	25	20	1	9	34	.292	.260	.289	5.56	1.47
Soriano, Larimel	R-R	5-11	160	1-28-00	2	2	8.14	16	0	0	0	21	27	25	19	1	14	17	.318	.368	.277	7.29	6.00
Soto, Hector	R-R	6-1	175	3-2-99	6	5	2.72	14	14	0	0	73	71	32	22	3	9	75	.247	.256	.241	9.29	
1.11 Suarez, Ronald	R-R	6-4	215	3-5-00	0	2	5.95	8	5	0	0	20	26	18	13	1	12	17	.306	—	—	7.78	5.49
Tabata, Sebastian	R-R	6-5	210	2-27-98	4	1	1.09	20	0	0	2	25	9	6	3	0	10	36	.107	—	—	13.14	3.65
Taveras, Leonardo	R-R	6-5	190	9-7-98	5	1	2.89	23	0	0	8	37	26	15	12	2	14	48	.203	.204	.203	10.61	5.79
Tena, Luis	R-R	5-11	172	10-21-99	0	3	5.29	15	0	0	1	17	15	11	10	3	12	13	.238	.310	.177	6.88	6.35
Trompiz, Anthony	R-R	6-3	214	11-20-97	2	1	4.44	19	0	0	3	26	38	17	13	0	10	13	.349	.436	.300	5.81	3.42
Ventura, Francis	R-R	6-2	195	7-22-99	4	2	3.65	14	14	0	0	74	81	38	30	1	21	59	.282	.303	.268	7.18	2.55
Victorino, Jhon	R-R	6-3	200	10-1-98	1	0	3.42	12	0	0	1	26	25	12	10	0	8	15	.258	—	—	5.13	2.73
Villanueva, Victor	R-R	6-1	170	3-26-01	1	0	2.45	9	0	0	0	11	10	4	3	1	4	5	.270	.177	.350	4.09	3.27
Yedis, Miguel	R-R	6-5	165	12-18-00	1	1	8.50	14	0	0	0	18	19	17	17	2	10	12	.275	.258	.290	6.00	5.00
Zamora, Dionis	R-R	6-2	193	8-2-96	2	0	1.93	3	2	0	0	14	14	9	3	0	5	19	.246	.276	.257	12.21	3.21

Fielding

C: Garcia 27, Longa 13, Orecchia 40, Rodriguez 37, Zapata 35. 1B: Andujar 2, De Jesus 52, Gomez 5, Longa 50, Nunez 5, Ramirez 21, Rosario 3, Selmo 15. 2B: Andujar 21, De Jesus 15, Gomez 32, Mendoza 18, Moquete 2, Mora 7, Pena 5, Soto 8. 3B: Andujar 12, Gomez 10, Hernandez 62, Longa 1, Mendoza 18, Mora 1, Nunez 30, Rosario 17. SS: Del Villar 32, Gomez 11, Moquete 1, Mora 11, Rosario 7, Soto 42. OF: Andujar 1, Burgos 50, Cruz 45, De Los Santos 60, Del Rio 17, Gomez 1, Montano 63, Moquete 50, Pena 5, Pena 18, Ramirez 25, Samuel 26, Selmo 31, Soler 32.

San Diego Padres

SEASON IN A SENTENCE: Another season of offensive ineptitude again sunk the Padres as they finished in the bottom three in runs (617), batting average (.235) and on-base percentage (.297) en route to a 66-96 record, their worst mark in 10 years.

HIGH POINT: Rookie catcher Francisco Mejia, acquired from the Indians for relievers Brad Hand and Adam Cimber at the trade deadline, homered in each of his first two-at bats in his first start as a Padre on Sept. 6 in Cincinnati. It was as promising a moment as any for the future of the club.

LOW POINT: The Padres arrived in Mexico City for a special three-game series against the Dodgers looking to showcase the club south of the border. Instead they got no-hit by four Dodgers pitchers in the series opener on May 4, striking out 13 times.

NOTABLE ROOKIES: Outfielder Franmil Reyes led the minors in home runs when he got called up in May and became the Padres' top offensive threat, batting .280 with 16 home runs in 87 games. Outfielder Franchy Cordero showcased tremendous power with a 489-foot home run in Arizona, the second-longest in the majors all season. He briefly held the Padres' left field job before suffering a season-ending elbow injury in late May. Lefties Joey Lucchesi (8-9, 4.08) and Eric Lauer (6-7, 4.34) became regulars in the rotation, and third baseman Christian Villanueva won the NL rookie of the month award for April after hitting eight home runs. Second baseman Luis Urias, shortstop Javier Guerra, righthanders Jacob Nix and Brett Kennedy and relievers Jose Castillo, Trey Wingenter and Robert Stock all made their big league debuts.

KEY TRANSACTIONS: The Padres signed first baseman Eric Hosmer to a six-year, $144 million deal before the season, the largest free-agent contract in club history, but he hit just .253/.322/.398 in a disappointing year. Sellers once again at the deadline, the Padres traded all-star closer Hand and rookie find Cimber to the Indians for the touted catcher Mejia.

DOWN ON THE FARM: The Padres asserted themselves as the No. 1 farm system with Mejia's acquisition. Chris Paddack and Luis Patino emerged as potential future aces and Fernando Tatis, Josh Naylor, Logan Allen, Hudson Potts and Buddy Reed all put up big numbers while ascending to the system's upper levels. Double-A San Antonio was the only championship finalist.

OPENING DAY PAYROLL: $73,716,532 (28th).

PLAYERS OF THE YEAR

MAJOR LEAGUE	MINOR LEAGUE
Kirby Yates RHP	**Chris Paddack** RHP
5-3, 2.14, 12 SV	(High Class A/Double-A)
90 SO, 17 BB in 63 IP	7-3, 2.10 in 17 GS
.181 AVG	120 SO, 8 BB in 90 IP

ORGANIZATION LEADERS

Batting		*Minimum 250 AB
MAJORS		
* AVG	Franmil Reyes	.280
* OPS	Franmil Reyes	.838
HR	Hunter Renfroe	26
RBI	Eric Hosmer	69
MINORS		
* AVG	Josh Naylor, San Antonio	.297
* OBP	Luis Urias, El Paso	.398
* SLG	Fernando Tatis Jr., San Antonio	.507
* OPS	Fernando Tatis Jr., San Antonio	.862
R	Ty France, San Antonio, El Paso	84
H	Josh Naylor, San Antonio	149
TB	Ty France, San Antonio, El Paso	236
2B	Luis Torrens, Lake Elsinore	36
3B	Edward Olivares, Lake Elsinore	10
3B	Agustin Ruiz, Padres 1, Tri-City, Fort Wayne	10
HR	Ty France, San Antonio, El Paso	22
HR	Austin Allen, San Antonio	22
RBI	Ty France, San Antonio, El Paso	96
BB	Luis Urias, El Paso	67
SO	Rod Boykin, San Antonio, Lake Elsinore	167
SB	Buddy Reed, Lake Elsinore, San Antonio	51

Pitching		#Minimum 75 IP
MAJORS		
W	Joey Lucchesi	8
W	Craig Stammen	8
# ERA	Craig Stammen	2.73
SO	Joey Lucchesi	145
SV	Brad Hand	24
MINORS		
W	Logan Allen, San Antonio, El Paso	14
L	Michel Baez, Lake Elsinore, San Antonio	10
# ERA	Logan Allen, San Antonio, El Paso	2.54
G	Rowan Wick, San Antonio, El Paso	49
GS	Cal Quantrill, San Antonio, El Paso	28
SV	Travis Radke, Ft. Wayne, San Antonio, Lake Elsinore, El Paso	16
IP	Logan Allen, San Antonio, El Paso	149
IP	Jerry Keel, San Antonio, El Paso	149
BB	Pedro Avila, Lake Elsinore	54
SO	Logan Allen, San Antonio, El Paso	151
# AVG	Logan Allen, San Antonio, El Paso	.205

2018 PERFORMANCE

General Manager: A.J. **Preller. Farm Director:** Sam Geaney. **Scouting Director:** Mark Conner.

Class	Team	League	W	L	PCT	Finish	Manager
Majors	San Diego Padres	National	66	96	.407	14th (15)	Andy Green
Triple-A	El Paso Chihuahuas	Pacific Coast	82	57	.590	t-2nd (16)	Rod Barajas
Double-A	San Antonio Missions	Texas	71	67	.514	3rd (8)	Phillip Wellman
High A	Lake Elsinore Storm	California	68	72	.486	5th (8)	Edwin Rodriguez
Low A	Fort Wayne TinCaps	Midwest	64	74	.464	t-11th (16)	Anthony Contreras
Short season	Tri-City Dust Devils	Northwest	35	41	.461	t-6th (8)	Mike McCoy
Rookie	AZL Padres 1	Arizona	27	29	.482	12th (18)	Vinny Lopez
Rookie	AZL Padres 2	Arizona	26	30	.464	13th (18)	Aaron Levin
Overall 2018 Minor League Record			345	330	.511	11th (30)	

ORGANIZATION STATISTICS

SAN DIEGO PADRES
NATIONAL LEAGUE

Batting	B-T	HT	WT	DOB	AVG	vLH	vRH	G	AB	R	H	2B	3B	HR	RBI	BB	HBP	SH	SF	SO	SB	CS	SLG	OBP
Asuaje, Carlos	L-R	5-9	158	11-2-91	.196	.111	.230	79	189	15	37	8	1	2	19	24	1	1	3	46	1	1	.280	.286
Cordero, Franchy	L-R	6-3	175	9-2-94	.237	.205	.253	40	139	19	33	5	1	7	19	14	0	1	0	55	5	2	.439	.307
Ellis, A.J.	R-R	6-2	225	4-9-81	.272	.294	.253	66	151	19	41	8	0	1	15	26	1	3	2	37	0	0	.344	.378
Galvis, Freddy	B-R	5-10	185	11-14-89	.248	.291	.228	162	602	62	149	31	5	13	67	45	2	1	6	147	8	6	.380	.299
Guerra, Javy	L-R	5-11	155	9-25-95	.125	.000	.182	13	16	2	2	0	0	0	1	3	0	0	0	9	0	0	.125	.263
Headley, Chase	B-R	6-2	215	5-9-84	.115	.077	.128	27	52	2	6	1	0	0	4	6	2	0	0	20	0	0	.135	.233
Hedges, Austin	R-R	6-1	206	8-18-92	.231	.214	.238	91	303	29	70	14	2	14	37	21	1	0	1	90	3	0	.429	.282
Hosmer, Eric	L-L	6-4	225	10-24-89	.253	.179	.295	157	613	72	155	31	2	18	69	62	1	0	7	142	7	4	.398	.322
Jankowski, Travis	L-R	6-2	185	6-15-91	.259	.188	.276	117	347	45	90	12	3	4	17	37	1	2	0	73	24	7	.346	.333
Lopez, Raffy	L-R	5-9	200	10-2-87	.177	.308	.157	37	102	11	18	2	0	3	13	13	0	0	2	43	1	0	.284	.265
Margot, Manuel	R-R	5-11	180	9-28-94	.245	.238	.249	141	477	50	117	26	8	8	51	32	2	1	7	88	11	10	.384	.292
Mejia, Francisco	B-R	5-10	180	10-27-95	.185	.185	.185	20	54	6	10	2	0	2	0	3	8	3	1	0	19	0	0	.389	.241
Myers, Wil	R-R	6-3	205	12-10-90	.253	.248	.257	83	312	39	79	25	1	11	39	30	0	0	1	94	13	1	.446	.318
Pirela, Jose	R-R	6-0	220	11-21-89	.249	.260	.243	146	438	54	109	23	2	5	32	30	3	0	2	89	6	3	.345	.300
Renfroe, Hunter	R-R	6-1	220	1-28-92	.248	.253	.245	117	403	53	100	23	1	26	68	30	3	0	5	109	2	1	.504	.302
Reyes, Franmil	R-R	6-5	275	7-7-95	.280	.349	.247	87	261	36	73	9	0	16	31	24	0	0	0	80	0	0	.498	.340
Spangenberg, Cory	L-R	6-0	195	3-16-91	.235	.141	.261	116	298	35	70	9	4	7	25	25	2	4	0	108	6	1	.362	.299
Szczur, Matt	R-R	6-0	200	7-20-89	.187	.172	.196	57	75	11	14	3	0	1	6	8	0	1	0	24	3	0	.267	.265
Urias, Luis	R-R	5-9	185	6-3-97	.208	.462	.114	12	48	5	10	1	0	2	5	3	1	0	1	10	1	0	.354	.264
Villanueva, Christian	R-R	5-11	210	6-19-91	.237	.336	.189	110	351	42	83	15	0	20	46	23	9	0	1	104	3	0	.450	.300

Pitching	B-T	HT	WT	DOB	W	L	ERA	G	GS	CG	SV	IP	H	R	ER	HR	BB	SO	AVG	vLH	vRH	K/9	BB/9
Baumann, Buddy	L-L	5-11	198	12-9-87	0	1	54.00	1	0	0	0	0	2	5	2	0	2	0	.667	1.000	.000	0.00	54.00
2-team total (3 New York)					0	2	27.00	4	0	0	0	3	9	13	10	1	7	4	.474	.571	.417	10.80	18.90
Brewer, Colten	R-R	6-4	230	10-29-92	1	0	5.59	11	0	0	0	10	15	10	6	0	7	10	.357	.350	.364	9.31	6.52
Castillo, Jose	L-L	6-5	246	1-10-96	3	3	3.29	37	0	0	0	38	23	14	14	3	12	52	.170	.133	.189	12.21	2.82
Cimber, Adam	R-R	6-4	180	8-15-90	3	5	3.17	42	0	0	0	48	42	19	17	2	10	51	.237	.293	.210	9.50	1.86
Diaz, Miguel	R-R	6-0	214	11-28-94	1	0	4.82	11	0	0	0	19	16	11	10	2	12	30	.225	.188	.256	14.46	5.79
Erlin, Robbie	R-L	6-0	190	10-8-90	4	7	4.21	39	12	0	0	109	112	57	51	12	12	88	.267	.265	.269	7.27	0.99
Hand, Brad	L-L	6-3	228	3-20-90	2	4	3.05	41	0	0	24	44	33	21	15	5	15	65	.203	.148	.229	13.20	3.05
Hughes, Phil	R-R	6-5	240	6-24-86	0	0	6.10	16	0	0	0	21	30	14	14	7	5	24	.326	.390	.275	10.45	2.18
Kennedy, Brett	R-R	6-0	200	8-4-94	1	2	6.75	6	6	0	0	27	36	20	20	6	12	18	.330	.250	.415	6.08	4.05
Lauer, Eric	R-L	6-3	205	6-3-95	6	7	4.34	23	23	0	0	112	127	61	54	15	46	100	.285	.293	.282	8.04	3.70
Lockett, Walker	R-R	6-5	225	5-3-94	0	3	9.60	4	3	0	0	15	22	16	16	4	10	12	.333	.395	.250	7.20	6.00
Lucchesi, Joey	L-L	6-5	204	6-6-93	8	9	4.08	26	26	0	0	130	125	64	59	23	43	145	.254	.245	.256	10.04	2.98
Lyles, Jordan	R-R	6-4	250	10-19-90	2	4	4.29	24	8	0	0	71	71	35	34	12	19	62	.259	.190	.314	7.82	2.40
2-team total (11 Milwaukee)					3	4	4.11	35	8	0	0	88	83	42	40	12	28	84	.249	.185	.300	8.62	2.87
Makita, Kazuhisa	R-R	5-10	181	11-10-84	0	1	5.40	27	0	0	0	35	32	23	21	7	12	37	.241	.274	.211	9.51	3.09
Maton, Phil	R-R	6-3	220	3-25-93	0	2	4.37	45	0	0	0	47	50	25	23	3	23	55	.269	.253	.283	10.46	4.37
McGrath, Kyle	L-L	6-2	185	7-31-92	0	0	4.50	4	0	0	0	4	3	2	2	2	3	4	.200	.125	.286	9.00	6.75
Mitchell, Bryan	L-R	6-3	210	4-19-91	2	4	5.42	16	11	0	0	73	85	45	44	12	43	38	.294	.260	.323	4.68	5.30
Nix, Jacob	R-R	6-4	220	1-9-96	2	5	7.02	9	9	0	0	42	52	33	33	8	13	21	.304	.320	.282	4.46	2.76
Perdomo, Luis	R-R	6-2	185	5-9-93	1	6	7.05	12	10	0	0	45	62	37	35	4	22	39	.328	.343	.310	7.86	4.43
Richard, Clayton	L-L	6-5	240	9-12-83	7	11	5.33	27	27	0	0	159	159	98	94	19	60	108	.263	.242	.269	6.13	3.40
Ross, Tyson	R-R	6-6	245	4-22-87	6	9	4.45	22	22	0	0	123	112	64	61	16	52	107	.240	.295	.177	7.81	3.79
2-team total (9 St. Louis)					8	9	4.15	31	23	0	0	150	132	73	69	17	62	122	.237	.294	.176	7.34	3.73
Stammen, Craig	R-R	6-4	230	3-9-84	8	3	2.73	73	0	0	0	79	65	25	24	3	17	88	.221	.248	.199	10.03	1.94
Stock, Robert	L-R	6-1	214	11-21-89	1	1	2.50	32	0	0	0	40	37	13	11	1	13	38	.247	.282	.215	8.62	2.95
Strahm, Matt	R-L	6-3	185	11-12-91	3	4	2.05	41	5	0	0	61	39	16	14	6	21	69	.178	.246	.149	10.13	3.08
Webb, Tyler	L-L	6-5	230	7-20-90	0	1	12.60	4	0	0	0	5	6	7	7	2	3	4	.286	.364	.200	7.20	5.40
2-team total (18 St. Louis)					0	1	4.43	22	0	0	0	22	22	15	10	3	9	15	.279	.238	.324	6.64	3.98
Wick, Rowan	L-R	6-3	234	11-9-92	0	1	6.48	10	0	0	0	8	13	6	6	1	1	7	.351	.278	.421	7.56	1.08
Wieck, Brad	L-L	6-9	255	10-14-91	0	0	1.29	5	0	0	0	7	3	1	1	0	10	.125	.083	.167	12.86	0.00
Wingenter, Trey	R-R	6-7	200	4-15-94	0	0	3.79	22	0	0	0	19	13	8	8	3	11	27	.191	.152	.229	12.79	5.21

Yates, Kirby	L-R	5-10	210	3-25-87	5	3	2.14	65	0	0	12	63	41	15	15	6	17	90	.181	.235	.137	12.86	2.43

SAN DIEGO PADRES

Fielding

Catcher	PCT	G	PO	A	E	DP	PB
Ellis	.997	44	321	22	1	2	3
Hedges	.986	83	748	34	11	3	4
Lopez	.996	30	254	20	1	2	1
Mejia	1.000	10	103	4	0	0	4

First Base	PCT	G	PO	A	E	DP
Headley	1.000	3	17	3	0	2
Hosmer	.997	157	1231	106	4	113
Lopez	1.000	1	1	0	0	1
Myers	1.000	2	11	1	0	1
Pirela	1.000	9	22	2	0	0
Villanueva	1.000	3	15	1	0	3

Second Base	PCT	G	PO	A	E	DP
Asuaje	.995	61	72	128	1	23
Galvis	1.000	5	7	9	0	1
Pirela	.973	77	99	158	7	34
Spangenberg	.986	49	60	77	2	20
Urias	1.000	12	18	29	0	9
Villanueva	.900	2	3	6	1	3

Third Base	PCT	G	PO	A	E	DP
Asuaje	.833	5	3	2	1	0
Guerra	.000	1	0	0	0	0
Headley	.947	11	6	12	1	4
Lopez	.000	1	0	0	0	0
Myers	.934	36	32	53	6	4
Spangenberg	.953	44	18	64	4	5
Villanueva	.947	96	49	167	12	17

Shortstop	PCT	G	PO	A	E	DP
Galvis	.986	160	222	399	9	80
Guerra	.920	7	12	11	2	3
Spangenberg	.000	1	0	0	0	0
Villanueva	1.000	4	1	4	0	0

Outfield	PCT	G	PO	A	E	DP
Cordero	.955	37	61	2	3	0
Ellis	.000	1	0	0	0	0
Jankowski	.989	101	185	2	2	0
Margot	.990	136	286	2	3	0
Myers	1.000	41	74	3	0	0
Pirela	.959	34	44	3	2	1
Renfroe	.961	103	192	6	8	1
Reyes	.982	75	107	2	2	0
Spangenberg	1.000	5	4	0	0	0
Szczur	1.000	32	22	1	0	0

EL PASO CHIHUAHUAS   TRIPLE-A
PACIFIC COAST LEAGUE

Batting	B-T	HT	WT	DOB	AVG	vLH	vRH	G	AB	R	H	2B	3B	HR	RBI	BB	HBP	SH	SF	SO	SB	CS	SLG	OBP
Allday, Forrestt	L-L	5-11	190	4-24-91	.281	.264	.287	80	288	54	81	16	3	4	35	34	14	0	1	52	11	2	.399	.383
Asuaje, Carlos	L-R	5-9	158	11-2-91	.314	.311	.315	47	175	33	55	10	5	2	19	16	5	2	1	26	0	1	.463	.386
Batten, Matthew	R-R	5-11	180	6-22-95	.167	1.000	.000	2	6	2	1	0	0	0	0	4	0	0	0	3	0	0	.167	.500
Bousfield, Auston	R-R	5-11	185	7-5-93	.239	.338	.198	87	272	42	65	17	2	2	26	38	3	1	5	63	3	5	.338	.333
Coleman, Dusty	R-R	6-2	205	4-20-87	.202	.167	.213	103	302	42	61	20	0	13	36	23	4	0	0	146	7	4	.397	.268
Cordero, Franchy	L-R	6-3	175	9-2-94	.259	.000	.412	7	27	3	7	1	0	1	1	4	0	0	0	10	3	0	.407	.355
Craig, Allen	R-R	6-2	215	7-18-84	.293	.325	.283	92	317	52	93	18	1	13	59	39	4	0	3	73	0	0	.480	.375
France, Ty	R-R	6-0	205	7-13-94	.287	.321	.273	25	94	18	27	8	0	5	19	13	2	0	1	19	0	0	.532	.382
Goris, Diego	R-R	5-11	200	11-8-90	.265	.247	.272	89	325	41	86	20	1	7	53	16	0	1	0	77	4	2	.397	.299
Guerra, Javy	L-R	5-11	155	9-25-95	.223	.230	.221	122	430	52	96	18	9	13	55	27	0	6	1	166	2	0	.398	.269
Hedges, Austin	R-R	6-1	206	8-18-92	.407	.400	.409	7	27	7	11	3	0	3	11	3	0	0	1	9	0	0	.852	.452
Jankowski, Travis	L-R	6-2	185	6-15-91	.363	.214	.394	22	80	17	29	4	0	1	11	11	2	1	0	21	4	3	.450	.452
Kennedy, A.J.	R-R	6-0	190	1-23-94	.152	.231	.121	20	46	3	7	3	0	1	3	0	0	0	1	19	0	0	.283	.149
Lopez, Raffy	L-R	5-9	200	10-2-87	.261	.268	.259	50	180	27	47	12	1	9	38	11	0	2		56	0	0	.489	.328
McGee, Stephen	R-R	6-3	215	2-7-91	.136	.167	.125	18	44	5	6	2	0	1	4	5	0	0	0	23	0	0	.250	.225
2-team total (14 Salt Lake)					.184	.286	.152	32	87	14	16	6	0	1	10	6	0	0	0	39	0	0	.287	.311
Mejia, Francisco	B-R	5-10	180	10-27-95	.328	.389	.302	31	122	22	40	8	1	7	23	7	1	0	2	25	0	0	.582	.364
Myers, Wil	R-R	6-3	205	12-10-90	.300	.300	.333	5	20	3	6	3	0	1	3	0	0	0	0	7	1	0	.600	.300
Nicholas, Brett	L-R	6-2	220	7-18-88	.291	.238	.309	117	412	65	120	30	1	16	83	37	4	0	3	86	1	1	.485	.353
Peterson, Shane	L-L	6-0	225	2-11-88	.286	.297	.283	126	426	61	122	31	3	11	74	35	2	2	1	113	1	0	.451	.343
Renfroe, Hunter	R-R	6-1	220	1-28-92	.220	.364	.167	10	41	6	9	1	0	2	4	2	0	0	0	10	0	0	.390	.256
Reyes, Franmil	R-R	6-5	275	7-7-95	.324	.359	.316	58	210	50	68	11	1	16	52	37	2	0	1	59	0	0	.614	.428
Roman, Luis	L-R	6-0	215	12-19-94	—	—	—	1	0	0	0	0	0	0	0	0	1	0	0	0	0	0	—	1.000
Schulz, Nick	R-R	6-3	210	5-3-91	.228	.237	.226	62	162	17	37	8	0	1	16	18	3	0	2	55	2	0	.296	.314
Spangenberg, Cory	L-R	6-0	195	3-16-91	.341	.313	.347	21	88	14	30	8	2	4	16	6	0	1	0	21	0	0	.614	.383
Stevens, River	R-R	6-0	185	1-10-92	.143	.000	.250	3	7	0	1	0	0	0	1	0	0	0	0	0	0	0	.143	.250
Szczur, Matt	R-R	6-0	200	7-20-89	.316	.250	.333	10	38	4	12	3	1	0	9	4	0	0	0	7	0	0	.447	.372
Urias, Luis	R-R	5-9	185	6-3-97	.296	.317	.289	120	450	83	133	30	7	8	45	67	11	3	2	109	2	1	.447	.398

Pitching	B-T	HT	WT	DOB	W	L	ERA	G	GS	CG	SV	IP	H	R	ER	HR	BB	SO	AVG	vLH	vRH	K/9	BB/9
Allen, Logan	R-L	6-3	200	5-23-97	4	0	1.63	5	5	0	0	28	21	7	5	4	13	26	.206	.143	.230	8.46	4.23
Aro, Jonathan	R-R	6-0	235	10-10-90	2	3	3.68	38	0	0	2	44	38	19	18	3	19	36	.241	.203	.274	7.36	3.89
Baumann, Buddy	L-L	5-11	198	12-9-87	0	0	0.00	3	0	0	1	7	2	0	0	0	5	9	.095	.083	.111	12.15	6.75
2-team total (26 Las Vegas)					1	0	4.78	34	0	0	1	32	29	20	17	5	17	35	.234	.211	.244	9.84	4.78
Blueberg, Colby	R-R	6-0	185	5-11-93	0	0	18.00	1	0	0	0	1	3	2	2	0	0	1	.500	.500	.500	9.00	0.00
Boushley, Caleb	R-R	6-3	188	10-1-93	0	0	9.00	1	0	0	0	1	1	1	1	0	0	0	.333	.500	.000	0.00	0.00
Brewer, Colten	R-R	6-4	230	10-29-92	3	4	3.75	37	0	0	3	48	40	24	20	3	15	63	.229	.186	.257	11.81	2.81
Capps, Carter	R-R	6-5	230	8-7-90	1	1	1.00	8	0	0	0	9	4	2	1	0	7	9	.121	.077	.150	9.00	7.00
Carkuff, Jared	R-R	6-3	180	8-25-93	0	0	27.00	1	0	0	0	1	3	3	3	0	2	1	.600	.500	.667	9.00	18.00
Castillo, Jose	L-L	6-5	246	1-10-96	1	0	0.79	10	0	0	3	11	6	3	1	1	2	13	.150	.100	.167	10.32	1.59
Diaz, Miguel	R-R	6-0	214	11-28-94	0	3	8.10	5	2	0	0	13	17	12	12	2	13	15	.304	.474	.216	10.13	8.78
Huffman, Chris	R-R	6-1	205	11-25-92	3	5	6.91	16	14	0	0	70	98	57	54	10	32	40	.343	.329	.357	5.12	4.09
Johnson, Erik	R-R	6-3	230	12-30-89	0	2	8.00	7	0	0	0	9	12	8	8	3	3	12	.316	.333	.300	12.00	3.00
Keel, Jerry	L-L	6-4	240	9-26-93	4	1	4.68	12	8	0	0	58	63	32	30	7	19	35	.278	.216	.307	5.46	2.97
Kennedy, Brett	R-R	6-0	200	8-4-94	10	2	2.72	16	16	0	0	89	77	32	27	6	23	80	.233	.296	.185	8.06	2.32
Lauer, Eric	R-L	6-3	205	6-3-95	2	1	2.53	4	4	0	0	21	13	6	6	1	9	18	.171	.208	.157	9.28	3.80
Lloyd, Kyle	R-R	6-4	220	10-16-90	3	2	5.59	15	9	0	0	47	51	29	29	5	19	42	.280	.303	.264	8.10	3.66
Lockett, Walker	R-R	6-5	225	5-3-94	5	9	4.73	23	23	0	0	133	145	87	70	17	33	118	.279	.324	.250	7.97	2.23
Lucchesi, Joey	L-L	6-5	204	6-6-93	0	1	23.63	1	1	0	0	3	7	7	7	1	4	5	.500	1.000	.250	6.75	13.50
Lyles, Jordan	R-R	6-4	230	10-19-90	0	2	17.47	2	2	0	0	6	14	11	11	4	2	4	.452	.556	.409	6.35	3.18
Makita, Kazuhisa	R-R	5-10	181	11-10-84	1	1	3.76	24	0	0	0	26	32	11	11	1	10	22	.235	.250	.227	7.52	3.42
Mariot, Michael	R-R	6-0	190	10-20-88	0	1	12.15	10	1	0	1	13	23	18	18	5	7	14	.377	.412	.333	9.45	4.73

	B-T	HT	WT	DOB	W	L	ERA	G	GS	CG	SV	IP	H	R	ER	HR	BB	SO	AVG	vLH	vRH	K/9	BB/9
2-team total (18 Omaha)					1	3	6.48	28	3	0	3	42	46	30	30	8	14	45	.277	.338	.235	9.72	3.02
Maton, Phil	R-R	6-3	220	3-25-93	0	0	2.84	6	0	0	2	6	5	2	2	0	1	10	.200	.273	.143	14.21	1.42
McGrath, Kyle	L-L	6-2	185	7-31-92	7	3	2.75	43	0	0	0	52	42	19	16	6	18	42	.219	.162	.254	7.22	3.10
Nix, Jacob	R-R	6-4	220	1-9-96	1	0	0.00	1	1	0	0	6	5	0	0	0	0	3	.250	.400	.200	4.50	0.00
Overton, Dillon	L-L	6-2	175	8-17-91	7	2	2.90	16	13	0	0	81	70	27	26	10	22	48	.234	.200	.249	5.36	2.45
Perdomo, Luis	R-R	6-2	185	5-9-93	6	3	3.72	13	13	1	0	75	72	33	31	12	21	61	.255	.282	.236	7.32	2.52
Quantrill, Cal	L-R	6-3	208	2-10-95	3	1	3.48	6	6	0	0	31	39	17	12	4	5	22	.300	.286	.311	6.39	1.45
Radke, Travis	L-L	6-4	237	3-6-93	0	0	0.00	3	0	0	1	4	0	0	0	0	1	0	.000	.000	.000	0.00	2.45
Ramirez, Emmanuel	R-R	6-2	190	7-15-94	0	0	2.25	1	0	0	0	4	3	1	1	0	2	5	.200	.250	.182	11.25	4.50
Rea, Colin	R-R	6-5	225	7-1-90	3	2	5.08	12	9	0	0	51	58	33	29	11	23	49	.293	.271	.310	8.59	4.03
Schlichtholz, Fred	R-L	6-3	215	9-18-95	0	0	0.00	1	0	0	0	3	2	0	0	0	4	0	.182	.250	.143	12.00	0.00
Scholtens, Jesse	R-R	6-4	230	4-6-94	1	4	8.38	8	6	0	0	29	39	29	27	4	10	21	.320	.283	.342	6.52	3.10
Simmons, Seth	R-R	5-9	170	6-14-88	1	1	4.12	13	6	0	1	39	38	20	18	10	20	23	.259	.276	.247	5.26	4.58
Stock, Robert	L-R	6-1	214	11-21-89	0	0	1.59	24	0	0	8	28	15	8	5	2	11	27	.158	.180	.143	8.58	3.49
Webb, Tyler	L-L	6-5	230	7-20-90	1	1	2.05	19	0	0	0	22	20	6	5	1	8	28	.244	.314	.192	11.45	3.27
2-team total (11 Memphis)					1	1	2.16	30	1	0	0	42	29	11	10	2	12	49	.200	.298	.136	10.58	2.59
Weir, T.J.	R-R	6-0	212	9-15-91	2	1	3.57	27	0	0	1	45	38	20	18	3	23	37	.232	.236	.228	7.35	4.57
Wick, Rowan	L-R	6-3	234	11-9-92	2	0	1.99	20	0	0	9	23	16	6	5	3	10	22	.193	.222	.170	8.74	3.97
Wieck, Brad	L-L	6-9	255	10-14-91	3	0	3.44	17	0	0	2	18	16	8	7	2	9	34	.229	.226	.231	16.69	4.42
Wingenter, Trey	R-R	6-7	200	4-15-94	3	3	3.45	40	0	0	4	44	29	19	17	4	24	53	.186	.193	.182	10.76	4.87
Yardley, Eric	R-R	6-0	165	8-18-90	3	0	5.40	14	0	0	1	22	25	13	13	2	7	10	.291	.242	.321	4.15	2.91

Fielding

Catcher	PCT	G	PO	A	E	DP	PB
Hedges	.981	6	46	6	1	1	0
Kennedy	.980	15	93	3	2	0	0
Lopez	.987	34	278	24	4	0	4
McGee	.989	12	84	5	1	2	1
Mejia	.995	26	174	11	1	1	1
Nicholas	.993	55	412	27	3	2	8

First Base	PCT	G	PO	A	E	DP
Craig	.993	63	530	36	4	52
France	.962	9	47	4	2	6
Goris	.995	29	204	13	1	18
Nicholas	.992	48	361	25	3	42

Second Base	PCT	G	PO	A	E	DP
Asuaje	.967	26	29	60	3	13
Batten	1.000	2	3	9	0	0

	PCT	G	PO	A	E	DP	PB
Coleman	.966	17	38	47	3	14	
Goris	1.000	2	3	6	0	1	
Guerra	1.000	2	4	3	0	0	
Spangenberg	1.000	5	4	9	0	3	
Stevens	1.000	2	4	5	0	2	
Urias	.990	90	136	250	4	65	

Third Base	PCT	G	PO	A	E	DP
Asuaje	.974	19	5	33	1	4
Coleman	.961	35	28	70	4	5
France	.982	19	12	43	1	2
Goris	.968	54	28	122	5	17
Spangenberg	.941	13	8	24	2	2
Urias	.893	11	7	18	3	3

Shortstop	PCT	G	PO	A	E	DP
Coleman	.958	9	5	18	1	3

	PCT	G	PO	A	E	DP
Guerra	.973	118	168	294	13	71
Urias	.975	20	33	45	2	8
Outfield	**PCT**	**G**	**PO**	**A**	**E**	**DP**
Allday	.962	75	148	5	6	0
Bousfield	1.000	78	193	6	0	2
Coleman	1.000	32	76	3	0	0
Cordero	1.000	6	6	0	0	0
Craig	1.000	8	14	0	0	0
Jankowski	.962	20	48	3	2	0
Myers	1.000	5	10	0	0	0
Peterson	.980	105	185	9	4	0
Renfroe	1.000	9	23	2	0	0
Reyes	.954	46	82	1	4	1
Schulz	.985	46	66	1	1	0
Spangenberg	1.000	2	3	0	0	0
Szczur	1.000	10	22	0	0	0

SAN ANTONIO MISSIONS
TEXAS LEAGUE

DOUBLE-A

Batting	B-T	HT	WT	DOB	AVG	vLH	vRH	G	AB	R	H	2B	3B	HR	RBI	BB	HBP	SH	SF	SO	SB	CS	SLG	OBP
Allday, Forrestt	L-L	5-11	190	4-24-91	.248	.317	.221	41	145	18	36	5	0	0	4	18	0	2	0	31	0	2	.283	.331
Allen, Austin	L-R	6-2	220	1-16-94	.291	.252	.305	119	451	59	131	31	0	22	56	37	7	0	3	97	0	3	.506	.351
Batten, Matthew	R-R	5-11	180	6-22-95	.260	.275	.254	63	181	22	47	6	1	2	18	29	2	3	0	55	11	2	.337	.368
Bousfield, Auston	R-R	5-11	185	7-5-93	.250	.368	.143	12	40	7	10	3	1	0	3	5	2	0	0	8	4	1	.375	.362
Boykin, Rod	R-R	6-1	175	4-17-95	.214	.233	.205	67	224	33	48	5	3	4	23	21	2	1	0	106	8	2	.317	.287
France, Ty	R-R	6-0	205	7-13-94	.263	.258	.265	112	415	66	109	22	2	17	77	33	25	1	5	70	3	4	.448	.349
Gettys, Michael	R-R	6-1	203	10-22-95	.230	.208	.239	125	431	51	99	22	3	15	53	31	6	4	1	160	17	6	.399	.290
Giron, Ruddy	R-R	6-0	205	1-4-97	.231	.000	.286	9	26	4	6	2	0	1	2	1	0	1	0	9	0	0	.423	.259
Kohlwey, Taylor	L-L	6-3	200	7-20-94	.265	.074	.294	72	204	25	54	8	4	6	22	25	6	3	2	58	4	4	.431	.359
Naylor, Josh	L-L	5-11	250	6-22-97	.297	.307	.294	128	501	72	149	22	1	17	74	64	7	0	2	69	5	5	.447	.383
Overstreet, Kyle	R-R	5-11	205	9-4-93	.272	.328	.250	124	470	45	128	23	1	9	46	32	3	0	2	75	2	0	.383	.322
Potts, Hudson	R-R	6-3	205	10-28-98	.154	.000	.185	22	78	5	12	0	0	2	5	10	1	0	0	33	1	0	.231	.258
Reed, Buddy	B-R	6-4	210	4-27-95	.179	.184	.177	43	179	21	32	7	0	1	15	12	0	1	3	63	18	3	.235	.227
Rivas, Webster	R-R	6-2	218	8-8-90	.277	.281	.275	57	217	19	60	7	1	4	23	13	1	1	1	47	1	1	.373	.319
Rosario, Eguy	R-R	5-9	150	8-25-99	.200	.000	.200	3	11	2	2	0	0	0	2	2	1	0	0	5	1	0	.182	.357
Schulz, Nick	R-R	6-3	210	5-3-91	.173	.194	.165	44	127	14	22	3	0	6	13	22	3	0	0	45	2	3	.339	.309
Stevens, River	L-R	6-0	185	1-10-92	.265	.245	.274	49	155	20	41	2	1	4	29	17	2	0	0	22	5	3	.368	.345
Tansel, Deion	R-R	5-8	155	6-4-94	.000	.000	.000	2	7	0	0	0	0	0	1	0	1	0	0	1	0	0	.000	.125
Tatis Jr., Fernando	R-R	6-3	185	1-2-99	.286	.255	.299	88	353	77	101	22	4	16	43	33	6	0	2	109	16	5	.507	.355
Van Gansen, Peter	L-R	5-9	175	3-4-94	.253	.232	.258	103	336	42	85	16	1	4	40	38	0	4	4	50	0	6	.342	.325

Pitching	B-T	HT	WT	DOB	W	L	ERA	G	GS	CG	SV	IP	H	R	ER	HR	BB	SO	AVG	vLH	vRH	K/9	BB/9
Allen, Logan	R-L	6-3	200	5-23-97	10	6	2.75	20	19	0	0	121	89	41	37	7	38	125	.205	.208	.204	9.30	2.83
Ashbeck, Elliot	L-R	6-3	220	11-16-93	1	2	7.50	7	1	0	0	12	18	10	10	1	4	13	.346	.400	.296	9.75	3.00
Bachar, Lake	R-R	6-3	215	6-3-95	3	7	5.59	20	14	0	1	87	99	56	54	15	38	62	.292	.289	.294	6.41	3.93
Baez, Michel	R-R	6-8	220	1-21-96	0	3	7.36	4	4	0	0	18	22	20	15	4	12	21	.301	.348	.280	10.31	5.89
Blueberg, Colby	R-R	6-0	185	5-11-93	1	1	3.91	16	0	0	0	25	29	13	11	3	9	31	.287	.435	.164	11.01	3.20
Carkuff, Jared	R-R	6-3	180	8-25-93	0	0	3.00	2	0	0	0	3	2	1	1	1	0	3	.182	.000	.222	9.00	0.00
Castillo, Jose	L-L	6-5	246	1-10-96	2	1	3.00	12	0	0	5	15	14	7	5	0	8	26	.246	.154	.273	15.60	4.80
Diaz, Miguel	R-R	6-0	214	11-28-94	5	2	2.35	19	9	0	2	65	45	21	17	4	30	66	.195	.205	.189	9.14	4.15
Frank, Trevor	R-R	6-0	195	6-23-91	1	0	2.11	12	0	0	1	21	18	6	5	2	4	15	.222	.200	.232	6.33	1.69
2-team total (10 Arkansas)					1	2	3.52	22	0	0	1	38	32	17	15	6	10	35	.219	.214	.222	8.22	2.35

Name	B-T	HT	WT	DOB	W	L	ERA	G	GS	CG	SV	IP	H	R	ER	HR	BB	SO	AVG	vLH	vRH	K/9	BB/9
Huffman, Chris	R-R	6-1	205	11-25-92	1	1	2.86	11	3	0	2	28	20	10	9	3	12	21	.202	.239	.170	6.67	3.81
Jester, Jason	R-R	5-11	205	5-4-91	2	4	4.33	40	0	0	0	60	69	34	29	2	13	56	.289	.287	.290	8.35	1.94
Johnson, Erik	R-R	6-3	230	12-30-89	3	3	2.84	19	0	0	0	32	27	12	10	4	9	33	.221	.245	.206	9.38	2.56
Keel, Jerry	L-L	6-6	240	9-26-93	6	3	4.55	16	16	0	0	91	99	46	46	9	22	73	.282	.214	.308	7.22	2.18
Maton, Phil	R-R	6-3	220	3-25-93	0	0	1.59	5	0	0	0	6	5	1	1	1	1	7	.227	.333	.188	11.12	1.59
Megill, Trevor	L-R	6-8	235	12-5-93	1	0	3.18	11	0	0	0	17	16	6	6	2	7	9	.254	.233	.273	4.76	3.71
Munoz, Andres	R-R	6-2	165	1-16-99	1	0	0.95	20	0	0	7	19	11	2	2	0	11	19	.175	.100	.242	9.00	5.21
Nix, Jacob	R-R	6-4	220	1-9-96	3	2	3.05	9	9	0	0	53	39	13	13	2	3	41	.211	.219	.207	7.01	1.54
Overton, Dillon	L-L	6-2	175	8-17-91	1	0	2.84	7	0	0	0	13	9	4	4	2	2	15	.192	.273	.167	10.66	1.42
Paddack, Chris	R-R	6-4	195	1-8-96	3	2	1.91	7	7	1	0	38	23	8	8	1	4	37	.177	.094	.234	8.84	0.96
Quantrill, Cal	L-R	6-3	208	2-10-95	6	5	5.15	22	22	0	0	117	135	78	67	12	38	101	.288	.311	.274	7.77	2.92
Radke, Travis	L-L	6-4	237	3-6-93	0	0	3.18	3	1	0	0	11	12	4	4	0	2	8	.300	.353	.261	6.35	1.59
Ramirez, Emmanuel	R-R	6-2	190	7-15-94	2	2	2.63	4	4	0	0	24	21	7	7	2	6	27	.241	.296	.186	10.13	2.25
Rea, Colin	R-R	6-5	225	7-1-90	0	3	7.13	6	6	0	0	24	32	21	19	3	13	21	.311	.290	.323	7.88	4.88
Reyes, Gerardo	R-R	5-11	160	5-13-93	1	2	3.00	31	0	0	1	39	32	20	13	1	17	49	.222	.193	.241	11.31	3.92
Scholtens, Jesse	R-R	6-4	230	4-6-94	7	4	3.00	19	18	0	0	108	95	43	36	5	24	98	.236	.241	.233	8.17	2.00
Sexton, Danny	R-L	6-0	195	6-30-95	0	0	40.50	1	0	0	0	1	5	6	6	0	2	2	.556	.750	.400	13.50	13.50
Simmons, Seth	R-R	5-9	170	6-14-88	1	1	3.00	5	2	0	0	15	12	5	5	1	4	13	.218	.286	.177	7.80	2.40
Stock, Robert	L-R	6-1	214	11-21-89	1	0	2.00	8	0	0	1	9	7	4	2	1	3	15	.200	.214	.191	15.00	3.00
Strahm, Matt	R-L	6-3	185	11-12-91	1	0	2.51	9	2	0	0	14	14	5	4	1	4	22	.259	.154	.293	13.81	2.51
Weir, T.J.	R-R	6-0	212	9-15-91	3	1	1.71	17	1	0	0	26	18	8	5	1	4	27	.192	.205	.180	9.23	1.37
Wick, Rowan	L-R	6-3	234	11-9-92	2	4	3.16	29	0	0	5	31	22	14	11	0	21	42	.198	.286	.158	12.06	6.03
Wieck, Brad	L-L	6-9	255	10-14-91	1	2	1.93	27	0	0	10	28	20	10	6	1	8	36	.191	.143	.214	11.57	2.57
Yardley, Eric	R-R	6-0	165	8-18-90	2	4	3.43	34	0	0	0	39	40	19	15	2	12	27	.276	.339	.236	6.18	2.75

Fielding

Catcher	PCT	G	PO	A	E	DP	PB
Allen	.994	91	745	80	5	5	3
Overstreet	.991	14	95	10	1	0	5
Rivas	.991	37	315	33	3	1	1

First Base	PCT	G	PO	A	E	DP
Allen	.980	19	137	12	3	7
Batten	1.000	3	10	1	0	3
France	1.000	1	1	0	0	1
Naylor	.986	29	198	10	3	12
Overstreet	.994	79	645	32	4	57
Rivas	.992	15	106	11	1	16

Second Base	PCT	G	PO	A	E	DP
Batten	.969	31	48	79	4	11

Catcher (cont.)	PCT	G	PO	A	E	DP
Giron	1.000	1	1	0	0	0
Overstreet	1.000	1	1	4	0	1
Rosario	1.000	3	5	7	0	1
Stevens	.981	26	52	54	2	10
Van Gansen	.983	82	132	206	6	43

Third Base	PCT	G	PO	A	E	DP
France	.951	101	71	161	12	10
Overstreet	.951	16	10	29	2	1
Potts	.932	21	15	40	4	4
Stevens	1.000	3	1	1	0	0

Shortstop	PCT	G	PO	A	E	DP
Batten	.950	23	43	53	5	15
Giron	1.000	4	5	15	0	5

(Catcher cont.)	PCT	G	PO	A	E	DP
Stevens	.988	18	33	52	1	18
Tatis Jr.	.961	83	117	207	13	34
Van Gansen	.980	15	14	35	1	3

Outfield	PCT	G	PO	A	E	DP
Allday	.974	30	35	2	1	0
Bousfield	1.000	2	2	2	0	1
Boykin	.984	62	119	1	2	0
Gettys	.989	118	254	16	3	5
Giron	.000	1	0	0	0	0
Kohlwey	.990	45	89	7	1	1
Naylor	.913	89	111	5	11	0
Reed	.984	43	121	4	2	2
Schulz	.971	24	34	0	1	0

LAKE ELSINORE STORM
CALIFORNIA LEAGUE

HIGH CLASS A

Batting	B-T	HT	WT	DOB	AVG	vLH	vRH	G	AB	R	H	2B	3B	HR	RBI	BB	HBP	SH	SF	SO	SB	CS	SLG	OBP
Baker, Chris	R-R	6-1	180	11-29-94	.248	.233	.251	64	218	30	54	10	2	4	27	13	4	2	1	68	3	0	.367	.301
Batten, Matthew	R-R	5-11	180	6-22-95	.342	.250	.351	13	41	7	14	2	0	0	4	6	0	0	0	12	1	0	.390	.426
Boykin, Rod	R-R	6-1	175	4-17-95	.203	.286	.187	36	128	13	26	5	2	2	17	4	2	1	1	61	2	3	.320	.237
Cantu, Michael	R-R	6-3	225	8-28-95	.194	.111	.222	11	36	4	7	0	0	2	4	3	0	0	0	13	0	0	.361	.256
Cordoba, Allen	R-R	6-1	175	12-6-95	.207	.069	.238	45	155	15	32	6	2	2	16	4	2	1	2	46	3	4	.310	.233
Curry, Michael	R-R	6-1	212	7-4-97	.375	—	.375	2	8	0	3	0	0	0	1	0	0	0	0	1	0	0	.375	.375
Easley, Nate	R-R	5-10	170	1-11-96	.273	.250	.280	102	355	51	97	26	4	5	44	37	1	0	3	90	10	4	.411	.341
Giron, Ruddy	R-R	6-0	205	1-4-97	.255	.326	.235	57	212	22	54	12	1	2	24	6	1	1	2	51	2	2	.349	.276
Greene Jr., Marcus	R-R	5-11	195	8-19-94	.256	.250	.257	51	168	21	43	7	0	2	21	17	1	0	0	45	0	0	.333	.328
Guzman, Luis	R-R	6-2	175	6-20-98	.150	.125	.156	14	40	4	6	2	1	0	3	7	0	0	0	11	1	0	.250	.277
Hedges, Austin	R-R	6-1	206	8-18-92	.333	1.000	.200	4	12	1	4	1	0	0	1	0	0	1	0	1	0	0	.417	.357
Jarmon, Hunter	R-R	6-0	195	3-2-95	.188	.000	.194	9	32	2	6	1	0	0	1	2	0	0	0	11	0	0	.219	.235
Kennedy, A.J.	R-R	6-0	190	1-23-94	.206	.214	.203	21	73	7	15	4	0	1	8	4	1	0	0	22	0	0	.301	.256
Kohlwey, Taylor	L-L	6-3	200	7-20-94	.196	.000	.214	17	46	7	9	3	0	2	9	5	1	1	1	17	1	0	.391	.283
Lambert, Greg	R-R	6-0	190	9-27-95	.065	.000	.087	10	31	3	2	0	0	0	1	3	0	1	0	17	0	0	.065	.147
Melean, Kelvin	R-R	6-0	165	9-5-98	.263	.533	.207	49	175	17	46	9	1	0	13	7	4	3	1	42	2	0	.326	.305
Myers, Wil	R-R	6-3	205	12-10-90	.143	.000	.167	4	14	2	2	0	0	2	3	1	0	0	0	3	0	0	.571	.200
Olivares, Edward	R-R	6-2	190	3-6-96	.277	.261	.281	129	531	79	147	25	10	12	62	29	8	1	6	102	21	8	.429	.321
Ona, Jorge	R-R	6-0	220	12-31-96	.239	.294	.223	100	368	44	88	24	2	8	44	33	7	0	2	110	0	2	.380	.312
Podorsky, Robbie	R-R	5-7	170	1-27-95	.211	.000	.235	5	19	4	4	0	1	0	2	0	0	0	0	4	1	1	.316	.211
Potts, Hudson	R-R	6-3	205	10-28-98	.281	.297	.276	106	406	66	114	35	1	17	58	37	7	1	2	112	3	1	.498	.350
Reed, Buddy	B-R	6-4	210	4-27-95	.324	.288	.332	79	315	54	102	21	7	12	47	24	1	1	2	84	33	7	.549	.371
Rosario, Eguy	R-R	5-9	150	8-25-99	.239	.220	.243	121	457	60	109	28	1	9	45	38	8	0	2	119	9	8	.363	.307
Tansel, Deion	R-R	5-8	155	6-4-94	.167	—	.167	2	6	0	1	0	0	0	0	0	0	0	0	1	0	0	.167	.286
Torrens, Luis	R-R	6-0	175	5-2-96	.280	.303	.274	122	475	62	133	36	3	6	73	26	6	0	8	77	1	1	.406	.320
Zunica, Brad	L-R	6-6	254	10-21-95	.251	.290	.243	123	431	55	108	20	3	17	60	53	8	0	5	148	0	0	.429	.340

Pitching	B-T	HT	WT	DOB	W	L	ERA	G	GS	CG	SV	IP	H	R	ER	HR	BB	SO	AVG	vLH	vRH	K/9	BB/9
Acevedo, Angel	R-R	6-1	180	9-19-98	0	1	5.06	1	1	0	0	5	5	3	3	2	2	3	.278	.300	.250	5.06	3.38
Anderson, Korey	R-R	6-2	205	9-11-94	0	0	4.05	5	0	0	0	7	7	3	3	1	2	9	.280	.375	.235	12.15	2.70
Ashbeck, Elliot	L-R	6-3	220	11-16-93	4	2	2.44	35	0	0	4	66	44	19	18	4	15	69	.191	.205	.184	9.36	2.04

	B-T	HT	WT	DOB	W	L	ERA	G	GS	CG	SV	IP	H	R	ER	HR	BB	SO	AVG	vLH	vRH	K/9	BB/9
Avila, Pedro	R-R	5-11	190	1-14-97	7	9	4.27	24	20	0	1	131	136	69	62	8	54	142	.270	.286	.260	9.78	3.72
Bachar, Lake	R-R	6-3	215	6-3-95	2	2	1.91	7	4	0	1	28	16	11	6	3	9	18	.167	.170	.163	5.72	2.86
Baez, Michel	R-R	6-8	220	1-21-96	4	7	2.91	17	17	0	0	87	73	32	28	5	33	92	.229	.260	.208	9.55	3.43
Bednar, David	L-R	6-1	220	10-10-94	2	4	2.73	47	0	0	10	69	65	29	21	4	29	96	.246	.227	.260	12.46	3.76
Blueberg, Colby	R-R	6-0	185	5-11-93	4	1	3.24	18	0	0	1	25	21	15	9	1	13	27	.226	.333	.158	9.72	4.68
Bolanos, Ronald	R-R	6-3	200	8-23-96	6	9	5.11	25	23	0	0	125	138	84	71	13	50	118	.282	.325	.254	8.50	3.60
Boushley, Caleb	R-R	6-3	188	10-1-93	1	1	3.09	6	1	0	0	12	10	4	4	2	1	12	.233	.278	.200	9.26	0.77
Capps, Carter	R-R	6-5	230	8-7-90	0	0	5.73	13	0	0	1	22	21	15	14	4	8	20	.247	.286	.220	8.18	3.27
Colletti, Tom	R-R	6-3	220	6-22-95	1	0	0.00	3	0	0	1	4	1	0	0	0	0	3	.091	.000	.125	7.36	0.00
Erb, Dalton	R-R	6-8	250	5-13-94	0	0	18.00	1	0	0	0	1	2	2	2	0	1	1	.400	.000	.500	9.00	9.00
Lauer, Eric	R-L	6-3	205	6-3-95	0	0	0.00	1	1	0	0	3	3	0	0	0	1	4	.300	.500	.167	12.00	0.00
Lawson, Reggie	R-R	6-4	205	8-2-97	8	5	4.69	24	22	0	0	117	130	69	61	11	51	117	.280	.279	.280	9.00	3.92
Leashar, Aaron	L-L	6-3	208	4-28-96	1	2	4.29	4	3	0	0	21	28	13	10	2	11	21	.329	.222	.379	9.00	4.71
Lopez, Diomar	R-R	6-0	165	12-15-96	0	0	9.90	6	0	0	0	10	16	13	11	3	4	7	.372	.313	.407	6.30	3.60
Lucchesi, Joey	L-L	6-5	204	6-6-93	0	0	0.00	1	1	0	0	4	0	0	0	0	0	6	.000	.000	.000	13.50	0.00
Margevicius, Nick	L-L	6-5	220	6-18-96	5	3	4.30	10	9	0	0	59	69	31	28	5	8	59	.297	.211	.340	9.05	1.23
Maton, Phil	R-R	6-3	220	3-25-93	0	0	0.00	1	0	0	0	1	2	0	0	0	1	2	.400	.000	.667	18.00	9.00
Megill, Trevor	L-R	6-8	235	12-5-93	1	1	3.20	13	0	0	1	20	13	7	7	3	1	22	.186	.200	.175	14.64	0.46
Mitchell, Bryan	R-R	6-3	210	4-19-91	1	3	4.13	6	6	0	0	28	23	19	13	6	12	28	.223	.163	.278	8.89	3.81
Morejon, Adrian	L-L	6-0	175	2-27-99	4	4	3.30	13	13	0	0	63	54	27	23	6	24	70	.233	.188	.252	10.05	3.45
Paddack, Chris	R-R	6-4	195	1-8-96	4	1	2.24	10	10	0	0	52	43	13	13	3	4	83	.223	.187	.246	14.27	0.69
Radke, Travis	L-L	6-4	237	3-6-93	0	1	2.70	4	0	0	1	7	7	3	2	0	2	6	.304	.143	.375	8.10	2.70
Ramirez, Emmanuel	R-R	6-2	190	7-15-94	5	4	5.43	23	9	0	0	71	72	52	43	13	24	78	.257	.280	.246	9.84	3.03
Reyes, Gerardo	R-R	5-11	160	5-13-93	0	1	2.20	14	0	0	1	16	11	4	4	0	12	20	.200	.120	.267	11.02	6.61
Rodriguez, Hansel	R-R	6-2	170	2-27-97	2	0	3.86	8	0	0	0	9	4	4	4	2	5	11	.129	.000	.174	10.61	4.82
Rogers, Blake	R-R	6-2	200	2-23-94	3	3	4.84	47	0	0	3	58	57	35	31	5	29	70	.253	.305	.224	10.92	4.53
Sheckler, Ben	L-L	6-8	276	5-12-95	0	0	10.38	2	0	0	0	4	9	5	5	1	2	5	.429	.571	.357	10.38	4.15
Smith, Austin	R-R	6-4	220	7-9-96	0	2	7.56	21	0	0	0	33	39	32	28	3	24	33	.293	.323	.268	8.91	6.48
Tyler, Cody	L-L	6-0	180	10-26-94	2	2	3.98	15	0	0	0	20	23	9	9	1	7	19	.284	.233	.314	8.41	3.15
Valdez, Dauris	R-R	6-8	221	10-22-95	1	4	4.39	48	0	0	13	53	46	32	26	4	29	76	.224	.167	.265	12.83	4.89
Wilson, Steven	R-R	6-3	185	8-24-94	0	0	18.00	2	0	0	0	3	8	6	6	2	3	3	.471	.500	.455	9.00	9.00

Fielding

Catcher	PCT	G	PO	A	E	DP	PB
Cantu	.985	6	61	3	1	0	0
Greene Jr.	.995	38	351	27	2	1	8
Hedges	1.000	3	31	3	0	0	1
Kennedy	1.000	13	133	14	0	0	2
Torrens	.984	85	765	76	14	8	21

First Base	PCT	G	PO	A	E	DP
Batten	1.000	2	11	0	0	1
Cantu	1.000	1	8	0	0	2
Giron	1.000	1	3	0	0	0
Greene Jr.	1.000	8	58	4	0	13
Potts	.946	8	32	3	2	5
Torrens	1.000	3	18	0	0	1
Zunica	.978	122	779	57	19	89

Second Base	PCT	G	PO	A	E	DP
Baker	.965	16	21	34	2	12
Batten	1.000	4	4	7	0	2

	PCT	G	PO	A	E	DP
Easley	1.000	6	14	9	0	2
Giron	.968	15	39	21	2	8
Guzman	.000	1	0	0	0	0
Melean	1.000	2	9	8	0	3
Rosario	.971	101	193	208	12	61
Tansel	1.000	1	2	2	0	1

Third Base	PCT	G	PO	A	E	DP
Batten	1.000	3	2	5	0	0
Giron	.929	14	6	20	2	3
Guzman	1.000	13	9	13	0	1
Melean	1.000	3	2	7	0	0
Myers	1.000	1	1	1	0	0
Potts	.954	99	76	150	11	19
Rosario	.880	14	9	13	3	3

Shortstop	PCT	G	PO	A	E	DP
Baker	.946	48	61	97	9	29
Batten	1.000	3	1	4	0	0
Cordoba	.963	32	47	58	4	20

	PCT	G	PO	A	E	DP
Giron	.854	15	16	25	7	6
Melean	.897	43	50	89	16	26
Rosario	1.000	1	4	1	0	0
Tansel	.667	1	0	2	1	0

Outfield	PCT	G	PO	A	E	DP
Batten	.000	1	0	0	0	0
Boykin	.958	35	67	3	3	0
Cordoba	1.000	4	6	1	0	0
Curry	1.000	2	2	0	0	0
Easley	.990	90	182	13	2	4
Jarmon	1.000	8	11	2	0	0
Kohlwey	.882	14	15	0	2	0
Lambert	.900	9	17	1	2	1
Myers	1.000	2	2	0	0	0
Olivares	.973	126	275	11	8	5
Ona	.973	59	103	5	3	1
Podorsky	.923	5	12	0	1	0
Reed	.987	78	141	8	2	1

FORT WAYNE TINCAPS

LOW CLASS A

MIDWEST LEAGUE

Batting	B-T	HT	WT	DOB	AVG	vLH	vRH	G	AB	R	H	2B	3B	HR	RBI	BB	HBP	SH	SF	SO	SB	CS	SLG	OBP
Almanzar, Luis	R-R	6-0	187	11-1-99	.177	.225	.163	63	221	27	39	10	0	2	16	23	2	0	3	79	3	2	.249	.257
Arias, Gabriel	R-R	6-1	201	2-27-00	.240	.275	.231	124	455	54	109	27	3	6	55	41	1	4	3	149	3	3	.352	.302
Basabe, Olivier	R-R	5-11	190	7-15-97	.258	.188	.280	17	66	7	17	1	1	1	4	3	1	0	1	8	1	0	.349	.296
Burgos, Aldemar	R-R	6-0	165	1-23-97	.195	.188	.197	27	77	10	15	2	0	1	3	6	1	2	1	27	0	0	.260	.259
Campusano, Luis	R-R	6-0	213	9-29-98	.289	.280	.291	70	260	26	75	11	0	3	40	19	4	0	1	43	0	1	.365	.345
Cantu, Michael	R-R	6-3	225	8-28-95	.207	.000	.214	10	29	4	6	1	0	3	6	6	0	0	0	8	0	0	.552	.343
Carter, Tre	L-R	6-2	181	3-22-97	.192	.125	.205	31	99	4	19	2	0	0	2	17	0	0	0	36	3	2	.212	.310
Feight, Nick	R-R	5-11	200	11-4-95	.223	.205	.228	47	175	14	39	14	1	2	17	5	0	0	1	23	1	0	.349	.243
Fernandez, Juan	R-R	5-11	200	3-7-99	.224	.180	.233	66	232	22	52	13	0	2	23	20	4	1	1	49	0	4	.306	.296
Ilarraza, Reinaldo	R-R	5-10	150	1-12-99	.180	.100	.190	28	89	8	16	2	0	0	9	7	0	4	1	29	7	1	.202	.237
Jarmon, Hunter	R-R	6-0	195	3-2-95	.150	.200	.133	7	20	4	3	1	0	0	4	2	2	1	0	7	2	1	.200	.292
Lopez, Justin	B-R	6-2	192	5-9-00	.224	.140	.245	68	246	23	55	9	3	6	25	19	1	2	2	80	0	0	.358	.280
Melean, Kelvin	R-R	6-0	165	9-5-98	.241	.346	.220	45	158	17	38	9	0	4	18	15	3	1	2	35	2	1	.373	.315
Miller, Owen	R-R	6-0	190	11-15-96	.336	.478	.298	26	107	18	36	11	0	2	13	4	2	0	1	17	0	0	.495	.368
Ornelas, Tirso	L-R	6-3	200	3-11-00	.252	.262	.250	86	309	45	78	13	3	8	40	40	3	0	3	68	5	1	.392	.341
Podorsky, Robbie	R-R	5-7	170	1-27-95	.366	.349	.370	57	205	34	75	7	5	1	25	12	7	5	0	24	23	5	.463	.420
Rosario, Jeisson	L-L	6-1	191	10-22-99	.271	.253	.275	117	436	79	118	17	5	3	34	66	5	8	6	108	18	12	.353	.368
Ruiz, Agustin	L-R	6-2	175	9-23-99	.267	.000	.308	4	15	2	4	3	0	0	2	2	0	0	0	5	0	0	.467	.353

Name	B-T	HT	WT	DOB	AVG	vLH	vRH	G	AB	R	H	2B	3B	HR	RBI	BB	HBP	SH	SF	SO	SB	CS	SLG	OBP
Ruíz, Esteury	R-R	6-0	169	2-15-99	.253	.235	.257	117	439	63	111	20	5	12	53	38	9	6	1	141	49	11	.403	.324
Seagle, Chandler	R-R	6-0	190	5-23-96	.042	.125	.000	8	24	0	1	0	0	0	0	2	1	0	0	12	0	0	.042	.148
Suwinski, Jack	L-L	6-2	206	7-29-98	.255	.209	.265	111	392	57	100	16	7	10	57	37	5	3	4	89	7	3	.408	.324
Washington, Jalen	R-R	5-11	190	2-28-95	.234	.237	.233	100	321	46	75	10	4	8	30	45	5	3	3	82	7	5	.365	.334

Pitching	B-T	HT	WT	DOB	W	L	ERA	G	GS	CG	SV	IP	H	R	ER	HR	BB	SO	AVG	vLH	vRH	K/9	BB/9
Anderson, Korey	R-R	6-2	205	9-11-94	2	0	3.24	5	0	0	0	8	8	3	3	1	3	6	.250	.250		6.48	3.24
Belen, Carlos	R-R	6-1	244	2-28-96	0	0	0.00	2	0	0	0	2	1	0	0	0	2		.143	.250	.000	9.00	9.00
Boushley, Caleb	R-R	6-3	188	10-1-93	5	3	2.54	31	0	0	0	60	50	23	17	4	13	60	.219	.272	.191	8.95	1.94
Cantillo, Joey	L-L	6-4	225	12-18-99	0	1	9.82	1	1	0	0	4	4	4	4	0	3	5	.286	.400		12.27	7.36
Carkuff, Jared	R-R	6-3	180	8-25-93	3	1	5.40	13	0	0	2	20	23	14	12	1	9	21	.303	.233	.348	9.45	4.05
Coleman, Dylan	R-R	6-5	215	9-16-96	1	2	3.24	13	0	0	3	17	14	7	6	0	9	22	.226	.087	.308	11.88	4.86
Cosgrove, Tom	L-L	6-2	190	6-14-96	3	6	3.71	24	21	0	0	116	129	59	48	6	34	122	.276	.233	.286	9.44	2.63
Dallas, Dan	L-L	6-2	180	12-24-97	0	1	3.00	7	0	0	1	9	8	3	3	0	6	11	.229	.000	.333	11.00	6.00
Galindo, Joe	R-R	6-4	225	5-16-95	0	1	6.75	2	0	0	0	3	0	3	2	0	4	1	.000	.000	.000	3.38	13.50
Gore, MacKenzie	L-L	6-3	191	2-24-99	2	5	4.45	16	16	0	0	61	61	35	30	5	18	74	.260	.300	.246	10.98	2.67
Guerrero, Jordan	R-R	6-5	296	8-1-96	0	1	3.60	20	0	0	0	20	19	8	8	1	11	17	.253	.231	.265	7.65	4.95
Henry, Henry	R-R	6-4	178	12-17-98	1	1	8.66	7	2	0	0	18	19	20	17	0	14	11	.279	.367	.211	5.60	7.13
Hernandez, Osvaldo	L-L	6-0	181	5-15-98	11	4	1.81	21	19	0	0	110	104	34	22	3	27	94	.254	.181	.273	7.71	2.22
Knehr, Reiss	L-R	6-2	205	11-3-96	0	1	4.02	8	1	0	0	16	14	8	7	1	7	20	.241	.333	.177	11.49	4.02
Kulman, Spencer	R-R	6-1	195	3-29-95	0	0	27.00	2	0	0	0	2	3	6	5	1	4	2	.333	.600	.000	10.80	21.60
Kuzia, Nick	R-R	6-4	190	2-7-96	0	0	4.05	2	0	0	0	7	5	3	3	3	1	4	.208	.300	.143	5.40	1.35
Leasher, Aaron	L-L	6-3	208	4-28-96	5	5	3.32	20	15	0	0	98	97	42	36	5	41	96	.260	.278	.254	8.85	3.78
Lopez, Diomar	R-R	6-0	165	12-15-96	0	0	18.00	2	0	0	0	2	3	5	4	1	2	4	.273	.200	.333	18.00	9.00
Margevicius, Nick	L-L	6-5	220	6-18-96	5	5	3.07	13	13	0	0	76	79	32	26	5	9	87	.261	.328	.243	10.26	1.06
Martinez, Adrian	R-R	6-2	195	12-10-96	0	1	9.87	8	1	0	1	17	28	20	19	2	12	26	.354	.389	.344	13.50	6.23
Miller, Evan	R-R	6-2	200	5-23-95	5	6	2.54	41	0	0	0	64	54	28	18	3	12	61	.236	.213	.247	8.62	1.70
Mosser, Gabe	R-R	6-4	179	6-8-96	1	1	0.00	3	1	0	0	12	8	1	0	0	3	18	.182	.125	.214	13.50	2.25
Patino, Luis	R-R	6-0	192	10-26-99	6	3	2.16	17	17	0	0	83	65	25	20	1	24	98	.220	.345	.140	10.58	2.59
Quezada, Jose	R-R	5-9	175	9-7-95	1	1	3.86	7	0	0	0	12	9	5	5	2	5	13	.200	.118	.250	10.03	3.86
Radke, Travis	L-L	6-4	237	3-6-93	2	4	1.74	35	0	0	14	57	36	16	11	3	9	77	.175	.214	.165	12.16	1.42
Ramirez, Emmanuel	R-R	6-2	190	7-15-94	1	2	2.20	3	3	0	0	16	14	4	4	1	5	26	.222	.100	.245	14.33	2.76
Schlichtholz, Fred	R-L	6-3	215	9-18-95	2	3	3.83	28	0	0	2	47	53	23	20	4	16	39	.283	.200	.310	7.47	3.06
Sexton, Danny	R-L	6-0	195	6-30-95	0	1	3.97	7	0	0	0	11	10	6	5	0	6	8	.250	.231	.259	6.35	4.76
Sheckler, Ben	L-L	6-8	276	5-12-95	1	5	4.29	32	6	0	2	80	90	45	38	8	23	52	.286	.321	.274	5.87	2.60
Smith, Austin	R-R	6-4	220	7-9-96	1	1	3.18	20	0	0	1	34	27	12	12	3	12	31	.214	.213	.215	8.21	3.18
Stillman, Will	R-R	6-4	175	11-2-93	0	0	14.29	4	0	0	0	6	11	9	9	1	6	3	.407	.273	.500	4.76	9.53
Thompson, Mason	R-R	6-7	223	2-20-98	6	8	4.94	22	20	0	0	93	95	61	51	8	37	97	.255	.270	.244	9.39	3.58
Weathers, Ryan	L-L	6-1	200	12-17-99	0	1	3.00	3	3	0	0	9	11	8	3	0	1	9	.282	.167	.303	9.00	1.00

Fielding

C: Campusano 38, Cantu 9, Fernandez 44, Seagle 8, Washington 42. **1B:** Belen 42, Campusano 4, Feight 38, Fernandez 1, Washington 57. **2B:** Basabe 4, Ilarraza 15, Lopez 25, Melean 22, Ruiz 74. **3B:** Almanzar 57, Arias 6, Basabe 5, Ilarraza 12, Lopez 15, Melean 18, Miller 13, Ruiz 16. **SS:** Arias 111, Lopez 21, Melean 3, Miller 7. **OF:** Basabe 8, Burgos 22, Carter 29, Jarmon 6, Ornelas 71, Podorsky 53, Rosario 114, Ruiz 4, Suwinski 109.

TRI-CITY DUST DEVILS
NORTHWEST LEAGUE

SHORT-SEASON

Batting	B-T	HT	WT	DOB	AVG	vLH	vRH	G	AB	R	H	2B	3B	HR	RBI	BB	HBP	SH	SF	SO	SB	CS	SLG	OBP
Alarcon, Kelvin	L-R	6-1	155	3-6-99	.173	.227	.155	52	173	22	30	5	2	0	13	14	1	1	1	53	2	2	.225	.238
Asuncion, Luis	R-R	6-4	205	2-27-97	.245	.219	.254	63	237	34	58	18	0	6	28	10	4	0	0	67	3	3	.397	.287
Basabe, Olivier	R-R	5-11	190	7-15-97	.313	.233	.339	40	150	18	47	13	0	4	28	12	3	1	2	26	5	3	.480	.371
Becker, Luke	L-R	5-11	190	4-8-96	.206	.257	.192	51	160	15	33	6	2	0	12	18	1	0	1	46	4	1	.269	.289
Benson, Tyler	L-R	5-11	180	6-17-96	.188	.000	.240	11	32	3	6	2	0	0	5	8	2	0	1	12	2	0	.250	.372
Burgos, Aldemar	R-R	6-0	165	1-23-97	.257	.278	.247	30	113	21	29	6	3	2	14	12	3	0	3	25	2	3	.416	.336
Carter, Tre	L-R	6-2	181	3-22-97	.219	.226	.217	67	233	33	51	5	5	5	28	21	2	1	4	63	10	3	.348	.285
Curry, Michael	R-R	6-1	212	7-4-97	.256	.237	.264	54	203	23	52	11	1	2	29	15	3	0	0	42	1	2	.350	.317
Edwards, Xavier	B-R	5-10	155	8-9-99	.314	.250	.333	24	86	21	27	4	0	0	5	18	1	2	0	15	10	0	.361	.438
Gatewood, Nick	L-R	6-1	190	7-17-97	.191	.000	.222	6	21	4	4	2	0	0	1	1	0	0	0	7	0	0	.286	.227
House, Mason	B-L	6-3	190	9-10-98	.121	.000	.175	18	58	5	7	3	0	2	9	12	2	0	1	32	0	0	.276	.288
Hunt, Blake	R-R	6-3	185	11-10-98	.271	.259	.275	56	207	34	56	13	0	3	25	27	8	0	3	56	2	1	.377	.371
Ilarraza, Reinaldo	B-R	5-10	150	1-12-99	.205	.158	.250	11	39	6	8	2	0	0	2	3	0	1	0	14	1	1	.256	.262
Kennedy, A.J.	R-R	6-0	190	1-23-94	.250	—	.250	2	4	0	1	0	0	0	0	0	0	0	0	1	0	0	.250	.250
Lezama, Jose	B-R	5-10	195	2-19-98	.158	.154	.160	15	38	1	6	1	0	0	4	6	0	1	1	7	1	0	.184	.267
Little, Grant	R-R	6-1	185	7-8-97	.262	.289	.250	39	149	16	39	8	0	0	17	20	2	1	3	28	9	2	.315	.351
Marcano, Tucupita	L-R	6-0	165	9-16-99	.314	.133	.364	17	70	12	22	1	2	1	9	4	1	1	1	6	5	0	.429	.355
Miller, Owen	R-R	6-0	190	11-15-96	.335	.347	.331	49	191	22	64	8	3	2	20	15	6	1	3	24	4	4	.440	.395
Paulsen, Justin	L-R	6-1	200	1-3-95	.230	.095	.265	55	204	28	47	8	2	5	25	21	5	1	0	59	1	1	.363	.317
Quintero, Alison	R-R	5-11	175	4-24-00	.286	.000	.333	2	7	0	2	0	0	0	0	0	0	0	0	2	0	0	.286	.286
Ruiz, Agustin	L-R	6-2	175	9-23-99	.200	.000	.286	2	10	1	2	0	0	0	0	1	0	0	0	5	0	0	.200	.200
Sabala, Elvis	R-R	6-1	180	9-26-97	.150	.200	.133	7	20	1	3	1	0	0	4	0	0	0	1	10	1	0	.200	.292
Seagle, Chandler	R-R	6-0	190	5-23-96	.213	.177	.233	16	47	6	10	2	0	0	5	8	4	0	1	16	2	0	.255	.367
Solarte, Angel	R-R	5-11	155	3-29-01	.200	.250	.182	5	15	2	3	0	0	0	1	0	0	0	0	2	0	0	.200	.250
Williams-Sutton, Dwanya	R-R	6-2	215	7-10-97	.256	.360	.215	27	90	14	23	5	1	2	14	5	1	2	1	4	0	1	.400	.320

Pitching	B-T	HT	WT	DOB	W	L	ERA	G	GS	CG	SV	IP	H	R	ER	HR	BB	SO	AVG	vLH	vRH	K/9	BB/9
Acevedo, Angel	R-R	6-1	180	9-19-98	3	3	3.88	12	11	0	0	65	55	30	28	1	16	54	.223	.241	.207	7.48	2.22
Anderson, Korey	R-R	6-2	205	9-11-94	0	1	2.84	12	0	0	0	19	18	7	6	2	3	29	.257	.281	.237	13.74	1.42

	B-T	HT	WT	DOB	W	L	ERA	G	GS	CG	SV	IP	H	R	ER	HR	BB	SO	AVG	vLH	vRH	K/9	BB/9
Belen, Carlos	R-R	6-1	244	2-28-96	1	0	0.00	2	0	0	0	3	0	0	0	0	2	2	.000	.000	.000	6.00	6.00
Bellinger, Cole	R-R	6-1	175	10-12-99	1	6	5.43	13	12	0	1	55	57	35	33	8	24	48	.273	.265	.278	7.90	3.95
Capps, Carter	R-R	6-5	230	8-7-90	0	1	1.29	6	0	0	1	7	5	1	1	0	2	10	.200	.000	.294	12.86	2.57
Coleman, Dylan	R-R	6-5	215	9-16-96	0	0	3.00	5	0	0	1	6	6	3	2	0	2	7	.273	.400	.235	10.50	3.00
Contreras, Efrain	R-R	5-10	185	1-2-00	1	0	0.00	2	0	0	0	6	1	0	0	0	2	7	.056	.111	.000	10.50	3.00
Cosme, Jean	R-R	6-2	155	5-24-96	0	1	13.50	1	0	0	0	3	5	4	4	1	2	1	.385	.167	.571	3.38	6.75
Cruz, Omar	L-L	6-0	170	1-26-99	1	0	2.01	6	5	0	0	22	16	5	5	0	16	29	.211	.267	.197	11.69	6.45
Dallas, Dan	L-L	6-2	180	12-24-97	1	1	2.03	16	0	0	1	27	12	6	6	0	12	45	.138	.211	.118	15.19	4.05
Galindo, Joe	R-R	6-4	225	5-16-95	2	0	2.28	23	0	0	1	24	16	9	6	1	14	30	.195	.250	.160	11.41	5.32
Garcia, Jeferson	R-R	6-0	165	2-4-00	0	1	9.00	1	1	0	0	3	5	3	3	0	3	4	.357	.375	.333	12.00	9.00
Guerrero, Jordan	R-R	6-5	296	8-1-96	0	1	0.00	22	0	0	8	22	9	3	0	0	7	29	.125	.138	.116	11.69	2.82
Guzman, Jonathan	R-R	5-10	180	2-8-95	3	1	3.41	20	0	0	1	34	27	18	13	1	17	45	.214	.196	.225	11.80	4.46
Guzman, Manny	R-R	6-4	180	11-1-99	1	1	6.14	2	2	0	0	7	7	6	5	0	5	3	.250	.294	.182	3.68	6.14
Henry, Henry	R-R	6-4	178	12-17-98	4	3	3.32	11	11	0	0	60	62	26	22	4	11	44	.271	.229	.289	6.64	1.66
Keating, Sam	R-R	6-3	190	8-31-98	3	6	5.20	12	12	0	0	55	56	39	32	5	28	34	.259	.222	.282	5.53	4.55
Kulman, Spencer	R-R	6-1	195	3-29-95	1	0	3.25	17	0	0	0	28	22	10	10	0	11	31	.216	.235	.206	10.08	3.58
Kuzia, Nick	R-R	6-4	190	2-7-94	1	2	4.26	22	1	0	3	32	36	21	15	1	14	33	.293	.381	.247	9.38	3.98
Lopez, Diomar	R-R	6-0	165	12-15-96	2	2	2.73	23	0	0	2	30	27	18	9	1	7	42	.248	.296	.215	12.74	2.12
Martinez, Adrian	R-R	6-2	195	12-10-96	4	5	6.00	13	13	0	0	57	84	45	38	3	14	52	.336	.338	.335	8.21	2.21
Mosser, Gabe	R-R	6-4	179	6-8-96	2	1	2.37	16	0	0	1	30	26	8	8	3	7	41	.230	.225	.233	12.16	2.08
Munoz, Andres	R-R	6-2	165	1-16-99	0	0	0.00	5	0	0	6	6	0	0	0	0	2	9	.000	.000	.000	14.29	3.18
Perez, Ramon	L-L	6-1	190	7-2-99	2	1	2.48	11	8	0	0	40	33	14	11	1	16	45	.228	.158	.252	10.13	3.60
Quezada, Jose	R-R	5-9	175	9-7-95	0	0	9.00	1	0	0	0	1	1	1	1	0	0	1	.400	—	.400	9.00	0.00
Sung, Wen-Hua	R-R	6-1	198	9-2-96	0	3	10.80	19	0	0	0	20	38	28	24	4	8	23	.396	.408	.385	10.35	3.60
Tyler, Cody	L-L	6-0	180	10-26-94	0	1	9.00	3	0	0	0	4	4	4	4	2	3	5	.250	.000	.286	11.25	6.75
Wilson, Steven	R-R	6-3	185	8-24-94	1	0	1.80	3	0	0	0	5	4	2	1	0	1	6	.235	.200	.250	10.80	1.80

Fielding

C: Hunt 47, Kennedy 2, Lezama 14, Quintero 2, Seagle 15. **1B:** Asuncion 27, Paulsen 52. **2B:** Alarcon 7, Basabe 21, Becker 26, Edwards 5, Ilarraza 9, Marcano 11. **3B:** Alarcon 43, Basabe 10, Becker 19, Lezama 1, Sabala 6. **SS:** Alarcon 1, Basabe 7, Edwards 19, Ilarraza 2, Marcano 6, Miller 44. **OF:** Asuncion 14, Benson 9, Burgos 30, Carter 66, Curry 38, House 15, Little 39, Ruiz 2, Solarte 4, Williams-Sutton 19.

AZL PADRES 1   ROOKIE
ARIZONA LEAGUE

Batting	B-T	HT	WT	DOB	AVG	vLH	vRH	G	AB	R	H	2B	3B	HR	RBI	BB	HBP	SH	SF	SO	SB	CS	SLG	OBP
Aguilar, Rainie	R-R	5-11	200	7-4-96	.174	.333	.118	23	1	4	0	0	0	4	3	1	0	2	14	0	0	.174	.276
Almanzar, Luis	R-R	6-0	187	11-1-99	.211	.313	.171	15	57	9	12	1	0	0	4	5	0	0	1	9	3	0	.228	.270
Benson, Tyler	L-R	5-11	180	6-17-96	.175	.158	.180	29	80	13	14	4	2	0	11	9	2	1	0	25	6	0	.275	.275
Cantu, Michael	R-R	6-3	225	8-28-95	.244	.500	.189	12	45	6	11	4	0	0	7	3	1	0	1	13	0	0	.333	.300
Dale, Jarryd	R-R	6-1	176	9-11-00	.207	.222	.203	29	87	12	18	5	0	0	6	7	2	0	0	28	3	0	.264	.281
2-team total (11 AZL Padres 2)					.183	.214	.174	40	120	14	22	6	0	0	6	7	4	0	0	47	3	1	.233	.252
Edwards, Xavier	B-R	5-10	155	8-9-99	.384	.381	.385	21	73	19	28	4	1	0	11	13	0	1	1	10	12	1	.466	.471
Gatewood, Nick	L-R	6-1	190	7-17-97	.283	.237	.300	54	219	28	62	18	1	5	37	13	1	0	2	52	0	0	.443	.323
Giron, Ruddy	R-R	6-0	205	1-4-97	.348	.500	.294	7	23	4	8	1	0	1	2	3	1	0	0	1	1	0	.522	.444
2-team total (2 AZL Padres 2)					.321	.375	.300	9	28	5	9	2	0	1	3	3	2	0	0	1	1	0	.500	.424
Guzman, Luis	R-R	6-2	175	6-20-98	.262	.191	.296	29	65	8	17	3	0	0	12	12	1	0	2	10	0	1	.308	.375
Harris, Jawuan	R-R	5-9	195	11-3-96	.225	.200	.232	49	160	23	36	7	4	3	20	29	7	1	4	50	14	6	.375	.360
Ilarraza, Reinaldo	B-R	5-10	150	1-12-99	.252	.231	.259	36	111	16	28	7	3	0	15	10	1	3	1	23	2	3	.369	.317
2-team total (4 AZL Padres 2)					.246	.241	.247	40	126	17	31	8	3	0	19	11	2	5	1	25	2	3	.357	.314
Lambert, Greg	R-R	6-0	190	9-27-95	.202	.263	.187	28	94	11	19	2	0	1	5	12	1	0	0	29	2	1	.255	.299
Landinez, Yerry	B-R	6-1	170	1-20-01	.185	.125	.211	21	54	8	10	1	0	1	4	7	5	0	0	23	0	1	.259	.333
Luis, Carlos	L-R	6-2	160	9-4-99	.238	.189	.252	45	160	22	38	4	1	0	16	16	0	0	0	39	0	1	.275	.307
McGee, Stephen	R-R	6-3	215	2-7-91	.333	.000	.500	2	6	0	2	0	0	0	0	1	0	0	0	2	0	0	.333	.429
2-team total (6 AZL Padres 2)					.222	.167	.250	8	18	0	4	0	0	0	0	6	1	0	0	6	0	0	.222	.440
Roman, Luis	L-R	6-0	215	12-19-94	.200	—	.200	4	10	0	2	1	0	0	0	1	0	0	0	2	0	0	.300	.273
2-team total (28 AZL Padres 2)					.258	.083	.284	32	93	7	24	6	0	3	19	15	0	0	0	21	1	0	.419	.361
Ruiz, Agustin	L-R	6-2	175	9-23-99	.290	.208	.317	53	193	39	56	11	10	1	28	27	3	0	1	66	2	3	.466	.384
Solomon, Lee	R-R	5-10	202	8-4-96	.298	.342	.283	41	151	27	45	8	2	7	30	15	1	0	0	38	6	4	.517	.365
Vizcarra, Gilberto	R-R	5-10	180	3-1-99	.148	.206	.124	37	115	11	17	2	0	2	11	21	2	0	1	24	0	0	.217	.288
Williams, Jaquez	L-R	6-3	215	11-16-97	.278	.174	.304	32	115	10	32	7	1	3	19	6	4	0	0	49	0	0	.435	.336

Pitching	B-T	HT	WT	DOB	W	L	ERA	G	GS	CG	SV	IP	H	R	ER	HR	BB	SO	AVG	vLH	vRH	K/9	BB/9
Arias, Luarbert	R-R	6-2	176	12-12-00	3	4	3.50	11	9	0	0	44	46	18	17	4	11	37	.274	.254	.284	7.63	2.27
Belen, Carlos	R-R	6-1	244	2-28-96	3	1	4.02	15	0	0	0	16	16	7	7	0	7	19	.254	.429	.167	10.91	4.02
Bencomo, Edwin	R-R	6-2	165	4-14-99	3	3	4.04	13	3	0	1	42	47	21	19	0	8	33	.280	.231	.302	7.02	1.70
Cabrera, Jose	L-L	6-0	170	9-26-98	1	1	2.52	14	0	0	0	25	22	8	7	2	12	16	.237	.143	.253	5.76	4.32
Carrasco, Martin	R-R	6-0	165	11-22-99	1	0	6.94	10	0	0	0	12	21	12	9	2	1	11	.396	.240	.536	8.49	0.77
Colletti, Tom	R-R	6-3	220	6-22-95	2	0	0.64	19	0	0	4	28	11	3	2	0	6	32	.120	.121	.119	10.16	1.91
Contreras, Efrain	R-R	5-10	185	1-2-00	1	3	2.72	9	4	0	0	43	36	15	13	3	9	44	.231	.259	.214	9.21	1.88
Cordero, Starlin	R-R	6-7	220	7-21-98	0	3	6.53	17	0	0	4	26	16	16	15	0	16	31	.211	.269	.180	13.50	6.97
Cosme, Jean	R-R	6-2	155	5-24-96	1	1	4.50	4	3	0	0	6	5	3	3	0	6	6	.238	.000	.294	9.00	0.00
2-team total (5 AZL Padres 2)					2	2	2.65	9	7	0	0	17	15	5	5	0	1	16	.246	.222	.256	8.47	0.53
Cruz, Omar	L-L	6-0	170	1-26-99	0	1	1.80	5	5	0	0	20	18	8	4	0	6	31	.231	.429	.188	13.50	2.70
Erb, Dalton	R-R	6-8	250	5-13-94	1	3	3.09	14	1	0	1	35	23	18	12	0	16	41	.177	.213	.157	10.54	4.11
2-team total (1 AZL Padres 2)					1	3	3.41	15	1	0	1	37	25	20	14	0	18	42	.184	.216	.165	10.22	4.38
Eusebio, Luis	R-R	6-0	180	3-15-96	0	0	15.00	1	0	0	0	3	4	5	5	1	3	2	.333	.000	.500	6.00	9.00

Pitching	B-T	HT	WT	DOB	W	L	ERA	G	GS	CG	SV	IP	H	R	ER	HR	BB	SO	AVG	vLH	vRH	K/9	BB/9
2-team total (12 AZL Padres 2)					1	1	5.77	13	0	0	0	39	38	28	25	2	22	30	.266	.255	.272	6.92	5.08
Fernandez, Omar	L-L	5-11	160	4-20-99	2	0	3.66	11	0	0	1	20	21	10	8	0	7	13	.288	.286	.288	5.95	3.20
Garcia, Jeferson	R-R	6-0	165	2-4-00	3	1	3.77	7	5	0	0	29	25	17	12	0	11	38	.227	.258	.215	11.93	3.45
2-team total (5 AZL Padres 2)					4	2	4.87	12	6	0	1	44	47	30	24	1	17	52	.266	.262	.267	10.56	3.45
Knehr, Reiss	L-R	6-2	205	11-3-96	3	0	2.84	12	0	0	2	19	12	8	6	2	8	25	.167	.167	.167	11.84	3.79
Lloyd, Kyle	R-R	6-4	220	10-16-90	0	0	0.00	5	4	0	0	8	4	1	0	1	1	15	.138	.182	.111	16.88	1.13
Lopez, Frank	R-R	6-1	170	4-23-01	1	4	4.38	9	7	0	0	25	24	16	12	1	18	29	.261	.306	.232	10.58	6.57
2-team total (1 AZL Padres 2)					1	4	3.86	10	8	0	0	28	26	17	12	1	22	35	.245	.275	.227	11.25	7.07
Lugo, Moises	R-R	6-1	185	1-20-99	0	1	24.00	2	2	0	0	3	10	8	8	0	4	1	.526	.750	.467	12.00	12.00
Miller, Vijay	L-R	6-3	190	11-8-97	0	0	6.00	2	0	0	0	3	4	2	2	0	2	4	.333	.333	.333	12.00	6.00
2-team total (13 AZL Padres 2)					1	1	5.90	15	0	0	0	29	30	21	19	2	15	31	.270	.283	.262	9.62	4.66
Minjarez, Felix	R-R	6-3	205	9-13-96	1	0	0.00	1	0	0	0	2	1	0	0	1	0	3	.333	.000	.400	0.00	5.40
2-team total (16 AZL Padres 2)					4	0	1.55	17	0	0	1	29	24	9	5	0	11	39	.222	.206	.206	12.10	3.41
Morejon, Adrian	L-L	6-0	175	2-27-99	0	1	6.75	1	1	0	0	3	5	2	2	0	0	4	.385	—	.385	13.50	0.00
Mortensen, Tyler	L-L	6-4	205	6-25-00	1	0	0.00	1	0	0	0	3	2	0	0	0	0	5	.167	.000	.200	15.00	0.00
2-team total (10 AZL Padres 2)					3	2	4.74	11	0	0	1	25	19	15	13	4	20	22	.209	.118	.230	8.03	7.30
Overton, Dillon	L-L	6-2	175	8-17-91	0	0	6.00	1	0	0	0	3	5	3	2	0	2	6	.357	1.000	.308	18.00	6.00
2-team total (1 AZL Padres 2)					0	0	3.00	2	1	0	0	6	8	3	2	0	2	9	.320	.250	.333	13.50	3.00
Rodriguez, Hansel	R-R	6-2	170	2-27-97	0	0	3.00	3	1	0	0	3	1	2	1	0	1	4	.077	.000	.125	12.00	3.00
2-team total (2 AZL Padres 2)					0	0	1.80	5	1	0	0	5	1	2	1	0	2	7	.053	.000	.100	12.60	3.60
Sims, Jake	L-R	6-2	215	3-8-97	0	0	7.64	15	0	0	0	18	18	20	15	0	18	31	.250	.172	.302	15.79	9.17
Thwaits, Nick	R-R	6-2	195	6-27-99	0	0	2.42	8	5	0	0	26	18	9	7	0	11	35	.190	.191	.189	12.12	3.81
Torres, Wilmer	R-R	6-3	190	5-31-96	0	0	9.00	2	0	0	0	2	1	2	2	0	4	1	.143	.000	.167	4.50	18.00
Tyler, Cody	L-L	6-0	180	10-26-94	0	0	6.75	4	0	0	0	5	7	4	4	0	3	5	.318	.000	.350	8.44	5.06
Vega, Alexuan	L-L	6-2	160	6-22-99	0	1	10.80	7	6	0	0	15	17	18	18	2	13	13	.283	.333	.275	7.80	7.80

Fielding

C: Aguilar 8, Cantu 11, Gatewood 3, McGee 2, Roman 1, Vizcarra 37. **1B:** Cantu 4, Gatewood 5, Lambert 10, Landinez 2, Luis 28, Roman 2, Solomon 13. **2B:** Dale 19, Guzman 11, Ilarraza 8, Landinez 6, Solomon 22. **3B:** Almanzar 15, Dale 4, Guzman 11, Landinez 10, Luis 18, Roman 1, Solomon 6. **SS:** Dale 5, Edwards 15, Giron 6, Guzman 5, Ilarraza 30, Landinez 3. **OF:** Benson 25, Harris 49, Lambert 18, Ruiz 53, Solomon 2, Williams 31.

AZL PADRES 2   *ROOKIE*
ARIZONA LEAGUE

Batting	B-T	HT	WT	DOB	AVG	vLH	vRH	G	AB	R	H	2B	3B	HR	RBI	BB	HBP	SH	SF	SO	SB	CS	SLG	OBP
Barley, Jordy	R-R	6-0	175	12-3-99	.200	.185	.206	54	195	30	39	9	2	4	20	15	5	0	3	59	12	7	.328	.271
Batista, Carlos	L-L	6-2	177	10-30-99	.000	.000	.000	2	3	0	0	0	0	0	0	0	0	0	0	3	0	0	.000	.000
Dale, Jarryd	R-R	6-1	176	9-11-00	.121	.200	.087	11	33	2	4	1	0	0	2	2	0	0	0	19	0	1	.152	.171
2-team total (29 AZL Padres 1)					.183	.214	.174	40	120	14	22	6	0	0	6	7	4	0	0	47	3	1	.233	.252
Francisco, Yordi	L-R	6-1	175	3-14-97	.262	.162	.303	38	126	19	33	6	0	2	22	12	6	2	0	33	6	4	.357	.354
Giron, Ruddy	R-R	6-0	205	1-4-97	.000	.000	.333	2	5	1	1	0	0	0	1	0	1	0	0	0	0	0	.400	.333
2-team total (7 AZL Padres 1)					.321	.375	.300	9	28	5	9	2	0	1	3	3	2	0	0	1	1	0	.500	.424
Guilbe, Sean	R-R	6-1	190	12-13-99	.218	.206	.222	40	133	19	29	10	1	5	15	40	3	0	0	62	6	0	.421	.409
Homza, Jonny	R-R	6-0	185	6-13-99	.226	.316	.197	44	155	25	35	7	1	3	21	26	4	0	0	37	0	0	.342	.351
House, Mason	B-L	6-3	190	9-10-98	.241	.273	.230	26	83	10	20	2	2	3	7	10	1	0	0	36	1	1	.422	.330
Ilarraza, Reinaldo	R-R	5-10	150	1-12-99	.200	.333	.167	4	15	1	3	1	0	0	4	1	1	2	0	2	0	0	.267	.294
2-team total (36 AZL Padres 1)					.246	.241	.247	40	126	17	31	8	3	0	19	11	2	5	1	25	2	3	.357	.314
Jarmon, Hunter	R-R	6-0	195	3-2-95	.229	.276	.209	34	96	16	22	4	2	1	7	13	5	0	0	32	4	1	.344	.351
Marcano, Tucupita	L-R	6-0	165	9-16-99	.395	.410	.388	35	124	33	49	4	1	0	17	26	2	5	3	10	10	7	.444	.497
McGee, Stephen	R-R	6-3	215	2-7-91	.167	.250	.125	6	12	0	2	0	0	0	0	5	1	0	0	4	0	0	.167	.444
2-team total (2 AZL Padres 1)					.222	.167	.250	8	18	0	4	0	0	0	6	1	0	0	0	21	0	0	.222	.440
Perez, Blinger	R-R	6-0	170	8-21-98	.229	.303	.194	34	105	20	24	4	0	3	17	15	4	0	2	35	0	0	.352	.341
Pineda, Jason	R-R	6-2	202	11-22-99	.210	.233	.202	47	162	21	34	11	1	2	22	30	4	0	5	67	0	0	.327	.342
Quintero, Alison	R-R	5-11	175	4-24-00	.288	.313	.280	38	132	19	38	9	0	0	19	10	3	0	0	22	0	1	.356	.352
Roman, Luis	L-R	6-0	215	12-19-94	.265	.083	.296	28	83	7	22	5	0	3	19	14	0	0	0	19	1	0	.434	.371
2-team total (4 AZL Padres 1)					.258	.083	.284	32	93	7	24	6	0	3	19	15	0	0	0	21	1	0	.419	.361
Sabala, Elvis	R-R	6-1	178	9-26-97	.262	.350	.222	24	65	13	17	4	0	2	18	14	0	0	1	15	1	1	.415	.388
Smith, Payton	R-R	6-5	225	5-22-00	.141	.273	.095	31	85	15	12	1	0	0	8	12	0	0	1	41	1	0	.153	.245
Solarte, Angel	R-R	5-11	155	3-29-01	.219	.244	.208	39	151	25	33	8	2	1	9	12	3	0	2	32	5	2	.318	.286
Stevens, River	L-R	6-0	185	1-10-92	.375	.667	.200	3	8	0	3	0	0	0	3	2	0	0	1	0	0	0	.375	.455
Suarez, Michael	L-L	6-2	200	5-21-00	.148	.177	.135	21	54	6	8	1	0	0	3	4	2	0	1	10	0	0	.167	.230

Pitching	B-T	HT	WT	DOB	W	L	ERA	G	GS	CG	SV	IP	H	R	ER	HR	BB	SO	AVG	vLH	vRH	K/9	BB/9
Anderson, Korey	R-R	6-2	205	9-11-94	1	0	2.70	1	0	0	0	3	3	1	1	0	0	4	.231	.000	.300	10.80	0.00
Cantillo, Joey	L-L	6-4	225	12-18-99	2	2	2.18	11	9	0	0	45	33	18	11	0	12	58	.198	.167	.206	11.51	2.38
Cosme, Jean	R-R	6-2	155	5-24-96	1	1	1.64	5	4	0	0	11	10	2	2	0	1	10	.250	.286	.231	8.18	0.82
2-team total (4 AZL Padres 1)					2	2	2.65	9	7	0	0	17	15	5	5	0	1	16	.246	.222	.256	8.47	0.53
Erb, Dalton	R-R	6-8	250	5-13-94	0	0	9.00	1	0	0	0	2	2	2	2	0	2	1	.333	.250	.500	4.50	9.00
2-team total (14 AZL Padres 1)					1	3	3.41	15	1	0	1	37	25	20	14	0	18	42	.184	.216	.165	10.22	4.38
Eusebio, Luis	R-R	6-0	180	3-15-96	1	1	5.00	12	0	0	0	36	34	23	20	1	19	28	.260	.277	.250	7.00	4.75
2-team total (1 AZL Padres 1)					1	1	5.77	13	0	0	0	39	38	28	25	2	22	30	.266	.255	.272	6.92	5.08
Fox, Mason	R-R	6-2	170	1-7-97	1	1	3.80	15	0	0	2	21	14	9	9	1	8	28	.182	.242	.136	11.81	3.38
Garcia, Jeferson	R-R	6-0	165	2-4-00	1	1	6.89	5	1	0	1	16	22	13	12	1	6	16	.328	.261	.358	8.04	3.45
2-team total (7 AZL Padres 1)					4	2	4.87	12	6	0	1	44	47	30	24	1	17	52	.266	.262	.267	10.56	3.45
Guzman, Manny	R-R	6-4	180	11-1-99	1	2	3.99	11	9	0	0	50	41	25	22	2	15	50	.224	.244	.208	9.06	2.72
Kulman, Spencer	R-R	6-1	195	3-29-95	0	1	3.18	4	0	0	0	4	4	2	2	0	4	6	.211	.200	.222	9.53	3.18
Lopez, Frank	R-R	6-1	170	4-23-01	0	0	0.00	1	0	0	0	3	2	1	0	0	4	6	.143	.000	.200	16.20	10.80

	B-T	HT	WT	DOB	W	L	ERA	G	GS	CG	SV	IP	H	R	ER	HR	BB	SO	AVG	vLH	vRH	K/9	BB/9
2-team total (9 AZL Padres 1)					1	4	3.86	10	8	0	0	28	26	17	12	1	22	35	.245	.275	.227	11.25	7.07
Megill, Trevor	L-R	6-8	235	12-5-93	0	0	9.00	1	0	0	0	1	2	1	1	0	0	1	.500	.500	.500	9.00	0.00
Miliano, Michell	R-R	6-3	185	12-22-99	1	3	9.21	11	11	0	0	28	35	33	29	2	19	34	.304	.333	.288	10.80	6.04
Miller, Vijay	L-R	6-3	190	11-8-97	1	1	5.88	13	0	0	0	26	26	19	17	2	13	27	.263	.275	.254	9.35	4.50
2-team total (2 AZL Padres 1)					1	1	5.90	15	0	0	0	29	30	21	19	2	15	31	.270	.283	.262	9.62	4.66
Minjarez, Felix	R-R	6-3	205	9-13-96	3	0	1.65	16	0	0	1	27	22	8	5	0	10	39	.216	.256	.191	12.84	3.29
2-team total (1 AZL Padres 1)					4	0	1.55	17	0	0	1	29	24	9	5	0	11	39	.222	.250	.206	12.10	3.41
Morales, Gabriel	L-L	6-3	175	4-14-99	1	0	3.79	11	7	0	0	36	28	16	15	2	26	44	.222	.129	.253	11.10	6.56
Mortensen, Tyler	L-L	6-4	205	6-25-00	2	2	5.40	10	0	0	1	22	17	15	13	4	20	17	.215	.133	.234	7.06	8.31
2-team total (1 AZL Padres 1)					3	2	4.74	11	0	0	1	25	19	15	13	4	20	22	.209	.118	.230	8.03	7.30
Newman, Chandler	R-R	6-2	175	2-5-97	0	2	12.27	9	0	0	0	7	2	12	10	0	16	6	.087	.000	.167	7.36	19.64
Overton, Dillon	L-L	6-2	175	8-17-91	0	0	0.00	1	1	0	0	3	3	0	0	0	0	3	.273	.000	.375	9.00	0.00
2-team total (1 AZL Padres 1)					0	0	3.00	2	1	0	0	6	8	3	2	0	2	9	.320	.250	.333	13.50	3.00
Quijada, Hazahel	R-R	6-2	185	9-18-97	2	3	2.59	15	0	0	0	24	12	11	7	0	14	34	.146	.150	.145	12.58	5.18
Rodriguez, Hansel	R-R	6-2	170	2-27-97	0	0	0.00	2	0	0	0	2	0	0	0	1	3	.000	.000	.000	13.50	4.50
2-team total (3 AZL Padres 1)					0	0	1.80	5	1	0	0	5	1	2	1	0	2	7	.053	.000	.100	12.60	3.60
Sexton, Danny	R-L	6-0	195	6-30-95	2	0	1.00	9	0	0	2	18	17	2	2	0	3	13	.262	.000	.315	6.50	1.50
Shelton, Trent	L-L	6-0	205	6-24-94	4	3	2.81	14	1	0	0	32	30	10	10	1	5	40	.244	.242	.244	11.25	1.41
Taccolini, Dominic	R-R	6-0	230	9-28-94	1	1	5.51	11	1	0	0	16	19	10	10	1	3	19	.312	.217	.368	10.47	1.65
Vela, Noel	L-L	6-1	165	12-21-98	1	4	4.19	11	7	0	0	34	43	32	16	3	22	41	.307	.148	.345	10.75	5.77
Weathers, Ryan	L-L	6-1	200	12-17-99	0	2	3.86	4	4	0	0	9	8	4	2	3	9	.211	.091	.259	8.68	2.89

Fielding

C: Homza 20, McGee 4, Quintero 32, Roman 9. **1B:** Pineda 43, Suarez 17. **2B:** Barley 15, Dale 6, Guilbe 20, Ilarraza 1, Marcano 18, Roman 2, Stevens 2. **3B:** Barley 1, Dale 3, Giron 1, Guilbe 20, Homza 15, Ilarraza 3, Marcano 1, Perez 1, Pineda 4, Roman 1, Sabala 17. **SS:** Barley 39, Dale 3, Marcano 18. **OF:** Batista 1, Francisco 33, Guilbe 4, House 25, Jarmon 34, Perez 23, Roman 1, Smith 29, Solarte 37.

DSL PADRES   ROOKIE
DOMINICAN SUMMER LEAGUE

Batting	B-T	HT	WT	DOB	AVG	vLH	vRH	G	AB	R	H	2B	3B	HR	RBI	BB	HBP	SH	SF	SO	SB	CS	SLG	OBP
Antunez, Adrian	R-R	6-3	195	1-17-99	.169	.170	.169	61	213	39	36	10	4	1	21	37	9	1	1	81	11	8	.268	.315
Arias, Andelson	B-R	6-1	170	6-14-00	.091	.000	.118	7	22	1	2	0	0	0	0	3	0	0	0	13	0	0	.091	.200
Batista, Carlos	L-L	6-2	177	10-30-99	.100	.111	.097	13	40	4	4	0	0	0	0	5	2	1	0	17	0	0	.100	.234
De La Cruz, Julio	R-R	6-3	170	1-29-01	.211	.083	.254	28	95	8	20	1	0	0	10	12	1	0	0	26	2	0	.221	.306
Echavarria, Vladimir	R-R	5-11	160	4-12-00	.205	.219	.201	60	176	32	36	7	2	2	20	55	8	1	1	70	16	8	.301	.413
Garcia, Juan	R-R	6-0	170	3-16-01	.093	.105	.090	34	86	14	8	2	0	1	7	20	8	0	1	52	3	2	.151	.313
Guerra, Emmanuel	R-R	6-3	185	11-16-00	.221	.224	.219	57	195	42	43	11	1	7	34	44	10	0	2	77	4	0	.395	.387
Heredia, Cristian	R-R	6-3		4-12-01	.240	.278	.226	54	200	27	48	9	0	4	24	26	1	0	0	63	1	3	.345	.330
Morales, Yanger	R-R	6-0	175	6-17-00	.190	.133	.203	30	79	13	15	3	0	0	10	18	9	0	3	28	1	0	.228	.385
Nova, Victor	B-R	5-9	160	1-6-00	.197	.261	.181	38	117	21	23	3	1	2	17	33	1	0	3	30	7	2	.291	.370
Paez, Luis	R-R	5-10	160	9-3-00	.256	.262	.253	60	227	42	58	6	1	0	20	50	3	0	0	32	11	9	.291	.396
Perez, Junior	R-R	6-1	165	7-4-01	.177	.113	.199	61	204	26	36	6	2	3	26	53	4	0	2	80	12	5	.270	.354
Polanco, Matias	L-R	5-11	175	9-18-00	.260	.192	.284	30	100	7	26	2	0	0	17	15	0	0	3	25	2	1	.280	.348
Santana, Yeison	R-R	5-11	160	12-7-00	.258	.290	.248	36	132	23	34	1	5	0	25	33	3	0	5	30	5	1	.341	.405
Torres, Bryan	R-R	5-9	165	12-11-99	.226	.264	.212	54	199	30	45	6	0	0	24	34	2	1	4	35	9	3	.256	.339
Valenzuela, Brandon	R-R	6-0		10-2-00	.253	.250	.256	54	198	34	50	7	2	1	27	39	3	0	3	59	1	3	.323	.379

Pitching	B-T	HT	WT	DOB	W	L	ERA	G	GS	CG	SV	IP	H	R	ER	HR	BB	SO	AVG	vLH	vRH	K/9	BB/9
Asencio, Eudi	R-R	6-1	170	6-18-99	2	2	4.50	15	12	0	0	52	54	36	26	1	30	50	.260	.333	.246	8.65	5.19
Batista, Bryan	L-L	6-3	175	1-1-99	0	2	8.10	14	0	0	0	13	9	19	12	0	28	11	.177	.231	.158	7.43	18.90
Carrizoza, Sergio	R-R	6-1	154	7-15-00	4	2	1.85	16	2	0	1	44	30	17	9	1	18	42	.189	.200	.185	8.66	3.71
Castaneda, Alfredo	R-R	6-2	175	7-10-00	2	2	4.00	14	0	0	0	18	10	11	8	0	13	17	.152	.182	.136	8.50	6.50
Cisneros, Jesus	R-R	6-0	155	12-7-00	2	2	4.38	11	3	0	0	25	22	21	12	1	13	24	.218	.102	.327	8.76	4.74
Contreras, Efrain	R-R	5-10	185	1-2-00	0	0	1.40	5	3	0	1	19	12	4	3	1	3	25	.171	.179	.167	11.64	1.40
Garcia, Jeferson	R-R	6-0	165	2-4-00	0	0	2.00	3	1	0	0	9	6	2	2	0	2	15	.177	.333	.161	15.00	2.00
Garcia, Jose	L-L	5-11	169	2-19-98	1	1	2.17	17	1	0	5	29	17	8	7	2	5	31	.168	.111	.181	9.62	1.55
Geraldo, Jose	R-R	6-3	200	1-30-99	1	0	4.74	16	0	0	1	19	17	11	10	1	7	18	.239	.313	.218	8.53	3.32
Gonzalez, Cesar	R-R	6-1	160	2-24-99	1	3	7.20	17	0	0	2	20	23	19	16	4	10	21	.284	.250	.302	9.45	4.50
Gonzalez, Jesus	L-L	5-10	160	6-12-01	4	2	2.20	13	7	0	0	49	43	17	12	1	7	45	.231	.103	.255	8.27	1.29
Guarate, Carlos	R-R	6-2	178	3-30-01	1	1	2.33	8	4	0	0	27	21	11	7	1	7	20	.219	.204	.234	6.67	2.33
Leo, Jorge	R-R	6-1	175	2-18-98	4	4	2.43	22	0	0	4	30	28	14	8	3	2	27	.257	.306	.233	8.19	0.91
Martinez, Edgar	R-R	5-10	155	2-26-01	2	2	2.01	13	5	0	1	49	47	13	11	2	14	40	.254	.254	.254	7.30	2.55
Mundo, Alan	R-R	6-2	170	5-27-00	2	4	6.09	16	4	0	0	34	37	27	23	4	24	29	.278	.308	.259	7.68	6.35
Partida, Manuel	L-L	6-1	175	9-25-00	2	4	2.31	13	12	0	0	58	48	20	15	0	11	58	.220	.278	.209	8.95	1.70
Rios, Nick	L-L	6-0		6-24-00	2	1	0.64	11	0	0	0	14	6	1	1	0	8	16	.136	.125	.139	10.29	5.14
Rodriguez, Mauricio	R-R	6-0	155	2-14-01	2	1	2.70	13	9	0	0	50	50	27	15	4	15	35	.263	.297	.232	6.30	2.70
Rondon, Miguel	R-R	5-11	150	1-26-01	2	1	2.52	13	9	0	0	50	39	19	14	0	12	50	.209	.205	.210	9.00	2.16
Sosa, Heriberto	R-R	6-0	170	11-9-98	1	2	5.70	16	0	0	1	24	22	19	15	1	14	26	.242	.300	.213	9.89	5.32

Fielding

C: Arias 1, Morales 13, Polanco 26, Valenzuela 37. **1B:** De La Cruz 21, Guerra 48, Valenzuela 6. **2B:** Garcia 9, Nova 5, Paez 46, Torres 16. **3B:** Echavarria 46, Nova 21, Torres 6. **SS:** Echavarria 10, Garcia 4, Santana 33, Torres 29. **OF:** Antunez 60, Batista 12, Echavarria 4, Garcia 3, Heredia 53, Morales 12, Nova 11, Paez 9, Perez 59.

San Francisco Giants

SEASON IN A SENTENCE: After trading for former all-stars Andrew McCutchen and Evan Longoria in the offseason, the Giants were bit by the injury bug (again), struggled offensively (again) and missed the playoffs for the first time in an "even year" since 2008.

HIGH POINT: The Giants won seven of eight from June 26 to July 1, including a three-game sweep of the D-backs, to jump to a season-high five games over .500. The Giants were one game ahead of the Dodgers and 3.5 games ahead of the Rockies in the NL West standings, and those two teams ended the regular season tied for the division title.

LOW POINT: Being swept by the Reds from Aug. 17-19 to fall three games below .500 was likely the end to the Giants' playoff hopes. But it was San Francisco's 11-game losing streak from Sept. 1-12, which came immediately after the organization traded McCutchen to the Yankees, that officially waved the white flag on the Giants' 2018 season.

NOTABLE ROOKIES: Lefthander Andrew Suarez started 29 games and logged a career-high 160.1 innings for the Giants. He ended his rookie campaign 7-13, 4.49 with 130 strikeouts, while righthander Dereck Rodriguez made 21 appearances (19 starts) and went 6-4, 2.81 in 118.1 innings. Prospects Chris Shaw and Tyler Beede also made their debuts in 2018. A first-round pick in 2015, Shaw hit .185/.274/.278 in a 54 at-bat sample, while Beede, a 2014 first-round righthander, made two starts. Center fielder Steven Duggar showed promise in 41 games, playing above-average defense and hitting .255/.303/.390 before suffering a season-ending shoulder injury.

KEY TRANSACTIONS: The Giants traded for McCutchen and Longoria in the offseason, and also signed outfielder Austin Jackson and lefthander Tony Watson, in an effort to get back to the postseason for the second time in three years. By the time the Aug. 31 waiver trade deadline came around, however, the Giants decided they were out of the mix and traded McCutchen to the Yankees for prospects Abiatal Avelino and Juan De Paula.

DOWN ON THE FARM: Only the Angels (.430) and Reds (.453) had a worse organizational winning percentage than the Giants, whose domestic minor league teams combined for a .457 mark. The Giants joined the Angels, Marlins and Orioles as the only organizations to have zero affiliates qualify for the playoffs.

OPENING DAY PAYROLL: $221,426,944 (1st).

ORGANIZATION LEADERS

Batting		*Minimum 250 AB
MAJORS		
* AVG	Buster Posey	.284
* OPS	Andrew McCutchen	.772
HR	Evan Longoria	16
RBI	Andrew McCutchen	55
MINORS		
* AVG	Diego Rincones, Salem-Keizer	.315
* OBP	Heath Quinn, San Jose	.376
* SLG	Chris Shaw, Sacramento	.505
* OPS	Heath Quinn, San Jose	.861
R	Jalen Miller, San Jose	73
H	Wander Franco, San Jose	143
H	Manuel Geraldo, Augusta	143
TB	Jalen Miller, San Jose	222
2B	Wander Franco, San Jose	39
3B	Logan Baldwin, Augusta	10
HR	Chris Shaw, Sacramento	24
RBI	Gio Brusa, San Jose	70
BB	Jacob Heyward, San Jose, Sacramento	62
SO	Gio Brusa, San Jose	149
SO	Logan Baldwin, Augusta	149
SB	Johneshwy Fargas, San Jose	47

Pitching		#Minimum 75 IP
MAJORS		
W	Chris Stratton	10
# ERA	Dereck Rodriguez	2.81
SO	Derek Holland	169
SV	Will Smith	14
SV	Hunter Strickland	14
MINORS		
W	Casey Kelly, Sacramento	10
L	Jordan Johnson, Richmond, Sacramento	13
# ERA	John Gavin, Augusta, San Jose	2.87
G	Tyler Rogers, Sacramento	51
GS	Conner Menez, San Jose, Sacramento, Richmond	28
SV	Frank Rubio, Augusta, Richmond, San Jose	19
IP	Shaun Anderson, Richmond, Sacramento	141
BB	Garrett Cave, Augusta	67
SO	Conner Menez, San Jose, Sacramento, Richmond	171
# AVG	John Gavin, Augusta, San Jose	.195

2018 PERFORMANCE

General Manager: Bobby Evans. **Farm Director:** David Bell. **Scouting Director:** John Barr.

Class	Team	League	W	L	PCT	Finish	Manager
Majors	San Francisco Giants	National	73	89	.451	12th (15)	Bruce Bochy
Triple-A	Sacramento River Cats	Pacific Coast	55	85	.393	15th (16)	Dave Brundage
Double-A	Richmond Flying Squirrels	Eastern	62	76	.449	12th (12)	Willie Harris
High A	San Jose Giants	California	59	81	.421	8th (8)	Lipso Nava
Low A	Augusta GreenJackets	South Atlantic	67	70	.489	8th (14)	Jolbert Cabrera
Short season	Salem-Keizer Volcanoes	Northwest	36	40	.474	5th (8)	Hector Borg
Rookie	AZL Giants Black	Arizona	30	25	.545	6th (18)	Carlos Valderrama
Rookie	AZL Giants Orange	Arizona	30	26	.536	t-8th (18)	Bill Horton
Overall 2018 Minor League Record			339	403	.457	28th (30)	

ORGANIZATION STATISTICS

SAN FRANCISCO GIANTS
NATIONAL LEAGUE

Batting	B-T	HT	WT	DOB	AVG	vLH	vRH	G	AB	R	H	2B	3B	HR	RBI	BB	HBP	SH	SF	SO	SB	CS	SLG	OBP
Avelino, Abiatal	R-R	5-11	195	2-14-95	.273	.222	.500	6	11	1	3	0	0	0	0	0	0	0	0	3	0	0	.273	.273
Belt, Brandon	L-L	6-4	235	4-20-88	.253	.221	.270	112	399	50	101	18	2	14	46	49	6	0	2	107	4	0	.414	.342
Blanco, Gregor	L-L	5-10	187	12-24-83	.217	.207	.219	68	189	19	41	7	3	2	12	12	0	1	1	58	6	2	.318	.262
Crawford, Brandon	L-R	6-2	227	1-21-87	.254	.274	.243	151	531	63	135	28	2	14	54	50	8	0	5	122	4	5	.394	.325
d'Arnaud, Chase	R-R	6-1	197	1-21-87	.215	.254	.115	42	93	9	20	5	0	3	9	4	1	1	1	37	2	1	.366	.253
Duggar, Steven	L-R	6-2	189	11-4-93	.255	.333	.222	41	141	20	36	11	1	2	17	10	0	0	1	44	5	1	.390	.303
Garcia, Aramis	R-R	6-2	220	1-12-93	.286	.227	.317	19	63	8	18	1	0	4	9	2	0	0	0	31	0	0	.492	.308
Gomez, Miguel	B-R	5-9	206	12-17-92	.267	.400	.200	9	15	3	4	0	0	0	1	0	0	0	0	5	0	0	.267	.267
Hanson, Alen	B-R	6-0	170	10-22-92	.252	.183	.274	110	294	36	74	17	5	8	39	9	1	3	3	71	7	3	.425	.274
Hernandez, Gorkys	R-R	6-1	196	9-7-87	.234	.227	.239	142	414	52	97	16	2	15	40	27	4	2	4	113	8	5	.391	.285
Hundley, Nick	R-R	6-0	203	9-8-83	.241	.280	.213	96	282	34	68	13	2	10	31	22	1	0	0	85	2	1	.408	.298
Jackson, Austin	R-R	6-1	198	2-1-87	.242	.288	.188	59	149	12	36	8	0	0	13	14	1	0	1	59	2	1	.295	.309
2-team total (57 New York)					.245	.252	.241	116	347	29	85	17	1	3	32	26	1	0	1	133	3	3	.326	.299
Jones, Ryder	L-R	6-2	221	6-7-94	.375	.000	.429	5	8	2	3	0	0	2	3	0	0	0	0	5	0	0	1.125	.375
Longoria, Evan	R-R	6-1	215	10-7-85	.244	.250	.241	125	480	51	117	25	4	16	54	22	5	0	5	101	3	1	.413	.281
McCutchen, Andrew	R-R	5-11	195	10-10-86	.255	.272	.246	130	482	65	123	28	2	15	55	73	7	0	6	123	13	6	.415	.357
Panik, Joe	L-R	6-1	200	10-30-90	.254	.191	.282	102	358	38	91	14	1	4	24	26	3	1	4	30	4	2	.332	.307
Pence, Hunter	R-R	6-4	230	4-13-83	.226	.192	.252	97	235	19	53	11	1	4	24	11	0	0	2	59	5	1	.332	.258
Posey, Buster	R-R	6-1	210	3-27-87	.284	.300	.276	105	398	47	113	22	1	5	41	45	3	0	2	53	3	2	.382	.359
Sandoval, Pablo	B-R	5-11	268	8-11-86	.248	.146	.280	92	230	22	57	10	1	9	40	19	2	0	1	52	0	0	.417	.310
Shaw, Chris	L-R	6-3	226	10-20-93	.185	.143	.192	22	54	1	10	2	0	1	7	7	0	0	1	23	1	0	.278	.274
Slater, Austin	R-R	6-2	197	12-13-92	.251	.273	.238	74	199	21	50	6	1	1	23	20	5	0	1	69	7	0	.307	.333
Tomlinson, Kelby	R-R	6-2	171	6-16-90	.207	.197	.217	63	140	9	29	4	2	0	10	9	2	1	0	35	0	2	.264	.265
Williamson, Mac	R-R	6-4	237	7-15-90	.213	.286	.182	28	94	14	20	4	0	4	11	11	0	0	0	27	1	1	.383	.295

Pitching	B-T	HT	WT	DOB	W	L	ERA	G	GS	CG	SV	IP	H	R	ER	HR	BB	SO	AVG	vLH	vRH	K/9	BB/9
Beede, Tyler	R-R	6-3	211	5-23-93	0	1	8.22	2	2	0	0	8	9	7	7	0	8	9	.290	.278	.308	10.57	9.39
Blach, Ty	R-L	6-1	213	10-20-90	6	7	4.25	47	13	0	0	119	133	62	56	8	41	75	.289	.289	.289	5.69	3.11
Black, Ray	R-R	6-5	225	6-26-90	2	2	6.17	26	0	0	0	23	17	16	16	4	10	33	.207	.261	.186	12.73	3.86
Bumgarner, Madison	R-L	6-4	242	8-1-89	6	7	3.26	21	21	0	0	130	118	51	47	14	43	109	.238	.247	.237	7.57	2.98
Cueto, Johnny	R-R	5-11	229	2-15-86	3	2	3.23	9	9	0	0	53	46	19	19	8	13	38	.238	.237	.240	6.45	2.21
Dyson, Sam	R-R	6-1	212	5-7-88	4	3	2.69	74	0	0	3	70	56	23	21	5	20	56	.228	.244	.219	7.17	2.56
Gearrin, Cory	R-R	6-1	205	4-14-86	1	1	4.20	35	0	0	1	30	33	14	14	5	13	31	.275	.333	.236	9.30	3.90
Gomez, Roberto	R-R	6-6	200	8-3-89	1	0	7.71	5	0	0	0	9	20	11	8	0	1	8	.426	.476	.385	7.71	0.96
Holland, Derek	B-L	6-2	213	10-9-86	7	9	3.57	36	30	0	0	171	154	74	68	19	67	169	.241	.168	.262	8.88	3.52
Johnson, Pierce	R-R	6-2	200	5-10-91	3	2	5.56	37	0	0	0	44	38	27	27	5	22	36	.236	.222	.245	7.42	4.53
Kelly, Casey	R-R	6-3	215	10-4-89	0	3	3.04	7	3	0	0	24	28	10	8	3	5	16	.292	.366	.236	6.08	1.90
Law, Derek	R-R	6-3	215	9-14-90	1	0	7.43	7	0	0	0	13	16	13	11	2	8	12	.286	.241	.333	8.10	5.40
Melancon, Mark	R-R	6-2	215	3-28-85	1	4	3.23	41	0	0	3	39	48	18	14	2	14	31	.302	.328	.287	7.15	3.23
Moronta, Reyes	R-R	5-11	241	1-6-93	5	2	2.49	69	0	0	1	65	34	20	18	4	37	79	.154	.188	.132	10.94	5.12
Okert, Steven	L-L	6-2	202	7-9-91	0	0	1.23	10	0	0	0	7	4	1	1	1	0	8	.148	.167	.133	9.82	0.00
Osich, Josh	L-L	6-3	232	9-3-88	0	0	8.25	12	0	0	0	12	20	11	11	2	7	10	.385	.474	.333	7.50	5.25
Rodriguez, Dereck	R-R	6-1	215	6-5-92	6	4	2.81	21	19	0	0	118	98	43	37	9	36	89	.223	.227	.220	6.77	2.74
Samardzija, Jeff	R-R	6-5	240	1-23-85	1	5	6.25	10	10	0	0	45	47	32	31	6	26	30	.270	.301	.248	6.04	5.24
Smith, Will	R-L	6-5	248	7-10-89	2	3	2.55	54	0	0	14	53	37	18	15	3	15	71	.194	.171	.207	12.06	2.55
Snelten, D.J.	L-L	6-6	240	5-29-92	0	0	10.38	4	0	0	0	4	9	6	5	2	3	4	.391	.455	.333	8.31	6.23
Stratton, Chris	R-R	6-2	211	8-22-90	10	10	5.09	28	26	1	0	145	153	87	82	19	54	112	.273	.289	.255	6.95	3.35
Strickland, Hunter	R-R	6-3	225	9-24-88	3	4	3.97	49	0	0	14	45	43	25	20	5	21	37	.247	.186	.307	7.35	4.17
Suarez, Andrew	L-L	6-0	187	9-11-92	7	13	4.49	29	29	0	0	160	163	85	80	23	45	130	.269	.208	.290	7.30	2.53
Valdez, Jose A.	R-R	5-11	210	3-1-90	0	0	12.60	4	0	0	0	5	8	7	7	3	1	4	.348	.417	.273	7.20	1.80
Watson, Tony	L-L	6-3	218	5-30-85	4	6	2.59	72	0	0	0	66	54	19	19	4	14	72	.224	.231	.219	9.82	1.91

Fielding

Catcher	PCT	G	PO	A	E	DP	PB
Garcia	1.000	7	54	3	0	0	0
Hundley	.990	83	566	27	6	2	6
Posey	.997	88	677	37	2	3	3
d'Arnaud	1.000	17	26	30	0		9
Gomez	1.000	3	4	8	0		3
Hanson	.975	45	70	88	4		24
Panik	.985	94	153	237	6		65
Sandoval	1.000	2	2	4	0		1
Tomlinson	.956	35	60	70	6		23

First Base	PCT	G	PO	A	E	DP
Belt	.991	104	786	93	8	92
d'Arnaud	1.000	4	12	0	0	3
Garcia	.988	10	80	3	1	9
Jones	1.000	2	1	0	0	0
Panik	1.000	1	10	0	0	1
Posey	1.000	13	87	8	0	9
Sandoval	.985	24	191	7	3	15
Slater	.989	21	165	9	2	18

Second Base	PCT	G	PO	A	E	DP
Avelino	.833	1	3	2	1	1

Third Base	PCT	G	PO	A	E	DP
d'Arnaud	1.000	10	2	13	0	0
Hanson	.947	10	5	13	1	1
Jones	1.000	1	1	0	0	0
Longoria	.950	123	72	213	15	25
Sandoval	.986	36	14	55	1	3
Tomlinson	1.000	3	1	7	0	0

Shortstop	PCT	G	PO	A	E	DP
Avelino	1.000	3	3	6	0	0
Crawford	.975	146	192	435	16	105
d'Arnaud	.000	1	0	0	0	0
Hanson	1.000	16	16	33	0	6
Tomlinson	1.000	13	15	28	0	8

Outfield	PCT	G	PO	A	E	DP
Belt	1.000	8	5	1	0	0
Blanco	.969	59	93	0	3	0
Duggar	.979	40	93	1	2	0
Hanson	1.000	20	24	1	0	0
Hernandez	.978	126	260	3	6	1
Jackson	.961	41	73	0	3	0
McCutchen	.992	128	245	8	2	1
Pence	.990	55	97	0	1	0
Shaw	1.000	15	18	1	0	0
Slater	.973	39	70	2	2	0
Williamson	1.000	27	40	3	0	0

SACRAMENTO RIVER CATS TRIPLE-A
PACIFIC COAST LEAGUE

Batting	B-T	HT	WT	DOB	AVG	vLH	vRH	G	AB	R	H	2B	3B	HR	RBI	BB	HBP	SH	SF	SO	SB	CS	SLG	OBP
Albertson, Will	R-R	5-11	190	6-26-94	.000	—	.000	2	2	0	0	0	0	0	0	0	0	0	0	2	0	0	.000	.000
Arnold, Jeff	R-R	6-2	210	1-13-88	.119	.143	.114	13	42	2	5	1	0	0	2	6	0	0	0	21	0	0	.143	.229
Avelino, Abiatal	R-R	5-11	195	2-14-95	.154	.000	.250	3	13	2	2	0	0	0	1	0	0	0	0	3	2	0	.154	.154
Belt, Brandon	L-L	6-4	235	4-20-88	.200	.000	.333	2	5	0	1	1	0	0	0	0	0	0	0	0	0	0	.400	.200
Blanco, Gregor	L-L	5-10	187	12-24-83	.247	.300	.231	60	170	20	42	7	2	4	13	23	0	1	0	40	2	1	.382	.337
Bourjos, Peter	R-R	6-1	175	3-31-87	.296	.407	.241	44	162	20	48	7	4	2	14	7	3	0	1	35	0	2	.426	.335
Brown, Trevor	R-R	6-2	193	11-15-91	.242	.174	.257	41	128	11	31	4	0	0	12	16	1	0	0	24	2	0	.273	.331
Calixte, Orlando	R-R	6-0	183	2-3-92	.270	.240	.280	125	400	52	108	15	3	11	48	32	1	0	4	96	14	1	.405	.323
d'Arnaud, Chase	R-R	6-1	197	1-21-87	.293	.327	.283	76	253	54	74	14	4	12	43	40	4	0	3	65	15	3	.522	.393
Davis, Dylan	R-R	6-0	205	7-20-93	.000	.000	.000	3	8	0	0	0	0	0	0	0	0	0	0	3	0	0	.000	.000
Duggar, Steven	L-R	6-2	189	11-4-93	.272	.179	.292	78	316	52	86	27	4	4	21	39	1	0	0	103	11	4	.421	.354
Freeman, Ronnie	R-R	6-1	190	1-8-91	.264	.317	.241	60	201	15	53	7	1	3	29	12	1	0	3	41	0	0	.353	.304
Garcia, Aramis	R-R	6-2	220	1-12-93	.237	.273	.222	10	38	5	9	1	0	0	4	2	0	0	1	12	0	0	.263	.268
Gindl, Caleb	L-L	5-7	210	8-31-88	.277	.143	.333	29	47	7	13	5	0	0	6	9	0	2	1	15	0	1	.383	.386
Gomez, Miguel	B-R	5-9	206	12-17-92	.273	.250	.281	63	231	20	63	14	1	2	23	2	1	0	2	35	0	0	.368	.280
Hanigan, Ryan	R-R	6-0	225	8-16-80	.175	.154	.182	18	57	2	10	1	0	0	8	5	1	0	0	11	0	0	.193	.254
Hanson, Alen	B-R	6-0	170	10-22-92	.403	.350	.414	18	62	17	25	5	1	3	9	8	1	0	0	7	6	1	.661	.479
Heyward, Jacob	R-R	6-3	215	4-1-95	.400	.500	.333	2	5	1	2	1	0	0	0	0	0	0	0	3	0	0	.600	.500
Jensen, Kyle	R-L	6-3	255	5-20-88	.196	.077	.227	52	189	15	37	6	1	5	27	15	0	0	3	70	0	0	.318	.251
Jones, Ryder	L-R	6-2	221	6-7-94	.274	.230	.290	116	441	57	121	22	4	11	59	30	7	0	4	106	2	2	.417	.328
Longoria, Evan	R-R	6-1	215	10-7-85	.214	.250	.200	4	14	2	3	1	0	0	2	1	1	0	0	0	0	0	.286	.313
Murphy, Tanner	R-R	6-1	215	2-27-95	.000	—	.000	1	3	0	0	0	0	0	0	0	0	0	0	0	0	0	.000	.000
Panik, Joe	L-R	6-1	200	10-30-90	.333	.375	.300	6	18	2	6	0	0	0	1	2	0	0	0	3	0	0	.333	.400
Pence, Hunter	R-R	6-4	230	4-13-83	.301	.400	.269	25	103	11	31	4	0	1	13	6	1	0	1	24	0	0	.369	.342
Perez, Eury	R-R	6-0	190	5-30-90	.264	.267	.263	52	144	21	38	7	2	1	20	7	1	4	1	19	8	3	.361	.301
Polonius, John	R-R	6-1	160	1-13-91	.211	.125	.273	8	19	0	4	2	0	0	1	0	1	0	0	5	0	0	.316	.250
Puello, Cesar	R-R	6-2	220	4-1-91	.289	.353	.250	13	45	5	13	1	0	1	3	0	0	4	5	1	0	1	.311	.365
2-team total (73 Reno)					.313	.307	.315	86	294	48	92	11	3	6	37	40	17	1	6	67	6	4	.432	.417
Rutledge, Josh	R-R	5-11	186	4-21-89	.077	.000	.087	18	52	2	4	0	0	0	0	2	0	0	0	21	0	1	.077	.111
Sanchez, Hector	B-R	6-2	255	11-17-89	.241	.500	.185	24	79	10	19	4	0	1	8	9	1	0	0	18	0	1	.329	.326
Sands, Jerry	R-R	6-4	225	9-28-87	.310	.500	.245	22	71	10	22	4	0	3	7	10	1	0	0	13	1	0	.493	.402
Schafer, Jordan	L-L	6-1	205	9-4-86	.000	—	.000	7	1	2	0	0	0	0	0	0	0	0	0	1	0	0	.000	.000
Schroder, Myles	B-R	5-11	180	8-1-87	.244	.264	.234	90	279	34	68	15	2	9	24	12	7	2	2	84	5	3	.409	.290
Shaw, Chris	L-R	6-3	226	10-20-93	.259	.204	.276	101	394	55	102	21	2	24	65	21	7	0	2	144	0	0	.505	.308
Slater, Austin	R-R	6-2	197	12-13-92	.344	.319	.351	53	195	32	67	24	2	5	32	21	5	0	2	39	8	2	.564	.417
Stassi, Brock	L-L	6-2	190	8-7-89	.391	.444	.370	21	64	11	25	10	0	0	11	19	1	0	0	14	0	0	.547	.536
Tomlinson, Kelby	R-R	6-2	171	6-16-90	.304	.354	.286	48	181	15	55	2	0	0	10	18	0	4	1	44	7	4	.315	.365
Williamson, Mac	R-R	6-4	237	7-15-90	.269	.146	.305	52	182	31	49	7	1	13	44	23	8	0	2	44	1	0	.533	.372

Pitching	B-T	HT	WT	DOB	W	L	ERA	G	GS	CG	SV	IP	H	R	ER	HR	BB	SO	AVG	vLH	vRH	K/9	BB/9
Anderson, Shaun	R-R	6-4	225	10-29-94	2	2	4.18	8	8	0	0	47	48	27	22	5	11	34	.261	.293	.235	6.46	2.09
Baragar, Caleb	R-L	6-3	210	4-9-94	0	0	2.45	2	0	0	0	4	3	1	1	1	0	0	.214	.400	.111	0.00	0.00
Beede, Tyler	R-R	6-3	211	5-23-93	4	9	7.05	33	10	0	0	74	82	67	58	10	56	75	.288	.274	.300	9.12	6.81
Black, Ray	R-R	6-5	225	6-26-90	3	0	3.16	26	0	0	1	26	15	10	9	2	8	46	.167	.273	.065	16.13	2.81
Bumgarner, Madison	R-L	6-4	242	8-1-89	0	0	0.00	1	1	0	0	4	0	0	0	0	0	0	.000	.000	.000	19.64	2.45
Camarena, Daniel	L-L	6-0	210	11-9-92	1	3	5.65	16	15	0	0	80	97	53	50	9	32	64	.299	.282	.309	7.23	3.62
Connolly, Mike	R-R	6-1	205	10-31-91	0	4	6.94	9	7	0	0	36	50	30	28	9	14	21	.325	.234	.416	5.20	3.47
Cueto, Johnny	R-R	5-11	229	2-15-86	0	0	0.00	2	2	0	0	8	5	0	0	0	1	10	.179	.111	.211	11.74	1.17
Flores, Jose A.	R-R	6-3	250	6-4-89	1	5	7.29	14	8	0	0	46	57	49	37	7	24	35	.305	.351	.274	6.90	4.73
Gage, Matt	R-L	6-4	240	2-11-93	4	7	6.45	11	10	0	0	53	83	45	38	4	15	32	.356	.416	.327	5.43	2.55
2-team total (2 Las Vegas)					5	8	6.43	13	12	0	0	63	96	52	45	4	19	48	.350	.393	.330	6.86	2.71
Gomez, Roberto	R-R	6-6	200	8-3-89	1	3	5.00	14	0	0	2	18	23	12	10	3	7	13	.307	.423	.245	6.50	3.50

Name	B-T	HT	WT	DOB	W	L	ERA	G	GS	CG	SV	IP	H	R	ER	HR	BB	SO	AVG	vLH	vRH	SO/9	BB/9
Gregorio, Joan	R-R	6-8	264	1-12-92	1	2	12.00	4	0	0	0	6	11	10	8	1	2	6	.355	.400	.313	9.00	3.00
Halstead, Ryan	L-R	6-5	220	5-13-92	0	0	12.27	3	0	0	0	4	9	9	5	4	2	4	.450	.400	.500	9.82	4.91
Herb, Tyler	R-R	6-3	200	4-28-92	2	8	5.35	13	13	0	0	71	85	45	42	9	28	59	.306	.355	.275	7.51	3.57
Heston, Chris	R-R	6-3	195	4-10-88	0	0	2.70	1	1	0	0	3	3	1	1	0	2	5	.231	.000	.375	13.50	5.40
Hill, Taylor	R-R	6-3	230	3-12-89	1	3	7.77	6	5	0	0	24	34	22	21	4	9	14	.327	.346	.308	5.18	3.33
Johnson, Jordan	R-R	6-3	200	9-15-93	1	6	4.66	11	11	0	0	58	56	32	30	3	33	37	.261	.213	.286	5.74	5.12
Johnson, Pierce	R-R	6-2	200	5-10-91	0	0	3.57	17	0	0	4	23	15	10	9	1	10	30	.183	.200	.170	11.91	3.97
Kelly, Casey	R-R	6-3	215	10-4-89	10	9	4.76	24	24	0	0	136	155	80	72	19	38	111	.286	.298	.273	7.35	2.51
Knight, Dusten	R-R	6-0	200	9-7-90	0	0	0.00	4	0	0	0	6	5	1	0	0	2	2	.227	.167	.300	3.18	3.18
LaMarche, Will	R-R	6-3	220	8-7-91	0	0	27.00	1	0	0	0	1	3	3	3	1	2	1	.500	.000	.750	9.00	18.00
Law, Derek	R-R	6-3	215	9-14-90	1	3	4.20	33	0	0	8	41	34	22	19	2	9	43	.233	.194	.266	9.52	1.99
McNamara, Dillon	R-R	6-3	230	10-6-91	0	0	9.00	6	0	0	0	8	10	9	8	1	6	13	.313	.333	.286	14.63	6.75
Melancon, Mark	R-R	6-2	215	3-28-85	0	0	0.00	4	0	0	0	4	2	0	0	0	0	4	.154	.000	.200	9.82	0.00
Menez, Conner	L-L	6-3	205	5-29-95	1	1	3.27	2	2	0	0	11	6	4	4	0	5	9	.162	.167	.160	7.36	4.09
Okert, Steven	L-L	6-2	202	7-9-91	2	1	4.55	33	0	0	1	32	37	20	16	3	8	43	.289	.197	.373	12.22	2.27
Osich, Josh	L-L	6-3	232	9-3-88	0	0	4.96	37	2	0	0	45	56	31	25	2	18	42	.300	.324	.286	8.34	3.57
Overton, Connor	R-R	6-0	190	7-24-93	0	0	6.23	2	0	0	0	4	3	3	3	0	3	6	.267	.286	.250	12.46	6.23
Parra, Manny	L-L	6-3	215	10-30-82	3	2	4.28	45	0	0	2	55	63	31	26	2	26	53	.294	.284	.303	8.73	4.28
Rheault, Dylan	R-R	6-9	245	3-21-92	0	0	0.00	1	0	0	0	2	0	0	0	0	1	1	.000	.000	.000	4.50	4.50
Riggs, Nolan	R-R	6-8	255	5-22-93	0	0	4.76	2	0	0	0	6	5	3	3	0	3	1	.250	.111	.364	1.59	4.76
Rodriguez, Dereck	R-R	6-1	215	6-5-92	4	1	3.40	9	9	0	0	50	49	24	19	11	11	53	.250	.222	.278	9.48	1.97
Rogers, Tyler	R-R	6-5	187	12-17-90	3	2	2.13	51	0	0	3	68	50	17	16	4	23	60	.207	.273	.161	7.98	3.06
Samardzija, Jeff	R-R	6-5	240	1-23-85	0	2	5.29	4	4	0	0	17	17	10	10	5	3	20	.254	.177	.333	10.59	1.59
Smith, Will	R-L	6-5	248	7-10-89	0	0	0.00	6	0	0	0	6	2	0	0	0	0	8	.105	.167	.077	12.71	0.00
Snelten, D.J.	L-L	6-6	240	5-29-92	1	1	4.08	13	0	0	0	18	14	12	8	0	9	15	.203	.217	.196	7.64	4.58
Stratton, Chris	R-R	6-2	211	8-22-90	3	0	3.00	4	4	0	0	24	25	9	8	3	8	24	.263	.278	.244	9.00	3.00
Strickland, Hunter	R-R	6-3	225	9-24-88	0	0	0.00	4	0	0	0	4	0	0	0	0	0	7	.000	.000	.000	15.75	0.00
Suarez, Andrew	L-L	6-0	187	9-11-92	2	0	1.08	3	3	0	0	17	10	4	2	0	7	16	.179	.273	.156	8.64	3.78
Valdez, Jose A.	R-R	5-11	210	3-1-90	3	4	4.93	37	0	0	1	49	44	29	27	3	35	58	.243	.256	.232	10.58	6.39
Younginer, Madison	R-R	6-3	209	11-3-90	1	1	8.53	18	1	0	0	25	40	27	24	1	22	24	.345	.295	.400	8.53	7.82
2-team total (3 Oklahoma City)					1	1	11.00	21	1	0	0	27	43	36	33	1	30	26	.347	.281	.417	8.67	10.00

Fielding

Catcher	PCT	G	PO	A	E	DP	PB
Arnold	1.000	13	77	5	0	0	3
Brown	1.000	32	255	24	0	2	5
Freeman	.989	52	418	41	5	4	5
Garcia	.976	10	74	9	2	1	1
Hanigan	1.000	14	123	10	0	0	2
Murphy	1.000	8	8	1	0	0	0
Sanchez	1.000	24	173	10	0	0	4

First Base	PCT	G	PO	A	E	DP
Belt	1.000	2	6	1	0	2
Brown	1.000	7	48	8	0	5
d'Arnaud	.981	16	101	5	2	11
Jensen	.986	41	266	18	4	26
Jones	1.000	6	51	2	0	3
Sands	.992	16	122	5	1	14
Schroder	.985	40	238	18	4	27
Slater	.976	13	77	6	2	4
Stassi	.994	19	147	15	1	16

Second Base	PCT	G	PO	A	E	DP
Calixte	1.000	4	8	10	0	3
d'Arnaud	.976	32	58	62	3	16

	PCT	G	PO	A	E	DP
Gomez	.968	57	83	130	7	38
Hanson	1.000	15	27	31	0	7
Panik	1.000	6	9	7	0	2
Polonius	.000	1	0	0	0	0
Rutledge	.941	14	18	30	3	5
Schroder	.928	19	31	33	5	8
Tomlinson	1.000	10	9	22	0	4

Third Base	PCT	G	PO	A	E	DP
Calixte	.895	20	8	26	4	3
d'Arnaud	1.000	5	3	5	0	0
Jones	.932	103	54	179	17	24
Longoria	.800	4	0	4	1	0
Polonius	.000	1	0	0	0	0
Rutledge	1.000	1	0	3	0	0
Sands	.000	1	0	0	0	0
Schroder	.944	12	4	13	1	0
Tomlinson	1.000	5	6	5	0	1

Shortstop	PCT	G	PO	A	E	DP
Avelino	1.000	3	7	7	0	1
Calixte	.945	83	127	180	18	37
d'Arnaud	.965	23	37	46	3	9

	PCT	G	PO	A	E	DP
Hanson	.667	2	1	1	1	1
Polonius	1.000	5	9	10	0	4
Schroder	1.000	2	3	5	0	1
Tomlinson	.971	34	48	84	4	26

Outfield	PCT	G	PO	A	E	DP
Blanco	1.000	45	70	1	0	0
Bourjos	.990	39	93	2	1	0
Calixte	.889	15	22	2	3	1
d'Arnaud	1.000	5	8	0	0	0
Davis	1.000	2	4	0	0	0
Duggar	.956	74	210	5	10	1
Gindl	.909	18	9	1	1	0
Hanson	1.000	1	2	0	0	0
Heyward	1.000	2	2	0	0	0
Pence	1.000	23	44	1	0	0
Perez	1.000	36	65	5	0	1
Puello	1.000	11	33	2	0	0
Schroder	1.000	18	30	2	0	0
Shaw	.959	86	137	4	6	0
Slater	.940	37	60	3	4	2
Stassi	.000	1	0	0	0	0
Williamson	.989	44	84	3	1	1

RICHMOND FLYING SQUIRRELS

DOUBLE-A

EASTERN LEAGUE

Batting	B-T	HT	WT	DOB	AVG	vLH	vRH	G	AB	R	H	2B	3B	HR	RBI	BB	HBP	SH	SF	SO	SB	CS	SLG	OBP
Arenado, Jonah	R-R	6-4	240	2-3-95	.200	.240	.182	102	340	28	68	20	0	5	39	19	2	0	4	72	1	2	.303	.244
Arnold, Jeff	R-R	6-2	210	1-13-88	.175	.194	.168	50	137	15	24	5	0	3	16	17	1	6	1	62	0	0	.277	.269
Brown, Tyler	R-R	6-1	180	1-18-95	.316	.429	.250	8	19	5	6	1	0	0	3	1	1	0	1	5	2	0	.368	.364
Carbonell, Daniel	R-R	6-3	200	3-29-91	.071	.000	.091	4	14	0	1	0	0	0	1	2	0	0	1	6	0	0	.071	.177
Castillo, Ali	R-R	5-9	180	6-19-89	.255	.303	.232	111	329	43	84	17	4	2	30	23	2	3	6	35	6	8	.350	.303
Davis, Dylan	R-R	6-0	205	7-20-93	.237	.183	.261	125	430	49	102	27	2	13	55	30	0	1	4	113	4	2	.400	.285
Dobson, Dillon	L-R	6-2	220	8-21-93	.172	.000	.198	71	180	24	31	7	0	6	15	25	2	0	1	65	2	3	.311	.279
Freeman, Ronnie	R-R	6-1	190	1-8-91	.194	.182	.200	12	31	1	6	0	0	0	2	5	0	0	0	8	0	0	.194	.306
Garcia, Aramis	R-R	6-2	220	1-12-93	.233	.217	.237	80	301	36	70	14	1	11	33	20	4	0	3	76	0	1	.395	.287
Gindl, Caleb	L-L	5-7	210	8-31-88	.304	.386	.282	68	207	24	63	14	1	3	28	22	0	0	4	33	0	1	.425	.365
Gomez, Miguel	B-R	5-9	206	12-17-92	.313	.302	.318	53	192	16	60	12	4	4	25	7	0	0	2	28	1	0	.479	.333
Hill, Nick	R-R	6-4	190	8-2-94	.250	1.000	.000	2	4	0	1	0	0	0	2	0	0	0	0	1	0	1	.250	.250
Hinojosa, C.J.	R-R	5-10	175	7-15-94	.261	.264	.260	67	253	26	66	14	1	3	26	24	2	2	2	28	5	3	.360	.327
Hobson, K.C.	L-L	6-2	230	8-22-90	.220	.250	.217	18	50	6	11	3	0	3	6	7	1	0	0	23	0	1	.460	.328

Name	B-T	HT	WT	DOB	AVG	vLH	vRH	G	AB	R	H	2B	3B	HR	RBI	BB	HBP	SH	SF	SO	SB	CS	SLG	OBP
Howard, Ryan	R-R	6-2	195	7-25-94	.273	.250	.282	117	422	44	115	32	4	4	50	39	4	5	5	55	9	5	.396	.336
Jebavy, Ronnie	R-R	6-2	205	5-17-94	.168	.244	.125	76	238	29	40	6	2	4	23	29	3	0	2	73	10	3	.261	.265
Lipka, Matt	R-R	6-1	190	4-15-92	.240	.207	.261	123	304	47	73	12	5	4	30	40	3	4	6	57	21	8	.352	.329
Polonius, John	R-R	6-1	160	1-13-91	.222	.229	.217	37	81	12	18	4	0	1	7	9	1	1	1	17	3	0	.309	.304
Riley, John	R-R	6-0	210	2-14-94	.250	.200	.286	26	60	8	15	3	1	1	8	7	1	0	0	26	1	0	.383	.338
Rodriguez, Luigi	L-R	5-11	160	11-13-92	.271	.213	.285	114	380	54	103	13	5	14	51	38	4	1	2	119	15	10	.442	.342
Sands, Jerry	R-R	6-4	225	9-28-87	.258	.284	.247	78	252	41	65	24	0	13	39	34	2	0	1	65	3	0	.508	.350
Winn, Matt	R-R	6-1	210	8-5-92	.255	.294	.235	19	51	4	13	6	0	1	4	6	0	1	0	21	0	0	.431	.333

Pitching	B-T	HT	WT	DOB	W	L	ERA	G	GS	CG	SV	IP	H	R	ER	HR	BB	SO	AVG	vLH	vRH	K/9	BB/9
Anderson, Shaun	R-R	6-4	225	10-29-94	6	5	3.45	17	16	0	0	94	93	42	36	9	22	93	.256	.258	.254	8.90	2.11
Black, Ray	R-R	6-5	225	6-26-90	0	0	0.90	10	0	0	4	10	4	2	1	0	4	20	.118	.100	.125	18.00	3.60
Camarena, Daniel	L-L	6-0	210	11-9-92	0	0	2.57	1	1	0	0	7	6	4	2	1	1	2	.231	.267	.182	2.57	1.29
Connolly, Mike	R-R	6-1	205	10-31-91	3	4	5.11	20	7	0	0	62	64	35	35	4	24	48	.271	.298	.241	7.01	3.50
Cyr, Tyler	R-R	6-2	211	5-5-93	0	1	6.00	8	0	0	3	9	7	6	6	0	6	8	.206	.214	.200	8.00	6.00
Diaz, Carlos	L-L	6-2	225	11-18-93	2	0	3.12	32	0	0	0	40	32	15	14	1	23	36	.218	.164	.256	8.03	5.13
Flores, Jose A.	R-R	6-3	250	6-4-89	0	1	6.94	6	2	0	0	12	20	10	9	0	5	9	.392	.364	.444	6.94	3.86
Gage, Dylan	R-R	6-4	240	2-11-93	0	2	3.18	4	4	0	0	23	24	12	8	3	15	25	.270	.238	.279	5.96	1.19
2-team total (3 Binghamton)					2	3	3.15	7	7	0	0	40	48	19	14	3	7	32	.300	.222	.316	7.20	1.58
Gardeck, Ian	R-R	6-2	220	11-21-90	0	0	0.00	6	0	0	0	6	5	3	0	0	3	6	.208	.375	.125	9.00	4.50
Halstead, Ryan	L-R	6-5	220	1-15-92	4	4	2.72	32	0	0	0	56	52	24	17	5	15	51	.251	.266	.239	8.15	2.40
Heston, Chris	R-R	6-3	195	4-10-88	1	0	5.00	3	1	0	0	9	10	5	5	1	3	7	.294	.381	.154	7.00	3.00
Hill, Taylor	R-R	6-3	230	3-12-89	0	8	5.40	14	10	0	0	52	66	38	31	10	11	37	.303	.246	.375	6.45	1.92
Johnson, Chase	R-R	6-4	192	1-9-92	2	5	3.86	18	18	0	0	58	52	31	25	3	21	37	.235	.220	.250	5.71	3.24
Johnson, Jordan	R-R	6-3	200	9-15-93	6	7	3.63	15	15	2	0	79	80	38	32	3	31	77	.261	.232	.290	8.74	3.52
Knight, Dusten	R-R	6-0	200	9-7-90	4	1	2.27	20	0	0	0	36	26	12	9	2	10	35	.206	.226	.192	8.83	2.52
LaMarche, Will	R-R	6-3	220	8-7-91	0	1	5.28	15	0	0	0	31	37	19	18	6	14	29	.298	.297	.300	8.51	4.11
Lannoo, Peter	R-R	6-6	220	11-13-94	0	0	0.00	1	0	0	0	2	2	0	0	0	0	2	.286	.250	.333	10.80	0.00
McCasland, Jake	R-R	6-2	225	9-13-91	4	7	4.66	32	14	0	0	106	117	61	55	7	43	75	.279	.280	.277	6.35	3.64
McNamara, Dillon	R-R	6-5	230	10-6-91	4	2	1.20	33	0	0	0	45	29	15	6	0	8	50	.186	.219	.157	10.00	1.60
Menez, Conner	L-L	6-3	205	5-29-95	4	6	4.38	15	15	0	0	74	73	37	36	1	34	92	.261	.198	.289	11.19	4.14
Overton, Connor	R-R	6-0	190	7-24-93	0	1	4.91	7	2	0	0	18	23	12	10	3	7	19	.303	.357	.235	9.33	3.44
Parra, Olbis	R-R	6-2	180	10-1-94	0	0	0.00	2	0	0	0	4	3	1	0	0	1	1	.200	.200	.200	2.25	2.25
Rheault, Dylan	R-R	6-9	245	3-21-92	0	0	3.38	2	0	0	0	3	4	2	1	0	4	4	.364	.333	.400	13.50	13.50
Riggs, Nolan	R-R	6-8	255	5-22-93	0	1	9.00	2	0	0	0	6	5	6	6	0	4	9	.217	.375	.133	13.50	6.00
Rubio, Frank	R-R	6-0	190	4-23-95	1	0	4.50	1	0	0	0	4	5	2	2	0	0	3	.313	.400	.273	6.75	0.00
Ruotolo, Patrick	R-R	5-10	220	1-16-95	1	1	2.42	23	0	0	4	26	18	7	7	5	10	36	.194	.151	.250	12.46	3.46
Samardzija, Jeff	R-R	6-5	240	1-23-85	0	0	0.00	1	1	0	0	4	1	0	0	0	1	1	.077	.000	.091	2.25	2.25
Simpson, Caleb	R-R	6-3	230	9-15-91	4	3	1.53	29	0	0	10	29	22	10	5	0	29	37	.210	.250	.175	11.35	8.90
Slania, Dan	R-R	6-5	275	5-24-92	1	3	2.43	47	1	0	1	70	51	20	19	7	21	69	.205	.222	.187	8.83	2.69
Taylor, Cory	R-R	6-2	255	12-14-93	8	1	3.95	11	11	0	0	55	53	24	24	8	27	31	.251	.284	.228	5.10	4.45
Van Gurp, Franklin	R-R	6-1	210	10-26-95	0	0	12.00	1	0	0	0	3	3	4	4	1	1	3	.250	.400	.143	9.00	3.00
Webb, Logan	R-R	6-2	220	11-18-96	1	2	3.82	6	6	0	0	31	30	16	13	4	11	26	.254	.392	.149	7.63	3.23
Williams, Garrett	L-L	6-1	200	9-15-94	3	9	6.06	33	15	0	1	82	96	63	55	6	61	73	.295	.274	.303	8.04	6.72
Wolff, Sam	R-R	6-1	204	4-14-91	1	2	6.91	22	0	0	5	27	36	24	21	1	16	38	.319	.364	.276	12.51	5.27

Fielding

Catcher	PCT	G	PO	A	E	DP	PB
Arnold	.990	40	281	28	3	3	0
Freeman	1.000	10	75	11	0	1	2
Garcia	.995	69	562	40	3	7	8
Riley	.981	9	47	5	1	0	2
Winn	.986	17	122	16	2	2	4

First Base	PCT	G	PO	A	E	DP
Arenado	.990	31	186	17	2	16
Arnold	1.000	1	1	0	0	0
Dobson	.984	26	180	9	3	21
Garcia	.987	11	70	7	1	7
Hobson	1.000	5	33	3	0	5
Polonius	1.000	2	5	0	0	0
Riley	1.000	10	72	7	0	10
Sands	.996	67	480	34	2	34

Second Base	PCT	G	PO	A	E	DP
Brown	1.000	5	6	13	0	3
Castillo	.978	30	34	54	2	10
Dobson	1.000	7	9	9	0	2
Gomez	.971	46	62	103	5	21
Hinojosa	.944	25	39	63	6	14
Howard	.986	21	34	35	1	10
Lipka	.700	2	4	3	3	1
Polonius	.938	14	21	24	3	9

Third Base	PCT	G	PO	A	E	DP
Arenado	.907	71	55	101	16	12
Brown	1.000	1	0	1	0	0
Castillo	.946	52	36	70	6	6
Dobson	.846	19	11	22	6	2
Hinojosa	.913	10	4	17	2	0
Lipka	.000	1	0	0	0	0

Shortstop	PCT	G	PO	A	E	DP
Castillo	.964	14	20	33	2	9
Hinojosa	.947	31	52	56	6	13
Howard	.952	93	131	207	17	43
Polonius	1.000	8	9	18	0	4

Outfield	PCT	G	PO	A	E	DP
Carbonell	1.000	3	7	0	0	0
Castillo	1.000	13	19	0	0	0
Davis	.984	110	173	10	3	1
Gindl	.988	45	80	3	1	1
Hill	1.000	1	2	0	0	0
Hobson	1.000	2	2	0	0	0
Jebavy	.970	73	158	6	5	1
Lipka	.981	113	198	10	4	1
Riley	.000	2	0	0	0	0
Rodriguez	.975	100	191	4	5	2
Sands	1.000	1	1	0	0	0

SAN JOSE GIANTS
CALIFORNIA LEAGUE

HIGH CLASS A

Batting	B-T	HT	WT	DOB	AVG	vLH	vRH	G	AB	R	H	2B	3B	HR	RBI	BB	HBP	SH	SF	SO	SB	CS	SLG	OBP
Arnold, Jeff	R-R	6-2	210	1-13-88	.261	.000	.353	6	23	2	6	2	0	0	3	2	0	0	0	7	0	0	.348	.320
Beltre, Kelvin	R-R	5-11	170	9-25-96	.236	.341	.204	56	191	18	45	4	0	5	15	22	2	0	0	71	1	3	.335	.321
Brusa, Gio	B-R	6-3	235	7-26-93	.238	.192	.249	107	408	62	97	23	5	19	70	35	2	1	5	149	8	0	.458	.298
Corbett, Chris	R-R	6-1	195	7-7-94	.200	.167	.211	15	50	5	10	3	0	0	3	3	0	0	0	14	0	0	.260	.245

Player	B-T	HT	WT	DOB	AVG	vLH	vRH	G	AB	R	H	2B	3B	HR	RBI	BB	HBP	SH	SF	SO	SB	CS	SLG	OBP
De La Rosa, Frandy	B-R	6-2	202	1-24-96	.227	.143	.247	49	181	19	41	2	3	6	23	13	3	3	0	59	0	1	.370	.289
Dobson, Dillon	L-R	6-2	220	8-21-93	.222	.150	.239	29	108	9	24	7	0	4	17	6	1	0	0	38	1	1	.398	.270
Fabian, Sandro	R-R	6-1	180	3-6-98	.200	.193	.201	112	406	47	81	19	1	10	35	26	9	3	5	107	1	2	.325	.260
Fargas, Johneshwy	R-R	6-1	180	12-15-94	.288	.308	.280	89	278	47	80	9	2	8	32	21	9	4	3	49	47	16	.421	.354
Franco, Wander	R-R	6-2	170	12-13-94	.277	.278	.277	124	516	55	143	39	1	5	65	11	4	1	2	113	4	3	.386	.296
Hanson, Alen	B-R	6-0	170	10-22-92	.300	.333	.286	3	10	1	3	0	0	1	2	0	0	0	0	2	0	0	.600	.300
Heyward, Jacob	R-R	6-3	215	8-1-95	.258	.313	.244	112	407	61	105	26	1	12	47	61	4	1	4	104	14	8	.415	.357
Hinojosa, C.J.	R-R	5-10	175	7-15-94	.308	.333	.304	7	26	2	8	1	0	0	2	2	0	0	0	6	1	0	.346	.357
Johnson, Bryce	B-R	6-1	190	10-27-95	.249	.279	.243	116	441	62	110	18	6	1	35	54	7	7	2	116	31	4	.324	.339
Manwaring, Dylan	R-R	6-3	210	9-27-94	.429	1.000	.000	3	7	1	3	3	0	0	0	1	0	0	0	1	0	0	.857	.500
Miller, Jalen	R-R	5-11	190	12-19-96	.276	.254	.282	123	511	73	141	35	2	14	62	27	8	5	3	121	11	4	.434	.321
Murphy, Tanner	R-R	6-1	215	2-27-95	.172	.250	.146	40	128	7	22	1	1	0	6	15	2	2	0	38	1	0	.195	.269
Panik, Joe	L-R	6-1	200	10-30-90	.286	.000	.333	2	7	1	2	1	0	0	1	2	0	0	0	1	0	0	.429	.375
Polonius, John	R-R	6-1	160	1-13-91	.125	.000	.154	5	16	2	2	1	0	0	1	0	0	1	0	0	0	0	.188	.222
Quinn, Heath	R-R	6-3	220	6-7-95	.300	.405	.270	96	357	53	107	24	0	14	51	42	4	0	4	98	4	1	.485	.376
Riley, John	B-R	6-0	210	2-14-94	.205	.385	.129	14	44	4	9	3	0	1	4	3	0	0	0	13	0	0	.341	.255
Rivera, Kevin	B-R	5-11	170	6-12-96	.238	.200	.250	8	21	2	5	3	0	0	4	4	0	0	1	10	0	0	.381	.346
Sabanosh, Connor	R-R	6-2	200	8-6-93	.200	.111	.250	8	25	3	5	0	0	0	3	5	0	0	1	6	0	0	.200	.222
Tomlinson, Kelby	R-R	6-2	171	6-16-90	.444	—	.444	2	9	1	4	1	0	0	2	0	0	0	0	0	0	0	.556	.444
Van Horn, Brandon	R-R	6-2	180	12-18-93	.211	.227	.206	104	369	36	78	19	1	10	39	29	1	3	3	108	8	8	.350	.269
Winn, Matt	R-R	6-1	210	8-5-92	.233	.333	.208	74	258	34	60	15	3	9	34	25	1	1	0	108	0	0	.419	.303

Pitching	B-T	HT	WT	DOB	W	L	ERA	G	GS	CG	SV	IP	H	R	ER	HR	BB	SO	AVG	vLH	vRH	K/9	BB/9
Adon, Melvin	R-R	6-3	235	6-9-94	2	5	4.87	16	15	0	0	78	82	46	42	6	34	71	.278	.283	.273	8.23	3.94
Bahr, Jason	R-R	6-5	190	2-15-95	2	0	1.69	3	3	0	0	16	12	3	3	3	2	15	.197	.077	.286	8.44	1.13
Baragar, Caleb	R-L	6-3	210	4-9-94	1	2	4.76	8	1	0	0	11	13	9	6	0	6	12	.260	.300	.233	9.53	4.76
Bartlett, Keenan	R-R	6-9	195	9-27-95	0	0	7.36	2	0	0	0	4	4	3	3	1	2	1	.333	.333	.333	2.45	4.91
Beede, Tyler	R-R	6-3	211	5-23-93	0	0	1.80	1	1	0	0	5	1	1	1	0	3	4	.067	.000	.100	7.20	5.40
Bumgarner, Madison	R-L	6-4	242	8-1-89	0	0	1.93	1	1	0	0	5	2	1	1	1	0	7	.133	.500	.077	13.50	0.00
Burke, Jeff	R-R	6-5	210	6-7-93	1	1	8.16	16	0	0	0	29	40	28	26	3	13	15	.342	.367	.324	4.71	4.08
Cabrera, Sandro	L-L	6-2	195	6-22-95	6	5	4.88	34	9	0	0	101	130	66	55	10	53	85	.311	.254	.341	7.55	4.71
Cederoth, Michael	R-R	6-6	215	11-25-92	0	0	2.70	6	0	0	0	10	6	4	3	0	13	11	.177	.222	.125	9.90	11.70
Coonrod, Sam	R-R	6-2	225	9-22-92	0	0	5.68	6	0	0	0	6	5	7	4	0	2	13	.200	.133	.300	18.47	2.84
Diaz, Carlos	L-L	6-2	225	11-18-93	1	1	1.69	8	0	0	0	16	10	3	3	0	2	13	.185	.217	.161	7.31	1.13
Gardeck, Ian	R-R	6-2	220	11-21-90	0	0	2.25	4	0	0	0	4	5	2	1	0	4	1	.313	.286	.333	4.50	2.25
Gavin, John	R-L	6-6	230	10-10-95	1	2	5.60	6	6	0	0	27	30	19	17	7	10	28	.278	.300	.265	9.22	3.29
Gettman, CJ	L-R	6-5	215	6-2-94	0	1	4.76	3	0	0	0	6	6	3	3	1	2	7	.316	.364	.250	11.12	3.18
Gudino, Norwith	R-R	6-2	200	11-22-95	0	0	0.00	1	0	0	0	3	0	0	0	0	0	2	.250	.500	.000	6.00	0.00
Horn, Trevor	R-R	6-1	200	12-25-95	0	0	2.57	4	0	0	0	7	3	2	2	0	1	5	.130	.250	.067	6.43	1.29
Lannoo, Peter	R-R	6-6	220	11-13-94	1	7	4.19	31	0	0	2	58	72	30	27	9	21	39	.295	.303	.290	6.05	3.26
Marciano, Joey	L-L	6-5	250	1-11-95	1	4	8.33	13	4	0	0	31	35	30	29	11	15	26	.280	.261	.291	7.47	4.31
Marshall, Mac	R-L	6-1	205	1-27-96	6	1	5.43	19	18	0	0	56	47	37	34	6	40	64	.227	.167	.259	10.22	6.39
Martinez, Rodolfo	R-R	6-2	200	4-4-94	3	9	5.76	45	0	0	5	55	67	54	35	6	31	48	.295	.349	.248	7.90	5.10
Mazza, Domenic	R-L	6-1	195	7-29-94	3	6	4.52	13	11	0	0	68	86	38	34	6	23	56	.311	.291	.323	7.45	3.06
Menez, Conner	L-L	6-3	205	5-29-95	2	5	4.83	11	11	0	0	50	48	29	27	2	21	70	.262	.244		12.52	3.75
Myers, DJ	L-R	6-5	265	12-24-94	6	4	4.86	24	9	0	0	96	107	54	52	8	22	94	.278	.207	.323	8.78	2.06
Overton, Connor	R-R	6-0	190	7-24-93	2	0	4.68	14	0	0	2	25	26	13	13	2	7	23	.263	.262	.263	8.28	2.52
Perry, Travis	R-R	6-4	190	3-8-97	0	0	3.00	2	0	0	0	3	2	1	1	0	1	2	.200	.500	.167	6.00	3.00
Quiroz, Orleny	L-L	6-3	180	7-21-93	1	0	2.00	11	0	0	1	18	15	4	4	0	8	12	.227	.143	.267	6.00	4.00
Rheault, Dylan	R-R	6-9	245	3-21-92	2	3	2.43	25	0	0	3	37	41	10	10	2	12	30	.275	.329	.224	7.30	2.92
Riggs, Nolan	R-R	6-8	255	5-22-93	5	5	4.08	41	0	0	6	64	53	33	29	5	33	73	.229	.190	.260	10.27	4.64
Roberts, Chris	R-R	6-0	210	7-3-97	0	0	108.00	1	0	0	0	0	3	4	4	1	3	1	.667	.667	—	27.00	81.00
Rubio, Frank	R-R	6-0	190	4-23-95	2	2	5.52	24	0	0	9	31	36	23	19	3	8	23	.290	.313	.276	6.68	2.32
Ruotolo, Patrick	R-R	5-10	220	1-16-95	3	0	1.47	14	0	0	6	18	12	5	3	0	7	26	.191	.172	.206	12.76	3.44
Russell, John	R-R	6-3	170	10-17-95	0	0	0.00	2	0	0	0	4	3	0	0	0	0	5	.200	.222	.167	11.25	0.00
Samardzija, Jeff	R-R	6-5	240	1-23-85	0	0	20.25	1	1	0	0	3	5	6	6	1	2	5	.385	.571	.167	16.88	6.75
Sano, Carlos	R-R	6-4	205	2-24-93	5	5	3.81	20	12	0	0	87	77	44	37	9	36	85	.237	.247	.228	8.76	3.71
Schimpf, Tyler	R-R	6-4	210	3-8-95	0	0	3.86	1	0	0	0	2	2	1	1	0	2	2	.250	.250	.250	7.71	0.00
Smith, Will	R-L	6-5	248	7-10-89	0	0	10.80	2	0	0	0	4	4	2	2	0	0	3	.444	.333	.667	16.20	0.00
Still, Doug	L-L	6-2	220	8-2-95	0	0	7.71	3	0	0	0	5	5	4	4	0	1	7	.375	.222	.467	13.50	1.93
Strickland, Hunter	R-R	6-3	225	9-24-88	0	0	13.50	1	0	0	0	1	1	1	1	1	1	1	.333	—	.333	13.50	13.50
Suarez, Andrew	L-L	6-0	187	9-11-92	0	1	1.35	1	1	0	0	7	8	1	1	0	2	7	.308	.143	.368	9.45	2.70
Van Gurp, Franklin	R-R	6-1	210	10-26-95	1	0	6.95	14	0	0	0	22	16	18	17	6	20	33	.198	.333	.118	13.50	8.18
Vizcaino, Raffi	R-R	6-1	235	12-2-95	5	5	4.65	17	16	0	0	79	70	45	41	11	52	85	.243	.229	.255	9.64	5.90
Walker, Ryan	R-R	6-2	200	11-26-95	1	0	1.69	4	0	0	0	5	5	1	1	1	2	3	.250	.250	.250	5.06	3.38
Webb, Logan	R-R	6-2	220	11-18-96	1	3	1.82	21	20	0	0	74	54	23	15	2	36	74	.207	.211	.204	9.00	4.38
Woods, Stetson	R-R	6-8	200	1-15-95	1	0	0.00	1	1	0	0	5	1	0	0	0	0	2	.063	.111	.000	3.60	0.00

Fielding

Catcher	PCT	G	PO	A	E	DP	PB
Arnold	1.000	6	54	4	0	1	1
Corbett	.978	15	129	3	3	0	3
Manwaring	.909	1	8	2	1	0	0
Murphy	.997	40	348	25	1	2	2
Riley	1.000	1	5	0	0	0	0
Sabanosh	.988	8	79	4	1	0	2
Winn	.989	73	596	54	7	5	18

First Base	PCT	G	PO	A	E	DP
Brusa	.976	87	627	28	16	65
De La Rosa	.973	25	208	10	6	27
Dobson	.957	14	65	2	3	9
Franco	1.000	6	37	1	0	6
Manwaring	1.000	2	8	0	0	0
Riley	1.000	12	69	6	0	6

Second Base	PCT	G	PO	A	E	DP
Beltre	.982	14	27	27	1	5
De La Rosa	.889	3	5	3	1	0
Hanson	1.000	1	3	3	0	1
Miller	.968	119	230	281	17	59
Panik	1.000	1	4	2	0	1
Polonius	1.000	1	2	3	0	0
Rivera	.917	2	2	9	1	0
Tomlinson	1.000	1	1	4	0	1
De La Rosa	.714	7	4	6	4	1
Dobson	.882	6	6	9	2	0
Franco	.933	103	69	168	17	19
Polonius	.000	1	0	0	0	0
Rivera	.857	3	1	5	1	0
Van Horn	1.000	2	2	4	0	0
Polonius	1.000	3	2	8	0	3
Tomlinson	1.000	1	5	4	0	3
Van Horn	.944	101	154	250	24	65

Third Base	PCT	G	PO	A	E	DP
Beltre	.885	20	18	28	6	5

Shortstop	PCT	G	PO	A	E	DP
Beltre	.945	22	35	51	5	9
Franco	.920	6	6	17	2	3
Hanson	1.000	2	6	7	0	3
Hinojosa	.889	6	9	15	3	4

Outfield	PCT	G	PO	A	E	DP
Fabian	.972	112	234	8	7	0
Fargas	.973	80	169	10	5	2
Heyward	.977	67	119	10	3	2
Johnson	1.000	112	244	7	0	0
Quinn	.976	58	78	4	2	0

AUGUSTA GREENJACKETS

LOW CLASS A

SOUTH ATLANTIC LEAGUE

Batting	B-T	HT	WT	DOB	AVG	vLH	vRH	G	AB	R	H	2B	3B	HR	RBI	BB	HBP	SH	SF	SO	SB	CS	SLG	OBP
Abrams, Trevor	R-R	6-4	215	4-23-95	.229	.226	.230	31	105	8	24	5	0	1	10	7	0	0	1	39	1	0	.305	.274
Angomas, Jean	L-R	6-0	170	6-5-95	.254	.368	.212	22	71	9	18	5	1	0	9	0	1	1	0	7	0	2	.352	.333
Baldwin, Logan	L-L	6-0	170	4-9-96	.249	.266	.244	121	429	60	107	22	10	6	44	28	10	6	1	149	26	10	.389	.310
Bennett, T.J.	L-R	6-3	215	7-22-92	.278	.000	.333	6	18	4	5	1	0	1	3	0	1	0	0	9	0	1	.500	.316
Bond, Aaron	L-R	6-5	195	2-16-97	.205	.191	.211	28	78	12	16	1	0	0	6	12	0	0	3	29	3	1	.218	.301
Brown, Tyler	R-R	6-1	180	1-18-95	.250	.129	.304	38	100	13	25	6	0	0	5	7	5	3	0	26	4	3	.310	.330
Calabrese, Rob	R-R	6-1	205	10-3-95	.193	.250	.170	67	197	24	38	6	2	5	21	19	7	1	3	67	3	1	.320	.283
DalPorto, Tim	R-R	6-2	190	5-8-96	.286	.333	.250	3	7	1	2	0	0	0	1	0	1	0	1	1	0	0	.286	.333
Garcia, Orlando	R-R	6-2	190	12-31-95	.244	.283	.228	123	423	59	103	17	2	8	40	57	10	4	7	137	9	6	.350	.342
Geraldo, Manuel	B-R	6-0	170	9-23-96	.294	.282	.300	124	486	71	143	15	1	9	52	30	3	3	3	121	24	9	.385	.337
Gonzalez, Jacob	R-R	6-3	190	6-26-98	.227	.226	.227	122	459	54	104	20	2	8	45	31	15	0	2	107	7	5	.331	.296
Hill, Nick	R-R	6-4	190	8-2-94	.259	.269	.254	59	189	19	49	9	0	1	17	16	8	1	1	79	13	3	.323	.341
Kirby, Ryan	L-R	6-2	180	1-25-95	.232	.183	.249	127	444	62	103	32	1	14	61	52	15	0	2	134	4	2	.403	.331
Layer, Abdiel	B-R	6-2	170	8-9-98	.000	.000	.000	4	11	1	0	0	0	0	0	2	0	0	0	6	0	1	.000	.154
Matheny, Shane	L-R	6-2	205	6-5-96	.205	.171	.216	92	317	38	65	4	2	6	33	36	5	0	5	109	2	4	.287	.292
McPherson, Kyle	R-R	5-11	180	2-9-96	.000	.000	.000	1	2	0	0	0	0	0	0	1	0	0	0	1	0	1	.000	.333
Munguia, Ismael	L-L	5-10	158	10-19-96	.226	.185	.236	37	133	9	30	1	3	1	17	6	1	5	2	22	2	0	.301	.261
Parra, Jeffry	R-R	6-0	195	1-24-98	.190	.180	.194	72	221	20	42	10	0	7	25	26	7	4	2	79	1	0	.330	.293
Ramos, Heliot	R-R	6-2	185	9-7-99	.245	.227	.253	124	485	61	119	24	8	11	52	35	13	1	1	136	8	7	.396	.313
Riley, John	R-R	6-0	210	2-14-94	.316	.167	.424	17	57	11	18	4	1	4	20	7	0	0	1	19	1	0	.632	.385
Vizcaino, Jose Jr.	R-R	6-2	220	4-5-94	.200	.200	—	1	5	0	1	0	0	0	0	0	0	0	0	1	0	0	.200	.200
Ziegler, Malique	R-R	6-2	170	9-8-96	.235	.177	.258	50	183	21	43	9	2	4	16	20	6	3	2	60	7	5	.372	.327

Pitching	B-T	HT	WT	DOB	W	L	ERA	G	GS	CG	SV	IP	H	R	ER	HR	BB	SO	AVG	vLH	vRH	K/9	BB/9
Bahr, Jason	R-R	6-5	190	2-15-95	6	4	2.75	13	13	1	0	69	52	22	21	5	21	88	.211	.221	.200	11.53	2.75
Baragar, Caleb	R-L	6-3	210	4-9-94	2	2	4.03	16	11	0	0	67	62	30	30	9	13	73	.244	.188	.289	9.81	1.75
Bartlett, Keenan	R-R	6-1	170	9-27-95	1	0	4.50	11	0	0	1	16	16	12	8	1	5	14	.258	.235	.286	7.88	2.81
Cave, Garrett	R-R	6-4	200	7-18-96	6	10	5.20	27	26	0	0	116	112	74	67	11	67	118	.251	.197	.311	9.16	5.20
De Paula, Juan	R-R	6-3	165	9-22-97	0	1	1.80	1	1	0	0	5	1	1	1	1	1	9	.133	.077	.500	16.20	1.80
Doval, Camilo	R-R	6-2	185	7-4-97	0	3	3.06	44	0	0	11	53	40	24	18	2	27	78	.205	.280	.137	13.25	4.58
Gavin, John	R-L	6-6	230	10-10-95	5	5	2.08	20	20	1	0	95	54	26	22	8	37	111	.167	.211	.150	10.52	3.51
Gettman, CJ	L-R	6-5	215	6-2-94	2	0	1.26	7	0	0	0	14	8	2	2	1	4	16	.160	.138	.191	10.05	2.51
Gudino, Norwith	R-R	6-2	200	11-22-95	4	2	3.45	6	6	0	0	31	24	13	12	2	7	33	.205	.206	.204	9.48	2.01
Hernandez, Rayan	R-R	6-4	230	9-24-95	0	0	7.36	3	0	0	0	4	6	3	3	0	0	3	.375	.500	.167	7.36	0.00
Jacknewitz, Greg	L-L	6-3	210	6-26-95	0	0	0.00	1	0	0	0	4	6	0	0	0	0	3	.400	.250	.571	6.75	0.00
Koziol, Ryan	L-R	6-3	185	10-4-93	0	0	2.55	15	0	0	0	25	23	7	7	3	6	14	.253	.282	.231	5.11	2.19
Labrador, Jorge	R-R	6-1	180	3-9-99	0	0	15.88	3	1	0	0	6	8	10	10	2	6	7	.320	.250	.385	11.12	9.53
Lannoo, Peter	R-R	6-2	220	11-13-94	1	2	3.38	9	0	0	0	19	18	7	7	2	4	19	.254	.257	.250	9.16	1.93
Marciano, Joey	L-L	6-5	250	1-11-95	4	3	2.58	15	14	0	0	80	74	30	23	3	22	71	.246	.253	.243	7.95	2.46
Marte, Jose	R-R	6-3	180	6-14-96	7	7	4.70	25	25	0	0	119	127	68	62	10	50	112	.276	.256	.295	8.49	3.79
Parra, Olbis	R-R	6-2	180	10-1-94	4	6	2.24	35	0	0	3	68	67	30	17	5	9	50	.252	.282	.225	6.59	1.19
Phillips, Aaron	R-R	6-5	215	10-11-96	6	7	3.72	19	18	0	0	102	94	51	42	13	16	120	.240	.212	.266	10.62	1.42
Quiroz, Orleny	L-L	6-3	180	7-21-93	1	1	3.91	14	0	0	1	25	32	13	11	4	6	20	.311	.386	.254	7.11	2.13
Rivera, Eduardo	L-R	6-5	190	9-24-92	0	2	10.80	5	0	0	0	10	12	12	12	3	4	17	.293	.227	.368	15.30	3.60
Rubio, Frank	R-R	6-0	190	4-23-95	0	1	1.55	17	0	0	10	29	23	7	5	0	6	32	.221	.250	.192	9.93	1.86
Russell, John	R-R	6-3	170	10-17-95	8	5	2.49	36	0	0	7	61	39	22	17	6	19	72	.188	.162	.213	10.57	2.79
Sano, Carlos	R-R	6-4	205	2-24-93	0	0	0.00	2	0	0	1	5	1	0	0	0	0	7	.063	.000	.167	12.60	0.00
Santa Cruz, JJ	L-L	6-7	210	1-15-96	0	2	2.16	11	0	0	0	17	12	5	4	2	2	16	.203	.238	.184	8.64	1.08
Schimpf, Tyler	R-R	6-4	210	8-7-95	4	4	5.45	24	0	0	0	38	38	28	23	1	17	44	.262	.222	.301	10.42	4.03
Still, Doug	L-L	6-2	220	8-2-95	0	0	3.00	2	0	0	0	3	5	1	1	0	1	1	.385	1.000	.200	3.00	3.00
Timmins, John	R-R	6-6	215	1-20-94	0	1	6.33	21	0	0	1	27	38	24	19	2	6	34	.330	.269	.381	11.33	2.00
Van Gurp, Franklin	R-R	6-1	210	10-26-95	4	0	1.77	18	1	0	4	41	24	9	8	1	16	48	.170	.139	.197	10.62	3.54
Woods, Stetson	R-R	6-8	200	1-15-95	2	2	3.58	9	1	0	0	28	27	13	11	2	10	28	.257	.245	.268	9.11	3.25

Fielding

C: Bond 1, Calabrese 66, DalPorto 3, Matheny 1, Parra 72, Riley 3. **1B:** Abrams 15, Bennett 1, Brown 5, Kirby 110, Riley 7. **2B:** Abrams 1, Brown 7, Garcia 91, Matheny 39, McPherson 1. **3B:** Abrams 5, Brown 3, Gonzalez 94, Matheny 36. **SS:** Garcia 14, Geraldo 118, Layer 4, Matheny 1. **OF:** Abrams 1, Angomas 14, Baldwin 112, Bennett 3, Bond 23, Brown 18, Hill 54, Munguia 35, Ramos 113, Ziegler 47.

SALEM-KEIZER VOLCANOES
NORTHWEST LEAGUE

SHORT-SEASON

Batting	B-T	HT	WT	DOB	AVG	vLH	vRH	G	AB	R	H	2B	3B	HR	RBI	BB	HBP	SH	SF	SO	SB	CS	SLG	OBP
Abrams, Trevor	R-R	6-4	215	4-23-95	.361	.500	.311	15	61	9	22	8	1	1	8	2	1	0	0	19	0	0	.574	.391
Albertson, Will	R-R	5-11	190	6-26-94	.243	.375	.207	12	37	1	9	1	0	0	2	0	0	1	0	11	0	0	.270	.243
Bart, Joey	R-R	6-3	220	12-15-96	.298	.356	.279	45	181	35	54	14	2	13	39	12	9	0	1	40	2	1	.613	.370
Bond, Aaron	L-R	6-5	195	2-16-97	.268	.235	.280	45	183	38	49	6	5	14	39	14	1	1	2	58	8	1	.585	.320
Burks, Christopher	L-R	5-10	180	6-24-94	.175	.100	.209	24	63	7	11	3	0	0	6	3	0	0	0	19	1	1	.222	.212
Cairo, Victor	R-R	6-0	180	9-10-97	.200	.000	.250	2	5	0	1	0	0	0	2	0	0	0	0	2	0	0	.200	.200
Combs, Dalton	L-L	6-3	200	10-29-94	.318	.208	.343	38	129	20	41	8	1	5	21	8	5	0	2	35	1	0	.512	.375
Corbett, Chris	R-R	6-1	195	7-7-94	.333	.143	.385	13	33	10	11	2	0	1	3	6	2	0	0	8	0	0	.485	.463
Edie, Mikey	R-R	5-11	175	7-3-97	.328	.349	.317	36	125	18	41	6	0	1	10	11	5	1	1	16	8	8	.400	.401
Franco, Wander	R-R	6-1	189	10-11-96	.314	.305	.318	56	210	36	66	24	2	5	36	13	0	0	2	41	0	1	.519	.351
Genoves, Ricardo	R-R	6-2	190	5-14-99	.243	.208	.256	50	177	22	43	9	0	1	13	14	9	1	1	39	0	0	.311	.328
Giarratano, Nico	B-R	5-11	172	12-15-94	.269	.432	.213	50	171	27	46	11	0	5	27	18	0	3	1	41	1	1	.421	.337
Hill, Nick	R-R	6-4	190	8-2-94	.222	.214	.226	13	45	5	10	1	1	1	4	3	1	0	0	19	1	0	.356	.286
Layer, Jose	R-R	6-0	160	5-28-97	.280	.317	.267	39	157	26	44	7	2	5	22	16	3	0	2	45	4	3	.446	.354
Manning, Jett	B-R	6-1	180	5-13-97	.182	.300	.156	15	55	2	10	1	0	0	5	4	0	0	0	16	0	0	.200	.237
Manwaring, Dylan	R-R	6-3	210	9-27-94	.231	.200	.250	4	13	2	3	1	0	0	1	0	1	0	0	5	0	0	.308	.286
McPherson, Kyle	R-R	5-11	180	2-9-96	.314	.321	.312	65	280	49	88	23	3	7	32	23	3	3	2	44	2	4	.493	.370
Medrano, Robinson	R-R	6-3	180	4-20-96	.230	.241	.225	54	196	27	45	6	2	9	23	26	6	0	0	66	0	0	.418	.338
Rincones, Diego	R-R	6-0	175	6-14-99	.315	.328	.311	61	257	30	81	15	0	7	34	10	8	0	2	32	0	0	.455	.357
Rivera, Kevin	B-R	5-11	170	6-12-96	.216	.231	.210	27	88	18	19	2	2	0	8	4	1	1	0	22	2	1	.284	.258
Villar, David	R-R	6-0	205	1-27-97	.279	.290	.274	56	226	36	63	22	0	13	42	16	3	0	2	67	0	0	.549	.332

Pitching	B-T	HT	WT	DOB	W	L	ERA	G	GS	CG	SV	IP	H	R	ER	HR	BB	SO	AVG	vLH	vRH	K/9	BB/9
Bartlett, Keenan	R-R	6-1	170	9-27-95	1	2	4.58	9	0	0	1	20	19	11	10	2	5	15	.247	.310	.208	6.86	2.29
Bates, Solomon	R-R	6-2	210	3-16-97	6	0	4.88	13	0	0	0	28	26	17	15	2	14	45	.245	.256	.239	14.64	4.55
Becherer, Zach	R-R	6-4	220	9-4-95	1	1	5.49	18	0	0	0	20	19	13	12	3	19	18	.253	.313	.209	8.24	8.69
Casad, Cooper	R-R	6-0	185	5-14-96	0	1	2.84	3	0	0	0	6	10	6	2	1	1	8	.357	.429	.286	11.37	1.42
Corry, Seth	L-L	6-2	195	11-3-98	1	2	5.49	5	5	0	0	20	14	15	12	1	15	17	.200	.143	.225	7.78	6.86
De La Rosa, Alejandro	R-R	6-0	165	2-14-95	0	0	11.57	5	1	0	0	7	11	10	9	2	5	5	.344	.429	.278	6.43	6.43
DuBord, Alex	R-R	6-5	225	12-4-96	0	2	10.32	10	0	0	0	23	37	29	26	5	13	15	.366	.417	.321	5.96	5.16
Duprey, Sidney	L-L	6-3	230	11-15-96	2	2	3.99	21	0	0	0	29	30	18	13	0	17	26	.261	.318	.225	7.98	5.22
Figueroa, Miguel	R-R	6-2	165	8-9-97	2	5	7.41	14	5	0	0	38	53	35	31	3	17	16	.356	.397	.326	3.82	4.06
Frisbee, Matt	R-R	6-5	215	11-18-96	4	1	2.96	20	0	0	0	27	18	12	9	1	13	36	.186	.175	.193	11.85	4.28
Gudino, Norwith	R-R	6-2	200	11-22-95	4	4	5.36	9	8	0	0	45	53	30	27	5	6	41	.287	.288	.286	8.14	1.19
Hjelle, Sean	R-R	6-11	225	5-7-97	0	0	5.06	12	12	0	0	21	24	16	12	4	4	22	.273	.250	.292	9.28	1.69
Horn, Trevor	R-R	6-1	200	12-25-95	1	1	6.43	8	0	0	0	14	16	10	10	3	6	8	.302	.167	.371	5.14	3.86
Jacknewitz, Greg	L-L	6-3	210	6-26-95	4	3	6.88	15	6	0	0	54	72	45	41	10	20	45	.324	.345	.317	7.55	3.35
Meyer, Mack	R-R	6-0	190	10-31-94	2	4	5.04	20	0	0	0	30	39	18	17	1	12	15	.317	.286	.343	4.45	3.56
Moreno, Luis	R-R	6-2	174	8-3-98	0	0	9.00	1	0	0	0	2	2	2	2	0	1	0	.250	.500	.167	0.00	4.50
Pena, Francis	R-R	6-3	175	6-2-97	0	0	0.00	1	0	0	0	1	0	0	0	0	1	0	.000	.000	.000	0.00	9.00
Quiroz, Orleny	L-L	6-3	180	7-21-93	0	0	4.32	4	0	0	0	8	8	5	4	1	0	9	.235	.000	.333	9.72	0.00
Rivera, Blake	R-R	6-4	225	1-9-98	0	0	6.16	9	8	0	0	19	20	14	13	2	11	14	.263	.281	.250	6.63	5.21
Santa Cruz, JJ	L-L	6-7	220	1-15-96	0	0	1.88	6	0	0	1	14	13	4	3	0	6	11	.265	.231	.278	6.91	3.77
Santos, Gregory	R-R	6-2	190	8-28-99	2	5	4.53	12	12	0	0	50	64	34	25	3	15	46	.311	.333	.295	8.34	2.72
Still, Doug	L-L	6-2	220	8-2-95	2	0	2.84	8	0	0	1	19	17	6	6	2	6	21	.250	.200	.279	9.95	2.84
Tona, Jesus	R-R	5-10	170	3-30-96	0	1	0.87	23	0	0	12	31	17	6	3	1	8	41	.160	.106	.203	11.90	2.32
Toplikar, Trent	R-R	6-4	210	5-21-96	1	2	1.23	17	1	0	0	37	28	8	5	0	10	25	.206	.170	.225	6.14	2.45
Walker, Ryan	R-R	6-2	200	11-26-95	1	0	3.15	12	0	0	2	20	18	8	7	3	2	19	.234	.333	.180	8.55	0.90
Winn, Keaton	R-R	6-4	205	2-20-98	3	1	4.81	15	5	0	0	43	49	33	23	4	13	36	.288	.312	.269	7.53	2.72
Wong, Jake	R-R	6-2	215	9-3-96	0	2	2.30	11	11	0	0	27	28	8	7	1	6	27	.259	.204	.315	8.89	1.98
Woods, Stetson	R-R	6-8	200	1-15-95	0	1	5.06	4	3	0	0	21	20	12	12	7	4	15	.247	.273	.229	6.33	1.69

Fielding

C: Albertson 12, Bart 32, Corbett 4, Genoves 33. **1B:** Abrams 5, Combs 2, Corbett 1, Franco 31, Manwaring 1, Medrano 40. **2B:** Giarratano 2, Manning 4, McPherson 48, Rivera 23. **3B:** Abrams 8, Franco 15, Villar 55. **SS:** Giarratano 47, Manning 11, McPherson 18, Rivera 1. **OF:** Bond 45, Burks 20, Combs 29, Edie 35, Hill 12, Layer 39, Medrano 6, Rincones 51.

AZL GIANTS BLACK
ARIZONA LEAGUE

ROOKIE

Batting	B-T	HT	WT	DOB	AVG	vLH	vRH	G	AB	R	H	2B	3B	HR	RBI	BB	HBP	SH	SF	SO	SB	CS	SLG	OBP
Adkins, Kwan	L-L	6-2	195	10-2-96	.190	.286	.162	35	95	21	18	2	2	1	12	21	5	1	0	32	6	2	.284	.364
Almanzar, Angeddy	R-R	6-2	180	6-30-98	.089	.071	.092	23	79	6	7	1	1	0	3	13	1	1	0	41	1	0	.127	.226
Bennett, T.J.	L-R	6-3	215	7-22-92	.250	—	.250	3	8	3	2	0	0	1	2	2	0	0	3	0	0	.625	.500
Brickhouse, Cody	R-R	6-3	210	12-23-96	.279	.333	.268	23	68	10	19	3	0	1	5	13	3	0	0	21	1	0	.368	.417
Campos, Marcos	R-R	5-11	205	10-29-96	.178	.167	.181	29	90	11	16	3	2	0	13	12	3	2	0	14	3	2	.256	.295
Canario, Alexander	R-R	6-1	165	5-7-00	.250	.296	.242	45	176	36	44	5	2	6	19	27	3	1	1	51	8	5	.403	.358
Clarke, Zander	R-R	6-5	225	1-19-95	.238	.250	.235	20	63	11	15	6	1	0	6	15	3	0	0	21	2	2	.365	.407
Frankfort, Braden	L-R	6-0	205	3-14-96	.267	.071	.312	23	75	10	20	3	1	0	15	6	1	0	1	23	0	0	.333	.325
2-team total (2 AZL Giants Orange)					.250	.071	.312	25	80	11	20	3	1	0	16	8	1	0	2	26	0	0	.313	.319
Gutierrez, Raiber	R-R	5-10	165	12-10-99	.118	.000	.133	5	17	0	2	1	0	0	0	1	0	0	0	7	0	0	.177	.167
Guzman, Angel	R-R	6-0	155	5-17-00	.289	.125	.324	19	45	2	13	2	1	0	9	8	2	0	0	18	0	0	.378	.418

SAN FRANCISCO GIANTS

	B-T	HT	WT	DOB	AVG	vLH	vRH	G	AB	R	H	2B	3B	HR	RBI	BB	HBP	SH	SF	SO	SB	CS	SLG	OBP
Labour, Franklin	R-R	6-1	190	5-11-98	.269	.441	.208	37	130	23	35	14	2	1	20	18	5	0	0	40	7	1	.431	.379
Layer, Abdiel	B-R	6-2	170	8-9-98	.289	.405	.254	43	159	24	46	9	2	3	25	15	2	1	0	43	9	2	.428	.358
Manning, Jett	B-R	6-1	180	5-13-97	.100	.000	.111	4	10	0	1	0	0	0	0	1	1	0	0	0	0	0	.100	.250
Medina, Francisco	R-R	6-1	165	3-20-98	.229	.207	.235	35	131	22	30	6	3	2	15	11	1	0	1	47	3	0	.366	.292
Norris, Randy	R-R	6-1	190	8-8-97	.262	.407	.228	42	141	18	37	3	2	0	17	12	2	0	0	33	10	3	.312	.329
Perez, Eury	R-R	6-0	190	5-30-90	.000	—	.000	1	2	0	0	0	0	0	0	0	0	0	0	0	0	0	.000	.000
Rivero, Jose	L-R	5-11	158	4-30-98	.272	.177	.289	34	114	17	31	2	0	0	15	13	2	0	2	26	4	0	.290	.351
Roby, Sean	R-R	6-2	215	7-8-98	.281	.438	.242	44	160	29	45	8	1	5	23	16	3	0	3	36	0	1	.438	.352
2-team total (1 AZL Giants Orange)					.288	.438	.242	45	163	29	47	8	1	5	23	17	3	0	3	36	0	1	.442	.360
Tostado, Frankie	L-L	6-2	205	3-8-98	.281	.182	.304	43	171	34	48	12	1	3	35	13	1	0	2	23	2	0	.415	.332
Villar, David	R-R	6-0	205	1-27-97	.316	.500	.267	6	19	3	6	1	0	0	5	4	1	0	1	5	0	0	.368	.440
Watts, Enoc	B-R	6-0	160	12-2-99	.176	.105	.200	22	74	5	13	0	0	0	5	5	5	1	1	25	0	1	.176	.271
Ziegler, Malique	R-R	6-2	170	9-8-96	.250	.250	.250		28	3	7	3	0	0	2	8	0	0	0	8	1	1	.357	.417

Pitching

	B-T	HT	WT	DOB	W	L	ERA	G	GS	CG	SV	IP	H	R	ER	HR	BB	SO	AVG	vLH	vRH	K/9	BB/9
Acosta, Aneudy	R-R	5-11	180	4-7-96	1	2	5.16	17	0	0	0	30	31	21	17	1	10	26	.267	.292	.250	7.89	3.03
Adames, Abel	R-R	6-5	190	12-8-95	0	0	6.06	14	0	0	0	16	15	14	11	0	18	9	.254	.000	.326	4.96	9.92
Amaya, Luis	L-L	5-11	160	8-26-98	2	0	5.40	16	0	0	1	22	19	13	13	0	15	27	.244	.167	.278	11.22	6.23
Becherer, Zach	R-R	6-4	220	9-4-95	0	0	0.00	1	0	0	0	2	0	0	0	0	0	2	.000	—	.000	0.00	54.00
Casad, Cooper	R-R	6-0	185	5-14-96	2	1	3.21	12	0	0	4	14	11	6	5	2	6	13	.229	.273	.216	8.36	3.86
Christman, Garrett	L-R	6-2	195	1-6-96	1	5	5.68	12	0	0	1	13	16	10	8	0	2	8	.320	.444	.250	5.68	1.42
Concepcion, Victor	R-R	6-0	170	11-23-96	1	1	2.25	9	0	0	0	8	9	2	2	0	2	9	.273	.500	.241	10.13	2.25
Coonrod, Sam	R-R	6-2	225	9-22-92	0	0	5.06	4	2	0	0	5	5	3	3	0	1	10	.261	.375	.200	16.88	1.69
Cruz, Israel	R-R	6-1	170	6-1-97	5	1	3.97	13	12	0	0	59	59	28	26	5	26	66	.262	.253	.268	10.07	3.97
De La Rosa, Alejandro	R-R	6-5	165	2-14-95	0	0	27.00	1	0	0	0	1	1	2	2	0	1	1	.333	1.000	.333	13.50	13.50
Dusek, Dylan	L-L	6-2	215	2-20-95	2	1	2.03	9	0	0	0	13	9	5	3	1	5	18	.180	.143	.186	12.15	3.38
Gomez, Roberto	R-R	6-6	200	8-3-89	0	0	0.00	4	1	0	0	5	3	0	0	0	1	5	.158	.143	.167	9.00	1.80
Gregorio, Joan	R-R	6-8	264	1-12-92	1	0	0.00	1	0	0	0	1	0	0	0	0	2	0	.000	.000	.000	18.00	0.00
Herb, Tyler	R-R	6-3	200	4-28-92	1	1	5.68	4	4	0	0	13	13	9	8		4	8	.241	.353	.189	5.68	2.84
Herrera, Johan	R-R	6-1	170	12-8-98	2	4	4.25	12	9	0	0	42	49	23	20	2	8	32	.285	.360	.254	6.80	1.70
Horn, Trevor	R-R	6-1	200	12-25-95	1	0	1.23	11	0	0	4	15	8	3	2	1	2	14	.167	.235	.129	8.59	1.23
Koziol, Ryan	L-R	6-3	185	10-4-93	0	0	0.00	1	0	0	0	1	1	0	0	0	0	1	.250	.000	.500	9.00	0.00
Maita, Jose	L-L	5-11	180	12-23-97	0	0	5.19	16	0	0	0	17	12	10	10	0	9	17	.194	.077	.225	8.83	4.67
Moreno, Luis	R-R	6-2	174	8-3-98	4	2	2.91	13	9	1	1	59	61	26	19	2	13	58	.264	.295	.248	8.90	1.99
Nurse, Conner	R-R	6-6	210	7-31-99	1	1	3.23	12	11	0	0	53	48	27	19	1	26	56	.240	.266	.228	9.51	4.42
Perry, Travis	R-R	6-4	190	3-8-97	0	1	4.15	5	0	0	2	4	7	3	2	0	1	9	.368	.250	.455	2.08	2.08
2-team total (10 AZL Giants Orange)					2	1	3.50	15	0	0	3	18	16	8	7	1	6	13	.232	.250	.455	6.50	3.00
Pinto, Oliver	R-R	6-0	175	9-9-96	4	1	5.92	15	0	0	0	24	31	17	16	0	9	14	.330	.382	.300	5.18	3.33
Santa Cruz, JJ	L-L	6-7	220	1-15-96	0	0	0.00	1	0	0	0	1	1	0	0	0	0	3	.333	—	.333	18.00	0.00
2-team total (2 AZL Giants Orange)					0	0	0.00	3	0	0	0	4	2	0	0	0	3	5	.154	—	.333	10.38	6.23
Scott, Jordan	R-R	6-3	195	4-3-95	0	0	4.50	11	5	0	0	26	24	13	13	2	10	27	.253	.280	.243	9.35	3.46
Severino, Jerson	R-R	6-3	191	7-30-98	0	1	5.40	3	1	0	0	18	12	7	6	0	7	3	.293	.250	.320	2.70	6.30
Strahm, Ben	R-R	6-5	210	12-16-96	2	3	3.79	15	0	0	1	19	19	11	8	1	10	20	.253	.200	.280	9.47	4.74
Strickland, Hunter	R-R	6-3	225	9-24-88	0	0	0.00	1	1	0	0	2	1	0	0	0	0	2	.400	.500	.333	18.00	0.00
Yan, Weilly	R-R	6-0	175	1-30-96	0	0	5.19	10	0	0	0	9	5	5	5	1	11	8	.156	.308	.053	8.31	11.42

Fielding

C: Brickhouse 22, Frankfort 22, Guzman 19. **1B:** Almanzar 23, Clarke 7, Medina 8, Tostado 20. **2B:** Bennett 3, Campos 11, Rivero 34, Watts 10. **3B:** Layer 27, Medina 13, Roby 14, Villar 5. **SS:** Campos 19, Layer 13, Manning 2, Medina 12, Watts 12. **OF:** Adkins 30, Canario 44, Clarke 7, Gutierrez 4, Labour 35, Norris 38, Perez 1, Tostado 12, Ziegler 7.

AZL GIANTS ORANGE   ROOKIE
ARIZONA LEAGUE

Batting	B-T	HT	WT	DOB	AVG	vLH	vRH	G	AB	R	H	2B	3B	HR	RBI	BB	HBP	SH	SF	SO	SB	CS	SLG	OBP
Alvarado, Luis	R-R	5-11	175	11-23-99	.200	—	—	4	10	0	2	0	0	0	0	1	0	0	0	2	0	0	.200	.273
Angulo, Andres	R-R	5-10	181	9-5-97	.346	—	—	25	78	14	27	10	0	0	14	7	0	0	3	24	3	1	.474	.386
Antunez, Robert	R-R	5-10	160	3-22-96	.170	—	—	21	53	11	9	2	0	0	4	10	0	0	0	15	4	0	.208	.302
Bart, Joey	R-R	6-3	220	12-15-96	.261	—	—	6	23	3	6	1	1	0	1	1	1	0	0	7	0	0	.391	.320
Bell, George	R-R	6-4	215	5-8-98	.285	—	—	45	158	22	45	4	1	0	20	16	1	1	4	39	9	1	.323	.346
DalPorto, Tim	R-R	6-2	190	5-8-96	.204	—	—	15	49	6	10	0	0	0	3	8	0	0	0	8	0	0	.204	.316
De Leon, Wascar	B-R	5-11	180	1-8-98	.191	—	—	23	68	5	13	1	1	0	7	10	0	2	0	25	0	2	.235	.295
Edgette, Austin	L-L	6-2	185	7-6-95	.286	—	—	23	70	15	20	2	0	0	11	15	0	0	2	15	4	0	.329	.402
Flores, Tyler	L-L	6-2	185	1-24-96	.296	—	—	45	159	22	47	7	1	2	28	26	1	0	3	29	3	1	.390	.392
Frankfort, Braden	L-R	6-0	205	3-14-96	.000	—	—	2	5	1	0	0	0	0	1	2	0	0	1	3	0	0	.000	.250
2-team total (23 AZL Giants Black)					.250	.071	.312	25	80	11	20	3	1	0	16	8	1	0	2	26	0	0	.313	.319
Hernandez, Bryan	R-R		178	12-24-99	.138	—	—	21	58	3	8	3	0	0	6	16	2	0	0	29	3	0	.190	.342
Hilson, Patrick	R-R	5-11	175	8-25-00	.186	—	—	45	161	25	30	6	3	4	19	14	7	0	0	67	5	2	.335	.280
Jebavy, Ronnie	R-R	6-2	205	5-17-94	.071	—	—	5	14	0	1	1	0	0	0	3	0	0	0	9	0	0	.143	.235
Mendoza, Beicker	R-R	6-2	185	2-14-98	.301	—	—	44	173	25	52	16	0	4	35	8	2	0	5	55	5	1	.462	.330
Mora, Edison	R-R	6-2	165	8-13-00	.156	—	—	37	135	16	21	3	0	0	6	9	3	0	0	53	2	1	.178	.225
Munguia, Ismael	L-L	5-10	158	10-19-98	.345	—	—	15	58	11	20	6	3	0	4	4	1	0	0	6	0	1	.552	.397
Patino, Jose	R-R	6-0	160	12-11-97	.225	—	—	27	71	13	16	0	0	0	8	5	0	1	1	19	1	0	.225	.273
Pena, Fabian	R-R	5-11	205	10-18-96	.309	—	—	28	97	21	30	10	1	5	24	11	0	1	1	20	0	0	.588	.376
Roby, Sean	R-R	6-2	215	7-8-98	.667	—	—	1	3	0	2	0	0	0	0	1	0	0	0	0	0	0	.667	.750
2-team total (44 AZL Giants Black)					.288	.438	.242	45	163	29	47	8	1	5	23	17	3	0	3	36	0	1	.442	.360

SAN FRANCISCO GIANTS

Name	B-T	HT	WT	DOB	AVG	vLH	vRH	G	AB	R	H	2B	3B	HR	RBI	BB	HBP	SH	SF	SO	SB	CS	SLG	OBP
Rodriguez, Yorlis	R-R	6-0	187	7-20-99	.323	—	—	41	155	30	50	9	2	2	26	19	5	2	2	25	6	6	.445	.409
Sabanosh, Connor	R-R	6-0	200	8-6-93	.143	—	—	4	14	1	2	0	1	1	1	0	0	0	0	6	0	0	.500	.143
Santiago, Hector	R-R	6-3	185	11-18-97	.250	—	—	23	76	9	19	4	0	0	7	2	2	1	1	33	0	1	.303	.284
Sivira, Anyesber	R-R	5-9	155	1-9-00	.267	—	—	43	161	30	43	11	0	1	14	10	16	0	1	31	2	0	.354	.367

Pitching	B-T	HT	WT	DOB	W	L	ERA	G	GS	CG	SV	IP	H	R	ER	HR	BB	SO	AVG	vLH	vRH	K/9	BB/9
Adon, Melvin	R-R	6-3	235	6-9-94	0	1	7.71	2	0	0	0	5	9	5	4	0	3	8	.409	—	—	15.43	5.79
Beede, Tyler	R-R	6-3	211	5-23-93	0	0	0.00	1	0	0	0	1	0	0	0	0	0	2	.000	—	—	18.00	0.00
Bolivar, Deiyerbert	L-L	5-11	155	4-3-96	0	0	0.00	6	0	0	0	6	4	2	0	0	4	6	.200	—	—	9.00	6.00
Bostic, Alex	L-L	6-3	195	11-14-94	0	1	3.86	5	0	0	0	7	5	3	3	0	3	12	.200	—	—	15.43	3.86
Brown, Matt	R-R	6-6	215	6-12-96	0	1	3.95	10	1	0	0	14	16	6	6	0	10	5	.340	—	—	3.29	6.59
Corry, Seth	L-L	6-2	195	11-3-98	3	1	2.61	9	9	0	0	38	38	18	11	1	17	42	.260	—	—	9.95	4.03
Gardeck, Ian	R-R	6-2	220	11-21-90	1	1	7.36	4	0	0	0	4	4	3	3	0	3	4	.267	—	—	9.82	7.36
Gonzalez, Marco	L-L	6-1	180	12-8-97	3	7	6.28	12	10	0	0	57	82	57	40	6	14	55	.322	—	—	8.63	2.20
Harasta, Logan	R-R	6-6	235	8-29-96	1	1	1.10	13	0	0	1	16	11	6	2	0	5	28	.186	—	—	15.43	2.76
Helvey, Clay	R-R	6-3	195	2-14-97	1	3	9.43	14	0	0	0	21	36	23	22	2	14	16	.400	—	—	6.86	6.00
Herrera, Jasier	R-R	6-5	190	1-1-98	1	4	3.88	12	11	0	0	56	56	34	24	1	15	49	.257	—	—	7.92	2.43
Heston, Chris	R-R	6-3	195	4-10-88	0	0	0.00	5	1	0	0	7	5	0	0	0	1	7	.192	—	—	9.00	1.29
Knight, Dusten	R-R	6-0	200	9-7-90	0	0	0.00	5	0	0	1	6	2	0	0	0	0	11	.100	—	—	16.50	0.00
Labrador, Jorge	R-R	6-1	180	3-9-99	3	0	4.33	11	0	0	0	27	26	16	13	1	4	25	.241	—	—	8.33	1.33
Lopez, Jacob	L-L	6-4	220	3-11-98	1	1	1.42	9	0	0	0	25	18	4	4	2	6	34	.202	—	—	12.08	2.13
Madison, Ben	R-R	6-3	205	9-15-97	0	0	3.38	9	0	0	0	16	14	9	6	0	9	23	.226	—	—	12.94	5.06
Mazza, Domenic	R-L	6-1	195	7-29-94	1	0	0.00	2	0	0	0	6	4	2	0	0	0	5	.182	—	—	7.50	0.00
Pena, Francis	R-R	6-3	175	6-2-97	3	0	3.17	12	11	0	0	54	60	29	19	0	20	39	.278	—	—	6.50	3.33
Perry, Travis	R-R	6-4	190	3-8-97	2	0	3.29	10	0	0	1	14	9	5	5	1	5	12	.180	—	—	7.90	3.29
2-team total (5 AZL Giants Black)					2	1	3.50	15	0	0	3	18	16	8	7	1	6	13	.232	.250	.455	6.50	3.00
Roberts, Chris	R-R	6-0	210	7-3-97	2	1	2.45	14	0	0	0	22	12	15	6	1	14	34	.154	—	—	13.91	5.73
Rodriguez, Julio	R-R	6-3	180	2-10-00	3	1	2.20	8	0	0	0	16	11	5	4	0	11	15	.200	—	—	8.27	6.06
Rohloff, Andy	R-R	6-2	180	7-17-96	1	1	3.00	17	0	0	0	24	19	11	8	3	6	28	.211	—	—	10.50	2.25
Santa Cruz, JJ	L-L	6-7	220	1-15-96	0	0	0.00	2	0	0	0	3	1	0	0	0	3	3	.100	—	—	8.10	8.10
2-team total (1 AZL Giants Black)					0	0	0.00	3	0	0	0	4	2	0	0	0	3	5	.154	—	.333	10.38	6.23
Veras, Yoel	R-R	6-0	175	10-2-96	2	0	4.12	15	0	0	2	20	16	14	9	3	5	28	.205	—	—	12.81	2.29
Walker, Ryan	R-R	6-2	200	11-26-95	0	1	1.29	4	0	0	1	7	5	1	1	0	2	9	.192	—	—	11.57	2.57
White, Preston	R-R	6-6	215	7-29-96	1	2	3.00	7	0	0	1	6	7	3	2	0	2	5	.304	—	—	7.50	3.00
Wolff, Sam	R-R	6-1	204	4-14-91	0	0	0.00	3	0	0	0	4	2	0	0	0	1	6	.154	—	—	13.50	2.25

Fielding

C: Alvarado 3, Angulo 21, Bart 4, DalPorto 9, Frankfort 2, Pena 18, Sabanosh 4. 1B: Edgette 3, Flores 18, Mendoza 40. 2B: Antunez 15, De Leon 19, Sivira 24. 3B: De Leon 3, Rodriguez 34, Santiago 19, Sivira 1. SS: Antunez 2, Mora 37, Santiago 1, Sivira 16. OF: Bell 43, Edgette 18, Flores 26, Hernandez 21, Hilson 43, Jebavy 3, Munguia 7, Patino 23.

DSL GIANTS   ROOKIE
DOMINICAN SUMMER LEAGUE

Batting	B-T	HT	WT	DOB	AVG	vLH	vRH	G	AB	R	H	2B	3B	HR	RBI	BB	HBP	SH	SF	SO	SB	CS	SLG	OBP
Alcantara, Ismael	L-R	6-3	190	4-15-00	.262	.212	.273	51	172	26	45	12	0	3	32	32	6	0	0	49	4	1	.384	.395
Batista, Robinson	B-R	5-11	167	10-11-98	.250	.367	.227	54	180	26	45	7	5	3	21	23	2	0	2	54	11	5	.394	.338
Bone, Rodolfo	R-R	5-11	170	3-22-00	.318	.231	.340	24	63	10	20	3	2	0	12	9	3	0	2	12	1	0	.429	.416
Caraballo, Andrew	R-R	6-0	175	4-29-00	.234	.258	.228	51	154	36	36	9	5	1	24	40	8	0	2	48	2	2	.377	.412
Doria, Martin	R-R	5-10	155	4-20-99	.241	.323	.219	47	145	29	35	4	1	0	13	18	7	0	1	19	8	3	.283	.351
Gomez, Robert	R-R	6-1	170	12-4-00	.172	.250	.156	32	93	18	16	5	0	1	8	14	4	0	0	43	2	3	.258	.306
Gonzalez, Cesar	R-R	5-11	206	5-8-01	.270	.333	.265	16	37	13	10	4	1	2	9	7	4	0	0	15	0	0	.595	.438
Hernandez, Jose	R-R	5-11	160	9-15-99	.198	.143	.213	39	101	16	20	2	1	0	10	10	4	0	1	26	8	4	.238	.293
Jorge, Samuel	R-R	6-2	190	9-9-99	.274	.194	.294	51	179	27	49	10	0	2	28	18	7	1	0	49	1	0	.363	.363
Juliana, Richgelon	R-R	6-0	170	5-30-00	.261	.278	.257	59	211	39	55	9	7	3	35	35	3	1	1	67	9	4	.412	.372
Medina, Omar	R-R	5-11	170	12-20-99	.235	.250	.231	37	98	12	23	6	0	0	17	24	6	1	1	28	1	2	.296	.411
Mejias, Keyberth	R-R	6-0	170	9-24-99	.256	.222	.265	31	86	13	22	1	1	4	12	7	2	0	1	17	3	2	.430	.323
Pena, Jean	R-R	5-11	150	12-22-00	.237	.130	.252	54	190	37	45	6	3	6	33	31	5	0	2	73	0	3	.395	.355
Peralta, Jose	B-R	5-11	160	7-4-01	.211	.167	.219	17	38	5	8	2	1	0	6	4	1	0	0	13	4	0	.316	.302
Pichardo, Luigi	R-R	5-10	185	6-9-00	.163	.333	.118	13	43	4	7	2	0	0	7	2	1	0	2	8	1	0	.209	.208
Polanco, Yohan	R-R	6-0	200	4-1-01	.209	.000	.243	14	43	5	9	1	0	0	4	4	1	0	0	20	2	0	.233	.292
Santos, Ghordy	R-R	6-1	177	9-2-99	.220	.158	.235	57	191	49	42	10	1	3	23	52	3	1	1	49	18	4	.330	.393
Toribio, Luis	L-R	6-1	165	9-24-00	.263	.310	.263	64	215	44	58	13	1	10	39	51	7	0	1	62	4	1	.479	.423
Watts, Enoc	B-R	6-0	160	12-2-99	.333	.200	.375	12	42	12	14	4	0	0	5	4	4	0	0	6	2	2	.429	.440

Pitching	B-T	HT	WT	DOB	W	L	ERA	G	GS	CG	SV	IP	H	R	ER	HR	BB	SO	AVG	vLH	vRH	K/9	BB/9
Acosta, Cristian	R-R	6-0	170	9-19-99	5	0	2.81	9	0	0	2	16	12	6	5	0	10	12	.222	.143	.250	6.75	5.63
Armstrong, Ivan	R-R	6-5	247	7-27-00	3	3	3.38	14	14	1	0	56	46	33	21	2	32	47	.223	.147	.261	7.55	5.14
Castillo, Wilkelma	R-R	6-0	170	1-6-00	0	0	6.75	7	0	0	1	12	11	10	9	0	4	10	.256	.100	.303	7.50	3.00
Castro, Kervin	R-R	6-0	185	2-7-99	0	0	0.00	1	0	0	0	1	0	0	0	0	1	2	.000	.000	.000	18.00	9.00
Cruz, Jose	R-R	6-1	178	5-18-00	2	2	4.88	20	0	0	5	31	27	21	17	4	15	31	.239	.333	.214	8.90	4.31
Ferreras, Alvaro	R-R	6-3	187	2-5-98	1	1	9.00	8	0	0	1	7	9	7	7	0	14	7	.371	.000	.394	11.00	14.00
Gomez, Jesus	L-L	6-2	180	4-1-01	5	0	2.68	17	4	0	3	44	32	16	13	2	25	60	.209	.286	.192	12.37	5.15
Lopez, Lylon	R-R	6-1	190	3-1-97	0	1	5.09	5	3	0	0	18	19	11	10	1	5	16	.279	.300	.276	8.15	2.55
Marcano, Josdeiker	R-R	6-2	170	8-20-99	2	0	1.76	21	0	0	3	31	22	7	6	2	8	29	.190	.192	.189	8.51	2.35
Martinez, Melvin	R-R	6-3	182	8-11-00	0	5	7.36	11	10	0	1	29	36	33	24	0	31	31	.316	.244	.362	9.51	

Martinez, Rafael	R-R	6-0	160	4-18-00	2	0	3.00	3	0	0	0	3	1	1	1	0	3	2	.091	.000	.125	6.00	9.00
Montero, Luis	R-R	5-11	198	3-29-98	0	2	6.16	16	3	0	0	31	28	26	21	2	28	20	.244	.258	.238	5.87	8.22
Moronta, Yovanny	R-R	6-1	175	5-22-96	0	3	8.02	18	0	0	1	21	18	23	19	0	32	18	.240	.313	.220	7.59	13.50
Paulino, Freddery	R-R	6-2	181	9-12-00	2	2	2.31	11	11	0	0	51	54	23	13	1	15	28	.273	.245	.283	4.97	2.66
Quintana, Samuel	L-L	6-5	215	11-29-00	1	2	4.74	13	1	0	0	25	33	17	13	0	9	29	.320	.316	.321	10.58	3.28
Ramirez, Yoniel	R-R	6-0	180	5-27-01	1	1	1.50	9	0	0	0	18	8	3	3	0	16	10	.143	.167	.132	5.00	8.00
Rodriguez, Randy	R-R	6-0	166	9-5-99	1	1	4.28	10	2	0	2	27	24	16	13	1	9	34	.233	.238	.230	11.20	2.96
Rojas, Yhonson	L-L	6-0	160	10-1-96	1	1	5.16	17	0	0	0	30	23	26	17	1	27	38	.213	.200	.215	11.53	8.19
Sanchez, Juan	L-L	6-2	165	11-12-00	4	6	3.39	13	13	0	0	61	63	30	23	5	13	63	.257	.276	.255	9.30	1.92
Suarez, Elian	L-L	5-11	165	4-6-00	0	0	0.00	1	0	0	0	1	0	0	0	0	1	1	.000	—	.000	9.00	9.00
Suarez, Willian	R-R	6-3	175	3-21-98	3	3	5.02	17	0	0	0	29	21	18	16	4	15	26	.204	.191	.207	8.16	4.71
Vargas, Sonny	L-L	6-2	180	11-8-00	4	2	3.12	15	11	0	0	58	46	26	20	1	14	48	.211	.172	.217	7.49	2.18

Fielding

C: Bone 21, Gonzalez 13, Medina 23, Mejias 31. **1B:** Alcantara 30, Gomez 2, Jorge 36, Medina 11, Peralta 1. **2B:** Caraballo 28, Doria 27, Hernandez 1, Medina 2, Pena 5, Peralta 14, Santos 1, Watts 5. **3B:** Caraballo 10, Doria 6, Jorge 9, Medina 2, Pena 1, Toribio 47, Watts 4. **SS:** Caraballo 4, Pena 33, Peralta 1, Santos 33, Watts 4. **OF:** Alcantara 20, Batista 54, Doria 13, Gomez 31, Hernandez 34, Juliana 58, Pichardo 12, Polanco 14.

Seattle Mariners

SEASON IN A SENTENCE: The Mariners were good in 2018, but they just weren't good enough, failing to capitalize on a hot first three months by finishing under .500 in the second half and missing the postseason for the 17th consecutive season.

HIGH POINT: After a three-game sweep of the Rays from June 1-3, which included arguably the best start of the season from veteran righthander Felix Hernandez, the Mariners were 37-22 and in first place in the AL West—a position they would hold at least a share of until mid-June.

LOW POINT: It would be easy to pinpoint the Mariners' clubhouse brawl on Sept. 4 after a loss to the Orioles as the low point. But the loss of second baseman Robinson Cano on May 13th, first to a broken hand followed days later by an 80-game suspension for a positive PED test, was the toughest blow for the Mariners to absorb. The impact wasn't immediate, because the Mariners went 24-9 right after his departure, but the second-half slide was largely due to a collapse of the team's offense with Cano not returning until mid-August.

NOTABLE ROOKIES: After eight of their Top 30 Prospects made contributions in 2017, it was a barren year for Mariners rookies in 2018. Matt Festa, the club's No. 7 prospect, made his major league debut late in the season and got into eight games. First baseman Daniel Vogelbach made the team after a hot spring training but failed to contribute much offense to the Mariners' attack. Reliever Nick Rumbelow was acquired from the Yankees, but injuries and ineffectiveness had the 27-year-old righthander shuttling between Triple-A Tacoma and Seattle.

KEY TRANSACTIONS: In the offseason, the Mariners traded a trio of prospects to the Marlins for Dee Gordon, who moved to center field to allow Cano to stay at second base. Cano's suspension led the Mariners to trade for Rays outfielder Denard Span, as well as reliever Alex Colome in May, with Gordon moving back to second base to make room for Span in the outfield. The offseason signing of lefthander Wade LeBlanc proved smart, as he filled a rotation spot for much of the year.

DOWN ON THE FARM: Double-A Arkansas was the only one of six Mariners affiliates to post a record above .500, finishing 71-68 and qualifying for the Texas League playoffs. First baseman Joey Curletta was the team's most productive hitter, leading the league in both RBIs (94) and OPS (.865) and claiming the TL MVP award.

OPENING DAY PAYROLL: $165,303,943 (8th).

PLAYERS OF THE YEAR

ANDY KUNO

JOSE CARLOS MAGANA

MAJOR LEAGUE	MINOR LEAGUE
Edwin Diaz	**Evan White**
RHP	**1B**
1.96 ERA, 15.2 SO/9	(High Class A/Triple-A)
Led the majors in	.300/.372/.453
saves (57)	11 HR, 66 RBIs

ORGANIZATION LEADERS

Batting		*Minimum 250 AB
MAJORS		
* AVG	Jean Segura	.304
* OPS	Mitch Haniger	.859
HR	Nelson Cruz	37
RBI	Nelson Cruz	97
MINORS		
* AVG	Bobby Honeyman, Everett, Modesto	.336
* OBP	Daniel Vogelbach, Tacoma	.434
* SLG	Daniel Vogelbach, Tacoma	.545
* OPS	Daniel Vogelbach, Tacoma	.979
R	Ariel Sandoval, Clinton	78
H	Chuck Taylor, Arkansas	149
TB	Joey Curletta, Arkansas	224
TB	Evan White, Modesto, Tacoma	224
2B	Nick Zammarelli III, Modesto	30
3B	Bryson Brigman, Modesto, Jupiter, Jacksonville	7
3B	Evan White, Modesto, Tacoma	7
HR	Joey Curletta, Arkansas	23
RBI	Joey Curletta, Arkansas	94
BB	Joey Curletta, Arkansas	81
SO	Gareth Morgan, Modesto, Mariners	187
SB	Ian Miller, Tacoma	33

Pitching		#Minimum 75 IP
MAJORS		
W	Marco Gonzales	13
# ERA	Wade LeBlanc	3.72
SO	James Paxton	208
SV	Edwin Diaz	57
MINORS		
W	Nick Wells, Clinton, Modesto	9
W	Spencer Herrmann, Arkansas, Modesto	9
W	Clay Chandler, Clinton	9
L	Anthony Misiewicz, Arkansas, Mariners	12
# ERA	Darren McCaughan, Modesto, Tacoma	3.08
G	Shawn Armstrong, Tacoma	49
GS	Nick Wells, Clinton, Modesto	28
SV	Matt Festa, Arkansas	20
IP	Darren McCaughan, Modesto, Tacoma	149
BB	Nick Wells, Clinton, Modesto	62
SO	Darren McCaughan, Modesto, Tacoma	129
# AVG	Clay Chandler, Clinton	.238

2018 PERFORMANCE

General Manager: Jerry Dipoto. **Farm Director:** Andy McKay. **Scouting Director:** Scott Hunter.

Class	Team	League	W	L	PCT	Finish	Manager
Majors	Seattle Mariners	American	89	73	.549	7th (15)	Scott Servais
Triple-A	Tacoma Rainiers	Pacific Coast	66	73	.475	11th (16)	Pat Listach
Double-A	Arkansas Travelers	Texas	71	68	.511	4th (8)	Daren Brown
High A	Modesto Nuts	California	62	78	.443	7th (8)	Mitch Canham
Low A	Clinton Lumberkings	Midwest	69	70	.496	8th (16)	Denny Hocking
Short season	Everett Aquasox	Northwest	38	38	.500	t3rd (8)	Jose Moreno
Rookie	AZL Mariners	Arizona	16	38	.296	t16th (18)	Zac Livingston
Overall 2018 Minor League Record			322	365	.469	24th (30)	

ORGANIZATION STATISTICS

SEATTLE MARINERS
AMERICAN LEAGUE

Batting	B-T	HT	WT	DOB	AVG	vLH	vRH	G	AB	R	H	2B	3B	HR	RBI	BB	HBP	SH	SF	SO	SB	CS	SLG	OBP
Andreoli, John	R-R	6-1	210	6-9-90	.200	.000	.333	3	5	0	1	0	0	0	0	1	0	0	0	2	0	0	.200	.333
2-team total (23 Baltimore)					.230	.226	.233	26	61	4	14	2	0	0	4	5	0	0	1	19	2	0	.262	.284
Beckham, Gordon	R-R	6-0	190	9-16-86	.182	.231	.161	22	44	3	8	1	0	0	1	4	0	2	0	11	1	0	.205	.250
Cano, Robinson	L-R	6-0	210	10-22-82	.303	.333	.287	80	310	44	94	22	0	10	50	32	4	0	2	47	0	0	.471	.374
Cruz, Nelson	R-R	6-2	230	7-1-80	.256	.266	.253	144	519	70	133	18	1	37	97	55	14	0	3	122	1	0	.509	.342
Freitas, David	R-R	6-3	225	3-18-89	.215	.194	.228	36	93	9	20	6	0	1	5	8	0	1	0	25	0	0	.312	.277
Gamel, Ben	L-L	5-11	185	5-17-92	.272	.222	.283	101	257	37	70	14	4	1	19	31	4	0	1	61	7	3	.370	.358
Gordon, Dee	L-R	5-11	170	4-22-88	.268	.261	.271	141	556	62	149	17	8	4	36	9	9	9	5	80	30	12	.349	.288
Haniger, Mitch	R-R	6-2	215	12-23-90	.285	.314	.274	157	596	90	170	38	4	26	93	70	10	0	7	148	8	2	.493	.366
Healy, Ryon	R-R	6-5	225	1-10-92	.235	.213	.246	133	493	51	116	15	0	24	73	27	2	0	2	113	0	0	.412	.277
Heredia, Guillermo	R-L	5-10	180	1-31-91	.236	.246	.228	125	292	29	69	14	1	5	19	32	4	7	2	52	2	4	.343	.318
Herrmann, Chris	L-R	6-0	200	11-24-87	.237	.273	.231	36	76	6	18	4	2	2	7	10	0	0	1	24	0	0	.421	.322
Marjama, Mike	R-R	6-2	205	7-20-89	.111	.167	.095	10	27	1	3	3	0	0	2	0	0	0	0	6	0	1	.222	.172
Maybin, Cameron	R-R	6-3	215	4-4-87	.242	.229	.256	30	91	12	22	2	1	1	8	6	0	0	0	20	2	0	.319	.289
Motter, Taylor	R-R	6-1	195	9-18-89	.267	.250	.333	7	15	2	4	0	0	1	1	2	0	0	0	5	0	0	.467	.353
2-team total (9 Minnesota)					.147	.191	.077	16	34	2	5	0	0	1	2	4	0	0	0	8	1	0	.235	.237
Negron, Kristopher	R-R	6-0	190	2-1-86	.207	.267	.143	19	29	6	6	0	0	1	3	1	0	0	0	9	2	0	.310	.233
Romine, Andrew	B-R	6-1	200	12-24-85	.210	.233	.197	72	119	15	25	2	1	0	2	7	1	4	0	39	1	0	.244	.260
Seager, Kyle	L-R	6-0	210	11-3-87	.221	.247	.208	155	583	62	129	36	1	22	78	38	5	0	4	138	2	2	.400	.273
Segura, Jean	R-R	5-10	205	3-17-90	.304	.313	.300	144	586	91	178	29	3	10	63	32	4	4	6	69	20	11	.415	.341
Span, Denard	L-R	6-0	210	2-27-84	.272	.310	.263	94	294	36	80	15	6	7	30	23	5	0	6	55	3	2	.435	.329
2-team total (43 Tampa Bay)					.261	.302	.251	137	437	63	114	22	7	11	58	51	6	0	7	79	9	4	.419	.341
Suzuki, Ichiro	L-R	5-11	175	10-22-73	.205	.500	.139	15	44	5	9	0	0	0	0	3	0	0	0	7	0	0	.205	.255
Vincej, Zach	R-R	6-0	190	5-1-91	.500	.667	.000	1	4	0	2	0	0	0	1	0	0	0	0	1	0	0	.500	.500
Vogelbach, Daniel	L-R	6-0	250	12-17-92	.207	.050	.254	37	87	9	18	2	0	4	13	13	2	0	0	26	0	0	.368	.324
Zunino, Mike	R-R	6-2	220	3-25-91	.201	.167	.217	113	373	37	75	18	0	20	44	24	6	0	2	150	0	0	.410	.259

Pitching	B-T	HT	WT	DOB	W	L	ERA	G	GS	CG	SV	IP	H	R	ER	HR	BB	SO	AVG	vLH	vRH	K/9	BB/9
Altavilla, Dan	R-R	5-11	200	9-8-92	3	2	2.61	22	0	0	0	21	11	7	6	2	15	23	.162	.094	.222	10.02	6.53
Armstrong, Shawn	R-R	6-2	225	9-11-90	0	1	1.23	14	0	0	1	15	9	2	2	1	3	15	.184	.154	.194	9.20	1.84
Bergman, Christian	R-R	6-1	195	5-4-88	0	1	5.79	3	2	0	0	14	12	9	9	4	3	7	.231	.138	.348	4.50	1.93
Bradford, Chasen	R-R	6-1	229	8-5-89	5	0	3.69	46	0	0	0	54	55	23	22	9	14	38	.262	.258	.264	6.37	2.35
Colome, Alex	R-R	6-2	220	12-31-88	5	0	2.53	47	0	0	1	46	35	14	13	6	13	49	.207	.149	.245	9.52	2.53
2-team total (23 Tampa Bay)					7	5	3.04	70	0	0	12	68	59	26	23	7	21	72	.230	.171	.274	9.53	2.78
Cook, Ryan	R-R	6-2	215	6-30-87	2	1	5.29	19	0	0	0	17	15	10	10	4	7	23	.234	.250	.225	12.18	3.71
Detwiler, Ross	R-L	6-3	210	3-6-86	0	1	4.50	1	0	0	0	6	8	3	3	1	2	2	.400	.500	.375	3.00	3.00
Diaz, Edwin	R-R	6-3	165	3-22-94	0	4	1.96	73	0	0	57	73	41	17	16	5	17	124	.160	.144	.171	15.22	2.09
Duke, Zach	L-L	6-2	210	4-19-83	2	1	5.52	27	0	0	0	15	13	9	9	1	6	12	.241	.188	.318	7.36	3.68
2-team total (45 Minnesota)					5	5	4.15	72	0	0	0	52	57	28	24	1	21	51	.271	.220	.311	8.83	3.63
Elias, Roenis	L-L	6-1	205	8-1-88	3	1	2.65	23	4	0	0	51	46	17	15	1	16	34	.242	.275	.223	6.00	2.82
Festa, Matt	R-R	6-2	195	3-11-93	0	0	2.16	8	1	0	0	8	13	2	2	0	2	4	.351	.357	.348	4.32	2.16
Goeddel, Erik	R-R	6-3	191	12-20-88	2	0	1.23	5	0	0	0	7	4	1	1	0	5	9	.167	.000	.222	11.05	6.14
Gonzales, Marco	L-L	6-1	195	2-16-92	13	9	4.00	29	29	1	0	167	172	76	74	17	32	145	.268	.263	.268	7.83	1.73
Grimm, Justin	R-R	6-3	210	8-16-88	0	0	1.93	5	0	0	0	5	2	1	1	0	3	.133	.000	.182	5.79	0.00
2-team total (16 Kansas City)					1	3	10.38	21	0	0	0	17	19	20	20	3	14	11	.297	.333	.275	5.71	7.27
Hernandez, Felix	R-R	6-3	225	4-8-86	8	14	5.55	29	28	0	0	156	159	107	96	27	59	125	.262	.251	.271	7.23	3.41
Lawrence, Casey	R-R	6-2	170	10-28-87	1	0	7.33	11	0	0	0	23	28	19	19	2	10	14	.298	.212	.344	5.40	3.86
Leake, Mike	R-R	5-10	170	11-12-87	10	10	4.36	31	31	0	0	186	207	98	90	23	34	119	.280	.288	.274	5.77	1.65
LeBlanc, Wade	L-L	6-1	205	8-7-84	9	5	3.72	32	27	0	0	162	151	74	67	24	40	130	.246	.245	.246	7.22	2.22
Miranda, Ariel	L-L	6-2	190	1-10-89	0	0	1.80	1	1	0	0	5	6	1	1	0	4	5	.300	.000	.353	9.00	7.20
Morin, Mike	R-R	6-4	220	5-3-91	0	0	6.75	3	0	0	0	4	6	3	3	0	1	6	.375	.333	.400	13.50	2.25
Nicasio, Juan	R-R	6-4	252	8-1-86	1	6	6.00	46	0	0	1	42	53	30	28	6	5	53	.308	.278	.330	11.36	1.07
Paxton, James	L-L	6-4	235	11-6-88	11	6	3.76	28	28	2	0	160	134	67	67	23	42	208	.224	.330	.202	11.68	2.36
Pazos, James	R-L	6-2	235	5-5-91	4	1	2.88	60	0	0	0	50	47	19	16	4	15	45	.249	.280	.228	8.10	2.70

Pitching	B-T	HT	WT	DOB	W	L	ERA	G	GS	CG	SV	IP	H	R	ER	HR	BB	SO	AVG	vLH	vRH	K/9	BB/9
Ramirez, Erasmo	R-R	5-10	215	5-2-90	2	4	6.50	10	10	0	0	46	52	35	33	14	12	33	.284	.296	.274	6.50	2.36
Rumbelow, Nick	R-R	6-0	190	9-6-91	0	0	6.11	13	0	0	0	18	19	12	12	6	6	16	.275	.222	.310	8.15	3.06
Rzepczynski, Marc	L-L	6-2	220	8-29-85	0	1	9.39	18	0	0	0	8	13	11	8	2	9	10	.342	.222	.636	11.74	10.57
2-team total (5 Cleveland)					0	1	6.97	23	0	0	0	10	16	11	8	2	10	11	.340	.258	.500	9.58	8.71
Tuivailala, Sam	R-R	6-3	225	10-19-92	1	0	1.69	5	0	0	0	5	6	1	1	0	1	4	.300	.600	.200	6.75	1.69
Vincent, Nick	R-R	6-0	185	7-12-86	4	4	3.99	62	1	0	0	56	50	28	25	7	15	56	.229	.217	.235	8.95	2.40
Warren, Adam	R-R	6-1	224	8-25-87	3	1	3.74	23	0	0	0	22	22	9	9	3	8	15	.256	.241	.263	6.23	3.32
2-team total (24 New York)					3	2	3.14	47	0	0	0	52	48	18	18	6	20	52	.240	.274	.216	9.06	3.48
Whalen, Rob	R-R	6-2	220	1-31-94	0	0	0.00	1	0	0	0	4	1	0	0	0	1	0	.077	.000	.167	0.00	2.25

Fielding

Catcher	PCT	G	PO	A	E	DP	PB
Freitas	.993	35	267	10	2	2	3
Herrmann	.993	28	126	7	1	1	0
Marjama	.985	10	61	4	1	0	0
Zunino	.998	111	880	43	2	5	10

First Base	PCT	G	PO	A	E	DP
Cano	.989	14	87	3	1	9
Freitas	1.000	1	1	0	0	0
Gamel	1.000	1	1	1	0	0
Healy	.993	131	1007	63	8	114
Herrmann	1.000	1	2	0	0	0
Motter	1.000	5	20	0	0	2
Romine	1.000	16	29	0	0	3
Vogelbach	1.000	20	121	11	0	13

Second Base	PCT	G	PO	A	E	DP
Beckham	1.000	13	18	38	0	5
Cano	.996	69	111	146	1	44
Gordon	.974	81	170	200	10	63
Negron	1.000	2	3	0	0	0
Romine	1.000	18	20	27	0	10
Seager	.000	1	0	0	0	0

Third Base	PCT	G	PO	A	E	DP
Beckham	1.000	6	0	6	0	0
Cano	1.000	2	2	2	0	1
Healy	1.000	2	0	2	0	0
Negron	1.000	4	2	3	0	0
Romine	.917	6	4	7	1	0
Seager	.968	154	98	325	14	49
Vincej	1.000	1	0	1	0	0

Shortstop	PCT	G	PO	A	E	DP
Beckham	1.000	2	3	8	0	1
Gordon	1.000	8	10	20	0	3
Negron	1.000	2	2	4	0	1
Romine	.978	18	18	27	1	7
Segura	.969	144	141	387	17	68

Outfield	PCT	G	PO	A	E	DP
Andreoli	1.000	2	5	0	0	0
Cruz	1.000	4	6	0	0	0
Gamel	.979	87	133	4	3	1
Gordon	.963	53	129	2	5	0
Haniger	.978	156	338	12	8	1
Heredia	1.000	120	219	3	0	2
Maybin	1.000	30	60	0	0	0
Motter	.000	1	0	0	0	0
Negron	1.000	5	9	1	0	0
Romine	1.000	5	11	1	0	0
Span	.973	87	144	1	4	0
Suzuki	1.000	12	21	0	0	0

TACOMA RAINIERS — TRIPLE-A
PACIFIC COAST LEAGUE

Batting	B-T	HT	WT	DOB	AVG	vLH	vRH	G	AB	R	H	2B	3B	HR	RBI	BB	HBP	SH	SF	SO	SB	CS	SLG	OBP
Andreoli, John	R-R	6-1	210	6-9-90	.288	.333	.274	89	327	54	94	18	5	3	36	55	5	0	1	86	19	5	.401	.397
Aplin, Andrew	L-L	6-0	205	3-21-91	.265	.322	.246	63	234	36	62	17	0	5	31	31	2	0	2	47	2	1	.402	.353
Beckham, Gordon	R-R	6-0	190	9-16-86	.302	.287	.306	94	358	64	108	24	1	10	51	57	5	0	5	52	6	2	.458	.400
Cano, Robinson	L-R	6-0	210	10-22-82	.286	.000	.400	2	7	1	2	0	0	0	1	0	0	0	0	0	0	0	.286	.375
Freitas, David	R-R	6-3	225	3-18-89	.349	.405	.327	39	146	15	51	12	1	4	23	17	3	0	0	27	0	0	.527	.428
Gamel, Ben	L-L	5-11	185	5-17-92	.349	.300	.365	21	83	19	29	8	3	1	16	10	0	0	1	12	4	0	.554	.415
Hague, Matt	R-R	6-3	225	8-20-85	.226	.250	.220	17	53	17	12	2	0	0	13	19	0	0	2	9	0	0	.264	.419
Heredia, Guillermo	R-L	5-10	180	1-31-91	.276	.714	.136	11	29	4	8	1	0	0	2	4	4	0	1	3	2	1	.310	.421
Hernandez, Cal	B-R	6-0	185	1-9-96	.182	.333	.000	3	11	1	2	0	0	0	0	1	0	0	0	3	0	1	.182	.250
Herrmann, Chris	L-R	6-0	200	11-24-87	.257	.290	.248	42	136	26	35	3	1	6	24	36	1	1	0	42	0	0	.427	.416
Hoover, Connor	L-R	5-10	185	7-18-96	—	—	—	1	0	1	0	0	0	0	0	0	0	0	0	0	0	0	—	—
Izturis Jr., Cesar	B-R	5-11	145	11-11-99	.200	.000	.300	5	15	2	3	2	0	0	2	1	0	0	0	5	0	0	.333	.250
Kennedy, Garrett	L-R	6-1	205	12-13-92	.211	.158	.225	31	90	11	19	2	1	2	11	12	0	0	0	29	0	0	.322	.304
Law, Adam	R-R	6-0	195	2-5-90	.260	.333	.235	62	223	27	58	14	1	3	24	10	3	2	2	42	3	0	.372	.298
Marjama, Mike	R-R	6-2	205	7-20-89	.247	.227	.254	43	158	22	39	9	2	5	23	11	2	0	1	35	2	0	.424	.302
Mejias-Brean, Seth	R-R	6-2	216	4-5-91	.266	.263	.267	96	350	45	93	13	3	8	44	42	4	0	4	67	4	2	.389	.348
Miller, Ian	L-R	6-0	175	2-21-92	.261	.231	.269	114	422	60	110	16	3	2	41	43	5	4	4	89	33	9	.327	.333
Motter, Taylor	R-R	6-1	195	9-18-89	.197	.125	.224	37	147	21	29	6	2	5	21	16	1	0	1	30	4	2	.367	.279
Muno, Danny	B-R	6-1	195	2-9-89	.155	.267	.174	61	200	20	39	9	1	1	23	36	2	1	2	63	1	1	.265	.321
Navarro, Rey	B-R	5-10	185	12-22-89	.148	.100	.177	7	27	2	4	1	0	1	6	3	0	0	1	5	0	0	.296	.226
Nieuwenhuis, Kirk	L-R	6-3	225	8-7-87	.214	.150	.232	80	271	39	58	17	2	4	31	48	3	0	2	99	5	0	.336	.336
Ochoa, Sebastian	R-R	6-1	180	5-8-98	.150	.167	.143	7	20	3	3	2	0	0	5	0	0	0	1	5	1	1	.250	.143
Odom, Joseph	R-R	6-2	225	1-9-92	.143	.000	.231	6	21	0	3	0	0	0	0	0	0	0	0	10	0	0	.143	.143
Ogren, Ryne	R-R	6-1	180	4-11-97	.000	.000	.000	1	4	0	0	0	0	0	0	0	0	0	0	1	0	0	.000	.000
Pazos, Manny	R-R	5-11	190	1-23-95	.000	—	.000	1	1	0	0	0	0	0	0	1	0	0	0	1	0	0	.000	.500
Perkins, Cameron	R-R	6-5	195	9-20-90	.257	.336	.224	94	362	51	93	25	2	10	48	25	6	0	4	68	8	4	.420	.312
Rivera, Jansiel	L-L	6-1	205	8-28-98	.500	1.000	.400	4	12	2	6	1	0	0	3	1	0	0	0	3	0	0	.583	.539
Rupp, Cameron	R-R	6-2	260	9-28-88	.218	.171	.240	33	110	15	24	5	1	4	12	18	0	0	0	30	0	0	.391	.328
2-team total (32 Round Rock)					.247	.222	.254	65	223	30	55	11	1	12	38	31	1	0	3	75	0	0	.466	.337
Taylor, Logan	R-R	6-1	200	9-22-93	.500	.500	.500	2	4	2	2	0	0	0	0	0	0	0	0	2	0	0	.500	.600
Vincej, Zach	R-R	6-0	190	5-1-91	.247	.265	.240	109	385	46	95	14	3	6	51	33	6	4	2	64	7	5	.346	.315
Vogelbach, Daniel	L-R	6-0	250	12-17-92	.290	.250	.301	84	297	54	86	16	0	20	60	77	1	0	3	59	0	1	.546	.434
Werth, Jayson	R-R	6-5	235	5-20-79	.206	.321	.174	36	126	16	26	11	0	4	19	15	2	0	2	33	0	0	.389	.297
White, Evan	R-L	6-3	205	4-26-96	.222	.333	.167	4	18	0	4	2	0	0	0	0	0	0	0	5	0	0	.333	.222
Zunino, Mike	R-R	6-2	225	3-25-91	.200	—	.200	2	5	1	1	0	0	0	1	0	0	0	0	1	0	0	.200	.167

Pitching	B-T	HT	WT	DOB	W	L	ERA	G	GS	CG	SV	IP	H	R	ER	HR	BB	SO	AVG	vLH	vRH	K/9	BB/9
Altavilla, Dan	R-R	5-11	200	9-8-92	0	0	9.45	9	1	0	0	7	8	7	2	4	7		.300	.300	.300	9.45	5.40
Alvarez, Dario	L-L	6-1	170	1-17-89	2	0	1.98	27	0	0	0	27	20	6	6	1	14	28	.202	.173	.234	9.22	4.61
Armstrong, Shawn	R-R	6-2	225	9-11-90	2	5	1.77	49	0	0	15	56	38	17	11	3	26	82	.192	.217	.170	13.18	4.18
Bannister, Nathan	R-R	6-3	224	12-17-93	0	0	4.15	1	0	0	0	4	5	2	2	0	0	3	.278	.375	.200	6.23	0.00
Beltran, Rigo	L-L	5-11	185	9-1-94	0	0	0.00	1	0	0	0	2	0	0	0	0	0	0	.000	.000	.000	0.00	0.00

Player	B-T	HT	WT	DOB																					
Bergman, Christian	R-R	6-1	195	5-4-88	8	10	5.08	26	25	0	0	142	169	86	80	15	39	113	.298	.252	.341	7.18	2.48
Bradford, Chasen	R-R	6-1	229	8-5-89	0	0	0.00	7	0	0	1	7	5	0	0	0	0	4	.200	.200	.200	5.40	0.00
Caughel, Lindsey	R-R	6-3	205	8-13-90	2	2	6.52	13	3	0	0	29	32	21	21	4	10	19	.276	.309	.246	5.90	3.10
Cook, Ryan	R-R	6-2	215	6-30-87	0	2	2.16	34	0	0	3	33	28	8	8	2	17	37	.224	.308	.164	9.99	4.59
Detwiler, Ross	R-L	6-3	210	3-6-86	2	5	4.89	16	13	1	0	85	94	46	46	10	25	52	.291	.235	.316	5.53	2.66
Elias, Roenis	L-L	6-1	205	8-1-88	2	4	4.54	10	7	0	0	34	32	20	17	1	15	31	.248	.229	.259	8.29	4.01
Evans, Bryan	R-R	6-2	200	2-25-87	6	3	4.40	14	14	0	0	78	83	42	38	14	15	71	.268	.265	.271	8.23	1.74
Frank, Trevor	R-R	6-0	195	6-23-91	1	0	0.00	1	0	0	0	3	0	0	0	0	1	4	.000	.000	.000	12.00	3.00
Garton, Ryan	R-R	5-10	190	12-5-89	1	0	3.16	35	0	0	4	43	27	15	15	2	24	43	.182	.177	.186	9.07	5.06
Gillies, Darin	R-R	6-4	220	11-6-92	1	1	5.44	26	0	0	1	43	40	26	26	7	17	45	.253	.312	.198	9.42	3.56
Goeddel, Erik	R-R	6-3	191	12-20-88	1	0	0.00	9	0	0	4	9	6	0	0	0	4	10	.188	.182	.191	10.00	4.00
Goudeau, Ashton	R-R	6-6	205	7-23-92	1	5	8.20	20	2	0	0	37	59	36	34	6	19	31	.362	.363	.361	7.47	4.58
Grimm, Justin	R-R	6-3	210	8-16-88	1	0	1.64	10	0	0	0	11	8	2	2	0	2	17	.211	.067	.304	13.91	1.64
2-team total (9 Omaha)					2	1	4.87	19	0	0	0	20	23	11	11	0	8	30	.291	.172	.360	13.28	3.54
Healy, Tucker	L-R	6-1	210	6-15-90	0	1	4.13	20	0	0	1	24	26	13	11	4	11	24	.271	.227	.308	9.00	4.13
Higgins, Tyler	R-R	6-3	215	4-22-91	1	1	2.83	28	0	0	3	35	32	12	11	4	9	38	.242	.321	.184	9.77	2.31
Hutchison, Austin	R-R	6-1	205	4-9-95	1	0	1.80	1	1	0	0	5	8	1	1	0	2	2	.348	.539	.100	3.60	3.60
Jackson, Tyler	R-R	6-6	210	10-22-93	0	1	12.54	5	0	0	0	9	13	13	13	3	5	6	.325	.300	.350	5.79	4.82
Lawrence, Casey	R-R	6-2	170	10-28-87	7	5	3.31	19	16	1	1	98	98	40	36	11	13	89	.255	.279	.234	8.17	1.19
Light, Pat	R-R	6-5	220	3-29-91	0	0	24.00	3	0	0	0	3	7	8	8	0	2	2	.467	.400	.500	6.00	24.00
McCaughan, Darren	R-R	6-1	195	3-18-96	1	1	3.48	2	2	0	0	10	10	4	4	1	7	8	.256	.063	.391	6.97	6.10
McIver, Anthony	L-L	6-5	210	4-8-92	1	0	1.50	6	0	0	0	6	6	2	1	0	1	5	.273	.286	.267	7.50	1.50
McKay, David	R-R	6-3	205	3-31-95	0	0	0.00	1	0	0	0	1	0	0	0	0	0	0	.000	.000	.000	0.00	0.00
Miranda, Ariel	L-L	6-2	190	1-10-89	5	0	3.97	10	9	0	0	45	44	20	20	3	24	40	.257	.257	.257	7.94	4.76
Morin, Mike	R-R	6-4	220	5-3-91	5	2	3.86	41	3	0	3	54	51	25	23	3	13	52	.250	.260	.241	8.72	2.18
Moyers, Steven	R-L	6-0	190	9-27-93	0	0	6.43	3	0	0	0	7	11	5	5	1	0	4	.355	.273	.400	5.14	0.00
Newsome, Ljay	R-R	5-11	210	11-8-96	0	0	5.40	1	1	0	0	5	3	3	3	0	1	2	.177	.200	.167	3.60	1.80
Pazos, James	R-L	6-2	235	5-5-91	0	0	0.00	3	0	0	0	3	1	0	0	0	1	2	.091	.167	.000	5.40	2.70
Perez, Williams	R-R	6-0	240	5-21-91	2	1	3.15	4	4	0	0	20	20	7	7	1	3	22	.279	.231	.325	9.90	1.35
Povse, Max	R-R	6-8	185	8-23-93	1	6	8.84	8	8	0	0	37	40	37	36	6	28	45	.280	.257	.301	11.05	6.87
Ramirez, Erasmo	R-R	5-10	215	5-2-90	0	2	2.41	5	5	0	0	19	14	7	5	1	3	17	.206	.208	.205	8.20	1.45
Rollins, David	L-L	6-1	210	12-21-89	0	3	9.61	4	4	0	0	20	35	21	21	5	3	17	.389	.308	.422	7.78	1.37
Rumbelow, Nick	R-R	6-0	190	9-6-91	1	0	2.04	13	0	0	2	18	13	4	4	1	8	25	.206	.125	.256	12.74	4.08
Rzepczynski, Marc	L-L	6-2	220	8-29-85	0	0	9.64	12	0	0	0	9	15	11	10	2	8	10	.357	.393	.286	9.64	7.71
Schlereth, Daniel	L-L	6-0	210	5-9-86	2	2	5.40	12	0	0	1	8	11	5	5	0	8	9	.333	.391	.200	9.72	8.64
Smith, Josh A.	R-R	6-2	220	8-7-87	0	2	6.10	4	1	0	0	10	17	17	7	3	3	14	.340	.333	.344	12.19	2.61
Tenuta, Matt	L-L	6-4	225	12-16-93	2	0	3.21	10	0	0	0	14	16	5	5	1	9	10	.276	.200	.357	6.43	5.79
Whalen, Rob	R-R	6-2	220	1-31-94	7	7	5.16	20	20	0	0	99	119	70	57	5	37	92	.290	.286	.294	8.34	3.35

Fielding

Catcher	PCT	G	PO	A	E	DP	PB
Freitas	1.000	29	250	13	0	0	2
Herrmann	.992	28	232	19	2	0	3
Kennedy	.979	30	212	18	5	1	3
Marjama	1.000	35	269	19	0	4	6
Odom	1.000	4	39	0	0	0	0
Pazos	1.000	1	1	0	0	0	0
Rupp	.993	22	143	8	1	2	1
Zunino	1.000	1	5	0	0	0	0

First Base	PCT	G	PO	A	E	DP
Beckham	1.000	19	140	7	0	18
Cano	1.000	1	10	2	0	1
Hague	.988	13	81	1	1	8
Law	1.000	1	5	0	0	1
Marjama	1.000	3	25	4	0	5
Mejias-Brean	1.000	6	42	4	0	3
Motter	1.000	1	7	0	0	0
Odom	1.000	2	7	0	0	0
Perkins	.988	42	302	17	4	30
Vogelbach	.986	53	393	24	6	35
White	1.000	4	28	5	0	2

Second Base	PCT	G	PO	A	E	DP
Beckham	1.000	32	39	76	0	17
Hernandez	1.000	3	4	12	0	1
Hoover	.000	1	0	0	0	0
Law	.972	46	59	115	5	25
Motter	.952	6	11	9	1	1
Muno	.963	35	42	88	5	16
Navarro	.957	7	6	16	1	5
Taylor	.000	1	0	0	0	0
Vincej	.986	15	29	43	1	9

Third Base	PCT	G	PO	A	E	DP
Beckham	.962	8	9	16	1	3
Hague	1.000	3	1	1	0	0
Law	1.000	4	4	2	0	0
Marjama	1.000	1	0	0	0	0
Mejias-Brean	.950	91	68	159	12	12
Motter	.944	9	2	15	1	2
Muno	.898	24	19	34	6	2
Taylor	1.000	1	0	3	0	0
Vincej	.000	1	0	0	0	0

Shortstop	PCT	G	PO	A	E	DP
Beckham	.964	27	34	74	4	13

	PCT	G	PO	A	E	DP
Izturis Jr.	1.000	5	4	6	0	2
Law	1.000	3	5	14	0	3
Mejias-Brean	1.000	1	0	1	0	1
Motter	.925	13	8	29	3	8
Ogren	1.000	1	1	1	0	0
Vincej	.973	93	115	210	9	49

Outfield	PCT	G	PO	A	E	DP
Andreoli	.995	80	191	4	1	1
Aplin	.993	60	146	3	1	1
Beckham	.944	6	15	2	1	0
Gamel	.971	15	32	1	1	0
Heredia	1.000	10	18	1	0	0
Law	1.000	10	19	0	0	0
Marjama	.000	1	0	0	0	0
Miller	.981	111	246	6	5	3
Motter	1.000	10	16	0	0	0
Muno	.000	1	0	0	0	0
Nieuwenhuis	.990	55	95	3	1	1
Ochoa	1.000	5	15	0	0	0
Perkins	.971	45	96	5	3	1
Rivera	.900	3	9	0	1	0
Werth	.949	24	33	4	2	1

ARKANSAS TRAVELERS
DOUBLE-A
TEXAS LEAGUE

Batting	B-T	HT	WT	DOB	AVG	vLH	vRH	G	AB	R	H	2B	3B	HR	RBI	BB	HBP	SH	SF	SO	SB	CS	SLG	OBP
Amaral, Beau	L-L	5-10	177	2-11-91	.250	.287	.237	102	384	57	96	18	1	3	53	33	4	4	7	84	10	2	.326	.311
Aplin, Andrew	L-L	6-0	205	3-21-91	.170	.056	.229	15	53	5	9	3	0	0	5	9	1	1	0	9	0	0	.226	.302
Bishop, Braden	R-R	6-1	190	8-22-93	.284	.295	.280	84	345	70	98	20	0	8	33	37	6	3	3	62	18	5	.412	.361
Curletta, Joey	R-R	6-4	245	3-8-94	.282	.287	.280	129	465	70	131	24	0	23	94	81	1	0	9	130	1	1	.482	.383
DeCarlo, Joe	R-R	5-10	210	9-13-93	.246	.179	.272	58	207	39	51	16	0	8	30	22	7	0	0	53	0	0	.440	.339
Filia, Eric	L-R	6-0	189	7-6-92	.274	.276	.273	79	296	44	81	14	1	2	38	44	3	0	2	30	1	0	.348	.371
Healy, Ryon	R-R	6-5	225	1-10-92	.333	.250	.364	4	15	3	5	0	0	1	6	3	0	0	0	0	0	0	.533	.444

Batting	B-T	HT	WT	DOB	AVG	vLH	vRH	G	AB	R	H	2B	3B	HR	RBI	BB	HBP	SH	SF	SO	SB	CS	SLG	OBP
Izturis Jr., Cesar	B-R	5-11	145	11-11-99	.000	—	.000	1	3	0	0	0	0	0	0	0	0	0	0	2	0	0	.000	.000
Law, Adam	R-R	6-0	195	2-5-90	.244	.245	.243	49	160	12	39	10	0	0	12	16	8	2	3	46	4	2	.306	.337
Lewis, Kyle	R-R	6-4	210	7-13-95	.220	.263	.202	37	132	18	29	8	0	4	20	17	1	0	2	32	1	0	.371	.309
Mariscal, Chris	R-R	5-10	170	4-26-93	.261	.263	.261	120	444	58	116	17	3	7	60	51	7	2	5	131	5	1	.360	.343
Mejias-Brean, Seth	R-R	6-2	216	4-5-91	.238	.158	.273	33	126	13	30	5	1	2	12	11	1	0	0	28	1	1	.341	.304
Mendoza, Yonathan	B-R	5-11	167	2-10-94	.261	.233	.271	97	333	61	87	10	0	0	26	46	0	2	4	48	5	1	.291	.347
Odom, Joseph	R-R	6-2	225	1-9-92	.241	.238	.242	76	266	27	64	17	0	5	36	22	1	0	1	73	0	0	.361	.300
Pizzano, Dario	L-R	5-11	200	4-25-91	.285	.261	.294	107	400	43	114	20	3	11	59	47	3	0	4	55	2	1	.433	.361
Sanders, Matt	R-R	5-8	175	6-7-96	.172	.273	.111	9	29	3	5	2	0	0	1	1	0	0	0	6	0	0	.241	.200
Scott, Ryan	R-R	6-1	180	2-7-95	.167	.222	.156	20	54	8	9	1	0	0	4	8	2	0	1	24	0	0	.185	.292
Shank, Zach	R-R	6-1	180	1-6-91	.294	.000	.333	6	17	3	5	0	0	0	2	6	1	0	0	5	0	1	.294	.500
Silva, Rainis	R-R	6-1	185	3-20-96	.667	.500	1.000	3	3	1	2	0	0	0	0	0	0	0	0	0	0	0	.667	.667
Taylor, Chuck	B-L	5-9	190	9-21-93	.297	.263	.312	126	502	70	149	25	3	3	60	61	7	0	5	79	2	2	.377	.377
Taylor, Logan	R-R	6-1	200	9-22-93	.270	.291	.263	66	226	24	61	9	1	7	31	20	1	0	3	67	0	0	.412	.328
Walton, Donnie	L-R	5-10	184	5-25-94	.236	.319	.211	62	208	22	49	14	1	1	22	21	7	1	1	34	3	1	.327	.325

Pitching	B-T	HT	WT	DOB	W	L	ERA	G	GS	CG	SV	IP	H	R	ER	HR	BB	SO	AVG	vLH	vRH	K/9	BB/9
Altavilla, Dan	R-R	5-11	200	9-8-92	0	0	0.00	1	0	0	0	1	0	0	0	0	0	2	.000	.000	.000	18.00	0.00
Bannister, Nathan	R-R	6-3	224	12-17-93	7	9	6.07	26	24	1	0	138	173	98	93	22	48	84	.305	.297	.309	5.48	3.13
Bonnell, Bryan	L-R	6-5	240	9-28-93	3	3	3.17	32	0	0	2	48	52	22	17	6	12	38	.274	.300	.262	7.08	2.23
Caughel, Lindsey	R-R	6-3	205	8-13-90	1	0	6.00	1	0	0	0	3	3	2	2	0	0	4	.250	.500	.200	12.00	0.00
De Jong, Chase	L-R	6-4	205	12-29-93	5	5	3.80	21	21	0	0	121	122	60	51	12	34	89	.265	.241	.278	6.64	2.54
Festa, Matt	R-R	6-2	195	3-11-93	5	2	2.76	44	0	0	20	49	50	18	15	6	12	67	.263	.290	.250	12.31	2.20
Frank, Trevor	R-R	6-0	195	6-23-91	0	2	5.29	10	0	0	0	17	14	11	10	4	6	20	.215	.226	.206	5.59	3.18
2-team total (12 San Antonio)					1	2	3.52	22	0	0	1	38	32	17	15	6	10	35	.219	.214	.222	8.22	2.35
Gillies, Darin	R-R	6-4	220	11-6-92	2	1	4.58	15	0	0	1	20	16	11	10	2	8	23	.225	.300	.196	10.53	3.66
Goudeau, Ashton	R-R	6-6	205	7-23-92	4	5	4.38	9	9	1	0	51	51	26	25	5	14	35	.264	.339	.227	6.14	2.45
Herrmann, Spencer	L-L	6-4	235	8-6-93	6	5	5.01	29	7	0	0	65	74	38	36	3	28	55	.289	.232	.305	7.65	3.90
Hutchison, Austin	R-R	6-1	205	4-9-95	0	0	4.50	1	0	0	0	2	5	1	1	0	0	1	.500	.000	.556	4.50	0.00
Jackson, Tyler	R-R	6-6	210	10-22-93	1	1	7.63	4	1	0	0	15	23	13	13	3	5	11	.329	.261	.362	6.46	2.93
Jiminian, Johendi	R-R	6-3	170	10-14-92	4	4	3.49	16	16	0	0	70	67	30	27	8	31	52	.254	.314	.225	6.72	4.00
Kuzminsky, Scott	R-R	6-2	195	11-1-91	1	1	3.86	14	0	0	0	28	27	16	12	4	20	16	.255	.297	.232	5.14	6.43
Mazza, Chris	R-R	6-4	180	10-15-89	1	0	1.33	4	4	0	0	27	15	6	4	1	4	23	.158	.238	.094	7.67	1.33
McIver, Anthony	L-L	6-5	210	4-8-92	0	0	13.03	6	0	0	0	10	14	14	14	2	6	8	.350	.214	.423	7.45	5.59
McKay, David	R-R	6-3	205	3-31-95	5	1	2.49	35	0	0	1	51	36	18	14	3	21	71	.199	.158	.218	12.61	3.73
Mills, Wyatt	R-R	6-3	175	1-25-95	0	2	10.13	9	0	0	0	11	18	13	12	0	4	16	.367	.381	.357	8.44	3.38
Misiewicz, Anthony	R-L	6-1	190	11-1-94	3	12	5.51	21	21	0	0	98	133	73	60	14	29	91	.319	.392	.290	8.36	2.66
Moore, Andrew	R-R	6-0	185	6-2-94	3	1	3.04	9	9	0	0	50	38	17	17	6	14	47	.210	.234	.197	8.40	2.50
Moyers, Steven	R-R	6-0	190	9-27-93	0	0	27.00	1	0	0	0	3	3	3	3	1	1	1	.600	—	.600	9.00	9.00
Perakslis, Stephen	R-R	6-1	185	1-15-91	3	2	6.05	28	0	0	0	42	48	32	28	6	11	27	.289	.319	.277	5.83	2.38
Perez, Williams	R-R	6-0	240	5-21-91	6	1	2.28	13	13	1	0	79	69	25	20	5	13	68	.231	.231	.231	7.75	1.48
Pistorese, Joe	L-L	6-2	175	10-15-92	0	0	9.53	3	0	0	0	6	8	6	6	2	4	2	.320	.417	.231	3.18	6.35
Povse, Max	R-R	6-8	185	8-23-93	4	3	3.41	10	10	0	0	61	62	24	23	2	19	60	.266	.307	.247	8.90	2.82
Ramirez, Erasmo	R-R	5-10	215	5-2-90	0	0	2.25	1	1	0	0	4	4	2	1	0	0	6	.267	.200	.400	13.50	0.00
Rumbelow, Nick	R-R	6-0	190	9-6-91	0	0	0.00	2	0	0	0	2	2	0	0	0	1	2	.250	.000	.500	4.50	0.00
Schlereth, Daniel	L-L	6-0	210	5-9-86	0	0	1.35	8	0	0	0	7	3	1	1	0	3	10	.160	.091	.214	13.50	4.05
Tenuta, Matt	L-L	6-4	225	12-16-93	1	3	2.98	28	0	0	1	45	43	18	15	0	14	52	.254	.245	.259	10.32	2.78
Vincent, Nick	R-R	6-0	185	7-12-86	0	0	0.00	1	1	0	0	1	1	0	0	0	0	0	.250	.333	.000	0.00	0.00
Walker, Matt	R-R	6-6	201	9-28-94	5	1	3.63	39	0	0	3	62	59	29	25	5	22	56	.247	.273	.237	8.13	3.19
Warren, Art	R-R	6-3	230	3-23-93	1	2	1.72	14	0	0	2	16	10	7	3	0	14	22	.185	.412	.081	12.64	8.04
Whalen, Rob	R-R	6-2	220	1-31-94	0	2	7.50	2	2	0	0	6	10	7	5	1	3	8	.357	.333	.364	12.00	4.50

Fielding

Catcher	PCT	G	PO	A	E	DP	PB
DeCarlo	.987	49	345	31	5	2	7
Odom	.990	75	581	35	6	4	7
Scott	.975	20	151	8	4	0	5
Silva	.000	1	0	0	0	0	0

First Base	PCT	G	PO	A	E	DP
Curletta	.993	118	907	39	7	81
Filia	1.000	3	27	1	0	3
Healy	1.000	2	14	0	0	2
Mejias-Brean	1.000	4	30	3	0	3
Pizzano	.980	13	97	1	2	6

Second Base	PCT	G	PO	A	E	DP
Izturis Jr.	1.000	1	1	0	0	0

	PCT	G	PO	A	E	DP
Law	.975	19	40	38	2	8
Mariscal	.995	49	89	129	1	35
Mendoza	.970	6	20	12	1	1
Shank	1.000	2	7	3	0	2
Taylor	.500	1	2	0	2	0
Walton	.979	62	123	160	6	28

Third Base	PCT	G	PO	A	E	DP
DeCarlo	.941	9	5	11	1	3
Law	.946	18	18	35	3	7
Mariscal	.963	29	18	59	3	4
Mejias-Brean	1.000	28	27	70	0	9
Shank	1.000	1	0	4	0	0
Taylor	.912	58	29	85	11	5

Shortstop	PCT	G	PO	A	E	DP

	PCT	G	PO	A	E	DP
Mariscal	.955	44	38	130	8	13
Mendoza	.961	90	110	238	14	46
Sanders	.895	8	2	15	2	5

Outfield	PCT	G	PO	A	E	DP
Amaral	.995	93	212	4	1	0
Aplin	1.000	10	19	0	0	0
Bishop	1.000	84	219	4	0	0
Filia	1.000	55	112	2	0	0
Law	1.000	9	11	0	0	0
Lewis	1.000	30	76	0	0	0
Pizzano	1.000	23	45	0	0	0
Shank	1.000	3	10	0	0	0
Taylor	.974	107	186	5	5	0
Taylor	1.000	6	13	0	0	0

MODESTO NUTS   HIGH CLASS A
CALIFORNIA LEAGUE

Batting	B-T	HT	WT	DOB	AVG	vLH	vRH	G	AB	R	H	2B	3B	HR	RBI	BB	HBP	SH	SF	SO	SB	CS	SLG	OBP
Baker, Tyler	L-R	5-9	179	3-8-93	.164	.233	.147	46	159	9	26	7	1	1	9	20	3	1	1	51	0	0	.239	.268
Boyd, Louis	R-R	5-11	169	5-4-94	.207	.159	.229	46	140	14	29	3	0	0	6	15	2	2	1	22	0	0	.229	.291
Branton, Beau	R-R	5-7	175	9-4-95	.247	.276	.235	28	97	12	24	2	1	0	6	7	0	0	0	19	2	0	.289	.336

Name	B-T	HT	WT	DOB	AVG	vLH	vRH	G	AB	R	H	2B	3B	HR	RBI	BB	HBP	SH	SF	SO	SB	CS	OBP	SLG
Brigman, Bryson	R-R	5-11	180	6-19-95	.305	.389	.285	98	381	47	116	13	7	2	38	37	5	1	1	58	15	6	.391	.373
Cowan, Jordan	L-R	6-0	160	4-13-95	.284	.188	.310	20	74	12	21	4	0	0	8	7	1	2	2	16	1	0	.338	.345
Gamel, Ben	L-L	5-11	185	5-17-92	.294	—	.294	5	17	6	5	1	0	0	0	4	0	0	0	2	1	1	.353	.429
Garcia, Ryan	L-L	6-2	205	7-8-95	.125	.500	.000	2	8	2	1	0	0	0	2	1	0	0	2	0	0	0	.125	.222
Honeyman, Bobby	L-R	6-1	185	5-25-96	.227	.333	.188	6	22	2	5	0	1	0	1	0	0	0	0	3	0	1	.318	.227
Jimenez, Anthony	R-R	5-11	165	10-21-95	.262	.292	.253	102	385	38	101	20	3	6	42	22	7	1	0	103	13	7	.377	.314
Joseph, Luis	B-R	5-9	160	9-20-96	.250	.333	.000	1	4	0	1	0	0	0	0	0	0	0	0	0	0	0	.250	.250
Kennedy, Garrett	L-R	6-1	205	12-13-92	.160	.000	.191	18	50	6	8	1	1	0	7	12	2	0	0	14	0	0	.220	.344
Larsen, Jack	L-L	6-1	195	1-13-95	.171	.222	.156	26	82	7	14	4	1	1	13	13	1	0	1	29	0	0	.281	.289
Lewis, Kyle	R-R	6-4	210	7-13-95	.260	.206	.272	49	196	21	51	18	0	5	32	11	2	0	2	55	0	0	.429	.303
Liberato, Luis	L-L	6-1	175	12-18-95	.250	.260	.247	87	328	48	82	20	2	11	44	34	0	4	4	63	2	5	.424	.317
Morales, Jhombeyker	R-R	6-0	170	7-17-94	.146	.000	.170	16	55	3	8	1	0	0	3	2	2	0	0	11	0	2	.164	.203
Morgan, Gareth	R-R	6-4	220	4-17-96	.158	.177	.153	84	298	42	47	7	2	19	39	30	6	0	0	180	7	1	.386	.249
Pazos, Manny	R-R	5-11	190	1-23-95	.223	.235	.217	45	148	14	33	4	2	2	21	9	1	1	1	47	0	1	.318	.270
Rivera, Jansiel	L-L	6-1	205	8-28-98	.133	.000	.182	5	15	2	2	0	0	0	0	1	1	0	0	7	0	0	.133	.235
Rizzo, Joe	L-R	5-9	194	3-31-98	.241	.226	.245	123	461	46	111	21	2	4	55	40	3	0	4	108	6	1	.321	.303
Santa, Kevin	L-R	5-11	175	3-9-95	.287	.338	.275	98	348	57	100	13	4	2	32	25	6	4	1	38	11	6	.365	.345
Scott, Ryan	R-R	6-1	180	2-7-95	.179	.000	.217	10	28	1	5	0	0	0	2	4	0	1	1	7	0	0	.179	.273
Scott, Zach	L-R	6-0	185	4-27-95	.167	.500	.000	2	6	0	1	0	0	0	0	0	0	0	0	3	0	0	.167	.167
Solano, Jorge	R-R	5-10	185	10-21-94	.174	.100	.194	19	46	11	8	1	1	0	4	6	1	1	0	24	2	0	.239	.283
Stroosma, Aaron	R-R	6-2	205	5-16-94	.118	.125	.111	6	17	1	2	0	0	0	5	3	0	0	0	6	0	0	.118	.250
Taylor, Logan	R-R	6-1	200	9-22-93	.291	.273	.295	35	127	18	37	9	1	3	22	12	1	0	1	44	4	1	.449	.397
Thurman, Nick	L-R	6-2	210	9-9-93	.205	.250	.192	39	122	8	25	5	0	1	11	10	1	0	1	44	0	1	.271	.269
Walton, Donnie	L-R	5-10	184	5-25-94	.309	.294	.312	57	217	35	67	12	3	3	19	30	5	2	2	37	8	3	.433	.402
White, Evan	R-L	6-3	205	4-26-96	.303	.352	.291	120	476	72	144	27	7	11	66	52	6	0	4	103	4	3	.458	.376
Zammarelli III, Nick	L-R	6-1	195	7-30-94	.274	.221	.286	124	457	60	125	30	6	10	60	39	6	2	4	136	5	1	.431	.336
Zunino, Mike	R-R	6-2	220	3-25-91	.091	.000	.111	3	11	1	1	1	0	0	1	0	0	0	0	4	0	0	.182	.167

Pitching

Name	B-T	HT	WT	DOB	W	L	ERA	G	GS	CG	SV	IP	H	R	ER	HR	BB	SO	AVG	vLH	vRH	K/9	BB/9
Anderson, Jack	R-R	6-3	210	1-10-94	2	4	2.68	44	0	0	2	54	54	25	16	0	14	57	.251	.306	.224	9.56	2.35
Bell, Randy	R-L	5-10	190	2-11-95	3	4	4.95	13	13	0	0	67	78	45	37	9	14	49	.286	.225	.315	6.55	1.87
Boches, Scott	R-R	6-5	205	10-17-94	1	0	0.00	1	1	0	0	6	6	0	0	0	2	4	.250	.000	.316	6.00	3.00
Desguin, Jordan	R-R	6-1	195	10-30-93	0	0	1.13	6	0	0	0	8	7	1	1	0	4	10	.226	.286	.177	11.25	4.50
Elledge, Seth	R-R	6-3	230	5-20-96	5	1	1.17	31	0	0	9	38	18	10	5	1	15	54	.140	.133	.143	12.68	3.52
Ellingson, David	R-R	6-2	200	1-23-95	1	0	4.76	12	0	0	1	17	18	10	9	1	10	21	.269	.238	.283	11.12	5.29
Espinal, Erik	R-R	5-9	155	11-14-96	0	1	20.25	1	1	0	0	3	7	6	6	0	1	2	.539	.667	.429	6.75	3.38
Espino, Elias	R-R	6-2	195	4-19-97	0	0	2.25	1	0	0	0	4	2	1	1	0	2	3	.154	.000	.182	6.75	4.50
Franks, AJ	R-R	6-2	170	6-25-95	1	0	6.04	17	0	0	0	25	31	17	17	3	10	11	.323	.389	.283	3.91	3.55
Garcia, Danny	L-L	6-1	195	2-21-94	1	5	6.27	34	10	0	1	93	125	70	65	12	23	89	.326	.327	.326	8.58	2.22
Goudeau, Ashton	R-R	6-6	205	7-23-92	1	1	4.50	3	3	0	0	14	14	8	7	2	6	12	.259	.333	.200	7.71	3.86
Haberer, Jake	R-R	6-2	225	2-9-95	0	0	4.15	4	0	0	0	4	5	2	2	0	2	7	.294	.333	.273	14.54	4.15
Hernandez, Carlos	R-R	6-3	195	2-8-96	0	0	10.80	1	0	0	0	2	1	2	2	0	2	2	.167	.000	.333	10.80	10.80
Herrmann, Spencer	L-L	6-4	235	8-6-93	0	0	0.96	6	0	0	1	9	3	1	1	0	6	14	.094	.250	.042	13.50	5.79
Hutchison, Austin	R-R	6-2	205	4-9-95	3	4	3.47	26	9	0	0	83	74	36	32	5	25	89	.235	.234	.235	9.65	2.71
Jackson, Tyler	R-R	6-6	210	10-22-93	0	1	9.00	1	1	0	0	4	7	4	4	0	3	0	.438	.250	.500	0.00	6.75
Kober, Collin	R-R	6-1	185	9-9-94	1	1	4.73	11	0	0	2	13	12	8	7	1	3	18	.240	.333	.188	12.15	2.03
Koval, Michael	R-R	6-1	180	4-20-95	0	3	3.55	24	0	0	0	38	48	21	15	1	12	32	.306	.344	.280	7.58	2.84
Kuzminsky, Scott	R-R	6-2	195	11-1-91	0	0	2.70	2	0	0	0	3	2	1	1	0	5	2	.222	.000	.400	5.40	13.50
McCaughan, Darren	R-R	6-1	195	3-18-96	6	10	3.05	25	25	0	0	139	152	61	47	6	30	121	.275	.279	.273	7.85	1.95
McClain, Reggie	R-R	6-2	180	11-16-92	6	11	5.01	24	23	0	0	133	160	89	74	16	28	108	.298	.317	.287	7.31	1.89
McIver, Anthony	L-L	6-5	210	4-8-92	0	5	4.62	19	0	0	0	25	33	16	13	4	5	28	.297	.167	.346	9.95	1.78
McKay, David	R-R	6-3	205	3-31-95	1	1	3.52	6	0	0	0	8	11	4	3	0	1	14	.324	.400	.263	16.43	1.17
Medina, Jefferson	R-R	6-2	184	5-31-94	3	3	3.73	39	0	0	1	72	63	38	30	1	34	66	.236	.267	.217	8.21	4.23
Mills, Wyatt	R-R	6-3	175	1-25-95	6	0	1.91	35	0	0	11	42	29	12	9	1	9	49	.193	.224	.169	10.42	1.91
Miranda, Ariel	L-L	6-2	190	1-10-89	1	0	1.80	1	1	0	0	5	5	1	1	0	2	5	.368	.546	.125	9.00	3.60
Moyers, Steven	R-L	6-0	190	9-27-93	0	0	0.00	1	0	0	0	0	0	0	0	0	1	0	—	.000	.000		27.00
Newsome, Ljay	R-R	5-11	210	11-8-96	6	10	4.87	26	26	0	0	139	169	79	75	24	13	123	.297	.299	.296	7.98	0.84
Onyshko, Benjamin	R-L	6-2	205	10-18-96	0	0	0.00	1	0	0	0	2	2	0	0	0	2	2	.286	1.000	.167	9.00	9.00
Ramirez, Erasmo	R-R	5-10	215	5-2-90	0	0	3.00	1	1	0	0	3	4	1	1	0	1	3	.400	.167	.750	9.00	3.00
Razo, Orlando	L-L	5-11	185	2-7-95	0	1	5.40	1	1	0	0	5	4	3	3	0	3	2	.235	—	.235	3.60	5.40
Richy, John	R-R	6-2	215	7-28-92	0	3	6.65	7	2	0	0	23	25	19	17	4	12	17	.275	.225	.314	6.65	4.70
Rodgers, Colin	L-L	6-0	181	12-2-93	3	5	5.59	21	9	0	0	68	78	48	42	6	26	67	.282	.316	.269	8.91	3.46
Salter, J.T.	R-R	6-8	295	6-10-96	0	0	0.00	3	0	0	0	4	0	0	0	0	0	4	.000	.000	.000	9.00	2.25
Wells, Nick	L-L	6-5	185	2-21-96	5	4	5.45	14	14	0	0	66	78	47	40	4	29	61	.293	.347	.272	8.32	3.95
Wilcox, Kyle	R-R	6-4	195	6-14-94	0	0	13.50	5	0	0	0	5	6	7	7	2	6	5	.333	.455	.143	9.64	11.57
Zavolas, Noah	R-R	6-1	190	5-11-96	3	0	0.00	3	0	0	0	4	2	0	0	0	2	4	.133	.167	.111	9.00	4.50

Fielding

Catcher	PCT	G	PO	A	E	DP	PB
Baker	.993	46	384	37	3	5	4
Kennedy	.992	17	117	9	1	0	1
Pazos	1.000	38	288	21	0	0	5
Scott	1.000	8	55	2	0	1	0
Thurman	.985	37	308	13	5	0	2
Zunino	1.000	2	12	1	0	0	0

First Base	PCT	G	PO	A	E	DP
Garcia	.952	2	19	1	1	2
Honeyman	1.000	1	15	1	0	2
Kennedy	.867	1	12	1	2	1
Morales	.909	2	10	0	1	0
Rizzo	1.000	5	36	4	0	0
White	.996	106	866	69	4	89
Zammarelli III	.980	25	190	9	4	18

Second Base	PCT	G	PO	A	E	DP
Boyd	.986	16	24	48	1	7
Branton	.957	24	40	48	4	4
Brigman	.949	7	13	24	2	3
Morales	1.000	2	2	4	0	1
Pazos	.955	4	8	13	1	6
Rizzo	1.000	6	13	14	0	6
Santa	.977	46	85	129	5	37

	PCT	G	PO	A	E	DP
Scott	.800	1	4	0	1	0
Walton	.979	36	65	73	3	20

Third Base	PCT	G	PO	A	E	DP
Boyd	.919	14	9	25	3	4
Branton	.500	1	0	1	1	0
Honeyman	1.000	4	5	1	0	0
Morales	1.000	1	1	1	0	0
Rizzo	.909	99	53	176	23	17
Santa	.929	25	24	41	5	2
Taylor	.857	3	2	4	1	0

Shortstop	PCT	G	PO	A	E	DP
Boyd	.977	13	11	32	1	4
Branton	.857	2	1	5	1	1
Brigman	.959	83	110	243	15	60
Santa	.933	25	34	50	6	10
Walton	.895	19	26	51	9	11

Outfield	PCT	G	PO	A	E	DP
Boyd	1.000	3	4	0	0	0
Gamel	1.000	2	5	0	0	0
Jimenez	.947	85	155	7	9	1

	PCT	G	PO	A	E	DP
Joseph	1.000	1	1	0	0	0
Larsen	1.000	26	46	4	0	0
Lewis	.961	36	69	4	3	0
Liberato	.976	74	158	6	4	1
Morales	.938	9	15	0	1	0
Morgan	.969	82	181	4	6	1
Rivera	1.000	5	7	1	0	0
Solano	.944	15	32	2	2	1
Stroosma	1.000	6	5	0	0	0
Taylor	1.000	27	39	5	0	0
Zammarelli III	.953	64	77	4	4	2

CLINTON LUMBERKINGS
MIDWEST LEAGUE   LOW CLASS A

Batting	B-T	HT	WT	DOB	AVG	vLH	vRH	G	AB	R	H	2B	3B	HR	RBI	BB	HBP	SH	SF	SO	SB	CS	SLG	OBP
Adams, Johnny	R-R	6-0	200	9-2-94	.219	.185	.227	132	471	63	103	20	2	11	44	44	3	2	2	134	8	4	.340	.289
Andrade, Greifer	R-R	6-0	170	1-27-97	.221	.207	.225	39	140	13	31	6	0	3	20	1	3	1	1	48	0	1	.329	.241
Boyd, Louis	R-R	5-11	169	5-4-94	.207	.323	.182	49	174	27	36	2	1	2	12	13	5	1	1	40	3	1	.264	.280
Camacho, Juan	R-R	6-3	215	4-19-96	.290	.282	.294	40	131	8	38	6	0	3	18	1	2	0	1	25	0	0	.405	.304
Cooke, Billy	R-R	5-10	175	9-26-95	.175	.226	.162	95	297	26	52	7	1	1	15	36	14	4	5	101	13	6	.216	.290
Costello, Ryan	L-R	6-2	200	6-13-96	.266	.325	.249	101	346	48	92	24	2	16	70	51	3	0	6	82	2	4	.486	.360
Helder, Eugene	R-R	5-11	165	2-26-96	.240	.270	.233	102	375	48	90	17	3	7	44	34	3	2	4	64	4	0	.357	.305
Hoover, Connor	L-R	5-10	185	7-18-96	.208	.250	.196	23	72	3	15	1	0	0	4	8	0	0	0	22	1	2	.222	.288
Larsen, Jack	L-L	6-1	195	1-13-95	.266	.246	.271	88	305	52	81	17	5	12	58	54	5	0	1	107	2	4	.472	.384
McGovern, Keegan	L-R	6-3	200	9-13-95	.268	.215	.287	65	239	35	64	12	2	15	44	28	3	1	0	66	1	1	.523	.351
Ojeda, Dimas	L-L	6-1	195	9-19-95	.272	.288	.268	108	382	50	104	24	1	8	45	34	2	1	0	103	1	1	.403	.335
Pena, Onil	R-R	6-0	180	11-6-96	.209	.204	.211	53	177	15	37	8	1	2	15	19	6	0	0	60	0	0	.299	.307
Rosa, Joseph	B-R	5-10	165	3-6-97	.217	.159	.231	114	428	61	93	7	2	6	22	46	5	2	2	117	20	17	.285	.299
Sanders, Matt	R-R	5-8	175	6-7-96	.259	.100	.353	24	27	4	7	0	0	3	4	1	0	0	0	2	1	0	.593	.286
Sandoval, Ariel	R-R	6-2	180	11-6-95	.242	.327	.216	129	472	78	114	19	3	18	56	47	3	0	3	173	14	7	.409	.312
Scott, Ryan	R-R	6-1	180	2-7-95	.206	.250	.198	35	107	13	22	5	1	0	9	19	1	1	0	36	1	1	.271	.331
Scott, Zach	L-R	6-0	185	4-27-95	.225	.273	.206	52	151	19	34	5	0	0	7	21	1	2	1	51	1	1	.258	.322
Silva, Rainis	R-R	6-1	185	3-20-96	.202	.286	.181	34	104	7	21	6	0	1	13	7	1	2	1	23	1	0	.289	.257
Thurman, Nick	L-R	6-2	210	9-9-93	.208	.263	.198	36	120	7	25	6	1	0	13	10	1	2	1	48	0	0	.275	.282

Pitching	B-T	HT	WT	DOB	W	L	ERA	G	GS	CG	SV	IP	H	R	ER	HR	BB	SO	AVG	vLH	vRH	K/9	BB/9
Anderson, Grant	R-R	6-0	180	6-21-97	1	0	0.00	1	0	0	0	2	0	0	0	0	0	4	.000	.000	.000	18.00	0.00
Bell, Randy	R-R	5-10	190	2-11-95	3	4	5.85	15	7	0	1	52	70	38	34	3	16	53	.321	.250	.366	9.11	2.75
Boches, Scott	R-R	6-5	205	10-17-94	2	5	3.39	26	10	0	2	82	86	37	31	3	17	79	.263	.250	.273	8.64	1.86
Castellanos, Chris	L-L	5-10	185	5-8-95	3	0	4.02	9	0	0	0	16	13	7	7	0	8	12	.213	.000	.232	6.89	4.60
Chandler, Clay	R-R	6-3	180	4-27-94	9	4	3.89	27	19	0	1	137	124	61	59	20	33	101	.238	.237	.239	6.65	2.17
Clancy, Matt	B-L	5-11	180	4-1-94	0	1	6.18	32	0	0	2	60	68	42	41	6	37	65	.286	.366	.252	9.80	5.58
De La Cruz, Adonis	R-R	6-2	170	12-20-94	3	4	4.71	34	0	0	1	57	54	37	30	3	19	75	.249	.237	.255	11.77	2.98
Delaplane, Sam	R-R	5-11	175	3-27-95	4	2	1.96	39	0	0	10	60	54	23	13	5	22	100	.234	.218	.242	15.08	3.32
Gerber, David	R-R	6-1	200	2-9-94	2	1	2.92	8	0	0	1	12	8	4	4	0	6	13	.191	.375	.147	9.49	4.38
Gerber, Joey	R-R	6-4	215	5-3-97	0	0	2.31	9	0	0	2	12	9	3	3	0	5	22	.220	.083	.276	16.97	3.86
Gorgas, Marvin	R-R	5-9	185	1-19-96	6	4	3.64	29	0	0	4	54	55	28	22	2	28	58	.268	.238	.288	9.61	4.64
Hutchinson, Austin	R-R	6-1	205	4-9-95	1	0	0.00	5	0	0	0	12	5	0	0	0	3	12	.128	.182	.107	9.26	2.31
Inman, Ryne	R-R	6-5	215	5-13-96	4	10	4.57	25	25	0	0	112	107	61	57	11	44	117	.249	.238	.255	9.37	3.53
Jackson, Tyler	R-R	6-6	210	10-22-93	1	3	6.07	13	0	0	0	43	57	37	29	9	11	37	.308	.290	.319	7.74	2.30
Jaskie, Oliver	L-L	6-3	210	11-17-95	4	8	6.60	18	16	0	0	76	92	62	56	7	49	77	.301	.371	.283	9.08	5.78
Kerr, Raymond	L-L	6-2	185	9-10-94	5	11	4.28	25	25	0	0	111	117	66	53	14	43	101	.272	.316	.260	8.16	3.48
Kober, Collin	R-R	6-1	185	9-8-94	5	0	1.93	27	0	0	7	47	35	20	10	1	12	64	.198	.258	.165	12.34	2.31
Moyers, Steven	R-L	6-0	190	9-27-93	4	2	3.24	21	7	0	1	75	74	31	27	6	14	56	.254	.212	.267	6.72	1.68
Razo, Orlando	L-L	5-11	185	2-7-95	0	0	0.00	1	0	0	0	5	4	1	0	0	0	6	.200	.167	.214	10.13	0.00
Romero, Tommy	L-R	6-2	225	7-8-97	3	3	2.45	9	9	0	0	44	41	12	12	1	15	54	.252	.233	.267	11.05	3.07
2-team total (16 Bowling Green)					11	4	2.95	25	25	1	0	128	111	42	42	11	51	131	.238	.264	.216	9.21	3.59
Sweet, Devin	B-R	5-11	183	9-6-96	0	0	9.00	2	0	0	0	3	5	3	3	1	0	7	.357	.400	.333	3.00	0.00
Watson, Tyler	L-L	5-11	200	6-9-93	0	0	12.00	2	0	0	0	3	6	4	4	1	1	4	.429	.400	.444	12.00	3.00
Wells, Nick	L-L	6-5	185	2-21-96	4	4	4.44	14	14	1	0	73	73	39	36	4	33	62	.265	.163	.283	7.64	4.07
Wilcox, Kyle	R-R	6-3	195	6-14-94	4	2	2.50	32	0	0	7	54	33	16	15	2	26	89	.174	.175	.173	14.83	4.33

Fielding

C: Camacho 39, Scott 35, Silva 34, Thurman 36. **1B:** Boyd 2, Costello 85, Helder 3, Ojeda 9, Pena 47. **2B:** Boyd 15, Hoover 5, Rosa 104, Sanders 6, Scott 13. **3B:** Boyd 14, Costello 4, Helder 97, Hoover 14, Scott 17. **SS:** Adams 126, Boyd 9, Scott 8. **OF:** Andrade 32, Boyd 10, Cooke 95, Larsen 80, McGovern 62, Ojeda 66, Rosa 1, Sandoval 79, Scott 7.

EVERETT AQUASOX
NORTHWEST LEAGUE   SHORT-SEASON

Batting	B-T	HT	WT	DOB	AVG	vLH	vRH	G	AB	R	H	2B	3B	HR	RBI	BB	HBP	SH	SF	SO	SB	CS	SLG	OBP
Anchia, Jake	R-R	6-1	210	3-5-97	.228	.222	.231	15	57	6	13	5	0	2	8	3	2	0	0	16	0	0	.386	.290
Cano, Robinson	L-R	6-0	210	10-22-82	.455	1.000	.400	3	11	3	5	1	0	2	6	1	0	0	0	0	0	0	1.091	.500
Dixon, Troy	L-R	6-2	205	4-26-95	.185	.333	.156	32	108	11	20	4	0	1	9	6	0	1	1	26	0	1	.250	.226
Garcia, Ryan	L-L	6-2	205	7-8-95	.222	.150	.242	54	189	24	42	10	1	5	22	21	1	0	2	33	2	0	.365	.301

Name	B-T	HT	WT	DOB	AVG	vLH	vRH	G	AB	R	H	2B	3B	HR	RBI	BB	HBP	SH	SF	SO	SB	CS	SLG	OBP
Gladfelter, Cash	L-R	6-4	200	11-9-96	.182	.100	.200	19	55	7	10	3	0	0	4	11	2	0	0	16	0	0	.236	.338
Honeyman, Bobby	L-R	6-1	185	5-25-96	.347	.340	.348	58	228	32	79	12	4	3	29	12	2	1	1	24	4	3	.474	.383
Hoover, Connor	L-R	5-10	185	7-18-96	.232	.182	.239	26	82	12	19	5	0	3	12	18	0	0	1	22	2	3	.402	.366
Izturis Jr., Cesar	B-R	5-11	145	11-11-99	.500	—	.500	1	4	0	2	1	0	0	2	0	0	0	0	0	0	0	.750	.500
Kopach, Connor	R-R	6-0	170	8-4-94	.274	.261	.277	61	212	36	58	15	3	2	27	27	3	1	1	58	14	4	.401	.362
McConnell, Charlie	L-R	6-2	195	1-7-96	.284	.400	.260	65	225	32	64	5	1	4	24	13	1	2	3	36	11	4	.369	.322
McGovern, Keegan	L-R	6-3	200	9-13-95	.313	.000	.417	4	16	2	5	2	0	0	2	0	1	0	0	3	0	1	.438	.353
Montilla, Geoandry	R-R	6-0	165	5-14-96	.215	.294	.184	35	121	19	26	8	0	3	11	8	3	1	0	47	1	2	.355	.280
Ogren, Ryne	R-R	6-1	180	4-11-97	.250	.353	.227	55	188	26	47	9	1	3	31	23	5	0	2	43	5	1	.356	.344
Pena, Onil	R-R	6-0	180	11-6-96	.200	.000	.250	4	15	1	3	0	0	0	2	2	1	0	0	3	0	0	.200	.333
Perkins, Cameron	R-R	6-5	195	9-27-90	.250	.000	.333	4	16	3	4	1	0	1	3	1	1	0	0	4	1	0	.500	.333
Raleigh, Cal	B-R	6-3	215	11-26-96	.288	.364	.274	38	146	25	42	10	1	8	29	18	1	0	1	29	1	1	.534	.368
Ramiz, Ryan	L-L	6-1	185	1-13-96	.241	.200	.254	47	166	24	40	5	2	2	13	32	1	2	2	47	4	3	.331	.363
Rivera, Jansiel	L-L	6-1	205	8-28-98	.217	.069	.254	49	143	16	31	5	0	5	21	19	2	0	1	57	3	3	.357	.315
Rodriguez, Nick	R-R	6-2	170	6-28-96	.256	.244	.260	57	195	34	50	10	0	7	24	12	2	0	1	46	2	1	.415	.305
Rosario, Ronald	L-L	6-2	165	2-8-97	.079	.000	.100	13	38	2	3	1	0	0	1	0	0	0	0	17	0	0	.105	.103
Sanders, Matt	R-R	5-8	175	6-7-96	.216	.291	.191	34	111	10	24	7	0	0	14	10	0	0	3	19	1	3	.279	.274
Silva, Rainis	R-R	6-1	185	3-20-96	.286	.000	.400	2	7	1	2	2	0	0	0	0	0	0	0	0	0	0	.571	.286
Stowers, Josh	R-R	6-1	200	2-25-97	.260	.313	.250	58	200	32	52	15	0	5	28	37	3	2	2	57	20	4	.410	.380

Pitching	B-T	HT	WT	DOB	W	L	ERA	G	GS	CG	SV	IP	H	R	ER	HR	BB	SO	AVG	vLH	vRH	K/9	BB/9
Alvarez, Dario	L-L	6-1	170	1-17-89	0	0	0.00	1	0	0	0	1	0	0	0	0	0	2	.000	.000	.000	18.00	0.00
Anderson, Grant	R-R	6-0	180	6-21-97	0	0	0.00	1	0	0	0	2	1	0	0	0	2	3	.167	.000	.250	13.50	9.00
Arias, Dayeison	R-R	6-1	160	1-7-97	2	0	1.69	19	0	0	1	32	19	6	6	5	10	45	.167	.146	.182	12.66	2.81
Benitez, Jorge	L-L	6-2	155	6-1-99	0	0	2.25	2	0	0	0	4	2	1	1	0	1	6	.143	.143	.143	13.50	2.25
Bonilla, Feliberto	R-R	6-2	165	4-21-98	0	0	6.75	1	0	0	0	1	1	1	1	0	1	2	.200	.333	.000	13.50	6.75
Brown, Cody	R-R	6-1	195	12-30-93	2	4	6.44	9	4	0	0	29	38	24	21	3	11	20	.325	.362	.300	6.14	3.38
Caraballo, Jheyson	R-R	6-0	170	10-16-95	4	5	5.12	14	14	0	0	63	69	40	36	6	25	48	.283	.232	.326	6.82	3.55
Ellingson, David	R-R	6-2	200	1-23-95	2	0	2.19	7	0	0	1	12	9	3	3	0	4	13	.209	.250	.194	9.49	2.92
Espino, Elias	R-R	6-2	195	4-19-97	0	0	1.93	1	1	0	0	5	7	2	1	1	2	3	.318	.313	.333	5.79	3.86
Fortunato, Ivan	R-R	6-1	170	12-1-98	4	3	3.83	14	3	0	0	52	50	30	22	6	19	45	.259	.236	.273	7.84	3.31
Franks, AJ	R-R	6-2	170	6-25-95	0	0	0.00	3	0	0	1	3	3	1	0	0	2	1	.273	.250	.286	2.70	5.40
Gerber, Joey	R-R	6-4	215	5-3-97	1	0	1.93	13	0	0	6	14	9	3	3	0	6	21	.188	.083	.222	13.50	3.86
Grimm, Justin	R-R	6-3	210	8-16-88	0	0	4.50	2	0	0	0	2	2	1	1	0	2	3	.286	.000	.333	13.50	9.00
Hernandez, Carlos	R-R	6-3	195	2-8-96	3	5	4.60	14	13	0	0	61	63	36	31	5	21	46	.275	.291	.266	6.82	3.12
Hoffman, Nolan	R-R	6-4	190	8-9-97	1	3	2.45	15	0	0	4	18	17	8	5	0	7	16	.254	.222	.275	7.85	3.44
Iwakuma, Hisashi	R-R	6-3	210	4-12-81	0	0	3.00	2	2	0	0	3	2	1	1	0	1	2	.222	.400	.000	6.00	3.00
Jackson, Tyler	R-R	6-6	210	10-22-93	0	0	0.00	3	0	0	1	6	5	1	0	0	6	8	.200	.200	.200	11.37	0.00
Mobley, Cody	R-R	6-3	190	9-23-96	3	1	5.09	16	1	0	0	35	24	20	20	4	20	40	.194	.122	.240	10.19	5.09
Murfee, Penn	R-R	6-2	195	5-2-94	3	2	6.55	19	0	0	0	33	35	25	24	6	12	23	.278	.233	.301	6.27	3.27
Onyshko, Benjamin	R-L	6-2	205	10-18-96	1	0	2.25	12	0	0	1	20	17	6	5	1	11	24	.221	.172	.250	10.80	4.95
Perez, Ulises	R-R	6-3	160	7-14-97	0	1	5.40	15	0	0	0	27	34	16	16	1	9	21	.306	.359	.278	7.09	3.04
Plassmeyer, Michael	L-L	6-2	197	11-5-96	0	1	2.25	13	12	0	0	24	16	7	6	1	4	44	.182	.227	.167	16.50	1.50
Razo, Orlando	L-L	5-11	185	2-7-95	5	3	3.24	15	10	0	0	72	74	34	28	10	25	65	.255	.183	.284	7.53	2.90
Roberts, Max	L-L	6-6	190	7-23-97	1	3	4.25	10	9	0	0	42	43	20	20	4	17	47	.272	.375	.254	9.99	3.61
Salter, J.T.	R-R	6-8	295	6-10-96	0	1	5.19	9	0	0	1	9	11	5	5	0	8	14	.324	.357	.300	14.54	8.31
Spranger, Grant	R-R	6-2	210	1-30-96	0	1	2.00	6	0	0	0	9	6	5	2	1	5	14	.167	.077	.217	14.00	5.00
Sweet, Devin	B-R	5-11	183	9-6-96	1	0	3.38	6	0	0	0	8	10	5	3	0	2	11	.313	.294	.333	12.38	2.25
Wade, Jamal	R-R	6-0	205	2-8-96	1	2	4.15	20	0	0	1	30	27	17	14	5	17	37	.237	.255	.224	10.98	5.04
Whalen, Rob	R-R	6-2	220	1-31-94	0	1	9.64	2	2	0	0	5	9	6	5	3	0	5	.375	.833	.222	9.64	0.00
Zavolas, Noah	R-R	6-2	190	5-11-96	2	1	3.38	16	0	0	0	35	29	15	13	3	9	37	.223	.133	.271	9.61	2.34

Fielding

C: Anchia 9, Dixon 29, Montilla 15, Raleigh 25, Silva 2. **1B:** Anchia 2, Cano 1, Garcia 36, Gladfelter 2, Honeyman 4, Hoover 1, Montilla 6, Ogren 1, Pena 4, Rodriguez 27. **2B:** Cano 1, Honeyman 6, Hoover 20, Izturis Jr. 1, Kopach 12, Ogren 10, Rodriguez 16, Sanders 16. **3B:** Cano 1, Gladfelter 9, Honeyman 41, Hoover 2, Ogren 11, Rodriguez 11, Sanders 5. **SS:** Gladfelter 2, Honeyman 1, Hoover 3, Kopach 39, Ogren 27, Sanders 7. **OF:** Garcia 12, Gladfelter 2, McConnell 61, McGovern 10, Montilla 10, Perkins 2, Ramiz 43, Rivera 48, Rosario 12, Stowers 47.

AZL MARINERS ROOKIE

ARIZONA LEAGUE

Batting	B-T	HT	WT	DOB	AVG	vLH	vRH	G	AB	R	H	2B	3B	HR	RBI	BB	HBP	SH	SF	SO	SB	CS	SLG	OBP
Andrade, Greifer	R-R	6-0	170	1-27-97	.500	1.000	.000	1	2	1	1	0	0	0	0	1	1	0	0	1	0	0	.500	.750
Branton, Beau	R-R	5-7	175	9-4-95	.423	.438	.418	21	71	18	30	3	3	0	12	11	5	0	0	6	13	3	.549	.529
Camacho, Juan	R-R	6-3	215	4-19-96	.286	.500	.200	2	7	1	2	0	0	0	0	1	0	0	0	1	0	0	.286	.375
Cano, Jose	R-R	5-11	190	12-18-96	.212	.125	.240	21	66	4	14	2	0	0	4	2	3	0	2	25	0	0	.242	.260
Contreras, Danny	L-L	6-3	195	5-21-98	.265	.167	.299	35	117	13	31	2	0	4	18	10	0	0	2	27	1	1	.385	.318
Cooke, Billy	R-R	5-10	175	9-26-95	.200	.250	.192	8	30	5	6	2	0	0	2	2	1	0	1	12	2	1	.267	.265
Cowan, Jordan	R-R	6-0	160	4-13-95	.423	.250	.455	7	26	2	11	0	0	0	5	2	0	0	0	5	0	0	.423	.464
Gamboa, Miguel	B-R	5-11	175	10-22-97	.056	.059	.055	30	72	6	4	1	0	0	7	13	1	0	0	43	1	1	.069	.209
Garcia, Jepherson	R-R	6-2	185	4-19-99	.253	.118	.282	27	95	14	24	3	3	2	15	8	1	0	1	39	0	2	.411	.314
Gladfelter, Cash	L-R	6-4	200	11-9-96	.241	.250	.240	11	29	6	7	0	0	0	1	8	0	0	0	9	1	1	.241	.405
Hernandez, Cal	B-R	6-0	185	1-9-96	.221	.188	.230	21	77	4	17	2	2	0	5	9	0	1	1	28	0	3	.299	.299
Izturis Jr., Cesar	B-R	5-11	145	11-11-99	.245	.316	.227	50	188	28	46	7	0	1	12	12	4	2	0	44	5	3	.298	.304
Joseph, Luis	R-R	5-9	160	9-20-96	.267	.179	.294	37	120	18	32	6	2	1	9	2	1	0	0	14	7	1	.375	.290
Morgan, Gareth	R-R	6-4	220	4-12-96	.125	.000	.167	2	8	0	1	1	0	0	2	0	0	0	0	7	0	0	.250	.125
Moses, DeAires	L-L	5-9	170	11-30-95	.300	.000	.375	4	10	1	3	0	0	0	3	0	0	0	0	2	3	0	.300	.462

	B-T	HT	WT	DOB	AVG	vLH	vRH	G	AB	R	H	2B	3B	HR	RBI	BB	HBP	SH	SF	SO	SB	CS	SLG	OBP
Mota, Ismerling	R-R	6-1	185	9-2-97	.328	.375	.311	23	61	8	20	4	0	1	10	7	1	0	0	22	0	0	.443	.406
Munoz, Oberto	R-R	6-0	170	2-18-97	.206	.222	.200	13	34	4	7	1	0	0	2	4	0	0	0	16	0	0	.235	.290
Nevarez, Dean	R-R	6-0	220	1-4-97	.237	.214	.243	41	131	12	31	4	0	3	15	20	5	0	3	34	1	0	.336	.352
Ochoa, Sebastian	R-R	6-1	180	5-8-98	.204	.300	.177	48	181	17	37	4	0	1	9	17	2	1	1	34	9	4	.243	.279
Perez, Nolan	B-R	6-1	190	5-9-99	.186	.243	.169	44	161	17	30	7	2	1	14	11	2	0	3	58	1	1	.273	.243
Ramiz, Ryan	L-L	6-1	185	1-13-96	.298	.222	.316	14	47	10	14	1	0	0	3	8	3	0	0	11	2	1	.319	.431
Rosario, Ronald	L-L	6-2	165	2-8-97	.169	.000	.197	27	89	7	15	1	1	1	8	7	0	0	0	39	1	1	.236	.229
Sheaffer, David	L-L	6-2	170	5-9-95	.202	.167	.212	37	134	19	27	5	2	4	17	10	1	0	2	29	3	0	.358	.259
Staab, Cody	L-L	6-1	170	7-3-96	.063	.143	.040	16	32	8	2	1	0	0	1	9	0	0	0	14	1	0	.094	.268
Trejo, Cesar	R-R	6-2	200	5-15-97	.375	.333	.400	2	8	3	3	2	0	0	1	0	0	0	0	1	0	0	.625	.375

Pitching	B-T	HT	WT	DOB	W	L	ERA	G	GS	CG	SV	IP	H	R	ER	HR	BB	SO	AVG	vLH	vRH	K/9	BB/9
Alvarez, Dario	L-L	6-1	170	1-17-89	1	0	0.00	2	0	0	0	2	0	0	0	0	2	2	.000	—	.000	9.00	9.00
Anderson, Grant	R-R	6-0	180	6-21-97	1	0	2.00	1	0	0	1	9	3	3	2	1	5	6	.094	.083	.100	6.00	5.00
Beltran, Rigo	L-L	5-11	185	9-1-94	2	1	7.01	15	0	0	0	26	34	23	20	2	9	35	.315	.160	.361	12.27	3.16
Benitez, Jorge	L-L	6-2	155	6-1-99	2	3	4.92	13	9	0	0	53	62	38	29	3	23	44	.293	.286	.294	7.47	3.91
Bonilla, Feliberto	R-R	6-2	165	4-21-98	0	1	3.89	10	3	0	0	35	41	22	15	5	20	21	.308	.365	.272	5.45	5.19
Canela, Jose	R-R	6-0	167	12-10-95	2	3	5.84	16	0	0	2	25	22	16	16	1	10	26	.234	.256	.218	9.49	3.65
Casetta-Stubbs, Damon	R-R	6-4	200	7-22-99	0	2	13.50	6	5	0	0	7	15	13	10	0	4	7	.429	.438	.421	9.45	5.40
Encarnacion, Frank	R-R	6-3	195	2-13-95	0	0	2.65	13	0	0	0	17	13	6	5	0	12	19	.203	.226	.182	10.06	6.35
Espinal, Erik	R-R	5-9	155	11-14-96	1	0	3.23	14	1	0	0	31	23	14	11	0	8	25	.205	.231	.192	7.34	2.35
Espino, Elias	R-R	6-2	195	4-19-97	1	5	3.76	10	8	0	0	38	41	17	16	2	14	35	.283	.279	.286	8.22	3.29
Gerber, David	R-R	6-1	200	9-24-94	0	1	9.00	1	0	0	0	1	3	1	1	0	1	1	.600	.667	.500	9.00	9.00
Guzman, Carlos	R-L	6-1	170	1-28-97	0	0	4.91	7	0	0	0	7	14	8	4	1	5	10	.400	.200	.433	12.27	6.14
Haberer, Jake	R-R	6-2	225	2-9-95	0	0	6.23	4	0	0	0	4	7	3	3	0	4	6	.333	.571	.214	12.46	8.31
Hoffman, Nolan	R-R	6-4	190	8-9-97	1	0	1.35	6	0	0	0	7	3	2	1	0	1	7	.136	.333	.063	9.45	1.35
Laws, Holden	L-L	6-2	166	12-8-99	0	3	4.76	5	0	0	0	11	17	12	6	2	1	9	.347	.462	.306	7.15	0.79
Marte, Cristhopher	R-R	6-2	170	4-2-99	0	2	5.40	5	4	0	0	12	13	13	7	0	9	10	.271	.143	.324	7.71	6.94
Martinez, Edwin	R-R	6-6	240	7-31-95	0	0	4.05	16	1	0	0	33	31	24	15	2	20	27	.252	.300	.229	7.29	5.40
Mayer, Jake	R-R	6-2	200	6-26-95	2	1	9.00	7	2	0	0	13	26	21	13	0	4	14	.388	.394	.382	9.69	2.77
Mercedes, Juan	R-R	6-2	190	4-3-00	0	1	6.00	2	0	0	0	6	8	4	4	1	2	4	.320	.143	.389	6.00	3.00
Misiewicz, Anthony	R-L	6-1	190	11-1-94	0	0	0.00	2	2	0	0	5	2	0	0	0	0	5	.118	.000	.143	7.20	0.00
O'Brien, Joey	R-R	6-2	215	11-28-97	0	1	4.05	6	6	0	0	7	6	4	3	1	2	8	.222	.182	.250	10.80	2.70
Onyshko, Benjamin	R-R	6-2	205	10-18-96	0	0	0.00	2	0	0	0	2	2	2	0	0	3	2	.222	.000	.250	13.50	0.00
Pedrol, Christian	R-R	5-11	190	6-15-00	0	0	0.00	2	2	0	0	2	0	0	0	1	0	0	.000	.000	.000		4.50
Quezada, Edwin	R-R	6-5	205	11-22-96	0	2	6.75	10	3	0	0	24	22	21	18	3	21	16	.262	.313	.231	6.00	7.88
Salter, J.T.	R-R	6-8	295	6-10-96	1	1	1.13	6	0	0	3	8	1	1	1	0	9	10	.000		.050	11.25	10.13
Spranger, Grant	L-L	6-2	210	1-30-96	0	1	12.00	6	0	0	0	6	11	8	8	2	2	10	.367	.200	.400	15.00	3.00
Suarez, Michael	L-L	6-2	180	3-21-95	0	0	6.00	3	1	0	0	3	5	3	2	1	0	3	.385	.000	.417	9.00	3.00
Suellentrop, Tyler	R-R	6-3	217	12-21-97	0	1	4.97	14	0	0	1	13	17	11	7	1	13	12	.309	.273	.333	8.53	9.24
Sweet, Devin	B-R	5-11	183	9-6-96	1	1	4.32	7	0	0	2	8	6	4	4	0	4	12	.214	.167	.227	12.96	4.32
Wegmann, Nick	L-L	6-1	195	4-26-96	1	4	7.89	15	0	0	0	22	27	23	19	3	7	25	.303	.214	.320	10.38	2.91
Willrodt, Matthew	**R-R**	**6-4**	**220**	**10-19-97**	**1**	**2**	**7.36**	**11**	**2**	**0**	**0**	**26**	**34**	**26**	**21**	**1**	**11**	**23**	**.318**	**.323**	**.316**	**8.06**	**3.86**

Fielding

C: Camacho 2, Hernandez 1, Mota 18, Munoz 12, Nevarez 24, Sheaffer 10. **1B:** Cano 15, Contreras 33, Gamboa 3, Hernandez 2, Mota 1, Nevarez 1, Sheaffer 6. **2B:** Branton 10, Gamboa 7, Gladfelter 2, Hernandez 9, Izturis Jr. 12, Joseph 10, Perez 9. **3B:** Branton 6, Cano 1, Gamboa 4, Gladfelter 7, Hernandez 8, Perez 33. **SS:** Branton 2, Gamboa 12, Gladfelter 1, Hernandez 3, Izturis Jr. 38, Perez 1. **OF:** Cooke 8, Gamboa 5, Garcia 18, Hernandez 1, Joseph 26, Moses 4, Ochoa 48, Ramiz 14, Rosario 27, Sheaffer 11, Staab 14, Trejo 2.

DSL MARINERS   ROOKIE
DOMINICAN SUMMER LEAGUE

Batting	B-T	HT	WT	DOB	AVG	vLH	vRH	G	AB	R	H	2B	3B	HR	RBI	BB	HBP	SH	SF	SO	SB	CS	SLG	OBP
Batista, Freuddy	R-R	6-0	182	12-12-99	.250	.265	.244	51	176	29	44	12	1	7	38	21	5	0	3	51	1	1	.449	.342
Branche, Steve	R-R	6-1	165	9-1-97	.097	.000	.125	12	31	4	3	2	0	0	5	5	0	1	0	17	0	1	.161	.222
Casilla, Yeral	R-R	6-2	175	11-9-00	.194	.116	.221	49	165	17	32	13	0	2	14	20	3	0	1	62	0	5	.309	.291
Castillo, Osiris	R-R	5-11	170	9-5-00	.294	.346	.278	61	231	27	68	9	0	0	20	24	2	1	1	31	6	5	.333	.364
Franco, Francis	R-R	6-1	160	3-27-00	.159	.278	.125	28	82	9	13	3	0	1	4	8	4	0	0	26	2	1	.232	.266
Gil, Edwin	R-R	6-0	194	7-22-99	.161	.037	.198	43	118	13	19	8	0	0	8	14	2	1	0	46	1	1	.229	.261
Gonzalez, Junior	R-R	5-11	186	5-10-00	.231	.250	.226	17	39	4	9	1	0	0	4	4	1	0	1	5	0	0	.256	.311
Guerrero, Arturo	R-R	6-3	165	9-21-00	.206	.231	.200	41	141	22	29	6	6	1	13	19	3	1	0	48	3	4	.355	.313
Hernandez, Jery	R-R	6-2	160	4-22-01	.186	.035	.224	45	145	19	27	5	0	2	14	16	1	2	2	51	4	2	.262	.268
Omosako, Gunn	R-R	6-4	190	5-12-01	.283	.160	.324	19	99	12	28	5	2	2	9	10	4	1	0	28	1	1	.434	.372
Perez, Miguel	R-R	6-2	170	8-21-00	.252	.346	.223	59	218	44	55	8	4	3	22	27	4	2	4	65	11	3	.367	.340
Perez, Robert	R-R	6-1	170	6-26-00	.248	.191	.262	32	105	14	26	6	0	5	18	18	4	0	0	34	1	3	.448	.378
Pieternella, Ortwin	R-R	6-2	184	5-19-99	.133	.000	.143	9	15	2	2	0	0	0	1	1	1	0	0	3	0	0	.133	.235
Querecuto, Jean	R-R	6-2	175	9-21-00	.243	.174	.270	64	243	37	59	8	2	3	29	25	8	2	2	54	3	6	.329	.331
Rodriguez, Julio	R-R	6-3	180	12-29-00	.315	.312	.317	59	219	50	69	13	9	5	36	30	4	0	2	40	10	0	.525	.404
Santos, Daniel	R-R	6-2	175	1-25-99	.293	.298	.292	53	191	31	56	11	2	5	42	21	5	0	3	44	3	2	.450	.373
Veloz, Luis	R-R	6-0	180	12-15-99	.260	.273	.258	51	195	32	51	9	4	3	35	26	2	0	4	44	3	1	.410	.313

Pitching	B-T	HT	WT	DOB	W	L	ERA	G	GS	CG	SV	IP	H	R	ER	HR	BB	SO	AVG	vLH	vRH	K/9	BB/9
Alcantara, Luis	R-R	6-0	180	9-30-99	3	0	1.50	7	0	0	2	6	3	1	1	0	4	8	.167	.143	.182	12.00	6.00
Alcantara, Raul	L-L	6-0	167	1-22-01	2	1	6.87	18	0	0	2	18	21	15	14	0	17	16	.300	.417	.276	7.85	8.35
Baez, Luis	R-R	6-3	165	2-6-01	1	2	5.90	19	2	0	3	29	35	19	19	0	12	25	.292	.250	.310	7.76	3.72
Bonilla, Feliberto	R-R	6-2	165	4-21-98	1	1	2.91	6	0	0	0	22	15	8	7	1	14	14	.221	.207	.231	5.82	5.82

Player	T	Ht	Wt	DOB	W	L	ERA	G	GS	CG	SV	IP	H	R	ER	HR	BB	SO	AVG	vLH	vRH	K/9	BB/9
Cuenca, Saul	R-R	6-5	195	3-22-98	1	1	3.86	18	0	0	2	28	20	13	12	0	17	36	.202	.211	.197	11.57	5.46
Curvelo, Luis	R-R	6-1	170	10-21-00	4	2	1.17	9	3	0	0	31	25	9	4	0	4	22	.223	.189	.240	6.46	1.17
De Los Santos, Josias	R-R	6-2	174	7-29-99	3	3	4.63	14	6	1	0	45	49	32	23	1	14	29	.269	.230	.289	5.84	2.82
De Los Santos, Yeisel	L-L	5-10	170	2-6-01	2	1	22.50	4	0	0	0	2	5	5	5	0	4	3	.455	.500	.444	13.50	18.00
Escobar, Melquiades	R-R	6-1	175	1-31-00	0	0	5.40	4	0	0	0	3	4	2	2	0	4	2	.308	.429	.167	5.40	10.80
Florido, Deivy	R-R	6-2	165	9-17-00	3	2	3.47	14	9	0	0	62	57	26	24	4	9	48	.241	.250	.237	6.93	1.30
German, Carlos	R-R	6-3	180	12-30-00	0	1	17.00	13	0	0	0	9	17	19	17	2	9	4	.378	.421	.346	4.00	9.00
Hernandez, Joseph	R-R	5-11	150	6-15-00	3	2	4.62	15	6	0	1	39	38	29	20	4	22	42	.248	.218	.265	9.69	5.08
Januario, Igor	L-R	6-7	260	1-20-98	2	1	2.16	6	0	0	0	8	5	2	2	0	3	11	.200	.250	.177	11.88	3.24
Mercedes, Anderson	L-L	6-0	178	12-23-98	1	2	4.00	22	0	0	5	27	28	18	12	0	12	20	.264	.333	.250	6.67	4.00
Mercedes, Juan	R-R	6-2	190	4-3-00	4	2	2.42	13	9	0	1	52	40	21	14	3	9	41	.206	.258	.180	7.10	1.56
Nunez, Kelvin	R-R	6-1	170	12-10-99	2	1	2.89	12	7	0	1	47	43	20	15	1	17	30	.244	.259	.238	5.79	3.28
Ozoria, Jesus	R-R	6-2	195	6-1-98	5	3	2.19	14	5	0	2	49	37	13	12	2	7	59	.207	.181	.224	10.76	1.28
Perez, Brayan	L-L	6-0	170	9-5-00	1	3	3.57	15	10	0	0	53	50	25	21	1	11	58	.248	.125	.278	9.85	1.87
Sanchez, Freiquik	L-L	6-6	200	3-16-99	0	0	0.00	1	0	0	0	1	0	0	0	0	3	1	.000	—	.000	9.00	27.00
Tatiz, Yeury	R-R	6-3	175	11-22-00	0	3	5.92	12	9	0	0	38	38	30	25	4	20	26	.268	.377	.202	6.16	4.74

Fielding

C: Batista 31, Gonzalez 7, Pieternella 1, Santos 38. **1B:** Batista 4, Branche 12, Casilla 42, Gil 3, Perez 10, Santos 12. **2B:** Castillo 43, Franco 5, Hernandez 24, Querecuto 3. **3B:** Castillo 15, Franco 22, Gil 38, Hernandez 3. **SS:** Gil 1, Hernandez 14, Querecuto 62. **OF:** Casilla 4, Gonzalez 1, Guerrero 37, Omosako 23, Perez 56, Perez 11, Rodriguez 50, Veloz 48.

Tampa Bay Rays

SEASON IN A SENTENCE: Baseball's innovators in 2018, the Rays dumped high-priced veterans in the offseason, endured a series of costly injuries and still surprised everyone by winning 90 games.

HIGH POINT: Despite having only lefthander Blake Snell as a rotation regular, the Rays finished a sweep of the Red Sox on Aug. 26 to cap an eight-game winning streak. They relied on the "opener," a scenario where they started the game with a reliever who was then followed an inning or two later by a pitcher who worked four or five innings.

LOW POINT: For a few weeks at the beginning of season, the Rays seemed to live up to the low expectations most national observers had for them. After winning on Opening Day, the Rays lost 12 of their next 14 games. A month later, the Rays turned to the "opener" for the first time and helped stabilize their pitching staff.

NOTABLE ROOKIES: Second baseman Joey Wendle was acquired in a seemingly minor off-season trade, but he turned out to be one of the best rookies in the American League. He hit .300/.345/.435 while playing second base, third base and left field. Lefthander Ryan Yarbrough was the beneficiary of the "opener" role. He won 16 games in 38 appearances. Willy Adames hit .278/.348/.406 as he took over as the every-day shortstop at the midpoint of the season. First baseman Jake Bauers got off to a fast start but then struggled to hit .201/.316/.384 in 323 at-bats. Second baseman Brandon Lowe started out slow but finished on a hot streak, hitting .233/.339/.450 with six home runs in 43 games.

KEY TRANSACTIONS: The Rays made the long-awaited Chris Archer trade at the July trade dead-line, sending Archer to the Pirates for righthander Tyler Glasnow, outfielder Austin Meadows and 2017 first-round righty Shane Baz. The Rays slowly worked Glasnow into their rotation, and he and Meadows will be a major part of the Rays' plans for 2019 and beyond. Trade acquisition C.J. Cron hit .253/.323/.493 with 30 home runs. Free agent signee Carlos Gomez struggled (.208/.298/.336).

DOWN ON THE FARM: Even in a season when they sent 23 rookies to the big leagues, the Rays left the season with a stronger farm system than they had when the year began. Having three first-round picks helped, but it was the dominance of 17-year-old shortstop Wander Franco that was most notable. Low Class A Bowling Green won the Midwest League title with a prospect-laden lineup.

OPENING DAY PAYROLL: $69,605,999 (29th).

PLAYERS OF THE YEAR

MAJOR LEAGUE

MINOR LEAGUE

Blake Snell LHP	**Wander Franco** SS
21-5, 1.89 in 31 GS	(Rookie)
Led majors in W and	.351/.418/.587
led AL in ERA	27 BB, 19 SO in 242 AB

ORGANIZATION LEADERS

Batting		*Minimum 250 AB
MAJORS		
* AVG	Joey Wendle	.300
* OPS	Wilson Ramos	.834
HR	C.J. Cron	30
RBI	C.J. Cron	74
MINORS		
	Nathaniel Lowe, Charlotte, FL, Mont., Durham	.330
	Nathaniel Lowe, Charlotte, FL, Mont., Durham	.416
	Nathaniel Lowe, Charlotte, FL, Mont., Durham	.568
	Nathaniel Lowe, Charlotte, FL, Mont., Durham	.985
	Vidal Brujan, Bowling Green, Charlotte, FL	112
	Nathaniel Lowe, Charlotte, FL, Mont., Durham	159
	Nathaniel Lowe, Charlotte, FL, Mont., Durham	274
	Tristan Gray, Charlotte, FL	38
	Thomas Milone, Montgomery	11
	Nathaniel Lowe, Charlotte, FL, Mont., Durham	27
	Nathaniel Lowe, Charlotte, FL, Mont., Durham	102
	Nathaniel Lowe, Charlotte, FL, Mont., Durham	68
	Nick Solak, Montgomery	68
	Brandon Snyder, Durham	146
	Vidal Brujan, Bowling Green, Charlotte, FL	55

Pitching		#Minimum 75 IP
MAJORS		
W	Blake Snell	21
# ERA	Blake Snell	1.89
SO	Blake Snell	221
SV	Sergio Romo	25
MINORS		
W	Zach Lee, Montgomery, Durham	12
L	J.D. Martin, Montgomery	10
# ERA	Josh Fleming, Bowling Green, Charlotte, FL	2.53
G	Jordan Harrison, Montgomery, Durham	50
GS	Zach Lee, Montgomery, Durham	25
SV	Ian Gibaut, Durham	14
IP	Zach Lee, Montgomery, Durham	146
BB	J.D. Martin, Montgomery	60
SO	Brock Burke, Charlotte, FL, Montgomery	158
# AVG	Genesis Cabrera, Montgomery, Springfield, MO, Memphis	.218

General Manager: Erik Neander. **Farm Director:** Mitch Lukevics. **Scouting Director:** R.J Harrison.

Class	Team	League	W	L	PCT	Finish	Manager
Majors	Tampa Bay Rays	American	90	72	.556	6th (15)	Kevin Cash
Triple-A	Durham Bulls	International	79	60	.568	2nd (14)	Jared Sandberg
Double-A	Montgomery Biscuits	Southern	79	61	.564	2nd (10)	Brady Williams
High A	Charlotte Stone Crabs	Florida State	74	62	.544	3rd (12)	Jim Morrison
Low A	Bowling Green Hot Rods	Midwest	90	49	.647	1st (16)	Reinaldo Ruiz
Short season	Hudson Valley Renegades	New York-Penn	45	30	.600	1st (14)	Craig Albernaz
Rookie	Princeton Rays	Appalachian	44	22	.667	1st (10)	Danny Sheaffer
Rookie	GCL Rays	Gulf Coast	33	23	.589	4th (18)	Tomas Francisco
Overall 2018 Minor League Record			444	307	.591	1st (30)	

ORGANIZATION STATISTICS

TAMPA BAY RAYS
AMERICAN LEAGUE

Batting	B-T	HT	WT	DOB	AVG	vLH	vRH	G	AB	R	H	2B	3B	HR	RBI	BB	HBP	SH	SF	SO	SB	CS	SLG	OBP
Adames, Willy	R-R	6-0	200	9-2-95	.278	.256	.286	85	288	43	80	7	0	10	34	31	1	1	2	95	6	5	.406	.348
Arroyo, Christian	R-R	6-1	180	5-30-95	.264	.250	.280	20	53	5	14	2	1	1	6	6	0	0	0	16	0	0	.396	.339
Bauers, Jake	L-L	6-1	195	10-6-95	.201	.176	.211	96	323	48	65	22	2	11	48	54	3	2	6	104	6	6	.384	.316
Choi, Ji-Man	L-R	6-1	230	5-19-91	.269	.111	.289	49	160	21	43	12	1	8	27	24	3	0	2	41	2	0	.506	.370
Ciuffo, Nick	L-R	6-1	205	3-7-95	.189	.250	.172	16	37	3	7	1	0	1	5	3	1	2	1	12	0	0	.297	.262
Cron, C.J.	R-R	6-4	235	1-5-90	.254	.307	.231	140	501	68	127	28	1	30	74	37	17	0	5	145	1	2	.493	.323
Duffy, Matt	R-R	6-2	170	1-15-91	.294	.288	.297	132	503	59	148	22	1	4	44	47	7	1	2	93	12	6	.366	.361
Field, Johnny	R-R	5-10	180	2-20-92	.213	.267	.184	62	169	20	36	9	0	6	14	7	2	1	0	58	4	0	.373	.253
2-team total (21 Minnesota)					.222	.239	.211	83	221	28	49	13	0	9	21	7	3	1	1	72	4	0	.403	.254
Gomez, Carlos	R-R	6-3	220	12-4-85	.208	.182	.222	118	360	42	75	15	2	9	32	25	21	2	0	103	12	3	.336	.298
Hechavarria, Adeiny	R-R	6-0	195	4-15-89	.258	.328	.231	61	217	29	56	7	0	3	26	12	0	2	6	37	1	0	.332	.289
2-team total (18 New York)					.249	.300	.230	79	253	32	63	7	0	5	28	13	0	2	6	47	2	0	.336	.279
Kiermaier, Kevin	L-R	6-1	215	4-22-90	.217	.179	.232	88	332	44	72	12	9	7	29	25	6	2	2	91	10	5	.371	.282
Lowe, Brandon	L-R	6-0	185	7-6-94	.233	.188	.247	43	129	16	30	6	2	6	25	16	2	0	1	38	2	1	.450	.324
Meadows, Austin	L-L	6-3	210	5-3-95	.250	.250	.250	10	24	3	6	1	0	1	4	2	0	0	0	5	1	0	.417	.308
Miller, Brad	L-R	6-2	215	10-18-89	.256	.265	.254	48	156	16	40	10	1	5	21	16	0	0	2	51	0	0	.430	.322
Moore, Adam	R-R	6-3	220	5-8-84	.222	.333	.200	8	18	2	4	1	0	1	2	1	0	1	0	7	0	0	.444	.263
Perez, Michael	L-R	5-11	180	8-7-92	.284	.385	.262	24	74	9	21	5	0	1	11	3	0	1	2	19	0	0	.392	.304
Pham, Tommy	R-R	6-1	210	3-8-88	.343	.351	.340	39	143	35	49	7	6	7	22	25	4	0	2	43	5	1	.622	.448
Ramos, Wilson	R-R	6-1	245	8-10-87	.297	.326	.285	78	293	30	87	14	0	14	53	22	0	0	6	61	0	0	.488	.346
Refsnyder, Rob	R-R	6-0	200	3-26-91	.167	.143	.200	40	84	10	14	3	0	2	5	18	0	0	0	26	0	2	.274	.314
Robertson, Daniel	R-R	5-11	200	3-22-94	.262	.256	.265	87	282	46	74	16	0	9	34	43	13	0	2	77	2	2	.415	.382
Smith, Mallex	L-R	5-10	180	5-6-93	.296	.337	.285	141	480	65	142	27	10	2	40	47	8	7	2	98	40	12	.406	.367
Snyder, Brandon	R-R	6-2	225	11-23-86	.167	.200	.000	2	6	0	1	1	0	0	0	0	0	0	0	2	0	0	.333	.167
Span, Denard	L-L	6-0	210	2-27-84	.238	.286	.226	43	143	27	34	7	1	4	28	28	1	0	1	24	6	2	.385	.364
2-team total (94 Seattle)					.261	.302	.251	137	437	63	114	22	7	11	58	51	6	0	7	79	9	4	.419	.341
Sucre, Jesus	R-R	6-0	200	4-30-88	.209	.155	.234	73	182	9	38	5	0	1	17	9	1	4	2	29	1	0	.253	.247
Velazquez, Andrew	B-R	5-10	160	7-14-94	.300	.333	.286	13	10	3	3	1	0	0	0	1	1	0	0	3	1	0	.400	.417
Wendle, Joey	L-R	6-1	190	4-26-90	.300	.299	.300	139	487	62	146	33	6	7	61	37	9	2	10	96	16	4	.435	.354
Williams, Justin	L-R	6-2	215	8-20-95	.000	.000	—	1	1	0	0	0	0	0	0	0	0	0	0	0	0	0	.000	.000

Pitching	B-T	HT	WT	DOB	W	L	ERA	G	GS	CG	SV	IP	H	R	ER	HR	BB	SO	AVG	vLH	vRH	K/9	BB/9
Alvarado, Jose	L-L	6-2	245	5-21-95	1	6	2.39	70	0	0	8	64	42	21	17	1	29	80	.183	.215	.167	11.25	4.08
Andriese, Matt	R-R	6-2	225	8-28-89	3	4	4.07	27	4	0	0	60	55	32	27	7	18	59	.240	.174	.285	8.90	2.72
Archer, Chris	R-R	6-2	195	9-26-88	3	5	4.31	17	17	0	0	96	102	50	46	11	31	102	.271	.283	.262	9.56	2.91
Banda, Anthony	L-L	6-2	190	8-10-93	1	0	3.68	3	1	0	0	10	10	5	5	1	8	10	.235	.333	.205	6.14	1.84
Beeks, Jalen	L-L	5-11	195	7-10-93	5	0	4.47	12	0	0	0	44	41	22	22	5	20	37	.249	.128	.286	7.51	4.06
2-team total (2 Boston)					5	1	5.51	14	1	0	0	51	52	31	31	6	24	42	.268	.196	.291	7.46	4.26
Castillo, Diego	R-R	6-3	240	1-18-94	4	2	3.18	43	11	0	0	57	36	21	20	6	18	65	.178	.146	.200	10.32	2.86
Chirinos, Yonny	R-R	6-2	235	12-26-93	5	5	3.51	18	7	0	0	90	84	40	35	7	25	75	.254	.240	.265	7.53	2.51
Colome, Alex	R-R	6-1	220	12-31-88	2	5	4.15	23	0	0	11	22	24	12	10	1	8	23	.273	.205	.341	9.55	3.32
2-team total (47 Seattle)					7	5	3.04	70	0	0	12	68	59	26	23	7	21	72	.230	.171	.274	9.53	2.78
Eovaldi, Nathan	R-R	6-2	225	2-13-90	3	4	4.26	10	10	0	0	57	48	27	27	11	8	53	.225	.247	.207	8.37	1.26
2-team total (12 Boston)					6	7	3.81	22	21	0	0	111	105	55	47	14	20	101	.246	.254	.239	8.19	1.62
Faria, Jake	R-R	6-4	235	7-30-93	4	4	5.40	17	12	0	0	60	60	39	39	9	33	56	.248	.250	.247	6.92	4.57
Font, Wilmer	R-R	6-4	265	5-24-90	2	1	1.67	9	5	0	0	27	15	5	5	2	11	20	.158	.152	.163	6.67	3.67
2-team total (4 Oakland)					2	1	4.28	13	5	0	0	34	28	16	16	7	15	29	.219	.175	.254	7.75	4.01
Glasnow, Tyler	L-R	6-8	220	8-23-93	1	5	4.20	11	11	0	0	56	42	27	26	10	19	64	.208	.190	.233	10.35	3.07
Hu, Chih-Wei	R-R	6-0	220	11-4-93	0	0	4.15	5	0	0	0	13	7	6	6	2	3	12	.149	.227	.080	8.31	2.08
Kittredge, Andrew	R-R	6-1	200	3-17-90	3	2	7.75	33	3	0	0	38	54	34	33	7	17	30	.338	.232	.394	7.04	3.99
Kolarek, Adam	L-L	6-3	205	1-14-89	1	0	3.93	31	0	0	2	34	38	15	15	0	5	19	.284	.208	.333	4.98	1.31
Milner, Hoby	L-L	6-2	165	1-13-91	0	0	6.75	4	0	0	0	3	4	2	2	2	4	2	.273	.200	.333	13.50	6.75
Nuno, Vidal	L-L	5-11	210	7-26-87	3	0	1.64	17	0	0	0	33	24	7	6	5	10	29	.198	.226	.189	7.91	2.73
Pruitt, Austin	R-R	5-10	180	8-31-89	2	3	4.65	23	0	0	4	70	72	40	36	7	16	42	.268	.245	.280	5.43	2.07

Name	B-T	HT	WT	DOB	W	L	ERA	G	GS	CG	SV	IP	H	R	ER	HR	BB	SO	AVG	vLH	vRH	K/9	BB/9
Roe, Chaz	R-R	6-5	190	10-9-86	1	3	3.58	61	0	0	1	50	35	21	20	6	16	53	.197	.225	.188	9.48	2.86
Romo, Sergio	R-R	5-11	185	3-4-83	3	4	4.14	73	5	0	25	67	65	31	31	11	20	75	.253	.239	.260	10.02	2.67
Schultz, Jaime	R-R	5-10	200	6-20-91	2	2	5.64	22	1	0	0	30	18	19	19	6	17	35	.175	.114	.220	10.38	5.04
Snell, Blake	L-L	6-4	200	12-4-92	21	5	1.89	31	31	0	0	181	112	41	38	16	64	221	.178	.135	.189	11.01	3.19
Stanek, Ryne	R-R	6-4	215	7-26-91	2	3	2.98	59	29	0	0	66	45	23	22	8	27	81	.192	.163	.208	10.99	3.66
Venters, Jonny	L-L	6-3	200	3-20-85	1	1	3.86	22	1	0	1	14	11	6	6	1	6	11	.212	.167	.250	7.07	3.86
Weber, Ryan	R-R	6-1	180	8-12-90	0	1	5.06	2	0	0	0	5	5	5	3	0	2	1	.238	.100	.364	1.69	3.38
Wood, Hunter	R-R	6-1	165	8-12-93	1	1	3.73	29	8	0	0	41	42	17	17	4	18	42	.264	.270	.260	9.22	3.95
Yarbrough, Ryan	R-L	6-5	205	12-31-91	16	6	3.91	38	6	0	0	147	140	70	64	18	50	128	.247	.201	.262	7.82	3.05

Fielding

Catcher	PCT	G	PO	A	E	DP	PB
Ciuffo	1.000	16	108	5	0	0	4
Moore	1.000	8	51	8	0	1	0
Perez	1.000	24	175	18	0	0	0
Ramos	.993	73	564	38	4	3	6
Sucre	.996	71	497	37	2	3	7

First Base	PCT	G	PO	A	E	DP
Alvarado	.000	1	0	0	0	0
Bauers	.992	76	557	29	5	57
Choi	1.000	1	3	0	0	0
Cron	.996	61	463	27	2	46
Miller	.990	35	303	8	3	22
Refsnyder	1.000	1	1	0	0	0
Robertson	1.000	1	2	0	0	0

Second Base	PCT	G	PO	A	E	DP
Adames	.981	10	20	31	1	6
Arroyo	1.000	8	15	18	0	7

	PCT	G	PO	A	E	DP
Gomez	.000	1	0	0	0	0
Lowe	.990	28	47	57	1	19
Miller	1.000	6	5	7	0	0
Robertson	.987	39	56	94	2	23
Velazquez	1.000	2	1	0	0	0
Wendle	.989	101	149	222	4	57

Third Base	PCT	G	PO	A	E	DP
Arroyo	.923	7	1	11	1	0
Duffy	.963	125	87	253	13	24
Robertson	.946	19	9	26	2	4
Romo	.000	1	0	0	0	0
Snyder	1.000	2	1	3	0	0
Velazquez	1.000	4	0	1	0	0
Wendle	1.000	20	13	39	0	4

Shortstop	PCT	G	PO	A	E	DP
Adames	.947	75	72	161	13	38
Duffy	.000	1	0	0	0	0
Hechavarria	.990	61	51	141	2	28

	PCT	G	PO	A	E	DP
Robertson	.932	29	14	68	6	9
Velazquez	1.000	2	0	6	0	0
Wendle	.935	10	5	24	2	7

Outfield	PCT	G	PO	A	E	DP
Bauers	1.000	20	27	1	0	0
Field	.991	54	105	4	1	0
Gomez	.967	103	201	5	7	2
Kiermaier	1.000	88	232	5	0	1
Lowe	1.000	15	16	0	0	0
O Meadows	1.000	8	6	1	0	0
Pham	1.000	37	63	2	0	0
Refsnyder	1.000	26	35	3	0	0
Robertson	1.000	4	5	0	0	0
Smith	.977	138	255	3	6	1
Span	1.000	34	59	2	0	1
Velazquez	1.000	4	2	0	0	0
Wendle	.950	17	18	1	1	0
Williams	1.000	1	1	0	0	0

DURHAM BULLS   TRIPLE-A
INTERNATIONAL LEAGUE

Batting	B-T	HT	WT	DOB	AVG	vLH	vRH	G	AB	R	H	2B	3B	HR	RBI	BB	HBP	SH	SF	SO	SB	CS	SLG	OBP
Adames, Willy	R-R	6-0	200	9-2-95	.286	.243	.304	64	245	36	70	9	5	4	34	27	1	0	5	66	3	3	.412	.353
Arroyo, Christian	R-R	6-1	180	5-30-95	.235	.268	.219	46	170	19	40	12	0	2	20	8	4	0	0	32	2	3	.341	.286
Bauers, Jake	L-L	6-1	195	10-6-95	.279	.309	.264	52	197	31	55	14	0	5	24	23	1	1	0	47	10	6	.426	.358
Casali, Curt	R-R	6-3	235	11-9-88	.274	.310	.258	28	95	13	26	5	0	4	20	7	1	0	1	19	0	0	.453	.327
Choi, Ji-Man	L-R	6-1	230	5-19-91	.270	.364	.254	22	74	9	20	4	0	2	14	11	0	0	1	18	0	0	.405	.361
Ciuffo, Nick	L-R	6-1	205	3-7-95	.262	.190	.288	60	221	26	58	11	0	5	28	13	0	0	2	62	0	0	.380	.301
Coats, Jason	R-R	6-2	200	7-24-90	.247	.293	.224	108	397	50	98	27	4	15	60	24	3	0	2	93	3	0	.446	.293
Cronenworth, Jake	L-R	6-1	185	1-21-94	.240	.333	.188	7	25	4	6	3	0	0	2	1	0	0	0	5	1	0	.360	.269
Field, Johnny	R-R	5-10	180	2-20-92	.351	.429	.304	10	37	6	13	3	0	0	4	2	1	0	0	7	1	1	.432	.400
3-team total (5 Columbus, 10 Rochester)					.258	.320	.234	25	89	14	23	6	0	1	9	2	0	0	0	18	2	1	.360	.340
Hazelbaker, Jeremy	L-R	6-3	190	8-14-87	.210	.185	.219	62	214	32	45	16	0	8	27	22	3	0	0	83	9	0	.397	.293
2-team total (35 Rochester)					.203	.177	.212	97	310	46	63	20	2	11	36	38	4	0	0	121	14	0	.387	.298
Hechavarria, Adeiny	R-R	6-0	175	4-15-89	.500	1.000	1.000	1	2	0	1	0	0	0	0	0	0	0	0	2	0	0	.500	.750
James, Mac	R-R	6-1	195	6-2-93	.143	.167	.125	15	42	3	6	0	0	0	3	1	0	0	1	7	0	0	.143	.159
Johnson, Micah	L-R	6-0	210	12-18-90	.198	.152	.217	74	232	25	46	13	3	5	31	15	1	5	0	74	3	4	.345	.250
Kiermaier, Kevin	L-R	6-1	215	4-22-90	.364	.000	.444	3	11	2	4	1	0	0	1	2	0	0	0	2	1	0	.455	.462
Lowe, Brandon	L-R	6-0	185	7-6-94	.304	.326	.296	46	181	36	55	14	0	14	35	22	1	0	1	47	0	1	.613	.381
Lowe, Nathaniel	L-R	6-4	235	7-7-95	.260	.258	.261	28	100	18	26	6	1	4	16	8	2	0	0	27	0	0	.460	.327
McCarthy, Joe	L-L	6-3	225	2-23-94	.269	.212	.296	47	160	31	43	13	1	8	25	25	4	0	2	43	3	1	.513	.377
Meadows, Austin	L-R	6-3	225	5-3-95	.344	.308	.357	27	96	19	33	11	0	6	23	8	1	0	1	13	1	1	.771	.396
2-team total (42 Indianapolis)					.303	.322	.293	69	261	46	79	24	0	12	43	17	2	3	2	37	12	2	.533	.348
Moore, Adam	R-R	6-3	220	5-8-84	.219	.200	.228	58	196	18	43	11	4	3	30	11	0	0	1	50	0	0	.347	.260
Pena, Roberto	R-R	6-0	225	6-8-92	.279	.231	.300	13	43	2	12	1	0	0	2	1	1	0	0	10	0	1	.302	.311
Refsnyder, Rob	R-R	6-0	200	3-26-91	.283	.359	.252	51	184	31	52	10	0	4	15	18	4	0	1	46	0	0	.402	.358
Russell, Michael	R-R	6-2	200	1-30-93	.250	.308	.224	42	124	17	31	4	1	0	3	6	3	0	1	29	4	2	.298	.299
Snyder, Brandon	R-R	6-2	225	11-23-86	.250	.216	.268	106	387	56	98	24	2	18	60	42	4	0	5	146	2	0	.465	.329
Velazquez, Andrew	B-R	5-10	160	7-14-94	.258	.310	.239	117	423	63	109	16	6	12	41	34	3	1	0	124	29	3	.409	.317
Williams, Justin	L-R	6-2	215	8-20-95	.258	.289	.246	94	356	41	92	18	0	8	46	25	3	2	0	81	4	3	.376	.313
Wong, Kean	L-R	5-11	190	4-17-95	.282	.241	.299	116	451	65	127	23	3	9	50	40	5	3	3	112	7	3	.406	.345

Pitching	B-T	HT	WT	DOB	W	L	ERA	G	GS	CG	SV	IP	H	R	ER	HR	BB	SO	AVG	vLH	vRH	K/9	BB/9
Alaniz, Ruben	R-R	6-4	219	6-14-91	1	3	4.00	20	0	0	3	27	27	15	12	1	8	35	.257	.277	.241	11.67	2.67
Banda, Anthony	L-L	6-2	190	8-10-93	4	3	3.64	8	8	0	0	42	43	17	17	3	18	49	.272	.339	.235	10.50	3.86
Bird, Kyle	L-L	6-2	175	4-12-93	3	1	1.94	27	5	0	0	56	38	13	12	4	26	65	.195	.164	.213	10.51	4.20
Castillo, Diego	R-R	6-3	240	1-18-94	0	1	1.03	19	0	0	4	26	15	4	3	1	7	32	.160	.200	.140	10.94	2.39
Chirinos, Yonny	R-R	6-2	235	12-26-93	0	2	5.28	8	8	0	0	31	35	20	18	7	7	31	.282	.263	.299	9.10	2.05
Eovaldi, Nathan	R-R	6-2	225	2-13-90	0	1	18.00	1	1	0	0	4	10	8	8	1	0	6	.455	.400	.500	13.50	0.00
Faria, Jake	R-R	6-4	225	7-16-93	2	1	4.60	7	5	0	0	29	25	19	15	5	13	28	.227	.234	.217	8.59	3.99
Franco, Mike	R-R	5-11	200	11-30-91	3	3	3.52	29	1	0	1	46	41	19	18	8	15	47	.234	.218	.247	9.20	2.93
Gibaut, Ian	R-R	6-3	250	11-19-93	4	3	2.09	48	0	0	14	56	35	14	13	3	21	75	.181	.226	.147	12.05	3.38

Name	B-T	HT	WT	DOB	W	L	ERA	G	GS	CG	SV	IP	H	R	ER	HR	BB	SO	AVG	vLH	vRH	K/9	BB/9
Hall, Cody	R-R	6-4	235	1-6-88	1	2	2.84	10	0	0	0	19	11	6	6	1	13	23	.172	.226	.121	10.89	6.16
Harrison, Jordan	R-L	6-1	180	4-9-91	0	0	1.65	14	0	0	0	16	11	3	3	0	9	15	.190	.250	.147	8.27	4.96
Hu, Chih-Wei	R-R	6-0	220	11-4-93	5	7	4.66	24	19	0	0	102	113	56	53	14	28	92	.276	.332	.215	8.09	2.46
Kittredge, Andrew	R-R	6-1	200	3-17-90	6	0	2.74	21	1	0	2	46	41	17	14	3	12	58	.220	.286	.193	11.35	2.35
Kolarek, Adam	L-L	6-3	205	1-14-89	5	1	1.61	31	1	0	4	45	35	8	8	1	12	52	.216	.123	.278	10.48	2.42
Lee, Zach	R-R	6-4	227	9-13-91	4	5	5.02	13	13	0	0	72	86	44	40	6	15	48	.297	.270	.320	6.03	1.88
Milner, Hoby	L-L	6-2	165	1-13-91	1	0	3.77	15	1	0	2	14	9	6	1	3	21	.259	.182	.313	13.19	1.88
2-team total (25 Lehigh Valley)					1	0	2.88	40	1	0	2	41	35	16	13	3	17	49	.233	.210	.250	10.84	3.76
Moore, Andrew	R-R	6-0	185	6-2-94	6	7	4.34	17	15	0	0	83	90	47	40	15	29	53	.270	.257	.284	5.75	3.14
Mujica, Jose	R-R	6-2	235	6-29-96	5	1	2.70	7	7	0	0	37	31	13	11	1	10	34	.226	.273	.183	8.35	2.45
Nuno, Vidal	L-L	5-11	210	7-26-87	3	1	3.57	8	7	0	0	40	38	17	16	6	3	37	.244	.149	.284	8.26	0.67
Ott, Travis	L-L	6-4	175	6-29-95	0	0	20.25	1	0	0	0	1	1	3	3	0	3	0	.200	.500	.000	0.00	20.25
Poche, Colin	L-L	6-3	185	1-17-94	5	0	1.08	28	2	0	1	50	29	7	6	2	17	78	.172	.179	.167	14.04	3.06
Pruitt, Austin	R-R	5-10	180	8-31-89	3	0	2.95	14	4	0	1	40	26	14	13	2	7	49	.182	.169	.192	11.12	1.59
Schultz, Jaime	R-R	5-10	200	6-20-91	2	1	5.75	32	1	0	3	36	44	27	23	5	23	58	.299	.281	.313	14.50	5.75
Snow, Forrest	R-R	6-6	220	12-30-88	5	8	4.82	26	20	0	0	118	116	73	63	22	37	112	.253	.241	.264	8.57	2.83
Stanek, Ryne	R-R	6-4	215	7-26-91	0	1	1.86	10	0	0	2	10	5	3	2	1	6	17	.152	.000	.238	15.83	5.59
Venters, Jonny	L-L	6-3	200	3-20-85	0	0	1.59	5	0	0	0	6	4	2	1	0	5	6	.191	.000	.308	9.53	7.94
Weber, Ryan	R-R	6-1	180	8-12-90	9	6	2.73	25	18	0	1	115	117	45	35	9	23	83	.264	.267	.261	6.48	1.79
Wood, Hunter	R-R	6-1	165	8-12-93	2	2	3.00	24	2	0	3	42	26	15	14	4	10	63	.172	.186	.161	13.50	2.14

Fielding

Catcher	PCT	G	PO	A	E	DP	PB
Casali	.984	26	238	13	4	1	4
Ciuffo	.996	55	442	39	2	4	5
James	.965	12	105	5	4	2	3
Moore	.991	44	424	19	4	2	1
Pena	.965	6	51	4	2	2	0
Snyder	1.000	2	1	0	0	0	0

First Base	PCT	G	PO	A	E	DP
Bauers	.987	46	345	30	5	25
Choi	.971	18	124	11	4	7
Lowe	.994	25	163	10	1	19
McCarthy	1.000	6	37	5	0	5
Pena	.750	1	2	1	1	0
Refsnyder	1.000	2	13	1	0	2
Russell	1.000	5	30	2	0	5
Snyder	.997	44	333	20	1	31

Second Base	PCT	G	PO	A	E	DP
Cronenworth	1.000	1	3	4	0	1

	PCT	G	PO	A	E	DP
Johnson	.936	14	17	27	3	3
Lowe	.983	31	39	79	2	20
Russell	.909	3	7	3	1	1
Snyder	1.000	3	3	4	0	1
Velazquez	.948	14	20	35	3	4
Wong	.976	80	108	178	7	39

Third Base	PCT	G	PO	A	E	DP
Arroyo	.988	34	27	55	1	4
Cronenworth	1.000	5	6	6	0	2
James	1.000	3	0	3	0	0
Johnson	.667	10	4	4	4	0
Russell	.973	30	26	45	2	4
Snyder	.937	54	32	72	7	8
Velazquez	1.000	1	1	0	0	0
Wong	.833	14	6	14	4	0

Shortstop	PCT	G	PO	A	E	DP
Adames	.958	62	68	160	10	33
Arroyo	.952	6	7	13	1	3
Cronenworth	1.000	1	1	1	0	1

	PCT	G	PO	A	E	DP
Hechavarria	1.000	1	1	0	0	0
Russell	1.000	2	1	5	0	0
Snyder	1.000	1	2	3	0	1
Velazquez	.960	69	80	162	10	34

Outfield	PCT	G	PO	A	E	DP
Bauers	.846	6	11	0	2	0
Choi	1.000	2	4	0	0	0
Coats	.970	76	123	5	4	2
Field	1.000	10	16	0	0	0
Hazelbaker	.988	43	84	0	1	0
Johnson	.976	45	79	4	2	1
Kiermaier	1.000	2	4	0	0	0
Lowe	1.000	13	29	0	0	0
McCarthy	1.000	33	56	4	0	0
Meadows	.980	23	48	0	1	0
Refsnyder	.971	37	63	3	2	0
Snyder	1.000	1	1	0	0	0
Velazquez	.988	33	76	3	1	2
Williams	.989	82	159	13	2	3
Wong	1.000	26	41	2	0	0

MONTGOMERY BISCUITS   DOUBLE-A
SOUTHERN LEAGUE

Batting	B-T	HT	WT	DOB	AVG	vLH	vRH	G	AB	R	H	2B	3B	HR	RBI	BB	HBP	SH	SF	SO	SB	CS	SLG	OBP
Boldt, Ryan	L-R	6-2	210	11-22-94	.274	.347	.243	62	241	40	66	12	6	7	34	24	5	0	3	58	12	2	.461	.348
Brosseau, Michael	R-R	5-10	210	3-15-94	.262	.314	.243	104	370	53	97	24	3	13	61	29	10	1	7	74	11	4	.449	.327
Cronenworth, Jake	L-R	6-1	185	1-21-94	.254	.250	.255	108	418	75	106	18	4	4	50	43	3	0	6	69	21	3	.345	.323
De La Calle, Daniel	R-R	6-3	220	9-18-92	.213	.412	.100	17	47	3	10	1	1	2	11	0	0	0	1	23	0	0	.404	.208
Fox, Lucius	B-R	6-1	180	7-2-97	.221	.333	.182	27	104	14	23	3	1	1	9	8	2	4	2	20	6	2	.298	.285
James, Mac	R-R	6-1	195	6-2-93	.208	.278	.180	39	125	13	26	3	0	0	11	23	0	0	1	20	1	2	.232	.329
Kelly, Dalton	L-L	6-3	180	8-4-94	.228	.268	.211	121	417	72	95	24	2	5	47	65	8	1	2	102	22	2	.331	.342
Lowe, Brandon	L-R	6-0	185	7-6-94	.292	.271	.300	54	199	37	58	10	1	8	41	35	3	0	3	55	8	2	.508	.400
Lowe, Nathaniel	L-R	6-4	235	7-7-95	.340	.296	.354	51	188	36	64	11	0	13	42	35	1	0	1	30	1	1	.606	.444
Lukes, Nathan	L-R	5-11	185	7-12-94	.278	.140	.319	115	435	62	121	29	3	6	51	31	6	6	6	93	9	4	.400	.331
Maris, Peter	L-R	5-10	175	6-6-94	.248	.310	.222	42	153	25	38	10	1	6	24	21	1	1	3	39	5	2	.444	.337
Mastrobuoni, Miles	L-R	5-11	175	10-31-95	.256	.077	.333	12	43	4	11	0	0	0	8	5	0	0	0	7	1	1	.256	.333
Milone, Thomas	L-L	5-11	190	1-26-95	.255	.215	.268	106	365	48	93	11	11	4	29	25	6	3	0	102	10	9	.378	.313
Palacios, Jermaine	R-R	6-0	145	7-12-96	.189	.191	.189	49	164	13	31	7	1	1	20	11	1	1	3	42	4	4	.262	.240
Rodriguez, David	R-R	6-1	215	2-25-96	.230	.294	.207	69	252	23	58	13	1	4	44	21	0	0	3	59	2	1	.337	.286
Russell, Michael	R-R	6-2	200	1-30-93	.249	.340	.213	45	177	24	44	10	2	3	17	12	0	0	1	42	5	3	.379	.295
Sanchez, Jesus	L-R	6-3	210	10-7-97	.214	.160	.233	27	98	14	21	8	0	1	11	11	1	0	0	21	1	1	.327	.300
Solak, Nick	R-R	5-11	175	1-11-95	.282	.297	.278	126	478	91	135	17	3	19	76	68	14	0	5	112	21	6	.450	.384
Sullivan, Brett	L-R	6-1	195	2-22-94	.266	.295	.256	111	421	47	112	19	4	7	65	34	4	0	7	55	17	7	.380	.322
Velazquez, Andrew	B-R	5-10	160	7-14-94	.229	.200	.240	8	35	5	8	2	1	2	4	1	0	0	0	11	2	0	.514	.250

Pitching	B-T	HT	WT	DOB	W	L	ERA	G	GS	CG	SV	IP	H	R	ER	HR	BB	SO	AVG	vLH	vRH	K/9	BB/9
Alaniz, Ruben	R-R	6-4	219	6-14-91	2	1	2.84	9	0	0	1	13	7	5	4	0	7	13	.159	.222	.115	9.24	4.97
Bird, Kyle	L-L	6-2	175	4-12-93	0	2	3.66	16	1	0	4	20	14	9	8	2	9	23	.206	.130	.244	10.53	4.12
Bivens, Blake	R-R	6-2	205	8-11-95	0	2	6.23	4	4	0	0	22	24	15	15	4	12	15	.289	.286	.292	6.23	4.98
Broadway, Mike	R-R	6-5	215	3-30-87	2	2	3.60	22	1	0	1	30	20	14	12	3	11	38	.182	.152	.195	11.40	3.30
Burke, Brock	L-L	6-4	200	8-4-96	6	1	1.95	9	9	0	0	55	39	12	12	2	14	71	.193	.188	.194	11.55	2.28
Cabrera, Genesis	L-L	6-1	170	10-10-96	7	6	4.12	21	20	0	0	114	90	53	52	11	57	124	.218	.211	.221	9.82	4.51
Espinal, Yoel	R-R	6-2	200	11-7-92	3	1	1.98	40	0	0	10	55	29	18	12	5	29	71	.153	.194	.133	11.69	4.77

Name	B-T	HT	WT	DOB	W	L	ERA	G	GS	CG	SV	IP	H	R	ER	HR	BB	SO	AVG	vLH	vRH		
Franco, Mike	R-R	5-11	200	11-30-91	1	0	2.16	12	0	0	3	17	7	4	4	0	6	20	.130	.067	.208	10.80	3.24
Hall, Cody	R-R	6-4	235	1-6-88	1	1	3.72	9	0	0	5	10	5	6	4	1	6	5	.167	.182	.158	4.66	5.59
Harrison, Jordan	R-L	6-1	180	4-9-91	0	1	1.56	36	0	0	2	40	26	9	7	2	21	38	.190	.122	.227	8.48	4.69
Jones, Spencer	R-R	6-5	205	9-22-94	1	1	4.11	10	2	0	0	15	19	8	7	2	5	7	.328	.417	.265	4.11	2.93
Karalus, Reece	R-R	6-3	245	6-14-94	1	1	7.77	12	0	0	1	22	24	20	19	4	11	21	.276	.226	.304	8.59	4.50
Krook, Matt	L-L	6-4	225	10-21-94	4	2	4.26	37	6	0	0	74	57	40	35	3	50	95	.218	.182	.231	11.55	6.08
Lawson, Brandon	R-R	6-3	205	12-13-94	3	1	4.25	14	5	0	0	42	53	24	20	4	17	33	.303	.279	.316	7.02	3.61
Lee, Zach	R-R	6-4	227	9-13-91	8	1	2.31	13	12	1	0	74	72	23	19	4	20	59	.254	.264	.247	7.18	2.43
Lopez, Eduar	R-R	6-0	180	2-21-95	5	2	4.32	12	11	0	0	58	53	28	28	3	29	38	.247	.263	.233	5.86	4.47
Martin, J.D.	R-R	6-4	220	1-2-83	8	10	4.49	25	22	0	0	124	127	66	62	10	60	71	.270	.242	.289	5.14	4.34
McWilliams, Sam	R-R	6-7	190	9-4-95	6	7	5.02	19	15	0	0	100	111	61	56	13	40	94	.282	.274	.287	8.43	3.59
Moats, Dalton	L-L	6-3	195	5-24-95	2	3	5.34	41	10	0	0	62	58	41	37	12	29	65	.238	.148	.282	9.39	4.19
Moss, Benton	R-R	6-2	193	2-21-93	8	5	2.75	18	15	1	0	101	85	32	31	13	22	75	.227	.200	.244	6.66	1.95
Ott, Travis	L-L	6-4	175	6-29-95	3	3	3.21	43	2	0	4	70	57	28	25	6	29	91	.222	.181	.238	11.70	3.73
Poche, Colin	L-L	6-3	185	1-17-94	1	0	0.00	3	0	0	0	5	1	0	0	0	0	9	.067	.167	.000	16.20	0.00
2-team total (9 Jackson)					1	0	0.00	12	0	0	1	16	4	0	0	0	2	32	.080	.143	.056	18.00	1.13
Ramirez, Roel	R-R	6-1	210	5-26-95	3	1	3.32	26	1	0	0	41	37	19	15	4	17	46	.243	.207	.266	10.18	3.76
Snow, Forrest	R-R	6-6	220	12-30-88	1	0	4.00	2	1	0	0	9	10	4	4	1	4	7	.278	.286	.273	7.00	4.00
Taylor, Curtis	R-R	6-6	215	7-25-95	3	4	2.37	30	4	0	6	61	34	16	16	6	26	74	.162	.163	.162	10.98	3.86
Wright, Austin	L-L	6-4	235	9-26-89	0	1	13.50	6	0	0	0	7	10	12	11	2	9	8	.345	.375	.333	9.82	11.05

Fielding

Catcher	PCT	G	PO	A	E	DP	PB
Brosseau	.000	1	0	0	0	0	0
De La Calle	1.000	3	26	3	0	1	1
James	1.000	18	150	18	0	1	8
Rodriguez	.995	44	392	29	2	2	2
Sullivan	.996	76	640	34	3	3	15

First Base	PCT	G	PO	A	E	DP
Brosseau	1.000	10	65	6	0	4
Cronenworth	1.000	1	8	1	0	1
De La Calle	1.000	2	14	0	0	3
James	1.000	13	78	6	0	12
Kelly	.998	75	538	34	1	53
Lowe	.990	39	276	15	3	23
Rodriguez	.941	2	16	0	1	3
Russell	1.000	4	27	4	0	1

Second Base	PCT	G	PO	A	E	DP
Brosseau	.982	16	26	30	1	12
Cronenworth	.931	18	24	30	4	10
Lowe	.990	24	49	47	1	16
Maris	.949	15	21	16	2	9
Mastrobuoni	1.000	5	5	7	0	0
Russell	1.000	4	11	10	0	5
Solak	.990	61	81	110	2	19

Third Base	PCT	G	PO	A	E	DP
Brosseau	.949	64	55	111	9	14
Cronenworth	.975	28	18	60	2	3
James	.909	5	1	9	1	1
Maris	.981	19	12	39	1	1
Mastrobuoni	1.000	1	1	1	0	0
Russell	.976	30	22	58	2	3

Shortstop	PCT	G	PO	A	E	DP
Brosseau	1.000	1	3	3	0	0
Cronenworth	.976	59	77	125	5	33
Fox	.947	26	29	60	5	9
Maris	1.000	8	11	17	0	5
Palacios	.933	48	55	111	12	26
Russell	1.000	2	3	4	0	1

Outfield	PCT	G	PO	A	E	DP
Boldt	.985	56	135	0	2	0
Kelly	1.000	34	66	2	0	1
Lowe	1.000	26	51	2	0	0
Lukes	1.000	107	258	8	0	4
Maris	1.000	2	2	0	0	0
Mastrobuoni	.929	6	12	1	1	0
Milone	.984	105	235	8	4	2
Sanchez	1.000	27	53	1	0	1
Solak	1.000	57	112	5	0	0
Velazquez	1.000	7	21	2	0	0

TAMPA BAY RAYS

CHARLOTTE STONE CRABS   HIGH CLASS A
FLORIDA STATE LEAGUE

Batting	B-T	HT	WT	DOB	AVG	vLH	vRH	G	AB	R	H	2B	3B	HR	RBI	BB	HBP	SH	SF	SO	SB	CS	SLG	OBP
Arroyo, Christian	R-R	6-1	180	5-30-95	.000	.000	.000	2	7	0	0	0	0	0	0	0	0	0	0	2	0	0	.000	.000
Bridgman, Justin	R-R	5-11	175	6-20-95	.111	.000	.200	4	9	1	1	0	0	3	1	0	0	1	1	0	0	.222	.182
Brujan, Vidal	B-R	5-9	155	2-9-98	.347	.333	.353	27	98	26	34	7	2	4	12	15	0	1	0	15	12	4	.582	.434
Cabrera, Eleardo	L-R	5-11	195	11-8-95	.206	.235	.196	20	63	8	13	2	0	0	5	5	3	0	1	13	1	2	.238	.292
Chester, Carl	R-R	6-0	200	12-12-95	.346	.348	.345	14	52	11	18	2	1	2	8	0	1	0	2	9	1	0	.539	.346
Ciuffo, Nick	L-R	6-1	205	3-7-95	.125	.333	.000	2	8	1	1	1	0	0	1	0	0	0	0	3	0	0	.250	.125
Duffy, Matt	R-R	6-2	170	1-15-91	.667	—	.667	1	3	0	2	0	0	0	1	0	0	0	0	0	0	0	.667	.667
Fox, Lucius	B-R	6-1	180	7-2-97	.282	.343	.256	89	351	54	99	17	1	2	30	42	8	2	1	79	23	7	.353	.371
Fraley, Jake	L-L	6-0	195	5-25-95	.347	.297	.371	66	225	39	78	19	7	4	41	26	4	0	5	44	11	8	.547	.415
Gray, Tristan	L-R	6-3	185	3-29-96	.238	.250	.234	118	449	71	107	38	2	13	69	39	3	0	5	113	5	5	.419	.300
Hechavarria, Adeiny	R-R	6-0	195	4-15-89	.125	.000	.143	2	8	0	1	0	0	0	1	0	0	0	0	3	0	0	.125	.125
Kiermaier, Kevin	L-R	6-1	215	4-22-90	.500	—	.500	2	6	1	3	0	1	0	0	2	0	0	0	0	0	0	.833	.625
Law, Zacrey	R-R	6-0	190	7-9-94	.283	.200	.283	27	88	8	22	2	2	1	9	7	4	1	3	14	3	0	.352	.324
Lowe, Josh	L-R	6-4	205	2-2-98	.238	.212	.248	105	399	62	95	25	3	6	47	47	4	1	4	117	18	6	.361	.322
Lowe, Nathaniel	L-R	6-4	235	7-7-95	.356	.359	.355	51	194	39	69	15	0	10	44	25	1	0	0	33	0	0	.588	.432
Maris, Peter	L-R	5-10	175	5-2-95	.300	.300	.325	29	100	15	32	7	3	5	19	14	1	0	1	19	0	1	.600	.405
Mastrobuoni, Miles	L-R	5-11	175	10-31-95	.289	.236	.307	91	287	49	83	14	3	1	31	50	0	6	2	59	8	3	.369	.392
McCarthy, Joe	L-L	6-3	225	2-23-94	.000	—	.000	3	10	0	0	0	0	0	0	3	0	0	0	4	1	0	.000	.231
McKay, Brendan	L-L	6-2	212	12-18-95	.210	.172	.222	32	119	19	25	6	1	5	21	16	3	0	1	38	0	0	.403	.317
Miller, Andrew	L-R	6-1	200	3-19-97	.091	.250	.000	6	11	0	1	0	0	0	1	0	0	0	0	4	0	0	.091	.167
Miller, Brad	L-R	6-2	215	10-18-89	.333	.333	.333	2	6	2	2	0	0	0	0	1	0	0	1	0	0	0	.333	.429
Olive, Russ	L-L	6-0	205	6-3-96	.385	.455	.333	9	26	3	10	1	0	0	3	4	0	0	2	8	2	0	.500	.438
Olmedo-Barrera, David	L-R	6-1	195	6-20-94	.242	.152	.273	40	132	25	32	9	2	2	17	7	1	0	2	33	2	0	.386	.282
Padlo, Kevin	R-R	6-2	205	7-15-96	.223	.231	.220	115	385	54	86	26	0	8	54	47	9	0	6	119	5	0	.353	.318
Palacios, Jermaine	R-R	6-0	145	7-19-96	.237	.221	.244	69	241	32	57	13	4	1	33	18	1	4	4	45	4	4	.336	.288
Pinto, Rene	R-R	5-11	195	11-24-96	.280	.346	.280	72	246	35	74	21	1	1	38	23	1	2	8	43	1	1	.407	.353
Roach, Joey	L-R	6-0	205	8-27-93	.274	.308	.264	30	113	14	31	1	1	0	19	6	2	1	1	16	1	1	.301	.320
Robertson, Daniel	R-R	5-11	200	3-22-94	.500	—	.500	1	2	0	1	0	0	0	0	0	0	1	0	0	0	0	.500	.667
Rodriguez, David	R-R	6-1	215	2-25-96	.317	.320	.317	28	104	18	33	8	1	2	20	8	4	0	1	23	1	0	.471	.385
Sanchez, Jesus	L-R	6-3	210	10-7-97	.301	.339	.283	90	359	56	108	24	2	10	64	15	2	0	2	71	6	3	.462	.331

	B-T	HT	WT	DOB	AVG	vLH	vRH	G	AB	R	H	2B	3B	HR	RBI	BB	HBP	SH	SF	SO	SB	CS	SLG	OBP
Smith, Mallex	L-R	5-10	180	5-6-93	.000	.000	—	1	4	0	0	0	0	0	0	1	0	0	0	1	0	0	.000	.200
Stone, Jake	L-R	6-0	200	1-31-95	.200	.286	.174	10	30	3	6	0	0	0	0	4	0	0	0	9	2	0	.200	.294
Tenerowicz, Robbie	R-R	6-1	185	1-6-95	.292	.320	.283	100	383	64	112	22	1	5	61	32	6	0	8	62	8	4	.394	.350

Pitching

	B-T	HT	WT	DOB	W	L	ERA	G	GS	CG	SV	IP	H	R	ER	HR	BB	SO	AVG	vLH	vRH	K/9	BB/9
Alaniz, Ruben	R-R	6-4	219	6-14-91	0	0	0.00	1	0	0	0	2	0	0	0	0	1	4	.000	.000	.000	18.00	4.50
Archer, Chris	R-R	6-2	195	9-26-88	0	0	0.00	1	1	0	0	4	0	0	0	0	1	7	.000	.000	.000	15.75	2.25
Bayer, Peter	R-R	6-4	195	3-6-94	0	0	18.00	5	0	0	0	4	7	8	8	2	6	6	.389	.333	.444	13.50	13.50
Bivens, Blake	R-R	6-2	205	8-11-95	6	4	2.83	12	10	1	0	57	47	21	18	2	14	48	.229	.230	.228	7.53	2.20
Burke, Brock	L-L	6-4	200	8-4-96	3	5	3.84	16	13	0	0	82	85	43	35	4	30	87	.263	.278	.257	9.55	3.29
Busfield, J.D.	R-R	6-7	235	5-5-95	3	4	6.34	23	5	0	0	44	58	36	31	5	10	27	.317	.290	.336	5.52	2.05
Charpie, Trevor	R-R	6-1	195	12-30-93	4	1	4.67	27	1	0	1	44	51	25	23	1	14	34	.293	.352	.229	6.90	2.84
Chirinos, Yonny	R-R	6-2	235	12-26-93	0	0	0.00	1	1	0	0	2	2	0	0	0	2	2	.333	.250	.500	9.00	9.00
Disla, Jose	R-R	6-2	165	3-11-96	2	1	4.66	10	0	0	0	19	19	11	10	0	7	15	.264	.317	.194	6.98	3.26
Eovaldi, Nathan	R-R	6-2	225	2-13-90	0	0	4.50	3	3	0	0	6	6	3	3	2	0	7	.250	.231	.273	10.50	0.00
Espinal, Yoel	R-R	6-2	200	11-7-92	0	1	3.86	6	0	0	0	9	12	6	4	1	3	8	.333	.611	.056	7.71	2.89
Faria, Jake	R-R	6-4	235	7-30-93	0	0	4.50	1	1	0	0	2	2	1	1	1	1	0	.286	.250	.333	0.00	4.50
Fleming, Josh	R-L	6-1	190	5-18-96	3	3	4.11	9	7	1	0	50	51	25	23	4	9	38	.258	.190	.303	6.79	1.61
Jones, Spencer	R-R	6-5	205	9-22-94	4	2	2.31	26	1	0	3	47	43	15	12	2	9	33	.249	.236	.257	6.36	1.74
Karalus, Reece	R-R	6-3	245	6-14-94	1	2	2.97	16	2	0	0	33	31	19	11	1	16	27	.254	.333	.170	7.29	4.32
Koch, Brandon	R-R	6-2	205	8-14-95	2	1	1.76	13	0	0	5	15	9	7	3	0	6	20	.167	.120	.207	11.74	3.52
Lawson, Brandon	R-R	6-3	205	12-13-94	3	6	4.09	14	13	1	0	70	75	35	32	7	17	45	.272	.292	.252	5.76	2.18
McWilliams, Sam	R-R	6-7	190	9-4-95	0	1	3.86	3	3	0	0	12	13	6	5	0	3	7	.277	.296	.250	5.40	2.31
Mendez, Deivy	R-R	6-2	190	10-27-95	0	2	8.76	11	0	0	0	12	11	12	12	1	12	17	.234	.222	.241	12.41	8.76
2-team total (11 Bradenton)					0	4	8.53	22	0	0	0	25	23	24	24	1	21	31	.240	.239	.240	11.01	7.46
Moss, Benton	R-R	6-2	193	2-21-93	1	1	3.75	3	3	0	0	12	13	5	5	1	1	13	.271	.286	.259	9.75	0.75
Mozingo, Zack	L-R	6-1	215	4-26-94	1	1	6.68	22	2	0	3	34	39	28	25	3	19	35	.285	.349	.225	9.36	5.08
Mujica, Jose	R-R	6-2	235	6-29-96	1	1	5.79	5	4	0	0	19	25	13	12	3	6	13	.325	.370	.258	6.16	2.84
Navas, Adrian	R-R	6-2	200	4-13-96	0	2	5.68	11	0	0	1	19	23	13	12	2	7	17	.291	.353	.244	8.05	3.32
Nuno, Vidal	L-L	5-11	210	7-26-87	0	0	4.91	3	3	0	0	7	12	4	4	2	1	8	.375	.250	.450	9.82	1.23
O'Brien, Riley	R-R	6-4	170	2-6-95	4	3	3.60	10	8	1	0	40	36	18	16	1	21	37	.240	.214	.279	8.33	4.73
Ortiz, Willy	R-R	6-1	180	7-20-95	6	2	3.74	18	14	1	0	84	72	37	35	10	33	73	.228	.225	.230	7.79	3.52
Pelaez, Ivan	L-L	5-11	155	2-1-94	6	3	2.05	36	0	0	7	53	51	17	12	4	8	40	.254	.235	.272	6.84	1.37
Raiden, Chandler	R-R	6-1	170	6-7-96	0	0	3.00	8	0	0	0	18	17	6	6	0	8	6	.250	.286	.192	3.00	4.00
Ramirez, Roel	R-R	6-1	210	5-26-95	0	0	0.00	8	0	0	1	13	4	0	0	0	0	14	.095	.125	.077	9.95	0.00
Ramos, Reimin	R-R	6-1	190	4-27-96	0	2	9.22	8	0	0	0	14	22	15	14	1	6	7	.344	.333	.353	4.61	3.95
Roe, Chaz	R-R	6-5	190	10-9-86	0	0	0.00	2	1	0	0	2	0	0	0	0	0	4	.000	.000	.000	18.00	0.00
Romero, Orlando	R-R	6-0	211	9-26-96	0	1	4.86	8	0	0	1	17	16	9	9	1	10	11	.246	.222	.276	5.94	5.40
Rosenberg, Kenny	L-L	6-1	195	7-9-95	11	2	4.86	25	17	0	0	113	119	67	61	10	49	106	.267	.270	.265	8.44	3.90
Salinas, Jhonleider	R-R	6-2	215	9-25-95	0	1	5.73	5	0	0	1	11	10	7	7	3	3	5	.244	.208	.294	4.09	2.45
Sanders, Phoenix	R-R	5-10	184	6-5-95	1	1	3.29	6	0	0	0	14	10	5	5	0	3	18	.196	.154	.240	11.85	1.98
Schryver, Hunter	L-L	6-1	198	4-3-95	0	1	2.92	10	1	0	0	12	13	6	4	1	4	11	.283	.292	.273	8.03	2.92
Shaffer, Brian	R-R	6-5	200	8-12-96	2	2	3.03	7	6	0	0	39	36	15	13	5	10	16	.238	.213	.281	3.72	2.33
Tapia, Alexis	R-R	6-2	240	8-10-95	0	2	4.19	7	1	0	0	19	13	9	9	1	7	16	.300	.359	.262	7.45	3.26
Taylor, Curtis	R-R	6-6	215	7-25-95	3	0	3.12	8	0	0	2	17	17	6	6	0	4	23	.254	.241	.263	11.94	2.08
Venters, Jonny	L-L	6-3	200	3-20-85	0	0	0.00	2	1	0	0	2	2	0	0	0	2	3	.286	.000	.500	13.50	9.00
York, Mikey	R-R	6-2	190	2-24-96	4	2	6.35	9	5	0	0	34	43	30	24	5	18	21	.312	.315	.310	5.56	4.76

Fielding

Catcher

	PCT	G	PO	A	E	DP	PB
Ciuffo	1.000	1	7	0	0	0	0
Law	.968	26	217	23	8	1	3
Miller	1.000	2	5	0	0	0	0
Pinto	.987	63	416	52	6	3	6
Roach	.979	22	134	7	3	0	6
Rodriguez	.985	26	180	19	3	1	1

First Base

	PCT	G	PO	A	E	DP
Lowe	.990	35	280	8	3	35
Maris	1.000	1	8	0	0	1
McCarthy	1.000	2	12	0	0	3
McKay	.989	18	167	5	2	14
Miller	1.000	1	5	0	0	0
Olive	1.000	9	67	5	0	2
Padlo	.992	18	121	7	1	9
Roach	1.000	2	8	0	0	0
Tenerowicz	.996	57	421	33	2	36

Second Base

	PCT	G	PO	A	E	DP
Arroyo	1.000	1	0	2	0	0
Bridgman	1.000	1	2	3	0	2
Brujan	.990	24	30	73	1	11
Gray	.964	64	111	157	10	42
Maris	1.000	15	25	42	0	14
Mastrobuoni	.968	18	24	36	2	6
Miller	1.000	1	1	2	0	0
Palacios	.983	14	16	41	1	3
Robertson	1.000	1	1	3	0	1
Tenerowicz	1.000	4	5	9	0	2

Third Base

	PCT	G	PO	A	E	DP
Bridgman	1.000	2	0	4	0	0
Duffy	.667	1	0	2	1	0
Gray	.833	16	4	11	3	0
Maris	.885	9	6	17	3	2
Mastrobuoni	1.000	8	6	8	0	2
Padlo	.952	87	54	123	9	14
Palacios	.973	18	8	28	1	1

Shortstop

	PCT	G	PO	A	E	DP
Fox	.966	79	90	191	10	43
Gray	.963	21	26	52	3	10
Hechavarria	1.000	2	2	1	0	0
Mastrobuoni	.750	2	1	2	1	0
Palacios	.979	36	47	92	3	20

Outfield

	PCT	G	PO	A	E	DP
Bridgman	.000	1	0	0	0	0
Cabrera	.982	20	53	2	1	0
Chester	.972	13	34	1	1	0
Fraley	.981	62	146	7	3	2
Kiermaier	1.000	1	1	0	0	0
Lowe	.984	102	245	9	4	4
Maris	.000	1	0	0	0	0
Mastrobuoni	1.000	65	155	2	0	0
McCarthy	1.000	1	1	0	0	0
Miller	1.000	2	2	0	0	0
Olive	.000	1	0	0	0	0
Olmedo-Barrera	.936	32	43	1	3	0
Roach	.983	84	170	4	3	0
Sanchez	.983	84	170	4	3	0
Smith	.000	1	0	0	0	0
Stone	.963	10	26	0	1	0
Tenerowicz	1.000	28	45	1	0	0

BOWLING GREEN HOT RODS   LOW CLASS A
MIDWEST LEAGUE

Batting

	B-T	HT	WT	DOB	AVG	vLH	vRH	G	AB	R	H	2B	3B	HR	RBI	BB	HBP	SH	SF	SO	SB	CS	SLG	OBP
Alvarez, Alexander	R-R	5-11	200	9-14-96	.237	.289	.206	32	118	13	28	4	2	3	11	5	0	3	0	38	0	1	.381	.268

Batting	B-T	HT	WT	DOB	AVG	vLH	vRH	G	AB	R	H	2B	3B	HR	RBI	BB	HBP	SH	SF	SO	SB	CS	SLG	OBP
Betts, Chris	L-R	6-2	215	3-10-97	.232	.000	.250	16	56	8	13	1	0	1	6	6	1	1	1	16	0	0	.304	.313
Bridgman, Justin	R-R	5-11	175	6-20-95	.303	.471	.254	22	76	11	23	3	0	0	6	4	0	1	1	8	4	2	.342	.333
Brujan, Vidal	B-R	5-9	155	2-9-98	.313	.259	.335	95	377	86	118	18	5	5	41	48	5	1	3	53	43	15	.427	.395
Cabrera, Eleardo	L-R	5-11	195	11-8-95	.220	.257	.206	76	259	28	57	10	0	4	31	26	4	2	3	71	7	1	.305	.298
Chester, Carl	R-R	6-0	200	12-12-95	.285	.296	.281	105	393	61	112	23	6	5	63	22	8	6	10	67	15	7	.412	.328
Davis, Devin	R-R	6-3	215	2-14-97	.284	.275	.288	96	342	31	97	17	0	6	47	30	7	1	5	67	1	5	.386	.349
Gomez, Moises	R-R	5-11	200	8-27-98	.280	.284	.279	122	471	67	132	34	7	19	82	34	3	0	8	137	4	3	.503	.328
Gustave, Emilio	R-R	6-2	200	1-26-95	.224	.188	.240	98	339	49	76	14	4	3	32	22	8	5	3	101	5	4	.316	.285
Hair, Trey	L-R	5-10	185	4-21-95	.290	.351	.269	58	217	34	63	17	3	3	22	18	7	0	1	42	5	3	.438	.362
Haley, Jim	R-R	6-1	195	2-23-95	.323	.312	.329	80	300	47	97	22	2	7	47	15	6	3	4	52	13	2	.480	.363
Hernandez, Ronaldo	R-R	6-1	185	11-11-97	.284	.223	.310	109	405	68	115	20	1	21	79	31	6	0	7	69	10	4	.494	.339
Law, Zacrey	R-R	6-0	190	7-8-96	.302	.261	.315	26	96	18	29	4	0	3	18	8	3	1	5	13	5	0	.438	.357
McKay, Brendan	L-L	6-2	212	12-18-95	.254	.500	.208	21	63	12	16	2	0	1	16	28	0	0	0	13	0	0	.333	.484
Rondon, Adrian	R-R	6-1	190	7-7-98	.170	.244	.146	47	171	17	29	13	0	0	14	9	0	0	1	57	1	0	.246	.210
Rutherford, Zach	R-R	6-2	180	3-13-96	.268	.280	.263	112	426	65	114	25	1	6	54	41	11	3	3	99	11	2	.373	.345
Seibert, Mac	R-R	6-0	195	11-17-93	.233	.385	.118	8	30	3	7	2	1	0	2	2	0	0	0	10	0	0	.367	.281
Stone, Jake	L-R	6-0	200	1-31-95	.203	.143	.217	22	74	13	15	4	2	1	8	9	0	1	1	15	1	1	.351	.286
Walls, Taylor	B-R	5-10	180	7-10-96	.304	.352	.283	120	467	87	142	28	6	6	57	66	4	0	3	80	31	12	.428	.393

Pitching	B-T	HT	WT	DOB	W	L	ERA	G	GS	CG	SV	IP	H	R	ER	HR	BB	SO	AVG	vLH	vRH	K/9	BB/9
Busfield, J.D.	R-R	6-7	235	5-5-95	1	1	3.42	5	5	0	0	24	19	10	9	3	3	18	.214	.273	.179	6.85	1.14
Campbell, Paul	L-R	6-0	190	7-26-95	4	1	2.70	7	6	0	1	37	31	12	11	2	12	22	.235	.174	.267	5.40	2.95
Day, Tyler	R-R	6-1	185	1-22-94	0	5	2.23	22	0	0	1	40	32	14	10	5	14	46	.218	.231	.211	10.26	3.12
Disla, Jose	R-R	6-2	165	3-11-96	0	1	2.95	22	0	0	3	40	29	19	13	4	13	56	.196	.200	.193	12.71	2.95
Fleming, Josh	R-L	6-2	190	5-18-96	6	1	1.20	10	10	0	0	60	41	9	8	1	10	42	.193	.211	.184	6.30	1.50
Franklin, Austin	R-R	6-3	215	10-2-97	6	5	3.62	16	15	0	0	82	77	35	33	6	31	65	.247	.230	.255	7.13	3.40
Gist, Andrew	R-L	5-10	192	3-28-95	0	2	4.44	13	0	0	1	24	28	16	12	1	8	14	.286	.188	.333	5.18	2.96
Goodbrand, Kyle	R-R	6-2	198	4-22-95	5	0	3.86	16	0	0	0	33	34	15	14	4	11	36	.274	.304	.256	9.92	3.03
Linares, Resly	L-L	6-2	170	12-11-97	7	3	3.20	17	17	0	0	84	69	37	30	6	25	97	.222	.188	.235	10.35	2.67
Marsden, Justin	R-R	6-4	175	1-27-97	1	0	3.38	3	0	0	0	8	6	3	3	1	2	8	.222	.308	.143	9.00	2.25
Myers, Tobias	R-R	6-0	193	8-5-98	10	6	3.71	23	21	0	0	119	127	59	49	11	41	101	.274	.254	.286	7.64	3.10
O'Brien, Riley	R-R	6-4	170	2-6-95	4	1	2.05	15	5	0	0	48	23	14	11	3	21	66	.143	.130	.150	12.29	3.91
Ortiz, Jesus	R-R	6-2	185	8-4-97	0	0	0.00	1	0	0	0	2	0	0	0	0	0	1	.000	.000	.000	4.50	0.00
Padilla, Nicholas	R-R	6-2	220	12-04-96	1	2	9.00	7	0	0	0	9	12	10	9	2	2	9	.423	.429	.419	9.00	2.00
Pelaez, Ivan	L-L	5-11	155	2-1-94	1	1	2.25	6	0	0	1	16	13	4	4	0	2	17	.220	.211	.225	9.56	1.13
Romero, Orlando	R-R	6-0	211	9-26-96	3	1	2.90	18	0	0	4	31	13	11	10	3	10	39	.125	.171	.095	11.32	2.90
Romero, Tommy	R-R	6-2	225	7-8-97	8	1	3.21	16	16	1	0	84	70	30	30	10	36	77	.230	.282	.189	8.25	3.86
2-team total (9 Clinton)					11	4	2.95	25	25	1	0	128	111	42	42	11	51	131	.238	.264	.216	9.21	3.59
Rosenblum-Larson, Simon	R-R	6-3	202	2-11-97	0	2	2.55	9	0	0	0	18	8	7	5	1	5	29	.138	.077	.188	14.77	2.55
Salinas, Jhonleider	R-R	6-7	215	9-25-95	3	2	2.70	28	2	0	5	60	39	23	18	3	42	63	.186	.206	.176	9.45	6.30
Sanders, Phoenix	R-R	5-10	184	6-5-95	5	3	3.02	28	0	0	3	51	44	22	17	2	19	71	.234	.167	.271	12.61	3.38
Schryver, Hunter	L-L	6-1	198	4-3-95	1	2	2.23	21	0	0	8	36	25	11	9	4	10	48	.188	.156	.198	11.89	2.48
Seelinger, Matt	R-R	6-0	205	4-19-95	1	0	2.19	8	0	0	3	12	10	4	3	1	5	15	.217	.250	.200	10.95	3.65
Strotman, Drew	R-R	6-3	195	9-3-96	3	0	3.52	9	9	0	0	46	40	21	18	0	18	43	.241	.305	.206	8.41	3.52
Valverde, Alex	R-R	6-2	185	9-26-96	8	7	4.56	24	21	0	0	109	120	69	55	15	57	79	.277	.272	.281	6.54	4.72
York, Mikey	R-R	6-2	190	2-24-96	2	0	2.77	14	6	0	2	39	39	18	12	0	13	39	.264	.250	.273	9.00	3.00
Zombro, Tyler	R-R	6-1	190	9-2-94	8	2	2.84	33	0	0	8	76	80	28	24	3	8	54	.271	.349	.228	6.39	0.95

Fielding

C: Alvarez 26, Betts 10, Hernandez 85, Law 20, Seibert 3. **1B:** Alvarez 4, Davis 75, Haley 55, McKay 9, Rutherford 1. **2B:** Bridgman 7, Brujan 88, Hair 24, Haley 9, Rutherford 17. **3B:** Bridgman 16, Hair 23, Haley 8, Rondon 46, Rutherford 48. **SS:** Rutherford 36, Walls 104. **OF:** Bridgman 1, Cabrera 76, Chester 103, Gomez 110, Gustave 98, Haley 12, Stone 21.

HUDSON VALLEY RENEGADES   SHORT-SEASON
NEW YORK-PENN LEAGUE

Batting	B-T	HT	WT	DOB	AVG	vLH	vRH	G	AB	R	H	2B	3B	HR	RBI	BB	HBP	SH	SF	SO	SB	CS	SLG	OBP
Aranda, Jonathan	L-R	5-10	173	5-23-98	.200	.250	.192	9	30	2	6	0	0	0	4	2	0	0	0	2	0	0	.200	.250
Berglund, Michael	L-R	6-2	175	7-18-97	.200	.000	.250	5	5	2	1	0	0	0	2	4	0	0	1	3	0	0	.200	.500
Betts, Chris	L-R	6-2	215	3-10-97	.248	.283	.238	56	206	29	51	16	0	9	36	27	1	0	3	44	0	0	.456	.333
Bridgman, Justin	R-R	5-11	175	6-20-95	.241	.353	.212	26	83	11	20	2	1	0	7	9	1	0	2	6	8	2	.289	.316
Brown, Bryce	R-R	6-1	185	3-29-97	.203	.222	.197	51	163	26	33	8	1	2	11	7	2	2	1	50	16	2	.301	.284
Dodson, Tanner	B-R	6-1	160	5-9-97	.273	.216	.286	49	198	30	54	7	3	2	19	20	3	0	3	34	8	3	.369	.344
Frank, Tyler	R-R	6-0	185	1-15-97	.288	.256	.299	51	177	37	51	14	1	2	22	33	12	0	4	28	3	3	.412	.425
Giovannelli, Garrett	R-R	6-0	178	4-10-95	.200	.208	.198	37	115	11	23	5	1	0	10	11	1	2	2	17	11	3	.261	.271
Hair, Trey	L-R	5-10	185	4-21-95	.471	.333	.500	4	17	2	8	2	0	1	3	1	0	0	0	3	1	1	.765	.500
Johnson, Kaleo	R-R	6-3	220	8-26-96	.265	.200	.276	9	34	5	9	1	0	1	8	3	2	0	1	10	0	0	.382	.350
Malone, Marvin	R-R	6-3	205	5-2-95	.205	.200	.207	37	117	17	24	3	1	3	15	9	0		1	45	5	1	.325	.338
McGowan, Jacson	R-R	6-2	212	6-18-97	.269	.326	.253	59	212	30	57	8	2	2	39	30	2	0	9	65	1	0	.354	.352
Ostberg, Erik	L-R	5-10	225	10-12-95	.287	.314	.281	51	174	25	50	13	2	2	30	22	2	0	2	44	1	1	.420	.370
Parrett, David	R-R	6-0	200	1-17-94	.162	.300	.111	14	37	6	6	1	0	0	5	5	0	0	0	21	0	0	.189	.262
Pham, Tommy	R-R	6-1	210	3-8-88	.750	—	.750	1	4	2	3	0	0	1	2	0	0	0	0	0	0	0	1.500	.750
Proctor, Ford	L-R	6-1	195	12-4-96	.256	.200	.271	60	227	36	58	12	1	1	24	32	2	2	5	50	4	2	.339	.346
Qsar, Jordan	L-R	6-3	195	12-2-95	.176	.083	.194	22	74	9	13	4	0	4	11	18	0	0	1	35	0	0	.392	.333
Rondon, Adrian	R-R	6-1	190	7-7-98	.195	.216	.189	46	164	16	32	10	0	4	23	16	2	0	1	39	0	0	.329	.273
Smith, Michael	L-L	5-11	165	5-30-97	.251	.195	.264	59	223	32	56	13	1	3	17	20	0	1	2	48	3	3	.359	.310
Smoot, Allen	L-R	6-2	200	4-6-94	.224	.167	.233	29	85	9	19	4	1	0	7	16	2	0	2	32	0	0	.294	.352

	B-T	HT	WT	DOB	AVG	vLH	vRH	G	AB	R	H	2B	3B	HR	RBI	BB	HBP	SH	SF	SO	SB	CS	SLG	OBP
Stone, Jake	L-R	6-0	200	1-31-95	.290	.308	.288	27	93	16	27	5	2	4	13	9	0	1	2	30	4	3	.516	.346

Pitching	B-T	HT	WT	DOB	W	L	ERA	G	GS	CG	SV	IP	H	R	ER	HR	BB	SO	AVG	vLH	vRH	K/9	BB/9
Campbell, Paul	L-R	6-0	190	7-26-95	3	1	1.67	6	6	0	0	32	23	7	6	2	5	35	.200	.196	.203	9.74	1.39
Cumbie, Trey	L-L	6-2	200	7-12-96	3	1	3.62	17	0	0	1	32	27	14	13	2	7	43	.225	.191	.244	11.97	1.95
Gist, Andrew	R-L	5-10	192	3-28-95	0	0	3.86	6	0	0	1	12	10	5	5	0	5	13	.222	.133	.267	10.03	3.86
Goodbrand, Kyle	R-R	6-2	198	4-22-95	0	1	5.68	3	0	0	2	6	8	4	4	1	0	6	.308	.364	.267	8.53	0.00
Hogan, Miller	R-R	6-2	200	7-18-96	2	4	4.76	11	8	0	0	34	34	18	18	3	8	32	.272	.296	.254	8.47	2.12
Labosky, Jack	R-R	6-3	235	7-19-96	3	2	2.63	17	0	0	3	38	37	14	11	2	5	34	.253	.190	.296	8.12	1.19
Lee, Nick	R-R	6-5	195	2-10-97	1	1	9.42	9	2	0	0	14	17	16	15	0	15	12	.288	.269	.303	7.53	9.42
McGee, Easton	R-R	6-6	205	12-26-97	7	3	5.23	13	13	0	0	64	73	39	37	4	13	37	.289	.333	.254	5.23	1.84
Mercado, Michael	R-R	6-4	160	4-15-99	1	2	5.22	11	11	0	0	50	55	34	29	6	16	38	.274	.237	.306	6.84	2.88
Montgomery, Justin	R-R	6-5	200	9-10-96	2	0	3.38	6	1	0	0	13	6	9	5	0	8	9	.140	.143	.138	6.08	5.40
Muller, Chris	R-R	6-5	210	4-22-96	0	1	2.25	5	0	0	0	8	4	2	2	0	2	7	.154	.111	.177	7.88	2.25
Myers, B.J.	R-R	6-0	195	4-28-95	4	0	4.81	17	0	0	4	24	31	18	13	2	10	29	.301	.386	.237	10.73	3.70
Ortiz, Jesus	R-R	6-2	185	8-4-97	3	2	3.38	14	0	0	0	45	40	19	17	5	9	35	.242	.246	.240	6.95	1.79
Padilla, Nicholas	R-R	6-2	220	12-24-96	3	5	3.30	13	12	0	0	60	54	27	22	3	12	44	.247	.253	.242	6.60	1.80
Pflughaupt, Blake	L-L	6-0	210	9-4-96	2	2	3.26	10	9	0	0	39	36	16	14	1	24	35	.255	.231	.265	8.15	5.59
Roca, Jose	R-R	6-0	195	8-27-96	0	1	10.50	2	1	0	0	6	10	7	7	0	0	3	.370	.333	.400	4.50	0.00
Rosenblum-Larson, Simon	R-R	6-3	202	2-11-97	1	1	0.00	9	0	0	5	21	11	3	0	0	4	33	.159	.148	.167	14.14	1.71
Ryan, Joe	R-R	6-1	185	6-5-96	2	1	3.72	12	7	0	0	36	26	15	15	3	14	51	.202	.177	.218	12.63	3.47
Sanchez, Cristopher	L-L	6-5	165	12-12-96	1	0	4.00	2	2	0	0	9	9	5	4	0	5	11	.273	.000	.409	11.00	5.00
Sprengel, Nick	L-L	6-2	220	6-4-97	3	1	1.09	12	0	0	2	25	18	6	3	1	8	20	.205	.129	.246	7.30	2.92
Strong, Alan	R-R	6-3	200	10-22-96	1	1	2.68	15	0	0	1	37	30	12	11	2	14	44	.216	.107	.289	10.70	3.41
Trageton, Zack	R-R	6-1	225	9-2-98	2	0	0.56	3	3	0	0	16	9	1	1	0	0	12	.161	.136	.177	6.75	0.00
Yancey, Stephen	L-R	6-1	190	11-8-95	0	0	1.50	3	0	0	0	6	5	1	1	0	2	5	.217	.200	.231	7.50	3.00

Fielding

C: Berglund 2, Betts 53, Ostberg 17, Parrett 5. **1B:** Johnson 1, McGowan 54, Ostberg 1, Rondon 1, Smoot 21. **2B:** Aranda 8, Bridgman 9, Frank 24, Giovannelli 35, Proctor 4. **3B:** Aranda 1, Bridgman 9, Frank 10, Hair 3, Johnson 8, Rondon 44, Smoot 3. **SS:** Bridgman 1, Frank 19, Giovannelli 3, Proctor 55. **OF:** Bridgman 7, Brown 49, Dodson 30, Malone 35, Parrett 2, Pham 1, Qsar 21, Smith 59, Smoot 1, Stone 27.

PRINCETON RAYS
APPALACHIAN LEAGUE
ROOKIE

Batting	B-T	HT	WT	DOB	AVG	vLH	vRH	G	AB	R	H	2B	3B	HR	RBI	BB	HBP	SH	SF	SO	SB	CS	SLG	OBP
Alvarez, Roberto	R-R	5-11	151	7-28-99	.320	.313	.322	44	169	19	54	12	1	2	13	8	0	0	16	2	1	.438	.350
Aranda, Jonathan	L-R	5-10	173	5-23-98	.286	.211	.299	36	126	24	36	8	4	1	25	12	3	0	2	18	0	1	.437	.357
Berglund, Michael	L-R	6-2	175	7-18-97	.250	—	.250	1	4	1	1	0	0	0	1	1	0	0	0	1	0	0	.250	.400
Brundage, Beau	L-R	6-3	170	4-29-97	.228	.412	.191	30	101	15	23	1	1	0	4	7	4	0	2	34	4	1	.257	.298
Byrd, Vincent	L-R	6-7	240	10-8-97	.275	.191	.296	29	102	19	28	4	0	10	27	10	1	0	0	40	0	0	.608	.345
Diaz, Pedro	R-R	6-3	210	1-9-99	.252	.255	.250	45	151	21	38	9	2	5	18	11	3	0	3	54	5	5	.437	.310
Franco, Wander	B-R	5-10	189	3-1-01	.351	.349	.352	61	242	46	85	10	7	11	57	27	2	0	2	19	4	3	.587	.418
Gregorio, Osmy	R-R	6-2	175	5-27-98	.245	.227	.253	39	143	25	35	6	2	3	21	15	4	1	2	31	6	2	.378	.329
Hollis, Connor	R-R	5-10	170	11-18-94	.365	.340	.374	48	170	48	62	11	0	7	26	28	7	0	2	30	8	3	.553	.469
Leon, Luis	R-R	6-0	175	9-10-98	.250	.000	.333	1	4	3	1	0	0	0	0	1	0	0	1	0	0		.250	.500
Muffley, Jordyn	R-R	6-1	195	4-14-97	.278	.083	.317	22	72	9	20	6	0	1	9	4	4	0	1	15	1	0	.403	.346
Palomaki, Jake	B-R	5-10	175	7-17-95	.258	.174	.289	45	167	37	43	4	2	3	15	25	4	4	3	26	10	2	.359	.362
Pena, Tony	R-R	5-11	180	9-24-97	.357	.138	.423	36	126	35	45	9	1	4	29	11	2	0	0	36	5	0	.540	.417
Qsar, Jordan	L-R	6-3	195	12-2-95	.350	.417	.327	40	137	32	48	8	3	10	32	32	0	0	1	45	4	1	.672	.471
Ramirez, Jean	R-R	6-0	210	4-27-93	.154	.118	.182	17	39	6	6	2	0	1	7	9	0	0	0	12	0	0	.282	.313
Tonton, Jose	R-R	6-2	205	4-4-96	.500	.667	.400	2	8	2	4	1	0	0	0	0	0	0	0	3	0	0	.625	.500
Torrealba, Jose	R-R	6-2	171	10-15-97	.155	.167	.150	19	58	10	9	3	1	1	5	4	1	0	0	27	0	0	.293	.222
Vargas, Carlos	R-R	6-3	170	3-18-99	.256	.255	.257	47	160	18	41	11	1	4	22	18	1	1	5	39	0	0	.413	.333
Witherspoon, Grant	L-L	6-3	200	9-27-96	.245	.190	.266	56	212	33	52	8	3	5	31	18	3	1	1	59	8	1	.382	.312

Pitching	B-T	HT	WT	DOB	W	L	ERA	G	GS	CG	SV	IP	H	R	ER	HR	BB	SO	AVG	vLH	vRH	K/9	BB/9
Arias, Juan Carlos	R-R	6-3	228	9-16-95	4	1	4.26	17	0	0	0	32	31	18	15	2	18	31	.254	.237	.262	8.81	5.12
Baz, Shane	R-R	6-3	190	6-17-99	0	2	7.71	2	2	0	0	7	11	7	6	1	6	5	.367	.222	.429	6.43	7.71
2-team total (10 Bristol)					4	5	4.47	12	12	0	0	52	56	30	26	3	29	59	.267	.247	.280	10.15	4.99
Costanzo, Michael	L-L	6-1	190	11-14-95	2	1	2.08	19	0	0	6	26	30	9	6	2	5	37	.283	.346	.263	12.81	1.73
Garcia, Wilson	R-R	6-3	205	10-14-96	0	0	2.25	1	1	0	0	4	2	1	1	0	2	5	.154	.143	.167	11.25	4.50
Gau, Christopher	R-R	6-2	205	2-3-97	5	1	2.92	13	0	0	0	25	21	10	8	3	7	30	.228	.206	.241	10.95	2.55
German, Francisco	R-R	6-2	160	12-26-96	2	1	3.86	14	0	0	4	14	13	12	6	0	12	21	.236	.067	.300	13.50	7.71
Gonzalez, Edisson	R-R	5-10	160	10-2-99	1	0	6.62	5	4	0	0	18	14	14	13	3	10	20	.212	.217	.209	10.19	5.09
Lara, Miguel	R-R	5-11	165	7-14-97	4	3	4.29	12	12	0	0	50	54	25	24	3	15	51	.276	.267	.281	9.12	2.68
Liberatore, Matthew	L-L	6-5	200	11-6-99	1	0	3.60	1	1	0	0	5	5	2	2	0	2	5	.294	.500	.267	9.00	3.60
Linares, Wanderson	R-R	6-1	160	9-28-96	2	2	6.07	12	9	0	0	46	48	34	31	9	17	44	.268	.214	.293	8.61	3.33
Marsden, Justin	R-R	6-4	175	1-27-97	2	0	3.52	13	0	0	2	31	19	18	12	5	18	36	.170	.214	.143	10.38	5.18
McClanahan, Shane	L-L	6-1	188	4-28-97	1	0	0.00	2	2	0	0	4	2	0	0	0	1	7	.154	.000	.182	15.75	2.25
Moncada, Luis	L-L	6-1	150	2-28-98	3	1	3.13	11	9	0	0	46	34	17	16	2	18	53	.200	.320	.179	10.37	3.52
Montgomery, Justin	R-R	6-5	200	9-10-96	2	0	3.38	10	0	0	2	21	17	8	8	2	9	19	.215	.136	.246	8.02	3.80
Moore, Steffon	R-R	6-3	185	6-25-97	1	0	2.31	14	0	0	5	23	14	6	6	1	11	27	.169	.143	.174	10.41	4.24
Peguero, Joe	R-R	5-11	160	5-5-97	1	2	7.44	14	0	0	0	33	43	32	27	4	18	38	.316	.350	.290	10.47	4.96
Renz, Heath	L-R	6-0	210	8-17-95	2	3	3.86	16	0	0	0	26	26	15	11	2	15	23	.263	.125	.307	8.06	5.26
Rodriguez, Angel	R-R	6-5	189	1-28-98	0	0	40.50	2	0	0	0	1	5	6	6	0	5	2	.625	1.000	.500	13.50	33.75
Rosa, Jeffrey	R-R	6-3	189	6-5-95	1	1	4.82	7	0	0	0	9	6	5	5	0	11	8	.188	.214	.167	7.71	10.61
Sanchez, Cristopher	L-L	6-5	165	12-12-96	3	2	4.60	10	10	0	0	43	53	25	22	3	22	34	.308	.250	.321	7.12	4.60

Sanchez, Rodolfo	R-R	5-10	165	1-12-00	1	0	0.00	1	0	0	0	5	0	0	0	0	1	7	.000	.000	.000	12.60	1.80
Trageton, Zack	R-R	6-1	225	9-2-98	2	1	4.29	9	9	0	0	42	51	23	20	4	8	35	.297	.349	.266	7.50	1.71
Yancey, Stephen	L-R	6-1	190	11-8-95	4	1	3.44	13	1	0	1	34	29	14	13	4	10	31	.228	.275	.197	8.21	2.65

Fielding

C: Alvarez 44, Berglund 1, Muffley 18, Ramirez 8. **1B:** Byrd 21, Ramirez 1, Vargas 47. **2B:** Aranda 25, Hollis 14, Leon 1, Palomaki 27. **3B:** Aranda 5, Gregorio 27, Hollis 24, Palomaki 10. **SS:** Franco 53, Gregorio 10, Palomaki 3. **OF:** Brundage 30, Diaz 38, Palomaki 1, Pena 27, Qsar 37, Ramirez 1, Tonton 2, Torrealba 15, Witherspoon 54.

GCL RAYS   ROOKIE
GULF COAST LEAGUE

Batting	B-T	HT	WT	DOB	AVG	vLH	vRH	G	AB	R	H	2B	3B	HR	RBI	BB	HBP	SH	SF	SO	SB	CS	SLG	OBP
Arcendo, Luis	L-R	6-1	160	11-1-99	.158	.133	.169	32	95	12	15	3	0	0	10	14	0	2	1	23	8	6	.190	.264
Berglund, Michael	L-R	6-2	178	7-18-97	.257	.214	.273	34	105	16	27	7	0	0	14	24	2	0	2	18	2	2	.324	.399
Brito, Raider	R-R	6-1	164	5-17-99	.242	.227	.247	29	95	12	23	5	1	1	9	3	2	0	0	24	1	4	.347	.280
Dimon, Dawson	R-R	6-1	185	5-17-99	.194	.222	.182	13	31	1	6	1	0	0	4	4	4	1	0	7	0	0	.226	.359
Edwards, K.V.	R-R	6-1	175	3-5-98	.247	.182	.273	24	77	11	19	4	1	0	8	8	3	2	0	25	4	1	.325	.341
Infante, Diego	R-R	6-2	178	10-22-99	.232	.265	.220	34	125	16	29	4	1	1	21	8	0	0	0	34	6	0	.304	.278
Johnson, Kaleo	R-R	6-3	220	8-26-96	.311	.304	.314	47	167	32	52	13	2	7	25	13	13	0	2	33	4	3	.539	.400
Leon, Luis	B-R	6-0	175	9-10-98	.230	.238	.226	40	148	17	34	5	0	2	14	21	1	0	0	26	2	3	.304	.329
Marte, Jelfry	B-R	5-10	130	3-27-01	.281	.212	.300	43	153	16	43	3	1	0	14	6	2	4	0	26	7	4	.314	.317
Martinez, Yunior	B-R	6-1	166	12-24-98	.255	.200	.272	41	149	24	38	7	2	1	10	10	2	2	0	39	8	5	.349	.311
McCarthy, Joe	L-L	6-3	225	2-23-94	.100	.250	.000	3	10	1	0	0	0	0	1	1	0	0	1	5	0	0	.100	.167
McKay, Brendan	L-L	6-2	212	12-18-95	.000	.000	.000	3	10	1	0	0	0	0	2	0	1	0	1	0	0	.000	.083
Melendez, Kevin	R-R	6-1	185	3-15-00	.217	.120	.250	31	97	17	21	4	0	1	12	12	4	0	2	29	2	2	.289	.322
Miller, Andrew	L-R	6-1	200	3-19-99	.136	.000	.214	6	22	3	3	1	0	0	1	2	0	0	0	8	0	0	.182	.208
Olive, Russ	L-L	6-3	205	6-3-96	.307	.238	.328	49	176	26	54	15	3	0	24	28	4	0	4	45	4	2	.426	.406
Pedroza, Cristhian	R-R	5-10	173	2-14-99	.268	.375	.236	27	71	10	19	5	0	0	9	8	3	0	0	17	2	1	.338	.366
Pena, Tony	R-R	5-11	180	9-24-97	.364	.167	.600	3	11	2	4	1	0	1	2	0	0	0	0	3	0	1	.727	.364
Sanchez, Aldenis	R-R	6-1	165	9-26-98	.281	.333	.267	47	185	27	52	4	2	0	22	16	1	2	1	34	16	4	.324	.340
Schnell, Nick	L-R	6-3	180	3-27-00	.239	.174	.273	19	67	8	16	4	1	1	4	14	1	0	0	23	2	6	.373	.378
Soria, Nate	R-R	5-10	175	11-24-95	.111	.167	.000	7	9	2	1	0	0	0	0	2	0	0	0	2	0	1	.111	.273

Pitching	B-T	HT	WT	DOB	W	L	ERA	G	GS	CG	SV	IP	H	R	ER	HR	BB	SO	AVG	vLH	vRH	K/9	BB/9
Alaniz, Ruben	R-R	6-4	219	6-14-91	0	0	0.00	1	0	0	0	1	0	0	0	0	0	1	.000	—	.000	9.00	0.00
Bernstein, Andrew	R-R	6-1	190	12-14-95	4	0	1.08	11	0	0	2	17	13	3	2	1	2	6	.228	.208	.242	3.24	1.08
Bradley, Taj	R-R	6-2	190	3-20-01	1	4	5.09	10	9	0	0	23	26	18	13	1	12	24	.277	.395	.196	9.39	4.70
Brito, Sandy	R-R	6-2	170	7-19-96	0	0	27.00	1	0	0	0	1	0	2	2	0	3	1	.000	.000	.000	13.50	40.50
Cedeno, Jhoanbert	R-R	6-6	170	2-12-98	0	2	5.40	14	0	0	3	23	23	15	14	1	7	28	.247	.200	.283	10.80	2.70
Felipe, Angel	R-R	6-5	190	8-30-97	1	1	6.17	12	0	0	0	23	30	17	16	0	15	26	.309	.302	.315	10.03	5.79
Fernandez, Christian	R-R	6-2	170	8-11-99	3	1	2.61	10	6	0	0	41	36	14	12	3	17	45	.231	.216	.244	9.80	3.70
Gonzalez, Edisson	R-R	5-10	160	10-2-99	2	1	1.83	8	6	0	0	34	28	12	7	1	18	30	.212	.152	.244	7.86	4.72
Herrera, Bryan	R-R	6-2	175	4-22-98	0	0	4.06	13	0	0	1	31	28	15	14	1	22	33	.255	.275	.237	9.58	6.39
Liberatore, Matthew	L-L	6-5	200	11-6-99	1	2	0.98	8	8	0	0	28	16	7	3	0	11	32	.170	.200	.156	10.41	3.58
Lopez, Jose	L-L	6-2	200	2-15-99	3	1	2.28	11	7	0	0	43	44	20	11	2	17	36	.246	.238	.248	7.48	3.53
McClanahan, Shane	L-L	6-1	188	4-28-97	0	0	0.00	2	2	0	0	3	1	0	0	0	6	6	.100	.000	.125	18.00	0.00
Moore, Steffon	L-L	6-3	185	6-29-96	0	0	0.00	3	0	0	1	5	2	1	0	0	6	5	.125	.000	.143	10.13	0.00
Mujica, Jose	R-R	6-2	235	6-29-96	0	0	3.86	1	1	0	0	2	4	1	1	0	0	4	.364	.286	.500	15.43	0.00
Muller, Chris	R-R	6-5	210	4-22-96	1	2	2.30	9	4	0	2	16	10	6	4	1	11	13	.179	.167	.192	7.47	6.32
Raiden, Chandler	R-R	6-1	170	6-7-96	0	0	0.00	4	0	0	1	3	1	0	0	0	1	3	.100	.000	.000	9.00	3.00
Ramirez, Wikelman	R-R	6-0	183	8-9-00	0	1	5.40	2	2	0	0	8	8	6	5	1	4	8	.235	.059	.412	8.64	4.32
Roca, Jose	R-R	6-0	195	8-27-96	4	0	1.96	7	0	0	1	18	24	6	4	0	4	14	.312	.429	.214	6.87	1.96
Rodriguez, Aldor	R-R	6-1	182	7-4-97	3	1	4.61	12	0	0	1	27	24	16	14	3	10	26	.222	.189	.255	8.56	3.29
Rodriguez, Angel	R-R	6-5	229	1-28-98	1	0	2.90	11	0	0	1	31	23	11	10	1	13	22	.205	.158	.255	6.39	3.77
Sabino, Stanly	L-L	6-0	150	9-26-97	4	0	2.45	15	0	0	3	26	22	8	7	0	13	32	.234	.308	.206	11.22	4.56
Sanchez, Francisco	L-L	6-1	180	4-24-98	0	0	40.50	2	1	0	0	1	9	6	6	0	2	1	.692	1.000	.636	6.75	13.50
Sanchez, Rodolfo	R-R	5-10	165	1-12-00	4	3	3.23	10	7	0	0	47	49	25	17	4	7	43	.263	.250	.276	8.18	1.33
Santos, Fraylin	R-R	6-3	195	10-3-98	1	0	3.52	2	2	0	0	8	8	7	3	1	7	2	.242	.222	.250	8.22	1.17
Sprengel, Nick	L-L	6-2	220	6-4-97	0	0	1.86	5	0	0	2	10	8	3	2	1	5	13	.216	.333	.179	12.10	4.66
Whittle, Daiveyon	R-R	6-1	236	11-11-99	0	0	7.71	7	0	0	0	7	8	6	6	1	4	6	.286	.429	.238	7.71	5.14

Fielding

C: Berglund 24, Dimon 12, Melendez 19, Miller 5, Soria 3. **1B:** Johnson 6, McKay 1, Olive 49. **2B:** Arcendo 22, Edwards 1, Leon 15, Pedroza 22. **3B:** Arcendo 4, Johnson 37, Leon 14, Pedroza 5. **SS:** Arcendo 5, Leon 13, Marte 43. **OF:** Brito 24, Edwards 16, Infante 28, Martinez 39, McCarthy 1, Pena 3, Sanchez 47, Schnell 18.

DSL RAYS   ROOKIE
DOMINICAN SUMMER LEAGUE

Batting	B-T	HT	WT	DOB	AVG	vLH	vRH	G	AB	R	H	2B	3B	HR	RBI	BB	HBP	SH	SF	SO	SB	CS	SLG	OBP
Arias, Amador	R-R	5-11	143	8-25-00	.236	.333	.214	63	220	46	52	11	2	6	36	38	5	0	3	41	16	7	.386	.357
Arrendoll, Johampher	L-R	6-2	165	10-15-98	.226	.269	.218	53	168	34	38	9	3	2	18	28	2	0	3	64	8	6	.351	.338
Balbuena, Alfredo	R-R	5-9	178	11-25-98	.245	.235	.247	53	200	35	49	9	4	2	27	20	2	1	4	39	13	4	.360	.314
Bolivar, Roimer	R-R	6-0	175	12-10-99	.267	.229	.275	53	202	46	54	6	0	2	24	20	13	2	2	33	12	7	.337	.367
Calmes, Nigel	R-R	6-1	175	9-21-99	.248	.053	.287	34	113	16	28	1	2	0	16	15	1	1	0	31	9	2	.292	.341
Candelario, Stir	R-R	6-0	185	9-3-00	.255	.222	.263	54	196	31	50	11	3	2	23	22	4	2	2	57	4	4	.372	.339
Castellanos, Daiwer	L-R	5-11	155	8-16-00	.277	.250	.282	47	159	37	44	3	4	1	17	18	7	1	1	15	10	4	.365	.373

Name	B-T	HT	WT	DOB	AVG	vLH	vRH	G	AB	R	H	2B	3B	HR	RBI	BB	HP	SH	SF	SO	SB	CS	SLG	OBP
Chevez, Freddvil	R-R	6-4	200	3-13-00	.214	.250	.205	63	243	30	52	11	1	5	37	15	9	0	2	52	2	0	.329	.283
Del Palacio, Jose	L-R	6-0	185	10-14-98	.228	.179	.242	38	123	16	28	8	2	1	13	17	5	0	0	39	4	2	.350	.345
Figuereo, Alberto	R-R	5-8	145	4-24-00	.282	.255	.289	64	234	49	66	8	6	0	25	32	9	2	4	38	36	3	.368	.384
Fortuna, Saul	R-R	6-3	185	8-3-00	.257	.255	.257	58	218	25	56	7	1	1	27	11	7	0	3	60	3	7	.312	.310
Garcia, Juan	R-R	6-0	191	1-6-99	.286	.160	.309	45	161	27	46	7	1	2	29	10	2	8	4	33	7	7	.379	.328
Johnson, Dahiandy	L-R	6-3	200	9-25-99	.216	.195	.221	51	181	26	39	7	1	3	26	20	3	0	3	39	1	2	.315	.300
Lopez, Angel	R-R	5-11	160	11-14-99	.225	.195	.233	51	187	35	42	11	3	3	22	23	5	0	3	41	11	6	.364	.321
Lopez, Johan	R-R	5-10	167	7-28-00	.240	.256	.236	52	183	35	44	12	0	2	23	20	8	6	3	28	12	5	.339	.336
Manzueta, Oneill	R-R	6-0	190	2-7-01	.224	.185	.231	47	161	28	36	7	1	4	25	33	3	0	0	43	5	2	.354	.366
Mata, Juan	R-R	6-0	165	8-1-01	.174	.231	.160	37	132	21	23	3	0	0	11	10	2	0	0	26	10	2	.197	.243
Meza, Julio	R-R	6-0	165	5-4-99	.306	.391	.291	47	170	30	52	9	1	1	26	9	5	3	3	25	5	5	.388	.353
Nelo, Angel	R-R	5-7	164	3-29-00	.266	.318	.255	38	124	11	33	3	0	0	11	17	3	1	1	18	4	5	.290	.366
Pereira, Jose	R-R	5-11	153	3-3-99	.154	.000	.200	5	13	2	2	0	0	0	1	3	0	1	0	5	0	0	.154	.313
Perez, Luis	R-R	6-0	241	6-16-97	.296	.188	.327	25	71	12	21	6	0	3	16	7	3	0	3	16	2	1	.507	.369
Ramirez, Abiezel	B-R	5-11	160	1-26-00	.291	.220	.310	66	237	53	69	9	7	2	50	37	7	1	8	33	27	8	.414	.391
Rodriguez, Edgardo	R-R	6-0	207	11-29-00	.330	.226	.350	51	191	34	63	11	1	6	34	12	8	0	5	19	1	1	.492	.384
Sangrona, Isaias	R-R	6-2	180	4-19-01	.091	.000	.111	7	22	1	2	0	0	0	2	2	1	0	1	9	1	0	.091	.192
Santos, Bryan	L-L	6-0	165	5-4-99	.279	.318	.268	31	104	12	29	8	0	1	11	11	1	2	1	14	1	0	.385	.350
Silvestre, Reissel	R-R	6-0	163	4-7-98	.244	.143	.265	42	123	25	30	6	0	0	10	21	3	1	0	36	7	13	.293	.367
Tejeda, Gioser	R-R	5-11	204	9-23-97	.252	.227	.258	32	111	18	28	7	0	0	12	10	5	1	1	15	1	2	.315	.339
Valera, Robert	R-R	6-0	165	9-6-98	.290	.250	.297	20	76	10	22	3	1	0	7	3	7	0	0	9	3	1	.355	.372
Vargas, Jhosner	B-R	5-11	158	1-24-99	.259	.279	.253	51	193	27	50	6	1	1	27	19	2	5	2	26	11	2	.316	.329
Verbel, Dewins	B-R	5-11	160	12-24-99	.239	.375	.208	31	88	24	21	5	1	1	11	28	1	0	2	19	7	1	.352	.420
Villasmil, Fermin	R-R	6-0		2-4-00	.000	.000	.000	4	8	0	0	0	0	0	0	3	0	0	0	3	0	0	.000	.111

Pitching

Name	B-T	HT	WT	DOB	W	L	ERA	G	GS	CG	SV	IP	H	R	ER	HR	BB	SO	AVG	vLH	vRH	K/9	BB/9
Alfonzo, Emilio	R-R	6-6	170	8-2-00	1	3	2.82	13	11	0	0	51	42	25	16	0	26	45	.225	.214	.233	7.94	4.59
Andujar, Gustavo	R-R	5-11	164	4-6-00	5	1	3.58	12	5	0	0	28	25	19	11	0	15	15	.236	.206	.250	4.88	4.88
Casilla, Marquito	R-R	6-2	180	11-12-99	1	0	6.35	15	0	0	0	17	10	19	12	1	27	13	.167	.200	.133	6.88	14.29
Cedeno, Jhoanbert	R-R	6-6	170	2-12-98	1	0	3.27	5	0	0	0	11	10	4	4	1	4	21	.238	.250	.240	17.18	3.27
Cerda, Jose	R-R	6-0	180	10-18-99	2	0	1.69	19	0	0	8	32	18	10	6	0	16	38	.175	.111	.197	10.69	4.50
Cordero, Dauris	R-R	6-3	186	7-18-99	1	1	3.68	15	13	0	0	64	56	33	26	0	30	47	.231	.194	.271	6.64	4.24
Cuevas, Johan	R-R	6-2	180	5-8-00	2	1	6.95	12	0	0	0	22	23	17	17	2	11	21	.274	.297	.255	8.59	4.50
Curbata, Yosmer	R-R	6-3	170	7-19-00	4	0	3.75	16	0	0	1	36	26	16	15	1	10	16	.226	.281	.179	4.00	2.50
Dacosta, Franklin	L-L	5-11	162	2-27-00	2	3	2.79	15	6	0	0	42	31	14	13	0	17	55	.204	.207	.203	11.79	3.64
De Los Santos, Jose	R-R	6-0	175	9-19-99	0	0	0.00	7	2	0	0	13	3	1	0	0	4	7	.077	.000	.150	4.97	2.84
Duran, Luis	R-R	6-1	160	3-4-00	2	1	3.94	14	0	0	0	30	26	18	13	2	21	19	.252	.241	.265	5.76	6.37
Fernandez, Christian	R-R	6-2	170	8-11-99	0	0	2.60	4	4	0	0	17	11	6	5	1	8	17	.183	.218	.217	8.83	4.15
Galan, Jeremy	R-R	6-2	190	10-30-98	2	0	5.02	10	1	0	0	14	15	10	8	1	6	8	.267	.367	.160	5.23	3.77
Galue, Over	R-R	6-2	188	7-31-01	0	0	6.75	3	3	0	0	4	4	3	3	0	4	3	.267	.000	.400	6.75	9.00
Garcia, Carlos	R-R	6-3	185	11-28-98	2	0	0.81	19	1	0	6	33	12	3	3	0	13	35	.113	.057	.141	9.45	3.51
Garcia, Yeury	R-R	6-4	190	1-18-00	1	1	21.00	5	0	0	0	3	2	7	7	0	15	2	.200	.400	.000	6.00	45.00
Genao, Joaquin	R-R	5-11	155	2-22-00	3	0	3.81	18	0	0	0	26	22	11	11	0	15	21	.230	.231	.239	7.27	5.19
Gomez, Carlos	R-R	6-0	170	9-30-99	5	2	2.83	17	8	0	0	35	28	12	11	1	13	26	.224	.289	.188	6.69	3.34
Hernandez, Jesus	R-R	6-4	167	7-10-01	3	0	2.53	10	0	0	0	11	6	5	3	0	16	5	.171	.154	.182	4.22	13.50
Herrera, Bryan	R-R	6-2	175	4-22-98	0	0	0.00	4	0	0	1	7	4	1	0	0	3	5	.174	.246	.237	6.75	4.05
Jimenez, Antonio	L-L	5-11	145	5-6-01	3	1	2.89	11	0	0	1	19	17	7	6	0	13	20	.246	.200	.259	9.64	6.27
Kimura, Igor	R-R	6-1	207	4-14-99	0	0	0.00	4	0	0	2	7	1	0	0	0	1	9	.048	.000	.111	11.57	1.29
King, Pedro	R-R	6-0	180	10-10-99	0	0	2.08	14	0	0	0	26	20	9	6	2	10	23	.211	.276	.182	7.96	3.46
Leon, Maicor	L-L	5-9	165	3-6-01	0	1	10.38	4	3	0	0	4	5	5	5	0	2	1	.313	.200	.364	2.08	4.15
Liriano, Argenis	R-R	6-0	185	9-30-96	4	3	3.96	16	4	1	1	52	48	25	23	0	20	42	.247	.250	.245	7.22	3.44
Lopez, Dauris	R-R	6-3	185	10-20-98	3	4	4.50	15	10	0	1	54	51	32	27	2	32	26	.267	.295	.240	4.33	5.33
Lopez, Janick	R-R	6-3	187	4-24-99	0	3	3.19	14	14	0	0	54	46	26	19	2	36	36	.237	.298	.212	6.04	6.04
Manrique, Endry	R-R	6-0	150	11-3-00	2	1	2.64	14	5	0	0	44	35	18	13	1	18	32	.229	.235	.226	6.50	3.65
Medina, Luis	R-R	6-2	175	6-18-95	5	0	2.70	17	0	0	6	30	21	9	9	2	21	32	.202	.170	.228	9.60	6.30
Melo, Fernando	L-L	6-6	200	12-31-99	1	4	5.82	14	10	0	0	39	36	33	25	3	37	31	.254	.182	.275	7.22	8.61
Munoz, Victor	R-R	6-3	160	12-25-00	4	2	5.06	16	0	0	0	32	25	24	18	3	18	28	.216	.234	.192	7.88	5.06
Peguero, Matthew	R-R	6-2	200	1-12-00	5	1	2.69	13	12	0	0	60	46	22	18	1	21	60	.217	.152	.247	8.95	3.13
Prensa, Rafael	R-R	6-4	190	2-15-98	0	0	6.27	13	1	0	3	19	26	16	13	3	6	18	.356	.372	.333	8.68	2.89
Ramirez, Angel	R-R	6-2	180	12-25-96	2	0	5.87	11	0	0	2	15	20	11	10	2	11	17	.323	.296	.343	9.98	6.46
Roca, Jose	R-R	6-0	195	8-27-96	2	0	0.91	8	4	0	0	30	21	5	3	0	7	23	.194	.329	.221	6.98	2.12
Sanchez, Leonardo	R-R	6-3	187	12-16-98	5	1	2.45	15	0	0	0	26	16	11	7	3	16	21	.176	.137	.225	7.36	5.61
Sanchez, Rodolfo	R-R	5-10	165	1-12-00	1	0	0.00	3	3	0	0	13	5	0	0	0	4	14	.111	.226	.214	9.45	2.70
Santana, Daniel	R-R	6-2	193	4-16-98	5	1	2.70	14	13	0	0	63	55	24	19	3	26	38	.242	.262	.233	3.98	2.84
Santodomingo, Roybell	R-R	6-2	170	5-6-01	1	1	4.01	11	0	0	0	25	20	13	11	1	18	25	.227	.180	.265	9.12	6.57
Torres, Henry	R-R	6-2	175	3-24-98	3	5	7.58	16	4	0	0	30	27	32	25	0	30	31	.248	.225	.261	9.40	9.10
Trinidad, Luis	R-R	6-0	165	5-16-98	4	0	2.73	19	1	0	5	30	12	11	9	1	14	33	.125	.196	.060	10.01	4.25
Urena, Wilfry	R-R	6-1	160	1-20-99	0	0	3.86	14	2	0	1	16	18	10	7	0	23	17	.277	.444	.213	9.37	12.67
Utrera, Joseph	L-L	6-3	185	9-24-99	0	0	27.00	5	0	0	0	3	4	11	10	2	10	2	.333	.333	.333	5.40	27.00
Valeriano, Shuruendy	R-R	6-0	160	2-26-98	6	3	2.38	16	0	0	5	34	22	9	9	1	12	32	.190	.303	.145	8.47	3.18

Fielding

C: Calmes 21, Meza 35, Nelo 13, Perez 1, Rodriguez 25, Sangrona 2, Tejeda 20, Valera 12, Villasmil 3. **1B:** Balbuena 23, Chevez 57, Del Palacio 35, Garcia 1, Meza 1, Perez 16, Santos 10, Valera 6. **2B:** Balbuena 20, Figuereo 59, Garcia 11, Lopez 7, Pereira 1, Ramirez 12, Vargas 36, Verbel 2. **3B:** Arias 36, Balbuena 9, Figuereo 4, Garcia 21, Lopez 42, Pereira 1, Ramirez 7, Verbel 28. **SS:** Arias 27, Figuereo 2, Garcia 10, Lopez 51, Ramirez 46, Vargas 11. **OF:** Arrendoll 51, Bolivar 54, Candelario 51, Castellanos 46, Del Palacio 2, Fortuna 55, Johnson 46, Manzueta 35, Mata 35, Pereira 3, Santos 17, Silvestre 42, Verbel 1.

Texas Rangers

SEASON IN A SENTENCE: At 67-95, not only did the Rangers finish in last place in the American League West, but their .414 winning percentage tied the 2014 club for the franchise's worst mark in the last 30 years.

HIGH POINT: On June 16, the Rangers beat the Rockies, 5-2—the start of a season-long, seven-game winning streak. They proceeded to sweep the Royals and win their next two games in Minnesota. The Rangers finished with a 14-11 record during June, their only month with a winning record.

LOW POINT: From July 1-26, the Rangers went 4-16. That stretch included a two-game sweep at home against the Astros, a three-game sweep in Boston and, finally, a four-game sweep at home against the Athletics—a series in which the Rangers were outscored 41-24.

NOTABLE ROOKIES: There wasn't much impact talent coming up from the farm system. A 23-year-old named Isiah Kiner-Falefa showcased his versatility by playing third base, catcher, second base and even a little shortstop, batting .261/.325/.357 in 111 games. Ronald Guzman managed to tread water at first base, where he provided a big target with his 6-foot-6 frame and ability to drop down into splits, though his .235/.306/.416 batting line was light for the position.

KEY TRANSACTIONS: With the Rangers well out of contention at the trade deadline, they sent veteran lefthander Cole Hamels to the Cubs for righthanders Eddie Butler, Rollie Lacy and a player to be named. A few days later, righthanded reliever Keone Kela was traded to the Pirates, who gave the Rangers lefthander Taylor Hearn and a player to be named. They also sent lefthander Jake Diekman to the D-backs for righthander Wei-Chieh Huang and yet another PTBN. Texas resolved all its PTBN trades by acquiring prospects who had played in the Dominican Summer League.

DOWN ON THE FARM: As rough as things were at the major league level, they weren't much better in the minor leagues. Willie Calhoun looked poised to break through with the major league team but instead struggled at Triple-A. Injuries bit the Rangers hard, erasing the seasons of lefthander Cole Ragans, righthander Kyle Cody and shortstop Chris Seise. Righthander Hans Crouse dominated the lower levels, and the Rangers added a promising Cuban outfielder, Julio Pablo Martinez, for $2.8 million in March.

OPENING DAY PAYROLL: $128,821,249 (17th).

PLAYERS OF THE YEAR

JENNIFER STEWART

JENNIFER STEWART

MAJOR LEAGUE

Mike Minor
LHP
12-8, 4.18 ERA
Led Rangers in SO
(132) and IP (157)

MINOR LEAGUE

Jonathan Hernandez
RHP
(High Class A/Double-A)
8-6, 3.63 ERA
134 SO in 121.1 IP

ORGANIZATION LEADERS

Batting		*Minimum 250 AB
MAJORS		
* AVG	Adrian Beltre	.273
* OPS	Shin-Soo Choo	.810
HR	Joey Gallo	40
RBI	Joey Gallo	92
MINORS		
* AVG	Hanser Alberto, Round Rock	.330
* OBP	Yonny Hernandez, Hickory, Frisco	.374
* SLG	Tommy Joseph, Frisco, Round Rock	.533
* OPS	Tommy Joseph, Frisco, Round Rock	.884
R	Anderson Tejeda, Down East	76
H	Scott Heineman, Frisco, Round Rock	137
TB	Anderson Tejeda, Down East	205
2B	Willie Calhoun, Round Rock	32
3B	Eric Jenkins, Hickory, Down East	7
3B	Leody Taveras, Down East	7
HR	Tommy Joseph, Frisco, Round Rock	21
RBI	Anderson Tejeda, Down East	74
BB	Christian Lopes, Round Rock	68
SO	Anderson Tejeda, Down East	142
SB	Yonny Hernandez, Hickory, Frisco	46

Pitching		#Minimum 75 IP
MAJORS		
W	Mike Minor	12
# ERA	Mike Minor	4.18
SO	Mike Minor	132
SV	Keone Kela	24
MINORS		
W	Tyler Phillips, Hickory, Down East	12
L	Emerson Martinez, Down East	11
# ERA	Tyler Phillips, Hickory, Down East	2.64
G	Reed Garrett, Round Rock, Frisco	51
GS	Emerson Martinez, Down East	24
SV	R.J. Alvarez, Round Rock	24
IP	Emerson Martinez, Down East	137
BB	Jonathan Hernandez, Down East, Frisco	53
SO	A.J. Alexy, Hickory	138
# AVG	Jonathan Hernandez, Down East, Frisco	.218

2018 PERFORMANCE

General Manager: Jon Daniels. **Farm Director:** Jayce Tingler. **Scouting Director:** Kip Fagg.

Class	Team	League	W	L	PCT	Finish	Manager
Majors	Texas Rangers	American	67	95	.414	11th (15)	Jeff Banister
Triple-A	Round Rock Express	Pacific Coast	65	73	.471	13th (16)	Jason Wood
Double-A	Frisco Roughriders	Texas	60	80	.429	8th (xx)	Joe Mikulik
High A	Down East Wood Ducks	Carolina	59	81	.421	10th (10)	Spike Owen
Low A	Hickory Crawdads	South Atlantic	70	68	.507	7th (12)	Matt Hagen
Short season	Spokane Indians	Northwest	38	38	.500	t3rd (8)	Kenny Holmberg
Rookie	AZL Rangers	Arizona	28	27	.509	11th (18)	Matt Siegel
Overall 2018 Minor League Record			320	367	.466	25th (30)	

ORGANIZATION STATISTICS

TEXAS RANGERS
AMERICAN LEAGUE

Batting	B-T	HT	WT	DOB	AVG	vLH	vRH	G	AB	R	H	2B	3B	HR	RBI	BB	HBP	SH	SF	SO	SB	CS	SLG	OBP
Alberto, Hanser	R-R	5-11	215	10-17-92	.185	.300	.118	13	27	0	5	2	0	0	0	2	0	1	0	4	0	1	.259	.241
Andrus, Elvis	R-R	6-0	200	8-26-88	.256	.252	.257	97	395	53	101	20	3	6	33	28	3	0	2	66	5	3	.367	.308
Beltre, Adrian	R-R	5-11	220	4-7-79	.273	.254	.281	119	433	49	118	23	1	15	65	34	6	0	8	96	1	0	.434	.329
Calhoun, Willie	L-R	5-8	187	11-4-94	.222	.167	.246	35	99	8	22	5	0	2	11	6	1	0	2	24	0	0	.333	.269
Centeno, Juan	L-R	5-9	195	11-16-89	.162	.333	.147	10	37	3	6	1	0	1	3	1	0	0	0	7	0	0	.270	.184
Chirinos, Robinson	R-R	6-1	210	6-5-84	.222	.226	.221	113	360	48	80	15	1	18	65	45	19	0	2	140	2	0	.419	.338
Choo, Shin-Soo	L-L	5-11	210	7-13-82	.264	.221	.285	146	560	83	148	30	1	21	62	92	10	1	2	156	6	1	.434	.377
DeShields, Delino	R-R	5-9	200	8-16-92	.216	.248	.199	106	334	52	72	14	1	2	22	43	3	12	1	83	20	4	.281	.310
Gallo, Joey	L-R	6-5	235	11-19-93	.206	.210	.204	148	500	82	103	24	1	40	92	74	3	0	0	207	3	4	.498	.312
Guzman, Ronald	L-L	6-5	225	10-20-94	.235	.208	.245	123	387	46	91	18	2	16	58	33	7	0	1	121	1	0	.416	.306
Kiner-Falefa, Isiah	R-R	5-10	176	3-23-95	.261	.288	.248	111	356	43	93	18	2	4	34	28	6	5	1	62	7	5	.357	.325
Mazara, Nomar	L-L	6-4	215	4-26-95	.258	.240	.268	128	489	61	126	25	1	20	77	40	4	0	3	116	1	0	.436	.317
Nunez, Renato	R-R	6-1	220	4-4-94	.167	.177	.158	13	36	2	6	1	0	1	2	3	1	0	1	12	0	0	.278	.244
2-team total (60 Baltimore)					.259	.247	.265	73	236	28	61	14	0	8	22	19	4	0	2	62	0	0	.420	.322
Odor, Rougned	L-R	5-11	195	2-3-94	.253	.257	.251	129	474	76	120	23	2	18	63	43	11	2	5	127	12	12	.424	.327
Perez, Carlos	R-R	6-0	210	10-27-90	.143	.056	.194	20	49	1	7	2	0	1	3	1	1	2	0	15	1	0	.245	.177
Profar, Jurickson	B-R	6-0	190	2-20-93	.254	.270	.247	146	524	82	133	35	6	20	77	54	12	0	4	88	10	0	.458	.335
Robinson, Drew	L-R	6-1	200	4-20-92	.184	.267	.170	47	109	20	20	3	0	3	9	16	0	0	0	57	2	1	.294	.288
Rua, Ryan	R-R	6-2	205	3-11-90	.194	.212	.178	61	139	17	27	3	1	6	12	5	0	2	1	53	3	1	.360	.221
Tocci, Carlos	R-R	6-2	160	8-23-95	.225	.271	.194	65	120	11	27	3	2	0	5	7	1	6	1	39	0	3	.283	.271
Trevino, Jose	R-R	5-11	211	11-28-92	.250	.250	.250	3	8	0	2	0	0	0	3	0	0	0	0	1	0	0	.250	.250

Pitching	B-T	HT	WT	DOB	W	L	ERA	G	GS	CG	SV	IP	H	R	ER	HR	BB	SO	AVG	vLH	vRH	K/9	BB/9
Barnette, Tony	R-R	6-1	190	11-9-83	2	0	2.39	22	0	0	0	26	19	11	7	2	5	26	.196	.167	.209	8.89	1.71
Bibens-Dirkx, Austin	R-R	6-1	210	4-29-85	2	3	6.20	13	6	0	0	45	56	33	31	9	14	33	.308	.301	.313	6.60	2.80
Bush, Matt	R-R	5-9	180	2-8-86	0	0	4.70	21	0	0	0	23	23	13	12	3	14	19	.256	.192	.281	7.43	5.48
Butler, Eddie	R-R	6-2	180	3-13-91	1	2	6.47	22	0	0	2	32	43	24	23	10	12	18	.316	.298	.326	5.06	3.38
Chavez, Jesse	R-R	6-2	175	8-21-83	3	1	3.51	30	0	0	1	56	58	23	22	10	12	50	.262	.274	.257	7.99	1.92
Claudio, Alex	L-L	6-3	180	1-31-92	4	2	4.48	66	1	0	1	68	91	35	34	4	13	41	.329	.244	.369	5.40	1.71
Colon, Bartolo	R-R	5-11	285	5-24-73	7	12	5.78	28	24	1	0	146	172	97	94	32	25	81	.291	.270	.308	4.98	1.54
Curtis, Zac	L-L	5-9	190	7-4-92	0	1	9.45	8	0	0	0	7	8	7	7	1	9	8	.250	.500	.200	10.80	12.15
Diekman, Jake	L-L	6-4	200	1-21-87	1	1	3.69	47	0	0	2	39	31	18	16	2	23	48	.215	.273	.190	11.08	5.31
Fister, Doug	L-R	6-8	210	2-4-84	1	7	4.50	12	12	0	0	66	73	40	33	11	19	40	.278	.246	.303	5.45	2.59
Gallardo, Yovani	R-R	6-2	205	2-27-86	8	8	5.77	18	18	0	0	92	99	60	59	13	43	56	.279	.241	.314	5.48	4.21
Gardewine, Nick	R-R	6-1	179	8-15-93	0	0	3.60	3	0	0	0	5	7	2	2	0	0	4	.333	.200	.375	7.20	0.00
Gearrin, Cory	R-R	6-1	205	4-14-86	1	0	2.53	21	0	0	0	21	13	6	6	2	6	20	.176	.039	.250	8.44	2.53
2-team total (6 Oakland)					1	0	3.29	27	0	0	0	27	23	10	10	2	8	22	.230	.128	.295	7.24	2.63
Hamels, Cole	L-L	6-4	205	12-27-83	5	9	4.72	20	20	0	0	114	115	70	60	23	42	114	.258	.290	.253	8.97	3.31
Hutchison, Drew	L-R	6-3	205	8-22-90	1	1	8.86	5	5	0	0	21	29	21	21	5	13	12	.333	.300	.362	5.06	5.48
Jepsen, Kevin	R-R	6-3	235	7-26-84	0	3	5.94	21	0	0	0	17	15	13	11	4	11	8	.238	.167	.255	4.32	5.94
Jurado, Ariel	R-R	6-1	180	1-30-96	5	5	5.93	12	8	0	0	55	66	36	36	7	18	22	.297	.365	.246	3.62	2.96
Kela, Keone	R-R	6-1	215	4-16-93	3	3	3.44	38	0	0	24	37	28	14	14	3	14	44	.206	.321	.125	10.80	3.44
Leclerc, Jose	R-R	6-0	190	12-19-93	2	3	1.56	59	0	0	12	58	24	16	10	1	25	85	.126	.114	.132	13.27	3.90
Mann, Brandon	L-L	6-2	200	5-16-84	0	0	5.40	7	0	0	0	8	7	5	5	1	4	3	.250	.000	.304	3.24	4.32
Martin, Chris	R-R	6-8	215	6-2-86	1	5	4.54	46	0	0	0	42	46	21	21	5	5	37	.274	.273	.274	7.99	1.08
Mendez, Yohander	L-L	6-5	200	1-17-95	2	2	5.53	8	5	0	0	28	28	18	17	4	15	18	.264	.364	.238	5.86	4.88
Minor, Mike	R-L	6-4	210	12-26-87	12	8	4.18	28	28	0	0	157	138	76	73	25	38	132	.235	.259	.230	7.57	2.18
Moore, Matt	L-L	6-3	210	6-18-89	3	8	6.79	39	12	0	0	102	128	82	77	19	41	86	.305	.304	.305	7.59	3.62
Pelham, C.D.	L-L	6-6	235	2-21-95	0	0	7.04	10	0	0	0	6	6	6	4	0	7	2	.353	.429	.300	8.22	4.70
Perez, Martin	L-L	6-0	200	4-4-91	2	7	6.22	22	15	0	0	85	116	68	59	16	36	52	.329	.271	.347	5.48	3.80
Rodriguez, Ricardo	R-R	6-2	220	8-31-92	0	0	4.05	4	0	0	0	7	11	3	3	0	1	3	.367	.500	.278	4.05	1.35
Sadzeck, Connor	R-R	6-7	240	10-1-91	0	0	0.96	13	2	0	0	9	6	2	1	0	11	7	.182	.091	.227	6.75	10.61
Sampson, Adrian	R-R	6-2	210	10-7-91	0	3	4.30	5	4	0	0	23	24	13	11	6	4	15	.270	.226	.333	5.87	1.57
Springs, Jeffrey	L-L	6-3	180	9-20-92	1	1	3.38	18	2	0	0	32	32	14	12	4	14	31	.256	.324	.231	8.72	3.94

Fielding

Catcher	PCT	G	PO	A	E	DP	PB
Centeno	1.000	10	67	0	0	0	1
Chirinos	.996	108	719	31	3	4	5
Kiner-Falefa	.996	35	227	15	1	2	4
Perez	.992	19	123	8	1	1	3
Trevino	1.000	3	15	0	0	0	0

First Base	PCT	G	PO	A	E	DP
Gallo	.996	35	248	15	1	29
Guzman	.994	117	909	54	6	102
Profar	1.000	24	201	7	0	23
Rua	1.000	7	33	2	0	3

Second Base	PCT	G	PO	A	E	DP
Alberto	1.000	4	6	8	0	3

Second Base (cont.)	PCT	G	PO	A	E	DP
Kiner-Falefa	.979	20	40	53	2	15
Odor	.984	127	218	336	9	96
Profar	.978	10	18	27	1	13
Robinson	.972	8	11	24	1	5

Third Base	PCT	G	PO	A	E	DP
Alberto	1.000	3	0	2	0	0
Beltre	.952	70	53	145	10	14
Kiner-Falefa	.960	46	23	98	5	8
Nunez	.821	8	3	20	5	4
Profar	.919	51	39	85	11	9
Robinson	1.000	3	0	1	0	0

Shortstop	PCT	G	PO	A	E	DP
Alberto	.944	5	7	10	1	3
Andrus	.973	97	139	263	11	77

Shortstop (cont.)	PCT	G	PO	A	E	DP
Kiner-Falefa	.923	2	6	6	1	3
Profar	.940	68	57	148	13	29
Robinson	.500	1	0	1	1	0

Outfield	PCT	G	PO	A	E	DP
Calhoun	.950	27	37	1	2	0
Choo	.964	59	105	2	4	0
DeShields	.976	102	275	6	7	2
Gallo	.990	108	194	8	2	1
Mazara	.991	115	216	7	2	0
Nunez	1.000	4	5	0	0	0
Profar	.000	1	0	0	0	0
Robinson	.970	30	63	2	2	0
Rua	1.000	45	69	2	0	0
Tocci	.991	61	111	1	1	0

ROUND ROCK EXPRESS

PACIFIC COAST LEAGUE

TRIPLE-A

Batting	B-T	HT	WT	DOB	AVG	vLH	vRH	G	AB	R	H	2B	3B	HR	RBI	BB	HBP	SH	SF	SO	SB	CS	SLG	OBP
Alberto, Hanser	R-R	5-11	215	10-17-92	.330	.275	.345	101	361	45	119	17	3	7	58	9	3	5	6	28	0	3	.452	.346
Andrus, Elvis	R-R	6-0	200	8-26-88	.000	.000	.000	2	6	0	0	0	0	0	0	0	0	0	0	1	0	0	.000	.250
Calhoun, Willie	L-R	5-8	187	11-4-94	.294	.266	.302	108	432	66	127	32	0	9	47	32	6	0	0	47	4	0	.431	.351
Cardona, Jose	R-R	6-1	175	3-16-94	.228	.222	.229	47	171	20	39	2	0	3	13	6	2	0	2	33	4	4	.292	.260
Centeno, Juan	L-R	5-9	195	11-16-89	.234	.233	.235	59	205	27	48	9	0	2	27	16	2	5	4	34	0	1	.307	.291
Cole, Hunter	R-R	6-1	190	10-3-92	.264	.333	.243	47	178	32	47	7	0	8	19	11	0	0	1	53	0	1	.438	.305
DeShields, Delino	R-R	5-9	200	8-16-92	.167	.000	.182	3	12	1	2	0	0	0	0	0	0	0	0	4	1	0	.167	.167
Garay, Carlos	R-R	6-0	210	10-5-94	.100	.200	.000	3	10	0	1	0	0	0	0	0	0	0	0	3	0	0	.100	.100
Guzman, Ronald	L-L	6-5	225	10-20-94	.412	.333	.429	5	17	5	7	2	0	1	4	0	0	0	0	4	0	0	.529	.524
Heineman, Scott	R-R	6-1	215	12-4-92	.295	.261	.304	107	424	68	125	20	2	11	57	32	9	1	3	93	16	8	.429	.355
Hood, Destin	R-R	6-2	205	4-3-90	.217	.095	.239	41	138	16	30	5	0	4	20	7	2	0	3	42	2	1	.341	.260
Ibanez, Andy	R-R	5-10	170	4-3-93	.283	.263	.289	125	463	62	131	21	1	12	55	40	5	3	4	74	1	6	.410	.344
Inoa, Cristian	R-R	5-10	165	7-4-99	.000	.000	.000	2	5	0	0	0	0	0	0	1	0	0	0	2	0	0	.000	.167
Joseph, Tommy	R-R	6-1	255	7-16-91	.284	.389	.253	84	317	47	90	21	0	21	67	28	8	0	4	77	0	0	.549	.353
Kiner-Falefa, Isiah	R-R	5-10	176	3-23-95	.200	.000	.214	5	15	2	3	0	0	0	1	3	0	0	0	3	1	0	.200	.333
Lopes, Christian	R-R	6-0	185	10-1-92	.261	.255	.263	123	429	62	112	21	3	12	52	68	5	1	5	74	16	9	.408	.365
Matta, Shaq	B-R	5-8	175		.000	.000	.000	2	3	1	0	0	0	0	0	0	0	0	0	1	0	0	.000	.000
Mazara, Nomar	L-L	6-4	215	4-26-95	.417	.500	.333	4	12	1	5	0	0	0	2	0	0	0	0	2	0	0	.417	.417
Mendez, Luis	B-R	5-10	188	1-1-93	.333	.333	.333	2	6	0	2	0	1	0	2	0	0	1	0	0	0	0	.667	.333
Noonan, Nick	L-R	6-1	185	5-4-89	.256	.320	.241	75	270	34	69	11	3	4	35	13	3	2	0	70	2	1	.363	.297
O'Neill, Michael	R-R	6-1	195	6-12-92	.182	.400	.118	6	22	3	4	3	0	0	1	2	0	0	0	8	0	0	.318	.250
Odor, Rougned	L-R	5-11	195	2-3-94	.167	.333	.111	3	12	1	2	0	0	0	1	0	0	0	0	4	0	0	.167	.231
Pennington, Cliff	B-R	5-11	195	6-15-84	.204	.346	.155	61	216	26	44	12	1	1	13	30	1	1	2	54	4	1	.282	.301
Perez, Carlos	R-R	6-0	210	10-27-90	.317	.316	.317	22	79	10	25	2	0	4	13	7	0	0	1	12	0	0	.494	.368
Plouffe, Trevor	R-R	6-2	215	6-15-86	.273	—	.273	4	11	4	3	1	0	1	2	6	0	0	0	4	1	0	.636	.529
Robinson, Drew	L-R	6-1	200	4-20-92	.303	.268	.316	53	211	40	64	16	5	10	28	27	0	1	2	84	5	6	.569	.379
Rollin, Franklin	R-R	5-11	165	8-26-95	.235	.118	.275	19	68	8	16	4	0	1	5	4	1	1	0	9	2	4	.338	.288
Rua, Ryan	R-R	6-2	205	3-11-90	.236	.177	.255	18	72	12	17	5	1	3	17	7	3	0	1	22	4	0	.458	.325
Rupp, Cameron	R-R	6-2	260	9-28-88	.274	.316	.266	32	113	15	31	6	0	8	26	13	1	0	3	45	0	0	.540	.346
2-team total (33 Tacoma)					.247	.222	.254	65	223	30	55	11	1	12	38	31	1	0	3	75	0	0	.466	.337
Sanchez, Tony	R-R	5-11	220	5-20-88	.300	.263	.313	62	220	28	66	11	1	7	31	17	2	1	2	54	0	0	.455	.353
Tocci, Carlos	R-R	6-2	160	8-23-95	.214	.100	.278	8	28	3	6	2	0	0	3	2	0	0	0	5	0	0	.286	.267
Torres, Nick	R-R	6-1	220	6-30-93	.195	.259	.176	35	118	7	23	2	0	0	10	4	2	0	1	37	1	0	.212	.232

Pitching	B-T	HT	WT	DOB	W	L	ERA	G	GS	CG	SV	IP	H	R	ER	HR	BB	SO	AVG	vLH	vRH	K/9	BB/9
Alvarez, R.J.	R-R	6-2	225	6-8-91	4	4	3.68	45	0	0	24	44	40	21	18	2	18	44	.247	.241	.250	9.00	3.68
Bibens-Dirkx, Austin	R-R	6-1	210	4-29-85	3	6	5.68	17	15	1	0	82	94	59	52	14	28	79	.283	.321	.259	8.64	3.06
Bush, Matt	R-R	5-9	180	2-8-86	1	1	2.00	8	0	0	0	9	9	2	2	0	4	14	.265	.188	.333	14.00	4.00
Curtis, Zac	L-L	5-9	190	7-4-92	1	0	4.00	9	0	0	0	9	5	4	4	1	6	12	.161	.125	.200	12.00	6.00
Delabar, Steve	R-R	6-5	215	7-17-83	0	0	4.76	5	0	0	0	6	5	5	3	0	5	3	.227	.375	.143	4.76	7.94
Espino, Paolo	R-R	5-10	215	1-10-87	0	0	15.00	3	0	0	0	6	10	11	10	2	4	6	.370	.600	.235	9.00	6.00
2-team total (19 Colorado Springs)					4	5	5.85	22	10	0	0	60	72	42	39	9	26	58	.301	.370	.266	8.70	3.90
Feigl, Brady	R-L	6-4	195	12-27-90	5	1	2.13	31	0	0	2	42	42	12	10	0	11	25	.268	.263	.270	5.31	2.34
Gallardo, Yovani	R-R	6-2	205	2-27-86	2	1	3.81	10	10	0	0	50	49	24	21	1	14	40	.262	.179	.333	7.25	2.54
Gardewine, Nick	R-R	6-1	179	8-15-93	2	1	7.30	12	0	0	1	12	15	11	10	1	7	17	.306	.263	.333	12.41	5.11
Garrett, Reed	R-R	6-2	210	1-2-93	1	1	2.84	16	0	0	5	19	25	14	6	1	6	15	.309	.310	.308	7.11	2.84
Guerra, Deolis	R-R	6-5	245	4-17-89	2	2	3.79	40	4	0	2	59	47	26	25	5	14	71	.216	.188	.233	10.77	2.43
Hurlbut, David	L-L	6-3	221	11-24-89	4	6	5.72	18	17	0	0	85	116	54	54	13	24	61	.327	.340	.322	6.46	2.54
Jensen, Chris	R-R	6-4	200	9-30-90	1	2	4.94	15	5	0	0	47	56	29	26	5	23	28	.301	.317	.289	5.32	4.37
2-team total (5 Albuquerque)					1	2	5.54	20	7	0	0	65	80	43	40	8	33	43	.309	.339	.284	5.95	4.57
Jones, James	L-L	6-4	200	9-24-88	0	0	10.29	5	0	0	0	7	11	8	8	2	5	2	.379	.429	.364	2.57	6.43
Leclerc, Jose	R-R	6-0	190	12-19-93	0	1	7.71	4	0	0	1	5	3	4	4	0	5	9	.177	.000	.250	17.36	9.64
Ledbetter, David	L-R	5-11	190	2-13-92	8	8	6.09	8	8	0	0	44	48	31	30	6	15	31	.279	.313	.259	6.29	3.05
Lincecum, Tim	L-R	5-11	170	6-15-84	1	1	5.68	10	0	0	0	13	14	12	8	2	9	10	.280	.273	.286	7.11	6.39

PITCHING (cont.)	B-T	HT	WT	DOB	W	L	ERA	G	GS	CG	SV	IP	H	R	ER	BB	SO	AVG	vLH	vRH	K/9	BB/9
Loewen, Adam	L-L	6-6	245	4-9-84	0	1	1.80	5	0	0	0	5	5	2	1	1	4	4	.250	.000	.385	7.20	7.20
Mann, Brandon	L-L	6-2	200	5-16-84	4	1	2.41	36	1	0	0	52	37	18	14	2	24	45	.195	.261	.157	7.74	4.13
Martin, Chris	R-R	6-8	215	6-2-86	0	0	0.00	1	0	0	0	1	2	0	0	0	0	1	.500	.667	.000	9.00	0.00
McGuire, Deck	R-R	6-6	220	6-23-89	0	0	27.00	1	0	0	0	2	5	5	5	1	4	0	.556	.500	.600	0.00	21.60
2-team total (6 Salt Lake)					1	1	7.82	7	3	0	0	13	14	11	11	3	9	10	.286	.188	.333	7.11	6.39
Mendez, Yohander	L-L	6-5	200	1-17-95	0	7	5.25	12	12	0	0	58	65	39	34	13	24	50	.286	.262	.295	7.71	3.70
Pena, Richelson	R-R	6-1	170	9-29-93	4	2	4.65	11	7	0	0	50	69	28	26	5	9	37	.322	.279	.352	6.62	1.61
Perez, Martin	L-L	6-0	200	4-4-91	1	0	1.42	1	1	0	0	6	6	1	1	1	0	6	.250	.222	.267	8.53	0.00
Rodriguez, Ricardo	R-R	6-2	220	8-31-92	1	2	2.45	22	0	0	3	26	20	8	7	1	4	27	.213	.209	.216	9.47	1.40
Roth, Michael	L-L	6-1	210	2-15-90	5	5	4.90	14	13	0	0	72	95	47	39	10	23	38	.329	.346	.322	4.77	2.89
2-team total (7 Iowa)					6	7	4.35	21	18	0	0	101	122	60	49	12	38	61	.312	.306	.314	5.42	3.38
Rowley, Chris	R-R	6-2	195	8-14-90	2	3	3.46	7	7	0	0	42	40	18	16	2	16	33	.252	.222	.276	7.13	3.46
Sadzeck, Connor	R-R	6-7	240	10-1-91	5	3	4.03	32	0	0	0	38	36	22	17	2	16	43	.254	.304	.221	10.18	3.79
Sampson, Adrian	R-R	6-2	210	10-7-91	8	4	3.77	33	19	0	0	127	137	61	53	12	24	85	.274	.214	.321	6.04	1.71
Scott, Tayler	R-R	6-3	185	6-1-92	5	5	3.26	44	0	0	1	61	60	25	22	4	25	52	.266	.259	.269	7.71	3.71
Springs, Jeffrey	L-L	6-3	180	9-20-92	1	2	2.79	13	0	0	1	19	12	6	6	0	12	30	.182	.158	.192	13.97	5.59
Tillman, Chris	R-R	6-5	200	4-15-88	0	1	9.00	4	4	0	0	9	11	10	9	1	8	5	.314	.357	.286	5.00	8.00
Vivas, Samir	R-R	5-11	170	2-1-95	1	0	1.50	2	0	0	0	6	5	1	1	0	3	7	.217	.222	.214	10.50	4.50
Wagner, Tyler	R-R	6-3	205	1-24-91	1	6	5.19	22	15	1	0	85	105	57	49	12	31	45	.309	.311	.308	4.76	3.28

Fielding

Catcher	PCT	G	PO	A	E	DP	PB
Centeno	.991	45	280	36	3	6	12
Garay	1.000	3	14	2	0	0	0
Kiner-Falefa	1.000	3	16	2	0	0	0
Perez	.989	10	79	7	1	1	1
Rupp	.992	30	243	19	2	1	4
Sanchez	.995	50	343	32	2	2	1

First Base	PCT	G	PO	A	E	DP
Alberto	.992	43	337	17	3	46
Cole	.875	1	7	0	1	0
Guzman	1.000	5	45	4	0	4
Hood	.979	4	47	0	1	7
Joseph	.989	71	613	32	7	55
Perez	1.000	2	13	0	0	0
Plouffe	1.000	1	11	0	0	2
Rua	1.000	4	34	4	0	4
Torres	1.000	11	86	3	0	11

Second Base	PCT	G	PO	A	E	DP
Alberto	1.000	9	14	29	0	5
Ibanez	.973	25	50	59	3	18

	PCT	G	PO	A	E	DP
Inoa	1.000	2	3	7	0	2
Kiner-Falefa	1.000	1	2	2	0	0
Lopes	.970	76	141	187	10	56
Matta	1.000	2	1	2	0	1
Mendez	.909	2	7	3	1	1
Noonan	.985	14	29	37	1	8
Odor	.857	2	1	11	2	1
Pennington	1.000	5	12	12	0	5
Robinson	1.000	4	11	19	0	4
Rua	1.000	1	2	2	0	0

Third Base	PCT	G	PO	A	E	DP
Alberto	.857	3	1	5	1	1
Ibanez	.973	91	66	183	7	22
Lopes	.886	17	6	33	5	3
Noonan	.951	24	13	45	3	6
Plouffe	.875	3	2	5	1	0

Shortstop	PCT	G	PO	A	E	DP
Alberto	.967	44	66	138	7	28
Andrus	1.000	1	3	1	0	0
Kiner-Falefa	1.000	1	1	2	0	1
Lopes	.907	9	12	27	4	7

	PCT	G	PO	A	E	DP
Noonan	.984	34	41	86	2	21
Pennington	.978	54	67	154	5	31

Outfield	PCT	G	PO	A	E	DP
Alberto	1.000	2	5	0	0	0
Calhoun	.978	91	131	5	3	0
Cardona	.989	43	84	4	1	1
Cole	1.000	39	87	2	0	1
DeShields	1.000	3	8	0	0	0
Feigl	.000	1	0	0	0	0
Heineman	.973	104	210	8	6	2
Hood	.969	23	28	3	1	0
Jones	1.000	1	1	0	0	0
Lopes	1.000	13	36	1	0	0
Mazara	1.000	2	1	0	0	0
O'Neill	1.000	5	10	2	0	1
Robinson	.992	44	118	6	1	1
Rollin	1.000	19	33	4	0	0
Rua	.960	10	23	1	1	0
Sanchez	.000	1	0	0	0	0
Scott	.000	1	0	0	0	0
Tocci	1.000	7	13	0	0	0
Torres	.979	20	44	3	1	0

FRISCO ROUGHRIDERS

DOUBLE-A

TEXAS LEAGUE

Batting	B-T	HT	WT	DOB	AVG	vLH	vRH	G	AB	R	H	2B	3B	HR	RBI	BB	HBP	SH	SF	SO	SB	CS	SLG	OBP
Alvarez, Eliezer	L-R	5-11	165	10-15-94	.228	.170	.245	108	408	68	93	17	6	12	43	42	2	4	3	124	26	2	.387	.301
Andrus, Elvis	R-R	6-0	200	8-26-88	.056	.250	.000	5	18	1	1	0	0	0	1	0	0	0	0	2	0	0	.056	.105
Beck, Preston	L-R	6-2	190	10-26-90	.260	.245	.264	122	442	58	115	21	3	13	53	38	7	0	1	94	0	3	.410	.328
Cardona, Jose	R-R	6-1	175	9-4-91	.268	.186	.291	54	194	28	52	8	0	5	16	22	3	0	2	33	9	4	.387	.348
Cole, Hunter	R-R	6-1	190	10-3-92	.330	.281	.353	53	200	27	66	9	2	8	28	29	1	0	3	55	1	2	.515	.412
De Leon, Michael	B-R	6-1	160	1-14-97	.262	.203	.281	135	503	54	132	21	0	4	49	21	4	4	6	69	1	1	.328	.295
DeShields, Delino	R-R	5-9	200	8-16-92	.278	.286	.273	7	18	2	5	0	0	0	0	0	0	0	0	2	2	2	.278	.500
Garay, Carlos	R-R	6-0	210	10-5-94	.313	.300	.316	56	208	23	65	12	0	2	21	8	1	1	0	23	0	1	.399	.341
Heineman, Scott	R-R	6-1	215	12-4-92	.522	.750	.474	7	23	6	12	2	0	1	10	7	0	0	1	5	2	1	.739	.613
Hernandez, Yonny	B-R	5-9	171	5-4-98	.273	.333	.200	4	11	3	3	0	0	0	1	4	0	1	0	3	2	0	.273	.438
Hood, Destin	R-R	6-2	205	4-3-90	.225	.326	.201	71	240	30	54	10	2	11	36	18	2	0	3	79	3	2	.421	.281
Inoa, Cristian	R-R	5-10	165	7-4-99	.143	.000	.167	3	7	0	1	0	0	0	0	1	0	0	0	1	0	0	.143	.250
Joseph, Tommy	R-R	6-1	255	7-16-91	.286	.200	.304	7	28	2	8	2	0	0	3	2	0	0	1	5	0	0	.357	.323
La O, Luis Yander	R-R	6-0	178	12-9-91	.290	.269	.297	77	286	31	83	9	2	3	43	17	3	0	4	45	6	4	.367	.332
Marte, Luis	R-R	6-1	188	12-15-93	.223	.186	.246	31	112	9	25	6	0	1	6	0	0	1	0	24	1	2	.304	.223
Mazara, Nomar	L-L	6-4	215	4-26-95	.125	.000	.143	2	8	0	1	0	0	0	0	0	0	0	0	4	0	0	.125	.125
Mendez, Luis	B-L	5-10	188	1-1-93	.242	.189	.259	75	227	31	55	11	0	5	35	24	2	2	2	52	4	2	.357	.318
Moorman, Chuck	R-R	5-11	200	1-9-94	.191	.250	.162	49	157	9	30	7	1	3	12	20	0	1	1	61	0	1	.306	.281
Morgan, Josh	R-R	5-11	185	11-16-95	.231	.279	.219	79	294	30	68	14	1	3	30	27	5	0	6	49	1	1	.316	.301
Noonan, Nick	L-R	6-1	185	5-4-89	.375	.500	.357	4	16	1	6	3	0	0	2	0	0	1	0	5	0	0	.563	.421
O'Banion, Austin	R-R	6-3	215	7-12-95	.188	.111	.286	4	16	2	3	0	0	0	1	1	0	0	0	7	0	0	.188	.235
O'Neill, Michael	R-R	6-1	195	6-12-92	.255	.265	.251	121	440	63	112	23	2	12	39	41	8	5	4	119	31	6	.398	.327
Odor, Rougned	L-R	5-11	190	2-3-94	.200	.500	.000	2	5	0	1	1	0	0	1	0	0	0	0	0	0	0	.400	.333
Perez, Carlos	R-R	6-0	210	10-27-90	.250	.000	.286	4	16	3	4	2	0	2	5	2	0	0	0	5	0	0	.750	.333
Perez, Yanio	R-R	6-2	205	8-10-95	.227	.250	.222	13	44	8	10	1	0	0	5	7	1	0	0	15	0	0	.250	.346
Prime, Correlle	R-R	6-5	222	2-18-94	.257	.333	.215	41	144	17	37	9	0	5	17	11	1	0	1	55	1	1	.424	.312
Profar, Juremi	R-R	6-1	185	1-30-96	.232	.286	.219	98	349	37	81	12	0	10	51	24	2	0	3	46	1	4	.352	.283

Batting	B-T	HT	WT	DOB	AVG	vLH	vRH	G	AB	R	H	2B	3B	HR	RBI	BB	HBP	SH	SF	SO	SB	CS	SLG	OBP
Robinson, Drew	L-R	6-1	200	4-20-92	.125	.000	.500	2	8	2	1	0	0	1	4	1	0	0	0	5	1	0	.500	.222
Rollin, Franklin	R-R	5-11	165	8-26-95	.303	.000	.333	10	33	5	10	3	1	1	5	2	1	0	0	8	3	0	.546	.361
Rua, Ryan	R-R	6-2	205	3-11-90	.250	.000	.333	3	8	1	2	0	0	0	1	1	0	0	0	2	0	0	.250	.333
Tocci, Carlos	R-R	6-2	160	8-23-95	.318	.200	.353	7	22	4	7	0	1	0	1	4	0	0	1	5	3	1	.409	.407
Trevino, Jose	R-R	5-11	211	11-28-92	.234	.264	.221	46	184	18	43	7	1	3	16	13	1	0	3	27	0	1	.332	.284

Pitching	B-T	HT	WT	DOB	W	L	ERA	G	GS	CG	SV	IP	H	R	ER	HR	BB	SO	AVG	vLH	vRH	K/9	BB/9
Arredondo, Edgar	R-R	6-3	190	5-16-97	0	4	4.80	9	8	0	1	45	50	24	24	4	10	27	.286	.275	.293	5.40	2.00
Barnette, Tony	R-R	6-1	190	11-9-83	0	0	0.00	3	0	0	0	4	4	0	0	0	0	1	.286	.250	.300	2.25	0.00
Benjamin, Wes	R-L	6-1	180	7-26-93	5	6	3.62	15	0	0	0	80	76	32	32	9	23	72	.249	.319	.220	8.13	2.60
Choplick, Adam	L-L	6-9	250	11-18-92	5	1	6.08	29	0	0	0	37	45	28	25	3	22	42	.313	.308	.314	10.22	5.35
Cook, Clayton	R-R	6-3	215	7-23-90	0	0	5.06	5	0	0	0	5	6	4	3	0	6	5	.261	.250	.267	8.44	10.13
Davis, Tyler	R-R	5-10	185	1-5-93	2	7	6.41	31	11	0	3	79	118	61	56	8	25	56	.344	.331	.329	6.41	2.86
Dykstra, James	R-R	6-4	195	11-22-90	0	2	14.85	5	0	0	0	7	16	11	11	2	2	7	.457	.375	.482	9.45	2.70
Fasola, John	R-R	6-2	195	12-12-91	1	2	4.05	21	0	0	1	27	28	14	12	0	11	27	.257	.282	.243	9.11	3.71
Feigl, Brady	R-L	6-4	195	12-27-90	1	0	0.00	11	0	0	2	16	7	0	0	0	4	12	.135	.000	.175	6.61	2.20
Filomeno, Joe	R-L	5-11	235	12-31-92	0	1	9.82	6	0	0	0	7	13	8	8	2	4	8	.382	.167	.429	9.82	4.91
Garrett, Reed	R-R	6-2	210	1-2-93	3	1	1.69	35	0	0	16	43	29	11	8	2	14	46	.204	.173	.222	9.70	2.95
Gose, Anthony	L-L	6-1	190	8-10-90	1	0	6.52	21	0	0	1	19	17	15	14	5	23	18	.243	.154	.296	8.38	10.71
Hearn, Taylor	L-L	6-5	210	8-30-94	1	2	5.04	5	5	0	0	25	29	14	14	5	9	33	.284	.333	.269	11.88	3.24
Hernandez, Jonathan	R-R	6-2	175	7-6-96	4	4	4.92	12	12	0	0	64	58	38	35	6	36	57	.247	.238	.254	8.02	5.06
Huang, Wei-Chieh	R-R	6-1	170	9-26-93	1	1	6.30	9	0	0	0	20	21	14	14	5	8	25	.269	.290	.250	11.25	3.60
Jensen, Chris	R-R	6-4	200	9-30-90	1	0	1.50	1	1	0	0	6	4	1	1	0	2	4	.191	.111	.250	6.00	3.00
Jones, James	L-L	6-4	200	9-24-88	0	0	10.50	1	0	0	0	6	10	8	7	2	3	7	.357	.286	.381	10.50	4.50
Jurado, Ariel	R-R	6-1	180	1-30-96	5	3	3.28	16	16	1	0	102	107	42	37	12	17	58	.272	.291	.261	5.13	1.50
Martin, Brett	L-L	6-4	190	4-28-95	2	10	7.28	29	15	0	0	89	138	78	72	7	29	96	.357	.412	.333	9.71	2.93
Martin, Chris	R-R	6-8	215	6-2-86	0	0	0.00	2	0	0	2	2	0	0	0	0	0	3	.250	.000	.400	13.50	0.00
Mendez, Yohander	L-L	6-5	200	1-17-95	1	1	4.91	6	6	0	0	33	33	19	18	6	10	32	.262	.194	.289	8.73	2.73
Palmquist, Cody	R-R	6-5	190	4-8-94	0	4	7.24	10	0	0	0	14	18	14	11	6	7	13	.333	.539	.268	8.56	4.61
Palumbo, Joe	L-L	6-2	168	10-26-94	1	0	1.93	2	2	0	0	9	6	2	2	0	3	10	.182	.500	.080	9.64	2.89
Parks, Adam	R-R	6-3	220	10-10-92	1	4	4.26	34	0	0	4	44	41	24	21	6	15	47	.237	.257	.223	9.54	3.05
Pelham, C.D.	L-L	6-6	235	2-21-95	2	0	6.16	24	0	0	2	19	20	14	13	1	13	19	.270	.276	.267	9.00	6.16
Pena, Richelson	R-R	6-1	170	9-29-93	4	3	2.43	11	11	1	0	67	64	22	18	7	12	54	.251	.263	.244	7.29	1.62
Perez, Martin	L-L	6-0	200	4-4-91	1	0	0.00	1	1	0	0	6	2	0	0	0	3	4	.095	—	.095	6.00	4.50
Rodriguez, Ricardo	R-R	6-2	220	8-31-92	0	0	3.00	3	0	0	0	3	2	1	1	0	1	1	.200	.200	.200	3.00	0.00
Rowland, Robby	B-R	6-4	215	12-15-91	0	0	9.00	1	0	0	0	2	2	1	0	0	1		.500	.000	.667	9.00	0.00
Slack, Ryne	L-L	6-2	239	7-22-92	2	3	6.84	34	1	0	1	49	56	37	37	8	26	39	.273	.297	.271	7.21	4.81
Springs, Jeffrey	L-L	6-3	180	9-20-92	3	2	4.82	20	0	0	1	37	39	20	20	2	7	68	.269	.292	.258	16.39	1.69
St. John, Locke	L-L	6-3	180	1-31-93	2	0	4.24	11	0	0	0	17	16	8	8	3	8	17	.254	.143	.310	9.00	4.24
Topa, Justin	R-R	6-4	200	3-7-91	2	3	5.71	9	6	0	0	41	53	26	26	4	13	34	.319	.347	.298	7.46	2.85
Vivas, Samir	R-R	5-11	170	2-1-95	1	0	2.25	6	0	0	0	8	6	2	2	0	2	12	.194	.188	.200	13.50	2.25
Wagner, Tyler	R-R	6-3	205	1-24-91	1	1	2.84	3	3	0	0	19	16	7	6	1	4	14	.219	.233	.209	6.63	1.89
Weickel, Walker	R-R	6-5	195	11-14-93	2	1	3.46	5	1	0	0	13	18	7	5	0	4	6	.333	.520	.172	4.15	2.77
Wiles, Collin	R-R	6-4	222	5-30-94	0	1	6.10	4	0	0	0	21	27	14	14	5	5	26	.314	.323	.309	11.32	2.18
Wiper, Cole	R-R	6-4	185	6-3-92	0	3	6.04	17	0	0	1	22	34	20	15	3	12	19	.354	.400	.314	7.66	4.84

Fielding

Catcher	PCT	G	PO	A	E	DP	PB
Garay	.996	31	235	21	1	4	3
Moorman	.992	36	228	21	2	2	1
Morgan	.983	38	333	9	6	1	2
Perez	1.000	4	35	3	0	1	0
Trevino	.997	38	307	28	1	7	2

First Base	PCT	G	PO	A	E	DP
Beck	.996	61	465	26	2	40
Garay	1.000	9	78	4	0	8
Joseph	1.000	3	23	1	0	3
La O	.986	8	68	3	1	7
Moorman	1.000	3	17	0	0	0
Prime	.990	35	288	15	3	38
Profar	.995	29	197	13	1	20

Second Base	PCT	G	PO	A	E	DP
Alvarez	.938	19	27	34	4	6
De Leon	.976	19	30	52	2	17
Hernandez	.947	3	10	8	1	4
Inoa	1.000	3	4	7	0	1
La O	.976	45	67	96	4	25

		PCT	G	PO	A	E	DP
Marte		1.000	1	2	4	0	1
Mendez		.985	18	32	34	1	15
Morgan		.980	26	36	60	2	19
Odor		1.000	1	1	1	0	0
Profar		.975	18	42	36	2	9

Third Base	PCT	G	PO	A	E	DP
De Leon	1.000	12	6	27	0	4
Hernandez	1.000	1	1	0	1	0
La O	.907	15	6	33	4	4
Marte	.971	12	10	24	1	2
Mendez	.969	56	34	89	4	8
Morgan	1.000	2	0	1	0	0
Perez	.893	12	5	20	3	0
Profar	.910	38	23	78	10	8

Shortstop	PCT	G	PO	A	E	DP
Andrus	.923	4	2	10	1	3
De Leon	.978	107	150	286	10	58
Marte	.989	19	32	59	1	14
Mendez	.000	1	0	0	0	0
Morgan	.936	11	16	28	3	7

	PCT	G	PO	A	E	DP
Noonan	.909	4	1	9	1	1

Outfield	PCT	G	PO	A	E	DP
Alvarez	.959	90	152	11	7	4
Beck	.990	47	91	4	1	1
Cardona	.984	52	114	8	2	4
Cole	.988	41	76	7	1	0
DeShields	1.000	5	12	0	0	0
Gose	1.000	5	16	0	0	0
Heineman	1.000	7	15	0	0	0
Hood	.967	45	86	1	3	0
Jones	1.000	2	1	0	0	0
Joseph	.000	1	0	0	0	0
La O	.000	1	0	0	0	0
Mazara	1.000	2	1	0	0	0
O'Banion	1.000	4	7	0	0	0
O'Neill	.990	113	204	4	2	2
Prime	1.000	7	10	0	0	0
Robinson	1.000	1	3	0	0	0
Rollin	1.000	10	22	1	0	0
Rua	1.000	2	3	0	0	0
Tocci	1.000	4	10	0	0	0

DOWN EAST WOOD DUCKS   HIGH CLASS A
CAROLINA LEAGUE

Batting	B-T	HT	WT	DOB	AVG	vLH	vRH	G	AB	R	H	2B	3B	HR	RBI	BB	HBP	SH	SF	SO	SB	CS	SLG	OBP
Altmann, Josh	R-R	6-3	190	7-6-94	.222	.213	.226	106	356	49	79	16	1	20	62	45	13	0	0	90	6	0	.441	.331
Clark, LeDarious	R-R	5-10	185	12-27-93	.227	.203	.239	62	216	37	49	8	2	9	21	43	6	1	2	74	20	4	.407	.367
Cordero, Andretty	R-R	6-1	170	5-3-97	.262	.285	.254	119	450	39	118	27	2	10	57	18	4	0	0	88	1	1	.398	.297

TEXAS RANGERS

Name	B-T	HT	WT	DOB	AVG	vLH	vRH	G	AB	R	H	2B	3B	HR	RBI	BB	HBP	SH	SF	SO	SB	CS	SLG	OBP
Davis, Brendon	R-R	6-4	185	7-28-97	.254	.221	.265	117	406	49	103	23	2	6	40	46	5	2	4	105	6	2	.365	.334
Jenkins, Eric	L-R	6-1	170	1-30-97	.223	.189	.231	85	274	36	61	6	4	1	14	21	2	3	1	79	19	5	.285	.282
Kowalczyk, Alex	R-R	6-3	205	10-17-93	.247	.297	.225	102	364	44	90	20	1	12	44	41	6	0	2	122	5	0	.407	.332
Leblanc, Charles	R-R	6-3	195	6-3-96	.274	.312	.260	131	468	65	128	27	4	10	72	56	2	0	7	120	7	3	.412	.349
Novoa, Melvin	R-R	5-11	224	6-17-96	.184	.167	.190	64	223	15	41	6	0	4	15	7	2	2	2	56	1	0	.265	.214
Perez, Yanio	R-R	6-2	205	8-10-95	.221	.214	.223	43	163	12	36	3	0	4	18	13	1	0	1	41	0	1	.313	.281
Prescott, Blaine	R-R	5-10	175	7-28-95	.221	.167	.241	37	113	23	25	7	0	6	12	9	3	1	1	40	5	0	.443	.294
Rollin, Franklin	R-R	5-11	165	8-26-95	.222	.211	.227	58	189	23	42	6	1	4	13	20	3	1	3	34	4	3	.328	.302
Scott, Preston	R-R	6-2	210	11-15-93	.198	.292	.158	24	81	7	16	2	2	1	12	6	3	0	0	39	1	1	.309	.278
Taveras, Leody	B-R	6-1	190	9-8-98	.246	.247	.245	132	521	65	128	16	7	5	48	51	0	7	1	96	19	11	.332	.312
Tejeda, Anderson	L-R	5-11	185	5-1-98	.259	.172	.292	121	467	76	121	17	5	19	74	49	3	0	3	142	11	4	.439	.331
Valencia, Ricardo	R-R	6-0	185	1-13-93	.245	.170	.281	47	143	21	35	10	0	3	12	16	1	0	3	39	0	0	.378	.319
Whatley, Matt	R-R	6-0	200	1-7-96	.175	.118	.193	45	143	11	25	5	2	2	13	12	4	1	2	48	1	1	.280	.255

Pitching	B-T	HT	WT	DOB	W	L	ERA	G	GS	CG	SV	IP	H	R	ER	HR	BB	SO	AVG	vLH	vRH	K/9	BB/9
Arredondo, Edgar	R-R	6-3	190	5-16-97	5	2	2.88	11	11	0	0	59	53	26	19	5	11	68	.233	.250	.221	10.31	1.67
Bahr, Jason	R-R	6-5	190	2-15-95	2	4	5.80	8	8	0	0	36	42	25	23	4	12	32	.292	.203	.373	8.07	3.03
Bass, Blake	R-R	6-2	250	6-3-93	1	1	2.92	16	0	0	1	25	28	11	8	0	10	21	.283	.292	.275	7.66	3.65
Bolinger, Royce	R-R	6-2	200	8-12-90	1	0	1.54	11	0	0	0	23	14	6	4	3	13	18	.180	.088	.250	6.94	5.01
Bruce, Steven	R-R	6-0	190	3-7-92	5	8	3.05	17	16	1	0	94	83	38	32	11	17	73	.240	.244	.237	6.96	1.62
Eibner, Brett	R-R	6-4	215	12-2-88	0	1	4.15	3	0	0	0	4	5	2	2	0	1	4	.278	.300	.250	8.31	2.08
Ferguson, Tyler	R-R	6-4	225	10-5-93	0	0	0.00	1	0	0	0	1	1	0	0	0	0	1	.333	.500	.000	9.00	1.00
Fontenot, Kaleb	R-R	6-1	180	6-23-93	2	3	3.25	35	1	0	1	69	71	36	25	4	25	58	.264	.236	.288	7.53	3.25
Gose, Anthony	L-L	6-1	190	8-10-90	1	0	1.35	7	0	0	0	7	6	1	1	0	2	6	.250	.400	.211	8.10	2.70
Hernandez, Jonathan	R-R	6-2	175	7-6-96	4	2	2.20	10	10	0	0	57	37	14	14	6	17	77	.184	.171	.195	12.09	2.67
Jones, James	L-L	6-4	200	9-24-88	1	1	5.93	10	0	0	0	14	20	14	9	0	9	10	.345	.250	.395	6.59	5.93
Lacy, Rollie	R-R	6-4	195	7-17-95	1	2	4.45	6	6	0	0	28	26	17	14	1	13	27	.250	.240	.259	8.58	4.13
2-team total (2 Myrtle Beach)					2	3	4.78	8	8	0	0	38	37	23	20	3	17	37	.262	.257	.268	8.84	4.06
Leal, Werner	R-R	6-1	160	7-8-95	1	0	1.80	1	1	0	0	5	3	1	1	1	1	4	.167	.000	.300	7.20	1.80
Lebron, David	R-R	6-0	190	9-7-93	0	0	3.00	3	0	0	0	6	4	2	2	0	1	3	.174	.273	.083	4.50	1.50
Lemoine, Jacob	R-R	6-5	220	11-28-93	3	4	2.40	38	0	0	4	56	48	19	15	6	26	54	.229	.226	.230	8.63	4.15
Martinez, Emerson	R-R	6-0	190	1-11-95	5	11	4.01	24	24	0	0	137	145	74	61	13	32	110	.271	.288	.257	7.23	2.10
Matuella, Michael	R-R	6-6	220	6-3-94	3	5	8.24	20	8	0	2	51	67	54	47	12	21	44	.307	.296	.315	7.71	3.68
Mendez, Sal	R-L	6-4	180	2-25-95	2	3	3.69	15	8	0	1	54	51	24	22	3	23	41	.250	.254	.248	6.88	3.86
Mendez, Yohander	L-L	6-5	200	1-17-95	1	2	3.48	5	1	0	0	31	29	15	12	3	6	27	.254	.177	.288	7.84	1.74
Palumbo, Joe	L-L	6-1	168	10-26-94	1	4	2.67	6	6	0	0	27	24	16	8	3	6	34	.226	.286	.205	11.33	2.00
Pelham, C.D.	L-L	6-6	235	2-21-95	0	0	1.95	23	0	0	11	28	23	9	6	0	13	34	.215	.147	.247	11.06	4.23
Pettibone, Austin	R-R	6-3	180	9-10-92	0	0	0.00	2	0	0	0	4	3	0	0	0	0	4	.200	.200	.200	9.82	0.00
Phillips, Tyler	R-R	6-5	200	10-27-97	1	0	1.80	1	1	0	0	5	2	1	1	0	2	3	.125	.000	.182	5.40	3.60
Rowland, Robby	B-R	6-4	215	12-15-91	1	2	8.40	4	3	0	0	15	24	15	14	0	2	10	.364	.310	.405	6.00	1.20
Shortslef, Jacob	R-R	6-5	235	12-29-94	2	1	4.97	20	0	0	1	29	31	18	16	5	12	32	.274	.275	.275	9.93	3.72
St. John, Locke	L-L	6-3	180	1-31-93	4	3	2.06	29	0	0	3	44	30	14	10	4	15	61	.203	.152	.244	12.57	3.09
Thomas, Tyler	R-L	6-1	175	12-22-95	0	2	2.65	4	3	0	1	17	11	5	5	0	8	13	.186	.167	.195	6.88	4.24
Topa, Justin	R-R	6-4	200	3-7-91	0	1	19.64	1	1	0	0	4	7	8	8	2	1	4	.412	.300	.571	9.82	2.45
Torres, Christian	L-L	6-0	160	9-7-93	5	6	3.36	20	9	0	0	62	65	33	23	3	19	55	.261	.224	.272	8.03	2.77
Vivas, Samir	R-R	5-11	170	2-1-95	0	1	9.95	7	0	0	0	13	14	14	14	5	9	9	.286	.130	.423	6.39	6.39
Weickel, Walker	R-R	6-6	195	11-14-93	2	8	4.92	19	19	0	0	101	100	67	55	12	34	96	.252	.242	.260	8.58	3.04
Wiper, Cole	R-R	6-4	185	6-3-92	2	0	3.83	21	0	0	1	40	47	21	17	2	13	39	.290	.411	.226	8.78	2.93

Fielding

Catcher	PCT	G	PO	A	E	DP	PB
Kowalczyk	.987	37	284	22	4	2	5
Novoa	.985	43	298	23	5	2	6
Valencia	.992	31	241	15	2	1	2
Whatley	.997	38	314	33	1	3	3

First Base	PCT	G	PO	A	E	DP
Altmann	.994	23	164	11	1	14
Cordero	.984	85	703	38	12	67
Leblanc	.978	6	43	2	1	4
Novoa	.971	12	63	4	2	2
Perez	.989	23	169	12	2	22
Valencia	1.000	1	6	0	0	0

Second Base	PCT	G	PO	A	E	DP
Altmann	.975	46	77	122	5	25
Davis	.954	17	24	38	3	17
Leblanc	.958	60	76	153	10	31
Prescott	.967	10	11	18	1	2
Tejeda	.981	12	20	32	1	8

Third Base	PCT	G	PO	A	E	DP
Altmann	1.000	7	4	8	0	0
Cordero	.894	16	11	31	5	5
Davis	.956	60	39	112	7	12
Leblanc	.885	52	37	86	16	4
Perez	.852	10	11	12	4	3

Shortstop	PCT	G	PO	A	E	DP
Davis	.927	36	55	98	12	26
Tejeda	.958	105	150	281	19	52

Outfield	PCT	G	PO	A	E	DP
Altmann	1.000	27	28	1	0	1
Clark	.929	57	74	5	6	0
Gose	1.000	3	12	0	0	0
Jenkins	.986	79	132	5	2	1
Kowalczyk	.917	40	52	3	5	1
Novoa	.000	1	0	0	0	0
Perez	1.000	5	10	3	0	0
Prescott	.944	21	33	1	2	0
Rollin	.990	53	95	6	1	2
Scott	.979	21	43	3	1	0
Taveras	.978	126	292	13	7	3

HICKORY CRAWDADS
SOUTH ATLANTIC LEAGUE

LOW CLASS A

Batting	B-T	HT	WT	DOB	AVG	vLH	vRH	G	AB	R	H	2B	3B	HR	RBI	BB	HBP	SH	SF	SO	SB	CS	SLG	OBP
Aparicio, Miguel	L-L	6-0	188	3-17-99	.214	.245	.200	81	294	37	63	9	5	8	28	16	4	0	1	65	4	6	.361	.264
Dorow, Ryan	R-R	6-0	195	8-21-95	.272	.275	.270	122	431	54	117	28	1	12	61	39	10	1	5	119	5	2	.425	.342
Enright, Kole	B-R	6-1	175	1-21-98	.224	.182	.247	77	254	25	57	8	0	4	26	19	4	4	1	80	5	2	.303	.288
Gonzalez, Pedro	R-R	6-5	190	10-27-97	.234	.253	.227	92	337	47	79	17	5	12	46	28	3	0	3	110	9	5	.421	.299
Hernandez, Yonny	B-T	5-9	171	5-4-98	.260	.246	.268	115	361	56	94	12	3	2	40	58	7	15	2	65	44	15	.327	.372
Huff, Sam	R-R	6-4	230	1-14-98	.241	.211	.253	118	415	53	100	22	3	18	55	23	8	0	2	140	9	1	.439	.292
Inoa, Cristian	R-R	5-10	165	7-4-99	.152	.182	.136	12	33	5	5	2	0	0	1	8	0	0	0	6	0	0	.212	.317

Batting	B-T	HT	WT	DOB	AVG	vLH	vRH	G	AB	R	H	2B	3B	HR	RBI	BB	HBP	SH	SF	SO	SB	CS	SLG	OBP
Jacobs, Justin	L-R	6-1	195	10-25-95	.230	.127	.257	80	257	27	59	12	0	5	25	29	5	0	1	80	1	2	.335	.319
Jenkins, Eric	L-R	6-1	170	1-30-97	.291	.219	.324	26	103	14	30	1	3	3	15	8	0	1	1	32	16	3	.447	.339
Middleton, Clayton	R-R	6-0	205	10-8-93	.206	.182	.217	26	68	11	14	3	0	2	5	13	0	0	0	23	1	0	.338	.333
Novoa, Melvin	R-R	5-11	224	6-17-96	.322	.276	.344	24	90	11	29	8	0	2	22	5	3	0	0	12	0	0	.478	.378
O'Banion, Austin	R-R	6-3	215	7-12-95	.192	.167	.207	31	94	12	18	3	1	1	8	9	2	0	1	45	1	0	.277	.274
Pozo, Yohel	R-R	6-0	220	6-14-97	.264	.295	.247	117	428	45	113	29	2	10	49	27	5	0	5	50	0	0	.411	.312
Ratliff, Tyler	R-R	6-2	210	11-2-95	.217	.208	.221	93	291	39	63	7	0	8	26	35	8	0	0	87	1	1	.323	.317
Reed, Tyreque	R-R	6-2	260	6-6-97	.267	.253	.274	97	344	48	92	27	0	18	53	32	8	0	1	102	1	0	.503	.343
Rollin, Franklin	R-R	5-11	165	8-26-95	.296	.364	.250	9	27	6	8	1	0	1	2	5	0	0	0	3	8	2	.444	.406
Scott, Preston	R-R	6-2	210	11-15-93	.250	.195	.275	73	248	24	62	13	1	6	26	16	7	0	3	59	8	1	.383	.310
Smith, Chad	L-L	6-2	200	9-30-97	.095	.067	.111	13	42	4	4	1	1	0	2	3	0	1	0	19	0	1	.167	.156
Thompson, Bubba	R-R	6-2	186	6-9-98	.289	.303	.281	84	332	52	96	18	5	8	42	23	6	0	2	104	32	7	.446	.344
Whatley, Matt	R-R	5-10	200	1-7-96	.211	.400	.143	7	19	3	4	0	0	1	1	2	0	0	0	7	0	0	.368	.286

Pitching	B-T	HT	WT	DOB	W	L	ERA	G	GS	CG	SV	IP	H	R	ER	HR	BB	SO	AVG	vLH	vRH	K/9	BB/9
Advocate, Josh	R-R	6-1	195	1-18-94	1	0	4.01	23	0	0	5	43	38	19	19	4	11	45	.236	.233	.240	9.49	2.32
Alexy, A.J.	R-R	6-4	217	4-21-98	6	8	3.58	22	20	0	0	108	89	50	43	5	52	138	.229	.234	.226	11.50	4.33
Anderson, Reid	R-R	6-3	213	8-22-95	8	6	3.22	23	19	1	0	117	102	55	42	2	30	102	.231	.185	.274	7.82	2.30
Barlow, Joe	R-R	6-2	223	9-8-95	3	3	1.68	38	0	0	8	59	22	14	11	3	41	91	.118	.191	.058	13.88	6.25
Beltre, Dario	R-R	6-3	170	11-19-92	1	0	6.75	4	0	0	0	9	8	7	1	7	13	.222	.250	.188	12.54	6.75
Bolinger, Royce	R-R	6-2	200	8-12-90	0	0	0.00	1	0	0	0	1	1	0	0	0	0	0	.333	.000	.500	0.00	0.00
Bremer, Noah	R-R	6-5	200	5-13-96	5	7	4.20	17	17	1	0	81	94	42	38	8	25	69	.298	.259	.333	7.64	2.77
Casanova, Jean	R-R	6-3	181	3-4-97	4	4	2.78	27	8	0	3	71	69	30	22	8	30	55	.253	.201	.306	6.94	3.79
Crouse, Hans	L-R	6-4	180	9-15-98	0	2	2.70	5	5	0	0	17	18	9	5	1	8	15	.273	.393	.184	8.10	4.32
Dease, Ryan	R-R	6-3	175	4-15-99	1	0	0.00	1	1	0	0	5	5	0	0	0	4	3	.263	.333	.231	5.40	0.00
Eubanks, Alex	R-R	6-2	180	9-13-95	8	6	5.38	26	16	0	0	112	126	70	67	12	30	106	.283	.346	.211	8.52	2.41
Evans, Demarcus	R-R	6-5	275	10-22-96	4	1	1.77	35	0	0	9	56	28	11	11	1	27	103	.149	.177	.128	16.55	4.34
Ferguson, Tyler	R-R	6-4	225	10-5-93	0	0	5.06	13	0	0	1	16	11	12	9	0	12	13	.190	.167	.206	7.31	6.75
Heffel, Derek	R-R	6-6	225	4-13-96	4	3	5.71	24	4	0	0	58	69	39	37	5	13	49	.296	.340	.263	7.56	2.01
Kuzia, Joe	R-R	6-5	190	10-3-93	1	3	4.35	31	0	0	2	60	68	37	29	4	21	60	.288	.339	.232	9.00	3.15
Leal, Werner	R-R	6-1	160	7-8-95	0	2	5.00	2	2	0	0	9	14	6	5	0	2	11	.400	.412	.389	11.00	2.00
Mendez, Sal	R-L	6-1	160	2-25-95	3	4	1.66	17	0	0	2	38	24	10	7	0	10	30	.179	.106	.218	7.11	2.37
Mendoza, Abdiel	R-R	5-10	160	9-19-98	0	0	0.00	1	0	0	0	3	2	0	0	0	1	1	.200	.333	.143	3.00	3.00
Perez, Martin	L-L	6-0	200	4-4-91	0	0	0.00	1	1	0	0	5	2	0	0	0	0	9	.250	.077	16.20	0.00	
Phillips, Tyler	R-R	6-5	200	10-27-97	11	5	2.67	22	22	1	0	128	117	41	38	4	14	124	.239	.265	.214	8.72	0.98
Speas, Alex	R-R	6-4	180	3-4-98	2	0	2.20	20	0	0	6	29	16	10	7	1	21	49	.155	.148	.163	15.38	6.59
Thomas, Tyler	R-L	6-1	175	12-22-95	0	2	4.15	3	3	0	0	13	8	6	6	2	4	14	.250	.154	.177	9.69	2.77
Thompson, Tyree	R-R	6-4	165	6-12-97	7	11	4.93	23	20	0	0	111	118	75	61	21	44	76	.274	.238	.308	6.14	3.56
Vivas, Samir	R-R	5-11	170	2-1-95	0	0	7.30	7	0	0	1	12	14	10	10	1	7	16	.280	.214	.364	11.68	5.11
Zawadzki, Grant	R-R	5-10	200	4-27-92	1	1	7.00	8	0	0	1	9	9	7	7	1	5	5	.265	.235	.294	5.00	5.00

Fielding

C: Huff 56, Middleton 11, Novoa 9, Pozo 63, Whatley 4. **1B:** Dorow 1, Huff 11, Jacobs 11, Middleton 11, Pozo 10, Ratliff 18, Reed 78, Scott 9. **2B:** Dorow 15, Enright 72, Hernandez 48, Inoa 2, Jacobs 8, Scott 1. **3B:** Dorow 42, Enright 5, Jacobs 46, Middleton 1, Ratliff 49, Scott 1. **SS:** Dorow 67, Hernandez 65, Inoa 10. **OF:** Aparicio 80, Dorow 1, Gonzalez 90, Hernandez 1, Jacobs 18, Jenkins 25, Middleton 3, O'Banion 29, Ratliff 25, Rollin 8, Scott 61, Smith 9, Thompson 84.

SPOKANE INDIANS

SHORT-SEASON

NORTHWEST LEAGUE

Batting	B-T	HT	WT	DOB	AVG	vLH	vRH	G	AB	R	H	2B	3B	HR	RBI	BB	HBP	SH	SF	SO	SB	CS	SLG	OBP
Aparicio, Miguel	L-L	6-0	188	3-17-99	.244	.200	.257	11	45	5	11	1	0	1	4	1	0	0	2	8	0	1	.333	.250
Apostel, Sherten	R-R	6-4	200	3-11-99	.351	.600	.259	12	37	7	13	1	0	1	10	9	1	0	2	8	0	1	.460	.469
Arias, Diosbel	R-R	6-2	190	7-21-96	.366	.397	.355	61	224	43	82	15	2	3	44	33	4	0	3	39	5	1	.491	.451
Biggers, Jax	R-R	5-11	175	4-7-97	.260	.238	.268	39	154	26	40	6	1	1	20	18	2	0	2	29	6	3	.331	.341
Depreta-Johnson, Tyler	R-R	5-9	180	5-10-96	.230	.222	.233	46	152	20	35	8	0	0	5	20	3	1	1	30	1	1	.283	.330
Dixon, Troy	L-R	6-0	185	2-25-97	.207	.063	.237	27	92	9	19	3	1	0	7	11	3	0	0	27	4	1	.261	.311
Gardner, Tanner	L-R	6-0	210	9-28-95	.247	.171	.265	51	186	23	46	6	1	5	30	17	1	0	3	47	6	3	.371	.309
Inoa, Cristian	R-R	5-10	165	7-4-99	.255	.216	.266	46	161	14	41	8	0	2	13	15	5	1	0	33	3	3	.342	.337
Joseph, Starling	R-R	6-3	209	8-1-98	.205	.286	.175	59	205	26	42	7	0	11	30	11	7	0	4	86	0	4	.400	.264
Kapers, Scott	R-R	5-11	175	11-27-96	.164	.286	.115	23	73	7	12	6	0	1	6	5	6	0	0	15	0	1	.288	.274
Martinez, Julio Pablo	L-L	5-9	174	3-21-96	.252	.207	.267	60	234	49	59	9	5	8	21	34	2	2	1	69	11	6	.436	.351
McReynolds, Jonah	R-R	5-11	165	12-16-95	.223	.283	.199	47	184	23	41	9	1	2	13	11	5	2	0	64	2	1	.315	.285
Mendoza, Kevin	R-R	5-10	155	8-16-95	.231	.200	.267	13	39	4	9	2	0	0	5	3	1	0	1	5	0	0	.282	.296
O'Banion, Austin	R-R	6-3	215	7-12-95	.103	.167	.080	21	68	5	7	2	0	0	6	11	1	0	1	24	1	0	.221	.235
Quiroz, Isaias	R-R	5-10	234	10-22-96	.224	.226	.224	37	107	15	24	7	0	4	15	15	3	0	1	42	0	0	.402	.333
Ricumstrict, Obie	R-R	6-2	175	7-20-98	.119	.188	.077	13	42	3	5	1	0	2	3	1	2	0	0	25	0	0	.286	.178
Terry, Curtis	R-R	6-3	264	10-6-96	.337	.284	.361	67	246	51	83	17	2	15	60	32	11	0	1	64	1	1	.606	.435
Ventura, Francisco	R-R	5-9	206	11-19-98	.227	.324	.192	37	141	16	32	5	0	5	22	14	0	0	1	37	0	0	.376	.295
Ventura, Juan	R-R	6-0	165	6-15-98	.111	.167	.083	10	36	1	4	1	0	0	1	2	0	0	0	10	0	0	.139	.158
Viera, Hasuan	L-L	5-9	179	1-30-96	.260	.233	.268	38	127	17	33	4	0	0	14	21	0	1	2	38	3	4	.291	.360

Pitching	B-T	HT	WT	DOB	W	L	ERA	G	GS	CG	SV	IP	H	R	ER	HR	BB	SO	AVG	vLH	vRH	K/9	BB/9
Bass, Blake	R-R	6-7	250	6-3-93	0	0	0.00	4	0	0	0	6	1	0	0	0	1	3	.053	.000	.100	4.50	1.50
Bolinger, Royce	R-R	6-2	200	8-12-90	0	3	3.14	7	1	0	0	14	18	7	5	0	3	20	.321	.235	.359	12.56	1.88
Chandler, Sean	R-R	6-5	200	1-24-97	0	0	1.27	17	0	0	3	21	16	6	3	0	8	22	.208	.207	.208	9.28	3.38
Clase, Emmanuel	R-R	6-2	206	3-18-98	1	1	0.64	22	0	0	12	28	16	4	2	0	6	27	.158	.188	.140	8.58	1.91

Name	B-T	HT	WT	DOB	W	L	ERA	G	GS	CG	SV	IP	H	R	ER	HR	BB	SO	AVG	vLH	vRH	K/9	BB/9
Crouse, Hans	L-R	6-4	180	9-15-98	5	1	2.37	8	8	0	0	38	25	11	10	2	11	47	.179	.148	.198	11.13	2.61
Dease, Ryan	R-R	6-3	175	4-15-99	5	4	5.34	12	11	0	0	56	79	36	33	9	11	39	.341	.317	.359	6.31	1.78
Eibner, Brett	R-R	6-4	215	12-2-88	1	1	0.00	5	0	0	0	5	1	0	0	0	2	7	.200	.300	.133	8.22	2.35
Engler, Scott	R-R	6-4	220	12-12-97	3	6	5.87	13	9	0	0	54	58	36	35	7	24	49	.276	.261	.288	8.22	4.02
Eveld, Bobby	L-R	6-5	200	12-4-91	0	1	2.81	14	0	0	0	16	11	6	5	1	9	15	.196	.292	.125	8.44	5.06
Gonzalez, Chi Chi	R-R	6-3	215	1-15-92	1	0	0.00	1	1	0	0	5	0	0	0	0	0	4	.000	.000	.000	7.20	0.00
Gonzalez, Kelvin	R-R	6-0	170	12-24-97	0	0	13.50	3	0	0	0	2	5	4	3	0	3	2	.417	.500	.375	9.00	13.50
Keith, Kyle	L-R	6-0	180	11-20-94	0	0	4.24	14	0	0	1	17	25	12	8	1	7	18	.313	.306	.318	9.53	3.71
King, John	L-L	6-2	195	9-14-94	0	0	6.00	1	1	0	0	3	5	2	2	0	0	2	.357	.400	.333	6.00	0.00
Latz, Jake	R-L	6-2	185	4-8-96	3	13	3.93	13	13	0	0	71	63	39	31	4	24	67	.233	.150	.256	8.49	3.04
Leal, Werner	R-R	6-1	160	7-8-95	3	3	5.90	13	4	0	0	29	35	21	19	3	9	37	.297	.255	.333	11.48	2.79
Lebron, David	R-R	6-0	190	9-7-93	0	0	0.61	7	0	0	0	15	8	1	1	0	5	16	.157	.235	.118	9.82	3.07
Linarez, Jesus	R-R	6-4	216	1-10-97	0	1	9.00	1	0	0	0	2	3	2	2	0	1	4	.333	1.000	.250	18.00	4.50
Mendoza, Kenny	R-L	6-2	215	3-12-98	0	0	0.00	1	0	0	0	2	1	0	0	0	2	3	.143	.333	.000	16.20	10.80
Meyer, Reggie	L-R	6-4	210	7-27-95	0	2	6.06	13	0	0	0	16	21	12	11	2	3	17	.304	.393	.244	9.37	1.65
Moore, Xavier	R-R	6-2	175	1-7-99	0	1	5.73	8	0	0	0	11	12	7	7	2	6	12	.286	.368	.217	10.64	4.91
Nordlin, Seth	R-R	6-4	205	9-4-97	3	1	3.82	13	12	0	0	68	63	31	29	7	14	79	.244	.290	.208	10.40	1.84
Pettibone, Austin	R-R	6-3	180	9-10-92	0	1	0.87	8	0	0	0	10	9	3	1	1	2	6	.231	.188	.261	5.23	1.74
Robertson, Wes	R-R	6-2	190	3-11-96	2	1	1.53	14	0	0	0	18	11	6	3	0	8	20	.169	.353	.182	6.62	4.08
Rodriguez, Yerry	R-R	6-2	198	10-15-97	3	0	1.82	4	0	0	0	25	22	6	5	2	5	27	.229	.167	.278	9.85	1.82
Rosario, Luis	R-R	5-11	165	2-8-97	0	1	19.29	1	0	0	0	2	8	7	5	0	1	1	.500	.600	.455	3.86	3.86
Sanburn, Chandler	R-R	6-2	200	7-8-95	0	1	7.45	9	0	0	0	10	11	9	8	2	7	11	.275	.294	.261	10.24	6.52
Suarez, Sergio	L-L	6-0	160	5-24-95	0	1	5.40	7	0	0	0	12	8	8	7	1	6	8	.200	.222	.194	6.17	4.63
Tiedemann, Tai	R-R	6-6	195	5-31-96	3	2	4.84	13	12	0	0	58	51	36	31	3	35	49	.232	.265	.203	7.65	5.46
Uvila, Cole	R-R	6-4	206	1-30-94	1	0	1.42	19	0	0	3	32	13	7	5	1	15	48	.128	.098	.148	13.64	4.26
Villegas, Francisco	L-L	6-2	175	8-31-97	0	1	5.00	14	0	0	0	18	14	10	10	1	14	17	.230	.100	.293	8.50	7.00

Fielding

C: Kapers 21, Mendoza 2, Quiroz 34, Ventura 24. **1B:** Gardner 3, McReynolds 6, Mendoza 3, Terry 38, Viera 30. **2B:** Arias 11, Biggers 5, Depreta-Johnson 16, Dixon 7, Inoa 24, McReynolds 14, Ventura 3. **3B:** Apostel 8, Arias 35, Depreta-Johnson 10, Inoa 12, McReynolds 3, Mendoza 3, Ricumstrict 4, Ventura 5. **SS:** Arias 11, Biggers 34, Depreta-Johnson 21, Inoa 11, McReynolds 1. **OF:** Aparicio 11, Dixon 11, Gardner 39, Joseph 57, Martinez 58, McReynolds 26, Mendoza 1, O'Banion 19, Ricumstrict 7, Viera 6.

AZL RANGERS   ROOKIE
ARIZONA LEAGUE

Batting	B-T	HT	WT	DOB	AVG	vLH	vRH	G	AB	R	H	2B	3B	HR	RBI	BB	HBP	SH	SF	SO	SB	CS	SLG	OBP
Almonte, Jose	R-R	6-3	205	9-9-96	.194	.200	.191	11	31	8	6	1	0	0	5	9	2	0	0	14	1	0	.226	.405
Anderson, Ryan	R-R	6-1	205	8-30-95	.250	.333	.229	37	136	26	34	7	2	3	17	8	3	0	0	27	8	1	.397	.306
Biggers, Jax	L-R	5-11	175	4-7-97	.000	.000	.000	1	4	0	0	0	0	0	0	1	0	0	1	0	1	0	.000	.200
Cardona, Jose	R-R	6-1	175	3-16-94	.444	1.000	.375	3	9	4	4	3	1	0	4	2	0	0	1	0	1	0	1.000	.500
Chavez, Frainyer	B-R	5-10	170	5-24-99	.306	.286	.313	45	173	30	53	7	2	2	31	19	2	0	2	37	23	6	.405	.378
Clark, LeDarious	R-R	5-10	185	12-27-93	.333	.500	.000	3	6	3	2	0	0	0	3	0	0	0	2	2	0	.333	.556
Dixon, Troy	L-R	6-0	185	2-25-97	.125	.250	.000	2	8	1	1	0	0	0	0	0	0	0	2	0	0	.125	.125
Easley, Jayce	B-R	5-8	145	8-2-99	.287	.429	.246	42	157	34	45	6	0	0	16	27	0	1	1	41	22	4	.325	.389
Enright, Kole	B-R	6-1	175	3-4-00	.308	.333	.300	4	13	2	4	1	0	1	4	1	1	0	0	6	2	0	.615	.400
Garcia, David	B-R	5-11	170	2-6-00	.269	.174	.292	34	119	10	32	8	0	1	20	9	0	1	0	26	0	1	.361	.320
Gutierrez, Beder	R-R	6-0	180	1-13-97	.261	.281	.253	38	115	19	30	8	2	2	13	15	1	0	1	31	1	0	.417	.349
Irizarry, Kenen	L-R	6-0	150	5-6-00	.195	.188	.200	17	41	8	8	1	1	0	2	6	0	1	1	10	1	1	.268	.320
Kapers, Scott	R-R	5-11	175	11-27-96	.375	.000	.600	2	8	0	3	1	0	0	0	0	0	0	0	0	1	0	.500	.375
Mack, Marcus	L-L	6-2	185	8-1-98	.121	.231	.050	14	33	3	4	0	0	0	3	3	2	1	0	11	1	1	.121	.237
Martinez, Stanley	R-R	6-0	176	1-5-97	.336	.303	.345	45	146	21	49	9	1	2	21	17	3	0	1	40	2	4	.452	.413
McKisic, Myles	R-R	6-2	185	11-3-97	.100	.063	.111	24	70	10	7	2	0	0	2	13	2	1	1	41	3	0	.129	.256
Mejia, Leuri	B-R	6-0	150	8-30-00	.100	.000	.136	12	30	5	3	0	0	0	0	7	2	0	0	14	6	0	.100	.308
Morales, Maxwell	B-R	6-0	190	9-28-97	.288	.324	.276	38	139	23	40	15	0	7	32	14	2	0	3	33	1	1	.547	.354
Morgan, Josh	R-R	5-11	185	11-16-95	.100	.000	.167	4	10	1	1	0	0	0	1	2	1	0	0	0	0	0	.100	.308
Noonan, Nick	L-R	6-1	185	5-4-89	.000	—	.000	1	2	0	0	0	0	0	0	2	0	0	0	1	0	1	.000	.500
Ornelas, Jonathan	R-R	6-1	178	5-26-00	.302	.308	.301	48	172	34	52	10	4	3	28	25	2	0	4	41	15	5	.459	.389
Pena, Yenci	R-R	6-2	190	11-14-98	.158	.250	.133	10	38	3	6	0	0	0	5	2	0	0	0	5	2	0	.211	.200
Perez, Yanio	R-R	6-2	205	8-10-95	.200	.000	.250	3	10	0	2	0	0	0	2	0	0	0	0	5	0	0	.200	.333
Pichardo, Reynaldo	R-R	5-10	190	12-29-98	.191	.200	.182	7	21	2	4	0	0	0	3	4	0	0	0	8	0	0	.191	.320
Ricumstrict, Obie	R-R	6-2	175	7-20-98	.236	.125	.268	20	72	13	17	2	1	2	8	7	2	0	1	32	4	1	.375	.317
Smith, Chad	L-L	6-2	200	9-30-97	.000	.000	.000	2	3	0	0	0	0	0	0	2	0	0	0	3	0	1	.000	.400
Taylor, Kobie	R-R	6-0	183	8-13-98	.155	.095	.175	28	84	14	13	3	2	2	8	5	3	0	0	41	6	0	.310	.228
Valdez, Fernando	R-R	5-11	185	11-14-98	.263	.188	.293	35	114	13	30	5	4	3	20	12	1	0	1	33	5	4	.456	.336
Valentin, Xavier	L-R	5-9	165	8-22-00	.149	.231	.118	16	47	1	7	2	2	1	5	1	0	0	1	23	1	0	.340	.163

Pitching	B-T	HT	WT	DOB	W	L	ERA	G	GS	CG	SV	IP	H	R	ER	HR	BB	SO	AVG	vLH	vRH	K/9	BB/9
Baker, Brandon	L-L	6-0	180	4-7-95	0	0	3.38	4	0	0	0	5	4	3	2	0	5	9	.222	.000	.267	15.19	8.44
Benjamin, Wes	R-L	6-1	180	7-26-93	0	0	0.00	3	3	0	0	7	3	0	0	0	1	9	.136	.167	.125	11.57	1.29
Bice, Dylan	L-R	6-4	220	8-17-97	0	0	0.00	4	0	0	0	3	1	0	0	0	1	4	.091	.143	.000	10.80	2.70
Castillo, Juan	R-R	6-3	166	9-18-95	0	1	10.24	11	0	0	0	10	15	13	11	0	13	8	.366	.294	.417	7.45	12.10
Castro, Ray	R-R	6-3	165	5-9-97	0	0	10.80	3	0	0	0	5	6	8	6	1	3	6	.300	.429	.231	10.80	5.40
Cody, Kyle	R-R	6-7	245	8-9-94	0	0	0.00	2	2	0	0	5	2	1	0	0	1	9	.118	.167	.091	16.20	1.80
Cohen, Tyler	R-R	6-2	205	6-20-95	2	0	4.96	15	0	0	2	16	17	10	9	1	6	15	.283	.167	.361	8.27	3.31
Cruz, Edwin	L-L	6-4	195	7-26-94	0	0	19.06	4	0	0	0	6	15	12	12	0	6	6	.484	.300	.571	9.53	9.53
Eibner, Brett	R-R	6-4	215	12-2-88	0	0	3.00	3	0	0	0	3	1	1	1	0	1	5	.100	.000	.143	15.00	3.00

					W	L	ERA	G	GS	CG	SV	IP	H	R	ER	HR	BB	SO	AVG	vLH	vRH		
Encarnacion, Ediberto	R-R	5-11	170	2-9-94	3	1	4.44	14	0	0	1	24	22	12	12	4	12	26	.239	.226	.246	9.62	4.44
Gonzalez, Chi Chi	R-R	6-3	215	1-15-92	1	0	0.00	2	1	0	0	5	2	0	0	0	0	4	.118	.125	.111	7.20	0.00
Gonzalez, Kelvin	R-R	6-0	170	12-24-97	0	0	0.00	1	0	0	0	1	0	0	0	0	2	2	.000	—	.000	18.00	18.00
Javier, Joshua	L-L	6-3	195	12-16-98	0	0	2.57	2	2	0	0	7	4	2	2	0	1	12	.160	.000	.174	15.43	1.29
2-team total (10 AZL D-backs)					3	1	2.76	12	6	0	0	42	31	16	13	1	16	45	.201	.094	.230	9.57	3.40
Jones, James	L-L	6-4	200	9-24-88	0	0	2.25	2	2	0	0	4	3	1	1	0	1	3	.200	.333	.167	6.75	2.25
King, John	L-L	6-2	215	9-14-94	0	0	5.40	1	1	0	0	2	3	2	1	0	1	1	.375	.333	.400	5.40	5.40
Layne Jr., Billy	R-R	6-4	185	12-19-96	1	1	1.63	10	5	0	1	28	22	10	5	1	4	36	.212	.152	.259	11.71	1.30
Linarez, Jesus	R-R	6-2	216	1-10-97	3	2	3.67	11	8	0	0	49	39	21	20	2	15	55	.217	.218	.216	10.10	2.76
McDowell, Theo	L-R	6-4	175	12-2-98	2	0	9.37	11	0	0	0	16	18	18	17	1	10	9	.273	.143	.333	4.96	5.51
Mendoza, Kenny	R-L	6-4	215	3-12-98	2	1	2.38	3	2	0	0	11	11	3	3	0	6	15	.275	.308	.259	11.91	4.76
Moore, Xavier	R-R	6-2	175	1-7-99	0	0	4.70	5	0	0	0	8	8	5	4	0	4	8	.258	.200	.286	9.39	4.70
Morris, Chris	R-R	6-2	180	1-11-96	0	0	67.50	4	0	0	0	1	2	5	5	0	0	8	.500	—	.500	0.00	108.00
Nunez, Jeifry	R-R	5-11	160	4-1-98	1	2	6.75	4	2	0	0	12	15	9	9	3	0	18	.294	.263	.313	13.50	0.00
Palumbo, Joe	L-L	6-1	168	10-26-94	0	0	4.00	3	3	0	0	9	5	4	4	1	1	15	.161	.500	.111	15.00	1.00
Pearson, Braden	R-L	6-3	185	2-26-96	3	2	6.50	16	0	0	0	18	23	15	13	1	6	16	.299	.250	.312	8.00	3.00
Penrod, Zach	L-L	6-2	210	6-16-97	0	2	6.17	4	3	0	0	12	12	10	8	3	6	16	.261	.143	.313	12.34	4.63
Pettibone, Austin	R-R	6-3	180	9-10-92	0	0	0.00	1	0	0	0	1	0	0	0	0	0	1	.000	—	.000	9.00	0.00
Reeg, Zach	R-R	6-2	210	11-10-95	0	1	5.40	4	1	0	0	8	9	5	5	0	4	8	.310	.500	.177	8.64	4.32
Robertson, Wes	R-R	6-2	190	3-11-96	0	0	0.00	2	0	0	1	2	0	0	0	0	1	6	.000	.000	.000	27.00	4.50
Rodriguez, Yerry	R-R	6-2	198	10-15-97	2	2	3.52	8	6	0	0	38	38	16	15	1	3	55	.252	.286	.227	12.91	0.70
Rosario, Luis	R-R	5-11	165	2-8-97	1	3	4.72	12	6	0	1	34	33	19	18	3	15	38	.252	.216	.275	9.96	3.93
Sadzeck, Connor	R-R	6-7	240	10-11-91	0	0	0.00	3	2	0	0	4	3	0	0	1	0	10	.177	.125	.222	20.77	2.08
Snyder, Nick	R-R	6-4	190	10-10-95	1	0	6.00	12	0	0	0	12	17	9	8	0	6	12	.309	.391	.250	9.00	4.50
Starr, Nick	R-R	6-3	225	12-3-96	0	1	2.70	4	0	0	0	3	3	1	1	0	0	4	.250	.333	.000	10.80	0.00
Suarez, Sergio	L-L	6-0	160	5-24-95	0	0	6.17	8	0	0	0	12	15	10	8	0	7	12	.306	.308	.308	9.26	5.00
Tejada, Leury	R-R	6-1	160	12-24-99	1	1	3.31	8	2	0	0	16	15	10	6	1	6	18	.231	.107	.324	9.92	3.31
Urriola, Elvis	L-L	5-11	180	9-9-97	0	0	13.50	3	0	0	0	3	9	7	5	1	3	5	.450	.500	.438	13.50	8.10
Valdes, Erne	L-L	5-10	170	3-14-94	1	2	3.86	16	0	0	2	28	16	16	12	3	13	42	.167	.100	.197	13.50	4.18
Vanasco, Ricky	R-R	6-3	180	10-13-98	3	3	4.38	7	3	0	0	25	25	12	12	1	13	25	.287	.296	.283	9.12	4.74
Ventura, Francis	R-L	6-0	185	5-13-93	1	0	7.56	6	1	0	0	8	9	10	7	0	9	10	.273	.357	.211	10.80	9.72
Wolfram, Grant	L-L	6-6	210	12-12-96	0	0	3.38	8	1	0	0	11	12	4	4	0	6	10	.308	.000	.375	8.44	5.06

Fielding

C: Garcia 33, Kapers 2, Morales 9, Morgan 3, Pichardo 2, Valentin 13. **1B:** Martinez 34, McKisic 6, Morales 12, Perez 2, Valdez 7. **2B:** Chavez 8, Easley 28, Enright 3, Irizarry 11, McKisic 5, Ornelas 3. **3B:** Chavez 9, Martinez 11, McKisic 3, Ornelas 31, Pena 2, Perez 1, Valdez 2. **SS:** Biggers 1, Chavez 27, Easley 11, Martinez 1, Noonan 1, Ornelas 12, Pena 8. **OF:** Almonte 9, Anderson 37, Cardona 2, Clark 2, Dixon 2, Gutierrez 35, Mack 12, Martinez 1, McKisic 10, Mejia 12, Ricumstrict 20, Smith 1, Taylor 14, Valdez 24.

DSL RANGERS   ROOKIE
DOMINICAN SUMMER LEAGUE

Batting	B-T	HT	WT	DOB	AVG	vLH	vRH	G	AB	R	H	2B	3B	HR	RBI	BB	HBP	SH	SF	SO	SB	CS	SLG	OBP
Almonte, Jeremia	B-R	5-7	170	5-7-00	.171	.238	.143	32	70	15	12	3	3	1	11	24	0	1	0	26	1	2	.343	.383
Aponte, Angel	R-R	6-0	170	2-3-00	.281	.208	.298	63	246	58	69	11	3	7	38	21	12	1	0	53	30	4	.435	.366
Baptista, Angel	R-R	5-8	150	3-21-01	.233	.667	.185	30	30	12	7	2	0	0	2	16	3	2	0	12	4	1	.300	.531
Barete, Rafy	B-R	5-11	160	1-15-99	.377	.294	.400	22	77	20	29	8	1	2	16	13	2	1	0	14	6	1	.584	.478
Barreto, Derwin	B-R	5-9	155	9-1-00	.224	.345	.200	54	174	33	39	6	3	3	25	38	5	1	4	38	9	4	.345	.371
Basabe, Osleivis	R-R	6-1	165	9-13-00	.344	.390	.331	52	192	37	66	16	3	1	34	23	2	2	3	25	12	6	.474	.414
Bidau, Juan	R-R	5-9	155	12-29-99	.253	.189	.266	64	225	42	57	7	4	0	20	39	7	9	3	32	8	5	.320	.376
Cardozo, Jose	R-R	6-2	180	9-8-99	.198	.133	.209	38	106	10	21	3	1	0	15	17	3	0	3	14	4	4	.245	.318
Chirinos, Michael	B-R	5-10	155	10-11-99	.318	.362	.308	69	242	47	77	7	3	2	42	49	2	1	4	20	13	4	.397	.431
De La Rosa, Darlin	R-R	6-1	195	1-2-01	.200	.100	.250	19	30	3	6	1	1	0	2	6	2	0	0	14	0	1	.300	.368
Drullard, Danny	L-L	6-1	175	5-8-00	.253	.242	.255	49	174	29	44	7	4	2	22	28	2	1	2	47	10	4	.374	.359
Favela, Samuel	R-R	5-11	160	5-15-98	—	—	—	2	0	0	0	0	0	0	0	0	1	0	0	0	0	0	—	—
Feliz, Luis	R-R	6-2	180	3-8-01	.300	.333	.294	21	40	5	12	2	0	0	6	4	0	0	0	15	1	3	.350	.440
Florentino, Randy	L-R	5-11	175	7-5-00	.309	.293	.313	60	191	48	59	18	5	6	35	53	1	0	4	51	8	8	.550	.454
George, Anyelo	R-R	6-1	165	9-3-00	.156	.100	.182	19	32	7	5	0	0	1	3	6	3	0	0	13	1	0	.250	.342
Gonzalez, Robert	R-R	6-0	175	6-19-01	.167	.207	.155	52	126	25	21	3	2	3	20	27	8	0	1	48	2	0	.294	.346
Guardo, Jose	R-R	6-0	180	2-6-99	.244	.217	.248	54	176	27	43	9	1	5	25	20	15	2	3	49	3	2	.392	.365
Gutierrez, Jember	R-R	5-11	160	9-8-99	.299	.256	.309	65	221	40	66	9	4	0	29	50	5	0	3	39	11	7	.376	.434
Guzman, Yaniery	R-R	5-11	185	5-30-98	.332	.300	.338	53	190	36	63	12	5	7	52	17	1	0	4	33	2	1	.558	.382
Hernandez, Heriberto	R-R	6-1	180	12-16-99	.292	.364	.276	60	178	56	52	15	5	12	49	53	6	0	2	41	5	5	.635	.464
Jeffry, William	R-R	6-1	170	5-11-99	.250	.250	.250	25	64	20	16	2	1	3	15	10	7	0	3	32	1	1	.453	.393
Lascarro, Ronier	L-L	5-10	155	1-31-01	.259	.317	.244	60	197	30	51	11	2	0	41	37	1	2	3	49	6	3	.335	.377
Leon, Isaias	R-R	6-2	182	8-23-99	.188	.146	.200	59	186	31	35	9	0	4	27	28	9	0	3	64	6	3	.301	.319
Linares, Brandon	R-R	6-0	165	8-14-00	.111	.111	.111	40	63	6	7	1	1	0	4	7	3	0	0	19	0	1	.159	.233
Martinez, Julio Pablo	L-L	5-9	174	3-21-96	.409	.213	.282	7	22	10	9	1	1	1	3	9	2	0	0	7	2	3	.682	.606
Mejia, Leuri	R-R	6-0	150	8-30-00	.141	.250	.103	22	64	9	9	2	0	0	2	12	1	1	0	33	4	1	.172	.286
Mendoza, Edilberto	L-R	6-0	180	7-2-99	.211	.042	.242	53	152	31	32	8	0	4	34	42	4	4	3	53	2	2	.342	.388
Moreno, Jesus	R-R	5-11	170	4-16-01	.222	.000	.267	10	18	2	4	0	0	0	2	3	1	0	0	9	0	2	.222	.364
Moss, Keithron	B-R	5-11	165	8-20-01	.196	.167	.203	51	163	29	32	11	1	0	23	35	4	1	1	62	8	7	.276	.350
Ortega, Cesar	L-R	5-11	180	10-16-00	.231	—	.231	13	13	0	3	0	0	0	0	4	1	0	1	2	1		.231	.421
Pernalete, Adrian	B-R	6-0	165	9-14-98	.345	.500	.286	11	29	3	10	2	0	1	2	0	0	0	8	0	1		.414	.387
Perozo, Rehybell	B-R	6-3	180	11-6-99	.242	.225	.247	64	207	32	50	8	4	2	31	31	2	1	1	62	5	0	.348	.344
Puerta, Freddy	R-R	5-11	165	1-17-01	.037	.000	.046	19	27	0	1	0	0	0	2	2	0	0	16	0	0		.037	.161

Name	B-T	HT	WT	DOB	AVG	vLH	vRH	G	AB	R	H	2B	3B	HR	RBI	BB	HBP	SH	SF	SO	SB	CS	OBP	SLG
Quiceno, Daniel	L-R	6-1	165	2-8-00	.142	.100	.151	41	113	15	16	2	1	1	11	19	3	0	1	29	3	0	.204	.279
Rodriguez, Josue	R-R	5-10	160	12-27-99	.181	.188	.179	33	83	11	15	3	0	2	9	21	2	0	3	35	0	1	.289	.349
Rodriguez, Keyber	B-R	5-9	160	10-24-00	.254	.310	.238	51	193	35	49	6	6	1	26	24	2	2	3	36	4	3	.363	.338
Smith, Courtney	R-R	6-0	207	12-9-96	.080	.000	.087	17	25	4	2	0	0	0	2	5	4	0	0	17	1	0	.080	.324
Velasquez, Emir	B-R	5-8	160	3-10-00	.229	.276	.219	52	175	38	40	7	3	0	16	40	2	2	3	25	10	6	.303	.373
Viera, Hasuan	L-L	6-0	195	1-30-96	.238	.200	.274	7	21	2	5	1	0	0	7	8	0	0	2	2	1	3	.286	.419
Zambrano, Abraham	B-R	5-9	160	1-2-01	.367	.286	.391	21	30	8	11	1	2	0	6	2	1	0	0	3	4	0	.533	.424

Pitching	B-T	HT	WT	DOB	W	L	ERA	G	GS	CG	SV	IP	H	R	ER	HR	BB	SO	AVG	vLH	vRH	K/9	BB/9
Abreu, Oscar	R-R	6-1	175	12-11-99	2	1	2.81	14	0	0	5	32	26	11	10	3	15	29	.228	.200	.254	8.16	4.22
Alcala, Jose	L-L	5-11	160	2-21-00	2	1	6.56	11	0	0	1	23	32	19	17	1	8	19	.333	.273	.351	7.33	3.09
Bautista, Kelvin	L-L	5-11	155	7-7-99	2	1	5.00	18	0	0	0	27	25	18	15	0	17	25	.253	.150	.279	8.33	5.67
Beard, Aneudis	R-R	6-1	185	1-30-98	6	1	3.22	12	12	0	0	59	49	24	21	1	17	57	.222	.200	.245	8.74	2.61
Betances, Emmanuel	R-R	6-5	189	2-5-96	4	2	2.61	12	0	0	0	21	22	17	6	3	3	14	.272	.310	.231	6.10	1.31
Buitimea, Martin	R-R	6-1	155	4-14-98	3	0	1.06	13	5	0	3	51	39	8	6	0	14	49	.219	.226	.213	8.65	2.47
Burgos, Samuel	R-R	6-3	205	6-7-99	2	2	3.68	11	1	0	1	22	29	12	9	0	12	21	.312	.340	.283	8.59	4.91
Castro, Ray	R-R	6-3	165	5-9-97	1	1	2.55	10	0	0	2	18	16	6	5	0	4	26	.239	.238	.267	13.25	2.04
Cruz, Juan	R-R	6-6	215	12-5-97	3	2	7.91	14	5	0	0	39	55	41	34	3	16	30	.335	.213	.385	6.98	3.72
De La Cruz, Yangely	R-R	6-3	175	9-14-99	4	1	1.85	16	0	0	3	34	27	16	7	0	10	24	.216	.175	.235	6.35	2.65
De Leon, Daniel	R-R	6-4	195	5-9-01	3	1	6.32	14	0	0	1	31	35	24	22	4	20	19	.285	.209	.325	5.46	5.74
Encarnacion, Yohan	R-R	6-3	180	1-19-96	1	0	4.50	3	0	0	0	6	5	3	3	0	3	7	.217	.333	.091	10.50	4.50
Escalona, Maikol	L-L	5-10	170	10-19-98	2	1	6.75	13	0	0	0	17	19	15	13	1	18	15	.284	.375	.255	7.79	9.35
Ferreira, Elian	R-R	6-1	175	4-12-00	4	3	1.73	13	11	1	0	62	54	20	12	2	18	42	.241	.216	.253	6.06	2.60
Frias, Ricardo	L-L	5-10	160	9-7-00	2	0	2.67	13	0	0	1	27	17	9	8	0	16	23	.177	.158	.182	7.67	5.33
Garcia, Jesus Rodolfo	R-R	6-2	155	7-3-99	1	1	3.55	6	6	0	0	25	13	13	10	1	13	26	.153	.206	.118	9.24	4.62
Gomez, Orceli	R-R	6-5	175	11-23-00	3	1	4.10	9	9	0	0	37	38	23	17	3	12	19	.270	.256	.276	4.58	2.89
Guzman, Stanley	R-R	6-3	170	12-28-99	1	0	2.81	14	1	0	0	26	22	16	8	0	15	23	.216	.304	.190	8.06	5.26
Henriquez, Ronny	R-R	5-10	155	6-20-00	5	0	1.55	11	11	0	0	58	37	18	10	2	8	79	.177	.172	.179	12.26	1.24
Hernandez, Alexander	L-L	6-1	170	3-20-98	1	3	5.08	13	1	0	1	28	28	20	16	1	11	27	.257	.270	.250	8.58	3.49
Herrera, Jeremis	R-R	6-1	175	7-3-99	0	2	2.08	6	0	0	2	13	11	4	3	0	2	11	.234	.240	.227	7.62	1.38
Inojosa, Rosmer	R-R	6-3	165	8-10-99	5	1	1.38	12	12	0	0	65	49	18	10	1	9	53	.208	.214	.200	7.34	1.25
Lopez, Abrahan	R-R	5-10	160	9-27-99	2	3	2.08	15	0	0	6	26	26	12	6	1	9	24	.255	.257	.254	8.31	3.12
Marine, Luis	R-R	6-4	210	2-12-01	5	3	3.58	12	12	1	0	60	48	28	24	3	16	44	.213	.189	.225	6.56	2.39
Mejia, Juan	L-L	5-11	160	1-9-99	7	2	2.15	12	12	2	0	71	69	23	17	3	8	48	.257	.317	.232	6.08	1.01
Mendoza, Damian	R-R	6-1	175	1-25-01	6	1	2.58	11	11	0	0	59	56	20	17	0	9	40	.253	.260	.250	6.07	1.37
Morel, Emmy	L-L	6-4	178	9-18-99	4	2	2.40	11	6	0	1	45	30	12	12	1	4	48	.190	.083	.221	9.60	0.80
Naveda, Carlos	R-R	6-2	190	7-5-99	5	4	3.22	12	12	0	0	64	60	30	23	1	11	65	.246	.254	.237	9.09	1.54
Nin, Ezequiel	R-R	5-11	170	11-22-99	1	1	2.52	15	0	0	3	25	25	14	7	1	8	15	.253	.212	.273	5.40	2.88
Ozuna, Fernery	R-R	5-8	170	11-9-95	0	0	2.25	7	0	0	0	12	10	4	3	0	2	10	.222	.238	.208	7.50	1.50
Pacheco, Sergio	R-R	6-1	170	8-17-99	4	2	2.07	13	11	0	1	65	54	21	15	0	9	59	.229	.218	.238	8.13	1.24
Paulino, Luis	L-L	5-10	135	5-2-98	4	0	4.50	14	0	0	3	26	27	13	13	1	4	33	.270	.050	.325	11.42	1.38
Santiago, Manuel	L-L	6-0	175	10-15-99	4	0	2.84	6	6	1	0	32	31	10	10	3	3	38	.256	.313	.236	10.80	0.85
Torres, Darel	R-R	5-11	160	1-5-99	2	3	2.83	17	0	0	6	35	27	12	11	0	10	36	.202	.194	.209	9.26	2.57

Fielding

C: Bidau 1, Favela 2, Florentino 37, Guardo 26, Hernandez 14, Mendoza 48, Moreno 3, Pernalete 5, Puerta 13, Rodriguez 22, Smith 5. **1B:** Almonte 3, Basabe 1, Chirinos 27, Florentino 12, George 5, Guardo 8, Gutierrez 27, Guzman 35, Hernandez 26, Linares 1, Mendoza 3, Moreno 2, Pernalete 4, Puerta 4, Quiceno 2, Rodriguez 4, Smith 6, Viera 1. **2B:** Almonte 18, Baptista 12, Barete 1, Barreto 27, Basabe 13, Bidau 1, Chirinos 1, George 1, Gutierrez 14, Guzman 1, Moss 30, Rodriguez 16, Velasquez 24, Zambrano 12. **3B:** Almonte 3, Baptista 6, Barete 2, Bidau 30, Chirinos 37, George 10, Gutierrez 19, Ortega 1, Perozo 48, Velasquez 11, Zambrano 1. **SS:** Almonte 11, Baptista 7, Barreto 25, Basabe 28, Bidau 11, Chirinos 7, Gutierrez 1, Moss 17, Perozo 13, Rodriguez 32, Smith 1, Velasquez 14, Zambrano 2. **OF:** Aponte 60, Baptista 2, Barete 1, Bidau 29, Cardozo 34, De La Rosa 16, Drullard 48, Feliz 17, Gonzalez 50, Jeffry 24, Lascarro 57, Leon 51, Linares 37, Martinez 7, Mejia 22, Moreno 1, Ortega 6, Pernalete 1, Quiceno 36, Viera 6, Zambrano 1.

Toronto Blue Jays

SEASON IN A SENTENCE: Just four teams in baseball allowed more runs than the Blue Jays, who combined bad pitching with a mediocre offense to slog their way to a second straight losing season and a fourth place finish in the AL East.

HIGH POINT: The Blue Jays jumped out to a 13-6 start, aided by a soft schedule where they beat up on the White Sox, Rangers, Orioles and Royals. In all, playing 19 games against the Orioles—and accumulating a 14-5 record against the AL East foe—accounted for 19 percent of Toronto's wins.

LOW POINT: After finishing April with a winning record, things quickly turned south for the Blue Jays, who went 9-19 for a .321 winning percentage in May. During that month, they lost five out of six games to the Red Sox and were swept in a four-game series at home against the Athletics.

NOTABLE ROOKIES: Lefthander Ryan Borucki mixed a solid fastball and a plus changeup to induce weak contact and perform capably at the back of Toronto's rotation. After an injury-shortened start to his Blue Jays tenure in 2017, middle infielder Lourdes Gurriel Jr. opened the year in Double-A New Hampshire but finished in Toronto, where he showed an aggressive approach with power while splitting time between shortstop and second base.

KEY TRANSACTIONS: The Josh Donaldson era in Toronto ended on Aug. 31. The Blue Jays traded Donaldson, who played just 36 games due to injuries, to the Indians for a player to be named. That PTBN turned out to be righthander Julian Merryweather. The sell-off started the previous month, with Roberto Osuna going to Houston for righthanders Hector Perez, David Paulino and Ken Giles, and reliever Seung-Hwan Oh going to the Rockies for outfielder Forrest Wall and first baseman Chad Spanberger.

DOWN ON THE FARM: With the major league team scuffling, the focus quickly turned to the farm system, where third baseman Vladimir Guerrero Jr. was annihilating minor league pitching. Guerrero won the BA Minor League Player of the Year award easily, dominating Double-A and Triple-A as a 19-year-old. In all, Guerrero hit .381/.437/.636 with 20 home runs. Meanwhile, Double-A New Hampshire went 76-62 in the regular season and eventually won the Eastern League title. The team featured at various points top prospects Guerrero, shortstop Bo Bichette, Gurriel, righthander Sean Reid-Foley and second baseman Cavan Biggio.

OPENING DAY PAYROLL: $164,122,200 (9th).

PLAYERS OF THE YEAR

ROBBIE ROGERS

TOM DiPACE

MAJOR LEAGUE	MINOR LEAGUE
Justin Smoak	**Vladimir Guerrero Jr**
1B	3B
.242/.350/.457	(Double-A/Triple-A)
Led Blue Jays in HR	.381/.437/.636
(25) and OPS (.808)	20 HR, 78 RBIs

ORGANIZATION LEADERS

Batting		*Minimum 250 AB
MAJORS		
* AVG	Aledmys Diaz	.263
* OPS	Justin Smoak	.808
HR	Randal Grichuk	25
HR	Justin Smoak	25
RBI	Justin Smoak	77
MINORS		
* AVG	Vladimir Guerrero Jr., New Hamp., Blue Jays, Dunedin, Buffalo	.381
* OBP	Vladimir Guerrero Jr., New Hamp., Blue Jays, Dunedin, Buffalo	.437
* SLG	Vladimir Guerrero Jr., New Hamp., Blue Jays, Dunedin, Buffalo	.636
* OPS	Vladimir Guerrero Jr., New Hamp., Blue Jays, Dunedin, Buffalo	1.073
R	Bo Bichette, New Hampshire	95
H	Kevin Smith, Lansing, Dunedin	158
TB	Kevin Smith, Lansing, Dunedin	276
2B	Bo Bichette, New Hampshire	43
3B	DJ Neal, Bluefield	9
3B	Chavez Young, Lansing	9
HR	Cavan Biggio, New Hampshire	26
RBI	Cavan Biggio, New Hampshire	99
BB	Ryan Noda, Lansing	109
SO	Cavan Biggio, New Hampshire	148
SB	Samad Taylor, Lansing	44
SB	Chavez Young, Lansing	44

Pitching		#Minimum 75 IP
MAJORS		
W	J.A. Happ	10
# ERA	Ryan Borucki	3.87
SO	J.A. Happ	130
SV	Ken Giles	14
MINORS		
W	Jon Harris, New Hampshire, Buffalo	13
L	Josh DeGraaf, Dunedin, New Hampshire, Buffalo	11
# ERA	Patrick Murphy, Dunedin, New Hampshire	2.65
G	Justin Shafer, New Hampshire, Buffalo	47
GS	Jon Harris, New Hampshire, Buffalo	27
GS	Patrick Murphy, Dunedin, New Hampshire	27
GS	T.J. Zeuch, Dunedin, New Hampshire	27
SV	Justin Shafer, New Hampshire, Buffalo	16
IP	T.J. Zeuch, Dunedin, New Hampshire	156
BB	Patrick Murphy, Dunedin, New Hampshire	53
BB	Yennsy Diaz, Lansing, Dunedin	53
SO	Sean Reid-Foley, New Hampshire, Buffalo	150
# AVG	Yennsy Diaz, Lansing, Dunedin	.210

2018 PERFORMANCE

General Manager: Ross Atkins. **Farm Director:** Gil Kim. **Scouting Director:** Steve Sanders.

Class	Team	League	W	L	PCT	Finish	Manager
Majors	Toronto Blue Jays	American	73	89	.451	10th (15)	John Gibbons
Triple-A	Buffalo Bisons	International	61	77	.442	14th (14)	Bobby Meacham
Double-A	N. Hampshire Fisher Cats	Eastern	78	62	.551	4th (12)	John Schneider
High A	Dunedin Blue Jays	Florida State	69	68	.504	8th (12)	Casey Candaele
Low A	Lansing Lugnuts	Midwest	80	60	.571	3rd (16)	Cesar Martin
Short season	Vancouver Canadians	Northwest	40	36	.526	2nd (8)	Dallas McPherson
Rookie	Bluefield Blue Jays	Appalachian	42	26	.618	2nd (10)	Dennis Holmberg
Rookie	GCL Blue Jays	Gulf Coast	24	29	.xxx	12th (18)	Luis Hurtado
Overall 2018 Minor League Record			392	358	.523	8th (30)	

ORGANIZATION STATISTICS

TORONTO BLUE JAYS
AMERICAN LEAGUE

Batting	B-T	HT	WT	DOB	AVG	vLH	vRH	G	AB	R	H	2B	3B	HR	RBI	BB	HBP	SH	SF	SO	SB	CS	SLG	OBP
Alford, Anthony	R-R	6-1	215	7-20-94	.105	.091	.125	13	19	3	2	0	0	0	1	2	0	0	0	9	1	0	.105	.191
Berti, Jon	R-R	5-10	195	1-22-90	.267	.250	.286	4	15	2	4	1	1	0	2	0	0	0	0	4	1	0	.467	.267
Davis, Jonathan	R-R	5-8	190	5-12-92	.200	.250	.154	20	25	3	5	1	0	0	1	1	0	0	0	6	3	0	.240	.259
Diaz, Aledmys	R-R	6-1	195	8-1-90	.263	.223	.276	130	422	55	111	26	0	18	55	23	3	0	4	62	3	4	.453	.303
Donaldson, Josh	R-R	6-1	210	12-8-85	.234	.279	.213	36	137	22	32	11	0	5	16	21	0	0	1	44	2	0	.423	.333
2-team total (16 Cleveland)					.246		.276	52	187	30	46	14	0	8	23	31	0	0	1	54	2	0	.449	.352
Drury, Brandon	R-R	6-2	210	8-21-92	.154	.154	.154	8	26	3	4	2	0	0	3	2	1	0	0	8	0	0	.231	.241
2-team total (18 New York)					.169	.167	.170	26	77	5	13	4	0	1	10	7	2	0	0	20	0	0	.260	.256
Granderson, Curtis	L-R	6-1	200	3-16-81	.245	.143	.253	104	302	48	74	21	1	11	35	42	3	1	1	96	2	1	.431	.342
Grichuk, Randal	R-R	6-1	205	8-13-91	.245	.263	.237	124	424	60	104	32	1	25	61	27	8	0	3	122	3	2	.502	.301
Gurriel Jr., Lourdes	R-R	6-2	185	10-10-93	.281	.310	.270	65	249	30	70	8	0	11	35	9	2	1	2	59	1	2	.446	.309
Hernandez, Teoscar	R-R	6-2	180	10-15-92	.240	.217	.250	134	476	67	114	29	7	22	57	41	3	0	3	163	5	5	.469	.302
Jansen, Danny	R-R	6-2	225	4-15-95	.247	.263	.242	31	81	12	20	6	0	3	8	9	4	0	1	17	0	0	.432	.347
Maile, Luke	R-R	6-3	225	2-6-91	.248	.259	.243	68	202	22	50	13	1	3	27	25	2	0	2	67	2	0	.366	.333
Martin, Russell	R-R	5-10	205	2-15-83	.194	.222	.184	90	289	37	56	8	0	10	25	56	7	0	0	82	0	3	.325	.338
McGuire, Reese	L-R	5-11	215	3-2-95	.290	.125	.348	14	31	5	9	3	0	2	4	2	0	0	0	9	1	0	.581	.333
McKinney, Billy	L-L	6-1	205	8-23-94	.252	.143	.277	36	115	14	29	7	0	6	13	11	1	0	1	32	1	0	.470	.320
2-team total (2 New York)					.252	.143	.276	38	119	14	30	7	0	6	13	11	1	0	1	33	1	0	.462	.318
Morales, Kendrys	R-R	6-1	225	6-20-83	.249	.199	.274	130	413	47	103	15	0	21	57	50	3	0	5	95	2	3	.438	.331
Ngoepe, Gift	R-R	5-8	200	1-18-90	.056	.000	.071	13	18	2	1	0	0	0	1	0	0	0	0	12	0	0	.056	.105
Pearce, Steve	R-R	5-11	200	4-13-83	.291	.306	.267	26	79	16	23	6	0	4	16	7	0	0	0	14	0	0	.519	.349
2-team total (50 Boston)					.284	.304	.266	76	215	35	61	14	1	11	42	29	5	0	2	41	0	0	.512	.379
Pillar, Kevin	R-R	6-0	205	1-4-89	.252	.235	.259	142	512	65	129	40	2	15	59	18	6	0	6	98	14	3	.426	.282
Pompey, Dalton	B-R	6-2	195	12-11-92	.200	.250	.167	5	10	0	2	0	0	0	1	0	0	0	0	6	0	0	.200	.273
Smith Jr., Dwight	L-R	5-11	195	10-26-92	.262	.083	.302	35	65	9	17	8	0	2	8	7	2	0	1	13	0	0	.477	.347
Smoak, Justin	B-L	6-4	220	12-5-86	.242	.235	.245	147	505	67	122	34	0	25	77	83	3	0	3	156	0	1	.457	.350
Solarte, Yangervis	B-R	5-11	205	7-3-87	.227	.225	.227	122	468	50	106	20	0	17	54	31	3	1	3	72	1	3	.378	.277
Sweeney, Darnell	B-R	6-1	205	2-1-91	.000	.000	.000	2	2	0	0	0	0	0	0	0	0	0	0	2	0	0	.000	.000
Tellez, Rowdy	L-L	6-4	220	3-16-95	.314	.100	.400	23	70	10	22	9	0	4	14	2	0	0	1	21	0	0	.614	.329
Travis, Devon	R-R	5-9	190	2-21-91	.233	.263	.221	103	357	41	83	14	3	11	44	16	5	0	0	64	3	2	.381	.275
Urena, Richard	B-R	6-0	185	2-26-96	.293	.318	.286	40	99	10	29	4	0	1	6	7	0	2	0	32	2	1	.364	.340
Urshela, Gio	R-R	6-0	215	10-11-91	.233	.250	.229	19	43	7	10	1	0	1	3	2	1	0	0	6	0	0	.326	.283

Pitching	B-T	HT	WT	DOB	W	L	ERA	G	GS	CG	SV	IP	H	R	ER	HR	BB	SO	AVG	vLH	vRH	K/9	BB/9
Axford, John	R-R	6-5	220	4-1-83	4	1	4.41	45	0	0	0	51	44	27	25	6	20	50	.234	.147	.283	8.82	3.53
Barnes, Danny	L-R	6-1	195	10-21-89	3	3	5.71	47	0	0	0	41	47	28	26	6	22	38	.285	.267	.300	8.34	4.83
Biagini, Joe	R-R	6-5	240	5-29-90	4	7	6.00	50	4	0	0	72	96	50	48	14	24	53	.323	.333	.315	6.63	3.00
Borucki, Ryan	L-L	6-4	175	3-31-94	4	6	3.87	17	17	0	0	98	96	48	42	7	33	67	.256	.242	.261	6.17	3.04
Clippard, Tyler	R-R	6-3	200	2-14-85	4	3	3.67	73	1	0	7	69	57	29	28	13	23	85	.223	.210	.234	11.14	3.01
Cruz, Rhiner	R-R	6-2	210	11-1-86	0	0	2.70	2	0	0	0	3	3	1	1	0	2	4	.231	.250	.222	10.80	5.40
Cumpton, Brandon	R-R	6-2	215	11-16-88	0	0	5.40	1	0	0	0	2	3	1	1	0	0	2	.375	.000	.600	10.80	10.80
Drake, Oliver	R-R	6-4	215	1-13-87	0	0	16.20	2	0	0	0	2	4	3	3	0	0	2	.444	.333	.667	10.80	0.00
4-team total (4 Cleveland, 8 Los Angeles, 19 Minnesota)					0	1	4.89	33	0	0	0	35	38	20	19	4	9	36	.270	.328	.221	9.26	2.31
Estrada, Marco	R-R	6-0	180	7-5-83	7	14	5.64	28	28	0	0	144	155	91	90	29	50	103	.274	.231	.306	6.45	3.13
Fernandez, Jose	L-L	6-3	170	2-13-93	0	0	6.10	13	0	0	0	10	11	7	7	2	4	6	.244	.240	.250	5.23	3.48
Garcia, Jaime	L-L	6-2	215	7-8-86	3	6	5.93	25	13	0	0	74	76	53	49	13	38	69	.261	.188	.289	8.35	4.60
Gaviglio, Sam	R-R	6-2	195	12-26-90	3	10	5.31	26	24	0	0	124	140	77	73	21	38	105	.281	.279	.283	7.64	2.77
Giles, Ken	R-R	6-2	205	9-20-90	0	1	4.12	21	0	0	14	20	18	11	9	4	4	22	.234	.163	.324	10.07	1.83
2-team total (34 Houston)					0	3	4.65	55	0	0	26	50	54	28	26	6	7	53	.266	.225	.305	9.48	1.25
Guerrieri, Taylor	R-R	6-2	210	12-1-92	0	0	4.66	9	0	0	0	10	9	5	5	1	4	8	.243	.200	.273	7.45	3.72
Guilmet, Preston	R-R	6-2	200	7-27-87	0	0	9.00	6	0	0	0	8	11	8	8	4	5	5	.324	.500	.200	5.63	4.50
Happ, J.A.	L-L	6-5	205	10-19-82	10	6	4.18	20	20	0	0	114	99	61	53	17	35	130	.229	.188	.239	10.26	2.76
2-team total (11 New York)					17	6	3.65	31	31	0	0	178	150	81	72	27	51	193	.225	.171	.238	9.78	2.58

Name	B-T	HT	WT	DOB	W	L	ERA	G	GS	CG	SV	IP	H	R	ER	HR	BB	SO	AVG	vLH	vRH		
Hauschild, Mike	R-R	6-3	210	1-22-90	1	1	4.32	2	1	0	0	8	7	4	4	0	4	5	.241	.200	.263	5.40	4.32
Leiter Jr., Mark	R-R	6-0	195	3-13-91	0	0	13.50	8	0	0	0	7	13	11	10	2	4	9	.394	.300	.539	12.15	5.40
Loup, Aaron	L-L	5-11	210	12-19-87	0	0	4.54	50	0	0	0	36	44	21	18	4	13	42	.299	.271	.325	10.60	3.28
Mayza, Tim	L-L	6-3	220	1-15-92	2	0	3.28	37	0	0	0	36	33	13	13	3	14	40	.244	.233	.253	10.09	3.53
McGuire, Deck	R-R	6-6	220	6-23-89	0	0	6.48	4	0	0	0	8	9	6	6	2	5	7	.265	.118	.412	7.56	5.40
2-team total (17 Los Angeles)					0	2	6.16	21	4	0	0	38	38	28	26	9	26	33	.266	.214	.315	7.82	6.16
Oh, Seunghwan	R-R	5-10	205	7-15-82	4	3	2.68	48	0	0	2	47	37	14	14	5	10	55	.214	.315	.168	10.53	1.91
Osuna, Roberto	R-R	6-2	215	2-7-95	0	0	2.93	15	0	0	9	15	16	5	5	0	1	13	.267	.280	.280	7.63	0.59
2-team total (23 Houston)					2	2	2.37	38	0	0	21	38	33	10	10	1	4	32	.234	.280	.182	7.58	0.95
Pannone, Thomas	L-L	6-0	195	4-28-94	4	1	4.19	12	6	0	0	43	37	20	20	7	15	29	.231	.311	.200	6.07	3.14
Paulino, David	R-R	6-7	222	2-6-94	1	0	1.35	7	0	0	0	7	6	2	1	1	2	6	.240	.111	.313	8.10	2.70
Petricka, Jake	R-R	6-5	220	6-5-88	3	1	4.53	41	0	0	0	46	59	28	23	6	16	41	.317	.257	.357	8.08	3.15
Ramirez, Carlos	R-R	6-5	205	4-24-91	0	0	3.86	2	0	0	0	2	1	1	1	0	5	3	.125	.167	.000	11.57	19.29
2-team total (3 Oakland)					0	0	3.24	5	0	0	0	8	3	3	3	0	9	5	.115	.100	.125	5.40	9.72
Reid-Foley, Sean	R-R	6-3	220	8-30-95	2	4	5.13	7	7	0	0	33	31	23	19	6	21	42	.244	.209	.283	11.34	5.67
Rowley, Chris	R-R	6-2	195	8-14-90	0	1	40.50	2	0	0	0	1	2	4	3	1	1	0	.400	.500	.333	0.00	13.50
Sanchez, Aaron	R-R	6-4	215	7-1-92	4	6	4.89	20	20	0	0	105	106	62	57	11	58	86	.262	.288	.237	7.37	4.97
Santos, Luis	R-R	6-0	185	2-11-91	1	1	7.20	15	1	0	0	20	26	16	16	4	10	24	.333	.378	.273	10.80	4.50
Shafer, Justin	R-R	6-2	195	9-18-92	0	0	3.24	6	0	0	0	8	6	4	3	1	7	2	.194	.091	.250	2.16	7.56
Smith, Murphy	R-R	6-3	210	8-25-87	0	0	8.10	3	0	0	0	3	5	3	3	0	1	0	.385	.500	.286	0.00	2.70
Stroman, Marcus	R-R	5-8	180	5-1-91	4	9	5.54	19	19	0	0	102	115	68	63	9	36	77	.283	.272	.295	6.77	3.17
Tepera, Ryan	R-R	6-2	195	11-3-87	5	5	3.62	68	0	0	7	65	55	27	26	9	24	68	.237	.274	.212	9.46	3.34

Fielding

Catcher	PCT	G	PO	A	E	DP	PB
Jansen	.989	29	169	13	2	1	0
Maile	.989	66	485	43	6	5	4
Martin	.992	71	591	38	5	4	3
McGuire	.987	11	72	3	1	0	1

First Base	PCT	G	PO	A	E	DP
Donaldson	.875	1	6	1	1	2
McKinney	1.000	1	1	0	0	0
Morales	.992	18	116	9	1	13
Pearce	1.000	3	22	1	0	1
Smoak	.999	134	1036	39	1	98
Solarte	1.000	4	5	1	0	0
Tellez	.984	17	113	10	2	11

Second Base	PCT	G	PO	A	E	DP
Berti	1.000	4	6	6	0	3
Drury	1.000	2	1	1	0	0
Gurriel Jr.	.982	24	43	65	2	15

	PCT	G	PO	A	E	DP
Ngoepe	1.000	5	3	5	0	1
Solarte	.991	28	47	59	1	12
Travis	.978	101	161	247	9	72
Urena	1.000	13	13	21	0	2

Third Base	PCT	G	PO	A	E	DP
Diaz	.973	38	18	53	2	4
Donaldson	.970	26	16	49	2	7
Drury	.923	6	2	10	1	4
Martin	.959	21	11	36	2	2
Morales	.000	1	0	0	0	0
Ngoepe	1.000	1	0	1	0	0
Solarte	.964	83	50	137	7	15
Sweeney	.000	1	0	0	0	0
Urena	1.000	3	1	3	0	0
Urshela	1.000	10	3	12	0	0

Shortstop	PCT	G	PO	A	E	DP
Diaz	.980	95	124	221	7	55
Drury	1.000	1	1	2	0	1

	PCT	G	PO	A	E	DP
Gurriel Jr.	.955	46	43	105	7	20
Martin	1.000	3	1	1	0	0
Ngoepe	1.000	6	5	11	0	5
Solarte	1.000	7	7	14	0	3
Urena	.944	20	16	35	3	6
Urshela	.941	8	5	11	1	0

Outfield	PCT	G	PO	A	E	DP
Alford	1.000	11	14	0	0	0
Davis	.952	16	19	1	1	1
Granderson	.966	71	109	4	4	1
Grichuk	.996	121	232	5	1	2
Hernandez	.965	119	211	11	8	2
Martin	1.000	1	2	0	0	0
McKinney	.984	34	62	0	1	0
Pearce	1.000	11	17	0	0	0
Pillar	.984	142	352	7	6	2
Pompey	1.000	3	5	0	0	0
Smith Jr.	1.000	25	36	1	0	0
Sweeney	1.000	1	2	0	0	0

BUFFALO BISONS   TRIPLE-A
INTERNATIONAL LEAGUE

Batting	B-T	HT	WT	DOB	AVG	vLH	vRH	G	AB	R	H	2B	3B	HR	RBI	BB	HBP	SH	SF	SO	SB	CS	SLG	OBP
Alford, Anthony	R-R	6-1	215	7-20-94	.240	.250	.236	105	375	52	90	22	1	5	34	30	10	0	2	112	17	7	.344	.312
Berti, Jon	R-R	5-10	195	1-22-90	.250	.000	.286	4	8	1	2	0	0	0	1	0	0	0	0	3	0	0	.250	.250
2-team total (25 Columbus)					.221	.300	.188	29	68	11	15	1	0	0	4	9	2	1	1	16	8	1	.235	.325
Davis, Jonathan	R-R	5-8	190	5-12-92	.249	.182	.277	46	185	26	46	7	2	5	23	12	4	1	0	41	7	1	.389	.309
De La Cruz, Michael	B-R	5-10	190	5-15-93	.186	.333	.129	14	43	4	8	5	1	0	4	6	0	1	0	17	0	0	.349	.286
Espinosa, Danny	B-R	6-0	205	4-25-87	.232	.231	.233	13	56	5	13	3	0	0	2	3	0	1	0	15	0	0	.286	.271
2-team total (31 Lehigh Valley)					.211	.154	.230	44	161	16	34	7	0	4	16	8	2	1	3	45	3	0	.329	.253
Fields, Roemon	L-L	5-11	180	11-28-90	.238	.191	.254	100	328	41	78	10	3	2	27	29	5	2	3	80	25	16	.305	.307
Grichuk, Randal	R-R	6-1	205	8-13-91	.250	.333	.200	2	8	1	2	0	0	1	2	1	0	0	0	3	0	0	.625	.333
Guerrero Jr., Vladimir	R-R	6-1	200	3-16-99	.336	.290	.361	30	110	15	37	7	0	6	16	15	1	0	2	10	0	0	.564	.414
Guillotte, Andrew	R-R	5-8	170	3-30-93	.091	.000	.100	7	11	1	1	0	0	0	0	0	0	0	0	4	1	0	.091	.091
Gurriel Jr., Lourdes	R-R	6-2	185	10-10-93	.293	.289	.294	37	147	20	43	8	0	5	30	4	3	0	2	34	3	2	.449	.321
Heidt, Gunnar	R-R	6-0	200	9-12-92	.286	.250	.298	18	63	8	18	5	0	2	6	7	0	0	0	27	1	0	.460	.357
Hernandez, Teoscar	R-R	6-2	180	10-15-92	.278	.250	.286	4	18	4	5	1	0	2	3	0	0	0	0	7	2	0	.667	.278
Jansen, Danny	R-R	6-2	225	4-15-95	.275	.302	.262	88	298	45	82	21	1	12	58	44	14	1	3	49	5	1	.473	.390
Ladendorf, Tyler	R-R	5-11	195	3-7-88	.000	.000	.000	2	6	0	0	0	0	0	0	0	0	0	0	1	0	0	.000	.000
Leblebijian, Jason	R-R	6-2	205	5-13-91	.220	.220	.220	84	282	40	62	8	1	10	41	36	4	0	2	98	5	3	.362	.315
Lopes, Tim	R-R	5-11	180	6-24-94	.277	.274	.278	104	354	41	98	19	3	2	29	26	1	0	4	58	18	8	.364	.325
McGuire, Reese	L-R	5-11	215	3-2-95	.233	.225	.236	96	322	31	75	9	2	7	37	33	6	4	4	77	3	2	.339	.312
McKinney, Billy	L-L	6-1	205	8-23-94	.203	.154	.237	20	64	10	13	3	2	3	8	6	0	0	0	16	0	0	.453	.292
2-team total (56 Scranton/Wilkes-Barre)					.221	.206	.229	76	276	37	61	11	7	16	40	29	1	0	0	72	0	0	.486	.297
Mineo, Alberto	L-R	5-10	170	7-23-94	.462	1.000	.417	4	13	2	6	0	0	1	3	2	0	0	0	0	0	0	.692	.533
Ngoepe, Gift	R-R	5-8	200	1-18-90	.180	.185	.156	48	131	15	22	3	1	2	8	25	1	1	1	63	2	1	.252	.304
Parmley, Ian	L-L	5-11	175	12-19-89	.263	.267	.261	40	118	15	31	3	3	0	14	4	1	1	0	30	2	1	.339	.293
Pearce, Steve	R-R	5-11	200	4-13-83	.364	.250	.667	4	11	1	4	0	0	1	3	3	1	0	0	1	0	0	.636	.533
Pompey, Dalton	B-R	6-2	195	12-11-92	.255	.167	.284	41	145	22	37	8	0	4	17	14	3	2	4	41	8	2	.393	.325

Name	B-T	HT	WT	DOB																				
Smith Jr., Dwight	L-R	5-11	195	10-26-92	.268	.282	.261	85	310	39	83	25	1	6	42	44	2	1	4	53	9	3	.413	.358
Sweeney, Darnell	B-R	6-1	205	2-1-91	.236	.221	.241	88	292	47	69	13	4	10	37	31	3	1	5	113	6	5	.411	.311
Tellez, Rowdy	L-L	6-4	220	3-16-95	.270	.277	.267	112	393	43	106	22	0	13	50	40	5	0	6	74	7	4	.425	.340
Travis, Devon	R-R	5-9	190	2-21-91	.210	.280	.162	14	62	9	13	1	0	1	4	2	0	0	0	7	1	0	.274	.234
Urena, Richard	B-R	6-0	185	2-26-96	.216	.207	.219	65	250	28	54	11	3	5	29	12	0	4	2	48	2	3	.344	.250
Urshela, Gio	R-R	6-0	215	10-11-91	.244	.118	.275	24	86	7	21	3	0	0	5	4	0	0	1	9	0	0	.279	.275
3-team total (11 Columbus, 27 Scranton/W-B)					.286	.300	.282	62	224	27	64	14	2	2	24	13	1	1	1	31	0	0	.393	.326

Pitching	B-T	HT	WT	DOB	W	L	ERA	G	GS	CG	SV	IP	H	R	ER	HR	BB	SO	AVG	vLH	vRH	K/9	BB/9
Alburquerque, Al	R-R	6-0	195	6-10-86	1	1	3.77	25	0	0	4	29	34	16	12	3	8	27	.301	.313	.292	8.48	2.51
Barnes, Danny	L-R	6-1	195	10-21-89	1	1	5.19	7	0	0	0	9	9	5	5	1	1	11	.257	.250	.261	11.42	1.04
Biagini, Joe	R-R	6-5	240	5-29-90	0	3	4.57	4	4	0	0	22	19	12	11	1	8	13	.232	.216	.244	5.40	3.32
Borucki, Ryan	L-L	6-4	195	3-31-94	6	5	3.27	13	13	1	0	77	62	29	28	6	28	58	.221	.191	.234	6.78	3.27
Breslow, Craig	L-L	6-0	190	8-8-80	1	1	5.59	21	0	0	0	19	29	13	12	3	15	21	.333	.350	.319	9.78	6.98
Case, Andrew	R-R	6-2	230	1-6-93	0	0	3.00	1	0	0	0	3	2	1	1	0	0	1	.182	.333	.125	3.00	0.00
Cruz, Rhiner	R-R	6-2	210	11-1-86	1	0	1.04	6	0	0	1	9	6	1	1	1	5	9	.200	.167	.222	9.35	5.19
Cumpton, Brandon	R-R	6-2	215	11-16-88	2	5	6.15	12	9	0	1	53	62	37	36	9	15	31	.293	.228	.342	5.30	2.56
Custodio, Claudio	R-R	5-10	155	10-30-90	0	0	4.50	5	0	0	0	10	9	6	5	0	4	8	.231	.238	.222	7.20	3.60
DeGraaf, Josh	R-R	6-4	195	1-28-93	0	0	7.36	1	1	0	0	4	4	3	3	1	2	2	.286	.143	.429	4.91	4.91
Dermody, Matt	R-L	6-5	190	7-4-90	0	0	7.20	5	0	0	0	5	7	4	4	0	4	6	.333	.125	.462	10.80	7.20
Dillon, Justin	R-R	6-3	225	9-5-93	2	1	0.79	4	3	1	1	23	10	3	2	2	2	19	.130	.105	.154	7.54	0.79
Eller, Connor	R-R	6-2	195	1-23-94	0	0	33.75	1	0	0	0	1	5	5	5	0	1	0	.625	.500	.667	0.00	6.75
Estrada, Marco	R-R	6-0	180	7-5-83	0	1	8.10	1	1	0	0	3	3	3	3	2	2	3	.250	.333	.167	8.10	5.40
Fernandez, Jose	L-L	6-3	170	2-13-93	1	2	2.45	21	0	0	2	29	23	10	8	2	8	32	.209	.256	.183	9.82	2.45
Fishman, Jake	L-L	6-3	195	2-8-95	0	0	0.00	1	0	0	0	1	0	0	0	0	0	1	.000	.000	.000	6.75	0.00
Fisk, Conor	R-R	6-2	210	4-4-92	3	4	2.81	34	1	0	1	58	56	21	18	4	18	46	.255	.272	.242	7.18	2.81
Gaviglio, Sam	R-R	6-2	195	5-22-90	0	0	1.86	5	5	0	0	29	21	6	4	4	4	29	.206	.125	.258	9.00	1.24
Girodo, Chad	L-L	6-1	190	2-6-91	0	1	12.27	3	0	0	0	4	7	5	5	3	0	3	.389	.286	.455	7.36	0.00
Guerrieri, Taylor	R-R	6-2	210	12-1-92	2	2	5.18	23	7	0	0	57	68	37	33	8	22	41	.294	.326	.273	6.44	3.45
Guilmet, Preston	R-R	6-2	200	7-27-87	0	0	5.79	3	0	0	0	5	7	3	3	2	1	2	.368	.500	.273	3.86	1.93
Harris, Jon	R-R	6-4	175	10-16-93	1	1	3.00	2	2	0	0	12	14	5	4	1	1	9	.298	.429	.192	6.75	0.75
Hauschild, Mike	R-R	6-3	210	1-22-90	1	1	4.98	4	4	0	0	22	23	13	12	3	8	10	.271	.387	.204	4.15	3.32
Higuera, Juliandry	L-L	6-1	180	9-6-94	0	1	7.71	1	0	0	0	2	1	2	2	0	2	1	.125	.000	.200	3.86	7.71
Isaacs, Dusty	R-R	6-1	190	8-7-91	1	0	6.30	6	0	0	0	10	15	8	7	1	5	8	.341	.370	.294	7.20	4.50
Mayza, Tim	L-L	6-3	220	1-15-92	6	2	4.56	20	0	0	1	26	26	14	13	2	11	36	.265	.370	.173	12.62	3.86
McGuire, Deck	R-R	6-6	220	6-23-89	4	2	3.22	8	8	0	0	45	33	18	16	3	19	40	.210	.242	.187	8.06	3.83
Moll, Sam	L-L	5-10	185	1-3-92	1	3	5.30	15	0	0	1	19	24	15	11	1	5	19	.293	.235	.333	9.16	2.41
Morimando, Shawn	L-L	6-0	200	11-20-92	1	3	4.50	4	4	0	0	20	21	11	10	5	2	11	.259	.214	.269	4.95	0.90
2-team total (5 Columbus)					2	6	5.89	9	9	0	0	44	65	33	29	6	12	22	.339	.250	.342	4.47	2.44
Osuna, Roberto	R-R	6-2	215	2-7-95	0	0	0.00	3	0	0	0	3	5	0	0	0	2	5	.385	.667	.300	15.00	6.00
Pannone, Thomas	L-L	6-0	195	4-28-94	3	0	4.91	6	6	0	0	37	40	21	20	8	7	40	.276	.273	.278	9.82	1.72
Petricka, Jake	R-R	6-5	220	6-5-88	0	0	0.78	16	0	0	2	23	20	5	2	1	5	14	.244	.333	.184	5.48	1.96
Ramirez, Carlos	R-R	6-5	205	4-24-91	0	1	5.40	7	0	0	1	8	2	5	5	0	8	10	.074	.182	.000	10.80	8.64
Reid-Foley, Sean	R-R	6-3	220	8-30-95	7	5	3.90	16	16	1	0	85	76	39	37	5	30	98	.235	.261	.211	10.34	3.16
Rodriguez, Dalton	R-R	6-1	180	8-20-96	0	0	16.20	1	0	0	0	2	2	3	3	1	2	3	.286	.400	.000	16.20	10.80
Romano, Jordan	R-R	6-4	200	4-21-93	1	0	3.60	1	1	0	0	5	4	2	2	0	4	3	.222	.300	.125	5.40	7.20
Rowley, Chris	R-R	6-2	195	8-14-90	5	6	3.30	17	17	0	0	101	98	48	37	11	42	63	.253	.246	.260	5.61	3.74
Santos, Luis	R-R	6-0	185	2-11-91	2	3	2.74	20	2	0	0	43	41	22	13	2	13	40	.241	.282	.207	8.44	2.74
Shafer, Justin	R-R	6-2	195	9-18-92	3	3	1.41	34	0	0	15	38	27	10	6	0	16	32	.202	.196	.205	7.51	3.76
Smith, Murphy	R-R	6-3	210	8-25-87	3	4	3.59	26	7	0	1	63	61	30	25	7	25	42	.255	.257	.254	6.03	3.59
Stewart, Zach	R-R	6-2	205	9-28-86	2	1	4.98	14	4	0	0	34	46	20	19	3	12	19	.322	.300	.337	4.98	3.15
Tepesch, Nick	R-R	6-4	240	10-12-88	1	6	7.90	10	8	0	0	41	58	39	36	12	13	20	.331	.356	.307	4.39	2.85
Tracy, Matt	L-L	6-3	215	11-26-88	1	1	2.40	11	9	0	0	49	42	14	13	0	20	32	.237	.163	.266	5.92	3.70
Waguespack, Jacob	R-R	6-6	225	11-5-93	2	4	5.03	7	6	1	0	39	47	26	22	3	10	33	.294	.260	.325	7.55	2.29
2-team total (14 Lehigh Valley)					5	9	5.05	21	14	1	1	93	101	60	52	7	30	81	.277	.282	.272	7.87	2.91

Fielding

Catcher	PCT	G	PO	A	E	DP	PB
De La Cruz	1.000	11	59	5	0	0	1
Jansen	.987	56	364	18	5	3	5
McGuire	.983	73	546	24	10	5	8
Mineo	.917	3	11	0	1	0	0

First Base	PCT	G	PO	A	E	DP
De La Cruz	1.000	4	32	0	0	1
Gurriel Jr.	1.000	1	1	1	0	1
Heidt	.982	7	49	5	1	4
Leblebijian	.992	18	121	10	1	18
McKinney	1.000	4	26	2	0	3
Tellez	.994	107	821	53	5	80
Urshela	1.000	7	44	4	0	1

Second Base	PCT	G	PO	A	E	DP
Guillotte	1.000	1	2	2	0	1
Gurriel Jr.	.956	9	17	26	2	6
Leblebijian	.972	7	13	22	1	8
Lopes	.986	69	95	180	4	38
Ngoepe	.952	4	6	14	1	3
Sweeney	.966	24	40	73	4	14
Travis	.983	12	16	41	1	7
Urena	.986	17	25	43	1	10

Third Base	PCT	G	PO	A	E	DP
Berti	1.000	3	2	2	0	0
Guerrero Jr.	.937	25	13	61	5	6
Heidt	1.000	1	1	1	0	0
Leblebijian	.932	48	31	92	9	13
Lopes	.973	18	9	27	1	0
Ngoepe	1.000	14	14	26	0	4
Sweeney	.923	21	7	29	3	1
Urena	1.000	3	4	5	0	0
Urshela	.917	14	5	17	2	3

Shortstop	PCT	G	PO	A	E	DP
Espinosa	.949	12	12	25	2	3
Gurriel Jr.	.990	23	37	60	1	13
Heidt	.956	12	14	29	2	7
Ladendorf	.857	2	2	4	1	1
Leblebijian	.957	5	7	15	1	0
Ngoepe	.948	29	43	67	6	18
Sweeney	.939	13	19	27	3	6
Urena	.982	43	55	110	3	24
Urshela	.875	2	3	4	1	2

Outfield	PCT	G	PO	A	E	DP
Alford	.973	97	212	4	6	1
Davis	1.000	44	99	1	0	0
Fields	.978	97	252	9	6	2
Grichuk	1.000	1	3	0	0	0
Guillotte	1.000	4	3	0	0	0
Hernandez	1.000	4	11	0	0	0

	PCT	G	PO	A	E	DP			PCT	G	PO	A	E	DP			PCT	G	PO	A	E	DP
Leblebijian	.667	3	2	0	1	0		Parmley	.973	37	71	2	2	0		Smith Jr.	.973	74	136	8	4	0
Lopes	.500	1	1	0	1	0		Pearce	1.000	2	4	0	0	0		Sweeney	.947	21	36	0	2	0
McKinney	.963	14	22	4	1	1		Pompey	1.000	38	54	1	0	0								

NEW HAMPSHIRE FISHER CATS DOUBLE-A
EASTERN LEAGUE

TORONTO BLUE JAYS

Batting	B-T	HT	WT	DOB	AVG	vLH	vRH	G	AB	R	H	2B	3B	HR	RBI	BB	HBP	SH	SF	SO	SB	CS	SLG	OBP
Berti, Jon	R-R	5-10	195	1-22-90	.314	.287	.328	72	277	55	87	13	7	8	42	29	10	0	0	46	21	9	.498	.399
Bichette, Bo	R-R	6-0	200	3-5-98	.286	.324	.271	131	539	95	154	43	7	11	74	48	2	1	5	101	32	11	.453	.343
Biggio, Cavan	L-R	6-1	203	4-11-95	.252	.276	.242	132	449	80	113	23	5	26	99	100	5	1	8	148	20	8	.499	.388
Cantwell, Patrick	R-R	6-2	210	4-10-90	.276	.147	.323	40	127	21	35	4	2	4	19	18	6	2	2	31	2	1	.433	.386
Davis, Jonathan	R-R	5-8	190	5-12-92	.302	.433	.265	78	305	68	92	22	3	5	33	35	11	2	5	53	19	3	.443	.388
Diaz, Aledmys	R-R	6-1	195	8-1-90	.400	.500	.333	3	10	3	4	3	0	0	0	0	0	0	0	0	0	0	.700	.400
Espinal, Santiago	R-R	5-10	175	11-13-94	.286	.304	.277	42	147	17	42	9	2	1	20	14	2	0	1	22	2	1	.395	.354
Grichuk, Randal	R-R	6-1	205	8-13-91	.143	—	.143	2	7	1	1	0	0	0	0	1	0	0	0	2	0	0	.143	.250
Guerrero Jr., Vladimir	R-R	6-1	200	3-16-99	.402	.405	.401	61	234	48	94	19	1	14	60	21	4	1	6	27	3	3	.671	.449
Guillotte, Andrew	R-R	5-8	170	3-30-93	.251	.250	.251	107	331	53	83	17	1	2	30	43	3	2	7	68	9	8	.326	.336
Gurriel Jr., Lourdes	R-R	6-2	185	10-10-93	.322	.308	.326	14	59	7	19	3	1	2	14	3	1	0	2	8	1	1	.509	.354
Heidt, Gunnar	R-R	6-0	200	9-12-92	.229	.278	.212	85	284	30	65	16	2	4	28	27	2	4	3	76	7	5	.342	.298
Hissey, Ryan	L-R	6-0	190	4-8-94	.173	.103	.198	34	110	12	19	3	0	2	7	6	0	2	0	28	0	0	.255	.216
Kelly, Juan	B-R	5-10	218	7-16-94	.221	.221	.221	87	290	37	64	15	0	13	40	40	2	0	2	89	2	3	.407	.317
Knight, Nash	B-R	6-0	195	9-20-92	.161	.154	.167	11	31	3	5	0	0	1	1	2	0	0	0	5	0	0	.258	.212
Palacios, Joshua	L-R	6-1	193	7-30-95	.000	.000	.000	1	3	0	0	0	0	0	0	0	0	0	0	2	0	0	.000	.000
Panas, Connor	L-R	6-2	218	2-11-93	.232	.247	.228	105	370	39	86	16	2	9	39	25	9	0	2	84	4	3	.360	.296
Pentecost, Max	R-R	6-2	191	3-10-93	.253	.337	.224	89	344	40	87	17	2	10	52	15	2	0	7	89	1	0	.401	.283
Pinto, Eduard	L-L	5-11	150	10-23-94	.218	.231	.212	35	124	15	27	3	0	2	8	4	0	2	0	17	3	2	.290	.242
Pompey, Dalton	B-R	6-2	195	12-11-92	.200	.333	.111	4	15	3	3	0	0	0	1	4	0	0	0	3	1	0	.200	.368
Ramirez, Harold	R-R	5-10	220	9-6-94	.320	.291	.330	120	463	60	148	37	0	11	70	27	9	1	5	88	16	2	.471	.365
Wall, Forrest	L-R	6-0	176	11-20-95	.271	.267	.274	35	129	19	35	7	2	1	13	13	0	0	1	46	10	3	.380	.354
2-team total (46 Hartford)					.234	.242	.231	81	299	46	70	13	3	7	25	30	7	0	1	88	18	6	.368	.318

Pitching	B-T	HT	WT	DOB	W	L	ERA	G	GS	CG	SV	IP	H	R	ER	HR	BB	SO	AVG	vLH	vRH	K/9	BB/9
Barrett, Jordan	L-L	6-4	225	6-24-95	0	0	2.70	1	1	0	0	3	2	1	1	0	2	2	.200	.000	.286	5.40	5.40
Bergen, Travis	L-L	6-1	205	10-8-93	4	1	0.50	27	0	0	7	36	26	8	2	2	9	43	.196	.217	.184	10.85	2.27
Bouchey, Brayden	R-R	6-6	212	9-20-95	0	0	1.59	4	0	0	0	6	4	1	1	0	3	5	.200	.182	.222	7.94	4.76
Breslow, Craig	L-L	6-0	190	8-8-80	1	0	5.63	11	0	0	0	8	4	5	5	0	9	8	.138	.143	.133	9.00	10.13
Case, Andrew	R-R	6-2	230	1-6-93	1	3	5.09	39	0	0	7	46	57	29	26	8	15	34	.302	.259	.337	6.65	2.93
Copping, Corey	R-R	6-1	175	1-11-94	0	1	1.93	10	0	0	3	14	7	5	3	1	9	20	.146	.167	.125	12.86	5.79
DeGraaf, Josh	R-R	6-4	195	1-28-93	7	6	4.33	19	15	0	0	81	90	44	39	12	23	77	.286	.288	.283	8.56	2.56
Dillon, Justin	R-R	6-3	225	9-5-93	2	4	6.84	14	7	0	0	50	60	41	38	6	22	22	.309	.360	.261	3.96	3.96
Fernandez, Jose	L-L	6-3	170	2-19-93	3	1	3.45	23	0	0	2	31	23	14	12	5	23	33	.204	.208	.200	9.48	6.61
Fisk, Conor	R-R	6-2	210	4-4-92	0	0	0.00	7	0	0	2	15	8	1	0	0	5	16	.167	.150	.179	9.60	3.00
Harris, Jon	R-R	6-4	175	10-16-93	12	5	4.75	25	25	0	0	136	152	76	72	21	31	99	.286	.278	.293	6.54	2.05
Hartman, Nick	R-R	6-2	180	10-24-94	2	1	5.40	18	0	0	0	28	36	22	17	3	16	21	.310	.352	.274	6.67	5.08
Isaacs, Dusty	R-R	6-1	190	8-7-91	3	4	4.86	38	0	0	2	50	40	29	27	7	32	56	.224	.274	.189	10.08	5.76
Jackson, Zach	R-R	6-4	215	12-25-94	2	3	2.47	43	0	0	2	62	29	20	17	2	51	75	.142	.191	.108	10.89	7.40
McClelland, Jackson	R-R	6-5	220	7-19-94	0	0	5.68	6	0	0	0	6	7	5	4	1	5	9	.259	.429	.077	12.79	7.11
Muren, Drew	L-R	6-6	225	11-22-88	1	0	0.00	1	0	0	0	1	1	0	0	0	0	2	.250	.000	.333	0.00	0.00
Murphy, Patrick	R-R	6-4	220	6-10-95	0	0	3.00	1	1	0	0	6	4	2	2	0	3	6	.200	.250	.188	9.00	4.50
Pannone, Thomas	L-L	6-0	195	4-28-94	2	2	3.00	2	2	0	0	9	9	3	3	1	5	12	.257	.222	.269	12.00	5.00
Perez, Hector	R-R	6-3	190	6-6-94	0	1	3.86	6	5	0	0	26	17	12	11	1	16	32	.193	.204	.177	11.22	5.61
Pondler, Randy	L-L	6-2	160	11-8-96	0	1	7.36	1	1	0	0	4	5	3	3	0	3	2	.357	.400	.333	4.91	7.36
Reid-Foley, Sean	R-R	6-3	220	8-30-95	5	0	2.03	8	8	0	0	44	27	10	10	3	20	52	.174	.231	.117	10.56	4.06
Rios, Francisco	R-R	6-1	180	5-6-95	1	4	7.15	14	8	0	0	39	47	33	31	9	21	29	.305	.341	.261	6.69	4.85
Rodriguez, Dalton	R-R	6-1	180	8-20-96	0	0	0.00	1	0	0	0	1	0	0	0	0	0	2	.000	—		0.00	18.00
Romano, Jordan	R-R	6-4	200	4-21-93	11	8	4.13	25	25	0	0	137	122	80	63	15	41	125	.237	.256	.216	8.19	2.69
Sanchez, Aaron	R-R	6-4	215	7-1-92	0	1	6.23	1	1	0	0	4	6	4	3	0	4	4	.316	.455	.125	8.31	8.31
Saucedo, Tayler	L-L	6-5	185	6-18-93	4	5	5.17	11	11	0	0	63	77	41	36	9	18	38	.300	.235	.323	5.46	2.59
Shafer, Justin	R-R	6-2	195	9-18-92	2	2	0.52	13	0	0	1	17	12	3	1	1	5	17	.203	.167	.229	8.83	2.60
Snead, Kirby	L-L	6-0	200	10-7-94	3	4	4.43	36	0	0	1	43	45	23	21	3	25	39	.262	.198	.319	5.27	5.27
Tepesch, Nick	R-R	6-4	240	10-12-88	1	2	5.21	10	8	0	1	48	55	31	28	6	16	30	.288	.293	.283	5.59	2.99
2-team total (4 Erie)					1	2	5.63	14	8	0	1	56	67	38	35	6	20	34	.298	.307	.290	5.46	3.21
Young, Danny	L-L	6-3	200	5-27-94	2	0	4.13	40	0	0	2	57	63	32	26	3	19	48	.283	.217	.328	7.62	3.02
Zeuch, T.J.	R-R	6-7	225	8-1-95	9	5	3.08	21	21	1	0	120	120	48	41	7	31	81	.258	.274	.241	6.08	2.33

Fielding

Catcher	PCT	G	PO	A	E	DP	PB
Cantwell	.990	36	275	31	3	1	7
Hissey	.996	28	213	26	1	3	1
Pentecost	.984	77	541	63	10	9	10

	PCT	G	PO	A	E	DP
Heidt	.990	37	284	19	3	33
Kelly	.987	73	559	37	8	59
Knight	1.000	2	13	1	0	1
Panas	1.000	10	61	4	0	4

	PCT	G	PO	A	E	DP
Biggio	.984	68	120	182	5	51
Espinal	1.000	16	28	42	0	13
Guillotte	.857	1	1	5	1	1
Gurriel Jr.	.970	7	16	16	1	10
Heidt	.982	23	46	61	2	15

First Base	PCT	G	PO	A	E	DP
Biggio	.984	22	173	8	3	20
Cantwell	1.000	1	1	1	0	1

Second Base	PCT	G	PO	A	E	DP
Berti	.938	20	22	54	5	10
Bichette	.944	9	14	20	2	2

Third Base	PCT	G	PO	A	E	DP
Berti	.942	27	21	44	4	7

	PCT	G	PO	A	E	DP		PCT	G	PO	A	E	DP		PCT	G	PO	A	E	DP
Biggio	.924	34	26	47	6	8	Diaz	1.000	2	1	5	0	1	Grichuk	1.000	1	2	0	0	0
Espinal	.919	12	11	23	3	2	Espinal	.946	12	13	22	2	2	Guillotte	1.000	100	217	14	0	2
Guerrero Jr.	.955	53	33	95	6	14	Guillotte	1.000	1	1	1	0	1	Heidt	1.000	3	4	0	0	0
Heidt	.968	10	10	20	1	2	Gurriel Jr.	1.000	5	8	6	0	2	Panas	.994	89	153	6	1	1
Kelly	.000	2	0	0	0	0	Heidt	.950	9	5	14	1	1	Pinto	.962	31	48	3	2	1
Knight	.917	7	4	7	1	2								Pompey	1.000	3	8	0	0	0

Shortstop	PCT	G	PO	A	E	DP	Outfield	PCT	G	PO	A	E	DP	Ramirez	.978	79	132	3	3	1
Bichette	.949	116	177	291	25	79	Berti	1.000	13	23	0	0	0	Wall	.971	34	66	2	2	0
Biggio	1.000	1	0	1	0	0	Biggio	1.000	2	6	1	0	1							
							Davis	.995	77	195	1	1	0							

DUNEDIN BLUE JAYS — HIGH CLASS A
FLORIDA STATE LEAGUE

Batting	B-T	HT	WT	DOB	AVG	vLH	vRH	G	AB	R	H	2B	3B	HR	RBI	BB	HBP	SH	SF	SO	SB	CS	SLG	OBP
Adams, Riley	R-R	6-4	225	6-26-96	.246	.242	.249	99	349	49	86	26	1	4	43	50	8	0	2	93	3	0	.361	.352
Alford, Anthony	R-R	6-1	215	7-20-94	.200	.000	.333	7	20	2	4	1	0	0	2	3	2	0	0	8	0	1	.250	.360
Cardenas, J.C.	B-R	6-0	185	6-27-94	.250	.000	1.000	1	4	0	1	0	0	0	1	0	0	0	0	2	0	0	.250	.250
Castillo, Ivan	B-R	5-9	173	5-30-95	.304	.353	.282	108	388	41	118	25	8	5	44	23	3	0	3	51	8	8	.449	.345
Clemens, Kacy	L-R	6-2	200	7-27-94	.211	.205	.214	93	336	46	71	15	1	5	40	38	3	0	6	94	1	0	.307	.292
Davis, D.J.	L-R	6-1	180	7-25-94	.239	.242	.237	36	109	16	26	5	1	2	5	9	2	0	0	35	2	1	.358	.308
Donaldson, Josh	R-R	6-1	210	12-8-85	.400	.500	.375	4	10	1	4	0	0	1	3	2	0	0	0	0	0	0	.700	.500
Espinal, Santiago	R-R	5-10	175	11-13-94	.262	.318	.233	17	65	9	17	3	1	2	8	6	1	1	0	10	0	3	.431	.333
Grichuk, Randal	R-R	6-1	205	8-13-91	.333	.000	.400	3	6	2	2	0	0	1	2	5	0	0	0	3	0	0	.833	.636
Gudino, Yeltsin	R-R	6-0	150	1-17-97	.238	.161	.279	53	160	17	38	2	0	0	23	17	3	1	7	26	4	0	.250	.310
Guerrero Jr., Vladimir	R-R	6-1	200	3-16-99	.500	.500	—	1	4	1	2	1	0	0	0	0	0	0	0	0	0	0	.750	.500
Jacob, David	L-L	6-4	225	6-19-95	.205	.227	.196	42	151	17	31	6	0	5	18	17	6	0	0	47	1	0	.344	.310
Jones, Bradley	R-R	6-1	180	6-12-95	.248	.256	.243	57	222	24	55	13	2	5	23	12	2	0	1	71	3	1	.392	.291
Knight, Nash	B-R	6-0	195	9-20-92	.246	.333	.211	99	350	44	86	14	1	3	44	39	9	0	2	67	0	3	.317	.335
La Prise, John	L-R	6-2	180	8-24-93	.230	.333	.172	40	135	19	31	4	1	1	7	19	1	0	1	52	2	0	.296	.327
Lundquist, Brock	L-R	5-11	190	1-23-96	.337	.286	.350	49	178	26	60	11	0	5	26	16	5	0	3	35	1	0	.483	.401
Mineo, Alberto	L-R	5-10	170	7-23-94	.294	.382	.276	57	197	34	58	14	1	2	23	25	3	1	3	40	0	0	.406	.377
Molina, Jonelvy	R-R	6-0	180	3-18-97	.500	.400	1.000	2	6	0	3	1	0	0	1	2	0	0	0	1	0	0	.667	.625
Orozco, Rodrigo	B-R	5-11	155	4-2-95	.304	.339	.288	112	378	70	115	23	3	1	39	40	3	3	0	53	18	4	.389	.375
Palacios, Joshua	L-R	6-1	193	7-30-95	.292	.299	.289	125	507	62	148	30	5	8	78	47	5	1	2	125	15	9	.418	.357
Pinto, Eduard	L-L	5-11	150	10-23-94	.308	.348	.291	63	227	34	70	15	1	2	30	15	3	4	2	15	8	8	.410	.356
Pompey, Dalton	B-R	6-2	195	12-11-92	.444	.400	.462	5	18	4	8	3	0	1	5	2	0	0	0	2	1	0	.778	.500
Smith, Kevin	R-R	6-1	188	7-4-96	.274	.233	.291	83	340	57	93	8	2	18	49	23	7	0	1	88	17	5	.468	.332
Sotillo, Andres	R-R	5-11	180	12-28-93	.143	.111	.200	4	14	1	2	0	0	1	2	0	0	0	1	3	0	0	.357	.133
Spanberger, Chad	L-R	6-3	235	11-1-95	.231	.240	.226	22	78	8	18	2	0	3	9	14	0	0	0	17	0	0	.372	.348
Spiwak, Owen	L-R	6-2	185	5-23-95	.000	—	.000	1	3	0	0	0	0	0	0	0	0	0	0	1	0	0	.000	.000
Urena, Richard	B-R	6-0	185	2-26-96	.148	.083	.200	7	27	1	4	1	0	0	2	1	0	0	1	6	0	0	.148	.172
Warmoth, Logan	R-R	6-0	190	9-6-95	.248	.310	.221	75	282	31	70	13	2	1	28	30	3	2	5	69	9	0	.319	.322

Pitching	B-T	HT	WT	DOB	W	L	ERA	G	GS	CG	SV	IP	H	R	ER	HR	BB	SO	AVG	vLH	vRH	K/9	BB/9
Baker, Bryan	R-R	6-6	220	12-2-94	1	1	2.84	6	0	0	1	6	5	2	2	2	3	9	.227	.250	.200	12.79	4.26
Bergen, Travis	L-L	6-1	205	10-8-93	0	1	1.71	16	0	0	1	21	16	4	4	0	6	31	.208	.241	.188	13.29	2.57
Buffo, Maverik	R-R	6-2	200	9-15-95	3	4	6.12	11	11	0	0	57	74	42	39	6	16	48	.308	.347	.266	7.53	2.51
Cheshire, Jonathan	L-R	6-1	185	11-15-94	6	1	2.47	33	1	0	0	51	42	19	14	2	12	45	.221	.286	.152	7.94	2.12
Custodio, Claudio	R-R	5-10	155	10-30-90	1	0	3.71	11	0	0	0	17	17	7	7	1	5	11	.254	.273	.235	5.82	2.65
DeGraaf, Josh	R-R	6-4	195	1-28-93	1	5	4.08	7	7	0	0	40	43	25	18	3	10	34	.276	.258	.287	7.71	2.27
Diaz, Yennsy	R-R	6-1	160	11-15-96	5	4	3.52	18	16	0	0	100	91	42	39	5	28	83	.242	.231	.254	7.49	2.53
Dillon, Justin	R-R	6-3	225	9-5-93	0	3	4.43	6	4	0	0	22	23	12	11	5	8	17	.258	.263	.255	6.85	3.22
Eller, Connor	R-R	6-1	195	1-23-94	7	7	4.18	34	12	0	0	80	96	44	37	3	29	54	.296	.306	.287	6.10	3.28
Espinal, Joel	R-R	6-1	185	8-15-96	0	0	0.00	1	0	0	0	3	0	0	0	0	2	3	.000	.000	.000	9.00	6.00
Fishman, Jake	L-L	6-3	195	2-8-95	2	3	2.68	44	0	0	8	57	46	22	17	2	11	56	.224	.203	.237	8.84	1.74
Garcia, Jaime	L-L	6-2	215	7-8-86	0	0	0.00	1	1	0	0	1	0	0	0	0	0	2	.000	—	.000	18.00	0.00
Gunter, Matt	L-L	6-1	190	2-7-94	0	0	3.55	3	2	0	0	13	9	7	5	2	3	11	.196	.235	.172	7.82	2.13
Hartman, Nick	R-R	6-2	180	10-24-94	2	1	4.80	21	0	0	2	30	41	18	16	0	10	38	.333	.321	.343	11.40	3.00
Higuera, Juliandry	L-L	6-1	180	9-6-94	2	3	6.07	28	1	0	0	43	48	31	29	3	24	35	.298	.286	.308	7.33	5.02
Law, Connor	R-R	6-4	195	4-27-94	0	0	0.00	2	0	0	0	4	3	0	0	0	1	2	.250	.286	.200	4.91	2.45
Logue, Zach	L-L	6-0	165	4-23-96	9	3	3.41	18	16	0	0	100	102	41	38	8	23	85	.264	.252	.272	7.62	2.06
McClelland, Jackson	R-R	6-5	220	7-19-94	1	4	4.10	33	0	0	8	37	27	23	17	4	16	48	.193	.203	.183	11.57	3.86
Murphy, Patrick	R-R	6-2	200	6-10-95	10	5	2.64	26	26	1	0	147	126	51	43	5	50	135	.233	.224	.244	8.28	3.07
Nunez, Anderson	R-R	6-1	190	12-23-97	0	0	20.25	2	0	0	0	1	2	3	3	0	1	1	.333	.000	.500	6.75	6.75
Osuna, Roberto	R-R	6-2	215	2-7-95	0	0	0.00	2	0	0	0	2	1	0	0	0	0	1	.143	.250	.000	4.50	0.00
Ouellette, William	R-R	6-1	195	6-30-93	0	1	4.14	35	0	0	4	46	63	29	21	3	13	27	.326	.347	.306	5.32	2.56
Pannone, Thomas	L-L	6-0	195	4-28-94	0	1	13.50	1	1	0	0	5	9	7	7	1	1	1	.450	.000	.500	1.93	1.93
Pearson, Nate	R-R	6-6	245	8-20-96	1	1	10.80	1	1	0	0	2	5	3	2	1	0	1	.500	.333	.571	5.40	0.00
Perdomo, Angel	L-L	6-6	200	5-7-94	1	5	3.63	26	12	0	1	79	68	38	32	5	35	100	.233	.204	.246	11.34	3.97
Pondler, Randy	L-L	6-2	195	10-12-94	1	0	1.93	1	0	0	0	5	6	1	1	0	2	6	.333	.000	.400	11.57	3.86
Ravel, Andy	R-R	6-2	165	10-12-94	0	0	6.85	16	1	0	0	24	29	19	18	1	9	18	.296	.229	.360	6.85	3.42
Sanchez, Aaron	R-R	6-4	215	7-1-92	0	0	2.45	1	1	0	0	4	2	1	1	0	4	3	.167	.000	.286	7.36	9.82
Saucedo, Tayler	L-L	6-5	185	6-18-93	6	4	3.49	15	15	1	0	85	78	44	33	7	18	66	.243	.248	.241	6.99	1.91
Snead, Kirby	L-L	6-0	200	10-7-94	1	1	1.08	8	0	0	2	8	3	1	1	0	6	12	.103	.000	.158	12.96	6.48

TORONTO BLUE JAYS

Stroman, Marcus	R-R	5-8	180	5-1-91	0	1	4.15	1	1	0	0	4	1	2	2	1	4	3	.077	.167	.000	6.23	8.31		
Tice, Ty	L-R	5-9	170	7-4-96	6	6	2.70	34	0	0	3	50	39	20	15	3	21	44	.220	.217	.223	7.92	3.78		
Zeuch, T.J.	R-R	6-7	225	8-1-95	3	3	3.47	6	6	1	0	36	34	15	14	4	9	24	.248	.250	.247	5.94	2.23		

Fielding

Catcher	PCT	G	PO	A	E	DP	PB
Adams	.992	93	702	75	6	7	11
Knight	.000	1	0	0	0	0	0
Mineo	.994	43	324	32	2	4	3
Sotillo	1.000	1	12	1	0	0	0
Spiwak	1.000	1	2	0	0	0	0

First Base	PCT	G	PO	A	E	DP
Adams	1.000	1	1	0	0	0
Clemens	.992	75	623	36	5	40
Gudino	1.000	1	1	0	0	1
Jacob	1.000	16	114	13	0	12
Jones	.993	15	135	3	1	0
Knight	.988	21	156	13	2	13
La Prise	1.000	1	3	0	0	0
Mineo	1.000	3	14	2	0	2
Spanberger	.978	11	80	8	2	11

Second Base	PCT	G	PO	A	E	DP
Castillo	.988	39	64	104	2	19
Espinal	1.000	6	8	14	0	2
Gudino	.974	26	44	69	3	10
Jones	.935	11	22	21	3	6

	PCT	G	PO	A	E	DP
Knight	1.000	2	2	4	0	1
La Prise	.979	29	37	100	3	16
Smith	.984	13	22	38	1	8
Urena	.947	3	9	9	1	3
Warmoth	1.000	14	28	39	0	10

Third Base	PCT	G	PO	A	E	DP
Castillo	.952	31	19	41	3	4
Clemens	.000	3	0	0	0	0
Donaldson	.750	3	2	4	2	0
Espinal	1.000	2	1	0	0	0
Gudino	.923	19	15	33	4	1
Guerrero Jr.	.000	1	0	0	1	0
Jones	.906	21	12	36	5	3
Knight	.942	52	36	78	7	7
La Prise	.778	10	8	13	6	0
Smith	1.000	6	4	6	0	1

Shortstop	PCT	G	PO	A	E	DP
Alford	1.000	1	1	2	0	0
Cardenas	1.000	1	1	1	0	0
Castillo	.957	11	13	31	2	7
Espinal	1.000	8	9	20	0	3

	PCT	G	PO	A	E	DP
Gudino	.971	7	11	23	1	4
Knight	.000	1	0	0	0	0
Smith	.963	63	94	189	11	32
Urena	1.000	3	1	8	0	0
Warmoth	.943	46	64	119	11	22

Outfield	PCT	G	PO	A	E	DP
Alford	1.000	5	7	0	0	0
Castillo	.952	19	39	1	2	0
Davis	.986	33	69	2	1	0
Grichuk	1.000	2	3	0	0	0
Gudino	.000	1	0	0	0	0
Jacob	1.000	7	8	0	0	0
Jones	1.000	4	8	0	0	0
Knight	1.000	4	5	0	0	0
La Prise	1.000	2	3	0	0	0
Lundquist	1.000	47	82	3	0	1
Orozco	.984	109	184	6	3	1
Ouellette	.000	1	0	0	0	0
Palacios	.972	121	267	6	8	0
Pinto	.983	59	109	5	2	1
Pompey	1.000	4	7	0	0	0
Spanberger	1.000	8	8	1	0	0

LANSING LUGNUTS

MIDWEST LEAGUE

LOW CLASS A

Batting	B-T	HT	WT	DOB	AVG	vLH	vRH	G	AB	R	H	2B	3B	HR	RBI	BB	HBP	SH	SF	SO	SB	CS	SLG	OBP
Capra, Vinny	R-R	5-8	175	7-7-96	.266	.250	.270	25	94	13	25	8	0	0	4	8	0	1	0	19	1	0	.351	.324
Clemens, Kacy	L-R	6-2	200	7-27-94	.301	.297	.304	27	93	25	28	5	2	7	25	25	1	0	0	22	1	1	.624	.454
Gold, Ryan	L-R	5-9	188	10-10-97	.264	.250	.268	56	208	21	55	9	1	2	26	11	4	0	4	46	3	0	.346	.308
Grudzielanek, Brandon	R-R	6-0	205	5-26-95	.245	.225	.252	88	322	43	79	12	4	5	35	35	4	0	5	84	9	2	.354	.322
Gudino, Yeltsin	R-R	6-0	150	1-17-97	.321	.292	.337	38	134	27	43	7	0	0	17	15	2	3	2	6	3	0	.373	.392
Hernandez, Javier	R-L	6-1	180	7-21-96	.093	.071	.103	14	43	4	4	0	0	0	5	6	3	0	2	10	0	0	.093	.241
Johnson, Reilly	R-R	5-9	160	9-26-96	.257	.100	.320	10	35	2	9	1	0	0	7	1	2	0	0	8	0	0	.286	.316
Large, Cullen	B-R	6-0	175	1-22-96	.316	.143	.365	27	95	32	30	9	0	5	18	13	3	0	1	18	3	0	.568	.411
Lizardo, Bryan	R-R	6-0	205	7-26-97	.266	.273	.264	18	64	6	17	3	0	0	6	8	0	0	0	13	0	0	.313	.347
Lundquist, Brock	L-R	6-1	190	1-23-96	.249	.273	.236	70	245	29	61	11	1	13	48	33	10	0	4	68	1	0	.461	.356
Morgan, Matt	R-R	5-11	160	1-27-96	.150	.231	.108	35	113	15	17	3	0	1	8	17	1	1	1	44	1	0	.204	.265
Navarro, Jesus	R-R	5-11	160	1-13-98	.288	.382	.267	54	184	17	53	10	0	1	22	20	2	0	5	33	4	1	.359	.356
Noda, Ryan	L-L	6-3	217	3-30-96	.256	.234	.266	124	403	78	103	24	4	20	80	109	10	0	5	135	14	4	.484	.421
Obeso, Norberto	R-R	5-11	175	7-9-95	.227	.245	.221	98	348	44	79	11	2	3	37	45	3	0	3	55	10	4	.296	.318
Polizzi, Brandon	R-R	5-10	170	3-16-96	.111	.000	.150	11	27	1	3	0	0	0	1	2	0	1	0	6	1	0	.111	.172
Pruitt, Reggie	R-R	6-0	169	5-7-97	.211	.260	.194	89	299	51	63	13	3	3	25	33	7	3	4	103	37	9	.304	.300
Rodriguez, Freddy	L-R	6-1	180	11-15-96	.205	.214	.202	36	127	13	26	4	1	0	10	10	2	0	0	32	2	2	.252	.273
Smith, Kevin	R-R	6-1	188	7-4-96	.355	.350	.358	46	183	36	65	23	4	7	44	17	1	0	3	33	12	1	.639	.407
Smith, Ridge	R-R	5-10	190	4-26-95	.286	.375	.167	4	14	1	4	0	0	1	3	0	0	0	0	3	0	0	.500	.286
Sotillo, Andres	R-R	5-11	180	12-28-93	.261	.300	.245	38	134	18	35	7	0	2	11	7	6	1	1	34	2	2	.358	.324
Spanberger, Chad	L-R	6-3	235	11-1-95	.278	.100	.346	9	36	6	10	0	1	2	6	1	0	0	1	6	0	0	.500	.290
Spiwak, Owen	L-R	6-2	185	5-23-95	.150	.000	.194	14	40	4	6	3	0	0	6	2	2	1	0	13	0	0	.225	.227
Taylor, Samad	R-R	5-10	160	7-11-98	.228	.206	.237	121	460	67	105	32	7	9	53	57	6	4	3	99	44	16	.387	.319
Vicuna, Kevin	R-R	6-0	140	1-14-98	.266	.281	.260	89	372	60	99	16	6	2	37	18	4	1	0	56	10	8	.358	.307
Williams, Christian	L-R	6-3	210	9-14-94	.285	.366	.244	32	123	19	35	10	0	4	18	10	1	0	1	34	0	0	.463	.341
Young, Chavez	B-R	6-0	175	7-8-97	.285	.256	.297	125	490	88	134	33	9	8	57	48	12	4	10	100	44	13	.445	.363

Pitching	B-T	HT	WT	DOB	W	L	ERA	G	GS	CG	SV	IP	H	R	ER	HR	BB	SO	AVG	vLH	vRH	K/9	BB/9
Barrett, Jordan	L-L	6-4	225	6-24-95	4	2	3.18	10	10	0	0	51	58	20	18	1	16	32	.289	.167	.315	5.65	2.82
Bouchey, Brayden	R-R	6-6	212	9-20-95	2	1	2.29	21	0	0	2	39	27	12	10	3	20	39	.202	.304	.148	8.92	4.58
Buffo, Maverick	R-R	6-2	200	9-15-95	3	3	4.26	16	14	0	0	82	101	40	39	11	16	62	.313	.321	.308	6.78	1.75
Castillo, Maximo	R-R	6-2	256	5-4-99	10	5	4.52	28	22	0	1	131	142	74	66	12	42	115	.277	.252	.288	7.88	2.88
Custodio, Claudio	R-R	5-10	155	10-30-90	1	2	2.66	13	0	0	3	20	18	9	6	1	4	13	.237	.208	.250	5.75	1.77
Deramo, Andrew	R-R	6-6	210	5-26-95	2	4	6.48	24	1	0	3	42	48	36	30	2	26	41	.286	.268	.295	8.86	5.62
Diaz, Yennsy	R-R	6-1	160	11-15-96	5	1	2.08	9	9	0	0	48	22	14	11	4	25	42	.135	.136	.135	7.93	4.72
Gunter, Matt	L-L	6-1	190	2-7-95	4	7	5.88	17	16	0	0	75	87	57	49	10	40	41	.293	.373	.273	4.92	4.80
Hinojosa, Yunior	R-R	6-2	190	12-21-99	0	1	7.36	5	0	0	0	7	7	7	6	1	2	4	.269	.250	.278	4.91	2.45
Jimenez, Dany	R-R	6-3	190	12-23-93	6	2	3.84	38	0	0	13	63	58	30	27	10	24	80	.237	.200	.256	11.37	3.41
Jimenez, Emerson	B-R	6-1	160	12-16-94	1	0	7.58	16	0	0	1	30	32	29	25	6	13	25	.258	.219	.272	7.58	3.94
Larkins, Turner	R-R	6-3	200	11-6-95	4	6	3.68	16	12	0	0	64	70	31	26	3	20	57	.285	.273	.293	8.06	2.83
Laws, Colton	R-R	6-7	215	11-20-95	4	4	6.19	12	10	0	0	48	64	34	33	10	7	39	.317	.351	.297	7.31	1.31
Logue, Zach	L-L	6-0	165	4-23-96	3	1	2.67	9	9	1	0	54	50	18	16	8	11	44	.250	.257	.249	7.33	1.83

TORONTO BLUE JAYS

Name	B-T	HT	WT	DOB	W	L	ERA	G	GS	CG	SV	IP	H	R	ER	HR	BB	SO	AVG	vLH	vRH	K/9	BB/9
Pascual, Orlando	R-R	6-3	210	11-7-95	0	2	4.57	14	0	0	1	22	20	13	11	3	16	21	.244	.281	.220	8.72	6.65
Ravel, Andy	R-R	6-2	165	10-12-94	0	0	3.80	13	0	0	0	21	25	10	9	0	7	16	.294	.250	.327	6.75	2.95
Rodning, Brody	R-L	6-1	185	1-14-96	5	3	3.89	35	0	0	5	69	67	36	30	3	24	60	.257	.203	.274	7.79	3.12
Rodriguez, Dalton	R-R	6-1	180	8-20-96	2	1	5.80	21	0	0	0	36	51	25	23	5	17	24	.340	.268	.383	6.06	4.29
Sellers, Donnie	R-R	6-1	190	7-26-95	7	3	3.98	22	13	0	1	93	98	46	41	10	27	71	.273	.271	.274	6.90	2.62
Shannon, Matt	R-R	6-3	220	5-31-95	3	5	5.03	29	0	0	7	48	62	33	27	1	24	35	.302	.388	.261	6.52	4.47
Spraker, Graham	R-R	6-3	200	3-19-95	4	3	3.26	18	15	0	1	91	83	37	33	8	26	66	.237	.233	.240	6.53	2.57
Tice, Ty	L-R	5-9	170	7-4-96	1	1	0.00	10	0	0	5	9	5	1	0	2	3	12	.161	.143	.167	12.00	3.00
Weatherly, Kyle	R-R	6-4	200	10-3-94	3	3	3.70	36	9	0	3	88	89	47	36	3	30	59	.262	.273	.256	6.06	3.08

Fielding

C: Gold 36, Hernandez 14, Johnson 7, Morgan 35, Smith 4, Sotillo 37, Spiwak 14. **1B:** Clemens 17, Gold 10, Grudzielanek 31, Gudino 2, Lizardo 4, Noda 60, Spanberger 7, Williams 17. **2B:** Gudino 6, Large 2, Navarro 8, Taylor 114, Vicuna 12. **3B:** Grudzielanek 42, Gudino 27, Large 21, Lizardo 10, Navarro 26, Smith 21, Vicuna 2. **SS:** Capra 42, Gudino 7, Navarro 22, Smith 24, Vicuna 68. **OF:** Lundquist 50, Noda 57, Obeso 84, Polizzi 8, Pruitt 88, Rodriguez 25, Young 118.

VANCOUVER CANADIANS   SHORT-SEASON
NORTHWEST LEAGUE

Batting	B-T	HT	WT	DOB	AVG	vLH	vRH	G	AB	R	H	2B	3B	HR	RBI	BB	HBP	SH	SF	SO	SB	CS	SLG	OBP
Bec, Christopher	R-R	5-11	190	12-30-95	.245	.226	.250	49	159	25	39	8	1	3	21	27	1	0	4	34	16	0	.365	.351
Brodt, Jake	R-R	6-4	220	1-23-96	.237	.296	.225	45	169	14	40	15	0	2	17	5	0	0	2	63	3	1	.361	.256
Capra, Vinny	R-R	5-8	175	7-7-96	.235	.214	.240	39	132	15	31	10	1	2	18	21	4	0	6	33	8	2	.371	.344
Conine, Griffin	L-R	6-1	200	7-11-97	.238	.238	.238	55	206	24	49	14	2	7	30	19	3	0	2	63	5	0	.427	.309
Contreras, Mc Gregory	R-R	6-1	170	8-30-98	.261	.273	.256	59	215	27	56	11	4	8	30	9	9	0	0	69	6	4	.461	.318
Guzman, Sterling	R-R	5-11	175	2-2-98	.225	.189	.235	49	169	17	38	8	0	2	10	17	2	1	1	46	6	3	.308	.302
Johnson, Reilly	R-R	5-9	160	9-26-96	.164	.133	.175	18	55	6	9	1	0	1	3	6	0	0	0	14	0	1	.236	.246
Kirwer, Tanner	R-R	6-0	160	3-15-96	.280	.213	.298	61	218	32	61	13	6	4	22	16	4	4	5	58	28	6	.450	.333
Lizardo, Bryan	R-R	6-0	205	7-26-97	.268	.179	.293	37	127	22	34	7	1	4	17	16	0	0	1	43	5	3	.433	.347
Lopez, Otto	R-R	5-10	160	10-1-98	.297	.250	.309	51	175	31	52	7	4	3	22	26	2	1	2	21	13	6	.434	.390
Navarro, Jesus	R-R	5-11	160	1-13-98	.143	.167	.136	9	28	1	4	1	0	0	2	2	0	0	0	3	3	0	.179	.200
Podkul, Nick	R-R	6-1	198	4-11-97	.222	.344	.192	50	162	22	36	10	2	3	18	28	4	1	2	38	1	1	.364	.347
Polizzi, Brandon	R-R	5-10	170	3-16-96	.224	.174	.234	52	134	17	30	2	1	0	9	18	2	2	1	31	19	2	.254	.323
Rodriguez, Freddy	L-R	6-1	180	11-15-96	.107	.000	.120	8	28	0	3	0	0	0	0	0	0	0	0	6	0	0	.107	.107
Rodriguez, Yorman	R-R	5-10	160	7-23-97	.267	.171	.298	45	172	22	46	8	1	1	30	7	4	0	1	24	2	3	.343	.310
Severino, Jesus	R-R	5-11	175	6-11-97	.270	.172	.294	42	148	21	40	15	0	2	19	11	1	0	1	34	1	1	.412	.323
Spiwak, Owen	L-R	6-2	185	5-23-95	.100	.500	.000	4	10	0	1	0	0	0	1	0	2	0	2	2	0	0	.100	.154
Steinmetz, Hunter	L-L	5-9	175	12-31-96	.179	.191	.175	26	84	12	15	5	2	0	4	5	2	0	2	23	6	1	.286	.237
Wright, Brett	R-R	6-0	210	8-5-95	.147	.154	.145	24	75	7	11	1	0	5	9	5	3	0	0	22	0	0	.360	.229

Pitching	B-T	HT	WT	DOB	W	L	ERA	G	GS	CG	SV	IP	H	R	ER	HR	BB	SO	AVG	vLH	vRH	K/9	BB/9
Allgeyer, Nick	L-L	6-3	210	2-3-96	0	2	2.73	15	6	0	1	26	19	11	8	3	8	31	.196	.206	.191	10.59	2.73
Barrett, Jordan	L-L	6-4	225	6-24-95	2	0	3.48	4	4	0	0	21	13	9	8	2	12	28	.181	.125	.196	12.19	5.23
Diaz, Denis	R-R	6-1	180	11-20-94	0	2	7.31	21	0	0	0	36	37	27	23	3	20	18	.305	.380	.250	5.72	6.35
Espada, Jose	R-R	6-0	170	2-22-97	3	7	4.88	13	13	0	0	59	50	36	32	5	26	70	.224	.218	.228	10.68	3.97
Johnson, Cobi	R-R	6-4	220	11-6-95	1	0	1.73	20	0	0	10	26	17	5	5	1	8	35	.183	.158	.200	12.12	2.77
Law, Connor	R-R	6-4	195	4-27-94	0	0	4.23	22	0	0	4	38	25	14	13	1	12	33	.238	.343	.186	10.73	3.90
McAffer, Will	R-R	6-2	185	5-30-97	7	2	3.68	21	0	0	0	29	22	15	12	3	17	37	.200	.204	.197	11.35	5.22
McKown, Mitch	R-R	6-4	195	5-21-96	0	0	3.00	2	0	0	0	3	3	1	1	0	2	2	.273	.333	.200	6.00	6.00
Miller, Troy	R-R	6-4	210	2-13-97	0	0	3.46	9	0	0	0	13	11	7	5	0	10	15	.225	.227	.222	10.38	6.92
Murray, Joey	R-R	6-2	195	9-23-96	1	1	1.75	13	6	0	0	26	19	5	5	1	10	39	.204	.214	.196	13.68	3.51
Nunez, Juan	R-R	6-2	185	1-23-96	0	1	5.20	17	2	0	1	45	47	32	26	6	26	41	.270	.346	.208	8.20	5.20
Pascual, Orlando	R-R	6-3	210	11-7-95	1	0	3.09	9	0	0	2	12	7	4	4	0	5	11	.167	.048	.286	8.49	3.86
Pondler, Randy	L-L	6-2	160	11-8-96	5	5	2.90	12	12	0	0	59	60	25	19	5	15	42	.267	.293	.258	6.41	2.29
Pulido, Joey	R-R	5-9	170	9-25-95	1	0	0.00	15	0	0	0	25	13	2	0	0	7	21	.148	.205	.091	7.66	2.55
Reyes, Marcus	L-L	5-11	180	3-10-95	1	2	1.35	23	0	0	2	33	31	8	5	2	8	31	.252	.344	.220	8.37	2.16
Rodriguez, Dalton	R-R	6-1	180	8-20-96	0	0	0.00	3	0	0	0	5	3	0	0	0	1	5	.177	.333	.091	9.00	1.80
Silva, Elio	L-L	5-11	160	8-21-95	3	4	3.82	14	13	0	0	66	56	33	28	6	20	40	.230	.194	.242	5.45	2.73
Stadler, Fitz	R-R	6-9	233	4-2-97	2	2	2.22	16	0	0	0	24	21	8	6	1	9	22	.241	.220	.251	8.14	3.33
Watts, Justin	R-R	6-3	215	9-8-93	5	0	2.45	21	0	0	0	37	24	10	10	1	10	52	.185	.231	.154	12.76	2.45
Winckowski, Josh	R-R	6-3	185	6-28-98	4	5	2.78	13	13	0	0	68	68	27	21	2	15	71	.255	.322	.204	9.40	1.99
Wymer, Sean	R-R	6-1	190	3-19-97	4	3	4.84	13	7	0	0	35	35	20	19	3	7	34	.257	.333	.192	8.66	1.78

Fielding

C: Bec 24, Johnson 6, Rodriguez 27, Spiwak 4, Wright 18. **1B:** Brodt 43, Guzman 22, Lizardo 6, Polizzi 1, Rodriguez 7, Severino 3. **2B:** Brodt 1, Guzman 6, Johnson 2, Lopez 13, Navarro 2, Podkul 43, Polizzi 15. **3B:** Guzman 13, Lizardo 27, Lopez 14, Navarro 5, Podkul 7, Severino 12. **SS:** Capra 39, Lopez 9, Navarro 3, Severino 28. **OF:** Conine 46, Contreras 51, Diaz 1, Johnson 6, Kirwer 59, Lopez 13, Polizzi 34, Rodriguez 7, Steinmetz 24.

BLUEFIELD BLUE JAYS   ROOKIE
APPALACHIAN LEAGUE

Batting	B-T	HT	WT	DOB	AVG	vLH	vRH	G	AB	R	H	2B	3B	HR	RBI	BB	HBP	SH	SF	SO	SB	CS	SLG	OBP
Abbadessa, Dominic	R-R	5-10	185	12-8-97	.311	.429	.280	59	238	42	74	14	3	2	29	14	8	2	2	47	18	5	.420	.366
Aiello, John	R-R	6-2	200	2-14-97	.273	.333	.257	12	44	8	12	3	0	1	7	8	4	0	0	12	1	1	.409	.429
Daniels, D.J.	R-R	6-3	205	12-17-97	.184	.294	.147	42	136	16	25	5	0	2	9	9	5	0	1	54	4	0	.265	.258
Danner, Hagen	R-R	6-2	185	9-30-98	.279	.300	.275	32	111	19	31	11	0	2	19	20	5	0	1	35	1	0	.432	.409

Batting	B-T	HT	WT	DOB	AVG	vLH	vRH	G	AB	R	H	2B	3B	HR	RBI	BB	HBP	SH	SF	SO	SB	CS	SLG	OBP
De Los Santos, Luis	R-R	6-1	160	6-9-98	.246	.200	.257	62	232	45	57	8	5	7	33	15	7	2	3	59	9	2	.414	.307
Groshans, Jordan	R-R	6-3	178	11-10-99	.182	.000	.258	11	44	4	8	1	0	1	4	2	1	0	1	8	0	0	.273	.229
Guerra, Andres	R-R	5-11	175	6-3-97	.225	.150	.255	29	71	9	16	2	0	3	11	10	1	0	1	21	0	0	.380	.325
Guerrero, Hector	L-R	6-0	155	9-11-97	.000	—	.000	9	19	1	0	0	0	0	2	0	2	0	7	0	0		.000	.095
Kirk, Alejandro	R-R	5-9	220	11-6-98	.354	.432	.333	58	206	31	73	10	1	10	57	33	2	0	3	21	2	0	.558	.443
Lantigua, Rafael	R-R	5-8	153	4-28-98	.303	.296	.304	48	165	28	50	7	1	1	23	30	4	1	0	33	7	5	.376	.422
Lopez, Otto	R-R	5-10	160	10-1-98	.364	.091	.500	7	33	8	12	5	2	0	6	0	1	0	0	5	1	0	.636	.382
Moreno, Gabriel	R-R	5-11	160	2-14-00	.279	.222	.289	17	61	10	17	5	0	2	14	3	0	0	2	13	1	0	.459	.303
Morris, Patrick	L-L	6-1	195	11-30-98	.216	.250	.210	51	181	27	39	8	1	4	19	30	1	3	3	58	1	1	.337	.326
Neal, DJ	R-R	6-3	201	1-11-97	.237	.244	.236	59	236	37	56	7	9	4	39	19	2	0	2	69	15	1	.394	.297
Schneider, Davis	R-R	5-10	190	1-26-99	.233	.167	.252	44	133	19	31	8	1	3	21	22	3	1	2	47	4	4	.376	.350
Severino, Jesus	R-R	6-1	175	6-11-97	.375	.000	.500	2	8	0	3	0	0	0	0	0	0	0	0	2	0	0	.375	.375
Steinmetz, Hunter	L-L	5-9	175	12-13-96	.238	.333	.200	6	21	5	5	1	0	0	1	4	1	0	1	4	2	0	.286	.370
Stevenson, Cal	L-L	5-10	175	9-12-96	.359	.467	.339	53	195	61	70	13	6	2	29	53	0	0	1	21	20	1	.518	.494
Theran, Jose	R-R	5-10	155	6-2-98	.260	.191	.280	35	96	16	25	4	3	1	11	7	1	2	0	20	2	1	.396	.317

Pitching	B-T	HT	WT	DOB	W	L	ERA	G	GS	CG	SV	IP	H	R	ER	HR	BB	SO	AVG	vLH	vRH	K/9	BB/9
Burland, Gage	R-R	6-2	195	6-27-95	0	0	4.50	2	0	0	0	2	5	1	1	0	0	1	.500	.500	.500	4.50	0.00
Castaneda, Felipe	R-R	6-1	194	1-4-00	2	1	6.69	10	10	0	0	38	41	31	28	5	28	29	.272	.213	.331	6.93	6.69
Cuevas, Adams	R-R	6-0	192	2-2-96	1	3	3.57	17	6	0	0	53	48	26	21	8	9	61	.245	.247	.243	10.36	1.53
DiBenedetto, Joe	L-L	5-9	180	5-25-95	0	0	15.43	10	0	0	0	7	14	12	12	1	14	9	.259	.111	.333	11.57	18.00
Espinal, Joel	R-R	6-2	185	8-15-96	1	0	3.18	3	2	0	0	11	9	4	4	0	5	14	.231	.278	.191	11.12	3.97
Finfrock, Cre	B-R	5-11	185	6-26-96	3	1	5.14	15	3	0	0	28	23	18	16	1	17	34	.271	.255	.186	10.93	5.46
Galindo, Alvaro	R-R	6-2	170	2-25-98	1	4	9.33	10	7	0	0	27	38	28	28	6	20	26	.342	.313	.365	8.67	6.67
Galva, Claudio	L-L	6-2	169	10-9-96	4	3	4.61	11	11	0	0	55	66	30	28	8	14	36	.304	.361	.293	5.93	2.30
Harris, Matt	R-R	6-0	175	7-10-94	0	0	2.45	4	0	0	1	7	6	2	2	2	1	8	.222	.385	.071	9.82	1.23
McGuire, Andy	R-R	6-0	178	12-2-94	1	2	3.09	18	0	0	2	23	16	11	8	2	8	22	.184	.189	.180	8.49	3.09
Medina, Nicolas	L-L	5-10	160	1-15-00	4	1	1.52	14	0	0	1	24	11	6	4	0	8	28	.138	.200	.109	10.65	3.04
Pardinho, Eric	R-R	5-10	155	1-5-01	4	3	2.88	11	11	0	0	50	37	16	16	5	16	64	.199	.181	.217	11.52	2.88
Pascoe, Mike	R-R	5-10	180	1-17-98	2	1	10.18	18	0	0	0	20	28	24	23	5	16	18	.326	.368	.292	7.97	7.08
Perez, Nathanael	R-R	6-1	160	6-5-98	3	1	4.47	12	12	0	0	56	63	31	28	6	21	59	.286	.330	.252	9.43	3.36
Price, Brennan	R-R	6-9	265	7-15-95	0	0	3.38	9	0	0	0	13	7	4	1	7	14	30	.302	.500	.160	11.81	5.91
Pulido, Joey	R-R	5-9	170	9-25-95	0	1	2.70	6	0	0	0	10	6	3	3	1	4	7	.182	.222	.167	6.30	3.60
Rackoski, Sean	R-R	6-7	210	5-12-95	7	3	4.21	23	0	0	6	26	30	15	12	3	9	33	.291	.390	.226	11.57	3.16
Rees, Jackson	R-R	6-4	205	7-30-94	0	1	4.63	8	0	0	0	12	13	10	6	1	5	12	.260	.217	.296	9.26	3.86
Stadler, Fitz	R-R	6-9	233	4-2-97	2	0	0.79	5	0	0	0	11	6	1	1	0	3	17	.150	.333	.071	13.50	2.38
Thurston, Ryan	L-L	6-2	175	10-8-94	0	0	0.00	1	0	0	0	1	0	0	0	0	0	1	.000	—	.000	9.00	0.00
Townsend, Grant	R-R	6-0	190	8-9-97	1	0	5.47	21	0	0	0	26	18	18	16	3	15	31	.190	.147	.213	10.59	5.13
Watson, Troy	R-R	6-2	180	6-11-97	3	0	1.67	9	6	0	0	27	13	5	5	1	8	20	.138	.162	.123	6.67	2.67
Wilson, Brad	R-R	6-1	260	8-15-96	3	0	1.63	22	0	0	7	28	14	6	5	1	9	30	.144	.135	.150	9.76	2.93

Fielding

C: Danner 9, Guerra 23, Kirk 32, Moreno 15. **1B:** Guerra 5, Guerrero 1, McGuire 11, Morris 51, Severino 1. **2B:** Lantigua 32, Lopez 3, Schneider 7, Theran 28. **3B:** Aiello 12, De Los Santos 4, Groshans 5, Guerrero 3, Lantigua 14, Schneider 33. **SS:** De Los Santos 56, Groshans 6, Lantigua 3, Lopez 2, Severino 1. **OF:** Abbadessa 55, Daniels 36, Lopez 1, McGuire 1, Neal 56, Steinmetz 6, Stevenson 50.

GCL BLUE JAYS — ROOKIE
GULF COAST LEAGUE

Batting	B-T	HT	WT	DOB	AVG	vLH	vRH	G	AB	R	H	2B	3B	HR	RBI	BB	HBP	SH	SF	SO	SB	CS	SLG	OBP
Barger, Addison	L-R	6-0	175	11-12-99	.194	.175	.200	49	180	28	35	10	2	3	18	25	8	0	1	38	0	0	.322	.318
Berroa, Steward	B-R	5-10	178	6-5-99	.282	.281	.282	39	142	30	40	9	1	0	11	23	1	1	0	36	17	6	.359	.386
Brodt, Jake	R-R	6-4	220	1-23-96	.000	—	.000	2	6	0	0	0	0	0	1	2	0	0	1	0	0	0	.000	.222
Conine, Griffin	L-R	6-1	200	7-11-97	.375	1.000	.167	2	8	1	3	1	0	0	3	1	0	0	0	2	0	0	.500	.444
Ferrer, Jose	R-R	5-11	175	3-1-99	.273	.000	.429	4	11	2	3	2	0	0	1	2	0	0	0	3	0	0	.455	.385
Groshans, Jordan	R-R	6-3	178	11-10-99	.331	.310	.336	37	142	17	47	12	0	4	39	13	2	0	2	29	0	0	.500	.390
Guerrero Jr., Vladimir	R-R	6-1	200	3-16-99	.333	.000	.429	3	9	3	3	2	0	0	1	0	0	0	1	0	0	0	.556	.400
Guerrero, Hector	L-R	6-0	155	9-11-97	.400	.444	.389	15	45	15	18	2	2	1	7	7	0	0	0	6	1	1	.600	.481
Hernandez, Jose Abel	R-R	6-5	201	12-4-95	.208	.077	.234	24	77	9	16	5	0	0	5	7	2	1	0	26	2	1	.273	.291
Hiraldo, Miguel	R-R	5-11	170	9-5-00	.263	.000	.273	10	39	3	9	4	0	0	3	1	0	0	0	12	3	0	.333	.250
Jimenez, Leonardo	R-R	5-11	160	5-17-01	.250	.240	.252	37	132	13	33	8	2	0	19	16	1	0	1	17	0	0	.341	.333
Kelly, Yhordegny	R-R	6-3	205	3-5-97	.288	.286	.289	20	73	12	21	6	2	2	8	5	5	0	0	27	1	0	.507	.374
Lantigua, Rafael	R-R	5-8	153	4-28-98	.212	.100	.261	8	33	7	7	3	1	0	3	3	1	0	0	7	1	0	.364	.297
Mauricio, Kenny	L-R	5-9	150	3-16-00	.000	—	.000	4	8	0	0	0	0	0	0	1	0	0	1	0	1	0	.000	.111
Molina, Jonelvy	R-R	6-0	180	3-18-97	.296	1.000	.240	10	27	5	8	1	0	0	2	7	1	0	1	8	0	0	.333	.444
Moreno, Gabriel	R-R	5-11	160	2-14-00	.413	.364	.420	23	92	14	38	12	2	2	22	4	4	0	1	7	1	1	.652	.455
Ovando, Aldo	R-R	6-5	195	4-6-97	.210	.238	.202	28	105	7	22	2	2	0	7	6	0	3	3	37	1	1	.267	.265
Pompey, Dalton	B-B	6-2	195	12-11-92	.333	.333	.333	2	6	1	2	1	0	0	0	2	0	0	0	3	1	0	.500	.500
Ramos, Adrian	R-R	5-10	160	6-18-98	.266	.378	.231	44	154	31	41	5	3	1	23	26	11	0	3	43	23	8	.357	.402
Reyes, Joseph	L-R	6-3	195	1-24-98	.273	.208	.287	38	132	26	36	9	1	6	27	27	3	0	2	45	1	3	.492	.402
Rivas, Jose	R-R	5-9	165	9-5-00	.429	.250	.471	6	21	3	9	1	2	0	2	0	0	0	0	3	2	0	.667	.429
Rodriguez, Yorman	R-R	5-10	160	7-23-97	.158	.200	.143	5	19	1	3	1	0	0	4	0	0	0	0	2	0	0	.211	.150
Ruiz, Francisco	R-R	6-0	195	1-30-99	.138	.071	.157	19	65	5	9	3	0	0	4	4	0	0	0	32	0	0	.185	.188
Squires, Troy	L-R	5-11	200	12-6-94	.211	.318	.188	35	123	16	26	0	1	0	8	22	5	2	0	14	2	0	.228	.353
Stevenson, Cal	L-L	5-10	175	9-12-96	.474	.800	.357	6	19	12	9	2	0	0	2	11	0	0	1	3	1	0	.579	.645
Valdez, Warnel	L-L	5-10	150	3-16-99	.240	.148	.266	33	121	14	29	9	1	2	15	2	0	0	1	32	2	0	.380	.250

	B-T	HT	WT	DOB	AVG	vLH	vRH	G	AB	R	H	2B	3B	HR	RBI	BB	HBP	SH	SF	SO	SB	CS	SLG	OBP
Warmoth, Logan	R-R	6-0	190	9-6-95	.273	.000	.375	4	11	4	3	0	0	0	0	2	3	0	0	4	0	0	.273	.500
Wright, Brett	R-R	6-0	210	8-5-95	.000	.000	.000	2	6	0	0	0	0	0	0	1	1	0	0	2	0	0	.000	.250

Pitching	B-T	HT	WT	DOB	W	L	ERA	G	GS	CG	SV	IP	H	R	ER	HR	BB	SO	AVG	vLH	vRH	K/9	BB/9
Acosta, Juan	R-R	6-2	185	4-5-00	0	1	4.50	1	0	0	0	2	2	1	1	0	0	0	.286	—	.286	0.00	0.00
Alvarez, Luis	L-R	6-0	170	2-8-00	1	0	4.42	12	0	0	1	18	12	10	9	1	6	17	.191	.235	.174	8.35	2.95
Barnes, Danny	L-R	6-1	195	10-21-89	0	0	9.00	1	1	0	0	1	3	1	1	0	0	2	.600	—	.600	18.00	0.00
Bello, Eliezer	R-R	6-5	230	2-12-99	0	0	3.00	6	0	0	0	9	10	4	3	0	5	6	.313	.222	.348	6.00	5.00
Breslow, Craig	L-L	6-0	190	8-8-80	1	0	0.00	1	0	0	0	1	1	0	0	0	0	1	.250	.000	.500	9.00	0.00
Burland, Gage	R-R	6-2	195	6-27-95	0	1	3.00	8	0	0	1	9	6	3	3	0	6	11	.188	.083	.250	11.00	6.00
Caballero, Elixon	R-R	5-9	160	7-9-00	1	0	1.15	9	1	0	1	16	10	2	2	0	6	18	.182	.214	.171	10.34	3.45
De Los Santos, Alvery	R-R	6-4	180	7-18-99	2	0	1.71	7	3	0	1	21	18	6	4	0	4	9	.234	.192	.255	3.86	1.71
Diaz, Juan	L-L	6-0	175	6-19-98	2	1	2.49	10	5	0	0	43	41	15	12	1	10	44	.250	.132	.286	9.14	2.08
Harris, Matt	R-R	6-0	175	7-10-94	0	0	0.00	1	0	0	0	1	2	0	0	0	0	1	.400	—	.400	9.00	0.00
Hernandez, Roither	R-R	6-4	185	3-5-98	1	0	9.82	2	0	0	0	4	4	4	4	1	3	7	.267	.333	.250	17.18	7.36
Hinojosa, Yunior	R-R	6-2	190	12-21-99	2	0	1.56	9	0	0	2	17	10	6	3	1	4	8	.156	.143	.163	4.15	2.08
Jose, Kelyn	L-L	6-4	195	5-19-95	0	0	9.00	2	0	0	0	2	1	2	2	1	2	4	.143	1.000	.000	18.00	9.00
Kloffenstein, Adam	R-R	6-5	243	8-25-00	0	0	0.00	2	2	0	0	2	1	0	0	0	2	4	.143	.000	.000	18.00	9.00
Magdaniel, Ronald	R-R	6-1	170	11-15-96	0	0	0.00	1	1	0	0	1	1	0	0	0	1	1	.250	—	.250	9.00	9.00
McKown, Mitch	R-R		195	5-21-96	0	0	0.00	1	1	0	0	1	1	0	0	0	0	0	.250	1.000	.000	0.00	0.00
Medina, Nicolas	L-L	5-10	160	1-15-00	1	1	3.72	5	0	0	1	10	5	5	4	0	4	8	.161	.167	.160	7.45	3.72
Mejia, Brayan	R-R	6-2	165	6-1-00	1	1	3.00	6	0	0	0	12	9	5	4	0	8	6	.205	.083	.250	4.50	6.00
Melean, Alejandro	R-R	6-0	175	10-11-00	1	3	4.68	9	7	0	0	33	36	24	17	5	22	31	.275	.432	.195	8.54	6.06
Molina, Alexander	R-R	6-1	155	2-17-00	0	1	4.50	12	0	0	0	16	16	19	8	2	10	7	.239	.375	.196	3.94	5.63
Monsion, Rafael	L-L	6-3	185	8-16-99	5	3	4.38	10	8	0	0	49	50	26	24	3	11	30	.272	.143	.302	5.47	2.01
Moreno, Williams	R-R	6-2	198	3-7-98	0	2	7.30	8	0	0	1	12	15	14	10	1	10	8	.283	.333	.263	5.84	7.30
Morimando, Shawn	L-L	6-0	200	11-20-92	0	0	1.29	4	4	0	0	7	6	1	1	0	1	10	.222	.333	.191	12.86	1.29
Nunez, Anderson	R-R	6-1	190	12-23-97	0	0	2.35	9	2	0	0	15	13	4	4	0	4	11	.224	.111	.275	6.46	2.35
Osuna, Roberto	R-R	6-2	215	2-7-95	0	0	0.00	1	0	0	0	1	1	0	0	0	0	1	.250	1.000	.000	9.00	0.00
Polanco, Franniel	R-R	6-5	180	10-23-97	1	2	1.59	9	0	0	1	17	12	6	3	0	4	14	.197	.368	.119	7.41	2.12
Price, Brennan	R-R	6-9	265	7-15-95	0	0	7.00	5	0	0	0	9	10	8	7	1	3	9	.303	.100	.391	9.00	3.00
Pulido, Joey	R-R	5-9	170	9-25-95	0	0	4.50	2	0	0	0	2	2	1	1	0	0	4	.222	.333	.167	18.00	0.00
Ramirez, Gaudy	R-R	6-2	175	9-11-97	0	1	5.40	8	0	0	2	12	10	7	7	1	3	8	.244	.111	.348	6.17	2.31
Rees, Jackson	R-R	6-4	205	7-30-94	2	1	5.59	8	0	0	0	10	12	8	6	1	2	11	.300	.333	.290	10.24	1.86
Reyes, Meliton	R-R	6-2	180	7-31-97	1	3	4.43	13	2	0	1	20	16	11	10	2	8	16	.219	.278	.200	7.08	3.54
Rios, Francisco	R-R	6-1	180	5-6-95	0	1	3.38	4	1	0	0	5	1	4	2	1	2	2	.059	.000	.083	3.38	3.38
Sanchez, Aaron	R-R	6-4	215	7-1-92	0	0	12.00	1	1	0	0	3	5	4	4	0	2	4	.357	—	.357	12.00	6.00
Spraker, Graham	R-R	6-3	200	3-19-95	0	1	4.15	2	2	0	0	4	6	3	2	0	1	3	.316	.250	.333	6.23	2.08
Thurston, Ryan	L-L	6-2	175	10-8-94	1	2	0.90	12	4	0	0	30	15	7	3	0	8	36	.144	.286	.122	10.80	2.40
Tracy, Matt	L-L	6-3	215	11-26-88	1	1	3.18	3	3	0	0	6	8	3	2	1	0	5	.320	.429	.278	7.94	0.00
Vizcaino, Emanuel	R-R	6-5	180	8-24-99	1	3	6.28	11	5	0	0	43	54	36	30	3	27	38	.318	.311	.320	7.95	5.65

Fielding

C: Ferrer 2, Molina 3, Moreno 17, Rodriguez 3, Ruiz 15, Squires 17, Wright 2. **1B:** Brodt 2, Guerrero 3, Hernandez 2, Kelly 13, Reyes 18, Ruiz 1, Squires 17. **2B:** Barger 18, Berroa 2, Guerrero 3, Jimenez 20, Lantigua 7, Mauricio 2, Rivas 6. **3B:** Barger 9, Groshans 16, Guerrero 8, Guerrero Jr. 2, Hiraldo 5, Lantigua 1, Mauricio 2, Reyes 18. **SS:** Barger 22, Groshans 15, Hiraldo 4, Jimenez 14, Warmoth 3. **OF:** Berroa 36, Conine 2, Hernandez 18, Ovando 28, Pompey 1, Ramos 41, Reyes 3, Stevenson 6, Valdez 28.

DSL BLUE JAYS   ROOKIE
DOMINICAN SUMMER LEAGUE

Batting	B-T	HT	WT	DOB	AVG	vLH	vRH	G	AB	R	H	2B	3B	HR	RBI	BB	HBP	SH	SF	SO	SB	CS	SLG	OBP
Acevedo, Hanley	R-R	6-0	185	9-28-99	.163	.188	.157	46	147	17	24	7	3	1	17	29	11	0	1	71	7	5	.272	.340
Celedonio, Erickvi	L-L	6-0	169	12-15-00	.257	.250	.260	61	237	36	61	11	2	0	32	23	2	0	1	64	16	2	.321	.327
Concepcion, Alonso	R-R	5-11	170	4-10-99	.110	.091	.117	27	82	11	9	1	0	0	6	15	0	1	1	32	5	3	.122	.245
Ferrer, Jose	R-R	5-11	175	3-1-99	.115	.000	.150	22	52	9	6	1	0	0	3	9	1	0	0	18	1	0	.135	.258
Hernandez, Jesus	R-R	6-0	175	10-30-99	.164	.105	.191	26	61	11	10	2	0	0	8	14	6	0	0	24	4	1	.197	.370
Hiraldo, Miguel	R-R	5-11	170	9-5-00	.313	.357	.298	54	214	41	67	18	3	2	33	23	1	0	1	30	15	6	.453	.381
Hurtado, Pedro	R-R	5-10	178	6-29-00	.259	.172	.298	59	205	24	53	8	3	1	27	25	2	3	3	44	4	2	.342	.340
Jimenez, Geyber	R-R	5-11	194	1-17-01	.246	.273	.241	41	130	14	32	5	1	1	14	16	0	0	1	35	2	3	.323	.327
Mauricio, Kenny	L-R	5-9	150	3-16-00	.202	.182	.212	30	99	14	20	1	1	1	7	15	0	0	1	21	4	2	.263	.304
Nunez, Rainer	R-R	6-3	180	12-4-00	.247	.224	.254	64	247	35	61	12	1	2	31	16	4	0	5	30	2	3	.328	.298
Rivas, Jose	R-R	5-9	165	9-5-00	.223	.255	.213	57	229	41	51	7	2	0	18	22	4	2	2	35	14	6	.271	.300
Rodriguez, Alberto	L-L	5-11	180	10-6-00	.254	.207	.271	61	228	44	58	9	1	5	34	32	2	0	1	55	21	6	.368	.350
Rodriguez, Anthony	R-R	6-2	195	7-23-96	.241	.200	.250	10	29	4	7	3	0	0	4	9	0	0	0	11	0	1	.345	.421
Rodriguez, Brayan	R-R	5-11	212	4-26-97	.143	.000	.167	5	14	2	2	1	0	0	1	3	1	0	0	5	0	0	.214	.333
Ruiz, Gustavo	R-R	6-0	175	3-22-00	.186	.000	.225	24	59	5	11	3	0	0	10	7	2	0	0	10	1	1	.237	.294
Solarte, Jhon	R-R	6-0	165	12-9-00	.295	.309	.291	68	271	52	80	14	4	0	29	37	8	0	2	54	27	10	.376	.393
Ventura, Pedro	R-R	5-11	188	3-14-97	.306	.571	.241	10	36	5	11	1	0	0	8	2	0	0	0	5	1	1	.333	.342
Zepeda, Jose	R-R	5-11	155	10-1-00	.304	.371	.371	15	46	9	14	4	0	0	4	6	0	2		5	3	1	.326	.414

Pitching	B-T	HT	WT	DOB	W	L	ERA	G	GS	CG	SV	IP	H	R	ER	HR	BB	SO	AVG	vLH	vRH	K/9	BB/9
Acosta, Juan	R-R	6-2	185	4-5-00	1	1	1.35	5	1	0	1	13	8	2	2	0	1	11	.170	.231	.147	7.43	0.68
Bello, Eliezer	R-R	6-5	230	2-12-99	0	0	4.26	10	0	0	1	13	9	8	6	0	12	10	.200	.250	.172	7.11	8.53
Brito, Jose	R-R	6-1	168	9-19-99	0	0	4.50	17	1	0	0	20	13	18	10	0	21	27	.176	.250	.140	12.15	9.45
Carmona, Alexis	R-R	6-4	160	3-24-01	2	2	3.36	13	12	0	0	59	67	36	22	2	16	50	.278	.271	.281	7.63	2.44

Contreras, Jeison	L-R	6-4	185	1-7-00	3	3	4.03	18	0	0	3	22	25	15	10	1	9	15	.281	.462	.206	6.04	3.63
De La Cruz, Moises	R-R	6-1	175	7-23-99	1	0	13.94	9	0	0	0	10	7	16	16	1	17	5	.194	.167	.200	4.35	14.81
Dominguez, Jhoan	L-L	6-4	225	1-29-00	3	0	5.73	14	0	0	0	22	26	18	14	1	13	18	.296	.231	.307	7.36	5.32
Estrada, Lazaro	R-R	5-10	180	4-24-99	3	3	2.06	14	14	0	0	70	48	20	16	4	12	87	.185	.169	.191	11.19	1.54
Gonzalez, William	R-R	5-9	165	1-8-99	2	4	4.33	22	0	0	3	27	20	26	13	0	20	35	.198	.222	.189	11.67	6.67
Govea, Ronald	R-R	6-3	175	10-10-00	4	1	2.30	14	13	0	0	59	56	25	15	0	13	42	.249	.270	.238	6.44	1.99
Guzman, Junior	R-R	6-3	187	12-4-97	2	6	5.50	14	9	1	0	52	61	34	32	3	16	37	.296	.324	.280	6.36	2.75
Guzman, Pedro	R-R	6-1	175	12-18-99	1	0	3.29	9	0	0	3	14	15	8	5	1	3	14	.259	.313	.238	9.22	1.98
Hernandez, Adrian	R-L	5-9	161	1-22-00	3	1	2.60	13	8	0	2	55	46	20	16	2	21	64	.222	.257	.215	10.41	3.42
Mejia, Brayan	R-R	6-2	165	6-1-00	2	0	3.06	8	0	0	0	18	14	7	6	0	11	10	.209	.231	.204	5.09	5.60
Moreno, Santos	R-R	5-9	165	2-17-00	2	3	2.04	14	14	0	0	71	59	25	16	2	16	69	.218	.151	.249	8.79	2.04
Moreno, Williams	R-R	6-4	198	3-17-98	2	0	0.71	6	0	0	0	13	8	2	1	1	7	12	.178	.077	.219	8.53	4.97
Olivo, Miguel	R-R	6-4	188	11-19-99	2	1	5.06	7	0	0	3	11	15	7	6	0	3	6	.326	.333	.324	5.06	2.53
Padilla, Pedro	R-R	6-1	170	10-27-99	1	2	4.12	14	0	0	0	20	11	12	9	0	18	15	.157	.191	.143	6.86	8.24
Polanco, Franniel	R-R	6-5	180	10-23-97	1	0	1.10	6	0	0	0	16	9	4	2	0	7	9	.155	.105	.180	4.96	3.86
Reyes, Christian	L-R	6-5	250	2-2-00	2	2	4.08	17	0	0	0	18	10	10	8	0	17	24	.167	.071	.196	12.23	8.66
Santos, Nelfi	L-L	6-1	165	3-21-99	1	0	6.00	3	0	0	0	3	3	3	2	0	2	5	.273	.000	.300	15.00	6.00
Teran, Erick	L-L	6-4	180	10-2-98	2	0	2.81	7	0	0	0	16	14	5	5	0	9	20	.255	.333	.239	11.25	5.06

Fielding

C: Ferrer 18, Hernandez 24, Jimenez 25, Rodriguez 4, Ruiz 22. **1B:** Ferrer 4, Hurtado 45, Jimenez 9, Nunez 1, Rodriguez 10, Ruiz 2, Zepeda 4. **2B:** Concepcion 10, Hurtado 15, Mauricio 9, Rivas 39, Zepeda 3. **3B:** Hiraldo 4, Mauricio 4, Nunez 61, Zepeda 5. **SS:** Concepcion 8, Hiraldo 46, Mauricio 8, Rivas 1, Ventura 10, Zepeda 2. **OF:** Acevedo 46, Celedonio 43, Concepcion 6, Rodriguez 59, Solarte 63.

TORONTO BLUE JAYS

Washington Nationals

SEASON IN A SENTENCE: Bryce Harper's final year before hitting free agency didn't go the way anyone expected in Washington, as the Nationals finished just two games over .500—eight games behind the division-winning Braves—and missed the postseason for the second time in five seasons.

HIGH POINT: Rookie left fielder Juan Soto made a rapid ascension through the minors after starting the year at low Class A Hagerstown. He was called up in mid-May and immediately established himself as one of the top young players in baseball, hitting .292/.406/.517 with a 142 OPS+. No other teenager in major league history had managed to post an on-base percentage over .400 with at least 50 games played.

LOW POINT: On Sept. 22, the Nationals beat the Mets 6-0 but were officially eliminated from the playoffs, leaving fans and front office executives alike wondering if the team built around Harper and Stephen Strasburg would have just four NL Division Series losses to show for an otherwise strong six years.

NOTABLE ROOKIES: The conversation about notable Nationals rookies starts with Soto, who figures to lead a dynamic outfield along with Victor Robles, the organization's current No. 1 prospect. After dealing with injuries that limited his season, Robles played 21 games for the Nationals in September, hitting .288/.348/.525 in that time. Righthander Wander Suero threw 47.2 innings in relief, posting a 3.59 ERA with solid strikeout and walk rates.

KEY TRANSACTIONS: Seven and a half games out of the NL East on Aug. 21, the Nationals began trading away veterans who had previously helped them make playoff runs. Daniel Murphy was traded to the Cubs, lefthander Gio Gonzalez was traded to the Brewers and righthander Ryan Madson was sent to the Dodgers. Washington received minor leaguers Andruw Monasterio, Gilbert Lara, K.J. Harrison and Andrew Istler in the deals.

DOWN ON THE FARM: Shortstop Carter Kieboom, the club's 2016 first-rounder, started the season on a roll at high Class A Potomac, hitting .298/.386/.494 in 61 games before earning a promotion to Double-A Harrisburg. The shortstop cooled down against the more advanced pitching of the Eastern League (.721 OPS) but still managed to put together a solid all-around campaign after dealing with several nagging injuries in 2017.

OPENING DAY PAYROLL: $167,846,918 (9th).

PLAYERS OF THE YEAR

MICHAEL IVINS

MIKE JANES/FOUR SEAM

MAJOR LEAGUE	MINOR LEAGUE
Max Scherzer	**Carter Kieboom**
RHP	SS
18-7, 2.53 in 33 GS	(High Class A/Double-A)
Led majors with both	.280/.357/.444
300 SO, 220.2 IP	16 HR, 31 2B

ORGANIZATION LEADERS

Batting		*Minimum 250 AB
MAJORS		
* AVG	Anthony Rendon	.308
* OPS	Juan Soto	.923
HR	Bryce Harper	34
RBI	Bryce Harper	100
MINORS		
* AVG	Ian Sagdal, Potomac	.318
* OBP	Austin Davidson, Potomac, Harrisburg	.374
* OBP	Hunter Jones, Syracuse, Harrisburg	.374
* SLG	Rhett Wiseman, Potomac	.484
* OPS	Austin Davidson, Potomac, Harrisburg	.856
R	Carter Kieboom, Potomac, Harrisburg	84
H	Luis Garcia, Hagerstown, Potomac	149
TB	Carter Kieboom, Potomac, Harrisburg	219
2B	Cole Freeman, Hagerstown	32
3B	Daniel Johnson, Harrisburg, Nationals	7
HR	Rhett Wiseman, Potomac	21
RBI	Jake Noll, Potomac, Harrisburg	72
BB	Rhett Wiseman, Potomac	63
SO	Armond Upshaw, Hagerstown	129
SB	Cole Freeman, Hagerstown	26

Pitching		#Minimum 75 IP
MAJORS		
W	Max Scherzer	18
# ERA	Max Scherzer	2.53
SO	Max Scherzer	300
SV	Sean Doolittle	25
MINORS		
W	Wil Crowe, Potomac, Auburn, Harrisburg	11
W	Sterling Sharp, Potomac, Harrisburg	11
L	Matthew Crownover, Potomac	9
L	Joan Baez, Potomac	9
L	Jaron Long, Syracuse, Harrisburg	9
L	Nick Raquet, Hagerstown, Potomac	9
L	Jackson Tetreault, Hagerstown, Potomac	9
# ERA	Ben Braymer, Hagerstown, Potomac	2.28
G	Chris Smith, Syracuse	49
GS	Sterling Sharp, Potomac, Harrisburg	27
SV	Roman Mendez, Harrisburg	11
IP	Brady Dragmire, Harrisburg, Syracuse	149
BB	Joan Baez, Potomac	69
SO	Kyle McGowin, Potomac, Harrisburg, Syracuse	152
# AVG	Kyle McGowin, Potomac, Harrisburg, Syracuse	.188

General Manager: Mike Rizzo. **Farm Director:** Doug Harris. **Scouting Director:** Kris Kline.

Class	Team	League	W	L	PCT	Finish	Manager
Majors	Washington Nationals	National	82	80	.506	t-8th (15)	Dave Martinez
Triple-A	Syracuse Chiefs	International	64	76	.457	t-11th (14)	Randy Knorr
Double-A	Harrisburg Senators	Eastern	72	65	.526	5th (12)	Matt LeCroy
High A	Potomac Nationals	Carolina	74	62	.544	3rd (10)	Tripp Keister
Low A	Hagerstown Suns	South Atlantic	52	81	.391	14th (14)	Patrick Anderson
Short season	Auburn Doubledays	New York-Penn	41	35	.539	4th (14)	Jerad Head
Rookie	GCL Nationals	Gulf Coast	23	33	.411	15th (18)	Mario Lisson
Overall 2018 Minor League Record			326	352	.481	19th (30)	

ORGANIZATION STATISTICS

WASHINGTON NATIONALS
NATIONAL LEAGUE

Batting	B-T	HT	WT	DOB	AVG	vLH	vRH	G	AB	R	H	2B	3B	HR	RBI	BB	HBP	SH	SF	SO	SB	CS	SLG	OBP
Adams, Matt	L-R	6-3	245	8-31-88	.257	.216	.264	94	249	37	64	9	0	18	48	24	4	0	0	55	0	0	.510	.332
2-team total (27 St. Louis)					.239	.220	.242	121	306	42	73	10	0	21	57	27	4	0	0	73	0	0	.477	.309
Bautista, Rafael	R-R	6-2	194	3-8-93	.000	.000	.000	9	6	1	0	0	0	0	0	0	0	0	0	1	0	0	.000	.000
Difo, Wilmer	B-R	5-11	200	4-2-92	.230	.154	.252	148	408	55	94	14	7	7	42	39	2	3	4	82	10	3	.351	.298
Eaton, Adam	L-L	5-9	176	12-6-88	.301	.222	.314	95	319	55	96	18	1	5	33	38	11	2	0	64	9	1	.411	.394
Goodwin, Brian	L-R	6-0	200	11-2-90	.200	.000	.217	48	65	9	13	1	0	3	12	10	2	1	1	26	3	1	.354	.321
Harper, Bryce	L-R	6-3	220	10-16-92	.249	.247	.250	159	550	103	137	34	0	34	100	130	6	0	9	169	13	3	.496	.393
Kendrick, Howie	R-R	5-11	220	7-12-83	.303	.250	.324	40	152	17	46	14	0	4	12	5	2	0	1	29	1	1	.474	.331
Kieboom, Spencer	R-R	6-0	210	3-16-91	.232	.294	.209	52	125	16	29	5	0	2	13	16	1	0	1	28	0	0	.320	.322
Montero, Miguel	L-R	5-11	221	7-9-83	.000	.000	.000	4	11	0	0	0	0	0	0	2	0	0	0	3	0	0	.000	.154
Murphy, Daniel	L-R	6-1	221	4-1-85	.300	.250	.317	56	190	17	57	9	0	6	29	13	0	0	2	17	1	0	.442	.342
2-team total (35 Chicago)					.299	.238	.319	91	328	40	98	15	0	12	42	20	0	0	3	40	3	0	.454	.336
Rendon, Anthony	R-R	6-1	200	6-6-90	.308	.285	.316	136	529	88	163	44	2	24	92	55	5	0	8	82	2	1	.535	.374
Reynolds, Mark	R-R	6-2	220	8-3-83	.248	.309	.217	86	206	26	51	8	0	13	40	24	2	0	3	64	0	0	.476	.328
Reynolds, Matt	R-R	6-1	200	12-3-90	.154	.250	.111	12	13	1	2	0	0	0	1	1	0	0	0	4	0	0	.154	.214
Robles, Victor	R-R	6-0	190	5-19-97	.288	.333	.257	21	59	8	17	3	1	3	10	4	2	0	1	12	3	2	.525	.349
Sanchez, Adrian	R-R	6-0	216	8-16-90	.276	.343	.174	28	58	8	16	2	1	0	3	1	0	0	0	8	0	0	.345	.288
Severino, Pedro	R-R	6-1	219	7-20-93	.168	.216	.151	70	190	14	32	9	0	2	15	18	4	0	1	47	1	0	.247	.254
Sierra, Moises	R-R	6-1	233	9-24-88	.167	.077	.250	27	54	4	9	2	0	0	4	2	2	0	2	20	1	1	.204	.217
Soto, Juan	L-L	6-1	185	10-25-98	.292	.279	.297	116	414	77	121	25	1	22	70	79	0	1	0	99	5	2	.517	.406
Stevenson, Andrew	L-L	6-0	192	6-1-94	.253	.200	.257	57	75	9	19	2	0	1	6	1	1	3	23	1	1	.320	.306
Taylor, Michael A.	R-R	6-4	212	3-26-91	.227	.217	.232	134	353	46	80	22	3	6	28	29	1	2	0	116	24	6	.357	.287
Turner, Trea	R-R	6-2	185	6-30-93	.271	.287	.266	162	664	103	180	27	6	19	73	69	5	2	0	132	43	9	.416	.344
Wieters, Matt	B-R	6-5	235	5-21-86	.238	.205	.246	76	235	24	56	8	0	8	30	30	3	1	2	45	0	1	.375	.330
Zimmerman, Ryan	R-R	6-3	215	9-28-84	.264	.377	.228	85	288	33	76	21	2	13	51	30	3	0	2	55	1	1	.486	.338

Pitching	B-T	HT	WT	DOB	W	L	ERA	G	GS	CG	SV	IP	H	R	ER	HR	BB	SO	AVG	vLH	vRH	K/9	BB/9
Adams, Austin L.	R-R	6-3	225	5-5-91	0	0	0.00	2	0	0	0	1	1	0	0	0	3	0	.250	.500	.000	0.00	27.00
Cole, A.J.	R-R	6-5	238	1-5-92	1	1	13.06	4	2	0	0	10	16	15	15	6	6	10	.356	.355	.357	8.71	5.23
Collins, Tim	L-L	5-7	168	8-21-89	0	0	4.37	38	0	0	0	23	23	11	11	-5	12	21	.264	.222	.310	8.34	4.76
Cordero, Jimmy	R-R	6-4	222	10-19-91	1	2	5.68	22	0	0	0	19	23	13	12	2	12	12	.288	.194	.347	5.68	5.68
Doolittle, Sean	L-L	6-2	204	9-26-86	3	3	1.60	43	0	0	25	45	21	8	8	3	6	60	.136	.033	.160	12.00	1.20
Fedde, Erick	R-R	6-4	195	2-25-93	2	4	5.54	11	11	0	0	50	55	31	31	8	22	46	.287	.302	.274	8.23	3.93
Glover, Koda	R-R	6-5	215	4-13-93	1	3	3.31	21	0	0	1	16	13	6	6	1	10	9	.217	.095	.282	4.96	5.51
Gonzalez, Gio	R-L	6-0	203	9-19-85	7	11	4.57	27	27	0	0	146	153	77	74	15	70	126	.272	.235	.281	7.78	4.32
2-team total (5 Milwaukee)					10	11	4.21	32	32	0	0	171	167	84	80	17	80	148	.256	.219	.265	7.79	4.21
Gott, Trevor	R-R	6-0	185	8-26-92	0	2	5.68	20	0	0	0	19	19	13	12	4	10	15	.271	.273	.271	7.11	4.74
Grace, Matt	L-L	6-4	215	12-14-88	1	1	2.87	56	0	0	0	60	55	22	19	5	13	48	.240	.258	.229	7.24	1.96
Hellickson, Jeremy	R-R	6-1	190	4-8-87	5	3	3.45	19	19	0	0	91	78	41	35	11	20	65	.230	.204	.260	6.41	1.97
Herrera, Kelvin	R-R	5-10	200	12-31-89	1	2	4.34	21	0	0	3	19	24	9	9	4	8	16	.304	.290	.317	7.71	3.86
Holland, Greg	R-R	5-10	205	11-20-85	2	0	0.84	24	0	0	3	21	9	2	2	1	10	25	.130	.077	.163	10.55	4.22
2-team total (32 St. Louis)					2	4	4.66	56	0	0	3	46	43	30	24	2	32	47	.242	.205	.270	9.13	6.22
Kelley, Shawn	R-R	6-2	237	4-26-84	1	0	3.34	35	0	0	0	32	26	12	12	7	5	32	.215	.225	.210	8.91	1.39
Kintzler, Brandon	R-R	6-0	194	8-1-84	1	2	3.59	45	0	0	2	43	40	17	17	2	13	31	.253	.242	.261	6.54	2.74
2-team total (25 Chicago Cubs)					3	3	4.60	70	0	0	2	61	67	31	31	5	22	43	.286	.264	.299	6.38	3.26
Madson, Ryan	L-R	6-6	234	8-28-80	2	5	5.28	49	0	0	4	44	48	28	26	6	15	41	.279	.263	.292	8.32	3.05
2-team total (9 Los Angeles)					2	5	5.47	58	0	0	4	53	58	34	32	7	16	54	.282	.289	.276	9.23	2.73
McGowin, Kyle	R-R	6-3	195	11-27-91	0	0	5.87	5	1	0	0	8	6	5	5	2	5	8	.214	.143	.286	9.39	5.87
Miller, Justin	R-R	6-3	215	6-13-87	7	1	3.61	51	0	0	2	52	42	22	21	10	17	60	.218	.233	.208	10.32	2.92
Milone, Tommy	L-L	6-0	215	2-16-87	1	1	5.81	5	4	0	0	26	37	17	17	1	23	.330	.192	.372	7.86	0.34
Roark, Tanner	R-R	6-2	229	10-5-86	9	15	4.34	31	30	0	0	180	181	90	87	24	50	146	.262	.265	.260	7.29	2.50
Rodriguez, Jefry	R-R	6-6	232	7-26-93	3	3	5.71	14	8	0	0	52	43	35	33	8	37	39	.228	.261	.198	6.75	6.40

WASHINGTON NATIONALS

Name	B-T	HT	WT	DOB	W	L	ERA	G	GS	CG	SV	IP	H	R	ER	HR	BB	SO	AVG	vLH	vRH	K/9	BB/9
Romero, Enny	R-L	6-3	232	1-24-91	0	0	13.50	2	0	0	0	2	5	3	3	1	1	2	.455	.429	.500	9.00	4.50
2-team total (2 Pittsburgh)					0	0	7.50	4	0	0	0	6	12	8	5	1	4	7	.387	.308	.444	10.50	6.00
Ross, Joe	R-R	6-4	220	5-21-93	0	2	5.06	3	3	0	0	16	17	10	9	3	4	7	.274	.242	.310	3.94	2.25
Scherzer, Max	R-R	6-3	215	7-27-84	18	7	2.53	33	33	2	0	221	150	66	62	23	51	300	.188	.197	.179	12.24	2.08
Solis, Sammy	R-L	6-5	251	8-10-88	1	2	6.41	56	0	0	0	39	43	28	28	7	18	44	.277	.329	.224	10.07	4.12
Strasburg, Stephen	R-R	6-5	235	7-20-88	10	7	3.74	22	22	0	0	130	118	59	54	18	38	156	.240	.250	.229	10.80	2.63
Suero, Wander	R-R	6-4	211	9-15-91	4	1	3.59	40	0	0	0	48	43	20	19	4	15	47	.240	.237	.243	8.87	2.83
Torres, Carlos	R-R	6-1	180	10-22-82	0	0	6.52	10	0	0	0	10	9	7	7	3	3	9	.243	.294	.200	8.38	2.79
Voth, Austin	R-R	6-2	201	6-26-92	1	1	6.57	4	2	0	0	12	12	9	9	3	6	11	.255	.250	.259	8.03	4.38
Williams, Austen	R-R	6-3	220	12-19-92	0	1	5.59	10	0	0	0	10	10	6	6	5	6	8	.270	.077	.375	7.45	5.59

Fielding

Catcher	PCT	G	PO	A	E	DP	PB
Kieboom	.991	49	297	21	3	2	3
Montero	1.000	4	28	0	0	0	1
Severino	1.000	67	534	31	0	3	4
Wieters	.995	73	579	24	3	5	2

First Base	PCT	G	PO	A	E	DP
Adams	.997	48	298	22	1	21
Harper	.000	1	0	0	0	0
Kendrick	1.000	2	3	1	0	0
Kieboom	1.000	3	4	0	0	0
Murphy	1.000	14	82	4	0	8
Reynolds	.994	45	316	20	2	35
Taylor	.000	1	0	0	0	0
Zimmerman	.997	73	538	39	2	41

Second Base	PCT	G	PO	A	E	DP
Difo	.992	112	147	214	3	45
Kendrick	.965	33	47	62	4	16
Murphy	.968	38	53	69	4	9
Reynolds	1.000	1	0	1	0	0
Sanchez	1.000	13	14	13	0	3

Third Base	PCT	G	PO	A	E	DP
Difo	.947	20	11	25	2	1
Kieboom	.000	1	0	0	0	0
Rendon	.981	136	88	222	6	23
Reynolds	.875	10	7	14	3	0
Reynolds	1.000	4	1	2	0	0
Sanchez	1.000	7	2	3	0	1

Shortstop	PCT	G	PO	A	E	DP
Difo	1.000	9	10	12	0	3
Turner	.980	159	204	399	12	70

Outfield	PCT	G	PO	A	E	DP
Adams	1.000	16	21	1	0	0
Bautista	1.000	7	4	0	0	0
Difo	.000	1	0	0	0	0
Eaton	.980	76	147	2	3	0
Goodwin	.962	26	24	1	1	0
Harper	.990	156	285	1	3	0
Kendrick	.917	6	11	0	1	0
Reynolds	.000	2	0	0	0	0
Robles	1.000	17	33	1	0	0
Sierra	1.000	17	16	0	0	0
Soto	.991	114	207	4	2	2
Stevenson	.950	20	19	0	1	0
Taylor	.996	113	232	6	1	2

SYRACUSE CHIEFS

TRIPLE-A

INTERNATIONAL LEAGUE

Batting	B-T	HT	WT	DOB	AVG	vLH	vRH	G	AB	R	H	2B	3B	HR	RBI	BB	HBP	SH	SF	SO	SB	CS	SLG	OBP
Almanzar, Michael	R-R	6-3	190	12-2-90	.207	.333	.174	18	58	3	12	2	0	0	4	2	0	0	0	12	0	0	.241	.246
Bautista, Rafael	R-R	6-2	194	3-8-93	.366	.222	.406	20	82	11	30	3	1	1	4	4	0	5	0	23	5	1	.463	.395
De Aza, Alejandro	L-L	6-0	195	4-11-84	.302	.400	.272	32	106	17	32	6	0	1	16	20	3	0	2	18	4	0	.387	.420
Decker, Jaff	L-L	5-9	190	2-23-90	.230	.048	.288	24	87	17	20	4	0	2	10	14	2	0	1	30	1	0	.345	.346
2-team total (15 Gwinnett)					.244	.139	.283	39	135	24	33	10	0	3	14	25	2	0	1	49	2	2	.385	.368
Dominguez, Chris	R-R	6-4	235	11-22-86	.243	.217	.255	84	276	31	67	16	1	9	45	16	6	0	6	83	7	4	.406	.293
Dunlap, Alex	R-R	6-2	195	10-6-94	.250	.000	.333	4	8	0	2	0	0	0	1	1	1	0	0	2	0	0	.250	.400
Falu, Irving	B-R	5-9	185	6-6-83	.276	.269	.278	108	381	45	105	16	2	4	53	34	2	1	2	32	12	4	.360	.337
Gonzalez, Bengie	B-R	5-11	160	1-16-90	.240	.242	.240	105	312	39	75	14	1	3	29	31	3	2	2	68	9	3	.321	.313
Gosewisch, Tuffy	R-R	5-11	200	8-17-83	.219	.279	.196	73	224	27	49	17	0	3	25	27	4	2	3	56	0	1	.335	.310
Gushue, Taylor	B-R	6-1	233	12-19-93	.250	—	.250	1	4	1	1	0	0	0	0	0	0	0	0	1	0	0	.500	.250
Hague, Matt	R-R	6-3	225	8-20-85	.242	.258	.235	28	99	9	24	5	0	1	7	12	0	0	1	18	0	1	.323	.321
Hernandez, Yadiel	L-R	5-9	185	10-9-87	.277	.247	.287	95	325	45	90	15	1	11	46	36	0	1	1	88	2	1	.431	.348
Jones, Hunter	R-R	6-2	185	8-17-91	.305	.324	.299	37	131	19	40	9	3	2	17	10	1	0	2	28	1	0	.466	.354
Kieboom, Spencer	R-R	6-0	210	3-16-91	.250	.118	.284	25	84	8	21	4	0	1	10	10	1	0	0	10	0	0	.333	.337
Lowery, Jake	L-R	6-0	200	7-21-90	.162	.167	.160	12	37	3	6	2	0	0	2	7	0	1	0	13	0	0	.216	.296
Marmolejos, Jose	L-L	6-1	225	1-2-93	.266	.315	.246	130	493	52	131	25	1	8	57	39	2	0	5	97	0	0	.369	.319
Martinson, Jason	R-R	6-1	210	10-15-88	.158	.143	.167	7	19	3	3	0	0	1	2	4	0	0	0	7	0	0	.316	.304
Read, Raudy	R-R	6-0	170	10-29-93	.260	.375	.206	13	50	2	13	2	0	0	2	1	0	0	1	8	0	0	.340	.269
Reistetter, Matt	L-R	5-10	180	5-5-92	.000	.000	.000	2	5	0	0	0	0	0	1	0	0	0	0	1	0	0	.000	.000
Reynolds, Mark	R-R	6-2	220	8-3-83	.231	.182	.250	10	39	3	9	1	0	1	4	3	0	0	0	13	0	0	.333	.286
Reynolds, Matt	R-R	6-1	200	12-3-90	.265	.234	.279	86	309	55	82	31	3	4	29	40	4	0	2	75	2	1	.424	.355
Robles, Victor	R-R	6-0	190	5-19-97	.279	.235	.290	40	158	25	44	9	1	2	10	18	2	1	2	26	14	6	.386	.356
Sanchez, Adrian	R-R	6-1	216	8-16-90	.234	.247	.228	70	269	21	63	15	2	4	27	16	3	3	4	42	10	6	.349	.281
Severino, Pedro	R-R	6-1	219	7-20-93	.269	.353	.240	33	130	14	35	5	1	6	13	5	0	0	1	23	0	0	.462	.294
Sierra, Moises	R-R	6-1	233	9-24-88	.243	.217	.255	67	226	29	55	12	0	6	32	23	4	0	2	50	3	4	.376	.322
Stevenson, Andrew	L-L	6-0	192	6-1-94	.236	.286	.210	77	293	40	69	10	1	6	28	31	5	1	1	75	12	6	.338	.318
Ward, Drew	L-R	6-3	215	11-25-94	.185	.150	.206	17	54	5	10	2	0	0	2	7	0	0	0	20	0	1	.222	.279
Wilson, Jacob	R-R	5-11	205	7-29-90	.282	.326	.265	89	316	37	89	24	1	3	42	33	6	1	8	63	1	1	.392	.353

Pitching	B-T	HT	WT	DOB	W	L	ERA	G	GS	CG	SV	IP	H	R	ER	HR	BB	SO	AVG	vLH	vRH	K/9	BB/9
Adams, Austin L.	R-R	6-3	225	5-5-91	1	4	3.50	41	0	0	9	46	47	24	18	1	20	78	.260	.273	.247	15.15	3.88
Collins, Tim	L-L	5-7	168	8-21-89	2	4	3.94	30	0	0	0	32	26	18	14	0	15	34	.230	.167	.277	9.56	4.22
Cordero, Jimmy	R-R	6-4	222	10-19-91	4	1	1.96	41	0	0	6	46	43	16	10	0	22	53	.243	.187	.284	10.37	4.30
Darnell, Logan	L-L	6-2	220	2-2-89	0	1	17.28	2	2	0	0	8	22	16	16	1	5	4	.500	.500	.500	4.32	5.40
Dragmire, Brady	R-R	6-1	185	2-5-93	1	6	6.16	14	11	1	0	69	81	48	47	11	21	47	.302	.358	.255	6.16	2.75
Edgin, Josh	R-L	6-1	245	12-17-86	1	3	2.96	35	0	0	0	24	22	11	8	4	16	39	.242	.146	.349	14.42	5.92
2-team total (12 Norfolk)					4	3	3.56	47	0	0	0	43	41	21	17	7	21	64	.253	.183	.325	13.40	4.40
Fedde, Erick	R-R	6-4	195	2-25-93	3	3	4.41	13	13	0	0	67	78	34	33	3	18	70	.298	.275	.317	9.36	2.41
Glover, Koda	R-R	6-5	215	4-13-93	1	0	2.25	8	0	0	2	8	7	2	2	0	2	10	.241	.154	.313	11.25	2.25

Pitcher	B-T	HT	WT	DOB	W	L	ERA	G	GS	CG	SV	IP	H	R	ER	HR	BB	SO	AVG	vLH	vRH	SO/9	BB/9
Goforth, David	R-R	5-11	205	10-11-88	3	4	3.46	38	4	0	2	68	62	27	26	6	23	45	.244	.262	.231	5.99	3.06
Gott, Trevor	R-R	6-0	185	8-26-92	1	1	3.68	28	0	0	3	29	23	16	12	1	8	38	.215	.255	.183	11.66	2.45
Grace, Matt	L-L	6-4	215	12-14-88	0	0	0.00	1	0	0	0	1	0	0	0	0	1	0	.000	.000	.000	0.00	9.00
Jackson, Edwin	R-R	6-2	215	9-9-83	4	2	3.40	10	10	0	0	56	51	22	21	4	22	47	.238	.250	.228	7.60	3.56
Long, Jaron	R-R	6-0	198	8-28-91	0	1	9.64	2	0	0	0	5	11	5	5	0	1	1	.458	.333	.533	1.93	1.93
McGowin, Kyle	R-R	6-3	195	11-27-91	3	2	1.20	8	8	0	0	53	26	7	7	3	9	44	.147	.121	.170	7.52	1.54
Miller, Justin	R-R	6-3	215	6-13-87	2	0	0.00	9	0	0	1	14	3	0	0	0	3	23	.070	.136	.000	15.15	1.98
Milone, Tommy	L-L	6-0	215	2-16-87	7	4	4.19	20	20	1	0	110	101	52	51	11	24	113	.243	.287	.225	9.27	1.97
Rodriguez, Jefry	R-R	6-6	232	7-26-93	2	2	3.58	6	6	0	0	33	32	14	13	0	15	30	.258	.217	.297	8.27	4.13
Ross, Joe	R-R	6-4	220	5-21-93	2	0	3.09	2	2	0	0	12	12	4	4	0	4	4	.250	.208	.292	3.09	3.09
Satterwhite, Cody	R-R	6-4	235	1-27-87	0	1	4.91	3	0	0	0	4	5	2	2	0	2	2	.333	.250	.364	4.91	4.91
Self, Derek	R-R	6-3	205	1-14-90	1	0	0.00	2	0	0	0	3	3	1	0	0	0	4	.231	.000	.375	10.80	0.00
Simms, John	R-R	6-3	205	1-17-92	2	4	3.69	24	6	0	2	63	62	31	26	8	28	57	.257	.214	.298	8.10	3.98
Smith, Chris	R-R	6-2	205	8-19-88	4	5	3.93	49	0	0	1	55	53	27	24	7	21	65	.255	.205	.292	10.64	3.44
Solis, Sammy	R-L	6-5	251	8-10-88	0	0	1.93	10	0	0	0	9	5	3	2	0	4	11	.161	.143	.177	10.61	3.86
Suero, Wander	R-R	6-4	211	9-15-91	1	2	3.71	14	0	0	1	17	16	9	7	1	4	16	.242	.192	.275	8.47	2.12
Torres, Carlos	R-R	6-1	180	10-22-82	4	4	3.02	36	3	0	3	51	36	20	17	3	17	51	.207	.168	.260	9.06	3.02
Valdez, Phillips	R-R	6-2	160	11-16-91	6	7	2.75	26	19	1	0	124	111	44	38	10	44	96	.239	.230	.248	6.95	3.18
Vargas, Cesar	R-R	6-2	237	12-30-91	1	7	5.92	13	12	0	0	65	83	49	43	9	30	39	.313	.326	.301	5.37	4.13
Voth, Austin	R-R	6-2	201	6-26-92	6	8	4.37	24	24	0	0	126	119	68	61	13	40	117	.247	.249	.245	8.38	2.86
Williams, Austen	R-R	6-2	220	12-19-92	0	0	0.55	8	0	0	1	16	6	1	1	0	4	20	.111	.111	.111	11.02	2.20

Fielding

Catcher	PCT	G	PO	A	E	DP	PB
Dunlap	1.000	3	19	1	0	0	1
Gosewisch	.995	65	559	39	3	3	2
Gushue	1.000	1	10	0	0	0	0
Kieboom	.984	21	173	17	3	4	1
Lowery	1.000	10	69	5	0	1	0
Read	.988	10	73	6	1	1	2
Reistetter	1.000	1	7	0	0	0	0
Severino	.983	32	264	28	5	3	6

First Base	PCT	G	PO	A	E	DP
Dominguez	.994	43	321	23	2	35
Gosewisch	1.000	2	13	1	0	1
Hague	.980	17	137	11	3	17
Kieboom	.941	3	15	1	1	0
Lowery	1.000	1	7	0	0	1
Marmolejos	.995	73	566	42	3	51
Reynolds	1.000	1	8	1	0	1
Reynolds	1.000	1	2	0	0	0
Wilson	1.000	9	65	3	0	5

Second Base	PCT	G	PO	A	E	DP
Falu	.994	90	136	225	2	55
Gonzalez	.969	17	21	42	2	9
Reynolds	.982	16	26	30	1	8
Sanchez	.975	20	27	52	2	12
Wilson	.980	12	19	30	1	8

Third Base	PCT	G	PO	A	E	DP
Almanzar	.870	16	4	16	3	2
Dominguez	.981	27	17	36	1	3
Gonzalez	.947	12	6	12	1	4
Martinson	1.000	6	2	9	0	1
Reynolds	.667	2	0	2	1	0
Reynolds	1.000	6	2	8	0	0
Sanchez	.912	23	19	33	5	1
Ward	.912	15	4	27	3	3
Wilson	.953	52	37	86	6	10

Shortstop	PCT	G	PO	A	E	DP
Falu	1.000	6	5	10	0	3
Gonzalez	.980	69	99	198	6	40
Reynolds	.969	43	52	106	5	25
Sanchez	.981	29	31	73	2	16

Outfield	PCT	G	PO	A	E	DP
Bautista	1.000	18	34	1	0	0
De Aza	.980	25	48	0	1	0
Decker	1.000	22	39	2	0	2
Dominguez	1.000	7	14	0	0	0
Gonzalez	.000	1	0	0	0	0
Hernandez	.984	71	119	4	2	1
Jones	1.000	32	60	1	0	0
Marmolejos	.987	49	74	1	1	1
Reynolds	1.000	5	8	0	0	0
Reynolds	1.000	18	39	0	0	0
Robles	1.000	39	81	2	0	0
Sanchez	1.000	1	1	0	0	0
Sierra	.972	60	101	3	3	2
Stevenson	.985	76	132	1	2	1
Wilson	1.000	11	16	2	0	1

HARRISBURG SENATORS

DOUBLE-A

EASTERN LEAGUE

Batting	B-T	HT	WT	DOB	AVG	vLH	vRH	G	AB	R	H	2B	3B	HR	RBI	BB	HBP	SH	SF	SO	SB	CS	SLG	OBP
Abreu, Osvaldo	R-R	6-0	195	6-13-94	.183	.207	.172	109	360	40	66	18	2	8	41	36	2	2	3	101	4	2	.311	.259
Adams, Matt	L-R	6-3	245	8-31-88	.000	.000	.000	1	3	0	0	0	0	0	0	0	0	0	0	2	0	0	.000	.000
Bautista, Rafael	R-R	6-2	194	3-8-93	.111	.222	.056	6	27	0	3	0	0	0	3	3	0	0	0	5	1	1	.111	.200
Collier, Zach	L-L	6-2	200	9-8-90	.212	.279	.189	102	307	38	65	17	5	6	40	43	6	2	3	97	5	3	.358	.318
Davidson, Austin	L-R	6-0	180	1-3-93	.285	.250	.296	94	267	38	76	17	3	10	42	33	1	0	2	46	1	1	.483	.363
Eaton, Adam	L-L	5-9	176	12-6-88	.000	.000	—	2	5	0	0	0	0	0	0	1	0	0	0	1	0	0	.000	.167
Gamache, Dan	L-R	5-11	205	11-20-90	.274	.234	.291	121	413	47	113	22	1	5	45	54	8	2	0	108	2	6	.368	.368
Goodwin, Brian	L-R	6-0	200	11-2-90	.200	.250	.182	4	15	4	3	0	0	1	3	3	0	0	0	3	1	0	.400	.333
Gushue, Taylor	B-R	6-1	233	12-19-93	.212	.252	.193	97	339	42	72	19	1	10	44	37	4	0	6	93	0	1	.363	.293
Gutierrez, Kelvin	R-R	6-3	215	8-28-94	.274	.279	.272	58	230	36	63	6	3	5	26	16	1	0	2	62	10	1	.391	.321
Hernandez, Yadiel	L-R	5-9	185	10-9-87	.315	.143	.356	29	108	17	34	3	0	7	22	20	1	0	0	18	2	1	.537	.426
Johnson, Daniel	L-L	5-10	185	7-11-95	.267	.163	.303	89	356	48	95	19	7	6	31	23	7	2	3	90	21	4	.410	.321
Jones, Hunter	R-R	6-2	185	8-17-91	.298	.333	.284	70	255	30	76	5	3	3	27	31	5	2	1	46	12	5	.377	.384
Keller, Alec	L-R	6-2	200	5-13-92	.336	.281	.355	61	223	34	75	12	3	2	21	14	2	1	1	30	1	2	.444	.379
Kieboom, Carter	R-R	6-2	190	9-3-97	.262	.276	.258	62	248	36	65	16	1	5	23	22	2	0	1	59	3	1	.395	.326
Lowery, Jake	L-R	6-0	200	7-21-90	.317	.250	.333	16	41	8	13	1	0	3	16	0	0	0	0	9	0	0	.561	.417
Murphy, Daniel	L-R	6-1	221	4-1-85	.243	.200	.273	10	37	8	9	2	0	2	7	6	1	0	0	4	0	0	.460	.364
Noll, Jake	R-R	6-2	195	3-8-94	.279	.239	.294	66	237	35	66	8	1	3	26	14	5	1	3	39	4	1	.359	.328
Norfork, Khayyan	R-R	5-10	190	1-19-89	.156	.208	.104	42	96	15	15	1	0	3	17	11	2	2	0	23	1	0	.260	.257
Perez, Stephen	B-R	5-11	185	12-16-90	.216	.258	.197	44	102	20	22	1	0	0	8	19	1	4	2	30	5	2	.226	.339
Read, Raudy	R-R	6-0	170	10-29-93	.286	.294	.283	40	147	14	42	9	2	3	24	11	1	0	2	30	0	0	.435	.335
Reistetter, Matt	L-R	5-10	180	5-5-92	.152	.000	.161	10	33	2	5	0	0	1	4	1	0	0	0	12	0	0	.242	.177
Soto, Juan	L-L	6-1	185	10-25-98	.323	.300	.333	8	31	4	10	2	0	2	10	4	0	0	0	7	1	0	.581	.400
Walker, Adam Brett	R-R	6-5	225	10-18-91	.200	.222	.187	41	120	17	24	6	2	4	17	22	1	0	2	51	1	0	.383	.324
Ward, Drew	L-R	6-3	215	11-25-94	.259	.217	.278	98	320	59	83	16	4	13	56	55	5	0	0	95	1	1	.456	.376
Wieters, Matt	B-R	6-5	235	5-21-86	.167	.200	.000	2	6	0	1	0	0	0	1	1	0	0	0	2	0	0	.333	.286
Wilson, Jacob	R-R	5-11	205	7-29-90	.246	.261	.237	15	61	9	15	3	0	4	8	7	0	0	3	13	0	1	.492	.310

Zimmerman, Ryan	R-R	6-3	215	9-28-84	.286	.500	.200	2	7	2	2	0	0	1	1	1	0	0	0	1	0	.714	.375

Pitching

Pitching	B-T	HT	WT	DOB	W	L	ERA	G	GS	CG	SV	IP	H	R	ER	HR	BB	SO	AVG	vLH	vRH	K/9	BB/9
Ames, Jeff	R-R	6-4	220	1-31-91	2	1	5.70	16	0	0	0	24	19	18	15	5	10	34	.226	.226	.226	12.93	3.80
Bacus, Dakota	R-R	6-2	200	4-2-91	2	1	3.89	26	0	0	2	37	36	19	16	1	13	48	.261	.297	.230	11.68	3.16
Bourque, James	R-R	6-4	190	7-9-93	1	0	0.92	15	0	0	1	20	11	2	2	0	14	24	.167	.122	.240	10.98	6.41
Crowe, Wil	R-R	6-2	240	9-9-94	0	5	6.15	5	5	0	0	26	31	25	18	4	16	15	.307	.418	.174	5.13	5.47
Darnell, Logan	L-L	6-2	220	2-2-89	8	6	3.91	24	19	0	0	113	123	53	49	14	24	82	.276	.207	.300	6.55	1.92
Dragmire, Brady	R-R	6-1	185	2-5-93	5	2	3.25	13	13	0	0	80	84	35	29	5	14	52	.265	.229	.290	5.83	1.57
Estevez, Wirkin	R-R	6-1	170	3-15-92	1	4	4.33	11	10	0	0	52	57	27	25	6	17	41	.256	.284	.237	7.10	2.94
Fedde, Erick	R-R	6-4	195	2-25-93	0	1	2.25	1	1	0	0	4	4	1	1	0	2	4	.267	.500	.182	9.00	4.50
Fleck, Kaleb	R-R	6-2	215	1-24-89	4	4	4.35	25	0	0	0	39	40	22	19	4	12	51	.263	.286	.250	11.67	2.75
Grace, Matt	L-L	6-4	215	12-14-88	0	0	0.00	3	1	0	0	3	4	1	0	0	4	3	.308	.200	.375	12.00	0.00
Guillon, Ismael	L-L	6-2	222	2-13-92	1	1	2.97	27	0	0	0	30	23	10	10	3	14	32	.217	.311	.148	9.49	4.15
Harper, Bryan	L-L	6-6	215	12-29-89	3	1	3.69	44	0	0	4	46	43	23	19	3	28	38	.246	.217	.264	7.38	5.44
Long, Jaron	R-R	6-0	198	8-28-91	6	8	3.65	25	19	2	0	123	136	57	50	9	27	77	.282	.277	.286	5.62	1.97
Mapes, Tyler	R-R	6-2	205	7-18-91	1	2	3.95	8	8	0	0	43	48	23	19	3	12	34	.273	.329	.236	7.06	2.49
McGowin, Kyle	R-R	6-3	195	11-27-91	4	3	3.69	13	13	0	0	78	62	34	32	7	19	94	.212	.213	.209	10.85	2.19
Mendez, Roman	R-R	6-3	245	7-25-90	6	4	3.67	44	0	0	11	54	46	27	22	8	20	59	.229	.220	.235	9.83	3.33
Mills, Jordan	L-L	6-5	215	5-11-92	2	1	2.29	15	0	0	0	20	13	6	5	0	7	20	.186	.286	.143	9.15	3.20
Milone, Tommy	L-L	6-0	215	2-16-87	0	0	0.00	1	1	0	0	2	2	0	0	1	1	2	.250	.500	.167	9.00	4.50
Pena, Ronald	R-R	6-4	195	9-19-91	1	2	4.68	21	0	0	5	25	21	15	13	5	16	30	.219	.156	.271	10.58	5.40
Reyes, Luis	R-R	6-2	175	9-26-94	5	6	5.18	12	12	0	0	64	67	39	37	9	32	36	.274	.296	.256	5.04	4.48
Rodriguez, Jefry	R-R	6-6	232	7-26-93	5	3	3.31	13	13	0	0	68	55	36	25	6	28	72	.222	.213	.229	9.53	3.71
Romero, Jhon	R-R	5-10	195	1-17-95	0	0	6.14	6	0	0	0	7	10	6	5	1	3	3	.313	.316	.308	3.68	3.68
Ross, Joe	R-R	6-4	220	5-21-93	0	1	5.40	1	1	0	0	5	4	3	3	1	0	6	.211	.000	.308	10.80	0.00
Self, Derek	R-R	6-3	205	1-14-90	5	2	3.05	42	0	0	6	56	52	21	19	5	7	39	.252	.241	.261	6.27	1.13
Sharp, Sterling	R-R	6-4	170	5-30-95	6	3	4.33	13	13	1	0	69	72	39	33	6	26	47	.268	.312	.221	6.16	3.41
Valdez, Phillips	R-R	6-2	160	11-16-91	0	0	2.53	5	0	0	0	11	9	3	3	0	2	8	.237	.300	.167	6.75	1.69
Vargas, Cesar	R-R	6-2	237	12-30-91	1	1	4.36	7	6	0	0	33	37	21	16	4	15	32	.278	.268	.286	8.73	4.09
Williams, Austen	R-R	6-3	220	12-19-92	3	3	1.39	24	2	0	1	52	34	10	8	0	13	69	.182	.235	.137	12.02	2.26

Fielding

Catcher	PCT	G	PO	A	E	DP	PB
Davidson	1.000	1	2	0	0	0	0
Gushue	.996	83	645	60	3	2	5
Lowery	.989	12	75	12	1	2	2
Read	.985	35	233	35	4	2	7
Reistetter	1.000	9	56	12	0	0	1
Wieters	1.000	2	10	0	0	0	0

First Base	PCT	G	PO	A	E	DP
Adams	1.000	1	4	0	0	1
Davidson	.993	20	129	5	1	15
Gamache	.997	36	280	30	1	26
Murphy	1.000	2	16	2	0	0
Noll	.900	1	8	1	1	0
Ward	.991	82	685	55	7	63
Wilson	1.000	2	9	1	0	0
Zimmerman	1.000	1	9	0	0	0

Second Base	PCT	G	PO	A	E	DP
Abreu	.975	42	81	116	5	27
Davidson	.912	8	13	18	3	5
Gamache	.970	60	90	166	8	42
Murphy	.793	8	9	14	6	3
Noll	.000	1	0	0	0	0
Norfork	.960	16	23	25	2	5
Perez	1.000	8	5	5	0	1
Wilson	.968	12	24	37	2	10

Third Base	PCT	G	PO	A	E	DP
Gamache	.000	1	0	0	1	0
Gutierrez	.930	56	47	126	13	12
Noll	.931	63	33	116	11	10
Norfork	.833	7	2	8	2	0
Perez	1.000	6	3	8	0	0
Ward	.769	11	3	7	3	2

Shortstop	PCT	G	PO	A	E	DP
Abreu	.952	65	78	141	11	34
Gutierrez	1.000	1	2	4	0	0
Kieboom	.956	62	86	176	12	31
Perez	1.000	13	19	30	0	5

Outfield	PCT	G	PO	A	E	DP
Bautista	.941	6	15	1	1	0
Collier	.990	94	198	1	2	1
Davidson	.939	28	31	0	2	0
Eaton	1.000	2	3	0	0	0
Gamache	1.000	4	6	0	0	0
Goodwin	1.000	4	5	0	0	0
Hernandez	.963	24	24	2	1	0
Johnson	.989	86	164	11	2	5
Jones	.993	65	135	5	1	1
Keller	.982	55	107	2	2	1
Norfork	1.000	16	17	0	0	0
Perez	.958	16	22	1	1	0
Soto	1.000	8	13	0	0	0
Walker	.981	29	50	1	1	0

POTOMAC NATIONALS

HIGH CLASS A

CAROLINA LEAGUE

Batting	B-T	HT	WT	DOB	AVG	vLH	vRH	G	AB	R	H	2B	3B	HR	RBI	BB	HBP	SH	SF	SO	SB	CS	SLG	OBP
Agustin, Telmito	L-L	5-10	160	10-9-96	.302	.313	.298	63	205	31	62	10	3	5	30	20	3	2	3	43	7	3	.454	.368
Banks, Nick	L-L	6-1	215	11-18-94	.263	.211	.289	64	232	27	61	11	2	4	30	14	3	1	3	52	1	0	.379	.310
Barrera, Tres	R-R	6-0	215	9-15-94	.263	.276	.256	68	259	36	68	14	0	6	24	22	6	1	0	53	3	0	.386	.335
Basto, Nick	R-R	6-2	210	4-4-94	.212	.150	.239	19	66	2	14	2	0	1	6	11	3	0	1	21	0	0	.288	.346
Boggetto, Branden	R-R	6-0	190	11-10-93	.122	.091	.132	18	49	3	6	2	0	0	7	6	3	0	0	20	1	0	.163	.271
Corredor, Aldrem	L-L	6-0	202	10-27-95	.311	.349	.295	59	219	24	68	17	0	5	37	19	0	0	4	46	0	0	.457	.360
Davidson, Austin	L-R	6-0	190	1-3-93	.319	.200	.352	18	69	9	22	4	2	1	13	10	2	0	1	7	4	1	.478	.415
Eaton, Adam	L-L	5-9	176	12-6-88	.250	.400	.143	3	12	3	3	0	0	1	3	2	1	0	0	3	0	0	.500	.400
Garcia, Luis	L-R	6-0	190	5-16-00	.299	.222	.341	49	204	34	61	7	2	4	23	12	1	2	2	33	4	1	.412	.338
Keller, Alec	L-R	6-2	200	5-19-92	.340	.333	.343	29	100	17	34	6	1	1	14	15	1	1	3	22	2	2	.450	.420
Kieboom, Carter	R-R	6-2	190	9-3-97	.298	.269	.309	61	245	48	73	15	0	11	46	36	1	0	3	50	6	1	.494	.386
Lora, Edwin	R-R	6-1	150	9-14-95	.180	.148	.194	64	178	20	32	8	0	0	15	13	6	7	2	68	4	1	.236	.256
Masters, David	R-R	6-1	185	4-3-94	.239	.262	.226	92	293	50	70	16	0	3	32	50	6	3	1	79	0	2	.355	.360
Mejia, Bryan	B-R	6-1	170	3-2-94	.266	.361	.223	101	388	46	103	28	0	6	54	23	3	0	5	81	8	9	.384	.308
Monasterio, Andruw	R-R	6-0	175	5-30-97	.308	.263	.350	13	39	6	12	0	1	0	5	7	0	0	1	6	2	3	.359	.404
2-team total (109 Myrtle Beach)					.267	.290	.259	122	408	58	109	14	3	3	36	59	5	7	4	70	12	6	.338	.363

Name	B-T	HT	WT	DOB	AVG	vLH	vRH	G	AB	R	H	2B	3B	HR	RBI	BB	HBP	SH	SF	SO	SB	CS	SLG	OBP
Noll, Jake	R-R	6-2	195	3-8-94	.302	.388	.273	66	265	47	80	12	3	8	46	19	3	0	2	51	3	1	.460	.353
Perkins, Blake	B-R	6-1	165	9-10-96	.234	.265	.223	65	252	39	59	11	0	1	21	42	3	3	5	67	12	5	.290	.344
2-team total (64 Wilmington)					.237	.245	.233	129	485	87	115	22	1	3	39	92	6	8	5	134	29	9	.305	.362
Reetz, Jakson	R-R	6-1	195	1-3-96	.224	.310	.195	69	232	25	52	8	0	5	27	35	7	1	1	46	1	4	.323	.342
Reistetter, Matt	L-R	5-10	180	5-5-92	.000	.000	.000	5	13	1	0	0	0	0	0	4	0	0	0	5	0	0	.000	.235
Rendon, Anthony	R-R	6-1	200	6-6-90	.625	.500	.667	2	8	3	5	2	0	0	1	0	1	0	0	0	0	0	.875	.667
Sagdal, Ian	L-R	6-3	190	1-6-93	.318	.344	.305	101	390	52	124	28	3	6	58	35	4	0	8	69	7	4	.451	.373
Soto, Juan	L-L	6-1	185	10-25-98	.371	.438	.348	15	62	17	23	3	1	7	18	11	0	0	8	0	1	.790	.466
Sundberg, Jack	L-R	5-11	195	7-21-93	.261	.217	.278	99	322	47	84	10	1	3	34	51	3	7	6	85	8	9	.326	.361
Wieters, Matt	B-R	6-5	235	5-21-86	.250	.333	.000	1	4	1	1	0	0	0	0	0	0	0	0	1	0	0	.250	.250
Wiseman, Rhett	L-R	6-0	200	6-22-94	.253	.219	.264	116	407	65	103	23	4	21	63	63	6	1	1	122	8	2	.484	.361
Zimmerman, Ryan	R-R	6-3	215	9-28-84	1.000	1.000	1.000	1	2	3	2	1	0	0	1	1	0	0	0	0	0	0	1.500	1.000

Pitching	B-T	HT	WT	DOB	W	L	ERA	G	GS	CG	SV	IP	H	R	ER	HR	BB	SO	AVG	vLH	vRH	K/9	BB/9
Acevedo, Carlos	R-R	6-3	200	9-27-94	1	3	3.62	13	1	0	0	27	24	12	11	2	5	19	.250	.208	.292	6.26	1.65
Baez, Joan	R-R	6-3	190	12-26-94	9	9	3.79	25	25	0	0	123	104	61	52	9	69	101	.231	.205	.257	7.37	5.04
Bogucki, A.J.	R-R	6-3	187	5-2-95	3	2	1.42	16	1	0	0	32	27	7	5	1	12	33	.229	.255	.209	9.38	3.41
Bourque, James	R-R	6-4	190	7-9-93	3	2	2.16	26	0	0	5	33	19	10	8	3	12	52	.170	.132	.203	14.04	3.24
Braymer, James	L-L	6-2	215	4-28-94	6	3	2.43	21	11	0	2	89	73	27	24	4	29	93	.223	.182	.239	9.40	2.93
Condra-Bogan, Jacob	R-R	6-3	220	8-30-94	1	2	2.40	11	0	0	2	15	8	5	4	0	3	13	.157	.300	.065	7.80	1.80
2-team total (1 Wilmington)					1	2	3.94	12	0	0	2	16	11	8	7	0	4	14	.196	.318	.118	7.88	2.25
Crowe, Wil	R-R	6-2	240	9-9-94	11	0	2.69	16	15	0	0	87	71	32	26	6	30	78	.220	.193	.239	8.07	3.10
Crownover, Matthew	R-L	5-11	205	3-5-93	5	9	4.42	24	21	1	0	118	124	65	58	11	33	80	.270	.217	.294	6.10	2.52
DeRosier, Matthew	R-R	6-2	200	7-13-94	0	2	6.48	6	3	0	0	17	19	12	12	3	8	12	.284	.296	.275	6.48	4.32
Fuentes, Steven	R-R	6-2	175	5-4-97	3	3	3.00	24	0	0	3	45	33	19	15	1	16	43	.201	.174	.221	8.60	3.20
Glover, Koda	R-R	6-5	215	4-13-93	0	0	10.80	1	0	0	0	2	5	2	2	1	1	2	.500	.400	.600	10.80	5.40
Guilbeau, Taylor	L-L	6-4	180	5-12-93	1	0	2.52	28	0	0	0	36	34	11	10	0	15	35	.248	.184	.284	8.83	3.79
Hellickson, Jeremy	R-R	6-1	190	4-8-87	0	1	21.21	1	1	0	0	5	9	11	11	2	3	4	.391	.313	.571	11.57	5.79
Howard, Hayden	R-L	6-5	193	3-26-94	3	1	2.87	35	0	0	1	63	56	24	20	4	24	61	.242	.193	.273	8.76	3.45
Johnston, Kyle	R-R	6-0	190	7-17-96	5	2	4.94	10	9	1	0	47	41	30	26	4	28	37	.237	.318	.159	7.04	5.32
Kelley, Shawn	R-R	6-2	237	4-26-84	0	0	0.00	1	1	0	0	1	0	0	0	0	0	1	.000	—	.000	9.00	0.00
Kintzler, Brandon	R-R	6-0	194	8-1-84	0	0	0.00	1	0	0	0	1	0	0	0	0	0	1	.000	.000	.000	9.00	0.00
Klobosits, Gabe	L-R	6-7	270	5-16-95	1	1	2.20	11	0	0	1	16	14	9	4	0	11	18	.226	.261	.205	9.92	6.06
Mapes, Tyler	R-R	6-2	205	7-19-94	6	1	1.76	12	12	1	0	66	52	14	13	0	15	52	.219	.250	.189	7.06	2.04
McGowin, Kyle	R-R	6-3	195	11-27-91	1	1	4.09	2	2	0	0	11	8	6	5	2	3	14	.200	.133	.240	11.45	2.45
McKinney, Jeremy	R-R	6-0	190	12-8-94	3	4	1.89	22	0	0	4	33	22	14	7	0	19	36	.190	.211	.170	9.72	5.13
Mills, Jordan	L-L	6-5	215	5-11-92	0	2	2.60	25	0	0	6	35	27	13	10	0	14	41	.213	.264	.176	10.64	3.63
Pantoja, Jorge	R-R	6-5	215	3-26-94	0	4	4.68	25	1	0	2	50	49	33	26	5	16	42	.254	.338	.198	7.56	2.88
Pena, Ronald	R-R	6-4	195	9-19-91	1	1	1.98	17	0	0	1	27	19	6	6	0	9	38	.196	.257	.161	12.51	2.96
Raquet, Nick	R-L	6-0	215	12-12-95	5	3	4.91	12	12	1	0	55	72	32	30	3	21	36	.319	.309	.322	5.89	3.44
Rivera, Mariano	R-R	5-11	155	10-4-93	0	1	8.49	9	0	0	0	12	16	12	11	3	4	12	.308	.412	.257	9.26	3.09
Romero, Jhon	R-R	5-10	195	1-17-95	0	0	0.00	4	0	0	0	5	2	0	0	2	7	.111	.000	.182	11.81	3.38
2-team total (32 Myrtle Beach)					1	2	2.92	36	0	0	9	49	42	19	16	1	19	64	.225	.240	.213	11.68	3.47
Ross, Joe	R-R	6-4	220	5-21-93	0	0	0.00	1	1	0	0	1	0	0	0	0	1	1	.083	.143	.000	2.45	2.45
Sharp, Sterling	R-R	6-4	170	5-30-95	5	3	3.16	14	14	0	0	80	82	32	28	4	21	58	.262	.293	.233	6.55	2.37
Strasburg, Stephen	R-R	6-5	235	7-20-88	0	1	1.00	2	2	0	0	9	7	4	1	1	1	12	.194	.217	.154	12.00	1.00
Tetreault, Jackson	R-R	6-5	170	6-3-96	1	1	4.37	4	4	1	0	23	21	12	11	2	7	20	.241	.218	.281	7.94	2.78

Fielding

Catcher	PCT	G	PO	A	E	DP	PB
Barrera	.991	67	521	53	5	4	2
Reetz	.986	67	508	39	8	3	5
Reistetter	1.000	4	24	2	0	0	0
Wieters	1.000	1	6	0	0	0	1

First Base	PCT	G	PO	A	E	DP
Basto	.968	7	59	2	2	6
Corredor	.997	47	355	17	1	33
Davidson	1.000	7	66	5	0	3
Masters	1.000	17	119	10	0	8
Noll	1.000	16	139	6	0	7
Sagdal	.992	45	326	26	3	30
Zimmerman	.875	1	6	1	1	4

Second Base	PCT	G	PO	A	E	DP
Boggetto	1.000	7	7	19	0	4
Davidson	.750	1	0	3	1	0
Lora	.904	27	28	47	8	8
Masters	1.000	12	24	23	0	10
Mejia	.968	90	162	204	12	44
Monasterio	1.000	6	6	20	0	3

Third Base	PCT	G	PO	A	E	DP
Boggetto	.960	12	4	20	1	2
Davidson	1.000	0	2	0	0	0
Masters	.919	39	28	74	9	5
Mejia	1.000	3	0	3	0	0
Noll	.938	42	22	68	6	5
Rendon	1.000	1	2	0	0	0
Sagdal	.941	44	18	77	6	3

Shortstop	PCT	G	PO	A	E	DP
Garcia	.960	40	58	87	6	24
Kieboom	.943	56	89	141	14	26
Lora	1.000	13	27	22	0	7
Masters	.988	25	17	64	1	12
Monasterio	1.000	3	5	9	0	4

Outfield	PCT	G	PO	A	E	DP
Agustin	.962	53	95	5	4	1
Banks	1.000	57	137	6	0	1
Basto	1.000	6	5	0	0	0
Eaton	1.000	2	1	0	0	0
Keller	1.000	16	24	0	0	0
Lora	.889	7	8	0	1	0
Perkins	.993	63	136	1	1	0
Sagdal	1.000	2	4	0	0	0
Soto	.967	15	28	1	1	0
Sundberg	.994	84	160	1	1	0
Wiseman	.983	109	223	9	4	1

HAGERSTOWN SUNS
SOUTH ATLANTIC LEAGUE

LOW CLASS A

Batting	B-T	HT	WT	DOB	AVG	vLH	vRH	G	AB	R	H	2B	3B	HR	RBI	BB	HBP	SH	SF	SO	SB	CS	SLG	OBP
Antuna, Yasel	B-R	6-0	170	10-26-99	.220	.165	.246	87	323	44	71	14	2	6	27	32	3	0	4	79	8	7	.331	.293
Baez, Jeyner	R-R	6-1	175	7-25-95	.200	.227	.191	27	90	10	18	3	0	0	4	7	1	2	0	14	2	0	.233	.265
Banks, Nick	L-L	6-1	215	11-18-94	.260	.167	.306	56	200	25	52	9	0	6	27	13	1	0	1	45	10	4	.395	.307
Boggetto, Branden	R-R	6-0	190	11-10-93	.344	.386	.308	29	96	17	33	10	2	2	13	11	2	0	0	0	1		.552	.422

WASHINGTON NATIONALS

BATTING	B-T	HT	WT	DOB	AVG	vLH	vRH	G	AB	R	H	2B	3B	HR	RBI	BB	HBP	SH	SF	SO	SB	CS	SLG	OBP
Canning, Gage	L-R	5-10	175	4-23-97	.223	.256	.206	31	112	15	25	9	0	4	16	11	1	2	2	36	2	0	.411	.294
Caulfield, Phil	L-R	5-8	170	12-30-94	.188	.160	.205	24	69	7	13	3	1	0	4	6	1	7	1	14	1	0	.261	.260
Choruby, Nick	L-R	6-0	190	11-8-94	.228	.200	.241	52	167	18	38	5	1	0	8	27	1	2	0	41	14	6	.270	.339
Corredor, Aldrem	L-L	6-0	202	10-27-95	.289	.203	.328	56	187	21	54	7	2	4	30	17	2	1	1	33	0	0	.412	.353
Dunlap, Alex	R-R	6-2	195	10-6-94	.277	.370	.212	35	112	15	31	9	0	5	13	6	1	3		26	0	0	.491	.373
Esthay, Kameron	L-L	6-0	215	12-5-94	.216	.250	.202	97	334	38	72	16	4	10	30	27	5	1	2	126	3	4	.377	.283
Flores, Alejandro	B-R	6-1	180	12-27-95	.216	.203	.222	66	213	22	46	13	3	6	29	24	5	2	1	44	3	1	.390	.309
Franco, Anderson	R-R	6-3	190	8-15-97	.237	.197	.255	63	228	21	54	14	0	3	34	25	2	0	5	45	2	1	.338	.312
Freeman, Cole	R-R	5-9	175	9-27-94	.266	.300	.249	122	447	78	119	32	3	3	43	47	16	8	4	59	26	8	.371	.354
Garcia, Luis	L-R	6-0	190	5-16-00	.297	.242	.323	78	296	48	88	14	4	3	31	19	0	4	4	49	8	5	.402	.335
Harris, Joey	L-R	6-0	200	2-13-94	.208	.200	.211	8	24	2	5	0	0	0	1	4	1	0	0	12	0	0	.208	.345
Meregildo, Omar	R-R	6-1	185	8-18-97	.268	.272	.265	65	228	23	61	19	0	7	34	19	3	0	4	70	0	0	.443	.327
Ortiz, Oliver	L-L	6-0	170	5-6-96	.120	.000	.177	8	25	2	3	2	0	0	2	3	0	0	1	7	0	0	.200	.207
Panaccione, Paul	R-R	5-10	190	12-6-93	.163	.161	.165	44	135	13	22	1	0	1	13	12	1	0	2	44	4	1	.193	.233
Pascal, Juan	R-R	6-1	175	10-6-94	.186	.167	.195	37	113	7	21	4	1	0	8	10	3	3	1	27	5	2	.239	.268
Perkins, Nic	R-R	6-4	215	2-19-96	.250	.000	1.000	1	4	1	1	0	0	0	0	0	0	0	0	0	0	0	.250	.250
Ruiz, Adderling	R-R	6-1	175	5-3-91	.000	—	.000	1	3	0	0	0	0	0	0	0	1	0	0	2	0	0	.000	.250
Scudder, Jake	L-R	6-0	210	3-23-95	.244	.222	.255	86	311	36	76	19	0	7	55	25	5	0	4	66	1	2	.373	.307
Soto, Juan	L-L	6-1	185	10-25-98	.373	.500	.317	16	59	12	22	5	3	5	24	14	0	0	1	13	2	0	.814	.487
Sundberg, Jack	L-R	5-11	195	7-21-93	.200	.188	.205	14	55	4	11	2	0	0	4	3	1	1	1	20	2	0	.236	.250
Upshaw, Armond	B-L	6-0	190	6-20-96	.234	.276	.213	113	363	48	85	13	1	2	25	42	3	9	2	129	24	9	.292	.317

Pitching	B-T	HT	WT	DOB	W	L	ERA	G	GS	CG	SV	IP	H	R	ER	HR	BB	SO	AVG	vLH	vRH	K/9	BB/9
Acevedo, Carlos	R-R	6-3	200	9-27-94	1	4	6.51	13	3	0	2	37	47	27	27	11	36		.301	.300	.303	8.28	2.65
Alastre, Tomas	R-R	6-4	170	6-11-98	4	8	5.32	23	23	0	0	118	135	86	70	21	44	80	.290	.240	.276	6.08	3.35
Bartow, Frankie	R-R	6-3	180	2-26-97	3	2	5.32	15	0	0	3	24	29	15	14	4	2	15	.309	.319	.298	5.70	0.76
Bogucki, A.J.	R-R	6-3	187	5-2-95	1	2	5.72	17	1	0	3	39	43	28	25	7	13	46	.269	.238	.300	10.53	2.97
Brasher, Jared	R-R	6-1	200	1-3-95	0	5	5.48	32	0	0	1	43	42	26	26	4	24	42	.261	.246	.272	8.86	5.06
Braymer, Ben	L-L	6-2	215	4-28-94	3	0	1.75	7	0	0	0	26	18	5	5	2	5	25	.205	.152	.236	8.77	1.75
Cate, Tim	L-L	6-0	185	9-30-97	0	3	5.57	4	4	0	0	21	23	15	13	4	6	19	.271	.323	.241	8.14	2.57
DeRosier, Matthew	R-R	6-2	200	7-13-94	3	4	3.79	7	7	0	0	40	32	19	17	7	11	37	.208	.173	.241	8.26	2.45
Engelbrekt, Max	L-L	6-3	197	9-30-93	0	2	7.50	5	0	0	0	6	9	7	5	1	3	4	.346	.333	.357	6.00	4.50
Fuentes, Steven	R-R	6-2	175	5-4-97	2	1	2.35	9	0	0	3	23	17	7	6	0	2	27	.198	.211	.188	10.57	0.78
German, Jhonatan	R-R	6-4	215	1-24-95	2	1	2.95	11	0	0	2	21	14	9	7	0	6	22	.180	.238	.111	9.28	2.53
Held, Sam	R-R	6-5	190	8-24-94	5	8	4.07	27	0	1	0	86	88	52	39	5	12	65	.264	.230	.298	6.78	1.25
Hill, Brigham	R-R	5-11	190	7-8-95	4	3	3.08	10	10	1	0	50	46	22	17	0	18	35	.250	.304	.196	6.34	3.26
Johnson, Jared	R-L	6-4	185	9-1-95	0	2	5.01	17	0	0	1	32	34	20	18	2	23	25	.281	.349	.244	6.96	6.40
Johnston, Kyle	R-R	6-0	190	7-17-96	2	3	3.42	18	7	0	2	55	50	27	21	3	25	59	.238	.231	.245	9.60	4.07
Lee, Andrew	L-R	6-5	225	12-2-93	4	5	4.28	20	10	0	0	67	39	38	32	4	57	86	.166	.191	.135	11.50	7.62
McKinney, Jeremy	R-R	6-0	190	12-8-94	1	0	0.00	9	0	0	1	11	7	1	0	0	1	10	.180	.111	.333	13.91	0.82
Morse, Phil	R-R	6-2	195	5-23-94	2	0	8.79	23	0	0	3	29	45	33	28	2	16	26	.352	.347	.354	8.16	5.02
Pantoja, Jorge	R-R	6-5	215	3-26-94	0	1	2.63	7	0	0	0	14	13	5	4	1	1	9	.250	.250	.250	5.93	0.66
Pena, Carlos	R-R	6-6	240	4-3-94	1	1	6.00	19	0	0	2	36	36	24	24	4	20	41	.259	.293	.235	10.25	5.00
Pena, Malvin	R-R	6-2	180	6-24-97	3	1	3.60	6	0	0	0	30	37	15	12	1	4	27	.289	.237	.333	8.10	1.20
Raquet, Nick	R-L	6-0	215	12-12-95	4	6	2.79	12	12	2	0	68	68	29	21	1	18	56	.262	.279	.253	7.45	2.39
Romero, Seth	L-L	6-3	240	4-19-96	0	1	3.91	7	7	0	0	25	20	13	11	3	8	34	.206	.278	.164	12.08	2.84
Smith, David	R-R	6-4	210	10-20-94	0	0	17.36	3	0	0	0	5	11	9	9	2	1	6	.458	.471	.429	11.57	1.93
Stoeckinger, Jackson	L-L	6-3	210	2-13-96	3	6	6.38	14	13	0	0	68	86	53	48	12	11	51	.306	.296	.312	6.78	1.46
Tetreault, Jackson	R-R	6-5	170	6-3-96	3	8	4.01	20	20	0	0	110	108	62	49	10	34	118	.255	.284	.229	9.65	2.78
Troop, Alex	L-L	6-5	210	7-19-96	1	3	4.76	4	3	0	0	17	21	12	9	5	5	16	.284	.286	.283	8.47	2.65
Zwetsch, Connor	R-R	6-5	230	5-6-95	0	1	12.60	5	0	0	1	5	9	8	7	1	1	6	.360	.429	.273	10.80	1.80

Fielding

C: Baez 27, Dunlap 34, Flores 66, Harris 7, Perkins 1, Ruiz 1. **1B:** Boggetto 5, Corredor 18, Franco 35, Meregildo 22, Scudder 56. **2B:** Antuna 9, Boggetto 2, Caulfield 9, Freeman 101, Garcia 11, Panaccione 4. **3B:** Boggetto 15, Caulfield 1, Franco 24, Freeman 7, Garcia 36, Meregildo 29, Panaccione 14, Pascal 9. **SS:** Antuna 67, Garcia 27, Panaccione 14, Pascal 27. **OF:** Banks 50, Canning 31, Caulfield 7, Choruby 51, Corredor 29, Esthay 82, Ortiz 8, Panaccione 1, Soto 16, Sundberg 14, Upshaw 113.

AUBURN DOUBLEDAYS   SHORT-SEASON
NEW YORK-PENN LEAGUE

Batting	B-T	HT	WT	DOB	AVG	vLH	vRH	G	AB	R	H	2B	3B	HR	RBI	BB	HBP	SH	SF	SO	SB	CS	SLG	OBP
Agustin, Telmito	L-L	5-10	160	10-9-96	.186	.174	.192	18	70	7	13	2	0	1	5	5	1	0	1	20	1	0	.257	.247
Blash, Jamori	R-R	6-4	225	11-9-95	.218	.318	.178	62	229	29	50	15	1	5	34	15	3	0	2	76	0	1	.358	.273
Canning, Gage	L-R	5-10	175	4-23-97	.315	.273	.326	14	54	13	17	3	3	2	7	5	0	0	0	18	0	2	.593	.373
Carrillo, Adalberto	R-R	5-11	185	6-1-95	.260	.320	.239	28	96	13	25	2	1	0	9	7	5	1	0	24	0	0	.302	.343
Caulfield, Phil	L-R	5-8	170	12-30-94	.263	.250	.265	14	38	4	10	4	2	0	6	4	2	0	0	7	0	0	.474	.364
Choruby, Nick	L-R	6-0	190	11-8-94	.300	.500	.167	3	10	2	3	0	1	0	1	1	0	0	0	1	1	0	.500	.364
Connell, Justin	R-R	6-1	185	3-11-99	.263	.429	.226	14	38	4	10	1	0	0	3	10	1	0	1	8	1	2	.290	.420
Cropley, Tyler	R-R	5-11	185	12-10-95	.167	.000	.200	4	12	3	2	1	0	0	1	1	0	0	1	5	0	0	.250	.286
Daily, Cole	L-R	5-11	170	11-28-94	.275	.304	.265	53	182	30	50	6	1	0	16	18	1	3	1	36	5	2	.324	.342
Marinconz, Kyle	L-R	5-10	185	5-24-96	.284	.341	.263	45	162	20	46	5	2	1	19	18	0	0	0	44	5	1	.358	.356
Martinson, Jason	R-R	6-1	210	10-15-88	.238	.286	.214	6	21	2	5	0	0	1	2	1	0	0	0	7	0	0	.381	.304
Mendez, Ricardo	L-R	6-0	165	1-24-00	.198	.235	.182	54	172	28	34	4	1	1	18	17	1	2	1	41	8	4	.250	.272
O'Connor, Pablo	R-R	6-0	195	9-6-95	.296	.300	.294	52	213	34	63	14	3	5	25	12	1	0	0	46	2	0	.460	.336
Ortiz, Oliver	L-L	6-0	170	5-6-96	.000	.000	.000	3	10	0	0	0	0	0	0	0	0	0	0	4	0	0	.000	.000

Name	B-T	HT	WT	DOB	AVG	vLH	vRH	G	AB	R	H	2B	3B	HR	RBI	BB	HBP	SH	SF	SO	SB	CS	SLG	OBP
Pascal, Juan	R-R	6-1	175	11-6-97	.227	.167	.250	14	44	3	10	2	0	0	4	1	1	1	0	11	2	0	.273	.261
Perez, Wilmer	R-R	5-10	186	4-16-98	.476	.333	.500	6	21	4	10	3	0	0	5	5	0	0	0	3	0	0	.619	.577
Perkins, Nic	R-R	6-4	215	2-19-96	.248	.200	.266	44	149	16	37	6	0	3	32	16	3	0	2	19	0	0	.349	.329
Pineda, Israel	R-R	5-11	190	4-3-00	.273	.235	.290	46	165	25	45	7	0	4	24	12	6	0	2	35	0	0	.388	.341
Pryor, Jonathan	L-L	6-1	190	4-28-94	.313	.200	.333	15	32	5	10	1	0	0	3	0	0	0	0	4	0	1	.344	.371
Reynolds, Matt	R-R	6-1	200	12-3-90	.500	.667	.333	2	6	1	3	0	0	0	2	0	0	0	0	1	0	0	.500	.625
Rhinesmith, Jacob	L-L	6-2	195	5-23-96	.283	.356	.266	63	237	39	67	12	4	1	32	27	2	0	2	40	6	0	.380	.358
Robles, Victor	R-R	6-0	190	5-19-97	.188	.000	.250	4	16	0	3	0	0	0	3	1	0	0	0	2	1	0	.188	.235
Sanchez, Jose	R-R	5-11	155	7-12-00	.230	.259	.219	64	209	20	48	9	1	0	23	24	1	2	2	56	1	0	.282	.309
Shaddy, Carson	R-R	5-11	185	8-19-94	.234	.313	.200	42	158	21	37	10	1	1	18	20	5	1	1	55	5	4	.329	.337
Sierra, Moises	R-R	6-1	233	9-24-88	.385	.100	.563	7	26	4	10	4	0	1	6	0	0	0	0	3	0	0	.654	.467
Wilson, Cody	R-R	6-2	200	7-4-96	.278	.220	.306	48	180	24	50	10	5	0	18	17	5	1	1	39	3	5	.389	.355

Pitching	B-T	HT	WT	DOB	W	L	ERA	G	GS	CG	SV	IP	H	R	ER	HR	BB	SO	AVG	vLH	vRH	K/9	BB/9
Adon, Joan	R-R	6-2	185	8-12-98	1	1	7.36	7	0	0	0	11	13	10	9	2	9	11	.310	.300	.318	9.00	7.36
Barrett, Aaron	R-R	6-3	230	1-2-88	2	0	1.74	20	0	0	0	21	13	6	4	0	8	26	.171	.258	.111	11.32	3.48
Bartow, Frankie	R-R	6-3	180	2-26-97	1	0	0.00	2	0	0	0	4	0	0	0	0	3		.000	.000	.000	6.75	0.00
Cate, Tim	L-L	6-0	185	9-30-97	2	3	4.65	9	8	0	0	31	34	18	16	1	10	26	.272	.405	.216	7.55	2.90
Chu, Gilberto	L-L	5-11	160	11-19-97	2	2	3.66	18	0	0	1	32	32	16	13	0	7	26	.254	.209	.277	7.31	1.97
Crowe, Wil	R-R	6-2	240	9-9-94	0	0	0.00	1	1	0	0	3	2	0	0	0	2	1	.222	.400	.000	3.00	6.00
Day, Chandler	R-R	6-5	175	5-24-97	1	2	3.68	10	0	0	2	29	24	13	12	3	9	24	.229	.281	.206	7.36	2.76
De Los Santos, Jose	R-R	6-3	190	1-14-97	1	0	9.00	6	0	0	0	8	9	9	8	0	8	5	.300	.214	.375	5.63	9.00
Driskill, Tanner	R-R	6-0	170	1-18-96	1	4	9.00	15	0	0	1	24	37	28	24	6	8	21	.352	.364	.344	7.88	3.00
Fletcher, Aaron	L-L	6-0	220	2-25-96	2	1	2.48	12	7	0	0	29	30	9	8	0	3	32	.266	.286	.256	9.93	0.93
Galindez, Nelson	L-L	6-3	220	7-26-98	0	1	13.06	3	2	0	0	10	19	15	15	0	8	7	.432	.571	.367	6.10	6.97
German, Jhonatan	R-R	6-4	215	1-24-95	1	1	2.63	7	0	0	2	14	6	5	4	0	7	16	.128	.222	.069	10.54	4.61
Gomez, Niomar	R-R	6-3	173	9-9-98	2	1	3.00	4	0	0	0	21	22	8	7	0	5	14	.275	.333	.250	6.00	2.14
Guillen, Angel	R-R	6-2	150	1-24-97	5	2	2.84	15	2	0	1	57	49	26	18	3	15	49	.240	.211	.263	7.74	2.37
Hernandez, Alfonso	L-L	5-11	162	8-3-99	1	0	2.77	3	0	0	0	13	7	4	4	0	6	10	.152	.147	.147	6.92	4.15
Irvin, Jake	R-R	6-6	225	2-18-97	0	0	2.25	4	4	0	0	8	6	2	2	0	4	6	.207	.250	.191	6.75	4.50
Karp, Andrew	R-R	6-1	204	9-9-95	0	0	0.00	1	1	0	0	3	1	0	0	0	0	2	.100	.250	.000	6.00	
Maley, Alec	R-R	6-1	185	8-15-95	0	0	10.13	2	0	0	1	3	5	3	3	0	0	2	.385	.400	.375	6.75	0.00
Morse, Colin	R-R	6-5	185	5-16-96	0	2	9.53	8	0	0	0	11	10	13	12	1	12	8	.238	.250	.231	6.35	9.53
Peguero, Francys	R-R	6-2	170	10-6-95	5	3	2.93	14	13	0	0	68	54	22	22	7	14	46	.217	.205	.226	6.12	1.86
Pena, Malvin	R-R	6-2	180	6-24-97	3	0	1.80	4	0	0	0	20	20	5	4	0	3	26	.253	.207	.280	9.00	1.35
Ramirez, Nector	R-R	6-0	170	9-4-96	1	3	6.08	16	0	0	1	24	33	18	16	3	12	12	.340	.343	.339	4.56	4.56
Ramirez, Yonathan	L-L	5-11	165	4-13-97	3	4	3.83	11	6	0	0	40	44	22	17	0	12	21	.275	.298	.266	4.73	2.70
Reyes, Luis	R-R	6-2	175	9-26-94	0	0	0.00	2	2	0	0	7	2	0	0	0	2	7	.087	.000	.118	9.00	2.57
Schaller, Reid	R-R	6-3	210	4-2-97	2	2	5.90	7	0	0	0	29	30	19	19	0	9	16	.268	.340	.203	4.97	2.79
Smith, David	R-R	6-4	210	10-20-94	1	0	1.71	15	0	0	0	26	23	8	5	0	10	19	.235	.209	.255	6.49	3.42
Stoeckinger, Jackson	L-L	6-3	210	2-13-96	3	1	2.08	7	6	0	0	35	31	8	8	1	6	29	.244	.167	.275	7.53	1.56
Tapani, Ryan	R-R	6-0	180	6-28-94	0	2	3.56	15	3	0	2	30	29	12	12	1	4	30	.250	.277	.232	8.90	1.19
Teel, Carson	L-L	6-0	160	12-17-95	1	0	2.20	12	4	0	1	33	31	9	8	1	6	23	.246	.268	.235	6.34	1.65
Turner, Trey	R-R	6-1	195	6-15-94	0	0	6.75	2	0	0	0	1	1	5	1	1	2	0	.143	.000	.250	9.00	13.50
Vargas, Cesar	R-R	6-2	237	12-30-91	0	0	0.00	2	0	0	0	5	2	0	0	0	0	5	.125	.125	.125	9.00	0.00
Zwetsch, Connor	R-R	6-5	230	5-6-95	0	0	1.13	7	0	0	5	8	6	1	1	0	3	6	.200	.211	.182	6.75	3.38

Fielding

C: Carrillo 23, Cropley 4, Perez 3, Perkins 24, Pineda 30. **1B:** Blash 61, Ortiz 1, Pascal 1, Perkins 17. **2B:** Caulfield 6, Daily 7, Marinconz 30, Pascal 1, Sanchez 1, Shaddy 32. **3B:** Carrillo 1, Caulfield 6, Daily 34, Marinconz 14, Martinson 5, Pascal 12, Reynolds 1, Shaddy 7. **SS:** Daily 13, Pascal 2, Reynolds 1, Sanchez 63. **OF:** Agustin 15, Canning 14, Choruby 3, Connell 13, Mendez 53, O'Connor 24, Ortiz 1, Pryor 12, Rhinesmith 55, Robles 4, Sierra 6, Wilson 48.

GCL NATIONALS
GULF COAST LEAGUE
ROOKIE

Batting	B-T	HT	WT	DOB	AVG	vLH	vRH	G	AB	R	H	2B	3B	HR	RBI	BB	HBP	SH	SF	SO	SB	CS	SLG	OBP
Aquino, Luis	R-R	6-1	157	4-28-99	.171	.083	.188	29	76	6	13	0	0	0	4	8	0	0	0	27	7	0	.171	.250
Bencosme, Bryan	R-R	6-1	196	12-18-97	.000	.000	.000	6	14	0	0	0	0	0	1	2	0	0	0	8	0	0	.000	.125
Chisolm, Blake	L-R	6-5	210	7-17-96	.296	.211	.311	40	125	20	37	11	3	2	25	21	9	0	2	31	3	1	.480	.427
Connell, Justin	R-R	6-1	185	3-11-99	.244	.167	.250	25	78	17	19	1	0	1	7	11	1	2	1	12	7	2	.295	.341
Cropley, Tyler	R-R	5-11	185	12-10-95	.367	.500	.357	10	30	3	11	1	0	0	8	8	1	0	0	2	1	0	.400	.513
De Aza, Alejandro	L-L	6-0	195	4-11-84	.276	.000	.296	9	29	2	8	2	0	0	4	3	0	0	0	5	0	0	.345	.344
Dunlap, Alex	R-R	6-2	195	10-6-94	.294	.000	.357	6	17	2	5	2	0	0	3	2	0	0	0	4	0	0	.412	.368
Emiliani, Leandro	L-L	6-1	180	3-22-00	.245	.091	.257	43	151	21	37	12	1	3	23	9	2	1	2	32	0	0	.397	.293
Franco, Anderson	R-R	6-3	190	8-19-97	.349	.250	.371	12	43	7	15	1	1	2	12	4	0	0	1	3	0	0	.558	.396
Harris, Joey	L-R	6-0	200	2-13-94	.143	.000	.154	7	14	2	2	1	0	0	2	0	0	0	0	7	0	0	.214	.333
Johnson, Daniel	L-L	5-10	185	7-11-95	.300	.000	.316	7	20	3	6	0	0	1	4	2	2	0	0	2	1	0	.450	.417
Marinconz, Kyle	L-R	5-10	185	5-24-96	.250	.000	.333	2	4	0	1	0	0	0	0	0	0	0	0	1	0	0	.250	.250
Matos, Wilfrido	R-R	5-10	160	9-8-00	.195	.000	.229	11	41	5	8	0	0	0	3	2	0	1	1	12	0	0	.195	.227
Morales, Jesus	R-R	5-10	173	12-22-97	.263	.278	.261	45	156	22	41	5	0	0	11	11	1	0	2	29	6	2	.295	.312
O'Connor, Pablo	R-R	6-0	195	9-6-95	.324	.000	.333	10	34	5	11	4	0	0	6	2	0	0	1	7	3	0	.441	.351
Pena, Landerson	R-R	6-0	194	10-14-97	.187	.200	.184	41	107	10	20	2	1	2	9	11	1	0	1	41	4	2	.280	.267
Perez, Wilmer	R-R	5-10	186	4-16-98	.310	.187	.317	29	100	21	31	6	0	1	21	6	2	0	5	14	2	0	.400	.345
Peroni, Anthony	R-R	5-11	175	12-12-96	.177	.154	.182	28	79	10	14	5	0	1	9	16	2	0	1	19	1	0	.279	.327
Pogue, Colton	R-R	6-1	195	2-1-96	.282	.191	.298	42	135	15	38	6	1	1	11	11	3	0	1	25	4	1	.363	.347
Quintana, Jonathan	R-R	6-0	205	11-23-94	.224	.100	.246	28	67	10	15	2	1	0	4	13	2	0	0	16	1	3	.284	.366

	B-T	HT	WT	DOB	AVG	vLH	vRH	G	AB	R	H	2B	3B	HR	RBI	BB	HBP	SH	SF	SO	SB	CS	SLG	OBP
Robles, Victor	R-R	6-0	190	5-19-97	.333	—	.333	8	18	7	6	1	0	0	1	7	2	0	0	4	4	1	.389	.556
Sanchez, Adrian	R-R	6-0	216	8-16-90	.467	—	.467	5	15	7	7	2	1	1	4	1	0	0	0	1	2	0	.933	.500
Sanfler, Caldioli	L-R	6-2	185	12-7-97	.221	.154	.233	23	86	14	19	1	3	0	6	7	1	1	1	23	7	2	.302	.284
Senior, Eric	R-R	6-2	170	9-29-99	.274	.357	.263	34	113	13	31	8	0	0	14	9	1	1	1	19	3	2	.345	.331
Sosa, Ronaldy	L-R	6-0	184	11-2-98	.184	.150	.192	35	114	11	21	6	0	0	12	8	1	0	1	24	0	0	.237	.242
Vega, Onix	R-R	5-10	200	9-7-98	.276	.125	.300	21	58	7	16	2	0	0	5	9	3	1	0	4	2	1	.310	.400
Vickers, Trey	R-R	6-1	185	9-17-95	.245	.333	.233	30	98	15	24	2	1	0	13	9	2	1	0	24	0	1	.286	.321
Wilson, Jacob	R-R	5-11	205	7-29-90	.333	.000	.385	4	15	2	5	1	0	0	5	1	0	0	0	1	0	0	.400	.375

Pitching	B-T	HT	WT	DOB	W	L	ERA	G	GS	CG	SV	IP	H	R	ER	HR	BB	SO	AVG	vLH	vRH	K/9	BB/9
Adon, Joan	R-R	6-2	185	8-12-98	2	0	2.29	13	0	0	2	20	20	16	5	0	13	29	.250	.200	.273	13.27	5.95
Cousins, Jake	R-R	6-4	185	7-14-94	0	0	4.09	7	1	0	0	11	13	5	5	0	2	8	.277	.308	.265	6.55	1.64
Cuello, Carlos	R-R	6-5	190	2-26-99	0	2	3.91	13	0	0	0	23	19	13	10	1	7	15	.216	.161	.246	5.87	2.74
Day, Chandler	R-R	6-5	175	5-24-97	0	0	1.80	2	0	0	0	5	3	1	1	0	1	5	.167	.200	.154	9.00	0.00
Driskill, Tanner	R-R	6-0	170	1-18-96	0	0	9.00	1	0	0	0	2	3	2	2	0	0	0	.333	—	.333	0.00	0.00
Fletcher, Aaron	L-L	6-0	220	2-25-96	0	0	9.00	1	0	0	0	2	4	2	2	0	1	2	.500	.333	.600	9.00	4.50
Galindez, Nelson	L-L	6-3	220	7-26-98	0	0	2.16	4	0	0	1	8	9	2	2	0	3	5	.257	.273	.250	5.40	3.24
Glover, Koda	R-R	6-5	215	4-13-93	0	0	0.00	2	0	0	0	2	0	0	0	0	1	4	.000	.000	.000	18.00	4.50
Gomez, Niomar	R-R	6-3	173	9-9-98	0	1	8.24	8	0	0	0	32	49	30	29	2	8	27	.360	.348	.367	7.67	2.27
Gomez, Rafael	R-R	6-0	178	6-15-98	3	4	6.12	11	5	0	0	43	54	32	29	2	10	26	.309	.255	.333	5.48	2.11
Gonzalez, Pedro	R-R	6-2	183	7-16-00	1	2	9.60	5	2	0	0	15	20	20	16	4	5	15	.313	.318	.310	9.00	3.00
Hernandez, Alfonso	L-L	5-11	162	8-3-99	2	0	2.14	13	0	0	2	34	29	10	8	0	8	31	.228	.156	.253	8.29	2.14
Hill, Brigham	R-R	5-11	190	7-8-95	0	2	4.50	2	2	0	0	6	8	4	3	0	4	5	.348	.556	.214	7.50	6.00
Irvin, Jake	R-R	6-6	225	2-18-97	1	0	1.42	7	3	0	0	13	10	6	2	0	3	9	.213	.200	.219	6.39	2.13
Jimenez, Jose	L-L	6-1	190	12-7-96	1	2	6.75	8	0	0	0	12	18	12	9	2	2	8	.321	.357	.310	6.00	1.50
Karp, Andrew	R-R	6-1	204	9-30-95	0	1	3.00	5	3	0	0	9	10	4	3	1	3	9	.278	.250	.300	9.00	3.00
Lee, Evan	L-L	6-1	200	6-18-97	0	0	5.40	2	0	0	0	2	1	1	1	0	4	1	.167	.000	.200	5.40	21.60
Maley, Alec	R-R	6-1	185	8-15-95	2	0	5.87	6	0	0	0	8	9	5	5	0	3	5	.300	.364	.263	5.87	3.52
Milacki, Bobby	R-R	6-2	210	11-6-96	2	1	3.95	7	0	0	1	14	16	9	6	0	5	9	.286	.333	.250	5.93	3.29
Morse, Colin	R-R	6-5	185	5-16-96	1	1	5.63	6	1	0	0	8	3	5	5	0	11	9	.125	.143	.118	10.13	12.38
Peguero, Jairon	L-L	6-0	177	6-14-97	0	0	1.74	5	0	0	0	10	10	2	2	0	4	8	.256	.500	.229	6.97	3.48
Perez, Fray	R-R	5-11	170	8-22-96	3	2	5.82	15	0	0	2	22	25	20	14	2	8	22	.284	.231	.307	9.14	3.32
Reyes, Luis	R-R	6-2	175	9-26-94	0	1	4.50	2	2	0	0	4	5	3	2	0	3	3	.278	.250	.300	6.75	0.00
Romero, Carlos	R-R	6-6	179	7-15-99	0	0	2.25	2	1	0	0	8	7	3	2	0	3	8	.226	.154	.278	9.00	3.38
Ross, Joe	R-R	6-4	220	5-21-93	0	0	0.00	2	2	0	0	6	0	0	0	0	3	8	.000	.000	.000	12.00	4.50
Schaller, Reid	R-R	6-3	210	4-2-97	0	1	1.54	5	5	0	0	12	9	2	2	1	3	16	.209	.417	.129	12.34	2.31
Segura, Fausto	R-R	6-3	191	10-24-96	1	3	6.60	7	0	0	0	15	17	13	11	1	9	13	.283	.389	.238	7.80	5.40
Strom, Leif	R-R	6-6	215	5-17-97	1	3	4.83	11	9	1	0	41	52	23	22	2	10	31	.304	.305	.304	6.80	2.20
Teel, Carson	L-L	6-0	160	12-17-95	0	0	3.60	2	2	0	0	5	4	2	2	0	1	7	.211	.250	.182	12.60	1.80
Theophile, Rodney	R-R	6-5	230	9-16-99	0	4	10.67	10	5	0	0	14	23	21	17	3	11	11	.359	.333	.375	6.91	6.91
Turner, Trey	R-R	6-1	195	6-15-96	1	1	5.19	14	0	0	1	17	16	15	10	0	20	24	.239	.250	.233	12.46	10.38
Vann, Chris	L-L	6-2	195	6-25-96	1	2	5.40	14	0	0	1	17	18	13	10	3	7	18	.257	.105	.314	9.72	3.78
Williamson, Ryan	L-L	6-2	190	4-28-95	1	1	2.53	7	5	0	0	21	18	7	6	2	4	23	.222	.150	.246	9.70	1.69

Fielding

C: Cropley 8, Dunlap 6, Harris 6, Perez 17, Peroni 17, Vega 16. **1B:** Chisolm 33, Emiliani 24, Peroni 1, Sosa 3. **2B:** Marinconz 2, Morales 25, Pogue 2, Sanchez 2, Sosa 32, Wilson 2. **3B:** Bencosme 6, Franco 11, Morales 8, Pogue 38, Vickers 1, Wilson 2. **SS:** Matos 11, Morales 18, Pogue 3, Sanchez 3, Vickers 29. **OF:** Aquino 29, Connell 3, De Aza 8, Emiliani 14, Johnson 6, O'Connor 6, Pena 35, Quintana 26, Robles 7, Sanfler 22, Senior 29.

DSL NATIONALS

ROOKIE

DOMINICAN SUMMER LEAGUE

Batting	B-T	HT	WT	DOB	AVG	vLH	vRH	G	AB	R	H	2B	3B	HR	RBI	BB	HBP	SH	SF	SO	SB	CS	SLG	OBP
Arias, Andry	L-L	6-3	180	6-19-00	.270	.238	.277	61	226	33	61	9	7	3	40	28	6	0	4	48	3	3	.412	.360
De La Cruz, Christopher	L-L	5-11	145	3-29-01	.179	.444	.119	49	145	29	26	1	2	0	11	22	3	3	1	23	4	2	.214	.298
Diaz, Geraldi	L-R	6-0	196	7-8-00	.244	.103	.275	53	160	20	39	12	3	1	28	29	13	1	1	31	3	2	.375	.399
Fernandez, Braian	R-L	6-1	170	4-15-99	.313	.351	.305	57	214	36	67	4	6	0	34	18	5	1	3	37	8	9	.388	.375
Hansack, Tristan	R-R	5-11	150	10-15-00	.211	.333	.176	32	95	20	20	1	3	0	4	13	0	0	0	17	7	2	.284	.306
Hernandez, Daniel	L-R	6-0	170	9-21-00	.255	.300	.247	58	196	32	50	11	3	2	17	25	9	1	2	55	12	3	.372	.362
Hurtado, Jorge	R-R	6-1	165	10-15-00	.277	.206	.292	54	195	27	54	11	7	2	43	16	3	0	3	60	3	3	.436	.336
Joseph, Diony	L-L	6-3	165	9-23-00	.164	.105	.185	23	73	8	12	2	0	0	6	5	2	0	0	27	3	1	.192	.238
Matias, Addiel	R-R	6-1	170	10-17-00	.095	.107	.091	36	116	8	11	4	0	0	9	14	0	0	1	39	0	0	.129	.191
Matos, Wilfrido	R-R	5-11	160	9-28-00	.243	.270	.235	45	173	27	42	2	5	1	20	5	4	1	0	29	3	4	.330	.280
Murzi, Ivan	R-R	6-0	165	5-28-01	.180	.278	.155	33	89	13	16	6	0	0	4	12	8	1	0	35	3	2	.247	.330
Pena, Viandel	B-R	5-8	148	11-22-00	.250	.216	.256	65	240	49	60	13	5	1	24	47	6	2	0	51	4	2	.358	.386
Sanchez, Wilfredo	R-R	6-2	170	12-4-98	.231	.231	.231	35	104	12	24	6	1	0	12	9	2	0	1	35	1	1	.308	.302
Tatis, Guillermo	R-R	6-1	180	6-3-00	.206	.243	.195	48	160	21	33	12	1	1	24	22	2	0	1	53	3	1	.313	.308
Tovar, Edangel	R-R	5-10	150	7-26-00	.268	.233	.275	51	168	30	45	8	1	3	18	11	3	0	1	30	7	10	.381	.322

Pitching	B-T	HT	WT	DOB	W	L	ERA	G	GS	CG	SV	IP	H	R	ER	HR	BB	SO	AVG	vLH	vRH	K/9	BB/9
Amoroso, Thony	R-R	6-0	154	8-2-98	2	0	3.07	16	0	0	7	29	18	11	10	0	21	38	.188	.286	.147	11.66	6.44
Caceres, Bryan	R-R	6-1	170	2-19-00	3	5	6.32	18	3	0	1	37	44	31	26	1	15	25	.299	.315	.290	6.08	3.65
Carty, Yimi	R-R	6-3	200	3-1-01	0	0	7.82	12	0	0	0	13	9	11	11	0	14	9	.214	.313	.154	6.39	9.95
De La Rosa, Manuel	R-R	6-3	182	6-8-99	3	1	3.51	17	0	0	0	26	18	15	10	0	25	18	.205	.270	.157	6.31	8.77
Ferrer, Jose A.	L-L	5-11	180	3-3-00	1	1	3.60	14	0	0	0	30	28	21	12	0	11	53	.230	.182	.240	15.90	3.30
Gonzalez, Pedro	R-R	6-2	183	7-16-00	3	1	1.46	7	7	0	0	37	27	8	6	1	8	39	.200	.204	.198	9.49	1.95

Name	B-T	Ht	Wt	DOB	W	L	ERA	G	GS	CG	SV	IP	H	R	ER	HR	BB	SO	AVG	vLH	vRH	K/9	BB/9
Hiraldo, Abrahan	R-R	6-0	171	10-7-98	4	3	3.65	12	7	0	0	44	35	27	18	2	27	55	.212	.196	.219	11.17	5.48
Jameson, Charls	R-R	6-1	175	1-27-01	1	2	0.31	17	0	0	2	29	25	4	1	0	8	18	.236	.191	.266	5.59	2.48
Martinez, Adrian	R-R	6-0	192	8-2-98	4	2	2.86	17	0	0	2	28	28	11	9	1	9	33	.255	.214	.268	10.48	2.86
Morel, Yohanse	R-R	6-0	170	8-23-00	0	0	8.10	1	1	0	0	3	6	4	3	0	1	5	.375	.250	.417	13.50	2.70
Oquel, Osvaldo	L-L	6-0	190	5-24-97	0	2	1.50	16	0	0	2	24	18	7	4	0	21	28	.207	.278	.188	10.50	7.88
Pena, Bryan	L-L	6-1	175	1-10-00	3	2	2.93	12	12	0	0	55	49	25	18	0	24	45	.239	.317	.220	7.32	3.90
Pena, Eric	R-R	6-0	155	6-29-99	1	0	0.00	2	0	0	1	9	2	1	0	0	3	6	.077	.167	.000	6.23	3.12
Pozo, Miguel	R-R	6-4	185	10-11-99	1	2	3.55	12	11	0	0	51	46	28	20	1	26	33	.249	.224	.263	5.86	4.62
Rodriguez, Jose	R-R	6-1	170	7-31-99	0	3	6.20	15	0	0	1	20	19	18	14	0	21	21	.260	.276	.250	9.30	9.30
Romero, Carlos	R-R	6-6	179	7-15-99	6	1	1.19	10	9	0	0	53	28	13	7	1	18	47	.154	.217	.123	7.98	3.06
Seijas, Karlo	R-R	6-1	185	9-6-00	2	7	5.47	12	12	0	0	54	53	43	33	2	26	48	.259	.296	.239	7.95	4.31
Severino, Wilson	R-R	6-4	188	6-7-98	1	2	6.00	15	0	0	3	21	14	16	14	1	20	20	.194	.177	.211	8.57	8.57
Vallejo, Alejandro	R-R	6-3	184	11-4-98	0	0	4.08	13	0	0	0	18	11	20	8	0	31	16	.167	.179	.158	8.15	15.79
Yean, Eddy	R-R	6-1	180	6-25-01	1	2	5.98	11	10	0	0	44	57	40	29	1	23	32	.322	.387	.287	6.60	4.74

Fielding

C: Diaz 39, Murzi 31, Sanchez 12. **1B:** Arias 39, De La Cruz 4, Diaz 8, Sanchez 14, Tatis 14. **2B:** Hernandez 28, Matias 8, Matos 4, Pena 37. **3B:** Fernandez 1, Hernandez 29, Matias 26, Tatis 23. **SS:** Hernandez 4, Matos 40, Pena 31. **OF:** Arias 22, De La Cruz 28, Fernandez 54, Hansack 23, Hurtado 47, Joseph 10, Tovar 44.

MINOR
LEAGUES

Top Prospects, Tim Tebow Lessen Attendance Dip

BY JOSH NORRIS

Fewer fans came to minor league games in 2018, continuing a trend that seems to have some staying power. By Minor League Baseball's official count, 40,450,337 fans attended minor league games during the 2018 season. That figure represents a drop of 1,382,027 fans compared to 2017.

The league was understandably quick to point out some explanations for why attendance fell. It was unusually cold this April, with 73 games that started with a game-time temperature below 40 degrees. There were zero games in April 2017 where the game-time temperature was below 40.

On top of that, there were also fewer games played. After a request by Major League Baseball, the Triple-A leagues and Double-A Eastern League cut their number of scheduled games from 142 to 140. Those lost dates can explain roughly 400,000 of the nearly 1.4 million attendance drop.

Those facts are undeniably true, but dig a little deeper and weather and lost dates don't fully explain the 2018 attendance report. The total attendance for 2018 was the worst overall mark in 14 seasons. The average per-game attendance of 3,922 fans is also the worst of the past 14 seasons.

MiLB president Pat O'Conner said he and his team will study the numbers and look for avenues of improvement, but he is not particularly worried by what MiLB views as an anomaly.

"There is no real grave concern going into the winter," O'Conner said. "We need to figure out what happened to us. The things we can deal with, we need to deal with."

The 2018 report appears to be another reminder that after years of explosive growth, Minor League Baseball's attendance seems to have found its high-water mark and has leveled off. Staying flat or generating modest growth compared to the previous year's attendance is a more realistic goal now.

At the end of the 20th century and into the start of the 21st century, Minor League Baseball attendance was a perpetual growth machine. In 1998 (the first year that Triple-A expanded to its current 30 teams), 32.3 million fans attended minor league games. Just two seasons later, 37.7 million fans came through the games. By 2008, 43.26 million fans came to minor league games.

But that steady growth has largely plateaued

After the weather warmed, fans came out to see Binghamton and Tim Tebow

over the past decade and now has dropped off. The 2008 all-time record seems far away—teams drew nearly 250 more fans per game per team that year than they did in 2018.

And it goes beyond a cold April or fewer home dates. April's average attendance numbers were easily worse than average attendance in any of the past five seasons. But May, June and July's average attendance numbers were also worse than in those respective months in any of the previous five seasons.

Of the 160 minor league teams in the U.S. and Canada, 105 (65 percent) had a lower average attendance in 2018 than 2017.

The rest of Minor League Baseball's measures are more positive than the attendance numbers. Merchandise sales are up. Gross revenues are up. O'Conner noted that teams are seeing fans spend more money when they come to the ballpark, even if there aren't more fans coming through the gates.

MINOR LEAGUES

DIAMOND IMAGES

America's Pastime ... Saved

In March, Major League Baseball and Minor League Baseball, through years of lobbying politicians on both sides of the aisle, got their wish when the Save America's Pastime Act was included as part of a massive omnibus spending bill.

The law cut off a lawsuit brought by former players that aimed to include minor leaguers under the Fair Labor Standards Act, which would have entitled them to the same minimum wage and overtime protections enjoyed by millions of workers across the country.

Once the law passed, those hopes were quashed. Instead, the bill required the players be paid the minimum wage for 40 hours a week during the regular season. Players would not be eligible for overtime and the bill spelled out that they will not be paid during spring training, which is the case under the current system as well.

MLB and MiLB have contended that baseball players are seasonal employees who are exempt from minimum wage and overtime rules. The players contend that they are protected by overtime and minimum wage laws and as such have been cheated out of earned overtime wages since they worked well more than 40 hours a week. During the season, players often play on six or seven days a week and have extensive work travel.

Because the bill included a provision that players must receive minimum wage for 40 hours a week in season, it actually gave a small pay increase to the lowest-paid affiliated minor leaguers, some of which currently make $1,100 a month. Under the new bill, they would make $290 a week.

O'Conner has said that without such a bill, minor leagues or teams could shut down because of increased labor costs. Player advocates have said that as a $10 billion a year industry, they believe baseball could easily afford paying minor league players higher wages.

Teams Tap Prospect Power

The Triple-A Charlotte Knights weren't sure when superstar prospect Eloy Jimenez was going to arrive in the Queen City, but they wanted to make sure they were ready.

As was the case 2017, when Yoan Moncada started the year in the International League, the team made sure to have plenty of jersey shirts on hand in their team store for the occasion. The move marked a departure from the team's past practices.

"I was hesitant. In my 37 years, it's never really warranted that," Knights COO Dan Rajkowski said. "I can't remember the last time that we did it.

AFFILIATION SHUFFLE

Which minor league teams are bringing a new parent organization into the fold next season?

TRIPLE-A

Team (League)	New Affiliate	Old Affiliate
Syracuse Chiefs (IL)	Mets	Nationals
Las Vegas 51s (PCL)	Athletics	Mets
Fresno Grizzlies (PCL)	Astros	Giants
Nashville Sounds (PCL)	Rangers	Athletics
*San Antonio (PCL)	Brewers	Brewers

*San Antonio moves from Double-A to Triple-A for 2019

DOUBLE-A

Team (League)	New Affiliate	Old Affiliate
Chattanooga Lookouts (SL)	Reds	Twins
Pensacola Blue Wahoos (SL)	Twins	Reds
*Amarillo (TL)	Padres	—

*Amarillo replaces San Antonio in the Texas League

LOW CLASS A

Team (League)	New Affiliate	Old Affiliate
Clinton Lumberkings (MWL)	Marlins	Mariners
Greensboro Grasshoppers (SAL)	Pirates	Marlins
West Virginia Power (SAL)	Mariners	Pirates

ROOKIE

Team (League)	New Affiliate	Old Affiliate
*Colorado Springs	Brewers	Brewers

*Colorado Springs moves from Triple-A to Rookie-level

You might order three dozen and you'd have two and a half dozen left, but Moncada was the exception. He had several re-orders. Then we did it with (Michael) Kopech this year, and we're doing it with Jimenez now, and it catches on."

The same was true in Buffalo with Vladimir Guerrero Jr., the game's top prospect. When he started scorching the competition in the Double-A Eastern League, the folks in the Bisons' front office knew it was only a matter of time before he made his way to the International League. The timetable was stunted by a knee injury that cost Guerrero roughly a month, but the Blue Jays committed to the move in August, after the younger Guerrero attended his father's Hall of Fame induction.

"It was exciting news, and the fact that the Blue Jays announced it the Saturday before he came was nice so we could build a little bit of momentum for his debut . . .," Bisons announcer Pat Malacaro said.

"We had a little advance warning, which made it nice so that we could have big crowds that week. He was the prospect who we'd hoped to see at some point this year. The fact that he was finally joining the team added a little extra juice to what was already a fun month of July."

Overall, Guerrero was part of 15 openings (16 games) with the Bisons and provided a significant spark to the team's attendance figures.

Buffalo drew 161,938 fans on days when Guerrero played, which amounted to 30.7 percent

DANNY PARKER

Selling Eloy Jimenez merchandise was a smart move for the Charlotte Knights

Cumulative domestic farm club records for major league organizations, with winning percentages going back five years. Most organizations have six affiliates.

		2018					
		W	L	PCT	2017	2016	2015	2014
1.	Rays	444	307	.591	.536	.529	.502	.505
2.	Astros	394	290	.576	.521	.513	.565	.519
3.	Dodgers	379	308	.552	.546	.527	.529	.458
4.	Phillies	404	332	.549	.528	.595	.542	.435
5.	D-backs	412	350	.541	.515	.507	.509	.561
6.	Cardinals	401	350	.534	.546	.520	.512	.545
7.	Indians	392	349	.529	.493	.550	.509	.507
8.	Blue Jays	392	358	.523	.505	.507	.485	.495
t-9.	White Sox	352	331	.515	.438	.427	.504	.456
t-9.	**Athletics**	354	333	.515	.494	.488	.483	.513
11.	Twins	345	330	.511	.581	.540	.534	.528
12.	Tigers	369	362	.505	.502	.474	.472	.516
t-13.	**Brewers**	345	342	.502	.504	.443	.439	.508
t-13.	**Padres**	373	370	.502	.505	.463	.476	.472
15.	Yankees	399	399	.500	.602	.595	.542	.435
16.	Pirates	368	369	.499	.499	.490	.547	.450
17.	Royals	370	382	.492	.466	.452	.497	.450
18.	Rockies	340	366	.482	.496	.477	.466	.466
19.	Nationals	326	352	.481	.456	.508	.469	.514
20.	Red Sox	326	359	.476	.497	.526	.469	.514
21.	Mets	350	392	.472	.456	.480	.532	.568
t-22.	**Braves**	314	352	.471	.471	.468	.489	.493
t-22.	**Orioles**	320	359	.471	.482	.455	.524	.465
24.	Mariners	322	365	.469	.487	.581	.435	.475
25.	Rangers	320	367	.466	.467	.491	.518	.546
26.	Marlins	315	363	.465	.483	.454	.427	.498
27.	Cubs	339	399	.459	.504	.539	.540	.522
28.	Giants	339	403	.457	.446	.483	.504	.509
29.	Reds	338	408	.453	.456	.502	.512	.489
30.	Angels	292	387	.430	.492	.451	.459	.486

League	Champion	Runner-Up
International	Durham	Scranton/W-B
Pacific Coast	Memphis	Fresno
Eastern	New Hampshire	Altoona
Southern	Jackson	Biloxi
Texas	Tulsa	San Antonio
California	Rancho Cucamonga	Visalia
Carolina	Buies Creek	Potomac
Florida State	Fort Myers	Daytona
Midwest	Bowling Green	Peoria
South Atlantic	Lexington	Lakewood
New York-Penn	Tri-City	Hudson Valley
Northwest	Eugene	Spokane
Appalachian	Elizabethton	Princeton
Pioneer	Great Falls	Grand Junction
Arizona	AZL Dodgers	AZL Cubs
Gulf Coast	GCL Tigers West	GCL Cardinals

MINOR LEAGUES

of their total attendance for the season. Overall, the Bisons averaged 8,250 fans per game in 2018, but that figure jumped to 10,796 on days when Guerrero was in the lineup.

The New Hamsphire Fisher Cats, for whom Guerrero played the bulk of the season, also saw an attendance boost from 2017. The team averaged 330 more fans per game from year over year and drew 5,065 more fans in total.

Prospects don't always equate to big-time figures at the box office, but Guerrero and Jimenez certainly helped their teams make money in 2018.

Shuffle Shakes Up Minors

Because 2018 was an even-numbered year, it also meant that it was time for another round of the Affiliation Shuffle, when major league teams have the chance to search for new minor league affiliates.

Although the framework of this version's shake-up was anticipated—everyone knew San Antonio was reclassifying to the Triple-A Pacific Coast League and that the Texas League was adding a new team in Amarillo, Texas, as its replacement—but where the merry-go-round would stop was still a big question mark.

The other certainties were Colorado Springs moving from a Triple-A team to a Rookie-level club in the Pioneer League while the Helena Brewers ceased operations. The Mets bought the Syracuse Chiefs in the 2017 offseason with plans to escape Las Vegas after the 2018 season. That left Las Vegas, which is slated to open a replacement for Cashman Field in 2019, without an affiliate to move into the digs.

It was widely speculated both in Baseball America and around the league that one of the most likely scenarios would have the Brewers sliding into Fresno, with the Astros moving to Round Rock and the Rangers taking over in San Antonio and sticking it out until Wolff Stadium (a Double-A park thrust into a Triple-A market) could either be updated or replaced.

That scenario would have left an avenue for the A's to move west into the shiny new Vegas ballpark while opening Nashville and its excellent park for the Nationals.

Although it all sounded good and made sense on paper, very little of that scenario wound up coming to fruition.

The A's moving to Vegas and the Astros taking over at Round Rock were on the money, but the rest of it blew up when the Rangers announced that they had reached a deal to affiliate with Nashville. The dominoes began to fall shortly thereafter.

Ready? Here it goes:

The Brewers moved into San Antonio. The Padres moved to Amarillo. Both of those moves left the Nationals as the odd team out, which means their Triple-A prospects and reinforcements will now have to travel from Fresno, Calif. and across the country whenever they get called to the big leagues in Washington, D.C.

The variable that threw the situation for a loop appears to have been the Brewers' loyalty to the Elmore Group, which owns Colorado Springs and San Antonio and also owned Helena before it was shuttered. The Brewers stayed loyal to the Elmores, settling in at San Antonio while the stadium situation gets resolved one way or another and leaving the rest of that arm of the shuffle to play itself out, accordingly.

There were a few other shifts as well. The Twins and Reds swapped Double-A affiliates at Chattanooga and Pensacola, and the Mariners, Marlins and Pirates scuttled their low Class A teams, with the Pirates taking over in Greensboro, the Mariners moving to West Virginia and the Marlins parking in Clinton for the next two seasons.

More Hurricane Havoc

A year after the Carolina, Florida State and Southern leagues had their playoffs scuttled by Hurricane Irma, the minor league postseason was once again whipped into disarray by hazardous weather.

The culprit this time was Hurricane Florence, which set its sights on the the Carolinas and the mid-Atlantic. As a result, the International League's division series between Scranton/Wilkes-Barre and Durham was relocated entirely to Scranton. Despite the inconvenience, Durham

Jonathan Arauz's sacrifice fly helped send Buies Creek out with a championship

CARL KLINE

prevailed in four games to win its second straight Governors Cup and advance to the Triple-A National Championship Game in Columbus.

A similar situation played out in the Carolina League, where the Buies Creek Astros and Potomac Nationals were both in Florence's crosshairs. Facing an imperfect set of solutions, the Carolina League decided to shorten the championship series to a single, winner-take-all game, to be played at Buies Creek.

The Astros prevailed in dramatic fashion, scoring on a walk-off sacrifice fly in the 11th inning from shortstop Jonathan Arauz to win the title.

Because Buies Creek's tenure in the CL is over, Arauz's sacrifice fly marked the second time in 2018 that a franchise was essentially walked off and out of existence, simultaneously. Mets slugger Peter Alonso's minor-league leading 36th and final home run of the season ended the final game in Las Vegas' history as a Mets affiliate and officially closed the book on Cashman Field in dramatic, walk-off fashion.

Extra, extra!

In its continuing effort to shorten game times across the sport, Minor League Baseball implemented an experimental rule aimed at curtailing

CONTINUED ON PAGE 358

MINOR LEAGUES

Vladimir Guerrero Jr.: Simply The Best

BY BEN BADLER

Every team wants to build a pipeline of homegrown talent to help the major league club. With Vladimir Guerrero Jr., the Blue Jays have a homegrown player with superstar potential, a player who just had one of the best minor league seasons ever for a teenage hitter en route to winning Baseball America's Minor League Player of the Year award.

Guerrero is a homegrown player in every sense of the term, and not just because he's on the verge of hitting in the middle of Toronto's lineup after signing with the Blue Jays for $3.9 million when he was 16. When Guerrero gets to Toronto next season, he will be going back to Canada, the country where he was born and where his Hall of Fame father burst on to the major league stage.

Vladimir Guerrero Jr.

When Vladimir Guerrero Sr. started with the Montreal Expos, Luciano del Rosario was one of the team's bat boys. Senior took it upon del Rosario to help take care of Junior, and the two built a close relationship.

By the time Vladdy Jr. was old enough to work out for major league clubs, del Rosario (known as "Negron") had become Toronto's area scout responsible for covering the south in the Dominican Republic. When it came to getting to know Vladdy Jr.'s makeup off the field, the Blue Jays had a thorough book.

Vladimir Sr.'s brother, Wilton Guerrero, played eight major league seasons from 1996-2004, mostly with the Dodgers and Expos. In his post-playing days, Guerrero, now 43, works as a trainer running a program in the town of Don Gregorio in the Dominican Republic.

Separate from the academy, the Guerrero family also runs a local league, the Guerrero Brothers league. When Vladdy Jr. was six, Wilton took him to play in the league.

"Sometimes, he played against kids his age, but sometimes he would play against older people," Wilton said. "When he was 12 years old, he faced kids who were 15, 17 years old. At 13, he would play against people who were 25.

"I saw his swing," Wilton said, "and I said,

'He's going to be like his father.' He swings hard all the time. Every pitch. No matter what you throw, he swings hard. You can throw everything. You might get him out one time, but you're not going to get him out with the same pitch twice … His dad was the same way—no matter what you throw, he can hit every pitch. The only thing is, Junior is a little bit more selective at the plate."

Those two themes—playing more advanced competition and showing a mature approach with sharp strike-zone awareness—have been central to Guerrero's career path. The Blue Jays skipping him over two levels to make his pro debut in the Rookie-level Appalachian League as a 17-year-old didn't faze him. Neither did going to Double-A at 19 or the promotion to Triple-A, where he walked more than he struck out.

"I remember his father used to take him to play against grown men," said Ismael Cruz, who led the international scouting for the Blue Jays at the time and now runs the Dodgers' international department. "He would take him at 14 and play against guys 25 and over. He loves the challenge. He never wanted to play with his peers—he was always playing ahead of his time. That helped him. It helped him see velocity, it helped him see breaking balls . . ."

To this day, Guerrero continues to toy with pitchers born a decade before him, getting pitched around as a 19-year-old just like he did when he was a kid playing against grown men.

PREVIOUS WINNERS

2008: Matt Wieters, Frederick/Bowie (Orioles)
2009: Jason Heyward, Myrtle Beach/Mississippi (Braves)
2010: Jeremy Hellickson, Montgomery/Durham (Rays)
2011: Mike Trout, Arkansas (Angels)
2012: Wil Myers, Northwest Arkansas/Omaha (Royals)
2013: Byron Buxton, Cedar Rapids/Fort Myers (Twins)
2014: Kris Bryant, Iowa (Cubs)
2015: Blake Snell, Charlotte/Montgomery/Durham (Rays)
2016: Yoan Moncada, Salem/Portland (Red Sox)
2017: Ronald Acuna Jr., Florida/Mississippi/Gwinnett (Braves)
Full list: BaseballAmerica.com/awards

MINOR LEAGUES

Bob Murphy Keeps 'Em Coming Back

BY J.J. COOPER

When Bob Murphy took the Dayton Dragons general manager's job nearly 20 years ago, there was no team. There wasn't even a stadium. But Murphy was confident that if the Dragons were going to be successful, they would be excellent at some simple core principles.

■ The Dragons would offer great family entertainment.

■ The Dragons wanted to offer affordable products.

■ The Dragons would have unsurpassed customer service.

■ The Dragons wanted to make sure they were impacting the community.

■ The Dragons wanted to create impactful sponsorships for corporate sponsors that would impact their businesses.

"When you look at what we decided 20 years ago would be our guiding lights, it has stayed exactly the same," Murphy said.

There is nothing among Murphy's manifesto that would seem out of place for any minor league team. But there's a difference between having these mantras as goals and having them as cornerstones of the business.

Customer service is something the organization stresses before a new staffer is hired. They look to attract problem solvers who want the freedom to do their job exceptionally well.

Anytime a customer reaches out to compliment the Dragons on excellent customer

EXECUTIVE OF THE YEAR

service, the Dragons save it. If it's a voicemail, it's transcribed. If it's an email, it's printed out. If it's a letter, it's saved. Murphy has binders full of these notes. And he and his staff make sure that new hires read some of them to understand just how important customer service is.

"I've always told people, 'Start with solving the problem. Treat people the way you would like to be treated,'" Murphy said.

"For us, we want to take a completely different approach. My gameday staff comes from all these jobs with all kinds of rules. Here they feel free and liberated to be in this environment. I told them, 'If you solve the problem and I think you have gone too far, I will reign you back in.'

"In 19 years, I've never had to reign them back in."

CONTINUED FROM PAGE 356

extra innings. Under the rule, every extra inning would begin with a runner on second base, giving each team a man in scoring position instantly.

Beyond the pace-of-play issues, Minor League Baseball also wanted to help its operators save money during extra-inning affairs. The extra frames are usually sparsely attended, but still require the use of lights and the payment of gameday staff, concession vendors and security. The longer the game, the bigger the hit to a team's bottom line.

Despite harsh, near-universal criticism on social media, the rule was a success on the field.

Thanks to those rules, extra-inning games took an average of 16 minutes less to play in 2018 than

in 2017. Where the average extra-inning game took 3 hours, 32 minutes in 2017, an average extra-inning game took 3 hours, 16 minutes in 2018.

"I'm happy to report, at least in the first go-around, (we) accomplished what we wanted it to," O'Conner said.

"I think that clearly demonstrates—especially with the extra-inning rule—it accomplished what we wanted it to accomplish. There were 1,000 less innings in extra innings. It opened to some critical fanfare, but as time went on, I know the players and the operators learned to like it a lot. I think the fans can appreciate what we did."

Beyond trimming games, the rule had some wild side effects. For example, the Tampa Tarpons lost a game to the Clearwater Threshers without

MINOR LEAGUES

Drew Saylor Helps Keep Quakes Afloat

BY KYLE GLASER

After Drew Saylor's playing career ended in 2010, he spent a year and a half working at Enterprise Rent-A-Car in his native Ohio.

Saylor kept a positive attitude, but his wife Amanda could tell he wasn't being fulfilled. So she encouraged him to get back into baseball as a coach. For both Saylor and the Dodgers, her advice proved to be a blessing.

Saylor led high Class A Rancho Cucamonga to 87 wins this season, tied for second-most in the minor leagues. He guided the Quakes to a 52-18 record in the second half, tied for the second-best half-season record in California League history, despite losing top prospects Gavin Lux, Dustin May and Tony Gonsolin to promotions as well as league MVP Rylan Bannon in the trade for Manny Machado. And he finished it off with a championship, skippering Rancho Cucamonga to a sweep of Visalia in the Cal League finals.

For that, Saylor is Baseball America's 2018 Minor League Manager of the Year.

"My wife knew what challenges that lied ahead if I get back into baseball," said Saylor, 34. "Every time I look back at that moment it becomes more inspiring to me. Just looking at the season, it was a gift every single day I got a chance to come to the ballpark."

Saylor lived that sentiment every day, perennially positive and always upbeat. That attitude filtered down to his players, creating a

MANAGER OF THE YEAR

PREVIOUS WINNERS

2008: Rocket Wheeler, Myrtle Beach (Braves)
2009: Charlie Montoyo, Durham (Rays)
2010: Mike Sarbaugh, Columbus (Indians)
2011: Ryne Sandberg, Lehigh Valley (Phillies)
2012: Dave Miley, Scranton/Wilkes-Barre (Yankees)
2013: Gary DiSarcina, Pawtucket (Red Sox)
2014: Mark Johnson, Kane County (Cubs)
2015: Tony DeFrancesco, Fresno (Astros)
2016: Dave Wallace, Akron (Indians)
2017: Stubby Clapp, Memphis (Cardinals)
Full list: BaseballAmerica.com/awards

clubhouse culture of perpetual optimism.

That came in handy early when Rancho Cucamonga opened the season 17-22.

"May 15 stands out to me," Saylor said. "It stands out to me because the way our team was performing wasn't the way we wanted to be. The attitude, the atmosphere wasn't where it wanted to be. So my staff and I decided to see it through a positive lens. We were going to start to celebrate the things they did well, and soon that permeated into the clubhouse and onto the field and guys were playing with more confidence, and then the wins started racking up and that positive enveloped everything we did."

With that attitude set by Saylor, the Quakes rallied to win the first-half division title and carried it through their historic second half.

MINOR LEAGUES

allowing a hit or a walk.

Here's how: After Tampa righthander Deivi Garcia spun seven perfect innings in a scoreless first game of a seven-inning doubleheader, the eighth inning began with Clearwater's Luke Williams on second base. An error moved Williams up to third, and a groundout one batter later brought him home with the game's only run.

No hits. No walks. One win.

The rule also helped the Rome Braves make their mark on the bizarro history books when they scored the first two-pitch inning in history. The West Virginia Power opened their extra inning with a line-drive double play, then finished it on the next pitch with a second consecutive lineout. Two pitches to complete an entire inning was that simple.

In Hillsboro, the rule, plus an experimental rule added in 2017, helped four runners reach base with only one pitch thrown. The extra inning began with a runner on second base before a first-pitch triple drove in a run. After that, the team decided to set up force plays by issuing to consecutive no-pitch intentional walks.

The pitch-clock rules also contributed to a speed-up around the minors. Minor League Baseball adopted pitch clocks and began strictly enforcing the time between innings after Double-A and Triple-A leagues averaged two hours and 53 minutes per regulation nine-inning game in 2014. The time of game dropped by 11 minutes for the Double-A and Triple-A leagues in 2015 and by six minutes across the majors.

Overall, the average nine-inning game across the

TRIPLE-A

Pos	Player	Age	AVG	OBP	SLG	G	AB	H	2B	3B	HR	BB	SO	SB
C	Danny Jansen, Buffalo (Blue Jays)	23	.275	.390	.473	88	298	82	21	1	12	44	49	5
1B	Dan Vogelbach, Tacoma (Mariners)	25	.290	.434	.545	84	297	86	16	0	20	77	59	0
2B	Brandon Lowe, Durham (Rays)	23	.304	.380	.613	46	181	55	14	0	14	22	47	0
3B	Taylor Ward, Salt Lake (Angels)	24	.352	.442	.537	60	227	80	18	0	8	36	61	10
SS	Kevin Newman, Indianapolis (Pirates)	24	.302	.350	.407	109	437	132	30	2	4	31	50	28
OF	Eloy Jimenez, Charlotte (White Sox)	21	.355	.399	.597	55	211	75	13	1	12	14	30	0
OF	Tyler O'Neill, Memphis (Cardinals)	23	.311	.385	.693	64	238	74	9	2	26	29	68	3
OF	Kyle Tucker, Fresno (Astros)	21	.332	.400	.590	100	407	135	27	3	24	48	84	20
DH	Franmil Reyes, El Paso (Padres)	22	.324	.428	.614	58	210	68	11	1	16	37	59	0

Pos	Pitcher	Age	W	L	ERA	G	GS	SV	IP	HR	BB	SO	AVG	SO/9
SP	Enyel de los Santos, Lehigh Valley (Phillies)	22	10	5	2.63	22	22	0	127	104	43	110	.226	7.8
SP	Dakota Hudson, Memphis (Cardinals)	23	13	3	2.50	19	19	0	112	107	38	87	.254	7.0
SP	Michael Kopech, Charlotte (White Sox)	22	7	7	3.70	24	24	0	126	101	60	170	.219	12.1
SP	Stephen Gonsalves, Rochester (Twins)	23	9	3	2.96	19	18	0	100	65	55	95	.187	8.6
SP	Cole Irvin, Lehigh Valley (Phillies)	24	14	4	2.57	26	25	0	161	135	35	131	.227	7.3
RP	Colin Poche, Durham (Rays)	24	5	0	1.08	28	2	1	50	29	17	78	.172	14.0

DOUBLE-A

Pos	Player	Age	AVG	OBP	SLG	G	AB	H	2B	3B	HR	BB	SO	SB
C	Austin Allen, San Antonio (Padres)	23	.290	.351	.506	119	451	131	31	0	22	37	97	0
1B	Nate Lowe, Montgomery (Rays)	22	.340	.444	.606	51	188	64	11	0	13	35	30	1
2B	Jeff McNeil, Binghamton (Mets)	26	.327	.402	.626	57	214	70	16	3	14	22	23	3
3B	Vladimir Guerrero Jr., New Hampshire (Blue Jays)	19	.402	.449	.671	61	234	94	19	1	14	21	27	3
SS	Fernando Tatis Jr., San Antonio (Padres)	19	.286	.355	.507	88	353	101	22	4	16	33	109	16
OF	Eloy Jimenez, Birmingham (White Sox)	21	.317	.368	.556	53	205	65	15	2	10	18	39	0
OF	Cedric Mullins, Bowie (Orioles)	23	.313	.362	.512	49	201	63	12	5	6	15	28	9
OF	Jason Martin, Altoona (Pirates)	22	.325	.392	.522	68	255	83	13	5	9	28	61	7
DH	Peter Alonso, Binghamton (Mets)	23	.314	.440	.573	65	220	69	12	0	15	43	50	0

Pos	Pitcher	Age	W	L	ERA	G	GS	SV	IP	HR	BB	SO	AVG	SO/9
SP	Jesus Luzardo, Midland (Athletics)	20	7	3	2.29	16	16	0	79	58	18	86	.204	9.8
SP	Taylor Widener, Jackson (D-backs)	23	5	8	2.75	26	25	0	137	99	43	176	.197	11.6
SP	Logan Allen, San Antonio (Padres)	21	10	6	2.75	20	19	0	121	89	38	125	.205	9.3
SP	Ryan Hartman, Corpus Christi (Astros)	24	11	4	2.69	25	18	0	121	104	26	143	.235	10.6
SP	Zack Brown, Biloxi (Brewers)	23	9	1	2.44	22	21	0	126	95	36	116	.207	8.3
RP	Travis Bergen, New Hampshire (Blue Jays)	24	4	1	0.50	27	0	7	36	26	9	43	.195	10.8

HIGH CLASS A

Pos	Player	Age	AVG	OBP	SLG	G	AB	H	2B	3B	HR	BB	SO	SB
C	Dominic Miroglio, Visalia (D-backs)	23	.327	.394	.460	76	278	91	23	1	4	20	42	5
1B	Roberto Ramos, Lancaster (Rockies)	23	.304	.411	.640	60	214	65	15	3	17	32	65	3
2B	Keston Hiura, Carolina (Brewers)	21	.320	.382	.529	50	206	66	16	3	7	14	47	4
3B	Bobby Dalbec, Salem (Red Sox)	23	.256	.372	.573	100	344	88	27	2	26	60	130	3
SS	Gavin Lux, Rancho Cucamonga (Dodgers)	20	.324	.396	.520	88	358	116	23	7	11	43	68	11
OF	Alex Kirilloff, Fort Myers (Twins)	20	.362	.393	.550	65	260	94	24	2	7	14	39	3
OF	Buddy Reed, Lake Elsinore (Padres)	22	.324	.371	.549	79	315	102	21	7	12	24	84	33
OF	Ryan McKenna, Frederick (Orioles)	21	.377	.467	.556	67	257	97	18	2	8	37	45	5
DH	Ibandel Isabel, Daytona (Reds)	23	.257	.332	.562	110	397	102	13	0	36	38	161	1

Pos	Pitcher	Age	W	L	ERA	G	GS	SV	IP	HR	BB	SO	AVG	SO/9
SP	Chris Paddack, Lake Elsinore (Padres)	22	4	1	2.24	10	10	0	52	43	4	83	.223	14.4
SP	Jonathan Hernandez, Down East (Rangers)	22	4	2	2.20	10	10	0	57	37	17	77	.184	12.2
SP	Ian Anderson, Florida (Braves)	20	2	6	2.52	20	20	0	100	73	40	118	.198	10.6
SP	Emilio Vargas, Visalia (Diamondbacks)	21	8	5	2.50	20	19	0	108	92	41	140	.230	11.7
SP	Patrick Murphy, Dunedin (Blue Jays)	23	10	5	2.64	26	26	0	147	126	50	135	.233	8.3
RP	Reid Humphreys, Lancaster (Rockies)	23	2	0	1.83	35	0	22	34	22	13	51	.179	13.5

minors was played in two hours and 48 minutes in 2018, down slightly from the two hours and 49 minutes it took in 2017.

More dramatically, games at Double-A and Triple-A (where the pitch clock is implemented) averaged two hours and 45 minutes this year, down two minutes a game from 2017.

Tebow Time Returns

After low Class A Columbia and high Class A St. Lucie got big-time boosts from former Heisman Trophy winner and NFL quarterback Tim Tebow's foray into baseball in 2017, it was Double-A Binghamton's turn in 2018.

LOW CLASS A

Pos	Player	Age	AVG	OBP	SLG	G	AB	H	2B	3B	HR	BB	SO	SB
C	Ronaldo Hernandez, Bowling Green (Rays)	20	.284	.339	.494	109	405	115	20	1	21	31	69	10
1B	Chad Spanberger, Asheville/Lansing (Rockies/Blue Jays)	22	.312	.356	.571	101	385	120	20	4	24	21	88	17
2B	Vidal Brujan, Bowling Green (Rays)	20	.313	.395	.427	95	377	118	18	5	5	48	53	43
3B	Elehuris Montero, Peoria (Cardinals)	19	.322	.381	.529	103	382	123	28	3	15	33	81	2
SS	Royce Lewis, Cedar Rapids (Twins)	19	.315	.368	.485	75	295	93	23	0	9	24	49	22
OF	Alex Kirilloff, Cedar Rapids (Twins)	20	.333	.391	.607	65	252	84	20	5	13	24	47	1
OF	Drew Waters, Rome (Braves)	19	.303	.353	.513	84	337	102	32	6	9	21	72	20
OF	Moises Gomez, Bowling Green (Rays)	19	.280	.328	.503	122	471	132	34	7	19	34	137	4
DH	Casey Golden, Asheville (Rockies)	23	.278	.359	.562	124	461	128	23	3	34	38	180	24

Pos	Pitcher	Age	W	L	ERA	G	GS	SV	IP	HR	BB	SO	AVG	SO/9
SP	Luis Patino, Fort Wayne (Padres)	18	6	3	2.16	17	17	0	83	65	24	98	.220	10.6
SP	D.L. Hall, Delmarva (Orioles)	19	2	7	2.10	22	20	0	94	68	42	100	.203	9.6
SP	David Parkinson, Lakewood (Phillies)	22	8	1	1.51	17	17	0	95	74	26	115	.210	10.9
SP	Denyi Reyes, Greenville (Red Sox)	21	10	3	1.89	21	18	0	124	92	13	122	.201	8.9
SP	Tyler Phillips, Hickory (Rangers)	20	11	5	2.67	22	22	0	128	117	14	124	.239	8.7
RP	Brian Glowicki, South Bend (Cubs)	23	5	5	1.20	45	0	18	68	52	24	66	.211	8.7

SHORT-SEASON

Pos	Player	Age	AVG	OBP	SLG	G	AB	H	2B	3B	HR	BB	SO	SB
C	Joey Bart, Salem-Keizer (Giants)	21	.298	.369	.613	45	181	54	14	2	13	12	40	2
1B	Curtis Terry, Spokane (Rangers)	21	.337	.434	.606	67	246	83	17	2	15	32	64	1
2B	Jarren Duran, Lowell (Red Sox)	21	.348	.393	.548	37	155	54	5	10	2	11	26	12
3B	Disobel Arias, Spokane (Rangers)	21	.366	.451	.491	61	224	82	15	2	3	33	39	5
SS	Tyler Freeman, Mahoning Valley (Indians)	19	.352	.405	.511	72	270	95	29	4	2	8	22	14
OF	Alex McKenna, Tri-City (Astros)	20	.328	.423	.534	32	116	38	7	1	5	11	24	6
OF	Gilberto Celestino, Tri-City (Astros)	19	.323	.387	.480	34	127	41	8	0	4	10	25	14
OF	Diego Rincones, Salem-Keizer (Giants)	19	.315	.357	.455	61	257	81	15	0	7	10	32	0
DH	Cal Raleigh, Everett (Mariners)	21	.288	.367	.534	38	146	42	10	1	8	18	29	1

Pos	Pitcher	Age	W	L	ERA	G	GS	SV	IP	HR	BB	SO	AVG	SO/9
SP	Luis Oviedo, Mahoning Valley (Indians)	19	4	2	1.88	9	9	0	48	34	10	61	.192	11.4
SP	Hans Crouse, Spokane (Rangers)	19	5	1	2.37	8	8	0	38	25	11	47	.179	11.1
SP	Juan De Paula, Staten Island (Yankees)	20	2	2	1.71	10	9	0	47	35	26	46	.207	8.8
SP	Ethan Lindow, Williamsport (Phillies)	19	3	2	2.19	13	13	0	70	58	19	63	.227	8.1
SP	Jaison Vilera, Brooklyn (Mets)	21	5	2	1.83	13	13	0	74	50	22	78	.191	9.5
RP	Simon Rosenblum-Larson, Hudson Valley (Rays)	21	1	1	0	9	0	5	21	11	4	33	.159	14.1

ROOKIE

Pos	Player	Age	AVG	OBP	SLG	G	AB	H	2B	3B	HR	BB	SO	SB
C	Ryan Jeffers, Elizabethton (Twins)	21	.422	.543	.578	28	102	43	7	0	3	20	16	0
1B	Grant Lavigne, Grand Junction (Rockies)	18	.343	.457	.512	56	201	69	12	2	6	37	40	10
2B	Blaze Alexander, Missoula (D-backs)	19	.345	.436	.563	52	197	68	18	5	5	31	48	10
3B	Nolan Gorman, Johnson City (Cardinals)	18	.350	.443	.664	38	143	50	10	1	11	24	37	1
SS	Wander Franco, Princeton (Rays)	17	.351	.418	.587	61	242	85	10	7	11	27	19	4
OF	Antonio Cabello, GCL Yankees	17	.321	.456	.555	137	137	44	9	4	5	21	34	5
OF	Jonah Davis, Bristol (Pirates)	20	.306	.398	.612	51	206	63	15	6	12	27	59	6
OF	Jordan Qsar, Princeton (Rays)	22	.350	.471	.672	40	137	48	8	3	10	32	45	4
DH	Leandro Cedeno, Johnson City (Cardinals)	19	.336	.419	.592	59	223	75	13	1	14	22	69	2

Pos	Pitcher	Age	W	L	ERA	G	GS	SV	IP	HR	BB	SO	AVG	SO/9
SP	Eric Pardinho, Bluefield (Blue Jays)	17	4	3	2.88	11	11	0	50	37	16	64	.199	11.5
SP	Matthew Liberatore, Princeton (Rays)	18	2	2	1.38	9	9	0	33	21	13	37	.189	10.1
SP	Josiah Gray, Greeneville (Reds)	20	2	2	2.58	12	12	0	52	29	17	59	.155	10.2
SP	Luis Gil, Pulaski (Yankees)	20	2	1	1.37	10	10	0	39	21	25	58	.154	13.4
SP	Marcelo Martinez, Burlington (Royals)	21	5	4	2.57	12	10	0	63	50	13	81	.214	11.6
RP	Rigo Fernandez, Great Falls (White Sox)	20	2	0	2.19	17	0	8	37	25	15	40	.189	9.7

Although the fans didn't truly start coming out until after the frigid weather in the northeast abated, Tebow's presence helped give the Rumble Ponies their best numbers at the box office in years.

With his help, the team cleared the 220,000-fan plateau for the eighth time in franchise history and reached its highest average attendance (3,533) since the team first opened its doors.

On the field, Tebow was also better than expected and might have had a shot at making the major leagues were it not for a season-ending broken hand. He put up a .734 OPS with six home runs over 84 games with the Rumble Ponies before the injury.

MINOR LEAGUES

The Mets' Peter Alonso tied for the minor league lead with 36 home runs

A's lefthander Jesus Luzardo blitzed his way to Triple-A as a 20-year-old

FIRST TEAM

Pos	Player, Organization (Highest Level)	Age	AVG	OBP	SLG	AB	R	H	HR	RBI	BB	SO
C	Danny Jansen, Blue Jays (AAA)	23	.275	.390	.473	298	45	82	12	58	44	49
1B	Peter Alonso, Mets (AAA)	23	.285	.395	.579	478	92	136	36	119	76	128
2B	Gavin Lux, Dodgers (AA)	20	.324	.399	.514	463	85	150	15	57	57	88
3B	Vladimir Guerrero Jr., Blue Jays (AAA)	19	.381	.437	.636	357	67	136	20	78	37	38
SS	Wander Franco, Rays (R)	17	.351	.418	.587	242	46	85	11	57	27	19
OF	Kyle Tucker, Astros (AAA)	21	.332	.400	.590	407	86	135	24	93	48	84
OF	Jo Adell, Angels (AA)	19	.290	.355	.543	396	83	115	20	77	32	111
OF	Alex Kirilloff, Twins (HiA)	20	.348	.392	.578	512	75	178	20	101	38	86
DH	Eloy Jimenez, White Sox (AAA)	21	.337	.384	.577	416	64	140	22	75	32	69

Pos	Pitcher, Organization (Highest Level)	Age	W	L	ERA	G	GS	IP	H	BB	SO	AVG
SP	Dylan Cease, White Sox (AA)	22	12	2	2.40	23	23	124	82	50	160	.189
SP	Touki Toussaint, Braves (AAA)	22	9	6	2.38	24	24	136	101	53	163	.202
SP	Justus Sheffield, Yankees (AAA)	22	7	6	2.48	25	20	116	82	50	123	.195
SP	Ian Anderson, Braves (AA)	20	4	7	2.49	24	24	119	87	49	142	.199
SP	Jesus Luzardo, Athletics (AAA)	20	10	5	2.88	23	23	109	89	30	129	.220
RP	Colin Poche, Rays (AAA)	24	6	0	0.82	40	2	66	33	19	119	.151

SECOND TEAM

Pos	Player (High Level)	Age	AVG	OBP	SLG	AB	R	H	HR	RBI	BB	SO
C	Austin Allen, Padres (AA)	24	.290	.351	.506	451	59	131	22	56	37	97
1B	Nate Lowe, Rays (AAA)	22	.330	.416	.578	482	93	159	27	102	68	90
2B	Brandon Lowe, Rays (AAA)	24	.297	.391	.558	380	73	113	22	76	57	102
3B	Taylor Ward, Angels (AA)	24	.349	.446	.531	375	68	131	14	60	65	94
SS	Royce Lewis, Twins (HiA)	19	.292	.352	.451	483	83	141	14	74	43	84
OF	Yordan Alvarez, Astros (AAA)	21	.293	.369	.534	335	63	98	20	74	42	92
OF	Alex Verdugo, Dodgers (AAA)	22	.329	.391	.472	343	44	113	10	44	34	47
OF	Tyler O'Neill, Cardinals (AAA)	23	.311	.385	.693	238	61	74	26	63	29	68
DH	Franmil Reyes, Padres (AAA)	22	.324	.428	.614	210	50	68	16	52	37	59

Pos	Pitcher (Highest Level)	Age	W	L	ERA	G	GS	IP	H	BB	SO	AVG
SP	Logan Allen, Padres (AAA)	21	14	6	2.54	25	24	149	110	51	151	.205
SP	Corbin Martin, Astros (AA)	22	9	2	2.51	25	21	122	88	35	122	.199
SP	Taylor Widener, D-backs (AA)	23	5	8	2.75	26	25	137	99	43	176	.197
SP	Michael King, Yankees (AAA)	23	11	5	1.79	25	24	161	118	29	152	.202
SP	Patrick Sandoval, Angels (AA)	22	11	1	2.06	26	20	122	88	29	145	.196
RP	Tommy Eveld, Marlins (AA)	24	4	3	1.07	45	0	50	36	11	61	.198

MINOR LEAGUES

Hot Rods Rolled Over Everyone

BY J.J. COOPER

What are the marks of a great minor league team?

You can measure them by their wins. If 100 wins is the demarcation line for greatness in Major League Baseball, 90 wins is a fair number to filter out all but the best of minor league teams. Winning 90 games over a 140-game season is the equivalent of winning 104 games in an 162-game MLB season.

The Bowling Green Hot Rods won 90 games this year, setting a Rays minor league record while also being the only team in the minors to clear the 90-win bar this season, although the Hot Rods players were equally excited to have avoided losing 50 games all year.

But to be remembered as a great team, a team also has to have a trophy, as winning a lot of games but no championship leaves a team short of greatness.

In the playoffs, the Hot Rods won seven of eight games, steamrolling the rest of the Midwest League to win the league title.

Ideally, a great team should be consistent. Most everyone playing in the Midwest League is playing a full 140-game season for the first time, which usually means teams run hot and cold as young players struggle to keep up their focus and effort level every night.

The Hot Rods did lose six straight in the first week of the season. But after that, they dominated week after week. From April 13 until the end of the season, Bowling Green never lost four games in a row. They only had two three-game losing streaks over the final 130 games. Over that stretch, they had an 11-game winning streak, another 10-game winning streak and another eight-game winning streak.

A great minor league team also will make its mark over the long term by producing major leaguers. When pro scouts talked about Bowling Green this year, they were almost unanimous in saying it was one of, or the most, talented minor league team they saw all year. But what was fascinating is depending on which scout was talking, they usually men-

Ronaldo Hernandez

tioned a different prospect as the one who most caught their eye.

Ronaldo Hernandez is a 20-year-old catcher who finished second in the Midwest League in home runs. Second baseman Vidal Brujan and shortstop Taylor Walls are a double play combo, both of whom will likely play in the major leagues. First baseman/lefthander Brendan McKay will likely fit in the middle of the Rays' rotation one day. Outfielder Moises Gomez has the best power potential of them all. And that's not counting pitchers like Tobias Myers, Tommy Romero, Simon Rosenblum-Larson, Drew Strotman or useful position players like Carl Chester, Jim Haley, Zack Law and Chris Betts.

"We had a lot of talented players. It all goes back to just a great group effort. Amateur scouting, international scouting. pro scouting," Bowling Green manager Craig Albernaz said. "To have all these talented guys, it was a fun effort. The talent jumps out at you, but the way they played the game jumped out even more."

Bowling Green was second in the league in runs scored (two behind Lansing) and second in the league in runs allowed (behind Quad Cities). It was a team that dominated from start to finish.

"It was a great season, It was a special year," Albernaz said.

And it was a great team.

PREVIOUS WINNERS

2008: Frisco/Texas League (Rangers)
2009: Akron/Eastern League (Indians)
2010: Northwest Arkansas/Texas League (Royals)
2011: Mobile BayBears/Southern League (Diamondbacks)
2012: Springfield Cardinals/Texas League (Cardinals)
2013: Daytona Cubs/Florida State League (Cubs)
2014: Portland Sea Dogs/Eastern League (Red Sox)
2015: Biloxi Shuckers/Southern League (Brewers)
2016: Rome Braves/South Atlantic League (Braves)
2017: Midland RockHounds/Texas League (Athletics)
Full list: BaseballAmerica.com/awards

MINOR LEAGUES

MINOR LEAGUES

BY J.J. COOPER

The Futures Game is supposed to be a sneak peek at baseball of the next decade. There were no shifts, which seemed kind of retro, but otherwise, we saw baseball in 2018 just amped up to the next level by an all-star atmosphere.

Lots of home runs. Lot of strikeouts, Lots of velocity. Lots of fun.

It's an all-star game, so you want stars. You want big flies and big fastballs and we got plenty of both. The Futures Game had a perfect formula for a lot of home runs. For one, the teams used the big league ball with its tighter seams and its tendencies to carry in ways minor league balls never do. But beyond that, you had pitchers who were showing off their fastballs and hitters who were going to show they could hit pretty much any fastball.

"Everyone was looking for fastballs. Pitchers wanted to show off their heaters, too. It was challenging guys. It was a fun atmosphere and it paid off in a fun game," Tigers righthander Matt Manning said.

Nowhere was that more apparent than when White Sox outfielder Luis Alexander Basabe took Hunter Greene deep. Greene showed off one of the hardest fastballs the Futures Game have ever seen—not one of his fastballs dipped below 100 and he touched 103 mph—but Basabe turned around a 102 mph fastball, driving it out to right center field.

Of the eight home runs hit, seven came on fastballs. In addition to the Greene 102.3 mph fastball, four other home runs came on pitches that were 95 mph or harder.

The pitchers didn't seem too bothered by being touched up and roughed up. They had their fun blowing gas (there were 16 strikeouts) and the hitters had even more fun.

Mets first baseman Peter Alonso may have had the most fun. He skied a 95 mph fastball by Adonis Medina that almost reached the concourse beyond left field. Alonso knew it as soon as he hit it. He didn't budge out of the batter's box until the ball was well on its way. When he did, he then did a half bat toss/half bat flip.

There have been Futures Games where there have been better defensive plays. There have been ones with better pitching, but there have been few Futures Games that were more fun.

"People go to watch baseball for entertainment . . . There were strikeouts, home runs, double plays. I don't know what more you would want in a baseball game from a fan standpoint . . . ," Alonso said.

FUTURES GAME BOX SCORE

U.S. 10, WORLD 6
JULY 15 IN WASHINGTON, D.C.

World	AB	R	H	RBI	U.S.	AB	R	H	RBI
Basabe, CF	3	1	1	2	Adell, CF-RF	4	1	1	1
Taveras, CF	2	0	0	0	Bichette, SS	3	0	1	0
Tatis Jr., SS-3B	5	1	2	0	Kieboom, SS	2	0	0	0
Diaz, LF	5	2	2	3	Rodgers, 2B	4	2	1	0
Matias, DH	3	1	2	1	Lowe, 1B	2	0	1	1
Ramos PH-DH	1	0	1	0	Alonso, 1B	2	1	1	2
Alvarez, 1B	3	0	1	0	Hiura, DH	2	0	0	0
Urias, 2B	2	0	0	0	Mountcastle, PH-DH	2	0	0	0
Garcia, 2B	0	0	0	0	Kirilloff, RF	2	1	2	0
Sanchez, RF	3	0	0	0	Reed, CF	2	0	1	0
Arozarena, RF	1	0	0	0	Jansen, C	2	1	1	2
Amaya, C	3	0	0	0	Knizner, C	2	0	0	0
Ruiz, C	1	0	0	0	Lewis, LF	1	1	0	0
Lugo, 3B	2	1	1	0	Trammell, LF	2	2	2	1
Gimenez, SS	2	0	0	0	Hayes, 3B	3	1	1	2
Totals	**36**	**6**	**10**	**6**	**Totals**	**35**	**10**	**12**	**9**

WORLD		012	020	100		6	10	1	
UNITED STATES		100	401	31x		10	12	1	

World: HR: Diaz 2 (2, 5th inn off Manning, 1 on, 2 out, 7th inn off Anderson, 0 on, 2 out); Matias (1, 2nd inn off Sheffield, 0 on, 0 out); Basabe (1, 3rd inn off Greene, 1 on, 1 out). **RBI:** Matias (1); Diaz (3); Basabe (2). **Team RISP:** 1-for-8. **Team LOB:** 6. **SB:** Tatis (1, 2nd base off Greene/Jansen). **E:** Garcia (1, throw). **Outfield assists:** Basabe (Lowe, 2nd base).

U.S.: 2B: Rodgers (1, Luzardo); Adell (1, Medina). **3B:** Trammell (1, Toussaint). **HR:** Alonso (1, 7th inn off Medina, 1 on, 1 out); Hayes (1, 4th inn off Thorpe, 1 on, 1 out); Jansen (1, 4th inn off Thorpe, 1 on, 1 out); Trammell (1, 6th inn off Lovegrove, 0 on, 2 out). **RBI:** Adell (1); Alonso (2); Hayes (2); Jansen (2); Lowe (1); Trammell (1). **Team RISP:** 2-for-8. **Team LOB:** 4. **SB:** Rodgers (1, 2nd base off Medina/Amaya). **E:** Alonso (1, fielding).

World	IP	H	R	ER	BB	SO	U.S.	IP	H	R	ER	BB	SO
Luzardo	2	3	1	1	0	2	Keller	1	0	0	0	0	1
Mata	1	1	0	0	1	1	Ortiz, L.	0.1	0	0	0	0	0
Thorpe	0.2	3	4	4	1	1	Sheffield	1.1	2	2	2	0	1
Tinoco	1	0	0	0	0	0	Greene	1.1	2	1	1	1	1
Lopez, Y.	0.1	0	0	0	0	1	Manning	1.1	4	2	2	0	2
Wells, A.	0.2	0	0	0	0	1	Hudson, D.	1	0	0	0	0	1
Lovegrove	0.1	1	1	1	0	0	Anderson (W)	1	1	1	1	0	0
Medina (L)	0.1	2	3	3	0	2	Pelham	0	0	0	0	1	0
Guzman, J.	0.2	1	0	0	0	1	Wright	1	0	0	0	0	0
Toussaint	1	1	1	1	0	1	Cease	0.2	0	0	0	0	0
Totals	8	12	10	10	2	10	Totals	9	10	6	6	2	6

Game Scores: Luzardo 45; Keller 47. **WP:** Mata; Medina; Manning. **HBP:** Urias (by Greene). **Pitches-strikes:** Luzardo 29-19; Mata 31-20; Thorpe 26-16; Tinoco 9-6; Lopez Y 4-3; Wells, A 9-6; Lovegrove 13-8; Medina 26-20; Guzman, J 10-7; Toussaint 14-9; Keller 14-9; Ortiz L 1-1; Sheffield 20-13; Greene 27-13; Manning 26-17; Hudson 11-10; Anderson 14-11; Pelham 8-3; Wright 5-4; Cease 8-4. **Inherited runners-scored:** Greene 1-1; Manning 1-0; Wright 2-0. **T:** 2:59

TRIPLE-A: Powered by Rockies prospect Josh Fuentes, the Pacific Coast League topped the International League in a 12-7 slugfest at Columbus' Huntington Park. Fuentes went 2-for-3 with a home run in a game that featured 19 runs, 29 hits and 22 pitchers. Hometown star Eric Haase collected the IL's lone longball, and Rangers prospect Scott Heineman stole four bags.

EASTERN: After Trenton's Trey Amburgey tied the game at 4-4 with an RBI double, the East seemed poised to walk off with a win at Trenton's Arm & Hammer Park. Instead, Amburgey was stranded at second and the tiebreaking scenario was triggered. Instead of extra innings, the teams held a sudden-death hitting competition that pitted Altoona's WIll Craig against Reading's Zach Green. Craig won, giving the West the victory.

Josh Fuentes

SOUTHERN: After Mississippi's Tyler Marlette tied the game in top of the ninth with a solo home run, Mobile's Zach Gibbons and Pensacola's Shed Long drove home three more runs to give the South Division the margin it needed to score a 9-5 win at Birmingham's Regions Field. Jackson's Taylor Widener, who finished second in the minors in strikeouts, pitched a scoreless top of the first for the North.

TEXAS: Much like the Eastern League, the Texas League also needed sudden death to settle their all-star festivities. The game was deadlocked at 2-2 after nine innings at Midland's Security Bank Ballpark, so the game was decided by a home run derby that matched Springfield's Victor Roache against Corpus Christi's Taylor Jones. Jones prevailed, giving the South the victory.

CALIFORNIA: Any game at The Hangar in Lancaster packs the potential for big-time offensive fireworks, and the North Division capitalized with eight runs in an 8-1 victory. Dairon Blanco went 4-for-5 with a home run to lead his team in the victory. Blanco was one of six players on his team to record a multi-hit game in the win. Rancho Cucamonga's Logan Landon went deep in the loss.

CAROLINA: Winston-Salem's Joel Booker opened the game with a long home run to left field and never looked back. The outfielder drove in four runs in the South Division's win 7-6 win at Carolina's Five County Stadium. Potomac's Carter Kieboom recorded the day's other three-hit game. His night included a home run. Kieboom's teammate Tres Barrera also went deep.

FLORIDA STATE: Clearwater's Austin Listi drove in three runs, but Tampa's Diego Castillo still walked away with the game's MVP honors in the North Division's 5-0 win at Tampa's Steinbrenner Field. Castillo's RBI double opened the game's scoring and a pair of hits from Listi gave the squad the insurance it needed.

MIDWEST: Two 2018 all-star games required sudden-death hitting competitions to decide their result, but Dayton's Montrell Marshall helped the Midwest League avoid that fate with a walk-off single in the bottom of the 10th inning at Lansing's Cooley Law School Stadium. Marshall's single gave the East Division a 3-2 win over the West. Twins top prospects Royce Lewis and Alex Kirilloff each had a hit in the game.

SOUTH ATLANTIC: Lexington's Nick Pratto hit one of the day's six home runs, and the South Division notched a 9-5 win at Greensboro's First National Bank Field. Hagerstown's Bret Boswell, Columbia's Jeremy Vasquez, Augusta's Manuel Geraldo, Delmarva's Trevor Craport and Kannapolis' Tate Blackman also went deep.

NEW YORK-PENN: Brooklyn's Ross Adolph swatted a triple and a home run in the South Division's 7-1 win at State College. West Virginia's Travis Swaggerty drove in two runs.

NORTHWEST-PIONEER: Grand Junction's Coco Montes swatted two home runs, helping the Pioneer League score a 13-10 win over the Northwest League at his home park. Salem-Keizer catcher Joey Bart, the No. 2 overall pick in the draft, went deep for the NWL. Idaho Falls' Nathan Eaton went 5-for-5 in the win.

MINOR LEAGUES

2018 OVERALL MINOR LEAGUE DEPARTMENT LEADERS

TEAM

(Bowling Green (Midwest)	90
Lakewood (South Atlantic)	87
R. Cucamonga (California)	87
Winston-Salem (Carolina)	84
Lehigh Valley (International)	84

LONGEST WINNING STREAK

Nashville (Pacific Coast)	15
R. Cucamonga (California)	15
Bowling Green (Midwest)	13
San Antonio (Texas)	11
Binghamton (Eastern)	11

LOSSES

Iowa (Pacific Coast)	88
Sacramento (Pacific Coast)	85
Burlington (Midwest)	84
Jacksonville (Southern)	82
San Jose (California)	81
Down East (Carolina)	81
Hagerstown (South Atlantic)	81

LONGEST LOSING STREAK*

Great Lakes (Midwest)	13
Greenville (South Atlantic)	13
Mobile (Southern)	12
Buffalo (International)	11
Frisco (Texas)	11
Down East (Carolina)	11
Bradenton (Florida State)	1
Augusta (South Atlantic)	11
Greensboro (South Atlantic)	11

BATTING AVERAGE*

Salt Lake (Pacific Coast)	.290
Albuquerque (Pacific Coast)	.285
Reno (Pacific Coast)	.284
Fresno (Pacific Coast)	.283
Lancaster (California)	.282

RUNS

R. Cucamonga (California)	841
Salt Lake (Pacific Coast)	824
Fresno (Pacific Coast)	802
Lancaster (California)	791
Las Vegas (Pacific Coast)	787

HOME RUNS

R. Cucamonga (California)	202
Tulsa (Texas)	184
Las Vegas (Pacific Coast)	173
Salt Lake (Pacific Coast)	173
Fresno (Pacific Coast)	164

STOLEN BASES

Cubs1 (Dominican Summer)	248
Lansing (Midwest)	203
Wilmington (Carolina)	184
D-backs (Dominican Summer)	183
Dayton (Midwest)	182
Corpus Christi (Texas)	181
NW Arkansas (Texas)	167

EARNED RUN AVERAGE*

Lakewood (South Atlantic)	2.74
Quad Cities (Midwest)	2.86
Buies Creek (Carolina)	3.07
Bowling Green (Midwest)	3.11
Trenton (Eastern)	3.25

STRIKEOUTS

Quad Cities (Midwest)	1514
R. Cucamonga (California)	1409
Visalia (California)	1368
Lake Elsinore (California)	1360
Inland Empire (California)	1334

INDIVIDUAL BATTING

BATTING AVERAGE

Guerrero Jr., Vladimir	
(GCL Blue Jays, Dunedin, New Hampshire, Buffalo)	.382
Ward, Taylor (Mobile, Salt Lake)	.349
Kiriloff, Alex (Cedar Rapids, Fort Myers)	.348
Dean, Austin (Jacksonville, New Orleans)	.345
Davis, J.D. (Fresno)	.342
Reed, Michael (Mississippi, Gwinnett)	.342
McNeil, Jeff (Binghamton, Las Vegas)	.342

RUNS

Brujan, Vidal (Bowling Green, Charlotte (FL)	112
Rengifo, Luis (Inland Empire, Mobile, Salt Lake)	109
Boswell, Bret (Asheville, Lancaster)	97
Bichette, Bo (New Hampshire)	95

McKenna, Ryan (Frederick, Bowie)	95
Straw, Myles (Corpus Christi, Fresno)	95
Davis, Jonathan (New Hampshire, Buffalo)	94

HITS

Fuentes, Josh (Albuquerque)	180
Kiriloff, Alex (Fort Myers, Cedar Rapids)	178
Vargas, Ildemaro (Reno)	167
Lowe, Nathaniel (Charlotte, Montgomery, Durham)	159
Smith, Kevin (Dunedin, Lansing)	158
Edman, Tommy (Springfield, Memphis)	156

TOP HITTING STREAKS

Cesar, Randy (Corpus Christi)	42
Vargas, Ildemaro (Reno)	35
Estevez, Omar (R. Cucamonga)	25
Bautista, Mariel (Billings)	25
Franco, Wander (Princeton)	25

MOST HITS (ONE GAME)

Kasser, Kyle (Idaho Falls)	6
De Los Santos, Joerlin (Cardinals)	6
107 Others	5

TOTAL BASES

Kiriloff, Alex (Cedar Rapids, Fort Myers)	296
Fuentes, Josh (Albuquerque)	285
Alonso, Peter (Las Vegas)	277
Smith, Kevin (Lansing, Dunedin)	276
Lowe, Nathaniel (Charlotte (FL), Montgomery, Durham)	274

EXTRA-BASE HITS

Kiriloff, Alex (Cedar Rapids, Fort Myers)	71
Dalbec, Bobby (Salem, Portland)	70
Alonso, Peter (Binghamton, Las Vegas)	68
Ray, Corey (Biloxi)	66
Fuentes, Josh (Albuquerque)	65

DOUBLES

Kiriloff, Alex (Cedar Rapids, Fort Myers)	44
Bichette, Bo (New Hampshire)	43
Estevez, Omar (R. Cucamonga)	43
Gonzalez, Luis (Kannapolis, Winston-Salem)	40
Barnes, Brandon (Columbus)	39
Franco, Wander (San Jose (39	
Fuentes, Josh (Albuquerque)	39
Waters, Drew (Rome, Florida)	39

TRIPLES

Mateo, Jorge (Nashville)	16
Del Rio, Diomedes (Cardinals Blue, Cardinals)	13
Rengifo, Luis (Inland Empire, Mobile, Salt Lake)	13
Adolph, Ross (Brooklyn)	12
Arias, Jean Carlos (Cedar Rapids, Elizabethton)	12
Eaton, Nathan (Idaho Falls)	12
Fuentes, Josh (Albuquerque)	12

HOME RUNS

Alonso, Peter (Binghamton, Las Vegas)	36
Isabel, Ibandel (R. Cucamonga, Daytona)	36
Golden, Casey (Asheville)	34
Dalbec, Bobby (Salem, Portland)	32
Ramos, Roberto (Lancaster, Hartford)	32

RUNS BATTED IN

Alonso, Peter (Binghamton, Las Vegas)	119
Dalbec, Bobby (Salem, Portland)	109
Santana, Cristian (R. Cucamonga)	109
Reed, AJ (Fresno)	108
Craig, Will (Altoona)	102
Lowe, Nathaniel	
(Charlotte (FL), Montgomery, Durham)	102

MOST RBIS (ONE GAME)

Urena, Jhoan (Binghamton)	9
Giambrone, Trent (Tennessee)	9
Perez, Luis (Rays1)	9
De La Cruz, Yeremi (Twins)	9
12 Others	8

WALKS

Noda, Ryan (Lansing)	109
Collins, Zack (Birmingham)	101
Biggio, Cavan (New Hampshire)	100
MacKinnon, David (Burlington, Inland Empire)	95
Perkins, Blake (Potomac, Wilmington)	92

INTENTIONAL WALKS

Naylor, Josh (San Antonio)	8
Filia, Eric (Arkansas)	7
Telis, Tomas (New Orleans)	7
Curletta, Joey (Arkansas)	6
Flores, Rudy (Jackson)	6
Lowe, Nathaniel (Charlotte (FL), Montgomery, Durham)	6
Martin, Troy (Tennessee, Iowa)	6
Qsar, Jordan (Princeton, Hudson Valley)	6
Yanqui, Yoel (Kane County)	6

Alex Kiriloff

BRACE HEMMELGARN

STRIKEOUTS

Harrison, Monte (Jacksonville)	215
Davidson, Braxton (Florida)	213
Peters, DJ (Tulsa)	192
Morgan, Gareth (AZL Mariners, Modesto)	187
Borenstein, Zach (Las Vegas)	182
Sparks, Taylor (Pensacola, Louisville)	182

STOLEN BASES

Straw, Myles (Corpus Christi, Fresno)	70
Cruz, Rochest (Cubs1)	56
Brujan, Vidal (Bowling Green, Charlotte (FL)	55
Reed, Buddy (Lake Elsinore, San Antonio)	51
Moesquit, Kirvin (Delmarva)	49
Ruiz, Esteury (Fort Wayne)	49

CAUGHT STEALING

Brujan, Vidal (Bowling Green, Charlotte (FL)	19
Duarte, Osvaldo (Buies Creek)	19
Montero, Alvaro (Marlins)	18
Booker, Joel (Winston-Salem, Birmingham)	17
Mejia, Erick (NW Arkansas)	17
Rosa, Joseph (Clinton)	17

ON-BASE PERCENTAGE*

Reed, Michael (Mississippi, Gwinnett)	.453
Ward, Taylor (Mobile, Salt Lake)	.446
Guerrero Jr., Vladimir	
(GCL Blue Jays, Dunedin, New Hampshire, Buffalo)	.438
Vogelbach, Daniel (Tacoma	.434
Noda, Ryan (Lansing)	.421

SLUGGING PERCENTAGE*

Guerrero Jr., Vladimir	
(GCL Blue Jays, Dunedin, New Hampshire, Buffalo)	.638
McNeil, Jeff (Binghamton, Las Vegas)	.617
Tucker, Kyle (Fresno)	.590
Davis, J.D. (Fresno)	.583
Alonso, Peter (Binghamton, Las Vegas)	.579

ON-BASE PLUS SLUGGING (OPS)*

Guerrero Jr., Vladimir	
(GCL Blue Jays, Dunedin, New Hampshire, Buffalo)	1.076
McNeil, Jeff (Binghamton, Las Vegas)	1.028
Tucker, Kyle (Fresno)	.989
Davis, J.D. (Fresno)	.988
Lowe, Nathaniel	
(Charlotte (FL), Montgomery, Durham)	.985

HIT BY PITCH

Jones, Travis (Lexington, Wilmington)	36
Locastro, Tim (AZL Dodgers, Oklahoma City)	28
France, Ty (San Antonio, El Paso)	27
Young, Andy (Palm Beach, Springfield (MO)	27
Downs, Jerry (Salem)	26

SACRIFICE BUNTS

Herrera, Carlos (Lancaster)	16
Valerio, Adrian (Bradenton)	16
Hernandez, Yonny (Frisco, Hickory)	15
Mejia, Erick (NW Arkansas)	14
Rivera, Laz (Kannapolis, Winston-Salem)	13
Vilade, Ryan (Asheville)	13

SACRIFICE FLIES

Chester, Carl (Bowling Green, Charlotte (FL)	12
Craig, Will (Altoona)	12
De La Trinidad, Ernie (Kane County, Fort Myers)	12
Michalczewski, Trey (Birmingham)	12
Welker, Colton (Lancaster)	11
Wilson, Jacob (Harrisburg, GCL Nationals, Syracuse)	11

GROUNDED INTO DOUBLE PLAY

Meneses, Joey (Lehigh Valley)	32
Balaguert, Yasiel (Tennessee) •	25
Castillo, Diego (Tampa)	24
France, Ty (San Antonio, El Paso)	22
Vargas, Kennys (Rochester)	21

BATTING AVERAGE * By Position

CATCHERS
Knizner, Andrew (Springfield, Memphis)	.313
Stubbs, Garrett (Fresno)	.310
Miroglio, Dominic (Visalia, Jackson)	.306
Martinez, Renae (Kane County, Visalia)	.305
Kruger, Jack (Inland Empire, Mobile)	.299

FIRST BASEMEN
Lowe, Nathaniel (Charlotte (FL), Montgomery, Durham)	.330
Nevin, Tyler (Lancaster)	.328
Haley, Jim (Bowling Green)	.323
Sagdal, Ian (Potomac)	.318
Nogowski, John (GCL Cardinals, Springfield)	.312

SECOND BASEMEN
Eaton, Nathan (Idaho Falls)	.354
McNeil, Jeff (Binghamton, Las Vegas)	.342
Fernandez, Jose (Salt Lake)	.333
Montes, Coco (Grand Junction)	.333
Medrano, Kevin (Reno, Jackson)	.331

THIRD BASEMEN
Guerrero Jr., Vladimir (GCL Blue Jays, Dunedin, New Hampshire, Buffalo)	.381
Ward, Taylor (Mobile, Salt Lake)	.349
Davis, J.D. (Fresno)	.342
Rodriguez, Ronny (Toledo)	.339
White, Tyler (Fresno)	.333
Welker, Colton (Lancaster)	.333

SHORTSTOPS
Freeman, Tyler (Mahoning Valley)	.352
Fletcher, David (Salt Lake)	.350
Miller, Owen (Tri-City, Fort Wayne)	.336
Alberto, Hanser (Round Rock)	.330
Solano, Donovan (AZL Dodgers, Oklahoma City)	.327

OUTFIELDERS
Kirilloff, Alex (Cedar Rapids, Fort Myers)	.348
Dean, Austin (Jacksonville, New Orleans)	.345
Reed, Michael (Mississippi, Gwinnett)	.342
Keller, Alec (Potomac, Harrisburg)	.338
Jimenez, Eloy (Birmingham, Charlotte)	.337

DESIGNATED HITTERS
Novoa, Melvin (Hickory)	.322
Chatham, C.J. (Greenville)	.307
McKay, Brendan (Bowling Green)	.254
Spires, Mitch (Mobile)	.246
Perry, Nathan (Astros)	.244

INDIVIDUAL PITCHING

Earned run average*
Parkinson, David (Lakewood, Clearwater)	1.45
King, Michael (Tampa, Trenton, Scranton/W-B)	1.79
Whitlock, Garrett (Charleston (SC), Trenton, Tampa)	1.86
Reyes, Denyi (Greenville, Salem)	1.97
Rosso, Ramon (Lakewood, Clearwater)	2.04

WORST ERA*
Kennedy, Nick (Asheville)	7.09
Pineyro, Ivan (Mobile, Salt Lake)	6.68
Conlon, P.J. (Las Vegas)	6.55
Strahan, Wyatt (Pensacola)	6.38
Tseng, Jen-Ho (Iowa)	6.27

WINS
Moss, Scott (Daytona)	15
Akin, Keegan (Bowie)	14
Allen, Logan (San Antonio, El Paso)	14
Irvin, Cole (Lehigh Valley)	14
Rosa, Adonis (Tampa, Trenton, Scranton/W-B)	14

LOSSES
Gonzalez, Harol (St. Lucie, Las Vegas, Binghamton)	16
Poteet, Cody (Jupiter, Jacksonville)	15
Tseng, Jen-Ho (Iowa)	15
Stankiewicz, Teddy (Pawtucket, Portland)	14
Adams, Spencer (Birmingham, Charlotte)	13
Dennis, Matt (Lancaster)	13
Eshelman, Tom (Lehigh Valley)	13
Johnson, Jordan (Richmond, Sacramento)	13
Kennedy, Nick (Asheville)	13
Lopez, Jose (Louisville)	13
Santos, Antonio (Asheville, Lancaster)	13
Thompson, Jake (Salem)	13
Woodford, Jake (Springfield (MO), Memphis)	13
Garcia, Danny (Clinton)	13
Jaye, Myles (Erie, Toledo)	13
Ross, Greg (Syracuse, Harrisburg)	13
Reyes, Mark (San Jose, Sacramento)	13
Pena, Luis (Inland Empire, Mobile)	13
Reyes, Luis (Potomac)	13
Aiken, Brady (Lake County)	13
Toussaint, Touki (Florida, Mississippi)	13
Knapp, Ricky (Las Vegas, Binghamton)	13

GAMES
Beato, Pedro (Lehigh Valley)	63
Schlitter, Brian (Oklahoma City)	58
Broussard, Joe (Oklahoma City)	57
Lawrence, Justin (Lancaster)	55
Pierpont, Matt (Hartford)	55

GAMES STARTED
Adams, Spencer (Birmingham, Charlotte)	28
Brady, Sean (Columbus, Akron)	28
Brubaker, J.T. (Altoona, Indianapolis)	28
Dennis, Matt (Lancaster)	28
Gagnon, Drew (Binghamton, Las Vegas)	28
Hernandez, Nelson (Wisconsin)	28
Menez, Conner (Sacramento, San Jose, Richmond)	28
Naughton, Packy (Dayton)	28
Quantrill, Cal (San Antonio, El Paso)	28
Stephens, Jordan (Birmingham, Charlotte)	28
Wells, Nick (Clinton, Modesto)	28
Woodford, Jake (Springfield (MO), Memphis)	28
Wright, Daniel (Pensacola)	28

COMPLETE GAMES
Dugger, Robert (Jupiter, Jacksonville)	3
Gonzalez, Harol (St. Lucie, Las Vegas, Binghamton)	3
Hernandez, Arnaldo (Wilmington, NW Arkansas, Omaha)	3
Marvel, James (Bradenton, Altoona)	3
Raquet, Nick (Hagerstown, Potomac)	3

SHUTOUTS
Dugger, Robert (Jupiter, Jacksonville)	2
Lillie, Ryan (Greensboro, GCL Marlins, Jupiter)	2
Milburn, Matt (Nashville, Stockton)	2
Stewart, Will (Lakewood)	2
Watson, Nolan (Lexington, Wilmington)	2

GAMES FINISHED
Beato, Pedro (Lehigh Valley)	56
Pierpont, Matt (Hartford)	49
Russ, Addison (Lakewood, Clearwater)	48
Griep, Nate (Biloxi)	46
Johnson, DJ (Albuquerque)	43

HOLDS
Cozart, Logan (Hartford)	16
Harrison, Jordan (Montgomery, Durham)	15
Ginkel, Kevin (Visalia, Jackson)	13
Horacek, Mitch (Hartford)	13
Patterson, Jacob (Palm Beach)	13
Scahill, Rob (Charlotte)	13
Wick, Rowan (San Antonio, El Paso)	13

SAVES
Beato, Pedro (Lehigh Valley)	35
Griep, Nate (Biloxi)	34
Pierpont, Matt (Hartford)	32
Russ, Addison (Lakewood, Clearwater)	27
Humphreys, Reid (Lancaster, Hartford)	26

INNINGS PITCHED
Marvel, James (Bradenton, Altoona)	167
Garcia, Rico (Lancaster, Hartford)	167
Wilk, Adam (Columbus)	165
Gagnon, Drew (Binghamton, Las Vegas)	164
Irvin, Cole (Lehigh Valley)	161
King, Michael (Tampa, Trenton, Scranton/W-B)	161

WALKS
Oviedo, Johan (Peoria)	79
Kelly, Michael (Norfolk, Bowie)	77
Dietz, Matthias (Delmarva, Frederick)	75
Diplan, Marcos (Carolina, Biloxi)	74
Garabito, Gerson (Wilmington)	73

STRIKEOUTS
Kremer, Dean (R. Cucamonga, Tulsa, Bowie)	178
Widener, Taylor (Jackson)	176
Gagnon, Drew (Binghamton, Las Vegas)	172
James, Josh (Corpus Christi, Fresno)	171
Menez, Conner (Sacramento, San Jose, Richmond)	171

HITS ALLOWED
Gold, Brandon (Lancaster)	204
Tomshaw, Matt (Charlotte, Birmingham)	200
Griffin, Foster (NW Arkansas)	197
Dennis, Matt (Lancaster)	195
Buchanan, Jake (Reno)	190

HOME RUNS ALLOWED
Kennedy, Nick (Asheville)	30
Wojciechowski, Asher (Norfolk, Charlotte)	26
Oberholtzer, Brett (Albuquerque)	25
Wright, Daniel (Pensacola)	25
Dennis, Matt (Lancaster)	24
Newsome, Ljay (Tacoma, Modesto)	24
Stankiewicz, Teddy (Pawtucket, Portland)	24

STRIKEOUTS PER NINE INNINGS (STARTERS)*
James, Josh (Corpus Christi, Fresno)	13.5
Kremer, Dean (R. Cucamonga, Tulsa, Bowie)	13.2
Kopech, Michael (Charlotte)	12.1
Javier, Cristian (Quad Cities, Buies Creek)	12.0
Howard, Spencer (Lakewood)	11.8

STRIKEOUT PER NINE INNINGS (RELIEVERS)*
Maples, Dillon (Iowa)	17.5
Black, Ray (Richmond, Sacramento)	16.7
Evans, Demarcus (Hickory)	16.6
Abreu, Bryan (Quad Cities)	16.0
Warren, Zach (Lakewood)	15.9

BATTING AVERAGE AGAINST (STARTERS)*
Gonsalves, Stephen (Chattanooga, Rochester)	.184
Stephenson, Robert (Louisville)	.184
Javier, Cristian (Quad Cities, Buies Creek)	.185
McGowin, Kyle (Potomac, Harrisburg, Syracuse)	.188
Cease, Dylan (Winston-Salem, Birmingham)	.189

BATTING AVERAGE AGAINST (RELIEVERS)*
Ginkel, Kevin (Visalia, Jackson)	.186
Lawrence, Justin (Lancaster)	.188
Russ, Addison (Lakewood, Clearwater)	.189
Pierpont, Matt (Hartford)	.209
Cozart, Logan (Hartford)	.213

MOST STRIKEOUTS (ONE GAME)
Gomber, Austin (Memphis)	16
Payamps, Joel (Jackson, Reno)	14
Rennie, Luc (Columbia)	14
16 others	13

WILD PITCHES
Antigua, Faustino (Angels)	32
Albertos, Jose (South Bend, Eugene)	27
Martinez, Justin (D-backs, D-backs2)	24
Gomez, Wilson (Angels)	23
Gonzalez, Edmar (Cubs1)	23
Houck, Tanner (Salem)	23
McAvoy, Kevin (Portland, Salem)	23
Pena, Elian (Angels)	23

BALKS
Cordero, Diego (GCL Cardinals, Palm Beach, State College)	7
De Los Santos, Enyel (Lehigh Valley)	6
Mendez, Yohander (Down East, Frisco, Round Rock)	6
Gonell, Rafi (Phillies West)	5
Huang, Wei-Chieh (Visalia, Jackson, Frisco)	5
Suarez, Jose (Inland Empire, Mobile, Salt Lake)	5
Weatherly, Kyle (Lansing)	5

HIT BATTERS
Stephan, Trevor (Tampa, Trenton)	21
McAvoy, Kevin (Portland, Salem)	19
Clifton, Trevor (Tennessee, Iowa)	17
Diaz, Jhonathan (Salem, Greenville)	17
Garcia, Danny (Modesto)	17
Javier, Odalvi (Rome)	17
Noguera, Luis (Rockies)	17
Payano, Pedro (Frisco)	17

GROUND BALL DOUBLE PLAYS
Naile, James (Midland, Nashville)	26
Irvin, Cole (Lehigh Valley)	25
Strahan, Wyatt (Pensacola)	22
Zeuch, T.J. (Dunedin, New Hampshire)	22
Brady, Sean (Columbus, Akron)	21
Copeland, Scott (Binghamton, Las Vegas)	21
Lovvorn, Zach (NW Arkansas, Omaha)	21

INDIVIDUAL FIELDING

ERRORS
Garcia, Wilkerman (Charleston)	35
Vilade, Ryan (Asheville)	34
Cruz, Oneil (West Virginia)	33
Encarnacion, Jean Carlos (Rome, Delmarva)	33
Guzman, Jeison (Lexington, Burlington)	32
Maitan, Kevin (Orem)	32
Gonzalez, Luis (Daytona, Pensacola)	32

MINOR LEAGUES

BY KEGAN LOWE

For the second consecutive year and sixth time in franchise history, the Durham Bulls took home the Governors' Cup as International League champions in 2018. The Rays' Triple-A affiliate since 1998, the Bulls defeated Scranton/Wilkes-Barre (Yankees), 6-2, in Game 5 of the best-of-five championship series, marking the first time in four attempts that the Bulls had won a winner-take-all Game 5 in the finals.

Although the Bulls successfully defended their Governors' Cup crown in 2018, they could not do the same in the Triple-A National Championship game in Columbus, Ohio. A year after defeating the Memphis Redbirds in the final game of the minor league season, the Bulls fell to the Cardinals' Triple-A affiliate in the rematch, giving Memphis its first national title in franchise history.

Despite the Bulls' postseason success, it was the Lehigh Valley IronPigs (Phillies) who became the first IL franchise in 23 years (Norfolk Tides, 1995) to sweep all of the league's major individual awards. The IronPigs, who had the league's best regular season record at 84-56, were led by first baseman Joey Meneses, who was named International League MVP and rookie of the year, lefthander Cole Irvin, the league's pitcher of the year, and manager Gary Jones, who was the first IronPigs skipper to win IL manager of the year.

In his age-26 season, Meneses hit .311/.360/.510 with a league-best 23 home runs and 82 RBIs, while Irvin, 24, set a single-season franchise record with 14 wins and led all qualifying pitchers in both ERA (2.57) and WHIP (1.05). After spending the previous four seasons as the Cubs' third base coach, Jones led Lehigh Valley to its first North Division

TOP 20 PROSPECTS

1. Eloy Jimenez, OF, Charlotte (White Sox)
2. Michael Kopech, RHP, Charlotte (White Sox)
3. Willy Adames, SS, Durham (Rays)
4. Austin Riley, 3B, Gwinnett (Braves)
5. Austin Meadows, OF, Indianapolis (Pirates)/Durham (Rays)
6. Nick Senzel, 2B/3B, Louisville (Reds)
7. Justus Sheffield, LHP, Scranton/Wilkes-Barre (Yankees)
8. Victor Robles, OF, Syracuse (Nationals)
9. Francisco Mejia, C, Columbus (Indians)
10. Touki Toussaint, RHP, Gwinnett (Braves)
11. Mitch Keller, RHP, Indianapolis (Pirates)
12. Lourdes Gurriel Jr., SS/2B, Buffalo (Blue Jays)
13. Shane Bieber, RHP, Columbus (Indians)
14. Kevin Kramer, 2B/3B, Indianapolis (Pirates)
15. Cedric Mullins, OF, Norfolk (Orioles)
16. Jake Bauers, 1B, Durham (Rays)
17. Christin Stewart, OF, Toledo (Tigers)
18. Enyel de los Santos, RHP, Lehigh Valley (Phillies)
19. Brandon Lowe, 2B/OF, Durham (Rays)
20. Kevin Newman, SS, Indianapolis (Pirates)

championship in the franchise's 11-year history.

In terms of prospect power, some of the best talent in Triple-A resided in the South Division, with many of the league's top prospects—including each of the league's top four prospects—making their way through Charlotte (White Sox), Gwinnett (Braves) and Durham.

Buffalo third baseman Vladimir Guerrero Jr. (Blue Jays) ended the season as Baseball America's No. 1 overall prospect and played in 30 games for the Bisons, but he did not accumulate enough plate apperances to qualify for the International League Top 20 prospects list. Gwinnett righthander Mike Soroka held the same distinction for pitchers, as he was the top pitching prospect to appear in the IL in 2018, but did not complete enough innings to crack the league's Top 20 Prospects list.

OVERALL STANDINGS

North Division	W	L	PCT	GB	Manager(s)	Attendance	Average	Last Pennant
Lehigh Valley IronPigs (Phillies)	84	56	.600	—	Gary Jones	561,745	8,511	1995
Scranton/W-B RailRiders (Yankees)	73	65	.529	10	Bobby Mitchell	386,819	6,140	2016
Pawtucket Red Sox (Red Sox)	66	73	.475	17 ½	Kevin Boles	394,811	5,982	2014
Rochester Red Wings (Twins)	64	76	.457	20	Joel Skinner	437,974	6,537	1997
Syracuse Chiefs (Nationals)	64	76	.457	20	Randy Knorr	277,332	4,202	1976
Buffalo Bisons (Blue Jays)	61	77	.442	22	Bob Meacham	527,988	8,250	2004
South Division								
Durham Bulls (Rays)	79	60	.568	—	Jared Sandberg	536,304	7,661	2018
Gwinnett Stripers (Braves)	70	69	.504	9	Damon Berryhill	195,955	3,062	2007
Norfolk Tides (Orioles)	69	71	.492	10 ½	Ron Johnson	341,369	5,334	1999
Charlotte Knights (White Sox)	64	75	.460	15	Mark Grudzielanek	619,639	8,980	1985
West Division								
Toledo Mud Hens (Tigers)	73	66	.525	—	Doug Mientkiewicz	507,965	7,362	2006
Columbus Clippers (Indians)	73	67	.521	½	Chris Tremie	587,067	8,633	2015
Indianapolis Indians (Indians)	73	67	.521	½	Brian Esposito	619,122	8,845	2000
Louisville Bats (Reds)	61	76	.445	11	Pat Kelly/Dick Schofield	466,026	6,658	2001

Semifinals: Durham defeated Toledo 3-1 and Scranton/W-B defeated Lehigh Valley 3-1 in best-of-five series. **Finals:** Durham defeated Scranton/W-B 3-2 in a best-of-five series.

CLUB BATTING

	AVG	G	AB	R	H	2B	3B	HR	RBI	BB	SO	SB	OBP	SLG
Indianapolis	.271	140	4624	625	1251	310	30	104	594	416	1044	111	.335	.418
Louisville	.260	137	4602	576	1195	256	36	113	537	390	1157	73	.321	.405
Durham	.259	139	4663	653	1209	269	27	141	613	398	1243	83	.322	.419
Scranton/W-B	.256	138	4558	578	1168	219	36	132	546	408	1050	49	.322	.407
Syracuse	.256	140	4639	565	1187	251	19	79	523	448	1005	84	.325	.369
Gwinnett	.254	139	4593	584	1165	246	24	101	551	388	1152	60	.315	.384
Toledo	.253	139	4671	577	1180	237	31	113	545	413	1075	66	.318	.389
Norfolk	.252	140	4618	601	1162	240	24	103	563	433	1095	61	.320	.381
Pawtucket	.249	139	4644	535	1158	224	10	101	499	440	1138	64	.318	.367
Buffalo	.249	138	4489	573	1119	217	28	105	533	435	1091	124	.321	.380
Columbus	.249	140	4609	602	1147	278	19	118	566	470	1290	91	.325	.394
Charlotte	.248	139	4621	533	1145	271	22	103	490	432	1204	80	.316	.383
Lehigh Valley	.245	140	4562	620	1119	230	21	145	590	489	1213	60	.322	.400
Rochester	.227	140	4491	485	1021	193	24	97	454	433	1061	78	.304	.346

CLUB PITCHING

	ERA	G	CG	SHO	SV	IP	H	R	ER	HR	BB	SO	AVG
Rochester	3.39	140	2	11	38	1216	1103	514	458	99	439	1151	.242
Pawtucket	3.43	139	1	9	39	1221	1127	544	465	117	413	1221	.242
Durham	3.54	139	0	7	41	1210	1111	545	476	127	380	1267	.242
Lehigh Valley	3.63	140	3	13	46	1221	1112	555	492	114	422	1072	.242
Scranton/W-B	3.71	138	6	7	29	1188	1056	540	490	112	436	1179	.236
Syracuse	3.77	140	3	8	31	1218	1149	573	510	96	424	1161	.250
Gwinnett	3.78	139	3	14	30	1196	1109	565	502	89	467	1174	.247
Indianapolis	3.88	140	3	15	33	1206	1225	586	520	88	482	1093	.265
Buffalo	3.94	138	4	5	31	1177	1169	590	515	121	410	953	.258
Toledo	4.05	140	9	12	48	1221	1210	595	550	105	402	1132	.260
Norfolk	4.05	140	2	10	31	1205	1218	610	542	109	444	1109	.260
Charlotte	4.11	139	1	9	34	1216	1173	611	556	113	478	1146	.254
Louisville	4.19	137	1	6	32	1197	1192	627	558	132	435	1080	.260
Columbus	4.34	140	3	11	37	1220	1272	652	588	133	361	1080	.269

CLUB FIELDING

	PCT	PO	A	E	DP		PCT	PO	A	E	DP
Lehigh Valley	.985	3663	1346	77	120	Norfolk	.982	3616	1143	88	100
Toledo	.985	3663	1250	76	132	Gwinnett	.981	3587	1280	94	130
Syracuse	.984	3655	1333	81	121	Scranton/W-B	.981	3565	1156	92	88
Indianapolis	.984	3617	1366	81	147	Louisville	.981	3592	1210	94	113
Charlotte	.983	3649	1350	87	131	Durham	.978	3629	1206	107	107
Columbus	.983	3662	1311	88	131	Pawtucket	.978	3662	1104	107	110
Rochester	.982	3647	1213	88	120	Buffalo	.977	3530	1252	112	120

INDIVIDUAL BATTING

Batter, Club	AVG	G	AB	R	H	2B	3B	HR	RBI	BB	SO	SB
Rusney Castillo, Pawtucket	.319	117	474	56	151	31	0	5	59	29	80	13
Kevin Kramer, Indianapolis	.311	129	476	73	148	35	3	15	59	38	127	13
Joey Meneses, Lehigh Valley	.311	130	492	75	153	27	1	23	82	40	110	0
Kevin Newman, Indianapolis	.302	109	437	74	132	30	2	4	35	31	50	28
Ryan McBroom, Scranton/W-B	.295	96	359	49	106	18	1	11	46	25	106	1
Yandy Diaz, Columbus	.293	98	348	53	102	24	0	3	40	70	75	2
Gabriel Guerrero, Louisville	.292	104	404	64	118	15	4	17	65	23	97	1
Jake Elmore, Charlotte	.289	100	329	47	95	18	1	1	27	55	58	11
Pablo Reyes, Indianapolis	.289	110	356	52	103	20	4	8	36	28	71	13
Kean Wong, Durham	.282	116	451	65	127	23	3	9	50	40	112	7

INDIVIDUAL PITCHING

Pitcher, Club	W	L	ERA	G	GS	CG	SV	IP	H	R	ER	BB	SO
Cole Irvin, Lehigh Valley	14	4	2.57	26	25	1	0	161	135	51	46	35	131
Enyel De Los Santos, Lehigh Valley	10	5	2.63	22	22	1	0	127	104	41	37	43	110
Kolby Allard, Gwinnett	6	4	2.72	19	19	0	0	112	102	37	34	34	89
Ryan Weber, Durham	9	6	2.73	25	18	0	1	115	117	45	35	23	83
Phillips Valdez, Syracuse	6	7	2.75	26	19	1	0	124	111	44	38	44	96
Robert Stephenson, Louisville	11	6	2.87	20	20	1	0	113	74	41	36	57	135
J.T. Brubaker, Indianapolis	8	4	3.10	22	22	0	0	119	121	47	41	36	96
William Cuevas, Pawtucket	10	7	3.39	23	23	0	0	135	120	59	51	38	121
Josh Rogers, Norfolk	8	9	3.54	24	24	1	0	139.2	144	62	55	36	101
Tyler Eppler, Indianapolis	13	6	3.59	28	25	0	0	153	160	63	61	39	118

ALL-STAR TEAM

C: Danny Jansen, Buffalo. **1B:** Joey Meneses, Lehigh Valley. **2B:** Kevin Kramer, Indianapolis. **3B:** Mitch Walding, Lehigh Valley. **SS:** Kevin Newman, Indianapolis. **OF:** Brandon Barnes, Columbus; Rusney Castillo, Pawtucket; Christin Stewart; Toledo. **DH:** Kenny Vargas, Rochester. **UT:** Kean Wong, Durham. **SP:** Cole Irvin, Lehigh Valley. **RP:** Pedro Beato, Lehigh Valley. **Most Valuable Player:** Joey Meneses, Lehigh Valley. **Most Valuable Pitcher:** Cole Irvin, Lehigh Valley. **Rookie of the Year:** Joey Meneses, Lehigh Valley. **Manager of the Year:** Gary Jones, Lehigh Valley.

DEPARTMENT LEADERS

BATTING

OBP	Diaz, Yandy, Columbus	.409
SLG	Meneses, Joey, Lehigh Valley	.510
OPS	Meneses, Joey, Lehigh Valley	.870
R	Barnes, Brandon, Columbus	75
H	Meneses, Joey, Lehigh Valley	153
TB	Meneses, Joey, Lehigh Valley	251
XBH	Barnes, Brandon, Columbus	55
2B	Barnes, Brandon, Columbus	39
3B	McKinney, Billy, Scranton/WB, Buffalo	7
HR	Stewart, Christin, Toledo	23
	Meneses, Joey, Lehigh Valley	23
RBI	Meneses, Joey, Lehigh Valley	82
SAC	Trahan, Blake, Louisville	12
	Anna, Dean, Lehigh Valley	12
BB	Walding, Mitch, Lehigh Valley	73
HBP	Anna, Dean, Lehigh Valley	18
SO	Franco, Carlos, Gwinnett	153
SB	Velazquez, Andrew, Durham	29
CS	Fields, Roemon, Buffalo	16
AB/SO	Falu, Irving, Syracuse	11.9

FIELDING

C PCT	Moore, Logan, Lehigh Valley	.995
PO	Haase, Eric, Columbus	654
A	Haase, Eric, Columbus	48
DP	Butler, Dan, Pawtucket	7
	Hernandez, Oscar, Pawtucket	7
	Lavarnway, Ryan, Indianapolis	7
E	McGuire, Reese, Buffalo	10
CS	Haase, Eric, Columbus	33
SB	Butler, Dan, Pawtucket	44
PB	Haase, Eric, Columbus	10
1B PCT	Meneses, Joey, Lehigh Valley	.997
PO	Tellez, Rowdy, Buffalo	821
A	Espinal, Edwin, Toledo	72
DP	Franco, Carlos, Gwinnett	104
E	Rosa, Garabez, Norfolk	9
2B PCT	Falu, Irving, Syracuse	.995
PO	Kramer, Kevin, Indianapolis	153
A	Falu, Irving, Syracuse	225
DP	Kramer, Kevin, Indianapolis	70
E	Mazzilli, L.J., Scranton/W-B	10
3B PCT	Leonard, Patrick, Charlotte	.968
PO	Walding, Mitch, Lehigh Valley	65
A	Walding, Mitch, Lehigh Valley	220
DP	Walding, Mitch, Lehigh Valley	21
E	Walding, Mitch, Lehigh Valley	18
SS PCT	Trahan, Blake, Louisville	.984
PO	Trahan, Blake, Louisville	150
A	Trahan, Blake, Louisville	335
DP	Trahan, Blake, Louisville	66
E	Adames, Willy, Durham	10
	Velazquez, Andrew, Durham	10
OF PCT	Castillo, Rusney, Pawtucket	1.000
PO	Barnes, Brandon, Columbus	260
A	Williams, Justin, Durham	13
DP	Williams, Mason, Columbus	5
E	Barnes, Brandon, Columbus	7
	Zehner, Zack, Scranton/W-B	7

PITCHING

G	Beato, Pedro, Lehigh Valley	63
GS	Wilk, Adam, Columbus	27
GF	Beato, Pedro, Lehigh Valley	56
SV	Beato, Pedro, Lehigh Valley	35
W	Irvin, Cole, Lehigh Valley	14
L	Eshelman, Tom, Lehigh Valley	13
	Lopez, Jose, Louisville	13
IP	Wilk, Adam, Columbus	165
H	Eshelman, Tom, Lehigh Valley	189
R	Eshelman, Tom, Lehigh Valley	105
ER	Eshelman, Tom, Lehigh Valley	91
HB	Smith, Josh D., Pawtucket	14
BB	Kopech, Michael, Charlotte	60
SO	Kopech, Michael, Charlotte	170
SO/9	Kopech, Michael, Charlotte	12.11
SO/9 (RP)	Anderson, Nick, Rochester	13.02
BB/9	Irvin, Cole, Lehigh Valley	1.87
WP	Fulmer, Carson, Charlotte	15
	Snow, Forrest, Durham	15
BK	De Los Santos, Enyel, Lehigh Valley	6
HRA	Wojciechowski, Asher, Charlotte	26
BAA	Stephenson, Robert, Louisville	.184

BY KYLE GLASER

Minor league dynasties are hard to come by, but the Memphis Redbirds have built the case as one. After winning the Pacific Coast League championship in 2017, Memphis led the league with 83 wins and cruised to its second straight PCL championship, knocking off Fresno (Astros) to win the title. The Redbirds followed by pounding Durham (Rays), 14-4, in the Triple-A National Championship Game, the first national championship in franchise history.

The Cardinals' affiliate accomplished its historic season despite massive roster turnover. Opening Day starter John Gant, PCL pitcher of the year Dakota Hudson, top three home run hitters Tyler O'Neill, Adolis Garcia and Patrick Wisdom and starters Austin Gomber and Daniel Poncedeleon were all playing for the Cardinals by August, and yet the Redbirds rolled on.

Aided by reinforcements from Double-A Springfield, headlined by shortstop Tommy Edman, outfielders Lane Thomas and Randy Arozarena and pitcher Jake Woodford, Memphis clinched the American Southern Division title and went 7-2 in the postseason. Arozarena hit two home runs and Woodford pitched 7.1 scoreless innings in the clinching 5-0 win over Fresno in Game 4 of the PCL championship series.

Then, in the national title game, Arozarena doubled twice, Thomas tripled and homered, and Alex Mejia went 5-for-5 to win MVP honors.

Memphis' Stubby Clapp was named PCL manager of the year for the second straight year, joining

Hudson as the Redbirds' award winners.

The other awards went to Albuquerque third baseman Josh Fuentes, who won PCL MVP and Rookie of the Year. The undrafted Missouri Baptist product led the PCL in runs (93), hits (180), doubles (39), total bases (285) and overall hit .327 with 14 home runs and an .871 OPS.

Las Vegas' Cashman Field closed its doors to baseball after 35 years, and Mets prospect Peter Alonso sent the old ballpark out in style. Alonso bashed a two-run, walk-off home run in the ninth off Sacramento's Tyler Beede on the final day of the season, giving Las Vegas an emotional 4-3 victory in the final game ever at Cashman Field.

TOP 20 PROSPECTS

1. Kyle Tucker, OF, Fresno (Astros)
2. Alex Verdugo, OF, Oklahoma City (Dodgers)
3. Luis Urias, 2B, El Paso (Padres)
4. Griffin Canning, RHP, Salt Lake (Angels)
5. Tyler O'Neill, OF, Memphis (Cardinals)
6. Yordan Alvarez, OF, Fresno (Astros)
7. Freddy Peralta, RHP, Colorado Springs (Brewers)
8. Willie Calhoun, OF, Round Rock (Rangers)
9. Corbin Burnes, RHP, Colorado Springs (Brewers)
10. Ryan McMahon, 1B/3B, Albuquerque (Rockies)
11. Sandy Alcantara, RHP, New Orleans (Marlins)
12. Ramon Laureano, OF, Nashville (Athletics)
13. Dakota Hudson, RHP, Memphis (Cardinals)
14. Peter Alonso, 1B, Las Vegas (Mets)
15. Jose Suarez, LHP, Salt Lake (Angels)
16. Josh James, RHP, Fresno (Astros)
17. Jeff McNeil, 2B/3B, Las Vegas (Mets)
18. Garrett Hampson, 2B/SS, Albuquerque (Rockies)
19. Austin Gomber, LHP, Memphis (Cardinals)
20. Franmil Reyes, OF, El Paso (Padres)

OVERALL STANDINGS

American Northern	W	L	PCT	GB	Manager(s)	Attendance	Average	Last Pennant
Oklahoma City Dodgers (Dodgers)	75	65	.536	—	Bill Haselman	463,195	6,713	1965
Colorado Springs Sky Sox (Brewers)	73	66	.525	1 ½	Rick Sweet	262,657	4,104	1995
Omaha Storm Chasers (Royals)	66	74	.471	9	Brian Poldberg	345,830	5,320	2014
Iowa Cubs (Cubs)	50	88	.362	24	Marty Pevey	463,399	7,356	Never

American Southern	W	L	PCT	GB	Manager(s)	Attendance	Average	Last Pennant
Memphis Redbirds (Cardinals)	83	57	.593	—	Stubby Clapp	340,476	5,007	2018
Nashville Sounds (Athletics)	72	68	.514	11	Fran Riordan	603,135	8,741	2005
New Orleans Baby Cakes (Marlins)	69	70	.496	13 ½	Arnie Beyeler	252,614	3,827	2001
Round Rock Express (Rangers)	65	73	.471	17	Jason Wood	616,636	8,809	Never

Pacific Northern	W	L	PCT	GB	Manager(s)	Attendance	Average	Last Pennant
Fresno Grizzlies (Astros)	82	57	.590	—	Rodney Linares	405,403	6,051	Never
Reno Aces (D-backs)	72	68	.514	10 ½	Greg Gross	351,298	5,019	2012
Tacoma Rainiers (Mariners)	66	73	.475	16	Pat Listach	372,780	5,403	2010
Sacramento River Cats (Giants)	55	85	.393	27 ½	Dave Brundage	538,785	7,808	2008

Pacific Southern	W	L	PCT	GB	Manager(s)	Attendance	Average	Last Pennant
El Paso Chihuahuas (Padres)	82	57	.590	—	Rod Barajas	539,520	7,819	2016
Salt Lake Bees (Angels)	71	68	.511	11	Keith Johnson	477,528	6,921	1979
Las Vegas 51s (Mets)	71	69	.507	11 ½	Tony DeFrancesco	332,224	4,746	1998
Albuquerque Isotopes (Rockies)	63	77	.450	19 ½	Glenallen Hill	556,330	7,948	1994

Semifinals: Memphis defeated Oklahoma City 3-1 and Fresno defeated El Paso 3-2 in best-of-five series. **Finals:** Memphis defeated Fresno 3-1 in a best-of-five series.

MINOR LEAGUES

CLUB BATTING

	AVG	G	AB	R	H	2B	3B	HR	RBI	BB	SO	SB	OBP	SLG
Salt Lake	.290	139	4832	824	1402	291	53	173	783	512	1071	96	.361	.480
Albuquerque	.285	140	4792	767	1366	287	67	154	733	422	1072	86	.347	.469
Reno	.284	140	4857	761	1377	262	54	156	716	448	1164	77	.347	.456
Fresno	.283	139	4782	802	1353	280	39	164	760	567	1104	124	.362	.461
Okla. City	.277	140	4718	653	1305	274	25	121	618	369	1103	62	.335	.422
Col. Springs	.271	139	4580	715	1243	254	45	142	660	473	1119	162	.345	.440
Round Rock	.271	138	4646	646	1258	232	21	128	606	392	982	64	.332	.412
Las Vegas	.270	140	4777	787	1288	313	33	173	739	524	1223	72	.346	.458
Memphis	.269	140	4727	688	1272	238	19	142	650	404	950	113	.332	.418
El Paso	.268	139	4746	739	1271	291	39	142	701	479	1329	44	.341	.435
New Orleans	.267	139	4668	660	1247	200	41	96	611	509	1014	98	.342	.389
Sacramento	.263	140	4768	605	1255	243	34	114	565	406	1242	84	.326	.400
Nashville	.260	140	4680	629	1215	227	47	101	587	515	1222	88	.337	.393
Omaha	.259	140	4649	611	1203	232	25	108	563	383	954	90	.318	.389
Tacoma	.258	139	4652	676	1198	250	32	104	621	623	1027	101	.349	.392
Iowa	.244	138	4512	526	1101	201	18	79	497	451	1188	90	.318	.349

CLUB PITCHING

	ERA	G	CG	SHO	SV	IP	H	R	ER	HR	BB	SO	AVG
Memphis	3.54	140	3	11	44	1230	1152	564	484	118	428	1160	.248
Okla. City	3.92	140	1	9	40	1216	1209	598	530	104	456	1144	.259
Nashville	3.96	140	2	9	37	1224	1225	625	539	106	374	1116	.260
New Orleans	4.07	139	0	12	40	1215	1260	622	550	130	385	1084	.268
El Paso	4.20	139	1	7	40	1227	1202	640	573	147	455	1063	.257
Fresno	4.27	139	2	9	29	1226	1184	636	581	118	477	1330	.252
Omaha	4.39	140	4	14	37	1208	1251	643	589	105	460	1037	.267
Round Rock	4.41	138	2	1	40	1199	1301	677	588	124	429	975	.278
Iowa	4.46	138	0	5	23	1180	1153	649	585	121	494	1069	.257
Tacoma	4.53	139	2	6	39	1211	1271	672	610	122	441	1135	.269
Col. Springs	4.60	139	2	9	23	1187	1252	687	607	104	492	1040	.272
Sacramento	4.91	140	0	5	22	1218	1317	768	665	129	500	1117	.275
Reno	5.18	140	0	3	40	1228	1319	768	707	155	542	1076	.276
Albuquerque	5.34	140	0	2	28	1217	1393	801	722	182	464	1081	.290
Las Vegas	5.83	140	4	5	37	1223	1424	867	792	174	516	1158	.292
Salt Lake	6.02	139	0	5	40	1226	1441	872	820	158	564	1179	.295

CLUB FIELDING

	PCT	PO	A	E	DP		PCT	PO	A	E	DP
El Paso	.983	3680	1379	87	128	Las Vegas	.981	3669	1332	96	124
Omaha	.983	3625	1272	85	125	Round Rock	.981	3598	1408	97	139
Salt Lake	.982	3679	1221	88	121	New Orleans	.981	3646	1290	97	115
Reno	.982	3683	1324	92	133	Colorado Springs	.981	3560	1360	97	133
Fresno	.982	3678	1220	91	102	Iowa	.981	3540	1289	96	120
Memphis	.982	3689	1225	92	116	Albuquerque	.980	3651	1428	102	160
Oklahoma City	.981	3648	1275	93	117	Nashville	.978	3671	1363	113	133
Tacoma	.981	3633	1203	92	112	Sacramento	.975	3655	1242	123	117

INDIVIDUAL BATTING

Batter, Club	AVG	G	AB	R	H	2B	3B	HR	RBI	BB	SO	SB
J.D. Davis, Fresno	.342	85	333	56	114	25	2	17	81	36	69	3
Jose Fernandez, Salt Lake	.333	91	357	66	119	19	1	17	59	33	34	2
Kyle Tucker, Fresno	.332	100	407	86	135	27	3	24	93	48	84	20
Hanser Alberto, Round Rock	.330	101	361	45	119	17	3	7	58	9	28	0
Alex Verdugo, Oklahoma City	.329	91	343	44	113	19	0	10	44	34	47	8
Josh Fuentes, Albuquerque	.327	135	551	93	180	39	12	14	95	21	103	3
Mike Tauchman, Albuquerque	.323	112	403	84	130	26	7	20	81	60	70	12
Socrates Brito, Reno	.318	114	428	85	136	34	5	17	69	44	104	15
Patrick Kivlehan, Las Vegas	.314	98	354	59	111	29	4	20	67	30	84	4
Eric Campbell, New Orleans	.313	95	326	54	102	21	2	6	68	58	61	8

INDIVIDUAL PITCHING

Pitcher, Club	W	L	ERA	G	GS	CG	SV	IP	H	R	ER	BB	SO
Trevor Oaks, Omaha	8	8	3.23	22	22	1	0	128	130	50	46	44	70
Zac Gallen, New Orleans	8	9	3.65	25	25	0	0	133	148	60	54	48	136
Rogelio Armenteros, Fresno	8	1	3.74	22	21	1	1	118	106	51	49	48	134
Adrian Sampson, Round Rock	8	4	3.77	33	19	0	0	127	137	61	53	24	85
Cy Sneed, Fresno	10	6	3.83	26	20	1	0	127	120	56	54	53	114
Sandy Alcantara, New Orleans	6	3	3.89	19	19	0	0	116	107	51	50	38	88
Jonathan Dziedzic, Omaha	8	9	3.94	25	24	0	1	139	141	68	61	43	96
Taylor Clarke, Reno	13	8	4.03	27	27	0	0	152	149	76	68	44	125
Eric Jokisch, Nashville	5	11	4.06	26	23	0	1	149	165	84	67	46	121
Trent Thornton, Fresno	9	8	4.42	24	22	0	0	124	118	67	61	31	122

ALL-STAR TEAM

C: Christian Bethancourt, Colorado Springs. **1B:** A.J. Reed, Fresno. **2B:** Luis Urias, El Paso. **3B:** Josh Fuentes, Albuquerque. **SS:** Ildemaro Vargas, Reno. **OF:** Tyler O'Neill, Memphis; Mike Tauchman, Albuquerque; Alex Verdugo, Oklahoma City. **DH:** Kevin Cron, Reno. **RHP:** Dakota Hudson, Memphis. **LHP:** Manny Banuelos, Oklahoma City. **RP:** R.J. Alvarez, Round Rock. **Most Valuable Player:** Josh Fuentes, Albuquerque. **Pitcher of the Year:** Dakota Hudson, Memphis. **Rookie of the Year:** Josh Fuentes, Albuquerque. **Manager of the Year:** Stubby Clapp, Memphis.

DEPARTMENT LEADERS

BATTING

OBP	Vogelbach, Daniel, Tacoma	.434
SLG	Blash, Jabari, Salt Lake	.700
OPS	Tucker, Kyle, Fresno	.989
R	Fuentes, Josh, Albuquerque	93
H	Fuentes, Josh, Albuquerque	180
TB	Fuentes, Josh, Albuquerque	285
XBH	Fuentes, Josh, Albuquerque	65
2B	Fuentes, Josh, Albuquerque	39
3B	Mateo, Jorge, Nashville	16
HR	Blash, Jabari, Salt Lake	29
RBI	Reed, AJ, Fresno	108
SAC	Burns, Billy, Omaha	11
BB	Borenstein, Zach, Las Vegas	81
HBP	Locastro, Tim, Oklahoma City	26
SO	Borenstein, Zach, Las Vegas	182
SB	Straw, Myles, Fresno	35
CS	Tauchman, Mike, Albuquerque	10
	Mateo, Jorge, Nashville	10
AB/SO	Alberto, Hanser, Round Rock	12.9

FIELDING

C PCT	Gale, Rocky, Oklahoma City	.995
PO	Gale, Rocky, Oklahoma City	706
A	Gale, Rocky, Oklahoma City	55
DP	Plaia, Colton, Las Vegas	8
E	Murphy, Tom, Albuquerque	9
CS	Nola, Austin, New Orleans	26
SB	Taylor, Beau, Nashville	61
PB	Centeno, Juan, Round Rock	12
1B PCT	Reed, AJ, Fresno	.984
PO	Reed, AJ, Fresno	623
A	Reed, AJ, Fresno	72
DP	Patterson, Jordan, Albuquerque	68
E	Reed, AJ, Fresno	11
2B PCT	Urias, LuisEl Paso	.990
PO	Lopes, Christian, Round Rock	141
A	Urias, LuisEl Paso	250
DP	Urias, LuisEl Paso	65
E	Lopes, Christian, Round Rock	10
3B PCT	Fuentes, Josh, Albuquerque	.966
PO	Neuse, Sheldon, Nashville	97
A	Neuse, Sheldon, Nashville	249
DP	Neuse, Sheldon, Nashville	25
	Fuentes, Josh, Albuquerque	25
E	Neuse, Sheldon, Nashville	24
SS PCT	Vargas, Ildemaro, Reno	.977
PO	Guerra, Javy, El Paso	168
A	Mateo, Jorge, Nashville	340
DP	Vargas, Ildemaro, Reno	73
E	Mateo, Jorge, Nashville	23
OF PCT	Taylor, Tyrone, Colorado Springs	.996
PO	Miller, Ian, Tacoma	246
A	Taylor, Tyrone, Colorado Springs	18
DP	Tucker, Kyle, Fresno	5
E	Duggar, Steven, Sacramento	10

PITCHING

G	Schlitter, Brian, Oklahoma City	58
GS	Clarke, Taylor, Reno	27
	Gagnon, Drew, Las Vegas	27
GF	Johnson, DJ, Albuquerque	43
SV	Alvarez, R.J., Round Rock	24
W	Clarke, Taylor, Reno	13
	Hudson, Dakota, Memphis	13
L	Tseng, Jen-Ho, Iowa	15
IP	Gagnon, Drew, Las Vegas	158
H	Buchanan, Jake, Reno	190
R	Tseng, Jen-Ho, Iowa	103
ER	Tseng, Jen-Ho, Iowa	95
HB	Whalen, Rob, Tacoma	12
BB	Miller, Jared, Reno	63
SO	Gagnon, Drew, Las Vegas	167
SO/9	Armenteros, Rogelio, Fresno	10.1
SO/9 (RP)	Armstrong, Shawn, Tacoma	13.2
BB/9	Herget, Kevin, Memphis	1.8
WP	Beede, Tyler, Sacramento	18
BK	Mendez, Yohander, Round Rock	5
	Suarez, Jose, Salt Lake	5
HRA	Oberholtzer, Brett, Albuquerque	25

BY JOSH NORRIS

The 2018 Eastern League season belonged to the New Hampshire Fisher Cats. The team started the year with a bejeweled roster that housed, among others, two of the 10 best prospects in the game in shortstop Bo Bichette and superstar-in-training Vladimir Guerrero Jr.

Those two, combined with EL home run leader Cavan Biggio, league batting champion Harold Ramirez and all-star game starter Jordan Romano helped, lead the Fisher Cats (Blue Jays) to a playoff sweep over Trenton and Altoona on their way to the team's first league championship since 2011.

Guerrero, Bichette and Biggio all placed among the league's Top 20 Prospects, and Guerrero ended the year ranked as BA's No. 1 prospect and Minor League Player of the Year.

About the only thing the Fisher Cats didn't claim was the Eastern Division title, which went to the Trenton Thunder (Yankees), who also hosted the league's all-star game at Arm & Hammer Park.

Beyond New Hampshire's dominance, Mets farmhand Tim Tebow, the former Heisman Trophy winner and NFL quarterback moved to Binghamton and blessed their box office with numbers it hadn't seen in years.

The team averaged 3,533 fans per game at NYSEG Stadium, its highest figure since the team's inaugural season in 1992. They also topped 220,000 fans for the eighth time in team history and set a franchise record with 7,488 fans through the turnstiles at NYSEG Stadium on July 20.

Ironically enough, that last record was set without Tebow in the lineup. He had broken his hand the day before, ending his season. When healthy, Tebow hit .273/.336/.399 with six homers and 36 RBIs. He also was named an EL all-star and collected a double against Tigers pitching prospect Beau Burrows.

TOP 20 PROSPECTS

1. Vladimir Guerrero Jr., 3B, New Hampshire (Blue Jays)
2. Bo Bichette, SS, New Hampshire (Blue Jays)
3. Brendan Rodgers, SS, Hartford (Rockies)
4. Ke'Bryan Hayes, 3B, Altoona (Pirates)
5. Carter Kieboom, SS, Harrisburg (Nationals)
6. Mitch Keller, RHP, Altoona (Pirates)
7. Daz Cameron, OF, Erie (Tigers)
8. Peter Alonso, 1B, Binghamton (Mets)
9. Peter Lambert, RHP, Hartford (Rockies)
10. Andres Gimenez, SS, Binghamton (Mets)
11. Triston McKenzie, RHP, Akron (Indians)
12. Justin Dunn, RHP, Binghamton (Mets)
13. Cedric Mullins, OF, Bowie (Orioles)
14. Cavan Biggio, 2B, New Hampshire (Blue Jays)
15. Ryan Mountcastle, 3B, Bowie (Orioles)
16. Isaac Paredes, SS, Erie (Tigers)
17. Beau Burrows, RHP, Erie (Tigers)
18. Michael King, RHP, Trenton (Yankees)
19. Taylor Hearn, LHP, Altoona (Pirates)
20. Jeff McNeil, 2B, Binghamton (Mets)

While Tebow was the most famous former Florida Gator on Binghamton's roster, he certainly wasn't the most productive. That honor belonged to Peter Alonso, the big-time bopper who spent the first part of his summer doing what he hopes to do more often in 2019: smashing baseballs over fences in New York. The first baseman tied for the MiLB-lead with 36 longballs in 2018, and he hit one of eight longballs at the annual Futures Game, held at Nationals Park in Washington D.C.

The Western division-champion Altoona Curve (Pirates) helped develop one of the league's best kept secrets: third baseman Ke'Bryan Hayes. Long known for his reputation as a stellar gloveman, Hayes slowly developed into a complete hitter with an all-fields approach and burgeoning power. That helped him earn a berth in the Futures Game and placed him among the league's best prospects.

Above all, 2018 in the Eastern League will always be known as the summer of the Fisher Cat.

OVERALL STANDINGS

Eastern Division	W	L	PCT	GB	Manager(s)	Attendance	Average	Last Pennant
Trenton Thunder (Yankees)	79	61	.564	—	Jay Bell	351,297	5,019	2013
New Hampshire Fisher Cats (Blue Jays)	76	62	.551	2	John Schneider	319,099	5,065	2018
Hartford Yard Goats (Rockies)	65	72	.474	12½	Warren Schaeffer	408,942	6,014	2001
Reading Fightin Phils (Phillies)	64	73	.467	13½	Greg Legg	388,510	5,713	2001
Binghamton Rumble Ponies (Mets)	64	76	.457	15	Luis Rojas	220,279	3,553	1994
Portland Sea Dogs (Red Sox)	63	76	.453	15½	Darren Fenster	346,341	5,678	2006

Western Division	W	L	PCT	GB	Manager(s)	Attendance	Average	Last Pennant
Altoona Curve (Pirates)	78	60	.565	—	Michael Ryan	297,118	4,571	2017
Akron RubberDucks (Indians)	78	62	.557	1	Tony Mansolino	344,754	4,996	2016
Harrisburg Senators (Nationals)	72	65	.526	5½	Matthew LeCroy	259,243	3,988	1999
Bowie Baysox (Orioles)	67	71	.486	11	Gary Kendall	230,347	3,438	Never
Erie SeaWolves (Tigers)	63	77	.450	16	Andrew Graham	205,055	3,204	Never
Richmond Flying Squirrels (Giants)	62	76	.449	16	Willie Harris	396,686	6,198	2014

Semifinals: New Hampshire defeated Trenton 3-0 and Akron defeated Altoona 3-1 in best-of-five series. **Finals:** New Hampshire defeated Akron 3-0 in a best-of-five series.

MINOR LEAGUES

CLUB BATTING

	AVG	G	AB	R	H	2B	3B	HR	RBI	BB	SO	SB	OBP	SLG
New Hampshire	.272	139	4648	706	1263	270	37	126	650	475	1033	153	.345	.427
Bowie	.263	138	4651	649	1224	231	29	135	606	405	917	72	.324	.412
Erie	.263	140	4617	647	1212	205	38	92	581	488	1187	118	.335	.383
Altoona	.255	138	4477	613	1142	202	38	93	568	467	1020	110	.332	.379
Portland	.254	139	4615	618	1174	224	25	116	571	466	1200	85	.329	.389
Akron	.250	140	4620	665	1155	245	34	110	618	506	1093	132	.332	.389
Binghamton	.250	140	4563	593	1140	226	24	114	548	499	1080	65	.331	.385
Harrisburg	.249	137	4536	613	1129	205	38	108	568	510	1138	76	.330	.382
Reading	.247	137	4476	600	1104	188	17	141	562	417	1158	62	.317	.391
Trenton	.246	140	4563	575	1124	227	26	102	525	498	1158	91	.324	.375
Hartford	.245	137	4459	548	1094	224	23	117	494	405	1121	146	.312	.385
Richmond	.240	139	4403	527	1056	240	30	97	500	409	1041	83	.306	.374

CLUB PITCHING

	ERA	G	CG	SHO	SV	IP	H	R	ER	HR	BB	SO	AVG
Trenton	3.25	140	1	11	34	1225	1030	513	442	86	473	1228	.228
Akron	3.59	140	1	13	38	1231	1119	580	491	94	454	1068	.242
Harrisburg	3.73	137	3	8	31	1185	1137	576	491	109	391	1051	.252
Altoona	3.85	138	3	11	39	1193	1067	567	510	103	465	1020	.240
Richmond	3.91	139	2	6	39	1173	1149	601	510	91	475	1079	.256
Reading	4.00	137	3	5	34	1190	1089	618	529	117	532	1129	.243
Erie	4.06	140	1	10	25	1209	1190	625	546	121	469	1182	.258
New Hampshire	4.12	139	1	8	31	1195	1163	630	547	127	485	1035	.256
Binghamton	4.34	140	2	7	35	1196	1251	656	577	111	424	1177	.271
Hartford	4.38	137	2	9	45	1195	1219	631	581	137	426	1031	.266
Portland	4.45	139	5	11	25	1196	1209	687	591	127	474	1057	.262
Bowie	4.52	138	3	5	33	1194	1194	670	599	128	477	1089	.261

CLUB FIELDING

	PCT	PO	A	E	DP		PCT	PO	A	E	DP
Altoona	.985	3580	1316	74	125	Bowie	.978	3581	1194	108	117
Hartford	.982	3585	1230	89	129	Reading	.977	3569	1269	114	96
Trenton	.981	3675	1206	94	126	Harrisburg	.977	3554	1366	118	118
Binghamton	.978	3587	1275	108	126	Erie	.976	3628	1210	120	114
New Hampshire	.978	3588	1314	110	135	Portland	.975	3589	1235	124	108
Akron	.978	3692	1429	115	114	Richmond	.974	3519	1182	126	107

INDIVIDUAL BATTING

Batter, Club	AVG	G	AB	R	H	2B	3B	HR	RBI	BB	SO	SB
Harold Ramirez, New Hampshire	.320	120	463	60	148	37	0	11	70	27	88	16
Daniel Woodrow, Erie	.313	92	342	48	107	13	3	3	37	31	71	19
Corban Joseph, Bowie	.312	122	459	73	143	30	2	17	68	52	43	8
Levi Michael, Binghamton	.305	103	387	72	118	30	2	10	36	35	93	13
Bryan Reynolds, Altoona	.302	88	331	56	100	18	3	7	46	43	73	4
Will Maddox, Erie	.300	102	397	59	119	17	5	4	41	24	67	7
Ryan Mountcastle, Bowie	.297	102	394	63	117	19	4	13	59	26	79	2
Damek Tomscha, Reading	.294	93	344	53	101	12	1	15	54	26	58	1
Ke'Bryan Hayes, Altoona	.293	117	437	64	128	31	7	7	47	57	84	12
Aderlin Rodriguez, Bowie	.286	128	483	76	138	20	2	23	92	29	95	1
Bo Bichette, New Hampshire	.286	131	539	95	154	43	7	11	74	48	101	32

INDIVIDUAL PITCHING

Pitcher, Club	W	L	ERA	G	GS	CG	SV	IP	H	R	ER	BB	SO
Jake Paulson, Akron	8	5	3.04	20	19	1	0	115	104	42	39	32	91
T.J. Zeuch, New Hampshire	9	5	3.08	21	21	1	0	120	120	48	41	31	81
Keegan Akin, Bowie	14	7	3.27	25	25	0	0	138	114	52	50	58	142
Mike Shawaryn, Portland	6	8	3.28	19	19	1	0	113	100	45	41	27	99
Kyle Hart, Portland	7	9	3.57	24	24	1	0	139	139	68	55	49	100
Matthew Kent, Portland	11	8	3.58	27	23	0	0	143	143	66	57	35	123
Mickey Jannis, Binghamton	10	6	3.60	24	23	1	0	142	157	65	57	36	114
Jaron Long, Harrisburg	6	8	3.65	25	19	2	0	123	136	57	50	27	77
Brian Keller, Trenton	10	9	3.74	22	21	0	0	125	120	55	52	37	114
Logan Darnell, Harrisburg	8	6	3.91	24	19	0	0	113	123	53	49	24	82

ALL-STAR TEAM

C: Deivi Grullon, Reading. **1B:** Will Craig, Altoona. **2B:** Cavan Biggio, New Hampshire. **3B:** Vladimir Guerrero Jr., New Hampshire; Ke'Bryan Hayes, Altoona. **SS:** Bo Bichette, New Hampshire. **OF:** Trey Amburgey, Trenton; Harold Ramirez, New Hampshire; Jonathan Davis, New Hampshire. **DH:** Corban Joseph, Bowie. **UT:** Levi Michael, Bingamton. **RHP:** Jordan Romano, New Hampshire. **LHP:** Keegan Akin, Bowie. **RP:** Matt Pierpont, Hartford. **Most Valuable Player:** Cavan Biggio, New Hampshire. **Pitcher of the Year:** Keegan Akin, Bowie. **Rookie of the Year:** Cavan Biggio, New Hampshire. **Manager of the Year:** John Schneider, New Hampshire.

DEPARTMENT LEADERS

BATTING

OBP	Michael, Levi, Binghamton	.391
SLG	Biggio, Cavan, New Hampshire	.499
OPS	Biggio, Cavan, New Hampshire	.887
R	Bichette, Bo, New Hampshire	95
H	Bichette, Bo, New Hampshire	154
TB	Bichette, Bo, New Hampshire	244
XBH	Bichette, Bo, New Hampshire	61
2B	Bichette, Bo, New Hampshire	43
3B	Hayes, Ke'Bryan, Altoona	7
	Mora, John, Binghamton	7
	Tucker, Cole, Altoona	7
	Johnson, Daniel, Harrisburg	7
	Berti, Jon, New Hampshire	7
	Bichette, Bo, New Hampshire	7
HR	Biggio, Cavan, New Hampshire	26
RBI	Craig, Will, Altoona	102
SAC	Castro, Willi, Akron, Erie	9
BB	Biggio, Cavan, New Hampshire	100
HBP	Calica, Andrew, Akron	22
SO	Hilliard, Sam, Hartford	151
SB	Tucker, Cole, Altoona	35
CS	Hilliard, Sam, Hartford	14
AB/SO	Joseph, Corban, Bowie	10.7

FIELDING

C PCT	Gushue, Taylor, Harrisburg	.996
PO	Rogers, Jake, Erie	857
A	Rogers, Jake, Erie	102
DP	Rabago, Chris, Hartford, Trenton	12
E	Grullon, Deivi, Reading	12
CS	Rogers, Jake, Erie	50
SB	Gushue, Taylor, Harrisburg	68
	Cervenka, Martin, Bowie	68
PB	Cervenka, Martin, Bowie	13
	Loopstok, Sicnarf, Akron	13
1B PCT	Craig, Will, Altoona	.993
PO	Craig, Will, Altoona	1021
A	Craig, Will, Altoona	87
DP	Craig, Will, Altoona	110
E	Ockimey, Josh, Portland	14
2B PCT	Mathias, Mark, Akron	.987
PO	Alemais, Stephen, Altoona	166
A	Alemais, Stephen, Altoona	334
DP	Alemais, Stephen, Altoona	71
E	Maddox, Will, Erie	14
3B PCT	Hayes, Ke'Bryan, Altoona	.978
PO	Hayes, Ke'Bryan, Altoona	72
A	Hayes, Ke'Bryan, Altoona	200
DP	Hayes, Ke'Bryan, Altoona	29
E	Mountcastle, Ryan, Bowie	16
SS PCT	Tucker, Cole, Altoona	.973
PO	Tucker, Cole, Altoona	182
A	Tucker, Cole, Altoona	315
DP	Bichette, Bo, New Hampshire	79
E	Bichette, Bo, New Hampshire	25
OF PCT	Guillotte, Andrew, New Hampshire	1.000
PO	Matheny, Tate, Portland	267
A	Guillotte, Andrew, New Hampshire	14
DP	Tom, Ka'ai, Akron	5
	Johnson, Daniel, Harrisburg	5
E	Tom, Ka'ai, Akron	8

PITCHING

G	Pierpont, Matt, Hartford	55
GS	Brady, Sean, Akron	27
GF	Pierpont, Matt, Hartford	49
SV	Pierpont, Matt, Hartford	32
W	Akin, Keegan, Bowie	14
L	Stankiewicz, Teddy, Portland	13
IP	Stankiewicz, Teddy, Portland	148
H	Jannis, Mickey, Binghamton	157
R	Stankiewicz, Teddy, Portland	87
ER	Castellani, Ryan, Hartford	82
HB	Stephan, Trevor, Trenton	14
BB	Castellani, Ryan, Hartford	70
SO	Akin, Keegan, Bowie	142
SO/9	Akin, Keegan, Bowie	9.3
SO/9 (RP)	Pierpont, Matt, Hartford	11.6
BB/9	Harris, Jon, New Hampshire	2.1
WP	Brown, Mitch, Akron	14
	Johnson, Jordan, Richmond	14
BK	Civale, Aaron, Akron	3
	Johnson, Jordan, Richmond	3
HRA	Stankiewicz, Teddy, Portland	23
	Tinoco, Jesus, Hartford	23
BAA	Akin, Keegan, Bowie	.225

MINOR LEAGUES

BY MATT EDDY

The Southern League sees less offense than any Double-A or Triple-A circuit and features the lowest batting average (.246) in full-season ball. Thus, it is a league where pitchers tend to excel at the expense of batters.

That's what makes the performances by Birmingham outfielder Eloy Jimenez and Biloxi second baseman Keston Hiura so impressive. These talented hitters ranked as the top prospects in the Southern League and should see improved results as they continue to advance, especially in terms of batting average and power production.

Jimenez hit .337/.384/.577 with 22 home runs, 28 doubles and 75 RBIs in 108 games for the Barons prior to his June 21 promotion to Triple-A Charlotte. His bat so impressed scouts and managers that he ranked as the No. 1 prospect in both the Southern and International leagues.

Hiura, whom the Brewers selected ninth overall in 2017 after a decorated career at UC Irvine, zoomed to Double-A a year after being drafted and hit .272/.339/.416 with six home runs and 18 doubles in 73 games. He settled in as the No. 3 hitter for Biloxi, who led the Southern League with 81 wins and advanced to the league finals.

Birmingham (White Sox) and Montgomery (Rays) each placed four players among the league's Top 20 Prospects ranking. The Barons nearly had a fifth in the form of 22-year-old outfielder Luis Basabe, but he just missed the cut. Birmingham had to "settle" for having the top position prospect (Jimenez) and top pitching prospect, righthander Dylan Cease, in the Southern League.

Montgomery scored the most runs in the league but lost in the first round of the playoffs to Jackson (D-backs), the eventual league champions.

Led by top manager prospect Shelley Duncan, Jackson succeeded on the strength of its pitching staff, which set an Southern League record with 1,300 strikeouts. Generals pitchers also led the league in opponent average (.229) and were paced

by D-backs prospect righthanders Taylor Widener and Jon Duplantier.

That duo was joined by California League pitcher of the year Emilio Vargas for the second half of the season and the playoffs, but he didn't pitch enough innings for the Generals to qualify for the Southern League Top 20 Prospects ranking.

TOP 20 PROSPECTS

1. Eloy Jimenez, OF, Birmingham (White Sox)
2. Keston Hiura, 2B, Biloxi (Brewers)
3. Dylan Cease, RHP, Birmingham (White Sox)
4. Griffin Canning, RHP, Mobile (Angels)
5. Bryse Wilson, RHP, Mississippi (Braves)
6. Tony Santillan, RHP, Pensacola (Reds)
7. Kyle Wright, RHP, Mississippi (Braves)
8. Touki Toussaint, RHP, Mississippi (Braves)
9. Taylor Widener, RHP, Jackson (Diamondbacks)
10. Brandon Lowe, 2B/OF, Montgomery (Rays)
11. Nate Lowe, 1B, Montgomery (Rays)
12. Brent Rooker, 1B/OF, Chattanooga (Twins)
13. Corey Ray, OF, Biloxi (Brewers)
14. Genesis Cabrera, LHP, Montgomery (Rays)
15. Dane Dunning, RHP, Birmingham (White Sox)
16. Jon Duplantier, RHP, Jackson (Diamondbacks)
17. Luis Rengifo, SS/2B, Mobile (Angels)
18. Nick Solak, 2B/OF, Montgomery (Rays)
19. Taylor Ward, 3B, Mobile (Angels)
20. Zack Collins, C, Birmingham (White Sox)

STANDINGS: SPLIT SEASON

FIRST HALF

North	W	L	PCT	GB	South	W	L	PCT	GB
Jackson	39	30	.565	—	Biloxi	41	29	.586	—
Montgomery	37	33	.529	2 ½	Mobile	37	31	.544	3
Chattanooga	36	33	.522	3	Pensacola	30	38	.441	10
Tennessee	36	34	.514	3 ½	Mississippi	29	41	.414	12
Birmingham	32	36	.471	6 ½	Jacksonville	28	40	.412	12

SECOND HALF

North	W	L	PCT	GB	South	W	L	PCT	GB
Montgomery	42	28	.600	—	Biloxi	40	30	.571	—
Jackson	36	34	.514	6	Pensacola	39	30	.565	½
Birmingham	34	36	.486	8	Mississippi	38	30	.559	1
Tennessee	31	37	.456	10	Mobile	29	39	.426	10
Chattanooga	29	39	.426	12	Jacksonville	27	42	.391	12 ½

Playoffs—Semifinals: Jackson defeated Montgomery 3-2 and Biloxi defeated Pensacola 3-1 in best-of-five series. **Finals:** Jackson defeated Biloxi 3-1 in best-of-five series.

OVERALL STANDINGS

Northern Division	W	L	PCT	GB	Manager	Attendance	Average	Last Pennant
Montgomery Biscuits (Rays)	79	61	.564	—	Brady Williams	238,538	3,408	2007
Jackson Generals (D-backs)	75	64	.540	3 ½	Shelley Duncan	110,798	1,654	2018
Tennessee Smokies (Cubs)	67	71	.486	11	Mark Johnson	308,069	4,668	2004
Birmingham Barons (White Sox)	66	72	.478	12	Ryan Newman	391,061	5,751	2013
Chattanooga Lookouts (Twins)	65	72	.474	12 ½	Tommy Watkins	214,811	3,206	2017

Southern Division	W	L	PCT	GB	Manager	Attendance	Average	Last Pennant
Biloxi Shuckers (Brewers)	81	59	.579	—	Mike Guerrero	160,364	2,430	Never
Pensacola Blue Wahoos (Reds)	69	68	.504	10 ½	Jody Davis	300,002	4,348	2017
Mississippi Braves (Braves)	67	71	.486	13	Chris Maloney	151,352	2,259	2008
Mobile BayBears (Angels)	66	70	.485	13	Lou Marson	69,504	1,121	2012
Jacksonville Jumbo Shrimp (Marlins)	55	82	.401	24 ½	Randy Ready	317,335	5,037	2014

CLUB BATTING

	AVG	G	AB	R	H	2B	3B	HR	RBI	BB	SO	SB	OBP	SLG
Jackson	.262	139	4704	627	1233	240	38	83	560	464	1123	122	.336	.382
Montgomery	.257	140	4730	699	1217	239	45	106	655	502	1034	159	.333	.394
Mobile	.256	136	4403	643	1126	217	36	101	588	527	1102	127	.340	.390
Chattanooga	.255	137	4540	601	1157	217	32	107	560	440	1064	64	.326	.387
Biloxi	.241	140	4489	581	1083	216	28	145	535	490	1164	129	.322	.399
Mississippi	.240	138	4396	541	1054	209	33	74	488	390	1185	73	.308	.353
Pensacola	.239	137	4478	572	1071	203	37	106	516	438	1248	102	.313	.372
Birmingham	.239	138	4471	572	1068	209	25	119	543	482	1346	82	.319	.377
Jacksonville	.235	137	4429	524	1040	199	23	104	471	445	1308	125	.312	.361
Tennessee	.230	138	4463	562	1025	224	21	111	514	516	1187	108	.315	.364

CLUB PITCHING

	ERA	G	CG	SHO	SV	IP	H	R	ER	HR	BB	SO	AVG
Biloxi	3.47	140	1	12	48	1214	1066	549	468	101	482	1194	.236
Mississippi	3.62	138	5	14	37	1169	1072	565	470	75	537	1205	.243
Montgomery	3.75	140	2	13	37	1242	1070	570	518	118	542	1211	.233
Jackson	3.76	139	2	12	32	1219	1029	571	509	100	492	1300	.229
Chattanooga	3.85	137	2	5	32	1184	1168	600	507	96	419	1272	.258
Tennessee	3.88	138	3	10	29	1209	1138	583	521	117	406	1083	.248
Birmingham	3.92	138	3	10	41	1203	1186	614	524	85	456	1136	.257
Pensacola	3.94	137	1	9	40	1194	1106	615	522	141	409	1140	.244
Jacksonville	4.18	137	5	4	26	1174	1149	623	545	138	430	1111	.257
Mobile	4.42	136	0	12	29	1155	1090	632	567	85	521	1109	.249

CLUB FIELDING

	PCT	PO	A	E	DP		PCT	PO	A	E	DP
Montgomery	.985	3725	1156	76	110	Mississippi	.976	3506	1219	117	95
Jackson	.980	3658	1165	99	103	Mobile	.976	3466	1197	117	127
Tennessee	.980	3628	1337	102	117	Biloxi	.974	3642	1329	132	130
Chattanooga	.977	3552	1201	110	122	Birmingham	.974	3610	1352	132	113
Jacksonville	.976	3528	1161	113	119	Pensacola	.974	3581	1219	129	134

INDIVIDUAL BATTING

Batter, Club	AVG	G	AB	R	H	2B	3B	HR	RBI	BB	SO	SB
Kevin Medrano, Jackson	.331	96	369	54	122	30	5	4	48	28	71	9
Zander Wiel, Chattanooga	.311	101	386	53	120	27	2	7	58	40	82	8
Jamie Westbrook, Jackson	.287	107	408	65	117	20	5	15	68	24	71	4
Luis Valenzuela, Mississippi	.282	114	369	42	104	22	2	2	42	13	66	5
Nick Solak, Montgomery	.282	126	478	91	135	17	3	19	76	68	112	21
Rudy Flores, Jacksonville	.281	126	438	60	123	25	3	17	75	57	124	2
Nathan Lukes, Montgomery	.278	115	435	62	121	29	3	6	51	31	93	9
Brett Sullivan, Montgomery	.266	111	421	47	112	19	4	7	65	34	55	17
Brennon Lund, Mobile	.264	100	401	63	106	20	6	8	59	43	102	21
Michael Brosseau, Montgomery	.262	104	370	53	97	24	3	13	61	29	74	11

INDIVIDUAL PITCHING

Pitcher, Club	W	L	ERA	G	GS	CG	SV	IP	H	R	ER	BB	SO
Zack Brown, Biloxi	9	1	2.44	22	21	1	0	126	95	44	34	36	116
Taylor Widener, Jackson	5	8	2.75	26	25	1	0	137	99	42	42	43	176
Nick Neidert, Jacksonville	12	7	3.24	26	26	0	0	153	142	63	55	31	154
Duncan Robinson, Tennessee	7	4	3.31	24	24	0	0	131	142	61	48	22	111
Seth Varner, Pensacola	9	3	3.39	25	17	0	0	119	104	56	45	31	99
Omar Bencomo, Chattanooga	8	6	3.45	26	17	0	2	120	128	56	46	17	102
Justin Donatella, Jackson	7	8	3.46	27	24	0	0	130	112	53	50	47	103
Kodi Medeiros, Birmingham	7	7	3.60	27	22	0	0	138	121	66	55	67	141
Michael Rucker, Tennessee	9	6	3.73	26	26	0	0	133	111	62	55	38	118
Thomas Hatch, Tennessee	8	6	3.82	26	26	2	0	144	127	62	61	61	117

ALL-STAR TEAM

C: Zack Collins, Birmingham. **1B:** Jose Rojas, Mobile. **2B:** Nick Solak, Montgomery. **3B:** Brian Schales, Jacksonville. **SS:** Zack Short, Tennessee. **OF:** Corey Ray, Biloxi; Zander Wiel, Chattanooga; Jamie Westbrook, Jackson; Monte Harrison, Jacksonville. **DH:** Brent Rooker, Chattanooga. **UT:** Kevin Medrano, Jackson. **RHP:** Zack Brown, Biloxi. **LHP:** Lewis Thorpe, Chattanooga. **RP:** Nate Griep, Biloxi. **Most Valuable Player:** Corey Ray, Biloxi. **Most Outstanding Pitcher:** Zack Brown, Biloxi. **Manager of the Year:** Mike Guerrero, Biloxi.

DEPARTMENT LEADERS

BATTING

OBP	Solak, Nick, Montgomery	.384
SLG	Rojas, Jose, Mobile	.554
OPS	Medrano, Kevin, Jackson	.849
R	Solak, Nick, Montgomery	91
H	Solak, Nick, Montgomery	135
TB	Ray, Corey, Biloxi	254
XBH	Ray, Corey, Biloxi	66
2B	Rooker, Brent, Chattanooga	32
	Ray, Corey, Biloxi	32
3B	Milone, Thomas, Montgomery	11
HR	Ray, Corey, Biloxi	27
RBI	Rooker, Brent, Chattanooga	79
SAC	Salazar, Alejandro, Mississippi	8
BB	Collins, Zack, Birmingham	101
HBP	Cribbs, Galli, Jackson	20
SO	Harrison, Monte, Jacksonville	215
SB	Ray, Corey, Biloxi	37
CS	Mendick, Danny, Birmingham	10
AB/SO	Sullivan, Brett, Montgomery	7.7

FIELDING

C PCT	Sullivan, Brett, Montgomery	.996
PO	Navarreto, Brian, Chattanooga	885
A	Navarreto, Brian, Chattanooga	88
DP	Vigil, Rodrigo, Jacksonville	9
E	Navarreto, Brian, Chattanooga	10
CS	Collins, Zack, Birmingham	38
SB	Collins, Zack, Birmingham	93
PB	Sullivan, Brett, Montgomery	15
1B PCT	LaValley, Gavin, Pensacola	.992
PO	Balaguert, Yasiel, Tennessee	898
A	Balaguert, Yasiel, Tennessee	77
DP	Balaguert, Yasiel, Tennessee	90
E	Balaguert, Yasiel, Tennessee	10
2B PCT	Long, Shed, Pensacola	.971
PO	Long, Shed, Pensacola	212
A	Long, Shed, Pensacola	283
DP	Long, Shed, Pensacola	90
E	Long, Shed, Pensacola	15
3B PCT	Erceg, Lucas, Biloxi	.924
PO	Schales, Brian, Jacksonville	97
A	Erceg, Lucas, Biloxi	204
DP	Schales, Brian, Jacksonville	29
E	Erceg, Lucas, Biloxi	23
SS PCT	Mendick, Danny, Birmingham	.968
PO	Mendick, Danny, Birmingham	171
A	Mendick, Danny, Birmingham	348
DP	Short, Zack, Tennessee	72
E	Gonzalez, Luis, Pensacola	30
OF PCT	Lukes, Nathan, Montgomery	1
PO	Ray, Corey, Biloxi	314
A	Norwood, John, Jacksonville	12
	Aquino, Aristides, Pensacola	12
DP	Norwood, John, Jacksonville	6
E	Fisher, Jameson, Birmingham	9

PITCHING

G	Griep, Nate, Biloxi	51
GS	Wright, Daniel, Pensacola	28
GF	Griep, Nate, Biloxi	46
SV	Griep, Nate, Biloxi	34
W	Neidert, Nick, Jacksonville	12
L	Poteet, Cody, Jacksonville	12
	Strahan, Wyatt, Pensacola	12
IP	Neidert, Nick, Jacksonville	153
H	Tomshaw, Matt, Birmingham	154
R	Strahan, Wyatt, Pensacola	95
ER	Strahan, Wyatt, Pensacola	85
HB	Gutierrez, Vladimir, Pensacola	16
BB	Medeiros, Kodi, Birmingham	67
SO	Widener, Taylor, Jackson	176
SO/9	Widener, Taylor, Jackson	11.6
SO/9 (RP)	Lopez, Yoan, Jackson	12.7
BB/9	Robinson, Duncan, Tennessee	1.5
WP	Krook, Matt, Montgomery	20
BK	Gutierrez, Vladimir, Pensacola	3
	Huang, Wei-Chieh, Jackson	3
HRA	Wright, Daniel, Pensacola	25
BAA	Widener, Taylor, Jackson	.193

MINOR LEAGUES

MINOR LEAGUES

BY KEGAN LOWE

For the first time since 2013, a team other than the Midland RockHounds, the Oakland Athletics' Double-A affiliate, claimed the Texas League championship. Breaking up Midland's streak of four consecutive Texas League titles were the Tulsa Drillers, which lost last year's best-of-five championship series in five games after initially jumping out to a 2-0 series lead.

This year, the Drillers, the Dodgers' Double-A affiliate, once again established a 2-0 series lead in the finals, this time on San Antonio, before finishing off the sweep with a 5-2 win over the Missions (Padres) in Game 3 of the championship series. It was Tulsa's first TL title since 1998, which ended the league's longest active championship drought.

While Tulsa's late-season triumph brought home the hardware, it was the Corpus Christi Hooks who were the Texas League's best team during the regular season. Led by top Astros prospects such as outfielder/first baseman Yordan Alvarez, righthander Corbin Martin and lefthander Cionel Perez, Corpus Christi went 82-56 during the regular season, 8.5 games better than Tulsa's 74-65 mark. The Hooks lost in the semifinals of the playoffs, dropping the best-of-five series to San Antonio despite winning the first two games.

The Arkansas Travelers were the fourth and final team to qualify for the Texas League playoffs in 2018, but the Mariners' Double-A affiliate, like Corpus Christi, also lost the best-of-five series in a win-or-go-home Game 5.

In terms of prospects, the Texas League stood out for its talented youth in 2018. The league's top two position prospects—shortstop Fernando Tatis Jr. (Padres) and catcher Keibert Ruiz (Dodgers)—were the only two 19-year-olds on Opening Day rosters in the TL, while Jesus Luzardo (Athletics) established himself as the top lefthanded pitching prospect in the minors at just 20 years old.

One year ago, righthanders Walker Buehler and Jack Flaherty ranked among the top five prospects in the TL before establishing themselves as two of the top rookies in the majors this season. A similar path could be on the horizon for Tatis Jr. and Luzardo, who rank inside the top 15 on Baseball America's current Top 100 Prospects list.

This season also marked the final year of San Antonio's relationship with the Texas League, as the Missions—which will no longer be affiliated with the Padres—will compete in the Triple-A Pacific Coast League beginning next season.

TOP 20 PROSPECTS

1. Fernando Tatis Jr., SS, San Antonio (Padres)
2. Jesus Luzardo, LHP, Midland (Athletics)
3. Keibert Ruiz, C, Tulsa (Dodgers)
4. Yordan Alvarez, 1B, Corpus Christi (Astros)
5. Yusniel Diaz, OF, Tulsa (Dodgers)
6. Sean Murphy, C, Midland (Athletics)
7. Logan Allen, LHP, San Antonio (Padres)
8. Corbin Martin, RHP, Corpus Christi (Astros)
9. Josh Naylor, LF/1B, San Antonio (Padres)
10. Will Smith, C/3B, Tulsa (Dodgers)
11. Cionel Perez, LHP, Corpus Christi (Astros)
12. Nicky Lopez, SS, Northwest Arkansas (Royals)
13. Mitchell White, RHP, Tulsa (Dodgers)
14. D.J. Peters, OF, Tulsa (Dodgers)
15. Cal Quantrill, RHP, San Antonio (Padres)
16. Andrew Knizner, C, Springfield (Cardinals)
17. Jonathan Hernandez, RHP, Frisco (Rangers)
18. Richie Martin, SS, Midland (Athletics)
19. Austin Allen, C, San Antonio (Padres)
20. Eli White, 2B/SS, Midland (Athletics)

STANDINGS: SPLIT SEASON

FIRST HALF

North	W	L	PCT	GB	South	W	L	PCT	GB
Arkansas	35	35	.500	—	Corpus Christi	43	26	.623	—
NW Arkansas	35	35	.500	—	San Antonio	42	28	.600	1 ½
Tulsa	34	36	.486	1	Midland	33	36	.478	10
Springfield	33	37	.471	2	Frisco	24	46	.343	19 ½

SECOND HALF

North	W	L	PCT	GB	South	W	L	PCT	GB
Tulsa	40	29	.580	—	Corpus Christi	39	30	.565	—
Arkansas	36	33	.522	4	Frisco	36	34	.514	3 ½
NW Arkansas	35	35	.500	5 ½	Midland	35	35	.500	4 ½
Springfield	27	42	.391	13	San Antonio	29	39	.426	9 ½

Playoffs—Semifinals: San Antonio defeated Corpus Christi 3-2 and Tulsa defeated Arkansas 3-2 in best-of-five series. **Finals:** Tulsa defeated San Antonio 3-0 in best-of-five series.

OVERALL STANDINGS

North Division	W	L	PCT	GB	Manager(s)	Attendance	Average	Last Pennant
Tulsa Drillers (Dodgers)	74	65	.532	—	Scott Hennessey	350,396	5,230	2018
Arkansas Travelers (Mariners)	71	68	.511	3	Daren Brown	296,847	4,498	2009
Northwest Arkansas Naturals (Royals)	70	70	.500	4 ½	Mike Rojas	304,526	4,478	2010
Springfield Cardinals (Cardinals)	60	79	.432	14	Johnny Rodriguez	326,362	4,871	2012

South Division	W	L	PCT	GB	Manager(s)	Attendance	Average	Last Pennant
Corpus Christi Hooks (Astros)	82	56	.557	—	Omar Lopez	340,607	4,866	2006
San Antonio Missions (Padres)	71	67	.486	11	Phillip Wellman	327,276	4,885	2013
Midland RockHounds (Athletics)	68	71	.486	14 ½	Scott Steinmann	263,024	3,868	2017
Frisco RoughRiders (Rangers)	60	80	.429	23	Joe Mikulik	468,259	6,886	2004

CLUB BATTING

	AVG	G	AB	R	H	2B	3B	HR	RBI	BB	SO	SB	OBP	SLG
Corpus Christi	.268	138	4640	662	1245	250	36	106	617	448	1080	181	.339	.406
NW Arkansas	.267	140	4693	660	1252	224	44	106	594	373	1044	167	.325	.401
Midland	.264	139	4704	643	1240	274	38	96	588	462	1152	124	.333	.399
Arkansas	.263	139	4668	651	1230	233	14	85	604	556	1004	40	.346	.374
Springfield	.260	139	4692	620	1218	205	21	149	592	378	1059	69	.319	.408
Tulsa	.257	139	4671	687	1201	223	25	184	641	460	1268	84	.334	.434
San Antonio	.256	138	4600	604	1176	206	23	130	551	445	1138	98	.330	.395
Frisco	.254	140	4694	579	1194	210	23	105	540	402	1033	102	.316	.376

CLUB PITCHING

	ERA	G	CG	SHO	SV	IP	H	R	ER	HR	BB	SO	AVG
Corpus Christi	3.44	138	0		9	1225	1070	535	468	97	502	1319	.235
San Antonio	3.58	138	1		14	1212	1119	557	482	94	391	1161	.246
Tulsa	4.00	139	1		11	1214	1147	642	540	127	450	1133	.247
Midland	4.10	139	3		7	1222	1271	634	557	113	371	1002	.268
Arkansas	4.21	139	3		5	1206	1256	643	564	123	401	1060	.268
NW Arkansas	4.56	140	1		9	1209	1334	692	613	138	461	1004	.280
Springfield	4.58	139	1		8	1202	1206	676	612	128	505	991	.262
Frisco	4.88	140	2		6	1226	1353	727	665	141	443	1108	.281

CLUB FIELDING

	PCT	PO	A	E	DP		PCT	PO	A	E	DP
Springfield	.982	3619	1318	93	123	San Antonio	.979	3636	1301	105	104
Corpus Christi	.981	3676	1219	94	136	Midland	.976	3668	1403	124	125
Arkansas	.980	3617	1213	98	102	NW Arkansas	.976	3628	1359	123	119
Frisco	.980	3679	1307	104	138	Tulsa	.971	3643	1262	145	109

INDIVIDUAL BATTING

Batter, Club	AVG	G	AB	R	H	2B	3B	HR	RBI	BB	SO	SB
Jecksson Flores, Northwest Arkansas	.314	122	459	74	144	31	3	7	52	30	72	27
Eli White, Midland	.306	130	504	81	154	30	8	9	55	62	116	18
Richie Martin, Midland	.300	118	453	68	136	29	8	6	42	44	86	25
Tommy Edman, Springfield	.299	109	452	71	135	23	3	6	36	35	76	27
Chuck Taylor, Arkansas	.297	126	502	70	149	25	3	3	60	61	79	2
Josh Naylor, San Antonio	.297	128	501	72	149	22	1	17	74	64	69	5
Randy Cesar, Corpus Christi	.296	116	446	59	132	25	2	10	62	36	112	3
Austin Allen, San Antonio	.290	119	451	59	131	31	0	22	56	37	97	0
Elier Hernandez, Northwest Arkansas	.287	91	355	45	102	22	1	3	50	14	71	10
Tyler Ramirez, Midland	.287	134	512	73	147	35	4	10	79	62	148	5

INDIVIDUAL PITCHING

Pitcher, Club	W	L	ERA	G	GS	CG	SV	IP	H	R	ER	BB	SO
Ryan Hartman, Corpus Christi	11	4	2.69	25	18	0	0	121	104	41	36	26	143
Logan Allen, San Antonio	10	6	2.75	20	19	0	0	121	89	41	37	38	125
Chase De Jong, Arkansas	5	5	3.80	21	21	0	0	121	122	60	51	34	89
Anthony Shew, Springfield	6	8	4.50	19	19	0	0	114	128	57	57	32	96
Norge Ruiz, Midland	5	9	4.69	21	21	1	0	121	142	66	63	34	76
Scott Blewett, Northwest Arkansas	8	6	4.79	26	25	1	0	148	164	84	79	49	100
Emilio Ogando, Northwest Arkansas	11	7	4.79	26	26	0	0	118	127	71	63	72	94
Joel Seddon, Midland	9	7	4.81	28	17	0	0	118	131	67	63	38	80
Foster Griffin, Northwest Arkansas	10	12	5.13	28	26	0	0	153	197	94	87	40	117
Cal Quantrill, San Antonio	6	5	5.15	22	22	0	0	117	135	78	67	38	101

ALL-STAR TEAM

C: Austin Allen, San Antonio. **1B:** Joey Curletta, Arkansas. **2B:** Eli White, Midland. **3B:** Randy Cesar, Corpus Christi. **SS:** Fernando Tatis Jr., San Antonio. **OF:** Josh Naylor, San Antonio; Lane Thomas, Springfield; Jacob Scavuzzo, Tulsa. **P:** Logan Allen, San Antonio; Matt Festa, Arkansas; Ryan Hartman, Corpus Christi; Reed Garrett, Frisco; Jesus Luzardo, Midland; Corbin Martin, Corpus Christi.
Most Valuable Player: Joey Curletta, Arkansas. **Pitcher of the Year:** Logan Allen, San Antonio.
Manager of the Year: Omar Lopez, Corpus Christi.

DEPARTMENT LEADERS

BATTING

OBP	Jones, Taylor, Corpus Christi	.409
SLG	Scavuzzo, Jacob, Tulsa	.550
OPS	Curletta, Joey, Arkansas	.865
R	White, Eli, Midland	81
H	White, Eli, Midland	154
TB	Peters, DJ, Tulsa	232
XBH	Peters, DJ, Tulsa	55
	Brown, Seth, Midland	55
2B	Brown, Seth, Midland	38
3B	White, Eli, Midland	8
	Martin, Richie, Midland	8
HR	Peters, DJ, Tulsa	29
RBI	Curletta, Joey, Arkansas	94
SAC	Mejia, Erick, NW Arkansas	14
BB	Curletta, Joey, Arkansas	81
HBP	France, Ty, San Antonio	25
SO	Peters, DJ, Tulsa	192
SB	Wrenn, Stephen, Corpus Christi	44
CS	Mejia, Erick, NW Arkansas	17
AB/SO	Ruiz, Keibert, Tulsa	11.4

FIELDING

C PCT	Ruiz, Keibert, Tulsa	.995
PO	Allen, Austin, San Antonio	745
A	Allen, Austin, San Antonio	80
DP	Trevino, Jose, Frisco	7
	de Oleo, Eduardo, Corpus Christi	7
E	Morgan, Josh, Frisco	6
	Odom, Joseph, Arkansas	6
CS	Allen, Austin, San Antonio	52
SB	Allen, Austin, San Antonio	93
PB	Ruiz, Keibert, Tulsa	11
1B PCT	Curletta, Joey, Arkansas	.993
PO	Brown, Seth, Midland	907
	Curletta, Joey, Arkansas	907
A	Nogowski, John, Springfield, MO	81
DP	Brown, Seth, Midland	85
E	Brown, Seth, Midland	12
2B PCT	Birk, Ryne, Corpus Christi	.987
PO	Birk, Ryne, Corpus Christi	167
A	Birk, Ryne, Corpus Christi	210
DP	Birk, Ryne, Corpus Christi	67
E	Jackson, Drew, Tulsa	12
3B PCT	France, Ty, San Antonio	.951
PO	Mendoza, Evan, Springfield, MO	76
A	France, Ty, San Antonio	161
DP	Mendoza, Evan, Springfield, MO	22
E	France, Ty, San Antonio	12
SS PCT	De Leon, Michael, Frisco	.978
PO	De Leon, Michael, Frisco	150
A	De Leon, Michael, Frisco	286
DP	De Leon, Michael, Frisco	58
E	Martin, Richie, Midland	16
OF PCT	Thomas, Lane, Springfield, MO	1.000
PO	Peters, DJ, Tulsa	294
A	Gettys, Michael, San Antonio	16
DP	Gettys, Michael, San Antonio	5
E	Naylor, Josh, San Antonio	11

PITCHING

G	Festa, Matt, Arkansas	44
	Terrero, Franco, NW Arkansas	44
GS	Griffin, Foster, NW Arkansas	26
	Ogando, Emilio, NW Arkansas	26
GF	Festa, Matt, Arkansas	41
SV	Festa, Matt, Arkansas	20
W	Hartman, Ryan, Corpus Christi	11
	Ogando, Emilio, NW Arkansas	11
L	Griffin, Foster, NW Arkansas	12
	Misiewicz, Anthony, Arkansas	12
IP	Griffin, Foster, NW Arkansas	153
H	Griffin, Foster, NW Arkansas	197
R	Bannister, Nathan, Arkansas	98
ER	Bannister, Nathan, Arkansas	93
HB	Payano, Pedro, Frisco	17
BB	Ogando, Emilio, NW Arkansas	72
SO	Hartman, Ryan, Corpus Christi	143
SO/9	Allen, Logan, San Antonio	9.2
SO/9 (RP)	Spitzbarth, Shea, Tulsa	11.9
BB/9	Griffin, Foster, NW Arkansas	2.4
WP	Martin, Corbin, Corpus Christi	14
BK	Arias, Estarlin, Springfield, MO	2
	Blewett, Scott, NW Arkansas	2
	11 others	2
HRA	Bannister, Nathan, Arkansas	22
	Ogando, Emilio, NW Arkansas	22
BAA	Allen, Logan, San Antonio	.207

MINOR LEAGUES

BY KYLE GLASER

As the Dodgers rolled to another division title at the major league level, their high Class A affiliate was similarly steamrolling the California League just 45 miles east. Rancho Cucamonga put together one of the most dominant seasons in Cal League history in 2018. The Quakes won the first half South Division title, went a remarkable 52-18 in the second half, and then went 6-1 in the postseason to secure the franchise's second championship in four seasons.

League MVP Rylan Bannon, shortstop Gavin Lux and righthanders Dean Kremer, Tony Gonsolin and Dustin May led the way in the first half. After the all-star break, third baseman Cristian Santana, shortstop Omar Estevez, catcher Connor Wong and pitcher Isaac Anderson carried Rancho Cucamonga to the record books.

After running through the league in the second half and dispatching Lancaster in four games in the semifinals, the Quakes outscored D-backs affiliate Visalia 23-8 in a three-game sweep for the title.

Jared Walker hit the tiebreaking home run in the top of ninth for a 5-4 win in Game 1. Cody Thomas hit a fifth-inning grand slam to kickstart a 9-3 victory in Game 2. And in Game 3, Anderson threw six scoreless innings while the offense hit four home runs for a 9-1 win to secure the title.

Santana, who finished tied for the league lead with 24 home runs during the regular season, was named postseason MVP after hitting .308 with a 1.154 OPS in the playoffs.

Overall, Rancho Cucamonga led the league in runs (841), home runs (202) and OPS (.825). And on the pitching side, the Quakes led the league in strikeouts (1409), tied for first in WHIP (1.29) and finished second in ERA (3.77).

The environment of the league was different than in previous seasons. In the second year after High Desert and Bakersfield—two of the three most-hitter friendly parks in the league—contracted, teams were less reticent to send their top pitching prospects to the circuit.

TOP 20 PROSPECTS

1. Jo Adell, OF, Inland Empire (Angels)
2. Adrian Morejon, LHP, Lake Elsinore (Padres)
3. Chris Paddack, RHP, Lake Elsinore (Padres)
4. Gavin Lux, SS, Rancho Cucamonga (Dodgers)
5. Dustin May, RHP, Rancho Cucamonga (Dodgers)
6. Jazz Chisholm, SS, Visalia (D-backs)
7. Michel Baez, RHP, Lake Elsinore (Padres)
8. Colton Welker, 3B, Lancaster (Rockies)
9. Hudson Potts, 3B, Lake Elsinore (Padres)
10. Daulton Varsho, C, Visalia (D-backs)
11. Brandon Marsh, OF, Inland Empire (Angels)
12. Tony Gonsolin, RHP, Rancho Cucamonga (Dodgers)
13. Luis Rengifo, SS, Inland Empire (Angels)
14. Evan White, 1B, Modesto (Mariners)
15. Dean Kremer, RHP, Rancho Cucamonga (Dodgers)
16. Buddy Reed, OF, Lake Elsinore (Padres)
17. Logan Webb, RHP, San Jose (Giants)
18. Tyler Nevin, 1B, Lancaster (Rockies)
19. Emilio Vargas, RHP, Visalia (D-backs)
20. Bryson Brigman, SS, Modesto (Mariners)

STANDINGS: SPLIT SEASON

FIRST HALF

North	W	L	PCT	GB	South	W	L	PCT	GB
Stockton	44	26	.629	—	R. Cucamonga	35	35	.500	—
Visalia	37	33	.529	7	Lake Elsinore	34	36	.486	1
San Jose	34	36	.486	10	Inland Empire	33	37	.471	2
Modesto	30	40	.429	14	Lancaster	33	37	.471	2

SECOND HALF

North	W	L	PCT	GB	South	W	L	PCT	GB
Stockton	33	37	.471	—	R. Cucamonga	52	18	.743	—
Visalia	33	37	.471	—	Lancaster	37	33	.529	15
Modesto	32	38	.457	1	Inland Empire	34	36	.486	18
San Jose	25	45	.357	8	Lake Elsinore	34	36	.486	18

Playoffs—Semifinals: Visalia defeated Stockton 3-2 and Rancho Cucamonga defeated Lancster 3-1 in best-of-five series. **Finals:** Rancho Cucamonga defeated Visalia 3-0 in a best-of-five series.

As such, lefthanders Jesus Luzardo and Adrian Morejon and righthanders Griffin Canning and Chris Paddack headlined a star-studded pitching crop that made its way through the league, while Cal League pitcher of the year Emilio Vargas (8-5, 2.50) led a group of breakout arms. With less hitter-friendly parks and standout pitchers aplenty, scoring in the Cal League dropped to 4.83 runs per game, the lowest mark since 1989.

OVERALL STANDINGS

North Division	W	L	PCT	GB	Manager(s)	Attendance	Average	Last Pennant
Stockton Ports (Athletics)	77	63	.550	—	Rick Magnante	187,966	2,724	2008
Visalia Rawhide (D-backs)	70	70	.500	7	Joe Mather	124,208	1,774	1978
Modesto Nuts (Mariners)	62	78	.443	15	Mitch Canham	145,028	2,072	2017
San Jose Giants (Giants)	59	81	.421	18	Lipso Nava	147,668	2,110	2010

South Division	W	L	PCT	GB	Manager(s)	Attendance	Average	Last Pennant
Rancho Cucamonga Quakes (Dodgers)	87	53	.564	—	Drew Saylor	171,767	2,454	2018
Lancaster JetHawks (Rockies)	70	70	.543	17	Fred Ocasio	155,573	2,222	2014
Lake Elsinore Storm (Padres)	68	72	.464	19	Edwin Rodriguez	214,955	3,071	2011
Inland Empire 66ers (Angels)	67	73	.457	20	Ryan Barba	193,992	2,771	2013

CLUB BATTING

	AVG	G	AB	R	H	2B	3B	HR	RBI	BB	SO	SB	OBP	SLG
Lancaster	.282	140	4795	791	1350	266	52	150	722	446	1257	156	.350	.453
Rancho Cucamonga	.274	140	4869	841	1334	281	44	202	776	528	1404	107	.351	.474
Lake Elsinore	.258	140	4752	630	1226	277	41	105	588	360	1268	93	.316	.400
Stockton	.257	140	4755	653	1220	248	48	102	608	515	1212	82	.333	.393
Visalia	.255	140	4759	652	1212	279	30	118	608	443	1188	112	.327	.400
Modesto	.251	140	4775	595	1200	224	45	81	546	456	1236	81	.324	.368
Inland Empire	.251	140	4735	642	1189	223	58	99	585	534	1310	114	.332	.385
San Jose	.248	140	4797	607	1191	259	26	119	555	405	1346	132	.312	.388

CLUB PITCHING

	ERA	G	CG	SHO	SV	IP	H	R	ER	HR	BB	SO	AVG
Visalia	3.73	140	0	11	35	1245	1178	608	516	109	429	1368	.248
Rancho Cucamonga	3.77	140	0	13	39	1237	1152	613	518	110	449	1409	.243
Stockton	3.95	140	2	11	37	1245	1241	608	546	129	391	1221	.259
Lake Elsinore	4.10	140	0	7	38	1235	1196	660	562	117	471	1360	.254
Modesto	4.31	140	0	6	32	1232	1338	699	590	103	362	1157	.275
San Jose	4.49	140	0	9	34	1236	1256	718	616	123	548	1192	.263
Inland Empire	4.55	140	0	14	30	1234	1173	721	624	117	589	1334	.249
Lancaster	5.08	140	0	3	36	1233	1388	784	696	168	448	1180	.283

CLUB FIELDING

	PCT	PO	A	E	DP		PCT	PO	A	E	DP
Lancaster	.979	3698	1318	108	122	Lake Elsinore	.971	3705	1124	143	128
Stockton	.977	3736	1337	117	110	Modesto	.971	3695	1345	152	123
Inland Empire	.976	3702	1231	122	89	R. Cucamonga	.970	3712	1232	152	106
Visalia	.975	3736	1259	128	100	San Jose	.969	3707	1207	159	123

INDIVIDUAL BATING

Batter, Club	AVG	G	AB	R	H	2B	3B	HR	RBI	BB	SO	SB
Colton Welker, Lancaster	.333	114	454	74	151	32	0	13	82	42	103	5
Tyler Nevin, Lancaster	.328	100	378	59	124	25	1	13	62	34	77	4
Gavin Lux, Rancho Cucamonga	.324	88	358	64	116	23	7	11	48	43	68	11
Bryson Brigman, Modesto	.304	98	381	47	116	13	7	2	38	37	58	15
Evan White, Modesto	.303	120	476	72	144	27	7	11	66	52	103	4
Heath Quinn, San Jose	.300	96	357	53	107	24	0	14	51	42	98	4
Rylan Bannon, Rancho Cucamonga	.296	89	338	58	100	17	6	20	61	59	103	4
Nate Mondou, Stockton	.291	88	344	64	100	20	5	8	61	33	58	8
Manuel Melendez, Lancaster	.291	119	499	76	145	18	11	5	66	25	81	17
Kevin Santa, Modesto	.287	98	348	57	100	13	4	2	32	25	38	11
Luke Persico, Stockton	.287	112	429	58	123	32	5	5	60	44	78	5

INDIVIDUAL PITCHING

Pitcher, Club	W	L	ERA	G	GS	CG	SV	IP	H	R	ER	BB	SO
Darren McCaughan, Modesto	6	10	3.05	25	25	0	0	139	152	61	47	30	121
Matt Milburn, Stockton	9	5	3.49	23	22	2	0	142	161	63	55	16	111
Riley Smith, Visalia	8	6	3.57	26	25	0	0	151	141	64	60	48	148
Isaac Anderson, Rancho Cucamonga	10	6	3.67	31	16	0	1	118	121	55	48	32	120
Pedro Avila, Lake Elsinore	7	9	4.27	24	20	0	1	131	136	69	62	54	142
Connor Grey, Visalia	10	9	4.54	27	27	0	0	141	154	92	71	38	131
Reggie Lawson, Lake Elsinore	8	5	4.69	24	22	0	0	117	130	69	61	51	117
Ljay Newsome, Modesto	6	10	4.87	26	26	0	0	139	169	79	75	13	123
Reggie McClain, Modesto	6	11	5.01	24	23	0	0	133	160	89	74	28	108
Ronald Bolanos, Lake Elsinore	6	9	5.11	25	23	0	0	125	138	84	71	50	118

ALL-STAR TEAM

C: Dominic Miroglio, Visalia. **1B:** Evan White, Modesto. **2B:** Jalen Miller, San Jose. **3B:** Colton Welker, Lancaster. **SS:** Gavin Lux, Rancho Cucamonga. **OF:** Vince Fernandez, Lancaster; Buddy Reed, Lake Elsinore; Cody Thomas, Rancho Cucamonga. **DH:** Hudson Potts, Lake Elsinore. **UT:** Rylan Bannon, Rancho Cucamonga. **P:** Rico Garcia, Lancaster; Reid Humphreys, Lancaster; Dustin May, Rancho Cucamonga; Emilo Vargas, Visalia. **Most Valuable Player:** Rylan Bannon, Rancho Cucamonga. **Pitcher of the Year:** Emilio Vargas, Visalia. **Manager of the Year:** Rick Magnante, Stockton.

DEPARTMENT LEADERS

BATTING

OBP	MacKinnon, David, Inland Empire	.408
SLG	Bannon, Rylan, Bowie	.559
OPS	Bannon, Rylan, Bowie	.961
R	Estevez, Omar, R. Cucamonga	87
H	Welker, Colton, Lancaster	151
TB	Thomas, Cody, R. Cucamonga	248
XBH	Thomas, Cody, R. Cucamonga	61
2B	Estevez, Omar, R. Cucamonga	43
3B	Melendez, Manuel, Lancaster	11
HR	Santana, Cristian, R. Cucamonga	24
	Fernandez, Vince, Lancaster	24
RBI	Santana, Cristian, R. Cucamonga	109
SAC	Herrera, Carlos, Lancaster	16
BB	Fernandez, Vince, Lancaster	65
HBP	George, Max, Lancaster	19
SO	Morgan, Gareth, Modesto	180
SB	Fargas, Johneshwy, San Jose	47
CS	Fargas, Johneshwy, San Jose	16
	Melendez, Manuel, Lancaster	16
AB/SO	Santa, Kevin, Modesto	9.2

FIELDING

C PCT	Serven, Brian, Lancaster	.990
PO	Torrens, Luis, Lake Elsinore	765
A	Torrens, Luis, Lake Elsinore	76
DP	Torrens, Luis, Lake Elsinore	8
E	Torrens, Luis, Lake Elsinore	14
CS	Torrens, Luis, Lake Elsinore	32
SB	Torrens, Luis, Lake Elsinore	63
	Kruger, Jack, Inland Empire	63
PB	Torrens, Luis, Lake Elsinore	21
1B PCT	White, Evan, Modesto	.996
PO	White, Evan, Modesto	866
A	Smith, Pavin, Visalia	79
DP	White, Evan, Modesto	89
	Zunica, Brad, Lake Elsinore	89
E	Zunica, Brad, Lake Elsinore	19
2B PCT	Rosario, Eguy, Lake Elsinore	.971
PO	Miller, Jalen, San Jose	230
A	Miller, Jalen, San Jose	281
DP	Miller, Jalen, San Jose	79
E	Miller, Jalen, San Jose	17
3B PCT	Potts, Hudson, Lake Elsinore	.954
PO	Ellis, Drew, Visalia	81
A	Rizzo, Joe, Modesto	176
DP	Potts, Hudson, Lake Elsinore	19
	Franco, Wander, San Jose	19
E	Rizzo, Joe, Modesto	23
SS PCT	Van Horn, Brandon, San Jose	.944
PO	Van Horn, Brandon, San Jose	154
A	Van Horn, Brandon, San Jose	250
DP	Van Horn, Brandon, San Jose	65
E	Van Horn, Brandon, San Jose	24
OF PCT	Johnson, Bryce, San Jose	1.000
PO	Olivares, Edward, Lake Elsinore	275
A	Easley, Nate, Lake Elsinore	13
DP	Olivares, Edward, Lake Elsinore	5
E	Jimenez, Anthony, Modesto	9

PITCHING

G	Lawrence, Justin, Lancaster	55
GS	Dennis, Matt, Lancaster	28
GF	Duno, Angel, Stockton	36
SV	Humphreys, Reid, Lancaster	22
W	Anderson, Isaac, R. Cucamonga	10
	Grey, Connor, Visalia	10
L	Dennis, Matt, Lancaster	13
IP	Gold, Brandon, Lancaster	154
H	Gold, Brandon, Lancaster	204
R	Dennis, Matt, Lancaster	105
ER	Dennis, Matt, Lancaster	95
HB	Garcia, Danny, Modesto	17
BB	Bertness, Nate, Inland Empire	66
SO	Smith, Riley, Visalia	148
SO/9	Avila, Pedro, Lake Elsinore	9.4
SO/9 (RP)	Holder, Heath, Lancaster	12.6
BB/9	Newsome, Ljay, Modesto	0.8
WP	Valdez, Dauris, Lake Elsinore	17
BK	Bell, Randy, Modesto	3
HRA	Dennis, Matt, Lancaster	24
	Newsome, Ljay, Modesto	24
BAA	Smith, Riley, Visalia	.245

MINOR LEAGUES

MINOR LEAGUES

BY J.J. COOPER

Carolina League president Geoff Lassiter faced a problem with no ideal solution.

With Hurricane Florence bearing down on the North Carolina and Virginia coasts, Lassiter knew that both Buies Creek and Potomac's home parks were likely to be inundated with rain for days. So, just hours before Game 1 of the best-of-three championship series began, Lassiter announced that the series would instead become a one-game, winner-takes-all affair.

The Buies Creek Astros responded by saying farewell to their temporary home with extra-inning heroics to win a championship. Jonathan Arauz hit a sacrifice fly to score the winning run in a 2-1 win over Potomac (Nationals) in the 11th inning. Astros first baseman Jake Adams had tied the game with a solo home run in the eighth inning.

The win gave Buies Creek a title in the final game of its two years spent playing on Campbell University's campus. The team is moving to Fayetteville, N.C. and will take on a new name for 2019, but it spent two seasons at Buies Creek while waiting for its new stadium to be completed.

Buies Creek battled the Winston-Salem Dash (White Sox) for supremacy in the Southern Division all season. The Dash edged Buies Creek by 3.5 games in the first half and then the two teams tied for first place in the division in the second half. While the Dash were the better team in the regular season, Buies Creek swept the Dash in three games in the first round of the playoffs.

The Dash boasted the most well-rounded group of prospects as well. Managed by long-time major league shortstop and Carolina League manager of the year Omar Vizquel, the Dash had a seemingly never-ending line of outfield prospects, including Blake Rutherford, Luis Gonzalez, Micker Adolfo, Luis Robert, Luis Basabe and Joel Booker.

Salem third baseman Bobby Dalbec was named the league's Most Valuable Player. Dalbec actually struggled early in the season, but after hitting

just .218/.351/.477 in the first half, Dalbec hit .319/.414/.747 with 10 home runs in just 26 games in July to earn an August promotion to Double-A. Despite being sent up with a month remaining in the season, Dalbec's 26 home runs still topped the league.

TOP 20 PROSPECTS

1. Dylan Cease, RHP, Winston-Salem (White Sox)
2. Carter Kieboom, SS, Potomac (Nationals)
3. Luis Garcia, SS, Potomac (Nationals)
4. Keston Hiura, 2B, Carolina (Brewers)
5. Micker Adolfo, Winston-Salem (White Sox)
6. Anderson Tejeda, SS, Down East (Rangers)
7. Khalil Lee, OF, Wilmington (Royals)
8. Bobby Dalbec, 3B, Salem (Red Sox)
9. Jonathan Hernandez, RHP, Down East (Rangers)
10. Luis Robert, OF, Winston-Salem (White Sox)
11. Sam Hentges, LHP, Lynchburg (Indians)
12. Hector Perez, RHP, Buies Creek (Astros)
13. Darwinzon Hernandez, LHP, Salem (Red Sox)
14. Brandon Bielak, RHP, Buies Creek (Astros)
15. C.J. Chatham, SS, Salem (Red Sox)
16. Meibrys Viloria, C, Wilmington (Royals)
17. Blake Rutherford, OF, Winston-Salem (White Sox)
18. Luis Gonzalez, OF, Winston-Salem (White Sox)
19. J.J. Matijevic, OF, Buies Creek (Astros)
20. Ryan McKenna, OF, Frederick (Orioles)

STANDINGS: SPLIT SEASON

FIRST HALF

North	W	L	PCT	GB	South	W	L	PCT	GB
Potomac	37	30	.552	—	W-Salem	41	29	.586	—
Frederick	35	34	.507	3	Buies Creek	37	32	.536	3 ½
Salem	32	36	.471	5 ½	Down East	35	35	.500	6
Wilmington	31	39	.443	7 ½	Carolina	34	36	.486	7
Lynchburg	29	38	.433	8	Myrtle Beach	34	36	.486	7

SECOND HALF

North	W	L	PCT	GB	South	W	L	PCT	GB
Lynchburg	42	28	.600	—	Buies Creek	43	25	.632	—
Potomac	37	32	.536	4 ½	W-Salem	43	25	.632	—
Wilmington	37	33	.529	5	Carolina	31	37	.456	12
Salem	31	39	.443	11	Myrtle Beach	27	42	.391	16 ½
Frederick	30	38	.441	11	Down East	24	46	.343	20

Playoffs—Semifinals: Potomac defeated Lynchburg 3-2 and Buies Creek defeated Winston-Salem 3-0 in best-of-five series.
Finals: Buies Creek defeated Potomac in one-game series.

OVERALL STANDINGS

Northern Division	W	L	PCT	GB	Manager(s)	Attendance	Average	Last Pennant
Potomac Nationals (Nationals)	74	62	.544	—	Tripp Keister	237,244	3,766	2014
Lynchburg Hillcats (Indians)	71	66	.518	3 ½	Rouglas Odor	112,228	1,781	2017
Wilmington Blue Rocks (Royals)	68	72	.486	8	Darryl Kennedy	249,746	3,842	1999
Frederick Keys (Orioles)	65	72	.474	9 ½	Ryan Minor	275,001	4,297	2011
Salem Red Sox (Red Sox)	63	75	.457	12	Joe Oliver	192,621	2,919	2013

Southern Division	W	L	PCT	GB	Manager(s)	Attendance	Average	Last Pennant
Winston-Salem Dash (White Sox)	84	54	.609	—	Omar Vizquel	292,774	4,436	2003
Buies Creek Astros (Astros)	80	57	.482	3 ½	Morgan Ensberg	24,068	359	2018
Carolina Mudcats (Brewers)	65	73	.450	19	Joe Ayrault	181,122	2,744	2006
Myrtle Beach Pelicans (Cubs)	61	78	.446	23 ½	Buddy Bailey	219,589	3,327	2016
Down East Wood Ducks (Rangers)	59	81	.400	26	Spike Owen	116,835	1,770	2017

CLUB BATTING

	AVG	G	AB	R	H	2B	3B	HR	RBI	BB	SO	SB	OBP	SLG
Winston-Salem	.273	138	4632	711	1265	263	44	101	661	429	1065	121	.341	.414
Potomac	.271	136	4515	656	1222	240	23	102	601	522	1028	80	.351	.402
Salem	.252	138	4426	583	1114	215	24	89	533	441	1036	98	.328	.371
Frederick	.251	137	4469	571	1121	239	13	102	514	409	865	37	.319	.379
Wilmington	.248	140	4417	602	1094	216	32	63	548	530	1145	184	.337	.354
Lynchburg	.247	137	4444	583	1096	247	26	74	520	499	1117	72	.329	.364
Buies Creek	.244	137	4354	605	1064	228	27	100	551	483	1075	155	.324	.378
Down East	.240	140	4597	574	1101	199	33	116	528	454	1222	106	.314	.373
Carolina	.235	138	4459	541	1049	224	33	84	479	521	1311	78	.322	.357
Myrtle Beach	.232	139	4360	468	1013	173	21	55	409	447	1052	101	.309	.319

CLUB PITCHING

	ERA	G	CG	SHO	SV	IP	H	R	ER	HR	BB	SO	AVG
Buies Creek	3.07	137	3	19	37	1184	878	458	404	73	498	1272	.205
Potomac	3.36	136	5	16	27	1166	1039	515	436	71	432	1052	.238
Myrtle Beach	3.51	139	1	16	36	1178	1065	565	460	67	433	1064	.240
Winston-Salem	3.66	138	2	12	36	1201	1117	575	488	87	426	1119	.247
Lynchburg	3.76	137	4	12	42	1171	1089	574	489	79	487	1190	.247
Down East	3.90	140	1	8	30	1208	1163	644	524	114	406	1149	.251
Carolina	4.06	138	4	10	34	1185	1129	601	534	102	540	1073	.253
Wilmington	4.18	140	5	7	43	1187	1235	625	551	92	509	903	.272
Salem	4.47	138	0	6	32	1177	1202	669	585	79	554	1090	.266
Frederick	4.58	137	3	9	34	1160	1222	668	590	122	450	1004	.271

CLUB FIELDING

	PCT	PO	A	E	DP		PCT	PO	A	E	DP
Buies Creek	.982	3553	1123	84	91	Wilmington	.976	3562	1355	121	133
Carolina	.980	3555	1321	102	101	Winston-Salem	.975	3604	1287	123	118
Potomac	.977	3499	1111	99		Lynchburg	.972	3514	1251	136	111
Frederick	.976	3479	1154	113	91	Down East	.971	3625	1336	147	121
Salem	.976	3531	1267	118	132	Myrtle Beach	.969	3536	1289	155	112

INDIVIDUAL BATTING

Batter, Club	AVG	G	AB	R	H	2B	3B	HR	RBI	BB	SO	SB
Ian Sagdal, Potomac	.318	101	390	52	124	28	3	6	58	35	69	7
C.J. Chatham, Salem	.315	95	362	42	114	14	1	3	43	21	72	10
Wilson Garcia, Frederick	.295	108	413	60	122	24	0	23	70	21	46	0
Blake Rutherford, Winston-Salem	.293	115	447	67	131	25	9	7	78	34	90	15
Gavin Sheets, Winston-Salem	.293	119	437	58	128	28	2	6	61	52	81	1
Yermin Mercedes, Winston-Salem	.289	103	360	58	104	24	1	14	64	40	67	4
Trenton Brooks, Lynchburg	.281	107	388	47	109	28	3	5	52	45	66	
Emmanuel Rivera, Wilmington	.280	99	375	45	105	25	6	6	61	29	59	3
D.J. Burt, Wilmington	.280	111	410	72	115	14	7	3	46	59	98	32
Osvaldo Duarte, Buies Creek	.276	132	486	68	134	22	9	7	52	44	120	21

INDIVIDUAL PITCHING

Pitcher, Club	W	L	ERA	G	GS	CG	SV	IP	H	R	ER	BB	SO
Gerson Garabito, Wilmington	8	6	3.16	26	26	1	0	142.1	117	59	50	73	116
Sam Hentges, Lynchburg	6	6	3.27	23	23	0	0	118.1	114	51	43	53	122
Ofreidy Gomez, Wilmington	6	10	3.40	27	22	0	1	135.0	134	65	51	61	104
Alex Wells, Frederick	7	8	3.47	24	24	0	0	135.0	142	56	52	33	101
Tyson Miller, Myrtle Beach	9	9	3.54	23	23	1	0	127.0	104	53	50	35	126
Alex Lange, Myrtle Beach	6	8	3.74	23	23	0	0	120.1	104	52	50	38	101
Joan Baez, Potomac	9	9	3.79	25	25	0	0	123.1	104	61	52	69	101
Emerson Martinez, Down East	5	11	4.01	24	24	0	0	137.0	145	74	61	32	110
Zach Plesac, Lynchburg	8	5	4.04	22	22	1	0	122.2	124	63	55	33	111
Cristian Alvarado, Frederick	12	11	4.18	26	26	0	0	155.0	173	78	72	23	119
Carson LaRue, Buies Creek	8	7	4.18	25	17	0	0	116.1	109	56	54	40	99

ALL-STAR TEAM

C: Yermin Mercedes, Winston-Salem. **1B:** Wilson Garcia, Frederick. **2B:** D.J. Burt, Wilmington.
3B: Bobby Dalbec, Salem. **SS:** Anderson Tejeda, Down East. **OF:** Blake Rutherford, Winston-Salem;
Rhett Wiseman, Potomac; Ryan McKenna, Frederick. **DH:** Micker Adolfo, Winston-Salem. **UT:** Ian
Sagdal, Potomac; J.J. Matijevic, Buies Creek. **SP:** Wil Crowe, Potomac. **RP:** Luke Barker, Carolina.
Most Valuable Player: Bobby Dalbec, Salem. **Pitcher of the Year:** Wil Crowe, Potomac.
Manager of the Year: Omar Vizquel, Winston-Salem.

DEPARTMENT LEADERS

BATTING

OBP	Hummel, Cooper, Carolina	.397
SLG	Dalbec, Bobby, Salem	.573
OPS	Dalbec, Bobby, Salem	.945
R	Perkins, Blake, Potomac, Wilmington	87
H	Duarte, Osvaldo, Buies Creek	134
TB	Garcia, Wilson, Frederick	215
XBH	Dalbec, Bobby, Salem	55
2B	Netzer, Brett, Salem	31
	Cancel, Gabriel, Wilmington	31
3B	Aguilar, Ryan, Carolina	9
	Rutherford, Blake, Winston-Salem	9
	Duarte, Osvaldo, Buies Creek	9
HR	Dalbec, Bobby, Salem	26
RBI	Dalbec, Bobby, Salem	85
SAC	Burt, D.J., Wilmington	12
BB	Perkins, Blake, Potomac, Wilmington	92
HBP	Downs, Jerry, Salem	26
SO	Tejeda, Anderson, Down East	142
SB	Burt, D.J., Wilmington	32
CS	Duarte, Osvaldo, Buies Creek	19
AB/SO	Garcia, Wilson, Frederick	9.0

FIELDING

C PCT	Robinson, Chuckie, Buies Creek	.994
PO	Pereda, Jhonny, Myrtle Beach	671
A	Viloria, Meibrys, Wilmington	86
DP	Pereda, Jhonny, Myrtle Beach	9
	Viloria, Meibrys, Wilmington	9
E	Chu, Li-Jen, Lynchburg	11
CS	Mercedes, Yermin, Winston-Salem	40
SB	Pereda, Jhonny, Myrtle Beach	64
PB	Mercedes, Yermin, Winston-Salem	11
	Collins, Gavin, Lynchburg	11
	Pereda, Jhonny, Myrtle Beach	11
1B PCT	Sheets, Gavin, Winston-Salem	.995
PO	Downs, Jerry, Salem	811
A	Downs, Jerry, Salem	57
DP	Downs, Jerry, Salem	99
E	Tapia, Emmanuel, Lynchburg	14
2B PCT	Palmeiro, Preston, Frederick	.975
PO	Netzer, Brett, Salem	213
A	Netzer, Brett, Salem	319
DP	Netzer, Brett, Salem	76
E	Netzer, Brett, Salem	14
3B PCT	Carroll, Dallas, Carolina	.929
PO	Rivera, Emmanuel, Wilmington	76
A	Carroll, Dallas, Carolina	194
DP	Dalbec, Bobby, Salem	29
E	Galindo, Wladimir, Myrtle Beach	29
SS PCT	Clare, Chris, Frederick	.974
PO	Clare, Chris, Frederick	196
A	Castellano, Angelo, Wilmington	312
DP	Castellano, Angelo, Wilmington	83
E	Ademan, Aramis, Myrtle Beach	23
OF PCT	Nichting, T.J., Frederick	.996
PO	Perkins, Blake, Potomac, Wilmington	306
A	Billingsley, Cole, Frederick	15
DP	Billingsley, Cole, Frederick	5
E	Capel, Conner, Lynchburg	8
	Hill, Tyler, Salem	8

PITCHING

G	Erwin, Tyler, Frederick	50
GS	Alvarado, Cristian, Frederick	26
GS	Garabito, Gerson, Wilmington	26
	2 others	26
GF	Barker, Luke, Carolina	38
SV	Barker, Luke, Carolina	20
W	Alvarado, Cristian, Frederick	12
L	Thompson, Jake, Salem	13
IP	Alvarado, Cristian, Frederick	155
H	Tully, Tanner, Lynchburg	176
R	Thompson, Jake, Salem	91
ER	Thompson, Jake, Salem	74
HB	McAvoy, Kevin, Salem	14
BB	Garabito, Gerson, Wilmington	73
SO	Miller, Tyson, Myrtle Beach	126
SO/9	Hentges, Sam, Lynchburg	9.3
SO/9 (RP)	Krauth, Ben, Lynchburg	13.2
BB/9	Tully, Tanner, Lynchburg	1.2
WP	Houck, Tanner, Salem	23
BK	Abbott, Cory, Myrtle Beach	3
BK	Erwin, Tyler, Frederick	3
	4 others	3
HRA	Alvarado, Cristian, Frederick	19
	Wells, Alex, Frederick	19
BAA	Miller, Tyson, Myrtle Beach	.220

MINOR LEAGUES

BY JOSH NORRIS

While the Eastern League was fronted by the prospect duo of Blue Jays top prospects Vladimir Guerrero Jr. and Bo Bichette, the Florida State League came close to matching that firepower when the Twins promoted two of its top prospects to Fort Myers for the second part of the season.

The arrivals of shortstop Royce Lewis—the No. 1 overall pick in the 2017 draft—and resurgent outfielder Alex Kirilloff gave the Miracle a one-two punch that powered it through the summer and all the way to the team's first title since 2014.

Lewis entered the season as more of a known commodity because of his draft status and the quick success he'd achieved in his first taste of pro ball, but Kirilloff, who had missed the 2017 season while recovering from Tommy John surgery, emerged as one of the best prospects not only in the FSL, but in the sport as a whole.

Kirilloff's 71 extra-base hits led all minor leaguers, and his .348 batting average and 101 RBIs paced all Twins minor leaguers. He and Lewis, along with fireballing righthander Brusdar Graterol, helped the Miracle defeat Daytona in four games for the FSL championship.

Although they fell in the championship round, Daytona had a record-breaking season. Slugger Ibandel Isabel tied with Mets prospect Peter Alonso for the most home runs in the minor leagues with 36. The mark also set an FSL record, topping the previous high of 35 set in 1950 and tied in 1971. Isabel spent a part of the season in the Dodgers organization before he and righthander Zach Neal were dealt to the Reds.

On the pitching side, Phillies righthander Sixto Sanchez wowed evaluators despite a season shortened by injury. He showcased potential front-line stuff with the Threshers, including a fastball and a changeup that could rank as 80s on the 20-to-80 scouting scale and a breaking ball that's not far behind. The league's best pitching prospect, Sanchez headed a trio of Clearwater players on the league's Top 20 list, including righthander Adonis Medina and outfielder Adam Haseley.

TOP 20 PROSPECTS

1. Royce Lewis, SS, Fort Myers (Twins)
2. Alex Kirilloff, OF, Fort Myers (Twins)
3. Cristian Pache, OF, Florida (Braves)
4. Sixto Sanchez, RHP, Clearwater (Phillies)
5. Taylor Trammell, OF, Daytona (Reds)
6. Matt Manning, RHP, Lakeland (Tigers)
7. Andres Gimenez, SS, St. Lucie (Mets)
8. Jesus Sanchez, OF, Charlotte (Rays)
9. Ian Anderson, RHP, Florida (Braves)
10. Kyle Muller, LHP, Florida (Braves)
11. Kevin Smith, SS, Dunedin (Blue Jays)
12. Brendan McKay, 1B/LHP, Charlotte (Rays)
13. Brusdar Graterol, RHP, Fort Myers (Twins)
14. Tony Santillan, RHP, Daytona (Reds)
15. Nathaniel Lowe, 1B, Charlotte (Rays)
16. Daz Cameron, OF, Lakeland (Tigers)
17. Dylan Carlson, OF, Palm Beach (Cardinals)
18. Tyler Stephenson, C, Daytona (Reds)
19. Adam Haseley, OF, Clearwater (Phillies)
20. Adonis Medina, RHP, Clearwater (Phillies)

STANDINGS: SPLIT SEASON

FIRST HALF

North	W	L	PCT	GB	South	W	L	PCT	GB
Daytona	37	29	.561	—	Palm Beach	39	25	.609	—
Lakeland	36	34	.514	3	Jupiter	41	28	.594	½
Tampa	35	35	.500	4	Bradenton	35	30	.538	4½
Clearwater	32	36	.471	6	Charlotte	34	33	.507	6½
Dunedin	31	37	.456	7	Fort Myers	28	40	.412	13
Florida	29	37	.439	8	St. Lucie	27	40	.403	13½

SECOND HALF

North	W	L	PCT	GB	South	W	L	PCT	GB
Clearwater	45	24	.652	—	Charlotte	40	29	.580	—
Lakeland	36	27	.571	6	Fort Myers	40	29	.580	—
Dunedin	38	31	.551	7	Palm Beach	36	33	.522	4
Tampa	35	32	.522	9	Jupiter	29	36	.446	9
Daytona	32	37	.464	13	St. Lucie	27	36	.429	10
Florida	22	43	.338	21	Bradenton	21	44	.323	17

Playoffs—Semifinals: Daytona defeated Clearwater 2-1 and Fort Myers defeated Palm Beach 2-0 in best-of-three series.
Finals: Fort Myers defeated Daytona 3-1 in a best-of-five series.

OVERALL STANDINGS

North Division	W	L	PCT	GB	Manager(s)	Attendance	Average	Last Pennant
Clearwater Threshers (Phillies)	77	60	.562	—	Shawn Williams	181,686	2,672	2007
Lakeland Flying Tigers (Tigers)	72	61	.541	3	Mike Rabelo	49,551	840	2012
Daytona Tortugas (Reds)	69	66	.511	7	Ricky Gutierrez	120,728	2,046	2011
Tampa Tarpons (Yankees)	70	67	.511	7	Pat Osborn	71,835	1,105	2010
Dunedin Blue Jays (Blue Jays)	69	68	.504	8	Casey Candaele	30,569	450	2017
Florida Fire Frogs (Braves)	51	80	.389	23	Luis Salazar	33,017	600	Never

South Division	W	L	PCT	GB	Manager(s)	Attendance	Average	Last Pennant
Palm Beach Cardinals (Cardinals)	75	58	.564	—	Dann Bilardello	64,008	1,032	2017
Charlotte Stone Crabs (Rays)	74	62	.544	2½	Reinaldo Ruiz	104,193	1,654	2015
Jupiter Hammerheads (Marlins)	70	64	.522	5½	Kevin Randel	69,095	1,063	1991
Fort Myers Miracle (Twins)	68	69	.496	9	Ramon Borrego	123,882	1,849	2018
Bradenton Marauders (Pirates)	56	74	.431	17½	Gerardo Alvarez	79,874	1,192	1963
St. Lucie Mets (Mets)	54	76	.415	19½	Chad Kreuter	98,823	1,520	2006

CLUB BATTING

	AVG	G	AB	R	H	2B	3B	HR	RBI	BB	SO	SB	OBP	SLG
Charlotte	.274	136	4518	710	1236	283	38	82	653	459	1001	115	.344	.407
Dunedin	.268	137	4564	617	1221	235	30	76	557	455	1014	93	.340	.382
Clearwater	.258	137	4588	592	1185	200	34	87	541	382	1021	66	.322	.374
Lakeland	.254	133	4289	565	1088	190	35	62	509	385	1078	117	.321	.358
Tampa	.253	137	4489	602	1136	191	33	110	569	450	1091	112	.327	.384
Palm Beach	.253	133	4436	592	1121	213	21	84	543	433	1004	55	.330	.367
Daytona	.252	135	4396	594	1107	193	31	99	538	457	1157	123	.330	.377
Bradenton	.250	130	4196	530	1049	202	27	84	471	366	1049	122	.320	.371
Fort Myers	.246	137	4467	570	1100	216	30	90	510	417	1067	73	.316	.368
Jupiter	.242	134	4333	519	1049	178	39	51	457	382	1085	124	.312	.336
St. Lucie	.238	130	4102	433	977	189	22	60	388	379	898	125	.306	.339
Florida	.233	131	4229	448	984	183	33	69	413	379	1139	78	.303	.341

CLUB PITCHING

	ERA	G	CG	SHO	SV	IP	H	R	ER	HR	BB	SO	AVG
Jupiter	3.43	134	2	10	37	1157	1064	542	441	84	377	1038	.245
Lakeland	3.51	133	4	8	36	1132	1024	510	441	68	405	1076	.241
Tampa	3.52	137	3	12	32	1190	1060	559	465	71	501	1257	.237
Clearwater	3.60	137	4	14	37	1193	1073	546	477	91	400	1212	.240
Fort Myers	3.61	137	2	11	36	1188	1173	546	477	68	362	1046	.258
Palm Beach	3.62	133	3	7	38	1161	1082	534	467	74	411	1059	.247
St. Lucie	3.68	130	4	4	33	1108	1039	527	453	67	415	965	.248
Dunedin	3.71	137	3	11	32	1183	1153	574	487	77	379	1054	.256
Florida	4.02	131	2	10	25	1109	1065	569	495	58	502	997	.254
Charlotte	4.09	136	5	12	27	1158	1173	605	527	88	391	976	.262
Daytona	4.11	135	3	5	38	1148	1180	626	525	86	407	997	.264
Bradenton	4.65	130	4	5	28	1115	1167	634	576	122	394	927	.272

CLUB FIELDING

	PCT	PO	A	E	DP		PCT	PO	A	E	DP
Bradenton	.983	3345	1229	81	134	Dunedin	.978	3548	1333	112	105
Clearwater	.982	3579	1237	87	83	Florida	.977	3327	1263	106	111
Palm Beach	.980	3483	1178	96	106	St. Lucie	.976	3324	1190	112	93
Fort Myers	.979	3565	1294	103	122	Tampa	.975	3569	1235	122	108
Lakeland	.979	3395	1204	99	108	Jupiter	.974	3471	1262	124	101
Charlotte	.978	3475	1187	105	111	Daytona	.973	3445	1210	127	103

INDIVIDUAL BATTING

Batter, Club	AVG	G	AB	R	H	2B	3B	HR	RBI	BB	SO	SB
Ivan Castillo, Dunedin	.304	108	388	41	118	25	8	5	44	23	51	8
Rodrigo Orozco, Dunedin	.304	112	378	70	115	23	3	1	39	40	53	18
Jesus Sanchez, Charlotte	.301	90	359	56	108	24	2	10	64	15	71	6
Jose Pujols, Clearwater	.301	95	352	56	106	16	4	18	58	33	127	1
Taylor Grzelakowski, Fort Myers	.298	95	332	46	99	23	3	8	40	37	98	1
Robbie Tenerowicz, Charlotte	.292	100	383	64	112	22	1	5	61	32	62	8
Joshua Palacios, Dunedin	.292	125	507	62	148	30	5	8	78	47	125	15
Dom Thompson-Williams, Tampa	.290	90	331	56	96	16	4	17	65	31	95	17
Cristian Pache, Florida	.285	93	369	46	105	20	5	8	40	15	69	7
Andres Gimenez, St. Lucie	.282	85	308	43	87	20	4	6	30	22	70	28
Lucius Fox, Charlotte	.282	89	351	54	99	17	1	2	30	42	79	23

INDIVIDUAL PITCHING

Pitcher, Club	W	L	ERA	G	GS	CG	SV	IP	H	R	ER	BB	SO
Spenser Watkins, Lakeland	8	4	2.24	22	13	2	1	112	91	31	28	33	89
Patrick Murphy, Dunedin	10	5	2.64	26	26	1	0	147	126	51	43	50	135
Charlie Barnes, Fort Myers	6	6	2.81	23	23	0	0	118	115	39	37	44	84
Anthony Castro, Lakeland	9	4	2.93	22	20	2	0	117	112	42	38	43	101
Nick Green, Tampa	7	5	3.28	20	20	1	0	115	104	57	42	57	93
James Marvel, Bradenton	9	6	3.68	22	21	0	0	134	132	64	55	31	100
Scott Moss, Daytona	15	4	3.68	25	25	0	0	132	135	66	54	41	112
Mauricio Llovera, Clearwater	8	7	3.72	23	22	1	0	121	100	59	50	34	137
Jeremy Walker, Florida	5	11	4.07	25	25	1	0	135	148	71	61	46	95
Adonis Medina, Clearwater	10	4	4.12	22	21	1	0	111	103	59	51	36	123

ALL-STAR TEAM

C: Tyler Stephenson, Daytona; Taylor Grzelakowski, Fort Myers. **1B:** Brandon Wagner, Tampa. **2B:** Andy Young, Palm Beach. **3B:** Michael Paez, St. Lucie. **SS:** Andres Gimenez, St. **Lucie**. **OF:** Jose Pujols, Clearwater; Jesus Sanchez, Charlotte; Joshua Palacios, Dunedin; Taylor Trammell, Daytona; Ibandel Isabel, Daytona. **UT:** Ivan Castillo, Dunedin. **SP:** Patrick Murphy, Dunedin; Spenser Watkins, Lakeland; Ian Anderson, Florida; Scott Moss, Daytona. **RP:** Ryan Hendrix, Daytona; Joel Kuhnel, Daytona.
Most Valuable Player: Jose Pujols, Clearwater. **Pitcher of the Year:** Patrick Murphy, Dunedin.
Manager of the Year: Dann Bilardello, Palm Beach.

DEPARTMENT LEADERS

BATTING

OBP	Park, Hoy Jun, Tampa	.387
SLG	Isabel, Ibandel, Daytona	.566
OPS	Isabel, Ibandel, Daytona	.900
R	Oliva, Jared, Bradenton	75
H	Palacios, Joshua, Dunedin	148
TB	Isabel, Ibandel, Daytona	213
XBH	Gray, Tristan, Charlotte, FL	53
2B	Gray, Tristan, Charlotte, FL	38
3B	Castillo, Ivan, Dunedin	8
HR	Isabel, Ibandel, Daytona	35
RBI	Palacios, Joshua, Dunedin	78
SAC	Valerio, Adrian, Bradenton	16
BB	Park, Hoy Jun, Tampa	68
HBP	Robertson, Kramer, Palm Beach	18
SO	Davidson, Braxton, Florida	213
SB	Hill, Derek Lakeland	35
CS	Ruta, Ben, Tampa	13
AB/SO	Castillo, Diego, Tampa	10.0

FIELDING

C PCT	Stephenson, Tyler, Daytona	.996
PO	Stephenson, Tyler, Daytona	703
A	Adams, Riley, Dunedin	75
DP	Hamilton, Caleb, Fort Myers	7
	Adams, Riley, Dunedin	7
	2 others	7
E	Law, Zacrey, Charlotte, FL	8
	Sthormes, Andres, Lakeland	8
CS	Adams, Riley, Dunedin	43
SB	Stephenson, Tyler, Daytona	79
PB	Hamilton, Caleb, Fort Myers	16
1B PCT	Yari, Bruce, Daytona	.997
PO	Yari, Bruce, Daytona	730
A	Diaz, Lewin, Fort Myers	50
	Davidson, Braxton, Florida	50
DP	Davidson, Braxton, Florida	75
E	Davidson, Braxton, Florida	11
2B PCT	Mahan, Riley, Jupiter	.971
PO	Mahan, Riley, Jupiter	160
A	Mahan, Riley, Jupiter	267
DP	Mahan, Riley, Jupiter	49
E	Mahan, Riley, Jupiter	13
3B PCT	Aguilar, Angel, Tampa	.954
PO	Paez, Michael, St. Lucie	73
A	Paez, Michael, St. Lucie	148
DP	Owen, Hunter, Bradenton	18
E	Paez, Michael, St. Lucie	20
SS PCT	Gamboa, Arquimedes, Clearwater	.971
PO	Robertson, Kramer, Palm Beach	170
A	Valerio, Adrian, Bradenton	294
DP	Valerio, Adrian, Bradenton	76
E	Robertson, Kramer, Palm Beach	18
OF PCT	Cone, Gene, St. Lucie	1.000
PO	Palacios, Joshua, Dunedin	267
A	Contreras, Mark, Fort Myers	11
	Pujols, Jose, Clearwater	11
DP	Lowe, Josh, Charlotte, FL	4
	Hughston, Casey, Bradenton	4
	Carlson, Dylan, Palm Beach	4
E	Strom, Ian, St. Lucie	9
	Pujols, Jose, Clearwater	9

PITCHING

G	Patterson, Jacob, Palm Beach	51
GS	Murphy, Patrick, Dunedin	26
GF	Kuhnel, Joel, Daytona	35
SV	Kuhnel, Joel, Daytona	17
W	Moss, Scott, Daytona	15
L	Walker, Jeremy, Florida	11
	Wallace, Mike, Bradenton	11
IP	Murphy, Patrick, Dunedin	147
H	Wallace, Mike, Bradenton	155
R	Romero, Wennington, Daytona	78
ER	Romero, Wennington, Daytona	70
HB	Llovera, Mauricio, Clearwater	14
	Nunez, Oddy, Bradenton	14
BB	Soto, Gregory, Lakeland	70
SO	Llovera, Mauricio, Clearwater	137
SO/9	Llovera, Mauricio, Clearwater	10.2
SO/9 (RP)	Hernandez, Jakob, Clearwater	11.7
BB/9	Marvel, James, Bradenton	2.0
WP	Anderson, Ian, Florida	18
	Green, Nick, Tampa	18
BK	Castro, Anthony, Lakeland	3
	Nunez, Oddy, Bradenton	3
	2 others	3
HRA	Wallace, Mike, Bradenton	18
BAA	Llovera, Mauricio, Clearwater	.222

MINOR LEAGUES

BY JUSTIN COLEMAN

The Bowling Green Hot Rods were the story of the Midwest League, posting a minor league-leading 90 wins. The Rays' low Class A affiliate posted a league-best .274 batting average and a .747 OPS. In addition to the offensive excellence, the pitching staff recorded a league-best 1.21 WHIP and the second-best team ERA (3.11).

The club featured a plethora of excellent prospects in 2018, including infielder Vidal Brujan, who had the second-highest batting average (.322) in the league, and teammates Moises Gomez and Ronaldo Hernandez, who combined for 40 home runs in the middle of the Hot Rods' lineup.

After splitting the first two games of the championship series against Peoria (Cardinals), Bowling Green outscored the Chiefs 12-3 over the next two games, leading to a league title for the first time since the Rays took over as its parent club in 2009.

From a prospect standpoint, two of the bright spots were third baseman Elehuris Montero (Cardinals), who was named Midwest League MVP, and shortstop Royce Lewis (Twins), who ranked as the league's top prospect. Montero hit 15 home runs and recorded a .910 OPS, while Lewis lived up to the hype as the No. 1 pick in 2017, slashing .315/.368/.485 before being promoted to high Class A Fort Myers in July. Both prospects were part of a strong Midwest League talent pool, deep in both positional and pitching prospects.

The Padres' 2017 first-round pick, lefthander MacKenzie Gore was the top pitching prospect in the Midwest League, striking out 74 hitters and surrendering five home runs in 60.2 innings. Fellow 2017 top-five pick and lefthander/first baseman Brendan McKay (Rays) also saw time in the Midwest League, going 2-0, 1.09 in six starts while also hitting .254/.484/.333 in 63 at-bats.

TOP 20 PROSPECTS

1. Royce Lewis, SS, Cedar Rapids (Twins)
2. MacKenzie Gore, LHP, Fort Wayne (Padres)
3. Alex Kirilloff, OF, Cedar Rapids (Twins)
4. Brendan McKay, 1B/LHP, Bowling Green (Rays)
5. Hunter Greene, RHP, Dayton (Reds)
6. Matt Manning, RHP, West Michigan (Tigers)
7. Ronaldo Hernandez, C, Bowling Green (Rays)
8. Jeter Downs, 2B/SS, Dayton (Reds)
9. Elehuris Montero, 3B, Peoria (Cardinals)
10. Luis Patino, RHP, Fort Wayne (Padres)
11. Vidal Brujan, 2B, Bowling Green (Rays)
12. Miguel Amaya, C, South Bend (Cubs)
13. Moises Gomez, OF, Bowling Green (Rays)
14. Lazaro Armenteros, OF, Beloit (Athletics)
15. Kevin Smith, SS, Lansing (Blue Jays)
16. Esteury Ruiz, 2B, Fort Wayne (Padres)
17. Johan Oviedo, RHP, Peoria (Cardinals)
18. Akil Baddoo, OF, Cedar Rapids (Twins)
19. Nolan Jones, 3B, Lake County (Indians)
20. Patrick Sandoval, LHP, Quad Cities (Astros)

STANDINGS: SPLIT SEASON

FIRST HALF

Eastern	W	L	PCT	GB	Western	W	L	PCT	GB
B. Green	47	22	.681	—	Quad Cities	40	30	.571	—
Lansing	43	27	.614	4 ½	Peoria	39	31	.557	1
W. Michigan	36	34	.514	11 ½	Clinton	39	31	.557	1
South Bend	34	35	.493	13	Kane County	35	34	.507	4 ½
Fort Wayne	32	37	.463	15	Beloit	32	37	.464	7 ½
Dayton	31	37	.456	15 ½	Cedar Rapids	32	37	.464	7 ½
Lake County	29	41	.414	18 ½	Wisconsin	31	38	.449	8 ½
Great Lakes	24	44	.353	22 ½	Burlington	30	39	.435	9 ½

SECOND HALF

Eastern	W	L	PCT	GB	Western	W	L	PCT	GB
B. Green	43	27	.614	—	Cedar Rapids	45	25	.643	—
Lansing	37	33	.529	6	Quad Cities	41	29	.586	4
Great Lakes	36	33	.522	6 ½	Beloit	37	32	.536	7 ½
W. Michigan	33	36	.478	9 ½	Kane County	37	32	.536	7 ½
Fort Wayne	32	37	.464	10 ½	Peoria	37	32	.536	7 ½
Lake County	31	38	.449	11 ½	Wisconsin	37	33	.529	8
South Bend	30	39	.435	12 ½	Clinton	30	39	.435	14 ½
Dayton	27	43	.386	16	Burlington	20	45	.308	22 ½

Playoffs—Semifinals: Bowling Green defeated West Michigan 2-0 and Peoria defeated Cedar Rapids 2-0 in best-of-three series.
Finals: Bowling Green defeated Peoria 3-1 in a best-of-five series.

OVERALL STANDINGS

Eastern Division	W	L	PCT	GB	Manager(s)	Attendance	Average	Last Pennant
Bowling Green Hot Rods (Rays)	90	49	.647	—	Craig Albernaz	178,329	2,702	2018
Lansing Lugnuts (Blue Jays)	80	60	.571	10 ½	Cesar Martin	313,592	4,612	2003
West Michigan Whitecaps (Tigers)	69	70	.496	21	Lance Parrish	386,609	5,770	2015
Fort Wayne TinCaps (Padres)	64	74	.464	25 ½	Anthony Contreras	376,422	5,703	2009
South Bend Cubs (Cubs)	64	74	.464	25 ½	Jimmy Gonzalez	343,763	4,911	2005
Great Lakes Loons (Dodgers)	60	77	.438	29	John Shoemaker	187,220	2,880	2017
Lake County Captains (Indians)	60	79	.432	30	Luke Carlin	202,124	3,062	2010
Dayton Dragons (Reds)	58	80	.420	31 ½	Luis Bolivar	550,725	7,868	Never

Western Division	W	L	PCT	GB	Manager(s)	Attendance	Average	Last Pennant
Quad Cities River Bandits (Astros)	81	59	.579	—	Mickey Storey	215,061	3,163	2013
Cedar Rapids Kernels (Twins)	77	62	.554	3 ½	Toby Gardenhire	160,165	2,355	1994
Peoria Chiefs (Cardinals)	76	63	.547	4 ½	Chris Swauger	208,275	3,156	2002
Kane County Cougars (D-backs)	72	66	.522	8	Blake Lalli	350,028	5,469	2014
Beloit Snappers (Athletics)	69	69	.500	11	Webster Garrison	64,574	1,025	1995
Clinton LumberKings (Mariners)	69	70	.496	11 ½	Denny Hocking	121,678	1,816	2016
Wisconsin Timber Rattlers (Brewers)	68	71	.489	12 ½	Matt Erickson	225,897	3,475	2012
Burlington Bees (Angels)	50	84	.373	28	Jack Howell/Chad Tracy	53,259	859	2008

CLUB BATTING

	AVG	G	AB	R	H	2B	3B	HR	RBI	BB	SO	SB	OBP	SLG
Bowling Green	.274	139	4682	718	1283	261	40	94	636	424	1010	156	.340	.407
Peoria	.267	139	4634	601	1236	242	40	95	540	434	1024	73	.335	.389
Cedar Rapids	.265	139	4688	665	1242	264	46	113	609	427	1153	93	.329	.413
Kane County	.262	138	4628	630	1211	234	39	79	574	460	1114	88	.335	.380
Beloit	.257	138	4594	562	1182	209	36	66	506	410	1031	99	.324	.362
South Bend	.256	138	4451	571	1163	218	32	69	513	410	1050	117	.322	.363
Lansing	.255	140	4666	720	1188	254	45	95	609	561	1085	203	.341	.389
Dayton	.248	138	4577	573	1133	221	44	89	503	406	1204	182	.318	.373
Fort Wayne	.246	138	4530	585	1115	206	37	79	500	452	1185	133	.320	.360
Lake County	.246	139	4679	568	1151	227	23	118	519	457	1171	110	.317	.380
Great Lakes	.244	137	4564	534	1115	204	42	84	488	433	1284	159	.319	.363
Quad Cities	.242	140	4537	577	1099	218	45	101	514	522	1237	91	.330	.377
Wisconsin	.241	139	4546	571	1097	229	34	86	511	459	1357	115	.317	.363
Burlington	.240	134	4400	537	1054	179	41	59	483	506	1343	95	.323	.339
West Michigan	.237	139	4464	525	1060	212	47	53	477	447	1167	117	.312	.342
Clinton	.234	139	4518	577	1059	192	25	108	513	474	1302	73	.314	.360

CLUB PITCHING

	ERA	G	CG	SHO	SV	IP	H	R	ER	HR	BB	SO	AVG
Quad Cities	2.86	140	0	17	50	1226	976	489	389	65	527	1514	.215
Bowling Green	3.11	139	1	11	44	1217	1053	515	421	92	421	1196	.233
Cedar Rapids	3.40	139	2	13	38	1206	1089	526	456	75	429	1161	.242
Kane County	3.46	138	2	7	31	1194	1130	556	459	81	441	1188	.248
West Michigan	3.46	139	2	9	38	1194	1143	562	459	78	428	1140	.252
Fort Wayne	3.54	138	0	9	32	1192	1158	578	469	73	391	1219	.253
Great Lakes	3.72	137	0	10	23	1194	1051	582	494	73	543	1135	.237
Peoria	3.73	139	2	8	36	1210	1147	583	502	91	501	1168	.251
South Bend	3.75	138	0	12	37	1204	1131	619	501	77	428	1156	.247
Burlington	3.92	134	0	8	23	1150	1099	602	501	75	543	1139	.253
Lake County	4.04	139	0	9	30	1215	1179	659	546	94	441	1182	.253
Beloit	4.05	138	1	8	37	1197	1133	624	538	103	456	1107	.250
Clinton	4.08	139	1	9	35	1205	1191	632	546	99	442	1263	.256
Wisconsin	4.14	139	1	11	33	1215	1275	618	559	87	416	1057	.271
Lansing	4.18	140	1	5	46	1231	1284	659	572	115	440	998	.269
Dayton	4.73	138	1	5	44	1205	1349	710	633	110	435	1094	.283

CLUB FIELDING

	PCT	PO	A	E	DP		PCT	PO	A	E	DP
Wisconsin	.979	3645	1349	108	140	Quad Cities	.973	3675	1142	134	78
Cedar Rapids	.978	3619	1385	115	139	Kane County	.969	3583	1283	154	109
Peoria	.976	3630	1206	121	128	Burlington	.969	3450	1267	150	118
Beloit	.975	3592	1261	124	114	Lake County	.969	3647	1279	157	113
Bowling	.974	3650	1312	130	109	Great Lakes	.969	3582	1213	155	109
Clinton	.974	3615	1229	130	99	West Michigan	.968	3583	1220	157	102
Dayton	.973	3615	1286	135	101	South Bend	.966	3612	1303	173	11
Lansing	.973	3694	1378	141	122	Fort Wayne	.964	3576	1260	183	101

INDIVIUAL BATTING

Batter, Club	AVG	G	AB	R	H	2B	3B	HR	RBI	BB	SO	SB
Elehuris Montero, Peoria	.322	103	382	68	123	28	3	15	69	33	81	2
Vidal Brujan, Bowling Green	.313	95	377	86	118	18	5	5	41	48	53	43
Ernie De La Trinidad, Kane County	.311	91	312	52	97	13	2	8	56	45	48	6
Yariel Gonzalez, Peoria	.311	107	395	51	123	23	1	11	64	31	58	3
Taylor Walls, Bowling Green	.304	120	467	87	142	28	6	6	57	66	80	31
Jancarlos Cintron, Kane County	.298	97	342	51	102	19	2	7	39	18	45	3
Austin Beck, Beloit	.296	123	493	58	146	29	4	2	60	30	117	8
Oscar Gonzalez, Lake County	.292	114	462	52	135	25	1	13	52	12	107	5
Hunter Hargrove, Beloit	.290	126	469	59	136	28	0	9	68	37	61	1
Yoel Yanqui, Kane County	.289	126	495	83	143	22	4	5	60	49	100	13

INDIVIDUAL PITCHING

Pitcher, Club	W	L	ERA	G	GS	CG	SV	IP	H	R	ER	BB	SO
Mitchell Jordan, Beloit	8	4	2.67	25	19	1	0	125	110	40	37	34	105
Tommy Romero, Bowling Green	11	4	2.95	25	25	0	0	128	111	42	42	51	131
Randy Dobnak, Cedar Rapids	10	5	3.14	24	20	1	0	129	138	51	45	25	84
Elvin Rodriguez, West Michigan	8	7	3.34	21	21	0	0	113	108	49	42	32	109
Christian Taugner, Wisconsin	7	7	3.49	22	22	0	0	124	136	52	48	19	90
Tobias Myers, Bowling Green	10	6	3.71	23	21	0	0	119	127	59	49	41	101
Tom Cosgrove, Fort Wayne	3	6	3.71	24	21	0	0	116	129	59	48	34	122
Austin Orewiler, Dayton	5	5	3.72	30	12	0	2	123	129	64	51	39	71
Clay Chandler, Clinton	9	4	3.89	27	19	0	1	137	124	61	59	33	101
Dylan File, Wisconsin	8	10	3.96	25	25	0	0	136	152	68	60	28	114

ALL-STAR TEAM

C: Moises Gomez, Bowling Green. **1B:** Yariel Gonzalez, Peoria. **2B:** Vidal Brujan, Bowling Green.
3B: Elehuris Montero, Bowling Green. **SS:** Royce Lewis, Cedar Rapids. **OF:** Alex Kirilloff, Cedar Rapids;
Ernie De La Trinidad, Kane County; Moises Gomez, Bowling Green. **DH:** Hendrik Clementina, Dayton.
RHP: Tommy Romero, Bowling Green; John Ghyzel, Dayton. **LHP:** Osvaldo Hernandez, Fort Wayne;
Travis Radke, Fort Wayne. **Most Valuable Player:** Elehuris Montero, Peoria. **Prospect of the
Year:** Royce Lewis, Cedar Rapids. **Manager of the Year:** Craig Albernaz.

DEPARTMENT LEADERS

BATTING

OBP	Noda, Ryan, Lansing	.421
SLG	Montero, Elehuris, Peoria	.529
OPS	Montero, Elehuris, Peoria	.910
R	Young, Chavez, Lansing	88
H	Beck, Austin, Beloit	146
TB	Gomez, Moises, Bowling Green	237
XBH	Gomez, Moises, Bowling Green	60
2B	Gomez, Moises, Bowling Green	34
3B	Baddoo, Akil, Cedar Rapids	11
HR	Benson, Will, Lake County	22
RBI	Gomez, Moises, Bowling Green	82
SAC	Singleton, Chris, South Bend	9
BB	Noda, Ryan, Lansing	109
HBP	Chiu, Marcus, Great Lakes	18
SO	Sandoval, Ariel, Clinton	173
SB	Ruiz, Esteury, Fort Wayne	49
CS	Rosa, Joseph, Clinton	17
AB/SO	Miranda, Jose, Cedar Rapids	7.9

FIELDING

C PCT	Henry, Payton, Wisconsin	.996
PO	Papierski, Michael, Quad Cities	956
A	Amaya, Miguel, South Bend	99
DP	Amaya, Miguel, South Bend	9
	Wenson, Harrison, Burlington	9
E	Wenson, Harrison, Burlington	14
CS	Pina, Keinner, Burlington	48
SB	Morgan, Joey, West Michigan	94
PB	Hernandez, Ronaldo, Bowling Green	19
1B PCT	Hargrove, Hunter, Beloit	.993
PO	Hargrove, Hunter, Beloit	931
A	Yanqui, Yoel, Kane County	82
DP	Hargrove, Hunter, Beloit	79
E	Yanqui, Yoel, Kane County	15
2B PCT	Taylor, Samad, Lansing	.979
PO	Taylor, Samad, Lansing	250
A	Taylor, Samad, Lansing	302
DP	Taylor, Samad, Lansing	74
E	Ruiz, Esteury, Fort Wayne	21
3B PCT	Bortles, Colby, West Michigan	.929
PO	Bortles, Colby, West Michigan	91
A	Bortles, Colby, West Michigan	169
DP	Bortles, Colby, West Michigan	18
	Bechtold, Andrew, Cedar Rapids	18
E	Filiere, Austin, South Bend	23
SS PCT	Rivas, Leonardo, Burlington	.966
PO	Arias, Gabriel, Fort Wayne	171
A	Allen, Nick, Beloit	315
DP	Arias, Gabriel, Fort Wayne	61
E	Arias, Gabriel, Fort Wayne	30
OF PCT	Chester, Carl, Bowling Green	.996
PO	Young, Chavez, Lansing	290
A	Cabrera, Eleardo, Bowling Green	17
DP	Beck, Austin, Beloit	4
	Cuadrado, Romer, Great Lakes	4
	2 others	4
E	Gonzalez, Oscar, Lake County	12

PITCHING

G	Nutof, Ryan, Dayton	46
	Thompson, Cory, Dayton	46
GS	Hernandez, Nelson, Wisconsin	28
	Naughton, Packy, Dayton	28
GF	Glowicki, Brian, South Bend	40
SV	Ghyzel, John, Dayton	19
W	Hernandez, Osvaldo, Fort Wayne	11
	Romero, Tommy, Bowling Green	11
L	Hillman, Juan, Lake County	12
	Ruiz, Jean, Beloit	12
IP	Naughton, Packy, Dayton	154
H	Naughton, Packy, Dayton	168
R	Hillman, Juan, Lake County	95
ER	Hernandez, Nelson, Wisconsin	74
	Hillman, Juan, Lake County	74
HB	Andueza, Ivan, Beloit	11
	Balestrieri, Paul, Peoria	11
	2 others	11
BB	Oviedo, Johan, Peoria	79
SO	Naughton, Packy, Dayton	137
SO/9	McCarty, Kirk, Lake County	10.3
SO/9 (RP)	Delaplane, Sam, Clinton	15.1
BB/9	Taugner, Christian, Wisconsin	1.4
WP	Hillman, Juan, Lake County	21
BK	Weatherly, Kyle, Lansing	5
HRA	Chandler, Clay, Clinton	20
BAA	Romero, Tommy, Clinton/Bowling Green	.238

MINOR LEAGUES

BY J.J. COOPER

By the midseason, it was clear that the Lexington Legends had a special group. By the end of the season, they had proven it.

The Legends placed four position players on the midseason all-star team, including all-star game Most Valuable Player Nick Pratto, but it was during the second half of the season that they truly put things together.

Lexington edged Greenville for the Southern Division's second-half title, then blitzed through the playoffs winning five of its six playoff games.

Cristian Perez's ninth-inning sacrifice fly scored Brewer Hicklen to clinch the title with a 2-1 win over Lakewood. The title was Lexington's third in league history and its first since 2001. Lexington had not even made the playoffs since 2006.

Lakewood had earned its own spot in the championship series with an impressive sweep of Kannapolis. Righthander Spencer Howard threw the first playoff no-hitter in league history as he struck out nine in a 1-0 nail biter.

Asheville first basemen Casey Golden earned MVP honors as he led the league with 32 homers, 57 extra-base hits, 90 RBIs and 86 runs scored.

Greenville righthander Denyi Reyes was named pitcher of the year after leading the league with a 1.86 ERA. Reyes had outstanding control as he walked only 13 batters in 123.2 innings.

Howard's no-hitter was one of four in the league this season. Greenville's Enmanuel De Jesus, Devon Fisher and Durbin Feltman combined for the first in July. Greensboro's Taylor Braley, Jeremy Ovalle and Michael Mertz pieced together a seven-inning no-hitter in August. And Charleston's Janson Junk, Austin DeCarr and Daniel Alvarez no-hit Delmarva in August as well.

TOP 20 PROSPECTS

1. D.L. Hall, LHP, Delmarva (Orioles)
2. Luis Garcia, 2B/SS, Hagerstown (Nationals)
3. Drew Waters, OF, Rome (Braves)
4. Oneil Cruz, SS, West Virginia (Pirates)
5. Bubba Thompson, OF, Hickory (Rangers)
6. M.J. Melendez, C, Lexington (Royals)
7. William Contreras, C, Rome (Braves)
8. Anthony Kay, LHP, Columbia (Mets)
9. Tyler Phillips, RHP, Hickory (Rangers)
10. Heliot Ramos, OF, Augusta (Giants)
11. Calvin Mitchell, OF, West Virginia (Pirates)
12. Spencer Howard, RHP, Lakewood (Phillies)
13. Jose Devers, SS, Greensboro (Marlins)
14. Will Stewart, LHP, Lakewood (Phillies)
15. Edward Cabrera, RHP, Greensboro (Marlins)
16. Huascar Ynoa, RHP, Rome (Braves)
17. Nick Pratto, 1B, Lexington (Royals)
18. Seuly Matias, OF, Lexington (Royals)
19. A.J. Alexy, RHP, Hickory (Rangers)
20. Yefri Del Rosario, RHP, Lexington (Royals)

STANDINGS: SPLIT SEASON

FIRST HALF

North	W	L	PCT	GB	South	W	L	PCT	GB
Lakewood	41	28	.594	—	Rome	40	29	.580	—
Kannapolis	39	28	.582	1	Augusta	37	31	.544	2 ½
West Virginia	37	29	.561	2 ½	Lexington	37	31	.544	2 ½
Delmarva	35	32	.522	5	Columbia	34	33	.507	5
Greensboro	34	45	.493	7	Charleston	33	35	.485	6 ½
Hickory	30	38	.441	10 ½	Asheville	27	42	.391	13
Hagerstown	27	41	.397	13 ½	Greenville	25	44	.362	15

SECOND HALF

North	W	L	PCT	GB	South	W	L	PCT	GB
Lakewood	46	23	.667	—	Lexington	39	29	.574	—
Hickory	40	30	.571	6 ½	Greenville	39	31	.557	1
West Virginia	34	33	.529	11	Asheville	37	31	.544	2
Kannapolis	35	35	.522	11 ½	Rome	31	36	.463	7 ½
Delmarva	33	34	.478	12	Charleston	31	37	.456	8
Greensboro	26	41	.435	19	Columbia	30	37	.448	8 ½
Hagerstown	25	40	.420	19	Augusta	30	39	.435	9 ½

Playoffs—Semifinals: Lakewood defeated Kannapolis 2-0 and Lexington defeated Rome 2-0 in best-of-three-series.
Finals: Lexington defeated Lakewood 3-1 in a best-of-five series.

OVERALL STANDINGS

Northern Division	W	L	PCT	GB	Manager(s)	Attendance	Average	Last Pennant
Lakewood BlueClaws (Phillies)	87	51	.630	—	Marty Malloy	293,413	4,657	2010
Kannapolis Intimidators (White Sox)	74	63	.540	12 ½	Justin Jirschele	64,688	1,115	2005
West Virginia Power (Pirates)	71	62	.534	13 ½	Wyatt Toregas	112,273	1,841	1990
Delmarva Shorebirds (Orioles)	68	66	.507	17	Buck Britton	201,329	3,097	2001
Hickory Crawdads (Rangers)	70	68	.507	17	Matt Hagen	125,394	1,900	2015
Greensboro Grasshoppers (Marlins)	60	76	.441	26	Todd Pratt	322,156	4,881	2011
Hagerstown Suns (Nationals)	52	81	.391	32 ½	Patrick Anderson	64,957	1,160	Never

Southern Division	W	L	PCT	GB	Manager(s)	Attendance	Average	Last Pennant
Lexington Legends (Royals)	76	60	.559	—	Scott Thorman	281,134	4,462	2018
Rome Braves (Braves)	71	65	.522	5	Rocket Wheeler	146,276	2,286	2016
Augusta GreenJackets (Giants)	67	70	.489	9 ½	Jolbert Cabrera	255,155	4,050	2008
Columbia Fireflies (Mets)	64	70	.478	11 ½	Pedro Lopez	251,586	3,755	2013
Charleston RiverDogs (Yankees)	64	72	.471	12	Julio Mosquera	305,040	4,486	Never
Asheville Tourists (Rockies)	64	73	.467	12 ½	Robinson Cancel	170,389	2,840	2014
Greenville Drive (Red Sox)	64	75	.460	13 ½	Iggy Suarez	313,507	4,823	2017

MINOR LEAGUES

CLUB BATTING

	AVG	G	AB	R	H	2B	3B	HR	RBI	BB	SO	SB	OBP	SLG
Greenville	.262	139	4681	619	1227	231	41	75	526	366	1199	90	.325	.377
Asheville	.260	137	4540	680	1180	231	35	156	619	331	1220	150	.321	.429
Lexington	.258	137	4463	682	1151	230	30	137	603	340	1276	164	.318	.415
Rome	.258	137	4561	578	1176	251	34	89	525	317	1137	78	.313	.386
Kannapolis	.254	137	4447	603	1128	245	27	85	545	393	1142	65	.321	.378
Lakewood	.251	138	4397	543	1103	230	28	95	492	355	1019	80	.313	.381
Delmarva	.250	134	4487	587	1120	214	31	81	523	365	1066	77	.313	.365
Hickory	.248	138	4468	573	1107	221	30	121	533	398	1208	145	.319	.392
West Virginia	.245	133	4329	611	1039	231	33	89	544	406	1168	104	.317	.378
Hagerstown	.243	133	4194	527	1021	223	27	74	478	411	1023	118	.317	.362
Charleston	.240	136	4398	501	1056	210	37	77	435	349	1066	86	.304	.357
Augusta	.239	137	4422	557	1055	191	35	86	481	401	1339	115	.315	.356
Columbia	.237	134	4357	538	1031	203	37	88	486	406	1003	70	.311	.361
Greensboro	.236	136	4260	525	1007	201	23	95	478	371	1229	113	.303	.361

CLUB PITCHING

	ERA	G	CG	SHO	SV	IP	H	R	ER	HR	BB	SO	AVG
Lakewood	2.74	138	7	23	49	1173	979	433	357	63	380	1305	.227
Charleston	3.29	136	1	6	40	1171	1040	519	428	77	339	1116	.236
Delmarva	3.39	134	2	10	30	1162	992	527	437	68	401	1100	.231
West Virginia	3.40	133	1	11	38	1129	1040	540	427	98	350	1066	.243
Kannapolis	3.41	137	5	11	36	1163	1022	529	440	78	417	1077	.237
Augusta	3.54	137	3	13	39	1176	1044	544	463	99	382	1258	.238
Lexington	3.61	137	2	11	36	1168	1119	591	469	129	349	1147	.250
Hickory	3.68	138	3	7	38	1172	1073	561	480	84	416	1197	.244
Rome	3.73	137	1	10	36	1171	1085	614	485	86	422	1143	.243
Columbia	3.81	134	2	7	29	1166	1136	591	494	79	376	1241	.255
Greenville	3.95	139	5	8	30	1198	1186	651	526	120	351	1154	.256
Greensboro	4.25	136	5	10	32	1143	1209	639	540	134	321	1130	.269
Hagerstown	4.58	133	3	11	25	1106	1127	667	563	110	382	1030	.262
Asheville	4.64	137	1	4	34	1178	1351	718	608	123	323	1131	.287

CLUB FIELDING

	PCT	PO	A	E	DP		PCT	PO	A	E	DP
Lakewood	.979	3518	1288	101	115	Asheville	.970	3536	1305	148	96
Augusta	.976	3527	1134	115	96	Greenville	.967	3594	1221	162	97
Delmarva	.976	3485	1321	120	112	Hagerstown	.967	3319	1178	152	94
Hickory	.976	3518	1347	122	98	Greensboro	.967	3429	1207	158	96
Columbia	.974	3498	1209	126	103	West Virginia	.966	3387	1217	163	97
Charleston	.971	3513	1344	143	103	Lexington	.966	3503	1236	169	95
Kannapolis	.971	3488	1348	144	117	Rome	.963	3513	1316	184	96

INDIVIDUAL BATTING

Batter, Club	AVG	G	AB	R	H	2B	3B	HR	RBI	BB	SO	SB
Chad Spanberger, Asheville	.315	92	349	65	110	20	3	22	75	20	82	16
Jake Scheiner, Lakewood	.296	122	453	65	134	30	5	13	67	49	81	10
Manuel Geraldo, Augusta	.294	124	486	71	143	15	1	9	52	30	121	24
Bret Boswell, Asheville	.288	97	379	69	109	20	4	17	50	21	103	7
Oneil Cruz, West Virginia	.286	103	402	66	115	25	7	14	59	34	100	11
Calvin Mitchell, West Virginia	.280	119	443	55	124	29	3	10	65	41	109	4
Nick Pratto, Lexington	.280	127	485	79	136	33	2	14	62	45	150	22
Casey Golden, Asheville	.278	124	461	92	128	23	3	34	95	38	180	24
Zach Jarrett, Delmarva	.277	129	501	74	139	26	6	14	72	41	136	4
Ryan Vilade, Asheville	.274	124	457	77	125	20	4	5	44	49	96	17

INDIVIDUAL PITCHING

Pitcher, Club	W	L	ERA	G	GS	CG	SV	IP	H	R	ER	BB	SO
Denyi Reyes, Greenville	10	3	1.89	21	18	2	0	124	92	33	26	13	122
Will Stewart, Lakewood	8	1	2.06	20	20	2	0	114	90	29	26	21	90
Tyler Phillips, Hickory	11	5	2.67	22	22	1	0	128	117	41	38	14	124
Brenan Hanifee, Delmarva	8	6	2.86	23	23	1	0	132	120	48	42	22	85
Cameron Bishop, Delmarva	9	7	2.94	22	22	1	0	126	107	47	41	20	99
Kutter Crawford, Greenville	5	4	2.96	21	21	0	0	112	104	45	37	34	120
Domingo Robles, West Virginia	9	6	2.97	21	21	0	0	115	118	60	38	26	88
Jhonathan Diaz, Greenville	11	8	3.00	26	26	1	0	153	123	60	51	39	147
Reid Anderson, Hickory	8	6	3.22	23	19	1	0	117	102	55	42	30	102
Damon Jones, Lakewood	10	7	3.41	23	22	0	0	113	105	53	43	50	123

ALL-STAR TEAM

C: William Contreras, Rome. **1B:** Chad Spanberger, Asheville. **2B:** Bret Boswell, Asheville. **3B:** Jean Carlos Encarnacion, Delmarva. **SS:** Oneil Cruz, West Virginia. **OF:** Drew Waters, Rome; Casey Golden, Asheville; Seuly Matias, Lexington. **UT:** Jake Scheiner, Lakewood; Zach Jarrett, Delmarva. **RHP:** Denyi Reyes, Greenville. **LHP:** Will Stewart, Lakewood. **RP:** Demarcus Evans, Hickory. **Most Valuable Player:** Casey Golden, Asheville. **Most Outstanding Pitcher:** Denyi Reyes, Greenville. **Most Outstanding Prospect:** Oneil Cruz, West Virginia. **Manager of the Year:** Marty Malloy, Lakewood.

DEPARTMENT LEADERS

BATTING

OBP	Scheiner, Jake, Lakewood	.372
SLG	Spanberger, Chad, Dunedin	.579
OPS	Spanberger, Chad, Dunedin	.942
R	Golden, Casey, Asheville	92
H	Geraldo, Manuel, Augusta	143
TB	Golden, Casey, Asheville	259
XBH	Golden, Casey, Asheville	60
2B	Bouchard, Sean, Asheville	34
3B	Baldwin, Logan, Augusta	10
	McCoy, Mason, Delmarva	10
HR	Golden, Casey, Asheville	34
RBI	Golden, Casey, Asheville	95
SAC	Hernandez, Yonny, Hickory	15
BB	Blackman, Tate, Kannapolis	62
	Winaker, Matt, Columbia	62
HBP	Manea, Scott, Columbia	24
SO	Golden, Casey, Asheville	180
SB	Moesquit, Kirvin, Delmarva	49
CS	Hernandez, Yonny, Hickory	15
AB/SO	Pozo, Yohel, Hickory	8.6

FIELDING

C PCT	Duran, Rodolfo, Lakewood	.995
PO	Duran, Rodolfo, Lakewood	723
A	Duran, Rodolfo, Lakewood	100
DP	Miranda, Samuel, Greenville	8
E	Melendez, MJ, Lexington	13
CS	Duran, Rodolfo, Lakewood	39
SB	Hernandez, Michael, Greensboro	68
PB	Duran, Rodolfo, Lakewood	18
1B PCT	Kirby, Ryan, Augusta	.994
PO	Pratto, Nick, Lexington	962
A	Pratto, Nick, Lexington	74
DP	Pratto, Nick, Lexington	78
E	Pratto, Nick, Lexington	14
2B PCT	Brito, Daniel, Lakewood	.990
PO	Freeman, Cole, Hagerstown	194
A	Cruz, Derian, Rome	309
DP	Brito, Daniel, Lakewood	64
E	Cruz, Derian, Rome	30
3B PCT	Encarnacion, Jean Carlos, Rome/Delmarva	.895
PO	Encarnacion, Jean Carlos, Rome/Delmarva	79
A	Encarnacion, Jean Carlos, Rome/Delmarva	203
DP	Nishioka, Tanner, Greenville	15
E	Encarnacion, Jean Carlos, Rome/Delmarva	33
SS PCT	Maton, Nick, Lakewood	.966
PO	Vilade, Ryan, Asheville	177
A	Vilade, Ryan, Asheville	277
DP	Vilade, Ryan, Asheville	63
E	Vilade, Ryan, Asheville	34
OF PCT	Ramos, Heliot, Augusta	.996
PO	Sanchez, Lolo, West Virginia	249
A	Dedelow, Craig, Kannapolis	17
DP	Baldwin, Logan, Augusta	6
E	Ortiz, Jhailyn, Lakewood	11

PITCHING

G	Doyle, Tommy, Asheville	52
GS	Rigler, Parker, Kannapolis	27
GF	Doyle, Tommy, Asheville	34
SV	Doyle, Tommy, Asheville	18
W	Diaz, Jhonathan, Greenville	11
	Phillips, Tyler, Hickory	11
L	Kennedy, Nick, Asheville	13
IP	Diaz, Jhonathan, Greenville	153
H	Kennedy, Nick, Asheville	180
R	Kennedy, Nick, Asheville	108
ER	Kennedy, Nick, Asheville	98
HB	Javier, Odalvi, Rome	17
BB	Cave, Garrett, Augusta	67
SO	Diaz, Jhonathan, Greenville	147
	Dibrell, Tony, Columbia	147
	Howard, Spencer, Lakewood	147
SO/9	Howard, Spencer, Lakewood	11.8
SO/9 (RP)	Evans, Demarcus, Hickory	16.6
BB/9	Phillips, Tyler, Hickory	1.0
WP	Stratton, Hunter, West Virginia	21
BK	Cubilete, Sergio, West Virginia	3
	Garcia, Rony, Charleston, SC	3
	7 others	3
HRA	Kennedy, Nick, Asheville	30
BAA	Stewart, Will, Lakewood	.218

MINOR LEAGUES

MINOR LEAGUES

BY JUSTIN COLEMAN

After returning to the New York-Penn League championship series for the third straight year, the Hudson Valley Renegades were dethroned as league champions by the Tri-City Valley Cats.

The Valley Cats (Astros) swept the three-games series, highlighted by a shutout performance from their pitching staff. Righthanders Shawn Dubin, Jose Alberto Rivera, Joey Gonzalez and R.J. Freure combined to strike out 17 hitters in a 2-0 victory, helping Tri-City hoist its first trophy since 2013.

While Tri-City didn't score the most runs in the league, they did manage to slug a league-best 56 home runs. The offense was anchored by outfielder Carlos Machado, who ranked third in the New York-Penn League with a .304 batting average, and infielder Luis Encarnacion, who blasted a team-high 10 home runs to help the Valley Cats win the Stedler Division with a 42-33 regular season record. The Tri-City pitching staff also played a strong role in the team's success, as they posted a league-best 741 strikeouts and 3.30 team ERA.

Five-tool outfielder and the New York-Penn League's No. 1 prospect Gilberto Celestino helped the Valley Cats with his .323 batting average before being traded to the Twins on July 27, along with fellow Astros prospect Jorge Alcala, in exchange for major league reliever Ryan Pressly.

Despite losing its offensive cog midway through the season, Tri-City was able to outscore Hudson Valley (Rays) 7-2 in the championship series.

While the league was void of elite prospect talent in 2018, there were still some impressive individual performances. A clear standout in the league was Mahoning Valley shortstop Tyler Freeman (Indians), who recorded a .352 batting average in 270 at-bats. Freeman's average remained above .350 late in the season despite the fact that he struggled to the tune of a .162 average over his final 37 at-bats of the season.

Pitching as a whole was quite good across the league, with the Brooklyn Cyclones (Mets) boasting a pair of rotation mates who put up impressive statistics during the season. Venezuelan righthander Jaison Vilera dominated with a league-best 1.83 ERA in 73.2 innings. He struck out 78 hitters and gave up just one home run, limiting opponents to a .191 average, while teammate and fellow righthander Christian James posted the league's second-best ERA (2.01) among qualified starters. James boasted a 1.13 WHIP and limited opponents to a .232 batting average.

TOP 20 PROSPECTS

1. Gilberto Celestino, OF, Tri-City (Astros)
2. Travis Swaggerty, OF, West Virginia (Pirates)
3. Luis Oviedo, RHP, Mahoning Valley (Indians)
4. Juan De Paula, RHP, Staten Island (Yankees)
5. Roansy Contreras, RHP, Staten Island (Yankees)
6. Tanner Dodson, OF/RHP, Hudson Valley (Rays)
7. Alex McKenna, OF, Tri-City (Astros)
8. Alec Bohm, 3B, Williamsport (Phillies)
9. Israel Pineda, C, Auburn (Nationals)
10. Tyler Freeman, SS, Mahoning Valley (Indians)
11. Jeremy Eierman, SS, Vermont (Athletics)
12. Rafael Marchan, C, Williamsport (Phillies)
13. Matt Sauer, RHP, Staten Island (Yankees)
14. Chris Betts, C, Hudson Valley (Rays)
15. Adam Hall, SS, Aberdeen (Orioles)
16. Jameson Hannah, OF, Vermont (Athletics)
17. Eduard Bazardo, RHP, Lowell (Red Sox)
18. Rafael Kelly, RHP, Vermont (Athletics)
19. Marcos Brito, 2B, Vermont (Athletics)
20. Jose Medina, OF, Brooklyn (Mets)

OVERALL STANDINGS

McNamara Division	W	L	PCT	GB	Manager(s)	Attendance	Average	Last Pennant
Hudson Valley Renegades (Rays)	45	30	.600	—	Blake Butera	148,156	4,004	2017
Brooklyn Cyclones (Mets)	40	35	.533	5	Edgardo Alfonzo	202,495	5,329	2001
Staten Island Yankees (Yankees)	37	36	.507	7	Lino Diaz	72,894	2,083	2011
Aberdeen IronBirds (Orioles)	38	37	.507	7	Kyle Moore	121,907	3,483	1983

Pinckney Division	W	L	PCT	GB	Manager(s)	Attendance	Average	Last Pennant
Mahoning Valley Scrappers (Indians)	42	33	.560	—	Jim Pankovits	97,204	2,700	2004
Auburn Doubledays (Nationals)	41	35	.539	1 ½	Jerad Head	43,343	1,204	2007
Batavia Muckdogs (Marlins)	36	40	.474	6 ½	Mike Jacobs	29,005	784	2008
State College Spikes (Cardinals)	36	40	.474	6 ½	Joe Kruzel	119,986	3,243	2016
West Virginia Black Bears (Pirates)	32	44	.421	10 ½	Kieran Mattison	69,430	1,827	2015
Williamsport Crosscutters (Phillies)	32	44	.421	10 ½	Pat Borders	68,475	1,902	2003

Stedler Division	W	L	PCT	GB	Manager(s)	Attendance	Average	Last Pennant
Tri-City ValleyCats (Astros)	42	33	.560	—	Jason Bell	140,036	4,119	2018
Vermont Lake Monsters (Athletics)	39	37	.513	3 ½	Aaron Nieckula	83,956	2,209	1996
Lowell Spinners (Red Sox)	37	38	.493	5	Corey Wimberly	118,319	3,381	Never
Connecticut Tigers (Tigers)	29	44	.397	12	Gary Cathcart	75,810	2,049	1998

Semifinals: Hudson Valley defeated Auburn 2-0 and Tri-City defeated Mahoning Valley 2-0 in best-of-three series. **Finals:** Tri-City defeated Hudson Valley 2-0 in a best-of-three series.

CLUB BATTING

	AVG	G	AB	R	H	2B	3B	HR	RBI	BB	SO	SB	OBP	SLG
Brooklyn	.259	75	2503	360	648	118	27	34	313	265	602	84	.338	.368
Auburn	.258	76	2550	351	658	121	25	27	311	246	601	41	.331	.357
Mahoning Valley	.253	75	2458	335	621	135	17	38	303	222	592	64	.326	.368
Aberdeen	.248	75	2410	307	598	131	12	26	266	200	587	54	.314	.345
Hudson Valley	.247	75	2438	353	601	128	18	41	300	310	600	75	.336	.364
Lowell	.244	75	2449	308	598	119	28	28	277	256	617	93	.321	.350
Williamsport	.244	76	2472	293	603	119	23	33	270	209	620	49	.310	.351
Tri-City	.243	75	2414	328	587	136	12	56	290	255	566	98	.324	.379
West Virginia	.242	76	2472	311	597	116	26	35	272	280	672	99	.325	.352
Batavia	.238	76	2488	320	592	121	19	43	282	237	693	74	.311	.354
Vermont	.233	76	2515	350	585	111	17	32	288	287	662	79	.321	.328
State College	.232	76	2535	294	587	111	19	27	254	260	603	59	.318	.322
Staten Island	.213	73	2249	253	479	117	12	37	225	202	683	39	.285	.325
Connecticut	.204	73	2283	241	466	93	14	18	207	239	710	69	.290	.281

CLUB PITCHING

	ERA	G	CG	SHO	SV	IP	H	R	ER	HR	BB	SO	AVG
Staten Island	2.60	73	0	8	22	629	526	238	182	24	201	684	.227
Brooklyn	3.21	75	0	7	16	657	571	289	234	39	241	668	.233
Tri-City	3.30	75	0	3	20	649	540	295	238	42	281	741	.223
Williamsport	3.45	76	1	6	21	650	585	304	249	32	264	674	.239
Lowell	3.49	75	1	4	14	648	579	327	251	33	275	642	.238
Hudson Valley	3.54	75	0	14	20	653	586	299	257	37	191	613	.240
Batavia	3.61	76	0	4	22	660	647	346	265	38	264	646	.254
Mahoning Valley	3.64	75	1	5	21	648	600	324	262	35	224	655	.245
Vermont	3.65	76	0	7	21	667	555	350	271	40	320	644	.224
Auburn	3.71	76	0	5	23	658	625	314	271	30	204	523	.250
State College	3.75	76	0	8	24	668	632	318	278	35	216	584	.248
Aberdeen	3.81	75	5	4	17	631	563	309	267	34	241	589	.237
Connecticut	4.02	73	1	2	18	622	570	347	278	29	283	563	.243
West Virginia	4.02	76	0	3	15	658	641	344	294	27	263	582	.257

CLUB FIELDING

	PCT	PO	A	E	DP		PCT	PO	A	E	DP
Hudson Valley	.979	1960	732	59	64	Connecticut	.969	1867	674	80	48
Auburn	.975	1973	754	70	58	State College	.969	2004	730	87	56
Brooklyn	.975	1971	709	69	52	Mahoning Valley	.969	1944	742	86	57
Staten Island	.974	1888	652	67	62	Tri-City	.967	1946	579	85	49
Williamsport	.974	1949	697	70	47	Lowell	.967	1943	750	91	79
Aberdeen	.970	1893	748	82	57	Batavia	.966	1981	729	95	55
West Virginia	.969	1974	823	88	68	Vermont	.962	2002	770	109	59

INDIVIDUAL BATTING

Batter, Club	AVG	G	AB	R	H	2B	3B	HR	RBI	BB	SO	SB
Tyler Freeman, Mahoning Valley	.352	72	270	49	95	29	4	2	38	8	22	14
J.C. Escarra, Aberdeen	.331	51	178	30	59	10	2	6	34	18	22	0
Carlos Machado, Tri-City	.304	52	194	25	59	10	1	3	28	14	26	5
Rafael Marchan, Williamsport	.301	51	196	28	59	8	2	0	12	11	18	9
Devlin Granberg, Lowell	.300	61	223	40	67	18	0	4	29	25	49	8
Pablo O'Connor, Auburn	.296	52	213	34	63	14	3	5	25	12	46	2
Adam Hall, Aberdeen	.293	62	222	35	65	9	3	1	24	17	58	22
Tyler Frank, Hudson Valley	.288	51	177	37	51	14	1	2	22	33	28	3
Jonah Bride, Vermont	.287	54	195	29	56	17	0	3	34	24	35	3
Stanley Espinal, State College	.286	64	241	34	69	9	4	8	41	19	47	1

INDIVIDUAL PITCHING

Pitcher, Club	W	L	ERA	G	GS	CG	SV	IP	H	R	ER	BB	SO
Jaison Vilera, Brooklyn	5	2	1.83	13	13	0	0	74	50	20	15	22	78
Christian James, Brooklyn	4	2	2.01	13	13	0	0	72	61	22	16	20	45
Ethan Lindow, Williamsport	3	2	2.19	13	13	1	0	70	58	20	17	19	63
Manuel Silva, Williamsport	2	5	2.60	13	12	0	0	62	54	22	18	27	60
Francys Peguero, Auburn	5	3	2.93	14	13	0	0	68	54	22	22	14	46
Zack Draper, Mahoning Valley	7	4	3.04	14	13	1	0	68	69	30	23	14	65
Humberto Mejia, Batavia	1	6	3.30	15	12	0	0	63	55	27	23	14	59
Nicholas Padilla, Hudson Valley	3	5	3.30	13	12	0	0	60	54	27	22	12	44
Jose Vasquez, Connecticut	5	4	3.45	13	13	1	0	60	61	36	23	23	42
Alberto Guerrero, Batavia	3	6	3.49	15	14	0	0	70	61	31	27	22	63

DEPARTMENT LEADERS

BATTING

OBP	Frank, Tyler, Hudson Valley	.425
SLG	Escarra, J.C., Aberdeen	.511
OPS	Escarra, J.C., Aberdeen	.929
R	Reynolds, Sean, Batavia	49
	Freeman, Tyler, Mahoning Valley	49
H	Freeman, Tyler, Mahoning Valley	95
TB	Freeman, Tyler, Mahoning Valley	138
XBH	Freeman, Tyler, Mahoning Valley	35
2B	Freeman, Tyler, Mahoning Valley	29
3B	Adolph, Ross, Brooklyn	12
HR	Reynolds, Sean, Batavia	17
RBI	Reynolds, Sean, Batavia	52
SAC	Torrealba, Eduardo, Staten Island	9
BB	Reynolds, Sean, Batavia	42
HBP	Figuera, Edwin, State College	20
SO	Reynolds, Sean, Batavia	133
SB	Amaral, Daniel, West Virginia	25
CS	Medina, Jose Miguel, Brooklyn	8
AB/SO	Freeman, Tyler, Mahoning Valley	12.3

FIELDING

C PCT	Betts, Chris, Hudson Valley	.992
PO	Betts, Chris, Hudson Valley	430
A	Marchan, Rafael, Williamsport	57
DP	Meyer, Nick, Brooklyn	5
	Marchan, Rafael, Williamsport	5
E	Meyer, Nick, Brooklyn	8
CS	Marchan, Rafael, Williamsport	20
SB	Marchan, Rafael, Williamsport	48
PB	McMillan, Sam, Connecticut	14
1B PCT	Whalen, Brady, State College	.990
PO	Reynolds, Sean, Batavia	585
A	Reynolds, Sean, Batavia	46
DP	Reynolds, Sean, Batavia	52
E	Reynolds, Sean, Batavia	11
2B PCT	Gonzalez, Brayan, Williamsport	.960
PO	Gonzalez, Brayan, Williamsport	80
A	Brito, Marcos, Vermont	134
DP	Torres, Alexis, Aberdeen	29
	Brito, Marcos, Vermont	29
E	Brito, Marcos, Vermont	13
3B PCT	Yahn, Willy, Aberdeen	.958
PO	Figuera, Edwin, State College	46
A	Yahn, Willy, Aberdeen	117
DP	Chaparro, Andres, Staten Island	14
E	Pujols, Henry, Mahoning Valley	17
SS PCT	Proctor, Ford, Hudson Valley	.969
PO	Perez, Delvin, State College	91
A	Sanchez, Jose, Auburn	177
DP	Proctor, Ford, Hudson Valley	38
E	Sanchez, Jose, Auburn	17
OF PCT	Aklinski, Ben, Williamsport	1.000
PO	Ynfante, Wadye, State College	183
A	Soto, Junior, Staten Island	11
DP	Soto, Junior, Staten Island	3
	Encarnacion, Jerar, Batavia	3
E	Encarnacion, Jerar, Batavia	6

PITCHING

G	Oxford, Billy, Brooklyn	26
GS	Manasa, Alex, West Virginia	15
	Mota, Juan, Mahoning Valley	15
GF	Chentouf, Yaya, Connecticut	18
	Hamann, Kevin, State College	18
SV	Hamann, Kevin, State College	10
	Killgore, Keylan, Williamsport	10
W	Oxford, Billy, Brooklyn	8
L	Manasa, Alex, West Virginia	7
IP	Manasa, Alex, West Virginia	80
H	Manasa, Alex, West Virginia	84
R	Mota, Juan, Mahoning Valley	48
ER	Mota, Juan, Mahoning Valley	42
HB	Mota, Juan, Mahoning Valley	12
BB	Mora, Jose, Vermont	39
SO	Vilera, Jaison, Brooklyn	78
SO/9	Vilera, Jaison, Brooklyn	9.5
SO/9 (RP)	Ross, Austin, Wilmington	14.5
BB/9	Cordero, Diego, State College	1.6
WP	Morales, Francisco, Williamsport	15
BK	Cordero, Diego, State College	6
HRA	Casadilla, Franyel, State College	8
	Mejia, Humberto, Batavia	8
BAA	Vilera, Jaison, Brooklyn	.191

MINOR LEAGUES

BY JOSH NORRIS

The 2018 Northwest League season can be divided neatly into two parts: the regular season and the postseason.

The regular season was dominated by the Hillsboro Hops, who whipped through the summer with a 51-25 record that was by far the best in the league. They won both halves, and over the last four seasons have taken seven of eight halves.

The Hops were led on the mound by right-hander Matt Tabor, with a 3.26 ERA that was good for fourth in the league. He was backed up by catcher Andy Yerzy and outfielder Jake McCarthy. All three players ranked among the league's Top 20 prospects.

Because the NWL utilizes a split-season format, however, things got very weird toward season's end. Hillsboro's opponent in the South Division Series was the Eugene Emeralds, who made the playoffs despite finishing with the league's worst overall record. The Emeralds snatched a postseason berth because the other two clubs in their division—Salem-Keizer and Boise—were slightly worse in the second half.

Naturally, Eugene flipped the script once the postseason began. The club, which had embraced its "Bad News Ems" persona, scored a two-game sweep of Hillsboro to move on to the team's second championship appearance in three seasons.

There, the Emeralds received even more good news. Spokane beat Everett in the North Division series, but its stadium was unavailable due to a previous commitment, meaning all five potential NWLCS games would be played at Eugene's PK Park.

The Indians were led by a stout offense that included Curtis Terry, who led the league in runs and homers, and Diosbel Arias, who won the NWL batting title with a .366 average. They also had Cuban import Julio Pablo Martinez, who brought speed and power to the top of the lineup.

After winning the first two games as the road team in Eugene, the Emeralds finished the

TOP 20 PROSPECTS

1. Joey Bart, C, Salem-Keizer (Giants)
2. Hans Crouse, RHP, Spokane (Rangers)
3. Brailyn Marquez, RHP, Eugene (Cubs)
4. Xavier Edwards, SS, Tri-City (Padres)
5. Geraldo Perdomo, SS, Hillsboro (D-backs)
6. Julio Pablo Martinez, OF, Spokane (Rangers)
7. Tucupita Marcano, 2B, Tri-City (Padres)
8. Nelson Velazquez, OF, Eugene (Cubs)
9. Diosbel Arias, 3B, Spokane (Rangers)
10. Gregory Santos, RHP, Salem-Keizer (Giants)
11. Jake Wong, RHP, Salem-Keizer (Giants)
12. Josh Stowers, OF, Everett (Mariners)
13. Cal Raleigh, C, Everett (Mariners)
14. Matt Tabor, RHP, Hillsboro (D-backs)
15. Andy Yerzy, C, Hillsboro (D-backs)
16. Owen Miller, SS, Tri-City (Padres)
17. Grant Little, OF, Tri-City (Padres)
18. Henry Henry, RHP, Tri-City (Padres)
19. Terrin Vavra, SS, Boise (Rockies)
20. Jake McCarthy, OF, Hillsboro (D-backs)

STANDINGS: SPLIT SEASON

FIRST HALF

North	W	L	PCT	GB	South	W	L	PCT	GB
Everett	20	18	.526	—	Hillsboro	24	14	.632	—
Vancouver	19	19	.500	1	Boise	21	17	.553	3
Tri-City	18	20	.474	2	Salem-Keizer	20	18	.526	4
Spokane	16	22	.421	4	Eugene	14	24	.368	10

SECOND HALF

North	W	L	PCT	GB	South	W	L	PCT	GB
Spokane	22	16	.579	—	Hillsboro	27	11	.711	—
Vancouver	21	17	.553	1	Eugene	17	21	.447	10
Everett	20	18	.474	4	Salem-Keizer	16	22	.421	11
Tri-City	17	21	.447	5	Boise	14	24	.368	13

Playoffs—Semifinals: Spokane defeated Everett 2-1 and Eugene defeated Hillsboro 2-0 in best-of-three series.
Finals: Eugene defeated Spokane 3-0 in a best-of-five series.

bizarre championship run when Spokane closer Emmanuel Clase's ninth-inning balk brought home the clinching run.

The Northwest League also was where Giants catcher Joey Bart, the No. 2 overall pick in the 2018 draft, got the bulk of his work during his pro debut. Bart, who spent his college career at Georgia Tech and was in the mix for the No. 1 overall pick, swatted 13 home runs, good for third on the circuit behind Spokane's Terry.

OVERALL STANDINGS

North Division	W	L	PCT	GB	Manager(s)	Attendance	Average	Last Pennant
Vancouver Canadians (Blue Jays)	40	36	.526	—	Dallas McPherson	239,086	6,292	2017
Everett AquaSox (Mariners)	38	38	.500	2	Jose Moreno	111,599	2,937	2010
Spokane Indians (Rangers)	38	38	.500	2	Kenny Holmberg	198,423	5,222	2008
Tri-City Dust Devils (Padres)	35	41	.461	5	Mike McCoy	86,283	2,332	Never

South Division	W	L	PCT	GB	Manager(s)	Attendance	Average	Last Pennant
Hillsboro Hops (D-backs)	51	25	.671	—	Shawn Roof	130,286	3,429	2015
Salem-Keizer Volcanoes (Giants)	36	40	.474	15	Hector Borg	72,094	1,897	2009
Boise Hawks (Rockies)	35	41	.461	16	Scott Little	126,192	3,321	2004
Eugene Emeralds (Cubs)	31	45	.408	20	Steve Lerud	125,967	3,315	2018

CLUB BATTING

	AVG	G	AB	R	H	2B	3B	HR	RBI	BB	SO	SB	OBP	SLG
Salem-Keizer	.281	76	2692	418	757	170	21	88	376	204	645	30	.343	.458
Boise	.257	76	2588	368	665	121	34	52	333	242	711	105	.327	.390
Everett	.253	76	2533	358	641	134	13	56	322	275	603	71	.331	.383
Hillsboro	.252	76	2555	349	643	136	26	54	303	254	678	125	.332	.389
Spokane	.250	76	2553	364	638	119	13	63	329	284	700	43	.335	.381
Tri-City	.246	76	2557	340	630	124	21	34	294	262	644	66	.324	.351
Vancouver	.241	76	2466	315	595	136	25	47	283	238	627	122	.315	.374
Eugene	.234	76	2496	278	583	125	14	38	243	213	666	97	.301	.341

CLUB PITCHING

	ERA	G	CG	SHO	SV	IP	H	R	ER	HR	BB	SO	AVG
Hillsboro	3.24	76	0	6	30	685	581	286	247	52	205	685	.230
Vancouver	3.37	76	0	8	20	668	580	299	250	45	248	678	.232
Spokane	3.80	76	0	4	19	666	625	331	281	49	244	671	.246
Tri-City	3.82	76	0	5	20	671	636	347	285	38	249	709	.250
Everett	3.97	76	0	3	19	664	632	339	293	70	253	666	.253
Eugene	4.13	76	0	3	13	669	623	367	307	51	281	665	.247
Boise	4.38	76	0	4	17	674	750	396	328	60	242	604	.282
Salem-Keizer	4.74	76	0	1	18	674	725	425	355	67	250	596	.274

CLUB FIELDING

	PCT	PO	A	E	DP		PCT	PO	A	E	DP
Hillsboro	.980	2056	745	58	67	Tri-City	.970	2032	672	85	50
Everett	.978	1991	784	63	64	Eugene	.969	2007	724	87	69
Spokane	.972	1997	689	77	53	Vancouver	.968	2005	664	88	56
Salem-Keizer	.970	2023	751	86	49	Boise	.967	2022	813	97	62

INDIVIDUAL BATTING

Batter, Club	AVG	G	AB	R	H	2B	3B	HR	RBI	BB	SO	SB
Diosbel Arias, Spokane	.366	61	224	43	82	15	2	3	44	33	39	5
Bobby Honeyman, Everett	.346	58	228	32	79	12	4	3	29	12	24	4
Curtis Terry, Spokane	.337	67	246	51	83	17	2	15	60	32	64	1
Owen Miller, Tri-City	.335	49	191	22	64	8	3	2	20	15	24	4
Diego Rincones, Salem-Keizer	.315	61	257	30	81	15	0	7	34	10	32	0
Wander Franco, Salem-Keizer	.314	56	210	36	66	24	2	5	36	13	41	0
Kyle McPherson, Salem-Keizer	.314	65	280	49	88	23	3	7	32	23	44	2
Luke Morgan, Boise	.312	67	260	46	81	17	4	39	24	60	16	9
Otto Lopez, Vancouver	.297	51	175	31	52	7	4	3	22	26	21	13
Andy Yerzy, Hillsboro	.297	63	239	30	71	11	1	8	34	28	67	0

INDIVIDUAL PITCHING

Pitcher, Club	W	L	ERA	G	GS	CG	SV	IP	H	R	ER	BB	SO
Faustino Carrera, Eugene	5	2	2.54	13	9	0	0	67	48	20	19	19	58
Josh Winckowski, Vancouver	4	5	2.78	13	13	0	0	68	68	27	21	15	71
Orlando Razo, Everett	5	3	3.24	15	15	0	0	78	74	34	28	25	65
Seth Nordlin, Spokane	4	1	3.82	13	12	0	0	68	63	31	29	14	79
Elio Silva, Vancouver	3	4	3.82	14	13	0	0	66	56	33	28	20	40
Angel Acevedo, Tri-City	4	3	3.88	12	11	0	0	65	55	30	28	16	54
Jake Latz, Spokane	6	2	3.93	13	13	0	0	71	63	39	31	24	67
Kenny Hernandez, Hillsboro	6	3	4.37	16	5	0	0	68	81	34	33	7	59
Jheyson Caraballo, Everett	4	5	5.12	14	14	0	0	63	69	40	36	25	48
Pearson McMahan, Boise	3	5	6.03	15	14	0	0	69	92	54	46	33	62

ALL-STAR TEAM

C: Joey Bart, Salem-Keizer. **1B:** Curtis Terry, Spokane. **2B:** Kyle McPherson, Salem-Keizer. **3B:** Bobby Honeyman, Everett. **SS:** Diosbel Arias, Spokane. **OF:** Luke Morgan, Boise; Diego Rincones, Salem-Keizer, Otto Lopez, Vancouver. **DH:** Andy Yerzy, Hillsboro. **P:** Josh Winckowski, Vancouver; Josh Green, Hillsboro; Brailyn Marquez, Eugene; Jordan Guerrero, Tri-City; Matt Tabor, Hillsboro. **Player of the Year:** Curtis Terry, Spokane. **Pitcher of the Year:** Josh Winckowski, Vancouver.

DEPARTMENT LEADERS

BATTING

OBP	Diosbel, Arias, Spokane	.451
SLG	Bart, Joey, Salem-Keizer	.613
OPS	Terry, Curtis, Spokane	1.040
R	Terry, Curtis, Spokane	51
H	McPherson, Kyle, Salem-Keizer	88
TB	Terry, Curtis, Spokane	149
XBH	Villar, David, Salem-Keizer	35
2B	Franco, Wander, Salem-Keizer	24
3B	Morgan, Luke, Boise	7
HR	Terry, Curtis, Spokane	15
RBI	Terry, Curtis, Spokane	60
SAC	Kirwer, Tanner, Vancouver	4
BB	Harris, Cade, Boise	43
HBP	Terry, Curtis, Spokane	11
SO	Martinez, Francis, Hillsboro	88
SB	Kelli, Fernando, Eugene	28
	Kirwer, Tanner, Vancouver	28
CS	Kelli, Fernando, Eugene	13
AB/SO	Honeyman, Bobby, Everett	9.5

FIELDING

C PCT	Yerzy, Andy, Hillsboro	.995
PO	Hunt, Blake, Tri-City	422
A	Hunt, Blake, Tri-City	55
DP	Yerzy, Andy, Hillsboro	5
E	Hunt, Blake, Tri-City	9
CS	Hunt, Blake, Tri-City	26
SB	Hunt, Blake, Tri-City	63
PB	Soto, Jonathan, Eugene	11
1B PCT	Paulsen, Justin, Tri-City	.990
PO	Martinez, Francis, Hillsboro	430
A	Paulsen, Justin, Tri-City	41
DP	Martinez, Francis, Hillsboro	36
E	Jipping, Daniel, Boise	8
2B PCT	Lynch, Keshawn, Hillsboro	.990
PO	Lynch, Keshawn, Hillsboro	93
A	McPherson, Kyle, Salem-Keizer	116
DP	Podkul, Nick, Vancouver	28
E	Podkul, Nick, Vancouver	8
3B PCT	Villar, David, Salem-Keizer	.920
PO	Villar, David, Salem-Keizer	39
A	Villar, David, Salem-Keizer	111
DP	Bohling, Jeff, Boise	7
	Caballero, Jose, Hillsboro	7
E	Villar, David, Salem-Keizer	13
SS PCT	Vazquez, Luis, Eugene	.970
PO	Vazquez, Luis, Eugene	88
A	Vazquez, Luis, Eugene	141
DP	Vazquez, Luis, Eugene	34
E	Kopach, Connor, Everett	12
OF PCT	McConnell, Charlie, Everett	1.000
PO	Martinez, Julio Pablo, Spokane	140
A	Rincones, Diego, Salem-Keizer	11
DP	McConnell, Charlie, Everett	2
	Edie, Mikey, Salem-Keizer	2
E	Velazquez, Nelson, Eugene	7

PITCHING

G	Valdez, Jefry, Boise	27
GS	Razo, Orlando, Everett	15
GF	Guerrero, Jordan, Tri-City	20
	Tona, Jesus, Salem-Keizer	20
SV	Clase, Emmanuel, Spokane	12
	Tona, Jesus, Salem-Keizer	12
W	McAffer, Will, Vancouver	7
L	Espada, Jose, Vancouver	7
IP	Razo, Orlando, Everett	78
H	McMahan, Pearson, Boise	92
R	McMahan, Pearson, Boise	54
ER	McMahan, Pearson, Boise	46
HB	Keating, Sam, Tri-City	12
	Tiedemann, Tai, Spokane	12
BB	Tiedemann, Tai, Spokane	35
SO	Nordlin, Seth, Spokane	79
SO/9	Nordlin, Seth, Spokane	10.4
SO/9 (RP)	Uvila, Cole, Spokane	13.6
BB/9	Nordlin, Seth, Spokane	1.7
WP	Albertos, Jose, Eugene	16
BK	Carrera, Faustino, Eugene	3
HRA	Hernandez, Kenny, Hillsboro	11
	Ocando, Jeffri, Boise	11
BAA	Acevedo, Angel, Tri-City	.220

MINOR LEAGUES

BY CARLOS COLLAZO

Elizabethton won the Rookie-level Appalachian League title for the second year in a row, topping Princeton two games to none in the finals. The Twins' Rookie-level affiliate now has 12 Appy League titles since 1974—the most of any team during that span.

While the 2017 edition of the Elizabethton club featured a handful of Top 20 Prospects, the 2018 version places only one: catcher/first baseman Ryan Jeffers. A 2018 second-round pick out of UNC Wilmington, Jeffers led the league in average (.422) and on-base percentage (.523).

Runner-up Princeton led the league in OPS and also employed the services of the consensus top prospect in the league: 17-year-old shortstop Wander Franco. He established himself as one of the top prospects in baseball in his first pro season.

Franco's presence alone makes the Appy League a stronger prospect crop than 2017, when Venezuelan shortstop Kevin Maitan topped the list. In addition to Franco, the 2018 group features an exciting combination of recent decorated draft picks, high-pedigree, high-ceiling international signees and a handful of college players who opened eyes.

The mix of promising talent from stateside players recently drafted, young international prospects having success and the breakout campaign of Franco allow the 2018 crop to top last year's, but you only have to go back to 2016—headlined by Blue Jays third baseman Vladimir Guerrerero Jr.—to get another class with as much talent, which speaks to the usual strength of the Appy League.

Following Franco are first-round high school draft picks, third baseman Nolan Gorman (Cardinals) and outfielder Jarred Kelenic (Mets), who both showcased big future potential with some of the best raw power in the league (Gorman) and an all-around toolset and polished approach in

TOP 20 PROSPECTS

1. Wander Franco, SS, Princeton (Rays)
2. Nolan Gorman, 3B, Johnson City (Cardinals)
3. Jarred Kelenic, OF, Kingsport (Mets)
4. Eric Pardinho, RHP, Bluefield (Blue Jays)
5. Trevor Larnach, OF, Elizabethton (Twins)
6. Mike Siani, OF, Greeneville (Reds)
7. Mark Vientos, 3B, Kingsport (Mets)
8. Shane Baz, RHP, Bristol (Pirates)/Princeton (Rays)
9. Everson Pereira, OF, Pulaski (Yankees)
10. Josiah Gray, RHP, Greeneville (Reds)
11. Shervyen Newton, SS, Kingsport (Mets)
12. Alejandro Kirk, C, Bluefield (Blue Jays)
13. Luis Medina, RHP, Pulaski (Yankees)
14. Luis Rijo, RHP, Pulaski (Yankees)/Elizabethton (Twins)
15. Ryan Jeffers, C/1B, Elizabethton (Twins)
16. Hagen Danner, C, Bluefield (Blue Jays)
17. C.J. Alexander, 3B, Danville (Braves)
18. Austin Cox, LHP, Burlington (Royals)
19. Luis Gil, RHP, Pulaski (Yankees)
20. Lyon Richardson, RHP, Greeneville (Reds)

the batter's box (Kelenic).

While most prospects who make the Appy League list will spend a good bit of time in the minors before debuting in the majors, there were a few impressive college hitters who stood out and could move through their respective farm systems quicker, including Jeffers, outfielder Trevor Larnach (Twins) and third baseman C.J. Alexander (Braves).

While Elizabethtown won back-to-back league championships, the Johnson City Cardinals were voted as Organization of the Year after setting a single-season attendance record of 68,881 fans. For his part, Johnson City first-year general manager Zac Clark was named the 2018 Executive of the Year. Pulaski Yankees general manager Betsy Haugh received the league's Woman of Excellence Award for the second straight year, helped lead the organization to a league-best attendance and was also the recipient of the Rawlings Woman Executive of the Year Award.

OVERALL STANDINGS

Eastern Division	W	L	PCT	GB	Manager(s)	Attendance	Average	Last Pennant
Princeton Rays (Rays)	44	22	.667	—	Danny Sheaffer	23,549	760	1994
Bluefield Blue Jays (Blue Jays)	42	26	.618	3	Dennis Holmberg	20,018	646	2001
Danville Braves (Braves)	33	35	.485	12	Barrett Kleinknecht	34,766	1,054	2009
Pulaski Yankees (Yankees)	32	36	.471	13	Nick Ortiz	91,226	2,764	2013
Burlington Royals (Royals)	25	43	.368	20	Brooks Conrad	36,541	1,142	1993
Western Division	**W**	**L**	**PCT**	**GB**	**Manager(s)**	**Attendance**	**Average**	**Last Pennant**
Elizabethton Twins (Twins)	39	27	.591	—	Ray Smith	15,329	529	2018
Kingsport Mets (Mets)	33	35	.485	7	Sean Ratliff	28,928	904	1995
Bristol Pirates (Pirates)	31	37	.456	9	Miguel Perez	21,941	708	2002
Johnson City Cardinals (Cardinals)	31	37	.456	9	Roberto Espinoza	68,881	2,222	2016
Greeneville Reds (Reds)	28	40	.412	12	Gookie Dawkins	48,021	1,549	2015

Semifinals: Princeton defeated Bluefield 2-1 and Elizabethwton defeated Kingsport 2-1 in best-of-three series. **Finals:** Elizabethton defeated Princeton 2-0 in a best-of-three series.

CLUB BATTING

	AVG	G	AB	R	H	2B	3B	HR	RBI	BB	SO	SB	OBP	SLG
Princeton	.288	66	2191	403	631	113	28	68	342	241	506	57	.366	.458
Elizabethton	.280	66	2222	375	623	110	12	58	329	239	502	50	.357	.419
Johnson City	.273	68	2274	394	620	126	11	75	343	298	598	42	.364	.437
Bluefield	.271	68	2270	395	615	116	32	45	336	291	547	88	.362	.410
Kingsport	.269	68	2285	438	614	113	18	52	377	328	572	87	.369	.402
Greeneville	.259	68	2284	350	592	101	17	52	311	234	572	24	.336	.387
Danville	.253	68	2275	314	575	106	23	27	278	244	598	43	.333	.355
Bristol	.250	68	2223	364	556	96	20	48	302	328	568	68	.354	.376
Burlington	.243	68	2249	322	546	112	23	37	275	244	572	63	.326	.362
Pulaski	.234	68	2271	325	531	94	23	48	277	277	712	53	.328	.359

CLUB PITCHING

	ERA	G	CG	SHO	SV	IP	H	R	ER	HR	BB	SO	AVG
Danville	3.74	68	1	2	14	589	565	304	245	38	250	545	.250
Pulaski	3.89	68	0	3	15	596	550	311	258	43	267	698	.241
Elizabethton	4.11	66	0	4	17	563	549	319	257	31	246	574	.253
Princeton	4.35	66	0	5	22	550	539	312	266	52	244	571	.254
Bluefield	4.60	68	0	3	17	581	539	336	297	62	262	600	.244
Kingsport	4.96	68	1	3	10	583	595	408	321	60	328	533	.264
Burlington	5.32	68	2	6	10	579	611	394	342	48	295	610	.266
Greeneville	5.47	68	0	0	12	580	619	424	353	51	327	574	.269
Johnson City	5.61	68	2	3	13	574	722	430	358	68	195	522	.307
Bristol	5.67	68	0	5	17	581	614	442	366	57	310	540	.267

CLUB FIELDING

	PCT	PO	A	E	DP		PCT	PO	A	E	DP
Bluefield	.973	1743	657	67	59	Burlington	.964	1737	641	88	43
Princeton	.967	1650	572	75	59	Pulaski	.963	1789	594	91	41
Danville	.967	1768	633	83	66	Bristol	.958	1744	698	107	75
Kingsport	.965	1749	646	86	73	Elizabethton	.958	1689	616	101	65
Johnson City	.964	1722	685	89	69	Greeneville	.958	1741	536	101	49

INDIVIDUAL BATTING

Batter, Club	AVG	G	AB	R	H	2B	3B	HR	RBI	BB	SO	SB
Connor Hollis, Princeton	.365	48	170	48	62	11	0	7	26	28	30	8
Cal Stevenson, Bluefield	.359	53	195	61	70	13	6	2	29	53	21	20
Alejandro Kirk, Bluefield	.354	58	206	31	73	10	1	10	57	33	21	2
Wander Franco, Princeton	.351	61	242	46	85	10	7	11	57	27	19	4
Luis Santana, Kingsport	.348	53	204	34	71	13	0	4	35	27	23	8
Leandro Cedeno, Johnson City	.336	59	223	47	75	13	1	14	47	22	69	2
Dominic Abbadessa, Bluefield	.311	59	238	42	74	14	3	2	29	14	47	18
Jonah Davis, Bristol	.306	51	206	46	63	15	6	12	34	27	59	6
Rafael Lantigua, Bluefield	.303	48	165	28	50	7	1	1	23	30	33	7
Guillermo Granadillo, Kingsport	.303	51	198	44	60	3	0	1	23	26	38	21

INDIVIDUAL PTICHING

Pitcher, Club	W	L	ERA	G	GS	CG	SV	IP	H	R	ER	BB	SO
Marcelo Martinez, Burlington	5	3	2.68	10	10	1	0	57	46	18	17	11	71
Dilmer Mejia, Danville	5	4	2.87	13	13	0	0	69	65	29	22	24	53
Tommy Parsons, Johnson City	5	1	3.00	13	9	1	1	57	59	23	19	10	43
Dionis Zamora, Johnson City	2	3	3.86	12	11	0	0	61	64	33	26	20	57
Jose Montilla, Danville	1	4	4.37	13	13	1	0	70	83	35	34	19	53
Nathanael Perez, Bluefield	3	1	4.47	12	12	0	0	56	63	31	28	21	59
Yerelmy Garcia, Burlington	5	2	4.58	11	8	1	0	55	55	31	28	14	35
Elvis Luciano, Burlington	3	5	4.66	11	11	0	0	56	55	30	29	20	56
Steven Jennings, Bristol	3	4	4.82	13	13	0	0	65	68	44	35	27	53
Kyle Leahy, Johnson City	4	3	5.52	13	10	0	2	59	88	48	36	11	45

ALL-STAR TEAM

C: Roberto Alvarez, Princeton. **1B:** Chris Williams, Elizabethton. **2B:** Luis Santana, Kingsport. **3B:** Nolan Gorman, Johnson City. **SS:** Wander Franco, Princeton. **OF:** Jonah Davis, Bristol; Jordan Qsar, Princeton; Cal Stevenson, Bluefield. **DH:** Alejandro Kirk, Bluefield. **UT:** Connor Hollis, Princeton; Guillermo Granadillo, Kingsport. **RHP:** Tommy Parsons, Johnson City. **LHP:** Dilmer Mejia, Danville. **RP:** Sean Rackoski, Bluefield. **Most Valuable Player:** Wander Franco, Princeton. **Pitcher of the Year:** Dilmer Mejia, Danville. **Manager of the Year:** Danny Sheaffer, Princeton.

DEPARTMENT LEADERS

BATTING

OBP	Stevenson, Cal, Bluefield	.494
SLG	Davis, Jonah, Bristol	.612
OPS	Hollis, Connor, Princeton	1.022
R	Stevenson, Cal, Bluefield	61
H	Franco, Wander, Princeton	85
TB	Franco, Wander, Princeton	142
XBH	Davis, Jonah, Bristol	33
2B	Newton, Shervyen, Kingsport	16
3B	Neal, DJ, Bluefield	9
	Alexander, Evan, Pulaski	9
HR	Williams, Chris	Elizabethton
15		
RBI	Franco, Wander, Princeton	57
	Kirk, Alejandro, Bluefield	57
SAC	Ngoepe, Victor, Bristol	6
BB	Stevenson, Cal, Bluefield	53
HBP	Cedeno, Leandro, Johnson City	11
SO	Gomez, Nelson, Pulaski	93
SB	Granadillo, Guillermo, Kingsport	21
CS	Granadillo, Guillermo, Kingsport	8
AB/SO	Franco, Wander, Princeton	12.7

FIELDING

C PCT	Alvarez, Roberto, Princeton	.991
PO	Alvarez, Roberto, Princeton	378
A	Alvarez, Roberto, Princeton	54
DP	Alvarez, Roberto, Princeton	7
	Fermin, Freddy, Burlington	7
E	Narvaez, Carlos, Pulaski	6
CS	Alvarez, Roberto, Princeton	20
SB	Oliver, Hunter, Greeneville	50
PB	Martinez, Domingo, Kingsport	10
1B PCT	Hernandez, Kenny, Kingsport	.988
PO	Williams, Chris, Elizabethton	454
A	Martin, Mason, Bristol	36
DP	Martin, Mason, Bristol	57
E	Tatis, Carlos, Pulaski	10
2B PCT	Cullen, Greg, Danville	.987
PO	Williams, Donivan, Johnson City	118
A	Santana, Luis, Kingsport	140
DP	Santana, Luis, Kingsport	42
E	Willems, Jonathan, Greeneville	19
3B PCT	Vientos, Mark, Kingsport	.902
PO	Robles, Alex, Elizabethton	33
A	Bewley, Brhet, Burlington	89
DP	Gorman, Nolan, Johnson City	20
E	Apostel, Sherten, Bristol	17
SS PCT	De Los Santos, Luis, Bluefield	.962
PO	Ngoepe, Victor, Bristol	78
A	Ngoepe, Victor, Bristol	171
DP	Ngoepe, Victor, Bristol	46
E	Ngoepe, Victor, Bristol	19
OF PCT	Stevenson, Cal, Bluefield	.992
PO	Siani, Mike, Greeneville	114
A	Negret, Juan Carlos, Burlington	7
	Stevenson, Cal, Bluefield	7
	Kelenic, Jarred, Kingsport	7
DP	Siani, Mike, Greeneville	2
	Stevenson, Cal, Bluefield	2
	4 others	2
E	Ozuna, Reniel, Greeneville	8

PITCHING

G	Rackoski, Sean, Bluefield	23
GS	Jennings, Steven, Bristol	13
GS	Mejia, Dilmer, Danville	13
	2 others	13
GF	Rackoski, Sean, Bluefield	21
SV	Wilson, Brad, Bluefield	7
W	Rackoski, Sean, Bluefield	7
L	Oca, David, Johnson City	6
	Santana, Roger, Bristol	6
IP	Montilla, Jose, Danville	70
H	Leahy, Kyle, Johnson City	88
R	Leahy, Kyle, Johnson City	48
ER	Santana, Roger, Bristol	38
HB	Almonte, Josh, Bluefield	11
BB	Medina, Luis, Pulaski	46
SO	Martinez, Marcelo, Burlington	71
SO/9	Martinez, Marcelo, Burlington	11.2
SO/9 (RP)	Hinton, Kyle, Burlington	13.5
BB/9	Martinez, Marcelo, Burlington	1.7
WP	McCall, Liam, Kingsport	18
BK	Garcia, Oliver, Bristol	4
HRA	Zamora, Dionis, Johnson City	12
BAA	Martinez, Marcelo, Burlington	.216

MINOR LEAGUES

BY BILL MITCHELL

The Great Falls Voyagers experienced quite the schizophrenic season in 2018, before eventually capturing its first league championship since 2011 with a two-game sweep of Grand Junction (Rockies) in the best-of-three championship series.

The White Sox affiliate started the season strong with a 22-16 first half record before slumping to a 12-25 record in the second half. Manager Tim Esmay's club rallied in the postseason, however, sweeping Billings (Reds) to move into the finals. Grand Junction bested 2017 Pioneer League champions Ogden (Dodgers) in the South division qualifier, taking two of three against the Raptors.

Grand Junction infielder Coco Montes earned league MVP honors by posting a .333/.413/.513 slash line and anchoring the left side of the Rockies infield, while Idaho Falls lefthander J.C. Cloney (Royals) was named the league's pitcher of the year after recording an outstanding 9-0, 1.93 record in his second pro season.

Great Falls infielder Amado Nunez led all hitters with a .357 batting average in his second try in the league, boosting his OPS from a meager .493 in 2017 to .962 in 2018. Grand Junction first baseman Grant Lavigne recorded the best on-base percentage (.477) while Missoula first baseman Zack Shannon (D-backs) was tops in all power categories (14 home runs, .677 slugging percentage, 1.116 OPS). Idaho Falls' Tyler James swiped 38 bases to easily lead in that category after also being the top basestealer in the Arizona League in 2017.

Cloney's nine wins led all pitchers, while Ogden righthander Jose Chacin finishing with the best ERA (2.85) among qualifying pitchers. Grand Junction's Alexander Martinez more than doubled the saves total (19) of any other reliever.

Lavigne turned an outstanding season in his pro debut into the No. 1 ranking on the league's prospects list, with the New Hampshire high school product showing advanced plate discipline and pitch recognition along with the projection to add more over-the-fence power.

Shortstop Brice Turang (Brewers) and lefthander Ryan Rolison (Rockies) were the only 2018 first-round picks to accrue enough playing time to rank on the league's Top 20 Prospects list. Fifth overall pick Jonathan India (Reds) made a circuitous stopover in Billings in between stints with Rookie-level Greeneville and low Class A Dayton, while outfielder Jordyn Adams (Angels) played in nine games with Orem before his season ended after an outfield collision resulted in a broken jaw.

TOP 20 PROSPECTS

1. Grant Lavigne, 1B, Grand Junction (Rockies)
2. Brice Turang, SS, Helena (Brewers)
3. Ryan Rolison, LHP, Grand Junction (Rockies)
4. Kyle Isbel, OF, Idaho Falls (Royals)
5. Kris Bubic, LHP, Idaho Falls (Royals)
6. Ryan Feltner, RHP, Grand Junction (Rockies)
7. Mariel Bautista, OF, Billings (Reds)
8. Miguel Vargas, 3B, Ogden (Dodgers)
9. Alek Thomas, OF, Missoula (D-backs)
10. Jeremiah Jackson, SS, Orem (Angels)
11. James Marinan, RHP, Billings (Reds)
12. Jacob Amaya, SS, Ogden (Dodgers)
13. Blaze Alexander, SS, Missoula (D-backs)
14. D'Shawn Knowles, OF, Orem (Angels)
15. Niko Decolati, OF, Grand Junction (Rockies)
16. Je'Von Ward, OF, Helena (Brewers)
17. Jean Carmona, SS, Helena (Brewers)
18. Jared Solomon, RHP, Billings (Reds)
19. Bryce Bush, 3B, Great Falls (White Sox)
20. Kevin Maitan, 3B, Orem (Angels)

STANDINGS: SPLIT SEASON

FIRST HALF

North	W	L	PCT	GB	South	W	L	PCT	GB
Great Falls	22	16	.579	—	Ogden	26	12	.684	—
Missoula	19	19	.500	3	Idaho	21	17	.553	5
Helena	17	21	.447	5	Grand Junct.	20	18	.526	6
Billings	15	23	.395	7	Orem	12	26	.316	14

SECOND HALF

North	W	L	PCT	GB	South	W	L	PCT	GB
Billings	25	13	.658	—	Grand Junct.	23	15	.605	—
Missoula	20	17	.541	4 ½	Idaho Falls	22	16	.579	1
Helena	19	19	.500	6	Ogden	20	18	.526	3
Great Falls	12	25	.324	12 ½	Orem	10	28	.263	13

Playoffs—Semifinals: Great Falls defeated Billings 2-0 and Grand Junction defeated Ogden 2-1 in best-of-three series. **Finals:** Great Falls defeated Grand Junction 2-0 in a best-of-three series.

OVERALL STANDINGS

North Division	W	L	PCT	GB	Manager(s)	Attendance	Average	Last Pennant
Billings Mustangs (Reds)	40	36	.526	—	Ray Martinez	93,466	2,670	2014
Missoula Osprey (D-backs)	39	36	.520	½	Mike Benjamin	65,919	1,883	2015
Helena Brewers (Brewers)	36	40	.474	4	Nestor Corredor	31,086	840	2010
Great Falls Voyagers (White Sox)	34	41	.453	5 ½	Tim Esmay	47,625	1,401	2018

South Division	W	L	PCT	GB	Manager(s)	Attendance	Average	Last Pennant
Ogden Raptors (Dodgers)	46	30	.605	—	Jeremy Rodriguez	129,285	3,402	2017
Grand Junction Rockies (Rockies)	43	33	.566	3	Jake Opitz	84,416	2,221	Never
Idaho Falls Chukars (Royals)	43	33	.566	3	Omar Ramirez	101,448	2,742	2013
Orem Owlz (Angels)	22	54	.289	24	Dave Stapleton	51,092	1,345	2016

CLUB BATTING

	AVG	G	AB	R	H	2B	3B	HR	RBI	BB	SO	SB	OBP	SLG
Idaho Falls	.301	76	2714	538	818	179	38	52	470	306	603	105	.377	.453
Ogden	.294	76	2707	591	796	164	36	82	518	362	627	99	.384	.472
Missoula	.290	75	2599	433	754	153	23	59	388	237	578	64	.354	.435
Grand Junction	.279	76	2624	451	732	151	34	77	398	257	587	87	.349	.450
Helena	.274	76	2602	409	712	133	29	55	356	228	633	80	.337	.410
Great Falls	.271	75	2612	419	709	151	24	75	373	209	636	39	.334	.434
Billings	.265	76	2560	404	678	126	19	49	363	213	604	68	.329	.386
Orem	.247	76	2580	373	638	128	20	57	322	254	657	52	.324	.379

CLUB PITCHING

	ERA	G	CG	SHO	SV	IP	H	R	ER	HR	BB	SO	AVG
Billings	4.26	76	0	1	18	663	657	391	314	54	241	695	.254
Grand Junction	4.58	76	0	1	25	668	690	425	340	70	279	591	.266
Great Falls	4.69	75	0	4	15	648	733	412	338	48	195	630	.283
Missoula	4.87	75	0	4	17	640	693	416	346	70	248	553	.275
Helena	5.06	76	0	3	14	657	734	447	369	61	249	589	.282
Idaho Falls	5.24	76	0	4	18	666	746	452	388	60	261	600	.278
Ogden	5.27	76	0	2	16	673	790	499	394	57	260	616	.291
Orem	6.52	76	0	2	11	658	794	576	477	86	333	651	.294

CLUB FIELDING

	PCT	PO	A	E	DP		PCT	PO	A	E	DP
Grand Junction	.967	2005	892	98	78	Helena	.960	1970	741	113	73
Idaho Falls	.966	1998	802	98	64	Great Falls	.960	1945	857	117	59
Billings	.961	1988	748	110	53	Ogden	.956	2020	847	133	89
Missoula	.961	1919	829	112	79	Orem	.945	1983	768	161	68

INDIVIDUAL BATTING

Batter, Club	AVG	G	AB	R	H	2B	3B	HR	RBI	BB	SO	SB
Amado Nunez, Great Falls	.357	60	241	39	86	21	6	6	52	15	71	3
Zack Shannon, Missoula	.354	54	189	45	67	17	1	14	55	28	43	0
Nathan Eaton, Idaho Falls	.354	66	260	59	92	20	12	5	53	33	60	19
Grant Lavigne, Grand Junction	.350	59	206	45	72	13	2	6	38	45	40	12
Zachery Almond, Missoula	.345	56	229	43	79	16	1	13	53	13	40	2
Coco Montes, Grand Junction	.333	69	267	55	89	18	3	8	42	35	69	7
Daniel Robinson, Ogden	.332	57	205	50	68	13	4	2	36	32	24	11
Mariel Bautista, Billings	.330	56	209	43	69	12	4	8	37	16	29	16
Buddy Kennedy, Missoula	.327	57	226	46	74	17	1	4	32	26	34	2
Niko Decolati, Grand Junction	.327	69	263	55	86	15	3	11	56	34	56	17

INDIVIDUAL PITCHING

Pitcher, Club	W	L	ERA	G	GS	CG	SV	IP	H	R	ER	BB	SO
Jose Chacin, Ogden	6	2	2.85	12	12	0	0	66	77	31	21	14	51
Deyni Olivero, Missoula	4	4	3.94	14	14	0	0	64	62	33	28	25	55
Max Lazar, Helena	3	3	4.37	14	14	0	0	68	74	37	33	15	55
Cristopher Molina, Orem	4	5	5.23	16	12	0	0	65	52	44	38	35	70
Wilfry Cruz, Missoula	5	5	5.27	14	14	0	0	68	68	43	40	31	60
Connor Mayes, Idaho Falls	5	2	5.52	13	11	0	0	62	81	40	38	25	52
Eris Filpo, Grand Junction	6	4	5.64	14	14	0	0	67	84	49	42	25	38
Kevin Malisheski, Ogden	3	2	5.88	16	16	0	0	64	89	61	42	31	51
Edgar Martinez, Missoula	5	6	5.94	15	15	0	0	67	86	52	44	19	32
C.J. Eldred, Idaho Falls	6	2	6.00	13	13	0	0	72	86	59	48	12	39

ALL-STAR TEAM

C: Zachery Almond, Missoula; David Fry, Helena. **1B:** Grant Lavigne, Grand Junction. **2B:** Coco Montes, Grand Junction. **3B:** Nathan Eaton, Idaho Falls. **SS:** Ronny Brito, Ogden. **OF:** Mariel Bautista, Billings. **DH:** Zack Shannon, Missoula. **P:** J.C. Cloney, Idaho Falls; Jared Solomon, Billings; Jose Chacin, Ogden; Luis Alecis, Billings; Alexander Martinez, Grand Junction. **Most Valuable Player:** Coco Montes, Grand Junction. **Pitcher of the Year:** J.C. Cloney. **Manager of the Year:** Tim Esmay, Great Falls.

DEPARTMENT LEADERS

BATTING

OBP	Lavigne, Grant, Grand Junction	.477
SLG	Shannon, Zack, Missoula	.677
OPS	Shannon, Zack, Missoula	1.116
R	Eaton, Nathan, Idaho Falls	59
	Rohlman, Reed, Idaho Falls	59
H	Eaton, Nathan, Idaho Falls	92
TB	Eaton, Nathan, Idaho Falls	151
XBH	Eaton, Nathan, Idaho Falls	37
2B	Rohlman, Reed, Idaho Falls	23
	Caraballo, Jose, Idaho Falls	23
3B	Eaton, Nathan, Idaho Falls	12
HR	Shannon, Zack, Missoula	14
RBI	Paulson, Dillon, Ogden	61
SAC	Coca, Yeison, Helena	9
BB	Lavigne, Grant, Grand Junction	45
HBP	Fitzpatrick, Ryan, Great Falls	14
SO	Sowers, Logan, Great Falls	82
SB	James, Tyler, Idaho Falls	38
CS	Golsan, Will, Grand Junction	10
AB/SO	Stovall, Hunter, Grand Junction	9.1

FIELDING

C PCT	Guevara, Javier, Grand Junction	.992
PO	Guevara, Javier, Grand Junction	329
A	Guevara, Javier, Grand Junction	57
DP	Guevara, Javier, Grand Junction	8
E	Alfaro, Jhoandro, Great Falls	9
CS	Guevara, Javier, Grand Junction	20
	Rodriguez, Ramon, Ogden	20
SB	Troutwine, Gunnar, Great Falls	45
PB	Schuyler, Jay, Billings	11
1B PCT	Rohlman, Reed, Idaho Falls	.994
PO	Lavigne, Grant, Grand Junction	523
A	Lavigne, Grant, Grand Junction	33
DP	Paulson, Dillon, Ogden	66
E	Shannon, Zack, Missoula	10
2B PCT	Arocho, Jeremy, Ogden	.978
PO	Coca, Yeison, Helena	102
A	Arocho, Jeremy, Ogden	167
DP	Arocho, Jeremy, Ogden	51
E	Nunez, Amado, Great Falls	17
3B PCT	Kennedy, Buddy, Missoula	.909
PO	Kennedy, Buddy, Missoula	32
A	Kennedy, Buddy, Missoula	98
DP	Egnatuk, Nick, Helena	11
E	Medina, Angel, Idaho Falls	17
SS PCT	Sosa, Lenyn, Great Falls	.975
PO	Navarro, Cristopher, Grand Junction	103
A	Navarro, Cristopher, Grand Junction	195
DP	Navarro, Cristopher, Grand Junction	43
E	Collado, Offerman, Idaho Falls	20
OF PCT	Mount, Drew, Billings	.984
PO	Abreu, Pablo, Helena	123
A	Sanchez, David, Missoula	11
DP	Dawkins, Ian, Great Falls	3
	Williams, Cam, Orem	3
	Isbel, Kyle, Idaho Falls	3
E	Abreu, Pablo, Helena	10

PITCHING

G	Martinez, Alexander, Grand Junction	28
GS	Malisheski, Kevin, Ogden	16
GF	Martinez, Alexander, Grand Junction	26
SV	Martinez, Alexander, Grand Junction	19
W	Cloney, J.C., Idaho Falls	9
L	Duensing, Cole, Orem	10
IP	Eldred, C.J., Idaho Falls	72
H	Comito, Chris, Great Falls	98
R	Mejia, Alejandro, Grand Junction	65
ER	Duensing, Cole, Orem	60
HB	Morell, Johnny, Orem	12
BB	Mejia, Alejandro, Grand Junction	38
SO	Molina, Cristopher, Orem	70
SO/9	Cruz, Wilfry, Missoula	7.9
SO/9 (RP)	Bruihl, Justin, Ogden	12.5
BB/9	Eldred, C.J., Idaho Falls	1.5
WP	Morell, Johnny, Orem	22
BK	Filpo, Eris, Grand Junction	2
BK	Gillaspie, Logan, Helena	2
	5 others	2
HRA	Cruz, Wilfry, Missoula	13
	Martinez, Edgar, Missoula	13
BAA	Olivero, Deyni, Missoula	.250

MINOR LEAGUES

BY BILL MITCHELL

D The biggest news from the Arizona League came when three more organizations added a second team, bringing the total number to 18. The Padres started the trend in 2017, with the Cubs, Giants and Indians following suit.

The Cubs 1 squad finished with the best overall record at 38-18, earning Carmelo Martinez manager of the year honors. But it was the Dodgers, that captured the league championship by defeating Cubs 1 in a best-of-three championship series.

Earning MVP honors was Indians slugger Miguel Jerez, who led the league in home runs (14) and slugging percentage (.577). Padres shortstop Tucupita Marcano paced hitters with a .395 batting average and .497 on-base percentage, while Rangers shortstop Frainyer Chavez was the league's top basestealer with 23 stolen bases. Athletics righthander Richard Morban led pitchers in ERA (1.92), while also tying Ezequiel De La Cruz (D-backs) and Peyton Remy (Cubs) with six wins.

The addition of three teams resulted in a deep crop of prospects. Shortstop Brayan Rocchio (Indians) has an impressive array of tools, excellent feel to hit and advanced instincts for the game that convinced observers he belonged at the top of the league's Top 20 Prospects list. Seven 2018 first-round picks made their professional debuts in the Arizona League, with Jordyn Adams (Angels), Brice Turang (Brewers) and Bo Naylor (Indians) getting enough playing time to rank in the league Top 20. Other first rounders who didn't accrue enough playing time to qualify included Joey Bart (Giants), Nick Madrigal (White Sox), Ryan Weathers (Padres), Nico Hoerner (Cubs) and Ethan Hankins (Indians).

TOP 20 PROSPECTS

1. Brayan Rocchio, SS, Indians
2. Jhon Torres, OF, Indians
3. Brice Turang, SS, Brewers
4. Xavier Edwards, SS, Padres
5. Bo Naylor, C/3B, Indians
6. Kristian Robinson, OF, D-backs
7. Cole Roederer, OF, Cubs
8. Jordyn Adams, OF, Angels
9. Alexander Canario, OF, Giants
10. Jonathan Ornelas, 3B/SS, Rangers
11. Carlos Vargas, RHP, Indians
12. Frank Lopez, RHP, Padres
13. Tahnaj Thomas, RHP, Indians
14. Geraldo Perdomo, SS, D-backs
15. Alek Thomas, OF, D-backs
16. Jeremiah Jackson, SS, Angels
17. Luis Verdugo, SS/3B, Cubs
18. Robinson Ortiz, LHP, Dodgers
19. Tucupita Marcano, SS, Padres
20. Blaze Alexander, SS, D-backs

STANDINGS: SPLIT SEASON

FIRST HALF					SECOND HALF				
East	W	L	PCT	GB	**East**	W	L	PCT	GB
Cubs 1	18	10	.643	—	Cubs 1	20	8	.714	—
D-backs	18	10	.643	—	Giants Black	16	11	.593	3 ½
Giants Oran.	16	12	.571	2	D-backs	15	11	.577	4
Athletics	15	12	.556	2 ½	Athletics	14	13	.519	5 ½
Giants Black	14	14	.500	4	Giants Oran.	14	14	.500	6
Angels	8	20	.286	10	Angels	8	18	.308	11
Central	W	L	PCT	GB	**Central**	W	L	PCT	GB
Indians 1	20	8	.714	—	Indians 1	16	10	.615	—
Indians 2	15	13	.536	5	Indians 2	17	11	.607	—
Cubs 2	14	13	.519	5 ½	White Sox	16	12	.571	1
White Sox	14	14	.500	6	Cubs 2	14	12	.538	2
Brewers	11	16	.407	8 ½	Brewers	11	17	.393	6
Reds	6	21	.222	13 ½	Reds	7	21	.250	10
West	W	L	PCT	GB	**West**	W	L	PCT	GB
Dodgers	18	10	.643	—	Dodgers	19	8	.704	—
Royals	15	12	.556	2 ½	Padres 1	17	11	.607	2 ½
Padres 2	15	13	.536	3	Rangers	14	13	.519	5
Rangers	14	14	.500	4	Padres 2	11	17	.393	8 ½
Padres 1	10	18	.357	8	Mariners	8	19	.296	11
Mariners	8	19	.296	9 ½	Royals	7	18	.280	11

Playoffs—Semifinals: Cubs 1 defeated D-backs and Dodgers defeated Indians 2 in one-game playoffs. **Finals:** Dodgers defeated Cubs 1 2-1 in a best-of-three series.

OVERALL STANDINGS

East Division	W	L	PCT	GB	Manager(s)	Last Pennant
Cubs 1	38	18	.679	—	Carmelo Martinez	2017
D-backs	33	21	.611	4	Darrin Garner	Never
Giants Black	30	25	.545	7 ½	Carlos Valderrama	2013
Athletics	29	25	.537	8	Eddie Menchaca	2001
Giants Orange	30	26	.536	8	Bill Horton	Never
Angels	16	38	.296	21	Jack Santora	Never

Central Division	W	L	PCT	GB	Manager(s)	Last Pennant
Indians 1	36	18	.667	—	Larry Day	2014
Indians 2	32	24	.571	5	Jerry Owens	Never
White Sox	30	26	.536	7	Tommy Thompson	2015
Cubs 2	28	25	.528	7 ½	Jonathan Mota	Never
Brewers	22	33	.400	14 ½	Rafael Neda	2010
Reds	13	42	.236	23 ½	Jose Nievas	Never

West Division	W	L	PCT	GB	Manager(s)	Last Pennant
Dodgers	37	18	.673	—	Mark Kertenian	2018
Rangers	28	27	.509	9	Matt Siegel	2012
Padres 1	27	29	.482	10 ½	Vinny Lopez	2006
Padres 2	26	30	.464	11 ½	Aaron Levin	Never
Royals	22	30	.423	13 ½	Tony Pena Jr.	Never
Mariners	16	38	.296	20 ½	Zac Livingston	2016

MINOR LEAGUES

CLUB BATTING

	AVG	G	AB	R	H	2B	3B	HR	RBI	BB	SO	SB	OBP	SLG
Indians 2	.273	56	1932	339	528	94	22	38	276	229	505	88	.359	.404
Indians 1	.268	54	1857	308	497	93	24	35	262	211	415	49	.351	.400
Cubs 2	.264	53	1802	283	475	84	15	14	224	214	425	65	.347	.350
Cubs 1	.257	56	1897	305	488	98	23	26	259	215	467	62	.338	.374
Giants Orange	.256	56	1849	283	473	97	14	19	239	198	520	47	.337	.354
Rangers	.252	55	1811	288	457	93	22	29	244	220	538	107	.340	.376
Dodgers	.251	55	1810	280	455	86	30	23	231	212	467	99	.335	.370
D-backs	.251	54	1863	312	467	91	27	20	257	219	470	83	.338	.361
Padres 1	.249	56	1841	267	459	90	25	24	242	213	507	51	.335	.364
White Sox	.248	54	1844	256	458	72	17	14	213	189	435	54	.331	.329
Giants Black	.245	55	1855	288	455	84	21	23	236	234	517	57	.342	.350
Reds	.244	55	1847	234	450	88	21	30	196	128	548	58	.303	.363
Athletics	.239	54	1824	298	436	78	29	18	235	255	523	60	.340	.343
Royals	.235	52	1716	221	404	66	21	18	175	187	508	75	.319	.330
Padres 2	.235	56	1825	282	428	88	12	29	232	261	538	48	.342	.344
Brewers	.234	55	1793	244	420	81	20	11	196	208	573	83	.322	.320
Mariners	.231	54	1796	225	415	59	15	19	172	177	520	52	.309	.312
Angels	.230	54	1764	202	405	63	19	12	166	188	554	62	.315	.307

CLUB PITCHING

	ERA	G	CG	SHO	SV	IP	H	R	ER	HR	BB	SO	AVG
Cubs 1	3.06	56	0	3	15	500	403	238	170	20	234	523	.219
Dodgers	3.07	55	0	4	16	483	388	202	165	25	201	568	.218
Indians 1	3.40	54	0	5	14	482	462	229	182	20	166	562	.251
D-backs	3.54	54	0	3	19	480	402	250	189	24	246	520	.224
Giants Orange	3.59	56	0	3	11	482	472	271	192	21	177	511	.253
Athletics	3.86	54	0	3	16	478	430	256	205	14	226	521	.238
Padres 1	3.99	56	0	4	13	481	444	262	213	17	200	534	.242
White Sox	4.04	56	0	4	16	483	476	263	217	39	155	517	.251
Giants Black	4.08	55	1	1	14	481	472	259	218	19	199	457	.256
Padres 2	4.10	56	0	5	7	481	429	273	219	22	197	425	.239
Royals	4.24	52	0	2	13	452	457	246	213	26	211	448	.261
Brewers	4.28	55	0	2	10	473	473	292	225	21	197	425	.256
Cubs 2	4.32	53	0	1	15	465	439	278	223	20	213	454	.246
Indians 2	4.32	56	0	1	12	498	486	289	239	16	214	535	.254
Rangers	4.66	55	0	5	11	473	457	283	245	28	201	563	.252
Angels	4.75	54	0	1	8	468	445	318	247	14	249	495	.245
Mariners	5.13	54	0	1	10	461	509	347	263	32	224	434	.279
Reds	5.43	55	0	1	8	470	526	359	284	24	221	427	.279

CLUB FIELDING

	PCT	PO	A	E	DP		PCT	PO	A	E	DP
Royals	.969	1355	503	59	39	Brewers	.957	1418	515	86	33
Giants Black	.969	1443	557	65	48	Cubs 2	.957	1394	534	86	40
Indians 1	.967	1447	563	69	46	Athletics	.957	1434	534	89	48
Rangers	.966	1421	522	69	46	Mariners	.956	1384	534	89	47
Dodgers	.965	1449	537	71	28	Giants Orange	.955	1446	562	94	39
White Sox	.965	1450	548	72	29	Reds	.954	1411	508	92	46
Cubs 1	.962	1501	577	82	49	Indians 2	.953	1495	563	101	39
Padres 2	.961	1443	557	82	49	Padres 1	.953	1442	476	95	45
D-backs	.958	1440	499	85	41	Angels	.944	1405	540	115	46

INDIVIDUAL BATTING

Batter, Club	AVG	G	AB	R	H	2B	3B	HR	RBI	BB	SO	SB
Tucupita Marcano, Padres 2	.395	35	124	33	49	4	1	0	17	26	10	10
Yainer Diaz, Indians 2	.355	41	155	27	55	9	4	2	28	7	18	1
Brayan Rocchio, Indians 2	.343	35	143	21	49	10	1	1	17	10	17	14
Stanley Martinez, Rangers	.336	45	146	21	49	9	1	2	21	17	40	2
Fidel Mejia, Cubs 2	.324	50	188	27	61	9	2	1	24	20	33	3
Yorlis Rodriguez, Giants Orange	.323	41	155	30	50	9	2	2	26	19	25	6
Yonathan Perlaza, Cubs 1	.317	50	183	34	58	9	2	1	26	15	40	9
Harvin Mendoza, White Sox	.314	39	137	18	43	9	2	0	23	12	12	3
Wilbis Santiago, Indians 1	.314	42	159	27	50	3	4	1	26	7	12	2
David Garza, D-backs	.307	38	127	31	39	11	3	2	26	16	17	4

INDIVIDUAL PITCHING

Pitcher, Club	W	L	ERA	G	GS	CG	SV	IP	H	R	ER	BB	SO
Richard Morban, Athletics	6	3	1.92	13	7	0	0	61	45	24	13	23	64
Taylor Varnell, White Sox	3	1	1.97	10	10	0	0	46	30	20	10	10	61
Joey Cantillo, Padres 2	2	2	2.18	11	9	0	0	45	33	18	11	12	58
Peyton Remy, Cubs 1	6	1	2.58	11	7	0	1	52	40	16	15	13	59
Brayan Herrera, White Sox	5	2	2.70	12	11	0	0	57	46	19	17	15	43
Jesus Tejada, Cubs 1	1	1	2.83	12	12	0	0	57	49	22	18	16	49
Yovanny Cruz, Cubs 2	4	2	2.86	10	10	0	0	44	36	18	14	13	50
Luis Moreno, Giants Black	4	2	2.91	13	9	1	1	59	61	26	19	13	58
Carter Love, White Sox	5	1	2.96	13	2	0	0	46	49	24	15	5	59
Ignacio Feliz, Indians 1	5	3	3.00	10	10	0	0	45	34	22	15	14	54

ALL-STAR TEAM

C: Yainer Diaz, Indians 2. **1B:** Stanley Martinez, Rangers. **2B:** Tucupita Marcano, Padres 2. **3B:** Fidel Mejia, Cubs 2. **SS:** Frainyer Chavez, Rangers; Brayan Rocchio, Indians 2. **OF:** Miguel Jerez, Indians 1; Ruben Cardenas, Indians 1; Anderson Comas, White Sox. **DH:** Nick Gatewood, Padres 1. **RHP:** Richard Morban, Athletics; Tom Colletti, Padres 1. **LHP:** Taylor Varnell, White Sox; Rigo Fernandez, White Sox. **Most Valuable Player:** Miguel Jerez, Indians 1. **Manager of the Year:** Carmelo Martinez, Cubs 1.

DEPARTMENT LEADERS

BATTING

OBP	Marcano, Tucupita, Padres 2	.497
SLG	Jerez, Miguel, Indians 1	.577
OPS	Marcano, Tucupita, Padres 2	.940
R	Wilson, Billy, Indians 2	40
H	Gatewood, Nick, Padres 1	62
TB	Jerez, Miguel, Indians 1	101
XBH	Lantigua, Danny, Reds	26
2B	Gatewood, Nick, Padres 1	18
3B	Ruiz, Agustin, Padres 1	10
HR	Jerez, Miguel, Indians 1	14
RBI	Jerez, Miguel, Indians 1	37
	Lantigua, Danny, Reds	37
	Gatewood, Nick, Padres 1	37
SAC	Garcia, Maikel, Royals	6
BB	Guilbe, Sean, Padres	40
HBP	Sivira, Anyesber, Giants Orange	16
SO	Lantigua, Danny, Reds	75
SB	Chavez, Frainyer, Rangers	23
CS	Rocchio, Brayan, Indians 2	8
AB/SO	Santiago, Wilbis, Indians 2, Indians 1	13.3

FIELDING

C PCT	Guerra, Alexander, Cubs 1	.995
PO	Garcia, David, Rangers	333
A	Guerra, Alexander, Cubs 1	48
DP	Vizcarra, Gilberto, Padres 1	5
E	Vizcarra, Gilberto, Padres 1	7
	Perez, Henderson, Cubs 2	7
	Fernandez, Felix, Indians 2, Indians 1	7
CS	Quintero, Alison, Padres 1	20
SB	Vizcarra, Gilberto, Padres 1	48
PB	Perez, Henderson, Cubs 2	13
1B PCT	Mendoza, Harvin, White Sox	1.000
PO	Pineda, Jason, Padres	340
A	De Oleo, Henderson, Indians 2	32
DP	Pineda, Jason, Padres	33
E	Dingcong, Gio, Athletics	9
2B PCT	Garcia, Reivaj, Cubs 2	.961
PO	Nacero, Kember, Royals	94
A	Santiago, Wilbis, Indians 2, Indians 1	95
DP	Santiago, Wilbis, Indians 2, Indians 1	25
E	Verrier, Jose, Angels	9
	Turner, Gionti, Indians 2	9
	Easley, Jayce, Rangers	9
3B PCT	Diaz, Jordan, Athletics	.886
PO	Santana, Debby, Reds	34
A	Santana, Debby, Reds	73
DP	Santana, Debby, Reds	10
	Lopez, Jonathan, Indians 2, Indians 1	10
E	Santana, Debby, Reds	17
SS PCT	Garcia, Maikel, Royals	.964
PO	Mora, Edison, Giants Orange	65
A	Mora, Edison, Giants Orange	106
DP	Verdugo, Luis, Cubs 2	24
E	Verdugo, Luis, Cubs 2	16
	Barley, Jordy, Angels	16
OF PCT	Anderson, Ryan, Rangers	1.000
	Norris, Randy, Giants Black	1.000
	Butler, Lawrence, Athletics	1.000
PO	Harris, Jawuan, Padres 1	113
A	Mieses, Luis, White Sox	8
DP	Ruiz, Agustin, Padres 1	4
E	Lantigua, Danny, Reds	8

PITCHING

G	Guerrero, Fauris, Cubs 1	21
GS	Cruz, Israel, Giants Black	12
	Noriega, Orlando, Reds	12
	Tejada, Jesus, Cubs 1	12
GF	Guerrero, Fauris, Cubs 1	19
SV	Fernandez, Rigo, White Sox	8
W	De La Cruz, Ezequiel, Diamondbacks	6
	Morban, Richard, Athletics	6
	Remy, Peyton, Cubs 1	6
L	Gonzalez, Marco, Giants Orange	7
IP	Morban, Richard, Athletics	61
H	Gonzalez, Marco, Giants Orange	82
R	Gonzalez, Marco, Giants Orange	57
ER	Gonzalez, Marco, Giants Orange	40
HB	Sweeney, Nathan, Cubs 2	10
BB	Rodriguez, Jose M., Angels	34
SO	Cruz, Israel, Giants Black	66
SO/9	Varnell, Taylor, White Sox	12.0
SO/9 (RP)	Aguiar, Maikel, Cubs 1	13.9
BB/9	Varnell, Taylor, White Sox	2.0
WP	Natera, Jose, Angels	16
BK	Linarez, Jesus, Rangers	4
HRA	Capellan, Delvin, Royals	8
	Soto, Aaron, White Sox	8
BAA	Varnell, Taylor, White Sox	.175

MINOR LEAGUES

BY BEN BADLER

When the Venezuelan Summer League shut down before 2016, the Tigers had to regroup. The Tigers, who had fielded a team in the VSL, decided to field two teams in the Gulf Coast League, rather than put two clubs on the field in the Dominican Summer League.

Despite splitting their players up between two teams in the league, the Tigers won the GCL championship with their Tigers West club, drawing on contributions from college and high school draft picks as well as international players throughout the season. Shortstop Wenceel Perez was the star of the team, batting .383/.462/.543 in 20 games before getting promoted. Outfielder Parker Meadows, a second-round pick, helped carry the lineup throughout the year, while the team's 3.06 combined ERA ranked third in the GCL.

The Tigers West won the championship by winning 9-2 over the Cardinals in the decisive Game 3 of the finals. The Cardinals had the best regular season record in the league, getting a huge boost in August when the organization acquired outfielder Jhon Torres, the No. 6 prospect in the league, from Cleveland. Torres went on to bat .397/.493/.683 in 17 games with the Cardinals.

Overall, it was a strong year for prospects in the GCL. Luis Garcia (Phillies, $2.5 million) and Ronny Mauricio (Mets, $2.1 million) both trained in the same program in San Pedro de Macoris in the Dominican Republic before signing in 2017, and they ranked as the top two prospects in

the league. Perez, Torres and outfielder Antonio Cabello, another big-ticket international signing from 2017, helped lead the way for a strong core of Latin American prospects in the league.

Four first-round picks also made their marks on the league. Rays lefthander Matthew Liberatore and Orioles righthander Grayson Rodriguez both showed promising stuff and polish, while Blue Jays infielder Jordan Groshans showed an advanced approach and exciting power potential. Among late-round sleepers, Pirates outfielder Jack Herman (30th round) and Phillies catcher Logan O'Hoppe (23rd round) both stood out as well.

TOP 20 PROSPECTS

1. Luis Garcia, SS, Phillies
2. Ronny Mauricio, SS, Mets
3. Matthew Liberatore, LHP, Rays
4. Wenceel Perez, SS, Tigers
5. Jordan Groshans, SS/3B, Blue Jays
6. Jhon Torres, OF, Cardinals
7. Antonio Cabello, OF, Yankees
8. Freudis Nova, SS, Astros
9. Ivan Herrera, C, Cardinals
10. Parker Meadows, OF, Tigers
11. Anthony Garcia, OF, Yankees
12. Nick Schnell, OF, Rays
13. Yoendrys Gomez, RHP, Yankees
14. Braxton Ashcraft, RHP, Pirates
15. Gabriel Moreno, C, Blue Jays
16. Jack Herman, OF, Pirates
17. Osiris Johnson, SS, Marlins
18. Will Banfield, C, Marlins
19. Leonardo Jimenez, SS, Blue Jays
20. Brandon Howlett, 3B, Red Sox

OVERALL STANDINGS

Eastern Division	W	L	PCT	GB	Manager(s)	Last Pennant
Cardinals	40	16	.714	—	Erick Almonte	2016
Astros	27	28	.491	12 ½	Wladimir Sutil	Never
Marlins	25	31	.446	15	John Pachot	Never
Mets	24	31	.436	15 ½	David Davalillo	Never
Nationals	23	33	.411	17	Mario Lisson	2009

Northeastern Division	W	L	PCT	GB	Manager(s)	Last Pennant
Phillies East	30	24	.556	—	Roly de Armas	2010
Tigers East	26	28	.481	4	Luis Lopez	Never
Braves	22	32	.407	8	Nestor Perez	2003
Yankees East	19	35	.352	11	Edgar Gonzalez	2017

Northwestern Division	W	L	PCT	GB	Manager(s)	Last Pennant
Tigers West	37	16	.698	—	Brayan Pena	2018
Phillies West	30	24	.556	7 ½	Luis Hurtado	Never
Pirates	27	25	.519	9 ½	Dave Turgeon	2012
Yankees West	25	27	.481	11 ½	David Adams	2011
Blue Jays	24	29	.453	13	Luis Hurtado	Never

Southern Division	W	L	PCT	GB	Manager(s)	Last Pennant
Red Sox	33	22	.600	—	Tom Kotchman	2015
Rays	33	23	.589	½	Tomas Francisco	Never
Twins	32	24	.571	1 ½	Dan Ramsay/Matt Borgschulte	Never
Orioles	13	42	.236	20	Carlos Tosca	Never

Semifinals: Cardinals defeated Phillies East and Tigers West defeated Red Sox in one-game playoffs. **Finals:** Tigers West defeated Cardinals 2-1 in a best-of-three series.

CLUB BATTING

	AVG	G	AB	R	H	2B	3B	HR	RBI	BB	SO	SB	OBP	SLG
Phillies West	.289	54	1743	301	503	92	10	10	235	167	346	94	.357	.370
Tigers West	.277	53	1670	292	463	100	16	40	257	187	389	66	.358	.428
Phillies East	.274	54	1764	288	484	90	15	37	254	178	393	38	.348	.405
Cardinals	.270	56	1890	347	511	100	28	30	307	214	493	40	.361	.401
Blue Jays	.260	53	1806	273	470	110	22	21	234	221	440	59	.354	.380
Pirates	.258	52	1739	294	449	83	29	20	244	199	339	60	.356	.374
Mets	.255	55	1834	253	467	91	25	20	214	157	438	71	.319	.364
Rays	.253	56	1803	252	457	86	14	15	206	194	422	68	.338	.342
Twins	.253	56	1841	252	466	86	7	14	216	180	393	44	.328	.330
Marlins	.252	56	1850	261	466	93	20	18	214	210	456	81	.338	.353
Nationals	.251	54	1837	257	461	84	13	15	227	197	397	58	.332	.335
Red Sox	.249	55	1810	236	450	91	18	18	201	229	448	18	.343	.349
Braves	.242	54	1821	251	441	86	12	37	211	174	454	27	.317	.364
Tigers East	.234	54	1777	244	415	83	12	35	204	199	514	78	.322	.353
Yankees East	.231	54	1686	203	389	71	20	23	175	174	487	86	.320	.337
Yankees West	.225	52	1586	188	357	66	18	32	164	190	428	43	.316	.350
Astros	.222	55	1752	211	389	85	19	17	183	203	452	78	.308	.321
Orioles	.219	55	1768	173	387	62	7	14	153	158	454	13	.298	.286

CLUB PITCHING

	ERA	G	CG	SHO	SV	IP	H	R	ER	HR	BB	SO	AVG
Red Sox	3.01	55	0	2	476	430	199	159	11	134	376	.240
Twins	3.04	56	0	8	486	421	214	164	12	206	468	.234
Tigers West	3.06	53	0	12	435	387	185	148	21	203	502	.236
Rays	3.23	56	0	1	485	447	226	174	23	200	475	.240
Cardinals	3.37	56	1	6	489	462	238	183	18	172	415	.250
Astros	3.52	55	0	4	473	409	227	185	14	205	486	.234
Blue Jays	3.72	53	0	2	465	425	251	192	26	179	395	.243
Mets	3.91	55	1	1	475	438	272	206	26	235	420	.243
Phillies East	3.93	54	0	8	447	464	265	195	25	149	425	.263
Yankees West	3.95	52	0	2	423	425	234	186	21	153	397	.258
Orioles	4.11	55	0	3	464	462	274	212	15	221	398	.262
Marlins	4.17	56	0	3	486	468	274	225	14	181	488	.250
Phillies West	4.28	54	1	2	450	452	262	214	30	188	419	.256
Tigers East	4.37	54	0	6	461	443	261	224	27	203	405	.250
Yankees East	4.70	54	0	2	444	447	293	232	40	191	423	.259
Braves	4.73	54	0	3	470	479	292	247	34	215	441	.260
Nationals	4.82	56	1	4	473	517	318	253	28	188	427	.273
Pirates	4.83	52	0	1	449	449	291	241	31	208	383	.260

CLUB FIELDING

	PCT	PO	A	E	DP		PCT	PO	A	E	DP
Red Sox	.974	1427	569	53	46	Yankees West	.963	1270	478	67	33
Tigers West	.972	1305	473	52	38	Marlins	.963	1457	552	78	38
Twins	.968	1458	537	66	51	Mets	.962	1424	524	77	42
Pirates	.966	1346	514	65	47	Braves	.961	1410	498	77	34
Tigers East	.966	1383	515	67	62	Rays	.959	1454	509	84	41
Phillies West	.966	1349	451	64	21	Astros	.959	1420	530	84	46
Cardinals	.966	1467	524	71	52	Yankees East	.957	1333	479	81	37
Blue Jays	.964	1394	474	69	46	Phillies East	.956	1340	474	83	38
Orioles	.964	1394	515	71	42	Nationals	.956	1430	489	89	25

INDIVIDUAL BATTING

Batter, Club	AVG	G	AB	R	H	2B	3B	HR	RBI	BB	SO	SB
Luis Garcia, Phillies West	.369	43	168	33	62	11	3	1	32	15	21	12
Juan Carlos Abreu, Red Sox	.351	45	171	38	60	6	8	1	12	21	28	4
Jack Herman, Pirates	.340	37	141	28	48	9	3	2	22	13	24	2
Jordan Groshans, Blue Jays	.331	37	142	17	47	12	0	4	39	13	29	0
William Jimenez, Cardinals	.329	41	143	27	47	6	4	2	25	17	33	3
Patrick Dorrian, Pirates	.328	40	137	28	45	10	6	1	34	24	24	2
Antonio Cabello, Yankees West	.321	40	137	21	44	9	4	5	20	21	34	5
Abrahan Gutierrez, Phillies West	.315	41	162	24	51	10	1	1	30	10	16	2
Vinny Esposito, Tigers West	.312	45	141	34	44	14	0	4	26	25	42	10
Kaleo Johnson, Rays	.311	47	167	32	52	13	2	7	25	13	33	4

INDIVIDUAL PITCHING

Pitcher, Club	W	L	ERA	G	GS	CG	SV	IP	H	R	ER	BB	SO
Yasel Santana, Red Sox	3	1	1.97	10	10	0	0	46	36	12	10	9	42
Perry DellaValle, Cardinals	0	2	1.97	11	7	0	1	46	43	13	10	7	67
Ramon Guzman, Mets	5	2	2.05	11	5	0	0	48	42	18	11	18	36
Carlos D. Rodriguez, Yankees West	4	3	2.44	10	5	0	0	44	34	17	12	12	44
Juan Diaz, Blue Jays	2	1	2.49	10	5	0	0	43	41	15	12	10	44
Juan Then, Yankees East	0	3	2.70	11	11	0	0	50	38	21	15	11	42
Brian Pirela, Cardinals	10	0	2.71	12	11	1	0	70	65	25	21	20	44
Xavier Javier, Tigers West	3	2	2.79	10	10	0	0	52	46	18	16	27	38
Victor Santos, Phillies East	6	1	3.03	11	11	0	0	59	63	21	20	4	65
Ben Brown, Phillies West	4	2	3.12	10	8	1	0	49	43	21	17	15	62
Angel De Jesus, Tigers West	4	3	3.12	11	11	0	0	43	32	19	15	17	54

ALL-STAR TEAM

C: Juan Aparicio, Phillies. **1B:** Russ Olive, Rays. **2B:** Nicolas Torres, Phillies. **3B:** Kaleo Johnson, Rays. **SS:** Luis Garcia, Phillies. **OF:** Juan Carlos Abreu, Red Sox; Antonio Cabello, Yankees; Jack Herman, Pirates. **DH:** Andrew Warner, Cardinals. **RHP:** Brian Pirela, Cardinals. **LHP:** Jose Lopez, Rays. **RP:** Edgar Escobar, Cardinals. **Most Valuable Player:** Andrew Warner, Cardinals. **Manager of the Year:** Erick Almonte, Cardinals.

DEPARTMENT LEADERS

BATTING

OBP	Mottice, Kyle, Pirates	.472
SLG	Warner, Andrew, Cardinals	.605
OPS	Cabello, Antonio, Yankees West	.981
R	Trejo, Yerwin, Phillies West	40
H	Garcia, Luis, Phillies West	62
TB	Fernandez, Jeremy, Braves	91
XBH	Reyes, Daniel, Tigers East	23
2B	Warner, Andrew, Cardinals	16
3B	Abreu, Juan Carlos, Red Sox	8
HR	Garcia, Anthony, Yankees2	10
RBI	Groshans, Jordan, Blue Jays	39
SAC	Cubillan, Ricardo, Red Sox	7
BB	Zoellner, Jack, Phillies East	32
HBP	Mottice, Kyle, Pirates	14
SO	Laurencio, Luis, Tigers East	89
SB	Trejo, Yerwin, Phillies West	23
	Ramos, Adrian, Blue Jays	23
CS	Trejo, Yerwin, Phillies West	9
AB/SO	Shaw, Josh, Cardinals	12.6

FIELDING

C PCT	Rodriguez, Nerio, Astros	.995
PO	Gutierrez, Abrahan, Phillies West	224
A	Berglund, Michael, Rays	27
DP	Hale, Austin, Twins	5
E	De Hoyos, Victor, Braves	6
CS	Banfield, Will, Marlins	18
SB	Gutierrez, Abrahan, Phillies West	38
PB	Mompierre, Nelson, Mets	14
1B PCT	Patten, Nick, Rays	.997
PO	Olive, Russ, Rays	394
A	Olive, Russ, Rays	21
DP	Laurencio, Luis, Tigers East	41
E	Snyder, Gabe, Twins	8
2B PCT	Espinal, Walner, Marlins	.974
PO	Espino, Sebastian, Mets	83
A	Espinal, Walner, Marlins	107
DP	Torres, Mike, Tigers East	24
E	Kreuter, Cole, Cardinals	9
3B PCT	Johnson, Kaleo, Rays	.906
PO	Stewart, D.J., Phillies West	32
A	Dorrian, Patrick, Pirates	79
DP	Pogue, Colton, Nationals	7
	Ramirez, Yeuris, Astros	7
E	Pogue, Colton, Nationals	15
	Pujols, Cristopher, Mets	15
SS PCT	Garcia, Luis, Phillies West	.969
PO	Mauricio, Ronny, Mets	75
A	Mauricio, Ronny, Mets	116
DP	Bello, Moises, Tigers East, Tigers West	20
	Gil, Mateo, Cardinals	20
E	Mercado, Jose, Phillies East	17
	Marte, Jeifry, Rays	17
OF PCT	Abreu, Juan Carlos, Red Sox	1.000
	Herman, Jack, Pirates	1.000
	3 others	1.000
PO	Trejo, Yerwin, Phillies West	123
A	Abreu, Wilyer, Astros	8
	Liniak, Kingston, Tigers West, Tigers East	8
	Abreu, Juan Carlos, Red Sox	8
DP	Liniak, Kingston, Tigers West, Tigers East	5
E	Valdez, Warnel, Blue Jays	5
E	Infante, Diego, Rays	5

PITCHING

G	Escobar, Edgar, Cardinals	19
GS	Toribio, Noe, Pirates	12
GF	Escobar, Edgar, Cardinals	16
SV	Escobar, Edgar, Cardinals	9
W	Pirela, Brian, Cardinals	10
L	Rodriguez, Leonardo, Orioles	7
IP	Pirela, Brian, Cardinals	70
H	Pirela, Brian, Cardinals	65
R	Martinez, Edgar, Marlins	43
ER	Martinez, Edgar, Marlins	40
HB	Martinez, Edgar, Marlins	10
BB	Arrieta, Luis, Pirates	29
SO	DellaValle, Perry, Cardinals	67
SO/9	De Jesus, Angel, Tigers West, Tigers East	11.2
SO/9 (RP)	De La Cruz, Sandel, Tigers West, Tigers East	14.0
BB/9	Santos, John, Phillies East	0.6
WP	Rodriguez, Elian, Astros	12
BK	Gonell, Rafi, Phillies West	5
HRA	Vargas, Victor, Phillies West	8
BAA	De Jesus, Angel, Tigers West, Tigers East	.199

MINOR LEAGUES

MINOR LEAGUES

	INTERNATIONAL LEAGUE	PACIFIC COAST LEAGUE	EASTERN LEAGUE	SOUTHERN LEAGUE	TEXAS LEAGUE	CALIFORNIA LEAGUE	CAROLINA LEAGUE	FLORIDA STATE LEAGUE	MIDWEST LEAGUE	SOUTH ATLANTIC LEAGUE
Best Batting Prospect	Ronald Acuna Jr. / Gwinnett	Kyle Tucker / Fresno	Vladimir Guerrero Jr. / New Hampshire	Eloy Jimenez / Birmingham	Fernando Tatis Jr. / San Antonio	Jo Adell / Inland Empire	Carter Kieboom / Potomac	Jesus Sanchez / Charlotte	Alex Kirilloff / Cedar Rapids	Chad Spanberger / Asheville
Best Power Prospect	Ronald Acuna Jr. / Gwinnett	Tyler O'Neill / Memphis	Peter Alonso / Binghamton	Eloy Jimenez / Birmingham	Austin Allen / San Antonio	Roberto Ramos / Lancaster	Bobby Dalbec / Salem	Ibandel Isabel / Daytona	Ronaldo Hernandez / Bowling Green	Seuly Matias / Lexington
Best Strike-Zone Judgment	Danny Jansen / Buffalo	Daniel Vogelbach / Tacoma	Vladimir Guerrero Jr. / New Hampshire	Zack Collins / Birmingham	Josh Naylor / San Antonio	Luis Rengifo / Inland Empire	Carter Kieboom / Potomac	T.J. Friedl / Daytona	Ryan Noda / Lansing	Jeremy Vasquez / Columbia
Best Baserunner	Kevin Newman / Indianapolis	Raimel Tapia / Albuquerque	Jonathan Davis / New Hampshire	Corey Ray / Biloxi	Myles Straw / Corpus Christi	Luis Rengifo / Inland Empire	D.J. Burt / Wilmington	Andres Gimenez / St. Lucie	Vidal Brujan / Bowling Green	Kirvin Moesquit / Delmarva
Fastest Baserunner	Andrew Velazquez / Durham	Terrance Gore / Omaha	Jonathan Davis / New Hampshire	Ben DeLuzio / Jackson	Myles Straw / Corpus Christi	Buddy Reed / Lake Elsinore	D.J. Burt / Wilmington	Andres Gimenez / St. Lucie	Brayan Morales / Great Lakes	Drew Waters / Rome
Best Pitching Prospect	Justus Sheffield / Scranton/W-B	Dakota Hudson / Memphis	Mitch Keller / Altoona	Griffin Canning / Mobile	Forrest Whitley / Corpus Christi	Chris Paddack / Lake Elsinore	Dylan Cease / Winston-Salem	Tony Santillan / Daytona	Hunter Greene / Dayton	Will Stewart / Lakewood
Best Fastball	Michael Kopech / Charlotte	Sandy Alcantara / New Orleans	Mitch Keller / Altoona	Dylan Cease / Birmingham	C.D. Pelham / Frisco	Melvin Adon / San Jose	Dylan Cease / Winston-Salem	Jorge Guzman / Jupiter	Hunter Greene / Dayton	Robert Tyler / Asheville
Best Breaking Pitch	Jalen Beeks / Pawtucket	Austin Gomber / Memphis	Mitch Keller / Altoona	Kyle Wright / Mississippi	Matt Festa / Arkansas	Tony Gonsolin / Rancho Cucamonga	Jonathan Hernandez / Down East	Ryan Hendrix / Daytona	Jorge Tavarez / Burlington	Kyle Dohy / Lakewood
Best Changeup	Cole Irvin / Lehigh Valley	Rogelio Armenteros / Fresno	Matt Pierpont / Hartford	Wei-Chieh Huang / Jackson	Forrest Whitley / Corpus Christi	Chris Paddack / Lake Elsinore	Jimmy Lambert / Winston-Salem	Joey Wentz / Florida	Jovani Moran / Cedar Rapids	Denyi Reyes / Greenville
Best Control	Cole Irvin / Lehigh Valley	Trent Thornton / Fresno	Peter Lambert / Hartford	Duncan Robinson / Tennessee	Logan Allen / San Antonio	Chris Paddack / Lake Elsinore	Tanner Tully / Lynchburg	Austin Warner / Palm Beach	Nick Margevicius / Fort Wayne	Denyl Reyes / Greenville
Best Reliever	Cody Carroll / Scranton/W-B	Jorge Lopez / Colorado Springs	Matt Pierpont / Hartford	Nate Griep / Biloxi	Matt Festa / Arkansas	Justin Lawrence / Lancaster	C.D. Pelham / Down East	Ryan Hendrix / Daytona	John Ghyzel / Dayton	Joe Barlow / Hickory
Best Defensive C	Eric Haase / Columbus	Rocky Gale / Oklahoma City	Jake Rogers / Erie	Brian Navaretto / Chattanooga	Sean Murphy / Midland	Brian Serven / Lancaster	Tres Barrera / Potomac	Rene Pinto / Charlotte	Miguel Amaya / South Bend	Sebastian Rivero / Lexington
Best Defensive 1B	Edwin Espinal / Toledo	Rangel Ravelo / Memphis	Will Craig / Altoona	Jake Gatewood / Biloxi	Taylor Jones / Corpus Christi	Evan White / Modesto	Gavin Sheets / Winston-Salem	Nate Lowe / Charlotte	Jared Young / South Bend	Nick Pratto / Lexington
Best Defensive 2B	Nick Senzel / Louisville	Luis Urias / El Paso	Stephen Alemais / Altoona	Isan Diaz / Jacksonville	Eli White / Midland	Max George / Lancaster	Brett Netzer / Salem	Diego Castillo / Tampa	Irving Lopez / Peoria	Bret Boswell / Asheville
Best Defensive 3B	Ronny Rodriguez / Toledo	Josh Fuentes / Albuquerque	Ke'Bryan Hayes / Altoona	Taylor Sparks / Pensacola	Evan Mendoza / Springfield	Colton Welker / Lancaster	Abraham Toro / Buies Creek	Evan Mendoza / Palm Beach	Nolan Jones / Lake County	Trevor Craport / Delmarva
Best Defensive SS	Kevin Newman / Indianapolis	Adalberto Mondesi / Omaha	Willi Castro / Akron	Zack Short / Tennessee	Nicky Lopez / NW Arkansas	Brandon Van Horn / San Jose	Luis Aviles / Carolina	Andres Gimenez / St. Lucie	Taylor Walls / Bowling Green	Jose Devers / Greensboro
Best Defensive OF	Rio Ruiz / Gwinnett	Jorge Mateo / Nashville	Brendan Rodgers / Hartford	Lucas Erceg / Biloxi	Fernando Tatis Jr. / San Antonio	Cristian Santana / Rancho Cucamonga	Anderson Tejeda / Down East	Andres Gimenez / Bradenton	Gabriel Arias / Fort Wayne	Oneil Cruz / West Virginia
Best Infield Arm	Ronald Acuna Jr. / Gwinnett	Magneuris Sierra / New Orleans	Jonathan Davis / New Hampshire	Monte Harrison / Jacksonville	Braden Bishop / Arkansas	Buddy Reed / Lake Elsinore	Leody Taveras / Down East	Cristian Pache / Florida	Jeison Rosario / Fort Wayne	Drew Waters / Rome
Best Outfield Arm	Gabby Guerrero / Louisville	Adolis Garcia / Memphis	Daniel Johnson / Harrisburg	Aristides Aquino / Pensacola	Myles Straw / Corpus Christi	Brandon Marsh / Inland Empire	Leody Taveras / Down East	Taylor Trammell / Daytona	Eleardo Cabrera / Bowling Green	Seuly Matias / Lexington
Most Exciting Player	Ronald Acuna Jr. / Gwinnett	Kyle Tucker / Fresno	Vladimir Guerrero Jr. / New Hampshire	Eloy Jimenez / Birmingham	Fernando Tatis Jr. / San Antonio	Jo Adell / Inland Empire	Carter Kieboom / Potomac	Cristian Pache / Florida	Royce Lewis / Cedar Rapids	Seuly Matias / Lexington
Best Manager Prospect	Kevin Boles / Pawtucket	Rodney Linares / Fresno	Tony Mansolino / Akron	Shelley Duncan / Jackson	Omar Lopez / Corpus Christi	Joe Mather / Visalia	Morgan Ensberg / Buies Creek	Mike Rabelo / Lakeland	Craig Albernaz / Bowling Green	Marty Malloy / Lakewood

BY BEN BADLER

The Rays have been one of the most productive teams recently when it comes to scouting in the Dominican Republic. Shortstop Wander Franco, outfielder Jesus Sanchez and second baseman Vidal Brujan are all top 10 prospects in their farm system and among the top prospects in the game.

There's more on the way.

The Rays split their Dominican Summer League players into two rosters. While DSL Rays2 finished 44-27, they finished second in the North division and missed the playoffs. DSL Rays1 went 51-20, then captured the DSL championship by winning 8-1 over the Rangers1 in the decisive Game 5. Strong pitching helped carry the Rays1, who led the league in ERA (2.64)

The league's best player was third baseman Malcom Nuñez, who didn't join the league until signing with the Cardinals for $300,000 on July 2. Nuñez won the league's triple crown and topped the DSL in batting average, OBP and slugging, hitting .415/.497/.774 in 44 games.

Both Rangers1 and Rangers 2 won their respective divisions. Rangers1 got a big contribution from shortstop Osleivis Basabe, one of the top 2017 signings from Venezuela and one of the DSL's better prospects.

Another one of the league's best prospects was Julio Rodriguez, a Dominican corner outfielder the Mariners signed for $1.75 million in 2017. Rodriguez showed a promising balance of hitting ability and power, batting .315/.404/.525 in 59 games.

PLAYOFFS—Semifinals: Rays 1 defeated Rangers 2 2-0 and Rangers 1 defeated Colorado 2-0 in best-of-three series. **Finals:** Rays 1 defeated Rangers 1 3-2 in a best-of-five series.

NORTH

Team	W	L	PCT	GB
Rangers 1	48	24	.667	—
Rays 2	42	28	.620	3 ½
Cubs 1	36	35	.569	7
Dodgers Guerrero	34	36	.486	13
Red Sox 2	33	38	.465	14 ½
Indians	32	40	.444	16
Pirates	32	40	.444	16
Indians/Brewers	21	49	.300	26

SOUTH

Team	W	L	PCT	GB
Cardinals Blue	44	28	.611	—
Twins	42	28	.600	1
Mets 1	36	35	.507	4
Nationals	36	36	.500	15
Phillies Red	31	40	.437	19 ½
Yankees	29	42	.408	21 ½
Rockies	22	50	.306	29
Angels	21	51	.292	30

NORTHWEST

Team	W	L	PCT	GB
Rays 1	51	20	.718	—
Marlins	42	30	.583	9 ½
Dodgers Robinson	39	30	.565	11
Royals 1	36	32	.529	13 ½
Athletics	30	39	.435	20
Astros	30	41	.423	21
Red Sox 1	30	41	.423	21
Braves	22	47	.319	28

BASEBALL CITY

Team	W	L	PCT	GB
D-backs 1	48	24	.667	—
Blue Jays	41	31	.569	7
Orioles	38	34	.528	10
Padres	37	35	.514	11
Reds	34	38	.472	14
White Sox	18	54	.250	30

SAN PEDRO

Team	W	L	PCT	GB
Rangers 2	51	21	.708	—
Cardinals Red	40	31	.563	10 ½
Brewers	40	32	.556	11
Phillies White	39	33	.542	12
Mets 2	34	37	.479	16 ½
Tigers 1	33	39	.458	18
Cubs 2	27	45	.375	24
D-backs 2	23	49	.319	28

NORTHEAST

Team	W	L	PCT	GB
Colorado	53	19	.736	—
Mariners	40	32	.556	13
Giants	37	35	.514	16
Tigers 2	34	38	.472	19
Pirates 2	27	45	.375	26
Royals 2	25	47	.347	28

INDIVIDUAL BATTING LEADERS

Player, Team	AVG	G	AB	R	H	2B	3B	HR	RBI	BB	SO	SB
Malcom Nunez, Cardinals Blue	.415	44	164	44	68	16	2	13	59	26	29	3
Joerlin De Los Santos, Cardinals Red	.359	64	234	66	84	18	6	1	28	41	36	30
Osleivis Basabe, Rangers 1	.344	52	192	37	66	16	3	1	34	23	25	12
Ronaiker Palma, Colorado	.340	51	191	25	65	6	1	1	33	12	13	9
Andres Regnault, Mets 1	.333	53	192	33	64	17	1	9	45	22	33	5
Yaniery Guzman, Rangers 1	.332	53	190	36	63	12	5	7	52	17	33	2
Edgardo Rodriguez, Rays 2	.330	51	191	34	63	11	1	6	34	12	19	1
Victor Heredia, Twins	.330	60	233	47	77	16	4	8	56	14	40	1
Ruben Santana, Twins	.324	51	173	44	56	15	6	0	30	23	19	15
Carlos Rodriguez, Brewers	.323	56	217	38	70	13	1	2	32	7	19	12

INDIVIDUAL PITCHING LEADERS

Player, Team	W	L	ERA	G	GS	CG	SV	IP	H	R	ER	BB	SO
Luis Rodriguez, Cubs 1	5	0	0.73	15	10	0	1	61	38	9	5	7	61
Luis Palacios, Marlins	8	0	0.85	15	4	0	0	64	34	9	6	4	62
Rodolfo Fajardo, Tigers 1	3	0	1.07	14	13	0	0	59	39	14	7	10	67
Rosmer Inojosa, Rangers 1	5	1	1.38	12	12	0	0	65	49	18	10	9	53
Henry Medina, Brewers	4	2	1.41	13	13	1	0	76	71	23	12	10	33
Cristofer Melendez, White Sox	4	4	1.54	15	11	0	0	70	39	22	12	28	93
Ronny Henriquez, Rangers 2	5	0	1.55	11	11	0	0	58	37	18	10	8	79
Livan Sanchez, Athletics	6	2	1.61	14	8	0	0	62	37	16	11	12	57
Jose Rodulfo, Dodgers Robinson	5	3	1.61	14	13	0	0	62	41	16	11	12	57
Kleiver Osorio, Colorado	6	2	1.63	16	8	0	2	61	48	16	11	7	54

Franchises Worth Honoring

Triple-A

OKLAHOMA CITY (PACIFIC COAST)

Complementing on-field success with a front office that continues to drive its organization forward on the back end, the Oklahoma City Dodgers have found a recipe for success.

Team president Michael Byrnes is particularly proud of the Dodgers Rookie League, which began in 2018. The program provided equipment and uniforms (Dodgers, of course) to 20 teams around the area. Those gifts allowed for a full, eight-week season a year after the league's season was cancelled due to lack of participation.

"They were able to wear Dodger uniforms and have the equipment provided to really minimize the cost of participation," Byrnes said. "Going out on some Saturdays and seeing those games was a lot of fun, to see people engaged with our brand and learning the game and doing it in an environment where kids can learn the sport . . . I think that's going to be a lasting legacy."

Double-A

TENNESSEE (SOUTHERN)

Since Chris Allen arrived in the front office of the Tennessee Smokies in 2013, the team has been a model for obtaining corporate sponsorship. The Double-A affiliate of the Chicago Cubs in the Southern League has generated close to $1.5 million in sponsorships that has allowed them to make significant upgrades around Smokies Stadium.

Allen, the President and COO, and his front office team have overseen the remodeling of an on-site restaurant, upgrades to the locker rooms and corporate suites and most recently the replacement of the field at Smokies Stadium.

Allen's arrival with the Smokies coincided with the acquisition of the team by Knoxville businessman Randy Boyd and his wife Jenny Boyd.

Class A

WINSTON-SALEM (CAROLINA))

In a state that's a hotbed for minor league baseball, the Winston-Salem Dash have established themselves as a forerunner. One of the top family-friendly options in North Carolina, the Dash led all of high Class A baseball in attendance in 2018 with 292,774 fans going through the gates of the downtown BB&T Ballpark.

The success of the Dash goes far beyond the playing field. They host 200 events year-round, not including home games. That includes nine high school proms and various holiday parties.

The ballpark has helped revitalize the downtown of the city and the Dash have benefitted from the foot traffic. Winston-Salem has finished either first or second in High Class A in overall and average attendance since the ballpark opened in 2010. Over the first nine seasons at BB&T Ballpark, 2,713,684 fans have entered, an average of 301,520 per season.

Short-Season

SPOKANE (NORTHWEST)

When the Spokane Indians decided to create a rally mascot, it became another chapter in the club's unique partnership with its community.

"I didn't want to introduce just some new animal or some new thing that didn't have depth, that didn't have a relevance to the team," Indians senior vice president Otto Klein explained.

Klein had the idea to highlight the redband trout, once a staple food for the team's namesake, the Spokane tribe of Native Americans. But that's not the only way the team honors the tribe.

"Even if we do a throwback uniform or a Star Wars uniform, anything we wear on-field has the Salish writing," he said. "We want to tell the story of the Spokane Tribe."

PREVIOUS 10 WINNERS

TRIPLE-A	DOUBLE-A	CLASS A	SHORT-SEASON
2008: Columbus (International)	2008: Birmingham (Southern)	2008: Greensboro (South Atlantic)	2008: Greeneville (Appalachian)
2009: Iowa (Pacific Coast)	2009: New Hamshire (Eastern)	2009: San Jose (California)	2009: Tri-City (New York-Penn)
2010: Louisville (International)	2010: Corpus Christi (Texas)	2010: Lynchburg (Carolina)	2010: Idaho Falls (Pioneer)
2011: Colo. Springs (Pacific Coast)	2011: Harrisburg (Eastern)	2011: Fort Wayne (Midwest)	2011: Vancouver (Northwest)
2012: Lehigh Valley (International)	2012: N-West Arkansas (Texas)	2012: Greenville (South Atlantic)	2012: Billings (Pioneer)
2013: Indianapolis (International)	2013: Tulsa (Texas)	2013: Clearwater (Florida State)	2013: State College (NY-Penn)
2014: Charlotte (International)	2014: Montgomery (Southern)	2014: West Michigan (Midwest)	2014: Brooklyn (NY-Penn)
2015: Salt Lake (Pacific Coast)	2015: Richmond (Eastern)	2015: Myrtle Beach (Carolina)	2015: Grand Junction (Pioneer)
2016: Round Rock (Pacific Coast)	2016: Pensacola (Southern)	2016: San Bernardino (California)	2016: Pulaski (Appalachian)
2017: Fresno (Pacific Coast)	2017: Reading (Eastern)	2017: Charleston (South Atlantic)	2017: Hillsboro (Northwest)

BY BILL MITCHELL

Long-time observers proclaimed the array of prospects in the 2018 Arizona Fall League to be one of the best in the league's 27-year history. The game's top hitting prospect and top pitching prospect—third baseman Vladimir Guerrero Jr. (Blue Jays) and righthander Forrest Whitley (Astros), respectively—were the marquee names to make it to Arizona, but each of the six AFL teams fielded an impressive array of blue-chip players. The best showcase of talent all fall, however, was at the annual Fall Stars Game, held at the end of the season's fourth week.

The 2018 version of the Fall Stars Game will be remembered for much more than just for the high-octane velocity flashed by many of the 21 pitchers appearing in the annual showcase. The West team scored a pair of runs in the bottom of the ninth inning—both coming with two outs—to eke out a 7-6 win over the East squad. Buddy Reed (Padres) drove in the tying run with a standup triple to left-center field that barely eluded the glove of Luis Barrera (Athletics). One batter later, Meibrys Viloria (Royals) ended the game with a single to center, scoring Reed for the winning run.

As for the premium velocity on display, five different pitchers touched 100 mph or more during their short stints, with righthander Nate Pearson (Blue Jays) touching as high as 104 mph.

This year's AFL championship game ended in equally dramatic fashion, although the ending turned out to be bittersweet for the hero of the game. Braxton Davidson (Braves) hit a 10th inning, walk-off home run that gave the Peoria Javelinas a 3-2 win over the Salt River Rafters, but on his way around the bases, somewhere between third base and home plate, he stepped wrong and suffered a mid-foot sprain in his left foot. Instead of continuing the celebration with his teammates, Davidson was helped to the clubhouse and later taken to the team bus, with his next destination being the X-Ray Room at a Phoenix-area hospital.

Earning their second straight AFL championship, the Javelinas also posted the league's best record at 21-9. Peoria players were told by their manager to just go into the game and stay loose, and they were able to stay close until their bats finally erupted late in the game.

"When you get to this point it's about having fun," said Peoria manager Daren Brown. "There wasn't much fun about it for the first eight innings, and then we got the two runs and ultimately got the home run in the 10th.

"It's a good group of guys, they seemed to come together and that's always a tough thing to do with five organizations coming together."

Davidson's home run to right-center off southpaw reliever Taylor Gilbeau (Nationals) marked just the second time in the AFL's 27-year history that the championship was decided by a walk-off home run. Davidson's championship-winning blast came 17 years after Mike Hessman hit a grand slam to cap a seven-run, ninth inning rally to give the Phoenix Desert Dogs a 12-8 win over the Grand Canyon Rafters.

Fall League Superlatives

Keston Hiura was presented with the Joe Black MVP Award as the AFL's Most Valuable Player prior to the championship game. The righthanded-hitting second baseman batted .323/371/.563 with five home runs and a league-leading 33 RBIs. Drafted by Milwaukee in 2017 with the ninth overall pick, Hiura made it to the Fall League in his first full season as a pro.

Salt River infielder Tyler Nevin (Rockies) was awarded the EyePromise Vizual EDGE Award as the league's leading hitter. The son of former big leaguer Phil Nevin led all AFL hitters in batting average (.426), on-base percentage (.535) and slugging percentage (.593). Nevin's performance this fall was even more impressive considering that he was one of the youngest players in the league, having just completed a year in high Class A.

Davidson's six home runs had him sharing the league lead with Scottsdale first baseman Peter Alonso (Mets) and Surprise first baseman Will Craig (Pirates). Four of Davidson's home runs occurred during a torrid two-day stretch over the final days of October when he had back-to-back two-homer games.

Surprise outfielder Nick Heath (Royals) was the league's leading base-stealer with 12 swiped bags.

Whitley paced all pitchers with 36 strikeouts. A pair of Royals pitchers with the Surprise team, Arnaldo Hernandez and Scott Blewett, were tops in ERA (1.10) and wins (four), respectively.

Surprise shortstop Cole Tucker (Pirates) was awarded the AFL's Dernell Stenson Sportsmanship Award prior to the championship game. Named in memory of the former AFL player who was tragically murdered in 2003 while a member of the Scottsdale Scorpions, the award has been given annually since 2004 to the league's player who best exemplifies unselfishness, hard work and leadership.

MINOR LEAGUES

STANDINGS

East	W	L	PCT	GB
Salt River Rafters	16	14	.533	—
Mesa Solar Sox	15	14	.517	½
Scottsdale Scorpions	14	15	.483	1 ½

West	W	L	PCT	GB
Peoria Javelinas	21	9	.700	—
Glendale Desert Dogs	12	18	.400	9
Surprise Saguaros	11	19	.367	10

INDIVIDUAL BATTING LEADERS
(Minimum 2 Plate Appearances/League Games)

Player, Team	AVG	G	AB	R	H	HR	RBI
Tyler Nevin, Salt River	.426	17	54	9	23	0	20
Daniel Woodrow, Mesa	.371	16	62	10	23	0	6
Cole Tucker, Surprise	.370	20	81	18	30	0	11
Vladimir Guerrero Jr., Surprise	.351	19	77	8	27	0	17
Abraham Toro, Scottsdale	.348	19	66	20	23	2	8
Ryan McKenna, Glendale	.344	17	61	16	21	1	9
Eli White, Mesa	.344	15	61	5	21	1	10
Daz Cameron, Mesa	.342	20	79	17	27	1	5
Nick Heath, Surprise	.338	21	77	21	26	0	4
Yu Chang, Glendale	.337	23	86	16	29	4	17
Nico Hoerner, Mesa	.337	21	89	10	30	1	11

INDIVIDUAL PITCHING LEADERS
(Minimum .4 Innings Pitched/League Games)

Player, Team	W	L	ERA	IP	H	BB	SO
Arnaldo Hernandez, Surprise	0	0	1.10	16	14	8	9
Eduardo Jimenez, Mesa	1	0	1.32	14	8	2	12
Jesus Tinoco, Salt River	0	0	1.72	16	11	6	14
Garrett Williams, Scottsdale	3	0	1.88	24	16	11	27
Evan Kruczynski, Surprise	2	2	1.99	23	26	11	20
Jordan Yamamoto, Salt River	3	0	2.08	26	15	13	27
Mike Shawaryn, Mesa	1	0	2.13	13	11	4	15
Forrest Whitley, Scottsdale	1	2	2.42	26	18	7	36
Scott Blewett, Surprise	4	0	2.49	25	21	8	21
Adam Bray, Salt River	1	0	2.63	14	10	5	14

GLENDALE DESERT DOGS

Name	AVG	AB	R	H	2B	3B	HR	RBI	BB	SO	SB
Ryan McKenna	.344	61	16	21	6	3	1	9	14	16	2
Yu Chang	.337	86	16	29	4	0	4	17	7	16	1
Luis Robert	.324	74	19	24	2	0	2	10	5	13	5
Connor Marabell	.294	85	11	25	7	2	0	10	1	13	0
Keibert Ruiz	.286	49	8	14	1	0	0	6	6	2	0
Steve Wilkerson	.282	71	8	20	4	0	0	9	11	16	0
Thairo Estrada	.238	80	9	19	2	0	0	7	4	15	0
Jared Walker	.226	53	6	12	1	0	3	10	11	24	0
Li-Jen Chu	.216	37	4	8	5	0	0	5	4	10	0
Laz Rivera	.215	65	8	14	2	0	0	7	3	14	1
Martin Cervenka	.212	52	6	11	4	0	1	9	2	7	1
Steven Sensley	.197	76	4	15	3	1	0	9	4	26	0
Errol Robinson	.191	47	4	9	1	1	0	4	7	16	3
Luis Alexander Basabe	.180	50	4	9	0	0	0	2	12	16	4
Estevan Florial	.178	73	10	13	2	2	0	8	12	29	2
Cody Thomas	.161	62	7	10	2	0	0	4	7	23	1

Name	W	L	ERA	G	GS	SV	IP	H	BB	SO	AVG
Zack Burdi	0	0	0.00	5	0	1	5	2	1	5	.111
Tanner Chleborad	1	1	1.46	10	0	0	12	14	4	12	.304
Matt Wivinis	0	1	1.50	11	0	1	12	6	6	14	.146
Rob Kaminsky	3	0	1.64	10	0	0	11	9	3	13	.220
Jordan Sheffield	1	1	1.93	10	0	1	9	6	4	7	.176
Zach Thompson	0	1	2.70	11	0	3	13	10	6	15	.200
Chris Lee	1	1	3.05	6	6	0	21	18	8	13	.237
Ben Holmes	1	2	3.97	6	6	0	23	22	10	24	.253
Hobie Harris	1	0	4.20	9	0	0	15	14	7	16	.250
Tanner Banks	2	1	4.43	6	5	0	22	30	5	10	.319
Jay Flaa	0	1	4.50	11	0	0	12	14	10	6	.292
Tyler Erwin	0	1	5.40	11	0	0	10	13	7	12	.302
Justin Garza	1	3	5.59	6	6	0	19	19	14	15	.268
Andre Scrubb	0	1	6.14	8	0	0	7	12	5	1	.364
Danny Dopico	0	0	6.57	10	0	0	12	10	12	15	.233
Dalbert Siri	1	0	7.84	11	0	1	10	14	3	10	.326

Name											
Jared Robinson	0	0	8.18	10	0	0	11	16	5	8	.320
Nolan Long	0	1	8.74	10	0	0	11	14	4	16	.292
Jordan Foley	0	2	9.15	7	7	0	20	20	19	20	.267
Kyle Zurak	0	1	11.57	9	0	0	9	16	10	3	.381

MESA SOLAR SOX

Name	AVG	AB	R	H	2B	3B	HR	RBI	BB	SO	SB
Daniel Woodrow	.371	62	10	23	1	0	0	6	6	11	12
Eli White	.344	61	5	21	2	1	1	10	4	18	3
Daz Cameron	.342	79	17	27	3	2	1	5	13	20	9
Nico Hoerner	.337	89	10	30	4	4	1	11	2	16	1
Trent Giambrone	.327	49	9	16	2	0	2	6	6	17	2
Jahmai Jones	.321	78	18	25	6	1	2	11	10	23	4
Jhonny Pereda	.276	29	2	8	2	0	0	3	3	6	0
Esteban Quiroz	.267	45	10	12	3	1	2	8	14	16	0
Luis Barrera	.263	57	10	15	1	1	1	12	6	13	6
Skye Bolt	.247	73	17	18	4	4	2	12	12	22	7
Bobby Dalbec	.219	73	9	16	6	0	3	16	15	32	0
Daniel Pinero	.216	37	5	8	1	0	0	3	7	9	3
D.J. Wilson	.190	63	12	12	3	0	0	4	7	20	6
David MacKinnon	.175	40	3	7	2	0	0	4	12	13	1
Josh Ockimey	.172	64	5	11	2	0	1	9	9	26	0
Jake Rogers	.167	48	8	8	5	0	0	1	3	11	0
P.J. Higgins	.158	38	4	6	0	0	1	6	7	7	0
Roberto Baldoquin	.093	43	6	4	0	0	0	5	6	17	0

Name	W	L	ERA	G	GS	SV	IP	H	BB	SO	AVG
Calvin Coker	0	1	0.00	9	0	0	11	7	5	11	.167
Aaron Wilkerson	0	0	0.00	3	0	0	4	2	3	3	.143
Eduardo Jimenez	1	0	1.32	8	0	0	14	8	2	12	.167
Darwinzon Hernandez	0	1	1.59	8	0	1	11	8	6	24	.195
Mike Shawaryn	1	0	2.13	9	1	1	13	11	4	15	.234
Erick Leal	2	1	2.66	6	6	0	20	16	11	20	.208
Jake Bray	0	1	3.09	9	0	1	12	5	4	10	.125
Gregory Soto	1	0	3.10	7	7	0	29	20	14	25	.206
Bailey Clark	0	0	3.75	9	0	1	12	13	8	8	.277
Sam Sheehan	0	1	4.76	9	0	0	11	3	14	12	.154
Manuel Rondon	0	1	4.76	8	2	0	11	6	8	7	.094
Daniel Procopio	0	0	4.85	9	0	0	13	11	10	8	.256
Justin Steele	1	1	5.79	6	6	0	19	22	11	16	.306
Jesus Castillo	3	1	5.82	6	6	0	22	33	7	11	.344
Josh Taylor	0	1	6.08	10	1	0	13	18	2	17	.300
John Schreiber	1	0	7.00	9	0	0	9	11	3	9	.314
Angel Duno	0	1	7.04	7	0	0	8	9	4	7	.290
Ryan Clark	1	0	7.36	9	0	1	11	14	5	6	.326
Brett Hanewich	2	2	9.00	11	0	0	11	14	13	11	.311
Sandy Baez	2	1	9.82	10	0	0	11	18	5	14	.353
Teddy Stankiewicz	0	1	13.50	1	1	0	2	4	1	1	.400

PEORIA JAVELINAS

Name	AVG	AB	R	H	2B	3B	HR	RBI	BB	SO	SB
Chris Mariscal	.381	42	7	16	2	1	0	6	5	9	1
Weston Wilson	.375	48	13	18	2	1	2	7	6	12	2
Ronaldo Hernandez	.357	14	5	5	0	1	0	2	2	1	0
Buddy Reed	.333	66	13	22	5	1	1	6	7	13	5
Lucius Fox	.326	86	18	28	2	0	1	11	16	19	7
Keston Hiura	.323	96	19	31	6	1	5	33	6	28	7
Cristian Pache	.279	86	14	24	3	2	0	9	6	18	3
Ryan Boldt	.278	18	3	5	0	0	0	1	2	6	0
Austin Allen	.263	57	10	15	3	0	2	13	8	19	0
Joe DeCarlo	.262	42	7	11	1	1	0	6	12	10	0
Evan White	.257	70	13	18	6	0	2	14	8	15	2
Mario Feliciano	.250	4	2	1	0	0	0	1	2	2	0
Ian Miller	.246	57	10	14	0	0	2	8	11	11	1
Joe McCarthy	.239	46	7	11	3	0	1	8	8	15	0
Ray-Patrick Didder	.228	57	7	13	1	0	0	2	7	13	5
Hudson Potts	.228	79	10	18	5	0	2	13	11	27	1
Braxton Davidson	.227	66	13	15	2	0	6	18	13	31	0
Izzy Wilson	.209	43	9	9	2	2	2	7	6	11	3
Trent Grisham	.150	60	4	9	0	1	1	6	13	25	0

Name	W	L	ERA	G	GS	SV	IP	H	BB	SO	AVG
Dalton Moats	0	0	0.84	7	0	0	11	4	1	15	.108
Blake Rogers	0	0	1.23	6	0	0	7	6	2	7	.240
Jon Olczak	1	0	1.50	10	0	0	12	8	5	13	.190
Wyatt Mills	1	0	1.93	8	0	0	9	8	3	7	.229

MINOR LEAGUES

Name	W	L	ERA	G	GS	SV	IP	H	BB	SO	AVG
Thomas Burrows	0	0	2.25	8	0	0	12	11	4	13	.244
Kyle Muller	1	0	2.53	7	0	0	11	8	8	15	.216
Anthony Misiewicz	1	1	2.76	5	5	0	16	13	4	13	.224
Travis Radke	0	0	2.81	7	0	0	16	15	7	17	.242
Daniel Brown	1	0	3.00	9	0	1	12	8	4	17	.190
Adam McCreery	2	0	3.38	7	0	1	8	5	3	7	.172
Miguel Sanchez	1	0	3.60	6	0	0	10	11	3	8	.268
David McKay	2	1	3.72	10	0	0	10	11	6	11	.289
Dauris Valdez	1	0	4.50	10	0	2	10	4		15	.250
Bubba Derby	1	1	4.78	7	7	0	26	32	9	18	.308
Miguel Diaz	2	1	4.87	6	6	0	20	20	9	19	.253
Matt Krook	1	1	5.93	6	4	0	14	11	10	20	.224
Brandon Lawson	2	2	7.47	8	2	0	16	21	7	16	.309
Phoenix Sanders	1	0	7.90	9	0	0	14	18	4	34	.327
Jeremy Walker	1	2	8.14	6	6	0	21	38	7	9	.388
Hansel Rodriguez	1	0	9.00	2	0	0	2	3	1	0	.333
Matt Walker	1	0	10.00	9	0	0	9	10	11	4	.278

SALT RIVER RAFTERS

Name	AVG	AB	R	H	2B	3B	HR	RBI	BB	SO	SB
Jazz Chisholm	.442	43	12	19	3	1	3	9	4	8	7
Tyler Nevin	.426	54	9	23	3	3	0	20	15	5	1
Sam Hilliard	.328	64	13	21	2	2	2	14	7	15	2
Josh Fuentes	.301	83	16	25	4	1	3	10	7	18	1
Renae Martinez	.300	30	5	9	3	0	2	5	3	2	0
Carter Kieboom	.295	78	18	23	1	1	1	5	17	18	4
Monte Harrison	.290	69	11	20	2	1	0	16	10	19	4
Jaylin Davis	.279	61	7	17	2	0	0	8	2	21	2
Brian Miller	.269	67	8	18	2	0	0	9	8	8	9
Jake Noll	.265	49	6	13	2	0	2	14	2	10	1
Daulton Varsho	.262	65	15	17	1	1	0	9	12	14	8
Bryson Brigman	.257	70	13	18	0	0	0	5	7	7	5
Tres Barrera	.255	47	5	12	2	0	0	6	1	9	0
Pavin Smith	.250	68	10	17	1	0	0	8	8	10	1
Drew Ellis	.231	52	6	12	4	0	2	12	7	16	0
Travis Blankenhorn	.224	58	12	13	1	0	0	6	10	13	3
Luke Raley	.214	14	3	3	0	1	0	3	3	4	1
Dominic Miroglio	.200	25	5	5	1	0	1	4	1	5	0
Daniel Johnson	.145	62	8	9	2	0	0	3	10	19	6

Name	W	L	ERA	G	GS	SV	IP	H	BB	SO	AVG
Jesus Tinoco	0	0	1.72	10	0	0	16	11	6	14	.190
Taylor Guilbeau	0	1	1.74	10	0	0	10	6	6	7	.188
Jordan Yamamoto	3	0	2.08	6	6	0	26	15	13	27	.172
Kevin Ginkel	1	0	2.53	10	0	1	11	10	2	17	.244
Adam Bray	1	0	2.63	10	0	1	14	10	5	14	.200
Jon Duplantier	1	1	3.32	6	6	0	22	23	10	32	.277
Justin Lawrence	0	0	3.38	10	0	3	11	10	6	13	.263
Jordan Mills	1	0	3.55	10	0	0	13	7	5	13	.167
Griffin Jax	1	1	3.86	6	5	0	21	21	11	14	.269
Kyle Keller	0	2	4.76	11	0	0	11	12	8	14	.279
Ryan Castellani	1	1	5.13	7	7	0	26	24	14	31	.235
Ben Braymer	1	0	5.40	9	0	0	10	8	5	13	.222
Hector Lujan	1	1	5.59	10	0	0	10	13	5	10	.317
Devin Smeltzer	1	0	5.87	8	0	0	8	14	4	7	.400
Bo Takahashi	1	2	6.94	8	2	0	12	12	6	11	.267
Chad Smith	0	2	7.45	10	0	0	10	12	6	5	.279
Mitch Horacek	1	0	8.74	11	0	0	11	17	6	12	.340
Tommy Eveld	1	1	9.39	7	0	0	8	9	6	6	.290
Tyler Mark	0	0	9.95	7	0	0	6	11	5	5	.393
Luis Reyes	1	2	11.37	4	4	0	13	22	6	6	.386

SCOTTSDALE SCORPIONS

Name	AVG	AB	R	H	2B	3B	HR	RBI	BB	SO	SB
Abraham Toro	.348	66	20	23	6	1	2	8	12	12	1
Taylor Trammell	.298	84	10	25	4	2	0	6	8	20	6
Ronnie Dawson	.291	79	8	23	5	3	1	10	15	26	10
Desmond Lindsay	.286	28	5	8	1	0	3	4	3	8	0
Peter Alonso	.255	98	16	25	7	0	6	27	11	28	4
Austin Listi	.250	76	10	19	2	1	0	7	8	8	0
Shed Long	.241	58	6	14	2	1	0	8	8	15	3
Darick Hall	.238	63	6	15	1	0	4	12	4	23	1
Mark Kolozsvary	.200	30	2	6	2	0	0	1	1	10	0
Arquimedes Gamboa	.186	59	4	11	2	0	0	3	12	19	2
Alfredo Rodriguez	.179	67	6	12	3	0	0	2	5	15	1
Drew Ferguson	.172	29	1	5	2	0	0	1	1	7	0

Name	AVG	AB	R	H	2B	3B	HR	RBI	BB	SO	SB
C.J. Hinojosa	.149	47	3	7	1	0	1	6	5	12	0
Heath Quinn	.128	39	4	5	0	0	0	4	4	17	1
Andres Gimenez	.125	48	7	6	3	1	1	7	8	15	0
Matt Winn	.122	41	6	5	0	1	2	4	12	20	1
Ali Sanchez	.120	25	3	3	1	0	0	1	3	5	0
Luke Williams	.097	31	4	3	0	1	0	1	3	10	0

Name	W	L	ERA	G	GS	SV	IP	H	BB	SO	AVG
Luke Leftwich	0	0	0.00	8	0	0	10	6	3	12	.162
Sam Wolff	1	0	0.00	10	0	3	10	2		14	.065
Jonathan Hennigan	1	0	1.29	8	0	1	7	6	5	9	.222
Garrett Williams	3	0	1.88	6	6	0	24	16	11	27	.184
Ty Boyles	1	0	2.16	10	0	0	8	6	3	10	.214
Seth McGarry	1	1	2.25	7	1	0	12	10	9	15	.227
Gerson Bautista	1	1	2.38	9	0	0	11	10	3	11	.250
Forrest Whitley	1	2	2.42	6	6	0	26	18	7	36	.189
Matt Blackham	0	1	2.70	9	0	0	10	9	9	11	.250
Melvin Adon	0	1	2.92	10	0	1	12	7	3	21	.163
Chase Johnson	0	0	3.00	9	0	0	9	7	7	10	.219
Erasmo Pinales	0	2	3.27	9	0	0	11	8	12	11	.205
J.B. Bukauskas	2	1	3.33	6	6	0	24	24	10	24	.270
Tyler Viza	1	1	3.47	6	6	0	23	23	7	20	.264
Stephen Nogosek	0	0	3.68	7	0	0	7	9	6	7	.300
Austin Orewiler	1	2	4.00	5	5	0	18	17	4	12	.258
Trent Thornton	0	0	4.02	9	0	0	15	14	4	20	.250
Joe Zanghi	0	1	4.50	9	0	0	10	11	2	9	.275
Alex Powers	0	1	5.23	9	0	2	10	10	4	15	.250
Wyatt Strahan	1	1	5.87	9	0	0	8	7	6	9	.233

SURPRISE SAGUAROS

Name	AVG	AB	R	H	2B	3B	HR	RBI	BB	SO	SB
Cole Tucker	.370	81	18	30	5	1	0	11	12	12	6
Vladimir Guerrero Jr.	.351	77	8	27	7	0	0	17	8	6	2
Nick Heath	.338	77	21	26	4	2	0	4	11	20	13
Julio Pablo Martinez	.327	52	9	17	5	1	1	6	6	13	4
Will Craig	.304	79	15	24	3	0	6	18	7	18	3
Andy Young	.301	73	13	22	5	1	3	15	14	17	1
Renae Martinez	.300	30	5	9	3	0	2	5	3	2	0
Charles Leblanc	.292	65	7	19	0	2	0	6	10	17	0
Lane Thomas	.262	61	11	16	1	0	1	10	14	18	8
Cavan Biggio	.262	65	7	17	4	0	2	10	15	15	2
Santiago Espinal	.250	56	7	14	3	1	0	4	7	7	2
Tommy Edman	.238	42	4	10	3	0	0	5	10	7	5
Jeremy Martinez	.231	39	3	9	1	0	0	2	8	6	0
Meibrys Viloria	.225	40	8	9	2	1	0	4	12	9	1
Yanio Perez	.190	42	4	8	2	0	0	9	2	9	0
Bryan Reynolds	.188	64	11	12	1	1	0	5	14	14	1
Khalil Lee	.157	83	9	13	3	0	1	10	8	27	3
Josh Morgan	.111	9	0	1	0	0	0	0	1	3	0

Name	W	L	ERA	G	GS	SV	IP	H	BB	SO	AVG
Arnaldo Hernandez	0	0	1.10	9	0	0	16	14	8	9	.259
Grant Gavin	0	0	1.50	9	0	1	12	9	5	7	.220
Evan Kruczynski	2	2	1.99	6	6	0	23	26	11	20	.299
Scott Blewett	4	0	2.49	6	6	0	25	21	8	21	.223
Blake Weiman	0	1	3.95	8	0	1	14	13	4	12	.250
Zach Jackson	1	1	4.05	9	0	0	13	6	9	17	.130
Connor Jones	0	0	4.11	9	1	0	15	16	8	17	.262
Jackson McClelland	1	1	4.91	8	0	0	11	6	9	15	.154
Nate Pearson	2	2	6.20	6	6	0	20	23	13	23	.284
Demarcus Evans	1	1	6.30	9	0	0	10	10	7	15	.270
Geoff Hartlieb	0	1	6.59	10	0	1	14	23	8	12	.383
Shawn Morimando	0	2	6.65	7	6	0	22	28	9	18	.304
Joe Barlow	0	2	6.94	11	0	0	12	12	11	14	.261
Tai Tiedemann	0	1	7.84	4	4	0	10	18	6	10	.391
Dario Agrazal	0	0	9.00	1	1	0	5	8	0	0	.400
Walker Sheller	0	0	9.64	5	0	3	5	4	2	0	.211
Will Latcham	0	1	10.32	10	0	0	11	13	8	8	.283
Conner Greene	0	2	11.17	9	0	1	10	13	15	6	.325
Matt Eckelman	0	2	13.00	9	0	0	9	13	11	3	.325
Joe Kuzia	0	0	21.60	5	0	0	5	12	5	3	.480
C.D. Pelham	1	0	22.50	4	0	0	4	8	7	0	.471

MINOR LEAGUES

INDEPENDENT
LEAGUES

Summer Leagues Throw A Curve At Indy Ball

INDEPENDENT LEAGUE ATTENDANCE

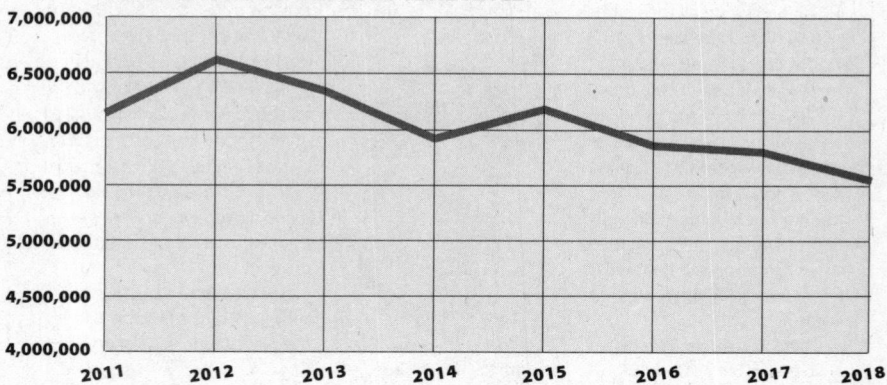

BY J.J. COOPER

In 1993 the independent leagues began because some forward-thinking baseball people had a clever idea.

They realized that there were many cities with baseball stadiums that were shut out of affiliated minor league baseball. Either their ballparks were too old, the cities were too small or their location fell within one of the many expansive territories of current majors and minor league teams.

So the Northern League and Frontier League were birthed to fill a gap in the baseball landscape. Now more than 25 years later, the independent leagues still exist at their roots because of that first original idea.

And the independent leagues are still solidly providing quality baseball to cities that may otherwise be without professional baseball. But in many ways they have been usurped by another original idea: what would happen if you can have baseball without having to pay the players?

The shift of independent league baseball from a growing business to a stable but relatively static one came about with the rise of summer wood-bat college leagues. Average attendance has dipped from 3,225 fans per game to 2,931 in the past seven seasons, but the biggest difference is the leagues are smaller.

Where once the independent leagues were looking to expand by adding new markets, now they are trying to find enough new markets to keep their overall franchise counts the same. The main reason for that is that poorer performing teams find the economics of summer college leagues, where players by the very rules of college baseball must play for free, make it much easier to make money.

And it's easier to make the economics of an older stadium work in a summer college league than it is in independent leagues these days. In some ways, indy ball has gone upscale, allowing someone else to move in to the very niche they filled 25 years ago.

For 2019, the Frontier League has announced that two teams are leaving to join summer college leagues, which will leave the league with 10 teams for 2019, down from 14 teams as recently as 2015 before Rockford left to take the summer college route. Of the six original Northern League franchises from 1993, three of the cities still have teams in the American Association (which split off from the now-defunct Northern League years ago). Three of the cities have teams in the summer college wood-bat Northwoods League.

There was other franchise movement in 2018. The Wichita Wingnuts have long been one of the strongest teams in the American Association. But they announced they were going dormant for 2019 because the city of Wichita paid to break their stadium lease to bring affiliated baseball to the city.

The Atlantic League will add an eighth franchise for 2019 as the High Point (N.C.) Rockers replace a travel team that filled the spot of the the now-defunct Bridgeport Bluefish for the 2018 season.

INDEPENDENT LEAGUES

Jordany Valdespin Outlives Old Reputation

Before he ever met Jordany Valdespin, Long Island Ducks manager Kevin Baez had heard all the stories.

And there were plenty of stories to tell. When he was a New York Met, Valdespin raised the ire of teammates and front office officials by violating dress codes, by celebrating a home run when his team was far, far behind and by reportedly yelling at his manager and demanding to be placed on the disabled list when he was being demoted to Triple-A.

There was also a 50-game suspension because of the Biogenesis scandal that eventually led to the Mets non-tendering him after the 2013 season. Valdespin did catch on with the Marlins for a few games in the majors in 2014 and 2015, but since then, he's bounced around. He spent 2016 in Triple-A for the Tigers and 2017 in the Mexican League.

But the independent leagues are a place for second chances, so Baez and the Ducks brought in Valdespin, 30, to see if he could help the team and what they found was a player who didn't match his previous reputation. He arrived for spring training with an enthusiasm that impressed Baez and a willingness to do whatever the Ducks needed.

"When he came to us, I had just heard about him. I didn't want to make any conclusions. I said 'let me see how he is with me,'" Baez said. "He's been good. He's been a good teammate and a good player."

Jordany Valdespin

Valdespin was more than a good player, he was the best player in the league and Baseball America's 2018 Independent Leagues Player of the Year. Valdespin hit .338/.399/.487 with 12 home runs, 30 stolen bases and a league-leading 94 runs scored. He also led the league in triples (7) and hits (154). He did so while providing reliable defense at second base.

"His range was good, his arm was good and he turned a very quick double play," Baez said. "He made a couple of double plays this year where I thought he had no chance."

But Valdespin's biggest contribution for the Ducks was at the plate. Valdespin collected hits in bunches. Valdespin had 55 multi-hit games. Valdespin reached base at least once in 100 of his 117 games played.

"He was our lead-off guy. He got things going. He caused havoc on the basepaths," Baez said. "He's got tremendous bat speed. The ball jumps off his bat. He can go the other way with some pop."

Valdespin helped Long Island reach the Atlantic League championship series for a third consecutive season. He then went off to play in the Dominican Winter League. Valdespin has returned home to play winter ball each of the past 10 seasons, including one year where he played in the Arizona Fall League and the Dominican Winter League.

"He comes every day ready to play and ready to win," Baez said. "I can't see why he won't get a shot (at affiliated ball). He's proven that he deserves another chance.

PREVIOUS WINNERS

1996: Darryl Motley, OF, Fargo-Moorhead (Northern)
1997: Mike Meggers, OF, Winnipeg/Duluth (Northern)
1998: Morgan Burkhart, 1B, Richmond (Frontier)
1999: Carmine Cappucio, OF, New Jersey (Northeast)
2000: Anthony Lewis, 1B, Duluth-Superior (Northern)
2001: Mike Warner, OF, Somerset (Atlantic)
2002: Bobby Madritsch, LHP, Winnipeg (Northern)
2003: Jason Shelley, RHP, Rockford (Frontier)
2004: Victor Rodriguez, SS, Somerset (Atlantic)
2005: Eddie Lantigua, 3B, Quebec (Can-Am)
2006: Ian Church, OF, Kalamazoo (Frontier)

2007: Darryl Brinkley, OF, Calgary (Northern)
2008: Patrick Breen, OF, Orange County (Golden)
2009: Greg Porter, OF, Wichita (American Association)
2010: Beau Torbert, OF, Sioux Falls (American Association)
2011: Chris Collabello, 1B, Worcester (Can-Am League)
2012: Blake Gailen, OF, Lancaster (Atlantic)
2013: C.J. Ziegler, 1B, Wichita (American Association)
2014: Balbino Fuenmayor, 1B, Quebec (Can-Am League)
2015: Joe Maloney, OF, Rocland (Can-Am League)
2016: Art Charles, 1B, New Jersey (Can-Am League)
2017: Alonzo Harris, OF, York (Atlantic League)

AMERICAN ASSOCIATION

Ever since joining the American Association in 2011, the Kansas City T-Bones had been on the outside looking in. The T-Bones were rarely awful, but until this year, they had never even made the league's playoffs. Led by manager of the year Joe Calfapietra and all-star outfielder Todd Cunningham, the T-Bones rolled past St. Paul in the championship series.

North Division	W	L	PCT	GB
Gary SouthShore RailCats	59	41	.590	—
St. Paul Saints	59	41	.590	—
Fargo-Moorhead RedHawks	51	49	.510	8
Chicago Dogs	45	54	.455	13 ½
Winnipeg Goldeyes	41	59	.410	18
Sioux Falls Canaries	40	60	.400	19

South Division	W	L	PCT	GB
Sioux City Explorers	71	29	.710	—
Kansas City T-Bones	62	37	.626	8 ½
Wichita Wingnuts	61	39	.610	10
Lincoln Saltdogs	51	48	.515	19 ½
Cleburne Railroaders	33	66	.333	37 ½
Texas AirHogs	25	75	.250	46

Playoffs: Semifinals: St. Paul defeated Gary 3-1 and Kansas City defeated Sioux City 3-2 in best-of-5 series. **Finals:** Kansas City defeated St. Paul 3-1 in best-of-5 series.

Attendance: St. Paul 408,921; Winnipeg 219,370; Kansas City 189,981; Gary SouthShore 167,152; Fargo-Moorhead 166,717; Lincoln 160,124. Chicago 138,855; Sioux Falls 124,121; Wichita 108,627; Texas 80,196; Cleburne 64,226; Sioux City 63,498.

ALL-Star Team: C: Justin O'Conner, St. Paul. **1B:** Brady Shoemaker, St. Paul. **2B:** Logan Watkins, Wichita. **3B:** Jose Sermo, Sioux City. **SS:** Nate Samson, Sioux City. **OF:** Todd Cunningham, Kansas City; Michael Lang, Sioux City; Dillon Thomas, Texas. **DH:** Curt Smith, Lincoln. **RHP:** Travis Banwart, Wichita. **RP:** Daniel Tillman, Wichita.

Player of the Year: Jose Sermo, 3B, Sioux City. **Manager of the Year:** Joe Calfapietra, Kansas City. **Rookie of the Year:** Justin Vernia, RHP, Sioux City.

BATTING LEADERS

Player	Team	AVG	AB	R	H	HR	RBI
Nate Samson	SC	.340	415	79	141	4	73
Logan Watkins	CLE	.338	420	63	142	3	51
Todd Cunningham	KC	.333	318	71	106	4	47
Dillon Thomas	TEX	.333	291	56	97	13	54
Dylan Tice	KC	.331	275	55	91	1	16
Edwin Arroyo	CHI	.325	363	54	118	4	35
Randolph Oduber	LIN	.324	349	60	113	8	57
Tim Colwell	FM	.320	325	47	104	3	41
Leobaldo Pina	FM	.319	367	46	117	8	56
Mason Davis	KC	.319	260	46	83	9	31

PITCHING LEADERS

Player	Team	W	L	ERA	IP	H	BB	SO
Travis Banwart	CLE	8	4	2.24	124	113	34	109
Daniel Minor	GARY	11	2	2.51	97	87	19	77
Eddie Medina	STP	9	5	2.80	116	99	43	104
Tommy Collier	KC	12	3	3.11	133	120	22	140
Taylor Jordan	SC	10	2	3.29	96	95	20	73
Justin Vernia	SC	12	3	3.32	119	122	22	91
James Dykstra	SC	9	4	3.49	108	106	26	84
Lars Liguori	GARY	4	7	3.52	95	117	16	45
Mitchell Lambson	WIN	8	6	3.81	116	120	24	81
Casey Harman	WIC	11	5	3.87	121	118	33	98

CHICAGO DOGS

Player	AVG	AB	R	H	HR	RBI	BB	SO	SB
Edwin Arroyo	.325	363	54	118	4	35	39	52	7
Kenny Wilson	.318	223	44	71	6	26	20	53	13
Joe Benson	.300	257	40	77	9	38	28	50	9
Trey Vavra	.299	368	41	110	16	65	37	55	5
Ryan Wagner	.298	47	4	14	0	6	4	10	0

	AVG	AB	R	H	HR	RBI	BB	SO	SB
Jonathan Moroney	.295	220	36	65	3	23	14	44	3
Stephen Perez	.293	167	22	49	3	37	18	41	6
Zach Racusin	.292	48	5	14	0	0	0	4	1
Rubi Silva	.286	192	27	55	5	30	4	50	3
Josh Goossen-Brown	.259	27	4	7	0	0	1	8	0
Dalton Blaser	.257	261	29	67	5	27	30	33	2
Tony Rosselli	.240	204	24	49	8	21	15	70	0
Matt Dean	.232	306	29	71	6	27	25	81	1
Craig Maddox	.227	97	7	22	1	12	4	29	1
Shawon Dunston	.226	31	5	7	0	6	1	6	1
Matt Telesco	.222	63	8	14	0	3	4	10	0
Michael Baca	.216	116	13	25	0	12	7	21	3
Kyle Gaedele	.213	47	5	10	2	6	2	19	0
Mike Falsetti	.186	161	24	30	3	16	38	58	1
Wilfredo Rodriguez	.163	49	2	8	0	4	3	7	1
Rey Gonzalez	.133	45	4	6	0	0	4	15	0

Player	W	L	ERA	G	SV	IP	H	BB	SO
Rich Mascheri	4	1	2.34	32	0	61.2	53	29	63
Brandon Shimo	1	0	2.44	34	0	48.0	28	14	41
Tommy Thorpe	4	4	2.53	38	1	74.2	67	23	60
Taylor Grover	1	2	2.63	43	14	48.0	36	20	63
Kaohi Downing	2	3	2.81	39	13	41.2	28	12	42
Trevor Simms	2	5	2.98	8	0	48.1	37	15	39
Wes Torrez	1	1	3.00	3	0	15.0	10	6	16
Jared Carkuff	6	5	3.12	26	0	66.1	62	14	68
Tyson Perez	3	2	4.32	20	0	25.0	24	13	28
Chad Girodo	2	0	4.37	22	0	22.2	31	6	19
Michael Wagner	2	3	4.44	11	0	46.2	49	24	39
Scott Barnes	2	4	4.46	16	0	84.2	84	47	73
Kylin Turnbull	4	4	4.62	13	0	64.1	75	8	40
Josh Goossen-Brown	7	8	5.09	20	0	116.2	141	38	60
Connor Root	2	8	5.43	12	0	59.2	78	22	42
Evan Smith	1	1	7.13	4	0	17.2	26	7	9

CLEBURNE RAILROADERS

Player	AVG	AB	R	H	HR	RBI	BB	SO	SB
Blake Grant-Parks	.312	125	17	39	3	19	9	25	4
Rafael Palmeiro	.301	103	10	31	6	21	20	25	0
Hunter Clanin	.286	98	14	28	2	16	11	13	4
Chase Simpson	.284	88	11	25	2	9	24	23	5
Angelo Gumbs	.276	225	21	62	4	21	11	44	6
Levi Scott	.270	356	52	96	15	55	52	128	1
Trevor Sealey	.267	330	56	88	6	30	29	53	9
Patrick Palmeiro	.255	377	36	96	9	48	26	115	1
KC Huth	.254	339	36	86	3	18	17	62	11
Angel Rosa	.251	211	45	53	14	36	19	48	8
Michael Pair	.250	40	4	10	0	5	5	13	0
Michael Gulino	.240	96	16	23	3	16	12	26	1
Justin Byrd	.235	34	6	8	0	2	6	7	3
Cameron Monger	.229	310	49	71	12	40	28	136	20
Axel Johnson	.194	36	1	7	0	5	0	8	0
Jake Simpson	.189	37	2	7	0	1	4	15	0
Dustin Williams	.185	27	6	5	1	7	7	13	0
Alex Polston	.176	278	24	49	1	20	28	74	5
Jordan Dean	.167	48	4	8	0	2	2	9	1
John Menken	.162	68	9	11	2	6	12	27	2
Quinn Irey	.138	29	2	4	0	0	3	9	0
Chevy Clarke	.105	38	6	4	0	2	3	8	1
Paul Ludden	.088	34	5	3	0	2	9	15	0

Player	W	L	ERA	G	SV	IP	H	BB	SO
James Williams	0	0	0.75	2	0	12.0	9	6	10
Jesus Sanchez	2	3	3.68	25	0	44.0	46	11	49
Shawn Blackwell	5	6	3.75	50	13	62.1	57	18	62
Tyler Wilson	2	2	3.86	16	1	21.0	18	13	20
Jared Mortensen	4	5	4.01	17	0	110.0	100	47	96
Dylan Mouzakes	2	6	4.84	16	0	80.0	95	31	71
Will Mathis	0	4	4.92	43	0	75.0	77	34	68
Cortland Cox	3	0	5.00	16	1	18.0	25	7	21
Patrick Mincey	3	9	5.59	20	0	120.2	161	30	70
Roman Gomez	0	7	5.61	30	0	67.1	81	26	47

INDEPENDENT LEAGUES

	W	L	ERA	G	SV	IP	H	BB	SO
Michael Gunn	3	8	5.69	22	0	87.0	100	53	61
Josh Hodges	5	6	5.71	21	0	86.2	109	33	55
Pat Young	3	6	6.14	31	1	63.0	54	57	68
John Hayes	0	3	10.97	11	0	10.2	16	11	12

	W	L	ERA	G	SV	IP	H	BB	SO
Alex Gunn	8	6	4.63	19	0	114.2	133	23	73
Chuck Weaver	0	1	4.97	3	0	12.2	16	6	12
Brendan Jenkins	2	1	6.00	9	0	12.0	17	4	

FARGO-MOORHEAD REDHAWKS

Player	AVG	AB	R	H	HR	RBI	BB	SO	SB
Chris Jacobs	.337	193	31	65	12	42	17	52	0
Tim Colwell	.320	325	47	104	3	41	22	42	24
Leobaldo Pina	.319	367	46	117	8	56	26	71	3
Devan Ahart	.295	387	61	114	11	48	38	61	12
Yhoxian Medina	.293	276	33	81	1	29	7	39	8
Maikol Gonzalez	.282	341	45	96	5	37	47	41	11
Brennan Metzger	.282	355	76	100	9	38	62	77	12
Keury De La Cruz	.275	335	36	92	15	58	33	65	3
Tommy Mendonca	.273	110	14	30	3	12	7	21	1
Charlie Valerio	.258	318	45	82	12	46	21	64	0
Randolph Oduber	.250	80	15	20	1	7	4	19	2
Jake Vieth	.242	33	5	8	0	2	4	6	0
Derrick Fox	.214	117	17	25	0	9	8	26	3
Quinn Irey	.208	72	8	15	1	7	4	16	1
Joe DeLuca	.170	47	5	8	1	2	4	17	3
Steve Zimmerman	.170	53	6	9	0	5	12	17	1

Player	W	L	ERA	G	SV	IP	H	BB	SO
Andrew Woeck	0	1	1.44	22	1	25.0	20	13	31
Sebastian Kessay	4	3	2.45	12	0	69.2	57	34	66
Geoff Broussard	0	1	2.67	23	5	27.0	23	7	27
Randy McCurry	3	3	3.38	36	17	37.1	33	19	44
Benji Waite	4	4	3.92	25	1	57.1	59	18	35
Travis Ballew	5	3	4.00	49	1	63.0	57	32	54
D.J. Brown	9	3	4.04	20	0	122.2	133	39	70
Anthony Pacillo	1	0	4.15	44	1	30.1	33	19	30
Will Solomon	10	7	4.18	19	0	114.0	127	39	58
Reese Gregory	3	5	4.34	24	0	74.2	92	10	35
Jose Nivar	0	1	4.35	9	0	10.1	10	3	12
Brandon Barker	3	6	4.85	12	0	68.2	86	15	54
Michael Tamburino	2	2	5.12	6	0	31.2	36	11	32
Trey McNutt	7	8	5.21	20	0	121.0	121	43	130

GARY SOUTHSHORE RAILCATS

Player	AVG	AB	R	H	HR	RBI	BB	SO	SB
Tillman Pugh	.357	157	27	56	7	24	21	31	5
Ronnie Mitchell	.316	133	14	42	1	21	9	22	2
D.K. Carey	.311	257	38	80	3	38	33	62	8
Will Savage	.309	136	24	42	1	16	15	26	4
Colin Willis	.297	330	50	98	9	50	48	60	4
Andy DeJesus	.290	293	32	85	1	39	13	55	11
Andy Paz	.283	251	30	71	1	40	13	42	3
Wilfredo Gimenez	.255	220	23	56	3	27	14	41	2
Randy Santiesteban	.255	271	50	69	9	40	20	43	0
Cole Fabio	.252	250	31	63	0	31	27	54	12
Alex Crosby	.249	349	51	87	6	36	32	36	8
KC Huth	.241	29	4	7	1	4	2	9	0
Mitch Glasser	.228	92	9	21	0	9	11	6	1
Reggie Wilson	.228	237	38	54	1	20	39	68	10
John Price	.217	46	4	10	0	1	0	11	0
Garrett Copeland	.193	197	27	38	3	20	29	67	3
Chris Bono	.121	58	5	7	0	2	5	20	0

Player	W	L	ERA	G	SV	IP	H	BB	SO
Scott Plaza	2	0	1.29	5	0	14.0	9	2	10
Myles Smith	4	1	1.36	33	4	46.1	33	15	51
Peyton Sanderlin	2	0	1.46	2	0	12.1	10	2	4
Mario Samuel	2	0	1.54	7	0	11.2	8	4	11
Adam Quintana	2	2	2.01	31	12	44.2	33	15	60
Dan Minor	11	2	2.51	15	0	97.0	87	19	77
Jorge De Leon	2	1	2.82	10	1	22.1	18	5	26
Gabe Perez	5	1	3.21	24	5	70.0	46	33	59
Keaton Steele	4	6	3.33	29	0	78.1	81	25	38
Lars Liguori	4	7	3.52	20	0	94.2	117	16	45
Austin Wright	1	1	3.66	4	0	19.2	19	6	22
Jack Fowler	1	1	4.15	33	1	43.1	44	10	39
Jeff McKenzie	6	9	4.51	24	1	137.2	161	23	69

KANSAS CITY T-BONES

Player	AVG	AB	R	H	HR	RBI	BB	SO	SB
Cal Towey	.341	85	16	29	3	18	9	26	1
Ryan Brett	.336	113	24	38	0	9	16	12	7
Todd Cunningham	.333	318	71	106	4	47	57	46	17
Dylan Tice	.331	275	55	91	1	16	41	41	12
Nick Torres	.329	231	40	76	5	43	20	63	2
Mason Davis	.319	260	46	83	9	31	10	41	26
Adrian Nieto	.313	291	40	91	6	44	34	40	3
Keith Curcio	.306	353	57	108	11	57	31	48	20
Anthony Phillips	.300	50	13	15	1	6	6	9	1
Noah Perio	.297	209	31	62	8	57	21	32	3
Alay Lago	.283	145	17	41	2	19	8	20	~3
Zach Walters	.279	190	29	53	6	34	10	34	0
Johnny Davis	.273	55	4	15	0	8	1	12	6
Colin Walsh	.268	164	34	44	8	31	41	41	4
Tucker Pennell	.267	180	14	48	2	21	15	33	0
Dexter Kjerstad	.247	215	30	53	4	30	18	43	8
Logan Moon	.232	69	5	16	0	1	5	23	0
Angel Rosa	.229	105	11	24	2	13	9	32	6
Jordan Edgerton	.222	36	4	8	0	0	2	10	0
Taylor Featherston	.202	99	17	20	5	15	10	31	2
Danny Hayes	.200	35	3	7	1	2	5	14	0

Player	W	L	ERA	G	SV	IP	H	BB	SO
Carlos Diaz	1	2	0.48	18	9	18.2	10	12	27
Joe Filomeno	4	2	1.31	35	1	41.1	24	10	48
Marcus Crescentini	5	0	1.32	25	1	27.1	11	17	36
Cody Winiarski	3	1	1.69	31	12	32.0	28	9	43
Scott Carroll	3	0	2.12	5	0	29.2	22	4	21
Tommy Collier	12	3	3.11	20	0	133.0	120	22	140
Jackson Lowery	1	0	3.18	32	0	45.1	32	24	56
Nick Lee	1	2	3.26	17	0	19.1	20	13	21
Luis Paula	1	1	3.68	3	0	14.2	11	1	4
Sam Street	0	1	4.03	19	1	22.1	18	8	20
Kevin Hill	1	1	4.30	21	1	23.0	22	7	20
Adam Bleday	1	1	4.50	10	0	30.0	31	14	30
Pasquale Mazzoccoli	4	2	4.53	27	2	53.2	54	35	46
Hunter Adkins	6	7	4.56	22	1	98.2	104	44	75
Francisco Gracesqui	1	2	5.74	24	2	31.1	25	28	36
Barrett Astin	10	3	5.80	19	0	102.1	119	35	69
Luke Irvine	5	4	5.99	15	0	85.2	110	20	48
Jayson Aquino	0	1	6.00	4	0	15.0	20	5	5
Jared Mortensen	0	1	6.14	4	0	22.0	30	9	26
James Buckelew	2	1	6.75	4	1	18.2	24	13	17

LINCOLN SALTDOGS

Player	AVG	AB	R	H	HR	RBI	BB	SO	SB
Randolph Oduber	.346	269	45	93	7	50	25	51	4
Omar Obregon	.316	38	6	12	0	1	2	7	0
Curt Smith	.315	365	53	115	18	74	26	51	2
Christian Ibarra	.299	345	76	103	20	64	62	68	2
Angel Reyes	.287	202	41	58	10	30	15	36	8
Chase Simpson	.277	141	25	39	6	22	32	38	0
Cesar Valera	.273	282	34	77	3	31	28	47	9
T.J. Bennett	.271	214	38	58	11	39	31	61	3
Dashenko Ricardo	.269	253	29	68	5	35	13	65	0
Brandon Jacobs	.260	361	65	94	22	68	49	120	5
Nathaniel Maggio	.257	179	19	46	2	15	15	47	0
Ivan Marin	.254	197	35	50	3	18	30	29	2
Dan Johnson	.250	72	6	18	1	9	10	16	0
Daniel Herrera	.241	54	3	13	0	3	4	18	0
Jamey Smart	.222	45	2	10	0	4	6	10	0
Alex Glenn	.202	109	15	22	4	16	12	30	7
Chad Hinshaw	.184	114	21	21	1	12	24	36	4
Brant Whiting	.178	90	15	16	3	9	6	18	0

Player	W	L	ERA	G	SV	IP	H	BB	SO
Dan Johnson	1	0	2.57	4	1	21.0	20	6	13
J.R. Bunda	3	0	2.73	25	8	26.1	18	9	28

INDEPENDENT LEAGUES

Eric Wooten	3	6	3.13	25	0	69.0	69	28	56
Derek Gordon	8	1	3.52	31	0	71.2	69	20	79
Jose Jose	3	3	3.80	34	11	42.2	39	14	40
Kyle Kinman	6	5	3.90	21	0	87.2	84	44	65
Brian Smith	1	0	3.95	9	0	13.2	15	8	11
Michael Tamburino	5	5	4.24	14	0	85.0	88	18	71
Joe Bircher	3	3	4.34	9	0	56.0	60	24	43
Austin Robichaux	5	7	4.40	20	0	110.1	120	47	82
Jake Hohensee	0	3	4.50	22	1	30.0	31	17	26
Shairon Martis	3	5	5.01	25	0	41.1	41	17	32
Dimitri Kourtis	2	2	5.05	17	0	35.2	43	25	30
Cortland Cox	1	1	5.25	18	1	24.0	25	11	16
Brad Thoutt	3	1	5.87	10	0	30.2	36	18	21
Tyler Herron	4	5	7.33	12	0	66.1	87	14	61
Leland Tilley	0	0	10.13	7	1	10.2	15	6	16
Mikey O'Brien	0	1	11.91	3	0	11.1	21	10	7

SIOUX CITY EXPLORERS

Player	AVG	AB	R	H	HR	RBI	BB	SO	SB
Blake Schmit	.370	127	27	47	1	17	10	12	7
Jay Austin	.364	206	43	75	3	36	23	14	13
Nate Samson	.340	415	79	141	4	73	28	28	22
Jose Sermo	.316	316	75	100	22	81	59	101	24
Michael Lang	.304	414	82	126	9	45	31	96	16
Dean Green	.303	76	16	23	3	17	9	8	1
Luis Durango	.303	412	71	125	0	34	53	40	24
Dylan Kelly	.297	320	35	95	2	65	26	43	7
Jay Baum	.285	365	72	104	8	77	55	72	9
Dexture McCall	.283	353	60	100	3	55	35	70	4
Daniel Jackson	.261	283	45	74	3	48	38	62	8
David Kerian	.237	97	15	23	2	14	11	34	0

Player	W	L	ERA	G	SV	IP	H	BB	SO
Tyler Fallwell	2	1	0.64	23	2	28.0	18	12	33
Jason Garcia	3	0	1.57	4	0	23.0	15	9	22
Patrick Schuster	4	1	1.64	46	0	33.0	20	9	47
Eric Karch	2	3	2.27	41	21	43.2	42	16	61
Ryan Flores	8	2	2.63	46	2	61.2	45	25	70
Dom Topoozian	1	1	2.93	11	1	30.2	32	5	19
Ryan Horstman	0	0	3.06	35	1	32.1	26	20	47
Ian McKinney	2	2	3.19	10	0	53.2	53	22	67
Taylor Jordan	10	2	3.29	15	0	95.2	95	20	73
Justin Vernia	12	2	3.32	20	0	119.1	122	22	91
James Dykstra	9	4	3.49	19	0	108.1	106	26	84
Parker Markel	1	1	4.14	37	4	41.1	38	21	62
Luis Mateo	11	5	4.21	21	0	124.0	144	42	112
Keith Picht	5	4	5.27	20	0	66.2	85	36	53
Geoff Broussard	0	0	5.40	15	1	15.0	11	11	22

SIOUX FALLS CANARIES

Player	AVG	AB	R	H	HR	RBI	BB	SO	SB
Mike Hart	.311	206	26	64	1	15	9	56	7
Mitch Glasser	.289	249	27	72	0	19	27	28	6
Chris Grayson	.281	324	51	91	8	41	19	53	27
Blake Schmit	.280	236	27	66	1	25	18	28	9
David Bergin	.278	291	47	81	12	51	44	99	1
Jordan Dean	.265	260	39	69	5	28	20	48	7
Dan Motl	.264	208	28	55	2	23	18	61	22
Patrick Fiala	.260	285	35	74	9	37	15	64	1
Jordan Smith	.253	300	44	76	4	30	30	59	25
Jabari Henry	.247	328	49	81	13	52	35	82	1
Tyler Wolfe	.246	65	8	16	1	6	7	15	0
Maxx Garrett	.241	282	39	68	12	40	36	111	4
Jeff Malm	.228	114	11	26	4	18	8	37	0
Chris Jacobs	.224	67	3	15	1	10	6	24	0
Aaron Gretz	.169	59	4	10	0	3	7	11	0

Player	W	L	ERA	G	SV	IP	H	BB	SO
Cesilio Pimentel	3	1	1.36	11	0	46.1	43	13	29
Ryan Fritze	5	2	3.06	42	0	50.0	43	25	60
Kyle Schepel	1	5	3.28	50	14	57.2	46	30	75
Kevin Folman	3	2	3.48	7	0	41.1	42	16	21
Luis Pollorena	0	2	3.56	14	1	30.1	27	2	19

Trevor Jaunich	2	1	3.86	28	1	37.1	47	15	33
Nicco Blank	3	1	4.15	41	1	43.1	31	38	50
Miles Nordgren	2	6	4.32	26	1	91.2	121	25	50
Jake Esch	5	4	4.33	12	0	72.2	77	28	44
Dylan Thompson	5	9	5.13	21	0	121.0	149	44	88
John Straka	3	5	5.26	13	0	49.2	69	21	41
Joe Bircher	3	4	5.37	10	0	58.2	67	26	36
Mark Seyler	2	4	5.40	8	0	41.2	43	20	26
Will LaMarche	0	1	6.35	11	0	11.1	12	7	17
Grady Wood	1	2	7.40	4	0	20.2	32	12	13
Tyler Wolfe	1	3	7.53	15	0	28.2	39	11	22
Bo Hellquist	0	0	7.53	10	0	14.1	15	12	12
James Jones	0	3	7.98	16	8	14.2	17	12	17
Dimitri Kourtis	1	0	10.80	9	0	10.0	14	2	9
Jim Patterson	0	3	11.81	5	0	16.0	31	13	11
Chad Martin	0	1	13.50	9	0	12.0	13	13	11

ST. PAUL SAINTS

Player	AVG	AB	R	H	HR	RBI	BB	SO	SB
Aaron Gretz	.350	60	13	21	2	12	8	5	0
Josh Allen	.344	90	17	31	4	11	8	18	2
Kyle Barrett	.338	234	44	79	4	29	24	32	17
Max Murphy	.319	427	70	136	7	68	32	80	10
Noah Perio	.311	183	26	57	0	17	18	22	1
Dante Bichette	.310	387	56	120	9	52	28	51	1
Brady Shoemaker	.309	346	58	107	14	69	47	42	2
Zach Walters	.300	207	33	62	9	38	13	40	1
Nathaniel Maggio	.297	138	23	41	4	21	15	32	0
Trevor Sealey	.280	25	4	7	0	3	2	2	0
Burt Reynolds	.280	207	37	58	15	43	32	59	12
Joey Wong	.272	81	17	22	1	12	13	16	0
Jayce Boyd	.270	100	10	27	1	11	11	12	1
Jake Smith	.254	63	14	16	0	12	4	20	0
Richard Prigatano	.254	130	19	33	1	14	19	29	8
Kes Carter	.250	152	14	38	4	18	15	44	6
Justin O'Conner	.250	292	44	73	17	41	13	86	1
Matt Snyder	.242	66	10	16	1	7	9	15	0
Anthony Phillips	.242	120	19	29	1	16	14	27	1
J.J. Gould	.237	93	11	22	2	11	11	33	0
Dan Motl	.200	25	4	5	0	2	6	6	2

Player	W	L	ERA	G	SV	IP	H	BB	SO
Zack Jones	1	0	2.03	27	10	26.2	19	10	38
Kenny Frosch	3	1	2.06	52	1	39.1	21	16	39
Beck Wheeler	3	1	2.21	46	1	61.0	46	15	94
Mike Devine	5	4	2.57	49	6	66.2	54	21	68
Evan Mitchell	2	0	2.57	9	0	14.0	12	3	13
Eddie Medina	9	5	2.80	20	0	115.2	99	43	104
Tom Wilhelmsen	1	2	2.89	18	7	18.2	14	7	14
Trevor Foss	4	2	3.04	11	0	71.0	79	18	44
Chris Nunn	7	3	3.05	11	0	59.0	59	13	49
Vinny Nittoli	3	2	3.21	5	0	28.0	25	6	38
Jake Matthys	9	8	4.10	34	1	90.0	92	25	66
Matt Solter	3	5	4.73	15	0	80.0	87	31	56
Ryan Boelter	2	1	4.75	20	0	30.1	34	8	24
Ryan Schlosser	2	1	4.82	23	0	37.1	44	16	21
John Straka	1	0	5.40	3	0	15.0	22	7	6
Jake Esch	3	2	6.96	7	0	32.1	44	17	32
Ryan Zimmerman	2	2	7.06	13	0	51.0	59	28	47
Jeff Malm	0	1	7.71	7	0	21.0	25	7	13
Andrew Thome	0	1	9.15	20	3	19.2	32	13	19

TEXAS AIRHOGS

Player	AVG	AB	R	H	HR	RBI	BB	SO	SB
Dillon Thomas	.333	291	56	97	13	54	36	71	14
Correlle Prime	.279	297	33	83	7	42	27	65	4
Stewart Ijames	.267	378	52	101	10	46	48	90	14
Casio Grider	.261	299	28	78	3	26	30	67	13
Javion Randle	.259	58	4	15	0	4	7	18	2
Greg Golson	.259	162	15	42	1	11	14	45	0
Luan Chenchen	.255	106	8	27	0	7	5	17	1
Chu Fujia	.245	110	15	27	0	5	6	13	5
Chen Junpeng	.244	123	6	30	0	14	5	22	0

Player	AVG	AB	R	H	HR	RBI	BB	SO	SB
Han Jichao	.238	42	3	10	0	2	3	15	0
Han Xiao	.235	34	3	8	0	3	1	8	1
Du Xiaolei	.233	90	4	21	0	4	6	19	1
Li Ning	.226	124	6	28	0	7	10	16	5
Yang Jin	.220	141	10	31	0	2	4	35	3
Luo Jinjun	.203	69	5	14	1	5	1	16	1
Lu Zhenhong	.196	148	12	29	0	8	10	47	0
Liang Pei	.191	68	8	13	0	4	6	22	1
Cao Jie	.188	48	3	9	1	4	4	23	0
Chen Chen	.187	198	13	37	0	10	17	52	0
Jesse Baker	.180	50	5	9	1	2	6	17	0
Ryan Wagner	.175	40	3	7	0	5	4	13	0
Song Yunqi	.171	129	8	22	0	3	3	34	2
Ni Ziyang	.167	30	0	5	0	3	1	7	0
Du Xiaoci	.152	46	1	7	0	3	7	15	0
Meng Weiqiang	.123	73	1	9	0	1	5	21	0
Cao Yijie	.121	33	1	4	0	0	1	6	0
Li Qi	.068	44	1	3	0	0	7	21	0

Player	W	L	ERA	G	SV	IP	H	BB	SO
Zheng Chaoqun	0	1	1.42	22	0	25.1	14	11	23
Carlos Contreras	2	0	1.52	24	14	23.2	14	6	31
Qi Xin	0	1	2.11	21	0	21.1	20	15	15
Taylor Wright	4	2	3.46	33	3	39.0	43	16	31
Chen Zhongyang	0	0	3.55	9	0	12.2	15	14	5
Cui Enting	1	0	4.11	10	0	15.1	19	2	9
Gan Quan	0	6	4.24	14	0	70.0	67	36	31
Lu Yusong	2	1	4.43	20	0	22.1	27	9	15
Meng Weiqiang	4	6	4.65	14	0	69.2	80	34	62
Calvin Drummond	0	0	5.23	8	0	10.1	11	3	12
Yang Yanyong	0	4	5.60	25	0	35.1	42	16	17
Zhang Tao	3	3	5.83	8	0	29.1	37	24	23
Miguel Rosario	2	12	5.87	20	0	96.2	97	58	80
Tyler Matzek	3	8	5.89	22	0	88.2	89	66	93
Liu Guoqing	1	0	6.00	8	0	15.0	20	2	11
Ran Song	1	1	6.27	22	0	18.2	24	15	13
Sun Jianzeng	1	5	7.34	10	0	41.2	64	17	18
Zhang Haonan	0	4	7.50	6	0	24.0	23	23	10
Zhu Jinghao	0	5	7.90	7	0	27.1	40	22	10
Sean Stutzman	0	5	8.20	17	0	37.1	49	35	34
Liu Yu	0	0	8.53	14	0	25.1	32	15	18
Cody White	0	4	9.00	6	0	23.0	32	13	17
Tu Jialun	0	0	12.15	16	0	13.1	18	16	11
Conner Camacho	0	1	14.40	9	0	15.0	27	13	12
Su Guangyao	0	0	15.30	8	0	10.0	19	16	11

WICHITA WINGNUTS

Player	AVG	AB	R	H	HR	RBI	BB	SO	SB
Logan Watkins	.338	420	63	142	3	51	44	66	26
Angel Reyes	.320	125	27	40	7	26	12	31	10
Zach Nehrir	.312	388	65	121	7	61	38	78	38
Abel Nieves	.300	380	59	114	4	47	58	46	7
Logan Trowbridge	.278	270	40	75	1	25	30	44	7
John Nester	.269	334	42	90	7	50	36	90	2
Nick Rotola	.263	156	20	41	1	18	12	41	8
Fernando Perez	.262	107	18	28	8	23	15	24	0
Chase Simpson	.261	115	16	30	5	16	19	28	2
Leo Vargas	.256	320	39	82	0	29	28	71	13
Tony Thomas	.249	398	72	99	23	74	28	121	10
Hunter Clanin	.240	125	14	30	2	24	4	26	4
Ryne Willard	.203	177	25	36	3	21	17	67	1
Isaiah Aluko	.167	36	5	6	1	5	8	18	1
Nick Kaye	.063	32	1	2	0	0	4	10	0

Player	W	L	ERA	G	SV	IP	H	BB	SO
Scott Kuzminsky	0	0	2.05	13	0	22.0	19	1	23
Travis Banwart	8	4	2.24	20	0	124.1	113	34	109
Daniel Tillman	1	4	2.27	40	27	39.2	33	11	54
Felix Carvallo	2	1	2.44	33	0	51.2	57	19	48
Austin Boyle	2	0	2.68	30	2	37.0	34	12	39
Seth Harvey	7	2	3.44	30	1	65.1	62	20	67
Casey Harman	11	5	3.87	21	1	121.0	118	33	98
Brady Bowen	2	1	3.91	39	2	48.1	69	12	50
Jordan Cooper	11	6	4.41	21	0	120.1	133	33	78
Tyler Kane	7	3	4.52	14	0	75.2	78	36	34

Player	W	L	ERA	G	SV	IP	H	BB	SO
Charlie Gillies	7	7	4.80	16	0	90.0	115	29	91
John Hayes	0	1	5.87	15	0	15.1	20	10	15
Corbin Osburn	2	1	7.56	4	0	16.2	28	9	6
James Campbell	0	3	8.50	19	2	18.0	23	13	11

WINNIPEG GOLDEYES

Player	AVG	AB	R	H	HR	RBI	BB	SO	SB
Reggie Abercrombie	.316	405	63	128	15	62	19	112	12
Josh Romanski	.313	278	39	87	4	30	28	27	2
Tucker Nathans	.288	264	43	76	12	33	30	68	4
Eric Aguilera	.286	63	12	18	1	7	13	22	0
Reynaldo Rodriguez	.281	89	15	25	3	17	11	9	3
Jordan Ebert	.280	232	35	65	0	20	27	30	12
Kevin Garcia	.273	132	17	36	1	18	13	15	1
Grant Heyman	.272	349	54	95	19	45	18	93	5
Tommy Mendonca	.269	26	4	7	2	5	1	4	0
Matt McCann	.258	221	25	57	0	21	37	40	6
Josh McAdams	.253	146	16	37	1	13	8	39	1
David Bergin	.250	32	6	8	1	5	6	14	0
Dave Sappelt	.250	116	18	29	2	14	17	9	2
Andrew Sohn	.250	224	26	56	1	30	24	51	11
Blake Adams	.245	49	5	12	1	3	4	7	2
Tyler Baker	.244	160	22	39	5	22	24	26	0
Gavin Stupienski	.236	72	9	17	0	8	5	24	0
Victor Cruzado	.233	86	9	20	0	8	12	22	1
Josh Mazzola	.233	361	45	84	20	75	33	75	1
Dexter Kjerstad	.200	50	2	10	0	1	2	8	0
J.J. Gould	.040	25	1	1	0	0	5	7	0

Player	W	L	ERA	G	SV	IP	H	BB	SO
Jack Charleston	2	3	2.63	60	1	51.1	44	19	34
Brandon Bingel	0	1	2.85	41	0	53.2	50	24	43
Cameron McVey	2	0	2.91	36	0	34.0	24	17	39
Brennan Bernardino	2	3	3.18	6	0	34.0	30	7	16
Tyler Herron	2	4	3.19	6	0	36.2	48	7	23
Victor Capellan	4	4	3.23	47	22	47.1	39	11	53
Shane Dawson	3	1	3.38	5	0	24.0	27	5	16
PJ Browne	1	0	3.74	16	0	33.2	34	11	17
Mitchell Lambson	8	6	3.81	18	0	115.2	120	24	81
Charle Rosario	2	2	3.94	8	0	48.0	52	21	39
Kevin McGovern	5	12	4.73	22	0	129.1	151	40	129
Edwin Carl	3	4	5.36	19	0	50.1	65	25	56
Alex Boshers	3	10	5.55	23	0	121.2	161	32	77
Juan Carlos Sulbaran	1	2	5.97	6	0	28.2	36	11	20
Carter Johnson	1	3	6.43	14	0	21.0	29	6	13
Zach Hartman	0	2	11.81	12	0	10.2	23	5	10

ATLANTIC LEAGUE

The Long Island Ducks are getting way too accustomed to watching other teams celebrate. For a third straight season the Ducks were league runners-up. Sugar Land knocked off the Ducks in the championship series giving Sugar Land its second title in three seasons.

Freedom Division	W	L	PCT	GB
* Sugar Land Skeeters	81	45	.643	—
^ Lancaster Barnstormers	74	52	.587	7
York Revolution	68	58	.540	13
Southern Maryland Blue Crabs	50	76	.397	31

Liberty Division	W	L	PCT	GB
* Somerset Patriots	72	54	.571	—
& Long Island Ducks	69	57	.548	3
New Britain Bees	61	65	.484	11
Road Warriors	29	97	.230	43

First-half champion. & Second-half champion. ^Wild-Card

Playoffs: Semifinals: Long Island defeated Somerset 3-2 and Sugar Land defeated Lancaster 3-2 in best-of-5 series. **Finals:** Sugar Land defeated Long Island 4-2 in best-of-7 series.

Attendance: Somerset 352,603; Long Island 349,058; Sugar Land 328,491; Lancaster 249,792; Southern Maryland 205,947; York 180,807; New Britain 183,147.

ALL-Star Team: C: Ryan Casteel, Lancaster. **1B:** Matt Chavez, Sugar Land; **2B:** Jordany Valdespin, Long Island. **3B:** Frank Martinez, Southern Maryland. **SS:** Alfredo Rodriguez, Somerset. **OF:** Blake Gailen,

Lancaster; Anthony Giansanti, Sugar Land; Melky Mesa, York. **DH:** Lew Ford, Long Island. **SP:** Nate Reed, Lancaster. **RP:** Mike Antonini, Somerset. **Closer:** Felipe Paulino, Sugar Land.

Player of the Year: Jordany Valdespin, Long Island. **Pitcher of the Year:** Nate Reed, Lancaster. **Defensive Player of the Year:** Edwin Garcia, Southern Maryland. **Manager of the Year:** Pete Incaviglia, Sugar Land.

BATTING LEADERS

Player	Team	AVG	AB	R	H	HR	RBI
Jordany Valdespin	LI	.338	456	94	154	12	55
Craig Massey	SOM	.338	328	56	111	3	40
Melky Mesa	YRK	.337	383	85	129	20	89
Alexi Casilla	YRK	.336	423	75	142	3	36
Frank Martinez	SMD	.321	436	45	140	11	62
Ryan Casteel	LAN	.321	365	51	117	16	70
Matt Chavez	SL	.320	472	59	151	12	72
Welington Dotel	YRK	.307	433	58	133	7	62
Angelys Nina	SMD	.304	358	41	109	2	40
Alfredo Rodriguez	SOM	.303	432	69	131	5	55

PITCHING LEADERS

Player	Team	W	L	ERA	IP	H	BB	SO
James Russell	SL	8	4	2.36	107	94	17	98
Vince Molesky	SOM	7	2	2.66	108	108	22	88
Nate Reed	LAN	13	3	2.75	115	92	40	104
Konner Wade	SL	8	6	3.10	137	144	19	79
Rainy Lara	NB	9	7	3.63	124	139	28	81
Craig Stem	SMD	7	8	3.70	107	107	34	86
Robert Carson	YRK	10	7	3.74	116	137	29	92
Jake Fisher	LI	8	7	3.92	133	148	25	107
Duane Below	SOM	9	6	3.99	129	150	22	94
Mitch Atkins	YRK	12	7	4.17	145	151	34	137

LANCASTER BARNSTORMERS

Player	AVG	AB	R	H	HR	RBI	BB	SO	SB
Jimmy Paredes	.363	80	15	29	3	14	5	20	1
Ryan Casteel	.321	365	51	117	16	70	34	53	3
Rico Noel	.305	295	50	90	2	31	18	50	53
Trayvon Robinson	.295	353	62	104	7	49	48	86	19
Vladimir Frias	.282	287	44	81	6	39	22	46	16
Blake Gailen	.282	444	80	125	28	91	72	82	14
Nate Coronado	.277	94	14	26	3	13	9	13	2
Joey Terdoslavich	.275	138	23	38	6	28	16	25	3
Carlos Garcia	.275	189	26	52	1	21	12	42	21
Darian Sandford	.274	471	74	129	0	35	57	109	82
K.C. Hobson	.244	291	36	71	10	46	20	86	1
Josh Bell	.237	156	21	37	6	29	25	49	7
Anderson De La Rosa	.229	240	21	55	1	15	6	46	2
Kyle Waldrop	.222	27	5	6	2	8	2	0	1
Stephen Perez	.216	37	9	8	0	5	12	10	1
Grant Desme	.215	121	8	26	1	6	6	31	3
Tyler Bortnick	.199	322	63	64	6	43	67	65	24
Keenyn Walker	.182	33	4	6	0	3	5	11	3

Player	W	L	ERA	G	SV	IP	H	BB	SO
Scott Shuman	2	0	0.98	29	0	27.2	13	9	52
Matt Marksberry	2	2	1.82	45	0	39.2	31	27	47
Huascar Brazoban	2	4	1.99	37	4	40.2	39	18	41
Garrett Granitz	1	1	2.72	45	1	43.0	40	23	31
Nate Reed	13	3	2.75	22	0	114.2	92	40	104
Kaleb Fleck	1	1	2.77	12	0	13.0	13	4	13
Matt Reynolds	0	1	2.86	45	25	44.0	41	13	43
Stephen Johnson	3	0	2.94	43	0	52.0	46	23	61
John Anderson	6	3	3.54	34	1	73.2	69	29	81
Kevin Munson	7	4	3.57	43	1	40.1	42	19	44
Jesus Sanchez	1	0	3.60	11	0	10.0	11	6	7
Jared Lakind	2	3	3.83	41	0	42.1	51	13	38
Jonathan Albaladejo	9	7	4.41	23	0	132.2	164	27	104
Luke Westphal	0	0	4.85	10	0	13.0	11	8	12
Brooks Hall	11	4	4.94	22	0	116.2	128	32	99
Steve Johnson	3	5	5.10	11	0	54.2	62	21	46
Joe Gardner	5	11	5.26	22	0	119.2	142	44	80
Ty'Relle Harris	2	1	5.32	6	0	23.2	27	15	27
Tommy Shirley	3	2	6.06	15	0	49.0	71	23	38

LONG ISLAND DUCKS

Player	AVG	AB	R	H	HR	RBI	BB	SO	SB
Emilio Bonifacio	.348	273	42	95	3	36	16	38	20
Jordany Valdespin	.338	456	94	154	12	55	46	58	30
Wilkin Castillo	.314	70	10	22	2	12	8	11	1
Lew Ford	.293	468	68	137	10	73	40	88	1
Travis Snider	.290	352	63	102	13	71	47	84	4
Steve Longo	.286	28	5	8	0	2	4	11	0
Taylor Ard	.271	361	46	98	16	61	25	99	0
Dioner Navarro	.268	71	10	19	3	13	4	5	0
Ramon Cabrera	.268	313	27	84	3	31	9	41	0
Daniel Fields	.267	341	48	91	9	40	38	112	12
Miles Williams	.259	112	13	29	4	14	6	42	2
Dan Lyons	.227	291	39	66	6	34	29	56	0
David Washington	.226	399	63	90	24	71	51	179	18
Cody Puckett	.222	302	35	67	7	37	22	63	0
Alec Sole	.219	64	14	14	0	8	8	14	4
Audie Afenir	.218	55	4	12	0	1	1	16	0
Rubi Silva	.217	46	4	10	2	5	1	12	0
Robert Garcia	.200	60	11	12	2	9	3	20	1
Anthony Vega	.176	187	27	33	4	12	19	70	23

Player	W	L	ERA	G	SV	IP	H	BB	SO
Fernando Abad	1	0	0.48	19	2	18.2	15	5	23
Logan Ondrusek	2	1	1.27	20	0	21.1	17	8	28
Jose Cuas	2	1	2.38	22	0	22.2	16	13	17
Francisco Rodriguez	2	1	2.76	44	27	42.1	30	22	42
Wander Perez	2	1	2.83	31	1	28.2	30	9	26
Bennett Parry	6	1	2.86	14	0	85.0	75	30	116
Carlos Pimentel	5	3	3.13	39	0	54.2	41	22	67
Matt Marsh	0	1	3.21	13	0	14.0	13	8	13
Tyler Badamo	3	2	3.38	7	0	40.0	44	8	26
Vinnie Pestano	1	1	3.50	18	2	18.0	11	9	19
Jair Jurrjens	3	3	3.55	9	0	50.2	52	12	32
Rob Rogers	0	0	3.75	13	0	12.0	10	5	16
Dennis O'Grady	6	4	3.82	52	0	63.2	63	22	41
Jake Fisher	8	7	3.92	21	0	133.1	148	25	107
Lorenzo Barcelo	2	1	4.20	12	0	30.0	35	5	23
Brett Marshall	1	1	4.26	3	0	12.2	14	11	12
Ashur Tolliver	2	2	4.34	49	2	47.2	44	25	56
Matt Larkins	7	5	4.56	19	0	102.2	133	21	66
John Brownell	9	11	4.66	22	0	129.1	143	45	88
Hector Silvestre	3	1	5.48	10	0	46.0	52	19	25
Colton Murray	0	2	6.86	24	0	21.0	20	13	24
Chris Pike	1	1	7.62	9	0	26.0	37	9	14
Jake Dunning	1	3	7.96	19	0	31.2	39	15	19
Lee Sosa	0	3	8.22	12	0	23.0	25	23	21
Branden Pinder	1	0	9.90	10	0	10.0	20	5	5

NEW BRITAIN BEES

Player	AVG	AB	R	H	HR	RBI	BB	SO	SB
Brock Stassi	.361	147	32	53	5	36	28	21	
Josh Thole	.317	60	7	19	0	10	11	12	
Jason Rogers	.297	390	53	116	5	65	64	45	
Reid Brignac	.295	220	29	65	1	23	26	41	
Jamar Walton	.280	375	54	105	12	54	20	101	
Jonathan Galvez	.277	405	50	112	10	47	38	97	
Darren Ford	.276	478	74	132	7	38	48	108	
Jovan Rosa	.263	194	16	51	6	25	15	46	
James Skelton	.255	267	45	68	3	33	56	84	
Deibinson Romero	.255	444	61	113	18	71	60	75	
Matt Tuiasosopo	.237	219	36	52	7	27	30	73	
Ryan Wagner	.235	102	12	24	1	7	10	18	
Ozney Guillen	.224	134	17	30	1	12	9	19	
Darrell Ceciliani	.212	66	4	14	0	2	5	11	
Vinny Siena	.207	193	24	40	4	26	18	78	
Conor Bierfeldt	.169	59	6	10	2	8	5	19	
Joe Poletsky	.167	30	3	5	1	2	2	10	
Angelo Songco	.167	78	4	13	1	6	12	22	
Vicente Conde	.165	170	18	28	2	20	27	50	
Manny Ramirez	.161	31	1	5	0	2	0	11	
Nate Irving	.160	25	3	4	0	0	0	11	
Angelys Nina	.140	43	1	6	1	3	1	12	

Player	W	L	ERA	G	SV	IP	H	BB	SO
Jared Carkuff	1	0	0.68	2	0	13.1	8	3	10

Player	W	L	ERA	G	SV	IP	H	BB	SO
Adam Loewen	3	0	1.64	26	0	22.0	19	4	28
Tyler Higgins	1	0	1.88	14	3	14.1	12	4	18
Jim Fuller	2	1	2.09	43	0	43.0	40	12	52
Evan Scribner	1	4	2.20	41	24	41.0	31	2	45
Sammy Gervacio	0	4	2.52	51	2	64.1	53	24	77
Zach Stewart	6	3	3.42	11	0	68.1	61	23	42
Andy Van Hekken	5	6	3.45	17	0	94.0	103	18	72
Tyler Badamo	1	1	3.49	5	0	28.1	25	6	14
Brandon Cunniff	2	0	3.54	26	1	28.0	28	6	25
Brandon Beachy	0	1	3.55	12	0	12.2	10	6	12
Rainy Lara	9	7	3.63	23	0	124.0	139	28	81
Elvin Ramirez	1	4	3.81	48	0	52.0	47	27	43
Chris Reed	0	3	3.91	21	0	23.0	25	12	29
Devin Burke	4	2	4.14	24	0	71.2	64	23	49
Matt Quintana	0	2	4.18	10	0	23.2	27	7	13
Kyle Simon	8	9	4.31	24	0	144.0	166	29	93
Mark Hamburger	10	8	4.39	21	0	127.0	128	44	86
Mike Hepple	0	1	4.79	21	0	20.2	19	14	17
Josh Outman	4	4	5.79	21	0	42.0	52	17	37
Manny Delcarmen	2	1	6.75	12	0	10.2	16	4	7

ROAD WARRIORS

Player	AVG	AB	R	H	HR	RBI	BB	SO	SB
Jose Julio-Ruiz	.299	304	32	91	4	33	18	53	0
Gustavo Pierre	.257	451	45	116	14	44	18	124	14
Osvaldo Martinez	.256	418	42	107	7	27	29	65	7
Anthony Ray	.250	240	27	60	0	13	21	63	15
Melvin Rodriguez	.248	391	30	97	4	32	22	86	5
Jorge Fernandez	.241	407	33	98	11	37	31	106	4
Isaac Wenrich	.235	179	15	42	3	14	20	47	1
Geraldo Valentin	.234	372	30	87	3	25	18	50	1
Edwin Gomez	.227	362	35	82	5	35	27	89	3
Ryde Rodriguez	.220	41	3	9	0	4	0	6	0
Ermindo Escobar	.217	120	7	26	1	9	2	19	1
Matt Hibbert	.217	189	25	41	2	13	21	69	13
Alfredo Silverio	.207	270	18	56	5	24	7	64	1
A.J. Jimenez	.204	49	4	10	1	6	0	12	0
Chris Rivera	.195	169	19	33	10	21	10	74	0
Daniel Aldrich	.189	127	13	24	3	9	8	56	0
Cody Bishop	.150	40	0	6	0	1	2	11	1

Player	W	L	ERA	G	SV	IP	H	BB	SO
Luis Cruz	1	2	2.51	44	2	71.2	64	25	79
Jailen Peguero	1	1	3.48	12	0	10.1	11	8	8
Christian Flecha	2	5	4.37	50	1	47.1	48	30	26
Andres Caceres	2	4	4.39	12	0	53.1	50	29	47
William Gabay	0	3	4.46	32	2	34.1	32	23	33
Jose Ortega	0	2	4.47	47	2	50.1	55	29	49
Mariel Checo	0	2	4.85	15	0	26.0	21	16	29
Raul Rivera	4	14	4.87	24	0	129.1	148	35	90
Giovanni Soto	1	3	4.95	9	0	43.2	52	15	40
Andrew Johnston	3	3	4.96	43	12	49.0	69	14	24
Zech Zinicola	0	3	4.98	19	0	21.2	19	11	20
Felix Baez	3	12	6.04	25	0	117.2	128	64	95
Mike Lee	2	10	6.25	13	0	63.1	85	18	51
Brandon Bargas	0	6	6.66	13	0	50.0	70	31	35
Kelvin Villa	6	12	6.69	26	0	117.0	153	72	72
Alberto Rodriguez	2	5	6.85	10	0	47.1	65	28	41
Julio DePaula	1	5	6.89	23	1	32.2	49	19	31
Chris Treibt	1	1	7.22	22	0	28.2	42	14	18
David Perez	0	3	9.26	3	0	11.2	21	7	9

SOMERSET PATRIOTS

Player	AVG	AB	R	H	HR	RBI	BB	SO	SB
Craig Massey	.338	328	56	111	3	40	43	72	24
Jayce Boyd	.316	133	19	42	5	22	13	26	2
Alfredo Rodriguez	.303	432	69	131	5	55	58	62	17
Julio Borbon	.301	229	39	69	5	33	20	32	19
Endy Chavez	.287	349	29	100	2	41	18	27	1
Nate Coronado	.283	180	27	51	7	26	18	42	5
Ramon Flores	.280	225	25	63	4	31	21	38	2
Justin Pacchioli	.280	257	50	72	0	25	31	50	34
Justin Trapp	.273	308	49	84	8	32	28	56	33

Player	AVG	AB	R	H	HR	RBI	BB	SO	SB
Alex Castellanos	.272	92	13	25	4	17	7	24	1
Mike Fransoso	.267	393	61	105	2	46	62	98	24
Yovan Gonzalez	.257	218	23	56	0	30	20	36	0
Danny Dorn	.246	191	15	47	1	22	13	41	0
Aaron Dudley	.237	156	15	37	2	19	14	41	0
Alfonso Reda	.231	26	1	6	0	1	3	6	0
Matt Oberste	.231	117	15	27	3	16	12	27	0
Kyle Roller	.205	156	22	32	7	22	28	67	0
Scott Kelly	.203	138	13	28	0	7	17	27	10
Adam Weisenburger	.198	111	16	22	4	18	9	26	1
Jermaine Curtis	.194	36	2	7	0	5	7	9	0
Mike Blanke	.143	98	8	14	1	5	11	26	0

Player	W	L	ERA	G	SV	IP	H	BB	SO
Mike Antonini	3	2	1.41	42	0	51.0	28	11	56
Vince Molesky	7	2	2.66	29	0	108.1	108	22	88
Zech Zinicola	2	1	2.87	12	0	15.2	13	9	16
Aaron Laffey	2	0	3.10	4	0	20.1	21	5	13
Cory Riordan	3	3	3.13	14	0	83.1	86	12	62
Ryan Kelly	2	3	3.16	46	23	42.2	33	10	57
Dustin Antolin	3	4	3.28	49	3	46.2	43	20	46
Stephen Perakslis	2	1	3.35	9	0	45.2	43	8	46
Dave Kubiak	8	3	3.40	14	0	82.0	76	31	95
Chase Huchingson	5	1	3.55	51	0	45.2	45	20	42
Dustin Molleken	4	2	3.58	43	1	55.1	54	18	58
Rick Teasley	4	5	3.60	16	0	80.0	80	24	71
Ryan Webb	0	0	3.60	6	0	10.0	6	9	10
Duane Below	9	6	3.99	22	0	128.2	150	22	94
Logan Kensing	3	4	4.00	55	0	54.0	47	17	55
Kyle Davies	6	8	4.50	21	0	104.0	103	43	90
Nate Roe	5	3	4.55	48	1	59.1	63	25	41
Trevor Foss	2	5	5.44	10	0	48.0	57	19	37

SOUTHERN MARYLAND BLUE CRABS

Player	AVG	AB	R	H	HR	RBI	BB	SO	SB
Johnny Bladel	.341	135	23	46	1	16	16	32	5
Angelys Nina	.327	315	40	103	1	37	27	43	6
Frank Martinez	.321	436	45	140	11	62	15	71	4
Devon Rodriguez	.288	437	53	126	6	42	21	67	1
Edwin Garcia	.288	458	55	132	3	34	36	71	9
Teodoro Martinez	.285	330	28	94	2	33	18	23	18
Jon Griffin	.280	257	42	72	11	39	27	71	2
Austin Green	.259	166	18	43	4	12	9	33	1
Jose Gonzalez	.253	150	12	38	1	21	9	40	0
Angelo Songco	.248	262	20	65	2	27	23	67	2
Ryan Strausborger	.247	368	52	91	10	44	31	92	11
Cory Vaughn	.241	353	65	85	18	51	53	120	11
Joey Wong	.239	71	10	17	0	5	10	11	0
Craig Maddox	.221	190	12	42	1	21	6	42	0
Francisco Rosario	.220	132	14	29	0	7	14	60	3
Dave Sappelt	.185	27	2	5	1	2	1	10	0
Kalaika Kahoohalahala	.102	49	1	5	0	4	2	14	1

Player	W	L	ERA	G	SV	IP	H	BB	SO
Chris Mazza	3	0	0.42	9	0	21.2	16	2	20
Jason Creasy	1	1	1.96	44	1	36.2	33	6	50
Daryl Thompson	5	4	3.38	16	0	96.0	88	18	67
Craig Stem	7	8	3.70	42	2	107.0	107	34	86
Ryan Chaffee	2	2	3.80	70	3	68.2	48	39	59
Cody Eppley	0	4	3.83	41	15	40.0	42	12	25
Tommy Shirley	1	1	4.08	11	0	17.2	15	3	23
Brandon Cumpton	4	3	4.11	11	0	65.2	66	20	44
Brett Marshall	3	5	4.24	13	0	76.1	74	43	60
Sam Runion	1	7	4.55	62	0	57.1	51	17	66
Casey Delgado	5	10	4.90	22	0	123.0	123	58	88
Paul Clemens	4	8	5.45	29	0	76.0	79	42	85
David Russo	3	7	5.85	33	0	72.1	82	44	48
Drake Britton	4	6	6.35	27	0	79.1	87	26	51
Shane Watson	5	0	6.40	43	0	45.0	54	25	43
Zac Westcott	0	0	6.75	3	0	12.0	16	4	8
Kyle Drabek	0	2	7.43	6	0	13.1	15	11	5
Joey Wagman	0	4	8.33	12	0	27.0	35	10	22
Alex Boshers	0	2	9.90	2	0	10.0	21	3	8

SUGAR LAND SKEETERS

Player	AVG	AB	R	H	HR	RBI	BB	SO	SB
Matt Chavez	.320	472	59	151	12	72	36	112	1
Juan Silverio	.310	197	36	61	8	37	10	39	3
Anthony Giansanti	.295	465	79	137	17	58	43	79	35
Courtney Hawkins	.285	323	54	92	18	72	25	79	12
Albert Cordero	.285	452	65	129	12	63	26	78	3
Colin Walsh	.281	135	24	38	1	15	33	28	2
Alvaro Rondon	.281	377	38	106	0	39	25	67	38
Denis Phipps	.265	351	49	93	9	37	37	101	6
Kyle Kubitza	.261	207	28	54	7	37	26	65	4
Derek Norris	.256	410	69	105	12	57	71	77	8
Barrett Barnes	.246	382	86	94	12	51	80	94	24
Luke Dykstra	.235	68	8	16	1	5	3	10	1
Daniel Robertson	.219	73	7	16	1	6	7	9	3
Javier Betancourt	.201	154	17	31	0	17	10	22	3
Slade Heathcott	.194	31	4	6	0	3	5	6	1
Welington Dotel	.172	29	0	5	0	2	3	6	1

Player	W	L	ERA	G	SV	IP	H	BB	SO
Dan Reynolds	2	0	0.00	11	0	15.0	6	2	21
Matt West	0	0	0.54	17	0	16.2	8	2	19
Jean Machi	2	0	0.84	22	1	21.1	10	11	21
Casey Coleman	3	0	0.96	7	0	37.1	24	10	38
Felipe Paulino	2	2	1.18	54	33	53.1	32	21	72
Hunter Cervenka	3	1	1.53	19	0	17.2	9	2	21
Alejandro Chacin	0	0	1.64	10	0	11.0	13	2	7
Mark Haynes	2	1	1.90	24	0	23.2	12	12	25
Mitch Talbot	3	1	1.93	5	0	28.0	22	6	19
Michael Mariot	0	0	1.93	4	0	14.0	13	5	8
Austin Adams	3	0	2.22	30	1	28.1	24	8	33
Dallas Beeler	8	2	2.29	19	0	90.1	70	16	73
James Russell	8	4	2.36	20	0	106.2	94	17	98
Luke Irvine	1	1	2.56	6	0	31.2	29	9	23
Dan Runzler	4	2	2.81	53	1	48.0	46	27	58
Konner Wade	8	6	3.10	27	0	136.2	144	19	79
Kraig Sitton	3	0	3.71	50	0	68.0	68	12	48
Alex Wimmers	3	0	3.77	20	0	28.2	22	10	34
Kyle Winkler	1	0	3.80	22	0	21.1	11	19	17
Tyler Levine	0	0	4.22	4	0	10.2	12	6	5
Ben Griset	2	3	4.35	12	0	41.1	50	24	32
Matt Sergey	4	5	4.47	13	0	58.1	56	14	54
Ben Rowen	3	1	4.50	15	0	16.0	20	2	13
Yasutomo Kubo	5	2	5.14	13	0	56.0	64	22	53
Brett Marshall	3	5	5.19	9	0	43.1	51	25	36
Derrick Loop	1	1	5.40	10	0	10.0	12	3	14
Vicente Campos	3	2	5.64	22	0	22.1	22	11	17
Logan Bawcom	1	1	6.75	3	0	13.1	16	1	13
Tyler Badamo	1	3	7.36	4	0	14.2	19	6	13

YORK REVOLUTION

Player	AVG	AB	R	H	HR	RBI	BB	SO	SB
Telvin Nash	.338	136	29	46	9	35	25	38	1
Melky Mesa	.337	383	85	129	20	89	24	88	2
Alexi Casilla	.336	423	75	142	3	36	27	51	16
Welington Dotel	.317	404	58	128	7	60	24	94	19
Henry Castillo	.310	142	23	44	2	22	11	40	0
Alonzo Harris	.304	138	33	42	3	16	18	16	14
Isaias Tejeda	.303	76	11	23	2	22	8	10	0
Ryan Dent	.279	365	48	102	16	59	29	85	4
Jared Mitchell	.275	436	80	120	6	44	64	103	33
Rubi Silva	.267	116	14	31	1	12	3	34	3
Luis Cruz	.262	206	22	54	3	31	9	51	0
Zach Wilson	.250	168	22	42	4	24	21	38	0
Travis Witherspoon	.246	337	35	83	6	26	25	108	21
Michael Burgess	.212	297	43	63	13	44	35	87	0
Jose Cuevas	.211	232	24	49	3	32	16	40	3
Roger Diaz	.186	59	3	11	0	5	3	15	1
Tyler Clark	.179	123	21	22	6	17	14	57	0
Tyson Gillies	.154	39	5	6	2	5	3	14	0

Player	W	L	ERA	G	SV	IP	H	BB	SO
Grant Sides	4	0	1.44	30	13	31.1	20	11	48

Player	W	L	ERA	G	SV	IP	H	BB	SO
Jay Gause	3	0	1.56	8	0	34.2	23	12	26
James Pugliese	5	1	2.29	29	0	35.1	26	9	36
Zac Grotz	2	1	2.53	7	1	32.0	24	10	33
Ross Detwiler	3	1	2.70	6	0	30.0	29	8	32
Michael Click	2	1	2.78	25	0	32.1	23	15	39
Dustin Richardson	0	0	2.87	13	4	15.2	14	4	27
Junior Rincon	1	4	2.93	43	10	43.0	35	22	37
Luke Westphal	1	2	3.29	28	0	27.1	21	11	39
Robert Carson	10	7	3.73	32	1	115.2	137	29	92
Ricardo Gomez	3	1	3.77	46	2	43.0	36	21	62
Joe Van Meter	5	3	3.93	36	0	84.2	96	26	86
Logan Williamson	7	5	4.13	17	0	89.1	102	31	50
Mitch Atkins	12	7	4.17	25	0	144.2	151	34	137
Jonathan Sanchez	0	1	4.43	6	0	22.1	23	13	19
Pat McCoy	1	4	4.54	7	0	35.2	37	15	17
Jailen Peguero	2	4	4.93	35	0	49.1	45	28	44
Troy Terzi	1	0	5.79	4	0	18.2	23	4	16
Carl Brice	0	1	6.04	8	0	22.1	26	18	19
Dominic Severino	4	8	6.45	18	0	75.1	100	17	40
Zac Treece	0	1	6.46	22	0	23.2	31	8	21
Estarlin Arias	0	2	8.16	11	0	14.1	20	8	11

CAN-AM LEAGUE

Martin Figueroa hit a three-run walk-off home run in the bottom of the ninth inning as Sussex County knocked off Quebec for the Can-Am League title. The win was Sussex County's first Can-Am League title since 2008.

Team	W	L	PCT	GB
Sussex County Miners	63	38	.624	—
Quebec Capitales	58	44	.569	5 ½
Rockland Boulders	54	48	.529	9 ½
Trois-Rivieres Aigles	53	49	.520	10 ½
New Jersey Jackals	50	52	.490	13 ½
Ottawa Champions	41	60	.406	22
Salina Stockade	3	15	.167	—
Hollywood Stars	1	8	.111	—
Dominican Republic	0	9	.000	—

Playoffs: Semifinals: Quebec defeated Rockland 3-1 and Sussex County defeated Trois Rivieres 3-2 in best-of-5 series. **Finals:** Sussex County defeated Quebec 3-1 in best-of-5 series.

Attendance: Rockland 129,599; Quebec 126,483; Ottawa 93,395; Trois-Rivieres 91,605; New Jersey 83,610; Sussex County 74,827.

ALL-Star Team: C: Luis Alen, Sussex County. **1B:** Audy Ciriaco, Sussex County. **2B:** Mikey Reynolds, Sussex County. **3B:** Taylor Brennan, Trois-Rivières. **SS:** Yordan Manduley, Québec. **OF:** David Harris, New Jersey; Kevin Krause, Rockland; Javier Herrera, Trois-Rivières. **DH:** Sébastien Boucher, Ottawa. **SP:** Jordan Kurokawa, Ottawa. **RP:** Alex Demchak, Sussex County.

Rookie of the Year: Martin Figueroa, 3B, Sussex County. **Rookie Pitcher of the Year:** Jordan Kurokawa, Ottawa. **Defensive Player of the Year:** Sam Dexter, Trois-Rivières. **Player of the Year:** Taylor Brennan, 3B, Trois-Rivières. **Manager of the Year:** Bobby Jones, Sussex County

BATTING LEADERS

Player	Team	AVG	AB	R	H	HR	RBI
Yordan Manduley	QUE	.337	303	43	102	4	37
Mikey Reynolds	SC	.335	355	78	119	1	52
David Harris	NJ	.331	344	77	114	23	68
Kevin Krause	ROC	.331	369	68	122	10	49
Martin Figueroa	SC	.328	308	65	101	5	50
Sebastian Boucher	OTT	.328	357	51	117	1	53
Sthervin Matos	DR	.323	31	3	10	0	.1
B. Luebcke	SAL	.319	69	11	22	0	4
Kalian Sams	QUE	.311	264	46	82	11	48
Conrad Gregor	ROC	.300	357	63	107	10	53

PITCHING LEADERS

Player	Team	W	L	ERA	IP	H	BB	SO
Jordan Kurokawa	OTT	12	5	2.21	118	116	25	90
David Rollins	SC	9	3	2.23	113	90	31	105
Kenny Koplove	SC	7	4	2.61	86	61	41	78
Jay Johnson	QUE	7	2	2.63	89	70	29	77

Hale, Jake	OTT	6	7	2.84	108	96	25	66
Blanco, Lazaro	QUE	5	3	3.36	88	80	29	81
McNorton, Kevin	TR	8	4	3.44	129	128	27	91
Murphy, Chris	TR	11	5	3.47	117	132	36	59
Gelinas, Karl	QUE	8	8	3.52	100	97	22	81
Jones, Cory	SC	11	3	3.55	112	113	48	62

QUEBEC CAPITALES

Player	AVG	AB	R	H	HR	RBI	BB	SO	SB
Zach Wilson	.348	141	26	49	6	32	21	16	1
Yordan Manduley	.337	303	43	102	4	37	26	8	17
Nick Van Stratten	.311	206	32	64	1	25	20	14	12
Kalian Sams	.311	264	46	82	11	48	36	67	12
James McOwen	.294	381	51	112	10	50	49	81	11
T.J. White	.287	300	51	86	11	46	23	71	3
Phildrick Llewellyn	.263	114	15	30	0	8	6	27	8
Maxx Tissenbaum	.255	278	28	71	4	36	34	30	1
Brad Antchak	.253	320	45	81	5	45	26	60	15
Stephen Gaylor	.247	81	14	20	1	6	3	8	8
Josh Vitters	.247	81	12	20	1	6	7	20	0
Adam Ehrlich	.247	259	29	64	2	31	31	33	0
Nick Gotta	.242	132	18	32	0	4	20	35	6
Edgar Lebron	.234	94	17	22	0	11	7	39	16
Lachlan Fontaine	.230	165	16	38	2	18	4	45	1
Jordan Serena	.197	117	13	23	1	10	11	27	2

Player	W	L	ERA	G	SV	IP	H	BB	SO
Nolan Becker	0	0	1.61	21	11	22.1	18	9	30
Trevor Bayless	4	5	2.30	42	12	47.0	32	13	50
Mike Hepple	1	0	2.37	16	0	19.0	9	18	13
Arik Sikula	8	2	2.58	12	0	80.1	71	10	82
Jay Johnson	7	2	2.63	28	1	89.0	70	29	77
Ryan Searle	7	3	3.13	13	0	72.0	65	26	60
Wendell Floranus	2	3	3.13	6	0	31.2	30	13	32
Bobby Blevins	1	0	3.27	3	0	11.0	6	4	9
Lazaro Blanco	5	3	3.36	15	0	88.1	80	29	81
Karl Gelinas	8	8	3.52	16	0	99.2	97	22	81
Andrew Elliott	2	0	3.60	37	0	50.0	41	17	65
Sean Donatello	1	2	3.90	24	5	27.2	31	9	34
Will Dennis	3	2	4.08	40	0	39.2	40	18	40
Brett Lee	4	6	4.14	17	0	87.0	85	46	68
Lachlan Fontaine	2	0	4.62	18	0	25.1	22	15	25
Juan Benitez	0	3	4.91	8	0	40.1	45	15	31
Brian Loconsole	0	0	5.91	9	0	10.2	10	6	7
Mark Vasquez	1	1	6.06	6	0	16.1	19	8	11
J.P. Stevenson	0	1	10.64	3	0	11.0	19	1	6

NEW JERSEY JACKALS

Player	AVG	AB	R	H	HR	RBI	BB	SO	SB
Dean Green	.355	217	38	77	13	43	21	22	1
David Harris	.331	344	77	114	23	68	57	92	15
Taylor Oldham	.322	115	20	37	2	20	16	28	11
Danny Canela	.302	308	42	93	10	49	20	46	0
John Ruettiger	.296	135	19	40	0	8	7	21	8
Jordan Hinshaw	.284	201	34	57	5	33	32	56	7
Seth Spivey	.281	338	44	95	5	44	40	47	2
Kevin Torres	.276	275	36	76	4	35	18	40	1
Carlos Triunfel	.266	353	55	94	7	38	16	44	1
Andy Mocahbee	.250	128	26	32	8	25	16	39	1
Connor Hofmann	.247	324	49	80	4	27	26	73	19
Nolan Meadows	.245	290	39	71	10	36	33	75	0
Rony Cabrera	.213	230	20	49	3	22	5	54	6
Gerald Bautista	.200	60	12	12	1	9	8	16	0

Player	W	L	ERA	G	SV	IP	H	BB	SO
Lendy Castillo	0	1	0.82	2	0	11.0	7	2	17
Jose Velez	5	1	1.67	40	0	54.0	38	25	68
Vin Mazzaro	3	4	1.76	34	10	46.0	33	10	44
Nate Gercken	2	2	2.08	30	0	34.2	29	17	38
Matt Vogel	1	1	3.14	4	0	14.1	6	8	17
Mat Latos	5	4	3.18	29	4	76.1	66	31	87
Eduar Lopez	1	3	3.60	4	0	25.0	20	14	9
Evan DeLuca	4	0	3.76	44	1	55.0	52	27	79
Yasmany Hernandez	6	6	3.93	18	0	94.0	98	43	74

Vic Black	2	4	4.37	15	1	55.2	59	38	37
Zach Arneson	2	1	4.82	13	0	28.0	35	8	30
Dylan Brammer	9	8	4.99	21	0	113.2	116	50	93
Tyler Levine	1	2	5.61	9	0	33.2	42	13	15
Alberto Rodriguez	3	5	6.17	12	0	65.2	81	32	56
Ricky Schafer	1	2	6.46	6	0	30.2	35	12	34
Jordan Wellander	0	1	6.62	9	0	17.2	26	6	22
Mariel Checo	2	3	7.58	9	0	38.0	36	29	42
Pete Perez	1	3	9.26	12	0	23.1	35	10	22

OTTAWA CHAMPIONS

Player	AVG	AB	R	H	HR	RBI	BB	SO	SB
Sebastien Boucher	.328	357	51	117	1	53	64	45	10
Zach Colby	.298	131	13	39	0	14	23	23	0
Chase Harris	.296	372	55	110	2	29	33	75	24
Vinny Guglietti	.292	319	46	93	9	45	33	59	6
Daniel Bick	.276	369	57	102	5	40	23	85	22
Steve Nyisztor	.254	138	16	35	3	17	19	24	5
Jordan Caillouet	.254	394	43	100	6	52	14	77	2
Steve Brown	.244	311	43	76	11	60	25	82	9
Mike Blanke	.242	66	13	16	2	6	17	14	0
Coco Johnson	.241	253	47	61	5	30	30	57	19
Kyle Zirbes	.222	63	9	14	0	6	10	24	4
Tyler Nordgren	.218	197	22	43	2	18	12	31	1
Ozney Guillen	.211	71	4	15	0	3	4	12	0
Michael Hungate	.211	123	13	26	2	6	5	40	6
Brian Portelli	.208	101	11	21	5	16	11	34	0

Player	W	L	ERA	G	SV	IP	H	BB	SO
Jordan Kurokawa	12	5	2.21	19	0	118.1	116	25	90
Jake Hale	6	7	2.84	18	0	107.2	96	25	66
Daniel Carela	1	2	3.41	30	1	34.1	24	21	52
James Jones	0	1	3.68	13	0	14.2	14	4	11
Austin Chrismon	8	10	4.00	19	0	117.0	133	28	60
Andrew Cooper	0	1	4.02	39	0	56.0	63	16	36
Miles Sheehan	1	6	4.33	26	1	54.0	50	23	39
Edilson Alvarez	3	4	4.39	13	0	84.0	93	31	53
Scott Maine	4	5	4.64	34	13	33.0	35	18	33
Steve Borkowski	4	9	5.13	21	0	114.0	130	38	86
Ryan Leach	0	0	5.32	17	1	22.0	20	18	21
Evan Rutckyj	2	6	5.64	26	0	67.0	69	29	65
Noah Gapp	0	2	8.31	4	0	17.1	23	13	7

ROCKLAND BOULDERS

Player	AVG	AB	R	H	HR	RBI	BB	SO	SB
Kevin Krause	.331	369	68	122	10	49	41	42	13
Conrad Gregor	.300	357	63	107	10	53	62	65	20
Jared McDonald	.288	240	37	69	6	26	22	38	3
Marcus Nidiffer	.287	328	47	94	21	60	46	63	0
Cody Regis	.270	367	55	99	22	62	39	89	4
Alex Herceg	.262	42	7	11	1	6	2	9	0
Conor Bierfeldt	.253	340	63	86	19	50	50	90	4
Reggie Wilson	.250	60	9	15	3	10	11	15	8
J.C. Rodriguez	.244	365	57	89	14	39	39	106	13
Mike Montville	.214	341	56	73	21	60	41	138	6
Mikael-Ali Mogues	.212	212	30	45	12	36	36	79	3
Rylan Sandoval	.209	86	13	18	2	12	10	30	3
Jason Agresti	.198	101	7	20	3	14	16	21	0
Matt Dacey	.171	35	6	6	2	6	2	12	0
Aaron Wilson	.150	60	5	9	0	6	7	27	4

Player	W	L	ERA	G	SV	IP	H	BB	SO
Ryan Deemes	3	1	2.48	5	0	29.0	29	7	28
Chris Pennell	1	0	2.55	3	0	17.2	14	4	12
Frankie Moscatiello	4	3	2.79	25	1	61.1	58	33	64
David Palladino	5	2	2.92	20	0	71.0	59	33	79
Bo Budkevics	1	1	3.07	3	0	14.2	13	8	8
Nick Kennedy	5	5	3.11	53	2	75.1	71	19	56
Nick Sarianides	2	1	3.20	6	0	19.2	14	18	21
Justin Brantley	4	4	3.58	9	0	50.1	52	13	53
Matt Kostalos	1	3	3.95	39	1	41.0	49	27	27
Kyle Hansen	5	1	4.10	42	18	41.2	42	12	54
Brian Ernst	4	2	4.20	10	0	49.1	48	14	39
Justin Topa	1	1	4.43	4	0	20.1	24	4	15

	W	L	ERA	G	SV	IP	H	BB	SO
Andy LaLonde	0	1	4.76	12	0	17.0	13	7	27
Travis Hissong	5	3	4.85	14	0	68.2	72	41	47
Garrett Johnson	5	2	4.97	16	1	58.0	63	17	72
Brad Schaenzer	2	4	5.40	12	0	50.0	60	14	22
Marc Huberman	2	1	6.88	12	0	17.0	25	14	17
Tommy Lawrence	2	4	6.90	30	1	60.0	75	26	41
Kagen Hopkins	1	3	7.24	8	0	41.0	53	16	24
Trey Haley	1	1	7.84	13	0	10.1	16	8	8

SALINA STOCKADE

Player	AVG	AB	R	H	HR	RBI	BB	SO	SB
William Salas	.375	32	6	12	2	3	6	7	3
Robert Garza	.355	31	2	11	0	3	2	8	2
Jeremy Delgado	.333	27	4	9	0	1	3	7	2
Brian Luebcke	.323	31	6	10	0	0	3	7	2
Steve Longo	.269	26	2	7	0	1	4	11	2
Tino Mention	.250	32	5	8	3	9	2	10	0
Ryan Retz	.207	29	3	6	0	1	2	8	0
Michael Hungate	.200	25	0	5	0	2	1	10	1
Aaron Stubblefield	.188	32	1	6	0	1	1	10	1
Bobby Webb	.160	25	3	4	2	2	2	9	1
Dominic Zaher	.160	25	1	4	0	3	2	9	0
Tom McKenna	.154	26	2	4	0	0	0	5	1
Daniel Williams	.154	39	2	6	0	2	0	15	2
Chris Kwitzer	.152	33	5	5	0	1	1	12	1
Scott Stetson	.115	26	4	3	0	4	3	8	1

Player	W	L	ERA	G	SV	IP	H	BB	SO
Tom Fazzini	0	0	3.48	6	0	10.1	11	5	10
Edilson Alvarez	2	0	4.50	2	0	14.0	17	6	15
Daniel Diaz	0	4	5.91	4	0	21.1	25	9	15
Cody Strayer	1	2	6.61	5	0	16.1	20	11	13
Jordan Cummings	0	4	7.66	4	0	22.1	24	8	19
Mason Mayberry	0	1	11.70	4	0	10.0	17	9	6

TROIS-RIVIERES AIGLES

Player	AVG	AB	R	H	HR	RBI	BB	SO	SB
Sam Dexter	.287	341	48	98	3	49	23	36	6
Alberth Martinez	.277	278	34	77	8	39	23	52	2
Javier Herrera	.261	387	59	101	16	63	44	100	13
Taylor Brennan	.259	332	67	86	32	82	70	120	17
David Glaude	.257	331	52	85	7	31	42	81	9
Alex Herceg	.256	133	18	34	2	8	7	29	0
Kevin Cornelius	.251	371	45	93	12	51	33	129	4
Taylor Oldham	.248	149	28	37	4	16	20	33	14
Michael Suchy	.246	354	49	87	12	50	48	98	11
Alexi Colon	.228	324	50	74	1	20	65	72	25
Anthony Hermelyn	.187	278	31	52	4	33	32	85	0

Player	W	L	ERA	G	SV	IP	H	BB	SO
Jacob Evans	2	1	1.14	5	0	31.2	19	8	37
Kyle Halbohn	2	2	3.08	16	1	61.1	61	16	70
Matt Rusch	1	2	3.21	4	0	14.0	13	5	16
Kevin McNorton	8	4	3.44	21	0	128.1	128	27	91
Chris Murphy	11	5	3.47	19	0	116.2	132	36	59
Philip Walby	1	2	3.47	20	2	23.1	18	15	17
Taylor Hyssong	5	1	3.54	41	0	40.2	41	14	27
Shaun Ellis	2	6	3.56	36	8	48.0	42	21	58
Ethan Elias	4	9	4.02	29	1	107.1	102	39	87
Yender Caramo	6	4	4.28	17	0	96.2	114	26	42
Tyler Garkow	7	5	4.72	19	0	87.2	106	32	63
Angel Rincon	3	4	4.91	40	9	47.2	56	18	29
Kramer Sneed	0	2	7.23	4	0	18.2	20	10	14
Jackson Zarubin	0	0	7.53	10	0	14.1	23	5	9
Fernando Fernandez	1	1	7.59	9	0	10.2	14	5	7
Owen Boon	0	0	7.62	5	0	13.0	19	9	9

FRONTIER LEAGUE

With the season on the line, Cody Clark stepped up and led the Joliet Slammers to their second Frontier League title. In a winner-takes-all Game 5, Clark came in as a reliever in the fourth inning and threw 5.1 perfect innings as Joliet held off Washington for a 4-2 victory.

East Division	W	L	PCT	GB
* Washington Wild Things	54	42	.563	—
^ Joliet Slammers	54	42	.563	—
Lake Erie Crushers	50	46	.521	4
Schaumburg Boomers	45	51	.469	9
Traverse City Beach Bums	44	51	.463	9 ½
Windy City ThunderBolts	41	54	.432	12 ½

West Division	W	L	PCT	GB
* River City Rascals	52	44	.542	—
^ Evansville Otters	51	45	.531	1
Florence Freedom	49	47	.510	3
Southern Illinois Miners	48	47	.505	3 ½
Normal CornBelters	48	47	.505	3 ½
Gateway Grizzlies	38	58	.396	14

Division Champ. ^Wild Card

Playoffs: Semifinals: Joliet defeated River City 3-2 and Washington defeated Evansville 3-0 in best-of-5 series. **Finals:** Joliet defeated Washington 3-2 in best-of-5 series.

Attendance: Schaumburg 149,255; Gateway 125,536; Southern Illinois 109,691; Florence 105,805; Lake Erie 101,229; Evansville 94,498; Joliet 88,198; Traverse City 88,176; Washington 87,534; River City 85,036; Normal 81,716; Windy City 78,177.

ALL-Star Team: C: Skyler Ewing, Florence. **1B:** Chris Iriart, Normal. **2B:** Jack Parenty, Schaumburg. **3B:** Ryan Long, Evansville. **SS:** Santiago Chirino, Normal. **OF:** Derrick Loveless, Normal; James Harris, Washington; Andrew Godbold, Normal. **DH:** Paul Kronenfeld, River City. **SP:** Thomas Dorminy, Washington. **RP:** Cody Mincey, River City.

Most Valuable Player: James Harris, Washington. **Pitcher of the Year:** Thomas Dorminy. **Rookie of the Year:** Aaron Hill, Lake Erie.

BATTING LEADERS

Player	Team	AVG	AB	R	H	HR	RBI
Santiago Chirino	NOR	.367	373	68	137	4	59
Omar Obregon	WC	.366	295	45	108	1	31
Zack Weigel	SCH	.330	261	55	86	10	52
Trenton Hill	JOL	.330	315	55	104	1	47
Derrick Loveless	NOR	.326	350	64	114	14	66
Jack Parenty	SCH	.324	358	57	116	0	27
Will Kengor	TC	.311	373	58	116	13	60
Hector Roa	WSH	.309	369	52	114	12	69
Andrew Godbold	NOR	.309	353	50	109	11	79
Ty Moore	SCH	.308	286	48	88	6	59

PITCHING LEADERS

Player	Team	W	L	ERA	IP	H	BB	SO
Thomas Dormin	WSH	9	5	2.45	132	112	39	109
Alex Romero	LE	11	6	2.77	123	97	40	105
Jonny Ortiz	RC	8	2	3.09	79	65	23	77
Liam O'Sullivan	JOL	11	4	3.15	123	111	22	77
Dan Ludwig	RC	5	4	3.31	84	86	16	63
Jack Landwehr	NOR	8	3	3.32	81	83	19	61
Geno Encina	SIL	5	8	3.32	125	128	29	108
Hector Hernandez	RC	10	7	3.46	117	112	49	107
Scot Hoffman	JOL	8	5	3.51	115	109	41	84
Randy Wynne	EVN	9	9	3.55	134	144	16	114

EVANSVILLE OTTERS

Player	AVG	AB	R	H	HR	RBI	BB	SO	SB
Carlos Castro	.333	78	12	26	0	7	2	15	1
Travis Harrison	.302	331	52	100	10	63	63	84	19
David Cronin	.296	294	57	87	3	37	49	49	8
Ryan Long	.292	346	59	101	12	55	48	70	5
Brant Whiting	.286	133	21	38	5	15	19	28	0
Luis Vilorio	.284	67	5	19	0	8	5	6	3
Daniel Spingola	.280	50	8	14	1	5	0	15	0
Taylor Lane	.275	51	9	14	0	9	9	11	2
Toby Thomas	.272	213	29	58	5	32	17	29	1
Joe DeLuca	.271	59	6	16	0	10	4	19	0
Jeff Gardner	.265	340	45	90	9	60	44	74	11
Manny Cruz	.262	122	18	32	1	15	14	25	4
J.J. Gould	.254	118	16	30	0	12	15	50	0
Brandon Dulin	.244	123	13	30	3	13	9	41	0

INDEPENDENT LEAGUES

Player	AVG	AB	R	H	HR	RBI	BB	SO	SB
Hunter Cullen	.240	233	38	56	3	23	24	54	12
Austin Bush	.231	65	6	15	2	12	3	13	0
Michael Rizzitello	.223	157	18	35	1	19	14	24	3
Joe Lytle	.214	42	3	9	0	3	4	3	0
Zach Welz	.214	154	23	33	3	15	17	43	8
Taylor Hillson	.186	59	10	11	0	6	11	9	1
Caleb Eldridge	.125	48	3	6	2	6	4	25	0

Player	W	L	ERA	G	SV	IP	H	BB	SO
Alex Phillips	1	0	1.23	16	6	22.0	11	3	41
Patrick McGuff	3	1	1.55	5	0	29.0	18	7	26
Luc Rennie	4	1	2.31	10	0	62.1	51	20	70
Matt Chavarria	4	1	3.42	13	4	23.2	26	8	28
Spencer Medick	4	2	3.54	10	0	61.0	49	28	64
Randy Wynne	9	9	3.55	23	0	134.1	144	16	114
Kyano Cummings	2	2	3.96	32	2	38.2	40	13	39
Austin Nicely	8	5	4.24	20	0	114.2	130	56	85
Tyler Beardsley	5	8	4.35	29	1	72.1	61	35	50
Garrett Harris	2	2	4.37	30	1	47.1	40	19	50
Mitchell Aker	1	5	4.66	34	19	36.2	35	23	33
Sean Adler	3	3	5.08	25	0	28.1	29	16	38
Ty Hensley	2	0	5.28	10	0	30.2	29	41	31
Tyler Vail	3	4	5.33	18	2	79.1	82	42	88

FLORENCE FREEDOM

Player	AVG	AB	R	H	HR	RBI	BB	SO	SB
John Price	.304	79	10	24	4	14	4	15	0
Skyler Ewing	.300	207	43	62	16	51	27	36	1
Caleb Lopes	.297	249	39	74	5	25	19	33	3
Austin Wobrock	.285	316	38	90	1	28	25	47	0
Keivan Berges	.281	338	51	95	18	65	27	71	5
Ricky Ramirez	.276	232	33	64	9	34	31	49	6
Andre Mercurio	.263	137	28	36	2	23	21	23	7
Xavier Turner	.259	212	40	55	4	26	16	23	20
Brandon Pugh	.256	82	14	21	0	4	6	19	9
Craig Lepre	.254	59	5	15	1	9	9	7	2
Jacob Wark	.249	237	39	59	7	37	10	71	6
Jimmy Heck	.246	126	18	31	0	9	17	29	2
Connor Crane	.244	119	18	29	3	17	9	34	6
Jose Brizuela	.234	77	10	18	4	18	6	10	0
Taylor Bryant	.231	52	6	12	1	8	9	13	0
Chandler Rodriguez	.222	27	3	6	1	3	0	9	0
Harrison White	.211	76	12	16	1	10	4	15	1
Ryan Rinsky	.165	103	12	17	1	12	22	34	0
Nick Crouse	.154	26	4	4	1	5	2	10	0
Cutter McDowell	.152	33	0	5	0	1	2	14	2
Mike Morris	.129	31	2	4	0	1	6	18	1

Player	W	L	ERA	G	SV	IP	H	BB	SO
Jake Haberer	0	1	1.80	17	3	20.0	18	3	19
Patrick McGrath	1	1	1.96	26	2	23.0	25	7	30
Tyler Gibson	4	5	2.42	28	0	74.1	81	15	43
Marty Anderson	2	2	2.45	9	0	25.2	14	11	43
Ryan Colegate	0	0	2.53	11	0	10.2	9	4	10
Johnathon Tripp	3	4	2.70	38	15	43.1	33	15	55
Evan Korson	1	1	2.81	15	0	16.0	17	7	23
Mike Castellani	2	1	3.50	22	0	36.0	41	11	16
Jordan Kraus	8	5	3.93	18	0	119.0	109	22	77
Christian DeLeon	7	5	4.17	16	0	77.2	72	23	48
Chuck Weaver	6	4	4.34	15	0	91.1	92	18	81
Steve Hagen	7	8	4.49	18	0	104.1	112	27	73
Sam Martin	0	0	4.71	22	0	21.0	26	3	21
Eric Gleese	1	0	5.13	31	0	33.1	39	11	27
Cody Gray	5	4	5.35	24	1	77.1	81	22	76
Zach Kirby	1	4	5.60	9	0	35.1	37	13	19

GATEWAY GRIZZLIES

Player	AVG	AB	R	H	HR	RBI	BB	SO	SB
Mitch Piatnik	.321	56	9	18	0	3	0	25	2
Audie Afenir	.306	72	7	22	1	10	5	21	0
Matt Hearn	.305	59	7	18	1	6	4	6	3
Trae Santos	.291	358	51	104	17	67	49	96	0
Paul Russo	.289	121	17	35	2	13	12	33	1
Shane Mardirosian	.288	208	37	60	3	20	29	42	12

Player	AVG	AB	R	H	HR	RBI	BB	SO	SB
Terry McClure	.277	159	26	44	3	22	8	26	4
Blake Brown	.272	367	66	100	18	59	51	103	13
Justin Ellison	.263	186	22	49	9	30	18	52	6
Cody Livesay	.262	302	42	79	0	23	39	52	18
Matt Gonzalez	.256	82	8	21	0	11	2	20	3
Cam Adams	.243	37	3	9	0	7	6	10	0
Jeff Cardenas	.242	186	23	45	3	21	30	39	1
Artemis Kadkhodaian	.234	218	34	51	5	22	33	60	4
Jonathan Piron	.231	108	12	25	5	24	3	42	0
Joel McKeithan	.226	106	15	24	3	14	13	34	6
Brent Sakurai	.218	243	27	53	0	21	19	55	6
Brennan Morgan	.217	120	14	26	0	9	13	33	2
Jhonniel Alvarez	.211	128	9	27	1	11	11	26	0
John Price	.200	45	6	9	1	2	1	11	0

Player	W	L	ERA	G	SV	IP	H	BB	SO
Chris Metrick	1	1	1.19	23	1	30.1	19	12	32
Max MacNabb	9	9	3.64	20	0	128.2	132	38	114
Kevin Simmons	0	3	3.66	28	7	32.0	25	11	41
Mike Elwood	6	8	4.12	19	0	115.2	117	39	99
Grant Black	1	4	4.38	35	7	49.1	49	21	63
Josh Glick	2	4	4.43	43	4	44.2	35	28	43
Taso Stathopoulos	2	6	4.57	12	0	61.0	63	23	48
Patrick Boyle	3	3	4.73	36	1	40.0	29	35	54
Alec Kisena	5	4	4.75	18	0	100.1	88	38	108
Colton Freeman	0	1	4.84	32	0	35.1	20	40	45
Connor Leedholm	0	0	4.86	15	0	16.2	17	9	17
Dakota Smith	2	2	6.18	6	0	27.2	29	22	19
Ryan McSweeney	1	1	6.23	13	1	17.1	20	10	15
Dalton Shalberg	2	2	6.91	7	0	28.2	31	25	33
Joe Hauser	1	2	7.45	4	0	19.1	29	6	4
Will Anderson	3	3	9.22	10	0	41.0	52	19	37
Trevor Lubking	0	1	9.82	7	0	11.0	15	8	10
Nelson Martz	0	1	9.90	5	0	10.0	13	5	9

JOLIET SLAMMERS

Player	AVG	AB	R	H	HR	RBI	BB	SO	SB
Trenton Hill	.330	315	55	104	1	47	54	65	9
L.J. Kalawaia	.300	263	35	79	1	32	35	46	9
Trey Fulton	.269	182	23	49	2	16	20	26	2
Chaz Meadows	.257	268	32	69	1	21	41	65	4
Justin Garcia	.255	337	57	86	23	75	33	114	2
R.J. Thompson	.249	209	22	52	2	29	21	42	3
Danny Zardon	.249	365	60	91	9	60	44	75	16
London Lindley	.239	293	60	70	1	18	18	42	32
Manny Cruz	.238	63	10	15	0	5	14	16	0
Ridge Hoopii-Haslam	.232	280	39	65	4	49	43	82	28
Travis Bolin	.210	324	45	68	10	46	23	106	16
Brian Parreira	.195	41	5	8	0	1	4	7	0
Dom Iero	.159	69	7	11	3	9	10	15	0
Cody Clark	.142	120	13	17	2	6	13	44	0

Player	W	L	ERA	G	SV	IP	H	BB	SO
Nate Antone	1	1	1.25	35	1	50.1	24	21	59
Ottavio Dattolo	0	0	1.53	13	1	17.2	9	7	9
Corey Kimber	6	6	2.50	25	0	72.0	52	48	67
Duke von Schamann	4	1	2.70	8	0	43.1	45	6	28
Keegan Long	2	5	2.79	35	9	42.0	37	14	48
Liam O'Sullivan	11	4	3.15	18	0	123.0	111	22	77
Andrew Zellner	3	2	3.38	22	1	45.1	43	19	37
Daren Osby	7	3	3.50	11	0	61.2	57	19	54
Scot Hoffman	8	5	3.51	20	0	115.1	109	41	84
Isaac Sanchez	3	0	3.86	21	9	21.0	15	5	30
Taylor Goshen	5	6	4.55	19	1	83.0	85	33	52
Austin Jones	0	0	5.06	5	0	10.2	12	3	13
Shane Bryant	1	5	5.72	15	0	67.2	85	26	59
Skylar Janisse	0	2	5.94	25	1	50.0	52	32	44

LAKE ERIE CRUSHERS

Player	AVG	AB	R	H	HR	RBI	BB	SO	SB
Derek Perry	.379	29	4	11	0	5	6	6	3
Dane Hutcheon	.305	282	30	86	3	29	18	59	16
Zach Racusin	.298	114	17	34	1	12	9	14	1
Aaron Hill	.297	347	63	103	5	28	58	98	14

Joel McKeithan	.291	158	22	46	6	21	20	35	8
Terry McClure	.278	97	6	27	0	9	6	19	2
Kewby Meyer	.271	144	13	39	0	23	4	15	2
Kevin Lachance	.267	131	16	35	2	18	14	27	10
Cameron Newell	.261	111	16	29	1	12	26	11	3
Cody Lenahan	.252	266	32	67	7	41	22	82	4
Bryan De La Rosa	.241	241	31	58	4	35	20	57	6
Dalton Wheat	.240	283	37	68	4	25	24	69	11
Doug Trimble	.226	235	29	53	6	26	20	57	4
Conner Simonetti	.215	79	4	17	2	5	6	30	1
Matt Dacey	.204	108	11	22	4	10	16	29	1
Tyler Cowles	.200	30	4	6	0	3	1	11	0
Sean Hurley	.199	186	25	37	5	19	38	50	2
Nick Roark	.174	92	7	16	1	7	17	19	3
Mason Brown	.171	82	7	14	0	5	5	17	0
Dustin Williams	.169	89	6	15	0	6	11	34	0

Player	W	L	ERA	G	SV	IP	H	BB	SO
Nick Deeg	2	0	0.47	3	0	19.1	8	8	14
Ethan Westphal	1	2	1.71	7	0	26.1	20	6	26
Austin Orvis	1	0	2.53	7	0	10.2	12	4	7
Alex Romero	11	6	2.77	19	0	123.1	97	40	105
Louis Cohen	4	1	2.79	32	2	48.1	41	19	56
Logan Lombana	1	1	2.81	17	11	16.0	12	3	11
Jake Repavich	1	2	2.86	9	0	34.2	31	2	24
Kent Hasler	0	1	3.08	32	3	38.0	46	20	44
Justin Sinibaldi	3	4	3.57	30	10	68.0	77	25	55
Mason Klotz	3	3	3.60	15	0	45.0	49	21	35
Oriel Caicedo	2	4	3.60	8	0	40.0	37	14	25
Sean Renzi	7	5	3.81	14	0	85.0	77	37	90
Max Biedrzycki	5	1	3.81	20	0	26.0	22	19	23
Micah Beyer	1	3	3.86	9	0	46.2	39	12	50
Luke Watts	0	2	4.26	16	0	25.1	29	12	18
Branden Nunn	1	3	4.44	38	2	48.2	52	15	48
Seth Lucio	1	2	4.44	26	2	24.1	20	18	37
Richard McWilliams	1	1	4.91	11	1	11.0	10	11	9
Donny Murray	3	4	5.13	10	0	54.1	58	30	33
Juan Perez	1	1	7.20	6	0	25.0	24	30	20

NORMAL CORNBELTERS

Player	AVG	AB	R	H	HR	RBI	BB	SO	SB
Santiago Chirino	.367	373	68	137	4	59	31	26	13
Derrick Loveless	.326	350	64	114	14	66	57	83	16
Sean Hurley	.318	85	16	27	3	12	28	19	1
Andrew Godbold	.309	353	50	109	11	79	32	67	6
James Davison	.302	179	31	54	1	16	15	42	12
Tanner Lubach	.276	170	25	47	8	25	8	51	0
Justin Fletcher	.273	330	53	90	1	27	24	29	8
Jacob Bissell	.269	26	4	7	2	3	3	13	0
Michael Baca	.265	166	31	44	1	21	6	20	12
Tony Holton	.259	58	12	15	1	8	9	21	5
Chris Iriart	.256	309	52	79	25	59	30	120	0
Sammy Vega	.247	81	15	20	0	10	11	11	3
Nick Cain	.242	120	14	29	2	16	8	37	0
Cody Erickson	.236	212	20	50	0	20	13	40	0
Tyler Beckwith	.222	27	4	6	0	5	3	7	0
Joel Davis	.211	76	11	16	0	4	6	13	0
Cam Adams	.185	65	11	12	0	7	11	21	1
Derek Bauer	.164	67	6	11	0	3	13	16	1
Michael Centeno	.048	42	4	2	0	2	2	15	1

Player	W	L	ERA	G	SV	IP	H	BB	SO
Thomas Nicoll	2	1	2.15	19	0	29.1	21	4	31
Jonathan de Marte	3	4	2.87	42	7	53.1	42	18	58
Mark Hendricks	0	1	2.87	17	1	37.2	49	18	35
Ryan Lawlor	0	2	3.15	5	0	20.0	13	5	31
Nick Bozman	6	2	3.18	31	0	65.0	45	44	49
Miles Moeller	0	0	3.18	14	0	22.2	18	14	24
Scott Sebald	3	2	3.30	5	0	30.0	35	4	25
Jack Landwehr	8	3	3.32	15	0	81.1	83	19	61
Matt Portland	3	2	3.55	7	0	38.0	32	15	44
Chance Simpson	1	1	3.60	2	0	10.0	8	6	6
Jess Amedee	0	0	3.86	11	1	11.2	11	7	11
Connor Root	4	3	4.09	10	0	44.0	43	14	28

Anthony Herrera	7	5	4.76	41	7	62.1	67	19	48
Trevor Simms	1	0	4.82	16	1	18.2	22	9	23
Jacinto Garcia	6	5	5.42	19	0	98.0	108	45	47
Billy Roth	0	1	5.54	3	0	13.0	10	12	8
Kuehl McEachern	0	3	6.00	21	4	27.0	36	11	20
Kevin Matthews	0	3	6.09	8	0	34.0	40	26	28
Zach Kirby	2	4	6.30	11	0	60.0	71	18	31

RIVER CITY RASCALS

Player	AVG	AB	R	H	HR	RBI	BB	SO	SB
Trevor Achenbach	.327	205	39	67	5	36	15	38	10
Paul Kronenfeld	.299	301	54	90	23	69	28	99	3
J.D. Hearn	.281	342	48	96	10	42	33	91	13
Dylan Woods	.273	33	7	9	0	3	2	11	2
Ransom LaLonde	.270	200	23	54	3	20	10	24	2
Mike Jurgella	.255	294	56	75	10	48	44	46	13
Clint Freeman	.254	386	49	98	14	54	24	75	7
Braxton Martinez	.252	301	45	76	12	51	56	80	9
Zach Lavy	.248	274	42	68	10	36	25	83	8
Stephen Kerr	.247	93	16	23	0	11	13	14	2
Gage West	.239	92	10	22	0	9	5	17	1
Kevin Suarez	.239	322	46	77	2	28	24	76	27
Gerrion Grim	.232	112	10	26	3	12	5	37	7
Ross Haffey	.180	50	2	9	2	5	2	19	0
Connor Oliver	.158	114	14	18	1	5	18	43	3

Player	W	L	ERA	G	SV	IP	H	BB	SO
Logan Fanning	1	1	0.59	14	0	15.1	13	7	5
Joe Iorio	5	1	1.46	45	3	49.1	36	7	55
Cody Mincey	5	2	2.20	43	23	49.0	27	20	69
Chris Chigas	0	1	2.95	21	0	21.1	22	4	15
Jonny Ortiz	8	2	3.09	30	0	78.2	65	23	77
Dan Ludwig	5	4	3.31	16	0	84.1	86	16	63
Hector Hernandez	10	7	3.46	19	0	117.0	112	49	107
Jackson Sigman	0	0	3.65	14	0	12.1	11	11	19
Tanner Wilt	2	1	4.15	30	0	34.2	27	18	30
Josh Kimborowicz	6	4	4.18	18	0	103.1	101	36	97
Ryan Orr	3	2	4.24	21	0	34.0	34	16	21
Justin Garcia	1	2	4.24	5	0	23.1	23	12	11
Dalton Roach	1	4	4.66	11	0	36.2	37	13	42
Scott Grist	2	3	4.98	8	0	43.1	48	12	25
Chad Gendron	1	3	5.35	31	0	33.2	40	15	29
Lucas Laster	1	4	5.40	8	0	35.0	36	22	20
Jake Gangelhoff	0	0	8.47	11	0	17.0	24	8	8

SCHAUMBURG BOOMERS

Player	AVG	AB	R	H	HR	RBI	BB	SO	SB
Zack Weigel	.330	261	55	86	10	52	58	32	5
Jack Parenty	.324	358	57	116	0	27	59	35	11
Ty Moore	.308	286	48	88	6	59	23	27	7
Nick Oddo	.292	209	28	61	4	24	10	33	1
Kewby Meyer	.265	68	5	18	0	3	5	12	1
Dylan Jones	.263	228	19	60	2	18	18	38	6
Michael Hartnagel	.259	143	18	37	1	10	6	31	0
Collin Ferguson	.253	308	34	78	7	50	32	54	5
Sean Godfrey	.253	332	51	84	6	32	32	62	12
Josh Gardiner	.242	190	21	46	0	12	4	39	4
Clint Hardy	.241	170	25	41	2	20	17	35	5
Darrell Miller	.238	80	4	19	1	12	5	12	0
Kenny Towns	.238	349	36	83	7	42	22	61	4
Tyler Wolfe	.179	28	2	5	0	0	3	9	0
James Keller	.168	119	13	20	1	13	9	36	0
Casey Scoggins	.150	40	3	6	0	4	6	6	1
Austin Byler	.077	52	2	4	0	1	1	20	1

Player	W	L	ERA	G	SV	IP	H	BB	SO
Chris Hall	2	1	1.21	25	4	29.2	13	9	47
Ivan Vieitez	1	1	2.03	38	1	44.1	36	15	33
Mitch Schulewitz	3	2	2.20	28	0	32.2	25	21	31
James Mulry	4	0	2.30	40	1	43.0	35	18	38
Jake Joyce	4	2	2.58	38	12	38.1	21	19	53
Chris Powell	0	4	2.83	5	0	28.2	22	12	24
Steven Ridings	4	2	3.40	7	0	39.2	35	18	42
Darrell Thompson	5	2	3.79	29	1	35.2	31	24	45

INDEPENDENT LEAGUES

Player	W	L	ERA	G	SV	IP	H	BB	SO
Sam Myers	0	1	4.22	3	0	10.2	15	4	8
Payton Lobdell	5	8	4.25	18	0	101.2	108	31	52
Gunnar Kines	6	4	4.34	16	0	93.1	92	26	81
Joe Hauser	7	7	4.50	18	0	106.0	119	37	46
Quinn DiPasquale	1	1	4.50	6	0	20.0	19	8	11
Kit Fowler	2	7	5.02	12	0	71.2	65	28	54
Dylan Stutsman	1	2	5.37	25	0	52.0	55	13	44
Keaton Conner	0	0	6.00	3	0	15.0	18	8	7
Hendry Rodriguez	0	2	7.04	3	0	15.1	19	9	8
Will Stillman	0	2	11.05	4	0	14.2	23	14	10

SOUTHERN ILLINOIS MINERS

Player	AVG	AB	R	H	HR	RBI	BB	SO	SB
Joe Duncan	.295	258	32	76	5	34	20	51	18
Ben Moore	.287	115	20	33	1	10	6	18	2
Romeo Cortina	.268	291	49	78	7	36	41	65	14
Nolan Earley	.265	339	50	90	13	43	57	50	3
Luke Bonfield	.258	66	5	17	0	10	7	17	0
Chance Shepard	.253	352	56	89	23	59	45	120	5
Joe Dudek	.252	222	25	56	8	28	18	59	0
Harrison Bragg	.247	146	19	36	6	19	5	51	0
John Holland	.246	114	7	28	0	17	10	24	1
Luis Jean	.244	82	10	20	1	5	6	12	1
Marc DiLeo	.242	124	10	30	0	13	15	27	1
Kurt Wertz	.231	143	15	33	6	18	24	43	3
Kyle Davis	.223	188	22	42	4	27	23	45	1
Austin Homan	.214	28	4	6	0	2	2	5	2
Anthony Critelli	.205	78	12	16	0	8	15	23	0
Dougie Parks	.194	31	4	6	0	3	2	11	0
Jake Willsey	.190	116	16	22	2	11	11	48	2
Chris Scura	.180	50	8	9	0	5	4	11	0
Daniel Comstock	.160	50	3	8	1	1	4	15	0
Max Dutto	.144	118	14	17	2	8	28	41	1
Corey Dempster	.123	73	10	9	1	8	10	22	3

Player	W	L	ERA	G	SV	IP	H	BB	SO
Zach Hartman	1	2	0.44	19	4	20.1	11	6	29
Williams Perez	0	1	1.64	2	0	11.0	8	4	10
Nick Durazo	2	1	2.01	23	0	22.1	8	13	24
Michael Starcevich	2	1	2.30	19	2	31.1	31	9	33
Robby Rowland	4	2	2.31	6	0	39.0	32	5	29
Geno Encina	5	8	3.32	19	0	124.2	128	29	108
John Werner	1	1	3.77	30	10	28.2	21	15	36
Kurt Heyer	8	7	3.96	19	0	104.2	127	19	88
Patrick Duester	2	3	4.08	31	0	39.2	45	17	21
Steven Ridings	5	5	4.16	14	0	84.1	79	18	73
Ryan Askew	1	0	4.22	19	0	21.1	32	2	13
Austin Dubsky	7	4	5.05	16	0	67.2	68	31	50
Aaron Rozek	3	3	5.10	12	0	60.0	55	28	38
Kyle Tinius	4	2	5.24	34	4	34.1	42	18	35
Jordan Brink	0	0	5.27	3	0	13.2	17	9	18
Chris Washington	1	1	5.70	10	1	23.2	29	8	24
James Carter	1	0	6.57	14	0	12.1	20	5	11
Billy Griffin	0	4	6.69	8	0	35.0	47	13	24
Kody Rock	1	2	9.20	12	0	14.2	23	2	14

TRAVERSE CITY BEACH BUMS

Player	AVG	AB	R	H	HR	RBI	BB	SO	SB
Will Kengor	.311	373	58	116	13	60	39	56	17
Connor Oliver	.299	137	19	41	6	22	19	36	7
Donald Glover	.294	85	12	25	1	12	7	18	3
Isaac Benard	.284	328	49	93	7	38	51	54	19
Steve Lohr	.282	238	33	67	7	35	47	52	0
Orlando Rivera	.273	194	23	53	2	25	14	11	7
Luke Lowery	.248	323	43	80	9	43	29	88	14
Ryan Kemp	.247	146	16	36	0	15	13	21	4
Noah McGowan	.235	170	22	40	0	14	20	47	0
Jason Heinrich	.214	28	3	6	0	0	2	12	0
Alec Olund	.207	174	20	36	0	16	11	50	4
Josh Hauser	.204	113	17	23	0	9	17	31	1
Alexis Rivera	.196	285	31	56	6	33	27	81	6
Kenny Peoples-Walls	.193	88	8	17	2	13	8	13	0
Arby Fields	.191	110	17	21	1	8	24	27	7

Player	AVG	AB	R	H	HR	RBI	BB	SO	SB
Max Dutto	.173	127	23	22	3	7	24	55	1
Kendall Patrick	.173	179	20	31	4	24	19	61	0

Player	W	L	ERA	G	SV	IP	H	BB	SO
Augie Gallardo	1	1	0.98	10	1	18.1	14	5	22
Matt Williams	5	2	2.73	42	7	56.0	34	34	48
Jordan Desguin	6	2	2.74	10	0	62.1	44	18	49
Tyler Thornton	1	2	2.86	4	0	22.0	14	11	15
Tyler Barss	1	1	3.08	23	0	38.0	37	12	40
Michael Knighton	3	4	3.30	38	16	46.1	45	15	50
John Havird	4	9	3.93	18	0	105.1	102	34	89
Reinaldo Lopez	8	4	4.17	20	0	121.0	147	19	57
Ken Knudsen	8	2	4.57	32	0	61.0	51	31	59
Matt Murphy	3	5	5.21	12	0	57.0	82	16	52
Andrew Click	1	1	6.75	20	0	30.2	35	33	27
Sam Burton	0	1	7.36	17	0	22.0	25	15	20
Adam Cornwell	0	4	7.57	6	0	27.1	29	18	18
Justin Finan	0	5	7.73	16	0	64.0	94	19	36
Kris Goodman	0	1	7.94	8	0	11.1	16	16	8
Seth Brenner	1	1	8.40	4	0	15.0	21	18	16
Luke DeVenney	1	5	8.49	9	0	35.0	54	20	18
Will Coursen-Carr	1	0	9.98	11	0	15.1	20	14	14

WASHINGTON WILD THINGS

Player	AVG	AB	R	H	HR	RBI	BB	SO	SB
Chase Simmons	.383	60	9	23	0	9	8	12	0
Hector Roa	.309	369	52	114	12	69	15	84	3
James Harris	.305	384	75	117	16	64	51	84	26
Roman Collins	.298	373	62	111	8	65	54	53	23
Louis Mele	.269	52	8	14	1	9	3	17	0
Reydel Medina	.269	327	50	88	6	43	21	82	15
Brett Marr	.268	228	39	61	1	30	21	52	3
Ryan Cox	.265	83	9	22	0	8	3	6	0
Kyle Pollock	.260	339	50	88	11	56	56	64	0
Carter McEachern	.256	348	44	89	4	51	19	46	8
Mike Hill	.240	271	47	65	14	43	39	106	4
Ramsey Romano	.232	56	9	13	1	3	2	14	1
Conner Simonetti	.218	142	20	31	4	12	10	51	0
Nick Fennell	.200	75	17	15	0	3	11	15	2
Jordan Edgerton	.191	68	5	13	2	8	4	24	4
Justin Bohn	.174	46	8	8	1	3	8	8	0
Austin Crutcher	.100	30	5	3	1	2	4	16	4

Player	W	L	ERA	G	SV	IP	H	BB	SO
Dillon Sunnafrank	1	0	1.15	5	0	15.2	7	8	16
Zach Strecker	6	5	1.48	51	21	60.2	60	17	47
Thomas Dorminy	9	5	2.45	21	0	132.1	112	39	109
Trevor Bradley	4	3	3.33	26	1	75.2	64	31	72
Aaron Burns	2	1	3.48	14	0	31.0	44	15	14
Jesus Balaguer	1	0	3.50	10	0	18.0	12	11	34
Jake Eaton	1	0	3.60	9	0	10.0	2	6	7
James Meeker	2	1	3.94	19	0	29.2	31	5	26
Michael Austin	3	3	4.08	14	0	70.2	67	25	63
Frank Trimarco	4	1	4.23	17	0	44.2	50	8	40
Sam Mersing	2	0	4.23	22	1	27.2	25	14	17
Chase Cunningham	7	6	4.45	20	0	117.1	122	49	63
Davis Adkins	4	4	4.47	40	0	46.1	41	25	44
Mike Anthony	0	2	5.63	5	0	16.0	19	7	14
Jake Belinda	1	2	5.79	5	0	18.2	18	19	16
Levi MaVorhis	2	3	5.90	6	0	29.0	40	15	16
Taylor Bloom	0	1	6.75	4	0	14.2	22	5	7
Jamal Wilson	1	0	7.24	9	0	13.2	22	5	19
Daniel Garmendia	2	4	7.71	7	0	28.0	35	19	22
Kellen Croce	2	0	8.71	8	0	10.1	11	11	11
B.J. Sabol	0	0	10.54	12	0	13.2	20	9	15

WINDY CITY THUNDERBOLTS

Player	AVG	AB	R	H	HR	RBI	BB	SO	SB
Omar Obregon	.366	295	45	108	1	31	20	31	15
Derek Bangert	.351	74	12	26	2	14	5	14	0
Joe Becht	.317	142	29	45	1	14	24	33	9
Axel Johnson	.303	271	30	82	8	43	17	71	8
Tyler Straub	.269	334	46	90	6	40	33	75	10
Tim Zier	.255	373	44	95	3	49	18	61	15

INDEPENDENT LEAGUES

David Oppenheim	.235	68	6	16	1	7	8	5	4
Will Krug	.230	74	9	17	0	3	4	17	7
Blair Beck	.230	313	42	72	10	40	28	75	9
Ronnie Healy	.224	107	8	24	1	12	9	31	0
Larry Balkwill	.221	289	36	64	13	46	35	94	0
Jonathan McCray	.216	88	16	19	2	10	9	14	8
Darius Day	.213	61	7	13	0	0	14	22	11
Riley Krane	.204	275	30	56	5	26	19	62	7
Terrance Robertson	.186	113	14	21	0	10	10	45	3
Matt Brown	.159	63	5	10	1	7	9	31	0
Brandon Rawe	.156	32	5	5	0	1	5	7	1
Ishmael Edwards	.138	29	2	4	0	1	0	12	3
Ransom LaLonde	.113	97	7	11	3	11	10	18	0

Player	W	L	ERA	G	SV	IP	H	BB	SO
Will Landsheft	2	0	1.04	5	0	26.0	17	9	22
Devin Raftery	0	2	1.22	36	15	44.1	28	14	70
Jack Andersen	3	5	2.39	42	5	49.0	37	17	49
Dan Hlad	2	1	2.88	26	0	34.1	16	22	32
Joel Toribio	1	3	3.26	40	0	38.2	40	26	52
Braulio Torres-Perez	3	6	3.39	9	0	58.1	67	25	48
Zac Westcott	7	8	3.67	20	0	132.1	127	36	121
Jake Welch	7	6	3.76	18	0	105.1	89	31	78
Drew Peden	3	2	3.86	28	3	37.1	44	11	32
Paddy Ledet	7	8	4.29	21	0	92.1	98	27	78
Eddie Avila	2	6	4.43	14	0	69.0	63	33	69
Connor Bach	3	1	4.70	15	0	51.2	46	44	74
Austin Sweet	0	0	7.31	14	0	16.0	24	7	13
Jaramy Jacobs	0	3	8.27	4	0	16.1	25	11	11

PACIFIC ASSOCIATION

Sonoma set a league record with 57 regular season wins, but it was San Rafael that once again hoisted the trophy. The Pacifics shut out Sonoma 6-0 in the championship game giving San Rafael its fourth title in the league's seven seasons.

Pacific Association	W	L	PCT	GB
* Sonoma Stompers	57	23	.713	—
^ San Rafael Pacifics	50	30	.625	7
^ Vallejo Admirals	37	43	.463	20
^ Pittsburg Diamonds	36	44	.450	21
Napa Silverados	31	49	.388	26
Martinez Clippers	29	51	.363	28

Regular season champion. ^Wild Card

Playoffs: Final: San Rafael defeated Sonoma.

Attendance: San Rafael 18,081; Sonoma 17,501; Martinez 9,015; Vallejo 8,095; Napa 6,264; Pittsburg 3,044.

BATTING LEADERS

Player	Team	AVG	AB	R	H	HR	RBI
Javion Randle	SRF	.402	251	69	101	12	63
Pedro Barrios	MAR	.365	249	61	91	6	26
Daniel Comstock	SON	.362	196	43	71	9	50
DonAndre Clark	SRF	.347	334	71	116	3	29
Ray Jones	NAP	.342	272	71	93	9	41
Alan Mocahbee	MAR	.332	241	58	80	19	6
Wilyns Jimenez	MAR	.327	211	30	69	8	31
Gabriel Bracamonte	PIT	.323	235	42	76	10	57
Brett Smith	PIT	.319	295	79	94	2	32
Jake Taylor	SRF	.308	299	56	92	16	68

PITCHING LEADERS

Player	Team	W	L	ERA	IP	H	BB	SO
Tyler Sharp	SON	6	2	2.90	81	68	33	79
Jared Koenig	SRF	11	1	3.54	97	77	51	140
Max Beatty	SRF	9	3	3.93	101	120	15	75
Ethan Gibbons	SON	8	1	3.95	93	98	28	77
Fernando Baez	SRF	8	3	4.09	73	43	60	101
Brett Solano	PIT	8	4	4.39	98	123	22	70
Juan Espinosa	SON	3	1	4.52	74	73	22	50
Jalen Miller	VAL	2	5	4.65	79	75	39	96
Scott Harkin	NAP	4	3	5.03	93	103	40	77
Vijay Patel	SON	9	3	5.04	84	78	43	92

PECOS LEAGUE

The departure of the California League from two cities has been very good for the Pecos League. In 2017, High Desert won the league in its inaugural year in the league while fellow California League refugee Bakersfield won the title this season.

SOUTHERN	W	L	PCT	GB
Tucson	41	18	.695	—
Roswell	41	19	.683	½
Ruidoso	26	34	.433	1 ½
White Sands	7	51	.121	33 ½

MOUNTAIN	W	L	PCT	GB
Alpine	47	15	.758	—
Trinidad	41	21	.661	6
Santa Fe	31	30	.508	1 ½
Garden City	11	50	.180	3 ½

PACIFIC	W	L	PCT	GB
Bakersfield	37	26	.587	—
California City	35	28	.556	2
High Desert	30	31	.492	6
Monterery	19	43	.306	17 ½

Playoffs: First Round: Bakersfield defeated California City and Trinidad defeated Roswell. **Semifinals:** Alpine defeated Trinidad and Bakersfield defeated Tucson. **Finals:** Bakersfield defeated Alpine.

U.S. PRO BASEBALL LEAGUE

The USPBL has managed to prove that a one-site league can succeed. Birmingham won its second consecutive league title after finishing the regular season with the best record as well.

East	W	L	PCT	GB
Eastside Diamond Hoppers	24	23	.510	—
Utica Unicorns	24	24	.500	½

West	W	L	PCT	GB
Birmingham Bloomfield Beavers	26	21	.552	—
Westside Woolly Mammoths	21	27	.438	5 ½

Playoffs: Quarterfinal: Westside defeated Utica. **Semifinal:** Eastside defeated Westside. **Final:** Birmingham defeated Eastside.

ALL-Star Team: C: Jackson Smith, Westside. **1B:** Jack Hranec, Birmingham. **2B:** Sebastian Diaz, Eastside. **SS:** Thomas Roulis, Birmingham. **3B:** Dan Ward, Utica. **OF:** Ethan Wiskur, Westside; Drew Kitson, Westside; Kody Ruedisili, Eastside. **SP:** Josh Mason, Westside; Cody Brown, Utica. **RP:** Michael Scimanico, Utica; Brian Heldman, Birmingham. **UT:** Jimmy Latona, Utica; Tyler Pagano, Westside.

MVP: Dan Ward, Utica and Ethan Wiskur, Westside. **Pitcher of the Year:** Josh Mason, Westside.

BATTING LEADERS

Player	Team	AVG	AB	R	H	HR	RBI
Thomas Roulis	BBB	.311	164	29	51	2	14
Ethan Wiskur	WWM	.304	181	31	55	10	34
Dan Ward	UU	.293	188	34	55	12	32
Jimmy Latona	UU	.291	141	21	41	3	26
Jack Hranec	BBB	.285	179	27	51	4	33
Jackson Smith	WWM	.271	166	26	45	4	15
Carter Grote	UU	.250	180	25	45	4	20
Gunnar Buhner	EDH	.250	156	21	39	1	18
Jake Barbee	WWM	.248	129	21	32	2	15
Kody Ruedisili	EDH	.245	159	22	39	6	23

PITCHING LEADERS

Player	Team	W	L	ERA	IP	H	BB	SO
Cody Brown	UU	4	3	2.25	56	48	15	65
Josh Mason	WWM	8	2	2.87	94	76	19	78
Jack Angus	WWM	3	6	3.39	72	60	42	56
Matt Dallas	BBB	3	4	3.59	48	43	37	46
Gerry Salisbury	BBB	4	4	3.70	66	59	12	58
Pete Grasso	EDH	4	1	3.97	57	66	20	43
Cameron MacKenzie	BBB	2	2	4.17	58	64	20	61
Michael Klein	WWM	2	4	4.42	53	56	21	35
Devin Alexander	EDH	2	4	4.57	43	38	28	46
Donald Wanner	EDH	2	1	4.62	49	43	32	52

INTERNATIONAL

United States Climbs To No. 1 In WBSC Rankings

BY J.J. COOPER

In 2018, the World Baseball Softball Confederation rankings finally caught up to reality. After winning nearly every major tournament over the past couple of years, USA Baseball remained stuck in second place in the WBSC rankings for all of 2017. But in February 2018, the WBSC announced that the U.S. had passed Japan to take the top spot in the world rankings.

The U.S. won four world championships at different age levels and has six first-place finishes among the last 12 world competitions. It has finished in the top three in all nine international tournaments in which it participated. The U.S. has skipped the past two U23 World Cups and the Premier12 tournament in 2015.

The U.S. remained on top of the rankings all year. USA Baseball's 15U team (comprised of players 15 years old and younger) won its first 15U World Cup title by beating Panama.

The U.S. finished the tournament with an 8-1 record. Team USA cruised through some very easy opening-round games (including a 27-0 win over China and a 10-0 win over Germany). Its lone loss was a 2-1 defeat to Taiwan. The U.S. beat Cuba 10-0 and Japan 8-2 to advance to the championship game.

USA's Andrew Painter was named the tournament's top starting pitcher. The rest of the all-tournament team included catcher Edgar Quero (Cuba), first baseman Brady House (USA), second baseman Seiya Fukuhara (Japan), shortstop Reginald Preciado (Panama), third baseman Luke Leto (USA), left fielder Ryan Spikes (USA), center fielder Luis Durango (Panama), right fielder Oscar Aude (Dominican Republic), designated hitter Aoi Sugishita (Japan) and relief pitcher Alexis Bernal (Panama).

The win continues an amazing run for USA Baseball in international competitions. The U.S. pro team currently holds the titles in the World Cups at the 12U, 15U and 18U levels and won the World Baseball Classic as well. The U.S. topped Puerto Rico by an 8-0 score to take home its first WBC crown.

The U.S. did not participate in the U23 World Cup, which was held in Nicaragua in October.

The 2019 season will include the WBSC's Premier12 tournament in November 2019 and

Japan's ace Ayami Sato was once again the top player at the Women's World Cup

baseball will return to the Olympics in Tokyo in 2020.

Japan Wows At Women's World Cup

Japan continued its domination of women's baseball with an easy and convincing win at the 2018 Women's World Cup for its sixth consecutive title.

Pitching on just two days of rest, Ayami Sato, the team's ace for much of this decade, once again helped lead the team to the title. She threw five scoreless innings against Taiwan in the gold medal game before handing the game over to Akino Tanaka. Tanaka threw two perfect innings for the save. Iori Mura and Yuki Kawabata each drove in two runs for Japan.

Japan has won 45 of 47 games over the past six World Cups. It outscored its opponents 64-4 on its way to its 9-0 record in the 2018 tournament. Japan has now won 30 consecutive World Cup games and has not allowed more than two runs in any game of its past three World Cups. Canada topped the United States in the bronze medal game.

U15 WORLD CUP

DAVID AND CHITRE, PANAMA

Rk. Team	W	L	Rk. Team	W	L
1. United States	8	1	7. Brazil	5	3
2. Panama	7	2	8. Netherlands	4	4
3. Taiwan	6	3	9. Australia	3	5
4. Japan	5	4	10. China	1	7
5. Cuba	5	3	11. Germany	1	7
6. Dominican Republic	4	4	12. South Africa	1	7

Playoffs—Gold Media Game: U.S. defeated Panama.
Bronze Medal Game: Taiwan defeated Japan.

BATTING LEADERS

PLAYER	TEAM	AVG	AB	R	H	2B	3B	HR	RBI	SB
Mao, Ying-Chieh	TPE	.500	24	5	12	6	0	0	6	0
Schrier, Cody Jackson	USA	.476	21	17	10	0	1	2	8	4
Wu, Ping-En	TPE	.474	19	4	9	2	1	0	5	0
Johnson, Quinn Adam	AUS	.471	17	5	8	2	0	0	6	1
House, Brady Hunter	USA	.448	29	10	13	2	1	1	16	1
Sugishita, Aoi	JPN	.438	16	6	7	0	0	0	8	3
Alcolea, Kevin	CUB	.429	21	4	9	2	0	0	5	1
Hanada, Asahi	JPN	.419	31	10	13	1	0	0	8	4
Lin, Yu-Min	TPE	.417	12	1	5	1	0	0	4	0
De Los Santos, Deyvison	DOM	.417	24	5	10	6	0	1	8	0
Aude Castillo, Oscar A.	DOM	.417	24	11	10	2	0	2	12	1
Collins, Charlie Joseph	AUS	.412	17	6	7	2	2	0	4	0
Velders, Jesse Maarten	NED	.409	22	7	9	2	2	0	8	1
Tiburtino, Juan	BRA	.400	20	4	8	2	0	0	4	0
Quero Aguila, Edgar Yoel	CUB	.400	15	4	6	1	0	0	6	0

PITCHING LEADERS

PLAYER	TEAM	W	L	ERA	G	IP	H	BB	SO
Dutton, Samuel Gary	USA	1	0	0.00	4	8	4	3	9
Xiao, Ziran	CHN	0	1	0.00	3	7	11	3	3
Lemos Da Costa, Pedro	BRA	2	0	0.54	4	13	9	7	18
Guevara, Valdes	CUB	1	0	0.66	2	11	7	7	12
Bernal Vega, Alexis	PAN	1	0	0.68	4	10	5	5	13
Painter, Andrew	USA	2	0	0.70	2	10	8	3	13
Sakurai Ferreira, João	BRA	0	1	1.31	3	11	2	10	12
Hartle, Joshua	USA	1	1	1.40	2	10	9	7	5
Hinoue, Sota	JPN	1	0	1.50	2	9	9	2	9

College National Team Cruises

USA Baseball's Collegiate National Team wrapped up an impressive summer slate with a series win in Cuba, completing their campaign with series wins against Taiwan, Japan and Cuba and a 12-3 overall record.

But it wasn't just the success that made the team memorable to manager Paul Mainieri, it was also the way the players conducted themselves.

"We just had an amazing group of young men," Mainieri said. "They obviously were very talented, but they were also very unselfish. Conducted themselves in a first-class way, like to think they forged relationships with teammates and coaches that will last a lifetime. For me, personally, it was a dream come true, something I can check off my bucket list."

The team won all five games against Taiwan and then took three out of five from Japan before traveling to Havana. Team USA won the first three games to win the series against Cuba for the fourth consecutive summer.

U23 WORLD CUP

MONTERIA AND BARRANQUILLA, COLUMBIA

FINAL STANDINGS

Rk. Team	W	L	Rk. Team	W	L
1. Mexico	7	2	7. Columbhia	5	3
2. Japan	8	1	8. Puerto Rico	4	4
3. Venezuela	7	2	9. Australia	4	4
4. South Korea	5	4	10 Netherlands	2	6
5. Taiwan	3	5	11. South Africa	1	7
6. D.R.	3	5	12. Czech Republic	1	7

Gold Medal Game: Mexico defeated Japan.
Bronze Medal Game: Venezuela defeated South Korea.
C: Orlano Pina, Mex. **1B:** Hisanori Yasuda, Japan. **2B:** Brallan Perez, Colum. **3B:** Dervin Pomare, Colum. **SS:** Jorma Rodriguez, Ven. **OF:** Norberto Obeso, Mex; Carlos Vidal, Col.; Bojarski Ulrich, Aus. **DH:** Leandro Cedeno, Ven. **SP:** Francisco Haro, Mex. **RP:** Kakeru Narita, Japan.
MVP: Hisanori Yasuda, Japan.
Outstanding Defensive Player: Gilberto Celestino, DR.

Catcher Adley Rutschman (Oregon State) finished an excellent campaign by going 5-for-12 in Cuba, walking three times and driving in two runs. Overall, Rutschman led all Team USA hitters with a .355 batting average.

Mainieri raved about Rutschman, who joined the team late following the Beavers' national championship run at the College World Series. Rutschman came to Team USA for the final two series and quickly made an impact.

"Adley is one of those guys that's just got the 'it' factor to the nth degree," Mainieri said. "When he joined our team following the Taiwan series he just brought so much to our team from an ability standpoint as a hitter and a catcher and as a leader. He's cut right out of central casting. He's got everything you look for in a ballplayer and a person.

"He made us better in a lot of ways. I think he picked everyone up around him. He was a true leader of our team. He caught great, hit great from both sides of the plate and he was a great manager of the pitching staff along with (Virginia head coach) Brian O'Connor. If I was a general manager of a team, I would have a tough time passing on him next year in the draft."

Outfielder Daniel Cabrera (Louisiana State) and shortstop Bryson Stott (Nevada-Las Vegas) were two of the other offensive standouts for Team USA. Cabrera, a sophomore, led the team in home runs (two) and finished second in RBIs with six. Stott raised his prospect status with an impressive summer both at the plate and at shortstop. He hit .262/.340/.333 and made several highlight-reel plays, showing impressive defensive ability.

"A lot of our success was due to the way Bryson Stott played defensively for us," Mainieri said. "By the second half he was swinging extremely well. I

MELBOURNE, FLA.

SUPER ROUND RESULTS

*Japan 5-0	^Canada 2-3
*Taiwan 4-1	Venezuela 1-4
^USA 3-2	Dom. Republic .. 0-5

Gold Medal Game: Japan defeated Taiwan.
Bronze Medal Game: Canada defeated the United States.

FIRST ROUND STANDINGS

Group A	W	L	Group B	W	L
* Taiwan	4	1	* Japan	5	0
United States	4	1	* Canada	4	1
* Venezuela	3	2	* Dominican Republic	2	3
Puerto Rico	3	2	Australia	2	3
Korea	1	4	Cuba	1	4
Netherlands	0	5	Hong Kong	1	4

MVP: Ayami Sato, Japan (3-0, 0.37, 19 IP, 14 H, 18 SO).

All-Tournament Team: C: Shih-Yun Lee (Taiwan). **1B:** Katherine Psota (Canada). **2B:** Torres Antiveros (Venezuela). **SS:** Paradizo Ramos (Puerto Rico). **3B:** Chia-Hui Yang (Taiwan). **LF:** Kelsey Lalor (Canada). **CF:** Iori Mura (Japan). **RF:** Chia-Wen Shen (Taiwan). **SP:** Chiao-Yun Huang (Taiwan). **RP:** Megan Meidlinger (United States). **DH:** Megan Baltzell (United States).

WBSC RANKINGS, OCT. 2018

1. USA	8. Australia
2. Japan	5. Taiwan
3. Korea	6. Mexico	9. Canada
4. Cuba	7. Netherlands	10. Puerto Rico

Charles Saum hoists the trophy after USA Baseball's 15U team won the World Cup.

think Bryson did himself an awful lot of good in the way he improved and to catch the eye of the pro scouting world."

Team USA received solid pitching performances all summer. As a team, they posted a 2.06 ERA and held opponents to a .184 batting average. Lefthander Mason Feole (Connecticut) was one of the stars on the mound. In three appearances, he pitched 11 innings, allowed just three hits and no runs and struck out nine batters. Lefthander Drew Parrish (Florida State) and righthander Zack Hess (LSU) were similarly strong, with neither pitcher allowing a run. Parrish struck out eight batters and walked just one in 10.1 innings of work, while Hess led the team with two wins and pitched nine innings across three appearances.

Closer Max Meyer (Minnesota) and lefthander Graeme Stinson (Duke) were part of an excellent bullpen for Team USA. Meyer, a sophomore, saved seven games and struck out 15 batters in eight innings. Stinson, a junior, struck out 10 batters in six innings and scattered two hits and five walks.

It was quite a run for the collegiate national team, and although Mainieri wishes his squad had won every game, he was happy with the results.

"I wish we would have won all 15 games," Mainieri said. "But we won all three series, beat the Cuban National Team three-of-four in Cuba. The Japan team, man they were a tough team to beat. I have so much respect for the way they play the game. The pitching Japan threw at us was almost shocking to me how quality it was. It was successful results-wise, but mostly it was successful because the young men had an experience that they'll never forget."

USA COLLEGE NATIONAL TEAM STATS

Player	AVG	OBP	SLG	AB	R	H	2B	3B	HR	RBI	SB	BB	SO
Rutschman, Adley	.355	.432	.516	31	2	11	5	0	0	2	0	5	5
Langeliers, Shea	.346	.393	.500	26	2	9	4	0	0	1	1	2	5
Packard, Bryant	.333	.350	.389	18	1	6	1	0	0	1	0	1	7
Cabrera, Daniel	.300	.375	.440	50	6	15	1	0	2	6	2	6	10
Torkelson, Spencer	.286	.422	.314	35	3	10	1	0	0	3	0	8	11
Jung, Josh	.293	.377	.377	53	6	15	3	1	0	3	0	8	12
Watson, Zach	.280	.333	.380	50	7	14	2	0	1	3	2	3	10
Stott, Bryson	.262	.340	.333	42	3	11	0	0	1	7	0	5	11
Bailey, Patrick	.250	.333	.375	8	0	2	1	0	0	3	0	0	2
Vaughn, Andrew	.224	.316	.367	49	5	11	4	0	1	4	1	4	12
Wilson, Will	.208	.208	.208	24	2	5	0	0	0	2	0	0	5
Fletcher, Dominic	.171	.256	.314	35	3	6	2	0	1	4	0	4	8
Wallner, Matt	.154	.313	.154	13	4	2	0	0	0	0	0	3	2
Shewmake, Braden	.136	.250	.205	44	3	6	1	1	0	2	2	6	8
Holland, Will	.000	.000	.000	6	1	0	0	0	0	0	1	1	2

Player	ERA	W	L	G	SV	IP	H	R	ER	BB	SO
Feole, Mason	0	1	0	3	0	11	3	0	0	6	9
Parrish, Drew	0	1	0	3	0	10	5	0	0	1	8
Carraci, Parker	0	1	0	6	2	10	3	1	0	4	8
Hess, Zack	0	2	0	3	0	9	3	0	0	0	6
Thompson, Zack	0	1	0	3	0	9	3	0	0	5	7
Stinson, Graeme	0	0	0	3	0	6	2	1	0	5	10
Bradford, Cody	0	1	0	2	0	5	1	0	0	1	5
Van Eyk, C.J.	0	1	0	2	0	4	2	0	0	5	4
Senger, Mitchell	0	0	0	2	0	3	4	0	0	2	3
Canterino, Matt	0	1	0	1	0	2	2	0	0	1	0
Fletcher, Dominic	0	0	0	1	0	1	2	2	0	1	1
Agnos, Jake	0.96	0	0	4	0	9	5	1	1	1	14
Yovan, Kenyon	1.08	0	1	5	0	8	5	2	1	2	7
Cronin, Matt	1.69	1	0	4	1	5	4	1	1	1	5
Brnovich, Kyle	2.7	1	1	3	0	7	3	2	2	3	10
Meyer, Max	3.38	0	0	8	7	8	5	4	3	4	15
Little, Jack	4.5	0	1	2	1	2	3	1	1	0	0
Burns, Tanner	5.87	0	0	4	0	8	9	5	5	1	6
Doxakis, John	6.75	1	1	3	0	9	9	7	7	1	6
Pallante, Andre	8.53	0	3	0	0	6	8	6	6	3	6
Zeferjahn, Ryan	10.8	0	0	2	0	3	4	4	4	2	4

HECTOR VIVAS/GETTY IMAGES

Monterrey, Yucatan Both Claim Titles

The Mexican League has decided that two leagues are better than one. Mexico already had the Mexican Pacific League where baseball is played all winter, but in 2018, Liga Mexicana Beisbol added a summer season as well, so it crowned two champions.

The two seasons are treated separately with separate batting and pitching leaders. But Monterrey was excellent in both seasons. The Sultanes lost to Yucatan in the deciding Game 7 of the spring season championship series. But the Sultanes bounced back to win the summer title.

Several ex-big leaguers had impressive seasons with Felix Pie, Daric Barton and Yuniesky Betancourt all standing out at the plate while Henderson Alvarez and Andre Rienzo starred on the mound.

SPRING SEASON

Northern Division	W	L	PCT	GB
Sultanes de Monterrey	37	20	.649	—
Toros de Tijuana	33	23	.589	3 ½
Rieleros de Aguascalientes	33	24	.579	4
Acereros del Norte	29	27	.518	7 ½
Saraperos de Saltillo	24	32	.429	12 ½
Generales de Durango	24	33	.421	13
Algodoneros Union Laguna	23	34	.404	14
Tecolotes de los Dos Laredos	18	39	.316	19

Southern Division	W	L	PCT	GB
Leones de Yucatan	40	17	.702	—
Diablos Rojos del Mexico	36	19	.655	3
Tigres de Quintana Roo	33	21	.611	5 ½
Bravos de Leon	27	29	.482	12 ½
Pericos de Puebla	25	30	.455	14
Olmecas de Tabasco	24	33	.421	16
Piratas de Campeche	22	34	.393	17 ½
Guerreros de Oaxaca	22	35	.386	18

Playoffs: Wild Card: Leon defeated Puebla in one-game playoff. **Quarterfinals:** Tijuana defeated Aguascalientes 4-0; Yucatan defeated Leon 4-1; Quintana Roo defeated Mexico 4-1, and Monterrey defeated Monclova 4-2 in best-of-7 series. **Semifinals:** Monterrey defeated Tijuana 4-2 and Yucatan defeated Quintana Roo 4-3 in best-of-7 series. **Finals:** Yucatan defeated Monterrey 4-3 in best-of-7 series.

BATTING LEADERS

Batter, Club	AVG	G	AB	R	H	HR	RBI
Rodriguez Salazar, Isaac, TIJ	.394	55	226	52	89	4	30
Hernandez, Brian, TIG	.379	53	219	35	83	2	46
Castillo, Jesus, MVA	.378	56	193	44	73	13	57
* Pie, Felix, LEO	.376	46	186	38	70	10	32
# Del Campo, Jon, DUR	.374	52	206	27	77	6	50
* Barton, Daric, PUE	.373	40	118	32	44	7	29
Juarez, Luis, YUC	.370	50	192	45	71	13	54
* Moncrief, Carlos, DUR	.369	36	157	30	58	2	19
Betancourt, Yuniesky, OAX	.367	56	237	41	87	11	36
Valdez, Jesus, YUC	.364	53	206	37	75	8	42

PITCHING LEADERS

Pitcher, Club	W-L	ERA	IP	H	BB	SO
Reyes, Jorge, MTY	3-0	1.97	46	45	15	45
Garza, Adrian, TAB	4-1	2.39	49	42	13	26
Castellanos, Jonathan, YUC	5-3	2.43	63	69	17	30
* Valdes, Raul, SAL	7-1	2.50	54	44	12	53
Samayoa, Jose, YUC	6-4	2.57	67	65	22	46
Lowey, Josh, MVA	8-2	2.58	73	61	21	79
Alvarez, Henderson, TIG	6-1	2.61	62	56	14	33
* Hernandez, Carlos, TIJ	8-2	2.64	58	54	5	30
Acosta, Octavio, MEX	5-1	2.84	57	45	24	40
Molina, Nestor LAR	4-4	2.85	54	48	17	45

SUMMER SEASON

Northern Division	W	L	PCT	GB
Acereros del Norte	42	14	.750	—
Toros de Tijuana	35	21	.625	7
Sultanes de Monterrey	34	23	.596	8 ½
Tecolotes de los Dos Laredos	33	24	.579	9 ½
Rieleros de Aguascalientes	25	30	.455	16 ½
Saraperos de Saltillo	24	31	.436	17 ½
Generales de Durango	22	32	.407	19
Algodoneros Union Laguna	18	39	.316	24 ½

South Division	W	L	PCT	GB
Leones de Yucatan	32	24	.571	—
Diablos Rojos del Mexico	31	24	.564	½
Pericos de Puebla	29	27	.518	3
Bravos de Leon	26	28	.481	5
Guerreros de Oaxaca	26	30	.464	6
Piratas de Campeche	25	32	.439	7 ½
Tigres de Quintana Roo	24	32	.429	8
Olmecas de Tabasco	20	35	.364	11 ½

Playoffs: Wild Card: Oaxaca defeated Leon in one-game playoff. **Quarterfinals:** Mexico defeated Puebla 4-1; Monclova defeated Dos Laredos 4-1; Monterrey defeated Tijuana 4-3, and Oaxaca defeated Yucatan 4-3 in best-of-7 series. **Semifinals:** Monterrey defeated Monclova 4-1 and Oaxaca defeated Mexico 4-2 in best-of-7 series. **Finals:** Monterrey defeated Oaxaca 4-2 in best-of-7 series.

BATTING LEADERS

Batter, Club	AVG	G	AB	R	H	HR	RBI
Rosario, Olmo, CAM	.408	56	218	32	89	6	38
Betancourt, Yuniesky, OAX	.406	56	224	27	91	4	49
Asencio, Yeison, MEX	.386	43	176	36	68	11	37
# Cabrera, Everth, YUC	.385	55	221	48	85	2	26
* Heras, Leo, YUC	.383	37	141	32	54	7	25
Fuenmayor, Balbino, LAR	.372	56	226	29	84	9	46
Peguero, Francisco, MVA	.368	52	212	42	78	13	60
* Urrutia, Henry, OAX	.360	37	136	26	49	3	28
Sanay, Oscar, PUE	.358	54	179	40	64	1	21
Hernandez, Brian, TIG	.356	56	225	36	80	9	46

PITCHING LEADERS

Pitcher, Club	W-L	ERA	IP	H	BB	SO
Rienzo, Andre, MVA	4-0	0.76	47	47	21	38
Marin, Terance, LAR	7-1	2.12	68	67	19	34
Del Rosario, Francisco, AGS	3-1	2.24	56	47	22	47
Gonzalez, Edgar, MTY	7-2	2.83	57	49	8	23
Rios, Wilmer, MVA	6-1	2.83	60	52	9	36
Martinez, Rogelio, LEO	4-2	2.93	46	44	14	31
De Leon, Carlos, MEX	6-2	3.00	51	49	18	31
Moscoso, Guillermo, LEO	2-2	3.15	66	63	24	58
Oyervides, Jose, LAR	4-1	3.29	55	59	20	36
Garza, Adrian, TAB	1-5	3.51	48.2	51	17	26

Fukuoka Wins Second Straight Title

The Fukuoka SoftBank Hawks continued to hold a firm grip over the rest of Japanese baseball with a second consecutive Japan Series title.

Rick Vanden Hurk struck out 10 in six shutout innings and a Yurisbel Gracial home run provided all the runs the Hawks needed in a 2-0 win over Hiroshima in the deciding Game 6.

The first game of the Japan Series ended in a tie, so Fukuoka won the series 4-1. Having finished in second place in the regular season, Fukuoka had a tough path to the title. It needed all three games to beat Hokkaido in the first round and then topped Seibu with four wins in five games in the Pacific League Climax Series.

Fukuoka's dominance stretches beyond back-to-back titles. The Hawks have won four of the last five league titles and five of the past eight. Because of Fukuoka's dominance, the Pacific League has won eight of the past 10 Japan Series.

With four titles in five years, the Hawks have dominated the league to an extent not seen since the Seibu Lions won six titles in a seven-year span from 1986-1992. The Yomiuri Giants won nine consecutive Japan Series titles from 1965-1973.

Hawks catcher Takuya Kai was named the Japan Series MVP largely because he completely shut down Hiroshima's running game. Kai threw out all six attempted basestealers in the series, setting a league record.

Fukuoka got useful seasons from former Mariners lefthander Ariel Miranda (6-1, 1.89) and longtime Cuba star Alfredo Despaigne (.238/.333/.494 with 29 home runs).

For Hiroshima, it was a disappointing ending, but the Carp have won three straight Central League regular season titles and have earned spots in the Japan Series in two of the past three seasons.

There were other heroics in the playoffs. Yomiuri advanced to the Central League Climax Series when Tomoyuki Sugano threw a clinching no-hitter to finish Yakult's season in the first round of the playoffs.

The season also was a finale for several notable players. Chunichi reliever Hitoki Iwase announced his retirement after a 20-season career, all with

Ariel Miranda

ANDY KUNO/GETTY IMAGES

the Dragons. Iwase holds the NPB record for saves (407) and games (1,001). He was a 10-time all-star.

Seibu infielder Kazuo Matsui, a longtime NPB star, announced his retirement after a long and storied career. Matsui, 42, was the NPB 1998 Most Valuable Player. He came the the U.S. to play for the Mets and Rockies, but returned to Japan and played another six seasons, finishing his playing career as a player-coach.

Lefthander Toshiya Sugiuchi also announced his retirement. Sugiuchi had been limited by injuries in recent years, but he was a star both in Japan and in international competitions for years. Sugiuchi finished with 142 wins. He played for three World Baseball Classic teams and also reprepresented Japan in the Olympics.

It's not clear if this will be the end in Japan for Sebiu lefthander Yusei Kikuchi. The 27-year-old is one of the best pitchers in Japan. After the season, Seibu announced that it will post Kikuchi, making him eligible to come to the U.S. Kikuchi finished second in the Pacific League with a 3.08 ERA in 2018.

There were several notable performances by imports from North and Central America. Former Reds infielder Neftali Soto had an excellent season. He hit a Central League-best 41 home runs for Yokohama. Former White Sox infielder Dayan Viciedo hit a Central League-best .348 for Chunichi.

Longtime MLB outfielder Nori Aoki, 36, had a smooth return to Japan, as he hit .327 with 10 home runs in his return. Seibu's Hotaka Yamakawa led all sluggers with 47 home runs over the course of the regular season. He also drove in 124 runs.

CENTRAL LEAGUE

Team	W	L	T	PCT	GB
Hiroshima Toyo Carp	82	59	2	.582	—
Yakult Swallows	75	66	2	.532	7
Yomiuri Giants	67	71	5	.486	13 ½
Yokohama DeNA BayStars	67	74	2	.475	15
Chunichi Dragons	63	78	2	.447	19
Hanshin Tigers	62	79	2	.440	20

Playoffs: First round: Yomiuri defeated Yakult 2-0 in best-of-3 series.
Climax Series: Hiroshima defeated Yomiuri 4-0 in best-of-7 series.
Japan Series: Fukuoka defeated Hiroshima 4-2 in best-of-7 series.

INTERNATIONAL

PACIFIC LEAGUE

Team	W	L	T	PCT	GB
Saitama Seibu Lions	88	53	2	.624	—
Fukuoka SoftBank Hawks	82	60	1	.577	6 ½
Hokkaido Nippon-Ham Fighters	74	66	3	.529	13 ½
Orix Buffaloes	65	73	5	.471	21 ½
Chiba Lotte Marines	59	81	3	.421	28 ½
Tohoku Rakuten Golden Eagles	58	82	3	.414	29 ½

Playoffs: First round: Fukuoka defeated Hokkaido 2-1 in best-of-three series. **Climax Series:** Fukuoka defeated Seibu 4-1 in best-of-seven series. **Japan Series:** Fukuoka defeated Hiroshima 4-1 in best-of-seven series.

CENTRAL LEAGUE BATTING LEADERS

Player, Team	AVG	AB	R	H	HR	RBI	SB
Viciedo, Dayan, Dragons	.348	512	91	178	26	99	3
Sakamoto, Hayato, Giants	.345	441	87	152	18	67	9
Hirata, Ryosuke, Dragons	.329	493	83	162	9	55	8
Aoki, Norichika, Swallows	.327	495	85	162	10	67	3
Almonte, Zoilo, Dragons	.321	498	56	160	15	77	1
Suzuki, Seiya, Carp	.320	422	86	135	30	94	4
Takai, Yuhei, Swallows	.318	446	50	142	6	67	6
Miyazaki, Toshiro, BayStars	.318	551	71	175	28	71	0
Sakaguchi, Tomotaka, Swallows	.317	508	64	161	3	37	9
Yamada, Tetsuto, Swallows	.315	524	130	165	34	89	33
Soto, Neftali, BayStars	.310	416	74	129	41	95	0
Okamoto, Kazuma, Giants	.309	540	82	167	33	100	2
Itoi, Yoshio, Tigers	.308	419	60	129	16	68	22
Maru, Yoshihiro, Carp	.306	432	109	132	39	97	10
Matsuyama, Ryuhei, Carp	.302	397	46	120	12	74	2
Tsutsugo, Yoshitomo, BayStars	.295	495	77	146	38	89	0
Lopez, Jose, BayStars	.288	441	46	127	26	77	0
Itohara, Kento, Tigers	.286	531	79	152	1	35	6
Noma, Takayoshi, Carp	.286	405	64	116	5	46	17
McGehee, Casey, Giants	.285	499	65	142	21	84	2
Fukudome, Kosuke, Tigers	.280	414	57	116	14	72	2
Oshima, Yohei, Dragons	.274	588	92	161	7	57	21
Balentien, Wladimir, Swallows	.268	514	72	138	38	131	1
Tanaka, Kosuke, Carp	.262	572	92	150	10	60	32
Fukuda, Nobumasa, Dragons	.261	440	50	115	13	63	0
Umeno, Ryutaro, Tigers	.259	386	45	100	8	47	5
Kamei, Yoshiyuki, Giants	.254	422	47	107	13	49	4
Takahashi, Shuhei, Dragons	.254	433	35	110	11	69	0
Nishiura, Naomichi, Swallows	.242	479	57	116	10	55	1
Kyoda, Yota, Dragons	.235	578	73	136	4	44	20
Kikuchi, Ryosuke, Carp	.233	557	85	130	13	60	10

CENTRAL LEAGUE PITCHING LEADERS

Pitcher, Team	W	L	ERA	IP	H	HR	BB	SO
Sugano, Tomoyuki, Giants	15	8	2.14	202	166	14	37	200
Azuma, Katsuki, BayStars	11	5	2.45	154	130	13	42	155
Osera, Daichi, Carp	15	7	2.62	182	143	22	41	159
Garcia, Onelki, Dragons	13	9	2.99	169	144	13	73	132
Johnson, Kris, Carp	11	5	3.11	145	137	9	48	113
Messenger, Randy, Tigers	11	7	3.63	174	160	13	58	149
Yamaguchi, Shun, Giants	9	9	3.68	154	127	18	60	144
Buchanan, David, Swallows	10	11	4.03	174	186	17	53	95

OTHER NOTABLE PITCHERS

Pitcher, Team	W	L	ERA	IP	H	HR	BB	SO
Franzua, Geronimo, Carp	3	4	1.66	65	38	3	34	81
Sato, Yu, Dragons	1	2	2.08	43	27	2	23	51
Ishiyama, Taichi, Swallows	3	2	2.08	74	63	6	15	62
Fujikawa, Kyuji, Tigers	5	3	2.32	54	29	3	37	67
Patton, Spencer, BayStars	5	1	2.57	56	53	3	16	67
Kuwahara, Kentaro, Tigers	5	3	2.68	57	52	6	12	65
Nakazaki, Shota, Carp	4	2	2.71	66	66	7	29	56
Yamasaki, Yasuaki, BayStars	2	4	2.72	56	40	5	18	63
Jackson, Jay, Carp	3	2	2.76	46	42	6	26	48
Dolis, Rafael, Tigers	1	7	2.85	54	50	4	17	56
Ichioka, Ryuji, Carp	5	6	2.88	56	46	7	22	61
Mathieson, Scott, Giants	0	3	2.97	33	21	3	13	41
Mikami, Tomoya, BayStars	1	1	3.05	56	55	3	20	40
Sunada, Yoshiki, BayStars	0	2	3.61	52	44	4	25	44
Kondo, Kazuki, Swallows	7	4	3.64	77	74	8	31	75
Adames, Samuel, Giants	0	2	3.94	32	30	2	20	19
Mishima, Kazuki, BayStars	7	2	3.97	68	61	8	31	82
Suzuki, Hiroshi, Carp	4	6	4.41	49	46	7	27	42
Sawamura, Hirokazu, Giants	1	6	4.64	52	55	4	27	54
Caminero, Arquimedes, Giants	1	1	5.79	19	27	1	6	19
Tajima, Shinji, Dragons	0	4	7.22	29	30	4	18	13

PACIFIC LEAGUE BATTING LEADERS

Player, Team	AVG	AB	R	H	HR	RBI	SB
Yanagita, Yuki, Hawks	.352	475	95	167	36	102	21
Kondo, Kensuke, Fighters	.323	462	59	149	9	69	5
Akiyama, Shogo, Lions	.323	603	107	195	24	82	15
Yoshida, Masataka, Buffaloes	.321	514	77	165	26	86	3
Asamura, Hideto, Lions	.310	565	104	175	32	127	4
Shimauchi, Hiroaki, Eagles	.292	394	53	115	11	53	11
Nakamura, Akira, Hawks	.292	506	57	148	14	57	1
Inoue, Seiya, Marines	.292	476	59	139	24	99	1
Tonosaki, Shuta, Lions	.287	453	70	130	18	67	25
Nakamura, Shogo, Marines	.284	552	82	157	8	57	39
Yamakawa, Hotaka, Lions	.281	541	115	152	47	124	0
Nishikawa, Haruki, Fighters	.278	528	90	147	10	48	44
Genda, Sosuke, Lions	.278	594	92	165	4	57	34
Akaminai, Ginji, Eagles	.276	492	45	136	5	48	1
Imae, Toshiaki, Eagles	.276	421	44	116	10	49	0
Mori, Tomoya, Lions	.275	473	67	130	16	80	7
Uebayashi, Seiji, Hawks	.270	551	88	149	22	62	13
Suzuki, Daichi, Marines	.266	477	44	127	8	49	8
Tanaka, Kazuki, Eagles	.265	423	67	112	18	45	21
Nakata, Sho, Fighters	.265	540	61	143	25	106	0
Kakunaka, Katsuya, Marines	.265	411	44	109	7	57	3
Nakashima, Takuya, Fighters	.261	391	57	102	1	23	29
Matsuda, Nobuhiro, Hawks	.248	517	72	128	32	82	3
Tamura, Tatsuhiro, Marines	.239	415	32	99	3	35	3
Despaigne, Alfredo, Hawks	.238	407	62	97	29	74	0
Romero, Stefen, Buffaloes	.237	443	63	105	25	63	7
Laird, Brandon, Fighters	.233	450	47	105	26	65	0
Fujioka, Yudai, Marines	.230	535	58	123	5	42	14
Adachi, Ryoichi, Buffaloes	.219	465	44	102	3	41	20

PACIFIC LEAGUE PITCHING LEADERS

Pitcher, Team	W	L	ERA	IP	H	HR	BB	SO
Kishi, Takayuki, Eagles	11	4	2.72	159	127	21	29	159
Kikuchi, Yusei, Lions	14	4	3.08	164	124	16	45	153
Uwasawa, Naoyuki, Fighters	11	6	3.16	165	146	15	38	151
Martinez, Nick, Fighters	10	11	3.51	162	168	16	40	93
Nishi, Yuki, Buffaloes	10	13	3.60	162	162	15	36	119
Norimoto, Takahiro, Eagles	10	11	3.69	180	171	18	51	187
Wakui, Hideaki, Marines	7	9	3.70	151	155	16	43	99
Tawata, Shinsaburo, Lions	16	5	3.81	173	173	12	47	102
Yamaoka, Taisuke, Buffaloes	7	12	3.95	146	137	21	49	121

OTHER NOTABLE PITCHERS

Pitcher, Team	W	L	ERA	IP	H	HR	BB	SO
Miyanishi, Naoki, Fighters	4	3	1.80	45	29	1	20	39
Aoyama, Koji, Eagles	4	1	1.85	48	35	2	21	37
Herrmann, Frank, Eagles	2	3	1.99	46	36	2	17	44
Urano, Hiroshi, Fighters	2	2	2.16	42	33	3	9	44
Kayama, Shinya, Hawks	2	1	2.45	33	17	3	11	28
Masui, Hirotoshi, Buffaloes	2	5	2.49	65	55	4	33	69
Heath, Deunte, Lions	4	1	2.50	40	28	4	8	53
Ishikawa, Naoya, Fighters	1	2	2.59	49	44	4	17	53
Mori, Yuito, Hawks	2	4	2.79	61	51	7	19	61
Yamamoto, Yoshinobu, Buffaloes	4	2	2.89	53	40	4	16	46
Matsunaga, Takahiro, Marines	2	3	3.15	40	40	1	18	35
Kajiya, Ren, Hawks	4	3	3.38	67	67	5	25	53
Hirai, Katsunori, Lions	3	1	3.40	53	40	9	19	54
Noda, Shogo, Lions	1	1	3.51	41	36	7	24	40
Matsui, Yuki, Eagles	5	8	3.65	67	53	4	29	91
Tonkin, Michael, Eagles	4	4	3.71	51	45	2	23	33
Tonkin, Michael, Fighters	4	4	3.71	51	45	2	23	33
Yoshida, Kazumasa, Buffaloes	3	4	3.83	56	47	4	18	53
Uchi, Tatsuya, Marines	3	5	3.84	59	51	5	19	54
Masuda, Tatsush, Lions	2	4	5.17	38	44	5	9	23

KOREA

Wyverns Win

Before the Korean Series began, SK Wyverns manager Trey Hillman announced that he would not return as the club's manager because he needed to return to the U.S. to be closer to his parents. His team gave him a wonderful parting gift as they beat regular season champion Doosan for a Korean Series title.

Han Dong Min was the MVP of the Korea Series. Han hit a walk-off home run in extra innings that finished off Nexen in the previous round, and then he homered in the 13th inning to put SK ahead against the Bears in the deciding Game 6 of the Korea Series.

The KBO adopted a new limit of $1 million for signing new foreign players. The restriction only applies to new players coming to Korea, as teams can go beyond the limit to re-sign their own imports for further seasons.

The KBO continues to be a slugger's league. Five different hitters hit 40 or more home runs as the league easily broke the single-season record for home runs.

STANDINGS & LEADERS

Team	W	L	T	PCT	GB
Doosan Bears	93	51	0	.646	—
SK Wyverns	78	65	1	.545	14 ½
Hanwha Eagles	77	67	0	.535	16
Nexen Heroes	75	69	0	.521	18
Kia Tigers	70	74	0	.486	23
Samsung Lions	68	72	4	.486	23
Lotte Giants	68	74	2	.479	24
LG Twins	68	75	1	.476	24 ½
KT Wiz	59	82	3	.418	32 ½
NC Dinos	58	85	1	.406	34 ½

BATTING LEADERS

Player, Team	AVG	AB	R	H	HR	RBI	SB
Kim Hyun Soo, Lg	.362	453	95	164	20	101	1
Yang Eui Ji, Doosan	.358	439	84	157	23	77	6
Lee Jung Hoo, Nexen	.355	459	81	163	6	57	11
Park Byung Ho, Nexen	.345	400	88	138	43	112	0
An Chi Hong, Kia	.342	494	88	169	23	118	5
Jeon Jun Woo, Lotte	.342	556	118	190	33	90	7
Kim Joo Chan, Kia	.340	429	71	146	18	93	8
Choi Hyoung Woo, Kia	.339	528	92	179	25	103	3
Yoo Han Joon, Kt	.339	428	59	145	20	83	1
Kim Jae Hwan, Doosan	.334	527	104	176	44	133	2

PITCHING LEADERS

Player, Team	W	L	ERA	IP	H	HR	BB	SO
Lindblom, Josh, Doosan	15	4	2.88	169	142	16	38	157
Wilson, Tyler, Lg	9	4	3.07	170	158	11	35	149
Sosa, Henry, Lg	9	9	3.52	181	192	16	28	181
Lee Yong Chan, Doosan	15	3	3.63	144	151	14	36	102
Frankoff Seth, Doosan	18	3	3.74	149	118	12	55	134
Brigham Jake, Nexen	11	7	3.84	199	188	19	50	175
Kelly Merrill, Sk	12	7	4.09	158	152	18	47	161
Yang Hyeon Jong, Kia	13	11	4.15	184	199	21	43	152
Park Jong Hun, Sk	14	8	4.18	159	158	16	54	133
Nippert Dustin, Kt	8	8	4.25	176	209	26	39	165

TAIWAN

Lamigo Claims CPBL Title

The Lamigo Monkeys continued to dominate the Chinese Professional Baseball League (CPBL), knocking off the Uni-President Lions, 4-2, in the best-of-seven CPBL Series. It was the Monkeys' second straight league title and their fifth in the past seven seasons.

During the season, UniLions lefthander Ryan Verdugo threw the first perfect game in the 29-year history of the CPBL. Even with the perfect game, Verdugo had to rely on a walk-off home run by Guo Fu-Lin in the ninth inning to pick up the win.

The CPBL has also approved adding a team from Australia to join the league's minor leagues. There is the possibility that in the long term an Australian team could join the CPBL's major leagues. Baseball Australia and the CPBL have developed closer ties in recent years, with the CPBL sending players to play in the Australian winter league as well.

STANDINGS & LEADERS

Team	W	L	T	PCT	GB
*Lamigo Monkeys	73	47	0	.608	—
^Uni President 7-Eleven Lions	64	55	1	.538	9
^Fubon Guardians	54	66	1	.450	19
Chinatrust Brothers	48	71	0	.403	24 ½

* First and second-half champion. ^Wild-card teams
Playoffs: UniLions defeated Fubon 3-1 in best-of-five series.
Finals: Lamigo defeated wthe UniLions 4-2 in best-of-seven series.

BATTING LEADERS

Player, Team	AVG	OBP	SLG	AB	R	H	HR	RBI	SB
Chen, Jun Shiu, Lamigo	.375	.439	.602	387	78	145	17	77	5
Fu, Chin Long, Fubon	.374	.414	.556	385	68	144	14	80	7
Chen, Chieh Shian, UniLions	.356	.428	.495	463	102	165	8	60	16
Wang, Bo Rong, Lamigo	.351	.446	.547	453	99	159	17	84	9
Wu, Chieh Ru, UniLions	.336	.395	.462	357	66	120	8	55	12
Wang, Wei Chen, Chinatrust	.335	.393	.387	489	74	164	0	42	44
Lan, Yin Liu, Lamigo	.335	.367	.489	436	71	146	15	64	6
Chiang, Chih Shein, Fubon	.331	.373	.545	429	63	142	18	89	2
Lin, Yee Chuan, Fubon	.315	.366	.458	349	45	110	8	54	2
Chou, Siz Chi, Chinatrust	.305	.359	.452	394	36	120	11	64	2

PITCHING LEADERS

Player, Team	W	L	ERA	G	IP	H	BB	SO
Josh Roenicke, UniLions	12	10	3.17	26	156	162	27	138
Bryan Woodall, Fubon	14	10	3.25	28	169	180	25	126
Bruce Kern, Lamigo	13	3	3.28	25	156	170	50	110
Mike Loree, Fubon	10	8	3.47	26	161	177	16	157
Nick Additon, Chinatrust	9	9	3.48	27	160	163	51	140
Michael Nix, Fubon	8	4	3.72	26	163	161	48	102
Mitch Lively, Chinatrust	7	8	4.05	28	151	176	41	119
Wang, Yi Cheng, Lamigo	8	8	4.25	22	140	152	36	103
Ryan Verdugo, UniLions	8	4	4.31	28	148	172	34	142

Bologna Wins Serie A1

BY HARVEY SAHKER

Bologna continued to dominate Serie A1 when it defeated Parma three games to one in the Italy Series. It was Bologna's third national title in five years.

Bologna advanced to the Series by sweeping SSD Nettuno three games to none in their best-of-five semifinal. Parma upset Rimini in the other semi-final, three games to two.

Veteran Cuban hurler Erly Casanova was outstanding for Parma in the semis (3-0, 0.87), going the distance and blanking Rimini 1-0 in the pivotal Game 4. It was Parma's first appearance in the Series since 2010.

Newcomer Jorge Martinez (8-1, 1.95) formed a formidable one-two punch with Raul Rivero (9-0, 2.13) on the Bologna pitching staff. Martinez is a former independent leaguer and winter leaguer. The Cuban righty was even better in the post-season (2-0, 1.33).

Seven Bologna regulars hit .300 or better. Among them was former Braves farmhand Osman Marval, who led all of Serie A1 in homers, RBIs, runs, total bases and slugging percentage. The team's .323 batting average was the best in the league. Bologna's regular season included a 22-game winning streak.

Three Rimini pitchers shared a no-hit, 11-0 victory over Parma in late June. Starter Alex Bassani went five inings. Bassani was followed by Southwestern Oklahoma State alumnus Kevin Kelly and Yuri Morellini, who threw one frame each.

On the last day of the regular season, three SSD Nettuno hurlers shared a seven-inning perfect game, a 19-0 rout of Padule. Former Blue Jay Scott Richmond started for SSD Nettuno and went four innings. Francesco Cozzolino pitched the fifth and Marcos Frias the sixth and seventh before the mercy rule was applied. Richmond topped the league in innings pitched and shared the lead in strikeouts with Casanova.

Richmond was not the only ex-Toronto player to make an impression in his first Serie A1 campaign. Chris Colabello joined San Marino late in the season and hit four home runs in just nine games. The day before Richmond pitched in the perfect game, Colabello knocked in seven runs in an 11-1 rout against Padova.

Colabello is a second-generation Serie A1 player.

Collabelo's father, Lou, won 94 games and batted .294 as a pitcher and first baseman for Rimini between 1977 and 1984. Father and son have both played for the Italian national team.

Chris Colabello

DAVID DUROCHIK/GETTY IMAGES

Chris has played for Italy in several competitions, including the World Baseball Classic. He wrapped up his 2018 season with a trip to Europe's Super Six tournament, which took place in Hoofddorp in the Netherlands. There, the junior Colabello hit .700 in 20 at bats with five homers and 14 RBIs in just five games. Italy finished second in the tournament, which was won by the host nation.

STANDINGS

Team	W	L	PCT	GB
Bologna	26	2	.929	—
Rimini	23	5	.821	3
Parma	16	12	.571	10
SSD Nettuno	16	12	.571	10
San Marino	13	15	.464	13
Padova	11	17	.393	15
Padule	5	23	.179	21
ASD Nettuno	2	26	.071	24

Semifinals: Bologna beat SSD Nettuno 3-0 and Parma beat Rimini 3-2 in best-of-5 series. **Finals:** Bologna beat Parma 3-1.

INDVIDUAL BATTING LEADERS

Player, Team	AVG	AB	R	H	2B	3B	HR	RBI	SB
Romero, G. A. Rafael, RIM	.430	100	31	43	9	0	3	16	4
Mazzanti, Giuseppe, BOL	.400	85	22	34	10	0	5	22	0
Perdomo, G. Carlos, PDO	.396	101	18	40	8	0	1	15	3
Russo, Alexander, PDO	.390	118	22	46	9	0	3	17	7
Vasquez, Andy W., NETC	.385	78	10	30	7	0	4	10	5
Angulo, G. O. David, RIM	.381	105	26	40	8	0	6	25	1
Alarcon, T. Yordanis, PDU	.380	92	15	35	4	0	3	14	3
Marval, G. Osman J., BOL	.378	111	36	42	9	0	9	31	0
Batista, D. Nathanael, RIM	.378	90	15	34	7	2	1	22	2
Nosti, Nicholas, BOL	.349	86	24	30	4	2	1	20	6

INDIVIDUAL PITCHING LEADERS

Player	W	L	ERA	IP	H	R	ER	BB	SO
Perez, P. Andres E., RSM	0	1	0.74	24	16	5	2	19	33
Ruiz, Seco R. Jose, RIM	6	1	1.60	56	37	19	10	24	62
Hernandez, Ricardo J., RIM	4	1	1.78	30	28	12	6	5	34
Richmond, S. Daniel, NET	4	3	1.81	89	57	23	18	22	105
Pirvu, Eduard, PAR	1	0	1.85	24	17	10	5	11	25
Casanova, Callaba Erl, PAR	8	2	1.87	82	53	21	17	19	105
Martinez, Jorge, PDU	8	1	1.95	74	58	17	16	12	84
Quevedo, Carlos, RSM	5	6	1.98	43	51	20	16	16	93
Rivero, Raul, BOL	9	0	2.13	55	44	14	13	9	81
Frias, Marcos, NET	8	4	2.54	74	58	23	21	25	77

NETHERLANDS

Neptunus Tops Amsterdam

BY HARVEY SAHKER

Neptunus won its sixth straight Holland Series, beating the Amsterdam Pirates four games to two. The Pirates won the first two games of the series, outscoring Neptunus 15-2. But the Rotterdam club came back with a vengeance, holding Amsterdam to just six runs the rest of the way. Neptunus has now won 19 Dutch championships.

Reliever Loek van Mil had an outstanding season for Neptunus. The 7-foot-1 righthander held opposing batters to a .140 average, allowed just two runs (one unearned) and had a 0.73 WHIP in 40 innings.

A minor leaguer for parts of 10 seasons, van Mil led the DML with 25 appearances and shared the lead with six saves.

Van Mil and Neptunus starters Diegomar Markwell and Orlando Yntema had a combined won-loss record of 26-1.

The Neptunus offense was led by Dwayne Kemp, who topped the DML in batting average, hits, total bases, slugging and RBIs. Kemp notched his 500th career DML hit during the 2018 campaign.

Amsterdam hurler Rob Cordemans (7-1, 2.17) broke the DML career strikeout record in June. Cordemans overtook Bart Volkerijk, whose 1,948 mark had stood for twenty-two years.

Veteran slugger Bryan Engelhardt made a successful return to the DML after spending the 2017 season in the second tier. Engelhardt, 36, batted .279 for Amersfoort and led the DML with 14 doubles, his single season best.

A pair of young ex-minor leaguers shared the DML home run crown. Sint Maarten native Denzel Richardson (Rockies) of DSS and Australian Sam Kennelly (Pirates) of the Oosterhout Twins hit six dingers each. Richardson, 24, and Kennelly, 22, were both DML newcomers in 2018.

At the bottom of the DML standings, the Hague Storks had a 22-game losing streak and were shut out nine times. The team batted .202 and the pitching staff had a 7.66 ERA in regular season play.

But the Storks defeated second-tier champs Kinheim three games to one in their best-of-five promotion/relegation playoff, so they will be back in 2019. Kinheim's lone win in the playoff

was a 3-2 decision that went 19 innings. The contest was suspended after twelve frames with the score 2-2, then completed six days later. In total, the marathon lasted almost six hours. Jurrian Koks pitched 9.1 innings of relief in the game for the Storks and logged 10 of his team's 20 strikeouts.

Loek van Mil

Neptunus also won the European Champions Cup to claim the club's 10th continental club title. The eight-team competition took place in Rotterdam. Markwell and Yntema were a combined 3-0 in the tournament and did not allow any runs in 23.2 innings.

STANDINGS

Team	G	W	L	T	GB
Neptunus	42	37	5		—
Amsterdam Pirates	42	32	9	1	4 ½
HCAW	42	21	18	3	14 ½
Osterhout Twins	42	18	21	3	17 ½
DSS	42	17	20	5	17 ½
Hoofddorp Pioniers	42	15	23	4	20
Amersfoort	42	14	25	3	21 ½
The Hague Storks	42	4	37	1	32 ½

Semifinal	G	W	L	GB
Amsterdam Pirates	9	8	1	—
Neptunus	9	5	4	3
HCAW	9	3	6	5
Osterhout Twins	9	2	7	6

Playoffs: Neptunus defeats Amsterdam 4-2 in best-of-7 series.

INDIVIDUAL BATTING LEADERS

Player, Team	AVG	AB	R	H	2B	3B	HR	RBI	SB
Kemp, Dwayne, NEP	.407	167	29	68	11	4	1	41	20
Takke, Tijmen, QUI	.381	105	23	40	7	1	1	24	0
Henrique, Roelie, HCA	.352	128	19	45	4	1	4	14	21
Richardson, Denzel, DSS	.343	166	27	57	8	1	6	30	20
Meer vd Stijn, NEP	.340	153	45	52	8	3	1	24	7
Daantji, Shaldimar, NEP	.331	121	25	40	4	5	1	11	9
Gerard, Rashid, AMS	.330	112	24	37	4	0	1	20	5
Englehardt, Rachid, QUI	.311	151	25	47	10	1	2	35	2
Sanden, vd Tommy, DSS	.310	158	28	49	7	4	0	21	5
Berkenbosch, Kenny, AMS	.308	143	33	44	12	2	4	29	5

INDIVIDUAL PITCHING LEADERS

Player, Team	W	L	ERA	IP	H	R	ER	BB	SO
Van Mil, Loek, NEP	4	0	0.22	40	18	2	1	10	52
Markwell, Diegomar, NEP	11	0	1.24	87	47	15	12	22	50
Huijer, Lars, PIO	5	4	1.35	93	62	21	14	13	101
Schel, Robin, AMS	5	0	1.41	57	41	12	9	14	44
Heijstek, Kevin, AMS	6	3	1.62	89	59	20	16	11	48
Ward, Kyle, AMS	7	0	1.72	63	55	13	12	8	56
Nakashima, Shogo, TWI	2	1	1.99	50	35	16	11	15	32
Cordemans, Rob, AMS	7	1	2.17	50	32	15	12	9	58
Yntema, Orlando, NEP	11	1	2.28	83	57	23	21	30	96
Pfau, Chris, HCA	5	2	2.34	85	59	31	22	35	103

Granma Wins Another Title

For decades, Granma could not compete with Industriales and other Cuban baseball powers. Now, everyone in Serie Nacional is consistently looking up at Bayamon's team.

Granma won its second consecutive (and second ever) Serie Nacional title when it rallied to edge Las Tunas in Game 7 of the championship series. Granma rallied after losing the first two games of the best-of-7 series.

The season meant yet another heartbreak for Matanzas. Amazingly, this was the fifth consecutive season Matanzas had the best regular season record in the league, but Matanzas is still looking for its first Serie Nacional title. This time Matanzas was swept by Granma in the semifinals.

STANDINGS

Team	W	L	PCT	GB
Matanzas	61	29	.678	—
Las Tunas	59	31	.656	2
Industriales	51	39	.567	10
Granma	49	39	.557	11
Artemisa	42	46	.478	18
Pinar del Rio	41	49	.456	20

ELIMINATED IN FIRST HALF

Team	W	L	PCT	GB
Ciego de Avila	24	21	.534	10
Villa Clara	23	22	.512	11
Santi Spiritus	23	22	.512	11
Santiago de Cuba	21	24	.467	13
Isla de la Juventud	20	25	.445	14
Camaguey	20	25	.445	14
Holguin	17	28	.378	17
Mayabeque	16	28	.364	17 ½
Guantanamo	14	30	.319	19 ½
Cienfuegos	11	34	.245	23

SECOND HALF BATTING LEADERS

Player, Team	AVG	AB	R	H	2B	3B	HR	RBI
Jorge A. Yhonson, LTU	.452	166	37	75	9	2	3	34
Yunior Paumier, LTU	.378	148	28	56	8	0	2	32
Yordan Manduley, ART	.375	128	20	48	10	1	3	21
Juan C. Torriente, IND	.372	113	15	42	8	0	0	8
Yurisbel Gracial, MTZ	.372	148	37	55	14	1	8	35
Yariel Duque, ART	.364	107	8	39	5	0	3	18
Carlos Benitez, GRA	.358	106	20	38	2	0	2	24
Yuniesky Larduet, LTU	.351	171	44	60	2	3	1	16
Yordanis Alarcon, LTU	.349	149	24	52	7	1	0	18
Rafael R. Viñales, LTU	.348	158	34	55	12	0	5	34

FIRST HALF BATTING LEADERS

Player, Team	AVG	AB	R	H	2B	3B	HR	RBI
Frederich Cepeda, SSP	.480	127	30	61	7	0	8	29
Yunier Mendoza, SSP	.445	173	26	77	14	0	2	33
Raul Glez, CAV	.391	151	35	59	8	0	7	27
Dennis Laza, MAY	.383	120	35	46	10	1	8	34

Player, Team								
Norel Gonzalez, VCL	.364	121	22	44	7	1	6	28
Alexander Pozo, MAY	.356	149	22	53	6	1	3	21
Yunior Paumier, HOL	.354	144	33	51	17	0	5	29
Michael Gonzalez, MAY	.353	136	22	48	7	0	2	20
Juan M. Soriano, CFG	.349	166	23	58	13	1	6	32
Gelkis Jimenez, SCU	.348	115	17	40	9	1	4	21
Humberto Morales, CAV	.342	117	15	40	7	0	6	15
Dariel Oliva, MAY	.342	149	19	51	6	0	2	26
Leonelquis Escalante, GTM	.342	152	18	52	11	1	1	17
Leonel Moas, CMG	.341	135	24	46	5	3	4	27
Edain Roman, MAY	.335	167	29	56	8	1	1	12
Pedro M. Leon, MAY	.333	117	21	39	8	0	6	25
Duniesky R. Barroso, SSP	.333	150	20	50	13	0	3	18
Orlando Acebey, SSP	.333	159	19	53	8	1	3	32
Yoelvis Fis, CAV	.328	134	23	44	2	1	4	19
Alberto Calderon, IJV	.327	156	26	51	3	1	2	18
Yeniet Perez, VCL	.321	131	19	42	7	0	8	28
Raudelin Legra, HOL	.321	168	15	54	8	0	2	30
Raul Reyes, VCL	.317	167	23	53	7	0	1	21
Orlando Lavandera, MAY	.314	137	24	43	1	1	4	16
Oscar J. Lopez, HOL	.310	100	22	31	2	0	0	12
Leonel Segura, CMG	.308	159	23	49	8	0	2	28
Luis F. Rivera, IJV	.307	150	23	46	5	1	0	16
Daniel Perez, CFG	.306	157	21	48	7	2	2	25
Robert L. Delgado, GTM	.303	155	20	47	13	0	5	25
Geydi Soler, HOL	.302	159	26	48	6	0	7	34

SECOND HALF PITCHING LEADERS

Player, Team	W	L	ERA	G	IP	H	HR	BB	SO
Roy Hernandez, MTZ	5	1	1.62	8	50	35	0	2	21
Vladimir Baños, PRI	3	2	2.72	8	50	49	0	2	10
Misael Villa, ART	5	3	2.73	9	56	65	0	4	25
Yoanni Yera, MTZ	4	4	3.24	10	67	62	0	4	14
Lazaro Blanco, GRA	5	3	3.27	10	66	63	0	3	20
Jonder Martinez, MTZ	5	2	3.38	9	51	47	0	2	16
Yosvany Torres, PRI	2	2	3.43	6	45	39	0	5	18
Erly Casanova, PRI	2	6	3.86	9	63	70	0	7	30
Geonel Gutierrez, ART	2	7	4.30	9	44	43	0	3	30
Yudiel Rodriguez, LTU	5	3	4.50	10	52	54	0	2	13

FIRST HALF PITCHING LEADERS

Player, Team	W	L	ERA	G	IP	H	HR	BB	SO
Luis A. Gomez, HOL	4	0	1.70	7	48	44	0	7	20
Jose R. Rodriguez, CMG	4	4	2.45	10	62	62	0	15	35
Alain Sanchez, VCL	5	3	2.47	11	62	50	0	18	45
Vladimir Garcia, CAV	6	2	2.61	9	62	59	0	25	49
Yoen Socarras, SSP	4	3	2.72	8	53	49	0	22	32
Irandy Castro, MTZ	4	2	2.83	10	48	38	0	30	20
Maikel Preval, GTM	3	2	2.86	15	50	47	0	21	17
Yariel Rodriguez, CMG	6	3	2.88	9	56	48	0	30	41
Carlos Font, SCU	2	4	3.04	11	53	50	0	47	32
Dariel Gongora D, CMG	3	3	3.15	8	46	38	0	19	31
Yosimar Cousin La, CMG	3	3	3.17	9	48	43	0	27	33
Freddy A. Alvarez, VCL	2	5	3.21	10	53	57	0	10	25
Javier Mirabal, VCL	2	1	3.35	10	51	43	0	30	26
Dachel Duquesne, CAV	4	4	3.38	11	80	71	0	24	50
Wilson Paredes, HOL	3	6	3.43	18	58	58	0	23	39
Yunier Gamboa, IJV	6	5	3.76	13	77	79	0	29	51
Pedro E. Aguero, GTM	2	7	3.77	12	60	72	0	38	8
Yosver J. Zulueta, VCL	4	3	3.79	12	59	55	0	44	54
Ulfrido Garcia, SCU	7	4	3.84	11	77	80	0	26	53
Jose N. Betancourt, MAY	5	5	4.33	11	60	64	0	23	21
Carlos D. Ramirez, CFG	3	6	4.34	12	58	68	0	31	24
Ariorky Hernandez, CAV	3	3	4.65	16	50	52	0	18	28
Yanielquis Duardo, SSP	3	1	4.72	20	48	57	0	17	31
Yadian Martinez, MAY	5	3	4.84	10	61	77	0	32	33
Adrian Bueno, CFG	3	5	5.11	11	56	70	0	26	25
Pedro A. Albares, SSP	2	5	5.36	10	45	38	0	24	18
Yasiel Morales, CFG	1	6	5.49	11	61	76	0	29	27
Yamichel Perez, SSP	1	4	5.74	10	47	69	0	17	20
Cesar Garcia, GRA	1	3	5.80	9	45	53	0	17	19
Angel Peña, SSP	4	4	5.96	9	45	52	0	22	27

Puerto Rico's Anthony Garcia (L) and teammate Jesmuel Valentin(R) celebrate the team's second straight Caribbean Series title.

Puerto Rico Defends Caribbean Series Crown

After winning the Caribbean Series for the first time this century in 2017, Puerto Rico successfully defended its title in 2018 by beating Cuba 7-4 in the semifinals and the Dominican Republic 9-4 in the championship game.

Jonathan Morales' three-run home run capped a five-run seventh inning as Puerto Rico rallied from a three-run deficit. The win was an emotional one for the entire team when it dedicated its title to the island, which had been devastated by Hurricane Maria the previous September.

Cuba had another solid effort, as league champion Granma went 3-1 during the preliminary round for the best record. Mexico's Culiacan club, the home club because the tournament was held in Guadalajara, was knocked out in the prelims thanks to a 1-3 record.

AUSTRALIAN BASEBALL LEAGUE

Team	W	L	PCT	GB
Brisbane Bandits	28	11	.718	—
Perth Heat	26	14	.650	2 ½
Canberra Cavalry	24	15	.615	4
Melbourne Aces	17	23	.425	11 ½
Sydney Blue Sox	13	27	.325	15 ½
Adelaide Bite	11	29	.275	17 ½

PLAYOFFS:

INDIVIDUAL BATTING LEADERS

Player, Team	AVG	AB	R	H	2B	3B	HR	RBI	BB	SO	SB
Baum, Jay, CAN	.439	139	41	61	18	2	9	41	12	18	7
Brosseau, Michael, PER	.427	96	25	41	11	0	6	32	12	12	6
Chiang, Chih-Hsien, SYD	.391	133	24	52	7	1	10	44	4	15	0
Kandilas, David, CAN	.380	158	46	60	14	0	12	44	13	22	5
Lohr, Stephen, ADE	.376	141	29	53	11	0	6	23	27	22	1
Younis, Jacob, SYD	.361	144	32	52	16	1	0	18	18	30	2
Fraley, Jake, PER	.361	169	50	61	13	1	13	39	27	26	39
Sutherland, David, BRI	.356	104	25	37	11	0	8	21	7	16	1
Kennelly, Tim, PER	.338	133	36	45	7	0	5	25	13	17	5
Bennett, T.J., BRI	.338	136	36	46	6	0	16	34	16	43	3

INDIVIDUAL PITCHING LEADERS

Player, Team	W	L	ERA	G	SV	IP	H	BB	SO	AVG
Gailey, Frank, CAN	4	0	1.80	9	0	50	26	19	59	.155
Bachar, Lake, CAN	5	1	2.91	10	0	56	47	23	49	.230
Bollinger, Ryan, BRI	5	1	3.48	9	0	54	58	12	75	.271
Grening, Brian, CAN	5	1	3.53	10	0	66	62	8	51	.247
Boshers, Alex, PER	1	6	3.97	12	0	57	67	12	52	.285
Atherton, Tim, BRI	3	1	4.15	8	0	35	31	11	45	.228
Tols, Josh, MEL	5	3	4.78	11	1	53	50	23	75	.246
Blackley, Travis, BRI	5	2	4.82	11	0	52	59	21	58	.286
Veale, Nick, PER	2	1	5.18	10	0	42	43	29	34	.262
Wilkins, Luke, SYD	4	3	5.29	12	0	48	62	14	32	.305

DOMINICAN LEAGUE

Team	W	L	PCT	GB
Gigantes del Cibao	29	21	.580	—
Aguilas Cibaenas	27	23	.540	2
Leones del Escogido	27	23	.540	2
Tigres del Licey	25	25	.500	4
Estrellas Orientales	23	27	.460	6
Toros del Este	19	31	.380	10

Playoffs:

INDIVIDUAL BATTING LEADERS

Player, Team	AVG	AB	R	H	2B	3B	HR	RBI	BB	SO	SB
Sierra, Moises, GIG	.353	150	17	53	10	1	1	22	15	23	4
Borbon, Julio, LIC	.333	135	24	45	9	2	3	21	22	22	8
Cordero, Franchy, ESC	.323	186	30	60	7	5	5	25	22	39	6
Navarro, Yamaico, LIC	.322	177	29	57	5	1	3	32	34	25	4
Nunez, Gustavo, EST	.320	125	20	40	4	2	0	10	10	22	7
Casilla, Alexi, TOR	.315	146	14	46	6	1	1	12	10	19	4
Avelino, Abiatal, GIG	.309	139	22	43	2	1	0	9	13	15	19
Brito, Socrates, EST	.301	163	23	49	9	5	3	12	17	35	8
Espinal, Edwin, AGU	.287	143	13	41	3	1	2	24	14	22	1
Guerrero, Gabriel, EST	.287	157	18	45	7	0	4	26	10	34	3

INDIVIDUAL PITCHING LEADERS

Player, Team	W	L	ERA	G	SV	IP	H	BB	SO	AVG
Pena, Richelson, AGU	4	0	1.55	12	0	41	34	8	32	.231
MacLane, Evan, GIG	3	2	1.72	11	0	47	53	7	18	.285
Lopez, Jorge, AGU	3	2	2.49	13	0	69	62	17	50	.245
Villanueva, Elih, AGU	3	2	2.54	10	0	50	52	8	35	.269
Valdes, Raul, GIG	1	7	2.74	10	0	62	70	17	47	.282
Bueno, Francisley, AGU	2	5	3.06	12	0	53	57	16	37	.270
Maya, Yunesky, AGU	2	2	3.38	11	0	48	46	10	32	.253
Jurrjens, Jair, LIC	3	4	3.44	11	0	50	47	16	30	.240
Evans, Bryan, LIC	2	2	3.67	11	0	42	49	22	27	.292
Johnson, Patrick, GIG	0	1	3.80	10	0	43	43	15	33	.264

MEXICAN PACIFIC LEAGUE

Team	W	L	PCT	GB
Aguilas de Mexicali	42	26	.618	—
Tomateros de Culiacan	39	29	.574	3
Mayos de Navojoa	38	30	.559	4
Vanados de Mazatlan	37	31	.544	5
Charros de Jalisco	35	32	.522	6 ½
Naranjeros de Hermosillo	33	34	.493	8 ½
Yaquis de Obregon	27	41	.397	15
Caneros de los Mochis	20	48	.294	22

Playoffs:

INDIVIDUAL BATTING LEADERS

Player, Team	AVG	AB	R	H	2B	3B	HR	RBI	BB	SO	SB
Elizalde, Sebastian, CUL	.380	250	42	95	17	2	5	36	27	29	16
Rodriguez, Manny, JAL	.371	256	50	95	25	0	10	58	16	26	4
Juarez, Luis, MXC	.358	190	27	68	9	0	8	38	16	13	1
Pineda, Jeremias, MAZ	.325	209	41	68	2	3	2	9	21	54	31
Urias, Ramon, MOC	.321	212	29	68	13	2	1	13	27	32	6
Roberson, Chris, MXC	.317	221	44	70	11	1	11	32	16	34	2
Castillo, Jesus, NAV	.314	223	36	70	8	0	9	40	43	43	0
Myers, D'Arby, CUL	.309	220	25	68	9	2	2	17	8	37	7
Rosario, Olmo, MXC	.308	266	28	82	12	0	5	33	20	40	7
Navarro, Efren, HER	.307	231	45	71	13	1	2	24	45	51	0

INDIVIDUAL PITCHING LEADERS

Player, Team	W	L	ERA	G	SV	IP	H	BB	SO	AVG
Valdes, Rolando, MXC	5	2	1.74	13	0	72.1	69	18	36	.257
Lively, Mitch, MAZ	9	2	2.50	12	0	79.1	63	13	63	.227
Lugo, Jaime, NAV	5	3	2.53	15	0	74.2	76	12	61	.264
Vasquez, Anthony, CUL	7	2	2.54	11	0	71	80	13	60	.282
Gonzalez, Edgar, CUL	3	3	2.55	12	0	74	78	12	36	.278
Gamboa, Eddie, NAV	6	2	2.85	13	0	79	70	16	52	.241
Alexander, Tyler, NAV	5	1	3.28	13	0	71.1	66	13	66	.244
Carrillo, Raul, NAV	4	6	3.89	13	0	69.1	67	25	43	.262
Dodson, Zack, NAV	4	5	3.95	13	0	68.1	84	22	41	.310
Solano, Javier, MXC	6	6	4.08	14	0	81.2	97	23	43	.309

PUERTO RICAN LEAGUE

Team	W	L	PCT	GB
Criollos de Caguas	11	7	.611	—
Cangrejeros de Santurce	9	9	.500	2
Indios de Mayaguez	9	9	.500	2
Gigantes de Carolina	7	11	.389	4

Playoffs:

INDIVIDUAL BATTING LEADERS

Player, Team	AVG	AB	R	H	2B	3B	HR	RBI	BB	SO	SB
Burgos, Aldemar, CAR	.403	62	9	25	0	1	1	10	2	13	3
Vidal, David, CAG	.373	51	14	19	2	0	4	12	11	3	0
Tomscha, Damek, SAN	.321	56	12	18	3	0	2	5	7	13	2
De Jesus Jr., Ivan, SAN	.315	54	5	17	3	0	0	3	7	7	1
Gomez, Edwin, SAN	.310	58	9	18	6	1	2	14	7	8	0
Garcia, Anthony, CAG	.310	58	10	18	3	0	2	14	8	8	2
Lopez, Jack, CAG	.302	53	6	16	1	0	1	6	3	4	1
Hernandez, Jan, SAN	.298	57	9	17	4	0	0	7	6	11	0
Hernandez, Yadiel, SAN	.288	59	6	17	3	0	0	7	6	8	2

Player, Team	AVG	AB	R	H	2B	3B	HR	RBI	BB	SO	SB
Gonzalez, Jay, MAY	.286	63	9	18	1	0	0	4	10	12	4

INDIVIDUAL PITCHING LEADERS

Player, Team	W	L	ERA	G	SV	IP	H	BB	SO	AVG
Flores, Adalberto, SAN	4	0	1.57	4	0	23	16	7	12	.195
Maldonado, Ivan, CAG	3	0	1.62	3	0	16.2	15	5	7	.242
Richardson, David, SAN	1	0	1.80	3	0	15	8	7	17	.163
Martinez, Miguel, CAR	0	0	1.84	6	0	14.2	12	5	9	.218
Soto Giovanni, CAG	2	1	1.93	4	0	23.1	15	3	16	.185
Cruz, Fernando, SAN	1	1	2.37	3	0	19	18	7	10	.261
Herron, Tyler, MAY	2	0	2.87	7	0	15.2	9	2	11	.164
Burgos, Hiram, MAY	1	1	3.28	4	0	24.2	24	5	13	.258
Gonzalez, Luis, CAG	2	1	3.45	3	0	15.2	16	4	5	.276
Rivera, Raul, CAR	2	3	3.50	5	0	18	22	4	7	.306

VENEZUELAN LEAGUE

Team	W	L	PCT	GB
Cardenales de Lara	38	25	.603	—
Leones del Caracas	35	28	.556	3
Navegantes del Magallanes	35	28	.556	3
Caribes de Anzoategui	32	31	.508	6
Tigres de Aragua	32	31	.508	6
Aguilas del Zulia	31	32	.492	7
Bravos de Margarita	25	38	.397	13
Tiburones de La Guaira	24	39	.381	14

Playoffs:

INDIVIDUAL BATTING LEADERS

Player, Team	AVG	AB	R	H	2B	3B	HR	RBI	BB	SO	SB
Urrutia, Henry, LAR	.385	195	38	75	12	1	5	41	27	35	2
Callaspo, Alberto, ARA	.351	188	32	66	11	0	2	30	36	24	0
Montero, Jesus, LAR	.351	211	30	74	10	0	7	47	24	49	1
Fuenmayor, Balbino, ORI	.341	211	30	72	18	0	7	40	19	40	0
Valdez, Jesus, MAG	.339	233	52	79	14	0	18	61	36	36	1
Gotta, Cade, ZUL	.335	212	40	71	14	2	1	19	38	39	21
Taylor, Chuck, LAR	.333	228	35	76	10	1	2	31	27	30	0
Rodriguez, Herlis, ZUL	.331	163	25	54	5	3	1	11	12	22	9
Cedeno, Ronny, MAG	.327	220	46	72	14	2	2	32	20	25	7
Ortega, Rafael, ORI	.320	178	38	57	7	3	4	29	38	21	5

INDIVIDUAL PITCHING LEADERS

Player, Team	W	L	ERA	G	SV	IP	H	BB	SO	AVG
Roibal, Reinier, ZUL	5	2	2.03	11	0	53	43	14	48	.224
Moscoso, Guillermo, ARA	5	2	2.05	14	0	70	64	16	42	.245
Martinez, Jorge, LAR	7	2	2.43	12	0	59	42	19	40	.201
Thompson, Daryl, ORI	2	2	2.79	14	0	68	73	10	50	.273
Rivero, Raul, LAR	7	2	3.07	11	0	56	57	10	32	.260
Darnell, Logan, ORI	3	6	3.32	13	0	65	68	19	47	.276
Poveda, Omar, MAR	3	3	3.42	12	0	53	56	24	47	.265
Castillo, Yeiper, ORI	5	5	3.43	17	0	63	58	22	30	.250
Diaz, Luis, CAR	4	4	3.82	13	0	64	62	23	57	.255
Molina, Nestor, LAR	7	5	3.98	13	0	63	66	17	44	.275

INTERNATIONAL

COLLEGE

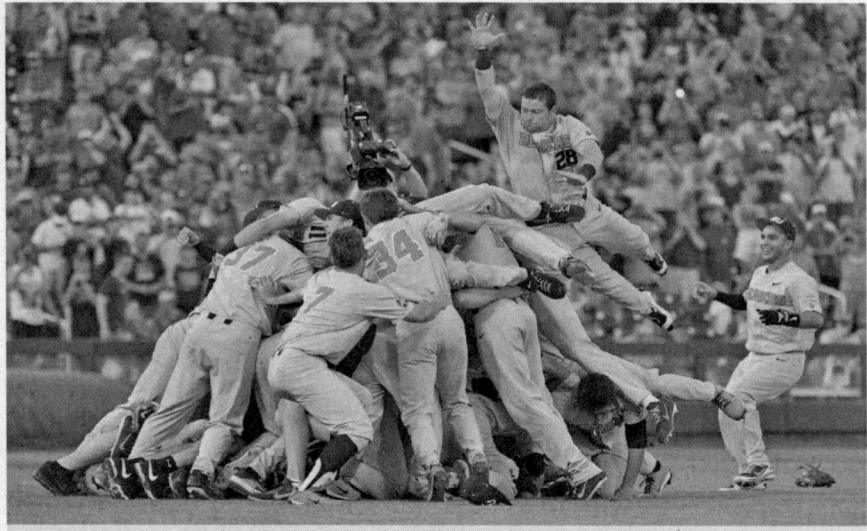

Oregon State celebrates after defeating Arkansas in the College World Series finals.

Oregon State Returns To CWS Summit

BY TEDDY CAHILL

All year long, Oregon State has broken its huddles to one word: Finish. The word, repeated so many times after practices and games and anytime the Beavers were together, was a reminder of the disappointing end to the 2017 season and a goal for the 2018 season.

Oregon State last year entered the NCAA Tournament as the No. 1 overall seed and one of the favorites at the College World Series. But its season came to a disappointing end when it lost back-to-back games against Louisiana State in the CWS semifinals. A team that had a chance to be one of the greatest of all time instead was knocked out before it even had a chance to play for the national title.

That loss fueled the Beavers this year. Second baseman Nick Madrigal said as soon as LSU eliminated Oregon State, he flipped a switch mentally to the 2018 season and did everything he could to get the Beavers back to Omaha to give them another chance. Shortstop Cadyn Grenier said the feeling at the end of last year's CWS was one that none of the Beavers wanted to experience again. Right fielder Trevor Larnach said it left a salty taste

in their mouths.

That taste was washed away Thursday night in Omaha. Oregon State defeated Arkansas, 5-0, in Game 3 of the CWS finals to claim the national championship. It is the third national title in program history and first since the Beavers won back-to-back championships in 2006-07.

Freshman righthander Kevin Abel threw a two-hit shutout and All-American catcher Adley Rutschman powered the offense with three hits and two RBIs. The victory saw Oregon State (55-12-1) complete a comeback that had started the night before, in Game 2, when it had been one strike away from being swept in the best-of-three series before pulling out an improbable victory to force Thursday's Game 3.

Above all, the Beavers had finished.

"All offseason long, from the first day, this has been our goal," Madrigal said. "We've said we've got to finish this year and we did exactly that. It took a total team effort. Not one guy could have won this by themselves. From top to bottom we needed every single guy on this team."

Oregon State really did need just about its whole roster in Omaha. It lost its opening game of the

COACHING CAROUSEL

School	In (Previous Job)	Out (Reason/New Job)
Abilene Christian	Rick McCarty (Dallas Baptist assistant)	Britt Bonneau (resigned)
Alabama A&M	Manny Lora (Alabama A&M assistant)	Mitch Hill (resigned)
Bethune-Cookman	Jonathan Hernandez (ASA Miami JC head coach)	Jason Beverlin (Blue Jays scout)
Central Michigan	Jordan Bischel (Northwood (Mich.) head coach)	Steve Jaksa (retired)
Davidson	Rucker Taylor (Davidson assistant)	Dick Cooke (retired)
Fairleigh Dickinson	Justin McKay* (Fairleigh Dickinson assistant)	Gary Puccio (retired)
Illinois State	Steve Holm (Purdue assistant)	Bo Durkac (fired)
Indiana	Jeff Mercer (Wright State head coach)	Chris Lemonis (Mississippi State head coach)
Iona	Paul Panik (Albany assistant)	Pat Carey (resigned)
Kansas State	Pete Hughes (Georgia assistant)	Brad Hill (retired)
Miami	Gino DiMare (Miami assistant)	Jim Morris (retired)
Middle Tennessee	Jim Toman (College of Charleston assistant)	Jim McGuire (fired)
Mississippi State	Chris Lemonis (Indiana head coach)	Andy Cannizaro (fired)
Murray State	Dan Skirka (Walters State (Tenn.) JC assistant)	Kevin Moulder (fired)
Oregon State	Pat Bailey* (Oregon State assistant)	Pat Casey (retired)
Pittsburgh	Mike Bell (Florida State assistant)	Joe Jordano (fired)
Rice	Matt Bragga (Tennessee Tech head coach)	Wayne Graham (fired)
San Jose State	Brad Sanfilippo (San Jose State assistant)	Jason Hawkins (fired)
Tennessee Tech	Justin Holmes (Tennessee Tech assistant)	Matt Bragga (Rice head coach)
UC Irvine	Ben Orloff (Irvine assistant)	Mike Gillespie (retired)
Wright State	Alex Sogard (Wright State assistant)	Jeff Mercer (Indiana head coach)

CWS against North Carolina, dropping it into the losers' bracket. But Oregon State fought through four straight elimination games, knocking out Washington, North Carolina and Mississippi State to get to the finals. Arkansas (48-21) beat Oregon State in the first game of the finals, putting the Beavers' backs against the walls again.

But, again, the Beavers found a way. Oregon State trailed Arkansas, 3-2, in the ninth inning of Game 2 and nearly saw its dream crushed again. Grenier lofted a pop up into foul ground up the first base line, a ball that he thought was going to be caught for the final out. Instead, it fell in and Grenier took advantage of his newfound life to drive in the game-tying run. Larnach followed with a two-run home run to send the series to a decisive Game 3, where the Beavers wouldn't be denied.

Grenier said the only time he ever doubted that Oregon State would win the championship was in the moment Wednesday night when his pop up was in the air.

"I thought for sure it was going to get caught," he said. "After I got that hit and Trevor hit that home run we came into today and I knew there was no way we were going to let that get away from us again."

Rutschman and Larnach led the way offensively for Oregon State in Omaha. Rutschman set a CWS record with 17 hits in the tournament and was named Most Outstanding Player. Larnach had 15 hits of his own, including that game-winning home run in Game 2 of the finals. On the mound, Abel won four games during the CWS—another

record. Lefthander Brandon Eisert, deployed as a longman out of the bullpen, often looked like Oregon State's best pitcher. All up and down Oregon State's roster, players found a way to contribute to the Beavers' success.

The depth of Oregon State's roster and the elite talent in its junior class—Madrigal, Larnach and Grenier were all earlier this month drafted in the top 40 picks—made it one of the dominant forces in college baseball over the last two years. The Beavers won 111 games, twice reached the final four of the CWS and produced six All-Americans.

As much talent as the Beavers have had the last two years, coach Pat Casey said the makeup and mentality of the team has been the real key to their success.

"We've won a lot of games in the last two years," he said. "I know it's a cliché people use all the time about their character and their guys. But it's really true. There's nothing that's going to come from anything if everybody isn't invested in on another."

Oregon State has been tested on the field time and again over the last few years. In 2016, it was perhaps the biggest snub from the NCAA Tournament. That slight fueled the Beavers during their magical 2017 run. The disappointment of last year then fed into this year's fire.

But this year wasn't easy for Oregon State. Madrigal, the 2017 Pac-12 player of the year, broke his hand in February and was sidelined for six weeks. During that time, the Beavers lost back-to-back conference series. Those losses ultimately cost them a chance at back-to-back conference titles and forced a reckoning within the team.

"We stubbed our toe pretty good there," Casey said. "We just didn't buy into the fact that we weren't going to be great. We came out and worked every day, talked about getting better. Everybody had to get better. I had to get better. The coaching staff had to get better. The players had to get better. We just weren't going to take no for an answer."

Oregon State has also been the subject of a harsh spotlight over the last year after The Oregonian reported last year that ace lefthander Luke Heimlich pled guilty to a sex crime he committed as a teenager. The report came last year following regionals and Heimlich did not pitch the rest of the year, removing himself from the team before the CWS. He returned to the mound this year and went 16-3, 2.92. Heimlich was not drafted in either of the last two years following the report and it is unclear whether he'll ever pitch again.

This Beavers team, unlike last year's, didn't come to Omaha with the chance to go down as one of the best ever. Their winning percentage isn't one of the four-best of all-time and they didn't rewrite the Pac-12 record book.

But they have something the 2017 team doesn't—a national championship, the goal they have all held since committing to Oregon State.

"This is the reason you come (to Oregon State)," Grenier said. "And that's aside of making a lot of lifetime friends and playing with some of the best players in the nation and getting some real good coaching. I can't explain this feeling."

The Beavers on Thursday did what they came to Omaha to do—they finished. And by doing so, they fulfilled the promise they came to Corvallis with, ending their careers in a dogpile at TD Ameritrade Park as fireworks burst in the fading evening twilight.

Martin Breaks Wins Record; Announces Retirement Following 2019 Season

College baseball has never had a more consistent winner than Mike Martin. For 39 years, like clockwork, the legendary coach known simply as "11"—his uniform number—has led Florida State to at least 40 wins and an appearance in the NCAA

COLLEGE WORLD SERIES CHAMPIONS

Year	Champion	Coach	Record	Runner-Up	Most Outstanding Player
1948	Southern California	Sam Barry	40-12	Yale	None selected
1949	Texas*	Bibb Falk	23-7	Wake Forest	Charles Teague, 2B, Wake Forest
1950	Texas	Bibb Falk	27-6	Washington State	Ray VanCleef, OF, Rutgers
1951	Oklahoma*	Jack Baer	19-9	Tennessee	Sid Hatfield, 1B/P, Tennessee
1952	Holy Cross	Jack Barry	21-3	Missouri	Jim O'Neill, P, Holy Cross
1953	Michigan	Ray Fisher	21-9	Texas	J.L. Smith, P, Texas
1954	Missouri	Hi Simmons	22-4	Rollins	Tom Yewcic, C, Michigan State
1955	Wake Forest	Taylor Sanford	29-7	Western Michigan	Tom Borland, P, Oklahoma State
1956	Minnesota	Dick Siebert	33-9	Arizona	Jerry Thomas, P, Minnesota
1957	California*	George Wolfman	35-10	Penn State	Cal Emery, 1B/P, Penn State
1958	Southern California	Rod Dedeaux	35-7	Missouri	Bill Thom, P, Southern California
1959	Oklahoma State	Toby Greene	27-5	Arizona	Jim Dobson, 3B, Oklahoma State
1960	Minnesota	Dick Siebert	34-7	Southern California	John Erickson, 2B, Minnesota
1961	Southern California*	Rod Dedeaux	43-9	Oklahoma State	Littleton Fowler, P, Oklahoma State
1962	Michigan	Don Lund	31-13	Santa Clara	Bob Garibaldi, P, Santa Clara
1963	Southern California	Rod Dedeaux	37-16	Arizona	Bud Hollowell, C, Southern California
1964	Minnesota	Dick Siebert	31-12	Missouri	Joe Ferris, P, Maine
1965	Arizona State	Bobby Winkles	54-8	Ohio State	Sal Bando, 3B, Arizona State
1966	Ohio State	Marty Karow	27-6	Oklahoma State	Steve Arlin, P, Ohio State
1967	Arizona State	Bobby Winkles	53-12	Houston	Ron Davini, C, Arizona State
1968	Southern California*	Rod Dedeaux	45-14	Southern Illinois	Bill Seinsoth, 1B, Southern California
1969	Arizona State	Bobby Winkles	56-11	Tulsa	John Dolinsek, OF, Arizona State
1970	Southern California	Rod Dedeaux	51-13	Florida State	Gene Ammann, P, Florida State
1971	Southern California	Rod Dedeaux	53-13	Southern Illinois	Jerry Tabb, 1B, Tulsa
1972	Southern California	Rod Dedeaux	50-13	Arizona State	Russ McQueen, P, Southern California
1973	Southern California*	Rod Dedeaux	51-11	Arizona State	Dave Winfield, OF/P, Minnesota
1974	Southern California	Rod Dedeaux	50-20	Miami	George Milke, P, Southern California
1975	Texas	Cliff Gustafson	56-6	South Carolina	Mickey Reichenbach, 1B, Texas
1976	Arizona	Jerry Kindall	56-17	Eastern Michigan	Steve Powers, DH/P, Arizona
1977	Arizona State	Jim Brock	57-12	South Carolina	Bob Horner, 3B, Arizona State
1978	Southern California*	Rod Dedeaux	54-9	Arizona State	Rod Boxberger, P, Southern California
1979	Cal State Fullerton	Augie Garrido	60-14	Arkansas	Tony Hudson, P, Cal State Fullerton
1980	Arizona	Jerry Kindall	45-21	Hawaii	Terry Francona, OF, Arizona
1981	Arizona State	Jim Brock	55-13	Oklahoma State	Stan Holmes, OF, Arizona State
1982	Miami	Ron Fraser	57-18	Wichita State	Dan Smith, P, Miami
1983	Texas	Cliff Gustafson	66-14	Alabama	Calvin Schiraldi, P, Texas

Tournament. Sixteen times the Seminoles have advanced to the College World Series. Eighteen times they have won the conference title.

Players and assistant coaches have come and gone. Dynasties have risen and fallen. Florida State has moved from the Metro Conference to the Atlantic Coast Conference. Rosenblatt Stadium has given way to TD Ameritrade Ballpark as home of the College World Series. Through it all, Martin has endured. And won.

Florida State and Martin won again Saturday, May 5, beating Clemson, 3-2, in 13 innings. The victory was the 1,976th of Martin's career and with it he became the all-time winningest coach in college baseball history, surpassing Augie Garrido's record in about 250 fewer games. No coach in college sports has more wins. Martin finished the year with a 1,987-713-4 record and will likely early next year become the first coach to reach 2,000 wins.

About six weeks after the record-breaking night, Florida State announced Martin would retire following the 2019 season. The university did not announce a succession plan for Martin.

"I'm glad that they want me to continue coaching next season," Martin said in a statement. "I thank all our former and current coaches, staff and most importantly our players for the consistent success of our baseball program. You don't win at our level without student-athletes who dedicate themselves to playing as a team and playing for something more than themselves."

Martin, 74, played for the Seminoles from 1965-66 and advanced to the College World Series in 1965. He returned to his alma mater in 1975 as an assistant coach and has remained in Tallahassee for the last 44 years.

Martin's first season as head coach was 1980 and he led the Seminoles to 51 wins and an appearance in Omaha. It was the start of an incredible run. Florida State won at least 50 games in Martin's first 12 seasons at the helm and made five trips to Omaha.

The Seminoles have never really slowed down. Martin, the 2012 Coach of the Year, has coached three Players of the Year and numerous big leaguers, including J.D. Drew, Stephen Drew, Doug Mientkiewicz and Buster Posey.

Year	Champion	Coach	Record	Runner-Up	MOST OUTSTANDING PLAYER
1984	Cal State Fullerton	Augie Garrido	66-20	Texas	John Fishel, OF, Cal State Fullerton
1985	Miami*	Ron Fraser	64-16	Texas	Greg Ellena, DH, Miami
1986	Arizona	Jerry Kindall	49-19	Florida State	Mike Senne, OF, Arizona
1987	Stanford	Mark Marquess	53-17	Oklahoma State	Paul Carey, OF, Stanford
1988	Stanford	Mark Marquess	46-23	Arizona State	Lee Plemel, P, Stanford
1989	Wichita State	Gene Stephenson	68-16	Texas	Greg Brummett, P, Wichita State
1990	Georgia	Steve Webber	52-19	Oklahoma State	Mike Rebhan, P, Georgia
1991	Louisiana State*	Skip Bertman	55-18	Wichita State	Gary Hymel, C, Louisiana State
1992	Pepperdine*	Andy Lopez	48-11	Cal State Fullerton	Phil Nevin, 3B, Cal State Fullerton
1993	Louisiana State	Skip Bertman	53-17	Wichita State	Todd Walker, 2B, Louisiana State
1994	Oklahoma*	Larry Cochell	50-17	Georgia Tech	Chip Glass, OF, Oklahoma
1995	Cal State Fullerton*	Augie Garrido	57-9	Southern California	Mark Kotsay, OF/P, Cal State Fullerton
1996	Louisiana State*	Skip Bertman	52-15	Miami	Pat Burrell, 3B, Miami
1997	Louisiana State*	Skip Bertman	57-13	Alabama	Brandon Larson, SS, Louisiana State
1998	Southern California	Mike Gillespie	49-17	Arizona State	Wes Rachels, 2B, Southern California
1999	Miami*	Jim Morris	50-13	Florida State	Marshall McDougall, 2B, Florida State
2000	Louisiana State*	Skip Bertman	52-17	Stanford	Trey Hodges, P, Louisiana State
2001	Miami*	Jim Morris	53-12	Stanford	Charlton Jimerson, OF, Miami
2002	Texas*	Augie Garrido	57-15	South Carolina	Huston Street, P, Texas
2003	Rice	Wayne Graham	58-12	Stanford	John Hudgins, P, Stanford
2004	Cal State Fullerton	George Horton	47-22	Texas	Jason Windsor, P, Cal State Fullerton
2005	Texas*	Augie Garrido	56-16	Florida	David Maroul, 3B, Texas
2006	Oregon State	Pat Casey	50-16	North Carolina	Jonah Nickerson, P, Oregon State
2007	Oregon State*	Pat Casey	49-18	North Carolina	Jorge Reyes, P, Oregon State
2008	Fresno State	Mike Batesole	47-31	Georgia	Tommy Mendonca, 3B, Fresno State
2009	Louisiana State	Paul Mainieri	56-17	Texas	Jared Mitchell, OF, Louisiana State
2010	South Carolina	Ray Tanner	54-16	UCLA	Jackie Bradley Jr., OF, South Carolina
2011	South Carolina*	Ray Tanner	55-14	Florida	Scott Wingo, 2B, South Carolina
2012	Arizona*	Andy Lopez	48-17	South Carolina	Robert Refsnyder, OF, Arizona
2013	UCLA*	John Savage	49-17	Mississippi State	Adam Plutko, P, UCLA
2014	Vanderbilt	Tim Corbin	51-21	Virginia	Dansby Swanson, 2B, Vanderbilt
2015	Virginia	Brian O'Connor	44-24	Vanderbilt	Josh Sborz, P, Virginia
2016	Coastal Carolina	Gary Gilmore	55-18	Arizona	Andrew Beckwith, P, Coastal Carolina
2017	Florida	Kevin O'Sullivan	52-19	Louisiana State	Alex Faedo, P, Florida
2018	Oregon State	Pat Casey	55-12-1	Arkansas	Adley Rutschman, C, Oregon State

The only area Martin has come up short in during his career is the College World Series. He has twice led the Seminoles to runner-up finishes in Omaha, but they have never won a national title. He is 21-32 in the CWS.

But now Martin is the game's winningest coach, a record that may never be broken. It took Martin less than two seasons to chase down Garrido, who stepped aside at Texas following the 2016 season. There are no active coaches today with more than 1,500 wins, however.

North Carolina's Mike Fox and Louisiana State's Paul Mainieri are the only two with even 1,400 wins, but it is unlikely either will coach for the 10 years or more that would be required to make up the more than 500-win gulf between them and Martin. Even Virginia's Brian O'Connor, who is just 47 years old and ranks third among active coaches in winning percentage (behind Martin and Fox), would need to win 40 games for the next 33 years to reach 1,975 wins.

Martin's record-breaking victory came about two months after Garrido's death. Martin and Garrido crossed paths plenty of times off the field over the years and Martin said his first meeting with Garrido was influential on his career. Martin and Garrido rarely met on the field, but they did face off in the CWS a few times. Garrido held a 5-1 edge against Martin.

"If it was, so called me against him, as we say in golf, I need to press because I'm really behind," Martin said. "Augie was a great ambassador for the game of college baseball."

Martin is the latest coach in his generation to head for retirement. In recent years, coaches such as Garrido, Stanford's Mark Marquess, UC Irvine's Mike Gillespie and Miami's Jim Morris, once an assistant under Martin, have all retired. All of them had won more than 1,000 games.

Regardless of how next season transpires, Martin's legacy in college baseball is already secured. As he prepares to exit the game, his impact on college baseball is sure to be celebrated over the next year.

Legendary Coach Augie Garrido Dies

Augie Garrido, the winningest baseball coach in NCAA history, died March 15 after suffering a stroke. He was 79.

By the time Garrido retired following the 2016 season, he had grown to be the largest figure in the sport and was perhaps the greatest coach of all time. He won five College World Series, compiled a 1,975-951-9 record in 48 years as a head coach

RPI RANKINGS

The Ratings Percentage Index is an important tool used by the NCAA in selecting at-large teams for the 64-team Division I regional tournament. The NCAA now releases its RPI rankings during the season. These were the top 100 finishers for 2018. A team's rank in the final Baseball America Top 25 is indicated in parentheses, and College World Series teams are in bold.

Rank School	Record	Rank School	Record
1. Arkansas (2)	48-21	51. South Alabama	32-25
2. Oregon St. (1)	55-12-1	52. West Virginia	29-27
3. Florida (3)	49-21	53. San Diego State	39-21
4. Mississippi (15)	48-17	54. Wichita State	35-21-1
5. N. Carolina (4)	44-20	55. Sam Houston State	39-20
6. Stanford (14)	46-12	56. Georgia Tech	31-27
7. Stetson (12)	48-13	57. Texas Christian	33-23
8. Texas Tech (5)	45-20	58. Louisiana-Lafayette	34-25
9. Auburn (13)	43-23	59. Kent State	40-18
10. Georgia (21)	39-21	60. UNC Wilmington	39-23
11. Florida State (20)	43-19	61. Louisiana Tech	39-20
12. Minnesota (8)	44-15	62. Creighton	34-16
13. Clemson (19)	47-16	63. Michigan	33-21
14. Duke (10)	45-18	64. Gonzaga	33-24
15. Tennessee Tech (11)	53-12	65. Miami	28-26
16. East Carolina (23)	44-18	66. Nevada	29-24
17. Texas A&M	40-22	67. UNC Greensboro	39-15
18. Mississippi St. (6)	39-29	68. Coll. of Charleston	36-19
19. Texas (7)	42-23	69. Wright State	39-17
20. Connecticut	37-22-1	70. Seton Hall	30-20-1
21. Louisville	45-19	71. Wake Forest	25-32
22. UCLA	38-21	72. California	32-22
23. Jacksonville	40-21	73. Indiana State	31-24
24. N.C. State (22)	42-18	74. Nevada-Las Vegas	35-24
25. Coastal Carolina (24)	43-19	75. Tennessee	29-27
26. Louisiana State	39-27	76. Wagner	38-18
27. Missouri State	40-17	77. Army	37-24
28. South Carolina (16)	37-26	78. Iowa	33-20
29. South Florida	36-22-1	79. Southeastern La.	37-22
30. Florida Atlantic	43-19-1	80. Charlotte	34-24
31. Kentucky	34-22	81. Georgia Southern	30-26
32. Vanderbilt (17)	35-27	82. Alabama	27-29
33. St. John's	40-17	83. Virginia	29-25
34. Indiana	40-19	84. Florida Gulf Coast	32-21
35. Baylor	37-21	85. Bradley	32-19
36. Oklahoma State	31-26-1	86. Tulane	25-33
37. Dallas Baptist	42-21	87. New Mexico State	40-22
38. So. Mississippi	44-18	88. Bryant	32-23-1
39. Northeastern	36-21	89. Rice	26-31-2
40. Purdue	38-21	90. Samford	37-26
41. Troy	42-21	91. Wofford	36-23
42. Houston (25)	38-25	92. Oregon	26-29
43. Oklahoma	38-25	93. Kansas	27-30
44. Cal St. Fullerton (18)	36-25	94. Northwestern State	38-24
45. Central Florida	35-21	95. Saint Louis	38-20
46. Ohio State	36-24	96. Cincinnati	28-28
47. Missouri	34-22	97. Arkansas-Little Rock	28-28
48. Arizona	34-22	98. Texas-San Antonio	32-24
49. Washington (9)	35-26	99. Davidson	33-21
50. Illinois	33-20	100. Morehead State	37-26

and was one of five men to have twice been named Coach of the Year. He in 2016 received Baseball America's Tony Gwynn Lifetime Achievement Award.

"Augie was a giant in our game," Texas coach David Pierce said. "His impact on baseball, on the Forty Acres, and on me and so many others will live on forever. My thoughts are with Jeannie,

COLLEGE ALL-AMERICA TEAM

FIRST TEAM

Pos.	Name	Year	AVG	OBP	SLG	AB	R	H	HR	RBI	BB	SO	SB
C	Joey Bart, Georgia Tech	Jr.	.359	.471	.632	220	55	79	16	38	41	56	3
1B	Bren Spillane, Illinois	Jr.	.389	.498	.903	175	57	68	23	60	36	57	16
2B	Kody Clemens, Texas	Jr.	.344	.437	.703	209	53	72	19	61	34	37	4
3B	Jonathan India, Florida	Jr.	.362	.502	.723	188	57	68	17	42	47	47	11
SS	Terrin Vavra, Minnesota	Jr.	.405	.477	.620	163	43	66	7	42	23	13	6
OF	Seth Beer, Clemson	Jr.	.316	.471	.656	209	60	66	20	52	52	31	1
OF	Trevor Larnach, Oregon State	Jr.	.324	.447	.637	204	52	66	17	64	40	50	3
OF	Bryant Packard, East Carolina	So.	.403	.460	.680	206	47	83	14	50	19	42	5
DH	Andrew Vaughn, California	So.	.402	.531	.819	199	59	80	23	63	44	18	4
UTL	Brooks Wilson, Stetson	Sr.	.287	.399	.437	167	28	48	3	26	31	39	8

Pos.	Name	Year	W	L	ERA	G	CG	SV	IP	H	BB	SO	AVG
SP	Logan Gilbert, Stetson	Jr.	10	1	2.52	14	0	0	100	60	20	143	.171
SP	Casey Mize, Auburn	Jr.	9	5	3.07	15	0	0	103	73	10	140	.209
SP	Nick Sandlin, Southern Mississippi	Jr.	9	0	1.13	14	0	0	95	51	15	134	.166
SP	Brady Singer, Florida	Jr.	10	1	2.25	13	1	0	88	59	18	92	.186
RP	Michael Byrne, Florida	Jr.	2	1	1.99	29	0	13	45	33	4	46	.200
RP	Jack LIttle, Stanford	So.	3	0	0.66	23	0	15	41	24	7	54	.170
UTL	Brooks Wilson, Stetson	Sr.	6	0	2.13	31	0	20	55	40	19	68	.197

SECOND TEAM

Pos.	Name	Year	AVG	OBP	SLG	AB	R	H	HR	RBI	BB	SO	SB
C	Adley Rutschman, Oregon State	So.	.391	.494	.594	197	44	77	6	63	44	30	1
1B	Spencer Torkelson, Arizona State	Fr.	.320	.440	.473	206	59	66	25	53	38	44	4
2B	Nick Dunn, Maryland	Jr.	.330	.419	.561	212	39	70	10	39	32	19	3
3B	Josh Jung, Texas Tech	So.	.381	.484	.650	226	63	86	11	73	33	29	4
SS	Cadyn Grenier, Oregon State	Jr.	.335	.420	.477	218	57	73	4	42	27	43	8
OF	Devlin Granberg, Dallas Baptist	Sr.	.426	.531	.651	235	65	100	11	65	50	41	23
OF	Grant Little, Texas Tech	So.	.378	.477	.675	209	58	79	12	67	37	30	9
OF	Steele Walker, Oklahoma	Jr.	.326	.441	.606	216	48	76	13	53	31	48	7
DH	Alec Bohm, Wichita State	Jr.	.339	.436	.625	224	57	76	16	55	39	28	9
UTL	Tanner Dodson, California	Jr.	.328	.389	.407	189	35	62	1	23	15	30	12

Pos.	Name	Year	W	L	ERA	G	CG	SV	IP	H	BB	SO	AVG
SP	Kyle Brnovich, Elon	So.	8	2	1.71	15	1	0	105	57	36	147	.159
SP	Colton Eastman, Cal State Fullerton	Jr.	9	3	2.26	15	1	0	104	73	26	108	.208
SP	Blaine Knight, Arkansas	Jr.	10	0	2.78	15	0	0	87	76	21	86	.234
SP	John Rooney, Hofstra	Jr.	8	2	1.23	13	3	0	95	51	27	108	.166
RP	Parker Caracci, Mississippi	R-So.	4	2	1.86	25	0	10	44	38	10	68	.246
RP	Ryley Gilliam, Clemson	Jr.	2	3	0.99	24	0	11	36	19	22	53	.153
UTL	Tanner Dodson, California	Jr.	2	1	2.48	19	0	11	40	36	7	35	.235

THIRD TEAM

Pos.	Name	Year	AVG	OBP	SLG	AB	R	H	HR	RBI	BB	SO	SB
C	Cal Raleigh, Florida State	Jr.	.330	.455	.593	221	44	73	13	54	51	40	2
1B	Chase Chambers, Tennessee Tech	Sr.	.400	.498	.652	230	71	92	15	76	41	24	0
2B	Nick Madrigal, Oregon State	Jr.	.395	.459	.563	119	29	47	2	27	12	5	9
3B	Luke Reynolds, Southern Mississippi	R-Jr.	.400	.562	.727	205	69	82	15	60	63	52	8
SS	Logan Davidson, Clemson	So.	.298	.411	.562	235	57	70	15	45	39	62	10
OF	Gage Canning, Arizona State	Jr.	.369	.426	.648	236	47	87	9	45	24	54	8
OF	Keegan McGovern, Georgia	Sr.	.325	.440	.630	200	63	65	15	44	36	42	7
OF	Andrew Moritz, UNC Greensboro	Jr.	.428	.492	.637	215	57	92	6	61	28	27	12
DH	Kevin Strohschein, Tennessee Tech	Jr.	.406	.463	.713	251	65	102	18	65	27	33	1
UTL	Jack Labosky, Duke	Sr.	.238	.391	.405	138	31	44	7	38	32	62	10

Pos.	Name	Year	W	L	ERA	G	CG	SV	IP	H	BB	SO	AVG
SP	Mason Feole, Connecticut	So.	9	1	2.50	15	0	0	94	75	47	114	.230
SP	Joey Murray, Kent State	Jr.	9	1	1.71	15	1	0	95	47	38	139	.146
SP	Andre Pallante, UC Irvine	So.	10	1	1.60	15	0	0	101	77	30	115	.220
SP	Adam Wolf, Louisville	Jr.	7	2	2.26	15	0	0	96	73	26	105	.209
RP	Robert Broom, Mercer	Jr.	10	4	1.70	31	0	2	74	57	24	111	.209
RP	Durbin Feltman, Texas Christian	Jr.	0	1	0.74	19	0	6	24	12	6	43	.156
UTL	Jack Labosky, Duke	Sr.	2	0	0.84	21	0	9	32	23	4	24	.211

his friends, his family, and all those who were lucky enough to have met him, played for him, or learned from him. His presence will be sorely missed but his legacy will never be forgotten."

Garrido's baseball life was truly legendary. He played at Fresno State and helped the Bulldogs advance to the 1959 College World Series, making him one of 11 men to reach Omaha as a player and a head coach. He went on to play five seasons in the minor leagues in the Indians' system, advancing to Triple-A.

Following his playing days, Garrido in 1969 began his coaching career at San Francisco State. After one season he moved on to Cal Poly for three years. Then, in 1973 he arrived at Cal State Fullerton.

It was at Fullerton that Garrido's legend was born. He led the Titans' transition to into Division I and led them to the CWS in 1975, their first season of playing at the highest level. Under Garrido's leadership, Fullerton quickly became a powerhouse. The Titans won the national championship in 1979 and another in 1984. After the second national championship, he won Coach of the Year for the first time.

In just 10 years, Garrido had turned Fullerton into an elite program and transformed the college baseball landscape as a result. But he grew frustrated at the lack of off-field progress at Fullerton and left in 1988 to take over at Illinois. His Midwestern venture lasted just three seasons before he returned to Fullerton. He lasted six seasons in his second stint and led the Titans to the 1995 national championship.

Garrido was lured away again after the 1996 season, this time by Texas, one of the sport's greatest powers. He succeeded Cliff Gustafson, a legend in his own right, in Austin and returned the Longhorns to prominence. Texas won national titles in 2002 and 2005 and finished as runner-up in 2004 and 2009. He won his second Coach of the Year award after the 2002 national championship.

But, eventually, Garrido's exceptional run ended. After making the 2011 CWS, Texas missed the NCAA Tournament the next two seasons. The Longhorns bounced back to make a surprise trip to Omaha in 2014 but needed to win the Big 12 Conference Tournament in 2015 to make it back to regionals. He entered the following season on the hot seat and after going 25-32, he retired from coaching and took a position as a special assistant to the athletic director.

During his time at Texas, Garrido set the Division I record for victories in 2003, and the all divisions mark in 2014. He also became the first coach to win a national championship at two different schools.

Garrido coached three players who won the Golden Spikes Award: Tim Wallach (1979), Phil Nevin (1992) and Mark Kotsay (1995). All three

COLLEGE WORLD SERIES

STANDINGS

Bracket One	W	L
Oregon State	4	1
Mississippi State	2	2
North Carolina	1	2
Washington	0	2

Bracket Two	W	L
Arkansas	3	0
Florida	2	2
Texas Tech	1	2
Texas	0	2

CWS FINALS (BEST OF THREE)
June 26: Arkansas 4, Oregon State 1
June 27: Oregon State 5, Arkansas 3
June 28: Oregon State 5, Arkansas 0

ALL-TOURNAMENT TEAM
C: *Adley Rutschman, Oregon State. **1B:** Jared Gates, Arkansas. **2B:** Hunter Stovall, Mississippi State. **3B:** Casey Martin, Arkansas. **SS:** Cadyn Grenier, Oregon State. **OF:** Dominic Fletcher, Arkansas; Heston Kjerstad, Arkansas; Trevor Larnach, Oregon State. **DH:** Tyler Malone, Oregon State. **P:** Kevin Abel, Oregon State; Blaine Knight, Arkansas.

*Named Most Outstanding Player.

BATTING
(Minimum 8 PA)

Player	AVG	R	H	2B	3B	HR	RBI	SB
Adley Rutschman, OSU	.567	8	17	3	0	2	13	0
Mason Cerrillo, UW	.500	2	4	0	0	0	0	0
Ashton McGee, UNC	.500	1	4	0	1	0	2	0
Ike Freeman, UNC	.462	2	6	0	0	0	1	0
Josh Jung, Texas Tech	.429	1	6	0	0	0	2	0
Trevor Larnach, OSU	.417	10	15	5	1	1	9	0
Levi Jordan, UW	.375	0	3	0	0	0	1	0
Casey Martin, Ark.	.357	7	10	2	0	0	3	0
Blake Reese, Florida	.357	4	5	3	0	0	0	2
Kyle Datres, UNC	.357	3	5	2	0	1	2	0

PITCHING
(Minimum 6 IP)

Pitcher	W-L	ERA	G	SV	IP	H	BB	SO
Barrett Loseke, Ark.	1-0	0.00	4	0	8	8	1	11
Cole Gordon, MSU	0-0	0.00	3	1	8	3	0	5
Joe DeMers, UW	0-0	0.00	1	0	7	7	1	2
Jackson Kowar, Florida	1-0	0.00	1	0	7	5	2	13
Kevin Abel, OSU	4-0	0.86	4	0	21	7	7	23
Brandon Eisert, OSU	1-0	1.88	3	0	14	11	2	14
Blaine Knight, Ark.	2-0	2.45	2	0	11	11	2	10
Chandler Champlain, OSU	0-0	2.79	3	0	10	5	8	15
Jack Leftwich, Florida	1-0	2.84	1	0	6	7	2	5
Konnor Pilkington, MSU	1-0	3.00	1	0	6	6	2	4

went on to find significant big league success. Other major leaguers he coached include Huston Street, Brandon Belt and Corey Knebel.

Beyond his own success, Garrido cultivated a large coaching tree. Oregon coach George Horton, who has won more than 1,000 games, and Fullerton coach Rick Vanderhook are among the current head coaches with ties to Garrido. The assistant coaching ranks are also filled with Garrido's former players, such as Arizona recruiting coordinator Sergio Brown and Stanford's Tommy Nicholson.

REGIONALS

JUNE 1-JUNE 4
64 teams, 16 four-team, double-elimination tournaments. Winners advance to super regionals.

GAINESVILLE, FLA.
Host: Florida (No. 1 national seed).
Participants: No. 1 Florida (42-17), No. 2 Jacksonville (39-19), No. 3 Florida Atlantic (40-17-1), No. 4 Columbia (20-28).
Champion: Florida (3-1).
Runner-up: Florida Atlantic (3-2).
Outstanding player: Jonah Girand, C, Florida.

STANFORD, CALIF..
Host: Stanford (No. 2 national seed).
Participants: No. 1 Stanford (44-10), No. 2 Baylor (36-19), No. 3 Cal State Fullerton (32-23), No. 4 Wright State (39-15).
Champion: Cal State Fullerton (3-0).
Runner-up: Stanford (2-2).
Outstanding player: Ruben Cardenas, OF, Cal State Fullerton.

CORVALLIS, ORE.
Host: Oregon State (No. 3 national seed).
Participants: No. 1 Oregon State (45-10-1), No. 2 Louisiana State (37-25), No. 3 San Diego State (39-19), No. 4 Northwestern State (37-23).
Champion: Oregon State (3-0).
Runner-up: Louisiana State (2-2).
Outstanding player: Nick Madirgal, 2B, Oregon State.

OXFORD, MISS.
Host: Mississippi (No. 4 national seed).
Participants: No. 1 Mississippi (46-15), No. 2 Tennessee Tech (48-9), No. 3 Missouri State (39-15), No. 4 St. Louis (38-18).
Champion: Tennessee Tech (4-1).
Runner-up: Mississippi (2-2).
Outstanding player: Chase Chambers, 1B, Tennessee Tech.

FAYETTEVILLE, ARK.
Host: Arkansas (No. 5 national seed).
Participants: No. 1 Arkansas (39-18), No. 2 Southern Mississippi (43-16), No. 3 Dallas Baptist (40-19), No. 4 Oral Roberts (38-18).
Champion: Arkansas (3-0).
Runner-up: Dallas Baptist (2-2).
Outstanding player: Devlin Granberg, OF, Dallas Baptist.

CHAPEL HILL, N.C.
Host: North Carolina (No. 6 national seed).
Participants: No. 1 North Carolina (38-18), No. 2 Purdue (37-19), No. 3 Houston (36-23), No. 4 North Carolina A&T (32-23).
Champion: North Carolina (3-0).
Runner-up: Houston (2-2).
Outstanding player: Michael Busch, 1B, North Carolina.

TALLAHASSEE, FLA.
Host: Florida State (No. 7 national seed).
Participants: No. 1 Florida State (43-17), No. 2 Mississippi State (31-25), No. 3 Oklahoma (36-23), No. 4 Samford (36-24).
Champion: Mississippi State (4-1).
Runner-up: Oklahoma (2-2).
Outstanding player: Elijah MacNamee, OF, Mississippi State.

ATHENS, GA.
Host: Georgia (No. 8 national seed).
Participants: No. 1 Georgia (39-17), No. 2 Duke (40-15), No. 3 Troy (41-19), No. 4 Campbell (35-24).
Champion: Duke (4-1).
Runner-up: Georgia (2-2).
Outstanding player: Chris Crabtree, DH, Duke.

LUBBOCK, TEXAS
Host: Texas Tech (No. 9 national seed).
Participants: No. 1 Texas Tech (39-17), No. 2 Louisville (43-17), No. 3 Kent State (39-16), No. 4 New Mexico State (39-20).
Champion: Texas Tech (3-0).
Runner-up: Louisville (2-2).
Outstanding player: Zach Rheams, DH, Texas Tech.

CLEMSON, S.C.
Host: Clemson (No. 10 national seed).
Participants: No. 1 Clemson (45-14), No. 2 Vanderbilt (31-25), No. 3 St. John's (39-15), No. 4 Morehead State (36-24).
Champion: Vanderbilt (3-0).
Runner-up: Clemson (2-2).
Outstanding player: Connor Kaiser, SS, Vanderbilt.

DELAND, FLA.
Host: Stetson (No. 11 national seed).
Participants: No. 1 Stetson (45-11), No. 2 South Florida (35-20-1), No. 3 Oklahoma State (29-24-1), No. 4 Hartford (26-29).
Champion: Stetson (3-0).
Runner-up: Oklahoma State (2-2).
Outstanding player: Brooks Wilson, RHP/DH, Stetson.

GREENVILLE, N.C.
Host: East Carolina (No. 12 national seed).
Participants: No. 1 East Carolina (43-16), No. 2 South Carolina (33-24), No. 3 Ohio State (36-22), No. 4 UNC Wilmington (37-21).
Champion: South Carolina (3-0).
Runner-up: UNC Wilmington (2-2).
Outstanding player: Danny Blair, OF, South Carolina.

AUSTIN, TEXAS
Host: Texas (No. 13 national seed).
Participants: No. 1 Texas (37-20), No. 2 Indiana (38-17), No. 3 Texas A&M (39-20), No. 4 Texas Southern (27-26).
Champion: Texas (3-0).
Runner-up: Indiana (2-2).
Outstanding player: Kody Clemens, 2B, Texas.

MINNEAPOLIS
Host: Minnesota (No. 14 national seed).
Participants: No. 1 Minnesota (41-13), No. 2 UCLA (36-19), No. 3 Gonzaga (32-22), No. 4 Canisius (35-20).
Champion: Minnesota (3-0).
Runner-up: UCLA (2-2).
Outstanding player: Terrin Vavra, SS, Minnesota.

CONWAY, S.C.
Host: Coastal Carolina (No. 15 national seed).
Participants: No. 1 Coastal Carolina (42-17), No. 2 Connecticut (35-20), No. 3 Washington (30-23), No. 4 LIU-Brooklyn (31-24).
Champion: Washington (3-0).
Runner-up: Connecticut (2-2).
Outstanding player: Joe Wainhouse, DH, Washington.

RALEIGH, N.C.
Host: North Carolina State (No. 16 national seed).
Participants: No. 1 North Carolina State (40-16), No. 2 Auburn (39-21), No. 3 Northeastern (36-19), No. 4 Army (36-22).
Champion: Auburn (3-0).
Runner-up: North Carolina State (2-2).
Outstanding player: Josh Anthony, 3B, Auburn.

SUPER REGIONALS

JUNE 8-11
16 teams, best-of-three series. Winners advance to College World Series.

AUBURN AT FLORIDA
Site: Gainesville, Fla.
Florida wins 2-1, advances to CWS.

WASHINGTON AT CAL STATE FULLERTON
Site: Fullerton, Calif.
Washington wins 2-1, advances to CWS.

MINNESOTA AT OREGON STATE
Site: Corvallis, Ore.
Oregon State wins 2-0, advances to CWS.

TENNESSEE TECH AT TEXAS
Site: Austin, Texas.
Texas wins 2-1, advances to CWS.

SOUTH CAROLINA AT ARKANSAS
Site: Fayetteville, Ark.
Arkansas wins 2-1, advances to CWS.

STETSON AT NORTH CAROLINA
Site: Chapel Hill, N.C.
North Carolina wins 2-0, advances to CWS.

MISSISSIPPI STATE AT VANDERBILT
Site: Nashville.
Mississippi State wins 2-1, advances to CWS.

DUKE AT TEXAS TECH
Site: Lubbock, Texas.
Texas Tech wins 2-1, advances to CWS.

Singer Shines As Florida's Ace

PLAYER OF THE YEAR

BY TEDDY CAHILL

Looking back on his remarkable regular season, Florida righthander Brady Singer is drawn all the way back to facing Siena on Opening Day. The junior took over as the Gators' ace and came into the year regarded as the top prospect in this year's draft class. The Gators were the defending national champions and all eyes were on Singer to get the season off to a strong start.

Singer did just that. He threw 89 pitches in seven innings and struck out eight batters while holding Siena to one run on two hits and a walk.

"Walking out there for the first time my junior year with all the pressure—you know the draft stuff and people are watching with the No. 1 tag on me," Singer said. "To go into that start and get it started on the right foot going into the next weekend with Miami, I think that was the toughest one."

Singer has carried that momentum through the rest of the season. As Florida's ace, he helped lead the Gators to the Southeastern Conference title and the top seed in the NCAA Tournament. He went 12-3, 2.55 with a 114-to-22 strikeout-to-walk ratio and held opposing hitters to a .203 batting average in 113 innings.

For his exemplary season and his premium talent, Singer is the 2018 Baseball America College Player of the Year.

After watching Singer pitch, his physical tools are readily apparent. What's more difficult to see is the hard work he puts in between starts to prepare. Coach Kevin O'Sullivan said Singer completely changed his body over his three years at Florida, filling out his lanky frame and getting stronger. Beyond those physical gains, Singer also spends a lot of time on the mental side of the game.

"He's a tremendously hard worker between starts," O'Sullivan said. "Forget just the weight room but the watching of video and preparation and understanding the game."

Singer's competitiveness is also a part of what makes him an elite college pitcher. That competitive fire famously spilled over last year in super regionals when his appearance was interrupted by the umpteenth rain delay of the weekend.

Singer's mentality on the mound helps him excel on big stages. He last year was at his best in the College World Series. This year he rose to the occasion time after time when facing the SEC's best pitchers, including Auburn's Casey Mize twice.

Singer said his competitive spirit comes from his parents, especially his mother.

"Even when we play board games we can't lose," he said. "She's a huge competitor and I get it from her."

All those pieces have come together for Singer to make him a true college ace and the leader of the best pitching staff in the country.

Brady Singer

PREVIOUS WINNERS

1982: Jeff Ledbetter, OF/LHP Florida St.
1983: Dave Magadan, 1B, Alabama
1984: Oddibe McDowell, OF, Arizona St.
1985: Pete Incaviglia, OF, Oklahoma State
1986: Casey Close, OF, Michigan
1987: Robin Ventura, 3B, Oklahoma State
1988: John Olerud, 1B/LHP, Washington St.
1989: Ben McDonald, RHP, Louisiana State
1990: Mike Kelly, OF, Arizona State
1991: David McCarthy, 1B, Stanford
1992: Phil Nevin, 3B, Cal State Fullerton
1993: Brooks Kieschnick, DH/RHP, Texas

1994: Jason Varitek, C, Georgia Tech
1995: Todd Helton, 1B/LHP, Tennessee
1996: Kris Benson, RHP, Clemson
1997: J.D. Drew, OF, Florida State
1998: Jeff Austin, RHP, Stanford
1999: Jason Jennings, RHP, Baylor
2000: Mark Teixeira, 3B, Georgia Tech
2001: Mark Prior, RHP, S. California
2002: Khalil Greene, SS, Clemson
2003: Rickie Weeks, 2B, Southern
2004: Jered Weaver, RHP, Long Beach St.
2005: Alex Gordon, 3B, Nebraska

2006: Andrew Miller, LHP, North Carolina
2007: David Price, LHP, Vanderbilt
2008: Buster Posey, C/RHP, Florida State
2009: Stephen Strasburg, RHP, San Diego St.
2010: Anthony Rendon, 3B, Rice
2011: Trevor Bauer, RHP, UCLA
2012: Mike Zunino, C, Florida
2013: Kris Bryant, 3B, San Diego
2014: A.J. Reed, 1B/LHP, Kentucky
2015: Andrew Benintendi, OF, Arkansas
2016: Klye Lewis, OF, Mercer
2017: Brendan McKay, LHP/1B, Louisville

Pierce Leads Texas Back To CWS

BY TEDDY CAHILL

Replacing Augie Garrido, who finished his career as the winningest coach in college baseball history, was never going to be easy. Texas went through a protracted search following the 2016 season when Garrido retired before landing on David Pierce, who was then the head coach at Tulane.

The choice has been an inspired one. Pierce this season, his second at the program's helm, led Texas to its first Big 12 Conference title since 2011 and to the College World Series for the first time since 2014. This wasn't a vintage Longhorns team loaded with elite prospects. It was a team that had to grind out results, that fought back from a disappointing 9-9 start against an ambitious nonconference schedule and was tested emotionally early, when Garrido passed away in March.

In the end, Texas won, something with which Pierce is very familiar. Since returning to the college game in 2001 as an assistant coach at Houston, his alma mater, he has not missed the NCAA Tournament. In seven years as a head coach, his teams have never won less than 35 games and he has taken three dif-

COACH OF THE YEAR

ferent teams to regionals.

This year at Texas was one of the best coaching jobs. The Longhorns caught fire down the stretch to win the Big 12 on the final weekend of the regular season. They went on to win the Austin Regional and Super Regional and finished the year 42-23. For those successes, Pierce is Baseball America's 2018 College Coach of the Year.

When Pierce arrived at Texas with his staff of assistant coaches Sean Allen, Phil Haig and

David Pierce

Philip Miller, who have been with him since he was head coach at Sam Houston State, he knew they had to embrace the expectations and history of one of college baseball's premier programs. In 2017, Pierce's first season, the Longhorns reached the Long Beach Regional final, a strong first step.

The Longhorns pushed beyond that this year. returning the program to heights it hadn't reached in recent seasons.

They weren't a team that was projected to reach Omaha and were just .500 going into Big 12 play. But they never gave in and continued to grow throughout the season before hitting their stride in the second half.

"You could see they were committed to each other," Pierce said. "When we won the conference championship and some things fell into place for us, you knew this team was doing things right and they were playing at a level for each other, they were playing with confidence. When that happened, you saw them feed off each other."

PREVIOUS WINNERS

1982: Gene Stephenson, Wichita State
1983: Barry Shollenberger, Alabama
1984: Augie Garrido, Cal State Fullerton
1985: Ron Polk, Mississippi State
1986: Skip Bertman, LSU/Dave Snow, LMU
1987: Mark Marquess, Stanford
1988: Jim Brock, Arizona State
1989: Dave Snow, Long Beach State
1990: Steve Webber, Georgia
1991: Jim Hendry, Creighton
1992: Andy Lopez, Pepperdine
1993: Gene Stephenson, Wichita State
1994: Jim Morris, Miami
1995: Pat Murphy, Arizona State
1996: Skip Bertman, Louisiana State
1997: Jim Wells, Alabama
1998: Pat Murphy, Arizona State
1999: Wayne Graham, Rice
2000: Ray Tanner, South Carolina
2001: Dave Van Horn, Nebraska
2002: Augie Garrido, Texas
2003: George Horton, Cal State Fullerton
2004: David Perno, Georgia
2005: Rick Jones, Tulane
2006: Pat Casey, Oregon State
2007: Dave Serrano, UC Irvine
2008: Mike Fox, North Carolina
2009: Paul Mainieri, Louisiana State
2010: Ray Tanner, South Carolina
2011: Kevin O'Sullivan, Florida
2012: Mike Martin, Florida State
2013: John Savage, UCLA
2014: Tim Corbin, Vanderbilt
2015: Brian O'Connor, Virginia
2016: Jim Schlossnagle, Texas Christian
2017: Dan McDonnell, Louisville

Abel Steps Up In Omaha

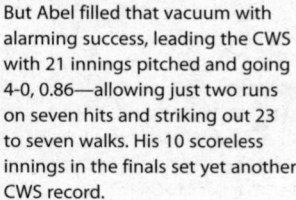

FRESHMAN OF THE YEAR

BY MICHAEL LANANNA

Oregon State could not have won the 2018 College World Series without Kevin Abel. On a team that has won 111 games over the last two seasons and this year produced three top-40 draft picks, it was the freshman righthander who proved indispensible in Omaha.

A day after earning his third win of the CWS in a 23-pitch relief outing, Abel hurled a 129-pitch two-hitter against Arkansas in Game 3 of the finals to clinch the national championship. Using a low-90s fastball, a devastating low-80s changeup and a biting upper-70s curveball, Abel retired the last 20 batters he faced. He struck out 10 and walked just two. He became the first pitcher in CWS history to win four games. No other pitcher has ever won two

Kevin Abel

games in the same three-game final series. Oregon State didn't receive a single quality start from the six combined outings starters Luke Heimlich and Bryce Fehmel made.

But Abel filled that vacuum with alarming success, leading the CWS with 21 innings pitched and going 4-0, 0.86—allowing just two runs on seven hits and striking out 23 to seven walks. His 10 scoreless innings in the finals set yet another CWS record.

All of that for a freshman who could barely find the strike zone in the first half of the season. Like many freshmen, Abel had trouble adjusting to the pressures of Division I baseball. Gradually, as Abel adjusted, the Beavers worked him into bigger and bigger situations and he eventually became one of their best starting pitchers.

Abel finished the year 8-1, 2.88 with 108 strikeouts in 81.1 innings and held opponents to a .188 batting average.

PREVIOUS WINNERS

1989: Alex Fernandez, RHP, Miami
1990: Jeffrey Hammonds, OF, Stanford
1991: Brooks Kieschnick, RHP/DH, Texas
1992: Todd Walker, 2B, Louisiana State
1993: Brett Laxton, RHP, Louisiana State
1994: R.A. Dickey, RHP, Tennessee
1995: Kyle Peterson, RHP, Stanford
1996: Pat Burrell, 3B, Miami
1997: Brian Roberts, SS, North Carolina
1998: Xavier Nady, 2B, California
1999: James Jurries, 2B, Tulane
2000: Kevin Howard, 3B, Miami
2001: Michael Aubrey, OF/LHP, Texas
2002: Stephen Drew, SS, Florida State
2003: Ryan Braun, SS, Miami
2004: Wade LeBlanc, LHP, Alabama
2005: Joe Savery, LHP, Rice
2006: Pedro Alvarez, 3B, Vanderbilt
2007: Dustin Ackley, 1B, North Carolina
2008: Chris Hernandez, LHP, Miami
2009: Anthony Rendon, 3B, Rice
2010: Matt Purke, LHP, Texas Christian
2011: Colin Moran, 3B, North Carolina
2012: Carlos Rodon, LHP, N.C. State
2013: Alex Bregman, SS, Louisiana State
2014: Zack Collins, C, Miami
2015: Brendan McKay, LHP/1B, Louisville
2016: Seth Beer, OF, Clemson
2017: Matt Wallner, OF/RHP, Southern Miss
Full list of winners can be found at BaseballAmerica.com/Stories/Baseball-America-Awards

FRESHMAN ALL-AMERICA TEAMS

FIRST TEAM

Pos.		AVG	OBP	SLG	AB	R	H	HR	RBI	SB
C	Patrick Bailey, N.C. State	.321	.419	.604	187	45	60	13	40	0
1B	Spencer Torkelson, Arizona St.	.320	.440	.743	206	59	66	25	53	4
2B	Gabe Holt, Texas Tech	.348	.440	.485	270	70	94	6	44	29
3B	Casey Martin, Arkansas	.345	.418	.556	252	50	87	13	49	8
SS	Nick Loftin, Baylor	.306	.370	.441	222	52	68	6	36	5
OF	Daniel Cabrera, Louisiana St.	.315	.405	.525	219	38	69	8	54	2
OF	Heston Kjerstad, Arkansas	.332	.419	.553	262	65	87	14	58	3
OF	Ryan Ward, Bryant	.409	.449	.636	247	51	101	8	52	9
DH	Edouard Julien, Auburn	.275	.398	.556	207	47	57	17	69	7
UT	Casey Schmitt, San Diego St.	.264	.302	.346	182	23	48	1	32	0

		W	L	ERA	G	SV	IP	H	BB	SO	BAA
SP	Kevin Abel, Oregon State	8	1	2.88	23	1	81	51	46	108	.181
SP	Tanner Burns, Auburn	7	4	3.01	17	0	87	73	37	77	.225
SP	Patrick Fredrickson, Minnesota	9	0	1.86	19	0	97	71	27	73	.209
SP	Zach Pettway, UCLA	8	4	3.35	16	0	97	85	19	78	.235
RP	Chris Mauloni, Jacksonville	3	2	2.97	29	20	33	27	12	48	.197
RP	Max Meyer, Minnesota	2	3	2.06	26	16	44	25	13	54	.163
UT	Casey Schmitt, San Diego St.	1	1	0.28	21	9	32	17	8	24	.157

SECOND TEAM

C: Adam Kerner, San Diego. **1B:** Jesse Franklin, Michigan. **2B:** Nick Gonzales, New Mexico State. **3B:** Tyler Keenan, Mississippi. **SS:** Jimmy Glowenke, Dallas Baptist. **OF:** Parker Chavers, Coastal Carolina; Austin Martin, Vanderbilt; Steven Williams, Auburn. **DH:** Le Bassett, Mercer. **UT:** Logan Allen, Florida International. **SP:** Nicholas Dombkowski, Hartford; Ma'Khaill Hillard, Louisiana State; Drey Jameson, Ball State; Samuel Strickland, Samford. **RP:** Andrew Abbott, Virginia; C.J. Van Eyk, Florida State.

HITTING (MINIMUM 140 AT-BATS)

BATTING AVERAGE

Rk.	Player, Team	Class	AVG	OBP	SLG	G	AB	2B	3B	HR	RBI	BB	SO	SB
1.	Greg Cullen, Niagara	Jr.	.458	.556	.655	49	177	17	3	4	42	38	22	13
2.	Devlin Granberg, Dallas Baptist	Sr.	.443	.541	.680	63	253	17	2	13	70	52	42	26
3.	Andrew Moritz, UNC Greensboro	Jr.	.428	.492	.637	54	215	7	10	6	61	28	27	12
4.	Ryan Ward, Bryant	R-Fr.	.409	.449	.636	56	247	22	5	8	52	21	10	9
5.	Adley Rutschman, Oregon State	So.	.408	.505	.628	67	250	22	3	9	83	53	40	1
6.	Bryant Packard, East Carolina	So.	.406	.462	.671	55	219	16	0	14	50	20	46	6
7.	Marshawn Taylor, Grambling	Sr.	.404	.470	.454	52	218	5	3	0	44	25	14	20
8.	Andrew Vaughn, California	So.	.402	.531	.819	54	199	14	0	23	63	44	18	4
9.	Chase Chambers, Tennessee Tech	Sr.	.395	.500	.652	65	256	13	1	17	84	49	24	0
10.	Joey Denison, Troy	Sr.	.393	.461	.591	63	247	25	3	6	81	29	31	21
11.	Josh Jung, Texas Tech	So.	.392	.491	.639	65	263	17	6	12	80	39	32	4
12.	Kamren Dukes, Texas Southern	Sr.	.391	.457	.538	55	238	22	2	3	42	15	43	30
13.	Quin Cotton, Grand Canyon	So.	.390	.462	.573	57	241	19	5	5	43	22	30	13
14.	Luke Reynolds, Southern Mississippi	R-Jr.	.389	.551	.699	62	216	20	1	15	61	65	52	8
15.	Bren Spillane, Illinois	Jr.	.389	.498	.903	50	175	17	2	23	60	36	57	16
16.	Matt Pita, Virginia Military Institute	Jr.	.389	.459	.721	53	226	21	6	14	48	23	30	23
17.	Grant Fennell, Nevada	Sr.	.389	.466	.562	51	203	16	2	5	52	27	50	8
18.	DaShawn Keirsey, Utah	Jr.	.386	.440	.609	50	202	23	5	4	22	15	32	7
19.	Terrin Vavra, Minnesota	Jr.	.386	.455	.614	58	223	13	4	10	59	30	22	8
20.	Nick Campana, Hartford	Sr.	.385	.467	.611	54	208	17	0	10	39	22	18	22
21.	Owen Miller, Illinois State	Jr.	.384	.433	.537	52	229	15	1	6	35	18	23	8
22.	Jordan Stoner, Tennessee-Martin	Jr.	.382	.465	.560	51	207	17	4	4	25	17	44	11
23.	Raul Hernandez, Jackson State	Jr.	.382	.425	.575	52	207	17	1	7	50	15	43	5
24.	Steven Kraft, Western Kentucky	Sr.	.382	.483	.494	44	170	13	0	2	33	29	27	7
25.	Ray Hernandez, Alabama State	Sr.	.381	.460	.604	50	202	12	0	11	44	23	32	21
26.	Ben Mezzenga, Minnesota	Jr.	.381	.464	.444	59	189	8	2	0	28	31	40	12
27.	Caleb Webster, UNC Greensboro	So.	.380	.417	.456	54	237	7	1	3	37	11	20	7
28.	Matt Sanders, Troy	Sr.	.378	.463	.538	63	262	19	4	5	28	44	33	26
29.	Beau Brundage, Portland	So.	.378	.452	.493	53	209	13	4	1	24	22	41	4
30.	Nick Grande, Stony Brook	So.	.377	.468	.560	56	207	18	1	6	28	28	43	32
31.	James Cilento, Bryant	So.	.377	.448	.518	47	191	14	2	3	31	16	32	5
32.	Trevor Ezell, Southeast Missouri State	Jr.	.377	.442	.558	56	231	16	4	6	50	25	38	11
33.	Tyler Lowe, Chicago State	Jr.	.376	.409	.537	54	205	5	2	8	41	12	46	7
34.	Grant Wood, Murray State	Fr.	.376	.520	.554	53	186	16	1	5	46	50	40	2
35.	Kevin Strohschein, Tennessee Tech	Jr.	.375	.433	.650	65	283	18	3	18	67	30	44	1
36.	Kyle Gray, West Virginia	Jr.	.374	.462	.677	55	198	12	3	14	38	34	41	10
37.	David Villar, South Florida	Jr.	.374	.463	.648	59	219	24	0	12	58	28	58	1
38.	Trey Truitt, Mercer	Sr.	.373	.457	.627	58	233	19	2	12	44	34	58	15
39.	Jesse Wilkening, Nebraska	Jr.	.372	.445	.588	52	199	14	1	9	56	24	36	0
40.	Matt Cogen, Belmont	So.	.372	.418	.586	55	239	15	3	10	51	20	21	12
41.	Gaudencio Lucca, Texas Southern	Sr.	.371	.488	.589	55	202	13	2	9	50	30	41	25
42.	Eddy Gonzalez, Incarnate Word	Jr.	.371	.440	.448	55	221	9	1	2	30	20	16	6
43.	Grant Little, Texas Tech	So.	.370	.462	.642	65	246	25	3	12	77	40	38	11
44.	Michael Helman, Texas A&M	Jr.	.369	.451	.526	62	249	17	2	6	36	28	31	12
45.	Scott Schreiber, Nebraska	Jr.	.369	.446	.692	52	214	13	1	18	48	28	48	4
46.	Gage Canning, Arizona State	Jr.	.369	.426	.648	55	236	17	11	9	45	24	54	8
47.	Luke Brown, Western Kentucky	Fr.	.369	.403	.405	48	168	6	0	0	14	9	27	11
48.	Braxton Morris, Morehead State	Sr.	.367	.443	.547	63	267	25	1	7	59	32	26	6
49.	Enrique Sanchez, Texas A&M-Corpus Christi	Jr.	.367	.397	.449	43	158	10	0	1	29	11	25	1
50.	Brennon Kaleiwahea, Tennessee Tech	Sr.	.367	.465	.540	64	237	15	1	8	55	36	48	1
51.	Bryson Stott, Nevada-Las Vegas	So.	.365	.442	.556	59	252	30	3	4	32	32	18	14
52.	Matthew Barefoot, Campbell	R-So.	.364	.484	.585	60	217	18	3	8	32	30	38	33
53.	Chris Cook, East Tennessee State	Sr.	.364	.444	.548	52	217	22	0	6	40	24	29	5
54.	Spencer Henson, Oral Roberts	So.	.364	.433	.541	54	209	7	0	10	58	23	53	1
55	Jameson Hannah, Dallas Baptist	Jr.	.363	.451	.554	59	251	24	3	6	48	39	39	9
56.	Chase Strumpf, UCLA	So.	.363	.475	.633	58	226	23	1	12	53	45	53	2
57.	Cesar Trejo, UNC Greensboro	Jr.	.363	.428	.569	53	204	15	6	5	50	24	41	22
58.	Garrett Giovannelli, Austin Peay	Sr.	.362	.437	.560	56	232	26	1	6	35	31	23	20
59.	Ben Anderson, Furman	Fr.	.361	.461	.530	52	202	11	7	3	39	35	48	5
60.	Jake Hammon, Morehead State	Jr.	.361	.471	.565	60	191	8	2	9	53	42	30	3
61.	John Valente, St. John's	Sr.	.360	.400	.483	56	236	8	3	5	40	18	11	11
62.	Andrew Penner, Cal State Bakersfield	Sr.	.360	.434	.440	57	225	12	0	2	24	19	19	6
63.	Will Haueter, North Kentucky	Jr.	.360	.451	.600	53	200	19	1	9	37	29	29	0
64.	Gabe Snyder, Wright State	Sr.	.359	.425	.668	56	223	20	2	15	73	24	27	15
65.	Russ Olive, Massachusetts-Lowell	Jr.	.359	.460	.641	54	198	13	2	13	37	32	33	3
66.	Joey Bart, Georgia Tech	Jr.	.359	.471	.632	57	220	12	0	16	38	41	56	3

			AVG	OBP	SLG	R	AB	2B	3B	HR	RBI	BB	SO	SB
67.	Ian Dawkins, Sacramento State	Sr.	.359	.415	.528	58	248	18	3	6	33	22	41	8
68.	Cole Krzmarzick, Nevada	Sr.	.359	.428	.425	48	167	8	0	1	19	17	14	4
69.	Will Brennan, Kansas State	So.	.359	.454	.427	54	220	13	1	0	23	32	11	19
70.	Nick Kanavas, Kent State	Sr.	.358	.440	.432	57	229	11	0	2	35	28	36	20
71.	Jonathan White, Presbyterian	Jr.	.358	.441	.519	54	212	10	0	8	39	23	37	2
72.	Corey Joyce, North Carolina Central	So.	.358	.456	.542	48	179	15	0	6	37	32	34	27
73.	Peter Battaglia, Niagara	So.	.357	.443	.595	47	168	15	2	7	49	22	30	4
74.	Davis Sims, Murray State	So.	.357	.434	.573	56	227	29	1	6	52	23	29	0
75.	Austin Embler, UNC Greensboro	Jr.	.357	.438	.467	53	227	15	2	2	32	30	47	9
76.	Hunter Wells, Louisiana Tech	So.	.357	.421	.443	59	255	12	2	2	32	29	34	6
77.	Kyle Isbel, Nevada-Las Vegas	Jr.	.357	.441	.643	59	238	18	4	14	56	34	43	6
78.	Matt Gorski, Indiana	So.	.356	.404	.554	59	222	14	3	8	40	18	37	24
79.	Pikai Winchester, Grand Canyon	Jr.	.355	.410	.461	57	217	13	2	2	38	20	29	0
80.	Reynaldo Pastrana, Marshall	Jr.	.355	.405	.616	50	203	14	0	13	50	18	50	4
81.	McClain Bradley, Wofford	Sr.	.355	.409	.526	58	251	10	3	9	49	22	51	20
82.	Rudy Rott, Ohio	Jr.	.355	.440	.654	53	214	15	2	15	50	30	38	3
83.	Joe Drpich, Siena	Sr.	.355	.403	.609	56	220	17	0	13	55	14	34	1
84.	Steven Kwan, Oregon State	Jr.	.355	.463	.457	66	256	8	6	2	41	50	18	14
85.	Joshua Zamora, Nevada	Fr.	.355	.430	.563	48	183	11	0	9	33	16	18	1
86.	Kyle Baker, Delaware	Jr.	.354	.397	.481	52	212	11	5	2	39	14	29	9
87.	Liam Wilson, Canisius	Sr.	.353	.434	.624	55	221	27	3	9	49	19	24	2
88.	Beau Branton, Stanford	Sr.	.353	.431	.418	53	170	6	1	1	22	19	28	2
89.	Vito Friscia, Hofstra	Jr.	.353	.431	.514	45	173	5	1	7	31	22	33	1
90.	Rafael Ramirez, Grambling State	Jr.	.353	.440	.735	47	170	17	0	16	66	24	43	3
91.	Kole Cottam, Kentucky	Jr.	.352	.438	.667	56	219	12	0	19	50	31	49	4
92.	Jake Garella, Saint Louis	So.	.352	.421	.458	58	227	14	2	2	47	25	57	2
93.	Steele Walker, Oklahoma	Jr.	.352	.441	.606	54	216	14	1	13	53	31	48	7
94.	Zach Ashford, Fresno State	Jr.	.352	.406	.489	52	219	18	3	2	24	15	24	7
95.	Spencer Holcomb, Western Carolina	Sr.	.352	.403	.523	56	199	13	0	7	27	14	40	1
96.	Alex Holderbach, Eastern Kentucky	Jr.	.352	.446	.657	60	230	12	2	18	79	40	42	2
97.	Kody Clemens, Texas	Jr.	.351	.444	.726	65	248	15	3	24	72	41	50	5
98.	Matt Wallner, Southern Mississippi	So.	.351	.474	.618	62	228	13	0	16	67	48	53	2
99.	Jackson Ware, Mercer	Sr.	.351	.446	.477	60	222	10	0	6	46	29	20	6
100.	Jonathan Engelmann, Michigan	Jr.	.351	.431	.521	54	211	14	2	6	44	25	41	21

ON-BASE PERCENTAGE

Rank Player, Pos., Team	OBP
1. Greg Cullen, INF, Niagara	.556
2. Luke Reynolds, 3B, Southern Miss.	.551
3. Devlin Granberg, OF, Dallas Baptist	.541
4. Andrew Vaughn, 1B, California	.531
5. Grant Wood, INF, Murray State	.520
6. Zach Heeke, INF, Central Michigan	.520
7. Adley Rutschman, C, Oregon State	.505
8. Chase Chambers, INF, Tennessee Tech	.500
9. Bren Spillane, 1B, Illinois	.498
10. Alexander Felder, INF, Grambling St.	.497

SLUGGING PERCENTAGE

Rank Player, Pos., Team	SLG
1. Bren Spillane, 1B, Illinois	.903
2. Andrew Vaughn, 1B, California	.819
3. Spencer Torkelson, 1B, Arizona State	.743
4. Rafael Ramirez, INF, Grambling State	.735
5. Kody Clemens, 2B, Texas	.726
6. Matt Pika, INF, Virginia Military Inst.	.721
7. Jonathan India, 3B, Florida	.717
8. Zach Rheams, INF, Texas Tech	.713
9. Luke Reynolds, 3B, Southern Miss.	.699
10. Nic Ready, INF, Air Force	.699

RUNS BATTED IN

Rank Player, Pos., Team	RBI
1. Chase Chambers, 1B, Tennessee Tech	84
2. Adley Rutschman, C, Oregon State	83
3. Joey Denison, INF, Troy	81
4. Josh Jung, 3B, Texas Tech	80
5. Alex Holderbach, OF, Eastern Kentucky	79
6. Trevor Larnach, OF, Oregon State	77
Grant Little, OF, Texas Tech	77
8. Nic Ready, INF, Air Force	74
9. Nick Ames, 1B, Nevada-Las Vegas	73
Trevor Putzig, INF, Tennessee Tech	73
Gabe Snyder, 1B, Wright State	73

HOME RUNS

Rank Player, Pos., Team	HR
1. Spencer Torkelson, 1B, Arizona State	25
2. Kody Clemens, 2B, Texas	24
3. Bren Spillane, 1B, Illinois	23
- Andrew Vaughn, 1B, California	23
5. Seth Beer, OF, Clemson	22
6. Jonathan India, 3B, Florida	21
7. Christian Jones, INF, Campbell	20
Seth Lancaster, SS, Coastal Carolina	20
Nic Ready, INF, Air Force	20
Albee Weiss, C, Cal State Northridge	20

DOUBLES

Rank Player, Pos., Team	2B
1. Bryson Stott, SS, Nevada-Las Vegas	30
2. Davis Sims, INF, Murray State	29
3. Jordan Verdon, INF, San Diego State	27
Liam Wilson, UTL, Canisius	27
5. David Fry, INF, Northwestern State	26
Garrett Giovannelli, INF, Austin Peay State	26
7. Joey Denison, INF, Troy	25
Grant Little, OF, Texas Tech	25
Braxton Morris, INF, Morehead State	25
10. Jameson Hannah, OF, Dallas Baptist	24
Michael Toglia, 1B, UCLA	24
David Villar, INF, South Florida	24

TRIPLES

Rank Player, Pos., Team	3B
1. Gage Canning, OF, Arizona State	11
2. Andrew Moritz, OF, UNC Greensboro	10
3. Jake Farrell, INF, Northeastern	8
Jackson Owens, OF, Tx. A&M-Corpus Christi	8
5. Ben Anderson, OF, Furman	7
Andrew Fregia, INF, Sam Houston State	7
Logan Knowles, OF, Navy	7
Hanke LoForte, INF, Cal State Fullerton	7
Brandon Lockridge, OF, Troy	7
Drew Mount, OF, Kansas State	7
Matt Munoz, OF, Abilene Christian	7
Scott Ota, OF, Illinois-Chicago	7
Isaiah Pasteur, INF, George Washington	7
Gage Workman, SS, Arizona State	7

STOLEN BASES

Rank Player, Pos., Team	SB
1. Jacob Hurtubise, OF, Army	42
2. Charlie McConnell, UTL, Northeastern	37
3. Nathan Eaton, INF, Va. Millitary Inst.	36
Josh Stowers, OF, Louisville	36
5. Ray Alejo, OF, Central Florida	34
Jake MacKenzie, INF, Fordham	34
Mason Mamarella, OF, Kent State	34
Cornell Nixon, INF, Eastern Kentucky	34
J.D. Orr, OF, Wright State	34
10. Matthew Barefoot, OF, Campbell	33
Bryce Kelley, OF, Michigan State	33
Connor Kopach, INF, Southern Illinois	33

RUNS

Rank Player, Pos., Team	R
1. Matt Sanders, INF, Troy	90
2. Alex Junior, OF, Tennessee Tech	81
Seth Lancaster, SS, Coastal Carolina	81
4. Chase Chambers, 1B, Tennessee Tech	80
5. Devlin Granberg, OF, Dallas Baptist	72
Trevor Larnach, OF, Oregon State	72
Josh Stowers, OF, Louisville	72
8. Trey Truitt, OF, Mercer	71
Kevin Woodall, 1B, Coastal Carolina	71
10. Michael Busch, 1B, North Carolina	70
Tyler Frank, SS, Florida Atlantic	70
Cadyn Grenier, SS, Oregon State	70

John Ham, INF, Tennessee Tech 70
Gabe Holt, 2B, Texas Tech 70
Luke Reynolds, 3B, Southern Miss. 70

HITS

Rank Player, Pos., Team	H
1. Devlin Granberg, OF, Dallas Baptist	112
2. Kevin Strohschein, OF, Tenn. Tech	106
3. Josh Jung, 3B, Texas Tech	103
4. Adley Rutschman, C, Oregon State	102
5. Chase Chambers, 1B, Tennessee Tech	101
Jake Mangum, OF, Mississippi State	101
Ryan Ward, OF, Bryant	101
8. Matt Sanders, INF, Troy	99
9. Braxton Morris, INF, Morehead State	98
10. Joey Denison, INF, Troy	97

TOTAL BASES

Rank Player, Pos., Team	TB
1. Kevin Strohschein, OF, Tenn. Tech	184
2. Kody Clemens, 2B, Texas	180
3. Devlin Granberg, OF, Dallas Baptist	172
4. Josh Jung, 3B, Texas Tech	168
5. Chase Chambers, 1B, Tennessee Tech	167
- Trevor Larnach, OF, Oregon State	167
7. Matt Pita, INF, Virginia Military Inst.	163
Andrew Vaughn, 1B, California	163
9. Jonathan India, 3B, Florida	162
10. Nic Ready, INF, Air Force	160

WALKS

Rank Player, Pos., Team	BB
1. Cade Harris, INF, Oklahoma	66

2. Luke Reynolds, 3B, Southern Miss.	65
3. Seth Lancaster, SS, Coastal Carolina	63
Logan Wyatt, 1B, Louisville	63
5. Jonathan India, 3B, Florida	60
Tre Todd, C, Liberty	60
7. Devin Mann, 2B, Louisville	59
8. Chas Hadden, C, Belmont	57
9. Alex Junior, OF, Tennessee Tech	56
10. Michael Busch, 1B, North Carolina	55
Reid Leonard, INF, Morehead State	55

TOUGHEST TO STRIKE OUT

Rank Player, Pos., Team	AB/SO
1. Clayton Andrews, OF, Long Beach St.	35.8
2. Bobby Honeyman, INF, Stony Brook	30.1
3. Clayton Daniel, INF, Jacksonville St.	25.5
4. Adan Ordonez, C, N.C. A&T	24.9
5. Ryan Ward, OF, Bryant	24.7
6. John Valente, 3B, St. John's	21.5
7. Ryan Kemp, 2B, Middle Tenn. State	20.6
8. Will Brennan, OF, Kansas State	20.0
9. Josh Shaw, 2B, St. John's	17.8
10. Michael Coritz, INF, Navy	16.9

HIT BY PITCH

Rank Player, Pos., Team	HBP
1. Dallas Oliver, OF, Florida A&M	28
2. Roberto Enriquez, OF, Indiana State	27
3. Ethan Valdez, INF, Nicholls State	26
Austen Zente, OF, High Point	26
5. Zach Heeke, INF, Central Michigan	25
6. Matthew Barefoot, OF, Campbell	23
Steven Curry, INF, Georgia Southern	23

Andrew Orzel, INF, Wofford	23
9. Tristen Carranza, INF, New Mexico St.	21
Joey Cooper, OF, Cal State Northridge	21
Brian Davis, INF, Florida A&M	21
Tyler Fris, OF, Maryland-Eastern Shore	21
Billy Godrick, OF, Fordham	21

SACRIFICE BUNTS

Rank Player, Pos., Team	SAC
1. Haiden Lamb, OF, Va. Commonwealth	23
2. Jonathan Weeks, INF, Hawaii	22
3. Mitchell Berryhill, OF, Cal St. Fullerton	21
4. J.T. Jarrett, INF, North Carolina State	20
Chris Lehane, OF, Jacksonville	20
6. Tyler Anshaw, INF, Campbell	16
Cadyn Grenier, SS, Oregon State	16
Devin Hager, INF, Eastern Michigan	16
Hal Hughes, INF, Louisiana State	16
Brett Rasso, OF, Saint Mary's	16

SACRIFICE FLYS

Rank Player, Pos., Team	SF
1. Ike Freeman, SS, North Carolina	11
Kyle Mendenhall, INF, Oklahoma	11
3. Peyton Burdick, OF, Wright State	10
Joey Denison, INF, Troy	10
Jimmy Glowenke, SS, Dallas Baptist	10
6. Nick Anderson, UTL, UC Irvine	9
James Bleming, SS, Lehigh	9
Garrett Chrstman, UTL, Butler	9
Devin Mann, 2B, Louisville	9
Trevor Putzig, INF, Tennessee Tech	9
Wesley Reyes, INF, Jackson State	9

PITCHING (MINIMUM 40 INNINGS PITCHED)

Rk. Pitcher, Team	Class	W	L	ERA	G	GS	SV	IP	H	R	ER	BB	SO
1. Nick Sandlin, Southern Mississippi	Jr.	10	0	1.06	15	15	0	102	55	15	12	18	144
2. John Rooney, Hofstra	Jr.	8	2	1.23	13	13	0	95	51	15	13	27	108
3. Carter Love, College of Charleston	Sr.	7	0	1.38	26	0	4	72	54	17	11	9	57
4. Ryan Campbell, Illinois-Chicago	Sr.	8	3	1.53	13	13	0	94	75	20	16	19	68
5. Frank German, North Florida	Jr.	8	4	1.58	14	14	0	91	62	20	16	14	108
6. Andre Pallante, UC Irvine	So.	10	1	1.60	15	15	0	101	77	24	18	30	115
7. Charlie Cerny, Illinois-Chicago	Jr.	5	3	1.63	21	5	1	55	32	19	10	12	64
8. Robert Broom, Mercer	Jr.	10	4	1.70	31	1	2	74	57	22	14	24	111
9. Danny Barlok, Holy Cross	Jr.	5	2	1.71	20	0	4	53	32	11	10	28	74
10. Kyle Brnovich, Elon	So.	8	2	1.71	15	15	0	105	57	31	20	36	147
11. Stephen Schoch, Maryland-Baltimore County	So.	2	6	1.72	24	0	10	58	42	12	11	19	71
12. Patrick Fredrickson, Minnesota	Fr.	9	0	1.86	19	15	0	97	71	26	20	27	73
13. Ricky DeVito, Seton Hall	So.	6	3	1.88	12	12	0	62	42	20	13	22	67
14. Jerry Maddox, Northwestern State	Jr.	8	3	1.88	16	15	0	86	54	23	18	37	66
15. Cole Whitney, Georgia Southern	Jr.	4	1	1.90	26	3	2	62	43	18	13	26	53
16. Noah Song, Navy	Jr.	6	5	1.92	14	14	0	89	55	26	19	41	121
17. Taso Stathopoulos, Rhode Island	Sr.	4	1	1.95	11	8	0	55	49	15	12	12	36
18. Clayton Andrews, Long Beach State	Jr.	7	7	1.99	15	15	0	100	78	27	22	17	118
19. Pauly Milto, Indiana	Jr.	8	2	2.03	14	13	0	80	66	22	18	24	66
20. John Barr, New Orleans	Jr.	6	3	2.04	30	0	0	66	48	24	15	25	68
21. Ken Waldichuk, St. Mary's	So.	8	4	2.05	14	14	0	92	68	25	21	21	118
22. Rion Murrah, High Point	Sr.	5	3	2.07	24	0	6	57	42	17	13	14	55
23. Joey Gonzalez, Stetson	Jr.	8	3	2.07	15	11	0	78	60	21	18	32	79
24. Reid Birlingmair, Illinois-Chicago	Jr.	6	1	2.12	10	8	0	51	39	12	12	21	57
25. Drew Reveno, Saint Louis	Jr.	10	2	2.13	18	11	0	68	48	20	16	29	52
26. Jack Maynard, UNC Greensboro	Sr.	5	3	2.13	29	0	0	63	57	17	15	11	81
27. Jake Bird, UCLA	Sr.	7	4	2.18	16	16	0	112	111	45	27	33	61
28. Wyatt Burns, Samford	Sr.	5	4	2.19	28	1	13	66	45	19	16	13	79
29. Aaron Fletcher, Houston	Jr.	7	3	2.19	16	15	0	94	86	30	23	18	78
30. Ryan Garcia, UCLA	So.	8	1	2.23	22	12	0	77	52	25	19	23	76
31. Logan Bailey, Louisiana Tech	Jr.	8	1	2.24	14	14	0	76	72	25	19	17	60
32. Josh Maciejewski, UNC Charlotte	Sr.	9	2	2.25	15	15	0	104	81	31	26	24	104
33. Daniel Federman, Miami	Fr.	2	4	2.25	23	4	0	60	45	27	15	22	54
34. David Leal, Louisiana Tech	Jr.	4	4	2.27	14	13	1	87	66	26	22	13	81
35. Seth Kinker, Ohio State	Sr.	6	2	2.27	30	0	15	63	57	25	16	5	60
36. Sean Mellen, Northeastern	So.	10	3	2.28	14	13	0	79	49	20	20	37	81
37. Ethan Roberts, Tennessee Tech	Jr.	6	1	2.30	28	1	15	78	65	21	20	22	103

Rank	Pitcher, Team	Class	W	L	ERA	G	GS	SV	IP	H	R	ER	BB	SO
38.	Tanner Foster, Northern Illinois	Jr.	2	4	2.33	12	11	0	70	63	33	18	22	76
39.	Samuel Strickland, Samford	Fr.	8	2	2.33	15	14	0	81	52	28	21	15	87
40.	Kent Klyman, North Carolina State	So.	8	2	2.34	31	0	4	62	46	22	16	25	67
41.	Connor Van Hoose, Bucknell	Sr.	8	4	2.36	12	12	0	76	54	24	20	31	108
42.	Darrius Wright, Alabama State	Jr.	8	1	2.36	12	12	0	72	61	38	19	41	56
43.	Colton Eastman, Cal State Fullerton	Jr.	10	4	2.37	17	17	0	118	89	38	31	28	124
44.	Ryan Tapani, Creighton	Sr.	10	1	2.38	14	14	0	95	83	27	25	25	95
45.	Reiss Knehr, Fordham	Jr.	6	3	2.40	15	15	0	90	72	27	24	48	93
46.	Josh Dye, Florida Gulf Coast	Jr.	8	4	2.40	14	14	0	94	79	33	25	16	74
47.	Ben Greenberg, Fordham	Sr.	6	2	2.41	15	15	0	82	68	25	22	31	65
48.	Parker Brahms, Sacramento State	So.	4	5	2.41	18	17	1	93	79	35	25	25	113
49.	Nick Allgeyer, Iowa	Jr.	5	4	2.41	15	15	0	97	85	35	26	28	95
50.	Joe DeMers, Washington	Jr.	7	3	2.42	20	17	3	130	103	39	35	21	94
51.	Addison Moss, Rice	So.	4	2	2.43	15	11	1	63	60	26	17	16	53
52.	Brendan Beck, Stanford	Fr.	8	0	2.43	17	12	1	67	56	19	18	12	38
53.	Sean Kamhoot, Navy	Sr.	5	1	2.44	14	14	0	85	85	26	23	22	55
54.	Joey Murray, Kent State	Jr.	9	2	2.45	16	16	0	96	54	27	26	40	141
55.	Colten Schmidt, Louisiana-Lafayette	Sr.	7	0	2.46	16	15	0	106	83	31	29	9	90
56.	Carlos Vega, Southeast Missouri State	Sr.	8	3	2.46	20	9	0	73	60	25	20	24	85
57.	Zach Mort, George Mason	Jr.	6	3	2.48	15	15	0	105	93	30	29	13	108
58.	Luke DeVenney, Eastern Michigan	Sr.	6	2	2.49	15	15	0	94	94	31	26	40	56
59.	Daniel Bies, Gonzaga	Jr.	7	4	2.49	16	16	0	112	93	33	31	25	124
60.	Mason Feole, Connecticut	So.	9	2	2.50	16	16	0	101	82	33	28	49	120
61.	Mitchell Senger, Stetson	So.	9	2	2.51	15	13	0	93	66	34	26	28	114
62.	Ryan Miller, Clemson	Sr.	7	1	2.51	26	0	4	72	63	22	20	17	64
63.	Cody Bradford, Baylor	So.	7	6	2.51	14	14	0	97	85	29	27	26	87
64.	Drew Parrish, Florida State	So.	5	1	2.52	16	16	0	107	71	35	30	37	128
65.	Justin Lasko, Massachusetts	Jr.	5	4	2.52	12	12	0	82	76	28	23	20	63
66.	J.J. Montgomery, Central Florida	Jr.	6	4	2.55	17	8	1	64	54	29	18	21	74
67.	Brady Singer, Florida	Jr.	12	3	2.55	17	17	0	113	84	42	32	22	114
68.	Robbie Baker, Richmond	Sr.	9	2	2.55	15	15	0	85	65	32	24	23	78
69.	Sean Mooney, St. John's	So.	11	3	2.56	16	16	0	95	74	28	27	28	104
70.	Connor Gillispie, Virginia Commonwealth	So.	7	3	2.57	18	18	0	74	62	25	21	20	97
71.	T.J. Stuart, Manhattan	So.	6	2	2.57	25	2	10	63	38	20	18	27	50
72.	Chris Gau, Jacksonville	Jr.	9	3	2.58	16	16	0	112	90	41	32	21	95
73.	Riley Ornido, San Francisco	So.	8	5	2.58	15	14	0	98	63	34	28	32	95
74.	Kris Bubic, Stanford	Jr.	8	1	2.62	15	15	0	86	60	28	25	32	101
75.	Ryan Pepiot, Butler	So.	6	0	2.62	15	12	1	76	55	23	22	32	101
76.	Adam Wolf, Louisville	Jr.	8	2	2.63	16	16	0	103	80	38	30	29	109
77.	Chance Kirby, Texas-San Antonio	Sr.	7	4	2.63	13	13	0	65	48	29	19	18	62
78.	Miller Hogan, Saint Louis	Jr.	10	4	2.64	16	16	0	106	82	38	31	14	133
79.	Sean Hunley, Tennessee	Fr.	7	3	2.64	15	14	0	75	77	25	22	18	53
80.	Cam Opp, Army	Jr.	5	2	2.66	25	6	4	61	48	29	18	25	72
81.	Jordan Wood, Brigham Young	Jr.	5	4	2.66	14	14	0	95	74	34	28	29	63
82.	Jahmon Taylor, Coppin State	Jr.	6	4	2.66	13	11	0	71	58	28	21	34	81
83.	Kevin Magee, St. John's	Sr.	7	3	2.67	15	14	0	78	73	28	23	15	92
84.	Jose Tirado, Jackson State	Sr.	6	2	2.67	31	0	13	64	40	20	19	13	74
85.	Kyle Bradish, New Mexico State	Jr.	9	3	2.67	17	17	0	101	72	43	30	55	140
86.	Carlisle Koestler, Southeastern Louisiana	Jr.	7	1	2.68	16	14	1	87	70	28	26	13	73
87.	Jonathan Pendergast, Pepperdine	Jr.	7	4	2.69	14	10	0	87	84	32	26	18	67
88.	John Doxakis, Texas A&M	So.	8	5	2.70	17	14	0	93	72	37	28	29	92
89.	Tommy Wilson, Cal State Fullerton	Jr.	7	0	2.71	20	13	0	90	81	31	27	22	81
90.	Simon Rosenblum-Larson, Harvard	Jr.	4	2	2.71	11	11	0	63	52	30	19	26	82
91.	Logan Gilbert, Stetson	Jr.	11	2	2.72	16	16	0	112	71	37	34	25	163
92.	J.P. Stevenson, Canisius	Sr.	10	2	2.73	17	16	0	99	71	38	30	21	93
93.	Allan Winans, Campbell	Sr.	6	4	2.73	15	14	0	82	71	32	25	24	96
94.	Brian Brown, North Carolina State	Sr.	7	2	2.74	16	16	0	99	84	38	30	26	98
95.	Andrew Crane, Troy	Sr.	7	4	2.74	16	16	0	99	87	34	30	34	87
96.	Tyler LaPlante, Missouri	Jr.	4	3	2.75	13	10	0	59	44	20	18	17	56
97.	Ben Dragani, Michigan	Fr.	6	2	2.76	16	11	0	75	61	27	23	26	54
98.	Elliott Raimo, George Washington	So.	3	4	2.76	12	12	0	72	56	28	22	14	72
99.	Eric Brodkowitz, Yale	Sr.	6	2	2.76	12	12	0	85	66	27	26	21	57
100.	Aaron Shortridge, California	Jr.	5	3	2.77	17	12	2	91	89	30	28	14	74

WINS

Rank Pitcher, Team	W
1. Luke Heimlich, Oregon State	16
2. Blaine Knight, Arkansas	14
3. Travis Moths, Tennessee Tech	13
4. Brady Singer, Florida	12
5. Logan Gilbert, Stetson	11
Jonathan Groff, New Mexico State	11
Sean Mooney, St. John's	11
Jack Perkins, Stetson	11
Austin Root, Sacramento State	11

SAVES

Rank Pitcher, Team	SV
1. Chris Mauloni, Jacksonville	20
Brooks Wilson, Stetson	20
3. Jack Little, Stanford	16
Max Meyer, Minnesota	16
Mac McCarty, Virginia Commonwealth	16
Jake Mulholland, Oregon State	16
P.J. Poulin, Connecticut	16
Michael Byrne, Florida	16
9. Zach Schneider, Florida Atlantic	15
Ethan Roberts, Tennessee Tech	15
Ross Learnard, Purdue	15
Seth Kinker, Ohio State	15

Dakota Mills, Sam Houston State   15

STRIKEOUTS

Rank Pitcher, Team	SO
1. Logan Gilbert, Stetson	163
2. Luke Heimlich, Oregon State	159
3. Casey Mize, Auburn	156
4. Kyle Brnovich, Elon	147
5. Nick Sandlin, Southern Mississippi	144
6. Joey Murray, Kent State	141
7. Kyle Bradish, New Mexico State	140
8. Adam Scott, Wofford	137
9. Miller Hogan, Saint Louis	133
10. Griffin Roberts, Wake Forest	130

STRIKEOUTS PER NINE

Rank Pitcher, Team	SO/9
1. R.J. Freure, Pittsburgh	14.57

Rank Pitcher, Team	
2. Shane McClanahan, South Florida	14.15
3. Robert Broom, Mercer	13.50
4. Jake Lee, Oakland	13.38
5. Joey Murray, Kent State	13.26
6. Andrew Wantz, UNC Greensboro	13.25
7. Logan Gilbert, Stetson	13.06
8. Austin Cox, Mercer	12.73
9. Connor Van Hoose, Bucknell	12.69
10. Nick Sandlin, Southern Mississippi	12.66

FEWEST HITS PER NINE

Rank Pitcher, Team	H/9
1. John Rooney, Hofstra	4.83
2. Nick Sandlin, Southern Mississippi	4.84
3. Kyle Brnovich, Elon	4.89
4. Joey Murray, Kent State	5.08
5. Charlie Cerny, Illinois-Chicago	5.20
6. T.J. Stuart, Manhattan	5.43

Rank Pitcher, Team	
7. Danny Barlok, Holy Cross	5.47
8. Jeff Belge, St. John's	5.54
9. Noah Song, Navy	5.56
10. Sean Mellen, Northeastern	5.58

FEWEST WALKS PER NINE

Rank Pitcher, Team	BB/9
1. Tim Brennan, Saint Joseph's	0.51
2. Seth Kinker, Ohio State	0.71
3. Jordan Silverman, Rider	0.73
4. Colten Schmidt, Louisiana-Lafayette	0.76
5. Garrett Stallings, Tennessee	0.92
6. Connor Thomas, Georgia Tech	0.93
7. Josh Agnew, Loyola Marymount	0.94
8. Matthew McCollough, Hou. Baptist	1.00
9. Zach Mort, George Mason	1.11
10. Carter Love, College of Charleston	1.13

TEAM LEADERS

SCORING

Rank Team	G	R	R/G
1. Tennessee Tech	65	639	9.8
2. Morehead State	63	529	8.4
3. Texas Tech	65	529	8.1
4. Coastal Carolina	62	499	8.0
5. Mercer	60	479	8.0
6. Southern Mississippi	62	493	8.0
New Mexico State	62	493	8.0
8. Wright State	56	435	7.8
9. Oregon State	68	518	7.6
10. Dallas Baptist	63	467	7.4
11. Air Force	54	400	7.4
12. Murray State	56	410	7.3
13. UNC Greensboro	54	394	7.3
14. Eastern Kentucky	61	445	7.3
15. Nevada-Las Vegas	59	423	7.2
16. Kentucky	56	397	7.1
17. Auburn	66	467	7.1
18. Jacksonville State	57	403	7.1
Austin Peay State	57	403	7.1
20. North Carolina	64	452	7.1
21. Northern Colorado	53	374	7.1
22. Troy	63	442	7.0
23. Arkansas	69	482	7.0
24. North Carolina State	60	419	7.0
25. Mississippi	65	451	6.9
26. UCLA	59	409	6.9
27. Alabama State	52	360	6.9
28. Louisville	64	443	6.9
29. Grambling State	52	359	6.9
30. Canisius	57	393	6.9
31. Arizona	56	385	6.9
32. Jackson State	52	357	6.9
33. Bradley	51	350	6.9
34. Kent State	58	394	6.8
35. Nevada	53	357	6.7
36. Minnesota	59	397	6.7
37. Texas Southern	55	370	6.7
38. South Alabama	57	383	6.7
39. Bryant	56	376	6.7
40. Saint Louis	58	388	6.7
41. Florida State	62	414	6.7
42. Wofford	59	393	6.7
43. Illinois State	52	346	6.7
44. Virginia Military Inst.	53	352	6.6
45. Indiana State	55	365	6.6
46. Duke	63	416	6.6
47. Wichita State	57	375	6.6
48. Niagara	51	335	6.6
49. Florida	70	459	6.6
50. California	54	353	6.5

BATTING AVERAGE

Rank Team	AVG
1. Tennessee Tech	.332
2. UNC Greensboro	.326
3. Oregon State	.321
4. Morehead State	.316
5. New Mexico State	.310
6. Nevada-Las Vegas	.310
7. Air Force	.310
8. Texas Tech	.309
9. Jackson State	.303
10. Bryant	.303

HOME RUNS

Rank Team	HR
1. Tennessee Tech	135
2. Florida	100
3. Clemson	98
Arkansas	98
5. North Carolina State	87
6. Dallas Baptist	86
7. Morehead State	83
8. Texas Tech	82
9. Kentucky	81
Coastal Carolina	81

DOUBLES

Rank Team	2B
1. Oregon State	151
2. Dallas Baptist	150
3. South Florida	147
4. Coastal Carolina	145
5. Morehead State	144
6. Texas Tech	142
7. Mississippi State	141
Tennessee Tech	141
Nevada-Las Vegas	141
10. Florida	134

TRIPLES

Rank Team	3B
1. Troy	30
UNC Greensboro	30
3. New Mexico State	25
4. Arizona State	24
Texas Tech	24
Navy	24
7. Stetson	23
Northeastern	23
9. Texas	22
Duke	22

SLUGGING PERCENTAGE

Rank Team	SLG
1. Tennessee Tech	.576
2. Texas Tech	.503
3. Morehead State	.498
4. Dallas Baptist	.495
5. Kentucky	.491
6. Oregon State	.488
7. Nevada-Las Vegas	.487
8. Coastal Carolina	.485
9. New Mexico State	.478
10. North Carolina State	.477

STOLEN BASES

Rank Team	SB
1. Fordham	169
2. Wofford	148
3. Southeastern Louisiana	136
4. Southern Illinois	131
5. Louisville	125
6. Troy	117
7. Texas Southern	115
8. Wright State	110
9. Central Florida	109
10. George Washington	105

WALKS

Rank Team	BB
1. Florida State	390
2. Tennessee Tech	371
3. Coastal Carolina	359
4. Liberty	356
5. Texas Tech	355
6. Clemson	350
7. North Carolina	346
8. Dallas Baptist	338
9. Oregon State	336
10. Louisville	333

PITCHING

EARNED RUN AVERAGE

Rank Team	ERA
1. Stetson	2.66
2. Stanford	2.83
3. Illinois-Chicago	2.98
4. College of Charleston	3.06
5. St. John's	3.08
6. UCLA	3.08
7. Indiana	3.09
8. Navy	3.10
9. Gonzaga	3.12
10. Minnesota	3.23
11. Baylor	3.24
12. Oregon State	3.29
13. Central Florida	3.32
14. Fordham	3.36
15. Elon	3.37
16. Texas A&M	3.38
17. East Carolina	3.41
18. Northwestern State	3.41
19. Saint Mary's	3.42
20. Cal State Fullerton	3.45
21. Texas Christian	3.45
22. Florida	3.46
23. Michigan	3.46
24. Saint Louis	3.47
25. Louisiana Tech	3.48
26. UNC Wilmington	3.50
27. Louisville	3.53
28. Texas-San Antonio	3.54
29. Arkansas	3.55
30. Hofstra	3.59
31. Virginia Commonwealth	3.61
32. Samford	3.61
33. North Carolina State	3.62
34. Southeastern Louisiana	3.62
35. Clemson	3.65
36. Sacramento State	3.66
37. Southern Mississippi	3.70
38. Richmond	3.70
39. Rhode Island	3.71
40. Miami	3.72
41. Missouri	3.73
42. North Carolina	3.75
43. UC Irvine	3.76
44. Kent State	3.76
45. Sam Houston State	3.78
46. Yale	3.78
47. San Francisco	3.78
48. Long Beach State	3.80
49. Wright State	3.80
50. Washington	3.81

STRIKEOUTS PER NINE

Rank Team	SO/9
1. Mercer	10.9
2. Virginia	10.5
3. Stetson	10.5
4. Florida State	10.2
5. South Florida	10.0
6. Ball State	9.9
7. Central Florida	9.8
8. UNC Greensboro	9.8
9. North Carolina	9.8
10. Elon	9.7

FEWEST WALKS PER NINE

Rank Team	BB/9
1. College of Charleston	2.32
2. Sacramento State	2.37
3. Southeastern Louisiana	2.47
4. Southern Mississippi	2.49
5. Cal State Fullerton	2.57
6. Dartmouth	2.75
7. East Carolina	2.79
8. Saint Mary's	2.82
9. Incarnate Word	2.86
10. Washington	2.93

FIELDING

FIELDING PERCENTAGE

Rank Team	PCT
1. Yale	.985
2. Gonzaga	.984
3. UCLA	.982
4. Virginia Commonwealth	.981
5. Vanderbilt	.981
6. Duke	.981
7. South Carolina	.980
8. Missouri	.980
9. Georgia	.979
10. Wright State	.979
11. Louisiana-Lafayette	.979
12. Oregon State	.979
13. College of Charleston	.979
14. Illinois	.979
15. Louisiana State	.979
16. Navy	.978
17. Southern California	.978
18. Mississippi	.978
19. San Jose State	.978
20. South Alabama	.978
21. Texas	.978
22. East Carolina	.978
23. Stanford	.978
24. Stony Brook	.978
25. UNC Greensboro	.978
26. New Mexico State	.977
27. Dallas Baptist	.977
28. Creighton	.977
29. Liberty	.977
30. Central Arkansas	.977
31. Washington	.977
32. Miami (Ohio)	.977
33. Loyola Marymount	.977
34. Florida	.977
35. Washington State	.977
36. Indiana	.977
37. Cal State Northridge	.977
38. Oregon	.977
39. Houston	.977
40. Sacramento State	.976
41. Illinois State	.976
42. Air Force	.976
43. Minnesota	.976
44. Troy	.976
45. Hofstra	.976
46. Saint Joseph's	.976
47. Kent State	.975
48. Missouri State	.975
49. Pittsburgh	.975
50. Illinois-Chicago	.975

DOUBLE PLAYS

Rank Team	DP
1. Texas	73
2. Cincinnati	71
3. Northwestern State	70
4. Morehead State	66
5. Mississippi State	63
6. Nicholls State	61
Duke	61
8. Arkansas	60
9. Air Force	58
San Francisco	58
Nevada-Las Vegas	58
Jacksonville State	58

1. OREGON STATE

Coach: Pat Casey. **Record:** 55-12-1

Player, Pos., Year	AVG	OBP	SLG	AB	R	2B	3B	HR	RBI	SB
Anderson, Jack, OF, R-Sr.	.268	.366	.333	168	36	9	1	0	15	1
Armstrong, Andy, INF, So.	.262	.333	.434	122	18	13	1	2	20	2
Casey, Joe, OF, R-Fr.	.500	.611	.643	14	5	2	0	0	2	0
Claunch, Troy, C, Fr.	.321	.512	.571	28	9	1	0	2	10	0
Clayton, Zach, INF/OF, Fr.	.000	.000	.000	6	1	0	0	0	0	0
Grenier, Cadyn, INF, Jr.	.319	.408	.462	273	70	17	2	6	47	9
Gretler, Michael, INF, Sr.	.305	.379	.473	262	43	21	1	7	51	1
Jones, Preston, OF, So.	.288	.342	.411	73	13	6	0	1	12	3
Kwan, Steven, OF, Jr.	.355	.463	.457	256	60	8	6	2	41	14
Larnach, Trevor, OF, Jr.	.348	.463	.652	256	72	19	1	19	77	4
Madrigal, Nick, INF, Jr.	.367	.428	.511	180	41	9	4	3	34	15
Malone, Tyler, INF, So.	.278	.405	.477	151	28	6	0	8	32	1
McMahan, Kyler, INF, Fr.	.000	.125	.000	7	3	0	0	0	0	0
Nobach, Kyle, OF, R-Sr.	.299	.413	.538	117	27	10	0	6	31	0
Ober, Ryan, INF, Fr.	.000	.222	.000	7	4	0	0	0	0	0
Rutschman, Adley, C/INF, So.	.408	.505	.628	250	56	22	3	9	83	1
Taylor, Zak, C/INF, Jr.	.274	.339	.366	164	31	7	1	2	22	0
Willy, Elliot, OF, R-Fr.	.333	.333	.667	3	0	1	0	0	1	0
Zalesky, Zack, C/INF, R-Fr.	.125	.182	.125	8	1	0	0	0	2	0

Pitcher, Year	W	L	ERA	G	GS	SV	IP	H	BB	SO
Abel, Kevin, Fr.	8	1	2.88	23	7	1	81	51	46	108
Britton, Jordan, Jr.	2	0	3.18	8	3	0	17	19	4	9
Burns, Nathan, Fr.	1	1	5.52	10	1	0	15	15	11	14
Chamberlain, Christian, Fr.	3	0	3.54	20	3	0	41	29	28	49
Donovan, Dakota, R-Fr.	0	0	3.86	4	0	1	7	4	6	6
Eisert, Brandon, So.	5	3	2.53	27	0	5	57	44	12	52
Fehmel, Bryce, Jr.	10	1	3.19	20	20	0	113	98	27	64
Gambrell, Grant, So.	5	1	4.40	14	12	0	57	53	29	57
Heimlich, Luke, Sr.	16	3	2.92	21	20	0	130	104	28	159
Mulholland, Jake, So.	2	2	2.20	31	0	16	45	30	11	42
Pearce, Dylan, Jr.	2	0	3.49	25	0	2	28	31	7	27
Tweedt, Sam, R-Jr.	1	0	7.16	10	2	0	16	15	12	9

2. ARKANSAS

Coach: Dave Van Horn. **Record:** 48-21

Player, Pos., Year	AVG	OBP	SLG	AB	R	2B	3B	HR	RBI	SB
Biggers, Jaxx, INF, Jr.	.280	.338	.382	207	35	9	0	4	26	7
Bonfield, Luke, OF, Sr.	.296	.426	.479	233	39	10	1	9	44	1
Cole, Eric, OF, Jr.	.313	.407	.520	281	64	14	1	14	52	4
Fletcher, Dominic, OF, So.	.288	.338	.468	267	43	16	1	10	49	1
Gates, Jared, INF, Sr.	.241	.348	.421	133	25	6	0	6	23	2
Kenley, Jack, INF, So.	.222	.389	.259	54	13	2	0	0	10	1
Kjerstad, Heston, OF, Fr.	.332	.419	.553	262	65	16	0	14	58	3
Koch, Grant, C, Jr.	.245	.358	.375	216	36	7	0	7	35	4
Lee, Evan, OF, So.	.300	.383	.520	50	11	2	0	3	15	1
Martin, Casey, INF, Fr.	.345	.418	.556	252	50	14	0	13	49	8
McFarland, Jordan, INF/OF, So.	.299	.379	.402	117	34	3	0	3	15	0
Murrell, Easton, INF, Fr.	.125	.462	.125	8	4	0	0	0	1	0
Opitz, Casey, C/INF, Fr.	.222	.303	.296	27	6	2	0	0	5	0
Plunkett, Zack, C, R-Jr.	.222	.300	.556	9	1	0	0	1	2	0
Shaddy, Carson, INF, R-Sr.	.330	.426	.609	197	45	12	2	13	55	4
Turney, Cole, OF, Fr.	.000	.222	.000	7	1	0	0	0	0	1
Wilson, Hunter, INF, R-Jr.	.283	.365	.391	46	10	2	0	1	12	2

Pitcher, Year	W	L	ERA	G	GS	SV	IP	H	BB	SO
Bolden, Caleb, Fr.	3	0	4.40	10	4	0	29	33	13	25
Bonnin, Bryce, Fr.	1	0	4.26	11	1	0	19	17	12	16
Campbell, Isaiah, R-So.	5	7	4.26	18	17	0	70	67	29	75
Cronin, Matt, So.	2	2	3.54	25	0	14	48	25	14	59
Knight, Blaine, Jr.	14	0	2.80	19	19	0	112	96	25	102
Kostyshock, Jacob, So.	0	0	6.43	9	0	1	14	19	8	10
Lee, Evan, So.	4	3	5.00	15	1	0	18	24	10	14
Loseke, Barrett, Jr.	4	2	2.68	27	2	4	54	37	27	68
McKinney, Keaton, R-Jr.	0	0	4.50	1	1	0	2	1	2	2
Milligan, Hunter, Jr.	0	0	4.50	3	2	0	4	2	3	4
Murphy, Kacey, Jr.	8	5	3.20	18	17	0	101	85	22	85
Ramage, Kole, Fr.	1	1	4.00	21	2	0	36	36	16	50
Reindl, Jake, Jr.	3	1	2.91	27	1	5	56	51	23	66
Rogers, Weston, Jr.	0	0	0.00	1	0	0	0	1	0	1
Rutledge, Jack, Fr.	3	0	3.45	12	2	1	16	13	11	14
Scroggins, Cody, R-So.	0	0	4.60	16	0	0	16	12	12	18
Vermillion, Zebulon, Fr.	0	0	4.82	7	0	1	9	12	0	11

3. FLORIDA

Coach: Kevin O'Sullivan. **Record:** 49-21

Player, Pos., Year	AVG	OBP	SLG	AB	R	2B	3B	HR	RBI	SB
Baker, Andrew, OF, So.	.250	.500	.375	8	8	1	0	0	0	1
Bell, Keenan, OF/INF, Jr.	.224	.301	.410	156	25	11	0	6	27	1
Butler, Jordan, INF/OF, Fr.	.308	.500	.385	13	3	1	0	0	2	0
Dalton, Wil, OF, So.	.262	.338	.542	275	60	18	1	19	60	8
Girand, Jonah, C, Jr.	.135	.238	.405	37	6	1	0	3	6	0
Greenfield, Cal, C, Fr.	.188	.278	.281	32	3	0	0	1	3	1
Horvath, Nick, INF, So.	.268	.339	.424	224	45	14	0	7	35	6
India, Jonathan, INF, Jr.	.350	.497	.717	226	66	12	4	21	52	15
Langworthy, Austin, OF, So.	.290	.404	.403	231	33	10	2	4	29	5
Liput, Deacon, INF, Jr.	.285	.375	.478	228	48	15	1	9	38	11
Maldonado, Nelson, OF, Jr.	.273	.359	.413	264	44	10	0	9	44	6
McConnell, Brady, INF, Fr.	.136	.136	.273	22	2	0	0	1	2	1
McMullen, Kirby, INF, So.	.250	.250	.375	8	1	1	0	0	1	0
Reese, Blake, INF, Jr.	.253	.375	.416	233	44	9	2	5	43	14
Schwarz, JJ, C/INF, Sr.	.308	.384	.575	221	51	16	2	13	48	4
Shifflett, Shane, INF/OF, Fr.	.256	.268	.282	39	2	1	0	0	7	0
Smith, Brady, C/INF, Fr.	.264	.322	.360	125	18	4	1	2	15	2

Pitcher, Year	W	L	ERA	G	GS	SV	IP	H	BB	SO
Baker, Andrew, So.	2	0	4.86	21	0	0	33	26	20	32
Butler, Jordan, Fr.	6	2	4.10	31	4	0	53	39	26	60
Byrne, Michael, Jr.	3	1	1.61	37	0	16	61	46	5	64
Churchill, Connor, Fr.	0	1	8.31	6	0	0	4	9	3	6
Dyson, Tyler, So.	5	3	4.47	14	11	0	50	50	28	51
Horvath, Nick, Sr.	0	0	9.82	3	0	0	4	4	1	2
Kowar, Jackson, Jr.	10	5	3.04	18	18	0	112	101	43	115
Langworthy, Austin, So.	0	1	2.70	4	0	0	7	10	0	1
Leftwich, Jack, Fr.	5	5	4.20	24	12	2	81	71	26	84
Long, Nick, So.	1	0	4.50	5	0	0	6	4	5	7
Mace, Tommy, Fr.	5	0	4.16	26	6	1	63	66	12	45
McMullen, Hunter, Fr.	0	0	4.76	17	2	0	23	24	14	17
McMullen, Kirby, So.	0	0	2.25	7	0	0	8	14	3	9
Singer, Brady, Jr.	12	3	2.55	17	17	0	113	84	22	114

4. NORTH CAROLINA

Coach: Mike Fox. **Record:** 44-20

Player, Pos., Year	AVG	OBP	SLG	AB	R	2B	3B	HR	RBI	SB
Brandenburg, Kip, OF/INF, So.	.296	.367	.481	27	3	2	0	1	9	0
Busch, Michael, INF, So.	.317	.465	.521	240	70	10	0	13	63	8
Casparius, Ben, INF, Fr.	.316	.409	.404	57	6	3	1	0	15	0
Datres, Kyle, INF, Jr.	.345	.438	.511	264	68	17	3	7	36	12
Enwiller, Dylan, OF/INF, Jr.	.239	.329	.310	71	17	2	0	1	7	4
Freeman, Ike, INF, So.	.305	.383	.377	223	37	5	1	3	51	3
Gahagan, Zack, INF, Sr.	.273	.365	.390	231	44	6	0	7	40	4
Hesterlee, Jackson, OF, Jr.	.316	.453	.439	57	10	4	0	1	10	0
Illies, Brendan, C, Jr.	.167	.375	.167	6	1	0	0	0	0	0
Inclan, Clemente, INF, Fr.	.267	.424	.311	45	8	2	0	0	10	0
Lancellotti, Joey, OF, Fr.	.500	.500	.500	2	1	0	0	0	0	0
Ladowski, Josh, OF, Jr.	.250	.333	.500	24	6	2	2	0	3	3
Martorano, Brandon, C/OF, So.	.246	.375	.491	171	34	11	2	9	36	0
McGee, Ashton, INF, So.	.257	.367	.366	191	26	7	4	2	28	2
Riley, Brandon, OF, Jr.	.284	.386	.416	250	43	14	2	5	55	6
Roberts, Cody, C/OF, Jr.	.278	.369	.403	216	49	12	0	5	41	4
Semper, Earl, OF, Fr.	.125	.300	.250	8	1	1	0	0	2	0
Tessar, Dallas, INF/OF, R-So.	.231	.319	.316	117	28	4	0	2	10	3
Zarate, Angel, OF, Fr.	.000	.125	.000	7	1	0	0	0	0	0

Pitcher, Year	W	L	ERA	G	GS	SV	IP	H	BB	SO
Baum, Tyler, So.	4	1	4.57	18	12	0	65	58	32	74
Bergner, Austin, So.	7	3	4.25	17	13	1	83	76	34	84
Blendinger, Kyle, Fr.	0	0	0.00	4	0	0	3	2	2	3

Player	W	L	ERA	G	GS	SV	IP	H	BB	SO
Butler, Hansen, R-Jr.	0	1	6.52	14	0	0	10	9	14	17
Casparius, Ben, Fr.	1	0	1.69	10	0	1	11	4	9	9
Criswell, Cooper, Jr.	6	2	2.99	26	9	1	75	71	12	86
Dalatri, Gianluca, So.	2	2	3.33	7	7	0	27	35	7	31
Daniels, Brett, Sr.	6	1	2.77	39	1	2	65	62	29	74
Gay, Trevor, Jr.	0	0	0.00	4	0	0	3	2	3	6
Hiatt, Josh, Jr.	3	2	3.73	31	0	6	51	46	19	52
Hutchison, Rodney, Jr.	3	3	4.55	23	10	0	59	65	16	56
Lancellotti, Joey, Fr.	3	3	3.96	28	1	1	39	26	18	43
O'Brien, Caden, Fr.	7	0	2.63	30	2	0	48	30	27	52
Sugg, Taylor, Jr.	2	1	5.40	12	9	0	33	36	19	32
Weiss, Bo, So.	0	0	3.37	6	0	0	3	3	7	4

5. TEXAS TECH

Coach: Tim Tadlock. **Record:** 45-20

Player, Pos., Year	AVG	OBP	SLG	AB	R	2B	3B	HR	RBI	SB
Beck, Connor, OF, Sr.	.086	.200	.086	35	5	0	0	0	2	2
Davis, Michael, INF, Sr.	.281	.371	.524	231	51	18	1	12	53	3
Farhat, Cody, OF, Jr.	.292	.418	.434	212	51	9	3	5	39	16
Fulford, Braxton, C, Fr.	.193	.324	.273	88	14	2	1	1	4	1
Holt, Gabe, INF, Fr.	.348	.440	.485	270	70	13	6	4	44	29
Jung, Josh, INF, So.	.392	.491	.639	263	69	17	6	12	80	4
Kelly, Parker, INF, Fr.	.083	.083	.083	12	1	0	0	0	0	0
Klein, Brian, INF, So.	.317	.422	.480	202	50	17	2	4	34	4
Koelzer, Clay, C, So.	.180	.333	.262	61	13	3	1	0	4	1
Little, Grant, INF, So.	.370	.462	.642	246	62	25	3	12	77	11
Masters, Cody, OF, Fr.	.258	.414	.364	66	23	5	1	0	14	2
McMillon, John, OF, So.	.143	.242	.286	28	6	1	1	0	6	0
Rheams, Zach, INF, Sr.	.341	.461	.713	167	40	11	0	17	55	0
Simonich, KC, INF/OF, Fr.	.444	.615	.444	9	2	0	0	0	7	0
Warren, Cameron, INF/OF, Jr.	.326	.444	.549	215	49	16	1	10	53	2
Willems, Zayne, C, Jr.	.250	.344	.357	84	16	4	1	1	9	0
Wilson, Kurt, INF, Fr.	.183	.296	.283	60	7	1	1	1	11	2

Pitcher, Year	W	L	ERA	G	GS	SV	IP	H	BB	SO
Candelari, Nick, Fr.	0	0	5.79	9	0	0	9	10	10	9
Davis, Andrew, So.	0	0	13.50	5	0	0	5	3	15	5
Dusek, Dylan, Sr.	3	0	2.18	20	5	0	33	29	13	31
Freeman, Caleb, So.	1	0	5.18	22	0	3	33	35	18	31
Gilbert, Richard, Fr.	0	0	17.36	7	0	0	5	7	9	5
Gingery, Steven, Jr.	0	0	0.00	1	1	0	2	0	0	3
Gonzalez, John Henry, So.	0	0	6.23	11	0	0	17	23	10	24
Herpenau, Ty, Jr.	7	2	3.59	27	0	4	58	45	26	55
Haveman, Dane, So.	0	1	11.12	14	0	3	11	12	13	14
Kelly, Parker, Fr.	0	0	0.00	2	0	0	2	3	1	0
Kilian, Caleb, So.	9	3	3.24	20	11	0	72	60	28	63
Lanning, Erikson, Jr.	0	0	6.75	2	2	0	5	7	4	3
Martin, Davis, Jr.	7	6	4.87	17	17	0	78	79	37	81
McMillon, John, So.	5	3	4.02	17	12	0	63	63	47	73
Queen, Connor, So.	1	0	4.20	18	1	0	30	29	17	11
Quezada, Jose, Sr.	5	2	2.21	22	0	2	37	19	21	41
Shetter, Ryan, Jr.	6	0	2.97	21	8	3	73	54	27	79
Sublette, Ryan, Fr.	0	3	9.49	13	0	0	25	39	22	20
Wilson, Kurt, Fr.	1	0	8.10	17	0	0	13	13	19	17

6. MISSISSIPPI STATE

Coach: Chris Lemonis. **Record:** 39-29

Player, Pos., Year	AVG	OBP	SLG	AB	R	2B	3B	HR	RBI	SB
Alexander, Luke, INF, Jr.	.221	.309	.326	267	37	10	0	6	49	1
Allen, Tanner, INF/OF, Fr.	.287	.353	.444	275	42	18	5	5	45	0
Anderson, Jordan, OF, Fr.	.313	.400	.313	16	11	0	0	0	3	0
Foscue, Justin, INF, Fr.	.241	.332	.353	187	24	12	0	3	20	0
Gilbert, Marshall, C, Jr.	.254	.341	.386	114	18	9	0	2	18	0
Hatcher, Josh, INF, Fr.	.259	.345	.333	174	25	4	0	3	16	4
Jordan, Rowdey, INF, Fr.	.321	.390	.518	193	39	15	1	7	37	2
MacNamee, Elijah, OF/INF, Jr.	.309	.377	.495	188	40	11	0	8	42	1
Mangum, Jake, OF, Sr.	.351	.434	.479	288	63	22	3	3	33	14
Pener, Alex, INF, Jr.	.000	.417	.000	7	1	0	0	0	0	0
Poole, Tanner, OF, R-Sr.	.227	.301	.320	75	13	1	0	2	7	2
Skelton, Dustin, C, So.	.238	.338	.320	122	18	7	0	1	13	0
Stovall, Hunter, INF, Jr.	.321	.369	.429	280	46	16	4	2	42	10
Vansau, Hunter, OF, Jr.	.191	.252	.282	110	13	5	1	1	12	0
Westburg, Jordan, INF, Fr.	.248	.319	.388	121	18	10	0	2	30	0

Pitcher, Year	W	L	ERA	G	GS	SV	IP	H	BB	SO
Barlow, Trysten, R-So.	0	0	13.50	4	0	0	3	3	4	3
Billingsley, Jacob, R-Sr.	5	4	5.57	19	18	0	73	81	41	71
Breaux, Kale, R-So.	0	0	5.40	4	0	0	2	0	6	3
France, JP, Gr.	5	5	3.77	25	2	2	60	57	26	65
Gordon, Cole, R-Jr.	4	3	4.26	30	1	4	61	51	32	68
Hatcher, Josh, Fr.	0	0	0.00	3	0	0	3	2	2	6
James, Keegan, R-So.	1	2	4.34	26	0	0	48	58	19	45
Liebelt, Jared, Jr.	0	0	13.15	12	1	0	13	21	8	7
Marsh, Cole, So.	1	0	4.70	9	2	0	15	15	4	8
McQuary, Denver, So.	2	2	5.54	19	6	2	39	50	26	31
Neff, Zach, Gr.	4	3	3.52	27	2	2	46	51	9	41
Pilkington, Konnor, Jr.	3	6	4.47	18	18	0	103	106	33	107
Self, Riley, So.	5	0	3.51	18	0	1	26	20	12	20
Small, Ethan, R-So.	5	4	3.20	18	18	0	101	93	33	122
Smith, Blake, R-Sr.	4	0	3.52	18	0	3	23	20	11	22

7. TEXAS

Coach: David Pierce. **Record:** 42-23

Player, Pos., Year	AVG	OBP	SLG	AB	R	2B	3B	HR	RBI	SB
Baker, Joe, INF, R-Jr.	.333	.500	.333	6	3	0	0	0	1	0
Bertelson, Sam, INF, Fr.	.000	.188	.000	13	1	0	0	0	0	0
Clemens, Kody, INF, Jr.	.351	.444	.726	248	58	15	3	24	72	5
Ellis, Duke, OF, So.	.289	.398	.353	201	39	4	3	1	27	16
Fields, Kamron, OF, Fr.	.000	.250	.000	12	4	0	0	0	0	0
Hamilton, David, INF, So.	.291	.404	.445	220	44	7	6	5	37	31
Hibbeler, Masen, INF, Jr.	.261	.357	.386	249	52	15	2	4	30	13
McCann, Michael, C, R-Jr.	.265	.383	.367	49	11	2	0	1	4	1
McGuire, Andy, OF, R-Jr.	.256	.375	.487	39	9	3	0	2	11	1
McKenzie, Jake, INF, Sr.	.252	.341	.311	151	19	9	0	0	14	1
Pappas, George, C, R-Jr.	.500	.750	.500	2	0	0	0	0	0	0
Petrinsky, DJ, C, Jr.	.257	.340	.452	210	35	10	2	9	29	1
Reynolds, Ryan, INF, So.	.247	.351	.370	227	24	16	0	4	37	1
Shaw, Tate, OF, Jr.	.252	.355	.364	206	38	13	5	0	22	5
Todd, Austin, OF, So.	.219	.352	.301	73	13	3	0	1	13	3
Zubia, Zach, INF, R-Fr.	.275	.407	.495	222	30	14	1	11	45	1

Pitcher, Year	W	L	ERA	G	GS	SV	IP	H	BB	SO
Bocchi, Matteo, Jr.	4	1	3.05	21	4	1	38	34	21	34
Elder, Bryce, Fr.	6	1	5.55	22	1	2	36	40	18	31
Fearon, Chris, Jr.	1	0	10.38	5	0	0	4	8	1	5
Fields, Kamron, Fr.	1	0	1.82	15	2	0	25	19	22	19
Henley, Blair, So.	6	7	3.32	18	16	1	87	94	37	64
Ivey, Brandon, Jr.	0	0	16.20	2	0	0	2	3	3	1
Kingham, Nolan, Jr.	8	5	4.57	20	16	3	100	126	24	81
McGuire, Andy, R-Jr.	1	2	1.93	28	0	7	33	23	13	29
McKenzie, Jake, So.	0	0	3.37	3	0	0	3	1	4	2
O'Donnell, Nico, Fr.	3	2	4.78	12	7	0	32	30	22	30
Ridgeway, Beau, Jr.	1	2	11.32	18	1	3	21	23	15	11
Robinson, Parker Joe, R-Jr.	3	0	1.71	22	0	0	32	25	9	31
Sawyer, Josh, R-Jr.	1	0	3.69	32	0	1	32	22	21	33
Shugart, Chase, Jr.	6	3	4.64	21	15	2	95	90	41	69
Stevenes, Tristan, R-Fr.	0	0	3.86	2	2	0	2	3	2	0
Verplank, Bryce, R-So.	0	0	9.00	9	0	0	6	5	9	8
Whelan, Matthew, Fr.	1	0	4.37	11	1	0	23	19	11	23

8. MINNESOTA

Coach: John Anderson. **Record:** 44-15

Player, Pos., Year	AVG	OBP	SLG	AB	R	2B	3B	HR	RBI	SB
Bertrand, Easton, OF, Fr.	.000	.000	.000	3	0	0	0	0	0	0
Boxwell, Alex, OF, Sr.	.258	.312	.412	182	32	8	1	6	34	21
Coffey, Micah, INF, Sr.	.278	.363	.409	230	32	11	2	5	34	0
Estrada Jr., Eduardo, OF, Jr.	.140	.288	.209	43	4	3	0	0	2	0
Hanson, Toby, 1B/OF, Sr.	.318	.398	.486	173	31	16	2	3	33	5
Hitz, Jacob, INF, Fr.	.273	.333	.545	11	3	0	0	1	1	0
Hmielewski, Drew, OF, R-Fr.	.333	.333	.500	6	3	1	0	0	0	0
Knowles, Gabe, OF, R-Fr.	.000	.125	.000	7	2	0	0	0	1	0
Kozicky, Jordan, INF/OF, R-So.	.271	.373	.422	199	28	13	1	5	38	3
McDevitt, Cole, C/INF, Jr.	.271	.395	.452	199	44	9	0	9	46	1
Meyer, Max, Fr.	.167	.324	.200	3	7	1	0	0	2	0
Mezzenga, Ben, OF, Fr.	.383	.466	.447	188	40	8	2	0	28	12
Pettersen, Luke, INF, Sr.	.322	.406	.397	242	58	13	1	1	27	13
Smith, Riley, INF/OF, Jr.	.268	.372	.366	71	19	2	1	1	8	5

Player, Pos., Year	AVG	OBP	SLG	AB	R	2B	3B	HR	RBI	SB
Vavra, Terrin, INF, Jr.	.386	.455	.614	223	55	13	4	10	59	8
Wassel, Jack, INF, R-Fr.	.282	.429	.308	39	10	1	0	0	7	0
Wilson, Eli, C/INF, So.	.289	.379	.428	173	41	9	0	5	37	0

Pitcher, Year	W	L	ERA	G	GS	SV	IP	H	BB	SO
Bridges, Sam, R-Fr.	0	0	12.00	2	0	0	3	3	1	2
Culliver, Joshua, Fr.	2	3	3.38	9	4	1	27	25	11	19
Duffy, Ryan, Fr.	0	1	1.17	5	0	0	8	5	3	9
Fasching, Jeff, R-Jr.	2	0	1.90	14	0	0	24	22	6	19
Fredrickson, Patrick, Fr.	9	0	1.86	19	15	0	97	71	27	73
Hmielewski, Drew, R-Fr.	0	0	0.00	1	0	0	1	0	0	0
Horton, Bubba, Fr.	0	0	4.05	9	0	0	13	8	10	15
Kapala, Danny, Fr.	0	0	13.50	2	0	0	1	2	3	3
Lackney, Nick, Jr.	4	2	5.48	13	10	0	48	55	15	47
Manke, Fred, Sr.	0	0	5.06	9	0	0	11	9	7	12
Meyer, Max, Fr.	2	3	2.06	26	0	16	44	25	13	54
Meyer, Reggie, R-Jr.	8	4	2.97	17	17	0	109	95	16	70
Rose, Jackson, Sr.	5	1	1.99	22	0	1	32	27	14	30
Schulze, Brett, So.	9	0	2.09	22	0	0	52	51	24	47
Stevenson, Jake, Fr.	1	1	6.32	13	8	0	31	32	18	15
Thoresen, Sam, Fr.	2	5	5.86	14	5	0	35	27	24	30

9. WASHINGTON
Coach: Lindsay Meggs. **Record:** 35-26

Player, Pos., Year	AVG	OBP	SLG	AB	R	2B	3B	HR	RBI	SB
Baird, Ben, INF, So.	.202	.279	.266	94	13	6	0	0	4	0
Brady, K.J., OF, Sr.	.143	.239	.221	77	11	3	0	1	3	1
Burton, Blake, OF, So.	.000	.333	.000	4	1	0	0	0	0	0
Cerrillo, Mason, OF, Jr.	.341	.395	.404	223	34	14	0	0	21	4
Graffanino, A.J., INF, Jr.	.364	.440	.455	110	16	6	2	0	19	5
Hsue, Noah, INF, Fr.	.202	.280	.214	84	5	1	0	0	9	1
Johnson, Jack, INF, Jr.	.105	.227	.105	19	6	2	0	0	1	0
Jones, Christian, INF/OF, So.	.262	.337	.378	164	13	7	3	2	13	0
Jordan, Levi, INF, Sr.	.305	.362	.489	233	46	17	1	8	43	5
Kahle, Nick, C, So.	.293	.392	.457	232	45	20	0	6	37	0
Leitgeb, Brandon, INF, Fr.	.000	.286	.000	5	0	0	0	0	0	0
Longaker, Casey, C, Jr.	.000	.000	.000	1	0	0	0	0	0	0
MacIver, Willie, INF/C, Jr.	.232	.312	.325	151	14	5	0	3	24	3
Petrie, Michael, C, R-Fr.	.000	.000	.000	4	0	0	0	0	0	0
Roberts, Nick, INF, So.	.120	.185	.160	25	3	1	0	0	2	0
Schiffer, Jonathan, INF, Fr.	.242	.318	.287	157	14	4	0	1	20	0
Wainhouse, Joe, INF, Sr.	.306	.352	.603	229	34	9	1	19	61	1
Ward, Braiden, OF, Fr.	.304	.401	.370	181	37	6	3	0	14	19
Weiss, Kaiser, INF, Jr.	.222	.343	.289	90	12	6	0	0	10	0

Pitcher, Year	W	L	ERA	G	GS	SV	IP	H	BB	SO
Burgmann, Josh, R-Fr.	2	2	3.19	16	1	1	31	36	13	21
DeCooman, Jack, Fr.	0	1	3.37	9	3	0	19	12	11	12
DeMers, Joe, Jr.	7	3	2.42	20	17	3	130	103	21	94
Emanuels, Stevie, Fr.	8	2	4.37	34	1	1	45	58	28	32
Enger, Jack, Fr.	0	0	4.76	2	0	0	6	5	5	9
Hardy, Alex, Sr.	5	4	2.80	37	0	8	61	50	23	47
Jones, Jordan, So.	6	4	3.98	19	18	0	104	107	19	83
Knowles, Lucas, R-Fr.	6	5	4.35	23	15	0	89	105	21	67
Lamb, Dylan, Fr.	1	0	3.95	18	0	0	27	24	10	22
Micheles, Chris, So.	0	2	9.25	11	6	0	24	37	15	20
Nierenberg, Leo, So.	0	3	6.75	15	0	0	15	11	13	17
Wainhouse, Joe, Sr.	0	0	0.00	2	0	0	2	0	1	1

10. DUKE
Coach: Chris Pollard. **Record:** 45-18

Player, Pos., Year	AVG	OBP	SLG	AB	R	2B	3B	HR	RBI	SB
Cheek, Chase, OF, So.	.158	.200	.211	19	7	1	0	0	3	2
Conine, Griffin, OF, Jr.	.286	.410	.608	227	54	15	2	18	52	0
Crabtree, Chris, INF, Fr.	.457	.548	.771	35	9	5	0	2	11	0
Dutra, Chris, C, So.	.000	.000	.000	1	0	0	0	0	0	0
Herron, Jimmy, OF, Jr.	.304	.419	.460	250	61	18	3	5	36	23
Kone, Zack, INF, Jr.	.300	.359	.449	267	45	19	3	5	42	6
Labosky, Jack, INF, So.	.226	.381	.382	212	34	12	0	7	40	10
Loperfido, Joey, INF, Fr.	.315	.408	.475	219	45	11	3	6	43	16
Mann, Steve, OF, Fr.	.182	.400	.182	22	6	0	0	0	1	0
Mervis, Matt, INF, So.	.250	.250	.250	4	0	0	0	0	0	0
Miller, Max, INF, Sr.	.280	.385	.336	211	43	5	2	1	36	10

Player, Pos., Year	AVG	OBP	SLG	AB	R	2B	3B	HR	RBI	SB
Nichols, Erikson, INF, So.	.211	.286	.211	19	3	0	0	0	0	0
Proctor, Chris, C, Jr.	.286	.364	.407	248	43	12	3	4	46	12
Rothenberg, Michael, C, Fr.	.253	.372	.385	91	18	4	1	2	17	2
Smiciklas, Michael, OF, Sr.	.211	.371	.267	90	9	3	1	0	9	1
Taylor, Kennie, OF, Jr.	.283	.347	.461	219	36	13	4	6	36	8
Therien, Aaron, C, Jr.	1.000	1.000	4.000	1	1	0	0	1	2	0
Wardwell, Tyler, INF, Fr.	.222	.364	.278	18	2	1	0	0	3	0
Zyla, Peter, OF/C, Sr.	.111	.273	.111	9	0	0	0	0	1	0

Pitcher, Year	W	L	ERA	G	GS	SV	IP	H	BB	SO
Chillari, Bill, So.	6	1	4.72	16	7	0	34	29	11	36
Davis, Hunter, Jr.	2	0	3.68	12	0	0	22	20	13	14
Day, Ryan, Sr.	5	4	5.08	15	13	0	67	81	22	51
DeCaster, Ethan, Gr.	6	0	1.34	27	0	5	54	43	6	57
Dockman, Matt, Fr.	0	1	2.13	24	1	0	25	26	9	21
Girard, Thomas, Fr.	0	0	4.91	8	0	0	11	12	3	10
Granoff, Sam, Gr.	0	0	10.12	3	0	0	3	5	1	0
Jarvis, Bryce, Fr.	5	1	2.45	25	5	1	48	23	22	67
Kovachik, Cameron, So.	0	0	13.50	1	0	0	1	1	2	1
Laskey, Adam, So.	6	4	5.47	16	15	0	76	79	38	61
Labosky, Jack, Sr.	3	1	1.11	26	0	10	41	31	7	32
Mervis, Matt, So.	3	0	4.91	20	0	0	26	21	10	21
Nifong, Josh, Fr.	0	0	13.50	5	0	0	4	6	9	4
Stallings, Mitch, Sr.	4	5	5.84	19	18	0	94	103	45	100
Stinson, Graeme, So.	5	1	1.89	23	4	0	62	43	19	98
Williams, Coleman, So.	0	0	9.00	2	0	0	1	1	2	2

11. TENNESSEE TECH
Coach: Matt Bragga. **Record:** 53-12

Player, Pos., Year	AVG	OBP	SLG	AB	R	2B	3B	HR	RBI	SB
Carrera, Anthony, OF, So.	.345	.438	.673	55	13	4	1	4	15	0
Chambers, Chase, INF, Sr.	.395	.500	.652	256	80	13	1	17	84	0
Elford, John, C, So.	.385	.438	1.077	13	5	0	0	3	7	0
Garza, David, INF, Sr.	.311	.399	.568	264	69	17	0	17	72	4
Ham, John, INF, Jr.	.317	.424	.576	243	70	18	3	13	62	0
Harris, Collin, OF, Sr.	.310	.405	.521	213	51	9	3	10	43	9
Higdon, Hunter, INF, R-Fr.	.500	.500	1.500	4	1	1	0	1	1	0
Hinchman, Jason, INF/OF, Fr.	.219	.342	.531	32	10	1	0	3	9	0
Junior, Alex, OF, Jr.	.316	.451	.465	269	81	13	3	7	35	4
Kaleiwahea, Brennon, C, Sr.	.367	.465	.540	237	67	15	1	8	55	1
Littlejohn, Cody, INF, So.	.289	.413	.605	38	14	3	0	3	17	0
Osborne, Nick, OF, Jr.	.312	.383	.584	202	41	17	1	12	48	7
Putzig, Trevor, INF, Sr.	.313	.424	.589	224	60	11	0	17	73	5
Strohschein, Kevin, OF, Jr.	.375	.433	.650	283	69	18	3	18	67	1
Walker, Zell, OF, R-Fr.	.189	.250	.378	37	8	1	0	2	9	0

Pitcher, Year	W	L	ERA	G	GS	SV	IP	H	BB	SO
Dye, Nic, So.	4	1	4.95	10	8	0	36	40	15	27
Evey, Marcus, Jr.	8	0	4.22	17	15	0	81	72	32	90
Hursey, Alex, Jr.	8	5	4.81	18	15	0	77	86	26	48
King, Ty, Jr.	0	0	15.92	10	0	1	13	19	14	13
Lancaster, Devin, So.	1	0	5.63	13	7	0	40	45	15	18
Moths, Travis, Sr.	13	3	3.96	20	17	0	102	97	40	109
Myers, Brock, Jr.	0	0	14.73	5	0	0	4	6	6	3
Noel, Seth, So.	1	0	6.59	13	0	0	14	19	12	12
O'Dwyer, Andrew, Jr.	1	0	11.05	9	0	0	7	9	5	6
Osborne, Nick, Jr.	2	0	5.82	11	2	0	22	20	11	23
Parham, Jacob, R-Fr.	0	0	3.38	3	0	0	3	0	4	7
Phillips, Grant, R-Fr.	1	0	4.11	12	0	0	15	14	5	12
Provey, Colton, Sr.	5	1	4.64	20	0	2	52	50	42	47
Roberts, Ethan, Jr.	6	1	2.30	28	1	15	78	65	22	103
Sylvester, Tyler, R-Fr.	3	1	5.04	21	0	4	25	20	13	25
Wilcox, Zack, Jr.	0	0	9.39	10	0	1	15	18	8	14

12. STETSON
Coach: Steve Trimper. **Record:** 48-13

Player, Pos., Year	AVG	OBP	SLG	AB	R	2B	3B	HR	RBI	SB
Arenas, Jorge, SS, So.	.233	.296	.363	223	32	11	3	4	39	10
Ball, Kyle, INF, Fr.	.230	.299	.295	61	12	0	2	0	3	0
Bogart, Austin, OF, So.	.260	.345	.380	100	18	6	0	2	12	5
Cardieri, Nick, C, Fr.	.207	.281	.310	29	3	3	0	0	4	0
Foggo, Eric, 1B/3B, Fr.	.236	.286	.407	123	17	4	1	5	25	1
Gonzalez, Jack, 1B/DH, Jr.	.154	.267	.154	13	0	0	0	0	1	0

Player, Pos., Year	AVG	OBP	SLG	AB	R	2B	3B	HR	RBI	SB
Hale, Austin, C, Sr.	.236	.340	.331	178	26	11	0	2	31	1
Koos, Jacob, OF, Jr.	.291	.387	.423	234	50	14	4	3	34	23
Liberatore, Jake, INF, Fr.	.000	.000	.000	2	0	0	0	0	0	0
MacNeil, Andrew, OF, So.	.263	.380	.388	152	35	5	1	4	26	9
Martin, Bruce, INF, Jr.	.178	.260	.244	45	5	1	1	0	9	2
Martin, Danny, C, Fr.	.200	.200	.200	5	0	0	0	0	0	0
Meola, Jonathan, INF, Jr.	.266	.362	.391	169	24	10	4	1	27	9
Murphy, Jake, OF, Fr.	.000	.000	.000	2	0	0	0	0	0	0
Shelton, Dee, INF, Fr.	.000	.333	.000	10	2	0	0	0	0	0
Sidwell, Kirk, OF, Jr.	.083	.083	.083	12	0	0	0	0	1	0
Sparks, Baylen, 1B/OF, Jr.	.221	.331	.302	149	26	7	1	1	12	6
Spooner, Mike, OF/1B, Jr.	.307	.381	.460	189	42	15	1	4	34	8
Torino, Nico, INF, Sr.	.259	.308	.429	112	19	7	3	2	12	0
Wilson, Brooks, DH, Sr.	.299	.413	.455	187	32	16	2	3	35	9

Pitcher, Year	W	L	ERA	G	GS	SV	IP	H	BB	SO
Bogart, Austin, So.	0	1	1.04	4	1	0	9	8	6	4
Gilbert, Logan, Jr.	11	2	2.72	16	16	0	112	71	25	163
Gonzalez, Chris, Fr.	0	0	4.82	8	1	0	9	14	3	6
Gonzalez, Joey, Jr.	8	3	2.07	15	11	1	78	60	32	79
Nunez, Vlad, Jr.	0	1	4.26	11	0	1	19	10	10	20
Onyshko, Ben, Sr.	2	1	2.60	22	2	0	35	26	14	46
Orbik, Jeremy, R-So.	0	0	6.00	4	0	0	3	1	8	0
Perkins, Jack, Jr.	11	3	2.80	18	17	0	106	98	32	108
Schwab, Zemp, Fr.	0	0	5.40	0	0	0	2	3	2	1
Senger, Mitchell, So.	9	2	2.51	15	13	0	93	66	28	114
Stark, Ryan, So.	0	0	8.44	6	0	0	5	7	4	2
Wiebke, Erik, R-So.	1	0	0.00	4	0	0	5	2	3	1
Wilson, Brooks, Sr.	6	0	2.08	32	0	20	56	40	19	69
Wood, Austin, Fr.	0	0	2.84	11	0	0	13	7	6	22

13. AUBURN

Coach: Butch Thompson. **Record:** 43-23

Player, Pos., Year	AVG	OBP	SLG	AB	R	2B	3B	HR	RBI	SB
Anthony, Josh, IF, Sr.	.301	.402	.417	216	43	13	0	4	40	7
Davis, Connor, OF, So.	.268	.371	.360	164	26	9	0	2	34	3
Estes, Jay, OF, Sr.	.329	.401	.409	237	52	19	0	0	33	13
Evans, Cade, IF/OF, Fr.	.333	.500	.333	3	8	0	0	0	0	0
Holland, Will, IF, So.	.313	.406	.530	249	61	18	0	12	52	9
Ingram, Dylan, IF, R-Sr.	.125	.393	.143	56	13	1	0	0	7	0
Jarvis, Luke, IF, R-Sr.	.253	.319	.367	229	49	13	2	3	28	7
Johnsons, Jere,my, OF, R-So.	.244	.404	.289	45	14	2	0	0	10	1
Julien, Edouard, IF/OF, Fr.	.275	.398	.556	207	47	7	0	17	69	7
McGuffin, Bowen, OF, So.	.083	.214	.083	12	0	0	0	0	1	0
Olson, Brett, IF, R-Jr.	.250	.400	.500	4	0	1	0	0	0	0
Rojas, Mike, C, Jr.	.154	.313	.154	13	2	0	0	0	0	0
Venter, Brendan, IF, Jr.	.307	.385	.510	251	44	15	0	12	45	1
Ward, Judd, Of, Fr.	.250	.344	.298	84	9	2	1	0	8	0
Williams, Steven, C, Fr.	.291	.409	.488	244	54	10	1	12	51	1
Wright, Brett, C, Jr.	.258	.388	.483	209	45	10	0	11	45	1

Pitcher, Year	W	L	ERA	G	GS	SV	IP	H	BB	SO
Anderson, Elliot, So.	5	0	3.64	24	0	1	30	25	15	32
Burns, Tanner, Fr.	7	4	3.01	17	17	0	87	73	37	77
Coker, Calvin, Sr.	3	2	4.78	29	1	7	58	59	21	54
Daniel, Davis, So.	3	4	4.86	19	10	0	67	74	32	70
Glavine, Peyton, Fr.	0	0	27.00	5	0	0	3	10	2	5
Greenhill, Cody, Fr.	6	3	2.30	21	0	5	59	53	19	55
Herndon, Corey, Sr.	1	0	2.87	14	0	0	16	13	11	13
Hoerter, Ryan, Fr.	0	0	6.23	7	2	0	9	9	7	5
Malczewski, Welby, R-Jr.	4	0	5.66	24	0	2	35	39	18	19
Mitchell, Andrew, R-Sr.	2	2	4.29	16	10	0	50	42	21	62
Mize, Casey, Jr.	10	6	3.30	17	17	0	115	84	16	156
Owen, Jack, Fr.	2	2	5.97	14	7	2	35	43	16	35
Schilleci, Blake, Jr.	0	0	9.53	6	0	0	6	8	3	3
Watson, Ryan, So.	0	0	4.76	7	2	0	11	13	5	9

14. STANFORD

Coach: David Esquer. **Record:** 46-12

Player, Pos., Year	AVG	OBP	SLG	AB	R	2B	3B	HR	RBI	SB
Bakst, Daniel, INF, So.	.204	.278	.306	49	7	5	0	0	4	1
Beck, Brendan, INF, Fr.	.286	.286	.286	7	1	0	0	0	2	0
Branton, Beau, INF, Sr.	.353	.431	.418	170	36	6	1	1	22	2
Brueser, Nick, INF, Fr.	.205	.300	.250	44	9	2	0	0	2	1
Carter, Bryce, C, Sr.	.172	.284	.276	58	5	4	1	0	4	0
Daschbach, Andrew, INF/OF, So.	.287	.358	.579	216	42	10	1	17	63	4
Decker, Matthew, C, R-Sr.	.214	.313	.286	14	4	1	0	0	2	0
Handley, Maverick, C, So.	.229	.360	.347	144	31	9	1	2	23	3
Hoerner, Nico, INF, Jr.	.345	.391	.496	232	45	17	6	2	40	15
Kuet, Jesse, INF, Jr.	.181	.278	.191	94	11	1	0	0	11	1
Matthiessen, Will, So.	.293	.414	.598	82	21	2	1	7	23	1
Molfetta, Christian, OF/INF/C, R-So.	.188	.317	.271	85	15	4	0	1	7	1
Oar, Nickolas, OF, R-So.	.333	.529	1.083	12	5	0	0	3	5	0
Robinson, Christian, OF, Fr.	.250	.303	.398	88	14	9	2	0	17	1
Stowers, Kyle, OF, So.	.286	.383	.510	206	39	10	3	10	42	6
Tawa, Tim, OF, Fr.	.296	.347	.498	223	44	18	3	7	41	7
Wilson, Alec, OF, Jr.	.272	.349	.368	114	21	6	1	1	15	8
Wulff, Brandon, OF, Jr.	.303	.420	.495	99	21	5	1	4	20	1

Pitcher, Year	W	L	ERA	G	GS	SV	IP	H	BB	SO
Bakst, Daniel, So.	1	0	3.52	14	0	0	15	12	4	12
Beck, Brendan, Jr.	8	0	2.43	17	12	1	67	56	12	38
Beck, Tristan, Jr.	8	4	2.98	15	15	0	91	79	31	73
Bubic, Kris, Jr.	8	1	2.62	15	15	0	86	60	32	101
Grech, Zach, So.	3	0	2.65	28	1	1	34	29	11	22
Little, Jack, So.	3	0	0.60	25	0	16	46	26	8	58
Matthiessen, Will, So.	2	1	2.00	13	0	0	18	12	11	17
Miller, Erik, So.	4	4	4.07	13	13	0	49	43	23	52
Palisch, Jacob, Fr.	4	1	1.72	26	0	4	47	33	12	36
Rudd, Carson, Fr.	0	0	6.60	15	0	0	15	23	7	9
Sleeper, Luke, R-Fr.	0	0	0.00	2	0	0	1	1	1	1
Stowers, Kyle, So.	0	0	0.00	4	0	1	4	0	3	3
Styles, John Henry, Sr.	0	0	11.42	10	0	0	9	9	9	4
Weiermiller, Austin, Fr.	5	1	3.29	23	2	0	38	31	15	27

15. MISSISSIPPI

Coach: Mike Bianco. **Record:** 48-17

Player, Pos. Year	AVG	OBP	SLG	AB	R	2B	3B	HR	RBI	SB
Adams, Jacob, INF, Jr.	.257	.392	.375	152	35	7	1	3	18	7
Cockrell, Chase, INF, Jr.	.317	.376	.539	180	37	13	0	9	38	1
Dillard, Thomas, C/OF, So.	.310	.439	.563	229	67	15	2	13	59	17
Elko, Tim, INF, Fr.	.216	.255	.333	51	10	3	0	1	5	2
Fitzsimmons, Michael, INF, R-Jr.	.440	.533	.960	25	6	4	0	3	11	0
Fortes, Nick, C, Jr.	.319	.435	.519	235	56	12	1	11	49	14
Gindl, Carl, OF, Fr.	.000	.300	.000	6	4	0	0	0	2	1
Golsan, Will, OF/OF, Jr.	.304	.371	.421	247	41	13	2	4	48	5
Johnson, Cooper, C, So.	.235	.329	.324	68	10	0	0	2	11	0
Keenan, Tyler, INF, Fr.	.301	.391	.520	173	35	11	0	9	38	1
Kessinger, Grae, INF, So.	.300	.370	.473	243	56	10	0	8	37	8
Olenek, Ryan, IF/OF, Jr.	.350	.388	.464	237	35	18	0	3	29	9
Rowe, Tim, OF, Jr.	.277	.338	.477	65	10	7	0	2	11	0
Seamster, Bryan, OF, So.	.000	.000	.000	0	0	0	0	0	0	0
Servideo, Anthony, INF, Fr.	.226	.314	.306	62	10	2	0	1	7	1
Spears, Michael, OF, Fr.	.118	.375	.176	17	5	1	0	0	4	0
Zabowski, Cole, INF, So.	.300	.370	.481	210	34	14	0	9	43	0

Pitcher, Year	W	L	ERA	G	GS	SV	IP	H	BB	SO
Caracci, Parker, Jr.	5	2	2.25	27	0	10	48	38	14	73
Cioffi, Max, Fr.	0	0	1.96	14	0	0	23	14	9	16
Coates, Colin, Jr.	0	0	13.50	2	0	0	1	1	3	1
Ethridge, Will, So.	1	3	3.91	26	0	3	51	49	14	53
Feigl, Brady, R-Jr.	8	5	4.03	16	16	0	92	91	26	93
Fowler, Jordan, Fr.	7	0	3.20	16	9	0	45	40	18	34
Green, Connor, Jr.	0	0	3.75	9	0	0	12	11	8	9
Holston, Greer, So.	2	1	3.27	24	0	0	33	36	9	35
McArthur, James, Jr.	6	1	4.48	16	16	0	66	58	38	58
Miller, Austin, So.	0	0	4.02	12	0	0	16	13	3	22
Rolison, Ryan, So.	10	4	3.70	17	16	0	97	88	45	120
Roth, Houston, So.	5	1	4.44	16	8	1	53	55	25	68
Smith, Pierce, Jr.	0	0	54.00	1	0	0	0	0	0	0
Stokes, Will, So.	1	1	8.39	20	0	1	25	33	9	23

16. SOUTH CAROLINA

Coach: Mark Kingston. **Record:** 37-26

Player, Pos., Year	AVG	OBP	SLG	AB	R	2B	3B	HR	RBI	SB
Blair, Danny, OF, Jr.	.230	.288	.361	61	13	2	0	2	7	2
Bride, Jonah, INF, Sr.	.301	.419	.415	229	40	12	1	4	31	1
Campbell, Noah, INF, Fr.	.270	.372	.380	163	34	3	3	3	13	7
Cortes, Carlos, INF/OF, So.	.265	.385	.500	230	53	9	0	15	44	8
Cullen, Chris, C, Jr.	.190	.294	.293	116	14	3	0	3	15	0
Hogan, Riley, 1B, So.	.216	.298	.275	51	3	3	0	0	7	0
Holladay, Jordan, INF, Fr.	.077	.143	.154	13	1	1	0	0	0	0
Hopkins, T.J., OF, Jr.	.345	.448	.496	119	31	8	2	2	24	14
Jacobsen, Kyle, OF, Fr.	.158	.289	.211	38	9	0	1	0	0	2
Olson, Jacob, UTIL, Jr.	.234	.290	.472	235	40	20	0	12	36	3
Row, Justin, INF, Sr.	.347	.418	.540	176	33	13	0	7	25	0
Stokes, Madison, INF, Sr.	.322	.414	.579	183	32	12	1	11	44	1
Streater, Mason, INF, Fr.	.167	.286	.167	6	1	0	0	0	0	0
Taylor, Hunter, C, Sr.	.261	.328	.485	165	23	10	0	9	34	1
Tolbert, L.T., INF, Jr.	.322	.401	.498	245	42	11	4	8	56	9
Williams, Matt, INF, Sr.	.214	.321	.307	140	21	4	0	3	21	0

Pitcher, Year	W	L	ERA	G	GS	SV	IP	H	BB	SO
Bridges, Sawyer, So.	2	1	1.35	21	0	5	33	27	9	25
Chapman, Logan, Fr.	3	3	5.85	16	14	0	60	60	34	55
Chapman, Ridge, Jr.	1	4	4.93	16	6	0	38	25	24	36
Coyne, Parker, Fr.	1	1	3.18	19	0	0	23	15	13	26
Demurias, Eddy, Jr.	7	1	4.87	31	1	3	65	70	30	51
Gilreath, John, Fr.	0	1	4.28	24	3	1	40	39	18	44
Hill, Adam, Jr.	7	5	4.12	16	16	0	83	55	55	101
Hinson, Gage, Jr.	0	0	3.18	3	0	0	6	2	3	2
Lawson, Graham, Jr.	1	1	5.60	22	0	3	27	26	10	26
Lee, Colby, So.	0	0	27.00	2	0	0	1	2	3	1
Lomas, Hunter, Jr.	0	0	7.58	15	0	1	19	20	6	17
Mlodzinski, Carmen, Fr.	3	6	5.52	19	7	1	46	47	21	43
Morris, Cody, So.	9	3	3.46	16	16	0	83	71	31	87
Shook, T.J., Fr.	3	0	2.33	21	0	0	27	32	15	27
Stone, Corey, Fr.	0	0	0.00	3	0	0	2	3	2	1

17. VANDERBILT

Coach: Tim Corbin. **Record:** 35-27

Player, Pos., Year	AVG	OBP	SLG	AB	R	2B	3B	HR	RBI	SB
Blaylock, Garrett, IF, Fr.	.231	.259	.308	26	4	2	0	0	6	0
Bieday, JJ, OF, So.	.368	.494	.511	133	26	5	1	4	15	22
Clarke, Philip, C, Fr.	.294	.382	.450	218	28	16	0	6	36	4
Davis, Cooper, OF, Jr.	.182	.286	.182	11	3	0	0	0	4	1
DeMarco, Pat, OF, Fr.	.277	.353	.479	242	48	12	2	11	43	10
Duvall, Ty, C, So.	.270	.405	.492	63	13	3	1	3	10	1
Fentress, Kiambu, OF, R-So.	.000	.000	.000	5	2	0	0	0	1	0
Gonzalaez, Jayson, IF, Fr.	.225	.287	.355	138	21	3	0	5	28	1
Grisanti, Walker, OF, Jr.	.139	.448	.250	36	12	1	0	1	5	2
Infante, Julian, IF, Jr.	.193	.276	.273	161	16	5	1	2	18	1
Jones, Alonzo, OF, Jr.	.236	.328	.382	110	23	4	3	2	9	16
Kaiser, Connor, If, Jr.	.293	.389	.446	222	46	14	1	6	46	12
Martin, Austin, IF, Fr.	.338	.452	.414	222	44	14	0	1	19	22
Paul, Ethan, IF, Jr.	.237	.358	.430	228	43	12	1	10	44	18
Ray, Harrison, IF, So.	.242	.307	.385	91	13	4	3	1	14	5
Scott, Stephen, OF/C, Jr.	.268	.420	.601	168	42	11	0	15	41	6
Solomon, Tyler IF, Fr.	.000	.333	.000	4	2	0	0	0	0	0

Pitcher, Year	W	L	ERA	G	GS	SV	IP	H	BB	SO
Brown, Aaron, Fr.	1	0	5.93	11	0	0	14	16	7	13
Brown, Tyler, Fr.	1	5	6.03	20	1	3	37	42	11	41
Conger, Maddux, Jr.	2	0	2.21	11	1	1	20	18	14	22
Day, Chandler, Jr.	2	1	3.46	20	3	4	42	28	18	47
Eder, Jake, Fr.	1	4	5.45	11	9	0	33	25	22	37
Fellows, Drake, So.	7	4	3.92	16	16	0	96	75	35	107
Fisher, Hugh, Fr.	2	0	1.93	8	0	0	9	6	6	8
Franklin, AJ, R-So.	0	0	0.00	3	0	0	0	0	1	2
Gillis, Jackson, So.	4	1	4.81	20	1	1	34	33	17	44
Hickman, Mason, Fr.	8	2	5.21	16	13	0	74	71	30	66
Kaiser, Erik, Fr.	0	0	0.00	2	0	0	2	1	0	3
King, Zach, Fr.	1	4	3.46	21	3	3	52	45	21	51
Raby, Patrick, Jr.	5	5	3.57	16	12	0	68	69	33	57
Schaller, Reid, R-Fr.	1	1	3.77	21	2	1	29	33	9	39

Stover, Paxton, Sr.	0	0	3.38	9	0	0	11	10	4	13
Willis, Justin, Fr.	0	0	7.59	10	0	0	11	12	7	8
Wilson, Justin, R-So.	0	0	2.84	7	0	0	6	2	4	9

18. CAL STATE FULLERTON

Coach: Rick Vanderhook. **Record:** 36-24

Player, Pos., Year	AVG	OBP	SLG	AB	R	2B	3B	HR	RBI	SB
Berryhill, Mitchell, OF, Jr.	.287	.382	.359	195	30	8	3	0	22	10
Borgogno, Brett, INF, Fr.	.230	.284	.292	161	17	10	0	0	18	2
Cardenas, Ruben, OF, Jr.	.294	.353	.443	228	33	14	4	4	36	8
Chamberlain, Jace, 1B, Fr.	.322	.396	.378	90	6	2	0	1	15	0
Ciandro, Nick, C, Jr.	.100	.167	.100	10	0	0	0	0	1	0
Conine, Brett, P, Jr.	.250	.250	.250	4	0	0	0	0	0	0
Cope, Daniel, C, So.	.280	.357	.412	216	26	13	0	5	43	4
Hernandez, Jordan, OF, Jr.	.154	.313	.192	26	4	1	0	0	3	0
Lasch, Tyler, C, Fr.	.150	.282	.200	60	6	3	0	0	5	0
LoForte, Hank, INF, Jr.	.333	.390	.432	222	42	5	7	1	32	3
Minnis, Cody, OF, Jr.	.167	.286	.167	6	2	0	0	0	0	0
Pevletich, Jacob, INF, R-Jr.	.285	.360	.333	207	24	10	0	0	20	5
Prescott, Chris, OF, Sr.	.213	.312	.298	94	20	2	0	2	13	1
Quezada, Andrew, P, Jr.	.000	.000	.000	1	0	0	0	0	0	0
Richards, Jairus, OF, Jr.	.243	.333	.333	111	20	6	2	0	12	2
Valenzuela, Sahid, INF, So.	.276	.319	.368	239	37	14	4	0	21	5
Weisz, Zach, OF, R-So.	.143	.268	.171	35	4	1	0	0	1	1
Weller, Zach, INF, So.	.048	.111	.048	42	2	0	0	0	3	0
Williams, Ryan, INF, Fr.	.100	.308	.100	10	1	0	0	0	1	0

Pitcher, Year	W	L	ERA	G	GS	SV	IP	H	BB	SO
Anderson, Landon, Fr.	1	0	2.70	7	1	0	10	12	6	5
Bibee, Tanner, Fr.	3	5	4.38	17	5	0	49	57	16	52
Brown, Dillon, So.	1	2	4.13	23	1	0	28	25	11	24
Cha, Erik, R-So.	1	0	3.52	8	0	0	8	7	1	4
Conine, Brett, Jr.	4	2	4.07	30	0	9	42	50	7	46
Eastman, Colton, Jr.	9	4	2.52	16	16	0	111	86	26	117
Endersby, Jimmy, R-Fr.	0	0	8.59	9	0	0	7	9	8	6
Josten, Timothy, Fr.	0	1	4.15	13	3	0	26	25	5	22
Pabich, Jack, Sr.	0	0	0.00	1	0	0	1	1	1	1
Quezada, Andrew, Jr.	4	5	3.90	14	14	0	83	89	19	58
Smith, Tyler, Fr.	0	0	6.00	1	1	0	3	4	1	3
Velasquez, Gavin, Jr.	0	1	9.95	4	1	0	6	7	5	1
Wills, Joe, Sr.	1	0	0.00	1	0	0	2	4	0	3
Wilson, Tommy, Jr.	6	0	2.90	18	12	0	81	72	21	70
Workman, Blake, Jr.	3	4	3.47	30	3	5	57	64	20	70

19. CLEMSON

Coach: Monte Lee. **Record:** 47-16

Player, Pos., Year	AVG	OBP	SLG	AB	R	2B	3B	HR	RBI	SB
Beer, Seth, OF/1B, Jr.	.301	.456	.642	226	64	11	0	22	54	1
Bowen, Bryce, 1B, Fr.	.000	.000	.000	1	0	0	0	0	0	0
Byrd, Grayson, INF, R-Jr.	.243	.309	.439	148	23	2	0	9	26	3
Cooper, Matt, C/OF/1B, Fr.	.286	.375	.286	7	0	0	0	0	0	0
Cromwell, Patrick, 3B/1B, Sr.	.224	.349	.358	201	36	6	0	7	26	1
Davidson, Logan, SS, So.	.292	.408	.544	250	60	18	0	15	46	10
Donathan, Drew, C, Fr.	.263	.400	.263	19	0	0	0	0	2	0
Greene, Jordan, 3B/2B, Jr.	.250	.398	.404	136	36	6	0	5	21	8
Hall, Sam, INF/OF, Fr.	.239	.341	.380	71	18	4	0	2	7	8
Hawkins, Justin, INF, R-Jr.	.200	.365	.425	40	7	3	0	2	8	0
Jolly, Robert, OF, Sr.	.228	.341	.289	149	18	6	0	1	17	3
Majkowski, OF, Fr.	.000	.000	.000	1	0	0	0	0	0	0
Meredith, Kier, OF, Fr.	.195	.411	.341	41	8	1	1	1	5	4
Renwick, Adam, INF, So.	.000	.167	.000	5	3	0	0	0	0	0
Teodosio, Bryce, OF, Fr.	.165	.283	.367	79	12	4	0	4	9	1
Wharton, Drew, OF, Sr.	.255	.337	.407	231	31	12	1	7	41	7
Wilkie, Kyle, C, So.	.324	.422	.440	216	35	10	0	5	40	2
Williams, Chris, INF/C, Sr.	.281	.401	.562	235	54	12	0	18	73	3
Weatherly, Sam, OF, Fr.	.100	.182	.100	10	1	0	0	0	1	1

Pitcher, Year	W	L	ERA	G	GS	SV	IP	H	BB	SO
Bowen, Bryce, Fr.	0	0	0.00	1	0	0	0	1	0	0
Mat, Clark, R-Fr.	4	0	1.69	19	1	0	21	18	4	23
Crawford, Brooks, Jr.	8	2	3.24	16	16	0	81	71	18	58
Gilliam, Ryley, Jr.	3	3	1.41	27	0	11	38	22	22	54
Gobin, Bo, R-Fr.	0	0	15.00	5	0	0	3	8	3	2

Griffith, Owen, So.	0	0	6.14	12	0	1	15	18	13	18
Hennessy, Jacob, So.	4	3	3.91	14	14	0	71	72	14	54
Higginbotham, Jake, R-So.	6	1	3.47	16	16	0	80	70	32	63
Huggins, Ryne, R-Fr.	0	0	9.82	10	0	0	4	5	2	3
Jones, Holt, Fr.	2	0	4.41	8	3	0	16	16	10	18
Marr, Travis, R-Fr.	6	2	6.04	22	2	0	45	54	21	33
Miller, Mitchell, So.	0	0	0.00	4	0	0	2	2	0	2
Miller, Ryan, Sr.	7	1	2.51	26	0	4	72	63	17	64
Schnell, Alex, Sr.	0	0	5.19	10	0	0	9	9	6	4
Spiers, Carson, So.	2	2	2.08	29	0	4	43	22	19	39
Strider, Spencer, Fr.	5	2	4.76	22	6	1	51	40	35	70
Weatherly, Sam, Fr.	0	0	6.64	8	5	0	20	24	17	17

20. FLORIDA STATE

Coach: Mike Martin. **Record:** 43-19

Player, Pos., Year	AVG	OBP	SLG	AB	R	2B	3B	HR	RBI	SB
Albert, Reese, OF, Fr.	.268	.360	.452	157	25	8	0	7	34	4
Aplin, Rhett, OF, Sr.	.301	.428	.416	226	37	18	1	2	35	3
Bournigal, Rafael, INF, Sr.	.189	.327	.295	132	22	8	0	2	19	3
Cavanaugh, Kyle, 1B, R-Sr.	.368	.489	.474	38	9	1	0	1	11	0
Derr, Nick, INF, So.	.212	.353	.401	137	30	8	0	6	24	0
Flowers, J.C., OF, So.	.218	.383	.273	110	26	6	0	0	14	2
Foster, Jonathan, C/1B, Jr.	.214	.353	.500	28	4	2	0	2	7	0
Frey, Skylar, OF, Jr.	.182	.419	.227	22	5	1	0	0	3	2
Herron, Jared, OF, R-Fr.	.297	.381	.459	37	8	3	0	1	6	0
Hutchinson, Gabe, P, R-Jr.	.000	.000	.000	1	1	0	0	0	0	0
Johnson, Cobi, P, R-Jr.	.250	.438	.667	12	4	0	1	1	7	0
Lueck, Jackson, OF, Jr.	.245	.364	.476	229	49	8	0	15	45	3
Mendoza, Drew, INF, So.	.313	.440	.491	224	44	17	1	7	44	3
Raleigh, Cal, C, Jr.	.326	.447	.583	230	44	18	1	13	54	2
Salvatore, Mike, INF, Jr.	.244	.333	.298	238	44	8	1	1	27	8
Swanson, Cooper, INF, Fr.	.255	.414	.436	55	12	4	0	2	4	3
Van Eyk, C.J., P, Fr.	.000	.000	.000	1	0	0	0	0	0	0
Wells, Steven, OF, Sr.	.261	.448	.466	176	50	13	1	7	28	3

Pitcher, Year	W	L	ERA	G	GS	SV	IP	H	BB	SO
Ahearn, Tyler, Fr.	1	0	5.50	11	0	0	18	14	18	13
Drohan, Shane, Fr.	0	0	20.77	6	0	0	4	3	10	1
Grady, Conor, Fr.	4	3	4.34	22	0	2	29	20	21	33
Holton, Tyler, Jr.	0	0	0.00	1	1	0	5	1	1	6
Hutchinson, Gage, R-Jr.	1	0	11.70	10	0	0	10	20	7	12
Johnson, Cobi, R-Jr.	0	1	3.54	14	0	1	20	16	13	27
Karp, Andrew, R-Jr.	8	4	3.97	16	15	0	82	81	17	97
Kwiatkowski, Clayton, So.	4	1	3.18	26	1	2	45	35	21	49
Parrish, Drew, So.	5	1	2.52	16	16	0	107	71	37	128
Pollock, Austin, Fr.	4	4	5.28	15	10	1	61	67	31	49
Sands, Cole, Jr.	7	4	4.54	14	14	0	75	59	25	88
Scolaro, Jonah, Fr.	2	1	3.43	27	0	6	45	46	18	60
Van Eyk, C.J., Fr.	7	0	2.86	19	5	2	57	42	30	71
Zirzow, Will, R-Sr.	0	0	0.00	1	0	0	1	0	0	1

21. GEORGIA

Coach: Scott Stricklin. **Record:** 39-21

Player, Pos., Year	AVG	OBP	SLG	AB	R	2B	3B	HR	RBI	SB
Biggar, Austin, C, So.	.182	.262	.218	55	3	2	0	0	7	1
Bradley, Tucker, OF, So.	.299	.350	.353	224	37	3	0	3	26	11
Curry, Michael, OF/C, Jr.	.322	.395	.532	233	44	10	0	13	53	1
Johnsin, Ivan, INF, Fr.	.239	.314	.283	46	11	2	0	0	4	6
King, Riley, INF, R-Fr.	.167	.375	.167	6	2	0	0	0	1	0
Logan, Trey, INF, Fr.	.143	.220	.143	7	1	0	0	0	1	0
Maxwell, Tucker, OF, So.	.216	.326	.310	116	20	5	0	2	13	10
McGovern, Keegan, OF, Sr.	.319	.431	.644	216	68	14	1	18	50	7
Meadows, Mason, C, R-Fr.	.289	.421	.387	142	23	5	0	3	25	1
Rogers, Chaney, OF/INF, Fr.	.375	.500	.500	8	1	1	0	0	1	0
Sasser, Adam, INF, Jr.	.317	.379	.508	183	29	5	0	10	44	0
Schunk, Aaron, INF, So.	.299	.340	.411	241	46	12	3	3	38	5
Smith, CJ, OF, Fr.	.300	.333	.363	80	12	2	0	1	9	0
Sullivan, Patrick, INF, R-So.	.196	.339	.196	46	7	0	0	0	5	0
Talley, LJ, INF, Jr.	.276	.365	.453	181	30	10	2	6	30	2
Tate, Cole, INF, Fr.	.188	.278	.188	16	3	0	0	0	3	0
Webb, Mitchell, INF, Sr.	.227	.346	.318	44	6	4	0	0	5	0
Shepherd, Cam, INF, So.	.244	.357	.385	221	42	12	2	5	37	2

Pitcher, Year	W	L	ERA	G	GS	SV	IP	H	BB	SO
Adkins, Chase, Sr.	5	0	4.30	16	16	0	82	83	29	65
Cairnes, Blake, Sr.	1	0	3.15	21	0	0	34	29	11	29
Elliott, Tim, So.	1	0	3.86	11	4	0	21	15	13	17
Glover, Justin, So.	0	0	14.54	5	0	0	4	10	3	3
Goodman, Adam, Jr.	0	1	3.00	13	0	0	9	7	5	10
Hancock, Emerson, Fr.	6	4	5.10	15	15	0	78	70	34	75
Kristofak, Zac, So.	4	2	3.83	31	0	4	42	38	22	58
Locey, Tony, So.	7	2	4.28	27	5	0	55	44	30	60
Moody, Logan, Jr.	0	0	0.00	0	0	0	0	0	0	0
Proctor, Will, So.	3	2	2.42	19	1	2	26	20	13	26
Ryder, Christian, So.	0	0	0.00	3	0	0	4	2	3	3
Schunk, Aaron, So.	2	2	3.00	20	0	8	30	25	5	31
Smith, CJ, Fr.	1	2	2.48	14	5	0	37	27	13	27
Smith, Kevin, Jr.	8	1	3.69	22	7	0	63	55	25	79
Tinder, Trevor, Jr.	0	0	0.00	1	0	0	1	0	1	1
Webb, Ryan, Fr.	1	5	4.50	23	7	4	54	49	29	48

22. N.C. STATE

Coach: Elliott Avent. **Record:** 42-18

PLAYER, POS., YEAR	AVG	OBP	SLG	AB	R	2B	3B	HR	RBI	SB
Bailey, Patrick, C, Fr.	.321	.419	.604	187	45	8	3	13	40	0
Brown, Devonte, INF, Fr.	.148	.343	.222	27	8	0	1	0	1	1
Conley, Jack, C, Fr.	.333	.476	.515	33	10	0	0	2	5	1
Cooper, Dillon, INF, R-So.	.256	.338	.286	133	20	4	0	0	24	5
Deatherage, Brock, OF, Sr.	.307	.397	.548	228	47	7	3	14	41	18
Debo, Brad, C, So.	.253	.361	.337	83	8	4	0	1	14	1
Edwards, Evan, INF, Jr.	.297	.419	.564	195	44	5	1	15	48	4
Gulakowski, Brady, C, R-Fr.	.000	.000	.000	5	0	0	0	0	0	0
Jarrett, J.T., INF, Fr.	.225	.306	.225	111	16	0	0	0	8	0
Kinneman, Brett, OF, Jr.	.274	.392	.581	234	52	13	4	17	61	10
McArthur, Lawson, OF, So.	.000	.500	.000	1	3	0	0	0	1	0
McLain, Josh, OF, Fr.	.344	.375	.458	273	51	13	3	4	40	12
Oakley, Steven, INF, R-So.	.222	.364	.222	9	0	0	0	0	0	0
Pitarra, Stephen, INF, Jr.	.271	.446	.353	85	19	7	0	0	6	2
Shepard, Shane, INF, Sr.	.200	.360	.440	75	14	3	0	5	23	1
Tatum, Terrell, OF, Fr.	.271	.427	.341	85	25	4	1	0	10	9
Vazquez, David, INF, Fr.	.263	.302	.447	38	7	4	0	1	7	0
Wilson, Will, INF, So.	.307	.376	.588	238	50	16	3	15	53	1

Pitcher, Year	W	L	ERA	G	GS	SV	IP	H	BB	SO
Bienlien, Michael, So.	3	3	5.35	16	7	0	34	51	11	30
Brown, Brian, Sr.	7	2	2.74	16	16	0	99	83	26	98
Centala, Connor, R-Fr.	1	0	3.65	11	0	0	12	17	4	9
Clenney, Nolan, R-Jr.	3	0	3.43	33	0	0	45	32	26	54
Gauthier, Mathieu, So.	0	0	4.01	17	4	1	43	39	15	34
Harrison, David, Fr.	1	4	5.72	14	9	0	39	42	22	30
Hooper, Cole, Fr.	0	0	18.00	2	0	0	1	1	2	0
Johnston, Reid, Fr.	7	1	3.06	21	10	4	65	54	15	49
Justice, Evan, Fr.	2	0	6.83	16	3	0	28	32	16	28
Kinneman, Brett, Jr.	0	0	0.00	2	0	0	1	2	4	1
Klyman, Kent, So.	8	2	2.34	31	0	4	62	46	25	67
O'Donnell, Joe, R-Sr.	1	3	1.48	24	0	11	31	18	13	40
Piedmonte, Johnny, Gr.	5	3	4.12	13	10	0	48	33	21	35
Pike, Josh, Fr.	0	0	0.00	1	0	0	0	0	0	0
Staley, Austin, R-Jr.	0	0	0.00	1	0	0	1	0	0	0
Swiney, Nick, Fr.	4	0	3.52	20	1	0	31	25	18	37

23. EAST CAROLINA

Coach: Cliff Godwin. **Record:** 44-18

Player, Pos., Year	AVG	OBP	SLG	AB	R	2B	3B	HR	RBI	SB
Baker, Dusty, OF, So.	.217	.390	.283	46	9	3	0	0	10	6
Barber, Nick, INF, So.	.210	.330	.235	81	16	2	0	0	7	3
Brickhouse, Spencer, 1B/DH, So.	.298	.382	.502	235	49	16	1	10	50	5
Brown, Turner, INF, Jr.	.230	.324	.337	178	28	7	0	4	28	8
Burleson, Alec, 1B, Fr.	.252	.325	.282	103	13	3	0	0	18	3
Caddell, Seth, C, Fr.	.237	.291	.395	76	11	3	0	3	13	0
Henrickson, Andrew, OF, Jr.	.291	.378	.358	179	33	6	3	0	26	6
Jenkins, Chandler, OF, Jr.	.219	.303	.323	96	17	4	0	2	15	1
Litton, Connor, INF, Jr.	.285	.383	.462	221	40	12	0	9	38	7
Lloyd, Brady, INF, Jr.	.322	.388	.402	214	41	11	0	2	25	16
Netterville, Josh, OF, Fr.	.000	.000	.000	2	0	0	0	0	0	0
Packard, Bryant, 1B/OF, So.	.406	.462	.671	219	51	16	0	14	50	6

Player, Pos., Year	AVG	OBP	SLG	AB	R	2B	3B	HR	RBI	SB
Washer, Jake, C, R-So.	.287	.395	.436	202	32	10	1	6	40	1
Watt, Collin, INF, Fr.	.000	.333	.000	2	1	0	0	0	0	0
Whitehead, Jeremy, OF, Fr.	.189	.233	.189	37	6	0	0	0	5	4
Williams-Sutton, Dwanya, OF, Jr.	.331	.477	.556	133	39	7	1	7	21	18
Worrell, Bryson, UTIL, Fr.	.256	.396	.487	39	7	4	1	1	10	0

Pitcher, Year	W	L	ERA	G	GS	SV	IP	H	BB	SO
Agnos, Jake, So.	4	4	4.10	22	14	1	64	61	38	86
Barnes, Zach, Jr.	2	0	4.21	24	0	2	26	26	7	20
Beavin, Cole, Fr.	0	0	21.60	3	0	0	2	4	2	2
Benton, Trey, So.	4	5	3.13	22	9	0	69	69	13	68
Bridges, Matt, Jr.	1	0	4.00	9	0	0	9	5	5	6
Burleson, Alec, Fr.	5	2	3.33	19	8	4	54	50	16	49
Colmore, Cam, R-So.	0	0	5.68	6	0	0	6	8	2	7
Covers, Austin, Jr.	0	0	10.38	9	0	0	4	5	4	4
Covington, West, R-Sr.	0	0	3.27	17	2	0	22	20	7	10
Holba, Chris, Jr.	9	1	2.99	15	15	0	81	86	20	60
Kirkpatrick, Davis, R-Sr.	2	0	0.95	29	0	3	38	29	14	34
Kuchmaner, Jake, Fr.	4	0	4.62	10	5	0	25	25	6	18
Lanier, Sam, Jr.	0	0	9.90	13	0	0	10	16	6	11
Ross, Ryan, Sr.	4	5	3.35	33	0	6	51	41	6	52
Smith, Tyler, So.	7	1	1.78	14	9	1	61	47	12	34
Strong, Willy, So.	0	0	12.86	7	0	0	7	12	5	9
Voliva, Evan, R-Jr.	2	0	0.00	4	0	0	4	1	0	2
Williams, Gavin, Fr.	0	0	1.15	15	0	0	16	9	7	9

24. COASTAL CAROLINA

Coach: Gary Gilmore. **Record:** 43-19

Player, Pos., Year	AVG	OBP	SLG	AB	R	2B	3B	HR	RBI	SB
Biermann, Zach, INF, Jr.	.302	.419	.561	212	57	14	1	13	57	2
Buis, Turner, OF, R-Jr.	.385	.468	.462	39	12	3	0	0	7	2
Chavers, Parker, INF, Fr.	.323	.435	.498	217	48	15	1	7	42	9
Damron, Trevor, P, Fr.	.000	.000	.000	1	0	0	0	0	0	0
Koenig, Michael, INF, Jr.	.269	.359	.373	67	13	5	1	0	12	1
Lancaster, Seth, INF, Sr.	.305	.454	.646	226	81	17	0	20	57	23
Pearcey, Cameron, OF, R-So.	.239	.393	.338	71	15	4	0	1	9	10
Rivers, Kieton, OF, Jr.	.285	.380	.453	214	31	15	3	5	50	10
Sehnert, Tor, OF, Fr.	.333	.500	.333	12	4	3	0	0	7	2
Sheppard, Garrett, C, Fr.	.400	.400	.600	5	2	1	0	0	4	0
Skeels, Kyle, C, So.	.301	.382	.538	93	22	7	0	5	28	0
Sponseller, Lee, OF, Gs	.290	.424	.516	155	30	13	2	6	42	3
Weisz, Keaton, INF, R-So.	.238	.307	.370	181	28	11	2	3	33	4
Wood, Cory, INF, So.	.296	.435	.390	223	61	19	1	0	22	17
Woodall Jr., Kevin, INF, Sr.	.298	.418	.576	245	71	9	1	19	62	3
Beaird, Matt, C, Sr.	.252	.320	.368	155	24	12	0	2	23	0

Pitcher, Year	W	L	ERA	G	GS	SV	IP	H	BB	SO
Bilous, Jason, Jr.	7	3	4.00	16	16	0	83	61	66	105
Causey, Jay, So.	2	2	2.28	24	1	5	43	30	20	39
Damron, Trevor, Jr.	1	1	8.22	11	0	1	15	21	10	20
Eardensohn, Matt, Jr.	7	0	2.18	20	1	6	58	38	14	51
Gentry, Dylan, Fr.	0	0	3.31	15	0	0	16	13	11	18
Hopeck, Zack, Sr.	6	4	4.15	16	16	0	87	84	34	71
Inman, Dave, So.	2	2	4.19	27	0	0	43	32	25	47
Kobos, Scott, Jr.	1	0	7.62	4	2	0	13	14	2	13
McCambley, Zach, Fr.	3	0	3.14	18	7	0	49	45	25	50
Orlando, Patrick, So.	2	2	3.73	18	0	0	31	29	10	20
Peavyhouse, Saddon, Fr.	2	3	6.00	18	1	2	27	30	17	32
Simonelli, Anthony, Fr.	3	1	7.00	9	6	0	27	28	10	13
Veneziano, Anthony, So.	7	1	3.73	15	12	0	59	50	25	36

25. HOUSTON

Coach: Todd Whitting. **Record:** 38-25

Player, Pos., Year	AVG	OBP	SLG	AB	R	2B	3B	HR	RBI	SB
Bartlett, Charlie, C, Rs-Fr.	.333	.600	.667	3	0	1	0	0	1	0
Bielamowicz, Tyler, OF, So.	.309	.449	.456	136	34	3	1	5	24	4
Brown, Ron, 1B/DH, Fr.	.135	.214	.189	37	2	2	0	0	1	0
Champion II, Wendell, OF, So.	.189	.362	.297	37	4	1	0	1	6	2
Coldiron, Cooper, INF, Sr.	.194	.285	.225	222	23	4	0	1	38	19
Davis, Joe, INF, Jr.	.318	.375	.554	242	40	18	0	13	62	0
Etzel, Landon, OF, So.	.238	.340	.377	122	21	2	3	3	15	9
Fuentes III, Rey, INF, Jr.	.222	.288	.259	54	3	2	0	0	4	2
Hollis, Connor, INF, Sr.	.302	.400	.420	245	50	19	2	2	25	6
Lockhart Jr., Lael, UTIL, Jr.	.297	.425	.419	229	43	17	1	3	44	2
Lovelace, Kyle, C, Fr.	.200	.265	.216	125	7	2	0	0	6	3
Minter, Drew, OF, Fr.	.200	.267	.333	90	13	9	0	1	12	3
Padgett, Grayson, OF, So.	.264	.353	.373	220	34	9	3	3	19	15
Redden, Tucker, C, Jr.	.182	.282	.197	66	4	1	0	0	5	0
Slaughter, Nick, C, So.	.163	.241	.163	49	4	0	0	0	8	3
Triolo, Jared, INF, So.	.344	.434	.457	247	45	11	1	5	28	17

Pitcher, Year	W	L	ERA	G	GS	SV	IP	H	BB	SO
Aguilar, Clay, Fr.	0	0	1.23	5	1	0	15	7	4	17
Bielamowicz, Tyler, So.	0	2	11.00	6	2	0	9	13	8	6
Bond, Nolan, Jr.	0	1	4.81	10	2	0	24	22	10	13
Cumbie, Trey, Jr.	7	4	3.47	16	16	0	104	81	26	110
Edwards, Hunter, Rs-Fr.	1	0	4.80	10	0	0	15	15	7	8
Fletcher, Aaron, Jr.	7	3	2.19	16	15	0	94	86	18	78
Hattingh, Griffin, Fr.	0	0	4.50	5	0	0	4	4	3	3
Henry, Carter, So.	5	1	2.09	28	0	6	47	36	23	51
Hurdsman, Brayson, So.	2	4	4.22	19	7	0	53	50	15	41
Juergens, Spencer, Jr.	0	0	0.00	1	0	0	0	0	3	0
Lester, Dylan, Rs-Fr.	0	0	5.40	6	0	0	5	4	5	4
Lockhart Jr., Lael, So.	1	2	6.64	13	5	3	20	19	14	22
Ott, Kyle, Sr.	3	0	4.15	23	0	0	22	16	17	21
Pulido, Joey, Sr.	6	2	3.55	28	1	6	51	43	19	53
Randel, Ryan, Jr.	5	4	4.58	17	13	0	73	67	31	53
Sundgren, Trevis, Fr.	0	0	30.86	5	0	0	2	5	7	1
Villarreal, Fred, Sr.	1	2	4.43	12	1	0	22	26	11	11

NCAA regional teams in bold. Conference category leaders in bold.
*Team won conference's automatic regional bid. #Category leader who did not qualify for batting or pitching title.

AMERICA EAST CONFERENCE

	Conference		Overall	
	W	L	W	L
* Hartford	16	8	26	31
Massachusetts-Lowell	13	11	25	29
Maryland-Baltimore County	12	11	22	29
Stony Brook	12	12	32	25
Maine	12	12	20	34
Albany	9	14	20	28
Binghamton	9	15	18	30

ALL-CONFERENCE TEAM: C: Christopher Bec, Sr., Maine. **1B:** T.J. Ward, Sr., Hartford. **2B:** A.J. Wright, Jr., UMBC. **3B:** Bobby Honeyman, Sr., Stony Brook. **SS:** Nick Grande, So., Stony Brook. **OF:** Ashton Bardzell, Jr., Hartford; Nick Campana, Sr., Hartford; Russ Olive, Jr., UMass-Lowell. **DH:** Chris Sullivan, Jr., Hartford. **SP:** Dominic Savino, Jr., Albany; Nicholas Dombkowski, Fr., Hartford; Andrew Ryan, Sr., UMass-Lowell; Greg Marino, So., Stony Brook. **RP:** Aaron Pinto, Sr., Stony Brook. **Player of the Year:** Nick Campana, Hartford. **Pitcher of the Year:** Nicholas Dombkowski, Hartford. **Coach of the Year:** Justin Blood, Hartford. **Rookie of the Year:** Nicholas Dombkowski, Hartford.

INDIVIDUAL BATTING LEADERS
(Minimum 140 at-bats)

	AVG	OBP	SLG	AB	2B	3B	HR	RBI	SB
Nick Campana, Hartford	.379	.464	.611	203	17	0	10	39	21
Nick Grande, Stony Brook	.377	.468	.560	207	18	1	6	28	32
Russ Olive, UMass-Lowell	.359	.460	.641	198	13	2	13	37	3
Bobby Honeyman, Stony Brook	.336	.387	.479	211	12	6	2	33	8
Christopher Bec, Maine	.318	.382	.547	179	11	3	8	29	16
Ashton Bardzell, Hartford	.313	.412	.540	198	9	3	10	41	9
Hernan Sardinas, Maine	.312	.360	.507	215	17	2	7	37	8
Jeremy Pena, Maine	.311	.396	.472	212	9	5	5	28	10
Jackson Olson, Hartford	.308	.348	.394	198	14	0	1	22	7
Andruw Gazzola, Stony Brook	.307	.394	.429	140	7	2	2	21	2
Patrick Lagravinese, Albany	.305	.429	.401	167	9	2	1	24	3
Steve Passatempo, UMass-Lowell	.304	.394	.500	184	10	1	8	32	2
Zack Bright, UMBC	.302	.340	.459	172	11	2	4	33	8
Danny Casals, Maine	.302	.405	.593	182	11	0	14	49	4
Zachary Ardito, Hartford	.295	.338	.389	193	12	3	0	29	10
Michael Wilson, Stony Brook	.293	.362	.498	205	20	5	4	40	4
Ryan Hernandez, Albany	.289	.353	.410	166	14	0	2	12	1
Christian Torres, UMBC	.282	.372	.409	149	11	1	1	23	3
Raven Beeman, UMBC	.282	.402	.380	163	5	1	4	25	7
AJ Wright, UMBC	.280	.367	.440	182	20	0	3	30	8
Kevin Doody, Maine	.278	.323	.307	176	3	1	0	14	14
Jason Agresti, Binghamton	.277	.391	.399	148	15	0	1	28	2
Colby Maiola, UMass-Lowell	.276	.401	.464	192	7	4	7	37	19
Travis Collins, Albany	.276	.380	.368	163	9	0	2	12	3

INDIVIDUAL PITCHING LEADERS
(Minimum 40 innings pitched)

	W	L	ERA	G	SV	IP	H	BB	SO
Aaron Pinto, Stony Brook	5	2	1.05	23	12	43	29	11	50
Stephen Schoch, UMBC	1	6	1.72	24	10	58	42	19	71
Nicholas Dombkowski, Hartford	6	4	2.90	14	0	87	70	23	68
Andrew Ryan, UMass-Lowell	5	4	3.18	15	0	91	86	35	83
Aaron Glickstein, Stony Brook	3	0	3.22	18	2	45	34	25	31
Mitchell Wilson, UMBC	3	1	3.40	12	1	42	34	24	28
Cody Laweryson, Maine	3	3	3.42	21	2	53	51	9	52
Nick Rand, UMass-Lowell	3	3	3.61	18	4	47	48	19	46
Dominic Savino, Albany	8	4	3.63	15	1	79	79	32	69
Nick Wegmann, Binghamton	3	7	3.71	14	0	70	75	21	56
Nathan Florence, Hartford	4	6	3.78	15	0	86	91	28	93
Brian Herrmann, Stony Brook	5	7	4.38	15	0	78	87	25	50
John Arel, Maine	5	4	4.41	15	0	65	52	35	57
Nick Gallagher, Binghamton	4	7	4.52	14	0	66	64	31	59

Clemson outfielder Seth Beer hit 22 home runs in an All-American junior season.

AMERICAN ATHLETIC CONFERENCE

	Conference		Overall	
	W	L	W	L
Houston	16	8	38	25
South Florida	14	9	36	22
Connecticut	14	10	37	22
* East Carolina	14	10	44	18
Central Florida	13	10	35	21
Cincinnati	12	12	28	28
Wichita State	9	14	35	21
Tulane	9	14	25	33
Memphis	5	19	20	36

ALL-CONFERENCE TEAM: C: Gunnar Troutwine, Sr., Wichita State. **1B:** Rylan Thomas, So., Central Florida. **2B:** Brady Lloyd, Jr., East Carolina. **3B:** David Villar, Jr., South Florida. **SS:** Manny Rodriguez, Sr., Cincinnati. **OF:** Isaac Feldstein, Sr., Connecticut; Bryant Packard, So., East Carolina; Grant Witherspoon, Jr., Tulane. **DH:** Spencer Brickhouse, So., East Carolina. **UTL:** Luke Ritter, Jr., Wichita State. **SP:** J.T. Perez, Sr., Cincinnati; Mason Feole, So., Connecticut; Chris Holba, Jr., East Carolina; Aaron Fletcher, Jr., Houston. **RP:** Thad Ward, Jr., Central Florida. **Player of the Year:** Bryant Packard, East Carolina. **Pitcher of the Year:** Aaron Fletcher, Houston. **Coach of the Year:** Todd Whitting, Houston. **Rookie of the Year:** Alec Burleson, East Carolina; Christian Fedko, Connecticut.

INDIVIDUAL BATTING LEADERS
(Minimum 140 at-bats)

	AVG	OBP	SLG	AB	2B	3B	HR	RBI	SB
Bryant Packard, East Carolina	.406	.462	.671	219	16	0	14	50	6
David Villar, South Florida	.374	.463	.648	219	24	0	12	59	1

	AVG	OBP	SLG	AB	2B	3B	HR	RBI	SB
Jared Triolo, Houston	.344	.434	.457	247	11	1	5	28	17
Rylan Thomas, Central Florida	.343	.447	.587	213	13	0	13	55	4
Luke Ritter, Wichita State	.341	.420	.484	223	12	1	6	31	6
Alec Bohm, Wichita State	.339	.436	.625	224	14	1	16	55	9
Zac Susi, Connecticut	.335	.429	.402	209	9	1	1	33	2
Kyle Mottice, Cincinnati	.335	.433	.443	221	11	2	3	29	20
Kyle Phillips, South Florida	.333	.403	.477	195	13	0	5	22	7
Coco Montes, South Florida	.331	.400	.487	236	23	1	4	40	7
Grant Witherspoon, Tulane	.330	.436	.587	230	19	2	12	53	13
Duke Stunkel Jr., South Florida	.330	.385	.442	224	16	0	3	24	2
Troy Stefanski, Connecticut	.325	.373	.442	231	10	1	5	35	14
Brady Lloyd, East Carolina	.322	.388	.402	214	11	0	2	25	16
Anthony Prato, Connecticut	.320	.384	.406	244	11	2	2	23	18
Joe Davis, Houston	.318	.375	.554	242	18	0	13	62	0
Tyler Osik, Central Florida	.310	.391	.485	200	6	1	9	56	4
Greyson Jenista, Wichita State	.309	.446	.475	204	7	0	9	38	12
Trevor Jensen, Tulane	.306	.369	.518	193	12	1	9	35	1
Joe Genord, South Florida	.306	.394	.633	180	11	0	16	53	0
Jonathon Artigues, Tulane	.303	.385	.420	231	16	1	3	38	10
Michael Woodworth, Connecticut	.302	.364	.395	205	5	1	4	22	13
Gunnar Troutwine, Wichita St.	.302	.413	.505	182	14	1	7	48	1
Connor Hollis, Houston	.302	.400	.420	245	19	2	2	25	6
Ray Alejo, Central Florida	.299	.379	.402	224	14	3	1	25	34
Garrett Zech, South Florida	.257	.327	.446	202	8	6	6	22	14

INDIVIDUAL PITCHING LEADERS
(Minimum 40 innings pitched)

	W	L	ERA	G	SV	IP	H	BB	SO
Aaron Fletcher, Houston	7	3	2.19	16	0	94	86	18	78
Mason Feole, Connecticut	9	2	2.50	16	0	101	82	49	120
J.J. Montgomery, Central Fla.	5	4	2.54	17	1	64	54	21	74
Chris Williams, Central Florida	4	3	2.81	15	0	93	76	17	79
J.T. Perez, Cincinnati	6	4	2.81	15	0	93	81	36	72
Chris Holba, East Carolina	9	1	2.99	15	0	81	86	20	60
Hunter Smith, Memphis	3	2	3.08	23	2	64	61	15	63
Trey Benton, East Carolina	4	5	3.13	22	0	69	69	13	68
Thad Ward, Central Florida	5	4	3.27	22	2	63	46	26	84
Joe Sheridan, Central Florida	3	3	3.36	12	0	56	46	37	49
Keagan Gillies, Tulane	6	6	3.36	14	0	80	67	31	57
Shane McClanahan, South Fla.	5	6	3.42	14	0	76	51	48	120
Trey Cumbie, Houston	7	4	3.47	16	0	104	81	26	110
Jonathan Bowlan, Memphis	2	9	3.71	14	0	85	93	18	104
P.J. Poulin, Connecticut	6	2	3.26	31	16	50	44	20	60

ATLANTIC COAST CONFERENCE

Atlantic Division	Conference W	L	Overall W	L
Clemson	22	8	47	16
North Carolina State	19	11	42	18
Louisville	18	12	45	19
* Florida State	16	13	43	19
Wake Forest	13	17	25	32
Notre Dame	12	18	24	30
Boston College	7	22	17	32

Coastal Division	Conference W	L	Overall W	L
North Carolina	22	8	44	20
Duke	18	11	45	18
Miami	16	13	28	26
Georgia Tech	14	16	31	27
Virginia	12	18	29	25
Pittsburgh	11	19	29	26
Virginia Tech	8	22	21	33

ALL-CONFERENCE TEAM: C: Cal Raleigh, Jr., Florida State; Joey Bart, Jr., Georgia Tech. **1B:** Logan Wyatt, So., Louisville. **2B:** Wade Bailey, Sr., Georgia Tech; Andy Weber, Jr., Virginia. **3B:** Kyle Datres, Jr., North Carolina. **SS:** Will Wilson, So., North Carolina State. **OF:** Seth Beer, Jr., Clemson; Josh Stowers, Jr., Louisville; Josh McLain, Sr., North Carolina State; Brett Kinneman, Sr., North Carolina State. **DH/UTL:** Tristin English, R-So., Georgia Tech. **SP:** Connor Thomas, So., Georgia Tech; Drew Parrish, So., Florida State; Brian Brown, Sr., North Carolina State. **RP:** Ryley Gilliam, Jr., Clemson. **Player of the Year:** Joey Bart, Georgia Tech.

Pitcher of the Year: Brian Brown, North Carolina State. **Coach of the Year:** Mike Fox, North Carolina. **Rookie of the Year:** Patrick Bailey, North Carolina State.

INDIVIDUAL BATTING LEADERS
(Minimum 140 at-bats)

	AVG	OBP	SLG	AB	2B	3B	HR	RBI	SB
Joey Bart, Georgia Tech	.359	.471	.632	220	12	0	16	38	3
Kyle Datres, North Carolina	.345	.438	.511	264	17	3	7	36	12
Josh McClain, North Carolina St.	.344	.375	.458	273	13	3	4	40	12
Andy Weber, Virginia	.344	.415	.536	209	19	3	5	49	4
Chase Murray, Georgia Tech	.343	.410	.510	210	11	3	6	39	4
Wade Bailey, Georgia Tech	.339	.420	.430	230	13	1	2	31	9
Logan Wyatt, Louisville	.339	.490	.522	230	22	1	6	69	1
Josh Stowers, Louisville	.336	.477	.559	220	14	4	9	60	36
Danny Oriente, Louisville	.331	.403	.416	178	10	1	1	41	5
Cal Raleigh, Florida State	.326	.447	.583	230	18	1	13	54	2
Kyle Wilkie, Clemson	.324	.422	.440	216	10	0	5	40	2
Patrick Bailey, North Carolina St.	.321	.419	.604	187	8	3	13	40	0
Brian Dempsey, Boston College	.319	.414	.337	163	3	0	0	20	7
Michael Busch, North Carolina	.317	.465	.521	240	10	0	13	63	8
Chris Galland, Boston College	.316	.403	.398	171	10	2	0	18	28
Jake Palomaki, Boston College	.315	.421	.445	200	13	2	3	32	19
Joey Loperfido, Duke	.315	.408	.475	219	11	3	6	43	16
Drew Mendoza, Florida State	.313	.440	.491	224	17	1	7	44	3
Nick Podkul, Notre Dame	.312	.433	.525	202	13	3	8	40	9
Matt Vierling, Notre Dame	.310	.402	.505	210	7	2	10	43	5
Brock Deatherage, N.C. St.	.307	.397	.548	228	7	3	14	41	18
Will Wilson, North Carolina St.	.307	.376	.588	238	16	3	15	53	1
Ike Freeman, North Carolina	.305	.383	.377	223	5	1	3	51	3
Jimmy Herron, Duke	.304	.419	.460	250	18	3	5	36	23
Devin Mann, Louisville	.303	.446	.504	228	17	4	7	52	15
Seth Beer, Clemson	.301	.456	.642	226	11	0	22	54	1
Alex Kerschner, Notre Dame	.284	.376	.439	155	8	5	2	24	0
Chris Williams, Clemson	.281	.401	.562	238	12	0	18	72	3

INDIVIDUAL PITCHING LEADERS
(Minimum 40 innings pitched)

	W	L	ERA	G	SV	IP	H	BB	SO
Daniel Federman, Miami	2	4	2.25	23	0	60	45	22	54
Kent Klyman, North Carolina St.	8	2	2.34	31	4	62	46	25	67
Ryan Miller, Clemson	7	1	2.51	26	4	72	63	17	64
Drew Parrish, Florida State	5	1	2.52	16	0	107	71	37	128
Adam Wolf, Louisville	8	2	2.63	16	0	103	80	29	109
Brian Brown, North Carolina St.	7	2	2.74	16	0	99	84	26	98
Brett Daniels, North Carolina	6	1	2.77	39	2	65	62	29	74
Nick Bennett, Louisville	8	2	2.84	14	0	73	54	27	72
Bryan Hoeing, Louisville	7	2	2.88	24	0	69	63	25	51
Bobby Miller, Louisville	6	1	2.97	17	0	67	49	21	55
Cooper Criswell, North Carolina	6	2	2.99	26	1	75	71	12	86
Matt Pidich, Pittsburgh	6	2	3.06	15	0	91	82	26	99
Reid Johnston, North Carolina St.	7	1	3.06	21	4	65	54	15	49
Brooks Crawford, Clemson	8	2	3.24	16	0	81	71	18	58
Jeb Bargfeldt, Miami	4	5	3.29	15	0	101	83	30	76
Connor Thomas, Georgia Tech	7	4	3.34	16	1	97	90	10	106
Jake Higginbotham, Clemson	6	1	3.47	16	0	80	70	32	63
Derek Casey, Virginia	7	4	3.48	14	0	96	98	25	106
Evan McKendry, Miami	7	6	3.52	14	0	87	79	33	114
Brian Rapp, Boston College	3	5	3.57	12	0	71	48	37	74
Griffin Roberts, Wake Forest	5	4	3.82	14	0	97	78	38	130
Colin Peluse, Wake Forest	6	2	3.87	16	0	84	74	26	63
Jacob Hennessy, Clemson	4	3	3.91	14	0	71	72	14	54
Daniel Lynch, Virginia	4	4	3.96	13	0	89	86	24	105
Andrew Cabezas, Miami	6	4	3.96	19	2	75	53	43	79
Andrew McDonald, Virginia Tech	1	8	4.45	29	5	55	68	27	67
Dan Metzdorf, Boston College	1	8	5.74	13	0	69	77	30	61

St. John's third baseman John Valente led the Big East Conference in batting.

	AVG	OBP	SLG	AB	2B	3B	HR	RBI	SB
Tyler Simon, Kennesaw State	.311	.371	.435	177	11	1	3	26	7
Mike Spooner, Stetson	.304	.380	.462	184	15	1	4	33	8
Grant Williams, Kennesaw St.	.304	.397	.458	214	16	1	5	37	2
Brooks Wilson, Stetson	.302	.417	.462	182	16	2	3	34	8
Jeffrey Crisan, Lipscomb	.301	.385	.494	166	5	0	9	38	0
Ruben Someillan, Jacksonville	.299	.400	.344	224	8	1	0	26	9
David Marcano, NJIT	.297	.368	.352	165	4	1	1	16	4
Gage Morey, Florida Gulf Coast	.296	.418	.369	179	11	1	0	19	6
LaDonis Bryant, Kennesaw St.	.294	.392	.418	170	7	4	2	19	13
Pat Raiff, USC Upstate	.292	.401	.370	192	4	4	1	21	2
Jacob Koos, Stetson	.288	.387	.424	229	14	4	3	34	23
Russel Schwertfeger, USC Upstate	.287	.357	.451	195	7	5	5	36	8
Jay Prather, North Florida	.286	.341	.372	199	6	1	3	34	4
Christian Proffitt, Fla. Gulf Coast	.284	.392	.310	155	4	0	0	25	1
Kohl Gilmore, Florida Gulf Coast	.282	.399	.525	202	14	1	11	43	0

INDIVIDUAL PITCHING LEADERS
(Minimum 40 innings pitched)

	W	L	ERA	G	SV	IP	H	BB	SO
Frank German, North Florida	8	3	1.58	14	0	91	62	14	108
Joey Gonzalez, Stetson	8	3	2.07	15	1	78	60	32	79
Jack Perkins, Stetson	11	2	2.34	17	0	104	89	31	106
Josh Dye, Florida Gulf Coast	8	4	2.40	14	0	94	79	16	74
Mitchell Senger, Stetson	9	2	2.56	14	0	88	61	27	110
Chris Gau, Jacksonville	9	3	2.58	16	0	112	90	21	95
Logan Gilbert, Stetson	11	2	2.72	16	0	112	71	25	163
Blake Whitney, USC Upstate	5	3	2.81	13	0	74	61	21	82
Tyler Stafflinger, NJIT	4	5	2.87	13	0	53	39	20	36
Noah Thompson, Lipscomb	3	4	3.02	11	0	60	50	24	26
Mario Leon, Florida Gulf Coast	5	6	3.05	14	0	83	81	30	83
Evan Lumbert, Fla. Gulf Coast	6	3	3.11	14	0	64	64	19	66
A.J. Moore, Kennesaw State	5	3	3.24	14	0	81	57	47	87
Robbie Knox, Lipscomb	4	5	3.29	29	5	55	58	13	37
Brooks Wilson, Stetson	6	0	2.13	31	20	55	40	19	68
Ryan Kennedy, Kennesaw State	2	7	7.89	14	0	43	63	24	35
Nicko Ortega, Lipscomb	4	1	3.53	27	0	43	34	29	39
Jacob Thiessen, USC Upstate	1	4	5.36	13	0	42	55	10	27

ATLANTIC SUN CONFERENCE

	Conference		Overall	
	W	L	W	L
* Stetson	15	3	48	13
Jacksonville	14	6	40	21
Kennesaw State	11	10	25	30
North Florida	10	11	28	28
Lipscomb	9	12	24	30
NJIT	9	12	22	25
Florida Gulf Coast	8	13	32	21
South Carolina-Upstate	5	14	23	28

ALL-CONFERENCE TEAM: C: Alex Brait, So., Florida Gulf Coast. **1B:** Angel Camacho, Jr., Jacksonville. **2B:** Chris Lehane, Sr., Jacksonville. **3B:** Richie Garica, So., Florida Gulf Coast. **SS:** Scott Dubrule, So., Jacksonville. **OF:** Tanner Murphy, So., North Florida; Terence Norman, So., Kennesaw State; Jesse Uttendorfer, Sr., NJIT. **DH:** Blake Voyles, Sr., North Florida. **SP:** Logan Gilbert, Jr., Stetson; Frank German, Jr., North Florida; Jack Perkins, Jr., Stetson. **RP:** Brooks Wilson, Sr., Stetson. **Player of the Year:** Brooks Wilson, Stetson. **Pitcher of the Year:** Logan Gilbert, Stetson. **Coach of the Year:** Steve Trimper, Stetson. **Rookie of the Year:** Christian Proffitt, Florida Gulf Coast.

INDIVIDUAL BATTING LEADERS
(Minimum 140 at-bats)

	AVG	OBP	SLG	AB	2B	3B	HR	RBI	SB
Scott Dubrule, Jacksonville	.348	.409	.418	244	11	3	0	54	5
Alex Brait, Florida Gulf Coast	.335	.404	.467	182	5	2	5	27	2
Terence Norman, Kennesaw St.	.333	.387	.402	189	7	0	2	32	3
Kyle Gensler, USC Upstate	.330	.420	.388	188	7	2	0	31	3
Angel Camacho, Jacksonville	.329	.394	.454	249	12	2	5	58	0
Jesse Uttendorfer, NJIT	.326	.387	.481	181	16	3	2	28	14
Tanner Murphy, North Florida	.326	.418	.534	221	12	2	10	40	15
Richie Garcia, Fla. Gulf Coast	.324	.411	.533	210	17	3	7	50	7
Charlie Carpenter, USC Upstate	.323	.445	.464	192	9	3	4	38	1
Blake Voyles, North Florida	.320	.366	.453	172	12	1	3	37	0
Chris Lehane, Jacksonville	.315	.412	.384	219	10	1	1	35	11

ATLANTIC 10 CONFERENCE

	Conference		Overall	
	W	L	W	L
* Saint Louis	19	4	38	20
Fordham	16	8	35	19
George Mason	16	8	29	27
Richmond	15	9	32	24
Davidson	14	10	33	21
Virginia Commonwealth	14	10	34	23
George Washington	13	11	32	26
Rhode Island	13	11	24	27
Dayton	10	14	21	31
Saint Joseph's	7	15	21	27
St. Bonaventure	6	15	10	32
Massachusetts	6	18	15	29
La Salle	4	20	14	41

ALL-CONFERENCE TEAM: C: Logan Driscoll, So., George Mason. **1B:** Nick Reeser, Sr., Saint Louis. **2B:** Jake MacKenzie, Fr., Fordham. **3B:** Isaiah Pasteur, Sr., George Washington. **SS:** Alex King, Sr., Saint Louis. **OF:** Mark Osis, Sr., George Washington; Jake Garella, So., Saint Louis; Parker Sniatynski, Sr., Saint Louis. **DH:** Dominic D'Alessandro, Jr., George Washington. **SP:** Robbie Baker, Sr., Richmond; Miller Hogan, Jr., Saint Louis. **RP:** Layne Looney, Jr., Richmond. **Player of the Year:** Isaiah Pasteur, George Washington. **Pitcher of the Year:** Miller Hogan, Saint Louis. **Coach of the Year:** Darin Hendrickson, Saint Louis. **Rookie of the Year:** Jake MacKenzie, Fordham.

INDIVIDUAL BATTING LEADERS
(Minimum 140 at-bats)

	AVG	OBP	SLG	AB	2B	3B	HR	RBI	SB
Jake Garella, Saint Louis	.352	.421	.458	221	14	2	2	47	2
Ben Faso, La Salle	.347	.391	.468	216	17	0	3	36	9
Hogan Brown, VCU	.344	.436	.429	154	11	1	0	21	7
Logan Driscoll, George Mason	.342	.407	.473	222	13	2	4	37	10

TOMASSO DeROSA

	AVG	OBP	SLG	AB	2B	3B	HR	RBI	SB
Eric Jones, Davidson	.333	.443	.577	201	14	1	11	60	2
Isaiah Pasteur, George Washington	.331	.398	.589	236	14	7	11	49	31
Nick Reeser, Saint Louis	.332	.417	.468	198	11	2	4	41	
1 Vinny Capra, Richmond	.327	.435	.485	202	13	2	5	41	9
Ryan MacCarrick, St. Bonaventure	.323	.390	.427	164	11	0	2	24	7
Mike Magnanti, St. Bonaventure	.321	.422	.359	156	4	1	0	12	6
Dominic D'Alessandro, George Washington	.318	.394	.544	195	15	1	9	47	1
Mark Osis, George Washington	.317	.388	.496	224	16	3	6	55	8
Charlie Concannon, St. Joseph's	.317	.393	.483	180	11	2	5	29	3
Trevor Kelly, George Mason	.313	.343	.534	233	18	2	9	48	2
Tyler Nelin, George Mason	.313	.425	.373	166	10	0	0	17	0
Parker Sniatsky, Saint Louis	.313	.416	.570	214	18	5	9	49	20
Steven Barmakian, George Washington	.310	.371	.354	229	8	1	0	27	14
Daane Berezo, VCU	.310	.412	.376	213	12	1	0	30	5
J Coutts, Rhode Island	.310	.388	.394	155	10	0	1	21	0
Robbie Metz, George Washington	.309	.340	.432	243	18	0	4	42	24
Michael Smith, George Mason	.307	.393	.413	150	6	5	0	19	6
Cole Dubet, Saint Louis	.303	.375	.438	201	11	1	4	23	7
Haiden Lamb, VCU	.303	.389	.332	208	6	0	0	16	26
Max Bazin, Davidson	.301	.390	.393	183	7	2	2	14	4
Austin Constantini, La Salle	.298	.378	.356	225	6	2	1	20	7
Alex King, Saint Louis	.287	.388	.569	209	13	2	14	51	12
Jake Mackenzie, Fordham	.291	.389	.523	199	10	6	8	42	34
Justin Bardwell, Fordham	.284	.351	.383	201	20	0	0	36	4

INDIVIDUAL PITCHING LEADERS
(Minimum 40 innings pitched)

	W	L	ERA	G	SV	IP	H	BB	SO
Drew Reveno, Saint Louis	10	2	1.84	17	0	64	45	27	47
Taso Stathopoulos, Rhode Island	4	1	1.95	11	0	55	49	12	36
Miller Hogan, Saint Louis	10	3	2.19	15	0	103	73	12	129
Reiss Knehr, Fordham	6	3	2.4	15	0	90	72	48	93
Ben Greenberg, Fordham	6	2	2.4	15	0	82	69	31	65
Zach Mort, George Mason	6	3	2.48	15	0	105	93	13	108
Justin Lasko, Massachusetts	4	4	2.52	12	0	82	76	20	63
Robbie Baker, Richmond	9	2	2.55	15	0	85	65	23	78
Connor Gillispie, VCU	7	3	2.57	18	0	74	62	20	97
Elliott Raimo, George Washington	3	4	2.76	12	0	72	56	14	72
Matt Murphy, Rhode Island	4	3	2.78	13	0	74	79	11	56
Tim Brennan, St. Joseph's	9	3	2.94	13	0	88	75	5	84
Sean Thompson, VCU	8	3	3.03	15	0	92	81	27	79
Tim Miller, Richmond	5	3	3.13	14	0	75	66	29	63
Justin Aungst, St. Joseph's	2	9	3.57	13	0	71	74	18	58

	AVG	OBP	SLG	AB	2B	3B	HR	RBI	SB
Gehrig Parker, Butler	.336	.424	.536	211	15	3	7	37	5
Will Robertson, Creighton	.333	.412	.641	198	17	4	12	59	4
Conor Grammes, Xavier	.330	.375	.517	209	7	1	10	27	1
Jamie Galazin, St. John's	.329	.419	.521	219	16	4	6	44	11
Rob Dadona, Seton Hall	.323	.383	.409	186	7	0	3	27	7
Clark Brinkman, Creighton	.317	.416	.471	208	13	2	5	28	24
Josh Shaw, St. John's	.316	.363	.424	231	17	1	2	46	3
Ryan Ramiz, Seton Hall	.316	.432	.427	171	13	3	0	32	8
Al Molina, Seton Hall	.314	.376	.490	194	17	1	5	29	5
Tyler Houston, Butler	.312	.382	.468	231	18	3	4	32	8
Jake Bernstein, Georgetown	.310	.413	.425	200	12	1	3	23	8
Garrett Christman, Butler	.310	.375	.381	197	7	2	1	48	5
Ryan M. Davis, Georgetown	.303	.359	.385	208	12	1	1	26	18
Mike Alescio, Seton Hall	.302	.399	.408	169	7	1	3	24	13
Ryan Toohers, Villanova	.298	.403	.472	178	14	1	5	31	0
Eddie McCabe, Georgetown	.297	.381	.411	209	12	3	2	36	1
Michael Hartnagel, Butler	.293	.400	.393	191	16	0	1	26	10
Alex Bernauer, Georgetown	.292	.366	.528	144	11	4	5	33	2
Allbry Major, Xavier	.291	.356	.386	158	9	0	2	21	5
Rob Boselli III, St. John's	.285	.395	.481	158	13	3	4	39	4
Michael Emodi, Creighton	.282	.376	.505	188	15	0	9	44	1
Matt Warkentin, Xavier	.252	.317	.490	202	6	0	14	40	3

INDIVIDUAL PITCHING LEADERS
(Minimum 40 innings pitched)

	W	L	ERA	G	SV	IP	H	BB	SO
Ricky DeVito, Seton Hall	6	3	1.88	12	0	62	42	22	67
Ryan Tapani, Creighton	10	1	2.38	14	0	95	83	25	95
Sean Mooney, St. John's	11	3	2.56	16	0	95	74	28	104
Ryan Pepiot, Butler	6	0	2.62	15	1	76	55	32	101
Kevin Magee, St. John's	7	3	2.67	15	0	78	73	15	92
Jeff Belge, St. John's	6	4	2.84	16	0	67	41	40	79
Brent Killam, Georgetown	6	4	3.06	16	0	82	63	26	97
Billy Layne, Seton Hall	5	1	3.09	15	0	55	54	12	63
Michael LoPresti, St. John's	4	3	3.16	17	0	77	71	29	55
Sam Hubbe, Butler	1	2	3.31	15	0	54	49	23	33
Garrett Christman, Butler	4	6	3.47	13	0	73	66	23	48
Mitch Ragan, Creighton	6	4	3.74	14	0	77	75	36	64
Shane McCarthy, Seton Hall	3	4	4.14	14	0	74	91	16	52
Ryan Doty, Villanova	2	9	4.23	11	0	66	68	24	63

BIG EAST CONFERENCE

Conference			Overall	
	W	L	W	L
* St. John's	15	3	40	17
Seton Hall	13	4	30	20
Butler	9	8	34	20
Creighton	8	9	34	16
Georgetown	8	9	25	30
Xavier	7	11	20	35
Villanova	1	17	9	39

ALL-CONFERENCE TEAM: C: Wyatt Mascarella, Jr., St. John's. **1B:** Luke Stampfl, R-Sr., St. John's; Ryan Toohers, So., Villanova. **2B:** Josh Shaw, Jr., St. John's. **3B:** John Valente, R-Sr., St. John's. **SS:** Michael Hartnagel, Sr., Butler. **OF:** Gehrig Parker, Sr., Butler; Will Robertson, So., Creighton; Jamie Galazin, Sr., St. John's; Ryan Ramiz, Sr., Seton Hall. **DH:** Ryan Mantle, Jr., Creighton. **SP:** Ryan Pepiot, So., Butler; Ryan Tapani, Sr., Creighton; Sean Mooney, So., St. John's; Ricky DeVito, So., Seton Hall. **RP:** Matt Leon, Sr., Seton Hall. **Player of the Year:** John Valente, St. John's. **Pitcher of the Year:** Ricky DeVito, Seton Hall. **Coach of the Year:** Ed Blankmeyer, St. John's. **Rookie of the Year:** Allbry Major, Xavier.

INDIVIDUAL BATTING LEADERS
(Minimum 140 at-bats)

	AVG	OBP	SLG	AB	2B	3B	HR	RBI	SB
John Valente, St. John's	.360	.400	.483	236	8	3	5	40	11
Chris Givin, Xavier	.342	.399	.511	219	13	6	4	45	5
Wyatt Mascarella, St. John's	.340	.394	.535	159	14	1	5	29	0
Luke Stampfl, St. John's	.336	.393	.498	211	11	1	7	34	0

BIG SOUTH CONFERENCE

	Conference		Overall	
	W	L	W	L
* Campbell	21	6	35	26
High Point	19	8	34	22
Liberty	17	10	32	26
Winthrop	15	12	25	31
Gardner-Webb	14	13	31	27
Radford	14	13	25	32
Charleston Southern	10	17	19	35
Longwood	9	18	17	38
Presbyterian	8	19	15	39
UNC Asheville	8	19	13	38

ALL-CONFERENCE TEAM: C: Daniel Millwee, R-Jr., High Point. **INF:** Mitch Spires, Sr., Winthrop; Hunter Lee, Sr., High Point; Jonathan White, Jr., Presbyterian; Corey Howard, Jr., Gardner-Webb; **OF:** Austen Zente, Sr., High Point; Matthew Barefoot, R-So., Campbell; D.J. Artis, Jr., Liberty. **DH:** Jeff Hahs, Sr., Campbell. **UTL:** Tre Todd, Jr., Liberty. **SP:** Allan Winans, R-Sr., Campbell; Austin Ross, R-Sr., Radford; Andrew Gottfried, Jr., High Point. **RP:** Rion Murrah, Sr., High Point; Logan Bender, R-Fr., Campbell. **Player of the Year:** Austen Zente, High Point. **Pitcher of the Year:** Allan Winans, Campbell. **Coach of the Year:** Justin Haire, Campbell. **Rookie of the Year:** Logan Bender, Campbell.

INDIVIDUAL BATTING LEADERS
(Minimum 140 at-bats)

	AVG	OBP	SLG	AB	2B	3B	HR	RBI	SB
Matthew Barefoot, Campbell	.364	.484	.585	217	18	3	8	32	33
Jonathan White, Presbyterian	.358	.441	.519	212	10	0	8	39	2
A.J. Priaulx, Presbyterian	.350	.376	.500	214	14	0	6	41	0
Corey Howard, Gardner-Webb	.347	.421	.449	225	15	1	2	34	7

	AVG	OBP	SLG	AB	2B	3B	HR	RBI	SB
Hunter Lee, High Point	.338	.460	.531	213	15	1	8	44	5
Tanner Wells, High Point	.329	.376	.452	155	7	0	4	20	7
Chris Clary, Garner-Webb	.322	.414	.537	149	6	1	8	20	20
Mitch Spires, Winthrop	.321	.383	.525	221	13	4	8	34	11
Mason Fox, Gardner-Webb	.321	.394	.488	209	13	2	6	40	21
Mickey Dugan, Gardner-Webb	.318	.407	.482	220	8	2	8	43	13
Tre Todd, Liberty	.315	.479	.553	197	11	3	10	52	4
Mike Sconzo, Charleston So.	.309	.363	.411	207	10	1	3	24	0
Tyler Halstead, Winthrop	.299	.340	.451	184	17	1	3	34	2
Austen Zente, High Point	.298	.424	.529	208	7	1	13	38	24
Danny Wilson, UNC Asheville	.293	.394	.371	167	7	0	2	24	4
D.J. Artis, Liberty	.292	.458	.457	219	16	4	4	23	26
Daniel Millwee, High Point	.292	.428	.468	154	10	1	5	30	0
Carson Jackson, High Point	.291	.355	.493	227	15	2	9	45	5
Spencer Horwitz, Radford	.288	.386	.443	219	13	0	7	43	6
Matt Roth, Radford	.287	.355	.441	202	11	1	6	37	4
Tyler Galazin, Liberty	.286	.389	.395	210	9	1	4	39	2
Travis Holt, High Point	.286	.366	.319	210	5	1	0	26	2
Jordan Sergent, High Point	.285	.330	.468	186	12	2	6	31	1
Sammy Miller, Longwood	.277	.415	.364	195	9	1	2	33	20
Eric Jones, Gardner-Webb	.276	.317	.358	232	7	0	4	44	3
Christian Jones, Campbell	.274	.365	.588	226	11	0	20	67	4

INDIVIDUAL PITCHING LEADERS
(Minimum 40 innings pitched)

	W	L	ERA	G	SV	IP	H	BB	SO
Rion Murrah, High Point	5	3	2.06	24	6	57	42	14	55
Allan Winans, Campbell	6	4	2.73	15	0	82	71	24	96
Andrew Gottfried, High Point	6	5	3.28	14	0	74	65	20	72
Cody Maw, Charleston So.	3	2	3.52	18	0	61	60	17	49
Austin Ross, Radford	9	4	3.54	17	0	69	60	22	69
Daniel Willcutt, Winthrop	3	7	3.58	23	0	75	74	19	63
Bradley Hallman, Gardner-Webb	6	2	3.60	16	0	95	97	32	68
Zach Peek, Winthrop	6	5	3.74	14	0	89	78	24	99
Michael Horrell, Campbell	6	4	3.75	14	0	72	69	32	48
Nate Pawelczyk, Winthrop	7	6	3.77	14	0	88	76	37	77
Tyler Weekley, Charleston So.	4	7	3.87	14	0	77	82	16	64
Jackson Bertsch, Liberty	4	4	3.94	21	3	76	.73	25	86
Garret Price, Liberty	7	4	3.99	23	5	65	64	22	75
Eric Miles, Presbyterian	6	5	4.20	20	0	64	65	31	64
Logan Bender, Campbell	5	2	3.42	29	3	47	33	31	64
Evan Nations, Charleston So.	1	3	4.28	16	0	55	75	9	37
Greg Gasparro, UNC Asheville	2	8	4.99	13	0	58	63	42	38

BIG TEN CONFERENCE

Conference			Overall	
	W	L	W	L
* Minnesota	18	4	44	15
Purdue	17	6	38	21
Michigan	15	8	33	21
Illinois	15	9	33	20
Indiana	14	9	40	19
Iowa	13	9	33	20
Ohio State	14	10	36	24
Michigan State	11	12	20	32
Maryland	9	14	24	30
Nebraska	8	14	24	28
Rutgers	7	16	25	25
Northwestern	6	18	17	32
Penn State	3	21	15	34

ALL-CONFERENCE TEAM: C: Tyler Cropley, Sr., Iowa. 1B: Bren Spillane, Jr., Illinois. 2B: Nick Dunn, Jr., Maryland. 3B: Noah McGowan, Sr., Ohio State. SS: Terrin Vavra, Jr., Minnesota. OF: Matt Gorski, So., Indiana; Robert Neustrom, Jr., Iowa; Jonathan Engelmann, Jr., Michigan. DH: Dominic Clementi, So., Michigan. UTL: Matt Lloyd, Jr., Indiana. SP: Jonathan Stiever, Jr., Indiana; Nick Allgeyer, Jr., Iowa; Patrick Fredrickson, Fr., Minnesota. RP: Max Meyer, Fr., Minnesota. Player of the Year: Bren Spillane, Illinois. Pitcher of the Year: Patrick Fredrickson, Minnesota. Coach of the Year: John Anderson, Minnesota. Rookie of the Year: Patrick Fredrickson, Minnesota.

INDIVIDUAL BATTING LEADERS
(Minimum 140 at-bats)

	AVG	OBP	SLG	AB	2B	3B	HR	RBI	SB
Bren Spillane, Illinois	.389	.498	.903	175	17	2	23	60	16
Terrin Vavra, Minnesota	.386	.455	.614	223	13	4	10	59	8
Ben Mezzenga, Minnesota	.386	.469	.450	189	8	2	0	28	12
Jesse Wilkening, Nebraska	.372	.445	.588	199	14	1	9	56	0
Scott Schrieber, Nebraska	.369	.446	.692	214	13	1	18	48	4
Matt Gorski, Indiana	.356	.404	.554	222	14	3	8	40	24
Noah McGowan, Ohio State	.351	.438	.561	228	19	1	9	55	0
Jonathan Engelmann, Michigan	.351	.431	.521	211	14	2	6	44	21
Tyler Cropley, Iowa	.342	.449	.578	199	20	0	9	50	4
Kobie Foppe, Ohio State	.335	.441	.385	200	6	2	0	29	8
Skyler Hunter, Purdue	.333	.385	.427	234	13	3	1	39	11
Nick Dunn, Maryland	.330	.419	.561	212	17	1	10	39	3
Jesse Franklin, Michigan	.327	.379	.588	165	11	1	10	47	4
Michael Massey, Illinois	.326	.369	.514	218	17	3	6	46	2
Dominic Canzone, Ohio State	.323	.395	.447	257	18	1	4	35	15
Luke Petterson, Ohio State	.322	.406	.397	242	13	1	1	27	13
Tyler Cowles, Ohio State	.322	.398	.522	230	20	1	8	49	1
Toby Hanson, Minnesota	.318	.398	.486	173	16	2	3	33	5
Jack Dunn, Northwestern	.314	.399	.381	194	8	1	1	22	21
Robert Neustrom, Iowa	.311	.386	.538	212	15	0	11	36	4
Luke Miller, Indiana	.309	.347	.586	181	11	0	13	34	1
Jack Claeys, Northwestern	.306	.386	.518	170	10	1	8	39	8
Ryan Sloniger, Penn State	.306	.404	.494	170	13	2	5	31	5
Jacson McGowan, Purdue	.304	.442	.544	204	10	0	13	59	2
Ben Nisle, Purdue	.304	.368	.495	184	12	1	7	43	6
Bryce Kelley, Michigan State	.271	.336	.312	199	6	1	0	16	33

INDIVIDUAL PITCHING LEADERS
(Minimum 40 innings pitched)

	W	L	ERA	G	SV	IP	H	BB	SO
Patrick Frederickson, Minnesota	9	0	1.86	19	0	97	71	27	73
Pauly Milto, Indiana	8	2	2.03	14	0	80	66	24	66
Seth Kinker, Ohio State	6	2	2.27	30	15	63	57	5	60
Nick Allgeyer, Iowa	5	4	2.41	15	0	97	85	28	95
Ben Dragani, Michigan	6	2	2.76	16	0	75	61	26	54
Quinn Snarskis, Illinois	6	1	2.84	13	0	73	63	26	34
Tanner Andrews, Purdue	7	5	2.94	17	0	98	102	41	78
Reggie Meyer, Minnesota	8	4	2.97	17	0	109	95	16	70
Karl Kauffman, Michigan	6	3	3.08	15	0	79	66	32	78
Tommy Henry, Michigan	7	3	3.09	15	0	82	71	26	77
Tim Herrin, Indiana	6	0	3.22	17	0	64	58	23	39
Cole McDonald, Iowa	3	2	3.23	11	0	56	52	17	52
Jonathan Stiever, Indiana	5	6	3.41	16	0	100	94	32	97
Hunter Parsons, Maryland	5	2	3.44	15	0	89	73	27	62
Max Meyer, Minnesota	2	3	2.27	26	16	44	25	13	54
Taylor Bloom, Maryland	3	8	4.99	12	0	79	83	27	50
Brady Schanuel, Iowa	5	7	5.94	14	0	53	51	43	65

BIG 12 CONFERENCE

Conference			Overall	
	W	L	W	L
Texas	17	7	42	23
Oklahoma State	16	8	31	26
Texas Tech	15	9	45	20
Oklahoma	14	10	38	25
* Baylor	13	11	37	21
Texas Christian	10	13	33	23
West Virginia	9	15	29	27
Kansas	8	15	27	30
Kansas State	5	19	23	31

ALL-CONFERENCE TEAM: C: Shea Langeliers, So., Baylor. INF: Josh Jung, So., Texas Tech; Davis Wendzel, So., Baylor; Kody Clemens, Jr., Texas; Gabe Holt, Fr., Texas Tech; Kyle Gray, Jr., West Virginia. OF: Steele Walker, Jr., Oklahoma; Duke Ellis, So., Texas; Grant Little, So., Texas Tech. DH: Zach Zubia, Fr., Texas; Zach Rheams, Sr., Texas Tech. UTL: Will Brennan, So., Kansas State. SP: Cody Bradford, So., Baylor; Jake Irvin, Jr., Oklahoma; Carson Teel, Jr., Oklahoma State; Caleb Kilian, So., Texas Tech. RP: Austin Hansen, Jr., Oklahoma; Durbin Feltman, Jr., Texas Christian. Player of the Year: Kody Clemens, Texas. Pitcher of the Year: Cody Bradford,

Baylor. **Coach of the Year:** David Pierce, Texas. **Newcomers of the Year:** Gabe Holt, Texas Tech; Matt Kroon, Oklahoma State.

INDIVIDUAL BATTING LEADERS
(Minimum 2.5 at-bats per team game)

	AVG	OBP	SLG	AB	2B	3B	HR	RBI	SB
Josh Jung, Texas Tech	.392	.491	.639	263	17	6	12	80	4
Kyle Gray, West Virginia	.374	.462	.677	198	12	3	14	38	10
Grant Little, Texas Tech	.370	.462	.642	246	25	3	12	77	11
Will Brennan, Kansas State	.359	.454	.427	220	13	1	0	23	19
Steele Walker, Oklahoma	.352	.441	.606	216	14	1	13	53	7
Kody Clemens, Texas	.351	.444	.726	248	15	3	24	72	5
Gabe Holt, Texas Tech	.348	.440	.485	270	13	3	6	44	29
Richard Cunningham, Baylor	.342	.396	.542	225	14	2	9	38	6
Zach Rheams, Texas Tech	.341	.461	.713	167	11	0	17	55	0
Brylie Ware, Oklahoma	.331	.411	.444	239	20	2	1	41	2
Devin Foyle, West Virginia	.330	.417	.578	206	17	2	10	42	12
Darius Hill, West Virginia	.329	.362	.479	240	20	2	4	36	2
Cameron Warren, Texas Tech	.326	.444	.549	215	16	1	10	53	2
Andy Thomas, Baylor	.324	.435	.384	216	10	0	1	34	4
Brendt Citta, Kansas	.322	.397	.473	205	17	1	4	34	3
Marques Inman, West Virginia	.319	.387	.529	191	20	1	6	40	1
Brian Klein, Texas Tech	.317	.422	.480	202	17	2	4	34	4
Jaxx Groshans, Kansas	.313	.355	.464	211	16	2	4	43	1
A.J. Balta, Texas Christian	.310	.408	.517	203	17	2	7	59	15
Davis Wendzel, Baylor	.310	.435	.532	216	22	1	8	49	4
Brett Vosik, Kansas	.309	.391	.376	178	10	1	0	26	2
Kyle Mendenhall, Oklahoma	.308	.352	.417	240	10	2	4	47	4
Nick Loftin, Baylor	.306	.370	.441	222	12	0	6	36	5
Josh Watson, Texas Christian	.305	.437	.495	210	10	3	8	32	8
Michael Landestoy, Tex. Christian	.304	.399	.397	204	10	0	3	42	4

INDIVIDUAL PITCHING LEADERS
(Minimum 1 IP per team game)

	W	L	ERA	G	SV	IP	H	BB	SO
Cody Bradford, Baylor	7	6	2.51	14	0	97	85	26	87
Kyle Tyler, Oklahoma	6	2	2.97	21	0	67	62	20	84
Ryan Shetter, Texas Tech	6	0	2.97	21	3	73	54	27	79
C. Kilian, Texas Tech	9	3	3.24	20	0	72	60	28	63
Blair Henley, Texas	6	7	3.32	18	1	87	94	37	64
Jake Irvin, Oklahoma	6	2	3.41	16	0	95	76	28	115
Nathan Wiles, Oklahoma	7	3	3.54	16	0	86	86	17	69
Sean Wymer, Texas Christian	6	3	3.65	15	0	74	69	14	69
Hayden Kettler, Baylor	8	4	3.81	16	0	87	84	36	56
B.J. Myers, Texas	2	2	4.19	19	1	77	86	25	59
Nick Lodolo, Texas Christian	7	4	4.32	16	0	77	80	28	93
Carson Teel, Oklahoma State	8	4	4.34	21	3	87	83	38	91
Ryan Zeferjahn, Kansas	8	5	4.48	14	0	80	66	39	100
Nolan Kingham, Texas	8	5	4.57	20	3	100	126	24	81
Chase Shugart, Texas	6	3	4.64	21	2	95	90	41	69
Kasey Ford, Kansas State	2	4	4.67	11	0	62	62	31	45
Davis Martin, Texas Tech	7	6	4.87	17	0	78	79	37	81
Joe Lienhard, Oklahoma State	5	3	5.30	18	1	70	82	40	62
Kade Strowd, West Virginia	4	7	5.74	15	0	63	67	36	61
Jonathan Heasley, Oklahoma St.	4	6	5.96	15	0	80	93	38	79
Justin Heskett, Kansas State	3	6	6.31	13	0	61	95	28	29
Taylor Turski, Kansas	2	9	6.84	16	0	78	87	36	81

BIG WEST CONFERENCE

Conference			Overall	
	W	L	W	L
* Cal State Fullerton	18	6	36	25
Cal Poly	15	9	30	27
UC Irvine	13	11	32	24
Cal State Northridge	13	11	28	30
Long Beach State	12	12	27	30
Hawaii	11	13	27	24
UC Santa Barbara	10	14	27	28
UC Davis	9	15	18	35
UC Riverside	7	17	19	33

ALL-CONFERENCE TEAM: C: Nick Meyer, Jr., Cal Poly. **1B:** Ryan Fitzpatrick, Sr., UC Irvine. **2B:** Hank LoForte, Jr., Cal State Fullerton. **3B:** Parker Coss, Sr., UC Irvine. **SS:** Maaki Yamazaki, Jr., Hawaii. **OF:** Ryan Anderson, Jr., UC Davis; Tommy Jew, So., UC Santa Barbara; Alex McKenna, Jr., Cal Poly; Albee Weiss, Sr., Cal State Northridge. **DH:** Connor Cannon, So., UC Riverside. **UTL:** Connor Cannon, So., UC Riverside; Clay Fisher, Jr., UC Santa Barbara. **SP:** Clayton Andrews, Jr., Long Beach State; Colton Eastman, Jr., Cal State Fullerton; Andre Pallante, So., UC Irvine; Blake Workman, Jr., Cal State Fullerton. **RP:** Dylan Thomas, So., Hawaii. **Player of the Year:** Alex McKenna, Cal Poly. **Pitcher of the Year:** Colton Eastman, Cal State Fullerton. **Coach of the Year:** Rick Vanderhook, Cal State Fullerton. **Rookie of the Year:** Tanner Murray, UC Davis; Cole Percival, UC Riverside.

INDIVIDUAL BATTING LEADERS
(Minimum 140 at-bats)

	AVG	OBP	SLG	AB	2B	3B	HR	RBI	SB
Ryan Anderson, UC Davis	.345	.384	.505	220	13	2	6	36	4
Trevor Casanova, CS Northridge	.345	.405	.480	223	18	0	4	32	1
Nick Meyer, Cal Poly	.344	.408	.428	215	14	2	0	29	3
Hank LoForte, CS Fullerton	.339	.397	.445	236	5	7	2	35	4
Alex McKenna, Cal Poly	.339	.424	.506	239	15	5	5	31	6
Tanner Murray, UC Davis	.333	.380	.411	192	10	1	1	22	6
Maaki Yamazaki, Hawaii	.325	.409	.408	191	10	0	2	19	2
Tommy Jew, UC Santa Barbara	.312	.386	.454	218	10	3	5	41	12
Colby Schultz, UC Riverside	.311	.378	.437	206	12	1	4	21	4
Brendan Brooks, UC Irvine	.308	.365	.349	172	4	0	1	23	1
Ryan Fitzpatrick, UC Irvine	.307	.436	.526	192	14	2	8	44	1
Konnor Zickefoose, UC Irvine	.306	.374	.469	196	13	2	5	27	2
Kyle Marinconz, Cal Poly	.305	.395	.438	226	14	2	4	30	3
Clayton Andrews, Long Beach St.	.302	.382	.377	215	6	5	0	26	13
Jarren Duran, Long Beach State	.302	.380	.392	222	8	3	2	22	17
Jake Palmer, UC Irvine	.298	.430	.340	141	6	0	0	17	2
Adam Fogel, Hawaii	.296	.378	.526	196	17	2	8	37	1
Cameron Briggs, UC Davis	.296	.380	.359	142	7	1	0	17	4
Mitchell Berryhill, CS Fullerton	.295	.384	.362	207	8	3	0	23	10
Ryan Hooper, UC Davis	.294	.390	.480	204	13	2	7	36	10
Clay Fisher, UC Santa Barbara	.294	.338	.425	221	10	5	3	34	13
Ruben Cardenas, CS Fullerton	.292	.355	.432	243	14	4	4	38	12
Nolan Bumstead, CS Northridge	.291	.373	.419	203	8	0	6	29	1
Albee Weiss, CS Northridge	.290	.324	.592	238	12	0	20	61	0
Christian Koss, UC Irvine	.287	.343	.379	195	9	3	1	17	4
Sahid Valenzuela, CS Fullerton	.272	.313	.358	254	14	4	0	22	5

INDIVIDUAL PITCHING LEADERS
(Minimum 40 innings pitched)

	W	L	ERA	G	SV	IP	H	BB	SO
Andre Pallante, UC Irvine	10	1	1.60	15	0	101	77	30	115
Clayton Andrews, Long Beach St.	7	7	1.99	15	0	100	78	17	118
Colton Eastman, CS Fullerton	10	4	2.37	17	0	118	89	28	124
Tommy Wilson, CS Fullerton	7	0	2.71	20	0	90	81	22	81
Stevie Ledesma, UC Santa Barbara	7	3	2.87	16	0	78	69	28	62
Taylor Rashi, UC Irvine	3	4	2.97	20	1	64	57	26	47
Cole Percival, UC Riverside	5	4	3.20	14	0	87	79	27	63
Trent Shelton, Cal Poly	6	3	3.34	13	0	84	97	15	68
Walker Armstrong, CS Northridge	3	4	3.42	17	0	92	92	26	62
Chris Lincoln, UC Santa Barbara	3	3	3.49	19	0	70	64	27	54
Zak Baayoun, Long Beach State	9	3	3.58	15	0	98	99	24	84
Isaiah Nunez, CS Northridge	1	2	3.65	23	2	67	84	11	46
Jackson Rees, Hawaii	5	3	3.86	15	0	79	84	35	57
Andrew Quezada, CS Fullerton	4	5	3.90	14	0	83	89	19	58
Brett Conine, CS Fullerton	4	4	4.07	30	9	42	50	7	46
Neil Uskali, Hawaii	6	2	4.12	11	0	55	55	18	32
Trenton Denholm, UC Irvine	4	8	4.72	15	0	74	83	25	48
Dylan Thomas, Hawaii	2	2	2.00	23	13	36	26	4	38
Jared Sasaki, UC Davis	4	6	4.34	16	0	77	99	10	33

COLONIAL ATHLETIC ASSOCIATION

	Conference		Overall	
	W	L	W	L
Northeastern	17	6	36	21
Elon	16	8	36	23
Charleston	15	8	36	19
* UNC-Wilmington	14	9	39	23

Delaware	12	11	31	27
Hofstra	12	12	23	23
James Madison	11	13	26	26
Towson	6	18	13	42
William & Mary	3	21	15	39

ALL-CONFERENCE TEAM: C: Ryan Jeffers, Jr., UNC Wilmington. **1B:** Mason Berne, Sr., UNC Wilmington. **2B:** Dupree Hart, Jr., Charleston. **3B:** Ryan Solomon, Jr., Northeastern. **SS:** Ryne Ogren, Jr., Elon. **OF:** Kyle Baker, Jr., Delaware; Charlie McConnell, Jr., Northeastern; Luke Morgan, Sr., Charleston. **DH:** Vito Friscia, Jr., Hofstra. **UTL:** Teddy Cillis, Sr., Hofstra. **SP:** Kyle Brnovich, So., Elon; Sean Mellen, So., Northeastern; John Rooney, Jr., Hofstra. **RP:** Clark Cota, Jr., UNC Wilmington. **Player of the Year:** Charlie McConnell, Northeastern. **Pitcher of the Year:** John Rooney, Hofstra. **Coach of the Year:** Mike Glavine, Northeastern. **Rookie of the Year:** Ian Fair, Northeastern; Billy Sullivan, Delaware.

INDIVIDUAL BATTING LEADERS
(Minimum 140 at-bats)

	AVG	OBP	SLG	AB	2B	3B	HR	RBI	SB
Kyle Baker, Delaware	.354	.397	.481	212	11	5	2	39	9
Jake Farrell, Northeastern	.353	.417	.622	241	16	8	11	64	6
Vito Friscia, Hofstra	.353	.431	.514	173	5	1	7	31	1
Charlie McConnell, Northeastern	.349	.427	.464	252	13	5	2	30	40
Mason Berne, UNC Wilmington	.347	.431	.559	236	14	0	12	56	2
Ryne Ogren, Elon	.338	.451	.457	219	17	0	3	53	6
Luke Morgan, Charleston	.321	.390	.489	221	10	3	7	28	20
Dupree Hart, Charleston	.319	.398	.431	216	14	2	2	21	13
Ryan Jeffers, UNC Wilmington	.312	.459	.619	215	21	0	15	57	2
Michael Morgan, James Madison	.311	.404	.385	148	8	0	1	18	3
Ian Fair, Northeastern	.306	.396	.415	183	8	3	2	28	6
Richie Palacios, Towson	.301	.457	.515	196	18	0	8	31	25
Zach Evers, Elon	.297	.401	.431	232	15	5	2	25	26
Calvin Scott, Delaware	.297	.389	.421	195	8	2	4	29	7
Josh Jones, James Madison	.296	.377	.385	179	11	1	1	24	10
Mason Koppens, Northeastern	.295	.383	.340	200	7	1	0	22	12
Fox Semones, James Madison	.291	.363	.460	189	9	1	7	32	10
Bradley Dixon, Charleston	.287	.332	.386	171	8	0	3	31	8
Cam Devanney, Elon	.287	.411	.433	157	6	1	5	23	1
Billy Lennox, Towson	.287	.384	.386	171	9	1	2	25	4
Kevin Mohollen, Delaware	.285	.402	.374	214	14	1	1	16	15
Adam Sisk, James Madison	.283	.387	.455	198	12	2	6	33	11
Max Burt, Northeastern	.281	.331	.372	253	14	0	3	35	11
Greg Jones, UNC Wilmington	.281	.415	.375	224	5	2	4	21	16
Logan McRae, Charleston	.275	.368	.466	193	14	1	7	34	3

INDIVIDUAL PITCHING LEADERS
(Minimum 40 innings pitched)

	W	L	ERA	G	SV	IP	H	BB	SO
John Rooney, Hofstra	8	2	1.23	14	0	95	51	27	108
Carter Love, Charleston	7	0	1.28	25	4	70	50	9	56
Kyle Brnovich, Elon	8	2	1.71	15	0	105	57	36	147
Austin Warren, UNC Wilmington	8	0	1.75	28	2	51	33	13	64
Colman Vila, Delaware	5	1	1.94	27	6	46	34	11	59
Nathan Ocker, Charleston	2	4	2.13	20	10	42	24	7	54
Sean Mellen, Northeastern	11	3	2.20	15	0	86	55	39	85
Robbie Welhaf, Elon	5	4	2.25	25	6	56	42	11	61
Gage Herring, UNC Wilmington	2	1	2.68	16	0	50	37	25	43
Kyle Hinton, Charleston	6	7	2.78	16	0	91	73	43	69
Andrew Misiaszek, Northeastern	2	2	2.79	31	12	61	53	13	69
Nick Stewart, James Madison	4	3	2.86	13	0	63	48	21	67
George Kirby, Elon	10	3	2.89	15	0	91	88	27	96
Evan Sisk, Charleston	10	3	2.96	15	0	91	74	24	78
David Marriggi, Towson	3	8	4.86	15	0	80	82	45	69
Clark Cota, UNC Wilmington	4	0	2.04	27	13	35	17	22	47
Nick Butts, William & Mary	3	1	3.83	34	0	40	33	15	32

CONFERENCE USA

	Conference		Overall	
	W	L	W	L
* Southern Mississippi	23	6	44	18
Louisiana Tech	21	9	39	20
Florida Atlantic	19	8	43	19

Charlotte	17	13	34	24
Texas-San Antonio	16	13	32	24
Florida International	15	13	26	28
Rice	12	15	26	31
Alabama-Birmingham	13	17	21	33
Middle Tennessee	12	17	27	27
Western Kentucky	11	18	21	31
Marshall	7	22	19	31
Old Dominion	7	22	15	37

ALL-CONFERENCE TEAM: C: Reynaldo Pastrana, Jr., Marshall. **INF:** Tyler Frank, Jr., Florida Atlantic; Ford Proctor, Jr., Rice; Luke Reynolds, Jr. Southern Mississippi; Eddie Silva, Jr., Florida International. **OF:** David Miranda, Sr., Florida Atlantic; Jacob Rhinesmith, Jr., Western Kentucky; Matt Wallner, So., Southern Mississippi. **DH:** Hunter Wells, So., Louisiana Tech. **UTL:** Austin Dennis, Jr., Middle Tennessee. **SP:** Logan Bailey, Jr., Louisiana Tech; Matt Canterino, So., Rice; Josh Maciejewski, Sr., Charlotte; Jake Miednik, Sr., Florida Atlantic; Nick Sandlin, Jr., Southern Mississippi. **RP:** Jonah Patten, Sr., Charlotte; Zach Schneider, Jr., Florida Atlantic. **Player of the Year:** Luke Reynolds, Southern Mississippi. **Pitcher of the Year:** Nick Sandlin, Southern Mississippi. **Coach of the Year:** Scott Berry, Southern Mississippi. **Newcomers of the Year:** Jose Garcia, Florida International; Luke Reynolds, Southern Mississippi.

INDIVIDUAL BATTING LEADERS
(Minimum 140 at-bats)

	AVG	OBP	SLG	AB	2B	3B	HR	RBI	SB
Ford Proctor, Rice	.406	.485	.582	249	18	1	8	63	5
Luke Reynolds, Southern Miss.	.389	.551	.699	216	20	1	15	61	8
Steven Kraft, Western Kentucky	.382	.483	.494	170	13	0	2	33	7
Jared DeSantolo, Fla. Atlantic	.373	.427	.528	161	13	0	4	36	1
Luke Brown, Western Kentucky	.369	.403	.405	168	6	0	0	14	11
Joe Montes, Florida Atlantic	.368	.385	.423	272	8	2	1	57	0
Hunter Wells, Louisiana Tech	.357	.421	.443	255	12	2	2	32	6
Reynaldo Pastrana, Marshall	.355	.406	.620	200	14	0	13	50	4
Matt Wallner, Southern Miss.	.351	.474	.618	228	13	0	16	67	2
Austin Shenton, Fla. Intl.	.348	.422	.517	207	11	0	8	25	2
Austin Dennis, Middle Tenn.	.345	.417	.485	229	11	3	5	35	25
Aaron Aucker, Middle Tenn.	.340	.418	.623	212	18	0	14	71	1
Matt Schwarz, Old Dominion	.335	.402	.456	158	9	2	2	24	9
Bryan Arias, UTSA	.335	.416	.543	221	16	3	8	35	12
Ryan Kemp, Middle Tennessee	.333	.402	.430	165	7	0	3	34	9
Derek Cartaya, Florida Intl.	.333	.426	.380	150	7	0	0	12	3
Erik Stock, Old Dominion	.331	.383	.480	148	13	0	3	20	0
Braden Comeaux, Rice	.331	.400	.412	272	14	1	2	36	8
Matthew Guidry, So. Miss.	.330	.449	.500	176	11	2	5	39	5
Jackson Mims, Charlotte	.328	.394	.511	235	12	2	9	40	7
Ryan Chandler, Rice	.325	.393	.394	249	11	3	0	26	13
David Miranda, Fla. Atlantic	.324	.406	.518	247	15	3	9	53	4
Harris Yett, Charlotte	.323	.395	.438	226	8	0	6	37	0
Trent Bowles, UTSA	.323	.376	.520	223	18	1	8	40	15
Ray Zuberer III, W. Kentucky	.315	.401	.430	165	4	3	3	22	6
Cody Wilson, Florida Atlantic	.274	.343	.468	299	12	2	14	41	22
Chace Sarchet, Rice	.307	.389	.475	244	15	7	4	44	6

INDIVIDUAL PITCHING LEADERS
(Minimum 40 innings pitched)

	W	L	ERA	G	SV	IP	H	BB	SO
Nick Sandlin, Southern Miss.	10	0	1.06	15	0	102	55	18	144
Derek Craft, UTSA	3	5	1.89	24	3	52	40	11	62
Josh Maciejewski, Charlotte	9	2	2.25	15	0	104	81	24	104
Addison Moss, Rice	2	4	2.25	22	1	68	63	22	62
David Leal, Louisiana Tech	4	4	2.27	14	1	87	66	13	81
Tyler Follis, Louisiana Tech	5	2	2.53	19	1	43	35	19	46
Chance Kirby, UTSA	4	4	2.63	13	0	65	48	18	62
Logan Bailey, Louisiana Tech	8	1	2.70	14	0	93	88	26	78
Mason Strickland, So. Miss.	2	1	2.74	24	2	49	47	6	29
Drew Peden, Florida Atlantic	9	1	2.82	36	4	73	58	31	70
Blake Sanderson, Fla. Atlantic	1	2	2.93	26	1	58	57	21	69
Mark Nowatnick, Fla. Atlantic	4	3	2.98	19	0	42	37	16	30
Steven Dressler, UTSA	5	4	3.05	15	0	91	86	29	53
Matt Horkey, Charlotte	0	0	3.12	24	3	40	43	7	22
Tanner Graham, UAB	3	9	3.86	15	0	89	94	31	55
Zach Schneider, Fla. Atlantic	7	1	2.61	24	15	31	30	14	21
Evan Kravetz, Rice	0	1	4.10	28	0	42	29	25	47

HORIZON LEAGUE

	Conference W	L	Overall W	L
* Wright State	22	6	39	17
Illinois-Chicago	15	9	30	18
Milwaukee	13	12	26	28
Oakland	12	14	15	32
Youngstown State	10	19	18	38
Northern Kentucky	9	21	14	39

ALL-CONFERENCE TEAM: C: Aaron Ackerman, R-So., Illinois-Chicago. **1B:** Gabe Snyder, R-Sr., Wright State. **2B:** Matt Morrow, Sr., Wright State. **3B:** Ben Chally, Sr., Milwaukee. **SS:** Chase Slone, Jr., Wright State. **OF:** Will Haueter, R-Jr., Northern Kentucky; Trey Bridis, Sr., Youngstown State; Peyton Burdick, R-So., Wright State. **DH:** Griffin Doersching, Fr., Northern Kentucky. **SP:** Austin Schulfer, Sr., Milwaukee; Ryan Campbell, Sr., Illinois-Chicago; Ryan Weiss, R-So., Wright State. **RP:** Charlie Cerny, Jr., Illinois-Chicago. **Player of the Year:** Gabe Snyder, Wright State. **Pitcher of the Year:** Ryan Campbell, Illinois-Chicago. **Coach of the Year:** Jeff Mercer, Wright State. **Rookie of the Year:** Griffin Doersching, Northern Kentucky.

INDIVIDUAL BATTING LEADERS
(Minimum 140 at-bats)

	AVG	OBP	SLG	AB	2B	3B	HR	RBI	SB
Will Haueter, No. Kentucky	.360	.451	.600	200	19	1	9	37	0
Gabe Snyder, Wright State	.359	.425	.668	223	20	2	15	73	15
Peyton Burdick, Wright State	.347	.437	.569	225	19	2	9	65	15
Devin Rybacki, Milwaukee	.336	.401	.418	146	5	2	1	15	4
Blaze Glenn, Youngstown St.	.325	.445	.558	197	13	0	11	43	16
Colin Kreiter, Milwaukee	.320	.404	.464	194	12	2	4	31	8
Trevor Schwecke, Milwaukee	.318	.376	.419	217	11	1	3	39	19
JD Orr, Wright State	.318	.465	.388	201	12	1	0	23	34
Mike Ferri, Milwaukee	.299	.381	.419	167	11	0	3	15	8
Mario Camilletti, Oakland	.299	.406	.364	184	6	0	2	22	9
Aaron Ackerman, Ill.-Chicago	.295	.360	.464	166	13	0	5	28	0
Trey Bridis, Youngstown State	.292	.417	.538	212	9	2	13	26	13
Chad Roberts, No. Kentucky	.291	.373	.520	196	9	0	12	50	1
Zach Weatherford, Wright St.	.284	.349	.432	148	7	3	3	28	18
Scott Ota, Illinois-Chicago	.283	.351	.481	187	8	7	5	34	1
Ben Hart, Oakland	.283	.317	.428	187	8	2	5	41	5
Chase Slone, Wright State	.280	.343	.372	207	15	1	3	47	0
Ben Chally, Milwaukee	.276	.338	.360	214	6	0	4	33	6
Emerson Misch, Oakland	.275	.345	.379	153	8	1	2	17	4
Matt Morrow, Wright State	.274	.413	.365	219	13	2	1	26	7
Bowen Ogata, Illinois-Chicago	.273	.333	.331	154	6	0	1	19	1
Dominic Mercurio, No. Kentucky	.273	.356	.344	154	5	0	2	11	0
Seth Gray, Wright State	.267	.378	.406	202	15	2	3	37	5
Matt Quartel, Milwaukee	.262	.349	.378	164	10	3	1	22	6
Mitch Buban, Milwaukee	.262	.355	.295	149	3	1	0	11	8

INDIVIDUAL PITCHING LEADERS
(Minimum 40 innings pitched)

	W	L	ERA	G	SV	IP	H	BB	SO
Ryan Campbell, Ill.-Chicago	8	3	1.53	13	0	94	75	19	68
Charlie Cerny, Ill.-Chicago	5	3	1.63	21	1	55	32	12	64
Reid Birlingmair, Ill.-Chicago	6	1	2.12	10	0	51	39	21	57
Jeremy Randolph, Wright St.	5	3	2.55	27	4	49	39	21	61
Austin Schulfer, Milwaukee	6	5	2.96	15	0	91	72	28	87
Jason Foster, Wright State	3	2	3.02	21	1	45	32	20	21
Caleb Sampen, Wright State	5	0	3.26	22	0	47	40	14	33
Daniel Kreuzer, Wright State	5	1	3.35	16	1	51	42	23	24
Ryan Weiss, Wright State	9	2	3.40	17	1	98	93	18	92
Nate Schweers, Oakland	3	3	3.42	22	3	47	45	16	52
Jacob Key, Illinois-Chicago	4	4	3.77	13	0	74	69	35	72
Zane Collins, Wright State	6	1	4.19	17	0	67	54	44	48
Collin Floyd, Youngstown St.	3	8	4.41	12	0	69	66	33	82
Jake Lee, Oakland	7	4	4.54	14	0	75	61	35	112
Nick Parr, Oakland	1	9	6.30	13	0	80	90	32	75

IVY LEAGUE

	Conference W	L	Overall W	L
Yale	15	6	22	20
* Columbia	13	8	19	29
Dartmouth	12	8	17	22
Harvard	12	9	22	20
Pennsylvania	9	11	16	25
Cornell	9	12	14	22
Princeton	7	14	10	27
Brown	6	15	11	26

ALL-CONFERENCE TEAM: C: Ellis Bitar, Sr., Cornell. **1B:** Chandler Bengston, Jr., Columbia. **2B:** Ryan Krainz, Sr., Cornell. **3B:** Matt McGeagh, Jr., Pennsylvania. **SS:** Joe Engel, Jr., Columbia. **OF:** Dustin Shirley, Sr., Dartmouth; Ben Skinner, Jr., Harvard; Jesper Horsted, Jr., Princeton. **DH:** Patrick Robinson, Jr., Harvard. **UTL:** Eduardo Malinowski, Fr., Pennsylvania. **SP:** Noah Zavolas, Sr., Harvard; Eric Brodkowitz, Sr., Yale; Scott Politz, Jr., Yale. **RP:** Benny Wanger, Jr., Yale. **Player of the Year:** Dustin Shirley, Dartmouth. **Pitcher of the Year:** Noah Zavolas, Harvard. **Coach of the Year:** Brett Boretti, Columbia. **Rookie of the Year:** Eduardo Malinowski, Pennsylvania.

INDIVIDUAL BATTING LEADERS
(Minimum 140 at-bats)

	AVG	OBP	SLG	AB	2B	3B	HR	RBI	SB
Eduardo Malinowski, Penn	.347	.389	.424	170	5	1	2	20	4
Sean Sullivan, Dartmouth	.340	.456	.388	147	5	1	0	12	4
Ben Skinner, Harvard	.320	.411	.408	169	12	0	1	16	17
Dustin Shirley, Dartmouth	.314	.365	.497	159	14	0	5	32	7
Joe Engel, Columbia	.312	.401	.376	189	7	1	1	29	3
Liam McGill, Columbia	.307	.386	.472	199	13	1	6	31	0
Griffin Dey, Yale	.306	.381	.476	170	6	1	7	35	0
Matt McGeagh, Penn	.299	.346	.508	177	12	2	7	43	0
Randell Kanemaru, Columbia	.299	.415	.473	184	13	2	5	19	0
Simon Whiteman, Yale	.298	.354	.320	178	4	0	0	31	9
Sean Phelan, Penn	.293	.398	.439	157	8	0	5	28	0
Chris Adams, Penn	.292	.365	.380	171	13	1	0	14	9
Will Simoneit, Cornell	.290	.358	.386	145	8	0	2	27	7
Ryan Krainz, Cornell	.285	.367	.323	158	4	1	0	14	11
Matt Rothenberg, Harvard	.285	.385	.431	144	4	1	5	24	2
Tim Degraw, Yale	.281	.378	.323	167	5	1	0	8	11
Andrew Murnane, Penn	.277	.327	.342	155	7	0	1	12	4
Matt Feinstein, Dartmouth	.271	.352	.347	170	7	0	2	19	2
Chandler Bengtson, Columbia	.271	.379	.489	188	9	1	10	34	1
Ellis Bitar, Cornell	.270	.387	.418	141	7	1	4	29	6
Jake Suddleson, Harvard	.268	.335	.451	153	8	1	6	23	1
Patrick McColl, Harvard	.267	.361	.388	165	7	2	3	37	5
Hunter Bigge, Harvard	.267	.351	.407	150	7	1	4	21	0
Garett Delano, Brown	.266	.338	.441	143	5	1	6	14	5
Nate Ostmo, Dartmouth	.262	.337	.407	145	5	2	4	17	5

INDIVIDUAL PITCHING LEADERS
(Minimum 40 innings pitched)

	W	L	ERA	G	SV	IP	H	BB	SO
Eric Brodkowitz, Yale	6	2	2.76	12	0	85	66	21	57
Si Rosenblum-Larson, Harvard	4	2	2.86	11	0	63	52	26	82
Will Tomlinson, Brown	3	2	2.91	8	0	43	27	23	29
Noah Zavolas, Harvard	6	1	2.96	11	0	70	66	24	77
Scott Politz, Yale	5	4	3.07	12	0	88	98	23	64
Austen Michel, Dartmouth	3	2	3.38	17	7	45	43	7	35
Collin Garner, Brown	1	3	3.94	10	0	59	57	22	30
Garett Delano, Brown	2	3	4.07	10	1	55	66	18	38
Gabe Kleiman, Penn	2	6	4.09	12	1	70	82	15	69
Mitchell Holcomb, Penn	0	4	4.17	11	0	54	54	28	50
Harrisen Egly, Columbia	3	3	4.25	12	0	59	59	26	45
Buddy Haywayd, Harvard	2	3	4.28	12	0	40	44	9	47
Jack Fossand, Dartmouth	4	4	4.41	12	0	65	66	23	51
Ben Gross, Princeton	4	5	4.47	9	0	52	54	7	52
Jordan Chriss, Columbia	2	7	6.33	15	0	54	75	14	40

METRO ATLANTIC ATHLETIC CONFERENCE

	Conference		Overall	
	W	L	W	L
Monmouth	16	7	30	25
Quinnipiac	16	8	26	30
* Canisius	16	8	35	22
Siena	14	10	21	35
Marist	14	10	27	23
Niagara	13	11	24	27
Manhattan	13	11	25	28
Iona	10	13	16	31
Fairfield	9	14	22	29
Rider	7	16	12	35
Saint Peter's	2	22	2	42

ALL-CONFERENCE TEAM: C: Phil Madonna, Sr., Siena. **1B:** Ben Gibson, Sr., Quinnipiac; Liam Wilson, Jr., Canisius. **2B:** Anthony Lazar, Jr., Marist. **3B:** Shaine Hughes, R-Sr., Monmouth. **SS:** Greg Cullen, Jr., Niagara. **OF:** Drew Arciuolo, Sr., Fairfield; Joe Simone, So., Rider; Liam Scafariello, So., Quinnipiac. **DH:** Tyler Kapuscinski, Jr., Marist. **UTL:** Ryan Stekl, Sr., Canisius; Mitch Williams, Sr., Fairfield. **SP:** J.P. Stevenson, Sr., Canisius; John Signore, Jr., Fairfield; Taylor Luciani, Sr., Quinnipiac; Tommy Miller, Jr., Siena. **Player of the Year:** Greg Cullen, Niagara. **Pitcher of the Year:** J.P. Stevenson, Canisius. **Coach of the Year:** John Delaney, Quinnipiac. **Rookie of the Year:** Dan Klepchick, Monmouth.

INDIVIDUAL BATTING LEADERS
(Minimum 140 at-bats)

	AVG	OBP	SLG	AB	2B	3B	HR	RBI	SB
Greg Cullen, Niagara	.458	.556	.655	177	17	3	4	42	13
Peter Battaglia, Niagara	.357	.443	.595	168	15	2	7	49	4
Joe Drpich, Siena	.355	.403	.609	220	17	0	13	55	1
Liam Wilson, Canisius	.353	.434	.624	221	27	3	9	49	2
Drew Arciuolo, Fairfield	.347	.430	.465	202	14	2	2	22	11
Mitch Williams, Fairfield	.346	.385	.464	153	9	0	3	29	1
Conner Morro, Canisius	.342	.448	.457	184	12	3	1	30	11
Mark McKenna, Canisius	.333	.406	.418	165	8	3	0	20	13
Joe Simone, Rider	.331	.446	.480	175	15	4	1	19	8
Marcos Campos, Siena	.322	.355	.402	239	17	1	0	25	9
Ben Gibson, Quinnipiac	.322	.387	.634	202	9	0	18	57	5
Phil Madonna, Siena	.319	.378	.372	191	10	0	0	24	6
Owen Dziados, Niagara	.316	.403	.418	177	9	0	3	50	1
Shane Hughes, Monmouth	.316	.442	.480	196	8	0	8	50	3
Kevin Radziewicz, Fairfield	.315	.407	.398	181	8	2	1	26	2
Sean Scales, Iona	.314	.385	.391	169	6	2	1	24	7
Brian Moskey, Quinnipiac	.312	.362	.437	215	13	1	4	33	10
Richie Barrella, Manhattan	.309	.379	.351	191	1	2	1	25	6
Randy Taveras, Marist	.308	.385	.440	159	8	2	3	21	14
Anthony Lazar, Marist	.305	.415	.506	154	11	1	6	28	4
Andrew Rouse, Marist	.301	.420	.382	186	12	0	1	23	9
Ryan Stekl, Canisius	.300	.410	.521	213	15	1	10	63	5
Matt Padre, Manhattan	.298	.417	.435	161	6	2	4	25	2
Evan Vulgamore, Quinnipiac	.298	.338	.495	208	11	0	10	40	9
Kyle Norman, Monmouth	.298	.412	.439	198	12	2	4	41	3
Julian Gallup, Niagara	.296	.390	.486	142	12	0	5	19	20

INDIVIDUAL PITCHING LEADERS
(Minimum 40 innings pitched)

	W	L	ERA	G	SV	IP	H	BB	SO
T.J. Stuart, Manhattan	6	2	2.57	25	10	63	38	27	50
J.P. Stevenson, Canisius	10	2	2.73	17	0	99	71	21	93
John Signore, Fairfield	6	4	2.93	13	0	83	77	19	91
Joe DeRosa, Iona	3	8	3.33	13	0	81	87	14	49
Dan Klepchick, Monmouth	5	1	3.47	14	0	86	75	18	78
Tommy Miller, Siena	9	6	3.70	15	0	105	115	28	84
Joe DiNizio, Manhattan	1	5	3.92	15	0	57	56	28	43
Romanelli, Marist	5	5	3.94	16	1	82	77	42	70
Taylor Luciani, Quinnipiac	8	3	3.99	14	0	86	77	45	62
Brendan White, Siena	3	9	4.08	16	0	90	93	18	61
Eli Oliphant, Fairfield	2	1	4.10	14	0	53	54	20	35
Matt Simonetti, Manhattan	4	5	4.11	16	0	77	93	22	76
Stephen Hansen, Iona	4	3	4.21	14	0	51	52	20	25

Brandon Shileikis, Quinnipiac	5	6	4.22	15	0	85	107	14	69
Mike Coss, Marist	5	2	3.38	27	8	48	38	15	54
Jordan Silverman, Rider	2	4	5.72	25	2	61	80	5	34

MID-AMERICAN CONFERENCE

	Conference		Overall	
	W	L	W	L
* Kent State	19	8	36	16
Miami (Ohio)	17	10	33	18
Ball State	17	10	32	24
Central Michigan	16	11	25	28
Toledo	14	13	21	31
Eastern Michigan	14	13	22	34
Western Michigan	12	13	23	25
Ohio	9	18	21	32
Northern Illinois	8	16	20	35
Bowling Green	6	19	11	39

ALL-CONFERENCE TEAM: C: Hayden Senger, Jr., Miami (Ohio). **1B:** Rudy Rott, Jr., Ohio. **2B:** Will Vogelgesang, So., Miami (Ohio). **3B:** Zachary Owings, So., Eastern Michigan. **SS:** Connor Smith, Jr., Western Michigan. **OF:** Ross Adolph, Jr., Toledo; Nick Kanavas, Sr., Kent State; Mason Mamarella, Sr., Kent State. **DH:** Griffin Lockwood-Powell, Fr., Central Michigan. **UTL:** Ross Haffey, Miami (Ohio). **SP:** Joey Murray, Jr., Kent State; Sam Shutes, Sr., Toledo; Drey Jameson, Fr., Ball State; Gus Graham, Jr., Miami. **RP:** Collin Romel, Fr., Kent State. **Player of the Year:** Rudy Rott, Ohio. **Pitcher of the Year:** Joey Murray, Kent State. **Coach of the Year:** Jeff Duncan, Kent State. **Rookie of the Year:** Drey Jameson, Ball State; John Servello, Toledo.

INDIVIDUAL BATTING LEADERS
(Minimum 140 at-bats)

	AVG	OBP	SLG	AB	2B	3B	HR	RBI	SB
Nick Kanavas, Kent State	.358	.440	.432	229	11	0	2	35	20
Rudy Rott, Ohio	.355	.440	.654	214	15	2	15	50	3
Zachary Owings, E. Michigan	.350	.440	.530	183	11	2	6	30	16
Zach Heeke, Central Michigan	.346	.520	.425	179	7	2	1	30	9
Hayden Senger, Miami (Ohio)	.344	.429	.511	180	17	2	3	34	8
John Servello, Toledo	.343	.424	.472	178	11	3	2	29	2
Connor Smith, W. Michigan	.338	.403	.460	198	14	2	2	30	8
Jeff Riedel, Ball State	.332	.413	.522	226	13	6	6	48	15
Mason Mamarella, Kent State	.324	.447	.381	210	10	1	0	42	34
Randy Righter, Bowling Green	.323	.349	.492	195	16	1	5	32	0
Ross Adolph, Toledo	.322	.445	.654	214	14	6	15	56	12
Will Vogelgesang, Miami (Ohio)	.322	.416	.411	180	5	4	1	22	18
Tim Dalporto, Kent State	.319	.378	.500	166	9	0	7	46	1
Noah Powell, Ball State	.319	.402	.473	182	12	2	4	35	3
Max Schuemann, E. Michigan	.317	.400	.441	227	16	0	4	30	24
Jimmy Roche, W. Michigan	.316	.364	.412	187	9	0	3	33	3
Ross Haffey, Miami (Ohio)	.315	.450	.650	200	14	4	15	43	1
Griffin Lockwood-Powell, C. Mich.	.311	.432	.425	167	7	0	4	36	0
Samuel Vega, Nothern Illinois	.309	.403	.396	217	6	2	3	26	8
Blake Dunn, Western Michigan	.308	.361	.371	143	9	0	0	18	6
Nate Grys, Western Michigan	.306	.406	.611	157	14	2	10	48	7
Daniel Robinson, C. Michigan	.300	.410	.410	217	7	1	5	43	11
Colin Brockhouse, Ball State	.298	.384	.522	228	16	1	11	42	3
Landon Stephens, Miami (Ohio)	.298	.358	.498	205	12	4	7	46	4
Derek Drewes, Miami (Ohio)	.297	.391	.367	158	8	0	1	21	1
Seth Freed, Ball State	.238	.308	.404	235	7	4	8	36	10

INDIVIDUAL PITCHING LEADERS
(Minimum 40 innings pitched)

	W	L	ERA	G	SV	IP	H	BB	SO
Tanner Foster, Northern Illinois	2	4	2.33	12	0	70	63	22	76
Joey Murray, Kent State	9	2	2.45	16	0	96	54	40	141
Luke Devenney, E. Michigan	6	2	2.49	15	0	94	94	40	56
Shane Smith, Miami (OH)	4	2	2.77	18	3	49	44	17	36
Sam Shutes, Toledo	10	2	2.97	15	0	97	84	30	82
Nolan Gazouski, Ball State	3	3	3.00	25	2	42	24	37	61
Jared Skolnicki, Kent State	5	1	3.19	15	0	68	71	17	57
Gus Graham, Miami (OH)	7	1	3.24	17	1	83	67	27	61
Jacob Piechota, W. Michigan	3	7	3.26	17	0	77	64	26	78
Cory Blessing, Ohio	3	4	3.35	28	1	48	39	18	42

	W	L	ERA	G	SV	IP	H	BB	SO
Kody Brown, Bowling Green	2	4	3.41	21	2	61	59	27	33
Pat Leatherman, C. Michigan	2	5	3.51	11	0	59	45	17	77
Eddie Kutt, Ohio	3	2	3.60	27	2	50	50	17	40
John Baker, Ball State	5	5	3.68	15	0	95	78	33	118
Andrew Reisinger, W. Michigan	8	1	4.33	29	2	52	57	32	43
Michael Jacob, Toledo	2	9	4.75	16	0	78	80	39	61
Zac Carey, Bowling Green	2	7	7.64	14	0	71	111	12	43

MID-EASTERN ATHLETIC CONFERENCE

Northern Division	Conference		Overall	
	W	L	W	L
Coppin State	18	4	21	24
Norfolk State	13	10	19	30
Maryland Eastern-Shore	8	16	12	41
Delaware State	7	16	9	35
Southern Division	**W**	**L**	**W**	**L**
* North Carolina A&T	16	8	32	25
Florida A&M	15	9	23	30
Bethune-Cookman	14	10	24	34
North Carolina Central	11	13	28	24
Savannah State	4	20	7	34

ALL-CONFERENCE TEAM: C: Jacky Miles Jr., R-Sr., Florida A&M. **1B:** Zach Michalski, Sr., North Carolina Central; Nazier McIlwain, Jr., Coppin State. **2B:** Corey Joyce, So., North Carolina Central. **3B:** Perry "A.J." Hunt, R-Jr., North Carolina A&T. **SS:** Derek Lohr, Fr., Coppin State. **OF:** Dawnoven Smith, Jr., North Carolina A&T; Jordan Curtis, Jr., Florida A&M; Justin Hayes, R-Jr., Norfolk State. **UTL:** Dallas Oliver, Sr., Florida A&M. **SP:** Michael Johnson, So., North Carolina A&T; Anthony Maldonado, So., Bethune-Cookman. **RP:** Dylan Carlson, So., Florida A&M. **Player of the Year:** Corey Joyce, North Carolina Central. **Pitcher of the Year:** Anthony Maldonado, Bethune-Cookman. **Coach of the Year:** Sherman Reed, Coppin State. **Rookie of the Year:** Derek Lohr, Coppin State.

INDIVIDUAL BATTING LEADERS
(Minimum 140 at-bats)

	AVG	OBP	SLG	AB	2B	3B	HR	RBI	SB
Corey Joyce, N.C. Central	.358	.456	.542	179	15	0	6	37	27
Justin Hayes, Norfolk State	.347	.438	.413	167	8	0	1	12	28
Jacky Miles, Florida A&M	.346	.435	.500	182	10	0	6	42	1
Greg White, N.C. A&T	.341	.413	.429	217	11	1	2	23	8
Caleb Duhay, Coppin State	.336	.381	.514	146	12	4	2	26	20
Dawnoven Smith, N.C. A&T	.335	.415	.600	170	19	1	8	45	3
Adonis Lao, Bethune-Cookman	.325	.420	.408	191	9	2	1	30	6
Nate Sterijevski, Bethune-Cookman	.325	.430	.433	194	7	1	4	28	8
Nazier McIlwain, Coppin State	.323	.404	.433	164	12	0	2	41	1
Zach Michalski, N.C. Central	.318	.376	.525	179	13	0	8	51	1
Jordan Curtis, Florida A&M	.317	.392	.415	183	6	3	2	27	20
Perry "A.J." Hunt, N.C. A&T	.316	.426	.487	193	11	2	6	35	5
Alsander Womack, Norfolk St.	.314	.393	.486	185	13	2	5	31	13
Dominic DeBlasie, UMES	.312	.416	.418	141	9	0	2	21	2
Dallas Oliver, Florida A&M	.310	.445	.386	197	9	0	2	40	10
Andres Santana, Coppin State	.308	.425	.343	143	5	0	0	21	22
Carter Williams, N.C. Central	.307	.407	.521	192	13	5	6	36	12
Brian Davis, Florida A&M	.306	.470	.468	173	13	0	5	38	0
Marcos Castillo, Coppin State	.303	.374	.467	152	9	5	2	31	12
Zach McLean, N.C. A&T	.294	.333	.482	170	14	0	6	38	0
Freddie Landers, Savannah St.	.293	.398	.407	150	8	0	3	29	1
Kyle Corbin, Bethune-Cookman	.289	.361	.400	180	6	4	2	22	9
Dominic Cuevas, N.C. Central	.285	.393	.380	179	10	2	1	26	13
Myles Sowell, N.C. A&T	.283	.355	.422	173	7	4	3	27	14
Zach Sivey, Bethune-Cookman	.282	.351	.376	202	6	2	3	27	15
Stephen Baughan, Norfolk St.	.259	.313	.470	185	10	2	9	30	2

INDIVIDUAL PITCHING LEADERS
(Minimum 40 innings pitched)

	W	L	ERA	G	SV	IP	H	BB	SO
Jahmon Taylor, Coppin State	6	4	2.66	13	0	71	58	34	81
Anthony Maldonado, Bethune-Cookman	7	2	2.81	11	0	64	50	18	74
Chris Kernen, N.C. Central	5	5	2.85	22	2	60	52	16	51
Chase Anderson, Norfolk State	7	5	3.12	16	0	98	100	38	78

	W	L	ERA	G	SV	IP	H	BB	SO
Jonathan Mahoney, Norfolk St.	7	5	3.71	17	0	87	98	32	64
Branden Redfern, Coppin State	4	1	3.75	12	0	46	59	13	27
Toby Hoskins, UMES	5	9	3.75	16	0	82	84	26	55
Michael Johnson, N.C. A&T	7	2	3.82	14	0	75	82	22	43
Seth Hockett, Norfolk State	2	2	3.98	24	1	52	51	32	39
Tim Luth, N.C. A&T	6	3	3.98	15	0	93	86	28	56
Trevor McKenna, Savannah St.	2	7	4.18	13	0	75	68	34	78
Jonathan Figueroa, N.C. Central	8	4	4.37	18	0	56	50	23	41
Aaron Rea, Coppin State	6	5	4.38	13	0	72	68	32	52
Marcello Betances, N.C. A&T	3	4	4.48	15	0	68	53	39	60
Devin Sweet, N.C. Central	5	4	4.54	16	0	85	88	20	87
Tyler Norris, Bethune-Cookman	4	6	4.62	15	0	86	87	24	70
Thomas Nicoll, Florida A&M	3	8	5.00	15	0	85	96	22	88
Alex Wright, Savannah State	2	6	5.85	11	0	52	59	29	66
Trey Hanchey, Norfolk State	1	7	5.93	13	0	61	87	30	44

MISSOURI VALLEY CONFERENCE

Team	Conference		Overall	
	W	L	W	L
*Missouri State	18	3	40	17
Dallas Baptist	16	5	42	21
Bradley	11	10	32	19
Indiana State	11	10	31	24
Southern Illinois	10	11	28	30
Illinois State	9	12	22	30
Valparaiso	6	15	19	34
Evansville	3	18	12	39

ALL-CONFERENCE TEAM: C: Matt Duce, Sr., Dallas Baptist. **1B:** Kody Funderburk, Jr., Dallas Baptist. **2B:** John Privitera, So., Missouri State. **3B:** Jake Means, Jr., Indiana State. **SS:** Owen Miller, Jr., Illinois State; Jimmy Glowenke, Fr., Dallas Baptist. **OF:** Devlin Granberg, Sr., Dallas Baptist; Jameson Hannah, Jr., Dallas Baptist; Blake Billinger, Jr., Valparaiso. **DH:** Drew Millas, So., Missouri State. **SP:** Michael Baird, Sr., Southern Illinois; Trevor Conn, Sr., Dallas Baptist; Dylan Coleman, Jr., Missouri State. **RP:** Connor Sechler, Fr., Missouri State; Kragen Kechely, So., Dallas Baptist. **Player of the Year:** Devlin Granberg, Dallas Baptist. **Pitcher of the Year:** Trevor Conn, Dallas Baptist. **Coach of the Year:** Keith Guttin, Missouri State. **Rookie of the Year:** Jimmy Glowenke, Dallas Baptist.

INDIVIDUAL BATTING LEADERS
(Minimum 140 at-bats)

	AVG	OBP	SLG	AB	2B	3B	HR	RBI	SB
Devlin Granberg, Dallas Baptist	.443	.541	.680	253	17	2	13	70	26
Owen Miller, Illinois State	.384	.433	.537	229	15	1	6	35	8
Jameson Hannah, Dallas Baptist	.363	.451	.554	251	24	3	6	48	9
John Rave, Illinois State	.347	.402	.571	219	19	3	8	49	5
Zack Leone, Valparaiso	.347	.449	.497	173	14	0	4	36	0
Jimmy Glowenke, Dallas Baptist	.336	.432	.546	229	16	1	10	50	5
Connor Kopach, S. Illinois	.336	.424	.522	226	16	4	6	44	33
Troy Beilsmith, Evansville	.335	.442	.564	179	18	1	7	28	10
Logan Blackfan, S. Illinois	.328	.390	.536	235	16	0	11	62	7
Andy Shadid, Bradley	.326	.404	.515	184	13	2	6	30	7
Luke Shadid, Bradley	.325	.407	.482	166	14	3	2	24	14
Brendan Dougherty, Bradley	.323	.406	.390	195	5	1	2	34	4
Blake Billinger, Valparaiso	.323	.391	.523	220	23	0	7	46	0
Luke Mangieri, Bradley	.322	.424	.510	202	15	4	5	34	8
Drew Milas, Missouri State	.321	.416	.500	212	13	2	7	61	3
Alex Lyon, Southern Illinois	.316	.374	.456	215	11	2	5	40	29
Kenton Crews, Evansville	.310	.367	.420	200	8	4	2	29	12
Hunter Steinmetz, Missouri St.	.307	.421	.469	192	12	2	5	37	8
Dalton Horstmeier, Evansville	.306	.361	.459	196	16	1	4	28	7
Jarrod Watkins, Indiana State	.305	.380	.376	226	12	2	0	18	7
Kody Funderburk, Dallas Baptist	.304	.429	.584	214	19	1	13	48	1
Dane Giesler, Indiana State	.304	.437	.597	191	9	1	15	47	5
Giovanni Garbella, Valparaiso	.304	.415	.512	168	11	0	8	41	0
Luke Fegen, Indiana State	.298	.409	.382	178	9	0	2	32	6
CJ Huntley, Indiana State	.293	.380	.429	191	13	2	3	33	3
Chase Dawson, Valparaiso	.265	.341	.389	234	10	5	3	28	10
Tim Millard, Dallas Baptist	.270	.386	.528	248	14	1	16	64	3

INDIVIDUAL PITCHING LEADERS
(Minimum 40 innings pitched)

	W	L	ERA	G	SV	IP	H	BB	SO
Trevor Conn, Dallas Baptist	8	2	3.15	17	0	69	64	22	57
Michael Baird, Southern Illinois	5	5	3.16	15	0	100	95	20	92
Triston Polley, Indiana State	7	2	3.53	15	0	94	78	43	55
Tyler Ward, Indiana State	6	3	3.66	9	0	64	61	13	55
Ethan Larrison, Indiana State	3	6	3.76	25	9	55	47	23	50
Dylan Coleman, Missouri St.	10	2	3.77	17	0	103	74	59	129
Logan Wiley, Missouri State	7	6	4.13	22	1	85	84	23	68
Alex Gray, Bradley	7	0	4.25	15	1	53	59	18	43
Brad Harrison, S. Illinois	5	5	4.25	15	0	83	72	29	75
Tristan Weaver, Indiana State	3	5	4.75	13	0	66	59	38	41
Ty Buckner, Missouri State	7	4	4.81	16	0	77	62	49	60
Cole Cook, Bradley	4	5	4.88	16	0	76	92	18	52
Mitch Janssen, Bradley	5	3	4.93	18	0	66	56	41	63
Brady Huffman, Illinois State	1	4	5.03	16	1	73	79	28	57
Alex Weigand, Evansville	1	4	5.09	17	0	58	54	28	48
Jon Tieman, Valparaiso	5	5	5.11	16	0	99	127	33	56
MD Johnson, Dallas Baptist	8	2	5.14	16	0	77	79	32	76
Sam Lund, Bradley	6	4	5.43	14	0	58	63	27	40
Matt Walker, Illinois State	5	2	5.49	15	0	62	71	41	57
Jamison Steege, S. Illinois	4	5	5.61	13	0	67	69	30	38
Wes Gordon, Valparaiso	2	8	7.32	13	0	68	89	13	38

Colby Brown, Air Force	.321	.392	.449	156	8	3	2	33	5
Matt Rudick, San Diego State	.319	.419	.363	226	4	3	0	19	5

INDIVIDUAL PITCHING LEADERS
(Minimum 40 innings pitched)

	W	L	ERA	G	SV	IP	H	BB	SO
Edgar Gonzalez, Fresno State	8	2	2.84	16	1	95	77	31	110
Nikoh Mitchell, Fresno State	4	3	3.28	24	1	58	40	29	53
Jacob Erickson, San Diego State	5	4	3.33	27	0	70	69	9	58
Jaime Arias, Fresno State	5	1	3.69	23	1	68	56	12	62
Andrew Mitchel, San Jose State	6	2	3.72	18	0	87	69	34	101
Alan Storng, UNLV	7	3	3.90	15	0	90	104	22	86
Garrett Hill, San Diego State	7	3	3.91	16	0	78	89	26	72
Chase Mddux, UNLV	4	7	4.14	15	0	72	93	20	30
Ryan Holloway, Air Force	3	5	4.50	14	0	60	58	35	47
Harrison Pyatt, San Diego State	4	4	4.69	17	0	73	58	38	40
Jorge Fernandez, San Diego St.	6	3	4.86	26	6	63	64	18	46
Dalton Gomez, Nevada	3	3	5.07	14	0	60	78	17	51
Nathaniel Garley, New Mexico	3	4	5.10	18	1	60	74	19	47
Mark Nowaczewski, Nevada	5	4	5.28	15	0	90	101	24	60
Ryan Jensen, Fresno State	2	6	5.35	18	2	67	83	36	66
Jake Jackson, Nevada	8	4	5.42	16	1	85	94	22	77
Cody Dye, New Mexico	5	6	5.63	14	0	86	108	29	71
Matt Hargreaves, Air Force	4	4	5.74	14	0	75	109	23	33
Trevor Horn, UNLV	5	5	5.96	15	0	77	106	25	43
Tyler Mortenson, Air Fore	4	7	6.98	14	0	68	100	35	54
Justin Slaten, New Mexico	2	9	7.02	15	0	67	89	30	62

MOUNTAIN WEST CONFERENCE

	Conference		Overall	
	W	L	W	L
Nevada	20	9	29	24
* San Diego State	18	12	39	21
San Jose State	16	14	27	30
UNLV	14	16	35	24
Fresno State	13	17	30	24
Air Force	12	17	24	30
New Mexico	11	19	20	33

ALL-CONFERENCE TEAM: C: Kaleb Foster, Jr., Nevada. **1B:** Nic Ready, Jr., Air Force; Jordan Verdon, Jr., San Diego State. **SS:** Bryson Stott, So., UNLV. **3B:** Joshua Zamora, Fr., Nevada. **OF:** Kyle Isbel, Jr., UNLV; Brett Bautista, Sr., San Jose State; Chase Calabuig, Sr., San Diego State; Grant Fennell, Sr., Nevada. **SP:** Garrett Hill, San Diego State; Edgar Gonzalez, Jr., Fresno State; Mark Nowaczewski, Sr., Nevada; Andrew Mitchel, Jr., San Jose State. **Player of the Year:** Grant Fennell, Nevada. **Pitcher of the Year:** Garrett Hill, San Diego State; Andrew Mitchel, San Jose State. **Coach of the Year:** T.J. Bruce, Nevada. **Rookie of the Year:** Joshue Zamora, Nevada.

INDIVIDUAL BATTING LEADERS
(Minimum 140 at-bats)

	AVG	OBP	SLG	AB	2B	3B	HR	RBI	SB
Grant Fennell, Nevada	.389	.466	.562	203	16	2	5	52	8
Bryson Stott, UNLV	.365	.442	.556	252	30	3	4	32	14
Cole Krzmarzick, Nevada	.359	.428	.425	167	8	0	1	19	4
Kyle Isbel, UNLV	.357	.441	.643	238	18	4	14	56	6
Joshua Zamora, Nevada	.355	.430	.563	183	11	0	9	33	1
Zach Ashford, Fresno State	.352	.406	.489	219	18	3	2	24	7
Rob Dau, Air Forcce	.350	.393	.520	223	19	2	5	52	3
Chase Calabuig, San Diego St.	.350	.421	.547	243	21	6	5	46	4
Hayden Schilling, New Mexico	.348	.453	.461	178	15	1	1	30	4
Brett Bautista, San Jose State	.343	.428	.464	207	7	3	4	34	5
Ryan Robb, Air Force	.342	.392	.437	231	9	5	1	33	19
Nic Ready, Air Force	.341	.400	.699	229	18	2	20	74	6
Jeremiah Burks, Fresno State	.340	.415	.544	206	15	0	9	39	12
Nick Rodriguez, UNLV	.337	.376	.542	249	17	2	10	56	2
Mike Echavia, Nevada	.337	.424	.540	202	17	3	6	50	3
Shane Timmons, San Jose St.	.333	.412	.510	210	9	2	8	55	7
Jordan Verdon, San Diego St.	.333	.386	.608	237	27	1	12	65	1
David Campbell, San Jose St.	.330	.371	.390	200	12	0	0	36	1
Dillon Johnson, UNLV	.328	.430	.404	235	13	1	1	43	2
Chad Bible, San Diego State	.327	.385	.523	214	11	2	9	42	2
Connor Mang, New Mexico	.326	.421	.453	172	10	3	2	27	2
Drew Wiss, Air Force	.326	.425	.507	215	17	2	6	35	16
Justin Watari, New Mexico	.321	.438	.434	159	11	2	1	25	6

NORTHEAST CONFERENCE

	Conference		Overall	
	W	L	W	L
Wagner	21	7	38	18
Bryant	21	7	32	23
* Long Island-Brooklyn	16	12	31	26
Mount St. Mary's	15	13	21	33
Sacred Heart	12	16	17	35
Central Connecticut	11	16	18	28
Fairleigh Dickinson	1	26	10	37

ALL-CONFERENCE TEAM: C: Mickey Gasper, Sr., Bryant. **1B:** Andrew Turner, Sr., Long Island-Brooklyn. **2B:** Dean Lockery, Sr., Central Connecticut. **3B:** Alex Briggs, Fr., Long Island-Brooklyn. **SS:** Sean Mazzio, Sr., Wagner. **OF:** Ryan Ward, R-Fr., Bryant; Dan Schock, Sr., Sacred Heart; James Ciliento, So., Bryant. **DH:** Freddy Sabido, So., Wagner. **SP:** Jack Patterson, Sr., Bryant; Neil Abbatiello, Jr., Wagner; Trey McGough, So., Mount St. Mary's. **RP:** Nick Robino, So., Wagner. **Player of the Year:** Ryan Ward, Bryant. **Pitcher of the Year:** Jack Patterson, Bryant. **Coach of the Year:** Jim Carone, Wagner. **Rookie of the Year:** Ryan Ward, Bryant.

INDIVIDUAL BATTING LEADERS
(Minimum 140 at-bats)

	AVG	OBP	SLG	AB	2B	3B	HR	RBI	SB
Ryan Ward, Bryant	.409	.449	.636	247	22	5	8	52	9
James Ciliento, Bryant	.377	.448	.518	191	14	2	3	31	5
Andrew Turner, LIU Brooklyn	.346	.493	.531	162	15	0	5	19	2
Mickey Gasper, Bryant	.340	.468	.539	206	13	2	8	43	3
Dean Lockery, C. Connecticut	.331	.443	.459	172	8	1	4	19	6
Patrick Causa, Mount St. Mary's	.316	.400	.511	190	17	1	6	47	2
Chris Wright, Bryant	.313	.405	.441	195	10	0	5	36	0
Phil Capra, Wagner	.312	.409	.551	205	13	0	12	58	2
Dan Schock, Sacred Heart	.311	.390	.623	183	14	2	13	45	7
Sean Mazzio, Wagner	.307	.412	.380	205	7	1	2	23	9
Jake Frasca, Sacred Heart	.307	.373	.391	179	10	1	1	25	1
Alex Kriss, Mount St. Mary's	.305	.375	.445	200	11	1	5	22	4
Gaby Cruz, Bryant	.302	.390	.360	139	8	0	0	26	0
Myles Nicholson, Mount St. Mary's	.301	.386	.363	193	8	2	0	12	22
Peyton Stephens, C. Conn.	.301	.390	.419	136	5	1	3	23	2
Freddy Sabido, Wagner	.300	.368	.500	210	16	4	6	44	8
Edward Modica Jr., LIU Brooklyn	.299	.364	.396	197	7	0	4	31	3
Shane Kelly, Bryant	.296	.411	.444	135	9	1	3	30	4
Joe Silverstrone, Wagner	.294	.337	.382	170	8	2	1	19	4
Andrew Smith, LIU Brooklyn	.293	.418	.491	167	8	5	5	34	11

	AVG	OBP	SLG	AB	2B	3B	HR	RBI	SB
Vaughn Parker II, Mt. St. Mary's	.292	.381	.455	178	14	0	5	36	1
Evan McDonald, Fairleigh Dickinson	.289	.383	.566	159	11	3	9	30	2
Nick Mascelli, Wagner	.280	.364	.445	218	16	1	6	25	8
Buddy Dewaine, C. Conn.	.279	.344	.355	172	8	1	1	24	5
Alex Briggs, LIU Brooklyn	.276	.361	.481	181	13	0	8	43	7
Anthony Warneke, LIU Brooklyn	.272	.373	.374	206	10	1	3	34	13
Tyler Panno, Bryant	.269	.348	.442	197	12	2	6	33	6

INDIVIDUAL PITCHING LEADERS
(Minimum 40 innings pitched)

	W	L	ERA	G	SV	IP	H	BB	SO
Neil Abbatiello, Wagner	8	0	3.30	15	0	87	78	33	79
Jackson Svete, LIU Brooklyn	4	2	3.75	23	1	58	57	30	38
Vito Morgese, Bryant	5	2	3.82	15	0	78	77	25	73
Jack Patterson, Bryant	6	3	3.84	14	0	82	75	46	101
Eric Ligda, Wagner	7	2	3.89	15	0	88	80	34	60
Zach Pederson, LIU Brooklyn	6	5	3.97	14	0	79	81	29	62
Steve Theetge, Bryant	6	7	4.02	15	0	87	92	33	70
Mike Appel, C. Connecticut	3	4	4.68	14	0	60	58	42	56
Patrick Clyne, LIU Brooklyn	5	5	4.73	15	0	86	84	41	89
James Taubl, Sacred Heart	2	5	5.21	14	0	76	94	24	50
Brent Teller, Sacred Heart	4	7	5.24	14	0	79	84	41	77
Trey McGough, Mount St. Mary's	4	7	5.31	14	0	76	80	41	62
Corey Zeller, Fairleigh Dickinson	2	8	5.35	12	0	69	92	24	51
Brandon Fox, C. Connecticut	1	3	5.40	10	0	47	55	13	29
Pat Gallagher, Wagner	4	3	5.67	16	0	60	71	34	37
Evan Raiburn, Fairleigh Dickinson	2	4	6.09	14	0	47	61	40	32

OHIO VALLEY CONFERENCE

	Conference		Overall	
	W	L	W	L
Tennessee Tech	27	3	53	12
Southeast Missouri State	20	10	27	30
* Morehead State	18	12	37	26
Jacksonville State	18	12	32	25
Austin Peay	17	13	30	27
Eastern Kentucky	15	15	30	31
Murray State	13	16	27	29
Eastern Illinois	12	18	23	31
Belmont	11	19	19	36
Tennessee-Martin	7	22	11	40
SIU Edwardsville	6	24	15	37

ALL-CONFERENCE TEAM: C: Alex Holderbach, Jr., Eastern Kentucky. 1B: Chase Chambers, Sr., Tennessee Tech. 2B: Trevor Ezell, R-Sr., Southeast Missouri; John Ham, Jr., Tennessee Tech. 3B: Trevor Putzig, Sr., Tennessee Tech. SS: Reid Leonard, Jr., Morehead State. OF: Justin Dirden, Jr., Southeast Missouri; Matt Cogen, R-So., Belmont; Connor Pauly, Jr., Morehead State; Jordan Stoner, Jr., Tennessee-Martin. DH: Kevin Strohschein, Jr., Tennessee Tech. UTL: Trent Simpson, Sr., Jacksonville State. SP: Travis Moths, Sr., Tennessee Tech; Carlos Vega, Sr., Southeast Missouri; Michael Costanzo, Sr., Austin Peay. RP: Ethan Roberts, Jr., Tennessee Tech. Player of the Year: Kevin Strohschein, Tennessee Tech. Pitcher of the Year: Travis Moths, Tennessee Tech. Coach of the Year: Matt Bragga, Tennessee Tech. Rookie of the Year: Grant Wood, Murray State.

INDIVIDUAL BATTING LEADERS
(Minimum 140 at-bats)

	AVG	OBP	SLG	AB	2B	3B	HR	RBI	SB
Chase Chambers, Tenn. Tech	.401	.506	.663	252	13	1	17	84	0
Jordan Stoner, Tenn.-Martin	.382	.465	.560	207	17	4	4	25	11
Trevor Ezell, SE Missouri State	.377	.442	.558	231	16	4	6	50	11
Grant Wodd, Murray State	.376	.520	.554	186	16	1	5	46	2
Kevin Strohschein, Tenn. Tech	.375	.432	.650	280	17	3	18	67	1
Brennon Kaleiwahea, Tenn. Tech	.373	.470	.549	233	15	1	8	55	1
Matt Cogen, Belmont	.372	.418	.586	239	15	3	10	51	12
Braxton Morris, Morehead St.	.367	.443	.547	267	25	1	7	59	6
Garrett Giovannelli, Austin Peay	.362	.437	.560	232	26	1	6	35	20
Jake Hammon, Morehead St.	.361	.471	.565	191	8	2	9	53	3
Davis Sims, Murray State	.357	.434	.573	227	29	1	6	52	0
Alex Holderbach, E. Kentucky	.352	.446	.657	230	12	2	18	79	2
Brandon Gutzler, Murray State	.351	.425	.571	191	12	0	10	51	1
Reid Leonard, Morehead State	.344	.468	.464	250	14	2	4	40	2

	AVG	OBP	SLG	AB	2B	3B	HR	RBI	SB
Tyler Niemann, Morehead St.	.340	.410	.592	206	21	5	7	43	5
Garrett Kueber, Austin Peay	.340	.465	.500	162	10	2	4	39	12
Justin Dirden, SE Missouri St.	.340	.437	.665	212	19	1	16	68	9
Connor Pauly, Morehead State	.339	.438	.526	230	17	1	8	53	5
Trevor Snyder, Morehead State	.335	.378	.606	251	14	0	18	69	0
Chase Urhahn, SE Missouri St.	.335	.380	.473	203	19	0	3	22	4
Tyler Romanik, E. Kentucky	.335	.408	.533	182	13	1	7	40	0
Nick Howie, Eastern Kentucky	.333	.420	.533	225	13	1	10	50	17
Jimmy Govern, Eastern Illinois	.331	.413	.528	178	12	1	7	38	8
Hunter Morris, Eastern Illinois	.326	.405	.572	187	9	2	11	55	0
Clayton Daniel, Jacksonville St.	.325	.397	.443	255	22	1	2	28	10
Parker Phillips, Austin Peay	.313	.408	.667	198	13	0	19	62	4
Cornell Nixon, E. Kentucky	.263	.394	.369	198	8	2	3	22	34

INDIVIDUAL PITCHING LEADERS
(Minimum 40 innings pitched)

	W	L	ERA	G	SV	IP	H	BB	SO
Ethan Roberts, Tennessee Tech	6	1	2.40	27	15	75	62	21	100
Carlos Vega, SW Missouri State	8	3	2.46	20	0	73	60	24	85
Tyler Jones, Eastern Illinois	7	3	3.52	13	0	69	67	25	54
Garrett Farmer, Jacksonville St.	7	2	3.80	15	0	90	95	24	107
Brett Newberg, Austin Peay	3	2	3.88	29	6	58	60	19	42
Travis Moths, Tennessee Tech	13	3	3.96	20	0	102	97	40	109
Colton Pate, Jacksonville State	5	5	3.96	19	0	86	73	35	92
Jacques Pucheu, Austin Peay	7	4	4.03	15	0	89	86	33	101
Casey Queener, Belmont	4	4	4.22	14	0	85	76	33	96
Marcus Evey, Tennessee Tech	8	0	4.22	17	0	81	72	32	90
Kenny Serwa, SIU Edwardsville	3	7	4.45	14	0	85	94	15	57
Alex Hursey, Tennessee Tech	8	4	4.52	17	0	74	81	25	45
Michael Costanzo, Austin Peay	9	2	4.62	15	0	90	94	28	104
Derrick Adams, Jacksonville St.	5	3	5.11	15	0	74	89	33	46
Trevor McMurray, Murray State	5	2	5.16	16	0	73	90	25	42
Tyler Vaughn, Belmont	3	7	5.27	12	0	67	78	15	57
Christian Vick, SE Missouri St.	5	5	5.68	17	0	63	82	18	50
Brandon Vial, Austin Peay	2	3	5.92	18	2	59	72	21	22
Kyle Cantu, Morehead State	4	1	6.17	21	2	66	93	23	51
Dalton Stambaugh, Morehead St.	7	3	6.17	18	1	89	108	33	87
Alex Stevenson, Eastern Illinois	3	8	6.45	15	1	68	81	24	46
Winston Cannon, Tenn.-Martin	1	8	7.66	14	0	72	99	36	67
Peyton Cain, Tennessee-Martin	0	5	6.31	18	2	56	76	14	37

PACIFIC-12 CONFERENCE

	Conference		Overall	
	W	L	W	L
* Stanford	22	8	46	12
Oregon State	20	9	55	12
Washington	20	10	35	26
UCLA	19	11	38	21
California	16	14	32	22
Arizona	14	16	34	22
Arizona State	13	17	23	32
Southern California	12	18	26	28
Oregon	12	18	26	29
Washington State	8	21	16	33
Utah	8	22	16	39

ALL-CONFERENCE TEAM: C: Nick Kahle, So., Washington; Cesar Salazar, Jr., Arizona. C/INF: Adley Rutschman, So., Oregon State. INF: Andrew Daschbach, So., Stanford; Michael Toglia, So., UCLA; Spencer Torkelson, Fr., Arizona State; Andrew Vaughn, So., California; Nick Madrigal, Jr., Oregon State; Cadyn Grenier, Jr., Oregon State; Chase Strumpf, So., UCLA; Nico Hoerner, Jr., Stanford; Levi Jordan, Sr., Washington; Nick Quintana, Jr., Arizona. OF: Gage Canning, Jr., Arizona State; Jonah Davis, Jr., California; Dashawn Keirsey Jr., Jr., Utah; Steven Kwan, Jr., Oregon State; Trevor Larnach, Jr., Oregon State; Alfonso Rivas, Jr., Arizona; Tim Tawa, Fr., Stanford; Jeremy Ydens, So., UCLA. DH: Joe Wainhouse, Jr., Washington. P/OF: Tanner Dodson, Jr., California. RHP: Tristan Beck, Jr., Stanford; Jake Bird, Sr., UCLA; Joe DeMers, Jr., Washington; Bryce Fehmel, Jr., Oregon State; Alex Hardy, Sr., Washington; Jack Little, So., Stanford; Kenyon Yovan, So., Oregon. LHP: Kris Bubic, Jr., Stanford; Luke Heimlich, Sr., Oregon State. Player of the Year: Andrew Vaughn, California. Pitcher of the Year: Luke Heimlich, Oregon State. Coach of the Year: David Esquer, Stanford. Rookie of the Year: Spencer Torkelson, Arizona State.

INDIVIDUAL BATTING LEADERS
(Minimum 140 at-bats)

	AVG	OBP	SLG	AB	2B	3B	HR	RBI	SB
Adley Rutschman, Oregon St.	.408	.505	.628	250	22	3	9	83	1
Andrew Vaughn, Calif.	.402	.531	.819	199	14	0	23	63	4
Dashawn Keirsey Jr., Utah	.386	.440	.609	202	23	5	4	22	7
Gage Canning, Arizona State	.369	.426	.648	236	17	11	9	45	8
Chaes Strumpf, UCLA	.363	.475	.633	226	23	1	12	53	2
Steven Kwan, Oregon State	.355	.463	.457	256	8	6	2	41	14
Beau Branton, Stanford	.353	.431	.418	170	6	1	1	22	2
Jeremy Ydens, UCLA	.350	.421	.558	217	17	5	6	38	13
Blake Clanton, Washington St.	.350	.430	.644	160	13	2	10	35	2
Trevor Larnach, Oregon State	.348	.463	.652	256	19	1	19	77	4
Alfonso Rivas, Arizona	.347	.429	.533	225	15	3	7	52	5
Nico Hoerner, Stanford	.345	.391	.496	232	17	6	2	40	15
Mason Cerrillo, Washington	.341	.395	.404	223	14	0	0	21	4
Cesar Salazar, Arizona	.339	.432	.471	189	11	1	4	42	2
Michael Toglia, UCLA	.336	.449	.588	226	24	0	11	58	5
Jonah Davis, Calif.	.321	.446	.606	193	9	2	14	58	6
Cameron Cannon, Arizona	.321	.427	.549	215	21	2	8	50	7
Spencer Torkelson, Arizona St.	.320	.440	.743	206	12	0	25	53	4
Tanner Dodson, Calif.	.320	.384	.386	228	12	0	1	27	12
Tyrus Greene, Calif.	.320	.414	.393	219	7	0	3	20	9
Oliver Dunn, Utah	.319	.426	.459	207	9	4	4	31	9
Cadyn Grenier, Oregon State	.319	.408	.462	273	17	2	6	47	9
Nick Quintana, Arizona	.313	.413	.592	211	17	0	14	55	0
Lyle Lin, Arizona State	.312	.344	.407	231	16	0	2	18	1
Jakob Goldfarb, Oregon	.308	.397	.487	195	13	2	6	29	14
Braiden Ward, Washington	.304	.401	.370	181	6	3	0	14	19

INDIVIDUAL PITCHING LEADERS
(Minimum 40 innings pitched)

	W	L	ERA	G	SV	IP	H	BB	SO
Jake Bird, UCLA	7	4	2.18	16	0	112	110	33	61
Ryan Garcia, UCLA	8	1	2.23	22	0	77	52	23	76
Joe DeMers, Washington	7	3	2.42	20	3	130	103	21	94
Brendan Beck, Stanford	8	0	2.43	17	1	67	56	12	38
Kris Bubic, Stanford	8	1	2.62	15	0	86	60	32	101
Aaron Shortridge, Calif.	5	3	2.77	17	2	91	89	14	74
Alex Hardy, Washington	5	4	2.80	37	8	61	50	23	47
Cody Deason, Arizona	6	5	2.87	14	0	91	70	37	84
Kevin Abel, Oregon State	8	1	2.88	23	1	81	51	46	108
Luke Heimlich, Oregon State	16	3	2.92	21	0	130	104	28	159
Kenyon Yovan, Oregon	6	4	2.98	21	5	85	61	37	98
Tristan Beck, Stanford	4	8	2.98	15	0	91	79	31	73
Solomon Bates, S. California	6	3	3.14	18	0	77	62	21	79
Bryce Fehmel, Oregon State	10	1	3.19	20	0	113	98	27	64
Jake Mulholland, Oregon State	2	2	2.20	31	16	45	30	11	42
Josh Tedeschi, Utah	2	10	5.42	16	0	81	103	31	66

PATRIOT LEAGUE

	Conference		Overall	
	W	L	W	L
Navy	18	7	38	16
* Army	18	7	37	24
Bucknell	13	11	17	27
Holy Cross	11	14	18	27
Lehigh	10	15	22	27
Lafayette	4	20	16	34

ALL-CONFERENCE TEAM: C: Jon Rosoff, Sr., Army. **1B:** Christian Hodge, Jr., Navy. **2B:** Zach Biggers, So., Navy. **3B:** Anthony Giachin, Fr., Army; John Marti, So., Lafayette. **SS:** Chris Rinaldi, Sr., Holy Cross. **OF:** Logan Knowles, Sr., Navy; Luke Robinson, Sr., Lafayette; Jacob Hurtubise, So., Army; Austin Masel, So., Holy Cross. **DH:** Liam Lowery, Jr., Navy. **SP:** Connor Van Hoose, Sr., Bucknell; Noah Song, Jr., Navy. **RP:** Danny Barlok, Jr., Holy Cross. **Player of the Year:** Jon Rosoff, Army. **Pitcher of the Year:** Connor Van Hoose, Bucknell. **Coach of the Year:** Paul Kostacopoulos, Navy. **Rookie of the Year:** Anthony Giachin, Army.

INDIVIDUAL BATTING LEADERS
(Minimum 140 at-bats)

	AVG	OBP	SLG	AB	2B	3B	HR	RBI	SB
John Marti, Lafayette	.348	.417	.459	181	10	2	2	25	4
Zach Biggers, Navy	.343	.403	.479	213	20	3	1	32	3
Jon Rosoff, Army	.340	.430	.442	215	15	2	1	47	3
Chris Kersey, Lehigh	.335	.435	.451	173	14	3	0	20	10
Austin Masel, Holy Cross	.322	.408	.477	149	7	2	4	25	8
Chris Rinaldi, Holy Cross	.320	.398	.453	150	10	2	2	13	13
Stephen Born, Navy	.318	.390	.429	217	12	6	0	44	16
Liam Lowery, Navy	.312	.383	.484	157	16	1	3	21	0
Trey Durrah, Lafayette	.306	.395	.463	134	9	0	4	27	2
Luke Robinson, Lafayette	.304	.408	.497	171	5	5	6	25	9
Michael Coritz, Navy	.303	.413	.382	152	10	1	0	17	1
Luke Johnson, Bucknell	.294	.367	.387	163	9	3	0	25	0
Josh White, Army	.290	.367	.396	217	11	6	0	38	6
Evan Madigan, Bucknell	.290	.348	.393	145	10	1	1	19	3
Logan Knowles, Navy	.287	.395	.407	209	8	7	1	28	13
Anthony Giachin, Army	.286	.371	.385	213	9	3	2	33	5
Domininc Toso, Bucknell	.284	.383	.459	148	15	4	1	21	1
Drake Titus, Army	.280	.416	.360	175	11	0	1	30	18
Jeff Shanfeldt, Lehigh	.280	.376	.367	150	5	1	2	20	1
Steven Cohen, Lafayette	.279	.346	.424	172	8	1	5	22	5
Thomas Russo, Holy Cross	.279	.368	.314	140	3	1	0	9	2
Jacob Hurtubise, Army	.278	.428	.325	212	4	3	0	22	42
Tyler Wincig, Bucknell	.277	.431	.346	130	6	0	1	15	2
Evan Lowery, Navy	.276	.371	.417	192	12	3	3	31	1
Jacob Williamson, Navy	.274	.333	.394	208	15	2	2	46	1
James Bleming, Lehigh	.256	.348	.360	172	5	2	3	36	12
Luke Hartman, Bucknell	.256	.447	.336	125	4	3	0	19	2
Cam O'Neill, Holy Cross	.222	.294	.380	158	7	0	6	26	3

INDIVIDUAL PITCHING LEADERS
(Minimum 40 innings pitched)

	W	L	ERA	G	SV	IP	H	BB	SO
Danny Barlok, Holy Cross	5	2	1.71	20	4	53	32	28	74
Noah Song, Navy	6	5	1.92	14	0	89	55	41	121
Connor Van Hoose, Bucknell	8	4	2.36	12	0	76	54	31	108
Sean Kamhoot, Navy	5	1	2.44	14	0	85	85	22	55
Cam Opp, Army	5	2	2.66	25	4	61	48	25	72
Jeff Gottesman, Bucknell	5	4	2.85	12	0	73	57	29	61
Daniel Burggraaf, Army	7	3	2.90	17	3	62	49	25	83
Levi Stoudt, Lehigh	3	8	3.03	12	0	65	66	22	67
Andrew Sauer, Navy	5	2	3.11	13	0	67	61	23	46
Pat McGowan, Holy Cross	2	6	3.22	12	0	73	50	26	57
Tyler Giovinco, Army	9	5	3.26	15	0	94	86	32	77
Liam Dvorak, Holy Cross	3	4	3.40	14	0	48	49	19	36
Matt Ball, Army	7	3	3.52	17	0	84	94	23	93
Jason Reynolds, Lehigh	4	5	3.60	12	0	65	61	25	51
Declan Cronin, Holy Cross	4	5	4.16	13	0	67	75	35	67
Brett Kreyer, Lafayette	2	7	5.04	17	0	64	59	31	53
Peter Moore, Lehigh	4	7	5.27	13	0	55	51	36	51
Jack Simpson, Bucknell	2	6	6.31	13	1	46	57	18	28
Jack Grabek, Bucknell	2	3	6.39	13	0	49	51	59	44
Mark Anderson, Lafayette	2	4	7.93	16	0	53	64	39	49

SOUTHEASTERN CONFERENCE

East Division	Conference		Overall	
	W	L	W	L
Florida	20	10	49	21
Georgia	18	12	39	21
South Carolina	17	13	37	26
Vanderbilt	16	14	35	27
Kentucky	13	17	34	22
Missouri	12	18	34	22
Tennessee	12	18	29	27

West Division	Conference		Overall	
	W	L	W	L
* Ole Miss	18	12	48	17
Arkansas	18	12	48	21
Auburn	15	15	43	23

	15	15	39	27
LSU	15	15	39	27
Mississippi State	15	15	39	29
Texas A&M	13	17	40	22
Alabama	8	22	27	29

ALL-CONFERENCE TEAM: C: J.J. Schwarz, Sr., Florida. **1B:** Kole Cottam, Jr., Kentucky. **2B:** Carson Shaddy, Sr., Arkansas. **3B:** Jonathan India, Jr., Florida. **SS:** Braden Shewmake, So., Texas A&M. **OF:** Jake Mangum, Jr., Mississippi State; Ryan Olenek, Jr., Ole Miss; Keegan McGovern, Sr., Georgia. **DH/UT:** Luke Heyer, Sr., Kentucky. **SP:** Brady Singer, Jr., Florida; Casey Mize, Jr., Auburn. **RP:** Michael Byrne, Jr., Florida. **Player of the Year:** Jonathan India, Florida. **Pitcher of the Year:** Brady Singer, Florida. **Coach of the Year:** Kevin O'Sullivan, Florida. **Rookie of the Year:** Heston Kjerstad, Arkansas.

INDIVIDUAL BATTING LEADERS
(Minimum 140 at-bats)

	AVG	OBP	SLG	AB	2B	3B	HR	RBI	SB
Michael Helman, Texas A&M	.369	.451	.526	249	17	2	6	36	12
Kole Cottam, Kentucky	.352	.438	.667	219	12	0	19	50	4
Jake Mangum, Mississippi St.	.351	.434	.479	288	22	3	3	33	14
Jonathan India, Florida	.350	.497	.717	226	12	4	21	52	15
Ryan Olenek, Ole Miss	.350	.388	.464	237	18	0	3	29	9
Luke Heyer, Kentucky	.348	.440	.691	207	17	0	18	57	9
Justin Row, South Carolina	.347	.418	.540	176	13	0	7	25	0
Casey Martin, Arkansas	.345	.418	.556	252	14	0	13	49	8
Austin Martin, Vanderbilt	.338	.452	.414	222	14	0	1	19	22
Tristan Pompey, Kentucky	.335	.448	.557	185	20	0	7	39	10
Heston Kjerstad, Arkansas	.332	.419	.553	262	16	0	14	58	3
Carson Shaddy, Arkansas	.330	.426	.609	197	12	2	13	55	4
Jay Estes, Auburn	.329	.401	.409	237	19	0	0	33	13
Antoine Duplantis, LSU	.328	.381	.443	271	13	6	2	48	19
Braden Shewmake, Texas A&M	.327	.395	.453	245	8	4	5	45	12
Michael Curry, Georgia	.322	.395	.532	233	10	0	13	53	1
Madison Stokes, S. Carolina	.322	.414	.579	183	12	1	11	44	1
LT Tolbert, South Carolina	.322	.401	.498	245	11	4	8	56	9
Brian Sharp, Missouri	.321	.418	.500	196	9	1	8	39	5
Hunter Stovall, Mississippi St.	.321	.369	.429	280	16	4	2	42	10
Rowdey Jordan, Mississippi St.	.321	.390	.518	193	15	1	7	37	2
Keegan McGovern, Georgia	.319	.431	.644	216	14	1	18	50	7
Nick Fortes, Ole Miss	.319	.435	.519	235	12	1	11	49	14
Adam Sasser, Georgia	.317	.379	.508	183	5	0	10	44	0
Chase Cockrell, Ole Miss	.317	.376	.539	180	13	0	9	38	1
Edouard Julien, Auburn	.275	.398	.556	207	7	0	17	69	7

INDIVIDUAL PITCHING LEADERS
(Minimum 40 innings pitched)

	W	L	ERA	G	SV	IP	H	BB	SO
Brady Singer, Florida	12	3	2.55	17	0	113	84	22	114
Sean Hunley, Tennessee	7	3	2.64	15	0	75	77	18	53
John Doxakis, Texas A&M	8	5	2.70	17	0	93	72	29	92
Tyler LaPlante, Missouri	4	3	2.75	13	0	59	44	17	56
Blaine Knight, Arkansas	14	0	2.80	19	0	112	96	25	102
Tanner Burns, Auburn	7	4	3.01	17	0	87	73	37	77
Jackson Kowar, Florida	10	5	3.05	18	0	112	101	43	115
Michael Plassmeyer, Missouri	5	4	3.06	14	0	91	86	17	103
Kacey Murphy, Arkansas	8	5	3.20	18	0	101	85	22	85
Ethan Small, Mississippi State	5	4	3.20	18	0	101	93	33	122
Casey Mize, Auburn	6	3	3.30	17	0	115	84	16	156
Mitchell Kilkenny, Texas A&M	8	5	3.34	16	0	97	89	24	92
TJ Sikkema, Missouri	3	5	3.34	16	0	70	75	20	76
Sean Hjelle, Kentucky	7	5	3.44	15	0	99	87	22	91
Cody Morris, South Carolina	9	3	3.46	16	0	83	71	31	87
Patrick Raby, Vanderbilt	5	5	3.57	16	0	68	69	33	57
Kevin Smith, Georgia	8	1	3.70	22	0	63	55	25	79
Ray Rolison, Ole Miss	10	4	3.70	17	0	97	88	45	120
Jake Walters, Alabama	4	5	3.73	14	0	82	73	35	82
Andy Toelken, Missouri	6	3	3.77	21	3	57	59	19	48
Ma'khail Hilliard, LSU	9	5	3.79	17	0	76	70	31	70
Drake Fellows, Vanderbilt	7	4	3.92	16	0	96	75	35	107
Brady Feigl, Ole Miss	8	5	4.03	16	0	92	91	26	93
Will Neely, Tennessee	4	2	4.09	14	0	84	86	21	52
Adam Hill, South Carolina	7	5	4.12	16	0	83	55	55	101
Isaiah Campbell, Arkansas	5	7	4.26	18	0	70	67	29	75
Eddy Demurias, South Carolina	7	1	4.87	31	3	65	70	30	51
Garrett Stallings, Tennessee	5	5	4.58	16	2	79	100	18	37

SOUTHERN CONFERENCE

	Conference		Overall	
	W	L	W	L
UNC Greensboro	18	3	39	15
* Samford	16	8	37	26
Wofford	15	9	36	23
Virginia Military Institute	12	12	26	27
Mercer	11	13	38	22
East Tennessee State	11	13	28	25
Furman	9	12	24	28
The Citadel	8	16	19	34
Western Carolina	5	19	11	47

ALL-CONFERENCE TEAM: C: Peyton Maddox, Sr., Virginia Military Institute. **1B:** Christian Bailey, Sr., East Tennessee State. **2B:** Austin Embler, R-Jr., UNC Greensboro. **3B:** Caleb Webster, So., UNC Greensboro. **SS:** Chris Cook, R-Sr., East Tennessee State. **OF:** Ben Anderson, Fr., Furman; Andrew Moritz, Jr., UNC Greensboro; Matt Pita, Jr., Virginia Military Institute. **DH:** Caleb Longley, Sr., East Tennessee State. **SP:** Matt Frisbee, Jr., UNC Greensboro; Samuel Strickland, Fr., Samford. **RP:** Robert Broom, Jr., Mercer. **Player of the Year:** Andrew Moritz, UNC Greensboro. **Pitcher of the Year:** Matt Frisbee, UNC Greensboro. **Coach of the Year:** Link Jarrett, UNC Greensboro. **Rookie of the Year:** R.J. Yeager, Mercer.

INDIVIDUAL BATTING LEADERS
(Minimum 140 at-bats)

	AVG	OBP	SLG	AB	2B	3B	HR	RBI	SB
Andrew Moritz, UNC Greensboro	.428	.492	.637	215	7	10	6	61	12
Matt Pita, Virginia Military Inst.	.389	.459	.721	226	21	6	14	48	23
Caleb Webster, UNC Greensboro	.380	.417	.465	237	7	1	3	37	7
Trey Truitt, UNC Greensboro	.373	.457	.627	233	19	2	12	44	15
Chris Cook, East Tennessee St.	.364	.444	.548	217	22	0	6	40	5
Cesar Trejo, UNC Greensboro	.363	.428	.569	204	15	6	5	50	22
Ben Anderson, Furman	.361	.461	.530	202	11	7	3	39	5
Austin Embler, UNC Greensboro	.357	.438	.467	227	15	2	2	32	9
McClain Bradley, Wofford	.355	.409	.526	251	10	3	9	49	20
Spencer Holcomb, W. Carolina	.352	.403	.523	199	13	0	7	27	1
Jackson Ware, Mercer	.351	.446	.477	222	10	0	6	46	6
Christian Bailey, E. Tenn. St.	.345	.420	.488	168	15	0	3	45	3
Brooks Carlosn, Samford	.343	.429	.552	230	16	1	10	47	1
Matt Dunleavy, Va. Military Inst.	.339	.457	.575	186	15	1	9	37	12
Mack Nathanson, Wofford	.338	.466	.602	216	20	2	11	55	20
William Kinney, The Citadel	.332	.412	.490	202	14	0	6	40	9
Dillon Stewart, UNC Greensboro	.325	.409	.522	203	13	3	7	38	13
Jeffery Brown, The Citadel	.325	.375	.373	169	4	2	0	11	20
RJ Yeager, Mercer	.324	.410	.458	225	12	0	6	42	6
Justice Bigbie, W. Carolina	.324	.358	.462	225	14	1	5	46	1
Alex Hanson, Mercer	.313	.415	.473	243	12	0	9	41	25
Jason Costa, Furman	.312	.415	.526	173	10	0	9	38	0
Caleb Longley E. Tennessee St.	.309	.399	.644	191	20	1	14	50	4
Aaron Maher, . Tennessee St.	.308	.365	.489	221	9	2	9	40	7
Anthony Mulrine, Samford	.307	.390	.446	231	8	0	8	49	1
Branden Fryman, Samford	.262	.333	.342	260	13	1	2	26	25
Nathan Eaton, Va. Military Inst.	.287	.402	.507	209	12	5	8	24	36

INDIVIDUAL PITCHING LEADERS
(Minimum 40 innings pitched)

	W	L	ERA	G	SV	IP	H	BB	SO
Robert Broom, Mercer	10	4	1.70	31	2	74	57	24	111
Jack Maynard, UNC Greensboro	5	3	2.13	29	9	63	57	11	81
Wyatt Burns, Samford	5	4	2.19	28	13	66	45	13	79
Samuel Strickland, Samford	8	2	2.33	15	0	81	52	15	87
Andrew Wantz, UNC Greensboro	6	0	2.95	26	10	55	42	18	81
Adam Scott, Wofford	8	5	3.14	18	2	103	94	18	137
Cody Shelton, Samford	2	4	3.29	16	0	82	81	32	70
Matt Frisbee, UNC Greensboro	10	2	3.45	15	0	91	86	23	116
Christian Vann, Mercer	5	3	3.93	22	2	69	57	39	83
Dylan Spence, The Citadel	3	5	4.00	16	0	92	109	20	62
Bryce Hensley, UNC Greensboro	6	2	4.21	15	0	83	95	19	82
Jake Lewis, UNC Greensboro	6	4	4.26	21	0	55	48	29	57
Thomas Byelick, The Citadel	3	6	4.45	15	0	63	68	42	56
Austin Higginbotham, Wofford	6	5	4.50	16	0	102	119	28	74
Nik Verbeke, Furman	5	5	4.50	15	0	68	86	30	47

	W	L	ERA	G	SV	IP	H	BB	SO
Austin Cox, Mercer	7	4	4.52	17	0	88	99	43	124
Matt Lazzaro, Furman	3	4	4.85	10	0	52	62	10	34
Chase Burks, Mercer	6	5	4.97	15	0	76	85	23	70
Grant Schuermann, Furman	4	8	4.98	14	1	81	98	18	5
Micah Kaczor, E. Tenn. State	5	4	5.01	14	0	83	84	29	75
Taylor Purus, Western Carolina	3	13	6.97	18	1	90	96	51	100

SOUTHLAND CONFERENCE

	Conference		Overall	
	W	L	W	L
Sam Houston State	24	6	39	20
Southeastern Louisiana	21	9	37	22
* Northwestern State	18	12	38	24
Houston Baptist	18	12	29	30
Central Arkansas	17	13	32	25
McNeese	15	15	25	33
Texas A&M-Corpus Christi	14	16	30	26
New Orleans	14	16	29	32
Nicholls	14	16	28	32
Incarnate Word	13	17	29	26
Lamar	13	17	19	36
Stephen F. Austin	9	21	17	36
Abilene Christian	5	25	21	33

ALL-CONFERENCE TEAM: C: William Hancock, Jr., Central Arkansas. **1B:** David Fry, Sr., Northwestern State. **2B:** Kyle Bergeron, So., Incarnate Word. **3B:** Owen Magee, Sr., New Orleans. **SS:** Andrew Fregia, Jr., Sam Houston State. **OF:** Matt Heck, Sr., Houston Baptist; Drew Avans, Sr., Southeastern Louisiana; Spencer Halloran, Sr., Houston Baptist. **DH:** Dalon Farkas, Jr., Abilene Christian. **UTL:** Jackson Owens, Sr., Texas A&M-Corpus Christi. **SP:** Tyler Gray, Sr., Central Arkansas; Bryan Warzek, Jr., New Orleans; Matthew McCollough, Sr., Houston Baptist. **Player of the Year:** David Fry, Northwestern State. **Pitcher of the Year:** Tyler Gray, Central Arkansas. **Coach of the Year:** Bobby Barbier, Northwestern State. **Newcomers of the Year:** Jerry Maddox, Northwestern State; Ridge Rogers, Incarnate Word.

INDIVIDUAL BATTING LEADERS
(Minimum 140 at-bats)

	AVG	OBP	SLG	AB	2B	3B	HR	RBI	SB
Eddy Gonzalez, Incarnate Word	.371	.440	.448	221	9	1	2	30	6
Enrique Sanchez Jr., Tx. A&M-Corpus Christi	.367	.397	.449	158	10	0	1	29	1
Ridge Rogers, Incarnate Word	.350	.439	.422	206	9	3	0	34	12
Matt Heck, Houston Baptist	.348	.415	.552	230	10	5	9	46	13
Joey Morales, Nicholls	.341	.399	.422	232	11	1	2	38	8
Hunter Strong, C. Arkansas	.338	.424	.519	231	19	4	5	45	3
Joe Provenzano, McNeese	.336	.428	.488	217	16	1	5	35	1
Jake Georgiades, Stephen F. Austin	.333	.423	.395	162	7	0	1	23	3
Drew Avans, SE Louisiana	.330	.462	.568	206	13	3	10	44	23
Brady Bell, Nicholls	.330	.375	.450	200	14	2	2	25	2
Ryan Flores, Incarnate Word	.329	.392	.416	161	9	1	1	23	3
Andrew Fregia, Sam Houston St.	.328	.384	.585	229	12	7	11	49	11
David Fry, Northwestern State	.327	.440	.604	245	26	3	12	55	2
Clayton Harp, Sam Houston St.	.323	.405	.460	198	10	1	5	29	13
Harrison Dinicola, Tx. A&M-Corpus Christi	.321	.406	.527	224	16	3	8	38	7
Kyle Bergeron, Incarnate Word	.321	.396	.466	234	14	1	6	50	5
Chet Niehaus, Nicholls	.321	.474	.488	209	12	1	7	46	9
Blake Chisolm, Sam Houston St.	.321	.429	.518	193	12	1	8	33	6
Kwan Adkins, NW State	.321	.396	.404	240	7	2	3	27	7
Owen Magee, New Orleans	.321	.368	.496	262	14	4	8	41	2
Spencer Halloran, Houston Baptist	.320	.377	.512	244	18	1	9	41	20
Rigo Aguilar, Central Arkansas	.319	.402	.397	204	11	1	1	38	3
Matt Munoz, Abilene Christian	.316	.427	.542	177	14	7	4	31	11
Beau Bratton, New Orleans	.315	.381	.432	241	12	5	2	41	1
Cody Grosse, SE Louisiana	.314	.394	.397	239	10	5	0	29	20
Jackson Owens, Tx. A&M-Corpus Christi	.303	.389	.473	201	12	8	2	40	12

INDIVIDUAL PITCHING LEADERS
(Minimum 40 innings pitched)

	W	L	ERA	G	SV	IP	H	BB	SO
Jerry Maddox, NW State	8	3	1.88	16	0	86	54	37	66
John Barr, New Orleans	6	3	2.04	30	0	66	48	25	68
Carlisle Koestler, SE Louisiana	7	1	2.68	16	1	87	70	13	73

	W	L	ERA	G	SV	IP	H	BB	SO
Bryan Warzek, New Orleans	5	2	2.82	16	0	96	75	41	127
Matthew McCollough, Houston Baptist	9	3	2.99	15	0	108	100	12	99
Noah Sills, Lamar	3	5	3.00	14	0	78	85	17	50
Seth Ballew, Sam Houston St.	6	1	3.00	18	0	81	71	29	57
Josh Green, SE Louisiana	6	6	3.14	15	0	92	87	16	59
Corey Gaconi, SE Louisiana	7	1	3.15	13	0	80	80	16	62
Aidan Anderson, McNeese	5	6	3.30	28	6	63	48	30	72
Tyler Gray, Central Arkansas	6	2	3.32	14	0	98	75	31	116
Ridge Heisler, NW State	7	3	3.40	16	0	95	94	25	77
Will Brand, Central Arkansas	2	5	3.46	23	3	68	60	17	53
Jason Blanchard, Lamar	1	6	3.49	13	0	59	61	20	50
Hayden Wesneski, Sam Houston St.	7	3	3.50	17	0	98	91	30	67
Riley Gossett, Sam Houston St.	2	1	3.66	21	0	59	64	10	48
Nathan Jones, Northwestern St.	4	6	3.85	16	0	103	112	25	72
Grant Anderson, McNeese	4	7	3.86	18	2	82	81	36	72
Zach Carter, Houston Baptist	4	5	3.87	15	0	109	113	27	80
Brennan Lewis, Abilene Christian	4	2	3.95	29	0	55	57	21	35
Christian Bahlinger, Nicholls	3	2	4.61	36	6	66	69	19	49
Jonathan Nicholson, Abilene Christian	2	8	5.60	20	0	72	85	25	44
Brock Barger, Abilene Christian	2	8	6.59	15	0	72	101	26	52

SOUTHWESTERN ATHLETIC CONFERENCE

East Division	Conference		Overall	
	W	L	W	L
Alabama State	18	6	30	22
Jackson State	17	7	34	18
Alabama A&M	9	15	12	37
Mississippi Valley State	9	15	11	35
Alcorn State	7	17	13	39

West Division	Conference		Overall	
	W	L	W	L
* Texas Southern	17	6	27	28
Grambling	14	10	26	26
Arkansas-Pine Bluff	12	10	20	25
Prairie View	8	16	14	40
Southern	6	15	9	33

ALL-CONFERENCE TEAM: C: Stephan Vidal, Sr., Jackson State. **1B:** Christian Sanchez, Jr., Texas Southern. **2B:** Gaudencio Lucca, R-Sr., Texas Southern. **3B:** Ray Hernandez, Sr., Alabama State. **SS:** Marshawn Taylor, R-Sr., Grambling State. **OF:** Kamren Dukes, Sr., Texas Southern; Joseph Estrada, Sr., Alabama State; Isaiah Torres, Jr., Grambling State. **SP:** Aaron Solis, Jr., Texas Southern; Darrius Wright, Jr., Alabama State. **RP:** Jose Tirado, Sr., Jackson State. **Player of the Year:** Kamren Dukes, Texas Southern. **Pitcher of the Year:** Aaron Solis, Texas Southern. **Coach of the Year:** Jose Vazques, Alabama State. **Newcomers of the Year:** Nickelle Galatas, Jackson State; Raul Hernandez, Jackson State.

INDIVIDUAL BATTING LEADERS
(Minimum 140 at-bats)

	AVG	OBP	SLG	AB	2B	3B	HR	RBI	SB
Marshwan Taylor, Grambling	.404	.470	.454	218	5	3	0	44	20
Kamren Dukes, Texas Southern	.391	.457	.538	238	22	2	3	42	30
Raul Hernandez, Jackson State	.382	.425	.575	207	17	1	7	50	5
Ray Hernandez, Alabama State	.379	.452	.601	203	12	0	11	45	20
Gaudencio Lucca, Texas So.	.371	.488	.589	202	13	2	9	50	25
Gustavo Rios, Alabama State	.357	.462	.516	157	10	0	5	47	2
Rafael Ramirez III, Grambling	.353	.440	.735	170	17	0	16	66	3
Daniel Lingua, Prairie View	.350	.489	.412	177	7	2	0	22	14
Christian Sanchez, Texas So.	.335	.423	.651	209	13	1	17	60	12
Stephan Vidal, Jackson State	.335	.449	.527	167	12	1	6	35	5
Lamar Briggs, Jackson State	.333	.412	.414	174	9	1	1	27	18
Ace Felder, Grambling	.333	.497	.412	114	7	1	0	11	13
Joseph Estrada, Alabama State	.332	.437	.495	214	14	3	5	36	7
Carson McGregory, Ala. A&M	.331	.427	.487	154	9	3	3	30	1
Jarficur Parker, Ark.-Pine Bluff	.331	.386	.402	127	4	1	1	17	3
J.T. O'Reel, Alabama A&M	.330	.405	.481	185	7	3	5	32	7
Isaiah Torres, Grambling	.325	.438	.446	166	11	0	3	36	7
Dezmond Chumley, Jackson St.	.320	.433	.483	172	11	1	5	34	11
Nick Kreutzer, Ark.-Pine Bluff	.319	.451	.543	138	16	0	5	29	1

	AVG	OBP	SLG	AB	2B	3B	HR	RBI	SB
Justin Barna, Alcorn State	.316	.349	.406	155	10	2	0	15	5
Noel Cheneau, Alabama State	.313	.385	.438	176	10	3	2	26	13
Dalton Mitchell, Alabama A&M	.309	.352	.406	175	11	3	0	20	4
Jarvis Warner, Jackson State	.309	.373	.370	181	5	3	0	22	26
Tyler LaPorte, SOuthern	.308	.339	.385	169	9	2	0	25	8
Wesley Reyes, Jackson State	.304	.360	.497	171	22	1	3	42	11
Sergio Esparza, Ark.-Pine Bluff	.303	.364	.448	165	10	1	4	38	6
Jesus Santana, Jackson State	.301	.374	.515	196	13	1	9	48	8
Hunter Allen, Alabama State	.297	.401	.471	172	12	0	6	36	3
Javeyan Williams, Southern	.262	.415	.362	141	1	5	1	16	21

INDIVIDUAL PITCHING LEADERS
(Minimum 40 innings pitched)

	W	L	ERA	G	SV	IP	H	BB	SO
Darrius Wright, Alabama State	8	1	2.36	12	0	72	61	41	56
Jose Tirado, Jackson State	6	2	2.67	31	13	64	40	13	74
Mark Watson, Jackson State	5	2	3.23	15	0	53	41	24	49
Dalton Wilder, Alabama State	3	4	3.44	14	0	65	68	27	64
Aaron Solis, Texas Southern	10	4	3.67	15	0	91	94	26	69
Chase Laney, Alabama State	6	1	4.07	23	2	66	73	16	44
Kevin Perez, Jackson State	11	4	4.36	19	0	93	101	25	74
Tim Reynolds, Ark.-Pine Bluff	2	5	4.47	16	0	58	64	16	38
Nikelle Galatas, Jackson State	9	3	4.59	18	0	88	97	38	53
Daniel Franklin, Southern	3	3	4.64	13	0	64	63	25	49
Ivanniel Vazquez, Alabama St.	1	5	4.86	21	4	67	87	21	62
Jaret Britt, Alabama A&M	4	7	4.88	16	0	76	93	23	33
Carlos Lopez, Alcorn State	4	3	4.90	13	0	79	85	28	91
Peyton Burks, Ark.-Pine Bluff	4	6	5.15	17	0	80	78	41	48
Raul Baduel, Grambling	4	3	5.60	13	0	63	66	32	34
Markaylon Boyd, Southern	1	4	5.79	16	0	42	43	21	16
Darrien Williams, Prairie View	2	6	5.80	15	0	76	84	39	69
Peyton Schneider, Texas So.	4	7	5.86	23	0	71	93	38	44
Jose Figueroa, Alabama A&M	2	5	6.16	23	1	69	82	43	40
Jahborus Smith, Alcorn State	2	12	6.18	16	1	74	73	53	79

SUMMIT LEAGUE

	Conference W	L	Overall W	L
* Oral Roberts	24	6	38	20
Western Illinois	14	12	17	31
North Dakota State	15	13	26	24
South Dakota State	14	13	18	32
Omaha	10	17	15	35
Fort Wayne	7	23	11	37

ALL-CONFERENCE TEAM: C: Riley Keizor, So., Oral Roberts. **1B:** Spencer Henson, So., Oral Roberts. **2B:** Nick Roark, Sr., Oral Roberts. **3B:** Cal Hernandez, Jr., Oral Roberts. **SS:** Tony Kjolsing, Sr., South Dakota State. **OF:** Noah Cummings, Sr., Oral Roberts; Steve McShane, Jr., Western Illinois; Nick Rotola, Sr., Oral Roberts. **DH:** Anthony Schneider, Sr., South Dakota State. **UTL:** Nick Smith, Jr., South Dakota State. **SP:** Miguel Ausua, Sr., Oral Roberts; Ian Koch, Jr., Western Illinois; Justin McGregor, Sr., Oral Roberts. **RP:** Kyler Stout, Sr., Oral Roberts. **Player of the Year:** Noah Cummings, Oral Roberts. **Pitcher of the Year:** Miguel Ausua, Oral Roberts. **Coach of the Year:** Ryan Folmar, Oral Roberts. **Rookie of the Year:** Riley Keizor, Oral Roberts.

INDIVIDUAL BATTING LEADERS
(Minimum 140 at-bats)

	AVG	OBP	SLG	AB	2B	3B	HR	RBI	SB
Spencer Henson, Oral Roberts	.364	.433	.541	209	7	0	10	58	1
Nick Rotola, Oral Roberts	.337	.376	.428	243	12	2	2	22	10
Cal Hernandez, Oral Roberts	.329	.426	.420	219	12	1	2	34	5
Noah Cummings, Oral Roberts	.318	.397	.537	201	11	3	9	55	6
Nick Roark, Oral Roberts	.318	.404	.436	236	11	4	3	32	7
Steve McShane, W. Illinois	.317	.359	.394	142	7	2	0	14	9
Gus Steiger, S. Dakota St.	.311	.338	.404	193	8	2	2	27	4
Anthony Schneider, S. Dakota St.	.295	.432	.532	156	9	2	8	37	9
Mason Pierzchalski, N. Dakota St.	.293	.359	.424	191	10	3	3	36	1
Riley Keizor, Oral Roberts	.293	.416	.441	188	8	1	6	41	2
Tony Kjolsing, S. Dakota State	.292	.423	.462	195	8	2	7	36	19
Bailey Montgomery, W. Illinois	.288	.373	.356	146	7	0	1	23	8
Shannon Baker, Fort Wayne	.287	.429	.360	150	9	1	0	20	0

	AVG	OBP	SLG	AB	2B	3B	HR	RBI	SB
Josh Falk, South Dakota State	.286	.377	.439	189	11	0	6	30	0
Jacob Dickson, Fort Wayne	.283	.331	.401	152	7	1	3	18	2
Matt Elsenpeter, N. Dakota St.	.282	.324	.382	170	8	0	3	28	4
Braden Rogers, Omaha	.280	.348	.339	189	4	2	1	23	3
Drew Fearing, N. Dakota State	.278	.379	.344	180	7	1	1	19	5
CJ Schaeffer, Western Illinois	.275	.349	.383	149	8	1	2	12	4
Landon Badger, S. Dakota St.	.273	.384	.327	150	6	1	0	17	10
Newt Johnson, S. Dakota St.	.273	.431	.432	183	8	0	7	45	10
Deion Thompson, W. Illinois	.271	.348	.424	177	9	0	6	30	17
Tucker Rohde, N. Dakota St.	.269	.342	.357	171	5	2	2	21	0
Thomas DeBonville, Omaha	.259	.343	.423	189	5	4	6	28	21
Brady Hettinger, Fort Wayne	.247	.298	.310	158	2	4	0	17	12
Bennett Hostetler, N. Dakota St.	.225	.351	.314	191	6	4	1	19	6
Jayse McLean, N, Dakota St.	.250	.366	.449	176	6	4	7	31	8

INDIVIDUAL PITCHING LEADERS
(Minimum 40 innings pitched)

	W	L	ERA	G	SV	IP	H	BB	SO
Justin McGregor, Oral Roberts	6	2	2.80	16	0	93	77	35	84
Miguel Ausua, Oral Roberts	8	2	3.67	16	0	91	84	34	69
Blake Stockert, N. Dakota State	5	3	3.71	13	0	68	68	27	63
Josh McMinn, Oral Roberts	6	5	3.86	16	0	77	63	37	68
Cal Hehnke, Omaha	0	4	3.86	20	4	61	50	20	58
Javin Drake, Western Illinois	2	6	3.96	12	0	50	47	25	53
Parker Harm, N. Dakota State	2	2	4.21	15	1	51	42	27	55
Joey Machado, Omaha	4	7	4.35	14	0	83	83	38	50
Ian Koch, Western Illinois	4	6	4.38	16	0	86	91	50	83
Riley Johnson, N. Dakota State	5	6	4.57	15	0	87	85	41	66
Tyler Olmstead, S. Dakota State	2	3	4.67	14	0	52	52	22	57
Ryan Dunne, Western Illinois	4	7	4.68	14	0	85	79	39	98
Andrew Brighton, Omaha	2	3	4.85	18	0	69	64	16	17
Chris Choles, N. Dakota State	3	0	5.19	21	2	50	62	25	30
Brandon Phelps, Fort Wayne	5	6	5.31	14	0	83	106	33	66
Brady Moxham, S. Dakota State	1	6	5.55	16	0	73	73	42	68
Chase Phelps, Fort Wayne	1	4	5.64	14	1	53	53	33	46
Taylor Varnell, Oral Roberts	3	4	5.95	16	0	59	58	30	62
Damian Helm, Fort Wayne	4	8	6.87	14	0	73	100	27	54
Shane Odzark, Fort Wayne	1	6	6.96	12	0	53	69	33	40
Jake Pennington, Omaha	2	8	7.43	16	0	46	63	22	24
Kevin Folman, N. Dakota State	0	4	3.18	18	6	45	42	11	49

SUN BELT CONFERENCE

East Division	Conference W	L	Overall W	L
* Coastal Carolina	23	7	43	19
Troy	19	11	42	21
South Alabama	18	11	32	25
Georgia Southern	18	11	30	26
Georgia State	10	19	26	29
Appalachian State	9	21	18	36

West Division	Conference W	L	Overall W	L
Louisiana	18	12	34	25
Texas State	16	14	30	28
Little Rock	15	14	29	27
Arkansas State	11	19	20	31
Texas-Arlington	11	19	22	35
Louisiana-Monroe	10	20	23	31

ALL-CONFERENCE TEAM: C: Nick Gatewood, Jr., Georgia State. **1B:** Kevin Woodall Jr., Sr., Coastal Carolina. **2B:** Cory Wood, So., Coastal Carolina. **3B:** Drew Frederic, So., Troy. **SS:** Seth Lancaster, Sr., Coastal Carolina. **OF:** Dylan Hardy, Jr., South Alabama; Travis Swaggerty, Jr., South Alabama; Joey Denison, Sr., Troy. **DH:** Zach Bierman, Jr., Coastal Carolina. **UTL:** Jeremy Brown, Sr., Arkansas State. **SP:** Jason Bilous, Jr., Coastal Carolina; Brian Eichhorn, Jr., Georgia Southern; Colten Schmidt, Sr., Louisiana. **RP:** Justin Garcia, Sr., Arkansas-Little Rock. **Player of the Year:** Joey Denison, Troy. **Pitcher of the Year:** Colten Schmidt, Louisiana. **Coach of the Year:** Gary Gilmore, Coastal Carolina. **Newcomers of the Year:** Kyle MacDonald, Arkansas State; Rigsby Mosley, Troy.

INDIVIDUAL BATTING LEADERS
(Minimum 140 at-bats)

	AVG	OBP	SLG	AB	2B	3B	HR	RBI	SB
Joey Denison, Troy	.393	.461	.591	247	25	3	6	81	21
Matt Sanders, Troy	.378	.463	.538	262	19	4	5	28	26
Kyle MacDonald, Appalachian St.	.344	.466	.640	186	12	2	13	47	0
Johnny De La Cruz, LMU	.338	.396	.454	207	18	0	2	24	12
Dylan Hardy, South Alabama	.335	.409	.449	236	11	2	4	27	18
Drew Frederic, Troy	.331	.432	.525	242	20	3	7	54	28
Parker Chavers, Coastal Carolina	.323	.435	.498	217	15	1	7	42	9
Rigsby Mosley, Troy	.322	.390	.505	202	12	5	5	51	8
Nick Gatewood, Georgia State	.322	.400	.568	199	10	0	13	49	2
Daniel Lahare, Louisiana	.321	.388	.470	215	12	4	4	21	6
Jeremy Brown, Appalachian St.	.319	.400	.495	188	19	1	4	28	1
Jaylen Hubbard, Texas State	.313	.398	.423	227	10	3	3	34	12
Gavin Bourgeois, Louisiana	.311	.402	.423	222	14	1	3	38	22
Brandon Lockridge, Troy	.307	.429	.480	244	16	7	4	39	25
Omar Salinas, UTA	.306	.395	.382	157	6	0	2	18	1
Seth Lancaster, Coastal Carolina	.305	.454	.646	226	17	0	20	57	23
Travis Swaggerty, S. Alabama	.303	.463	.538	208	10	0	13	38	9
Brody Binder, Troy	.303	.388	.398	211	9	1	3	37	0
Avant Christian, Georgia So.	.302	.401	.365	159	2	1	2	17	11
Justin Jones, Georgia State	.302	.412	.468	205	14	1	6	28	7
Zach Biermann, Coastal Carolina	.300	.419	.559	213	14	1	13	57	2
Wells Davis, South Alabama	.299	.456	.492	187	10	1	8	56	1
Brendan Donovan, S. Alabama	.298	.453	.470	198	17	1	5	53	4
Chase Coker, Little Rock	.297	.381	.479	192	11	6	4	22	12

INDIVIDUAL PITCHING LEADERS
(Minimum 40 innings pitched)

	W	L	ERA	G	SV	IP	H	BB	SO
Cole Whitney, Georgia So.	4	1	1.90	26	2	62	43	26	53
Levi Thomas, Troy	2	0	1.96	15	1	41	23	16	56
Matt Eardensohn, Coastal Carolina	7	0	2.19	20	6	58	38	14	51
Jay Causey, Coastal Carolina	2	2	2.28	24	5	43	30	20	39
Colten Schmidt, Louisiana	7	0	2.45	16	0	106	83	9	90
Hogan Harris, Louisiana	5	2	2.62	12	0	58	52	30	54
Andrew Cane, Troy	7	4	2.74	16	0	99	87	34	87
Hunter Gaddis, Georgia State	9	4	2.95	17	0	101	95	24	98
Will Sprinkle, Appalachian St.	2	1	2.96	12	0	49	40	17	28
Nicholas Fraze, Texas State	6	4	2.97	14	0	79	63	26	71
Logan Austin, UTA	4	0	3.02	25	1	51	53	21	43
Jared Proctor, South Alabama	5	1	3.11	19	0	55	44	27	49
Zach McCambley, Coastal Carolina	3	0	3.14	18	0	49	45	25	50
Brian Eichhorn, Georgia So.	4	3	3.15	15	0	89	70	29	106
Justin Garcia, Little Rock	4	5	3.38	36	10	59	46	26	39
Donavin Buck, Little Rock	6	1	3.46	31	1	52	57	16	39
Hayden Arnold, Little Rock	1	2	3.53	23	0	51	38	21	53
Tyler Carr, South Alabama	8	3	3.57	14	0	88	97	21	59
Connor Reich, Texas State	6	3	3.57	15	0	86	87	30	63
Peyton Culbertson, Appalachian St.	2	5	3.73	16	0	51	48	31	48

WEST COAST CONFERENCE

	Conference		Overall	
	W	L	W	L
Pepperdine	17	10	31	24
* Gonzaga	16	11	33	23
Loyola Marymount	15	12	25	30
San Francisco	15	12	28	30
Saint Mary's	14	13	31	23
Santa Clara	12	15	26	26
Portland	12	15	23	30
San Diego	12	15	23	32
Pacific	11	16	22	27
Brigham Young	11	16	22	28

ALL-CONFERENCE TEAM: C: Riley Helland, Jr., San Francisco. **INF:** Mike Perri, Sr., San Francisco; Jamey Smart, Sr., Loyola Marymount. **OF:** Brock Hale, Jr., Brigham Young; Cody Hawken, Jr., Portland; Matt Kanfer, Jr., Pepperdine. **OF/RHP:** Jordan Qsar, Jr., Pepperdine. **RHP:** Daniel Bies, Jr., Gonzaga; Casey Legumina, So., Gonzaga; Riley Ornido, So., San Francisco; Jonathan Pendergast, Jr., Pepperdine; Jordan Wood, Jr., Brigham Young. **LHP:** Ken Waldichuk, So., Saint Mary's. **Player of the Year:** Jordan Qsar,

Pepperdine. **Pitcher of the Year:** Jonathan Pendergast, Pepperdine. **Coach of the Year:** Rick Hirtensteiner, Pepperdine. **Rookie of the Year:** Cooper Chandler, Pepperdine.

INDIVIDUAL BATTING LEADERS
(Minimum 140 at-bats)

	AVG	OBP	SLG	AB	2B	3B	HR	RBI	SB
Beau Brundage, Portland	.378	.452	.493	209	13	4	1	24	4
Brock Hale, BYU	.342	.425	.551	196	15	1	8	31	7
Jay Schuyler, San Diego	.341	.413	.486	220	9	1	7	38	5
Adam Kerner, San Diego	.338	.415	.480	148	15	0	2	23	2
Michael Perri, San Francisco	.336	.382	.547	232	22	0	9	46	9
Riley Helland, San Francisco	.329	.398	.441	222	19	0	2	34	1
Nick Sogard, Loyola Marymount	.324	.438	.395	185	5	1	2	21	11
Ernie Yake, Gonzaga	.324	.371	.375	216	11	0	0	23	5
Jason Dicochea, Santa Clara	.323	.402	.415	195	15	0	1	25	6
Brandt Belk, Pepperdine	.318	.361	.418	170	12	1	1	20	5
Matthew Kanfer, Pepperdine	.317	.343	.477	218	12	1	7	35	7
Tora Otsuka, San Diego	.316	.380	.362	174	6	1	0	16	10
Cody Hawken, San Diego	.316	.404	.547	190	12	1	10	36	6
Jonathan Allen, San Francisco	.308	.393	.480	227	16	1	7	32	12
Kevin Sandri, Pacific	.305	.371	.326	190	4	0	0	19	5
Keaton Kringlen, BYU	.305	.360	.401	177	12	1	1	19	1
Kevin Milam, Saint Mary's	.302	.430	.455	189	12	1	5	29	1
Paul Kunst, San Diego	.299	.373	.375	224	11	0	2	19	5
Cory Wills, Pepperdine	.291	.353	.437	158	6	1	5	24	5
David Clawson, BYU	.291	.359	.383	141	11	1	0	14	0
Brhet Bewley, San Diego	.291	.376	.468	203	8	2	8	44	0
Joe Becht, Santa Clara	.290	.421	.419	186	9	3	3	22	15
Gunnar Schubert, Gonzaga	.290	.394	.360	200	3	1	3	32	2
Jake Vieth, Gonzaga	.290	.421	.464	183	11	0	7	28	0
Joey Fiske, Saint Mary's	.288	.381	.341	208	9	1	0	21	9
Jake Brodt, Santa Clara	.270	.335	.555	211	15	0	15	56	5
Jordan Qsar, Pepperdine	.277	.339	.539	206	11	2	13	63	1
Billy Wilson, Loyola Marymount	.270	.356	.447	215	11	6	5	32	15

INDIVIDUAL PITCHING LEADERS
(Minimum 40 innings pitched)

	W	L	ERA	G	SV	IP	H	BB	SO
Ken Waldichuk, Saint Mary's	8	4	2.05	14	0	92	68	21	118
Daniel Bies, Gonzaga	7	4	2.50	15	0	104	88	23	115
Riley Ornido, San Francisco	8	5	2.58	15	0	98	63	32	95
Mac Lardner, Gonzaga	6	3	2.63	13	0	82	77	26	55
Jordan Wood, BYU	4	4	2.66	14	0	95	74	29	63
Jonath Pendergast, Pepperdine	7	4	2.69	14	0	87	84	18	67
Alek Jakob, Gonzaga	6	5	2.94	16	0	95	65	28	90
Landen Bourassa, San Francisco	8	4	3.02	14	0	83	79	33	61
Nick Frasso, Loyola Marymount	4	4	3.15	16	1	60	52	17	74
Shelby Lackey, Pacific	6	3	3.48	18	0	88	79	23	87
Eli Morse, Portland	3	7	3.62	14	0	82	89	22	71
Penn Murfee, Santa Clara	6	3	3.65	24	4	67	72	31	57
Tate Budnick, Portland	5	1	3.65	19	3	62	58	13	61
Kevin Milam, Saint Mary's	6	4	3.68	14	0	86	76	25	81
Thomas Ponticelli, San Francisco	6	4	3.68	14	0	95	92	17	78
Cooper Casad, Pacific	3	6	3.93	18	3	73	71	21	46
Cooper Chandler, Pepperdine	6	3	3.99	16	0	70	79	28	44
Nick Frank, Saint Mary's	5	4	4.01	14	0	83	96	16	85
Codie Paiva, Loyola Marymount	6	6	4.17	15	0	86	87	26	65
Chris Murphy, San Diego	6	5	4.20	13	0	81	72	37	91
Casey Legumina, Gonzaga	3	3	2.77	26	13	49	45	7	52
Brendan Jenkins, San Francisco	2	3	2.60	30	9	52	41	15	47
Corbin Powers, Portland	4	7	5.12	13	0	72	87	33	70
Josh Agnew, Loyola Marymount	5	6	5.78	17	3	67	84	7	33

WESTERN ATHLETIC CONFERENCE

	Conference		Overall	
	W	L	W	L
Grand Canyon	19	5	33	24
* New Mexico State	17	7	40	22
Sacramento State	17	7	35	25
Seattle	13	11	34	23
Northern Colorado	11	13	29	24

Cal State Bakersfield	10	14	21	36
Texas-Rio Grande Valley	8	16	23	31
Chicago State	7	17	13	41
Utah Valley	6	18	15	37

ALL-CONFERENCE TEAM: C: Mason Fishback, Sr., New Mexico State. **1B:** Caleb Henderson, Jr., New Mexico State. **2B:** Nick Gonzales, Fr., New Mexico State. **3B:** Zach Malis, Jr., Grand Canyon. **SS:** Joey Ortiz, So., New Mexico State. **OF:** Quin Cotton, So., Grand Canyon; Ian Dawkins, Sr., Sacramento State; Tyler Wyatt, Jr., Grand Canyon. **DH:** Pikai Winchester, Jr., Grand Canyon. **UTL:** Trevor Peterson, Sr., Utah Valley. **SP:** Kyle Bradish, Jr., New Mexico State; Jonathan Groff, Sr., New Mexico State; Parker Brahms, So., Sacramento State. **RP:** Austin Roberts, So., Sacramento State. **Player of the Year:** Quin Cotton, Grand Canyon. **Pitcher of the Year:** Jonathan Groff, New Mexico State. **Coach of the Year:** Andy Stankiewicz, Grand Canyon. **Rookie of the Year:** Nick Gonzales, New Mexico State.

INDIVIDUAL BATTING LEADERS
(Minimum 140 at-bats)

	AVG	OBP	SLG	AB	2B	3B	HR	RBI	SB
Cotton Quin, Grand Canyon	.390	.462	.573	241	19	5	5	43	13
Tyler Lowe, CSU	.376	.409	.537	205	5	2	8	41	7
Andrew Penner, CSUB	.360	.434	.440	225	12	0	2	24	6
Ian Dawkins, SAC	.359	.415	.528	248	18	3	6	33	8
Pikai Winchester, GCU	.355	.410	.461	217	13	2	2	38	0
Nick Gonzales, NMSU	.347	.425	.596	193	17	2	9	36	2
Caleb Henderson, NMSU	.341	.436	.585	229	20	3	10	65	1
Jack Pauley, NC	.338	.433	.483	207	13	4	3	39	12
Dean Lawson, NC	.335	.450	.475	179	17	1	2	30	12
Ian Evans, GCU	.333	.407	.451	213	10	3	3	53	3
Coleman Grubbs, UTRGV	.329	.388	.428	222	11	1	3	26	5
Sean Sutton, SU	.328	.442	.469	192	9	0	6	51	0
Marcus Still, NMSU	.328	.423	.406	180	6	4	0	27	8
Tristen Carranza, NMSU	.325	.429	.517	209	11	1	9	53	0
Matt Paciello, CSU	.324	.408	.457	188	16	0	3	26	4
Tyler Wyatt, GCU	.324	.342	.382	173	10	0	0	30	8
Austin Lively, SU	.316	.446	.413	206	10	2	2	25	8
Logan Ehnes, NMSU	.314	.429	.515	204	10	5	7	40	3
Logan Bottrell, NMSU	.310	.407	.372	145	6	0	1	16	6
Matt Smith, SAC	.310	.377	.452	210	15	3	3	38	13
Dalton Hurd, SU	.309	.353	.507	217	17	1	8	43	8
Matt Burkart, NC	.307	.412	.547	192	16	3	8	38	6
Mason Fishback, NMSU	.307	.403	.500	202	15	0	8	43	0
James Outman, SAC	.253	.363	.489	229	15	3	11	40	12
Preston Pavlica, GCU	.247	.377	.397	174	9	1	5	28	16

INDIVIDUAL PITCHING LEADERS
(Minimum 40 innings pitched)

	W	L	ERA	G	SV	IP	H	BB	SO
Austin Roberts, SAC	4	2	1.83	29	2	54	37	13	55
Parker Brahms, SAC	4	5	2.41	18	1	93	79	25	113
Kyle Bradish, NMSU	9	3	2.67	17	0	101	72	55	140
Jake Wong, GCU	9	3	2.81	15	0	90	88	29	88
Jonathan Groff, NMSU	11	3	2.83	17	0	102	103	31	89
Austin Root, SAC	11	3	2.93	18	1	95	82	16	70
Brock Whittlesey, NMSU	3	5	2.95	28	12	61	66	22	60
Tanner Dalton, SAC	1	2	3.02	32	10	42	37	15	43
Ryan Jackson, UTRGV	3	3	3.13	27	7	46	38	5	41
Connor Leedholm, NC	3	3	3.30	27	12	44	43	12	48
Alex Pinedo, NMSU	5	3	3.34	20	0	70	69	31	53
Scott Randall, SAC	7	3	3.48	17	0	75	82	14	47
Ethan Evanko, GCU	5	1	3.51	16	0	59	60	19	62
Jake Mayer, UVU	2	9	3.51	14	0	97	96	18	70
Zach Wolf, SU	4	1	3.72	29	10	46	36	14	55
Jake Prizina, SU	8	1	3.82	19	1	99	100	17	92
Naithen Dewsnap, CSUB	3	5	3.84	23	6	63	68	15	60
Tarik Skubal, SU	8	2	4.16	19	0	80	66	56	106
Zach Thomas, CSU	3	5	4.19	12	0	62	67	27	58
Jorge Flores, UTRGV	6	6	4.22	17	0	79	82	35	81

SMALL COLLEGES

NCAA DIVISION II

Augustana (S.D.) won the first Division II College World Series in program history, defeating Columbus State (Ga.), 3-2, in the championship game. Senior righthander Jacob Blank threw a complete game and struck out 12 against Columbus State.

The Vikings lost just one game in the entire postseason, going 12-1 through their conference tournament, regionals and the CWS. They became the northernmost team to ever win the Division II title.

Righthander Tyler Mitzel was named CWS MVP after twice beating Southern New Hampshire in the tournament.

The World Series in 2018 returned to USA Baseball's National Training Complex in Cary, N.C. The 2017 version was moved to Grand Prairie, Texas, by the NCAA due to a controversial North Carolina law that was later repealed.

DIVISION II WORLD SERIES

Site: Cary, N.C.
Participants: 1. Florida Southern; 2. Columbus State (Ga.); 3. UC San Diego; 4. Southern New Hampshire; 5. Augustana (S.D.); 6. Texas A&M-Kingsville; 7. Mercyhurst (Pa.); 8. Southern Indiana.
Champion: Augustana.
Runner-up: Columbus State.

LEADERS: BATTING AVERAGE
(Minimum 140 at bats)

Rk. Player, Pos., Team	Class	AVG	OBP	SLG
1. Jared Melone, 1B, West Chester (Pa.)	Jr.	.469	.524	.743
2. Austin Edgette, OF, Bloomsburg (Pa.)	Sr.	.439	.530	.689
3. Randy Norris, INF, Winston-Salem (N.C.)	Jr.	.437	.475	.574
4. Reed Hjelle, 1B, Minnesota-Crookston	Jr.	.435	.510	.757
5. Matt Diesel, OF, Felician (N.J.)	Sr.	.435	.500	.700
6. Colin Kaucher, C, Ohio Dominican	Jr.	.430	.514	.676
7. Cody Bridges, OF, Kentucky Wesleyan	Jr.	.429	.485	.575
8. Justin Smith, UTL, Shepherd (W.V.)	Sr.	.429	.515	.773
9. Darrin Zombro, INF, Fairmont State (W.V.)	Jr.	.426	.490	.601
10. Darrell Langston, OF, Claflin (S.C.)	Sr.	.419	.468	.758

EARNED RUN AVERAGE
(Minimum 40 innings pitched)

Rk. Pitcher, Team	Class	W	L	ERA
1. Dan Wirchansky, Pace (N.Y.)	Jr.	5	1	0.71
2. Gus Varland, Concordia-St. Paul (Minn.)	Jr.	7	1	1.04
3. Josiah Gray, Le Moyne (N.Y.)	Jr.	11	0	1.25
4. Louie Varland, Concordia-St. Paul (Minn.)	So.	5	1	1.41
5. Griffin Bremer, Southern Conn. State	Sr.	6	1	1.55
6. Joe Ryan, Stanislaus State (Calif.)	Sr.	8	1	1.65
7. Michael Stout, Fairmont State (W.V.)	Jr.	8	3	1.68
8. Michael Bryja, Seton Hill (Pa.)	So.	6	2	1.72
9. Nick Arnold, Post (Conn.)	Sr.	9	2	1.76
10. J.T. Hintzen, Florida Southern	Sr.	14	0	1.77

CATEGORY LEADERS: BATTING
*Minimum 140 at bats

Dept.	Player, Pos., Team	Class	G	Total
OBP*	Justin Childers, INF, Ohio Dominican	Sr.	50	.540
SLG*	Zack Shannon, 1B, Delta State (Miss.)	Sr.	53	.955
R	Trevor Kehe, OF, Colorado School of Mines	So.	50	80

H	Brenton Doyle, OF, Shepherd (W.V.)	So.	55	98
2B	Trey Jacobs, INF, UNC Pembroke	So.	54	28
3B	Alec Craig, INF, Chestnut Hill (Pa.)	Sr.	44	11
HR	Zack Shannon, 1B, Delta State (Miss.)	Sr.	53	31
RBI	Zack Shannon, 1B, Delta State (Miss.)	Sr.	53	93
SB	Alec Craig, INF, Chestnut Hill (Pa.)	Sr.	44	47

CATEGORY LEADERS: PITCHING
*Minimum 40 innings

Dept.	Pitcher, Team	Class	Total
W	J.T. Hintzen, Florida Southern	Sr.	14
L	Will Rutledge, Christian Brothers	Sr.	10
SV	Peyton Isaacson, Saint Leo (Fla.)	Jr.	14
	Trevor Dudar, Northwest Missouri State	Jr.	14
G	Kellan Richards, Missouri Western	Jr.	35
IP	Kolton Ingram, Columbus State (Ga.)	Jr.	136
SO	Kolton Ingram, Columbus State (Ga.)	Jr.	150
SO/9*	Chris Vallimont, Mercyhurst (Pa.)	Jr.	16.47
BB/9*	Pablo Arevalo, Barry (Fla.)	So.	0.69
WHIP*	Dan Wirchansky, Pace (N.Y.)	Jr.	0.57

NCAA Division III

Texas-Tyler swept Texas Lutheran in the finals of the Division III College World Series to win its first ever national championship.

The Patriots completed an improbable journey to the national championship with a 9-6 victory to clinch the title. They had to win five straight elimination games in regionals to reach the CWS, where they again had to stave off elimination with a win in the bracket final.

Senior righthander Simon Sedillo was named the tournament's most outstanding player after winning two games in the CWS.

DIVISION III WORLD SERIES

Site: Appleton, Wisc.
Participants: Concordia-Chicago; Misericordia (Pa.); Oswego State (N.Y.); Randolph-Macon (Va.); Swarthmore (Pa.); Texas Lutheran; Texas-Tyler; Wooster (Ohio).
Champion: Texas-Tyler.
Runner-up: Texas Lutheran.

LEADERS: BATTING AVERAGE
(Minimum 120 at bats)

RK. Player, Pos., Team	Class	AVG	OBP	SLG
1. Jake Schuster, So., Marywood (Pa.)	So.	.481	.550	.822
2. Daytona Bryden, OF, Wisconsin-Whitewater	Sr.	.479	.546	.855
3. Chris Seibert, INF, Wesley (Del.)	Sr.	.475	.552	.850
4. Garrett Wilson, OF, Spalding (Ky.)	So.	.470	.525	.689
5. Andrew Mink, INF, Oglethorpe (Ga.)	Jr.	.462	.538	.727
6. Scott Sada, INF, Penn State-Behrend	Jr.	.459	.524	.767
7. Derek Manning, OF, Elizabethtown (Pa.)	So.	.457	.506	.675
8. Grant Myers, OF, Monmouth (Ill.)	Sr.	.453	.531	.767
9. Wesley Moss, OF, Sul Ross State (Texas)	Jr.	.451	.589	.542
10. Cal Aldridge, INF, Wisconsin-Whitewater	Jr.	.451	.505	.882

EARNED RUN AVERAGE
(Minimum 30 innings pitched)

Rk. Pitcher, Team	Class	W	L	ERA
1. Bob Hamel, Western New England (Mass.)	Jr.	7	0	0.95
2. Matt Cronin, Massachusetts-Dartmouth	Sr.	6	1	0.99
3. Nick Powers, New England College (N.H.)	So.	8	0	0.99
4. John Howard, Washington-St. Louis	Jr.	6	3	1.01

5.	Alex Sir Louis, Heidelberg (Ohio)	Jr.	6 0	1.10
6.	Carson Selin, Bethel (Minn.)	Sr.	5 0	1.14
7.	Connor Reeves, Salisbury (Md.)	Sr.	14 3	1.19
8.	Tanner Eckhart, Wartburg (Iowa)	Sr.	7 2	1.20
9.	Austin Ver Steeg, Concordia-Moorhead (Minn.)	So.	3 0	1.25
10.	Danny Serreino, Rowan (N.J.)	Jr.	7 2	1.25

CATEGORY LEADERS: BATTING
Minimum 120 at bats

Dept.	Player, Pos., Team	Class	G	Total
OBP*	Wesley Moss, Sul Ross State (Texas)	Jr.	41	.589
SLG*	Cal Aldridge, INF, Wisconsin-Whitewater	Jr.	40	.882
R	Michael Wielansky, INF, Wooster (Ohio)	Jr.	50	76
H	Riley Schaefer, INF, Texas Lutheran	Sr.	54	95
2B	David Boehme, INF, Penn State-Behrend	Sr.	42	25
3B	Daytona Bryden, OF, Wisconsin-Whitewater	Sr.	41	9
	Joe Maugeri, OF, Ramapo (N.J.)	Sr.	50	9
HR	Frank Podkul, INF, Franklin (Ohio)	Sr.	43	16
RBI	Mike Wisz, INF, North Central (Ill.)	So.	43	73
SB	Michael DeDonaton, 2B, Endicott (Mass.)	Sr.	44	41

CATEGORY LEADERS: PITCHING
Minimum 30 innings

Dept.	Pitcher, Team	Class	Total
W	Connor Reeves, Salisbury (Md.)	Sr.	14
L	Drake Black, Brevard (N.C.)	Sr.	12
SV	Nick Bosma, Rhodes (Tenn.)	Jr.	16
IP	Dylan Drgac, Texas Lutheran	Sr.	121
SO	Colin Selby, Randolph-Macon (Va.)	Jr.	126
SO/9*	Victor Cavalieri, Houghton (N.Y.)	Sr.	15
BB/9*	Austin Frey, Ohio Northern	Jr.	0.31
WHIP*	Connor Reeves, Salisbury (Md.)	Sr.	0.73

NAIA

Southeastern (Fla.) defeated Freed-Hardman (Tenn.), 6-3, in the championship game of the NAIA World Series to claim the first national title in program history.

The Fire became the first team since 2013 to sweep through the World Series. They are also the first team from Florida to ever win the NAIA national title.

Outfielder Manuel Mesa was named MVP after going 13-for-25 in the tournament.

NAIA WORLD SERIES
Site: Lewiston, Idaho.
Participants: Antelope Valley (Calif.); Freed-Hardeman (Tenn.); Lewis-Clark State (Idaho); Northwest Ohio; Oklahoma City; Reinhardt (Ga.); St. Thomas (Fla.); Southeastern (Fla.).
Champion: Southeastern.
Runner-up: Freed-Hardeman.

LEADERS: BATTING AVERAGE
(Minimum 140 at bats)

RK.	Player, Pos., Team	Class	AVG	OBP	SLG
1.	Walter Coursey, INF, Geogia-Gwinnett	R-Fr.	.485	.530	.598
2.	Kiki Menendez, OF, Texas Wesleyan	Sr.	.466	.512	.995
3.	Lane Milligan, OF, Oklahoma City	Sr.	.462	.540	.843
4.	Andrew Wilson, 3B, Marymount California	Jr.	.451	.502	.641
5.	Kyle Kolb, SS, Trinity Christian (Ill.)	Jr.	.449	.513	.633

EARNED RUN AVERAGE
(Minimum 40 innings pitched)

Rk.	Pitcher, Team	Class	W	L	ERA
1.	Vinny Schmidt, Hastings (Neb.)	Fr.	8	0	0.50
2.	Kyle Fulton, Central Methodist (Mo.)	Jr.	10	0	1.09

3.	Tyson Cronin, Oklahoma Wesleyan	Jr.	10 1	1.21
4.	Mason Swegarden, Mayville State (N.D.)	Sr.	9 1	1.48
5.	Erik Barron, Mayville State (N.D.)	Sr.	4 0	1.62

CATEGORY LEADERS: BATTING
Minimum 140 at bats

Dept.	Player, Pos., Team	Class	G	Total
OBP*	Andrew Warner, C, Columbia (Mo.)	Sr.	49	.580
SLG*	Kiki Menendez, OF, Texas Wesleyan	Sr.	52	.995
HR	Kiki Menendez, OF, Texas Wesleyan	Sr.	52	26
RBI	Lane Milligan, OF, Oklahoma City	Sr.	59	90
SB	Christian Smith, OF,B83 William Carey (Miss.)	Sr.	61	57

CATEGORY LEADERS: PITCHING

Dept.	Pitcher, Team	Class	Total
W	Jonathan Bermudez, Southeastern (Fla.)	Jr.	15
SV	Beau Caviness, Freed-Hardeman (Tenn.)	Sr.	18
IP	Zak Spivy, Webber International (Fla.)	Jr.	122
SO	Ben Madison, Central Baptist (Ark.)	Jr.	172

NJCAA Division I

Chipola (Fla.) defeated Walters State (Tenn.), 10-7, in the championship game of the DI Junior College World Series. The Indians repeated as national champions, becoming the first team to do so since Grayson (Texas) did so in 1999-2000.

Shortstop Morgan McCullough was named tournament MVP. He hit .591 with two home runs during the World Series.

NJCAA DIVISION I WORLD SERIES
Site: Grand Junction, Colo.
Participants: Barton (Kan.); Chattahoochee Valley (Ala.); Chipola (Fla.); Iowa Western; Jefferson (Mo.); Monroe (N.Y.); San Jacinto (Texas); Southern Idaho; Temple (Texas); Walters State (Tenn.).
Champion: Chipola.
Runner-up: Walters State.

LEADERS: BATTING AVERAGE
Minimum 140 at bats)

Rk.	Player, Pos., Team	Class	AVG	OBP	SLG
1.	Conrado Diaz, C, Trinidad State (Colo.)	So.	.491	.624	.848
2.	Blake Mattey, OF, Trinidad State (Colo.)	So.	.473	.545	.847
3.	Dayan Reinoso, C, Chesapeake (Md.)	Fr.	.472	.535	.872
4.	Luis Pelayo, OF, Connors State (Okla.)	So.	.469	.547	.684
5.	DeShawn Lookout, OF, Seminole St. (Okla.)	So.	.461	.524	.783

EARNED RUN AVERAGE
(Minimum 40 innings pitched)

Rk.	Pitcher, Team	Class	W	L	ERA
1.	Sean Chandler, Iowa Western	R-So.	11	0	1.34
2.	Cole Larsen, Cowley (Kan.)	Fr.	6	2	1.46
3.	Indigo Diaz, Iowa Western	So.	11	1	1.52
4.	Kaleb Huxford, Lincoln Trail (Ill.)	So.	5	1	1.53
5.	Cole Ganopulos, Chattahoochee Valley (Ala.)	So.	10	0	1.62

CATEGORY LEADERS: BATTING

Minimum 140 at bats Pos., Team	Dept.P l a y e r, Class	G	Total
OBP* Conrado Diaz, C, Trinidad State (Colo.)	So.	58	.624
SLG* Mark Castelblanco, OF, Clarendon (Texas)	So.	51	1.017
HR Joey Polak, INF, Jefferson (Mo.)	R-Fr.	66	32
RBI Joey Polak, INF, Jefferson (Mo.)	R-Fr.	66	107
SB Joseph Locascio, INF, Kishwaukee (Ill.)	So.	52	54

CATEGORY LEADERS: PITCHING

Dept.	Pitcher, Team	Class	Total
W	Hayden Lehman, Walters State (Tenn.)	So.	13

	Landon Knack, Walters State (Tenn.)	So.	13
SV	Tallon Thomason, South Mountain (Ariz.)	So.	16
IP	Phillip Sanderson, Chipola (Fla.)	R-Fr.	116
SO	Aaron Ashby, Crowder (Mo.)	So.	156

NJCAA Division II

Slate Fuller hit a two-out, two-run, walk-off home run to send LSU-Eunice to a 5-3 victory over Parkland (Ill.) to win the Division II Junior College World Series. It was the Bengals' sixth national title, the most in DII junior college history.

Shortstop Koi Westbrook was named tournament MVP after hitting .375 with two home runs. He was also named the tournament's defensive MVP.

NJCAA DIVISION II WORLD SERIES
Site: Enid, Okla.
Participants: 1. LSU-Eunice; 2. Parkland (Ill.); 3. Kirkwood (Iowa); 4. Northern Oklahoma; 5. Sinclair (Ohio); 6. Madison (Wisc.); 7. Scottsdale (Ariz.); 8. Brunswick (N.C.); 9. Monroe (N.Y.); 10. CCBC Essex.
Champion: LSU-Eunice.
Runner-up: Parkland.

LEADERS: BATTING AVERAGE
(Minimum 120 at bats)

RK. Player, Pos., Team	Class	AVG	OBP	SLG
1. Trevor Feeney, 3B, Dakota (N.D.)	So.	.507	.603	.813
2. Andrew Beesley, INF, Hinds (Miss.)	So.	.473	.540	.723
3. Izaya Fullard, 3B, Kirkwood (Iowa)	Fr.	.470	.520	.642
4. Austin Murr, Des Moines Area (Iowa)	Fr.	.470	.531	.717
5. Parker Murdie, INF, Jackson (Mich.)	So.	.469	.553	.547

EARNED RUN AVERAGE
(Minimum 40 innings pitched)

Rk. Pitcher, Team	Class	W	L	ERA
1. Matt Lundh, Phoenix	So.	6	1	1.29
2. Chas Sagedahl, Southeastern (Iowa)	Fr.	9	2	1.41
3. Joey Baran, Lackawanna (Pa.)	R-So.	6	1	1.58
4. Blake Flint, Paradise Valley (Ariz.)	So.	12	4	1.59
5. Kyle McCann, Rhode Island	So.	3	1	1.93

CATEGORY LEADERS: BATTING
*Minimum 120 at bats

Dept.	Player, Pos., Team	Class	G	Total
OBP*	Trevor Feeney, 3B, Dakota (N.D.)	So.	42	.603
SLG*	Dalton Bealmer, UTL, Metro. CC-Longview (Mo.)	So.	38	1.058
HR	Dalton Bealmer, UTL, Metro. CC-Longview (Mo.)	So.	38	26
RBI	Brandon Parker, OF, Mississippi Gulf Coast	Fr.	52	81
SB	Masen Prososki, INF, Southeast (Neb.)	So.	57	49

CATEGORY LEADERS: PITCHING

Dept.	Pitcher, Team	Class	Total
W	Zach Hester, LSU-Eunice	So.	13
SV	Trace Hoffman, Southeastern (Iowa)	So.	13
IP	Blake Flint, Paradise Valley (Ariz.)	So.	102
SO	Zach Hester, LSU-Eunice	So.	134

NJCAA Division III

Oakton (Ill.) defeated Tyler (Texas), 14-11, in 13 innings in the decisive third game of the championship seires to win its first ever national title. Tyler was the four-time defending national champion, but lost two close games against Oakton in

the finals.

Lefthander Tommy Gertner was named tournament MVP after striking out 12 batters in 14.1 innings in the World Series.

NJCAA DIVISION III WORLD SERIES
Site: Greeneville, Tenn.
Participants: 1. Hackimer (N.Y.); 2. Rowan-Gloucester (N.J.); 3. Tyler (Texas); 4. Oakton (Ill.); 5. Northampton (Pa.); 6. Northern Essex (Mass.); 7. St. Cloud Tech (Minn.); 8. Rockingham (N.C.).
Champion: Oakton.
Runner-up: Tyler.

LEADERS: BATTING AVERAGE
(Minimum 120 at bats)

RK. Player, Pos., Team	Class	AVG	OBP	SLG
1. Jack Goan, C, Rowan-Gloucester (N.J.)	So.	.486	.552	.850
2. Brian Rodriguez, SS, Brookdale (N.J.)	So.	.486	.516	.718
3. Nick Powell, OF, Schoolcraft (Mich.)	Fr.	.464	.525	.762
4. Jeffrey Towle, C, Suffolk County (N.Y.)	So.	.463	.543	.862
5. Jackson Wenstrom, OF, Hudson Valley (N.Y.)	Fr.	.462	.542	.909

EARNED RUN AVERAGE
(Minimum 40 innings pitched)

Rk. Pitcher, Team	Class	W	L	ERA
1. Ryan Sandberg, Queensborough (N.Y.)	Fr.	5	0	1.37
2. Joel Barker, Minnesota West	Fr.	5	2	1.63
3. Christopher Berte, Suffolk County (N.Y.)	So.	6	1	1.64
4. Tyler Schmid, Suffolk County (N.Y.)	Fr.	5	3	1.89
5. Aryed Garcia, Bergen (N.J.)	Fr.	7	3	1.96

California Junior Colleges

San Joaquin Delta defeated rival Sacramento City, 7-5, to win the California CC Athletic Association state championship.

The conference foes faced each other six times over the course of the year—three times in the regular season and three times in the playoffs—with San Joaquin Delta earning ultimate bragging rights and its first title since 2011.

Righthander Kevin Kyle and Jordan Vujovich shared tournament MVP honors.

CALIFORNIA CC ATHLETIC ASSOCIATION
Site: Fresno.
Participants: Mount San Antonio; Orange Coast; Sacramento City; San Joaquin Delta.
Champion: San Joaquin Delta.
Runner-up: Sacramento City.

LEADERS: BATTING AVERAGE
(Minimum 140 at bats)

RK. Player, Pos., Team	Class	AVG	OBP	SLG
1. Calvin Estrada, INF, Canyons	So.	.434	.526	.834
2. Eric De la Rosa, OF, Grossmont	So.	.434	.527	.875
3. Elijah Greene, OF, Mount San Antonio	R-Fr.	.428	.496	.668
4. John Mook, OF, Folsom Lake	So.	.424	.530	.493
5. A.J. Curtis, INF, Ohlone	So.	.421	.531	.743

EARNED RUN AVERAGE
(Minimum 40 innings pitched)

Rk. Pitcher, Team	Class	W	L	ERA
1. Brendan Talonen, Feather River	Fr.	4	0	0.69
2. Chris Allen, Marin	So.	13	0	1.34
3. Shane Gustafson, Folsom Lake	So.	7	3	1.55
4. Jacob Lopez, Canyons	So.	9	2	1.62
5. Ethan Skuija, Ohlone	So.	13	2	1.70

COLLEGE SUMMER BASEBALL

BY CHRIS HILBURN-TRENKLE

USA Baseball's Collegiate National Team wrapped up an impressive summer slate in late July with a series win in Cuba, completing their campaign with series wins against Taiwan, Japan and Cuba and a 12-3 overall record.

But it wasn't just the success that made the team memorable to manager Paul Mainieri, it was also the way the players conducted themselves.

"We just had an amazing group of young men," Mainieri said. "They obviously were very talented, but they were also very unselfish. Conducted themselves in a first-class way, like to think they forged relationships with teammates and coaches that will last a lifetime. For me, personally, it was a dream come true, something I can check off my bucket list."

The team won all five games against Taiwan and then took three out of five from Japan before traveling to Havana. Team USA won the first three games to win the series against Cuba for the fourth consecutive summer.

Catcher Adley Rutschman (Oregon State) finished an excellent campaign by going 5-for-12 in Cuba, walking three times and driving in two runs. Overall, Rutschman led all Team USA hitters with a .355 batting average.

Outfielder Daniel Cabrera (Louisiana State) and shortstop Bryson Stott (Nevada-Las Vegas)

were two of the other offensive standouts for Team USA. Cabrera, a sophomore, led the team in home runs (two) and finished second in RBIs with six. Stott raised his prospect status with an impressive summer both at the plate and at shortstop.

Team USA received solid pitching performances all summer. As a team, they posted a 2.06 ERA and held opponents to a .184 batting average. Lefthander Mason Feole (Connecticut) was one of the stars on the mound. Lefthander Drew Parrish (Florida State) and righthander Zack Hess (LSU) were similarly strong, as none of the trio allowed a run all summer.

Closer Max Meyer (Minnesota) and lefthander Graeme Stinson (Duke) were part of an excellent bullpen for Team USA.

It was quite a run for the collegiate national team, and although Mainieri wished his squad had won every game, he was happy with the results.

"I wish we would have won all 15 games," Mainieri said. "But we won all three series, beat the Cuban National Team three-of-four in Cuba. The Japan team, man they were a tough team to beat. I have so much respect for the way they play the game. The pitching Japan threw at us was almost shocking to me how quality it was. It was successful results-wise, but mostly it was successful because the young men had an experience that they'll never forget."

COLLEGIATE NATIONAL TEAM STATS

Year indicates 2017-18 class standing

Player, Pos.	Year	School	AVG	OBP	SLG	G	AB	R	H	2B	3B	HR	RBI	BB	SO	SB
Adley Rutschman, C	Jr.	Oregon State	.355	.432	.516	9	31	2	11	5	0	0	2	5	5	0
Shea Langeliers, C	Jr.	Baylor	.346	.393	.500	8	26	2	9	4	0	0	1	2	5	1
Bryant Packard, OF	Jr.	East Carolina	.333	.350	.389	6	18	1	6	1	0	0	1	1	7	0
Daniel Cabrera, OF	Jr.	Louisiana State	.300	.375	.440	14	50	6	15	1	0	2	6	6	10	2
Spencer Torkelson, OF	So.	Arizona State	.286	.422	.314	12	35	3	10	1	0	0	3	8	11	0
Josh Jung, 3B	Jr.	Texas Tech	.283	.377	.377	15	53	6	15	3	1	0	3	8	12	0
Zach Watson, OF	Jr.	Louisiana State	.280	.333	.380	14	50	7	14	2	0	1	3	3	10	2
Bryson Stott, SS	Jr.	Nevada-Las Vegas	.262	.340	.333	13	42	3	11	0	0	1	7	5	11	0
Andrew Vaughn, 1B	Jr.	California	.224	.316	.367	13	49	5	11	4	0	1	4	4	12	1
Will Wilson, SS	Jr.	North Carolina State	.208	.208	.208	10	24	2	5	0	0	0	2	0	5	0
Dominic Fletcher, OF	Jr.	Arkansas	.171	.256	.314	10	35	3	6	2	0	1	4	4	8	0
Braden Shewmake, 2B	Jr.	Texas A&M	.136	.250	.205	15	44	3	6	1	1	0	2	6	8	2

Pitcher, Pos.	Year	School	W	L	ERA	G	SV	IP	H	R	ER	BB	SO	AVG
Mason Feole, LHP	Jr.	Connecticut	1	0	0.00	3	0	11	3	0	0	6	9	.097
Drew Parrish, LHP	Jr.	Florida State	1	0	0.00	3	0	10	5	0	0	1	8	.147
Parker Carraci, RHP	R-Jr.	Mississippi	1	0	0.00	6	2	10	3	1	0	4	8	.094
Zack Hess, RHP	Jr.	Louisiana State	2	0	0.00	3	0	9	3	0	0	0	6	.097
Zack Thompson, LHP	Jr.	Kentucky	1	0	0.00	3	0	9	3	0	0	4	7	.107
Graeme Stinson, LHP	Jr.	Duke	0	0	0.00	3	0	6	2	1	0	5	10	.111
Cody Bradford, RHP	Jr.	Baylor	1	0	0.00	2	0	5	1	0	0	1	5	.063
Jake Agnos, LHP	Jr.	East Carolina	0	0	0.96	4	0	9	5	1	1	1	14	.152
Kenyon Yovan, RHP	Jr.	Oregon	0	1	1.08	5	0	8	5	2	1	2	7	.192
Matt Cronin, LHP	Jr.	Arkansas	1	0	1.69	4	1	5	4	1	1	1	5	.211
Kyle Brnovich, RHP	Jr.	Elon	1	1	2.70	3	0	7	3	2	2	3	10	.150
Max Meyer, RHP	So.	Minnesota	0	0	3.38	8	7	8	5	4	3	4	15	.179
Tanner Burns, RHP	So.	Auburn	0	0	5.87	4	0	8	9	5	5	1	6	.290

Wareham Wins Cape Title

Wareham swept through the Cape Cod League playoffs to win its first championship since 2012, defeating Chatham in the finals.

The Gatemen went 6-0 in the playoffs, led by third baseman Austin Shenton (Florida International). He homered three times in six playoff games and was named MVP of the championship series.

The decisive game of the championship series, a 9-3 win by the Gatemen, required two days to be completed. Fog rolled into Chatham's Veterans Field during the sixth inning of the game, forcing it to be suspended with Wareham leading, 4-1. The Gatemen added to their lead when the game resumed the next day, finishing off their run through the playoffs.

Shenton was one of the breakout stars of the Cape. He hit .349/.450/.490 during the regular season and played even better during the playoffs. He went 12-for-23 with a double, a triple, three home runs and 12 RBIs in six playoff games.

Shenton's success was part of a larger trend this summer. The Cape's strength was sluggers at corner positions. Andrew Vaughn, Spencer Torkelson and Matt Wallner were just a few of the league's standouts who fit that profile. There were fewer athletic, up-the-middle standouts, making for a more powerful summer.

Pitching was also down this summer, a reflection in part of the overall 2019 class. Still, the league figures to again produce several first-round picks for the 2019 draft.

Summer League Roundup

There is a dynasty brewing in Palmer, Alaska, as the Mat-Su Miners won their third straight Alaska Baseball League championship, sweeping the Anchorage Bucs in the best-of-three "Top of The World Series". After sneaking out a 1-0 victory in the first game of the series behind a dominant performance from starter Asa Lacy (Texas A&M) and a fourth-inning home run from slugger Spencer Henson (Oral Roberts), the Miners left no doubt in Game 2, racing to a 5-0 lead after the first inning and cruising to a 7-1 victory. The championship was also the third straight for Miners head coach Ben Taylor, whose team has made Palmer a very difficult place to play.

Led by dynamic corner infielders Jordan McFarland and Brandon Lewis—both top league prospects—the Conejo Oaks won their first California Collegiate League title in their 13th year as a program. The Oaks defeated the Orange County Riptide in the title game, 6-2. McFarland

posted four hits, and Lewis hit a two-run homer to pace the offense.

The Southern Ohio Copperheads won a franchise-record 31 games en route to a Great Lakes Summer Baseball League championship.

For the first time in Hamptons Collegiate Baseball League history, the Riverhead Tomcats won the title, defeating the Long Island Road Warriors, 8-4, in the three-game championship series. Of the seven teams in the league, the Tomcats were the only team that hadn't yet won a title.

The Duluth Huskies and the Fond du Lac Dock Spiders played a spectacular championship series, but it was the Dock Spiders that emerged victorious. The final game of the series went back and forth, before the Spiders pulled away for good in the bottom of the seventh inning. Alex Henwood and Cole Zabowski each recorded multiple hits for the Dock Spiders.

Taking the lead on a go-ahead, seventh-inning grand slam by right fielder Adan Fernandez, the New Market Rebels defeated Charlottesville, 8-5, to win their fourth title in Valley League history—and first since 2002.

For the second straight season, the Valley Blue Sox won the New England Collegiate League title, sweeping the Ocean State Waves in two games. That concluded a perfect 4-0 postseason for the Blue Sox, who went undefeated in last summer's playoffs, as well.

The Baltimore Redbirds ended their 10th—and final—season in the Cal Ripken League with a bang, winning the league title against Bethesda.

It was a hard fought season in the South Florida Collegiate Baseball League, with many teams showing a case for the title. However, a dominant performance from the West Boca Snappers took home the SFCBL by a count of two games to none over the Palm Beach Diamond Ducks. Francisco Urbaez (Florida Atlantic University) was brilliant in the championship series. The third baseman went 3-8 over the two games with a pair of runs and RBIs. His performance ultimately netted him the championship series MVP award. Snapper arm Colton Tyson (Southeastern University) was sensational in their 4-2 Game 1 win, while the bats—led by Urbaez—carried the the team to the 9-7 championship clincher.

Hays won the Jayhawk League, finishing five games ahead of Dodge City. It ended up being the last year of the league's existence, as the league disbanded with half the teams going to the Kansas Collegiate League and half going to the Sunflower League.

For players who played for multiple teams: 1: Stats with first team. 2: Stats with second team. 3: Stats with third team. T: combined stats.

CAPE COD LEAGUE

East Division

	W	L	T	PTS
Yarmouth-Dennis Red Sox	27	12	5	59
Chatham Anglers	22	19	3	47
Harwich Mariners	18	24	2	38
Brewster Whitecaps	13	27	4	30
Orleans Firebirds	14	29	1	29

West Division

	W	L	T	PTS
Wareham Gatemen	25	17	2	52
Hyannis Harbor Hawks	24	17	3	51
Falmouth Commodores	24	19	1	49
Cotuit Kettleers	22	18	4	48
Bourne Braves	18	25	1	37

CHAMPIONSHIP: Wareham Gatemen defeated Chatham Anglers, 2-0, in best-of-three championship series.

TOP 50 PROSPECTS: 1. Andrew Vaughn, 1B, Wareham (Jr., California). **2.** Spencer Torkelson, OF/1B, Chatham (So., Arizona State). **3.** Will Holland, SS, Hyannis (Jr., Auburn). **4.** Alek Manoah, RHP, Chatham (Jr., West Virginia). **5.** Ryne Nelson, RHP, Yarmouth-Dennis (Jr., Oregon). **6.** Noah Campbell, 2B/SS, Yarmouth-Dennis (So., South Carolina). **7.** Tyler Dyson, RHP, Falmouth (Jr., Florida). **8.** Matt Wallner, OF/RHP, Falmouth (Jr., Southern Mississippi). **9.** Logan Davidson, SS, Falmouth (Jr., Clemson). **10.** J.J. Bleday, OF, Orleans (Jr., Vanderbilt). **11.** Logan Wyatt, 1B, Orleans (Jr., Louisville). **12.** Michael Busch, 1B, Chatham (Jr., North Carolina). **13.** Greg Jones, SS/OF, Chatham (So., UNC Wilmington). **14.** Kyle Stowers, OF, Falmouth (Jr., Stanford). **15.** Michael Toglia, 1B/OF, Cotuit (Jr., UCLA). **16.** Ricky DeVito, RHP, Harwich (Jr., Seton Hall). **17.** Bryant Packard, OF, Wareham (Jr., East Carolina). **18.** Steven Williams, OF, Falmouth (So., Auburn). **19.** Adam Laskey, LHP, Falmouth (Jr., Duke). **20.** Matt Canterino, RHP, Falmouth (Jr., Rice). **21.** Jesse Franklin, OF/1B, Brewster (So., Michigan). **22.** Blake Sabol, C/OF, Chatham (Jr., Southern California). **23.** Christian Koss, SS, Yarmouth-Dennis (Jr., UC Irvine). **24.** Austin Bergner, RHP, Chatham (Jr., North Carolina). **25.** Drew Mendoza, 3B, Chatham (Jr., Florida State). **26.** David Hamilton, SS, Yarmouth-Dennis (Jr., Texas). **27.** Cameron Cannon, 3B/2B, Falmouth (Jr., Arizona). **28.** Kenyon Yovan, RHP/1B, Orleans (Jr., Oregon). **29.** Hunter Gaddis, RHP, Chatham (Jr., Georgia State). **30.** Tanner Morris, SS, Harwich (So., Virginia). **31.** Will Robertson, OF, Cotuit (Jr., Creighton). **32.** Erik Miller, LHP, Orleans (Jr., Stanford). **33.** Jeff Belge, LHP, Chatham (Jr., St. John's). **34.** Austin Langworthy, OF, Falmouth (Jr., Florida). **35.** Austin Shenton, 3B, Wareham (Jr., Florida International). **36.** Mitchell Senger, LHP, Orleans (Jr., Stetson). **37.** Gabe Holt, OF/2B, Bourne (So., Texas Tech). **38.** Spencer Brickhouse, 1B, Bourne (Jr., East Carolina). **39.** Andrew Daschbach, 1B, Yarmouth-Dennis (Jr., Stanford). **40.** Kyle Hurt, RHP, Chatham (So., Southern California). **41.** Greg Veliz, RHP, Chatham (Jr., Miami). **42.** Garrett Stallings, RHP, Harwich (Jr., Tennessee). **43.** Trent Denholm, RHP, Yarmouth-Dennis (So., UC Irvine). **44.** Chris Murphy, LHP, Brewster (Jr., San Diego). **45.** John Rave, OF, Chatham (Jr., Illinois State). **46.** Hunter Bishop, OF, Brewster (Jr., Arizona State). **47.** Matthew Barefoot, OF, Hyannis (R-Jr., Campbell). **48.** Brady Smith, C/3B, Cotuit (So., Florida). **49.** Spencer Steer, 3B/2B, Orleans (Jr., Oregon). **50.** George Kirby, RHP, Harwich (Jr., Elon).

INDIVIDUAL BATTING LEADERS

	AVG	AB	R	H	2B	3B	HR	RBI	SB
Matthew Barefoot, OF, Hyannis	.379	140	24	53	9	1	3	26	6
Noah Campbell, 2B, Y-D	.364	107	19	39	7	2	6	26	7
Austin Shenton, 3B, Wareham	.349	149	31	52	9	0	4	30	1
Blake Sabol, C/OF, Chatham	.340	103	28	35	3	0	7	22	14
Tanner Morris, SS, Harwich	.331	136	24	45	8	1	2	20	5
Kyle Stowers, OF, Falmouth	.326	138	29	45	13	1	6	24	5
Ashton Bardzell, OF, Bourne	.316	114	25	36	5	3	3	14	4
Zach Ashford, OF, Y-D	.314	137	27	43	5	0	0	9	8
Andre Lipcius, 1B, Harwich	.313	160	20	50	11	0	4	27	2
J.J. Bleday, OF, Orleans	.311	148	29	46	9	2	5	15	2

INDIVIDUAL PITCHING LEADERS

Player, Team	W	L	ERA	G	SV	IP	H	BB	SO
Trent Denholm, Y-D	2	0	0.00	9	1	22	14	8	29
Joey Matulovich, Wareham	2	0	0.38	5	0	24	16	7	21
Adam Elliott, Hyannis	1	1	0.44	16	4	21	13	11	13
Garrett Gayle, Cotuit	1	0	0.60	10	1	15	11	8	11
Stephen Schoch, Cotuit	2	1	0.95	14	1	19	16	6	21
Derek West, Wareham	2	0	1.10	5	0	16	8	6	15
Andrew Misiaszek, Harwich	3	0	1.11	17	5	24	13	7	27
Troy Miller, Chatham	0	0	1.14	9	1	24	9	9	29
Adam Laskey, Falmouth	5	0	1.19	6	0	30	19	11	26
Dylan Thomas, Hyannis	3	0	1.19	17	9	23	18	2	33

BOURNE

Batting	AVG	AB	R	H	2B	3B	HR	RBI	SB
Ashton Bardzell, OF	.316	114	25	36	5	3	3	14	4
Spencer Brickhouse, 1B	.247	150	19	37	5	1	4	26	0
Daniel Cabrera, OF	.091	11	0	1	0	0	0	0	1
Hunter Coleman, C	.000	5	0	0	0	0	0	0	0
Danny DiGeorgio, INF	.273	22	4	6	0	0	0	2	0
Tyler Fitzgerald, SS	.298	171	28	51	14	0	2	20	9
Jake Garella, OF	.214	42	1	9	4	0	0	4	0
Greer Holston, RHP	.000	0	0	0	0	0	0	0	0
Gabe Holt, 2B	.315	54	6	17	1	0	0	3	2
Spencer Horwitz, 1B	.279	68	10	19	2	1	1	8	2
Cooper Johnson, C	.155	58	6	9	0	0	0	3	1
Grae Kessinger, SS	.000	3	0	0	0	0	0	0	0
David Langer, INF	.222	27	3	6	2	0	0	3	0
Lyle Lin, C	.253	91	7	23	4	1	1	16	0
Jake MacKenzie, INF	.286	14	2	4	1	0	0	0	0
Chase Murray, OF	.317	101	16	32	5	1	2	14	2
Danny Oriente, OF	.222	45	1	10	0	0	0	3	0
Thaddeus Phillips, C	.141	71	7	10	1	1	0	7	0
Anthony Prato, SS	.261	119	24	31	4	1	2	10	8
Oscar Serratos, SS	.250	68	3	17	3	0	0	4	1
Tyler Shedler-McAvoy, OF	.083	12	0	1	1	0	0	1	0
William Simoneit, C	1.000	1	1	1	0	0	0	0	0
Jared Triolo, 3B	.276	156	21	43	9	1	4	27	4
Alika Williams, SS	.245	49	8	12	3	0	1	6	4
Pitching	W	L	ERA	G	SV	IP	H	BB	SO
Ben Anderson	0	0	0.00	1	0	1	1	0	1
Andy Archer	1	1	7.90	6	1	14	20	3	17
Trey Benton	0	3	2.02	9	2	22	21	10	19
Caleb Bolden	0	0	5.87	5	0	8	6	6	12
Jared DiCesare	3	1	2.95	7	0	37	34	2	28
Bryan Hoeing	2	3	7.62	7	0	28	43	9	24
Greer Holston	1	2	3.60	11	1	20	11	13	15
Jared Lasko	3	2	3.76	8	0	41	42	8	28
Casey Legumina	0	0	0.00	2	0	9	10	1	9
Kyle Martin	0	2	5.91	12	2	21	21	15	25
Michael McAvene	1	1	3.97	11	1	11	11	12	14
Sam Messina	0	0	2.46	4	0	4	3	2	7
Nick Morreale	1	3	2.95	14	0	21	19	11	33
Zachary Peek	0	1	5.89	8	0	26	31	10	27
Austin Pope	1	3	5.67	7	0	27	29	12	35
Mike Ruff	4	1	3.64	12	0	17	18	8	18
Harrison Rutkowski	0	2	6.65	6	0	22	25	10	16
Andrew Saalfrank	0	0	6.00	1	0	3	2	3	2
Oscar Serratos	0	0	6.75	1	0	1	3	1	2
Trey Van Der Weide	1	0	3.81	11	0	26	21	11	16
Jacob Wallace	0	0	0.00	12	6	14	10	5	25
Benjamin Wereski	0	0	9.00	1	0	2	4	1	2
Gavin Williams	0	0	12.00	4	0	3	4	6	3
Connor Wollersheim	0	0	27.00	2	0	1	3	3	1

BREWSTER

Batting	AVG	AB	R	H	2B	3B	HR	RBI	SB
Ray Alejo, OF	.262	107	15	28	6	3	2	11	9
Justin Ammons, OF	.258	62	7	16	2	0	1	3	2
Darren Baker, 2B	.222	18	2	4	1	0	0	2	1
Randy Bednar, OF	.125	8	1	1	0	0	0	0	0
Hunter Bishop, OF	.233	120	19	28	2	0	4	19	9
Dominic Canzone, OF	.276	116	16	32	3	1	1	11	2
Brett Centracchio, 3B	.600	5	0	3	1	0	0	3	0
Joe Donovan, C	.309	68	11	21	1	0	0	8	1
Cameron Eden, SS	.254	114	14	29	2	0	2	17	6
Jesse Franklin, 1B	.302	96	17	29	5	0	2	17	0
Ike Freeman, SS	.250	68	9	17	1	0	3	6	0
Connor Grammes, 3B/RHP	.253	79	16	20	3	1	7	16	1
Ryan Hogan, C	.000	6	0	0	0	0	0	0	0
Jeremy Houston, SS	.111	9	2	1	1	0	0	1	0
Jarrod Huber, C	.111	9	0	1	0	0	0	0	0
Austin Lively, INF	.226	31	1	7	2	0	0	2	2
Allbry Major, OF	.095	21	2	2	0	0	0	0	0
Brandon Martorano, C	.241	58	8	14	5	0	2	5	0
Michael Massey, INF	.280	82	9	23	4	0	1	8	7
Jared Melone, INF	.111	9	1	1	0	0	0	0	0
Christian Molfetta, INF	.136	59	4	8	2	0	0	2	2
Hernen Sardinas, INF	.308	13	1	4	1	0	0	0	0
Randy Taveras, INF	.400	10	1	4	1	0	0	2	1
Johnny Tuccillo, C	.000	6	0	0	0	0	0	0	0
Paul Witt, SS	.333	6	1	2	0	0	0	0	0
Gage Workman, SS	.163	98	9	16	3	1	3	12	6
Christopher Wright, 1B/LHP	.187	75	4	14	0	1	0	0	0
Brandon Wulff, OF	.194	67	8	13	2	0	1	6	1

Pitching	W	L	ERA	G	SV	IP	H	BB	SO
James Acuna	0	5	8.10	7	0	20	25	15	15
Brady Basso	0	2	3.06	9	0	18	21	6	13
John Cain	0	0	27.00	1	0	1	3	1	1
Kyle Cameron	0	1	5.32	6	0	22	28	5	15
Carson Coleman	0	0	1.00	8	1	9	5	6	9
Jeff Criswell	1	0	4.34	10	0	19	16	11	18
Reid Detmers	1	3	4.55	7	0	28	31	7	29
Benjamin Dragani	1	2	4.5	6	0	20	25	8	15
Evan Flynn	0	0	9.00	1	0	3	3	1	5
Connor Grammes	2	0	5.79	7	1	9	9	9	13
Owen Griffith	1	0	3.52	8	1	15	19	5	10
Jacob Hennessy	1	2	3.13	7	1	23	27	2	18
Chance Hroch	0	0	0.00	1	0	3	2	3	2
Zach Linginfelter	2	1	4.40	8	0	31	24	18	
29 Seth Lonsway	0	0	7.20	2	0	5	5	7	6
Chris Machamer	1	1	1.13	2	0	8	7	3	5
Allbry Major	0	1	0.00	1	0	0	1	3	0
Connor Manous	0	2	6.16	6	0	19	22	11	20
Conor McNamara	0	0	0.00	1	0	2	1	0	2
Morgan McSweeney	1	0	2.46	2	0	4	3	4	5
Bobby Miller	0	0	5.06	4	0	16	18	7	10
Chris Murphy	1	2	5.01	8	0	23	23	18	34
Jack Owen	0	0	1.80	2	0	5	8	0	4
Ashton Raines	0	1	45.00	1	0	1	6	0	1
Zach Schneider	1	0	2.35	3	0	8	7	3	9
Andrew Schultz	0	3	3.54	10	1	20	13	25	23
Steven Theetge	0	1	9.64	1	0	5	8	3	5
Ryan Thompson	0	0	12.15	3	0	7	14	5	3
Zack Thompson	0	0	3.18	2	0	6	5	3	4
Brayden Weyer	0	0	6.75	3	0	4	7	0	3
Brandon Wilkes	0	0	2.70	2	0	3	1	1	4
Taylor Williams	0	0	12.00	4	0	3	3	8	2
Christopher Wright	1	0	2.31	6	0	12	6	5	21

CHATHAM

Batting	AVG	AB	R	H	2B	3B	HR	RBI	SB
Jorge Arenas, SS	.214	98	14	21	2	0	0	9	1
Michael Busch, 1B	.322	90	19	29	4	0	6	17	3
Tristin English, 1B/RHP	.300	100	16	30	6	0	5	19	6

Batting	AVG	AB	R	H	2B	3B	HR	RBI	SB
Adam Fogel, OF	.169	59	4	10	2	0	0	2	3
Branden Fryman, INF	.267	30	7	8	2	0	0	0	5
Cole Heavilin, INF	.000	1	0	0	0	0	0	0	0
Greg Jones, SS/OF	.259	116	23	30	0	1	3	9	20
Nick Kahle, C	.125	16	0	2	1	0	0	0	0
Kyle McCann, C	.219	96	9	21	6	0	2	11	0
Ashton McGee, 2B	.140	43	4	6	1	0	0	3	2
Jonathan McMillon, OF/RHP	.154	13	2	2	1	0	1	2	0
Drew Mendoza, DH	.232	69	9	16	2	0	2	12	1
Ben Ramirez, SS	.228	92	6	21	1	0	0	12	6
John Rave, OF	.304	125	23	38	6	1	4	16	5
Brock Riley, RHP	.000	1	0	0	0	0	0	0	0
Blake Sabol, C/OF	.340	103	28	35	3	0	7	22	14
Colin Simpson, C	.275	138	24	38	8	2	5	27	3
Jake Snider, INF	.222	9	1	2	0	0	0	0	0
Jake Taylor, C	.122	49	5	6	0	0	0	2	1
Rylan Thomas, 1B	.200	5	1	1	0	0	1	0	0
Spencer Torkelson, OF	.333	81	18	27	9	0	7	25	2
Benny Wanger, 1B	.000	5	0	0	0	0	0	0	0
Austin Wilhite, SS	.000	3	0	0	0	0	0	0	0
Rankin Woley, INF	.100	20	5	2	0	0	0	0	2
Dan Valerio, 2B	.217	23	2	5	2	0	0	0	0

Pitching	W	L	ERA	G	SV	IP	H	BB	SO
Jorge Arenas	0	1	9.00	2	0	2	2	3	4
Jeff Belge	1	2	3.53	9	1	36	30	19	46
Austin Bergner	2	1	2.38	4	0	23	22	7	26
Cody Bradford	0	0	2.25	2	0	8	5	4	8
Jack Conlon	2	1	5.54	9	1	26	26	14	23
C.J. Dandeneau	0	0	0.00	1	0	1	1	0	1
Davis Daniel	0	1	2.30	4	0	16	9	4	15
Tristin English	1	1	2.31	4	0	12	12	1	8
R.J. Freure	0	0	0.00	1	0	1	0	3	1
Hunter Gaddis	3	1	2.00	5	0	18	11	4	13
Dan Hammer	2	0	2.16	6	0	25	20	5	20
Kyle Hurt	1	1	3.47	8	1	23	19	9	22
Cam Jabara	0	0	4.15	4	1	4	6	1	4
Zach King	1	0	7.04	3	0	8	7	3	9
Michael Kirian	0	0	0.00	3	0	2	4	1	3
Joseph Lowder	0	0	8.10	3	0	3	3	2	2
Alek Manoah	3	2	2.70	7	0	33	15	11	48
Reeves Martin	1	0	9.00	3	0	3	3	2	5
John McMillon	1	2	7.94	7	1	17	19	15	24
Andrew Miller	0	0	3.00	2	0	3	2	0	2
Troy Miller	0	0	1.14	9	1	24	9	9	29
Colby Morris	0	0	4.50	1	0	2	4	0	0
Zack Noll	1	2	9.28	6	0	11	12	8	11
Colin Peluse	0	0	2.57	2	0	7	3	4	10
Brock Riley	0	0	3.86	5	0	7	9	5	7
Nick Scheidler	0	1	2.00	8	0	9	6	11	7
Spencer Van Scoyoc	1	1	7.71	12	0	21	23	15	26
Gregory Veliz	2	1	2.57	13	4	21	16	8	32
Benny Wanger	0	0	54.00	1	0	1	1	3	2
Jackson Wark	0	1	15.75	2	0	4	9	3	5

COTUIT

Batting	AVG	AB	R	H	2B	3B	HR	RBI	SB
Zachary Biermann, 1B	.291	127	14	37	8	0	6	25	2
Beau Brundage, OF	.273	55	6	15	2	0	1	8	3
Peyton Burdick, OF	.252	115	19	29	4	1	5	24	6
Raphael Chaumette, OF	.000	4	0	0	0	0	0	0	0
Thomas Dillard, OF	.250	104	19	26	5	0	3	16	5
Drew Ellis, OF	.279	86	17	24	0	0	0	6	10
Jakob Goldfarb, OF	.053	19	3	1	0	1	0	1	0
Nick Gonzalez, 2B	.000	5	1	0	0	0	0	0	0
Zach Humphreys, C	.232	82	17	19	3	0	3	7	4
Trey Jacobs, 3B	.333	6	0	2	0	0	0	1	0
Eric Jones, C	.239	71	6	17	1	0	0	7	0
Corey Joyce, 2B	.000	6	0	0	0	0	0	0	0
Matt McCourt, INF	.125	8	1	1	0	0	0	2	0
Morgan McCullough, SS	.000	3	0	0	0	0	0	0	0
Adam Oviedo, SS	.197	71	11	14	3	1	3	12	1
Rey Pastrana, C	.286	14	1	4	3	0	0	3	0

Batting	AVG	AB	R	H	2B	3B	HR	RBI	SB
Ryan Reynolds, 3B	.227	44	5	10	3	0	1	7	0
Will Robertson, OF	.300	170	30	51	11	0	4	28	2
Mike Salvatore, SS	.287	101	16	29	5	1	2	14	2
Armani Smith, OF	.500	2	0	1	0	0	0	0	0
Brady Smith, 3B/C	.333	72	11	24	4	0	1	10	0
Michael Toglia, 1B/OF	.209	134	25	28	3	0	7	23	1
Keaton Weisz, INF	.250	4	2	1	0	0	0	0	0
Garrett Wolforth, C	.278	36	4	10	2	0	1	4	0
Cory Wood, 2B	.213	108	20	23	6	0	2	6	5

Pitching	W	L	ERA	G	SV	IP	H	BB	SO
John Baker	3	2	2.38	6	0	34	37	2	31
Bryce Bonnin	0	1	7.20	2	0	5	9	2	5
Joe Boyle	0	0	12.60	7	0	5	5	11	11
Luke Chevalier	3	0	3.70	10	0	32	30	9	25
Zane Collins	1	0	3.90	11	0	30	27	16	19
Jake Dexter	0	0	4.50	1	0	2	1	1	1
Mathieu Gauthier	0	1	9.00	8	0	10	14	7	6
Garrett Gayle	1	1	0.44	16	4	21	13	11	13
Keagan Gillies	0	0	2.70	2	0	3	4	2	1
Trey Holland	1	0	0.00	1	0	3	1	2	1
Bryce Jarvis	1	2	5.34	10	0	29	29	14	22
Ryan Lefner	2	0	5.26	14	1	26	27	9	22
Chris Lincoln	0	0	4.50	1	0	2	4	0	2
Griffin McLarty	1	3	5.28	8	0	31	44	11	23
Deacon Medders	1	0	4.77	15	2	28	32	12	32
Addison Moss	0	0	11.81	2	0	5	10	3	5
Jason Reynolds	0	0	9.00	2	0	6	8	0	5
Stephen Schoch	2	1	0.95	15	1	19	16	6	21
Seth Shuman	1	3	3.86	8	0	33	38	7	24
Ryan Smith	1	0	4.71	14	0	21	21	19	17
Ted Stuka	0	0	0.00	1	0	2	1	1	0
Anthony Veneziano	1	1	4.30	4	0	15	12	8	10
Joseph Walsh	3	2	5.68	14	0	19	23	6	18
Colby White	0	1	9.00	3	0	3	5	3	1
Michael Young	0	0	0.00	1	1	2	0	0	3

FALMOUTH

Batting	AVG	AB	R	H	2B	3B	HR	RBI	SB
Will Brennan, OF	.233	150	15	35	2	0	0	6	8
Jordan Butler, LHP/OF	.200	5	0	1	0	0	0	0	0
Cameron Cannon, 3B	.263	160	15	42	6	0	2	28	3
Hayden Cantrelle, INF	.174	86	12	15	0	3	0	11	7
Marc Coffers, OF	.267	15	0	4	0	0	0	2	0
James Cosentino, 2B	.192	26	5	5	0	0	1	2	3
Logan Davidson, SS	.194	139	19	27	4	0	2	11	3
Logan Foster, OF	.179	28	2	5	2	0	0	2	0
Nic Gaddis, C	.333	6	0	2	0	0	0	1	0
Maverick Handley, C	.252	103	21	26	6	0	2	12	11
Herbert Iser, C	.219	32	4	7	1	0	2	7	0
Edouard Julien, 2B/OF	.205	78	9	16	7	0	2	11	0
Austin Langworthy, OF	.206	102	20	21	1	0	7	16	3
Austin Masel, C	.143	21	2	3	0	0	0	1	1
Terrance Norman, OF	.091	11	2	1	1	0	0	1	0
C.J. Schaeffer, C	.132	38	4	5	1	0	0	3	0
Davis Sims, INF	.252	147	18	37	5	0	8	27	0
Kyle Stowers, OF	.326	138	29	45	13	1	6	24	5
Matt Trehub, C	.000	1	1	0	0	0	0	0	0
Alexander Volpi, INF	.200	5	1	1	0	0	1	2	0
Matt Wallner, OF	.250	84	13	21	2	0	4	11	4
Steven Williams, OF	.303	66	14	20	3	0	1	6	0
R.J. Yeager, INF	.200	5	1	1	0	0	0	0	0

Pitching	W	L	ERA	G	SV	IP	H	BB	SO
A.J. Block	1	1	6.40	10	0	13	17	8	20
Matt Canterino	2	1	2.59	5	0	24	16	10	29
Cal Coughlin	0	0	1.59	4	0	6	4	0	4
Declan Cronin	0	0	4.91	5	0	4	6	3	2
Tyler Dyson	1	1	2.37	3	0	19	12	9	23
Will Ethridge	0	1	9.31	4	0	10	17	3	9
Peyton Glavine	0	0	0.00	1	0	1	1	0	1
Pete Hamot	0	0	4.50	1	0	2	3	1	3
Brent Killiam	1	1	3.44	10	0	18	17	8	22
Ian Koch	1	1	2.66	10	1	24	13	12	22

Pitching	W	L	ERA	G	SV	IP	H	BB	SO
Owen Lamon	0	0	9.00	2	0	2	4	1	2
Adam Laskey	5	0	1.19	6	0	30	19	11	26
Jack Little	1	1	5.40	8	4	8	10	1	18
Patrick McGowan	2	1	4.15	9	0	30	28	11	28
Daniel Metzdorf	0	0	3.38	2	0	5	5	5	3
Nick Mikolajchak	1	0	1.84	8	1	15	16	2	20
Mitchell Miller	1	1	3.80	10	0	24	16	12	30
Scott Politz	2	2	4.60	6	0	29	32	7	22
Logan Rinehart	1	0	3.00	11	0	15	10	4	16
Tommy Sheehan	0	0	0.00	3	0	3	1	1	3
T.J. Sikkema	1	3	1.72	5	0	31	23	8	23
Carson Spiers	1	1	0.84	7	0	11	5	6	5
Mitchell Stone	0	2	3.38	7	0	29	31	16	28
Spencer Strider	2	2	3.38	6	0	27	22	19	28
Zach Stromberg	0	0	13.5	2	0	1	4	1	2
Taylor Wilkes	0	0	6.00	2	0	3	2	5	5

HARWICH

Batting	AVG	AB	R	H	2B	3B	HR	RBI	SB
Justin Ammons, OF	.000	3	0	0	0	0	0	0	0
Danny Casals, INF	.201	144	18	29	11	1	3	22	2
Brad Debo, C	.250	72	8	18	5	0	0	8	0
Brian Dempsey, INF	.286	7	1	2	1	0	0	2	0
Logan Driscoll, C	.204	98	6	20	3	0	0	8	1
Nate Eikhoff, INF	.220	132	14	29	6	0	1	7	1
Rob Emery, C	.000	1	0	0	0	0	0	0	0
Chris Galland, OF	.262	103	16	27	7	1	1	11	2
Ramon Garza, INF	.222	9	3	2	1	0	1	4	0
Ray Gil, 3B	.115	26	3	3	1	0	0	0	0
Matt Gorski, OF	.286	70	11	20	3	0	0	6	1
Jordan Greene, 2B	.063	16	4	1	0	0	0	0	0
Andre Lipcius, 1B	.313	160	20	50	11	0	4	27	2
Will Matthiessen, RHP/1B	.000	17	0	0	0	0	0	1	0
Mason Meadows, C	.108	37	2	4	3	0	0	0	0
Tanner Morris, SS	.331	136	24	45	8	1	2	20	5
Ben Norman, OF	.201	134	16	27	7	0	1	11	4
Steve Passatempo, C	.000	2	0	0	0	0	0	2	0
Gabe Rivera, OF	.163	98	8	16	4	2	0	5	2
Aaron Schunk, 3B	.287	122	18	35	6	0	0	19	1
John Stanton, OF	.167	12	3	2	0	0	0	0	0
Alex Tappen, OF	.667	3	1	2	0	0	0	2	1
Cam Thompson, 2B	.340	50	7	17	3	0	0	2	2
Zach Watson, OF	.382	34	4	13	1	0	1	9	4

Pitching	W	L	ERA	G	SV	IP	H	BB	SO
Jake Agnos	1	0	0.00	1	0	6	3	2	10
Tyler Baum	0	0	0.75	3	0	12	13	2	12
Michael Bienlien	0	1	3.86	9	1	21	14	8	17
Peter Bovenzi	0	0	0.00	1	0	2	1	1	1
Jacob Bradley	0	1	10.13	3	0	5	9	6	0
Kyle Brnovich	0	0	0.00	2	1	5	0	2	6
Ty Buckner	1	3	3.74	5	0	22	24	12	19
Jon Clines	0	1	11.57	1	0	2	4	2	1
Matt Cronin	0	1	4.05	4	0	7	7	4	1
Xzavion Curry	0	1	10.61	3	0	9	14	6	7
Ricky DeVito	1	1	2.46	8	0	29	27	13	35
Jack Dreyer	0	1	3.50	5	0	18	17	7	17
Caleb Freeman	0	0	3.38	9	0	19	13	10	15
Gage Gillian	0	0	8.31	3	0	4	4	4	3
Jackson Gillis	1	1	4.70	4	0	8	11	2	6
Zack Hess	1	0	0.00	2	0	7	1	1	8
George Kirby	0	1	1.39	10	2	13	13	1	24
Cal Krueger	0	0	3.68	7	0	7	12	4	5
Joe LaSorsa	3	2	5.79	12	0	23	26	9	25
Andre Lipcius	0	0	0.00	1	0	2	1	0	1
Will Matthiessen	1	1	3.51	6	0	26	29	13	20
Andrew Misiaszek	3	0	1.11	17	5	24	13	7	27
Kyle Mora	1	1	2.13	3	0	13	11	5	14
Kyle Murphy	0	1	13.5	2	0	2	2	2	2
Garrett Pearson	0	0	5.40	1	0	3	3	1	1
Danny Poidomani	2	1	3.91	7	0	23	14	9	12
Nick Rand	1	0	0.00	2	0	3	2	1	2
Christian Santana	1	0	0.00	2	0	4	3	1	3

	W	L	ERA	G	SV	IP	H	BB	SO
Ben Shields	0	0	4.50	1	0	2	1	1	3
Garrett Stallings	1	0	2.50	3	0	18	18	0	21
Tom Sutera	0	2	3.25	10	0	28	27	10	28
Jacob Westphal	0	1	19.29	3	0	2	7	0	2
Austin Wood	0	3	12.18	11	0	17	20	22	22

HYANNIS

Batting	AVG	AB	R	H	2B	3B	HR	RBI	SB
Matthew Barefoot, OF	.379	140	24	53	9	1	3	26	6
Braden Comeaux, 3B	.299	107	12	32	3	0	0	11	3
Nick Derr, 2B	.000	5	0	0	0	0	0	0	0
Griffin Dey, INF	.111	18	0	2	0	0	0	1	0
Adam Elliott, LHP/OF	.125	16	1	2	1	0	0	3	0
Taylor Garris, 3B	.186	59	7	11	0	0	0	3	1
Michael Geaslen, C	.000	2	0	0	0	0	0	0	0
Seth Gray, 3B	.246	126	15	31	6	1	1	18	1
Colin Hall, OF	.167	30	7	5	1	0	0	2	0
Trevor Hauver, INF	.267	75	8	20	3	0	1	11	0
Will Holland, SS	.341	44	7	15	2	1	0	4	4
Tommy Jew, OF	.245	98	21	24	3	1	2	11	11
Brady Lindsly, C	.196	92	7	18	2	0	0	8	0
Todd Lott, OF/1B	.293	147	19	43	8	0	6	21	5
Liam McGill, C	1.000	1	0	1	0	0	0	1	0
Pedro Pages, C/1B	.258	132	17	34	7	0	3	17	0
Vinnie Pasquantino, 1B	.111	9	1	1	1	0	0	1	0
Anthony Pecora, 3B	.000	0	1	0	0	0	0	0	0
Eric Rivera, OF	.250	100	15	25	1	0	1	13	11
Alec Trela, SS	.214	28	3	6	0	0	0	1	0
Davis Wendzel, 3B	.236	161	19	38	11	2	3	14	2
Kyle Wilkie, C	.226	62	11	14	0	0	0	7	3

Pitching	W	L	ERA	G	SV	IP	H	BB	SO
Braden Comeaux	0	0	9.00	2	0	2	1	2	2
Griffin Dey	0	0	0.00	1	0	1	1	2	0
Connor Donahue	0	0	18.00	1	0	1	3	0	0
Adam Elliott	1	0	0.60	10	1	15	11	8	11
Wes Engle	0	0	2.81	11	0	16	6	16	9
Jordan Fowler	1	2	8.80	5	0	15	22	12	16
A.J. Franklin	0	0	0.00	1	0	1	1	0	0
Gavin Hollowell	1	1	5.03	6	1	20	25	9	18
Keegan James	1	1	2.89	8	1	19	16	7	13
Kyle Kemp	1	1	2.77	13	0	13	10	8	12
Hayden Kettler	1	0	0.00	1	0	4	3	0	6
Zach Kohn	1	1	4.73	9	0	32	26	19	36
Michael Kreiger	0	0	0.00	1	0	1	1	0	3
Brandon LaManna	0	0	0.00	1	0	1	0	0	1
Nick MacDonald	2	1	4.59	8	0	33	37	15	33
Travis Marr	0	2	9.90	3	0	10	16	4	8
Matthew Marsili	0	0	0.00	1	0	1	2	0	0
Dom Masullo	0	0	54.00	2	0	1	0	7	2
Mitch McIntyre	0	0	0.00	1	0	1	0	0	1
Mike Mokma	1	2	9.70	10	0	21	37	12	14
Ryan Pepiot	3	0	4.91	14	0	22	17	11	33
Jacques Pucheu	0	1	1.50	5	0	6	4	2	3
Casey Queener	1	0	9.82	3	0	4	6	2	4
Joseph Quintal	1	0	6.75	2	0	7	10	2	5
Jeremy Randolph	2	0	3.00	8	0	33	37	11	46
Houston Roth	0	0	5.91	8	0	32	40	13	33
Brett Schulze	1	3	7.11	11	3	19	24	8	15
Riley Self	2	1	2.35	9	1	15	8	6	18
Dylan Thomas	3	0	1.19	17	9	23	18	2	33
Parker Towns	1	1	2.79	8	0	10	13	3	8

ORLEANS

Batting	AVG	AB	R	H	2B	3B	HR	RBI	SB
Carter Aldrete, INF	.252	127	9	32	8	0	5	17	2
J.J. Bleday, OF	.311	148	29	46	9	2	5	15	2
Alex Brickman, 1B	.000	1	0	0	0	0	0	0	0
Phillip Clarke, C	.232	95	8	22	2	0	1	11	1
Pat DeMarco, OF	.265	170	23	45	4	1	2	14	10
Matt Frazier, OF	.165	91	6	15	2	0	0	6	6

	AVG	AB	R	H	2B	3B	HR	RBI	SB
James Free, C	.187	91	7	17	4	0	2	10	0
Alex Gamache, C	.000	5	1	0	0	0	0	0	0
Sal Gozzo, SS	.200	80	6	16	1	0	1	1	2
Jaxx Groshans, C/OF	.262	84	13	22	3	0	3	10	1
Isaiah Kearns, RHP	.000	1	0	0	0	0	0	0	0
Justin Lavey, 3B	.200	105	9	21	5	0	0	10	4
Andrew Martinez, SS	.167	36	4	6	1	0	0	1	2
Ricky Martinez, SS	.192	26	6	5	0	0	0	1	2
Quincy McAfee, INF	.200	15	1	3	1	0	0	0	0
Eddie McCabe, INF	.500	4	2	2	0	1	0	2	1
Kevin Milam, RHP/1B	.000	6	0	0	0	0	0	0	1
Nick Osborne, OF/RHP	.300	70	13	21	3	0	8	17	1
Spencer Steer, INF	.304	135	20	41	9	0	5	25	3
Brandon White, OF	.200	40	7	8	0	0	0	1	1
Logan Wyatt, 1B	.305	128	20	39	5	0	4	18	0
Kenyon Yovan, RHP/1B	.192	26	3	5	1	0	0	2	0

Pitching	W	L	ERA	G	SV	IP	H	BB	SO
Andrew Abbott	0	2	1.74	5	0	21	14	6	13
Tyler Brown	0	0	4.77	4	0	6	7	2	3
Anthony DiMeglio	0	0	8.53	4	0	5	11	2	2
Adam Erickson	0	0	1.59	8	0	11	7	5	12
Corey Gaconi	0	2	4.41	7	0	16	23	3	6
Lucas Hall	0	1	13.50	1	0	1	1	2	0
Josh Hendrickson	2	0	4.88	10	0	28	29	10	25
Elijah Herrick	0	1	9.00	5	0	9	13	3	4
Isaiah Kearns	1	1	3.86	4	0	7	9	4	7
Kevin Kelly	1	1	1.25	13	0	36	23	4	27
Carlisle Koestler	0	0	5.14	6	0	7	12	4	6
Zac Kristofak	1	0	3.86	6	0	9	9	6	9
Joey Lancellotti	1	1	3.38	4	0	13	14	3	17
Michael Mahony	1	0	9.82	4	0	4	4	5	5
Kade Mechals	1	0	3.86	5	0	19	13	7	19
Kevin Millam	0	0	0.00	1	0	1	1	0	0
Erik Miller	0	4	7.71	8	0	23	31	15	32
Aaron Ochsenbein	1	2	3.42	18	7	24	16	12	43
Riley Ornido	0	0	2.19	3	0	12	8	3	15
Nick Osborne	1	2	9.82	10	0	11	17	7	15
Mitchell Senger	2	2	9.30	5	0	20	19	10	19
Justin Showalter	0	1	5.06	2	0	5	7	2	4
Shay Smiddy	1	2	3.96	15	0	25	27	13	24
Noah Song	0	1	3.38	2	0	8	7	1	9
Enso Stefanoni	0	0	7.56	3	0	8	13	2	7
Graeme Stinson	0	0	0.00	1	0	5	3	1	12
Levi Stoudt	0	3	4.26	8	0	25	32	16	26
Kenyon Yovan	1	3	6.46	4	0	15	15	4	15

WAREHAM

Batting	AVG	AB	R	H	2B	3B	HR	RBI	SB
Michael Amditis, C	.333	21	4	7	0	0	0	2	1
Dante Baldelli, OF	.000	4	0	0	0	0	0	0	0
Cade Cavalli, RHP/INF	.167	6	0	1	0	0	0	0	0
Dominic Clementi, OF	.048	21	3	1	0	0	0	1	0
Isaac Collins, 2B	.308	120	27	37	2	1	1	13	5
Oliver Dunn, 2B	.243	70	15	17	4	1	1	8	1
Eric Gilgenbach, OF	.000	1	0	0	0	0	0	0	0
Jakob Goldfarb, OF	.268	41	9	11	2	1	0	5	4
Skyler Hunter, OF	.205	117	9	24	4	0	0	10	4
Ryan Kreidler, SS	.229	109	20	25	3	0	3	15	4
Lael Lockhart, OF/LHP	.218	101	12	22	0	2	3	16	2
Gian Martellini, C	.243	37	5	9	4	0	1	6	0
Drew Millas, C	.261	92	11	24	3	0	0	7	1
Bryant Packard, OF	.305	59	14	18	2	1	4	10	3
Pavin Parks, INF/RHP	.210	81	7	17	4	0	1	13	3
Parker Phillips, 1B	.179	28	3	5	1	0	1	4	0
Luke Roskam, C	.242	66	8	16	3	0	0	8	0
Austin Shenton, 3B	.349	149	31	52	9	0	4	30	1
Bryson Stott, SS	.275	40	9	11	2	0	0	3	4
Sahid Valenzuela, SS	.286	105	18	30	7	0	2	14	0
Andrew Vaughn, 1B	.308	52	7	16	3	0	5	14	1
Jeremy Ydens, OF	.304	148	25	45	8	1	3	34	3

Pitching	W	L	ERA	G	SV	IP	H	BB	SO
Tyler Ahearn	0	2	5.40	7	0	15	20	6	8
Carter Bach	0	0	0.00	1	0	1	1	1	2
Joseph Baran	1	0	1.35	4	0	7	6	0	10
Serafino Brito	0	0	0.00	1	0	1	2	0	0
Cody Carroll	1	2	4.80	9	0	15	17	9	19
Cade Cavalli	0	1	4.15	4	0	13	12	15	15
Brendan Cellucci	0	0	0.00	1	0	1	0	1	0
Mason Feole	0	0	3.86	2	0	7	4	1	10
Nathan Florence	0	1	5.75	6	0	16	13	13	19
Ryan Garcia	2	0	1.29	7	0	28	24	9	33
Justin Glover	0	0	6.75	1	0	4	4	1	2
Zach Hart	1	0	1.54	11	1	23	18	4	16
MacGregor Hines	0	0	6.14	4	0	7	8	5	6
Jared Horn	1	2	5.08	9	0	28	34	19	36
Tyler Keysor	2	2	4.95	11	1	20	22	5	24
Lael Lockhart	1	0	11.25	3	0	4	7	0	3
Easton Lucas	1	2	2.28	7	2	24	20	8	17
Connor Lunn	3	1	2.29	5	0	20	12	6	13
Joseph Matulovich	2	0	0.38	5	0	24	16	7	21
Thomas Miller	1	0	4.50	3	0	2	3	2	3
McKinley Moore	0	0	10.8	1	0	2	3	0	1
Pavin Parks	1	0	1.80	6	1	10	6	4	15
Will Proctor	2	1	2.84	8	0	32	31	11	25
Jack Ralston	0	0	7.11	5	0	6	8	6	4
Anthony Romanelli	1	0	0.00	1	0	1	0	0	1
Dominic Savino	0	0	3.00	3	1	3	4	0	1
Alex Stiegler	0	0	0.00	1	0	1	2	2	2
Ryan Stoudemire	0	2	2.60	10	2	17	7	7	11
Ken Waldichuk	1	1	4.91	5	0	18	18	7	20
Derek West	2	0	1.10	4	0	16	8	6	15
Brendan White	1	1	6.43	9	0	14	15	11	13
Tyler Yeh	0	0	0.00	1	1	2	0	0	0

YARMOUTH-DENNIS

Batting	AVG	AB	R	H	2B	3B	HR	RBI	SB
Reese Albert, OF	.277	83	9	23	4	0	2	14	1
Zach Ashford, OF	.314	137	27	43	5	0	0	9	8
Patrick Bailey, C	.235	17	3	4	2	0	1	3	0
Bradlee Beesley, OF	.368	68	11	25	4	2	1	8	2
Noah Campbell, 2B	.364	107	19	39	7	2	6	26	7
Charlie Concannon, OF	.333	12	2	4	0	0	0	3	0
Quin Cotton, OF	.286	147	21	42	8	2	0	21	3
Andrew Dashbach, 1B	.306	134	28	41	13	0	5	27	1
Jonny DeLuca, OF	.296	125	19	37	4	1	1	18	6
Matthew Dyer, C	.250	60	10	15	4	0	0	6	0
Kale Emshoff, C	.000	6	0	0	0	0	0	0	0
Vito Friscia, C	.375	32	5	12	4	0	0	2	0
Jim Govern, 2B	.222	27	4	6	2	0	0	1	4
David Hamilton, SS	.200	50	9	10	2	0	0	5	11
Adam Kerner, C	.233	60	3	14	1	0	1	7	1
Christian Koss, SS	.263	114	21	30	3	1	1	18	1
Andrew Martinez, SS	.241	29	3	7	2	0	0	3	1
Gabe Matthews, 1B	.500	4	0	2	0	0	0	2	0
Micah Pries, OF	.364	11	2	4	0	0	0	0	0
Nick Quintana, 3B	.259	108	18	28	4	0	5	23	1
Luke Robinson, C	.333	3	0	1	0	0	0	0	0
Matthew Toke, INF	.000	3	1	0	0	0	0	0	0
Luke Waddell, INF	.243	74	11	18	1	0	0	11	3
Taylor Young, INF	.200	5	2	1	0	0	0	0	0
Zach Zubia, 1B	.250	60	8	15	1	0	3	10	1
Pitching	W	L	ERA	G	SV	IP	H	BB	SO
Tristan Baker	1	0	2.61	9	3	21	19	7	22
Brady Batten	1	0	0.87	2	0	10	4	7	6
Mike Cowell	0	0	4.50	1	0	2	2	1	3
Trent Denholm	2	0	0.00	9	1	22	14	8	29
Jensen Elliott	4	1	3.38	5	0	24	25	6	15
Mason Erla	0	0	7.20	1	0	5	7	0	5
Chandler Fidel	2	1	3.00	13	0	18	18	9	27
Braidyn Fink	1	1	1.96	13	0	23	16	12	29
William Frank	0	0	0.00	3	0	5	1	2	8
Justin Friedman	0	0	3.86	1	0	2	3	1	2

	W	L	ERA	G	SV	IP	H	BB	SO
Michael Henley	1	0	4.05	3	0	13	16	7	16
Tommy Henry	1	1	4.03	7	0	22	19	11	21
Brant Hurter	2	1	3.09	8	0	32	28	9	33
Gordon Ingebritson	1	0	0.00	2	0	5	3	1	2
Michael James	0	0	0.00	3	0	3	5	3	6
Karl Kauffmann	2	2	5.40	7	0	27	24	18	20
Sam Kessler	0	0	3.50	12	1	18	11	7	19
Tommy Mace	2	1	5.87	4	0	15	18	9	9
Ty Madrigal	0	0	1.44	11	0	25	25	5	20
Alec Marsh	0	0	1.59	5	0	11	9	6	20
Ryne Nelson	2	0	2.65	14	6	17	8	9	26
Brent Teller	0	1	13.5	1	0	3	4	1	2
Mitchell Tyranski	3	0	4.21	15	1	26	29	8	29
Luke Waddell	0	0	0.00	1	0	1	1	1	0
Nathan Wiles	2	3	6.84	6	0	26	37	4	19
Zach Zubia	0	0	0.00	1	0	1	0	1	0

ALASKA LEAGUE

	W	L	PCT	GB
Mat—Su Miners	27	17	.614	—
Anchorage Bucs	25	19	.568	2
Peninsula Oilers	23	21	.523	4
Chugiak Chinooks	18	26	.409	9
Anchorage Glacier Pilots	17	27	.386	10

CHAMPIONSHIP: Mat-Su Miners defeated Anchorage Bucs, 2-0, in best-of-three championship series.

TOP 10 PROSPECTS: 1. Asa Lacy, LHP, Mat-Su (So., Texas A&M) 2. Bryce Tassin, RHP, Mat-Su (R-Jr., Southeastern Louisiana), 3. Tevin Murray, LHP, Peninsula (Jr., Rutgers), 4. Ian Churchill, LHP, Mat-Su, (So., Santa Barbara City JC), 5. Spencer Henson, 1B, Mat-Su (Jr., Oral Roberts), 6. Jared Reklaitis, RHP, Chugiak (Sr., Wisconsin-Whitewater), 7. Jonathan Guardado, RHP, Mat-Su (So., Arizona), 8. J.C. Correa, 2B/3B, Anchorage (Jr., Lamar), 9. Adam Seminaris, LHP, Anchorage (So., Long Beach State), 10. Drew Swift, SS, Mat-Su (So., Arizona State).

INDIVIDUAL BATTING LEADERS

	AVG	AB	R	H	2B	3B	HR	RBI	SB
Jake Vieth, 1B, Bucs	.364	132	28	48	18	1	6	33	32
Spencer Henson, RHP/1B, Mat-Su	.336	146	27	49	12	1	7	33	20
Marc Mumper, INF, Pilots	.314	118	18	37	7	4	1	18	18
Kona Quiggle, OF, Mat-Su	.309	165	29	51	7	3	2	19	33
Ryan Knowles, INF, Pilots	.304	92	12	28	3	1	2	6	13
Jordan Arruda, INF, Pilots	.299	147	34	44	5	1	.0	8	28
J.C. Correa, 2B, Bucs	.289	159	20	46	11	1	1	16	18
Anthony Forte, OF, Chugiak	.285	130	16	37	7	1	3	25	24
Zack Zalesky, C, Peninsula	.283	53	11	15	2	2	0	5	10
Troy Claunch, C, Bucs	.280	50	5	14	3	0	0	3	9

INDIVIDUAL PITCHING LEADERS

	W	L	ERA	G	SV	IP	H	BB	SO
Adrian Mardueno, Bucs	2	1	0.00	15	7	20	8	5	26
Adam Seminaris, Bucs	4	1	0.38	8	0	47	21	6	35
Matt Amrhein, Peninsula	3	0	0.56	7	0	16	7	4	10
Mike Lopez, Peninsula	3	1	0.81	8	0	44	32	12	27
Bryce Tassin, Mat-Su	1	3	0.82	20	10	22	16	7	26
John Altman, Bucs	0	1	1.06	11	1	17	10	8	8
Cole Cook, Pilots	3	1	1.25	6	1	36	28	6	32
Alex Stiegler, Pilots	1	0	1.42	13	3	19	12	4	18
Tre Brown, Peninsula	2	1	1.46	14	1	25	27	8	19
Kyle Wullenweber, Bucs	5	0	1.50	14	1	24	18	11	32

ATLANTIC COLLEGIATE LEAGUE

	W	L	PCT	GB
Allentown Railers	22	9	.710	—
North Jersey Eagles	20	13	.606	3
Jersey Pilots	17	20	.459	8
Quakertown Blazers	16	19	.457	8
Trenton Generals	13	19	.406	9 ½
Ocean Gulls	14	22	.389	10 ½

CHAMPIONSHIP: Quakertown Blazers defeated Jersey Pilots, 2-0, in best-of-three championship series.

INDIVIDUAL BATTING LEADERS

	AVG	AB	R	H	2B	3B	HR	RBI	SB
Charles Barebo, OF, Allentown	.391	110	20	43	11	4	2	21	17
Patrick O'Hare, INF, Jersey	.381	97	10	37	4	0	1	10	2
Brainy Rojas, INF, Allentown	.367	79	20	29	4	2	0	18	4
Shayne Fontana, OF, Allentown	.359	117	31	42	4	5	6	26	17
Bret Williams, OF, Allentown	.351	77	23	27	5	0	7	17	6
Tatem Levins, C, Trenton	.342	79	12	27	3	2	6	24	1
Max Felsenstein, OF, Jersey	.325	114	17	37	3	1	0	8	8
Chance DiFebbo, OF, Quakertown	.324	105	26	34	4	2	1	10	11
Matt Hand, INF, Quakertown	.318	110	15	35	5	1	0	11	7
Vinny Carlesi, OF, Jersey	.275	91	16	25	4	0	0	6	3

INDIVIDUAL PITCHING LEADERS

	W	L	ERA	G	SV	IP	H	BB	SO
Ethan Frohman, Trenton	2	2	1.50	6		30	30	9	36
Sean Pavlik, Allentown	3	0	1.75	5		26	22	11	32
Corey Martinez, North Jersey	2	2	2.13	8		38	28	9	44
C.J. Kilgarriff, Quakertown	3	0	2.54	9		28	18	10	30
Jimmy Kingsbury, Quakertown	6	1	2.73	7		33	25	19	35
Brennan O'Neill, Jersey	3	2	3.09	7		35	37	18	35
Mike Gibbons, Jersey	2	5	3.16	8		43	35	16	42
Sean Roberts, Jersey	3	2	3.18	6		34	25	11	38
Nick Snyder, Trenton	1	1	3.18	6		28	16	22	47
J.J. Spehrley, Quakertown	2	3	3.29	9		38	32	20	37

CAL RIPKEN COLLEGIATE LEAGUE

North Division	W	L	PCT	GB
Baltimore Redbirds	31	9	.775	—
Gaithersburg Giants	20	20	.500	11
Silver Spring—Tacoma T Bolts	18	22	.450	13
Rockville Express	18	22	.450	13
Baltimore Dodgers	12	27	.308	18½
South Division	W	L	PCT	GB
Bethesda Big Train	34	6	.850	—
D.C. Grays	19	20	.487	14½
FCA Braves	18	21	.462	15½
Alexandria Aces	17	22	.436	16½
Loudoun Riverdogs	11	29	.275	23

CHAMPIONSHIP: Baltimore Redbirds defeated Bethesda Big Train in championship series.

TOP 10 PROSPECTS: 1. Anthony Servideo, SS, Baltimore Redbirds (So., Mississippi), 2. Saul Garza, C, Gaithersburg (So., Louisiana State), 3. Alex Tappen, INF/OF, Baltimore Redbirds (So., Virginia), 4. Hunter Brown, RHP, Bethesda (Jr., Wayne State), 5. Jason Reynolds, RHP, Baltimore Dodgers (Jr., Lehigh), 6. William Fleming, RHP, Baltimore Redbirds (So., Wake Forest), 7. Carlos Lomeli, RHP, Bethesda (So., St. Mary's), 8. Jahleel Sewer, OF, DC (Sr., Virginia State), 9. Mike YaSenka, RHP, Rockville (Jr., Eastern Illinois), 10. Fox Semones, INF, Bethesda (Jr., James Madison).

INDIVIDUAL BATTING LEADERS

	AVG	AB	R	H	2B	3B	HR	RBI	SB
Justin Wylie, OF, Bethesda	.417	108	27	45	12	1	7	25	5
Anthony Servideo, INF, Redbirds	.391	110	35	43	6	8	2	29	11
Carl Gindl, OF, Redbirds	.383	107	25	41	8	0	0	18	20
Alec Burleson, LHP/1B, Bethesda	.383	107	22	41	12	0	10	44	1
Jahleel Sewer, OF, D.C.	.374	99	29	37	7	2	4	21	20
Brett Norwood, INF, FCA	.364	129	31	47	8	1	2	16	23
Jared Melone, INF, Dodgers	.363	102	17	37	7	2	2	28	3
Alex Tappen, OF, Redbirds	.340	150	30	51	19	0	2	24	10
Matthew Thomas, C, Loudoun	.336	116	21	39	7	0	0	23	3
Mitch McIntyre, OF/LHP, D.C.	.336	131	21	44	10	0	4	23	7

INDIVIDUAL PITCHING LEADERS

	W	L	ERA	G	SV	IP	H	BB	SO
William Fleming, Redbirds	3	0	1.13	7	0	32	22	6	22
Carter Bosch, Alexandria	3	1	1.32	7	0	34	23	14	37
Andy Rozylowicz, SS-T	4	1	1.83	7	0	39	37	5	25
Anthony Amoroso, D.C.	3	1	2.23	8	0	32	22	20	18
J.P. Woodward, D.C.	2	2	2.42	7	0	41	28	19	30
John Farley, Rockville	3	3	2.53	8	0	43	35	16	35

Jason Reynolds, Dodgers	3	2	2.87	7	0	38	25	14	44
Isaac Olson, D.C.	3	2	3.16	7	0	37	24	15	38
Huei-Sheng Lin, SS-T	3	2	3.31	7	0	33	29	20	25
Robert Hamby, FCA	4	1	3.55	6	0	33	28	13	35

CALIFORNIA COLLEGIATE LEAGUE

	W	L	PCT	GB
Santa Barbara Foresters	25	5	.833	—
Orange County Riptide	20	12	.625	6
Healdsburg Prune Packers	14	10	.583	8
Conejo Oaks	17	13	.567	8
San Luis Obispo Blues	15	13	.536	9
Arroyo Seco Saints	12	23	.343	15½
Academy Barons	12	25	.324	16½
Southern California Catch	9	23	.281	17

CHAMPIONSHIP: Conejo Oaks defeated Orange Coast Riptide, 6-2, in championship game.

TOP 10 PROSPECTS: 1. Jackson Wolf, LHP, Santa Barbara (So., West Virginia), 2. Garrett Crochet, LHP, Santa Barbara (So., Tennessee), 3. Hunter Breault, RHP, Santa Barbara (So., Oregon), 4. Caleb Sloan, RHP, Santa Barbara (So., Texas Christian), 5. Michael Hobbs, RHP, Santa Barbara (So., St. Mary's), 6. Brandon Lewis, 3B, Conejo (Jr., UC Irvine), 7. Chase Ellig, C, Santa Barbara (R-Jr., West Virginia), 8. Elliott Anderson, LHP, Santa Barbara (So., Auburn), 9. Jordan McFarland, 1B, Conejo (Jr., Arkansas), 10. Kamron Fields, RHP/OF, Santa Barbara (So., Texas).

INDIVIDUAL BATTING LEADERS

	AVG	AB	R	H	2B	3B	HR	RBI	SB
Brandon Lewis, CO	.397	121	34	48	20	19	1	8	5
Ryan Cash, SBF	.365	96	18	35	29	2	4	0	13
Chase Illig, SBF	.355	93	26	33	15	11	1	6	3
Bryan Arias, HPP	.347	95	14	33	27	2	0	4	2
Joseph Argumedo, AB	.341	88	16	30	22	5	0	3	3
Drew Cowley, AS	.336	116	23	39	26	10	1	2	1
Jay Charleston, SLO	.333	99	27	33	28	0	4	1	19
Chase Cockrell, CO	.330	88	17	29	18	7	1	3	0
Daniel Jung, SCC	.327	107	14	35	26	5	1	2	1
Elijah Alexander, CO	.326	95	15	31	21	6	2	2	7

INDIVIDUAL PITCHING LEADERS

	W	L	ERA	G	SV	IP	H	BB	SO
Hunter Breault, SBF	3	0	0.00	8	0	21	14	7	21
Ryan Shreve, HPP	3	0	0.98	5	0	18	8	0	18
Jordan Chriss, SLO	1	0	1.17	6	0	23	15	4	27
Gabe Constantine, SLO	1	0	1.31	6	0	21	12	8	19
Angus Denton, CO	2	2	1.35	11	3	20	10	4	18
Hayden Jorgenson, SCC	0	0	1.50	4	0	18	17	4	13
Caleb Sloan , SBF	1	0	1.93	6	0	19	13	6	20
Corey Dawson, OCR	0	0	2.29	11	0	20	20	5	17
Michael Hobbs, SBF	1	0	2.51	8	0	29	24	7	31
Dylan Francis, CO	3	2	2.73	6	0	33	21	8	32

COASTAL PLAINS LEAGUE

North Division	W	L	PCT	GB
Peninsula Pilots	27	17	.614	—
Wilson Tobs	22	23	.489	5½
Edenton Steamers	24	26	.480	6
Martinsville Mustangs	21	26	.447	7½
South Division	W	L	PCT	GB
Savannah Bananas	37	14	.740	—
Macon Bacon	22	25	.468	11½
Florence RedWolves	22	26	.458	14
Lexington County Blowfish	17	31	.354	19
East Division	W	L	PCT	GB
Morehead City Marlins	34	14	.708	—
Fayetteville SwampDogs	24	25	.490	10½
Holly Springs Salamanders	21	30	.412	14½
Wilmington Sharks	17	34	.333	18½
West Division	W	L	PCT	GB
High Point-Thomasville HiToms	30	18	.625	—
Forest City Owls	29	20	.592	1½
Gastonia Grizzlies	23	26	.469	7½
Asheboro Copperheads	16	32	.333	14

CHAMPIONSHIP: Morehead City Marlins defeated High Point-Thomasville HiToms , 2-0, in best-of-three championship series.

INDIVIDUAL BATTING LEADERS

	AVG	AB	R	H	2B	3B	HR	RBI	SB
Chase Dawson, 2B, Martinsville	.395	167	31	66	10	0	3	27	12
Kendall McGowan, OF, FC	.392	148	39	58	20	1	5	36	22
Clay Dugan, 2B/SS, Savannah	.354	161	36	57	10	2	2	34	13
Austin Pharr, UTL, HPT	.352	159	43	56	11	3	15	49	6
Joe Simone, OF, Florence	.338	151	29	51	14	1	0	20	12
Sean Phelan, 1B, Asheboro	.337	166	24	56	7	1	6	40	0
Jake Sullivan, C, Savannah	.336	131	22	44	5	0	2	25	5
Jordan Eckard, OF, FC	.331	142	27	47	5	0	6	36	11
Derek Perry, 2B, Forest City	.329	152	46	50	5	0	5	20	32
Jonathan Embry, INF, Peninsula	.320	128	41	41	10	1	3	19	7

INDIVIDUAL PITCHING LEADERS

	W	L	ERA	G	SV	IP	H	BB	SO
Addison Domingo, Martinsville	4	1	1.59	9	0	51	32	15	52
Kristopher Kuhn, Florence	4	0	2.08	10	0	56	46	16	58
Octavio Mirabal, Morehead City	5	0	2.30	12	0	55	31	12	48
Jonathan Hughes, Florence	2	2	2.49	9	1	51	41	11	41
James Williams, Macon	2	2	2.49	8	0	47	30	19	46
Sam Luchansky, Wilmington	4	4	2.83	15	1	54	60	8	35
John Alan Kendrick, Asheboro	2	1	3.06	9	0	50	38	14	50
Jake Miller, Edenton	5	2	3.16	9	0	51	31	18	64
Brett Fulk, Lexington County	4	4	5.14	10	0	49	54	32	41
Bobby Hampton, Forest City	3	3	5.82	13	0	51	59	14	37

FLORIDA COLLEGIATE SUMMER LEAGUE

	W	L	PCT	GB
Leesburg Lightning	28	13	.683	—
DeLand Suns	22	16	.579	4½
Winter Park Diamond Dawgs	18	20	.474	8½
Sanford River Rats	18	20	.462	8½
Seminole County Scorpions	16	24	.400	11½
Winter Garden Squeeze	14	23	.368	12

CHAMPIONSHIP: DeLand Suns defeated Winter Park Diamond Dawgs, 2-1, in best-of-three championship series.

INDIVIDUAL BATTING LEADERS

	AVG	AB	R	H	2B	3B	HR	RBI	SB
Aaron Anderson, 1B, WG	.434	113	24	49	7	1	1	17	9
Jay Prather, INF, Leesburg	.350	137	22	48	4	0	0	28	4
Collin Morrill, 2B, Sanford	.347	101	16	35	5	0	0	14	6
Kerry Carpenter, OF, SC	.336	116	17	39	6	1	4	16	3
Luke Brown, OF, Leesburg	.328	137	37	45	6	0	0	9	10
Nick DeTringo, SS, DeLand	.318	107	23	34	8	2	1	24	9
Brayden Sisson, 3B, DeLand	.311	119	25	37	5	0	1	22	1
Anthony George, C, SC	.298	94	20	28	3	0	1	7	7
Trace Thornal, 3B, SC	.294	109	13	32	7	2	2	25	1
Scout McFalls, OF, DeLand	.291	117	24	34	7	0	0	21	13

INDIVIDUAL PITCHING LEADERS

	W	L	ERA	G	SV	IP	H	BB	SO
Vladimir Nunez, Sanford	2	0	1.03	7	0	35	20	14	39
Devin Meyer, Sanford	4	1	1.45	7	0	37	30	3	30
Jesus Valoy, DeLand	7	0	2.15	9	0	46	40	9	37
Hunter Caudelle, Leesburg	3	2	2.59	9	0	42	38	21	40
Nicholas Chiseri, DeLand	4	1	2.68	9	0	37	39	8	35
Ryan Ashworth, Winter Garden	3	3	2.72	9	0	43	35	6	23
Andrew Smith, DeLand	2	1	3.83	11	1	40	45	7	25
Tyler Fagler, Winter Garden	0	2	3.86	8	0	37	35	12	27
Ross Korosec, SC	1	3	4.13	8	0	33	32	9	36
Brooks Brophy, Winter Park	1	2	4.28	9	0	40	47	8	34

FUTURES COLLEGIATE LEAGUE

	W	L	PCT	GB
Marthas Vineyard Sharks	36	17	.679	—
Worcester Bravehearts	33	19	.635	2½
Bristol Blues	29	23	.558	6½
Brockton Rox	27	29	.482	10½
Nashua Silver Knights	21	32	.396	15

Pittsfield Suns	20	31	.392	15
North Shore Navigators	20	35	.364	17

CHAMPIONSHIP: Martha's Vineyard Sharks tied Worcester Bravehearts, and were declared co-champions when Game 3 of best-of-three championship series was rained out.

INDIVIDUAL BATTING LEADERS

	AVG	AB	R	H	2B	3B	HR	RBI	SB
Chris Rinaldi, INF, Worcester	.379	161	45	61	8	1	1	19	11
Collin Shapiro, OF, MVS	.365	104	34	38	6	0	0	17	10
Sal Frelick, INF, NSN	.361	133	35	48	6	2	7	36	22
Charlie Maxwell, 3B, Brockton	.353	153	42	54	10	1	1	19	16
Dylan Reynolds, OF, Bristol	.339	109	19	37	7	0	0	18	11
Michael Dellicarri, OF, Worcester	.339	192	48	65	13	4	7	45	12
Cody Morissette, INF, Nashua	.310	145	20	45	5	2	1	17	5
Matt Chamberlain, OF, MVS	.307	140	36	43	6	1	3	29	26
Dustin Harris, INF, Worcester	.306	173	29	53	12	2	2	42	7
Joe Lomuscio, OF, Brockton	.306	180	28	55	9	7	1	26	12

INDIVIDUAL PITCHING LEADERS

	W	L	ERA	G	SV	IP	H	BB	SO
Henry Ennen, Worcester	5	0	2.14	8	0	42	34	14	43
Shayne Audet, NSN	4	2	2.23	10	0	44	33	26	56
Brian Johnson, Pittsfield	2	3	2.83	8	0	41	30	28	38
Dalton Ponce, MVS	4	2	3.45	10	0	47	57	14	18
Shawn Babineau, MVS	3	2	3.53	8	0	43	50	7	36
Bryan Ketchie, MVS	5	0	3.54	11	0	53	61	6	48
Zach Begin, NSN	1	1	3.55	14	1	56	39	24	44
Michael Genaro, Bristol	2	2	3.58	9	0	50	51	6	39
Luke Dawson, Nashua	5	1	3.78	10	0	48	44	21	41
Gage Feeney, Pittsfield	4	0	3.99	9	0	47	45	12	23

GREAT LAKES LEAGUE

Northern Division	W	L	PCT	GB
St. Clair Green Giants	26	16	.619	—
Lima Locos	26	16	.619	—
Saginaw Sugar Beets	24	16	.598	1
Muskegon Clippers	24	18	.571	2
Irish Hills Leprechauns	19	22	.463	6½
Lake Erie Monarchs	17	23	.427	8
Grand Lake Mariners	17	24	.415	8½
Southern Division	**W**	**L**	**PCT**	**GB**
S. Ohio Copperheads	31	10	.756	—
Cincinnati Steam	30	12	.714	1½
Hamilton Joes	22	20	.524	9½
Galion Graders	19	22	.463	12
Richmond Jazz	16	26	.381	15½
Xenia Scouts	10	32	.238	21½
Licking County Settlers	9	33	.214	22½

CHAMPIONSHIP: Southern Ohio Copperheads defeated Saginaw Sugar Beets, 2-0, in best-of-three championship series.

TOP 10 PROSPECTS: 1. Jordan Nwogu, OF, Lake Erie (So., Michigan), 2. Michael Darrell-Hicks, RHP, Southern Ohio (Jr., Western Kentucky), 3. Miguel Cienfuegos, LHP, St. Clair (So., Northwest Florida State JC), 4. Cade Beloso, LHP, Lima (Fr., Louisiana State), 5. Ryan Jungbauer, RHP, Saginaw Valley (So., Northwestern Ohio), 6. Blake Holub, RHP/1B, Southern Ohio (So., St. Edward's (Texas)), 7. Adam Proctor, C, Saginaw (So., Michigan State), 8. Griffin Doersching, 1B, Hamilton (So., Northern Kentucky), 9. Tanner Hall, LHP, Lima (Jr., Mercer), 10. Blaine Crim, 3B, Southern Ohio (Sr. Mississippi College).

INDIVIDUAL BATTING LEADERS

	AVG	AB	R	H	2B	3B	HR	RBI	SB
Blaine Crim, INF, S. Ohio	.404	178	39	72	26	1	7	52	1
Jacob Reimold, OF, Gailon	.392	125	34	49	9	1	9	30	6
Brad Croy, OF, Lima	.386	114	23	44	8	1	1	21	1
Griffin Bernardo, 3B, Cincinnati	.376	149	43	56	13	2	7	44	1
Connor Charping, C, Saginaw	.372	129	26	48	7	1	2	33	22
Chris Hamilton, OF, Hamilton	.366	153	34	56	7	5	5	30	6
Cooper Marshall, INF, Saginaw	.364	140	35	51	8	3	7	34	10
Blake Holub, RHP, S. Ohio	.362	127	18	46	12	2	4	21	1

Tommy Pellis, INF, Irish Hills	.357	143	32	51	6	0	5	31	4
James Roche, SS, Muskegon	.353	167	32	59	12	0	9	40	4

INDIVIDUAL PITCHING LEADERS

	W	L	ERA	G	SV	IP	H	BB	SO
Jacob Moskowitz, St. Clair	6	1	1.21	9	0	52	36	17	26
Maxwell Ludka, Muskegon	6	0	1.34	10	0	47	24	24	64
Nicholas Smith, Galion	2	2	3.38	12	0	35	31	13	33
Tanner Hall, Lima	3	2	3.40	8	0	42	43	9	51
Branden Schlick, Galion	2	3	3.43	7	0	42	38	18	29
Jacob Gilhaus, Muskegon	3	1	3.43	13	1	39	37	15	29
Johnny Putnam, Licking County	0	3	3.47	10	2	49	52	17	43
Miguel Cienfuegos, St. Clair	3	3	3.48	9	0	52	46	16	56
Caleb Eder, Xenia	1	2	3.50	9	0	44	40	31	24
Wesley Pyles, S. Ohio	3	1	3.55	7	0	38	31	15	33

HAMPTONS COLLEGIATE LEAGUE

	W	L	T	PTS
Riverhead Tomcats	24	13	3	51
Long Island Road Warriors	25	15	0	50
Westhampton Aviators	20	19	1	41
Shelter Island Bucks	19	19	2	40
Sag Harbor Whalers	17	18	5	39
North Fork Ospreys	14	22	4	32
Southampton Breakers	13	26	1	27

CHAMPIONSHIP: Riverhead Tomcats defeated Long Island Road Warriors, 2-1, in best-of-three championship series.

TOP 10 PROSPECTS: 1. Carson Seymour, RHP, Southampton (So., Kansas State), 2. Nick Thornquist, C, Sag Harbor (Jr., Texas-San Antonio), 3. Jake McKenzie, 2B/SS, Shelter Island (So., Fordham), 4. Beau Keathley, RHP, Riverhead (So., Oakland), 5. Alex Volpi, 1B, Shelter Island (Jr., Holy Cross), 6. Curtis Robinson, OF, Westhampton (So., Penn State), 7. Dominic Savino, RHP, Long Island (Sr., Albany), 8. Tyler Thorington, RHP, Westhampton (Jr., Western Michigan), 9. Tyler Becker, SS, Westhampton (Jr., Adelphi (N.Y.)), 10. Eduardo Malinowski, SS/2B, Riverhead (So., Pennsylvania).

INDIVIDUAL BATTING LEADERS

	AVG	AB	R	H	2B	3B	HR	RBI	SB
Louis Antos, INF, Riverhead	.425	106	28	45	12	1	3	20	4
Nick Thornquist, C, Sag Harbor	.421	126	27	53	9	0	4	29	7
Alex Baratta, INF, Riverhead	.391	138	35	54	6	0	1	26	15
Curtis Robison, OF, WA	.374	139	28	52	7	0	9	29	6
Eduardo Malinowski, INF, RT	.371	151	27	56	12	4	3	36	11
Dylan Robertson, INF, SIB	.364	88	18	32	6	1	4	19	11
Mike Nyisztor, OF, SIB	.351	151	34	53	7	1	4	26	16
Jake MacKenzie, INF, SIB	.345	148	45	51	10	3	10	34	35
Mike Casaleggio, INF, SIB	.336	134	28	45	5	2	1	27	21
Brian Picone, OF, SB	.333	114	21	38	11	0	1	6	9

INDIVIDUAL PITCHING LEADERS

	W	L	ERA	G	SV	IP	H	BB	SO
Tyler Thorington, WA	3	0	1.87	10	0	34	22	13	46
Jordan Schulefand, SB	3	0	2.03	10	1	40	38	11	37
Tyler Henry, Riverhead	3	0	2.31	9	0	39	43	6	25
Enzo Stefanoni, North Fork	2	0	2.58	7	0	38	44	8	36
Carson Seymour, SB	5	0	2.63	9	0	41	30	23	40
Patrick Webler, SIB	4	1	2.78	14	1	32	32	15	16
Max Spencer, Sag Harbor	1	1	3.21	11	0	34	32	20	23
David Gately, Sag Harbor	2	2	3.25	7	0	36	36	12	32
Michael Marzonie, Sag Harbor	2	4	3.65	9	0	37	34	12	27
Joseph Quintal, SIB	3	2	3.86	8	0	42	42	9	48

JAYHAWK LEAGUE

	W	L	PCT	GB
Hays Larks	26	9	.743	—
Dodge City A's	21	14	.600	5
Liberal BeeJays	20	15	.571	6
Derby Twins	19	17	.528	7½
El Dorado Broncos	15	21	.417	11½
Great Bend	12	23	.343	14
Haysville Aviators	11	25	.306	15½

CHAMPIONSHIP: Hays won regular season title.

INDIVIDUAL BATTING LEADERS

	AVG	AB	R	H	2B	3B	HR	RBI	SB
Easton Kirk, C, Hays	.407	91	30	37	7	0	5	28	3
Ryne Randle, UTL, Hays	.364	129	32	47	15	0	1	18	7
Peyton Johnson, UTL, Liberal	.364	88	18	32	9	0	2	18	1
Dane Simon, UTL, Liberal	.358	109	33	39	7	3	2	16	19
Blaine Ray, OF, Great Bend	.354	82	21	29	2	0	2	21	2
Owen Jansen, INF, Dodge City	.347	95	26	33	11	0	3	19	2
Chris Swanberg, INF, Great Bend	.344	122	24	42	6	0	0	24	0
Dayton Cook, INF, Dodge City	.337	83	19	28	7	0	0	10	3
Brandan Madsen, OF, Great Bend	.333	105	19	35	3	0	0	21	4
Colton Eager, UTL, Derby	.333	129	27	43	12	2	1	22	1

INDIVIDUAL PITCHING LEADERS

	W	L	ERA	G	SV	IP	H	BB	SO
Michael Wong, Hays	3	0	1.95	6	0	37	29	8	35
Daniel Nelson, El Dorado	2	0	2.40	5	0	30	23	11	30
Fabian Muniz, Hays	5	1	2.52	10	1	36	59	9	32
Peyton Bauer, Liberal	3	2	2.83	8	0	41	37	10	35
Walter Pennington, Hays	2	0	3.66	7	1	32	32	20	24
Nolen McCarthy, Dodge City	3	1	3.73	6	0	31	29	6	31
Tyler Blomster, Hays	4	2	3.89	7	0	42	41	5	57
Connor Dove, Derby	4	3	3.89	9	0	39	36	20	27
Josh Zanger, Liberal	2	1	4.00	10	1	36	43	18	25
Neil Lemmons, Great Bend	1	3	4.05	11	0	33	37	14	22

MINK LEAGUE

North Division	W	L	PCT	GB
Sedalia Bombers	29	16	.644	—
Clarinda A's	21	23	.477	7½
St. Joseph Mustangs	20	23	.465	8
Chillicothe Mudcats	17	25	.405	10½
South Division	W	L	PCT	GB
Ozark Generals	26	18	.591	—
Nevada Griffons	24	18	.571	1
Jefferson City	20	24	.455	6
Joplin Outlaws	16	26	.381	9

CHAMPIONSHIP: Sedalia Bombers defeated Ozark Generals, 2-0, in best-of-three championship series.

INDIVIDUAL BATTING LEADERS

	AVG	AB	R	H	2B	3B	HR	RBI	SB
Ashanti Wheatley, OF, Sedalia	.355	121	48	43	6	2	2	26	10
Logan Hudson, INF, JC	.355	166	48	59	11	0	5	30	3
Alex Phillips, INF, St. Joseph	.350	157	37	55	15	0	8	37	7
Santiago Garcia, C, Sedalia	.346	130	24	45	10	0	8	50	0
Zachary Smith, OF, St. Joseph	.345	145	28	50	9	1	5	30	13
Zion Mayberry, OF, Nevada	.336	137	29	46	6	0	4	20	11
Connor Gage, INF, Nevada	.333	150	39	50	14	0	6	43	11
Reid Bonner, UTL, Clarinda	.329	164	34	54	6	0	3	23	20
Austin Blazevic, INF, JC	.329	158	41	52	12	0	3	34	0
Fernando Villegas, C, Ozark	.327	110	18	36	3	0	1	15	1

INDIVIDUAL PITCHING LEADERS

	W	L	ERA	G	SV	IP	H	BB	SO
Adam Link, Sedalia	0	1	1.20	11	4	15	6	4	11
Dalton Erger, JC	2	0	1.53	3	0	18	17	5	20
Jack Cavanaugh, Chillicothe	1	0	2.00	8	0	18	10	8	22
Aaron Celestino, Sedalia	3	0	2.06	8	0	35	22	8	35
Josiah Imhoff, Sedalia	2	0	2.19	15	1	25	20	8	19
Derek Kennell, Ozark	5	0	2.30	7	0	47	40	13	47
Peyton Warren, Nevada	4	2	2.30	8	0	43	35	8	35
Zach Parish, Joplin	1	2	2.46	6	0	37	24	16	39
Dakota Cortese, Sedalia	2	2	2.49	7	0	25	25	7	15
Joe Lewis, Ozark	5	1	2.72	10	0	43	40	19	33

NEW ENGLAND COLLEGIATE LEAGUE

Northern Division	W	L	PCT	GB
Valley Blue Sox	30	12	.714	—
Sanford Mainers	24	18	.571	6
Keene Swamp Bats	24	20	.545	7

	W	L	PCT	GB
Upper Valley Nighthawks	22	21	.512	8½
Vermont Mountaineers	21	23	.477	10
North Adams SteepleCats	15	28	.349	15½
Winnipesaukee Muskrats	14	29	.326	16½
Southern Division	**W**	**L**	**PCT**	**GB**
Plymouth Pilgrims	25	16	.610	—
Ocean State Waves	25	19	.568	1½
Mystic Schooners	22	21	.512	4
Newport Gulls	21	23	.477	5½
Danbury Westerners	18	23	.439	7
New Bedford Bay Sox	18	26	.409	8½

CHAMPIONSHIP: Valley Blue Sox defeated Ocean State Waves, 2-0, in best-of-three championship series.

TOP 10 PROSPECTS: 1. Tim Tawa, OF, Newport (So., Stanford), 2. Jared Shuster, LHP, New Bedford (So., Wake Forest), 3. Cameron Junker, RHP, Plymouth (Jr., Notre Dame), 4. Jack Weisenberger, RHP, Sanford (Jr., Michigan), 5. Dalton Reed, 1B, Newport (Jr., Kentucky), 6. Nick Mondak, LHP, Ocean State (R-So., St. John's), 7. Johnny Rizer, OF, Sanford (Sr., Texas Christian), 8. Kody Hoese, 3B, Newport (Jr., Tulane), 9. Eddie McCabe, SS, Danbury (So., Georgetown), 10. Griff McGarry, RHP, Keene (So., Virginia).

INDIVIDUAL BATTING LEADERS

	AVG	AB	R	H	2B	3B	HR	RBI	SB
Cam Walsh, OF, Plymouth	.378	143	33	54	9	0	4	23	2
Brandon Smith, 1B, Keene	.376	157	33	59	11	2	11	49	5
Tyler Kapucinski, INF, Valley	.376	109	15	41	10	0	3	19	1
Jackson Coutts, INF, NA	.376	133	16	50	8	0	3	28	0
Eddie McCabe, SS, Danbury	.368	125	31	46	7	1	3	21	13
Raphael Chaumette, OF, NBBS	.362	116	19	42	7	1	1	12	1
Garrett Hodges, OF, Ocean State	.361	158	35	57	9	0	7	40	13
Gregory Hardison, SS, UVN	.349	146	20	51	4	2	1	20	4
Christopher Berry, INF, UVN	.339	124	25	42	12	0	6	17	1
Tim Tawa, OF, Newport	.336	125	23	42	14	0	7	21	12

INDIVIDUAL PITCHING LEADERS

	W	L	ERA	G	SV	IP	H	BB	SO
Endy Morales, Valley	5	0	1.13	7	0	40	30	13	32
Sam Williams, Plymouth	4	3	1.48	8	0	43	42	11	39
Kumar Nambiar, Mystic	4	1	1.85	7	0	39	30	10	38
R.J. Hall, Sanford	3	0	2.14	8	0	34	29	7	25
Cooper Bradford, Valley	5	1	2.14	6	0	42	16	19	58
Austin Kullman, Plymouth	6	1	2.15	9	0	46	41	19	33
Jesse Slinger, Ocean State	2	2	2.19	8	0	37	36	9	38
Cameron Junker, Plymouth	6	1	2.34	8	0	42	32	16	46
Nick Robinson, Ocean State	2	2	2.43	10	0	37	24	12	34
Buddy Hayward, New Bedford	3	2	2.47	10	0	44	39	24	32

NORTHWOODS LEAGUE

North Division	**W**	**L**	**PCT**	**GB**
Willmar Stingers	26	11	.703	—
Mankato MoonDogs	25	11	.694	½
Duluth Huskies	23	13	.639	2½
La Crosse Loggers	23	14	.622	3
St. Cloud Rox	21	15	.583	4½
Rochester Honkers	17	19	.472	8½
Eau Claire Express	15	21	.419	10½
Bismarck Larks	12	23	.347	13
Waterloo Bucks	10	27	.270	16
Thunder Bay Border Cats	9	27	.250	16½
South Division	**W**	**L**	**PCT**	**GB**
Kenosha Kingfish	28	10	.737	—
Battle Creek Bombers	23	14	.622	4½
Madison Mallards	21	15	.583	6
Wisconsin Rapids Rafters	19	17	.528	8
Fond du Lac Dock Spiders	18	18	.500	9
Wisconsin Woodchucks	18	19	.486	9½
Kalamazoo Growlers	17	20	.459	10½
Green Bay Bullfrogs	16	20	.444	11
Lakeshore Chinooks	13	23	.361	14
Rockford Rivets	10	27	.270	17½

CHAMPIONSHIP: Fond du Lac Dock Spiders defeated Duluth Huskies,

2-1, in best-of-three championship series.

TOP 10 PROSPECTS: 1. Joe Boyle, RHP, Kalamazoo (So., Notre Dame), 2. Shane McGuire, C/1B, La Crosse (So., San Diego), 3. Mike Rothenberg, C, La Crosse (So., Duke), 4. Justin Slaten, RHP, Eau Claire (So., New Mexico), 5. Bobby Seymour, 1B, St. Cloud (So., Wake Forest), 6. Christian Robinson, OF, Rochester (So., Stanford), 7. Jake Randa, OF, Madison (So., Northwest Florida State JC), 8. Zach DeLoach, OF, Wisconsin (So., Texas A&M), 9. Baron Radcliff, OF, Kalamazoo (So., Georgia Tech), 10. Jaren Shelby, OF, Wisconsin (Jr., Kentucky).

INDIVIDUAL BATTING LEADERS

	AVG	AB	R	H	2B	3B	HR	RBI	SB
Augie Isaacson, INF, Duluth	.364	247	59	90	9	5	1	28	39
Alex Erro, INF, Fond du Lac	.348	178	23	62	7	0	1	35	5
Jordan Swiss, INF, Battle Creek	.339	168	35	57	6	3	4	31	7
Shane McGuire, C, La Crosse	.337	178	38	60	12	0	4	46	16
Tyler Reichenborn, OF, Willmar	.327	214	48	70	10	4	5	21	9
Mike Rothenberg, C, La Crosse	.326	175	28	57	7	1	5	26	0
Zach DeLoach, OF, Wisconsin	.323	198	38	64	17	1	5	38	10
Chris Gilbody, C, Duluth	.320	256	44	82	12	1	0	31	14
Jake Randa, OF, Madison	.318	261	57	83	22	1	9	53	6
Alex McGarry, INF, Rochester	.318	176	31	56	9	0	8	32	3

INDIVIDUAL PITCHING LEADERS

	W	L	ERA	G	SV	IP	H	BB	SO
Jon Young, Fond du Lac	4	2	1.71	12	1	58	52	17	40
Evan Johnson, St. Cloud	5	0	1.80	13	1	60	46	21	57
Kyle Virbitsky, Kalamazoo	4	1	2.48	12	0	69	63	20	42
Michael McCraith, Battle Creek	5	3	2.63	12	0	68	59	25	62
Hendry Rodriguez, Bismarck	5	4	2.71	11	0	63	43	39	68
Hayden Shenefield, Duluth	4	1	2.79	10	0	68	58	14	62
Kevin Tibor, Lakeshore	4	7	3.04	11	0	71	58	11	40
Kaleb Schmidt, Kenosha	3	4	3.32	14	0	60	48	39	52
Troy Newell, Duluth	6	2	3.32	11	0	60	35	40	51
Corey Binger, Willmar	4	2	3.64	14	0	59	57	17	38

PERFECT GAME COLLEGIATE LEAGUE

East Division	**W**	**L**	**PCT**	**GB**
Amsterdam Mohawks	29	17	.630	—
Albany Dutchmen	26	17	.605	1½
Saugerties Stallions	24	24	.500	6
Glens Falls Dragons	16	28	.364	12
Oneonta Outlaws	16	29	.356	12½
Central Division	**W**	**L**	**PCT**	**GB**
Mohawk Valley DiamondDawgs	26	19	.578	—
Watertown Rapids	26	21	.553	1
Utica Blue Sox	25	21	.543	1½
Adirondack Trail Blazers	19	26	.422	7
West Division	**W**	**L**	**PCT**	**GB**
Jamestown Jammers	31	14	.689	—
Geneva Red Wings	23	24	.489	9
Elmira Pioneers	21	26	.447	11
Newark Pilots	14	30	.318	16½

CHAMPIONSHIP: Jamestown Jammers defeated Amsterdam Mohawks, 2-1, in best-of-three championship series.

INDIVIDUAL BATTING LEADERS

	AVG	AB	R	H	2B	3B	HR	RBI	SB
Ryan Hernandez, INF, MV	.423	149	45	63	10	0	6	39	0
Ryan Toohers, INF, MV	.391	156	40	61	13	1	10	57	1
Austin Pollack, OF, MV	.386	153	37	59	9	0	1	24	21
Michael Russell, INF, WR	.376	133	32	50	11	0	6	32	1
Luis DeLeon, INF, Utica	.371	116	28	43	10	1	1	19	5
Allen Murphy, RHP, Newark	.369	111	27	41	10	6	6	41	4
Khalyd Cox, OF, Utica	.368	152	35	56	12	3	9	32	15
Julian Kurych, OF, WR	.365	126	37	46	13	0	2	21	11
Cameron Masterman, INF, AD	.357	126	23	45	6	1	1	27	9
Joseph Castellanos, INF, MV	.351	185	52	65	13	1	0	33	2

INDIVIDUAL PITCHING LEADERS

	W	L	ERA	G	SV	IP	H	BB	SO
Mason Hazelwood, Elmira	5	1	1.80	11	0	50	35	19	84
Deaven Phillips, AD	4	1	1.90	7	0	38	33	15	23

	W	L	ERA	G	SV	IP	H	BB	SO
Zack Durant, Amsterdam	3	1	1.96	11	0	41	34	20	47
Jack Buckley, WR	5	1	1.97	9	0	50	38	13	51
Mike Sansone, Adirondack	3	1	2.43	6	0	41	43	7	38
Blaise Lomon, Utica	3	0	2.70	9	0	43	30	30	54
R.J. Kuruts, Utica	1	3	2.98	15	0	42	41	11	40
Logan Moody, Oneonta	3	1	3.13	8	0	37	33	27	34
Rhyse Dee, Elmira	4	3	3.35	9	0	43	40	17	34
Jack Collins, Geneva	3	1	3.38	8	0	40	29	17	37

PROSPECT LEAGUE

East Division	W	L	PCT	GB
Kokomo Jackrabbits	37	22	.627	—
Chillicothe Paints	34	26	.567	3½
West Virginia Miners	30	29	.508	7
Champion City Kings	26	33	.441	11
Butler BlueSox	21	39	.350	16½
West Division	W	L	PCT	GB
Danville Dans	35	23	.603	—
Terre Haute Rex	35	24	.593	0½
Quincy Gems	33	27	.550	3
Springfield Sliders	28	30	.483	7
Hannibal Hoots	25	35	.417	11
Lafayette Aviators	22	38	.367	14

CHAMPIONSHIP: Terre Haute Rex defeated Kokomo Jackrabbits, 2-0, in best-of-three championship series.

INDIVIDUAL BATTING LEADERS

	AVG	AB	R	H	2B	3B	HR	RBI	SB
Richard Miller, INF, Springfield	.373	185	43	69	18	6	17	48	3
Joe Acker, OF, CC	.368	193	36	71	11	4	1	34	28
Kam Smith, INF, Lafayette	.358	159	35	57	20	3	7	34	8
Francisco Rodriguez, OF, Quincy	.347	199	47	69	13	4	7	33	18
Kobe Kato, INF, Danville	.346	156	35	54	9	1	2	19	27
Cody Klotz, RHP/OF, Quincy	.341	217	52	74	12	5	13	50	16
Andrew Czech, INF, Chillicothe	.340	215	45	73	21	2	9	56	5
Zachary Santoro, OF, CC	.333	159	32	53	7	4	1	15	10
Lorenzo Elion, INF, Terre Haute	.331	139	29	46	6	0	1	21	12
Ian Walters, INF, Kokomo	.329	219	39	72	11	2	3	35	11

INDIVIDUAL PITCHING LEADERS

	W	L	ERA	G	SV	IP	H	BB	SO
Chandler Coates, Kokomo	8	1	1.79	10	0	55	45	17	50
Chris Modrzynski, Chillicothe	4	2	2.47	10	0	58	52	10	37
Ben Stephens, Springfield	5	1	2.66	17	3	47	32	25	59
Alec Harris, Springfield	3	3	2.96	10	1	52	37	36	55
Michael Jacob, Chillicothe	5	1	3.06	10	1	53	38	16	58
Zack Harvey, Chillicothe	6	2	3.12	10	0	58	54	11	53
Adam Polansky, Terre Haute	4	3	4.53	9	0	58	61	19	47
Adam Nelson, Quincy	3	3	4.53	13	0	54	57	24	48
Taylor Perrett, Chillicothe	3	2	4.71	10	0	50	68	10	52
Alex McCune, CC	2	3	5.02	9	0	52	55	22	36

SOUTH FLORIDA COLLEGIATE LEAGUE

North Division	W	L	PCT	GB
Palm Beach Diamond Ducks	27	12	.692	—
Boynton Beach Buccaneers	20	20	.500	7½
Delray Beach Lightning	21	22	.488	8
Phipps Park Barracudas	10	20	.333	12½
Boca Raton Blazers	12	26	.321	14½
South Division	W	L	PCT	GB
West Boca Snappers	28	15	.651	—
Pompano Beach Clippers	21	11	.652	1½
Palm Beach Xtreme	22	21	.512	6
Fort Lauderdale Royals	16	18	.471	7½
Florida Pokers	11	23	.324	12½

CHAMPIONSHIP: West Boca Snappers defeated Palm Beach Diamond Dawgs, 2-0, in best-of-three championship series.

TOP 10 PROSPECTS: 1. Keegan Collett, RHP, Palm Beach Xtreme (Jr., Florida Gulf Coast), 2. Ryan Watson, RHP, Pompano Beach (Jr., Auburn), 3. Bryce Hulett, 1B, Boca Raton (So., State JC of Florida), 4. Matheu Nelson, C, Delray Beach (Fr., Florida State), 5. Vincent Martinez, C, Boca Raton (Fr., Stanford), 6. Jorge Iza, SS, Pompano Beach (Jr., New Orleans), 7. Matt Sellers, RHP, Boca Raton (Jr., Nova Southeastern, Fla.), 8. Emmanuel Fernandez, LHP, Fort Lauderdale (R-Fr., Santa Fe JC, Fla.), 9. Matt Mackey, C/OF, Florida (Jr., Eastern Illinois), 10. Justin Lara, OF, Florida (Sr., Keiser, Fla.).

INDIVIDUAL BATTING LEADERS

	AVG	AB	R	H	2B	3B	HR	RBI	SB
Owen Von Esslinger, C, BBB	.406	69	11	28	5	0	0	18	2
Keith Stevens, C, PBX	.403	77	18	31	11	1	4	33	5
Francisco Urbaez, INF, WBS	.397	116	32	46	7	0	0	16	10
Kohl Gilmore, INF, PBX	.386	70	17	27	8	0	1	13	1
A.J. Orrico, INF, BBB	.383	81	32	31	3	1	0	13	19
Anthony Harrold, INF, PBX	.380	100	24	38	9	2	3	26	1
Bryce Hulett, INF, Boca Raton	.375	112	20	42	9	1	2	23	5
Justin Lara, OF, Florida	.373	102	36	38	5	5	1	15	24
Matt Mackey, UTL, Florida	.371	97	29	36	10	1	9	36	6
Parker Stephens, INF, WBS	.364	88	11	32	6	0	0	17	3

INDIVIDUAL PITCHING LEADERS

	W	L	ERA	G	SV	IP	H	BB	SO
William Gibbons, BBB	3	2	1.25	10	0	36	30	6	36
Havier Sans, WBS	4	0	2.11	12	1	43	27	10	50
Nik Constantakos, Florida	1	2	2.38	8	0	34	21	12	53
Brant Brown, PBX	4	0	3.05	14	1	38	28	16	37
Gavin Gillespie, WBS	4	2	3.07	8	0	44	35	10	51
Justin Ricard, Fort Lauderdale	1	1	3.27	7	0	33	25	7	30
J.T. Eggert, BBB	3	1	3.27	11	0	33	27	23	50
Andrew Garbarini, PBX	3	1	3.49	12	0	39	25	27	24
Devin Adams, Florida	2	5	3.54	13	2	28	19	28	41
Sam Boies, Pompano Beach	3	1	3.67	11	1	27	19	27	30

SUNBELT LEAGUE

	W	L	PCT	GB
Norcross Astros	22	11	.667	—
Atlanta Crackers	20	12	.625	1½
Brookhaven Bucks	21	13	.618	1½
Marietta Patriots	18	17	.514	5
Gwinnett Tides	8	21	.276	12
Alpharetta Aviators	7	22	.241	13

CHAMPIONSHIP: Brookhaven Bucks defeated Marietta Patriots, 2-0, in best-of-three championship series.

INDIVIDUAL BATTING LEADERS

	AVG	AB	R	H	2B	3B	HR	RBI	SB
Jonathan Martin, OF, Gwinnett	.325	83	12	27	6	0	0	6	8
Zavier Lushington, OF, BB	.309	94	17	29	8	1	1	15	11
Matthew Vaccaro, 1B, Marietta	.304	92	11	28	3	0	1	15	0
Nick Wilhite, OF, Norcross	.304	115	21	35	8	0	0	10	15
Brandon Grover, OF, Marietta	.290	107	20	31	4	1	6	26	2
Kel Johnson, OF, Norcross	.281	96	14	27	8	1	6	27	1
Brock Maxwell, OF, Atlanta	.276	98	16	27	4	1	0	9	8
Nate Stinson, OF, Marietta	.276	105	26	29	8	0	2	9	6
Sam Freitas, INF, Norcross	.276	98	12	27	4	0	1	15	4
Roury Glanton, OF, Atlanta	.270	89	16	24	4	0	4	18	5

INDIVIDUAL PITCHING LEADERS

	W	L	ERA	G	SV	IP	H	BB	SO
Zach Williams, BB	4	0	0.99	6	0	27	22	13	30
Michael Mayuski, Atlanta	3	0	1.39	19	0	32	21	7	25
Jordan Ward, BB	5	2	1.57	8	0	46	34	6	34
Harrison Osborn, Marietta	3	0	1.78	8	0	30	29	6	18
William Griffin, Marietta	2	1	2.41	9	0	37	23	11	43
Harrison Fant, BB	3	2	2.43	8	0	41	25	19	42
Brock Carter, Atlanta	3	3	2.46	10	0	37	29	8	37
Jay Pendley, Atlanta	5	1	2.84	9	0	38	31	13	48
Tate Stone-Frisina, Norcross	0	2	2.91	13	0	34	29	8	42
Austin Hunter, BB	2	1	2.93	9	0	43	26	20	38

TEXAS COLLEGIATE LEAGUE

	W	L	PCT	GB
Brazos Valley Bombers	48	7	.873	—
Acadiana Cane Cutters	33	24	.579	16
Victoria Generals	28	28	.500	20½

Woodlands Strykers	16	40	.286	32 ½
Texas Marshals	15	41	.268	33 ½

CHAMPIONSHIP: Victoria Generals defeated Acadiana Cane Cutters, 2-1, in best-of-three championship series.

INDIVIDUAL BATTING LEADERS

	AVG	AB	R	H	2B	3B	HR	RBI	SB
Thomas Jeffries, INF, Victoria	.385	156	39	60	5	4	2	37	41
Rhett McCall, C, Acadiana	.361	155	30	56	7	0	2	28	10
Michael Williams, OF, Victoria	.343	178	32	61	6	8	0	27	22
Ben Rowden, 2B, Texas	.319	135	30	43	8	2	2	20	9
Luis Vargas, OF, Victoria	.315	143	26	45	7	3	3	22	7
Cole Secrest, OF, Acadiana	.313	176	38	55	10	0	4	30	6
Cole Coker, OF, Brazos Valley	.312	173	28	54	9	2	2	28	16
Robin Adames, 3B, Brazos Valley	.299	157	23	47	9	0	4	25	13
Mason Corbett, OF, Acadiana	.283	145	26	41	7	1	0	18	3
Zavier Moore, 3B, Texas	.283	152	19	43	12	0	4	26	9

INDIVIDUAL PITCHING LEADERS

	W	L	ERA	G	SV	IP	H	BB	SO
Ben Butler, Brazos Valley	0	1	0.50	16	0	18	21	7	8
Jared Biddy, Brazos Valley	5	0	0.59	9	0	15	10	1	18
Cody Collins, Brazos Valley	1	0	0.84	9	0	21	11	6	19
Jake Woodland, Victoria	0	2	1.65	10	0	16	11	5	14
Chandler Jozwiak, Brazos Valley	1	1	2.14	4	0	21	15	8	24
Matthew Beck, Acadiana	3	2	2.27	8	0	32	14	26	47
Brayson Smith, Acadiana	3	0	2.32	5	0	31	23	11	38
Austin Hendrix, Brazos Valley	4	1	2.38	9	0	45	32	16	58
Gabriel Sequeira, Victoria	2	0	2.46	4	0	22	21	7	18
Dylan Lester, Brazos Valley	2	2	2.49	6	0	22	21	7	22

VALLEY LEAGUE

North Division	W	L	PCT	GB
Purcellville Cannons	25	17	.595	—
Front Royal Cardinals	24	18	.571	1
New Market Rebels	24	18	.571	1
Winchester Royals	22	20	.524	3
Strasburg Express	17	25	.405	8
Woodstock River Bandits	5	37	.119	20
South Division	**W**	**L**	**PCT**	**GB**
Covington Lumberjacks	26	16	.619	—
Charlottesville TomSox	24	18	.571	2
Waynesboro Generals	24	18	.571	2
Staunton Braves	20	22	.476	6
Harrisonburg Turks	20	22	.476	6

CHAMPIONSHIP: New Market Rebels defeated Charlottesville TomSox, 2-0, in best-of-three championship series.

TOP 10 PROSPECTS: 1. Jeremy Cook, LHP, Staunton (So., Miami), 2. Andrew Eyster, OF, New Market (So., South Carolina), 3. Fred Villarreal, RHP, Waynesboro (Jr., Houston), 4. Anu Oraj, OF, New Market (So., Wallace State JC, Ala.), 5. Kyle Arjona, RHP, Harrisonburg (Sr., New Orleans), 6. Trevin Eubanks, RHP, New Market (Sr., Southern Mississippi), 7. Dominic D'Alessandro, UTL, Charlottesville (Sr., George Washington), 8. Rafe Schindler, RHP, Harrisonburg (So., New Orleans), 9. Anthony ZImmerman, RHP, Purcellville (Sr., Fordham), 10. Jared Wetherbee, LHP, Charlottesville (So., Elon).

INDIVIDUAL BATTING LEADERS

	AVG	AB	R	H	2B	3B	HR	RBI	SB
Andrew Eyster, OF, New Market	.421	114	32	48	14	0	9	35	6
Chase Cheek, OF, Waynesboro	.394	109	20	43	11	1	1	19	12
Austin Embler, INF, HT	.388	116	26	45	7	4	4	23	2
Andrew Burden, 1B, FRC	.385	135	34	52	12	2	5	32	4
Trey Jacobs, INF, Staunton	.376	141	27	53	13	0	8	37	3
Patrick McColl, 1B, CTS	.368	136	29	50	7	1	3	27	3
Oraj Anu, OF, New Market	.358	123	32	44	8	1	8	26	8
Kendall Small, 1B, Front Royal	.354	130	15	46	10	0	2	24	1
J.D. Mundy, 3B, Covington	.353	139	36	49	7	0	14	48	0
Bennett Hostetler, SS, Covington	.353	136	26	48	14	0	1	21	5

INDIVIDUAL PITCHING LEADERS

	W	L	ERA	G	SV	IP	H	BB	SO
Gabriel Ponce, Front Royal	3	0	2.27	9	0	40	27	22	32
Evan McAndrew, Covington	4	1	2.65	10	0	34	32	18	39
Chance Hroch, Strasburg	2	1	2.92	9	0	37	28	10	33
Chase Best, Covington	6	3	3.38	17	3	35	32	14	39
Justin Showalter, Staunton	3	1	3.43	12	0	42	40	13	30
Jordyn Eglite, Covington	3	1	3.79	16	2	38	33	8	42
Luke Scherzer, Harrisonburg	2	3	3.82	9	0	38	40	5	32
Ryan Kennedy, Winchester	2	3	3.95	7	0	41	47	9	36
Jacob Bradley, Woodstock	2	3	3.98	12	0	41	44	29	42
Evan Richardson, Winchester	4	2	4.32	7	0	42	37	22	33

WEST COAST LEAGUE

North Division	W	L	PCT	GB
Bellingham Bells	35	19	.648	—
Kelowna Falcons	28	26	.519	7
Victoria HarbourCats	27	27	.500	8
Yakima Valley Pippins	27	27	.500	8
Wenatchee AppleSox	26	28	.481	9
Port Angeles Lefties	21	33	.389	14
South Division	**W**	**L**	**PCT**	**GB**
Portland Pickles	37	17	.685	—
Corvallis Knights	36	18	.667	1
Walla Walla Sweets	28	26	.519	9
Cowlitz Black Bears	20	34	.370	17
Bend Elks	12	42	.222	25

CHAMPIONSHIP: Corvallis Knights defeated Kelowna Falcons, 2-0, in best-of-three championship series.

INDIVIDUAL BATTING LEADERS

	AVG	AB	R	H	2B	3B	HR	RBI	SB
Kyle Dean, OF, Yakima Valley	.374	139	24	52	8	4	2	24	1
Trent Tinglestad, OF, Kelowna	.350	157	30	55	13	0	9	40	0
Connor McCord, INF, Wenatchee	.346	162	27	56	9	1	6	37	1
Jason Dichochea, 2B, Port Angeles	.336	140	29	47	11	0	7	23	5
Dan Pruitt, INF, Kelowna	.331	130	24	43	7	0	7	26	6
Cody Hawken, OF, Corvallis	.331	172	37	57	10	1	3	30	12
Johnny Sage, OF, Wenatchee	.326	138	22	45	10	0	0	19	5
Carson Breshears, INF, Portland	.325	120	28	39	7	2	1	24	7
Chad Stevens, INF, Corvallis	.322	208	42	67	9	6	3	28	15
Gio Diaz, SS, Portland	.320	197	45	63	12	0	5	31	18

INDIVIDUAL PITCHING LEADERS

	W	L	ERA	G	SV	IP	H	BB	SO
Landen Bourassa, Corvallis	5	1	1.96	8	0	46	36	9	39
Bryce Moyle, Walla Walla	4	2	2.09	11	0	47	45	20	50
Cullen Kafka, Yakima Valley	3	3	2.37	9	0	46	49	10	50
Zach Heaton, Cowlitz	3	2	2.53	9	0	53	47	7	35
Curtis Bafus, Wenatchee	4	5	2.88	11	0	66	64	17	72
Sam Muskat, Bend	3	3	2.89	11	0	44	44	17	31
Trevor Brigden, Kelowna	4	4	2.95	11	0	58	63	22	69
Jack Gonzales, Yakima Valley	2	1	3.04	22	0	47	48	21	39
Garrett Goodall, Victoria	2	1	3.05	9	0	44	49	7	33
Chase Farrell, Yakima Valley	2	2	3.46	10	0	52	41	11	57

HIGH
SCHOOL

Parkview Dynasty Pushes Forward

Parkview High won its seventh Georgia state title with a 36-6 record in 2018.

BY CARLOS COLLAZO

The expectations at Parkview High School are high.

The Lilburn, Ga., program has had just two head baseball coaches since the school opened, and that consistency in leadership has translated into consistent success on the field.

From 1996 to 2015, the school won six state championships and was named the Baseball America High School Team of the Year in 2012 and 2015.

That's why a 2017 season, when the team went 31-6 and made it to the quarterfinals of the 7-A state championship, is considered by most to be a disappointment.

"Last year we lost in the quarterfinals with a team that should have won it, to be honest with you," Parkview head coach Chan Brown said.

Parkview lost in a three-game series to Woodstock (Ga.) High, which made the championship game. Prior to the 2018 season, Brown sat down with his seniors to discuss the upcoming season.

"We kind of hash things out, as far as expectations and that type of stuff," Brown said. "Their motto they came up with was 'Unfinished Business.'"

Parkview had a few bumps in the road early in the season—including losses to North Gwinnett (Suwanee, Ga.) High and Mill Creek (Hoschton, Ga.) High—but followed their top pitchers, lefthanders Robert Bennett and Braden Hays—to a 25-5 record in the regular season.

"(They) were our vocal leaders in the locker room and on the field," Brown said of the two southpaws, who each recorded 12 wins on the season. "They really showed up big-time as far as leadership goes."

Hays, a Georgia Southern commit, posted a 0.79 ERA and led the team with 108 strikeouts and just 16 walks. Bennett, a Chipola (Fla.) JC commit, posted a 1.19 ERA with 94 strikeouts and was also a crucial bat in the lineup, with a .381/529/.680 slash line and six home runs.

Eventually, Parkview made its way back into the 7-A state playoffs and found a familiar oppenent waiting in the semifinals. The day the semifinals started, Brown and his coaching staff put up signs in the batting cages, in the locker room, in the weight room—anywhere the team would see them. The signs read: "Woodstock 1, Parkview 0."

Unfinished business indeed.

"That was the first thing those kids did was go around and take those signs down when that happened," Brown said.

Shortly thereafter, Parkview took down the actual team that haulted their season a year before, beating Woodstock in a three-game series, 2-1, after losing Game 1 and pulling out an extra-inning victory in Game 2.

After taking down Woodstock, Parkview was matched up in the championship series with Mill Creek, who beat Parkview in the fifth game of the season. The Tigers made even shorter work in the championship, taking down Mill Creek in two games.

Hays and Bennett combined for 13.1 innings with 11 strikeouts and just one earned run over two games, while senior catcher and outfielder

Logan Cerny went 4-for-6 with two home runs, including a walk-off homer to win Game 1.

"(When it comes to) just leading by example and kind of putting it all on the line," Brown said, "especially the last half of the season, that would be Logan Cerny. He hit six home runs in the playoffs."

Cerny, a Troy commit, led the team with 10 home runs during the seaon and hit .397/.517/.767 with a team-high 43 runs and 46 RBI.

Cerny's offensive efforts helped Parkview avenge their 2017 disappointments and win the 2018 Georgia 7-A state championship. It was the team's seventh state title. For that, Parkview earned Baseball America's High School Team of the Year award for the third time since 2012, when current Athletics first baseman Matt Olson was leading Parkview to a fifth state title.

It's just the latest achievement in Parkview's ongoing dynasty.

"2011 was our first state championship under myself," Brown said. "And we started off 3-5 that year. So it was one of those years that was ugly at the beginning. We actually won the state championship with a 26-10 record. So that honestly, the 2010 and 2011 teams, I think the way I look back at them have kind of started this run that we've been on. And I think those senior classes kind of a put a staple on a new beginning.

"In 2005 when I took over we went to the semifinals and then we went to the quarterfinals (the next year), (and then the) quarterfinals (the year after that)—we just couldn't get over the hump. In 2010, our coaching staff and the program as a whole kind of revamped, got some new energy, some new ideas and since then we've taken off a little bit."

Three state titles in seven years and more Baseball America High School Team of the Year awards than any high school program in the nation.

The program responsible for Olson and Jeff Keppinger and former first-round pick and Braves No. 1 prospect Jeff Francoeur, has always had high expectations.

After yet another title in 2018, those expectations might have just gotten higher.

Florida Burn Takes Jupiter

At the 2017 Perfect Game World Wood Bat Association (WWBA) World Championship, Florida Burn Platinum was eliminated in the first round of bracket play.

Shortstop and third baseman Joshua Rivera—one of the most talented players on the team as a junior—struggled mightily at the plate and went hitless across four games and 12 plate appearances.

HIGH SCHOOL TOP 50

Rank School	Record
1. Parkview HS, Lilburn, Ga.	36-6
2. Har-Ber HS, Springdale, Ark.	30-4
3. Riverdale Baptist HS, Marlboro, Md.	32-1
4. Mountain Vista HS, Highlands Ranch, Col.	26-1
5. Valley Christian HS, San Jose, Calif.	29-3
6 St. Vianney HS, Kirkwood, Mo.	36-2
7 La Cueva HS, Albuqurque, N.M.	27-3
8 Pope HS, Marietta, Ga.	34-8
9 DeSoto Central HS, Southaven, Miss.	27-8
10 St. Xavier HS, Louisville	35-2
11 St. Thomas Aquinas HS, Fort Lauderdale, Fla.	25-3
12 Capistrano Valley HS, Mission Viejo, Calif.	25-10
13 Argyle (Texas) HS	37-0
14 Union HS, Tulsa, Okla.	24-13
15 Monsignor Pace HS, Miami	22-6
16 Yucaipa (Calif.) HS	28-5
17 Central HS, Baton Rouge, La.	26-12
18 De La Salle HS, Concord, Calif.	26-4
19 Auburn (Ala.) HS	35-7
20 Nogales (Ariz.) HS	30-5
21 Carroll HS, Southlake, Texas	33-6
22 Jupiter (Fla.) HS	19-11
23 Torrey Pines HS, San Diego	29-6
24 Eaton HS, Fort Worth, Texas	34-9
25 Jefferson HS, Tampa, Fla.	22-8
26 Olentangy Liberty HS, Powell, Ohio	30-4
27 Maranatha HS, Pasadena, Calif.	27-4
28 Bishop Kelley HS, Tulsa, Okla.	21-7
29 Blue Valley HS, Stilwell, Kan.	22-3
30 Mills Creek HS, Hoschton, Ga.	34-8
31 Orange (Calif.) Lutheran HS	25-8
32 Calvary Christian HS, Clearwater, Fla.	30-1
33 Pascack Hills HS, Montvale, N.J.	23-2
34 Aurora (Ill.) Christian HS	33-2
35 Venice (Fla.) HS	23-7
36 Foothills HS, Santa Ana, Calif.	25-8
37 Fishers (Ind.) HS	28-7
38 Monroe Campus HS, Bronx, N.Y.	23-1
39 Sulphur (La.) HS	35-10
40 Greenwood (Ark.) HS	31-0
41 Seaman HS, Topeka, Kan.	25-4
42 Beckman HS, Irvine, Calif.	26-4
43 Reagan HS, San Antonio, Texas	38-10
44 St. Francis HS, Mountain View, Calif.	24-8
45 Eastlake HS, Chula Vista, Calif.	28-5
46 Forney (Texas) HS	29-14
47 Dorman HS, Roebuck, S.C.	25-9
48 Aurora (Mo.) HS	31-1
49 Loganville (Ga.) HS	35-6
50 Stillwater (Minn.) HS	21-5

One year later at the 2018 edition of the tournament, those two facts couldn't be further away in the rear-view mirror.

Florida Burn Platinum played twice as many games in the 20th year of the event, winning all eight of their games and outscoring their opponents 25-9, including a 2-0 championship game victory over Canes National—all with Rivera, the co-MVP of the tournament, leading the way.

"Josh is the most talented player on our team, no doubt about it," said Florida Burn general manager Mark Guthrie, who pitched 15 years in the major leagues. "He's physical, but he is competitive. There's a lot of talented guys who are not winning today. But you have to have that guy to rally around. The kids have to be able to see that. And he makes everyone around him better."

Hitting in the three-hole and playing shortstop for Florida Burn during the five-day tournament, Rivera hit .438/.545/.625 with a home run, six RBIs and six runs, tacking on four stolen bases in four attempts for good measure. A 6-foot-2, 205-pound infielder, Rivera has some strength currently with plenty of more coming in the future as he continues to develop.

"I'm more of a consistent hitter," said Rivera, who is committed to Florida. "Power is going to come, but what my dad always tells me (is) homers will come by themselves. So I try to stick with my consistency. Just step in there, stick to my approach, try to barrel anything.

"Any pitch that's there I just try to put the barrel on it and stick opposite field mostly. Because I have an inside-out swing, but if it's an inside pitch I'll pull the hands onto it."

Rivera had a quiet championship game, going 0-for-2 at the plate, but it's hard to envision the team making the championship in the first place without his efforts at the plate, in the field, and—more surprisingly—on the mound.

"(Rivera) pitched the other day and was battling through against the East Cobb ST team," Guthrie said of the 1.2 relief innings Rivera threw in the second round. "And again, he's a talented kid, he throws 88-90 mph, but he doesn't pitch a lot. He came in to shut a game down for us, and (he's) very emotional in a good way—a competitive emotional.

"But you have to have that guy. You can have a bunch of gritty guys, but that one leader gets you to the next level."

Rivera helped elevate Florida Burn to the championship level, but from there, his teammates helped shoulder the load. First baseman William Bartlett—an Arizona commit who also plays high school ball with Rivera at IMG Academy in Bradenton, Fla.—got Florida Burn on the scoreboard in the first inning with a hard-hit, RBI single down the first base line.

Bartlett went 1-for-1 with a walk in the championship game and hit .400/.526/.600 with one home run and six RBIs over the course of the tournament, giving the Burn a powerful 3-4 punch in the middle of their lineup.

Bartlett also flashed the leather at first base, snagging a hard line drive that started a double play in the second inning, and in the seventh inning he threw his large, 6-foot-3, 220-pound frame to the left to make a difficult diving catch that prevented an extra-base hit, which could have

gotten the Canes back in the game.

Thin on arms, a pair of primary position players toed the rubber in relief for the Burn against one of the deepest lineups in the tournament. Outfielder Cameron Waderman threw 2.1 innings and allowed just two hits, while leadoff hitter Mac Guscette closed out the final 2.1 innings without allowing a hit.

"We were short on pitchers because we don't really have all of our pitchers with us," Rivera said. "So we just threw some position guys in and they went out there and did their job. Pounded the strike zone, got the batters guessing at what was coming and we just made all the routine plays and did everything we needed to do situationally."

Guthrie agreed.

"We had guys pitching at the end who don't get to pitch a lot," he said. "But we put our best competitors on the mound and winners win. Those guys are going to compete."

In addition to his work on the mound, Guscette went 1-for-3 at the plate and had a two-out, RBI single in the sixth inning that gave the Burn a much-needed insurance run to make the score 2-0. Predominantly a catcher, Guscette is a member of the 2020 draft class and, like Rivera, also committed to Florida.

"Mac is a winner," Guthrie said. "He is an unbelievable catcher. He is probably the most underrated player in his class. Whether he goes to pro ball or to the University of Florida, he's going to lead his team wherever he goes and we're fortunate enough to have him for another year."

After getting eliminated early in 2017, the Burn managed to put everything together and go a perfect 8-0, winning the biggest travel ball tournament in the country against plenty of teams who were the supposed favorites.

"It's an amazing feeling," Rivera said, in between taking celebration pictures with his teammates and his new MVP trophy. "As a team we've always been ruled the underdog, every tournament we've played in. Everybody usually thought it was an easy game against us, but then we started advancing. ... It was tough—for both teams. It's big time. It's big for our organization."

It's certainly a big accomplishment for the Florida Burn, but for Guthrie—who spent several innings of the championship game receiving and passing along encouraging texts from former players—it was about something else.

"You know what, it's more important for the kids, really, than the program," Guthrie said. "I love the memory of it for them, going forward.

"When they are juniors in college, hopefully we have another team here one day, they take pride in

AMATEUR/YOUTH CHAMPIONS 2018

ALL-AMERICAN AMATEUR BASEBALL ASSOCIATION (AAABA)

Event	Site	Champion	Runner-up
World Series (21U)	Johnstown, Pa.	Martella's Pharmacy	New Orleans Boosters

AMERICAN LEGION BASEBALL

Event	Site	Champion	Runner-up
World Series (19U)	Shelby, N.C.	Wilmington, Del.	Las Vegas, Nev.

BABE RUTH BASEBALL

Event	Site	Champion	Runner-up
Cal Ripken (10U)	Vincennes, Ind.	Hawaii	Lexington, Ken.
Cal Ripken 12-year-old (60 feet)	Phoenix City, Ala.	Kingsburg	Palm Beach Gardens, Fla.
Cal Ripken 13-year-old (70 feet)	Branson, Mo.	Japan	Glen Allen, Va.
13-year-old	Mt. Home, Ark.	Five Cities, Calif.	Eagle Pass, Texas
14-year-old	Eagle Pass, Texas	Atlantic Shore, N.J.	Honolulu, Hawaii
13-15-year-olds	Longview, Wash.	Tallahassee, Fla.	Mifflin County, Pa.
16-18-year-olds	Jamestown, N.Y.	Charleston, S.C.	Alabama

LITTLE LEAGUE BASEBALL

Event	Site	Champion	Runner-up
Little League (11-12)	Williamsport, Pa.	Honolulu, Hawaii	South Korea
Junior League (12-14)	Taylor, Mich.	Taoyuan City, Chinese Taipei	Lufkin, Texas
Senior League (13-16)	Easley, S.C.	Willemstad, Curacao	Wilmington, Del.
Intermediate (50/70)	Livermore, Calif.	Seoul, South Korea	Livermore/Granada

NATIONAL AMATEUR BASEBALL FEDERATION (NBAF)

Event	Site	Champion	Runner-up
Rookie (10U)	Tuxedo Park, N.Y.	New Jersey Renedaes, New York Devil Cats (Co-Champs)	
Freshman (12U)	Tuxedo Park, N.Y.	New York Devil Cats	New York Phenoms
Sophomore (14U)	Struthers, Ohio	Roth Brothers, Ohio	Astro Falcons, Ohio
Junior (16U)	Struthers, Ohio	Astro Falcons, Ohio	Brooklyn Bonnie Rockets, N.Y.
High School (17U)	Ellicott, Ohio.	Bonnie Cougars, N.Y.	Brooklyn Cougars, N.Y.
Senior (18U)	Struthers, Ohio	Baird Brothers, Ohio	Michigan College Connect

PERFECT GAME/BCS FINALS

Event	Site	Champion	Runner-up
11U	Fort Myers, Fla.	ESP Matrix	Legit Baseball Club 11U
12U	Fort Myers, Fla.	Team Elite South	Naples Cyclones
13U	Fort Myers, Fla.	Canes Florida Prime 2023	Elite Squad Outlaws
14U	Fort Myers, Fla.	5 Star National 14U King	East Cobb Astros 14U
15U	Fort Myers, Fla.	Molina Stars	Sticks Baseball Academy 2021 Elite
16U	Fort Myers, Fla.	5 Star National Buress	Top Tier Roos 16U Americans
17U	Fort Myers, Fla.	Elite Squad 17U American	Florida Burn 2019 Platinum
18U	Fort Myers, Fla.	Top Tier Hoffmann	Academy Baseball Canada

it and it's something for them. It's an experience, hopefully, that they can remember forever."

Notable 2018 Performances

■ RHP **Gunnar Hoglund** showcased impeccable command for a prep pitcher throughout the spring season with Fivay High in Hudson, Fla. The 6-foot-4, 210-pound righthander walked just two batters during the season, and both of those walks came in his final outing. He finished the year with 105 strikeouts, good for a ludicrous strikeout-to-walk ratio of 52.5-to-1 over 52 innings against solid Florida competition. Hoglund was later drafted by the Pirates in the supplemental first round, but the two could not come to terms on a signing bonus, leaving Hoglund to make his way to campus at Mississippi.

■ RHP **Grayson Rodriguez** completely changed his image on the mound after an intensive offseason workout routine, cutting bad weight from his large, 6-foot-5 frame and seeing jumps across the board in his stuff. After throwing in the upper 80s and low 90s during summer showcases, Rodriguez wowed Texas scouts during the spring by ramping his fastball up into the upper-90s. Rodriguez struck out 156 batters over 75 innings for his Central Heights High School, in Nacogdoches, Texas, and was later drafted in the first round by the Orioles, with the 11th overall pick. Rodriguez and the team agreed to a signing bonus of $4.3 million—the third-richest prep bonus of the draft.

■ OF **Nick Schnell** was one of the most impressive hitters in the country, despite getting off to a late start during the spring, thanks to the weather that's inevitable in the Upper Midwest, but was particularly difficult this spring. The Roncalli High (Indianapolis) outfielder hit .541 with 15 home runs and 19 stolen bases and wound

PERFECT GAME/WORLD WOOD BAT ASSOCIATION SUMMER CHAMPIONSHIPS

Event	Site	Champion	Runner-up
14U	Cartersville, Ga.	Canes National 14U	Dulins Dodgers-Wright
15U	Cartersville, Ga.	Louisiana Knights Black	Sheets Baseball 15U
16U	Cartersville, Ga.	Team Elite Prime 16U	MWE 16U
17U	Cartersville, Ga.	Team GA/MBA 17U Gold	CBA Marucci National
18U	Cartersville, Ga.	East Cobb Astros	Team Elite 17U Prime

PONY BASEBALL

Event	Site	Champion	Runner-up
Mustang 9U	Walnut, Calif.	Mililani, Hawaii	Tijuana, Mexico
Mustang 10U	Youngsville, La.	Tijuana, Mexico	Placentia, Calif.
Bronco 11U	Chesterfield, Va.	Chicago (AFCA), Ill.	California
Bronco 12U	Los Alamitos, Calif.	Kaohsiung City, Chinese Taipei	Mexico City, Mexico
Pony 13U	Whittier, Calif.	Seoul, South Korea	Placentia, Calif.
Pony 14U	Washington, Pa.	Taipei County, Chinese Taipei	Long Beach, Calif.
Colt (15-16)	Lafayette, Ind.	Levittown, Puerto Rico	Seoul, South Korea
Palomino (17-18)	Santa Clara, Calif.	Taoyuan County, Chinese Taipei	Los Angeles, Calif.

REVIVING BASEBALL IN INNER CITIES (RBI)

Event	Site	Champion	Runner-up
Junior (13-15)	Minnesota	Tampa Rays (West) RBI	Philadelphia Phillies (East) RBI
Senior (16-18)	Minnesota	Chicago White Sox (West) RBI	Arizona (West) RBI

U.S. SPECIALTY SPORTS ASSOCIATION (USSSA)

Event	Site	Champion	Runner-up
10U/Majors Elite	Viera, Fla.	Easton Elite	Midwest Elite Kemp
11U/Majors Elite	Viera, Fla.	MVP Hustle Prieto	SGSA Sharks
12U/Majors Elite	Viera, Fla.	Team Dirty South Bats	Team Clutch
13U/Majors Elite	Viera, Fla.	Louisiana Sox	Elite Squad Outlaws
14U/Majors Elite	Viera, Fla.	Sand Baseball	El Paso Sun Kings

USA BASEBALL

Event	Site	Champion	Runner-up
Tournament of Stars (18 & Under)	Cary, N.C.	Braves	United
USA Baseball 17U—East	Palm Beach County, Fla.	Rawlings Stealth Florida Underclass	16U KC Royals Scout Team
USA Baseball 17U—West	Peoria, Ariz.	San Diego Show	CBA Marucci
USA Baseball 15U—East	Palm Beach County, Fla.	Team Elite American	Louisiana Knights
USA Baseball 15U—West	Peoria, Ariz.	Pacific Baseball Academy	NCTB Prime
USA Baseball 14U—East	Palm Beach County, Fla.	Kangaroo Court Roos 14U	Kangaroo Court Roos 13U
USA Baseball 14U—West	Peoria, Ariz.	3D Gold	Pacific Baseball Academy

up being selected with the 32nd overall pick in the draft by the Rays. Schnell signed for a bonus of $2.3 million.

■ RHP **Carter Stewart** was a member of Baseball America's All-American First Team, along with Hoglund and Rodriguez, matching up with fellow first round pick RHP Mason Denaburg in a heavily scouted high school game to start the season in Merritt Island, Fla. After showcasing one of the best breaking balls that major league teams have seen at the prep level in years—with a spin rate regularly north of 3,000 rpm—over the summer, Stewart increased his fastball velocity in the spring to give the Mississippi State commit a pair of potential 70-grade offerings. That was enough for the Braves to make Stewart the first prep righthander off the board, at No. 8 overall, though the two sides failed to come to an agreement on a signing bonus after a medical caused Atlanta to lower its offer. Stewart struck out 128 batters and walked just 18 in 62 innings for Eau Gallie High in Melbourne, Fla.

■ OF **Jordyn Adams** was the biggest pop-up player on the hitting side for the 2018 class. While his talents were enough to get him invited to the 2017 Under Armour All-America Game—where he hit a walk-off single—most major league teams were hesitant to put a Day 1 draft grade on the athletic outfielder thanks a short track record of hitting. A four-star wide receiver committed to North Carolina to play both football and baseball, many teams believed his price tag would be higher than his present talent on the baseball field warranted. That all changed when Adams shined on a national stage at the 2018 National High School Invitational at USA Baseball's Training Complex in Cary, N.C. Playing for Green Hope High as the host school just a mile away from the USA Baseball Complex, Adams showcased a hit tool that was much more polished than both area scouts and scouting directors expected to see. In a field that included no-doubt Day One prospects like SS Brice Turang, 3B Nolan Gorman, 3B Triston Casas and OF Alek Thomas, Adams more than held his own and was arguably the most impressive hitter. The Angels rewarded him by taking him with pick No. 17 and signing him for $4.1 million.

Cole Winn Coasts In California

BY CARLOS COLLAZO

When Eric Borba first heard that Cole Winn would potentially be transferring to his program, he wasn't sure what to think.

Initially, he didn't even know the name of the uber-talented Colorado righthander who was pondering a move to the most prestigious region in the country for high school baseball.

"I got a call from my assistant coach about late July," said Borba, the head coach of Orange (Calif.) Lutheran High. "It was about a week before the Area Code [Games] and he just said, 'Hey, there's a pitcher from Colorado who is potentially going to be coming out to OLu.' I said, 'What's his name?' He didn't even know it at the time."

It took no time at all for Borba and the rest of the program to realize the sort of talent that the Lancers would be getting with Winn's transfer. Borba went to the Area Code Games to watch Winn pitch and saw one of the most dominant performances of any pitcher over the summer.

"Talking to his dad at the Area Codes, I said, 'Man, that's first-round stuff.' "

It was also Baseball America High School Player of the Year stuff. Winn joins MacKenzie Gore (2017), Dylan Bundy (2011) and Ethan Martin (2008) as the only pitchers to win the award in the past 10 years.

Winn's move out west was part baseball, part business. His father Randy worked with a lot of clients in Orange County and decided that he would open up an office in the area. If Cole were going to move to the top prep baseball hotbed in the country along with that, well, that was just fine.

"The guy moved 1,000 miles and just had a tremendous impact on our program," Borba said. "Not just the quality of our team, but he changed the culture in our program.

"His desire to win and his desire to be great just raised the level of the rest of the team. You could see the competitive fire in the guy when he takes the mound. It just seemed like no moment was too big for him, and every challenge that came in front of him he rose up and it just really set a tone for our program."

Winn helped lead Orange Lutheran to its second straight National High School Invitational championship and was the most impressive pitcher in a field that included fellow first-round

PLAYER OF THE YEAR

PREVIOUS WINNERS

1992: Preston Wilson, of/rhp, Bamberg-Ehrhardt (S.C.) HS
1993: Trot Nixon, of/lhp, New Hanover HS, Wilmington, N.C.
1994: Doug Million, lhp, Sarasota (Fla.) HS
1995: Ben Davis, c, Malvern (Pa.) Prep
1996: Matt White, rhp, Waynesboro Area (Pa.) HS
1997: Darnell McDonald, of, Cherry Creek HS, Englewood, Colo.
1998: Drew Henson, 3b/rhp, Brighton (Mich.) HS
1999: Josh Hamilton, of/lhp, Athens Drive HS, Raleigh, N.C.
2000: Matt Harrington, rhp, Palmdale (Calif.) HS
2001: Joe Mauer, c, Cretin-Derham Hall HS, St. Paul, Minn.
2002: Scott Kazmir, lhp, Cypress Falls HS, Houston
2003: Jeff Allison, rhp, Veterans Memorial HS, Peabody, Mass.
2004: Homer Bailey, rhp, LaGrange (Texas) HS
2005: Justin Upton, ss, Great Bridge HS, Chesapeake, Va.
2006: Adrian Cardenas, ss/2b, Mons. Pace HS, Opa Locka, Fla.
2007: Mike Moustakas, ss, Chatsworth (Calif.) HS
2008: Ethan Martin, rhp/3b, Stephens County HS, Toccoa, Ga.
2009: Bryce Harper, c, Las Vegas HS
2010: Kaleb Cowart, rhp/3b, Cook HS, Adel, Ga.
2011: Dylan Bundy, rhp, Owasso (Okla.) HS
2012: Byron Buxton, of, Appling County HS, Baxley, Ga.
2013: Clint Frazier, of, Loganville (Ga.) HS
2014: Alex Jackson, OF, Rancho Bernardo (Calif.) HS
2015: Kyle Tucker, OF, Plant HS, Tampa
2016: Mickey Moniak, OF, La Costa Canyon HS, Carlsbad, Calif.
2017: MacKenzie Gore, LHP, Whiteville (N.C.) HS

pick Matthew Liberatore. He struck out nine batters in Orange Lutheran's opening round game against Florence (Ala.) High and didn't allow a ball to leave the infield.

It wasn't just the one high-profile event that established Winn's credentials. He routinely took the ball for the Lancers and was arguably the most consistent pitcher in the nation. He went 6-2, 0.25 through 55 innings, with 93 strikeouts and just eight walks. Winn allowed just two earned runs on 21 hits

His consistent dominance compelled the Rangers to make him the 15th overall pick in the 2018 draft. He was the first player selected out of California .

"The way he performed with the expectations on him, he did such a great job," Randy Winn said. "He really did. He never let the stuff bother him and he had every right to. I was waiting for one game for him to not make it out of the second or third inning, just blow it. But he just never did.

"He stayed consistent, and I think it's a testament to him on how hard he really worked to get there."

ALL-AMERICA TEAM

Cole Winn

DONN PARRIS/FOUR SEAM

Anthony Seigler

BILL MITCHELL

FIRST TEAM

Pos.	Player, School	YR.	AVG	AB	R	H	2B	3B	HR	RBI	SB	Drafted
C	Anthony Seigler, Cartersville (Ga.) HS	Sr.	.424	99	48	42	10	2	12	32	16	Yankees (1)
CI	Triston Casas, American Heritage School, Plantation, Fla.	Sr.	.393	61	26	24	5	4	6	29	3	Red Sox (1)
MI	Jeremiah Jackson, St. Luke's Episcopal School, Mobile, Ala.	Sr.	.644	90	54	58	9	4	15	49	21	Angels (2)
MI	Bobby Witt Jr., Colleyville (Texas) Heritage HS	Jr.	.466	103	51	48	13	5	10	44	15	Undrafted
CI	Nolan Gorman, O'Connor HS, Phoenix	Sr.	.419	74	41	31	6	0	10	32	3	Cardinals (1)
OF	Alek Thomas, Mount Carmel HS, Chicago	Sr.	.433	104	48	45	6	3	7	30	12	D-backs (2)
OF	Nick Schnell, Roncalli HS, Indianapolis	Sr.	.541	85	50	46	6	4	15	36	19	Rays (1s)
OF	Joe Gray, Hattiesburg (Miss.) HS	Sr.	.485	103	57	50	15	5	6	34	19	Brewers (2)
UT	Simeon Woods-Richardson, Kempner (Texas) HS	Sr.	.446	65	14	29	5	3	6	22	N/A	Mets (2)

Pos.	Player, School	Year	W	L	ERA	IP	H	R	ER	BB	SO	Drafted
SP	Cole Winn, Orange (Calif.) Lutheran HS	Sr.	6	2	0.25	55	21	7	2	8	93	Rangers (1)
SP	Ryan Weathers, Loretto (Tenn.) HS	Sr.	9	0	0.13	52	17	4	4	7	101	Padres (1)
SP	Grayson Rodriguez, Central Heights HS, Necogdoches, Texas	Sr.	12	0	0.19	75	21	4	2	17	156	Orioles (1)
SP	Carter Stewart, Eau Gallie HS, Melbourne, Fla.	Sr.	6	3	0.91	62	26	13	8	18	128	Braves (1)
SP	Gunnar Hoglund, Fivay HS, Hudson, Fla.	Sr.	7	0	0.27	52	17	3	2	2	105	Pirates (1s)
UT	Simeon Woods-Richardson, Kempner (Texas) HS	Sr.	5	4	0.84	59	38	15	7	13	107	Mets (2)

SECOND TEAM

Pos.	Player, School	Year	AVG	AB	R	H	2B	3B	HR	RBI	SB	Drafted
C	Will Banfield, Brookwood HS, Snellville, Ga.	Sr.	.398	113	37	45	15	2	9	49	N/A	Marlins (2s)
CI	Grant Lavigne, Bedford (N.H.) HS	Sr.	.639	36	26	23	5	0	7	26	15	Rockies (1s)
MI	Jordan Groshans, Magnolia (Texas) HS	Sr.	.444	99	43	44	11	3	11	36	N/A	Blue Jays (1)
MI	Osiris Johnson, Envinal HS, Alameda, Calif.	Sr.	.535	86	30	46	15	2	6	24	16	Marlins (2)
CI	Rece Hinds, Niceville (Fla.) Senior HS	Jr.	.494	83	45	41	8	4	13	53	4	Undrafted
OF	Brennen Davis, Basha HS, Chandler, Ariz.	Sr.	.444	63	27	28	7	2	3	20	13	Cubs (2)
OF	Jordyn Adams, Green Hope HS, Cary, N.C.	Sr.	.453	75	29	34	5	3	1	15	31	Angels (1)
OF	Elijah Cabell, TNXL Academy, Altamonte Springs, Fla.	Sr.	.402	87	33	35	6	3	10	20	14	Brewers (14)
UT	Connor Scott, Plant HS, Tampa	Sr.	.527	55	19	29	4	2	5	17	6	Marlins (1)

Pos.	Player, School	Year	W	L	ERA	IP	H	R	ER	BB	SO	Drafted
SP	Matthew Liberatore, Mountain Ridge HS, Glendale, Ariz.	Sr.	8	1	0.93	60	28	18	8	25	104	Rays (1)
SP	Kumar Rocker, North Oconee (Ga.) HS, Bogart, Ga.	Sr.	6	2	0.91	46	19	9	6	13	90	Rockies (38)
SP	J.T. Ginn, Brandon (Miss.) HS	Sr.	5	1	0.36	39	10	5	2	9	78	Dodgers (1)
SP	Owen White, Carson HS, China Grove, N.C.	Sr.	10	1	0.22	64	28	3	2	15	101	Rangers (2)
SP	Jonathan Childress, Forney (Texas) HS	Sr.	8	1	1.08	71	42	18	11	21	142	Undrafted
UT	Connor Scott, Plant HS, Tampa	Sr.	3	0	2.13	23	14	7	7	7	28	Marlins (1)

Casey Mize Tops Draft Heavy In College Bats

BY CARLOS COLLAZO

In the weeks, days and even minutes leading up to MLB commissioner Rob Manfred announcing the Tigers' first overall selection to kick off the 2018 Draft, rumors floated around that Detroit was thinking about options other than the consensus No. 1 talent. When the pick was finally announced though, the best player in the 2018 class—Auburn righthander Casey Mize—heard his name called.

"You never really know until you hear your name called," Mize said in a conference call after he was picked. "That's what I believed until the last second. I honestly don't think I ever bought into the fact that I could possibly even go 1-1. I think I kind of kept telling myself, 'No, it's not going to happen, just keep working, get as high as you can, but that's not going to happen.'

"So I think I was kind of in denial a little bit for the longest time. I don't know. I think that was a strategy that I needed to do for it to work. I don't think there was an actual point where I realized that this was pretty possible, that I could go 1-1."

The selection rewarded an incredible spring for Mize, as he showed the best pure stuff and pitchability of any player in the class en route to a 9-5,

The consensus top player in the draft, Casey Mize, went No. 1 to the Tigers.

3.07 season with Auburn, with 140 strikeouts to just 10 walks. Following Mize were four college bats who stood out in their own ways, but each can lean back on a strong track record of offensive performance.

FIRST-ROUND BONUS PROGRESSION

After first round bonus prices rose for three years straight, culminating in a first-round record average bonus of $3,880,723 in 2017, the 2018 average fell 3.37 percent to $3,754,123. It's the biggest drop in percentage since 2012, the first year that the Collective Bargaining Agreement instituted penalties on teams going above bonus pool allotments. The 2018 average is still 28.6 percent higher than the average first round bonuses from 2012-2016 ($2,680,263), likely thanks to a 2016 CBA update that redistributed bonus pool money from the highest picks into the rest of the first round, which took effect with the 2017 draft.

After the first draft in 1965, first-round bonuses rose by an average of just 0.6 percent annually for the rest of the 1960s and 5.2 percent per year in the 1970s. Bonus inflation picked up in the 1980s, averaging 10.2 percent annually, and soared to 26.9 percent per year in the 1990s.

Below are the annual averages for first-round bonuses since the draft started in 1965. The 1996 total does not include four players who became free agents through a loophole in the draft rules.

Year	Average	Change	Year	Average	Change	Year	Average	Change	Year	Average	Change
1965	$42,516	—	1979	$68,094	0.20%	1993	$613,037	27.20%	2007	$2,098,083	8.50%
1966	$44,430	4.50%	1980	$74,025	8.70%	1994	$790,357	28.90%	2008	$2,458,714	17.20%
1967	$42,898	-3.40%	1981	$78,573	6.10%	1995	$918,019	16.10%	2009	$2,434,800	-1.00%
1968	$43,850	2.20%	1982	$82,615	5.10%	1996*	$944,404	2.90%	2010	$2,220,966	-8.80%
1969	$43,504	-0.80%	1983	$87,236	5.60%	1997	$1,325,536	40.40%	2011	$2,653,375	19.50%
1970	$45,230	3.90%	1984	$105,391	20.80%	1998	$1,637,667	23.10%	2012	$2,475,167	-6.70%
1971	$45,197	-0.10%	1985	$118,115	12.10%	1999	$1,809,767	10.50%	2013	$2,641,538	6.70%
1972	$44,952	-0.50%	1986	$116,300	-1.60%	2000	$1,872,586	3.50%	2014	$2,612,109	-1.10%
1973	$48,832	8.60%	1987	$128,480	10.50%	2001	$2,154,280	15.00%	2015	$2,774,945	6.23%
1974	$53,333	9.20%	1988	$142,540	10.90%	2002	$2,106,793	-2.20%	2016	$2,897,557	4.42%
1975	$49.33	-7.50%	1989	$176,008	23.50%	2003	$1,765,667	-16.20%	2017	$3,880,723	25.4%
1976	$49,631	0.60%	1990	$252,577	43.50%	2004	$1,958,448	10.90%	2018	$3,754,123	-3.37%
1977	$48,813	-1.60%	1991	$365,396	44.70%	2005	$2,018,000	3.00%			
1978	$67,892	39.10%	1992	$481,893	31.90%	2006	$1,933,333	-4.20%			

DRAFT

CLIFF WELCH/GETTY IMAGES

The Giants selected Georgia Tech catcher Joey Bart, who could be the heir apparent to Buster Posey.

The Phillies moved away from the small, up-the-middle outfield type they had taken in the previous two drafts and went for power with Wichita State third baseman Alec Bohm.

At No. 4 the White Sox zigged while the Phillies zagged, taking Oregon State infielder Nick Madrigal, who's listed at just 5-foot-7, 165-pounds but is one of the best pure hitters in the class.

Rounding out the top five was Cincinnati, who jumped on Florida third baseman Jonathan India, who had one of the best seasons of any hitter in the country, playing against SEC competition.

With the Tigers' first choice, Mize became the first pitcher taken 1-1 since 2014, when Brady Aiken was selected by the Astros (though he didn't sign) and the first righthander taken with the first pick since 2013, when the Astros selected Stanford righthander Mark Appel.

Mize will hope that his professional career gets off to a better start than either of the aforementioned players.

Mize was drafted just after Auburn advanced through the Raleigh Regional in the NCAA Tournament and talked about how he was able to handle the stresses of his draft season, with the rigors of holding down a Friday Night starting job for the Tigers after being selected.

"It is a relief to kind of have it out the way, I'm not going to lie to you," Mize said. "It definitely is a relief. I've been looking forward to this day for a long time. I'm very happy with how everything turned out.

"But the past month or so, or the past few weeks, have been really fun honestly. I've tried to enjoy it as much as I can. It's definitely been stressful a little bit, but I've tried to enjoy it as much as I can and just try to soak up the last month or so that I have here at Auburn University playing with my teammates. I've had a lot of fun, tried to enjoy it as much as I can and I think I did."

Out Of The Pocket At No. 9

As Baseball America attempted to gather information on players and teams for mock drafts leading up to the first round, the Athletics proved to be one of the more difficult teams to gauge. Understandably so, as Oakland shook the draft up in a big way with the No. 9 selection, taking Oklahoma center fielder Kyler Murray—who ranked as the No. 77 player on the BA 500.

Coming out of high school, Murray could have been a first-round talent if teams thought he was

BONUS SPENDING BY TEAM

Teams combined to spend $294.6 million on draft bonuses in 2018, blowing away the previous draft spending record of $267.4 million that was set in 2016. Teams' total expenditure on draft bonuses initially fell when a new Collective Bargaining Agreement changed the draft rules when it went into effect in 2012, but bonuses have now exceeded the level they reached under the old system.

The CBA that went into effect in 2012 curtailed spending by instituting harsh penalties for teams that exceeded their bonus pools by more than five percent. It also ended the practice of awarding major league contracts to draftees. But as revenues within the game have increased, so too have the bonus pools MLB allocates to teams for the first 10 rounds. As a results, overall spending in the draft has been allowed to increase over time.

The Tigers spent the most in 2018, thanks mostly to having the first overall pick and signing Casey Mize to a $7.5 million bonus that is tied for the second-highest bonus of all time. Both the Royals and Rays make the top five as well, despite their first picks coming in the mid to late teens. The two teams had the largest overall bonus pools, as the Rays had five picks on the first day of the draft, while the Royals also had five, including three first round picks. No team spent less than $5 million, compared to 2017, when three teams fell under that mark.

TEAM	2018	2017	2016
Tigers	$14,784,100	$6,837,300	$6,712,300
Royals	$14,768,200	$8,369,000	$5,047,000
Giants	$13,935,000	$6,456,400	$4,825,200
Rays	$13,786,100	$10,912,800	$7,765,700
Reds	$12,952,000	$13,665,300	$14,679,100
Padres	$12,565,515	$12,354,700	$14,886,045
White Sox	$12,284,400	$7,957,000	$10,061,500
Phillies	$11,342,900	$8,933,400	$14,990,300
Indians	$11,222,459	$3,828,870	$8,934,100
Mets	$11,017,238	$6,064,500	$8,654,501
Athletics	$10,888,200	$11,950,600	$11,001,300
Orioles	$10,433,500	$6,404,300	$8,106,900
Marlins	$10,415,200	$9,375,000	$7,219,900
Pirates	$10,402,600	$10,418,300	$6,472,700
Blue Jays	$9,890,300	$8,642,500	$7,871,100
Cardinals	$9,534,100	$2,248,100	$10,493,300
Cubs	$9,218,950	$7,655,100	$2,959,900
Rangers	$9,150,500	$7,893,200	$6,860,900
Angels	$8,760,000	$8,251,000	$7,322,600
Mariners	$8,655,200	$6,732,800	$7,574,700
Rockies	$8,549,000	$4,477,600	$11,649,200
Yankees	$8,148,400	$6,937,800	$7,123,600
Brewers	$7,747,400	$10,968,900	$11,136,264
Red Sox	$7,252,900	$5,927,000	$7,947,500
Nationals	$6,908,000	$5,533,800	$8,724,000
Twins	$6,876,700	$14,090,300	$8,532,900
Astros	$6,440,800	$8,913,300	$6,910,700
Braves	$5,815,000	$10,372,100	$15,516,300
D-backs	$5,769,400	$10,330,300	$6,116,900
Dodgers	$5,139,540	$6,048,000	$11,275,800
Total	**$294,653,602**	**$248,549,270**	**$267,372,210**
Average	**$9,821,787**	**$8,284,976**	**$8,912,407**

signable, but as an elite athlete on the football field Murray told teams not to select him and he made his way to Texas A&M.

Since then, Murray has transferred to Oklahoma, where he became the starting quarterback for the 2018 season. He also improved his game on the diamond tremendously.

His routes and instincts in the outfield have improved, allowing his plus speed to make him a potential impact defender in the grass, with an improved approach at the plate and potential for 20-25 home runs down the line.

Murray's arm plays well below-average on the baseball field now, though he has the arm strength that should allow it to tick up once he starts to focus on baseball and his throwing mechanics on the diamond full-time.

Which leads to the most interesting aspect of this Murray selection at No. 9. The Athletics are going to let Murray go back to school and play football during his redshirt junior season. Playing a contact sport will open himself up to more injury risk than any other first-round position player.

It's certainly a high-risk, high-reward pick for the Athletics for a number of reasons, but they seemed to mitigate that somewhat when they picked Dallas Baptist outfielder Jameson Hannah and Missouri State shortstop Jeremy Eierman with their other Day 1 picks.

Eierman entered the year with a chance to go in the middle of the first round, but slipped a bit when he underperformed compared to his excellent sophomore season.

DANNY KARNIK

The Giants were linked to Joey Bart as early as February and got him at No. 2.

HIGHEST BONUSES EVER

The first five picks of the 2017 draft joined the top 10 highest bonuses ever signed, with the 2018 class falling short of that mark. Only two players joined the top 10 this year with signing bonuses over $7 million. Just one additional player signed for more than $6 million to join the list of highest bonuses ever.

Player, Pos.	Team, Year (Pick)	Bonus
Gerrit Cole, rhp	Pirates, 2011 (No. 1)	$8,000,000
Stephen Strasburg, rhp	Nationals, 2009 (No. 1)	* $7,500,000
Bubba Starling, of	Royals, 2011 (No. 5)	+ $7,500,000
Casey Mize, rhp	Tigers, 2018 (No. 1)	$7,500,000
Hunter Greene, rhp/ss	Reds, 2017 (No. 2)	$7,230,000
Joey Bart, c	Giants, 2018 (No. 2)	$7,025,000
Brendan McKay, 1b/lhp	Rays, 2017 (No. 4)	$7,005,000
Kyle Wright, rhp	Braves, 2017 (No. 5)	$7,000,000
Royce Lewis, ss	Twins, 2017 (No. 1)	$6,725,000
Kris Bryant, 3b	Cubs, 2013 (No. 2)	$6,708,400
MacKenzie Gore, lhp	Padres, 2017 (No. 3)	$6,700,000
Carlos Rodon, lhp	White Sox, 2014 (No. 3)	$6,582,000
Jameson Taillon, rhp	Pirates, 2010 (No. 2)	$6,500,000
Dansby Swanson, ss	D-backs, 2015 (No. 1)	$6,500,000
Nick Madrigal, ss	White Sox, 2018 (No. 4)	$6,411,000
Danny Hultzen, lhp	Marinters, 2011 (No. 2)	* $6,350,000
Mark Appel, rhp	Astros, 2013 (No. 1	$6,350,000
Donavan Tate, of	Padres, 2009 (No. 3)	+ $6,250,000
Bryce Harper, of	Nationals, 2010 (No. 1)	* $6,250,000
Buster Posey, c	Giants, 2008 (No. 5)	$6,200,000
Nick Senzel, 3b	Reds, 2016 (No. 2)	$6,200,000
Tim Beckham, ss	Rays, 2008 (No. 1)	+ $6,150,000
Justin Upton, ss	D-backs, 2005 (No. 1)	+ $6,100,000
Mickey Moniak, of	Phillies, 2016 (No. 1)	$6,100,000
Matt Wieters, c	Orioles, 2007 (No. 5)	$6,000,000
Pedro Alvarez, 3b	Pirates, 2008 (No. 2)	* $6,000,000
Eric Hosmer, 1b	Royals, 2008 (No. 3)	$6,000,000

Part of major league contract. +Bonus spread over multiple years under MLB two-sport provisions

Money Talks

Once the top ten picks came and went, it seemed like Singer and prep lefthander Matthew Liberatore were sliding more than expected.

The two were still on the board after the first 15 picks of the first round, only for Liberatore—the No. 2 player on the BA 500—to get selected with the first of five Day 1 picks with the Rays at No. 16. Two selections later, Singer heard his name called with the first pick of the Royals, who had the highest bonus pool of any team in the draft and also had five Day 1 selections.

While it has become more difficult to slide players under the current CBA, both the Rays and the Royals were able to secure top-five talents despite picking outside of the top-15.

Each team continued to take players later than their talent would have seemed to suggest, with the Rays nabbing a sliding Shane McClanahan at pick No. 31 to secure the top two lefthanded pitchers in the 2018 draft class.

Tampa Bay rounded out its day one selections with prep outfielder Nick Schnell (No. 32), Florida Atlantic shortstop Tyler Frank (No. 73) and California righthanded pitcher/outfielder Tanner Dodson (No. 86).

The Royals opted to go all-in on college pitchers after struggling with high school arms in recent years, taking Singer's Florida roommate,

Jackson Kowar, with their second pick at No. 33 and Virginia lefthander Daniel Lynch at No. 34. Kowar has long been considered a first-round talent and Lynch got first-round buzz late this spring when his stuff started to tick up. Following Lynch, Kansas City grabbed another college lefthander in Stanford's Kris Bubic (No. 40) and rounded out the evening with Memphis righthander Jonathan Bowlan at No. 58.

NO. 1 OVERALL PICKS

Year Team: Player, Pos., School	Bonus
1965 Athletics: Rick Monday, of, Arizona State	$100,000
1966 Mets: Steve Chilcott, c, Antelope Valley HS, Lancaster, Calif.	$75,000
1967 Yankees: Ron Blomberg, 1b, Druid Hills HS, Atlanta	$65,000
1968 Mets: Tim Foli, ss, Notre Dame HS, Sherman Oaks, Calif.	$74,000
1969 Senators: Jeff Burroughs, of, Centennial HS, Long Beach	$88,000
1970 Padres: Mike Ivie, c, Walker HS, Atlanta	$75,000
1971 White Sox: Danny Goodwin, c, Peoria (Ill.) HS	Did Not Sign
1972 Padres: Dave Roberts, 3b, Oregon	$70,000
1973 Rangers: David Clyde, lhp, Westchester HS, Texas	*$65,000
1974 Padres: Bill Almon, ss, Brown	*$90,000
1975 Angels: Danny Goodwin, c, Southern	*$125,000
1976 Astros: Floyd Bannister, lhp, Arizona State	$100,000
1977 White Sox: Harold Baines, of, St. Michaels (Md.) HS	$32,000
1978 Braves: Bob Horner, 3b, Arizona State	*$162,000
1979 Mariners: Al Chambers, 1b, Harris HS, Harrisburg, Pa.	$60,000
1980 Mets: Darryl Strawberry, of, Crenshaw HS, Los Angeles	$152,500
1981 Mariners: Mike Moore, rhp, Oral Roberts	$100,000
1982 Cubs: Shawon Dunston, ss, Jefferson HS, New York	$135,000
1983 Twins: Tim Belcher, rhp, Mount Vernon Nazarene (Ohio)	Did Not Sign
1984 Mets: Shawn Abner, of, Mechanicsburg (Pa.) HS	$150,500
1985 Brewers: B.J. Surhoff, c, North Carolina	$150,000
1986 Pirates: Jeff King, 3b, Arkansas	$180,000
1987 Mariners: Ken Griffey Jr., of, Moeller HS, Cincinnati	$160,000
1988 Padres: Andy Benes, rhp, Evansville	$235,000
1989 Orioles: Ben McDonald, rhp, Louisiana State	*$350,000
1990 Braves: Chipper Jones, ss, The Bolles School, Jacksonville	$275,000
1991 Yankees: Brien Taylor, lhp, East Carteret HS, Beaufort, N.C.	$1,550,000
1992 Astros: Phil Nevin, 3b, Cal State Fullerton	$700,000
1993 Mariners: Alex Rodriguez, ss, Westminster Christian HS, Miami	*$1,000,000
1994 Mets: Paul Wilson, rhp, Florida State	$1,550,000
1995 Angels: Darin Erstad, of, Nebraska	$1,575,000
1996 Pirates: Kris Benson, rhp, Clemson	$2,000,000
1997 Tigers: Matt Anderson, rhp, Tigers	$2,505,000
1998 Phillies: Pat Burrell, 3b, Miami	*$3,150,000
1999 Devil Rays: Josh Hamilton, of, Athens Drive HS, Raleigh	$3,960,000
2000 Marlins: Adrian Gonzalez, 1b, Eastlake HS, Chula Vista, Calif.	$3,000,000
2001 Twins: Joe Mauer, c, Cretin-Derham Hall, St. Paul	$5,150,000
2002 Pirates: Bryan Bullington, rhp, Ball State	$4,000,000
2003 Devil Rays: Delmon Young, of, Camarillo (Calif.) HS	*$3,700,000
2004 Padres: Matt Bush, ss, Mission Bay HS, San Diego	$3,150,000
2005 Diamondbacks: Justin Upton, ss, Great Bridge HS, Chesapeake, Va.	$6,100,000
2006 Royals: Luke Hochevar, rhp, Fort Worth (American Assoc.)	*$3,500,000
2007 Devil Rays: David Price, lhp, Vanderbilt	*$5,600,000
2008 Rays: Tim Beckham, ss, Griffin (Ga.) HS	$6,150,000
2009 Nationals: Stephen Strasburg, rhp, San Diego State	*$7,500,000
2010 Nationals: Bryce Harper, of, JC of Southern Nevada	*$6,250,000
2011 Pirates: Gerrit Cole, rhp, UCLA	$8,000,000
2012 Astros: Carlos Correa, ss, Puerto Rico Baseball Acad., Gurabo, P.R.	$4,800,000
2013 Astros: Mark Appel, rhp, Stanford	$6,350,000
2014 Astros: Brady Aiken, lhp, Cathedral Catholic, San Diego	Did Not Sign
2015 Diamondbacks: Dansby Swanson, ss, Vanderbilt	$6,500,000
2016 Phillies: Mickey Moniak, La Costa Canyon HS, Carlsbad, Calif.	$6,100,000
2017 Twins: Royce Lewis, JSerra Catholic HS, San Juan Capistrano, Calif.	$6,750,000
2018 Tigers: Casey Mize, Auburn	$7,500,000

*Part of major league contract.

Prep Arms Reach Campus

How teams would deal with the incredible depth of prep pitchers was one of the storylines to watch throughout the draft. The 2018 class featured an extremely deep pool of talented prep pitchers, but many teams have started to factor in the huge risk that comes with that demographic—specifically high school righthanders.

With an abundance of arms to select at the position, there were sure to be a few who fell and weren't able to have their price tags met.

The most prominent examples were both Georgia righthanders. Kumar Rocker ranked as the No. 13 prospect on the BA 500, while Cole Wilcox ranked No. 37. Both players will end up in college, at Vanderbilt and Georgia, respectively, after sliding out of day one consideration. Both players were selected in the very late rounds by teams who assuredly knew they would not be signing.

That appeared to be the case for Texas-based righthander Adam Kloffenstein as well, after the No. 35 prospect on the BA 500 didn't hear his name called on day one.

However, the Blue Jays, after drafting Kloffenstein's high school teammate, shortstop Jordan Groshans with their first overall selection at No. 12, grabbed Kloffenstein with their first pick on day two, and signed him to a $2,450,000 overslot bonus in the third round that was more than twice the next-largest third round signing bonus.

In addition to Rocker, Vanderbilt also benefitted by watching righthander Austin Becker fall to the 37th round, where the No. 65 prospect passed on signing and will instead focus on a collegiate career with Tim Corbin, who has a wealth of incoming freshman pitching at his disposal.

By The Numbers

What the draft teaches us is that if you want to be selected, be a pitcher. Major league organizations need arms, and they always will.

Of the 1,214 players selected in the 2018 draft, 54 percent were pitchers. Specifically, they were righthanded pitchers, who accounted for 41 percent of all players drafted.

On the other hand, amateur first basemen and second basemen face long odds of being drafted, largely because teams expect that many of their future first and second basemen will begin their professional careers at more difficult defensive positions. Just 33 first basemen were drafted in 40 rounds this year.

California continues to be the state that produces the most draftees, but Florida is steadily gaining on the Golden State. This year, 149 players were drafted out of California and 133 were drafted out of Florida. Following California and Florida come Texas (105), North Carolina (68), Georgia (50), Alabama (41), Tennessee (38), South Carolina (33), Arizona (32), Mississippi (31) and New York (31).

As is almost always the case, the vast majority of draftees were picked out of four-year colleges. Roughly two out of every three players (66.3 percent) came from a four-year college, compared to 25 percent coming from the high school ranks and 8.5 percent being selected out of junior colleges.

This year's draft class saw the highest number of four-year college players selected since 2012, which marks the beginning of the "bonus pool allotment" era of the draft. The previous high occurred in 2015, when 776 college players (or 63.9 percent) were taken.

On the flip side, this year saw the fewest high school players picked under the current draft format. The previous low was 312 (or 25.7 percent) in 2017.

Overall, the 2018 draft distribution fell in line with the three-year averages for 2015-17, which were 63 percent college, 26 percent high school, 10 percent junior college and a handful of "other."

Digging a little deeper, it's quite clear that high school players are either picked very early (where they will land large signing bonuses) or quite late (where they may or may not sign).

In the first and supplemental first rounds of 2018, there were more high school players picked (53.5 percent) than college players (46.5 percent).

By the second and third rounds, the preference shifts back to college players, by a margin of 67 percent to 31 percent.

And from the fourth through the 10th rounds, where lower-cost college senior signs become popular, high school draftees are scarce. Collegians account for 81 percent and high schoolers 15 per-

THE BONUS RECORD

Rick Monday, the No. 1 overall pick in baseball's first draft in 1965, signed with the Athletics for $100,000—a figure that no draftee bettered for a decade. The record has been broken many times since, with Gerrit Cole setting a new standard in 2011 when he signed for $8 million with the Pirates as the No. 1 overall pick. No draftee has eclipsed him under the CBA, allowing his record to stand for seven years—the longest bonus record stretch dating back to Todd Demeter, whose $208,000 bonus in 1979 held the mark for nin years until 1988 when Andy Benes topped him with a $235,000 bonus. 2018 first overall pick Casey Mize came the closest in years with a $7,500,000 bonus that's tied for second all-time along with Stephen Strasburg and Bubba Starling.

The list below represents only cash bonuses and doesn't include guaranteed money from major league deals, college scholarship plans or incentives. It also considers only players who signed with the clubs that drafted them and doesn't include draft picks who signed after being granted free agency.

Year	Player, Pos. , Cwlub (Round)	Bonus
1965	Rick Monday, of, Athletics (1)	$100,000
1975	Danny Goodwin, c, Angels (1)	$125,000
1978	Kirk Gibson, of, Tigers (1)	$150,000
	*Bob Horner, 3b, Braves (1)	$162,000
1979	Todd Demeter, 1b, Yankees (2)	$208,000
1988	Andy Benes, rhp, Padres (1)	$235,000
1989	Tyler Houston, c, Braves (1)	$241,500
	*Ben McDonald, rhp, Orioles (1)	$350,000
	*John Olerud, 1b, Blue Jays (3)	$575,000
1991	Mike Kelly, of, Braves (1)	$575,000
	Brien Taylor, lhp, Yankees (1)	$1,550,000
1994	Paul Wilson, rhp, Mets (1)	$1,550,000
	Josh Booty, 3b, Marlins (1)	$1,600,000
1996	Kris Benson, rhp, Pirates (1)	$2,000,000
1997	Rick Ankiel, lhp, Cardinals (2)	$2,500,000
	Matt Anderson, rhp, Tigers (1)	$2,505,000
1998	*J.D. Drew, of, Cardinals (1)	$3,000,000
	*Pat Burrell, 3b, Phillies (1)	$3,150,000
	Mark Mulder, lhp, Athletics (1)	$3,200,000
	Corey Patterson, of, Cubs (1)	$3,700,000
1999	Josh Hamilton, of, Devil Rays (1)	$3,960,000
2000	Joe Borchard, of, White Sox (1)	$5,300,000
2005	Justin Upton, ss, Diamondbacks (1)	$6,100,000
2008	Tim Beckham, ss, Rays (1)	$6,150,000
	Buster Posey, c, Giants (1)	$6,200,000
2009	Donavan Tate, cf, Padres (1)	$6,250,000
	*Stephen Strasburg, rhp, Nationals (1)	$7,500,000
2011	Gerrit Cole, rhp, Pirates (1)	$8,000,000

*Part of major league contract.

cent during these rounds.

Once the 11th round is reached, where there are no longer any slot allotment penalties, teams start picking high school players again. Some of them will be taken in the 11th-15th rounds to land significant signing bonuses. Others will be picked in the later rounds even though teams know there is very little chance they will sign. There also are occasionally some hidden gems that can be unearthed by a shrewd area scout. The distribution from rounds 11-40 looks like this:

Four-year universities: 581 players, 63.8 percent. High school: 233 players, 25.6 percent. Junior college: 94 players, 10.3 percent. Other:

BONUSES VS. PICK VALUES

The assigned slots for the 2018 draft increased 4.2 percent from 2017 slots, as increases come in MLB's recenues. The first overall pick in the 2017 draft was assigned a value of $7,770,700, while the Tigers' No. 1 pick was assigned a bonus value of $8,096,300. While first overall pick Casey Mize signed underslot, he still signed the largest bonussince the 2012 CBA and the largest since Bubba Starling in 2011, who also signed for $7.5M.

The top 50 bonuses added up to $154.2 million, while the first 50 pick values totaled 149.6 million, $4.6 million more than what MLB assigned. By comparison, when MLB unilaterally determined slot recommendations in the last year of the previous Collective Bargaining Agreement (2011) but had no enforcement mechanism, the total of the first 50 bonuses ($120.5 million) dwarfed that of the top 50 slots ($70 million).

Player, Pos., Team (Round/Overall Pick)	Bonus	Pick Value
1. Casey Mize, RHP, Auburn (1st round/No. 1)	$7,500,000	$8,096,300
2. Joey Bart, C, Georgia Tech (1st round/No. 2)	$7,025,000	$7,494,600
3. Nick Madrigal, SS, Oregon State (1st round/No. 4)	$6,411,400	$6,411,400
4. Alec Bohm, 3B, Wichita State (1st round/No.3)	$5,850,000	$6,947,500
5. Jonathan India, 3B, Florida (1st round/No. 5)	$5,297,500	$5,946,400
6. Ryan Weathers, LHP, Loretto (Tenn.) HS (1st round/No. 7)	$5,226,500	$5,226,500
7. Kyler Murray, OF, Oklahoma (1st round/No. 9)	$4,660,000	$4,761,500
8. Jarred Kelenic, OF, Waukesha (Wis.) West HS (1st round/No. 6)	$4,500,000	$5,525,200
9. Travis Swaggerty, OF, South Alabama (1st round/No. 10)	$4,400,000	$4,560,200
10. Grayson Rodriguez, RHP, C. Heights HS, Nacogdoches, Tex. (1st round/No. 11)	$4,300,000	$4,375,100
11. Brady Singer, RHP, Florida (1st round/No. 18)	$4,247,500	$3,349,300
12. Jordyn Adams, OF, Green Hope HS, Cary, N.C. (1st round/No. 17)	$4,100,000	$3,472,900
13. Connor Scott, OF, Plant HS, Tampa (1st round/No. 13)	$4,038,200	$4,038,200
14. Logan Gilbert, RHP, Stetson (1st round/No. 14)	$3,883,800	$3,883,800
15. Matthew Liberatore, LHP, Mtn. Ridge HS, Glendale, Ariz. (1st round/No. 16)	$3,497,500	$3,603,500
16. Brice Turang, SS, Santiago HS, Corona, Calif. (1st round/No. 21)	$3,411,100	$3,013,600
17. Jordan Groshans, SS, Magnolia (Texas) HS (1st round/No. 12)	$3,400,000	$4,200,900
18. Nolan Gorman, 3B, O'Connor HS, Phoenix (1st round/No. 19)	$3,231,700	$3,231,700
19. Cole Winn, RHP, Orange (Calif.) Lutheran HS (1st round/No. 15)	$3,150,000	$3,738,500
20. Mason Denaburg, RHP, Merritt Island (Fla.) HS (1st round/No. 27)	$3,000,000	$2,472,700
21. Ryan Rolison, LHP, Mississippi (1st round/No. 22)	$2,912,300	$2,912,300
22. Anthony Seigler, C, Cartersville (Ga.) HS (1st round/No. 23)	$2,815,900	$2,815,900
23. Nico Hoerner, SS, Stanford (1st round/No. 24)	$2,724,000	$2,724,000
24. Xavier Edwards, SS, N.Broward Prep HS, Coconut Creek, Fla. (supp. 1st/No. 38)	$2,600,000	$1,878,300
25. Noah Naylor, C, St. Joan of Arc Catholic SS, Mississauga, Ont. (1st round/No. 29)	$2,578,137	$2,332,700
26. Triston Casas, 3B, American Heritage School, Plantation, Fla. (1st round/No. 26)	$2,552,800	$2,552,800
27. Trevor Larnach, OF, Oregon State (1st round/No. 20)	$2,550,000	$3,120,000
28. Parker Meadows, OF, Grayson HS, Loganville, Ga. (2nd round/No. 44	$2,500,000	$1,625,500
29. Adam Kloffenstein, RHP, Magnolia (Texas) HS (3rd round/No. 88)	$2,450,000	$652,900
30. Nick Schnell, OF, Roncalli HS, Indianapolis (1st round/No. 32) $2297500	$2,297,500	$2,171,700
31. Seth Beer, OF, Clemson (1st round/No. 28) $2250000	$2,250,000	$2,399,400
32. Ethan Hankins, RHP, Forsyth C. HS, Cumming, Ga. (1st round/No. 35)	$2,246,022	$2,016,400
33. Shane McClanahan, LHP, South Florida (1st round/No. 31) $2230100	$2,230,100	$2,224,400
34. Jackson Kowar, RHP, Florida (1st round/No. 33) $2147500	$2,147,500	$2,118,700
35. Grant Lavigne, 1B, Bedford (N.H.) HS (supp. 1st/No. 42) $2000000	$2,000,000	$1,704,000
36. Steele Walker, OF, Oklahoma (2nd round/No. 46) $2000000	$2,000,000	$1,556,100
37. Mike Siani, OF, Penn Charter HS, Philadelphia (4th round/No. 109)	$2,000,000	$512,800
38. Lyon Richardson, RHP, Jensen Beach (Fla.) HS (2nd round/No. 47)	$1,997,500	$1,520,300
39. Simeon Woods-Richardson, RHP, Kempner HS, Sugar Land, Tex. (2nd round/No. 48)	$1,850,000	$1,485,100
40. Braxton Ashcraft, RHP, Robinson (Texas) HS (2nd round/No. 51	$1,825,000	$1,382,400
41. Cadyn Grenier, SS, Oregon State (supp. 1st/No. 37) $1800000	$1,800,000	$1,923,500
42. Jameson Hannah, OF, Dallas Baptist (2nd round/No. 50) $1800000	$1,800,000	$1,414,200
43. Will Banfield, C, Brookwood HS, Snellville, Ga. (supp. 2nd/No. 69)	$1,800,000	$894,600
44. Daniel Lynch, LHP, Virginia (1st round/No. 34) $1697500	$1,697,500	$2,066,700
45. Griffin Roberts, RHP, Wake Forest (supp. 1st/No. 43) $1664200	$1,664,200	$1,664,200
46. Jake McCarthy, OF, Virginia (supp. 1st/No. 39) $1650000	$1,650,000	$1,834,500
47. Kris Bubic, LHP, Stanford (supp. 1st/No. 40) $1597500	$1,597,500	$1,786,300
48. Sean Hjelle, RHP, Kentucky (2nd round/No. 45) $1500000	$1,500,000	$1,587,600
49. Owen White, RHP, Carson HS, China Grove, N.C. (2nd round/No. 55)	$1,500,000	$1,257,500
50. Josh Breaux, C, McLennan (Texas) JC (2nd round/No. 61)	$1,497,500	$1,086,900
Total	**$154,163,659**	**$149,571,500**

two players, 0.2 percent.

Kentucky led all schools in 2018 with 13 draftees. Here are the top 20 college programs by number of draftees. Once again, teams show their preference for Southeastern Conference and Atlantic Coast Conference players.

Kentucky (13), Arkansas (11), Texas Tech (11), Wichita State (11), North Carolina (10), South Carolina (10), Oklahoma (9), Arizona (8), Louisville (8), Mississippi (8), Tennessee Tech (8), Vanderbilt (8), Auburn (7), Cal State Fullerton (7), Clemson (7), Dallas Baptist (7), Duke (7), Florida (7), Florida State (7), Louisiana State (7), Mississippi State (7).

Team, Player, Pos., School	Bonus
1. Tigers, Casey Mize, RHP, Auburn	7,500,000
2. Giants, Joey Bart, C, Georgia Tech	7,025,000
3. Phillies, Alec Bohm, 3B, Wichita State	5,850,000
4. White Sox, Nick Madrigal, SS, Oregon State	6,411,400
5. Reds, Jonathan India, 3B, FL	5,297,500
6. Mets, Jarred Kelenic, OF, Waukesha West HS, WS	4,500,000
7. Padres, Ryan Weathers, LHP, Loretto HS, TN	5,226,500
8. Braves, Carter Stewart, RHP, Eau Gallie HS, Melbourne, Fla. . Did not sign
9. Athletics, Kyler Murray, OF, Oklahoma	4,660,000
10. Pirates, Travis Swaggerty, OF, South Alabama	4,400,000
11. Orioles, Grayson Rodriguez, RHP, C. Hts. HS, Nacogdoches, Tex.	4,300,000
12. Blue Jays, Jordan Groshans, SS, Magnolia (Texas) HS	3,400,000
13. Marlins, Connor Scott, OF, Plant HS, Tampa	4,038,200
14. Mariners, Logan Gilbert, RHP, Stetson	3,883,800
15. Rangers, Cole Winn, RHP, Orange (Calif.) Lutheran HS	3,150,000
16. Rays, Matthew Liberatore, LHP, Mtn. Ridge HS, Glendale, Ariz	3,497,500
17. Angels, Jordyn Adams, OF, Green Hope HS, Cary, N.C.	4,100,000
18. Royals, Brady Singer, RHP, Florida	4,247,500
19. Cardinals, Nolan Gorman, 3B, O'Connor HS, Phoenix	3,231,700
20. Twins, Trevor Larnach, OF, Oregon State	2,550,000
21. Brewers, Brice Turang, SS, Santiago HS, Corona, Calif.	3,411,100
22. Rockies, Ryan Rolison, LHP, Mississippi	2,912,300
23. Yankees, Anthony Seigler, C, Cartersville (Ga.) HS	2,815,900
24. Cubs, Nico Hoerner, SS, Stanford	2,724,000
25. Dbacks, Matt McLain, SS, Beckman HS, Irvine, Calif.	Did not sign
26. Red Sox, Triston Casas, 3B, Am. Heritage School, Plantation, Fla.	2,552,800
27. Nationals, Mason Denaburg, RHP, Merritt Island (Fla.) HS	3,000,000
28. Astros, Seth Beer, OF, Clemson	2,250,000
29. Indians, Noah Naylor, C, St. Joan of Arc Catholic SS, Mississauga, Ont.	2,578,137
30. Dodgers, J.T. Ginn, RHP, Brandon (Miss.) HS	Did not sign
31. Rays, Shane McClanahan, LHP, South Florida	2,230,100
32. Rays, Nick Schnell, OF, Roncalli HS, Indianapolis	2,297,500
33. Royals, Jackson Kowar, RHP, Florida	2,147,500
34. Royals, Daniel Lynch, LHP, Virginia	1,697,500
35. Indians, Ethan Hankins, RHP, Forsyth C. HS, Cumming, Ga	2,246,022
36. Pirates, Gunnar Hoglund, RHP, Fivay HS, Hudson, Fla.	Did not sign
37. Orioles, Cadyn Grenier, SS, Oregon State	1,800,000
38. Padres, Xavier Edwards, SS, N. Broward Prep HS, Coconut Creek, Fla.	2,600,000
39. Dbacks, Jake McCarthy, OF, Virginia	1,650,000
40. Royals, Kris Bubic, LHP, Stanford	1,597,500
41. Indians, Lenny Torres, RHP, Beacon (N.Y.) HS	1,350,000
42. Rockies, Grant Lavigne, 1B, Bedford (N.H.) HS	2,000,000
43. Cardinals, Griffin Roberts, RHP, Wake Forest	1,664,200
44. Tigers, Parker Meadows, OF, Grayson HS, Loganville, Ga	2,500,000
45. Giants, Sean Hjelle, RHP, Kentucky	1,500,000
46. White Sox, Steele Walker, OF, Oklahoma	2,000,000
47. Reds, Lyon Richardson, RHP, Jensen Beach (Fla.) HS	1,997,500
48. Mets, Simeon Woods-Richardson, RHP, Kempner HS, Sugar Land, Tx.	1,850,000
49. Braves, Greyson Jenista, OF, Wichita State	1,200,000
50. Athletics, Jameson Hannah, OF, Dallas Baptist	1,800,000
51. Pirates, Braxton Ashcraft, RHP, Robinson (Texas) HS	1,825,000
52. Blue Jays, Griffin Conine, OF, Duke	1,350,000
53. Marlins, Osiris Johnson, SS, Encinal HS, Alameda, Calif.	1,350,000
54. Mariners, Josh Stowers, OF, Louisville	1,100,000
55. Rangers, Owen White, RHP, Carson HS, China Grove, N.C.	1,500,000
56. Rays, Tyler Frank, SS, Florida Atlantic	997,500
57. Angels, Jeremiah Jackson, SS, St. Luke's Episcopal School, Mobile, Ala	194,000
58. Royals, Jonathan Bowlan, RHP, Memphis	697,500
59. Twins, Ryan Jeffers, C, UNC Wilmington	800,000
60. Brewers, Joe Gray, OF, Hattiesburg (Miss.) HS	1,113,500
61. Yankees, Josh Breaux, C, McLennan (Texas) JC	1,497,500
62. Cubs, Brennen Davis, OF, Basha HS, Chandler, Ariz	1,100,000
63. Dbacks, Alek Thomas, OF, Mount Carmel HS, Chicago	1,200,000
64. Red Sox, Nick Decker, OF, Seneca HS, Tabernacle, NJ	1,250,000
65. Nationals, Tim Cate, LHP, Connecticut	986,200
66. Astros, Jayson Schroeder, RHP, Juanita HS, Kirkland, Wash.	1,200,000.

The White Sox took Nick Madrigal at No. 4

BILL MITCHELL

67. Indians, Nick Sandlin, RHP, Southern Mississippi	750,000
68. Dodgers, Michael Grove, RHP, West Virginia	1,229,500
69. Marlins, Will Banfield, C, Brookwood HS, Snellville, GA	1,800,000
70. Athletics, Jeremy Eierman, SS, Missouri State	1,232,000
71. Rays Tanner Dodson, RHP, CA	772,500
72. Reds, Josiah Gray, RHP, Le Moyne (N.Y.)	772,500
73. Brewers, Micah Bello, OF, Hilo (Hawaii) HS	550,000
74. Padres, Grant Little, OF, Texas Tech	800,000
75. Cardinals, Luken Baker, 1B, Texas Christian	800,000
76. Rockies, Mitchell Kilkenny, RHP, Texas A&M	550,000
77. Cubs, Cole Roederer, OF, Hart HS, Santa Clarita, Calif.	1,200,000
78. Cubs, Paul Richan, RHP, San Diego	450,000
79. Tigers, Kody Clemens, 2B, Texas	600,000
80. Giants, Jake Wong, RHP, Grand Canyon	850,000
81. White Sox, Konnor Pilkington, LHP, Mississippi State	650,000
82. Reds, Bren Spillane, OF, Illinois	597,500
83. Mets, Carlos Cortes, 2B, South Carolina	1,000,038
84. Padres, Owen Miller, SS, Illinois State	500,000
85. Athletics, Hogan Harris, LHP, Louisiana-Lafayette	660,000
86. Pirates, Connor Kaiser, SS, Vanderbilt	625,000
87. Orioles, Blaine Knight, RHP, Arkansas	1,100,000
88. Blue Jays, Adam Kloffenstein, RHP, Magnolia (Texas) HS	2,450,000
89. Marlins, Tristan Pompey, OF, Kentucky	645,000
90. Mariners, Cal Raleigh, C, Florida State	854,000
91. Rangers, Jonathan Ornelas, SS, Kellis HS, Glendale, Ariz	622,800
92. Rays, Ford Proctor, SS, Rice	572,500
93. Angels, Aaron Hernandez, RHP, Texas A&M-Corpus Christi	547,500
94. Royals, Kyle Isbel, 2B, Nevada-Las Vegas	592,300
95. Cardinals, Mateo Gil, SS, Timber Creek HS, Fort Worth	900,000
96. Rockies, Terrin Vavra, SS, Minnesota	550,000
97. Yankees, Ryder Green, OF, Karns HS, Knoxville	997,500
98. Cubs, Jimmy Herron, OF, Duke	520,000
99. Dbacks, Jackson Goddard, RHP, Kansas	550,000
100. Red Sox, Durbin Feltman, RHP, Texas Christian	559,600

Order Of Selection In Parentheses   Players Signed In Bold

DRAFT

ATLANTA BRAVES (8)

1. Carter Stewart, RHP, Eau Gallie HS, Melbourne, Fla.
2. **Greyson Jenista, OF, Wichita State**
4. **Tristan Beck, RHP, Stanford**
5. **Trey Riley, RHP, John A. Logan (Ill.) JC**
6. **Andrew Moritz, OF, UNC Greensboro**
7. **Brooks Wilson, RHP, Stetson**
8. **A.J. Graffanino, SS, Washington**
9. **Ryan Shetter, RHP, Texas Tech**
10. **Brett Langhorne, 3B, Carson-Newman (Tenn.)**
11. **Jake Higginbotham, LHP, Clemson**
12. **Nolan Kingham, RHP, Texas**
13. **Brendan Venter, 3B, Auburn**
14. **Victor Vodnik, RHP, Rialto (Calif.) HS**
15. **Greg Cullen, 2B, Niagara**
16. **Ty Harpenau, RHP, Texas Tech**
17. **Justin Dean, OF, Lenoir-Rhyne (N.C.)**
18. **Cameron Kurz, RHP, UC San Diego**
19. **Zach Daniels, RHP, Iowa**
20. **C.J. Alexander, 3B, State JC of Florida**
21. **Tanner Lawson, LHP, St. Edward's (Texas)**
22. **Ray Soderman, C, Oregon**
23. **William Woods, RHP, Dyersburg State (Tenn.) JC**
24. **Rusber Estrada, C, Faulkner (Ala.)**
25. **Michael Mateja, 3B, North Central (Ill.)**
26. **Zach Guth, LHP, Harford (Md.) JC**
27. **Zach Seipel, RHP, Minnesota-Crookston**
28. Derek West, RHP, Pittsburgh
29. **Ray Hernandez, 3B, Alabama State**
30. **Mitch Stallings, LHP, Duke**
31. **Gabriel Rodriguez, LHP, Miami Dade JC**
32. **Trey Harris, OF, Missouri**
33. **Mason Berne, 1B, UNC Wilmington**
34. Zack Hess, RHP, Louisiana State
35. **Logan Brown, C, Southern Indiana**
36. **Victor Cavalieri, LHP, Houghton (N.Y.)**
37. **Alex Camacho, RHP, Vanguard (Calif.)**
38. Franco Aleman, RHP, Alonso HS, Tampa
39. **Jack Perkins, RHP, Kokomo (Ind.) HS**
40. **Micky Mangan, C, Pinecrest Academy, Cumming, Ga.**

BALTIMORE ORIOLES (11)

1. **Grayson Rodriguez, RHP, Central Heights HS, Nacogdoches, Tx.**
1s. **Cadyn Grenier, SS, Oregon State**
3. **Blaine Knight, RHP, Arkansas**
4. **Drew Rom, LHP, Highlands HS, Fort Thomas, Ky.**
5. **Robert Neustrom, OF, Iowa**
6. **Yeankarlos Lleras, RHP, Leadership Christian Academy, Guaynabo, P.R.**
7. **J.J. Montgomery, RHP, Central Florida**
8. **Ryan Conroy, RHP, Elon**
9. **Kevin Magee, LHP, St. John's**
10. **Dallas Litscher, RHP, St. Katherine (Calif.)**
11. **Cody Roberts, C, North Carolina**
12. **Clay Fisher, SS, UC Santa Barbara**
13. **Andrew Fregia, SS, Sam Houston State**
14. **Doran Turchin, OF, Illinois**
15. **Cody Hacker, LHP, Holt HS, Wentzville, Mo.**
16. **Parker McFadden, RHP, Washington State**
17. **Trevor Putzig, 3B, Tennessee Tech**
18. **Jake Zebron, RHP, Colonel Richardson HS, Federalsburg, Md.**
19. **Andrew Jayne, OF, Sanford HS, Fayetteville, N.C.**
20. Caleb Kilian, RHP, Texas Tech
21. **Nick Meservey, LHP, Seattle**

22. Garrett Martin, 3B, Standley Lake HS, Westminster, Colo.
23. Bradley Brehmer, RHP, Decatur Central HS, Indianapolis
24. Herbert Iser, C, San Jacinto (Texas) JC
25. **Nick Horvath, OF, Florida**
26. **Ian Evans, 1B, Grand Canyon**
27. **Jason Montville, LHP, St. Katherine (Calif.)**
28. **Trey Whitley, OF, North Johnston HS, Kenly, N.C.**
29. **Jared Denning, C, Solano (Calif.) JC**
30. **Tyler Joyner, RHP, North Alabama**
31. **John Ham, SS, Tennessee Tech**
32. **Jayvien Sandridge, LHP, Mercersburg (Pa.) Academy**
33. **Zach McLeod, SS, Colorado Mesa**
34. **Trey Truitt, OF, Mercer**
35. Conor Grammes, RHP, Xavier
36. **Matt Beaird, C, Coastal Carolina**
37. **Andrew Ciolli, RHP, Mercyhurst (Pa.)**
38. Slade Cecconi, RHP, Trinity Prep School, Winter Park, Fla.
39. **Ted Stuka, RHP, UC San Diego**
40. **Sam Grace, RHP, Howell North HS, St. Charles, Mo.**

BOSTON RED SOX (26)

1. **Triston Casas, 3B, American Heritage School, Plantation, Fla.**
2. **Nick Decker, OF, Seneca HS, Tabernacle, N.J.**
3. **Durbin Feltman, RHP, Texas Christian**
4. **Kole Cottam, C, Kentucky**
5. **Thad Ward, RHP, Central Florida**
6. **Devlin Granberg, OF, Dallas Baptist**
7. **Jarren Duran, OF, Long Beach State**
8. **Elih Marrero, C, St. Thomas (Fla.)**
9. **Brian Brown, LHP, North Carolina State**
10. **Grant Williams, 2B, Kennesaw State**
11. **Nick Northcut, 3B, Mason (Ohio) HS**
12. **Chase Shugart, RHP, Texas**
13. **Dylan Hardy, OF, South Alabama**
14. Nick Lucky, 2B, Cocalico HS, Denver, Pa.
15. **Andrew Politi, RHP, Seton Hall**
16. **Chris Machamer, RHP, Kentucky**
17. **Lane Milligan, C, Oklahoma City**
18. **Eddie Jimenez, RHP, Southeastern (Fla.)**
19. **Jonathan Ortega, 2B, Texas State**
20. Kason Howell, OF, Liberty Christian HS, Argyle, Texas
21. **Brandon Howlett, 3B, Jenkins HS, Lakeland, Fla.**
22. **Yusniel Padron, RHP, Miami Dade JC**
23. **Ryan Fernandez, RHP, Hillsborough (Fla.) JC**
24. **Logan Browning, LHP, Florida Southern**
25. **Caleb Ramsey, OF, Heritage HS, Conyers, Ga.**
26. **Korby Batesole, SS, Fresno State**
27. **Gregorio Reyes, LHP, Camuy, P.R. (no school)**
28. **Kris Jackson, RHP, Corban (Ore.)**
29. Mason Ronan, LHP, Penn Cambria HS, Cresson, Pa.
30. Ryan Bliss, SS, Troup County HS, LaGrange, Ga.
31. **Connor Berry, RHP, Oklahoma**
32. **Bramdon Perez, OF, Miami Beach HS**
33. Adrian Torres, OF, Americas HS, El Paso
34. Jared Poland, 2B, Cathedral HS, Indianapolis
35. Jeremiah Boyd, C, Hickory Ridge HS, Harrisburg, N.C.
36. Jake Dukart, SS, Lake Oswego (Ore.) HS
37. Davis Wendzel, SS, Baylor
38. Art Joven, LHP, JC of the Sequoias (Calif.)
39. Shane Selman, OF, McNeese State
40. **Zach Watson, OF, Louisiana State**

CHICAGO CUBS (24)

1. **Nico Hoerner, SS, Stanford**
2. **Brennen Davis, OF, Basha HS, Chandler, Ariz.**
2s. **Cole Roederer, OF, Hart HS, Santa Clarita, Calif.**
2s. **Paul Richan, RHP, San Diego**

3. Jimmy Herron, OF, Duke
4. Ethan Roberts, RHP, Tennessee Tech
5. Andy Weber, 2B, Virginia
6. Kohl Franklin, RHP, Broken Arrow (Okla.) HS
7. D.J. Artis, OF, Liberty
8. Zach Mort, RHP, George Mason
9. Derek Casey, RHP, Virginia
10. Luke Reynolds, 3B, Southern Mississippi
11. Riley Thompson, RHP, Louisville
12. Cam Sanders, RHP, Louisiana State
13. Ezequiel Pagan, OF, Pro Baseball HS Academy, Cayey, P.R.
14. Riley McCauley, RHP, Michigan State
15. Tyler Durna, 1B, UC San Diego
16. Josh Sawyer, LHP, Texas
17. Jake Reindl, RHP, Arkansas
18. Jake Slaughter, 3B, Louisiana State
19. Layne Looney, RHP, Richmond
20. Chris Allen, LHP, JC of Marin (Calif.)
21. Carlos Vega, RHP, Southeast Missouri State
22. Jamie Galazin, OF, St. John's
23. Hunter Taylor, C, South Carolina
24. Blake Whitney, RHP, South Carolina-Upstate
25. Dalton Hurd, OF, Seattle
26. Julian Boyd, OF, St. John Bosco HS, Bellflower, Calif.
27. Niels Stone, RHP, Indian River State (Fla.) JC
28. Mitchell Parker, LHP, Manzano HS, Albuquerque
29. Levi Jordan, SS, Washington
30. Drew Wharton, OF, Clemson
31. Clayton Daniel, 2B, Jacksonville State
32. Jack Patterson, LHP, Bryant
33. Tyler Ras, RHP, Middletown North HS, Middletown, N.J.
34. Miguel Pabon, SS, Leadership Christian Academy, Guaynabo, P.R.
35. Edmond Americaan, OF, Chipola (Fla.) JC
36. Jacob Campbell, C, Craig HS, Janesville, Wis.
37. Henry Vilar, SS, Westminster Christian School, Palmetto Bay, Fla.
38. Chase Hanson, OF, Edison HS, Huntington Beach, Calif.
39. Pierson Gibis, C, Wauconda (Ill.) HS
40. Itamar Steiner, 1B, Niles North HS, Skokie, Ill.

CHICAGO WHITE SOX (4)

1. Nick Madrigal, SS, Oregon State
2. Steele Walker, OF, Oklahoma
3. Konnor Pilkington, LHP, Mississippi State
4. Lency Delgado, SS, Doral (Fla.) Academy Prep HS
5. Jonathan Stiever, RHP, Indiana
6. Codi Heuer, RHP, Wichita State
7. Caberea Weaver, OF, South Gwinnett HS, Snellville, Ga.
8. Andrew Perez, LHP, South Florida
9. Gunnar Troutwine, C, Wichita State
10. Bennett Sousa, LHP, Virginia
11. Kelvin Maldonado, SS, Pro Baseball HS Academy, Cayey, P.R.
12. Isaiah Carranza, RHP, Azusa Pacific (Calif.)
13. Jason Bilous, RHP, Coastal Carolina
14. Davis Martin, RHP, Texas Tech
15. Luke Shilling, RHP, Illinois
16. Ty Greene, C, California
17. Travis Moniot, SS, Arizona
18. Romy Gonzalez, OF, Miami
19. Gabriel Ortiz, C, PJ Educational HS, Carolina, P.R.
20. Jimmy Galusky, SS, West Virginia
21. Nick Johnson, RHP, Rhode Island
22. Ryan Fitzpatrick, 1B, UC Irvine
23. Lane Ramsey, RHP, Oklahoma
24. Rigo Fernandez, LHP, Cal State Dominguez Hills
25. Jack Maynard, RHP, UNC Greensboro
26. Devon Perez, RHP, Oklahoma
27. Ian Dawkins, OF, Sacramento State
28. Logan Sowers, OF, Indiana
29. Taylor Varnell, LHP, Oral Roberts
30. Michah Coffey, SS, Minnesota

31. Austin Conway, RHP, Louisville
32. Aaron Soto, LHP, Florida International
33. Bryce Bush, OF, De La Salle Collegiate HS, Warren, Mich.
34. Alec Valenzuela, C, Great Oak HS, Temecula, Calif.
35. Jason Morgan, RHP, North Carolina
36. Adrian Del Castillo, C, Gulliver Schools, Pinecrest, Fla.
37. Cannon King, 1B, Beverly Hills (Calif.) HS
38. Matt Klug, OF, Brookwood HS, Snellville, Ga.
39. Mason Montgomery, LHP, Leander (Texas) HS
40. Kyle Salley, LHP, Homewood-Flossmoor HS, Flossmoor, Ill.

CINCINNATI REDS (5)

1. Jonathan India, 3B, Florida
2. Lyon Richardson, RHP, Jensen Beach (Fla.) HS
2s. Josiah Gray, RHP, Le Moyne (N.Y.)
3. Bren Spillane, OF, Illinois
4. Mike Siani, OF, Penn Charter HS, Philadelphia
5. Ryan Campbell, RHP, Illinois-Chicago
6. Yomil Maysonet, RHP, PJ Educational HS, Carolina, P.R.
7. Jay Schuyler, C, San Diego
8. Matt Pidich, RHP, Pittsburgh
9. Andrew McDonald, RHP, Virginia Tech
10. A.J. Moore, RHP, Kennesaw State
11. Noah Davis, RHP, UC Santa Barbara
12. Josiah Sightler, LHP, Swansea (S.C.) HS
13. Brian Rey, OF, Miami Dade JC
14. Michael Byrne, RHP, Florida
15. Chris Williams, OF, River Ridge HS, Woodstock, Ga.
16. Drew Mount, OF, Kansas State
17. Noah Dickerson, OF, TNXL Academy, Altamonte Springs, Fla.
18. Alberto Gonzalez, RHP, Alexander HS, Laredo, Texas
19. Nick Starr, RHP, Southern Arkansas
20. Evan Marquardt, RHP, Ball State
21. Hunter Oliver, C, Cleveland State (Tenn.) JC
22. Peter Serruto, C, Millburn (N.J.) HS
23. A.J. Curtis, 1B, Ohlone (Calif.) JC
24. Connor Curlis, LHP, Ohio State
25. Ricky Salinas, RHP, Rice
26. Rylan Thomas, 1B, Central Florida
27. Eddy Demurias, RHP, South Carolina
28. Brandt Stallings, OF, Georgia College & State
29. John Schneider, RHP, Palm Beach Atlantic
30. Jake Wyrick, LHP, Middle Tennessee State
31. Justin McGregor, RHP, Oral Roberts
32. Edward Guzman, C, Leadership Christian Acad., Guaynabo, P.R.
33. Luis Lopez, SS, Medina HS, Yabucoa, P.R.
34. Cory Heitler, RHP, Ramapo (N.J.)
35. Max Dineen, OF, Pennsville (N.J.) Memorial HS
36. Zaid Walker, OF, Homewood-Flossmoor HS, Flossmoor, Ill.
37. Robert Boselli, C, St. John's
38. Adam Jacques, 2B, Interlake HS, Bellevue, Wash.
39. Sam Knowlton, RHP, Corner HS, Dora, Ala.
40. Ryan Cusick, RHP, Avon (Conn.) Old Farms School

CLEVELAND INDIANS (29)

1. Noah Naylor, C, St. Joan of Arc Catholic SS, Mississauga, Ont.
1. Ethan Hankins, RHP, Forsyth Central HS, Cumming, Ga.
2. Lenny Torres, RHP, Beacon (N.Y.) HS
2s. Nick Sandlin, RHP, Southern Mississippi
3. Richie Palacios, 2B, Towson
4. Adam Scott, LHP, Wofford
5. Steven Kwan, OF, Oregon State
6. Raynel Delgado, SS, Calvary Christian Academy, Fort Lauderdale
7. Cody Morris, RHP, South Carolina
8. Alex Royalty, RHP, UNC Wilmington
9. Brian Eichhorn, RHP, Georgia Southern
10. Robert Broom, RHP, Mercer
11. Jack DeGroat, RHP, Liberty
12. Thomas Ponticelli, RHP, San Francisco

13. Kyle Marman, RHP, Florida Atlantic
14. Korey Holland, OF, Langham Creek HS, Houston
15. Bryan Lavastida, C, Hillsborough (Fla.) JC
16. Ruben Cardenas, OF, Cal State Fullerton
17. Liam Jenkins, RHP, Louisville
18. Shane McCarthy, RHP, Seton Hall
19. Antoine Duplantis, OF, Louisiana State
20. Jake Miednik, LHP, Florida Atlantic
21. Eric Rodriguez, C, Wallace (Ala.) JC
22. Eli Lingos, LHP, Arizona State
23. Cody Farhat, OF, Texas Tech
24. Aaron Pinto, RHP, Stony Brook
25. Kellen Rholl, LHP, Angelo State (Texas)
26. Gunnar Halter, SS, Seminole State (Okla.) JC
27. Gionti Turner, SS, Watson Chapel HS, Pine Bluff, Ark.
28. Billy Wilson, OF, Loyola Marymount
29. Tim Herrin, LHP, Indiana
30. Connor Smith, 2B, Western Michigan
31. Jonathan Engelmann, OF, Michigan
32. Andrew Eyster, OF, Santa Fe (Fla.) JC
33. Daniel Schneemann, SS, Brigham Young
34. Spencer Schwellenbach, RHP, Heritage HS, Saginaw, Mich.
35. Casey Legumina, RHP, Gonzaga
36. Jose Gutierrez, 1B, Lamar HS, Arlington, Texas
37. Tim Borden, SS, Our Lady of Providence HS, Clarksville, Ind.
38. Zack Gelof, SS, Cape Henlopen HS, Lewes, Del.
39. Kaleb Hill, LHP, Watson Chapel HS, Pine Bluff, Ark.
40. Braxton Cottongame, LHP, Perry Central HS, Hazard, Ky.

COLORADO ROCKIES (22)

1. Ryan Rolison, LHP, Mississippi
1s. Grant Lavigne, 1B, Bedford (N.H.) HS
2s. Mitchell Kilkenny, RHP, Texas A&M
3. Terrin Vavra, SS, Minnesota
4. Ryan Feltner, RHP, Ohio State
5. Jake Bird, RHP, UCLA
6. Niko Decolati, OF, Loyola Marymount
7. Andrew Quezada, RHP, Cal State Fullerton
8. Nick Bush, LHP, Louisiana State
9. Willie MacIver, C, Washington
10. Cade Harris, OF, Oklahoma
11. P.J. Poulin, LHP, Connecticut
12. Kyle Datres, 3B, North Carolina
13. Rayne Supple, RHP, Wake Forest
14. Will Tribucher, LHP, Michigan
15. Coco Montes, SS, South Florida
16. Boby Johnson, RHP, Bradley
17. Reese Berberet, 3B, Long Beach JC
18. Shelby Lackey, RHP, Pacific
19. Zach Hall, OF, Colorado-Colorado Springs
20. Luke Morgan, OF, College of Charleston
21. Hunter Stovall, 2B, Mississippi State
22. Jacob Barnwell, C, Ohio State
23. Colten Schmidt, LHP, Louisiana-Lafayette
24. Trent Fennell, RHP, Barton (N.C.)
25. Robbie Metz, 2B, George Washington
26. Will Golsan, OF, Mississippi
27. Eric Hepple, RHP, Central Florida
28. John Cresto, 3B, Santa Clara
29. Miguel Ausua, LHP, Oral Roberts
30. Colton Harlow, LHP, James Madison
31. Joel Condreay, RHP, Whitworth (Wash.)
32. Reagan Todd, LHP, Colorado Mesa
33. Nick Pogue, RHP, Eau Gallie HS, Melbourne, Fla.
34. Jake Moberg, SS, Vista Murrieta HS, Murrieta, Calif.
35. Sean Mullen, RHP, Stockdale HS, Bakersfield, Calif.
36. Cayden Zimmerman, SS, Rock Canyon HS, Lone Tree, Colo.
37. Easton McMurray, LHP, Liberty HS, Bakersfield, Calif.
38. Kumar Rocker, RHP, North Oconee HS, Bogart, Ga.
39. Isaiah Thomas, OF, The Benjamin School, North Palm Beach, Fla.
40. Brett Auerbach, C, Saddleback (Calif.) JC

DETROIT TIGERS (1)

1. Casey Mize, RHP, Auburn
2. Parker Meadows, OF, Grayson HS, Loganville, Ga.
3. Kody Clemens, 2B, Texas
4. Kingston Liniak, OF, Mission Hills HS, San Marcos, Calif.
5. Adam Wolf, LHP, Louisville
6. Hugh Smith, RHP, Whitworth (Wash.)
7. Eric De La Rosa, OF, Grossmont (Calif.) JC
8. Jeremiah Burks, 2B, Fresno State
9. Tarik Skubal, LHP, Seattle
10. Brock Deatherage, OF, North Carolina State
11. Kacey Murphy, LHP, Arkansas
12. Reece Hampton, OF, Charlotte
13. Chris Proctor, C, Duke
14. Luke Sherley, SS, Texas State
15. Nick Ames, 1B, Nevada-Las Vegas
16. Dayton Dugas, OF, Wichita State
17. Avery Tuck, OF, New Mexico JC
18. Ethan DeCaster, RHP, Duke
19. Angel Reyes, RHP, Science and Arts of Oklahoma
20. Kelvin Smith, SS, Redan HS, Stone Mountain, Ga.
21. John Valente, 3B, St. John's
22. Maddux Conger, RHP, Vanderbilt
23. Jordan Verdon, 1B, San Diego State
24. Zach Malis, 3B, Grand Canyon
25. Chance Kirby, RHP, Texas-San Antonio
26. Garrett Hill, RHP, San Diego State
27. Stevie Ledesma, RHP, UC Santa Barbara
28. Daniel Reyes, OF, Miami
29. Jeb Bargfeldt, LHP, Miami
30. Jared Tobey, RHP, Wayne State
31. Jayce Vancena, RHP, Michigan
32. Clark Brinkman, OF, Creighton
33. Justin Childers, 1B, Ohio Dominican
34. Vinny Esposito, OF, Sacramento State
35. Chavez Fernander, RHP, Polk State (Fla.) JC
36. Yaya Chentouf, RHP, Pittsburgh
37. Matthew Jarecki, OF, Benedictine (Kan.)
38. Cole Henry, RHP, Florence (Ala.) HS
39. Cory Acton, 2B, American Heritage School, Plantation, Fla.
40. Kevynn Arias, C, Montreat (N.C.)

HOUSTON ASTROS (28)

1. Seth Beer, OF, Clemson
2. Jayson Schroeder, RHP, Juanita HS, Kirkland, Wash.
3. Jeremy Pena, SS, Maine
4. Alex McKenna, OF, Cal Poly
5. Cody Deason, RHP, Arizona
6. R.J. Freure, RHP, Pittsburgh
7. Cesar Salazar, C, Arizona
8. Austin Hansen, RHP, Oklahoma
9. Scott Schreiber, OF, Nebraska
10. Chandler Taylor, OF, Alabama
11. Brett Conine, RHP, Cal State Fullerton
12. Mark Moclair, RHP, Tampa
13. Shawn Dubin, RHP, Georgetown (Ky.)
14. J.P. France, RHP, Mississippi State
15. Trey Dawson, SS, Kentucky
16. Alex Holderbach, C, Eastern Kentucky
17. Brett Daniels, RHP, North Carolina
18. Michael Wielansky, SS, Wooster (Ohio)
19. Devin Conn, RHP, Nova Southeastern (Fla.)
20. Austin Dennis, OF, Middle Tennessee State
21. Dalton Roach, RHP, Minnesota State
22. Marty Costes, OF, Maryland
23. Jonathan Bermudez, LHP, Southeastern Louisiana
24. Miguel Figueroa, RHP, Oklahoma City
25. Logan Mattix, OF, Georgia College & State
26. David Hensley, SS, San Diego State
27. Juan Paulino, C, Western Oklahoma State JC
28. Joey Gonzalez, RHP, Stetson

29. Lyle Lin, C, Arizona State
30. **Layne Henderson, RHP, Azusa Pacific (Calif.)**
31. **Riley Cabral, RHP, Memphis**
32. **Jacob Billingsley, RHP, Mississippi State**
33. J.C. Correa, 2B, Alvin (Texas) JC
34. Ben Gross, RHP, Princeton
35. **A.J. Bregman, LHP, Albuquerque Academy**
36. **Cole Ayers, RHP, West Clermont HS, Batavia, Ohio**
37. Antonio Cruz, OF, Episcopal HS, Bellaire, Texas
38. **Cole Stilwell, C, Rockwall-Heath HS, Rockwall, Texas**
39. Brandon Birdsell, RHP, Willis (Texas) HS
40. Nathan Duarte, SS, Lancaster (Calif.) HS

KANSAS CITY ROYALS (18)

1. **Brady Singer, RHP, Florida**
1. **Jackson Kowar, RHP, Florida**
1. **Daniel Lynch, LHP, Virginia**
1s. **Kris Bubic, LHP, Stanford**
2. **Jonathan Bowlan, RHP, Memphis**
3. **Kyle Isbel, 2B, Nevada, Las Vegas**
4. **Eric Cole, OF, Arkansas**
5. **Austin Cox, LHP, Mercer**
6. **Zach Haake, RHP, Kentucky**
7. **Tyler Gray, RHP, Central Arkansas**
8. **Jackson Lueck, OF, Florida State**
9. **Kevon Jackson, OF, Queen Creek (Ariz.) HS**
10. **Austin Lambright, LHP, Central Oklahoma**
11. **Michael Emodi, C, Creighton**
12. **Rylan Kaufman, LHP, San Jacinto (Texas) JC**
13. **Jon Heasley, RHP, Oklahoma State**
14. **Christian Cosby, RHP, Chapman (Calif.)**
15. Milan Walla, OF, Tivy HS, Kerrville, Texas
16. **Kyle Hinton, RHP, Delaware**
17. **Noah Bryant, RHP, Georgia Highlands JC**
18. R.J. Dabovich, RHP, Central Arizona JC
19. Hunter Wolfe, SS, Walters State (Tenn.) JC
20. Josh Hendrickson, LHP, Barton (Kan.) JC
21. **Nathan Eaton, C, Virginia Military Institute**
22. **Bryce Hensley, LHP, UNC Greensboro**
23. **Josh Dye, LHP, Florida Gulf Coast**
24. **Gage Hughes, SS, Greenup (Ky.) County HS**
25. **Hunter Strong, OF, Central Arkansas**
26. **Daniel James, RHP, Texas-Arlington**
27. **Derrick Adams, LHP, Jacksonville State**
28. **Rhett Aplin, 1B, Florida State**
29. **Andres Nunez, RHP, Florida International**
30. **Kyle Kasser, 2B, Oregon**
31. **William Hancock, C, Central Arkansas**
32. **Brhet Bewley, 3B, San Diego**
33. **Teddy Cillis, LHP, Hofstra**
34. Ty Madden, RHP, Cypress (Texas) Ranch HS
35. **Kody Hoese, 3B, Tulane**
36. Elijah Pleasants, RHP, Rossview HS, Clarksville, Tenn.
37. **David Hollie, OF, Cross Creek HS, Augusta, Ga.**
38. Trae Robertson, LHP, Hickman HS, Columbia, Mo.
39. Adam Hackenberg, C, The Miller School, Charlottesville, Va.
40. Ky Bush, LHP, Fremont HS, Plain City, Utah

LOS ANGELES ANGELS (17)

1. **Jordyn Adams, OF, Green Hope HS, Cary, N.C.**
2. **Jeremiah Jackson, SS, St. Luke's Episcopal School, Mobile, Ala.**
3. **Aaron Hernandez, RHP, Texas A&M-Corpus Christi**
4. **Kyle Bradish, RHP, New Mexico State**
5. **William English, RHP, Western International HS, Detroit**
6. **Austin Warren, RHP, UNC Wilmington**
7. **Andrew Wantz, RHP, UNC Greensboro**
8. **Tyler Smith, RHP, Canisius**
9. **Jake Lee, RHP, Oakland**
10. **Ben Morrison, RHP, Western Kentucky**
11. **Connor Van Scoyoc, RHP, Jefferson HS, Cedar Rapids, Iowa**

12. **Daniel Nunan, LHP, Ocean City (N.J.) HS**
13. **Cooper Criswell, RHP, North Carolina**
14. **Drevian Nelson, OF, North Shore HS, Houston**
15. **Nick Frank, RHP, St. Mary's**
16. **Chase Chaney, RHP, Mountain View HS, Lawrenceville, Ga.**
17. **Luis Alvarado, RHP, Nebraska**
18. **Dylan King, RHP, Belmont**
19. **Datren Bray, OF, Gordon State (Ga.) JC**
20. **Kyle Tyler, RHP, Oklahoma**
21. **Cristian Reyes, RHP, Miami (no school)**
22. Hunter Milam, LHP, Russell County HS, Seale, Ala.
23. **William Rivera, OF, Puerto Rico Baseball Academy, Gurabo, P.R.**
24. Isaiah Campbell, RHP, Arkansas
25. **Dazon Cole, RHP, Central Michigan**
26. **Darrien Williams, RHP, Prairie View A&M**
27. **Jacob Voss, RHP, Creighton**
28. **Mitch Spires, SS, Winthrop**
29. Seth Caldwell, RHP, Oak Ridge (Tenn.) HS
30. **Connor Higgins, LHP, Arizona State**
31. Mitchell Miller, LHP, Clemson
32. Jared Janczak, RHP, Texas Christian
33. **Wade Bailey, 2B, Georgia Tech**
34. Paul McIntosh, C, Motlow State (Tenn.) JC
35. **Tim Millard, 3B, Dallas Baptist**
36. Hueston Morrill, RHP, Suwannee HS, Live Oak, FL
37. **D.C. Clawson, C, Brigham Young**
38. Chandler Champlain, RHP, Santa Margarita, Rancho Santa Margarita, CA
39. Max Alba, RHP, Franklin (Wis.) HS
40. Sam Stoutenborough, RHP, Palma HS, Salinas, Calif.

LOS ANGELES DODGERS (30)

1. **J.T. Ginn, RHP, Brandon (Miss.) HS**
2. **Michael Grove, RHP, West Virginia**
3. **John Rooney, LHP, Hofstra**
4. **Braydon Fisher, RHP, Clear Falls HS, League City, Texas**
5. **Devin Mann, SS, Louisville**
6. **Bryan Warzek, LHP, New Orleans**
7. **James Outman, OF, Sacramento State**
8. **Luke Heyer, 2B, Kentucky**
9. **Josh McLain, OF, North Carolina State**
10. **Deacon Liput, 2B, Florida**
11. **Stephen Kolek, RHP, Texas A&M**
12. **Hunter Feduccia, C, Louisiana State**
13. **Dillon Paulson, 1B, Southern California**
14. Brandon White, RHP, West HS, Chehalis, Wash.
15. **Julian Smith, LHP, Catawba Valley (N.C.) JC**
16. Trey Dillard, RHP, San Jacinto (Texas) JC
17. **Aldrich De Jongh, OF, Hillsborough (Fla.) JC**
18. **Niko Hulsizer, OF, Morehead State**
19. **Sam McWilliams, OF, Meridian (Miss.) JC**
20. **Caleb Sampen, RHP, Wright State**
21. **Tre Todd, C, Liberty**
22. **Simon Landry, 1B, Pearl River (Miss.) JC**
23. **Justin Hagenman, RHP, Penn State**
24. Jacen Roberson, OF, Garces Memorial HS, Bakersfield, Calif.
25. **Hunter Speer, RHP, William Carey (Miss.)**
26. **Aaron Ackerman, C, Illinois-Chicago**
27. **Connor Mitchell, LHP, Butler**
28. **Reza Aleaziz, RHP, Oklahoma State**
29. **Daniel Robinson, OF, Central Michigan**
30. **Matt Cogen, OF, Belmont**
31. **Andrew Shaps, LHP, William Jessup (Calif.)**
32. **Jacob Gilliland, RHP, Next Level Academy, Montgomery, Ala.**
33. **Drew Avans, OF, Southeastern Louisiana**
34. **Austin Drury, LHP, North Florida**
35. Tyler Reichenborn, OF, Iowa Western JC
36. **Jeremiah Vison, OF, Golden West (Calif.) JC**
37. **Jon Littell, OF, Oklahoma State**
38. Connery Peters, RHP, Joshua (Texas) HS
39. Jordan Myrow, OF, San Jacinto (Texas) JC

40. Ben Specht, RHP, Evangelical Christian School, Fort Myers, Fla.

MIAMI MARLINS (13)

1. **Connor Scott, OF, Plant HS, Tampa**
2. **Osiris Johnson, SS, Encinal HS, Alameda, Calif.**
2s. **Will Banfield, C, Brookwood HS, Snellville, Ga.**
3. **Tristan Pompey, OF, Kentucky**
4. **Nick Fortes, C, Mississippi**
5. **Chris Vallimont, RHP, Mercyhurst (Pa.)**
6. **Cameron Barstad, C, Serra HS, San Mateo, Calif.**
7. **Cason Sherrod, RHP, Texas A&M**
8. **Peyton Culbertson, RHP, Arkansas State**
9. **Jake Walters, RHP, Alabama**
10. **Tanner Andrews, RHP, Purdue**
11. **Davis Bradshaw, OF, Meridian (Miss.) JC**
12. **Zack Leban, RHP, Kansas**
13. **Keegan Fish, C, Lakota West HS, West Chester, Ohio**
14. **Eli Villalobos, RHP, Long Beach State**
15. Zach Greene, RHP, South Alabama
16. **Sam Bordner, RHP, Louisville**
17. **Alex Vesia, LHP, Cal State East Bay**
18. **Zach Wolf, RHP, Seattle**
19. **Justin Evans, RHP, Columbus State (Ga.)**
20. **Cam Baird, RHP, Texas State**
21. **Connor Grant, OF, North Greenville (S.C.)**
22. **Milton Smith, OF, Meridian (Miss.) JC**
23. **Giovanni Lopez, RHP, Missouri**
24. **Nathan Alexander, RHP, Texas-San Antonio**
25. **Luke Jarvis, SS, Auburn**
26. **Tyler Jones, RHP, Wichita State**
27. **Harrison DiNicola, OF, Texas A&M-Corpus Christi**
28. **Gunnar Schubert, SS, Gonzaga**
29. **C.J. Carter, RHP, Troy**
30. Garrett McDaniels, LHP, Pee Dee Academy, Mullins, S.C.
31. Steve Scott, OF, Vanderbilt
32. **Jake Norton, RHP, Stephen F. Austin State**
33. Andrew Martinez, SS, UC Santa Barbara
34. **Joe Strzelecki, RHP, Nova Southeastern (Fla.)**
35. **Jackson Rose, RHP, Minnesota**
36. Riley Egloff, RHP, Heritage HS, Littleton, Colo.
37. Robby Martin, OF, Jefferson HS, Tampa
38. Bryce Miller, RHP, Blinn (Texas) JC
39. **Andrew Turner, 3B, Long Island**
40. **Andrew Miller, LHP, Kentucky**

MILWAUKEE BREWERS (21)

1. **Brice Turang, SS, Santiago HS, Corona, Calif.**
2. **Joe Gray, OF, Hattiesburg (Miss.) HS**
2s. **Micah Bello, OF, Hilo (Hawaii) HS**
4. **Aaron Ashby, LHP, Crowder (Mo.) JC**
5. **Justin Jarvis, RHP, Lake Norman HS, Mooresville, N.C.**
6. **Drew Rasmussen, RHP, Oregon State**
7. **David Fry, C, Northwestern State**
8. **Luis Gonzalez, RHP, PJ Educational HS, Carolina, P.R.**
9. **Arbert Cipion, OF, Passaic County Technical Institute, Wayne, N.J.**
10. **J.T. Hintzen, RHP, Florida Southern**
11. Davis Daniel, RHP, Auburn
12. **Korry Howell, SS, Kirkwood (Iowa) JC**
13. **Reese Olson, RHP, North Hall HS, Gainesville, Ga.**
14. Elijah Cabell, OF, TNXL Academy, Altamonte Springs, Fla.
15. **Nick Trogrlic-Iverson, RHP, Central Arizona JC**
16. **Alec Barger, RHP, Polk State (Fla.) JC**
17. **Clayton Andrews, LHP, Long Beach State**
18. **Scotty Sunitsch, LHP, Washington State**
19. Peyton Zabel, RHP, Riggs HS, Pierre, S.D.
20. **Joey Matulovich, RHP, California**
21. Steve Hajjar, LHP, Central Catholic HS, Lawrence, Mass.
22. Joey Baran, LHP, Lackawanna (Pa.) JC
23. Jared Platero, RHP, Beckman HS, Irvine, Calif.
24. **Wade Beasley, RHP, Horatio (Ark.) HS**
25. **Pablo Garabitos, OF, Lakewood Ranch HS, Bradenton, Fla.**

26. Connor Sparks, RHP, Graham Collegiate HS, Saskatoon, Sask.
27. **Brady Schanuel, RHP, Iowa**
28. **Kekai Rios, C, Hawaii**
29. Nander De Sedas, SS, Montverde (Fla.) Academy
30. Basilio Pacheco, LHP, Segerstrom HS, Santa Ana, Calif.
31. Matt Dillard, LHP, St. Pius X HS, Houston
32. Johnny Cuevas, 3B, Palm Desert (Calif.) HS
33. Brandon Hylton, 1B, Ridge HS, Basking Ridge, N.J.
34. **Michael Mediavilla, LHP, Miami**
35. Josh Watson, OF, Texas Christian
36. Brandon Williamson, LHP, North Iowa Area JC
37. **Franklin Hernandez, RHP, JC of Central Florida**
38. Aidan Maldonado, RHP, Rosemount (Minn.) HS
39. **Caleb Marquez, C, Blue Springs (Mo.) HS**
40. Wes Clarke, C, Liberty Christian Academy, Lynchburg, Va.

MINNESOTA TWINS (20)

1. **Trevor Larnach, OF, Oregon State**
2. **Ryan Jeffers, C, UNC Wilmington**
4. **DaShawn Keirsey, OF, Utah**
5. **Cole Sands, RHP, Florida State**
6. **Charles Mack, 3B, Williamsville East HS, East Amherst, N.Y.**
7. **Josh Winder, RHP, Virginia Military Institute**
8. **Chris Williams, C, Clemson**
9. **Joe Garry, OF, Pascagoula (Miss.) HS**
10. **Regi Grace, RHP, Madison (Miss.) Central HS**
11. **Michael Helman, 2B, Texas A&M**
12. **Jon Olsen, RHP, UCLA**
13. **Trevor Casanova, C, Cal State Northridge**
14. **Erick Rivera, OF, Superior Urbana HS, Salinas, P.R.**
15. **Kody Funderburk, LHP, Dallas Baptist**
16. Anthony Tuionetoa, RHP, Baldwin HS, Wailuku, Hawaii
17. **Erik Cha, LHP, Cal State Fullerton**
18. **Andrew Cabezas, RHP, Miami**
19. **Austin Schulfer, RHP, Wisconsin-Milwaukee**
20. **Seth Pinkerton, RHP, Hartford**
21. **Gabe Snyder, 1B, Wright State**
22. **Jacob Blank, RHP, Augustana (S.D.)**
23. **Albee Weiss, C, Cal State Northridge**
24. **Michael Davis, 3B, Texas Tech**
25. **LaRon Smith, C, Foothills Composite HS, Okotoks, Alb.**
26. **Brian Rapp, RHP, Boston College**
27. **Hunter Lee, RHP, High Point**
28. **Austin Hale, C, Stetson**
29. **J.T. Perez, LHP, Cincinnati**
30. Seth Halvorsen, RHP, Heritage Christian Academy, Maple Grove, Minn.
31. **Zach Neff, LHP, Mississippi State**
32. Ryan Holgate, OF, Davis (Calif.) HS
33. **Denny Bentley, LHP, Howard (Texas) JC**
34. **Dylan Stowell, RHP, California Baptist**
35. **Tanner Howell, RHP, Dixie State (Utah)**
36. Zac Taylor, OF, Illinois
37. **Luke Ritter, OF, Wichita State**
38. **Dylan Thomas, RHP, Hawaii**
39. Bryce Collins, RHP, Hart HS, Santa Clarita, Calif.
40. **Tyler Webb, OF, Memphis**

NEW YORK METS (6)

1. **Jarred Kelenic, OF, Waukesha (Wis.) West HS**
2. **Simeon Woods-Richardson, RHP, Kempner HS, Sugar Land, Texas**
3. **Carlos Cortes, 2B, South Carolina**
4. **Adam Hill, RHP, South Carolina**
5. **Ryley Gilliam, RHP, Clemson**
6. **Nick Meyer, C, Cal Poly**
7. **Kevin Smith, LHP, Georgia**
8. **Tylor Megill, RHP, Arizona**
9. **Bryce Montes de Oca, RHP, Missouri**
10. **Manny Rodriguez, SS, Cincinnati**
11. **Franklin Parra, LHP, Copiague (N.Y.) HS**
12. **Ross Adolph, OF, Toledo**
13. **Christian Tripp, RHP, New Mexico**

14. **Andrew Mitchell, LHP, Auburn**
15. **Phil Capra, C, Wagner**
16. **L.A. Woodard, SS, Middle Tennessee State**
17. **Allan Winans, RHP, Campbell**
18. **Chase Chambers, 1B, Tennessee Tech**
19. **Tommy Wilson, RHP, Cal State Fullerton**
20. Brooks Warren, LHP, East Central (Miss.) JC
21. **Zachary Hammer, RHP, Alexander Central HS, Taylorsville, N.C.**
22. **Jaylen Palmer, SS, Holy Cross HS, Flushing, N.Y.**
23. **Saul Gonzalez, RHP, Montverde (Fla.) Acedmy**
24. **Hayden Senger, C, Miami (Ohio)**
25. **David Miranda, OF, Florida Atlantic**
26. **Brian Sharp, 3B, Missouri**
27. **Zach Rheams, OF, Texas Tech**
28. **Mitch Hickey, RHP, UC San Diego**
29. **Nelson Mompierre, C, St. Thomas (Fla.)**
30. **Chandler Avant, SS, Alabama**
31. **Brendan Hardy, RHP, Harrison Central HS, Gulfport, Miss.**
32. Jake Mangum, OF, Mississippi State
33. Mike Picollo, RHP, Blue Valley North HS, Overland Park, Kan.
34. **Duke Kinamon, 2B, Stanford**
35. Ian Mejia, RHP, Sahuarita (Ariz.) HS
36. Denzel Clarke, OF, Everest Academy, Thornhill, Ont.
37. Zachary Fascia, C, Indian Hills (Iowa) JC
38. Nick Zona, SS, Hanover HS, Mechanicsville, Va.
39. Kody Darcy, SS, Kentridge HS, Kent, Wash.
40. **Brian Metoyer, RHP, Louisiana State-Alexandira**

NEW YORK YANKEES (23)

1. **Anthony Seigler, C, Cartersville (Ga.) HS**
2. **Josh Breaux, C, McLennan (Texas) JC**
3. **Ryder Green, OF, Karns HS, Knoxville**
4. **Frank German, RHP, North Florida**
5. **Brandon Lockridge, OF, Troy**
6. **Rodney Hutchison, RHP, North Carolina**
7. **Daniel Bies, RHP, Gonzaga**
8. **Connor Van Hoose, RHP, Bucknell**
9. **Mick Vorhof, RHP, Grand Canyon**
10. **Josh Maciejewski, LHP, Charlotte**
11. **Tanner Myatt, RHP, Florence-Darlington Tech (S.C.) JC**
12. **Matt Pita, OF, Virginia Military Institute**
13. **Isaiah Pasteur, OF, George Washington**
14. **Kyle Gray, 2B, West Virginia**
15. **Nick Ernst, RHP, Miami (Ohio)**
16. **Derek Craft, RHP, Texas-San Antonio**
17. **Barrett Loseke, RHP, Arkansas**
18. **Alex Guerrero, C, Eagle (Idaho) HS**
19. **Alex Junior, OF, Tennessee Tech**
20. **Marcus Evey, RHP, Tennessee Tech**
21. **Mitch Robinson, 3B, British Columbia**
22. **Keegan Curtis, RHP, Louisiana-Monroe**
23. **Justin Wilson, RHP, Vanderbilt**
24. **Blakely Brown, RHP, Georgia Southern**
25. **Sean Boyle, RHP, Dallas Baptist**
26. **Jack Thoreson, C, St. Mary's**
27. **Mickey Gasper, 1B, Bryant**
28. **Max Burt, 3B, Northeastern**
29. **Jackson Bertsch, RHP, Liberty**
30. **Tyler Johnson, RHP, Gardner-Webb**
31. Patrick Winkel, C, Amity Regional HS, Woodbridge, Conn.
32. **Sincere Smith, SS, East Bladen HS, Elizabethtown, N.C.**
33. **Charlie Ruegger, RHP, Stevens Inst.of Technology, Hoboken, N.J.**
34. **Matt McGarry, 2B, Belmont Abbey (N.C.)**
35. Austin Wells, C, Bishop Gorman HS, Las Vegas
36. Jack Anderson, RHP, Jesuit HS, Tampa
37. Landon Marceaux, RHP, Destrehan (La.) HS
38. Dan Metzdorf, LHP, Boston College
39. Brady Allen, OF, Jenkins HS, Lakeland, Fla.
40. **Reid Anderson, RHP, Brown**

OAKLAND ATHLETICS (9)

1. **Kyler Murray, OF, Oklahoma**
2. **Jameson Hannah, OF, Dallas Baptist**
2s. **Jeremy Eierman, SS, Missouri State**
3. **Hogan Harris, LHP, Louisiana-Lafayette**
4. **Alfonso Rivas, 1B, Arizona**
5. **Brady Feigl, RHP, Mississippi**
6. **Lawrence Butler, OF, Westlake HS, Atlanta**
7. **Charlie Cerny, RHP, Illinois-Chicago**
8. **J.J. Schwarz, C, Florida**
9. **Chase Cohen, RHP, Georgia Southern**
10. **Clark Cota, RHP, UNC Wilmington**
11. **Joe DeMers, RHP, Washington**
12. **Noah Vaughan, OF, Texas-Arlington**
13. **Dallas Woolfolk, RHP, Mississippi**
14. **Gus Varland, RHP, Concordia (Minn.)**
15. **Calvin Coker, RHP, Auburn**
16. **Bryce Nightengale, RHP, George Mason**
17. **Devin Foyle, OF, Kansas**
18. **Cobie Vance, 2B, Alabama**
19. **Matt Cross, C, Niagara County (N.Y.) JC**
20. **Max Schuemann, 2B, Eastern Michigan**
21. **Daniel Martinez, RHP, Riverside (Calif.) JC**
22. **Aiden McIntyre, RHP, Holy Names (Calif.)**
23. **Jonah Bride, 3B, South Carolina**
24. **Dakota Mills, RHP, Sam Houston State**
25. **Alonzo Jones, OF, Vanderbilt**
26. **Leudeny Pineda, RHP, Advanced Software Analysis-Miami**
27. **Chase Calabuig, OF, San Diego State**
28. **Reid Birlingmair, RHP, Illinois-Chicago**
29. **Austin Briggs, LHP, McNeese State**
30. **Gio Dingcong, 1B, St. Thomas Aquinas (N.Y.)**
31. **Alex Pantuso, RHP, Slippery Rock (Pa.)**
32. **John Jones, C, North Greenville (S.C.)**
33. **Joseph Pena, SS, St. Thomas Aquinas (N.Y.)**
34. **Nick Ward, 2B, West Chester (Pa.)**
35. Brandon White, RHP, Simsbury (Conn.) HS
36. Chad Bryant, RHP, Pensacola State (Fla.) JC
37. Andrew Miller, OF, Casa Grande HS, Pentaluma, Calif.
38. **Austin Piscotty, OF, St. Mary's**
39. Hudson Haskin, OF, Avon (Conn.) Old Farms School
40. Lyndon Weaver, OF, Redan HS, Stone Mountain, Ga.

PHILADELPHIA PHILLIES (3)

1. **Alec Bohm, 3B, Wichita State**
4. **Colton Eastman, RHP, Cal State Fullerton**
5. **Matt Vierling, OF, Notre Dame**
6. **Logan Simmons, SS, Tattnall Square Academy, Macon, Ga.**
7. **Gabriel Cotto, LHP, Puerto Rico Baseball Academy, Gurabo, P.R.**
8. **Seth Lancaster, SS, Coastal Carolina**
9. **Dominic Pipkin, RHP, Pinole Valley HS, Pinole, Calif.**
10. **Madison Stokes, 3B, South Carolina**
11. **Jack Perkins, RHP, Stetson**
12. **James McArthur, RHP, Mississippi**
13. **Jose Mercado, SS, Beltran Baseball Academy, Florida, P.R.**
14. **Jesse Wilkening, C, Nebraska**
15. Daniel Carpenter, RHP, King HS, Riverside, Calif.
16. **Tyler McKay, RHP, Howard (Texas) JC**
17. **Keylan Killgore, LHP, Wichita State**
18. **Matt Kroon, 3B, Oklahoma State**
19. **Mark Potter, RHP, JC of Central Florida**
20. **Connor Litton, 3B, East Carolina**
21. Jake Smith, RHP, Chapel Hill (N.C.) HS
22. **Luke Miller, OF, Indiana**
23. **Logan O'Hoppe, C, St. John the Baptist HS, West Islip, N.Y.**
24. **Corbin Williams, OF, JC of the Canyons (Calif.)**
25. **Adam Cox, RHP, Montana State**
26. **Eric White, RHP, Southern Arkansas**
27. **Jack Conley, C, North Carolina State**
28. Jonathan Jones, RHP, Manvel (Texas) HS

29. Jaylen Smith, LHP, Copperas Cove (Texas) HS
30. Brandon Ramey, RHP, King HS, Riverside, Calif.
31. Tyler Carr, RHP, South Alabama
32. Ben Aklinski, OF, Kentucky
33. Jake Kinney, RHP, Tallahassee (Fla.) JC
34. Nick Matera, C, Rutgers
35. Austin Ross, RHP, Radford
36. Trent Bowles, OF, Texas-San Antonio
37. Ryan Rijo, 1B, New Mexico JC
38. Stephen Jones, RHP, Samford
39. Mat Nelson, C, Calvary Christian HS, Clearwater, Fla.
40. Waylon Richardson, RHP, Kankakee (Ill.) JC

PITTSBURGH PIRATES (10)

1. Travis Swaggerty, OF, South Alabama
1s. Gunnar Hoglund, RHP, Fivay HS, Hudson, Fla.
2. Braxton Ashcraft, RHP, Robinson (Texas) HS
3. Connor Kaiser, SS, Vanderbilt
4. Aaron Shortridge, RHP, California
5. Grant Koch, C, Arkansas
6. Michael Flynn, RHP, Arizona
7. Brett Kinneman, OF, North Carolina State
8. Zach Spears, LHP, Miami (Ohio)
9. Logan Stoelke, RHP, Louisiana-Lafayette
10. Mike Gretler, 3B, Oregon State
11. Michael Burrows, RHP, Waterford (Conn.) HS
12. Zac Susi, C, Connecticut
13. Zack Kone, SS, Duke
14. Daniel Amaral, OF, UCLA
15. Jonah Davis, OF, California
16. Colin Selby, RHP, Randolph-Macon (Va.)
17. Brad Case, RHP, Rollins (Fla.)
18. Michael Lopresti, RHP, St. John's
19. Will Kobos, RHP, George Washington
20. Conner Loeprich, RHP, St. Mary's
21. Will Gardner, RHP, Carson-Newman (Tenn.)
22. Jason Brandow, OF, Vintage HS, Napa, Calif.
23. Tyler Miller, SS, Spanish Fort (Ala.) HS
24. Cam Alldred, LHP, Cincinnati
25. Luke Mangieri, OF, Bradley
26. Ethan Paul, 2B, Vanderbilt
27. Ryan Haug, C, Arizona
28. Nick Patten, 1B, Delaware
29. Giovanni DiGiacomo, OF, Canterbury School, Fort Myers, Fla.
30. Jack Herman, OF, Eastern Regional HS, Voorhees Township, N.J.
31. Chase Lambert, SS, Pepperdine
32. Dean Lockery, 2B, Central Connecticut State
33. Joe Jacques, LHP, Manhattan
34. Davis Sharpe, RHP, Mill Creek HS, Hoschton, Ga.
35. Justin Harrer, OF, Washington State
36. Emanuel Andrews, OF, Long Beach Poly HS
37. Lavoisier Fisher, OF, North Gwinnett HS, Suwanee, Ga.
38. Brendt Citta, OF, Kansas
39. Cody Smith, RHP, Charleston Southern
40. Jake Mielock, RHP, Colorado Mesa

SAN DIEGO PADRES (7)

1. Ryan Weathers, LHP, Loretto (Tenn.) HS
1s. Xavier Edwards, SS, North Broward Prep HS, Coconut Creek, Fla.
2s. Grant Little, OF, Texas Tech
3. Owen Miller, SS, Illinois State
4. Dylan Coleman, RHP, Missouri State
5. Dwanya Williams-Sutton, OF, East Carolina
6. Alexuan Vega, LHP, Rodriguez HS, Lajas, P.R.
7. Jawuan Harris, OF, Rutgers
8. Steven Wilson, RHP, Santa Clara
9. Luke Becker, 2B, Kentucky
10. Jose Quezada, RHP, Texas Tech
11. Nick Gatewood, C, Georgia State
12. Sean Guilbe, 2B, Muhlenberg HS, Laureldale, Pa.

13. Antoine Kelly, LHP, Maine East HS, Park Ridge, Ill.
14. Erik Sabrowski, LHP, Cloud County (Kan.) JC
15. Nick Thwaits, RHP, Fort Recovery (Ohio) HS
16. Michael Curry, OF, Georgia
17. Hazahel Quijada, LHP, UC Riverside
18. Dylan Smith, RHP, Stafford (Texas) HS
19. Ian Villers, RHP, Northgate HS, Walnut Creek, Calif.
20. Reiss Knehr, RHP, Fordham
21. Mason Fox, RHP, Gardner-Webb
22. Payton Smith, OF, Thurmond HS, Johnston, S.C.
23. Nelson Alvarez, RHP, Miami Dade JC
24. Pavin Parks, 3B, Kent State
25. Lee Solomon, 2B, Lipscomb
26. Tyler Mortensen, LHP, Davis (Calif.) HS
27. Gabe Mosser, RHP, Shippensburg (Pa.)
28. Jake Plastiak, 3B, Andrew HS, Tinley Park, Ill.
29. William Duncan, RHP, Richardson (Texas) HS
30. Cullen Dana, LHP, Seton Hall
31. Jake Sims, RHP, St Leo (Fla.)
32. Cody Tyler, LHP, Wichita State
33. Rainier Aguilar, C, Redlands (Calif.)
34. George Arias, RHP, Tuscon Magnet HS
35. Jake Pfennigs, RHP, Post Falls (Idaho) HS
36. Will Freeman, RHP, Jones County (Miss.) JC
37. Ben Abram, RHP, Georgetown (Ont.) District HS
38. Michael Suarez, 1B, Miami Sunset HS
39. Seth Mayberry, RHP, Dinwiddie (Va.) HS
40. Michael Knorr, RHP, Carlsbad (Calif.) HS

SAN FRANCISCO GIANTS (2)

1. Joey Bart, C, Georgia Tech
2. Sean Hjelle, RHP, Kentucky
3. Jake Wong, RHP, Grand Canyon
4. Blake Rivera, RHP, Wallace State (Ala.) JC
5. Keaton Winn, RHP, Iowa Western JC
6. P.J. Hilson, RHP, Nettleton HS, Jonesboro, Ark.
7. Edison Mora, SS, Puerto Rico Baseball Academy, Gurabo, P.R.
8. Solomon Bates, RHP, Southern California
9. Ben Madison, RHP, Central Baptist (Ark.)
10. Alex DuBord, RHP, Faulkner (Ala.)
11. David Villar, 3B, South Florida
12. Sean Roby, 3B, Arizona Western JC
13. George Bell, OF, Connors State (Okla.) JC
14. Bryce Tucker, LHP, Central Florida
15. Matt Frisbee, RHP, UNC Greensboro
16. Trenton Toplikar, RHP, UC Riverside
17. Ryan Olenek, OF, Mississippi
18. Bryan Hernandez, OF, Such HS, San Juan, P.R.
19. Randy Norris, OF, Winston-Salem State (N.C.)
20. Jett Manning, SS, Alabama
21. Angel Guzman, C, Beltran Baseball Academy, Florida, P.R.
22. Clay Helvey, RHP, Tampa
23. Ben Strahm, RHP, Northeastern State (Okla.)
24. Preston White, RHP, The Master's (Calif.)
25. Fabian Pena, C, Manhattan
26. Jacob Lopez, LHP, JC of the Canyons (Calif.)
27. Dylan Dusek, LHP, Texas Tech
28. Travis Perry, RHP, Indian River State JC
29. Marcos Campos, SS, Siena
30. Kwan Adkins, OF, Northwestern State
31. Ryan Walker, RHP, Washington State
32. Braden Frankfort, C, Fresno Pacific
33. Austin Edgette, OF, Bloomsburg (Pa.)
34. Lucas Krull, LHP, Jefferson (Mo.) JC
35. Chris Roberts, RHP, San Jacinto (Texas) JC
36. Bryan Hoeing, RHP, Louisville
37. Ryan McDonald, RHP, JC of Southern Nevada
38. Brett Hansen, LHP, Foothill HS, Pleasanton, Calif.
39. Trevor Horn, RHP, Nevada-Las Vegas
40. Abdiel Layer, 3B, Miami Dade JC

SEATTLE MARINERS (14)

1. Logan Gilbert, RHP, Stetson
2. Josh Stowers, OF, Louisville
3. Cal Raleigh, C, Florida State
4. Michael Plassmeyer, LHP, Missouri
5. Nolan Hoffman, RHP, Texas A&M
6. Joey O'Brien, RHP, JC of Southern Nevada
7. Jake Anchia, C, Nova Southeastern (Fla.)
8. Joey Gerber, RHP, Illinois
9. Keegan McGovern, OF, Georgia
10. Matt Sanders, SS, Troy
11. Damon Casetta-Stubbs, RHP, Kings Way Christian Schools, Vancouver, Wash.
12. Ryne Ogren, 2B, Elon
13. Charlie McConnell, OF, Northeastern
14. Tyler Suellentrop, RHP, Indian River State (Fla.) JC
15. Matt Willrodt, RHP, Cisco (Texas) JC
16. Holden Laws, LHP, South Granville HS, Creedmoor, N.C.
17. Cesar Trejo, SS, UNC Greensboro
18. Noah Zavolas, RHP, Harvard
19. Dean Nevarez, C, San Diego State
20. J.T. Salter, RHP, West Alabama
21. Grant Anderson, RHP, McNeese State
22. Nick Rodriguez, SS, Nevada-Las Vegas
23. Ryan Ramiz, OF, Seton Hall
24. Ben Onyshko, LHP, Stetson
25. Connor Kopach, 2B, Southern Illinois
26. Cal Hernandez, 3B, Oral Roberts
27. Cash Gladfelter, 2B, Shippensburg (Pa.)
28. Beau Branton, 2B, Stanford
29. Bobby Honeyman, 3B, Stony Brook
30. Cody Staab, OF, Rice
31. Rigo Beltran, LHP, Lynn (Fla.)
32. Zach Scott, 2B, St. Leo (Fla.)
33. Penn Murfee, RHP, Santa Clara
34. Nick Wegmann, LHP, Binghamton
35. Will Gambino, RHP, Paul VI HS, Haddonfield, N.J.
36. Justin Wrobleski, LHP, Sequoyah HS, Canton, Ga.
37. Parker Towns, RHP, Dallas Baptist
38. Jack Montgomery, 2B, Simsbury (Conn.) HS
39. Jacob Maton, RHP, Glenwood HS, Chatham, Ill.
40. David Rhodes, RHP, Langley (B.C.) SS

ST. LOUIS CARDINALS (19)

1. Nolan Gorman, 3B, O'Connor HS, Phoenix
1s. Griffin Roberts, RHP, Wake Forest
2s. Luken Baker, 1B, Texas Christian
3. Mateo Gil, SS, Timber Creek HS, Fort Worth
4. Steven Gingery, LHP, Texas Tech
5. Nick Dunn, 2B, Maryland
6. Edgar Gonzalez, RHP, Fresno State
7. Brendan Donovan, 3B, South Alabama
8. Lars Nootbaar, OF, Southern California
9. Matt Duce, C, Dallas Baptist
10. Kevin Woodall, 1B, Coastal Carolina
11. Chris Holba, RHP, East Carolina
12. Francisco Justo, RHP, Monroe (N.Y.) JC
13. Colin Schmid, LHP, Appalachian State
14. Brandon Riley, 2B, North Carolina
15. Mike Brettell, RHP, Central Michigan
16. Evan Sisk, LHP, College of Charleston
17. Kyle Leahy, RHP, Coloardo Mesa
18. Cole Aker, RHP, Tampa
19. Josh Shaw, 2B, St. John's
20. Parker Kelly, RHP, Oregon
21. Michael Perri, SS, San Francisco
22. Kevin Vargas, SS, International Baseball Academy, Ceiba, P.R.
23. Michael Baird, RHP, Southern Illinois
24. Eli Kraus, LHP, Kent State
25. Troy Montemayor, RHP, Baylor

26. Connor Coward, RHP, Virginia Tech
27. Perry DellaValle, RHP, Seton Hill (Pa.)
28. Justin Toerner, OF, Cal State Northridge
29. Alerick Soularie, OF, San Jacinto (Texas) JC
30. Kendrick Calilao, OF, The First Academy, Orlando
31. Ty Cohen, RHP, Florida Tech
32. Brandon Purcell, C, Georgia College & State
33. Chris Rivera, RHP, Long Beach State
34. Benito Santiago, C, Tennessee
35. Liam Sabino, 3B, Pittsburgh
36. Cole Kreuter, 3B, UC Irvine
37. Christian Caudle, C, Texas A&M-Kingsville
38. Jaden Hill, RHP, Ashdown (Ark.) HS
39. Zack Gahagan, 3B, North Carolina
40. Andrew Warner, OF, Columbia (Mo.)

TAMPA BAY RAYS (16)

1. Matthew Liberatore, LHP, Mountain Ridge HS, Glendale, Ariz.
1. Shane McClanahan, LHP, South Florida
1. Nick Schnell, OF, Roncalli HS, Indianapolis
2. Tyler Frank, SS, Florida Atlantic
2s. Tanner Dodson, RHP, California
3. Ford Proctor, SS, Rice
4. Grant Witherspoon, OF, Tulane
5. Taj Bradley, RHP, Redan HS, Stone Mountain, Ga.
6. Miller Hogan, RHP, Saint Louis
7. Joe Ryan, RHP, Cal State Stanislaus
8. Michael Berglund, C, Midland (Texas) JC
9. Nick Lee, RHP, Louisiana-Lafayette
10. Alan Strong, RHP, Nevada-Las Vegas
11. Jacson McGowan, 1B, Purdue
12. Kevin Melendez, C, Puerto Rico Baseball Academy, Gurabo, P.R.
13. Trey Cumbie, LHP, Houston
14. Chris Gau, RHP, Jacksonville
15. Nick Sprengel, LHP, San Diego
16. Marvin Malone, OF, Southeastern (Fla.)
17. Justin Montgomery, RHP, California Baptist
18. Jake Palomaki, SS, Boston College
19. Simon Rosenblum-Larson, RHP, Harvard
20. Stephen Yancey, RHP, Texas Wesleyan
21. Kerry Wright, RHP, Montverde (Fla.) Academy
22. Jack Labosky, RHP, Duke
23. Daiveyon Whittle, RHP, Fresno JC
24. Keegan McCarville, RHP, South Mountain (Ariz.) JC
25. Jordan Qsar, OF, Pepperdine
26. Steffon Moore, LHP, West Alabama
27. Heath Renz, RHP, Wisconsin-Whitewater
28. Tanner Brubaker, RHP, Saddleback (Calif.) JC
29. Russ Olive, 1B, Massachusetts-Lowell
30. Eric Cerantola, RHP, Holy Trinity Catholic SS, Oakville, Ont.
31. Michael Costanzo, LHP, Austin Peay State
32. Kaleo Johnson, 3B, Montana State
33. Beau Brundage, OF, Portland
34. Dawson Dimon, C, Quartz Hill HS, Lancaster, Calif.
35. B.J. Myers, RHP, West Virginia
36. K.V. Edwards, SS, Cowley County (Kan.) JC
37. John Rodriguez, SS, Douglas HS, Parkland, Fla.
38. Garrett Wade, LHP, Hartselle (Ala.) HS
39. C.J. Willis, C, Ruston (La.) HS
40. David Luethje, RHP, Vero Beach (Fla.) HS

TEXAS RANGERS (15)

1. Cole Winn, RHP, Orange (Calif.) Lutheran HS
2. Owen White, RHP, Carson HS, China Grove, N.C.
3. Jonathan Ornelas, SS, Kellis HS, Glendale, Ariz.
4. Mason Englert, RHP, Forney (Texas) HS
5. Jayce Easley, SS, O'Connor HS, Phoenix
6. Sean Chandler, RHP, Iowa Western JC
7. Tim Brennan, RHP, St. Joseph's
8. Jax Biggers, SS, Arkansas

9. **Chandler Sanburn, RHP, Wichita State**
10. **Leury Tejada, RHP, Walton HS, Bronx, N.Y.**
11. **Billy Layne, RHP, Seton Hall**
12. **Destin Dotson, LHP, Scotlandville Magnet HS, Baton Rouge**
13. **Kenen Irizarry, SS, Quiles Claudio HS, Guanica, P.R.**
14. **Theo McDowell, RHP, Salisbury (Conn.) School**
15. Cameron Simmons, OF, Virginia
16. Jonathan Edwards, RHP, Eagle's Landing HS, McDonough, Ga.
17. **Scott Kapers, C, Valparaiso**
18. **Grant Wolfram, LHP, Davenport (Mich.)**
19. **Xavier Valentin, C, Leadership Christian Academy, Guaynabo, P.R.**
20. **Nic Laio, RHP, Western Michigan**
21. Cody Hawthorne, LHP, Parkland (Ill.) JC
22. **Frainyer Chavez, SS, Midland (Texas) JC**
23. **Wyatt Sparks, RHP, Aurora (Mo.) HS**
24. **Troy Dixon, OF, Samford**
25. **Josh Smith, LHP, Grand Valley State (Mich.)**
26. **David Lebron, RHP, Tampa**
27. Antonio Knowles, RHP, Key West (Fla.) HS
28. Renton Poole, RHP, Indiana-Kokomo
29. **Glen Richardson, RHP, Sinclair (Ohio) JC**
30. Evan Reifert, RHP, North Iowa Area JC
31. **Ryan Anderson, OF, UC Davis**
32. Owen Sharts, RHP, Simi Valley (Calif.) HS
33. **Reynaldo Pichardo, C, Dawson (Mont.) JC**
34. **Noah Burkholder, RHP, Waubonsee (Ill.) JC**
35. **Tyler Depreta-Johnson, SS, Houston Baptist**
36. William Corcoran, RHP, Malvern (Pa.) Prep School
37. Austin Becker, RHP, Big Walnut HS, Sunbury, Ohio
38. **Reggie Meyer, RHP, Minnesota**
39. **Shea Patterson, 3B, Michigan**
40. **Cole Uvila, RHP, Georgia Gwinnet**

TORONTO BLUE JAYS (12

1. **Jordan Groshans, SS, Magnolia (Texas) HS**
2. **Griffin Conine, OF, Duke**
3. **Adam Kloffenstein, RHP, Magnolia (Texas) HS**
4. **Sean Wymer, RHP, Texas Christian**
5. **Chris Bec, C, Maine**
6. **Addison Barger, SS, King HS, Tampa**
7. **Nick Podkul, 2B, Notre Dame**
8. **Joey Murray, RHP, Kent State**
9. **Jake Brodt, 1B, Santa Clara**
10. **Cal Stevenson, OF, Arizona**
11. **Hunter Steinmetz, OF, Missouri State**
12. **Nick Allgeyer, LHP, Iowa**
13. **Brad Wilson, RHP, Ohio Dominican**
14. **John Aiello, 3B, Wake Forest**
15. **Troy Watson, RHP, Northern Colorado**
16. **Josh Hiatt, RHP, North Carolina**
17. **Austin Havekost, RHP, Kent State**
18. **Fitz Stadler, RHP, Arizona State**
19. **Adrian Ramos, OF, Miami Dade JC**
20. **Vinny Capra, SS, Richmond**
21. Kobby Lopez, LHP, Imperial (Calif.) HS
22. **Gage Burland, RHP, Lewis-Clark State (Idaho)**
23. **Troy Squires, C, Kentucky**
24. **Mike Pascoe, RHP, San Jacinto (Texas) JC**
25. **Will McAffer, RHP, Tulane**
26. **Brett Wright, C, Auburn**
27. Kyle Luckham, RHP, El Dorado HS, Placentia, Calif.
28. **Andy McGuire, RHP, Texas**
29. **Cre Finfrock, RHP, Central Florida**
30. **Cobi Johnson, RHP, Florida State**
31. Austin Easter, RHP, UNC Wilmington
32. **Joey Pulido, RHP, Houston**
33. **Matt Harris, RHP, Florida Atlantic**
34. **Grant Townsend, RHP, Oral Roberts**
35. Damiano Palmegiani, 3B, Vauxhall (Alb.) HS
36. Kameron Guangorena, C, St. John Bosco HS, Bellflower, Calif.

37. Parker Caracci, RHP, Mississippi
38. **Francisco Ruiz, C, Beltran Baseball Academy, Florida, P.R.**
39. Cole Beverlin, RHP, Spruce Creek HS, Port Orange, Fla.
40. Drew Labounty, SS, South Alabama

WASHINGTON NATIONALS (27)

1. **Mason Denaburg, RHP, Merritt Island (Fla.) HS**
2. **Tim Cate, LHP, Connecticut**
3. **Reid Schaller, RHP, Vanderbilt**
4. **Jake Irvin, RHP, Oklahoma**
5. **Gage Canning, OF, Arizona State**
6. **Andrew Karp, RHP, Florida State**
7. **Chandler Day, RHP, Vanderbilt**
8. **Tyler Cropley, C, Iowa**
9. **Tanner Driskill, RHP, Lamar**
10. **Carson Shaddy, 2B, Arkansas**
11. **Frankie Bartow, RHP, Miami**
12. Graham Lawson, RHP, South Carolina
13. **Cody Wilson, OF, Florida Atlantic**
14. **Aaron Fletcher, LHP, Houston**
15. **Evan Lee, LHP, Arkansas**
16. **Carson Teel, LHP, Oklahoma State**
17. Ridge Chapman, RHP, South Carolina
18. **Jacob Rhinesmith, OF, Western Kentucky**
19. Zach Linginfelter, RHP, Tennessee
20. **Onix Vega, C, Broward (Fla.) JC**
21. **Ryan Tapani, RHP, Creighton**
22. **Cole Daily, SS, Notre Dame**
23. Cole Hamilton, C, Linn-Benton (Ore.) JC
24. **Kyle Marinconz, SS, Cal Poly**
25. **Chris Vann, LHP, Mercer**
26. **Colin Morse, RHP, Shenandoa (Va.)**
27. **Pablo O'Connor, OF, Azusa Pacific (Calif.)**
28. **Blake Chisolm, 1B, Sam Houston State**
29. **Colton Pogue, SS, Pittsburg State (Kan.)**
30. **Trey Vickers, SS, Wichita State**
31. **Jonathan Quintana, OF, Barry (Fla.)**
32. **Alec Maley, RHP, Kentucky**
33. Jack Haney, C, Cedartown (Ga.) HS
34. Tyler Baca, OF, Linfield Christian School, Temecula, Calif.
35. Alex Binelas, 1B, Oak Creek (Wis.) HS
36. Bo Blessie, RHP, Lee HS, Midland, Texas
37. Cole Wilcox, RHP, Heritage HS, Ringgold, Ga.
38. **Bobby Milacki, RHP, Arizona Christian**
39. Andrew Nardi, LHP, Moorpark (Calif.) JC
40. Mike Menhart, RHP, Richmond Hill (Ga.) HS

APPENDIX

OBITUARIES

Rodolfo "Rudy" Arias, a lefthander who made 34 major league appearances for the White Sox during the 1959 season, died Jan. 12 in Miami. He was 86.

George Alusik, an outfielder and first baseman who played for the Tigers and Kansas City Athletics in 1958 and from 1961-64, died April 20 in Woodbridge, N.J. He was 83.

Alusik played in 298 major league games, including 279 with the Kansas City Athletics, and hit .256/.333/.416 with 23 home runs and 93 RBIs in 652 at-bats.

Bob Bailey, who played third base, left field and first base for the Pirates, Dodgers, Montreal Canadians, Reds and Red Sox from 1962-78, died Jan. 9 in Las Vegas. He was 75.

Bailey was a member of the 1976 World Series-winning Reds and finished his career with more than 1,500 hits and 750 RBIs. Bailey also coached in the Montreal Expos organization after his playing career was over.

Raymond "Ray" Barker, a first baseman who played for the Orioles in 1960 and the Indians and Yankees from 1965-67, died May 29 in Martinsburg, W.Va. He was 82.

Barker played in 192 major league games, hitting .214/.283/.358 with 10 home runs and 44 RBIs in 318 at-bats during his four seasons in the majors.

Anthony "Tony" Bartirome, a first baseman who played for the Pirates in 1952, died June 22 in Bradenton, Fla. He was 86.

In Bartirome's lone season in the majors, he hit .220/.273/.265 with 13 extra-base hits in 124 games and 355 at-bats.

Robert "Bob" Barton, a catcher who played in 10 major league seasons for the Giants, Padres and Reds from 1965-74, died Jan. 15 in Vista, Calif. He was 76.

Bob Borkowski, an outfielder who played for the Cubs, Reds and Brooklyn Dodgers from 1950-55, died Nov. 18, 2017 in Dayton, Ohio. He was 91.

Borkowski played in 470 major league games during his career—318 of which came with the Reds—and hit .251/.298/.346 with 16 home runs and 112 RBIs.

Clinton "Clint" Brown, the owner and president of the Independent Frontier League's Florence Freedom since 2005, died Jan. 16 in Phoenix. He was 63.

Marcos Carvajal, a righthander who pitched in 42 major league games for the Rockies and Marlins during the 2005 and 2007 seasons, died Jan. 24 in Bolivar, Venezuela. He was 34.

Edwin "Ed" Charles, a third baseman who played for the Kansas City Athletics and Mets from 1962-69, died March 15 in Queens, N.Y. He was 84.

During his eight-year major league career, Charles hit .263/.330/.397 with 86 home runs and 86 stolen bases in 1,005 games. As a rookie in 1962, Charles set career highs in batting average (.288), slugging percentage (.454), home runs (17) and stolen bases (20).

Tony Cloninger, a righthander who pitched for the Braves, Reds and Cardinals from 1961-1972, died July 24 in Denver, N.C. He was 77 years old.

After making his major league debut in June 1961 at the age of 20, Cloninger went on to pitch in 352 games during his 12-year big league career, accumulating a 113-97, 4.07 record with 1,120 strikeouts in 1,767.2 innings pitched.

Donald "Don" Colpoys, a minor leaguer who played for the Cardinals organization from 1954-56, served as the head baseball coach at Canisius from 1977-2001 and worked as the general manager of the Buffalo Bisons from 1979-84, died March 30 in Buffalo. He was 83.

Colpoys, who also worked as a scout for the Phillies from 1976-77, accumulated a 325-489-2 record as Canisius' head coach. He was inducted to the Buffalo Baseball Hall of Fame in 2007, the Greater Buffalo Sports Hall of Fame in 2011 and the Canisius College Sports Hall of Fame in 2012.

William "Billy" Connors, a righthander who pitched for the Cubs and Mets from 1966-68 and also spent more than 30 years as a major league coach and front office executive, most notably with the Yankees, died on June 18. He was 76.

Connors made 26 major league appearances (one start) in his three seasons in the big leagues, finishing his career 0-2, 7.53 with 24 strikeouts and seven walks in 43 innings. Connors then spent more than 15 years as a major league coach, including stops with the Royals, Cubs, Mariners and Yankees. From 1996-2012, Connors worked in the Yankees' front office as the vice president of player personnel and was widely considered the organization's "pitching guru," helping the likes of Mariano Rivera, Andy Pettitte and C.C. Sabathia master the cut fastball.

■ **Roger Coryell**, a longtime amateur scout for the Texas Rangers and the organization's Scout of the Year in 2014, died on April 5. He was 70.

Before joining the Rangers organization in 2009, Coryell was previously the head coach at Eastern Michigan, where he was a two-time Mid-American Conference Coach of the Year.

■ **Andre Derouen Jr.**, a redshirt freshman on the Galveston (Texas) JC baseball team, died March 23 in League City, Texas. He was 19.

Derouen Jr. drowned after swimming out to rescue his younger brother, who had become submerged in a pond. Derouen Jr. successfully rescued his brother before drowning.

■ **Leroy "Roy" Dietzel**, an infielder who appeared in nine games and made 25 plate appearances for the Washington Senators during the 1954 season, died Feb. 3 in Charlotte. He was 87.

■ **James "Jim" Dobson**, the 1959 College World Series Most Outstanding Player with Oklahoma State and an outfielder and third baseman who played in the South Atlantic and California leagues for the Houston Colt .45's organization from 1961-62, died Feb. 26 in Bethany, Okla. He was 78.

■ **John Duffie**, a righthander who pitched for the Dodgers in 1967, died April 19 in Douglas, Ga. He was 72.

Duffie made two appearances—both starts—for the Dodgers, striking out six batters in 9.2 innings.

■ **Donald "Don" Eddy**, a lefthander who pitched for the White Sox in 1970 and 1971, died Oct. 10 in Rockwell, Iowa. He was 71.

Eddy made 29 relief appearances in his majors, ending his career 0-2, 2.36 with 23 strikeouts in 34.1 innings. In Eddy's only major league plate appearance, he hit a double off the Brewers' Billy Parsons, ending his big league career with a 1.000 batting average.

■ **Howard "Doc" Edwards**, a catcher who played for the Indians, Kansas City Athletics, Yankees and Phillies from 1962-65 and 1970, died Aug. 20 in San Angelo, Texas. He was 81.

After his playing career, Edwards served as the Indians' manager from 1987-89, winning 173 of his 380 games in charge. During his five major league seasons as a player, Edwards hit .238/.287/.325 with 15 home runs and 87 RBIs in 906 at-bats.

■ **Samuel "Sammy" Esposito**, an infielder who played for the White Sox (1952, 1955-63) and the Kansas City Athletics (1963) across 10 major league seasons, died July 9 in Newland, N.C. He was 86.

In addition to his 10-year major league career, in which he hit .207/.330/.277 with eight home runs in 792 at-bats, Esposito was the head baseball coach at North Carolina State from 1967-87. During his 21 years as Wolfpack head coach, Esposito led N.C. State to 513 wins and the program's first-trip to the College World Series in 1968. Esposito was also an assistant coach with the N.C. State basketball team for 12 years, helping the Wolfpack to the 1974 National Championship.

■ **Ernie Fazio**, who played both second base and shortstop for the Houston Colt .45s from 1962-63 and the Kansas City Athletics during the 1966 season, died Dec. 1, 2017 in Danville, Calif. He was 75.

Fazio played in 141 major league games during his career, including a career-high 102 games in 1963, when he hit his only two major league home runs off of left-handers Denny Lemaster and Hall of Famer Warren Spahn of the Brewers.

■ **William "Bill" Fischer**, a righthander who pitched for the White Sox, Tigers, Washington Senators, Kansas City Athletics and Twins, died Oct. 30 in Council Bluffs, Iowa. He was 88.

During his nine major league seasons, Fischer made 281 appearances (78 starts), posting a 45-58, 4.34 record with 313 strikeouts in 831.1 innings.

■ **Tom Fletcher**, a lefthander who pitched for the Tigers in 1962, died May 9 in Oakwood, Ill. He was 75.

Fletcher made his one and only major league appearance on Sept. 12, 1962, when he pitched two scoreless innings against the Red Sox. He allowed two hits, two walks and struck out one batter.

OBITUARIES

■ **Oscar Gamble**, an outfielder and designated hitter who played in 17 major league seasons for the Cubs, Phillies, Indians, Yankees, White Sox, Padres and Rangers from 1969-1985, died Jan. 31 in Birmingham, Ala. He was 68.

Gamble, who was well known for his big, Afro hairstyle, finished his major league career with 200 home runs and 666 RBIs, while hitting .265/.356/.454 in more than 1,500 games.

■ **David Garcia**, a former major league coach, scout and manager who managed the California Angels from 1977-78 and the Indians from 1979-82, died May 21 in San Diego, Calif. He was 97.

Garcia won 307 of his 618 games as a major league manager, including a 247-244 record during his four seasons as the Indians' manager.

■ **August "Augie" Garrido Jr.**, the winningest baseball coach in NCAA history best known for his five national championship-winning seasons at Cal State Fullerton and Texas, died Mar. 15 in Newport Beach, Calif. He was 79.

Garrido retired after 48 years as a head coach following 2016, ending his illustrious career with a 1,975-951-9 record. Garrido was one of only five men to have twice been named Coach of the Year and in 2016 he received Baseball America's Tony Gwynn Lifetime Achievement Award.

Before his coaching career, Garrido played at Fresno State and helped the Bulldogs advance to the 1959 College World Series, making him one of just 11 men to reach Omaha as both a player and head coach. Garrido went on to play five seasons in the minor leagues for the Indians organization, advancing as high as Triple-A.

Garrido coached at San Francisco State (1969), Cal Poly (1970-72), Cal State Fullerton (1973-87, 1991-96), Illinois (1988-90) and Texas (1997-2016). Garrido's teams advanced to the College World Series 15 times, winning the national championship with Cal State Fullerton in 1979, 1984 and 1995 and with Texas in 2002 and 2005. Garrido was the first head coach in NCAA history to win a national title at two different schools.

■ **Dick Gernert**, a first baseman and left fielder for the Red Sox, Cubs, Tigers, Reds and Astros from 1952-62, died Nov. 30, 2017 in Reading, Penn. He was 89.

Gernert played the majority of his 10-year career with the Red Sox, including his rookie season in 1952, when he hit 19 home runs and fin-

ished 25th in the American League MVP voting.

■ **Miguel Alfredo Gonzalez**, a righthander who pitched in six games for the Phillies during the 2014 season, died in a car crash on Nov. 23, 2017 in Havana, Cuba. He was 34.

Gonzalez played for the Vaqueros de La Habana team in Cuba from 2004-12, completing nearly 600 innings before signing a three-year, $12-million contract with the Phillies in 2013. Gonzalez struck out five batters in 5.1 innings during his major league career.

■ **Viola Griffin**, a lefthander who played in the All-American Girls Professional Baseball League from 1944-47 and participated in the 1992 movie "A League of Their Own" died Dec. 31, 2017 in Belton, S.C. She was 95.

■ **John Hope**, a righthander who pitched for the Pirates from 1993-96, died April 18 in Lauderhill, Fla. He was 47.

A second-round pick by the Pirates in 1989, Hope made 24 appearances (11 starts) during his four seasons in the majors, finishing his career 1-5, 5.99 with 29 strikeouts in 73.2 innings.

■ **Kenneth "Ken" Hottman**, a left fielder who played for the White Sox in 1971, died April 16 in Sacramento. He was 69.

Hottman appeared in six games for the White Sox, recording two hits and drawing one walk in 17 plate appearances.

■ **Harry "Wayne" Huizenga**, who owned the Florida Marlins from the time of their inception in 1993 until he sold the team in 1998, died March 22 in Fort Lauderdale, Fla. He was 80.

Huizenga was also the original owner of the NHL's Florida Panthers, which also began play in 1993, and he was the first entrepreneur to ever launch three Fortune 500 companies: Waste Management, Blockbuster Entertainment and Auto Nation.

■ **Manny Jimenez**, a leftfielder for the Kansas City Athletics from 1962-64 and the Pirates and Cubs from 1966-69, died Dec. 11, 2017 in New York. He was 79.

Jimenez hit .272/.337/.401 in 429 major league games during his career, including his career-best year in 1962, when, as a rookie with the Kansas City Athletics, Jimenez hit .301/.354/.428 with 11 home runs and 69 RBIs in 139 games.

APPENDIX

■ **Michael "Mike" Kilkenny**, a lefthander who pitched for the Tigers, Athletics, Padres and Indians from 1969-73, died June 28 in St. Thomas, Canada. He was 73.

During Kilkenny's five seasons in the majors, he made 139 appearances (54 starts) and finished his career 23-18, 4.43 with 301 strikeouts in 410 innings. Kilkenny is also known for being the pitcher who surrendered Frank Robinson's 500th career home run on Sept. 13, 1971.

■ **Jerry Kindall**, a major league infielder with the Cubs, Indians and Twins from 1956-65 and former head baseball coach for the Arizona Wildcats from 1973-96, died Dec. 24, 2017 in Tucson, Ariz. He was 82.

Kindall played in more than 740 major league games across nine seasons before eventually taking over the Arizona baseball program in 1973.

A member of the American Baseball Coaches Association Hall of Fame, Kindall led the Wildcats to three College World Series championships during his 23-year stint at Arizona.

Kindall, who also won a College World Series as a player at Minnesota in 1956, was the first person ever to win the College World Series as both a player and coach. Kindall also hit for the cycle in a victory against Mississippi during the 1956 College World Series, and that cycle still stands as the first and only cycle in CWS history.

As Arizona's head coach, Kindall tutored future big leaguers such as Terry Francona, who won the 1980 Golden Spikes Award, Trevor Hoffman and Kenny Lofton. Francona, who currently serves as the manager for the Cleveland Indians, is one of several of Kindall's pupils who has gone into coaching, joining Utah coach Bil Kinneberg and former Astros manager Brad Mills.

■ **Bruce Kison**, a righthander who pitched for the Pirates, California Angels and Red Sox from 1971-85, died June 2 in Bradenton, Fla. He was 68.

Kison made 380 appearances (246 starts) in the major leagues, ending his 15-year career 115-88, 3.66 with 12 saves, 1,073 strikeouts and 662 walks in 1,809.2 innings. Kison won two World Series with the Pirates in 1971 and 1979.

■ **Wayne Krenchicki**, a corner infielder for the Orioles, Reds, Tigers and Montreal Expos from 1979-86, died Oct. 16 in Pittsfield, Ill. He was 64.

A three-year letterman at the University of Miami, where he helped the Hurricanes to a runner-up finish at the 1974 College World Series, Krenchicki played in 550 major league games over his eight-year big league career, hitting .266/.330/.359 with 15 home runs and 124 RBIs in 1,063 at-bats. Krenchicki was inducted into the University of Miami Sports Hall of Fame in 1990.

■ **Joseph "Joe" Landrum**, a righthander who pitched for the Brooklyn Dodgers in 1950 and 1952, died Aug. 19 in Columbia, S.C. He was 89.

In his two seasons in the majors, Landrum made 16 appearances (five starts) and struck out 22, walked 11 and allowed 28 earned runs in 44.2 career innings. Landrum's son, Bill, also pitched in the big leagues, playing for the Reds, Cubs, Pirates and Montreal Expos from 1986-93.

■ **Frank Lary**, a righthander who pitched for the Tigers, Mets, Montreal Expos and White Sox from 1954-65, died Dec. 13, 2017 in Tuscaloosa, Ala. He was 87.

Lary was a two-time all-star with the Tigers in 1960 and 1961, when he combined to win 38 of his 72 starts. For his career, Lary, who finished third in the American League Cy Young voting in 1961, won 128 games and struck out 1,099 batters in 2,162.1 innings.

■ **Richard "Dick" LeMay**, a lefthander who pitched for the Giants and Cubs from 1961-63, died March 19 in Kansas City, Mo. He was 79.

LeMay made 45 appearances (six starts) in his three-year major league career, recording a 4.17 ERA with 69 strikeouts in 108 innings.

■ **Johnny Lewis**, a right fielder who played for the Cardinals and Mets from 1964-67, died July 29 in Pensacola, Fla. He was 78.

Lewis appeared in 266 games during his four-year big league career, hitting .227/.313/.359 with 22 home runs and eight stolen bases in 771 at-bats.

■ **Willie Lee McCovey**, a Hall of Fame slugger and 1969 National League Most Valuable Player who played for the Giants, Padres and Athletics from 1959-80, died Oct. 31 in Stanford, Calif. He was 80.

A six-time All-Star with the Giants, McCovey was the 1959 NL Rookie of the Year and helped San Francisco to the National League pennant in 1962. Nicknamed "Stretch" for his lengthy, 6-foot-4 frame, McCovey finished his 22-year big league career hitting .270/.374/.515 with 521 home runs and 1,555 RBIs. During his MVP season in 1969,

McCovey hit a career-high 45 home runs, drove in MLB-best 126 RBIs and led the league with a 1.108 on-base plus slugging percentage.

The Giants retired McCovey's famous No. 44 during his final season in 1980, and then he was inducted into the National Baseball Hall of Fame in 1986, which was the first year he was eligible.

■ **Wallace "Wally" Moon**, the 1954 National League Rookie of the Year and two-time All-Star who played for the Cardinals and Dodgers from 1954-65, died Feb. 9 in Bryan, Texas. He was 87.

Moon, who spent most of his 12-year career playing in the outfield, won a Gold Glove in 1960 and won the World Series as a member of the Dodgers in 1959, 1963 and 1965. Moon finished his career with a .289/.371/.445 slash line and 142 home runs.

■ **Gerald "Jerry" Moses**, a catcher who played for the Red Sox, California Angels, Indians, Yankees, Tigers, Padres and White Sox in 1965 and from 1968-75, died March 26 in Haverhill, Mass. He was 71.

During his nine-year major league career, Moses hit .295/.381/.676 with 25 home runs and 109 RBIs in 386 games. Moses was selected as an All-Star with the Red Sox in 1970, when he hit .263/.313/.384 with six home runs and 35 RBIs in 92 games.

■ **Jose Mota**, a longtime minor league coach who spent 22 years in the Braves organization and was most recently with Triple-A Gwinnett from 2016-18, died Nov. 6 in the Dominican Republic. He was 53.

■ **James "Jim" Napier**, a minor league catcher and outfielder who played in 1,174 games for the White Sox and Cardinals organizations from 1958-65 and from 1967-72, died Feb. 11 in Tucson, Ariz. He was 79.

Napier also worked as a minor league manager for 11 seasons, managing in the White Sox organization from 1973-77, in the Cubs organization from 1979-80 and 1982-84, and in the Indians organization in 1986. Napier's career minor league managerial record was 744-772.

■ **David "Dave" Nelson**, a second baseman and third baseman for the Indians, Washington Senators, Rangers and Royals from 1968-77, died April 23 in Milwaukee. He was 73.

An All-Star in 1973, Nelson ended his 10-year major league career hitting .244/.305/.312 with 20 home runs and 187 stolen bases. After his playing career, Nelson had major league coaching stops with the Athletics, Montreal Expos, Indians and Brewers. He also worked as a pregame television analyst and radio broadcaster for the Brewers.

■ **Charles "C.M." Newton**, a minor league right-hander who pitched in the Yankees organization from 1951-52 and 1955, died June 4 in Tuscaloosa, Ala. He was 88.

Newton also coached Division I college basketball for 20 seasons at Alabama and Vanderbilt. He won three SEC regular season championships and went to two NCAA Tournaments in 12 seasons at Alabama, while advancing to two NCAA Tournaments in eight seasons at Vanderbilt. After his career as a college basketball coach, Newton was the Athletic Director at Kentucky from 1989-2000.

■ **Wayne Norton**, a longtime and well-respected international scout with the Mariners organization who was also a minor league outfielder with the Yankees and Athletics organization from 1961-70, died on Jan. 6. He was 75.

Norton, who had battled amyotrophic lateral sclerosis (ALS) since being diagnosed with Lou Gehrig's disease in 2015, was named the Mariners International Scout of the Year in 2007 and Canadian Scout of the Year by the Canadian Baseball Network in 1998 and 2013. Elected to the Canadian Baseball Hall of Fame in 2016, Norton founded Baseball Canada's Junior National Team in the mid-1970s and established the National Baseball Insitute (NBI) in Vancouver in 1986 — a program responsible for producing numerous Major League players over the last 30 years.

■ **William "Billy" O'Dell**, a lefthander who pitched for the Orioles, Giants, Braves and Pirates in 1954 and from 1956-67, died Sept. 12 in Newberry, S.C. He was 85.

An All-Star with the Orioles in 1958 and 1959, O'Dell finished his 13-year major league career with 105 wins, a 3.29 ERA and 1,133 strikeouts in 1,817 innings. O'Dell won a career-high 19 games with the Giants in 1962, when he also started Game 1 of the World Series against the Yankees.

■ **Leonard "Len" Okrie**, a catcher who played for the Washington Senators in 1948 and from 1950-51, as well as the Red Sox in 1952, died April 12 in Hope Mills, N.C. He was 94.

Over his four seasons in the majors, Okrie hit .218/.307/.256 in 89 plate appearances. The son of Frank Okrie, a lefthander who pitched for the Tigers in 1920, Len was also a minor league manager and major league bullpen coach for both the Red Sox and Tigers.

■ **Ryan Owens**, a minor league second baseman, third baseman and outfielder for the Diamondbacks, Rockies, Twins and Reds organizations from 1999-2005, died on Feb. 10. He was 39.

Owens led Cal State Fullerton to the College World Series in 1999, when he paced the team in home runs (23) and RBIs (85). Owens, who also played for the USA Collegiate National Team, ranks 10th in Cal State Fullerton history in home runs (34), RBIs (163) and slugging percentage (.581).

■ **Lyle Palmer**, an outfielder who played in the Western International, Pacific Coast and West Texas-New Mexico leagues from 1948-53, died June 17 in Walnut Creek, Calif. He was 93.

Palmer was also a member of the first College World Series championship team at California in 1947. After his playing career, Palmer coached baseball at Pleasant Hill (Calif.) High until his retirement in 1982.

■ **Martin "Marty" Pattin**, a righthander who pitched for the California Angels, Seattle Pilots, Brewers, Red Sox and Royals from 1968-80, died Oct. 3 in Charleston, Ill. He was 75.

An American League All-Star as a member of the 1971 Brewers, Pattin finished his 13-year major league career with 114 wins, a 3.62 ERA and 1,179 strikeouts in 2,038.2 innings. After his playing career, Pattin served as the head baseball coach at the University of Kansas from 1982-87.

■ **Hugh "Laurin" Pepper**, a righthander who pitched in parts of four major league seasons and made 44 appearances (17 starts) for the Pirates from 1954-57, died on Feb. 4 in Ocean Springs, Miss. He was 88.

■ **Rob Picciolo**, an infielder for the Athletics, Brewers and California Angels from 1977-85 who spent 20 years in the San Diego Padres organization and served as the bench coach for the Angels from 2010-13, died Jan. 3 in Los Angeles. He was 64.

■ **Rance Pless**, a corner infielder for the Kansas City Athletics during the 1956 season and later a scout with the Atlanta Braves for 25 years, died Nov. 11, 2017 in Greeneville, Tenn. He was 91.

Pless played in 48 games during his only major league season, recording 23 hits and nine RBIs during his 85 at-bats.

■ **Frank Quilici**, who played both second base and third base for the Twins in 1965 and from 1967-70, died May 14 in Burnsville, Minn. He was 79.

Quilici played in 405 games during his five seasons in the majors, hitting .214/.281/.287 with five home runs, 53 RBIs and three stolen bases in 682 at-bats.

■ **Marvin "Marv" Rackley**, an outfielder who played for the Brooklyn Dodgers, Pirates and Reds from 1947-50, died April 24 in Greenville, S.C. He was 96.

Rackley played in 185 career games, including 169 with the Brooklyn Dodgers, and hit .317/.365/.390 with 27 extra-base hits and 35 RBIs in 477 at-bats.

■ **Jim Rivera**, an outfielder with the St. Louis Browns, White Sox and Kansas City Athletics from 1952-61, died Nov. 13, 2017 in Fort Wayne, Ind. He was 96.

Over the course of his 10-year major league career, the majority of which came with the White Sox, Rivera hit .256/.328/.402. He led the American League in triples in 1953, when he hit 16 for Chicago, which was followed by an American League-best 25 stolen bases in 1955.

■ **Daryl Robertson**, a shortstop and third baseman who played in nine games for the Cubs in 1962, died July 31 in Salt Lake City. He was 82.

Robertson made his major league debut on May 4, 1962 against the Giants and eventually ended his big league career with two hits, two RBIs and two walks in 19 at-bats.

■ **Ed Roebuck**, a righthander who pitched for the Dodgers, Washington Senators and Phillies from 1955-58 and 1960-66, died June 14 in Lakewood, Calif. He was 86.

During his 11 seasons in the major leagues, Roebuck made 460 appearances (one start), ending his career 52-31, 3.35 with 477 strikeouts and 302 walks in 791 innings. He received National League MVP votes during a career-best 1962 season, when he went 10-2, 3.09 and recorded nine saves in 64 appearances with the Dodgers over 119.1 innings.

■ **Edward "Ed" Samcoff**, a second baseman who played in four games for the Philadelphia Athletics in 1951, died March 29 in Concord, Calif. He was 93.

Samcoff made his major league debut on April 21, 1951, when he appeared as a pinch-hitter against the Red Sox at Fenway Park. In 12 career plate appearances, Samcoff drew one walk and struck out twice.

■ **Jose Santiago**, a righthander who pitched for the Indians and Kansas City Athletics from 1954-56, died Oct. 9 in San Juan, Puerto Rico. He was 90.

Santiago appeared in 27 major league games (five starts) during his three-year big league career, posting a 3-2, 4.66 record with 29 strikeouts in 56 innings. In 2003, Santiago was inducted into the Caribbean Baseball Hall of Fame.

■ **Carl Scheib**, a righthander who pitched for the Philadelphia Athletics and Cardinals from 1943-54, died March 24 in San Antonio. He was 91.

In his 11-year major league career, Scheib made 267 appearances (107 starts) and finished 45-65, 4.88 with 290 strikeouts in 1,070.2 innings.

■ **Albert "Red" Schoendienst**, a Hall of Fame second baseman, manager and coach for the Cardinals who had a major league career spanning six decades, died June 6 in Town & Country, Mo., just outside of St. Louis. He was 95.

The oldest living member of the Hall of Fame before his death, Schoendienst was a 10-time all-star and three-time World Series champion. As a player, Schoendienst was a .289/.337/.387 hitter with 2,449 hits in 2,216 games over 19 years from 1945-63. While he played for the Cardinals from 1945-56 and 1961-63, Schoendienst also played for the New York Giants (1956-57) and Milwaukee Braves (1957-60).

Schoendienst, who has a statue of his likeness outside of Busch Stadium, managed the Cardinals from 1965-76 and for brief stints in both 1980 and 1990. Over his 14 seasons at the helm, Schoendienst accumulated a 1,041-955 record, winning the National League pennant in 1967 and 1968 and winning the World Series in 1967.

■ **Jerald "Jerry" Schoonmaker**, an outfielder who played for the Washington Senators in 1955 and 1957, died March 18 in Dyer, Ind. He was 84.

Schoonmaker played in 50 games during his two-year big league career, hitting .130/.211/.217 with one home run and one stolen base while logging innings at all three outfield positions.

■ **Al Stanek**, a lefthander who pitched for the Giants in 1963, died May 8 in Holyoke, Mass. He was 74.

Stanek made 11 relief appearances during his major league career, recording a 4.73 ERA in 13.1 innings with five strikeouts and 12 walks.

■ **Evart "Tracy" Stallard**, a righthander who pitched for the Red Sox, Mets and Cardinals from 1960-66, died Dec. 6, 2017 in Kingsport, Tenn. He was 80.

Stallard, who may be most remembered for giving up New York Yankees slugger Roger Maris' 61st home run in 1961, won 30 games in his seven-year major league career.

■ **Jack Stallings**, a minor league second baseman who played for the Red Sox organization from 1953-54 and then served as the head baseball coach for Wake Forest (1960-68), Florida State (1969-74) and Georgia Southern (1976-1999), died June 20 in Tallahassee, Fla. He was 87.

■ **Albert "Lee" Stange**, a righthander who pitched for the Twins, Indians, Red Sox and White Sox from 1961-70, died Sept. 21 in Riverview, Fla. He was 81.

Stange finished his 10-year major league career with 62 wins, a 3.56 ERA and 718 strikeouts in 1,216 innings. After his playing days were over, Stange served as the pitching coach for the Red Sox (1972-74; 1981-84), Twins (1975) and Athletics (1977-79).

■ **Joe Stanka**, a righthander who pitched in two games for the White Sox in 1959, died Oct. 15 in Katy, Texas. He was 87.

Stanka ended his major league career with a 1-0, 3.38 record, striking out three hitters in 5.1 innings across two relief appearances.

■ **Daniel "Rusty" Staub**, a six-time all-star who played right field and first base for the Astros, Montreal Expos, Mets, Tigers and Rangers from 1963-85, died March 29 in West Palm Beach, Fla. He was 73.

APPENDIX

Staub finished his 23-year major league career with 2,716 hits and 299 home runs. He was selected to five consecutive all-star games from 1967-71 while playing for the Astros and Expos and selected again with the Tigers in 1976. Staub finished fifth in AL MVP voting in 1978, when he hit .273/.347/.435 with 24 home runs, 30 doubles and 121 RBIs.

■ **Rick Stelmaszek**, who was a catcher for the Washington Senators in 1971 and for the Rangers, California Angels and Cubs from 1973-74, died Nov. 6, 2017 in Chicago. He was 69.

Stelmaszek, who was an 11th-round pick by the Washington Senators in the 1967 MLB Draft, played in 60 major league games during his career, hitting .170/.302/.239 in 88 at-bats.

■ **Charles "Chuck" Stevens**, a first baseman who played in parts of three major league seasons for the St. Louis Browns in 1941, 1946 and 1948, died May 28 in Long Beach, Calif. He was 99.

Stevens appeared in 211 major league games, hitting .251/.333/.329 with four home runs, 55 RBIs and six stolen bases in 732 at-bats.

■ **Darragh "Dean" Stone**, a lefthander who pitched for the Washington Senators, Red Sox, Cardinals, Astros, White Sox and Orioles from 1953-57, 1959 and 1962-63, died Aug. 21 in East Moline, Ill. He was 87.

An American League All-Star with the Washington Senators in 1954, Stone made 215 appearances (85 starts) during his eight seasons in the majors. Stone retired from baseball with 29 wins and 380 strikeouts in 686 career innings.

■ **Lawrence "Moose" Stubing**, who appeared in five games for the California Angels during the 1967 season and also worked as a minor league manager, major league third base coach and professional baseball scout for more than 30 years, died Jan. 19 in San Marino, Calif. He was 79.

Stubing, who was also a well-known college basketball referee in the PAC-12, Southwest and Western Athletic conferences, served as the California Angels' interim manager for the final eight games of the 1988 season.

■ **Paul Stuffel**, a righthander who pitched for the Phillies in 1950 and 1952-53, died Sept. 9 in Canton, Ohio. He was 91.

Stuffel made seven appearances (one start) in three major league seasons, finishing 1-0, 5.73 with three strikeouts in 11 career innings.

■ **Charles "Chuck" Taylor**, a righthander who pitched for the Cardinals, Mets, Brewers and Montreal Expos from 1969-76, died June 5 in Murfreesboro, Tenn. He was 76.

Taylor made 305 appearances in the majors, ending his eight-year career 28-20, 3.07 with 31 saves, 282 strikeouts and 162 walks in 607 innings.

■ **Kevin Towers**, a Major League Baseball general manager with the Padres from 1995-2009 and then with the D-backs from 2010-2014, died Jan 30 in San Diego. He was 56.

A standout righthander at BYU, Towers was selected with the No. 1 overall pick in the seconday phase of the 1982 draft by the Padres. He pitched in the Padres organization from 1982-89, reaching as high as Triple-A Las Vegas in 1988. He served as the pitching coach at short-season Spokane for two seasons before moving into scouting.

Towers eventually took over as the Padres' pro scouting director and was then promoted to the organization's general manager role all within a six-year span.

As GM of both the Padres and D-backs, Towers oversaw a combined five division titles and a World Series appearance with the 1998 Padres.

Towers most recently worked as a Reds scout and special assistant to the general manager, and he also worked for the Yankees in 2010.

■ **Benjamin "Benny" Valenzuela**, a third baseman who played in 10 games for the Cardinals in 1958, died Oct. 24. He was 85.

In 15 career plate appearances at the major league level, Valenzuela was 3-for-14 with a double and one walk. After his brief stint in the majors, Valenzuela played professionally in Mexico from 1962-71.

■ **Camille "Ozzie" Van Brabant**, a righthander who pitched for the Philadelphia and Kansas City Athletics in 1954 and 1955, died Aug. 18 in La Jolla, Canada. He was 91.

In his two seasons in the majors, Van Brabant made 11 appearances (two starts) and struck out 11 and allowed 25 earned runs in 28.2 innings.

■ **Roy Wright**, a righthander who pitched for the New York Giants in 1956, died May 5 in Chickamauga, Ga. He was 84.

Wright made his one and only major league appearance on Sept. 30, 1956, when he pitched 2.2 innings against the Phillies, allowing five runs on eight hits with zero strikeouts and two walks.

STATISTICS INDEX

MAJOR LEAGUES

AMERICAN LEAGUE

Baltimore	66
Boston	75
Chicago	96
Cleveland	115
Detroit	134
Houston	146
Kansas City	155
Los Angeles	165
Minnesota	206
New York	227
Oakland	240
Seattle	301
Tampa Bay	311
Texas	321
Toronto	331

NATIONAL LEAGUE

Arizona	45
Atlanta	56
Chicago	85
Cincinnati	105
Colorado	126
Los Angeles	175
Miami	186
Milwaukee	196
New York	216
Philadelphia	249
Pittsburgh	260
St. Louis	270
San Diego	280
San Francisco	290
Washington	342

TRIPLE-A

INTERNATIONAL LEAGUE

Buffalo	333
Charlotte	98
Columbus	117
Durham	313
Gwinnett	58
Indianapolis	262
Lehigh Valley	251
Louisville	107
Norfolk	68
Pawtucket	77
Rochester	208
Scranton/W-B	229
Syracuse	344
Toledo	136

PACIFIC COAST LEAGUE

Albuquerque	128
Colorado Springs	198
El Paso	282
Fresno	148
Iowa	87
Las Vegas	218
Memphis	272
Nashville	242
New Orleans	188
Oklahoma City	177
Omaha	157
Reno	47
Round Rock	323
Sacramento	292
Salt Lake	167
Tacoma	303

DOUBLE-A

EASTERN LEAGUE

Akron	118
Altoona	263
Binghamton	219
Bowie	69
Erie	137
Harrisburg	345
Hartford	129
New Hampshire	335
Portland	78
Reading	252
Richmond	293
Trenton	230

SOUTHERN LEAGUE

Biloxi	199
Birmingham	99
Chattanooga	209
Jackson	48
Jacksonville	189
Mississippi	59
Mobile	168
Montgomery	314
Pensacola	108
Tennessee	88

TEXAS LEAGUE

Arkansas	304
Corpus Christi	149
Frisco	324
Midland	243
NW Arkansas	158
San Antonio	283
Springfield	273
Tulsa	178

HIGH CLASS A

CALIFORNIA LEAGUE

Inland Empire	170
Lake Elsinore	284
Lancaster	130
Modesto	305
Rancho	180
San Jose	294
Stockton	244
Visalia	49

CAROLINA LEAGUE

Buies Creek	150
Carolina	200
Down East	325
Frederick	70
Lynchburg	120
Myrtle Beach	89
Potomac	346
Salem	79
Wilmington	159
Winston-Salem	100

FLORIDA STATE

Bradenton	264
Charlotte	315
Clearwater	253
Daytona	109
Dunedin	336
Florida	60
Fort Myers	211
Jupiter	190
Lakeland	138
Palm Beach	274
St. Lucie	221
Tampa	232

LOW CLASS A

MIDWEST LEAGUE

Beloit	245
Bowling Green	316
Burlington	171
Cedar Rapids	212
Clinton	307
Dayton	111
Fort Wayne	285
Great Lakes	181
Kane County	50
Lake County	121
Lansing	337
Peoria	275
Quad Cities	151
South Bend	90
West Michigan	139
Wisconsin	201

SOUTH ATLANTIC LEAGUE

Asheville	131
Augusta	296
Charleston	233
Columbia	222
Delmarva	71
Greensboro	192
Greenville	80
Hagerstown	347
Hickory	326
Kannapolis	101
Lakewood	254
Lexington	160
Rome	62
West Virginia	265

SHORT-SEASON

NEW YORK-PENN LEAGUE

Aberdeen	72
Auburn	348
Batavia	193
Brooklyn	223
Connecticut	140
Hudson Valley	317
Lowell	81
Mahoning Valley	121
State College	276
Staten Island	234
Tri-City	152
Vermont	246
West Virginia	266
Williamsport	255

NORTHWEST LEAGUE

Boise	131
Eugene	91
Everett	307
Hillsboro	51
Salem-Keizer	297
Spokane	327
Tri-City	286
Vancouver	338

ROOKIE

APPALACHIAN LEAGUE

Bluefield	338
Bristol	267
Burlington	161
Danville	63
Elizabethton	213
Greeneville	112
Johnson City	277
Kingsport	224
Princeton	318
Pulaski	235

PIONEER LEAGUE

Billings	111
Grand Junction	132
Great Falls	102
Helena	202
Idaho Falls	162
Missoula	52
Ogden	182
Orem	172

ARIZONA LEAGUE

Angels	173
Athletics	247
Brewers	203
Cubs	92
D-backs	53
Dodgers	183
Giants	297
Indians	122
Mariners	308
Padres	287
Rangers	328
Reds	113
Royals	163
White Sox	103

GULF COAST LEAGUE

Astros	153
Blue Jays	339
Braves	63
Cardinals	278
Marlins	194
Mets	224
Nationals	350
Orioles	73
Phillies	256
Pirates	267
Rays	319
Red Sox	82
Tigers	141
Twins	213
Yankees East	236